2011
SEC Handbook

Rules and Forms for Financial Statements and Related Disclosures

Wolters Kluwer Editorial Staff Publication

Law & Business

RELATED PUBLICATIONS

2011
SEC Handbook

Rules and Forms for Financial Statements and Related Disclosures

As of November 2010

Wolters Kluwer

Law & Business

Editorial Staff

Amanda Maine, J.D.

Ted Trautmann, J.D.

Production Staff

Leslie Stoken

Carmen Kane

4025 W. Peterson Ave.
Chicago, IL 60645-6085
1-800-248-3248
http://www.wolterskluwerlb.com/

Printed in the United States of America

ISBN: 978-0-8080-2573-3

SUSTAINABLE FORESTRY INITIATIVE

Certified Fiber Sourcing

www.sfiprogram.org

FOREWORD

2011 SEC Handbook: Rules and Forms for Financial Statements and Related Disclosures reproduces SEC regulations, forms, and staff interpretations necessary for preparing a company's financial disclosures. Now in its 21th edition, the Handbook is a compendium of requirements for drafting and filing financial statements and related disclosures with the Commission. The Handbook therefore includes Regulations S-X, S-K and S-T, forms and instructions for selected registration statements and Exchange Act reports, selected Exchange Act rules, and interpretative materials such as the codification of financial reporting policies, staff accounting bulletins, and staff legal bulletins.

The new edition reflects amendments to forms and rules adopted since the previous edition, as of November 2010. These include amendments to Regulations S-K, S-X and S-T, as well as to many forms (including Forms 8-K, 10-K, 10-Q, 20-F and 40-F). New rules featured in this edition include Exchange Act Rules 14a-11, 14a-18, 14n-1–14n-3 and Schedule 14N, relating to shareholder nominations to the board (and subject, as of this writing, to a stay of effectiveness pending a court challenge). Also featured is new Staff Legal Bulletin No. 18 on suspension of reporting obligations under Exchange Act Section 15(d). In addition, the work includes changes to the Codification of Financial Reporting Policies at sections 501.03.a.i. (liquidity and capital resources disclosure) and 501.15 (climate change-related disclosure). Finally, the new edition features the SEC staff's Compliance and Disclosure Interpretations for non-GAAP financial measures (Regulation G).

November 2010

TABLE OF CONTENTS

Electronic Filing and the EDGAR System: A Regulatory Overview

➤➤➤ *Reproduced below is a document that the SEC posted on its website (www.sec.gov/info/edgar/ regoverview.htm) as a general introduction to the Commission's EDGAR filing system.*

An outline of the SEC's EDGAR rules as applied to filings processed by the Divisions of Corporation Finance and Investment Management

Updated by:

- Mauri L. Osheroff, Associate Director (Regulatory Policy), Division of Corporation Finance
- Mark W. Green, Senior Special Counsel (Regulatory Policy), Division of Corporation Finance
- Ruth Armfield Sanders, Senior Special Counsel (Legal and Disclosure), Division of Investment Management

October 3, 2006

The Securities and Exchange Commission disclaims responsibility for any private publication or statement of any of its employees. This outline was prepared by members of the staff of the Divisions of Corporation Finance and Investment Management and does not necessarily represent the views of the Commission, the Commissioners, or other members of the staff.

This outline was prepared by employees of the Securities and Exchange Commission as an aid to those who are subject to mandated electronic filing. The outline is available to the public at large and may be reproduced without restriction or charge by any party at any time.

Electronic Filing and the EDGAR System: A Regulatory Overview

In early 1993, the Commission began to mandate electronic filings through its Electronic Data Gathering, Analysis, and Retrieval system, EDGAR. This system is intended to benefit electronic filers, enhance the speed and efficiency of SEC processing, and make corporate and financial information available to investors, the financial community and others in a matter of minutes. Electronic dissemination generates more informed investor participation and more informed securities markets.

In 2006, the Commission awarded contracts to:

- Keane Federal Systems, Inc. to modernize and maintain the EDGAR database (the new system will use interactive data technologies such as XBRL (eXtensible Business Reporting Language) and XML (eXtensible Markup Language) to enable filers to tag key facts to create machine-readable documents from which computers can extract quickly desired data);
- XBRL US, Inc. to complete the writing of XBRL "taxonomies" or computer labels used to tag data so that companies in all industries can file their financial reports in XBRL; and both
- Rivet Software Inc. and Wall Street on Demand to provide interactive investor tools on the Commission's website to enable investors to view and analyze companies' financial statements that are filed in XBRL.

A. Chronology of EDGAR Releases

The Commission began developing an electronic disclosure system in 1983. By the fall of 1984, a pilot system was opened for volunteers filing with both the Division of Corporation Finance and the Division of Investment Management. On July 15, 1992, the operational EDGAR system was made available to those filers, still on a voluntary basis.

On February 23, 1993, the Commission issued four releases adopting rules, on an interim basis, that required filers to file electronically, by direct transmission, diskette, or magnetic tape, most documents processed by the Divisions of Corporation Finance and Investment Management. The following releases also contained phase-in schedules to bring filers onto the EDGAR system, a process that began on April 26, 1993:

- Release No. 33-6977 (explaining the EDGAR system generally and setting forth rules and procedures that apply to electronic submissions processed by the Division of Corporation Finance and in some cases, to those processed by the Division of Investment Management)
- Release No. IC-19284 (adopting rules specific to electronic submissions made by investment companies under the Investment Company Act of 1940 and institutional investment managers under Section 13(f) of the Exchange Act)
- Release No. 35-25746 (adopting rules specific to electronic submissions made by public utility holding companies and their subsidiaries under the Public Utility Holding Company Act of 1935 which was repealed as of early 2006)

- Release No. 33-6980 (relating to the payment of filing fees, by both paper and electronic filers, to the Commission's lockbox depository at Mellon Bank in Pittsburgh, Pennsylvania, under Rule 3a of the Rules Relating to Informal and Other Procedures).

After completing the phase-in of a statutorily mandated significant test group in December 1993, the Commission refrained from further phase-in of EDGAR filers while the staff evaluated EDGAR's performance during a six-month test period, which ran from January 1, 1994 to June 30, 1994. The evaluation resulted in a positive assessment of the EDGAR system, based on data gathered from within the Commission as well as from the filers and other members of the public. Consequently, the staff recommended that the Commission proceed with full implementation of mandated electronic filing.

Since that time, the Commission has issued a number of releases updating and making technical and other changes to the EDGAR filing requirements:

- On December 19, 1994, the Commission issued Release No. 33-7122, which made the EDGAR interim rules final and applicable to all domestic registrants and third parties filing with respect to those registrants. Phase-in recommenced on January 30, 1995 and proceeded as set forth in a revised phase-in schedule. The Commission also adopted minor amendments to the electronic filing rules to reflect the staff's experience with the rules since mandated filing began in 1993.

- On July 1, 1997, the Commission adopted a number of minor and technical amendments to its rules governing electronic filing, including the elimination of the transition rules applicable to the phase-in period. See Release No. 33-7427.

- On October 24, 1997, the Commission adopted Rule 14 of Regulation S-T. See Release No. 33-7472 (effective January 1, 1998). This rule provides that the Commission will not accept in paper format filings required to be submitted electronically, absent a hardship exemption.

- On January 12, 1999, the Commission adopted a rule requiring Form 13F reports to be filed in electronic format. See Release No. 34-40934. Filers must submit Forms 13F electronically, unless a hardship exemption is available.

- On April 15, 1999, the Commission adopted a rule requiring Form N-8F and applications for deregistration under Investment Company Act Rule 0-2 to be filed in electronic format. See Release No. IC-23786.

- On May 17, 1999, the Commission issued Release No. 33-7684 adopting new rules and amendments to existing rules and forms in connection with the first stage of EDGAR modernization. On June 28, 1999, the Commission began accepting live filings submitted to EDGAR in HyperText Markup Language (HTML) as well as documents submitted in American Standard Code for Information Interchange (ASCII) format. The Commission gave filers the option of accompanying their required filings with unofficial copies in Portable Document Format (PDF).

- On April 24, 2000, the Commission issued Release No. 33-7855 adopting amendments to existing rules and forms to reflect changes in filing requirements resulting from the implementation of the next stage of EDGAR modernization. The rules provided for use of the Internet as a means of filing, acceptance of HTML documents with graphic and image files, and expanded use of hyperlinks. These features became available on the system on May 30, 2000. The release also eliminated the Financial Data Schedule requirement, effective January 1, 2001, and removed diskettes as an available means of transmitting filings to the EDGAR system, effective July 10, 2000.

- On May 14, 2002, the Commission issued Release No. 33-8099 adopting rules requiring foreign issuers to make their Commission filings via EDGAR. The rules also eliminate the requirement that any first-time EDGAR filer, domestic or foreign, submit a paper copy of its electronic filing to the Commission. The rules became effective November 4, 2002, except that the rules eliminating the paper filing requirement were effective on May 24, 2002.

- On May 7, 2003, the Commission issued Release No. 33-8230 adopting rules requiring the electronic filing of beneficial ownership reports on Forms 3, 4 and 5 filed by officers, directors and principal security holders (insiders) under Section 16(a) of the Exchange Act, and requiring issuers with corporate websites to post these reports. The release also removed magnetic cartridges as an available means of transmitting filings to the EDGAR system. The changes became effective June 30, 2003.

- On April 21, 2004, the Commission issued Release No. 33-8410 adopting rule and form amendments requiring the electronic filing of applications on Form ID for access codes to file on EDGAR. The changes became effective April 26, 2004.

- On February 3, 2005, the Commission issued Release No. 33-8529 adopting rule amendments to enable registrants to participate in its interactive data initiative by submitting voluntarily supplemental tagged financial information using the XBRL format as exhibits to specified EDGAR filings under the Exchange Act and the Investment Company Act. Registrants choosing to participate in the voluntary program also continue to file their financial information in HTML or ASCII format, as currently required. The changes became effective March 16, 2005.

- On July 18, 2005, the Commission issued Release No. 33-8590 adopting rule amendments that require certain open-end management investment companies and insurance company separate accounts to identify in their EDGAR submissions information relating to their series and classes (or contracts, in the case of separate accounts). These provisions became effective February 6, 2006. The amendments also made filings under Section 17(g) of the Investment Company Act and sales literature filed by non-NASD members with the Commission under Section 24(b) mandatory electronic filings effective June 12, 2006. The amendments also made several minor and technical amendments, that became effective September 19, 2005.

B. EDGAR Rules

Most of the EDGAR rules apply to all electronic filers, whether the filings are processed by the Division of Corporation Finance or the Division of Investment Management. The most significant differences in the rules applicable to filings made with respect to investment companies and institutional investment managers relate to the treatment of exhibits and annual reports to security holders. The following discussion addresses the rules as applicable to all filers; where applicable, differences in treatment are noted.

1. Regulation S-T and EDGAR Filer Manual

The cornerstone of the EDGAR rules is Regulation S-T, a separate regulation containing rules prescribing requirements for filing electronically and the procedures for making such filings. Regulation S-T supersedes a number of the procedural requirements set forth in the Commission's rules and forms, for example, requirements relating to paper size and number of copies. The Commission amended its rules and forms as necessary to make references to specific electronic filing provisions. Electronic filers that obtain an exemption from the electronic filing provisions of Regulation S-T continue to file in paper in accordance with the paper filing requirements. In addition, as discussed below, the rules permit or require certain filings to be submitted in paper.

Instructions for electronic filing, including technical formatting requirements, are set forth in the EDGAR Filer Manual. See Rule 301 of Regulation S-T. The EDGAR Filer Manual and EDGARLink are available on the EDGAR Database section of the SEC's website at *http://www.sec.gov/info/edgar.shtml*.

a. Filing Medium and Filing Format

The EDGAR system accepts electronic submissions by direct transmission via the Internet, dial-up lines or leased lines. Most filers currently make EDGAR submissions via the Internet by linking to the EDGARFILING or EDGAR On-Line websites. A few filers use a dial-up modem connection to EDGAR and some EDGAR filing agents have leased lines that connect directly to the EDGAR system.

On May 5, 2003, a new on-line filing system was implemented as the method for insiders to file electronically their Forms 3, 4 and 5. As a result, EDGARLink (the filer assistance software that is provided to filers filing on EDGAR) support is no longer available for these forms. Persons need the same codes as are required to transmit using EDGARLink, however, to file on the new system. Each insider filing a Form 3, 4 or 5 needs a Central Index Key (CIK) and CIK Confirmation Code (CCC) for validation. This is true whether the insider is filing individually or as a joint filer. Each insider needs and should request only one set of codes even if he or she is an insider of more than one issuer. Persons can acquire the codes only by submitting a Form ID. The Commission's website posts frequently asked questions regarding the system at *http://www.sec.gov/divisions/corpfin/sec16faq.htm*.

On April 26, 2004, a new on-line filing system accessed through the EDGAR Filer Management website was implemented as the method for applicants to file their applications on Form ID for access codes to file on EDGAR. As before the new system began, the Commission assigns the following access codes in response to a Form ID:

- Central Index Key (CIK) — The CIK uniquely identifies each filer, filing agent, and training agent. An applicant cannot change this code. The CIK is a public number.

- CIK Confirmation Code (CCC) — The applicant will use the CCC in the header of the applicant's filings in conjunction with the applicant's CIK to ensure that the applicant authorized the filing.

- Password (PW) — The PW allows the applicant to log onto the EDGAR system, submit filings, and change the applicant's CCC.

- Password Modification Authorization Code (PMAC) — The PMAC allows the applicant to change the applicant's password.

In addition, modifications to EDGAR in connection with establishing the new system require not only applicants who file Form ID, but also users who log onto EDGAR for filing for the first time on or after April 26, 2004, to choose a passphrase. A passphrase enables a user to change access codes other than a CIK and remains valid unless and until the user changes it.

b. Use of HTML

The EDGAR system accepts both ASCII and HTML documents as official filings. The Commission is not now requiring the use of HTML. However, the Commission expects to require HTML for most filings in the future, so it encourages filers to use it and gain experience with this format if they do not have it already. If HTML is used, each EDGAR document may consist of no more than one HTML file.

The EDGAR system imposes certain limitations on HTML documents, as discussed below. Filers may not submit Form N-SAR and Form 13F as HTML documents. These documents have standard formats and tagging designed for presentation in ASCII, and their current format facilitates their downloading and use in other computer applications. However, filers may submit exhibits to Form N-SAR in HTML. See Rule 105 of Regulation S-T.

c. Use of PDF

In addition to permitting the use of HTML in filings, the Commission permits filers to submit a single unofficial PDF copy of each electronic document other than a Form 3, 4, 5 or ID. See Rule 104 of Regulation S-T. Filers may *not* use PDF documents instead of HTML or ASCII documents to meet filing requirements. Unofficial PDF copies of filings will be disseminated publicly. The unofficial PDF copy is optional, but if a filer submits an unofficial PDF copy of a document, that PDF document must be the same as the official document (the HTML or ASCII document of which it is a copy) in all respects except for the formatting and inclusion of graphics (instead of the narrative and/or tabular description of the graphics). The text of the two documents must be identical. Further, filers may not make a submission consisting solely of PDF documents; filers must include unofficial PDF copies only in submissions containing official documents in HTML or ASCII format.

The substantively equivalent requirement does not apply to non-public correspondence submissions. Filers may submit unofficial PDF copies of correspondence documents that differ from the contents of the associated ASCII or HTML correspondence documents. This enables filers to submit redlined copies of official filings in unofficial PDF copies of EDGAR correspondence documents. If a filer submits an unofficial PDF copy of a correspondence document that differs from the text of the ASCII or HTML document, the text of the ASCII or HTML correspondence document should identify and briefly describe the contents of the unofficial PDF copy.

d. Use of XBRL

The Commission generally permits registrants that file financial information in ASCII or HTML format to participate in its interactive data initiative by submitting that information voluntarily as supplemental tagged financial information in XBRL format as exhibits to specified EDGAR filings under the Exchange Act and the Investment Company Act. The XBRL submission must contain specified mandatory content (which may be accompanied by specified optional content) and appear in a prescribed format.

In early 2006, the Commission staff began to offer expedited processing of registration statements or annual reports that may be selected for review to companies that volunteer to participate in a new interactive data test group. Participants will furnish financial data contained in their periodic reports in XBRL format for at least one year and provide feedback on their experiences including the costs and benefits associated with reporting in the interactive data format.

Because the voluntary XBRL program is experimental, contains other appropriate safeguards, and should not unnecessarily deter volunteers from participating, the related rules provide limited protections from liability under the federal securities laws.

Also in 2006, the Commission awarded contracts to facilitate filer and investor use on EDGAR of interactive data technologies such as XBRL.

e. Limitation on Hypertext Links

Filers who choose to use HTML may include hyperlinks between sections of the same HTML document. They also may include hyperlinks to other documents within the same filing (*i.e.*, exhibits) or to other official filings in the EDGAR database on our public website at *http://www.sec.gov/index.htm*. For example, filers may link from within a document to previously filed documents that are incorporated by reference. The EDGAR system permits links to specific filings only, not to specific information within these documents. Links outside the EDGAR database, including links to websites, are prohibited.

Hyperlinks may not be used as a substitute for providing information required in the filed document when incorporation by reference is not available. For example, a Form S-1 for which incorporation by reference is unavailable may contain a hyperlink to the filer's Form 10-K, but the filer still must provide all required business and financial information in the Form S-1.

If incorporation by reference is available, the filer must comply with all related requirements even if the filer chooses to use hyperlinks. For example, a Form S-3 may contain a hyperlink to the previously filed Exchange Act reports incorporated by reference, but the Form S-3 still must make the required statements about which documents are incorporated by reference.

Linking material does not make it part of the official filing for determining compliance with reporting obligations. Such material, however, is subject to the civil liability and anti-fraud provisions of the federal securities laws, whether or not the hyperlink is permitted by the Commission's rules. Moreover, if a company hyperlinks to a hyperlink, which, in turn, links to another hyperlink, the company will be treated as making all the hyperlinked material its own. Also, if a hyperlinked document is corrected or updated by means of a new filing, the document containing the hyperlink also may have to be amended.

f. HTML Standard; Permissible Tags

The Commission has adopted a specific HTML standard for HTML documents submitted on the EDGAR system. Because different Internet browsers used by filers or the public may display the information presented in an HTML document in a different fashion, a document viewed through one browser may have a different appearance and layout from the same filing viewed through a different browser. To maximize the likelihood of consistent document appearance across different browsers, and eliminate active content, the rules specify a set of HTML tags permissible in HTML documents. The tag list is included in the EDGAR Filer Manual. In general, the EDGAR system will suspend submissions that contain tags that are not permitted. The EDGAR system will accept a subset of HTML 3.2/4.0 tags.

EDGAR submissions may not contain tags used to include executable code, in official submissions or unofficial submissions of PDF copies or XBRL-related documents (see Rule 106 of Regulation S-T). In addition, filers may not include tables within tables (nested tables) in their HTML documents. This is because users of EDGAR information may find it difficult to locate and use information in documents with nested tables.

2. Mandated, Excluded and Permitted Electronic Submissions

Rules 100 and 101 of Regulation S-T require filers, with certain exceptions, to submit electronically all documents, including filings, correspondence, and supplemental information, submitted by or relating to registrants under the Securities Act, the Exchange Act, the Trust Indenture Act, and the Investment Company Act.

Except as noted below, the electronic filing requirement also applies to third party filings, whether the filings are made by business entities or individuals. For example, the following kinds of filings must be made on EDGAR, absent a hardship exemption: proxy materials (whether or not filed by the company), tender offer materials, Forms 13F, and Schedules 13D/G. Effective June 30, 2003, filers are required to submit their Forms 3, 4 and 5 electronically. See Release No. 33-8230 (May 7, 2003). Before then, electronic filing of these forms was optional.

The Commission will not accept in paper format filings required to be submitted electronically, absent a hardship exemption. (See Rule 14 of Regulation S-T.) If the staff inadvertently accepts a paper filing not permitted by the EDGAR rules, the filer is subject to certain penalties: ineligibility to use Securities Act forms incorporating by reference Exchange Act reports; inability to incorporate the paper filing by reference (Rule 303 of Regulation S-T); and tolling of certain tender offer dates.

Some documents may not be filed on EDGAR. Among the documents that are excluded are: confidential treatment applications; interpretive, no-action and exemptive requests; filings pertaining to Regulation A and most other offerings exempt from Securities Act registration; shareholder proposal filings; and filings under Section 8(f) of the Investment Company Act (except Forms N-8F and applications for deregistration filed under Investment Company Act Rule 0-2).

Electronic filers should exercise special care when submitting documents or parts of documents that are the subject of a confidential treatment request, including preliminary proxy materials relating to business combinations to which the Commission may give confidential treatment if marked appropriately for such treatment under the proxy rules. Filers must submit these documents in paper or they will become available to the public immediately upon acceptance.

The Commission permits, but does not require, Corporation Finance filers to submit several types of documents electronically. Examples include: the "glossy" annual report to security holders furnished to the Commission for its information under the proxy rules (see no. 9, below, for the treatment of an annual report to security holders that is a part of a filing); the Notice of Exempt Solicitation, the submission that indicates reliance by certain security holders on the Exchange Act Rule 14a-2(b) exemption from proxy material filing requirements under the revised proxy rules; and Form 11-K, the report for employee benefit plans. Another example is Form 144, the notice of proposed sale of securities under Rule 144 under the Securities Act. See Release No. 33-7241 (November 13, 1995). Filers may submit Forms 144 electronically only if the issuer of the securities is a public company. The Commission has solicited comment on the concept of requiring more filings to be made electronically, such as Form 144 and exemptive application filings made by investment companies. See Release No. 33-7855 (April 24, 2000).

Effective April 26, 2004, filers are required to submit their Forms ID electronically. See Release No. 33-8410 (April 21, 2004). Before then, filers were required to submit Forms ID in paper.

Investment companies must file their Forms N-8F (and applications for deregistration under Investment Company Act Rule 0-2) electronically. See Release No. IC-23786 (April 15, 1999).

Effective February 6, 2006, filers who filed their latest registration statements or amendments on Form N-1A, N-3, N-4 or N-6 (S/C Funds) must, for EDGAR submissions specified in the EDGAR Filer Manual, include in the EDGAR template for the specified submissions all series and/or class (or contract) identifiers of each series and/or class (or contract) on behalf of which the filing is made. For new series and/or classes (contracts), filers must enter the respective names in the EDGAR submission template of the filing by which they are substantively added to generate the associated identifiers, which will appear on the acceptance message for the filing.

S/C Funds must use the series and class page on the EDGARFILING website (*https://www.edgarfiling.sec.gov/*) to update information for their series and classes (contracts) and to add ticker symbols. Effective February 6, 2006:

- Filings that require series and class (contract) identifiers will be suspended if they do not include identifiers or do not include the correct identifiers for that registrant (CIK); and

- Series and class (contract) identifiers are part of the official filing: a filing made under an incorrect identifier is a filing for the wrong series and/or class (contract), *i.e.*, it is a filing on behalf of the series and/or class (contract) for which an identifier is used and a filing for which an identifier is not included is not a filing for the series and class (contract) for which an identifier is omitted.

S/C Funds are required by Rule 313 of Regulation S-T to keep current their information concerning their existing and new series and/or classes (or contracts, in the case of separate accounts), including series and/or class (or contract) name and ticker symbol, if any; if a class (or contract) does not have but later obtains a ticker symbol, the company must update the information for the class (or contract) to add the ticker symbol.

S/C Funds are also required by Rule 313 to mark as inactive for EDGAR purposes any series and/or class (or contract, in the case of separate accounts) that are no longer offered, go out of existence, or deregister after the last filing for that series and/or class (or contract, in the case of separate accounts) is made, but the registrant must not mark as inactive the last remaining series unless the registrant deregisters.

Effective June 12, 2006, investment companies must submit electronically fidelity bonds under Section 17(g) and sales literature filed with the Commission under Section 24(b). See Release No. 33-8590 (July 18, 2005). Filers should be aware that Rule 304(e) prohibits filers from using graphic or image material to submit information, such as text or tables, that users must be able to search and/or download into spreadsheet form (for example, financial statements). Instead, filers must submit such information as text in an ASCII document, or as text or an HTML table in an HTML document. See Section 8 below.

3. Hours of Operation/Date of Filing

Rule 12 of Regulation S-T provides that electronic filings may be submitted by direct transmission via the Internet, dial-up lines or leased lines to the Commission each business day from 8:00 a.m. to 10:00 p.m. Eastern time. Currently, however, filings may be submitted electronically as early as 6 a.m. Rule 13(a) of Regulation S-T provides that any direct transmission filing that commences after 5:30 p.m. will be dated the following business day. The exceptions to this rule are that registration statements filed to increase the number of shares, as provided by Securities Act Rule 462(b), and, effective June 30, 2003, Forms 3, 4 and 5, receive the same day's filing date if transmitted by 10:00 p.m. See Rule 13(a) of Regulation S-T and Release Nos. 33-7168 (May 11, 1995) and 33-8230 (May 7, 2003), respectively. Any direct transmission filing commencing before 5:30 p.m., if accepted, will receive that day's filing date.

4. Exhibits

Rule 102 of Regulation S-T provides that filers are not required to refile in electronic format exhibits previously filed in paper when incorporated by reference into an electronic filing. After becoming subject to mandated electronic filing, a filer must file any new exhibits electronically, absent a hardship exemption. Where an electronic amendment is filed to an exhibit previously filed in paper, the filer must submit electronically only the amendment; the filer will not have to refile electronically the previously filed paper exhibit to which the amendment relates, except for the articles of incorporation, by-laws, and investment advisory contract of the registrant, which must be restated in their entirety upon amendment.

The rules for investment companies differ. In general, filers must submit all investment company exhibits, including exhibits to Form N-SAR, electronically. In addition, investment companies may incorporate by reference only to documents filed electronically. See Rule 102(e) of Regulation S-T.

5. Hardship Exemptions/Adjustment of the Filing Date

Two hardship exemptions are available to permit a filing or other submission to be made in paper rather than electronic format. First, Rule 201 of Regulation S-T provides a temporary hardship exemption for electronic filers, generally for unanticipated technical difficulties in submitting an electronic document. The exemption may be appropriate, for example, for a particular document that a filer is unable to file electronically because of problems with the filer's computer equipment that had been used previously to transmit either test or required electronic filings successfully. Under that exemption, the filer may make the filing in paper (with a legend on the cover page identifying it as being submitted under Rule 201) and then follow it with a confirming electronic copy within six business days so that the electronic database will be complete. An electronic filer may take advantage of the exemption simply by filing the subject document in paper under cover of Form TH, Notification of Reliance on Temporary Hardship Exemption. No Commission staff involvement is required. If the filing is an exhibit only, then filers must submit the documents under cover of both Form TH and Form SE. The sanctions for violating electronic filing requirements mentioned above also apply where a filer is required to submit a confirming electronic copy of a document filed in paper under a temporary hardship exemption but fails to do so. A temporary hardship exemption is not available for Forms 3, 4, 5 or ID.

Second, under Rule 202 of Regulation S-T, a continuing hardship exemption is available to electronic filers under limited circumstances for exhibits or a filing or group of filings. For example, this exemption might be appropriate for an exhibit consisting of another government agency's voluminous form that a filer cannot convert into electronic format without causing the filer undue hardship. Unlike the temporary hardship exemption, the staff must act upon a written application for a continuing hardship exemption. If the staff grants the exemption, the filer may make the submission in paper. A continuing hardship exemption is not available for Forms ID.

In most cases, a filer need not follow up a paper filing under a continuing hardship exemption with an electronic copy. However, under some circumstances, the staff believes that it would be in the public interest for the electronic database to contain the document in question. Rule 202(d) allows the grant of a continuing hardship exemption for a limited time only. When the time is up, the filer must submit a confirming electronic copy.

A paper filing submitted under a continuing hardship exemption must include a legend on the cover page of the document identifying it as being submitted in paper under Rule 202 of Regulation S-T. If the filing is an exhibit only, then filers must submit the document under both Form TH and Form SE. Corporation Finance filers should direct inquiries concerning continuing hardship exemptions to the Office of EDGAR and Information Analysis in the Division of Corporation Finance at (202) 551-3610. Investment company filers should direct their inquiries to the EDGAR contact in the Division of Investment Management at (202) 551-6989.

In addition to the two hardship exemptions, Rule 13 of Regulation S-T permits an electronic filer to request an adjustment of the filing date of an electronic document when the filer encounters technical problems beyond its control that prevent electronic submission by the due date specified by the applicable form or rule. Filers should direct requests for filing date adjustments to the contacts listed in the previous paragraph.

6. Signatures

Rule 302 of Regulation S-T provides that required signatures in electronic filings must be submitted in typed form. Required signatures must be typed to ensure legibility of these signatures. Electronic filers must retain a manually signed signature page or other document authenticating, acknowledging or otherwise adopting the signatures that appear in typed form within an electronic filing. Filers must make this document available to the Commission or its staff upon request for a period of five years. Each signatory to the filing must execute the manually signed authentication document before or at the time the filing is made.

Signatures in HTML documents that are not required by statute or regulation may appear as script. The same is true of signatures in unofficial PDF copies, which are not required signatures.

Following a recommendation of the Task Force on Disclosure Simplification, in May 1996 the Commission changed its rules governing signatures to allow typed signatures on all filed documents, with limited exceptions, both paper and electronic. Manually signed signature authentication documents are required whenever typed signatures are filed with the Commission.

7. Safe Harbor

Rule 103 of Regulation S-T provides a safe harbor against liability for errors in, or omissions from, documents filed electronically that result solely from electronic transmission errors beyond the control of the electronic filer. The safe harbor is available where the electronic filer takes corrective action as soon as reasonably practicable after becoming aware of the error or omission.

8. Graphic, Image, Audio, and Video Material

EDGAR does not accommodate electronic submission of graphic, image, audio, or video material in ASCII filings. EDGAR does, however, accommodate graphic and image material, but not audio or video material, in

HTML documents. Rule 304 of Regulation S-T governs the treatment of graphic, image, audio, and video information that is used in the version of the document disseminated to investors but omitted from the electronic filing. This rule requires that fair and accurate descriptions or transcripts of omitted material be included either at the point in the text where the omission occurs or in an appendix to the electronic filing. A note to Rule 304(a) provides that, if the omitted material includes data, filers must include a tabular representation or other appropriate representation of that data in the electronically filed version of the document. Rule 304 applies only to official filings, not to unofficial PDF copies, which may contain graphic and image material (but not animated graphics, audio or video material).

The graphic, image, audio, and video material in the version of the document distributed to investors is deemed part of the filing and is subject to the liability and antifraud provisions of the federal securities laws. Filers do not need to describe immaterial differences between the distributed and electronically filed versions of a document, such as type size or font, pagination or corporate logos. A safe harbor provides that, to the extent such descriptions or transcripts represent a good faith effort to fairly and accurately describe omitted material, they will not be subject to the civil liability and antifraud provisions of the federal securities laws.

The filer must retain any document containing graphic, image, audio, or video material that is omitted from an electronic filing for five years after the filing date of the document or the date appearing on the document, whichever is later. Filers must make such documents available to the Commission staff upon request.

Rule 304(d) of Regulation S-T gives special treatment to the performance line graph required by Regulation S-K (Release No. 33-8732A, August 29, 2006) moves the performance line graph requirement from Item 402(l) to Item 201(e) of Regulation S-K) and the line graph required by Item 22(b)(7)(ii) of Form N-1A for investment companies. ASCII filers must present the numerical data from which these graphs are created in the body of the electronic document in tabular or chart form. Of course, the paper version of the document disseminated to security holders must include the prescribed line graph. See Release No. 33-7427 (July 1, 1997).

Although the EDGAR system *permits* graphic or image material in HTML documents, filers are not *required* to submit graphics in HTML documents, except in the limited instances when our rules require graphics. Under Rule 304(e), filers submitting HTML documents must use graphics for the performance graph required by Regulation S-K (Release No. 33-8732A (August 29, 2006) moves the performance line graph requirement from Item 402(l) to Item 201(e) of Regulation S-K) and the line graph required by Item 22(b)(7)(ii) of Form N-1A.

Rule 304(e) prohibits filers from using graphic or image material to submit information, such as text or tables, that users must be able to search and/or download into spreadsheet form (for example, financial statements). Instead, filers must submit such information as text in an ASCII document, or as text or an HTML table in an HTML document.

The EDGAR system does not support animated graphics (*e.g.*, files with moving corporate logos or other animation), either in any official document or any unofficial PDF copy or XBRL-related document.

Please note that filers should not place non-public information in graphic files associated with non-public documents within a public submission, since these graphic files are disseminated, even if the associated HTML or unofficial PDF document is non-public and not disseminated.

9. Annual Reports to Security Holders and Certain Proxy Materials

The treatment of annual reports differs for Corporation Finance and investment company filers.

Annual reports to security holders ("glossy" reports) for Corporation Finance filers frequently contain extensive graphic information that is difficult to prepare in electronic format. Accordingly, the rules provide special treatment for these documents. As discussed above, Rule 101 of Regulation S-T provides that filers may furnish glossy reports for the Commission's information as required by the proxy and information statement rules (*e.g.*, Exchange Act Rule 14a-3(c)) in either paper or electronic format. In contrast, Rule 303 of Regulation S-T states that if the glossy report is incorporated by reference into any filing — for example, a Form 10-K — filers must file the portions incorporated by reference in electronic format as an exhibit. The same is true for a quarterly report to security holders incorporated by reference into a filing.

Investment company filers are required to file all annual and semi-annual reports to security holders electronically.

Form 10-K and Form 10-KSB both require issuers reporting under Section 15(d) of the Exchange Act to furnish to the Commission for its information any annual report to security holders covering the registrant's last fiscal year and every proxy statement, form of proxy or other proxy soliciting material sent to more than ten of the registrant's security holders with respect to any annual or other meeting of security holders. When these issuers submit this information with their Exchange Act annual reports, it is not deemed filed with the Commission unless it is incorporated by reference into the report itself. Filers should submit these proxy materials electronically. Consistent with the requirements to furnish annual reports to security holders under the proxy rules, registrants have the option to submit their annual report to security holders under these annual reporting provisions either in paper or in electronic format.

10. Schedules 13D and 13G

As noted above, Rules 100 and 101 of Regulation S-T require third party filers to transmit their Schedules 13D and 13G via EDGAR. In addition, Rule 101 of Regulation S-T provides that, where these schedules originally were filed in paper, the first electronic amendment must restate the entire text of the schedule, as amended. Where the amendment is made to report a transaction that would allow the filer to exit the reporting system, the filer need only file the amendment. Consistent with the general treatment of exhibits filed electronically, if any exhibit to a Schedule 13D or 13G is amended, the filer need only file the text of the amendment.

Filers filing Schedules 13D and 13G with respect to foreign private issuers should include in the EDGAR submission header all zeroes (*i.e.*, 00-0000000) for the IRS tax identification number. See the note to paragraph (a)(1)(iii) of Rule 101 of Regulation S-T.

11. Foreign Issuers

On May 14, 2002, the Commission issued Release No. 33-8099 to require foreign private issuers and foreign governments to make their filings via EDGAR. The rules became effective on November 4, 2002. The rules require the electronic filing of:

- Foreign private issuers' Securities Act registration statements and Exchange Act registration statements and reports;

- Foreign governments' Securities Act registration statements and Exchange Act registration statements and reports;

- Multijurisdictional Disclosure System (MJDS) forms filed by Canadian issuers;

- Statements of beneficial ownership on Schedules 13D and 13G and tender offer schedules that pertain to the securities of a foreign issuer, whether filed by a foreign or domestic person;

- Form CB, the form used for cross-border rights offers, exchange offers and business combinations that are exempt from the tender offer rules or Securities Act registration, if the filer is an Exchange Act reporting company;

- Form 6-K reports, except as noted below; and

- Most Trust Indenture Act forms.

The amendments also:

- Permit, but do not require, the electronic filing of Forms 6-K used to submit a company's "glossy" annual report to security holders, or used to provide information that has not been furnished to the press or the company's security holders and does not contain new material information;

- Generally require all filings to be in the English language, but permit specified information in foreign language exhibits to be summarized in English instead of fully translated, and provide guidance regarding what constitutes an adequate summary;

- Permit, but do not require, supranational entities such as the World Bank to file their reports electronically; and

- Continue to require documents submitted under Exchange Act Rule 12g3-2(b) to be in paper only.

12. Modular Submissions/Segmented Filings

The EDGAR system and Rule 501 of Regulation S-T are designed to facilitate electronic filing by allowing filers to submit in advance of an intended filing information intended to become part of that filed document by its subsequent inclusion in the electronic filing. A modular submission feature allows a filer to submit information, such as financial statements, to a non-public EDGAR database for inclusion in as many filings as the filer designates, so long as the information remains current.

A similar feature is segmented filing, in which a filer may submit various segments of a document to be filed with the Commission to the EDGAR non-public data storage area up to six business days in advance of the anticipated filing date. For example, filers may submit voluminous exhibits in advance of a filing. On the anticipated filing date, the electronic filer may submit a master segment instructing EDGAR to assemble the desired filing from the previously submitted segments and file it. Filers may use segments only once.

Regulation S-T provides that neither modular submissions nor segments will be deemed "filed" or subject to liability under the federal securities laws until the filer includes the information in an electronic filing.

13. EDGAR Forms

There are three forms used in connection with EDGAR filings. (A fourth, Form ET, was rescinded effective June 30, 2003.)

- Form ID is used to request access codes to file on EDGAR. Effective April 26, 2004, this form must be filed electronically through a new on-line system accessed through the EDGAR Filer Management website. For verification purposes, the requestor also must file in paper by fax within two business days before or after filing Form ID a notarized document, manually signed by the requestor over its typed signature, that includes the information contained in the Form ID filed or to be filed and confirms the authenticity of the Form ID.

- Electronic filers must use Form SE as a paper cover sheet attached to any paper format exhibit, including exhibits filed under a temporary or continuing hardship exemption.

- Filers use Form TH as a paper cover sheet accompanying documents filed in paper under a temporary hardship exemption, as described in Section 5 above. If the subject of a temporary hardship exemption is an exhibit only, a filer must file the exhibit and the Form TH under cover of Form SE. (See Release No. 33-8590 (July 18, 2005).)

14. Filing Fees; Lockbox

Rule 3a of the Commission's rules governing Informal and Other Procedures requires all electronic filers to pay fees via the lockbox at the U.S. Treasury designated lockbox depository maintained by the Commission at the Mellon Bank in Pittsburgh, Pennsylvania. Filers may pay by direct wire transfer or by mailing or delivering a check or cash to the lockbox. Rule 13(c) of Regulation S-T requires electronic filers to pay filing fees in accordance with the lockbox procedures, including those pertaining to documents filed in paper under a hardship exemption. Thus, persons subject to electronic filing must tender all fees to the lockbox at Mellon Bank — not to the Commission's filing desk — even when physically filing a paper document at the Commission's filing desk.

The Commission will deem a Securities Act registration statement (including a Securities Act filing by an investment company) filed as of its date of receipt, provided that all of the conditions of acceptance are satisfied, including verification of any fee payment required. If payment is not confirmed until the day following receipt by the Commission, the Commission will assign the filing a filing date as of the date of confirmation of payment, not the date of receipt. For information relating to fee confirmation with respect to registration statements filed for the purpose of increasing the number of shares, as provided under Securities Act Rule 462(b), see Release No. 33-7168 (May 11, 1995). If the Commission staff cannot verify payment, EDGAR will place the filing in a suspense file for up to six business days, and the staff will so notify the filer. Since EDGAR verifies fee payments made via wire transfer on a near real-time basis (every 15 minutes), while it verifies those made by check on a daily basis, a filer may wish to pay fees with respect to a time-sensitive Securities Act registration statement by wire transfer to expedite acceptance processing.

Filers should direct questions concerning fee payment to Filer Support at (202) 551-8900.

15. Other Electronic Document Issues

The EDGAR rules apply only to filings made with the Commission; the rules do not affect the obligation of filers to deliver to security holders or potential investors documents such as prospectuses, tender offer materials and proxy or information statements. As the ability to send and receive information in electronic form has become more prevalent, issuers and other market participants have requested interpretive guidance regarding the electronic delivery of these documents. Currently, many issuers provide information through electronic means, primarily through the Internet.

- On October 6, 1995, the Commission issued an interpretive release (1995 Interpretive Release) more fully addressing electronic delivery issues. See Release No. 33-7233. The 1995 Interpretive Release is based on the determination that information distributed through electronic means may be viewed as satisfying the delivery or transmission requirements of the federal securities laws if such distribution results in the delivery to the intended recipients of substantially equivalent information as these recipients would have had if the information were delivered to them in paper form. The use of electronic media should be at least an equal alternative to the use of paper delivery. However, until such time as electronic media becomes more universally accessible and accepted, paper delivery of information will continue to be available. The release provides guidance regarding the manner in which filers may achieve electronic delivery and includes many illustrative examples.

- To facilitate electronic delivery, the Commission adopted rule changes to codify some of the interpretations regarding Commission rules that are premised on the distribution of paper documents. See Release No. 33-7289 (May 9, 1996). The Commission has revised the rules to make it clear that filers may modify paper-based requirements relating to font size, bold-face type, red ink, graphics, and mailing as appropriate for documents delivered in electronic format. These rule changes are not intended to affect any substantive requirement. On the same date, the Commission issued an interpretive release primarily addressing issues relating to the use of electronic media by broker-dealers, transfer agents and investment advisers for delivery of information, but also expanding on some issues addressed in the 1995 Interpretive Release. See Release No. 33-7288 (May 9, 1996).

- The Commission also issued an interpretive release relating to the use of Internet websites to offer securities, solicit securities transactions, or advertise investment services offshore. See Release No. 33-7516 (March 23, 1998).

- On April 28, 2000, the Commission issued an interpretive release (2000 Interpretive Release) addressing the use of electronic media in three areas. See Release No. 33-7856. First, the Commission updated the 1995 Interpretive Release. Second, the Commission discussed an issuer's liability for website content. Third, the Commission outlined basic legal principles that issuers and market intermediaries should consider in conducting online offerings.

- To facilitate electronic delivery, the 2000 Interpretive Release clarifies the following: investors may consent to electronic delivery telephonically; intermediaries may request consent to electronic delivery on a "global," multiple-issuer basis; and issuers and intermediaries may deliver documents in portable document format, or PDF, with appropriate measures to assure that investors can easily access the documents. It also clarifies that an embedded hyperlink within a Section 10 prospectus or any other document required to be filed or delivered under the federal securities laws causes the hyperlinked information to be part of the document. (The Commission issued a further clarification that this view does not extend to a mutual fund's responsibility for hyperlinks to third-party websites from fund advertisements or sales literature. See Release No. 33-7877 (July 27, 2000).) The 2000 Interpretive Release also clarifies that the close proximity of information on a website to a Section 10 prospectus does not, by itself, make that information an "offer to sell," "offer for sale" or "offer" within the meaning of Section 2(a)(3) of the Securities Act.

- The 2000 Interpretive Release clarifies some of the facts and circumstances that may result in an issuer having adopted information on a third-party website to which the issuer has established a hyperlink for purposes of the antifraud provisions of the federal securities laws. Also, it clarifies the general legal principles that govern permissible website communications by issuers when in registration.

- To facilitate online offerings, the 2000 Interpretive Release clarifies the general legal principles that broker-dealers should consider when developing and implementing procedures for online public offerings. Also, it clarifies the circumstances under which a third-party service provider may establish a website to facilitate online private offerings.

- On July 19, 2005, the Commission issued a release adopting amendments to facilitate the securities offering process. The release generally reaffirms the 2000 Interpretive Release regarding information on an issuer's website and provides further related guidance. See Release No. 33-8591 at Part III.D.3.b.iii.(E).

C. Common Filing Concerns for EDGAR Filers

Since the adoption of the interim rules in February 1993, the Commission staff has been working with electronic filers to help them satisfy their electronic filing obligations. The following is a list of staff suggestions to help electronic filers avoid some of the more common errors associated with electronic filing. Filers should direct technical questions relating to filing on EDGAR to EDGAR Filer Support at (202) 551-8900.

- The registrant, not the filing agent or data transcriber, is responsible for complying with the electronic filing rules. Registrants are responsible for ensuring that correct information is given to and submitted by the filing agent. Registrants making EDGAR submissions "in-house" should not assign this responsibility to the least experienced person.

- Filers should review documents in electronic format and error check using EDGARLink before transmitting documents for filing. For example, filers should check to make sure that they have specified the correct EDGAR submission type (including a "/A" where it is needed to designate an amendment); that they have included all documents within the submission; and that each document is complete.

- Use the correct CIK. A submission under an incorrect CIK is a submission for the wrong registrant. The filer will have to resubmit for the correct registrant. Some filings require additional steps. Do not assume that incorrect submissions will be deleted.

- Use the correct file numbers in submissions, when required.

- Allow sufficient time to submit filings. Filers should not wait until the last minute to make a time-sensitive filing. Adjustments to filing dates of "late" filings are granted only for the circumstances set forth in Rule 13(b) of Regulation S-T.

- Use the correct EDGAR submission type. The staff, upon written request from the registrant, can correct some, but not all, erroneous submission types. Sometimes the registrant must formally withdraw and re-submit the filing. All requests for changes of submission types must be from the filer.

- Follow the procedures of Rule 3a of the Commission's Informal and Other Procedures in making fee payments. Filers must pay filing fees in connection with Securities Act registration statements to the lockbox before or at the time the filing is made except to the extent they are eligible to defer payment and do so in compliance with Rule 456(b) under the Securities Act as the rule was revised effective December 1, 2005. See Release No. 33-8591 (July 19, 2005). Filers should allow time for wire transfers before filing. EDGAR will not accept filings requiring fees until the fee payment is received. Include the correct CIK when making check or wire payment.

- Take care not to designate submissions incorrectly as TEST and CONFIRMING-COPY; submissions with these designations are not official Commission filings.

- Make sure the submission contains the text of the correct document (and not an earlier draft or different document).

- Filers have an obligation to confirm the status of their filings after transmitting them to the Commission. The staff may grant filing date adjustments under Rule 13(b) of Regulation S-T as warranted, for Exchange Act reports, but generally will not adjust a filing date over an extended period of time. It is not staff policy to grant filing date adjustments for Securities Act registration statements or other transactional filings, since shareholder rights may be affected.

- Carefully read the message sent by EDGAR in response to each submission. If a filer uses an Internet address for notification, the filer should carefully read all filing acceptance and suspension notices. If a message doesn't include a FILING DATE, then an official filing has not been made.

- Do not file material intended for confidential treatment on EDGAR. All material submitted via EDGAR is made public, except that cover letters and correspondence are non-public to the extent described immediately below.

- Submit all correspondence related to an electronic filing via EDGAR, and include a cover letter with submissions of public filings whenever appropriate. Cover letters submitted under document type "COVER" and correspondence submitted under document type "CORRESP" are treated initially as non-public and are not immediately disseminated. The staff may release all or parts of these documents electronically if they relate to the staff's review process not less than 45 days after the staff completes a filing review. See Press Release 2005-72, "SEC Staff to Begin Publicly Releasing Comment Letters and Responses."

- Letterheads on cover letters and correspondence will not appear in EDGAR documents unless typed.

- Please label exhibits as indicated in Appendix C of the EDGAR Filer Manual.

- Make sure all co-registrants are identified in the submission. Each co-registrant needs its own CIK and CCC.

Investment Companies:

- A new registered investment company *must* submit its "N-8A" *before* its initial registration statement. This submission assigns the registrant's Investment Company Act (811-) reporting file number, which the EDGAR system "looks up" in subsequent submissions. (A business development company must file its N-6F or N-54A first and is assigned an "814-" reporting number, since it is not registered under the Investment Company Act and does not make its filings under the Investment Company Act.)

- Registrants under the Investment Company Act must submit their filings under only one Investment Company Act file number (811-) and under one CIK. (Registrants may have multiple Securities Act file numbers under a single CIK.) Any Investment Company Act registrant having more than one Investment Company Act file number or more than one CIK should contact the IM EDGAR Inquiry Line at 202-551-6989 for assistance.

- Where appropriate, designate the correct ACT value(s). For a filing under both the Securities Act and the Investment Company Act, designate "33 40." Failure to make the required designation may result in a submission under only one Act and the need to re-submit the filing under the other Act.

- Usually, the file number required in an investment company submission will NOT be the Investment Company Act number (811-) but the Securities Act number or some other specialized number. The following submissions require the Securities Act number (either 2-, 33-, or 333-): "485APOS," "485BPOS," "485BXT," "24F-2NT," and "N-14/A." An "N-14/A" (a pre-effective amendment to Form N-14) always requires the Securities Act file number assigned to the initial Form N-14 filed for the particular offering in question.

- Fee-bearing filings must be made using an EDGAR submission type that allows for inclusion of a fee in the template. For example, the filing by a closed-end fund of a registration statement to register new securities under paragraph (a) or (b) of Rule 486 of the Securities Act must be filed using EDGAR submission type N-2.

- Fee payment is particularly critical for "24F-2NT" submissions, which cannot be accepted until fee payment is made.

- Fidelity bond filings, EDGAR submission type "40-17G," are now mandatory electronic filings. ASCII and HTML are the only acceptable formats for official filings.

  ○ All information should go in the primary EDGAR document named "40-17G," i.e., not in exhibit documents.

  ○ If the document is an HTML document, it may not consist entirely of graphics. That means that the information that comprises the substance of the filing, such as text and numbers that are of the kind normally searchable, may not be presented as graphics. Rule 304(e) of Regulation S-T prohibits filers from using graphic or image material to submit information, such as text or tables, that users must be able to search and/or download into spreadsheet form (for example, financial statements). Instead, filers must submit such information as text in an ASCII document, or as text or an HTML table in an HTML document.

  ○ The filer may attach an optional "unofficial" PDF copy of the filing if it wishes. See Rule 104 of Regulation S-T.

  ○ If a filer uses graphics incorrectly in contravention of the rule, the filer needs to file an amendment in compliance with the rule.

- The 40-17F1, 40-17F1/A, 40-17F2, 40-17F2/A, N-27D-1, and N-27D-1/A submission types now display the following subject company fields: CIK, IRS Number, File Number (when applicable), and Company Name. These changes were made to allow either the investment company or the accountant preparing the filing to make the submission. The "Subject" company will always be the investment company, whether the filing is submitted by the investment company or the accountant. The IRS number will be the IRS number of the company, or any series of the company, that is on file in the EDGAR database; the IRS number provides a double check that the correct subject company CIK is included in the submission.

- Future period dates are now allowed for the following submission types:

  N-23C-2, N-23C-2/A, N-23C3A, N-23C3A/A, N-23C3B, N-23C3B/A, N-23C3C, and N-23C3C/A.

- Please use the correct EDGAR submission type.

Use:	To Submit:
497K1, 497K2, 497K3A, or 497K3B, as appropriate	profiles for open-end management investment companies
485BXT	a filing under rule 485(b) to extend the effective date of a previous 485(a)
POS 8C	Post-effective amendments under the Securities Act, or under both the Securities and Investment Company Acts, filed by registrants filing on Forms N-2 and N-5
N-14 8C	Form N-14 registration statements filed by closed-end investment companies; a registration fee is required
N-CSR	certified annual shareholder report
N-CSRS	certified semi-annual shareholder report
NT-NCSR	Notice under Exchange Act Rule 12b-25 of inability to timely file Form N-CSR (annual or semi-annual report)

- Complete the facing sheets of registration statements and amendments correctly. Check the appropriate box(es) on the facing sheets of filings under Rule 485 and make sure all EDGAR header tags correspond to those boxes.

- Correctly label investment company exhibit documents. See Appendix C of the EDGAR Filer Manual. Please use the fourteen characters following the decimal point to include a descriptive label.

- Form N-PX must contain the registrant's proxy voting record for the most recent twelve-month period ended June 30, and must be filed no later than August 31 of each year. A registrant offering multiple series of shares must provide the information required by Item 1 of Form N-PX separately for each series. Registrants with multiple series may file a separate Form N-PX for each series.

- File as an exhibit to the Form N-Q submission the certifications called for by the form. The exhibit to the "N-Q" submission should be labeled "EX-99.CERT." If more than one certification is to be filed, all such certifications should be included in one EX-99.CERT exhibit document in the Form N-Q submission on EDGAR.

- Refer to "FAQ: EDGAR Filing of Certified Shareholder Reports by Registered Management Investment Companies" on the Commission's website at *http://www.sec.gov/info/edgar/certinvco.htm* for information on filing exhibits to Form N-CSR.

http://www.sec.gov/info/edgar/regoverview.htm

Electronic Form Types by Act

⟫⟩→ *Reproduced below is a document adapted from the EDGAR Filer Manual that the SEC posted on its website (www.sec.gov/info/edgar/forms/edgform.pdf) as a general resource for understanding its various forms. Not all forms mentioned here are reproduced in the Handbook.*

List of Tables

Table 3-1: Securities Act Submission Types Accepted by EDGAR

CFR Form/ Schedule/Rule	Description	Submission Type	Tool/Template Number	Filer-Constructed Form Spec.
D	Official notice of an offering of securities that is made without registration under the Securities Act in reliance on an exemption provided by Regulation D and Section 4(6) under the Act	D	Online Forms	N/A
	Amendment	D/A	Online Forms	N/A
F-1	Registration statement for securities of certain foreign private issuers	F-1	EDGARLink Template 1	XFDL Technical Specification
	Pre-effective amendment	F-1/A	EDGARLink Template 1	XFDL Technical Specification
	Post-effective amendment to a registration statement that is not immediately effective upon filing	POS AM	EDGARLink Template 1	XFDL Technical Specification
F-1MEF	A new registration statement filed under Rule 462(b) to add securities to a prior related effective registration statement filed on Form F-1	F-1MEF	EDGARLink Template 1	XFDL Technical Specification
	Post-effective amendment to Securities Act Rule 462(b) registration statement	POS462B	EDGARLink Template 3	XFDL Technical Specification
F-3	Registration statement for specified transactions by certain foreign private issuers	F-3	EDGARLink Template 1	XFDL Technical Specification
	Pre-Effective amendment	F-3/A	EDGARLink Template 1	XFDL Technical Specification

CFR Form/ Schedule/Rule	Description	Submission Type	Tool/Template Number	Filer- Constructed Form Spec.
	Post-effective amendment to a registration statement that is not immediately effective upon filing	POS AM	EDGARLink Template 1	XFDL Technical Specification
	Automatic shelf registration statement of securities of wellknown seasoned issuers	F-3ASR	EDGARLink Template 1	XFDL Technical Specification
	Post-effective Amendment to an automatic shelf registration statement on Form S-3ASR or Form F-3ASR	POSASR	EDGARLink Template 1	XFDL Technical Specification
	Registration statement for dividend or interest reinvestment plan securities of foreign private issuers	F-3D	EDGARLink Template 1	XFDL Technical Specification
	Post-Effective amendment to a F-3D registration	F-3DPOS	EDGARLink Template 1	XFDL Technical Specification
F-3MEF	A new registration statement filed under Rule 462(b) to add securities to a prior related effective registration statement filed on Form F-3	F-3MEF	EDGARLink Template 1	XFDL Technical Specification
	Post-effective amendment to Securities Act Rule 462(b) registration statement	POS462B	EDGARLink Template 3	XFDL Technical Specification
F-4	Registration statement for securities issued by foreign private issuers in certain business combination transactions	F-4	EDGARLink Template 1	XFDL Technical Specification
	Pre-effective amendment	F-4/A	EDGARLink Template 1	XFDL Technical Specification
	Post-effective amendment to a registration statement that is not immediately effective upon filing	POS AM	EDGARLink Template 1	XFDL Technical Specification
	Auto effective registration statement for securities by certain foreign private issuers in connection with certain business combination transactions	F-4EF	EDGARLink Template 1	XFDL Technical Specification
	Post-effective amendment to a F-4EF registration	F-4 POS	EDGARLink Template 1	XFDL Technical Specification
F-4MEF	A new registration statement filed under Rule 462(b) to add securities to a prior related effective registration statement filed on Form F-4	F-4MEF	EDGARLink Template 1	XFDL Technical Specification
	Post-effective amendment to Securities Act Rule 462(b) registration statement	POS462B	EDGARLink Template 3	XFDL Technical Specification

CFR Form/ Schedule/Rule	Description	Submission Type	Tool/Template Number	Filer-Constructed Form Spec.
F-6	Registration statement for American Depositary Receipts representing securities of certain foreign private issuers	F-6	EDGARLink Template 1	XFDL Technical Specification
	Pre-effective amendment	F-6/A	EDGARLink Template 1	XFDL Technical Specification
	Post-effective amendment to a registration statement that is not immediately effective upon filing	POS AM	EDGARLink Template 1	XFDL Technical Specification
	Auto effective registration statement for American Depositary Receipts representing securities of certain foreign private issuers	F 6EF	EDGARLink Template 1	XFDL Technical Specification
	Post-effective amendment to a F-6EF registration	F-6 POS	EDGARLink Template 1	XFDL Technical Specification
F-7	Registration statement for securities of certain Canadian issuers offered for cash upon the exercise of rights granted to existing security holders under the Securities Act of 1933	F-7	EDGARLink Template 1	XFDL Technical Specification
	Pre-effective amendment	F-7/A	EDGARLink Template 1	XFDL Technical Specification
	Post-effective amendment to a F-7 registration	F-7 POS	EDGARLink Template 1	XFDL Technical Specification
F-8	Registration statement for securities of certain Canadian issuers to be issued in exchange offers or a business combination under the Securities Act of 1933	F-8	EDGARLink Template 1	XFDL Technical Specification
	Pre-effective amendment	F-8/A	EDGARLink Template 1	XFDL Technical Specification
	Post-effective amendment to a F-8 registration	F-8 POS	EDGARLink Template 1	XFDL Technical Specification
F-9	Registration of securities of certain investment grade debt or investment grade preferred securities of certain Canadian issuers under the Securities Act of 1933	F-9	EDGARLink Template 1	XFDL Technical Specification
	Pre-effective amendment	F-9/A	EDGARLink Template 1	XFDL Technical Specification

CFR Form/ Schedule/Rule	Description	Submission Type	Tool/Template Number	Filer-Constructed Form Spec.
	Auto effective registration of securities of certain investment grade debt or investment grade preferred securities of certain Canadian issuers under the Securities Act of 1933	F-9EF	EDGARLink Template 1	XFDL Technical Specification
	Post-effective amendment to a F-9EF registration	F-9 POS	EDGARLink Template 1	XFDL Technical Specification
F-10	Registration statement for securities of certain Canadian issuers under the Securities Act of 1933	F-10	EDGARLink Template 1	XFDL Technical Specification
	Pre-effective amendment	F-10/A	EDGARLink Template 1	XFDL Technical Specification
	Auto effective registration statement for securities of certain Canadian issuers under the Securities Act of 1933	F-10EF	EDGARLink Template 1	XFDL Technical Specification
	Post-effective amendment to a F10EF registration	F-10POS	EDGARLink Template 1	XFDL Technical Specification
F-80	Registration of securities of certain Canadian issuers to be issued in exchange offers or a business combination under the Securities Act of 1933	F-80	EDGARLink Template 1	XFDL Technical Specification
	Pre-effective amendment	F-80/A	EDGARLink Template 1	XFDL Technical Specification
	Post-effective amendment to a F-80 registration	F-80POS	EDGARLink Template 1	XFDL Technical Specification
S-1	General form of registration statement for all companies including face-amount certificate companies	S-1	EDGARLink Template 1	XFDL Technical Specification
	Pre-effective amendment	S-1/A	EDGARLink Template 1	XFDL Technical Specification
	Post-effective amendment to a registration statement that is not immediately effective upon filing	POS AM	EDGARLink Template 1	XFDL Technical Specification
S-1MEF	A new registration statement filed under Rule 462(b) to add securities to a prior related effective registration statement filed on Form S-1	S-1MEF	EDGARLink Template 1	XFDL Technical Specification
	Post-effective amendment to Securities Act Rule 462(b) registration statement	POS462B	EDGARLink Template 3	XFDL Technical Specification

CFR Form/ Schedule/Rule	Description	Submission Type	Tool/Template Number	Filer-Constructed Form Spec.
S-3	Registration statement for specified transactions by certain issuers	S-3	EDGARLink Template 1	XFDL Technical Specification
	Pre-effective amendment	S-3/A	EDGARLink Template 1	XFDL Technical Specification
	Post-effective amendment to a registration statement that is not immediately effective upon filing	POS AM	EDGARLink Template 1	XFDL Technical Specification
	Automatic shelf registration statement of securities of well-known seasoned issuers	S-3ASR	EDGARLink Template 1	XFDL Technical Specification
	Post-effective Amendment to an automatic shelf registration statement on Form S-3ASR or Form F-3ASR	POSASR	EDGARLink Template 1	XFDL Technical Specification
	Automatically effective registration statement for securities issued pursuant to dividend or interest reinvestment plans	S-3D	EDGARLink Template 1	XFDL Technical Specification
	Post-effective amendment to a S-3D registration statement	S-3DPOS	EDGARLink Template 1	XFDL Technical Specification
S-3MEF	A new registration statement filed under Rule 462(b) to add securities to a prior related effective registration statement filed on Form S-3	S-3MEF	EDGARLink Template 1	XFDL Technical Specification
	Post-effective amendment to Securities Act Rule 462(b) registration statement	POS462B	EDGARLink Template 3	XFDL Technical Specification
S-4	Registration of securities issued in business combination transactions	S-4	EDGARLink Template 1	XFDL Technical Specification
	Pre-effective amendment	S-4/A	EDGARLink Template 1	XFDL Technical Specification
	Post-effective amendment to a registration statement that is not immediately effective upon filing	POS AM	EDGARLink Template 1	XFDL Technical Specification
	Auto effective registration statement for securities issued in connection with the formation of a bank or savings and loan holding company in compliance with General Instruction G	S-4EF	EDGARLink Template 1	XFDL Technical Specification
	Post-effective amendment to a S-4EF registration statement	S-4 POS	EDGARLink Template 1	XFDL Technical Specification

CFR Form/ Schedule/Rule	Description	Submission Type	Tool/Template Number	Filer-Constructed Form Spec.
S-4MEF	A new registration statement filed under Rule 462(b) to add securities to a prior related effective registration statement filed on Form S-4	S-4MEF	EDGARLink Template 1	XFDL Technical Specification
	Post-effective amendment to Securities Act Rule 462(b) registration statement	POS462B	EDGARLink Template 3	XFDL Technical Specification
S-8	Initial registration statement for securities to be offered to employees pursuant to employee benefit plans	S-8	EDGARLink Template 1	XFDL Technical Specification
	Post-effective amendment to a S-8 registration statement	S-8 POS	EDGARLink Template 1	XFDL Technical Specification
S-11	Registration statement for securities to be issued by real estate companies	S-11	EDGARLink Template 1	XFDL Technical Specification
	Pre-effective amendment	S-11/A	EDGARLink Template 1	XFDL Technical Specification
	Post-effective amendment to a registration statement that is not immediately effective upon filing	POS AM	EDGARLink Template 1	XFDL Technical Specification
S-11MEF	A new registration statement filed under Rule 462(b) to add securities to a prior related effective registration statement filed on Form S-11	S-11MEF	EDGARLink Template 1	XFDL Technical Specification
	Post-effective amendment to Securities Act Rule 462(b) registration statement	POS462B	EDGARLink Template 3	XFDL Technical Specification
S-20	Registration statement for standardized options	S-20	EDGARLink Template 1	XFDL Technical Specification
	Pre-effective amendment	S-20/A	EDGARLink Template 1	XFDL Technical Specification
	Post-effective amendment to a registration statement that is not immediately effective upon filing	POS AM	EDGARLink Template 1	XFDL Technical Specification
S-B	Registration statement for securities of foreign governments and subdivisions thereof under the Securities Act of 1933 (Schedule B)	S-B	EDGARLink Template 1	XFDL Technical Specification
	Pre-effective amendment	S-B/A	EDGARLink Template 1	XFDL Technical Specification

CFR Form/ Schedule/Rule	Description	Submission Type	Tool/Template Number	Filer- Constructed Form Spec.
	Post-effective amendment to a registration statement that is not immediately effective upon filing	POS AM	EDGARLink Template 1	XFDL Technical Specification
S-BMEF	A new registration statement filed under Rule 462(b) to add securities to a prior related effective registration statement filed on Form S-B	S-BMEF	EDGARLink Template 1	XFDL Technical Specification
	Post-effective amendment to Securities Act Rule 462(b) registration statement	POS462B	EDGARLink Template 3	XFDL Technical Specification
POS462B	Post-effective amendment to Securities Act Rule 462(b) registration statement	POS462B	EDGARLink Template 3	XFDL Technical Specification
POS462C	Post-effective amendment to a registration statement filed under Rule 462(c)	POS462C	EDGARLink Template 3	XFDL Technical Specification
POS AM	Post-effective amendment to a registration statement that is not immediately effective upon filing	POS AM	EDGARLink Template 1	XFDL Technical Specification
POS EX	Post-effective amendment filed solely to add exhibits to a registration statement	POS EX	EDGARLink Template 3	XFDL Technical Specification

PROSPECTUSES FILED PURSUANT TO RULE 424

CFR Form/ Schedule/Rule	Description	Submission Type	Tool/Template Number	Filer- Constructed Form Spec.
	Prospectus filed pursuant to Rule 424(a)	424A	EDGARLink Template 3	XFDL Technical Specification
	Prospectus filed pursuant to Rule 424(b)(1)	424B1	EDGARLink Template 1	XFDL Technical Specification
	Prospectus filed pursuant to Rule 424(b)(2)	424B2	EDGARLink Template 1	XFDL Technical Specification
	Prospectus filed pursuant to Rule 424(b)(3)	424B3	EDGARLink Template 1	XFDL Technical Specification
	Prospectus filed pursuant to Rule 424(b)(4)	424B4	EDGARLink Template 1	XFDL Technical Specification
	Prospectus filed pursuant to Rule 424(b)(5)	424B5	EDGARLink Template 1	XFDL Technical Specification
	Prospectus filed pursuant to Rule 424(b)(7)	424B7	EDGARLink Template 1	XFDL Technical Specification

CFR Form/ Schedule/Rule	Description	Submission Type	Tool/Template Number	Filer-Constructed Form Spec.
	Prospectus filed pursuant to Rule 424(b)(8)	424B8	EDGARLink Template 1	XFDL Technical Specification

FREE WRITING PROSPECTUS

	Description	Submission Type	Tool/Template Number	Filer-Constructed Form Spec.
	Filing under Securities Act Rules 163/433 of free writing prospectuses	FWP	EDGARLink Template 2	XFDL Technical Specification

FILINGS PURSUANT TO THE TRUST INDENTURE ACT

CFR Form	Description	Submission Type	Tool/Template Number	Filer-Constructed Form Spec.
305B2	Application for designation of a new trustee under the Trust Indenture Act	305B2	EDGARLink Template 3	XFDL Technical Specification
	Amendment	305B2/A	EDGARLink Template 3	XFDL Technical Specification
T-3	Initial application for qualification of trust indentures	T-3	EDGARLink Template 1	XFDL Technical Specification
	Pre-effective amendment	T-3/A	EDGARLink Template 1	XFDL Technical Specification
T-6	Application for determination of eligibility of a foreign person to act as institutional trustee filed pursuant to Section 310(a)(1) of the Trust Indenture Act of 1939	T-6	EDGARLink Template 1	XFDL Technical Specification
	Pre-effective amendment	T-6/A	EDGARLink Template 1	XFDL Technical Specification

Note: "Submission types" T-1 and T-2 are not used as stand-alone submission types on the EDGAR system. They are filed as EX-25 to registration statements.

FILINGS PURSUANT TO RULE 144

CFR Form	Description	Submission Type	Tool/Template Number	Filer-Constructed Form Spec.
144	Filing for proposed sale of securities under Rule 144	144	EDGARLink Template 2	XFDL Technical Specification
	Amendment to Form 144 **Note:** Form 144 may be filed electronically on a voluntary basis if the issuer of the securities is a public company.	144/A	EDGARLink Template 2	XFDL Technical Specification

MISCELLANEOUS FILINGS

CFR Form	Description	Submission Type	Tool/Template Number	Filer-Constructed Form Spec.
DEL AM	Separately filed delaying amendment under Securities Act Rule 473 to delay effectiveness of a 1933 Act registration statement	DEL AM	EDGARLink Template 3	XFDL Technical Specification
UNDER	Initial undertaking to file reports	UNDER	EDGARLink Template 3	XFDL Technical Specification

CFR Form/ Schedule/Rule	Description	Submission Type	Tool/Template Number	Filer-Constructed Form Spec.
	Amendment	UNDER/A	EDGARLink Template 3	XFDL Technical Specification
SUPPL	Voluntary supplemental material filed pursuant to Section 11(a) of the Securities Act of 1933 by foreign issuers	SUPPL	EDGARLink Template 2	XFDL Technical Specification
RW	Registration Withdrawal Request	RW	EDGARLink Template 3	XFDL Technical Specification
RW WD	Withdrawal of a Registration Withdrawal Request	RW WD	EDGARLink Template 1	XFDL Technical Specification
AW	Withdrawal of amendment to a registration statement filed under the Securities Act	AW	EDGARLink Template 3	XFDL Technical Specification
AW WD	Withdrawal of a request for withdrawal of an amendment to a registration statement	AW WD	EDGARLink Template 1	XFDL Technical Specification
425	Filing under Securities Act Rule 425 of certain prospectuses and communications in connection with business combination transactions	425	EDGARLink Template 2	XFDL Technical Specification
	Note: Form 425 can be filed as part of Form 8-K. For filers subject to 8K filing requirements, we recommend the use of the 8-K combined form type as the easiest method for fulfilling your filing requirement for both forms			
F-X	For appointment of agent for service of process by issuers registering securities (if filed on Form F-8, F-9, F-10 or F-80, or registering securities or filing periodic reports on Form 40-F, or by any person filing certain tender offer documents, or by any person acting as trustee with respect to securities registered on form F-7, F-8, F-9 or F-10	F-X	EDGARLink Template 2	XFDL Technical Specification
	Amendment	F-X/A	EDGARLink Template 2	XFDL Technical Specification
F-N	Notification of the appointment of an agent for service by certain foreign institutions	F-N	EDGARLink Template 2	XFDL Technical Specification
	Amendment	F-N/A	EDGARLink Template 2	XFDL Technical Specification

Table 3-2: Securities Exchange Act - Proxy Materials and Information Statements Filed Pursuant to Section 14 Submission Types Accepted by EDGAR

CFR Form/ Schedule/Rule	Description	Submission Type	Tool/Template Number	Filer-Constructed Form Spec.
PRELIMINARY PROXY SOLICITING MATERIALS				
	Preliminary proxy statements relating to merger or acquisition	PREM14A	EDGARLink Template 2	XFDL Technical Specification
	Preliminary proxy statement in connection with contested solicitations	PREC14A	EDGARLink Template 2	XFDL Technical Specification
	Preliminary proxy statement filed by non-management	PREN14A	EDGARLink Template 2	XFDL Technical Specification
	Preliminary proxy statement not related to a contested matter or merger / acquisition	PRE 14A	EDGARLink Template 2	XFDL Technical Specification
PRELIMINARY INFORMATION STATEMENTS				
	Preliminary information statements relating to merger or acquisition	PREM14C	EDGARLink Template 2	XFDL Technical Specification
	Preliminary information statements - contested solicitations	PREC14C	EDGARLink Template 2	XFDL Technical Specification
	Preliminary information statement not related to a contested matter or merger/ acquisition	PRE 14C	EDGARLink Template 2	XFDL Technical Specification
REVISED PRELIMINARY MATERIALS				
	Preliminary revised proxy soliciting materials	PRER14A	EDGARLink Template 2	XFDL Technical Specification
	Revised preliminary proxy statement filed by nonmanagement	PRRN14A	EDGARLink Template 2	XFDL Technical Specification
	Preliminary revised information statements	PRER14C	EDGARLink Template 2	XFDL Technical Specification
DEFINITIVE MATERIALS (PROXY MATERIALS)				
	Definitive proxy statement relating to merger or acquisition	DEFM14A	EDGARLink Template 2	XFDL Technical
	Definitive proxy statement in connection with contested solicitations	DEFC14A	EDGARLink Template 2	XFDL Technical Specification
	Definitive proxy statement filed by non-management	DEFN14A	EDGARLink Template 2	XFDL Technical Specification
	Revised definitive proxy statement filed by nonmanagement	DFRN14A	EDGARLink Template 2	XFDL Technical Specification
	Definitive revised proxy soliciting materials	DEFR14A	EDGARLink Template 2	XFDL Technical Specification
	Definitive additional proxy soliciting materials including Rule 14(a)(12) material	DEFA14A	EDGARLink Template 2	XFDL Technical Specification

CFR Form/ Schedule/Rule	Description	Submission Type	Tool/Template Number	Filer-Constructed Form Spec.
	Note: Submission type DEFA14A can be filed as part of Form 8-K. For filers subject to 8-K filing requirements, we recommend the use of the 8-K combined form type as the easiest method for fulfilling your filing requirement for both forms			
	Definitive additional proxy soliciting materials filed by nonmanagement including Rule 14(a)(12) material	DFAN14A	EDGARLink Template 2	XFDL Technical Specification
	Note: Submission type DFAN14A can be filed as part of Form 8-K. For filers subject to 8-K filing requirements, we recommend the use of the 8-K combined form type as the easiest method for fulfilling your filing requirement for both forms			
	Definitive proxy statements	DEF 14A	EDGARLink Template 2	XFDL Technical Specification
	Notice of exempt solicitation	PX14A6G	EDGARLink Template 2	XFDL Technical Specification
	Notice of exempt solicitation for the purpose of determining whether to solicit proxies, consents, or authorizations in opposition to a proposed rollup transaction filed pursuant to Rule 14a6(g) of the Securities Exchange Act of 1934	PX14A6N	EDGARLink Template 2	XFDL Technical Specification

DEFINITIVE MATERIALS (INFORMATION STATEMENTS)

	Description	Submission Type	Tool/Template Number	Filer-Constructed Form Spec.
	Definitive information statement relating to merger or acquisition	DEFM14C	EDGARLink Template 2	XFDL Technical Specification
	Definitive information statement - contested solicitations	DEFC14C	EDGARLink Template 2	XFDL Technical Specification
	Definitive information statements	DEF 14C	EDGARLink Template 2	XFDL Technical Specification
	Definitive additional information statement materials including Rule 14(a)(12) material	DEFA14C	EDGARLink Template 2	XFDL Technical Specification
	Definitive revised information statement materials	DEFR14C	EDGARLink Template 2	XFDL Technical Specification

Table 3-3: Securities Exchange Act - Registration and Report Submission Types Accepted by EDGAR

CFR Form/Schedule/ Rule	Description	Submission Type	Tool/Template Number	Filer-Constructed Form Spec.

REGISTRATION STATEMENTS

CFR Form/Schedule/Rule	Description	Submission Type	Tool/Template Number	Filer-Constructed Form Spec.
8-A	Form for the registration / listing of a class of securities on a national securities exchange pursuant to section 12(b)	8-A12B	EDGARLink Template 3	XFDL Technical Specification
	Amendment	8-A12B/A	EDGARLink Template 3	
	Form for registration of a class of securities pursuant to section 12(g)	8-A12G	EDGARLink Template 3	XFDL Technical Specification
	Amendment	8-A12G/A	EDGARLink Template 3	
10	Initial general form for registration of a class of securities pursuant to section 12(b)	10-12B	EDGARLink Template 3	XFDL Technical Specification
	Amendment	10-12B/A	EDGARLink Template 3	
	Initial general form for registration of a class of securities pursuant to section 12(g)	10-12G	EDGARLink Template 3	XFDL Technical Specification
	Amendment	10-12G/A	EDGARLink Template 3	
20-F	Form for initial registration of a class of securities of foreign private issuers pursuant to section 12(b)	20FR12B	EDGARLink Template 3	XFDL Technical Specification
	Amendment	20FR12B/A	EDGARLink Template 3	
	Form for initial registration of a class of securities of foreign private issuers pursuant to section 12(g)	20FR12G	EDGARLink Template 3	XFDL Technical Specification
	Amendment	20FR12G/A	EDGARLink Template 3	
40-F	Registration of a class of securities of certain Canadian issuers pursuant to Section 12(b) of the 1934 Act	40FR12B	EDGARLink Template 3	XFDL Technical Specification
	Amendment	40FR12B/A	EDGARLink Template 3	
	Registration of a class of securities of certain Canadian issuers pursuant to Section 12(g) of the 1934 Act	40FR12G	EDGARLink Template 3	XFDL Technical Specification
	Amendment	40FR12G/A	EDGARLink Template 3	
18	Form for initial registration of securities of foreign governments or political subdivisions pursuant to section 12(b)	18-12B	EDGARLink Template 3	XFDL Technical Specification
	Amendment	18-12B/A	EDGARLink Template 3	
	Form for initial registration of securities of foreign governments or political subdivisions thereof pursuant to section 12(g)	18-12G	EDGARLink Template 3	XFDL Technical Specification

CFR Form/Schedule/Rule	Description	Submission Type	Tool/Template Number	Filer-Constructed Form Spec.
	Amendment	18-12G/A	EDGARLink Template 3	

ANNUAL, QUARTERLY, AND PERIODIC REPORTS

CFR Form/Schedule/Rule	Description	Submission Type	Tool/Template Number	Filer-Constructed Form Spec.
ARS	Annual report to security holders	ARS	EDGARLink Template 3	XFDL Technical Specification
	Amendment	ARS/A	EDGARLink Template 3	
	Note: Use this submission type when furnishing the annual report to security holders for the information of the Commission pursuant to Rule 14a-3(c) or Rule 14c-3(b). Portions of the annual report to security holders filed with the Commission as part of a registration statement or periodic report should be filed as Exhibit 13, as provided by Item 601 of Regulation S-K and S-B.			
6-K	Current report of foreign issuer pursuant to Rules 13a-16 and 15d-16	6-K	EDGARLink Template 3	XFDL Technical Specification
	Amendments	6-K/A	EDGARLink Template 3	
10-Q	Quarterly report pursuant to sections 13 or 15(d)	10-Q	EDGARLink Template 3	XFDL Technical Specification
	Amendment	10-Q/A	EDGARLink Template 3	
	Transition report pursuant to Rule 13a-10 or 15d-10	10-QT	EDGARLink Template 3	XFDL Technical Specification
10-K	Annual report pursuant to section 13 and 15(d)	10-K	EDGARLink Template 3	XFDL Technical Specification
	Amendment	10-K/A	EDGARLink Template 3	
	Transition report pursuant to Rule 13a-10 or 15d-10	10-KT	EDGARLink Template 3	XFDL Technical Specification
	Amendment	10-KT/A	EDGARLink Template 3	
10KSB	Optional form for annual and transition reports of small business issuers under section 13 or 15(d) Will no longer be accepted as of March 16, 2009	10KSB	EDGARLink Template 3	XFDL Technical Specification
	Amendment	10KSB/A	EDGARLink Template 3	

CFR Form/Schedule/Rule	Description	Submission Type	Tool/Template Number	Filer-Constructed Form Spec.
	Will no longer be accepted as of March 16, 2009			
10-D	Periodic distribution reports by Asset-Backed issuers pursuant to Rule 13a-17 or 15d-17	10-D	EDGARLink Template 3	XFDL Technical Specification
	Amendment	10-D/A	EDGARLink Template 3	
8-K	Current report filing	8-K	EDGARLink Template 3	XFDL Technical Specification
	Amendment	8-K/A	EDGARLink Template 3	
	Notification that a class of securities of successor issuer is deemed to be registered pursuant to section 12(g)	8-K12G3	EDGARLink Template 3	XFDL Technical Specification
	Amendment	8-K12G3/A	EDGARLink Template 3	
	Notification of assumption of duty to report by successor issue under section 15(d)	8-K15D5	EDGARLink Template 3	XFDL Technical Specification
	Amendment	8-K15D5/A	EDGARLink Template 3	
11-K	Annual report of employee stock purchase, savings and similar plans	11-K	EDGARLink Template 3	XFDL Technical Specification
	Amendment	11-K/A	EDGARLink Template 3	
	Transition report pursuant to rule 13a-10 or 15d-10	11-KT	EDGARLink Template 3	XFDL Technical Specification
	Amendment	11-KT/A	EDGARLink Template 3	
18-K	Annual report for foreign governments and political subdivisions	18-K		XFDL Technical Specification
	Amendment	18-K/A		
20-F	Annual and transition report of foreign private issuers pursuant to sections 13 or 15(d)	20-F	EDGARLink Template 3	XFDL Technical Specification
	Amendment	20-F/A	EDGARLink Template 3	
40-F	Annual report filed by certain Canadian issuers pursuant to Section 15(d) and Rule 15d-4	40-F	EDGARLink Template 3	XFDL Technical Specification
	Amendment	40-F/A	EDGARLink Template 3	
12b-25	Notice under Rule 12b25 of inability to timely file all or part of a form 10-Q or 10-QSB	NT 10-Q	EDGARLink Template 3	XFDL Technical Specification

CFR Form/Schedule/ Rule	Description	Submission Type	Tool/Template Number	Filer-Constructed Form Spec.
	Amendment	NT 10-Q/A	EDGARLink Template 3	
	Notice under Rule 12b25 of inability to timely file all or part of a form 10-K, 10-KSB, or 10-KT	NT 10-K	EDGARLink Template 3	XFDL Technical Specification
	Amendment	NT 10-K/A	EDGARLink Template 3	
	Notice under Rule 12b25 of inability to timely file all or part of a Form 10-D	NT 10-D	EDGARLink Template 3	XFDL Technical Specification
	Amendment	NT 10-D/A	EDGARLink Template 3	
	Notice under Rule 12b25 of inability to timely file all or part of a form 11-K	NT 11-K	EDGARLink Template 3	XFDL Technical Specification
	Amendment	NT 11-K/A	EDGARLink Template 3	
	Notice under Rule 12b25 of inability to timely file a special report pursuant to section 15d-2	NT 15D2	EDGARLink Template 3	XFDL Technical Specification
	Amendment	NT 15D2/A	EDGARLink Template 3	
	Notice under Rule 12b25 of inability to timely file all or part of an annual report of form 20-F	NT 20-F	EDGARLink Template 3	XFDL Technical Specification
	Amendment	NT 20-F/A	EDGARLink Template 3	
15	Notice of termination of registration of a class of securities under Section 12(b)	15-12B	EDGARLink Template 3	XFDL Technical Specification
	Amendment	15-12B/A	EDGARLink Template 3	
	Notice of termination of registration of a class of securities under Section 12(g)	15-12G	EDGARLink Template 3	XFDL Technical Specification
	Amendment	15-12G/A	EDGARLink Template 3	
	Notice of suspension of duty to file reports pursuant to Section 13 and 15(d) of the Act	15-15D	EDGARLink Template 3	XFDL Technical Specification
	Amendment	15-15D/A	EDGARLink Template 3	
See Rule 15d-2	Special Financial Report filed under Rule 15d-2	SP 15D2	EDGARLink Template 3	XFDL Technical Specification
	Amendment	SP 15D2/A	EDGARLink Template 3	
15F	Notice of termination of a foreign private issuer's registration of a class of securities under Section 12(b)	15F-12B	EDGARLink Template 3	XFDL Technical Specification

CFR Form/Schedule/Rule	Description	Submission Type	Tool/Template Number	Filer-Constructed Form Spec.
	Amendment	15F-12B/A	EDGARLink Template 3	
	Notice of termination of a foreign private issuer's registration of a class of securities under Section 12(g)	15F-12G	EDGARLink Template 3	XFDL Technical Specification
	Amendment	15-12G/A	EDGARLink Template 3	
15F	Notice of a foreign private issuer's suspension of duty to file reports pursuant to Section 13 and 15(d) of the Act	15F-15D	EDGAR Link Template 3	XFDL Technical Specification
	Amendment	15-15D/A	EDGAR Link Template 3	

MISCELLANEOUS SUBMISSION TYPES/FILLINGS

CFR Form/Schedule/Rule	Description	Submission Type	Tool/Template Number	Filer-Constructed Form Spec.
Form 13 F	Initial Quarterly Form 13F Holdings report filed by institutional managers	13F-HR	EDGAR Link Template 3	XFDL Technical Specification
	Amendment	13F-HR/A	EDGAR Link Template 3	
	Initial Quarterly Form 13F Notice Report filed by institutional managers	13F-NT	EDGAR Link Template 3	XFDL Technical Specification
	Amendment	13F-NT/A	EDGAR Link Template 3	
Form SH	Weekly Form SH Entries Report Filed by Institutional Investment Managers	SH-ER	EDGAR Link Template 3	SH-ER Information table only: SH-ER Information Table XML Technical Specification; XFDL Technical Specification
	Amendment	SH-ER/A	EDGAR Link Template 3	SH-ER/A Information table only: SH-ER Information Table XML Technical Specification; XFDL Technical Specification
	Weekly Form SH Notice Report Filed by Institutional Investment Managers	SH-NT	EDGAR Link Template 3	XFDL Technical Specification
	Amendment	SH-NT/A	EDGAR Link Template 3	XFDL Technical Specification

CFR Form/Schedule/ Rule	Description	Submission Type	Tool/Template Number	Filer-Constructed Form Spec.
Form RW	Registration Withdrawal Request	RW	EDGAR Link Template 3	XFDL Technical Specification
	Withdrawal of a registration withdrawal statement	RW WD	EDGAR Link Template 3	XFDL Technical Specification
Form AW	Withdrawal of an amendment to a registration statement filed under the Securities Act	AW	EDGAR Link Template 3	XFDL Technical Specification
	Withdrawal of an amendment registration withdrawal statement	AW WD	EDGAR Link Template 3	XFDL Technical Specification
Form 425	Filing under Securities Act Rule 425 of certain prospectuses and communications in connection with business combination transactions	425	EDGAR Link Template 3	XFDL Technical Specification
	Note: Form 425 can be filed as part of Form 8-K. For filers subject to 8K filing requirements, we recommend the use of the 8-K combined form type as the easiest method for fulfilling your filing requirement for both forms.			
Form 25	Notification filed by issuer to voluntarily withdraw a class of securities from listing and registration on a national securities exchange	25	EDGAR Link Template 3	XFDL Technical Specification
	Amendment	25/A	EDGAR Link Template 3	
Form 25	Notification filed by national security exchange to report the removal from listing and registration of matured, redeemed or retired securities	25-NSE	Distributed to National Securities Exchanges only	Distributed to National Securities Exchanges only
	Amendment	25-NSE/A	Distributed to National Securities Exchanges only	Distributed to National Securities Exchanges only

SECTION 16 OWNERSHIP FORMS/FILINGS

CFR Form/Schedule/ Rule	Description	Submission Type	Tool/Template Number	Filer-Constructed Form Spec.
Form 3	Initial statement of beneficial ownership of securities	3	Online Forms	Ownership XML Technical Specification
	Amendment	3/A	Online Forms	Ownership XML Technical Specification
Form 4	Statement of changes in beneficial ownership of securities	4	Online Forms	Ownership XML Technical Specification

CFR Form/Schedule/Rule	Description	Submission Type	Tool/Template Number	Filer-Constructed Form Spec.
	Amendment	4/A	Online Forms	Ownership XML Technical Specification
Form 5	Annual statement of changes in beneficial ownership of securities	5	Online Forms	Ownership XML Technical Specification
	Amendment	5/A	Online Forms	Ownership XML Technical Specification

SECTION 17A TRANSFER AGENT FORMS/FILINGS

CFR Form/Schedule/Rule	Description	Submission Type	Tool/Template Number	Filer-Constructed Form Spec.
TA-1	Application for registration as a transfer agent filed pursuant to the Securities Exchange Act of 1934	TA-1	EDGAR Lite TA-1 Template	TA-1 XML Technical Specification
	Amendment	TA-1/A	EDGAR Lite TA-1 Template	TA-1 XML Technical Specification
TA-2	Annual report of transfer agent activities filed pursuant to the Securities Exchange Act of 1934	TA-2	EDGAR Lite TA-1 Template	TA-1 XML Technical Specification
	Amendment	TA-2/A	EDGAR Lite TA-1 Template	TA-1 XML Technical Specification
TA-W	Notice of withdrawal from registration as transfer agent filed pursuant to the Securities Exchange Act of 1934	TA-W	EDGAR Lite TA-1 Template	TA-1 XML Technical Specification

Table 3-4: Williams Act Filing Submission Types Accepted by EDGAR

CFR Form/Schedule/Rule	Description	Submission Type	Tool/Template Number	Filer-Constructed Form Spec.
Schedule 13D	Schedule filed to report acquisition of beneficial ownership of 5% or more of a class of equity securities	SC 13D	EDGARLink Template 2	XFDL Technical Specification
	Amendment	SC 13D/A	EDGARLink Template 2	
Schedule 13-E1	Schedule 13-E1 statement of issuer required by Rule 13e-1	SC 13E1	EDGARLink Template 2	XFDL Technical Specification
	Amendment	SC 13E1/A	EDGARLink Template 2	
Schedule 13E-3	Schedule filed to report going private transactions	SC 13E3	EDGARLink Template 2	XFDL Technical Specification
	Amendment	SC 13E3/A	EDGARLink Template 2	

CFR Form/ Schedule/Rule	Description	Submission Type	Tool/Template Number	Filer- Constructed Form Spec.
Schedule 13E4F	Issuer tender offer statement filed pursuant to Rule 13(e)(4) by foreign issuers	SC13E4F	EDGARLink Template 2	XFDL Technical Specification
	Amendment	SC13E4F/A	EDGARLink Template 2	
Schedule 13G	Schedule filed to report acquisition of beneficial ownership of 5% or more of a class of equity securities by passive investors and certain institutions	SC 13G	EDGARLink Template 2	XFDL Technical Specification
	Amendment	SC 13G/A	EDGARLink Template 2	
Schedule TO-I	Issuer tender offer statement	SC TO-I SC	EDGARLink Template 2	XFDL Technical Specification
	Amendment	TO-I/A SC	EDGARLink Template 2	
Schedule TO-T	Third party tender offer statement	TO-T SC	EDGARLink Template 2	XFDL Technical Specification
	Amendment	TO-T/A	EDGARLink Template 2	
Schedule TO-C	Written communication relating to an issuer or third party tender offer **Note:** Form Schedule TO-C can be filed as part of Form 8-K. For filers subject to 8-K filing requirements, we recommend the use of the 8-K combined form type as the easiest method for fulfilling your filing requirement for both forms	SC TO-C	EDGARLink Template 2	XFDL Technical Specification
Schedule 14D1F	Third party tender offer statement filed pursuant to Rule 14d-1(b) by foreign issuers	SC14D1F	EDGARLink Template 2	XFDL Technical Specification
	Amendment	SC14D1F/A	EDGARLink Template 2	
Schedule 14D9-C	Written communication by the subject company relating to a third party tender offer	SC14D9C	EDGARLink Template 2	XFDL Technical Specification
Schedule 14D9	Tender offer solicitation / recommendation statements filed under Rule 14-d9	SC 14D9	EDGARLink Template 2	XFDL Technical Specification
	Amendment	SC 14D9/A	EDGARLink Template 2	
Schedule 14D9F	Solicitation/recommendation statement pursuant to Section 14(d)(4) of the Securities Exchange Act of 1934 and Rules 14d-1(b) and 14e-2(c) by foreign issuers	SC14D9F	EDGARLink Template 2	XFDL Technical Specification
	Amendment	SC14D9F/A	EDGARLink Template 2	

CFR Form/ Schedule/Rule	Description	Submission Type	Tool/Template Number	Filer-Constructed Form Spec.
Schedule 14f-1	Statement regarding change in majority of directors pursuant to Rule 14f-1	SC 14F1	EDGARLink Template 2	XFDL Technical Specification
	Amendment	SC 14F1/A	EDGARLink Template 2	
CB	Notification form filed in connection with certain tender offers, business combinations and rights offerings, in which the subject company is a foreign private issuer of which less than 10% of its securities are held by U.S. persons	CB	EDGARLink Template 2	XFDL Technical Specification
	Amendment	CB/A	EDGARLink Template 2	

Table 3-5: Investment Company Submission Types Accepted by EDGAR

CFR Form/ Schedule/Rule	Description	Submission Type	Tool/Template Number	Filer-Constructed Form Spec.
Forms S-1 & S-3	Registration statement for faceamount certificate companies			
	General form of registration statement for all companies including face-amount certificate companies	S-1	EDGARLink Template 1	XFDL Technical Specification
	Pre-effective amendment	S-1/A	EDGARLink Template 1	
	Registration statement for specified transactions by certain issuers including face-amount certificate companies	S-3	EDGARLink Template 1	XFDL Technical Specification
	Pre-effective amendment	S-3/A	EDGARLink Template 1	
	Post-effective amendment to a registration statement that is not immediately effective upon filing	POS AM	EDGARLink Template 1	XFDL Technical Specification
	Definitive materials filed under paragraph (a), (b), (c), (d), (e) or (f) of Securities Act Rule 497	497	EDGARLink Template 3	XFDL Technical Specification
	Certification of no change in definitive materials under paragraph (j) of Securities Act Rule 497	497J	EDGARLink Template 3	XFDL Technical Specification
Forms N-1 & N-1A	Registration statement for openend management investment companies			
	Initial registration statement filed on Form N-1A for open-end management investment companies	N-1A	EDGARLink Template 1	XFDL Technical Specification
	Pre-effective amendment to a registration statement filed on Form N-1A for open-end management investment companies (this filing cannot be submitted as a 1940 Act only filing)	N-1A/A	EDGARLink Template 1	XFDL Technical Specification

CFR Form/ Schedule/Rule	Description	Submission Type	Tool/Template Number	Filer-Constructed Form Spec.
	Initial registration statement filed on Form N-1 for open-end management investment companies	N-1	EDGARLink Template 1	XFDL Technical Specification
	Pre-effective amendment to a registration statement filed on Form N-1 for open-end management investment companies (this filing cannot be submitted as a 1940 Act only filing)	N-1/A	EDGARLink Template 1	XFDL Technical Specification
	Post-effective amendment filed pursuant to Securities Act Rule 485(a) (this filing cannot be submitted as a 1940 Act only filing)	485APOS	EDGARLink Template 3	XFDL Technical Specification
	Post-effective amendment filed pursuant to Securities Act Rule 485(b) (this filing cannot be submitted as a 1940 Act only filing)	485BPOS	EDGARLink Template 3	XFDL Technical Specification
	Post-effective amendment (for filings made under the 1940 Act only)	POS AMI	EDGARLink Template 3	XFDL Technical Specification
	Post-effective amendment filed pursuant to Securities Act Rule 485(b)(1)(iii) to designate a new effective date for a post-effective amendment previously filed pursuant to Securities Act Rule 485(a) (this filing cannot be submitted as a 1940 Act only filing)	485BXT	EDGARLink Template 3	XFDL Technical Specification
	Definitive materials filed under paragraph (a), (b), (c), (d), (e) or (f) of Securities Act Rule 497	497	EDGARLink Template 3	XFDL Technical Specification
	Certification of no change in definitive materials under paragraph (j) of Securities Act Rule 497	497J	EDGARLink Template 3	XFDL Technical Specification
Rule 498	Summary Prospectus for certain open-end management investment companies filed pursuant to Securities Act Rule 497(k) Cannot be used until March 31, 2009.	497K	EDGARLink Template 3	XFDL Technical Specification
	Profiles for certain open-end management investment companies filed pursuant to Securities Act Rule 497(k)(1)(i) Will no longer be accepted after close of business (5:30 PM EST) on March 30, 2009.	497K1	EDGARLink Template 3	XFDL Technical Specification
	Profiles for certain open-end management investment companies filed pursuant to Securities Act Rule 497(k)(1)(ii) Will no longer be accepted after close of business (5:30 PM EST) on March 30, 2009.	497K2	EDGARLink Template 3	XFDL Technical Specification
	Profiles for certain open-end management investment companies filed pursuant to Will no longer be accepted after close of business (5:30 PM EST) on March 30, 2009. Securities Act Rule 497(k)(1)(iii)(A)	497K3A	EDGARLink Template 3	XFDL Technical Specification

CFR Form/ Schedule/Rule	Description	Submission Type	Tool/Template Number	Filer-Constructed Form Spec.
	Profiles for certain open-end management investment companies filed pursuant to Securities Act Rule 497(k)(1)(iii)(B) Will no longer be accepted after close of business (5:30 PM EST) on March 30, 2009.	497K3B	EDGARLink Template 3	XFDL Technical Specification
Form N-2	Initial filing of a registration statement on Form N-2 for closed-end investment companies	N-2	EDGARLink Template 1	XFDL Technical Specification
	Pre-effective amendment to a registration statement on Form N-2 for closed-end investment companies (this filing cannot be submitted as a 1940 Act only filing)	N-2/A	EDGARLink Template 1	XFDL Technical Specification
	Post-effective amendment (for filings made under the 1940 Act only)	POS AMI	EDGARLink Template 3	XFDL Technical Specification
	Post-effective amendment filed under the 1933 Act only or under both the 1933 and 1940 Acts pursuant to Section 8(c) of the 1933 Act by closed-end investment companies (this filing cannot be submitted as a 1940 Act only filing)	POS 8C	EDGARLink Template 3	XFDL Technical Specification
	Initial filing of a registration statement on Form N-2 for closed-end investment companies filed pursuant to Securities Act Rule 486(a)	N-2	EDGARLink Template 1	XFDL Technical Specification
	Post-effective amendment to filing filed pursuant to Securities Act Rule 486(a)	486APOS	EDGARLink Template 3	XFDL Technical Specification
	Initial filing of a registration statement on Form N-2 for closed-end investment companies filed pursuant to Securities Act Rule 486(b)	N-2	EDGARLink Template 1	XFDL Technical Specification
	Post-effective amendment to filing filed pursuant to Securities Act Rule 486(b)	486BPOS	EDGARLink Template 3	XFDL Technical Specification
	Definitive materials filed under paragraph (a), (b), (c), (d), (e) or (f) of Securities Act Rule 497	497	EDGARLink Template 3	XFDL Technical Specification
	Certification of no change in definitive materials	497J	EDGARLink Template 3	XFDL Technical Specification
	A new registration statement on Form N-2 filed under Securities Act Rule 462(b) by closed-end investment companies of up to an additional 20% of securities for an offering that was registered on Form N-2	N-2MEF	EDGARLink Template 1	XFDL Technical Specification
	Post-effective amendment to Securities Act Rule 462(b) registration statement	POS462B	EDGARLink Template 3	XFDL Technical Specification
	Post-effective amendment to a registration statement filed under Securities Act Rule 462(c)	POS462C	EDGARLink Template 3	XFDL Technical Specification

CFR Form/ Schedule/Rule	Description	Submission Type	Tool/Template Number	Filer-Constructed Form Spec.
	Post-effective amendment filed solely to add exhibits to a registration statement	POS EX	EDGARLink Template 3	XFDL Technical Specification
	Definitive materials filed under paragraph (a), (b), (c), (d), (e) or (f) of Securities Act Rule 497	497	EDGARLink Template 3	XFDL Technical Specification
	Filings made pursuant to Rule 497(h)(2)	497H2	EDGARLink Template 3	XFDL Technical Specification
Form N-3	Initial registration statement on Form N-3 for separate accounts (management investment companies)	N-3	EDGARLink Template 1	XFDL Technical Specification
	Pre-effective amendment to a registration statement on Form N-3 for separate accounts (management investment companies) (this filing cannot be submitted as a 1940 Act only filing)	N-3/A	EDGARLink Template 1	XFDL Technical Specification
	Post-effective amendment filed pursuant to Securities Act Rule 485(a) (this filing cannot be submitted as a 1940 Act only filing)	485APOS	EDGARLink Template 3	XFDL Technical Specification
	Post-effective amendment filed pursuant to Securities Act Rule 485(b) (this filing cannot be submitted as a 1940 Act only filing)	485BPOS	EDGARLink Template 3	XFDL Technical Specification
	Post-effective amendment (for filings made under the 1940 Act only)	POS AMI	EDGARLink Template 3	XFDL Technical Specification
	Post-effective amendment filed pursuant to Securities Act Rule 485(b)(1)(iii) to designate a new effective date for a post-effective amendment previously filed pursuant to Securities Act Rule 485(a) (this filing cannot be submitted as a 1940 Act only filing)	485BXT	EDGARLink Template 3	XFDL Technical Specification
	Definitive materials filed under paragraph (a), (b), (c), (d), (e) or (f) of Securities Act Rule 497	497	EDGARLink Template 3	XFDL Technical Specification
	Certification of no change in definitive materials under paragraph (j) of Securities Act Rule 497	497J	EDGARLink Template 3	XFDL Technical Specification
Form N-4	Initial registration statement on Form N-4 for separate accounts (unit investment trusts)	N-4	EDGARLink Template 1	XFDL Technical Specification
	Pre-effective amendment to a registration statement on Form N-4 for separate accounts (unit investment trusts) (this filing cannot be submitted as a 1940 Act only filing)	N-4/A	EDGARLink Template 1	XFDL Technical Specification
	Pre-effective pricing amendment filed pursuant to Securities Act Rule 487	487	EDGARLink Template 1	XFDL Technical Specification

CFR Form/ Schedule/Rule	Description	Submission Type	Tool/Template Number	Filer- Constructed Form Spec.
	Post-effective amendment filed pursuant to Securities Act Rule 485(a) (this filing cannot be submitted as a 1940 Act only filing)	485APOS	EDGARLink Template 3	XFDL Technical Specification
	Post-effective amendment filed pursuant to Securities Act Rule 485(b) (this filing cannot be submitted as a 1940 Act only filing)	485BPOS	EDGARLink Template 3	XFDL Technical Specification
	Post-effective amendment filed pursuant to Securities Act Rule 485(b)(1)(iii) to designate a new effective date for a post-effective amendment previously filed pursuant to Securities Act Rule 485(a) (this filing cannot be submitted as a 1940 Act only filing)	485BXT	EDGARLink Template 3	XFDL Technical Specification
	Post-effective amendment (for filings made under the 1940 Act only)	POS AMI	EDGARLink Template 3	XFDL Technical Specification
	Definitive materials filed under paragraph (a), (b), (c), (d), (e) or (f) of Securities Act Rule 497	497	EDGARLink Template 3	XFDL Technical Specification
	Certification of no change in definitive materials under paragraph (j) of Securities Act Rule 497	497J	EDGARLink Template 3	XFDL Technical Specification
Form N-6	Registration statement for separate accounts (unit investment trusts)	N-6	EDGARLink Template 1	XFDL Technical Specification
	Pre-effective amendment to a registration statement filed on Form N-6 for separate accounts (unit investment trusts)	N-6/A	EDGARLink Template 1	XFDL Technical Specification
	Pre-effective pricing amendment filed pursuant to Securities Act Rule 487	487	EDGARLink Template 1	XFDL Technical Specification
	Post-effective amendment filed pursuant to Securities Act Rule 485(a) (this filing cannot be submitted as a 1940 Act only filing)	485APOS	EDGARLink Template 3	XFDL Technical Specification
	Post-effective amendment filed pursuant to Securities Act Rule 485(b) (this filing cannot be submitted as a 1940 Act only filing)	485BPOS	EDGARLink Template 3	XFDL Technical Specification
	Post-effective amendment filed pursuant to Securities Act Rule 485(b)(1)(iii) to designate a new effective date for a post-effective amendment previously filed pursuant to Securities Act Rule 485(a) (this filing cannot be submitted as a 1940 Act only filing)	485BXT	EDGARLink Template 3	XFDL Technical Specification
	Post-effective amendment (for filings made under the 1940 Act only)	POS AMI	EDGARLink Template 3	XFDL Technical Specification
	Definitive materials filed under paragraph (a), (b), (c), (d), (e) or (f) of Securities Act Rule 497	497	EDGARLink Template 3	XFDL Technical Specification

CFR Form/ Schedule/Rule	Description	Submission Type	Tool/Template Number	Filer-Constructed Form Spec.
	Certification of no change in definitive materials under paragraph (j) of Securities Act Rule 497	497J	EDGARLink Template 3	XFDL Technical Specification
Form S-6	Initial registration statement filed on Form S-6 for unit investment trusts	S-6	EDGARLink Template 1	XFDL Technical Specification
	Pre-effective amendment	S-6/A	EDGARLink Template 1	XFDL Technical Specification
	Pre-effective pricing amendment filed pursuant to Securities Act Rule 487	487	EDGARLink Template 1	XFDL Technical Specification
	Initial undertaking to file reports	UNDER	EDGARLink Template 3	XFDL Technical Specification
	Amendment	UNDER/A	EDGARLink Template 3	XFDL Technical Specification
	Post-effective amendment filed pursuant to Securities Act Rule 485(a) (this filing cannot be submitted as a 1940 Act only filing)	485APOS	EDGARLink Template 3	XFDL Technical Specification
	Post-effective amendment filed pursuant to Securities Act Rule 485(b) (this filing cannot be submitted as a 1940 Act only filing)	485BPOS	EDGARLink Template 3	XFDL Technical Specification
	Post-effective amendment filed pursuant to Securities Act Rule 485(b)(1)(iii) to designate a new effective date for a post-effective amendment previously filed pursuant to Securities Act Rule 485(a) (this filing cannot be submitted as a 1940 Act only filing)	485BXT	EDGARLink Template 3	XFDL Technical Specification
	Definitive materials filed under paragraph (a), (b), (c), (d), (e) or (f) of Securities Act Rule 497	497	EDGARLink Template 3	XFDL Technical Specification
	Certification of no change in definitive materials under paragraph (j) of Securities Act Rule 497	497J	EDGARLink Template 3	XFDL Technical Specification
Form N-5	Registration statement for small business investment companies	N-5	EDGARLink Template 1	XFDL Technical Specification
	Pre-effective amendment to a registration statement on Form N-5 for small business investment companies (this filing cannot be submitted as a 1940 Act only filing)	N-5/A	EDGARLink Template 1	
	Post-effective amendment (for filings made under the 1940 Act only)	POS AMI	EDGARLink Template 3	XFDL Technical Specification

CFR Form/ Schedule/Rule	Description	Submission Type	Tool/Template Number	Filer-Constructed Form Spec.
	Post-effective amendment filed under the 1933 Act only or under both the 1933 and 1940 Acts pursuant to Section 8(c) of the 1933 Act by closed-end investment companies (this filing cannot be submitted as a 1940 Act only filing)	POS 8C	EDGARLink Template 3	XFDL Technical Specification
	Definitive materials filed under paragraph (a), (b), (c), (d), (e) or (f) of Securities Act Rule 497	497	EDGARLink Template 3	XFDL Technical Specification
	Certification of no change in definitive materials under paragraph (j) of Securities Act Rule 497	497J	EDGARLink Template 3	XFDL Technical Specification
Form N-14	Initial registration statement filed on Form N-14 for open-end investment company, including those filed with automatic effectiveness under Rule 488 (business combinations)	N-14	EDGARLink Template 1	XFDL Technical Specification
	Pre-effective amendment	N-14/A	EDGARLink Template 1	
	Post-effective amendment filed pursuant to Securities Act Rule 485(a) (this filing cannot be submitted as a 1940 Act only filing)	485APOS	EDGARLink Template 3	XFDL Technical Specification
	Post-effective amendment filed pursuant to Securities Act Rule 485(b) (this filing cannot be submitted as a 1940 Act only filing)	485BPOS	EDGARLink Template 3	XFDL Technical Specification
	Initial registration statement filed on Form N-14 by closed-end investment company (business combinations)	N-14 8C	EDGARLink Template 1	XFDL Technical Specification
	Pre-effective amendment	N-14 8C/A	EDGARLink Template 1	
	Post-effective amendment filed under the 1933 Act only or under both the 1933 and 1940 Acts pursuant to Section 8(c) of the 1933 Act by closed-end investment companies (this filing cannot be submitted as a 1940 Act only filing)	POS 8C	EDGARLink Template 3	XFDL Technical Specification
	Definitive materials filed under paragraph (a), (b), (c), (d), (e) or (f) of Securities Act Rule 497	497	EDGARLink Template 3	XFDL Technical Specification
	Certification of no change in definitive materials under paragraph (j) of Securities Act Rule 497	497J	EDGARLink Template 3	XFDL Technical Specification
	A new registration statement filed on Form N-14 by closed end investment companies filed under Securities Act Rule 462(b) of up to an additional 20% of securities for an offering that was registered on Form N-14	N-14MEF	EDGARLink Template 1	XFDL Technical Specification
	Post-effective amendment to Securities Act Rule 462(b) registration statement	POS462B	EDGARLink Template 3	XFDL Technical Specification
	Post-effective amendment to Securities Act Rule 462(c) registration statement	POS462C	EDGARLink Template 3	

CFR Form/ Schedule/Rule	Description	Submission Type	Tool/Template Number	Filer- Constructed Form Spec.
	Definitive materials filed under paragraph (a), (b), (c), (d), (e) or (f) of Securities Act Rule 497	497	EDGARLink Template 3	XFDL Technical Specification
MISCELLANEOUS FILINGS UNDER THE SECURITIES ACT				
Rule 425	Filing under Securities Act Rule 425 of certain prospectuses and communications in connection with business combination transactions **Note:** Form 425 can be filed as part of Form 8-K. For filers subject to 8-K filing requirements, we recommend the use of the 8-K combined form type as the easiest method for fulfilling your filing requirement for both forms	425	EDGARLink Template 2	XFDL Technical Specification
Rule 473	Separately filed delaying amendment under Securities Act Rule 473 to delay effectiveness of a 1933 Act registration statement	DEL AM	EDGARLink Template 3	XFDL Technical Specification
Rule 477	Registration Withdrawal Request	RW	EDGARLink Template 3	XFDL Technical Specification
	Withdrawal of a request for withdrawal of a registration statement	RW WD	EDGARLink Template 1	XFDL Technical Specification
	Withdrawal of amendment to a registration statement filed under the Securities Act	AW	EDGARLink Template 3	XFDL Technical Specification
	Withdrawal of a request for withdrawal of an amendment to a registration statement	AW WD	EDGARLink Template 1	XFDL Technical Specification
Rule 482	Filing by certain investment companies of Securities Act Rule 482 advertising in accordance with Securities Act Rule 497 and the Note to Rule 482(c)	497AD	EDGARLink Template 3	XFDL Technical Specification
REGISTRATION OF SECURITIES BY CERTAIN INVESTMENT COMPANIES PURSUANT TO RULE 24F-2				
Rule 24F-2	Rule 24f-2 notice filed on Form 24F-2	24F-2NT	EDGARLink Template 1	XFDL Technical Specification
	Amendment	24F-2NT/A	EDGARLink Template 1	XFDL Technical Specification
OTHER COMPANY ACT REGISTRATION STATEMENTS				
Form N-8A	Initial notification of registration under section 8(a) filed on Form N-8A	N-8A	EDGARLink Template 2	XFDL Technical Specification
	Amendment	N-8A/A	EDGARLink Template 2	

CFR Form/ Schedule/Rule	Description	Submission Type	Tool/Template Number	Filer-Constructed Form Spec.
Form N-8B-2	Initial registration statement for unit investment trusts filed on Form N-8B-2	N-8B-2	EDGARLink Template 2	XFDL Technical Specification
	Amendment	N-8B-2/A	EDGARLink Template 2	
Form N-8B-3	Initial registration statement for periodic payment plans filed on Form N-8B-3	N-8B-3	EDGARLink Template 2	XFDL Technical Specification
	Amendment	N-8B-3/A	EDGARLink Template 2	
Form N-8B-4	Initial registration statement for face-amount certificate companies filed on Form N-8B-4	N-8B-4	EDGARLink Template 2	XFDL Technical Specification
	Amendment	N-8B-4/A	EDGARLink Template 2	

SUBMISSION TYPES FOR BUSINESS DEVELOPMENT COMPANIES

CFR Form/ Schedule/Rule	Description	Submission Type	Tool/Template Number	Filer-Constructed Form Spec.
Form N-6F	Notice of intent by business development companies to elect to be subject to Sections 55 through 65 of the 1940 Act filed on Form N-6F	N-6F	EDGARLink Template 2	XFDL Technical Specification
	Amendment	N-6F/A	EDGARLink Template 2	
Form N-54A	Notification of election by business development companies filed on Form N-54A	N-54A	EDGARLink Template 2	XFDL Technical Specification
	Amendment	N-54A/A	EDGARLink Template 2	
Form N-54C	Notification of withdrawal by business development companies filed on Form N-54C	N-54C	EDGARLink Template 2	XFDL Technical Specification
	Amendment	N-54C/A	EDGARLink Template 2	

OTHER INVESTMENT COMPANY SUBMISSION TYPES

CFR Form/ Schedule/Rule	Description	Submission Type	Tool/Template Number	Filer-Constructed Form Spec.
Rule 8b-25(a)	Filing by investment company of application under Investment Company Act Rule 8b-25(a) requesting extension of time for filing certain information, document or report	40-8B25	EDGARLink Template 2	XFDL Technical Specification
Form 17F-1	Initial certificate of accounting of securities and similar investments in the custody of management investment companies filed pursuant to Rule 17f-1 of the Investment Company Act of 1940 filed on Form N-17F-1	40-17F1	EDGARLink Template 2	XFDL Technical Specification
	Amendment	40-17F1/A	EDGARLink Template 2	

CFR Form/ Schedule/Rule	Description	Submission Type	Tool/Template Number	Filer-Constructed Form Spec.
Form 17F-2	Initial certificate of accounting of securities and similar investments in the custody of management investment companies filed pursuant to Rule 17f-2 of the Investment Company Act of 1940 filed on Form N-17F-2	40-17F2	EDGARLink Template 2	XFDL Technical Specification
	Amendment	40-17F2/A	EDGARLink Template 2	
Rule 17g-1(g)(1)	Fidelity bond filed pursuant to Rule 17g-1(g)(1) of the Investment Company Act of 1940	40-17G	EDGARLink Template 2	XFDL Technical Specification
	Amendment	40-17G/A	EDGARLink Template 2	
Rule 17g-1(g)(2) or (3)	Filings of claim or settlement pursuant to rule 17g-1(g)(1)(2) or (3) of the Investment Company Act of 1940	40-17GCS	EDGARLink Template 2	XFDL Technical Specification
	Amendment	40-17GCS/A	EDGARLink Template 2	
Rule 24b-2	Filing of sales literature pursuant to Rule 24b-2 under the Investment Company Act of 1940	40-24B2	EDGARLink Template 2	XFDL Technical Specification
	Amendment	40-24B2/A	EDGARLink Template 2	
ICA Section 33	Copies of all stockholder derivative actions filed with a court against an investment company or an affiliate thereof pursuant to Section 33 of the Investment Company Act of 1940	40-33	EDGARLink Template 2	XFDL Technical Specification
	Amendment **Note:** May be filed electronically on a voluntary basis.	40-33/A	EDGARLink Template 2	
Form N-18F-1	Initial notification of election pursuant to Rule 18f-1 filed on Form N-18F-1	N-18F1	EDGARLink Template 2	XFDL Technical Specification
	Amendment	N-18F1/A	EDGARLink Template 2	XFDL Technical Specification
Rule 23c-2(b)	Notice by closed-end investment companies of intention to call or redeem their own securities under Investment Company Act Rule 23c-2	N-23C-2	EDGARLink Template 2	XFDL Technical Specification
	Amendment	N-23C-2/A	EDGARLink Template 2	XFDL Technical Specification
Form N-23C-3	Notification of periodic repurchase offer Filed pursuant to Rule 23c-3(b) only	N-23C3A	EDGARLink Template 2	XFDL Technical Specification
	Amendment	N-23C3A/A	EDGARLink Template 2	

CFR Form/ Schedule/Rule	Description	Submission Type	Tool/Template Number	Filer-Constructed Form Spec.
	Filing pursuant to Rule 23c-3(c) only on Form N-23C-3	N-23C3B	EDGARLink Template 2	XFDL Technical Specification
	Amendment	N-23C3B/A	EDGARLink Template 2	
	Filing pursuant to Rule 23c-3(b) and (c) on Form N-23C-3	N-23C3C	EDGARLink Template 2	XFDL Technical Specification
	Amendment	N-23C3C/A	EDGARLink Template 2	
Form N-27D-1	Accounting for segregated trust accounts on Form N-27D-1	N-27D-1	EDGARLink Template 2	XFDL Technical Specification
	Amendment	N-27D-1/A	EDGARLink Template 2	

PERIODIC REPORTS FOR REGISTERED INVESTMENT COMPANIES

CFR Form/ Schedule/Rule	Description	Submission Type	Tool/Template Number	Filer-Constructed Form Spec.
Form N-SAR	Semi-annual report for management companies filed on Form N-SAR	NSAR-A	EDGARLink Template 3	XFDL Technical Specification
	Amendment	NSAR-A/A		
	Transitional semi-annual report filed on Form N-SAR	NSAR-AT	EDGARLink Template 3	XFDL Technical Specification
	Amendment	NSAR-AT/A		
	Annual report for management companies filed on Form N-SAR	NSAR-B	EDGARLink Template 3	XFDL Technical Specification
	Amendment	NSAR-B/A	EDGARLink Template 3	
	Transitional annual report filed on Form N-SAR	NSAR-BT	EDGARLink Template 3	XFDL Technical Specification
	Amendment	NSAR-BT/A	EDGARLink Template 3	
	Annual report for unit investment trusts filed on Form N-SAR	NSAR-U	EDGARLink Template 3	XFDL Technical Specification
	Amendment	NSAR-U/A	EDGARLink Template 3	
Form N-CSR	Certified annual shareholder report of registered management investment companies filed on Form N-CSR	N-CSR	EDGARLink Template 3	XFDL Technical Specification
	Amendment	N-CSR/A	EDGARLink Template 3	
	Certified semi-annual shareholder report of registered management investment companies filed on Form NCSR	N-CSRS	EDGARLink Template 3	XFDL Technical Specification
	Amendment	N-CSRS/A	EDGARLink Template 3	

CFR Form/ Schedule/Rule	Description	Submission Type	Tool/Template Number	Filer-Constructed Form Spec.
Form N-PX	Annual Report of Proxy Voting Record of Registered Management Investment Companies filed on Form N-PX	N-PX	EDGARLink Template 3	XFDL Technical Specification
	Amendment	N-PX/A	EDGARLink Template 3	
Form N-Q	Quarterly Schedule of Portfolio Holdings of Registered Management Investment Company filed on Form N-Q	N-Q	EDGARLink Template 3	XFDL Technical Specification
	Amendment	N-Q/A	EDGARLink Template 3	
Rule 12b-25	Notice under Exchange Act Rule 12b-25 of inability to timely file Form NSAR	NT-NSAR	EDGARLink Template 3	XFDL Technical Specification
	Amendment	NT-NSAR/A	EDGARLink Template 3	
	Notice under Exchange Act Rule 12b25 of inability to timely file Form NCSR (annual or semiannual report)	NT-NCSR	EDGARLink Template 3	XFDL Technical Specification
	Amendment	NT-NCSR/A	EDGARLink Template 3	
Rule 30b2-1	Initial annual and semi-annual reports mailed to investment company shareholders pursuant to Rule 30e-1 (other than those required to be submitted as part of Form N-CSR)	N-30D	EDGARLink Template 3	XFDL Technical Specification
	Amendment	N-30D/A	EDGARLink Template 3	
	Periodic and interim reports mailed to investment company shareholders (other than annual and semi-annual reports mailed to shareholders pursuant to Rule 30e-1)	N-30B-2	EDGARLink Template 3	XFDL Technical Specification

REGULATION E FILINGS

Regulation E	Notification under Regulation E by small business investment companies and business development companies filed on Form 1-E.	1-E	EDGARLink Template 3	XFDL Technical Specification
	Amendment to a notification under Regulation E by small business investment companies and business development companies filed on Form 1-E	1-E/A	EDGARLink Template 3	XFDL Technical Specification
	Sales material filed pursuant to Rule 607 under Regulation E	1-E AD	EDGARLink Template 3	XFDL Technical Specification
	Amendment to sales material filed pursuant to Rule 607 under Regulation E	1-E AD/A	EDGARLink Template 3	XFDL Technical Specification
	Report of sales of securities pursuant to Rule 609 under Regulation E filed on Form 2-E	2-E	EDGARLink Template 3	XFDL Technical Specification

CFR Form/ Schedule/Rule	Description	Submission Type	Tool/Template Number	Filer-Constructed Form Spec.
	Amendment of a report of sales of securities pursuant to Rule 609 under Regulation E filed on Form 2-E	2-E/A	EDGARLink Template 3	XFDL Technical Specification

APPLICATION FOR AN ORDER UNDER THE INVESTMENT COMPANY ACT

CFR Form/ Schedule/Rule	Description	Submission Type	Tool/Template Number	Filer-Constructed Form Spec.
Rule 0-2	Application under the Investment Company Act submitted pursuant to Investment Company Act Rule 0-2 reviewed by the Office of Insurance Products	40-OIP	EDGARLink Template 3	XFDL Technical Specification
	Amendment to an application under the Investment Company Act submitted pursuant to Investment Company Act Rule 0-2 reviewed by the Office of Insurance Products	40-OIP/A	EDGARLink Template 3	XFDL Technical Specification
	Application under the Investment Company Act by an employees' securities company submitted pursuant to Investment Company Act Rule 0-2	40-6B	EDGARLink Template 3	XFDL Technical Specification
	Amendment to an application under the Investment Company Act by an employees' securities company submitted pursuant to Investment Company Act Rule 0-2	40-6B/A	EDGARLink Template 3	XFDL Technical Specification
	Application under the Investment Company Act submitted pursuant to Investment Company Act Rule 0-2 other than those reviewed by Office of Insurance Products	40-APP	EDGARLink Template 3	XFDL Technical Specification
	Amendment to an application under the Investment Company Act submitted pursuant to Investment Company Act Rule 0-2 other than those reviewed by Office of Insurance Products	40-APP/A	EDGARLink Template 3	XFDL Technical Specification

APPLICATION FOR DEREGISTRATION OF INVESTMENT COMPANIES

CFR Form/ Schedule/Rule	Description	Submission Type	Tool/Template Number	Filer-Constructed Form Spec.
Form N-8F	Application for deregistration made on Form N-8F	N-8F	EDGARLink Template 2	
	Amendment	N-8F/A	EDGARLink Template 2	
Rule 0-2	Initial application for deregistration pursuant to Investment Company Act Rule 0-2	40-8F-2	EDGARLink Template 2	XFDL Technical Specification
	Amendment	40-8F-2/A	EDGARLink Template 2	

Table 3-6: Development Bank Submission Types Accepted by EDGAR

CFR Form/ Schedule/Rule	Description	Submission Type	Tool/Template Number	Filer-Constructed Form Spec.
QRTLYRPT	Periodic Development Bank filing, submitted quarterly	QRTLYRPT	EDGARLink Template 2	XFDL Technical Specification
	Amendment	QRTLYRPT/A	EDGARLink Template 2	
ANNLRPT	Periodic Development Bank filing, submitted annually	ANNLRPT	EDGARLink Template 2	XFDL Technical Specification
	Amendment	ANNLRPT/A	EDGARLink Template 2	
DSTRBRPT	Distribution of primary obligations Development Bank report	DSTRBRPT	EDGARLink Template 2	XFDL Technical Specification
	Amendment	DSTRBRPT/A	EDGARLink Template 2	

Notes: (1) These submission types are to be filed ONLY by the Development Banks. BW-2 and BW-3 submission types have been rescinded; please use QRTLYRPT, ANNLRPT, and DSTRBRPT Form Types.

Table 3-7: Correspondence Submission Types

CFR Form/ Schedule/Rule	Description	Submission Type	Tool/Template Number	Filer-Constructed Form Spec.
Correspondence	A correspondence can be sent as a document with another submission type or can be sent as a separate submission. Correspondence is not publicly disseminated immediately. The SEC staff may release all or portions of these documents electronically if they relate to the staff's review process. See SEC Press Release 2004-89, "SEC Staff to Publicly Release Comment Letters and Responses."	CORRESP	EDGARLink Template 4	XFDL Technical Specification

»»→ *Reproduced below is a document that the SEC posted on its website (www.sec.gov/info/edgar/ fedwire.htm) as a resource for making fee payments to the Commission's designated financial agent.*

New Fee Payment Instructions, Effective Feb. 4, 2008

United States Securities and Exchange Commission

NOTICE: NEW SEC Financial Agent!

The U.S. Department of Treasury's Financial Management Service has designated U.S. Bank of St. Louis, Missouri as the new Financial Agent for General Lockbox Services for the SEC. US Bank will take over this responsibility from Mellon Bank on **February 4, 2008.** All fee payments (wires and checks) must be submitted to US Bank on and after this date. No payments should be submitted to Mellon Bank after **February 1, 2008**

Introduction

All companies that sell their securities to investors in United States markets are required to file certain information about their finances, ownership, and management with the SEC on a periodic basis. Other companies, such as mutual funds, and certain individuals who own securities are required to file reports with the SEC as well. There is a fee involved in many of these filings; the information that follows is designed for filers who anticipate submitting fee payments via wire transfer. The language is fairly technical.

Filers should note that inputting the special characters used to configure the wire in a readable format is the responsibility of the Federal Reserve or the bank and/or wire service.

- The tags used for wire transfer are numeric (e.g., 2000, 3000, and 4320). The FEDWIRE guide, which follows, provides explanations for each required numeric tag.
- The SEC adds a specific field to identify the payor, regardless of whether the payor is the registrant (see tag 6000)

Note: Filers should be aware that inputting the special characters used to configure the wire in a readable format is the responsibility of the Federal Reserve or the bank and/or wire service.

Instructions

These instructions provide direction regarding remitting fees to the SEC by wire transfer (FEDWIRE), check or money order. You may contact the Fee Account Services Branch in the Office of Financial Management at (202) 551-8989 for additional information if you have questions.

Instructions for Wire Transfer (FEDWIRE)

General Information

- US Bank in St. Louis, Missouri, is the U.S. Treasury designated financial agent for SEC filing fee payments. The hours of operation at US Bank are 8:30a.m. to 6:00p.m. eastern time for wires.
- Any bank or wire transfer service may initiate wire transfers of filing fee payments through the FEDWIRE system to US Bank. A filing entity does **not** need to establish an account at US Bank in order to remit filing fee payments.
- To ensure proper credit and prompt filing acceptance, it is critical to include:
- the **SEC's account number at US Bank (152307768324)** and
- the **payor's SEC-assigned CIK (Central Index Key) number (also known as the SEC-assigned registrant or payor account number) in all wire transfers of SEC filing fees.** You may refer to the *examples below* for the proper format.

Wire transfers are not instantaneous. The time required to process a wire transfer through the FEDWIRE system, from origination to receipt by US Bank, varies substantially. It is important that all filers discuss with their bank or wire transfer service their unique procedures and timing.

The SEC advises filers to allow sufficient time to complete all transactions prior to submission of filings registering securities. These filings will not be accepted if sufficient funds have not been received by the SEC at the time of filing. Such filings include:

- Registration statements pursuant to 6(b) of the Securities Act of 1933 that provides for the registration of securities and mandates the receipt of the appropriate fee payment upon filing (*e.g.*, filing submission types such as S-1, S-2, S-3, N-1A, N-2, F-1, F-2, and 24F-2NT); and

- Transactional filings pursuant to the Securities Exchange Act of 1934 (*e.g.*, form types such as PRE CON, PREM14A* and PREM14C* (*except when filed by a registered investment company)).

- All filers are advised to obtain from their bank or wire transfer service the **"FED" reference number** of the wire transfer. Having this number can greatly facilitate tracing the funds if any problems do occur.

If a wire transfer of SEC filing fees does not contain the required information in the proper format, the SEC may not be able to identify the payor and **the acceptance of filings may be delayed**. To ensure proper credit, it is critical that all required information be provided to the sending bank or wire transfer service. SEC data must be inserted in the proper fields. The most critical data are the SEC's account number at US Bank and the SEC-assigned account number identified as the CIK number. For additional information on filing fee procedures, please refer to 17 CFR 202.3a, Instructions for Filing Fees. If you have any questions, please contact the Fee Account Services Branch in the Office of Financial Management at (202) 551-8989.

FEDWIRE Field Tags and Terminology

Tag	Terminology	Format
{2000}	Transaction Dollar Amount - Total Wire Value (Example: $250.00 formatted is 000000025000)	Total wire amount, no commas or decimals. The last two positions of the transaction dollar amount are for cents. 12 positions total.
{3100}	Sending (Initiating) Bank's ABA Number and Sending (Initiating) Bank's Name	000123790 (9 positions) XYZ Bank
{3400}	ABA = American Bankers Association Receiving Bank's ABA Number and Receiving Bank's Name	081000210 (9 positions) US BANK
{4200}	Beneficiary Information (SEC's Account number at US Bank, which should always be 152307768324), Name of the beneficiary (which should always be Securities and Exchange Commission).	152307768324 Securities and Exchange Commission
{4320}	Reference to Beneficiary. Only use this field if the SEC registrant and the payor are different. In this field, the unique CIK number is used for the registrant. In this field, the initials "CIK" should be entered immediately followed by the registrant's CIK number. (If the registrant and payor are the same, use only the {6000} field.)	CIK9999999995
{5000}	Originator Information - Originating customer account number from sending bank, name of originating company address, city, state, and zip code.	12345 ABC CO 123 ABC PLAZA NEW YORK NY 10258
{6000}	Originator **(Payor)** to Beneficiary Information. This is the unique SEC identifier known as the CIK of the payor. Enter the initials "CIK" followed immediately by payor's CIK number. (If the registrant is not the payor, enter the registrant's CIK in the {4320} field, as shown above).	CIK9999999998

NOTE: The numeric tags displayed in bold contain the wire information that you provide to the banks and/or wire service sending the wire. Your bank and/or wire service or the Federal Reserve will automatically enter the required special characters where appropriate prior to sending the wire to US Bank.

Example and Description of the Fedwire Format

Definition of Fed Tag Values	Fed Tag	Value
Transaction Dollar Amount (total wire value) with no decimal, no comma(s) (12 positions) (Example: $250.00 = 000000025000)	{2000}	000000025000
Sending Bank's ABA Number (9 positions), and **Sending Bank's Name**	{3100}	000123790 XYZ BANK
Receiving Bank's ABA Number (9 positions), and **Receiving Bank's Name**	{3400}	081000210 US BANK
Beneficiary Information (BNF) (SEC's Account Number at US Bank) Beneficiary Name	{4200}	152307768324 Securities & Exchange Commission
Reference to Beneficiary (RFB) Registrant's SEC-assigned CIK number if payor and registrant are different. In this field, enter the initials "CIK" followed immediately by the SEC-assigned CIK number. An example of this is CIK9999999995. (Do not use spaces, blanks, or special characters).	{4320}	CIK9999999995
Originator Information (ORG) Originating customer account number from sending bank; name of originating company; and originator's address, city, state, and zip code.	{5000}	12345 ABC COMPANY 123 ABC PLAZA NEW YORK NY 10258
Originator to Beneficiary Information, (OBI) used to identify the SEC CIK number of the payor. In this field, enter the initials as "CIK" followed immediately by the SEC-assigned CIK number. An example of this is CIK9999999998. (Do not use spaces, blanks, or special characters.)	{6000}	CIK9999999998

Examples

Fedwire Format — Third Party Payor Submitting Payment for Filing

In this example: ABC Company, CIK9999999998 is the payor having its wire payment submitted to US Bank, and XYZ Company, CIK 9999999995 is the registrant. See Tags {4320} (use when registrant and payor are not the same, and therefore have different CIK numbers) and {6000} (always payor's CIK).

Fed Tag	Value
{2000}	000000025000
{3100}	000123790 XYZ BANK
{3400}	081000210 US BANK
{4200}	152307768324 SECURITIES AND EXCHANGE COMMISSION
{4320}	CIK9999999995
{5000}	12345 ABC CO 123 ABC PLAZA NEW YORK NY 10258
{6000}	CIK9999999998

Fedwire Format — Registrant is the Payor

In this example: JJJ CO, CIK9999999998 is the payor and the registrant; therefore, tag {4320} is not used. Tag {6000} contains the CIK information for payment to match with the right account at the SEC.

SEC Handbook

Fed Tag	Value
{2000}	000000025000
{3100}	00034690 NEW BANK
{3400}	081000210 US BANK
{4200}	152307768324 SECURITIES AND EXCHANGE COMMISSION
{5000}	37774 JJJ CO 100 BIG PLAZA ALBANY NEW YORK NY 12714
{6000}	CIK9999999998

Instructions for Check Payments

To remit your SEC filing fee payment by check or money order, you must make them payable to the Securities and Exchange Commission, omitting the name or title of any official of the Commission. On the front of the check or money order, you must include the SEC's account number (152307768324) and CIK number of the account to which the fee is to be applied.

You must mail checks (certified or cashier's check) or money orders to the following U.S. Bank addresses. U.S. Bank does not support walk-in deliveries by individuals.

For USPS remittances, they MUST be sent to the following PO Box address.

Securities & Exchange Commission
P.O. Box 979081
St. Louis, MO 63197-9000

The following address can be used for common carriers such as FedEx, Airborne, DHL, and UPS.

U.S. Bank
Government Lockbox 979081
1005 Convention Plaza
SL-MO-C2-GL
St. Louis, MO 63101

http://www.sec.gov/info/edgar/fedwire.htm

SECURITIES ACT FORMS (selected)

SECURITIES ACT FORMS (SELECTED)

TABLE OF CONTENTS

SECURITIES ACT FORMS

[¶ 7501]
FORM F-1

[As last amended in Release No. 33-8959, effective December 6, 2008, 73 F.R 58300.]

SECURITIES AND EXCHANGE COMMISSION

Washington, D.C. 20549

FORM F-1

REGISTRATION STATEMENT UNDER THE SECURITIES ACT OF 1933

Form F-1

SECURITIES AND EXCHANGE COMMISSION

Washington, D.C. 20549

FORM F-1

REGISTRATION STATEMENT UNDER THE SECURITIES ACT OF 1933

. . . .

(Exact name of Registrant as specified in its charter)

. . . .

(Translation of Registrant's name into English)

(State or other jurisdiction of incorporation or organization)	(Primary Standard Industrial Classification Code Number)	(I.R.S. Employer Identification No.)

. . . .

(Address, including zip code, and telephone number, including area code, of registrant's principal executive offices)

. . . .

(Name, address, including zip code, and telephone number, including area code, of agent for service)

Approximate date of commencement of proposed sale to the public . . . .

If any of the securities being registered on this Form are to be offered on a delayed or continuous basis pursuant to Rule 415 under the Securities Act, check the following box. ☐

If this Form is filed to register additional securities for an offering pursuant to Rule 462(b) under the Securities Act, check the following box and list the Securities Act registration statement number of the earlier effective registration statement for the same offering. ☐ . . . .

If this Form is a post-effective amendment filed pursuant to Rule 462(c) under the Securities Act, check the following box and list the Securities Act registration statement number of the earlier effective registration statement for the same offering. ☐ . . . .

If this Form is a post-effective amendment filed pursuant to Rule 462(d) under the Securities Act, check the following box and list the Securities Act registration statement number of the earlier effective registration statement for the same offering. ☐ . . . .

Calculation of Registration Fee

Title of each class of securities to be registered	Amount to be registered	Proposed maximum offering price per unit	Proposed maximum aggregate offering price	Amount of registration fee

Note: Specific details relating to the fee calculation shall be furnished in notes to the table, including references to provisions of Rule 457 relied upon, if the basis of the calculation is not otherwise evident from the information presented in the table. If the filing fee is calculated pursuant to Rule 457(o) under the Securities Act, only the title of the class of securities to be registered, the proposed maximum aggregate offering price for that class of securities and the amount of registration fee need to appear in the Calculation of Registration Fee table. Any difference between the dollar amount of securities registered for such offerings and the dollar amount of securities sold may be carried forward on a future registration statement pursuant to Rule 429 under the Securities Act.

GENERAL INSTRUCTIONS

I. Eligibility Requirements for Use of Form F-1

A. Form F-1 shall be used for registration under the Securities Act of 1933 ("Securities Act") of securities of all foreign private issuers as defined in Rule 405 (§ 230.405 of this chapter) for which no other form is authorized or prescribed.

In addition, this form shall not be used for an offering of asset-backed securities, as defined in 17 CFR 229.1101.

B. If a registrant is a majority-owned subsidiary, which does not itself meet the conditions of these eligibility requirements, it shall nevertheless be deemed to have met such conditions if its parent meets the conditions and if the parent fully guarantees the securities being registered as to principal and interest. Note: In such an instance the parent-guarantor is the issuer of a separate security consisting of the guarantee which must be concurrently registered but may be registered on the same registration statement as are the guaranteed securities. Both the parent-guarantor and the subsidiary shall each disclose the information required by this Form as if each were the only registrant except that if the subsidiary will not be eligible to file annual reports on Form 20-F after the effective date of the registration statement, then it shall disclose the information specified in Forms S-1 (§ 239.11 of this chapter). Rule 3-10 of Regulation S-X (§ 210.3-10 of this chapter) specifies the financial statements required.

II. Application of General Rules and Regulations

A. Attention is directed to the General Rules and Regulations under the Securities Act, particularly Regulation C (§ 230.400 et seq. of this chapter) thereunder. That Regulation contains general requirements regarding the preparation and filing of registration statements.

B. Attention is directed to Regulation S-K (§ 229.22 of this chapter) and Form 20-F (§ 249.220f of this chapter) for the requirements applicable to the content of registration statements under the Securities Act. Where this Form directs the registrant to furnish information required by Regulation S-K or Form 20-F and the item of Regulation S-K or Form 20-F so provides, information need only be furnished to the extent appropriate.

C. A registrant must file the Form F-1 registration statement in electronic format via the Commission's Electronic Data Gathering and Retrieval System (EDGAR) in accordance with the EDGAR rules set forth in Regulation S-T (17 CFR Part 232), except that a registrant that has obtained a hardship exception under Regulation S-T Rule 201 or 202 (17 CFR 232.201 or 232.202) may file the registration statement in paper. For assistance with technical questions about EDGAR or to request an access code, call the EDGAR Filer Support Office at (202) 942-8900. For assistance with questions about the EDGAR rules, call the Office of EDGAR and Information Analysis at (202) 942-2940.

D. The Form F-1 registration statement must be in the English language, as required by Regulation S-T Rule 306 (17 CFR 232.306) for electronic filings and Securities Act Rule 403(c) (17 CFR 230.403(c)), generally. If the registration statement requires the inclusion, as an exhibit or attachment, of a document that is in a foreign language, the registrant must provide instead either an English translation or an English summary of the foreign language document in accordance with Securities Act Rule 403(c) (17 CFR 230.403(c)) for both electronic and paper filings. The registrant may submit a copy of the unabridged foreign language document along with the English translation or English summary as permitted by Regulation S-T Rule 306(b) (17 CFR 232.306(b)) for electronic filings or by Securities Act Rule 403(c)(4) (17 CFR 230.403(c)(4)) for paper filings.

III. Exchange Offers

If any of the securities being registered are to be offered in exchange for securities of any other issuer the prospectus shall also include the information which would be required by Item 4 if the securities of such other issuer were registered on this Form. If such other issuer is not eligible to use this Form F-1, then the prospectus shall include the information which would be required by Item 11 of Form S-1 (§ 239.11 of this chapter) if the securities of such other issuer were being registered on Form S-1. There shall also be included the information concerning such securities of such other issuer which would be called for by Items 10.A and 10.B of Form 20-F or Item 12 of Form 20-F, as applicable if such securities were being registered. In connection with this instruction, reference is made to Rule 409 (§ 229.501 of this chapter).

IV. Roll-up Transactions

If the securities to be registered on this Form will be issued in a roll-up transaction as defined in Item 901(c) of Regulation S-K (17 CFR 229.901(c)), attention is directed to the requirements of Form S-4 applicable to roll-up transactions, including, but not limited to, General Instruction l.

V. Registration of Additional Securities

With respect to the registration of additional securities for an offering pursuant to Rule 462(b) under the Securities Act, the registrant may file a registration statement consisting only of the following: the facing page; a statement that the contents of the earlier registration statement, identified by file number, are incorporated by reference; required opinions and consents; the signature page; and any price-related information omitted from the earlier registration statement in reliance on Rule 430A that the registrant chooses to include in the new registration statement. The information contained in such a Rule 462(b) registration statement shall be deemed to be a part of the earlier registration statement as of the date of effectiveness of the Rule 462(b) registration statement. Any opinion or consent required in the Rule 462(b) registration statement may be incorporated by reference from the earlier registration statement with respect to the offering, if: (i) such opinion or consent expressly provides for such incorporation; and (ii) such opinion relates to the securities registered pursuant to Rule 462(b). *See* Rule 411(c) and Rule 439(b) under the Securities Act.

VI. Eligibility to Use Incorporation by Reference

If a registrant meets the following requirements immediately prior to the time of filing a registration statement on this Form, it may elect to provide information required by Item 3 and Item 4 of this Form in accordance with Item 4A and Item 5 of this Form:

A. The registrant is subject to the requirement to file reports pursuant to Section 13 or Section 15(d) of the Securities Exchange Act of 1934 ("Exchange Act");

B. The registrant has filed all reports and other materials required to be filed by Section 13(a) or 15(d) of the Exchange Act during the preceding 12 months (or for such shorter period that the registrant was required to file such reports and materials);

C. The registrant has filed an annual report required under Section 13(a) or 15(d) of the Exchange Act for its most recently completed fiscal year;

D. The registrant is not:

1. And during the past three years neither the registrant nor any of its predecessors was:

(a) A blank check company as defined in Rule 419(a)(2) (§ 230.419(a)(2) of this chapter);

(b) A shell company, other than a business combination related shell company, each as defined in Rule 405 (§ 230.405 of this chapter); or

(c) A registrant for an offering of penny stock as defined in Rule 3a51-1 of the Exchange Act (§ 240.3a51-1 of this chapter);

2. Registering an offering that effectuates a business combination transaction as defined in Rule 165(f)(1) (§ 230.165(f)(1) of this chapter);

E. If a registrant is a successor registrant it shall be deemed to have satisfied conditions A., B., C., and D.2. above if:

1. Its predecessor and it, taken together, do so, provided that the succession was primarily for the purpose of changing the state or other jurisdiction of incorporation of the predecessor or forming a holding company and that the assets and liabilities of the successor at the time of succession were substantially the same as those of the predecessor; or

2. All predecessors met the conditions at the time of succession and the registrant has continued to do so since the succession; and

F. The registrant makes its reports filed pursuant to Sections 13 or 15(d) of the Exchange Act that are incorporated by reference pursuant to Item 4A or Item 5 of this Form readily available and accessible on a Web site maintained by or for the registrant and containing information about the registrant.

PART I

INFORMATION REQUIRED IN PROSPECTUS

Item 1. Forepart of Registration Statement and Outside Front Cover Page of Prospectus

Set forth in the forepart of the registration statement and on the outside front cover page of the prospectus the information required by Item 501 of Regulation S-K (§ 229.501 of this chapter).

Item 2. Inside Front and Outside Back Cover Pages of Prospectus

Set forth on the inside front cover page of the prospectus or, where permitted, on the outside back cover page the information required by Item 502 of Regulation S-K (§ 229.502 of this chapter).

Item 3. Summary Information, Risk Factors and Ratio of Earnings to Fixed Charges

Furnish the information required by Item 503 of Regulation S-K (§ 229.503 of this chapter).

Item 4. Information with Respect to the Registrant and the Offering.

Furnish the following information with respect to the Registrant.

(a) Information required by Part I of Form 20-F (§ 249.220f of this chapter);

(b) Information required by Item 18 of Form 20-F (Schedules required under Regulation S-X shall be filed as "Financial Statement Schedules" Pursuant to Item 8, Exhibit and Financial Statement Schedules, of this Form), as well as any information required by Rule 3-05 and Article 11 of Regulation S-X (§ 210 of this chapter), except as permitted by (c) below:

(c) For the registrant's fiscal years ending before December 15, 2011, information required by Item 17 of Form 20-F may be furnished in lieu of the information specified by Item 18 thereof if the only securities being registered are non-convertible securities that are "investment grade securities," as defined below, or the only securities to be registered are to be offered:

1. upon the exercise of outstanding rights granted by the issuer of the securities to be offered, if such rights are granted on a pro rata basis to all existing security holders of the class of securities to which the rights attach and there is no standby underwriting in the United States or similar arrangement; or

2. pursuant to a dividend or interest reinvestment plan; or

3. upon the conversion of outstanding convertible securities or upon the exercise of outstanding transferable warrants issued by the issuer of the securities to be offered, or by an affiliate of such issuer.

(d) For the registrant's fiscal years ending on or after December 15, 2009, information required by Item 16F of Form 20-F.

Instructions

1. Attention is directed to section 10(a)(3) of the Securities Act.

2. A non-convertible security is an *investment grade security* if, at the time of sale, at least one nationally recognized statistical rating organization (as that term is used in Rule 15c3-1(c)(2)(vi)(F) under the Exchange Act (§ 240.15c3-1(c)(2)(vi)(F) of this chapter) has rated the security in one of its generic rating categories that signifies investment grade; typically, the four highest rating categories (within which there may be sub-categories or gradations indicating relative standing) signify investment grade.

Item 4A. Material Changes.

(a) If the registrant elects to incorporate information by reference pursuant to General Instruction VI., describe any and all material changes in the registrant's affairs which have occurred since the end of the latest fiscal year for which audited financial statements were included in accordance with Item 5 of this Form and which have not been described in a report on Form 6-K, Form 10-Q or Form 8-K filed under the Exchange Act and incorporated by reference pursuant to Item 5 of this Form.

(b)1. Include in the prospectus contained in the registration statement, if not included in the reports filed under the Exchange Act which are incorporated by reference into the prospectus contained in the registration statement pursuant to Item 5:

i. Information required by Rule 3-05 and Article 11 of Regulation S-X (§ 210.3-05 and § 210.11 *et seq.* of this chapter);

ii. Restated financial statements if there has been a change in accounting principles or a correction of an error where such change or correction requires material retroactive restatement of financial statements;

iii. Restated financial statements where one or more business combinations accounted for by the pooling of interest method of accounting have been consummated subsequent to the most recent fiscal year and the acquired businesses, considered in the aggregate, are significant under Rule 11-01(b) (§ 210.11-01(b) of this chapter); or

iv. Any financial information required because of a material disposition of assets outside the normal course of business.

2. If the financial statements included in this registration statement in accordance with Item 5 are not sufficiently current to comply with the requirements of Item 8.A of Form 20-F, financial statements necessary to comply with that Item shall be presented:

i. Directly in the prospectus;

ii. Through incorporation by reference and delivery of a Form 6-K identified in the prospectus as containing such financial statements; or

iii. Through incorporation by reference of an amended Form 20-F, Form 40-F, or Form 10-K, in which case the prospectus shall disclose that the Form 20-F, Form 40-F, or Form 10-K has been so amended.

Instruction.

Financial statements or information required to be furnished by this Item shall be reconciled pursuant to either Item 17 or Item 18 of Form 20-F, whichever is applicable to the primary financial statements.

For the registrant's fiscal years ending before December 15, 2011, financial statements or information required to be furnished by this Item shall be reconciled pursuant to either Item 17 or Item 18 of Form 20-F, whichever is applicable to the primary financial statements. For the registrant's fiscal years ending on or after December 15, 2011, financial statements or information required to be furnished by this Item shall be reconciled pursuant to Item 18 of Form 20-F.

Item 5. Incorporation of Certain Information by Reference.

If the registrant elects to incorporate information by reference pursuant to General Instruction VI.:

(a) It must specifically incorporate by reference into the prospectus contained in the registration statement the following documents by means of a statement to that effect in the prospectus listing all such documents:

1. The registrant's latest annual report on Form 20-F, Form 40-F or Form 10-K filed under the Exchange Act.

2. Any report on Form 10-Q or Form 8-K filed since the date of filing of the annual report. The registrant may also incorporate by reference any Form 6-K meeting the requirements of this Form.

Note to Item 5(a). Attention is directed to Rule 439 (§ 230.439) regarding consent to use of material incorporated by reference.

(b)1. The registrant must state:

i. That it will provide to each person, including any beneficial owner, to whom a prospectus is delivered, a copy of any or all of the reports or documents that have been incorporated by reference in the prospectus contained in the registration statement but not delivered with the prospectus;

ii. That it will provide these reports or documents upon written or oral request;

iii. That it will provide these reports or documents at no cost to the requester;

iv. The name, address, telephone number, and e-mail address, if any, to which the request for these reports or documents must be made; and

v. The registrant's Web site address, including the uniform resource locator (URL) where the incorporated reports and other documents may be accessed.

Note to Item 5.(b)1. If the registrant sends any of the information that is incorporated by reference in the prospectus contained in the registration statement to security holders, it also must send any exhibits that are specifically incorporated by reference in that information.

2. The registrant must:

i. Identify the reports and other information that it files with the SEC; and

ii. State that the public may read and copy any materials it files with the SEC at the SEC's Public Reference Room at 100 F Street, N.E., Washington, DC 20549. State that the public may obtain information on the operation of the Public Reference Room by calling the SEC at 1-800-SEC-0330. If the registrant is an electronic filer, state that the SEC maintains an Internet site that contains reports, proxy and information statements, and other information regarding issuers that file electronically with the SEC and state the address of that site (http://www.sec.gov).

Item 5A. Disclosure of Commission Position on Indemnification for Securities Act Liabilities.

Furnish the information required by Item 510 of Regulation S-K (§ 229.510 of this chapter).

PART II

INFORMATION NOT REQUIRED IN PROSPECTUS

Item 6. Indemnification of Directors and Officers

Furnish the information required by Item 702 of Regulation S-K (§ 229.702 of this chapter).

Item 7. Recent Sales of Unregistered Securities

Furnish the information required by Item 701 of Regulation S-K (§ 229.701 of this chapter).

Item 8. Exhibits and Financial Statement Schedules

(a) Subject to the rules regarding incorporation by reference, furnish the exhibits required by Item 601 of Regulation S-K (§ 229.601 of this chapter).

(b) Furnish financial statement schedules required by Regulation S-X (§ 210 of this chapter) and Item 4 (b) of this Form. These schedules shall be lettered or numbered in the manner described for exhibits in paragraph (a).

Item 9. Undertakings

Furnish the undertakings required by Item 512 of Regulation S-K (§ 229.512 of this chapter).

SIGNATURES

Pursuant to the requirements of the Securities Act of 1933, the registrant certifies that it has reasonable grounds to believe that it meets all of the requirements for filing on Form F-1 and has duly caused this registration statement to be signed on its behalf by the undersigned, thereunto duly authorized, in the City of _____, State of . . . . on . . . ., 19 . . . . . . (Registrant) . . . .

. . . .

By (Signature and Title) . . . .

Pursuant to the requirements of the Securities Act of 1933, this registration statement has been signed by the following persons in the capacities and on the dates indicated.

(Signature) . . . .

(Title) . . . .

(Date) . . . .

Instructions.

1. The registration statement shall be signed by the registrant, its principal executive officer or officers, its principal financial officer, its controller or principal accounting officer, at least a majority of the board of directors or persons performing similar functions, and its authorized representative in the United States. Where the registrant is a limited partnership, the registration statement shall be signed by a majority of the board of directors of any corporate general partner signing the registration statement.

2. The name of each person who signs the registration statement shall be typed or printed beneath his signature. Any person who occupies more than one of the specified positions shall indicate each capacity in which he signs the registration statement. Attention is directed to Rule 402 concerning manual signatures and Item 601 of Regulation S-K concerning signatures pursuant to powers of attorney.

INSTRUCTIONS AS TO SUMMARY PROSPECTUSES

1. A summary prospectus used pursuant to Rule 431 (§ 230.431 of this chapter), shall at the time of its use contain such of the information specified below as is then included in the registration statement. All other information and documents contained in the registration statement may be omitted.

(a) As to Item 1, the aggregate offering price to the public, the aggregate underwriting discounts and commissions and the offering price per unit to the public;

(b) As to Item 2, a statement concerning the enforceability of civil liabilities against foreign persons (Item 502 (f) of Regulation S-K (§ 229.502 of this chapter));

(c) (i) A brief statement of the principal purposes for which the proceeds are to be used;

(c) (ii) A statement as to the amount of the offering, if any, to be made for the account of security holders;

(c) (iii) The[1] name of the managing underwriter or underwriters and a brief statement as to the nature of the underwriter's obligation to take the securities; if any securities to be registered are to be offered otherwise than through underwriters, a brief statement as to the manner of distribution; and, if securities are to be offered otherwise than for cash, a brief statement as to the general purposes of the distribution, the basis upon which the securities are to be offered, the amount of compensation and other expenses of distribution and by whom they are to be borne;

(c) (iv) A brief statement as to dividend rights, voting rights, conversion rights, interest, maturity, exchange controls, tax treaties, limitations on ownership or voting;

(c) (v) As to Item 4, a brief statement of the general character of the business done and intended to be done, the Selected Financial Data (Item 3.A of Form 20-F (§ 249.220f of this chapter)) and a brief statement of the nature and pre-

---

[1] Release No. 33-7745, Text of Amendments No. 21, states that Instructions as to Summary Prospectives 1.(c) (iii) should begin with the word "A." The SEC most likely intended

1.(c) (iii) to begin with the word "The," which the text above reflects. CCH.

sent status of any material pending legal proceedings; and

(d) A tabular presentation of notes payable, long term debt, deferred credits, minority interests, if material, and the equity section of the latest balance sheet filed, as may be appropriate.

2. The summary prospectus shall not contain a summary or condensation of any other required financial information except as provided above.

3. Where securities being registered are to be offered in exchange for securities of any other issuer, the summary prospectus also shall contain that information specified in paragraphs 1.(c)(iv)and 1.(c)(v) above which would be re-quired if the securities of such other issuer were registered on this Form or Form S-1 according to General Instruction III.

4. The Commission may, upon request of the registrant, and where consistent with the protection of investors, permit the omission of any of the information herein required or the furnishing in substitution thereof of appropriate information of comparable character. The Commission may also require the inclusion of other information in addition to, or in substitution for, the information herein required in any case where such information is necessary or appropriate for the protection of investors.

FORM F-3

[As last amended Release No. 33-9026, effective April 23, 2009, 74 F.R. 18612.]

SECURITIES AND EXCHANGE COMMISSION

Form F-3

REGISTRATION STATEMENT UNDER THE SECURITIES ACT OF 1933

SECURITIES AND EXCHANGE COMMISSION
Form F-3
REGISTRATION STATEMENT UNDER THE SECURITIES ACT OF 1933
....
(Exact name of Registrant as specified in its charter)
....
(Translation of Registrant's name into English)

....
(State or other jurisdiction   (I.R.S. Employer Identification
of incorporation or organization)   Number

....
(Address and telephone number of Registrant's principal executive offices)
....
(Name, address, and telephone number of agent for service)

Approximate date of commencement of proposed sale to the public . . . .

If the only securities being registered on this Form are being offered pursuant to dividend or interest reinvestment plans, please check the following box. [ ]

If any of the securities being registered on this Form are to be offered on a delayed or continuous basis pursuant to Rule 415 under the Securities Act of 1933, check the following box. [ ]

If this Form is filed to register additional securities for an offering pursuant to Rule 462(b) under the Securities Act, please check the following box and list the Securities Act registration statement number of the earlier effective registration statement for the same offering. [ ] __

If this Form is a registration statement pursuant to General Instruction I.C. or a post-effective amendment thereto that shall become effective upon filing with the Commission pursuant to Rule 462(e) under the Securities Act, check the following box. [ ]

If this Form is a post-effective amendment to a registration statement filed pursuant to General Instruction I.C. filed to register additional securities or additional classes of securities pursuant to Rule 413(b) under the Securities Act, check the following box. [ ]

Calculation of Registration Fee

Title of each class of securities to be registered	Amount to be registered	Proposed maximum aggregate offering price	Amount of registration fee

Notes to the "Calculation of Registration Fee" Table ("Fee Table"):

1. Specific details relating to the fee calculation shall be furnished in notes to the Fee Table, including references to provisions of Rule 457 (§ 230.457 of this chapter) relied upon, if the basis of the calculation is not otherwise evident from the information presented in the Fee Table.

2. If the filing fee is calculated pursuant to Rule 457(o) under the Securities Act, only the title of the class of securities to be registered, the proposed maximum aggregate offering price for that class of securities, and the amount of registration fee need to appear in the Fee Table. Where two or more classes of securities are being registered pursuant to General Instruction II.C., however, the Fee Table need only specify the maximum aggregate offering price for all classes; the Fee Table need not specify by each class the proposed maximum aggregate offering price (see General Instruction II.C.).

3. If the filing fee is calculated pursuant to Rule 457(r) of this chapter) under the Securities Act, the Fee Table must state that it registers an unspecified amount of securities of each identified class of securities and must provide that the issuer is relying on Rule 456(b) and Rule 457(r). If the Fee Table is

amended in a post-effective amendment to the registration statement or in a prospectus filed in accordance with Rule 456(b)(1)(ii) (§ 230.456(b)(1)(ii) of this chapter), the Fee Table must specify the aggregate offering price for all classes of securities in the referenced offering or offerings and the applicable registration fee.

4. Any difference between the dollar amount of securities registered for such offerings and the dollar amount of securities sold may be carried forward on a future registration statement pursuant to Rule 457 under the Securities Act.

GENERAL INSTRUCTIONS

I. Eligibility Requirements for Use of Form F-3

This instruction sets forth registrant requirements and transaction requirements for the use of Form F-3. Any foreign private issuer, as defined in Rule 405 (§ 230.405 of this chapter), which meets the requirements of I.A. below (the "Registrant Requirements") may use this Form for the registration of securities under the Securities Act of 1933 (the "Securities Act") which are offered in any transaction specified in I.B. below (the "Transaction Requirements"), provided that the requirements applicable to the specified Transaction are met. With respect to majority-owned subsidiaries, see Instruction I.A.5 below. With respect to well-known seasoned issuers and majority-owned subsidiaries of well-known seasoned issuers, see Instruction I.C. below. In addition, this Form shall not be used for an offering of asset-backed securities, as defined in 17 CFR 229.1101.

A. *Registrant Requirements*

Except as set forth below, all registrants must meet the following conditions in order to use this Form F-3 for registration under the Securities Act of securities offered in the transactions specified in I.B. below:

1. The registrant has a class of securities registered pursuant to Section 12(b) of the Securities Exchange Act of 1934 ("Exchange Act") or has a class of equity securities registered pursuant to Section 12(g) of the Exchange Act or is required to file reports pursuant to Section 15(d) of the Exchange Act and has filed at least one annual report on Form 20-F, on Form 10-K, or, in the case of registrants described in General Instruction A(2) of Form 40-F, on Form 40-F under the Exchange Act.

2. The registrant: (a) has been subject to the requirements of Section 12 or 15(d) of the Exchange Act and has filed all the material required to be filed pursuant to Sections 13, 14 or 15(d) of the Exchange Act for a period of at least twelve calendar months immediately preceding the filing of the registration statement on this Form; and (b) has filed in a timely manner all reports required to be filed during the twelve calendar months and any portion of a month immediately preceding the filing of the registration statement and, if the registrant has used (during those twelve calendar months and that portion of a month) Rule 12b-25(b) (§ 240.12b-25(b) of this chapter) under the Exchange Act with respect to a report or a portion of a report, that report or portion thereof has actually been filed within the time period prescribed by the Rule.

3. Neither the registrant nor any of its consolidated or unconsolidated subsidiaries have, since the end of their last fiscal year for which certified financial statements of the registrant and its consolidated subsidiaries were included in a report filed pursuant to Section 13(a) or 15(d) of the Exchange Act: (a) failed to pay any dividend or sinking fund installment on preferred stock; or (b) defaulted (i) on any installment or installments on indebtedness for borrowed money, or (ii) on any rental on one or more long term leases, which defaults in the aggregate are material to the financial position of the registrant and its consolidated and unconsolidated subsidiaries, taken as a whole.

4. If the registrant is a successor registrant, it shall be deemed to have met conditions 1, 2, and 3 above if: (a) its predecessor and it, taken together, do so, provided that the succession was primarily for the purpose of changing the state or other jurisdiction of incorporation of the predecessor or forming a holding company and that the assets and liabilities of the successor at the time of succession were substantially the same as those of the predecessor; or (b) all predecessors met the conditions at the time of succession and the registrant has continued to do so since the succession.

5. *Majority-owned Subsidiaries*

If a registrant is a majority-owned subsidiary, security offerings may be registered on this Form if:

(i) The registrant-subsidiary itself meets the Registrant Requirements and the applicable Transaction Requirement;

(ii) The parent of the registrant-subsidiary meets the Registrant Requirements and the conditions of Transaction Requirement B.2. (Offerings of Certain Debt or Preferred Securities) are met;

(iii) the parent of the registrant-subsidiary meets the Registrant Requirements and the applicable Transaction Requirement, and provides a full and unconditional guarantee, as defined in Rule 3-10 of Regulation S-X (§ 210.3-10 of this chapter), of the payment obligations on the securities being registered, and the securities being registered are non-convertible securities, other than common equity;

(iv) the parent of the registrant-subsidiary meets the Registrant Requirements and the applicable Transaction Requirement, and the securities of the registrant-subsidiary being registered are full and unconditional guarantees, as defined in Rule 3-10 of Regulation S-X, of the payment obligations on the parent's non-convertible securities, other than common equity, being registered; or

(v) the parent of the registrant-subsidiary meets the Registrant Requirements and the applicable Transaction Requirement, and the securities of the registrant-subsidiary being registered are guarantees of the payment obligations on the non-convertible securities, other than common equity, being registered by another majority-owned subsidiary of the parent where the parent provides a full and unconditional guarantee, as defined in Rule 3-10 of Regulation S-X, of such non-convertible securities.

Note: In the situation described in paragraphs I.A.5(iii), I.A.5(iv), and I.A.5(v) above, the parent or majority-owned subsidiary guarantor is the issuer of a separate security consisting of the guarantee, which must be concurrently registered, but may be registered on the same registration statement as are the guaranteed non-convertible securities. Both the parent or majority-owned subsidiary shall each disclose the information required by this Form as if each were the only registrant except that if the majority-owned subsidiary will not be eligible to file annual reports on Form 20-F or Form 40-F after the effective date of the registration statement, then it shall disclose the information specified in Form S-3. Rule 3-10 of Regulation S-X specifies the financial statements required.

6. *Electronic filings.* In addition to satisfying the foregoing conditions, a registrant subject to the electronic filing requirements of Rule 101 of Regulation S-T (§ 232.101 of this chapter) shall have:

(i) Filed with the Commission all required electronic filings, including electronic copies of documents submitted in paper pursuant to a hardship exemption as provided by Rule 201 or Rule 202(d) of Regulation S-T (§ 232.201 or § 232.202(d) of this chapter); and

(ii) Submitted electronically to the Commission and posted on its corporate Web site, if any, all Interactive Data Files required to be submitted and posted pursuant to Rule 405 of Regulation S-T (§ 232.405 of this chapter) during the twelve calendar months and any portion of a month immediately preceding the filing of the registration statement on this Form (or for such shorter pe-

riod of time that the registrant was required to submit and post such files).

B. *Transaction Requirements*

Security offerings meeting any of the following conditions and made by registrants meeting the Registrant Requirements above may be registered on this Form:

1. *Primary Offerings by Certain Registrants.* Securities to be offered for cash by or on behalf of a registrant, *provided* that the aggregate market value worldwide of the voting and non-voting common equity held by non-affiliates of the registrant is the equivalent of $75 million or more. In the case of securities registered pursuant to this paragraph, the financial statements included in this registration statement must comply with Item 18 of Form 20-F.

Instruction

For the purposes of this Form, "common equity" is as defined in Securities Act Rule 405 (§ 230.405 of this chapter). The aggregate market value of the registrant's outstanding voting and non-voting common equity shall be computed by use of the price at which the common equity was last sold, or the average of the bid and asked prices of such common equity, in the principal market for such common equity as of a date within 60 days prior to the date of filing. See the definition of "affiliate" in Securities Act Rule 405.

2. *Primary Offerings of Non-convertible Investment Grade Securities.* Non-convertible securities to be offered for cash if such securities are "investment grade securities." A non-convertible security is an "investment grade security" if, at the time of sale, at least one nationally recognized statistical rating organization (as that term is used in Rule 15c3-1(c)(2)(vi)(F) under the Exchange Act (§ 240.15c3-1(c)(2)(vi)(F) of this chapter)) has rated the security in one of its generic rating categories that signifies investment grade; typically, the four highest rating categories (within which there may be subcategories or gradations indicating relative standing) signify investment grade. For the registrant's fiscal years ending before December 15, 2011, in the case of securities registered pursuant to this paragraph, the financial statements included in this registration statement may comply with Item 17 or 18 of Form 20-F. For the registrant's fiscal years ending on or after December 15, 2011, in the case of securities registered pursuant to this paragraph, the financial statements included in this registration statement must comply with Item 18 of Form 20-F.

3. *Transactions Involving Secondary Offerings.* Outstanding securities to be offered for the account of any person other than the issuer, including securities acquired by standby underwriters in connection with the call or redemption by the

issuer of warrants or a class of convertible securities. In the case of such securities, the financial statements included in this registration statement may comply with Item 17 or 18 of Form 20-F for a registrant's fiscal years ending before December 15, 2011; and for the registrant's fiscal years ending on or after December 15, 2011, the financial statements included in this registration statement must comply with Item 18 of Form 20-F. In addition, Form F-3 may be used by affiliates to register securities for resale pursuant to the conditions specified in General Instruction C to Form S-8 (§ 239.16b of this chapter). In the case of such securities, the financial statements included in this registration statement must comply with Item 18 of Form 20-F (§ 249.220f of this chapter).

4. *Rights Offerings, Dividend or Interest Reinvestment Plans, and Conversions or Warrants.* Securities to be offered: (a) upon the exercise of outstanding rights granted by the issuer of the securities to be offered, if such rights are granted pro rata to all existing security holders of the class of securities to which the rights attach; or (b) pursuant to a dividend or interest reinvestment plan; or (c) upon the conversion of outstanding convertible securities or upon the exercise of outstanding transferable warrants issued by the issuer of the securities to be offered, or by an affiliate of such issuer. In the case of securities registered pursuant to this paragraph, the financial statements included in this registration statement may comply with Item 17 or 18 of Form 20-F for the registrant's fiscal years ending before December 15, 2011; and for the registrant's fiscal years ending on or after December 15, 2011, the financial statements included in this registration statement must comply with Item 18 of Form 20-F. The registration of securities to be offered or sold in a standby underwriting in the United States or similar arrangement is not permitted pursuant to this paragraph. See paragraphs B.1., B.2., and B.3. of this Instruction.

5. *Limited Primary Offerings by Certain Other Registrants.* Securities to be offered for cash by or on behalf of a registrant; *provided that*:

(a) the aggregate market value of securities sold by or on behalf of the registrant pursuant to this Instruction I.B.5. during the period of 12 calendar months immediately prior to, and including, the sale is no more than one-third of the aggregate market value worldwide of the voting and non-voting common equity held by non-affiliates of the registrant;

(b) the registrant is not a shell company (as defined in § 230.405 of this chapter) and has not been a shell company for at least 12 calendar months previously and if it has been a shell company at any time previously, has filed current Form 10 information with the Commission at least

12 calendar months previously reflecting its status as an entity that is not a shell company; and

(c) the registrant has at least one class of common equity securities listed and registered on a national securities exchange.

Instructions.

1. "Common equity" is as defined in Securities Act Rule 405 (§ 230.405 of this chapter). For purposes of computing the aggregate market value of the registrant's outstanding voting and non-voting common equity pursuant to General Instruction I.B.5., registrants shall use the price at which the common equity was last sold, or the average of the bid and asked prices of such common equity, in the principal market for such common equity as of a date within 60 days prior to the date of sale. See the definition of "affiliate" in Securities Act Rule 405 (§ 230.405 of this chapter).

2. For purposes of computing the aggregate market value of all securities sold by or on behalf of the registrant in offerings pursuant to General Instruction I.B.5. during any period of 12 calendar months, registrants shall aggregate the gross proceeds of such sales; *provided*, that, in the case of derivative securities convertible into or exercisable for shares of the registrant's common equity, registrants shall calculate the aggregate market value of any underlying equity shares in lieu of the market value of the derivative securities. The aggregate market value of the underlying equity shall be calculated by multiplying the maximum number of common equity shares into which the derivative securities are convertible or for which they are exercisable as of a date within 60 days prior to the date of sale, by the same per share market price of the registrant's equity used for purposes of calculating the aggregate market value of the registrant's outstanding voting and non-voting common equity pursuant to Instruction 1 to General Instruction I.B.5. If the derivative securities have been converted or exercised, the aggregate market value of the underlying equity shall be calculated by multiplying the actual number of shares into which the securities were converted or received upon exercise, by the market price of such shares on the date of conversion or exercise.

3. If the aggregate market value of the registrant's outstanding voting and nonvoting common equity computed pursuant to General Instruction I.B.5. equals or exceeds $75 million subsequent to the effective date of this registration statement, then the onethird limitation on sales specified in General Instruction I.B.5(a) shall not apply to additional sales made pursuant to this registration statement on or subsequent to such date and instead the registration statement shall be considered filed pursuant to General Instruction I.B.1.

4. The term "Form 10 information" means the information that is required by Form 10 or Form 20-F (§ 249.210 or § 249.220f of this chapter), as applicable to the registrant, to register under the Securities Exchange Act of 1934 each class of securities being registered using this form. A registrant may provide the Form 10 information in another Commission filing with respect to the registrant.

5. The date used in Instruction 2 to General Instruction I.B.5. shall be the same date used in Instruction 1 to General Instruction I.B.5.

6. A registrant's eligibility to register a primary offering on Form F-3 pursuant to General Instruction I.B.5. does not mean that the registrant meets the requirements of Form F-3 for purposes of any other rule or regulation of the Commission apart from Rule 415(a)(1)(x) (§ 230.415(a)(1)(x) of this chapter).

7. Registrants must set forth on the outside front cover of the prospectus the calculation of the aggregate market value of the registrant's outstanding voting and nonvoting common equity pursuant to General Instruction I.B.5. and the amount of all securities offered pursuant to General Instruction I.B.5. during the prior 12 calendar month period that ends on, and includes, the date of the prospectus.

8. For purposes of General Instruction I.B.5(c), a "national securities exchange" shall mean an exchange registered as such under Section 6(a) of the Securities Exchange Act of 1934.

C. *Automatic Shelf Offerings by Well-Known Seasoned Issuers*

Any registrant that is a well-known seasoned issuer, as defined in Rule 405, at the most recent eligibility determination date specified in paragraph (2) of that definition may use this Form for registration under the Securities Act of securities offerings, other than pursuant to Rule 415(a)(1)(vii) or (viii) (§ 230.415(a)(1)(vii) or (viii) of this chapter), as follows:

1. The securities to be offered are:

(a) Any securities to be offered pursuant to Rule 415, Rule 430A, or Rule 430B (§ 230.415, § 230.430A, or § 230.430B of this chapter) by:

(i) A registrant that is a well-known seasoned issuer by reason of paragraph (1)(i)(A) of the definition in Rule 405; or

(ii) A registrant that is a well-known seasoned issuer only by reason of paragraph (1)(i)(B) of the definition in Rule 405 if the registrant also is eligible to register a primary offering of its securities pursuant to Transaction Requirement I.B.1 of this Form;

(b) Non-convertible securities, other than common equity, to be offered pursuant to Rule 415, Rule 430A, or Rule 430B by a registrant that is a well-known seasoned issuer only by reason of paragraph (1)(i)(B) of the definition in Rule 405 and does not fall within General Instruction I.B.1 of this Form;

(c) Securities of majority-owned subsidiaries of the parent registrant to be offered pursuant to Rule 415, Rule 430A, or Rule 430B if the parent registrant is a well-known seasoned issuer and the securities of the majority-owned subsidiary being registered meet the following requirements:

(i) Securities of a majority-owned subsidiary that is a well-known seasoned issuer at the time it becomes a registrant, other than by virtue of paragraph (1)(ii) of the definition of well-known seasoned issuer in Rule 405;

(ii) Securities of a majority-owned subsidiary that are non-convertible securities, other than common equity, and the parent registrant provides a full and unconditional guarantee, as defined in Rule 3-10 of Regulation S-X, of the payment obligations on such non-convertible securities;

(iii) Securities of a majority-owned subsidiary that are a guarantee of:

(A) Non-convertible securities, other than common equity of the parent registrant being registered;

(B) Non-convertible securities, other than common equity, of another majority-owned subsidiary being registered and the parent has provided a full and unconditional guarantee, as defined in Rule 3-10 of Regulation S-X, of the payment obligations on such non-convertible securities; or

(iv) Securities of a majority-owned subsidiary that meet the conditions of Transaction Requirement I.B.2. of this Form (Primary Offerings of Non-Convertible Investment Grade Securities).

(d) Securities to be offered for the account of any person other than the issuer ("selling security holders"), provided that the registration statement and the prospectus are not required to separately identify the selling security holders or the securities to be sold by such persons until the filing of a prospectus, prospectus supplement, posteffective amendment to the registration statement, or report under the Exchange Act that is incorporated by reference into the registration statement and prospectus, identifying the selling security holders and the amount of securities to be sold by each of them, and if included in a report under the Exchange Act that is incorporated by reference, a prospectus or prospectus supplement is filed, as required by Rule 430B, pursuant to Rule 424(b)(7) (§ 230.424(b)(7) of this chapter).

2. The registrant pays the registration fee pursuant to Rules 456(b) and 457(r) or in accordance with Rule 456(a).

3. If the registrant is a majority-owned subsidiary, it is required to file and has filed reports pursuant to Section 13 or Section 15(d) of the Exchange Act and satisfies the requirements of the Form with regard to incorporation by reference or information about the majority-owned subsidiary is included in the registration statement (or a post-effective amendment to the registration statement).

4. The registrant may register additional securities or classes of its or its majority-owned subsidiaries' securities on a post-effective amendment pursuant to Rule 413(b) (§ 203.413(b) of this chapter).

5. An automatic shelf registration statement and post-effective amendment will become effective immediately pursuant to Rule 462(e) and (f) (§ 230.462(e) and (f) of this chapter) upon filing. All filings made on or in connection with automatic shelf registration statements on this Form become public upon filing with the Commission.

II. Application of General Rules and Regulations

A. Attention is directed to the General Rules and Regulations under the Securities Act, particularly Regulation C (§ 230.400 et seq. of this chapter) thereunder. That Regulation contains general requirements regarding the preparation and filing of registration statements.

B. Attention is directed to Regulation S-K (§ 229 of this chapter) and Form 20-F (§ 249.220f of this chapter) for the requirements applicable to the content of registration statements under the Securities Act. Where this Form directs the registrant to furnish information required by Regulation S-K or Form 20-F and the Item of Regulation S-K or Form 20-F so provides, information need only be furnished to the extent appropriate. Notwithstanding Items 501 and 502 of Regulation S-K, no table of contents and cross-reference sheet are required to be included in the prospectus or the registration statement prepared on this Form. In addition to the information expressly required to be included in a registration statement on this Form F-3, registrants also may provide such other information as they deem appropriate.

A. Attention is directed to the General Rules and Regulations under the Securities Act, particularly Regulation C (§ 230.400 et seq. of this chapter) thereunder. That Regulation contains general requirements regarding the preparation and filing of registration statements.

B. Attention is directed to Regulation S-K (§ 229 of this chapter) and Form 20-F (§ 249.220f of this chapter) for the requirements applicable to the content of registration statements under the

Securities Act. Where this Form directs the registrant to furnish information required by Regulation S-K or Form 20-F and the Item of Regulation S-K or Form 20-F so provides, information need only be furnished to the extent appropriate. Notwithstanding Items 501 and 502 of Regulation S-K, no table of contents and cross-reference sheet are required to be included in the prospectus or the registration statement prepared on this Form. In addition to the information expressly required to be included in a registration statement on this Form F-3, registrants also may provide such other information as they deem appropriate.

C. Non-Automatic Shelf Registration Statements. Where two or more classes of securities being registered on this Form pursuant to General Instruction I.B.1.or I.B.2. are to be offered pursuant to Rule 415(a)(1)(x) (§ 230.415(a)(1)(x)), and where this Form is not an automatic shelf registration statement, Rule 457(o) permits the registration fee to be calculated on the basis of the maximum offering price of all the securities listed in the Fee Table. In this event, while the Fee Table would list each of the classes of securities being registered and the aggregate proceeds to be raised, the Fee Table need not specify by each class information as to the amount to be registered, proposed maximum offering price per unit, and proposed maximum aggregate offering price.

D. A registrant must file the Form F-3 registration statement in electronic format via the Commission's Electronic Data Gathering and Retrieval System (EDGAR) in accordance with the EDGAR rules set forth in Regulation S-T (17 CFR Part 232), except that a registrant that has obtained a hardship exception under Regulation S-T Rule 201 or 202 (17 CFR 232.201 or 232.202) may file the registration statement in paper. For assistance with technical questions about EDGAR or to request an access code, call the EDGAR Filer Support Office at (202) 551-8900. For assistance with questions about the EDGAR rules, call the Office of EDGAR and Information Analysis at (202) 551-3610.

E. The Form F-3 registration statement must be in the English language, as required by Regulation S-T Rule 306 (17 CFR 232.306) for electronic filings and Securities Act Rule 403(c) (17 CFR 230.403(c)), generally. If the registration statement requires the inclusion, as an exhibit or attachment, of a document that is in a foreign language, the registrant must provide instead either an English translation or an English summary of the foreign language document in accordance with Securities Act Rule 403(c) (17 CFR 230.403(c)) for both electronic and paper filings. The registrant may submit a copy of the unabridged foreign language document along with the English translation or English summary as permitted by Regulation S-T Rule 306(b) (17 CFR

232.306(b)) for electronic filings or by Securities Act Rule 403(c)(4) (17 CFR 230.403(c)(4)) for paper filings.

F. Automatic Shelf Registration Statements. Where securities are being registered on this Form pursuant to General Instruction I.C., Rule 456(b) permits, but does not require, the registrant to pay the registration fee on a pay-as-you-go basis and Rule 457(r) permits, but does not require, the registration fee to be calculated on the basis of the aggregate offering price of the securities to be offered in an offering or offerings off the registration statement. If a registrant elects to pay all or a portion of the registration fee on a deferred basis, the Fee Table in the initial filing must identify the classes of securities being registered and provide that the registrant elects to rely on Rule 456(b) and Rule 457(r), but the Fee Table does not need to specify any other information. When the registrant amends the Fee Table in accordance with Rule 456(b)(1)(ii), the amended Fee Table must include either the dollar amount of securities being registered if paid in advance of or in connection with an offering or offerings or the aggregate offering price for all classes of securities referenced in the offerings and the applicable registration fee.

G. Information in Automatic and Non-Automatic Shelf Registration Statements. Where securities are being registered on this Form pursuant to General Instruction I.A.5, I.B.1, I.B.2, or I.C., information is only required to be furnished as of the date of initial effectiveness of the registration statement to the extent required by Rule 430A or Rule 430B. Required information about a specific transaction must be included in the prospectus in the registration statement by means of a prospectus that is deemed to be part of and included in the registration statement pursuant to Rule 430A or Rule 430B, a post-effective amendment to the registration statement, or an Exchange Act report incorporated by reference into the registration statement and the prospectus and identified in a prospectus filed, as required by Rule 430B, pursuant to Rule 424(b) (§ 230.424(b) of this chapter).

H. Selling Security Holder Offerings. Where a registrant eligible to register primary offerings on this Form pursuant to General Instruction I.B.1 registers securities offerings on this Form pursuant to General Instruction I.B.1 or I.B.3 for the account of persons other than the registrant, if the offering of the securities, or securities convertible into such securities, that are being registered on behalf of the selling security holders was completed and the securities, or securities convertible into such securities, were issued and outstanding prior to the original date of filing the registration statement covering the resale of the securities, the registrant may, as permitted by Rule 430B(b), in lieu of identifying

selling security holders prior to effectiveness of the resale registration statement, refer to unnamed selling security holders in a generic manner by identifying the initial transaction in which the securities were sold. Following effectiveness, the registrant must include in a prospectus filed pursuant to Rule 424(b)(7), a post-effective amendment to the registration statement, or an Exchange Act report incorporated by reference into the prospectus that is part of the registration statement (which Exchange Act report is identified in a prospectus filed, as required by Rule 430B, pursuant to Rule 424(b)(7)), the names of previously unidentified selling security holders and amounts of securities that they intend to sell. If this Form is being filed pursuant to General Instruction I.C. by a well-known seasoned issuer to register securities being offered for the account of persons other than the issuer, the registration statement and the prospectus included in the registration statement do not need to designate the securities that will be offered for the account of such persons, identify them, or identify the initial transaction in which the securities, or securities convertible into such securities, were sold until the registrant files a post-effective amendment to the registration statement, a prospectus pursuant to Rule 424(b), or an Exchange Act report (and prospectus filed, as required by Rule 430B, pursuant to Rule 424(b)(7)) containing information for the offering on behalf of such persons.

III. Dividend or Interest Reinvestment Plans: Filing and Effectiveness of Registration Statement; Requests for Confidential Treatment

Original registration statements on this Form F-3 solely with respect to securities offered pursuant to dividend or interest reinvestment plans shall become effective automatically upon filing (Rule 456, § 230.456 of this chapter) pursuant to the provisions of Section 8(a) of the Act (Rule 462, § 230.462 of this chapter). Post-effective amendments to such a registration statement on this Form shall become effective upon the date of filing (Rule 464, § 230.464 of this chapter). Delaying amendments are not permitted in connection with either original filings or amendments on such a registration statement (Rule 473(d), § 239.473(d) of this chapter), and any attempt to interpose a delaying amendment of any kind will be ineffective. All filings made on or in connection with this Form become public upon filing with the Commission. As a result, requests for confidential treatment made under Rule 406 (§ 230.406 of this chapter) must be processed with the Commission staff prior to the filing of the registration statement. The number of copies of the registration statement and of each amendment required by Rules 402 and 472 (§ § 230.402 and 230.472 of this chapter) shall be filed with the Commission; *Provided however,* that the number of additional copies referred to in Rule 402(b) may be reduced from ten to three and the number of additional copies referred to in Rule 472(a) may be reduced from eight to three, one of which shall be marked clearly and precisely to indicate changes.

IV. Registration of Additional Securities and Additional Classes of Securities

A. Registration of Additional Securities Pursuant to Rule 462(b). With respect to the registration of additional securities for an offering pursuant to Rule 462(b) under the Securities Act, the registrant may file a registration statement consisting only of the following: the facing page; a statement that the contents of the earlier registration statement, identified by file number, are incorporated by reference; required opinions and consents; the signature page; and any price-related information omitted from the earlier registration statement in reliance on Rule 430A that the registrant chooses to include in the new registration statement. The information contained in such a Rule 462(b) registration statement shall be deemed to be a part of the earlier registration statement as of the date of effectiveness of the Rule 462(b) registration statement. Any opinion or consent required in the Rule 462(b) registration statement may be incorporated by reference from the earlier registration statement with respect to the offering, if: (i) such opinion or consent expressly provides for such incorporation; and (ii) such opinion relates to the securities registered pursuant to Rule 462(b). *See* Rule 411(c) and Rule 439(b) under the Securities Act.

B. Registration of Additional Securities or Classes of Securities or Additional Registrants After Effectiveness. A well-known seasoned issuer relying on General Instruction I.C. of this Form may register additional securities or classes of securities, pursuant to Rule 413(b) by filing a post-effective amendment to the effective registration statement. The well-known seasoned issuer may add majority-owned subsidiaries as additional registrants whose securities are eligible to be sold as part of the automatic shelf registration statement by filing a post-effective amendment identifying the additional registrants, and the registrant and the additional registrants and other persons required to sign the registration statement must sign the post-effective amendment. The post-effective amendment must consist of the facing page; any disclosure required by this Form that is necessary to update the registration statement to reflect the additional securities, additional classes of securities, or additional registrants; any required opinions and consents; and the signature page. Required information, consents or opinions may be included in the prospectus and the registration statement through a post-effective amendment or may be provided through a document incorporated or deemed incorporated by reference into the registration statement and the prospectus that is part of the registration statement, or, as to the required information only, contained in a prospectus filed pursuant to Rule 424(b) that is deemed part of and included in the registration statement and prospectus that is part of the registration statement.

PART I—INFORMATION REQUIRED IN PROSPECTUS

Item 1. Forepart of the Registration Statement and Outside Front Cover Page of Prospectus

Set forth in the forepart of the registration statement and on outside front cover page of the prospectus the information required by Item 501 of Regulation S-K (§ 229.501 of this chapter).

Item 2. Inside Front and Outside Back Cover Pages of Prospectus

Set forth on the inside front cover page of the prospectus or, where permitted, on the outside back cover page, the information required by Item 502 of Regulation S-K (§ 229.502 of this chapter).

Item 3. Summary Information, Risk Factors and Ratio of Earnings to Fixed Charges

Furnish the information required by Item 503 of Regulation S-K (§ 229.503 of this chapter).

Item 4. Information About the Offering

Furnish the information about the offering required by the following items of Form 20-F: Item 2 (Offer Statistics and Expected Timetable), Item 3.B (Capitalization and Indebtedness), Item 3.C (Reasons for the Offer and Use of Proceeds), Item 7.C (Interests of Experts and Counsel), Item 9 (Offer and Listing), Item 10 (Additional Information) and Item 12 (Description of Securities Other than Equity Securities). You do not have to repeat in the prospectus any information called for by these items if the same information is contained in a report being incorporated by reference into this registration statement.

Item 5. Material Changes

(a) Describe any and all material changes in the registrant's affairs that have occurred since the end of the latest fiscal year for which certified financial statements are included in this registration statement in accordance with Item 6 of this Form and that have not been described in a report on Form 6-K (§ 249.306 of this chapter), Form 10-Q (§ 249.308a of this chapter) or Form 8-K (§ 249.308 of this chapter) filed under the Exchange Act and incorporated by reference pursuant to Item 6 of this Form.

(b)(1) Include in the prospectus, if not included in documents incorporated by reference into the prospectus pursuant to Item 6 or a prospectus previously filed pursuant to Rule 424(b) or (c) under the Securities Act or, where no prospectus was required to be filed pursuant to Rule 424(b), the prospectus included in the registration statement at effectiveness, or a Form 6-K filed during either of the two preceding years: (i) information required by Rule 3-05 and Article 11 of Regulation S-X (§ 210 of this chapter) where the registrant has effected or is about to effect a transaction for which such information is required; (ii) restated financial statements if there has been a change in accounting principles or a correction of an error where such change or correction requires a material retroactive restatement of financial statements; (iii) restated financial statements where a combination of entities under common control has been consummated subsequent to the most recent fiscal year and the transferred businesses, considered in the aggregate, are significant under Rule 11-01(b) of Regulation S-X; or; (iv) any financial information required because of a material disposition of assets outside the normal course of business.

(2) If the financial statements included in this registration statement in accordance with Item 6 are not sufficiently current to comply with the requirements of Item 8.A of Form 20-F, financial statements necessary to comply with that Item shall be presented (i) directly in the prospectus, (ii) through incorporation by reference of a Form 6-K identified in the prospectus as containing such financial statements, or (iii) through incorporation by reference of an amended Form 20-F, Form 40-F or Form 10-K, in which case the prospectus shall disclose that the Form 20-F, Form 40-F or Form 10-K has been so amended.

Instructions.

1. For a registrant's fiscal years ending before December 15, 2011, financial statements or information required to be furnished by this Item shall be reconciled pursuant to either Item 17 or 18 of Form 20-F, whichever is applicable to the primary financial statements. For a registrant's fiscal years ending on or after December 15, 2011, financial statements or information required to be furnished by this Item shall be reconciled pursuant to Item 18 of Form 20-F.

2. Material changes to be disclosed pursuant to Item 5(a) include changes in and disagreements with registrant's certifying accountant. For the registrant's fiscal years ending on or after December 15, 2009, disclosure pursuant to Item 16F of Form 20-F should be provided as of the date of the registration statement or prospectus.

Item 6. Incorporation of Certain Information by Reference

(a) The registrant's latest Form 20-F, Form 40-F, Form 10-K or Form 10 filed pursuant to the Exchange Act shall be incorporated by reference. Any report on Form 10-Q or Form 8-K filed since the date of filing of the annual report incorporated by reference also shall be incorporated by reference. If capital stock is to be registered and securities of the same class are registered under Section 12 of the Exchange Act, the description of such class of securities which is contained in a registration statement filed under the Exchange Act, including any amendment or reports filed for the purpose of updating such description shall be incorporated by reference.

Instruction. If the registrant's latest filing on Form 20-F, Form 40-F or Form 10-K is amended to include the information specified in Item 18 of Form 20-F, the prospectus shall state that the Form 20-F, Form 40-F or Form 10-K has been so amended. Reference is made to the Transaction Requirements in General Instruction I.B. that, in some cases, require the financial statements in the Form 20-F, Form 40-F or Form 10-K to comply with Item 18 of Form 20-F as a condition for eligibility to use Form F-3.

(b) The prospectus shall also state that all subsequent annual reports filed on Form 20-F, Form 40-F or Form 10-K, and all subsequent filings on Forms 10-Q and 8-K filed by the registrant pursuant to the Exchange Act, prior to the termination of the offering, shall be deemed to be incorporated by reference into the prospectus.

(c) The registrant may incorporate by reference any Form 6-K meeting the requirements of this Form. If the registrant intends to incorporate any Form 6-K subsequently submitted to the Commission, the prospectus shall state that the registrant may incorporate such Forms 6-K by identifying in such Forms that they are being incorporated by reference into this Form.

(d) You must state (1) that you will provide to each person, including any beneficial owner, to whom a prospectus is delivered, a copy of any or all of the information that has been incorporated by reference in the prospectus but not delivered with the prospectus;

(2) that you will provide this information upon written or oral request;

(3) that you will provide this information at no cost to the requester; and

(4) the name, address, and telephone number to which the request for this information must be made.

Note to Item 6(d)

If you send any of the information that is incorporated by reference in the prospectus to security holders, you also must send any exhibits that are specifically incorporated by reference in that information.

(e) You must (1) identify the reports and other information that you file with the SEC; and

(2) state that the public may read and copy any materials you file with the SEC at the SEC's Public Reference Room at 100 F Street, N.E., Washington, D.C. 20549. State that the public may obtain information on the operation of the Public Reference Room by calling the SEC at 1-800-SEC-0330. If you are an electronic filer, state that the SEC maintains an Internet site that contains reports, proxy and information statements, and other information regarding issuers that file electronically with the SEC and state the address of that site (http://www.sec.gov). You are encouraged to give your Internet address, if available.

(f) Any information required in the prospectus in response to Item 3 through Item 5 of this Form may be included in the prospectus through documents filed pursuant to Sections 13(a), 14, or 15(d) of the Exchange Act that are incorporated or deemed incorporated by reference into the prospectus that is part of the registration statement.

Instructions.

1. Attention is directed to the requirements of Section 10(a)(3) of the Securities Act.

2. Attention is directed to Rule 439 (§ 230.439 of this chapter) regarding consent to use material incorporated by reference.

Item 7. Disclosure of Commission Position on Indemnification for Securities Act Liabilities

Furnish the information required by Item 510 of Regulation S-K (§ 229.510 of this chapter).

PART II—INFORMATION NOT REQUIRED IN PROSPECTUS

Item 8. Indemnification of Directors and Officers

Furnish the information required by Item 702 of Regulation S-K (§ 229.702 of this chapter).

Item 9. Exhibits

Subject to the rules regarding incorporation by reference, furnish the exhibits required by

Item 601 of Regulation S-K (§ 229.601 of this chapter).

Item 10. Undertakings

Furnish the undertakings required by Item 512 of Regulation S-K (§ 229.512 of this chapter).

SIGNATURES

Pursuant to the requirements of the Securities Act of 1933, the registrant certifies that it has reasonable grounds to believe that it meets all of the requirements for filing on Form F-3 and has duly

caused this registration statement to be signed on its behalf by the undersigned, thereunto duly authorized, in the City of . . . . , State of . . . .
. . . . , on . . . . , 19 . . . . (Registrant) . . . .
. . . .

By (Signature and Title) . . . .

Pursuant to the requirements of the Securities Act of 1933, this registration statement has been signed by the following persons in the capacities and on the dates indicated.

(Signature) . . . .

(Title) . . . .

(Date) . . . .

Instructions.

1. The registration statement shall be signed by the registrant, its principal executive officer or officers, its principal financial officer, its controller or principal accounting officer, at least a majority of the board of directors or persons performing similar functions, and its authorized representative in the United States. Where the registrant is a limited partnership, the registration statement shall be signed by a majority of the board of directors of any corporate general partner signing the registration statement.

2. The name of each person who signs the registration statement shall be typed or printed beneath his signature. Any person who occupies more than one of the specified positions shall indicate each capacity in which he signs the registration statement. Attention is directed to Rule 402 concerning manual signatures and Item 601 of Regulation S-K concerning signatures pursuant to powers of attorney.

3. Where eligibility for use of the Form is based on the assignment of a security rating pursuant to General Instruction I.B.2., the registrant may sign the registration statement notwithstanding the fact that such security rating has not been assigned by the filing date, provided that the registrant reasonably believes, and so states, that the security rating requirement will be met by the time of sale.

[¶ 7531]

FORM F-4

[As last amended in Release No. 33-8959, effective December 6, 2008, 73 F.R. 58300.]

SECURITIES AND EXCHANGE COMMISSION

Washington, D.C. 20549

Form F-4

REGISTRATION STATEMENT UNDER THE SECURITIES ACT OF 1933

Form F-4

SECURITIES AND EXCHANGE COMMISSION

Washington, D.C. 20549

REGISTRATION STATEMENT UNDER THE SECURITIES ACT OF 1933

. . . .

(Exact name of registrant as specified in its charter)

. . . .

(Translation of registrant's name into English)

. . . .

(State or other jurisdiction of incorporation or organization)

. . . .

(Primary Standard Industrial Classification Code Number)

. . . .

(I.R.S. Employer Identification Number)

. . . .

(Address, including zip code, and telephone number, including area code, of registrant's principal executive offices)

. . . .

(Name, address, including Zip Code, and telephone number, including area code, of agent for service)

Approximate date of commencement of proposed sale to the public . . . .

If this Form is filed to register additional securities for an offering pursuant to Rule 462(b) under the Securities Act, check the following box and list the Securities Act registration statement number of the earlier effective registration statement for the same offering. ☐ . . . .

If this Form is a post-effective amendment filed pursuant to Rule 462(d) under the Securities Act, check the following box and list the Securities Act registration statement number of the earlier effective registration statement for the same offering. ☐ . . . .

If applicable, place an X in the box to designate the appropriate rule provision relied upon in conducting this transaction:

Exchange Act Rule 13e-4(i) (Cross-Border Issuer Tender Offer) ☐

Exchange Act Rule 14d-1(d) (Cross-Border Third-Party Tender Offer) ☐

Calculation of Registration Fee

Title of each class of securities to be registered	Amount to be registered	Proposed maximum offering price per unit	Proposed maximum aggregate offering price	Amount of registration fee

Note: Specific details relating to the fee calculation shall be furnished in notes to the table, including references to provisions of Rule 457 (§ 230.457 of this chapter) relied upon, if the basis of the calculation is not otherwise evident from the information presented in the table.

GENERAL INSTRUCTIONS

A. Rule as to Use of Form F-4

1. This Form may be used by any foreign private issuer, as defined in Rule 405, for registration under the Securities Act of 1933 ("Securities Act") of securities to be issued: (1) in a transaction of the type specified in paragraph (a) of Rule 145; (2) in a merger in which the applicable law would not require the solicitation of the votes or consents of all of the securityholders of the company being acquired; (3) in an exchange offer for securities of the issuer or another entity; (4) in a public reoffering or resale of any such securities acquired pursuant to this registration statement; or (5) in more than one of the kinds of transactions listed in (1) through (4) registered on one registration statement.

2. If the registrant meets the requirements of and elects to comply with the provisions in any item of this Form or Form S-4 (§ 239.25) that provides for incorporation by reference of information about the registrant or the company being acquired, the prospectus must be sent to the security holders no later than 20 business days prior to the date on which the meeting of such security holders is held or, if no meeting is held, the earlier of 20 business days prior to either (1) the date the votes, consents or authorizations may be used to effect the corporate action or (2) if votes, consents or authorizations are not used, the date the transaction is consummated. Attention is directed to Sections 13(e), 14(d) and 14(e) of the Securities Exchange Act of 1934 ("Exchange Act") and the rules and regulations thereunder regarding other time periods in connection with exchange offers and going private transactions.

3. This form shall not be used if the registrant is a registered investment company.

B. Information with Respect to the Registrant

1. Information with respect to the registrant shall be provided in accordance with the items referenced in one of the following subparagraphs:

(a) Items 10 and 11 of this Form, if the registrant elects this alternative and meets the following requirements for use of Form F-3 (§ 239.33 of this chapter) (hereinafter, with respect to the registrant, "meets the requirements for use of Form F-3") for this offering of securities:

(i) The registrant meets the requirements of General Instruction I.A. of Form F-3, and

(ii) One of the following is met:

A. The registrant meets the aggregate market value requirement of General Instruction I.B. 1. of Form F-3; or

B. Non-convertible debt or preferred securities are to be offered pursuant to this registration statement and are "investment grade securities" as defined in General Instruction I.B. 2. of Form F-3; or

C. The registrant is a majority-owned subsidiary and one of the conditions of General Instruction I.A.5. of Form F-3 is met.

(b) Items 12 and 13 of this Form, if the registrant meets the requirements for use of Form F-3 and elects this alternative; or

(c) Item 14 of this Form, if the registrant does not meet the requirements for use of Form F-3, or if it otherwise elects this alternative.

2. If the registrant is a real estate entity of the type described in General Instruction A to Form S-11 (§ 239.18 of this chapter), the information prescribed by Items 12, 13, 14, 15 and 16 of the Form S-11 shall be furnished about the registrant in addition to the information provided pursuant to Items 10 through 14 of this Form. The information prescribed by such Items of Form S-11 may be incorporated by reference into the prospectus if (a) a registrant qualifies for and elects to provide information pursuant to alternative 1.a. or 1.b. of this instruction and (b) the documents incorporated by reference pursuant to such elected alternative contain such information.

C. Information With Respect to the Company Being Acquired

1. Information with respect to the company whose securities are being acquired (hereinafter including, where securities of the registrant are being offered in exchange for securities of another company, such other company) shall be provided in accordance with the items referenced in one of the following subparagraphs:

(a) Item 15 of this Form, if the company being acquired meets requirements of General Instruction I.A. and I.B. (hereinafter, with respect to the company being acquired, "meets the requirements for use of Form F-3") for use of Form F-3 and this alternative is elected;

(b) Item 16 of this Form, if the company being acquired meets the requirements for use of Form F-3 and this alternative is elected; or

(c) Item 17 of this Form, if the company being acquired does not meet the requirements for use of Form F-3, or if this alternative is otherwise elected.

(d) If the company to be acquired is a U.S. company, the registrant shall present information about such other company pursuant to Instructions C and F of Form S-4 (§ 239.25 of this chapter).

2. If the company being acquired is a real estate entity of the type described in General Instruction A to Form S-11, the information that would be required by Items 13, 14, 15 and 16(a) of Form S-11 if securities of such company were being registered shall be furnished about such company being acquired in addition to the information provided pursuant to this Form. The information prescribed by such Items of Form S-11 may be incorporated by reference into the prospectus if: (a) the company being registered would qualify for use of the level of disclosure prescribed by alternative 1.a. or 1.b. of this instruction and such alternative is elected; and (b) the documents incorporated by reference pursuant to such elected alternative contain such information.

D. Application of General Rules and Regulations

1. Attention is directed to the General Rules and Regulations under the Securities Act, particularly those comprising Regulation C thereunder (§ 230.400 et seq. of this chapter). That Regulation contains general requirements regarding the preparation and filing of registration statements.

2. Attention is directed to Regulation S-K (Part 229 of this chapter) and Form 20-F for the requirements applicable to the content of non-financial statement portions of registration statements under the Securities Act. Where this Form directs the registrant to furnish information required by Regulation S-K or Form 20-F and the item of Regulation S-K or Form 20-F so provides, information need only be furnished to the extent appropriate.

3. Where two or more classes of securities being registered on this Form are to be offered on a delayed or continuous basis pursuant to Rule 415(a)(1)(viii) (§ 230.415(a)(1)(viii) of this chapter), Rule 457(o) (§ 230.457(o) of this chapter) permits the registration fee to be calculated on the basis of the maximum offering price of all the securities listed in the "Calculation of Registration Fee" table ("Fee Table") if the securities are being registered by an issuer eligible to use Form F-3. In this event, while the Fee Table would list each of the classes of securities being registered and the aggregate proceeds to be raised, the Fee Table need not specify for each class information as to the amount to be registered, proposed maximum

offering price per unit and proposed maximum aggregate offering price.

4. A registrant must file the Form F-4 registration statement in electronic format via the Commission's Electronic Data Gathering and Retrieval System (EDGAR) in accordance with the EDGAR rules set forth in Regulation S-T (17 CFR Part 232), except that a registrant that has obtained a hardship exception under Regulation S-T Rule 201 or 202 (17 CFR 232.201 or 232.202) may file the registration statement in paper. For assistance with technical questions about EDGAR or to request an access code, call the EDGAR Filer Support Office at (202) 551-8900. For assistance with questions about the EDGAR rules, call the Office of EDGAR and Information Analysis at (202) 551-3610.

5. The Form F-4 registration statement must be in the English language, as required by Regulation S-T Rule 306 (17 CFR 232.306) for electronic filings and Securities Act Rule 403(c) (17 CFR 230.403(c)), generally. If the registration statement requires the inclusion, as an exhibit or attachment, of a document that is in a foreign language, the registrant must provide instead either an English translation or an English summary of the foreign language document in accordance with Securities Act Rule 403(c) (17 CFR 230.403(c)) for both electronic and paper filings. The registrant may submit a copy of the unabridged foreign language document along with the English translation or English summary as permitted by Regulation S-T Rule 306(b) (17 CFR 232.306(b)) for electronic filings or by Securities Act Rule 403(c)(4) (17 CFR 230.403(c)(4)) for paper filings.

E. Compliance With Exchange Act Rules

1. If a corporation or other person submits a proposal to its security holders entitled to vote on, or consent to, the transaction in which the securities being registered are to be issued, and such person's submission to its security holders is subject to Regulation 14A (§§ 240.14a-1 through 14a-101 of this chapter) or 14C (§§ 240.14c-1 through 14c-101 of this chapter) under the Exchange Act, then the provisions of such Regulations shall apply in all respects to such person's submission, except that: (a) The prospectus may be in the form of a proxy or information statement and may contain the information required by this Form in lieu of that required by Schedule 14A (§ 240.14a-101) or 14C (§ 240.14c-101) of Regulation 14A or 14C under the Exchange Act; and (b) copies of the preliminary and definitive proxy or information statement, form of proxy or other material filed as a part of the registration statement shall be deemed filed pursuant to such person's obligations under such Regulations.

2. If the proxy or information statement material sent to security holders is not subject to Regulation 14A or 14C, all such material shall be filed as a part of the registration statement at the time the statement is filed or as an amendment thereto prior to the use of such material.

3. If the transaction in which the securities being registered are to be issued is subject to Section 13(e), 14(d) or 14(e) of the Exchange Act, the provisions of those sections and the rules and regulations thereunder shall apply to the transaction in addition to the provisions of this Form.

F. Registration Statements Subject to Rule 415(a)(1)(viii) (§ 230.415(a)(1)(viii) of this chapter)

If the registration statement relates to offerings of securities pursuant to Rule 415(a)(1)(viii), required information about the type of contemplated transaction (and the company being acquired) need only be furnished as of the date of initial effectiveness of the registration statement to the extent practicable. The required information about the specific transaction and the particular company being acquired must be included in the prospectus by means of a post-effective amendment.

G. Roll-Up Transactions

1. If securities to be registered on this Form will be issued in a roll-up transaction as defined in Item 901(c) of Regulation S-K, then the disclosure provisions of Subpart 229.900 of Regulation S-K shall apply to the transaction in addition to the provisions of this Form. To the extent that the disclosure requirements of Subpart 229.900 are inconsistent with the disclosure requirements of any other applicable forms or schedules, the requirements of Subpart 229.900 are controlling.

2. If securities to be registered on this Form will be issued in a roll-up transaction as defined in Item 901(c) of Regulation S-K, the prospectus must be distributed to security holders no later than the lesser of 60 calendar days prior to the date on which action is to be taken or the maximum number of days permitted for giving notice under applicable state law.

3. Attention is directed to the proxy rules and Rule 14e-7 of the tender offer rules if securities to be registered on this Form will be issued in a roll-up transaction. Such rules contain provisions specifically applicable to roll-up transactions, whether or not the entities involved have securities registered pursuant to Section 12 of the Exchange Act.

H. Registration of Additional Securities

With respect to the registration of additional securities for an offering pursuant to Rule 462(b) under the Securities Act, the registrant may file a registration statement consisting only of the following: the facing page; a statement that the contents of the earlier registration statement, identified by file number, are incorporated by reference; required opinions and consents; the signature page; and any price-related information omitted from the earlier registration statement in reliance on Rule 430A that the registrant chooses to include in the new registration statement. The information contained in such a Rule 462(b) registration statement shall be deemed to be a part of the earlier registration statement as of the date of effectiveness of the Rule 462(b) registration statement. Any opinion or consent required in the Rule 462(b) registration statement may be incorporated by reference from the earlier registration statement with respect to the offering, if: (i) such opinion or consent expressly provides for such incorporation; and (ii) such opinion relates to the securities registered pursuant to Rule 462(b). See Rule 411(c) and Rule 439(b) under the Securities Act.

PART I—INFORMATION REQUIRED IN THE PROSPECTUS

A. INFORMATION ABOUT THE TRANSACTION

Item 1. Forepart of Registration Statement and Outside Front Cover Page of Prospectus

Set forth in the forepart of the registration statement and on the outside front cover page of the prospectus the information required by Item 501 of Regulation S-K (§ 229.501 of this chapter).

Item 2. Inside Front and Outside Back Cover Pages of Prospectus

Provide the information required by Item 502 of Regulation S-K. In addition, on the inside front cover page, you must state (1) that the prospectus incorporates important business and financial information about the company that is not included in or delivered with the document; and

(2) that this information is available without charge to security holders upon written or oral request. Give the name, address, and telephone number to which security holders must make this request. In addition, you must state that to obtain timely delivery, security holders must request the information no later than five business days before the date they must make their investment decision. Specify the date by which security holders must request this information. You must highlight this statement by print type or otherwise.

Note to Item 2.

If you send any of the information that is incorporated by reference in the prospectus to security holders, you also must send any exhibits that are specifically incorporated by reference in that information.

Item 3. Risk Factors, Ratio of Earnings to Fixed Charges and Other Information

Provide in the forepart of the prospectus a summary containing the information required by Item 503 of Regulation S-K (§ 229.503 of this chapter) and the following:

(a) The name, complete mailing address (including the Zip Code), and telephone number (including the area code) of the principal executive offices of the registrant and the company being acquired;

(b) A brief description of the general nature of the business conducted by the registrant and by the company being acquired;

(c) A brief description of the transaction in which the securities being registered are to be offered;

(d) The information required by Item 3.A of Form 20-F (selected financial data) for the registrant and the company being acquired. If the information is required to be presented in the prospectus pursuant to Items 12, 14, 16 or 17, it need not be presented pursuant to this Item.

(e) If material, the information required by Item 3.A of Form 20-F for the registrant on a pro forma basis, giving effect to the transaction. If the information is required to be presented in the prospectus pursuant to Items 12 or 14, it need not be presented pursuant to this Item.

(f) In comparative columnar form, historical and pro forma per share data of the registrant and historical and equivalent per share data of the company being acquired for the following items:

(1) book value per share as of the date financial data is presented pursuant to Item 3.A. of Form 20-F (selected financial data);

(2) cash dividends declared per share for the periods for which financial data is presented pursuant to Item 3.A. of Form 20-F (selected financial data); and

(3) income (loss) per share from continuing operations for the periods for which financial data is presented pursuant to Item 3.A. of Form 20-F (selected financial data).

Instructions to paragraphs (e) and (f).

1. For a business combination accounted for as a purchase, the financial information required

by paragraphs (e) and (f) shall be presented only for the most recent fiscal year and interim period. For a business combination accounted for as a pooling, the financial information required by paragraphs (e) and (f) (except for information with regard to book value) shall be presented for the most recent three fiscal years and interim period. For a business combination accounted for as a pooling, information with regard to book value shall be presented as of the end of the most recent fiscal year and interim period. Equivalent pro forma per share amounts shall be calculated by multiplying the pro forma income (loss) per share before non-recurring charges or credits directly attributable to the transaction, pro forma book value per share, and the pro forma dividends per share of the registrant by the exchange ratio so that the per share amounts are equated to the respective values for one share of the company being acquired.

2. Instructions to Item 3.A. of Form 20-F is applicable to the financial information presented hereunder to the extent that this Form requires reconciliation of financial statements of foreign private issuers to United States generally accepted accounting principles ("U.S. GAAP") and Regulation S-X (Part 210 of this chapter).

(g) In comparative columnar form, the market value of securities of the company being acquired (on an historical and equivalent per share basis) and the market value of the securities of the registrant (on an historical basis) as of the date preceding public announcement of the proposed transaction, or, if no such public announcement was made, as of the day preceding the day the agreement with respect to the transaction was entered into;

(h) With respect to the registrant and the company being acquired, a brief statement comparing the percentage of outstanding shares entitled to vote held by directors, executive officers and their affiliates and the vote required for approval of the proposed transaction;

(i) A statement as to whether any regulatory requirements other than the U.S. federal securities laws, must be complied with or approval must be obtained in connection with the transaction, and if so, the status of such compliance or approvals;

(j) A statement about whether or not dissenters' rights of appraisal exist, including a cross-reference to the information provided pursuant to Item 18 or 19 of this Form; and

(k) A brief statement about the tax consequences of the transaction or if appropriate, consisting of a cross-reference to the information provided pursuant to Item 4 of this Form.

Item 4. Terms of the Transaction

(a) Furnish a summary of the material features of the proposed transaction. The summary shall include, where applicable:

(1) A brief summary of the terms of the acquisition agreement;

(2) The reasons of the registrant and of the company being acquired for engaging in the transaction;

(3) The information required by Items 10.A. and 10.B. of Form 20-F or Item 12 of Form 20-F as applicable, description of registrant's securities, unless: (i) the registrant would meet the requirements for use of Form F-3 and elects to furnish information pursuant to Item 10, (ii) capital stock is to be registered, and (iii) securities of the same class are registered under Section 12 of the Exchange Act and listed for trading on a national exchange, or are securities for which bid and offer quotations are reported in an automated quotations system operated by a national securities association;

(4) An explanation of any material differences between the rights of security holders of the company being acquired and the rights of holders of the securities being offered;

(5) A brief statement as to the accounting treatment of the transaction;

(6) The tax consequences of the transaction; and

(7) A discussion of any material differences in the corporate laws of the country of the company to be acquired and the country of the surviving company. The discussion should include, but not necessarily be limited to: corporate governance, board structure, quorums, class action suits, shareholder derivative suits, rights to inspect corporate books and records, rights to inspect the shareholder list, and rights of directors and officers to obtain indemnification from the company.

(b) If a report, opinion or appraisal materially relating to the transaction has been received from an outside party, and such report, opinion or appraisal is referred to in the prospectus, furnish the information called for by Item 1015(b) of Regulation M-A (§ 229.1015(b) of this chapter).

(c) Incorporate the acquisition agreement by reference into the prospectus, by means of a statement to that effect.

Item 5. Pro Forma Financial Information

Furnish financial information required by Article 11 of Regulation S-X (§ 210.11-01 et seq. of this chapter) with respect to this transaction.

Instructions

1. Any other Article 11 information required to be presented (rather than incorporated by reference) pursuant to other Items of this Form shall be presented together with the information provided pursuant to Item 5, but the presentation shall clearly distinguish between this transaction and any other.

2. If pro forma financial information with respect to all other transactions is incorporated by reference pursuant to Item 11 or 15 of this Form only the pro forma results need be presented as part of the pro forma financial information required by this Item.

Item 6. Material Contacts With the Company Being Acquired

Describe any past, present or proposed material contracts, arrangements, understandings, relationships, negotiations or transactions during the periods for which financial statements are presented or incorporated by reference pursuant to Part I. B. or C. of this Form between the company being acquired or its affiliates and the registrant or its affiliates, such as those concerning: a merger, consolidation or acquisition; a tender offer or other acquisition of securities; an election of directors; or a sale or other transfer of a material amount of assets.

Item 7. Additional Information Required for Reoffering by Persons and Parties Deemed To Be Underwriters

If any of the securities are to be reoffered to the public by any person or party who is deemed to be an underwriter thereof, furnish the following information in the prospectus at the time it is being used for the reoffer of the securities, to the extent it is not already furnished therein:

(a) The information required by Item 9.D. of Form 20-F (§ 249.220f of this chapter); and

(b) Information with respect to the consummation of the transaction pursuant to which the securities were acquired and any material change in the registrant's affairs subsequent to the transaction.

Item 8. Interests of Named Experts and Counsel

Furnish the information required by Item 7.C. of Form 20-F (§ 249.220f of this chapter).

Item 9. Disclosure of Commission Position on Indemnification for Securities Act Liabilities

Furnish the information required by Item 510 of Regulation S-K (§ 229.510 of this chapter).

B. INFORMATION ABOUT THE REGISTRANT

Item 10. Information With Respect to F-3 Companies

If the registrant meets the requirements for use of Form F-3 and elects to furnish information in accordance with the provisions of this Item, furnish information as required below:

(a) Describe any and all material changes in the registrant's affairs that have occurred since the end of the latest fiscal year for which audited financial statements are incorporated by reference in accordance with Item 11 of this Form and that have not been described in a report on Form 6-K (§ 249.306 of this chapter), Form 10-Q (§ 249.308a of this chapter) or Form 8-K (§ 249.308 of this chapter) filed under the Exchange Act;

(b) If the financial statements incorporated by reference in accordance with Item 11 of this Form are not sufficiently current to comply with Item 8.A. of Form 20-F, financial statements necessary to comply with that rule shall be presented either in the prospectus, in an amended Form 20-F, 40-F or 10-K (in which case the prospectus shall disclose that such form has been so amended), or in a Form 6-K, Form 10-Q or Form 8-K; and

(c) Include in the prospectus, if not incorporated by reference from the documents filed under the Exchange Act specified in Item 11 of this Form, from a prospectus previously filed pursuant to Rule 424(b) or (c) under the Securities Act (§ 230.424 of this chapter) or, where no prospectus was required to be filed pursuant to Rule 424(b), the prospectus included in the registration statement at effectiveness, or from a Form 6-K filed during either of the two preceding fiscal years:

(1) Financial information required by Rule 3-05 (§ 210.3-05 of this chapter) and Article 11 of Regulation S-X with respect to transactions other than that pursuant to which the securities being registered are to be issued;

(2) Restated financial statements prepared in accordance with or, if prepared using a basis of accounting other than International Financial Reporting Standards ("IFRS") as issued by the International Accounting Standards Board ("IASB"), reconciled to U.S. GAAP and Regulation S-X if there has been a change in accounting principles or a correction of an error where such change or correction requires a material retroactive restatement of financial statements;

(3) Restated financial statements prepared in accordance with or, if prepared using a basis of accounting other than IFRS as issued by the IASB, reconciled to U.S. GAAP and Regulation S-X where one or more business combinations accounted for by the pooling of interest method of accounting have been consummated subsequent to the most recent fiscal year and the acquired businesses, considered in the aggregate, are sig-

nificant pursuant to Rule 11-01(b) of Regulation S-X (§ 210.11-01(b) of this chapter); or

(4) Any financial information required because of a material disposition of assets outside the normal course of business.

Instruction

Reference is made to Rules 4-01(a) (2) and 10-01 of Regulation S-X (§ § 210.4-01(a)(2) and 210.10-01 of this chapter).

Item 11. Incorporation of Certain Information by Reference

If the registrant furnishes information in accordance with the provisions of Item 10 of this Form:

(a) Incorporate by reference into the prospectus, by means of a statement to that effect listing all documents so incorporated, the documents listed in paragraph (1) below and, if applicable, (2) and (3) below.

(1) The registrant's latest annual report on Form 20-F, on Form 10-K or, in the case of registrants described in General Instruction A.(2) of Form 40-F, on Form 40-F filed pursuant to section 13(a) or 15(d) of the Exchange Act which contains financial statements for the registrant's latest fiscal year for which a Form 20-F, Form 10-K or Form 40-F was required to be filed;

(2) All reports filed pursuant to sections 13(a) or 15(d) of the Exchange Act since the end of the fiscal year covered by the financial statements in the report or registration statement incorporated pursuant to Item 11(a)(1) of this Form; and

(3) If capital stock is to be registered and securities of the same class are registered under section 12 of the Exchange Act, and (i) listed for trading or admitted to unlisted trading privileges on a national securities exchange; or (ii) are securities for which bid and offer quotations are reported on an automated quotations system operated by a national securities association the description of such class of securities which is contained in a registration statement filed under the Exchange Act, including any amendment or reports filed for the purpose of updating such description.

Instructions

1. For the registrant's fiscal years ending before December 15, 2011, all annual reports or registration statements incorporated by reference pursuant to Item 11 of this Form shall contain financial statements that comply with Item 18 of Form 20-F, except that financial statements of the registrants may comply with Item 17 of Form 20-F if the only securities being registered are investment grade securities as defined in the General Instructions to Form F-3. For the registrant's fiscal years ending

on or after December 15, 2011, all annual reports or registration statements incorporated by reference pursuant to Item 11 of this Form shall contain financial statements that comply with Item 18 of Form 20-F.

2. Where common equity securities are being issued, the information required by Item 9.A.4. of Form 20-F, nature of trading markets, should be updated, to cover any subsequent interim periods for which interim financial statements are required to be included to comply with Item 8.A. of Form 20-F. Such updating may be made in the prospectus, in an amended Form 20-F, Form 10-K or, in the case of registrants described in General Instruction A.(2) of Form 40-F, Form 40-F, or in a Form 6-K, Form 10-Q or Form 8-K, as applicable.

3. The registrant may incorporate by reference any Form 6-K meeting the requirements of Form F-3. See Rules 4-01 (a) (2) and 10-01 of Regulation S-X and Item 18 of Form 20-F.

(b) The prospectus also shall state that all annual reports on Form 20-F, on Form 10-K or, in the case of registrants described in General Instruction A. (2) of Form 40-F, on Form 40-F and all Forms 10-Q and 8-K, and any Form 6-K so designated, subsequently filed by the registrant pursuant to sections 31(a), 13(c) or 15(d) of the Exchange Act, prior to one of the following dates, whichever is applicable, shall be deemed to be incorporated by reference into the prospectus:

(1) If a meeting of securityholders is to be held, the date on which such meeting is held;

(2) If a meeting of securityholders is not to be held, the date on which the transaction is consummated;

(3) If securities of the registrant are being offered in exchange for securities of any other issuer, the termination of the offering; or

(4) If securities are being offered in a reoffering or resale of securities acquired pursuant to this registration statement, the termination of such reoffering.

Instruction

Attention is directed to Rule 439 (§ 230.439 of this chapter) regarding consent to the use of material incorporated by reference.

(b) You must (1) identify the reports and other information that you file with the SEC; and

(c) You must (1) identify the reports and other information that you file with the SEC; and

(2) state that the public may read and copy any materials you file with the SEC at the SEC's Public Reference Room at 100 F Street, N.E., Washington, D.C. 20549. State that the public may obtain information on the operation of the Public Reference Room by calling the SEC at 1-800-SEC-0330. If you are an electronic filer, state that the SEC maintains an Internet site that contains reports, proxy and information statements, and other information regarding issuers that file electronically with the SEC and state the address of that site (http://www.sec.gov). You are encouraged to give your Internet address, if available.

Item 12. Information with Respect to F-3 Registrants.

If the registrant meets the requirements for use of Form F-3 or Form S-3 and elects to comply with this Item, furnish the information required by either paragraph (a) or (b) of this Item. However, the registrant shall not provide prospectus information in the manner allowed by paragraph (a) of this Item if the financial statements incorporated by reference pursuant to Item 13 reflect: (1) restated financial statements prepared in accordance with or reconciled to U.S. GAAP and Regulation S-X if there has been a change in accounting principles or a correction of an error where such change or correction requires a material retroactive restatement of financial statements; (2) restated financial statements prepared in accordance with or reconciled to U.S. GAAP and Regulation S-X where one or more business combinations accounted for by the pooling of interest method of accounting have been consummated subsequent to the most recent fiscal year and the acquired businesses, considered in the aggregate, are significant pursuant to Rule 11-01(b) of Regulation S-X; or (3) any financial information required because of a material disposition of assets outside of the normal course of business.

(a) If the registrant elects to deliver this prospectus together with the annual report incorporated by reference pursuant to Item 13, or a complete and legible facsimile thereof:

(1) Indicate that the prospectus is accompanied by such annual report or registration statement.

(2) If the financial statements incorporated by reference pursuant to Item 13 of this Form are not sufficiently current to comply with Item 8.A. of Form 20-F, provide the information required by Rule 10-01 of Regulation S-X and Item 5 of Form 20-F by one of the following means:

(i) Including such information in the prospectus;

(ii) Providing without charge to whom a prospectus is delivered a copy of the registrant's Form 10-Q, Form 8-K or Form 6-K report that contains such later information; or

(iii) In an amended Form 20-F, Form 40-F or Form 10-K in which case the prospectus shall disclose that the Form 20-F, Form 40-F or Form 10-K has been so amended.

(3) If not reflected in the registrant's annual report incorporated by reference in accordance with Item 13 of this Form, provide information required by Rule 3-05 and Article 11 of Regulation S-X with respect to transactions other than that pursuant to which the securities being registered are to be issued.

(4) Describe any and all material changes in the registrant's affairs that have occurred since the end of the latest fiscal year for which audited financial statements are incorporated by reference in accordance with Item 13 of this Form and that have not been described in a report on Form 6-K, Form 10-Q or Form 8-K delivered with the prospectus in accordance with paragraph (2)(ii) of this Item.

(5) Where common equity securities are being issued, the information required by Item 9.A.4. of Form 20-F, nature of trading markets, should be updated to cover any subsequent interim periods for which interim financial statements are required to be included to comply with Item 8.A. of Form 20-F. Such updating may be made in the prospectus, in an amended Form 20-F, Form 10-K or Form 40-F, or in a Form 6-K, Form 10-Q or Form 8-K.

(b) If the registrant elects not to deliver its annual report incorporated by reference pursuant to Item 13 to the securityholders of the company to be acquired:

(1) Furnish a brief description of the business done by the registrant and its subsidiaries during the most recent fiscal year based on the requirements of Item 4 of Form 20-F. The description shall also take into account changes in the registrant's business that have occurred between the end of the latest fiscal year and the effective date of the registration statement.

(2) For the registrant's fiscal years ending before December 15, 2011, include financial statements and information as required by Item 18 of Form 20-F, except that financial statements of the registrant may comply with Item 17 of Form 20-F if the only securities being registered are investment grade securities as defined in the General Instructions to Form F-3. For the registrant's fiscal years ending on or after December 15, 2011, include financial statements and information as required by Item 18 of Form 20-F. In addition, provide:

(i) The interim financial information as required by Rule 10-01 of Regulation S-X sufficient to meet the requirements of Item 8.A. of Form 20-F;

(ii) Financial information required by Rule 3-05 and Article 11 of Regulation S-X with respect to transactions other than that pursuant to which the securities being registered are to be issued;

(iii) Restated financial statements prepared in accordance with or, if prepared using a basis of accounting other than IFRS as issued by the IASB, reconciled to U.S. GAAP and Regulation S-X if there has been a change in accounting principles or a correction of an error where such change or correction requires a material retroactive restatement of financial statements;

(iv) Restated financial statements prepared in accordance with or, if prepared using a basis of accounting other than IFRS as issued by the IASB, reconciled to U.S. GAAP and Regulation S-X where one or more business combinations accounted for by the pooling of interest method of accounting have been consummated subsequent to the most recent fiscal year and the acquired businesses, considered in the aggregate, are significant pursuant to Rule 11-01(b) of Regulation S-X; and

(v) Any financial information required because of a material disposition of assets outside the normal course of business.

Instruction

Reference is made to Item 4-01(a)(2) of Regulation S-X.

(3) Furnish the information required by the following:

(i) Items 4.B., 4.B.2., and 4.B.5. of Form 20-F, principal products, principal markets, methods of distribution, sales and revenues by categories of activity and into geographical markets;

(ii) Item 4.D of Form 20-F, properties if the registrant is engaged significantly in extractive industries;

(iii) Item 10.D. of Form 20-F, exchange controls;

(iv) Item 10.E. of Form 20-F, taxation;

(v) Item 3.A. of Form 20-F, selected financial data;

(vi)(A) Item 5. of Form 20-F, operating and financial review;

(B) Item 11 of Form 20-F, quantitative and qualitative disclosures of market risk;

(vii) For the registrant's fiscal years ending before December 15, 2011, financial statements required by Item 18 of Form 20-F, except that financial statements of the registrant may comply with Item 17 of Form 20-F if the only securities being registered are investment grade securities as defined in the General Instructions to Form F-3, and financial information required by Rule 3-05 and Article 11 of Regulation S-X with respect to transactions other than that pursuant to which the securities being registered are to be issued. (Schedules required under Regulation S-X shall be filed as "Financial Statement Schedules" pursuant to Item 21 of this Form, but need not be provided with respect to the company being acquired if information is being furnished pursuant to Item 17(a) of this Form.) For the registrant's fiscal years ending on or after December 15, 2011, financial statements required by Item 18 of Form 20-F, and financial information required by Rule 3-05 and Article 11 of Regulation S-X with respect to transactions other than that pursuant to which the securities being registered are to be issued;

(viii) Where common equity securities are being issued, Item 9.A.4. of Form 20-F, nature of trading markets, updated to cover any subsequent interim periods for which interim financial statements are required to comply with Item 8.A. of Form 20-F; and

(ix) For the registrant's fiscal years ending on or after December 15, 2009, Item 16F of Form 20-F, change in registrant's certifying accountant.

Item 13. Incorporation of Certain Information by Reference

If the registrant furnishes information in accordance with the provisions of Item 12 of this Form, incorporate by reference into the prospectus, by means of a statement to that effect in the prospectus listing all documents so incorporated, the documents listed in paragraphs (a) and, if applicable, (b) below:

(a) The registrant's latest annual report on Form 20-F, on Form 10-K or, in the case of registrants described in General Instruction A.(2) of Form 40-F, on Form 40-F filed pursuant to Section 13(a) or 15(d) of the Exchange Act which contains audited financial statements for the registrant's latest fiscal year for which a Form 20-F, Form 10-K or Form 40-F was required to be filed; and

(b) All other reports filed pursuant to Section 13(a) or 15(d) of the Exchange Act since the end of the fiscal year covered by the financial statements in the report incorporated pursuant to Item 13(a) of this Form.

Instructions

1. For the registrant's fiscal years ending before December 15, 2011, all annual reports incorporated by reference pursuant to Item 13 of this Form shall contain financial statements that comply with Item 18 of Form 20-F, except that financial statements of the registrants may comply with Item 17 of Form 20-F if the only securities being registered are investment grade securities as defined in the General Instructions to Form F-3. For the registrant's fiscal years ending on or after December 15, 2011, all annual reports incorporated by reference pursuant to Item 13 of this Form shall contain financial statements that comply with Item 18 of Form 20-F.

2. Where common equity securities are being issued, the information required by Item 9.A.4. of Form 20-F, nature of trading markets, should be updated to cover any subsequent interim periods for which interim financial statements are required to be included to comply with Item 8.A. of Form 20-F. Such updating may be made in the prospectus, in an amended Form 20-F, Form 10-K or Form 40-F or in a Form 6-K, Form 10-Q or Form 8-K.

3. The registrant may incorporate by reference and deliver with the prospectus any Form 6-K, Form 10-Q or Form 8-K containing information eligible to be incorporated by reference into Form F-1. See Rules 4-01(a)(2) and 10-01 of Regulation S-X and Item 18 of Form 20-F.

4. Attention is directed to Rule 439 regarding consent to the use of material incorporated by reference.

(c) You must (1) identify the reports and other information that you file with the SEC; and

(2) state that the public may read and copy any materials you file with the SEC at the SEC's Public Reference Room at 100 F Street, N.E., Washington, D.C. 20549. State that the public may obtain information on the operation of the Public Reference Room by calling the SEC at 1-800-SEC-0330. If you are an electronic filer, state that the SEC maintains an Internet site that contains reports, proxy and information statements, and other information regarding issuers that file electronically with the SEC and state the address of that site (http://www.sec.gov). You are encouraged to give your Internet address, if available.

Item 14. Information with Respect to Registrants Other Than F-3 Registrants.

If the foreign registrant does not meet the requirements for use of Form F-3, or otherwise elects to comply with this Item in lieu of Items 10 and 11 or Items 12 and 13, furnish the following information:

(a) Items 4.A., 4.B., and 4.C. of Form 20-F, information on the company;

(b) Item 4.D. of Form 20-F, property, plant and equipment;

(c) Item 8.A.7. of Form 20-F, legal proceedings;

(d) Item 10.D. of Form 20-F, exchange controls;

(e) Item 10.E. of Form 20-F, taxation;

(f) Item 3.A. of Form 20-F, selected financial data;

(g)(1) Item 5 of Form 20-F, operational and financial review;

(2) Item 11 of Form 20-F, quantitative and qualitative disclosures of market risk.

(h) For the registrant's fiscal years ending before December 15, 2011, financial statements required by Item 18 of Form 20-F, except that financial statements of the registrants may comply with Item 17 of Form 20-F if the only securities being registered are investment grade securities as defined in the General Instructions to Form F-1; and for the registrant's fiscal years ending on or after December 15, 2011, financial statements required by Item 18 of Form 20-F. In addition, financial information required by Rule 3-05 and Article 11 of Regulation S-X with respect to transactions other than that pursuant to which the securities being registered are to be issued. (Schedules required by Regulation S-X shall be filed as "Financial Statement Schedules" pursuant to Item 21 of this Form.);

(i) Where common equity securities are being issued, the information required by Item 9.A.4. of Form 20-F, nature of trading markets, should be updated to cover any subsequent interim periods for which interim financial statements are required to be included to comply with Item 8.A. of Form 20-F; and

(j) For the registrant's fiscal years ending on or after December 15, 2009, Item 16F of Form 20-F, change in registrant's certifying accountant.

Instructions

The financial statements required herein shall comply with Item 8.A. of Form 20-F. See also Rules 4-01(a)(2) and 10-01 of Regulation S-X.

C. INFORMATION ABOUT THE COMPANY BEING ACQUIRED

Item 15. Information With Respect to F-3 Companies

If the company being acquired meets the requirements for use of Form F-3 and compliance with this Item is elected, furnish the information that would be required by Items 10 and 11 of this Form if securities of such company were being registered.

Instruction

Notwithstanding the requirements of Items 10 and 11, the financial statements of the company being acquired need only comply with the reconciliation requirements of Item 17 of Form 20-F.

Item 16. Information with Respect to F-3 Companies.

If the company being acquired meets the requirements for use of Form F-3 and compliance with this Item is elected, furnish the information that would be required by Items 12 and 13 of this Form if securities of such company were being registered.

Instruction

Notwithstanding the requirements of Items 10 and 11, the financial statements of the company being acquired need only comply with the reconciliation requirements of Item 17 of Form 20-F.

Item 17. Information with Respect to Foreign Companies Other Than F-3 Companies.

If the company being acquired does not meet the requirements for use of Form F-3, or compliance with this Item is otherwise elected in lieu of Item 15 or 16, furnish the information required by paragraph (a) or (b) of this Item, whichever is applicable.

(a) If the company being acquired is subject to the reporting requirements of Section 13(a) or 15(d) of the Exchange Act, and compliance with this subparagraph in lieu of subparagraph (b) of this Item is elected, furnish the information that would be required by Item 14 of this Form if securities of such company were being registered; *however,* only financial statements complying with the reconciliation requirements of Item 17 of Form 20-F, and those schedules required by Rules 12-15, 28, and 29 of Regulation S-X (§ 210.12-15, 28, 29 of this chapter) need be provided with respect to the company being acquired.

(b) If the company being acquired is not subject to the reporting requirements of either Section 13(a) or 15(d) of the Exchange Act, furnish the information that would be required by the following if securities of such company were being registered:

(1) A brief description of the business done by the company which indicates the general nature and scope of the business;

(2) Where common equity securities are being issued, the information required by Item 9.A.4. of Form 20-F, nature of trading markets, updated to cover any subsequent interim periods for which interim financial statements are required to be included to comply with Item 8.A. of Form 20-F. Such updating may be made in the prospectus, in an amended Form 20-F, Form 10-K or, in the case of registrants described in General Instruction A.(2) of Form 40-F, Form 40-F, or in a Form 6-K, Form 10-Q or Form 8-K;

(3) Item 3.A. of Form 20-F, selected financial data;

(4)(i) Item 5 of Form 20-F, operating and financial review;

(ii) Item 11 of Form 20-F, quantitative and qualitative disclosures of market risk.

(5) Financial statements that would have been required to be included in an annual report on Form 20-F (§ 249.220f of this chapter) had the company being acquired been required to prepare such a report. If the registrant's security holders are not voting, the transaction is not a roll-up transaction (as described by Item 901 of Regulation S-K (§ 229.901 of this chapter)), and:

(i) the company being acquired is significant to the registrant in excess of the 20% level as determined under § 210.3-05(b)(2), provide financial statements of the company being acquired for the latest fiscal year in conformity with GAAP. In addition, if the company being acquired has provided its security holders with financial statements prepared in conformity with GAAP for either or both of the two fiscal years before the latest fiscal year, provide the financial statements for those years; or

(ii) the company being acquired is significant to the registrant at or below the 20% level, no financial information (including pro forma and comparative per share information) for the company being acquired need be provided; and

Instructions:

1. The financial statements required by this paragraph for the latest fiscal year need be audited only to the extent practicable. The financial statements for the fiscal years before the latest fiscal year need not be audited if they were not previously audited.

2. If this Form is used to register resales to the public by any person who is deemed an underwriter within the meaning of Rule 145(c) (§ 230.145(c) of this chapter) with respect to the securities being reoffered, the financial statements must be audited for the fiscal years required to be presented under paragraph (b)(2) of Rule 3-05 of Regulation S-X (17 CFR 210.3-05(b)(2)).

3. In determining the significance of an acquisition for purposes of this paragraph, apply the tests prescribed in Rule 1-02(w) (§ 210.1-02(w) of this chapter).

(6) For the registrant's fiscal years ending on or after December 15, 2009, Item 16F of Form 20-F, change in registrant's certifying accountant.

(7) Schedules required by Rules 12-15, 28 and 29 of Regulation S-X.

Instruction to paragraphs (b)(5) and (b)(6):

If the financial statements required by paragraphs (b)(5) and (b)(6) are prepared on the basis of a comprehensive body of accounting principles other than U.S. GAAP or IFRS as issued by the IASB, provide a reconciliation to U.S. GAAP in accordance with Item 17 of Form 20-F (§ 249.220f of this chapter) unless a reconciliation is unavailable or not obtainable without unreasonable cost or expense. At a minimum, provide a narrative description of all material variations in accounting principles, practices and methods used in preparing the non-U.S. GAAP financial statements from those accepted in the U.S. when the financial statements are prepared on a basis other than U.S. GAAP.

D. VOTING AND MANAGEMENT INFORMATION

Item 18. Information if Proxies, Consents or Authorizations Are To Be Solicited

(a) If proxies, consents or authorizations are to be solicited, furnish the following information, except as provided by paragraph (b) of this Item:

(1) The information required by Item 1 of Schedule 14A, date, time and place information;

(2) The information required by Item 2 of Schedule 14A, revocability of proxy;

(3) The information required by Item 3 of Schedule 14A, dissenters' rights of appraisal;

(4) The information required by Item 4 of Schedule 14A, persons making the solicitation;

(5) With respect to both the registrant and the company being acquired, the information required by:

(i) Item 5 of Schedule 14A, interest of certain persons in matters to be acted upon; and

(ii) Item 6 of Schedule 14A, voting securities and principal holders thereof.

Instruction

The information specified in Item 7.A. of Form 20-F may be provided in lieu of the information specified in Item 6(d) of Schedule 14A.

(6) The information required by Item 21 of Schedule 14A, vote required for approval;

(7) With respect to each person who will serve as a director or an executive officer of the surviving or acquiring company, the information required by:

(i) Item 6.A. of Form 20-F, directors and senior management of the registrant;

(ii) Items 6.B. and 6.E. of Form 20-F, compensation and share ownership; and

(iii) Item 7.B. of Form 20-F, related party transactions.

(b) If the registrant or the company being acquired meets the requirements for use of Form F-3, any information required by paragraphs (a)(5)(ii) and (7) of this Item with respect to such company may be incorporated by reference from its latest annual report on Form 20-F.

Item 19. Information if Proxies, Consents or Authorizations Are Not to Be Solicited or in an Exchange Offer.

(a) If the transaction is an exchange offer or if proxies, consents or authorizations are not to be solicited, furnish the following information, except as provided by paragraph (b) of this Item:

(1) The information required by Item 2 of Schedule 14C, statement that proxies are not to be solicited:

(2) The date, time and place of the meeting of security holders, unless such information is otherwise disclosed in material furnished to security holders with or preceding the prospectus.

(3) The information required by Item 3 of Schedule 14A, dissenters' rights of appraisal;

(4) With respect to both the registrant and the company being acquired, a brief description of any material interest, direct or indirect, by security holdings or otherwise, of affiliates of the registrant and of the company being acquired, in the proposed transaction.

Instruction

This subparagraph shall not apply to any interest arising from the ownership of securities of the registrant where the security holder receives no extra or special benefit not shared on a pro rata basis by all other holders of the same class.

(5) With respect to both the registrant and the company being acquired, the information required by Item 6 of Schedule 14A, voting securities and principal holders thereof.

Instruction

The information specified in Item 7.A. of Form 20-F may be provided in lieu of the information specified in Item 6(d) of Schedule 14A.

(6) The information required by Item 21 of Schedule 14A, vote required for approval, and

(7) With respect to each person who will serve as a director or an executive officer of the surviving or acquiring company, the information required by:

(i) Item 6.A. of Form 20-F, directors and senior management of the registrant;

(ii) Items 6.B. and 6.E. of Form 20-F, compensation and share ownership; and

(iii) Item 7.B. of Form 20-F, related party transactions.

(b) If the transaction is an exchange offer, furnish the information required by paragraph (a) (4), (a) (5), and (a) (7) of this Item, except as provided by paragraph (c) of this Item.

(c) If the registrant or the company being acquired meets the requirements for use of Form F-3, any information required by paragraphs (a) (5) (ii) and (7) of this Item with respect to such company may be incorporated by reference from its latest annual report on Form 20-F.

PART II

INFORMATION NOT REQUIRED IN PROSPECTUS

Item 20. Indemnification of Directors and Officers

Furnish the information required by Item 702 of Regulation S-K (§ 229.702 of this chapter).

Item 21. Exhibits and Financial Statement Schedules

(a) Subject to the rules regarding incorporation by reference, furnish the exhibits as required by Item 601 of Regulation S-K (§ 229.601 of this chapter).

(b) Furnish the financial statement schedules required by Regulation S-X and Item 14(e), Item 17(a) or Item 17(b) (7) of this Form. These schedules should be lettered or numbered in the manner described for exhibits in paragraph (a) of this Item.

(c) If information is provided pursuant to Item 4(b) of this Form, furnish the report, opinion or appraisal as an exhibit hereto, unless it is furnished as part of the prospectus.

Item 22. Undertakings

(a) Furnish the undertakings required by Item 512 of Regulation S-K (§ 229.512 of this chapter).

(b) Furnish the following undertaking: The undersigned registrant hereby undertakes: (i) to respond to requests for information that is incorporated by reference into the prospectus pursuant to Items 4, 10(b), 11, or 13 of this Form, within one business day of receipt of such request, and to send the incorporated documents by first class mail or other equally prompt means; and (ii) to arrange or provide for a facility in the U.S. for the purpose of responding to such requests. The undertaking in subparagraph (i) above include information contained in documents filed subsequent to the effective date of the registration statement through the date of responding to the request.

(c) Furnish the following undertaking: The undersigned registrant hereby undertakes to supply by means of a post-effective amendment all information concerning a transaction and the company being acquired involved therein, that was not the subject of and included in the registration statement when it became effective.

SIGNATURES

Pursuant to the requirements of the Securities Act, the registrant has duly caused this registration statement to be signed on its behalf by the undersigned, thereunto duly authorized, in the City of . . . . , State of . . . . , on . . . . ,19. . . .

(Registrant) . . . .

By (Signature and Title) . . . .

Pursuant to the requirements of the Securities Act of 1933, this registration statement has been signed by the following persons in the capacities and on the dates indicated.

(Signature) . . . .

(Title) . . . .

(Date) . . . .

Instructions

1. The registration statement shall be signed by the registrant, its principal executive officer or officers, its principal financial officer, its controller or principal accounting officer, at least a majority of the board of directors or persons performing similar functions and its authorized representative in the United States. Where registrant is a limited partnership, the registration statement shall be signed by a majority of the board of directors of any corporate general partner signing the registration statement.

2. The name of each person who signs the registration statement shall be typed or printed beneath his signature. Any person who occupies more than one of the specified positions shall indicate each capacity in which he signs the regis-

tration statement. Attention is directed to Rule 402 (§ 230.402 of this chapter) concerning manual signatures and Item 601 of Regulation S-K (§ 229.601 of this chapter) concerning signatures pursuant to powers of attorney.

3. If the securities to be offered are those of a corporation not yet in existence at the time the registration statement is filed which will be a party to a consolidation involving two or more existing corporations, then each such existing corporation shall be deemed a registrant and shall be so designated on the cover page of this Form, and the registration statement shall be signed by each such existing corporation and by the officers and directors of each such existing corporation as if each such existing corporation were the registrant.

[¶ 7551]   FORM F-6

[As last amended in Release No. 34-58465, effective October 10, 2008, 73 F.R. 52752.]

SECURITIES AND EXCHANGE COMMISSION

FORM F-6

REGISTRATION STATEMENT UNDER THE SECURITIES ACT OF 1933 FOR DEPOSITARY SHARES EVIDENCED BY AMERICAN DEPOSITARY RECEIPTS

....

(Exact name of issuer of deposited securities as specified in its charter)

....

(Translation of issuer's name into English)

....

(Jurisdiction of incorporation or organization of issuer)

....

(Exact name of depositary as specified in its charter)

....

(Address, including zip code, and telephone number, including area code, of depositary's principal executive offices)

....

(Address, including zip code, and telephone number, including area code, of agent for service)

It is proposed that this filing become effective under Rule 466

(check appropriate box)

[ ] immediately upon filing

[ ] on (Date) at (Time).

If a separate registration statement has been filed to register the deposited shares, check the following box. [ ]

Calculation of Registration Fee

Title of each class of securities to be registered	Amount to be registered	Proposed maximum aggregate price per unit	Proposed maximum aggregate offering price	Amount of registration fee

GENERAL INSTRUCTIONS

I. Eligibility Requirements for Use of Form F-6

A. General. Form F-6 may be used for the registration under the Securities Act of 1933 (the "Securities Act") of Depositary Shares evidenced by American Depositary Receipts ("ADRs") issued by a depositary against the deposit of the securities of a foreign issuer (regardless of the physical location of the certificates) if the following conditions are met:

(1) The holder of the ADRs is entitled to withdraw the deposited securities at any time subject only to (i) temporary delays caused by closing transfer books of the depositary or the issuer of the deposited securities or the deposit of shares in connection with voting at a shareholders' meeting, or the payment of dividends, (ii) the payment of fees, taxes, and similar charges, and (iii) compliance with any laws or governmental regulations relating to ADRs or to the withdrawal of deposited securities;

(2) The deposited securities are offered or sold in transactions registered under the Securities Act or in transactions that would be exempt therefrom if made in the United States; and

(3) As of the filing date of this registration statement, the issuer of the deposited securities is reporting pursuant to the periodic reporting requirements of section 13(a) or 15(d) of the Securi-

ties Exchange Act of 1934 or the deposited securities are exempt therefrom by Rule 12g3-2(b) (§ 240.12g3-2(b) of this chapter) unless the issuer of the deposited securities concurrently files a registration statement on another form for the deposited securities.

B. Registration of Deposited Securities. Form F-6 is available for registration of the Depositary Shares only. The registration of the deposited securities, if necessary, shall be on any other form the registrant is eligible to use. Alternatively, Depositary Shares may also be registered on any form used to register the deposited securities if such registration statement also conforms to the requirements of Parts I and II of Form F-6 and either the depositary or the legal entity created by the agreement for the issuance of ADRs signs the registration statement with respect to the disclosure and undertakings made in response to such requirements. The amount of fees charged need not be disclosed in the prospectus if the depositary makes and follows the undertakings in Item 4(c) and if the prospectus lists the various services for which fees may be charged, states that such fees may differ from those other depositaries charge, states that the fee schedule is available without charge from the depositary, and states that each registered holder of an ADR will receive thirty days notice of a change in the fee schedule.

II. Amount of Securities; Filing Fee

An ADR evidences one or more Depositary Shares, as defined in Rule 405 (§ 230.405 of this chapter). The registration statement relates to Depositary Shares, not the number of physical certificates issued. For example, if an ADR is issued against a Depositary Share, which equals two common shares in a foreign issuer, the registration of 100,000 Depositary Shares represents 200,000 common shares. If the depositary issues a certificate for 10,000 Depositary Shares and another for 15,000 Depositary Shares, then 75,000 (100,000 minus 25,000) Depositary Shares (not

99,998) remain available for distribution under the registration statement.

Rule 457(k) (§ 230.457(k) of this chapter) describes the method of computing the filing fee.

III. Application of General Rules and Regulations

A. Attention is directed to the General Rules and Regulations under the Securities Act, particularly Regulation C (§ 230.400 et seq. of this chapter). That Regulation contains general requirements regarding the preparation and filing of registration statements.

B. The prospectus may consist of the ADR certificate if it includes the information required in Part I of this Form. Such prospectus need not conform to the requirements of Rule 420 (§ 240.420 of this chapter) except that the type shall be roman type at least as large as 5½-point modern type.

C. You must file the Form F-6 registration statement in electronic format via the Commission's Electronic Data Gathering, Analysis, and Retrieval (EDGAR) system in accordance with the EDGAR rules set forth in Regulation S-T (17 CFR Part 232). For assistance with technical questions about EDGAR or to request an access code, call the EDGAR Filer Support Office at (202) 942-8900. For assistance with the EDGAR rules, call the Office of EDGAR and Information Analysis at (202) 942-2940.

If filing the registration statement in paper under a hardship exemption in Rule 201 or 202 of Regulation S-T (17 CFR 232.201 or 232.202), or as otherwise permitted, you must file the number of copies of the registration statement and of each amendment required by Securities Act Rules 402 and 472 (17 CFR 230.402 and 230.472), except that you need only file three additional copies instead of the ten referred to in Rule 402(b) (17 CFR 230.402(b)). You may also file only three additional copies instead of the eight referred to in Securities Act Rule 472(a) (17 CFR 230.472(a)).

PART I—INFORMATION REQUIRED IN PROSPECTUS

Item 1. Description of Securities to be Registered

Furnish the information required by Item 12.E. of Form 20-F (§ 249.220f of this chapter).

Item 2. Available Information. Provide the information in either (a) or (b) below, whichever is applicable.

(a) State that the foreign issuer publishes information in English required to maintain the exemption from registration under Rule 12g3-2(b) under the Securities Exchange of 1934 on its Internet Web site or through an electronic information delivery system generally available to the public in its primary trading market. Then dis-

close the address of the foreign issuer's Internet Web site or the electronic information delivery system in its primary trading market.

(b) State that the foreign issuer is subject to the periodic reporting requirements of the Securities Exchange Act of 1934 and accordingly files reports with the Commission. Then disclose that these reports are available for inspection and copying through the Commission's EDGAR system or at public reference facilities maintained by the Commission in Washington, D.C.

Note to Item 2: In the case of an unsponsored ADR facility, you may base your representation that the issuer publishes information in English required to maintain the exemption from registration under Exchange Act Rule 12g3-2(b) upon your reasonable, good faith belief after exercising reasonable diligence.

PART II—INFORMATION NOT REQUIRED IN PROSPECTUS

Item 3. Exhibits

Subject to the rules as to incorporation by reference, the exhibits specified below shall be filed as a part of the registration statement. Exhibits shall be appropriately lettered or numbered for convenient reference. Exhibits incorporated by reference may bear the designation given in the previous filing. Instruction 1 to Item 601 of Regulation S-K applies to this paragraph.

(a) A copy of the Deposit Agreement or Deposit Agreements under which the securities registered hereunder are issued. If the Deposit Agreement is amended during the offering of the Depositary Shares, such amendments shall be filed as amendments to the registration statement.

(b) Any other agreement, to which the depositary is a party relating to the issuance of the Depositary Shares registered hereby or the custody of the deposited securities represented thereby.

(c) Every material contract relating to the deposited securities between the depositary and the issuer of the deposited securities in effect at any time within the last three years.

(d) An opinion of counsel as to the legality of the securities being registered, indicating whether they will when sold be legally issued, and entitle the holders thereof to the rights specified therein.

(e) If the procedure in Rule 466 is being used, a certification in the following form:

Certification under Rule 466

The depositary, ..., represents and certifies the following:

(1) That it previously had filed a registration statement on Form F-6 (Name and File No.),

which the Commission declared effective, with terms of deposit identical to the terms of deposit of this registration statement except for the number of foreign securities a Depositary Share represents.

(2) That is ability to designate the date and time of effectiveness under Rule 466 has not been suspended.

[Depositary] . . . .

By [Signature and Title] . . . .

Item 4. Undertakings

Notwithstanding the provisions of Rule 415(a)(2) (§ 230.415(a)(2) of this chapter), the undertakings in Item 512(a) of Regulation S-K are not required. Furnish the following undertakings:

(a) The depositary hereby undertakes to make available at the principal office of the depositary in the United States, for inspection by holders of the ADRs, any reports and communications received from the issuer of the deposited securities which are both (1) received by the depositary as the holder of the deposited securities; and (2) made generally available to the holders of the underlying securities by the issuer.

(b) If the amounts of fees charged are not disclosed in the prospectus, the depositary undertakes to prepare a separate document stating the amount of any fee charged and describing the service for which it is charged and to deliver promptly a copy of such fee schedule without charge to anyone upon request. The depositary undertakes to notify each registered holder of an ADR thirty days before any change in the fee schedule.

SIGNATURES

Pursuant to the requirements of the Securities Act of 1933, the registrant certifies that it has reasonable grounds to believe that all the requirements for filing on Form F-6 are met and has duly caused this registration statement to be signed on its behalf by the undersigned, thereunto duly authorized, in the City of . . . ., State of . . . ., on . . . ., 19. . . . . . .

[Legal entity created by the agreement

for the issuance of American Depositary

Receipts for shares of . . . .]   . . . .

By [Signature and Title] . . . .

[Registrant] . . . .

By [Signature and Title] . . . .

Pursuant to the requirements of the Securities Act of 1933, this registration statement has been signed by the following persons in the capacities and on the dates indicated.

[Signature] ....

[Title] ....

[Date] ....

Instructions 1. The legal entity created by the agreement for the issuance of ADRs shall sign the registration statement as registrant. The depositary may sign on behalf of such entity, but the depositary for the issuance of ADRs itself shall not be deemed to be an issuer, a person signing the registration statement, or a person controlling such issuer. If the issuer of the deposited securities sponsors the ADR arrangement, the registration statement shall also be signed by the issuer and its principal executive officer or officers, its principal financial officer, its controller or principal accounting officer, at least a majority of the board of directors or persons performing similar functions, and its authorized representative in the United States.

2. The name of each person who signs the registration statement shall be typed or printed beneath his signature. Any person who occupies more than one of the specified positions shall indicate each capacity in which he signs the registration statement. Attention is directed to Rule 402 concerning manual signatures and Item 601 of Regulation S-K concerning signatures pursuant to powers of attorney.

[¶ 7561]   **FORM F-7**

[As last amended in Release No. 33-8099, effective November 4, 2002, 67 F.R. 36678.]

U.S. Securities and Exchange Commission
Washington, D.C. 20549

Form F-7

REGISTRATION STATEMENT UNDER THE SECURITIES ACT OF 1933

. . . .
(Exact name of Registrant as specified in its charter)

. . . .
(Translation of Registrant's name into English (if applicable))

. . . .
(Province or other jurisdiction of incorporation or organization)

. . . .
(Primary Standard Industrial Classification Code Number (if applicable))

. . . .
(I.R.S. Employer Identification Number (if applicable))

. . . .
(Address and telephone number of Registrant's principal executive offices)

. . . .
(Name, address (including zip code) and telephone number (including area code) of agent for
service in the United States)

Approximate date of commencement of proposed sale of the securities to the public . . . .

This registration statement and any amendment thereto shall become effective upon filing with the Commission in accordance with Rule 467(a).

If any of the securities being registered on this Form are to be offered on a delayed or continuous basis pursuant to the home jurisdiction's shelf prospectus offering procedures, check the following box. []

CALCULATION OF REGISTRATION FEE*

Title of each class of securities to be registered	Amount to be registered	Proposed maximum offering price per unit	Proposed maximum aggregate offering price	Amount of registration fee

* See General Instruction II.F. for rules as to calculation of the registration fee.

If, as a result of stock splits, stock dividends or similar transactions, the number of securities purported to be registered on this registration statement changes, the provisions of Rule 416 shall apply to this registration statement.

GENERAL INSTRUCTIONS

I. Eligibility Requirements for Use of Form F-7

A. Form F-7 may be used for the registration under the Securities Act of 1933 (the "Securities Act") of the Registrant's securities offered for cash upon the exercise of rights to purchase or subscribe for such securities that are granted to its existing securityholders in proportion to the number of securities held by them as of the record date for the rights offer.

B. Form F-7 is available to any Registrant that:

(1) is incorporated or organized under the laws of Canada or any Canadian province or territory;

(2) is a foreign private issuer; and

(3) has had a class of its securities listed on The Montreal Exchange, The Toronto Stock Exchange or the Senior Board of the Vancouver Stock Exchange for the 12 calendar months immediately preceding the filing of this Form, has been subject to the continuous disclosure requirements of any securities commission or equivalent regulatory authority in Canada for a period of at least 36 calendar months immediately preceding the filing of this Form, and is currently in compliance with obligations arising from such listing and reporting.

Instruction For purposes of this Form, "foreign private issuer" shall be construed in accordance with Rule 405 under the Securities Act.

C. If the Registrant is a successor Registrant subsisting after a statutory amalgamation, merger, arrangement or other reorganization requiring the vote of shareholders of the participating companies (a "business combination"), the Registrant shall be deemed to meet the 36-month reporting requirement and the 12-month listing requirement of I.B.(3) above if: (1) the time the successor Registrant has been subject to the continuous disclosure requirements of any securities commission or equivalent regulatory authority in Canada, when added separately to the time each predecessor had been subject to such requirements at the time of the business combination, in each case equals at least 36 calendar months, *provided, however,* that any predecessor need not be considered for purposes of the reporting history calculation if the reporting histories of predecessors whose assets and gross revenues, respectively, would contribute at least 80 percent of the total assets and gross revenues from continuing operations of the successor Registrant, as measured based on pro forma combination of such participating companies' most recently completed fiscal years immediately prior to the business combination, when combined with the reporting history of the successor Registrant in each case satisfy such 36-month reporting requirement; (2) the time the successor Registrant has been subject to the listing requirements of the specified exchanges, when added separately to the time each predecessor had been subject to such requirements at the time of the business combination, in each case equals at least 12 calendar months, *provided, however,* that any predecessor need not be considered for purposes of the listing history calculation if the listing histories of predecessors whose assets and gross revenues, respectively, would contribute at least 80 percent of the total assets and gross revenues from continuing operations of the successor Registrant, as measured based on pro forma combination of such participating companies' most recently completed fiscal years immediately prior to the business combination, when combined with the listing history of the successor Registrant in each case satisfy such 12-month listing requirement; and (3) the successor Registrant has been subject to such continuous disclosure requirements and listing requirements since the business combination, and is currently in compliance with its obligations thereunder.

D. The rights in connection with the transaction granted to securityholders that are U.S. holders shall be granted upon terms and conditions not less favorable than those extended to any other holders of the same class of securities. The securities offered or sold upon exercise of rights granted to U.S. holders may not be registered on this Form if such rights are transferable other than in accordance with Regulation S under the Securities Act.

Instruction For purposes of this Form, the term "U.S. holder" shall mean any person whose address appears on the records of the Registrant, any voting trustee, any depositary, any share transfer agent or any person acting on behalf of the Registrant as being located in the United States.

E. This Form shall not be used if the Registrant is an investment company registered or required to be registered under the Investment Company Act of 1940.

II. Application of General Rules and Regulations

A. The Rules comprising Regulation C under the Securities Act shall not apply to filings on this Form unless specifically referred to in this Form. Instead, the rules and regulations applicable in the home jurisdiction regarding form and method of preparation of disclosure documents shall apply to filings on this Form. Securities Act rules and regulations other than Regulation C apply to filings on this Form unless specifically excluded in this Form.

B. Rule 408 under the Securities Act, which provides that in addition to the information expressly required to be included in the registration statement, there shall be added such further material information, if any, as may be necessary to make the required statements, in light of the circumstances under which they are made, not misleading, shall apply to filings on this Form.

C. A registrant must file the registration statement in electronic format via the Commission's Electronic Data Gathering, Analysis, and Retrieval (EDGAR) system in accordance with the EDGAR rules set forth in Regulation S-T (17 CFR Part 232). For assistance with technical questions about EDGAR or to request an access code, call the EDGAR Filer Support Office at (202) 942-8900. For assistance with the EDGAR rules, call the Office of EDGAR and Information Analysis at (202) 942-2940.

If filing the registration statement in paper under a hardship exemption in Rule 201 or 202 of Regulation S-T (17 CFR 232.201 or 232.202), or as otherwise permitted, a registrant must file with the Commission at its principal office five copies of the complete registration statement and any amendments, including exhibits and all other documents filed as a part of the registration statement or amendment. The registrant must bind, staple or otherwise compile each copy in one or more parts without stiff covers. The registrant must further bind the registration statement or amendment on the side or stitching margin in a manner that leaves the reading matter legible. The registrant must provide three additional copies of the registration statement or amendment without exhibits to the Commission.

D. Any amendment to a registration statement on this Form shall be filed under cover of an appropriate facing sheet, shall be numbered consecutively in the order in which filed, and shall indicate on the facing sheet the applicable registration form on which the amendment is prepared and the file number of the registration statement.

If, however, an amendment to the home jurisdiction document(s) is filed after effectiveness of this registration statement that increases the number of securities that may be sold, in lieu of filing a post-effective amendment hereto, a new registration statement shall be filed on this Form. As provided in Rule 429, the prospectus included in the new registration statement shall be deemed to include a prospectus covering unsold securities registered previously. If this is the case, the following legend shall appear at the bottom of the facing page of the registration statement: "Pursuant to Rule 429 under the Securities Act, the prospectus contained in this registration statement relates to registration statement[s] 33-[insert file number[s] of previous registration statement[s]]."

E. An electronic filer must provide the signatures required for the registration statement or amendment in accordance with Regulation S-T Rule 302 (17 CFR 232.302). A registrant filing in paper must have at least one copy of the registration statement or amendment signed in accordance with Securities Act Rule 402(e) (17 CFR 230.402(e)) by the persons whose signatures are required for this registration statement. A registrant must also conform the unsigned copies.

F. At the time of filing this registration statement, the Registrant shall pay to the Commission in accordance with Rule 111 under the Securities Act a fee in U.S. dollars in the amount prescribed by Section 6 of the Securities Act. The amount of securities to be registered on this Form need not exceed the amount to be offered in the United States as part of the offering.

The registration fee is to be calculated at the price at which the rights may be exercised if known at the time of filing the registration statement, or, if not known, at the market value of outstanding securities of the same class included in the registration statement. If the fee is to be calculated upon the basis of the price at which the rights may be exercised and they are exercisable over a period of time at progressively higher prices, the fee shall be calculated on the basis of the highest price at which they may be exercised.

Instruction. The market value of the Registrant's outstanding securities shall be the average of the high and low prices reported or the average of the bid and asked price of such securities, in the principal market for such securities as of a date within 30 days prior to the date of filing.

G. A registrant must file the registration statement or amendment in electronic format in the English language in accordance with Regulation S-T Rule 306 (17 CFR 232.306). A registrant may file part of the prospectus or exhibit or other attachment to the registration statement or amendment in both French and English if it included the French text to comply with the requirements of the Canadian securities administrator or other Canadian authority and, for an electronic filing, if the filing is an HTML document, as defined in Regulation S-T Rule 11 (17 CFR 232.11). For both an electronic filing and a paper filing, a registrant may provide an English translation or English summary of a foreign language document as an exhibit or other attachment to the registration statement or amendment as permitted by the rules of the applicable Canadian securities administrator.

H. For a paper filing, one signed original of the registration statement or amendment must be numbered sequentially (in addition to any internal numbering that otherwise may be present) by handwritten, typed, printed or other legible form of notation from the first page through the last page of the registration statement or amendment, including any exhibits or attachments. A paper filer must disclose the total number of pages on the first page of the sequentially numbered registration statement or amendment.

I. Where the offering registered on this Form is being made pursuant to the home jurisdiction's shelf prospectus offering procedures or procedures for pricing offerings after the final receipt has been issued, three copies of each supplement to, or supplemented version of, the home jurisdiction disclosure document(s) prepared under such procedures shall be filed with the Commission within one business day after such supplement or supplemented version is filed with any Canadian jurisdiction. Such filings shall be deemed not to constitute amendments to this registration statement. Each such filing shall contain in the upper right corner of the cover page the following legend, which may be set forth in longhand if legible: "Filed pursuant to General Instruction II.I. of Form F-7; File No. 33-[insert number of the registration statement]."

J. Registrants are required to name an agent for service in the United States as required by the cover page of the registration statement even though not required to file a Form F-X.

Note: Offerings registered on this Form, whether or not made contemporaneously in Canada, may be made pursuant to National Policy Statement No. 44 shelf prospectus offering procedures and procedures for pricing offerings after the final receipt has been issued. Rules 415 and 430A under the Securities Act are not available for offerings registered on this Form.

III. Compliance with Exchange Act

A. Pursuant to Rule 12h-4 under the Securities Exchange Act of 1934 (the "Exchange Act"), a Registrant shall be exempt from reporting obligations under Section 15(d) of the Exchange Act if such reporting obligations would have arisen solely from registration of securities on this Form.

The Registrant's attention is directed, however, towards other provisions of the Exchange Act that may be applicable, and specifically to the provisions of Section 12(b) and 12(g) of the Exchange Act and Regulation M (17 CFR 242.100 through 242.105).

B. The Commission's rules on auditor independence, as codified in Section 600 of the Codification of Financial Reporting Policies, shall not apply to auditor reports on financial statements included in this registration statement.

PART I—INFORMATION REQUIRED TO BE SENT TO SHAREHOLDERS

Item 1. Home Jurisdiction Document

The prospectus shall consist of the entire disclosure document or documents used to offer the rights and underlying securities to holders in any Canadian jurisdiction. Such disclosure document(s) shall include all information used to make such offers, without regard to whether such information has previously been provided to shareholders. Except as noted hereinafter, such disclosure document(s) shall be prepared in accordance with the disclosure requirements of such jurisdiction as interpreted and applied by the securities commission or other regulatory authority in such jurisdiction.

Such prospectus used in the United States shall contain additional information and legends required by this Form. It need not include any documents incorporated by reference into disclosure documents used in Canada and not required to be delivered to securityholders pursuant to Canadian law.

Notwithstanding the foregoing, such prospectus used in the United States need not contain any disclosure applicable solely to Canadian offerees or purchasers that would not be material to offerees or purchasers in the United States, including, without limitation, (i) any Canadian "red herring" legend; (ii) any discussion of Canadian tax considerations other than those material to U.S. offerees or purchasers; (iii) the names of any Canadian underwriters not acting as underwriters in the United States or a description of the Canadian plan of distribution (except to the extent necessary to describe the material facts of the U.S. plan of distribution); (iv) any description of offerees' or purchasers' statutory rights under applicable Canadian, provincial or territorial securities legislation (except to the extent such rights are available to U.S. offerees or purchasers); or (v) certificates of the issuer or any underwriter.

Item 2. Information Legends

The following legends, to the extent applicable, shall appear on the outside front cover page of the prospectus (or on a sticker thereto) in bold-face roman type at least as high as ten-point modern type and at least two points leaded:

> "This offering is made by a foreign issuer, that is permitted, under a multijurisdictional disclosure system adopted by the United States, to prepare this prospectus in accordance with the disclosure requirements of its home country. Prospective investors should be aware that such requirements are different from those of the United States. Financial statements included or incorporated herein, if any, have been prepared in accordance with foreign generally accepted accounting principles, and are subject to foreign auditing and auditor independence standards, and thus may not be comparable to financial statements of United States companies."

> "Prospective investors should be aware that the acquisition of the securities described herein may have tax consequences both in the United States and in the home country of the Registrant. Such consequences for investors who are resident in, or citizens of, the United States may not be described fully herein."

> "The enforcement by investors of civil liabilities under the federal securities laws may be affected adversely by the fact that the Registrant is incorporated or organized under the laws of a foreign country, that some or all of the underwriters or experts named in the registration statement may be residents of a foreign country, and that all or a substantial portion of the assets of the Registrant and said persons may be located outside the United States."

> "THESE SECURITIES HAVE NOT BEEN APPROVED OR DISAPPROVED BY THE SECURITIES AND EXCHANGE COMMISSION NOR HAS THE COMMISSION PASSED UPON THE ACCURACY OR ADEQUACY OF THIS PROSPECTUS. ANY REPRESENTATION TO THE CONTRARY IS A CRIMINAL OFFENSE."

The Registrant should also include in the prospectus any legend or information required by the laws of any jurisdiction in which the securities are to be offered.

Note to Item 2. If the home-jurisdiction document(s) are delivered through an electronic medium, the issuer may satisfy the legibility requirements for the required legends relating to type size and font by presenting the legends in any manner reasonably calculated to draw investor attention to it.

Item 3. Incorporation of Certain Information by Reference

Information called for by this Form, including exhibits, may be incorporated by reference at the Registrant's option from documents that the Registrant has filed previously with the Commission pursuant to Section 13(a) or 15(d) of the Exchange Act or submitted to the Commission pursuant to Rule 12g3-2(b) under the Exchange Act. Any such incorporation by reference shall be done in accordance with Item 10(d) of Regulation S-K. If any information is incorporated by reference into the prospectus, the prospectus shall provide the name, address and telephone number of an officer of the Registrant from whom copies of such information may be obtained upon request without charge.

Item 4. List of Documents Filed with the Commission

There shall be set forth in or attached to the prospectus a list of all documents filed with the Commission as part of the registration statement.

PART II—INFORMATION NOT REQUIRED TO BE SENT TO SHAREHOLDERS

The exhibits specified below shall be filed as part of the registration statement. Exhibits shall be appropriately lettered or numbered for convenient reference.

(1) Any reports or information that, in accordance with the requirements of the jurisdiction of incorporation or organization of the Registrant, must be made publicly available in connection with the transaction.

(2) Copies of any documents incorporated by reference into the registration statement, and any publicly available documents filed with any other Canadian regulatory authority concurrently with the prospectus.

(3) If any accountant, engineer or appraiser, or any person whose profession gives authority to a statement made by him, is named as having prepared or certified any part of the offering document, or is named as having prepared or certified a report or valuation for use in connection with the offering document, the manually signed, written consent of such person.

If any such person is named as having prepared or certified any other report or valuation (other than a public official document or statement) which is used in connection with the registration statement, but is not named as having prepared or certified such report or valuation for use in connection with the registration statement, the manually signed, written consent of such person, unless the Commission dispenses with such filing as impracticable or as involving undue hardship in accordance with Rule 437 under the Securities Act.

Any other consent required by Rule 436, 438 or 439 under the Securities Act. Every amendment relating to a certified financial statement shall include the manually signed, written consent of the certifying accountant to the use of his certificate in connection with the amended financial statements in the registration statement or prospectus and to being named as having certified such financial statements.

NOTE: The consents required by this item shall specifically indicate consent regarding use of the report or valuation in the registration statement filed in the United States.

(4) If any name is signed to the registration statement or amendment pursuant to a power of attorney, manually signed copies of such power of attorney and, if the name of any officer signing on behalf of the Registrant is signed pursuant to a power of attorney, certified copies of a resolution of the Registrant's board of directors or similar governing body authorizing such signature.

(5) A copy of any indenture relating to the registered securities.

PART III—CONSENT TO SERVICE OF PROCESS

(a) At the time of filing Form F-7, any non-U.S. person acting as trustee with respect to the registered securities shall file with the Commission a written irrevocable consent and power of attorney on Form F-X.

(b) Any change to the name or address of the agent for service of the trustee shall be communicated promptly to the Commission by amendment to Form F-X referencing the file number of the relevant registration statement.

SIGNATURES

Pursuant to the requirements of the Securities Act, the Registrant certifies that it has reasonable grounds to believe that it meets all of the requirements for filing on Form F-7 and has duly caused this registration statement to be signed on its behalf by the undersigned, thereunto duly authorized, in the City of . . . ., Country of . . . ., on . . . .(date), ...

Registrant . . . .

By (Signature and Title) . . . .

Pursuant to the requirements of the Securities Act, this registration statement has been signed by the following persons in the capacities and on the dates indicated.

(Signature) . . . .

(Name and Title) . . . .

(Date) . . . .

Instructions

A. The registration statement shall be signed by the Registrant, its principal executive officer or officers, its principal financial officer, its comptroller or principal accounting officer, at least a majority of the board of directors or persons performing similar functions and its authorized representative in the United States. Where the Registrant is a limited partnership, the registration statement shall be signed by a majority of the board of directors of any corporate general partner signing the registration statement.

B. The name of each person who signs the registration statement shall be typed or printed beneath his signature. Any person who occupies more than one of the specified positions shall indicate each capacity in which the registration statement is signed.

[¶ 7571]   FORM F-8

[As last amended in Release No. 34-55146A, effective April 1, 2008, 73 F.R.17809
(technical correction).]

U.S. Securities and Exchange Commission

Washington, D.C. 20549

Form F-8

REGISTRATION STATEMENT UNDER THE SECURITIES ACT OF 1933

. . . .
(Exact name of Registrant as specified in its charter)

. . . .
(Translation of Registrant's name into English (if applicable))

. . . .
(Province or other jurisdiction of incorporation or organization)

. . . .
(Primary Standard Industrial Classification Code Number (if applicable))

. . . .
(I.R.S. Employer Identification Number (if applicable))

. . . .
(Address and telephone number of Registrant's principal executive offices)

. . . .
(Name, address (including zip code) and telephone number (including area code) of
agent for service in the United States)

Approximate date of commencement of proposed sale of the securities to the public . . . .

This registration statement and any amendment thereto shall become effective upon filing with the Commission in accordance with Rule 467(a).

If any of the securities being registered on this Form are to be offered on a delayed or continuous basis pursuant to the home jurisdiction's shelf prospectus offering procedures, check the following box. [ ]

CALCULATION OF REGISTRATION FEE*

Title of each class of securities to be registered	Amount to be registered	Proposed maximum offering price per unit	Proposed maximum aggregate offering price	Amount of registration fee

* See General Instructions IV.F.-IV.H. for rules as to calculation of the registration fee.

If, as a result of stock splits, stock dividends or similar transactions, the number of securities purported to be registered on this registration statement changes, the provisions of Rule 416 shall apply to this registration statement.

GENERAL INSTRUCTIONS

1. General Eligibility Requirements for Use of Form F-8

A. Form F-8 may be used for registration under the Securities Act of 1933 ("Securities Act") of securities to be issued in an exchange offer or in connection with a statutory amalgamation, merger, arrangement or other reorganization re-quiring the vote of shareholders of the participating companies (a "business combination"). Securities may be registered on this Form whether they constitute the sole consideration for such exchange offer or business combination, or are offered in conjunction with cash.

B. This Form shall not be used for registra-tion of securities if no takeover bid circular or issuer bid circular (in the case of an exchange offer) or information circular (in the case of a business combination) is prepared pursuant to the requirements of any Canadian jurisdiction due to the availability of an exemption from such requirements.

C. This Form may not be used for registration of derivative securities except:

(1) warrants, options and rights, provided that such securities and the underlying securities to which they relate are issued by the Registrant, its parent or an affiliate of either; and

(2) convertible securities, provided that such securities are convertible only into securities of the Registrant, its parent or an affiliate of either.

Instruction For purposes of this Form, an "affiliate" of a person is anyone who beneficially owns, directly or indirectly, or exercises control or direction over, more than 10 percent of the outstanding equity shares of such person. The determination of a person's affiliates shall be made as of the end of such person's most recently completed fiscal year.

D. This Form shall not be used if the Registrant or, in the case of an exchange offer, the issuer of securities to be exchanged (the "subject securities") for securities of the Registrant is an investment company registered or required to be registered under the Investment Company Act of 1940.

II. Eligibility Requirements for Exchange Offers

A. In the case of an exchange offer, Form F-8 is available to any Registrant that:

(1) is incorporated or organized under the laws of Canada or any Canadian province or territory;

(2) is a foreign private issuer;

(3) has had a class of its securities listed on The Montreal Exchange, The Toronto Stock Exchange or the Senior Board of the Vancouver Stock Exchange for the 12 calendar months immediately preceding the filing of this Form, has been subject to the continuous disclosure requirements of any securities commission or equivalent regulatory authority in Canada for a period of at least 36 calendar months immediately preceding the filing of this Form, and is currently in compliance with obligations arising from such listing and reporting; and

(4) has an aggregate market value of the public float of its outstanding equity shares of (CN) $75 million or more; *provided, however,* that such public float requirement need not be satisfied if the issuer of the securities to be exchanged is also the Registrant on this Form.

Instructions

1. For purposes of this Form, "foreign private issuer" shall be construed in accordance with Rule 405 under the Securities Act.

2. For purposes of this Form, "equity shares" shall mean common shares, non-voting equity shares and subordinate or restricted voting equity shares, but shall not include preferred shares.

3. For purposes of this form, the "public float" of specified securities shall mean only such securities held by persons other than affiliates of the issuer.

4. For the purposes of this Form, the market value of the public float of outstanding equity shares shall be computed by use of the price at which such shares were last sold, or the average of the bid and asked prices of such shares, in the principal market for such shares as of a date within 60 days prior to the date of filing. If there is no market for any of such securities, the book value of such securities computed as of the latest practicable date prior to the filing of this Form shall be used for purposes of calculating the market value, unless the issuer of such securities is in bankruptcy or receivership or has an accumulated capital deficit, in which case one-third of the principal amount, par value or stated value of such securities shall be used.

B. In the case of an exchange offer, the securities to be registered on this Form shall be offered to U.S. holders upon terms and conditions not less favorable than those offered to any other holder of the same class of the subject securities.

C. In the case of an exchange offer, if the Registrant is a successor Registrant subsisting after a business combination, the Registrant shall be deemed to meet the 36-month reporting requirement and the 12-month listing requirement of 11.A.(3) above if: (1) the time the successor registrant has been subject to the continuous disclosure requirements of any securities commission or equivalent regulatory authority in Canada, when added separately to the time each predecessor had been subject to such requirements at the time of the business combination, in each case equals at least 36 calendar months, *provided, however,* that any predecessor need not be considered for purposes of the reporting history calculation if the reporting histories of predecessors whose assets and gross revenues, respectively, would contribute at least 80 percent of the total assets and gross revenues from continuing operations of the successor Registrant, as measured based on pro forma combination of such participating companies' most recently completed fiscal years immediately prior to the business combination, when combined with the reporting history of the successor Registrant in each case satisfy such 36-month reporting requirement; (2) the time the successor Registrant has been subject to the listing requirements of the specified exchanges, when added separately to the time each predecessor had been subject to such requirements at the time of the business combination, in each case equals at least 12 calendar months, *provided, however,* that any predecessor need not be considered for purposes of the listing history calculation if the listing histories of predecessors whose assets and gross revenues, respectively, would contribute at least 80 percent of the total assets and gross revenues from continuing operations of the successor Registrant, as measured based on pro forma combination of such participating companies' most recently compl eted fiscal years immediately prior to the business combination, when combined with the listing history of the successor Registrant in each case satisfy such 12-month listing requirement; and (3) the successor Registrant has been subject to such continuous disclosure requirements and listing requirements since the business combination, and is currently in compliance with its obligations thereunder.

D. In the case of an exchange offer, the issuer of the subject securities shall be incorporated or organized under the laws of Canada or any Canadian province or territory and be a foreign private issuer, and less than 25 percent of the class of subject securities outstanding shall be held by U.S. holders.

Instructions

1. For purposes of exchange offers, the term "U.S. holder" shall mean any person whose address appears on the records of the issuer of the subject securities, any voting trustee, any depositary, any share transfer agent or any person acting in a similar capacity on behalf of the issuer of the subject securities as being located in the United States.

2. With respect to any tender offer, including any exchange offer, otherwise eligible to proceed in accordance with Rule 14d-1(b) under the Securities Exchange Act of 1934 (the "Exchange Act"), the issuer of the subject securities will be presumed to be a foreign private issuer and U.S. holders will be presumed to hold less than 25 percent of such outstanding securities, *unless* (1) the aggregate trading volume of that class on national securities exchanges in the United States and on NASDAQ exceeded its aggregate trading volume on securities exchanges in Canada and on the Canadian Dealing Network, In. ("CDN") over the 12 calendar month period prior to commencement of this offer, or if commenced in response to a prior offer, over the 12 calendar month period prior to commencement of the initial offer (based on volume figures published by such exchanges, NASDAQ and CDN); (b) the most recent annual report or annual information form filed or submitted by the issuer with securities regulators of Ontario, Quebec, British Columbia or Alberta (or, if the issuer of the subject securities is not a reporting issuer in any of such provinces, with any other Canadian securities regulator) or with the Commission indicates that U.S. holders hold 25 percent or more of the outstanding subject class of securities; or (c) the offeror has actual knowledge that the level of U.S. ownership equals or exceeds 25 percent of such securities.

3. For purposes of this Form, if this Form is filed during the pendency of one or more ongoing cash tender or exchange offers for securities of the class subject to the offer that was commenced or was eligible to be commenced on Schedule 13E-4F, Schedule 14D-1F, and/or Form F-8 or Form F-80, the date for calculation of U.S. ownership shall be the same as that date used by the initial bidder or issuer.

4. For purposes of this Form, the class of subject securities shall not include any securities that may be converted into or are exchangeable for the subject securities.

5. For purposes of exchange offers, the calculation of U.S. holders shall be made as of the end of the subject issuer's last quarter or, if such quarter terminated within 60 days of the filing date, as of the end of such issuer's preceding quarter.

III. Eligibility Requirements for Business Combinations

A. In the case of a business combination, Form F-8 is available if:

(1) each company participating in the business combination, including the successor Registrant, is incorporated or organized under the laws of Canada or any Canadian province or territory and is a foreign private issuer;

(2) each company participating in the business combination other than the successor Registrant has had a class of its securities listed on The Montreal Exchange, The Toronto Stock Exchange or the Senior Board of the Vancouver Stock Exchange for the 12 calendar months immediately preceding the filing of this Form, has been subject to the continuous disclosure requirements of any securities commission or equivalent regulatory authority in Canada for a period of at least 36 calendar months immediately preceding the filing of this Form, and is currently in compliance with obligations arising from such listing and reporting; *provided, however,* that any such participating company shall not be required to meet such 36-month reporting requirement or 12-month listing requirement if other participating companies whose assets and gross revenues, respectively, would contribute at least 80 percent of the total assets and gross revenues from continuing operations of the successor Registrant, as measured based on pro forma combination of the participating companies' most recently completed fiscal

years, each meet such reporting and listing requirements; and

(3) the aggregate market value of the public float of the outstanding equity shares of each company participating in the business combination other than the successor Registrant is (CN) $75 million or more; provided, however, that any such participating company shall not be required to meet such public float requirement if other participating companies whose assets and gross revenues, respectively, would contribute at least 80 percent of the total assets and gross revenues from continuing operations of the successor Registrant, as measured based on pro forma combination of the participating companies' most recently completed fiscal years, each meet such public float requirement; and, *provided further,* that such public float requirement shall be deemed satisfied in the case of a participating company whose equity shares were the subject of an exchange offer that was registered or would have been eligible for registration on Form F-8, Form F-9, Form F-10 or Form F-80, or a tender offer in connection with which Schedule 13E-4F or 14D-1F was filed or could have been filed, that terminated within the last 12 months, if the participating company would have satisfied such public float requirement immediately prior to commencement of such exchange or tender offer.

B. In the case of a business combination, less than 25 percent of the class of securities to be offered by the successor Registrant shall be held by U.S. holders, as if measured immediately after completion of the business combination.

Instructions

1. For purposes of business combinations, the term "U.S. holder" shall mean any person whose address appears on the records of a participating company, any voting trustee, any depositary, any share transfer agent or any person acting in a similar capacity on behalf of a participating company as being located in the United States.

2. For purposes of business combinations, the calculation of U.S. holders shall be made by a participant as of the end of such participant's last quarter or, if such quarter terminated within 60 days of the filing date, as of the end of such participant's preceding quarter.

C. In the case of a business combination, the securities to be registered on this Form shall be offered to U.S. holders upon terms and conditions not less favorable than those offered to any other holder of the same class of such securities of the participating company.

IV. Application of General Rules and Regulations

A. The rules comprising Regulation C under the Securities Act shall not apply to filings on this Form unless specifically referred to in the Form.

Instead, the rules and regulations applicable in the home jurisdiction, regarding the form and method of preparation of disclosure documents shall apply to filings on this Form. Securities Act rules and regulations other than Regulation C shall apply to filings on this Form unless specifically excluded in this Form.

B. Rule 408 under the Securities Act, which provides that in addition to the information expressly required to be included in the registration statement, there shall be added such further material information, if any, as may be necessary to make the required statements, in light of the circumstances under which they are made, not misleading, shall apply to filings on this Form.

C. A registrant must file the registration statement in electronic format via the Commission's Electronic Data Gathering, Analysis, and Retrieval (EDGAR) system in accordance with the EDGAR rules set forth in Regulation S-T (17 CFR Part 232). For assistance with technical questions about EDGAR or to request an access code, call the EDGAR Filer Support Office at (202) 551-8900. For assistance with the EDGAR rules, call the Office of EDGAR and Information Analysis at (202) 551-3610.

If filing the registration statement in paper under a hardship exemption in Rule 201 or 202 of Regulation S-T (17 CFR 232.201 or 232.202), or as otherwise permitted, a registrant must file with the Commission at its principal office five copies of the complete registration statement and any amendments, including exhibits and all other documents filed as a part of the registration statement or amendment. The registrant must bind, staple or otherwise compile each copy in one or more parts without stiff covers. The registrant must further bind the registration statement or amendment on the side or stitching margin in a manner that leaves the reading matter legible. The registrant must provide three additional copies of the registration statement or amendment without exhibits to the Commission.

D. Any amendment to a registration statement on this Form shall be filed under cover of an appropriate facing sheet, shall be numbered consecutively in the order in which filed, and shall indicate on the facing sheet the applicable registration form on which the amendment is prepared and the file number of the registration statement.

If, however, an amendment to the home jurisdiction document(s) is filed after effectiveness of this registration statement that increases the number of securities that may be sold, in lieu of filing a post-effective amendment hereto, a new registration statement shall be filed on this form. As provided in Rule 429, the prospectus included in the new registration statement shall be deemed to include a prospectus covering unsold securities registered previously. If this is the case, the following legend shall appear at the bottom of the facing page of the registration statement: "Pursuant to Rule 429 under the Securities Act, the prospectus contained in this registration statement relates to registration statement[s] 33-[insert file number of previous registration statements."

E. An electronic filer must provide the signatures required for the registration statement or amendment in accordance with Regulation S-T Rule 302 (17 CFR 232.302). A registrant filing in paper must have at least one copy of the registration statement or amendment signed in accordance with Securities Act Rule 402(e) (17 CFR 230.402(e)) by the persons whose signatures are required for this registration statement. A registrant must also conform the unsigned copies.

F. At the time of filing this registration statement, the Registrant shall pay to the Commission in accordance with Rule 111 under the Securities Act, a fee in U.S. dollars in the amount prescribed by Section 6 of the Securities Act. The amount of securities to be registered on this Form need not exceed the amount to be offered in the United States as part of the offering.

G. In the case of an exchange offer, the registration fee is to be calculated as follows:

(1) Upon the basis of the market value of the securities that may be received by the Registrant or cancelled in the exchange offer from United States residents as established by the price of securities of the same class, as determined in accordance with paragraph (4) of this section.

(2) If there is no market for the securities to be received by the Registrant or cancelled in the exchange offer, the book value of such securities computed as of the latest practicable date prior to the date of filing the registration statement shall be used, unless the issuer of such securities is in bankruptcy or receivership or has an accumulated capital deficit, in which case one-third of the principal amount, par value or stated value of such securities shall be used.

(3) If any cash may be received by the Registrant from United States residents in connection with the exchange offer, the amount thereof shall be added to the value of the securities to be received by the Registrant or cancelled as computed in accordance with paragraph (1) or (2) of this section. If any cash is to be paid by the Registrant in connection with the exchange offer, the amount thereof shall be deducted from the value of the securities to be received by the Registrant in exchange as computed in accordance with paragraph (1) or (2) of this section.

(4) For purposes of the registration fee, the market value of the securities received or cancelled shall be the average of the high and low prices reported or the average of the bid and asked prices of such stock, in the principal market for such stock as of a date within 30 days prior to the date of filing.

H. In the case of a business combination, the registration fee is to be calculated as follows:

(1) Upon the basis of the market value of the equity securities of the predecessor companies held by United States residents being offered the Registrant's securities, as established by the price of the predecessors' securities of the same class determined in accordance with paragraph (4) of this section.

(2) If there is no market for the securities of the predecessor companies, the book value of such securities computed as of the latest practicable date prior to the date of filing the registration statement shall be used, unless the issuer of such securities is in bankruptcy or receivership or has an accumulated capital deficit, in which case one-third of the principal amount, par value or stated value of such securities shall be used.

(3) If any cash may be received by the Registrant from United States residents in connection with the business combination, the amount thereof shall be added to the value of the securities as computed in accordance with paragraph (1) or (2) of this section. If any cash is to be paid by the Registrant in connection with the business combination, the amount thereof shall be deducted from the value of the securities as computed in accordance with paragraph (1) or (2) of this section.

(4) For purposes of the registration fee, the market value of a predecessor's equity securities shall be the average of this high and low prices reported or the average of the bid and asked prices of such securities, in the principal market for such securities as of a date within 30 days prior to the date of filing.

I. A registrant must file the registration statement or amendment in electronic format in the English language in accordance with Regulation S-T Rule 306 (17 CFR 232.306). A registrant may file part of the prospectus or exhibit or other attachment to the registration statement or amendment in both French and English if it included the French text to comply with the requirements of the Canadian securities administrator or other Canadian authority and, for an electronic filing, if the filing is an HTML document, as defined in Regulation S-T Rule 11 (17 CFR 232.11). For both an electronic filing and a paper filing, a registrant may provide an English translation or English summary of a foreign language document as an exhibit or other attachment to the registration statement or amendment as permitted by the rules of the applicable Canadian securities administrator.

J. A paper filer must number sequentially one signed original of the registration statement or amendment (in addition to any internal numbering that otherwise may be present) by handwritten, typed, printed or other legible form of notation from the first page through the last page of the registration statement or amendment, including any exhibits or attachments. A paper filer must disclose the total number of pages on the first page of the sequentially numbered registration statement or amendment.

K. Where the offering registered on this Form is being made pursuant to the home jurisdiction's shelf prospectus offering procedures or procedures for pricing offerings after the final receipt has been issued, three copies of each supplement to, or supplemented version of, the home jurisdiction disclosure document(s) prepared under such procedures shall be filed with the Commission within one business day after such supplement or supplemented version is filed with any Canadian jurisdiction. Such filings shall be deemed not to constitute amendments to this registration statement. Each such filing shall contain in the upper right corner of the cover page the following legend, which may be set forth in longhand if legible: "Filed pursuant to General Instruction IV.K. of Form F-8; File No. 33-[insert number of the registration statement]."

Note: Offerings registered on this Form, whether or not made contemporaneously in Canada, may be made pursuant to National Policy Statement No. 44 shelf prospectus offering procedures and procedures for pricing offerings after the final receipt has been issued. Rules 405 and 430A under the Securities Act are not available for offerings registered on this Form.

V. Compliance with Exchange Act and Auditor Independence and Reporting Requirements

A. Pursuant to Rule 12h-4 under the Securities Exchange Act of 1934 (the "Exchange Act"), a Registrant shall be exempt from reporting obligations under Section 15(d) of the Exchange Act if such reporting obligation would have arisen solely from registration of securities on this Form. Registrants' attention is directed, however, towards other provisions of the Exchange Act that may be applicable, and specifically to the provisions of Sections 12(b) and 12(g) of the Exchange Act and Regulation M (17 CFR 242.100 through 242.105) and Rule 10b-13 under the Exchange Act. [*See* Exchange Act Release No. 29355 (June 21, 1991) containing an exemption from Rule 10b-13.]

B. The Commission's rules on auditor independence, as codified in section 600 of the Codification of Financial Reporting Policies, apply to auditor reports on all financial statements that are included in this registration statement, except that such rules do not apply with respect to periods prior to the most recent fiscal year for which financial statements are included in the registration statement under the Securities Act filed by the issuer on Form F-8, Form F-9, Form F-10 or Form F-80 or under the Exchange Act filed by the issuer on Form 40-F. Notwithstanding the exception in the previous sentence, such rules do apply with respect to any periods prior to the most recent fiscal year if the issuer previously was required to file with the Commission a report or registration statement containing an audit report on financial statements for such prior periods as to which the Commission's rules on auditor independence applied.

C. Independent accountants reporting on financial statements included in the registration statement should consider Canadian auditing guidelines pertaining to the Canada-U.S. reporting conflict with respect to contingencies and going concern considerations. If additional comments for U.S. readers are appropriate under those guidelines but are not included in the prospectus itself, those comments should be included with the legends required by Item 2 of Part 1 hereof. In addition, the accountant's consent specifically should refer to any additional comments provided for U.S. readers.

D. Pursuant to Rule 13e-4(g) under the Exchange Act, the provisions of Rule 13e-4 are not applicable, and pursuant to Rule 14d-1(b) under the Exchange Act, the provisions of Sections 14(d)(1) through 14(d)(7) of the Exchange Act, Regulation 14D under the Exchange Act and Schedule TO thereunder, and Rule 14e-1 under Regulation 14E, are not applicable to a transaction involving offerings of securities that may be registered on this Form in connection with exchange offers, *provided that,* if an exemption has been granted from the requirements of Canadian federal, provincial and/or territorial laws, regulations or policies, and the tender offer does not comply with requirements that otherwise would be required by Commission tender offer rules, the Registrant shall comply with such provisions of the Exchange Act. Such transaction is not exempt from the antifraud provisions of Section 10(b), 13(e) of the Exchange Act or Rule 10b-5, 13e-4(b)(1) or 14e-3 thereunder, if the transaction otherwise is subject to those sections.

PART I—INFORMATION REQUIRED TO BE DELIVERED TO OFFEREES OR PURCHASERS

Item 1. Home Jurisdiction Document

In the case of an exchange offer, the prospectus shall consist of the entire disclosure document or documents used to offer the securities of the Registrant in any Canadian jurisdiction. Except as noted hereinafter, such disclosure document(s) shall be prepared in accordance with the disclosure requirements of such jurisdiction(s) as interpreted and applied by the securities commission(s) or other regulatory authorities in such jurisdiction(s).

In the case of a business combination, the prospectus shall consist of the entire disclosure document or documents used to solicit votes of securityholders in connection with the proposed business combination in any Canadian jurisdiction. Except as noted hereinafter, such disclosure documents(s) shall be prepared in accordance with the disclosure requirements of the jurisdiction(s) governing such solicitation as interpreted and applied by the securities commission(s) or other regulatory authorities in such jurisdiction(s).

The prospectus used in the United States shall contain additional information and legends required by this Form. It need not include any documents incorporated by reference into the disclosure document(s) used in Canada and not required to be delivered to offerees or purchasers (in the case of an exchange offer) or securityholder being solicited (in the case of a business combination) pursuant to Canadian law.

Notwithstanding the foregoing, such prospectus used in the United States need not contain any disclosure applicable solely to Canadian offerees or purchasers that would not be material to offerees or purchasers in the United States, including, without limitation, (i) any Canadian "red herring" legend; (ii) any discussion of Canadian tax considerations other than those material to U.S. offerees or purchasers; (iii) the names of any Canadian underwriters not acting as underwriters in the United States or a description of the Canadian plan of distribution (except to the extent necessary to describe the material facts of the U.S. plan of distribution); (iv) any description of offerees' or purchasers' statutory rights under applicable Canadian, provincial or territorial securities legislation (except to the extent such rights are available to U.S. offerees or purchasers); or (v) certificates of the issuer or any underwriter.

Item 2. Informational Legends

The following legends, to the extent applicable, shall appear on the outside front cover page of the prospectus (or on a sticker thereto) in bold-face roman type at least as high as ten-point modern type and at least two points leaded:

"This offering is made by a foreign issuer that is permitted, under a multijurisdictional disclosure system adopted by the United States, to prepare this prospectus in accordance with the disclosure requirements of its home country. Prospective investors should be aware that such requirements are different from those of the United States. The financial statements included or incorporated herein, if any, have been prepared in accordance with foreign generally accepted accounting principles, and may be subject to foreign auditing and auditor independence standards, and, thus, may not be comparable to financial statements of United States companies."

"Prospective investors should be aware that acquisition of the securities described herein may have tax consequences both in the United States and in the home country of the Registrant. Such consequences for investors who are resident in, or citizens of, the United States may not be described fully herein."

"The enforcement by investors of civil liabilities under the federal securities laws may be affected adversely by the fact that the Registrant is incorporated or organized under the laws of a foreign country, that some or all of its officers and directors may be residents of a foreign country, that some or all of the underwriters or experts named in the registration statement may be residents of a foreign country, and that all or a substantial portion of the assets of the Registrant and said persons may be located outside the United States."

"THESE SECURITIES HAVE NOT BEEN APPROVED OR DISAPPROVED BY THE SECURITIES AND EXCHANGE COMMISSION NOR HAS THE COMMISSION PASSED UPON THE ACCURACY OR ADEQUACY OF THIS PROSPECTUS. ANY REPRESENTATION TO THE CONTRARY IS A CRIMINAL OFFENSE."

The following legend shall appear in the manner noted above in any prospectus relating to an exchange offer.

"Prospective investors should be aware that, during the period of the exchange offer, the Registrant or its affiliates, directly or indirectly, may bid for or make purchases of the securities to be distributed or to be exchanged, or certain related securities, as permitted by applicable laws or regulations of Canada or its provinces or territories."

The Registrant should also include in the prospectus any legend or information requried by the laws of any jurisdiction in which the securities are to be offered.

Note to Item 2. If the home-jurisdiction document(s) are delivered through an electronic medium, the issuer may satisfy the legibility requirements for the required legends relating to type size and font by presenting the legends in any manner reasonably calculated to draw investor attention to it.

Item 3. Incorporation of Certain Information by Reference

Information called for by this Form, including exhibits, may be incorporated by reference at the Registrant's option from documents that the Registrant has filed previously with the Commission pursuant to Section 13(a) or 15(d) of the Exchange Act or submitted to the Commission pursuant to Rule 12g3-2(b) under the Exchange Act. Any such incorporation by reference shall be done in accordance with Item 10(d) of Regulation S-K. If any information is incorporated by reference into the prospectus, the prospectus shall provide the name, address and telephone number of an officer of the Registrant from whom copies of such information may be obtained upon request without charge.

Item 4. List of Documents Filed with the Commission

There shall be set forth in or attached to the prospectus a list of all documents filed with the Commission as part of the registration statement.

PART II—INFORMATION NOT REQUIRED TO BE DELIVERED TO OFFEREES OR PURCHASERS

Provide a brief description of the indemnification provisions relating to directors, officers and controlling persons of the Registrant against liability arising under the Securities Act (including any provision of the underwriting agreement which relates to indemnification of the underwriter or its controlling persons by the Registrant against such liabilities where a director, officer or controlling person of the Registrant is such an underwriter or controlling person thereof or a member of any firm which is such an underwriter), together with a statement in substantially the following form:

Insofar as indemnification for liabilities arising under the Securities Act of 1933 may be permitted to directors, officers or persons controlling the Registrant pursuant to the foregoing provisions, the Registrant has been informed that in the opinion of the U.S. Securities and Exchange Commission such indemnification is against public policy as expressed in the Act and is therefore unenforceable.

The exhibits specified below shall be filed as part of the registration statement. Exhibits shall be appropriate lettered or numbered for convenient reference.

(1) Any reports or information that, in accordance with the requirements of the jurisdiction of incorporation or organization of the subject issuer or, in the case of a business combination, in accordance with the requirements of the jurisdiction(s) of incorporation or organization of companies involved in the transaction other than the Registrant, must be made publicly available by the Registrant in connection with the transaction.

(2) A copy of any agreement relating to the proposed acquisition or business combination, as applicable.

(3) Copies of any documents incorporated by reference into the registration statement and any publicly available documents filed with any other Canadian regulatory authority concurrently with the prospectus.

(4) If any accountant, engineer or appraiser, or any person whose profession gives authority to a statement made by him, is named as having prepared or certified any part of the registration statement, or is named as having prepared or certified a report or valuation for use in connection with the offering document, the manually signed, written consent of such person.

If any such person is named as having prepared or certified any other report or valuation (other than a public official document or statement) which is used in connection with the registration statement, but is not named as having prepared or certified such report or valuation for use in connection with the registration statement, the manually signed, written consent of such person, unless the Commission dispenses with such filing as impracticable or as involving undue hardship in accordance with Rule 437 under the Securities Act.

Any other consent required by Rule 436, 438 or 439 under the Securities Act. Every amendment relating to a certified financial statement shall include the manually signed, written consent of the certifying accountant to the use of his certificate in connection with the amended financial statements in the registration statement and to being named as having certified such financial statements.

NOTE: The consents required by this item shall specifically indicate consent regarding use of the report or valuation in the registration statement filed in the United States.

(5) If any name is signed to the registration statement pursuant to power of attorney, manually signed copies of such power of attorney and, if the name of any officer signing on behalf of the Registrant is signed pursuant to a power of attorney, certified copies of a resolution of the Registrant's board of directors or similar governing body authorizing such signature.

(6) A copy of any indenture relating to the registered securities.

PART III—UNDERTAKINGS AND CONSENT TO SERVICE OF PROCESS

Item 1. Undertakings

This Form shall set forth the following undertakings of the Registrant:

(a) Registrant undertakes to make available, in person or by telephone, representatives to respond to inquiries made by the Commission staff, and to furnish promptly, when requested to do so by the Commission staff, information relating to the securities registered pursuant to Form F-8 or to transactions in said securities.

(b) In the case of an exchange offer, Registrant further undertakes to disclose in the United States, on the same basis as it is required to make such disclosure pursuant to any applicable Canadian federal and/or provincial or territorial law, regulation or policy, information regarding purchases of the Registrant's securities or of the subject issuer's securities during the exchange offer. Such information shall be set forth in amendments to this Form.

Item 2. Consent to Service of Process

(a) At the time of filng Form F-8, the Registrant shall file with the Commission a written irrevocable consent and power of attorney on Form F-X.

(b) At the time of filing Form F-8, any non-U.S. person acting as trustee with respect to the registered securities shall file with the Commission a written irrevocable consent and power of attorney on Form F-X.

(c) Any change to the name or address of the agent for service of the Registrant or the trustee shall be communicated promptly to the Commission by amendment to Form F-X referencing the file number of the relevant registration statement.

SIGNATURES

Pursuant to the requirements of the Securities Act, the Registrant certifies that it has reasonable grounds to believe that it meets all of the requirements for filing on Form F-8 and has duly caused this registration statement to be signed on its behalf by the undersigned, thereunto duly authorized, in the City of ...., Country of ...., on .... (date), ...

Registrant ....

By (Signature and Title) ....

Pursuant to the requirements of the Securities Act, this registration statement has been signed by the following persons in the capacities and on the dates indicated.

(Signature) ....

(Name and Title) ....

(Date) ....

Instructions

A. The registration statement shall be signed by the Registrant, its principal executive officer or officers, its principal financial officer, its controller or principal accounting officer, at least a majority of the board of directors or persons performing similar functions and its authorized representative in the United States. Where the Registrant is a limited partnership, the registration statement shall be signed by a majority of the board of directors of any corporate general partner signing the registration statement.

B. The name of each person who signs the registration statement shall be typed or printed beneath his signature. Any person who occupies more than one of the specified positions shall indicate each capacity in which the registration statement is signed.

C. If the securities to be offered are those of a corporation not yet in existence at the time the registration statement is filed and which will be a party to a consolidation involving two or more existing corporations, then each such existing corporation shall be deemed a Registrant and shall be so designated on the cover page of this Form, and the registration statement shall be signed by each such existing corporation and by the officers and directors of each such existing corporation as if each such existing corporation were the sole Registrant.

D. By signing this Form, the Registrant consents without power of revocation that any administrative subpoena may be served, or any administrative proceeding, civil suit or civil action where the cause of action arises out of or relates to or concerns any offering made or purported to be made in connection with the securities registered pursuant to Form F-8 or any purchases or sales of any security in connection therewith, may be commenced against it in any administrative tribunal or in any appropriate court in any place subject to the jurisdiction of any state or of the United States or of the District of Columbia or Puerto Rico by service of said subpoena or process upon the Registrant's designated agent.

[¶ 7581] FORM F-9

[As last amended in Release No. 33-9002, effective April 13, 2009, 74 F.R. 6776 and corrected in Release No. 33-9002A, 74 F.R. 15666.]

U.S. Securities and Exchange Commission

Washington, D.C. 20549

Form F-9

REGISTRATION STATEMENT UNDER THE SECURITIES ACT OF 1933

U.S. Securities and Exchange Commission
Washington, D.C. 20549
Form F-9
REGISTRATION STATEMENT UNDER THE SECURITIES ACT OF 1933

. . . .
(Exact name of Registrant as specified in its charter)
. . . .
(Translation of Registrant's name into English (if applicable))
. . . .
(Province or other jurisdiction of incorporation or organization)
. . . .
(Primary Standard Industrial Classification Code Number (if applicable))
. . . .
(I.R.S. Employer Identification Number (if applicable))
. . . .
(Address and telephone number of Registrant's principal executive offices)
. . . .
(Name, address (including zip code) and telephone number (including area code) of agent for service in the United States)

Approximate date of commencement of proposed sale of the securities to the public . . . . . .
. . . .
(Principal jurisdiction regulation this offering)

It is proposed that this filing shall become effective (check appropriate box)

A. [] upon filing with the Commission pursuant to Rule 467(a) (if in connection with an offering being made contemporaneously in the United States and Canada).

B. [] at some future date (check the appropriate box below)

1. [] pursuant to Rule 467(b) on *(date)* at *(time)* (designate a time not sooner than 7 calendar days after filing).

2. [] pursuant to Rule 467(b) on *(date)* at *(time)* (designate a time 7 calendar days or sooner after filing) because the securities regulatory authority in the review jurisdiction has issued a receipt or notification of clearance on *(date)*.

3. [] pursuant to Rule 467(b) as soon as practicable after notification of the Commission by the Registrant or the Canadian securities regulatory authority of the review jurisdiction that a receipt or notification of clearance has been issued with respect hereto.

4. [] after the filing of the next amendment to this Form (if preliminary material is being filed).

If any of the securities being registered on this Form are to be offered on a delayed or continuous basis pursuant to the home jurisdiction's shelf prospectus offering procedures, check the following box. []

CALCULATION OF REGISTRATION FEE*

Title of each class of securities to be registered	Amount to be registered	Proposed maximum offering price per unit	Proposed maximum aggregate offering price	Amount of registration fee

* See General Instruction II.G.-II.H. for rules as to calculation of the registration fee.

If, as a result of stock splits, stock dividends or similar transactions, the number of securities purported to be registered on this registation statement changes, the provisions of Rule 416 shall apply to this registration statement.

If it is proposed that this filing become effective pursuant Rule 467(b), the following legend shall appear on the cover page of this Form:

"The Registrant hereby amends this registration statement on such date or dates as may be necessary to delay its effective date until the registration statement shall become effective as provided in Rule 467 under the Securities Act of 1933 or on such date as the Commission, acting pursuant to Section 8(a) of the Act, may determine."

GENERAL INSTRUCTIONS

I. Eligibility Requirements for Use of Form F-9

A. Form F-9 may be used for the registration under the Securities Act of 1933 (the "Securities Act") of investment grade debt or investment grade preferred securities that are: (1) offered for cash or in connection with an exchange offer; and (2) either non-covertible or not convertible for a period of at least one year from the date of issuance and, except as noted in E. below, are thereafter only convertible into a security of another class of the issuer.

Instruction. Securities shall be "investment grade" if, at the time of sale at least one nationally recognized statistical rating organization (as that term is used in relation to Rule 15c3-1(c)(2)(vi)(F) under the Securities Exchange Act of 1934 (the "Exchange Act") or at least one Approved Rating Organization (as defined in National Policy Statement No. 45 of the Canadian Securities Administrator, as the same may be amended from time to time) has rated the security in one of its generic rating categories that signifies investment grade; typically the four highest rating categories (within which there may be subcategories or gradations indicating relative standing) signify investment grade.

B. Form F-9 is available to any Registrant that:

(1) is incorporated or organized under the laws of Canada or any Canadian province or territory;

(2) is a foreign private issuer or a crown corporation;

(3) has been subject to the continuous disclosure requirements of any securities commission or equivalent regulatory authority in Canada for a period of at least 12 calendar months immediately preceding the filing of this Form, and is currently in compliance with such obligations; and

(4) has an aggregate market value of the public float of its outstanding equity shares of $75 million or more; *provided, however,* that the requirements set forth in B.(4) above shall not apply if the securities being registered on this Form are not convertible into another security.

Instructions

1. For purposes of this Form, "foreign private issuer" shall be construed in accordance with Rule 405 under the Securities Act.

2. For purposes of this Form, the term "crown corporation" shall mean a corporation all of whose common shares or comparable equity is owned directly or indirectly by the Government of Canada or a Province or Territory of Canada.

3. For purposes of this Form, the "public float" of specified securities shall mean only such securities held by persons other than affiliates of the issuer.

4. For purposes of this Form, an "affiliate" of a person is anyone who beneficially owns, directly or indirectly, or exercises control or direction over, more than 10 percent of the outstanding equity shares of such person. The determination of a person's affiliates shall be made as of the end of such person's most recently completed fiscal year.

5. For purposes of this Form, "equity shares" shall mean common shares, non-voting equity shares and subordinate or restricted voting equity shares, but shall not include preferred shares.

6. For purposes of this Form, the market value of outstanding equity shares (whether or not held by affiliates) shall be computed by use of the price at which such shares were last sold, or the average of the bid and asked prices of such shares, in the principal market for such shares as of a date within 60 days prior to the date of filing. If there is not market for any of such securities, the book value of such securities computed as of the latest practicable date prior to the filing of this Form shall be used for purposes of calculating the market value, unless the issuer of such securities is in bankrutpcy or receivership or has an accumulated capital deficit, in which case one-third of the principal amount, par value or stated value of such securities shall be used.

C. In the case of an exchange offer, the securities to be registered on this Form shall be offered to U.S. holders upon terms and conditions not less favorable than those offered to any other holder of the same class of securities to be exchanged (the "subject securities") for the securities of the Registrant.

D. In the case of an exchange offer, the issuer of the subject securities shall be incorporated or organized under the laws of Canada or any Canadian province or territory and be a foreign private issuer or a crown corporation.

Instructions

1. For purposes of this Form, the term "U.S. holder" shall mean any person whose address appears on the records of the issuer of the subject securities, any voting trustee, any depositary, any share transfer agent or any person acting in a similar capacity on behalf of the issuer of the subject securities as being located in the United States.

2. For purposes of this Form, the class of subject securities shall not include any securities that may be converted into or are exchangeable for the subject securities.

E. If the Registrant is a majority-owned subsidiary offering debt securities or preferred securities, it shall be deemed to meet the requirements of I.B.(3) and (4) above if the parent of the Registrant-subsidiary meets the requirements of I.B. above, as applicable, and fully and unconditionally guarantees the securities being registered as to principal and interest (if debt securities) or as to liquidation preference, redemption price and dividends (if preferred securities); *provided, however,* that the securities of the subsidiary are only convertible or exchangeable, if at all, for the securities of the parent.

F. If the Registrant is a successor registrant subsisting after a statutory amalgamation, merger, arrangement, or other reorganization requiring the vote of shareholders of the participating companies (a "business combination"), the Registrant shall be deemed to meet the 12-month reporting requirement of I.B.(3) above if: (1) the time the successor registrant has been subject to the continuous disclosure requirements of any securities commission or equivalent regulatory authority in Canada, when added separately to the time each predecessor had been subject to such requirements at the time of the business combination, in each case equals at least 12 calendar months, *provided, however,* that any predecessor need not be considered for purposes of the reporting history calculation if the reporting histories of predecessors whose assets and gross revenues, respectively, would contributed at least 80 percent of the total assets and gross revenues from continuing operations of the successor Registrant, as measured based on pro forma combination of such participating companies' most recently completed fiscal years immediately prior to the business combination, when combined with the reporting history of the successor Registrant in each case satisfy such 12-month reporting requirement; and (2) the successor Registrant has been subject to such continuous disclosure requirements since the business combination, and is currently in compliance with its obligations thereunder.

G. This Form shall not be used for registration of securities if not takeover bid circular or issuer bid circular (in the case of an exchange offer) or prospectus (in all other cases) is prepared pursuant to the requirements of any Canadian jurisdiction due to the availability of an exemption from such requirements.

H. This Form shall not be used if the Registrant or, in the case of an exchange offer, the issuer of the subject securities is an investment company registered or required to be registered under the Investment Company Act of 1940.

II. Application of General Rules and Regulations

A. A registration statement on this Form, and any amendment thereto, shall become effective in accordance with Rule 467 under the Securities Act.

B. The rules comprising Regulation C under the Securities Act shall not apply to filings on this Form unless specifically referred to in the Form. Instead, the rules and regulations applicable in the home jurisdiction regarding the form and method of preparation of disclosure documents shall apply to filings on this Form. A registration statement or amendment thereto on this Form shall be deemed to be filed on the proper form unless objection to the Form is made by the Commission prior to the effective date. Securities Act rules and regulations other than Regulation C shall apply to filings on this Form unless specifically excluded in this Form.

C. Rule 408 under the Securities Act, which provides that in addition to the information expressly required to be included in the registration statement, there shall be added such further material information, if any, as may be necessary to make the required statements, in light of the circumstances under which they are made, not misleading, shall apply to filings on this Form.

D. A registrant must file the registration statement in electronic format via the Commission's Electronic Data Gathering, Analysis, and Retrieval (EDGAR) system in accordance with the EDGAR rules set forth in Regulation S-T (17 CFR Part 232). For assistance with technical questions about EDGAR or to request an access code, call the EDGAR Filer Support Office at (202) 551-8900. For assistance with the EDGAR rules, call the Office of EDGAR and Information Analysis at (202) 551-3610.

If filing the registration statement in paper under a hardship exemption in Rule 201 or 202 of Regulation S-T (17 CFR 232.201 or 232.202), or as otherwise permitted, a registrant must file with the Commission at its principal office five copies of the complete registration statement and any amendments, including exhibits and all other documents filed as a part of the registration statement or amendment. The registrant must bind, staple or otherwise compile each copy in one or more parts without stiff covers. The registrant must further bind the registration statement or amendment on the side or stitching margin in a manner that leaves the reading matter legible. The registrant must provide three additional copies of the registration statement or amendment without exhibits to the Commission.

E. Any amendment to a registration statement on this Form shall be filed under cover of an appropriate facing sheet, shall be numbered consecutively in the order in which filed, and shall indicate on the facing sheet the applicable registration form on which the amendment is prepared and the file number of the registration statement.

If, however, an amendment to the home jurisdiction document(s) is filed after effectiveness of this registration statement that increases the number of securities that may be sold, in lieu of filing a post-effective amendment hereto, a new registration statement shall be filed on this Form. As provided in Rule 429, the prospectus, included in the new registration statement shall be deemed to include a prospectus covering unsold securities registered previously. If this is the case, the following legend shall appear at the bottom of the facing page of the registration statement: "Pursuant to Rule 429 under the Securities Act, the prospectus contained in this registration statement relates to registration statement[s] 33-[insert file number[s] of previous registration statement[s]]."

F. An electronic filer must provide the signatures required for the registration statement or amendment in accordance with Regulation S-T Rule 302 (17 CFR 232.302). A registrant filing in paper must have at least one copy of the registration statement or amendment signed in accordance with Securities Act Rule 402(e) (17 CFR 230.402(e)) by the persons whose signatures are required for this registration statement. A registrant must also conform the unsigned copies.

G. At the time of filing this registration statement, the Registrant shall pay to the Commission in accordance with Rule 111 under the Securities Act a fee in U.S. dollars in the amount prescribed by Section 6 of the Securities Act. The amount of securities to be registered on this Form need not exceed the amount to be offered in the United States as part of the offering.

H. In the case of an exchange offer, the registration fee is to be calculated as follows:

(1) Upon the basis of the market value of the securities that may be received by the Registrant or cancelled in the exchange offer from United States residents as established by the price of securities of the same class, as determined in accordance with paragraph (4) of this section.

(2) If there is no market for the securities to be received by the Registrant or cancelled in the exchange offer, the book value of such securities computed as of the latest practicable date prior to the date of filing the registration statement shall be used, unless the issuer of such securities is in bankruptcy or receivership or has an accumulated capital deficit, in which case one-third of the principal amount, par value or stated value of such securities shall be used.

(3) If any cash may be received by the Registrant from United States residents in connection with the exchange offer, the amount thereof shall be added to the value of the securities to be received by the Registrant or cancelled as computed in accordance with paragraph (1) or (2) of this section. If any cash is to be paid by the Registrant in connection with the exchange offer, the amount thereof shall be deducted from the value of the securities to be received by the Registrant in exchange as computed in accordance with paragraph (1) or (2) of this section.

(4) For purposes of the registration fee, the market value of the securities received or cancelled shall be the average of the high and low prices reported or the average of the bid and asked prices of such stock, in the principal market for such stock as of a date within 30 days prior to the date of filing.

I. A registrant must file the registration statement or amendment in electronic format in the English language in accordance with Regulation S-T Rule 306 (17 CFR 232.306). A registrant may file part of the prospectus or exhibit or other attachment to the registration statement or amendment in both French and English if it included the French text to comply with the requirements of the Canadian securities administrator or other Canadian authority and, for an electronic filing, if the filing is an HTML document, as defined in Regulation S-T Rule 11 (17 CFR 232.11). For both an electronic filing and a paper filing, a registrant may provide an English translation or English summary of a foreign language document as an exhibit or other attachment to the registration statement or amendment as permitted by the rules of the applicable Canadian securities administrator.

J. A paper filer must number sequentially one signed original of the registration statement or amendment (in addition to any internal numbering that otherwise may be present) by handwritten, typed, printed or other legible form of notation from the first page through the last page of the registration statement or amendment, including any exhibits or attachments. A paper filer must disclose the total number of pages on the first page of the sequentially numbered registration statement or amendment.

K. Where the offering registered on this Form is being made pursuant to the home jurisdiction's shelf prospectus offering procedures or procedures for pricing offerings after the final receipt has been issued, three copies of each supplement to, or supplemented version of, the home jurisdiction disclosure document(s) prepared under such procedures shall be filed with the Commission within one business day after such supplement or supplemented version is filed with the principal jurisdiction. Such filings shall be deemed not to constitute amendments to this registration statement. Each such filings shall contain in the upper right corner of the cover page of the following legend, which may be set forth in longhand if legible: "Filed pursuant to General Instruction II.K. of Form F-9; File No. 33-[insert number of the registration statement]."

Note: Offerings registered on this Form, whether or not made contemporaneously in Canada, may be made pursuant to National Policy Statement No. 44 shelf prospectus offering procedures and procedures for pricing offerings after the final receipt has been issued. Rules 415 and 430A under the Securities Act are not available for offerings registered on this Form.

L. If the offering to be registered on this Form is not being made contemporaneously in Canada, the registration statement on this Form and any amendments hereto shall be prepared and filed as if the offering were being made contemporaneously in Canada. The Commission has been advised that the principal jurisdiction in Canada designated by the Registrant in connection with such an offering will require the filing of such documents and may select them for review.

III. Compliance with Exchange Act and Auditor Independence and Reporting Requirements

A. Pursuant to Rule 15d-4 under the Exchange Act, reporting obligations under Section 15(d) of the Exchange Act (and the requirements of Regulation 15D thereunder) arising solely from an offering of securities registered on this Form may be met by filing with the Commission, under cover of Forms 40-F and 6-K, certain home jurisdiction documents. Registrants' attention is directed, however, towards other provisions of the Exchange Act that may be applicable, and specifically to the provisions of Sections 12(b) and 12(g) of the Exchange Act and Regulation M (17 CFR 242.100 through 242.105).

B. The Commission's rules on auditor independence, as codified in Section 600 of the Codification of Financial Reporting Policies, apply to auditor reports on all financial statements that are included in this registration statement, except that such rules do not apply with respect to periods prior to the most recent fiscal year for which financial statements are included in the registration statement under the Securities Act filed by the issuer on Form F-8, Form F-9, Form F-10 or Form F-80 or under the Exchange Act filed by the issuer on Form 40-F. Notwithstanding the exception in the previous sentence, such rules do apply with respect to any periods prior to the most recent fiscal year if the issuer previously was required to file with the Commission a report or registration statement containing an audit report on financial statements for such prior periods as to which the Commission's rules on auditor independence applied.

C. Independent accountants reporting on financial statements included in the registration statement should consider Canadian auditing guidelines pertaining to the Canada-U.S. reporting conflict with respect to contingencies and going concern considerations. If additional comments for U.S. readers are appropriate under those guidelines but are not included in the prospectus itself, those comments should be included with the legends required by Item 2 of Part I hereof. In addition, the accountant's consent specifically should refer to any additional comments provided for U.S. readers.

D. Pursuant to Rule 13e-4(g) under the Exchange Act, the provisions of Rule 13e-4 are not applicable, and pursuant to Rule 14d-1(b) under the Exchange Act, the provisions of Sections 14(d)(1) through 14(d)(7) of the Exchange Act, Regulation 14D under the Exchange Act and Schedule TO thereunder, the Rule 14e-1 under Regulation 14E, are not applicable to a transaction involving offerings of securities that may be registered on this Form in connection with ex change offers; *provided that*, if an exemption has been granted from the requirements of Canadian federal, provincial and/or territorial laws, regulations or policies, and the tender offer does not comply with requirements that otherwise would be required by Commission tender offer rules, the Registrant shall comply with such provisions of the Exchange Act. Such transaction is not exempt from the antifraud provisions of Section 10(b), 13(e) or 14(e) of the Exchange Act or Rule 10b-5, 13e-4(b)(1) or 14e-3 thereunder, if the transaction otherwise is subject to those sections.

PART I—INFORMATION REQUIRED TO BE DELIVERED TO OFFEREES OR PURCHASERS

Item 1. Home Jurisdiction Document

In the case of an exchange offer, the prospectus shall consist of the entire disclosure document or documents used to offer securities in any Canadian jurisdiction. Except as noted hereinafter, such disclosure documents shall be prepared in accordance with the disclosure requirements of such jurisdiction(s) as interpreted and applied by the securities commission(s) or other regulatory authorities in such jurisdiction(s).

In all other cases, the prospectus shall consist of the entire disclosure document or documents used to offer the securities of the Registrant in the principal jurisdiction (or, if the offering is not being made contemporaneously in Canada, as if the offering were made in such jurisdiction). Except as noted hereinafter, such disclosure document(s) shall be prepared in accordance with the disclosure requirements of such jurisdiction as interpreted and applied by the securities commission or other regulatory authority in such jurisdiction.

Such prospectus used in the United States shall contain additional information and legends required by this Form. It need not include any documents incorporated by reference into disclosure document(s) used in Canada and not required to be delivered to offerees or purchasers (in the case of an exchange offer) pursuant to Canadian law or to offerees or purchasers (in all other cases) pursuant to the laws of the principal jurisdiction.

Notwithstanding the foregoing, such prospectus used in the United States need not contain any disclosure applicable solely to Canadian offerees or purchasers that would not be material to offerees or purchasers in the United States, including, without limitation, (i) any Canadian "red herring" legend; (ii) any discussion of Canadian tax considerations other than those material to U.S. offerees or purchasers; (iii) the names of any Canadian underwriters not acting as underwriters in the United States or a description of the Canadian plan of distribution (except to the extent necessary to describe the material facts of the U.S. plan of distribution); (iv) any description of offerees' or purchasers' statutory rights under applicable Canadian, provincial or territorial securities legislation (except to the extent such rights are available to U.S. offerees or purchasers); and (v) certificates of the issuer or any underwriters.

Item 2. Informational Legends

The following legends, to the extent applicable, shall appear on the outside front cover page of the prospectus (or on a sticker thereto) in bold-face roman type at least as high as ten-point modern type and at least two points leaded:

"This offering is made by a foreign issuer that is permitted, under a multijurisdictional disclosure system adopted by the United States, to prepare this prospectus in accordance with the disclosure requirements of its home country. Prospective investors should be aware that such requirements are different from those of the United States. The financial statements included or incorporated herein, if any, have been prepared in accordance with foreign generally accepted accounting principles, and may be subject to foreign auditing and auditor independence standards, and thus may not be comparable to financial statements of United States companies."

Prospective investors should be aware that the acquisition of the securities described herein may have tax consequences both in the United States and in the home country of the Registrant. Such consequences for investors who are resident in, or citizens of, the United States may not be described fully herein."

"The enforcement by investors of civil liabilities under the federal securities laws may be affected adversely by the fact that the Registrant is incorporated or organized under the laws of a foreign country, that some or all of its officers and directors may be residents of a foreign country, that some or all of the underwriters or experts named in the registration statement may be residents of a foreign country and that all or a substantial portion of the assets of the Registrant and said persons may be located outside the United States."

"THESE SECURITIES HAVE NOT BEEN APPROVED OR DISAPPROVED BY THE SECURITIES AND EXCHANGE COM-

MISSION NOR HAS THE COMMISSION PASSED UPON THE ACCURACY OR ADEQUACY OF THIS PROSPECTUS. ANY REPRESENTATION TO THE CONTRARY IS A CRIMINAL OFFENSE."

The following legend shall appear in the manner noted above in any prospectus relating to an exchange offer.

"Prospective investors should be aware that, during the period of the exchange offer, the Registrant or its affiliates, directly or indirectly, may bid for or make purchases of the securities to be distributed or to be exchanged, or certain related securities, as permitted by applicable laws or regulations of Canada or its provinces or territories."

Any prospectus to be used before the effective date of the registration statement shall contain, on the outside front cover page (or on a sticker thereto) the following statement printed in red ink in types as large as that generally used in the body of the prospectus:

"Information contained herein is subject to completion or amendment. A registration statement relating to these securities has been filed with the Securities and Exchange Commission. These securities may not be sold nor may offers to buy be accepted prior to the time the registration statement becomes effective. This prospectus shall not constitute an offer to sell or the solicitation of an offer to buy nor shall there be any sale of these securities in any state in which such offer, solicitation or sale would be unlawful prior to registration or

qualification under the securities laws of any such State."

The Registrant should also include in the prospectus any legend or information required by the laws of any jurisdiction in which the securities are to be offered.

Note to Item 2. If the home-jurisdiction document(s) are delivered through an electronic medium, the issuer may satisfy the legibility requirements for the required legends relating to type size and font by presenting the legends in any manner reasonably calculated to draw investor attention to it.

Item 3. Incorporation of Certain Information by Reference

Information called for by this Form, including exhibits, may be incorporated by reference at the Registrant's option from documents that the Registrant has filed previously with the Commission pursuant to Section 13(a) or 15(d) of the Exchange Act or submitted to the Commission pursuant to Rule 12g3-2(b) under the Exchange Act. Any such incorporation by reference shall be done in accordance with Item 10(d) of Regulation S-K. If any information is incorporated by reference into the prospectus, the prospectus shall provide the name, address and telephone number of an officer of the Registrant from whom copies of such information may be obtained upon request without charge.

Item 4. List of Documents Filed with the Commission

There shall be set forth in or attached to the prospectus a list of all documents filed with the Commission as part of the registration statement.

PART II—INFORMATION NOT REQUIRED TO BE DELIVERED TO OFFEREES OR PURCHASERS

Provide a brief description of the indemnification provisions relating to directors, officers and controlling persons of the Registrant against liability arising under the Securities Act (including any provision of the underwriting agreement which relates to indemnification of the underwriter or its controlling persons by the Registrant against such liabilities where a director, officer or controlling person of the Registrant is such an underwriter or controlling person thereof or a member of any firm which is such an underwriter), together with a statement in substantially the following form:

Insofar as indemnification for liabilities arising under the Securities Act of 1933 may be permitted to directors, officers or persons controlling the Registrant pursuant to the foregoing provisions, the Registrant has been informed that in the opinion of

the U.S. Securities and Exchange Commission such indemnification is against public policy as expressed in the Act and is therefore unenforceable.

The exhibits specified below shall be filed as part of the registration statement. Exhibits shall be appropriately lettered or numbered for convenient reference.

(1) In the case of an exchange offer, any reports or information that, in accordance with the requirements of the jurisdiction of incorporation or organization of the subject issuer, must be made publicly available by the Registrant in connection with the transaction.

(2) In all other cases, any reports or information that in accordance with the requirements of the principal jurisdiction must be made publicly

available in connection with the offering (or, if the offering is not being made contemporaneously in Canada, the reports or information that would be required to be made publicly available by the principal jurisdiction if the offering were made in Canada).

(3) In connection with an exchange offer, a copy of any agreement relating to the proposed acquisition.

(4) Copies of any documents incorporated by reference into the registration statement and any publicly available documents filed with the principal jurisdiction or any other Canadian regulatory authority concurrently with the prospectus.

(5) If any accountant, engineer or appraiser, or any person whose profession gives authority to a statement made by him, is named as having prepared or certified any part of the offering document, or is named as having prepared or certified a report or valuation for use in connection with the offering document, the manually signed, written consent of such person.

If any such person is named as having prepared or certified any other report or valuation (other than a public official document or statement) which is used in connection with the registration statement, but is not named as having prepared or certified such report or valuation for use in connection with the registration statement, the manually signed, written consent of such person, unless the Commission dispenses with such filing as impracticable or as involving undue hardship in accordance with Rule 437 under the Securities Act.

Any other consent required by Rule 436, 438 or 439 under the Securities Act. Every amendment relating to a certified financial statement shall include the manually signed, written consent of the certifying accountant to the use of his certificate in connection with the amended financial statements in the registration statement or prospectus and to being named as having certified such financial statements.

NOTE: The consents required by this item shall specifically indicate consent regarding the use of the report or valuation in the registration statement filed in the United States.

(6) If any name is signed to the registration statement or amendment pursuant to power of attorney, manually signed copies of such power of attorney and, if the name of any officer signing on behalf of the Registrant is signed pursuant to a power of attorney, certified copies of a resolution of the Registrant's board of directors or similar governing body authorizing such signature.

(7) A copy of any indenture relating to the registered securities.

(8) through (100) [Reserved]

(101) An Interactive Data File (§ 232.11 of this chapter) is:

(a) *Required to be submitted and posted.* Required to be submitted to the Commission and posted on the registrant's corporate Web site, if any, in the manner provided by Rule 405 of Regulation S-T (§ 232.405 of this chapter) if the Registrant does not prepare its financial statements in accordance with Article 6 of Regulation S-X (17 CFR 210.6-01 *et. seq.*) and is described in subparagraph (a)(i), (ii), or (iii) of this paragraph (101), except that an Interactive Data File: first is required for a periodic report on Form 10-Q (§ 249.308a of this chapter), Form 20-F (§ 249.220f of this chapter) or Form 40-F (§ 249.240f of this chapter), as applicable; and is required for a registration statement under the Securities Act only if the registration statement contains a price or price range:

(i) a large accelerated filer (§ 240.12b-2 of this chapter) that had an aggregate worldwide market value of the voting and non-voting common equity held by non-affiliates of more than $5 billion as of the last business day of the second fiscal quarter of its most recently completed fiscal year that prepares its financial statements in accordance with generally accepted accounting principles as used in the United States and the filing contains financial statements of the registrant for a fiscal period that ends on or after June 15, 2009;

(ii) A large accelerated filer not specified in subparagraph (a)(i) of this paragraph (101) that prepares its financial statements in accordance with generally accepted accounting principles as used in the United States and the filing contains financial statements of the registrant for a fiscal period that ends on or after June 15, 2010; or

(iii) A filer not specified in subparagraph (a)(i) or (a)(ii) of this paragraph (101) that prepares its financial statements in accordance with either generally accepted accounting principles as used in the United States or International Financial Reporting Standards as issued by the International Accounting Standards Board, and the filing contains financial statements of the registrant for a fiscal period that ends on or after June 15, 2011.

(b) *Permitted to be submitted.* Permitted to be submitted to the Commission in the manner provided by Rule 405 of Regulation S-T (§ 232.405 of this chapter) if the:

(i) Registrant prepares its financial statements:

(A) In accordance with either:

(*1*) Generally accepted accounting principles as used in the United States; or

(2) International Financial Reporting Standards as issued by the International Accounting Standards Board; and

(B) Not in accordance with Article 6 of Regulation S-X (17 CFR 210.6-01 *et. seq.*); and

(ii) Interactive Data File is not required to be submitted to the Commission under subparagraph (a) of this paragraph (101).

(c) *Not permitted to be submitted.* Not permitted to be submitted to the Commission if the registrant prepares its financial statements in accordance with Article 6 of Regulation S-X (17 CFR 210.6-01 *et. seq.*).

PART III—UNDERTAKING AND CONSENT TO SERVICE OF PROCESS

This Form shall set forth the following undertaking of the Registrant:

Item 1. Undertaking

The Registrant undertakes to make available, in person or by telephone, representatives to respond to inquiries made by the Commission staff, and to furnish promptly, when requested to do so by the Commission staff, information relating to the securities registered pursuant to Form F-9 or to transactions in said securities.

Item 2. Consent to Service of Process

(a) At the time of filing Form F-9, the Registrant shall file with the Commission a written irrevocable consent and power of attorney on Form F-X.

(b) At the time of filing Form F-9, any non-U.S. person acting as trustee with respect to the registered securities shall file with the Commission a written irrevocable consent and power of attorney on Form F-X.

(c) Any change to the name or address of the agent for service of the Registrant or the trustee shall be communicated promptly to the Commission by amendment to Form F-X referencing the file number of the relevant registration statement.

SIGNATURES

Pursuant to the requirements of the Securities Act, the Registrant certifies that it has reasonable grounds to believe that it meets all of the requirements for filing on Form F-9 and has duly caused this registration statement to be signed on its behalf by the undersigned, thereunto duly authorized, in the City of . . . ., Country of . . . ., on . . . . (date), ...

Registrant . . . .

By (Signature and Title) . . . .

Pursuant to the requirements of the Securities Act, this registration statement has been signed by the following persons in the capacities and on the dates indicated.

(Signature) . . . .

(Name and Title) . . . .

(Date) . . . .

Instructions

A. The registration statement shall be signed by the Registrant, its principal executive officer or officers, its principal financial officer, its controller or principal accounting officer, at least a majority of the board of directors or persons performing similar functions and its authorized representative in the United States. Where the Registrant is a limited partnership, the registration statement shall be signed by a majority of the board of directors of any corporate general partner signing the registration statement.

B. The name of each person who signs the registration statement shall be typed or printed beneath his signature. Any person who occupies more than one of the specified positions shall indicate each capacity in which he signs the registration statement.

C. By signing this Form, the Registrant consents without power of revocation that any administrative subpoena may be served, or any administrative proceeding, civil suit or civil action where the cause of action arises out of or relates to or concerns any offering made or purported to be made in connection with the securities registered pursuant to Form F-9 or any purchases or sales of any security in connection therewith, may be commenced against it in any administrative tribunal or in any appropriate court in any place subject to the jurisdiction of any state or of the United States or of the District of Columbia or Puerto Rico by service of said subpoena or process upon the Registrant's designated agent.

D. Where eligibility for use of this Form is based on the assignment of a security rating, the Registrant may sign the registration statement notwithstanding the fact that such security rating has not been assigned by the filing date, provided that the Registrant reasonably believes, and so states, that the security rating requirement will be met by the time of sale.

[¶ 7591]   FORM F-10

[As last amended in Release No. 33-9002, effective April 13, 2009, 74 F.R. 6776 and
corrected in Release No. 33-9002A, 74 F.R. 15666.]

U.S. Securities and Exchange Commission

Washington, D.C. 20549

Form F-10

REGISTRATION STATEMENT UNDER THE SECURITIES ACT OF 1933

U.S. Securities and Exchange Commission

Washington, D.C. 20549

Form F-10

REGISTRATION STATEMENT UNDER THE SECURITIES ACT OF 1933

. . . .
(Exact name of Registrant as specified in its charter)
. . . .
(Translation of Registrant's name into English (if applicable))
. . . .
(Province or other jurisdiction of incorporation or organization)
. . . .
(Primary Standard Industrial Classification Code Number (if applicable))
. . . .
(I.R.S. Employer Identification Number (if applicable))
. . . .
(Address and telephone number of Registrant's principal executive offices)
. . . .
(Name, address (including zip code) and telephone number (including area code) of
agent for service in the United States)

Approximate date of commencement of proposed sale of the securities to the public
. . . .
(Principal jurisdiction regulating this offering (if applicable))

It is proposed that this filing shall become effective (check appropriate box)

A. [] upon filing with the Commission, pursuant to Rule 467(a) (if in connection with an offering being made contemporaneously in the United States and Canada).

B. [] at some future date (check the appropriate box below)

1. [] pursuant to Rule 467(b) on (*date*) at (*time*) (designate a time not sooner than 7 calendar days after filing).

2. [] pursuant to Rule 467(b) on (*date*) at (*time*) (designate a time 7 calendar days or sooner after filing) because the securities regulatory authority in the review jurisdiction has issued a receipt or notification of clearance on (*date*).

3. [] pursuant to Rule 467(b) as soon as practicable after notification of the Commission by the Registrant or the Canadian securities regulatory authority of the review jurisdiction that a receipt or notification of clearance has been issued with respect hereto.

4. [] after the filing of the next amendment to this Form (if preliminary material is being filed).

If any of the securities being registered on this Form are to be offered on a delayed or continuous basis pursuant to the home jurisdiction's shelf prospectus offering procedures, check the following box. []

CALCULATION OF REGISTRATION FEE*

Title of each class of securities to be registered	Amount to be registered	Proposed maximum offering price per unit	Proposed maximum aggregate offering price	Amount of registration fee

* See General Instructions II.G.-II.I. for rules as to calculation of the registration fee.

If, as a result of stock splits, stock dividends or similar transactions, the number of securities purported to be registered on this registration statement changes, the provisions of Rule 416 shall apply to this registration statement.

If it is proposed that this filing become effective pursuant to Rule 467(b), the following legend shall appear on the cover page of this Form:

> "The Registrant hereby amends this registration statement on such date or dates as may be necessary to delay its effective date until the registration statement shall become effective as provided in Rule 467 under the Securities Act of 1933 or on such date as the Commission, acting pursuant to Section 8(a) of the Act, may determine."

GENERAL INSTRUCTIONS

I. General Eligibility Requirements for Use of Form F-10

A. Form F-10 may be used for the registration of securities under the Securities Act of 1933 (the "Securities Act"), including securities to be issued in an exchange offer or in connection with a statutory amalgamation, merger, arrangement or other reorganization requiring the vote of shareholders of the participating companies (a "business combination").

B. This form may not be used for registration of derivative securities except: (1) warrants, options and rights, provided that such securities and the underlying securities to which they relate are issued by the Registrant, its parent or an affiliate of either; and (2) convertible securities, provided that such securities are convertible only into securities of the Registrant, its parent or an affiliate of either.

Instruction For purposes of this Form, an "affiliate" of a person is anyone who beneficially owns, directly or indirectly, or exercises control or direction over, more than 10 percent of the outstanding equity shares of such person. The determination of a person's affiliates shall be made as of the end of such person's most recently completed fiscal year.

C. Form F-10 is available to any Registrant that:

(1) is incorporated or organized under the Laws of Canada or any Canadian province or territory;

(2) is a foreign private issuer;

(3) has been subject to the continuous disclosure requirements of any securities commission or equivalent regulatory authority in Canada for a period of at least 12 calendar months immediately preceding the filing of this form, and is currently in compliance with such obligations, *provided, however,* that in case of a business combination, each participating company other than the successor Registrant must meet such 12-month reporting obligation, except that any such participating company shall not be required to meet such reporting requirement if other participating companies whose assets and gross revenues, respectively, would contribute at least 80 percent of the total assets and gross revenues from continuing operations of the successor Registrant, as measured based on pro forma combination of the participating companies' most recently completed fiscal years, each meet such reporting requirement; and

(4) has an aggregate market value of the public float of its outstanding equity shares of $75 million or more; *provided however,* that in the case of a business combination, the aggregate market value of the public float of the outstanding equity shares of each participating company other than the successor Registrant is $75 million or more, except that any such participating company shall not be required to meet such public float requirement if other participating companies whose assets and gross revenues, respectively, would contribute at least 80 percent of the total assets and gross revenues from continuing operations of the successor Registrant, as measured based on pro forma combination of the participating companies' most recently completed fiscal years, each

meet such public float requirement; and *provided further,* that in the case of a business combination, such public float requirement shall be deemed satisfied in the case of a participating company whose equity shares were the subject of an exchange offer that was registered or would have been eligible for registration on Form F-8, Form F-9, Form F-10 or Form F-80, or a tender offer in connection with which Schedule 13E-4F or 14D-1F was filed or could have been filed, that terminated within the last twelve months, if the participating company would have satisfied such public float requirement immediately prior to commencement of such exchange or tender offer.

Instructions

1. For purposes of this Form, "foreign private issuer" shall be construed in accordance with Rule 405 under the Securities Act.

2. For purposes of this Form, the "public float" of specified securities shall mean only such securities held by persons other than affiliates of the issuer.

3. For purposes of this Form, "equity shares" shall mean common shares, non-voting equity shares and subordinate or restricted voting equity shares, but shall not include preferred shares.

4. For purposes of this Form, the market value of outstanding equity shares (whether or not held by affiliates) shall be computed by use of the price at which such shares were last sold, or the average of the bid and asked prices of such shares, in the principal market for such shares as of a date within 60 days prior to the date of filing. If there is no market for any of such securities, the book value of such securities computed as of the latest practicable date prior to the filing of this Form shall be used for purposes of calculating the market value, unless the issuer of such securities is in bankruptcy or receivership or has an accumulated capital deficit, in which case one-third of the principal amount, par value or stated value of such securities shall be used.

D. In the case of an exchange offer, the issuer of the securities to be exchanged (the "subject securities") for securities of the Registrant shall be incorporated or organized under the laws of Canada or any Canadian province or territory and be a foreign private issuer.

E. In the case of a business combination, each participating company shall be incorporated or organized under the laws of Canada or any Canadian province or territory and be a foreign private issuer.

F. In the case of an exchange offer, the securities to be registered on this form shall be offered to U.S. holders upon terms and conditions not less favorable than those offered to any other holder of the same class of subject securities.

G. In the case of a business combination, the securities to be registered on this Form shall be offered to U.S. holders upon terms and conditions not less favorable than those offered to any other holder of the same class of such securities of the participating company.

Instructions

1. For purposes of exchange offers, the term "U.S. holder" shall mean any person whose address appears on the records of the issuer of the subject securities, any voting trustee, any depositary, any share transfer agent or any person acting in a similar capacity on behalf of the issuer of the subject securities as being located in the United States.

2. For purposes of business combinations, the term "U.S. holder" shall mean any person whose address appears on the records of a participating company, any voting trustee, any depositary, any share transfer agent or any person acting in a similar capacity on behalf of a participating company as being located in the United States.

3. For purposes of this Form, the class of subject securities shall not include any securities that may be converted into or are exchangeable for the subject securities.

H. With respect to registration of debt securities or preferred securities on this Form, if the Registrant is a majority-owned subsidiary, it shall be deemed to meet the requirements of I.C. (3) and (4) above if the parent of the Registrant-subsidiary meets the requirements of I.C. above and fully and unconditionally guarantees the securities being registered as to principal and interest (if debt securities) or as to liquidation preference, redemption price and dividends (if preferred securities); *provided, however,* that the securities of the subsidiary are only convertible or exchangeable, if at all, for the securities of the parent.

I. If the Registrant is a successor Registrant subsisting after a business combination, it shall be deemed to meet the 12-month reporting reuirement of I.C.(3) above if: (1) the time the successor Registrant has been subject to the continuous disclosure requirements of any securities commission or equivalent regulatory authority in Canada, when added separately to the time each predecessor had been subject to such requirements at the time of the business combination, in each case equals at least 12 calendar months, *provided, however,* that any predecessor need not be considered for purposes of the reporting history calculation if the reporting histories of predecessors whose assets and gross revenues, respectively, would contribute at least 80 percent of the total assets and gross revenues from continuing operations of the successor Registrant, as measured based on pro forma combination of such participating companies' most recently completed fiscal years immediately prior to the business combination, when combined with the reporting history of the successor Registrant in each case satisfy such 12-month reporting requirement and (2) the successor Registrant has been subject to such continuous disclosure requirements since the business combination, and is currently in compliance with its obligations thereunder.

J. This Form shall not be used for registration of securities if no takeover bid circular or issuer bid circular (in the case of an exchange offer) or information circular (in the case of a business combination) or rights offering circular (in the case of exempt rights offerings) or prospectus (in all other cases) is prepared pursuant to the requirements of any Canadian jurisdiction due to the availability of an exemption from such requirements.

K. This form shall not be used if the Registrant or, in the case of an exchange offer, the issuer of the subject securities is an investment company registered or required to be registered under the Investment Company Act of 1940.

II. Application of General Rules and Regulations

A. A registration statement on this Form, and any amendment thereto, shall become effective in accordance with Rule 467 under the Securities Act.

B. The rules comprising Regulation C under the Securities Act shall not apply to filings on this Form unless specifically referred to in the Form. Instead, the rules and regulations applicable in the home jurisdiction regarding the Form and method of preparation of disclosure documents shall apply to filings on this Form. A registration statement or amendment thereto on this Form shall be deemed to be filed on the proper form unless objection to the Form is made by the Commission prior to the effective date. Securities Act rules and regulations other than Regulation C shall apply to filings on this Form unless specifically excluded in this Form.

C. Rule 408 under the Securities Act, which provides that in addition to the information expressly required to be included in the registration statement, there shall be added such further material information, if any, as may be necessary to make the required statements, in light of the circumstances under which they are made, not misleading, shall apply to filings on this Form.

D. A registrant must file the registration statement in electronic format via the Commission's Electronic Data Gathering, Analysis, and Retrieval (EDGAR) system in accordance with the EDGAR rules set forth in Regulation S-T (17 CFR Part 232). For assistance with technical questions about EDGAR or to request an access code, call

the EDGAR Filer Support Office at (202) 551-8900. For assistance with the EDGAR rules, call the Office of EDGAR and Information Analysis at (202) 551-3610.

If filing the registration statement in paper under a hardship exemption in Rule 201 or 202 of Regulation S-T (17 CFR 232.201 or 232.202), or as otherwise permitted, a registrant must file with the Commission at its principal office five copies of the complete registration statement and any amendments, including exhibits and all other documents filed as a part of the registration statement or amendment. The registrant must bind, staple or otherwise compile each copy in one or more parts without stiff covers. The registrant must further bind the registration statement or amendment on the side or stitching margin in a manner that leaves the reading matter legible. The registrant must provide three additional copies of the registration statement or amendment without exhibits to the Commission.

E. Any amendment to a registration statement on this Form shall be filed under cover of an appropriate facing sheet, shall be numbered consecutively in the order in which filed, and shall indicate on the facing sheet the applicable registration form on which the amendment is prepared and the file number of the registration statement.

If, however, an amendment to the home jurisdiction document(s) is filed after effectiveness of this registration statement that increases the number of securities that may be sold, in lieu of filing a post-effective amendment hereto, a new registration statement shall be filed on this Form. As provided in Rule 429, the prospectus included in the new registration statement shall be deemed to include a prospectus covering unsold securities registered previously. If this is the case, the following legend shall appear at the bottom of the facing page of the registration statement: "Pursuant to Rule 429 under the Securities Act, the prospectus contained in this registration statement relates to registration statement[s] 33-[insert file numbers of previous registration statements]."

F. An electronic filer must provide the signatures required for the registration statement or amendment in accordance with Regulation S-T Rule 302 (17 CFR 232.302). A registrant filing in paper must have at least one copy of the registration statement or amendment signed in accordance with Securities Act Rule 402(e) (17 CFR 230.402(e)) by the persons whose signatures are required for this registration statement. A registrant must also conform the unsigned copies.

G. At the time of filing this registration statement, the Registrant shall pay to the Commission in accordance with Rule 111 under the Securities Act a fee in U.S. dollars in the amount prescribed by Section 6 of the Securities Act. The amount of securities to be registered on this Form need not exceed the amount to be offered in the United States as part of the offering.

H. In the case of an exchange offer, the registration fee is to be calculated as follows:

(1) Upon the basis of the market value of the securities that may be received by the Registrant or cancelled in the exchange offer from United States residents as established by the price of securities of the same class, as determined in accordance with paragraph (4) of this section.

(2) If there is no market for the securities to be received by the Registrant or cancelled in the exchange offer, the book value of such securities computed as of the latest practicable date prior to the date of filing the registration statement shall be used, unless the issuer of such securities is in bankruptcy or receivership or has an accumulated capital deficit, in which case one-third of the principal amount, par value or stated value of such securities shall be used.

(3) If any cash may be received by the Registrant from United States residents in connection with the exchange offer, the amount thereof shall be added to the value of the securities to be received by the Registrant or cancelled as computed in accordance with paragraph (1) or (2) of this section. If any cash is to be paid by the Registrant in connection with the exchange offer, the amount thereof shall be deducted from the value of the securities to be received by the Registrant in exchange as computed in accordance with paragraph (1) or (2) of this section.

(4) For purposes of the registration fee, the market value of the securities received or cancelled shall be the average of the high and low prices reported or the average of the bid and asked prices of such stock, in the principal market for such stock as of a date within 30 days prior to the date of filing.

I. In the case of a business combination, the registration fee is to be calculated as follows:

(1) Upon the basis of the market value of the equity securities of the predecessor companies held by United States residents being offered the Registrant's securities, as established by the price of the predecessors' securities of the same class determined in accordance with paragraph (4) of this section.

(2) If there is no market for the securities of the predecessor companies, the book value of such securities computed as of the latest practicable date prior to the date of filing the registration statement shall be used, unless the issuer of such securities is in bankruptcy or receivership or has an accumulated capital deficit, in which case one-third of the principal amount, par value or stated value of such securities shall be used.

(3) If any cash may be received by the Registrant from United States residents in connection with the business combination, the amount thereof shall be added to the value of the securities as computed in accordance with paragraph (1) or (2) of this section. If any cash is to be paid by the Registrant in connection with the business combination, the amount thereof shall be deducted from the value of the securities as computed in accordance with paragraph (1) or (2) of this section.

(4) For purposes of the registration fee, the market value of a predecessor's equity securities shall be the average of the high and low prices reported or the average of the bid and asked prices of such securities, in the principal market for such securities as of a date within 30 days prior to the date of filing.

J. A registrant must file the registration statement or amendment in electronic format in the English language in accordance with Regulation S-T Rule 306 (17 CFR 232.306). A registrant may file part of the prospectus or exhibit or other attachment to the registration statement or amendment in both French and English if it included the French text to comply with the requirements of the Canadian securities administrator or other Canadian authority and, for an electronic filing, if the filing is an HTML document, as defined in Regulation S-T Rule 11 (17 CFR 232.11). For both an electronic filing and a paper filing, a registrant may provide an English translation or English summary of a foreign language document as an exhibit or other attachment to the registration statement or amendment as permitted by the rules of the applicable Canadian securities administrator.

K. A paper filer must number sequentially one signed original of the registration statement or amendment (in addition to any internal numbering that otherwise may be present) by handwritten, typed, printed or other legible form of notation from the first page through the last page of the registration statement or amendment, including any exhibits or attachments. A paper filer must disclose the total number of pages on the first page of the sequentially numbered registration statement or amendment.

L. Where the offering registered on this Form is being made pursuant to the home jurisdiction's shelf prospectus offering procedures or procedures for pricing offerings after the final receipt has been issued, three copies of each supplement to, or supplemented version of, the home jursidiction disclosure document(s) prepared under such procedures shall be filed with the Commission within one business day after such supplement or supplemented version is filed with the principal jurisdiction. Such filings shall be deemed not to constitute amendments to this registration statement. Each such filing shall contain in the upper right hand corner of the cover page the following legend, which may be set forth in longhand if legible: "Filed pursuant to General Instruction II.L. of Form F-10; File No. 33- [insert number of the registration statement]."

Note: Offerings registered on this Form, whether or not made contemporaneously in Canada, may be made pursuant to National Policy Statement No. 44 shelf prospectus offering procedures and procedures for pricing offerings after the final receipt has been issued. Rules 415 and 430A under the Securities Act are not available for offerings registered on this Form.

M. If the offering to be registered on this Form is not being made contemporaneously in Canada, the registration statement on this Form and any amendments hereto shall be prepared and filed as if the offering were being made contemporaneously in Canada. The Commission has been advised that the principal jurisdiction in Canada designated by the Registrant in connection with such an offering will require the filing of such documents and may select them for review.

III. Compliance with Exchange Act and Auditor Independence and Reporting Requirements

A. Pursuant to Rule 15d-4 under the Securities Exchange Act of 1934 (the "Exchange Act"), reporting obligations under section 15(d) of the Exchange Act (and the requirements of Regulation 15D thereunder) arising solely from an offering of securities registered on this Form may be met by filing with the Commission, under cover of Forms 40-F and 6-K, certain home jurisdiction documents. Registrants' attention is directed, however, towards other provisions of the Exchange Act that may be applicable, and specifically to the provisions of Sections 12(b) and 12(g) and Regulation M (17 CFR 242.100 through 242.105).

B. The Commission's rules on auditor independence, as codified in Section 600 of the Codification of Financial Reporting Policies, apply to auditor reports on all financial statements that are included in this registration statement, except that such rules do not apply with respect to periods prior to the most recent fiscal year for which

financial statements are included in the registration statement under the Securities Act filed by the issuer on Form F-8, Form F-9, Form F-10 or Form F-80 or under the Exchange Act filed by the issuer on Form 40-F. Notwithstanding the exception in the previous sentence, such rules do apply with respect to any periods prior to the most recent fiscal year if the issuer previously was required to file with the Commission a report or registration statement containing an audit report on financial statements for such prior periods as to which the Commission's rules on auditor independence applied.

C. Independent accountants reporting on financial statements included in the registration statement should consider Canadian auditing guidelines pertaining to the Canada-U.S. reporting conflict with respect to contingencies and going concern considerations. If additional comments for U.S. readers are appropriate under those guidelines but are not included in the prospectus itself, those comments should be included with the Legends required by Item 3 of Part I hereof. In addition, the accountant's consent specifically should refer to any additional comments provided for U.S. readers.

D. Pursuant to Rule 13e-4(g) under the Exchange Act, the provisions of Rule 13e-4 are not applicable and pursuant to Rule 14d-1(b) under the Exchange Act, the provisions of Sections 14(d)(1) through 14(d)(7) of the Exchange Act, Regulation 14D under the Exchange Act and Schedule TO thereunder, and Rule 14e-1 under Regulation 14E, are not applicable to a transaction involving offerings of securities that may be registered on this Form in connection with exchange offers; *provided that,* if an exemption has been granted from the requirements of Canadian federal, provincial and/or territorial laws, regulations or policies, and the tender offer does not comply with requirements that otherwise would be required by Commission tender offer rules, the Registrant shall comply with such provisions of the Exchange Act. Such transaction is not exempt from the antifraud provisions of Section 10(b), 13(e) and 14(e) of the Exchange Act or Rule 10b-5, 13e-4(b)(1) or 14e-3 thereunder, if the transaction otherwise is subject to those sections.

PART I—INFORMATION REQUIRED TO BE DELIVERED TO OFFEREES OR PURCHASERS

Item 1. Home Jurisdiction Document

In the case of a business combination, the prospectus shall consist of the entire disclosure document or documents used to solicit votes of security holders in connection with the proposed business combination in any Canadian jurisdiction. Except as noted hereinafter, such disclosure document(s) shall be prepared in accordance with

the disclosure requirements of such jurisdiction(s) as interpreted and applied by the securities commission(s) or other regulatory authorities in such jurisdiction(s).

In the case of an exchange offer, the prospectus shall consist of the entire disclosure document or documents used to offer securities in any Canadian jurisdiction. Except as noted hereinafter, such disclosure documents shall be prepared in accordance with the disclosure requirements of such jurisdiction(s) as interpreted and applied by the securities commission(s) or other regulatory authorities in such jurisdiction(s).

In all other cases, the prospectus shall consist of the entire disclosure document or documents used to offer the securities of the Registrant in the principal jurisdiction (or, if the offering is not being made contemporaneously in Canada, as if the offering were made in such jurisdiction). Except as noted hereinafter, such disclosure document(s) shall be prepared in accordance with the disclosure requirements of such jurisdiction as interpreted and applied by the securities commission or other regulatory authority in such jurisdiction.

The prospectus used in the United States shall contain additional information and Legends required by this Form. It need not include any documents incorporated by reference into disclosure document(s) used in Canada and not required to be delivered to offerees or purchasers (in the case of an exchange offer) or to securityholders being solicited (in the case of a business combination) pursuant to Canadian Law or to offerees or purchasers (in all other cases) pursuant to the laws of the principal jurisdiction.

Notwithstanding the foregoing, such prospectus used in the United States need not contain any disclosure applicable solely to Canadian offerees or purchasers that would not be material to offerees or purchasers in the United States, including, without limitation, (i) any Canadian "red herring" legend; (ii) any discussion of Canadian tax considerations other than those material to U.S. offerees or purchasers; (iii) the names of any Canadian underwriters not acting as underwriters in the United States or a description of the Canadian plan of distribution (except to the extent necessary to describe the material facts of the U.S. plan of distribution); (iv) any description of offerees' or purchasers' statutory rights under applicable Canadian, provincial or territorial securities legislation (except to the extent such rights are available to U.S. offerees or purchasers); or (v) certificates of the issuer or any underwriter.

Item 2. Additional Information

The following information also shall be provided to offerees as part of the prospectus.

Financial Statements.

Any financial statements included in the home jurisdiction document must be reconciled to U.S. GAAP as required by Item 18 of Form 20-F under the Exchange Act.

Item 3. Informational Legends

The following legends, to the extent applicable, shall appear on the outside front cover page of the prospectus (or on a sticker thereto) in bold-face roman type at least as high as ten-point modern type and at least two points leaded:

"This offering is made by a foreign issuer that is permitted, under a multijurisdictional disclosure system adopted by the United States, to prepare this prospectus in accordance with the disclosure requirements of its home country. Prospective investors should be aware that such requirements are different from those of the United States. Financial statements included or incorporated herein, if any, have been prepared in accordance with foreign generally accepted accounting principles, and may be subject to foreign auditing and auditor independence standards, and thus may not be comparable to financial statements of United States companies."

"Prospective investors should be aware that the acquisition of the securities described herein may have tax consequences both in the United States and in the home country of the Registrant. Such consequences for investors who are resident in, or citizens of, the United States may not be described fully herein."

"The enforcement by investors of civil liabilities under the federal securities Laws may be affected adversely by the fact that the Registrant is incorporated or organized under the laws of a foreign country, that some or all of its officers and directors may be residents of a foreign country, that some or all of the underwriters or experts named in the registration statement may be residents of a foreign country, and that all or a substantial portion of the assets of the Registrant and said persons may be located outside the United States."

"THESE SECURITIES HAVE NOT BEEN APPROVED OR DISAPPROVED BY THE SECURITIES AND EXCHANGE COMMISSION NOR HAS THE COMMISSION PASSED THE ACCURACY OR ADEQUACY OF THIS PROSPECTUS. ANY REPRESENTATION TO THE CONTRARY IS A CRIMINAL OFFENSE."

The following legend shall appear in the manner noted above in any prospectus relating to an exchange offer.

"Prospective investors should be aware that, during the period of the exchange offer, the Registrant or its affiliates, directly or indirectly, may bid for or make purchases of the securities to be distributed or to be exchanged, or certain related securities, as permitted by applicable laws or regulations of Canada or its provinces or territories."

Any prospectus to be used before the effective date of the registration statement shall contain, on the outside front cover page (or on a sticker thereto) the following statement printed in red ink in type as large as that generally used in the body of the prospectus:

"Information contained herein is subject to completion or amendment. A registration statement relating to these securities has been filed with the Securities and Exchange Commission. These securities may not be sold nor may offers to buy be accepted prior to the time the registration statement becomes effective. This prospectus shall not constitute an offer to sell or the solicitation of an offer to buy nor shall there be any sale of these securities in any State in which such offer, solicitation or sale would be unlawful prior to registration or qualification under the securities laws of any such State."

The Registrant should also include in the prospectus any legend or information required by the laws of any jurisdiction in which the securities are to be offered.

Note to Item 3. If the home-jurisdiction document(s) are delivered through an electronic medium, the issuer may satisfy the legibility requirements for the required legends relating to type size and font by presenting the legends in any manner reasonably calculated to draw investor attention to it.

Item 4. Incorporation of Certain Information by Reference

Information called for by this Form, including exhibits, may be incorporated by reference at the Registrant's option from documents that the Registrant has filed previously with the Commission pursuant to Section 13(a) or 15(d) of the Exchange Act or submitted to the Commission pursuant to Rule 12g3-2(b) under the Exchange Act. Any such incorporation by reference shall be done in accordance with Item 10(d) of Regulation S-K. If any information is incorporated by reference into the prospectus, the prospectus shall provide the name, address and telephone number of an officer of the Registrant from whom copies of such information may be obtained upon request without charge.

Item 5. List of Documents Filed with the Commission

There shall be set forth in or attached to the prospectus a list of all documents filed with the Commission as part of the registration statement.

PART II—INFORMATION NOT REQUIRED TO BE DELIVERED TO OFFEREES OR PURCHASERS

Provide a brief description of the indemnification provisions relating to directors, officers and controlling persons of the Registrant against liability arising under the Securities Act (including any provision of the underwriting agreement which relates to indemnification of the underwriter or its controlling persons by the Registrant against such liabilities where a director, officer or controlling person of the Registrant is such an underwriter or controlling person thereof or a member of any firm which is such an underwriter), together with a statement in substantially the following form:

Insofar as indemnification for liabilities arising under the Securities Act of 1933 may be permitted to directors, officers or persons controlling the Registrant pursuant to the foregoing provisions, the Registrant has been informed that in the opinion of the U.S. Securities and Exchange Commission such indemnification is against public policy as expressed in the Act and is therefore unenforceable.

The exhibits specified below shall be filed as part of the registration statement. Exhibits shall

be appropriately lettered or numbered for convenient reference.

(1) In the case of an exchange offer or business combination, any reports or information that, in accordance with the requirements of the jurisdiction of incorporation or organization of the subject issuer or, in the case of a business combination, in accordance with the requirements of the jurisdiction(s) of incorporation or organization of companies involved in the transaction other than the Registrant, must be made publicly available by the Registrant in connection with the transaction.

(2) In the case of an exchange offer or a business combination, a copy of any agreement relating to the proposed acquisition or business combination, as applicable.

(3) In all other cases, any reports or information that in accordance with the requirements of the principal jurisdiction must be made publicly available in connection with the offering (or, if the offering is not being made contemporaneously in Canada, the reports or information that would be required to be made publicly available by the prin-

cipal jurisdiction if the offering were made in Canada).

(4) Copies of any documents incorporated by reference into the registration statement and any publicly available documents filed with the principal jurisdiction or any other Canadian regulatory authority concurrently with the prospectus.

(5) If any accountant, engineer or appraiser, or any person whose profession gives authority to a statement made by him, is named as having prepared or certified any part of the offering document, or is named as having prepared or certified a report or valuation for use in connection with the offering document, the manually signed, written consent of such person.

If any such person is named as having prepared or certified any other report or valuation (other than a public official document or statement) which is used in connection with the registration statement, but is not named as having prepared or certified such report or valuation for use in connection with the registration statement, the manually signed, written consent of such person, unless the Commission dispenses with such filing as impracticable or as involving undue hardship in accordance with Rule 437 under the Securities Act.

Any other consent required by Rule 436, 438 or 439 under the Securities Act. Every amendment relating to a certified financial statement shall include the manually signed, written consent of the certifying accountant to the use of his certificate in connection with the amended financial statements in the registration statement or prospectus and to being named as having certified such financial statements.

NOTE: The consents required by this item shall specifically indicate consent regarding use of the report or valuation in the registration statement filed in the United States.

(6) If any name is signed to the registration statement or amendment pursuant to power of attorney, manually signed copies of such power of attorney and, if the name of any officer signing on behalf of the Registrant is signed pursuant to a power of attorney, certified copies of a resolution of the Registrant's board of directors or similar governing body authorizing such signature.

(7) A copy of any indenture relating to the registered securities.

(8) through (100) [Reserved]

(101) An Interactive Data File (§ 232.11 of this chapter) is:

(a) *Required to be submitted and posted.* Required to be submitted to the Commission and posted on the registrant's corporate Web site, if any, in the manner provided by Rule 405 of Regulation S-T (§ 232.405 of this chapter) if the Registrant does not prepare its financial statements in accordance with Article 6 of Regulation S-X (17 CFR 210.6-01 *et. seq.*) and is described in subparagraph (a)(i), (ii), or (iii) of this paragraph (101), except that an Interactive Data File first is required for a periodic report on Form 10-Q (§ 249.308a of this chapter), Form 20-F (§ 249.220f of this chapter) or Form 40-F (§ 249.240f of this chapter), as applicable; and is required for a registration statement under the Securities Act only if the registration statement contains a price or price range:

(i) a large accelerated filer (§ 240.12b-2 of this chapter) that had an aggregate worldwide market value of the voting and non-voting common equity held by non-affiliates of more than $5 billion as of the last business day of the second fiscal quarter of its most recently completed fiscal year that prepares its financial statements in accordance with generally accepted accounting principles as used in the United States and the filing contains financial statements of the registrant for a fiscal period that ends on or after June 15, 2009;

(ii) A large accelerated filer not specified in subparagraph (a)(i) of this paragraph (101) that prepares its financial statements in accordance with generally accepted accounting principles as used in the United States and the filing contains financial statements of the registrant for a fiscal period that ends on or after June 15, 2010; or

(iii) A filer not specified in subparagraph (a)(i) or (a)(ii) of this paragraph (101) that prepares its financial statements in accordance with either generally accepted accounting principles as used in the United States or International Financial Reporting Standards as issued by the International Accounting Standards Board, and the filing contains financial statements of the registrant for a fiscal period that ends on or after June 15, 2011.

(b) *Permitted to be submitted.* Permitted to be submitted to the Commission in the manner provided by Rule 405 of Regulation S-T (§ 232.405 of this chapter) if the:

(i) Registrant prepares its financial statements:

(A) In accordance with either:

(*1*) Generally accepted accounting principles as used in the United States; or

(*2*) International Financial Reporting Standards as issued by the International Accounting Standards Board; and

(B) Not in accordance with Article 6 of Regulation S-X (17 CFR 210.6-01 *et. seq.*); and

(ii) Interactive Data File is not required to be submitted to the Commission under subparagraph (a) of this paragraph (101).

(c) *Not permitted to be* submitted. Not permitted to be submitted to the Commission if the registrant prepares its financial statements in accordance with Article 6 of Regulation S-X (17 CFR 210.6-01 *et. seq.*).

PART III—UNDERTAKING AND CONSENT TO SERVICE OF PROCESS

Item 1. Undertaking

This Form shall set forth the following undertaking of the Registrant:

The Registrant undertakes to make available, in person or by telephone, representatives to respond to inquiries made by the Commission staff, and to furnish promptly, when requested to do so by the Commission staff, information relating to the securities registered pursuant to Form F-10 or to transactions in said securities.

Item 2. Consent to Service of Process

(a) At the time of filing Form F-10, the Registrant shall file with the Commission a written irrevocable consent and power of attorney on Form F-X.

(b) At the time of filing Form F-10, any non-U.S. person acting as trustee with respect to the registered securities shall file with the Commission a written irrevocable consent and power of attorney on Form F-X.

(c) Any change to the name or address of the agent for service of the Registrant or the trustee shall be communicated promptly to the Commission by amendment to Form F-X referencing the file number of the relevant registration statement.

SIGNATURES

Pursuant to the requirements of the Securities Act, the Registrant certifies that it has reasonable grounds to believe that it meets all of the requirements for filing on Form F-10 and has duly caused this registration statement to be signed on its behalf by the undersigned, thereunto duly authorized, in the City of . . . ., Country of . . . ., on . . . . (date), ...

Registrant . . . .

By (Signature and Title) . . . .

Pursuant to the requirements of the Securities Act, this registration statement has been signed by the following persons in the capacities and on the dates indicated.

(Signature) . . . .

(Name and Title) . . . .

(Date) . . . .

Instructions

A. The registration statement shall be signed by the Registrant, its principal executive officer or officers, its principal financial officer, its controller or principal accounting officer, at least a majority of the board of directors or persons performing similar functions and its authorized representative in the United States. Where the Registrant is a limited partnership, the registration statement shall be signed by a majority of the board of directors of any corporate general partner signing the registration statement.

B. The name of each person who signs the registration statement shall be typed or printed beneath his signature. Any person who occupies more than one of the specified positions shall indicate each capacity in which the registration statement is signed.

C. If the securities to be offered are those of a corporation not yet in existence at the time the registration statement is filed and which will be a party to a consolidation involving two or more existing corporations, then each such existing corporation shall be deemed a Registrant and shall be designated on the cover page of this Form, and the registration statement shall be signed by each such existing corporation and by the officers and directors of each such existing corporation as if each such existing corporation were the sole Registrant.

D. By signing this Form, the Registrant consents without power of revocation that any administrative subpoena may be served, or any administrative proceeding, civil suit or civil action where the cause of action arises out of or relates to or concerns any offering made or purported to be made in connection with the securities registered pursuant to Form F-10 or any purchases or sales of any security in connection therewith, may be commenced against it in any administrative tribunal or in any appropriate court in any place subject to the jurisdiction of any state or of the United States of the District of Columbia or Puerto Rico by service of said subpoena or process upon the Registrant's designated agent.

[¶ 7751] FORM F-80

[As last amended in Release No. 34-55146A, effective April 1, 2008, 73 F.R.17809 (technical correction).]

U.S. Securities and Exchange Commission

Washington, D.C. 20549

Form F-80

REGISTRATION STATEMENT UNDER THE SECURITIES ACT OF 1933

. . . .

(Exact name of Registrant as specified in its charter)

. . . .

(Translation of Registrant's name into English (if applicable))

. . . .

(Province or other jurisdiction of incorporation or organization)

. . . .

(Primary Standard Industrial Classification Code Number (if applicable))

. . . .

(I.R.S. Employer Identification Number (if applicable))

. . . .

(Address and telephone number of Registrant's principal executive offices)

. . . .

(Name, address (including zip code) and telephone number (including area code) of agent for service in the United States)

Approximate date of commencement or proposed sale of the securities to the public ____

This registration statement and any amendment thereto shall become effective upon filing with the Commission in accordance with Rule 467(a).

If any of the securities being registered on this Form are to be offered on a delayed or continuous basis pursuant to the home jurisdiction's shelf prospectus offering procedures, check the following box. []

CALCULATION OF REGISTRATION FEE*

Title of each class of securities to be registered	Amount to be registered	Proposed maximum offering price per unit	Proposed maximum aggregate offering price	Amount of registration fee

* See General Instructions IV.F.-IV.H. for rules as to calculation of the registration fee.

If, as a result of stock splits, stock dividends or similar transactions, the number of securities purported to be registered on this registration statement changes, the provisions of Rule 416 shall apply to this registration statement.

GENERAL INSTRUCTIONS

I. General Eligibility Requirements for Use of Form F-80

A. Form F-80 may be used for registration under the Securities Act of 1933 ("Securities Act") of securities to be issued in an exchange offer or in connection with a statutory amalgamation, merger, arrangement or other reorganization requiring the vote of shareholders of the participating companies (a "business combination"). Securities may be registered on this Form whether they constitute the sole consideration for such exchange offer or business combination, or are offered in conjunction with cash.

B. This Form shall not be used for registration of securities if no takeover bid circular or issuer bid circular (in the case of an exchange offer) or information circular (in the case of a business combination) is prepared pursuant to the requirements of any Canadian jurisdiction due to the availability of an exemption from such requirements.

C. This Form may not be used for registration of derivative securities except:

(1) warrants, options and rights, provided that such securities and the underlying securities to which they relate are issued by the Registrant, its parent or an affiliate of either; and

(2) convertible securities, provided that such securities are convertible only into securities of the Registrant, its parent or an affiliate of either.

Instruction For purposes of this Form, an "affiliate" of a person is anyone who beneficially owns, directly or indirectly, or exercises control or direction over, more than 10 percent of the outstanding equity shares of such person. The determination of a person's affiliates shall be made as of the end of such person's most recently completed fiscal year.

D. This Form shall not be used if the Registrant or, in the case of an exchange offer, the issuer of the securities to be exchanged (the "subject securities") for securities of the Registrant is an investment company registered or required to be registered under the Investment Company Act of 1940.

II. Eligibility Requirements for Exchange Offers

A. In the case of an exchange offer, Form F-80 is available to any Registrant that:

(1) is incorporated or organized under the laws of Canada or any Canadian province or territory;

(2) is a foreign private issuer;

(3) has had a class of its securities listed on The Montreal Exchange, The Toronto Stock Exchange or the Senior Board of the Vancouver Stock Exchange for the 12 calendar months immediately preceding the filing of this Form, has been subject to the continuous disclosure requirements of any securities commission or equivalent regulatory authority in Canada for a period of at least 36 calendar months immediately preceding the filing of this Form, and is currently in compliance with obligations arising from such listing and reporting; and

(4) has an aggregate market value of the public float of its outstanding equity shares of (CN) $75 million or more; *provided, however*, that such public float requirement need not be satis-

fied if the issuer of the securities to be exchanged is also the Registrant on this Form.

Instructions

1. For purposes of this Form, "foreign private issuer" shall be construed in accordance with Rule 405 under the Securities Act.

2. For purposes of this Form, "equity shares" shall mean common shares, non-voting equity shares and subordinate or restricted voting equity shares, but shall not include preferred shares.

3. For purposes of this Form, the "public float" of specified securities shall mean only such securities held by persons other than affiliates of the issuer.

4. For the purposes of this Form, the market value of the public float of outstanding equity shares shall be computed by use of the price at which such shares were last sold, or the average of the bid and asked prices of such shares, in the principal market for such shares as of a date within 60 days prior to the date of filing. If there is no market for any of such securities, the book value of such securities computed as of the latest practicable date prior to the filing of this Form shall be used for purposes of calculating the market value, unless the issuer of such securities is in bankruptcy or receivership or has an accumulated capital deficit, in which case one-third of the principal amount, par value or stated value of such securities shall be used.

B. In the case of an exchange offer, the securities to be registered on this Form shall be offered to U.S. holders upon terms and conditions not less favorable than those offered to any other holder of the same class of subject securities.

C. In the case of an exchange offer, if the Registrant is a successor Registrant subsisting after a business combination, the Registrant shall be deemed to meet the 36-month reporting requirement and the 12-month listing requirement of II.A.(3) above if: (1) the time the successor registrant has been subject to the continuous disclosure requirements of any securities commission or equivalent regulatory authority in Canada, when added separately to the time each predecessor had been subject to such requirements at the time of the business combination, in each case equals at least 36 calendar months, *provided, however,* that any predecessor need not be considered for purposes of the reporting history calculation if the reporting histories of predecessors whose assets and gross revenues, respectively, would contribute at least 80 percent of the total assets and gross revenues from continuing operations of the successor Registrant, as measured based on pro forma combination of such participating companies' most recently completed fiscal years immediately prior to the business combination, when combined with the reporting history of the successor Registrant in each case satisfy such 36-month reporting requirement; (2) the time the successor registrant has been subject to the listing requirements of the specified exchanges, when added separately to the time each predecessor had been subject to such requirements at the time of the business combination, in each case equals at least 12 calendar months, *provided, however,* that any predecessor need not be considered for purposes of the listing history calculation if the listing histories of predecessors whose assets and gross revenues, respectively, would contribute at least 80 percent of the total assets and gross revenues from continuing operations of the successor Registrant, as measured based on pro forma combination of such participating companies' most recently compl eted fiscal years immediately prior to the business combination, when combined with the listing history of the successor Registrant in each case satisfy such 12-month listing requirement; and (3) the successor Registrant has been subject to such continuous disclosure requirements and listing requirements since the business combination, and is currently in compliance with its obligations thereunder.

D. In the case of an exchange offer, the issuer of the subject securities shall be incorporated or organized under the laws of Canada or any Canadian province or territory and be a foreign private issuer, and less than 40 percent of the class of subject securities outstanding shall be held by U.S. holders.

Instructions

1. For purposes of exchange offers, the term "U.S. holder" shall mean any person whose address appears on the records of the issuer of the subject securities, any voting trustee, any depositary, any share transfer agent or any person acting in a similar capacity on behalf of the issuer of the subject securities as being located in the United States.

2. With respect to any tender offer, including any exchange offer, otherwise eligible to proceed in accordance with Rule 14d-1(b) under the Securities Exchange Act of 1934 (the "Exchange Act"), the issuer of the subject securities will be presumed to be a foreign private issuer and U.S. holders will be presumed to hold less than 40 percent of such outstanding securities, *unless* (a) the aggregate trading volume of that class on national securities exchanges in the United States and on NASDAQ exceeded its aggregate trading volume on securities exchanges in Canada and on the Canadian Dealing Network, Inc. ("CDN") over the 12 calendar month period prior to commencement of this offer, or if commenced in response to a prior offer, over the 12 calendar month period prior to commencement of the initial offer (based on volume figures published by such exchanges, NASDAQ and CDN); (b) the most recent annual report or annual information form filed or submitted by the issuer with securities regulators of Ontario, Quebec, British Columbia or Alberta (or, if the issuer of the subject securities is not a reporting issuer in any of such provinces, with any other Canadian securities regulator) or with the Commission indicates that U.S. holders hold 40 percent or more of the outstanding subject class of securities; or (c) the offeror has actual knowledge that the level of U.S. ownership equals or exceeds 40 percent of such securities.

3. For purposes of this Form, if this Form is filed during the pendency of one or more ongoing cash tender or exchange offers for securities of the class subject to the offer that was commenced or was eligible to be commenced on Schedule 13D-4F, Schedule 14D-1F, and/or Form F-8 or Form F-80, the date for calculation of U.S. ownership shall be the same as that date used by the initial bidder or issuer.

4. For purposes of this Form, the class of subject securities shall not include any securities that may be converted into or are exchangeable for the subject securities.

5. For purposes of exchange offers, the calculation of U.S. holders shall be made as of the end of the subject issuer's last quarter or, if such quarter terminated within 60 days of the filing date, as of the end of such issuer's preceding quarter.

III. Eligibility Requirements for Business Combinations

A. In the case of a business combination, Form F-80 is available if:

(1) each company participating in the business combination, including the successor Registrant, is incorporated or organized under the laws of Canada or any Canadian province or territory and is a foreign private issuer;

(2) each company participating in the business combination other than the successor Registrant has had a class of its securities listed on The Montreal Exchange, The Toronto Stock Exchange or the Senior Board of the Vancouver Stock Exchange for the 12 calendar months immediately preceding the filing of this Form, has been subject to the continuous disclosure requirements of any securities commission or equivalent regulatory authority in Canada for a period of at least 36 calendar months immediately preceding the filing of this Form, and is currently in compliance with obligations arising from such listing and reporting; *provided, however*, that any such participating company shall not be required to meet such 36-month reporting requirement or 12-month listing requirement if other participating companies whose assets and gross revenues, respectively, would contribute at least 80 percent of the total assets and gross revenues from continuing opera-

tions of the successor Registrant, as measured based on pro forma combination of the participating companies' most recently completed fiscal years, each meet such reporting and listing requirements; and

(3) the aggregate market value of the public float of the outstanding equity shares of each company participating in the business combination other than the successor Registrant is (CN) $75 million or more; *provided, however,* that any such participating company shall not be required to meet such public float requirement if other participating companies whose assets and gross revenues, respectively, would contribute at least 80 percent of the total assets and gross revenues from continuing operations of the successor Registrant, as measured based on pro forma combination of the participating companies' most recently completed fiscal years, each meet such public float requirement; and, *provided further,* that such public float requirement shall be deemed satisfied in the case of a participating company whose equity shares were the subject of an exchange offer that was registered or would have been eligible for registration on Form F-8, Form F-9, Form F-10 or Form F-80, or a tender offer in connection with which Schedule 13E-4F or 14D-1F was filed or could have been filed, that terminated within the last 12 months, if the participating company would have satisfied such public float requirement immediately prior to commencement of such exchange or tender offer.

B. In the case of a business combination, less than 40 percent of the class of securities to be offered by the successor Registrant shall be held by U.S. holders, as if measured immediately after completion of business combination.

Instructions

1. For purposes of business combinations, the term "U.S. holder" shall mean any person whose address appears on the records of a participating company, any voting trustee, any depositary, any share transfer agent or any person acting in a similar capacity on behalf of a participating company as being located in the United States.

2. for purposes of business combinations, the calculation of U.S. holders shall be made by a participant as of the end of such participant's last quarter or, if such quarter terminated within 60 days of the filing date, as of the end of such participant's preceding quarter.

C. In the case of a business combination, the securities to be registered on this Form shall be offered to U.S. holders upon terms and conditions not less favorable than those offered to any other holder of the same class of such securities of the participating company.

IV. Application of General Rules and Regulations

A. The rules comprising Regulation C under the Securities Act shall not apply to filings on this Form unless specifically referred to in the Form. Instead, the rules and regulations applicable in the home jurisdiction regarding the form and method of preparation of disclosure documents shall apply to filings on this Form. Securities Act rules and regulations other than Regulation C shall apply to filings on this Form unless specifically excluded in this Form.

B. Rule 408 under the Securities Act, which provides that in addition to the information expressly required to be included in the registration statement, there shall be added such further material information, if any, as may be necessary to make the required statements, in light of the circumstances under which they are made, not misleading, shall apply to filings on this Form.

C. A registrant must file the registration statement in electronic format via the Commission's Electronic Data Gathering, Analysis, and Retrieval (EDGAR) system in accordance with the EDGAR rules set forth in Regulation S-T (17 CFR Part 232). For assistance with technical questions about EDGAR or to request an access code, call the EDGAR Filer Support Office at (202) 551-8900. For assistance with the EDGAR rules, call the Office of EDGAR and Information Analysis at (202) 551-3610.

If filing the registration statement in paper under a hardship exemption in Rule 201 or 202 of Regulation S-T (17 CFR 232.201 or 232.202), or as otherwise permitted, a registrant must file with the Commission at its principal office five copies of the complete registration statement and any amendments, including exhibits and all other documents filed as a part of the registration statement or amendment. The registrant must bind, staple or otherwise compile each copy in one or more parts without stiff covers. The registrant must further bind the registration statement or amendment on the side or stitching margin in a manner that leaves the reading matter legible. The registrant must provide three additional copies of the registration statement or amendment without exhibits to the Commission.

D. Any amendment to a registration statement on this Form shall be filed under cover of an appropriate facing sheet, shall be numbered consecutively in the order in which filed, and shall indicate on the facing sheet the applicable registration form on which the amendment is prepared and the file number of the registration statement.

If, however, an amendment to the home jurisdiction document(s) is filed after effectiveness of this registration statement that increases the number of securities that may be sold, in lieu of filing a post-effective amendment hereto, a new registration statement shall be filed on this Form. As provided in Rule 429, the prospectus included in the new registration statement shall be deemed to include a prospectus covering unsold securities registered previously. If this is the case, the following legend shall appear at the bottom of the facing page of the registration statement: "Pursuant to Rule 429 under the Securities Act, the prospectus contained in this registration statement relates to registration statement[s] 33-[insert file numbers of previous registration statements]."

E. An electronic filer must provide the signatures required for the registration statement or amendment in accordance with Regulation S-T Rule 302 (17 CFR 232.302). A registrant filing in paper must have at least one copy of the registration statement or amendment signed in accordance with Securities Act Rule 402(e) (17 CFR 230.402(e)) by the persons whose signatures are required for this registration statement. A registrant must also conform the unsigned copies.

F. At the time of filing this registration statement, the Registrant shall pay to the Commission in accordance with Rule 111 under the Securities Act, a fee in U.S. dollars in the amount prescribed by Section 6 of the Securities Act. The amount of securities to be registered on this Form need not exceed the amount to be offered in the United States as part of the offering.

G. In the case of an exchange offer, the registration fee is to be calculated as follows:

(1) Upon the basis of the market value of the securities that may be received by the Registrant or cancelled in the exchange offer from United States residents as established by the price of securities of the same class, as determined in accordance with paragraph (4) of this section.

(2) If there is no market for the securities that may be received by the Registrant or cancelled in the exchange offer, the book value of such securities computed as of the latest practicable date prior to the date of filing the registration statement shall be used, unless the issuer of such securities is in bankruptcy or receivership or has an accumulated capital deficit, in which case one-third of the principal amount, par value or stated value of such securities shall be used.

(3) If any cash may be received by the Registrant from United States residents in connection with the exchange offer, the amount thereof shall be added to the value of the securities to be received by the Registrant or cancelled as computed in accordance with paragraph (1) or (2) of this section. If any cash is to be paid by the Registrant in connection with the exchange offer, the amount thereof shall be deducted from the value of the securities to be received by the Registrant in exchange as computed in accordance with paragraph (1) or (2) of this section.

(4) For purposes of the registration fee, the market value of the securities received or cancelled shall be the average of the high and low prices reported or the average of the bid and asked prices of such stock, in the principal market for such stock as of a date within 30 days prior to the date of filing.

H. In the case of a business combination, the registration fee is to be calculated as follows:

(1) Upon the basis of the market value of the equity securities of the predecessor companies held by United States residents being offered the Registrant's securities, as established by the price of the predecessors' securities of the same class determined in accordance with paragraph (4) of this section.

(2) If there is no market for the securities of the predecessor companies, the book value of such securities computed as of the latest practicable date prior to the date of filing the registration statement shall be used, unless the issue of such securities is in bankruptcy or receivership or has an accumulated capital deficit, in which case one-third of the principal amount, par value or stated value of such securities shall be used.

(3) If any cash may be received by the Registrant from United States residents in connection with the business combination, the amount thereof shall be added to the value of the securities as computed in accordance with paragraph (1) or (2) of this section. If any cash is to be paid by the Registrant in connection with the business combination, the amount thereof shall be deducted from the value of the securities as computed in accordance with paragraph (1) or (2) of this section.

(4) For purposes of the registration fee, the market value of a predecessor's equity securities shall be the average of the high and low prices reported or the average of the bid and asked prices of such securities, in the principal market for such securities as of a date with 30 days prior to the date of filing.

I. A registrant must file the registration statement or amendment in electronic format in the English language in accordance with Regulation S-T Rule 306 (17 CFR 232.306). A registrant may file part of the prospectus or exhibit or other attachment to the registration statement or amendment in both French and English if it included the French text to comply with the requirements of the Canadian securities administrator or other Canadian authority and, for an electronic filing, if the filing is an HTML document, as defined in Regulation S-T Rule 11 (17 CFR 232.11). For both an electronic filing and a paper filing, a registrant may provide an English translation or English summary of a foreign language document as an exhibit or other attachment to the registration statement or amendment as permitted by the rules of the applicable Canadian securities administrator.

J. A paper filer must number sequentially one signed original of the registration statement or amendment (in addition to any internal numbering that otherwise may be present) by handwritten, typed, printed or other legible form of notation from the first page through the last page of the registration statement or amendment, including any exhibits or attachments. A paper filer must disclose the total number of pages on the first page of the sequentially numbered registration statement or amendment.

K. Where the offering registered on this Form is being made pursuant to the home jurisdiction's shelf procedures or procedures for pricing offereings after the final receipt has been issued, three copies of each supplement to, or supplemented version of, the home jurisdiction disclosure document(s) prepared under such procedures shall be filed with the commission within one business day after such supplement or supplemented versions is filed with any Canadian jurisdiction. Such filings shall be deemed not to constitute amendments to this registration statement. Each such filing shall contain in the upper right corner of the cover page the following legend, which may be set forth in longhand if legible: "Filed pursuant to General Instruction IV.K. of Form F-80; File No. 33—[insert number of the registration statement]."

Note: Offerings registered on this Form, whether or not made contemporaneously in Canada, may be made pursuant to National Policy Statement No. 44 shelf procedures and procedures for pricing offerings after the final receipt has been issued. Rules 415 and 430A under the Securities Act are not available for offerings registered on this Form.

V. Compliance with Exchange Act and Auditor Independence and Reporting Requirements

A. Pursuant to Rule 12h-4 under the Exchange Act, a Registrant shall be exempt from reporting obligations under Section 15(d) of the Exchange Act if such reporting obligation would have arisen solely from registration of securities on this Form. Registrants' attention is directed, however, towards other provisions of the Exchange Act that may be applicable, and specifically to the provisions of Sections 12(b) and 12(g) of the Exchange Act and Rules 10b-6, 10b-7 and 10b-13 under the Exchange Act. [*See* Exchange Act Release No. 29355 (June 21, 1991) containing exemptions from Rules 10b-6 and 10b-13.]

B. The Commission's rules on auditor independence, as codified in Section 600 of the Codification of Financial Reporting Policies, apply to auditor reports on all financial statements that are included in this registration statement, except that such rules do not apply with respect to periods prior to the most recent fiscal year for which financial statements are included in the registration statement under the Securities Act filed by the issuer on Form F-8, Form F-9, Form F-10 or Form F-80 or under the Exchange Act filed by the issuer on Form 40-F. Notwithstanding the exception in the previous sentence, such rules do apply with respect to any periods prior to the most recent fiscal year if the issuer previously was required to file with the Commission on a report or registration statement containing an audit report on financial statements for such prior periods as to which the Commission's rules on auditor independence applied.

C. Independent accountants reporting on financial statements included in the registration statement should consider Canadian auditing guidelines pertaining to the Canada-U.S. reporting conflict with respect under those guidelines but are not included in the prospectus itself, those comments should be included with the legends required by Item 2 of Part I hereof. In addition, the accountant's consent specifically should refer to any additional comments provides for U.S. readers.

D. Pursuant to Rule 13e-4(g) under the Exchange Act, the provisions of Rule 13e-4 are not applicable, and pursuant to Rule 14d-1(b) under the Exchange Act, the provisions of Sections 14(d)(1) through 14(d)(7) of the Exchange Act, Regulation 14D under the Exchange Act and Schedule TO thereunder, and Rule 14e-1 under Regulation 14E, are not applicable to a transaction involving offerings of securities that may be registered on this Form in connection with exchange offers, *provided that*, if an exemption has been granted from the requirements of Canadian federal, provincial and/or territorial laws, regulations or policies, and offer rules, the Registrant shall comply with such provisions of the Exchange Act. Such transaction is not exempt from the antifraud provisions of Section 10(b), 13(e) or 14(e) of the Exchange Act or Rule 10b-5, 13e-4(b)(1) or 14e-3 thereunder, if the transaction otherwise is subject to those sections.

PART I—INFORMATION REQUIRED TO BE DELIVERED TO OFFEREES OR PURCHASERS

Item 1. Home Jursidiction Document

In the case of an exchange offer, the prospectus shall consist of the entire disclosure document or documents used to offer the securities of the Registrant in any Canadian jurisdiction. Except as noted hereinafter, such disclosure document(s) shall be prepared in accordance with the disclosure requirements of such jurisdiction(s) as interpreted and applied by the securities commission(s) or other regulatory authorities in such jurisdiction(s).

In the case of a business combination, the prospectus shall consist of the entire disclosure document or documents used to solicit votes of security holders in connection with the proposed business combination in any Canadian jurisdiction. Except as noted hereinafter, such disclosure document(s) governing such solicitation as interpreted and applied by the securities commission(s) or other regulatory authorities in such jurisdiction(s).

The prospectus used in the United States shall contain additional information and legends required by this Form. It need not include any documents incorporated by reference into the disclosure document(s) used in Canada and not required to be delivered to offerees or purchasers (in the case of an exchange offer) or securityholders being solicited (in the case of a business combination) pursuant to Canadian law.

Notwithstanding the foregoing, such prospectus used in the United States need not contain any disclosure applicable solely to Canadian offerees or purchasers that would not be material to offerees or purchasers in the United States, including, without limitation, (i) any Canadian "red herring" legend; (ii) any discussion of Canadian tax considerations other than those material to U.S. offerees or purchasers; (iii) the names of any Canadian underwriters not acting as underwriters in the United States or a description of the Canadian plan of distribution (except to the extent necessary to describe the material facts of the U.S. plan of distribution); (iv) any description of offerees' or purchasers' statutory rights under applicable Canadian, provincial or territorial securities legislation (except to the extend such rights are available to U.S. offerees or purchasers); or (v) certificates of the issuer or any underwriter.

Item 2. Informational Legends

The following legends, to the extent applicable, shall appear on the outside front cover page of the prospectus (or on a sticker thereto) in bold-face roman type at least as high as ten-point modern type and at least two points leaded:

"This offering is made by a foreign issuer that is permitted, under a multijurisdictional disclosure system adopted by the United States, to prepare this prospectus in accordance with the disclosure requirements of its home country. Prospective investors should be aware that such requirements are different from those of the United States. The financial statements included or incorporated herein, if any, have been prepared in accordance with foreign generally accepted accounting principles, and may be subject to foreign auditing and auditor independence standards, and, thus, may not be comparable to financial statements of United States companies."

"Prospective investors should be aware that acquisition of the securities described herein may have tax consequences both in the United States and in the home country of the Registrant. Such consequences for investors who are resident in, or citizens of, the United States may not be described fully herein."

"The enforcement by investors of civil liabilities under the federal securities laws may be affected adversely by the fact that the Registrant is incorporated or organized under the laws of a foreign country, that some or all of its officers and directors may be residents of a foreign country, that some or all of the underwriters or experts named in the registration statement may be residents of a foreign country, and that all or a substantial portion of the assets of the Registrant and said persons may be located outside the United States."

"THESE SECURITIES HAVE NOT BEEN APPROVED OR DISAPPROVED BY THE SECURITIES AND EXCHANGE COMMISSION NOR HAS THE COMMISSION PASSED UPON THE ACCURACY OR ADEQUACY OF THIS PROSPECTUS. ANY REPRESENTATION TO THE CONTRARY IS A CRIMINAL OFFENSE."

The following legend shall appear in the manner noted above in any prospectus relating to an exchange offer.

"Prospective investors ahould be aware that, during the period of the exchange offer, the Registrant or its affiliates, directly or indirectly, may bid for or make purchases of the securities to be distributed or to be exchanged, or certain related securities, as permitted by applicable laws or regulations of Canada or its provinces or territories."

The Registrant should also include in the prospectus any legend or information required by the laws of any jurisdiction in which the securities are to be offered.

Note to Item 2. If the home-jurisdiction document(s) are delivered through an electronic medium, the issuer may satisfy the legibility requirements for the required legends relating to type size and font by presenting the legends in any manner reasonably calculated to draw investor attention to it.

Item 3. Incorporation of Certain Information by Reference

Information called for by this Form, including exhibits, may be incorporated by reference at the

Registrant's option from documents that the Registrant has filed previously with the Commission pursuant to Section 13(a) or 15(d) of the Exchange Act or submitted to the Commission pursuant to Rule 12g3-2(b) under the Exchange Act. Any such incorporation by reference shall be done in accordance with Item 10(d) of Regulation S-K. If any information is incorporated by reference into the prospectus, the prospectus shall provide the name, address and telephone number of an officer of the Registrant from whom copies of such information may be obtained upon request without charge.

Item 4. List of Documents Filed with the Commission

There shall be set forth in or attached to the prospectus a list of all documents filed with the Commission as part of the registration statement.

PART II—INFORMATION NOT REQUIRED TO BE DELIVERED TO OFFEREES OR PURCHASERS

Provide a brief description of the indemnification provisions relating to directors, officers and controlling persons of the Registrant against liability arising under the Securities Act (including any provision of the underwriting agreement which relates to indemnification of the underwriter or its controlling persons by the Registrant against such liabilities where a director, officer or controlling person of the Registrant is such an underwriter or controlling person thereof or a member of any firm which is such an underwriter), together with a statement in substantially the following form:

> Insofar as indemnification for liabilities arising under the Securities Act of 1933 may be permitted to directors, officers or persons controlling the Registrant pursuant to the foregoing provision, the Registrant has been informed that the opinion of the U.S. Securities and Exchange Commission such indemnification is against public policy as expressed in the Act and is therefore unenforceable.

The exhibits specified below shall be filed as part of the registration statement. Exhibits shall be appropriately lettered or numbered for convenient reference.

(1) Any reports or information that, in accordance with the requirements of the jurisdiction of incorporation or organization of the subject issuer or, in the case of a business combination, in accordance with the requirements of the jurisdiction(s) of incorporation or organization of companies involved in the transaction other than the Registrant, must be made publicly available by the Registrant in connection with the transaction.

(2) A copy of any agreement relating to the proposed acquisition or business combination, as applicable.

(3) Copies of any documents incorporated by reference into the registration statement and any publicly available documents filed with any other Canadian regulatory authority concurrently with the prospectus.

(4) If any accountant, engineer or appraiser, or any person whose profession gives authority to a statement made by him, is named as having prepared or certified any part of the registration statement, or is named as having prepared or certified a report or valuation for use in connection with the offering document, the manually signed, written consent of such person.

If any such person is named as having prepared or certified any other report or valuation (other than a public official document or statement) which is used in connection with the registration statement, but is not named as having prepared or certified such report or valuation for use in connection with the registration statement, the manually signed, written consent of such person, unless the Commission dispenses with such filing as impracticable or as involving undue hardship in accordance with Rule 437 under the Securities Act.

Any other consent required by Rule 436, 438 or 439 under the Securities Act. Every amendment relating to a certified financial statement shall include the manually signed, written consent of the certifying account to the use of his certificate in connection with the amended financial statements in the registration statement and to being named as having certified such financial statements.

NOTE: The consents required by this item shall specifically indicate consent regarding use of the report or valuation in the registration statement filed in the United States.

(5) If any name is signed to the registration statement pursuant to power of attorney, manually signed copies of such power of attorney and, if the name of any officer signing on behalf of the Registrant is signed pursuant to a power of attorney, certified copies of a resolution of the Registrant's board of directors or similar governing body authorizing such signature.

(6) A copy of any indenture relating to the registered securities.

PART III—UNDERTAKINGS AND CONSENT TO SERVICE OF PROCESS

Item 1. Undertakings

This Form shall set forth the following undertakings of the Registrant:

(a) Registrant undertakes to make available, in person or by telephone, representatives to respond to inquires made by the Commission staff, and to furnish promptly, when requested to do so by the Commission staff, information relating to the securities registered pursuant to Form F-80 or to transactions in said securities.

(b) In the case of an exchange offer, Registrant further undertakes to disclose in the United States, on the same basis as it is required to make such disclosure pursuant to any applicable Canadian federal and/or provincial or territorial law, regulation or policy, information regarding purchases of the Registrant's securities or of the subject issuer's securities during the exchange offer. Such information shall be set forth in amendments to this Form.

Item 2. Consent to Service of Process

(a) At the time of filing Form F-80, the Registrant shall file with the Commission a written irrevocable consent and power of attorney on Form F-X.

(b) At the time of filing Form F-80, any non-U.S. person acting as trustee with respect to the registered securities shall file with the Commission a written irrevocalbe consent and power of attorney on Form F-X.

(c) Any change to the name or address of the agent for service of the Registrant or the trustee shall be communicated promptly to the commission by amendment to Form F-X referencing the file number of the relevant registration statement.

SIGNATURES

Pursuant to the requirements of the Securities Act, the Registrant certifies that it has reasonable grounds to believe that it meets all of the requirements for filing on Form F-80 and has duly caused this registration statement to be signed on its behalf by the undersigned, thereunto duly authorized, in the City of . . . ., Country of . . . ., on . . . . (date), ...

Registrant . . . .

By (Signature and Title) . . . .

Pursuant to the requirements of the Securities Act, this registration statement has been signed by the following persons in the capacities and on the dates indicated.

(Signature) . . . .

(Name and Title) . . . .

(Date) . . . .

Instructions

A. The registration statement shall be signed by the Registrant, its principal executive officer or officers, its principal financial officer, its controller or principal accounting officer, at least a majority of the board of directors or persons performing similar functions and its authorized representative in the United States. Where the Registrant is a limited partnership, the registration statement shall be signed by a majority of the board of directors of any corporate general partner signing the registration statement.

B. The name of each person who signs the registration statement shall be typed or printed beneath his signature. Any person who occupies more than one of the specified positions shall indicate each capacity in which the registration statement is signed.

C. If the securities to be offered are those of a corporation not yet in existence at the time the registration statement is filed and which will be a party to a consolidation involving two or more existing corporations, then each such existing corporation shall be deemed a Registrant and shall be so designated on the cover page of this Form, and the registration statement shall be signed by each such existing corporation and by the officers and directors of each such existing corporation as if each such existing corporation were the sole Registrant.

D. By signing this Form, the Registrant consents without power of revocation that any administrative subpoena may be served, or any administrative proceeding, civil suit or civil action where the cause of action arises out of or relates to or concerns any offering made or purported to be made in connection with the securities registered pursuant to Form F-80 or any purchases or sales of any security in connection therewith, may be commenced against it in any administrative tribunal or in any appropriate court in any place subject to the jurisdiction of any state or of the United States or of the District of Columbia or Puerto Rico by service of said subpoena or process upon the Registrant's designated agent.

[¶ 7791]   FORM F-X

[As last amended in Release No. 33-8957, effective December 8, 2008, 73 F.R. 60050.]

U.S. Securities and Exchange Commission
Washington, D.C. 20549

Form F-X

APPOINTMENT OF AGENT FOR SERVICE OF PROCESS AND UNDERTAKING
GENERAL INSTRUCTIONS

I. Form F-X shall be filed with the Commission:

   (a) by any issuer registering securities on Form F-8, F-9, F-10 or F-80 under the Securities Act of 1933;

   (b) by any issuer registering securities on Form 40-F under the Securities Exchange Act of 1934 (the "Exchange Act");

   (c) by any issuer filing a periodic report on Form 40-F, if it has not previously filed a Form F-X in connection with the class of securities in relation to which the obligation to file a report on Form 40-F arises;

   (d) by any issuer or other non-U.S. person filing tender offer documents on Schedule 13E-4F, 14D-1F or 14D-9F;

   (e) by any non-U.S. person acting as trustee with respect to securities registered on Form F-7, F-8, F-9, F-10, or F-80; and

   (f) by a Canadian issuer qualifying an offering statement pursuant to the provisions of Regulation A, or registering securities on Form SB-2.

   (g) by any non-U.S. issuer providing Form CB to the Commission in connection with a tender offer, rights offering or business combination.

A Form F-X filed in connection with any other Commission form should not be bound together with or be included only as an exhibit to, such other form.

II. Six copies of the Form F-X, one of which must be manually signed, shall be filed with the Commission at its principal office.

   A. Name of issuer or person filing ("Filer"): . . . .

   B. (1) This is [check one]

   ☐ an original filing for the Filer

   ☐ an amended filing for the Filer

   (2) Check the following box if you are filing the Form F-X in paper in accordance with Regulation S-T Rule 101(b)(9) ☐

   Note: Regulation S-T Rule 101(b)(9) only permits the filing of the Form F-X in paper:

      (a) if the party filing or submitting the Form CB is not subject to the reporting requirements of Section 13 or 15(d) of the Exchange Act; or

      (b) if filed by a Canadian issuer when qualifying an offering statement pursuant to the provisions of Regulation A (230.251 - 230.263 of this chapter).

   Note: Regulation S-T Rule 101(b)(8) only permits the filing of the Form F-X in paper if filed by a Canadian issuer when qualifying an offering statement pursuant to the provisions of Regulation A (§§ 230.251 - 230.263 of this chapter).

   (3) A filer may also file the Form F-X in paper under a hardship exemption provided by Regulation S-T Rule 201 or 202 (17 CFR 232.201 or 232.202). When submitting the Form F-X in paper under a hardship exemption, a filer must provide the legend required by Regulation S-T Rule 201(a)(2) or 202(c) (17 CFR 232.201(a)(2) or 232.202(c)) on the cover page of the Form F-X.

   C. Identify the filing in conjunction with which this Form is being filed:

   Name of registrant . . . .

Form type . . . .

File Number (if known) . . . .

Filed by . . . .

Date Filed (if filed concurrently, so indicate) . . . .

D. The Filer is incorporated or organized under the laws of (Name of the jurisdiction under whose laws the issuer is organized or incorporated . . and has its principal place of business at (Address in full and telephone number)

. . . .

. . . .

E. The Filer designates and appoints (Name of United States person serving as agent) . . . .
. . . . ("Agent") Located at (Address in full in the United States and telephone number)

. . . .

. . . .

as the agent of the Filer upon whom may be served any process, pleadings, subpoenas, or other papers in

(a) any investigation or administrative proceeding conducted by the Commission; and

(b) any civil suit or action brought against the Filer or to which the Filer has been joined as defendant or respondent, in any appropriate court in any place subject to the jurisdiction of any state or of the United States or of any of its territories or possessions or of the District of Columbia, where the investigation, proceeding or cause of action arises out of or relates to or concerns (i) any offering made or purported to be made in connection with the securities registered or qualified by the Filer on Form (Name of form) . . . . on (Date) . . . . or any purchases or sales of any security in connection therewith; (ii) the securities in relation to which the obligation to file an annual report on Form 40-F arises, or any purchases or sales of such securities; (iii) any tender offer for the securities of a Canadian issuer with respect to which filings are made by the Filer with the Commission on Schedule 13E-4F, 14D-1F or 14D-9F; or (iv) the securities in relation to which the Filer acts as trustee pursuant to an exemption under Rule 10a-5 under the Trust Indenture Act of 1939. The Filer stipulates an agrees that any such civil suit or action or administrative proceeding may be commenced by the service of process upon, and that service of an administrative subpoena shall be effected by service upon such agent for service of process, and that service as aforesaid shall be taken and held in all courts and administrative tribunals to be valid and binding as if personal service thereof had been made.

F. Each person filing this Form in connection with:

(a) the use of Form F-9, F-10, or 40-F or Schedule 13E-4F, 14D-1F, or 14D-9F stipulates and agrees to appoint a successor agent for service of process and file an amended Form F-X if the Filer discharges the Agent or the Agent is unwilling or unable to accept service on behalf of the Filer at any time until six years have elapsed from the date the issuer of the securities to which such Forms and Schedules relate has ceased reporting under the Exchange Act;

(b) the use of Form F-8, Form F-80 or Form CB stipulates and agrees to appoint a successor agent for service of process and file an amended Form F-X if the Filer discharges the Agent or the Agent is unwilling or unable to accept service on behalf of the Filer at any time until six years have elapsed following the effective date of the latest amendment to such Form F-8, Form F-80 or Form CB;

(c) its status as trustee with respect to securities registered on Form F-7, F-8, F-9, F-10, or F-80 stipulates and agrees to appoint a successor agent for service of process and file an amended Form F-X if the Filer discharges the Agent or the Agent is unwilling or unable to accept service on behalf of the Filer at any time during which any of the securities subject to the indenture remain outstanding; and

(d) the use of Form 1-A or other Commission form for an offering pursuant to Regulation A stipulates and agrees to appoint a successor agent for service of process and file an amended Form F-X if the Filer discharges the Agent or the Agent is unwilling or unable to accept service on behalf of the Filer at any time until six years have elapsed from the date of the last sale of securities in reliance upon the Regulation A exemption.

Each filer further undertakes to advise the Commission promptly of any change to the Agent's name and address during the applicable period by amendment of this Form, referencing the file number of the relevant form in conjunction with which the amendment is being filed.

¶7791   **Form F-X**

G. Each person filing this Form, other than a trustee filing in accordance with General Instruction I. (e) of this Form, undertakes to make available, in person or by telephone, representatives to respond to inquiries made by the Commission staff, and to furnish promptly, when requested to do so by the Commission staff, information relating to: the Forms, Schedules and offering statements described in General Instructions I. (a), I. (b), I. (c), I. (d) and I. (f) of this Form, as applicable; the securities to which such Forms, Schedules and offering statements relate; and the transactions in such securities.

The Filer certifies that it has duly caused this power of attorney, consent, stipulation and agreement to be signed on its behalf by the undersigned, thereunto duly authorized, in the City of . . . . Country of . . . . this . . . . day of . . . . , ...
. . . .

. . . .

Filer: By:(Signature and Title)

This statement has been signed by the following persons in the capacities and on the dates indicated.

(Signature) . . . .

(Title) . . . .

(Date) . . . .

Instructions

1. The power of attorney, consent, stipulation and agreement shall be signed by the Filer and its authorized Agent in the United States.

2. The name of each person who signs Form F-X shall be typed or printed beneath such person's signature. Any person who occupies more than one of the specified positions shall indicate each capacity in which such person signs Form F-X. If any name is signed pursuant to a board resolution, a copy of the resolution shall be filed with each copy of Form F-X. A certified copy of such resolution shall be filed with the manually signed copy of Form F-X. If any name is signed pursuant to a power of attorney, a copy of the power of attorney shall be filed with each copy of Form F-X. A manually signed copy of such power of attorney shall be filed with the manually signed copy of Form F-X.

[¶ 7792]　　　　　　　　　　**FORM F-N**

[As adopted in Release No. IC-18381, October 29, 1991, 56 F. R. 56294.]

U.S. Securities and Exchange Commission

Washington, D.C. 20549

Form F-N

APPOINTMENT OF AGENT FOR SERVICE OF PROCESS BY FOREIGN BANKS AND FOREIGN INSURANCE COMPANIES AND CERTAIN OF THEIR HOLDING COMPANIES AND FINANCE SUBSIDIARIES MAKING PUBLIC OFFERINGS OF SECURITIES IN THE UNITED STATES

GENERAL INSTRUCTIONS

I. Form F-N shall be filed with the Commission in connection with the filing of a registration statement under the Securities Act of 1933 by:

1. a foreign issuer that is a foreign bank or foreign insurance company excepted from the definition of an investment company by rule 3a-6 [17 CFR 270.3a-6] under the Investment Company Act of 1940 (the "1940 Act");

2. a foreign issuer that is a finance subsidiary of a foreign bank or foreign insurance company, as those terms are defined in rule 3a-6 under the 1940 Act, if such finance subsidiary is excepted from the definition of investment company by rule 3a-5 [17 CFR 270.3a-5]under the 1940 Act; or

3. a foreign issuer that is excepted from the definition of investment company by rule 3a-1 [17 CFR 270.3a-1] under the 1940 Act because some or all of its majority-owned subsidiaries are foreign banks or foreign insurance companies excepted from the definition of investment company by rule 3a-6 under the 1940 Act.

II. Notwithstanding paragraph (I), the following foreign issuers are not required to file Form F-N:

1. a foreign issuer that has filed Form F-X [17 CFR 239.42]under the Securities Act of 1933 with the Commission with respect to the securities being offered; and

2. a foreign issuer filing a registration statement relating to debt securities or non-voting preferred stock that has on file with the Commission a currently accurate Form N-6C9 [17 CFR 274.304, rescinded] under the 1940 Act.

III. Six copies of the Form F-N, one of which shall be manually signed, shall be filed with the Commission at its principal office. A Form F-N filed in connection with any other Commission form should not be bound together with or be included only as an exhibit to, such other form.

A. Name of issuer or person filing ("Filer"): . . . .

B. This is (select one):

[] an original filing for the Filer

[]an amended filing for the Filer

C. Identify the filing in conjunction with which this Form is being filed:

Name of registrant . . . .

Form type . . . .

File Number (if known) . . . .

Filed by . . . .

Date Filed (if filed concurrently, so indicate) . . . .

D. The Filer is incorporated or organized under the laws of (Name of the jurisdiction under whose laws the filer is organized or incorporated)

. . . .

and has its principal place of business at (Address in full and telephone number)

. . . .

E. The Filer designates and appoints (Name of United States person serving as agent)

. . . . ("Agent") located at (Address in full in the United States and telephone number)

. . . . as the agent of the Filer upon whom may be served any process; pleadings, subpoenas, or other papers in:

(a) any investigation or administrative proceeding conducted by the Commission, and

(b) any civil suit or action brought against the Filer or to which the Filer has been joined as defendant or respondent, in any appropriate court in any place subject to the jurisdiction of any state or of the United States or any of its territories or possessions or of the District of Columbia,

arising out of or based on any offering made or purported to be made in connection with the securities registered by the Filer on Form (Name of Form) . . . . filed on (Date) . . . . or any purchases or sales of any security in connection therewith. The Filer stipulates and agrees that any such civil suit or action or administrative proceeding may be commenced by the service of process upon, and that service of an administrative subpoena shall be effected by service upon, such agent for service of process, and that the service as aforesaid shall be taken and held in all courts and administrative tribunals to be valid and binding as if personal service thereof had been made.

F. Each person filing this Form stipulates and agrees to appoint a sucessor agent for service of process and file an amended Form F-N if the Filer discharges the Agent or the Agent is unwilling or unable to accept service on behalf of the Filer at any time until six years have elapsed from the date of the Filer's last registration statement or report, or amendment to any such registration statement or report, filed with the Commission under the Securities Act of 1933 or Securities Exchange Act of 1934. Filer further undertakes to advise the Commission promptly of any change to the Agent's name or address during the applicable period by amendment of this Form referencing the file number of the relevant registration form in conjunction with which the amendment is being filed.

G. Each person filing this form undertakes to make available, in person or by telephone, representatives to respond to inquiries made by the Commission staff, and to furnish promptly, when requested to do so by the Commission staff, information relating to the securities registered pursuant to the form referenced in paragraph E or transactions in said securities.

The Filer certifies that it has duly caused this power of attorney, consent, stipulation and agreement to be signed on its behalf by the undersigned, thereunto duly authorized, in the

City of . . . . Country of . . . .

this . . . . day of . . . . 19. . . . A.D.

    Filer: By (Signature and Title):

. . . .

This statement has been signed by the following persons in the capacities and on the dates indicated.

(Signature) . . . .

(Title) . . . .

(Date) . . . .

Instructions

1. The power of attorney, consent, stipulation and agreement shall be signed by the Filer and its authorized Agent in the United States.

2. The name of each person who signs Form F-N shall be typed or printed beneath his signature. Where any name is signed pursuant to a board resolution, a certified copy of the resolution shall be filed with each copy of the Form. If any name is signed pursuant to a power of attorney, a manually signed copy of each power of attorney shall be filed with each copy of the Form.

[¶ 8001]   **FORM S-1**

[As last amended in Release No. 33-8876, effective February 4, 2008, 73 F.R. 934.]

UNITED STATES SECURITIES AND EXCHANGE COMMISSION

Washington, D.C. 20549

FORM S-1

REGISTRATION STATEMENT UNDER THE SECURITIES ACT OF 1933

UNITED STATES SECURITIES AND EXCHANGE COMMISSION

Washington, D.C. 20549

FORM S-1

REGISTRATION STATEMENT UNDER THE SECURITIES ACT OF 1933

. . . .

(Exact name of registrant as specified in its charter)

. . . .

(State or other jurisdiction of incorporation or organization)

. . . .

(Primary Standard Industrial Classification Code Number)

. . . .

(I.R.S. Employer Identification Number)

(Address, including zip code, and telephone number, including area code, of registrant's
principal executive offices)

. . . .

(Name, address, including zip code, and telephone number, including area code, of agent
for service)

. . . .

(Approximate date of commencement of proposed sale to the public)

If any of the securities being registered on this Form are to be offered on a delayed or continuous basis pursuant to Rule 415 under the Securities Act, check the following box: ☐

If this Form is filed to register additional securities for an offering pursuant to Rule 462(b) under the Securities Act, please check the following box and list the Securities Act registration statement number of the earlier effective registration statement for the same offering. ☐

If this Form is a post-effective amendment filed pursuant to Rule 462(c) under the Securities Act, check the following box and list the Securities Act registration statement number of the earlier effective registration statement for the same offering. ☐

If this Form is a post-effective amendment filed pursuant to Rule 462(d) under the Securities Act, check the following box and list the Securities Act registration statement number of the earlier effective registration statement for the same offering. ☐

Indicate by check mark whether the registrant is a large accelerated filer, an accelerated filer, a non-accelerated filer, or a smaller reporting company. See the definitions of "large accelerated filer," "accelerated filer" and "smaller reporting company" in Rule 12b-2 of the Exchange Act. (Check one):

[ ] Large accelerated filer

[ ] Accelerated filer

[ ] Non-accelerated filer (do not check if a smaller reporting company)

[ ] Smaller reporting company

Calculation of Registration Fee

Title of each class of securities to be registered	Amount to be registered	Proposed maximum offering price per unit	Proposed maximum aggregate offering price	Amount of registration fee

Note: Specific details relating to the fee calculation shall be furnished in notes to the table, including references to provisions of *Rule 457* (§ 230.457 of this chapter) relied upon, if the basis of the calculation is not otherwise evident from the information presented in the table. If the filing fee is calculated pursuant to Rule 457(o) under the Securities Act, only the title of the class of securities to be registered, the proposed maximum aggregate offering price for that class of securities and the amount of registration fee need to appear in the Calculation of Registration Fee table. Any difference between the dollar amount of securities registered for such offerings and the dollar amount of securities sold may be carried forward on a future registration statement pursuant to *Rule 429* under the Securities Act.

GENERAL INSTRUCTIONS

I. Eligibility Requirements for Use of Form S-1

This Form shall be used for the registration under the Securities Act of 1933 ("Securities Act") of securities of all registrants for which no other form is authorized or prescribed, except that this Form shall not be used for securities of foreign governments or political subdivisions thereof.

II. Application of General Rules and Regulations

A. Attention is directed to the General Rules and Regulations under the Securities Act, particularly those comprising *Regulation C* (17 CFR 230.400 to 230.494) thereunder. That Regulation contains general requirements regarding the preparation and filing of the registration statement.

B. Attention is directed to *Regulation S-K* (17 CFR Part 229) for the requirements applicable to the content of the non-financial statement portions of registration statements under the Securities Act. Where this Form directs the registrant to furnish information required by Regulation S-K and the item of Regulation S-K so provides, information need only be furnished to the extent appropriate.

III. Exchange Offers

If any of the securities being registered are to be offered in exchange for securities of any other issuer, the prospectus shall also include the information which would be required by item 11 if the securities of such other issuer were registered on this Form. There shall also be included the information concerning such securities of such other issuer which would be called for by Item 9 if such securities were being registered. In connection with this instruction, reference is made to *Rule 409*.

IV. Roll-up Transactions

If the securities to be registered on this Form will be is[s]ued in a roll-up trans[a]ction as defined in *Item 901(c)* of Regulation S-K (17 CFR 229.901(c)), attention is directed to the requirements of Form S-4 applicable to roll-up transactions, including, but not limited to, General Instruction I.

V. Registration of Additional Securities

With respect to the registration of additional securities for an offering pursuant to *Rule 462(b)* under the Securities Act, the registrant may file a registration statement consisting only of the following: the facing page; a statement that the contents of the earlier registration statement, identified by file number, are incorporated by reference; required opinions and consents; the signature page; and any price-related information omitted from the earlier registration statement in reliance on *Rule 430A* that the registrant chooses to include in the new registration statement. The information contained in such a Rule 462(b) registration statement shall be deemed to be a part of the earlier registration statement as of the date of effectiveness of the Rule 462(b) registration statement. Any opinion or consent required in the Rule 462(b) registration statement may be incorporated by reference from the earlier registration statement with respect to the offering, if: (i) such opinion or consent expressly provides for such incorporation; and (ii) such opinion relates to the securities registered pursuant to Rule 462(b). *See Rule 411(c)* and *Rule 439(b)* under the Securities Act.

VI. Offerings of Asset-Backed Securities

The following applies if a registration statement on this Form S-1 is being used to register an offering of asset-backed securities. Terms used in this General Instruction VI. have the same meaning as in Item 1101 of Regulation AB (17 CFR 229.1101).

A. *Items that may be Omitted.*

Such registrants may omit the information called for by Item 11, Information with Respect to the Registrant.

B. *Substitute Information to be Included.*

In addition to the Items that are otherwise required by this Form, the registrant must furnish in the prospectus the information required by Items 1102 through 1120 of Regulation AB (17 CFR 229.1102 through 229.1120).

C. *Signatures.*

The registration statement must be signed by the depositor, the depositor's principal executive officer or officers, principal financial officer and controller or principal accounting officer, and by at least a majority of the depositor's board of directors or persons performing similar functions.

VII. Eligibility to Use Incorporation by Reference

If a registrant meets the following requirements immediately prior to the time of filing a registration statement on this Form, it may elect to provide information required by Items 3 through 11 of this Form in accordance with Item 11A and Item 12 of this Form:

A. The registrant is subject to the requirement to file reports pursuant to Section 13 or Section 15(d) of the Securities Exchange Act of 1934 ("Exchange Act").

B. The registrant has filed all reports and other materials required to be filed by Sections 13(a), 14, or 15(d) of the Exchange Act during the preceding 12 months (or for such shorter period that the registrant was required to file such reports and materials).

C. The registrant has filed an annual report required under Section 13(a) or Section 15(d) of the Exchange Act for its most recently completed fiscal year.

D. The registrant is not:

1. And during the past three years neither the registrant nor any of its predecessors was:

(a) A blank check company as defined in Rule 419(a)(2) (§ 230.419(a)(2));

(b) A shell company, other than a business combination related shell company, each as defined in Rule 405 (§ 230.405); or

(c) A registrant for an offering of penny stock as defined in Rule 3a51-1 of the Exchange Act (§ 240.3a51-1 of this chapter).

2. Registering an offering that effectuates a business combination transaction as defined in Rule 165(f)(1) (§ 230.165(f)(1) of this chapter).

E. If a registrant is a successor registrant it shall be deemed to have satisfied conditions A., B., C., and D.2 above if:

1. Its predecessor and it, taken together, do so, provided that the succession was primarily for the purpose of changing the state of incorporation of the predecessor or forming a holding company and that the assets and liabilities of the successor at the time of succession were substantially the same as those of the predecessor; or

2. All predecessors met the conditions at the time of succession and the registrant has continued to do so since the succession.

F. The registrant makes its periodic and current reports filed pursuant to Section 13 or Section 15(d) of the Exchange Act that are incorporated by reference pursuant to Item 11A or Item 12 of this Form readily available and accessible on a Web site maintained by or for the registrant and containing information about the registrant.

PART I—INFORMATION REQUIRED IN PROSPECTUS

Item 1. Forepart of the Registration Statement and Outside Front Cover Page of Prospectus.

Set forth in the forepart of the registration statement and on the outside front cover page of the prospectus the information required by *Item 501* of Regulation S-K (§ 229.501 of this chapter).

Item 2. Inside Front and Outside Back Cover Pages of Prospectus.

Set forth on the inside front cover page of the prospectus or, where permitted, on the outside back cover page, the information required by *Item 502* of Regulation S-K (§ 229.502 of this chapter).

Item 3. Summary Information, Risk Factors and Ratio of Earnings to Fixed Charges.

Furnish the information required by *Item 503* of Regulation S-K (§ 229.503 of this chapter).

Item 4. Use of Proceeds.

Furnish the information required by *Item 504* of Regulation S-K (§ 229.504 of this chapter).

Item 5. Determination of Offering Price.

Furnish the information required by *Item 505* of Regulation S-K (§ 229.505 of this chapter).

Item 6. Dilution.

Furnish the information required by *Item 506* of Regulation S-K (§ 229.506 of this chapter).

Item 7. Selling Security Holders.

Furnish the information required by *Item 507* of Regulation S-K (§ 229.507 of this chapter).

Item 8. Plan of Distribution.

Furnish the information required by *Item 508* of Regulation S-K (§ 229.508 of this chapter).

Item 9. Description of Securities to be Registered.

Furnish the information required by *Item 202* of Regulation S-K (§ 229.202 of this chapter).

Item 10. Interests of Named Experts and Counsel.

Furnish the information required by *Item 509* of Regulation S-K (§ 229.509 of this chapter).

Item 11. Information with Respect to the Registrant.

Furnish the following information with respect to the registrant:

(a) Information required by *Item 101* of Regulation S-K (§ 229.101 of this chapter), description of business;

(b) Information required by *Item 102* of Regulation S-K (§ 229.102 of this chapter), description of property;

(c) Information required by *Item 103* of Regulation S-K (§ 229.103 of this chapter), legal proceedings;

(d) Where common equity securities are being offered, information required by *Item 201* of Regulation S-K (§ 229.201 of this chapter), market price of and dividends on the registrant's common equity and related stockholder matters;

(e) Financial statements meeting the requirements of Regulation S-X (17 CFR Part 210) (Schedules required under Regulation S-X shall be filed as "Financial Statements Schedules" pursuant to Item 15, Exhibits and Financial Statement Schedules, of this form), as well as any financial information required by Rule 3-05 and Article 11 of Regulation S-X. A smaller reporting company may provide the information in Rule 8-04 and 8-05 of Regulation S-X in lieu of the financial information required by Rule 3-05 and Article 11 of Regulation S-X;

(f) Information required by *Item 301* of Regulation S-K (§ 229.301 of this chapter), selected financial data;

(g) Information required by *Item 302* of Regulation S-K (§ 229.302 of this chapter), supplementary financial in formation;

(h) Information required by *Item 303* of Regulation S-K (§ 229.303 of this chapter), management's discussion and analysis of financial condition and results of operations;

(i) Information required by *Item 304* of Regulation S-K (§ 229.304 of this chapter), changes in and disagreements with accountants on accounting and financial disclosure;

(j) Information required by *Item 305* of Regulation S-K (§ 229.305 of this chapter), quantitative and qualitative disclosures about market risk.

(k) Information required by *Item 401* of Regulation S-K (§ 229.401 of this chapter), directors and executive officers;

(l) Information required by *Item 402* of Regulation S-K (§ 229.402 of this chapter), executive compensation, and information required by paragraph (e)(4) of Item 407 of Regulation S-K (§ 229.407 of this chapter), corporate governance;

(m) Information required by *Item 403* of Regulation S-K (§ 229.403 of this chapter), security ownership of certain beneficial owners and management; and

(n) Information required by *Item 404* of Regulation S-K (§ 229.404 of this chapter), transactions with related persons, promoters and certain control persons, and Item 407(a) of Regulation S-K (§ 229.407(a) of this chapter), corporate governance.

Item 11A. Material Changes.

If the registrant elects to incorporate information by reference pursuant to General Instruction VII, describe any and all material changes in the registrant's affairs that have occurred since the end of the latest fiscal year for which audited financial statements were included in the latest Form 10-K and that have not been described in a Form 10-Q or Form 8-K filed under the Exchange Act.

Item 12. Incorporation of Certain Information by Reference.

If the registrant elects to incorporate information by reference pursuant to General Instruction VII.:

(a) It must specifically incorporate by reference into the prospectus contained in the registration statement the following documents by means of a statement to that effect in the prospectus listing all such documents:

(1) The registrant's latest annual report on Form 10-K filed pursuant to Section 13(a) or Section 15(d) of the Exchange Act that contains financial statements for the registrant's latest fiscal year for which a Form 10-K was required to have been filed; and

(2) All other reports filed pursuant to Section 13(a) or 15(d) of the Exchange Act or proxy or information statements filed pursuant to Section 14 of the Exchange Act since the end of the fiscal

year covered by the annual report referred to in paragraph (a)(1) above.

Note to Item 12(a). Attention is directed to Rule 439 (§ 230.439) regarding consent to use of material incorporated by reference.

(b)(1) The registrant must state:

(i) That it will provide to each person, including any beneficial owner, to whom a prospectus is delivered, a copy of any or all of the reports or documents that have been incorporated by reference in the prospectus contained in the registration statement but not delivered with the prospectus;

(ii) That it will provide these reports or documents upon written or oral request;

(iii) That it will provide these reports or documents at no cost to the requester;

(iv) The name, address, telephone number, and e-mail address, if any, to which the request for these reports or documents must be made; and

(v) The registrant's Web site address, including the uniform resource locator (URL) where the incorporated reports and other documents may be accessed.

Note to Item 12(b)(1). If the registrant sends any of the information that is incorporated by reference in the prospectus contained in the registration statement to security holders, it also must send any exhibits that are specifically incorporated by reference in that information.

(2) The registrant must:

(i) Identify the reports and other information that it files with the SEC; and

(ii) State that the public may read and copy any materials it files with the SEC at the SEC's Public Reference Room at 100 F Street, N.E., Washington, DC 20549. State that the public may obtain information on the operation of the Public Reference Room by calling the SEC at 1-800-SEC-0330. If the registrant is an electronic filer, state that the SEC maintains an Internet site that contains reports, proxy and information statements, and other information regarding issuers that file electronically with the SEC and state the address of that site (http://www.sec.gov).

Item 12A. Disclosure of Commission Position on Indemnification for Securities Act Liabilities.

Furnish the information required by *Item 510* of Regulation S-K (§ 229.510 of this chapter.)

PART II—INFORMATION NOT REQUIRED IN PROSPECTUS

Item 13. Other Expenses of Issuance and Distribution.

Furnish the information required by *Item 511* of Regulation S-K (§ 229.511 of this chapter).

Item 14. Indemnification of Directors and Officers.

Furnish the information required by *Item 702* of Regulation S-K (§ 229.702 of this chapter).

Item 15. Recent Sales of Unregistered Securities.

Furnish the information required by *Item 701* of Regulation S-K (§ 229.701 of this chapter).

Item 16. Exhibits and Financial Statement Schedules.

(a) Subject to the rules regarding incorporation by reference, furnish the exhibits as required by *Item 601* of Regulation S-K (§ 229.601 of this chapter).

(b) Furnish the financial statement schedules required by *Regulation S-X* (17 CFR Part 210) and Item 11(e) of this Form. These schedules shall be lettered or numbered in the manner described for exhibits in paragraph (a).

Item 17. Undertakings.

Furnish the undertakings required by *Item 512* of Regulation S-K (§ 229.512 of this chapter).

SIGNATURES

Pursuant to the requirements of the Securities Act of 1933, the registrant has duly caused this registration statement to be signed on its behalf by the undersigned, thereunto duly authorized in the City of ————————————————————, State of ————————————————————, on ——————————, 19———.

_____

(Registrant)

_____

By (Signature and Title)

Pursuant to the requirements of the Securities Act of 1933, this registration statement has been signed by the following persons in the capacities and on the dates indicated.

¶8001   Form S-1

(Signature)

_____

(Title)

_____

(Date)

Instructions.

1. The registration statement shall be signed by the registrant, its principal executive officer or officers, its principal financial officer, its controller or principal accounting officer and by at least a majority of the board of directors or persons performing similar functions. If the registrant is a foreign person, the registration statement shall also be signed by its authorized representative in the United States. Where the registrant is a limited partnership, the registration statement shall be signed by a majority of the board of directors of any corporate general partner signing the registration statement.

2. The name of each person who signs the registration statement shall be typed or printed beneath his signature. Any person who occupies more than one of the specified positions shall indicate each capacity in which he signs the registration statement. Attention is directed to *Rule 402* concerning manual signatures and to *Item 601* of Regulation S-K concerning signatures pursuant to powers of attorney.

INSTRUCTIONS AS TO SUMMARY PROSPECTUSES

1. A summary prospectus used pursuant to *Rule 431* (§ 230.431 of this chapter), shall at the time of its use contain much of the information specified below as is then included in the registration statement. All other information and documents contained in the registration statement may be omitted.

(a) As to Item 1, the aggregate offering price to the public, the aggregate underwriting discounts and commissions and the offering price per unit to the public;

(b) As to Item 4, a brief statement of the principal purposes for which the proceeds are to be used;

(c) As to Item 7, a statement as to the amount of the offering, if any, to be made for the account of security holders;

(d) As to Item 8, the name of the managing underwriter or underwriters and a brief statement as to the nature of the underwriter's obligation to take the securities; if any securities to be registered are to be offered otherwise than through underwriters, a brief statement as to the manner of distribution; and, if securities are to be offered otherwise than for cash. a brief statement as to the general purposes of the distribution, the basis upon which the securities are to be offered, the amount of compensation and other expenses of distribution, and by whom they are to be borne;

(e) As to Item 9, a brief statement as to dividend rights, voting rights, conversion rights, interest, maturity;

(f) As to Item 11, a brief statement of the general character of the business done and intended to be done, the selected financial data (*Item 301* of Regulation S-K (§ 229.301 of this chapter)) and a brief statement of the nature and present status of any material pending legal proceedings; and

(g) A tabular presentation of notes payable, long term debt, deferred credits, minority interests, if material, and the equity section of the latest balance sheet filed, as may be appropriate.

2. The summary prospectus shall not contain a summary or condensation of any other required financial information except as provided above.

3. Where securities being registered are to be offered in exchange for securities of any other issuer, the summary prospectus also shall contain that information as to Items 9 and 11 specified in paragraphs (e) and (f) above which would be required if the securities of such other issuer were registered on this Form.

4. The Commission may, upon the request of the registrant, and where consistent with the protection of investors, permit the omission of any of the information herein required or the furnishing in substitution therefor of appropriate information of comparable character. The Commission may also require the inclusion of other information in addition to, or in substitution for, the information herein required in any case where such information is necessary or appropriate for the protection of investors.

[¶ 8061]   **FORM S-3**

[As last amended in Release No. 33-9026, effective April 23, 2009, 74 F.R. 18612.]

UNITED STATES SECURITIES AND EXCHANGE COMMISSION

Washington, D.C. 20549

UNITED STATES SECURITIES AND EXCHANGE COMMISSION
Washington, D.C. 20549
FORM S-3

REGISTRATION STATEMENT UNDER THE SECURITIES ACT OF 1933

....
(Exact name of registrant as specified in its charter)

....
(State or other jurisdiction of incorporation or organization)

....
(I.R.S. Employer Identification No.)

....
(Address, including zip code, and telephone number, including area code, of registrant's principal
executive offices)

....
(Name, address, including zip code, and telephone number, including area code, of agent for
service)

Approximate date of commencement of proposed sale to the public . . . .

If the only securities being registered on this Form are being offered pursuant to dividend or interest reinvestment plans, please check the following box. [ ]

If any of the securities being registered on this Form are to be offered on a delayed or continuous basis pursuant to Rule 415 under the Securities Act of 1933, other than securities offered only in connection with dividend or interest reinvestment plans, check the following box. [ ]

If this Form is filed to register additional securities for an offering pursuant to Rule 462(b) under the Securities Act, please check the following box and list the Securities Act registration statement number of the earlier effective registration statement for the same offering. [ ] __

If this Form is a post-effective amendment filed pursuant to Rule 462(c) under the Securities Act, check the following box and list the Securities Act registration statement number of the earlier effective registration statement for the same offering. [ ] __

If this Form is a registration statement pursuant to General Instruction I.D. or a post-effective amendment thereto that shall become effective upon filing with the Commission pursuant to Rule 462(e) under the Securities Act, check the following box. [ ]

If this Form is a post-effective amendment to a registration statement filed pursuant to General Instruction I.D. filed to register additional securities or additional classes of securities pursuant to Rule 413(b) under the Securities Act, check the following box. [ ]

Indicate by check mark whether the registrant is a large accelerated filer, an accelerated filer, a non-accelerated filer, or a smaller reporting company. See the definitions of "large accelerated filer," "accelerated filer" and "smaller reporting company" in Rule 12b-2 of the Exchange Act. (Check one):

[ ] Large accelerated filer

[ ] Accelerated filer

[ ] Non-accelerated filer (Do not check if a smaller reporting company)

[ ] Smaller reporting company

Calculation of Registration Fee

Title of each class of securities to be registered	Amount to be registered	Proposed maximum offering price per unit	Proposed maximum aggregate offering price	Amount of registration fee

Note: Specific details relating to the fee calculation shall be furnished in notes to the table, including references to provisions of Rule 457 (§ 230.457 of this chapter) relied upon, if the basis of the calculation is not otherwise evident from the information presented in the table. If the filing fee is calculated pursuant to Rule 457(o) under the Securities Act, only the title of the class of securities to be registered, the proposed maximum aggregate offering price for that class of securities and the amount of registration fee need to appear in the "Calculation of Registration Fee" Table ("Fee Table"). Where two or more classes of securities are being registered pursuant to General Instruction II.D, however, the Fee Table need only specify the maximum aggregate offering price for all classes; the Fee Table need not specify by each class the proposed maximum aggregate offering price (See General Instruction II.D). Any difference between the dollar amount of securities registered for such offerings and the dollar amount of securities sold may be carried forward on a future registration statement pursuant to Rule 429 under the Securities Act.

Notes to the "Calculation of Registration Fee" Table ("Fee Table"):

1. Specific details relating to the fee calculation shall be furnished in notes to the Fee Table, including references to provisions of Rule 457 (§ 230.457 of this chapter) relied upon, if the basis of the calculation is not otherwise evident from the information presented in the Fee Table.

2. If the filing fee is calculated pursuant to Rule 457(o) under the Securities Act, only the title of the class of securities to be registered, the proposed maximum aggregate offering price for that class of securities, and the amount of registration fee need to appear in the Fee Table. Where two or more classes of securities are being registered pursuant to General Instruction II.D., however, the Fee Table need only specify the maximum aggregate offering price for all classes; the Fee Table need not specify by each class the proposed maximum aggregate offering price (see General Instruction II.D.).

3. If the filing fee is calculated pursuant to Rule 457(r) under the Securities Act, the Fee Table must state that it registers an unspecified amount of securities of each identified class of securities and must provide that the issuer is relying on Rule 456(b) and Rule 457(r). If the Fee Table is amended in a post-effective amendment to the registration statement or in a prospectus filed in accordance with Rule 456(b)(1)(ii) (§ 230.456(b)(1)(ii) of this chapter), the Fee Table must specify the aggregate offering price for all classes of securities in the referenced offering or offerings and the applicable registration fee.

4. Any difference between the dollar amount of securities registered for such offerings and the dollar amount of securities sold may be carried forward on a future registration statement pursuant to Rule 457 under the Securities Act.

GENERAL INSTRUCTIONS

I. Eligibility Requirements for Use of Form S-3

This instruction sets forth registrant requirements and transaction requirements for the use of Form S-3. Any registrant which meets the requirements of I.A. below ("Registrant Requirements") may use this Form for the registration of securities under the Securities Act of 1933 ("Securities Act") which are offered in any transaction specified in I.B. below ("Transaction Requirement") provided that the requirement applicable to the specified transaction are met. With respect to majority-owned subsidiaries, see Instruction I.C. below. With respect to well-known seasoned issuers and majority-owned subsidiaries of well-known seasoned issuers, see Instruction I.D. below.

A. *Registrant Requirements.* Registrants must meet the following conditions in order to use this Form for registration under the Securities Act of securities offered in the transactions specified in I.B. below:

1. The registrant is organized under the laws of the United States or any State or Territory or the District of Columbia and has its principal business operations in the United States or its territories.

2. The registrant has a class of securities registered pursuant to Section 12(b) of the Securities Exchange Act of 1934 ("Exchange Act") or a class of equity securities registered pursuant to Section 12(g) of the Exchange Act or is required to file reports pursuant to Section 15(d) of the Exchange Act.

3. The registrant:

(a) has been subject to the requirements of Section 12 or 15(d) of the Exchange Act and has filed all the material required to be filed pursuant to Section 13, 14 or 15(d) for a period of at least twelve calendar months immediately preceding the filing of the registration statement on this Form; and

(b) has filed in a timely manner all reports required to be filed during the twelve calendar months and any portion of a month immediately preceding the filing of the registration statement, other than a report that is required solely pursuant to Item 1.01, 1.02, 2.03, 2.04, 2.05, 2.06, 4.02(a) or 5.02(e) of Form 8-K (§ 249.308 of this chapter). If the registrant has used (during the twelve calendar months and any portion of a month immediately preceding the filing of the registration statement) Rule 12b-25(b) (§ 240.12b-25(b) of this chapter) under the Exchange Act with respect to a report or a portion of a report, that report or portion thereof has actually been filed within the time period prescribed by that rule.

4. The provisions in paragraphs A.2. and A.3.(a) above do not apply to any registered offerings of securities described in I.B.5 below. However, for such offerings of asset-backed securities, to the extent the depositor or any issuing entity previously established, directly or indirectly, by the depositor or any affiliate of the depositor (as defined in Item 1101 of Regulation AB (17 CFR 229.1101)) are or were at any time during the twelve calendar months and any portion of a month immediately preceding the filing of the registration statement on this Form subject to the requirements of section 12 or 15(d) of the Exchange Act (15 U.S.C. 78*l* or 78o(d)) with respect to a class of asset-backed securities involving the same asset class, such depositor and each such issuing entity must have filed all material required to be filed regarding such asset-backed securities pursuant to section 13, 14 or 15(d) of the Exchange Act (15 U.S.C. 78m, 78n or 78o(d)) for such period (or such shorter period that each such entity was required to file such materials). In addition, such material must have been filed in a timely manner, other than a report that is required solely pursuant to Item 1.01, 1.02, 2.03, 2.04, 2.05, 2.06, 4.02(a), 6.01, 6.03 or 6.05 of Form 8-K (17 CFR 249.308). If Rule 12b-25(b) (17 CFR 240.12b-25(b)) under the Exchange Act was used during such period with respect to a report or a portion of a report, that report or portion thereof has actually been filed within the time period prescribed by that rule. Regarding an affiliated depositor that became an affiliate as a result of a business combination transaction during such period, the filing of any material prior to the business combination transaction relating to asset-backed securities of an issuing entity previously established, directly or indirectly, by such affiliated depositor is excluded from this section, provided such business combination transaction was not part of a plan or scheme to evade the requirements of the Securities Act or the Exchange Act.

See the definition of "affiliate" in Securities Act Rule 405 (17 CFR 230.405).

5. Neither the registrant nor any of its consolidated or unconsolidated subsidiaries have, since the end of the last fiscal year for which certified financial statements of the registrant and its consolidated subsidiaries were included in a report filed pursuant to Section 13(a) or 15(d) of the Exchange Act: (a) failed to pay any dividend or sinking fund installment on preferred stock; or (b) defaulted (i) on any installment or installments on indebtedness for borrowed money, or (ii) on any rental on one or more long term leases, which defaults in the aggregate are material to the financial position of the registrant and its consolidated and unconsolidated subsidiaries, taken as a whole.

6. A foreign issuer, other than a foreign government, which satisfies all of the above provisions of these registrant eligibility requirements except the provisions in I.A. 1. relating to organization and principal business shall be deemed to have met these registrant eligibility requirements provided that such foreign issuer files the same reports with the Commission under Section 13(a) or 15(d) of the Exchange Act as a domestic registrant pursuant to I.A. 3. above.

7. If the registrant is a successor registrant, it shall be deemed to have met conditions 1., 2., 3., and 5, above if: (a) its predecessor and it, taken together, do so, provided that the succession was primarily for the purpose of changing the state of incorporation of the predecessor or forming a holding company and that the assets and liabilities of the successor at the time of succession were substantially the same as those of the predecessor, or (b) if all predecessors met the conditions at the time of succession and the registrant has continued to do so since the succession.

8. *Electronic filings.* In addition to satisfying the foregoing conditions, a registrant subject to the electronic filing requirements of Rule 101 of Regulation S-T (§ 232.101 of this chapter) shall have:

(a) Filed with the Commission all required electronic filings, including electronic copies of documents submitted in paper pursuant to a hardship exemption as provided by Rule 201 or Rule 202(d) of Regulation S-T (§ 232.201 or § 232.202(d) of this chapter); and

(b) Submitted electronically to the Commission and posted on its corporate Web site, if any, all Interactive Data Files required to be submitted and posted pursuant to Rule 405 of Regulation S-T (§ 232.405 of this chapter) during the twelve calendar months and any portion of a month immediately preceding the filing of the registration statement on this Form (or for such shorter period of time that the registrant was required to submit and post such files).

B. *Transaction Requirements.* Security offerings meeting any of the following conditions and made by a registrant meeting the Registrant Requirements specified in I.A. above may be registered on this Form:

1. *Primary Offerings by Certain Registrants.* Securities to be offered for cash by or on behalf of a registrant, or outstanding securities to be offered for cash for the account of any person other than the registrant, including securities acquired by standby underwriters in connection with the call or redemption by the registrant of warrants or a class of convertible securities; *provided* that the aggregate market value of the voting and non-voting common equity held by non-affiliates of the registrant is $75 million or more.

Instruction. For the purposes of this Form, "common equity" is as defined in Securities Act Rule 405 (§ 230.405 of this chapter). The aggregate market value of the registrant's outstanding voting and non-voting common equity shall be computed by use of the price at which the common equity was last sold, or the average of the bid and asked prices of such common equity, in the principal market for such common equity as of a date within 60 days prior to the date of filing. See the definition of "affiliate" in Securities Act Rule 405.

2. *Primary Offerings of Non-convertible Investment Grade Securities.* Non-convertible securities to be offered for cash by or on behalf of a registrant, provided such securities at the time of sale are "investment grade securities," as defined below. A non-convertible security is an "investment grade security" if, at the time of sale, at least one nationally recognized statistical rating organization (as that term is used in Rule 15c3-1(c)(2)(vi)(F) under the Securities Exchange Act of 1934 (§ 240.15c3-1(c)(2)(vi)(F) of this chapter) has rated the security in one of its generic rating categories which signifies investment grade; typically, the four highest rating categories (within which there may be sub-categories or gradations indicating relative standing) signify investment grade.

3. *Transactions Involving Secondary Offerings.*

Outstanding securities to be offered for the account of any person other than the issuer, including securities acquired by standby underwriters in connection with the call or redemption by the issuer of warrants or a class of convertible securities, if securities of the same class are listed and registered on a national securities exchange or are quoted on the automated quotation system of a national securities association. (In addition, attention is directed to General Instruction C to Form S-8 (§ 239.16b) for the registration of employee benefit plan securities for resale.)

4. *Rights Offerings, Dividend or Interest Reinvestment Plans, and Conversions, Warrants and Options.*

(a) Securities to be offered (1) upon the exercise of outstanding rights granted by the issuer of the securities to be offered, if such rights are granted on a pro rata basis to all existing security holders of the class of securities to which the rights attach, (2) under a dividend or interest reinvestment plan, or (3) upon the conversion of outstanding convertible securities or the exercise of outstanding warrants or options issued by the issuer of the securities to be offered, or an affiliate of that issuer.

(b) However, Form S-3 is available for registering these securities only if the issuer has sent, within the twelve calendar months immediately before the registration statement is filed, material containing the information required by Rule 14a-3(b) (§ 240.14a-3(b) of this chapter) under the Exchange Act to:

(1) all record holders of the rights,

(2) all participants in the plans, or

(3) all record holders of the convertible securities, warrants or options, respectively.

(c) The issuer also must have provided, within the twelve calendar months immediately before the Form S-3 registration statement is filed, the information required by Items 401, 402, 403 and 407(c)(3), (d)(4), (d)(5) and (e)(4) of Regulation S-K (§ 229.401 – § 229.403 and § 229.407(c)(3), (d)(4), (d)(5) and (e)(4) of this chapter) to:

(1) holders of rights exercisable for common stock,

(2) holders of securities convertible into common stock, and

(3) participants in plans that may invest in common stock, securities convertible into common stock, or warrants or options exercisable for common stock, respectively.

5. *Offerings of Investment grade Asset-backed Securities.*

(a) Asset-backed securities (as defined in 17 CFR 229.1101) to be offered for cash, provided:

(i) The securities are "investment grade securities," as defined in I.B.2 above (Primary Offerings of Non-convertible Investment Grade Securities);

(ii) Delinquent assets do not constitute 20% or more, as measured by dollar volume, of the asset pool as of the measurement date; and

(iii) With respect to securities that are backed by leases other than motor vehicle leases, the portion of the securitized pool balance attributable to the residual value of the physical property underlying the leases, as determined in accordance with the transaction agreements for the securities, does not constitute 20% or more, as measured by dollar volume, of the securitized pool balance as of the measurement date.

Instruction. For purposes of making the determinations required by paragraphs (a)(ii) and (a)(iii) of this General Instruction I.B.5, refer to the Instructions to Item 1101(c) of Regulation AB (17 CFR 229.1101(c)).

(b) Securities relating to an offering of asset-backed securities registered in accordance with paragraph (a) of this General Instruction I.B.5 where those securities represent an interest in or the right to the payments of cash flows of another asset pool and meet the requirements of Securities Act Rule 190(c)(1) through (4) (17 CFR 230.190(c)(1) through (4)).

6. *Limited Primary Offerings by Certain Other Registrants.* Securities to be offered for cash by or on behalf of a registrant; *provided that*:

(a) the aggregate market value of securities sold by or on behalf of the registrant pursuant to this Instruction I.B.6. during the period of 12 calendar months immediately prior to, and including, the sale is no more than one-third of the aggregate market value of the voting and non-voting common equity held by non-affiliates of the registrant;

(b) the registrant is not a shell company (as defined in §230.405 of this chapter) and has not been a shell company for at least 12 calendar months previously and if it has been a shell company at any time previously, has filed current Form 10 information with the Commission at least 12 calendar months previously reflecting its status as an entity that is not a shell company; and

(c) the registrant has at least one class of common equity securities listed and registered on a national securities exchange.

Instructions.

1. "Common equity" is as defined in Securities Act Rule 405 (§230.405 of this chapter). For purposes of computing the aggregate market value of the registrant's outstanding voting and non-voting common equity pursuant to General Instruction I.B.6., registrants shall use the price at which the common equity was last sold, or the average of the bid and asked prices of such common equity, in the principal market for such common equity as of a date within 60 days prior to the date of sale. See the definition of "affiliate" in Securities Act Rule 405 (§230.405 of this chapter).

2. For purposes of computing the aggregate market value of all securities sold by or on behalf of the registrant in offerings pursuant to General Instruction I.B.6. during any period of 12 calendar months, registrants shall aggregate the gross proceeds of such sales; *provided*, that, in the case of derivative securities convertible into or exercisa-

ble for shares of the registrant's common equity, registrants shall calculate the aggregate market value of any underlying equity shares in lieu of the market value of the derivative securities. The aggregate market value of the underlying equity shall be calculated by multiplying the maximum number of common equity shares into which the derivative securities are convertible or for which they are exercisable as of a date within 60 days prior to the date of sale, by the same per share market price of the registrant's equity used for purposes of calculating the aggregate market value of the registrant's outstanding voting and non-voting common equity pursuant to Instruction 1 to General Instruction I.B.6. If the derivative securities have been converted or exercised, the aggregate market value of the underlying equity shall be calculated by multiplying the actual number of shares into which the securities were converted or received upon exercise, by the market price of such shares on the date of conversion or exercise.

3. If the aggregate market value of the registrant's outstanding voting and nonvoting common equity computed pursuant to General Instruction I.B.6. equals or exceeds $75 million subsequent to the effective date of this registration statement, then the one third limitation on sales specified in General Instruction I.B.6(a) shall not apply to additional sales made pursuant to this registration statement on or subsequent to such date and instead the registration statement shall be considered filed pursuant to General Instruction I.B.1.

4. The term "Form 10 information" means the information that is required by Form 10 or Form 20-F (§249.210 or §249.220f of this chapter), as applicable to the registrant, to register under the Securities Exchange Act of 1934 each class of securities being registered using this form. A registrant may provide the Form 10 information in another Commission filing with respect to the registrant.

5. The date used in Instruction 2 to General Instruction I.B.6. shall be the same date used in Instruction 1 to General Instruction I.B.6.

6. A registrant's eligibility to register a primary offering on Form S-3 pursuant to General Instruction I.B.6. does not mean that the registrant meets the requirements of Form S-3 for purposes of any other rule or regulation of the Commission apart from Rule 415(a)(1)(x) (§230.415(a)(1)(x) of this chapter).

7. Registrants must set forth on the outside front cover of the prospectus the calculation of the aggregate market value of the registrant's outstanding voting and nonvoting common equity pursuant to General Instruction I.B.6. and the amount of all securities offered pursuant to General Instruction I.B.6. during the prior 12 calendar

month period that ends on, and includes, the date of the prospectus.

8. For purposes of General Instruction I.B.6(c), a "national securities exchange" shall mean an exchange registered as such under Section 6(a) of the Securities Exchange Act of 1934.

C. *Majority-owned Subsidiaries.* If a registrant is a majority-owned subsidiary, security offerings may be registered on this Form if:

1. the registrant-subsidiary itself meets the Registrant Requirements and the applicable Transaction Requirement;

2. the parent of the registrant-subsidiary meets the Registrant Requirements and the conditions of Transaction Requirements B.2. (Primary Offerings of Non-convertible Investment Grade Securities) are met;

3. the parent of the registrant-subsidiary meets the Registrant Requirements and the applicable Transaction Requirement, and provides a full and unconditional guarantee, as defined in Rule 3-10 of Regulation S-X (§ 210.3-10 of this chapter), of the payment obligations on the securities being registered, and the securities being registered are non-convertible securities, other than common equity;

Note: In such an instance, the parent-guarantor is the issuer of a separate security consisting if the guarantee which must be concurrently registered but may be registered on the same registration statement as are the guaranteed securities.

4. the parent of the registrant-subsidiary meets the Registrant Requirements and the applicable Transaction Requirement, and the securities of the registrant-subsidiary being registered are full and unconditional guarantees, as defined in Rule 3-10 of Regulation S-X, of the payment obligations on the parent's non-convertible securities, other than common equity, being registered; or

5. the parent of the registrant-subsidiary meets the Registrant Requirements and the applicable Transaction Requirement, and the securities of the registrant-subsidiary being registered are guarantees of the payment obligations on the non convertible securities, other than common equity, being registered by another majority-owned subsidiary of the parent where the parent provides a full and unconditional guarantee, as defined in Rule 3-10 of Regulation S-X, of such non-convertible securities.

Note to General Instruction I.C.: With regard to paragraphs I.C.3, I.C.4, and I.C.5 above, the guarantor is the issuer of a separate security consisting of the guarantee, which must be concurrently registered, but may be registered on the same registration statement as are the non-convertible guaranteed securities.

D. *Automatic Shelf Offerings by Well-Known Seasoned Issuers.* Any registrant that is a well-known seasoned issuer, as defined in Rule 405, at the most recent eligibility determination date specified in paragraph (2) of that definition may use this Form for registration under the Securities Act of securities offerings, other than pursuant to Rule 415(a)(1)(vii) or (viii) (§ 230.415(a)(1)(vii) or (viii) of this chapter), as follows:

1. The securities to be offered are:

(a) Any securities to be offered pursuant to Rule 415, Rule 430A, or Rule 430B (§ 230.415, § 230.430A, or § 230.430B of this chapter) by:

(i) A registrant that is a well-known seasoned issuer by reason of paragraph (1)(i)(A) of the definition in Rule 405; or

(ii) A registrant that is a well-known seasoned issuer only by reason of paragraph (1)(i)(B) of the definition in Rule 405 if the registrant also is eligible to register a primary offering of its securities pursuant to Transaction Requirement I.B.1 of this Form;

(b) Non-convertible securities, other than common equity, to be offered pursuant to Rule 415, Rule 430A, or Rule 430B by a registrant that is a well-known seasoned issuer only by reason of paragraph (1)(i)(B) of the definition in Rule 405 and does not fall within Transaction Requirement I.B.1 of this Form;

(c) Securities of majority-owned subsidiaries of the parent registrant to be offered pursuant to Rule 415, Rule 430A, or Rule 430B if the parent registrant is a well-known seasoned issuer and the securities of the majority-owned subsidiary being registered meet the following requirements:

(i) Securities of a majority-owned subsidiary that is a well-known seasoned issuer at the time it becomes a registrant, other than by virtue of paragraph (1)(ii) of the definition of well-known seasoned issuer in Rule 405;

(ii) Securities of a majority-owned subsidiary that are non-convertible securities, other than common equity, and the parent registrant provides a full and unconditional guarantee, as defined in Rule 3-10 of Regulation S-X, of the payment obligations on the non-convertible securities;

(iii) Securities of a majority-owned subsidiary that are a guarantee of:

(A) Non-convertible securities, other than common equity, of the parent registrant being registered;

(B) Non-convertible securities, other than common equity, of another majority-owned subsidiary being registered and the parent registrant has provided a full and unconditional guarantee, as defined in Rule 3-10 of Regulation S-X, of the payment obligations on such non-convertible securities; or

(iv) Securities of a majority-owned subsidiary that meet the conditions of Transaction Requirement I.B.2. of this Form (Primary Offerings of Non-Convertible Investment Grade Securities).

(d) Securities to be offered for the account of any person other than the issuer ("selling security holders"), provided that the registration statement and the prospectus are not required to separately identify the selling security holders or the securities to be sold by such persons until the filing of a prospectus, prospectus supplement, posteffective amendment to the registration statement, or periodic or current report under the Exchange Act that is incorporated by reference into the registration statement and prospectus, identifying the selling security holders and the amount of securities to be sold by each of them and, if included in a periodic or current report, a prospectus or prospectus supplement is filed, as required by Rule 430B, pursuant to Rule 424(b)(7) (§ 230.424(b)(7) of this chapter).

2. The registrant pays the registration fee pursuant to Rules 456(b) and 457(r) or in accordance with Rule 456(a).

3. If the registrant is a majority-owned subsidiary, it is required to file and has filed reports pursuant to Section 13 or Section 15(d) of the Exchange Act and satisfies the requirements of the Form with regard to incorporation by reference or information about the majority-owned subsidiary is included in the registration statement (or a post-effective amendment to the registration statement).

4. The registrant may register additional securities or classes of its or its majority-owned subsidiaries' securities on a post-effective amendment pursuant to Rule 413(b) (§ 203.413(b) of this chapter).

5. An automatic shelf registration statement and post-effective amendment will become effective immediately pursuant to Rule 462(e) and (f) (§ 230.462(e) and (f) of this chapter) upon filing. All filings made on or in connection with automatic shelf registration statements on this Form become public upon filing with the Commission.

II. Application of General Rules and Regulations

A. Attention is directed to the General Rules and Regulations under the Securities Act, particularly Regulation C thereunder (17 CFR 230.400 to 230.494). That Regulation contains general requirements regarding the preparation and filing of registration statements

B. Attention is directed to Regulation S-K (17 CFR Part 229) for the requirements applicable to the content of the non-financial statement portions of registration statements under the Securities Act. Where this Form directs the registrant to furnish information required by Regulation S-K and the item of Regulation S-K so provides, information need only be furnished to the extent appropriate. Notwithstanding Item 501 and 502 of Regulation S-K, no table of contents is required to be included in the prospectus or registration statement prepared on this form. In addition to the information expressly required to be included in a registration statement on this Form S-3, registrants also may provide such other information as they deem appropriate.

C. A smaller reporting company, defined in Rule 405 (17 CFR 230.405), that is eligible to use Form S-3 shall use the disclosure items in Regulation S-K (17 CFR 229.10 *et seq.*) with specific attention to the scaled disclosure provided for smaller reporting companies, if any. Smaller reporting companies may provide the financial information called for by Article 8 of Regulation S-X in lieu of the financial information called for by Item 11 in this form.

D. Non-Automatic Shelf Registration Statements. Where two or more classes of securities being registered on this Form pursuant to General Instruction I.B.1. or I.B.2. are to be offered pursuant to Rule 415(a)(1)(x) (§ 230.415(a)(1)(x) of this chapter), and where this Form is not an automatic shelf registration statement, Rule 457(o) permits the registration fee to be calculated on the basis of the maximum offering price of all the securities listed in the Fee Table. In this event, while the Fee Table would list each of the classes of securities being registered and the aggregate proceeds to be raised, the Fee Table need not specify by each class information as to the amount to be registered, proposed maximum offering price per unit, and proposed maximum aggregate offering price.

E. Automatic Shelf Registration Statements. Where securities are being registered on this Form pursuant to General Instruction I.D., Rule 456(b) permits, but does not require, the registrant to pay the registration fee on a pay-as-you-go basis and Rule 457(r) permits, but does not require, the registration fee to be calculated on the basis of the aggregate offering price of the securities to be offered in an offering or offerings off the registration statement. If a registrant elects to pay all or a portion of the registration fee on a deferred basis, the Fee Table in the initial filing must identify the classes of securities being registered and provide that the registrant elects to rely on Rule 456(b) and Rule 457(r), but the Fee Table does not need to specify any other information. When the registrant amends the Fee Table in accordance with Rule Rule 456(b)(ii), the amended Fee Table must include either the dollar amount of securities being registered if paid in advance of or in connection with an offering or offerings or the aggregate offering price for all classes of securities referenced in the offerings and the applicable registration fee.

F. Information in Automatic and Non-Automatic Shelf Registration Statements. Where securities are being registered on this Form pursuant to General Instruction I.B.1, I.B.2, I.B.5, I.C., or I.D., information is only required to be furnished as of the date of initial effectiveness of the registration statement to the extent required by Rule 430A or Rule 430B. Required information about a specific transaction must be included in the prospectus in the registration statement by means of a prospectus that is deemed to be part of and included in the registration statement pursuant to Rule 430A or Rule 430B, a post-effective amendment to the registration statement, or a periodic or current report under the Exchange Act incorporated by reference into the registration statement and the prospectus and identified in a prospectus filed, as required by Rule 430B, pursuant to Rule 424(b) (§ 230.424(b) of this chapter).

G. Selling Security Holder Offerings. Where a registrant eligible to register primary offerings on this Form pursuant to General Instruction I.B.1 registers securities offerings on this Form pursuant to General Instruction I.B.1 or I.B.3 for the account of persons other than the registrant, if the offering of the securities, or securities convertible into such securities, that are being registered on behalf of the selling security holders was completed and the securities, or securities convertible into such securities, were issued and outstanding prior to the original date of filing the registration statement covering the resale of the securities, the registrant may, as permitted by Rule 430B(b), in lieu of identifying selling security holders prior to effectiveness of the resale registration statement, refer to unnamed selling security holders in a generic manner by identifying the initial transaction in which the securities were sold. Following effectiveness, the registrant must include in a prospectus filed pursuant to Rule 424(b)(7), a post-effective amendment to the registration statement, or an Exchange Act report incorporated by reference into the prospectus that is part of the registration statement (which Exchange Act report is identified in a prospectus filed, as required by Rule 430B, pursuant to Rule 424(b)(7)) the names of previously unidentified selling security holders and amounts of securities that they intend to sell. If this Form is being filed pursuant to General Instruction I.D. by a well-known seasoned issuer to register securities being offered for the account of persons other than the issuer, the registration statement and the prospectus included in the registration statement do not need to designate the securities that will be offered for the account of such persons, identify them, or identify the initial transaction in which the securities, or securities

convertible into such securities, were sold until the registrant files a post-effective amendment to the registration statement, a prospectus pursuant to Rule 424(b), or an Exchange Act report (and prospectus filed, as required by Rule 430B, pursuant to Rule 424(b)(7)) containing information for the offering on behalf of such persons.

III. Dividend or Interest Reinvestment Plans: Filing and Effectiveness of Registration Statement; Requests for Confidential Treatment

A registration statement on this Form S-3 relating solely to securities offered pursuant to a dividend or interest reinvestment plan will become effective automatically (Rule 462, § 230.462 of this chapter) upon filing (Rule 456, § 230.456 of this chapter). Post-effective amendments to such a registration statement on this Form shall become effective upon filing (Rule 464, § 230.464 of this chapter). Delaying amendments are not permitted in connection with either original filings or amendments on such a registration statement (Rule 473(d), § 230.473(d) of this chapter), and any attempt to interpose a delaying amendment of any kind will be ineffective. All filings made on or in connection with this Form become public upon filing with the Commission. As a result, requests for confidential treatment made under Rule 406 (§ 230.406 of this chapter) must be processed with the Commission staff prior to the filing of such a registration statement. The number of copies of the registration statement and of each amendment required by rules 402 and 472 (§§ 230.402 and 230.472 of this chapter) shall be filed with the Commission: *provided, however,* That the number of additional copies referred to in Rule 402(b) may be reduced from ten to three and the number of additional copies referred to in Rule 472(a) may be reduced from eight to three, one of which shall be marked clearly and precisely to indicate changes.

IV. Registration of Additional Securities and Additional Classes of Securities

A. Registration of Additional Securities Pursuant to Rule 462(b). With respect to registration of additional securities for an offering pursuant to Rule 462(b) under the Securities Act, the registrant may file a registration statement consisting only of the following: the facing page; a statement that the contents of the earlier registration statement, identified by file number, are incorporated by reference; required opinions and consents; the signature page; and any price-related information omitted from the earlier registration statement in reliance on Rule 430A that the registrant chooses to include in the new registration statement. The information contained in such a Rule 462(b) registration statement shall be deemed to be a part of the earlier registration statement as of the date of effectiveness of the Rule 462(b) registration statement. Any opinion or consent required in the Rule

462(b) registration statement may be incorporated by reference from the earlier registration statement with respect to the offering, if: (i) such opinion or consent expressly provides for such incorporation; and (ii) such opinion relates to the securities registered pursuant to Rule 462(b). *See* Rule 411(c) and Rule 439(b) under the Securities Act.

B. Registration of Additional Securities or Classes of Securities or Additional Registrants After Effectiveness. A well-known seasoned issuer relying on General Instruction I.D. of this Form may register additional securities or classes of securities, pursuant to Rule 413(b) by filing a post-effective amendment to the effective registration statement. The well-known seasoned issuer may add majority-owned subsidiaries as additional registrants whose securities are eligible to be sold as part of the automatic shelf registration statement by filing a post-effective amendment identifying the additional registrants, and the registrant and the additional registrants and other persons required to sign the registration statement must sign the post-effective amendment. The post-effective amendment must consist of the facing page; any disclosure required by this Form that is necessary to update the registration statement to reflect the additional securities, additional classes of securities, or additional registrants; any required opinions and consents; and the signature page. Required information, consents, or opinions may be included in the prospectus and the registration statement through a post-effective amendment or may be provided through a document incorporated or deemed incorporated by reference into the registration statement and the prospectus that is part of the registration statement, or, as to the required information only, contained in a prospectus filed pursuant to Rule 424(b) that is deemed part of and included in the registration statement and prospectus that is part of the registration statement.

V. Offerings of Asset-Backed Securities

The following applies if a registration statement on this Form S-3 is being used to register an offering of asset-backed securities. Terms used in this General Instruction V. have the same meaning as in Item 1101 of Regulation AB (17 CFR 229.1101).

A. *Disclosure.*

1. For a registration statement on this Form S-3 relating to an offering of asset-backed securities, in addition to the Items that are otherwise required by this Form, the registrant must furnish in the prospectus the information required by Items 1102 through 1120 of Regulation AB (17 CFR 229.1102 through 229.1120).

2. For registered offerings pursuant to Securities Act Rule 415(a)(1)(x) (17 CFR 230.415(a)(1)(x)) that include a base prospectus and form of prospectus supplement, a separate base prospectus and form of prospectus supplement must be presented for each asset class that may be securitized in a discrete pool in a takedown of asset-backed securities under the registration statement. A separate base prospectus and form of prospectus supplement also must be presented for each country of origin or country of property securing pool assets that may be securitized in a discrete pool in a takedown of asset-backed securities under the registration statement. For both separate asset classes and jurisdictions of origin or property, a separate base prospectus and form of supplement is not required for transactions that principally consist of a particular asset class or jurisdiction which also describe one or more potential additional asset classes or jurisdictions, so long as the pool assets for the additional classes or jurisdictions in the aggregate are below 10% of the pool, as measured by dollar volume, for any particular takedown. When a preliminary prospectus is required under this Form pursuant to Securities Act Rule 190(b)(7) (17 CFR 230.190(b)(7)), the information to be included in the base prospectus and prospectus supplement is to be substantially similar to that which would be included if the preliminary prospectus was required under Form S-1 (17 CFR 239.11) pursuant to such rules.

B. *Signatures.*

The registration statement must be signed by the depositor, the depositor's principal executive officer or officers, principal financial officer and controller or principal accounting officer, and by at least a majority of the depositor's board of directors or persons performing similar functions.

PART I
INFORMATION REQUIRED IN PROSPECTUS

Item 1. Forepart of the Registration Statement and Outside Front Cover Page of Prospectus.

Set forth in the forepart of the registration statement and on the outside from cover page of the prospectus the information required by Item 501 of Regulation S-K (§ 229.501 of this chapter).

Item 2. Inside Front and Outside Back Cover Pages of Prospectus.

Set forth on the inside front cover page of the prospectus or, where permitted, on the outside back cover page, the information required by Item 502 of Regulation S-K (§ 229.502 of this chapter).

Item 3. Summary Information, Risk Factors and Ratio of Earnings to Fixed Charges.

Furnish the information required by Item 503 of Regulation S-K (§ 229.503 of this chapter).

Item 4. Use of Proceeds.

Furnish the information required by Item 504 of Regulation S-K (§ 229.504 of this chapter).

Item 5. Determination of Offering Price.

Furnish the information required by Item 505 of Regulation S-K (§ 229.505 of this chapter).

Item 6. Dilution.

Furnish the information required by Item 506 of Regulation S-K (§ 229.506 of this chapter).

Item 7. Selling Security Holders.

Furnish the information required by Item 507 of Regulation S-K (§ 229.507 of this chapter).

Item 8. Plan of Distribution.

Furnish the information required by Item 508 of Regulation S-K (§ 229.508 of this chapter).

Item 9. Description of Securities to be Registered.

Furnish the information required by Item 202 of Regulation S-K (§ 229.202 of this chapter), unless capital stock is to be registered and securities of the same class are registered pursuant to Section 12 of the Exchange Act.

Item 10. Interests of Named Experts and Counsel.

Furnish the information required by Item 509 of Regulation S-K (§ 229.509 of this chapter).

Item 11. Material Changes.

(a) Describe any and all material changes in the registrant's affairs that have occurred since the end of the latest fiscal year for which certified financial statements were included in the latest annual report to security holders and that have not been described in a report on Form 10-Q (§ 249.308a of this chapter) or Form 8-K (§ 249.308 of this chapter) filed under the Exchange Act.

(b) Include in the prospectus, if not incorporated by reference therein from the reports filed under the Exchange Act specified in Item 12(a), a proxy or information statement filed pursuant to Section 14 of the Exchange Act, a prospectus previously filed pursuant to Rule 424(b) or (c) under the Securities Act (§ 230.424(b) or (c) of this chapter) or, where no prospectus was required to be filed pursuant to Rule 424(b), the prospectus included in the registration statement at effectiveness, or a Form 8-K filed during either of the two preceding years:

(i) information required by Rule 3-05 and Article 11 of Regulation S-X (17 CFR Part 210);

(ii) restated financial statements prepared in accordance with Regulation S-X if there has been a change in accounting principles or a correction in an error where such change or correction requires a material retroactive restatement of financial statements;

(iii) restated financial statements prepared in accordance with Regulation S-X where a combination of entities under common control has been consummated subsequent to the most recent fiscal year and the transferred businesses, considered in the aggregate, are significant pursuant to Rule 11-01(b), or

(iv) any financial information required because of a material disposition of assets outside the normal course of business.

Item 12. Incorporation of Certain Information by Reference.

(a) the documents listed in (1) and (2) below shall be specifically incorporated by reference into the prospectus, by means of a statement to that effect in the prospectus listing all such documents.

(1) the registrant's latest annual report on Form 10-K (17 CFR 249.310) filed pursuant to Section 13(a) or 15(d) of the Exchange Act that contains financial statements for the registrant's latest fiscal year for which a Form 10-K was required to be filed; and

(2) all other reports filed pursuant to Section 13(a) or 15(d) of the Exchange Act since the end of the fiscal year covered by the annual report referred to in (1) above; and

(3) if capital stock is to be registered and securities of the same class are registered under Section 12 of the Exchange Act, the description of such class of securities which is contained in a registration statement filed under the Exchange Act, including any amendment or reports filed for the purpose of updating such description.

(b) The prospectus shall also state that all documents subsequently filed by the registrant pursuant to Sections 13(a), 13(c), 14 or 15(d) of the Exchange Act, prior to the termination of the offering shall be deemed to be incorporated by reference into the prospectus.

(c)(1) You must state (i) that you will provide to each person, including any beneficial owner, to whom a prospectus is delivered, a copy of any or all of the information that has been incorporated by reference in the prospectus but not delivered with the prospectus;

(ii) that you will provide this information upon written or oral request;

(iii) that you will provide this information at no cost to the requester; and

(iv) the name, address, and telephone number to which the request for this information must be made.

Note to Item 12(c)(1)

If you send any of the information that is incorporated by reference in the prospectus to security holders, you also must send any exhibits that are specifically incorporated by reference in that information.

(2) You must (i) identify the reports and other information that you file with the SEC; and

(ii) state that the public may read and copy any materials you file with the SEC at the SEC's Public Reference Room at 100 F Street, N.E., Washington, D.C. 20549. State that the public may obtain information on the operation of the Public Reference Room by calling the SEC at 1-800-SEC-0330. If you are an electronic filer, state that the SEC maintains an Internet site that contains reports, proxy and information statements,

and other information regarding issuers that file electronically with the SEC and state the address of that site (http://www.sec.gov). You are encouraged to give your Internet address, if available.

Instruction Attention is directed to Rule 439 (§ 230.439 of this chapter) regarding consent to use of material incorporated by reference.

(d) Any information required in the prospectus in response to Item 3 through Item 11 of this Form may be included in the prospectus through documents filed pursuant to Section 13(a), 14, or 15(d) of the Exchange Act that are incorporated or deemed incorporated by reference into the prospectus that is part of the registration statement.

Item 13. Disclosure of Commission Position on Indemnification for Securities Act Liabilities.

Furnish the information required by Item 510 of Regulation S-K (§ 229.510 of this chapter).

PART II
INFORMATION NOT REQUIRED IN PROSPECTUS

Item 14. Other Expenses of Issuance and Distribution.

Furnish the information required by Item 511 of Regulation S-K (§ 229.511 of this chapter).

Item 15. Indemnification of Directors and Officers.

Furnish the information required by Item 702 of Regulation S-K (§ 229.702 of this chapter).

Item 16. Exhibits.

Subject to the rules regarding incorporation by reference, furnish the exhibits required by Item 601 of Regulation S-K (§ 229.601 of this chapter).

Item 17. Undertakings.

Furnish the undertakings required by Item 512 of Regulation S-K (§ 229.512 of this chapter).

SIGNATURES

Pursuant to the requirements of the Securities Act of 1933, the registrant certifies that it has reasonable grounds to believe that it meets all of the requirements for filing on Form S-3 and has duly caused this registration statement to be signed on its behalf by the undersigned, thereunto duly authorized in the City of . . . . , State of . . . . , on . . . . , 19. . . . . . .

(Registrant) . . . .

By (Signature and Title) . . . .

Pursuant to the requirements of the Securities Act of 1933, this registration statement has been signed by the following persons in the capacities and on the dates indicated.

(Signature) . . . .

(Title) . . . .

(Date) . . . .

Instructions. 1. The registration statement shall be signed by the registrant, its principal executive officer or officers, its principal financial officer, its controller or principal accounting officer, and by at least a majority of the board of directors or persons performing similar functions. If the registrant is a foreign person, the registration statement shall also be signed by its authorized representative in the United States. Where the

registrant is a limited partnership, the registration statement shall be signed by a majority of the board of directors of any corporate general partner signing the registration statement.

2. The name of each person who signs the registration statement shall be typed or printed beneath his signature. Any person who occupies more than one of the specified positions shall

indicate each capacity in which he signs the registration statement. Attention is directed to Rule 402 concerning manual signatures and Item 601 of Regulation S-K concerning signatures pursuant to powers of attorney.

3. Where eligibility for use of the Form is based on the assignment of a security rating pursuant to

Transaction Requirement B.2 or B.5., the registrant may sign the registration statement notwithstanding the fact that such security rating has not been assigned by the filing date, provided that the registrant reasonably believes, and so states, that the security rating requirement will be met by the time of sale.

[¶ 8071]   FORM S-4

[As last amended in Release No. 33-9026, effective April 23, 2009, 74 F.R. 18612.]

UNITED STATES SECURITIES AND EXCHANGE COMMISSION

Washington, D.C. 20549

FORM S-4

REGISTRATION STATEMENT UNDER THE SECURITIES ACT OF 1933

UNITED STATES SECURITIES AND EXCHANGE COMMISSION
Washington, D.C. 20549
FORM S-4

REGISTRATION STATEMENT UNDER THE SECURITIES ACT OF 1933

. . . .
(Exact name of registrant as specified in its charter)
. . . .
(State or other jurisdiction of incorporation or organization)
. . . .
(Primary Standard Industrial Classification Code Number)
. . . .
(I.R.S. Employer Identification No.)
. . . .
(Address, including ZIP Code, and telephone number, including area code, of
registrant's principal executive offices)
. . . .
(Name, address, including ZIP Code, and telephone number, including area code, of
agent for service)

Approximate date of commencement of proposed sale of the securities to the public . . . .
. . . .

If the securities being registered on this Form are being offered in connection with the formation of a holding company and there is compliance with General Instruction G, check the following box. []

If this Form is filed to register additional securities for an offering pursuant to Rule 462(b) under the Securities Act, check the following box and list the Securities Act registration statement number of the earlier effective registration statement for the same offering. [ ]

If this Form is a post-effective amendment filed pursuant to Rule 462(d) under the Securities Act, check the following box and list the Securities Act registration statement number of the earlier effective registration statement for the same offering. [ ]

Indicate by check mark whether the registrant is a large accelerated filer, an accelerated filer, a non-accelerated filer, or a smaller reporting company. See the definitions of "large accelerated filer," "accelerated filer" and "smaller reporting company" in Rule 12b-2 of the Exchange Act. (Check one):

[ ] Large accelerated filer
[ ] Accelerated filer
[ ] Non-accelerated filer (Do not check if a smaller reporting company)
[ ] Smaller reporting company

If applicable, place an X in the box to designate the appropriate rule provision relied upon in conducting this transaction:

[ ] Exchange Act Rule 13e-4(i) (Cross-Border Issuer Tender Offer)
[ ] Exchange Act Rule 14d-1(d) (Cross-Border Third-Party Tender Offer)

Calculation of Registration Fee

Title of each class of securities to be registered	Amount to be registered	Proposed maximum offering price per unit	Proposed maximum aggregate offering price	Amount of registration fee

Note: Specific details relating to the fee calculation shall be furnished in notes to the table, including references to provisions of Rule 457 (§ 230.457 of the chapter) relied upon, if the basis of the calculation is not otherwise evident from the information presented in the table.

GENERAL INSTRUCTIONS

A. Rule as to Use of Form S-4.

1. This Form may be used for registration under the Securities Act of 1933 ("Securities Act") of securities to be issued (1) in a transaction of the type specified in paragraph (a) of Rule 145 (§ 230.145 of this chapter); (2) in a merger in which the applicable state law would not require the solicitation of the votes or consents of all of the security holders of the company being acquired; (3) in an exchange offer for securities of the issuer or another entity; (4) in a public reoffering or resale of any such securities acquired pursuant to this registration statement; or (5) in more than one of the kinds of transaction listed in (1) through (4) registered on one registration statement.

2. If the registrant meets the requirements of and elects to comply with the provisions in any item of this Form or Form F-4 (§ 239.34 of this chapter) that provides for incorporation by reference of information about the registrant or the company being acquired, the prospectus must be sent to the security holders no later than 20 business days prior to the date on which the meeting of such security holders is held or, if no meeting is held, at least 20 business days prior to either (1) the date the votes, consents or authorizations may be used to effect the corporate action or, (2) if votes, consents or authorizations are not used, the date the transaction is consummated. Attention is directed to Sections 13(e), 14(d) and 14(e) of the Securities Exchange Act of 1934 ("Exchange Act") the rules and regulations thereunder regarding other time periods in connection with exchange offers and going private transactions.

3. This Form shall not be used if the registrant is a registered investment company or a business development company as defined in Section 2(a)(48) of the Investment Company Act of 1940.

B. Information with Respect to the Registrant.

1. Information with respect to the registrant shall be provided in accordance with the items referenced in one of the following subparagraphs:

a. Items 10 and 11 of this Form, if the registrant elects this alternative and meets the following requirements of Form S-3 (§ 239.13 of this chapter) (hereinafter, with respect to the registrant, "meets the requirements for use of Form S-3") for this offering of securities:

(i) the registrant meets the requirements of General Instruction I.A. of Form S-3; and

(ii) one of the following is met

A. The registrant meets the aggregate market value requirement of General Instruction I.B.1. of Form S-3; or

B. Non-convertible debt or preferred securities are to be offered pursuant to this registration statement and are "investment grade securities" as defined in General Instruction I.B.2. of Form S-3; or

C. The registrant is a majority-owned subsidiary and one of the conditions of General Instruction I.C. of Form S-3 is met.

b. Items 12 and 13 of this Form, if the registrant meets the requirements for use of Form S-3 and elects this alternative; or

c. Item 14 of this Form, if the registrant does not meet the requirements for use of Form S-3, or if it otherwise elects to use this alternative.

2. If the registrant is a real estate entity of the type described in General Instruction A to Form S-11 (§ 239.18 of this chapter), the information prescribed by Items 12, 13, 14, 15 and 16 of Form S-11 shall be furnished about the registrant in addition to the information provided pursuant to Items 10 through 14 of this Form. The information prescribed by such Items of Form S-11 may be incorporated by reference into the prospectus if (a) a registrant qualifies for and elects to provide information pursuant to alternative 1. a. or 1.b. of this instruction and (b) the documents incorporated by reference pursuant to such elected alternative contain such information.

C. Information With Respect to the Company Being Acquired.

1. Information with respect to the company whose securities are being acquired (hereinafter including, where securities of the registrant are being offered in exchange for securities of another

company, such other company) shall be provided in accordance with the items referenced in one of the following subparagraphs:

a. Item 15 of this Form, if the company being acquired meets the requirements of General Instructions I.A. and I.B. 1. of Form S-3 (hereinafter, with respect to the company being acquired, "meets the requirements for use of Form S-3") of Form S-3 and this alternative is elected;

b. Item 16 of this Form, if the company being acquired meets the requirements for use of Form S-3 and this alternative is elected; or

c. Item 17 of this Form, if the company being acquired does not meet the requirements for use of Form S-3, or if this alternative is otherwise elected.

2. If the company being acquired is a real estate entity of the type described in General Instruction A to Form S-11, the information that would be required by Items 13, 14, 15 and 16(a) of Form S-11 if securities of such company were being registered shall be furnished about such company being acquired in addition to the information provided pursuant to this Form. The information prescribed by such Items of Form S-11 may be incorporated by reference into the prospectus if (a) the company being acquired would qualify for use of the level of disclosure prescribed by alternative 1.a. or 1.b. of this instruction and such alternative is elected and (b) the documents incorporated by reference pursuant to such elected alternative contain such information.

D. Application of General Rules and Regulations.

1. Attention is directed to the General Rules and Regulations under the Securities Act, particularly those comprising Regulation C thereunder (§ 230.400 et seq. of this chapter). That Regulation contains general requirements regarding the preparation and filing of registration statements.

2. Attention is directed to Regulation S-K (Part 229 of this chapter) for the requirements applicable to the content of non-financial statement portions of registration statements under the Securities Act. Where this Form directs the registrant to furnish information required by Regulation S-K and the item of Regulation S-K so provides, information need only be furnished to the extent appropriate.

3. A "small business issuer," defined in § 230.405, shall refer to the disclosure items in Regulation S-B (17 CFR 228.10 *et seq.*) and not Regulation S-K except with respect to disclosure called for by subpart 900 of Regulation S-K. Small business issuers shall provide or incorporate by reference the information called for by Item 310 of Regulation S-B.

(b) Registrants and Companies to be Acquired which relied upon Alternative 1 in their most recent Form 10-KSB:

(i) Part 1.A.—furnish the information required by Part 1.A. of this Form;

(ii) Part I.B.—in lieu of the information required in Item 14, furnish the information required in (a) Questions 3, 4, 11, 43 and 47-50 of Model A of Form 1-A, and (b) Item 14(d) and 14(i) of this Form;

(iii) Part 1.C.—in lieu of the information required in Item 17, furnish the information required in (a) Item 17(a), 17(b)(1), 17(b)(2), 17(b)(6), 17(b)(7) and 17(b)(8) of this Form, and (b) Questions 4, 11 and 47-50 of Model A of Form 1-A;

(iv) Part 1.D.—(1) in lieu of providing the information required in Item 18, furnish the information required in (a) Items 18(a)(1)—18(a)(6) and (b) Questions 29-36 and 39-42 of Model A of Form 1-A; and (2) in lieu of providing the information required in Item 19(a), furnish the information required in (a) Items 19(a)(1)—19(a)(6) of this Form and Questions 29-36 and 39-42 of Model A of Form 1-A; (3) in lieu of providing the information required in Item 19(b), furnish the information required in (a) Items 19(a)(4)—19(a)(6) of this Form and Questions 29-36 and 39-42 of Model A of Form 1-A.

(v) Part II—in lieu of the exhibits required by Item 21(a) and 21(b), furnish the exhibits required in Part II of Form S8-1.

(c) Registrants and Companies to be Acquired which relied upon Alternative 2 in their most recent Form 10-KSB:

(i) Part 1.A.—furnish the information required by Part 1.A. of this Form;

(ii) Part I.B.—in lieu of the information required in Item 14, furnish the information required in (a) Items 6 and 7 of Model B of Form 1-A, and (b) Items 14(c), (d), and (i) of this Form;

(iii) Part 1.C.—in lieu of the information required in Item 17, furnish the information required in (a) Item 17(a), 17(b)(1), 17(b)(2), 17(b)(6), 17(b)(7) and 17(b)(8) of this Form, and (b) Item 6(a)(3)(i) of Model B of Form 1-A;

(iv) Part 1.D.—(1) in lieu of providing the information required in Item 18, furnish the information required in (a) Items 18(a)(1) - 18(a)(6) and (b) Items 8, 9 and 11 of Model B of Form 1-A; (2) in lieu of providing the information required in Item 19(a), furnish the information required in (a) Items 19(a)(1) - 19(a)(6) of this Form and Items 8, 9 and 11 of Model 8 of Form 1-A; and (3) in lieu of providing the information required in Item 19(b), furnish the information required in (a) Items 19(a)(4) - 19(a)(6) of this Form and Questions Items 8, 9 and 11 of Model 8 of Form 1-A.

¶8071   Form S-4

(v) Part II—in lieu of the exhibits required by Item 21(a) and 21(b), furnish the exhibits required in Part II of Form SB-1.

E. Compliance with Exchange Act Rules.

1. If a corporation or other person submits a proposal to its security holders entitled to vote on, or consent to, the transaction in which the securities being registered are to be issued, and such person's submission to its security holders is subject to Regulation 14A (§ § 240.14a-1 through 14b-1 of this chapter) or 14C (§ § 240.14c-1 through 14c-101 of this chapter) under the Exchange Act, then the provisions of such Regulations shall apply in all respects to such person's submission, except that (a) the prospectus may be in the form of a proxy or information statement and may contain the information required by this Form in lieu of that required by Schedule 14A (§ 240.14a-1) or 14C (§ 240.14c-101) of Regulation 14A or 14C under the Exchange Act; and (b) copies of the preliminary and definitive proxy or information statement, form of proxy or other material filed as a part of the registration statement shall be deemed filed pursuant to such person's obligations under such Regulations.

2. If the proxy or information material sent to security holders is not subject to Regulation 14A or 14C, all such material shall be filed as a part of the registration statement at the time the statement is filed or as an amendment thereto prior to the use of such material.

3. If the transaction in which the securities being registered are to be issued is subject to Section 13(e), 14(d) or 14(e) of the Exchange Act, the provisions of those sections and the rules and regulations thereunder shall apply to the transaction in addition to the provisions of this Form.

F. Transactions Involving Foreign Private Issuers.

If a U.S. registrant is acquiring a foreign private issuer, as defined by Rule 405 (§ 230.405 of this chapter), such registrant may use this Form and may present information about the foreign private issuer pursuant to Form F-4. If the registrant is a foreign private issuer, such registrant may use Form F-4 and

(1) if the company being acquired is a foreign private issuer, may present information about such foreign company pursuant to Form F-4 or

(2) if the company being acquired is a U.S. company, may present information about such company pursuant to this Form; and

G. Filing and Effectiveness of Registration Statement Involving Formation of Holding

Companies; Requests for Confidential Treatment; Number of Copies.

Original registration statements on this Form S-4 will become effective automatically on the twentieth day after the date of filing (Rule 456, § 230.456 of this chapter), pursuant to the provisions of Section 8(a) of the Act (Rule 459, § 230.459 of this chapter) provided:

1. The transaction in connection with which securities are being registered involves the organization of a bank or savings and loan holding company for the sole purpose of issuing common stock to acquire all of the common stock of the company that is organizing the holding company; and

2. The following conditions are met:

a. the financial institution furnishes its security holders with an annual report that includes financial statements prepared on the basis of generally accepted accounting principles;

b. there are no anticipated changes in the security holders' relative equity ownership interest in the underlying company's assets except for redemption of no more than a nominal number of shares of unaffiliated persons who dissent;

c. in the aggregate, only nominal borrowings are to be incurred for such purposes as organizing the holding company to pay non-affiliated persons who dissent, or to meet minimum capital requirements;

d. there are no new classes of stock authorized other than those corresponding to the stock of the company being acquired immediately prior to the reorganization;

e. there are no plans or arrangements to issue any additional shares to acquire any business other than the company being acquired; and

f. there has been no material adverse change in the financial condition of the company being acquired since the latest fiscal year end included in the annual report to security holders.

Pre-effective amendments with respect to such a registration statement may be filed prior to effectiveness, and such amendments will be deemed to have been filed with the consent of the Commission (Rule 475a, § 230.475a of this chapter). Accordingly, the filing of a pre-effective amendment to such a registration statement will not commence a new twenty-day period. Post-effective amendments to such a registration statement on this Form shall become effective upon the date of filing (Rule 464, § 230.464 of this chapter). Delaying amendments are not permitted in connection with either original filings or amendments on such a registration statement (Rule 473(d), § 230.473(d) of this chapter), and any attempt to interpose a delaying amendment of any kind will be ineffective. All filings made on or in connection with this Form pursuant to this instruction become public upon filing with the Commission. As a result, requests for confidential treatment made under Rule 406 (§ 230.406 of this chapter) must be processed by the Commissions staff prior to the filing of such a registration statement. The number of copies of such a registration statement and of each amendment required by Rules 402 and 472 (§ § 230.402, 472 of this chapter) shall be filed with the Commission; *provided, however,* that the number of additional copies referred to in Rule 402(b) may be reduced from ten to three and the number of additional copies referred to in Rule 472(a) may be reduced from eight to three, one of which shall be marked to clearly and precisely indicate changes.

H. Registration Statements Subject to Rule 415(a)(1)(viii) (§ 230.415(a)(1)-(viii) of this chapter).

If the registration statement relates to offerings of securities pursuant to Rule 415(a)(1)(viii), required information about the type of contemplated transaction or the company to be acquired only need be furnished as of the date of initial effectiveness of the registration statement to the extent practicable. The required information about the specific transaction and the particular company being acquired, however, must be included in the prospectus by means of a post-effective amendment; *Provided, however,* that where the transaction in which the securities are being offered pursuant to a registration statement under the Securities Act of 1933 would itself qualify for an exemption from Section 5 of the Act, absent the existence of other similar (prior or subsequent) transactions, a prospectus supplement could be used to furnish the information necessary in connection with such transaction.

I. Roll-Up Transactions

1. If securities to be registered on this Form will be issued in a roll-up transaction as defined in Item 901(c) of Regulation S-K (17 CFR 229.901(c)), then the disclosure provisions of Subpart 229.900 of Regulation S-K (17 CFR 229.900) shall apply to the transaction in addition to the provisions of this Form. A smaller reporting company, defined in § 230.405, that is engaged in a roll-up transaction shall refer to the disclosure items in subpart 900 of Regulation S-K. To the extent that the disclosure requirements of Subpart 229.900 are inconsistent with the disclosure requirements of any other applicable forms or schedules, the requirements of Subpart 229.900 are controlling.

2. If securities to be registered on this Form will be issued in a roll-up transaction as defined in

Item 901(c) of Regulation S-K (17 CFR 229.901(c)), the prospectus must be distributed to security holders no later than the lesser of 60 calendar days prior to the date on which action is to be taken or the maximum number of days permitted for giving notice under applicable state law.

3. Attention is directed to the proxy rules (17 CFR 240.14a-1 *et seq.*) and Rule 14e-7 of the tender offer rules (17 CFR 240.14e-7) if securities to be registered on this Form will be issued in a roll-up transaction. Such rules will contain provisions specifically applicable to roll-up transactions, whether or not the entities involved have securities registered pursuant to Section 12 of the Exchange Act.

J. Where two or more classes of securities being registered on this Form pursuant to General Instruction H. are to be offered on a delayed or continuous basis pursuant to § 230.415(a)(1)(viii), § 230.457(*o*) under the Securities Act permits the registration fee to be calculated on the basis of the maximum offering price of all the securities listed in the "Calculation of Registration Fee" Table ("Fee Table"). In this event, while the Fee Table would list each of the classes of securities being registered and the aggregate proceeds to be raised, the Fee Table need not specify by each class information as to the amount to be registered, proposed maximum offering price per unit, and proposed maximum aggregate offering price.

K. Registration of Additional Securities.

With respect to the registration of additional securities for an offering pursuant to Rule 462(b) under the Securities Act, the registrant may file a registration statement consisting only of the following: the facing page; a statement that the contents of the earlier registration statement, identified by file number, are incorporated by reference; required opinions and consents; the signature page; and any price-related information omitted from the earlier registration statement in reliance on Rule 430A that the registrant chooses to include in the new registration statement. The information contained in such a Rule 462(b) registration statement shall be deemed to be a part of the earlier registration statement as of the date of effectiveness of the Rule 462(b) registration statement. Any opinion or consent required in the Rule 462(b) registration statement may be incorporated by reference from the earlier registration statement with respect to the offering, if: (i) such opinion or consent expressly provides for such incorporation; and (ii) such opinion relates to the securities registered pursuant to Rule 462(b). See Rule 411(c) and Rule 439(b) under the Securities Act.

PART I

INFORMATION REQUIRED IN THE PROSPECTUS

A. INFORMATION ABOUT THE TRANSACTION

Item 1. Forepart of Registration Statement and Outside Front Cover Page of Prospectus.

Set forth in the forepart of the registration statement and on the outside front cover page of the prospectus the information required by Item 501 of Regulation S-K (§ 229.501 of this chapter).

Item 2. Inside Front and Outside Back Cover Pages of Prospectus.

Provide the information required by Item 502 of Regulation S-K. In addition, on the inside front cover page, you must state (1) that the prospectus incorporates important business and financial information about the company that is not included in or delivered with the document; and

(2) that this information is available without charge to security holders upon written or oral request. Give the name, address, and telephone number to which security holders must make this request. In addition, you must state that to obtain timely delivery, security holders must request the information no later than five business days before the date they must make their investment decision. Specify the date by which security holders must request this information. You must highlight this statement by print type or otherwise.

Note to Item 2.

If you send any of the information that is incorporated by reference in the prospectus to security holders, you also must send any exhibits that are specifically incorporated by reference in that information.

Item 3. Risk Factors, Ratio of Earnings to Fixed Charges and Other Information.

Provide in the forepart of the prospectus a summary containing the information required by Item 503 of Regulation S-K (§ 229.503 of this chapter) and the following:

(a) The name, complete mailing address (including the Zip Code), and telephone number (including the area code) of the principal executive offices of the registrant and the company being acquired;

(b) A brief description of the general nature of the business conducted by the registrant and by the company being acquired;

(c) A brief description of the transaction in which the securities being registered are to be offered;

(d) The information required by Item 301 of Regulation S-K (§ 229.301 of this chapter) (selected financial data) for the registrant and the company being acquired. To the extent the information is required to be presented in the prospectus pursuant to Items 12, 14, 16 or 17, it need not be repeated pursuant to this Item.

(e) If material, the information required by Item 301 of Regulation S-K for the registrant on a pro forma basis, giving effect to the transaction. To the extent the information is required to be presented in the prospectus pursuant to Items 12 or 14, it need not be repeated pursuant to this Item.

(f) In comparative columnar form, historical and pro forma per share data of the registrant and historical and equivalent pro forma per share data of the company being acquired for the following items:

(1) book value per share as of the date financial data is presented pursuant to Item 301 of Regulation S-K (§ 229.301 of this chapter) (selected financial data);

(2) Cash dividends declared per share for the periods for which financial data is presented pursuant to Item 301 of Regulation S-K (§ 229.301 of this chapter) (selected financial data);

(3) income (loss) per share from continuing operations for the periods for which financial data is presented pursuant to Item 301 of Regulation S-K (§ 229.301 of this chapter) (selected financial data).

Instruction to paragraphs (e) and (f).

For a business combination, the financial information required by paragraphs (e) and (f) shall be presented only for the most recent fiscal year and interim period. For a combination between entities under common control, the financial information required by paragraphs (e) and (f) (except for information with regard to book value) shall be presented for the most recent three fiscal years and interim period. For a combination between entities under common control, information with regard to book value shall be presented as of the end of the most recent fiscal year and interim period. Equivalent pro forma per share amounts shall be calculated by multiplying the pro forma income (loss) per share before non-recurring charges or credits directly attributable to the transaction, pro forma book value per share, and the pro forma dividends per share of the registrant by the exchange ratio so that the per share amounts are equated to the respective values for one share of the company being acquired.

(g) In comparative columnar form, the market value of securities of the company being acquired (on an historical and equivalent per share basis) and the market value of the securities of the registrant (on an historical basis) as of the date preceding public announcement of the proposed transaction, or, if no such public announcement was made, as of the day preceding the day the agreement with respect to the transaction was entered into;

(h) With respect to the registrant and the company being acquired, a brief statement comparing the percentage of outstanding shares entitled to vote held by directors, executive officers and their affiliates and the vote required for approval of the proposed transaction;

(i) A statement as to whether any federal or state regulatory requirements must be complied with or approval must be obtained in connection with the transaction, and if so, the status of such compliance or approval;

(j) A statement about whether or not dissenters' rights of appraisal exist, including a cross-reference to the information provided pursuant to Item 18 or 19 of this Form; and

(k) A brief statement about the tax consequences of the transaction, or if appropriate, consisting of a cross-reference to the information provided pursuant to Item 4 of this Form.

Item 4. Terms of the Transaction.

(a) Furnish a summary of the material features of the proposed transaction. The summary shall include, where applicable:

(1) A brief summary of the terms of the acquisition agreement;

(2) The reasons of the registrant and of the company being acquired for engaging in the transaction;

(3) The information required by Item 202 of Regulation S-K (§ 229.202 of this chapter), description of registrant's securities, unless: (i) the registrant would meet the requirements for use of Form S-3 and elects to furnish information pursuant to Item 10, (ii) capital stock is to be registered and (iii) securities of the same class are registered under Section 12 of the Exchange Act and (i) listed for trading or admitted to unlisted trading privileges on a national securities exchange; or (ii) are securities for which bid and offer quotations are reported in an automated quotations system operated by a national securities association;

(4) An explanation of any material differences between the rights of security holders of the company being acquired and the rights of holders of the securities being offered;

(5) A brief statement as to the accounting treatment of the transaction; and

(6) The federal income tax consequences of the transaction.

(b) If a report, opinion or appraisal materially relating to the transaction has been received from an outside party, and such report, opinion or appraisal is referred to in the prospectus, furnish the same information as would be required by Item 1015(b) of Regulation M-A (§ 229.1015(b) of this chapter).

(c) Incorporate the acquisition agreement by reference into the prospectus by means of a statement to that effect.

Item 5. Pro Forma Financial Information.

Furnish financial information required by Article 11 of Regulation S-X (§ 210.11-01 *et.seq.* of this chapter) with respect to this transaction. A smaller reporting company may provide the information in Rule 8-05 of Regulation S-X (§ 210.8-05 of this chapter) in lieu of the financial information required by Article 11 of Regulation S-X.

Instruction.

1. Any other Article 11 information that is presented (rather than incorporated by reference) pursuant to other Items of this Form shall be presented together with the information provided pursuant to Item 5, but the presentation shall clearly distinguish between this transaction and any other.

2. If pro forma financial information with respect to all other transactions is incorporated by reference pursuant to Item 11 or 15 of this Form only the pro forma results need be presented as part of the pro forma financial information required by this Item.

Item 6. Material Contacts with the Company Being Acquired.

Describe any past, present or proposed material contracts, arrangements, understandings, relationships, negotiations or transactions during the periods for which financial statements are presented or incorporated by reference pursuant to Part I. B. or C. of this Form between the company being acquired or its affiliates and the registrant or its affiliates, such as those concerning: a merger, consolidation or acquisition; a tender offer or other acquisition of securities; an election of directors; or a sale or other transfer of a material amount of assets.

Item 7 Additional Information Required for Reoffering by Persons and Parties Deemed to Be Underwriters.

If any of the securities are to be reoffered to the public by any person or party who is deemed to be an underwriter thereof, furnish the following information in the prospectus, at the time it is being used for the reoffer of the securities to the extent it is not already furnished therein:

(a) The information required by Item 507 of Regulation S-K (§ 229.507 of this chapter), selling security holders; and

(b) Information with respect to the consummation of the transaction pursuant to which the securities were acquired and any material change in the registrant's affairs subsequent to the transaction.

Item 8. Interests of Named Experts and Counsel.

Furnish the information required by Item 509 of Regulation S-K (§ 229.509 of this chapter).

Item 9. Disclosure of Commission Position on Indemnification for Securities Act Liabilities.

Furnish the information required by Item 510 of Regulation S-K (§ 229.510 of this chapter).

B. INFORMATION ABOUT THE REGISTRANT

Item 10. Information with Respect to S-3 Registrants.

If the registrant meets the requirements for use of Form S-3 and elects to furnish information in accordance with the provisions of this Item, furnish information as required below:

(a) Describe any and all material changes in the registrant's affairs that have occurred since the end of the latest fiscal year for which audited financial statements were included in the latest annual report to security holders and that have not been described in a report on Form 10-Q and Form 10-QSB (§ 249.308a and § 249.308b of this chapter) or Form 8-K (§ 249.308 of this chapter) filed under the Exchange Act.

(b) Include in the prospectus, if not incorporated by reference from the reports filed under the Exchange Act specified in Item 11 of this Form, a proxy or information statement filed pursuant to Section 14 of the Exchange Act, a prospectus previously filed pursuant to Rule 424 under the Securities Act (§ 230.424 of this chapter) or, where no prospectus was required to be filed pursuant to Rule 424(b), the prospectus included in the registration statement at effectiveness, or a Form 8-K filed during either of the two preceding fiscal years:

(1) Financial information required by Rule 3-05 (§ 210.3-05 of this chapter) and Article 11 of Regulation S-X with respect to transactions other than that pursuant to which the securities being registered are to be issued;

(2) Restated financial statements prepared in accordance with Regulation S-X (Part 210 of this chapter), if there has been a change in accounting principles or a correction of an error where such change or correction requires a material retroactive restatement of financial statements;

(3) Restated financial statements prepared in accordance with Regulation S-X where one or more business combinations accounted for by the pooling of interest method of accounting have been consummated subsequent to the most recent fiscal year and the acquired businesses, considered in the aggregate, are significant pursuant to Rule 11-01(b) of Regulation S-X (§ 210.11-01(b) of this chapter); or

(4) Any financial information required because of a material disposition of assets outside the normal course of business.

Item 11. Incorporation of Certain Information by Reference.

If the registrant meets the requirements of Form S-3 and elects to furnish information in accordance with the provisions of Item 10 of this Form:

(a) Incorporate by reference into the prospectus, by means of a statement to that effect listing all documents so incorporated, the documents listed in paragraphs (1), (2) and, if applicable, (3) below.

(1) The registrant's latest annual report on Form 10-K and Form 10-KSB (§ 249.310 and § 249.310b of this chapter) filed pursuant to Section 13(a) or 15(d) of the Exchange Act which contains financial statements for the registrant's latest fiscal year for which a Form 10-K was required to be filed;

(2) All other reports filed pursuant to Section 13(a) or 15(d) of the Exchange Act since the end of the fiscal year covered by the annual report referred to in Item 11(a)(1) of this Form; and

(3) If capital stock is to be registered and securities of the same class are registered under Section 12 of the Exchange Act and: (i) listed for trading or admitted to unlisted trading privileges on a national securities exchange; or (ii) are securities for which bid and offer quotations are reported in an automated quotations system operated by a national securities association, the description of such class of securities which is contained in a registration statement filed under the Exchange Act, including any amendment or reports filed for the purpose of updating such description.

(b) The prospectus also shall state that all documents subsequently filed by the registrant pursuant to Sections 13(a), 13(c), 14 or 15(d) of the Exchange Act, prior to one of the following dates, whichever is applicable, shall be deemed to be incorporated by reference into the prospectus:

(1) If a meeting of security holders is to be held, the date on which such meeting is held;

(2) If a meeting of security holders is not to be held, the date on which the transaction is consummated;

(3) If securities of the registrant are being offered in exchange for securities of any other issuer, the date the offering is terminated; or

(4) If securities are being offered in a reoffering or resale of securities acquired pursuant to this registration statement, the date the reoffering is terminated.

(c) You must (1) identify the reports and other information that you file with the SEC; and

(2) state that the public may read and copy any materials you file with the SEC at the SEC's Public Reference Room at 100 F Street, N.E., Washington, D.C. 20549. State that the public may obtain information on the operation of the Public Reference Room by calling the SEC at 1-800-SEC-0330. If you are an electronic filer, state that the SEC maintains an Internet site that contains reports, proxy and information statements, and other information regarding issuers that file electronically with the SEC and state the address of that site (http://www.sec.gov). You are encouraged to give your Internet address, if available.

Instruction.

Attention is directed to Rule 439 (§ 230.439 of this chapter) regarding consent to the use of material incorporated by reference.

Item 12. Information with Respect to S-3 Registrants.

If the registrant meets the requirements for use of Form S-3 and elects to comply with this Item, furnish the information required by either paragraph (a) or paragraph (b) of this Item. The information required by paragraph (b) shall be furnished if the registrant satisfies the conditions of paragraph (c) of this Item.

(a) If the registrant elects to deliver this prospectus together with a copy of either its latest Form 10-K filed pursuant to Section 13(a) or 15(d) of the Exchange Act or its latest annual report to security holders, which at the time of original preparation met the requirements of either Rule 14a-3 or Rule 14c-3:

(1) Indicate that the prospectus is accompanied by either a copy of the registrant's latest Form 10-K or a copy of its latest annual report to security holders, whichever the registrant elects to deliver pursuant to paragraph (a) of this Item.

(2) Provide financial and other information with respect to the registrant in the form required by Part I of Form 10-Q as of the end of the most recent fiscal quarter which ended after the end of the latest fiscal year for which certified financial

statements were included in the latest Form 10-K or the latest report to security holders (whichever the registrant elects to deliver pursuant to paragraph (a) of this Item), and more than forty-five days before the effective date of this registration statement (or as of a more recent date) by one of the following means:

(i) including such information in the prospectus;

(ii) providing without charge to each person to whom a prospectus is delivered a copy of the registrant's latest Form 10-Q; or

(iii) providing without charge to each person to whom a prospectus is delivered a copy of the registrant's latest quarterly report that was delivered to security holders and included the required financial information.

(3) If not reflected in the registrant's latest Form 10-K or its latest annual report to security holders (whichever the registrant elects to deliver pursuant to paragraph (a) of this Item) provide information required by Rule 3-05 (§ 210.3-05 of this chapter) and Article 11 (§ 210.11-01 through 210.11-03 of this chapter) of Regulation S-X. Smaller reporting companies may provide the information required by Rules 8-04 and 8-05 of Regulation S-X.

(4) Describe any and all material changes in the registrant's affairs that have occurred since the end of the latest fiscal year for which audited financial statements were included in the latest Form 10-K or latest annual report to security holders (whichever the registrant elects to deliver pursuant to paragraph (a) of this Item) and that were not described in a Form 10-Q or quarterly report delivered with the prospectus in accordance with paragraph (a)(2)(ii) or (iii) of this Item.

Instruction. Where the registrant elects to deliver the documents identified in paragraph (a) with a preliminary prospectus, such documents need not be redelivered with the final prospectus.

(b) If the registrant does not elect to deliver its latest Form 10-K or its latest annual report to security holders:

(1) Furnish a brief description of the business done by the registrant and its subsidiaries during the most recent fiscal year as required by Rule 14a-3 to be included in an annual report to security holders. The description also should take into account changes in the registrant's business that have occurred between the end of the latest fiscal year and the effective date of the registration statement.

(2) Include financial statements and information as required by Rule 14a-3(b)(1) (240.14a-3(b)(1) of this chapter) to be included in an annual report to security holders. In addition, provide:

(i) the interim financial information required by Rule 10-01 of Regulation S-X (§ 210.10-01 of this chapter) for a filing on Form 10-Q and Form 10-QSB;

(ii) financial information required by Rule 3-05 and Article 11 of Regulation S-X with respect to transactions other than that pursuant to which the securities being registered are to be issued;

(iii) restated financial statements prepared in accordance with Regulation S-X if there has been a change in accounting principles or a correction of an error where such change or correction requires a material retroactive restatement of financial statements;

(iv) restated financial statements prepared in accordance with Regulation S-X where a combination under common control has been consummated subsequent to the most recent fiscal year and the businesses transferred, considered in the aggregate, are significant pursuant to Rule 11-01(b) of Regulation S-X; and

(v) Any financial information required because of a material disposition of assets outside of the normal course of business.

(3) Furnish the information required by the following:

(i) Item 101(b), (c)(1)(i) and (d) of Regulation S-K (§ 229.101 of this chapter), industry segments, classes of similar products or services, foreign and domestic operations and export sales;

(ii) where common equity securities are being offered, Item 201 of Regulation S-K (§ 229.201 of this chapter), market price of and dividends on the registrant's common equity and related stockholder matters;

(iii) Item 301 of Regulation S-K (§ 229.301 of this chapter), selected financial data;

(iv) Item 302 of Regulation S-K (§ 229.302 of this chapter), supplementary financial information;

(v) Item 303 of Regulation S-K (§ 229.303 of this chapter), management's discussion and analysis of financial condition and results of operations;

(vi) Item 304 of Regulation S-K (§ 229.304 of this chapter), changes in and disagreements with accountants on accounting and financial disclosure; and

(vii) Item 305 of Regulation S-K (§ 229.305 of this chapter), quantitative and qualitative disclosures about market risk.

(c) The registrant shall furnish the information required by paragraph (b) of this Item if:

(1) the registrant was required to make a material retroactive restatement of financial statements because of

(i) a change in accounting principles; or

(ii) a correction of an error; or

(iii) a consummation of one or more business combinations accounted for by the pooling of interest method of accounting was effected subsequent to the most recent fiscal year and the acquired businesses considered in the aggregate meet the test of a significant subsidiary;

OR

(2) the registrant engaged in a material disposition of assets outside the normal course of business;

AND

(3) such restatement of financial statements or disposition of assets was not reflected in the registrant's latest annual report to security holders and/or in its latest Form 10-K filed pursuant to Section 13(a) or 15(d) of the Exchange Act.

Item 13. Incorporation of Certain Information by Reference.

If the registrant meets the requirements for use of Form S-3 and elects to furnish information in accordance with the provisions of Item 12 of this Form:

(a) Incorporate by reference into the prospectus, by means of a statement to that effect in the prospectus listing all documents so incorporated, the documents listed in paragraphs (1) and (2) of this Item and, if applicable, the portions of the documents listed in paragraphs (3) and (4) thereof.

(1) The registrant's latest annual report on Form 10-K and Form 10-KSB filed pursuant to Section 13(a) or 15(d) of the Exchange Act which contains audited financial statements for the registrant's latest fiscal year for which a Form 10-K was required to be filed.

(2) All other reports filed pursuant to Section 13(a) or 15(d) of the Exchange Act since the end of the fiscal year covered by the annual report referred to in paragraph (a)(1) of this Item.

(3) If the registrant elects to deliver its latest annual report to security holders pursuant to Item 12 of this Form, the information furnished in accordance with the following:

(i) Item 101(b), (c)(1)(i) and (d) of Regulation S-K, segments, classes of similar products or services, foreign and domestic operations and export sales;

(ii) Where common equity securities are being issued, Item 201 of Regulation S-K, market price of and dividends on the registrant's common equity and related stockholder matters;

(iii) Item 301 of Regulation S-K, selected financial data;

(iv) Item 302 of Regulation S-K, supplementary financial information;

(v) Item 303 of Regulation S-K, management's discussion and analysis of financial condition and results of operations;

(vi) Item 304 of Regulation S-K, changes in and disagreements with accountants on accounting and financial disclosure; and

(vii) Item 305 of Regulation S-K (§ 229.305 of this chapter) quantitative and qualitative disclosures about market risk.

(4) If the registrant elects, pursuant to Item 12(a)(2)(iii) of this Form, to provide a copy of its latest quarterly report which was delivered to security holders, financial information equivalent to that required to be presented in Part I of Form 10-Q.

Instruction.

Attention is directed to Rule 439 regarding consent to the use of material incorporated by reference.

(b) The registrant also may state, if it so chooses, that specifically described portions of its annual or quarterly report to security holders, other than those portions required to be incorporated by reference pursuant to paragraphs (a)(3) and (4) of this Item, are not part of the registration statement. In such case, the description of portions that are not incorporated by reference or that are excluded shall be made with clarity and in reasonable detail.

(c) *Electronic filings.* Electronic filers electing to deliver and incorporate by reference all, or any portion, of the quarterly or annual report to security holders pursuant to this Item shall file as an exhibit such quarterly or annual report to security holders, or such portion thereof that is incorporated by reference, in electronic format.

(d) You must (1) identify the reports and other information that you file with the SEC; and

(2) state that the public may read and copy any materials you file with the SEC at the SEC's Public Reference Room at 100 F Street, N.E., Washington, D.C. 20549. State that the public may obtain information on the operation of the Public Reference Room by calling the SEC at 1-800-SEC-0330. If you are an electronic filer, state that the SEC maintains an Internet site that contains reports, proxy and information statements, and other information regarding issuers that file electronically with the SEC and state the address of that site (http://www.sec.gov). You are encouraged to give your Internet address, if available.

Item 14. Information with Respect to Registrants Other Than S-3 Registrants.

If the registrant does not meet the requirements for use of Form S-3, or otherwise elects to comply with this Item in lieu of Item 10 or 12, furnish the information required by:

(a) Item 101 of Regulation S-K, description of business;

(b) Item 102 of Regulation S-K, description of property;

(c) Item 103 of Regulation S-K, legal proceedings;

(d) Where common equity securities are being issued, Item 201 of Regulation S-K, market price of and dividends on the registrant's common equity and related stockholder matters;

(e) Financial statements meeting the requirements of Regulation S-X, (schedules required by Regulation S-X shall be filed as "Financial Statement Schedules" pursuant to Item 21 of this Form), as well as financial information required by Rule 3-05 and Article 11 of Regulation S-X with respect to transactions other than that pursuant to which the securities being registered are to be issued.

(f) Item 301 of Regulation S-K, selected financial data;

(g) Item 302 of Regulation S-K, supplementary financial information;

(h) Item 303 of Regulation S-K, management's discussion and analysis of financial condition and results of operations;

(i) Item 304 of Regulation S-K, changes in and disagreements with accountants on accounting and financial disclosure; and

(j) Item 305 of Regulation S-K (§ 229.305 of this chapter), quantitative and qualitative disclosures about market risk.

C. INFORMATION ABOUT THE COMPANY BEING ACQUIRED

Item 15. Information with Respect to S-3 Companies.

If the company being acquired meets the requirements for use of Form S-3 and compliance with this Item is elected, furnish the information that would be required by Items 10 and 11 of this Form if securities of such company were being registered.

Item 16. Information with Respect to S-3 Companies.

(a) If the company being acquired meets the requirements for use of Form S-3 and elects to comply with this Item, furnish the information that would be required by Items 12 and 13 of this Form if securities of such company were being registered.

(b) *Electronic filings.* In addition to satisfying the requirements of paragraph (a) of this Item, electronic filers that elect to deliver and incorporate by reference all, or any portion, of the quarterly or annual report to security holders of a company being acquired pursuant to this Item shall file as an exhibit such quarterly or annual report to security holders, or such portion thereof that is incorporated by reference, in electronic format.

Item 17. Information with Respect to Companies Other Than S-3 Companies.

If the company being acquired does not meet the requirements for use of Form S-3, or compliance with this Item is otherwise elected in lieu of Item 15 or 16, furnish the information required by paragraph (a) or (b) of this Item, whichever is applicable.

(a) If the company being acquired is subject to the reporting requirements of Section 13(a) or 15(d) of the Exchange Act, or compliance with this subparagraph in lieu of subparagraph (b) of this Item is selected, furnish the information that would be required by Item 14 of this Form if the securities of such company were being registered; *however,* only those schedules required by Rules 12-15, 28 and 29 of Regulation S-X (§ 210.12-15, 28, 29 of this chapter) need be provided with respect to the company being acquired.

(b) If the company being acquired is not subject to the reporting requirements of either Section 13(a) or 15(d) of the Exchange Act; or, because of Section 12(i) of the Exchange Act, has not furnished an annual report to security holders pursuant to Rule 14a-3 (§ 240.14a-3 of this chapter) or Rule 14c-3 (§ 240.14c-3 of this chapter) for its latest fiscal year; furnish the information that would be required by the following if securities of such company were being registered:

(1) a brief description of the business done by the company which indicates the general nature and scope of the business;

(2) Item 201 of Regulation S-K, market price of and dividends on the registrant's common equity and related stockholder matters;

(3) Item 301 of Regulation S-K, selected financial data;

(4) Item 302 of Regulation S-K, supplementary financial information;

(5) Item 303 of Regulation S-K, management's discussion and analysis of financial condition and results of operations;

(6) Item 304(b) of Regulation S-K (§ 229.304 of this chapter), changes in and disagreements

with accountants on accounting and financial disclosure.

(7) Financial statements that would be required in an annual report sent to security holders under Rule 14a-3(b)(1) and (b)(2) (§ 240.14b-3 of this chapter), if an annual report was required. If the registrant's security holders are not voting, the transaction is not a roll-up transaction (as described by Item 901 of Regulation S-K (§ 229.901 of this chapter)), and:

(i) the company being acquired is significant to the registrant in excess of the 20% level as determined under § 210.3-05(b)(2), provide financial statements of the company acquired for the latest fiscal year in conformity with GAAP. In addition, if the company being acquired has provided its security holders with financial statements prepared in conformity with GAAP for either or both of the two fiscal years before the latest fiscal year, provide the financial statements for those years; or

(ii) the company being acquired is significant to the registrant at or below the 20% level, no financial information (including pro forma and comparative per share information) for the company being acquired need be provided.

Instructions:

1. The financial statements required by this paragraph for the latest fiscal year need be audited only to the extent practicable. The financial statements for the fiscal years before the latest fiscal year need not be audited if they were not previously audited.

2. If the financial statements required by this paragraph are prepared on the basis of a comprehensive body of accounting principles other than U.S. GAAP or International Financial Reporting Standards as issued by the International Accounting Standards Board, provide a reconciliation to U.S. GAAP in accordance with Item 17 of Form 20-F (§ 249.220f of this chapter) unless a reconciliation is unavailable or not obtainable without unreasonable cost or expense. At a minimum, provide a narrative description of all material variations in accounting principles, practices and methods used in preparing the non-U.S. GAAP financial statements from those accepted in the U.S. when the financial statements are prepared on a basis other than U.S. GAAP.

3. If this Form is used to register resales to the public by any person who is deemed an underwriter within the meaning of Rule 145(c) (§ 230.145(c) of this chapter) with respect to the securities being reoffered, the financial statements must be audited for the fiscal years required to be presented under paragraph (b)(2) of Rule 3-05 of Regulation S-X (17 CFR 210.3-05(b)(2)).

4. In determining the significance of an acquisition for purposes of this paragraph, apply the tests prescribed in Rule 1-02(w) (§ 210.1-02(w) of this chapter).

(8) the quarterly financial and other information that would have been required had the company being acquired been required to file Part I of Form 10-Q (§ 249.308a of this chapter) for the most recent quarter for which such a report would have been on file at the time the registration statement becomes effective or for a period ending as of a more recent date.

(9) schedules required by Rules 12-15, 28 and 29 of Regulation S-X.

(10) Item 305 of Regulation S-K (§ 229.305 of this chapter), quantitative and qualitative disclosures about market risk.

D. VOTING AND MANAGEMENT INFORMATION

Item 18. Information if Proxies, Consents or Authorizations are to be Solicited.

(a) If proxies, consents or authorizations are to be solicited, furnish the following information, except as provided by paragraph (b) of this Item:

(1) The information required by Item 1 of Schedule 14A, date, time and place information;

(2) The information required by Item 2 of Schedule 14A, revocability of proxy;

(3) The information required by Item 3 of Schedule 14A, dissenters' rights of appraisal;

(4) The information required by Item 4 of Schedule 14A, persons making the solicitation;

(5) With respect to both the registrant and the company being acquired, the information required by:

(i) Item 5 of Schedule 14A, interest of certain persons in matters to be acted upon; and

(ii) Item 6 of Schedule 14A, voting securities and principal holders thereof;

(6) The information required by Item 21 of Schedule 14A, vote required for approval; and [Paragraphs (a) (1-6) as amended in Release No. 33-6676, effective January 20, 1987, 51 F. R. 42048.]

(7) With respect to each person who will serve as a director or an executive officer of the surviving or acquiring company, the information required by:

(i) Item 401 of Regulation S-K (§ 229.401 of this chapter), directors and executive officers;

(ii) Item 402 of Regulation S-K (§ 229.402 of this chapter), executive compensation, and paragraph (e)(4) of Item 407 of Regulation S-K

(§ 229.407(e)(4) of this chapter), corporate governance;

(iii) Item 404 of Regulation S-K (§ 229.404 of this chapter), transactions with related persons, promoters and certain control persons, and Item 407(a) of Regulation S-K (§ 229.407(a) of this chapter), corporate governance.

(b) If the registrant or the company being acquired meets the requirements for use of Form S-3, any information required by paragraphs (a)(5)(ii) and (7) of this Item with respect to such company may be incorporated by reference from its latest annual report on Form 10-K.

Item 19. Information if Proxies, Consents or Authorizations are not to be Solicited or in an Exchange Offer.

(a) If the transaction is an exchange offer or if proxies, consents or authorizations are not to be solicited, furnish the following information, except as provided by paragraph (c) of this Item;

(1) The information required by Item 2 of Schedule 14C, statement that proxies are not to be solicited;

(2) The date, time and place of the meeting of security holders, unless such information is otherwise disclosed in material furnished to security holders with the prospectus.

(3) The information required by Item 3 of Schedule 14A, dissenters' rights of appraisal;

(4) With respect to both the registrant and the company being acquired, a brief description of any material interest, direct or indirect, by security holdings or otherwise, of affiliates of the registrant and of the company being acquired, in the proposed transaction;

Instruction.

This subparagraph shall not apply to any interest arising from the ownership of securities of the registrant where the security holder receives no extra or special benefit not shared on a pro rata basis by all other holders of the same class.

(5) With respect to both the registrant and the company being acquired, the information required by Item 6 of Schedule 14A, voting securities and principal holders thereof;

(6) The information required by Item 21 of Schedule 14A, vote required for approval;

(7) With respect to each person who will serve as a director or an executive officer of the surviving or acquiring company, the information required by:

(i) Item 401 of Regulation S-K, directors and executive officers;

(ii) Item 402 of Regulation S-K (§ 229.402 of this chapter), executive compensation, and paragraph (e)(4) of Item 407 of Regulation S-K (§ 229.407(e)(4) of this chapter), corporate governance;

(iii) Item 404 of Regulation S-K (§ 229.404), transactions with related persons, promoters and certain controls persons, and Item 407(a) of Regulation S-K (§ 229.407(a)), corporate governance.

(b) If the transaction is an exchange offer, furnish the information required by paragraphs (a)(4), (a)(5), (a)(6) and (a)(7) of this Item, except as provided by paragraph (c) of this Item.

(c) If the registrant or the company being acquired meets the requirements for use of Form S-3, any information required by paragraphs (a)(5) and (7) of this Item with respect to such company may be incorporated by reference from its latest annual report on Form 10-K.

PART II

INFORMATION NOT REQUIRED IN PROSPECTUS

Item 20. Indemnification of Directors and Officers.

Furnish the information required by Item 702 of Regulation S-K (§ 229.702 of this chapter).

Item 21. Exhibits and Financial Statement Schedules.

(a) Subject to the rules regarding incorporation by reference, furnish the exhibits as required by Item 601 of Regulation S-K (§ 229.601 of this chapter).

(b) Furnish the financial statement schedules required by Regulation S-X and Item 14(e), Item 17(a) or Item 17(b)(9) of this Form. These schedules should be lettered or numbered in the manner described for exhibits in paragraph (a) of this Item.

(c) If information is provided pursuant to Item 4(b) of this Form, furnish the report, opinion or appraisal as an exhibit hereto, unless it is furnished as part of the prospectus.

Item 22. Undertakings.

(a) Furnish the undertakings required by Item 512 of Regulation S-K (§ 229.512 of this chapter).

(b) Furnish the following undertaking:

The undersigned registrant hereby undertakes to respond to requests for information that is incorporated by reference into the prospectus pursuant to Items 4, 10(b), 11, or 13 of this Form, within one business day of receipt of such request, and to send the incorporated documents by first class mail or other equally prompt means. This includes information contained in documents filed subsequent to the effective date of the registration statement through the date of responding to the request.

(c) Furnish the following undertaking:

The undersigned registrant hereby undertakes to supply by means of a post-effective amendment all information concerning a transaction, and the company being acquired involved therein, that was not the subject of and included in the registration statement when it became effective.

SIGNATURES

Pursuant to the requirements of the Securities Act, the registrant has duly caused this registration statement to be signed on its behalf by the undersigned, thereunto duly authorized, in the City of . . . ., State of . . . ., on . . . ., 20 . . . .

(Registrant) . . . .

By (Signature and Title) . . . .

Pursuant to the requirements of the Securities Act of 1933, this registration statement has been signed by the following persons in the capacities and on the dates indicated.

(Signature) . . . .

(Title) . . . .

(Date) . . . .

Instructions.

1. The registration statement shall be signed by the registrant, its principal executive officer or officers, its principal financial officer, its controller or principal accounting officer, and by at least a majority of the board of directors or persons performing similar functions. If the registrant is a foreign person, the registration statement shall also be signed by its authorized representative in the United States. Where the registrant is a lim-

ited partnership, the registration statement shall be signed by a majority of the board of directors of any corporate general partner signing the registration statement.

2. The name of each person who signs the registration statement shall be typed or printed beneath his signature. Any person who occupies more than one of the specified positions shall indicate each capacity in which he signs the registration statement. Attention is directed to Rule 402 (§ 230.402 of this chapter) concerning manual signatures and Item 601 concerning signatures pursuant to powers of attorney.

3. If the securities to be offered are those of a corporation not yet in existence at the time the registration statement is filed which will be a party to a consolidation involving two or more existing corporations, then each such existing corporation shall be deemed a registrant and shall be so designated on the cover page of this Form, and the registration statement shall be signed by each such existing corporation and by the officers and directors of each such existing corporation as if each such existing corporation were the registrant.

[¶ 8100]   FORM S-6

[As last amended in Release No. 33-7684, effective June 28, 1999, 64 F.R. 27888.]

UNITED STATES SECURITIES AND EXCHANGE COMMISSION
Washington, D.C. 20549

FORM S-6

FOR REGISTRATION UNDER THE SECURITIES ACT OF 1933 OF SECURITIES OF UNIT INVESTMENT TRUSTS REGISTERED ON FORM N-8B-2

A. Exact name of trust:

B. Name of depositor:

C. Complete address of depositor's principal executive offices:

D. Name and complete address of agent for service:

   It is proposed that this filing will become effective (check appropriate box)

   ☐ immediately upon filing pursuant to paragraph (b)

   ☐ on (date) pursuant to paragraph (b)

   ☐ 60 days after filing pursuant to paragraph (a)(1)

   ☐ on (date) pursuant to paragraph (a)(1) of Rule 485.

If appropriate, check the following box:

   ☐ this post-effective amendment designates a new effective date for a previously filed post-effective amendment.

E. Title of securities being registered:

F. Approximate date of proposed public offering:

   ☐ Check box if it is proposed that this filing will become effective on (date) at (time) pursuant to Rule 487.

GENERAL INSTRUCTIONS

Instruction 1. Rule as to Use of Form S-6

This form may be used for registration under the Securities Act of 1933 of securities of any unit investment trust registered under the Investment Company Act of 1940 on form N-8B-2.

Instruction 2. Compliance with Requirements

The registrant should read carefully every provision of this form and should consider the applicability of the General Rules and Regulations under the Act, particularly regulation C thereof. The registration statement will not be accepted for filing unless it is prepared, executed and filed substantially in accordance with the requirements contained in this form and in the General Rules and Regulations.

Instruction 3. Contents of Registration Statement

(a) The registration statement shall consist of the following:

(1) The facing sheet.

(2) A prospectus containing the information specified in the instructions hereinafter set forth.

(3) The undertaking required by Section 15(d) of the Securities Exchange Act of 1934, the form of which is hereinafter set forth.

(4) A list of the papers and documents comprising the registration statement.

(5) The signatures to the registration statement.

(6) The written consents referred to in instruction 4, below.

(7) The exhibits specified in the instructions as to exhibits set forth at the end of the form.

(b) The papers and documents comprising the registration statement shall be assembled and filed in the order indicated above. Two extra copies of the prospectus shall be filed to make up the five copies required by rule 800(a). [Now Reg. § 230.424 (¶ 10,611) which supersedes this requirement and now requires 5 copies in addition to the three copies included in the body of the registration statement.—CCH.]

(c) These general instructions and the instructions as to the prospectus and as to exhibits are to be entirely omitted from the registration statement as filed with the Commission.

Instruction 4. Written Consents

(a) Section 7 of the Securities Act of 1933 requires the filing of written consents of certain experts. Rule 670 and 671 [now Reg. § § 230.436—230.437 (¶ 10,691—10,695)] govern respectively the filing of such written consents and application to dispense with the filing thereof. Any such expert who is referred to or quoted in the prospectus shall specifically consent to such reference or quotation.

(b) Rule 672 [now Reg § 230.438 (¶ 10,701)] requires the filing of written consents of persons who have not signed the registration statement but who are named therein as about to become directors of the registrant.

INSTRUCTIONS AS TO THE PROSPECTUS

Instruction 1. Information to be Contained in Prospectus

A prospectus for securities registered on this form shall contain the following information:

(a) The information which would be required by the items of form N-8B-2 if a registration statement on that form were currently being filed, except items 7, 8, 36, 41 (b) and (c), 56, 57, 58 and 59.

(b) The following financial statements for the trust, prepared in accordance with the applicable provisions of regulation S-X:

(1) A statement of condition as of a date within 90 days prior to the date of filing. If this statement is not certified, there shall also be included a certified statement of condition as of a date within one year prior to the date of filing.

(2) Statements of income and other distributable funds for the last three fiscal years and any subsequent period up to the date of the latest statement of condition, certified to the date of the latest certified statement of condition.

Notwithstanding paragraphs (1) and (2), all schedules may be omitted from the prospectus, except the information required by columns A, F, G and H of Schedule I, and Schedules II, IV and V in support of the most recent financial statements filed for the trust.

(c) The following financial statements for each depositor prepared in accordance with the provisions of item 59 (d) of form N-8B-2 and the applicable provisions of regulation S-X.

(1) A balance sheet as of a date within 90 days prior to the date of filing. If this balance sheet is not certified there shall also be included a certified balance sheet as of a date within one year prior to the date of filing.

(2) A profit and loss statement for the last fiscal year and for any subsequent period up to the date of the latest balance sheet, certified to the date of the latest certified balance sheet.

Notwithstanding paragraphs (1) and (2), all schedules may be omitted from the prospectus.

(d) If any expert named in the registration statement as having prepared or certified any part thereof was employed for such purpose on a contingent basis or, at the time of such preparation or certification or at any time thereafter, had a substantial interest in the Company or any affiliated person or was connected with the Company or any affiliated person as a promoter, underwriter, voting trustee, director, officer, employee or affiliated person, furnish a brief statement of the nature of such contingent basis, interest or connection.

(e) The information, including financial statements, furnished pursuant to instruction 5 of the instructions as to exhibits, which would be required to be included in a prospectus for securities registered on the form on which the information is furnished.

Instruction 2. Presentation of Information

The information required to be included in the prospectus need not follow the numerical sequence of the items of form N-8B-2. However, the information required by items 10, 11 and 13 of form N-8B-2 shall be set forth not further back than page three of the prospectus.

Instruction 3. Negative Answers

If the answer to any item of form N-8B-2 required by instruction 1, above, to be included in the prospectus is "Not applicable", "None", or "No", or otherwise in the negative and is not material, it may be omitted from the prospectus.

Instruction 4. Reconciliation and Tie

A reconciliation and tie similar to that required by rule 801, giving a complete reconciliation and tie of the information shown in the prospectus with the items of form N-8B-2, shall be filed.

(Note.—None of the following matter is required to be included in the prospectus.)

UNDERTAKING TO FILE REPORTS

Subject to the terms and conditions of Section 15 (d) of the Securities Exchange Act of 1934, the undersigned registrant hereby undertakes to file with the Securities and Exchange Commission such supplementary and periodic information, documents, and reports as may be prescribed by any rule or regulation of the Commission heretofore or hereafter duly adopted pursuant to authority conferred in that section.

CONTENTS OF REGISTRATION STATEMENT

This registration statement comprises the following papers and documents:

The facing sheet.

The prospectus consisting of . . . . pages.

The undertaking of file reports.

The signatures.

Written consents of the following persons:

The following exhibits:

SIGNATURES

Pursuant to the requirements of the Securities Act of 1933, the registrant, ..., (certifies that it meets all of the requirements for effectiveness of this Registration Statement pursuant to rule (485(b)) under the Securities Act of 1933 and) has duly caused this registration statement to be signed on its behalf by the undersigned thereunto duly authorized, and its seal to be hereunto affixed and attested, all in the city of . . . ., and State of . . . ., on the . . . . day of . . . . , 20 . . . .

ALTERNATIVE FORM OF SIGNATURE FOR FILINGS UNDER RULE 487

The registrant, ..., hereby identifies series (number(s) and type) of the trust for purposes of the representations required by rule 487 and represents the following:

1) That the portfolio securities deposited in the series as to the securities of which this registration statement is being filed do not differ materially in type or quality from those deposited in such previous series;

2) That, except to the extent necessary to identify the specific portfolio securities deposited in, and to provide essential financial information for, the series with respect to the securities of which this registration statement is being filed, this registration statement does not contain disclosures that differ in any material respect from those contained in the registration statement(s) for such previous series as to which the effective date was determined by the Commission or the staff; and

3) That it has complied with rule 460 under the Securities Act of 1933.

Pursuant to the requirements of the Securities Act of 1933, the registrant has duly caused this registration statement to be signed on its behalf by the undersigned thereunto duly authorized, and its seal to be hereunto affixed and attested, all in the city of . . . . , and State of . . . . , on the . . . . day of . . . . , 19 . . . .

Pursuant to the requirements of the Securities Act of 1933, this registration statement has been signed below by the following persons in the capacities and on the dates indicated.

Signature . . . . *Title*

Date

Instruction. 1. The registration statement shall be signed by the registrant and its principal executive officer or officers, its principal financial officer, its comptroller or principal accounting officer, and by at least a majority of its board of directors or persons performing similar functions.

2. If the registrant is a foreign or territorial person the registration statement shall also be signed by its duly authorized representative in the United States.

3. The name of each person signing the registration statement shall be typed or printed beneath his signature. Any person who occupies more than one of the specified positions shall sign separately in each capacity.

INSTRUCTIONS AS TO EXHIBITS

Subject to the rules as to incorporation by reference, the exhibits specified below shall be filed as a part of the registration statement. Exhibits shall be appropriately numbered or lettered for convenient reference. Exhibits incorporated by reference may bear the designation given in the previous filing.

1. Copies of all exhibits which would be required by paragraph A of the instructions as to exhibits in form N-8B-2 if a registration statement on that form were currently being filed.

2. An opinion of counsel as to the legality of the securities being registered.

3. All financial statements omitted from the prospectus pursuant to instruction 1 (b) or 1 (c) of the instructions as to the prospectus.

4. If more than 25% of the trust property underlying any class of securities being registered consists or is to consist of securities of a single issuer, or of two or more affiliated issuers, which are not registered and are not being registered under the Securities Act of 1933, furnish the information which would be required if the underlying securities were being registered. The information shall be furnished on the form appropriate for registration of the underlying securities and shall be accompanied by the financial statements, exhibits and other documents specified in that form. However, the facing sheet, the undertaking to file reports and the signatures required by the form on which the information is furnished may be omitted.

[¶ 8141]   FORM S-8

[As last amended in Release No. 33-9002, effective April 13, 2009, 74 F.R. 6776.]

UNITED STATES SECURITIES AND EXCHANGE COMMISSION

Washington, D.C. 20549

UNITED STATES SECURITIES AND EXCHANGE COMMISSION
Washington, D.C. 20549
FORM S-8
REGISTRATION STATEMENT UNDER THE SECURITIES ACT OF 1933

(Exact name of registrant as specified in its charter)

(State or other jurisdiction of incorporation or organization)　　(I.R.S. Employer Identification No.)

(Address of Principal Executive Offices)　　(Zip Code)

(Full title of the plan)

(Name and address of agent for service)

(Telephone number, including area code, of agent for service)

Indicate by check mark whether the registrant is a large accelerated filer, an accelerated filer, a non-accelerated filer, or a smaller reporting company. See the definitions of "large accelerated filer," "accelerated filer" and "smaller reporting company" in Rule 12b-2 of the Exchange Act. (Check one):

[ ] Large accelerated filer

[ ] Accelerated filer

[ ] Non-accelerated filer (Do not check if a smaller reporting company)

[ ] Smaller reporting company

CALCULATION OF REGISTRATION FEE

Title of securities to be registered	Amount to be registered	Proposed maximum offering price per share	Proposed maximum aggregate offering price	Amount of registration fee

Notes:

1. If plan interests are being registered, include the following: In addition, pursuant to Rule 416(c) under the Securities Act of 1933, this registration statement also covers an indeterminate amount of interests to be offered or sold pursuant to the employee benefit plan(s) described herein.

2. Specific details relating to the fee calculation shall be furnished in notes to the table, including references to provisions of Rule 457 (§ 230.457 of this chapter) relied upon, if the basis of the calculation is not otherwise evident from the information presented in the table.

GENERAL INSTRUCTIONS

A. Rule as to Use of Form S-8

1. Any registrant that, immediately prior to the time of filing a registration statement on this Form, is subject to the requirement to file reports pursuant to Section 13 (15 U.S.C. 78m) or 15(d) (15 U.S.C. 78o(d)) of the Securities Exchange Act of 1934 ("Exchange Act"); has filed all reports and other materials required to be filed by such requirements during the preceding 12 months (or for such shorter period that the registrant was

required to file such reports and materials); is not a shell company (as defined in § 230.405 of this chapter) and has not been a shell company for at least 60 calendar days previously (subject to the exception in paragraph (a)(7) of this Instruction A.1.); and if it has been a shell company at any time previously, has filed current Form 10 information with the Commission at least 60 calendar days previously reflecting its status as an entity that is not a shell company (subject to the exception in paragraph (a)(7) of this Instruction A.1.), may use this Form for registration under the Securities Act of 1933 ("Act") (15 U.S.C. 77a *et seq.*) of the following securities:

(a) Securities of the registrant to be offered under any employee benefit plan to its employees or employees of its subsidiaries or parents. For purposes of this form, the term "employee benefit plan" is defined in Rule 405 of Regulation C (§ 230.405).

(1) For purposes of this form, the term "employee" is defined as any employee, director, general partner, trustee (where the registrant is a business trust), officer, or consultant or advisor. Form S-8 is available for the issuance of securities to consultants or advisors only if:

(i) they are natural persons;

(ii) They provide bona fide services to the registrant; and

(iii) the services are not in connection with the offeror sale of securities in a capital-raising transaction, and do not directly or indirectly promote or maintain a market for the registrant's securities.

(2) In addition, the term "employee" includes insurance agents who are exclusive agents of the registrant, its subsidiaries or parents, or derive more than 50% of their annual income from those entities.

(3) The term "employee" also includes former employees as well as executors, administrators or beneficiaries of the estates of deceased employees, guardians or members of a committee for incompetent former employees, or similar persons duly authorized by law to administer the estate or assets of former employees. The inclusion of all individuals described in the preceding sentence in the term "employee" is only to permit registration on Form S-8 of:

(i) the exercise of employee benefit plan stock options and the subsequent sale of the securities, if these exercises and sales are permitted under the terms of the plan; and

(ii) the acquisition of registrant securities pursuant to intra-plan transfers among plan funds, if these transfers are permitted under the terms of the plan.

(4) The term "registrant" as used in this Form means the company whose securities are to be offered pursuant to the plan, and also may mean the plan itself.

(5) The form also is available for the exercise of employee benefit plan options and the subsequent resale of the underlying securities by an employee's family member who has acquired the options from the employee through a gift or a domestic relations order. For purposes of this form, "family member" includes any child, stepchild, grandchild, parent, stepparent, grandparent, spouse, former spouse, sibling, niece, nephew, mother-in-law, father-in-law, son-in-law, daughter-in-law, brother-in-law, or sister-in-law, including adoptive relationships, any person sharing the employees household (other than a tenant or employee), a trust in which these persons have more than fifty percent of the beneficial interest, a foundation in which these persons (or the employee) control the management of assets, and any other entity in which these persons (or the employee) own more than fifty percent of the voting interests. Form S-8 is not available for the exercise of options transferred for value. The following transactions are not prohibited transfers for value:

(i) a transfer under a domestic relations order in settlement of marital property rights; and

(ii) a transfer to an entity in which more than fifty percent of the voting interests are owned by family members (or the employee) in exchange for an interest in that entity.

(6) The term "Form 10 information" means the information that is required by Form 10 or Form 20-F (§ 249.210 or § 249.210 of this chapter), as applicable to the registrant, to register under the Securities Exchange Act of 1934 each class of securities being registered using this form. A registrant may provide the Form 10 information in another Commission filing with respect to the registrant.

(7) Notwithstanding the last two clauses of the first paragraph of this Instruction A.1., a business combination related shell company may use this form immediately after it:

(i) Ceases to be a shell company; and

(ii) Files current Form 10 information with the Commission reflecting its status as an entity that is not a shell company.

(b) Interests in the above plans, if such interests constitute securities and are required to be registered under the Act. (*See* Release No. 33-6188 (February 1, 1980) and Section 3(a)(2) of the Act.)

2. Where interests in a plan are being registered and the plan's latest annual report filed pursuant to 15(d) of the Exchange Act is to be

incorporated by reference pursuant to the requirements of Form S-8, the plan shall either: (i) have been subject to the requirement to file reports pursuant to Section 15(d) and shall have filed all reports required to be filed by such requirements during the preceding 12 months (or for such shorter period that the plan was required to file such reports); or (ii) if the plan has not previously been subject to the reporting requirements of Section 15(d), concurrently with the filing of the registration statement on Form S-8, the plan shall file an annual report for its latest fiscal year (or if the plan has not yet completed its first fiscal year, then for a period ending not more than 90 days prior to the filing of this registration statement), *provided that* if the plan has not been in existence for at least 90 days prior to the filing date, the requirement to file an employee plan annual report concurrently with the Form S-8 registration statement shall not apply.

3. *Electronic filings.* In addition to satisfying the foregoing conditions, a registrant subject to the electronic filing requirements of Rule 101 of Regulation S-T (§ 232.101 of this chapter) shall have:

(a) Filed with the Commission all required electronic filings, including electronic copies of documents submitted in paper pursuant to a hardship exemption as provided by Rule 201 or Rule 202(d) of Regulation S-T (§ 232.201 or § 232.202(d) of this chapter); and

(b) Submitted electronically to the Commission and posted on its corporate Web site, if any, all Interactive Data Files required to be submitted and posted pursuant to Rule 405 of Regulation S-T (§ 232.405 of this chapter) during the twelve calendar months and any portion of a month immediately preceding the filing of the registration statement on this Form (or for such shorter period of time that the registrant was required to submit and post such files).

B. Application of General Rules and Regulations

1. Attention is directed to the General Rules and Regulations under the Act, particularly those comprising Regulation C thereunder (17 CFR §§ 230.400 to 230.499). That Regulation contains general requirements regarding the preparation and filing of registration statements. However, any provision in this Form covering the same subject matter as any such requirement shall be controlling unless otherwise specifically provided in Regulation C (*see* § 230.400).

2. Attention is directed to Regulation S-K (17 CFR Part 229) for the requirements applicable to the content of the non-financial portions of registration statements under the Act. Where this Form directs the registrant to furnish information required by any item of Regulation S-K, information need only be furnished to the extent appropriate.

3. A "smaller reporting company," defined in § 230.405, shall use the disclosure items in Regulation S-K (17 CFR 229.10 *et seq.*) with specific attention to the scaled disclosure provided for smaller reporting companies, if any.

C. Reoffers and Resales

1. *Securities.* Reoffers and resales of the following securities may be made on a continuous or delayed basis in the future, as provided by Rule 415 (§ 230.415), pursuant to a registration statement on this Form by means of a separate prospectus ("reoffer prospectus"), which is prepared in accordance with the requirements of Part I of Form S-3 (or, if the registrant is a foreign private issuer, in accordance with Part I of Form F-3), and filed with the registration statement on Form S-8 or, in the case of control securities, a post-effective amendment thereto:

(a) *Control securities,* which are defined for purposes of this General Instruction C as securities acquired under a Securities Act registration statement held by affiliates of the registrant as defined in Rule 405 (§ 230.405). Control securities may be included in a reoffer prospectus only if they have been or will be acquired by the selling security holder pursuant to an employee benefit plan; or

(b) *Restricted securities,* which are defined for purposes of this General Instruction C as securities issued under any employee benefit plan of the registrant meeting the definition of, "restricted securities" in Rule 144(a)(3) (§ 230.144(a)(3)), whether or not held by affiliates of the registrant. Restricted securities may be included in a reoffer prospectus only if they have been acquired by the selling security holder prior to the filing of the registration statement.

2. *Limitations.* The reoffer prospectus may be used as follows:

(a) If the registrant, at the time of filing such prospectus, satisfies the registrant requirements for use of Form S-3 (or if the registrant is a foreign private issuer, the registrant requirements for use of Form F-3), then control and restricted securities may be registered for reoffer and resale without any limitations.

(b) If the registrant, at the time of filing such prospectus, does not satisfy the registrant requirements for use of Form S-3 or F-3, as appropriate, then the following limitation shall apply with respect to both control securities and restricted securities: the amount of securities to be offered or resold by means of the reoffer prospectus, by each person, and any other person with whom he or she is acting in concert for the purpose of selling securities of the registrant, may not exceed, during any three month period, the amount specified in Rule 144(e) (§ 230. 144(e)).

3. *Selling Security Holders.*

(a) *Control Securities.* If the names of the security holders who intend to resell are not known by the registrant at the time of filing the Form S-8 registration statement, the registrant may either: (1) refer to the selling security holders in a generic manner in the reoffer prospectus; later, as their names and the amounts of securities to be reoffered become known, the registrant must supplement the reoffer prospectus with that information; or (2) name in the reoffer prospectus all persons eligible to resell and the amounts of securities available to be resold, whether or not they have a present intent to do so; any additional persons must be added by prospectus supplement. Prospectus supplements must be filed with the Commission as required by Rule 424(b) (§ 230.424(b)). The registrant may file a reoffer prospectus covering control securities as part of the initial registration statement or by means of a post-effective amendment to the Form S-8 registration statement.

(b) *Restricted Securities.* All persons (including non-affiliates) holding restricted securities registered for reoffer or resale pursuant to a reoffer prospectus are to be named as selling shareholders in the reoffer prospectus; *provided, however,* that any non-affiliate who holds less than the lesser of 1000 shares or 1% of the shares issuable under the plan to which the Form S-8 registration statement relates need not be named if the reoffer prospectus indicates that certain unnamed non-affiliates, each of whom may sell up to that amount, may use the reoffer prospectus for reoffers and resales. The reoffer prospectus covering restricted securities must be filed with the initial registration statement, not a post-effective amendment thereto.

Notes to General Instruction C

1. The term "person" as used in this General Instruction C shall be the same as set forth in Rule 144(a)(2) (§ 230.144(a)(2)).

2. If the conditions of this General Instruction C are not satisfied, registration of reoffers or resales must be made by means of a separate registration statement using whichever form is applicable.

D. Filing and Effectiveness of Registration Statement; Requests for Confidential Treatment; Number of Copies

A registration statement on this Form S-8 will become effective automatically (Rule 462, § 230.462) upon filing (Rule 456, § 230.456). In addition, post-effective amendments on this Form shall become effective upon filing (Rules 464, § 230.464 and 456). Delaying amendments are not permitted in connection with any registration statement on this Form (Rule 473(d), § 230.473(d)), and any attempt to interpose a delaying amendment of any kind will be ineffective. All filings made on or in connection with this Form become public upon filing with the Commission. As a result, requests for confidential treatment made under either Rule 406 (§ 230.406), or Exchange Act Rule 24b-2 (§ 240.24b-2) in connection with documents incorporated by reference, must be acted upon, *i.e.*, granted or denied, by the Commission staff prior to the filing of the registration statement. The number of copies of the filing required by Rules 402(c) and 472(d) (§ 230.402(c), § 230.472(d)) shall be filed with the Commission.

E. Registration of Additional Securities

With respect to the registration of additional securities of the same class as other securities for which a registration statement filed on this Form relating to an employee benefit plan is effective, the registrant may file a registration statement consisting only of the following: the facing page; a statement that the contents of the earlier registration statement, identified by file number, are incorporated by reference, required opinions and consents; the signature page; and any information required in the new registration statement that is not in the earlier registration statement. If the new registration statement covers restricted securities being offered for resale, it shall include the required reoffer prospectus. If the earlier registration statement included a reoffer prospectus, the new registration statement shall be deemed to include that reoffer prospectus, *provided, however,* that a revised reoffer prospectus shall be filed. if the reoffer prospectus is substantively different from that filed in the earlier registration statement. The filing fee required by the Act and Rule 457 (§ 230.457) shall be paid with respect to the additional securities only.

F. Registration of Plan Interests

Where a registration statement on this Form relates to securities to be offered pursuant to an employee stock purchase, savings, or similar plan, the registration statement shall be deemed to register an indeterminate amount of interests in such plan that are separate securities and required to be registered under the Securities Act. *See* Rule 416(c) (§ 230.416(c)).

G. Updating

Updating of information constituting the Section 10(a) prospectus pursuant to Rule 428(a) (§ 230.428(a)) during the offering of the securities shall be accomplished as follows:

1. Plan information specified by Item 1 of Form S-8 required to be sent or given to employees shall be updated as specified in Rule 428(b)(1) (§ 230.428(b)(1)). Such information need not be filed with the Commission.

¶8141   Form S-8

2. Registrant information shall be updated by the filing of Exchange Act reports, which are incorporated by reference in the registration statement and the Section 10(a) prospectus. Any material changes in the registrant's affairs required to be disclosed in the registration statement but not required to be included in a specific Exchange Act report shall be reported on Form 8-K (§ 249.308) pursuant to Item 5 thereof (or, if the registrant is a foreign private issuer, on Form 6-K (§ 249.306)).

3. An employee plan annual report incorporated by reference in the registration statement from Form 11-K (or Form 10-K, as permitted by Rule 15d-21 (§ 240.15d-21)) shall be updated by the filing of a subsequent plan annual report on Form 11-K or 10-K.

Part I
INFORMATION REQUIRED IN THE SECTION 10(a) PROSPECTUS

Note:

The document(s) containing the information specified in this Part I will be sent or given to employees as specified by Rule 428(b)(1) (§ 230.428(b)(1)). Such documents need not be filed with the Commission either as part of this registration statement or us prospectuses or prospectus supplements pursuant to Rule 424 (§ 230.424). These documents and the documents incorporated by reference in the registration statement pursuant to Item 3 of Part II of this Form, taken together, constitute a prospectus that meets the requirements of Section 10(a) of the Securities Act. See Rule 428 (§ 230.428(a)(1)).

Item 1. Plan Information.

The registrant shall deliver or cause to be delivered to each participant material information regarding the plan and its operations that will enable participants to make an informed decision regarding investment in the plan. This information shall include, to the extent material to the particular plan being described, but not be limited to, the disclosure specified in (a) through (j) below. Any unusual risks associated with participation in the plan not described pursuant to a specified item shall be prominently disclosed, as, for example, when the plan imposes a substantial restriction on the ability of a participant to withdraw contributions, or when plan participation may obligate the participant's general credit in connection with purchases on a margin basis. The information may be in one or several documents, provided that it is presented in a clear, concise and understandable manner. *See* Rule 421 (§ 230.421).

(a) General Plan Information

(1) Give the title of the plan and the name of the registrant whose securities are to be offered pursuant to the plan.

(2) Briefly state the general nature and purpose of the plan, its duration, and any provisions for its modification, earlier termination or extension to the extent that they affect the participants.

(3) Indicate whether the plan is subject to any provisions of the Employee Retirement Income Security Act of 1974 ("ERISA"), and if so, the general nature of those provisions to which it is subject.

(4) Give an address and a telephone number, including area code, which participants may use to obtain additional information about the plan and its administrators. State the capacity in which the plan administrators act (*e.g.*, trustees or managers) and the functions that they perform. If any person other than a participating employee has discretion with respect to the investment of all or any part of the assets of the plan in one or more investment media, name such person and describe the policies followed and to be followed with respect to the type and proportion of securities or other property in which funds of the plan may be invested. If the plan is not subject to ERISA: (i) state the nature of any material relationship between the administrators and the employees, the registrant or its affiliates; and (ii) describe the manner in which the plan administrators are selected, their term of office, and the manner in which they may be removed from office.

(b) Securities to be Offered

(1) State the title and total amount of securities to be offered pursuant to the plan.

(2) Furnish the information required by Item 202 of Regulation S-K (§ 229.202), except that if common stock registered under Section 12 of the Exchange Act is offered, such information is unnecessary. If plan interests are being registered, they need not be described pursuant to this item.

(c) Employees Who May Participate In the Plan

Indicate each class or group of employees that may participate in the plan and the basis upon which the eligibility of employees to participate therein is to be determined.

(d) Purchase of Securities Pursuant to the Plan and Payment for Securities Offered

(1) State the period of time within which employees may elect to participate in the plan, the price at which the securities may be purchased or the basis upon which such price is to be determined, and any terms regarding the amount of securities that an eligible employee can purchase.

(2) State when and the manner in which employees are to pay for the securities purchased pursuant to the plan, if payment is to be made by payroll deductions or other installment payments, state the percentage of wages or salaries or other basis for computing such payments, and the time and manner in which an employee may alter the amount of such deduction or payment.

(3) State the amount each employee is required or permitted to contribute or, if not a fixed amount, the percentage of wages or salaries or other basis of computing contributions.

(4) If contributions are to be made under the plan by the registrant or any employer, state who is to make such contributions, when they are to be made and the nature and amount of each contribution: If such contributions are not a fixed amount, state the basis for computing contributions.

(5) State the nature and frequency of any reports to be made to participating employees as to the amount and status of their accounts.

(6) If the plan is not subject to ERISA, state whether securities are to be purchased in the open market or otherwise. If they are not to be purchased in the open market, then state from whom they are to be purchased and describe the fees, commissions or other charges paid. If the employer or any of its affiliates, or any person having a material relationship with the employer or any of its affiliates, directly or indirectly, receives any part of the aggregate purchase price (including fees, commissions or other charges), explain the basis for compensation.

Note:

If the plan is one under which credit is extended to finance the acquisition of securities, consideration should be given to the applicability of Regulation G (12 CFR Part 207) or T (12 CFR Part 220).

(e) Resale Restrictions

Describe briefly any restriction on resale of the securities purchased under the plan which may be imposed upon the employee purchaser.

(f) Tax Effects of Plan Participation

Describe briefly the tax effect that may accrue to employees as a result of plan participation as well as the tax effects, if any, upon the registrant and whether or not the plan is qualified under Section 401(a) of the Internal Revenue Code.

Note:

If the plan is not qualified under Section 401 of the Internal Revenue Code of 1986, as amended, consideration should be given to the applicability of the Investment Company Act of

1940. *See* Securities Act Release No. 4790 (July 13, 1965).

(g) Investment of Funds

If participating employees may direct all or any part of the assets under the plan to two or more investment media, furnish a brief description of the provisions of the plan with respect to the alternative investment media; and provide a tabular or other meaningful presentation of financial data for each of the past three fiscal years (or such lesser period for which the data with respect to each investment medium is available) that, in the opinion of the registrant, will apprise employees of material trends and significant changes in the performance of alternative investment media and enable them to make informed investment decisions. Financial data shall be presented for any additional fiscal years necessary to keep the information from being misleading or that the registrant deems appropriate, but the total period presented need not exceed five years.

(h) Withdrawal from the Plan; Assignment of Interest

(1) Describe the terms and conditions under which a participating employee may (i) withdraw from the plan and terminate his or her interest therein; or (ii) withdraw funds or investments held for the employee's account without terminating his or her interest in the plan.

(2) State whether, and the terms and conditions upon which, the plan permits an employee to assign or hypothecate his or her interest in the plan.

(3) No information need be provided as to the effect of a qualified domestic relations order as defined in ERISA Section 206(d) (29 U.S.C. 1056(d)).

(i) Forfeitures and Penalties

Describe briefly every event which could, under the plan, result in a forfeiture by, or a penalty to, a participant, and the consequences thereof.

(j) Charges and Deductions and Liens Therefor

(1) Describe all charges and deductions (other than deductions described in paragraph (d) and taxes) that may be made against employees participating in the plan or against funds. securities or other property held under the plan and indicate who will receive, directly or indirectly, any part thereof. Such description should include charges and deductions that may be made upon the termination of an employee's interest in the plan, or upon partial withdrawals from the employee's account thereunder.

(2) State whether or not under the plan, or pursuant to any contract in connection therewith,

any person has or may create a lien on any funds, securities, or other property held under the plan. If so, describe fully the circumstances under which the lien was or may be created.

(3) No information need be provided as to the effect of a qualified domestic relations order as defined in ERISA Section 206(d) (29 U.S.C. 1056(d)).

Item 2. Registrant Information and Employee Plan Annual Information.

The registrant shall provide a written statement to participants advising them of the availabil-ity without charge, upon written or oral request, of the documents incorporated by reference in Item 3 of Part II of the registration statement, and stating that these documents are incorporated by reference in the Section 10(a) prospectus. The statement also shall indicate the availability with-out charge, upon written or oral request, of other documents required to be delivered to employees pursuant to Rule 428(b) (§ 230.428(b)). The state-ment shall include the address (giving title or department) and telephone number to which the request is to be directed.

Part II
INFORMATION REQUIRED IN THE REGISTRATION STATEMENT

Item 3. Incorporation of Documents by Reference.

The registrant, and where interests in the plan are being registered, the plan, shall state that the documents listed in (a) through (c) below are incorporated by reference in the registration state-ment; and shall state that all documents subse-quently filed by it pursuant to Sections 13(a), 13(c), 14 and 15(d) of the Securities Exchange Act of 1934, prior to the filing of a post-effective amendment which indicates that all securities of-fered have been sold or which deregisters all securities then remaining unsold, shall be deemed to be incorporated by reference in the registration statement and to be part thereof from the date of filing of such documents. Copies of these docu-ments are not required to be filed with the regis-tration statement.

(a) The registrant's latest annual report. and where interests in the plan are being registered, the plan's latest annual report, filed pursuant to Section 13(a) or 15(d) of the Exchange Act, or in the case of the registrant either (1) the latest prospectus filed pursuant to Rule 424(b) under the Act that contains audited financial statements for the registrant's latest fiscal year for which such statements have been filed, or (2) the registrant's effective registration statement on Form 10, Form 20-F or, in the case of registrants described in General Instruction A.(2) of Form 40-F, on Form 40-F filed under the Exchange Act containing au-dited financial statements for the registrant's latest fiscal year.

(b) All other reports filed pursuant to Section 13(a) or 15(d) of the Exchange Act since the end of the fiscal year covered by the registrant docu-ment referred to in (a) above.

(c) If the class of securities to be offered is registered under Section 12 of the Exchange Act, the description of such class of securities con-tained in a registration statement filed under such Act, including any amendment or report filed for the purpose of updating such description.

Item 4. Description of Securities.

If the class of securities to be offered is not registered under Section 12 of the Exchange Act, set forth the information required by Item 202 of Regulation S-K (§ 229.202 of this chapter). If plan interests are being registered, they need not be described pursuant to this item.

Item 5. Interests of Named Experts and Counsel.

Furnish the information required by Item 509 of Regulation S-K (§ 229.509 of this chapter).

Item 6. Indemnification of Directors and Officers.

Furnish the information required by Item 702 of Regulation S-K (§ 229.702 of this chapter).

Item 7. Exemption from Registration Claimed.

With respect to restricted securities to be reoffered or resold pursuant to this registration statement, the registrant shall indicate the section of the Act or Rule of the Commission under which exemption from registration was claimed and set forth briefly the facts relied upon to make the exemption available.

Item 8. Exhibits.

Furnish the exhibits required by Item 601 Regulation S-K (§ 229.601 of this chapter), except that with respect to Item 601(b)(5):

(a) An opinion of counsel as to the legality of the securities being registered is required only with respect to original issuance securities.

(b) Neither an opinion of counsel concerning compliance with the requirements of ERISA nor an Internal Revenue Service determination letter that the plan is qualified under Section 401 of the Internal Revenue Code shall be required if, in lieu thereof, the response to this Item 8 includes an undertaking that the registrant will submit or has submitted the plan and any amendment thereto to the Internal Revenue Service ("IRS") in a timely manner and has made or will make all changes required by the IRS in order to qualify the plan.

Item 9. Undertakings.

Furnish the undertakings required by Item 512(a), (b) and (h) of Regulation S-K (§ 229.512(a), (b) and (h) of this chapter), as well as any other applicable undertakings in Item 512.

Notes to Item 9:

(1) The Regulation S-K Item 512(a) undertakings are usually required pursuant to this item since most registration statements on Form S-8 involve the continuous offering and sale of securities under Rule 415 (§ 230.415 of this chapter).

(2) With respect to registration statements filed on this Form, foreign private issuers are not required to furnish the Item 512(a)(4) undertaking.

SIGNATURES

The Registrant. Pursuant to the requirements of the Securities Act of 1933, the registrant certifies that it has reasonable grounds to believe that it meets all of the requirements for filing on Form S-8 and has duly caused this registration statement to be signed on its behalf by the undersigned, thereunto duly authorized, in the City of _____

State of _____,

on _____, 19 _____.

(Registrant) _____

By (Signature and Title) _____

Pursuant to the requirements of the Securities Act of 1933, this registration statement has been signed by the following persons in the capacities and on the date indicated.

(Signature) _____

(Title) _____

(Date) _____

The Plan. Pursuant to the requirements of the Securities Act of 1933, the trustees (or other persons who administer the employee benefit plan) have duly caused this registration statement to be signed on its behalf by the undersigned, thereunto duly authorized,

in the City of _____

State of _____,

on _____ 19 _____

(Plan) _____

By (Signature and Title) _____

Instructions.

1. The registration statement shall be signed by the registrant, its principal executive officer or officers, its principal financial officer, its controller or principal accounting officer, and at least a majority of the board of directors or persons performing similar functions. Where interests in the plan are being registered, the registration statement shall be signed by the plan. If the signing person is a foreign person, the registration statement shall also be signed by its authorized representative in the United States. Where the signing person is a limited partnership, the registration statement shall be signed by a majority of the board of directors of any corporate general partner signing the registration statement.

2. The name of each person who signs the registration statement shall be typed or printed beneath the signature. Any person who occupies more than one of the specified positions shall indicate each capacity in which he or she signs the registration statement. Attention is directed to Rule 402 (§ 230.402) concerning manual signatures and Item 601 (§ 229.601) of Regulation S-K concerning signatures pursuant to powers of attorney.

[¶ 8251] FORM S-11

[As last amended in Release No. 33-8909, effective April 15, 2008, 73 F.R. 20512.]

UNITED STATES SECURITIES AND EXCHANGE COMMISSION

Washington, D.C. 20549

GENERAL INSTRUCTIONS

A. Rule as to Use of Form S-11.

This form shall be used for registration under the Securities Act of 1933 of (i) securities issued by real estate investment trust, as defined in Section 856 of the Internal Revenue Code, or (ii) securities issued by other issuers whose business is primarily that of acquiring and holding for investment real estate or interests in real estate or interests in other issuers whose business is primarily that of acquiring and holding real estate or interest in real estate for investment. This form shall not be used, however, by any issuer which is an investment company registered or required to register under the Investment Company Act of 1940.

In addition, this form shall not be used for an offering of asset-backed securities, as defined in 17 CFR 229.1101.

B. Application of General Rules and Regulations.

(a) Attention is directed to the General Rules and Regulations under the Securities Act, particularly those comprising Regulation C thereunder (17 CFR 230.400 to 230.494). That Regulation contains general requirements regarding the preparation and filing of registration statements.

(b) Attention is directed to Regulation S-K (17 CFR Part 229) for the requirements applicable to the content of the non-financial statement portions of registration statements under the Securities Act. Where this Form directs the registrant to furnish information required by Regulation S-K and the item of Regulation S-K so provides, information need only be furnished to the extent appropriate.

C. Exchange Offers.

If any of the securities being registered are to be offered in exchange for securities of any other issuer, the prospectus also shall include the information which would be required by Items 9 to 16, and Item 18 if securities of such other issuer were being registered on this form. Item 26 also shall be answered as to any promoter, director, officer or security holder of such other issuer who is an affiliated person of the registrant.

D. Definitions.

Unless the context clearly indicates the contrary, the following definitions apply:

Affiliated person. The term "affiliated person" means any of the following persons: (i) any director or officer of the registrant; (ii) any person directly or indirectly controlling or under direct or indirect common control with the registrant; (iii) any person owning of record or known by the registrant to own beneficially 10 percent or more of any class of equity securities or the registrant; (iv) any promoter of the registrant directly or indirectly connected with the registrant in any capacity; (v) any principal underwriter of the securities being registered; (vi) any person performing general management or advisory services for the registrant; and (vii) any associate of any of the foregoing persons.

Director. The term "director" means any director of a corporation, trustee of a trust, general partner of a partnership, or any person who performs for an organization functions similar to those performed by the foregoing persons.

Governing instruments. The term "governing instruments" means the Charter, trust agreement, partnership agreement, bylaws or other instruments under which the registrant was organized or created or under which it will operate.

Mortgage. The term "mortgage" means any mortgage, deed of trust or other evidence of indebtedness secured by a lien upon real estate or upon any interest in real estate.

Share. The term "share" means a share of stock in a corporation, a share or other unit of beneficial interest in a trust or unincorporated association, a limited partnership interest, or any similar equity interest in any other type of organization.

E. Foreign Issuers.

A foreign private issuer may comply with Items 19, 20, 21, 22 and 26 of this Form by furnishing the information specified in Items 6, 7.A, 8.A.7, and 18 of Form 20-F (§ 249.220f of this chapter).

F. Roll-up Transactions.

If the securities to be registered on this Form will be issued in a roll-up transaction as defined in Item 901(c) of Regulation S-K (17 CFR 229.901(c)), attention is directed to the requirements of Form S-4 applicable to roll-up transactions, including, but not limited to, General Instruction 1.

G. Registration of Additional Securities

With respect to the registration of additional securities for an offering pursuant to Rule 462(b) under the Securities Act, the registrant may file a registration statement consisting only of the following: the facing page; a statement that the contents of the earlier registration statement, identified by file number, are incorporated by reference; required opinions and consents; the signature page; and any price-related information omitted from the earlier registration statement in reliance on Rule 430A that the registrant chooses to include in the new registration statement. The information contained in such a Rule 462(b) registration statement shall be deemed to be a part of the earlier registration statement as of the date of effectiveness of the Rule 462(b) registration statement. Any opinion or consent required in the Rule 462(b) registration statement may be incorporated by reference from the earlier registration statement with respect to the offering, if: (i) such opinion or consent expressly provides for such incorporation; and (ii) such opinion relates to the securities registered pursuant to Rule 462(b). *See* Rule 411(c) and Rule 439(b) under the Securities Act.

H. Eligibility to Use Incorporation by Reference

If a registrant meets the following requirements immediately prior to the time of filing a registration statement on this Form, it may elect to provide information required by Items 3 through 28 of this Form in accordance with Item 28A and Item 29 of this Form:

1. The registrant is subject to the requirement to file reports pursuant to Section 13 or Section 15(d) of the Securities Exchange Act of 1934.

2. The registrant has filed all reports and other materials required to be filed by Section 13(a), 14, or 15(d) of the Exchange Act during the preceding 12 months (or for such shorter period

that the registrant was required to file such reports and materials).

3. The registrant has filed an annual report required under Section 13(a) or Section 15(d) of the Exchange Act for its most recently completed fiscal year.

4. The registrant is not:

(a) And during the past three years neither the registrant nor any of its predecessors was:

(i) A blank check company as defined in Rule 419(a)(2) (§ 230.419(a)(2) of this chapter);

(ii) A shell company, other than a business combination related shell company, each as defined in Rule 405 (§ 230.405 of this chapter); or

(iii) A registrant for an offering of penny stock as defined in Rule 3a51-1 of the Exchange Act (§ 240.3a51-1 of this chapter).

(b) Registering an offering that effectuates a business combination transaction as defined in Rule 165(f)(1) (§ 230.165(f)(1) of this chapter).

5. If a registrant is a successor registrant it shall be deemed to have satisfied conditions 1, 2, 3, and 4(b) above if:

(a) Its predecessor and it, taken together, do so, provided that the succession was primarily for the purpose of changing the state of incorporation of the predecessor or forming a holding company and that the assets and liabilities of the successor at the time of succession were substantially the same as those of the predecessor; or

(b) All predecessors met the conditions at the time of succession and the registrant has continued to do so since the succession.

6. The registrant makes its periodic and current reports filed pursuant to Section 13 or Section 15(d) of the Exchange Act that are incorporated by reference pursuant to Item 28A or Item 29 of this Form readily available and accessible on a Web site maintained by or for the registrant and containing information about the registrant.

UNITED STATES SECURITIES AND EXCHANGE COMMISSION

Washington, D.C. 20549

FORM S-11

REGISTRATION STATEMENT UNDER THE SECURITIES ACT OF 1933

UNITED STATES SECURITIES AND EXCHANGE COMMISSION

Washington, D.C. 20549

REGISTRATION STATEMENT UNDER THE SECURITIES ACT OF 1933

. . . .

(Exact name of registrant as specified in governing instruments)

. . . .

(Address, including zip code, and telephone number, including area code, of registrant's principal executive offices)

. . . .

(Name, address, including zip code, and telephone number, including area code, of agent for service)

Approximate date of commencement of proposed sale to the public . . . .

If any of the Securities being registered on this Form are to be offered on a delayed or continuous basis pursuant to Rule 415 under the Securities Act, check the following box: []

If this Form is filed to register additional securities for an offering pursuant to Rule 462(b) under the Securities Act, check the following box and list the Securities Act registration statement number of the earlier effective registration statement for the same offering.   ☐ . . . .

If this Form is a post-effective amendment filed pursuant to Rule 462(c) under the Securities Act, check the following box and list the Securities Act registration statement number of the earlier effective registration statement for the same offering.   ☐ . . . .

If this Form is a post-effective amendment filed pursuant to Rule 462(d) under the Securities Act, check the following box and list the Securities Act registration statement number of the earlier effective registration statement for the same offering.   ☐ . . . .

If delivery of the prospectus is expected to be made pursuant to Rule 434, please check the following box.   ☐

Indicate by check mark whether the registrant is a large accelerated filer, an accelerated filer, a non-accelerated filer, or a smaller reporting company. See the definitions of "large accelerated filer," "accelerated filer" and "smaller reporting company" in Rule 12b-2 of the Exchange Act. (Check one):
[ ] Large accelerated filer
[ ] Accelerated filer
[ ] Non-accelerated filer (do not check if a smaller reporting company)
[ ] Smaller reporting company

Calculation of Registration Fee

Title of securities being registered	Amount being registered	Proposed maximum offering price per unit	Proposed maximum aggregate offering price	Amount of registration fee

Note: Specific details relating to the fee calculation shall be furnished in notes to the table, including references to provisions of Rule 457 (§ 230.457 of this chapter) relied upon, if the basis of the calculation is not otherwise evident from the information presented in the table. If the filing fee is calculated pursuant to Rule 457(o) under the Securities Act, only the title of the class of securities to be registered, the proposed maximum aggregate offering price for that class of securities and the amount of registration fee need to appear in the Calculation of Registration Fee table. Any difference between the dollar amount of securities registered for such offerings and the dollar amount of securities sold may be carried forward on a future registration statement pursuant to Rule 429 under the Securities Act.

The registrant hereby amends this registration statement on such date or dates as may be necessary to delay its effective date until the registrant shall file a further amendment which specifically states that this registration statement shall thereafter become effective in accordance with Section 8(a) of the Securities Act of 1933 or until the registration statement shall become effective on such date as the Commission, acting pursuant to said Section 8(a), may determine.[*]

PART I. INFORMATION REQUIRED IN PROSPECTUS

Item 1. Forepart of Registration Statement and Outside Front Cover Page of Prospectus.

(a) Set forth on the outside front cover page of the prospectus the information required by Item 501 of Regulation S-K (§ 229.501 of this chapter).

(b) If there are any limitations on the transferability of the securities being registered, so state on the outside front cover page of the prospectus and refer to a statement elsewhere in the prospectus as to the nature of such limitations. If there is no market for securities of the same class as those being registered, so state on the outside front cover page of the prospectus; otherwise, state elsewhere in the prospectus the nature of the market for such securities and the market price thereof as of the latest practicable date prior to the filing of the registration statement or amendment thereto.

Item 2. Inside Front and Outside Back Cover Pages of Prospectus.

Set forth on the inside front cover page of the prospectus or, where permitted, on the outside back cover page, the information required by Item 502 of Regulation S-K (§ 229.502 of this chapter).

Item 3. Summary Information, Risk Factors and Ratio of Earnings to Fixed Charges.

(a) Furnish the information required by Item 503 of Regulation S-K (§ 229.503 of this chapter).

(b) Where appropriate to a clear understanding by investors, an introductory statement shall be made in the forepart of the prospectus, in a series of short, concise paragraphs, summarizing the principal factors which make the offering speculative. Where appropriate, statements with respect to the following shall also be set forth:

(1) A comparison in percentages of the securities being offered to the public and those issued or to be issued to affiliated persons;

(2) The extent to which security holders may be liable for the acts or obligations of the registrant;

(3) Allocation of cash distributions between the public security holders and security holders who are affiliated persons;

(4) The compensation and other forms of compensation and benefits to be received, directly or indirectly, by affiliated persons, including in the case of underwriters a comparison of the aggregate compensation to be received by them with the aggregate net proceeds from the sale of the securities being registered.

Item 4. Determination of Offering Price.

Furnish the information required by Item 505 of Regulation S-K (§ 229.505 of this chapter).

Item 5. Dilution.

Furnish the information required by Item 506 of Regulation S-K (§ 229.506 of this chapter).

Item 6. Selling Security Holders.

Furnish the information required by Item 507 of Regulation S-K (§ 229.507 of this chapter).

---

[*] Inclusion of this paragraph is optional. See Rule 473.

Item 7. Plan of Distribution.

Furnish the information required by Item 508 of Regulation S-K (§ 229.508 of this chapter).

Item 8. Use of Proceeds.

Furnish the information required by Item 504 of Regulation S-K (§ 229.504 of this chapter).

Item 9. Selected Financial Data.

Furnish the information required by Item 301 of Regulation S-K (§ 229.301 of this chapter).

Instruction. If, pursuant to this Item, a statement showing the pro forma taxable operating results of the registrant is included in the registration statement, the Commission or its staff may request as supplemental information, which the registrant should be prepared to furnish promptly upon request, a schedule reconciling such pro forma results with the historical operating results (*see* Rule 3-14 of Regulation S-X).

Item 10. Management's Discussion and Analysis of Financial Condition and Results of Operations.

Furnish the information required by Item 303 of Regulation S-K (§ 229.303 of this chapter).

Item 11. General Information as to Registrant.

(a) State the name and form of organization of the registrant and the name of the State or other jurisdiction the laws of which govern with respect to the organization of the registrant.

(b) State the date on which the governing instruments became operative and the date on which they will expire. If the duration of the registrant may be sooner terminated or may be extended, outline briefly the pertinent provisions.

(c) If the registrant is not a corporation state briefly the provisions of the governing instruments with respect to the holding of annual or other meetings of security holders. If the governing instruments do not provide for such meetings state the policy or proposed policy of the registrant with respect to holding annual or other meetings of security holders.

(d) If the registrant was organized within the last five years, give the full names of all promoters and indicate all positions and offices with the registrant now held or intended to be held by each such promoter.

Instruction. If any person named as a promoter is no longer connected with the registrant in any capacity, so state.

Item 12. Policy with Respect to Certain Activities.

Describe the policy of the registrant with respect to each of the following types of activities, indicating whether such policy may be changed by the officers and directors without a vote of security holders. Indicate the extent to which the registrant proposes to engage in such activities and the extent to which it has engaged in such activities during the past three years.

(a) To issue senior securities.

(b) To borrow money.

(c) To make loans to other persons.

(d) To invest in the securities of other issuers for the purpose of exercising control.

(e) To underwrite securities of other issuers.

(f) To engage in the purchase and sale (or turnover) of investments.

(g) To offer securities in exchange for property.

(h) To repurchase or otherwise reacquire its shares or other securities.

(i) To make annual or other reports to security holders, indicating the nature and scope of such reports and whether they will contain financial statements certified by independent public accountants.

Instructions. 1. The policy or proposed policy of the registrant with respect to each activity shall be described separately. If the registrant does not propose to engage in a particular activity, a specific statement to that effect shall be made. The information shall be given in such manner and detail as will be meaningful to investors.

2. For the purpose of (c), the purchasing of a portion of publicly distributed bonds, debentures or other securities, whether or not the purchase was made upon the original issuance of the securities, is not to be considered the making of a loan by the registrant.

Item 13. Investment Policies of Registrant.

Describe the policy of the registrant with respect to investing in each of the following types of investments, indicating whether such policy may be changed by the directors without a vote of security holders, the percentage of assets which the registrant may invest in any one type of investment and, in the case of securities, the percentage of securities of any one issuer which the registrant may acquire and the principles and procedures the registrant will employ in connection with the acquisition of assets.

(a) *Investments in real estate or interests in real estate.*

Instructions. 1. Indicate the geographic area or areas in which the registrant proposes to acquire real estate or interests in real estate.

2. The types of real estate and interests in real estate in which the registrant may invest shall be

indicated; for example, office buildings, apartment buildings, shopping centers, industrial and commercial properties, special purpose buildings and undeveloped acreage.

3. The method or proposed method of operating and financing the registrant's real estate shall be briefly described. Indicate any limitations on the number or amount of mortgages which may be placed on any one piece of property.

4. The answer to this item shall be such as will be appropriate in view of the nature of the registrant's business, its history and its experience and the proposed nature of its business and activities.

5. Include a specific statement as to whether or not it is the registrant's policy to acquire assets primarily for possible capital gain or primarily for income.

6. State the registrant's policy as to the amount or percentage of assets which will be invested in any specific property.

7. Include a statement with respect to any other material policy with respect to real estate activities.

(b) *Investments in real estate mortgages.*

Instructions. 1. Indicate the types of mortgages; for example, first or second mortgages and whether such mortgages are to be insured by the Federal Housing Administration or guaranteed by the Veterans Administration or otherwise guaranteed or insured, and the proportion of assets which may be invested in each type of mortgage or in any single mortgage.

2. Include a description of each type of mortgage activity in which the registrant intends to engage such as originating, servicing and warehousing of mortgages and its portfolio turnover policy.

3. Indicate the types of properties subject to mortgages in which the registrant invests or proposes to invest; for example, single family dwellings, apartment buildings, office buildings, bowling alleys, commercial properties and unimproved land.

(c) *Securities of or interests in persons primarily engaged in real estate activities.*

Instructions. 1. Indicate separately the types of securities of or interests in persons engaged in real estate activities (for example, common stock, interests in real estate investment trusts, partnership interests, joint venture interests) in which the registrant may invest and the proportion of its assets which may be invested in each such type of security or interest.

2. Indicate the primary activities of persons in which the registrant will invest such as mortgage sales, investment in office buildings or investments in undeveloped acreage and the investment policies of such persons.

3. State the criteria followed in the purchase of such securities and interests (for example, securities listed on a national securities exchange, minimum net income requirements, period of operation of issuer).

(d) *Investments in other securities.*

Instructions. 1. Indicate the type of securities (for example, bonds, preferred stocks, common stocks) and the industry groups in which the registrant may invest and the percentage of its assets which it may invest in each such type or industry group.

2. Instruction 3 to paragraph (c) shall also apply to this paragraph.

Item 14. Description of Real Estate.

(a) State the location and describe the general character of all materially important real properties now held or intended to be acquired by or leased to the registrant or its subsidiaries. Include information as to the present or proposed use of such properties and their suitability and adequacy for such use. Properties not yet acquired shall be identified as such.

(b) State the nature of the registrant's or subsidiary's title to, or other interest in such properties and the nature and amount of all material mortgages, or other liens or encumbrances against such properties. Set forth briefly the current principal amount of each such material encumbrance, its interest and amortization provisions, its pre-payment provisions and its maturity date and balance to be due at maturity assuming no payment has been made on principal in advance of its due date.

(c) Outline briefly the principal terms of any lease of any of such properties or any option or contract to purchase or sell any of such properties.

(d) Outline briefly any proposed program for the renovation, improvement or development of such properties, including the estimated cost thereof and the method of financing to be used. If there are no present plans for the improvement or development of any unimproved or undeveloped property, so state and indicate the purpose for which the property is to be held or acquired.

(e) Describe the general competitive conditions to which the properties described above are or may be subject.

Instructions. 1. What is required is information essential to an investor's understanding of the securities being registered. Detailed descriptions of the physical characteristics of individual properties or legal descriptions by metes and bounds are not required and should not be given. If the registrant has a number of properties, the information may be given in tabular form to the extent that it is practicable to do so.

2. The information shall be furnished separately as to each property the book value of which amounts to ten percent or more of the total assets of the registrant and its consolidated subsidiaries or the gross revenue from which for the last fiscal year amounted to ten percent or more of the aggregate gross revenues of the registrant and its consolidated subsidiaries for the registrant's last fiscal year. With respect to other properties the information shall be given by such classes or groups and in such detail as will reasonably convey the information required.

3. Include a statement as to whether, in the opinion of the management of the registrant the properties are adequately covered by insurance.

Item 15. Operating Data.

Furnish the following information with respect to each improved property which is separately described in answer to Item 14.

(a) Occupancy rate expressed as a percentage for each of the last five years.

(b) Number of tenants occupying ten percent or more of the rentable square footage and principal nature of business of such tenant.

(c) Principal business, occupations and professions carried on in, or from the building.

(d) The principal provisions of the leases between the tenants referred to in (b) above including, but not limited to: rental per annum, expiration date, and renewal options.

(e) The average effective annual rental per square foot or unit for each of the last five years prior to the date of filing.

(f) Schedule of the lease expirations for each of the ten years starting with the year in which the registration statement is filed, stating (i) the number of tenants whose leases will expire, (ii) the total area in square feet covered by such leases, (iii) the annual rental represented by such leases, and (iv) the percentage of gross annual rental represented by such leases.

(g) Each of the properties and components thereof upon which depreciation is taken, setting forth the (i) Federal tax basis, (ii) rate, (iii) method, and (iv) life claimed with respect to such property or component thereof for purposes of depreciation.

(h) The realty tax rate, annual realty taxes and estimated taxes on any proposed improvements.

Instruction. Instruction 3 to Item 14 shall apply to this Item.

Item 16. Tax Treatment of Registrant and Its Security Holders.

(a) Briefly describe the material aspects of the tax treatment of registrant under Federal income tax laws and the Federal tax treatment of registrant's security holders with respect to distributions by registrant, including the tax treatment of gains from the sale of securities or property and distributions in excess of annual net income.

(b) If any of the securities being registered are to be offered in exchange for other securities or property indicate the tax effect upon such exchanges of the Federal income tax laws.

Item 17. Market Price of and Dividends on the Registrant's Common Equity and Related Stockholder Matters.

Furnish the information required by Item 201 of Regulation S-K (§ 229.201 of this chapter).

Item 18. Description of Registrant's Securities.

Furnish the information required by Item 202 of Regulation S-K (§ 229.202 of this chapter).

Item 19. Legal Proceedings.

Furnish the information required by Item 103 of the Regulation S-K (§ 229.103 of this chapter).

Item 20. Security Ownership of Certain Beneficial Owners and Management.

Furnish the information required by Item 403 of Regulation S-K (§ 229.403 of this chapter).

Item 21. Directors and Executive Officers.

Furnish the information required by Item 401 of Regulation S-K (§ 229.401 of this chapter).

Item 22. Executive Compensation.

Furnish the information required by Item 402 of Regulation S-K (§ 229.402 of this chapter), and the information required by paragraph (e)(4) of Item 407 of Regulation S-K (§ 229.407(e)(4) of this chapter).

Item 23. Certain Relationships and Related Transactions.

Furnish the information required by Items 404 and 407(a) of Regulation S-K (§ § 229.404 and 229.407(a) of this chapter). If a transaction involves the purchase or sale of assets by or to the registrant, otherwise than in the ordinary course of business, state the cost of the assets to the purchaser and, if acquired by the seller within two years prior to the transaction, the cost thereof to the seller. Furthermore, if the assets have been acquired by the seller within five years prior to the transaction, disclose the aggregate depreciation claimed by the seller for federal income tax purposes. Indicate the principle followed in determining the registrant's purchase or sale price and the name of the person making such determination.

Item 24. Selection, Management and Custody of Registrant's Investments.

(a) Describe the arrangements made or proposed to be made by the registrant with respect to the following:

(1) Management of the registrant's real estate, including arranging for purchases, sales, leases, maintenance and insurance.

(2) The purchase, sale and servicing of mortgages for the registrant.

(3) Investment advisory services.

(b) If any of the services specified in paragraph (a) are performed or to be performed by any affiliated person, furnish the following information as to such person:

(1) Name and address.

(2) Nature of principal business.

(3) Principal occupations during the last five years.

(4) Nature of all existing direct or indirect material interests in or business connections with the registrant or any of its other affiliated persons.

(5) Nature of all services rendered to the registrant and its subsidiaries.

(6) Aggregate compensation received from the registrant and its subsidiaries, directly or indirectly, during the registrant's last fiscal year and the capacities in which such remuneration was received.

Instructions. 1. If any person whose principal occupations during the last five years are described in answer to paragraph (b)(3) is a corporation or other organization, include the name and principal occupations during the last five years of each principal executive officer of such corporation or other organization.

2. The information required by paragraph (b) need not be furnished with respect to any director or officer of the registrant who performs the services specified solely in his capacity as such director or officer and who receives no additional compensation directly or indirectly for such services.

Item 25. Policies with Respect to Certain Transactions.

Outline briefly any provisions of the governing instruments limiting any director, officer, security holder or affiliate of the registrant, or any other person in the following respects. If the governing instruments contain no such provisions, describe the policy of the registrant with respect to such matters.

(a) Having any direct or indirect pecuniary interest in any investment to be acquired or disposed of by the registrant or any of its subsidiaries or in any transaction to which the registrant or any of its subsidiaries is a party or has an interest.

(b) Engaging for their own account in business activities of the types conducted or to be conducted by the registrant and its subsidiaries.

Item 26. Limitations of Liability.

Outline briefly the principal provisions of the governing instruments or of any contract or arrangement to which the registrant or a subsidiary is a party with respect to limitations on the liability of affiliated persons or any of their directors, officers or employees.

Instructions. If any of such provisions are broad enough to cover liability arising under the Securities Act of 1933, the effect of Section 14 of that Act upon such provisions should be indicated.

Item 27. Financial Statements and Information.

Include in the prospectus the financial statements required by Regulation S-X, the supplementary financial information required in Item 302 of Regulation S-K (§ 229.302 of this chapter) and the information concerning changes in and disagreements with accountants on accounting and financial disclosure required by Item 304 of Regulation S-K (§ 229.304 of this chapter). Although all schedules required by Regulation S-X are to be included in the registration statement, all such schedules other than those prepared in accordance with Rules 12-12, 12-28, and 12-29 of Regulation S-X (§§ 210.12-12, 12-28, and 12-29 of this chapter) may be omitted from the prospectus. A smaller reporting company may provide the information in Article 8 of Regulation S-X (§ 210.8 of this chapter) in lieu of the financial information required by other parts of Regulation S-X, and need not provide the supplementary financial information required in Item 302 of Regulation S-K.

Item 28. Interests of Named Experts and Counsel.

Furnish the information required by Item 509 of Regulation S-K (§ 229.509 of this chapter).

Item 28A. Material Changes.

If the registrant elects to incorporate information by reference pursuant to General Instruction H, describe any and all material changes in the registrant's affairs which have occurred since the end of the latest fiscal year for which audited financial statements were included in the latest Form 10-K and which have not been described in a Form 10-Q or Form 8-K filed under the Exchange Act.

Item 29. Incorporation of Certain Information by Reference.

If the registrant elects to incorporate information by reference pursuant to General Instruction H:

(a) It must specifically incorporate by reference into the prospectus contained in the registration statement the following documents by means of a statement to that effect in the prospectus listing all such documents:

(1) The registrant's latest annual report on Form 10-K filed pursuant to Section 13(a) or Section 15(d) of the Exchange Act which contains financial statements for the registrant's latest fiscal year for which a Form 10-K was required to have been filed; and

(2) All other reports filed pursuant to Section 13(a) or Section 15(d) of the Exchange Act or proxy or information statements filed pursuant to Section 14 of the Exchange Act since the end of the fiscal year covered by the annual report referred to in paragraph (a)(1) of this Item.

Note to Item 29(a). Attention is directed to Rule 439 (§ 230.439 of this chapter) regarding consent to use of material incorporated by reference.

(b)(1) The registrant must state:

(i) That it will provide to each person, including any beneficial owner, to whom a prospectus is delivered, a copy of any or all of the reports or documents that have been incorporated by reference in the prospectus contained in the registration statement but not delivered with the prospectus;

(ii) That it will provide these reports or documents upon written or oral request;

(iii) That it will provide these reports or documents at no cost to the requester;

(iv) The name, address, telephone number, and e-mail address, if any, to which the request for these reports or documents must be made; and

(v) The registrant's Web site address, including the uniform resource locator (URL) where the incorporated reports and other documents may be accessed.

Note to Item 29(b)(1). If the registrant sends any of the information that is incorporated by reference in the prospectus contained in the registration statement to security holders, it also must send any exhibits that are specifically incorporated by reference in that information.

(2) The registrant must:

(i) Identify the reports and other information that it files with the SEC; and

(ii) State that the public may read and copy any materials it files with the SEC at the SEC's Public Reference Room at 100 F Street, NE, Washington, DC 20549. State that the public may obtain information on the operation of the Public Reference Room by calling the SEC at 1-800-SEC-0330. If the registrant is an electronic filer, state that the SEC maintains an Internet site that contains reports, proxy and information statements, and other information regarding issuers that file electronically with the SEC and state the address of that site (*http://www.sec.gov*).

Item 29A. Disclosure of Commission Position on Indemnification for Securities Act Liabilities.

Furnish the information required by Item 510 of Regulation S-K (§ 229.510 of this chapter).

Item 30. Quantitative and Qualitative Disclosures About Market Risk.

Furnish the information required by Item 305 of Regulation S-K (§ 229.305 of this chapter).

PART II. INFORMATION NOT REQUIRED IN PROSPECTUS

Item 31. Other Expenses of Issuance and Distribution.

Furnish the information required by Item 511 of Regulation S-K (§ 229.511 of this chapter).

Item 32. Sales to Special Parties.

Name each person or specify each class of persons (other than underwriters or dealers, as such) to whom any securities have been sold within the past six months, or are to be sold, by the registrant or any security holder for whose account any of the securities being registered are to be offered, at a price varying from that at which securities of the same class are to be offered to the general public pursuant to this registration. State the consideration given or to be given by each such person or class.

Item 33. Recent Sales of Unregistered Securities.

Furnish the information required by Item 701 of Regulation S-K (§ 229.701 of this chapter).

Item 34. Indemnification of Directors and Officers.

Furnish the information required by Item 702 of Regulation S-K (§ 229.702 of this chapter).

Item 35. Treatment of Proceeds from Stock Being Registered.

If the capital shares are being registered hereunder and any portion of the consideration to be received by the registrant for such shares is to be credited to an account other than the appropriate capital share account, state to what other account such portion is to be credited and the estimated amount per share. If the consideration from the sale of par value shares is less than par value, state the amount per share involved and its treatment in the accounts.

Item 36. Financial Statements and Exhibits.

(a) List all financial statements filed as part of the registration statement, indicating those included in the prospectus.

(b) Furnish the exhibits required by Item 601 of Regulation S-K (§ 229.601 of this chapter).

Item 37. Undertakings.

Furnish the information required by Item 512 of Regulation S-K (§ 229.512 of this chapter).

SIGNATURES

Pursuant to the requirements of the Securities Act of 1933, the registrant certifies that it has reasonable grounds to believe that it meets all of the requirements for filing on Form S-11 and has duly caused this registration statement to be signed on its behalf by the undersigned, thereunto duly authorized, in the City of . . . . , State of . . . . , on . . . . , 20. . . . . .

(Issuer) . . . .

By (Signature and Title) . . . .

Pursuant to the requirements of the Securities Act of 1933, this registration statement has been signed by the folowing persons in the capacities and on the dates indicated.

(Signature) . . . .

(Title) . . . .

(Date) . . . .

Instructions. 1. The registration statement shall be signed by the registrant, its principal executive officer or officers, its principal financial officer, its controller or principal accounting officer, and by at least a majority of the board of directors or persons performing similar functions. If the registrant is a foreign person, the registration statement shall also be signed by its authorized representative in the United States. Where the registrant is a limited partnership, the registration statement shall be signed by a majority of the board of directors of any corporate general partner signing the registration statement.

2. The name of each person who signs the registration statement shall be typed or printed beneath his signature. Any person who occupies more than one of the specified positions shall indicate each capacity in which he signs the registration statement. Attention is directed to Rule 402 concerning manual signatures and Item 601 of Regulation S-K concerning signatures pursuant to powers of attorney.

[¶ 8471]   **FORM S-20**

[As last amended in Release No. 33-7497, January 28, 1998, effective October 1, 1998, 63 F.R. 6370.]

UNITED STATES SECURITIES AND EXCHANGE COMMISSION

FORM S-20

REGISTRATION STATEMENT UNDER THE SECURITIES ACT OF 1933

. . . .

(Exact name of registrant as specified in its charter)

. . . .

(Address, including zip code, and telephone number, including area code, or registrant's principal executive offices)

. . . .

(Name, address, including zip code, and telephone number, including area code, of agent for service)

Approximate date of commencement of proposed sale to public . . . .

Calculation of Registration Fee

Title of securities to be registered	Amount to be registered	Proposed maximum fee or charge per unit	Proposed maximum aggregate fee or charge	Amount of registration fee

Note: Specific details relating to the fee calculation shall be furnished in notes to the table, including references to provisions of Rule 457 (§§ 230.457 of this chapter) relied upon, if the basis of the calculation is not otherwise evident from the information presented in the table.

GENERAL INSTRUCTIONS

I. Eligibility Requirement for Use of Form S-20

This form may be used for registration of standardized options under the Securities Act of 1933 ("Securities Act") provided that the registrant undertakes not to issue, clear, guarantee or accept an option registered on Form S-20 unless there is a definitive options disclosure document meeting the requirements of Rule 9b-1 of the Securities Exchange Act of 1934 with respect to the options class.

II. Application of General Rules and Regulations

A. Attention is directed to the General Rules and Regulations under the Securities Act, particu- larly those comprising Regulation C [17 CFR 230.400 to 230.494] thereunder. That Regulation contains general requirements regarding the prep- aration and filing of the registration statement.

B. Attention is directed to Regulation S-K [17 CFR Part 229] for the requirements applicable to the content of the nonfinancial statement portions of registration statements under the Securities Act. Where this Form directs the registration to furnish information required by Regulation S-K and the item of Regulation S-K so provides, infor- mation need only be furnished to the extent appropriate.

PART I

INFORMATION REQUIRED IN PROSPECTUS

Item 1. Forepart of the Registration Statement and Outside Front Cover Page of Prospectus

Set forth in the forepart of the registration statement and on the outside front cover page of the prospectus the information required by Item

501 of Regulation S-K [§ 229.501 of this chapter]. In the case of a foreign registrant, the information required by Item 101(g) of Regulation S-K [§ 229.101(g) of this chapter] also shall be in- cluded. In addition, the outside front cover page of

the prospectus shall contain a statement to the effect that (1) an options disclosure document containing a description of the risks of options transactions is required to be furnished to option investors and stating from whom such a document may be obtained; (2) the financial statements and certain additional information required by Part II of the registration statement, other than exhibits, can be obtained without charge upon request from the registrant; and (3) the exhibits required by Part II of the registration statement can be inspected at the offices of the registrant or obtained from the registrant or the Securities and Exchange Commission upon payment of an appropriate fee.

Item 2. Description of Registrant

(a) State the year in which the registrant was organized, its form of organization and the name of the State or other jurisdiction under the laws of which it was organized.

(b) List all the parents of the registrant showing the basis of control.

(c) Briefly describe the business of the registrant and the services rendered by it.

Item 3. Description of Securities to be Registered

State the title of the securities to be registered, the rights evidenced by such securities, whether certificates representing these securities are issued, the contractual obligations of the registrant with respect to such securities and any restriction on the purchase of such securities.

Instruction. This item only requires a brief summary of the provisions of the security. A complete legal description of the provisions referred to is not required and should not be given; only a succinct resume is required.

PART II

INFORMATION NOT REQUIRED IN PROSPECTUS

Item 4. Directors and Executive Officers

Furnish the information required by Item 401 of Regulation S-K [§ 229.401 of this chapter].

Item 5. Legal Proceedings

Furnish the information required by Item 103 of Regulation S-K [§ 229.103 of this chapter].

Item 6. Legal Opinions and Experts

Furnish the information required by Items 601(b)(5) and 601(b)(24) of Regulation S-K [§ 229.601 of this chapter].

Item 7. Financial Statements

Include financial statements meeting the requirements of Regulation S-X [17 CFR Part 210] and the supplementary financial information specified by Item 12 of Regulation S-K [17 CFR 229.20].

Item 8. Undertakings

Furnish the following undertakings:

1. The undersigned registrant hereby undertakes to file a post-effective amendment, not later than 120 days after the end of each fiscal year subsequent to that covered by the financial statements presented herein, containing financial statements meeting the requirements of Regulation S-X [17 CFR 210] and the supplementary financial information specified by Item 12 of Regulation S-K [17 CFR 229.20].

2. The undersigned registrant hereby undertakes not to issue, clear, guarantee or accept any security registered herein until there is a definitive options disclosure document meeting the requirements of Rule 9b-1 of the Securities Exchange Act of 1934 with respect to the class options.

SIGNATURES

Pursuant to the requirements of the Securities Act of 1933, the registrant certifies that it has reasonable grounds to believe that it meets all of the requirements for filing on Form S-20 and has duly caused this registration statement to be signed on its behalf by the undersigned, thereunto duly authorized, in the City of . . . . , State of . . . . , on . . . ., 20. . . . .

(Registrant) . . . .

by (Signature and Title) . . . .

Pursuant to the requirements of the Securities Act of 1933, this registration statement has been signed by the following persons in the capacities and on the dates indicated.

(Signature) . . . .

(Title) ....

(Date) ....

Instructions: 1. The registration statement shall be signed by the registrant, its principal executive officer or officers, its principal financial officer, its controller or principal accounting officer and by at least a majority of the board of directors or persons performing similar functions. If the registrant is a foreign person, the registration statement shall also be signed by its authorized representative in the United States.

2. The name of each person who signs the registration statement shall be typed or printed beneath his signature. Any person who occupies more than one of the specified positions shall indicate each capacity in which he signs the registration statement. Attention is directed to Rule 402 concerning manual signatures and to Item 601 of Regulation S-K concerning signatures pursuant to powers of attorney.

[¶ 8551]   FORM 1-A

[As last amended in Release No. 33-9026, effective April 23, 2009, 74 F.R. 18612.]

UNITED STATES SECURITIES AND EXCHANGE COMMISSION

Washington, D.C. 20549

FORM 1-A

REGULATION A OFFERING STATEMENT UNDER THE SECURITIES ACT OF 1933
UNITED STATES SECURITIES AND EXCHANGE COMMISSION

FORM 1-A

REGULATION A OFFERING STATEMENT
UNDER THE SECURITIES ACT OF 1933

. . . .

(Exact name of issuer as specified in its charter)

. . . .

(State or other jurisdiction of incorporation or organization)

. . . .

(Address, including zip code, and telephone number,
including area code of issuer's principal executive offices)

. . . .

(Name, address, including zip code, and telephone number,
including area code, of agent for service)

. . . .

(Primary standard Industrial Classification Code Number)	(I.R.S. Employer Identification Number)

The following delaying notation is optional, but see Rule 252 (g) before omitting it:

This offering statement shall only be qualified upon order of the Commission, unless a subsequent amendment is filed indicating the intention to become qualified by operation of the terms of Regulation A.

GENERAL INSTRUCTIONS

I. Eligibility Requirements for Use of Form 1-A

This form is to be used for securities offerings made pursuant to Regulation A, 17 CFR 230.251 *et seq.* Careful attention should be directed to the terms, conditions and requirements of the regulation, especially Rule 251, inasmuch as the exemption is not available to all issuers or to every type of securities transaction. Further, the aggregate offering amount of securities which may be sold in any 12 month period is strictly limited to $5 million.

II. Preparation and Filing of the Offering Statement

An offering statement shall be prepared by all persons seeking exemption pursuant to the provisions of Regulation A. Parts I, II and III shall be addressed by all issuers. Part II of the form which relates to the content of the required offering circular provides several alternate formats depending upon the nature and/or business of the issuer; only one format needs to be followed and provided in the offering statement. General information regarding the preparation, format, content of, and where to file the offering statement is contained in Rule 252. Requirements relating to the offering circular are contained in Rules 253 and 255. The offering statement may be printed, mimeographed, lithographed, or typewritten or prepared by any similar process which will result in clearly legible copies.

III. Supplemental Information

The following information shall be furnished to the Commission as supplemental information:

(1) A statement as to whether or not the amount of compensation to be allowed or paid to the underwriter has been cleared with the NASD.

(2) Any engineering, management or similar report referenced in the offering circular.

(3) Such other information as requested by the staff in support of statements, representations and other assertions contained in the offering statement.

PART I—NOTIFICATION

The information requested shall be provided in the order which follows specifying each item number; the text of each item as presented in this form may be omitted. All items shall be addressed and negative responses should be included.

ITEM 1. Significant Parties

List the full names and business and residential addresses, as applicable, for the following persons:

(a) the issuer's directors;

(b) the issuer's officers;

(c) the issuer's general partners;

(d) record owners of 5 percent or more of any class of the issuer's equity securities;

(e) beneficial owners of 5 percent or more of any class of the issuer's equity securities;

(f) promoters of the issuer;

(g) affiliates of the issuer;

(h) counsel to the issuer with respect to the proposed offering;

(i) each underwriter with respect to the proposed offering;

(j) the underwriter's directors;

(k) the underwriter's officers;

(l) the underwriter's general partners; and

(m) counsel to the underwriter.

ITEM 2. Application of Rule 262

(a) State whether any of the persons identified in response to Item 1 are subject to any of the disqualification provisions set forth in Rule 262.

(b) If any such person is subject to these provisions, provide a full description including pertinent names, dates and other details, as well as whether or not an application has been made pursuant to Rule 262 for a waiver of such disqualification and whether or not such application has been granted or denied.

ITEM 3. Affiliate Sales

If any part of the proposed offering involves the resale of securities by affiliates of the issuer, confirm that the following description does not apply to the issuer.

The issuer has not had a net income from operations of the character in which the issuer intends to engage for at least one of its last two fiscal years.

ITEM 4. Jurisdictions in Which Securities Are to be Offered

(a) List the jurisdiction in which the securities are to be offered by underwriters, dealers or salespersons.

(b) List the jurisdictions in which the securities are to be offered other than by underwriters, dealers or salesmen and state the method by which such securities are to be offered.

ITEM 5. Unregistered Securities Issued or Sold Within One Year

(a) As to any unregistered securities issued by the issuer or any of its predecessors or affiliated issuers within one year prior to the filing of this Form 1-A, state:

(1) the name of such issuer;

(2) the title and amount of securities issued;

(3) the aggregate offering price or other consideration for which they were issued and the basis for computing the amount thereof;

(4) the names and identities of the persons to whom the securities were issued.

(b) As to any unregistered securities of the issuer or any of its predecessors or affiliated issuers which were sold within one year prior to the filing of this Form 1-A by or for the account of any person who at the time was a director, officer, promoter or principal security holder of the issuer of such securities, or was an underwriter of any securities of such issuer, furnish the information specified in subsections (1) through (4) of paragraph (a).

(c) Indicate the section of the Securities Act or Commission rule or regulation relied upon for exemption from the registration requirements of such Act and state briefly the facts relied upon for such exemption.

ITEM 6. Other Present or Proposed Offerings

State whether or not the issuer or any of its affiliates is currently offering or contemplating the offering of any securities in addition to those covered by this Form 1-A. If so, describe fully the present or proposed offering.

ITEM 7. Marketing Arrangements

(a) Briefly describe any arrangement known to the issuer or to any person named in response to Item 1 above or to any selling securityholder in the offering covered by this Form 1-A for any of the following purposes:

(1) To limit or restrict the sale of other securities of the same class as those to be offered for the period of distribution;

—— (2) To stabilize the market for any of the securities to be offered;

(3) For withholding commissions, or otherwise to hold each underwriter or dealer responsible for the distribution of its participation.

(b) Identify any underwriter that intends to confirm sales to any accounts over which it exercises discretionary authority and include an estimate of the amount of securities so intended to be confirmed.

ITEM 8. Relationship with Issuer of Experts Named in Offering Statement

If any expert named in the offering statement as having prepared or certified any part thereof was employed for such purpose on a contingent basis or, at the time of such preparation or certification or at any time thereafter, had a material interest in the issuer or any of its parents or subsidiaries or was connected with the issuer or any of its subsidiaries as a promoter, underwriter, voting trustee, director, officer or employee furnish a brief statement of the nature of such contingent basis, interest or connection.

ITEM 9. Use of a Solicitation of Interest Document

Indicate whether or not a written document or broadcast script authorized by Rule 254 was used prior to the filing of this notification. If so, indicate the date(s) of such use.

PART II—OFFERING CIRCULAR

Financial Statement requirements, regardless of the applicable disclosure model, are specified in Part F/S of this Form 1-A.

The Commission encourages the use of management's projections of future economic performance that have a reasonable basis and are presented in an appropriate format. See 17 CFR 228.10(e), 17 CFR 229.10. The Commission's safe harbor provision relative to projections is contained in Rule 175, 17 CFR 230.175.

The narrative disclosure contents of offering circulars are specified as follows:

A: For all corporate issuers—the information required by Model A of this Part II of Form 1-A.

B. For all other issuers and for any issuer that so chooses—the information required by either Part I of Form S-1, (17 CFR 239.11), except for the financial statements called for there, or Model B of this Part II of Form 1-A. Offering circulars prepared pursuant to this instruction need not follow the order of the items or other requirements of the disclosure form. Such information shall not, however, be set forth in such a fashion as to obscure any of the required information or information necessary to keep the required information from being incomplete or misleading. Information requested to be presented in a specified tabular format shall be given in substantially the tabular form specified in the item.

OFFERING CIRCULAR MODEL A

Each question in each paragraph of this part shall be responded to; and each question and any notes, but not any instructions thereto, shall be restated in its entirety. If the question or series of questions is inapplicable, so state. If the space provided in the format is insufficient, additional space should be created by cutting and pasting the format to add more lines.

Be very careful and precise in answering all questions. Give full and complete answers so that they are not misleading under the circumstances involved. Do not discuss any future performance or other anticipated event unless you have a reasonable basis to believe that it will actually occur within the foreseeable future. If any answer requiring significant information is materially inaccurate, incomplete or misleading, the Company, its management and principal shareholders may have liability to investors. The selling agents should exercise appropriate diligence to determine that no such inaccuracy or incompleteness has occurred, or they may be liable.

COVER PAGE

. . . .

(Exact name of Company as set forth in Charter)

Type of securities offered: . . . .

Maximum number of securities offered: . . . .

Minimum number of securities offered: . . . .

Price per security: $ . . . .

Total proceeds: If maximum sold: $ . . . . If minimum sold: $ . . . .

(See Questions 9 and 10)

Is a commissioned selling agent selling the securities in this offering?

 [ ] Yes [ ] No

If yes, what percent is commission of price to public? . . . . %.

Is there other compensation to selling agent(s)?

 [ ] Yes [ ] No

Is there a finder's fee or similar payment to any person?

 [ ] Yes [ ] No (See Question No. 22)

Is there an escrow of proceeds until minimum is obtained?

 [ ] Yes [ ] No (See Question No. 26)

Is this offering limited to members of a special group, such as employees of the Company or individuals?

 [ ] Yes [ ] No (See Question No. 25)

Is transfer of the securities restricted?

 [ ] Yes [ ] No (See Question No. 25)

INVESTMENT IN SMALL BUSINESSES INVOLVES A HIGH DEGREE OF RISK, AND INVESTORS SHOULD NOT INVEST ANY FUNDS IN THIS OFFERING UNLESS THEY CAN AFFORD TO LOSE THEIR ENTIRE INVESTMENT. SEE QUESTION NO. 2 FOR THE RISK FACTORS THAT MANAGEMENT BELIEVES PRESENT THE MOST SUBSTANTIAL RISKS TO AN INVESTOR IN THIS OFFERING.

IN MAKING AN INVESTMENT DECISION INVESTORS MUST RELY ON THEIR OWN EXAMINATION OF THE ISSUER AND THE TERMS OF THE OFFERING, INCLUDING THE MERITS AND RISKS INVOLVED. THESE SECURITIES HAVE NOT BEEN RECOMMENDED OR APPROVED BY ANY FEDERAL OR STATE SECURITIES COMMISSION OR REGULATORY AUTHORITY. FURTHERMORE, THESE AUTHORITIES HAVE NOT PASSED UPON THE ACCURACY OR ADEQUACY OF THIS DOCUMENT. ANY REPRESENTATION TO THE CONTRARY IS A CRIMINAL OFFENSE.

THE U.S. SECURITIES AND EXCHANGE COMMISSION DOES NOT PASS UPON THE MERITS OF ANY SECURITIES OFFERED OR THE TERMS OF THE OFFERING, NOR DOES IT PASS UPON

THE ACCURACY OR COMPLETENESS OF ANY OFFERING CIRCULAR OR SELLING LITERATURE. THESE SECURITIES ARE OFFERED UNDER AN EXEMPTION FROM REGISTRATION; HOWEVER, THE COMMISSION HAS NOT MADE AN INDEPENDENT DETERMINATION THAT THESE SECURITIES ARE EXEMPT FROM REGISTRATION.

This Company:

    [ ] Has never conducted operations.

    [ ] Is in the development stage.

    [ ] Is currently conducting operations.

    [ ] Has shown a profit in the last fiscal year.

    [ ] Other (Specify): . . . .

(Check at least one, as appropriate)

This offering has been registered for offer and sale in the following states:

State	State File No.	Effective Date
. . . .	. . . .	. . . .
. . . .	. . . .	. . . .
. . . .	. . . .	. . . .

INSTRUCTION: The Cover Page of the Offering Circular is a summary of certain essential information and should be kept on one page if at all possible. For purposes of characterizing the Company on the cover page, the term "development stage" has the same meaning as that set forth in Statement of Financial Accounting Standards No. 7 (June 1, 1975).

TABLE OF CONTENTS

THIS OFFERING CIRCULAR CONTAINS ALL OF THE REPRESENTATIONS BY THE COMPANY CONCERNING THIS OFFERING, AND NO PERSON SHALL MAKE DIFFERENT OR BROADER STATEMENTS THAN THOSE CONTAINED HEREIN. INVESTORS ARE CAUTIONED NOT TO RELY UPON ANY INFORMATION NOT EXPRESSLY SET FORTH IN THIS OFFERING CIRCULAR.

This Offering Circular, together with Financial Statements and other Attachments, consists of a total of . . . . pages.

¶8551   **Form 1-A**

THE COMPANY

1. Exact corporate name: . . . .

   State and date of incorporation: . . . .

   Street address of principal office:

    . . . .

   Company Telephone Number: (   ) . . . .

               Fiscal year: . . . .

                                                                      (month)   (day)

Person(s) to contact at Company with respect to offering:

    . . . .

Telephone Number (if different from above): (   ) . . . .

RISK FACTORS

2. List in the order of importance the factors which the Company considers to be the most substantial risks to an investor in this offering in view of all facts and circumstances or which otherwise make the offering one of high risk or speculative (i.e., those factors which constitute the greatest threat that the investment will be lost in whole or in part, or not provide an adequate return).

   (1) . . . .

   (2) . . . .

   (3) . . . .

   (4) . . . .

   (5) . . . .

   (6) . . . .

   (7) . . . .

   (8) . . . .

   (9) . . . .

   (10) . . . .

   (11) . . . .

   (12) . . . .

   (13) . . . .

   (14) . . . .

   (15) . . . .

   (16) . . . .

Note: In addition to the above risks, businesses are often subject to risks not foreseen or fully appreciated by management. In reviewing this Offering Circular potential investors should keep in mind other possible risks that could be important.

INSTRUCTION: The Company should avoid generalized statements and include only those factors which are unique to the Company. No specific number of risk factors is required to be identified. If more than 16 significant risk factors exist, add additional lines and number as appropriate. Risk factors may be due to such matters as cash flow and liquidity problems, inexperience of management in managing a business in the particular industry, dependence of the Company on an unproven product, absence of an existing market for the product (even though management may believe a need exists), absence of an operating history of the Company, absence of profitable operations in recent periods, an erratic financial history, the financial position of the Company, the nature of the business in which the Company is engaged or proposes to engage, conflicts of interest with management, arbitrary establishment of offering price, reliance on the efforts of a single individual, or absence of a trading market if a trading market is not expected to develop. Cross references should be made to the Questions where details of the risks are described.

BUSINESS AND PROPERTIES

3. With respect to the business of the Company and its properties:

(a) Describe in detail *what* business the Company does and proposes to do, including what products or goods are or will be produced or services that are or will be rendered.

(b) Describe *how* these products or services are to be produced or rendered and how and when the Company intends to carry out its activities. If the Company plans to offer a new product(s), state the present stage of development, including whether or not a working prototype(s) is in existence. Indicate if completion of development of the product would require a material amount of the resources of the Company, and the estimated amount. If the Company is or is expected to be dependent upon one or a limited number of suppliers for essential raw materials, energy or other items, describe. Describe any major existing supply contracts.

(c) Describe the industry in which the Company is selling or expects to sell its products or services and, where applicable, any recognized trends within that industry. Describe that part of the industry and the geographic area in which the business competes or will compete.

Indicate whether competition is or is expected to be by price, service, or other basis. Indicate (by attached table if appropriate) the current or anticipated prices or price ranges for the Company's products or services, or the formula for determining prices, and how these prices compare with those of competitiors' products or services, including a description of any variations in product or service features. Name the principal competitors that the Company has or expects to have in its area of competition. Indicate the relative size and financial and market strengths of the Company's competitors in the area of competition in which the Company is or will be operating. State why the Company believes it can effectively compete with these and other companies in its area of competition.

Note: Because this Offering Circular focuses primarily on details concerning the Company rather than the industry in which the Company operates or will operate, potential investors may wish to conduct their own separate investigation of the Company's industry to obtain broader insight in assessing the Company's prospects.

(d) Describe specifically the marketing strategies the Company is employing or will employ in penetrating its market or in developing a new market. Set forth in response to Question 4 below the timing and size of the results of this effort which will be necessary in order for the Company to be profitable. Indicate how and by whom its products or services are or will be marketed (such as by advertising, personal contact by sales representatives, etc.), how its marketing structure operates or will operate and the basis of its marketing approach, including any market studies. Name any customers that account for, or based upon existing orders will account for a major portion (20% or more) of the Company's sales. Describe any major existing sales contracts.

(e) State the backlog of written firm orders for products and/or services as of a recent date (within the last 90 days) and compare it with the backlog of a year ago from that date.

    As of:. . ./. . ./. . . $. . . .

       (a recent date)

    As of:. . ./. . ./. . . $. . . .

       (one year earlier)

Explain the reason for significant variations between the two figures, if any. Indicate what types and amounts of orders are included in the backlog figures. State the size of typical orders. if the Company's sales are seasonal or cyclical, explain.

(f) State the number of the Company's present employees and the number of employees it anticipates it will have within the next 12 months. Also, indicate the number by type of employee (i.e., clerical, operations, administrative, etc.) the Company will use, whether or not any of them are subject to collective bargaining agreements, and the expiration date(s) of any collective bargaining agreement(s). If the Company's employees are on strike, or have been in the past three years, or are threatening to strike, describe the dispute. Indicate any supplemental benefits or incentive arrangements the Company has or will have with its employees.

(g) Describe generally the principal properties (such as real estate, plant and equipment, patents, etc.) that the Company owns, indicating also what properties it leases and a summary of the terms under those leases, including the amount of payments, expiration dates and the terms of any renewal options. Indicate what properties the Company intends to acquire in the immediate future, the cost of such acquisitions and the sources of financing it expects to use in obtaining these properties, whether by purchase, lease or otherwise.

(h) Indicate the extent to which the Company's operations depend or are expected to depend upon patents, copyrights, trade secrets, know-how or other proprietary information and the steps undertaken to secure and protect this intellectual property, including any use of confidentiality agreements, covenants-not-to-compete and the like. Summarize the principal terms and expiration dates of any significant license agreements. Indicate the amounts expended by the Company for research and development during the last fiscal year, the amount expected to be spent this year and what percentage of revenues research and development expenditures were for the last fiscal year.

(i) If the Company's business, products, or properties are subject to material regulation (including environmental regulation) by federal, state, or local governmental agencies, indicate the nature and extent of regulation and its effects or potential effects upon the Company.

(j) State the names of any subsidiaries of the Company, their business purposes and ownership, and indicate which are included in the Financial Statements attached hereto. If not included, or if included but not consolidated, please explain.

(k) Summarize the material events in the development of the Company (including any material mergers or acquisitions) during the past five years, or for whatever lesser period the Company has been in existence. Discuss any pending or anticipated mergers, acquisitions, spin-offs or recapitalizations. If the Company has recently undergone a stock split, stock dividend or recapitalization in anticipation of this offering, describe (and adjust historical per share figures elsewhere in this Offering Circular accordingly).

4.(a) If the Company was not profitable during its last fiscal year, list below in chronological order the events which in management's opinion must or should occur or the milestones which in management's opinion the Company must or should reach in order for the Company to become profitable, and indicate the expected manner of occurrence or the expected method by which the Company will achieve the milestones.

Event or Milestone	Expected manner of occurrence or method of achievement	Date or number of months after receipt of proceeds when should be accomplished
(1)		
(2)		
(3)		
(4)		
(5)		

(b) State the probable consequences to the Company of delays in achieving each of the events or milestones within the above time schedule, and particularly the effect of any delays upon the Company's liquidity in view of the Company's then anticipated level of operating costs. (See Question Nos. 11 and 12)

Note: After reviewing the nature and timing of each event or milestone, potential investors should reflect upon whether achievement of each within the estimated time frame is realistic and should assess the consequences of delays or failure of achievement in making an investment decision.

INSTRUCTION: The inquiries under Business and Properties elicit information concerning the nature of the business of the Company and its properties. Make clear what aspects of the business are presently in operation and what aspects are planned to be in operation in the future. The description of principal properties should provide information which will reasonably inform investors as to the suitability, adequacy, productive capacity and extent of utilization of the facilities used in the enterprise. Detailed descriptions of the physical characteristics of the individual properties or legal descriptions by metes and bounds are not required and should not be given.

As to Question 4, if more than five events or milestones exist, add additional lines as necessary. A "milestone" is a significant point in the Company's development or an obstacle which the Company must overcome in order to become profitable.

OFFERING PRICE FACTORS

If the securities offered are common stock, or are exercisable for or convertible into common stock, the following factors may be relevant to the price at which the securities are being offered.

5. What were net, after-tax earnings for the last fiscal year?

Total $ . . . . ($ . . . . per share)

6. If the Company had profits, show offering price as a multiple of earnings. Adjust to reflect for any stock splits or recapitalizations, and use conversion or exercise price in lieu of offering price, if applicable.

$$\frac{\text{Offering Price Per Share}}{\text{Net After-Tax Earnings Last Year Per Share}} = \frac{}{\text{(price/earnings multiple)}}$$

7.(a) what is the net tangible book value of the Company? (If deficit, show in parenthesis.) For this purpose, net tangible book value means total assets (exclusive of copyrights, patents, goodwill, research and development costs and similar intangible items) minus total liabilities.

$ . . . . ($ . . . . per share)

If the net tangible book value per share is substantially less than this offering (or exercise or conversion) price per share, explain the reasons for the variation.

(b) State the dates on which the Company sold or otherwise issued securities during the last 12 months, the amount of such securities sold, the number of persons to whom they were sold, any relationship of such persons to the company at the time of sale, the price at which they were sold and, if not sold for cash, a concise description of the consideration. (Exclude bank debt.)

8.(a) What percentage of the outstanding shares of the Company will the investors in this offering have? Assume exercise of outstanding options, warrants or rights and conversion of convertible securities, if the respective exercise or conversion prices are at or less than the offering price. Also assume exercise of any options, warrants or rights and conversions of any convertible securities offered in this offering.)

If the maximum is sold: . . . . %

If the minimum is sold: . . . . %

(b) What post-offering value is management implicitly attributing to the entire Company by establishing the price per security set forth on the cover page (or exercise or conversion price if common stock is not offered)? (Total outstanding shares after offering times offering price, or exercise or conversion price if common stock is not offered.)

If maximum is sold: $ . . . . *

If minimum is sold: $ . . . . *

(For above purposes, assume outstanding options are exercised in determining "shares" if the exercise prices are at or less than the offering price. All convertible securities, including outstanding convertible securities, shall be assumed converted and any options, warrants or rights in this offering shall be assumed exercised.)

   * These values assume that the Company's capital structure would be changed to reflect any conversions of outstanding convertible securities and any use of outstanding securities as payment in

the exercise of outstanding options, warrants or rights included in the calculation. The type and amount of convertible or other securities thus eliminated would be: . . . . These values also assume an increase in cash in the Company by the amount of any cash payments that would be made upon cash exercise of options, warrants or rights included in the calculations. The amount of such cash would be: $ . . .

Note: After reviewing the above, potential investors should consider whether or not the offering price (or exercise or conversion price, if applicable) for the securities is appropriate at the present stage of the Company's development.

INSTRUCTION: Financial information in response to Questions 5, 6 and 7 should be consistent with the Financial Statements. Earnings per share for purposes of Question 5 should be calculated by dividing earnings for the last fiscal year by the weighted average of outstanding shares during that year. No calculations should be shown for periods of less than one year or if earnings are negative or nominal. For purposes of Question 8, the "offering price" of any options, warrants or rights or convertible securities in the offering is the respective exercise or conversion price.

USE OF PROCEEDS

9. (a) The following table sets forth the use of the proceeds from this offering:

	If Minimum Sold		If Maximum Sold	
	Amount	%	Amount	%
Total Proceeds	$_____		$_____	
Less: Offering Expenses		100%		100%
Commissions & Finders Fees				
Legal & Accounting	_____		_____	
Copying & Advertising	_____		_____	
Other (Specify):	_____		_____	
	_____		_____	
Net Proceeds from Offering	_____		_____	
Use of Net Proceeds	_____		_____	
	_____		_____	
	$_____		$_____	
	_____		_____	
	_____		_____	
	_____		_____	
	$_____		_____	
	_____		_____	
Total Use of Net Proceeds	_____		_____	
	_____		_____	
	_____		_____	
	_____		_____	
	_____		_____	
	$_____		$_____	
	100%		100%	

(b) If there is no minimum amount of proceeds that must be raised before the Company may use the proceeds of the offering, describe the order of priority in which the proceeds set forth above in the column "If Maximum Sold" will be used.

Note: After reviewing the portion of the offering allocated to the payment of offering expenses, and to the immediate payment to management and promoters of any fees, reimbursements, past salaries or similar payments, a potential investor should consider whether the remaining portion of his investment, which would be that part available for future development of the Company's business and operations, would be adequate.

10.(a) If material amounts of funds from sources other than this offering are to be used in conjunction with the proceeds from this offering, state the amounts and sources of such other funds, and whether funds are firm or contingent. If contingent, explain.

(b) If any material part of the proceeds is to be used to discharge indebtedness, describe the terms of such indebtedness, including interest rates. If the indebtedness to be discharged was incurred within the current or previous fiscal year, describe the use of proceeds of such indebtedness.

(c) If any material amount of proceeds is to be used to acquire assets, other than in the ordinary course of business, briefly describe and state the cost of the assets and other material terms of the acquisitions. If the assets are to be acquired from officers, directors, employees or principal stockholders of the Company or their associates, give the names of the persons from whom the assets are to be acquired and set forth the cost to the Company, the method followed in determining the cost, and any profit to such persons.

(d) If any amount of the proceeds is to be used to reimburse any officer, director, employee or stockholder for services already rendered, assets previously transferred, or monies loaned or advanced, or otherwise, explain:

11. Indicate whether the Company is having or anticipates having within the next 12 months any cash flow or liquidity problems and whether or not it is in default or in breach of any note, loan, lease or other indebtedness or financing arrangement requiring the Company to make payments. Indicate if a significant amount of the Company's tradepayables have not been paid within the stated trade term. State whether the Company is subject to any unsatisfied judgments, liens or settlement obligations and the amounts thereof. Indicate the Company's plans to resolve any such problems.

12. Indicate whether proceeds from this offering will satisfy the Company's cash requirements for the next 12 months, and whether it will be necessary to raise additional funds. State the source of additional funds, if known.

INSTRUCTION: Use of net proceeds should be stated with a high degree of specificity. Suggested (but not mandatory) categories are: leases, rent, utilities, payroll (by position or type), purchase or lease of specific items of equipment or inventory, payment of notes, accounts payable, etc., marketing or advertising costs, taxes, consulting fees, permits, professional fees, insurance and supplies. Categories will vary depending on the Company's plans. Use of footnotes or other explanation is recommended where appropriate. Footnotes should be used to indicate those items of offering expenses that are estimates. Set forth in separate categories all payments which will be made immediately to the Company's executive officers, directors and promoters, indicating by footnote that these payments will be so made to such persons. If a substantial amount is allocated to working capital, set forth separate sub-categories for use of the funds in the Company's business.

If any substantial portion of the proceeds has not been allocated for particular purposes, a statement to that effect as one of the Use of Net Proceeds categories should be included together with a statement of the amount of proceeds not so allocated and a footnote explaining how the Company expects to employ such funds not so allocated.

CAPITALIZATION

13. Indicate the capitalization of the Company as of the most recent balance sheet date (adjusted to reflect any subsequent stock splits, stock dividends, recapitalizations or refinancings) and as adjusted to reflect the sale of the minimum and maximum amount of securities in this offering and the use of the net proceeds therefrom:

| | Amount Outstanding | | |
| | As of: | As Adjusted | |
	/ / (date)	Minimum	Maximum
Debt:			
Short-term debt (average interest rate ___%)	$_____	$_____	$_____
Long-term debt (average interest rate ___%)	$_____	$_____	$_____
Total debt	$_____	$_____	$_____
Stockholders equity (deficit):			
Preferred stock - par or stated value (by class of preferred in order of preferences)			
_____	$_____	$_____	$_____
_____	$_____	$_____	$_____
_____	$_____	$_____	$_____
Common stock - par or stated value	$_____	$_____	$_____
Additional paid in capital	$_____	$_____	$_____
Retained earnings (deficit)	$_____	$_____	$_____
Total stockholders equity (deficit)	$_____	$_____	$_____
Total Capitalization	$_____	$_____	$_____

Number of preferred shares authorized to be outstanding:

Class of Preferred	Number of Shares Authorized	Par Value Per Share
_____	_____	$_____
_____	_____	$_____
_____	_____	$_____

Number of common shares authorized: . . . . shares. Par or stated value per share, if any: $ . . . . .

Number of common shares reserved to meet conversion requirements or for the issuance upon exercise of options, warrants or rights: . . . . shares.

INSTRUCTION: Capitalization should be shown as of a date no earlier than that of the most recent Financial Statements provided pursuant to Question 46. If the Company has mandatory redeemable preferred stock, include the amount thereof in "long term debt" and so indicate by footnote to that category in the capitalization table.

DESCRIPTION OF SECURITIES

14. The securities being offered hereby are:

[ ] Common Stock

[ ] Preferred or Preference Stock

[ ] Notes or Debentures

[ ] Units of two or more types of securities composed of: . . . .

[ ]Other: . . . .

15. These securities have:

Yes No

[ ] [ ] Cumulative voting rights

[ ] [ ] Other special voting rights

[ ] [ ] Preemptive rights to purchase in new issues of shares

[ ] [ ] Preference as to dividends or interest

[ ] [ ] Preference upon liquidation

[ ] [ ] Other special rights or preferences (specify):

Explain:

16. Are the securities convertible? [ ] Yes [ ]No

    If so, state conversion price or formula. . . . .

    Date when conversion becomes effective: . . ./ . . . / . . .

    Date when conversion expires: . . ./ . . .

17. (a) If securities are notes or other types of debt securities:

    (1) What is the interest rate? . . . . . .%

    If interest rate is variable or multiple rates, describe: . . . .

    (2) What is the maturity date? . . ./ . . ./ . . .

    If serial maturity dates, describe: . . . .

    (3) Is there a mandatory sinking fund?

    [ ] Yes [ ]No

    Describe: . . . .

    (4) Is there a trust indenture? [ ] Yes [ ] No

    Name, address and telephone number of Trustee

    (5) Are the securities callable or subject to redemption? [] Yes [ ] No

    Describe, including redemption prices: . . . .

    (6) Are the securities collateralized by real or personal property?

    [ ] Yes [ ] No Describe: . . . .

    (7) If these securities are subordinated in right of payment of interest or principal, explain the terms of such subordination.

How much currently outstanding indebtedness of the Company is senior to the securities in right of payment of interest or principal? $ . . . .

How much indebtedness shares in right of payment on an equivalent (pari passu) basis? $ . . . .

How much indebtedness is junior (subordinated) to the securities? $ . . . .

    (b) If notes or other types of debt securities are being offered and the Company had earnings during its last fiscal year, show the ratio of earnings to fixed charges on an actual and pro forma basis for that fiscal year. "Earnings" means pretax income from continuing operations plus fixed charges and capitalized interest. "Fixed charges" means interest (including capitalized interest), amortization of debt discount, premium and expense, preferred stock dividend requirements of majority owned subsidiary, and such portion of rental expense as can be demonstrated to be representative of the interest factor in the particular case. The pro forma ratio of earnings to fixed charges should include incremental interest expense as a result of the offering of the notes or other debt securities.

	Last Fiscal Year		
	Actual	Pro Forma	
		Minimum	Maximum
"Earnings" =			
————	———	———	———
"Fixed Charges"			
If no earnings show "Fixed Charges" only			
	———	———	———

Note: Care should be exercised in interpreting the significance of the ratio of earnings to fixed charges as a measure of the "coverage" of debt service, as the existence of earnings does not necessarily mean that the Company's liquidity at any given time will permit payment of debt service requirements to be timely made. See Question Nos. 11 and 12. See also the Financial Statements and especially the Statement of Cash Flows.

18. If securities are Preference or Preferred stock:

Are unpaid dividends cumulative? [ ] Yes [ ] No

Are securities callable? [ ] Yes [ ] No

Explain:

Note: Attach to this Offering Circular copies or a summary of the charter, bylaw or contractual provision or document that gives rise to the rights of holders of Preferred or Preference Stock, notes or other securities being offered.

19. If securities are capital stock of any type, indicate restrictions on dividends under loan or other financing arrangements or otherwise:

20. Current amount of assets available for payment of dividends if deficit must be first made up, show deficit in parenthesis): $ . . . .

PLAN OF DISTRIBUTION

21. The selling agents (that is, the persons selling the securities as agent for the Company for a commission or other compensation) in this offering are:

Name: . . . .   Name: . . . .

Address: . . . .   Address: . . . .

Telephone No.(   )   Telephone No. (   )

22. Describe any compensation to selling agents or finders, including cash, securities, contracts or other consideration, in addition to the cash commission set forth as a percent of the offering price on the cover page of this Offering Circular. Also indicate whether the Company will indemnify the selling agents or finders against liabilities under the securities laws. ("Finders" are persons who for compensation act as intermediaries in obtaining selling agents or other-wise making introductions in furtherance of this offering.)

23. Describe any material relationships between any of the selling agents or finders and the Company or its management.

Note: After reviewing the amount of compensation to the selling agents or finders for selling the securities, and the nature of any relationship between the selling agents or finders and the Company, a potential investor should assess the extent to which it may be inappropriate to rely upon any recommendation by the selling agents or finders to buy the securities.

24. If this offering is not being made through selling agents, the names of persons at the Company through which this offering is being made:

Name: . . . .   Name: . . . .

Address: . . . .   Address: . . . .

Telephone No.(   )   Telephone No. (   )

25. If this offering is limited to a special group, such as employees of the Company, or is limited to a certain number of individuals (as required to qualify under Subchapter S of the Internal Revenue Code) or is subject to any other limitations, describe the limitations and any restrictions on resale that apply:

Will the certificates bear a legend notifying holders of such restrictions?

[ ] Yes [ ] No

26. (a) Name, address and telephone number of independent bank or savings and loan association or other similar depository institution acting as escrow agent if proceeds are escrowed until minimum proceeds are raised:

(b) Date at which funds will be returned by escrow agent if minimum proceeds are not raised:

Will interest on proceeds during escrow period be paid to investors? [ ] Yes [ ] No

27. Explain the nature of any resale restrictions on presently outstanding shares, and when those restrictions will terminate, if this can be determined:

Note: Equity investors should be aware that unless the Company is able to complete a further public offering or the Company is able to be sold for cash or merged with a public company that their investment in the Company may be illiquid indefinitely.

DIVIDENDS, DISTRIBUTIONS AND REDEMPTIONS

28. If the Company has within the last five years paid dividends, made distributions upon its stock or redeemed any securities, explain how much and when:

OFFICERS AND KEY PERSONNEL OF THE COMPANY

29. Chief Executive Officer: Title: . . . .

Name: . . . .   Age: . . . .

Office Street Address: Telephone No.:

. . . . ( )

Name of employers, titles and dates of positions held during past five years with an indication of job responsibilities.

Education (degrees, schools, and dates):

Also a Director of the Company [ ] Yes [ ] No

Indicate amount of time to be spent on Company matters if less than full time:

30. Chief Operating Officer: Title: . . . .

Name: . . . .   Age: . . . .

Office Street Address: Telephone No.:

. . . . ( )

Names of employers, titles and dates of positions held during past five years with an indication of job responsibilities.

Education (degrees, schools, and dates): . . . .

Also a Director of the Company? [ ] Yes [ ] No

Indicate amount of time to be spent on Company matters if less than full time:

31. Chief Financial Officer: Title: . . . .

Name: . . . .   Age: . . . .

Office Street Address: Telephone No.:

. . . . ( )

Names of employers, titles and dates of positions held during past five years with an indication of job responsibilities.

Education (degrees, schools, and dates): . . . .

Also a Director of the Company? [ ] Yes [ ] No

Indicate amount of time to be spent on Company matters if less than full time:

32. Other Key Personnel:

(A) Name: . . . .   Age: . . . .

Title: . . . .

Office Street Address: Telephone No.:

. . . . ( )

Names of employers, titles and dates of positions held during past five years with an indication of job responsibilities.

Education (degrees, schools, and dates): . . . .

Also a Director of the Company? [ ] Yes [ ] No

Indicate amount of time to be spent on Company matters if less than full time:

(B) Name: . . . .   Age: . . . .

    Title: . . . .

    Office Street Address: Telephone No.:

    . . . . (   )   -

Names of employers, titles and dates of positions held during past five years with an indication of job responsibilities.

    Education (degrees, schools, and dates): . . . .

    Also a Director of the Company? [ ] Yes [ ] No

    Indicate amount of time to be spent on Company matters if less than full time:

INSTRUCTION: The term "Chief Executive Officer" means the officer of the Company who has been delegated final authority by the board of directors to direct all aspects of the Company's affairs. The term "Chief Operating Officer" means the officer in charge of the actual day-to-day operations of the Company's business. The term "Chief Financial Officer" means the officer having accounting skills who is primarily in charge of assuring that the Company's financial books and records are properly kept and maintained and financial statements prepared.

The term "key personnel" means persons such as vice presidents, production managers, sales managers, or research scientists and similar persons, who are not included above, but who make or are expected to make significant contributions to the business of the Company, whether as employees, independent contractors, consultants or otherwise.

DIRECTORS OF THE COMPANY

33. Number of Directors: . . If Directors are not elected annually, or are elected under a voting trust or other arrangement, explain:

34. Information concerning outside or other Directors (i.e. those not described above):

   (A) Name: . . . .   Age: . . . .

    Office Street Address: Telephone No.:

    . . . . (   )   -

Names of employers, titles and dates of positions held during past five years with an indication of job responsibilities.

    Education (degrees, schools, and dates): . . . .

   (B) Name: . . . .   Age: . . . .

    Office Street Address: Telephone No.:

    . . . . (   )   -

Names of employers, titles and dates of positions held during past five years with an indication of job responsibilities.

    Education (degrees, schools, and dates): . . . .

   (C) Name: . . . .   Age: . . . .

    Office Street Address: Telephone No.:

    . . . . (   )   -

Names of employers, titles and dates of positions held during past five years with an indication of job responsibilities.

    Education (degrees, schools, and dates): . . . .

35. (a) Have any of the Officers or Directors ever worked for or managed a company (including a separate subsidiary or division of a larger enterprise) in the same business as the Company?

    [ ] Yes [ ] No

Explain:

   (b) If any of the Officers, Directors or other key personnel have ever worked for or managed a company in the same business or industry as the Company or in a related business or industry, describe what precautions, if any, (including the obtaining of releases or consents from prior employers) have been taken to preclude claims by prior employers for conversion or theft of trade secrets, know-how or other proprietary information.

(c) If the Company has never conducted operations or is otherwise in the development stage, indicate whether any of the Officers or Directors has ever managed any other company in the startup or development stage and describe the circumstances, including relevant dates.

(d) If any of the Company's key personnel are not employees but are consultants or other independent contractors, state the details of their engagement by the Company.

(e) If the Company has key man life insurance policies on any of its Officers, Directors or key personnel, explain, including the names of the persons insured, the amount of insurance, whether the insurance proceeds are payable to the Company and whether there are arrangements that require the proceeds to be used to redeem securities or pay benefits to the estate of the insured person or a surviving spouse.

36. If a petition under the Bankruptcy Act or any State insolvency law was filed by or against the Company or its Officers, Directors or other key personnel, or a receiver, fiscal agent or similar officer was appointed by a court for the business or property of any such persons, or any partnership in which any of such persons was a general partner at or within the past five years, or any corporation or business association of which any such person was an executive officer at or within the past five years, set forth below the name of such persons, and the nature and date of such actions.

Note: After reviewing the information concerning the background of the Company's Officers, Directors and other key personnel, potential investors should consider whether or not these persons have adequate background and experience to develop and operate this Company and to make it successful. In this regard, the experience and ability of management are often considered the most significant factors in the success of a business.

PRINCIPAL STOCKHOLDERS

37. Principal owners of the Company (those who beneficially own directly or indirectly 10% or more of the common and preferred stock presently outstanding) starting with the largest common stockholder. Include separately all common stock issuable upon conversion of convertible securities (identifying them by asterisk) and show average price per share as if conversion has occurred. Indicate by footnote if the price paid was for a consideration other than cash and the nature of any such consideration.

Class of Shares	Average Price Per Share	No. of Shares Now Held	% of Total	No. of Shares Held After Offering if All Securities Sold	% of Total

Name:

_____   _____   _____   _____   _____

_____   _____   _____   _____   _____

Office Street Address:

_____

_____

_____

Telephone No.
(_____) _____-_____

Principal occupation:

_____

38. Number of shares beneficially owned by Officers and Directors as a group:

Before offering: . . . . shares (. . . . .% of total outstanding)

After offering: a) Assuming minimum securities sold:

. . . . shares (. . . . .% of total outstanding)

b) Assuming maximum securities sold:

. . . . shares (. . . . .% of total outstanding)

(Assume all options exercised and all convertible securities converted.)

INSTRUCTION: If shares are held by family members, through corporations or partnerships, or otherwise in a manner that would allow a person to direct or control the voting of the shares (or share in such direction or control—as, for example, a co-trustee) they should be included as being "beneficially owned." An explanation of these circumstances should be set forth in a footnote to the "Number of Shares Now Held."

MANAGEMENT RELATIONSHIPS, TRANSACTIONS AND REMUNERATION

39. (a) If any of the Officers, key personnel or principal stockholders are related by blood or marriage, please describe.

(b) If the Company has made loans to or is doing business with any of its Officers, Directors, key personnel or 10% stockholders, or any of their relatives (or any entity controlled directly or indirectly by any such persons) within the last two years, or proposes to do so within the future, explain. (This includes sales or lease of goods, property or services to or from the Company, employment or stock purchase contracts, etc.) State the principal terms of any significant loans, agreements, leases, financing or other arrangements.

(c) If any of the Company's Officers, Directors, key personnel or 10% stockholders has guaranteed or co-signed any of the Company's bank debt or other obligations, including any indebtedness to be retired from the proceeds of this offering, explain and state the amounts involved.

40. (a) List all remuneration by the Company to Officers, Directors and key personnel for the last fiscal year:

	Cash	Other
Chief Executive Officer	$_____	$_____
Chief Operating Officer	_____	_____
Chief Accounting Officer	_____	_____
Key Personnel:		
_____	_____	_____
_____	_____	_____
_____	_____	_____
Others:		
_____	_____	_____
_____	_____	_____
_____	_____	_____
Total:	$_____	$_____
Directors as a group (number of persons__)	$_____	$_____

(b) If remuneration is expected to change or has been unpaid in prior years, explain:

(c) If any employment agreements exist or are contemplated, describe:

41. (a) Number of shares subject to issuance under presently outstanding stock purchase agreements, stock options, warrants or rights: . . . . . . shares (. . . . .% of total shares to be outstanding after the completion of the offering if all securities sold, assuming exercise of options and conversion of convertible securities). Indicate which have been approved by shareholders. State the expiration dates, exercise prices and other basic terms for these securities:

(b) Number of common shares subject to issuance existing stock purchase or option plans but not yet covered by outstanding purchase agreements, options or warrants: . . . . . . shares.

(c) Describe the extent to which future stock purchase agreements, stock options, warrants or rights must be approved by shareholders.

42. If the business is highly dependent on the services of certain key personnel, describe any arrangement to assure that these persons will remain with the Company and not compete upon any termination:

Note: After reviewing the above, potential investors should consider whether or not the compensation to management and other key personnel directly or indirectly, is reasonable in view of the present stage of the Company's development.

INSTRUCTION: For purposes of Question 39(b), a person directly or indirectly controls an entity if he is part of the group that directs or is able to direct the entity's activities or affairs. A person is typically a member of a control group if he is an officer, director, general partner, trustee or beneficial owner of a 10% or greater interest in the entity. In Question 40, the term "Cash" should indicate salary, bonus, consulting fees, non-accountable expense accounts and the like. The column captioned "Other" should include the value of any options or securities given, any annuity, pension or retirement benefits, bonus or profit-sharing plans, and personal benefits (club memberships, company cars, insurance benefits not generally available to employees, etc.). The nature of these benefits should be explained in a footnote to this column.

LITIGATION

43. Describe any past, pending or threatened litigation or administrative action which has held or may have a material effect upon the Company's business, financial condition, or operations, including any litigation or action involving the Company's Officers, Directors or other key personnel. State the names of the principal parties, the nature and current status of the matters, and amounts involved. Give an evaluation by managment or counsel, to the extent feasible, of the merits of the proceedings or litigation and the potential impact on the Company's business, financial condition, or operations.

FEDERAL TAX ASPECTS

44. If the Company is an S corporation under the Internal Revenue Code of 1986, and it is anticipated that any significant tax benefits will be available to investors in the offering, indicate the nature and amount of such anticipated tax benefits and the material risks of their disallowance. Also, state the name, address and telephone number of any tax advisor that has passed upon these tax benefits. Attach any opinion or description of the tax consequences of an investment in the securities by the tax advisor.

Name of Tax Advisor: . . . .

Address: . . . .

Telephone No. (   )   -

Note: Potential investors are encouraged to have their own personal tax consultant contact the tax advisor to review details of the tax benefits and the extent that the benefits would be available and advantageous to the particular investor.

MISCELLANEOUS FACTORS

45. Describe any other material factors, either adverse or favorable, that will or could affect the Company or its business (for example, discuss any defaults under major contracts, any breach of bylaw provisions, etc.) or which are necessary to make any other information in this Offering Circular not misleading or incomplete.

FINANCIAL STATEMENTS

46. Provide the financial statements required by Part F/S of this Offering Circular section of Form 1-A.

MANAGEMENT'S DISCUSSION AND ANALYSIS OF CERTAIN RELEVANT FACTORS

47. If the Company's financial statements show losses from operations, explain the causes underlying these losses and what steps the Company has taken or is taking to address these causes.

48. Describe any trends in the Company's historical operating results. Indicate any changes now occurring in the underlying economics of the industry or the Company's business which, in the opinion of Management, will have a significant impact (either favorable or adverse) upon the Company's results of operations within the next 12 months, and give a rough estimate of the probable extent of the impact, if possible.

49. If the Company sells a product or products and has had significant sales during its last fiscal year, state the existing gross margin (net sales less cost of such sales as presented in accordance with generally accepted accounting principles) as a percentage of sales for the last fiscal year: . . %. What is the anticipated gross margin for next year of operations? Approximately . . . . %. If this is expected to change, explain. Also, if reasonably current gross margin figures are available for the industry, indicate these figures and the source or sources from which they are obtained.

50. Foreign sales as a percent of total sales for last fiscal year: . . . . %. Domestic government sales as a percent of total domestic sales for last fiscal year: . . . . %. Explain the nature of these sales, including any anticipated changes:

OFFERING CIRCULAR MODEL B.

Item 1. Cover Page

The cover page of the offering circular shall include the following information:

(a) Name of the issuer;

(b) The mailing address of the issuer's principal executive offices including the zip code and the issuer's telephone number;

(c) Date of the offering circular;

(d) Description and amount of securities offered (*Note:* this description should include, for example, appropriate disclosure of redemption and conversion features of debt securities);

(e) The statement required by Rule 253;

(f) The table(s) required by Item 2;

(g) The name of the underwriter or underwriters;

(h) Any materials required by the law of any state in which the securities are to be offered;

(i) If applicable, identify material risks in connection with the purchase of the securities; and

(j) Approximate date of commencement of proposed sale to the public.

Instruction: Where the name of the issuer is the same as the name of another well-known company or indicates a line of business in which the issuer is not engaged or is engaged to only a limited extent, a statement should be furnished to that effect. In some circumstances, however, disclosure may not be sufficient, and a change of name may be the only way to cure its misleading character.

Item 2. Distribution Spread

(a) The information called for by the following table shall be given, in substantially the tabular form indicated, on the outside front cover page of the offering circular as to all securities being offered (estimate, if necessary).

	Price to public	Underwriting discount and commissions	Proceeds to issuer or other persons
Per unit	_____	_____	_____
Total	_____	_____	_____

If the securities are to be offered on a best efforts basis, the cover page should set forth the termination date, if any, of the offering, any minimum required sale and any arrangements to place the funds received in an escrow, trust, or similar arrangement. The following tabular presentation of the total maximum and minimum securities to be offered should be combined with the table required above.

	Price to public	Underwriting discount and commissions	Proceeds to issuer or other persons
Total Minimum	_____	_____	_____
Total Maximum	_____	_____	_____

Instructions

1. The term "commissions" shall include all cash, securities, contracts, or anything else of value, paid, to be set aside, disposed of, or understandings with or for the benefit of any other persons in which any underwriter is interested, made in connection with the sale of such security.

2. Only commissions paid by the issuer in cash are to be indicated in the table. Commissions paid by other persons or any form of non-cash compensation shall be briefly identified in a note to the table with a cross-reference to a more complete description elsewhere in the offering circular.

3. Prior to the commencement of sales pursuant to Regulation A, the issuer shall inform the Commission whether or not the amount of compensation to be allowed or paid to the underwriters, as described in the offering statement, has been cleared with the National Association of Securities Dealers, Inc.

4. If the securities are not to be offered for cash, state the basis upon which the offering is to be made.

5. If it is impracticable to state the price to the public, the method by which it is to be determined shall be explained.

(b) Any finder's fees or similar payments shall be disclosed on the cover page with a reference to a more complete discussion in the offering circular. Such disclosure should identify the finder, the nature of the services rendered and the nature of any relationship between the finder and the issuer, its officers, directors, promoters, principal stockholders and underwriters (including any affiliates thereof.)

(c) The amount of the expenses of the offering borne by the issuer, including underwriting expenses to be borne by the issuer, should be disclosed in a footnote to the table.

Item 3. Summary Information, Risk Factors and Dilution

(a) Where appropriate to a clear understanding by investors, there should be set forth in the forepart of the offering circular, under an appropriate caption, a carefully organized series of short, concise paragraphs, summarizing the principal factors which make the offering one of high risk or speculative. *Note:* These factors may be due to such matters as an absence of an operating history of the issuer, an absence of profitable operations in recent periods, an erratic financial history, the financial position of the issuer, the nature of the business in which the issuer is engaged or proposed to engage, conflicts of interest with management, reliance on the efforts of a single individual, or the method of determining the market price where no market currently exists. Issuers should *avoid* generalized statements and include only those factors which are unique to the issuer.

(b) Where there is a material disparity between the public offering price and the effective cash cost to officers, directors, promoters and affiliated persons for shares acquired by them in a transaction during the past three years, or which they have a right to acquire, there should be included a comparison of the public contribution under the proposed public offering and the effective cash contribution of such persons. In such cases, and in other instances where the extent of the dilution makes is appropriate, the following shall be given: (1) the net tangible book value per share before and after the distribution; (2) the amount of the increase in such net tangible book value per share attributable to the cash payment made by purchasers of the shares being offered,; and (3) the amount of the immediate dilution from the public offering price which will be absorbed by such purchasers.

Item 4. Plan of Distribution

(a) If the securities are to be offered through underwriters, give the names of the principal underwriters, and state the respective amounts underwritten. Identify each such underwriter having a material relationship to the issuer and state the nature of the relationship. State briefly the nature of the underwriters' obligation to take the securities.

(b) State briefly the discounts and commissions to be allowed or paid to dealers, including all cash, securities, contracts or other consideration to be received by any dealer in connection with the sale of the securities.

(c) Outline briefly the plan of distribution of any securities being issued which are to be offered through the selling efforts of brokers or dealers or otherwise than through underwriters.

(d) If any of the securities are to be offered for the account of security holders, indicate on the cover page the total amount to be offered for their account and include a cross-reference to a fuller discussion elsewhere in the offering circular. Such discussion should identify each selling security holder, state the amount owned by him, the amount offered for his account and the amount to be owned after the offering.

(e)(1) Describe any arrangements for the return of funds to subscribers if all of the securities to be offered are not sold; if there are no such arrangements, so state.

(2) If there will be a material delay in the payment of the proceeds of the offering by the underwriter to the issuer, the salient provisions in this regard and the effects on the issuer should be stated.

Instruction:

Attention is directed to the provisions of Rules 10b-9 [17 CFR § 240.10b-9] and 15c2-4 [17 CFR § 240.15c2-4] under the Securities Exchange Act of 1934. These rules outline, among other things, antifraud provisions concerning the return of funds to subscribers and the transmission of proceeds of an offering to a seller.

Item 5. Use of Proceeds to Issuer

State the principal purposes for which the net proceeds to the issuer from the securities to be offered are intended to be used, and the approximate amount intended to be used for each such purpose.

Instructions:

1. If any substantial portion of the proceeds has not been allocated for particular purposes, a statement to that effect shall be made together with a statement of the amount of proceeds not so allocated and how the registrant expects to employ such funds not so allocated.

2. Include a statement as to the use of the actual proceeds if they are not sufficient to accomplish the purpose set forth and the order of priority in which they will be applied. However, such statement need not be made if the underwriting arrangements are such that, if any securities are sold to the public, it can be reasonably expected that the actual proceeds of the issue will not be substantially less than the estimated aggregate proceeds to the issuer as shown under Item 2.

3. If any material amounts of other funds are to be used in conjunction with the proceeds, state the amounts and sources of such other funds.

4. If any material part of the proceeds is to be used to discharge indebtedness, describe the terms of such indebtedness. If the indebtedness to be discharged was incurred within one year, describe the use of the proceeds of such indebtedness.

5. If any material amount of the proceeds is to be used to acquire assets, otherwise than in the ordinary course of business, briefly describe and state the cost of the assets. If the assets are to be acquired from affiliates of the issuer or their associates, give the names of the persons from whom they are to be acquired and set forth the principle followed in determining the cost to the issuer.

6. The issuer may reserve the right to change the use of proceeds provided that such reservation is due to certain contingencies which are adequately disclosed.

Item 6. Description of Business

(a) Narrative description of business.

(1) Describe the business done and intended to be done by the issuer and its subsidiaries and the general development of the business during the past five years or such shorter period as the issuer may have been in business. Such description should include, but not be limited to, a discussion of the following factors if such factors are material to an understanding of the issuer's business:

(i) The principal products produced and services rendered and the principal markets for and method of distribution of such products and services.

(ii) The status of a product or service if the issuer has made public information about a new product or service which would require the investment of a material amount of the assets of the issuer or is otherwise material.

(iii) The estimated amount spent during each of the last two fiscal years on company-sponsored research and development activities determined in accordance with generally accepted accounting principles. In addition, state the estimated dollar amount spent during each of such years on material customer-sponsored research activities relating to the development of new products, services or techniques or the improvement of existing products, services or techniques.

(iv) The number of persons employed by the issuer, indicating the number employed full time.

(v) The material effects that compliance with Federal, State and Local provisions which have been enacted or adopted regulating the discharge of materials into the environment, may have upon the capital expenditures, earnings and competitive position of the issuer and its subsidiaries. The issuer shall disclose any material estimated capital expenditures for environmental control facilities for the remainder of its current fiscal year and for such further periods as the issuer may deem material.

(2) The issuer should also describe those distinctive or special characteristics of the issuer's operation or industry which may have a material impact upon the issuer's future financial performance. Examples of factors which might be discussed include dependence on one or a few major customers or

suppliers (including suppliers of raw materials or financing), existing or probable governmental regulation, material terms of and/or expiration of material labor contracts or patents, trademarks, licenses,
franchises, concessions or royalty agreements, unusual competitive conditions in the industry, cyclicality
of the industry and anticipated raw material or energy shortages to the extent management may not be
able to secure a continuing source of supply.

(3) The following requirement in subparagraph (i) applies only to issuers (including predecessors)
which have not received revenue from operations during each of the three fiscal years immediately prior
to the filing of the offering statement.

(i) Describe, if formulated, the issuer's plan of operation for the twelve months following the
commencement of the proposed offering. If such information is not available, the reasons for its
unavailability shall be stated. Disclosure relating to any plan should include, among other things, a
statement indicating whether, in the issuer's opinion, the proceeds from the offering will satisfy its cash
requirements and whether, in the next six months, it will be necessary to raise additional funds.

(ii) Any engineering, management or similar reports which have been prepared or provided for
external use by the issuer or by a principal underwriter in connection with the proposed offering should
be furnished to the Commission at the time of filing the offering statement or as soon as practicable
thereafter. There should also be furnished at the same time a statement as to the actual or proposed use
and distribution of such report or memorandum. Such statement should identify each class of persons
who have received or will receive the report or memorandum, and state the number of copies distributed
to each such class. If no such report or memorandum has been prepared, the Commission should be so
informed in writing at the time the report or memorandum would otherwise have been submitted.

(b) Segment Data. If the issuer is required to include segment information in its financial
statements, an appropriate cross-reference shall be included in the description of business.

Item 7. Description of Property

State briefly the location and general character of the principal plants, and other materially
important physical properties of the issuer and its subsidiaries. If any such property is not held in fee or
is held subject to any major encumbrance, so state and briefly describe how held.

Instruction:

What is required is information essential to an investor's appraisal of the securities being offered.
Such information should be furnished as will reasonably inform investors as to the suitability, adequacy,
productive capacity and extent of utilization of the facilities used in the enterprise. Detailed descriptions
of the physical characteristics of individual properties or legal descriptions by metes and bounds are not
required and should not be given.

Item 8. Directors, Executive Officers and Significant Employees

(a) List the names and ages of each of the following persons stating his term of office and any
periods during which he has served as such and briefly describe any arrangement or understanding
between him and any other person(s) (naming such person(s)) pursuant to which he was or is to be
selected to his office or position:

(1) directors;

(2) persons nominated to become directors;

(3) executive officers;

(4) persons chosen to become executive officers;

(5) significant employees.

Instructions:

1. No nominee or person chosen to become a director or person chosen to be an executive officer who
has not consented to act as such should be named in response to this item.

2. The term "executive officer" means the president, secretary, treasurer, any vice-president in charge of
a principal business function (such as sales, administration, or finance) and any other person who
performs similar policy making functions for the issuer.

3. The term "significant employee" means persons such as production managers, sales managers, or
research scientists, who are not executive officers, but who make or are expected to make significant
contributions to the business of the issuer.

(b) Family relationships. State the nature of any family relationship between any director, executive officer, person nominated or chosen by the issuer to become a director or executive officer or any significant employee.

Instruction:

The term "family relationship" means any relationship by blood, marriage, or adoption, not more remote than first cousin.

(c) Business experience. Give a brief account of the business experience during the past five years of each director, person nominated or chosen to become a director or executive officer, and each significant employee, including his principal occupations and employment during that period and the name and principal business of any corporation or other organization in which such occupations and employment were carried on. When an executive officer or significant employee has been employed by the issuer for less than five years, a brief explanation should be included as to the nature of the responsibilities undertaken by the individual in prior positions to provide adequate disclosure of this prior business experience. What is required is information relating to the level of his professional competence which may include, depending upon the circumstances, such specific information as the size of the operation supervised.

(d) Involvement in certain legal proceedings. Describe any of the following events which occurred during the past five years and which are material to an evaluation of the ability or integrity of any director, person nominated to become a director or executive officer of the issuer.

(1) A petition under the Bankruptcy Act or any State insolvency law was filed by or against, or a receiver, fiscal agent or similar officer was appointed by a court for the business or property of such person, or any partnership in which he was general partner at or within 2 years before the time of such filing, or any corporation or business association of which he was an executive officer at or within two years before the time of such filing;

(2) Such person was convicted in a criminal proceeding (excluding traffic violations and other minor offenses).

Item 9. Remuneration of Directors and Officers

(a) Furnish, in substantially the tabular form indicated, the aggregate annual remuneration of each of the three highest paid persons who are officers or directors as a group during the issuer's last fiscal year. State the number of persons in the group referred to above without naming them.

Name of individual or identity of group	Capacities in remuneration was received	Aggregate remuneration

Instructions:

1. In case of remuneration paid or to be paid otherwise than in cash, if it is impracticable to determine the cash value thereof, state in a note to the table the nature and amount thereof.

2. This item is to be answered on an accrual basis if practicable; if not so answered, state the basis used.

(b) Briefly describe all remuneration payments proposed to be made in the future pursuant to any ongoing plan or arrangement to the individuals and group specified in Item 9(a). The description should include a summary of how each plan operates, any performance formula or measure in effect (or the criteria used to determine payment amounts), the time periods over which the measurements of benefits will be determined, payment schedules, and any recent material amendments to the plan. Information need not be furnished with respect to any group life, health, hospitalization, or medical reimbursement plans which do not discriminate in scope, terms or operation in favor of officers or directors of the registrant and which are available generally to all salaried employees.

Item 10. Security Ownership of Management and Certain Securityholders

(a) Voting securities and principal holders thereof. Furnish the following information, in substantially the tabular form indicated, with respect to voting securities held of record by:

(1) each of the three highest paid persons who are officers and directors of the issuer; *Note*—In the event none of the issuer's officers or directors have received a salary in the past twelve months, this item should be responded to for every officer and director;

(2) all officers and directors as a group;

(3) each shareholder who owns more than 10% of any class of the issuer's securities, including those shares subject to outstanding options.

(1) Title of Class	(2) Name and address of owner	(3) Amount owned before the offering	(4) Amount owned after the offering	(5) Percent of Class

Instruction:

Column (4) need not be responded to if the information would be the same as that appearing under column (3).

(b) If, to the knowledge of the issuer, any other person holds or shares the power to vote or direct the voting of securities described pursuant to subsection (a) above, appropriate disclosure should be made. In addition, if any person other than those named pursuant to subsection (a) holds or shares the power to vote 10% or more of the issuer's voting securities, the information required by the table should be provided with respect to such person.

(c) Non-voting securities and principal holders thereof. Furnish the same information as required in subsection (a) above with respect to securities that are not entitled to vote.

(d) Options, warrants, and rights. Furnish the information required by the table as to options, warrants or rights to purchase securities from the issuer or any of its subsidiaries held by each of the individuals and referred to in subsection (a) above:

Name of holder	Title and amount securities called for by options, warrants or rights	Exercise price	Date of Exercise

Instruction:

Where the total market value of securities called for by all outstanding options, warrants or rights does not exceed $10,000 for any officer, director, or principal shareholder named in answer to this item, or $50,000 for all officers and directors as a group, this item need not be answered with respect to options, warrants or rights held by such person or group. If the issuer cannot ascertain the market value of its securities, the offering price may be used for purposes of this subsection. If, as is the case with offerings of debt securities, the offering price cannot be determined at the time of filing the offering statement, the issuer may utilize any reasonable method of valuation.

(e) List all parents of the issuer, showing the basis of control and as to each parent the percentage of voting securities owned or other basis of control by its immediate parent, if any.

Item 11. Interest of Management and Others in Certain Transactions

Describe briefly any transactions during the previous two years or any presently proposed transactions, to which the issuer or any of its subsidiaries was or is to be a party, in which any of the following persons had or is to have a direct or indirect material interest, naming such person and stating his relationship to the issuer, the nature of his interest in the transaction and, where practicable, the amount of such interest:

(1) Any director or officer of the issuer;

(2) Any nominee for election as a director;

(3) Any principal securityholder named in answer to Item 10(a);

(4) If the issuer was incorporated or organized within the past three years, any promoter of the issuer;

(5) Any relative or spouse of any of the foregoing persons, or any relative of such spouse, who has the same house as such person or who is a director or officer of any parent or subsidiary of the issuer.

Instructions:

1. No information need be given in answer to this item as to any transaction where:

(a) The rates of charges involved in the transaction are determined by competitive bids, or the transaction involves the rendering of services as a common or contract carrier fixed in conformity with law or governmental authority;

(b) The transaction involves services as a bank depositary of funds, transfer agent, registrar, trustee under a trust indenture, or similar services;

(c) The amount involved in the transaction or a series of similar transactions, including all periodic installments in the case of any lease or other agreement providing for periodic payments or installments does not exceed $50,000; or

(d) The interest of the specified person arises solely from the ownership of securities of the issuer and the specified person receives no extra or special benefit not shared on a pro-rata basis by all of the holders of securities of the class.

2. It should be noted that this Item calls for disclosure of indirect as well as direct material interests in transactions. A person who has a position or relationship with a firm, corporation, or other entity which engages in a transaction with the issuer or its subsidiaries may have an indirect interest in such transaction by reason of such position or relationship. However, a person shall be deemed not to have a material indirect interest in a transaction within the meaning of this Item where:

(a) the interest arises only (i) from such person's position as a director of another corporation or organization (other than a partnership) which is a party to the transaction, or (ii) from the direct or indirect ownership by such person and all other persons specified in subparagraphs (1) through (5) above, in the aggregate, of less than a 10 percent equity interest in another person (other than a partnership) which is a party to the transaction, or (iii) from both such position and ownership;

(b) the interest arises only from such person's position as a limited partner in a partnership in which he and all other persons specified in (1) through (5) above had an interest of less than 10 percent; or

(c) the interest of such person arises solely from the holding of an equity interest (including a limited partnership interest but excluding a general partnership interest) or a creditor interest in another person which is a party to the transaction with the issuer or any of its subsidiaries and the transaction is not material to such other person.

3. Include the name of each person whose interest in any transaction is described and the nature of the relationships by reason of which such interest is required to be described. The amount of the interest of any specified person shall be computed without regard to the amount of the profit or loss involved in the transaction. Where it is not practicable to state the approximate amount of the interest, the approximate amount involved in the transaction shall be disclosed.

4. Information should be included as to any material underwriting discounts and commissions upon the sale of securities by the issuer where any of the specified persons was or is to be a principal underwriter or is a controlling person, or member, of a firm which was or is to be a principal underwriter. Information need not be given concerning ordinary management fees paid by underwriters to a managing underwriter pursuant to an agreement among underwriters the parties to which do not include the issuer or its subsidiaries.

5. As to any transaction involving the purchase or sale of assets by or to any issuer or any subsidiary, otherwise than in the ordinary course of business, state the cost of the assets to the purchaser and, if acquired by the seller within two years prior to the transaction, the cost thereof to the seller.

6. Information shall be furnished in answer to this Item with respect to transactions not excluded above which involve remuneration from the issuer or its subsidiaries, directly or indirectly, to any of the specified persons for services in any capacity unless the interest of such persons arises solely from the ownership individually and in the aggregate of less than 10 percent of any class of equity securities of another corporation furnishing the services to the issuer or its subsidiaries.

Item 12. Securities Being Offered

(a) If capital stock is being offered, state the title of the class and furnish the following information:

(1) Outline briefly: (i) dividend rights; (ii) voting rights; (iii) liquidation rights; (iv) preemptive rights; (v) conversion rights; (vi) redemption provisions; (vii) sinking fund provisions; and (viii) liability to further calls or to assessment by the issuer.

(2) Briefly describe potential liabilities imposed on shareholders under state statutes or foreign law, e.g., to laborers, servants or employees of the registrant, unless such disclosure would be immaterial because the financial resources of the registrant are such as to make it unlikely that the liability will ever be imposed.

(b) If debt securities are being offered, outline briefly the following:

(1) Provisions with respect to interest, conversion, maturity, redemption, amortization, sinking fund or retirement.

(2) Provisions with respect to the kind and priority of any lien securing the issue, together with a brief identification of the principal properties subject to such lien.

(3) Provisions restricting the declaration of dividends or requiring the maintenance of any ratio of assets, the creation or maintenance of reserves or the maintenance of properties.

(4) Provisions permitting or restricting the issuance of additional securities, the withdrawal of cash deposited against such issuance, the incurring of additional debt, the release or substitution of assets securing the issue, the modification of the terms of the security, and similar provisions.

Instruction:

In the case of secured debt there should be stated (i) the approximate amount of unbonded property available for use against the issuance of bonds, as of the most recent practicable date, and (ii) whether the securities being issued are to be issued against such property, against the deposit of cash, or otherwise.

(c) If securities described are to be offered pursuant to warrants, rights, or convertible securities, state briefly:

(1) the amount of securities called for by such warrants, convertible securities or rights;

(2) the period during which and the price at which the warrants, convertible securities or rights are exercisable;

(3) the amounts of warrants, convertible securities or rights outstanding; and

(4) any other material terms of such securities.

(d) In the case of any other kind of securities, appropriate information of a comparable character.

PART F/S

The following financial statements of the issuer, or the issuer and its predecessors or any businesses to which the issuer is a successor shall be filed as part of the offering statement and included in the offering circular which is distributed to investors.

Such financial statements shall be prepared in accordance with generally accepted accounting principles (GAAP) in the United States. If the issuer is a Canadian company, a reconciliation to GAAP in the United States shall be filed as part of the financial statements.

Issuers which have audited financial statements because they prepare them for other purposes, shall provide them.

The Commission's Regulation S-X, 17 CFR 210.1 et seq. relating to the form, content of and requirements for financial statements shall not apply to the financial statements required by this part, except that if audited financial statements are filed, the qualifications and reports of an independent auditor shall comply with the requirements of Article 2 of Regulation S-X.

Issuers which are limited partners are required to also file the balance sheets of general partners: (1) if such general partner is a corporation, the balance sheet shall be as of the end of its most recently completed fiscal year; receivables from a parent or affiliate of such general partner (including notes receivable, but excluding trade receivables) should be deductions from shareholders equity of the general partner; where a parent or affiliate has committed to increase or maintain the general partner's capital, there shall also be filed the balance sheet of such parent or affiliate as of the end of its most recently completed fiscal year; (2) if such general partner is a partnership, its balance sheet as of the end of its most recently completed fiscal year; (3) if such general partner is a natural person, the net worth of such general partner(s) based on the estimated fair market value of their assets and liabilities, singly or in the aggregate shall be disclosed in the offering circular, and balance sheets of each of the individual general partners supporting such net worth shall be provided as supplemental information.

(1) Balance Sheet—as of a date within 90 days prior to filing the offering statement or such longer time, not exceeding 6 months, as the Commission may permit at the written request of the issuer upon a showing of good cause; for filings made after 90 days subsequent to the issuer's most recent fiscal year, the balance sheet shall be dated as of the end of the most recent fiscal year.

(2) Statements of income, cash flows, and other stockholders equity—for each of the 2 fiscal years preceding the date of the most recent balance sheet being filed, and for any interim period between the end of the most recent of such fiscal years and the date of the most recent balance sheet being filed, or for the period of the issuer's existence if less than the period above.

Income statements shall be accompanied by a statement that in the opinion of management all adjustments necessary for a fair statement of results for the interim period have been included. If all such adjustments are of a normal recurring nature, a statement to that effect shall be made. If otherwise, there shall be furnished as supplemental information and not as part of the offering statement, a letter describing in detail the nature and amount of any adjustments other than normal recurring adjustments entering into the determination of results shown.

(3) Financial Statements of Businesses Acquired or to be Acquired.

(a) Financial statements for the periods specified in (c) below should be furnished if any of the following conditions exist:

(i) A significant business combination has occurred or is probable (for purposes of this rule, this encompasses the acquisition of an interest in a business accounted for by the equity method); or

(ii) Consummation of a combination between entities under common control.

(b) A business combination shall be considered significant if a comparison of the most recent annual financial statements of the business acquired or to be acquired and the registrant's most recent annual consolidated financial statements filed at or prior to the date of acquisition indicates that the business would be a significant subsidiary pursuant to the conditions specified in Rule 405 of Regulation C, 17 CFR § 230.405.

(c)(i) The financial statements shall be furnished for the periods up to the date of acquisition, for those periods for which the registrant is required to furnish financial statements.

(ii) These financial statements need not be audited.

(iii) The separate balance sheet of the acquired business is not required when the registrant's most recent balance sheet filed is for a date after the acquisition was consummated.

(iv) If none of the conditions in the definitions of significant subsidiary in Rule 405 exceeds 40%, income statements of the acquired business for only the most recent fiscal year and interim period

need be filed, unless such statements are readily available. [Amended in Release No. 33-6996 (¶ 85,134), effective June 3, 1993, 58 F.R. 26509.]

(d) If consummation of more than one transaction has occurred or is probable, the tests of significance shall be made using the aggregate impact of the businesses and the required financial statements may be presented on a combined basis, if appropriate.

(e) This paragraph (3) shall not apply to a business which is totally held by the registrant prior to consummation of the transaction.

(4) Pro Forma Financial Information.

(a) Pro forma information shall be furnished if any of the following conditions exist (for purposes of this rule, "business combination" encompasses the acquisition of an interest in a business accounted for by the equity method):

(i) During the most recent fiscal year or subsequent interim period for which a balance sheet of the registrant is required, a significant business combination has occurred.

(ii) After the date of the registrant's most recent balance sheet, consummation of a significant business combination or a combination between entities under common control has occurred or is probable.

(b) The provisions of paragraph (3)(b), (d) and (e) apply to this paragraph (4).

(c) Pro forma statements shall ordinarily be in columnar form showing condensed historical statements, pro forma adjustments, and the pro forma results and should include the following:

(i) If the transaction was consummated during the most recent fiscal year or in the subsequent interim period, pro forma statements of income reflecting the combined operations of the entities for the latest fiscal year and interim period, if any, or

(ii) If consummation of the transaction has occurred or is probable after the date of the most recent balance sheet, a pro forma balance sheet giving effect to the combination as of the date of the most recent balance sheet required by paragraph (b). For a purchase, pro forma statements of income reflecting the combined operations of the entities for the latest fiscal year and interim period, if any, and for a pooling of interests, pro forma statements of income for all periods for which income statements of the registrant are required.

PART III—EXHIBITS

Item 1. Index to Exhibits

(a) An index to the exhibits filed should be presented immediately following the cover page to Part III.

(b) Each exhibit should be listed in the exhibit index according to the number assigned to it under Item 2 below.

(c) The index to exhibits should identify the location of the exhibit under the sequential page numbering system for this Form 1-A.

(d) Where exhibits are incorporated by reference, the reference shall be made in the index of exhibits.

Instructions:

1. Any document or part thereof filed with the Commission pursuant to any Act administered by the Commission may, subject to the limitations of Rule 24 of the Commission's Rule of Practice, be incorporated by reference as an exhibit to any offering statement.

2. If any modification has occurred in the text of any document incorporated by reference since the filing thereof, the issuer shall file with the reference a statement containing the text of such modification and the date thereof.

3. Procedurally, the techniques specified in Rule 411(d) of Regulation C shall be followed.

Item 2. Description of Exhibits

As appropriate, the following documents should be filed as exhibits to the offering statement.

(1) *Underwriting Agreement*—Each underwriting contract or agreement with a principal underwriter or letter pursuant to which the securities are to be distributed; where the terms have yet to be finalized, proposed formats may be provided.

(2) *Charter and by-laws*—The charter and by-laws of the issuer or instruments corresponding thereto as presently in effect and any amendments thereto.

(3) *Instruments defining the rights of security holders*—(a) All instruments defining the rights of any holder of the issuer's securities, including but not limited to (i) holders of equity or debt securities being issued; (ii) holders of long-term debt of the issuer, and of all subsidiaries for which consolidated or unconsolidated financial statements are required to be filed.

(b) The following instruments need not be filed if the issuer agrees to provide them to the Commission upon request: (i) instruments defining the rights of holders of long-term debt of the issuer and all of its subsidiaries for which consolidated financial statements are required to be filed if such debt is not being issued pursuant to this Regulation A offering and the total amount of such authorized issuance does not exceed 5% of the total assets of the issuer and its subsidiaries on a consolidated basis; (ii) any instrument with respect to a class of securities which is to be retired or redeemed prior to the issuance or upon delivery of the securities being issued pursuant to this Regulation A offering and appropriate steps have been taken to assure such retirement or redemption; and (iii) copies of instruments evidencing scrip certificates or fractions of shares.

(4) *Subscription agreement*—The form of any subscription agreement to be used in connection with the purchase of securities in this offering.

(5) *Voting trust agreement*—Any voting trust agreements and amendments thereto.

(6) *Material contracts*—(a) Every contract not made in the ordinary course of business which is material to the issuer and is to be performed in whole or in part at or after the filing of the offering statement or was entered into not more than 2 years before such filing. Only contracts need be filed as to which the issuer or subsidiary of the issuer is a party or has succeeded to a party by assumption or assignment or in which the issuer or such subsidiary has a beneficial interest.

(b) If the contract is such as ordinarily accompanies the kind of business conducted by the issuer and its subsidiaries, it is made in the ordinary course of business and need not be filed unless it falls within one or more of the following categories, in which case it should be filed except where immaterial in amount or significance: (i) any contract to which directors, officers, promoters, voting trustees, security holders named in the offering statement, or underwriters are parties except where the contract merely involves the purchase or sale of current assets having a determinable market price, at such market price; (ii) any contract upon which the issuer's business is substantially dependent, as in the case of continuing contracts to sell the major part of the issuer's products or services or to purchase the major part of the issuer's requirements of goods, services or raw materials or any franchise or license or other agreement to use a patent, formula, trade secret, process or trade name upon which the issuer's business depends to a material extent; (iii) any contract calling for the acquisition or sale of any property, plant or equipment for a consideration exceeding 15% of such fixed assets of the issuer on a consolidated basis; or (iv) any material lease under which a part of the property described in the offering statement is held by the issuer.

(c) Any management contract or any compensatory plan, contract or arrangement including but not limited to plans relating to options, warrants or rights, pension, retirement or deferred compensation or bonus, incentive or profit sharing (or if not set forth in any formal document, a written description thereof) shall be deemed material and shall be filed except for the following: (i) ordinary purchase and sales agency agreements; (ii) agreements with managers of stores in a chain organization or similar organization; (iii) contracts providing for labor or salesmen's bonuses or payments to a class of security holders, as such; (iv) any compensatory plan, contract or arrangement which pursuant to its terms is available to employees generally and which in operation provides for the same method of allocation of benefits between management and non-management participants.

(7) *Material foreign patents*—Each material foreign patent for an invention not covered by a United States patent. If a substantial part of the securities to be offered or if the proceeds therefrom have been or are to be used for the particular purposes of acquiring, developing or exploiting one or more material foreign patents or patent rights, furnish a list showing the number and a brief identification of each such patent or patent right.

(8) *Plan of acquisition, reorganization, arrangement, liquidation, or succession*—Any material plan of acquisition, disposition, reorganization, readjustment, succession, liquidation or arrangement and any amendments thereto described in the offering statement. Schedules (or similar attachments) to these exhibits shall not be filed unless such schedules contain information which is material to an investment decision and which is not otherwise disclosed in the agreement or the offering statement. The plan filed shall contain a list briefly identifying the contents of all omitted schedules, together with an agreement to furnish supplementally a copy of any omitted schedule to the Commission upon request.

(9) *Escrow agreements*—Any escrow agreement or similar arrangement which has been executed in connection with the Regulation A offering.

(10) *Consents*—(a) Experts: The written consent of (i) any account, engineer, geologist, appraiser or any person whose profession gives authority to a statement made by them and who is named in the offering statement as having prepared or certified any part of the document or is named as having prepared or certified a report or evaluation whether or not for use in connection with the offering statement; (ii) the expert that authored any portion of a report quoted or summarized as such in the offering statement, expressly stating their consent to the use of such quotation or summary; (iii) any persons who are referenced as having reviewed or passed upon any information in the offering statement, and that such information is being included on the basis of their authority or in reliance upon their status as experts.

(b) Underwriters: A written consent and certification in the form which follows signed by each underwriter of the securities proposed to be offered. All underwriters may, with appropriate modifications, sign the same consent and certification or separate consents and certifications may be signed by any underwriter or group of underwriters.

CONSENT AND CERTIFICATION BY UNDERWRITER

1. The undersigned hereby consents to being named as underwriter in an offering statement filed with the Securities and Exchange Commission by [insert name of issuer] pursuant to Regulation A in connection with a proposed offering of [insert title of securities] to the public.

2. The undersigned hereby certifies that it furnished the statements and information set forth in the offering statement with respect to the undersigned, its directors and officers or partners, that such statements and information are accurate, complete and fully responsive to the requirements of Parts I, II and III of the Offering Statement thereto, and do not omit any information required to be stated therein with respect of any such persons, or necessary to make the state-

ments and information therein with respect to any of them not misleading.

3. If Preliminary Offering Circulars are distributed, the undersigned hereby undertakes to keep an accurate and complete record of the name and address of each person furnished a Preliminary Offering Circular and, if such Preliminary Offering Circular is inaccurate or inadequate in any material respect, to furnish a revised Preliminary Offering Circular or a Final Offering Circular to all persons to whom the securities are to be sold at least 48 hours prior to the mailing of any confirmation of sale to such persons, or to send such a circular to such persons under circumstances that it would normally be received by them 48 hours prior to their receipt of confirmation of the sale.

. . . .

                    (Underwriter)

By . . . .

Date   /   /

(c) All written consents shall be dated and manually signed.

(11) *Opinion re legality*—An opinion of counsel as to the legality of the securities covered by theOffering Statement, indicating whether they will, when sold, be legally issued, fully paid and non-assessable, and if debt securities, whether they will be binding obligations of the issuer.

(12) *Sales Material*—Any material required to be filed by virtue of Rule 256.

(13) *"Test the Water" Material*—Any written document or broadcast script used under the authorization of Rule 254.

(14) *Appointment of Agent for Service of Process*—A Canadian issuer shall provide Form F-X.

(15) *Additional exhibits*—Any additional exhibits which the issuer may wish to file, which shall be so marked to indicate clearly the subject matters to which they refer.

SIGNATURES

The issuer has duly caused this offering statement to be signed on its behalf by the undersigned, thereunto duly authorized, in the City of . . . ., State of . . . ., on . . . ., 19 . . . .

(Issuer) . . . .

By (Signature and Title) . . . .

This offering statement has been signed by the following persons in the capacities and on the dates indicated.

(Signature) . . . .

(Title) . . . .

(Selling security holder) . . . .

(Date) . . . .

Instructions:

1. The offering statement shall be signed by the issuer, its Chief Executive Officer, Chief Financial Officer, a majority of the members of its board of directors or other governing instrumentality, and each person, other than the issuer, for whose account any of the securities are to be offered. If a signature is by a person on behalf of any other person, evidence of authority to sign shall be filed with the offering statement, except where an exec-

utive officer signs on behalf of the issuer. If the issuer is Canadian, its authorized representative in the United States also shall sign. Where the issuer is a limited partnership, the offering statement shall also be signed by a majority of the board of directors of any corporate general partner.

2. The name of each person signing the offering statement shall be typed or printed beneath the signature.

[¶ 8561]   FORM 2-A

[As last amended in Release No. 33-7373, December 16, 1996, effective January 21,
1997, 61 F.R. 67200.]

UNITED STATES SECURITIES AND EXCHANGE COMMISSION

Washington, D.C. 20549

FORM 2-A

REPORT OF SALES AND USES OF PROCEEDS PURSUANT TO RULE 257 OF REGULATION A

File No. 24-_____ _

For period ending   /   /_
    Indicate whether the report is an   initial report [   ]
        amendment [   ]
        or final report [   ]
    If the report is an amendment, indicate the number of such amendment. ☐ ☐
        If the offering has terminated, indicate the date of termination   /   /

General Instructions:

The report shall be filed in accordance with the provisions of Rule 257 of Regulation A.

Answer each item in the box(es) or spaces provided. If additional space is required for any response, continue the response on an attached sheet.

If the issuer is required to file any report(s) on this form subsequent to its initial filing, each subsequent filing shall be deemed to be an amendment to the initial filing. Do not report in any amendment responses to Items 3-11 unless the information has changed.

No fee is required to accompany this filing.

Seven copies of the form shall be filed with the main office of the Commission in Washington, D.C. At least one copy of the form shall be manually signed; other copies may bear typed or printed signatures.

1. . . . .
    Exact name of issuer as specified in its charter.
2. Date of qualification of the offering statement:
    ☐☐☐☐☐☐
3. Has the offering commenced? [ ] Yes [ ] No.
    If yes, date of commencement: ☐☐☐☐☐
    If no, explain briefly:
. . . .
4. Did the offering terminate before any securities were sold? [ ] Yes [ ] No.
    If yes, explain briefly:

. . . .
    If "yes", do not answer Items 5-11.
5. Did the offering terminate prior to the sale of all the securities qualified under Regulation A? [ ] Yes [ ] No.
    If yes, explain briefly:
. . . .

6. Indicate the total number of shares or other units offered and sold to date:
    . . . . (issuer's account) . . . . (selling securityholders)
    Indicate the number of shares or other units still being offered:
    . . . . (issuer's account)   . . . . (selling securityholders)
7. Total amount of dollars received from the public to date. $ . . . .
    Total amount allocable to selling securityholders: $ . . . .
        Underwriting discount or commission allowed $ . . . .
        Underwriting expenses paid $ . . . .
        Finders' Fees $ . . . .
        Other expenses paid to date by or for issuer:

Legal (including organization) $. . . . .

Accounting $. . . . .

Engineering $. . . . .

Printing and Advertising $. . . . .

Other (specify)_____ $. . . . .

. . . . $. . . . .

. . . . $. . . . .

Total costs and expenses $. . . . .

Total net proceeds remaining. $. . . . .

8. Uses of net proceeds to date.

Instructions:

1. Do not include any amount in "working capital" to which a more specific category is applicable.

2. Round all amounts to the nearest dollar.

3. Specify under "other purposes" any purpose for which at least 5% of the issuer's proceeds or $50,000, whichever is less,   has been used.

Salaries and fees $. . . . .

Construction of plant, building and facilities $. . . . .

Purchases and installation of machinery and equipment $. . . . .

Purchase of real estate $. . . . .

Acquisition of other business(es) $. . . . .

Repayment of indebtedness $. . . . .

Working capital $. . . . .

Development expense (product development, research, patent costs, etc.) $. . . . .

Temporary investment (specify) . . . . $. . . . .

. . . . $. . . . .

. . . . $. . . . .

Other purposes (specify)

. . . . $. . . . .

. . . . $. . . . .

. . . . $. . . . .

. . . . $. . . . .

. . . . $. . . . .

. . . . $. . . . .

. . . . $. . . . .

9. Do the use(s) of proceeds in Item 8 represent a material change in the use(s) of proceeds described in the offering circular? [ ] Yes [ ] No.

If yes, explain briefly:

. . . .

10. State the number of shares held by each promoter, director, officer or controlling person of the issuer, if different from the amount stated in the offering circular.

. . . .

11. List the names and addresses of all brokers and dealers who have, to the knowledge of the issuer or underwriters, participated in the distribution of the securities during the period covered by this report.

. . . .

SIGNATURE

Pursuant to the requirements of Rule 257 and Regulation A, ... has caused this report to be signed on its behalf by the undersigned thereunto duly authorized.

. . . .

Issuer

. . . . By . . . .

Date   Signature

¶8561   **Form 2-A**

Instruction:

The report shall be signed by an executive officer, general partner or counsel of the issuer or by any other duly authorized person. The name and any title of the person who signs the report shall be typed or printed beneath the signature.

[¶ 8701]   FORM 1-E

[As last amended in Release No. 33-6546, August 30, 1984, 49 F.R. 35342.]

UNITED STATES SECURITIES AND EXCHANGE COMMISSION

Washington D.C.

FORM 1-E

NOTIFICATION UNDER REGULATION E

Item 1. The Issuer

State the exact name of the issuer and the address (street, city and State) of its principal business office.

Item 2. Affiliates and Principal Security Holders of Issuer

List the full name and complete address of each of the following persons:

(a) Each affiliate of the issuer, indicating the nature of the affiliation.

(b) Each person who owns of record, or is known to own beneficially, ten percent or more of the outstanding securities of any class of the issuer, stating the title and amount owned by each such person.

Item 3. Directors and Officers

List the full name and complete residence address of each of the following persons:

(a) Each director of the issuer;

(b) Each officer of the issuer, indicating all positions and offices held with the issuer;

(c) Each investment adviser.

Item 4. Counsel for Issuer and Underwriters

Give the name and address of counsel for the issuer in connection with the proposed offering. Furnish similar information as to any counsel for the underwriters.

Item 5. Events Making Exemption Unavailable

State whether or not any event specified in Rule 602(b), (c) or (d) [Reg. § 230.602] has occurred which would make an exemption under this regulation unavailable for securities of the issuer in the absence of a waiver by the Commission pursuant to Rule 602(e) [Reg. § 230.602].

Item 6. Jurisdictions in which Securities are to be Offered

(a) List the names of the States and other jurisdictions in which the securities covered by this notification are proposed to be offered through underwriters, dealers or salesmen in such jurisdictions.

(b) If the offering is to be made by advertisements, mail, telephone or otherwise in States or other jurisdictions other than those listed under (a) above, describe the methods proposed to be employed in making the offering therein and list such States or other jurisdictions to the extent that they are known.

Note. No securities shall be offered or sold in any other State or jurisdiction until an amendment to the notification has been filed listing the names of the additional jurisdictions.

Item 7. Unregistered Securities Issued or Sold Within One Year

(a) As to any unregistered securities issued by the issuer within one year prior to the filing of this notification, state (i) the title and amount of securities issued; (ii) the aggregate offering price or other consideration for which they were issued and the basis for computing the amount thereof; and (iii) the names of the persons or the identity of the class of persons to whom the securities were issued.

(b) As to any unregistered securities of the issuer which were sold within one year prior to the filing of this notification by or for the account of any person who at the time was a director, officer, or principal security holder of the issuer, or was an underwriter of any securities of such issuer, furnish the information specified in (i) through (iii) of paragraph (a).

(c) Indicate the section of the Act or rule or regulation of the Commission under which exemption from registration was claimed with respect to such securities and state briefly the facts relied upon for the exemption.

Item 8. Other Present or Proposed Offerings

State whether or not the issuer is presently offering or presently contemplates the offering of any securities, in addition to those covered by this notification. If so, describe fully the present or proposed offering.

Item 9. Exhibits

Four copies of each of the documents specified below shall be filed as exhibits to the notification. List under this item all such documents filed.

(a) Any indenture or other instruments defining the rights of holders of debt securities to be offered hereunder. If equity securities are to be offered, furnish copies of the provisions of the governing instruments defining the rights of holders of such securities.

(b) All underwriting contracts relating to the securities to be offered hereunder.

(c) If any of the securities proposed to be offered hereunder are to be offered for the account of any person other than the issuer, a written statement signed by the issuer representing that the proposed offering will not interfere with any needed financing by the issuer under this regulation.

(d) The offering circular or if the offering is to be made pursuant to Rule 606 [Reg. §230.606], the statement required by paragraph (a) of that rule and any offering circular to be used in connection with such offering.

(e) A written consent and certification, signed by each underwriter of the securities proposed to be offered hereunder. All underwriters may, with appropriate modifications, sign the same consent and certification or separate consents and certifications may be signed by any underwriter or group of underwriters. At least one copy of each consent and certification shall be signed manually.

"1. The undersigned hereby consents to being named as underwriter in a notification and offering circular filed with the Securities and Exchange Commission by *(name of issuer)* pursuant to Regulation E in connection with a proposed offering of *(title of securities)* to the public.

"2. The undersigned hereby certifies that it furnished the statements and information set forth in such notification and offering circular with respect to the undersigned, its directors and officers or partners, that such statements and information are accurate, complete and fully responsive to the requirements of Form 1-E and Schedule A and do not omit any information required to be stated therein with respect of any of such persons, or necessary to make the statements and information therein with respect to any of them not misleading."

3. If a Preliminary Offering Circular will be distributed as permitted by Rule 605(f), the Consent and Certification by Underwriter shall include the following additional paragraph:

The undersigned hereby undertakes, in connection with any distribution of the Preliminary Offering Circular as permitted by Rule 605(f), (a) to keep an accurate and complete record of the name and address of each person furnished such Preliminary Offering Circular and (b) if such Preliminary Offering Circular is inaccurate or inadequate in any material respect, to furnish a revised Preliminary Offering Circular or an offering circular of the type referred to in Rule 605(f)(4) to all persons to which the securities are to be sold at least 48 hours prior to the mailing of any confirmation of sale to such persons under circumstances that it would normally be received by them 48 hours prior to their receipt of confirmation of the sale.

(f) If the issuer is a small business investment company as defined in §230.602(a) of this chapter and has not yet obtained a license from the Small Business Administration, copies of any contract or arrangement made to assure that the funds paid in by investors for the securities to be offered will be returned to them in the event such license is not obtained.

SIGNATURE[2]

This notification has been signed in the City of ...., State of ...., on ...., 19......

....
(Issuer)

By ....
(Name and Title)

---

[2] The notification shall be signed in accordance with Rule 604 [Reg. §230.604]. At least one copy shall be signed manually by or on behalf of the issuer and each selling security holder. Any copies not manually signed shall bear typed or printed signatures.

....

(Selling Security Holder)

[¶ 8711]   FORM 2-E

[As adopted in Release No. 33-4005, December 17, 1958.]

UNITED STATES SECURITIES AND EXCHANGE COMMISSION

Washington D.C.

FORM 2-E

REPORT PURSUANT TO RULE 609 OF REGULATION E

1. Name of issuer . . . .

2. Name of underwriter . . . .

3. Date of this report . . . .

4. (a) Date offering commenced . . . .

   (b) Date offering completed, if completed . . . .

   (c) If offering has not commenced, state reasons briefly . . . .

5. (a) Total number of shares or other units offered hereunder . . . .

   (b) Number of such shares or other units sold from commencement of offering to date . . .

   (c) Number of such shares or other units still being offered . . . .

6. (a) Total amount received from public from commencement of offering to date . . . . $. . . . . .

   (b) Underwriting discount allowed . . . . $. . . . . .

   (c) Expenses paid to or for the account of the underwriters . . . . . $. . . . . .

   (d) Other expenses paid to date by or for the account of the issuer:

       (1) Legal (including organization) . . . . $. . . . . .

       (2) Accounting . . . . $. . . . . .

       (3) Printing and advertising . . . . $. . . . . .

       (4) Other . . . . $. . . . . .

   (e) Total costs and expenses ((b), (c) and (d)) . . . . $. . . . . .

   (f) Proceeds to issuer after above deductions ((a) minus (e)) . . . . $. . . . . .

7. State briefly the nature and extent of each type of the issuer's principal activities to date.

8. State whether the offering has been discontinued, and if so, state the date and describe briefly the reasons for such discontinuance.

9. List the names and addresses of all brokers and dealers who have, to the knowledge of the issuer or underwriters, participated in the distribution of the securities offered during the period covered by this report.

Instruction. In reports made subsequent to the initial report, the information need be given only with respect to persons not previously reported.

. . . .

(Issuer)*

Date. . . . .   By. . . . .

(Name and Title)*

. . . .

(Selling Security Holder)*

Date. . . . .

* At least one copy of the report shall be signed manually by each person whose signature is required. Any copies not manually signed shall bear typed or printed signatures.

[¶ 8801]   Form 144

[As last amended in Release No. 33-8869, effective February 15, 2008, 72 F.R. 71546.]

UNITED STATES
SECURITIES AND EXCHANGE COMMISSION
Washington, D.C. 20549

FORM 144
NOTICE OF PROPOSED SALE OF SECURITIES
PURSUANT TO RULE 144 UNDER THE SECURITIES ACT OF 1933

ATTENTION: *Transmit for filing 3 copies of this form concurrently with either placing an order with a broker to execute sale or executing a sale directly with a market maker.*

1 (a) NAME OF ISSUER (*Please type or print*)

(b) IRS IDENT. NO.

(c) S.E.C. FILE NO.

1 (d) ADDRESS OF ISSUER   STREET   CITY   STATE   ZIP CODE

2 (a) NAME OF PERSON FOR WHOSE ACCOUNT THE SECURITIES ARE TO BE SOLD

(b) RELATIONSHIP TO ISSUER

(c) ADDRESS STREET   CITY   STATE   ZIP CODE

SEC USE ONLY
DOCUMENT SEQUENCE NO.

CUSIP NUMBER

WORK LOCATION

(d) TELEPHONE NO.   AREA CODE   NUMBER

INSTRUCTION: *The person filing this notice should contact the issuer to obtain the I.R.S. Identification Number and the S.E.C. File Number.*

3 (a) Title of the Class of Securities To Be Sold	(b) Name and Address of Each Broker Through Whom the Securities are to be Offered or of Each Market Maker who is Acquiring the Securities	SEC USE ONLY Broker–Dealer File Number	(c) Number of Shares or Other Units To Be Sold (*See instr. 3(c)*)	(d) Aggregate Market Value (*See instr. 3(d)*)	(e) Number of Shares or Other Units Outstanding (*See instr. 3(c)*)	(f) Approximate Date of Sale (*See instr. 3(f)*) (MO. DAY. YR.)	(g) Name of Each Securities Exchange (*See instr. 3(g)*)

3. (a) Title of the class of securities to be sold
   (b) Name and address of each broker through whom the securities are intended to be sold
   (c) Number of shares or other units to be sold (if debt securities, give the aggregate face amount)
   (d) Aggregate market value of the securities to be sold as of a specified date within 10 days prior to filing of this notice
   (e) Number of shares or other units of the class outstanding, or if debt securities the face amount thereof outstanding, as shown by the most recent report or statement published by the issuer
   (f) Approximate date on which the securities are to be sold
   (g) Name of each securities exchange, if any, on which the securities are intended to be sold

INSTRUCTIONS:
1. (a) Name of issuer
   (b) Issuer's I.R.S. Identification Number
   (c) Issuer's S.E.C. file number, if any
   (d) Issuer's address, including zip code
   (e) Issuer's telephone number, including area code

2. (a) Name of person for whose account the securities are to be sold
   (b) Such person's I.R.S. identification number, if such person is an entity
   (c) Such person's relationship to the issuer (e.g., officer, director, 10% stockholder, or member of immediate family of any of the foregoing)
   (d) Such person's address, including zip code

TABLE I — SECURITIES TO BE SOLD

Furnish the following information with respect to the acquisition of the securities to be sold and with respect to the payment of all or any part of the purchase price or other consideration therefor:

Title of the Class	Date you Acquired	Nature of Acquisition Transaction	Name of Person from Whom Acquired (If gift, also give date donor acquired)	Amount of Securities Acquired	Date of Payment	Nature of Payment

INSTRUCTIONS: If the securities were purchased and full payment therefor was not made in cash at the time of purchase, explain in the table or in a note thereto the nature of the consideration given. If the consideration consisted of any note or other obligation, or if payment was made in installments describe the arrangement and state when the note or other obligation was discharged in full or the last installment paid.

TABLE II — SECURITIES SOLD DURING THE PAST 3 MONTHS

Furnish the following information as to all securities of the issuer sold during the past 3 months by the person for whose account the securities are to be sold.

Name and Address of Seller	Title of Securities Sold	Date of Sale	Amount of Securities Sold	Gross Proceeds

REMARKS:

INSTRUCTIONS:

See the definition of "person" in paragraph (a) of Rule 144. Information is to be given not only as to the person for whose account the securities are to be sold but also as to all other persons included in that definition. In addition, information shall be given as to sales by all persons whose sales are required by paragraph (e) of Rule 144 to be aggregated with sales for the account of the person filing this notice.

_____
DATE OF NOTICE

_____
DATE OF PLAN ADOPTION OR GIVING OF INSTRUCTION,
IF RELYING ON RULE 10B5-1

ATTENTION:

The person for whose account the securities to which this notice relates are to be sold hereby represents by signing this notice that he does not know any material adverse information in regard to the current and prospective operations of the issuer of the securities to be sold which has not been publicly disclosed. If such person has adopted a written trading plan or given trading instructions to satisfy Rule 10b5-1 under the Exchange Act, by signing the form and indicating the date that the plan was adopted or the instruction given, that person makes such representation as of the plan adoption or instruction date.

_____
(SIGNATURE)

The notice shall be signed by the person for whose account the securities are to be sold. At least one copy of the notice shall be manually signed. Any copies not manually signed shall bear typed or printed signatures.

ATTENTION: Intentional misstatements or omission of facts constitute Federal Criminal Violations (See 18 U.S.C. 1001)

[¶ 8871]   FORM D

[As last amended in Release No. 33-8891, effective September 15, 2008, 73 F.R. 10592.]

UNITED STATES
SECURITIES AND EXCHANGE COMMISSION
Washington, DC 20549

FORM D

NOTICE OF EXEMPT OFFERING OF SECURITIES

Intentional misstatements or omissions of fact constitute federal criminal violations. See 18 U.S.C. 1001.

You must follow the accompanying <u>instructions</u> in submitting this notice.

---

1.   <u>**Issuer's Identity**</u>

   <u>**Name of Issuer**</u> _____

   <u>**Previous Name(s)**</u> _____ ☐ None

   <u>**Jurisdiction of Incorporation/Organization**</u> (dropdown or other list selection feature)

   <u>**Entity Type**</u> (dropdown or other list selection feature)

   <u>**Year of Incorporation/Organization**</u> (dropdown or other list selection feature to select year or "Yet to Be Formed")

[Add Issuer]

2.   **Principal Place of Business and Contact Information**

Street Address _____

City _____ State/Province __ (<u>dropdown</u> or other list selection feature)

Zip/Postal Code _____

Country
- ⊙ U.S.
- ⊙ Canada
- ⊙ Other (<u>dropdown</u> or other list selection feature for countries if answer is "Other" than U.S. or Canada)

Telephone Number _____

Add Information for Additional Issuer(s)

3.   **Related Persons**

Full Name	Relationship	Address
_____	[ ] Executive Officer	_____
	[ ] Director	_____
	[ ] Promoter	_____

Clarification of Response (if Necessary): _____

Add Related Person

4.   **Industry Group (dropdown or other list selection feature)**

5.   **Issuer Size**

Revenue Range (for issuers that do not specify "Hedge Fund" or "Other Investment Fund" in response to Item 4)
- ⊙ No Revenues
- ⊙ $1 - $1,000,000
- ⊙ $1,000,001 - $5,000,000
- ⊙ $5,000,001 - $25,000,000
- ⊙ $25,000,001 - $100,000,000
- ⊙ Over $100,000,000
- ⊙ Decline to Disclose
- ⊙ Not Applicable

Aggregate Net Asset Value Range (for issuers that specify "Hedge Fund" or "Other Investment Fund" in response to Item 4)
- ⊙ No Aggregate Net Asset Value
- ⊙ $1 - $5,000,000

⊙ $5,000,001 - $25,000,000
⊙ $25,000,001 - $50,000,000
⊙ $50,000,001 - $100,000,000
⊙ Over $100,000,000
⊙ Decline to Disclose
⊙ Not Applicable

6.   **Federal Exemption(s) and Exclusion(s) Claimed** (select all that apply)

[ ] Rule 504(b)(1) (not (i), (ii) or (iii))   [ ] Rule 506
[ ] Rule 504(b)(1)(i)   [ ] Securities Act Section 4(6)
[ ] Rule 504(b)(1)(ii)   [ ] Investment Company Act Section 3(c)[1]
[ ] Rule 504(b)(1)(iii)
[ ] Rule 505

7.   **Type of Filing**

[ ] New Notice (dropdown or other feature to select "Date of First Sale" or "First Sale Yet to Occur")
[ ] Amendment

8.   **Duration of Offering**

Does the issuer intend this offering to last more than one year?
⊙ Yes
⊙ No

9.   **Type(s) of Securities Offered** (select all that apply)

[ ] Equity
[ ] Debt
[ ] Option, Warrant or Other Right to Acquire Another Security
[ ] Security to be Acquired Upon Exercise of Option, Warrant or Other Right to Acquire Security
[ ] Pooled Investment Fund Interests
[ ] Tenant-in-Common Securities
[ ] Mineral Property Securities
[ ] Other (Describe: _____)

10.   **Business Combination Transaction**

Is this offering being made in connection with a business combination transaction, such as a merger, acquisition or exchange offer?
⊙ Yes
⊙ No
Clarification of Response (if Necessary): _____

11.   **Minimum Investment**

---

[1] If the filer selects the Investment Company Act Section 3(c) checkbox, a pop-up or other feature will require the filer to select all claimed exclusions from the definition of "investment company" from among Sections 3(c)(1) through Section 3(c)(14) (except for Section 3(c)(8)).

Minimum investment accepted from any outside investor $_____

12.   **Sales Compensation**

Recipient	Recipient CRD Number	Associated Broker or Dealer	Broker or Dealer CRD Number	Street Address	State(s) of Solicitation
					(dropdown or other list selection feature)

    Add Recipient

13.   **Offering and Sales Amounts**
      Total Offering Amount $_____ or [ ] Indefinite
      Total Amount Sold $_____
              Total Remaining to be Sold $[auto subtract]_____ or [ ] Indefinite
      Clarification of Response (if Necessary): _____

14.   **Investors**
      [ ] Select if securities in the offering have been or may be sold to persons who do not
          qualify as accredited investors, and enter the number of such non-accredited investors
          who already have invested in the offering: _____

      Regardless whether securities in the offering have been or may be sold to persons who do
          not qualify as accredited investors, enter the total number of investors who already
          have invested in the offering: _____

15.   **Sales Commissions and Finders' Fees Expenses**
      Provide separately the amounts of sales commissions and finders' fees expenses, if any.
      If the amount of an expenditure is not known, provide an estimate and check the box next
      to the amount(s).

      Sales Commissions $_____ [ ] Estimate
      Finders' Fees $_____ [ ] Estimate
      Clarification of Response (if Necessary): _____

16.   **Use of Proceeds**
      Provide the amount of the gross proceeds of the offering that has been or is proposed to
      be used for payments to any of the persons required to be named as executive officers,
      directors or promoters in response to Item 3 above. If the amount is unknown, provide an
      estimate and check the box next to the amount.

      $_____ [ ] Estimate
      Clarification of Response (if Necessary): _____

Signature and Submission

Terms of Submission: Please verify the information you have entered and review the Terms of Submission below before signing and clicking SUBMIT below to file this notice.

Printable Version

In submitting this notice, each issuer named above is:

- Notifying the SEC and/or each State in which this notice is filed of the offering of securities described and undertaking to furnish them, upon written request in accordance with applicable law, the information furnished to offerees.[*]

- Irrevocably appointing each of the Secretary of the SEC and the Securities Administrator or other legally designated officer of the State in which the issuer maintains its principal place of business and any State in which this notice is filed, as its agents for service of process, and agreeing that these persons may accept service on its behalf, of any notice, process or pleading, and further agreeing that such service may be made by registered or certified mail, in any Federal or state action, administrative proceeding, or arbitration brought against the issuer in any place subject to the jurisdiction of the United States, if the action, proceeding or arbitration (a) arises out of any activity in connection with the offering of securities that is the subject of this notice, and (b) is founded, directly or indirectly, upon the provisions of: (i) the Securities Act of 1933, the Securities Exchange Act of 1934, the Trust Indenture Act of 1939, the Investment Company Act of 1940, or the Investment Advisers Act of 1940, or any rule or regulation under any of these statutes; or (ii) the laws of the State in which the issuer maintains its principal place of business or any State in which this notice is filed.

- Certifying that, if the issuer is claiming a Rule 505 exemption, the issuer is not disqualified from relying on Rule 505 for one of the reasons stated in Rule 505(b)(2)(iii).

Each issuer identified above has read this notice, knows the contents to be true, and has duly caused this notice to be signed on its behalf by the undersigned duly authorized person.

Signature

---

[*] This undertaking does not affect any limits Section 102(a) of the National Securities Markets Improvement Act of 1996 ("NSMIA") [Pub. L. No. 104-290, 110 Stat. 3416 (Oct. 11, 1996)] imposes on the ability of States to require information. As a result, if the securities that are the subject of this Form D are "covered securities" for purposes of NSMIA, whether in all instances or due to the nature of the offering that is the subject of this Form D, States cannot routinely require offering materials under this undertaking or otherwise and can require offering materials only to the extent NSMIA permits them to do so under NSMIA's preservation of their anti-fraud authority.

Signature: _____ Title: _____ Date: _____

By clicking on SUBMIT below, you are agreeing to the Terms of Submission above.

| **SUBMIT** |

Persons who respond to the collection of information contained in this form are not required to respond unless the form displays a currently valid OMB control number.

Instructions for Submitting Notice

General Instructions

- **Who must file:**

  - Each issuer of securities that sells its securities in reliance on an exemption provided in Regulation D or Section 4(6) of the Securities Act of 1933 must file this notice containing the information requested with the U.S. Securities and Exchange Commission (SEC) and with the state(s) requiring it. If more than one issuer has sold its securities in the same transaction, all issuers should be identified in one filing with the SEC, but some states may require a separate filing for each issuer or security sold.

- **When to file:**

  - An issuer must file a new notice with the SEC for each new offering of securities no later than 15 calendar days after the "date of first sale" of securities in the offering as explained in Instruction 7. For this purpose, the date of first sale is the date on which the first investor is irrevocably contractually committed to invest, which, depending on the terms and conditions of the contract, could be the date on which the issuer receives the investor's subscription agreement or check. An issuer may file the notice at any time before that if it has determined to make the offering. An issuer must file a new notice with each state that requires it at the time set by the state. For state filing information, go to www.NASAA.org. A

mandatory capital commitment call does not constitute a new offering, but is

made under the original offering, so no new Form D filing is required.

o An issuer may file an amendment to a previously filed notice at any time.

o An issuer must file an amendment to a previously filed notice for an offering:

- to correct a material mistake of fact or error in the previously filed notice,

    as soon as practicable after discovery of the mistake or error;

- to reflect a change in the information provided in the previously filed

    notice, except as provided below, as soon as practicable after the change;

    and

- annually, on or before the first anniversary of the most recent previously

    filed notice, if the offering is continuing at that time.

- **When amendment is not required:** An issuer is not required to file an amendment to a

previously filed notice to reflect a change that occurs after the offering terminates or a

change that occurs solely in the following information:

o the address or relationship to the issuer of a related person identified in response

    to Item 3;

o an issuer's revenues or aggregate net asset value;

o the minimum investment amount, if the change is an increase, or if the change,

    together with all other changes in that amount since the previously filed notice,

    does not result in a decrease of more than 10%;

o any address or state(s) of solicitation shown in response to Item 12;

- the total offering amount, if the change is a decrease, or if the change, together with all other changes in that amount since the previously filed notice, does not result in an increase of more than 10%;
- the amount of securities sold in the offering or the amount remaining to be sold;
- the number of non-accredited investors who have invested in the offering, as long as the change does not increase the number to more than 35;
- the total number of investors who have invested in the offering;
- the amount of sales commissions, finders' fees or use of proceeds for payments to executive officers, directors or promoters, if the change is a decrease, or if the change, together with all other changes in that amount since the previously filed notice, does not result in an increase of more than 10%.

- **Saturdays, Sundays and Holidays:** If the date on which a notice or an amendment to a previously filed notice is required to be filed falls on a Saturday, Sunday or holiday, the due date is the first business day following.

- **Amendment content:** An issuer that files an amendment to a previously filed notice must provide current information in response to all items of this Form D, regardless of why the amendment is filed.

- **How to File:** Issuers must file this notice with the SEC in electronic format. For state filing information, go to www.NASAA.org.

- **Filing Fee:** There is no federal filing fee. For information on state filing fees, go to www.NASAA.org.

- **Definitions of Terms:** Terms used but not defined in this form that are defined in Rule 405 and Rule 501 under the Securities Act of 1933, 17 CFR 230.405 and 230.501, have the meanings given to them in those rules.

Item-by-Item Instructions

1.   **Issuer's Identity.** Identify each legal entity issuing any securities being reported as being offered by entering its full name; any previous name used within the past five years; and its jurisdiction of incorporation or organization, type of legal entity, and year of incorporation or organization within the past five years or status as formed over five years ago or not yet formed. If more than one entity is issuing the securities, identify a primary issuer in the first fields shown and identify additional issuers in the fields that appear.

2.   **Principal Place of Business and Contact Information.** Enter a full street address of the issuer's principal place of business. Post office box numbers and "In care of" addresses are not acceptable. Enter a contact telephone number for the issuer. If you identified more than one issuer in response to Item 1, enter the requested information for the primary issuer you identified in response to that item and, at your option, for any or all of the other issuers you identified in the fields that appear.

3.   Related Persons. Enter the full name and address of each person having the specified relationships with any issuer and identify each relationship:

   - Each <u>executive officer</u> and <u>director</u> of the issuer and person performing similar functions (title alone is not determinative) for the issuer, such as the general and managing partners of partnerships and managing members of limited liability companies; and

   - Each person who has functioned directly or indirectly as a <u>promoter</u> of the issuer within the past five years of the later of the first sale of securities or the date upon which the Form D filing was required to be made.

If necessary to prevent the information supplied from being misleading, also provide a clarification in the space provided.

4. **Industry Group.** Select the issuer's industry group. If the issuer or issuers can be categorized in more than one industry group, select the industry group that most accurately reflects the use of the bulk of the proceeds of the offering. For purposes of this filing, use the ordinary dictionary and commonly understood meanings of the terms identifying the industry group.

5. **Issuer Size.**

- Revenue Range (for issuers that do not specify "Hedge Fund" or "Other Investment Fund" in response to Item 4): Enter the revenue range of the issuer or of all the issuers together for the most recently completed fiscal year available, or, if not in existence for a fiscal year, revenue range to date. Domestic SEC reporting companies should state revenues in accordance with Regulation S-X under the Securities Exchange Act of 1934. Domestic non-reporting companies should state revenues in accordance with U.S. Generally Accepted Accounting Principles (GAAP). Foreign issuers should calculate revenues in U.S. dollars and state them in accordance with U.S. GAAP, home country GAAP or International Financial Reporting Standards. If the issuer(s) declines to disclose its revenue range, enter "Decline to Disclose." If the issuer's(s')business is intended to produce revenue but did not, enter "No Revenues." If the business is not intended to produce revenue (for example, the business seeks asset appreciation only), enter "Not Applicable."

- Aggregate Net Asset Value (for issuers that specify "Hedge Fund" or "Other Investment Fund" in response to Item 4): Enter the aggregate net asset value range of the issuer or of all the issuers together as of the most recent practicable date. If the issuer(s) declines to disclose its aggregate net asset value range, enter "Decline to Disclose."

6. **Federal Exemption(s) and Exclusion(s) Claimed.** Select the provision(s) being claimed to exempt the offering and resulting sales from the federal registration requirements under the Securities Act of 1933 and, if applicable, to exclude the issuer from the definition of "investment company" under the Investment Company Act of 1940. Select "Rule 504(b)(1) (not (i), (ii) or (iii))" only if the issuer is relying on the exemption in the introductory sentence of Rule 504 for offers and sales that satisfy all the terms and conditions of Rules 501 and 502(a), (c) and (d).

7. **Type of Filing.** Indicate whether the issuer is filing a new notice or an amendment to a notice that was filed previously. If this is a new notice, enter the date of the first sale of securities in the offering or indicate that the first sale has "Yet to Occur." For this purpose, the date of first sale is the date on which the first investor is irrevocably contractually committed to invest, which, depending on the terms and conditions of the contract, could be the date on which the issuer receives the investor's subscription agreement or check.

8. **Duration of Offering.** Indicate whether the issuer intends the offering to last for more than one year.

9. **Type(s) of Securities Offered.** Select the appropriate type or types of securities offered as to which this notice is filed. If the securities are debt convertible into other securities, however, select "Debt" and any other appropriate types of securities except for "Equity." For purposes of this filing, use the ordinary dictionary and commonly understood meanings of these categories. For instance, equity securities would be securities that represent proportional ownership in an issuer, such as ordinary common and preferred

stock of corporations and partnership and limited liability company interests; debt

securities would be securities representing money loaned to an issuer that must be repaid

to the investor at a later date; pooled investment fund interests would be securities that

represent ownership interests in a pooled or collective investment vehicle; tenant-in-

common securities would be securities that include an undivided fractional interest in real

property other than a mineral property; and mineral property securities would be

securities that include an undivided interest in an oil, gas or other mineral property.

10. **Business Combination Transaction.** Indicate whether or not the offering is being made

in connection with a business combination, such as an exchange (tender) offer or a

merger, acquisition, or other transaction of the type described in paragraph (a)(1), (2) or

(3) of Rule 145 under the Securities Act of 1933. Do not include an exchange (tender)

offer for a class of the issuer's own securities. If necessary to prevent the information

supplied from being misleading, also provide a clarification in the space provided.

11. **Minimum Investment.** Enter the minimum dollar amount of investment that will be

accepted from any outside investor. If the offering provides a minimum investment

amount for outside investors that can be waived, provide the lowest amount below which

a waiver will not be granted. If there is no minimum investment amount, enter "0."

Investors will be considered outside investors if they are not employees, officers,

directors, general partners, trustees (where the issuer is a business trust), consultants,

advisors or vendors of the issuer, its parents, its majority owned subsidiaries, or majority

owned subsidiaries of the issuer's parent.

12. **Sales Compensation.** Enter the requested information for each person that has been or

will be paid directly or indirectly any commission or other similar compensation in cash

or other consideration in connection with sales of securities in the offering, including finders. Enter the CRD number for every person identified and any broker and dealer listed that has a CRD number. CRD numbers can be found at http://brokercheck.finra.org. A person that does not have a CRD number need not obtain one in order to be listed, and must be listed when required regardless of whether the person has a CRD number. In addition, enter the State(s) in which the named person has solicited or intends to solicit investors. If more than five persons to be listed are associated persons of the same broker or dealer, enter only the name of the broker or dealer, its CRD number and street address, and the State(s) in which the named person has solicited or intends to solicit investors.

13.   **Offering and Sales Amounts**. Enter the dollar amount of securities being offered under a claim of federal exemption identified in Item 6 above. Also enter the dollar amount of securities sold in the offering as of the filing date. Select the "Indefinite" box if the amount being offered is undetermined or cannot be calculated at the present time, such as if the offering includes securities to be acquired upon the exercise or exchange of other securities or property and the exercise price or exchange value is not currently known or knowable. If an amount is definite but difficult to calculate without unreasonable effort or expense, provide a good faith estimate. The total offering and sold amounts should include all cash and other consideration to be received for the securities, including cash to be paid in the future under mandatory capital commitments. In offerings for consideration other than cash, the amounts entered should be based on the issuer's good faith valuation of the consideration. If necessary to prevent the information supplied from being misleading, also provide a clarification in the space provided.

14. **Investors.** Indicate whether securities in the offering have been or may be sold to persons who do not qualify as accredited investors as defined in Rule 501(a) and provide the number of such investors who already have already invested in the offering. In addition, regardless whether securities in the offering have been or may be sold to persons who do not qualify as accredited investors, specify the total number of investors who already have invested.

15. **Sales Commission and Finders' Fees Expenses.** The information on sales commissions and finders' fees expenses may be given as subject to future contingencies.

16. **Use of Proceeds.** No additional instructions.

Signature and Submission. An individual who is a duly authorized representative of each issuer identified must sign, date and submit this notice for the issuer. The capacity in which the individual signed should be set forth in the "Title" space.

Each individual must:

- sign with a typed signature; and

- manually sign a signature page or other document authenticating, acknowledging or otherwise adopting the signature that appears in typed form in the Form D filing on or before the time of filing the Form D.

Each issuer must:

- retain the manually signed document signed on its behalf for five years; and

- provide a copy of the manually signed document to the SEC or its staff upon request.

<u>**Entity Type (for Item 1)**</u>

[ ] Corporation
[ ] Limited Partnership
[ ] Limited Liability Company
[ ] General Partnership
[ ] Business Trust

[ ] Other (Specify)

Year of Incorporation/Organization (for Item 1)

[ ] Yet to Be Formed
[ ] Within Last Five Years (Specify Year)
[ ] Over Five Years Ago

Industry Groups (for Item 4)

[ ] Agriculture

Banking & Financial Services

       [ ] Commercial Banking
       [ ] Insurance
       [ ] Investing
       [ ] Investment Banking
       [ ] Pooled Investment Fund*
          [ ] Hedge Fund
          [ ] Private Equity Fund
          [ ] Venture Capital Fund
          [ ] Other Investment Fund
       [ ] Other Banking & Financial Services

[ ] Business Services

Energy

       [ ] Coal Mining
       [ ] Electric Utilities
       [ ] Energy Conservation
       [ ] Environmental Services
       [ ] Oil & Gas
       [ ] Other Energy

Health Care

       [ ] Biotechnology
       [ ] Health Insurance
       [ ] Hospitals & Physicians

---

* If the Pooled Investment Fund checkbox is selected, pop-ups or other features also will require the filer to select one of the lower level checkboxes designating a specific type of investment fund and select a "yes" or "no" checkbox as to whether the filer is registered as an investment company under the Investment Company Act of 1940. If the "Hedge Fund" or "Other Investment Fund" option is selected, the filer will be asked to specify its aggregate net asset value range or to "Decline to Disclose" that value or specify that the information request is "Not Applicable."

[ ] Pharmaceuticals
[ ] Other Health Care

[ ] Manufacturing

Real Estate

[ ] Commercial
[ ] Construction
[ ] REITS & Finance
[ ] Residential
[ ] Other Real Estate

[ ] Retailing

[ ] Restaurants

Technology

[ ] Computers
[ ] Telecommunications
[ ] Other Technology

Travel

[ ] Airlines & Airports
[ ] Lodging & Conventions
[ ] Tourism & Travel Services
[ ] Other Travel

[ ] Other

[¶ 8891]

FORM ID

[As last amended in Release No. 33-9013, effective March 16, 2009, 74 F.R. 10836.]

United States
Securities and Exchange Commission
Washington, D.C. 20549

OMB APPROVAL

OMB Number: 3235-0328

Expires: April 30, 2009

Estimated average burden
hours per response: . . .0.15

FORM ID

UNIFORM APPLICATION FOR ACCESS CODES TO FILE ON EDGAR

PART I — APPLICATION FOR ACCESS CODES TO FILE ON EDGAR

Name of applicant (applicant's name as specified in its charter, except, if individual, last name, first name, middle name, suffix (e.g., "Jr.")

Mailing Address or Post Office Box No.

City   State or Country   Zip

Telephone number (Include Area and, if Foreign, Country Code) (   )

Applicant is (see definitions in the General Instructions)

☐ Filer   ☐ Filing Agent   ☐ Training Agent   ☐ Transfer Agent   ☐ Individual (if you check this box, you must also check either Filer, Filing Agent, Training Agent or Transfer Agent box)

PART II — FILER INFORMATION (To be completed only by filers that are not individuals)

Filer's Tax Number or Federal Identification Number (Do Not Enter a Social Security Number)

Doing Business As

Foreign Name (if Foreign Issuer Filer and applicable)

Primary Business Address or Post Office Box No. (if different from mailing address)

City   State or County   Zip

State of Incorporation   Fiscal Year End (mm/yy)

PART III — CONTACT INFORMATION (To be completed by all applicants)

Person to receive EDGAR Information, Inquiries and Access Codes

---

Telephone Number (Include Area and, if foreign, Country Code) (   )

Mailing Address or Post Office Box No. (if different from applicant's mailing address)

City   State or Country   Zip

E-Mail Address

PART IV — ACCOUNT INFORMATION (To be completed by filers and filing agents only)

Person to receive SEC Account Information and Billing Invoices

Telephone Number (Include Area and, if Foreign, Country Code) (   )

Mailing Address or Post Office Box No. (if different from applicant's mailing address)

City   State or Country   Zip

PART V — SIGNATURE (To be Completed by all Applicants)

Signature: Type or Print Name:

Position or Title: Date:

Intentional misstatements or omissions of facts constitute federal criminal violations. See 18 U.S.C. 1001.

Section 19(a) of the Securities Act of 1933 (15 U.S.C. 77s(a)), sections 13(a) and 23(a) of the Securities Exchange Act of 1934 (15 U.S.C. 78m(a) and 78w(a)), section 319 of the Trust Indenture Act of 1939 (15 U.S.C. 77sss), and sections 30 and 38 of the Investment Company Act of 1940 (15 U.S.C. 80a-29 and 80a-37) authorize solicitation of this information. We will use this information to assign system identification to filers, filing agents, and training agents. This will allow the Commission to identify persons sending electronic submissions and grant secure access to the EDGAR system.

SEC 2084 (05-06) Previous form obsolete

Persons who potentially are to respond to the collection of information contained in this form are not required to respond unless the form displays a currently valid OMB control number.

FORM ID GENERAL INSTRUCTIONS

USING AND PREPARING FORM ID

Form ID must be filed by registrants, third party filers, or their agents, to whom the Commission previously has not assigned a Central Index Key (CIK) code, to request the following access codes to permit filing on EDGAR:

- Central Index Key (CIK) - The CIK uniquely identifies each filer, filing agent, and training agent. We assign the CIK at the time you make an initial application. You may not change this code. The CIK is a public number.

- CIK Confirmation Code (CCC) - You will use the CCC in the header of your filings in conjunction with your CIK to ensure that you authorized the filing.

- Password (PW) - The PW allows you to log onto the EDGAR system, submit filings, and change your CCC.

- Password Modification Authorization Code (PMAC) - The PMAC allows you to change your password.

An applicant must file the information required by this form in electronic format via the Commission's EDGAR Filer Management website. Please see Regulation S-T (17 CFR Part 232) and the EDGAR Filer Manual for instructions on how to file electronically, including how to use the access codes.

The applicant must complete the Form ID electronic filing by also submitting to the Commission a copy of a notarized paper "authenticating" document. The authenticating document must include the information required to be included in the Form ID filing, be manually signed by the applicant over the applicant's typed signature, and confirm the authenticity of the Form ID filing. Applicants may fulfill the authenticating document requirement by making a copy of the applicant's electronic Form ID filing, adding the necessary confirming language, signing it, and having the signature notarized.

If the applicant has prepared the authenticating document before making its electronic Form ID filing, it may submit the document as an uploaded Portable Document Format (PDF) attachment to the electronic filing. An applicant also may submit the authenticating document by faxing it to the Commission at (202) 504-2474 or (703) 914-4240 within two business days before or after its electronic Form ID filing. If submitted by fax after the electronic Form ID filing, the authenticating document must contain the accession number assigned to the electronic Form ID filing. If the fax is not received timely, the Form ID filing and application for access codes will not be processed, and the applicant will receive an e-mail message at the contact e-mail address included in the Form ID filing informing the applicant of the failure to process and providing further guidance. The message will state why the application was not processed.

For assistance with technical questions about electronic filing, call Filer Support at (202) 551-8900. For assistance with questions about the EDGAR rules, Division of Corporation Finance filers may call the Office of Information Technology at (202) 551-3600; and Division of Investment Management filers may call the IM EDGAR Inquiry Line at (202) 551-6989.

You must complete all items in any parts that apply to you. If any item in any part does not apply to you, please leave it blank.

PART I—APPLICANT INFORMATION (to be completed by all applicants)

Provide the applicant's name in English.

Please check one of the boxes to indicate whether you will be sending electronic submissions as a filer, filing agent, or training agent. Mark only one of these boxes per application. If you are an individual, however, also mark the "Individual" box.

- "Filer" - Any individual or entity on whose behalf an electronic filing is made.

- "Filing Agent" - A financial printer, law firm, or other party, which will be using these access codes to send a filing or portion of a filing on behalf of a filer.

- "Training Agent" - Any individual or entity that will be sending only test filings in conjunction with training other persons.

- "Transfer Agent" - Any individual or entity planning to register as a Transfer Agent on whose behalf an electronic filing is made.

- "Individual" - A natural person.

PART II—FILER INFORMATION (to be completed only by filers that are not individuals)

The filer's tax or federal identification number is the number issued by the Internal Revenue Service. This section does not apply to individuals. Accordingly, do not enter a Social Security number. If an investment company filer is organized as a series company, the investment company may use the tax or federal identification number of any one of its constituent series. Issuers that have applied for but not yet received their tax or federal identification number and foreign issuers that do not have a tax or federal identification number must include all zeroes. A "foreign issuer" is an entity so defined by the Securities Act of 1933 (15 U.S.C. 77a *et seq.*) Rule 405 (17 CFR 230.405) and the Securities Exchange Act of 1934 (15 U.S.C. 78a *et seq.*) Rule 3b-4(b) (17 CFR 240.3b-4(b)). Foreign issuers should include their country of organization.

A foreign issuer filer must provide its "doing business as" name in the language of the name under which it does business and must provide its foreign language name, if any, in the space so marked.

If the filer's fiscal year does not end on the same date each year (*e.g.*, falls on the last Saturday in December), the filer must enter the date the current fiscal year will end.

PART III—CONTACT INFORMATION (to be completed by all applicants)

In this section, identify the individual who should receive the access codes and other EDGAR-related information. Please include an e-mail address that will become your default notification address for EDGAR filings; it will be stored in the Company Contact Information on the EDGAR Database. EDGAR will send all subsequent filing notifications automatically to that address. You can have one e-mail address in the EDGAR Company Contact Information. For information on including additional e-mail addresses on a per filing basis, refer to Volume 1, Section 3.2.2 of the EDGAR Filer Manual.

PART IV—ACCOUNT INFORMATION (to be completed by filers and filing agents only)

Identify in this section the individual who should receive account information and/or billing invoices from us. We will use this information to process electronically fee payments and billings. If the address changes, update it via the EDGAR filing Web site, or your account statements may be returned to us as undeliverable.

PART V—SIGNATURE (to be completed by all applicants)

If the applicant is a corporation, partnership, trust or other entity, state the capacity in which the representative individual, who must be duly authorized, signs the Form on behalf of the applicant.

If the applicant is an individual, the applicant must sign the Form.

If another person signs on behalf of the representative individual or the individual applicant, confirm the authority of the other person to sign in writing in an electronic attachment to the Form. The confirming statement need only indicate that the representative individual or individual applicant authorizes and designates the named person or persons to file the Form on behalf of the applicant and state the duration of the authorization.

[¶ 8901]   **FORM SE**

[As last amended in Release No. 33-8876, effective February 4, 2008, 73 F.R. 934.]

UNITED STATES SECURITIES AND EXCHANGE COMMISSION

Washington, D.C. 20549

FORM SE

FORM FOR SUBMISSION OF PAPER FORMAT EXHIBITS BY ELECTRONIC FILERS

_____   _____

Exact name of registrant as specified in charter   Registrant CIK Number

_____   _____

Electronic report, schedule or registration statement of which the
documents are a part   SEC filer number, if available

S-_____   _____

(Series identifier(s) and names(s), if applicable; add more lines as needed)

C-_____   _____

(Class (contract) identifier(s) and names(s), if applicable; add more lines as needed)

_____

Report period (if applicable)

_____

Name of person filing this exhibit (if other than the registrant)

Identify the provision of Regulation S-T (§ 232 of this chapter) under which this exhibit is being filed in paper (check *only* one):

____ Rule 201 (Temporary Hardship Exemption)

____ Rule 202 (Continuing Hardship Exemption)

____ Rule 311 (Permitted Paper Exhibit)

SIGNATURES

Filings Made by the Registrant:

   The registrant has duly caused this form to be signed on its behalf by the undersigned, duly authorized, in the City of _____, State of _____, on _____ 20___.

_____

Registrant

By: _____

(Name)

_____

(Title)

Filings Made by Person Other than the Registrant:

   After reasonable inquiry and to the best of my knowledge and belief, I certify on _____ 20___, that the information set forth in this statement is true and complete.

   By: _____

(Name)

_____

(Title)

FORM SE GENERAL INSTRUCTIONS

1. Rule as to Use of Form SE.

A. Electronic filers must use this form to submit any paper format exhibit under the Securities Act of 1933, the Securities Exchange Act of 1934, the Public Utility Holding Company Act of 1935, the Trust Indenture Act of 1939, or the Investment Company Act of 1940, *provided that* the submission of such exhibit in paper is permitted under Rule 201, 202, or 311 of Regulation S-T (§§ 232.201, 232.202, or 232.311 of this chapter).

B. Electronic filers are subject to Regulation S-T (Part 232 of this chapter) and the EDGAR Filer Manual. We direct your attention to the General Rules and Regulations under the Securities Act of 1933, the Securities Exchange Act of 1934, the Public Utility Holding Company Act of 1935, the Trust Indenture Act of 1939, the Investment Company Act of 1940, and the electronic filing rules and regulations under these Acts.

2. Preparation of Form SE.

Submit in paper format four complete copies of both the Form SE and the exhibit filed under cover of the Form SE.

3. Filing of Form SE.

A. If you are filing the exhibit under a temporary hardship exemption, submit the exhibit and a Form TH (§§ 239.65, 249.447, 259.604, 269.10, and 274.404 of this chapter) under cover of this Form SE no later than one business day after the date on which the exhibit was to have been filed electronically. See Rule 201 of Regulation S-T (§ 232.201 of this chapter).

B. If you are filing the exhibit under a continuing hardship exemption under Rule 202 of Regulation S-T (§ 232.202 of this chapter), or as allowed by Rule 311 of Regulation S-T (§ 232.311 of this chapter), you may file the exhibit in paper under cover of Form SE up to six business days before or on the date of filing of the electronic format document to which it relates; you may not file the exhibit after the filing date of the electronic document to which it relates. Exhibits filed under a continuing hardship exemption must include the legend required by Rule 202(c) (§ 232.202(c) of this chapter). If you submit the paper exhibit in this manner, you will have satisfied any requirements that you file the exhibit with, provide the document with, or have the document accompany the electronic filing. This instruction does not affect any requirement that you deliver or furnish the information in the exhibit to persons other than the Commission.

C. Identify the exhibit being filed. Attach to the Form SE the paper format exhibit and an exhibit index if required by Item 601 of Regulation S-K (§ 229.601 of this chapter).

4. Signatures.

A. Submit one copy signed by each person on whose behalf you are submitting the form or by that person's authorized representative. If the form is signed by the authorized representative of a person (other than an executive officer or general partner), file with the form the evidence of the authority of the representative to sign on behalf of such person, except that you may incorporate by reference a power of attorney for this purpose that is already on file with the Commission.

B. Signatures may be in typed form rather than manual format.

[¶ 8911]   **FORM TH**

[As last amended in Release No. 33-8590, effective February 6, 2006, 70 F.R. 43558.]

UNITED STATES SECURITIES AND EXCHANGE COMMISSION

Washington, DC

FORM TH NOTIFICATION OF RELIANCE ON TEMPORARY HARDSHIP EXEMPTION

Report, schedule or registration statement to which   SEC file number(s) under which filing made
the hardship exemption relates (give period of   (Required, if assigned)
report, if applicable)

CIK of filer or subject company CIK, as applicable

Name of Filer or subject company, as applicable

Filed-by CIK (for subject company filings only)

Name of "filed-by" entity (for subject company filings only)
S-

(Series identifier(s) and names(s), if applicable; add more lines as needed)
C-

(Class (contract) identifier(s) and names(s), if applicable; add more lines as needed)

Part I—Filer Information

Full Name of Filer

Address of Principal Office

Street and Number

City, State, and Postal Code; Country, if other than US

Part II—Information Relating to the Hardship

Furnish the following information:

1. A description of the nature and extent of the temporary technical difficulties experienced by the electronic filer in attempting to submit the document in electronic format.

2. A description of the extent to which the electronic filer has successfully submitted documents previously in electronic format with the same hardware and software, in test of required filings.

3. A description of the burden and expense involved to employ alternative means to submit the electronic submission in a timely manner.

4. Any other reasons an exemption is warranted.

Part III—Representation of Intent to Submit Confirming Electronic Copy. The filer shall include a representation that it shall cause to be filed a confirming electronic copy of the document filed in paper under cover of the Form TH and that its filing will be in accordance with Rule 201(b) of Regulation S-T (§ 232.201(b) of this chapter) and appropriately designated as a "confirming electronic copy" in accordance with the requirements of the EDGAR Filer Manual.

¶8911   Form TH

Part IV—Contact Person

Name, telephone number, and e-mail address of person to contact in regard to this filing under Form TH:

_____   (___)_____   _____

Name   (Area code) Phone number   e-mail address

Part V—Signature

_____

Name of Filer (if registrant, name as it appears in charter) has caused this Form TH to be signed on its behalf by the undersigned, being duly authorized:

Date: _____   By:_____

Instruction: This form my be signed by an executive officer of the registrant or by any other duly authorized representative.

has caused this notification to be signed on its behalf by the undersigned, being duly authorized:

Date: _____ By: _____

Instruction: This form may be signed by an executive officer of the registrant or by any other duly authorized representative. Signatures may be in typed form rather than in manual format.

GENERAL INSTRUCTIONS

1. Rule 201(a) of Regulation S-T (§ 232.201(a) of this chapter) requires an electronic filer relying on a temporary hardship exemption to file this Form TH in addition to filing a paper copy of a document otherwise required to be filed in electronic format.

2. Four signed copies of this Form TH must accompany the paper format document being filed pursuant to Rule 201; filers must file under Form TH within one business day after the date upon which the filer was originally to file the document electronically.

3. Signatures to the paper format document being filed with Form TH may be in typed form rather than in manual format. See Rule 302 of Regulation S-T (§ 232.302 of this chapter). Filers must satisfy all other requirements relating to paper format filings, including number of copies to be filed.

[¶ 8921]　　　　　　FORM CB

[As last amended in Release No. 34-55146A, effective April 1, 2008, 73 F.R. 17809 (technical correction).]

UNITED STATES SECURITIES AND EXCHANGE COMMISSION

Washington, D.C. 20549

FORM CB

TENDER OFFER/RIGHTS OFFERING NOTIFICATION FORM (AMENDMENT NO. ———)

Please place an X in the box(es) to designate the appropriate rule provision(s) relied upon to file this Form:

Securities Act Rule 801 (Rights Offering) ☐

Securities Act Rule 802 (Exchange Offer) ☐

Exchange Act Rule 13e-4(h)(8) (Issuer Tender Offer) ☐

Exchange Act Rule 14d-1(c) (Third Party Tender Offer) ☐

Exchange Act Rule 14e-2(d) (Subject Company Response) ☐

Filed or submitted in paper if permitted by Regulation S-T Rule 101(b)(8) ☐

Note: Regulation S-T Rule 101(b)(8) only permits the filing or submission of a Form CB in paper by a party that is not subject to the reporting requirements of Section 13 or 15(d) of the Exchange Act.

. . . .
(Name of Subject Company)

. . . .
(Translation of Subject Company's Name into English (if applicable))

. . . .
(Jurisdiction of Subject Company's Incorporation or Organization)

. . . .
(Name of Person(s) Furnishing Form)

. . . .
(Title of Class of Subject Securities)

. . . .
(CUSIP Number of Class of Securities (if applicable))

. . . .
(Name, Address (including zip code) and Telephone Number (including area code) of Person(s) Authorized to Receive Notices and Communications on Behalf of Subject Company)

. . . .
(Date Tender Offer/Rights Offering Commenced)

GENERAL INSTRUCTIONS

I. *Eligibility Requirements for Use of Form CB*

A. Use this Form to furnish information pursuant to Rules 13e-4(h)(8), 14d-1(c) and 14e-2(d) under the Securities Exchange Act of 1934 ("Exchange Act"), and Rules 801 and 802 under the Securities Act of 1933 ("Securities Act").

Instructions:

1. For the purposes of this Form, the term "subject company" means the issuer of the securities in a rights offering and the company whose securities are sought in a tender offer.

2. For the purposes of this Form, the term "tender offer" includes both cash and securities tender offers.

B. The information and documents furnished on this Form are not deemed "filed" with the Commission or otherwise subject to the liabilities of Section 18 of the Exchange Act.

II. *Instructions for Submitting Form*

A.(1) If the party filing or submitting the Form CB has reporting obligations under Exchange Act Section 13 or 15(d), Regulation S-T Rule 101(a)(1)(vi) (17 CFR 232.101(a)(1)(vi)) requires the submission of the Form CB in electronic format via the Commission's Electronic Data Gathering and Retrieval System (EDGAR) in accordance with the EDGAR rules set forth in Regulation S-T (17 CFR Part 232). For assistance with technical questions about EDGAR or to request an access code, call the EDGAR Filer Support Office at (202) 551-8900. For assistance with the EDGAR rules, call the Office of EDGAR and Information Analysis at (202) 551-3610.

(2) If the party filing or submitting the Form CB is not an Exchange Act reporting company, Regulation S-T Rule 101(b)(8) (17 CFR 232.101(b)(8)) permits the submission of the Form CB either via EDGAR or in paper. When filing or submitting the Form CB in electronic format, either voluntarily or as a mandated EDGAR filer, a party must also file or submit on EDGAR all home jurisdiction documents required by Parts I and II of this Form, except as provided by the Note following paragraph (2) of Part II.

(3) A party may also file a Form CB in paper under a hardship exemption provided by Regulation S-T Rule 201 or 202 (17 CFR 232.201 or 232.202). When submitting a Form CB in paper under a hardship exemption, a party must provide the legend required by Regulation S-T Rule 201(a)(2) or 202(c) (17 CFR 232.201(a)(2) or 232.202(c)) on the cover page of the Form CB.

(4) If filing the Form CB in paper in accordance with Rule 101(b)(8) or a hardship exemption, you must furnish two copies of this Form and any amendment to the Form (see Part I, Item 1.(b)), including all exhibits and any other paper or document furnished as part of the Form, to the Commission at its principal office. You must bind, staple or otherwise compile each copy in one or more parts without stiff covers. You must make the binding on the side or stitching margin in a manner that leaves the reading matter legible.

B. When submitting the Form CB in electronic format, the persons specified in Part IV must provide signatures in accordance with Regulation S-T Rule 302 (17 CFR 232.302). When submitting the Form CB in paper, the persons specified in Part IV must sign the original of the Form and any amendments. You must conform any unsigned copies. The specified persons may provide typed or facsimile signatures in accordance with Securities Act Rule 402(e) (17 CFR 230.402(e)) or Exchange Act Rule 12b-11(d) (17 CFR 240.12b-11(d)) as long as the filer retains copies of signatures manually signed by each of the specified persons for five years.

C. You must furnish this Form to the Commission no later than the next business day after the disclosure documents submitted with this Form are published or otherwise disseminated in the subject company's home jurisdiction.

D. If filing in paper, in addition to any internal numbering you may include, sequentially number the signed original of the Form and any amendments by handwritten, typed, printed or other legible form of notation from the first page of the document through the last page of the document and any exhibits or attachments. Further, you must set forth the total number of pages contained in a numbered original on the first page of the document.

III. *Special Instructions for Complying with Form CB*

Under Sections 3(b), 7, 8, 10, 19 and 28 of the Securities Act of 1933, and Sections 12, 13, 14, 23 and 36 of the Exchange Act of 1934 and the rules and regulations adopted under those Sections, the Commission is authorized to solicit the information required to be supplied by this form by certain entities conducting a tender offer, rights offer or business combination for the securities of certain issuers.

Disclosure of the information specified in this form is mandatory. We will use the information for the primary purposes of assuring that the offeror is entitled to use the Form and that investors have information about the transaction to enable them to make informed investment decisions. We will make this Form a matter of public record. Therefore, any information given will be available for inspection by any member of the public.

Because of the public nature of the information, the Commission can use it for a variety of purposes. These purposes include referral to other governmental authorities or securities self-regulatory organizations for investigatory purposes or in connection with litigation involving the Federal securities laws or other civil, criminal or regulatory statutes or provisions.

PART I—INFORMATION SENT TO SECURITY HOLDERS

Item 1. *Home Jurisdiction Documents*

(a) You must attach to this Form the entire disclosure document or documents, including any amendments thereto, in English, that you have delivered to holders of securities or published in the subject company's home jurisdiction that are required to be disseminated to U.S. security holders or published in the United States. The Form need not include any documents incorporated by reference into those disclosure document(s) and not published or distributed to holders of securities.

(b) Furnish any amendment to a furnished document or documents to the Commission under cover of this Form. Indicate on the cover page the number of the amendment.

Item 2. *Informational Legends*

You may need to include legends on the outside cover page of any offering document(s) used in the transaction. See Rules 801(b) and 802(b).

Note to Item 2. If you deliver the home jurisdiction document(s) through an electronic medium, the required legends must be presented in a manner reasonably calculated to draw attention to them.

PART II—INFORMATION NOT REQUIRED TO BE SENT TO SECURITY HOLDERS

The exhibits specified below must be furnished as part of the Form, but need not be sent to security holders unless sent to security holders in the home jurisdiction. Letter or number all exhibits for convenient reference.

(1) Furnish to the Commission either an English translation or English summary of any reports or information that, in accordance with the requirements of the home jurisdiction, must be made publicly available in connection with the transaction but need not be disseminated to security holders. Any English summary submitted must meet the requirements of Regulation S-T Rule 306(a) (17 CFR 232.306(a)) if submitted electronically or of Securities Act Rule 403(c)(3) (17 CFR 230.403(c)(3)) or Exchange Act Rule 12b-12(d)(3) (17 CFR 240.12b-12(d)(3)) if submitted in paper.

(2) Furnish copies of any documents incorporated by reference into the home jurisdiction document(s).

Note to paragraphs (1) and (2) of Part II: In accordance with Regulation S-T Rule 311(f) (17 CFR 232.311(f)), a party may submit a paper copy under cover of Form SE (17 CFR 239.64, 249.444, 259.603, 269.8, and 274.403) of an unabridged foreign language document when submitting an English summary in electronic format under paragraph (1) of this Part or when furnishing a foreign language document that has been incorporated by reference under paragraph (2) of this Part.

(3) If any of the persons specified in Part IV has signed the Form CB under a power of attorney, a party submitting the Form CB in electronic format must include a copy of the power of attorney signed in accordance with Regulation S-T Rule 302 (17 CFR 232.302). A party submitting the Form CB in paper must also include a copy of the signed power of attorney.

PART III—CONSENT TO SERVICE OF PROCESS

(1) When this Form is furnished to the Commission, the person furnishing this Form (if a non-U.S. person) must also file with the Commission a written irrevocable consent and power of attorney on Form F-X.

(2) Promptly communicate any change in the name or address of an agent for service to the Commission by amendment of the Form F-X.

PART IV—SIGNATURES

(1) Each person (or its authorized representative) on whose behalf the Form is submitted must sign the Form. If a person's authorized representative signs, and the authorized representative is someone other than an executive officer or general partner, provide evidence of the representative's authority with the Form.

¶8921   Form CB

(2) Type or print the name and any title of each person who signs the Form beneath his or her signature.

After due inquiry and to the best of my knowledge and belief, I certify that the information set forth in this statement is true, complete and correct.

_____

(Signature)

_____

(Name and Title)

(Date)

INDUSTRY GUIDES

INDUSTRY GUIDES

TABLE OF CONTENTS

INDUSTRY GUIDES

SECURITIES ACT INDUSTRY GUIDES

[¶ 12,001]   Guide 1—Disclosure by Electric and Gas Utilities

Guide 1. [Removed and reserved in Release No. 33-7300, May 31, 1996, effective July 15, 1996, 61 F.R. 30397.]

≫→ *Caution: Guide 2 has been removed by Release No. 33-8995, effective January 1, 2010, 74 F.R. 2157. The oil and gas disclosure requirements have been revised and codified into Regulation S-K at Subpart 229.1200.*

[¶ 12,011]   Guide 2—Disclosure of Oil and Gas Operations

Guide 2. If oil and gas operations are material to the registrant's and its subsidiaries' business operations or financial position, the disclosure specified in this Guide should be included under appropriate captions (in tabular form, if practicable, and with cross references, where applicable, to related information disclosed in financial statements). *Provided however,* That limited partnerships or joint ventures that conduct, operate, manage, or report upon oil and gas drilling or income programs, that acquire properties either for drilling and production, or for production of oil, gas, or geothermal steam or water, need not include such disclosure and, *Provided further,* That any registrant qualifying for the exemption provided in § 210.4-10(k) of Regulation S-X need not provide any such information.

Note—Limited partnerships exempted from the disclosure required in this Guide by the first proviso above remain subject to disclosure requirements of § 210.4-10(k) of Regulation S-X. See discussion in Accounting Series Release No. 257 (Dec. 19, 1978) [43 FR 60404]; and Staff Accounting Bulletin No. 40, Topic 6(d)(3)(c) [17 CFR 211] (Jan. 23, 1981).

[Item 1 deleted. CCH.]

2. RESERVES REPORTED TO OTHER AGENCIES

Any estimates of total, proved net oil or gas reserves filed with or included in reports to any other Federal authority or agency since the beginning of the last fiscal year (or a statement that there were none), together with the name of the authority or agency and an explanation of the reasons for differences, if any, between such estimates and the estimates included in the document. This requirement should not apply if the difference between the total reserve estimate included in the Commission filing and the total reserve estimate filed with the Federal authority or agency does not exceed five percent. However, a statement that the difference does not exceed five percent should be included.

3. PRODUCTION

A. For each of the last three fiscal years by the same geographic areas for which production data are required by Statement of Financial Accounting Standards (SFAS) No. 69.

(i) the average sales price (including transfers) per unit of oil produced and of gas produced;

(ii) the average production cost (lifting cost) per unit of production.

B. *Instructions.* Generally, net production should include only production that is owned by the registrant and produced to its interest, less royalties and production due others. However, in special situations (e.g., foreign production) net production before royalties may be provided, if more appropriate. If "net before royalty" production figures are furnished, the change from the usage of "net production" should be noted.

Any part of natural gas liquids production obtained through or from processing plant ownership rather than through leasehold ownership should be reported separately, if material.

Production of natural gas should include only marketable production of gas on an "as sold" basis. Production will include dry, residue, and wet gas, depending on whether liquids have been extracted before the registrant passed title. Flared gas, injected gas and gas consumed in operations should be omitted. Recovered gas-lift gas and reproduced gas should not be included until sold.

The transfer price of oil and gas produced should be determined in accordance with SFAS No. 69.

The average production cost per unit of production should be computed using production costs disclosed pursuant to SFAS No. 69. Units of production should be expressed in common units of production with oil or gas converted to a common unit of measure on the basis used in computing amortization (relative energy content or gross revenue method). *See* § 210.4-10(e)(3) or § 210.4-10(i)(3)(iii) of Regulation S-X, whichever is appropriate.

4. PRODUCTIVE WELLS AND ACREAGE.

A. As of a reasonably current date or as of the end of the most recent fiscal year, the total gross and net productive wells, expressed separately for oil and gas, and the total gross and net developed acres (i.e., acres spaced or assignable to productive wells) by the geographic areas for which production data are required pursuant to paragraph 3 of this Guide.

B. *Instructions.* For purposes of this paragraph, one or more completions in the same bore hole should be counted as one well. A footnote should disclose the number of wells with multiple completions. If one of the multiple completions in a given well is an oil completion, the well should be classified as an oil well.

A gross well or acre is a well or acre in which a working interest is owned. The number of gross wells is the total number of wells in which a working interest is owned.

A net well or acre is deemed to exist when the sum of fractional ownership working interests in gross wells or acres equals one. The number of net well or acres is the sum of the fractional working interests owned in gross wells or acres expressed as whole numbers and fractions thereof.

For those unusual situations in which gross and net data cannot be supplied, alternative disclosure should be furnished that adequately describes the registrant's productive wells and developed acreage.

Productive wells are producing wells and wells capable of production.

5. UNDEVELOPED ACREAGE

As of a reasonably current date or as of the end of the most recent fiscal year, the amounts of undeveloped acreage, both leases and concessions, if any, expressed in both gross and net acres by appropriate geographic area, together with an indication of acreage concentrations, and, if material, the minimum remaining terms of leases and concessions. Undeveloped acreage is considered to be those lease acres on which wells have not been drilled or completed to a point that would permit the production of commercial quantities of oil and gas regardless of whether or not such acreage contains proved reserves. Undeveloped acreage should not be confused with undrilled acreage Held by Production under the terms of a lease.

6. DRILLING ACTIVITY

A. For each of the last three fiscal years by appropriate geographic areas:

(i) the number of net productive and dry exploratory wells drilled; and

(ii) the number of net productive and dry development wells drilled.

B. *Instructions.* A dry well (hole) is an exploratory or a development well found to be incapable of producing either oil or gas in sufficient quantities to justify completion as an oil or gas well.

A Productive well is an exploratory or a development well that is not a dry well.

The number of wells drilled refers to the number of wells (hole) completed at any time during the fiscal years, regardless of when drilling was initiated.

The term "completion" refers to the installation of permanent equipment for the production of oil or gas, or, in the case of a dry hole, to the reporting of abandonment to the appropriate agency.

7. PRESENT ACTIVITIES

Present activities, such as the number of wells in process of drilling (including wells temporarily suspended), waterfloods in process of installation, pressure maintenance operations, and any other related operations of material importance by appropriate geographic areas. This description of present activities should be provided for an "as of" date as close to the date of filing the document as reasonably possible or as of the end of the most recent fiscal year. The disclosure of wells in the process of being drilled should include only those wells actually being drilled at the "as of" date and should be expressed in terms of both gross and net wells. The disclosure should not include wells planned but not commenced unless there are factors which make such information material.

8. DELIVERY COMMITMENTS

If the registrant is obligated to provide a fixed and determinable quantity of oil or gas in the future under existing contracts or agreements, material information concerning the estimated availability of oil and gas from any principal sources.

A. Such information should be furnished as to current and future reserves and supplies, and should:

(i) identify the principal sources of oil and gas to be relied upon and the total available amounts expected to be received from each principal source and from all sources combined;

(ii) disclose the total quantities of oil and gas which are subject to delivery commitments; and

(iii) indicate steps taken to insure available reserves and supplies are sufficient to meet such commitments. Such future information should be provided for an appropriate period of one to three years.

B. The term "availability" is used herein to mean an estimate of that quantity of oil and gas which can be produced from current proved developed reserves using presently installed equipment under existing economic and operating conditions and an estimate of amounts that can be delivered to the registrant under long-term contracts or agreements on a per-day, per-month or per-year basis.

C. The registrant should develop disclosure based upon the facts and circumstances of its particular situation, including disclosure by appropriate geographic areas. Such disclosure should be in a form understandable to investors and should include, but not be limited to, a description of the following factors:

(i) significant supplies dedicated or contracted to the registrant;

(ii) any significant amounts of reserves or supplies subject to priorities or curtailments which may affect quantities delivered to certain classes of customers, such as customers receiving services under low priority and interruptible contracts;

(iii) any priority allocations or price limitations imposed by Federal or State regulatory agencies, as well as other factors beyond the control of the registrant which may affect the ability of the registrant to meet its contractual obligations (detailed discussions of price regulation need not be furnished);

(iv) any other factors beyond the control of the registrant, such as other parties having control over the drilling of new wells, competition for the acquisition of reserves and supplies, and the availability of foreign reserves and supplies which may affect the ability of the registrant to acquire additional reserves and supplies, or to maintain or increase the availability of reserves and supplies; and

(v) any impact on the registrant's earnings and financing needs resulting from its inability to meet short or long-term contractual obligations. See Item 303 of Regulation S-K.

D. If within the last three years the registrant has been unable to meet any significant delivery commitments, describe the circumstances concerning such events and the impact on the registrant.

[As last amended in Release No. 33-6444, December 15, 1982, effective for companies with fiscal years beginning after December 14, 1982, 47 F.R. 57911.]

[¶ 12,021] Guide 3—Statistical Disclosure by Bank Holding Companies

General Instructions

Guide 3. 1. This Guide applies to the description of business portions of those bank holding company registration statements for which financial statements are required.

2. Information furnished in accordance with this Guide should generally be presented in tabular form in the order appearing below. However, an alternative presentation, such as inclusion of the information in Management's Discussion and Analysis, may be used if in management's opinion such presentation would be more meaningful to investors.

3. When the term "reported period" is used in the Guide, it refers to each of the periods described below:

(a) each of the last three fiscal years of the registrant, except as is provided in paragraphs (b) and (c) below;

(b) each of the last five fiscal years of the registrant with respect to Items III and IV, except as is provided in paragraph (c) below;

(c) each of the last two fiscal years with respect to all items, if the registrant had assets of less than $200,000,000 or net worth of $10,000,000 or less as of the end of its latest fiscal year; and

(d) any additional interim period necessary to keep the information from being misleading.

The reported period shall not include an additional interim period under paragraph (d) above merely because an income statement is presented for such additional interim period, but the reported period shall include such an additional period if a material change in the information presented or the trend evidenced thereby has occurred.

4. Unless otherwise indicated, averages called for by the Guide are daily averages. Where the collection of data on a daily average basis would involve unwarranted or undue burden or expense, weekly or month-end averages may be used, provided such averages are representative of the operations of the registrant. The basis used for presenting averages need be stated only if not presented on a daily average basis.

5. Some of the information called for by the Guide which is prospective in nature may not be available on a historical basis. The staff should be advised of such situations prior to filing and if the requested information is unavailable and cannot be compiled without unwarranted or undue burden or expense, the requirement that such information be furnished may be waived. If possible, reasonably comparable data should be furnished

instead. If certain requested information will not be available with respect to periods to be covered in future filings subject to the Guide, this should also be brought to the staff's attention.

6. The disclosure requirements of the Guide are also applicable to foreign registrants to the extent the requested information is available. If the information is unavailable and cannot be compiled without unwarranted or undue burden or expense, this should be brought to the staff's attention.

[NOTE: In evaluating the reasonableness of assertions by registrants that the compilation of requested information, such as historical data or daily averages, would involve an unwarranted or undue burden or expense, the staff takes into consideration, among other factors, the size of the registrant, the estimated costs of compiling the data, the electronic data processing capacity of the registrant, and efforts in process to obtain the information in future periods.]

7. In various places throughout this Guide, disclosure is called for regarding certain "foreign" data. For purposes of this Guide, this information need not be presented unless the registrant is required to make separate disclosures concerning its foreign activities in its consolidated financial statements pursuant to the test set forth in § 210.9-05 of Regulation S-X.

I. *Distribution of Assets, Liabilities and Stockholders' Equity; Interest Rates and Interest Differential*

A. For each reported period, present average balance sheets. The format of the average balance sheets may be condensed from the detail required by the financial statements provided that the condensed average balance sheets indicate the significant categories of assets and liabilities, including all major categories of interest-earning assets and interest-bearing liabilities. Major categories of interest-earning assets should include loans, taxable investment securities, non-taxable investment securities, interest bearing deposits in other banks. Federal funds sold and securities purchased with agreements to resell, other short-term investments, and other (specify if significant). Major categories of interest-bearing liabilities should include savings deposits, other time deposits, short-term debt, long-term debt and other (specify if significant).

B. For each reported period, present an analysis of net interest earnings as follows:

1. For each major category of interest-earning asset and each major category of interest-bearing liability, the average amount outstanding during the period and the interest earned or paid on such amount.

2. The average yield for each major category of interest-bearing asset.

3. The average rate paid for each major category of interest-bearing liability.

4. The average yield on all interest-earning assets and the average effective rate paid on all interest-bearing liabilities.

5. The net yield on interest-earning assets (net interest earnings divided by total interest-earning assets, with net interest earnings equaling the difference between total interest earned and total interest paid).

6. This analysis may, at the option of the registrant, be presented in connection with the average balance sheet required by paragraph A.

C. For the latest two fiscal years, present (1) the dollar amount of change in interest income and (2) the dollar amount of change in interest expense. The changes should be segregated for each major category of interest-earning asset and interest-bearing liability into amounts attributable to (a) changes in volume (change in volume times old rate), (b) changes in rates (change in rate times old volume), and (c) changes in rate/volume (change in rate times the change in volume). The rate/volume variances should be allocated on a consistent basis between rate and volume variances and the basis of allocation disclosed in a note to the table.

Instructions. (1) Explain how non-accruing loans have been treated for purposes of the analyses required by paragraph B.

(2) In the calculation of the changes in the interest income and interest expense, any out-of-period items and adjustments should be excluded and the types and amounts of items excluded disclosed in a note to the table.

(3) If loan fees are included in the interest income computation, the amount of such fees should be disclosed, if material.

(4) Tax exempt income may be calculated on a tax equivalent basis. A brief note should describe the extent of recognition of exemption from Federal, state and local taxation and the combined marginal or incremental rate used.

(5) If disclosure regarding foreign activities is required pursuant to General Instruction 7 of this Guide, the information required by paragraphs A, B and C of Item I should be further segregated between domestic and foreign activities for each significant category of assets and liabilities disclosed pursuant to paragraph A. In addition, for each reported period, present separately, on the basis of averages, the percentage of total assets and total liabilities attributable to foreign activities.

II. *Investment Portfolio*

A. As of the end of each reported period, present the book value of investments in obligations of (1) the U.S. Treasury and other U.S. Government agencies and corporations; (2) States of the U.S. and political subdivisions; and (3) other securities including bonds, notes, debentures and stock of business corporations, foreign governments and political subdivisions, intergovernmental agencies and the Federal Reserve bank.

B. As of the end of the latest reported period, present the amount of each investment category listed above which is due (1) in one year or less, (2) after one year through five years, (3) after five years through ten years, and (4) after ten years. In addition, state the weighted average yield for each range of maturities.

Instruction. State whether yields on tax exempt obligations have been computed on a tax equivalent basis. (See Instruction (4) to Item I.) Any major changes in the taxexempt portfolio should be discussed hereunder.

C. As of the end of the latest reported period, state the name of any issuer, and the aggregate book value and aggregate market value of the securities of such issuer, when the aggregate book value of such securities exceeds ten percent of stockholders' equity.

Instruction. The term "issuer" has the meaning given in Section 2(4) of the Securities Act of 1933, except that debt securities issued by a state of the United States and its political subdivisions and agencies which are payable from and secured by the same source of revenue or taxing authority shall be considered to be securities of a single issuer. This information does not have to be provided for securities of the U.S. Government and U.S. Government agencies and corporations. Consideration should be given to disclosure of risk characteristics of the securities of an issuer and of differences in risk characteristics of different issues of securities of an issuer as may be appropriate.

III. *Loan Portfolio*

A. *Types of Loans*

As of the end of each reported period, present separately the amount of loans in each category listed below. Also show the total amount of all loans for each reported period which amounts should be the same as those shown on the balance sheets.

Domestic:

1. Commercial, financial and agricultural;

2. Real estate—construction;

3. Real estate—mortgage;

4. Installment loans to individuals;

5. Lease financing

Foreign:

6. Governments and official institutions;

7. Banks and other financial institutions;

8. Commercial and industrial;

9. Other loans.

Instructions. A series of categories other than those specified above may be used to present details of loans if considered a more appropriate presentation.

B. *Maturities and Sensitivities of Loans to Changes in Interest Rates*

As of the end of the latest fiscal year reported on, present separately the amount of loans in each category listed in paragraph A (except that this information need not be presented for categories 3, 4 and 5, and categories 6 through 9 may be aggregated) which are: (1) due in one year or less, (2) due after one year through five years and (3) due after five years. In addition, present separately the total amount of all such loans due after one year which (a) have predetermined interest rates and (b) have floating or adjustable interest rates.

Instructions. (1) Scheduled repayments should be reported in the maturity category in which the payment is due.

(2) Demand loans, loans having no stated schedule of repayments and no stated maturity, and overdrafts should be reported as due in one year or less.

(3) Determinations of maturities should be based upon contract terms. However, such terms may vary due to the registrant's "rollover policy," in which case the maturity should be revised as appropriate and the rollover policy should be briefly discussed.

C. Risk Elements

1. *Nonaccrual, Past Due and Restructured Loans.* As of the end of each reported period, state separately the aggregate amount of loans in each of the following categories:

(a) Loans accounted for on a nonaccrual basis;

(b) Accruing loans which are contractually past due 90 days or more as to principal *or* interest payments; and

(c) Loans not included above which are "troubled debt restructurings" as defined in Statement of Financial Accounting Standards No. 15 ("FAS 15"), "Accounting by Debtors and Creditors for Troubled Debt Restructurings."

Instructions. (1) The information required by this Item should be provided separately for domestic and for foreign loans for each reported period.

(2) As of the most recent reported period, state separately as to foreign and domestic loans included in (a) and (c) above the following information: (i) the gross interest income that would have been recorded in the period then ended if the loans had been current in accordance with their original terms and had been outstanding throughout the period or since origination, if held for part of the period; and (ii) the amount of interest income on those loans that was included in net income for the period.

(3) A discussion of the registrant's policy for placing loans on nonaccrual status should be provided.

(4) No loans shall be excluded from the amounts presented, except that loans to foreign borrowers which are restructured for reasons other than concerns as to ultimate collectibility and which are included in amounts disclosed pursuant to Instruction (6)(d) to Item III.C.3. need not be included in amounts reported pursuant to Item III.C.1.(c). Supplemental disclosures may be made to facilitate understanding of the aggregate amounts reported. These disclosures may include, for example, information as to the nature of the loans, any guarantees, the extent of collateral, or amounts in process of collection.

2. *Potential Problem Loans.* As of the end of the most recent reported period, describe the nature and extent of any loans which are not now disclosed pursuant to Item III.C.1. above, but where known information about possible credit problems of borrowers (which are not related to transfer risk inherent in cross-border lending activities) causes management to have serious doubts as to the ability of such borrowers to comply with the present loan repayment terms and which may result in disclosure of such loans pursuant to Item III.C.1.

3. *Foreign Outstandings.* As of the end of each of the last three reported periods, state the name of the country and aggregate amount of cross-border outstandings to borrowers in each foreign country where such outstandings exceed 1% of total assets.

Instructions. (1) Cross-border outstandings are defined as loans (including accrued interest), acceptances, interest-bearing deposits with other banks, other interest-bearing investments and any other monetary assets which are denominated in dollars or other non-local currency. To the extent that material local currency outstandings are not hedged or are not funded by local borrowings, such amounts should be included in cross-border outstandings. Commitments such as irrevocable letters of credit should not be included in outstandings; however, where such items are material, the amounts should be separately disclosed.

(2) Disclose separately the amounts of cross-border outstandings by type of foreign borrower as set forth in Item III.A. above.

(3) If a material amount of the outstandings to any foreign country disclosed herein is included in the amounts disclosed pursuant to Item III.C.1. or 2. identify each such country and the related amounts disclosed pursuant to those Items.

(4) Amounts of any legally enforceable, written guarantees of principal or interest by domestic or other non-local third parties may be netted against cross-border outstandings of a country. If such a guarantee is made by a foreign guarantor, the guarantee amount shall be reflected as an outstanding of such guarantor. The value of any tangible, liquid collateral may also be netted against cross-border outstandings of a country if it is held and realizable by the lender outside of the borrower's country.

(5) For purposes of determining the amount of outstandings to be reported, loans made to, or deposits placed with, a branch of a foreign bank located outside the foreign bank's home country should be considered as loans to, or deposits with, the foreign bank.

(6) Where current conditions in a foreign country give rise to liquidity problems which are expected to have a material impact on the timely repayment of principal or interest on the country's private or public sector debt, furnish:

(a) a description of the nature and impact of such developments.

(b) an analysis of the changes in aggregate outstandings to borrowers in each such country (except that a country need not be included if aggregate outstandings to all borrowers in the country at the end of the most recent reported period do not exceed 1% of total assets), for the most recent reported period, in the following format:

	Country A	Country B
Aggregate outstandings at (beginning of period)	$X	X
Net change in short-term outstandings:	X	X
Changes in other outstandings:		
Additional outstandings	X	X
Interest income accrued	X	X
Collections of: Principal	X	X
Accrued interest	X	X
Other changes	X	X
Aggregate outstandings at (end of period)	$X	X

For purposes of the above table, short-term outstandings are trade credits and interbank deposits (and similar items) which, at the time they were extended, had maturities of one year or less. This table should be supplemented with the amounts of short-term outstandings that are included in the end-of-period aggregate amounts reported for each country.

(c) the total amounts recognized as interest income and the total amounts of interest collected during the most recent reported period on all outstandings to each country disclosed pursuant to subpart (b) of this Instruction, if such totals are significantly different from the amounts disclosed pursuant to subpart (b) on the lines entitled "Interest income accrued" and "Collections of accrued interest", respectively. (The amounts might be different if, for example, all or a portion of the outstandings were on a nonaccrual basis.)

(d) the following information, if a material portion of the outstandings to any country that is identified pursuant to subpart (b) of this Instruction is restructured during or subsequent to the most recent reported period, or if a material portion may be subject to restructuring pursuant to an agreement in principle (or its equivalent) which has been reached between the debtor and the registrant (or a committee organized by creditor banks to negotiate such an agreement in principle or its equivalent):

(i) information describing the pre- and post-restructuring repayment terms of the affected outstandings, including at a minimum the following (in tabular format such as the following):

	Country A	Country B
Amount restructured (or subject to restructuring)	$X	X
Wieghted average year of maturity (including any grace periods):		
Pre-restructuring	19XX	19XX
Post-restructuring	19YY	19YY
Wieghted average interest rate:		
Pre-restructuring	X %	X %
Post-restructuring	Y %	Y %

Alternative tabular formats are not precluded, provided that the minimum data presented above (or their equivalent) is presented. Supplementing weighted average maturities and interest rates with ranges of maturities and interest rates is not precluded; however, ranges should not be presented without also presenting weighted averages (unless the ranges are very narrow). Alternatively, individual years of maturities could be disclosed with respect to discernable portions of restructured outstandings, along with the interest rates on those portions. If interest rates are variable, the applicable index and the weighted average spread from the index should be disclosed in lieu of the actual rates as of any particular date.

(ii) a description of commitments (e.g., new money provisions; agreements to relend, or to maintain on deposit, repayments of principal or interest within the country) arising or expected to arise in connection with the restructuring(s).

(iii) the amount of outstandings, separately as to each country, that has been removed or is expected to be removed from nonaccrual status as a result of the restructuring(s).

Disclosures pursuant to subpart (d) should be in reasonable proximity to disclosures pursuant to other subparts of this Instruction, and should be described as subject to change, if applicable.

(7) For countries whose outstandings are between .75% and 1% of total assets, disclose the names of the countries and the aggregate amount of outstandings attributable to all such countries.

(8) The disclosure threshold set forth in this Item is for disclosure guidance and is not intended as an indicator of a prudent level of lending to any one country by an individual bank.

4. *Loan Concentrations.* As of the end of the most recent reported period, describe any concentration of loans exceeding 10% of total loans which are not otherwise disclosed as a category of loans pursuant to Item III.A. of this Guide. Loan concentrations are considered to exist when there are amounts loaned to a multiple number of borrowers engaged in similar activities which would cause them to be similarly impacted by economic or other conditions.

Instructions. (1) If a material amount of the loan concentrations disclosed herein or pursuant to Item III.3.A. is included in the amounts disclosed pursuant to Item III.C.1. or 2., that fact should be discussed

(2) The disclosure threshold in this Item is for disclosure guidance and is not intended as an indicator of a prudent level of lending.

D. *Other Interest Bearing Assets.* As of the end of the most recent reported period, disclose the nature and amounts of any other interest bearing assets that would be required to be disclosed under Item III.C.1. or 2. if such assets were loans.

IV *Summary of Loan Loss Experience*

A. An analysis of loss experience shall be furnished in the following format for each reported period:

Analysis of the Allowance for Loan Losses

	Reported Period
Balance at beginning of period	$ X
Charge-offs:	
Domestic:	
Commerical, financial and agricultural	
Real estate—construction	X
Real estate—mortgage	X
Installment loans to individuals	X
Lease financing	X
Foreign	X
	X
Recoveries:	
Domestic:	X
Commercial, financial and agricultural	X
Real estate—construction	X
Real estate—mortgage	X
Installment loans to individuals	X
Lease financing	X
Foreign	X
	X
Net charge-offs	X
Additions charge to operations	X
Balance at end of period	$ X
Ratio of net charge-offs during the period to average loans outstanding during the period	X

Instructions. (1) The above table is not intended to mandate a specific format for disclosure of this information. Registrants are encouraged to experiment with various disclosure formats in the interest of effective communication of this data; however, all the required information must be given.

(2) For each period presented, describe briefly the factors which influenced management's judgment in determining the amount of the additions to the allowance charged to operating expense. A statement that the amount is based on management's judgment will not be sufficient.

(3) If, in accordance with the instructions to paragraph III-A, information concerning loans has been presented in categories other than those specified in that paragraph, those other categories should be used to present the disclosures called for under this paragraph.

(4) If the registrant is required to present separate data as to its foreign activities pursuant to General Instruction 7 to this Guide, disclosure must be provided as to the changes in the allowance for loan losses applicable to loans related to foreign activities, including the balances at the beginning and end of the periods, charge-offs, recoveries, and additions charged to operations.

B. At the end of each reported period, furnish a breakdown of the allowance for loan losses in the following format:

Allocation of the Allowance for Loan Losses

		Reported Period
Balance at End of Period Applicable to:	Amount	Percent of loans in each category to total loans
Domestic	$ X	X%
Commercial, financial and agricultural	X	X%
Real estate—construction	X	X%
Real estate—mortgage	X	X%
Installment loans to individuals	X	X%
Lease financing	X	X%
Foreign	X	X%
Unallocated	X	N/A
	$ X	100%

Instructions. (1) See instructions (1) and (3) to paragraph A above.

(2) In lieu of the breakdown of the allowance for loan losses by loan category called for above, the registrant may furnish a narrative discussion of the risk elements in the loan portfolio and the factors considered in determining the amount of the allowance for loan losses. The discussion may be extended to risk elements associated with particular loan categories or subcategories. Information should also be furnished as to the approximate anticipated amount of charge-offs by category during the next full year of operation.

V. *Deposits*

A. For each reported period, present separately the average amount of and the average rate paid on each of the following deposit categories which are in excess of 10 percent of average total deposits:

Deposits in domestic bank offices:

(1) Noninterest bearing demand deposits.

(2) Interest bearing demand deposits.

(3) Savings deposits.

(4) Time deposits.

Deposits in foreign banking offices:

(5) Banks located in foreign countries (including foreign branches of other U.S. banks).

(6) Foreign governments and official institutions.

(7) Other foreign demand deposits.

(8) Other foreign time and savings deposits.

B. Categories other than those specified for deposits in domestic bank offices above may be used to present the types of domestic deposits if they more appropriately describe the nature of the deposits.

C. If material, the registrant should disclose separately the aggregate amount of deposits by foreign depositors in domestic offices. Identification of the nationality of the depositors is not required.

D. As of the end of the latest reported period, state the amount outstanding of 1) time certificates of deposit in amounts of $100,000 or more and 2) other time deposits of $100,000 or more issued by domestic offices by time remaining until maturity of 3 months or less; over 3 through 6 months; over 6 through 12 months; and over 12 months.

E. As of the end of the latest reported period, state the amount outstanding of time certificates of deposits and other time deposits in amount of $100,000 or more issued by foreign offices. If the aggregate of such certificates of deposit and time deposits in amounts exceeding $100,000 represents a majority of total foreign deposit liabilities, the disclosure need not be given, provided that there is a statement that a majority of deposits were in amounts in excess of $100,000.

VI. *Return on Equity and Assets*

For each reported period, present the following:

(1) Return on assets (net income divided by average total assets).

(2) Return on equity (net income divided by average equity).

(3) Dividend payout ratio (dividends declared per share divided by net income per share).

(4) Equity to assets ratio (average equity divided by average total assets).

Instructions. (1) If mandatorily redeemable preferred stock is outstanding, furnish the ratios required under (2) and (4) above in a dual presentation including and excluding such stock in the calculations.

(2) Registrants should supply any other ratios which they deem necessary to explain their operations.

VII. *Short-Term Borrowings*

For each reported period, present the following information for each category of short-term borrowings reported in the financial statements pursuant to § 210.9-04.11:

(1) The amounts outstanding at the end of the reported period, the weighted average interest rate thereon, and the general terms thereof;

(2) The maximum amount of borrowings in each category outstanding at any month-end during each reported period;

(3) The approximate average amounts outstanding during each reported period and the approximate weighted average interest rate thereon.

Instruction. This information is not required to be given for any category of short-term borrowings for which the average balance outstanding during the period was less than 30 percent of stockholders' equity at the end of the period.

[As last amended in Release No. 33-6478, August 11, 1983, 48 F.R. 37609.]

[¶ 12,031]   Guide 4—Prospectus Relating to Interests in Oil and Gas Programs

Guide 4. The following disclosures should be included under appropriate captions:

1. *Summary of Program.* There should be set forth briefly on the cover page of the prospectus a summary which should include the following: (1) *Terms of Offering:* State the title and general nature of the securities being offered; the maximum aggregate amount of the offering; the minimum aggregate amount necessary to initiate the program; the disposition of the funds raised if they are not sufficient for that purpose; the minimum subscription price; the period of the offering; any provisions for additional assessments; and a brief description of the proposed method of distribution, including the amount of any commission to be paid. If funds received from investors are not to be held in trust or in special account pending expenditure in the program, appropriate disclosures should be set forth including when appropriate reference to exposure to claims of creditors of the custodian of the funds. The tabular presentation specified in Item 501(c)(7) of Regulation S-K (§ 229.501(c)(7) may be omitted; (2) *Compensation:* Describe generally all cash or property interests that will be paid as compensation in connection with the program, including underwriting commission; (3) *Participation in Costs and Revenues:* Show the percentages of expenditures to be borne, respectively, by the investors and by other parties, who should be briefly identified, and the percentages of revenues to be payable, respectively, to investors and to other parties, who should be briefly identified; and (4) *Application of Proceeds:* Indicate the minimum dollar amount of net proceeds (excluding additional assessments) that will be available to finance the program and the proposed estimated percentages thereof to be used for financing the principal activities of the program, such as acreage acquisition, drilling of exploratory wells, drilling of development wells and purchase of producing properties.

2. *The Risk Factors.* The investor should be advised in a carefully organized series of short, concise paragraphs, under subcaptions where appropriate, of the risks he should consider before making an investment

in the program and should include cross-reference to where in the prospectus further information may be found.

3. *Definitions.* Include an appropriate glossary of terms used in the prospectus which should not be inconsistent with their customary usage in the oil and gas industry.

4. *Terms of the Offering.* Describe the interests and the amount and terms of offering.

5. *Additional Assessments.* Describe those assessments which may be later required from investors either for completion of wells or for the drilling of additional wells and where available, historical information relating to past programs, of the registrant or its associates, should be shown, in tabular form, indicating for each program, the aggregate amount (excluding assessments) paid by investors, the aggregate amount of additional assessments separately required for (a) the completion of wells and (b) the drilling of additional wells.

6. *Plan of Distribution.* Describe how the interests being offered are to be sold, as well as arrangements for compensation.

7. *Proposed Activities.* Describe the proposed activities of the program in which the interests are being offered.

8. *Application of Proceeds.* Include an appropriate percentage estimate of the proceeds to be applied to the different purposes within each of the principal activities of the program, such as acreage acquisition, drilling of exploratory wells, drilling of development wells and the purchase of producing properties. Where possible, the information should be set forth in tabular form.

9. *Participation in Costs and Revenues.* Describe the arrangements and understandings with respect to the provision of funds for expenditures in connection with the program and with respect to participation in revenues from any production of minerals which may be realized. Where possible, the information should be set forth in tabular form.

10. *Compensation.* Describe, whether in the form of cash or property interests, the compensation for underwriting, managerial, and operational services to be rendered in connection with the program, as well as the sources from which such compensation will be paid. Where possible, the information should be set forth in tabular form.

11. *Management.* Furnish the information required by Items 401 through 403 of Regulation S-K (§ § 229.401 through 403) as to the management and operating companies.

12. *Conflict of Interest.* Describe all conflicts of interest which may arise in the operations of the program involving parties engaged in the management and operation of the program.

13. *Prior Activities.* Describe in tabular form the results of programs during at least the past ten years of the registrant or its associates, indicating in appropriate detail for each of the programs (1) the drilling results thereof, and (2) for, respectively, (a) the public investors and (b) others, the total investment in each of such programs and the recovery on investment to date and for the last three months of the period covered, together with any other information as may be appropriate.

14. *Tax Aspects.* Discuss the tax consequences of oil and gas exploration, drilling and production, as well as Federal tax legislation which has been proposed. This may include, in tabular form, only historical information relating to past programs of the registrant or its associates, showing expenses deductible and income taxable.

15. Other captions should then follow, such as *Competition, Limited Partnership Agreement, Agent Agreement, Exploration Agreement,* and *Operating Agreement,* under which other required information is set forth.

[As last amended in Release No. 33-7168, May 11, 1995, 60 F.R. 26604.]

[¶ 12,041]   Guide 5—Preparation of Registration Statements Relating to Interests in Real Estate Limited Partnerships

Guide 5. References to the General Partner and its affiliates, also referred to as sponsors, are intended to include references to the General Partner(s), promoters of the partnership, and all persons that, directly or indirectly through one or more intermediaries, control or are controlled by, or are under common control with, such General Partner(s) or promoters.

It is suggested that where appropriate, the information in the prospectus be presented in the same order as the following comments. Where the registrant believes that specific comments are not relevant or are otherwise inappropriate, the registrant should bring this to the staff's attention in a letter indicating the reasons therefor.

1. *COVER PAGE*

A. The disclosure on the cover page should be as succinct and brief as possible.

B. The cover page should set forth, in addition to basic information about the offering, the termination date of the offering, any minimum required purchase and any arrangements to place the funds received in an escrow trust or similar arrangement.

C. The cover page should contain a tabular presentation of the total maximum and minimum interests to be offered:

	Price to Public	Selling Commissions	Proceeds to the Partnership
Per Limited Partnership Interest			
Total Minimum			
Total Maximum			

D. The cover page also should contain brief identification of the material risks involved in the purchase of the securities with cross-reference to further discussion in the prospectus. The most significant risk factors should be identified where applicable, for example:

i) Tax Aspects

For example:

There are material income tax risks associated with the offering.

ii) Use of Proceeds

For example:

The proceeds of the offering are insufficient to meet the requirements for funds as set forth in the partnership's investment objectives.

iii) Conflicts of Interests

For example:

The operation of the partnership involves transactions between the partnership and the General Partner or its affiliates which may involve conflicts of interest.

2. SUITABILITY STANDARDS

Standards, if any, to be utilized by the registrant ("suitability standards") in determining the acceptance of subscription agreements should be described immediately following the cover page. Suitability standards should include those established by the registrant, if any, or by any self-regulatory organization or state agency having jurisdiction over the offering of the securities. Registrant should disclose the method(s) it intends to employ to assure adherence to the suitability standards by persons selling the interests and should briefly discuss the factors pertaining to the need for such standards such as lack of liquidity (resale or assignment of securities), importance of the investor's Federal income tax bracket in terms of the tax-benefits to be derived, the long term nature of the investment and possible adverse tax consequences of premature sale of the interests. If suitability standards apply to resale of the interests, this should be discussed.

3. SUMMARY OF THE PARTNERSHIP AND USE OF PROCEEDS

A two-part, concise outline summary relating to the partnership and a tabular summary of use of proceeds should follow the Suitability section of the prospectus. These summaries may replace the Introductory Statement and Use of Proceeds Sections required by the relevant Form if such sections would merely repeat the information in the summaries.

A. *Summary of the Partnership.* The following information should be disclosed in outline form with appropriate cross-references, where applicable:

i) Name, address and telephone number of the General Partner and names of persons making investment decisions for the partnership;

ii) The intended termination date of the partnership;

iii) State, if true, that the General Partner and its affiliates will receive substantial fees and profits in connection with the offering;

iv) If current distributions are an investment objective, state the estimated maximum time from the closing date that the investor might have to wait to receive such distributions;

v) Describe briefly the properties to be purchased. If a material portion of the minimum net proceeds of the offering (allowing for reserves) is not committed to specific properties, so indicate;

vi) Describe the depreciation method to be used;

vii) State the maximum leverage expected to be used by the partnership as a whole and on individual properties, where it may differ;

viii) Include a cross-reference to the Glossary.

B. *Use of Proceeds.* The use of proceeds tabular summary will vary according to the partnership but should include, where appropriate, estimates of the public offering expenses (both organizational and sales), the amount available for investment, non-recurring initial investment fees, prepaid items and financing fees, cash down payments, reserves, and acquisition fees including those paid by the seller. Estimated amounts to be paid to the General Partner and its affiliates should be identified. The summary should include both dollar amounts and percentages of the maximum and minimum proceeds of the offering. Inclusion of percentages of the estimated maximum and minimum total assets is optional. An example of a summary of Use of Proceeds is attached as Appendix I, but the summary will vary according to the circumstances.

4. *COMPENSATION AND FEES TO THE GENERAL PARTNERS AND AFFILIATES*

A. This section should include a summary tabular presentation, itemizing by category and specifying dollar amounts where possible, of all compensation, fees, profits, and other benefits (including reimbursement of out-of-pocket expenses) which the General Partner and its affiliates may earn or receive in connection with the offering or operation of the partnership. If more detailed information is required it should be located in the Summary of Partnership Agreement section with cross-reference to that Summary. The presentation should identify the person, including affiliations with the General Partner, who will receive such compensation, fees, profits or benefits and the services to be performed by such person.

The summary should be organized so as to indicate clearly whether the compensation relates to the offering and organizational stage, the developmental or acquisition stage, the operational stage or the termination and liquidation stage of the partnership. Separate subcaptions are recommended.

The type of compensation, fees, profits or other benefits that should be disclosed includes, but is not limited to, the following: disbursements incident to the purchase and sale of the limited partnership interests, including sales commissions, reimbursements for expenses, and real estate commissions; finder's fees; fees for property acquisitions, marketing or leasing up of properties, financing or refinancing, management of properties, insurance and miscellaneous services; commissions and other fees to be paid upon sale of the partnership's properties; participation by the General Partner in cash flow or profits and losses or capital gains and losses arising out of the operation, refinancing or sale of properties; fees or builder's profits; overhead absorption and/or land write-ups; and all profits on the purchase of investments for the partnership from the General Partner or its affiliates. If the partnership agreement limits the losses the General Partner and its affiliates can sustain, this should be discussed.

B. Maximum aggregate dollar front-end fees to be paid during the first fiscal year of operations should be disclosed based upon the assumption that the partnership's maximum leverage is utilized.

C. Where compensation arrangements are based upon a formula or percentage, the terms of such arrangements should be disclosed and illustrated. The assumptions underlying the dollar figures should be disclosed and the calculations underlying the figures should be submitted to the staff supplementally with the initial filing. Compensation based upon a given return (percentage of contributed investor capital) to investors should disclose whether such return is cumulative or non-cumulative.

D. Where the General Partner or an affiliate receives a disproportionate interest in the partnership in relation to its own contribution, registrants attention is directed to Item 506 of Regulation S-K. A bar chart comparison of the various interests and contributors should be provided.

5. *CONFLICTS OF INTEREST*

A. This section should include a summary of each type of transaction which may result in a conflict between the interests of the public investors and those of the General Partner and its affiliates, and of the proposed method of dealing with such conflict. The types of conflicts of interest which should be disclosed and discussed, if appropriate, include, but are not limited to:

i) The General Partner is a general partner or an affiliate of the general partner in other investment entities (public and/or private) engaged in making similar investments or otherwise makes or arranges for similar investments.

ii) The General Partner has the authority to invest the partnership's funds in other partnerships in which the General Partner or an affiliate is the general partner or has an interest.

iii) Properties in which the General Partner or its affiliates have an interest are bought from or partnership properties are sold to the General Partner or its affiliates or entities in which they have an interest. Where appraisals are used in connection with any such transaction, it should be made clear that appraisals are only estimates of value and should not be relied on as measures of realized value. If the appraiser is named as an expert, a consent to the use of his name should be furnished. If specific appraised values are included in the registration statement, the appraiser should be named as an expert, his consent furnished and the appraisals filed as exhibits to the registration statement. If a statement that the purchase price of the property does not exceed its appraised value is included and the appraiser is not named and specific values are not cited, there need not be furnished a consent to use the appraiser's name. In that event, a copy of the appraisal should be submitted supplementally with the registration statement. If any relationship exists between the appraiser and the General Partner or its affiliates this should be stated. If the General Partner intends to buy any properties in which the general partner or any of its affiliates have a material interest, such properties should be appropriately described in the prospectus along with the investment objectives of the partnership (see paragraph 10, Investment Objectives and Policies). If it is disclosed in the prospectus that the partnership may purchase properties in which the General Partner or its affiliates have a material interest, but no properties are described, and such properties are thereafter purchased for the partnership, the General Partner will have the heavy burden of demonstrating that it did not intend to purchase such property at the time the registration statement became effective.

iv) The General Partner or its affiliates own or have an interest in properties adjacent to those to be purchased and developed by the partnership.

v) Affiliates of the General Partner who act as underwriters, real estate brokers or managers for the partnership, act in such capacities for other partnerships or entities.

vi) An affiliate of the General Partner places mortgages for the partnership or otherwise acts as a finance broker or as insurance agent or broker receiving commissions for such services.

vii) An affiliate of the General Partner acts (a) as an underwriter for the offering, or (b) as a principal underwriter for the offering thereby creating conflicts in performance of the underwriter's due diligence inquiries under the Securities Act.

viii) The compensation plan for the General Partner may create a conflict between the interests of the General Partner and those of the partnership.

B. An organization chart should be included in this section showing the relationship between the various organizations managed or controlled by the General Partner or its affiliates that will do business with the partnership where the relationships are so complex that a graphic display would assist investors in understanding such relationships.

6. FIDUCIARY RESPONSIBILITY OF THE GENERAL PARTNER

A. A discussion of the fiduciary obligation owed by the General Partner to the Limited Partners should be set forth. The following disclosure is suggested with appropriate modification for the laws of the state of organization:

A General Partner is accountable to a limited partnership as a fiduciary and consequently must exercise good faith and integrity in handling partnership affairs. This is a rapidly developing and changing area of the law and Limited Partners who have questions concerning the duties of the General Partner should consult with their counsel.

B. Where the limited partnership agreement contains an exculpatory provision and/or the right to indemnification, the following disclosure is suggested, as modified to reflect the substance of such provisions:

Exculpation

i) The General Partner may not be liable to the Partnership or Limited Partners for errors in judgment or other acts or omissions not amounting to willful misconduct or gross negligence, since provision has been made in the Agreement of Limited Partnership for exculpation of the General Partner. Therefore, purchasers of the interests have a more limited right of action than they would have absent the limitation in the Partnership Agreement.

Indemnification

ii) The Partnership Agreement provides for indemnification of the General Partner by the Partnership for liabilities he incurs in dealings with third parties on behalf of the partnership. To the extent that the indemnification provisions purport to include indemnification for liabilities arising under the Securities Act of 1933, in the opinion of the Securities and Exchange Commission, such indemnification is contrary to public policy and therefore unenforceable.

Registrant's attention is also directed to Items 510 and 512(i) of Regulation S-K relating to disclosure of indemnification agreements.

7. RISK FACTORS

A. This section should include a carefully organized series of short, concise subcaptioned paragraphs, with cross-references to fuller discussion where appropriate, summarizing the principal risk factors applicable to the offering and to the partnership's particular plan of operations. The risk factors section should be brief.

B. This subsection should summarize each material risk of adverse tax consequences with appropriate cross-references to fuller discussions in the Federal tax section. For example:

i) Where no Internal Revenue Service (IRS) ruling as to partnership tax status has been applied for or obtained, the risk that the IRS may on audit determine that for tax purposes the partnership is an association taxable as a corporation, in which case, investors would be deprived of the tax benefits associated with the offering. As part of this disclosure, it should be stated that a material risk of IRS classification as a corporate association may exist even though registrant relies on an opinion of counsel as to partnership tax status as such opinion is not binding on the IRS. It may also be stated that IRS classification of the partnership as a corporate association would deprive investors of the tax benefits of the offering only if the IRS determination is upheld in court or otherwise becomes final. Any such additional disclosure should explain that contesting an IRS determination may impose representation expenses on investors. (See Federal tax section, p. 12.)

ii) Where the IRS has advised registrant that it proposes not to rule, or to rule adversely, on any tax issue as to which a ruling was applied for, the risk that investors may lose some or all tax benefits associated with the offering. (See Federal tax section, p. 12.)

iii) The risk that after some years of partnership operations an investor's tax liabilities may exceed his cash distributions in corresponding years and that to the extent of such excess the payment of such taxes will be out-of-pocket expenses.

iv) Upon a sale or other disposition (*e.g.,* by gift) of a partnership interest or, upon a sale (including a foreclosure sale) or other disposition of partnership property, the risk that an investor's tax liabilities may exceed the cash he receives and that to the extent of such excess the payment of such taxes will be out-of-pocket expenses. The disclosure should indicate to what extent the gain may be taxed as ordinary income, to what extent as capital gain. (See Federal tax section, p. 19.)

v) The risk that an audit of the partnership's information return may result in an audit of an investor's own tax return. (See Federal tax section, p. 20.)

C. Risk factors relating to the specific partnership might include, where applicable:

i) Management's lack of relevant experience, or management's lack of success with similar partnerships or other real estate investments;

ii) Where the proceeds of the offering will be insufficient to meet the requirements of the partnership's investment objectives, a discussion of the additional sources of capital for the partnership and of the risk of not being able to satisfy the partnership's objectives as a result of not obtaining additional necessary funds;

iii) Where the partnership has high risk investment objectives, including high leveraging, these should be explained;

iv) The risk that no public market for interests is likely to develop and that holders of interests may not be able to liquidate their investment quickly;

v) Risks associated with contemplated rent stabilization programs, fuel or energy requirements or regulations, and construction in areas that are subject to environmental or other federal, state or local regulations, actual or pending;

vi) Where a material portion of the minimum net proceeds of the offering is not committed to specific properties, disclosure of the particular risk associated with an investment in such an offering. Such disclosure should include the increased uncertainty and risk to investors since they are unable to evaluate the manner in which the proceeds are to be invested and the economic merit of the particular real estate projects prior to investment. Also it should be disclosed that there may be a substantial period of time before the proceeds of the offering are invested and therefore a delay to investors in receiving a return on their investment.

D. Risk factors relating to real estate limited partnership offerings in general should be briefly discussed after those relating to the specific partnership. Such risks might include, where applicable: the risks associated with the ownership of real estate, including uncertainty of cash flow to meet fixed and maturing obligations, adverse local market conditions, risks of "leveraging," and uninsured losses.

8. PRIOR PERFORMANCE OF THE GENERAL PARTNER AND AFFILIATES

A narrative summary of the "track record" or prior performance of programs sponsored by the General Partner and its affiliates ("sponsors") containing the information set forth below should be included in the text of the prospectus. Tables following the format of those in Appendix II, relating to historical use of proceeds of prior programs, compensation to the sponsors, operations of prior programs, and acquisitions and sales of properties by prior programs, should be included at the back of the prospectus or in Part II of the registration statement as specified in paragraph B "Prior Performance Tables" hereunder.

Sponsors are urged not to include in the prospectus information about prior performance beyond that required by this Guide except for such further material information as may be necessary to make the required statements, in light of the circumstances under which they are made, not misleading.

Terms used in the Guide. "Public" programs include all offerings registered under the Securities Act of 1933, all programs required to report under Section 15(d) of the Securities Exchange Act of 1934 ("Exchange Act"), all programs with a class of equity securities registered pursuant to Section 12(g) of the Exchange Act, and all other programs with at least 300 security holders of record that initially raised at least $1 million.

Programs with "similar investment objectives" are those with similar objectives as set forth in the prospectus. Generally, the sponsor has the responsibility to determine which previous programs had "similar investment objectives," taking into consideration the materiality of information about the prior programs in analyzing the registrant's proposed activities.

A sponsor would be considered to have a "public track record" if it has sponsored at least three programs with investment objectives similar to those of the registrant that file reports under Section 13(a) or Section 15(d) of the Exchange Act and at least two public programs with investment objectives similar to those of the registrant that had three years of operations after investments of 90% of the amount available for investment. In addition, at least two of the public offerings for programs with investment objectives to those of the registrant must have closed in the previous three years.

A. *Narrative Summary.*

1. The narrative summary in the text of the prospectus should include a description of the sponsor's experience in the last ten years with all other programs, both public and nonpublic, that have invested primarily in real estate, regardless of the investment objectives of the programs. This summary should include at least (a) the number of programs sponsored, (b) the total amount of money raised from investors, (c) the total number of investors, (d) the number of properties purchased and location by region, (e) the aggregate dollar amount of property purchased, (f) the percentage (based on purchase prices rather than on number) of properties that are commercial (broken out by shopping centers, office buildings and others) and residential, (g) the percentage (based on purchase prices) of new, used or construction properties, and (h) the number of properties sold. Aggregate figures should be presented separately for public and nonpublic programs. In addition, the narrative should indicate the approximate percentage of the overall data that represents activities of programs with investment objectives similar to those of the registrant. The summary also should cross-reference the prior performance tables.

2. The narrative summary should include a discussion of those major adverse business developments or conditions experienced by any prior program, either public or nonpublic, that would be material to investors in this program. The narrative summary also should include a cross-reference to further information that may be found in Appendix II as part of Table III.

3. The narrative summary should include a list of all prior public programs sponsored by the General Partner and its affiliates and an undertaking to provide upon request, for no fee, the most recent Form 10-K Annual Report filed with the Commission by any prior public program that has reported to the Commission within the last twenty-four months and to provide, for a reasonable fee, the exhibits to each such Form 10-K.

4. The narrative summary should include a summary of acquisitions of properties by programs in the most recent three years as set forth in Table VI of Appendix II. The summary should include the number of properties purchased, the type, location and method of financing. Reference should be made to the more detailed description of these acquisitions in Part II of the registration statement, and the registrant should undertake to provide the more detailed description from Part II without fee upon request.

B. *Prior Performance Tables.* The information required by the tables set forth in Appendix II should be included in the format shown. Tables should appear at the back of the prospectus except for Table VI, which should appear only in Part II of the registration statement. The instructions to the tables specify the programs and time periods about which information is required.

9. MANAGEMENT

A. If a material portion of the maximum net proceeds (allowing for reserves) is not committed to specific properties, disclosure should be made of the identity of the individuals who will make the investment decisions with appropriate background information including that required by Item 401(f) of Regulation S-K.

B. Any substantial reliance on a nonaffiliate in running the operations of the partnership should be disclosed and any relevant prior experience should be discussed. If material amounts of compensation or fees are to be paid to nonaffiliates, a separate heading should be provided entitled, "Fees and Compensation Arrangements with Nonaffiliates" and a tabular presentation describing such fees should be provided.

C. If there is provision in the partnership agreement or otherwise for a change in the management of the partnership, a description of how such change could be accomplished should be included.

D. The amount of, and reason for, any contingent liabilities of the General Partner and its affiliates with regard to prior programs now in existence should be disclosed. If this information appears in the financial statements it may be incorporated hereunder by reference.

10. *INVESTMENT OBJECTIVES AND POLICIES*

A. Disclosure should be made of the nature of the property intended to be purchased (*e.g.,* commercial, residential) and the criteria (*e.g.,* method of depreciation, location) to be utilized in evaluating proposed investments.

B. If there is provision in the partnership agreement or otherwise for change in the investment objectives of the partnership, a description of how such change could be made should be included.

C. Generally, where the net proceeds of the offering will be invested in non-specified properties or in properties that do not have any significant operating histories, it is not appropriate to make any statement setting forth a rate of return on the investment.

11. *DESCRIPTION OF REAL ESTATE INVESTMENTS*

A. Risks associated with specified properties, such as competitive factors, environmental regulation, rent control regulation, fuel or energy requirements and regulation should be noted.

B. If a material portion of the minimum net proceeds (allowing for reasonable reserves) is not committed to specific properties, the issuer should clearly so indicate in the prospectus.

Where a reasonable probability exists that a property will be acquired and the funds to be expended represent a material portion of the net proceeds of the minimum offering, the issuer should describe such property in the registration statement at the time of filing. Where after the registration statement has been filed but prior to its effectiveness a reasonable probability arises that a property will be acquired, a description of such property should be included in a pre-effective amendment to the registration statement. Where a reasonable probability that a property will be acquired arises after the effectiveness of the registration statement and during the distribution period, a 424(c) supplement or post-effective amendment, as appropriate, should be promptly filed. (See Undertaking D.)[*] Whether adequate disclosure of properties to be acquired has been timely made can only be determined by an examination of the facts in each case. This may vary due to different business practices particular to each issuer. Thus, as in all other situations, the burden of making adequate and timely disclosure rests solely with the issuer.

12. *FEDERAL TAXES*

A. *General Instructions.* This section should summarize under a series of appropriate headings all material Federal income tax aspects of the offering. State tax aspects need usually be summarized only to the extent required by Subsection L, below. Proper citations should be used whenever reference is made to sections of the Internal Revenue Code (the "Code"), the Treasury regulations, decided cases or other sources. An opinion of counsel as to all material tax aspects of the offering should be filed as an exhibit. Such opinion should cite relevant authority for any conclusions expressed. The tax sections of the prospectus should summarize or restate the tax information contained in the opinion.

The function of the tax opinion is to inform investors of the tax consequences they can reasonably expect from an investment in the partnership. If, with respect to an intended tax benefit, counsel are unable to express an opinion that such benefit will be available because of uncertainty in the law or for other reasons, the opinion should so state and also disclose that there is or may be a material tax risk the particular benefit will be disallowed on audit. The tax effect of such disallowance should be explained. Each material risk of disallowance of an intended tax benefit should be disclosed in the tax opinion and under the appropriate heading in the prospectus.

Tax counsel should be aware that their opinion speaks as of the effective date of the registration statement. Such opinion should be updated for any material changes or events occurring subsequent to filing and prior to the effective date. Ruling requests (including amendments) and rulings should also be filed as exhibits with the original filing, or by amendment as soon thereafter as available.

B. *Partnership Status.* This subsection should state whether an IRS ruling has been requested as to the entity's classification as a partnership for Federal income tax purposes. The contents of any ruling, including any conditions therein, should be summarized. Where a ruling or opinion of counsel as to partnership status is conditioned on the maintenance of certain net worth or other standards, there should be disclosure as to how these standards will be maintained in the future. If no IRS ruling as to partnership tax status has been requested or obtained, counsel's opinion as to partnership tax status should be summarized and the risk of IRS classification of the entity as a corporate association, referred to in the Risk Factors section, should be discussed.

C. *Taxation of Limited Partners.* Insofar as necessary to an understanding of the intended tax benefits and any material risks of their disallowance, this subsection should summarize basic rules of partnership taxation, e.g., that a partnership is not a taxable entity, that a partner will be required to report on his Federal tax return his

---

[*] It has come to the staff's attention that on a number of occasions issuers have identified properties to be purchased and have delayed proceeding with the purchase in order to avoid the necessary disclosure. In the staff's opinion, such practice is not consistent with the obligation of the issuer to disclose material facts relating to the offering.

distributive share of partnership income, gain, loss, deductions or credits, whether or not any actual distribution is made to such partner during his taxable year. The tax treatment of cash distributions to partners should also be explained.

If the partnership agreement provides special allocations among partners of distributive shares of income, gain, loss, deductions or credits, this subsection should set forth an opinion of counsel to the effect that the principal purpose of the allocations is not tax avoidance or evasion under Code Sec. 704(b)(2), and/or a risk disclosure to the effect that the IRS may on audit disallow any special allocation which it determines to have tax avoidance or evasion as its principal purpose. The tax consequences to partners of disallowance of a special allocation should be explained. Where applicable, the tax consequences of retroactive allocations to new partners should be discussed.

D. *Basis.* This subsection should explain that a partner may deduct his share of partnership losses only to the extent of the adjusted basis of his interest in the partnership. Inclusion of a partner's share of the partnership's nonrecourse debt in the adjusted basis of his partnership interest should be explained. If there is a question as to whether the partnership's nonrecourse debt will enter into bases of the limited partners' interests, that should be disclosed.

Where appropriate, there should be an explanation of the consequences to a limited partner of a reduction in his share of the partnership's nonrecourse debt as may result, for example, from a change in his profit sharing ratio.

E. *Depreciation and Recapture.* This subsection should explain the method or methods of depreciation to be used by the partnership on its depreciable property as well as the basis for determining useful lives of such property. Any material risks that the IRS may challenge useful lives chosen by the partnership should be disclosed together with an explanation of the possible tax consequences of applying longer useful lives to partnership property. If methods of depreciation available only to a "first-user" are to be utilized, the basis of such "first-user" status should be explained. Depreciation recapture may be explained here with appropriate cross-reference to subsections on Sale or Other Disposition of Partnership Property and Sale or Other Disposition of a Partnership Interest.

F. *Deductibility of Prepaid and Other Expenses.* As to prepaid interest, possible nondeductibility in the year of payment should be discussed. It should be explained that if a partnership takes a large deduction for prepaid interest in its first year of operation, having little or no income in such year, the IRS may determine that the prepayment created a material distortion of income at the partnership level and require that it be allocated over the term of the loan.

As to other material partnership expenses (e.g., interim commitment fees, management fees, permanent mortgage fees, etc.) it should be stated which are deductible, which are nondeductible and as to which deductibility is uncertain. Where applicable, the possible nondeductibility of guaranteed payments under Code Sec. 707(c) should be discussed.

G. *Tax Liabilities in Later Years.* This subsection should discuss the Risk Factors disclosure that after some years of partnership operations an investor's tax liabilities may exceed cash distributions in corresponding years. The tax problems that will arise after partnership property reaches the point when the partnership's nondeductible mortgage amortization payments exceed its depreciation deductions (the crossover point) should be explained.

It should also be explained that where partnership losses offset an investor's earned income taxable at a 50 percent rate, partnership income in later years may be taxed to the investor at a higher rate.

H. *Sale or Other Disposition of a Partnership Interest.* This subsection should begin with a restatement of the Risk Factors disclosure that an investor may be unable to sell his partnership interest as there may be no market for it. The subsection should then discuss the Risk Factors disclosure that taxes payable on a sale of a partnership interest may exceed cash received. The discussion should explain the tax effect on a partner of being relieved from his share of the partnership's nonrecourse liabilities. The discussion should also state to what extent the gain recognized will be taxed as ordinary income, to what extent as capital gain.

Whether or not the partnership plans to make the Sec. 754 election should be disclosed together with an explanation of the possible tax consequences on a transferee Limited Partner should the election not be made.

This subsection should also explain that a gift of an interest in a partnership holding leveraged property may result in Federal income tax (as well as Federal gift tax) liability to the donor. It should be explained that the IRS is likely to consider that a partner who gives away his partnership interest is relieved of his share of the partnership's nonrecourse liabilities and that he may realize a taxable gain on the gift to the extent that his share of such liabilities exceeds his adjusted basis in his partnership interest. It should be stated to what extent the gain will be taxed as ordinary income, to what extent as capital gain.

I. *Sale or Other Disposition of Partnership Property.* This subsection may use cross-reference to, or be combined with, subsection H in order to avoid repetition.

The subsection should discuss the Risk Factors disclosure that upon a sale (including a foreclosure sale) or other disposition of partnership property an investor's tax liability may exceed cash he would receive. The discussion should explain that the amount received by the partnership on sale (including a foreclosure sale) or other disposition of property will include any nonrecourse indebtedness to which the property was subject. It should be stated to what extent the gain will be taxed as ordinary income, to what extent as capital gain.

If appropriate, the tax treatment of dealer property should be explained. Should the sale of condominium units by the partnership be contemplated, it should be pointed out such units may be treated as dealer property.

J. *Section 183*. The possible impact of this Code section on investors lacking a profit objective in investing in any tax shelter program which is expected to generate annual net losses for tax purposes for a period of years should be discussed. The discussion should note that the section may apply to the Limited Partners of a partnership notwithstanding any profit objective the partnership itself may be deemed to have.

K. *Liquidation or Termination of the Partnership*. The tax consequences to a Limited Partner of partnership liquidation or termination should be explained.

L. *State, Local and Foreign Taxes*. It should be disclosed whether partners will be required to file tax returns and/or be subject to tax in any state or states other than their state of residence, or in any foreign countries. Where applicable, state and foreign tax rates should be noted.

M. *Tax Returns and Tax Information*. It should be disclosed what kind of tax information will be supplied to Limited Partners and when, and whether the same kind of information will also be supplied to assignees who are not substitute limited partners.

It should be explained that the information return filed by the partnership may be audited and that such audit may result in adjustments or proposed adjustments. Any adjustment of the partnership information return would normally result in adjustments or proposed adjustments of a partner's own return. Any audit of a partner's return could result in adjustments of nonpartnership as well as partnership income and losses.

N. *Other Headings*. Where applicable the tax section should also discuss the limitation on deductions of investment interest, the minimum tax on tax preference income, the impact of tax preference items on the maximum tax on earned income, and any other tax information deemed material in the particular offering.

13. *GLOSSARY*

If terms are used in the prospectus that are technical in nature or are susceptible to varying methods of computation, e.g., acquisition fees, book value, capital contribution, cash flow, cash available for distribution, construction fees, cost of property, development fee, net worth, organization and offering expenses, profit, partnership management fee and property management fee, definitions should be provided. For purposes of uniformity, it is suggested that these definitions conform to those that appear in the Statement of Policy Regarding Real Estate Programs of the North American Securities Administrators Association, or that any variations, and the economic effect thereof, be disclosed.

14. *SUMMARY OF PARTNERSHIP AGREEMENT*

A brief summary of the material provisions of the Limited Partnership Agreement should be included.

15. *REPORTS TO LIMITED PARTNERS*

The registrant should identify all reports and other documents that will be furnished to Limited Partners as required by the partnership's Limited Partnership Agreement and the undertakings to the registration statement. In particular, registrant should disclose: (1) whether the financial information contained in such reports will be prepared on an accrual basis in accordance with generally accepted accounting principles, with a reconciliation with respect to information furnished to limited partners for income tax purposes; (2) whether independent certified public accountants will audit the financial statements to be included in the annual report; (3) whether the annual report will be provided to limited partners within 90 days following the close of the partnership's fiscal year; (4) that a detailed statement of any transactions with the General Partner or its affiliates, and of fees, commissions, compensation and other benefits paid, or accrued to the General Partner or its affiliates for the fiscal year completed, showing the amount paid or accrued to each recipient and the services performed, will be furnished to each limited partner at least on an annual basis pursuant to the registrant's undertaking; (5) that the information specified by Form 10-Q (if such report is required to be filed with the Commission) will be furnished to limited partners within 45 days after the close of each quarterly fiscal period pursuant to the registrant's undertaking; and (6) if the registrant has applied for, but not received an IRS ruling as to the tax status at the time of effectiveness of the registration statement, that the registrant will promptly notify each limited partner, in writing, pursuant to its undertaking of the receipt of the ruling or of an adverse ruling or refusal to rule by the IRS.

16. *THE OFFERING—DESCRIPTION OF THE UNITS*

In addition to the disclosure required by the relevant items of Form S-1 or S-11, disclosure should be made of all restrictions on transfer of the interests, including those in the Partnership Agreement, those imposed by state suitability standards or blue sky laws, and those resulting from the tax laws.

17. REDEMPTION, REPURCHASE AND RIGHT OF PRESENTMENT AGREEMENTS

There should be a discussion of any provisions in the partnership agreement that allow the General Partner or its affiliates to redeem or repurchase the offered security or that allow the investor to seek redemption or repurchase. The conditions or formulae used, *e.g.*, purchase price less capital returns, should also be disclosed. Registrant should be careful to appropriately describe the investor's right—whether it be redemption, repurchase, or merely a right of presentment. The discussion should include the following factors:

(1) That appraisals are simply estimates of value and may not necessarily correspond to realizable value;

(2) The order in which redemption requests will be honored (post mark or other objective standard);

(3) Whether the General Partner and its affiliates will defer their redemption requests until requests for redemption by the Limited Partner public investors have been met;

(4) The source and amount of funds (together with any legal or practical limitations) available for this purpose;

(5) The circumstances under which a later request will be honored, while an earlier request is still pending;

(6) Tax consequences related to redemption;

(7) The period of time during which a redemption request may be pending prior to its being granted or rejected;

(8) Whether there is to be allocation of funds among partners requesting redemption in circumstances where redemption requests exceed funds available for this purpose. If so, state and briefly describe the allocation process;

(9) Whether Limited Partners must hold an interest in the partnership for a specified period prior to making a redemption request; and

(10) A detailed statement of the procedure that must be followed in order to redeem or seek repurchase of the interest, including the forms that must be presented, and whether signature guarantees will be required.

18. PLAN OF DISTRIBUTION

A. If there is an understanding or arrangement, whether written or oral, between the registrant and any broker or dealer, relating to the distribution of the interests, which is intended to be finalized after effectiveness of the registration statement, such understanding or arrangement should be disclosed.

B. If, after the registration statement becomes effective, the registrant enters into any selling arrangement which calls for the payment of more than the usual and customary compensation, a sticker supplement (Rule 424(c)) describing such arrangement should be filed.

C. If the registrant intends to pay referral or similar fees to any professional or other persons in connection with the distribution of the interests, this fact should be disclosed.

D. If the General Partner or its affiliates intend to purchase interests, and such interests will be included in satisfying the minimum offering requirements, it should be disclosed whether such interests are intended to be resold, and if so, the period of time these interests will be held prior to being resold. Depending on the circumstances, such interests may be considered to be unsold allotments under Section 4(3) of the Act. (See Securities Act Release 4150.)

19. SUMMARY OF PROMOTIONAL AND SALES MATERIAL

A. The sales material should present a balanced discussion of both risk and reward. The contents of the sales material or sales meetings or seminars should be consistent with the representations in the prospectus.

B. A section which identifies all written sales material proposed to be transmitted to prospective investors orally or in writing should be included. The sales material should be appropriately identified by title and character and should be separately categorized either as the registrant's material or that of another person. If material provided by the latter is to be used, state the name of the author and publication and the date of prior publication, if any, identify any persons who are quoted without being identified, and, except in the case of a public official document or statement, state whether or not the consent of the author and publication have been obtained for the use of the material as sales material. Sales materials include memoranda, summary descriptions, graphics, supplemental exhibits, media advertising, charts and pictures relating to the offering of the security and proposed to be transmitted to prospective investors.

C. If any other material is to be used subsequent to the effective date, a "sticker" supplement (424(c) prospectus) should be filed to describe any such sales material.

D. Any sales material that is intended to be furnished to investors orally or in writing, other than that which is used for internal purposes of the registrant, and including all material described in paragraph B above, should be submitted to the staff supplementally, prior to its use. For purposes of this paragraph only, sales material includes all marketing memoranda that are sent by the General Partner or its affiliates to broker/dealers or other sales personnel and may include material labeled "for broker/dealer use only." Staff comments, if any, will be promptly communicated to the registrant. Registrant should check with the staff before using sale material that has been submitted to the staff.

E. Wherever public sales meetings or seminars are to be employed to discuss the offering, individually or in conjunction with other tax sheltered offerings, the staff should be provided, as supplemental information, copies of any written scripts or outlines which are prepared for use in such meetings a reasonable time prior to their use.

F. Reference in sales material or at such sales meetings or seminars to Federal income tax treatment of the partnership and its investors should refer to either a ruling of the IRS or an opinion of counsel. Counsel should be named, his acknowledgement furnished supplementally with respect to such use, and any qualification contained in counsel's opinion should be referred to in such material by cross-referencing to the prospectus. Where the program has not sought a ruling as to the tax status (partnership) from the IRS and is relying on an opinion of counsel, it should be indicated that an opinion of counsel is not binding on the IRS.

20. *UNDERTAKINGS*

A. The following undertaking should be included in the registration statement if the securities to be registered are to be offered in a continuous offering over an extended period of time:

The registrant undertakes (a) to file any prospectuses required by Section 10(a)(3) as post-effective amendments to the registration statement, (b) that for the purpose of determining any liability under the Act each such post-effective amendment may be deemed to be a new registration statement relating to the securities offered therein and the offering of such securities at that time may be deemed to be the initial bona fide offering thereof, (c) that all post-effective amendments will comply with the applicable forms, rules and regulations of the Commission in effect at the time such post-effective amendments are filed, and (d) to remove from registration by means of a post-effective amendment any of the securities being registered which remain at the termination of the offering.

B. The following undertaking should be included in every registration statement:

The registrant undertakes to send to each limited partner at least on an annual basis a detailed statement of any transactions with the General Partner or its affiliates, and of fees, commissions, compensation and other benefits paid, or accrued to the General Partner or its affiliates for the fiscal year completed, showing the amount paid or accrued to each recipient and the services performed.

C. The following undertaking should be included in every registration statement:

The registrant undertakes to provide to the limited partners the financial statements required by Form 10-K for the first full fiscal year of operations of the partnership.

D. The following undertakings relating to investment of the proceeds of an offering in which a material portion of the maximum net proceeds (allowing for reasonable reserves) is not committed (i.e., subject to a binding purchase agreement) to specific properties should be included in the registration statement:

The registrant undertakes to file a sticker supplement pursuant to Rule 424(c) under the Act during the distribution period describing each property not identified in the prospectus at such time as there arises a reasonable probability that such property will be acquired and to consolidate all such stickers into a post-effective amendment filed at least once every three months, with the information contained in such amendment provided simultaneously to the existing Limited Partners. Each sticker supplement should disclose all compensation and fees received by the General Partner(s) and its affiliates in connection with any such acquisition. The post-effective amendment shall include audited financial statements meeting the requirements of Rule 3-14 of Regulation S-X only for properties acquired during the distribution period.

The registrant also undertakes to file, after the end of the distribution period, a current report on Form 8-K containing the financial statements and any additional information required by Rule 3-14 of Regulation S-X, to reflect each commitment (i.e., the signing of a binding purchase agreement) made after the end of the distribution period involving the use of 10% or more (on a cumulative basis) of the net proceeds of the offering and to provide the information contained in such report to the Limited Partners at least once each quarter after the distribution period of the offering has ended.

Note—Offers and sales of the interests may continue after the filing of a post-effective amendment containing information previously disclosed in sticker supplements to the prospectus, as long as the information disclosed in a current sticker supplement accompanying the prospectus is as complete as the information contained in the most recently filed post-effective amendment.

E. If the registrant has applied for a ruling from the IRS as to tax status, and has not received it at the time of effectiveness:

The registrant undertakes to promptly notify each limited partner, in writing, of the receipt of the ruling or of an adverse ruling or refusal to rule by the IRS, and undertakes to file with the Commission a Form 8-K describing such event.

APPENDIX I
EXAMPLE OF SUMMARY OF THE USE OF PROCEEDS SECTION
Estimated Application of Proceeds of This Offering

	Minimum Dollar Amount	Per Cent	Maximum Dollar Amount	Per Cent
Gross Offering Proceeds	$	100.00 %	$	100.00 %
Public Offering Expenses:				
Underwriting Discount and Commissions				
Paid to Affiliate				
Organizational Expenses (1)				
Amount Available for investment	$	%	$	%
Prepaid Terms and Fees Related to Purchase of Property (2)				
Cash Down Payment (Equity)				
Acquisition Fees (Real Estate Commissions) (3)				
Working Capital Reserve				
Proceeds Invested				
Public Offering Expenses				
Total Application of Proceeds	$	%	$	100.00 %

The Corporate General Partner and its affiliates may receive a maximum of $ (%) if the minimum dollar amount is sold and $ (%) if the maximum dollar amount is sold from the sellers of the properties as Real Estate Commissions on purchases of properties. Real estate commissions are normally paid by the seller of a property rather than the buyer. However, the price of a property will generally be adjusted upward to take into account this obligation of the seller so that in effect the Partnership, as purchaser, will bear all or a portion of the commission in the purchase price of the property. The partnership also expects to pay commissions in connection with the sale of properties which will reduce the net proceeds to the Partnership of any such sales.

(1) Includes a $ non-recurring organization fee to be received by the Corporate General Partner and legal, accounting, printing and other expenses of this offering. To the extent, if any, that expenses of the offering exceed $ per interest, the excess will be paid by.

(2) Includes prepaid interest, points, loan commitment fees and legal and other costs of acquisition. The percentage of such items to be capitalized is ... %.

(3) "Real Estate Commission" is defined as the total of all fees and commissions paid by any person to any person, including the Corporate General Partner or affiliates in connection with the selection, purchase, construction or development of any property by the Partnership, whether designated as real estate commission, acquisition fees, finders fees, selection fees, development fees, construction fees, non-recurring management fees, consulting fees or any other similar fees or commissions howsoever designated and howsoever treated for tax or accounting purposes. (See "Compensation to Management." Page.)

APPENDIX II
PRIOR PERFORMANCE TABLES
Instructions to Appendix II

1. The prior performance tables should be preceded by a narrative introduction that cross-references the narrative summary in the text, explains the significance of the track record and the tables, explains where additional information (Part II of the registration statement or Form 10-K Annual Reports for prior programs) can be obtained on request and includes a glossary of terms used in the tables.

This introduction also should include a discussion of the factors the sponsor considered in determining which previous programs had "similar investment objectives" to those of the registrant.

2. Each of the tables should be introduced by a brief narrative explaining the objective of the table and what it covers so that the investor will be able to understand the significance of the information presented. There also should be set forth with or in each table any further material information that may be necessary to make the required tabular data, in light of the circumstances under which it is presented, not misleading.

Table I. Experience in Raising and Investing Funds (on a percentage basis)

Instructions: 1. Include information only for programs the offering of which closed in the most recent three years.

2. Sponsors with a "public track record" should include information relating only to public programs with investment objectives similar to those of the registrant.

3. If the sponsor does not have a "public track record," information must be given for each prior program, public or nonpublic, with investment objectives similar to those of the registrant. If the sponsor has not sponsored at least five such programs, then information must be given for each prior program, public or nonpublic, even if the investment objectives for those programs are not similar to those of the registrant. In that case, nonpublic programs with investment objectives that are not similar to those of the registrant should be grouped together according to investment objective and information about those programs presented on an aggregate basis by year. If so presented, the number of programs that have been aggregated should be disclosed. The sponsor also should indicate by note if the investment objectives of any program are not similar to those of the registrant and should briefly describe those investment objectives.

	Program X	Program Y
Dollar amount offered		
Dollar amount raised (100%)		
Less offering expenses:		
Selling commissions and discounts Retained by affiliates		
Organizational expenses		
Other (explain)		
Reserves		
Percent available for investment		
Acquisition costs:		
Prepaid items and fees related to purchase of property		
Cash down payment		
Acquisition fees		
Other (explain)		
Total acquisition cost		
Percent leverage (mortgage financing divided by total acquisition cost)		
Date offering began		
Length of offering (in months)		
Months to invest 90% of amount available for investment (measured from beginning of offering)		

Table II. Compensation to Sponsor

Instructions: 1. Include in a separate column for each program aggregated payments made to the sponsor only by real estate programs the offering of which closed in the most recent three years. Include in another separate column aggregate payments to the sponsor in the most recent three years from all other programs and indicate the number of programs involved.

2. Sponsors with a "public track record" should include information relating only to public programs with investment objectives similar to those of the registrant.

3. If the sponsor does not have a "public track record," information must be given for each prior program, public or nonpublic, with investment objectives similar to those of the registrant. If the sponsor has not sponsored at least five such programs, then information must be given for each prior program, public or nonpublic, even if the investment objectives for those programs are not similar to those of the registrant. In that case, nonpublic programs with investment objectives that are not similar to those of the registrant should be grouped together according to investment objective and information about those programs presented on an aggregate basis by year. If so presented, the number of programs that have been aggregated should be disclosed. The sponsor also should indicate by note if the investment objectives of any program are not similar to those of the registrant and should briefly describe those investment objectives.

4. The table should include any real estate commissions and other fees paid to the sponsor in connection with the acquisition or disposition of any properties by the program by entities other than the program itself.

Type of Compensation	Program X	Program Y	*Other Programs*
Date offering commenced			
Dollar amount raised			
Amount paid to sponsor from proceeds of offering:			

Type of Compensation	Program X	Program Y	Other Programs
Underwriting fees			
Acquisition fees			
—real estate commissions			
—advisory fees			
—other (identify and quantify)			
Other			
Dollar amount of cash generated from operations before deducting payments to sponsor			
Amount paid to sponsor from operations:			
Property management fees			
Partnership management fees			
Reimbursements			
Leasing commissions			
Other (identify and quantify)			
Dollar amount of property sales and refinancing before deducting payments to sponsor			
—cash			
—notes			
Amount paid to sponsor from property sales and refinancing:			
Real estate commissions			
Incentive fees[1]			
Other (identify and quantify)			

[1] Explain subordinated commissions in a note.

Table III. Operating Results of Prior Programs

Instructions:

1. Include information only for programs the offerings of which closed in the most recent five years. Financial data for each program should be presented separately for each year.

2. Sponsors with a "public track record" should include information relating only to public programs with investment objectives similar to those of the registrant.

3. If the sponsor does not have a "public track record," information must be given for each program, public or nonpublic, with investment objectives similar to those of the registrant. If the sponsor has not sponsored at least five such programs, then information must be given for each prior program, public or nonpublic, even if the investment objectives for those programs are not similar to those of the registrant. In that case, nonpublic programs with investment objectives that are not similar to those of the registrant should be grouped together according to investment objective and information about those programs presented on an aggregate basis by year. If so presented, the number of programs that have been aggregated should be disclosed. The sponsor also should indicate by note if the investment objectives of any program are not similar to those of the registrant and should briefly describe those investment objectives.

4. Information should be presented on the basis of generally accepted accounting principles ("GAAP") where indicated. However, where information about nonpublic programs is required to be included, such information may be presented on a tax basis if the program's books have not been kept on a GAAP basis. If there are any significant differences in operating results between accounting on a tax and GAAP basis, they should be explained. This explanation should provide the reader with any additional information about the particular programs presented that may be necessary to make the information contained in the Table not materially misleading in light of the circumstances under which the information is given.

	Program X		
	year 1	year 2	year 3
Gross Revenues			
Profit on sale of properties			
Less: Operating expenses			

¶12,041   Guide 5

	Program X		
	year 1	year 2	year 3

Interest expense
Depreciation
Net Income—GAAP Basis
Taxable Income
 —from operations
 —from gain on sale
Cash generated from operations[1]
Cash generated from sales
Cash generated from refinancing
Cash generated from operations, sales and refinancing
Less: Cash distributions to investors
  —from operating cash flow
  —from sales and refinancing
  —from other
Cash generated (deficiency) after cash distributions
Less: Special items (not including sales and refinancing) (identify and quantify)
Cash generated (deficiency) after cash distributions and special items
Tax and Distribution Data Per $1000 Invested
Federal Income Tax Results:
 Ordinary income (loss)
 —from operations
 —from recapture
 Capital gain (loss)
Cash Distributions to Investors Source (on GAAP basis)
  —Investment income
  —Return of capital
 Source (on cash basis)
  —Sales
  —Refinancing
  —Operations
  —Other
Amount (in percentage terms) remaining invested in program properties at the end of the last year reported in the Table (original total acquisition cost of properties retained divided by original total acquisition cost of all properties in program).

---

[1] Indicate in a note what amount is from sources other than operations, such as guaranteed rents or interest.

Table IV. Results of Completed Programs

Instructions:

1. Include programs that have completed operations (no longer hold properties) in the most recent five years, even if they still hold notes.

2. Sponsors with a "public track record" should include information relating only to public programs with investment objectives similar to those of the registrant.

3. If the sponsor does not have a "public track record," information must be given for each prior program, public or nonpublic, with investment objectives similar to those of the registrant. If the sponsor has not sponsored at least five such programs, then information must be given for each prior program, public or nonpublic, even if the investment objectives for those programs are not similar to those of the registrant. In that case, nonpublic programs with investment objectives that are not similar to those of the registrant should be grouped together according to investment objective and information about those programs presented on an

aggregate basis by year. If so presented, the number of programs that have been aggregated should be disclosed. The sponsor also should indicate by note if the investment objectives of any program are not similar to those of the registrant and should briefly describe those investment objectives.

Program Name

    Dollar Amount Raised

    Number of Properties Purchased

    Date of Closing of Offering

    Date of First Sale of Property

    Date of Final Sale of Property

Tax and Distribution Data Per $1000 Investment Through . . .

    Federal Income Tax Results:

    Ordinary income (loss)

        —from operations

        —from recapture

    Capital Gain (loss)[1]

    Deferred Gain[2]

    Capital

    Ordinary

Cash Distributions to Investors

    Source (on GAAP basis)

        —Investment income

        —Return of capital

    Source (on cash basis)

        —Sales

        —Refinancing

        —Operations

        —Other

Receivable on Net Purchase Money Financing[3]

---

[1] Note 60% capital gain exclusion.
[2] Explain in a note deferred capital gain.

[3] Explain in a note the terms of notes taken back and annual payments, and the fact that the amounts presented are face amounts and do not represent discounted current value.

Table V. Sales or Disposals of Properties

Instructions:

1. Include all sales or disposals of property by programs with similar investment objectives within the most recent three years.

2. Sponsors with a "public track record" should only include information relating to public programs. If the sponsor does not have a "public track record," then information should be given about sales or disposals of properties by public and nonpublic programs. Where properties held by nonpublic programs are included, information should be on a GAAP basis where feasible without undue effort or expense.

Property	Date acquired	Date of Sale [1]	Selling Price, Net of Closing Costs and GAAP Adjustments					Cost of Properties Including Closing and Soft Costs			Excess (Deficiency) of Property Operating Cash Receipts Over Cash Expenditures [6]
			Cash received net of closing costs	Mortgage balance at time of sale	Purchase money mortgage taken back by program[2]	Adjustments resulting from application of GAAP[3]	Total[4]	Original mortgage financing	Total acquisition cost, capital improvement, closing and soft costs[5]	Total	

[1] Note if sales of properties are to related parties.

[2] Indicate in a note that the amounts shown are face amounts and do not represent discounted current value. In addition, describe the terms of purchase money mortgages taken by the partnership, including the interest rate, any balloon payment requirements and other special provisions. Also, describe those sales made with a leaseback or any other guarantees which require continued seller involvement.

[3] Include an explanation of any GAAP adjustments.

[4] Note the allocation of the taxable gain between ordinary and capital, and identify those sales that are being reported for tax purposes on the installment basis.

[5] Identify real estate commissions carried but not taken. Indicate that the amounts shown do not include pro rata share of original offering costs.

[6] Do not include amounts otherwise included under "Selling Price, Net of Closing Costs and GAAP Adjustments" or "Cost of Properties including Closing and Soft Costs." Costs incurred in the administration of the partnership not related to the operation of properties need not be included in a note to the Table.

Table VI. Acquisitions of Properties by Programs

Instructions:

   1. Include the following table only in Part II of the registration statement.

   2. Include all properties acquired by any prior programs with similar investment objectives in the most recent three years.

   3. Sponsors with a "public track record" should only include information relating to public programs. If the sponsor does not have a "public track record," then information should be given about properties acquired by public and nonpublic programs.

Program X

   Name, location, type of property

   Gross leasable space (sq. ft.) or number of units and total square feet of units

   Date of purchase

   Mortgage financing at date of purchase

   Cash down payment

   Contract purchase price plus acquisition fee

   Other cash expenditures expensed

   Other cash expenditures capitalized

   Total acquisition cost

   [As last amended in Release No. 33-6465, April 22, 1983, 48 F.R. 19873.]

[¶ 12,051] Guide 6—Disclosures Concerning Unpaid Claims and Claim Adjustment Expenses of Property-Casualty Insurance Underwriters

1. General Instructions:

Guide 6. The Guide applies to the description of business portions of registration statements of companies with property-casualty ("P/C") insurance reserves for which financial statements are required.

The information should be furnished if reserves for unpaid P/C claims and claim adjustment expenses of the registrant and its consolidated subsidiaries, its unconsolidated subsidiaries and its 50%-or-less-owned equity basis investees, taken in the aggregate after intercompany eliminations, exceed one-half of the common stockholder's equity of the registrant and its consolidated subsidiaries as of the beginning of the latest fiscal year. For purposes of this test, only the proportionate share of the registrant and its other subsidiaries in the unpaid claims and claim adjustment expenses of 50%-or-less-owned equity basis investees shall be taken into account.

Information should be presented separately for (a) the registrant and its consolidated subsidiaries, (b) unconsolidated subsidiaries and (c) 50%-or-less-owned equity investees. If ending reserves in category (a), (b), or the proportionate share of the registrant and its other subsidiaries in (c) above are less than 5% of the total ending reserves in (a), (b), and the proportionate share in (c), the information called for by Instruction 2B with respect to that category may be omitted.

Information furnished in accordance with this Guide should generally be presented in the form appearing below. However, an alternative presentation, such as inclusion of the information in Management's Discussion and Analysis, may be used if in management's opinion such presentation would be more meaningful to investors.

Except where noted, the information furnished pursuant to this Guide shall be for the latest annual period for which financial statements are required. However, information for any additional interim periods should be provided to the extent necessary to keep the annual information from being misleading, such as where a material change in the information presented or the trend evidenced thereby has occurred.

2. Description of the Business

A. Discussion Topics

   The following should be among the matters discussed in the description of business.

   (1) The nature of current year adjustments to loss reserves recorded in prior years.

   (2) Reinsurance transactions (including "swaps" of reserves, portfolio loss transfers, etc.) which have a material effect on earnings or reserves.

¶12,051   Guide 6

(3) Significant reserving assumptions and recent changes therein.

(4) The nature of recent changes in the terms under which reinsurance is ceded to other insurers.

(5) Changes in the mix of business, including but not limited to changes in the location of business, geographic mix, and types of risks assumed.

(6) Changes in payment patterns due to portfolio loss transfers, structured settlements and other transactions and circumstances.

(7) Unusually large losses or gains.

(8) The effect of currency fluctuations.

B. Disclosures

The following (all presented in accordance with generally accepted accounting principles) should be among the items included in the description of business.

(1) *Reconciliation of claims reserves.*

An analysis of changes in aggregate reserves for property casualty insurance claims and claim adjustment expenses for each of the latest three one-year periods in the following tabular format:

(a) Amount of reserves for unpaid claims and claim adjustment expenses at the beginning of each year.

(b) Incurred claims and claim adjustment expenses:

(i) Provision for insured events of the current year

(ii) Increases (decrease) in provision for insured events of prior years

Total incurred claims and claim adjustment expenses

(c) Payments

(i) Claims and claim adjustment expenses attributable to insured events of the current year

(ii) Claims and claim adjustment expenses attributable to insured events of prior years

(d) Other (provide an explanation of each material item)

(e) Amount of reserves for unpaid claims and claim adjustment expenses at the end of each year.

(2) *Loss reserve development*

A table that presents

(a) Amounts of reserves for unpaid claims and claim adjustment expenses as of the end of each of the ten years prior to the latest fiscal year.

(b) The cumulative amount paid as of the end of each succeeding year with respect to each of the reserve amounts presented in response to (a) above.

(c) The retroactively reestimated liability for unpaid claims and claim adjustment expenses as of the end of each succeeding year with respect to each of the reserve amounts presented in response to (a) above.

(d) The difference between the latest reestimated liability presented in response to (c) with respect to each of the year-ends reflected in (a) above and the liabilities set forth in (a).

The amounts presented in (b), (c), and (d) above may be in dollars or expressed as a percentage of the amounts in (a).

The registrant should include an explanation of the data which will disclose the effects of unusual circumstances, for example changes in reinsurance agreements, which might distort the data.

(3) If the registrant makes explicit provision for the effects of inflation or for the combined effects of a number of factors (including inflation) that are expected to cause future changes in claims severities, describe briefly registrant's method of estimating the amount of that provision. An explicit provision is one in which the reserving system requires the estimation of a separate provision for inflation. The rates may be generated by the system or obtained from other appropriate sources. If the registrant makes implicit provision for the effects of inflation or for the combined effects of a number of factors (including inflation) that are expected to cause future changes in claims severities describe the circumstances on which management relies in concluding that the implicit provision is adequate. Provisions for inflation for this purpose may be taken to mean provision for any change in average claim severities if this permits more meaningful disclosure.

(4) State the amount of the difference, if any, between GAAP basis P/C reserves for claims and claim adjustment expenses for each of the groups mentioned in the next to last paragraph of Item 1 of this Guide and statutory P/C reserves for claims and claim adjustment expenses in total for each of those groups. Explain briefly the nature and amount of principal differences.

(5) State the amount (estimated if necessary) by which GAAP basis claim reserves have been discounted. State also the effect (estimated if necessary) on pre-tax income (loss) of discounts accrued and the effect of discounts amortized. Describe briefly the principal types of business for which reserves are discounted.

[As adopted in Release No. 33-6559, November 27, 1984, 49 F.R. 47594.]

[¶ 12,061] Guide 7—Description of Property by Issuers Engaged or to be Engaged in Significant Mining Operations

Guide 7. (a) *Definitions.* The following definitions apply to registrants engaged or to be engaged in significant mining operations:

(1) *Reserve.* That part of a mineral deposit which could be economically and legally extracted or produced at the time of the reserve determination.

Note: Reserves are customarily stated in terms of "ore" when dealing with metalliferous minerals; when other materials such as coal, oil, shale, tar, sands, limestone, etc. are involved, an appropriate term such as "recoverable coal" may be substituted.

(2) *Proven (Measured) Reserves.* Reserves for which (a) quantity is computed from dimensions revealed in outcrops, trenches, workings or drill holes; grade and/or quality are computed from the results of detailed sampling and (b) the sites for inspection, sampling and measurement are spaced so closely and the geologic character is so well defined that size, shape, depth and mineral content of reserves are well-established.

(3) *Probable (Indicated) Reserves.* Reserves for which quantity and grade and/or quality are computed from information similar to that used for proven (measure) reserves, but the sites for inspection, sampling, and measurement are farther apart or are otherwise less adequately spaced. The degree of assurance, although lower than that for proven (measured) reserves, is high enough to assume continuity between points of observation.

(4) (i) *Exploration Stage*—includes all issuers engaged in the search for mineral deposits (reserves) which are not in either the development or production stage.

(ii) *Development Stage*—includes all issuers engaged in the preparation of an established commercially minable deposit (reserves) for its extraction which are not in the production stage.

(iii) *Production Stage*—includes all issuers engaged in the exploitation of a mineral deposit (reserve).

Instruction to paragraph (a).

1. Mining companies in the exploration stage should not refer to themselves as development stage companies in the financial statements, even though such companies should comply with FASB Statement No. 7, if applicable.

(b) *Mining Operations Disclosure.* Furnish the following information as to each of the mines, plants and other significant properties owned or operated, or presently intended to be owned or operated, by the registrant:

(1) The location and means of access to the property;

(2) A brief description of the title, claim, lease or option under which the registrant and its subsidiaries have or will have the right to hold or operate the property, indicating any conditions which the registrant must meet in order to obtain or retain the property. If held by leases or options, the expiration dates of such leases or options should be stated. Appropriate maps may be used to portray the locations of significant properties;

(3) A brief history of previous operations, including the names of previous operators, insofar as known;

(4) (i) A brief description of the present condition of the property, the work completed by the registrant on the property, the registrant's proposed program of exploration and development, and the current state of exploration and/or development of the property. Mines should be identified as either open-pit or underground. If the property is without known reserves and the proposed program is exploratory in nature, a statement to that effect shall be made;

(ii) The age, details as to modernization and physical condition of the plant and equipment, including subsurface improvements and equipment. Further, the total cost for each property and its associated plant and equipment should be stated. The source of power utilized with respect to each property should also be disclosed.

(5) A brief description of the rock formations and mineralization of existing or potential economic significance on the property, including the identity of the principal metallic or other constituents insofar as known. If proven (measured) or probable (indicated) reserves have been established, state (i) the estimated tonnages and grades (or quality, where appropriate) of such classes of reserves, and (ii) the name of the person making the estimates and the nature of his relationship to the registrant.

Instructions to paragraph (b)(5).

1. It should be stated whether the reserve estimate is of in-place material or of recoverable material. Any inplace estimate should be qualified to show the anticipated losses resulting from mining methods and beneficiation or preparation.

2. The summation of proven (measured) and probable (indicated) ore reserves is acceptable if the difference in degree of assurance between the two classes of reserves cannot be readily defined.

3. Estimates other than proved (measured) or probable (indicated) reserves, and any estimated values of such reserves shall not be disclosed unless such information is required to be disclosed by foreign or state law; provided, however, that where such estimates previously have been provided to a person (or any of its affiliates) that is offering to acquire, merge, or consolidate with, the registrant or otherwise to acquire the registrant's securities, such estimates may be included.

(6) If technical terms relating to geology, mining or related matters whose definition cannot readily be found in conventional dictionaries (as opposed to technical dictionaries or glossaries) are used, an appropriate glossary should be included in this report.

(7) Detailed geographic maps and reports, feasibility studies and other highly technical data should not be included in the report but should be, to the degree appropriate and necessary for the Commission's understanding of the registrant's presentation of business and property matters, furnished as supplemental information.

(c) Supplemental Information.

(1) If an estimate of proven (measured) or probable (indicated) reserves is set forth in the report, furnish:

(i) maps drawn to scale showing any mine workings and the outlines of the reserve blocks involved together with the pertinent sample-assay thereon.

(ii) all pertinent drill data and related maps.

(iii) the calculations whereby the basic sample-assay or drill data were translated into the estimates made of the grade and tonnage of reserves in each block and in the complete reserve estimate.

Instructions to paragraph (c)(1).

1. Maps and drawings submitted to the staff should include:

    (a) A legend or explanation showing, by means of pattern or symbol, every pattern or symbol used on the map or drawing; the use of the symbols used by the U.S. Geological Survey is encouraged;

    (b) A graphical bar scale should be included; additional representations of scale such as "one inch equals one mile" may be utilized provided the original scale of the map has not been altered;

    (c) A north arrow on the maps;

    (d) An index map showing where the property is situated in relationship to the state or province, etc., in which it was located;

    (e) A title of the map or drawing and the date on which it was drawn;

    (f) In the event interpretive data is submitted in conjunction with any map, the identity of the geologist or engineer that prepared such data; and

    (g) Any drawing should be simple enough or of sufficiently large scale to clearly show all features on the drawing.

(2) Furnish a complete copy of every material engineering, geological or metallurgical report concerning the registrant's property, including governmental reports, which are known and available to the registrant. Every such report should include the name of its author and the date of its preparation, if known to the registrant.

Instruction to paragraph (c)(2).

1. Any of the above-required reports as to which the staff has access need not be submitted. In this regard, issuers should consult with the staff prior to filing the report. Any reports not submitted should be identified in a list furnished to the staff. This list should also identify any known governmental reports concerning the registrant's property.

(3) Furnish copies of all documents such as title documents, operating permits and easements needed to support representations made in the report.

[As adopted in Release No. FR-39, July 30, 1992, effective August 13, 1992, 57 F.R. 36442.]

EXCHANGE ACT INDUSTRY GUIDES

[¶ 12,501]   Guide 1—Disclosure by Electric and Gas Utilities

Guide 1. [Removed and reserved in Release No. 33-7300, May 31, 1996, effective July 15, 1996, 61 F.R. 30397.]

≫→ *Caution: Guide 2 has been removed by Release No. 33-8995, effective January 1, 2010, 74 F.R. 2157. The oil and gas disclosure requirements have been revised and codified into Regulation S-K at Subpart 229.1200.*

[¶ 12,511]   Guide 2—Disclosure of Oil and Gas Operations

Guide 2. [The text of this Guide is the same as Securities Act Industry Guide 2 which is reproduced at ¶ 12,011. CCH.]

[As adopted in Release No. 34-18525, March 3, 1982, effective May 24, 1982, 47 F.R. 11476.]

[¶ 12,521]   Guide 3—Statistical Disclosure by Bank Holding Companies

Guide 3. This Guide applies to the description of business portion of bank holding company registration statements filed on Form 10 (Item 1) [17 CFR 249.210], in proxy and information statements relating to mergers, consolidations, acquisitions and similar matters (Item 14 of Schedule 14A and Item 1 of Schedule 14C) [17 CFR 240.14a-101 and 240.14c-101], and in reports filed on Form 10-K (Item 1) [17 CFR 249.310].

[The balance of Guide 3 is identical to Securities Act Industry Guide 3 which is reproduced at ¶ 12,021. CCH.]

[As last amended in Release No. 34-23846, November 25, 1986, 51 F.R. 43594.]

[¶ 12,531]   Guide 4—Disclosures Concerning Unpaid Claims and Claim Adjustment Expenses of Property Casualty Underwriters

Guide 4. The Guide applies to the description of business portion of registration statements filed on Form 10 (Item 1) [17 CFR 249.210], in proxy and information statements relating to mergers, consolidations, acquisitions, and similar matters (Item 14 of Schedule 14A and Item 1 of Schedule 14C) [17 CFR 240.14a-101 and 240.14c-101], and in reports filed on Form 10-K (Item 1) [17 CFR 249.310].

[The balance of the Guide is identical to Securities Act Industry Guide 6.]

[As adopted in Release No. 33-6559, November 27, 1984, 49 F.R. 47594.]

[¶ 12,561]   Guide 7—Description of Property by Issuers Engaged or to Be Engaged in Significant Mining Operations

Guide 7. [The text of this Guide is the same as Securities Act Industry Guide 7 which is reproduced at ¶ 12,061. CCH.]

¶ 12,501   Guide 7

REGULATIONS S-K, M-A AND AB

REGULATIONS S-K, M-A and AB

TABLE OF CONTENTS

REGULATION M-A

Subpart 229.1000—Mergers and Acquisitions (Regulation M-A)

REGULATION AB

Subpart 229.1100—Asset-Backed Securities (Regulation AB)

REGULATION S-K

PART 229—STANDARD INSTRUCTIONS FOR FILING FORMS UNDER SECURITIES ACT OF 1933, SECURITIES EXCHANGE ACT OF 1934 AND ENERGY POLICY AND CONSERVATION ACT OF 1975—

REGULATION S-K

Subpart 229.1—General

ATTENTION ELECTRONIC FILERS

THIS REGULATION SHOULD BE READ IN CONJUNCTION WITH REGULATION S- T (PART 232 OF THIS CHAPTER), WHICH GOVERNS THE PREPARATION AND SUBMISSION OF DOCUMENTS IN ELECTRONIC FORMAT. MANY PROVISIONS RELATING TO THE PREPARATION AND SUBMISSION OF DOCUMENTS IN PAPER FORMAT CONTAINED IN THIS REGULATION ARE SUPERSEDED BY THE PROVISIONS OF REGULATION S-T FOR DOCUMENTS REQUIRED TO BE FILED IN ELECTRONIC FORMAT.

[¶ 13,001] General

Reg. § 229.10. (Item 10). (a) *Application of Regulation S-K.* This part (together with the General Rules and Regulations under the Securities Act of 1933, 15 U.S.C. 77a et seq., as amended ("Securities Act"), and the Securities Exchange Act of 1934, 15 U.S.C. 78a et seq., as amended ("Exchange Act") (Parts 230 and 240 of this chapter), the Interpretative Releases under these Acts (Parts 231 and 241 of this chapter) and the forms under these Acts (Parts 239 and 249 of this chapter)) states the requirements applicable to the content of the non-financial statement portions of:

(1) Registration statements under the Securities Act (Part 239 of this chapter) to the extent provided in the forms to be used for registration under such Act; and

(2) Registration statements under section 12 (subpart C of part 249 of this chapter), annual or other reports under sections 13 and 15(d) (subparts D and E of part 249 of this chapter), going-private transaction statements under section 13 (part 240 of this chapter), tender offer statements under sections 13 and 14 (part 240 of this chapter), annual reports to security holders and proxy and information statements under section 14 (part 240 of this chapter), and any other documents required to be filed under the Exchange Act, to the extent provided in the forms and rules under that Act.

(b) *Commission policy on projections.* The Commission encourages the use in documents specified in Rule 175 under the Securities Act (§ 230.175 of this chapter) and Rule 3b-6 under the Exchange Act (§ 240.3b-6 of this chapter) of management's projections of future economic performance that have a reasonable basis and are presented in an appropriate format. The guidelines set forth herein represent the Commission's views on important factors to be considered in formulating and disclosing such projections.

(1) *Basis for projections.* The Commission believes that management must have the option to present in Commission filings its good faith assessment of a registrant's future performance. Management, however, must have a reasonable basis for such an assessment. Although a history of operations or experience in projecting may be among the factors providing a basis for management's assessment, the Commission does not believe that a registrant always must have had such a history or experience in order to formulate projections with a reasonable basis. An outside review of management's projections may furnish additional support for having a reasonable basis for a projection. If management decides to include a report of such a review in a Commission filing, there also should be disclosure of the qualifications of the reviewer, the extent of the review, the relationship between the reviewer and the registrant, and other material factors concerning the process by which any outside review was sought or obtained. Moreover, in the case of a registration statement under the Securities Act, the reviewer would be deemed an expert and an appropriate consent must be filed with the registration statement.

(2) *Format for projections.* In determining the appropriate format for projections included in Commission filings, consideration must be given to, among other things, the financial items to be projected, the period to be covered, and the manner of presentation to be used. Although traditionally projections have been given for three financial items generally considered to be of primary importance to investors (revenues, net income (loss) and earnings (loss) per share), projection information need not necessarily be limited to these three items. However, management should take care to assure that the choice of items projected is not susceptible of misleading inferences through selective projection of only favorable items. Revenues, net income (loss) and earnings (loss) per share usually are presented together in order to avoid any misleading inferences that may arise when the individual items reflect

contradictory trends. There may be instances, however, when it is appropriate to present earnings (loss) from continuing operations, or income (loss) before extraordinary items in addition to or in lieu of net income (loss). It generally would be misleading to present sales or revenue projections without one of the foregoing measures of income. The period that appropriately may be covered by a projection depends to a large extent on the particular circumstances of the company involved. For certain companies in certain industries, a projection covering a two or three year period may be entirely reasonable. Other companies may not have a reasonable basis for projections beyond the current year. Accordingly, management should select the period most appropriate in the circumstances. In addition, management, in making a projection, should disclose what, in its opinion, is the most probable specific amount or the most reasonable range for each financial item projected based on the selected assumptions. Ranges, however, should not be so wide as to make the disclosures meaningless. Moreover, several projections based on varying assumptions may be judged by management to be more meaningful than a single number or range and would be permitted.

(3) *Investor understanding.* (i) When management chooses to include its projections in a Commission filing, the disclosures accompanying the projections should facilitate investor understanding of the basis for and limitations of projections. In this regard investors should be cautioned against attributing undue certainty to management's assessment, and the Commission believes that investors would be aided by a statement indicating management's intention regarding the furnishing of updated projections. The Commission also believes that investor understanding would be enhanced by disclosure of the assumptions which in management's opinion are most significant to the projections or are the key factors upon which the financial results of the enterprise depend and encourages disclosure of assumptions in a manner that will provide a framework for analysis of the projection.

(ii) Management also should consider whether disclosure of the accuracy or inaccuracy of previous projections would provide investors with important insights into the limitations of projections. In this regard, consideration should be given to presenting the projections in a format that will facilitate subsequent analysis of the reasons for differences between actual and forecast results. An important benefit may arise from the systematic analysis of variances between projected and actual results on a continuing basis, since such disclosure may highlight for investors the most significant risk and profit-sensitive areas in a business operation.

(iii) With respect to previously issued projections, registrants are reminded of their responsibility to make full and prompt disclosure of material facts, both favorable and unfavorable, regarding their financial condition. This responsibility may extend to situations where management knows or has reason to know that its previously disclosed projections no longer have a reasonable basis.

(iv) Since a registrant's ability to make projections with relative confidence may vary with all the facts and circumstances, the responsibility for determining whether to discontinue or to resume making projections is best left to management. However, the Commission encourages registrants not to discontinue or to resume projections in Commission filings without a reasonable basis.

(c) *Commission policy on security ratings.* In view of the importance of security ratings ("ratings") to investors and the marketplace, the Commission permits registrants to disclose, on a voluntary basis, ratings assigned by rating organizations to classes of debt securities, convertible debt securities and preferred stock in registration statements and periodic reports. In addition, the Commission permits, pursuant to Rule 134(a)(14) under the Securities Act (§230.134(a)(14) of this chapter), voluntary disclosure of ratings assigned by any nationally recognized statistical rating organizations ("NRSROs") in certain communications deemed not to be a prospectus ("tombstone advertisements").

Set forth herein are the Commission's views on important matters to be considered in disclosing security ratings.

(1) *Securities Act filings.* (i) If a registrant includes in a registration statement filed under the Securities Act any rating(s) assigned to a class of securities, it should consider including: (A) any other rating intended for public dissemination assigned to such class by a NRSRO ("additional NRSRO rating") that is available on the date of the initial filing of the document and that is materially different from any rating disclosed; and (B) the name of each rating organization whose rating is disclosed; each such rating organization's definition or description of the category in which it rated the class of securities; the relative rank of each rating within the assigning rating organization's overall classification system; and a statement informing investors that a security rating is not a recommendation to buy, sell or hold securities, that it may be subject to revision or withdrawal at any time by the assigning rating organization, and that each rating should be evaluated independently of any other rating. The registrant also should include the written consent of any rating organization that is not a NRSRO whose rating is included. With respect to the written consent of any NRSRO whose rating is included, see Rule 436(g) under the Securities Act (§230.436(g) of this chapter). When the registrant has filed a registration statement on Form F-9 (§239.39 of this chapter), see Rule 436(g) (§230.436(g) of this chapter) under

the Securities Act with respect to the written consent of any rating organization specified in the Instruction to paragraph (a)(2) of General Instruction I of Form F-9.

(ii) If a change in a rating already included is available subsequent to the filing of the registration statement, but prior to its effectiveness, the registrant should consider including such rating change in the final prospectus. If the rating change is material or if a materially different rating from any disclosed becomes available during this period, the registrant should consider amending the registration statement to include the rating change or additional rating and recirculating the preliminary prospectus.

(iii) If a materially different additional NRSRO rating or a material change in a rating already included becomes available during any period in which offers or sales are being made, the registrant should consider disclosing such additional rating or rating change by means of a post-effective amendment or sticker to the prospectus pursuant to Rule 424(b) under the Securities Act (§ 230.424(b) of this chapter), unless, in the case of a registration statement on Form S-3 (§ 239.13 of this chapter), it has been disclosed in a document incorporated by reference into the registration statement subsequent to its effectiveness and prior to the termination of the offering.

(2) *Exchange Act filings.* (i) If a registrant includes in a registration statement or periodic report filed under the Exchange Act any rating(s) assigned to a class of securities, it should consider including the information specified in paragraphs (c)(1)(i)(A) and (B) of this section.

(ii) If there is a material change in the rating(s) assigned by any NRSRO(s) to any outstanding class(es) of securities of a registrant subject to the reporting requirements of section 13(a) or 15(d) of the Exchange Act, the registrant should consider filing a report on Form 8-K (§ 249.308 of this chapter) or other appropriate report under the Exchange Act disclosing such rating change.

(d) *Incorporation by Reference.* Where rules, regulations, or instructions to forms of the Commission permit incorporation by reference, a document may be so incorporated by reference to the specific document and to the prior filing or submission in which such document was physically filed or submitted. Except where a registrant or issuer is expressly required to incorporate a document or documents by reference (or for purposes of Item 1100(c) of Regulation AB (§ 229.1100(c)) with respect to an asset-backed issuer, as that term is defined in Item 1101 of Regulation AB (§ 229.1101)), reference may not be made to any document which incorporates another document by reference if the pertinent portion of the document containing the information or financial statements to be incorporated by reference includes an incorporation by reference to another document. No document on file with the Commission for more than five years may be incorporated by reference except:

(1) Documents contained in registration statements, which may be incorporated by reference as long as the registrant has a reporting requirement with the Commission; or

(2) Documents that the registrant specifically identifies by physical location by SEC file number reference, provided such materials have not been disposed of by the Commission pursuant to its Records Control Schedule (17 CFR 200.80f).

(e) *Use of non-GAAP financial measures in Commission filings.* (1) Whenever one or more non-GAAP financial measures are included in a filing with the Commission:

(i) The registrant must include the following in the filing:

(A) A presentation, with equal or greater prominence, of the most directly comparable financial measure or measures calculated and presented in accordance with Generally Accepted Accounting Principles (GAAP);

(B) A reconciliation (by schedule or other clearly understandable method), which shall be quantitative for historical non-GAAP measures presented, and quantitative, to the extent available without unreasonable efforts, for forward-looking information, of the differences between the non-GAAP financial measure disclosed or released with the most directly comparable financial measure or measures calculated and presented in accordance with GAAP identified in paragraph (e)(1)(i)(A) of this section;

(C) A statement disclosing the reasons why the registrant's management believes that presentation of the non-GAAP financial measure provides useful information to investors regarding the registrant's financial condition and results of operations; and

(D) To the extent material, a statement disclosing the additional purposes, if any, for which the registrant's management uses the non-GAAP financial measure that are not disclosed pursuant to paragraph (e)(1)(i)(C) of this section; and

(ii) A registrant must not:

(A) Exclude charges or liabilities that required, or will require, cash settlement, or would have required cash settlement absent an ability to settle in another manner, from non-GAAP liquidity measures, other than the measures earnings before interest and taxes (EBIT) and earnings before interest, taxes, depreciation, and amortization (EBITDA);

(B) Adjust a non-GAAP performance measure to eliminate or smooth items identified as non-recurring, infrequent or unusual, when the nature of the charge or gain is such that it is reasonably likely to recur within two years or there was a similar charge or gain within the prior two years;

(C) Present non-GAAP financial measures on the face of the registrant's financial statements prepared in accordance with GAAP or in the accompanying notes;

(D) Present non-GAAP financial measures on the face of any pro forma financial information required to be disclosed by Article 11 of Regulation S-X (17 CFR 210.11-01 through 210.11-03); or

(E) Use titles or descriptions of non-GAAP financial measures that are the same as, or confusingly similar to, titles or descriptions used for GAAP financial measures; and

(iii) If the filing is not an annual report on Form 10-K or Form 20-F (17 CFR 249.220f), a registrant need not include the information required by paragraphs (e)(1)(i)(C) and (e)(1)(i)(D) of this section if that information was included in its most recent annual report on Form 10-K or Form 20-F or a more recent filing, provided that the required information is updated to the extent necessary to meet the requirements of paragraphs (e)(1)(i)(C) and (e)(1)(i)(D) of this section at the time of the registrant's current filing.

(2) For purposes of this paragraph (e), a non-GAAP financial measure is a numerical measure of a registrant's historical or future financial performance, financial position or cash flows that:

(i) Excludes amounts, or is subject to adjustments that have the effect of excluding amounts, that are included in the most directly comparable measure calculated and presented in accordance with GAAP in the statement of income, balance sheet or statement of cash flows (or equivalent statements) of the issuer; or

(ii) Includes amounts, or is subject to adjustments that have the effect of including amounts, that are excluded from the most directly comparable measure so calculated and presented.

(3) For purposes of this paragraph (e), GAAP refers to generally accepted accounting principles in the United States, except that (i) in the case of foreign private issuers whose primary financial statements are prepared in accordance with non-U.S. generally accepted accounting principles, GAAP refers to the principles under which those primary financial statements are prepared; and (ii) in the case of foreign private issuers that include a non-GAAP financial measure derived from or based on a measure calculated in accordance with U.S. generally accepted accounting principles, GAAP refers to U.S. generally accepted accounting principles for purposes of the application of the requirements of this paragraph (e) to the disclosure of that measure.

(4) For purposes of this paragraph (e), non-GAAP financial measures exclude:

(i) operating and other statistical measures; and

(ii) ratios or statistical measures calculated using exclusively one or both of:

(A) Financial measures calculated in accordance with GAAP; and

(B) Operating measures or other measures that are not non-GAAP financial measures.

(5) For purposes of this paragraph (e), non-GAAP financial measures exclude financial measures required to be disclosed by GAAP, Commission rules, or a system of regulation of a government or governmental authority or self-regulatory organization that is applicable to the registrant. However, the financial measure should be presented outside of the financial statements unless the financial measure is required or expressly permitted by the standard-setter that is responsible for establishing the GAAP used in such financial statements.

(6) The requirements of paragraph (e) of this section shall not apply to a non-GAAP financial measure included in disclosure relating to a proposed business combination, the entity resulting therefrom or an entity that is a party thereto, if the disclosure is contained in a communication that is subject to § 230.425 of this chapter, § 240.14a-12 or § 240.14d-2(b)(2) of this chapter or § 229.1015 of this chapter.

(7) The requirements of paragraph (e) of this section shall not apply to investment companies registered under Section 8 of the Investment Company Act of 1940 (15 U.S.C. 80a-8).

Note to paragraph (e).

A non-GAAP financial measure that would otherwise be prohibited by paragraph (e)(1)(ii) of this section is permitted in a filing of a foreign private issuer if:

1. The non-GAAP financial measure relates to the GAAP used in the registrant's primary financial statements included in its filing with the Commission;

2. The non-GAAP financial measure is required or expressly permitted by the standard-setter that is responsible for establishing the GAAP used in such financial statements; and

3. The non-GAAP financial measure is included in the annual report prepared by the registrant for use in the jurisdiction in which it is domiciled, incorporated or organized or for distribution to its security holders.

(f) *Smaller reporting companies.* The requirements of this part apply to smaller reporting companies. A smaller reporting company may comply with either the requirements applicable to smaller reporting companies or the requirements applicable to other companies for each item, unless the requirements for smaller reporting companies specify that smaller reporting companies must comply with the smaller reporting company requirements. The following items of this part set forth requirements for smaller reporting companies that are different from requirements applicable to other companies:

Index of Scaled Disclosure Available to Smaller Reporting Companies

Item 101	Description of business
Item 201	Market price of and dividends on registrant's common equity and related stockholder matters
Item 301	Selected financial data
Item 302	Supplementary financial information
Item 303	Management's discussion and analysis of financial condition and results of operations
Item 305	Quantitative and qualitative disclosures about market risk
Item 402	Executive compensation
Item 404	Transactions with related persons, promoters and certain control persons
Item 407	Corporate governance
Item 503	Prospectus summary, risk factors, and ratio of earnings to fixed charges
Item 504	Use of proceeds
Item 601	Exhibits

(1) *Definition of smaller reporting company.* As used in this part, the term *smaller reporting company* means an issuer that is not an investment company, an asset-backed issuer (as defined in § 229.1101), or a majority-owned subsidiary of a parent that is not a smaller reporting company and that:

(i) Had a public float of less than $75 million as of the last business day of its most recently completed second fiscal quarter, computed by multiplying the aggregate worldwide number of shares of its voting and non-voting common equity held by non-affiliates by the price at which the common equity was last sold, or the average of the bid and asked prices of common equity, in the principal market for the common equity; or

(ii) In the case of an initial registration statement under the Securities Act or Exchange Act for shares of its common equity, had a public float of less than $75 million as of a date within 30 days of the date of the filing of the registration statement, computed by multiplying the aggregate worldwide number of such shares held by non-affiliates before the registration plus, in the case of a Securities Act registration statement, the number of such shares included in the registration statement by the estimated public offering price of the shares; or

(iii) In the case of an issuer whose public float as calculated under paragraph (i) or (ii) of this definition was zero, had annual revenues of less than $50 million during the most recently completed fiscal year for which audited financial statements are available.

(2) *Determination:* Whether or not an issuer is a smaller reporting company is determined on an annual basis.

(i) For issuers that are required to file reports under section 13(a) or 15(d) of the Exchange Act, the determination is based on whether the issuer came within the definition of smaller reporting company, using the amounts specified in paragraph (f)(2)(iii) of this Item, as of the last business day of the second fiscal quarter of the issuer's previous fiscal year. An issuer in this category must reflect this determination in the information it provides in its quarterly report on Form 10-Q for the first fiscal quarter of the next year, indicating on the cover page of that filing, and in subsequent filings for that fiscal year, whether or not it is a smaller reporting company, except that, if a determination based on public float indicates that the issuer is newly eligible to be a smaller reporting company, the issuer may choose to reflect this determination beginning with its first quarterly report on Form 10-Q following the determination, rather than waiting until the first fiscal quarter of the next year.

(ii) For determinations based on an initial Securities Act or Exchange Act registration statement under paragraph (f)(1)(ii) of this Item, the issuer must reflect the determination in the information it provides in the registration statement and must appropriately indicate on the cover page of the filing, and subsequent filings for the fiscal year in which the filing is made, whether or not it is a smaller reporting company. The issuer must redetermine its status at the end of its second fiscal quarter and then reflect any change in status as provided in paragraph (f)(2)(i) of this Item. In the case of a determination based on an initial Securities Act registration statement, an issuer that was not determined to be a smaller reporting company has the option to redetermine its status at the conclusion of the offering covered by the registration statement based on the actual offering price and number of shares sold.

(iii) Once an issuer fails to qualify for smaller reporting company status, it will remain unqualified unless it determines that its public float, as calculated in accordance with paragraph (f)(1) of this Item, was less than $50 million as of the last business day of its second fiscal quarter or, if that calculation results in zero because the issuer had no public equity outstanding or no market price for its equity existed, if the issuers had annual revenues of less than $40 million during its previous fiscal year.

[As last amended in Release No. 33-8876, effective February 4, 2008, 73 F.R. 934.]

Subpart 229.100—Business

[¶ 13,011] Description of Business

Reg. § 229.101. Item 101. (a) *General development of business.* Describe the general development of the business of the registrant, its subsidiaries and any predecessor(s) during the past five years, or such shorter period as the registrant may have been engaged in business. Information shall be disclosed for earlier periods if material to an understanding of the general development of the business.

(1) In describing developments, information shall be given as to matters such as the following: the year in which the registrant was organized and its form of organization; the nature and results of any bankruptcy, receivership or similar proceedings with respect to the registrant or any of its significant subsidiaries; the nature and results of any other material reclassification, merger or consolidation of the registrant or any of its significant subsidiaries; the acquisition or disposition of any material amount of assets otherwise than in the ordinary course of business; and any material changes in the mode of conducting the business.

(2) Registrants:

(i) Filing a registration statement on Form S-1 (§ 239.11 of this chapter) under the Securities Act or on Form 10 (§ 249.210 of this chapter) under the Exchange Act;

(ii) Not subject to the reporting requirements of section 13(a) or 15(d) of the Exchange Act immediately before the filing of such registration statement; and

(iii) That (including predecessors) have not received revenue from operations during each of the three fiscal years immediately before the filing of such registration statement, shall provide the following information:

(A) (A) if the registration statement is filed prior to the end of the registrant's second fiscal quarter, a description of the registrant's plan of operation for the remainder of the fiscal year; or

(B) if the registration statement is filed subsequent to the end of the registrant's second fiscal quarter, a description of the registrant's plan of operation for the remainder of the fiscal year and for the first six months of the next fiscal year. If such information is not available, the reasons for its not being available shall be stated. Disclosure relating to any plan shall include such matters as:

(*1*) In the case of a registration statement on Form S-1, a statement in narrative form indicating the registrant's opinion as to the period of time that the proceeds from the offering will satisfy cash requirements and whether in the next six months it will be necessary to raise additional funds to meet the expenditures required for operating the business of the registrant; the specific reasons for such opinion shall be set forth and categories of expenditures and sources of cash resources shall be identified; however, amounts of expenditures and cash resources need not be provided; in addition, if the narrative statement is based on a cash budget, such budget shall be furnished to the Commission as supplemental information, but not as part of the registration statement;

(*2*) An explanation of material product research and development to be performed during the period covered in the plan;

(*3*) Any anticipated material acquisition of plant and equipment and the capacity thereof;

(*4*) Any anticipated material changes in number of employees in the various departments such as research and development, production, sales or administration; and

(*5*) Other material areas which may be peculiar to the registrant's business.

(b) *Financial information about segments.* Report for each segment, as defined by generally accepted accounting principles, revenues from external customers, a measure of profit or loss and total assets. A registrant must report this information for each of the last three fiscal years or for as long as it has been in business, whichever period is shorter. If the information provided in response to this paragraph (b) conforms with generally accepted accounting principles, a registrant may include in its financial statements a cross reference to this data in lieu of presenting duplicative information in the financial statements; conversely, a registrant may cross reference to the financial statements.

(1) If a registrant changes the structure of its internal organization in a manner that causes the composition of its reportable segments to change, the registrant must restate the corresponding information for earlier periods, including interim periods, unless it is impracticable to do so. Following a change in the composition of its reportable segments, a registrant shall disclose whether it has restated the corresponding items of segment information for earlier periods. If it has not restated the items from earlier periods, the registrant shall disclose in the year in which the change occurs segment information for the current period under both the old basis and the new basis of segmentation, unless it is impracticable to do so.

(2) If the registrant includes, or is required by Article 3 of Regulation S-X (17 CFR 210) to include, interim financial statements, discuss any facts relating to the performance of any of the segments during the period which, in the opinion of management, indicate that the three year segment financial data may

not be indicative of current or future operations of the segment. Comparative financial information shall be included to the extent necessary to the discussion.

(c) *Narrative description of business.* (1) Describe the business done and intended to be done by the registrant and its subsidiaries, focusing upon the registrant's dominant segment or each reportable segment about which financial information is presented in the financial statements. To the extent material to an understanding of the registrant's business taken as a whole, the description of each such segment shall include the information specified in paragraphs (c)(1)(i) through (x) of this Item. The matters specified in paragraphs (c)(1)(xi) through (xiii) of this Item shall be discussed with respect to the registrant's business in general; where material, the segments to which these matters are significant shall be identified.

(i) The principal products produced and services rendered by the registrant in the segment and the principal markets for, and methods of distribution of, the segment's principal products and services. In addition, state for each of the last three fiscal years the amount or percentage of total revenue contributed by any class of similar products or services which accounted for 10 percent or more of consolidated revenue in any of the last three fiscal years or 15 percent or more of consolidated revenue, if total revenue did not exceed $50,000,000 during any of such fiscal years.

(ii) A description of the status of a product or segment (*e.g.* whether in the planning stage, whether prototypes exist, the degree to which product design has progressed or whether further engineering is necessary), if there has been a public announcement of, or if the registrant otherwise has made public information about, a new product or segment that would require the investment of a material amount of the assets of the registrant or that otherwise is material. This paragraph is not intended to require disclosure of otherwise nonpublic corporate information the disclosure of which would affect adversely the registrant's competitive position.

(iii) The sources and availability of raw materials.

(iv) The importance to the segment and the duration and effect of all patents, trademarks, licenses, franchises and concessions held.

(v) The extent to which the business of the segment is or may be seasonal.

(vi) The practices of the registrant and the industry (respective industries) relating to working capital items (*e.g.,* where the registrant is required to carry significant amounts of inventory to meet rapid delivery requirements of customers or to assure itself of a continuous allotment of goods from suppliers; where the registrant provides rights to return merchandise; or where the registrant has provided extended payment terms to customers).

(vii) The dependence of the segment upon a single customer, or a few customers, the loss of any one or more of which would have a material adverse effect on the segment. The name of any customer and its relationship, if any, with the registrant or its subsidiaries shall be disclosed if sales to the customer by one or more segments are made in an aggregate amount equal to 10 percent or more of the registrant's consolidated revenues and the loss of such customer would have a material adverse effect on the registrant and its subsidiaries taken as a whole. The names of other customers may be included, unless in the particular case the effect of including the names would be misleading. For purposes of this paragraph, a group of customers under common control or customers that are affiliates of each other shall be regarded as a single customer.

(viii) The dollar amount of backlog orders believed to be firm, as of a recent date and as of a comparable date in the preceding fiscal year, together with an indication of the portion thereof not reasonably expected to be filled within the current fiscal year, and seasonal or other material aspects of the backlog. (There may be included as firm orders government orders that are firm but not yet funded and contracts awarded but not yet signed, provided an appropriate statement is added to explain the nature of such orders and the amount thereof. The portion of orders already included in sales or operating revenues on the basis of percentage of completion or program accounting shall be excluded.)

(ix) A description of any material portion of the business that may be subject to renegotiation of profits or termination of contracts or subcontracts at the election of the Government.

(x) Competitive conditions in the business involved including, where material, the identity of the particular markets in which the registrant competes, an estimate of the number of competitors and the registrant's competitive position, if known or reasonably available to the registrant. Separate consideration shall be given to the principal products or services or classes of products or services of the segment, if any. Generally, the names of competitors need not be disclosed. The registrant may include such names, unless in the particular case the effect of including the names would be misleading. Where, however, the registrant knows or has reason to know that one or a small number of competitors is dominant in the industry it shall be identified. The principal methods of competition (*e.g.,* price, service, warranty or product performance) shall be identified, and positive and negative factors pertaining to the competitive position of the registrant, to the extent that they exist, shall be explained if known or reasonably available to the registrant.

(xi) If material, the estimated amount spent during each of the last three fiscal years on company-sponsored research and development activities determined in accordance with generally accepted accounting principles. In addition, state, if material, the estimated dollar amount spent during each of such years on customer-sponsored research activities relating to the development of new products, services or techniques or the improvement of existing products, services or techniques.

(xii) Appropriate disclosure also shall be made as to the material effects that compliance with Federal, State and local provisions which have been enacted or adopted regulating the discharge of materials into the environment, or otherwise relating to the protection of the environment, may have upon the capital expenditures, earnings and competitive position of the registrant and its subsidiaries. The registrant shall disclose any material estimated capital expenditures for environmental control facilities for the remainder of its current fiscal year and its succeeding fiscal year and for such further periods as the registrant may deem material.

(xiii) The number of persons employed by the registrant.

(d) *Financial information about geographic areas.* (1) State for each of the registrant's last three fiscal years, or for each fiscal year the registrant has been engaged in business, whichever period is shorter:

(i) Revenues from external customers attributed to:

(A) The registrant's country of domicile;

(B) All foreign countries, in total, from which the registrant derives revenues; and

(C) Any individual foreign country, if material. Disclose the basis for attributing revenues from external customers to individual countries.

(ii) Long-lived assets, other than financial instruments, long-term customer relationships of a financial institution, mortgage and other servicing rights, deferred policy acquisition costs, and deferred tax assets, located in:

(A) The registrant's country of domicile;

(B) All foreign countries, in total, in which the registrant holds assets; and

(C) Any individual foreign country, if material.

(2) A registrant shall report the amounts based on the financial information that it uses to produce the general-purpose financial statements. If providing the geographic information is impracticable, the registrant shall disclose that fact. A registrant may wish to provide, in addition to the information required by paragraph (d)(1) of this section, subtotals of geographic information about groups of countries. To the extent that the disclosed information conforms with generally accepted accounting principles, the registrant may include in its financial statements a cross reference to this data in lieu of presenting duplicative data in its financial statements; conversely, a registrant may cross-reference to the financial statements.

(3) A registrant shall describe any risks attendant to the foreign operations and any dependence on one or more of the registrant's segments upon such foreign operations, unless it would be more appropriate to discuss this information in connection with the description of one or more of the registrant's segments under paragraph (c) of this item.

(4) If the registrant includes, or is required by Article 3 of Regulation S-X (17 CFR 210), to include, interim financial statements, discuss any facts relating to the information furnished under this paragraph (d) that, in the opinion of management, indicate that the three year financial data for geographic areas may not be indicative of current or future operations. To the extent necessary to the discussion, include comparative information.

(e) *Available information.* Disclose the information in paragraphs (e)(1), (e)(2) and (e)(3) of this section in any registration statement you file under the Securities Act (15 U.S.C. 77a *et seq.*), and disclose the information in paragraphs (e)(3) and (e)(4) of this section if you are an accelerated filer or a large accelerated filer (as defined in § 240.12b-2 of this chapter) filing an annual report on Form 10-K (§ 249.310 of this chapter):

(1) Whether you file reports with the Securities and Exchange Commission. If you are a reporting company, identify the reports and other information you file with the SEC.

(2) That the public may read and copy any materials you file with the SEC at the SEC's Public Reference Room at 100 F Street, NE, Washington, DC 20549. State that the public may obtain information on the operation of the Public Reference Room by calling the SEC at 1-800-SEC-0330. If you are an electronic filer, state that the SEC maintains an Internet site that contains reports, proxy and information statements, and other information regarding issuers that file electronically with the SEC and state the address of that site (http://www.sec.gov).

(3) You are encouraged to give your Internet address, if available, except that if you are an accelerated filer filing your annual report on Form 10-K, you must disclose your Internet address, if you have one.

(4) (i) Whether you make available free of charge on or through your Internet website, if you have one, your annual report on Form 10-K, quarterly reports on Form 10-Q (§ 249.308a of this chapter), current reports on Form 8-K (§ 249.308 of this chapter), and amendments to those reports filed or furnished pursuant to Section 13(a) or 15(d) of the Exchange Act (15 U.S.C. 78m(a) or 78o(d)) as soon as reasonably practicable after you electronically file such material with, or furnish it to, the SEC;

(ii) If you do not make your filings available in this manner, the reasons you do not do so (including, where applicable, that you do not have an Internet website); and

(iii) If you do not make your filings available in this manner, whether you voluntarily will provide electronic or paper copies of your filings free of charge upon request.

(f) *Reports to Security Holders.* Disclose the following information in any registration statement you file under the Securities Act:

(1) If the SEC's proxy rules or regulations, or stock exchange requirements, do not require you to send an annual report to security holders or to holders of American depository receipts, describe briefly the nature and frequency of reports that you will give to security holders. Specify whether the reports that you give will contain financial information that has been examined and reported on, with an opinion expressed "by" an independent public or certified public accountant.

(2) For a foreign private issuer, if the report will not contain financial information prepared in accordance with U.S. generally accepted accounting principles, you must state whether the report will include a reconciliation of this information with U.S. generally accepted accounting principles.

(g) *Enforceability of Civil Liabilities Against Foreign Persons.* Disclose the following if you are a foreign private issuer filing a registration statement under the Securities Act:

(1) Whether or not investors may bring actions under the civil liability provisions of the U.S. federal securities laws against the foreign private issuer, any of its officers and directors who are residents of a foreign country, any underwriters or experts named in the registration statement that are residents of a foreign country, and whether investors may enforce these civil liability provisions when the assets of the issuer or these other persons are located outside of the United States. The disclosure must address the following matters:

(i) The investor's ability to effect service of process within the United States on the foreign private issuer or any person;

(ii) The investor's ability to enforce judgments obtained in U.S. courts against foreign persons based upon the civil liability provisions of the U.S. federal securities laws;

(iii) The investor's ability to enforce, in an appropriate foreign court, judgments of U.S. courts based upon the civil liability provisions of the U.S. federal securities laws; and

(iv) The investor's ability to bring an original action in an appropriate foreign court to enforce liabilities against the foreign private issuer or any person based upon the U.S. federal securities laws.

(2) If you provide this disclosure based on an opinion of counsel, name counsel in the prospectus and file as an exhibit to the registration statement a signed consent of counsel to the use of its name and opinion.

(h) *Smaller reporting companies.* A smaller reporting company, as defined by § 229.10(f)(1), may satisfy its obligations under this Item by describing the development of its business during the last three years. If the smaller reporting company has not been in business for three years, give the same information for predecessor(s) of the smaller reporting company if there are any. This business development description should include:

(1) Form and year of organization;

(2) Any bankruptcy, receivership or similar proceeding; and

(3) Any material reclassification, merger, consolidation, or purchase or sale of a significant amount of assets not in the ordinary course of business.

(4) *Business of the smaller reporting company.* Briefly describe the business and include, to the extent material to an understanding of the smaller reporting company:

(i) Principal products or services and their markets;

(ii) Distribution methods of the products or services;

(iii) Status of any publicly announced new product or service;

(iv) Competitive business conditions and the smaller reporting company's competitive position in the industry and methods of competition;

(v) Sources and availability of raw materials and the names of principal suppliers;

(vi) Dependence on one or a few major customers;

(vii) Patents, trademarks, licenses, franchises, concessions, royalty agreements or labor contracts, including duration;

(viii) Need for any government approval of principal products or services. If government approval is necessary and the smaller reporting company has not yet received that approval, discuss the status of the approval within the government approval process;

(ix) Effect of existing or probable governmental regulations on the business;

(x) Estimate of the amount spent during each of the last two fiscal years on research and development activities, and if applicable, the extent to which the cost of such activities is borne directly by customers;

(xi) Costs and effects of compliance with environmental laws (federal, state and local); and

(xii) Number of total employees and number of full-time employees.

(5) *Reports to security holders.* Disclose the following in any registration statement you file under the Securities Act of 1933:

(i) If you are not required to deliver an annual report to security holders, whether you will voluntarily send an annual report and whether the report will include audited financial statements;

(ii) Whether you file reports with the Securities and Exchange Commission. If you are a reporting company, identify the reports and other information you file with the Commission; and

(iii) That the public may read and copy any materials you file with the Commission at the SEC's Public Reference Room at 100 F Street, NE, Washington, DC 20549, on official business days during the hours of 10:00 am to 3:00 pm. State that the public may obtain information on the operation of the Public Reference Room by calling the Commission at 1-800-SEC-0330. State that the Commission maintains an Internet site that contains reports, proxy and information statements, and other information regarding issuers that file electronically with the Commission and state the address of that site (http://www.sec.gov). You are encouraged to give your Internet address, if available.

(6) *Foreign issuers.* Provide the information required by Item 101(g) of Regulation S-K (§ 229.101(g)).

Instructions to Item 101. 1. In determining what information about the segments is material to an understanding of the registrant's business taken as a whole and therefore required to be disclosed pursuant to paragraph (c) of this Item, the registrant should take into account both quantitative and qualitative factors such as the significance of the matter to the registrant (*e.g.,* whether a matter with a relatively minor impact on the registrant's business is represented by management to be important to its future profitability), the pervasiveness of the matter (*e.g.,* whether it affects or may affect numerous items in the segment information), and the impact of the matter (*e.g.,* whether it distorts the trends reflected in the segment information). Situations may arise when information should be disclosed about a segment, although the information in quantitative terms may not appear significant to the registrant's business taken as a whole.

2. Base the determination of whether information about segments is required for a particular year upon an evaluation of interperiod comparability. For instance, interperiod comparability would require a registrant to report segment information in the current period even if not material under the criteria for reportability of SFAS No. 131 if a segment has been significant in the immediately preceding period and the registrant expects it to be significant in the future.

3. The Commission, upon written request of the registrant and where consistent with the protection of investors, may permit the omission of any of the information required by this Item or the furnishing in substitution thereof of appropriate information of comparable character.

[As last amended by Release No. 33-8876, effective February 4, 2008, 73 F.R. 934.]

[¶ 13,012] Description of Property

Reg. § 229.102. Item 102. State briefly the location and general character of the principal plants, mines and other materially important physical properties of the registrant and its subsidiaries. In addition, identify the segment(s), as reported in the financial statements, that use the properties described. If any such property is not held in fee or is held subject to any major encumbrance, so state and describe briefly how held.

Instructions to Item 102. 1. What is required is such information as reasonably will inform investors as to the suitability, adequacy, productive capacity and extent of utilization of the facilities by the registrant. Detailed descriptions of the physical characteristics of individual properties or legal descriptions by metes and bounds are not required and shall not be given.

2. In determining whether properties should be described, the registrant should take into account both quantitative and qualitative factors. See Instruction 1 to Item 101 of Regulation S-K (§ 229.101).

3. In the case of an extractive enterprise, not involved in oil and gas producing activities, material information shall be given as to production, reserves, locations, development, and the nature of the registrant's interest. If individual properties are of major significance to an industry segment:

A. More detailed information concerning these matters shall be furnished; and

B. Appropriate maps shall be used to disclose location data of significant properties except in cases for which numerous maps would be required.

4. A registrant engaged in oil and gas producing activities shall provide the information required by Subpart 1200 of Regulation S-K.

5. In the case of extractive reserves other than oil and gas reserves, estimates other than proven or probable reserves (and any estimated values of such reserves) shall not be disclosed in any document publicly filed with the Commission, unless such information is required to be disclosed in the document by foreign or state law; provided, however, that where such estimates previously have been provided to a person (or any of its affiliates) that is offering to acquire, merge, or consolidate with the registrant, or otherwise to acquire the registrant's securities, such estimates may be included in documents relating to such acquisition.

6. The definitions in § 210.4-10(a) of Regulation S-X [17 CFR 210] shall apply to this Item with respect to oil and gas operations.

7. The attention of issuers engaged in significant mining operations is directed to the information called for in Guide 7 (§ 229.801(g) and § 229.802(g)).

8. The attention of certain issuers engaged in oil and gas producing activities is directed to the information called for in Securities Act Industry Guide 4 (referred to in § 229.801(d)).

9. The attention of issuers engaged in real estate activities is directed to the information called for in Guide 5 (§ 229.801(e) of this chapter).

[Amended in Release No. 33-8995, effective January 1, 2010, 74 F.R. 2157.]

[¶ 13,013] Legal Proceedings

Reg. § 229.103. Item 103. Describe briefly any material pending legal proceedings, other than ordinary routine litigation incidental to the business, to which the registrant or any of its subsidiaries is a party or of which any of their property is the subject. Include the name of the court or agency in which the proceedings are pending, the date instituted, the principal parties thereto, a description of the factual basis alleged to underlie the proceeding and the relief sought. Include similar information as to any such proceedings known to be contemplated by governmental authorities.

Instructions to Item 103. 1. If the business ordinarily results in actions for negligence or other claims, no such action or claim need be described unless it departs from the normal kind of such actions.

2. No information need be given with respect to any proceeding that involves primarily a claim for damages if the amount involved, exclusive of interest and costs, does not exceed 10 percent of the current assets of the registrant and its subsidiaries on a consolidated basis. However, if any proceeding presents in large degree the same legal and factual issues as other proceedings pending or known to be contemplated, the amount involved in such other proceedings shall be included in computing such percentage.

3. Notwithstanding Instructions 1 and 2, any material bankruptcy, receivership, or similar proceeding with respect to the registrant or any of its significant subsidiaries shall be described.

4. Any material proceedings to which any director, officer or affiliate of the registrant, any owner of record or beneficially of more than five percent of any class of voting securities of the registrant, or any associate of any such director, officer, affiliate of the registrant, or security holder is a party adverse to the registrant or any of its subsidiaries or has a material interest adverse to the registrant or any of its subsidiaries also shall be described.

5. Notwithstanding the foregoing, an administrative or judicial proceeding (including, for purposes of A and B of this Instruction, proceedings which present in large degree the same issues) arising under any Federal, State or local provisions that have been enacted or adopted regulating the discharge of materials into the environment or primary [primarily] for the purpose of protecting the environment shall not be deemed "ordinary routine litigation incidental to the business" and shall be described if:

A. Such proceeding is material to the business or financial condition of the registrant;

B. Such proceeding involves primarily a claim for damages, or involves potential monetary sanctions, capital expenditures, deferred charges or charges to income and the amount involved, exclusive of interest and costs, exceeds 10 percent of the current assets of the registrant and its subsidiaries on a consolidated basis; or

C. A governmental authority is a party to such proceeding and such proceeding involves potential monetary sanctions, unless the registrant reasonably believes that such proceeding will result in no monetary sanctions, or in monetary sanctions, exclusive of interest and costs, of less than $100,000; provided, however, that such proceedings which are similar in nature may be grouped and described generically.

[As last amended in Release No. AS-306, March 3, 1982, effective May 24, 1982, 47 F.R. 11380.]

Subpart 229.200—Securities of the Registrant

[¶ 13,021] Market Price of and Dividends on the Registrant's Common Equity and Related Stockholder Matters

Reg. § 229.201. Item 201. (a) *Market information.* (1) (i) Identify the principal United States market or markets in which each class of the registrant's common equity is being traded. Where there is no established public trading market for a class of common equity, furnish a statement to that effect. For purposes of this Item the existence of limited or sporadic quotations should not of itself be deemed to constitute an "established public trading market." In the case of foreign registrants, also identify the principal established foreign public trading market, if any, for each class of the registrant's common equity.

(ii) If the principal United States market for such common equity is an exchange, state the high and low sales prices for the equity for each full quarterly period within the two most recent fiscal years and any subsequent interim period for which financial statements are included, or are required to be included by Article 3-01 through 3-04 of Regulation S-X (§ 210.3-01 through 3-04 of this chapter), or Article 8-02 through 8-03 of Regulation S-X (§ 210.8-02 through 8-03 of this chapter) in the case of smaller reporting companies, as reported in the consolidated transaction reporting system or, if not so reported, as reported on the principal exchange market for such equity.

(iii) If the principal United States market for such common equity is not an exchange, state the range of high and low bid information for the equity for each full quarterly period within the two most recent fiscal years and any subsequent interim period for which financial statements are included, or are required to be included by Article 3 of Regulation S-X, as regularly quoted in the automated quotation system of a registered securities association, or where the equity is not quoted in such a system, the range of reported high and low bid quotations, indicating the source of such quotations. Indicate, as applicable, that such over-the-counter market quotations reflect inter-dealer prices, without retail mark-up, mark-down or commission and may not necessarily represent actual transactions. Where there is an absence of an established public trading market, reference to quotations shall be qualified by appropriate explanation.

(iv) Where a foreign registrant has identified a principal established foreign trading market for its common equity pursuant to paragraph (a) (1) of this Item, also provide market price information comparable, to the extent practicable, to that required for the principal United States market, including the source of such information. Such prices shall be stated in the currency in which they are quoted. The registrant may translate such prices into United States currency at the currency exchange rate in effect on the date the price disclosed was reported on the foreign exchange. If the primary United States market for the registrant's common equity trades using American Depositary Receipts, the United States prices disclosed shall be on that basis.

(v) If the information called for by this Item is being presented in a registration statement filed pursuant to the Securities Act or a proxy or information statement filed pursuant to the Exchange Act, the document also shall include price information as of the latest practicable date, and, in the case of securities to be issued in connection with an acquisition, business combination or other reorganization, as of the date immediately prior to the public announcement of such transaction.

(2) If the information called for by this paragraph (a) is being presented in a registration statement on Form S-1 (§ 239.11 of this chapter) under the Securities Act or on Form 10 (§ 249.210 of this chapter) under the Exchange Act relating to a class of common equity for which at the time of filing there is no established United States public trading market, indicate the amount(s) of common equity:

(i) That is subject to outstanding options or warrants to purchase, or securities convertible into, common equity of the registrant;

(ii) That could be sold pursuant to § 230.144 of this chapter or that the registrant has agreed to register under the Securities Act for sale by security holders; or

(iii) That is being, or has been publicly proposed to be, publicly offered by the registrant (unless such common equity is being offered pursuant to an employee benefit plan or dividend reinvestment plan), the offering of which could have a material effect on the market price of the registrant's common equity.

(b) *Holders.* (1) Set forth the approximate number of holders of each class of common equity of the registrant as of the latest practicable date.

(2) If the information called for by this paragraph (b) is being presented in a registration statement filed pursuant to the Securities Act or a proxy statement or information statement filed pursuant to the Exchange Act that relates to an acquisition, business combination or other reorganization, indicate the effect of such transaction on the amount and percentage of present holdings of the registrant's common equity owned beneficially by (i) any person (including any group as that term is used in section 13(d)(3) of the Exchange Act) who is known to the registrant to be the beneficial owner of more than five percent

of any class of the registrant's common equity and (ii) each director and nominee and (iii) all directors and officers as a group, and the registrant's present commitments to such persons with respect to the issuance of shares of any class of its common equity.

(c) *Dividends.* (1) State the frequency and amount of any cash dividends declared on each class of its common equity by the registrant for the two most recent fiscal years and any subsequent interim period for which financial statements are required to be presented by §210.3 of Regulation S-X. Where there are restrictions (including, where appropriate, restrictions on the ability of registrant's subsidiaries to transfer funds to the registrant in the form of cash dividends, loans or advances) that currently materially limit the registrant's ability to pay such dividends or that the registrant reasonably believes are likely to limit materially the future payment of dividends on the common equity so state and either (i) describe briefly (where appropriate quantify) such restrictions, or (ii) cross reference to the specific discussion of such restrictions in the Management's Discussion and Analysis of financial condition and operating results prescribed by Item 303 of Regulation S-K (§229.303) and the description of such restrictions required by Regulation S-X in the registrant's financial statements.

(2) Where registrants have a record of paying no cash dividends although earnings indicate an ability to do so, they are encouraged to consider the question of their intention to pay cash dividends in the foreseeable future and, if no such intention exists, to make a statement of that fact in the filing. Registrants which have a history of paying cash dividends also are encouraged to indicate whether they currently expect that comparable cash dividends will continue to be paid in the future and, if not, the nature of the change in the amount or rate of cash dividend payments.

(d) *Securities authorized for issuance under equity compensation plans.* (1) In the following tabular format, provide the information specified in paragraph (d)(2) of this Item as of the end of the most recently completed fiscal year with respect to compensation plans (including individual compensation arrangements) under which equity securities of the registrant are authorized for issuance, aggregated as follows:

(i) All compensation plans previously approved by security holders; and

(ii) All compensation plans not previously approved by security holders.

Equity Compensation Plan Information

Plan category	Number of securities to be issued upon exercise of outstanding options, warrants and rights	Weighted-average exercise price of outstanding options, warrants and rights	Number of securities remaining available for future issuance under equity compensation plans (excluding securities reflected in column (a))
	(a)	*(b)*	*(c)*
Equity compensation plans approved by security holders			
Equity compensation plans not approved by security holders			
Total			

(2) The table shall include the following information as of the end of the most recently completed fiscal year for each category of equity compensation plan described in paragraph (d)(1) of this Item:

(i) The number of securities to be issued upon the exercise of outstanding options, warrants and rights (column (a));

(ii) The weighted-average exercise price of the outstanding options, warrants and rights disclosed pursuant to paragraph (d)(2)(i) of this Item (column (b)); and

(iii) Other than securities to be issued upon the exercise of the outstanding options, warrants and rights disclosed in paragraph (d)(2)(i) of this Item, the number of securities remaining available for future issuance under the plan (column (c)).

(3) For each compensation plan under which equity securities of the registrant are authorized for issuance that was adopted without the approval of security holders, describe briefly, in narrative form, the material features of the plan.

Instructions to Paragraph (d).

1. Disclosure shall be provided with respect to any compensation plan and individual compensation arrangement of the registrant (or parent, subsidiary or affiliate of the registrant) under which equity securities of the registrant are authorized for issuance to employees or non-employees (such as

directors, consultants, advisors, vendors, customers, suppliers or lenders) in exchange for consideration in the form of goods or services as described in Statement of Financial Accounting Standards No. 123, *Accounting for Stock-Based Compensation*, or any successor standard. No disclosure is required with respect to

(i) any plan, contract or arrangement for the issuance of warrants or rights to all security holders of the registrant as such on a pro rata basis (such as a stock rights offering) or

(ii) any employee benefit plan that is intended to meet the qualification requirements of Section 401(a) of the Internal Revenue Code (26 U.S.C. § 401(a)).

2. For purposes of this paragraph, an "individual compensation arrangement" includes, but is not limited to, the following: a written compensation contract within the meaning of "employee benefit plan" under § 230.405 of this chapter and a plan (whether or not set forth in any formal document) applicable to one person as provided under Item 402(a)(6)(ii) of Regulation S-K (§ 229.402(a)(6)(ii)).

3. If more than one class of equity security is issued under its equity compensation plans, a registrant should aggregate plan information for each class of security.

4. A registrant may aggregate information regarding individual compensation arrangements with the plan information required under paragraph (d)(1)(i) and (ii) of this item, as applicable.

5. A registrant may aggregate information regarding a compensation plan assumed in connection with a merger, consolidation or other acquisition transaction pursuant to which the registrant may make subsequent grants or awards of its equity securities with the plan information required under paragraph (d)(1)(i) and (ii) of this item, as applicable. A registrant shall disclose on an aggregated basis in a footnote to the table the information required under paragraph (d)(2)(i) and (ii) of this item with respect to any individual options, warrants or rights assumed in connection with a merger, consolidation or other acquisition transaction.

6. To the extent that the number of securities remaining available for future issuance disclosed in column (c) includes securities available for future issuance under any compensation plan or individual compensation arrangement other than upon the exercise of an option, warrant or right, disclose the number of securities and type of plan separately for each such plan in a footnote to the table.

7. If the description of an equity compensation plan set forth in a registrant's financial statements contains the disclosure required by paragraph (d)(3) of this item, a cross-reference to such description will satisfy the requirements of paragraph (d)(3) of this item.

8. If an equity compensation plan contains a formula for calculating the number of securities available for issuance under the plan, including, without limitation, a formula that automatically increases the number of securities available for issuance by a percentage of the number of outstanding securities of the registrant, a description of this formula shall be disclosed in a footnote to the table.

9. Except where it is part of a document that is incorporated by reference into a prospectus, the information required by this paragraph need not be provided in any registration statement filed under the Securities Act.

(e) *Performance graph.* (1) Provide a line graph comparing the yearly percentage change in the registrant's cumulative total shareholder return on a class of common stock registered under section 12 of the Exchange Act (as measured by dividing (i) the sum of (A) the cumulative amount of dividends for the measurement period, assuming dividend reinvestment, and (B) the difference between the registrant's share price at the end and the beginning of the measurement period; by (ii) the share price at the beginning of the measurement period) with:

(i) The cumulative total return of a broad equity market index assuming reinvestment of dividends, that includes companies whose equity securities are traded on the same exchange or are of comparable market capitalization; *provided, however*, that if the registrant is a company within the Standard & Poor's 500 Stock Index, the registrant must use that index; and

(ii) The cumulative total return, assuming reinvestment of dividends, of:

(A) A published industry or line-of-business index;

(B) Peer issuer(s) selected in good faith. If the registrant does not select its peer issuer(s) on an industry or line-of-business basis, the registrant shall disclose the basis for its selection; or

(C) Issuer(s) with similar market capitalization(s), but only if the registrant does not use a published industry or line-of-business index and does not believe it can reasonably identify a peer group. If the registrant uses this alternative, the graph shall be accompanied by a statement of the reasons for this selection.

(2) For purposes of paragraph (e)(1) of this Item, the term "measurement period" shall be the period beginning at the "measurement point" established by the market close on the last trading day before the beginning of the registrant's fifth preceding fiscal year, through and including the end of the registrant's last completed fiscal year. If the class of securities has been registered under section 12 of

the Exchange Act (15 U.S.C. 78l) for a shorter period of time, the period covered by the comparison may correspond to that time period.

(3) For purposes of paragraph (e)(1)(ii)(A) of this Item, the term "published industry or line-of-business index" means any index that is prepared by a party other than the registrant or an affiliate and is accessible to the registrant's security holders; *provided, however,* that registrants may use an index prepared by the registrant or affiliate if such index is widely recognized and used.

(4) If the registrant selects a different index from an index used for the immediately preceding fiscal year, explain the reason(s) for this change and also compare the registrant's total return with that of both the newly selected index and the index used in the immediately preceding fiscal year.

Instructions to Item 201(e):

1. In preparing the required graphic comparisons, the registrant should:

a. Use, to the extent feasible, comparable methods of presentation and assumptions for the total return calculations required by paragraph (e)(1) of this Item; *provided, however,* that if the registrant constructs its own peer group index under paragraph (e)(1)(ii)(B), the same methodology must be used in calculating both the registrant's total return and that on the peer group index; and

b. Assume the reinvestment of dividends into additional shares of the same class of equity securities at the frequency with which dividends are paid on such securities during the applicable fiscal year.

2. In constructing the graph:

a. The closing price at the measurement point must be converted into a fixed investment, stated in dollars, in the registrant's stock (or in the stocks represented by a given index) with cumulative returns for each subsequent fiscal year measured as a change from that investment; and

b. Each fiscal year should be plotted with points showing the cumulative total return as of that point. The value of the investment as of each point plotted on a given return line is the number of shares held at that point multiplied by the then-prevailing share price.

3. The registrant is required to present information for the registrant's last five fiscal years, and may choose to graph a longer period; but the measurement point, however, shall remain the same.

4. Registrants may include comparisons using performance measures in addition to total return, such as return on average common shareholders' equity.

5. If the registrant uses a peer issuer(s) comparison or comparison with issuer(s) with similar market capitalizations, the identity of those issuers must be disclosed and the returns of each component issuer of the group must be weighted according to the respective issuer's stock market capitalization at the beginning of each period for which a return is indicated.

6. *Smaller reporting companies.* A registrant that qualifies as a smaller reporting company, as defined by § 229.10(f)(1), is not required to provide the information required by paragraph (e) of this Item.

7. The information required by paragraph (e) of this Item need not be provided in any filings other than an annual report to security holders required by Exchange Act Rule 14a-3 (17 CFR 240.14a-3) or Exchange Act Rule 14c-3 (17 CFR 240.14c-3) that precedes or accompanies a registrant's proxy or information statement relating to an annual meeting of security holders at which directors are to be elected (or special meeting or written consents in lieu of such meeting). Such information will not be deemed to be incorporated by reference into any filing under the Securities Act or the Exchange Act, except to the extent that the registrant specifically incorporates it by reference.

8. The information required by paragraph (e) of this Item shall not be deemed to be "soliciting material" or to be "filed" with the Commission or subject to Regulation 14A or 14C (17 CFR 240.14a-1 - 240.14a-104 or 240.14c-1 - 240.14c-101), other than as provided in this item, or to the liabilities of section 18 of the Exchange Act (15 U.S.C. 78r), except to the extent that the registrant specifically requests that such information be treated as soliciting material or specifically incorporates it by reference into a filing under the Securities Act or the Exchange Act.

Instructions to Item 201. 1. Registrants, the common equity of which is listed for trading on more than one securities exchange registered under the Exchange Act, are required to indicate each such exchange pursuant to paragraph (a)(1)(i) of this Item; such registrants, however, need only report one set of price quotations pursuant to paragraph (a)(1)(ii) of this Item; where available, these shall be the prices as reported in the consolidated transaction reporting system and, where the prices are not so reported, the prices on the most significant (in terms of volume) securities exchange for such shares.

2. Market prices and dividends reported pursuant to this Item shall be adjusted to give retroactive effect to material changes resulting from stock dividends, stock splits and reverse stock splits.

3. The computation of the approximate number of holders of registrant's common equity may be based upon the number of record holders or also may include individual participants in security position listings. See Rule 17Ad-8 under the Exchange Act. The method of computation that is chosen shall be indicated.

4. If the registrant is a foreign issuer, describe briefly:

A. Any governmental laws, decrees or regulations in the country in which the registrant is organized that restrict the export or import of capital, including, but not limited to, foreign exchange controls, or that affect the remittance of dividends or other payments to nonresident holders of the registrant's common equity; and

B. All taxes, including withholding provisions, to which United States common equity holders are subject under existing laws and regulations of the foreign country in which the registrant is organized. Include a brief description of pertinent provisions of any reciprocal tax treaty between such foreign country and the United States regarding withholding. If there is no such treaty, so state.

5. If the registrant is a foreign private issuer whose common equity of the class being registered is wholly or partially in bearer form, the response to this Item shall so indicate together with as much information as the registrant is able to provide with respect to security holdings in the United States. If the securities being registered trade in the United States in the form of American Depositary Receipts or similar certificates, the response to this Item shall so indicate together with the name of the depositary issuing such receipts and the number of shares or other units of the underlying security representing the trading units in such receipts.

[As last amended in Release No. 33-8876, effective February 4, 2008, 73 F.R. 934.]

[¶ 13,022] Description of Registrant's Securities

Reg. § 229.202. Item 202. Note.—If the securities being described have been accepted for listing on an exchange, the exchange may be identified. The document should not however, convey the impression that the registrant may apply successfully for listing of the securities on an exchange or that, in the case of an underwritten offering, the underwriters may request the registrant to apply for such listing, unless there is reasonable assurance that the securities to be offered will be acceptable to a securities exchange for listing.

(a) *Capital stock.* If capital stock is to be registered, state the title of the class and describe such of the matters listed in paragraphs (a)(1) through (5) as are relevant. A complete legal description of the securities need not be given.

(1) Outline briefly: (i) dividend rights; (ii) terms of conversion; (iii) sinking fund provisions; (iv) redemption provisions; (v) voting rights, including any provisions specifying the vote required by security holders to take action; (vi) any classification of the Board of Directors, and the impact of such classification where cumulative voting is permitted or required; (vii) liquidation rights; (viii) preemption rights; and (ix) liability to further calls or to assessment by the registrant and for liabilities of the registrant imposed on its stockholders under state statutes (*e.g.,* to laborers, servants or employees of the registrant), unless such disclosure would be immaterial because the financial resources of the registrant or other factors make it improbable that liability under such state statutes would be imposed; (x) any restriction on alienability of the securities to be registered; and (xi) any provision discriminating against any existing or prospective holder of such securities as a result of such security holder owning a substantial amount of securities.

(2) If the rights of holders of such stock may be modified otherwise than by a vote of a majority or more of the shares outstanding, voting as a class, so state and explain briefly.

(3) If preferred stock is to be registered, describe briefly any restriction on the repurchase or redemption of shares by the registrant while there is any arrearage in the payment of dividends or sinking fund installments. If there is no such restriction, so state.

(4) If the rights evidenced by, or amounts payable with respect to, the shares to be registered are, or may be, materially limited or qualified by the rights of any other authorized class of securities, include the information regarding such other securities as will enable investors to understand such limitations or qualifications. No information need be given, however, as to any class of securities all of which will be retired, provided appropriate steps to ensure such retirement will be completed prior to or upon delivery by the registrant of the shares.

(5) Describe briefly or cross-reference to a description in another part of the document, any provision of the registrant's charter or by-laws that would have an effect of delaying, deferring or preventing a change in control of the registrant and that would operate only with respect to an extraordinary corporate transaction involving the registrant [or any of its subsidiaries], such as a merger, reorganization, tender offer, sale or transfer of substantially all of its assets, or liquidation. Provisions and arrangements required by law or imposed by governmental or judicial authority need not be described or discussed pursuant to this paragraph (a)(5). Provisions or arrangements adopted by the registrant to effect, or further, compliance with laws or governmental or judicial mandate are not subject to the immediately preceding sentence where such compliance did not require the specific provisions or arrangements adopted.

(b) *Debt securities.* If debt securities are to be registered, state the title of such securities, the principal amount being offered, and, if a series, the total amount authorized and the total amount outstanding as of the most recent practicable date; and describe such of the matter listed in paragraphs (b)(1) through (10) as are relevant. A complete legal description of the securities need not be given. For purposes solely of this Item, debt securities that differ from one another only as to the interest rate or maturity shall be regarded as securities of the same class. Outline briefly:

(1) Provisions with respect to maturity, interest, conversion, redemption, amortization, sinking fund, or retirement;

(2) Provisions with respect to the kind and priority of any lien securing the securities, together with a brief identification of the principal properties subject to such lien;

(3) Provisions with respect to the subordination of the rights of holders of the securities to other security holders or creditors of the registrant; where debt securities are designated as subordinated in accordance with Instruction 1 to this Item, set forth the aggregate amount of outstanding indebtedness as of the most recent practicable date that by the terms of such debt securities would be senior to such subordinated debt and describe briefly any limitation on the issuance of such additional senior indebtedness or state that there is no such limitation;

(4) Provisions restricting the declaration of dividends or requiring the maintenance of any asset ratio or the creation or maintenance of reserves;

(5) Provisions restricting the incurrence of additional debt or the issuance of additional securities; in the case of secured debt, whether the securities being registered are to be issued on the basis of unbonded bondable property, the deposit of cash or otherwise; as of the most recent practicable date, the approximate amount of unbonded bondable property available as a basis for the issuance of bonds; provisions permitting the withdrawal of cash deposited as a basis for the issuance of bonds; and provisions permitting the release or substitution of assets securing the issue; *Provided, however,* That provisions permitting the release of assets upon the deposit of equivalent funds or the pledge of equivalent property, the release of property no longer required in the business, obsolete property, or property taken by eminent domain or the application of insurance moneys, and other similar provisions need not be described;

(6) The general type of event that constitutes a default and whether or not any periodic evidence is required to be furnished as to the absence of default or as to compliance with the terms of the indenture;

(7) Provisions relating to modification of the terms of the security or the rights of security holders;

(8) If the rights evidenced by the securities to be registered are, or may be, materially limited or qualified by the rights of any other authorized class of securities, the information regarding such other securities as will enable investors to understand the rights evidenced by the securities[;] to the extent not otherwise disclosed pursuant to this Item; no information need be given, however, as to any class of securities all of which will be retired, provided appropriate steps to ensure such retirement will be completed prior to or upon delivery by the registrant of the securities;

(9) If debt securities are to be offered at a price such that they will be deemed to be offered at an "original issue discount" as defined in paragraph (a) of Section 1273 of the Internal Revenue Code (26 U.S.C. 1273), or if a debt security is sold in a package with another security and the allocation of the offering price between the two securities may have the effect of offering the debt security at such an original issue discount, the tax effects thereof pursuant to sections 1271—1278; and

(10) The name of the trustee(s) and the nature of any material relationship with the registrant or with any of its affiliates; the percentage of securities of the class necessary to require the trustee to take action; and what indemnification the trustee may require before proceeding to enforce the lien.

(c) *Warrants and rights.* If the securities described are to be offered pursuant to warrants or rights state:

(1) The amount of securities called for by such warrants or rights;

(2) The period during which and the price at which the warrants or rights are exercisable;

(3) The amount of warrants or rights outstanding;

(4) Provisions for changes to or adjustments in the exercise price; and

(5) Any other material terms of such rights on [or]warrants.

(d) *Other securities.* If securities other than capital stock, debt, warrants or rights are to be registered, include a brief description (comparable to that required in paragraphs (a), (b) and (c) of Item 202) of the rights evidenced thereby.

(e) *Market information for securities other than common equity.* If securities other than common equity are to be registered and there is an established public trading market for such securities (as that term is used in Item 201 of Regulation S-K (§ 229.201 of this chapter)) provide market information with respect to such securities comparable to that required by paragraph (a) of Item 201 of Regulation S-K (§ 229.201).

(f) *American Depositary Receipts.* If Depositary Shares represented by American Depositary Receipts are being registered, furnish the following information:

(1) The name of the depositary and the address of its principal executive office.

(2) State the title of the American Depositary Receipts and identify the deposited security. Describe briefly the terms of deposit, including the provisions, if any, with respect to: (i) the amount of deposited securities represented by one unit of American Depositary Receipts; (ii) the procedure for voting, if any, the deposited securities; (iii) the collection and distribution of dividends; (iv) the transmission of notices, reports and proxy soliciting material; (v) the sale or exercise of rights; (vi) the deposit or sale of securities resulting from dividends, splits or plans of reorganization; (vii) amendment, extension or termination of the deposit; (viii) rights of holders of receipts to inspect the transfer books of the depositary and the list of holders of receipts; (ix) restrictions upon the right to deposit or withdraw the underlying securities; (x) limitation upon the liability of the depositary.

(3) Describe all fees and charges which may be imposed directly or indirectly against the holder of the American Depositary Receipts, indicating the type of service, the amount of fee or charges and to whom paid.

Instructions to Item 202. 1. Wherever the title of securities is required to be stated, there shall be given such information as will indicate the type and general character of the securities, including the following:

A. In the case of shares, the par or stated value, if any; the rate of dividends, if fixed, and whether cumulative or non-cumulative; a brief indication of the preference, if any; and if convertible or redeemable, a statement to that effect;

B. In the case of debt, the rate of interest; the date of maturity or, if the issue matures serially, a brief indication of the serial maturities, such as "maturing serially from 1955 to 1960"; if the payment of principal or interest is contingent, an appropriate indication of such contingency; a brief indication of the priority of the issue; and, if convertible or callable, a statement to that effect; or

C. In the case of any other kind of security, appropriate information of comparable character.

2. If the registrant is a foreign registrant, include (to the extent not disclosed in the document pursuant to Item 201 of Regulation S-K (§ 229.201) or otherwise) in the description of the securities:

A. A brief description of any limitations on the right of nonresident or foreign owners to hold or vote such securities imposed by foreign law or by the charter or other constituent document of the registrant, or if no such limitations are applicable, so state;

B. A brief description of any governmental laws, decrees or regulations in the country in which the registrant is organized affecting the remittance of dividends, interest and other payments to nonresident holders of the securities being registered;

C. A brief outline of all taxes, including withholding provisions, to which United States security holders are subject under existing laws and regulations of the foreign country in which the registrant is organized; and

D. A brief description of pertinent provisions of any reciprocal tax treaty between such foreign country and the United States regarding withholding or, if there is no such treaty, so state.

3. Section 305(a)(2) of the Trust Indenture Act of 1939, 15 U.S.C. 77aaa et seq., as amended ("Trust Indenture Act"), shall not be deemed to require the inclusion in a registration statement or in a prospectus of any information not required by this Item.

4. Where convertible securities or stock purchase warrants are being registered that are subject to redemption or call, the description of the conversion terms of the securities or material terms of the warrants shall disclose:

A. Whether the right to convert or purchase the securities will be forfeited unless it is exercised before the date specified in a notice of the redemption or call;

B. The expiration or termination date of the warrants;

C. The kinds, frequency and timing of notice of the redemption or call, including the cities or newspapers in which notice will be published (where the securities provide for a class of newspapers or group of cities in which the publication may be made at the discretion of the registrant, the registrant should describe such provision); and

D. In the case of bearer securities, that investors are responsible for making arrangements to prevent loss of the right to convert or purchase in the event of redemption of call, for example, by reading the newspapers in which the notice of redemption or call may be published.

5. The response to paragraph (f) shall include information with respect to fees and charges in connection with (A) the deposit or substitution of the underlying securities; (B) receipt and distribution of dividends; (C) the sale or exercise of rights; (D) the withdrawal of the underlying security; and (E) the transferring, splitting or grouping of receipts. Information with respect to the right to collect the fees and charges against dividends received and deposited securities shall be included in response to this item.

6. For asset-backed securities, see also Item 1113 of Regulation AB (§ 229.1113).

[As last amended in Release No. 33-8518, effective March 8, 2005 (Compliance dates are triggered by initial bona fide offer date or registration statement filing date and extend out to March 31, 2006. Complete compliance date details can be found in the "Dates" section of the release.), 70 F.R. 1506.]

Subpart 229.300—Financial Information

[¶ 13,031] Selected Financial Data

Reg. § 229.301. Item 301. Furnish in comparative columnar form the selected financial data for the registrant referred to below, for

(a) Each of the last five fiscal years of the registrant (or for the life of the registrant and its predecessors, if less), and

(b) Any additional fiscal years necessary to keep the information from being misleading.

(c) *Smaller reporting companies.* A registrant that qualifies as a smaller reporting company, as defined by § 229.10(f)(1), is not required to provide the information required by this Item.

Instructions to Item 301. 1. The purpose of the selected financial data shall be to supply in a convenient and readable format selected financial data which highlight certain significant trends in the registrant's financial condition and results of operations.

2. Subject to appropriate variation to conform to the nature of the registrant's business, the following items shall be included in the table of financial data: net sales or operating revenues; income (loss) from continuing operations; income (loss) from continuing operations per common share; total assets; long-term obligations and redeemable preferred stock (including long-term debt, capital leases, and redeemable preferred stock as defined in § 210.5-02.27(a) of Regulation S-X [17 CFR 210]; and cash dividends declared per common share. Registrants may include additional items which they believe would enhance an understanding of and would highlight other trends in their financial condition and results of operations.

Briefly describe, or cross-reference to a discussion thereof, factors such as accounting changes, business combinations or dispositions of business operations, that materially affect the comparability of the information reflected in selected financial data. Discussion of, or reference to, any material uncertainties should also be included where such matters might cause the data reflected herein not to be indicative of the registrant's future financial condition or results of operations.

3. All references to the registrant in the table of selected financial data and in this Item shall mean the registrant and its subsidiaries consolidated.

4. If interim period financial statements are included, or are required to be included by Article 3 of Regulation S-X, registrants should consider whether any or all of the selected financial data need to be updated for such interim periods to reflect a material change in the trends indicated; where such updating information is necessary, registrants shall provide the information on a comparative basis unless not necessary to an understanding of such updating information.

5. A foreign private issuer shall disclose also the following information in all filings containing financial statements:

A. In the forepart of the document and as of the latest practicable date, the exchange rate into U.S. currency of the foreign currency in which the financial statements are denominated;

B. A history of exchange rates for the five most recent years and any subsequent interim period for which financial statements are presented setting forth the rates for period end, the average rates, and the range of high and low rates for each year, and

C. If equity securities are being registered, a five year summary of dividends per share stated in both the currency in which the financial statements are denominated and United States currency based on the exchange rates at each respective payment date.

6. A foreign private issuer shall present the selected financial data in the same currency as its financial statements. The issuer may present the selected financial data on the basis of the accounting principles used in its primary financial statements but in such case shall present this data also on the basis of any reconciliations of such data to United States generally accepted accounting principles and Regulation S-X made pursuant to Rule 4-01 of Regulation S-X (§ 210.4-01 of this chapter).

7. For purposes of this rule, the rate of exchange means the noon buying rate in New York City for cable transfers in foreign currencies as certified for customs purposes by the Federal Reserve Bank of New York. The average rate means the average of the exchange rates on the last day of each month during a year.

[As last amended in Release No. 33-9026, effective April 23, 2009, 74 F.R. 18612.]

[¶ 13,032] Supplementary Financial Information

Reg. § 229.302 Item 302. (a) *Selected quarterly financial data.* Registrants specified in paragraph (a)(5) of this Item shall provide the information specified below.

(1) Disclosure shall be made of net sales, gross profit (net sales less costs and expenses associated directly with or allocated to products sold or services rendered), income (loss) before extraordinary items and cumulative effect of a change in accounting, per share data based upon such income (loss),

net income (loss) and net income (loss) attributable to the registrant, for each full quarter within the two most recent fiscal years and any subsequent interim period for which financial statements are included or are required to be included by Article 3 of Regulation S-X (Part 17 CFR 210 of this chapter).

(2) When the data supplied pursuant to paragraph (a) of this section vary from the amounts previously reported on the Form 10-Q (§ 249.308a of this chapter) filed for any quarter, such as would be the case when a combination between entities under common control occurs or where an error is corrected, reconcile the amounts given with those previously reported and describe the reason for the difference.

(3) Describe the effect of any disposals of segments of a business, and extraordinary, unusual or infrequently occurring items recognized in each full quarter within the two most recent fiscal years and any subsequent interim period for which financial statements are included or are required to be included by Article 3 of Regulation S-X, as well as the aggregate effect and the nature of year-end or other adjustments which are material to the results of that quarter.

(4) If the financial statements to which this information relates have been reported on by an accountant, appropriate professional standards and procedures, as enumerated in the Statements of Auditing Standards issued by the Auditing Standards Board of the American Institute of Certified Public Accountants, shall be followed by the reporting accountant with regard to the data required by this paragraph (a).

(5) This paragraph (a) applies to any registrant, except a foreign private issuer, that has securities registered pursuant to sections 12(b) (15 U.S.C. § 78*l*(b)) (other than mutual life insurance companies) or 12(g) of the Exchange Act (15 U.S.C. § 78*l*(g)).

(b) *Information about oil and gas producing activities.* Registrants engaged in oil and gas producing activities shall present the information about oil and gas producing activities (as those activities are defined in Regulation S-X, § 210.4-10(a)) specified in paragraphs 9-34 of Statement of Financial Accounting Standards ("SFAS") No. 69, "Disclosures about Oil and Gas Producing Activities," if such oil and gas producing activities are regarded as significant under one or more of the tests set forth in paragraph 8 of SFAS No. 69.

Instructions to Paragraph (b). 1. (a) SFAS No. 69 disclosures that relate to annual periods shall be presented for each annual period for which an income statement is required, (b) SFAS No. 69 disclosures required as of the end of an annual period shall be presented as of the date of each audited balance sheet required, and (c) SFAS No. 69 disclosures required as of the beginning of an annual period shall be presented as of the beginning of each annual period for which an income statement is required.

2. This paragraph, together with § 210.4-10 of Regulation S-X, prescribes financial reporting standards for the preparation of accounts by persons engaged, in whole or in part, in the production of crude oil or natural gas in the United States, pursuant to Section 503 of the Energy Policy and Conservation Act of 1975 [42 U.S.C. 6383] ("EPCA") and Section 11(c) of the Energy Supply and Environmental Coordination Act of 1974 [15 U.S.C. 796] ("ESECA") as amended by Section 506 of EPCA. The application of this paragraph to those oil and gas producing operations of companies regulated for ratemaking purposes on an individual-company-cost-of-service basis may, however, give appropriate recognition to differences arising because of the effect of the ratemaking process.

3. Any person exempted by the Department of Energy from any recordkeeping or reporting requirements pursuant to Section 11(c) of ESECA, as amended, is similarly exempted from the related provisions of this paragraph in the preparation of accounts pursuant to EPCA. This exemption does not affect the applicability of this paragraph to filings pursuant to the federal securities laws.

(c) *Smaller reporting companies.* A registrant that qualifies as a smaller reporting company, as defined by § 229.10(f)(1), is not required to provide the information required by this Item.

[As last amended in Release No. 33-9026, effective April 23, 2009, 74 F.R. 18612.]

[¶ 13,033] Management's Discussion and Analysis of Financial Condition and Results of Operations

Reg. § 229.303. Item 303. (a) *Full fiscal years.* Discuss registrant's financial condition, changes in financial condition and results of operations. The discussion shall provide information as specified in paragraphs (a)(1) through (5) of this item and also shall provide such other information that the registrant believes to be necessary to an understanding of its financial condition, changes in financial condition and results of operations. Discussions of liquidity and capital resources may be combined whenever the two topics are interrelated. Where in the registrant's judgment a discussion of segment information or of other subdivisions of the registrant's business would be appropriate to an understanding of such business, the discussion shall focus on each relevant, reportable segment or other subdivision of the business and on the registrant as a whole.

(1) *Liquidity.* Identify any known trends or any known demands, commitments, events or uncertainties that will result in or that are reasonably likely to result in the registrant's liquidity increasing or

decreasing in any material way. If a material deficiency is identified, indicate the course of action that the registrant has taken or proposes to take to remedy the deficiency. Also identify and separately describe internal and external sources of liquidity, and briefly discuss any material unused sources of liquid assets.

(2) *Capital resources.* (i) Describe the registrant's material commitments for capital expenditures as of the end of the latest fiscal period, and indicate the general purpose of such commitments and the anticipated source of funds needed to fulfill such commitments.

(ii) Describe any known material trends, favorable or unfavorable, in the registrant's capital resources. Indicate any expected material changes in the mix and relative cost of such resources. The discussion shall consider changes between equity, debt and any off-balance sheet financing arrangements.

(3) *Results of operations.* (i) Describe any unusual or infrequent events or transactions or any significant economic changes that materially affected the amount of reported income from continuing operations and, in each case, indicate the extent to which income was so affected. In addition, describe any other significant components of revenues or expenses that, in the registrant's judgment, should be described in order to understand the registrant's results of operations.

(ii) Describe any known trends or uncertainties that have had or that the registrant reasonably expects will have a material favorable or unfavorable impact on net sales or revenues or income from continuing operations. If the registrant knows of events that will cause a material change in the relationship between costs and revenues (such as known future increases in costs of labor or materials or price increases or inventory adjustments), the change in the relationship shall be disclosed.

(iii) To the extent that the financial statements disclose material increases in net sales or revenues, provide a narrative discussion of the extent to which such increases are attributable to increases in prices or to increases in the volume or amount of goods or services being sold or to the introduction of new products or services.

(iv) For the three most recent fiscal years of the registrant, or for those fiscal years in which the registrant has been engaged in business, whichever period is shortest, discuss the impact of inflation and changing prices on the registrant's net sales and revenues and on income from continuing operations.

(4) *Off-balance sheet arrangements.* (i) In a separately-captioned section, discuss the registrant's off-balance sheet arrangements that have or are reasonably likely to have a current or future effect on the registrant's financial condition, changes in financial condition, revenues or expenses, results of operations, liquidity, capital expenditures or capital resources that is material to investors. The disclosure shall include the items specified in paragraphs (a)(4)(i)(A), (B), (C) and (D) of this Item to the extent necessary to an understanding of such arrangements and effect and shall also include such other information that the registrant believes is necessary for such an understanding.

(A) The nature and business purpose to the registrant of such off-balance sheet arrangements;

(B) The importance to the registrant of such off-balance sheet arrangements in respect of its liquidity, capital resources, market risk support, credit risk support or other benefits;

(C) The amounts of revenues, expenses and cash flows of the registrant arising from such arrangements; the nature and amounts of any interests retained, securities issued and other indebtedness incurred by the registrant in connection with such arrangements; and the nature and amounts of any other obligations or liabilities (including contingent obligations or liabilities) of the registrant arising from such arrangements that are or are reasonably likely to become material and the triggering events or circumstances that could cause them to arise; and

(D) Any known event, demand, commitment, trend or uncertainty that will result in or is reasonably likely to result in the termination, or material reduction in availability to the registrant, of its off-balance sheet arrangements that provide material benefits to it, and the course of action that the registrant has taken or proposes to take in response to any such circumstances.

(ii) As used in this paragraph (a)(4), the term *off-balance sheet arrangement* means any transaction, agreement or other contractual arrangement to which an entity unconsolidated with the registrant is a party, under which the registrant has:

(A) Any obligation under a guarantee contract that has any of the characteristics identified in paragraph 3 of FASB Interpretation No. 45, *Guarantor's Accounting and Disclosure Requirements for Guarantees, Including Indirect Guarantees of Indebtedness of Others* (November 2002) ("FIN 45"), as may be modified or supplemented, and that is not excluded from the initial recognition and measurement provisions of FIN 45 pursuant to paragraphs 6 or 7 of that Interpretation;

(B) A retained or contingent interest in assets transferred to an unconsolidated entity or similar arrangement that serves as credit, liquidity or market risk support to such entity for such assets;

(C) Any obligation, including a contingent obligation, under a contract that would be accounted for as a derivative instrument, except that it is both indexed to the registrant's own stock and classified in stockholders' equity in the registrant's statement of financial position, and therefore excluded from the scope of FASB Statement of Financial Accounting Standards No. 133, *Accounting for Derivative Instruments and Hedging Activities* (June 1998), pursuant to paragraph 11(a) of that Statement, as may be modified or supplemented; or

(D) Any obligation, including a contingent obligation, arising out of a variable interest (as referenced in FASB Interpretation No. 46, *Consolidation of Variable Interest Entities* (January 2003), as may be modified or supplemented) in an unconsolidated entity that is held by, and material to, the registrant, where such entity provides financing, liquidity, market risk or credit risk support to, or engages in leasing, hedging or research and development services with, the registrant.

(5) *Tabular disclosure of contractual obligations.* (i) In a tabular format, provide the information specified in this paragraph (a)(5) as of the latest fiscal year end balance sheet date with respect to the registrant's known contractual obligations specified in the table that follows this paragraph (a)(5)(i). The registrant shall provide amounts, aggregated by type of contractual obligation. The registrant may disaggregate the specified categories of contractual obligations using other categories suitable to its business, but the presentation must include all of the obligations of the registrant that fall within the specified categories. A presentation covering at least the periods specified shall be included. The tabular presentation may be accompanied by footnotes to describe provisions that create, increase or accelerate obligations, or other pertinent data to the extent necessary for an understanding of the timing and amount of the registrant's specified contractual obligations.

Contractual Obligations	Total	Payments due by period			
		Less than 1 year	1–3 years	3–5 years	More than 5 years
[Long–Term Debt Obligations]					
[Capital (Finance) Lease Obligations]					
[Operating Lease Obligations]					
[Purchase Obligations]					
[Other Long–Term Liabilities Reflected on the Registrant's Balance Sheet under GAAP]					
Total					

(ii) *Definitions* : The following definitions apply to this paragraph (a)(5):

(A) *Long-Term Debt Obligation* means a payment obligation under long-term borrowings referenced in FASB Statement of Financial Accounting Standards No. 47 *Disclosure of Long-Term Obligations* (March 1981), as may be modified or supplemented.

(B) *Capital Lease Obligation* means a payment obligation under a lease classified as a capital lease pursuant to FASB Statement of Financial Accounting Standards No. 13 *Accounting for Leases* (November 1976), as may be modified or supplemented.

(C) *Operating Lease Obligation* means a payment obligation under a lease classified as an operating lease and disclosed pursuant to FASB Statement of Financial Accounting Standards No. 13 *Accounting for Leases* (November 1976), as may be modified or supplemented.

(D) *Purchase Obligation* means an agreement to purchase goods or services that is enforceable and legally binding on the registrant that specifies all significant terms, including: fixed or minimum quantities to be purchased; fixed, minimum or variable price provisions; and the approximate timing of the transaction.

Instructions to paragraph 303(a): 1. The registrant's discussion and analysis shall be of the financial statements and other statistical data that the registrant believes will enhance a reader's understanding of its financial condition, changes in financial condition and results of operations. Generally, the discussion shall cover the three-year period covered by the financial statements and shall use year-to-year comparisons or any other formats that in the registrant's judgment enhance a reader's understanding. However, where trend information is relevant, reference to the five-year selected financial data appearing pursuant to Item 301 of Regulation S-K (§ 229.301) may be necessary. A smaller reporting company's discussion shall cover the two-year period required in Article 8 of Regulation S-X and shall use year-to-year comparisons or any other formats that in the registrant's judgment enhance a reader's understanding.

2. The purpose of the discussion and analysis shall be to provide to investors and other users information relevant to an assessment of the financial condition and results of operations of the

registrant as determined by evaluating the amounts and certainty of cash flows from operations and from outside sources.

3. The discussion and analysis shall focus specifically on material events and uncertainties known to management that would cause reported financial information not to be necessarily indicative of future operating results or of future financial condition. This would include descriptions and amounts of (A) matters that would have an impact on future operations and have not had an impact in the past, and (B) matters that have had an impact on reported operations and are not expected to have an impact upon future operations.

4. Where the consolidated financial statements reveal material changes from year to year in one or more line items, the causes for the changes shall be described to the extent necessary to an understanding of the registrant's businesses as a whole; *Provided, however,* That if the causes for a change in one line item also relate to other line items, no repetition is required and a line-by-line analysis of the financial statements as a whole is not required or generally appropriate. Registrants need not recite the amounts of changes from year to year which are readily computable from the financial statements. The discussion shall not merely repeat numerical data contained in the consolidated financial statements.

5. The term "liquidity" as used in this Item refers to the ability of an enterprise to generate adequate amounts of cash to meet the enterprise's needs for cash. Except where it is otherwise clear from the discussion, the registrant shall indicate those balance sheet conditions or income or cash flow items which the registrant believes may be indicators of its liquidity condition. Liquidity generally shall be discussed on both a long-term and short-term basis. The issue of liquidity shall be discussed in the context of the registrant's own business or businesses. For example a discussion of working capital may be appropriate for certain manufacturing, industrial or related operations but might be inappropriate for a bank or public utility.

6. Where financial statements presented or incorporated by reference in the registration statement are required by § 210.4-08(e)(3) of Regulation S-X [17 CFR Part 210] to include disclosure of restrictions on the ability of both consolidated and unconsolidated subsidiaries to transfer funds to the registrant in the form of cash dividends, loans or advances, the discussion of liquidity shall include a discussion of the nature and extent of such restrictions and the impact such restrictions have had and are expected to have on the ability of the parent company to meet its cash obligations.

7. Any forward-looking information supplied is expressly covered by the safe harbor rule for projections. See Rule 175 under the Securities Act [17 CFR 230.175], Rule 3b-6 under the Exchange Act [17 CFR 240.3b-6] and Securities Act Release No. 6084 (June 25, 1979) (44 FR 33810).

8. Registrants are only required to discuss the effects of inflation and other changes in prices when considered material. This discussion may be made in whatever manner appears appropriate under the circumstances. All that is required is a brief textual presentation of management's views. No specific numerical financial data need be presented except as Rule 3-20(c) of Regulation S-X (§ 210.3-20(c) of this chapter) otherwise requires. However, registrants may elect to voluntarily disclose supplemental information on the effects of changing prices as provided for in Statement of Financial Accounting Standards No. 89, "Financial Reporting and Changing Prices" or through other supplemental disclosures. The Commission encourages experimentation with these disclosures in order to provide the most meaningful presentation of the impact of price changes on the registrant's financial statements.

9. Registrants that elect to disclose supplementary information on the effects of changing prices as specified by SFAS No. 89, "Financial Reporting and Changing Prices," may combine such explanations with the discussion and analysis required pursuant to this Item or may supply such information separately with appropriate cross reference.

10. All references to the registrant in the discussion and in this Item shall mean the registrant and its subsidiaries consolidated.

11. Foreign private registrants also shall discuss briefly any pertinent governmental economic, fiscal, monetary, or potential policies or factors that have materially affected or could materially affect, directly or indirectly, their operations or investments by United States nationals.

12. If the registrant is a foreign private issuer, the discussion shall focus on the primary financial statements presented in the registration statement or report. There shall be a reference to the reconciliation to United States generally accepted accounting principles, and a discussion of any aspects of the difference between foreign and United States generally accepted accounting principles, not discussed in the reconciliation, that the registrant believes is necessary for an understanding of the financial statements as a whole.

13. The attention of bank holding companies is directed to the information called for in Guide 3 (§ 229.801(c) and § 229.802(c)).

14. The attention of property-casualty insurance companies is directed to the information called for in Guide 6 (§ 229.801(f)).

Instructions to Paragraph 303(a)(4):

1. No obligation to make disclosure under paragraph (a)(4) of this Item shall arise in respect of an off-balance sheet arrangement until a definitive agreement that is unconditionally binding or subject only to customary closing conditions exists or, if there is no such agreement, when settlement of the transaction occurs.

2. Registrants should aggregate off-balance sheet arrangements in groups or categories that provide material information in an efficient and understandable manner and should avoid repetition and disclosure of immaterial information. Effects that are common or similar with respect to a number of off-balance sheet arrangements must be analyzed in the aggregate to the extent the aggregation increases understanding. Distinctions in arrangements and their effects must be discussed to the extent the information is material, but the discussion should avoid repetition and disclosure of immaterial information.

3. For purposes of paragraph (a)(4) of this Item only, contingent liabilities arising out of litigation, arbitration or regulatory actions are not considered to be off-balance sheet arrangements.

4. Generally, the disclosure required by paragraph (a)(4) shall cover the most recent fiscal year. However, the discussion should address changes from the previous year where such discussion is necessary to an understanding of the disclosure.

5. In satisfying the requirements of paragraph (a)(4) of this Item, the discussion of off-balance sheet arrangements need not repeat information provided in the footnotes to the financial statements, provided that such discussion clearly cross-references to specific information in the relevant footnotes and integrates the substance of the footnotes into such discussion in a manner designed to inform readers of the significance of the information that is not included within the body of such discussion.

(b) *Interim periods.* If interim period financial statements are included or are required to be included by Article 3 of Regulations S-X (17 CFR 210), a management's discussion and analysis of the financial condition and results of operations shall be provided so as to enable the reader to assess material changes in financial condition and results of operations between the periods specified in paragraphs (b)(1) and (2) of this Item. The discussion and analysis shall include a discussion of material changes in those items specifically listed in paragraph (a) of this Item, except that the impact of inflation and changing prices on operations for interim periods need not be addressed.

(1) *Material changes in financial condition.* Discuss any material changes in financial condition from the end of the preceding fiscal year to the date of the most recent interim balance sheet provided. If the interim financial statements include an interim balance sheet as of the corresponding interim date of the preceding fiscal year, any material changes in financial condition from that date to the date of the most recent interim balance sheet provided also shall be discussed. If discussions of changes from both the end and the corresponding interim date of the preceding fiscal year are required, the discussions may be combined at the discretion of the registrant.

(2) *Material changes in results of operations.* Discuss any material changes in the registrant's results of operations with respect to the most recent fiscal year-to-date period for which an income statement is provided and the corresponding year-to-date period of the preceding fiscal year. If the registrant is required to or has elected to provide an income statement for the most recent fiscal quarter, such discussion also shall cover material changes with respect to that fiscal quarter and the corresponding fiscal quarter in the preceding fiscal year. In addition, if the registrant has elected to provide an income statement for the twelve-month period ended as of the date of the most recent interim balance sheet provided, the discussion also shall cover material changes with respect to that twelve-month and the twelve-month period ended as of the corresponding interim balance sheet date of the preceding fiscal year. Notwithstanding the above, if for purposes of a registration statement a registrant subject to paragraph (b) of § 210.3-03 of Regulation S-X provides a statement of income for the twelve-month period ended as of the date of the most recent interim balance sheet provided in lieu of the interim income statements otherwise required, the discussion of material changes in that twelve-month period will be in respect to the preceding fiscal year rather than the corresponding preceding period.

Instructions to paragraph 303(b): 1. If interim financial statements are presented together with financial statements for full fiscal years, the discussion of the interim financial information shall be prepared pursuant to this paragraph (b) and the discussion of the full fiscal year's information shall be prepared pursuant to paragraph (a) of this Item. Such discussions may be combined.

2. In preparing the discussion and analysis required by this paragraph (b), the registrant may presume that users of the interim financial information have read or have access to the discussion and analysis required by paragraph (a) for the preceding fiscal year.

3. The discussion and analysis required by this paragraph (b) is required to focus only on material changes. Where the interim financial statements reveal material changes from period to period in one or more significant line items, the causes for the changes shall be described if they have not already been disclosed: *Provided, however,* That if the causes for a change in one line item also relate to other line items, no repetition is required. Registrants need not recite the amounts of changes from period to period which are readily computable from the financial statements. The discussion shall not merely repeat numerical data contained in the financial statements. The information provided shall include that which is available to the registrant without undue effort or expense and which does not clearly appear in the registrant's condensed interim financial statements.

4. The registrant's discussion of material changes in results of operations shall identify any significant elements of the registrant's income or loss from continuing operations which do not arise from or are not necessarily representative of the registrant's ongoing business.

5. The registrant shall discuss any seasonal aspects of its business which have had a material effect upon its financial condition or results of operation.

6. Any forward-looking information supplied is expressly covered by the safe harbor rule for projections. See Rule 175 under the Securities Act (17 CFR 230.175), Rule 3b-6 under the Exchange Act (17 CFR 249.3b-6) and Securities Act Release No. 6084 (June 25, 1979) (44 FR 38810).

7. The registrant is not required to include the table required by paragraph (a) (5) of this Item for interim periods. Instead, the registrant should disclose material changes outside the ordinary course of the registrant's business in the specified contractual obligations during the interim period.

(c) *Safe harbor.* (1) The safe harbor provided in Section 27A of the Securities Act of 1933 (15 U.S.C. 77z-2) and Section 21E of the Securities Exchange Act of 1934 (15 U.S.C. 78u-5) ("statutory safe harbors") shall apply to forward-looking information provided pursuant to paragraphs (a) (4) and (5) of this Item, provided that the disclosure is made by: an issuer; a person acting on behalf of the issuer; an outside reviewer retained by the issuer making a statement on behalf of the issuer; or an underwriter, with respect to information provided by the issuer or information derived from information provided by the issuer.

(2) For purposes of paragraph (c) of this Item only:

(i) All information required by paragraphs (a) (4) and (5) of this Item is deemed to be a *forward looking statement* as that term is defined in the statutory safe harbors, except for historical facts.

(ii) With respect to paragraph (a) (4) of this Item, the meaningful cautionary statements element of the statutory safe harbors will be satisfied if a registrant satisfies all requirements of that same paragraph (a) (4) of this Item.

(d) *Smaller reporting companies.* A smaller reporting company, as defined by § 229.10(f) (1), may provide the information required in paragraph (a) (3) (iv) of this Item for the last two most recent fiscal years of the registrant if it provides financial information on net sales and revenues and on income from continuing operations for only two years. A smaller reporting company is not required to provide the information required by paragraph (a) (5) of this Item.

[As last amended in Release No. 33-8876, effective February 4, 2008, 73 F.R. 934.]

[¶ 13,034] Changes in and Disagreements with Accountants on Accounting and Financial Disclosure

Reg. § 229.304. Item 304. (a) (1) If during the registrant's two most recent fiscal years or any subsequent interim period, an independent accountant who was previously engaged as the principal accountant to audit the registrant's financial statements, or an independent accountant who was previously engaged to audit a significant subsidiary and on whom the principal accountant expressed reliance in its report, has resigned (or indicated it has declined to stand for re-election after the completion of the current audit) or was dismissed, then the registrant shall:

(i) State whether the former accountant resigned, declined to stand for re-election or was dismissed and the date thereof.

(ii) State whether the principal accountant's report on the financial statements for either of the past two years contained an adverse opinion or a disclaimer of opinion, or was qualified or modified as to uncertainty, audit scope, or accounting principles; and also describe the nature of each such adverse opinion, disclaimer of opinion, modification, or qualification.

(iii) State whether the decision to change accountants was recommended or approved by:

(A) any audit or similar committee of the board of directors, if the issuer has such a committee; or

(B) the board of directors, if the issuer has no such committee.

(iv) State whether during the registrant's two most recent fiscal years and any subsequent interim period preceding such resignation, declination or dismissal there were any disagreements with the former accountant on any matter of accounting principles or practices, financial statement disclosure, or auditing scope of procedure, which disagreement(s), if not resolved to the satisfaction of the former accountant, would have caused it to make reference to the subject matter of the disagreement(s) in connection with its report. Also, (A) describe each such disagreement; (B) state whether any audit or similar committee of the board of directors, or the board of directors, discussed the subject matter of each of such disagreements with the former accountant; and (C) state whether the registrant has authorized the former accountant to respond fully to the inquiries of the successor accountant concerning the subject matter of each of such disagreements and, if not, describe the nature of any limitation thereon and the reason therefore. The disagreements required to be reported in response to this Item include both those resolved to the former accountant's satisfaction and those not resolved to the former accountant's satisfaction. Disagreements contemplated by this Item are those that occur at the decision-making level, i.e., between personnel of the registrant responsible for presentation of its financial statements and personnel of the accounting firm responsible for rendering its report.

(v) Provide the information required by paragraphs (a)(1)(iv) of this Item for each of the kinds of events (even though the registrant and the former accountant did not express a difference of opinion regarding the event) listed in paragraphs (A) through (D) below, that occurred within the registrant's two most recent fiscal years and any subsequent interim period preceding the former accountant's resignation, declination to stand for re-election, or dismissal ("reportable events"). If the event led to a disagreement or difference of opinion, then the event should be reported as a disagreement under paragraph (a)(1)(iv) and need not be repeated under this paragraph.

(A) The accountant's having advised the registrant that the internal controls necessary for the registrant to develop reliable financial statements do not exist;

(B) the accountant's having advised the registrant that information has come to the accountant's attention that has led it to no longer be able to rely on management's representations, or that has made it unwilling to be associated with the financial statements prepared by management;

(C) (*1*) the accountant's having advised the registrant of the need to expand significantly the scope of its audit, or that information has come to the accountant's attention during the time period covered by Item 304(a)(1)(iv), that if further investigated may (*i*) materially impact the fairness or reliability of either: a previously issued audit report or the underlying financial statements; or the financial statements issued or to be issued covering the fiscal period(s) subsequent to the date of the most recent financial statements covered by an audit report (including information that may prevent it from rendering an unqualified audit report on those financial statements), or (*ii*) cause it to be unwilling to rely on management's representations or be associated with the registrant's financial statements, and (*2*) due to the accountant's resignation (due to audit scope limitations or otherwise) or dismissal, or for any other reason, the accountant did not so expand the scope of its audit or conduct such further investigation; or

(D) (*1*) the accountant's having advised the registrant that information has come to the accountant's attention that it has concluded materially impacts the fairness or reliability of either (*i*) a previously issued audit report or the underlying financial statements, or (*ii*) the financial statements issued or to be issued covering the fiscal period(s) subsequent to the date of the most recent financial statements covered by an audit report (including information that, unless resolved to the accountant's satisfaction, would prevent it from rendering an unqualified audit report on those financial statements), and (*2*) due to the accountant's resignation, dismissal or declination to stand for re-election, or for any other reason, the issue has not been resolved to the accountant's satisfaction prior to its resignation, dismissal or declination to stand for re-election.

(2) If during the registrant's two most recent fiscal years or any subsequent interim period, a new independent accountant has been engaged as either the principal accountant to audit the registrant's financial statements, or as an independent accountant to audit a significant subsidiary and on whom the principal accountant is expected to express reliance in its report, then the registrant shall identify the newly engaged accountant and indicate the date of such accountant's engagement. In addition, if during the registrant's two most recent fiscal years, and any subsequent interim period prior to engaging that accountant, the registrant (or someone on its behalf) consulted the newly engaged accountant regarding (i) either: the application of accounting principles to a specified transaction, either completed or proposed; or the type of audit opinion that might be rendered on the registrant's financial statements, and either a written report was provided to the registrant or oral advice was provided that the new accountant concluded was an important factor considered by the registrant in reaching a decision as to the accounting, auditing or financial reporting issue; or (ii) any matter that was either the subject of a

disagreement (as defined in paragraph 304(a)(1)(iv) and the related instructions to this item) or a reportable event (as described in paragraph 304(a)(1)(v)), then the registrant shall:

(A) so state and identify the issues that were the subjects of those consultations;

(B) briefly describe the views of the newly engaged accountant as expressed orally or in writing to the registrant on each such issue and, if written views were received by the registrant, file them as an exhibit to the report or registration statement requiring compliance with this Item 304(a);

(C) state whether the former accountant was consulted by the registrant regarding any such issues, and if so, provide a summary of the former accountant's views; and

(D) request the newly engaged accountant to review the disclosure required by this Item 304(a) before it is filed with the Commission and provide the new accountant the opportunity to furnish the registrant with a letter addressed to the Commission containing any new information, clarification of the registrant's expression of its views, or the respects in which it does not agree with the statements made by the registrant in response to Item 304(a). The registrant shall file any such letter as an exhibit to the report or registration statement containing the disclosure required by this Item.

(3) The registrant shall provide the former accountant with a copy of the disclosures it is making in response to this Item 304(a) that the former accountant shall receive no later than the day that the disclosures are filed with the Commission. The registrant shall request the former accountant to furnish the registrant with a letter addressed to the Commission stating whether it agrees with the statements made by the registrant in response to this Item 304(a) and, if not, stating the respects in which it does not agree. The registrant shall file the former accountant's letter as an exhibit to the report or registration statement containing this disclosure. If the former accountant's letter is unavailable at the time of filing such report or registration statement, then the registrant shall request the former accountant to provide the letter as promptly as possible so that the registrant can file the letter with the Commission within ten business days after the filing of the report or registration statement. Notwithstanding the ten business day period, the registrant shall file the letter by amendment within two business days of receipt; if the letter is received on a Saturday, Sunday or holiday on which the Commission is not open for business, then the two business day period shall begin to run on and shall include the first business day thereafter. The former accountant may provide the registrant with an interim letter highlighting specific areas of concern and indicating that a more detailed letter will be forthcoming within the ten business day period noted above. If not filed with the report or registration statement containing the registrant's disclosure under this Item 304(a), then the interim letter, if any, shall be filed by the registrant by amendment within two business days of receipt.

(b) If, (1) in connection with a change in accountants subject to paragraph (a) of this Item 304, there was any disagreement of the type described in paragraph (a)(1)(iv) or any reportable event as described in paragraph (a)(1)(v) of this Item; (2) during the fiscal year in which the change in accountants took place or during the subsequent fiscal year, there have been any transactions or events similar to those which involved such disagreement or reportable event and (3) such transactions or events were material and were accounted for or disclosed in a manner different from that which the former accountants apparently would have concluded was required, the registrant shall state the existence and nature of the disagreement or reportable event and also state the effect on the financial statements if the method had been followed which the former accountants apparently would have concluded was required. These disclosures need not be made if the method asserted by the former accountants ceases to be generally accepted because of authoritative standards or interpretations subsequently issued.

Instructions to Item 304: 1. The disclosure called for by paragraph (a) of this Item need not be provided if it has been previously reported (as that term is defined in Rule 12b-2 under the Exchange Act (§ 240.12b-2 of this chapter); the disclosure called for by paragraph (a) must be provided, however, notwithstanding prior disclosure, if required pursuant to Item 9 of Schedule 14A (§ 240.14a-101 of this chapter). The disclosure called for by paragraph (b) of this section must be furnished, where required, notwithstanding any prior disclosure about accountant changes or disagreements.

2. When disclosure is required by paragraph (a) of this section in an annual report to security holders pursuant to Rule 14a-3 (§ 240.14a-3 of this chapter) or Rule 14c-3 (§ 240.14c-3 of this chapter), or in a proxy or information statement filed pursuant to the requirements of Schedule 14A or 14C (§ 240.14a-101 or § 240.14c-101 of this chapter), in lieu of a letter pursuant to paragraph (a)(2)(D) or (a)(3), prior to filing such materials with or furnishing such materials to the Commission, the registrant shall furnish the disclosure required by paragraph (a) of this section to any former accountant engaged by the registrant during the period set forth in paragraph (a) of this section and to the newly engaged accountant. If any such accountant believes that the statements made in response to paragraph (a) of this section are incorrect or incomplete, it may present its views in a brief statement, ordinarily expected not to exceed 200 words, to be included in the annual report or proxy or information statement. This statement shall be submitted to the registrant within ten business days of the date the accountant

receives the registrant's disclosure. Further, unless the written views of the newly engaged accountant required to be filed as an exhibit by paragraph (a)(2)(B) of this Item 304 have been previously filed with the Commission the registrant shall file a Form 8-K concurrently with the annual report or proxy or information statement for the purpose of filing the written views as exhibits thereto.

3. The information required by Item 304(a) need not be provided for a company being acquired by the registrant that is not subject to the filing requirements of either section 13(a) or 15(d) of the Exchange Act, or, because of section 12(i) of the Exchange Act, has not furnished an annual report to security holders pursuant to Rule 14a-3 Rule 14c-3 for its latest fiscal year.

4. The term 'disagreements' as used in this Item shall be interpreted broadly, to include any difference of opinion concerning any matter of accounting principles or practices, financial statement disclosure, or auditing scope or procedure which (if not resolved to the satisfaction of the former accountant) would have caused it to make reference to the subject matter of the disagreement in connection with its report. It is not necessary for there to have been an argument to have had a disagreement, merely a difference of opinion. For purposes of this Item, however, the term disagreements does not include initial differences of opinion based on incomplete facts or preliminary information that were later resolved to the former accountant's satisfaction by, and providing the registrant and the accountant do not continue to have a difference of opinion upon, obtaining additional relevant facts or information.

5. In determining whether any disagreement or reportable event has occurred, an oral communication from the engagement partner or another person responsible for rendering the accounting firm's opinion (or their designee) will generally suffice as the accountant advising the registrant of a reportable event or as a statement of a disagreement at the "decision-making level" within the accounting firm and require disclosure under this Item.

[As last amended in Release No. FR-34, March 2, 1989, 54 F. R. 9770.]

[¶ 13,035] Quantitative and Qualitative Disclosures About Market Risk

Reg. § 229.305. Item 305. (a) *Quantitative information about market risk.* (1) Registrants shall provide, in their reporting currency, quantitative information about market risk as of the end of the latest fiscal year, in accordance with one of the following three disclosure alternatives. In preparing this quantitative information, registrants shall categorize market risk sensitive instruments into instruments entered into for trading purposes and instruments entered into for purposes other than trading purposes. Within both the trading and other than trading portfolios, separate quantitative information shall be presented, to the extent material, for each market risk exposure category (i.e., interest rate risk, foreign currency exchange rate risk, commodity price risk, and other relevant market risks, such as equity price risk). A registrant may use one of the three alternatives set forth below for all of the required quantitative disclosures about market risk. A registrant also may choose, from among the three alternatives, one disclosure alternative for market risk sensitive instruments entered into for trading purposes and another disclosure alternative for market risk sensitive instruments entered into for other than trading purposes. Alternatively, a registrant may choose any disclosure alternative, from among the three alternatives, for each risk exposure category within the trading and other than trading portfolios. The three disclosure alternatives are:

(i)(A)(1) Tabular presentation of information related to market risk sensitive instruments; such information shall include fair values of the market risk sensitive instruments and contract terms sufficient to determine future cash flows from those instruments, categorized by expected maturity dates.

(2) Tabular information relating to contract terms shall allow readers of the table to determine expected cash flows from the market risk sensitive instruments for each of the next five years. Comparable tabular information for any remaining years shall be displayed as an aggregate amount.

(3) Within each risk exposure category, the market risk sensitive instruments shall be grouped based on common characteristics. Within the foreign currency exchange rate risk category, the market risk sensitive instruments shall be grouped by functional currency and within the commodity price risk category, the market risk sensitive instruments shall be grouped by type of commodity.

(4) See the Appendix to this Item for a suggested format for presentation of this information; and

(B) Registrants shall provide a description of the contents of the table and any related assumptions necessary to understand the disclosures required under paragraph (a)(1)(i)(A) of this Item 305; or

(ii)(A) Sensitivity analysis disclosures that express the potential loss in future earnings, fair values, or cash flows of market risk sensitive instruments resulting from one or more selected hypothetical changes in interest rates, foreign currency exchange rates, commodity prices, and other relevant market rates or prices over a selected period of time. The magnitude of selected hypothetical changes in rates or prices may differ among and within market risk exposure categories; and

(B) Registrants shall provide a description of the model, assumptions, and parameters, which are necessary to understand the disclosures required under paragraph (a) (1) (ii) (A) of this Item 305; or

(iii) (A) Value at risk disclosures that express the potential loss in future earnings, fair values, or cash flows of market risk sensitive instruments over a selected period of time, with a selected likelihood of occurrence, from changes in interest rates, foreign currency exchange rates, commodity prices, and other relevant market rates or prices;

(B) (1) For each category for which value at risk disclosures are required under paragraph (a) (1) (iii) (A) of this Item 305, provide either:

(i) The average, high and low amounts, or the distribution of the value at risk amounts for the reporting period; or

(ii) The average, high and low amounts, or the distribution of actual changes in fair values, earnings, or cash flows from the market risk sensitive instruments occurring during the reporting period; or

(iii) The percentage or number of times the actual changes in fair values, earnings, or cash flows from the market risk sensitive instruments exceeded the value at risk amounts during the reporting period;

(2) Information required under paragraph (a) (1) (iii) (B) (1) of this Item 305 is not required for the first fiscal year end in which a registrant must present Item 305 information; and

(C) Registrants shall provide a description of the model, assumptions, and parameters, which are necessary to understand the disclosures required under paragraphs (a) (1) (iii) (A) and (B) of this Item 305.

(2) Registrants shall discuss material limitations that cause the information required under paragraph (a) (1) of this Item 305 not to reflect fully the net market risk exposures of the entity. This discussion shall include summarized descriptions of instruments, positions, and transactions omitted from the quantitative market risk disclosure information or the features of instruments, positions, and transactions that are included, but not reflected fully in the quantitative market risk disclosure information.

(3) Registrants shall present summarized market risk information for the preceding fiscal year. In addition, registrants shall discuss the reasons for material quantitative changes in market risk exposures between the current and preceding fiscal years. Information required by this paragraph (a) (3), however, is not required if disclosure is not required under paragraph (a) (1) of this Item 305 for the current fiscal year. Information required by this paragraph (a) (3) is not required for the first fiscal year end in which a registrant must present Item 305 information.

(4) If registrants change disclosure alternatives or key model characteristics, assumptions, and parameters used in providing quantitative information about market risk (e.g., changing from tabular presentation to value at risk, changing the scope of instruments included in the model, or changing the definition of loss from fair values to earnings), and if the effects of any such change is material, the registrant shall:

(i) Explain the reasons for the change; and

(ii) Either provide summarized comparable information, under the new disclosure method, for the year preceding the current year or, in addition to providing disclosure for the current year under the new method, provide disclosures for the current year and preceding fiscal year under the method used in the preceding year.

Instructions to Paragraph 305(a).

1. Under paragraph 305(a) (1):

A. For each market risk exposure category within the trading and other than trading portfolios, registrants may report the average, high, and low sensitivity analysis or value at risk amounts for the reporting period, as an alternative to reporting year-end amounts.

B. In determining the average, high, and low amounts for the fiscal year under instruction 1.A. of the Instructions to Paragraph 305(a), registrants should use sensitivity analysis or value at risk amounts relating to at least four equal time periods throughout the reporting period (e.g., four quarter-end amounts, 12 month-end amounts, or 52 week-end amounts).

C. Functional currency means functional currency as defined by generally accepted accounting principles (see, e.g., FASB, Statement of Financial Accounting Standards No. 52, "Foreign Currency Translation", ("FAS 52") paragraph 20 (December 1981)).

D. Registrants using the sensitivity analysis and value at risk disclosure alternatives are encouraged, but not required, to provide quantitative amounts that reflect the aggregate market risk inherent in the trading and other than trading portfolios.

2. Under paragraph 305(a) (1) (i):

A. Examples of contract terms sufficient to determine future cash flows from market risk sensitive instruments include, but are not limited to:

i. Debt instruments—principal amounts and weighted average effective interest rates;

ii. Forwards and futures—contract amounts and weighted average settlement prices;

iii. Options—contract amounts and weighted average strike prices;

iv. Swaps—notional amounts, weighted average pay rates or prices, and weighted average receive rates or prices; and

v. Complex instruments—likely to be a combination of the contract terms presented in 2.A.i. through iv. of this Instruction;

B. When grouping based on common characteristics, instruments should be categorized, at a minimum, by the following characteristics, when material:

i. Fixed rate or variable rate assets or liabilities;

ii. Long or short forwards and futures;

iii. Written or purchased put or call options with similar strike prices;

iv. Receive fixed and pay variable swaps, receive variable and pay fixed swaps, and receive variable and pay variable swaps;

v. The currency in which the instruments' cash flows are denominated;

vi. Financial instruments for which foreign currency transaction gains and losses are reported in the same manner as translation adjustments under generally accepted accounting principles (see, e.g., FAS 52 paragraph 20 (December 1981)); and

vii. Derivatives used to manage risks inherent in anticipated transactions;

C. Registrants may aggregate information regarding functional currencies that are economically related, managed together for internal risk management purposes, and have statistical correlations of greater than 75% over each of the past three years;

D. Market risk sensitive instruments that are exposed to rate or price changes in more than one market risk exposure category should be presented within the tabular information for each of the risk exposure categories to which those instruments are exposed;

E. If a currency swap (see, e.g., FAS 52 Appendix E for a definition of currency swap) eliminates all foreign currency exposures in the cash flows of a foreign currency denominated debt instrument, neither the currency swap nor the foreign currency denominated debt instrument are required to be disclosed in the foreign currency risk exposure category. However, both the currency swap and the foreign currency denominated debt instrument should be disclosed in the interest rate risk exposure category; and

F. The contents of the table and related assumptions that should be described include, but are not limited to:

i. The different amounts reported in the table for various categories of the market risk sensitive instruments (e.g., principal amounts for debt, notional amounts for swaps, and contract amounts for options and futures);

ii. The different types of reported market rates or prices (e.g., contractual rates or prices, spot rates or prices, forward rates or prices); and

iii. Key prepayment or reinvestment assumptions relating to the timing of reported amounts.

3. Under paragraph 305(a)(1)(ii):

A. Registrants should select hypothetical changes in market rates or prices that are expected to reflect reasonably possible near-term changes in those rates and prices. In this regard, absent economic justification for the selection of a different amount, registrants should use changes that are not less than 10 percent of end of period market rates or prices;

B. For purposes of instruction 3.A. of the Instructions to Paragraph 305(a), the term reasonably possible has the same meaning as defined by generally accepted accounting principles (see, e.g., FASB, Statement of Financial Accounting Standards No. 5, "Accounting for Contingencies," ("FAS 5") paragraph 3 (March 1975));

C. For purposes of instruction 3.A. of the Instructions to Paragraph 305(a), the term near term means a period of time going forward up to one year from the date of the financial statements (see generally AICPA, Statement of Position 94-6, "Disclosure of Certain Significant Risks and Uncertainties," ("SOP 94-6") at paragraph 7 (December 30, 1994));

D. Market risk sensitive instruments that are exposed to rate or price changes in more than one market risk exposure category should be included in the sensitivity analysis disclosures for each market risk category to which those instruments are exposed;

E. Registrants with multiple foreign currency exchange rate exposures should prepare foreign currency sensitivity analysis disclosures that measure the aggregate sensitivity to changes in all foreign currency exchange rate exposures, including the effects of changes in both transactional currency/ functional currency exchange rate exposures and functional currency/reporting currency exchange rate exposures. For example, assume a French division of a registrant presenting its financial statements in U.S. dollars ($US) invests in a deutschmark(DM)-denominated debt security. In these circumstances, the $US is the reporting currency and the DM is the transactional currency. In addition, assume this division determines that the French franc (FF) is its functional currency according to FAS 52. In preparing the foreign currency sensitivity analysis disclosures, this registrant should report the aggregate potential loss from hypothetical changes in both the DM/FF exchange rate exposure and the FF/ $US exchange rate exposure; and

F. Model, assumptions, and parameters that should be described include, but are not limited to, how loss is defined by the model (e.g., loss in earnings, fair values, or cash flows), a general description of the modeling technique (e.g., duration modeling, modeling that measures the change in net present values arising from selected hypothetical changes in market rates or prices, and a description as to how optionality is addressed by the model), the types of instruments covered by the model (e.g., derivative financial instruments, other financial instruments, derivative commodity instruments, and whether other instruments are included voluntarily, such as certain commodity instruments and positions, cash flows from anticipated transactions, and certain financial instruments excluded under instruction 3.C.ii. of the General Instructions to Paragraphs 305(a) and 305(b)), and other relevant information about the model's assumptions and parameters, (e.g., the magnitude and timing of selected hypothetical changes in market rates or prices used, the method by which discount rates are determined, and key prepayment or reinvestment assumptions).

4. Under paragraph 305(a)(1)(iii):

A. The confidence intervals selected should reflect reasonably possible near-term changes in market rates and prices. In this regard, absent economic justification for the selection of different confidence intervals, registrants should use intervals that are 95 percent or higher;

B. For purposes of instruction 4.A. of the Instructions to Paragraph 305(a), the term reasonably possible has the same meaning as defined by generally accepted accounting principles (see, e.g., FAS 5, paragraph 3 (March 1975));

C. For purposes of instruction 4.A. of the Instructions to Paragraphs 305(a), the term near term means a period of time going forward up to one year from the date of the financial statements (see generally SOP 94-6, at paragraph 7 (December 30, 1994));

D. Registrants with multiple foreign currency exchange rate exposures should prepare foreign currency value at risk analysis disclosures that measure the aggregate sensitivity to changes in all foreign currency exchange rate exposures, including the aggregate effects of changes in both transactional currency/functional currency exchange rate exposures and functional currency/reporting currency exchange rate exposures. For example, assume a French division of a registrant presenting its financial statements in U.S. dollars ($US) invests in a deutschmark(DM)-denominated debt security. In these circumstances, the $US is the reporting currency and the DM is the transactional currency. In addition, assume this division determines that the French franc (FF) is its functional currency according to FAS 52. In preparing the foreign currency value at risk disclosures, this registrant should report the aggregate potential loss from hypothetical changes in both the DM/FF exchange rate exposure and the FF/$US exchange rate exposure; and

E. Model, assumptions, and parameters that should be described include, but are not limited to, how loss is defined by the model (e.g., loss in earnings, fair values, or cash flows), the type of model used (e.g., variance/covariance, historical simulation, or Monte Carlo simulation and a description as to how optionality is addressed by the model), the types of instruments covered by the model (e.g., derivative financial instruments, other financial instruments, derivative commodity instruments, and whether other instruments are included voluntarily, such as certain commodity instruments and positions, cash flows from anticipated transactions, and certain financial instruments excluded under instruction 3.C.ii. of the General Instructions to Paragraphs 305(a) and 305(b)), and other relevant information about the model's assumptions and parameters, (e.g., holding periods, confidence intervals, and, when appropriate, the methods used for aggregating value at risk amounts across market risk exposure categories, such as by assuming perfect positive correlation, independence, or actual observed correlation).

5. Under paragraph 305(a)(2), limitations that should be considered include, but are not limited to:

A. The exclusion of certain market risk sensitive instruments, positions, and transactions from the disclosures required under paragraph 305(a)(1) (e.g., derivative commodity instruments not permitted by contract or business custom to be settled in cash or with another financial instrument, commodity positions, cash flows from anticipated transactions, and certain financial instruments excluded under instruction 3.C.ii. of the General Instructions to Paragraphs 305(a) and 305(b)). Failure to include such instruments, positions, and transactions in preparing the disclosures under paragraph 305(a)(1) may be a limitation because the resulting disclosures may not fully reflect the net market risk of a registrant; and

B. The ability of disclosures required under paragraph 305(a)(1) to reflect fully the market risk that may be inherent in instruments with leverage, option, or prepayment features (e.g., options, including written options, structured notes, collateralized mortgage obligations, leveraged swaps, and options embedded in swaps).

(b) *Qualitative information about market risk.* (1) To the extent material, describe:

(i) The registrant's primary market risk exposures;

(ii) How those exposures are managed. Such descriptions shall include, but not be limited to, a discussion of the objectives, general strategies, and instruments, if any, used to manage those exposures; and

(iii) Changes in either the registrant's primary market risk exposures or how those exposures are managed, when compared to what was in effect during the most recently completed fiscal year and what is known or expected to be in effect in future reporting periods.

(2) Qualitative information about market risk shall be presented separately for market risk sensitive instruments entered into for trading purposes and those entered into for purposes other than trading.

Instructions to Paragraph 305(b).

1. For purposes of disclosure under paragraph 305(b), primary market risk exposures means:

A. The following categories of market risk: interest rate risk, foreign currency exchange rate risk, commodity price risk, and other relevant market rate or price risks (e.g., equity price risk); and

B. Within each of these categories, the particular markets that present the primary risk of loss to the registrant. For example, if a registrant has a material exposure to foreign currency exchange rate risk and, within this category of market risk, is most vulnerable to changes in dollar/yen, dollar/pound, and dollar/peso exchange rates, the registrant should disclose those exposures. Similarly, if a registrant has a material exposure to interest rate risk and, within this category of market risk, is most vulnerable to changes in short-term U.S. prime interest rates, it should disclose the existence of that exposure.

2. For purposes of disclosure under paragraph 305(b), registrants should describe primary market risk exposures that exist as of the end of the latest fiscal year, and how those exposures are managed.

General Instructions to Paragraphs 305(a) and 305(b).

1. The disclosures called for by paragraphs 305(a) and 305(b) are intended to clarify the registrant's exposures to market risk associated with activities in derivative financial instruments, other financial instruments, and derivative commodity instruments.

2. In preparing the disclosures under paragraphs 305(a) and 305(b), registrants are required to include derivative financial instruments, other financial instruments, and derivative commodity instruments.

3. For purposes of paragraphs 305(a) and 305(b), derivative financial instruments, other financial instruments, and derivative commodity instruments (collectively referred to as "market risk sensitive instruments") are defined as follows:

A. Derivative financial instruments has the same meaning as defined by generally accepted accounting principles (see, e.g., FASB, Statement of Financial Accounting Standards No. 119, "Disclosure about Derivative Financial Instruments and Fair Value of Financial Instruments," ("FAS 119") paragraphs 5-7 (October 1994)), and includes futures, forwards, swaps, options, and other financial instruments with similar characteristics;

B. Other financial instruments means all financial instruments as defined by generally accepted accounting principles for which fair value disclosures are required (see, e.g., FASB, Statement of Financial Accounting Standards No. 107, "Disclosures about Fair Value of Financial Instruments," ("FAS 107") paragraphs 3 and 8 (December 1991)), except for derivative financial instruments, as defined above;

C.i. Other financial instruments include, but are not limited to, trade accounts receivable, investments, loans, structured notes, mortgage-backed securities, trade accounts payable, indexed debt instruments, interest-only and principal-only obligations, deposits, and other debt obligations;

ii. Other financial instruments exclude employers and plans obligations for pension and other post-retirement benefits, substantively extinguished debt, insurance contracts, lease contracts, warranty obligations and rights, unconditional purchase obligations, investments accounted for under the equity method, noncontrolling interests in consolidated enterprises, and equity instruments issued by the registrant and classified in stockholders' equity in the statement of financial position (see, e.g., FAS 107, paragraph 8 (December 1991)). For purposes of this item, trade accounts receivable and trade accounts payable need not be considered other financial instruments when their carrying amounts approximate fair value; and

D. Derivative commodity instruments include, to the extent such instruments are not derivative financial instruments, commodity futures, commodity forwards, commodity swaps, commodity options, and other commodity instruments with similar characteristics that are permitted by contract or business custom to be settled in cash or with another financial instrument. For purposes of this paragraph, settlement in cash includes settlement in cash of the net change in value of the derivative commodity instrument (e.g., net cash settlement based on changes in the price of the underlying commodity).

4.A. In addition to providing required disclosures for the market risk sensitive instruments defined in instruction 2. of the General Instructions to Paragraphs 305(a) and 305(b), registrants are encouraged to include other market risk sensitive instruments, positions, and transactions within the disclosures required under paragraphs 305(a) and 305(b). Such instruments, positions, and transactions might include commodity positions, derivative commodity instruments that are not permitted by contract or business custom to be settled in cash or with another financial instrument, cash flows from anticipated transactions, and certain financial instruments excluded under instruction 3.C.ii. of the General Instructions to Paragraphs 305(a) and 305(b).

B. Registrants that voluntarily include other market risk sensitive instruments, positions and transactions within their quantitative disclosures about market risk under the sensitivity analysis or value at risk disclosure alternatives are not required to provide separate market risk disclosures for any voluntarily selected instruments, positions, or transactions. Instead, registrants selecting the sensitivity analysis and value at risk disclosure alternatives are permitted to present comprehensive market risk disclosures, which reflect the combined market risk exposures inherent in both the required and any voluntarily selected instruments, position, or transactions. Registrants that choose the tabular presentation disclosure alternative should present voluntarily selected instruments, positions, or transactions in a manner consistent with the requirements in Item 305(a) for market risk sensitive instruments.

C. If a registrant elects to include voluntarily a particular type of instrument, position, or transaction in their quantitative disclosures about market risk, that registrant should include all, rather than some, of those instruments, positions, or transactions within those disclosures. For example, if a registrant holds in inventory a particular type of commodity position and elects to include that commodity position within their market risk disclosures, the registrant should include the entire commodity position, rather than only a portion thereof, in their quantitative disclosures about market risk.

5.A. Under paragraphs 305(a) and 305(b), a materiality assessment should be made for each market risk exposure category within the trading and other than trading portfolios.

B. For purposes of making the materiality assessment under instruction 5.A. of the General Instructions to Paragraphs 305(a) and 305(b), registrants should evaluate both:

i. The materiality of the fair values of derivative financial instruments, other financial instruments, and derivative commodity instruments outstanding as of the end of the latest fiscal year; and

ii. The materiality of potential, near-term losses in future earnings, fair values, and/or cash flows from reasonably possible near-term changes in market rates or prices.

iii. If either paragraphs B.i. or B.ii. in this instruction of the General Instructions to Paragraphs 305(a) and 305(b) are material, the registrant should disclose quantitative and qualitative information about market risk, if such market risk for the particular market risk exposure category is material.

C. For purposes of instruction 5.B.i. of the General Instructions to Paragraphs 305(a) and 305(b), registrants generally should not net fair values, except to the extent allowed under generally accepted accounting principles (see, e.g., FASB Interpretation No. 39, "Offsetting of Amounts Related to Certain Contracts" (March 1992)). For example, under this instruction, the fair value of assets generally should not be netted with the fair value of liabilities.

D. For purposes of instruction 5.B.ii. of the General Instructions to Paragraphs 305(a) and 305(b), registrants should consider, among other things, the magnitude of:

i. Past market movements;

ii. Reasonably possible, near-term market movements; and

iii. Potential losses that may arise from leverage, option, and multiplier features.

E. For purposes of instructions 5.B.ii and 5.D.ii of the General Instructions to Paragraphs 305(a) and 305(b), the term near term means a period of time going forward up to one year from the date of the financial statements (see generally SOP 94-6, at paragraph 7 (December 30, 1994)).

F. For the purpose of instructions 5.B.ii. and 5.D.ii. of the General Instructions to Paragraphs 305(a) and 305(b), the term reasonably possible has the same meaning as defined by generally accepted accounting principles (see, e.g., FAS 5, paragraph 3 (March 1975)).

6. For purposes of paragraphs 305(a) and 305(b), registrants should present the information outside of, and not incorporate the information into, the financial statements (including the footnotes to the financial statements). In addition, registrants are encouraged to provide the required information in one location. However, alternative presentation, such as inclusion of all or part of the information in

Management's Discussion and Analysis, may be used at the discretion of the registrant. If information is disclosed in more than one location, registrants should provide cross-references to the locations of the related disclosures.

7. For purposes of the instructions to paragraphs 305(a) and 305(b), trading purposes has the same meaning as defined by generally accepted accounting principles (see, e.g., FAS 119, paragraph 9a (October 1994)). In addition, anticipated transactions means transactions (other than transactions involving existing assets or liabilities or transactions necessitated by existing firm commitments) an enterprise expects, but is not obligated, to carry out in the normal course of business (see, e.g., FASB, Statement of Financial Accounting Standards No. 80, "Accounting for Futures Contracts," paragraph 9, (August 1984)).

(c) *Interim periods.* If interim period financial statements are included or are required to be included by Article 3 of Regulation S-X (17 CFR 210), discussion and analysis shall be provided so as to enable the reader to assess the sources and effects of material changes in information that would be provided under Item 305 of Regulation S-K from the end of the preceding fiscal year to the date of the most recent interim balance sheet.

Instructions to Paragraph 305(c).

1. Information required under paragraph (c) of this Item 305 is not required until after the first fiscal year end in which this Item 305 is applicable.

(d) *Safe Harbor.* (1) The safe harbor provided in Section 27A of the Securities Act of 1933 (15 U.S.C. 77z-2) and Section 21E of the Securities Exchange Act of 1934 (15 U.S.C. 78u-5) ("statutory safe harbors") shall apply, with respect to all types of issuers and transactions, to information provided pursuant to paragraphs (a), (b), and (c) of this Item 305, provided that the disclosure is made by: an issuer; a person acting on behalf of the issuer; an outside reviewer retained by the issuer making a statement on behalf of the issuer; or an underwriter, with respect to information provided by the issuer or information derived from information provided by the issuer.

(2) For purposes of paragraph (d) of this Item 305 only:

(i) All information required by paragraphs (a), (b)(1)(i), (b)(1)(iii), and (c) of this Item 305 is considered forward looking statements for purposes of the statutory safe harbors, except for historical facts such as the terms of particular contracts and the number of market risk sensitive instruments held during or at the end of the reporting period; and

(ii) With respect to paragraph (a) of this Item 305, the meaningful cautionary statements prong of the statutory safe harbors will be satisfied if a registrant satisfies all requirements of that same paragraph (a) of this Item 305.

(e) *Smaller reporting companies.* A smaller reporting company, as defined by § 229.10(f)(1), is not required to provide the information required by this Item.

General Instructions to Paragraphs 305(a), 305(b), 305(c), 305(d), and 305(e).

1. Bank registrants, thrift registrants, and non-bank and non-thrift registrants with market capitalizations on January 28, 1997 in excess of $2.5 billion should provide Item 305 disclosures in filings with the Commission that include annual financial statements for fiscal years ending after June 15, 1997. Non-bank and non-thrift registrants with market capitalizations on January 28, 1997 of $2.5 billion or less should provide Item 305 disclosures in filings with the Commission that include financial statements for fiscal years ending after June 15, 1998.

2.A. For purposes of instruction 1. of the General Instructions to Paragraphs 305(a), 305(b), 305(c), 305(d), and 305(e), bank registrants and thrift registrants include any registrant which has control over a depository institution.

B. For purposes of instruction 2.A. of the General Instructions to Paragraphs 305(a), 305(b), 305(c), 305(d), and 305(e), a registrant has control over a depository institution if:

i. The registrant directly or indirectly or acting through one or more other persons owns, controls, or has power to vote 25% or more of any class of voting securities of the depository institution;

ii. The registrant controls in any manner the election of a majority of the directors or trustees of the depository institution; or

iii. The Federal Reserve Board or Office of Thrift Supervision determines, after notice and opportunity for hearing, that the registrant directly or indirectly exercises a controlling influence over the management or policies of the depository institution.

C. For purposes of instruction 2.B. of the General Instructions to Paragraphs 305(a), 305(b), 305(c), 305(d), and 305(e), a depository institution means any of the following:

i. An insured depository institution as defined in section 3(c)(2) of the Federal Deposit Insurance Act (12 U.S.C.A. Sec. 1813(c));

ii. An institution organized under the laws of the United States, any State of the United States, the District of Columbia, any territory of the United States, Puerto Rico, Guam, American Samoa, or the

Virgin Islands, which both accepts demand deposits or deposits that the depositor may withdraw by check or similar means for payment to third parties or others and is engaged in the business of making commercial loans.

D. For purposes of instruction 1. of the General Instructions to Paragraphs 305(a), 305(b), 305(c), 305(d) and 305(e), market capitalization is the aggregate market value of common equity as set forth in General Instruction I.B.1. of Form S-3; provided however, that common equity held by affiliates is included in the calculation of market capitalization; and provided further that instead of using the 60 day period prior to filing referenced in General Instruction I.B.1. of Form S-3, the measurement date is January 28, 1997.

Appendix to Item 305—Tabular Disclosures

The tables set forth below are illustrative of the format that might be used when a registrant elects to present the information required by paragraph (a)(1)(i)(A) of Item 305 regarding terms and information about derivative financial instruments, other financial instruments, and derivative commodity instruments. These examples are for illustrative purposes only. Registrants are not required to display the information in the specific format illustrated below. Alternative methods of display are permissible as long as the disclosure requirements of the section are satisfied. Furthermore, these examples were designed primarily to illustrate possible formats for presentation of the information required by the disclosure item and do not purport to illustrate the broad range of derivative financial instruments, other financial instruments, and derivative commodity instruments utilized by registrants.

Interest Rate Sensitivity

The table below provides information about the Company's derivative financial instruments and other financial instruments that are sensitive to changes in interest rates, including interest rate swaps and debt obligations. For debt obligations, the table presents principal cash flows and related weighted average interest rates by expected maturity dates. For interest rate swaps, the table presents notional amounts and weighted average interest rates by expected (contractual) maturity dates. Notional amounts are used to calculate the contractual payments to be exchanged under the contract. Weighted average variable rates are based on implied forward rates in the yield curve at the reporting date. The information is presented in U.S. dollar equivalents, which is the Company's reporting currency. The instrument's actual cash flows are denominated in both U.S. dollars ($US) and German deutschmarks (DM), as indicated in parentheses.

| | December 31, 19X1 | | | | | | | |
| | Expected maturity date | | | | | | | |
Liabilities	*19X2*	*19X3*	*19X4*	*19X5*	*19X6*	*Thereafter*	*Total*	*Fair value*
(7) (US$ Equivalent in millions)								
Long-term Debt:								
Fixed Rate ($US)	$XXXX	$XXXX	$XXXX	$XXXX	$XXXX	$XXXX	$XXXX	$X
Average interest rate	XX %	XX %	XX %	XX %	XX %	XX %	XX %	
Fixed Rate (DM)	XXX	XXX	XXX	XXX	XXX	XXX	XXX	X
Average interest rate	XX %	XX %	XX %	XX %	XX %	XX %	XX %	
Variable Rate ($US)	XXX	XXX	XXX	XXX	XXX	XXX	XXX	X
Average interest rate	XX %	XX %	XX %	XX %	XX %	XX %	XX %	
Interest Rate Derivatives								
(7) (In millions)								
Interest Rate Swaps:								
Variable to Fixed ($US)	$XXX	$XXX	$XXX	$XXX	$XXX	$XXX	$XXXX	$SX
Average pay rate	XX %	XX %	XX %	XX %	XX %	XX %	XX %	
Average receive rate	XX %	XX %	XX %	XX %	XX %	XX %	XX %	
Fixed to Variable ($US)	XXX	XXX	XXX	XXX	XXX	XXX	XXX	X
Average pay rate	XX %	XX %	XX %	XX %	XX %	XX %	XX %	
Average receive rate	XX %	XX %	XX %	XX %	XX %	XX %	XX %	

Exchange Rate Sensitivity

The table below provides information about the Company's derivative financial instruments, other financial instruments, and firmly committed sales transactions by functional currency and presents such information in U.S. dollar equivalents.[1] The table summarizes information on instruments and transactions that are sensitive to foreign currency exchange rates, including foreign currency forward exchange agreements, deutschmark (DM)-denominated debt obligations, and firmly committed DM sales transactions. For debt obligations, the table presents principal cash flows and related weighted average interest rates by expected maturity dates. For firmly committed DM-sales transactions, sales amounts are presented by the expected transaction date, which are not expected to exceed two years. For foreign currency forward exchange agreements, the table presents the notional amounts and weighted average exchange rates by expected (contractual) maturity dates. These notional amounts generally are used to calculate the contractual payments to be exchanged under the contract.

---

[1] The information is presented in U.S. dollars because that is the registrant's reporting currency.

December 31, 19X1

On-Balance Sheet Financial Instruments	Expected maturity date							
(7) (US$ Equivalent in millions)	19X2	19X3	19X4	19X5	19X6	Thereafter	Total	Fair value
$US Functional Currency[2]:								
Liabilities								
Long-Term Debt:								
Fixed Rate (DM)	$XXX	$XXX	$XXX	$XXX	$XXX	$XXX	$XXXX	$XX
Average interest rate	XX	XX	XX	XX	XX	XX	XX	

(7) Expected maturity or transaction date								
Anticipated Transactions and Related Derivatives[3]	19X2	19X3	19X4	19X5	19X6	Thereafter	Total	Fair value
(7) (US$ Equivalent in millions)								
$US Functional Currency:								
Firmly committed Sales Contracts (DM)	$XXX	$XXX	$XXX	—	—	—	$XXXX	$X
Forward Exchange Agreements (Receive $US/Pay DM):								
Contract Amount	XXX	XXX	XXX	—	—	—	XXX	X
Average Contractual Exchange Rate	XX	XX	XX	—	—	—	XX	—

[2] Similar tabular information would be provided for other functional currencies.

[3] Pursuant to General Instruction 4. to Items 305(a) and 305(b) of Regulation S-K, registrants may include cash flows from anticipated transactions and operating cash flows resulting from non-financial and non-commodity instruments.

Commodity Price Sensitivity

The table below provides information about the Company's corn inventory and futures contracts that are sensitive to changes in commodity prices, specifically corn prices. For inventory, the table presents the carrying amount and fair value at December 31, 19x1. For the futures contracts the table presents the notional amounts in bushels, the weighted average contract prices, and the total dollar contract amount by expected maturity dates, the latest of which occurs one year from the reporting date. Contract amounts are used to calculate the contractual payments and quantity of corn to be exchanged under the futures contracts.

December 31, 19X1

	Carrying amount	Fair value
(1) (In millions)		
On Balance Sheet Commodity Position and Related Derivatives Corn Inventory[4]	$XXX	$XXX

	Expected maturity 1992	Fair value
Related Derivatives		
Futures Contracts (Short):		
Contract Volumes (100,000 bushels)	XXX	—
Weighted Average Price (Per 100,000 bushels)	$X.XX	—
Contract Amount ($US in millions)	$XXX	$XXX

---

[4] Pursuant to General Instruction 4. to Items 305(a) and 305(b) of Regulation S-K, registrants may include information on commodity positions, such as corn inventory.

[As last amended in Release No. 33-9026, effective April 23, 2009, 74 F.R. 18612.]

⋙→ *§ 229.306 is removed and reserved, effective November 7, 2006. See below and Release No. 33-8732, 71 F.R. 53158.*

[¶ 13,036] Audit Committee Report

Reg. § 229.306. (Item 306) [Removed and reserved in Release No. 33-8732, effective November 7, 2006, 71 F.R. 53158.]

[¶ 13,037] Disclosure Controls and Procedures

Reg. § 229.307 (Item 307). Disclose the conclusions of the registrant's principal executive and principal financial officers, or persons performing similar functions, regarding the effectiveness of the registrant's disclosure controls and procedures (as defined in 240.13a-15(e) or 240.15d-15(e) of this chapter) as of the end of the period covered by the report, based on the evaluation of these controls and procedures required by paragraph (b) of § 240.13a-15 or § 240.15d-15 of this chapter.

[As last amended in Release No. 33-8238, effective August 14, 2003, (Compliance dates vary from the effective date of the amendment through April 15, 2005. See text of release ``Dates'' section and Sections II.I and III.E for details about compliance requirements), 68 F.R. 36636.]

[¶ 13,038] Internal Control Over Financial Reporting

Reg. § 229.308 (Item 308). (a) *Management's annual report on internal control over financial reporting.* Provide a report of management on the registrant's internal control over financial reporting (as defined in § 240.13a-15(f) or 240.15d-15(f) of this chapter) that contains:

(1) A statement of management's responsibility for establishing and maintaining adequate internal control over financial reporting for the registrant;

(2) A statement identifying the framework used by management to evaluate the effectiveness of the registrant's internal control over financial reporting as required by paragraph (c) of § 240.13a-15 or 240.15d-15 of this chapter;

(3) Management's assessment of the effectiveness of the registrant's internal control over financial reporting as of the end of the registrant's most recent fiscal year, including a statement as to whether or not internal control over financial reporting is effective. This discussion must include disclosure of any material weakness in the registrant's internal control over financial reporting identified by management. Management is not permitted to conclude that the registrant's internal control over financial reporting is effective if there are one or more material weaknesses in the registrant's internal control over financial reporting; and

(4) If the registrant is an accelerated filer or a large accelerated filer (as defined in § 240.12b-2 of this chapter), or otherwise includes in its annual report a registered public accounting firm's attestation report on internal control over financial reporting, a statement that the registered public accounting firm

that audited the financial statements included in the annual report containing the disclosure required by this Item has issued an attestation report on the registrant's internal control over financial reporting.

(b) *Attestation report of the registered public accounting firm.* If the registrant is an accelerated filer or a large accelerated filer (as defined in § 240.12b-2 of this chapter), provide the registered public accounting firm's attestation report on the registrant's internal control over financial reporting in the registrant's annual report containing the disclosure required by this Item.

(c) *Changes in internal control over financial reporting.* Disclose any change in the registrant's internal control over financial reporting identified in connection with the evaluation required by paragraph (d) of § 240.13a-15 or 240.15d-15 of this chapter that occurred during the registrant's last fiscal quarter (the registrant's fourth fiscal quarter in the case of an annual report) that has materially affected, or is reasonably likely to materially affect, the registrant's internal control over financial reporting.

Instructions to Item 308

1. A registrant need not comply with paragraphs (a) and (b) of this Item until it either had been required to file an annual report pursuant to section 13(a) or 15(d) of the Exchange Act (15 U.S.C. 78m or 78o(d)) for the prior fiscal year or had filed an annual report with the Commission for the prior fiscal year. A registrant that does not comply shall include a statement in the first annual report that it files in substantially the following form: "This annual report does not include a report of management's assessment regarding internal control over financial reporting or an attestation report of the company's registered public accounting firm due to a transition period established by rules of the Securities and Exchange Commission for newly public companies."

2. The registrant must maintain evidential matter, including documentation, to provide reasonable support for management's assessment of the effectiveness of the registrant's internal control over financial reporting.

[As last amended in Release No. 33-9142, effective September 21, 2010, 75 F.R. 57385.]

[¶ 13,038F] Internal Control Over Financial Reporting

Reg. § 229.308T (Item 308T). *Note to Item 308T:* This is a special temporary section that applies only to a registrant that is neither a "large accelerated filer" nor an "accelerated filer" as those terms are defined in § 240.12b-2 of this chapter and only with respect to a fiscal period ending on or after December 15, 2007, but before June 15, 2010.

(a) *Management's annual report on internal control over financial reporting.* Provide a report of management on the registrant's internal control over financial reporting (as defined in § 240.13a-15(f) or § 240.15d-15(f) of this chapter). This report shall not be deemed to be filed for purposes of Section 18 of the Exchange Act or otherwise subject to the liabilities of that section, unless the registrant specifically states that the report is to be considered "filed" under the Exchange Act or incorporates it by reference into a filing under the Securities Act or the Exchange Act. The report must contain:

(1) A statement of management's responsibility for establishing and maintaining adequate internal control over financial reporting for the registrant;

(2) A statement identifying the framework used by management to evaluate the effectiveness of the registrant's internal control over financial reporting as required by paragraph (c) of § 240.13a-15 or § 240.15d-15 of this chapter; and

(3) Management's assessment of the effectiveness of the registrant's internal control over financial reporting as of the end of the registrant's most recent fiscal year, including a statement as to whether or not internal control over financial reporting is effective. This discussion must include disclosure of any material weakness in the registrant's internal control over financial reporting identified by management. Management is not permitted to conclude that the registrant's internal control over financial reporting is effective if there are one or more material weaknesses in the registrant's internal control over financial reporting.

(4) A statement in substantially the following form: "This annual report does not include an attestation report of the company's registered public accounting firm regarding internal control over financial reporting. Management's report was not subject to attestation by the company's registered public accounting firm pursuant to temporary rules of the Securities and Exchange Commission that permit the company to provide only management's report in this annual report."

(b) *Changes in internal control over financial reporting.* Disclose any change in the registrant's internal control over financial reporting identified in connection with the evaluation required by paragraph (d) of § 240.13a-15 or § 240.15d-15 of this chapter that occurred during the registrant's last fiscal quarter (the registrant's fourth fiscal quarter in the case of an annual report) that has materially affected, or is reasonably likely to materially affect, the registrant's internal control over financial reporting.

Instructions to paragraphs (a) and (b) of Item 308T

1. A registrant need not comply with paragraph (a) of this Item until it either had been required to file an annual report pursuant to section 13(a) or 15(d) of the Exchange Act (15 U.S.C. 78m or 78o(d)) for the prior fiscal year or previously had filed an annual report with the Commission for the prior fiscal year. A registrant that does not comply shall include a statement in the first annual report that it files in substantially the following form: "This annual report does not include a report of management's assessment regarding internal control over financial reporting or an attestation report of the company's registered public accounting firm due to a transition period established by rules of the Securities and Exchange Commission for newly public companies."

2. The registrant must maintain evidential matter, including documentation, to provide reasonable support for management's assessment of the effectiveness of the registrant's internal control over financial reporting.

(c) This temporary Item 308T, and accompanying note and instructions, will expire on December 15, 2010.

[As last amended in Release No. 33-9072, effective December 18, 2009, 74 F.R. 53628.]

Subpart 229.400—Management and Certain Security Holders

[¶ 13,041] Directors, Executive Officers, Promoters and Control Persons

Reg. § 229.401. Item 401.

(Item 401). (a) *Identification of directors.* List the names and ages of all directors of the registrant and all persons nominated or chosen to become directors; indicate all positions and offices with the registrant held by each such person; state his term of office as director and any period(s) during which he has served as such; describe briefly any arrangement or understanding between him and any other person(s) (naming such person(s)) pursuant to which he was or is to be selected as a director or nominee.

Instructions to Paragraph (a) of Item 401. 1. Do not include arrangements or understandings with directors or officers of the registrant acting solely in their capacities as such.

2. No nominee or person chosen to become a director who has not consented to act as such shall be named in response to this Item. In this regard, with respect to proxy statements, see Rule 14a-4(d) under the Exchange Act (§ 240.14a-4(d) of this chapter).

3. If the information called for by this paragraph (a) is being presented in a proxy or information statement, no information need be given respecting any director whose term of office as a director will not continue after the meeting to which the statement relates.

4. With regard to proxy statements in connection with action to be taken concerning the election of directors, if fewer nominees are named than the number fixed by or pursuant to the governing instruments, state the reasons for this procedure and that the proxies cannot be voted for a greater number of persons than the number of nominees named.

5. With regard to proxy statements in connection with action to be taken concerning the election of directors, if the solicitation is made by persons other than management, information shall be given as to nominees of the persons making the solicitation. In all other instances, information shall be given as to directors and persons nominated for election or chosen by management to become directors.

(b) *Identification of executive officers.* List the names and ages of all executive officers of the registrant and all persons chosen to become executive officers; indicate all positions and offices with the registrant held by each such person; state his term of office as officer and the period during which he has served as such and describe briefly any arrangement or understanding between him and any other person(s) (naming such person) pursuant to which he was or is to be selected as an officer.

Instructions to Paragraph (b) of Item 401. 1. Do not include arrangements or understandings with directors or officers of the registrant acting solely in their capacities as such.

2. No person chosen to become an executive officer who has not consented to act as such shall be named in response to this Item.

3. The information regarding executive officers called for by this Item need not be furnished in proxy or information statements prepared in accordance with Schedule 14A under the Exchange Act (§ 240.14a-101 of this chapter) by registrants relying on General Instruction G of Form 10-K under the Exchange Act (§ 249.310 of this chapter); *Provided*, that such information is furnished in a separate item captioned "Executive officers of the registrant" and included in Part I of the registrant's annual report on Form 10-K.

(c) *Identification of certain significant employees.* Where the registrant employs persons such as production managers, sales managers, or research scientists who are not executive officers but who make or are expected to make significant contributions to the business of the registrant, such persons shall be identified and their background disclosed to the same extent as in the case of executive officers. Such disclosure need not be made if the registrant was subject to section 13(a) or 15(d) of the Exchange Act or was exempt from section 13(a) by section 12(g)(2)(G) of such Act immediately prior to the filing of the registration statement, report, or statement to which this Item is applicable.

(d) *Family relationships.* State the nature of any family relationship between any director, executive officer, or person nominated or chosen by the registrant to become a director or executive officer.

Instruction to Paragraph 401(d). The term "family relationship" means any relationship by blood, marriage, or adoption, not more remote than first cousin.

(e) *Business experience.* (1) *Background.* Briefly describe the business experience during the past five years of each director, executive officer, person nominated or chosen to become a director or executive officer, and each person named in answer to paragraph (c) of Item 401, including: each person's principal occupations and employment during the past five years; the name and principal business of any corporation or other organization in which such occupations and employment were carried on; and whether such corporation or organization is a parent, subsidiary or other affiliate of the registrant. In addition, for each director or person nominated or chosen to become a director, briefly discuss the specific experience, qualifications, attributes or skills that led to the conclusion that the person should serve as a director for the registrant at the time that the disclosure is made, in light of the registrant's business and structure. If material, this disclosure should cover more than the past five years, including information about the person's particular areas of expertise or other relevant qualifications. When an executive officer or person named in response to paragraph (c) of Item 401 has been employed by the registrant or a subsidiary of the registrant for less than five years, a brief explanation shall be included as to the nature of the responsibility undertaken by the individual in prior positions to provide adequate disclosure of his or her prior business experience. What is required is information relating to the level of his or her professional competence, which may include, depending upon the circumstances, such specific information as the size of the operation supervised.

(2) *Directorships.* Indicate any other directorships held, including any other directorships held during the past five years, held by each director or person nominated or chosen to become a director in any company with a class of securities registered pursuant to section 12 of the Exchange Act or subject to the requirements of section 15(d) of such Act or any company registered as an investment company under the Investment Company Act of 1940, 15 U.S.C. 80a-1, et seq., as amended, naming such company.

Instruction to Paragraph (e) of Item 401.

For the purposes of paragraph (e)(2), where the other directorships of each director or person nominated or chosen to become a director include directorships of two or more registered investment companies that are part of a "fund complex" as that term is defined in Item 22(a) of Schedule 14A under the Exchange Act (§ 240.14a-101 of this chapter), the registrant may, rather than listing each such investment company, identify the fund complex and provide the number of investment company directorships held by the director or nominee in such fund complex.

(f) *Involvement in certain legal proceedings.* Describe any of the following events that occurred during the past ten years and that are material to an evaluation of the ability or integrity of any director, person nominated to become a director or executive officer of the registrant:

(1) A petition under the Federal bankruptcy laws or any state insolvency law was filed by or against, or a receiver, fiscal agent or similar officer was appointed by a court for the business or property of such person, or any partnership in which he was a general partner at or within two years before the time of such filing, or any corporation or business association of which he was an executive officer at or within two years before the time of such filing;

(2) Such person was convicted in a criminal proceeding or is a named subject of a pending criminal proceeding (excluding traffic violations and other minor offenses);

(3) Such person was the subject of any order, judgment, or decree, not subsequently reversed, suspended or vacated, of any court of competent jurisdiction, permanently or temporarily enjoining him from, or otherwise limiting, the following activities:

(i) Acting as a futures commission merchant, introducing broker, commodity trading advisor, commodity pool operator, floor broker, leverage transaction merchant, any other person regulated by the Commodity Futures Trading Commission, or an associated person of any of the foregoing, or as an investment adviser, underwriter, broker or dealer in securities, or as an affiliated person, director or employee of any investment company, bank, savings and loan association or insurance company, or engaging in or continuing any conduct or practice in connection with such activity;

(ii) Engaging in any type of business practice; or

(iii) Engaging in any activity in connection with the purchase or sale of any security or commodity or in connection with any violation of Federal or State securities laws or Federal commodities laws;

(4) Such person was the subject of any order, judgment or decree, not subsequently reversed, suspended or vacated, of any Federal or State authority barring, suspending or otherwise limiting for more than 60 days the right of such person to engage in any activity described in paragraph (f)(3)(i) of this Item, or to be associated with persons engaged in any such activity;

(5) Such person was found by a court of competent jurisdiction in a civil action or by the Commission to have violated any Federal or State securities law, and the judgment in such civil action or finding by the Commission has not been subsequently reversed, suspended, or vacated;

(6) Such person was found by a court of competent jurisdiction in a civil action or by the Commodity Futures Trading Commission to have violated any Federal commodities law, and the judgment in such civil action or finding by the Commodity Futures Trading Commission has not been subsequently reversed, suspended or vacated;

(7) Such person was the subject of, or a party to, any Federal or State judicial or administrative order, judgment, decree, or finding, not subsequently reversed, suspended or vacated, relating to an alleged violation of:

(i) Any Federal or State securities or commodities law or regulation; or

(ii) Any law or regulation respecting financial institutions or insurance companies including, but not limited to, a temporary or permanent injunction, order of disgorgement or restitution, civil money penalty or temporary or permanent cease-and-desist order, or removal or prohibition order; or

(iii) Any law or regulation prohibiting mail or wire fraud or fraud in connection with any business entity; or

(8) Such person was the subject of, or a party to, any sanction or order, not subsequently reversed, suspended or vacated, of any self-regulatory organization (as defined in Section 3(a)(26) of the Exchange Act (15 U.S.C. 78c(a)(26))), any registered entity (as defined in Section 1(a)(29) of the Commodity Exchange Act (7 U.S.C. 1(a)(29))), or any equivalent exchange, association, entity or organization that has disciplinary authority over its members or persons associated with a member.

Instructions to Paragraph (f) of Item 401. 1. For purposes of computing the ten-year period referred to in this paragraph, the date of a reportable event shall be deemed the date on which the final order, judgment or decree was entered, or the date on which any rights of appeal from preliminary orders, judgments, or decrees have lapsed. With respect to bankruptcy petitions, the computation date shall be the date of filing for uncontested petitions or the date upon which approval of a contested petition became final.

2. If any event specified in this paragraph (f) has occurred and information in regard thereto is omitted on the grounds that it is not material, the registrant may furnish to the Commission, at time of filing (or at the time preliminary materials are filed, or ten days before definitive materials are filed if preliminary filing is not required, pursuant to Rule 14a-6 or 14c-5 under the Exchange Act (§§ 240.14a-6 and 240.14c-5 of this chapter), as supplemental information and not as part of the registration statement, report, or proxy or information statement, materials to which the omission relates, a description of the event and a statement of the reasons for the omission of information in regard thereto.

3. The registrant is permitted to explain any mitigating circumstances associated with events reported pursuant to this paragraph.

4. If the information called for by this paragraph (f) is being presented in a proxy or information statement, no information need be given respecting any director whose term of office as a director will not continue after the meeting to which the statement relates.

5. This paragraph (f)(7) shall not apply to any settlement of a civil proceeding among private litigants.

(g)*Promoters and control persons.* (1) Registrants, which have not been subject to the reporting requirements of section 13(a) or 15(d) of the Exchange Act (15 U.S.C. 78m(a) or 78o(d)) for the twelve months immediately prior to the filing of the registration statement, report, or statement to which this Item is applicable, and which had a promoter at any time during the past five fiscal years, shall describe with respect to any promoter, any of the events enumerated in paragraphs (f)(1) through (f)(6) of this Item that occurred during the past five years and that are material to a voting or investment decision.

(2) Registrants, which have not been subject to the reporting requirements of Section 13(a) or 15(d) of the Exchange Act for the twelve months immediately prior to the filing of the registration statement, report, or statement to which this Item is applicable, shall describe with respect to any control person, any of the events enumerated in paragraphs (f)(1) through (f)(6) of this section that occurred during the past five years and that are material to a voting or investment decision.

Instructions to Paragraph (g) of Item 401. 1. Instructions 1. through 3. to paragraph (f) shall apply to this paragraph (g).

2. Paragraph (g) shall not apply to any subsidiary of a registrant which has been reporting pursuant to Section 13(a) or 15(d) of the Exchange Act for the twelve months immediately prior to the filing of the registration statement, report or statement.

[As last amended in Release No. 33-9089, effective February 28, 2010, 74 F.R. 68334.]

[¶ 13,042] Executive Compensation

Reg. § 229.402. Item 402. (a) *General.*

(1) *Treatment of foreign private issuers.* A foreign private issuer will be deemed to comply with this Item if it provides the information required by Items 6.B and 6.E.2 of Form 20-F (17 CFR 249.220f), with more detailed information provided if otherwise made publicly available or required to be disclosed by the issuer's home jurisdiction or a market in which its securities are listed or traded.

(2) *All compensation covered.* This Item requires clear, concise and understandable disclosure of all plan and non-plan compensation awarded to, earned by, or paid to the named executive officers designated under paragraph (a)(3) of this Item, and directors covered by paragraph (k) of this Item, by any person for all services rendered in all capacities to the registrant and its subsidiaries, unless otherwise specifically excluded from disclosure in this Item. All such compensation shall be reported

pursuant to this Item, even if also called for by another requirement, including transactions between the registrant and a third party where a purpose of the transaction is to furnish compensation to any such named executive officer or director. No amount reported as compensation for one fiscal year need be reported in the same manner as compensation for a subsequent fiscal year; amounts reported as compensation for one fiscal year may be required to be reported in a different manner pursuant to this Item.

(3) *Persons covered.* Disclosure shall be provided pursuant to this Item for each of the following (the "named executive officers"):

(i) All individuals serving as the registrant's principal executive officer or acting in a similar capacity during the last completed fiscal year ("PEO"), regardless of compensation level;

(ii) All individuals serving as the registrant's principal financial officer or acting in a similar capacity during the last completed fiscal year ("PFO"), regardless of compensation level;

(iii) The registrant's three most highly compensated executive officers other than the PEO and PFO who were serving as executive officers at the end of the last completed fiscal year; and

(iv) Up to two additional individuals for whom disclosure would have been provided pursuant to paragraph (a)(3)(iii) of this Item but for the fact that the individual was not serving as an executive officer of the registrant at the end of the last completed fiscal year.

Instructions to Item 402(a)(3).

1. *Determination of most highly compensated executive officers.* The determination as to which executive officers are most highly compensated shall be made by reference to total compensation for the last completed fiscal year (as required to be disclosed pursuant to paragraph (c)(2)(x) of this Item) reduced by the amount required to be disclosed pursuant to paragraph (c)(2)(viii) of this Item, *provided, however,* that no disclosure need be provided for any executive officer, other than the PEO and PFO, whose total compensation, as so reduced, does not exceed $100,000.

2. *Inclusion of executive officer of subsidiary.* It may be appropriate for a registrant to include as named executive officers one or more executive officers or other employees of subsidiaries in the disclosure required by this Item. See Rule 3b-7 under the Exchange Act (17 CFR 240.3b-7).

3. *Exclusion of executive officer due to overseas compensation.* It may be appropriate in limited circumstances for a registrant not to include in the disclosure required by this Item an individual, other than its PEO or PFO, who is one of the registrant's most highly compensated executive officers due to the payment of amounts of cash compensation relating to overseas assignments attributed predominantly to such assignments.

(4) *Information for full fiscal year.* If the PEO or PFO served in that capacity during any part of a fiscal year with respect to which information is required, information should be provided as to all of his or her compensation for the full fiscal year. If a named executive officer (other than the PEO or PFO) served as an executive officer of the registrant (whether or not in the same position) during any part of the fiscal year with respect to which information is required, information shall be provided as to all compensation of that individual for the full fiscal year.

(5) *Omission of table or column.* A table or column may be omitted if there has been no compensation awarded to, earned by, or paid to any of the named executive officers or directors required to be reported in that table or column in any fiscal year covered by that table.

(6) *Definitions.* For purposes of this Item:

(i) The term *stock* means instruments such as common stock, restricted stock, restricted stock units, phantom stock, phantom stock units, common stock equivalent units or any similar instruments that do not have option-like features, and the term option means instruments such as stock options, stock appreciation rights and similar instruments with option-like features. The term *stock appreciation rights* ("*SARs*") refers to SARs payable in cash or stock, including SARs payable in cash or stock at the election of the registrant or a named executive officer. The term *equity* is used to refer generally to stock and/or options.

(ii) The term *plan* includes, but is not limited to, the following: Any plan, contract, authorization or arrangement, whether or not set forth in any formal document, pursuant to which cash, securities, similar instruments, or any other property may be received. A plan may be applicable to one person. Registrants may omit information regarding group life, health, hospitalization, or medical reimbursement plans that do not discriminate in scope, terms or operation, in favor of executive officers or directors of the registrant and that are available generally to all salaried employees.

(iii) The term *incentive plan* means any plan providing compensation intended to serve as incentive for performance to occur over a specified period, whether such performance is measured by reference to financial performance of the registrant or an affiliate, the registrant's stock price, or any other performance measure. An *equity incentive plan* is an incentive plan or portion of an incentive plan under which awards are granted that fall within the scope of Financial Accounting Standards Board Statement of

Financial Accounting Standards No. 123 (revised 2004), *Share-Based Payment*, as modified or supplemented ("FAS 123R"). A *non-equity incentive plan* is an incentive plan or portion of an incentive plan that is not an equity incentive plan. The term *incentive plan award* means an award provided under an incentive plan.

(iv) The terms *date of grant* or *grant date* refer to the grant date determined for financial statement reporting purposes pursuant to FAS 123R.

(v) *Closing market price* is defined as the price at which the registrant's security was last sold in the principal United States market for such security as of the date for which the closing market price is determined.

(b) *Compensation discussion and analysis.*

(1) Discuss the compensation awarded to, earned by, or paid to the named executive officers. The discussion shall explain all material elements of the registrant's compensation of the named executive officers. The discussion shall describe the following:

(i) The objectives of the registrant's compensation programs;

(ii) What the compensation program is designed to reward;

(iii) Each element of compensation;

(iv) Why the registrant chooses to pay each element;

(v) How the registrant determines the amount (and, where applicable, the formula) for each element to pay; and

(vi) How each compensation element and the registrant's decisions regarding that element fit into the registrant's overall compensation objectives and affect decisions regarding other elements.

(2) While the material information to be disclosed under Compensation Discussion and Analysis will vary depending upon the facts and circumstances, examples of such information may include, in a given case, among other things, the following:

(i) The policies for allocating between long-term and currently paid out compensation;

(ii) The policies for allocating between cash and non-cash compensation, and among different forms of non-cash compensation;

(iii) For long-term compensation, the basis for allocating compensation to each different form of award (such as relationship of the award to the achievement of the registrant's long-term goals, management's exposure to downside equity performance risk, correlation between cost to registrant and expected benefits to the registrant);

(iv) How the determination is made as to when awards are granted, including awards of equity-based compensation such as options;

(v) What specific items of corporate performance are taken into account in setting compensation policies and making compensation decisions;

(vi) How specific forms of compensation are structured and implemented to reflect these items of the registrant's performance, including whether discretion can be or has been exercised (either to award compensation absent attainment of the relevant performance goal(s) or to reduce or increase the size of any award or payout), identifying any particular exercise of discretion, and stating whether it applied to one or more specified named executive officers or to all compensation subject to the relevant performance goal(s);

(vii) How specific forms of compensation are structured and implemented to reflect the named executive officer's individual performance and/or individual contribution to these items of the registrant's performance, describing the elements of individual performance and/or contribution that are taken into account;

(viii) Registrant policies and decisions regarding the adjustment or recovery of awards or payments if the relevant registrant performance measures upon which they are based are restated or otherwise adjusted in a manner that would reduce the size of an award or payment;

(ix) The factors considered in decisions to increase or decrease compensation materially;

(x) How compensation or amounts realizable from prior compensation are considered in setting other elements of compensation (*e.g.*, how gains from prior option or stock awards are considered in setting retirement benefits);

(xi) With respect to any contract, agreement, plan or arrangement, whether written or unwritten, that provides for payment(s) at, following, or in connection with any termination or change-in-control, the basis for selecting particular events as triggering payment (*e.g.*, the rationale for providing a single trigger for payment in the event of a change-in-control);

(xii) The impact of the accounting and tax treatments of the particular form of compensation;

(xiii) The registrant's equity or other security ownership requirements or guidelines (specifying applicable amounts and forms of ownership), and any registrant policies regarding hedging the economic risk of such ownership;

(xiv) Whether the registrant engaged in any benchmarking of total compensation, or any material element of compensation, identifying the benchmark and, if applicable, its components (including component companies); and

(xv) The role of executive officers in determining executive compensation.

Instructions to Item 402(b).

1. The purpose of the Compensation Discussion and Analysis is to provide to investors material information that is necessary to an understanding of the registrant's compensation policies and decisions regarding the named executive officers.

2. The Compensation Discussion and Analysis should be of the information contained in the tables and otherwise disclosed pursuant to this Item. The Compensation Discussion and Analysis should also cover actions regarding executive compensation that were taken after the registrant's last fiscal year's end. Actions that should be addressed might include, as examples only, the adoption or implementation of new or modified programs and policies or specific decisions that were made or steps that were taken that could affect a fair understanding of the named executive officer's compensation for the last fiscal year. Moreover, in some situations it may be necessary to discuss prior years in order to give context to the disclosure provided.

3. The Compensation Discussion and Analysis should focus on the material principles underlying the registrant's executive compensation policies and decisions and the most important factors relevant to analysis of those policies and decisions. The Compensation Discussion and Analysis shall reflect the individual circumstances of the registrant and shall avoid boilerplate language and repetition of the more detailed information set forth in the tables and narrative disclosures that follow.

4. Registrants are not required to disclose target levels with respect to specific quantitative or qualitative performance-related factors considered by the compensation committee or the board of directors, or any other factors or criteria involving confidential trade secrets or confidential commercial or financial information, the disclosure of which would result in competitive harm for the registrant. The standard to use when determining whether disclosure would cause competitive harm for the registrant is the same standard that would apply when a registrant requests confidential treatment of confidential trade secrets or confidential commercial or financial information pursuant to Securities Act Rule 406 (17 CFR 230.406) and Exchange Act Rule 24b-2 (17 CFR 240.24b-2), each of which incorporates the criteria for non-disclosure when relying upon Exemption 4 of the Freedom of Information Act (5 U.S.C. 552(b)(4)) and Rule 80(b)(4) (17 CFR 200.80(b)(4)) thereunder. A registrant is not required to seek confidential treatment under the procedures in Securities Act Rule 406 and Exchange Act Rule 24b-2 if it determines that the disclosure would cause competitive harm in reliance on this instruction; however, in that case, the registrant must discuss how difficult it will be for the executive or how likely it will be for the registrant to achieve the undisclosed target level or other factors.

5. Disclosure of target levels that are non-GAAP financial measures will not be subject to Regulation G (17 CFR 244.100 - 102) and Item 10(e) (§ 229.10(e)); however, disclosure must be provided as to how the number is calculated from the registrant's audited financial statements.

(c) *Summary compensation table.*

(1) *General.* Provide the information specified in paragraph (c)(2) of this Item, concerning the compensation of the named executive officers for each of the registrant's last three completed fiscal years, in a Summary Compensation Table in the tabular format specified below.

SUMMARY COMPENSATION TABLE

Name and Principal Position	Year	Salary ($)	Bonus ($)	Stock Awards ($)	Option Awards ($)	Non-Equity Incentive Plan Compensation ($)	Change in Pension Value and Nonqualified Deferred Compensation Earnings ($)	All Other Compensation ($)	Total ($)
(a)	(b)	(c)	(d)	(e)	(f)	(g)	(h)	(i)	(j)
PEO	——								
	——								
	——								
PFO	——								
	——								
	——								

Name and Principal Position	Year	Salary ($)	Bonus ($)	Stock Awards ($)	Option Awards ($)	Non-Equity Incentive Plan Compensation ($)	Change in Pension Value and Nonqualified Deferred Compensation Earnings ($)	All Other Compensation ($)	Total ($)
(a)	(b)	(c)	(d)	(e)	(f)	(g)	(h)	(i)	(j)
A									
B									
C									

(2) The Table shall include:

(i) The name and principal position of the named executive officer (column (a));

(ii) The fiscal year covered (column (b));

(iii) The dollar value of base salary (cash and non-cash) earned by the named executive officer during the fiscal year covered (column (c));

(iv) The dollar value of bonus (cash and non-cash) earned by the named executive officer during the fiscal year covered (column (d));

Instructions to Item 402(c)(2)(iii) and (iv).

1. If the amount of salary or bonus earned in a given fiscal year is not calculable through the latest practicable date, a footnote shall be included disclosing that the amount of salary or bonus is not calculable through the latest practicable date and providing the date that the amount of salary or bonus is expected to be determined, and such amount must then be disclosed in a filing under Item 5.02(f) of Form 8-K (17 CFR 249.308).

2. Registrants shall include in the salary column (column (c)) or bonus column (column (d)) any amount of salary or bonus forgone at the election of a named executive officer under which stock, equity-based or other forms of non-cash compensation instead have been received by the named executive officer. However, the receipt of any such form of non-cash compensation instead of salary or bonus must be disclosed in a footnote added to the salary or bonus column and, where applicable, referring to the Grants of Plan-Based Awards Table (required by paragraph (d) of this Item) where the stock, option or non-equity incentive plan award elected by the named executive officer is reported.

(v) For awards of stock, the aggregate grant date fair value computed in accordance with FASB ASC Topic 718 (column (e));

(vi) For awards of options, with or without tandem SARs (including awards that subsequently have been transferred), the aggregate grant date fair value computed in accordance with FASB ASC Topic 718 (column (f));

Instruction 1 to Item 402(c)(2)(v) and (vi). For awards reported in columns (e) and (f), include a footnote disclosing all assumptions made in the valuation by reference to a discussion of those assumptions in the registrant's financial statements, footnotes to the financial statements, or discussion in the Management's Discussion and Analysis. The sections so referenced are deemed part of the disclosure provided pursuant to this Item.

Instruction 2 to Item 402(c)(2)(v) and (vi). If at any time during the last completed fiscal year, the registrant has adjusted or amended the exercise price of options or SARs previously awarded to a named executive officer, whether through amendment, cancellation or replacement grants, or any other means ("repriced"), or otherwise has materially modified such awards, the registrant shall include, as awards required to be reported in column (f), the incremental fair value, computed as of the repricing or modification date in accordance with FASB ASC Topic 718, with respect to that repriced or modified award.

Instruction 3 to Item 402(c)(2)(v) and (vi). For any awards that are subject to performance conditions, report the value at the grant date based upon the probable outcome of such conditions. This amount should be consistent with the estimate of aggregate compensation cost to be recognized over the service period determined as of the grant date under FASB ASC Topic 718, excluding the effect of estimated forfeitures. In a footnote to the table, disclose the value of the award at the grant date assuming that the highest level of performance conditions will be achieved if an amount less than the maximum was included in the table.

(vii) The dollar value of all earnings for services performed during the fiscal year pursuant to awards under non-equity incentive plans as defined in paragraph (a)(6)(iii) of this Item, and all earnings on any outstanding awards (column (g));

Instructions to Item 402(c)(2)(vii).

1. If the relevant performance measure is satisfied during the fiscal year (including for a single year in a plan with a multi-year performance measure), the earnings are reportable for that fiscal year, even if not payable until a later date, and are not reportable again in the fiscal year when amounts are paid to the named executive officer.

2. All earnings on non-equity incentive plan compensation must be identified and quantified in a footnote to column (g), whether the earnings were paid during the fiscal year, payable during the period but deferred at the election of the named executive officer, or payable by their terms at a later date.

(viii) The sum of the amounts specified in paragraphs (c)(2)(viii)(A) and (B) of this Item (column (h)) as follows:

(A) The aggregate change in the actuarial present value of the named executive officer's accumulated benefit under all defined benefit and actuarial pension plans (including supplemental plans) from the pension plan measurement date used for financial statement reporting purposes with respect to the registrant's audited financial statements for the prior completed fiscal year to the pension plan measurement date used for financial statement reporting purposes with respect to the registrant's audited financial statements for the covered fiscal year; and

(B) Above-market or preferential earnings on compensation that is deferred on a basis that is not tax-qualified, including such earnings on nonqualified defined contribution plans;

Instructions to Item 402(c)(2)(viii).

1. The disclosure required pursuant to paragraph (c)(2)(viii)(A) of this Item applies to each plan that provides for the payment of retirement benefits, or benefits that will be paid primarily following retirement, including but not limited to tax-qualified defined benefit plans and supplemental executive retirement plans, but excluding tax-qualified defined contribution plans and nonqualified defined contribution plans. For purposes of this disclosure, the registrant should use the same amounts required to be disclosed pursuant to paragraph (h)(2)(iv) of this Item for the covered fiscal year and the amounts that were or would have been required to be reported for the executive officer pursuant to paragraph (h)(2)(iv) of this Item for the prior completed fiscal year.

2. Regarding paragraph (c)(2)(viii)(B) of this Item, interest on deferred compensation is above-market only if the rate of interest exceeds 120% of the applicable federal long-term rate, with compounding (as prescribed under section 1274(d) of the Internal Revenue Code, (26 U.S.C. 1274(d))) at the rate that corresponds most closely to the rate under the registrant's plan at the time the interest rate or formula is set. In the event of a discretionary reset of the interest rate, the requisite calculation must be made on the basis of the interest rate at the time of such reset, rather than when originally established. Only the above-market portion of the interest must be included. If the applicable interest rates vary depending upon conditions such as a minimum period of continued service, the reported amount should be calculated assuming satisfaction of all conditions to receiving interest at the highest rate. Dividends (and dividend equivalents) on deferred compensation denominated in the registrant's stock ("deferred stock") are preferential only if earned at a rate higher than dividends on the registrant's common stock. Only the preferential portion of the dividends or equivalents must be included. Footnote or narrative disclosure may be provided explaining the registrant's criteria for determining any portion considered to be above-market.

3. The registrant shall identify and quantify by footnote the separate amounts attributable to each of paragraphs (c)(2)(viii)(A) and (B) of this Item. Where such amount pursuant to paragraph (c)(2)(viii)(A) is negative, it should be disclosed by footnote but should not be reflected in the sum reported in column (h).

(ix) All other compensation for the covered fiscal year that the registrant could not properly report in any other column of the Summary Compensation Table (column (i)). Each compensation item that is not properly reportable in columns (c) - (h), regardless of the amount of the compensation item, must be included in column (i). Such compensation must include, but is not limited to:

(A) Perquisites and other personal benefits, or property, unless the aggregate amount of such compensation is less than $10,000;

(B) All "gross-ups" or other amounts reimbursed during the fiscal year for the payment of taxes;

(C) For any security of the registrant or its subsidiaries purchased from the registrant or its subsidiaries (through deferral of salary or bonus, or otherwise) at a discount from the market price of such security at the date of purchase, unless that discount is available generally, either to all security holders or to all salaried employees of the registrant, the compensation cost, if any, computed in accordance with FAS 123R;

(D) The amount paid or accrued to any named executive officer pursuant to a plan or arrangement in connection with:

(1) Any termination, including without limitation through retirement, resignation, severance or constructive termination (including a change in responsibilities) of such executive officer's employment with the registrant and its subsidiaries; or

(2) A change in control of the registrant;

(E) Registrant contributions or other allocations to vested and unvested defined contribution plans;

(F) The dollar value of any insurance premiums paid by, or on behalf of, the registrant during the covered fiscal year with respect to life insurance for the benefit of a named executive officer; and

(G) The dollar value of any dividends or other earnings paid on stock or option awards, when those amounts were not factored into the grant date fair value required to be reported for the stock or option award in column (e) or (f); and

Instructions to Item 402(c)(2)(ix).

1. Non-equity incentive plan awards and earnings and earnings on stock and options, except as specified in paragraph (c)(2)(ix)(G) of this Item, are required to be reported elsewhere as provided in this Item and are not reportable as All Other Compensation in column (i).

2. Benefits paid pursuant to defined benefit and actuarial plans are not reportable as All Other Compensation in column (i) unless accelerated pursuant to a change in control; information concerning these plans is reportable pursuant to paragraphs (c)(2)(viii)(A) and (h) of this Item.

3. Any item reported for a named executive officer pursuant to paragraph (c)(2)(ix) of this Item that is not a perquisite or personal benefit and whose value exceeds $10,000 must be identified and quantified in a footnote to column (i). This requirement applies only to compensation for the last fiscal year. All items of compensation are required to be included in the Summary Compensation Table without regard to whether such items are required to be identified other than as specifically noted in this Item.

4. Perquisites and personal benefits may be excluded as long as the total value of all perquisites and personal benefits for a named executive officer is less than $10,000. If the total value of all perquisites and personal benefits is $10,000 or more for any named executive officer, then each perquisite or personal benefit, regardless of its amount, must be identified by type. If perquisites and personal benefits are required to be reported for a named executive officer pursuant to this rule, then each perquisite or personal benefit that exceeds the greater of $25,000 or 10% of the total amount of perquisites and personal benefits for that officer must be quantified and disclosed in a footnote. The requirements for identification and quantification apply only to compensation for the last fiscal year. Perquisites and other personal benefits shall be valued on the basis of the aggregate incremental cost to the registrant. With respect to the perquisite or other personal benefit for which footnote quantification is required, the registrant shall describe in the footnote its methodology for computing the aggregate incremental cost. Reimbursements of taxes owed with respect to perquisites or other personal benefits must be included in column (i) and are subject to separate quantification and identification as tax reimbursements (paragraph (c)(2)(ix)(B) of this Item) even if the associated perquisites or other personal benefits are not required to be included because the total amount of all perquisites or personal benefits for an individual named executive officer is less than $10,000 or are required to be identified but are not required to be separately quantified.

5. For purposes of paragraph (c)(2)(ix)(D) of this Item, an accrued amount is an amount for which payment has become due.

(x) The dollar value of total compensation for the covered fiscal year (column (j)). With respect to each named executive officer, disclose the sum of all amounts reported in columns (c) through (i).

Instructions to Item 402(c).

1. Information with respect to fiscal years prior to the last completed fiscal year will not be required if the registrant was not a reporting company pursuant to section 13(a) or 15(d) of the Exchange Act (15 U.S.C. 78m(a) or 78o(d)) at any time during that year, except that the registrant will be required to provide information for any such year if that information previously was required to be provided in response to a Commission filing requirement.

2. All compensation values reported in the Summary Compensation Table must be reported in dollars and rounded to the nearest dollar. Reported compensation values must be reported numerically, providing a single numerical value for each grid in the table. Where compensation was paid to or

received by a named executive officer in a different currency, a footnote must be provided to identify that currency and describe the rate and methodology used to convert the payment amounts to dollars.

3. If a named executive officer is also a director who receives compensation for his or her services as a director, reflect that compensation in the Summary Compensation Table and provide a footnote identifying and itemizing such compensation and amounts. Use the categories in the Director Compensation Table required pursuant to paragraph (k) of this Item.

4. Any amounts deferred, whether pursuant to a plan established under section 401(k) of the Internal Revenue Code (26 U.S.C. 401(k)), or otherwise, shall be included in the appropriate column for the fiscal year in which earned.

(d) *Grants of plan-based awards table.* (1) Provide the information specified in paragraph (d)(2) of this Item, concerning each grant of an award made to a named executive officer in the last completed fiscal year under any plan, including awards that subsequently have been transferred, in the following tabular format:

GRANTS OF PLAN-BASED AWARDS

Name	Grant Date	Estimated Future Payouts Under Non-Equity Incentive Plan Awards			Estimated Future Payouts Under Equity Incentive Plan Awards			All Other Stock Awards: Number of Shares of Stock or Units (#)	All Other Option Awards: Number of Securities Underlying Options (#)	Exercise or Base Price of Option Awards ($/Sh)	Grant Date Fair Value of Stock and Option Awards
		Threshold ($)	Target ($)	Maximum ($)	Threshold (#)	Target (#)	Maximum (#)				
(a)	(b)	(c)	(d)	(e)	(f)	(g)	(h)	(i)	(j)	(k)	(l)
PEO											
PFO											
A											
B											
C											

(2) The Table shall include:

(i) The name of the named executive officer (column (a));

(ii) The grant date for equity-based awards reported in the table (column (b)). If such grant date is different than the date on which the compensation committee (or a committee of the board of directors performing a similar function or the full board of directors) takes action or is deemed to take action to grant such awards, a separate, adjoining column shall be added between columns (b) and (c) showing such date;

(iii) The dollar value of the estimated future payout upon satisfaction of the conditions in question under non-equity incentive plan awards granted in the fiscal year, or the applicable range of estimated payouts denominated in dollars (threshold, target and maximum amount) (columns (c) through (e));

(iv) The number of shares of stock, or the number of shares underlying options to be paid out or vested upon satisfaction of the conditions in question under equity incentive plan awards granted in the fiscal year, or the applicable range of estimated payouts denominated in the number of shares of stock, or the number of shares underlying options under the award (threshold, target and maximum amount) (columns (f) through (h)).

(v) The number of shares of stock granted in the fiscal year that are not required to be disclosed in columns (f) through (h) (column (i));

(vi) The number of securities underlying options granted in the fiscal year that are not required to be disclosed in columns (f) through (h) (column (j));

(vii) The per-share exercise or base price of the options granted in the fiscal year (column (k)). If such exercise or base price is less than the closing market price of the underlying security on the date of the grant, a separate, adjoining column showing the closing market price on the date of the grant shall be added after column (k); and

(viii) The grant date fair value of each equity award computed in accordance with FAS 123R (column (*l*)). If at any time during the last completed fiscal year, the registrant has adjusted or amended the exercise or base price of options, SARs or similar option-like instruments previously awarded to a named executive officer, whether through amendment, cancellation or replacement grants, or any other means ("repriced"), or otherwise has materially modified such awards, the incremental fair value, computed as of the repricing or modification date in accordance with FAS 123R, with respect to that repriced or modified award, shall be reported.

Instructions to Item 402(d).

1. Disclosure on a separate line shall be provided in the Table for each grant of an award made to a named executive officer during the fiscal year. If grants of awards were made to a named executive officer during the fiscal year under more than one plan, identify the particular plan under which each such grant was made.

2. For grants of incentive plan awards, provide the information called for by columns (c), (d) and (e), or (f), (g) and (h), as applicable. For columns (c) and (f), *threshold* refers to the minimum amount payable for a certain level of performance under the plan. For columns (d) and (g), *target* refers to the amount payable if the specified performance target(s) are reached. For columns (e) and (h), *maximum* refers to the maximum payout possible under the plan. If the award provides only for a single estimated payout, that amount must be reported as the *target* in columns (d) and (g). In columns (d) and (g), registrants must provide a representative amount based on the previous fiscal year's performance if the target amount is not determinable.

3. In determining if the exercise or base price of an option is less than the closing market price of the underlying security on the date of the grant, the registrant may use either the closing market price as specified in paragraph (a)(6)(v) of this Item, or if no market exists, any other formula prescribed for the security. Whenever the exercise or base price reported in column (k) is not the closing market price, describe the methodology for determining the exercise or base price either by a footnote or accompanying textual narrative.

4. A tandem grant of two instruments, only one of which is granted under an incentive plan, such as an option granted in tandem with a performance share, need be reported only in column (i) or (j), as applicable. For example, an option granted in tandem with a performance share would be reported only as an option grant in column (j), with the tandem feature noted either by a footnote or accompanying textual narrative.

5. Disclose the dollar amount of consideration, if any, paid by the executive officer for the award in a footnote to the appropriate column.

6. If non-equity incentive plan awards are denominated in units or other rights, a separate, adjoining column between columns (b) and (c) shall be added quantifying the units or other rights awarded.

7. Options, SARs and similar option-like instruments granted in connection with a repricing transaction or other material modification shall be reported in this Table. However, the disclosure required by this Table does not apply to any repricing that occurs through a pre-existing formula or mechanism in the plan or award that results in the periodic adjustment of the option or SAR exercise or base price, an antidilution provision in a plan or award, or a recapitalization or similar transaction equally affecting all holders of the class of securities underlying the options or SARs.

8. For any equity awards that are subject to performance conditions, report in column (l) the value at the grant date based upon the probable outcome of such conditions. This amount should be consistent with the estimate of aggregate compensation cost to be recognized over the service period determined as of the grant date under FASB ASC Topic 718, excluding the effect of estimated forfeitures.

(e) *Narrative disclosure to summary compensation table and grants of plan-based awards table.*

(1) Provide a narrative description of any material factors necessary to an understanding of the information disclosed in the tables required by paragraphs (c) and (d) of this Item. Examples of such factors may include, in given cases, among other things:

(i) The material terms of each named executive officer's employment agreement or arrangement, whether written or unwritten;

(ii) If at any time during the last fiscal year, any outstanding option or other equity-based award was repriced or otherwise materially modified (such as by extension of exercise periods, the change of vesting or forfeiture conditions, the change or elimination of applicable performance criteria, or the change of the bases upon which returns are determined), a description of each such repricing or other material modification;

(iii) The material terms of any award reported in response to paragraph (d) of this Item, including a general description of the formula or criteria to be applied in determining the amounts payable, and the vesting schedule. For example, state where applicable that dividends will be paid on stock, and if so, the applicable dividend rate and whether that rate is preferential. Describe any performance-based conditions, and any other material conditions, that are applicable to the award. For purposes of the Table required by paragraph (d) of this Item and the narrative disclosure required by paragraph (e) of this Item, performance-based conditions include both performance conditions and market conditions, as those terms are defined in FAS 123R; and

(iv) An explanation of the amount of salary and bonus in proportion to total compensation.

Instructions to Item 402(e)(1).

1. The disclosure required by paragraph (e)(1)(ii) of this Item would not apply to any repricing that occurs through a pre-existing formula or mechanism in the plan or award that results in the periodic adjustment of the option or SAR exercise or base price, an antidilution provision in a plan or award, or a recapitalization or similar transaction equally affecting all holders of the class of securities underlying the options or SARs.

2. Instructions 4 and 5 to Item 402(b) apply regarding disclosure pursuant to paragraph (e)(1) of target levels with respect to specific quantitative or qualitative performance-related factors considered by the compensation committee or the board of directors, or any other factors or criteria involving confidential trade secrets or confidential commercial or financial information, the disclosure of which would result in competitive harm for the registrant.

(2) [Reserved.]

(f) *Outstanding equity awards at fiscal year-end table.* (1) Provide the information specified in paragraph (f)(2) of this Item, concerning unexercised options; stock that has not vested; and equity incentive plan awards for each named executive officer outstanding as of the end of the registrant's last completed fiscal year in the following tabular format:

OUTSTANDING EQUITY AWARDS AT FISCAL YEAR-END

	Option Awards					Stock Awards			
Name	Number of Securities Underlying Unexercised Options (#) Exercisable	Number of Securities Underlying Unexercised Options (#) Unexercisable	Equity Incentive Plan Awards: Number of Securities Underlying Unexercised Unearned Options (#)	Option Exercise Price ($)	Option Expiration Date	Number of Shares or Units of Stock That Have Not Vested (#)	Market Value of Shares or Units of Stock That Have Not Vested ($)	Equity Incentive Plan Awards: Number of Unearned Shares, Units or Other Rights That Have Not Vested (#)	Equity Incentive Plan Awards: Market or Payout Value of Unearned Shares, Units or Other Rights That Have Not Vested ($)
(a)	(b)	(c)	(d)	(e)	(f)	(g)	(h)	(i)	(j)
PEO									
PFO									
A									
B									
C									

(2) The Table shall include:

(i) The name of the named executive officer (column (a));

(ii) On an award-by-award basis, the number of securities underlying unexercised options, including awards that have been transferred other than for value, that are exercisable and that are not reported in column (d) (column (b));

(iii) On an award-by-award basis, the number of securities underlying unexercised options, including awards that have been transferred other than for value, that are unexercisable and that are not reported in column (d) (column (c));

(iv) On an award-by-award basis, the total number of shares underlying unexercised options awarded under any equity incentive plan that have not been earned (column (d));

(v) For each instrument reported in columns (b), (c) and (d), as applicable, the exercise or base price (column (e));

(vi) For each instrument reported in columns (b), (c) and (d), as applicable, the expiration date (column (f));

(vii) The total number of shares of stock that have not vested and that are not reported in column (i) (column (g));

(viii) The aggregate market value of shares of stock that have not vested and that are not reported in column (j) (column (h));

(ix) The total number of shares of stock, units or other rights awarded under any equity incentive plan that have not vested and that have not been earned, and, if applicable the number of shares underlying any such unit or right (column (i)); and

(x) The aggregate market or payout value of shares of stock, units or other rights awarded under any equity incentive plan that have not vested and that have not been earned (column (j)).

Instructions to Item 402(f)(2).

1. Identify by footnote any award that has been transferred other than for value, disclosing the nature of the transfer.

2. The vesting dates of options, shares of stock and equity incentive plan awards held at fiscal-year end must be disclosed by footnote to the applicable column where the outstanding award is reported.

3. Compute the market value of stock reported in column (h) and equity incentive plan awards of stock reported in column (j) by multiplying the closing market price of the registrant's stock at the end of the last completed fiscal year by the number of shares or units of stock or the amount of equity incentive plan awards, respectively. The number of shares or units reported in columns (d) or (i), and the payout value reported in column (j), shall be based on achieving threshold performance goals, except that if the previous fiscal year's performance has exceeded the threshold, the disclosure shall be based on the next higher performance measure (target or maximum) that exceeds the previous fiscal year's performance. If the award provides only for a single estimated payout, that amount should be reported. If the target amount is not determinable, registrants must provide a representative amount based on the previous fiscal year's performance.

4. Multiple awards may be aggregated where the expiration date and the exercise and/or base price of the instruments is identical. A single award consisting of a combination of options, SARs and/or similar option-like instruments shall be reported as separate awards with respect to each tranche with a different exercise and/or base price or expiration date.

5. Options or stock awarded under an equity incentive plan are reported in columns (d) or (i) and (j), respectively, until the relevant performance condition has been satisfied. Once the relevant performance condition has been satisfied, even if the option or stock award is subject to forfeiture conditions, options are reported in column (b) or (c), as appropriate, until they are exercised or expire, or stock is reported in columns (g) and (h) until it vests.

(g) *Option exercises and stock vested table.* (1) Provide the information specified in paragraph (g)(2) of this Item, concerning each exercise of stock options, SARs and similar instruments, and each vesting of stock, including restricted stock, restricted stock units and similar instruments, during the last completed fiscal year for each of the named executive officers on an aggregated basis in the following tabular format:

OPTION EXERCISES AND STOCK VESTED

	Option Awards		Stock Awards	
Name	Number of Shares Acquired on Exercise (#)	Value Realized on Exercise ($)	Number of Shares Acquired on Vesting (#)	Value Realized on Vesting ($)
(a)	(b)	(c)	(d)	(e)
PEO				
PFO				
A				
B				

	Option Awards		Stock Awards	
Name	Number of Shares Acquired on Exercise (#)	Value Realized on Exercise ($)	Number of Shares Acquired on Vesting (#)	Value Realized on Vesting ($)
(a)	(b)	(c)	(d)	(e)
C				

(2) The Table shall include:

(i) The name of the executive officer (column (a));

(ii) The number of securities for which the options were exercised (column (b));

(iii) The aggregate dollar value realized upon exercise of options, or upon the transfer of an award for value (column (c));

(iv) The number of shares of stock that have vested (column (d)); and

(v) The aggregate dollar value realized upon vesting of stock, or upon the transfer of an award for value (column (e)).

Instruction to Item 402(g)(2).

Report in column (c) the aggregate dollar amount realized by the named executive officer upon exercise of the options or upon the transfer of such instruments for value. Compute the dollar amount realized upon exercise by determining the difference between the market price of the underlying securities at exercise and the exercise or base price of the options. Do not include the value of any related payment or other consideration provided (or to be provided) by the registrant to or on behalf of a named executive officer, whether in payment of the exercise price or related taxes. (Any such payment or other consideration provided by the registrant is required to be disclosed in accordance with paragraph (c)(2)(ix) of this Item.) Report in column (e) the aggregate dollar amount realized by the named executive officer upon the vesting of stock or the transfer of such instruments for value. Compute the aggregate dollar amount realized upon vesting by multiplying the number of shares of stock or units by the market value of the underlying shares on the vesting date. For any amount realized upon exercise or vesting for which receipt has been deferred, provide a footnote quantifying the amount and disclosing the terms of the deferral.

(h) *Pension benefits.*

(1) Provide the information specified in paragraph (h)(2) of this Item with respect to each plan that provides for payments or other benefits at, following, or in connection with retirement, in the following tabular format:

PENSION BENEFITS

Name	Plan Name	Number of Years Credited Service (#)	Present Value of Accumulated Benefit ($)	Payments During Last Fiscal Year ($)
(a)	(b)	(c)	(d)	(e)
PEO				
PFO				
A				
B				
C				

(2) The Table shall include:

(i) The name of the executive officer (column (a));

(ii) The name of the plan (column (b));

(iii) The number of years of service credited to the named executive officer under the plan, computed as of the same pension plan measurement date used for financial statement reporting purposes with respect to the registrant's audited financial statements for the last completed fiscal year (column (c));

(iv) The actuarial present value of the named executive officer's accumulated benefit under the plan, computed as of the same pension plan measurement date used for financial statement reporting purposes with respect to the registrant's audited financial statements for the last completed fiscal year (column (d)); and

(v) The dollar amount of any payments and benefits paid to the named executive officer during the registrant's last completed fiscal year (column (e)).

Instructions to Item 402(h)(2).

1. The disclosure required pursuant to this Table applies to each plan that provides for specified retirement payments and benefits, or payments and benefits that will be provided primarily following retirement, including but not limited to tax-qualified defined benefit plans and supplemental executive retirement plans, but excluding tax-qualified defined contribution plans and nonqualified defined contribution plans. Provide a separate row for each such plan in which the named executive officer participates.

2. For purposes of the amount(s) reported in column (d), the registrant must use the same assumptions used for financial reporting purposes under generally accepted accounting principles, except that retirement age shall be assumed to be the normal retirement age as defined in the plan, or if not so defined, the earliest time at which a participant may retire under the plan without any benefit reduction due to age. The registrant must disclose in the accompanying textual narrative the valuation method and all material assumptions applied in quantifying the present value of the current accrued benefit. A benefit specified in the plan document or the executive's contract itself is not an assumption. Registrants may satisfy all or part of this disclosure by reference to a discussion of those assumptions in the registrant's financial statements, footnotes to the financial statements, or discussion in the Management's Discussion and Analysis. The sections so referenced are deemed part of the disclosure provided pursuant to this Item.

3. For purposes of allocating the current accrued benefit between tax qualified defined benefit plans and related supplemental plans, apply the limitations applicable to tax qualified defined benefit plans established by the Internal Revenue Code and the regulations thereunder that applied as of the pension plan measurement date.

4. If a named executive officer's number of years of credited service with respect to any plan is different from the named executive officer's number of actual years of service with the registrant, provide footnote disclosure quantifying the difference and any resulting benefit augmentation.

(3) Provide a succinct narrative description of any material factors necessary to an understanding of each plan covered by the tabular disclosure required by this paragraph. While material factors will vary depending upon the facts, examples of such factors may include, in given cases, among other things:

(i) The material terms and conditions of payments and benefits available under the plan, including the plan's normal retirement payment and benefit formula and eligibility standards, and the effect of the form of benefit elected on the amount of annual benefits. For this purpose, normal retirement means retirement at the normal retirement age as defined in the plan, or if not so defined, the earliest time at which a participant may retire under the plan without any benefit reduction due to age;

(ii) If any named executive officer is currently eligible for early retirement under any plan, identify that named executive officer and the plan, and describe the plan's early retirement payment and benefit formula and eligibility standards. For this purpose, early retirement means retirement at the early retirement age as defined in the plan, or otherwise available to the executive under the plan;

(iii) The specific elements of compensation (*e.g.*, salary, bonus, etc.) included in applying the payment and benefit formula, identifying each such element;

(iv) With respect to named executive officers' participation in multiple plans, the different purposes for each plan; and

(v) Registrant policies with regard to such matters as granting extra years of credited service.

(i) *Nonqualified defined contribution and other nonqualified deferred compensation plans.*

(1) Provide the information specified in paragraph (i)(2) of this Item with respect to each defined contribution or other plan that provides for the deferral of compensation on a basis that is not tax-qualified in the following tabular format:

NONQUALIFIED DEFERRED COMPENSATION

Name	Executive Contributions in Last FY ($)	Registrant Contributions in Last FY ($)	Aggregate Earnings in Last FY ($)	Aggregate Withdrawals/ Distributions ($)	Aggregate Balance at Last FYE ($)
(a)	(b)	(c)	(d)	(e)	(f)
PEO					
PFO					
A					
B					
C					

(2) The Table shall include:

(i) The name of the executive officer (column (a));

(ii) The dollar amount of aggregate executive contributions during the registrant's last fiscal year (column (b));

(iii) The dollar amount of aggregate registrant contributions during the registrant's last fiscal year (column (c));

(iv) The dollar amount of aggregate interest or other earnings accrued during the registrant's last fiscal year (column (d));

(v) The aggregate dollar amount of all withdrawals by and distributions to the executive during the registrant's last fiscal year (column (e)); and

(vi) The dollar amount of total balance of the executive's account as of the end of the registrant's last fiscal year (column (f)).

Instruction to Item 402(i)(2).

Provide a footnote quantifying the extent to which amounts reported in the contributions and earnings columns are reported as compensation in the last completed fiscal year in the registrant's Summary Compensation Table and amounts reported in the aggregate balance at last fiscal year end (column (f)) previously were reported as compensation to the named executive officer in the registrant's Summary Compensation Table for previous years.

(3) Provide a succinct narrative description of any material factors necessary to an understanding of each plan covered by tabular disclosure required by this paragraph. While material factors will vary depending upon the facts, examples of such factors may include, in given cases, among other things:

(i) The type(s) of compensation permitted to be deferred, and any limitations (by percentage of compensation or otherwise) on the extent to which deferral is permitted;

(ii) The measures for calculating interest or other plan earnings (including whether such measure(s) are selected by the executive or the registrant and the frequency and manner in which selections may be changed), quantifying interest rates and other earnings measures applicable during the registrant's last fiscal year; and

(iii) Material terms with respect to payouts, withdrawals and other distributions.

(j) *Potential payments upon termination or change-in-control.* Regarding each contract, agreement, plan or arrangement, whether written or unwritten, that provides for payment(s) to a named executive officer at, following, or in connection with any termination, including without limitation resignation, severance, retirement or a constructive termination of a named executive officer, or a change in control of the registrant or a change in the named executive officer's responsibilities, with respect to each named executive officer:

(1) Describe and explain the specific circumstances that would trigger payment(s) or the provision of other benefits, including perquisites and health care benefits;

(2) Describe and quantify the estimated payments and benefits that would be provided in each covered circumstance, whether they would or could be lump sum, or annual, disclosing the duration, and by whom they would be provided;

(3) Describe and explain how the appropriate payment and benefit levels are determined under the various circumstances that trigger payments or provision of benefits;

(4) Describe and explain any material conditions or obligations applicable to the receipt of payments or benefits, including but not limited to non-compete, nonsolicitation, non-disparagement or confidentiality agreements, including the duration of such agreements and provisions regarding waiver of breach of such agreements; and

(5) Describe any other material factors regarding each such contract, agreement, plan or arrangement.

Instructions to Item 402(j).

1. The registrant must provide quantitative disclosure under these requirements, applying the assumptions that the triggering event took place on the last business day of the registrant's last completed fiscal year, and the price per share of the registrant's securities is the closing market price as of that date. In the event that uncertainties exist as to the provision of payments and benefits or the amounts involved, the registrant is required to make a reasonable estimate (or a reasonable estimated range of amounts) applicable to the payment or benefit and disclose material assumptions underlying such estimates or estimated ranges in its disclosure. In such event, the disclosure would require forward-looking information as appropriate.

2. Perquisites and other personal benefits or property may be excluded only if the aggregate amount of such compensation will be less than $10,000. Individual perquisites and personal benefits shall be identified and quantified as required by Instruction 4 to paragraph (c)(2)(ix) of this Item. For purposes of quantifying health care benefits, the registrant must use the assumptions used for financial reporting purposes under generally accepted accounting principles.

3. To the extent that the form and amount of any payment or benefit that would be provided in connection with any triggering event is fully disclosed pursuant to paragraph (h) or (i) of this Item, reference may be made to that disclosure. However, to the extent that the form or amount of any such payment or benefit would be enhanced or its vesting or other provisions accelerated in connection with any triggering event, such enhancement or acceleration must be disclosed pursuant to this paragraph.

4. Where a triggering event has actually occurred for a named executive officer and that individual was not serving as a named executive officer of the registrant at the end of the last completed fiscal year, the disclosure required by this paragraph for that named executive officer shall apply only to that triggering event.

5. The registrant need not provide information with respect to contracts, agreements, plans or arrangements to the extent they do not discriminate in scope, terms or operation, in favor of executive officers of the registrant and that are available generally to all salaried employees.

(k) *Compensation of directors.*

(1) Provide the information specified in paragraph (k)(2) of this Item, concerning the compensation of the directors for the registrant's last completed fiscal year, in the following tabular format:

DIRECTOR COMPENSATION

Name	Fees Earned or Paid in Cash ($)	Stock Awards ($)	Option Awards ($)	Non-Equity Incentive Plan Compensation ($)	Change in Pension Value and Nonqualified Deferred Compensation Earnings	All Other Compensation ($)	Total ($)
(a)	(b)	(c)	(d)	(e)	(f)	(g)	(h)
A							
B							
C							
D							
E							

(2) The Table shall include:

(i) The name of each director unless such director is also a named executive officer under paragraph (a) of this Item and his or her compensation for service as a director is fully reflected in the Summary Compensation Table pursuant to paragraph (c) of this Item and otherwise as required pursuant to paragraphs (d) through (j) of this Item (column (a));

(ii) The aggregate dollar amount of all fees earned or paid in cash for services as a director, including annual retainer fees, committee and/or chairmanship fees, and meeting fees (column (b));

(iii) For awards of stock, the aggregate grant date fair value computed in accordance with FASB ASC Topic 718 (column (c));

(iv) For awards of options, with or without tandem SARs (including awards that subsequently have been transferred), the aggregate grant date fair value computed in accordance with FASB ASC Topic 718 (column (d));

Instruction to Item 402(k)(2)(iii) and (iv).

For each director, disclose by footnote to the appropriate column: the grant date fair value of each equity award computed in accordance with FAS 123R; for each option, SAR or similar option like instrument for which the registrant has adjusted or amended the exercise or base price during the last completed fiscal year, whether through amendment, cancellation or replacement grants, or any other means ("repriced"), or otherwise has materially modified such awards, the incremental fair value, computed as of the repricing or modification date in accordance with FAS 123R; and the aggregate number of stock awards and the aggregate number of option awards outstanding at fiscal year end. However, the disclosure required by this Instruction does not apply to any repricing that occurs through a pre-existing formula or mechanism in the plan or award that results in the periodic adjustment of the option or SAR exercise or base price, an antidilution provision in a plan or award, or a recapitalization or similar transaction equally affecting all holders of the class of securities underlying the options or SARs.

(v) The dollar value of all earnings for services performed during the fiscal year pursuant to non-equity incentive plans as defined in paragraph (a)(6)(iii) of this Item, and all earnings on any outstanding awards (column (e));

(vi) The sum of the amounts specified in paragraphs (k)(2)(vi)(A) and (B) of this Item (column (f)) as follows:

(A) The aggregate change in the actuarial present value of the director's accumulated benefit under all defined benefit and actuarial pension plans (including supplemental plans) from the pension plan measurement date used for financial statement reporting purposes with respect to the registrant's audited financial statements for the prior completed fiscal year to the pension plan measurement date used for financial statement reporting purposes with respect to the registrant's audited financial statements for the covered fiscal year; and

(B) Above-market or preferential earnings on compensation that is deferred on a basis that is not tax-qualified, including such earnings on nonqualified defined contribution plans;

(vii) All other compensation for the covered fiscal year that the registrant could not properly report in any other column of the Director Compensation Table (column (g)). Each compensation item that is not properly reportable in columns (b) - (f), regardless of the amount of the compensation item, must be included in column (g). Such compensation must include, but is not limited to:

(A) Perquisites and other personal benefits, or property, unless the aggregate amount of such compensation is less than $10,000;

(B) All "gross-ups" or other amounts reimbursed during the fiscal year for the payment of taxes;

(C) For any security of the registrant or its subsidiaries purchased from the registrant or its subsidiaries (through deferral of salary or bonus, or otherwise) at a discount from the market price of such security at the date of purchase, unless that discount is available generally, either to all security holders or to all salaried employees of the registrant, the compensation cost, if any, computed in accordance with FAS 123R;

(D) The amount paid or accrued to any director pursuant to a plan or arrangement in connection with:

(1) The resignation, retirement or any other termination of such director; or

(2) A change in control of the registrant;

(E) Registrant contributions or other allocations to vested and unvested defined contribution plans;

(F) Consulting fees earned from, or paid or payable by the registrant and/or its subsidiaries (including joint ventures);

(G) The annual costs of payments and promises of payments pursuant to director legacy programs and similar charitable award programs;

(H) The dollar value of any insurance premiums paid by, or on behalf of, the registrant during the covered fiscal year with respect to life insurance for the benefit of a director; and

(I) The dollar value of any dividends or other earnings paid on stock or option awards, when those amounts were not factored into the grant date fair value required to be reported for the stock or option award in column (c) or (d); and

Instructions to Item 402(k)(2)(vii).

1. Programs in which registrants agree to make donations to one or more charitable institutions in a director's name, payable by the registrant currently or upon a designated event, such as the retirement or death of the director, are charitable awards programs or director legacy programs for purposes of the disclosure required by paragraph (k)(2)(vii)(G) of this Item. Provide footnote disclosure of the total dollar amount payable under the program and other material terms of each such program for which tabular disclosure is provided.

2. Any item reported for a director pursuant to paragraph (k)(2)(vii) of this Item that is not a perquisite or personal benefit and whose value exceeds $10,000 must be identified and quantified in a footnote to column (g). All items of compensation are required to be included in the Director Compensation Table without regard to whether such items are required to be identified other than as specifically noted in this Item.

3. Perquisites and personal benefits may be excluded as long as the total value of all perquisites and personal benefits for a director is less than $10,000. If the total value of all perquisites and personal benefits is $10,000 or more for any director, then each perquisite or personal benefit, regardless of its amount, must be identified by type. If perquisites and personal benefits are required to be reported for a director pursuant to this rule, then each perquisite or personal benefit that exceeds the greater of $25,000 or 10% of the total amount of perquisites and personal benefits for that director must be quantified and disclosed in a footnote. Perquisites and other personal benefits shall be valued on the basis of the aggregate incremental cost to the registrant. With respect to the perquisite or other personal benefit for which footnote quantification is required, the registrant shall describe in the footnote its methodology for computing the aggregate incremental cost. Reimbursements of taxes owed with respect to perquisites or other personal benefits must be included in column (g) and are subject to separate quantification and identification as tax reimbursements (paragraph (k)(2)(vii)(B) of this Item) even if the associated perquisites or other personal benefits are not required to be included because the total amount of all perquisites or personal benefits for an individual director is less than $10,000 or are required to be identified but are not required to be separately quantified.

(viii) The dollar value of total compensation for the covered fiscal year (column (h)). With respect to each director, disclose the sum of all amounts reported in columns (b) through (g).

Instruction to Item 402(k)(2).

Two or more directors may be grouped in a single row in the Table if all elements of their compensation are identical. The names of the directors for whom disclosure is presented on a group basis should be clear from the Table.

(3) *Narrative to director compensation table.*

Provide a narrative description of any material factors necessary to an understanding of the director compensation disclosed in this Table. While material factors will vary depending upon the facts, examples of such factors may include, in given cases, among other things:

(i) A description of standard compensation arrangements (such as fees for retainer, committee service, service as chairman of the board or a committee, and meeting attendance); and

(ii) Whether any director has a different compensation arrangement, identifying that director and describing the terms of that arrangement.

Instruction to Item 402(k).

In addition to the Instruction to paragraphs (k)(2)(iii) and (iv) and the Instructions to paragraph (k)(2)(vii) of this Item, the following apply equally to paragraph (k) of this Item: Instructions 2 and 4 to paragraph (c) of this Item; Instructions to paragraphs (c)(2)(iii) and (iv) of this Item; Instructions to paragraphs (c)(2)(v) and (vi) of this Item; Instructions to paragraph (c)(2)(vii) of this Item; Instructions to paragraph (c)(2)(viii) of this Item; and Instructions 1 and 5 to paragraph (c)(2)(ix) of this Item. These Instructions apply to the columns in the Director Compensation Table that are analogous to the columns in the Summary Compensation Table to which they refer and to disclosures under paragraph (k) of this Item that correspond to analogous disclosures provided for in paragraph (c) of this Item to which they refer.

(*l*) *Smaller reporting companies.* A registrant that qualifies as a "smaller reporting company," as defined by Item 10(f) (§ 229.10(f)(1)), may provide the scaled disclosure in paragraphs (m) through (r) instead of paragraphs (a) through (k) and (s) of this Item.

(m) *Smaller reporting companies - General*

(1) *All compensation covered.* This Item requires clear, concise and understandable disclosure of all plan and non-plan compensation awarded to, earned by, or paid to the named executive officers designated under paragraph (m)(2) of this Item, and directors covered by paragraph (r) of this Item, by any person for all services rendered in all capacities to the smaller reporting company and its subsidiaries, unless otherwise specifically excluded from disclosure in this Item. All such compensation shall be reported pursuant to this Item, even if also called for by another requirement, including transactions between the smaller reporting company and a third party where a purpose of the transaction is to furnish compensation to any such named executive officer or director. No amount reported as compensation for one fiscal year need be reported in the same manner as compensation for a subsequent fiscal year; amounts reported as compensation for one fiscal year may be required to be reported in a different manner pursuant to this Item.

(2) *Persons covered.* Disclosure shall be provided pursuant to this Item for each of the following (the "named executive officers"):

(i) All individuals serving as the smaller reporting company's principal executive officer or acting in a similar capacity during the last completed fiscal year ("PEO"), regardless of compensation level;

(ii) The smaller reporting company's two most highly compensated executive officers other than the PEO who were serving as executive officers at the end of the last completed fiscal year; and

(iii) Up to two additional individuals for whom disclosure would have been provided pursuant to paragraph (m)(2)(ii) of this Item but for the fact that the individual was not serving as an executive officer of the smaller reporting company at the end of the last completed fiscal year.

Instructions to Item 402(m)(2).

1. *Determination of most highly compensated executive officers.* The determination as to which executive officers are most highly compensated shall be made by reference to total compensation for the last completed fiscal year (as required to be disclosed pursuant to paragraph (n)(2)(x) of this Item) reduced by the amount required to be disclosed pursuant to paragraph (n)(2)(viii) of this Item, *provided, however,* that no disclosure need be provided for any executive officer, other than the PEO, whose total compensation, as so reduced, does not exceed $100,000.

2. *Inclusion of executive officer of a subsidiary.* It may be appropriate for a smaller reporting company to include as named executive officers one or more executive officers or other employees of subsidiaries in the disclosure required by this Item. See Rule 3b-7 under the Exchange Act (17 CFR 240.3b-7).

3. *Exclusion of executive officer due to overseas compensation.* It may be appropriate in limited circumstances for a smaller reporting company not to include in the disclosure required by this Item an individual, other than its PEO, who is one of the smaller reporting company's most highly compensated executive officers due to the payment of amounts of cash compensation relating to overseas assignments attributed predominantly to such assignments.

(3) *Information for full fiscal year.* If the PEO served in that capacity during any part of a fiscal year with respect to which information is required, information should be provided as to all of his or her compensation for the full fiscal year. If a named executive officer (other than the PEO) served as an executive officer of the smaller reporting company (whether or not in the same position) during any part of the fiscal year with respect to which information is required, information shall be provided as to all compensation of that individual for the full fiscal year.

(4) *Omission of table or column.* A table or column may be omitted if there has been no compensation awarded to, earned by, or paid to any of the named executive officers or directors required to be reported in that table or column in any fiscal year covered by that table.

(5) *Definitions.* For purposes of this Item:

(i) The term *stock* means instruments such as common stock, restricted stock, restricted stock units, phantom stock, phantom stock units, common stock equivalent units or any similar instruments that do not have option-like features, and the term *option* means instruments such as stock options, stock appreciation rights and similar instruments with option-like features. The term *stock appreciation rights* ("*SARs*") refers to SARs payable in cash or stock, including SARs payable in cash or stock at the election of the smaller reporting company or a named executive officer. The term *equity* is used to refer generally to stock and/or options.

(ii) The term *plan* includes, but is not limited to, the following: Any plan, contract, authorization or arrangement, whether or not set forth in any formal document, pursuant to which cash, securities, similar instruments, or any other property may be received. A plan may be applicable to one person. Smaller reporting companies may omit information regarding group life, health, hospitalization, or medical reimbursement plans that do not discriminate in scope, terms or operation, in favor of executive officers or directors of the smaller reporting company and that are available generally to all salaried employees.

(iii) The term *incentive plan* means any plan providing compensation intended to serve as incentive for performance to occur over a specified period, whether such performance is measured by reference to financial performance of the smaller reporting company or an affiliate, the smaller reporting company's stock price, or any other performance measure. An equity incentive plan is an incentive plan or portion of an incentive plan under which awards are granted that fall within the scope of Financial Accounting Standards Board Statement of Financial Accounting Standards No. 123 (revised 2004), *Share-Based Payment*, as modified or supplemented ("FAS 123R"). A *non-equity incentive plan* is an incentive plan or portion of an incentive plan that is not an equity incentive plan. The term *incentive plan award* means an award provided under an incentive plan.

(iv) The terms *date of grant* or *grant date* refer to the grant date determined for financial statement reporting purposes pursuant to FAS 123R.

(v) *Closing market price* is defined as the price at which the smaller reporting company's security was last sold in the principal United States market for such security as of the date for which the closing market price is determined.

(n) *Smaller reporting companies - Summary compensation table* (1) *General.* Provide the information specified in paragraph (n)(2) of this Item, concerning the compensation of the named executive officers for each of the smaller reporting company's last two completed fiscal years, in a Summary Compensation Table in the tabular format specified below.

Summary Compensation Table

Name and principal position	Year	Salary ($)	Bonus ($)	Stock awards ($)	Option awards ($)	Nonequity incentive plan compensation ($)	Nonqualified deferred compensation earnings ($)	All other compensation ($)	Total ($)
(a)	(b)	(c)	(d)	(e)	(f)	(g)	(h)	(i)	(j)
PEO									
A									
B									

(2) The Table shall include:

(i) The name and principal position of the named executive officer (column (a));

(ii) The fiscal year covered (column (b));

(iii) The dollar value of base salary (cash and non-cash) earned by the named executive officer during the fiscal year covered (column (c));

(iv) The dollar value of bonus (cash and non-cash) earned by the named executive officer during the fiscal year covered (column (d));

Instructions to Item 402(n)(2)(iii) and (iv).

1. If the amount of salary or bonus earned in a given fiscal year is not calculable through the latest practicable date, a footnote shall be included disclosing that the amount of salary or bonus is not calculable through the latest practicable date and providing the date that the amount of salary or bonus is expected to be determined, and such amount must then be disclosed in a filing under Item 5.02(f) of Form 8-K (17 CFR 249.308).

2. Smaller reporting companies shall include in the salary column (column (c)) or bonus column (column (d)) any amount of salary or bonus forgone at the election of a named executive officer under which stock, equity-based or other forms of non-cash compensation instead have been received by the named executive officer. However, the receipt of any such form of non-cash compensation instead of salary or bonus must be disclosed in a footnote added to the salary or bonus column and, where applicable, referring to the narrative disclosure to the Summary Compensation Table (required by paragraph (o) of this Item) where the material terms of the stock, option or non-equity incentive plan award elected by the named executive officer are reported.

(v) For awards of stock, the aggregate grant date fair value computed in accordance with FASB ASC Topic 718 (column (e));

(vi) For awards of options, with or without tandem SARs (including awards that subsequently have been transferred), the aggregate grant date fair value computed in accordance with FASB ASC Topic 718 (column (f));

Instruction 1 to Item 402(n)(2)(v) and (n)(2)(vi). For awards reported in columns (e) and (f), include a footnote disclosing all assumptions made in the valuation by reference to a discussion of those assumptions in the smaller reporting company's financial statements, footnotes to the financial statements, or discussion in the Management's Discussion and Analysis. The sections so referenced are deemed part of the disclosure provided pursuant to this Item.

Instruction 2 to Item 402(n)(2)(v) and (n)(2)(vi). If at any time during the last completed fiscal year, the smaller reporting company has adjusted or amended the exercise price of options or SARs previously awarded to a named executive officer, whether through amendment, cancellation or replacement grants, or any other means ("repriced"), or otherwise has materially modified such awards, the smaller reporting company shall include, as awards required to be reported in column (f), the incremental fair value, computed as of the repricing or modification date in accordance with FASB ASC Topic 718, with respect to that repriced or modified award.

Instruction 3 to Item 402(n)(2)(v) and (vi). For any awards that are subject to performance conditions, report the value at the grant date based upon the probable outcome of such conditions. This amount should be consistent with the estimate of aggregate compensation cost to be recognized over the service period determined as of the grant date under FASB ASC Topic 718, excluding the effect of estimated forfeitures. In a footnote to the table, disclose the value of the award at the grant date assuming that the highest level of performance conditions will be achieved if an amount less than the maximum was included in the table.

(vii) The dollar value of all earnings for services performed during the fiscal year pursuant to awards under non-equity incentive plans as defined in paragraph (m)(5)(iii) of this Item, and all earnings on any outstanding awards (column (g));

Instructions to Item 402(n)(2)(vii).

1. If the relevant performance measure is satisfied during the fiscal year (including for a single year in a plan with a multi-year performance measure), the earnings are reportable for that fiscal year, even if not payable until a later date, and are not reportable again in the fiscal year when amounts are paid to the named executive officer.

2. All earnings on non-equity incentive plan compensation must be identified and quantified in a footnote to column (g), whether the earnings were paid during the fiscal year, payable during the period but deferred at the election of the named executive officer, or payable by their terms at a later date.

(viii) Above-market or preferential earnings on compensation that is deferred on a basis that is not tax-qualified, including such earnings on nonqualified defined contribution plans (column (h));

Instruction to Item 402(n)(2)(viii). Interest on deferred compensation is above-market only if the rate of interest exceeds 120% of the applicable federal long-term rate, with compounding (as prescribed under section 1274(d) of the Internal Revenue Code, (26 U.S.C. 1274(d))) at the rate that corresponds most closely to the rate under the smaller reporting company's plan at the time the interest rate or formula is set. In the event of a discretionary reset of the interest rate, the requisite calculation must be made on the basis of the interest rate at the time of such reset, rather than when originally established. Only the above-market portion of the interest must be included. If the applicable interest rates vary depending upon conditions such as a minimum period of continued service, the reported amount should be calculated assuming satisfaction of all conditions to receiving interest at the highest rate. Dividends (and dividend equivalents) on deferred compensation denominated in the smaller reporting company's stock ("deferred stock") are preferential only if earned at a rate higher than dividends on the smaller reporting company's common stock. Only the preferential portion of the dividends or equivalents must be included. Footnote or narrative disclosure may be provided explaining the smaller reporting company's criteria for determining any portion considered to be above-market.

(ix) All other compensation for the covered fiscal year that the smaller reporting company could not properly report in any other column of the Summary Compensation Table (column (i)). Each compensation item that is not properly reportable in columns (c) through (h), regardless of the amount of the compensation item, must be included in column (i). Such compensation must include, but is not limited to:

(A) Perquisites and other personal benefits, or property, unless the aggregate amount of such compensation is less than $10,000;

(B) All "gross-ups" or other amounts reimbursed during the fiscal year for the payment of taxes;

(C) For any security of the smaller reporting company or its subsidiaries purchased from the smaller reporting company or its subsidiaries (through deferral of salary or bonus, or otherwise) at a discount from the market price of such security at the date of purchase, unless that discount is available generally, either to all security holders or to all salaried employees of the smaller reporting company, the compensation cost, if any, computed in accordance with FAS 123R;

(D) The amount paid or accrued to any named executive officer pursuant to a plan or arrangement in connection with:

(1) Any termination, including without limitation through retirement, resignation, severance or constructive termination (including a change in responsibilities) of such executive officer's employment with the smaller reporting company and its subsidiaries; or

(2) A change in control of the smaller reporting company;

(E) Smaller reporting company contributions or other allocations to vested and unvested defined contribution plans;

(F) The dollar value of any insurance premiums paid by, or on behalf of, the smaller reporting company during the covered fiscal year with respect to life insurance for the benefit of a named executive officer; and

(G) The dollar value of any dividends or other earnings paid on stock or option awards, when those amounts were not factored into the grant date fair value required to be reported for the stock or option award in column (e) or (f).

Instructions to Item 402(n)(2)(ix).

1. Non-equity incentive plan awards and earnings and earnings on stock or options, except as specified in paragraph (n)(2)(ix)(G) of this Item, are required to be reported elsewhere as provided in this Item and are not reportable as All Other Compensation in column (i).

2. Benefits paid pursuant to defined benefit and actuarial plans are not reportable as All Other Compensation in column (i) unless accelerated pursuant to a change in control; information concerning these plans is reportable pursuant to paragraph (q)(1) of this Item.

3. Reimbursements of taxes owed with respect to perquisites or other personal benefits must be included in the columns as tax reimbursements (paragraph (n)(2)(ix)(B) of this Item) even if the associated perquisites or other personal benefits are not required to be included because the aggregate amount of such compensation is less than $10,000.

4. Perquisites and other personal benefits shall be valued on the basis of the aggregate incremental cost to the smaller reporting company.

5. For purposes of paragraph (n)(2)(ix)(D) of this Item, an accrued amount is an amount for which payment has become due.

(x) The dollar value of total compensation for the covered fiscal year (column (j)). With respect to each named executive officer, disclose the sum of all amounts reported in columns (c) through (i).

Instructions to Item 402(n).

1. Information with respect to the fiscal year prior to the last completed fiscal year will not be required if the smaller reporting company was not a reporting company pursuant to section 13(a) or 15(d) of the Exchange Act (15 U.S.C. 78m(a) or 78o(d)) at any time during that year, except that the smaller reporting company will be required to provide information for any such year if that information previously was required to be provided in response to a Commission filing requirement.

2. All compensation values reported in the Summary Compensation Table must be reported in dollars and rounded to the nearest dollar. Reported compensation values must be reported numerically, providing a single numerical value for each grid in the table. Where compensation was paid to or received by a named executive officer in a different currency, a footnote must be provided to identify that currency and describe the rate and methodology used to convert the payment amounts to dollars.

3. If a named executive officer is also a director who receives compensation for his or her services as a director, reflect that compensation in the Summary Compensation Table and provide a footnote

identifying and itemizing such compensation and amounts. Use the categories in the Director Compensation Table required pursuant to paragraph (r) of this Item.

4. Any amounts deferred, whether pursuant to a plan established under section 401(k) of the Internal Revenue Code (26 U.S.C. 401(k)), or otherwise, shall be included in the appropriate column for the fiscal year in which earned.

(o) *Smaller reporting companies - Narrative disclosure to summary compensation table.* Provide a narrative description of any material factors necessary to an understanding of the information disclosed in the Table required by paragraph (n) of this Item. Examples of such factors may include, in given cases, among other things:

(1) The material terms of each named executive officer's employment agreement or arrangement, whether written or unwritten;

(2) If at any time during the last fiscal year, any outstanding option or other equity-based award was repriced or otherwise materially modified (such as by extension of exercise periods, the change of vesting or forfeiture conditions, the change or elimination of applicable performance criteria, or the change of the bases upon which returns are determined), a description of each such repricing or other material modification;

(3) The waiver or modification of any specified performance target, goal or condition to payout with respect to any amount included in non-stock incentive plan compensation or payouts reported in column (g) to the Summary Compensation Table required by paragraph (n) of this Item, stating whether the waiver or modification applied to one or more specified named executive officers or to all compensation subject to the target, goal or condition;

(4) The material terms of each grant, including but not limited to the date of exercisability, any conditions to exercisability, any tandem feature, any reload feature, any tax-reimbursement feature, and any provision that could cause the exercise price to be lowered;

(5) The material terms of any non-equity incentive plan award made to a named executive officer during the last completed fiscal year, including a general description of the formula or criteria to be applied in determining the amounts payable and vesting schedule;

(6) The method of calculating earnings on nonqualified deferred compensation plans including nonqualified defined contribution plans; and

(7) An identification to the extent material of any item included under All Other Compensation (column (i)) in the Summary Compensation Table. Identification of an item shall not be considered material if it does not exceed the greater of $25,000 or 10% of all items included in the specified category in question set forth in paragraph (n)(2)(ix) of this Item. All items of compensation are required to be included in the Summary Compensation Table without regard to whether such items are required to be identified.

Instruction to Item 402(o). The disclosure required by paragraph (o)(2) of this Item would not apply to any repricing that occurs through a pre-existing formula or mechanism in the plan or award that results in the periodic adjustment of the option or SAR exercise or base price, an antidilution provision in a plan or award, or a recapitalization or similar transaction equally affecting all holders of the class of securities underlying the options or SARs.

(p) *Smaller reporting companies - Outstanding equity awards at fiscal year-end table.* (1) Provide the information specified in paragraph (p)(2) of this Item, concerning unexercised options; stock that has not vested; and equity incentive plan awards for each named executive officer outstanding as of the end of the smaller reporting company's last completed fiscal year in the following tabular format:

Outstanding Equity Awards at Fiscal Year-End

| | Option awards | | | | | Stock awards | | | |
Name	Number of securities underlying unexercised options (#) exercisable	Number of securities underlying unexercised options (#) unexercisable	Equity incentive plan awards: Number of securities underlying unexercised unearned options (#)	Option exercise price ($)	Option expiration date	Number of shares or units of stock that have not vested (#)	Market value of shares of units of stock that have not vested ($)	Equity incentive plan awards: Number of unearned shares, units or other rights that have not vested (#)	Equity incentive plan awards: Market or payout value of unearned shares, units or other rights that have not vested ($)
(a)	(b)	(c)	(d)	(e)	(f)	(g)	(h)	(i)	(j)
PEO									
A									
B									

(2) The Table shall include:

(i) The name of the named executive officer (column (a));

(ii) On an award-by-award basis, the number of securities underlying unexercised options, including awards that have been transferred other than for value, that are exercisable and that are not reported in column (d) (column (b));

(iii) On an award-by-award basis, the number of securities underlying unexercised options, including awards that have been transferred other than for value, that are unexercisable and that are not reported in column (d) (column (c));

(iv) On an award-by-award basis, the total number of shares underlying unexercised options awarded under any equity incentive plan that have not been earned (column (d));

(v) For each instrument reported in columns (b), (c) and (d), as applicable, the exercise or base price (column (e));

(vi) For each instrument reported in columns (b), (c) and (d), as applicable, the expiration date (column (f));

(vii) The total number of shares of stock that have not vested and that are not reported in column (i) (column (g));

(viii) The aggregate market value of shares of stock that have not vested and that are not reported in column (j) (column (h));

(ix) The total number of shares of stock, units or other rights awarded under any equity incentive plan that have not vested and that have not been earned, and, if applicable the number of shares underlying any such unit or right (column (i)); and

(x) The aggregate market or payout value of shares of stock, units or other rights awarded under any equity incentive plan that have not vested and that have not been earned (column (j)).

Instructions to Item 402(p)(2).

1. Identify by footnote any award that has been transferred other than for value, disclosing the nature of the transfer.

2. The vesting dates of options, shares of stock and equity incentive plan awards held at fiscal-year end must be disclosed by footnote to the applicable column where the outstanding award is reported.

3. Compute the market value of stock reported in column (h) and equity incentive plan awards of stock reported in column (j) by multiplying the closing market price of the smaller reporting company's stock at the end of the last completed fiscal year by the number of shares or units of stock or the amount of equity incentive plan awards, respectively. The number of shares or units reported in column (d) or

(i), and the payout value reported in column (j), shall be based on achieving threshold performance goals, except that if the previous fiscal year's performance has exceeded the threshold, the disclosure shall be based on the next higher performance measure (target or maximum) that exceeds the previous fiscal year's performance. If the award provides only for a single estimated payout, that amount should be reported. If the target amount is not determinable, smaller reporting companies must provide a representative amount based on the previous fiscal year's performance.

4. Multiple awards may be aggregated where the expiration date and the exercise and/or base price of the instruments is identical. A single award consisting of a combination of options, SARs and/or similar option-like instruments shall be reported as separate awards with respect to each tranche with a different exercise and/or base price or expiration date.

5. Options or stock awarded under an equity incentive plan are reported in columns (d) or (i) and (j), respectively, until the relevant performance condition has been satisfied. Once the relevant performance condition has been satisfied, even if the option or stock award is subject to forfeiture conditions, options are reported in column (b) or (c), as appropriate, until they are exercised or expire, or stock is reported in columns (g) and (h) until it vests.

(q) *Smaller reporting companies - Additional narrative disclosure.* Provide a narrative description of the following to the extent material:

(1) The material terms of each plan that provides for the payment of retirement benefits, or benefits that will be paid primarily following retirement, including but not limited to tax-qualified defined benefit plans, supplemental executive retirement plans, tax-qualified defined contribution plans and nonqualified defined contribution plans.

(2) The material terms of each contract, agreement, plan or arrangement, whether written or unwritten, that provides for payment(s) to a named executive officer at, following, or in connection with the resignation, retirement or other termination of a named executive officer, or a change in control of the smaller reporting company or a change in the named executive officer's responsibilities following a change in control, with respect to each named executive officer.

(r) *Smaller reporting companies - Compensation of directors.* (1) Provide the information specified in paragraph (r)(2) of this Item, concerning the compensation of the directors for the smaller reporting company's last completed fiscal year, in the following tabular format:

Director Compensation

Name	Fees earned or paid in cash ($)	Stock awards ($)	Option awards ($)	Non-equity incentive plan compensation ($)	Nonqualified deferred compensation earnings ($)	All other compensation ($)	Total ($)
(a)	(b)	(c)	(d)	(e)	(f)	(g)	(h)
A							
B							
C							
D							
E							

(2) The Table shall include:

(i) The name of each director unless such director is also a named executive officer under paragraph (m) of this Item and his or her compensation for service as a director is fully reflected in the Summary Compensation Table pursuant to paragraph (n) of this Item and otherwise as required pursuant to paragraphs (o) through (q) of this Item (column (a));

(ii) The aggregate dollar amount of all fees earned or paid in cash for services as a director, including annual retainer fees, committee and/or chairmanship fees, and meeting fees (column (b));

(iii) For awards of stock, the aggregate grant date fair value computed in accordance with FASB ASC Topic 718 (column (c));

(iv) For awards of options, with or without tandem SARs (including awards that subsequently have been transferred), the aggregate grant date fair value computed in accordance with FASB ASC Topic 718 (column (d));

Instruction to Item 402(r)(2)(iii) and (iv). For each director, disclose by footnote to the appropriate column, the aggregate number of stock awards and the aggregate number of option awards outstanding at fiscal year end.

(v) The dollar value of all earnings for services performed during the fiscal year pursuant to non-equity incentive plans as defined in paragraph (m)(5)(iii) of this Item, and all earnings on any outstanding awards (column (e));

(vi) Above-market or preferential earnings on compensation that is deferred on a basis that is not tax-qualified, including such earnings on nonqualified defined contribution plans (column (f));

(vii) All other compensation for the covered fiscal year that the smaller reporting company could not properly report in any other column of the Director Compensation Table (column (g)). Each compensation item that is not properly reportable in columns (b) through (f), regardless of the amount of the compensation item, must be included in column (g) and must be identified and quantified in a footnote if it is deemed material in accordance with paragraph (o)(7) of this Item. Such compensation must include, but is not limited to:

(A) Perquisites and other personal benefits, or property, unless the aggregate amount of such compensation is less than $10,000;

(B) All "gross-ups" or other amounts reimbursed during the fiscal year for the payment of taxes;

(C) For any security of the smaller reporting company or its subsidiaries purchased from the smaller reporting company or its subsidiaries (through deferral of salary or bonus, or otherwise) at a discount from the market price of such security at the date of purchase, unless that discount is available generally, either to all security holders or to all salaried employees of the smaller reporting company, the compensation cost, if any, computed in accordance with FAS 123R;

(D) The amount paid or accrued to any director pursuant to a plan or arrangement in connection with:

(*1*) The resignation, retirement or any other termination of such director; or

(*2*) A change in control of the smaller reporting company;

(E) Smaller reporting company contributions or other allocations to vested and unvested defined contribution plans;

(F) Consulting fees earned from, or paid or payable by the smaller reporting company and/or its subsidiaries (including joint ventures);

(G) The annual costs of payments and promises of payments pursuant to director legacy programs and similar charitable award programs;

(H) The dollar value of any insurance premiums paid by, or on behalf of, the smaller reporting company during the covered fiscal year with respect to life insurance for the benefit of a director; and

(I) The dollar value of any dividends or other earnings paid on stock or option awards, when those amounts were not factored into the grant date fair value required to be reported for the stock or option award in column (c) or (d); and

Instruction to Item 402(r)(2)(vii). Programs in which smaller reporting companies agree to make donations to one or more charitable institutions in a director's name, payable by the smaller reporting company currently or upon a designated event, such as the retirement or death of the director, are charitable awards programs or director legacy programs for purposes of the disclosure required by paragraph (r)(2)(vii)(G) of this Item. Provide footnote disclosure of the total dollar amount payable under the program and other material terms of each such program for which tabular disclosure is provided.

(viii) The dollar value of total compensation for the covered fiscal year (column (h)). With respect to each director, disclose the sum of all amounts reported in columns (b) through (g).

Instruction to Item 402(r)(2). Two or more directors may be grouped in a single row in the Table if all elements of their compensation are identical. The names of the directors for whom disclosure is presented on a group basis should be clear from the Table.

(3) *Narrative to director compensation table.* Provide a narrative description of any material factors necessary to an understanding of the director compensation disclosed in this Table. While material factors will vary depending upon the facts, examples of such factors may include, in given cases, among other things:

(i) A description of standard compensation arrangements (such as fees for retainer, committee service, service as chairman of the board or a committee, and meeting attendance); and

(ii) Whether any director has a different compensation arrangement, identifying that director and describing the terms of that arrangement.

Instruction to Item 402(r). In addition to the Instruction to paragraph (r)(2)(vii) of this Item, the following apply equally to paragraph (r) of this Item: Instructions 2 and 4 to paragraph (n) of this Item; the Instructions to paragraphs (n)(2)(iii) and (iv) of this Item; the Instructions to paragraphs (n)(2)(v) and (vi) of this Item; the Instructions to paragraph (n)(2)(vii) of this Item; the Instruction to paragraph (n)(2)(viii) of this Item; the Instructions to paragraph (n)(2)(ix) of this Item; and paragraph (o)(7) of this Item. These Instructions apply to the columns in the Director Compensation Table that are analogous to the columns in the Summary Compensation Table to which they refer and to disclosures under paragraph (r) of this Item that correspond to analogous disclosures provided for in paragraph (n) of this Item to which they refer.

(s) *Narrative disclosure of the registrant's compensation policies and practices as they relate to the registrant's risk management.* To the extent that risks arising from the registrant's compensation policies and practices for its employees are reasonably likely to have a material adverse effect on the registrant, discuss the registrant's policies and practices of compensating its employees, including non-executive officers, as they relate to risk management practices and risk-taking incentives. While the situations requiring disclosure will vary depending on the particular registrant and compensation policies and practices, situations that may trigger disclosure include, among others, compensation policies and practices: at a business unit of the company that carries a significant portion of the registrant's risk profile; at a business unit with compensation structured significantly differently than other units within the registrant; at a business unit that is significantly more profitable than others within the registrant; at a business unit where compensation expense is a significant percentage of the unit's revenues; and that vary significantly from the overall risk and reward structure of the registrant, such as when bonuses are awarded upon accomplishment of a task, while the income and risk to the registrant from the task extend over a significantly longer period of time. The purpose of this paragraph (s) is to provide investors material information concerning how the registrant compensates and incentivizes its employees that may create risks that are reasonably likely to have a material adverse effect on the registrant. While the information to be disclosed pursuant to this paragraph (s) will vary depending upon the nature of the registrant's business and the compensation approach, the following are examples of the issues that the registrant may need to address for the business units or employees discussed:

(1) The general design philosophy of the registrant's compensation policies and practices for employees whose behavior would be most affected by the incentives established by the policies and practices, as such policies and practices relate to or affect risk taking by employees on behalf of the registrant, and the manner of their implementation;

(2) The registrant's risk assessment or incentive considerations, if any, in structuring its compensation policies and practices or in awarding and paying compensation;

(3) How the registrant's compensation policies and practices relate to the realization of risks resulting from the actions of employees in both the short term and the long term, such as through policies requiring claw backs or imposing holding periods;

(4) The registrant's policies regarding adjustments to its compensation policies and practices to address changes in its risk profile;

(5) Material adjustments the registrant has made to its compensation policies and practices as a result of changes in its risk profile; and

(6) The extent to which the registrant monitors its compensation policies and practices to determine whether its risk management objectives are being met with respect to incentivizing its employees.

Instruction to Item 402. Specify the applicable fiscal year in the title to each table required under this Item which calls for disclosure as of or for a completed fiscal year.

[As last amended in Release No. 33-9089, effective February 28, 2010, 74 F.R. 68334.]

[¶ 13,043] Security Ownership of Certain Beneficial Owners and Management

Reg. § 229.403. Item 403. (a) *Security ownership of certain beneficial owners.* Furnish the following information, as of the most recent practicable date, in substantially the tabular form indicated, with respect to any person (including any "group" as that term is used in section 13(d)(3) of the Exchange Act) who is known to the registrant to be the beneficial owner of more than five percent of any class of the registrant's voting securities. The address given in column (2) may be a business, mailing or residence address. Show in column (3) the total number of shares beneficially owned and in column (4) the percentage of class so owned. Of the number of shares shown in column (3), indicate by footnote or otherwise the amount known to be shares with respect to which such listed beneficial owner has the right to acquire beneficial ownership, as specified in Rule 13d-3(d)(1) under the Exchange Act (§ 240.13d-3(d)(1) of this chapter).

(1) Title of class	(2) Name and address of beneficial owner	(3) Amount and nature of beneficial ownership	(4) Percent of class

(b) *Security ownership of management.* Furnish the following information, as of the most recent practicable date, in substantially the tabular form indicated, as to each class of equity securities of the registrant or any of its parents or subsidiaries, including directors' qualifying shares, beneficially owned by all directors and nominees, naming them, each of the named executive officers as defined in Item 402(a)(3) (§ 229.402(a)(3)), and directors and executive officers of the registrant as a group, without naming them. Show in column (3) the total number of shares beneficially owned and in column (4) the percent of the class so owned. Of the number of shares shown in column (3), indicate, by footnote or otherwise, the amount of shares that are pledged as security and the amount of shares with respect to which such persons have the right to acquire beneficial ownership as specified in § 240.13d-3(d)(1) of this chapter.

(1) Title of Class	(2) Name of Beneficial Owner	(3) Amount and Nature of Beneficial Ownership	(4) Percent of Class

(c) *Changes in control.* Describe any arrangements, known to the registrant, including any pledge by any person of securities of the registrant or any of its parents, the operation of which may at a subsequent date result in a change in control of the registrant.

Instructions to Item 403. 1. The percentages are to be calculated on the basis of the amount of outstanding securities, excluding securities held by or for the account of the registrant or its subsidiaries, plus securities deemed outstanding pursuant to Rule 13d-3(d)(1) under the Exchange Act [17 CFR 240.13d-3(d)(1)]. For purposes of paragraph (b), if the percentage of shares beneficially owned by any director or nominee, or by all directors and officers of the registrant as a group, does not exceed one percent of the class so owned, the registrant may, in lieu of furnishing a precise percentage, indicate this fact by means of an asterisk and explanatory footnote or other similar means.

2. For the purposes of this Item, beneficial ownership shall be determined in accordance with Rule 13d-3 under the Exchange Act (§ 240.13d-3 of this chapter). Include such additional subcolumns or other appropriate explanation of column (3) necessary to reflect amounts as to which the beneficial owner has (A) sole voting power, (B) shared voting power, (C) sole investment power, or (D) shared investment power.

3. The registrant shall be deemed to know the contents of any statements filed with the Commission pursuant to section 13(d) or 13(g) of the Exchange Act. When applicable, a registrant may rely upon information set forth in such statements unless the registrant knows or has reason to believe that such information is not complete or accurate or that a statement or amendment should have been filed and was not.

4. For purposes of furnishing information pursuant to paragraph (a) of this Item, the registrant may indicate the source and date of such information.

5. Where more than one beneficial owner is known to be listed for the same securities, appropriate disclosure should be made to avoid confusion. For purposes of paragraph (b), in computing the aggregate number of shares owned by directors and officers of the registrant as a group, the same shares shall not be counted more than once.

6. Paragraph (c) of this Item does not require a description of ordinary default provisions contained in the charter, trust indentures or other governing instruments relating to securities of the registrant.

7. Where the holder(s) of voting securities reported pursuant to paragraph (a) hold more than five percent of any class of voting securities of the registrant pursuant to any voting trust or similar agreement, state the title of such securities, the amount held or to be held pursuant to the trust or agreement (if not clear from the table) and the duration of the agreement. Give the names and addresses of the voting trustees and outline briefly their voting rights and other powers under the trust or agreement.

[As last amended in Release No. 33-8732, effective November 7, 2006, 71 F.R. 53158.]

[¶ 13,044] Transactions With Related Persons, Promoters and Certain Control Persons.

Reg. § 229.404. Item 404. (a) *Transactions with related persons.* Describe any transaction, since the beginning of the registrant's last fiscal year, or any currently proposed transaction, in which the registrant was or is to be a participant and the amount involved exceeds $120,000, and in which any related person had or will have a direct or indirect material interest. Disclose the following information regarding the transaction:

(1) The name of the related person and the basis on which the person is a related person.

(2) The related person's interest in the transaction with the registrant, including the related person's position(s) or relationship(s) with, or ownership in, a firm, corporation, or other entity that is a party to, or has an interest in, the transaction.

(3) The approximate dollar value of the amount involved in the transaction.

(4) The approximate dollar value of the amount of the related person's interest in the transaction, which shall be computed without regard to the amount of profit or loss.

(5) In the case of indebtedness, disclosure of the amount involved in the transaction shall include the largest aggregate amount of principal outstanding during the period for which disclosure is provided, the amount thereof outstanding as of the latest practicable date, the amount of principal paid during the periods for which disclosure is provided, the amount of interest paid during the period for which disclosure is provided, and the rate or amount of interest payable on the indebtedness.

(6) Any other information regarding the transaction or the related person in the context of the transaction that is material to investors in light of the circumstances of the particular transaction.

Instructions to Item 404(a).

1. For the purposes of paragraph (a) of this Item, the term *related person* means:

a. Any person who was in any of the following categories at any time during the specified period for which disclosure under paragraph (a) of this Item is required:

i. Any director or executive officer of the registrant;

ii. Any nominee for director, when the information called for by paragraph (a) of this Item is being presented in a proxy or information statement relating to the election of that nominee for director; or

iii. Any immediate family member of a director or executive officer of the registrant, or of any nominee for director when the information called for by paragraph (a) of this Item is being presented in a proxy or information statement relating to the election of that nominee for director, which means any child, stepchild, parent, stepparent, spouse, sibling, mother-in-law, father-in-law, son-in-law, daughter-in-law, brother-in-law, or sister-in-law of such director, executive officer or nominee for director, and any person (other than a tenant or employee) sharing the household of such director, executive officer or nominee for director; and

b. Any person who was in any of the following categories when a transaction in which such person had a direct or indirect material interest occurred or existed:

i. A security holder covered by Item 403(a) (§ 229.403(a)); or

ii. Any immediate family member of any such security holder, which means any child, stepchild, parent, stepparent, spouse, sibling, mother-in-law, father-in-law, son-inlaw, daughter-in-law, brother-in-law, or sister-in-law of such security holder, and any person (other than a tenant or employee) sharing the household of such security holder.

2. For purposes of paragraph (a) of this Item, a *transaction* includes, but is not limited to, any financial transaction, arrangement or relationship (including any indebtedness or guarantee of indebtedness) or any series of similar transactions, arrangements or relationships.

3. The amount involved in the transaction shall be computed by determining the dollar value of the amount involved in the transaction in question, which shall include:

a. In the case of any lease or other transaction providing for periodic payments or installments, the aggregate amount of all periodic payments or installments due on or after the beginning of the registrant's last fiscal year, including any required or optional payments due during or at the conclusion of the lease or other transaction providing for periodic payments or installments; and

b. In the case of indebtedness, the largest aggregate amount of all indebtedness outstanding at any time since the beginning of the registrant's last fiscal year and all amounts of interest payable on it during the last fiscal year.

4. In the case of a transaction involving indebtedness:

a. The following items of indebtedness may be excluded from the calculation of the amount of indebtedness and need not be disclosed: amounts due from the related person for purchases of goods and services subject to usual trade terms, for ordinary business travel and expense payments and for other transactions in the ordinary course of business;

b. Disclosure need not be provided of any indebtedness transaction for the related persons specified in Instruction 1.b. to paragraph (a) of this Item; and

c. If the lender is a bank, savings and loan association, or broker-dealer extending credit under Federal Reserve Regulation T (12 CFR part 220) and the loans are not disclosed as nonaccrual, past due, restructured or potential problems (see Item III.C.1. and 2. of Industry Guide 3, Statistical Disclosure by

Bank Holding Companies (17 CFR 229.802(c))), disclosure under paragraph (a) of this Item may consist of a statement, if such is the case, that the loans to such persons:

i. Were made in the ordinary course of business;

ii. Were made on substantially the same terms, including interest rates and collateral, as those prevailing at the time for comparable loans with persons not related to the lender; and

iii. Did not involve more than the normal risk of collectibility or present other unfavorable features.

5.a. Disclosure of an employment relationship or transaction involving an executive officer and any related compensation solely resulting from that employment relationship or transaction need not be provided pursuant to paragraph (a) of this Item if:

i. The compensation arising from the relationship or transaction is reported pursuant to Item 402 (§ 229.402); or

ii. The executive officer is not an immediate family member (as specified in Instruction 1 to paragraph (a) of this Item) and such compensation would have been reported under Item 402 (§ 229.402) as compensation earned for services to the registrant if the executive officer was a named executive officer as that term is defined in Item 402(a)(3) (§ 229.402(a)(3)), and such compensation had been approved, or recommended to the board of directors of the registrant for approval, by the compensation committee of the board of directors (or group of independent directors performing a similar function) of the registrant.

b. Disclosure of compensation to a director need not be provided pursuant to paragraph (a) of this Item if the compensation is reported pursuant to Item 402(k) (§ 229.402(k)).

6. A person who has a position or relationship with a firm, corporation, or other entity that engages in a transaction with the registrant shall not be deemed to have an indirect material interest within the meaning of paragraph (a) of this Item where:

a. The interest arises only:

i. From such person's position as a director of another corporation or organization that is a party to the transaction; or

ii. From the direct or indirect ownership by such person and all other persons specified in Instruction 1 to paragraph (a) of this Item, in the aggregate, of less than a ten percent equity interest in another person (other than a partnership) which is a party to the transaction; or

iii. From both such position and ownership; or

b. The interest arises only from such person's position as a limited partner in a partnership in which the person and all other persons specified in Instruction 1 to paragraph (a) of this Item, have an interest of less than ten percent, and the person is not a general partner of and does not hold another position in the partnership.

7. Disclosure need not be provided pursuant to paragraph (a) of this Item if:

a. The transaction is one where the rates or charges involved in the transaction are determined by competitive bids, or the transaction involves the rendering of services as a common or contract carrier, or public utility, at rates or charges fixed in conformity with law or governmental authority;

b. The transaction involves services as a bank depositary of funds, transfer agent, registrar, trustee under a trust indenture, or similar services; or

c. The interest of the related person arises solely from the ownership of a class of equity securities of the registrant and all holders of that class of equity securities of the registrant received the same benefit on a pro rata basis.

(b) *Review, approval or ratification of transactions with related persons.*

(1) Describe the registrant's policies and procedures for the review, approval, or ratification of any transaction required to be reported under paragraph (a) of this Item. While the material features of such policies and procedures will vary depending on the particular circumstances, examples of such features may include, in given cases, among other things:

(i) The types of transactions that are covered by such policies and procedures;

(ii) The standards to be applied pursuant to such policies and procedures;

(iii) The persons or groups of persons on the board of directors or otherwise who are responsible for applying such policies and procedures; and

(iv) A statement of whether such policies and procedures are in writing and, if not, how such policies and procedures are evidenced.

(2) Identify any transaction required to be reported under paragraph (a) of this Item since the beginning of the registrant's last fiscal year where such policies and procedures did not require review, approval or ratification or where such policies and procedures were not followed.

Instruction to Item 404(b).

Disclosure need not be provided pursuant to this paragraph regarding any transaction that occurred at a time before the related person became one of the enumerated persons in Instruction 1.a.i., ii., or iii. to Item 404(a) if such transaction did not continue after the related person became one of the enumerated persons in Instruction 1.a.i., ii., or iii. to Item 404(a).

(c) *Promoters and certain control persons.*

(1) Registrants that are filing a registration statement on Form S-1 under the Securities Act (§ 239.11 of this chapter) or on Form 10 under the Exchange Act (§ 249.210 of this chapter) and that had a promoter at any time during the past five fiscal years shall:

(i) State the names of the promoter(s), the nature and amount of anything of value (including money, property, contracts, options or rights of any kind) received or to be received by each promoter, directly or indirectly, from the registrant and the nature and amount of any assets, services or other consideration therefore received or to be received by the registrant; and

(ii) As to any assets acquired or to be acquired by the registrant from a promoter, state the amount at which the assets were acquired or are to be acquired and the principle followed or to be followed in determining such amount, and identify the persons making the determination and their relationship, if any, with the registrant or any promoter. If the assets were acquired by the promoter within two years prior to their transfer to the registrant, also state the cost thereof to the promoter.

(2) Registrants shall provide the disclosure required by paragraphs (c)(1)(i) and (c)(1)(ii) of this Item as to any person who acquired control of a registrant that is a shell company, or any person that is part of a group, consisting of two or more persons that agree to act together for the purpose of acquiring, holding, voting or disposing of equity securities of a registrant, that acquired control of a registrant that is a shell company. For purposes of this Item, *shell company* has the same meaning as in Rule 405 under the Securities Act (17 CFR 230.405) and Rule 12b-2 under the Exchange Act (17 CFR 240.12b-2).

(d) Smaller reporting companies. A registrant that qualifies as a "smaller reporting company," as defined by § 229.10(f)(1), must provide the following information in order to comply with this Item:

(1) The information required by paragraph (a) of this Item for the period specified there for a transaction in which the amount involved exceeds the lesser of $120,000 or one percent of the average of the smaller reporting company's total assets at year end for the last two completed fiscal years;

(2) The information required by paragraph (c) of this Item; and

(3) A list of all parents of the smaller reporting company showing the basis of control and as to each parent, the percentage of voting securities owned or other basis of control by its immediate parent, if any.

Instruction to Item 404(d)

1. Include information for any material underwriting discounts and commissions upon the sale of securities by the smaller reporting company where any of the persons specified in paragraph (a) of this Item was or is to be a principal underwriter or is a controlling person or member of a firm that was or is to be a principal underwriter.

2. For smaller reporting companies information shall be given for the period specified in paragraph (a) of this Item and, in addition, for the fiscal year preceding the small reporting company's last fiscal year.

Instructions to Item 404.

1. If the information called for by this Item is being presented in a registration statement filed pursuant to the Securities Act or the Exchange Act, information shall be given for the periods specified in the Item and, in addition, for the two fiscal years preceding the registrant's last fiscal year, unless the information is being incorporated by reference into a registration statement on Form S-4 (17 CFR 239.25), in which case, information shall be given for the periods specified in the Item.

2. A foreign private issuer will be deemed to comply with this Item if it provides the information required by Item 7.B. of Form 20-F (17 CFR 249.220f) with more detailed information provided if otherwise made publicly available or required to be disclosed by the issuer's home jurisdiction or a market in which its securities are listed or traded.

[As last amended in Release No. 33-8876, effective February 4, 2008, 73 F.R. 934.]

[¶ 13,045] Compliance With Section 16(a) of the Exchange Act

Reg. § 229.405. Item 405. Every registrant having a class of equity securities registered pursuant to Section 12 of the Exchange Act (15 U.S.C. 78*l*), every closed-end investment company registered under the Investment Company Act of 1940 (15 U.S.C. § 80a-1 *et seq.*), and every holding company registered pursuant to the Public Utility Holding Company Act of 1935 (15 U.S.C. § 79a *et seq.*) shall:

(a) Based solely upon a review of Forms 3 and 4 (17 CFR 249.103 and 249.104) and amendments thereto furnished to the registrant under 17 CFR 240.16a-3(e) during its most recent fiscal year and

Forms 5 and amendments thereto (17 CFR 249.105) furnished to the registrant with respect to its most recent fiscal year, and any written representation referred to in paragraph (b)(1) of this section:

(1) Under the caption "Section 16(a) Beneficial Ownership Reporting Compliance," identify each person who, at any time during the fiscal year, was a director, officer, beneficial owner of more than ten percent of any class of equity securities of the registrant registered pursuant to section 12 of the Exchange Act, or any other person subject to section 16 of the Exchange Act with respect to the registrant because of the requirements of section 30 of the Investment Company Act or section 17 of the Public Utility Holding Company Act ("reporting person") that failed to file on a timely basis, as disclosed in the above Forms, reports required by section 16(a) of the Exchange Act during the most recent fiscal year or prior fiscal years.

(2) For each such person, set forth the number of late reports, the number of transactions that were not reported on a timely basis, and any known failure to file a required Form. A known failure to file would include, but not be limited to, a failure to file a Form 3, which is required of all reporting persons, and a failure to file a Form 5 in the absence of the written representation referred to in paragraph (b)(1) of this section, unless the registrant otherwise knows that no Form 5 is required.

Note: The disclosure requirement is based on a review of the forms submitted to the registrant during and with respect to its most recent fiscal year, as specified above. Accordingly, a failure to file timely need only be disclosed once. For example, if in the most recently concluded fiscal year a reporting person filed a Form 4 disclosing a transaction that took place in the prior fiscal year, and should have been reported in that year, the registrant should disclose that late filing and transaction pursuant to this Item 405 with respect to the most recently concluded fiscal year, but not in material filed with respect to subsequent years.

(b) With respect to the disclosure required by paragraph (a) of this section, if the registrant:

(1) Receives a written representation from the reporting person that no Form 5 is required; and

(2) Maintains the representation for two years, making a copy available to the Commission or its staff upon request, the registrant need not identify such reporting person pursuant to paragraph (a) of this section as having failed to file a Form 5 with respect to that fiscal year.

[As last amended in Release No. 33-8600, effective September 8, 2005, 70 F.R. 46080.]

[¶ 13,046] Code of Ethics

Reg. § 229.406 Item 406. (a) Disclose whether the registrant has adopted a code of ethics that applies to the registrant's principal executive officer, principal financial officer, principal accounting officer or controller, or persons performing similar functions. If the registrant has not adopted such a code of ethics, explain why it has not done so.

(b) For purposes of this Item 406, the term *code of ethics* means written standards that are reasonably designed to deter wrongdoing and to promote:

(1) Honest and ethical conduct, including the ethical handling of actual or apparent conflicts of interest between personal and professional relationships;

(2) Full, fair, accurate, timely, and understandable disclosure in reports and documents that a registrant files with, or submits to, the Commission and in other public communications made by the registrant;

(3) Compliance with applicable governmental laws, rules and regulations;

(4) The prompt internal reporting of violations of the code to an appropriate person or persons identified in the code; and

(5) Accountability for adherence to the code.

(c) The registrant must:

(1) File with the Commission a copy of its code of ethics that applies to the registrant's principal executive officer, principal financial officer, principal accounting officer or controller, or persons performing similar functions, as an exhibit to its annual report;

(2) Post the text of such code of ethics on its Internet website and disclose, in its annual report, its Internet address and the fact that it has posted such code of ethics on its Internet website; or

(3) Undertake in its annual report filed with the Commission to provide to any person without charge, upon request, a copy of such code of ethics and explain the manner in which such request may be made.

(d) If the registrant intends to satisfy the disclosure requirement under Item 10 of Form 8-K regarding an amendment to, or a waiver from, a provision of its code of ethics that applies to the registrant's principal executive officer, principal financial officer, principal accounting officer or controller, or persons performing similar functions and that relates to any element of the code of ethics definition enumerated in paragraph (b) of this Item by posting such information on its Internet website, disclose the registrant's Internet address and such intention.

Instructions to Item 406.

1. A registrant may have separate codes of ethics for different types of officers. Furthermore, a *code of ethics* within the meaning of paragraph (b) of this Item may be a portion of a broader document that addresses additional topics or that applies to more persons than those specified in paragraph (a). In satisfying the requirements of paragraph (c), a registrant need only file, post or provide the portions of a broader document that constitutes a *code of ethics* as defined in paragraph (b) and that apply to the persons specified in paragraph (a).

2. If a registrant elects to satisfy paragraph (c) of this Item by posting its code of ethics on its website pursuant to paragraph (c)(2), the code of ethics must remain accessible on its website for as long as the registrant remains subject to the requirements of this Item and chooses to comply with this Item by posting its code on its website pursuant to paragraph (c)(2).

[As added in Release No. 33-8518, effective March 8, 2005 (Compliance dates are triggered by initial bona fide offer date or registration statement filing date and extend out to March 31, 2006. Complete compliance date details can be found in the "Dates" section of the release.), 70 F.R. 1506.]

[¶ 13,049] Corporate Governance

Reg. § 229.407 Item 407. (a) *Director independence.* Identify each director and, when the disclosure called for by this paragraph is being presented in a proxy or information statement relating to the election of directors, each nominee for director, that is independent under the independence standards applicable to the registrant under paragraph (a)(1) of this Item. In addition, if such independence standards contain independence requirements for committees of the board of directors, identify each director that is a member of the compensation, nominating or audit committee that is not independent under such committee independence standards. If the registrant does not have a separately designated audit, nominating or compensation committee or committee performing similar functions, the registrant must provide the disclosure of directors that are not independent with respect to all members of the board of directors applying such committee independence standards.

(1) In determining whether or not the director or nominee for director is independent for the purposes of paragraph (a) of this Item, the registrant shall use the applicable definition of independence, as follows:

(i) If the registrant is a listed issuer whose securities are listed on a national securities exchange or in an inter-dealer quotation system which has requirements that a majority of the board of directors be independent, the registrant's definition of independence that it uses for determining if a majority of the board of directors is independent in compliance with the listing standards applicable to the registrant. When determining whether the members of a committee of the board of directors are independent, the registrant's definition of independence that it uses for determining if the members of that specific committee are independent in compliance with the independence standards applicable for the members of the specific committee in the listing standards of the national securities exchange or inter-dealer quotation system that the registrant uses for determining if a majority of the board of directors are independent. If the registrant does not have independence standards for a committee, the independence standards for that specific committee in the listing standards of the national securities exchange or inter-dealer quotation system that the registrant uses for determining if a majority of the board of directors are independent.

(ii) If the registrant is not a listed issuer, a definition of independence of a national securities exchange or of an inter-dealer quotation system which has requirements that a majority of the board of directors be independent, and state which definition is used. Whatever such definition the registrant chooses, it must use the same definition with respect to all directors and nominees for director. When determining whether the members of a specific committee of the board of directors are independent, if the national securities exchange or national securities association whose standards are used has independence standards for the members of a specific committee, use those committee specific standards.

(iii) If the information called for by paragraph (a) of this Item is being presented in a registration statement on Form S-1 (§ 239.11 of this chapter) under the Securities Act or on a Form 10 (§ 249.210 of this chapter) under the Exchange Act where the registrant has applied for listing with a national securities exchange or in an inter-dealer quotation system that has requirements that a majority of the board of directors be independent, the definition of independence that the registrant uses for determining if a majority of the board of directors is independent, and the definition of independence that the registrant uses for determining if members of the specific committee of the board of directors are independent, that is in compliance with the independence listing standards of the national securities exchange or inter-dealer quotation system on which it has applied for listing, or if the registrant has not adopted such definitions, the independence standards for determining if the majority of the board of directors is independent and if members of the committee of the board of directors are independent of that national securities exchange or inter-dealer quotation system.

(2) If the registrant uses its own definitions for determining whether its directors and nominees for director, and members of specific committees of the board of directors, are independent, disclose whether these definitions are available to security holders on the registrant's Web site. If so, provide the registrant's Web site address. If not, include a copy of these policies in an appendix to the registrant's proxy statement or information statement that is provided to security holders at least once every three fiscal years or if the policies have been materially amended since the beginning of the registrant's last fiscal year. If a current copy of the policies is not available to security holders on the registrant's Web site, and is not included as an appendix to the registrant's proxy statement or information statement, identify the most recent fiscal year in which the policies were so included in satisfaction of this requirement.

(3) For each director and nominee for director that is identified as independent, describe, by specific category or type, any transactions, relationships or arrangements not disclosed pursuant to Item 404(a) (§ 229.404(a)), or for investment companies, Item 22(b) of Schedule 14A (§ 240.14a-101 of this chapter), that were considered by the board of directors under the applicable independence definitions in determining that the director is independent.

Instructions to Item 407(a).

1. If the registrant is a listed issuer whose securities are listed on a national securities exchange or in an inter-dealer quotation system which has requirements that a majority of the board of directors be independent, and also has exemptions to those requirements (for independence of a majority of the board of directors or committee member independence) upon which the registrant relied, disclose the exemption relied upon and explain the basis for the registrant's conclusion that such exemption is applicable. The same disclosure should be provided if the registrant is not a listed issuer and the national securities exchange or inter-dealer quotation system selected by the registrant has exemptions that are applicable to the registrant. Any national securities exchange or inter-dealer quotation system which has requirements that at least 50 percent of the members of a small business issuer's board of directors must be independent shall be considered a national securities exchange or inter-dealer quotation system which has requirements that a majority of the board of directors be independent for the purposes of the disclosure required by paragraph (a) of this Item.

2. Registrants shall provide the disclosure required by paragraph (a) of this Item for any person who served as a director during any part of the last completed fiscal year, except that no information called for by paragraph (a) of this Item need be given in a registration statement filed at a time when the registrant is not subject to the reporting requirements of section 13(a) or 15(d) of the Exchange Act (15 U.S.C. 78m(a) or 78o(d)) respecting any director who is no longer a director at the time of effectiveness of the registration statement.

3. The description of the specific categories or types of transactions, relationships or arrangements required by paragraph (a)(3) of this Item must be provided in such detail as is necessary to fully describe the nature of the transactions, relationships or arrangements.

(b) *Board meetings and committees; annual meeting attendance.*

(1) State the total number of meetings of the board of directors (including regularly scheduled and special meetings) which were held during the last full fiscal year. Name each incumbent director who during the last full fiscal year attended fewer than 75 percent of the aggregate of:

(i) The total number of meetings of the board of directors (held during the period for which he has been a director); and

(ii) The total number of meetings held by all committees of the board on which he served (during the periods that he served).

(2) Describe the registrant's policy, if any, with regard to board members' attendance at annual meetings of security holders and state the number of board members who attended the prior year's annual meeting.

Instruction to Item 407(b)(2).

In lieu of providing the information required by paragraph (b)(2) of this Item in the proxy statement, the registrant may instead provide the registrant's Web site address where such information appears.

(3) State whether or not the registrant has standing audit, nominating and compensation committees of the board of directors, or committees performing similar functions. If the registrant has such committees, however designated, identify each committee member, state the number of committee meetings held by each such committee during the last fiscal year and describe briefly the functions performed by each such committee. Such disclosure need not be provided to the extent it is duplicative of disclosure provided in accordance with paragraph (c), (d) or (e) of this Item.

(c) *Nominating committee.* (1) If the registrant does not have a standing nominating committee or committee performing similar functions, state the basis for the view of the board of directors that it is appropriate for the registrant not to have such a committee and identify each director who participates in the consideration of director nominees.

(2) Provide the following information regarding the registrant's director nomination process:

(i) State whether or not the nominating committee has a charter. If the nominating committee has a charter, provide the disclosure required by Instruction 2 to this Item regarding the nominating committee charter;

(ii) If the nominating committee has a policy with regard to the consideration of any director candidates recommended by security holders, provide a description of the material elements of that policy, which shall include, but need not be limited to, a statement as to whether the committee will consider director candidates recommended by security holders;

(iii) If the nominating committee does not have a policy with regard to the consideration of any director candidates recommended by security holders, state that fact and state the basis for the view of the board of directors that it is appropriate for the registrant not to have such a policy;

(iv) If the nominating committee will consider candidates recommended by security holders, describe the procedures to be followed by security holders in submitting such recommendations;

(v) Describe any specific minimum qualifications that the nominating committee believes must be met by a nominating committee-recommended nominee for a position on the registrant's board of directors, and describe any specific qualities or skills that the nominating committee believes are necessary for one or more of the registrant's directors to possess;

(vi) Describe the nominating committee's process for identifying and evaluating nominees for director, including nominees recommended by security holders, and any differences in the manner in which the nominating committee evaluates nominees for director based on whether the nominee is recommended by a security holder, and whether, and if so how, the nominating committee (or the board) considers diversity in identifying nominees for director. If the nominating committee (or the board) has a policy with regard to the consideration of diversity in identifying director nominees, describe how this policy is implemented, as well as how the nominating committee (or the board) assesses the effectiveness of its policy;

(vii) With regard to each nominee approved by the nominating committee for inclusion on the registrant's proxy card (other than nominees who are executive officers or who are directors standing for re-election), state which one or more of the following categories of persons or entities recommended that nominee: security holder, nonmanagement director, chief executive officer, other executive officer, third-party search firm, or other specified source. With regard to each such nominee approved by a nominating committee of an investment company, state which one or more of the following additional categories of persons or entities recommended that nominee: security holder, director, chief executive officer, other executive officer, or employee of the investment company's investment adviser, principal underwriter, or any affiliated person of the investment adviser or principal underwriter;

(viii) If the registrant pays a fee to any third party or parties to identify or evaluate or assist in identifying or evaluating potential nominees, disclose the function performed by each such third party; and

(ix) If the registrant's nominating committee received, by a date not later than the 120th calendar day before the date of the registrant's proxy statement released to security holders in connection with the previous year's annual meeting, a recommended nominee from a security holder that beneficially owned more than 5% of the registrant's voting common stock for at least one year as of the date the recommendation was made, or from a group of security holders that beneficially owned, in the aggregate, more than 5% of the registrant's voting common stock, with each of the securities used to calculate that ownership held for at least one year as of the date the recommendation was made, identify the candidate and the security holder or security holder group that recommended the candidate and disclose whether the nominating committee chose to nominate the candidate, *provided, however,* that no such identification or disclosure is required without the written consent of both the security holder or security holder group and the candidate to be so identified.

Instructions to Item 407(c)(2)(ix).

1. For purposes of paragraph (c)(2)(ix) of this Item, the percentage of securities held by a nominating security holder may be determined using information set forth in the registrant's most recent quarterly or annual report, and any current report subsequent thereto, filed with the Commission pursuant to the Exchange Act (or, in the case of a registrant that is an investment company registered under the Investment Company Act of 1940, the registrant's most recent report on Form N-CSR (§§ 249.331 and 274.128 of this chapter)), unless the party relying on such report knows or has reason to believe that the information contained therein is inaccurate.

2. For purposes of the registrant's obligation to provide the disclosure specified in paragraph (c)(2)(ix) of this Item, where the date of the annual meeting has been changed by more than 30 days from the date of the previous year's meeting, the obligation under that Item will arise where the registrant receives the security holder recommendation a reasonable time before the registrant begins to print and mail its proxy materials.

3. For purposes of paragraph (c)(2)(ix) of this Item, the percentage of securities held by a recommending security holder, as well as the holding period of those securities, may be determined by the registrant if the security holder is the registered holder of the securities. If the security holder is not the registered owner of the securities, he or she can submit one of the following to the registrant to evidence the required ownership percentage and holding period:

a. A written statement from the "record" holder of the securities (usually a broker or bank) verifying that, at the time the security holder made the recommendation, he or she had held the required securities for at least one year; or

b. If the security holder has filed a Schedule 13D (§ 240.13d-101 of this chapter), Schedule 13G (§ 240.13d-102 of this chapter), Form 3 (§ 249.103 of this chapter), Form 4 (§ 249.104 of this chapter), and/or Form 5 (§ 249.105 of this chapter), or amendments to those documents or updated forms, reflecting ownership of the securities as of or before the date of the recommendation, a copy of the schedule and/or form, and any subsequent amendments reporting a change in ownership level, as well as a written statement that the security holder continuously held the securities for the one-year period as of the date of the recommendation.

4. For purposes of the registrant's obligation to provide the disclosure specified in paragraph (c)(2)(ix) of this Item, the security holder or group must have provided to the registrant, at the time of the recommendation, the written consent of all parties to be identified and, where the security holder or group members are not registered holders, proof that the security holder or group satisfied the required ownership percentage and holding period as of the date of the recommendation.

Instruction to Item 407(c)(2).

For purposes of paragraph (c)(2) of this Item, the term *nominating committee* refers not only to nominating committees and committees performing similar functions, but also to groups of directors fulfilling the role of a nominating committee, including the entire board of directors.

(3) Describe any material changes to the procedures by which security holders may recommend nominees to the registrant's board of directors, where those changes were implemented after the registrant last provided disclosure in response to the requirements of paragraph (c)(2)(iv) of this Item, or paragraph (c)(3) of this Item.

Instructions to Item 407(c)(3).

1. The disclosure required in paragraph (c)(3) of this Item need only be provided in a registrant's quarterly or annual reports.

2. For purposes of paragraph (c)(3) of this Item, adoption of procedures by which security holders may recommend nominees to the registrant's board of directors, where the registrant's most recent disclosure in response to the requirements of paragraph (c)(2)(iv) of this Item, or paragraph (c)(3) of this Item, indicated that the registrant did not have in place such procedures, will constitute a material change.

(d) *Audit committee.*

(1) State whether or not the audit committee has a charter. If the audit committee has a charter, provide the disclosure required by Instruction 2 to this Item regarding the audit committee charter.

(2) If a listed issuer's board of directors determines, in accordance with the listing standards applicable to the issuer, to appoint a director to the audit committee who is not independent (apart from the requirements in § 240.10A-3 of this chapter), including as a result of exceptional or limited or similar circumstances, disclose the nature of the relationship that makes that individual not independent and the reasons for the board of directors' determination.

(3)(i) The audit committee must state whether:

(A) The audit committee has reviewed and discussed the audited financial statements with management;

(B) The audit committee has discussed with the independent auditors the matters required to be discussed by the statement on Auditing Standards No. 61, as amended (AICPA, *Professional Standards*, Vol. 1. AU section 380), as adopted by the Public Company Accounting Oversight Board in Rule 3200T;

(C) The audit committee has received the written disclosures and the letter from the independent accountant required by applicable requirements of the Public Company Accounting Oversight Board regarding the independent accountant's communications with the audit committee concerning independence, and has discussed with the independent accountant the independent accountant's independence; and

(D) Based on the review and discussions referred to in paragraphs (d)(3)(i)(A) through (d)(3)(i)(C) of this Item, the audit committee recommended to the board of directors that the audited financial statements be included in the company's annual report on Form 10-K (17 CFR 249.310) (or, for closed-end investment companies registered under the Investment Company Act of 1940 (15 U.S.C. 80a-1 *et seq.*), the annual report to shareholders required by section 30(e) of the Investment Company Act of 1940 (15 U.S.C. 80a-29(e)) and Rule 30d-1 (17 CFR 270.30d-1) thereunder) for the last fiscal year for filing with the Commission.

(ii) The name of each member of the company's audit committee (or, in the absence of an audit committee, the board committee performing equivalent functions or the entire board of directors) must appear below the disclosure required by paragraph (d)(3)(i) of this Item.

(4)(i) If the registrant meets the following requirements, provide the disclosure in paragraph (d)(4)(ii) of this Item:

(A) The registrant is a listed issuer, as defined in § 240.10A-3 of this chapter;

(B) The registrant is filing an annual report on Form 10-K (§ 249.310 of this chapter) or a proxy statement or information statement pursuant to the Exchange Act (15 U.S.C. 78a *et seq.*) if action is to be taken with respect to the election of directors; and

(C) The registrant is neither:

(*1*) A subsidiary of another listed issuer that is relying on the exemption in § 240.10A-3(c)(2) of this chapter; nor

(*2*) Relying on any of the exemptions in § 240.10A-3(c)(4) through (c)(7) of this chapter.

(ii)(A) State whether or not the registrant has a separately-designated standing audit committee established in accordance with section 3(a)(58)(A) of the Exchange Act (15 U.S.C. 78c(a)(58)(A)), or a committee performing similar functions. If the registrant has such a committee, however designated, identify each committee member. If the entire board of directors is acting as the registrant's audit committee as specified in section 3(a)(58)(B) of the Exchange Act (15 U.S.C. 78c(a)(58)(B)), so state.

(B) If applicable, provide the disclosure required by § 240.10A-3(d) of this chapter regarding an exemption from the listing standards for audit committees.

(5) *Audit committee financial expert.*

(i)(A) Disclose that the registrant's board of directors has determined that the registrant either:

(*1*) Has at least one audit committee financial expert serving on its audit committee; or

(*2*) Does not have an audit committee financial expert serving on its audit committee.

(B) If the registrant provides the disclosure required by paragraph (d)(5)(i)(A)(*1*) of this Item, it must disclose the name of the audit committee financial expert and whether that person is *independent*, as independence for audit committee members is defined in the listing standards applicable to the listed issuer.

(C) If the registrant provides the disclosure required by paragraph (d)(5)(i)(A)(*2*) of this Item, it must explain why it does not have an audit committee financial expert.

Instruction to Item 407(d)(5)(i).

If the registrant's board of directors has determined that the registrant has more than one audit committee financial expert serving on its audit committee, the registrant may, but is not required to, disclose the names of those additional persons. A registrant choosing to identify such persons must indicate whether they are independent pursuant to paragraph (d)(5)(i)(B) of this Item.

(ii) For purposes of this Item, an *audit committee financial expert* means a person who has the following attributes:

(A) An understanding of generally accepted accounting principles and financial statements;

(B) The ability to assess the general application of such principles in connection with the accounting for estimates, accruals and reserves;

(C) Experience preparing, auditing, analyzing or evaluating financial statements that present a breadth and level of complexity of accounting issues that are generally comparable to the breadth and complexity of issues that can reasonably be expected to be raised by the registrant's financial statements, or experience actively supervising one or more persons engaged in such activities;

(D) An understanding of internal control over financial reporting; and

(E) An understanding of audit committee functions.

(iii) A person shall have acquired such attributes through:

(A) Education and experience as a principal financial officer, principal accounting officer, controller, public accountant or auditor or experience in one or more positions that involve the performance of similar functions;

(B) Experience actively supervising a principal financial officer, principal accounting officer, controller, public accountant, auditor or person performing similar functions;

(C) Experience overseeing or assessing the performance of companies or public accountants with respect to the preparation, auditing or evaluation of financial statements; or

(D) Other relevant experience.

(iv) *Safe harbor.*

(A) A person who is determined to be an audit committee financial expert will not be deemed an *expert* for any purpose, including without limitation for purposes of section 11 of the Securities Act (15 U.S.C. 77k), as a result of being designated or identified as an audit committee financial expert pursuant to this Item 407.

(B) The designation or identification of a person as an audit committee financial expert pursuant to this Item 407 does not impose on such person any duties, obligations or liability that are greater than the duties, obligations and liability imposed on such person as a member of the audit committee and board of directors in the absence of such designation or identification.

(C) The designation or identification of a person as an audit committee financial expert pursuant to this Item does not affect the duties, obligations or liability of any other member of the audit committee or board of directors.

Instructions to Item 407(d)(5).

1. The disclosure under paragraph (d)(5) of this Item is required only in a registrant's annual report. The registrant need not provide the disclosure required by paragraph (d)(5) of this Item in a proxy or information statement unless that registrant is electing to incorporate this information by reference from the proxy or information statement into its annual report pursuant to General Instruction G(3) to Form 10-K (17 CFR 249.310).

2. If a person qualifies as an audit committee financial expert by means of having held a position described in paragraph (d)(5)(iii)(D) of this Item, the registrant shall provide a brief listing of that person's relevant experience. Such disclosure may be made by reference to disclosures required under Item 401(e) (§229.401(e)).

3. In the case of a foreign private issuer with a two-tier board of directors, for purposes of paragraph (d)(5) of this Item, the term *board of directors* means the supervisory or non-management board. In the case of a foreign private issuer meeting the requirements of §240.10A-3(c)(3) of this chapter, for purposes of paragraph (d)(5) of this Item, the term *board of directors* means the issuer's board of auditors (or similar body) or statutory auditors, as applicable. Also, in the case of a foreign private issuer, the term *generally accepted accounting principles* in paragraph (d)(5)(ii)(A) of this Item means the body of generally accepted accounting principles used by that issuer in its primary financial statements filed with the Commission.

4. A registrant that is an Asset-Backed Issuer (as defined in §229.1101) is not required to disclose the information required by paragraph (d)(5) of this Item.

Instructions to Item 407(d).

1. The information required by paragraphs (d)(1) - (3) of this Item shall not be deemed to be "soliciting material," or to be "filed" with the Commission or subject to Regulation 14A or 14C (17 CFR 240.14a-1 through 240.14b-2 or 240.14c-1 through 240.14c-101), other than as provided in this Item, or to the liabilities of section 18 of the Exchange Act (15 U.S.C. 78r), except to the extent that the registrant specifically requests that the information be treated as soliciting material or specifically incorporates it by reference into a document filed under the Securities Act or the Exchange Act. Such information will not be deemed to be incorporated by reference into any filing under the Securities Act or the Exchange Act, except to the extent that the registrant specifically incorporates it by reference.

2. The disclosure required by paragraphs (d)(1) - (3) of this Item need only be provided one time during any fiscal year.

3. The disclosure required by paragraph (d)(3) of this Item need not be provided in any filings other than a registrant's proxy or information statement relating to an annual meeting of security holders at which directors are to be elected (or special meeting or written consents in lieu of such meeting).

(e) *Compensation committee.*

(1) If the registrant does not have a standing compensation committee or committee performing similar functions, state the basis for the view of the board of directors that it is appropriate for the registrant not to have such a committee and identify each director who participates in the consideration of executive officer and director compensation.

(2) State whether or not the compensation committee has a charter. If the compensation committee has a charter, provide the disclosure required by Instruction 2 to this Item regarding the compensation committee charter.

(3) Provide a narrative description of the registrant's processes and procedures for the consideration and determination of executive and director compensation, including:

(i)(A) The scope of authority of the compensation committee (or persons performing the equivalent functions); and

(B) The extent to which the compensation committee (or persons performing the equivalent functions) may delegate any authority described in paragraph (e)(3)(i)(A) of this Item to other persons, specifying what authority may be so delegated and to whom;

(ii) Any role of executive officers in determining or recommending the amount or form of executive and director compensation; and

(iii) Any role of compensation consultants in determining or recommending the amount or form of executive and director compensation (other than any role *limited* to consulting on any broad-based plan that does not discriminate in scope, terms, or operation, in favor of executive officers or directors of the registrant, and that is available generally to all salaried employees; or providing information that either is not customized for a particular registrant or that is customized based on parameters that are not developed by the compensation consultant, and about which the compensation consultant does not provide advice) during the registrant's last completed fiscal year, identifying such consultants, stating whether such consultants were engaged directly by the compensation committee (or persons performing the equivalent functions) or any other person, describing the nature and scope of their assignment, and the material elements of the instructions or directions given to the consultants with respect to the performance of their duties under the engagement:

(A) If such compensation consultant was engaged by the compensation committee (or persons performing the equivalent functions) to provide advice or recommendations on the amount or form of executive and director compensation (other than any role *limited* to consulting on any broad-based plan that does not discriminate in scope, terms, or operation, in favor of executive officers or directors of the registrant, and that is available generally to all salaried employees; or providing information that either is not customized for a particular registrant or that is customized based on parameters that are not developed by the compensation consultant, and about which the compensation consultant does not provide advice) and the compensation consultant or its affiliates also provided additional services to the registrant or its affiliates in an amount in excess of $120,000 during the registrant's last completed fiscal year, then disclose the aggregate fees for determining or recommending the amount or form of executive and director compensation and the aggregate fees for such additional services. Disclose whether the decision to engage the compensation consultant or its affiliates for these other services was made, or recommended, by management, and whether the compensation committee or the board approved such other services of the compensation consultant or its affiliates.

(B) If the compensation committee (or persons performing the equivalent functions) has not engaged a compensation consultant, but management has engaged a compensation consultant to provide advice or recommendations on the amount or form of executive and director compensation (other than any role *limited* to consulting on any broad-based plan that does not discriminate in scope, terms, or operation, in favor of executive officers or directors of the registrant, and that is available generally to all salaried employees; or providing information that either is not customized for a particular registrant or that is customized based on parameters that are not developed by the compensation consultant, and about which the compensation consultant does not provide advice) and such compensation consultant or its affiliates has provided additional services to the registrant in an amount in excess of $120,000 during the registrant's last completed fiscal year, then disclose the aggregate fees for determining or recommending the amount or form of executive and director compensation and the aggregate fees for any additional services provided by the compensation consultant or its affiliates.

(4) Under the caption "Compensation Committee Interlocks and Insider Participation":

(i) Identify each person who served as a member of the compensation committee of the registrant's board of directors (or board committee performing equivalent functions) during the last completed fiscal year, indicating each committee member who:

(A) Was, during the fiscal year, an officer or employee of the registrant;

(B) Was formerly an officer of the registrant; or

(C) Had any relationship requiring disclosure by the registrant under any paragraph of Item 404 (§ 229.404). In this event, the disclosure required by Item 404 (§ 229.404) shall accompany such identification.

(ii) If the registrant has no compensation committee (or other board committee performing equivalent functions), the registrant shall identify each officer and employee of the registrant, and any former officer of the registrant, who, during the last completed fiscal year, participated in deliberations of the registrant's board of directors concerning executive officer compensation.

(iii) Describe any of the following relationships that existed during the last completed fiscal year:

(A) An executive officer of the registrant served as a member of the compensation committee (or other board committee performing equivalent functions or, in the absence of any such committee, the entire board of directors) of another entity, one of whose executive officers served on the compensation committee (or other board committee performing equivalent functions or, in the absence of any such committee, the entire board of directors) of the registrant;

(B) An executive officer of the registrant served as a director of another entity, one of whose executive officers served on the compensation committee (or other board committee performing equivalent functions or, in the absence of any such committee, the entire board of directors) of the registrant; and

(C) An executive officer of the registrant served as a member of the compensation committee (or other board committee performing equivalent functions or, in the absence of any such committee, the entire board of directors) of another entity, one of whose executive officers served as a director of the registrant.

(iv) Disclosure required under paragraph (e)(4)(iii) of this Item regarding a compensation committee member or other director of the registrant who also served as an executive officer of another entity shall be accompanied by the disclosure called for by Item 404 with respect to that person.

Instruction to Item 407(e)(4).

For purposes of paragraph (e)(4) of this Item, the term *entity* shall not include an entity exempt from tax under section 501(c)(3) of the Internal Revenue Code (26 U.S.C. 501(c)(3)).

(5) Under the caption "Compensation Committee Report:"

(i) The compensation committee (or other board committee performing equivalent functions or, in the absence of any such committee, the entire board of directors) must state whether:

(A) The compensation committee has reviewed and discussed the Compensation Discussion and Analysis required by Item 402(b) (§ 229.402(b)) with management; and

(B) Based on the review and discussions referred to in paragraph (e)(5)(i)(A) of this Item, the compensation committee recommended to the board of directors that the Compensation Discussion and Analysis be included in the registrant's annual report on Form 10-K (§ 249.310 of this chapter), proxy statement on Schedule 14A (§ 240.14a-101 of this chapter) or information statement on Schedule 14C (§ 240.14c-101 of this chapter).

(ii) The name of each member of the registrant's compensation committee (or other board committee performing equivalent functions or, in the absence of any such committee, the entire board of directors) must appear below the disclosure required by paragraph (e)(5)(i) of this Item.

Instructions to Item 407(e)(5).

1. The information required by paragraph (e)(5) of this Item shall not be deemed to be "soliciting material," or to be "filed" with the Commission or subject to Regulation 14A or 14C (17 CFR 240.14a-1 through 240.14b-2 or 240.14c-1 through 240.14c-101), other than as provided in this Item, or to the liabilities of section 18 of the Exchange Act (15 U.S.C. 78r), except to the extent that the registrant specifically requests that the information be treated as soliciting material or specifically incorporates it by reference into a document filed under the Securities Act or the Exchange Act.

2. The disclosure required by paragraph (e)(5) of this Item need not be provided in any filings other than an annual report on Form 10-K (§ 249.310 of this chapter), a proxy statement on Schedule 14A (§ 240.14a-101 of this chapter) or an information statement on Schedule 14C (§ 240.14c-101 of this chapter). Such information will not be deemed to be incorporated by reference into any filing under the Securities Act or the Exchange Act, except to the extent that the registrant specifically incorporates it by reference. If the registrant elects to incorporate this information by reference from the proxy or information statement into its annual report on Form 10-K pursuant to General Instruction G(3) to Form 10-K, the disclosure required by paragraph (e)(5) of this Item will be deemed furnished in the annual report on Form 10-K and will not be deemed incorporated by reference into any filing under the Securities Act or the Exchange Act as a result as a result of furnishing the disclosure in this manner.

3. The disclosure required by paragraph (e)(5) of this Item need only be provided one time during any fiscal year.

(f) *Shareholder communications.*

(1) State whether or not the registrant's board of directors provides a process for security holders to send communications to the board of directors and, if the registrant does not have such a process for security holders to send communications to the board of directors, state the basis for the view of the board of directors that it is appropriate for the registrant not to have such a process.

(2) If the registrant has a process for security holders to send communications to the board of directors:

(i) Describe the manner in which security holders can send communications to the board and, if applicable, to specified individual directors; and

(ii) If all security holder communications are not sent directly to board members, describe the registrant's process for determining which communications will be relayed to board members.

Instructions to Item 407(f).

1. In lieu of providing the information required by paragraph (f)(2) of this Item in the proxy statement, the registrant may instead provide the registrant's Web site address where such information appears.

2. For purposes of the disclosure required by paragraph (f)(2)(ii) of this Item, a registrant's process for collecting and organizing security holder communications, as well as similar or related activities, need not be disclosed provided that the registrant's process is approved by a majority of the independent directors or, in the case of a registrant that is an investment company, a majority of the directors who are not "interested persons" of the investment company as defined in section 2(a)(19) of the Investment Company Act of 1940 (15 U.S.C. 80a-2(a)(19)).

3. For purposes of this paragraph, communications from an officer or director of the registrant will not be viewed as "security holder communications." Communications from an employee or agent of the registrant will be viewed as "security holder communications" for purposes of this paragraph only if those communications are made solely in such employee's or agent's capacity as a security holder.

4. For purposes of this paragraph, security holder proposals submitted pursuant to § 240.14a-8 of this chapter, and communications made in connection with such proposals, will not be viewed as "security holder communications."

(g) *Smaller reporting companies.* A registrant that qualifies as a "smaller reporting company," as defined by § 229.10(f)(1), is not required to provide:

(1) The disclosure required in paragraph (d)(5) of this Item in its first annual report filed pursuant to section 13(a) or 15(d) of the Exchange Act (15 U.S.C. 78m (a) or 78o(d)) following the effective date of its first registration statement filed under the Securities Act (15 U.S.C. 77a *et seq.*) or Exchange Act (15 U.S.C. 78a *et seq.*); and

(2) Need not provide the disclosures required by paragraphs (e)(4) and (e)(5) of this Item.

(h) *Board leadership structure and role in risk oversight.* Briefly describe the leadership structure of the registrant's board, such as whether the same person serves as both principal executive officer and chairman of the board, or whether two individuals serve in those positions, and, in the case of a registrant that is an investment company, whether the chairman of the board is an "interested person" of the registrant as defined in section 2(a)(19) of the Investment Company Act (15 U.S.C. 80a-2(a)(19)). If one person serves as both principal executive officer and chairman of the board, or if the chairman of the board of a registrant that is an investment company is an "interested person" of the registrant, disclose whether the registrant has a lead independent director and what specific role the lead independent director plays in the leadership of the board. This disclosure should indicate why the registrant has determined that its leadership structure is appropriate given the specific characteristics or circumstances of the registrant. In addition, disclose the extent of the board's role in the risk oversight of the registrant, such as how the board administers its oversight function, and the effect that this has on the board's leadership structure.

Instructions to Item 407.

1. For purposes of this Item:

a. *Listed issuer* means a listed issuer as defined in § 240.10A-3 of this chapter;

b. *National securities exchange* means a national securities exchange registered pursuant to section 6(a) of the Exchange Act (15 U.S.C. 78f(a));

c. *Inter-dealer quotation system* means an automated inter-dealer quotation system of a national securities association registered pursuant to section 15A(a) of the Exchange Act (15 U.S.C. 78o-3(a)); and

d. *National securities association* means a national securities association registered pursuant to section 15A(a) of the Exchange Act (15 U.S.C. 78o-3(a)) that has been approved by the Commission (as that definition may be modified or supplemented).

2. With respect to paragraphs (c)(2)(i), (d)(1) and (e)(2) of this Item, disclose whether a current copy of the applicable committee charter is available to security holders on the registrant's Web site, and if so, provide the registrant's Web site address. If a current copy of the charter is not available to security holders on the registrant's Web site, include a copy of the charter in an appendix to the registrant's proxy or information statement that is provided to security holders at least once every three fiscal years, or if the charter has been materially amended since the beginning of the registrant's last fiscal year. If a current copy of the charter is not available to security holders on the registrant's Web site, and is not included as an appendix to the registrant's proxy or information statement, identify in which of the prior fiscal years the charter was so included in satisfaction of this requirement.

[As amended in Release No. 33-9089, effective February 28, 2010, 74 F.R. 68334.]

Subpart 229.500—Registration Statement and Prospectus Provisions

[¶ 13,051] Forepart of Registration Statement and Outside Front Cover Page of Prospectus

Reg. § 229.501. Item 501. The registrant must furnish the following information in plain English. See § 230.421(d) of Regulation C of this chapter.

(a) *Front Cover Page of the Registration Statement.* Where appropriate, include the delaying amendment legend from § 230.473 of Regulation C of this chapter.

(b) *Outside Front Cover Page of the Prospectus.* Limit the outside cover page to one page. If the following information applies to your offering, disclose it on the outside cover page of the prospectus.

(1) *Name.* The registrant's name. A foreign registrant must give the English translation of its name.

Instruction to paragraph 501(b)(1).

If your name is the same as that of a company that is well known, include information to eliminate any possible confusion with the other company. If your name indicates a line of business in which you are not engaged or you are engaged only to a limited extent, include information to eliminate any misleading inference as to your business. In some circumstances, disclosure may not be sufficient and you may be required to change your name. You will not be required to change your name if you are an established company, the character of your business has changed, and the investing public is generally aware of the change and the character of your current business.

(2) *Title and amount of securities.* The title and amount of securities offered. Separately state the amount of securities offered by selling security holders, if any. If the underwriter has any arrangement with the issuer, such as an over-allotment option, under which the underwriter may purchase additional shares in connection with the offering, indicate that this arrangement exists and state the amount of additional shares that the underwriter may purchase under the arrangement. Give a brief description of the securities except where the information is clear from the title of the security. For example, you are not required to describe common stock that has full voting, dividend and liquidation rights usually associated with common stock.

(3) *Offering price of the securities.* Where you offer securities for cash, the price to the public of the securities, the underwriter's discounts and commissions, the net proceeds you receive, and any selling shareholder's net proceeds. Show this information on both a per share or unit basis and for the total amount of the offering. If you make the offering on a minimum/maximum basis, show this information based on the total minimum and total maximum amount of the offering. You may present the information in a table, term sheet format, or other clear presentation. You may present the information in any format that fits the design of the cover page so long as the information can be easily read and is not misleading;

Instructions to paragraph 501(b)(3)

1. If a preliminary prospectus is circulated and you are not subject to the reporting requirements of Section 13(a) or 15(d) of the Exchange Act, provide, as applicable:

(A) A bona fide estimate of the range of the maximum offering price and the maximum number of securities offered; or

(B) A bona fide estimate of the principal amount of the debt securities offered.

2. If it is impracticable to state the price to the public, explain the method by which the price is to be determined. If the securities are to be offered at the market price, or if the offering price is to be determined by a formula related to the market price, indicate the market and market price of the securities as of the latest practicable date.

3. If you file a registration statement on Form S-8, you are not required to comply with this paragraph (b)(3).

(4) *Market for the Securities.* Whether any national securities exchange or the Nasdaq Stock Market lists the securities offered, naming the particular market(s), and identifying the trading symbol(s) for those securities;

(5) *Risk Factors.* A cross-reference to the risk factors section, including the page number where it appears in the prospectus. Highlight this cross-reference by prominent type or in another manner;

(6) *State Legend.* Any legend or statement required by the law of any state in which the securities are to be offered. You may combine this with any legend required by the SEC, if appropriate;

(7) *Commission Legend.* A legend that indicates that neither the Securities and Exchange Commission nor any state securities commission has approved or disapproved of the securities or passed upon the accuracy or adequacy of the disclosures in the prospectus and that any contrary representation is a criminal offense. You may use one of the following or other clear, plain language:

Example A: Neither the Securities and Exchange Commission nor any state securities commission has approved or disapproved of these securities or passed upon the adequacy or accuracy of this prospectus. Any representation to the contrary is a criminal offense.

Example B: Neither the Securities and Exchange Commission nor any state securities commission has approved or disapproved of these securities or determined if this prospectus is truthful or complete. Any representation to the contrary is a criminal offense.

(8) *Underwriting.* (i) Name(s) of the lead or managing underwriter(s) and an identification of the nature of the underwriting arrangements;

(ii) If the offering is not made on a firm commitment basis, a brief description of the underwriting arrangements. You may use any clear, concise, and accurate description of the underwriting arrangements. You may use the following descriptions of underwriting arrangements where appropriate:

Example A: Best efforts offering. The underwriters are not required to sell any specific number or dollar amount of securities but will use their best efforts to sell the securities offered.

Example B: Best efforts, minimum-maximum offering. The underwriters must sell the minimum number of securities offered (insert number) if any are sold. The underwriters are required to use only their best efforts to sell the maximum number of securities offered (insert number).

(iii) If you offer the securities on a best efforts or best efforts minimum/maximum basis, the date the offering will end, any minimum purchase requirements, and any arrangements to place the funds in an escrow, trust, or similar account. If you have not made any of these arrangements, state this fact and describe the effect on investors;

(9) *Date of Prospectus.* The date of the prospectus;

(10) *Prospectus "Subject to Completion" Legend.* If you use the prospectus before the effective date of the registration statement, a prominent statement that:

(i) The information in the prospectus will be amended or completed;

(ii) A registration statement relating to these securities has been filed with the Securities and Exchange Commission;

(iii) The securities may not be sold until the registration statement becomes effective; and

(iv) The prospectus is not an offer to sell the securities and it is not soliciting an offer to buy the securities in any state where offers or sales are not permitted. The legend may be in the following or other clear, plain language:

> The information in this prospectus is not complete and may be changed. We may not sell these securities until the registration statement filed with the Securities and Exchange Commission is effective. This prospectus is not an offer to sell these securities and it is not soliciting an offer to buy these securities in any state where the offer or sale is not permitted.

(11) If you use § 230.430A of this chapter to omit pricing information and the prospectus is used before you determine the public offering price, the information and legend in paragraph (b)(10) of this section.

Instruction to Item 501. For asset-backed securities, see also Item 1102 of Regulation AB (§ 229.1102).

[As last amended in Release No. 33-8518, effective March 8, 2005 (Compliance dates are triggered by initial bona fide offer date or registration statement filing date and extend out to March 31, 2006. Complete compliance date details can be found in the "Dates" section of the release.), 70 F.R. 1506.]

[¶ 13,052] Inside Front and Outside Back Cover Pages of Prospectus

Reg. § 229.502. Item 502. The registrant must furnish this information in plain English. See § 230.421(d) of Regulation C of this chapter.

(a) *Table of Contents.* On either the inside front or outside back cover page of the prospectus, provide a reasonably detailed table of contents. It must show the page number of the various sections or subdivisions of the prospectus. Include a specific listing of the risk factors section required by Item 503 of this Regulation S-K (17 CFR 229.503). You must include the table of contents immediately following the cover page in any prospectus you deliver electronically.

(b) *Dealer Prospectus Delivery Obligation.* On the outside back cover page of the prospectus, advise dealers of their prospectus delivery obligation, including the expiration date specified by Section 4(3) of the Securities Act (15 U.S.C. 77d(3)) and § 230.174 of this chapter. If you do not know the expiration date on the effective date of the registration statement, include the expiration date in the copy of the prospectus you file under § 230.424(b) of this chapter. You do not have to include this information if dealers are not required to deliver a prospectus under § 230.174 of this chapter or Section 24(d) of the Investment Company Act (15 U.S.C. 80a-24). You may use the following or other clear, plain language:

> Dealer Prospectus Delivery Obligation
>
> Until (insert date), all dealers that effect transactions in these securities, whether or not participating in this offering, may be required to deliver a prospectus. This is in addition to the dealers' obligation to deliver a prospectus when acting as underwriters and with respect to their unsold allotments or subscriptions.

[As last amended in Release No. 33-7497, January 28, 1998, effective October 1, 1998, 63 F.R. 6370.]

[¶ 13,053] Prospectus Summary, Risk Factors, and Ratio of Earnings to Fixed Charges

Reg. § 229.503. Item 503. The registrant must furnish this information in plain English. See § 230.421(d) of Regulation C of this chapter.

(a) *Prospectus Summary.* Provide a summary of the information in the prospectus where the length or complexity of the prospectus makes a summary useful. The summary should be brief. The summary should not contain, and is not required to contain, all of the detailed information in the prospectus. If you provide summary business or financial information, even if you do not caption it as a summary, you still must provide that information in plain English.

Instruction to paragraph 503(a).

The summary should not merely repeat the text of the prospectus but should provide a brief overview of the key aspects of the offering. Carefully consider and identify those aspects of the offering that are the most significant and determine how best to highlight those points in clear, plain language.

(b) *Address and Telephone Number.* Include, either on the cover page or in the summary section of the prospectus, the complete mailing address and telephone number of your principal executive offices.

(c) *Risk Factors.* Where appropriate, provide under the caption "Risk Factors" a discussion of the most significant factors that make the offering speculative or risky. This discussion must be concise and organized logically. Do not present risks that could apply to any issuer or any offering. Explain how the risk affects the issuer or the securities being offered. Set forth each risk factor under a subcaption that adequately describes the risk. The risk factor discussion must immediately follow the summary section. If you do not include a summary section, the risk factor section must immediately follow the cover page of the prospectus or the pricing information section that immediately follows the cover page. Pricing information means price and price-related information that you may omit from the prospectus in an effective registration statement based on § 230.430A(a) of this chapter. The risk factors may include, among other things, the following:

(1) Your lack of an operating history;

(2) Your lack of profitable operations in recent periods;

(3) Your financial position;

(4) Your business or proposed business; or

(5) The lack of a market for your common equity securities or securities convertible into or exercisable for common equity securities.

(d) *Ratio of Earnings to Fixed Charges.* If you register debt securities, show a ratio of earnings to fixed charges. If you register preference equity securities, show the ratio of combined fixed charges and preference dividends to earnings. Present the ratio for each of the last five fiscal years and the latest interim period for which financial statements are presented in the document. If you will use the proceeds from the sale of debt or preference securities to repay any of your outstanding debt or to retire other securities and the change in the ratio would be ten percent or greater, you must include a ratio showing the application of the proceeds, commonly referred to as the pro forma ratio.

Instructions to paragraph 503(d)

1. *Definitions.* In calculating the ratio of earnings to fixed charges, you must use the following definitions:

(A) *Fixed charges.* The term "fixed charges" means the sum of the following: (a) interest expensed and capitalized, (b) amortized premiums, discounts and capitalized expenses related to indebtedness, (c) an estimate of the interest within rental expense, and (d) preference security dividend requirements of consolidated subsidiaries.

(B) *Preference security dividend.* The term "preference security dividend" is the amount of pre-tax earnings that is required to pay the dividends on outstanding preference securities. The dividend requirement must be computed as the amount of the dividend divided by (1 minus the effective income tax rate applicable to continuing operations).

(C) *Earnings.* The term "earnings" is the amount resulting from adding and subtracting the following items. Add the following: (a) pre-tax income from continuing operations before adjustment for income or loss from equity investees; (b) fixed charges; (c) amortization of capitalized interest; (d) distributed income of equity investees; and (e) your share of pre-tax losses of equity investees for which charges arising from guarantees are included in fixed charges. From the total of the added items, subtract the following: (a) interest capitalized; (b) preference security dividend requirements of consolidated subsidiaries; and (c) the noncontrolling interest in pre-tax income of subsidiaries that have not incurred fixed charges. Equity investees are investments that you account for using the equity method of accounting. Public utilities following SFAS 71 should not add amortization of capitalized interest in determining earnings, nor reduce fixed charges by any allowance for funds used during construction.

2. *Disclosure*. Disclose the following information when showing the ratio of earnings to fixed charges:

(A) *Deficiency*. If a ratio indicates less than one-to-one coverage, disclose the dollar amount of the deficiency.

(B) *Pro forma ratio*. You may show the pro forma ratio only for the most recent fiscal year and the latest interim period. Use the net change in interest or dividends from the refinancing to calculate the pro forma ratio.

(C) *Foreign private issuers*. A foreign private issuer must show the ratio based on the figures in the primary financial statement. A foreign private issuer must show the ratio based on the figures resulting from the reconciliation to U.S. generally accepted accounting principles if this ratio is materially different.

(D) *Summary Section*. If you provide a summary or similar section in the prospectus, show the ratios in that section.

3. *Exhibit*. File an exhibit to the registration statement to show the figures used to calculate the ratios. See paragraph (b)(12) of Item 601 of Regulation S-K (17 CFR 229.601(b)(12)).

(e) *Smaller reporting companies*. A registrant that qualifies as a smaller reporting company, as defined by § 229.10(f), need not comply with paragraph (d) of this Item.

Instruction to Item 503. For asset-backed securities, see also Item 1103 of Regulation AB (§ 229.1103).

[As last amended in Release No. 33-9026, effective April 23, 2009, 74 F.R. 18612.]

[¶ 13,054] Use of Proceeds

Reg. § 229.504. Item 504. State the principal purposes for which the net proceeds to the registrant from the securities to be offered are intended to be used and the approximate amount intended to be used for each such purpose. Where registrant has no current specific plan for the proceeds, or a significant portion thereof, the registrant shall so state and discuss the principal reasons for the offering.

Instructions to Item 504. 1. Where less than all the securities to be offered may be sold and more than one use is listed for the proceeds, indicate the order of priority of such purposes and discuss the registrant's plans if substantially less than the maximum proceeds are obtained. Such discussion need not be included if underwriting arrangements with respect to such securities are such that, if any securities are sold to the public, it reasonably can be expected that the actual proceeds will not be substantially less than the aggregate proceeds to the registrant shown pursuant to Item 501 of Regulation S-K (§ 229.501).

2. Details of proposed expenditures need not be given; for example, there need be furnished only a brief outline of any program of construction or addition of equipment. Consideration should be given as to the need to include a discussion of certain matters addressed in the discussion and analysis of registrant's financial condition and results of operations, such as liquidity and capital expenditures.

3. If any material amounts of other funds are necessary to accomplish the specified purposes for which the proceeds are to be obtained, state the amounts and sources of such other funds needed for each such specified purpose and the sources thereof.

4. If any material part of the proceeds is to be used to discharge indebtedness, set forth the interest rate and maturity of such indebtedness. If the indebtedness to be discharged was incurred within one year, describe the use of the proceeds of such indebtedness other than short-term borrowings used for working capital.

5. If any material amount of the proceeds is to be used to acquire assets, otherwise than in the ordinary course of business, describe briefly and state the cost of the assets and, where such assets are to be acquired from affiliates of the registrant or their associates, give the names of the persons from whom they are to be acquired and set forth the principle followed in determining the cost to the registrant.

6. Where the registrant indicates that the proceeds may, or will, be used to finance acquisitions of other businesses, the identity of such businesses, if known, or, if not known, the nature of the businesses to be sought, the status of any negotiations with respect to the acquisition, and a brief description of such business shall be included. Where, however, pro forma financial statements reflecting such acquisition are not required by Regulation S-X (17 CFR 210.01 through 210.12-29), including Rule 8-05 for smaller reporting companies, to be included in the registration statement, the possible terms of any transaction, the identification of the parties thereto or the nature of the business sought need not be disclosed, to the extent that the registrant reasonably determines that public disclosure of such information would jeopardize

the acquisition. Where Regulation S-X, including Rule 8-04 for smaller reporting companies, as applicable, would require financial statements of the business to be acquired to be included, the description of the business to be acquired shall be more detailed.

7. The registrant may reserve the right to change the use of proceeds, provided that such reservation is due to certain contingencies that are discussed specifically and the alternatives to such use in that event are indicated.

[As amended in Release No. 33-8876, effective February 4, 2008, 73 F.R. 934.]

[¶ 13,055] Determination of Offering Price

Reg. § 229.505. Item 505. (a) *Common equity.* Where common equity is being registered for which there is no established public trading market for purposes of paragraph (a) of Item 201 of Regulation S-K (§ 229.201(a)) or where there is a material disparity between the offering price of the common equity being registered and the market price of outstanding shares of the same class, describe the various factors considered in determining such offering price.

(b) *Warrants, rights and convertible securities.* Where warrants, rights or convertible securities exercisable for common equity for which there is no established public trading market for purposes of paragraph (a) of Item 201 of Regulation S-K (§ 229.201(a)) are being registered, describe the various factors considered in determining their exercise or conversion price.

[As adopted in Release No. AS-306, March 3, 1982, effective May 24, 1982, 47 F.R. 11380.]

[¶ 13,056] Dilution

Reg. § 229.506. Item 506. Where common equity securities are being registered and there is substantial disparity between the public offering price and the effective cash cost to officers, directors, promoters and affiliated persons of common equity acquired by them in transactions during the past five years, or which they have the right to acquire, and the registrant is not subject to the reporting requirements of section 13(a) or 15(d) of the Exchange Act immediately prior to filing of the registration statement, there shall be included a comparison of the public contribution under the proposed public offering and the effective cash contribution of such persons. In such cases, and in other instances where common equity securities are being registered by a registrant that has had losses in each of its last three fiscal years and there is a material dilution of the purchasers' equity interest, the following shall be disclosed:

(a) The net tangible book value per share before and after the distribution;

(b) The amount of the increase in such net tangible book value per share attributable to the cash payments made by purchasers of the shares being offered; and

(c) The amount of the immediate dilution from the public offering price which will be absorbed by such purchasers.

[As adopted in Release No. AS-306, March 3, 1982, effective May 24, 1982, 47 F.R. 11380.]

[¶ 13,057] Selling Security Holders

Reg. § 229.507. Item 507. If any of the securities to be registered are to be offered for the account of security holders, name each such security holder, indicate the nature of any position, office, or other material relationship which the selling security holder has had within the past three years with the registrant or any of its predecessors or affiliates, and state the amount of securities of the class owned by such security holder prior to the offering, the amount to be offered for the security holder's account, the amount and (if one percent or more) the percentage of the class to be owned by such security holder after completion of the offering.

[As adopted in Release No. AS-306, March 3, 1982, effective May 24, 1982, 47 F.R. 11380.]

[¶ 13,058] Plan of Distribution

Reg. § 229.508. Item 508. (a) *Underwriters and underwriting obligation.* If the securities are to be offered through underwriters, name the principal underwriters, and state the respective amounts underwritten. Identify each such underwriter having a material relationship with the registrant and state the nature of the relationship. State briefly the nature of the obligation of the underwriter(s) to take the securities.

Instruction to Paragraph 508(a). All that is required as to the nature of the underwriters' obligation is whether the underwriters are or will be committed to take and to pay for all of the securities if any are taken, or whether it is merely an agency or the type of "best efforts" arrangement under which the underwriters are required to take and to pay for only such securities as they may sell to the public. Conditions precedent to the underwriters' taking the securities, including "market-outs," need not be described except in the case of an agency or "best efforts" arrangement.

(b) *New underwriters.* Where securities being registered are those of a registrant that has not previously been required to file reports pursuant to section 13(a) or 15(d) of the Exchange Act, or where a prospectus is required to include reference on its cover page to material risks pursuant to Item 501 of Regulation S-K (§ 229.501), and any one or more of the managing underwriter(s) (or where there are no managing underwriters, a majority of the principal underwriters) has been organized, reactivated, or first registered as a broker-dealer within the past three years, these facts concerning such underwriter(s) shall be disclosed in the prospectus together with, where applicable, the disclosures that the principal business function of such underwriter(s) will be to sell the securities to be registered, or that the promoters of the registrant have a material relationship with such underwriter(s). Sufficient details shall be given to allow full appreciation of such underwriter(s) experience and its relationship with the registrant, promoters and their controlling persons.

(c) *Other distributions.* Outline briefly the plan of distribution of any securities to be registered that are to be offered otherwise than through underwriters.

(1) If any securities are to be offered pursuant to a dividend or interest reinvestment plan the terms of which provide for the purchase of some securities on the market, state whether the registrant or the participant pays fees, commissions, and expenses incurred in connection with the plan. If the participant will pay such fees, commissions and expenses, state the anticipated cost to participants by transaction or other convenient reference.

(2) If the securities are to be offered through the selling efforts of brokers or dealers, describe the plan of distribution and the terms of any agreement, arrangement, or understanding entered into with broker(s) or dealer(s) prior to the effective date of the registration statement, including volume limitations on sales, parties to the agreement and the conditions under which the agreement may be terminated. If known, identify the broker(s) or dealer(s) which will participate in the offering and state the amount to be offered through each.

(3) If any of the securities being registered are to be offered otherwise than for cash, state briefly the general purposes of the distribution, the basis upon which the securities are to be offered, the amount of compensation and other expenses of distribution, and by whom they are to be borne. If the distribution is to be made pursuant to a plan of acquisition, reorganization, readjustment or succession, describe briefly the general effect of the plan and state when it became or is to become operative. As to any material amount of assets to be acquired under the plan, furnish information corresponding to that required by Instruction 5 of Item 504 of Regulation S-K (§ 229.504).

(d) *Offerings on exchange.* If the securities are to be offered on an exchange, indicate the exchange. If the registered securities are to be offered in connection with the writing of exchange-traded call options, describe briefly such transactions.

(e) *Underwriter's compensation.* Provide a table that sets out the nature of the compensation and the amount of discounts and commissions to be paid to the underwriter for each security and in total. The table must show the separate amounts to be paid by the company and the selling shareholders. In addition, include in the table all other items considered by the National Association of Securities Dealers to be underwriting compensation for purposes of that Association's Rules of Fair Practice.

Instructions to paragraph 508(e)

1. The term "commissions" is defined in paragraph (17) of Schedule A of the Securities Act. Show separately in the table the cash commissions paid by the registrant and selling security holders. Also show in the table commissions paid by other persons. Disclose any finder's fee or similar payments in the table.

2. Disclose the offering expenses specified in Item 511 of Regulation S-K (17 CFR 229.511).

3. If the underwriter has any arrangement with the issuer, such as an over-allotment option, under which the underwriter may purchase additional shares in connection with the offering, indicate that this arrangement exists and state the amount of additional shares that the underwriter may purchase under the arrangement. Where the underwriter has such an arrangement, present maximum-minimum information in a separate column to the table, based on the purchase of all or none of the shares subject to the arrangement. Describe the key terms of the arrangement in the narrative.

(f) *Underwriter's representative on board of directors.* Describe any arrangement whereby the underwriter has the right to designate or nominate a member or members of the board of directors of the registrant. The registrant shall disclose the identity of any director so designated or nominated, and indicate whether or not a person so designated or nominated, or allowed to be designated or nominated by the underwriter is or may be a director, officer, partner, employee or affiliate of the underwriter.

(g) *Indemnification of underwriters.* If the underwriting agreement provides for indemnification by the registrant of the underwriters or their controlling persons against any liability arising under the Securities Act, furnish a brief description of such indemnification provisions.

(h) *Dealers' compensation.* State briefly the discounts and commissions to be allowed or paid to dealers, including all cash, securities, contracts or other considerations to be received by any dealer in connection with the sale of the securities. If any dealers are to act in the capacity of sub-underwriters and are to be allowed or paid any additional discounts or commissions for acting in such capacity, a general statement to that effect will suffice without giving the additional amounts to be sold.

(i) *Finders.* Identify any finder and, if applicable, describe the nature of any material relationship between such finder and the registrant, its officers, directors, principal stockholders, finders or promoters or the principal underwriter(s), or if there is a managing underwriter(s), the managing underwriter(s) (including, in each case, affiliates or associates thereof).

(j) *Discretionary accounts.* If the registrant was not, immediately prior to the filing of the registration statement, subject to the requirements of section 13(a) or 15(d) of the Exchange Act, identify any principal underwriter that intends to sell to any accounts over which it exercises discretionary authority and include an estimate of the amount of securities so intended to be sold. The response to this paragraph shall be contained in a pre-effective amendment which shall be circulated if the information is not available when the registration statement is filed.

(k) *Passive market making.* If the underwriters or any selling group members intend to engage in passive market making transactions as permitted by Rule 103 of Regulation M (§ 242.103 of this chapter), indicate such intention and briefly describe passive market making.

(l) *Stabilization and other transactions.* (1) Briefly describe any transaction that the underwriter intends to conduct during the offering that stabilizes, maintains, or otherwise affects the market price of the offered securities. Include information on stabilizing transactions, syndicate short covering transactions, penalty bids, or any other transaction that affects the offered security's price. Describe the nature of the transactions clearly and explain how the transactions affect the offered security's price. Identify the exchange or other market on which these transactions may occur. If true, disclose that the underwriter may discontinue these transactions at any time;

(2) If the stabilizing began before the effective date of the registration statement, disclose the amount of securities bought, the prices at which they were bought and the period within which they were bought. If you use § 230.430A of this chapter, the prospectus you file under § 230.424(b) of this chapter or include in a post-effective amendment must contain information on the stabilizing transactions that took place before the determination of the public offering price; and

(3) If you are making a warrants or rights offering of securities to existing security holders and any securities not purchased by existing security holders are to be reoffered to the public, disclose in a supplement to the prospectus or in the prospectus used in connection with the reoffering:

(i) The amount of securities bought in stabilization activities during the offering period and the price or range of prices at which the securities were bought;

(ii) The amount of the offered securities subscribed for during the offering period;

(iii) The amount of the offered securities subscribed for by the underwriter during the offering period;

(iv) The amount of the offered securities sold during the offering period by the underwriter and the price or price ranges at which the securities were sold; and

(v) The amount of the offered securities that will be reoffered to the public and the public offering price.

[As last amended in Release No. 33-7497, January 28, 1998, effective October 1, 1998, 63 F.R. 6370.]

[¶ 13,059] Interests of Named Experts and Counsel

Reg. § 229.509. Item 509. If (a) any expert named in the registration statement as having prepared or certified any part thereof (or is named as having prepared or certified a report or valuation for use in connection with the registration statement), or (b) counsel for the registrant, underwriters or selling security holders named in the prospectus as having given an opinion upon the validity of the securities being registered or upon other legal matters in connection with the registration or offering of such securities, was employed for such purpose on a contingent basis, or at the time of such preparation, certification or opinion or at any time thereafter through the date of effectiveness of the registration statement or that part of the registration statement to which such preparation, certification or opinion relates, had, or is to receive in connection with the offering, a substantial interest, direct or indirect, in the registrant or any of its parents or subsidiaries or was connected with the registrant or any of its parents or subsidiaries as a promoter, managing underwriter (or any principal underwriter, if there are no managing underwriters), voting trustee, director, officer, or employee, furnish a brief statement of the nature of such contingent basis, interest, or connection.

Instructions to Item 509. 1. The interest of an expert (other than an accountant) or counsel will not be deemed substantial and need not be disclosed if the interest, including the fair market value of all securities of the registrant owned, received and to be received, or subject to options, warrants or rights received or to be received by the expert or counsel does not exceed $50,000. For the purpose of this Instruction, the term "expert" or counsel includes the firm, corporation, partnership or other entity, if any, by which such expert or counsel is employed or of which he is a member or of counsel to and all attorneys in the case of counsel, and all nonclerical personnel in the case of named experts, participating in such matter on behalf of such firm, corporation, partnership or entity.

2. Accountants, providing a report on the financial statements, presented or incorporated by reference in the registration statement, should note § 210.2-01 of Regulation S-X (17 CFR 210) for the Commission's requirements regarding "Qualification of Accountants" which discusses disqualifying interests.

[As adopted in Release No. AS-306, March 3, 1982, effective May 24, 1982, 47 F.R. 11380.]

[¶ 13,060] Disclosure of Commission Position on Indemnification for Securities Act Liabilities

Reg. § 229.510. Item 510. In addition to the disclosure prescribed by Item 702 of Regulation S-K (§ 229.702), if the undertaking required by paragraph (h) of Item 512 of Regulation S-K (§ 229.512) is not required to be included in the registration statement because acceleration of the effective date of the registration statement is not being requested, and if waivers have not been obtained comparable to those specified in paragraph (h), a brief description of the indemnification provisions relating to directors, officers and controlling persons of the registrant against liability arising under the Securities Act (including any provision of the underwriting agreement which relates to indemnification of the under-writer or its controlling persons by the registrant against such liabilities where a director, officer or controlling person of the registrant is such an underwriter or controlling person thereof or a member of any firm which is such an underwriter) shall be included in the prospectus, together with a statement in substantially the following form:

> Insofar as indemnification for liabilities arising under the Securities Act of 1933 may be permitted to directors, officers or persons controlling the registrant pursuant to the foregoing provisions, the registrant has been informed that in the opinion of the Securities and Exchange Commission such indemnification is against public policy as expressed in the Act and is therefore unenforceable.

[As last amended in Release No. 33-6910, September 17, 1991, 56 F.R. 48103.]

[¶ 13,061] Other Expenses of Issuance and Distribution

Reg. § 229.511. Item 511. Furnish a reasonably itemized statement of all expenses in connection with the issuance and distribution of the securities to be registered, other than underwriting discounts and commissions. If any of the securities to be registered are to be offered for the account of security holders, indicate the portion of such expenses to be borne by such security holder.

> *Instruction to Item 511.* Insofar as practicable, registration fees, Federal taxes, States taxes and fees, trustees' and transfer agents' fees, costs of printing and engraving, and legal, accounting, and engineering fees shall be itemized separately. Include as a separate item any premium paid by the registrant or any selling security holder on any policy obtained in connection with the offering and sale of the securities being registered which insures or indemnifies directors or officers against any liabilities they may incur in connection with the registration, offering, or sale of such securities. The information may be given as subject to future contingencies. If the amounts of any items are not known, estimates, identified as such, shall be given.

[As adopted in Release No. AS-306, March 3, 1982, effective May 24, 1982, 47 F.R. 11380.]

[¶ 13,062] Undertakings

Reg. § 229.512. Item 512. Include each of the following undertakings that is applicable to the offering being registered.

(a) *Rule 415 offering.*[1] Include the following if the securities are registered pursuant to Rule 415 under the Securities Act (§ 230.415 of this chapter):

The undersigned registrant hereby undertakes:

(1) To file, during any period in which offers or sales are being made, a post-effective amendment to this registration statement:

(i) To include any prospectus required by section 10(a)(3) of the Securities Act of 1933;

(ii) To reflect in the prospectus any facts or events arising after the effective date of the registration statement (or the most recent post-effective amendment thereof) which, individually or in the aggregate, represent a fundamental change in the information set forth in the registration statement. Notwithstanding the foregoing, any increase or decrease in volume of securities offered (if the total dollar value of

---

[1] Paragraph (a) reflects proposals made in Securities Act Release No. 6334 (Aug. 6, 1981).

securities offered would not exceed that which was registered) and any deviation from the low or high end of the estimated maximum offering range may be reflected in the form of prospectus filed with the Commission pursuant to Rule 424(b) (§ 230.424(b) of this chapter) if, in the aggregate, the changes in volume and price represent no more than a 20% change in the maximum aggregate offering price set forth in the "Calculation of Registration Fee" table in the effective registration statement;

(iii) To include any material information with respect to the plan of distribution not previously disclosed in the registration statement or any material change to such information in the registration statement;

Provided, however, That:

(A) Paragraphs (a)(1)(i) and (a)(1)(ii) of this section do not apply if the registration statement is on Form S-8 (§ 239.16b of this chapter), and the information required to be included in a post-effective amendment by those paragraphs is contained in reports filed with or furnished to the Commission by the registrant pursuant to section 13 or section 15(d) of the Securities Exchange Act of 1934 (15 U.S.C. 78m or 78o(d)) that are incorporated by reference in the registration statement; and

(B) Paragraphs (a)(1)(i), (a)(1)(ii) and (a)(1)(iii) of this section do not apply if the registration statement is on Form S-3 (§ 239.13 of this chapter) or Form F-3 (§ 239.33 of this chapter) and the information required to be included in a post-effective amendment by those paragraphs is contained in reports filed with or furnished to the Commission by the registrant pursuant to section 13 or section 15(d) of the Securities Exchange Act of 1934 that are incorporated by reference in the registration statement, or is contained in a form of prospectus filed pursuant to Rule 424(b) (§ 230.424(b) of this chapter) that is part of the registration statement.

(C) *Provided further, however,* that paragraphs (a)(1)(i) and (a)(1)(ii) do not apply if the registration statement is for an offering of asset-backed securities on Form S-1 (§ 239.11 of this chapter) or Form S-3 (§ 239.13 of this chapter), and the information required to be included in a post-effective amendment is provided pursuant to Item 1100(c) of Regulation AB (§ 239.1100(c)).

(2) That, for the purpose of determining any liability under the Securities Act of 1933, each such post-effective amendment shall be deemed to be a new registration statement relating to the securities offered therein, and the offering of such securities at that time shall be deemed to be the initial bona fide offering thereof.

(3) To remove from registration by means of a post-effective amendment any of the securities being registered which remain unsold at the termination of the offering.

(4) If the registrant is a foreign private issuer, to file a post-effective amendment to the registration statement to include any financial statements required by Item 8.A of Form 20-F (17 CFR 249.220f) at the start of any delayed offering or throughout a continuous offering. Financial statements and information otherwise required by Section 10(a)(3) of the Act need not be furnished, *provided* that the registrant includes in the prospectus, by means of a post-effective amendment, financial statements required pursuant to this paragraph (a)(4) and other information necessary to ensure that all other information in the prospectus is at least as current as the date of those financial statements. Notwithstanding the foregoing,with respect to registration statements on Form F-3 (§ 239.33 of this chapter), a post-effective amendment need not be filed to include financial statements and information required by Section 10(a)(3) of the Act or § 210.3-19 of this chapter if such financial statements and information are contained in periodic reports filed with or furnished to the Commission by the registrant pursuant to section 13 or section 15(d) of the Securities Exchange Act of 1934 that are incorporated by reference in the Form F-3.

(5) That, for the purpose of determining liability under the Securities Act of 1933 to any purchaser:

(i) If the registrant is relying on Rule 430B (§ 230.430B of this chapter):

(A) Each prospectus filed by the registrant pursuant to Rule 424(b)(3) (§ 230.424(b)(3) of this chapter) shall be deemed to be part of the registration statement as of the date the filed prospectus was deemed part of and included in the registration statement; and

(B) Each prospectus required to be filed pursuant to Rule 424(b)(2), (b)(5), or (b)(7) (§ 230.424(b)(2), (b)(5), or (b)(7) of this chapter) as part of a registration statement in reliance on Rule 430B relating to an offering made pursuant to Rule 415(a)(1)(i), (vii), or (x) (§ 230.415(a)(1)(i), (vii), or (x) of this chapter) for the purpose of providing the information required by section 10(a) of the Securities Act of 1933 shall be deemed to be part of and included in the registration statement as of the earlier of the date such form of prospectus is first used after effectiveness or the date of the first contract of sale of securities in the offering described in the prospectus. As provided in Rule 430B, for liability purposes of the issuer and any person that is at that date an underwriter, such date shall be deemed to be a new effective date of the registration statement relating to the securities in the registration statement to which that prospectus relates, and the offering of such securities at that time shall be deemed to be the initial bona fide offering thereof. *Provided, however,* that no statement made in a registration statement or prospectus that is part of the registration statement or made in a document incorporated or deemed incorporated by reference into the registration statement or prospectus that is part of the registration statement will, as to a purchaser with a time of contract of sale prior to such effective date, supersede or modify any statement that was made in the registration statement or prospectus that was part of the registration statement or made in any such document immediately prior to such effective date; or

(ii) If the registrant is subject to Rule 430C (§ 230.430C of this chapter), each prospectus filed pursuant to Rule 424(b) as part of a registration statement relating to an offering, other than registration statements relying on Rule 430B or other than prospectuses filed in reliance on Rule 430A (§ 230.430A of this chapter), shall be deemed to be part of and included in the registration statement as of the date it is first used after effectiveness. *Provided, however,* that no statement made in a registration statement or prospectus that is part of the registration statement or made in a document incorporated or deemed incorporated by reference into the registration statement or prospectus that is part of the registration statement will, as to a purchaser with a time of contract of sale prior to such first use, supersede or modify any statement that was made in the registration statement or prospectus that was part of the registration statement or made in any such document immediately prior to such date of first use.

(6) That, for the purpose of determining liability of the registrant under the Securities Act of 1933 to any purchaser in the initial distribution of the securities:

The undersigned registrant undertakes that in a primary offering of securities of the undersigned registrant pursuant to this registration statement, regardless of the underwriting method used to sell the securities to the purchaser, if the securities are offered or sold to such purchaser by means of any of the following communications, the undersigned registrant will be a seller to the purchaser and will be considered to offer or sell such securities to such purchaser:

(i) Any preliminary prospectus or prospectus of the undersigned registrant relating to the offering required to be filed pursuant to Rule 424 (§ 230.424 of this chapter);

(ii) Any free writing prospectus relating to the offering prepared by or on behalf of the undersigned registrant or used or referred to by the undersigned registrant;

(iii) The portion of any other free writing prospectus relating to the offering containing material information about the undersigned registrant or its securities provided by or on behalf of the under-signed registrant; and

(iv) Any other communication that is an offer in the offering made by the undersigned registrant to the purchaser.

(b) *Filings incorporating subsequent Exchange Act documents by reference.* Include the following if the registration statement incorporates by reference any Exchange Act document filed subsequent to the effective date of the registration statement:

The undersigned registrant hereby undertakes that, for purposes of determining any liability under the Securities Act of 1933, each filing of the registrant's annual report pursuant to section 13(a) or section 15(d) of the Securities Exchange Act of 1934 (and, where applicable, each filing of an employee benefit plan's annual report pursuant to section 15(d) of the Securities Exchange Act of 1934) that is incorporated by reference in the registration statement shall be deemed to be a new registration statement relating to the securities offered therein, and the offering of such securities at that time shall be deemed to be the initial bona fide offering thereof.

(c) *Warrants and rights offerings.* Include the following, with appropriate modifications to suit the particular case, if the securities to be registered are to be offered to existing security holders pursuant to warrants or rights and any securities not taken by security holders are to be reoffered to the public:

The undersigned registrant hereby undertakes to supplement the prospectus, after the expira-tion of the subscription period, to set forth the results of the subscription offer, the transactions by the underwriters during the subscription period, the amount of unsubscribed securities to be purchased by the underwriters, and the terms of any subsequent reoffering thereof. If any public offering by the underwriters is to be made on terms differing from those set forth on the cover page of the prospectus, a post-effective amendment will be filed to set forth the terms of such offering.

(d) *Competitive bids.* Include the following, with appropriate modifications to suit the particular case, if the securities to be registered are to be offered at competitive bidding:

The undersigned registrant hereby undertakes (1) to use its best efforts to distribute prior to the opening of bids, to prospective bidders, underwriters, and dealers, a reasonable number of copies of a prospectus which at that time meets the requirements of section 10(a) of the Act, and relating to the securities offered at competitive bidding, as contained in the registration statement, together with any supplements thereto, and (2) to file an amendment to the registration statement reflecting the results of bidding, the terms of the reoffering and related matters to the extent required by the applicable form, not later than the first use, authorized by the issuer after the opening of bids, of a prospectus relating to the securities offered at competitive bidding, unless no further public offering of such securities by the issuer and no reoffering of such securities by the purchasers is proposed to be made.

(e) *Incorporated annual and quarterly reports.* Include the following if the registration statement specifically incorporates by reference (other than by indirect incorporation by reference through a Form 10-K (§ 249.310 of this chapter) report) in the prospectus all or any part of the annual report to security holders meeting the requirements of Rule 14a-3 or Rule 14c-3 under the Exchange Act (§ 240.14a-3 or § 240.14c-3 of this chapter):

> The undersigned registrant hereby undertakes to deliver or cause to be delivered with the prospectus, to each person to whom the prospectus is sent or given, the latest annual report to security holders that is incorporated by reference in the prospectus and furnished pursuant to and meeting the requirements of Rule 14a-3 or Rule 14c-3 under the Securities Exchange Act of 1934; and, where interim financial information required to be presented by Article 3 of Regulation S-X are not set forth in the prospectus, to deliver, or cause to be delivered to each person to whom the prospectus is sent or given, the latest quarterly report that is specifically incorporated by reference in the prospectus to provide such interim financial information.

(f) *Equity offerings of nonreporting registrants.* Include the following if equity securities of a registrant that prior to the offering had no obligation to file reports with the Commission pursuant to section 13(a) or 15(d) of the Exchange Act are being registered for sale in an underwritten offering:

> The undersigned registrant hereby undertakes to provide to the underwriter at the closing specified in the underwriting agreements certificates in such denominations and registered in such names as required by the underwriter to permit prompt delivery to each purchaser.

(g) *Registration on Form S-4 or F-4 of securities offered for resale.* Include the following if the securities are being registered on Form S-4 or F-4 (§ 239.23, 25 or 34 of this chapter) in connection with a transaction specified in paragraph (a) of Rule 145 (§ 230.145 of this chapter).

(1) The undersigned registrant hereby undertakes as follows: that prior to any public reoffering of the securities registered hereunder through use of a prospectus which is a part of this registration statement, by any person or party who is deemed to be an underwriter within the meaning of Rule 145(c), the issuer undertakes that such reoffering prospectus will contain the information called for by the applicable registration form with respect to reofferings by persons who may be deemed underwriters, in addition to the information called for by the other Items of the applicable form.

(2) The registrant undertakes that every prospectus (i) that is filed pursuant to paragraph (1) immediately preceding, or (ii) that purports to meet the requirements of section 10(a)(3) of the Act and is used in connection with an offering of securities subject to Rule 415 (§ 230.415 of this chapter), will be filed as a part of an amendment to the registration statement and will not be used until such amendment is effective, and that, for purposes of determining any liability under the Securities Act of 1933, each such post-effective amendment shall be deemed to be a new registration statement relating to the securities offered therein, and the offering of such securities at that time shall be deemed to be the initial bona fide offering thereof.

(h) *Request for acceleration of effective date or filing of registration statement becoming effective upon filing.* Include the following if acceleration is requested of the effective date of the registration statement pursuant to Rule 461 under the Securities Act (§ 230.461 of this chapter), if a Form S-3 or Form F-3 will become effective upon filing with the Commission pursuant to Rule 462 (e) or (f) under the Securities Act (§ 230.462 (e) or (f)), or if the registration statement is filed on Form S-8, and:

(1) any provision or arrangement exists whereby the registrant may indemnify a director, officer or controlling person of the registrant against liabilities arising under the Securities Act, or (2) the underwriting agreement contains a provision whereby the registrant indemnifies the underwriter or controlling persons of the underwriter against such liabilities and a director, officer or controlling person of the registrant is such an underwriter or controlling person thereof or a member of any firm which is such an underwriter, and (3) the benefits of such indemnification are not waived by such persons:

> Insofar as indemnification for liabilities arising under the Securities Act of 1933 may be permitted to directors, officers and controlling persons of the registrant pursuant to the foregoing provisions, or otherwise, the registrant has been advised that in the opinion of the Securities and Exchange Commission such indemnification is against public policy as expressed in the Act and is, therefore, unenforceable. In the event that a claim for indemnification against such liabilities (other than the payment by the registrant of expenses incurred or paid by a director, officer or controlling person of the registrant in the successful defense of any action, suit or proceeding) is asserted by such director, officer or controlling person in connection with the securities being registered, the registrant will, unless in the opinion of its counsel the matter has been settled by controlling precedent, submit to a court of appropriate

jurisdiction the question whether such indemnification by it is against public policy as expressed in the Act and will be governed by the final adjudication of such issue.

(i) Include the following in a registration statement permitted by Rule 430A under the Securities Act of 1933 [§ 230.430A of this chapter]:

The undersigned registrant hereby undertakes that:

(1) For purposes of determining any liability under the Securities Act of 1933, the information omitted from the form of prospectus filed as part of this registration statement in reliance upon Rule 430A and contained in a form of prospectus filed by the registrant pursuant to Rule 424(b)(1) or (4) or 497(h) under the Securities Act shall be deemed to be part of this registration statement as of the time it was declared effective.

(2) For the purpose of determining any liability under the Securities Act of 1933, each post-effective amendment that contains a form of prospectus shall be deemed to be a new registration statement relating to the securities offered therein, and the offering of such securities at that time shall be deemed to be the initial bona fide offering thereof.

(j) *Qualification of trust indentures under the Trust Indenture Act of 1939 for delayed offerings.* Include the following if the registrant intends to rely on Section 305(b)(2) of the Trust Indenture Act of 1939 for determining the eligibility of the trustee under indentures for securities to be issued, offered, or sold on a delayed basis by or on behalf of the registrant:

"The undersigned registrant hereby undertakes to file an application for the purpose of determining the eligibility of the trustee to act under subsection (a) of Section 310 of the Trust Indenture Act ('Act') in accordance with the rules and regulations prescribed by the Commission under Section 305(b)(2) of the Act."

(k) *Filings regarding asset-backed securities incorporating by reference subsequent Exchange Act documents by third parties.* Include the following if the registration statement incorporates by reference any Exchange Act document filed subsequent to the effective date of the registration statement pursuant to Item 1100(c) of Regulation AB (§ 229.1100(c)):

The undersigned registrant hereby undertakes that, for purposes of determining any liability under the Securities Act of 1933, each filing of the annual report pursuant to section 13(a) or section 15(d) of the Securities Exchange Act of 1934 of a third party that is incorporated by reference in the registration statement in accordance with Item 1100(c)(1) of Regulation AB (17 CFR 229.1100(c)(1)) shall be deemed to be a new registration statement relating to the securities offered therein, and the offering of such securities at that time shall be deemed to be the initial bona fide offering thereof.

(l) *Filings regarding asset-backed securities that provide certain information through an Internet Web site.* Include the following if the registration statement is to provide information required by Item 1105 of Regulation AB (§ 229.1105) through an Internet Web site in accordance with Rule 312 of Regulation S-T (§ 232.312 of this chapter):

The undersigned registrant hereby undertakes that, except as otherwise provided by Item 1105 of Regulation AB (17 CFR 229.1105), information provided in response to that Item pursuant to Rule 312 of Regulation S-T (17 CFR 232.312) through the specified Internet address in the prospectus is deemed to be a part of the prospectus included in the registration statement. In addition, the undersigned registrant hereby undertakes to provide to any person without charge, upon request, a copy of the information provided in response to Item 1105 of Regulation AB pursuant to Rule 312 of Regulation S-T through the specified Internet address as of the date of the prospectus included in the registration statement if a subsequent update or change is made to the information.

[As last amended in Release No. 33-8876, effective February 4, 2008, 73 F.R. 934.]

Subpart 229.600—Exhibits

[¶ 13,071] Exhibits

Reg. § 229.601. **Item 601.** (1) Subject to Rule 411(c) (§ 230.411(c) of this chapter) under the Securities Act and Rule 12b-32 (§ 240.12b-32 of this chapter) under the Exchange Act regarding incorporation of exhibits by reference, the exhibits required in the exhibit table shall be filed as indicated, as part of the registration statement or report.

(2) Each registration statement or report shall contain an exhibit index, which shall precede immediately the exhibits filed with such registration statement. For convenient reference, each exhibit shall be listed in the exhibit index according to the number assigned to it in the exhibit table. The exhibit index shall indicate, by handwritten, typed, printed, or other legible form of notation in the manually signed original registration statement or report, the page number in the sequential numbering system where such exhibit can be found. Where exhibits are incorporated by reference, this fact shall be noted in the exhibit index referred to in the preceding sentence. Further, the first page of the manually signed registration statement shall list the page in the filing where the exhibit index is located. For a description of each of the exhibits included in the exhibit table, see paragraph (b) of this Item.

(3) This Item applies only to the forms specified in the exhibit table. With regard to forms not listed in that table, reference shall be made to the appropriate form for the specific exhibit filing requirements applicable thereto.

(4) If a material contract or plan of acquisition, reorganization, arrangement, liquidation or succession is executed or becomes effective during the reporting period reflected by a Form 10-Q or Form 10-K, it shall be filed as an exhibit to the Form 10-Q or Form 10-K filed for the corresponding period. Any amendment or modification to a previously filed exhibit to a Form 10, 10-K or 10-Q document shall be filed as an exhibit to a Form 10-Q and Form 10-K. Such amendment or modification need not be filed where such previously filed exhibit would not be currently required.

Instructions to Item 601. 1. If an exhibit to a registration statement (other than an opinion or consent), filed in preliminary form, has been changed only (A) to insert information as to interest, dividend or conversion rates, redemption or conversion prices, purchase or offering prices, underwriters' or dealers' commissions, names, addresses or participation of underwriters or similar matters, which information appears elsewhere in an amendment to the registration statement or a prospectus filed pursuant to Rule 424(b) under the Securities Act [§ 230.424(b) of this chapter], or (B) to correct typographical errors, insert signatures or make other similar immaterial changes, then, notwithstanding any contrary requirement of any rule or form, the registrant need not refile such exhibit as so amended. Any such incomplete exhibit may not, however, be incorporated by reference in any subsequent filing under any Act administered by the Commission.

2. In any case where two or more indentures, contracts, franchises, or other documents required to be filed as exhibits are substantially identical in all material respects except as to the parties thereto, the dates of execution, or other details, the registrant need file a copy of only one of such documents, with a schedule identifying the other documents omitted and setting forth the material details in which such documents differ from the document a copy of which is filed. The Commission may at any time in its discretion require filing of copies of any documents so omitted.

3. Only copies, rather than originals, need be filed of each exhibit required except as otherwise specifically noted.

4. *Electronic filings.* Whenever an exhibit is filed in paper pursuant to a hardship exemption (§ § 232.201 and 232.202 of this chapter), the letter "P" (paper) shall be placed next to the exhibit in the list of exhibits required by Item 601(a)(2) of this Rule. Whenever an electronic confirming copy of an exhibit is filed pursuant to a hardship exemption (§ 232.201 or § 232.202(d) of this chapter), the exhibit index should specify where the confirming electronic copy can be located; in addition, the designation "CE" (confirming electronic) should be placed next to the listed exhibit in the exhibit index.

Exhibit Table

Instructions to the Exhibit Table. 1. The exhibit table indicates those documents that must be filed as exhibits to the respective forms listed.

2. The "X" designation indicates the documents which are required to be filed with each form even if filed previously with another document. *Provided, however,* that such previously filed documents may be incorporated by reference to satisfy the filing requirements.

3. The number used in the far left column of the table refers to the appropriate subsection in paragraph (b) where a description of the exhibit can be found. Whenever necessary, alphabetical or numerical subparts may be used.

EXHIBIT TABLE

	Securities Act Forms								Exchange Act Forms				
	S-1	S-3	S-4[1]	S-8	S-11	F-1	F-3	F-4[1]	10	8-K[2]	10-D	10-Q	10-K
(1) Underwriting agreement	X	X	X	—	X	X	X	X	—	X	—	—	—
(2) Plan of acquisition, reorganization, arrangement, liquidation or succession	X	X	X	—	X	X	X	X	X	X	—	X	X
(3) (i) Articles of incorporation	X	—	X	—	X	X	—	X	X	X	X	X	X
(ii) Bylaws	X	—	X	—	X	X	—	X	X	X	X	X	X
(4) Instruments defining the rights of security holders, including indentures	X	X	X	X	X	X	X	X	X	X	X	X	X
(5) Opinion re legality	X	X	X	X	X	X	X	X	—	—	—	—	—
(6) [Reserved]	N/A	N/A	N/A	N/A	N/A	N/A	N/A	N/A	N/A	N/A	N/A	N/A	N/A
(7) Correspondence from an independent accountant regarding non-reliance on a previously issued audit report or completed interim review	—	—	—	—	—	—	—	—	—	X	—	—	—
(8) Opinion re tax matters	X	X	X	—	X	X	X	X	—	—	—	—	—
(9) Voting trust agreement	X	—	X	—	X	X	—	X	X	—	—	—	X
(10) Material contracts	X	—	X	—	X	X	—	X	X	—	X	X	X
(11) Statement re computation of per share earnings	X	—	X	—	X	X	—	X	X	—	—	X	X
(12) Statements re computation of ratios	X	X	X	—	X	X	—	X	X	—	—	—	X
(13) Annual report to security holders, Form 10-Q or quarterly report to security holders[3]	—	—	X	—	—	—	—	—	—	—	—	—	X
(14) Code of Ethics	—	—	—	—	—	—	—	—	—	X	—	—	X
(15) Letter re unaudited interim financial information	X	X	X	X	X	X	X	X	—	—	—	X	—
(16) Letter re change in certifying accountant[4]	X	—	X	—	X	—	—	—	X	X	—	—	X
(17) Correspondence on departure of director	—	—	—	—	—	—	—	—	—	X	—	—	—

EXHIBIT TABLE

	Securities Act Forms								Exchange Act Forms				
	S-1	S-3	S-4[1]	S-8	S-11	F-1	F-3	F-4[1]	10	8-K[2]	10-D	10-Q	10-K
(18) Letter re change in accounting principles	—	—	—	—	—	—	—	—	—	—	—	X	X
(19) Report furnished to security holders	—	—	—	—	—	—	—	—	—	—	—	X	—
(20) Other documents or statements to security holders	—	—	—	—	—	—	—	—	—	X	—	—	—
(21) Subsidiaries of the registrant	X	—	X	—	X	X	—	X	X	—	—	—	X
(22) Published report regarding matters submitted to vote of security holders	—	—	—	—	—	—	—	—	—	—	X	X	X
(23) Consents of experts and counsel	X	X	X	X	X	X	X	X	—	X[5]	X[5]	X[5]	X[5]
(24) Power of attorney	X	X	X	X	X	X	X	X	X	X	—	X	X
(25) Statement of eligibility of trustee	X	X	X	—	X	X	X	X	—	—	—	—	—
(26) Invitation for competitive bids	X	X	X	—	X	X	X	X	—	—	—	—	—
(27) through (30) [Reserved]													
(31) (i) Rule 13a-14(a)/15d-14(a) Certifications (ii) Rule 13a-14/15d-14 Certifications	—	—	—	—	—	—	—	—	—	—	—	X	X
													X
(32) Section 1350 Certifications[6]	—	—	—	—	—	—	—	—	—	—	—	X	X
(33) Report on assessment of compliance with servicing criteria for asset-backed issuers	—	—	—	—	—	—	—	—	—	—	—	—	X
(34) Attestation report on assessment of compliance with servicing criteria for asset-backed securities	—	—	—	—	—	—	—	—	—	—	—	—	X
(35) Servicer compliance statement	—	—	—	—	—	—	—	—	—	—	—	—	X
(36) through (98) [Reserved]	N/A	N/A	N/A	N/A	N/A	N/A	N/A	N/A	N/A	N/A	N/A	N/A	N/A
(99) Additional exhibits	X	X	X	X	X	X	X	X	X	X	X	X	X
(100) XBRL-Related Documents									X	X		X	X

EXHIBIT TABLE

	Securities Act Forms								Exchange Act Forms				
	S-1	S-3	S-4[1]	S-8	S-11	F-1	F-3	F-4[1]	10	8-K[2]	10-D	10-Q	10-K
(101) Interactive Data File	X	X	X	—	X	X	X	X	—	X	—	X	X

[1] An exhibit need not be provided about a company if: (1) With respect to such company an election has been made under Form S-4 or F-4 to provide information about such company at a level prescribed by Form S-3 or F-3; and (2) the form, the level of which has been elected under Form S-4 or F-4, would not require such company to provide such exhibit if it were registering a primary offering.

[2] A Form 8-K exhibit is required only if relevant to the subject matter reported on the Form 8-K report. For example, if the Form 8-K pertains to the departure of a director, only the exhibit described in paragraph (b)(17) of this section need be filed. A required exhibit may be incorporated by reference from a previous filing.

[3] Where incorporated by reference into the text of the prospectus and delivered to security holders along with the prospectus as permitted by the registration statement; or, in the case of the Form 10-K, where the annual report to security holders is incorporated by reference into the text of the Form 10-K.

[4] If required pursuant to Item 304 of Regulation S-K.

[5] Where the opinion of the expert or counsel has been incorporated by reference into a previously filed Securities Act registration statement.

[6] Pursuant to §§ 240.13a-13(b)(3) and 240.15d-13(b)(3) of this chapter, asset-backed issuers are not required to file reports on Form 10-Q.

(b) *Description of exhibits.* Set forth below is a description of each document listed in the exhibit tables.

(1) *Underwriting agreement*—Each underwriting contract or agreement with a principal underwriter pursuant to which the securities being registered are to be distributed; if the terms of such documents have not been determined, the proposed forms thereof. Such agreement may be filed as an exhibit to a report on Form 8-K (§ 249.308 of this chapter) which is incorporated by reference into a registration statement subsequent to its effectiveness.

(2) *Plan of acquisition, reorganization, arrangement, liquidation or succession*—Any material plan of acquisition, disposition, reorganization, readjustment, succession, liquidation or arrangement and any amendments thereto described in the statement or report. Schedules (or similar attachments) to these exhibits shall not be filed unless such schedules contain information which is material to an investment decision and which is not otherwise disclosed in the agreement or the disclosure document. The plan filed shall contain a list briefly identifying the contents of all omitted schedules, together with an agreement to furnish supplementally a copy of any omitted schedule to the Commission upon request.

(3)(i) *Articles of incorporation.* The articles of incorporation of the registrant or instruments corresponding thereto as currently in effect and any amendments thereto. Whenever the registrant files an amendment to its articles of incorporation, it must file a complete copy of the articles as amended. However, if such amendment is being reported on Form 8-K (§ 249.308 of this chapter), the registrant is required to file only the text of the amendment as a Form 8-K exhibit. In such case, a complete copy of the articles of incorporation as amended must be filed as an exhibit to the next Securities Act registration statement or periodic report filed by the registrant to which this exhibit requirement applies. Where it is impracticable for the registrant to file a charter amendment authorizing new securities with the appropriate state authority prior to the effective date of the registration statement registering such securities, the registrant may file as an exhibit to the registration statement the form of amendment to be filed with the state authority. In such a case, if material changes are made after the copy is filed, the registrant must also file the changed copy.

(ii) *Bylaws.* The bylaws of the registrant or instruments corresponding thereto as currently in effect and any amendments thereto. Whenever the registrant files an amendment to the bylaws, it must file a complete copy of the amended bylaws. However, if such amendment is being reported on Form 8-K (§ 249.308 of this chapter), the registrant is required to file only the text of the amendment as a Form 8-K exhibit. In such case, a complete copy of the bylaws as amended must be filed as an exhibit to the next Securities Act registration statement or periodic report filed by the registrant to which this exhibit requirement applies.

(4) *Instruments defining the rights of security holders, including indentures*—(i) All instruments defining the rights of holders of the equity or debt securities being registered including, where applicable, the relevant portion of the articles of incorporation or by-laws of the registrant.

(ii) Except as set forth in paragraph (b)(4)(iii) of this Item for filings on Forms S-1, S-4, S-11, N-14, and F-4 under the Securities Act (§ 239.11, 239.25, 239.18, 239.23 and 239.34 of this chapter) and Forms 10 and 10-K under the Exchange Act (§§ 249.210 and 249.310 of this chapter) all instruments defining the rights of holders of long-term debt of the registrant and its consolidated subsidiaries and for any of its unconsolidated subsidiaries for which financial statements are required to be filed.

(iii) Where the instrument defines the rights of holders of long-term debt of the registrant and its consolidated subsidiaries and for any of its unconsolidated subsidiaries for which financial statements are required to be filed, there need not be filed:

(A) Any instrument with respect to long-term debt not being registered if the total amount of securities authorized thereunder does not exceed 10 percent of the total assets of the registrant and its subsidiaries on a consolidated basis and if there is filed an agreement to furnish a copy of such agreement to the Commission upon request;

(B) Any instrument with respect to any class of securities if appropriate steps to assure the redemption or retirement of such class will be taken prior to or upon delivery by the registrant of the securities being registered; or

(C) Copies of instruments evidencing scrip certificates for fractions of shares.

(iv) If any of the securities being registered are, or will be, issued under an indenture to be qualified under the Trust Indenture Act, the copy of such indenture which is filed as an exhibit shall include or be accompanied by:

(A) A reasonably itemized and informative table of contents; and

(B) A cross-reference sheet showing the location in the indenture of the provisions inserted pursuant to sections 310 through 318(a) inclusive of the Trust Indenture Act of 1939.

(v) With respect to Forms 8-K and 10-Q under the Exchange Act that are filed and that disclose, in the text of the Form 10-Q, the interim financial statements, or the footnotes thereto the creation of a new class of securities or indebtedness or the modification of existing rights of security holders, file all instruments defining the rights of holders of these securities or indebtedness. However, there need not be filed any instrument with respect to long-term debt not being registered which meets the exclusion set forth in paragraph (b)(4)(iii)(A) of this Item.

Instruction 1 to paragraph (b)(4). There need not be filed any instrument which defines the rights of participants (not as security holders) pursuant to an employee benefit plan.

Instruction 2 to paragraph (b)(4) (for electronic filings). If the instrument defining the rights of security holders is in the form of a certificate, the text appearing on the certificate shall be reproduced in an electronic filing together with a description of any other graphic and image material appearing on the certificate, as provided in Rule 304 of Regulation S-T (§ 232.304 of this chapter).

(5) *Opinion re legality*—(i) An opinion of counsel as to the legality of the securities being registered, indicating whether they will, when sold, be legally issued, fully paid and non-assessable, and, if debt securities, whether they will be binding obligations of the registrant.

(ii) If the securities being registered are issued under a plan and the plan is subject to the requirements of ERISA furnish either:

(A) An opinion of counsel which confirms compliance of the provisions of the written documents constituting the plan with the requirements of ERISA pertaining to such provisions; or

(B) A copy of the Internal Revenue Service determination letter that the plan is qualified under section 401 of the Internal Revenue Code; or

(iii) If the securities being registered are issued under a plan which is subject to the requirements of ERISA and the plan has been amended subsequent to the filing of (ii)(A) or (B) above, furnish either:

(A) An opinion of counsel which confirms compliance of the amended provisions of the plan with the requirements of ERISA pertaining to such provisions; or

(B) A copy of the Internal Revenue Service determination letter that the amended plan is qualified under section 401 of the Internal Revenue Code.

Note: Attention is directed to Item 8 of Form S-8 for exemptions to this exhibit requirement applicable to that Form.

(6) [Reserved.]

(7) *Correspondence from an independent accountant regarding non-reliance on a previously issued audit report or completed interim review.* Any written notice from the registrant's current or previously engaged independent accountant that the independent accountant is withdrawing a previously issued audit report or that a previously issued audit report or completed interim review, covering one or more years or interim periods for which the registrant is required to provide financial statements under Regulation S-X (part 210 of this chapter), should no longer be relied upon. In addition, any letter, pursuant to Item 4.02(c) of Form 8-K (§ 249.308 of this chapter), from the independent accountant to the

Commission stating whether the independent accountant agrees with the statements made by the registrant describing the events giving rise to the notice.

(8) *Opinion re tax matters*—For filings on Form S-11 under the Securities Act (§ 239.18) or those to which Securities Act Industry Guide 5 applies, an opinion of counsel or of an independent public or certified public accountant or, in lieu thereof, a revenue ruling from the Internal Revenue Service, supporting the tax matters and consequences to the shareholders as described in the filing when such tax matters are material to the transaction for which the registration statement is being filed. This exhibit otherwise need only be filed with the other applicable registration forms where the tax consequences are material to an investor and a representation as to tax consequences is set forth in the filing. If a tax opinion is set forth in full in the filing, an indication that such is the case may be made in lieu of filing the otherwise required exhibit. Such tax opinions may be conditioned or may be qualified, so long as such conditions and qualifications are adequately described in the filing.

(9) *Voting trust agreement* —Any voting trust agreements and amendments thereto.

(10) *Material contracts*—(i) Every contract not made in the ordinary course of business which is material to the registrant and is to be performed in whole or in part at or after the filing of the registration statement or report or was entered into not more than two years before such filing. Only contracts need be filed as to which the registrant or subsidiary of the registrant is a party or has succeeded to a party by assumption or assignment or in which the registrant or such subsidiary has a beneficial interest.

(ii) If the contract is such as ordinarily accompanies the kind of business conducted by the registrant and its subsidiaries, it will be deemed to have been made in the ordinary course of business and need not be filed unless it falls within one or more of the following categories, in which case it shall be filed except where immaterial in amount or significance:

(A) Any contract to which directors, officers, promoters, voting trustees, security holders named in the registration statement or report, or underwriters are parties other than contracts involving only the purchase or sale of current assets having a determinable market price, at such market price;

(B) Any contract upon which the registrant's business is substantially dependent, as in the case of continuing contracts to sell the major part of registrant's products or services or to purchase the major part of registrant's requirements of goods, services or raw materials or any franchise or license or other agreement to use a patent, formula, trade secret, process or trade name upon which registrant's business depends to a material extent;

(C) Any contract calling for the acquisition or sale of any property, plant or equipment for a consideration exceeding 15 percent of such fixed assets of the registrant on a consolidated basis; or

(D) Any material lease under which a part of the property described in the registration statement or report is held by the registrant.

(iii) (A) Any management contract or any compensatory plan, contract or arrangement, including but not limited to plans relating to options, warrants or rights, pension, retirement or deferred compensation or bonus, incentive or profit sharing (or if not set forth in any formal document, a written description thereof) in which any director or any of the named executive officers of the registrant, as defined by Item 402(a)(3) (§ 229.402(a)(31), participates shall be deemed material and shall be filed; and any other management contract or any other compensatory plan, contract, or arrangement in which any other executive officer of the registrant participates shall be filed unless immaterial in amount or significance.

(B) Any compensatory plan, contract or arrangement adopted without the approval of security holders pursuant to which equity may be awarded, including, but not limited to, options, warrants or rights (or if not set forth in any formal document, a written description thereof), in which any employee (whether or not an executive officer of the registrant) participates shall be filed unless immaterial in amount or significance. A compensation plan assumed by a registrant in connection with a merger, consolidation or other acquisition transaction pursuant to which the registrant may make further grants or awards of its equity securities shall be considered a compensation plan of the registrant for purposes of the preceding sentence.

(C) Notwithstanding paragraph (iii)(A) above, the following management contracts or compensatory plans, contracts or arrangements need not be filed:

(*1*) Ordinary purchase and sales agency agreements.

(*2*) Agreements with managers of stores in a chain organization or similar organization.

(*3*) Contracts providing for labor or salesmen's bonuses or payments to a class of security holders, as such.

(*4*) Any compensatory plan, contract or arrangement which pursuant to its terms is available to employees, officers or directors generally and which in operation provides for the same method of allocation of benefits between management and nonmanagement participants.

(5) Any compensatory plan, contract or arrangement if the registrant is a foreign private issuer that furnishes compensatory information under Item 402(a)(1) (§ 229.402(a)(1)) and the public filing of the plan, contract or arrangement, or portion thereof, is not required in the registrant's home country and is not otherwise publicly disclosed by the registrant.

(6) Any compensatory plan, contract, or arrangement if the registrant is a wholly owned subsidiary of a company that has a class of securities registered pursuant to section 12 or files reports pursuant to section 15(d) of the Exchange Act and is filing a report on Form 10-K or registering debt instruments or preferred stock that are not voting securities on Form S-1.

Instruction 1 to paragraph (b)(10). With the exception of management contracts, in order to comply with paragraph (iii) above, registrants need only file copies of the various remunerative plans and need not file each individual director's or executive officer's personal agreement under the plans unless there are particular provisions in such personal agreements whose disclosure in an exhibit is necessary to an investor's understanding of that individual's compensation under the plan.

Instruction 2 to paragraph (b)(10). If a material contract is executed or becomes effective during the reporting period reflected by a Form 10-Q or Form 10-K, it shall be filed as an exhibit to the Form 10-Q or Form 10-K filed for the corresponding period. *See* paragraph (a)(4) of this Item. With respect to quarterly reports on Form 10-Q, only those contracts executed or becoming effective during the most recent period reflected in the report shall be filed.

(11) *Statement re computation of per share earnings.* A statement setting forth in reasonable detail the computation of per share earnings, unless the computation can be clearly determined from the material contained in the registration statement or report. The information with respect to the computation of per share earnings on both primary and fully diluted bases, presented by exhibit or otherwise, must be furnished even though the amounts of per share earnings on the fully diluted basis are not required to be presented in the income statement under the provisions of Accounting Principles Board Opinion No. 15. That Opinion provides that any reduction of less than 3% need not be considered as dilution (see footnote to paragraph 14 of the Opinion) and that a computation on the fully diluted basis which results in improvement of earnings per share not be taken into account (see paragraph 40 of the Opinion).

(12) *Statements re computation of ratios*—A statement setting forth in reasonable detail the computation of any ratio of earnings to fixed charges, any ratio of earnings to combined fixed charges and preferred stock dividends or any other ratios which appear in the registration statement or report. See Item 503(d) of Regulation S-K (§ 229.503(d)).

(13) *Annual report to security holders, Form 10-Q or quarterly report to security holders*—(i) The registrant's annual report to security holders for its last fiscal year, its Form 10-Q (if specifically incorporated by reference in the prospectus) or its quarterly report to security holders, if all or a portion thereof is incorporated by reference in the filing. Such report, except for those portions thereof that are expressly incorporated by reference in the filing, is to be furnished for the information of the Commission and is not to be deemed "filed" as part of the filing. If the financial statements in the report have been incorporated by reference in the filing, the accountant's certificate shall be manually signed in one copy. *See* Rule 411(b) (§ 230.411(b) of this chapter).

(ii) *Electronic filings.* If all, or any portion, of the annual or quarterly report to security holders is incorporated by reference into any electronic filing, all, or such portion of the annual or quarterly report to security holders so incorporated, shall be filed in electronic format as an exhibit to the filing.

(14)*Code of ethics.* Any code of ethics, or amendment thereto, that is the subject of the disclosure required by Item 406 of Regulation S-K (-229.406) or Item 10 of Form 8-K (-249.308 of this chapter), to the extent that the registrant intends to satisfy the Item 406 or Item 10 requirements through filing of an exhibit.

(15) *Letter re unaudited interim financial information.* A letter, where applicable, from the independent accountant that acknowledges awareness of the use in a registration statement of a report on unaudited interim financial information that pursuant to Rule 436(c) under the Securities Act (§ 230.436(c) of this chapter) is not considered a part of a registration statement prepared or certified by an accountant or a report prepared or certified by an accountant within the meaning of sections 7 and 11 of that Act. Such letter may be filed with the registration statement, an amendment thereto, or a report on Form 10-Q which is incorporated by reference into the registration statement.

(16) *Letter re change in certifying accountant* —A letter from the registrant's former independent accountant regarding its concurrence or disagreement with the statements made by the registrant in the current report concerning the resignation or dismissal as the registrant's principal accountant.

(17) *Correspondence on departure of director.* Any written correspondence from a former director concerning the circumstances surrounding the former director's retirement, resignation, refusal to stand for re-election or removal, including any letter from the former director to the registrant stating whether

the former director agrees with statements made by the registrant describing the former director's departure.

(18) *Letter re change in accounting principles*—Unless previously filed, a letter from the registrant's independent accountant indicating whether any change in accounting principles or practices followed by the registrant, or any change in the method of applying any such accounting principles or practices, which affected the financial statements being filed with the Commission in the report or which is reasonably certain to affect the financial statements of future fiscal years is to an alternative principle which in his judgment is preferable under the circumstances. No such letter need be filed when such change is made in response to a standard adopted by the Financial Accounting Standards Board that creates a new accounting principle, that expresses a preference for an accounting principle, or that rejects a specific accounting principle.

(19) *Report furnished to security holders.* If the registrant makes available to its security holders or otherwise publishes, within the period prescribed for filing the report, a document or statement containing information meeting some or all of the requirements of Part I of Form 10-Q, the information called for may be incorporated by reference to such published document or statement, provided copies thereof are included as an exhibit to the registration statement or to Part I of the Form 10-Q report.

(20) *Other documents or statements to security holders*—If the registrant makes available to its stockholders or otherwise publishes, within the period prescribed for filing the report, a document or statement containing information meeting some or all of the requirements of this form the information called for may be incorporated by reference to such published document or statement provided copies thereof are filed as an exhibit to the report on this form.

(21) *Subsidiaries of the registrant* —(i) List all subsidiaries of the registrant, the state or other jurisdiction of incorporation or organization of each, and the names under which such subsidiaries do business. This list may be incorporated by reference from a document which includes a complete and accurate list.

(ii) The names of particular subsidiaries may be omitted if the unnamed subsidiaries, considered in the aggregate as a single subsidiary, would not constitute a significant subsidiary as of the end of the year covered by this report. (See the definition of "significant subsidiary" in Rule 1-02(w) (17 CFR 210.1-02(w)) of Regulation S-X.) The names of consolidated wholly-owned multiple subsidiaries carrying on the same line of business, such as chain stores or small loan companies, may be omitted, provided the name of the immediate parent, the line of business, the number of omitted subsidiaries operating in the United States and the number operating in foreign countries are given. This instruction shall not apply, however, to banks, insurance companies, savings and loan associations or to any subsidiary subject to regulation by another Federal agency.

(22) *Published report regarding matters submitted to vote of security holders.* Published reports containing all of the information called for by Item 4 of Part II of Form 10-Q or Item 4 of Part I of Form 10-K that is referred to therein in lieu of providing disclosure in Form 10-Q or 10-K, that are required to be filed as exhibits by Rule 12b-23(a)(3) under the Exchange Act (§ 240.12b-23(a)(3) of this chapter).

(23) *Consents of experts and counsel* —(i) Securities Act filings—All written consents required to be filed shall be dated and manually signed. Where the consent of an expert or counsel is contained in his report or opinion or elsewhere in the registration statement or document filed therewith, a reference shall be made in the index to the report, the part of the registration statement or document or opinion, containing the consent.

(ii) Exchange Act reports—where the filing of a written consent is required with respect to material incorporated by reference in a previously filed registration statement under the Securities Act, such consent may be filed as an exhibit to the material incorporated by reference. Such consents shall be dated and manually signed.

(24) *Power of attorney*—If any name is signed to the registration statement or report pursuant to power of attorney, manually signed copies of such power of attorney shall be filed. Where the power of attorney is contained elsewhere in the registration statement or documents filed therewith a reference shall be made in the index to the part of the registration statement or document containing such power of attorney. In addition, if the name of any officer signing on behalf of the registrant is signed pursuant to a power of attorney, certified copies of a resolution of the registrant's board of directors authorizing such signature shall also be filed. A power of attorney that is filed with the Commission shall relate to a specific filing or an amendment thereto, provided, however, that a power of attorney relating to a registration statement under the Securities Act or an amendment thereto also may relate to any registration statement for the same offering that is to be effective upon filing pursuant to Rule 462(b) under the Securities Act (§ 230.462(b) of this chapter). A power of attorney that is filed with the Commission shall relate to a specific filing or an amendment thereto. A power of attorney that confers general authority shall not be filed with the Commission.

(25) *Statement of eligibility of trustee*—(i) A statement of eligibility and qualification of each person designated to act as trustee under an indenture to be qualified under the Trust Indenture Act of 1939. Such statement of eligibility shall be bound separately from the other exhibits.

(ii) *Electronic filings.* The requirement to bind separately the statement of eligibility and qualification of each person designated to act as a trustee under the Trust Indenture Act of 1939 from other exhibits shall not apply to statements submitted in electronic format. Rather, such statements must be submitted as exhibits in the same electronic submission as the registration statement to which they relate, or in an amendment thereto, except that electronic filers that rely on Trust Indenture Act Section 305(b)(2) for determining the eligibility of the trustee under indentures for securities to be issued, offered or sold on a delayed basis by or on behalf of the registrant shall file such statements separately in the manner prescribed by § 260.5b-1 through § 260.5b-3 of this chapter and by the EDGAR Filer Manual.

(26) *Invitations for competitive bids*—If the registration statement covers securities to be offered at competitive bidding, any form of communication which is an invitation for competitive bid which will be sent or given to any person shall be filed.

(27) through (30) [Reserved]

(31)(i) *Rule 13a-14(a)/15d-14(a) Certifications.* The certifications required by Rule 13a-14(a) (17 CFR 240.13a-14(a)) or Rule 15d-14(a) (17 CFR 240.15d-14(a)) exactly as set forth below:

CERTIFICATIONS

I, [identify the certifying individual], certify that:

1. I have reviewed this [specify report] of [identify registrant];

2. Based on my knowledge, this report does not contain any untrue statement of a material fact or omit to state a material fact necessary to make the statements made, in light of the circumstances under which such statements were made, not misleading with respect to the period covered by this report;

3. Based on my knowledge, the financial statements, and other financial information included in this report, fairly present in all material respects the financial condition, results of operations and cash flows of the registrant as of, and for, the periods presented in this report;

4. The registrant's other certifying officer(s) and I are responsible for establishing and maintaining disclosure controls and procedures (as defined in Exchange Act Rules 13a-15(e) and 15d-15(e)) and internal control over financial reporting (as defined in Exchange Act Rules 13a-15(f) and 15d-15(f)) for the registrant and have:

(a) Designed such disclosure controls and procedures, or caused such disclosure controls and procedures to be designed under our supervision, to ensure that material information relating to the registrant, including its consolidated subsidiaries, is made known to us by others within those entities, particularly during the period in which this report is being prepared;

(b) Designed such internal control over financial reporting, or caused such internal control over financial reporting to be designed under our supervision, to provide reasonable assurance regarding the reliability of financial reporting and the preparation of financial statements for external purposes in accordance with generally accepted accounting principles;

(c) Evaluated the effectiveness of the registrant's disclosure controls and procedures and presented in this report our conclusions about the effectiveness of the disclosure controls and procedures, as of the end of the period covered by this report based on such evaluation; and

(d) Disclosed in this report any change in the registrant's internal control over financial reporting that occurred during the registrant's most recent fiscal quarter (the registrant's fourth fiscal quarter in the case of an annual report) that has materially affected, or is reasonably likely to materially affect, the registrant's internal control over financial reporting; and

5. The registrant's other certifying officer(s) and I have disclosed, based on our most recent evaluation of internal control over financial reporting, to the registrant's auditors and the audit committee of the registrant's board of directors (or persons performing the equivalent functions):

(a) All significant deficiencies and material weaknesses in the design or operation of internal control over financial reporting which are reasonably likely to adversely affect the registrant's ability to record, process, summarize and report financial information; and

(b) Any fraud, whether or not material, that involves management or other employees who have a significant role in the registrant's internal control over financial reporting.

Date: . . . .

[Signature]

[Title]

* Provide a separate certification for each principal executive officer and principal financial officer of the registrant. See Rules 13a-14(a) and 15d-14(a).

(ii) *Rule 13a-14(d)/15d-14(d) Certifications.* If an asset-backed issuer (as defined in § 229.1101), the certifications required by Rule 13a-14(d) (17 CFR 240.13a-14(d)) or Rule 15d-14(d) (17 CFR 240.15d-14(d)) exactly as set forth below:

CERTIFICATIONS[1]

I, [identify the certifying individual], certify that:

1. I have reviewed this report on Form 10-K and all reports on Form 10-D required to be filed in respect of the period covered by this report on Form 10-K of [identify the issuing entity] (the "Exchange Act periodic reports");

2. Based on my knowledge, the Exchange Act periodic reports, taken as a whole, do not contain any untrue statement of a material fact or omit to state a material fact necessary to make the statements made, in light of the circumstances under which such statements were made, not misleading with respect to the period covered by this report;

3. Based on my knowledge, all of the distribution, servicing and other information required to be provided under Form 10-D for the period covered by this report is included in the Exchange Act periodic reports;

4. [I am responsible for reviewing the activities performed by the servicer(s) and based on my knowledge and the compliance review(s) conducted in preparing the servicer compliance statement(s) required in this report under Item 1123 of Regulation AB, and except as disclosed in the Exchange Act periodic reports, the servicer(s) [has/have]fulfilled [its/their] obligations under the servicing agreement(s) in all material respects; and]

[Based on my knowledge and the servicer compliance statement(s) required in this report under Item 1123 of Regulation AB, and except as disclosed in the Exchange Act periodic reports, the servicer(s) [has/have] fulfilled [its/their] obligations under the servicing agreement(s) in all material respects; and]

5. All of the reports on assessment of compliance with servicing criteria for asset-backed securities and their related attestation reports on assessment of compliance with servicing criteria for asset-backed securities required to be included in this report in accordance with Item 1122 of Regulation AB and Exchange Act Rules 13a-18 and 15d-18 have been included as an exhibit to this report, except as otherwise disclosed in this report. Any material instances of noncompliance described in such reports have been disclosed in this report on Form 10-K.[3]

[In giving the certifications above, I have reasonably relied on information provided to me by the following unaffiliated parties [name of servicer, sub-servicer, co-servicer, depositor or trustee].][4]

Date: . . . .

—————————
[Signature]
[Title]

(32) Section 1350 Certifications.

(i) The certifications required by Rule 13a-14(b) (17 CFR 240.13a-14(b)) or Rule 15d-14(b) (17 CFR 240.15d-14(b)) and Section 1350 of Chapter 63 of Title 18 of the United States Code (18 U.S.C. 1350).

(ii) A certification furnished pursuant to this item will not be deemed "filed" for purposes of Section 18 of the Exchange Act (15 U.S.C. 78r), or otherwise subject to the liability of that section. Such certification will not be deemed to be incorporated by reference into any filing under the Securities Act or the Exchange Act, except to the extent that the registrant specifically incorporates it by reference.

(33) through (98) [Reserved]

---

[1] With respect to asset-backed issuers, the certification must be signed by either:

(1) The senior officer in charge of securitization of the depositor if the depositor is signing the report on Form 10-K; or

(2) The senior officer in charge of the servicing function of the servicer if the servicer is signing the report on Form 10-K on behalf of the issuing entity. See Rules 13a-14(e) and 15d-14(e) (§§ 240.13a-14(e) and 240.15d-14(e)). If multiple servicers are involved in servicing the pool assets, the senior officer in charge of the servicing function of the master servicer (or entity performing the equivalent function) must sign if a representative of the servicer is to sign the certification. If there is a master servicer and one or more underlying servicers, the references in the certification relate to the master servicer. A natural person must sign the certification in his or her individual capacity, although the title of that person in the

organization of which he or she is an officer may be included under the signature.

[3] The certification refers to the reports prepared by parties participating in the servicing function that are required to be included as an exhibit to the Form 10-K. See Item 1122 of Regulation AB (§ 229.1122) and Rules 13a-18 and 15d-18 (§§ 240.13a-18 and 240.15d-18 of this chapter). If a report is otherwise required to be included is not attached, disclosure that the report is not included and an associated explanation must be provided in the Form 10-K report.

[4] Because the signer of the certification must rely in certain circumstances on information provided by unaffiliated parties outside of the signer's control, this paragraph must be included if the signer is reasonably relying on information that unaffiliated trustees, depositors, servicers, sub-servicers or co-servicers have provided.

(33) *Report on assessment of compliance with servicing criteria for asset-backed securities.* Each report on assessment of compliance with servicing criteria required by § 229.1122(a).

(34) *Attestation report on assessment of compliance with servicing criteria for asset-backed securities.* Each attestation report on assessment of compliance with servicing criteria for asset-backed securities required by § 229.1122(b).

(35) *Servicer compliance statement.* Each servicer compliance statement required by § 229.1123.

(36) through (98) [Reserved]

(99) *Additional exhibits*—(i) Any additional exhibits which the registrant may wish to file shall be so marked as to indicate clearly the subject matters to which they refer. (ii) Any document (except for an exhibit) or part thereof which is incorporated by reference in the filing and is not otherwise required to be filed by this Item or is not a Commission filed document incorporated by reference in a Securities Act registration statement.

(iii) If pursuant to Section 11(a) of the Securities Act (15 U.S.C. 77k(a)) an issuer makes generally available to its security holders an earnings statement covering a period of at least 12 months beginning after the effective date of the registration statement, and if such earnings statement is made available by "other methods" than those specified in paragraph (a) or (b) of § 230.158 of this chapter, it must be filed as an exhibit to the Form 10-Q or the Form 10-K, as appropriate, covering the period in which the earnings statement was released.

(100) *XBRL-Related Documents.* Only an electronic filer that prepares its financial statements in accordance with Article 6 of Regulation S-X (17 CFR 210.6-01 et. seq.) is permitted to participate in the voluntary XBRL (eXtensible Business Reporting Language) program and, as a result, may submit XBRL-Related Documents (§ 232.11 of this chapter) in electronic format as an exhibit to: the filing to which they relate; an amendment to such filing; or a Form 8-K (§ 249.308 of this chapter) that references such filing, if the Form 8-K is submitted no earlier than the date of filing. Rule 401 of Regulation S-T (§ 232.401 of this chapter) sets forth further details regarding eligibility to participate in the voluntary XBRL program.

(101) *Interactive Data File.* An Interactive Data File (§ 232.11 of this chapter) is:

(i) *Required to be submitted and posted.* Required to be submitted to the Commission and posted on the registrant's corporate Web site, if any, in the manner provided by Rule 405 of Regulation S-T (§ 232.405 of this chapter) if the registrant does not prepare its financial statements in accordance with Article 6 of Regulation S-X (17 CFR 210.6-01 et. seq.) and is described in paragraph (b)(101)(i)(A), (B) or (C) of this Item, except that an Interactive Data File: first is required for a periodic report on Form 10-Q (§ 249.308a of this chapter), Form 20-F (§ 249.220f of this chapter) or Form 40-F (§ 249.240f of this chapter), as applicable; is required for a registration statement under the Securities Act only if the registration statement contains a price or price range; and is required for a Form 8-K (§ 249.308 of this chapter) only when the Form 8-K contains audited annual financial statements that are a revised version of financial statements that previously were filed with the Commission that have been revised pursuant to applicable accounting standards to reflect the effects of certain subsequent events, including a discontinued operation, a change in reportable segments or a change in accounting principle, and, in such case, the Interactive Data File would be required only as to such revised financial statements regardless whether the Form 8-K contains other financial statements:

(A) A large accelerated filer (§ 240.12b-2 of this chapter) that had an aggregate worldwide market value of the voting and non-voting common equity held by non-affiliates of more than $5 billion as of the last business day of the second fiscal quarter of its most recently completed fiscal year that prepares its financial statements in accordance with generally accepted accounting principles as used in the United States and the filing contains financial statements of the registrant for a fiscal period that ends on or after June 15, 2009;

(B) A large accelerated filer not specified in paragraph (b)(101)(i)(A) of this Item that prepares its financial statements in accordance with generally accepted accounting principles as used in the United States and the filing contains financial statements of the registrant for a fiscal period that ends on or after June 15, 2010; or

(C) A filer not specified in paragraph (b)(101)(i)(A) or (B) of this Item that prepares its financial statements in accordance with either generally accepted accounting principles as used in the United States or International Financial Reporting Standards as issued by the International Accounting Standards Board, and the filing contains financial statements of the registrant for a fiscal period that ends on or after June 15, 2011.

(ii) *Permitted to be submitted.* Permitted to be submitted to the Commission in the manner provided by Rule 405 of Regulation S-T (§ 232.405 of this chapter) if the:

(A) Registrant prepares its financial statements:

(*1*) In accordance with either:

(*i*) Generally accepted accounting principles as used in the United States; or

(*ii*) International Financial Reporting Standards as issued by the International Accounting Standards Board; and

(2) Not in accordance with Article 6 of Regulation S-X (17 CFR 210.6-01 et. seq.); and

(B) Interactive Data File is not required to be submitted to the Commission under paragraph (b)(101)(i) of this Item.

(iii) *Not permitted to be submitted.* Not permitted to be submitted to the Commission if the registrant prepares its financial statements in accordance with Article 6 of Regulation S-X (17 CFR 210.6-01 *et. seq.*).

(c) *Smaller reporting companies.* A smaller reporting company need not provide the disclosure required in paragraph (b)(12) of this Item, Statements re computation of ratios.

[As last amended in Release No. 33-9002, effective April 13, 2009, 74 F.R. 6776.]

Subpart 229.700—Miscellaneous

[¶ 13,081] Recent Sales of Unregistered Securities; Use of Proceeds from Registered Securities

Reg. § 229.701. Item 701. Furnish the following information as to all securities of the registrant sold by the registrant within the past three years which were not registered under the Securities Act. Include sales of reacquired securities, as well as new issues, securities issued in exchange for property, services, or other securities, and new securities resulting from the modification of outstanding securities.

(a) *Securities sold.* Give the date of sale and the title and amount of securities sold.

(b) *Underwriters and other purchasers.* Give the names of the principal underwriters, if any. As to any such securities not publicly offered, name the persons or identify the class of persons to whom the securities were sold.

(c) *Consideration.* As to securities sold for cash, state the aggregate offering price and the aggregate underwriting discounts or commissions. As to any securities sold otherwise than for cash, state the nature of the transaction and the nature and aggregate amount of consideration received by the registrant.

(d) *Exemption from registration claimed.* Indicate the section of the Securities Act or the rule of the Commission under which exemption from registration was claimed and state briefly the facts relied upon to make the exemption available.

(e) *Terms of conversion or exercise.* If the information called for by this paragraph (e) is being presented on Form 8-K, Form 10-Q, Form 10-K, or Form 10-D under the Exchange Act (§ 249.308, § 249.308(a), § 240.310 or § 249.312) of this chapter, and where the securities sold by the registrant are convertible or exchangeable into equity securities, or are warrants or options representing equity securities, disclose the terms of conversion or exercise of the securities.

(f) *Use of Proceeds.* As required by § 230.463 of this chapter, following the effective date of the first registration statement filed under the Securities Act by an issuer, the issuer or successor issuer shall report the use of proceeds on its first periodic report filed pursuant to sections 13(a) and 15(d) of the Exchange Act (15 U.S.C. 78m(a) and 78o(d)) after effectiveness of its Securities Act registration statement, and thereafter on each of its subsequent periodic reports filed pursuant to sections 13(a) and 15(d) of the Exchange Act through the later of disclosure of the application of all the offering proceeds, or disclosure of the termination of the offering. If a report of the use of proceeds is required with respect to the first effective registration statement of the predecessor issuer, the successor issuer shall provide such a report. The information provided pursuant to paragraphs (f)(2) through (f)(4) of this Item need only be provided with respect to the first periodic report filed pursuant to sections 13(a) and 15(d) of the Exchange Act after effectiveness of the registration statement filed under the Securities Act. Subsequent periodic reports filed pursuant to sections 13(a) and 15(d) of the Exchange Act need only provide the information required in paragraphs (f)(2) through (f)(4) of this Item if any of such required information has changed since the last periodic report filed. In disclosing the use of proceeds in the first periodic report filed pursuant to the Exchange Act, the issuer or successor issuer should include the following information:

(1) The effective date of the Securities Act registration statement for which the use of proceeds information is being disclosed and the Commission file number assigned to the registration statement;

(2) If the offering has commenced, the offering date, and if the offering has not commenced, an explanation why it has not;

(3) If the offering terminated before any securities were sold, an explanation for such termination; and

(4) If the offering did not terminate before any securities were sold, disclose:

(i) Whether the offering has terminated and, if so, whether it terminated before the sale of all securities registered;

(ii) The name(s) of the managing underwriter(s), if any;

(iii) The title of each class of securities registered and, where a class of convertible securities is being registered, the title of any class of securities into which such securities may be converted;

(iv) For each class of securities (other than a class of securities into which a class of convertible securities registered may be converted without additional payment to the issuer) the following information, provided for both the account of the issuer and the account(s) of any selling security holder(s): the amount registered, the aggregate price of the offering amount registered, the amount sold and the aggregate offering price of the amount sold to date;

(v) From the effective date of the Securities Act registration statement to the ending date of the reporting period, the amount of expenses incurred for the issuer's account in connection with the issuance and distribution of the securities registered for underwriting discounts and commissions, finders' fees, expenses paid to or for underwriters, other expenses and total expenses. Indicate if a reasonable estimate for the amount of expenses incurred is provided instead of the actual amount of expense. Indicate whether such payments were:

(A) Direct or indirect payments to directors, officers, general partners of the issuer or their associates; to persons owning ten (10) percent or more of any class of equity securities of the issuer; and to affiliates of the issuer; or

(B) Direct or indirect payments to others;

(vi) The net offering proceeds to the issuer after deducting the total expenses described in paragraph (f)(4)(v) of this Item;

(vii) From the effective date of the Securities Act registration statement to the ending date of the reporting period, the amount of net offering proceeds to the issuer used for construction of plant, building and facilities; purchase and installation of machinery and equipment; purchases of real estate; acquisition of other business(es); repayment of indebtedness; working capital; temporary investments (which should be specified); and any other purposes for which at least five (5) percent of the issuer's total offering proceeds or $100,000 (whichever is less) has been used (which should be specified). Indicate if a reasonable estimate for the amount of net offering proceeds applied is provided instead of the actual amount of net offering proceeds used. Indicate whether such payments were:

(A) Direct or indirect payments to directors, officers, general partners of the issuer or their associates; to persons owning ten (10) percent or more of any class of equity securities of the issuer; and to affiliates of the issuer; or

(B) Direct or indirect payments to others; and

(viii) If the use of proceeds in paragraph (f)(4)(vii) of this Item represents a material change in the use of proceeds described in the prospectus, the issuer should describe briefly the material change.

Instructions. 1. Information required by this Item 701 need not be set forth as to notes, drafts, bills of exchange, or bankers' acceptances which mature not later than one year from the date of issuance.

2. If the sales were made in a series of transactions, the information may be given by such totals and periods as will reasonably convey the information required.

[As last amended in Release No. 33-8876, effective February 4, 2008, 73 F.R. 934.]

[¶ 13,082] Indemnification of Directors and Officers

Reg. § 229.702. Item 702. State the general effect of any statute, charter provisions, by-laws, contract or other arrangements under which any controlling persons, director or officer of the registrant is insured or indemnified in any manner against liability which he may incur in his capacity as such.

[As last amended in Release No. 33-7300, May 31, 1996, effective July 15, 1996, 61 F.R. 30397.]

[¶ 13,083] Purchases of Equity Securities by the Issuer and Affiliated Purchasers

Reg. § 229.703. Item 703. (a) In the following tabular format, provide the information specified in paragraph (b) of this Item with respect to any purchase made by or on behalf of the issuer or any "affiliated purchaser," as defined in § 240.10b-18(a)(3) of this chapter, of shares or other units of any class of the issuer's equity securities that is registered by the issuer pursuant to section 12 of the Exchange Act (15 U.S.C. 78*l*).

Period	(a) Total Number of Shares (or Units) Purchased	(b) Average Price Paid per Share (or Unit)	(c) Total Number of Shares (or Units) Purchased as Part of Publicly Announced Plans or Programs	(d) Maximum Number (or Approximate Dollar Value) of Shares (or Units) that May Yet Be Purchased Under the Plans or Programs
Month #1 (identify beginning and ending dates)				
Month #2 (identify beginning and ending dates)				
Month #3 (identify beginning and ending dates)				
Total				

(b) The table shall include the following information for each class or series of securities for each month included in the period covered by the report:

(1) The total number of shares (or units) purchased (column (a));

Instruction to paragraph (b)(1) of Item 703

Include in this column all issuer repurchases, including those made pursuant to publicly announced plans or programs and those not made pursuant to publicly announced plans or programs. Briefly disclose, by footnote to the table, the number of shares purchased other than through a publicly announced plan or program and the nature of the transaction (*e.g.*, whether the purchases were made in open-market transactions, tender offers, in satisfaction of the company's obligations upon exercise of outstanding put options issued by the company, or other transactions).

(2) The average price paid per share (or unit) (column (b));

(3) The total number of shares (or units) purchased as part of publicly announced repurchase plans or programs (column (c)); and

(4) The maximum number (or approximate dollar value) of shares (or units) that may yet be purchased under the plans or programs (column (d)).

Instructions to paragraphs (b)(3) and (b)(4) of Item 703

1. In the table, disclose this information in the aggregate for all plans or programs publicly announced.

2. By footnote to the table, indicate:

a. The date each plan or program was announced;

b. The dollar amount (or share or unit amount) approved;

c. The expiration date (if any) of each plan or program;

d. Each plan or program that has expired during the period covered by the table; and

e. Each plan or program the issuer has determined to terminate prior to expiration, or under which the issuer does not intend to make further purchases.

Instruction to Item 703

Disclose all purchases covered by this Item, including purchases that do not satisfy the conditions of the safe harbor of § 240.10b-18 of this chapter.

[Added by Release No. 33-8335, effective December 17, 2003, 68 F.R. 64952.]

Subpart 229.800—List of Industry Guides

»»→ For the text of the Securities Act Industry Guides, see ¶ 12,001—12,041

[¶ 13,091] Securities Act Industry Guides

Reg. § 229.801. .(a) Guide 1. [Removed and reserved in Release No. 33-7300, effective July 15, 1996, 61 F.R. 30397.]

(b) Guide 2. [Removed and reserved in Release No. 33-8995, effective January 1, 2010.]

(c) Guide 3. Statistical disclosure by bank holding companies.

(d) Guide 4. Prospectuses relating to interests in oil and gas programs.

(e) Guide 5. Preparation of registration statements relating to interests in real estate limited partnerships.

(f) Guide 6. Disclosures concerning unpaid claims and claim adjustment expenses of property-casualty underwriters.

(g) Guide 7. Description of Property by Issuers Engaged or To Be Engaged in Significant Mining Operations.

[As last amended in Release No. 33-8995, effective January 1, 2010, 74 F.R. 2157.]

»»→ For the text of the Exchange Act Industry Guides, see ¶ 12,501—12,521

[¶ 13,092] Exchange Act Industry Guides

Reg. § 229.802. (Item 802).(a) Guide 1. [Removed and reserved in Release No. 33-7300, effective July 15, 1996, 61 F.R. 30397.]

(b) Guide 2. [Removed and reserved in Release No. 33-8995, effective January 1, 2010.]

(c) Guide 3. Statistical disclosure by bank holding companies.

(d) Guide 4. Disclosures concerning unpaid claims and claim adjustment expenses of property-casualty underwriters. [Added in Release No. FR-20, effective for fiscal years ending after December 15, 1984, 49 F.R. 47594.]

(e) [Reserved].

(f) [Reserved].

(g) Guide 7. Description of Property by Issuers Engaged or To Be Engaged in Significant Mining Operations. [Added in Release No. FR-39, effective August 13, 1992, 57 F.R. 36442.]

[As last amended in Release No. 33-8995, effective January 1, 2010, 74 F.R. 2157.]

Subpart 229.900—Roll-up Transactions

[¶ 13,101] Definitions

Reg. § 229.901. (Item 901). For the purposes of subpart 229.900:

(a) "General partner" means the person or persons responsible under state law for managing or directing the management of the business and affairs of a partnership that is the subject of a roll-up transaction including, but not limited to, a general partner(s), board of directors, board of trustees, or other person(s) having a fiduciary duty to such partnership.

(b) (1) "Partnership" means any:

(i) Finite-life limited partnership; or

(ii) Other finite-life entity.

(2) (i) Except as provided in subparagraph (b)(2)(ii) of this Item (§ 229.901(b)(2)(ii)), a limited partnership or other entity is "finite-life" if:

(A) It operates as a conduit vehicle for investors to participate in the ownership of assets for a limited period of time; and

(B) It has as a policy or purpose distributing to investors proceeds from the sale, financing or refinancing of assets or cash from operations, rather than reinvesting such proceeds or cash in the business (whether for the term of the entity or after an initial period of time following commencement of operations).

(ii) A real estate investment trust as defined in I.R.C. § 856 is not "finite-life" solely because of the distribution to investors of net income as provided by the I.R.C. if its policies or purposes do not include the distribution to investors of proceeds from the sale, financing or refinancing of assets, rather than the reinvestment of such proceeds in the business.

(3) "Partnership" does not include any entity registered under the Investment Company Act of 1940 [15 U.S.C. 80a-1 et seq.]or any Business Development Company as defined in § 2(a)(48) of that Act [15 U.S.C. 80a-2(a)(48)].

(c) (1) Except as provided in paragraph (c)(2) or (c)(3) of this Item, *roll-up transaction* means a transaction involving the combination or reorganization of one or more partnerships, directly or indirectly, in which some or all of the investors in any of such partnerships will receive new securities, or securities in another entity.

(2) Notwithstanding paragraph (c)(1) of this Item, *roll-up transaction* shall not include:

(i) A transaction wherein the interests of all of the investors in each of the partnerships are repurchased, recalled, or exchanged in accordance with the terms of the preexisting partnership agreement for securities in an operating company specifically identified at the time of the formation of the original partnership;

(ii) A transaction in which the securities to be issued or exchanged are not required to be and are not registered under the Securities Act of 1933 (15 U.S.C. 77a *et seq.*);

(iii) A transaction that involves only issuers that are not required to register or report under Section 12 of the Securities Exchange Act of 1934 (15 U.S.C. 78*l*), both before and after the transaction;

(iv) A transaction that involves the combination or reorganization of one or more partnerships in which a non-affiliated party succeeds to the interests of a general partner or sponsor, if:

(A) Such action is approved by not less than 66⅔% of the outstanding units of each of the participating partnerships; and

(B) As a result of the transaction, the existing general partners will receive only compensation to which they are entitled as expressly provided for in the preexisting partnership agreements;

(v) A transaction in which the securities offered to investors are securities of another entity that are reported under a transaction reporting plan declared effective before December 17, 1993 by the Commission under Section 11A of the Securities Exchange Act of 1934 (15 U.S.C. 78k-1), if:

(A) Such other entity was formed, and such class of securities was reported and regularly traded, not less than 12 months before the date on which soliciting material is mailed to investors; *and*

(B) The securities of that entity issued to investors in the transaction do not exceed 20% of the total outstanding securities of the entity, exclusive of any securities of such class held by or for the account of the entity or a subsidiary of the entity;

(C) For purposes of paragraph (c)(2)(v) of this Item (§ 229.901(c)(2)(v)), a *regularly traded* security means any security with a minimum closing price of $2.00 or more for a majority of the business days during the preceding three-month period and a six-month minimum average daily trading volume of 1,000 shares.

(vi) A transaction in which all of the investors' partnership securities are reported under a transaction reporting plan declared effective before December 17, 1993 by the Commission under

Section 11A of the Securities Exchange Act of 1934 (15 U.S.C. 78k-1) and such investors receive new securities or securities in another entity that are reported under a transaction reporting plan declared effective before December 17, 1993 by the Commission under Section 11A of the Securities Exchange Act of 1934 (15 U.S.C. 78k-1), except that, for purposes of this paragraph, securities that are reported under a transaction reporting plan declared effective before December 17, 1993 by the Commission under Section 11A of the Securities Exchange Act of 1934 shall not include securities listed on the American Stock Exchange's Emerging Company Marketplace;

(vii) A transaction in which the investors in any of the partnerships involved in the transaction are not subject to a significant adverse change with respect to voting rights, the terms of existence of the entity, management compensation or investment objectives; or

(viii) A transaction in which all investors are provided an option to receive or retain a security under substantially the same terms and conditions as the original issue.

(3) The Commission, upon written request or upon its own motion, may exempt by rule or order any security or class of securities, any transaction or class of transactions, or any person or class of persons, in whole or in part, conditionally or unconditionally, from the definition of roll-up transaction or the requirements imposed on roll-up transactions by Items 902—915 of Regulation S-K (§§ 229.902—915), if it finds such action to be consistent with the public interest and the protection of investors.

(d) "Sponsor" means the person proposing the roll-up transaction.

(e) "Successor" means the surviving entity after completion of the roll-up transaction or the entity whose securities are being offered or sold to, or acquired by, limited partners of the partnerships or the limited partnerships to be combined or reorganized.

Instruction to Item 901. If a transaction is a roll-up transaction as defined in Item 901(c) of this subpart (§ 229.901(c)), the requirements of this subpart apply to each entity proposed to be included in the roll-up transaction, whether or not the entity is a "partnership" as defined in Item 901(b) of this subpart (§ 229.901(b)).

[As last amended in Release No. 33-7113, December 1, 1994, 59 F.R. 63676.]

[¶ 13,102] Individual Partnership Supplements

Reg. § 229.902. (Item 902). (a) If two or more entities are proposed to be included in the roll-up transaction, provide the information specified in this Item (§ 229.902) in a separate supplement to the disclosure document for each entity.

(b) The separate supplement required by paragraph (a) of this Item (§ 229.902) shall be filed as part of the registration statement, shall be delivered with the prospectus to investors in the partnership covered thereby, and shall include:

(1) A statement in the forepart of the supplement to the effect that:

(i) Supplements have been prepared for each partnership;

(ii) The effects of the roll-up transaction may be different for investors in the various partnerships; and

(iii) Upon receipt of a written request by an investor or his representative who has been so designated in writing, a copy of any supplement will be transmitted promptly, without charge, by the general partner or sponsor.

This statement must include the name and address of the person to whom investors should make their request.

(2) A brief description of each material risk and effect of the roll-up transaction, including, but not limited to, federal income tax consequences, for investors in the partnership, with appropriate cross references to the discussions of the risks, effects and tax consequences of the roll-up transaction required in the principal disclosure document pursuant to Items 904 and 915 of this subpart (§ 229.904 and § 229.915). Such discussion shall address the effect of the roll-up transaction on the partnership's financial condition and results of operations.

(3) A statement concerning whether the general partner reasonably believes that the roll-up transaction is fair or unfair to investors in the partnership, together with a brief discussion of the bases for such relief, with appropriate cross references to the discussion of the fairness of the roll-up transaction required in the principal disclosure document pursuant to Item 910 of this subpart (§ 229.910). If there are material differences between the fairness analysis for the partnership and for the other partnerships, such differences shall be described briefly in the supplement.

(4) A brief, narrative description of the method of calculating the value of the partnership and allocating interests in the successor to the partnership, and a table showing such calculation and allocation. Such table shall include the following information (or other information of a comparable character necessary to a thorough understanding of the calculation and allocation):

(i) The appraised value of each separately appraised significant asset (as defined in Item 911(c)(5) of this subpart (§ 229.911(c)(5)) held by the partnership, or, if appraisals have not been obtained for each significant asset, the value assigned for purposes of the valuation of the partnership to each significant asset for which an appraisal has not been obtained;

(ii) The dollar amount of any mortgages or other similar liabilities to which each of such assets is subject;

(iii) Cash and cash equivalent assets held by the partnership;

(iv) Other assets held by the partnership;

(v) Other liabilities of the partnership;

(vi) The value assigned to the partnership;

(vii) The value assigned to the partnership per interest held by holders of interests in the partnership (on an equivalent interest basis, such as per $1,000 original investment);

(viii) The aggregate number of interests in the successor to be allocated to the partnership and the percentage of the total interests of the successor;

(ix) The number of interests in the successor to be allocated to investors in the partnership for each interest held by such investors (on an equivalent interest basis, such as per $1,000 original investment); and

(x) The value assigned to the general partner's interest in the partnership, and the number of interests in the successor or other consideration to be allocated in the roll-up transaction to the general partner for such general partnership interest or otherwise as compensation or reimbursement for claims against or interests in the partnership, such as foregone fees, unearned fees and for fees to be earned on the sale or refinancing of an asset.

(5) The amounts of compensation paid, and cash distributions made, to the general partner and its affiliates by the partnership for the last three fiscal years and the most recently completed interim period and the amounts that would have been paid if the compensation and distributions structure to be in effect after the roll-up transaction had been in effect during such period. If any proposed change(s) in the business or operations of the successor after the roll-up transaction would change materially the compensation and distributions that would have been paid by the successor (e.g., if properties will be sold or purchased after the roll-up transaction and no properties were sold or purchased during the period covered by the table), describe such changes and the effects thereof on the compensation and distributions to be paid by the successor.

(6) Cash distributions made to investors during each of the last five fiscal years and most recently completed interim period, identifying any such distributions which represent a return of capital.

(7) An appropriate cross reference to selected financial information concerning the partnership and the pro forma financial statements included in the principal disclosure document in response to Item 914(b)(2) of this subpart (§ 229.914(b)(2)).

[As adopted in Release No. FR-38, October 30, 1991, 56 F.R. 57237.]

[¶ 13,103] Summary

Reg. § 229.903. (Item 903). (a) Provide in the forepart of the disclosure document a clear, concise and comprehensible summary of the roll-up transaction.

(b) The summary required by paragraph (a) of this Item (§ 229.903) shall include a summary description of each of the following items, as well as any other material terms or consequences of the roll-up transaction necessary to an understanding of such transaction:

(1) Each material risk and effect on investors, including, but not limited to:

(i) Changes in the business plan, voting rights, cash distribution policies, form of ownership interest or management compensation;

(ii) The general partner's conflicts of interest in connection with the roll-up transaction and in connection with the successor's future operations; and

(iii) The likelihood that securities received by investors in the roll-up transaction will trade at prices substantially below the value assigned to such securities in the roll-up transaction and/or the value of the successor's assets;

(2) The material terms of the roll-up transaction, including the valuation method used to allocate securities in the successor to investors in the partnerships;

(3) Whether the general partner reasonably believes that the roll-up transaction is fair or unfair to investors in each partnership, including a brief discussion of the bases for such belief;

(4) Any opinion from an outside party concerning the fairness of the roll-up transaction, including whether the opinion addresses the fairness of all possible combinations of partnerships or portions of partnerships, and contacts with any outside party concerning fairness opinions, valuations or reports in

connection with the roll-up transaction required to be disclosed pursuant to Item 911(a)(5) of this subpart (§ 229.911(a)(5));

(5) The background of and reasons for the roll-up transaction, as well as alternatives to the roll-up transaction described in response to Item 908(b) of this subpart (§ 229.908(b));

(6) Rights of investors to exercise dissenters' or appraisal rights or similar rights and to obtain a list of investors in the partnership in which the investor holds an interest; and

(7) If any affiliates of the general partner or the sponsor may participate in the business of the successor or receive compensation from the successor, an organizational chart showing the relationships between the general partner, the sponsor and their affiliates.

Instruction to Item 903. The description of the material risks and effects of the roll-up transaction required by paragraph (b)(1) of this Item (§ 229.903) must be presented prominently in the forepart of the summary.

[As adopted in Release No. FR-38, October 30, 1991, 56 F.R. 57237.]

[¶ 13,104] Risk Factors and Other Considerations

Reg. § 229.904. (Item 904). (a) Immediately following the summary required by Item 903 of this subpart (§ 229.903), describe in reasonable detail each material risk and effect of the roll-up transaction on investors in each partnership, including, but not limited to:

(1) The potential risks, adverse effects and benefits of the roll-up transaction for investors and for the general partner, including those partner, including those which result from each matter described in response to Item 905 of this subpart (§ 229.905), with appropriate cross references to the comparative information required by Item 905;

(2) The material risks arising from an investment in the successor; and

(3) The likelihood that securities of the successor received by investors in the roll-up transaction will trade in the securities markets at a price substantially below the value assigned to such securities in the roll-up transaction and/or the value of the assets of the successor, and the effects on investors of such a trading market discount.

(b) Quantify each risk or effect to the extent practicable.

(c) State whether any of such risks or effects may be different for investors in any partnership and, if so, identify such partnership(s) and describe such difference(s).

Instruction to Item 904. The requirement to quantify the effects of the roll-up transaction shall include, but not be limited to:

(i) If cost savings resulting from combined administration of the partnerships is identified as a potential benefit of the roll-up transaction, the amount of cost savings and a comparison of such amount to the costs of the roll-up transaction; and

(ii) If there may be a material conflict of interest of the sponsor or general partner arising from its receipt of payments or other consideration as a result of a the roll-up transaction, the amount of such payments and other consideration to be obtained in the roll-up transaction and a comparison of such amounts to the amounts to which the sponsor or general partner would be entitled without the roll-up transaction.

[As adopted in Release No. FR-38, October 30, 1991, 56 F.R. 57237.]

[¶ 13,105] Comparative Information

Reg. § 229.905 (Item 905). (a)(1) Describe the voting and other rights of investors in the successor under the successor's governing instruments and under applicable law. Compare such rights to the voting and other rights of investors in each partnership subject to the transaction under the partnerships' governing instruments and under applicable law. Describe the effects of the change(s) in such rights.

(2) Describe the duties owed by the general partner of the successor to investors in the successor under the successor's governing instruments and under applicable law. Compare such duties to the duties owed by the general partner of each partnership to investors in the partnership under the partnership's governing instruments and under applicable law. Describe the effects of the change(s) in such duties.

(b)(1) Describe each item of compensation (including reimbursement of expenses) payable by the successor after the roll-up transaction to the general partner and its affiliates or to any affiliate of the successor. Compare such compensation to the compensation currently payable to the general partner and its affiliates by each partnership. Describe the effects of the change(s) in compensation arrangements.

(2) Describe each instance in which cash or other distributions may be made by the successor to the general partner and its affiliates or to any affiliate of the successor. Compare such distributions to the

distributions currently paid or payable to the general partner and its affiliates by each partnership. Describe the effects of the change(s) in distribution arrangements. If distributions similar to those currently paid or payable by any partnership to the general partner or its affiliates will not be made by the successor, state whether or not other compensation arrangements with the successor described in response to paragraph (b)1) of this Item (§ 229.905) (e.g., incentive fees payable upon sale of a property) will, in effect, replace such distributions.

(3) Provide a table demonstrating the changes in such compensation and distributions setting forth among other things:

(i) The actual amounts of compensation and distributions, separately identified, paid by the parnterships on a combined basis to the general partner and its affiliates for the partnerships' last three fiscal years and most recently ended interim periods; and

(ii) The amounts of compensation and distributions that would have been paid if the compensation and distributions structure to be in effect after the roll-up transaction had been in effect during such period.

(4) If any proposed change(s) in the business or operations of the successor after the roll-up transaction would change materially the compensation and distributions that would have been paid by the successor from that shown in the table provided in response to paragraph (b)(3)(ii) of this Item (§ 229.905) (e.g., if properties will be sold or purchased after the roll-up transaction and no properties were sold or purchased during the period covered by the table), describe such changes and the effects thereof on the compensation and distributions to be paid by the successor.

(5) Describe the material conflicts that may arise between the interests of the sponsor or general partner and the interests of investors in the successor as a result of the compensation and distribution arrangements described in response to paragraphs (b)(1) and (2) of this Item (§ 229.905) and describe any steps that will be taken to resolve any such conflicts.

(c) Describe any provisions in the governing instruments of the successor and any policies of the general partner of the successor relating to distributions to investors of cash from operations, proceeds from the sale, financing or refinancing of assets, and any other distributions. Compare such provisions and policies to those of each of the partnerships. Describe the effects of any change(s) in such provisions or policies.

(d)(1) Describe each material investment policy of the successor, including, without limitation, policies with respect to borrowings by the successor. Compare such investment policies to the investment policies of each of the partnerships. Describe the effects of any change(s) in such policies.

(2) Describe any plans of the general partner, sponsor or of any person who will be an affiliate of the successor with respect to:

(i) A sale of any material assets of the partnerships;

(ii) A purchase of any material assets; and

(iii) Borrowings.

(3)(i) State whether or not specific assets have been identified for sale, financing, refinancing or purchase following the roll-up transaction.

(ii) If specific assets have been so identified, describe the assets and the proposed transaction.

(e) Describe any other similar terms or policies of the successor that are material to an investment in the successor. Compare any such terms or policies to those of each of the partnerships. Describe the effects of any change(s) in any such terms or policies.

Instructions to Item 905. (1) The information provided in response to this Item (§ 229.905) should be illustrated in tables or other readily understandable formats, which should be included together with the disclosures required by this Item.

The information required by this Item (§ 229.905) shall be set forth in appropriate separate sections of the principal disclosure document.

[As adopted in Release No. FR-38, October 30, 1991, 56 F.R. 57237.]

[¶ 13,106] Allocation of Roll-Up Consideration

Reg. § 229.906. (Item 906). (a) Describe in reasonable detail the method used to allocate interests in the successor to investors in the partnerships and the reasons why such method was used.

(b) Provide a table showing the calculation of the valuation of each partnership and the allocation of interests in the successor to investors. Such table shall include for each partnership the following information (or other information of a comparable character necessary to an understanding of the calculation and allocation):

(1) The value assigned to each significant category of assets of the partnership and the total value assigned to the partnership;

(2) The total value assigned to all partnerships;

(3) The aggregate amount of interests in the successor to be allocated to each partnership and the percentage of the total amount of all such interests represented thereby; and

(4) The amount of interests of the successor to be issued to investors per interest held in each partnership (on an equivalent interest basis, such as per $1,000 invested).

(c) If interests in the successor will be allocated to the general partner in exchange for its general partner interest or otherwise or if the general partner will receive other consideration in connection with the roll-up transaction:

(1) Describe in reasonable detail the method used to allocate interests in the successor to the general partner or to determine the amount of consideration payable to the general partner and the reasons such method(s) was used; and

(2) Identify the consideration paid by the general partner for interests in the partnerships that will be changed in the roll-up transaction.

[As adopted in Release No. FR-38, October 30, 1991, 56 F.R. 57237.]

[¶ 13,107] Background of the Roll-Up Transaction

Reg. § 229.907. (Item 907). (a)(1) Furnish a summary of the background of the transaction. Such summary shall include, but not be limited to, a description of any contacts, negotiations or transactions concerning any of the following matters:

(i) A merger, consolidation, or combination of any of the partnerships;

(ii) An acquisition of any of the partnerships of a material amount of any of their assets;

(iii) A tender offer for or other acquisition of securities of any class issued by any of the partnerships; or

(iv) A change in control of any of the partnerships.

(2) The summary required by paragraph (a)(1) shall:

(i) Cover the period beginning with each partnership's second full fiscal year preceding the date of the filing of the roll-up transaction;

(ii) Include contacts, negotiations or transactions between the general partner or its affiliates and any person who would have a direct interest in the matters listed in (a)(1)(i)—(iv); and

(iii) Identify the person who initiated such contacts, negotiations or transactions.

(b) Briefly describe the background of each partnership, including, but not limited to:

(1) The amount of capital raised from investors, the extent to which net proceeds from the original offering of interests have been invested, the extent to which funds have been invested as planned and the amount not yet invested; and

(2) The partnership's investment objectives, and the extent to which the partnership has achieved its investment objectives.

(c) Discuss whether the general partner (including any affiliated person materially dependent on the general partner's compensation arrangement with the partnership) or any partnership has experienced since the commencement of the most recently completed fiscal year or is likely to experience any material adverse financial developments. If so, describe such developments and the effect of the transaction on such matters.

[As adopted in Release No. FR-38, October 30, 1991, 56 F.R. 57237.]

[¶ 13,108] Reasons for and Alternatives to the Roll-Up Transaction

Reg. § 229.908. (Item 908). (a) Describe the reason(s) for the roll-up transaction.

(b)(1) if the general partner or sponsor considered alternatives to the roll-up transaction being proposed, describe such alternative(s) and state reason(s) for their rejection.

(2) Whether or not described in response to paragraph (b)(1) of this Item (§ 229.908), describe in reasonable detail the potential alternative of continuation of the partnerships in accordance with their existing business plans, including the effects of such continuation and the material risks and benefits that likely would rise in connection therewith, and, if applicable, the general partner's reasons for not considering such alternative.

(3) Whether or not described in response to paragraph (b)(1) of this Item (§ 229.908), describe in reasonable detail the potential alternative of liquidation of the partnerships, the procedures required to accomplish liquidation, the effects of liquidation, the material risks and benefits that likely would arise in connection with liquidation, and, if applicable, the general partner's reasons for not considering such alternative.

(c) State the reasons for the structure of the roll-up transaction and for undertaking such transaction at this time.

(d) State whether the general partner initiated the roll-up transaction and, if not, whether the general partner participated in the structuring of the transaction.

(e) State whether the general partner recommends the roll-up transaction and briefly describe the reasons for such recommendation.

[As adopted in Release No. FR-38, October 30, 1991, 56 F.R. 57237.]

[¶ 13,109] Conflicts of Interests

Reg. § 229.909. (Item 909). (a) Briefly describe the general partner's fiduciary duties to each partnership subject to the roll-up transaction and each actual or potential material conflict of interest between the general partner and the investors relating to the roll-up transaction.

(b) (1) State whether or not the general partner has retained an unaffiliated representative to act on behalf of investors for purposes of negotiating the terms of the roll-up transaction. If no such representative has been retained, describe the reasons therefor and the risks arising from the absence of separate representation.

(2) If an unaffiliated representative has been retained to represent investors:

(i) Identify such unaffiliated representative;

(ii) Briefly describe the representative's qualifications, including a brief description of any other transaction similar to the roll-up transaction in which the representative has served in a similar capacity within the past five years;

(iii) Describe the method of selection of such representative, including a statement as to whether or not any investors were consulted in the selection of the representative and, if so, the names of such investors;

(iv) Describe the scope and terms of the engagement of the representative, including, but not limited to, what party will be responsible for paying the representative's fees and whether such fees are contingent upon the outcome of the roll-up transaction;

(v) Describe any material relationship between the representative or its affiliates and:

(A) The general partner, sponsor, any affiliate of the general partner or sponsor; or

(B) Any other person having a material interest in the roll-up transaction,

which existed during the past two years or is mutually understood to be contemplated and any compensation received or to be received as a result of such relationship;

(vi) Describe in reasonable detail the actions taken by the representative on behalf of investors; and

(vii) Describe the fiduciary duties or other legal obligations of the representative to investors in each of the partnerships.

[As adopted in Release No. FR-38, October 30, 1991, 56 F.R. 57237.]

[¶ 13,110] Fairness of the Transaction

Reg. § 229.910. (Item 910). (a) State whether the general partner reasonably believes that the roll-up transaction is fair or unfair to investors and the reasons for such belief. Such discussion must address the fairness of the roll-up transaction to investors in each of the partnerships and as a whole. If the roll-up transaction may be completed with a combination of partnerships consisting of less than all partnerships, or with portions of partnerships, the belief stated must address each possible combination.

(b) Discuss in reasonable detail the material factors upon which the belief stated in paragraph (a) of this Item (§ 229.910) is based and, to the extent practicable, the weight assigned to each such factor. Such discussion should include an analysis of the extent, if any, to which such belief is based on the factors set forth in Instructions (2) and (3) to this Item (§ 229.910), paragraph (b) (1) of Item 909 of this subpart (§ 229.909(b) (1)) and Item 911 of this subpart (§ 229.911). This discussion also must:

(1) Compare the value of the consideration to be received in the roll-up transaction to the value of the consideration that would be received pursuant to each of the alternatives discussed in response to Item 908(b) of this subpart (§ 229.908(b)); and

(2) Describe any material differences among the partnerships (e.g., different types of assets or different investment objectives) relating to the fairness of the transaction.

(c) If any offer of the type described in Instruction (2) (viii) to this Item (§ 229.910) has been received, describe such offer and state the reason(s) for its rejection.

(d) Describe any factors known to the general partner that may affect materially the value of the consideration to be received by investors in the roll-up transaction, the values assigned to the partnerships for purposes of the comparisons to alternatives required by paragraph (b) of this Item (§ 229.910) and the fairness of the transaction to investors.

(e) State whether the general partner's statements in response to paragraphs (a) and (b) of this Item (§ 229.910) are based, in whole or in part, on any report, opinion or appraisal described in response to Item 911 of this subpart (§ 229.911). If so, describe any material uncertainties known to the general partner that relate to the conclusions in any such report, opinion or appraisal including, but not limited to, developments or trends that have affected or are reasonably likely to affect materially such conclusions.

Instructions to Item 910. (1) A statement that the general partner has no reasonable belief as to the fairness of the roll-up transaction to investors will not be considered sufficient disclosure in response to paragraph (a) of this Item (§ 229.910(a)).

(2) The factors which are important in determining the fairness of a roll-up transaction to investors and the weight, if any, which should be given to them in a particular context will vary. Normally such factors will include, among others, those referred to in paragraph (b)(1) of Item 909 (§ 229.909(b)(1)) and whether the consideration offered to investors constitutes fair value in relation to:

    (a) Current market prices, if any;

    (b) Historic market prices, if any;

    (c) Net book value;

    (d) Going concern value;

    (e) Liquidation value;

    (f) Purchases of limited partnership interests by the general partner or sponsor or their affiliates since the commencement of the partnership's second full fiscal year preceding the date of filing of the disclosure document for the roll-up transaction;

    (g) Any report, opinion, or appraisal described in Item 911 of this subpart (§ 229.911); and

    (h) Offers of which the general partner or sponsor is aware made during the preceding eighteen months for a merger, consolidation, or combination of any of the partnerships; an acquisition of any of the partnerships or a material amount of their assets; a tender offer for or other acquisition of securities of any class issued by any of the partnerships; or a change in control of any of the partnerships.

(3) The discussion concerning fairness should specifically address material terms of the transaction including whether the consideration offered to investors constitutes fair value in relation to:

    (a) The form and amount of consideration to be received by investors and the sponsor in the roll-up transaction;

    (b) The methods used to determine such consideration; and

    (c) The compensation to be paid to the sponsor in the future.

(4) Conclusory statements, such as "The roll-up transaction is fair to investors in relation to net book value, going concern value, liquidation value and future prospects of the partnership," will not be considered sufficient disclosure in response to paragraph (b) of this Item (§ 229.910(b)).

(5) Consideration should be given to presenting the comparative numerical data as to the value of the consideration being received by investors, liquidation value and other values in a tabular format. Financial and other information concerning the partnerships should be prepared based upon the most recent available information, such as, in the case of financial information, the periods covered by interim selected financial information included in the prospectus in accordance with Item 914 of this subpart (§ 229.914).

[As adopted in Release No. FR-38, October 30, 1991, 56 F.R. 57237.]

[¶ 13,111] Reports, Opinions and Appraisals

Reg. § 229.911. (Item 911). (a) *All Material Reports, Opinions or Appraisals*: State whether or not the general partner or sponsor has received any report, opinion (other than an opinion of counsel) or appraisal from an outside party which is materially related to the roll-up transaction including, but not limited to, any such report, opinion or appraisal relating to the consideration or the fairness of the consideration to be offered to investors in connection with the roll-up transaction or the fairness of such transaction to the general partner or investors.

(2) With respect to any report, opinion or appraisal described in paragraph (a)(1) of this Item (§ 229.911):

    (i) Identify such outside party;

    (ii) Briefly describe the qualifications of such outside party;

    (iii) Describe the method of selection of such outside party;

    (iv) Describe any material relationship between:

    (A) The outside party or its affiliates; and

(B) The general partner, sponsor, the successor or any of their affiliates,

which existed during the past two years or is mutually understood to be contemplated and any compensation received or to be received as a result of such relationship;

(v) If such report, opinion or appraisal relates to the fairness of the consideration, state whether the general partner, sponsor or affiliate determined the amount of consideration to be paid or whether the outside party recommended the amount of consideration to be paid.

(vi) Furnish a summary concerning such report, opinion or appraisal which shall include, but not be limited to, the procedures followed; the findings and recommendations; the bases for and methods of arriving at such findings and recommendations; instructions received from the general partner, sponsor or its affiliates; and any limitation imposed by the general partner, sponsor or affiliate on the scope of the investigation. If any limitation was imposed by the general partner, sponsor or affiliate on the scope of the investigation, including, but not limited to, access to its personnel, premises, and relevant books and records, state the reasons therefor.

(vii) State whether any compensation paid to such outside party is contingent on the approval or completion of the roll-up transaction and, if so, the reasons for compensating such parties on a contingent basis.

(3) Furnish a statement to the effect that upon written request by an investor or his representative who has been so designated in writing, a copy of any such report, opinion or appraisal shall be transmitted promptly, without charge, by the general partner or sponsor. The statement also must include the name and address of the person to whom investors or their representatives should make their request.

(4) All reports, opinions or appraisals referred to in paragraph (a)(1) of this Item (§ 229.911) shall be filed as exhibits to the registration statement.

(5)(i) Describe any contacts in connection with the roll-up transaction between the sponsor or the general partner and any outside party with respect to the preparation by such party of an opinion concerning the fairness of the roll-up transaction, a valuation of a partnership or its assets, or any other report with respect to the roll-up transaction. No description is required, however, of contacts with respect to reports, opinions or appraisals filed as exhibits pursuant to paragraph (a)(4) of this Item (§ 229.911).

(ii) The description of contacts with any outside party required by paragraph (a)(5)(i) of this Item (§ 229.911) shall include the following:

(A) The identity of each such party;

(B) The nature of the contact;

(C) The actions taken by such party;

(D) Any views, preliminary or final, expressed on the proposed subject matter of the report, opinion or appraisal; and

(E) Any reasons such party did not provide a report, opinion or appraisal.

(b) *Fairness Opinions:* (1) If any report, opinion or appraisal relates to the fairness of the roll-up transaction to investors in the partnerships, state whether or not the report, opinion or appraisal addresses the fairness of:

(i) The roll-up transaction as a whole and to investors in each partnership; and

(ii) All possible combinations of partnerships in the roll-up transaction (including portions of partnerships if the transaction is structured to permit portions of partnerships to participate). If all possible combinations are not addressed:

(A) Identify the combinations that are addressed;

(B) Identify the person(s) that determined which combinations would be addressed and state the reasons for the selection of the combinations; and

(C) State that if the roll-up transaction is completed with a combination of partnerships not addressed, no report, opinion or appraisal concerning the fairness of the roll-up transaction will have been obtained.

(2) If the sponsor or the general partner has not obtained any opinion on the fairness of the proposed roll-up transaction to investors in each of the affected partnerships, state the sponsor's or general partner's reasons for concluding that such an opinion is not necessary in order to permit the limited partners or shareholders to make an informed decision on the proposed transaction.

(c) *Appraisals:* If the report, opinion or appraisal consists of an appraisal of the assets of the partnerships:

(1) Describe the purpose(s) for which the appraisals were obtained and their use in connection with the roll-up transaction;

(2) Describe which assets are covered by the appraisals and state the aggregate appraised value of the assets covered by the appraisals (including such value net of associated indebtedness). Provide a description of, and valuation of, any assets subject to any material qualifications by the appraiser and a summary of such qualifications;

(3) Identify the date as of which the appraisals were prepared. State whether and in what circumstances the appraisals will be updated. State whether any events have occurred or conditions have changed since the date of the appraisals that may have caused a material change in the value of the assets;

(4) Include as an appendix to the prospectus one or more tables setting forth the following information:

(i) The appraised value of any separately appraised asset that is significant to the partnership holding such asset;

(ii) If the appraiser considered different valuation approaches in preparing the appraisals of the assets identified in response to paragraph (c)(4)(i) of this Item (§ 229.911(c)(4)(i)), the value of each such asset under each valuation approach considered by the appraiser, identifying the valuation approach used by the appraiser in determining the appraised value and the reason such approach was chosen; and

(iii) All material assumptions used by the appraiser in appraising the assets identified in response to paragraph (c)(4)(i) of this Item (§ 229.911(c)(4)(i)), and, if the appraiser used different assumptions for any of such assets, the reasons the different assumptions were chosen.

(5) For purposes of this Item and Item 902 of this Subpart (§ 229.902), an asset is "significant" to a partnership if it represents more than 10% of the value of the partnership's assets as of the end of the most recently-completed fiscal year or recently-completed interim period or if 10% or more of the partnership's cash flow or net income for the most recently-completed fiscal year or most recently-completed subsequent interim period was derived from such asset.

Instructions to Item 911. (1) The reports, opinions and appraisals required to be identified in response to paragraph (a) of this Item (§ 229.911) include any reports, opinions and appraisals which materially relate to the roll-up transaction whether or not relied upon, such as reports or opinions regarding alternatives to the roll-up transaction whether or not the alternatives were rejected.

(2) The information called for by paragraph (a)(2) of this Item (§ 229.911) should be given with respect to the firm which provides the report, opinion or appraisal rather than the employees of such firm who prepared it.

(3) With respect to appraisals, a summary prepared by the appraisers should not be included in lieu of the description of the appraisals required by paragraph (c) of this Item (§ 229.911). A clear and concise summary description of the appraisals is required.

[As last amended in Release No. 33-7113, December 1, 1994, 59 F.R. 63676.]

[¶ 13,112] Source and Amount of Funds and Transactional Expenses

Reg. § 229.912. (Item 912). (a) State the source and total amount of funds or other consideration to be used in the roll-up transaction.

(b)(1) Furnish a reasonably itemized statement of all expenses incurred or estimated to be incurred in connection with the roll-up transaction including, but not limited to, filing fees, legal, financial advisory, accounting and appraisal fees, solicitation expenses and printing costs. Identify the persons responsible for paying any or all of such expenses.

(2) State whether or not any partnership subject to the roll-up transaction will be, directly or indirectly, responsible for any or all of the expenses of the transaction. If any partnership will be so responsible, state the amount to be provided by each partnership and the sources of capital to finance such amount.

(c) If all or any part of the consideration to be used by the sponsor or successor in the roll-up transaction is expected to be, directly or indirectly, provided by any partnership, state the amount to be provided by each partnership and the sources of capital to finance such amount.

(d) If all or any part of the funds or other consideration is, or is expected to be, directly or indirectly borrowed by the sponsor or successor for the purpose of the roll-up transaction:

(1) Provide a summary of each such loan agreement containing the identity of the parties, the term, the collateral, the stated and effective interest rates, and other material terms or conditions; and

(2) Briefly describe any plans or arrangements to finance or repay such borrowing, or, if no plans or arrangements have been made, make a statement to that effect.

(e) If the source of all or any part of the funds to be used in the roll-up transaction is a loan made in the ordinary course of business by a bank as defined by Section 3(a)(6) of the Exchange Act and Section 13(d) or 14(d) is applicable to such transaction, the name of such bank shall not be made available to the public if the person filing the statement so requests in writing and files such request, naming such bank, with the Secretary of the Commission.

[As adopted in Release No. FR-38, October 30, 1991, 56 F.R. 57237.]

[¶ 13,113] Other Provisions of the Transaction

Reg. § 229.913. (Item 913). (a) State whether or not appraisal rights are provided under applicable state law, under the partnership's governing instruments or will be voluntarily accorded by the successor, the general partner or the sponsor (or any of their affiliates) in connection with the roll-up transaction. If so, summarize such appraisal rights. If appraisal rights will not be available to investors who object to the transaction, briefly outline the rights which may be available to such investors under such law.

(b) If any provision has been made to allow investors to obtain access to the books and records of the partnership or to obtain counsel or appraisal services at the expense of the successor, the general partner, the partnership, the sponsor (or any of their affiliates), describe such provision.

(c) Discuss the investors' rights under federal and state law to obtain a partnership's list of investors.

[As adopted in Release No. FR-38, October 30, 1991, 56 F.R. 57237.]

[¶ 13,114] Pro Forma Financial Statements; Selected Financial Data

Reg. § 229.914. (Item 914). (a) In addition to the information required by Item 301 of Regulation S-K, Selected Financial Data (§ 229.301), and Item 302 of Regulation S-K, Supplementary Financial Information (§ 229.302), for each partnership proposed to be included in a roll-up transaction provide: ratio of earnings to fixed charges, cash and cash equivalents, total assets at book value, total assets at the value assigned for purposes of the roll-up transaction (if applicable), total liabilities, general and limited partners' equity, net increase (decrease) in cash and cash equivalents, net cash provided by operating activities, distributions; and per unit data for net income (loss), book value, value assigned for purposes of the roll-up transaction (if applicable), and distributions (separately identifying distributions that represent a return of capital). This information should be provided for the same period(s) for which Selected Financial Data and Supplementary Financial Information are required to be provided. Additional or other information should be provided if material to an understanding of each partnership proposed to be included in a roll-up transaction.

(b) Provide pro forma financial information (including oil and gas reserves and cash flow disclosure, if appropriate), assuming:

(1) All partnerships participate in the roll-up transaction; and

(2) Participation in a roll-up transaction of those partnerships that on a combined basis have the lowest combined net cash provided by operating activities for the last fiscal year of such partnerships, *provided* participation by such partnerships satisfies any conditions to consummation of the roll-up transaction. If the combination of all partnerships proposed to be included in a roll-up transaction results in such lowest combined net cash provided by operating activities, this shall be noted and no separate pro forma financial statements are required.

(c) The pro forma financial statements required by paragraph (b) of this Item (§ 229.914) shall disclose the effect of the roll-up transaction on the successor's:

(1) Balance sheet as of the later of the end of the most recent fiscal year or the latest interim period;

(2) Statement of income (with separate line items to reflect income (loss) excluding *and* including the roll-up expenses and payments), earnings per share amounts, and ratio of earnings to fixed charges for the most recent fiscal year and the latest interim period;

(3) Statement of cash flows for the most recent fiscal year and the latest interim period; and

(4) Book value per share as of the later of the end of the most recent fiscal year or the latest interim period.

Instruction to Item 914. (1) Notwithstanding the provisions of this Item (§ 229.914), any or all of the information required by paragraphs (b) and (c) of this Item (§ 229.914) that is not material for the exercise of prudent judgment in regard to the matter to be acted upon, may be omitted.

(2) If the roll-up transaction is structured to permit participation by portions of partnerships, consideration should be given to the effect of such participation in preparing the pro forma financial statements reflecting a partial roll-up.

[As adopted in Release No. FR-38, October 30, 1991, 56 F.R. 57237.]

[¶ 13,115] Federal Income Tax Consequences

Reg. § 229.915. (Item 915). (a) Provide a brief, clear and understandable summary of the material federal income tax consequences of the roll-up transaction and an investment in the successor. Where a tax opinion has been provided, briefly summarize the substance of such opinion, including identification of the material consequences upon which counsel has not been asked, or is unable, to opine. If any of the material federal income tax consequences are not expected to be the same for investors in all partnerships, the differences shall be described.

(b) State whether or not the opinion of counsel is included as an appendix to the prospectus. If filed as an exhibit to the registration statement and not included as an appendix to the prospectus, include a statement to the effect that, upon receipt of a written request by an investor or his representative who has been so designated in writing, a copy of the opinion of counsel will be transmitted promptly, without charge, by the general partner or sponsor. The statement should include the name and address of the person to whom investors should make their request.

[As adopted in Release No. FR-38, October 30, 1991, 56 F.R. 57237.]

Subpart 229.1000—Mergers and Acquisitions (Regulation M-A)

[¶ 13,121] Definitions

Reg. § 229.1000 (Item 1000). The following definitions apply to the terms used in Regulation M-A (§§ 229.1000 through 229.1016), unless specified otherwise:

(a) *Associate* has the same meaning as in § 240.12b-2 of this chapter;

(b) *Instruction C* means General Instruction C to Schedule 13E-3 (§ 240.13e-100 of this chapter) and General Instruction C to Schedule TO (§ 240.14d-100 of this chapter);

(c) *Issuer tender offer* has the same meaning as in § 240.13e-4(a)(2) of this chapter;

(d) *Offeror* means any person who makes a tender offer or on whose behalf a tender offer is made;

(e) *Rule 13e-3 transaction* has the same meaning as in § 240.13e-3(a)(3) of this chapter;

(f) *Subject company* means the company or entity whose securities are sought to be acquired in the transaction (*e.g.*, the target), or that is otherwise the subject of the transaction;

(g) *Subject securities* means the securities or class of securities that are sought to be acquired in the transaction or that are otherwise the subject of the transaction; and

(h) *Third-party tender offer* means a tender offer that is not an issuer tender offer.

[As adopted in Release No. 33-7760, effective January 24, 2000, 64 F.R. 61408.]

[¶ 13,122] Summary Term Sheet

Reg. § 229.1001 (Item 1001). *Summary term sheet.* Provide security holders with a summary term sheet that is written in plain English. The summary term sheet must briefly describe in bullet point format the most material terms of the proposed transaction. The summary term sheet must provide security holders with sufficient information to understand the essential features and significance of the proposed transaction. The bullet points must cross-reference a more detailed discussion contained in the disclosure document that is disseminated to security holders.

Instructions to Item 1001:

1. The summary term sheet must not recite all information contained in the disclosure document that will be provided to security holders. The summary term sheet is intended to serve as an overview of all material matters that are presented in the accompanying documents provided to security holders.

2. The summary term sheet must begin on the first or second page of the disclosure document provided to security holders.

3. Refer to Rule 421(b) and (d) of Regulation C of the Securities Act (§ 230.421 of this chapter) for a description of plain English disclosure.

[As adopted in Release No. 33-7760, effective January 24, 2000, 64 F.R. 61408.]

[¶ 13,123] Subject Company Information

Reg. § 229.1002 (Item 1002). (a) *Name and address.* State the name of the subject company (or the issuer in the case of an issuer tender offer), and the address and telephone number of its principal executive offices.

(b) *Securities.* State the exact title and number of shares outstanding of the subject class of equity securities as of the most recent practicable date. This may be based upon information in the most recently available filing with the Commission by the subject company unless the filing person has more current information.

(c) *Trading market and price.* Identify the principal market in which the subject securities are traded and state the high and low sales prices for the subject securities in the principal market (or, if there is no principal market, the range of high and low bid quotations and the source of the quotations) for each quarter during the past two years. If there is no established trading market for the securities (except for limited or sporadic quotations), so state.

(d) *Dividends.* State the frequency and amount of any dividends paid during the past two years with respect to the subject securities. Briefly describe any restriction on the subject company's current or future ability to pay dividends. If the filing person is not the subject company, furnish this information to the extent known after making reasonable inquiry.

(e) *Prior public offerings.* If the filing person has made an underwritten public offering of the subject securities for cash during the past three years that was registered under the Securities Act of 1933 or exempt from registration under Regulation A (§ 230.251 through § 230.263 of this chapter), state the date of the offering, the amount of securities offered, the offering price per share (adjusted for stock splits, stock dividends, etc. as appropriate) and the aggregate proceeds received by the filing person.

(f) *Prior stock purchases.* If the filing person purchased any subject securities during the past two years, state the amount of the securities purchased, the range of prices paid and the average purchase price for each quarter during that period. Affiliates need not give information for purchases made before becoming an affiliate.

[As adopted in Release No. 33-7760, effective January 24, 2000, 64 F.R. 61408.]

[¶ 13,124] Identity and Background of Filing Person

Reg. § 229.1003 (Item 1003). (a) *Name and address.* State the name, business address and business telephone number of each filing person. Also state the name and address of each person specified in Instruction C to the schedule (except for Schedule 14D-9 (§ 240.14d-101 of this chapter)). If the filing person is an affiliate of the subject company, state the nature of the affiliation. If the filing person is the subject company, so state.

(b) *Business and background of entities.* If any filing person (other than the subject company) or any person specified in Instruction C to the schedule is not a natural person, state the person's principal business, state or other place of organization, and the information required by paragraphs (c)(3) and (c)(4) of this section for each person.

(c) *Business and background of natural persons.* If any filing person or any person specified in Instruction C to the schedule is a natural person, provide the following information for each person:

(1) Current principal occupation or employment and the name, principal business and address of any corporation or other organization in which the employment or occupation is conducted;

(2) Material occupations, positions, offices or employment during the past five years, giving the starting and ending dates of each and the name, principal business and address of any corporation or other organization in which the occupation, position, office or employment was carried on;

(3) A statement whether or not the person was convicted in a criminal proceeding during the past five years (excluding traffic violations or similar misdemeanors). If the person was convicted, describe the criminal proceeding, including the dates, nature of conviction, name and location of court, and penalty imposed or other disposition of the case;

(4) A statement whether or not the person was a party to any judicial or administrative proceeding during the past five years (except for matters that were dismissed without sanction or settlement) that resulted in a judgment, decree or final order enjoining the person from future violations of, or prohibiting activities subject to, federal or state securities laws, or a finding of any violation of federal or state securities laws. Describe the proceeding, including a summary of the terms of the judgment, decree or final order; and

(5) Country of citizenship.

(d) *Tender offer.* Identify the tender offer and the class of securities to which the offer relates, the name of the offeror and its address (which may be based on the offeror's Schedule TO (§ 240.14d-100 of this chapter) filed with the Commission).

Instruction to Item 1003:

If the filing person is making information relating to the transaction available on the Internet, state the address where the information can be found.

[As adopted in Release No. 33-7760, effective January 24, 2000, 64 F.R. 61408.]

[¶ 13,125] Terms of the Transaction

Reg. § 229.1004 (Item 1004). (a) *Material terms.* State the material terms of the transaction.

(1) *Tender offers.* In the case of a tender offer, the information must include:

(i) The total number and class of securities sought in the offer;

(ii) The type and amount of consideration offered to security holders;

(iii) The scheduled expiration date;

(iv) Whether a subsequent offering period will be available, if the transaction is a third-party tender offer;

(v) Whether the offer may be extended, and if so, how it could be extended;

(vi) The dates before and after which security holders may withdraw securities tendered in the offer;

(vii) The procedures for tendering and withdrawing securities;

(viii) The manner in which securities will be accepted for payment;

(ix) If the offer is for less than all securities of a class, the periods for accepting securities on a pro rata basis and the offeror's present intentions in the event that the offer is oversubscribed;

(x) An explanation of any material differences in the rights of security holders as a result of the transaction, if material;

(xi) A brief statement as to the accounting treatment of the transaction, if material; and

(xii) The federal income tax consequences of the transaction, if material.

(2) *Mergers or Similar Transactions.* In the case of a merger or similar transaction, the information must include:

(i) A brief description of the transaction;

(ii) The consideration offered to security holders;

(iii) The reasons for engaging in the transaction;

(iv) The vote required for approval of the transaction;

(v) An explanation of any material differences in the rights of security holders as a result of the transaction, if material;

(vi) A brief statement as to the accounting treatment of the transaction, if material; and

(vii) The federal income tax consequences of the transaction, if material.

Instruction to Item 1004(a):

If the consideration offered includes securities exempt from registration under the Securities Act of 1933, provide a description of the securities that complies with Item 202 of Regulation S-K (§ 229.202). This description is not required if the issuer of the securities meets the requirements of General Instructions I.A, I.B.1 or I.B.2, as applicable, or I.C. of Form S-3 (§ 239.13 of this chapter) and elects to furnish information by incorporation by reference; only capital stock is to be issued; and securities of the same class are registered under section 12 of the Exchange Act and either are listed for trading or admitted to unlisted trading privileges on a national securities exchange; or are securities for which bid and offer quotations are reported in an automated quotations system operated by a national securities association.

(b) *Purchases.* State whether any securities are to be purchased from any officer, director or affiliate of the subject company and provide the details of each transaction.

(c) *Different terms.* Describe any term or arrangement in the Rule 13e-3 transaction that treats any subject security holders differently from other subject security holders.

(d) *Appraisal rights.* State whether or not dissenting security holders are entitled to any appraisal rights. If so, summarize the appraisal rights. If there are no appraisal rights available under state law for security holders who object to the transaction, briefly outline any other rights that may be available to security holders under the law.

(e) *Provisions for unaffiliated security holders.* Describe any provision made by the filing person in connection with the transaction to grant unaffiliated security holders access to the corporate files of the filing person or to obtain counsel or appraisal services at the expense of the filing person. If none, so state.

(f) *Eligibility for listing or trading.* If the transaction involves the offer of securities of the filing person in exchange for equity securities held by unaffiliated security holders of the subject company, describe whether or not the filing person will take steps to assure that the securities offered are or will be eligible for trading on an automated quotations system operated by a national securities association.

[As adopted in Release No. 33-7760, effective January 24, 2000, 64 F.R. 61408.]

[¶ 13,126] Past Contacts, Transactions, Negotiations and Agreements

Reg. § 229.1005 (Item 1005). (a) *Transactions.* Briefly state the nature and approximate dollar amount of any transaction, other than those described in paragraphs (b) or (c) of this section, that occurred during the past two years, between the filing person (including any person specified in Instruction C of the schedule) and;

(1) The subject company or any of its affiliates that are not natural persons if the aggregate value of the transactions is more than one percent of the subject company's consolidated revenues for:

(i) The fiscal year when the transaction occurred; or

(ii) The past portion of the current fiscal year, if the transaction occurred in the current year; and

Instruction to Item 1005(a)(1):

The information required by this Item may be based on information in the subject company's most recent filing with the Commission, unless the filing person has reason to believe the information is not accurate.

(2) Any executive officer, director or affiliate of the subject company that is a natural person if the aggregate value of the transaction or series of similar transactions with that person exceeds $60,000.

(b) *Significant corporate events.* Describe any negotiations, transactions or material contacts during the past two years between the filing person (including subsidiaries of the filing person and any person specified in Instruction C of the schedule) and the subject company or its affiliates concerning any:

(1) Merger;

(2) Consolidation;

(3) Acquisition;

(4) Tender offer for or other acquisition of any class of the subject company's securities;

(5) Election of the subject company's directors; or

(6) Sale or other transfer of a material amount of assets of the subject company.

(c) *Negotiations or contacts.* Describe any negotiations or material contacts concerning the matters referred to in paragraph (b) of this section during the past two years between:

(1) Any affiliates of the subject company; or

(2) The subject company or any of its affiliates and any person not affiliated with the subject company who would have a direct interest in such matters.

Instruction to paragraphs (b) and (c) of Item 1005:

Identify the person who initiated the contacts or negotiations.

(d) *Conflicts of interest.* If material, describe any agreement, arrangement or understanding and any actual or potential conflict of interest between the filing person or its affiliates and:

(1) The subject company, its executive officers, directors or affiliates; or

(2) The offeror, its executive officers, directors or affiliates.

Instruction to Item 1005(d):

If the filing person is the subject company, no disclosure called for by this paragraph is required in the document disseminated to security holders, so long as substantially the same information was filed with the Commission previously and disclosed in a proxy statement, report or other communication sent to security holders by the subject company in the past year. The document disseminated to security holders, however, must refer specifically to the discussion in the proxy statement, report or other communication that was sent to security holders previously. The information also must be filed as an exhibit to the schedule.

(e) *Agreements involving the subject company's securities.* Describe any agreement, arrangement, or understanding, whether or not legally enforceable, between the filing person (including any person specified in Instruction C of the schedule) and any other person with respect to any securities of the subject company. Name all persons that are a party to the agreements, arrangements, or understandings and describe all material provisions.

Instructions to Item 1005(e):

1. The information required by this Item includes: the transfer or voting of securities, joint ventures, loan or option arrangements, puts or calls, guarantees of loans, guarantees against loss, or the giving or withholding of proxies, consents or authorizations.

2. Include information for any securities that are pledged or otherwise subject to a contingency, the occurrence of which would give another person the power to direct the voting or disposition of the subject securities. No disclosure, however, is required about standard default and similar provisions contained in loan agreements.

[As adopted in Release No. 33-7760, effective January 24, 2000, 64 F.R. 61408.]

[¶ 13,127] Purpose of the Transaction and Plans or Proposals

Reg. § 229.1006 (Item 1006). (a) *Purposes.* State the purposes of the transaction.

(b) *Use of securities acquired.* Indicate whether the securities acquired in the transaction will be retained, retired, held in treasury, or otherwise disposed of.

(c) *Plans.* Describe any plans, proposals or negotiations that relate to or would result in:

(1) Any extraordinary transaction, such as a merger, reorganization or liquidation, involving the subject company or any of its subsidiaries;

(2) Any purchase, sale or transfer of a material amount of assets of the subject company or any of its subsidiaries;

(3) Any material change in the present dividend rate or policy, or indebtedness or capitalization of the subject company;

(4) Any change in the present board of directors or management of the subject company, including, but not limited to, any plans or proposals to change the number or the term of directors or to fill any existing vacancies on the board or to change any material term of the employment contract of any executive officer;

(5) Any other material change in the subject company's corporate structure or business, including, if the subject company is a registered closed-end investment company, any plans or proposals to make any changes in its investment policy for which a vote would be required by Section 13 of the Investment Company Act of 1940 (15 U.S.C. 80a-13);

(6) Any class of equity securities of the subject company to be delisted from a national securities exchange or cease to be authorized to be quoted in an automated quotations system operated by a national securities association;

(7) Any class of equity securities of the subject company becoming eligible for termination of registration under Section 12(g)(4) of the Act (15 U.S.C. 78*l*);

(8) The suspension of the subject company's obligation to file reports under Section 15(d) of the Act (15 U.S.C. 78o);

(9) The acquisition by any person of additional securities of the subject company, or the disposition of securities of the subject company; or

(10) Any changes in the subject company's charter, bylaws or other governing instruments or other actions that could impede the acquisition of control of the subject company.

(d) *Subject company negotiations.* If the filing person is the subject company:

(1) State whether or not that person is undertaking or engaged in any negotiations in response to the tender offer that relate to:

(i) A tender offer or other acquisition of the subject company's securities by the filing person, any of its subsidiaries, or any other person; or

(ii) Any of the matters referred to in paragraphs (c)(1) through (c)(3) of this section; and

(2) Describe any transaction, board resolution, agreement in principle, or signed contract that is entered into in response to the tender offer that relates to one or more of the matters referred to in paragraph (d)(1) of this section.

Instruction to Item 1006(d)(1):

If an agreement in principle has not been reached at the time of filing, no disclosure under paragraph (d)(1) of this section is required of the possible terms of or the parties to the transaction if in the opinion of the board of directors of the subject company disclosure would jeopardize continuation of the negotiations. In that case, disclosure indicating that negotiations are being undertaken or are underway and are in the preliminary stages is sufficient.

[As adopted in Release No. 33-7760, effective January 24, 2000, 64 F.R. 61408.]

[¶ 13,128] Source and Amount of Funds or Other Consideration

Reg. § 229.1007 (Item 1007). (a) *Source of funds.* State the specific sources and total amount of funds or other consideration to be used in the transaction. If the transaction involves a tender offer, disclose the amount of funds or other consideration required to purchase the maximum amount of securities sought in the offer.

(b) *Conditions.* State any material conditions to the financing discussed in response to paragraph (a) of this section. Disclose any alternative financing arrangements or alternative financing plans in the event the primary financing plans fall through. If none, so state.

(c) *Expenses.* Furnish a reasonably itemized statement of all expenses incurred or estimated to be incurred in connection with the transaction including, but not limited to, filing, legal, accounting and appraisal fees, solicitation expenses and printing costs and state whether or not the subject company has paid or will be responsible for paying any or all expenses.

(d) *Borrowed funds.* If all or any part of the funds or other consideration required is, or is expected, to be borrowed, directly or indirectly, for the purpose of the transaction:

(1) Provide a summary of each loan agreement or arrangement containing the identity of the parties, the term, the collateral, the stated and effective interest rates, and any other material terms or conditions of the loan; and

(2) Briefly describe any plans or arrangements to finance or repay the loan, or, if no plans or arrangements have been made, so state.

Instruction to Item 1007(d):

If the transaction is a third-party tender offer and the source of all or any part of the funds used in the transaction is to come from a loan made in the ordinary course of business by a bank as defined by Section 3(a)(6) of the Act (15 U.S.C. 78c), the name of the bank will not be made available to the public if the filing person so requests in writing and files the request, naming the bank, with the Secretary of the Commission.

[As adopted in Release No. 33-7760, effective January 24, 2000, 64 F.R. 61408.]

[¶ 13,129] Interest in Securities of the Subject Company

Reg. § 229.1008 (Item 1008). (a) *Securities ownership.* State the aggregate number and percentage of subject securities that are beneficially owned by each person named in response to Item 1003 of Regulation M-A (§ 229.1003) and by each associate and majority-owned subsidiary of those persons. Give the name and address of any associate or subsidiary.

Instructions to Item 1008(a):

1. For purposes of this section, beneficial ownership is determined in accordance with Rule 13d-3 (§ 240.13d-3 of this chapter) under the Exchange Act. Identify the shares that the person has a right to acquire.

2. The information required by this section may be based on the number of outstanding securities disclosed in the subject company's most recently available filing with the Commission, unless the filing person has more current information.

3. The information required by this section with respect to officers, directors and associates of the subject company must be given to the extent known after making reasonable inquiry.

(b) *Securities transactions.* Describe any transaction in the subject securities during the past 60 days. The description of transactions required must include, but not necessarily be limited to:

(1) The identity of the persons specified in the Instruction to this section who effected the transaction;

(2) The date of the transaction;

(3) The amount of securities involved;

(4) The price per share; and

(5) Where and how the transaction was effected.

Instructions to Item 1008(b):

1. Provide the required transaction information for the following persons:

(a) The filing person (for all schedules);

(b) Any person named in Instruction C of the schedule and any associate or majority-owned subsidiary of the issuer or filing person (for all schedules except Schedule 14D-9 (§ 240.14d-101 of this chapter));

(c) Any executive officer, director, affiliate or subsidiary of the filing person (for Schedule 14D-9 (§ 240.14d-101 of this chapter);

(d) The issuer and any executive officer or director of any subsidiary of the issuer or filing person (for an issuer tender offer on Schedule TO (§ 240.14d-100 of this chapter)); and

(e) The issuer and any pension, profit-sharing or similar plan of the issuer or affiliate filing the schedule (for a going-private transaction on Schedule 13E-3 (§ 240.13e-100 of this chapter)).

2. Provide the information required by this Item if it is available to the filing person at the time the statement is initially filed with the Commission. If the information is not initially available, it must be obtained and filed with the Commission promptly, but in no event later than three business days after the date of the initial filing, and if material, disclosed in a manner reasonably designed to inform security holders. The procedure specified by this instruction is provided to maintain the confidentiality of information in order to avoid possible misuse of inside information.

[As adopted in Release No. 33-7760, effective January 24, 2000, 64 F.R. 61408.]

[¶ 13,130] Persons/Assets, Retained, Employed, Compensated or Used

Reg. § 229.1009 (Item 1009). (a) *Solicitations or recommendations.* Identify all persons and classes of persons that are directly or indirectly employed, retained, or to be compensated to make solicitations or recommendations in connection with the transaction. Provide a summary of all material terms of employment, retainer or other arrangement for compensation.

(b) *Employees and corporate assets.* Identify any officer, class of employees or corporate assets of the subject company that has been or will be employed or used by the filing person in connection with the transaction. Describe the purpose for their employment or use.

Instruction to Item 1009(b):

Provide all information required by this Item except for the information required by paragraph (a) of this section and Item 1007 of Regulation M-A (§ 229.1007).

[As adopted in Release No. 33-7760, effective January 24, 2000, 64 F.R. 61408.]

[¶ 13,131] Financial Statements

Reg. § 229.1010 (Item 1010). (a) *Financial information.* Furnish the following financial information:

(1) Audited financial statements for the two fiscal years required to be filed with the company's most recent annual report under Sections 13 and 15(d) of the Exchange Act (15 U.S.C. 78m; 15 U.S.C. 78o);

(2) Unaudited balance sheets, comparative year-to-date income statements and related earnings per share data, statements of cash flows, and comprehensive income required to be included in the company's most recent quarterly report filed under the Exchange Act;

(3) Ratio of earnings to fixed charges, computed in a manner consistent with Item 503(d) of Regulation S-K (§ 229.503(d)), for the two most recent fiscal years and the interim periods provided under paragraph (a)(2) of this section; and

(4) Book value per share as of the date of the most recent balance sheet presented.

(b) *Pro forma information.* If material, furnish pro forma information disclosing the effect of the transaction on:

(1) The company's balance sheet as of the date of the most recent balance sheet presented under paragraph (a) of this section;

(2) The company's statement of income, earnings per share, and ratio of earnings to fixed charges for the most recent fiscal year and the latest interim period provided under paragraph (a)(2) of this section; and

(3) The company's book value per share as of the date of the most recent balance sheet presented under paragraph (a) of this section.

(c) *Summary Information.* Furnish a fair and adequate summary of the information specified in paragraphs (a) and (b) of this section for the same periods specified. A fair and adequate summary includes:

(1) The summarized financial information specified in § 210.1-02(bb)(1) of this chapter;

(2) Income per common share from continuing operations (basic and diluted, if applicable);

(3) Net income per common share (basic and diluted, if applicable);

(4) Ratio of earnings to fixed charges, computed in a manner consistent with Item 503(d) of Regulation S-K (§ 229.503(d));

(5) Book value per share as of the date of the most recent balance sheet; and

(6) If material, pro forma data for the summarized financial information specified in paragraph (c) (1) through (c)(5) of this section disclosing the effect of the transaction.

[As adopted in Release No. 33-7760, effective January 24, 2000, 64 F.R. 61408.]

[¶ 13,132] Additional information

Reg. § 229.1011 (Item 1011). (a) *Agreements, regulatory requirements and legal proceedings.* If material to a security holder's decision whether to sell, tender or hold the securities sought in the tender offer, furnish the following information:

(1) Any present or proposed material agreement, arrangement, understanding or relationship between the offeror or any of its executive officers, directors, controlling persons or subsidiaries and the subject company or any of its executive officers, directors, controlling persons or subsidiaries (other than any agreement, arrangement or understanding disclosed under any other sections of Regulation M-A (§ § 229.1000 through 229.1016));

Instruction to paragraph (a)(1):

In an issuer tender offer disclose any material agreement, arrangement, understanding or relationship between the offeror and any of its executive officers, directors, controlling persons or subsidiaries.

(2) To the extent known by the offeror after reasonable investigation, the applicable regulatory requirements which must be complied with or approvals which must be obtained in connection with the tender offer;

(3) The applicability of any anti-trust laws;

(4) The applicability of margin requirements under Section 7 of the Act (15 U.S.C. 78g) and the applicable regulations; and

(5) Any material pending legal proceedings relating to the tender offer, including the name and location of the court or agency in which the proceedings are pending, the date instituted, the principal parties, and a brief summary of the proceedings and the relief sought.

Instruction to Item 1011(a)(5):

A copy of any document relating to a major development (such as pleadings, an answer, complaint, temporary restraining order, injunction, opinion, judgment or order) in a material pending legal proceeding must be furnished promptly to the Commission staff on a supplemental basis.

(b) *Other material information.* Furnish such additional material information, if any, as may be necessary to make the required statements, in light of the circumstances under which they are made, not materially misleading.

[As adopted in Release No. 33-7760, effective January 24, 2000, 64 F.R. 61408.]

[¶ 13,133] The Solicitation or Recommendation

Reg. § 229.1012 (Item 1012). (a) *Solicitation or recommendation.* State the nature of the solicitation or the recommendation. If this statement relates to a recommendation, state whether the filing person is advising holders of the subject securities to accept or reject the tender offer or to take other action with respect to the tender offer and, if so, describe the other action recommended. If the filing person is the subject company and is not making a recommendation, state whether the subject company is expressing no opinion and is remaining neutral toward the tender offer or is unable to take a position with respect to the tender offer.

(b) *Reasons.* State the reasons for the position (including the inability to take a position) stated in paragraph (a) of this section. Conclusory statements such as "The tender offer is in the best interests of shareholders" are not considered sufficient disclosure.

(c) *Intent to tender.* To the extent known by the filing person after making reasonable inquiry, state whether the filing person or any executive officer, director, affiliate or subsidiary of the filing person currently intends to tender, sell or hold the subject securities that are held of record or beneficially owned by that person.

(d) *Intent to tender or vote in a going-private transaction.* To the extent known by the filing person after making reasonable inquiry, state whether or not any executive officer, director or affiliate of the issuer (or any person specified in Instruction C to the schedule) currently intends to tender or sell subject securities owned or held by that person and/or how each person currently intends to vote subject securities, including any securities the person has proxy authority for. State the reasons for the intended action.

Instruction to Item 1012(d):

Provide the information required by this section if it is available to the filing person at the time the statement is initially filed with the Commission. If the information is not available, it must be filed with the Commission promptly, but in no event later than three business days after the date of the initial filing, and if material, disclosed in a manner reasonably designed to inform security holders.

(e) *Recommendations of others.* To the extent known by the filing person after making reasonable inquiry, state whether or not any person specified in paragraph (d) of this section has made a recommendation either in support of or opposed to the transaction and the reasons for the recommendation.

[As adopted in Release No. 33-7760, effective January 24, 2000, 64 F.R. 61408.]

[¶ 13,134] Purposes, Alternatives, Reasons and Effects in a Going-Private Transaction

Reg. § 229.1013 (Item 1013). (a) *Purposes.* State the purposes for the Rule 13e-3 transaction.

(b) *Alternatives.* If the subject company or affiliate considered alternative means to accomplish the stated purposes, briefly describe the alternatives and state the reasons for their rejection.

(c) *Reasons.* State the reasons for the structure of the Rule 13e-3 transaction and for undertaking the transaction at this time.

(d) *Effects.* Describe the effects of the Rule 13e-3 transaction on the subject company, its affiliates and unaffiliated security holders, including the federal tax consequences of the transaction.

Instructions to Item 1013:

1. Conclusory statements will not be considered sufficient disclosure in response to this section.

2. The description required by paragraph (d) of this section must include a reasonably detailed discussion of both the benefits and detriments of the Rule 13e-3 transaction to the subject company, its affiliates and unaffiliated security holders. The benefits and detriments of the Rule 13e-3 transaction must be quantified to the extent practicable.

3. If this statement is filed by an affiliate of the subject company, the description required by paragraph (d) of this section must include, but not be limited to, the effect of the Rule 13e-3 transaction on the affiliate's interest in the net book value and net earnings of the subject company in terms of both dollar amounts and percentages.

[As adopted in Release No. 33-7760, effective January 24, 2000, 64 F.R. 61408.]

[¶ 13,135] Fairness of the Going-Private Transaction

Reg. § 229.1014 (Item 1014). (a) *Fairness.* State whether the subject company or affiliate filing the statement reasonably believes that the Rule 13e-3 transaction is fair or unfair to unaffiliated security holders. If any director dissented to or abstained from voting on the Rule 13e-3 transaction, identify the director, and indicate, if known, after making reasonable inquiry, the reasons for the dissent or abstention.

(b) *Factors considered in determining fairness.* Discuss in reasonable detail the material factors upon which the belief stated in paragraph (a) of this section is based and, to the extent practicable, the weight assigned to each factor. The discussion must include an analysis of the extent, if any, to which the filing person's beliefs are based on the factors described in Instruction 2 of this section, paragraphs (c), (d) and (e) of this section and Item 1015 of Regulation M-A (§ 229.1015).

(c) *Approval of security holders.* State whether or not the transaction is structured so that approval of at least a majority of unaffiliated security holders is required.

(d) *Unaffiliated representative.* State whether or not a majority of directors who are not employees of the subject company has retained an unaffiliated representative to act solely on behalf of unaffiliated security holders for purposes of negotiating the terms of the Rule 13e-3 transaction and/or preparing a report concerning the fairness of the transaction.

(e) *Approval of directors.* State whether or not the Rule 13e-3 transaction was approved by a majority of the directors of the subject company who are not employees of the subject company.

(f) *Other offers.* If any offer of the type described in paragraph (viii) of Instruction 2 to this section has been received, describe the offer and state the reasons for its rejection.

Instructions to Item 1014:

1. A statement that the issuer or affiliate has no reasonable belief as to the fairness of the Rule 13e-3 transaction to unaffiliated security holders will not be considered sufficient disclosure in response to paragraph (a) of this section.

2. The factors that are important in determining the fairness of a transaction to unaffiliated security holders and the weight, if any, that should be given to them in a particular context will vary. Normally such factors will include, among others, those referred to in paragraphs (c), (d) and (e) of this section and whether the consideration offered to unaffiliated security holders constitutes fair value in relation to:

(i) Current market prices;

(ii) Historical market prices;

(iii) Net book value;

(iv) Going concern value;

(v) Liquidation value;

(vi) Purchase prices paid in previous purchases disclosed in response to Item 1002(f) of Regulation M-A (§ 229.1002(f));

(vii) Any report, opinion, or appraisal described in Item 1015 of Regulation M-A (§ 229.1015); and

(viii) Firm offers of which the subject company or affiliate is aware made by any unaffiliated person, other than the filing persons, during the past two years for:

(A) The merger or consolidation of the subject company with or into another company, or *vice versa*;

(B) The sale or other transfer of all or any substantial part of the assets of the subject company; or

(C) A purchase of the subject company's securities that would enable the holder to exercise control of the subject company.

3. Conclusory statements, such as "The Rule 13e-3 transaction is fair to unaffiliated security holders in relation to net book value, going concern value and future prospects of the issuer" will not be considered sufficient disclosure in response to paragraph (b) of this section.

[As adopted in Release No. 33-7760, effective January 24, 2000, 64 F.R. 61408.]

[¶ 13,136] Reports, Opinions, Appraisals and Negotiations

Reg. § 229.1015 (Item 1015). (a) *Report, opinion or appraisal.* State whether or not the subject company or affiliate has received any report, opinion (other than an opinion of counsel) or appraisal from an outside party that is materially related to the Rule 13e-3 transaction, including, but not limited to: any report, opinion or appraisal relating to the consideration or the fairness of the consideration to be offered to security holders or the fairness of the transaction to the issuer or affiliate or to security holders who are not affiliates.

(b) *Preparer and summary of the report, opinion or appraisal.* For each report, opinion or appraisal described in response to paragraph (a) of this section or any negotiation or report described in response to Item 1014(d) of Regulation M-A (§ 229.1014) or Item 14(b)(6) of Schedule 14A (§ 240.14a-101 of this chapter) concerning the terms of the transaction:

(1) Identify the outside party and/or unaffiliated representative;

(2) Briefly describe the qualifications of the outside party and/or unaffiliated representative;

(3) Describe the method of selection of the outside party and/or unaffiliated representative;

(4) Describe any material relationship that existed during the past two years or is mutually understood to be contemplated and any compensation received or to be received as a result of the relationship between:

(i) The outside party, its affiliates, and/or unaffiliated representative; and

(ii) The subject company or its affiliates;

(5) If the report, opinion or appraisal relates to the fairness of the consideration, state whether the subject company or affiliate determined the amount of consideration to be paid or whether the outside party recommended the amount of consideration to be paid; and

(6) Furnish a summary concerning the negotiation, report, opinion or appraisal. The summary must include, but need not be limited to, the procedures followed; the findings and recommendations; the bases for and methods of arriving at such findings and recommendations; instructions received from the subject company or affiliate; and any limitation imposed by the subject company or affiliate on the scope of the investigation.

Instruction to Item 1015(b):

The information called for by paragraphs (b)(1), (2) and (3) of this section must be given with respect to the firm that provides the report, opinion or appraisal rather than the employees of the firm that prepared the report.

(c) *Availability of documents.* Furnish a statement to the effect that the report, opinion or appraisal will be made available for inspection and copying at the principal executive offices of the subject company or affiliate during its regular business hours by any interested equity security holder of the subject company or representative who has been so designated in writing. This statement also may provide that a copy of the report, opinion or appraisal will be transmitted by the subject company or affiliate to any interested equity security holder of the subject company or representative who has been so designated in writing upon written request and at the expense of the requesting security holder.

[As adopted in Release No. 33-7760, effective January 24, 2000, 64 F.R. 61408.]

[¶ 13,137] Exhibits

Reg. § 229.1016 (Item 1016). File as an exhibit to the schedule:

(a) Any disclosure materials furnished to security holders by or on behalf of the filing person, including:

(1) Tender offer materials (including transmittal letter);

(2) Solicitation or recommendation (including those referred to in Item 1012 of Regulation M-A (§ 229.1012));

(3) Going-private disclosure document;

(4) Prospectus used in connection with an exchange offer where securities are registered under the Securities Act of 1933; and

(5) Any other disclosure materials;

(b) Any loan agreement referred to in response to Item 1007(d) of Regulation M-A (§ 229.1007(d));

Instruction to Item 1016(b):

If the filing relates to a third-party tender offer and a request is made under Item 1007(d) of Regulation M-A (§ 229.1007(d)), the identity of the bank providing financing may be omitted from the loan agreement filed as an exhibit.

(c) Any report, opinion or appraisal referred to in response to Item 1014(d) or Item 1015 of Regulation M-A (§ 229.1014(d) or § 229.1015);

(d) Any document setting forth the terms of any agreement, arrangement, understanding or relationship referred to in response to Item 1005(e) or Item 1011(a)(1) of Regulation M-A (§ 229.1005(e) or § 229.1011(a)(1));

(e) Any agreement, arrangement or understanding referred to in response to § 229.1005(d), or the pertinent portions of any proxy statement, report or other communication containing the disclosure required by Item 1005(d) of Regulation M-A (§ 229.1005(d));

(f) A detailed statement describing security holders' appraisal rights and the procedures for exercising those appraisal rights referred to in response to Item 1004(d) of Regulation M-A (§ 229.1004(d));

(g) Any written instruction, form or other material that is furnished to persons making an oral solicitation or recommendation by or on behalf of the filing person for their use directly or indirectly in connection with the transaction; and

(h) Any written opinion prepared by legal counsel at the filing person's request and communicated to the filing person pertaining to the tax consequences of the transaction.

Exhibit Table to Item 1016 of Regulation M-A

	13E-3	TO	14D-9
Disclosure Material	x	x	x
Loan Agreement	x	x	
Report, Opinion or Appraisal	x		

Exhibit Table to Item 1016 of Regulation M-A

	13E-3	TO	14D-9
Contracts, Arrangements or Understandings	x	x	x
Statement re: Appraisal Rights	x		
Oral Solicitation Materials	x	x	x
Tax Opinion	x		

[As adopted in Release No. 33-7760, effective January 24, 2000, 64 F.R. 61408.]

Subpart 229.1100—Asset-Backed Securities (Regulation AB)

[¶ 13,201] General

Reg. § 229.1100 (Item 1100). (a) *Application of Regulation AB.* Regulation AB (§§ 229.1100 through 229.1123) is the source of various disclosure items and requirements for "asset-backed securities" filings under the Securities Act of 1933 (15 U.S.C. 77a *et seq.*) (the "Securities Act") and the Securities Exchange Act of 1934 (the "Exchange Act") (15 U.S.C. 78a *et seq.*). Unless otherwise specified, definitions to be used in this Regulation AB, including the definition of "asset-backed security," are set forth in Item 1101.

(b) *Presentation of historical delinquency and loss information.* Several Items in Regulation AB call for the presentation of historical information and data on delinquencies and loss information. In providing such information:

(1) Present delinquency experience in 30 or 31 day increments, as applicable, beginning at least with assets that are 30 or 31 days delinquent, as applicable, through the point that assets are written off or charged off as uncollectable. At a minimum, present such information by number of accounts and dollar amount. Present statistical information in a tabular or graphical format, if such presentation will aid understanding.

(2) Disclose the total amount of delinquent assets as a percentage of the aggregate asset pool.

(3) Present loss and cumulative loss information, as applicable, regarding charge-offs, charge-off rate, gross losses, recoveries and net losses (with a description of how these terms are defined), the number and amount of assets experiencing a loss and the number and amount of assets with a recovery, the ratio of aggregate net losses to average portfolio balance and the average of net loss on all assets that have experienced a net loss.

(4) Categorize all delinquency and loss information by pool asset type.

(5) In a registration statement under the Securities Act or the Exchange Act or in a prospectus to be filed pursuant to § 230.424, describe how delinquencies, charge-offs and uncollectable accounts are defined or determined, addressing the effect of any grace period, re-aging, restructure, partial payments considered current or other practices on delinquency and loss experience.

(6) Describe any other material information regarding delinquencies and losses particular to the pool asset type(s), such as repossession information, foreclosure information and real estate owned (REO) or similar information.

(c) *Presentation of certain third party financial information.*

If financial information of a third party is required in a filing by Item 1112(b) of this Regulation AB (Information regarding significant obligors) or Items 1114(b)(2) or 1115(b) of this Regulation AB (Information regarding significant provider of enhancement or other support), such information, in lieu of including such information, may be provided as follows:

(1) *Incorporation by reference.* If the following conditions are met, you may incorporate by reference (by means of a statement to that effect) the reports filed by the third party (or the entity that consolidates the third party) pursuant to section 13(a) or 15(d) of the Exchange Act (15 U.S.C. 78m(a) or 78o(d)):

(i) Such third party or the entity that consolidates the third party is required to file reports with the Commission pursuant to section 13(a) or 15(d) of the Exchange Act.

(ii) Such third party or the entity that consolidates the third party has filed all reports and other materials required to be filed by such requirements during the preceding 12 months (or such shorter period that such party was required to file such reports and materials).

(iii) The reports filed by such third party, or entity that consolidates the third party, include (or properly incorporate by reference) the financial statements of such third party.

(iv) If incorporated by reference into a prospectus or registration statement, the prospectus also states that all documents subsequently filed by such third party, or the entity that consolidates the third party, pursuant to section 13(a) or 15(d) of the Exchange Act prior to the termination of the offering also shall be deemed to be incorporated by reference into the prospectus.

Instructions to Item 1100(c)(1).

1. In addition to the conditions in paragraph (c)(1) of this section, any information incorporated by reference must comply with all applicable Commission rules pertaining to incorporation by reference, such as Item 10(d) of Regulation S-K (§ 229.10(d)), Rule 303 of Regulation S-T (§ 232.303 of this chapter), Rule 411 of Regulation C (§ 230.411 of this chapter), and Rules 12b-23 and 12b-32 under the Exchange Act (§§ 240.12b-23 and 240.12b-32 of this chapter).

2. In addition, any applicable requirements under the Securities Act or the rules and regulations of the Commission regarding the filing of a written consent for the use of incorporated material apply to the material incorporated by reference. See, for example, § 230.439 of this chapter.

3. Any undertakings set forth in Item 512 of Regulation S-K (§ 229.512) apply to any material incorporated by reference in a registration statement or prospectus.

4. If neither the third party nor any of its affiliates has had a direct or indirect agreement, arrangement, relationship or understanding, written or otherwise, relating to the ABS transaction, and neither the third party nor any of its affiliates is an affiliate of the sponsor, depositor, issuing entity or underwriter of the ABS transaction, then paragraph (c)(1)(ii) of this section is qualified by the knowledge of the registrant.

5. If you are relying on paragraph (c)(1) of this section to provide information required by Item 1112 of this Regulation AB regarding a significant obligor that is an asset-backed issuer and the pool assets relating to such significant obligor are asset-backed securities, then for purposes of paragraph (c)(1)(iii) of this section, the term "financial statements" means the information required by Instruction 3 of Item 1112 of this Regulation AB. Such information required by Instruction 3.a. of Item 1112 of this Regulation AB may be incorporated by reference from a prospectus that contains such information and is included in an effective Securities Act registration statement or filed pursuant to § 230.424 of this chapter.

(2) *Reference information for significant obligors.* If the third party information relates to a significant obligor and the following conditions are met, you may include a reference to the third party's periodic reports (or the third party's parent with respect to paragraph (c)(2)(ii)(C) of this section) under section 13(a) or 15(d) of the Exchange Act (15 U.S.C. 78m(a) or 78o(d)) that are on file with the Commission (or otherwise publicly available with respect to paragraph (c)(2)(ii)(F) of this section), along with a statement of how those reports may be accessed, including the third party's name and Commission file number, if applicable (See, *e.g.*, Item 1118 of this Regulation AB):

(i) Neither the third party nor any of its affiliates has had a direct or indirect agreement, arrangement, relationship or understanding, written or otherwise, relating to the asset-backed securities transaction, and neither the third party nor any of its affiliates is an affiliate of the sponsor, depositor, issuing entity or underwriter of the asset-backed securities transaction.

(ii) To the knowledge of the registrant, any of the following is true:

(A) The third party is eligible to use Form S-3 or F-3 (§ 239.13 or 239.33 of this chapter) for a primary offering of non-investment grade securities pursuant to General Instruction I.B.1 of such forms.

(B) The third party meets the requirements of General Instruction I.A. of Form S-3 or General Instructions 1.A.1, 2, 3, 4 and 6 of Form F-3 and the pool assets relating to such third party are non-convertible investment grade securities, as described in General Instruction 1.B.2 of Form S-3 or Form F-3.

(C) If the third party does not meet the conditions of paragraph (c)(2)(ii)(A) or (c)(2)(ii)(B) of this section and the pool assets relating to the third party are fully and unconditionally guaranteed by a direct or indirect parent of the third party, General Instruction I.C.3 of Form S-3 or General Instruction I.A.5(iii) of Form F-3 is met with respect to the pool assets relating to such third party and the requirements of Rule 3-10 of Regulation S-X (§ 210.3-10 of this chapter) are satisfied regarding the information in the reports to be referenced.

(D) If the pool assets relating to the third party are guaranteed by a wholly owned subsidiary of the third party and the subsidiary does not meet the conditions of paragraph (c)(2)(ii)(A) or (c)(2)(ii)(B) of this section, the criteria in either paragraph (c)(2)(ii)(A) or paragraph (c)(2)(ii)(B) of this section are met with respect to the third party and the requirements of Rule 3-10 of Regulation S-X (§ 210.3-10 of this chapter) are satisfied regarding the information in the reports to be referenced.

(E) The pool assets relating to such third party are asset-backed securities and the third party is filing reports pursuant to section 12 or 15(d) of the Exchange Act (15 U.S.C. 78l or 78o(d)) and has filed all the material that would be required to be filed pursuant to section 13, 14 or 15(d) of the Exchange Act (15 U.S.C. 78m, 78n or 78o(d)) for a period of at least twelve calendar months and any portion of a month immediately preceding the filing referencing the third party's reports (or such shorter period that such third party was required to file such materials).

(F) The third party is a U.S. government-sponsored enterprise, has outstanding securities held by non-affiliates with an aggregate market value of $75 million or more, and makes information publicly available on an annual and quarterly basis, including audited financial statements prepared in accordance with generally accepted accounting principles covering the same periods that would be required for audited financial statements under Regulation S-X (§§ 210.1-01 through 210.12-29 of this chapter) and non-financial information consistent with that required by Regulation S-K (§§ 229.10 through 229.1123).

Instruction to Item 1100(c)(2). If you are relying on paragraph (c)(2)(ii)(E) of this section because the pool assets relating to such third party are asset-backed securities, then for purposes of a registration statement under the Securities Act or the Exchange Act or a prospectus to be filed pursuant to § 230.424 for your securities, you also must include a reference (including Commission reporting number and filing date) to the prospectus for the third party asset-backed securities that: (a) is either included in an effective Securities Act registration statement or filed pursuant to §230.424 of this chapter; and (b) contains the information required by Instruction 3.a. of Item 1112 of this Regulation AB.

(d) *Other participants to the transaction and pool assets representing interests in certain other asset pools.*

(1) If the asset-backed securities transaction involves additional or intermediate parties not specifically identified in this Regulation AB, the disclosure required by this Regulation AB includes information to the extent material regarding any such party and its role, function and experience in relation to the asset-backed securities and the asset pool. Describe the material terms of any agreement with such party regarding the transaction, and file such agreement as an exhibit.

(2) If the asset pool backing the asset-backed securities includes one or more pool assets representing an interest in or the right to the payments or cash flows of another asset pool, then for purposes of this Regulation AB and §§240.13a-18 and 240.15d-18 of this chapter, references to the asset pool and the pool assets of the issuing entity also include the other asset pool and its pool assets if the following conditions are met:

(i) Both the issuing entity for the asset-backed securities and the entity issuing the pool asset to be included in the issuing entity's asset pool were established under the direction of the same sponsor or depositor.

(ii) The pool asset was created solely to satisfy legal requirements or otherwise facilitate the structuring of the asset-backed securities transaction.

Instruction to Item 1100(d)(2).

Reference to the underlying asset pool includes, without limitation, compliance with applicable servicing criteria referenced in §§240.13a-18 and 240.15d-18 of this chapter and the servicer compliance statement required by Item 1123 of this Regulation AB. In addition, provide clear and concise disclosure, including by flow chart or other illustration, of the transaction and the various parties involved.

(e) *Foreign asset-backed securities.* If the asset-backed securities are issued by a foreign issuer (as defined in §230.405 of this chapter), backed by pool assets that are foreign assets, or affected by enhancement or support contemplated by Items 1114 or 1115 of this Regulation AB provided by a foreign entity, then in providing the disclosure required by this Regulation AB (including, but not limited to, Items 1104 and 1110 of this Regulation AB regarding origination and securitization practices, Item 1107 of this Regulation AB regarding the sale or transfer of the pool assets, bankruptcy remoteness and collateral protection, Item 1108 of this Regulation AB regarding servicing, Item 1109 of this Regulation AB regarding the rights, duties and responsibilities of the trustee, Item 1111 of this Regulation AB regarding the terms, nature and treatment of the pool assets and Items 1114 or 1115 of this Regulation AB, as applicable, regarding the enhancement provider), the filing must describe any pertinent governmental, legal or regulatory or administrative matters and any pertinent tax matters, exchange controls, currency restrictions or other economic, fiscal, monetary or potential factors in the applicable home jurisdiction that could materially affect payments on, the performance of, or other matters relating to, the assets contained in the pool or the asset-backed securities. See also Instruction 2 to Item 202 of Regulation S-K (§229.202). In addition, in a registration statement under the Securities Act, provide the information required by Item 101(g) of Regulation S-K (§229.101(g)). Disclosure also is required in Forms 10-D (§249.312 of this chapter) and 10-K (§249.310 of this chapter) with respect to the asset-backed securities regarding any material impact caused by foreign legal and regulatory developments during the period covered by the report which have not been previously described in a Form 10-D, 10-K or 8-K (§249.308 of this chapter) filed under the Exchange Act.

(f) *Filing of required exhibits.* Where agreements or other documents in this Regulation AB are specified to be filed as exhibits to a Securities Act registration statement, such final agreements or other documents, if applicable, may be incorporated by reference as an exhibit to the registration statement, such as by filing a Form 8-K in the case of offerings registered on Form S-3 (§239.13 of this chapter).

[As last amended by Release No. 33-5818A, effective December 5, 2005, 70 F.R. 72372.]

[¶ 13,215] Definitions

Reg. §229.1101 (Item 1101). The following definitions apply to the terms used in Regulation AB (§§229.1100 through 229.1123), unless specified otherwise:

(a) *ABS informational and computational material* means a written communication consisting solely of one or some combination of the following:

(1) Factual information regarding the asset-backed securities being offered and the structure and basic parameters of the securities, such as the number of classes, seniority, payment priorities, terms of payment, the tax, Employment Retirement Income Security Act of 1974, as amended, (29 U.S.C. 1001 *et seq.*) ("ERISA") or other legal conclusions of counsel, and descriptive information relating to each class (*e.g.*, principal amount, coupon, minimum denomination, anticipated price, yield, weighted average life,

credit enhancements, anticipated ratings, and other similar information relating to the proposed structure of the offering);

(2) Factual information regarding the pool assets underlying the asset-backed securities, including origination, acquisition and pool selection criteria, information regarding any prefunding or revolving period applicable to the offering, information regarding significant obligors, data regarding the contractual and related characteristics of the underlying pool assets (*e.g.*, weighted average coupon, weighted average maturity, delinquency and loss information and geographic distribution) and other factual information concerning the parameters of the asset pool appropriate to the nature of the underlying assets, such as the type of assets comprising the pool and the programs under which the loans were originated;

(3) Identification of key parties to the transaction, such as servicers, trustees, depositors, sponsors, originators and providers of credit enhancement or other support, including a brief description of each such party's roles, responsibilities, background and experience;

(4) Static pool data, as referenced in Item 1105 of this Regulation AB, such as for the sponsor's and/or servicer's portfolio, prior transactions or the asset pool itself;

(5) Statistical information displaying for a particular class of asset-backed securities the yield, average life, expected maturity, interest rate sensitivity, cash flow characteristics, total rate of return, option adjusted spread or other financial or statistical information relating to the class or classes under specified prepayment, interest rate, loss or other hypothetical scenarios. Examples of such information under the definition include:

(i) Statistical results of interest rate sensitivity analyses regarding the impact on yield or other financial characteristics of a class of securities from changes in interest rates at one or more assumed prepayment speeds;

(ii) Statistical information showing the cash flows that would be associated with a particular class of asset-backed securities at a specified prepayment speed; and

(iii) Statistical information reflecting the financial impact of losses based on a variety of loss or default experience, prepayment, interest rate and related assumptions.

(6) The names of underwriters participating in the offering of the securities, and their additional roles, if any, within the underwriting syndicate;

(7) The anticipated schedule for the offering (including the approximate date upon which the proposed sale to the public will begin) and a description of marketing events (including the dates, times, locations, and procedures for attending or otherwise accessing them); and

(8) A description of the procedures by which the underwriters will conduct the offering and the procedures for transactions in connection with the offering with an underwriter or participating dealer (including procedures regarding account-opening and submitting indications of interest and conditional offers to buy).

(b) *Asset-backed issuer* means an issuer whose reporting obligation results from either the registration of an offering of asset-backed securities under the Securities Act, or the registration of a class of asset-backed securities under section 12 of the Exchange Act (15 U.S.C. 78*l*).

(c) (1) *Asset-backed security* means a security that is primarily serviced by the cash flows of a discrete pool of receivables or other financial assets, either fixed or revolving, that by their terms convert into cash within a finite time period, plus any rights or other assets designed to assure the servicing or timely distributions of proceeds to the security holders; provided that in the case of financial assets that are leases, those assets may convert to cash partially by the cash proceeds from the disposition of the physical property underlying such leases.

(2) The following additional conditions apply in order to be considered an *asset-backed security*:

(i) Neither the depositor nor the issuing entity is an investment company under the Investment Company Act of 1940 (15 U.S.C. 80a-1 *et seq.*) nor will become an investment company as a result of the asset-backed securities transaction.

(ii) The activities of the issuing entity for the asset-backed securities are limited to passively owning or holding the pool of assets, issuing the asset-backed securities supported or serviced by those assets, and other activities reasonably incidental thereto.

(iii) No non-performing assets are part of the asset pool as of the measurement date.

(iv) Delinquent assets do not constitute 50% or more, as measured by dollar volume, of the asset pool as of the measurement date.

(v) With respect to securities that are backed by leases, the portion of the securitized pool balance attributable to the residual value of the physical property underlying the leases, as determined in accordance with the transaction agreements for the securities, does not constitute:

(A) For motor vehicle leases, 65% or more, as measured by dollar volume, of the securitized pool balance as of the measurement date.

(B) For all other leases, 50% or more, as measured by dollar volume, of the securitized pool balance as of the measurement date.

(3) Notwithstanding the requirement in paragraph (c)(1) of this section that the asset pool be a discrete pool of assets, the following are considered to be a discrete pool of assets for purposes of being considered an *asset-backed security*.

(i) *Master trusts.* The offering related to the securities contemplates adding additional assets to the pool that backs such securities in connection with future issuances of asset-backed securities backed by such pool. The offering related to the securities also may contemplate additions to the asset pool, to the extent consistent with paragraphs (c)(3)(ii) and (c)(3)(iii) of this section, in connection with maintaining minimum pool balances in accordance with the transaction agreements for master trusts with revolving periods or receivables or other financial assets that arise under revolving accounts.

(ii) *Prefunding periods.* The offering related to the securities contemplates a prefunding account where a portion of the proceeds of that offering is to be used for the future acquisition of additional pool assets, if the duration of the prefunding period does not extend for more than one year from the date of issuance of the securities and the portion of the proceeds for such prefunding account does not involve in excess of:

(A) For master trusts, 50% of the aggregate principal balance of the total asset pool whose cash flows support the securities; and

(B) For other offerings, 50% of the proceeds of the offering.

(iii) *Revolving periods.* The offering related to the securities contemplates a revolving period where cash flows from the pool assets may be used to acquire additional pool assets, provided, that, for securities backed by receivables or other financial assets that do not arise under revolving accounts, the revolving period does not extend for more than three years from the date of issuance of the securities and the additional pool assets are of the same general character as the original pool assets.

Instructions to Item 1101(c)

1. For purposes of determining non-performing, delinquency and residual value thresholds, the "measurement date" means either:

a. The designated cut-off date for the transaction (*i.e.*, the date on and after which collections on the pool assets accrue for the benefit of asset-backed security holders), if applicable; or

b. In the case of master trusts, the date as of which delinquency and loss information or securitized pool balance information, as applicable, is presented in the prospectus for the asset-backed securities to be filed pursuant to § 230.424(b) of this chapter.

2. Non-performing and delinquent assets that are not funded or purchased by proceeds from the securities and that are not considered in cash flow calculations for the securities need not be considered as part of the asset pool for purposes of determining non-performing and delinquency thresholds.

3. For purposes of determining non-performing, delinquency and residual value thresholds for master trusts, calculations are to be measured against the total asset pool whose cash flows support the securities.

4. For purposes of determining residual value thresholds, residual values need not be included in measuring against the thresholds to the extent a separate party is obligated for such amounts (*e.g.*, through a residual value guarantee, residual value insurance or where the lessee is obligated to cover any residual losses).

(d) *Delinquent*, for purposes of determining if a pool asset is delinquent, means if a pool asset is more than 30 or 31 days or a single payment cycle, as applicable, past due from the contractual due date, as determined in accordance with any of the following:

(1) The transaction agreements for the asset-backed securities;

(2) The delinquency recognition policies of the sponsor, any affiliate of the sponsor that originated the pool asset or the servicer of the pool asset; or

(3) The delinquency recognition policies applicable to such pool asset established by the primary safety and soundness regulator of any entity listed in paragraph (d)(2) of this section or the program or regulatory entity that oversees the program under which the pool asset was originated.

(e) *Depositor* means the depositor who receives or purchases and transfers or sells the pool assets to the issuing entity. For asset-backed securities transactions where there is not an intermediate transfer of the assets from the sponsor to the issuing entity, the term *depositor* refers to the sponsor. For asset-backed securities transactions where the person transferring or selling the pool assets is itself a trust, the *depositor* of the issuing entity is the depositor of that trust.

(f) *Issuing entity* means the trust or other entity created at the direction of the sponsor or depositor that owns or holds the pool assets and in whose name the asset-backed securities supported or serviced by the pool assets are issued.

(g) *Non-performing*, for purposes of determining if a pool asset is non-performing, means a pool asset if any of the following is true:

(1) The pool asset would be treated as wholly or partially charged-off under the requirements in the transaction agreements for the asset-backed securities;

(2) The pool asset would be treated as wholly or partially charged-off under the charge-off policies of the sponsor, an affiliate of the sponsor that originates the pool asset or a servicer that services the pool asset; or

(3) The pool asset would be treated as wholly or partially charged-off under the charge-off policies applicable to such pool asset established by the primary safety and soundness regulator of any entity listed in paragraph (g)(2) of this section or the program or regulatory entity that oversees the program under which the pool asset was originated.

(h) *NRSRO* has the same meaning as the term "nationally recognized statistical rating organization" as used in § 240.15c3-1(c)(2)(vi)(F) of this chapter.

(i) *Obligor* means any person who is directly or indirectly committed by contract or other arrangement to make payments on all or part of the obligations on a pool asset.

(j) *Servicer* means any person responsible for the management or collection of the pool assets or making allocations or distributions to holders of the asset-backed securities. The term *servicer* does not include a trustee for the issuing entity or the asset-backed securities that makes allocations or distributions to holders of the asset-backed securities if the trustee receives such allocations or distributions from a servicer and the trustee does not otherwise perform the functions of a servicer.

(k) *Significant obligor* means any of the following:

(1) An obligor or a group of affiliated obligors on any pool asset or group of pool assets if such pool asset or group of pool assets represents 10% or more of the asset pool.

(2) A single property or group of related properties securing a pool asset or a group of pool assets if such pool asset or group of pool assets represents 10% or more of the asset pool.

(3) A lessee or group of affiliated lessees if the related lease or group of leases represents 10% or more of the asset pool.

Instructions to Item 1101(k).

1. Regarding paragraph (k)(3) of this section, the calculation must focus on the leases whose cash flow supports the asset-backed securities directly or indirectly (including the residual value of the physical property underlying the leases if a portion of the securitized pool balance is attributable to the residual value of such property), regardless of whether the asset pool contains the leases themselves, mortgages on properties that are the subject of the leases or other assets related to the leases.

2. If separate pool assets, or properties underlying pool assets, are cross-defaulted and/or cross-collateralized, such pool assets are to be aggregated and considered together in determining concentration levels.

3. If the pool asset is a mortgage or lease relating to real estate, the pool asset is non-recourse to the obligor, and the obligor does not manage the property or does not own other assets and has no other operations, then the obligor need not be considered a separate significant obligor from the real estate. Otherwise, the obligor is a separate significant obligor.

4. The determination of significant obligors is to be made as of the designated cut-off date for the transaction (*i.e.*, the date on and after which collections on the pool assets accrue for the benefit of asset-backed security holders), provided, that, in the case of master trusts, the determination is to be made as of the cut-off date (or issuance date if there is not a cut-off date) for each issuance of asset-backed securities backed by the same asset pool. In addition, if disclosure is required pursuant to either Item 6.05 of Form 8-K (17 CFR 249.308) or in a Form 10-D (17 CFR 249.312) pursuant to Item 1121(b) of this Regulation AB, the determination of significant obligors is to be made against the asset pool described in such report. However, if the percentage concentration regarding an obligor falls below 10% subsequent to the determination dates discussed in this Instruction, the obligor no longer need be considered a significant obligor.

(l) *Sponsor* means the person who organizes and initiates an asset-backed securities transaction by selling or transferring assets, either directly or indirectly, including through an affiliate, to the issuing entity.

[As adopted in Release No. 33-8518, effective March 8, 2005 (Compliance dates are triggered by initial bona fide offer date or registration statement filing date and extend out to March 31, 2006. Complete compliance date details can be found in the "Dates" section of the release.), 70 F.R. 1506.]

[¶ 13,231] Forepart of registration statement and outside cover page of the prospectus

Reg. § 229.1102 (Item 1102). (a) Identify the sponsor, the depositor and the issuing entity (if known).

(b) In identifying the title of the securities, include the series number, if applicable. If there is more than one class of securities offered, state the class designations of the securities offered.

(c) Identify the asset type(s) being securitized.

(d) Include a statement, if applicable and appropriately modified to the transaction, that the securities represent the obligations of the issuing entity only and do not represent the obligations of or interest in the sponsor, depositor or any of their affiliates.

(e) Identify the aggregate principal amount of all securities offered and the principal amount, if any, of each class of securities offered. If a class has no principal amount, disclose that fact, and, if applicable, state the notional amount, clearly identifying that the amount is a notional one. If the amounts are approximate, disclose that fact.

(f) Indicate the interest rate or specified rate of return of each class of security offered. If a class of securities does not bear interest or a specified return, disclose that fact. If the rate is based on a formula or is calculated in reference to a generally recognized interest rate index, such as a U.S. Treasury securities index, either provide the formula on the cover, or indicate that the rate is variable, indicate the index upon which the rate is based and indicate that further disclosure of how the rate is determined is included in the transaction summary.

(g) Identify the distribution frequency, by class or series where applicable, and the first expected distribution date for the asset-backed securities.

(h) Briefly describe any credit enhancement or other support for the transaction and identify any enhancement or support provider referenced in Items 1114(b) or 1115 of this Regulation AB.

Instruction to Item 1102. Also see Item 1113(f)(2) of this Regulation AB regarding the title of any class of securities with an optional redemption or termination feature that may be exercised when 25% or more of the original principal balance of the pool assets are still outstanding.

[As adopted in Release No. 33-8518, effective March 8, 2005 (Compliance dates are triggered by initial bona fide offer date or registration statement filing date and extend out to March 31, 2006. Complete compliance date details can be found in the "Dates" section of the release.), 70 F.R. 1506.]

[¶ 13,245] Transaction summary and risk factors

Reg. § 229.1103 (Item 1103). (a) *Prospectus summary.* In providing the information required by Item 503(a) of Regulation S-K (§ 229.503(a)), provide the following information in the prospectus summary, as applicable. Present information regarding multiple classes in tables if doing so will aid understanding. Consider using diagrams to illustrate the relationships among the parties, the structure of the securities offered (including, for example, the flow of funds or any subordination features) and any other material features of the transaction.

(1) Identify the participants in the transaction, including the sponsor, depositor, issuing entity, trustee and servicers contemplated by Item 1108(a)(2) of this Regulation AB, and their respective roles. Describe the roles briefly if they are not apparent from the title of the role. Identify any originator contemplated by Item 1110 of this Regulation AB and any significant obligor.

(2) Briefly identify the pool assets and summarize briefly the size and material characteristics of the asset pool. Identify the cut-off date or similar date for establishing the composition of the asset pool, if applicable.

(3) State briefly the basic terms of each class of securities offered. In particular:

(i) Identify the classes offered by the prospectus and any classes issued in the same transaction or residual or equity interests in the transaction that are not being offered by the prospectus.

(ii) State the interest rate or rate of return on each class of securities offered, to the extent that the rates on any class of securities were not disclosed in full on the prospectus cover page.

(iii) State the expected final and final scheduled maturity or principal distribution dates, if applicable, of each class of securities offered.

(iv) Identify the denominations in which the securities may be issued.

(v) Identify the distribution frequency on the securities.

(vi) Summarize the flow of funds, payment priorities and allocations among the classes of securities offered, the classes of securities that are not offered, and fees and expenses, to the extent necessary to understand the payment characteristics of the classes that are offered by the prospectus.

(vii) Identify any events in the transaction agreements that can trigger liquidation or amortization of the asset pool or other performance triggers that would alter the transaction structure or the flow of funds.

(viii) Identify any optional or mandatory redemption or termination features.

(ix) Identify any credit enhancement or other support for the transaction, as referenced in Items 1114(a) and 1115 of this Regulation AB, and briefly describe what protection or support is provided by the enhancement. Identify any enhancement provider referenced in Items 1114(b) and 1115 of this

Regulation AB. Summarize how losses not covered by credit enhancement or support will be allocated to the securities.

(4) Identify any outstanding series or classes of securities that are backed by the same asset pool or otherwise have claims on the pool assets. In addition, state if additional series or classes of securities may be issued that are backed by the same asset pool and briefly identify the circumstances under which those additional securities may be issued. Specify if security holder approval is necessary for such issuances and if security holders will receive notice of such issuances.

(5) If the transaction will include prefunding or revolving periods, indicate:

(i) The term or duration of the prefunding or revolving period.

(ii) For prefunding periods, the amount of proceeds to be deposited in the prefunding account.

(iii) For revolving periods, the maximum amount of additional assets that may be acquired during the revolving period, if applicable.

(iv) The percentage of the asset pool and any class or series of the asset-backed securities represented by the prefunding account or the revolving period, if applicable.

(v) Any limitation on the ability to add pool assets.

(vi) The requirements for assets that may be added to the pool.

(6) If pool assets can otherwise be added, removed or substituted (for example, in the event of a breach in representations or warranties regarding pool assets), summarize briefly the circumstances under which such actions can occur.

(7) Summarize the amount or formula for calculating the fee that the servicer will receive for performing its duties, and identify from what source those fees will be paid and the distribution priority of those fees.

(8) Summarize the federal income tax issues material to investors of each class of securities offered.

(9) Indicate whether the issuance or sale of any class of offered securities is conditioned on the assignment of a rating by one or more rating agencies. If so, identify each rating agency and the minimum rating that must be assigned.

(b) *Risk factors.* In providing the information required by Item 503(c) of Regulation S-K (§ 229.503(c)), identify any risks that may be different for investors in any offered class of asset-backed securities, and if so, identify such classes and describe such difference(s).

[As adopted in Release No. 33-8518, effective March 8, 2005 (Compliance dates are triggered by initial bona fide offer date or registration statement filing date and extend out to March 31, 2006. Complete compliance date details can be found in the "Dates" section of the release.), 70 F.R. 1506.]

[¶ 13,261] Sponsors

Reg. § 229.1104 (Item 1104). Provide the following information about the sponsor:

(a) State the sponsor's name and describe the sponsor's form of organization.

(b) Describe the general character of the sponsor's business.

(c) Describe the sponsor's securitization program and state how long the sponsor has been engaged in the securitization of assets. The description must include, to the extent material, a general discussion of the sponsor's experience in securitizing assets of any type as well as a more detailed discussion of the sponsor's experience in and overall procedures for originating or acquiring and securitizing assets of the type included in the current transaction. Include to the extent material information regarding the size, composition and growth of the sponsor's portfolio of assets of the type to be securitized and information or factors related to the sponsor that may be material to an analysis of the origination or performance of the pool assets, such as whether any prior securitizations organized by the sponsor have defaulted or experienced an early amortization triggering event.

(d) Describe the sponsor's material roles and responsibilities in its securitization program, including whether the sponsor or an affiliate is responsible for originating, acquiring, pooling or servicing the pool assets, and the sponsor's participation in structuring the transaction.

[As adopted in Release No. 33-8518, effective March 8, 2005 (Compliance dates are triggered by initial bona fide offer date or registration statement filing date and extend out to March 31, 2006. Complete compliance date details can be found in the "Dates" section of the release.), 70 F.R. 1506.]

[¶ 13,275] Static pool information

Reg. § 229.1105 (Item 1105). (a) For amortizing asset pools, unless the registrant determines that such information is not material:

(1) Provide static pool information, to the extent material, regarding delinquencies, cumulative losses and prepayments for prior securitized pools of the sponsor for that asset type.

(2) If the sponsor has less than three years of experience securitizing assets of the type to be included in the offered asset pool, consider providing instead static pool information, to the extent

material, regarding delinquencies, cumulative losses and prepayments by vintage origination years regarding originations or purchases by the sponsor, as applicable, for that asset type. A vintage origination year represents assets originated during the same year.

(3) In providing the information required by paragraphs (a)(1) and (a)(2) of this section:

(i) Provide the requested information for prior pools or vintage origination years, as applicable, relating to the following time period, to the extent material:

(A) Five years, or

(B) For so long as the sponsor has been either securitizing assets of the same asset type (in the case of paragraph (a)(1) of this section) or making originations or purchases of assets of the same asset type (in the case of paragraph (a)(2) of this section) if less than five years.

(ii) Present delinquency, cumulative loss and prepayment data for each prior securitized pool or vintage origination year, as applicable, in periodic increments (*e.g.*, monthly or quarterly), to the extent material, over the life of the prior securitized pool or vintage origination year. The most recent periodic increment for the data must be as of a date no later than 135 days of the date of first use of the prospectus.

(iii) Provide summary information for the original characteristics of the prior securitized pools or vintage origination years, as applicable and material. While the material summary characteristics may vary, these characteristics may include, among other things, the following: number of pool assets; original pool balance; weighted average initial loan balance; weighted average interest or note rate; weighted average original term; weighted average remaining term; weighted average and minimum and maximum standardized credit score or other applicable measure of obligor credit quality; product type; loan purpose; loan-to-value information; distribution of assets by loan or note rate; and geographic distribution information.

(b) For revolving asset master trusts, unless the registrant determines that such information is not material, provide, to the extent material, data regarding delinquencies, cumulative losses, prepayments, payment rate, yield and standardized credit scores or other applicable measure of obligor credit quality in separate increments based on the date of origination of the pool assets. While the material increments may vary, consider presenting such data at a minimum in 12-month increments through the first five years of the account's life (*e.g.*, 0-12 months, 13-24 months, 25-36 months, 37-48 months, 49-60 months and 61 months or more).

(c) If the information that would otherwise be required by paragraph (a)(1), (a)(2) or (b) of this section is not material, but alternative static pool information would provide material disclosure, provide such alternative information instead. Similarly, information contemplated by paragraph (a)(1), (a)(2) or (b) of this section regarding a party or parties other than the sponsor may be provided in addition to or in lieu of such information regarding the sponsor if appropriate to provide material disclosure. In addition, other explanatory disclosure, including disclosure explaining the absence of any static pool information, may be provided.

(d) The following information provided in response to this section shall not be deemed to be a prospectus or part of a prospectus for the asset-backed securities nor shall such information be deemed to be part of the registration statement for the asset-backed securities:

(1) With respect to information regarding prior securitized pools of the sponsor that do not include the currently offered pool, information regarding prior securitized pools that were established before January 1, 2006; and

(2) With respect to information regarding the currently offered pool, information about the pool for periods before January 1, 2006.

(e) For prospectuses to be filed pursuant to § 230.424 of this chapter that include information specified in paragraph (d)(1) or (d)(2) of this section, the prospectus shall disclose that such information is not deemed to be part of that prospectus or the registration statement for the asset-backed securities.

(f) If any of the information identified in paragraph (d)(1) or (d)(2) of this section that is to be provided in response to this section is unknown and not available to the registrant without unreasonable effort or expense, such information may be omitted, provided the registrant provides the information on the subject it possesses or can acquire without unreasonable effort or expense, and the registrant includes a statement in the prospectus showing that unreasonable effort or expense would be involved in obtaining the omitted information.

[As last amended in Release No. 33-5818A, effective December 5, 2005, 70 F.R. 72372.]

[¶ 13,290] Depositors

Reg. § 229.1106 (Item 1106). If the depositor is not the same entity as the sponsor, provide separately the information regarding the depositor called for by paragraphs (a) and (b) of Item 1104 of this Regulation AB, and, to the extent the information would be material and materially different from the sponsor, paragraphs (c) and (d) of Item 1104 of this Regulation AB. In addition, provide the following information:

(a) The ownership structure of the depositor.

(b) The general character of any activities the depositor is engaged in other than securitizing assets and the time period during which it has been so engaged.

(c) Any continuing duties of the depositor after issuance of the asset-backed securities being registered regarding the asset-backed securities or the pool assets.

[As adopted in Release No. 33-8518, effective March 8, 2005 (Compliance dates are triggered by initial bona fide offer date or registration statement filing date and extend out to March 31, 2006. Complete compliance date details can be found in the "Dates" section of the release.), 70 F.R. 1506.]

[¶ 13,301] Issuing Entities

Reg. § 229.1107 (Item 1107). Provide the following information about the issuing entity:

(a) State the issuing entity's name and describe the issuing entity's form of organization, including the State or other jurisdiction under whose laws the issuing entity is organized. File the issuing entity's governing documents as an exhibit.

(b) Describe the permissible activities and restrictions on the activities of the issuing entity under its governing documents, including any restrictions on the ability to issue or invest in additional securities, to borrow money or to make loans to other persons. Describe any provisions in the issuing entity's governing documents allowing for modification of the issuing entity's governing documents, including its permissible activities.

(c) Describe any specific discretionary activities with regard to the administration of the asset pool or the asset-backed securities, and identify the person or persons authorized to exercise such discretion.

(d) Describe any assets owned or to be owned by the issuing entity, apart from the pool assets, as well as any liabilities of the issuing entity, apart from the asset-backed securities. Disclose the fiscal year end of the issuing entity.

(e) If the issuing entity has executive officers, a board of directors or persons performing similar functions, provide the information required by Items 401, 402, 403 404 and 407(a), (c)(3), (d)(4), (d)(5) and (e)(4) of Regulation S-K (§ § 229.401, 229.402, 229.403, 229.404 and 229.407(a), (c)(3), (d)(4), (d)(5) and (e)(4)) for the issuing entity.

(f) Describe the terms of any management or administration agreement regarding the issuing entity. File any such agreement as an exhibit.

(g) Describe the capitalization of the issuing entity and the amount or nature of any equity contribution to the issuing entity by the sponsor, depositor or other party.

(h) Describe the sale or transfer of the pool assets to the issuing entity as well as the creation (and perfection and priority status) of any security interest in favor of the issuing entity, the trustee, the asset-backed security holders or others, including the material terms of any agreement providing for such sale, transfer or creation of a security interest. File any such agreements as an exhibit. In addition to an appropriate narrative description, also provide this information graphically or in a flow chart if it will aid understanding.

(i) If the pool assets are securities, as defined under the Securities Act, state the market price of the securities and the basis on which the market price was determined.

(j) If expenses incurred in connection with the selection and acquisition of the pool assets are to be payable from offering proceeds, disclose the amount of such expenses. If such expenses are to be paid to the sponsor, servicer contemplated by Item 1108(a)(2) of this Regulation AB, depositor, issuing entity, originator contemplated by Item 1110 of this Regulation AB, underwriter, or any affiliate of the foregoing, separately identify the type and amount of expenses paid to each such party.

(k) Describe to the extent material any provisions or arrangements included to address any one or more of the following issues:

(1) Whether any security interests granted in connection with the transaction are perfected, maintained and enforced.

(2) Whether declaration of bankruptcy, receivership or similar proceeding with respect to the issuing entity can occur.

(3) Whether in the event of a bankruptcy, receivership or similar proceeding with respect to the sponsor, originator, depositor or other seller of the pool assets, the issuing entity's assets will become part of the bankruptcy estate or subject to the bankruptcy control of a third party.

(4) Whether in the event of a bankruptcy, receivership or similar proceeding with respect to the issuing entity, the issuing entity's assets will become subject to the bankruptcy control of a third party.

(*l*) If applicable law prohibits the issuing entity from holding the pool assets directly (for example, an "eligible lender" trustee must hold student loans originated under the Federal Family Education Loan Program of the Higher Education Act of 1965 (20 U.S.C. 1001 *et seq.*)), describe the arrangements instituted to hold the pool assets on behalf of the issuing entity. Include disclosure regarding the arrangements taken, as applicable, regarding the items in paragraph (k) of this section with respect to any such additional entity that holds such assets on behalf of the issuing entity.

[As last amended in Release No. 33-8732, effective November 7, 2006, 71 F.R. 53158.]

[¶ 13,315] Servicers

Reg. § 229.1108 (Item 1108). Provide the following information for the servicer.

(a) *Multiple servicers.* Where servicing of the pool assets utilizes multiple servicers (*e.g.*, master servicers that oversee the actions of other servicers, primary servicers that have primary contact with the obligor, or special servicers for specific servicing functions):

(1) Provide a clear introductory description of the roles, responsibilities and oversight requirements of the entire servicing structure and the parties involved. In addition to an appropriate narrative discussion of the allocation of servicing responsibilities, also consider presenting the information graphically if doing so will aid understanding.

(2) Identify:

(i) Each master servicer;

(ii) Each affiliated servicer;

(iii) Each unaffiliated servicer that services 10% or more of the pool assets; and

(iv) Any other material servicer responsible for calculating or making distributions to holders of the asset-backed securities, performing work-outs or foreclosures, or other aspect of the servicing of the pool assets or the asset-backed securities upon which the performance of the pool assets or the asset-backed securities is materially dependent.

(3) Provide the information in paragraphs (b), (c) and (d) of this section, as applicable depending on the servicer's role, for each servicer identified in paragraph (a)(2)(i), (ii) and (iv) of this section and each unaffiliated servicer identified in paragraph (a)(2)(iii) of this section that services 20% or more of the pool assets

(b) *Identifying information and experience.*

(1) State the servicer's name and describe the servicer's form of organization.

(2) State how long the servicer has been servicing assets. Provide, to the extent material, a general discussion of the servicer's experience in servicing assets of any type as well as a more detailed discussion of the servicer's experience in, and procedures for the servicing function it will perform in the current transaction for assets of the type included in the current transaction. Include to the extent material information regarding the size, composition and growth of the servicer's portfolio of serviced assets of the type included in the current transaction and information on factors related to the servicer that may be material to an analysis of the servicing of the assets or the asset-backed securities, as applicable.

(3) Describe any material changes to the servicer's policies or procedures in the servicing function it will perform in the current transaction for assets of the same type included in the current transaction during the past three years.

(4) Provide information regarding the servicer's financial condition to the extent that there is a material risk that the effect on one or more aspects of servicing resulting from such financial condition could have a material impact on pool performance or performance of the asset-backed securities.

(c) *Servicing agreements and servicing practices.*

(1) Describe the material terms of the servicing agreement and the servicer's duties regarding the asset-backed securities transaction. File the servicing agreement as an exhibit.

(2) Describe to the extent material the manner in which collections on the assets will be maintained, such as through a segregated collection account, and the extent of commingling of funds that occurs or may occur from the assets with other funds, serviced assets or other assets of the servicer.

(3) Describe to the extent material any special or unique factors involved in servicing the particular type of assets included in the current transaction, such as subprime assets, and the servicer's processes and procedures designed to address such factors.

(4) Describe to the extent material the terms of any arrangements whereby the servicer is required or permitted to provide advances of funds regarding collections, cash flows or distributions, including interest or other fees charged for such advances and terms of recovery by the servicer of such advances. To the extent material, provide statistical information regarding servicer advances on the pool assets and the servicer's overall servicing portfolio for the past three years.

(5) Describe to the extent material the servicer's process for handling delinquencies, losses, bankruptcies and recoveries, such as through liquidation of the underlying collateral, note sale by a special servicer or borrower negotiation or workouts.

(6) Describe to the extent material any ability of the servicer to waive or modify any terms, fees, penalties or payments on the assets and the effect of any such ability, if material, on the potential cash flows from the assets.

(7) If the servicer has custodial responsibility for the assets, describe material arrangements regarding the safekeeping and preservation of the assets, such as the physical promissory notes, and procedures to reflect the segregation of the assets from other serviced assets. If no servicer has custodial responsibility for the assets, disclose that fact, identify the party that has such responsibility and provide the information called for by this paragraph for such party.

(8) Describe any limitations on the servicer's liability under the transaction agreements regarding the asset-backed securities transaction.

(d) *Back-up servicing.* Describe the material terms regarding the servicer's removal, replacement, resignation or transfer, including:

(1) Provisions for selection of a successor servicer and financial or other requirements that must be met by a successor servicer.

(2) The process for transferring servicing to a successor servicer.

(3) Provisions for payment of expenses associated with a servicing transfer and any additional fees charged by a successor servicer. Specify the amount of any funds set aside for a servicing transfer.

(4) Arrangements, if any, regarding a back-up servicer for the assets and the identity of any such back-up servicer.

[As adopted in Release No. 33-8518, effective March 8, 2005 (Compliance dates are triggered by initial bona fide offer date or registration statement filing date and extend out to March 31, 2006. Complete compliance date details can be found in the "Dates" section of the release.), 70 F.R. 1506.]

[¶ 13,331] Trustees

Reg. § 229.1109 (Item 1109). Provide the following information for each trustee:

(a) State the trustee's name and describe the trustee's form of organization.

(b) Describe to what extent the trustee has had prior experience serving as a trustee for asset-backed securities transactions involving similar pool assets, if applicable.

(c) Describe the trustee's duties and responsibilities regarding the asset-backed securities under the governing documents and under applicable law. In addition, describe any actions required by the trustee, including whether notices are required to investors, rating agencies or other third parties, upon an event of default, potential event of default (and how defined) or other breach of a transaction covenant and any required percentage of a class or classes of asset-backed securities that is needed to require the trustee to take action.

(d) Describe any limitations on the trustee's liability under the transaction agreements regarding the asset-backed securities transaction.

(e) Describe any indemnification provisions that entitle the trustee to be indemnified from the cash flow that otherwise would be used to pay the asset-backed securities.

(f) Describe any contractual provisions or understandings regarding the trustee's removal, replacement or resignation, as well as how the expenses associated with changing from one trustee to another trustee will be paid.

Instruction to Item 1109. If multiple trustees are involved in the transaction, provide a description of the roles and responsibilities of each trustee.

[As adopted in Release No. 33-8518, effective March 8, 2005 (Compliance dates are triggered by initial bona fide offer date or registration statement filing date and extend out to March 31, 2006. Complete compliance date details can be found in the "Dates" section of the release.), 70 F.R. 1506.]

[¶ 13,345] Originators

Reg. § 229.1110 (Item 1110). (a) Identify any originator or group of affiliated originators, apart from the sponsor or its affiliates, that originated, or is expected to originate, 10% or more of the pool assets.

(b) Provide the following information for any originator or group of affiliated originators, apart from the sponsor or its affiliates, that originated, or is expected to originate, 20% or more of the pool assets:

(1) The originator's form of organization.

(2) To the extent material, a description of the originator's origination program and how long the originator has been engaged in originating assets. The description must include a discussion of the originator's experience in originating assets of the type included in the current transaction. In providing

the description, include, if material, information regarding the size and composition of the originator's origination portfolio as well as information material to an analysis of the performance of the pool assets, such as the originator's credit-granting or underwriting criteria for the asset types being securitized.

[As adopted in Release No. 33-8518, effective March 8, 2005 (Compliance dates are triggered by initial bona fide offer date or registration statement filing date and extend out to March 31, 2006. Complete compliance date details can be found in the "Dates" section of the release.), 70 F.R. 1506.]

[¶ 13,361] Pool assets

Reg. § 229.1111 (Item 1111). Describe the pool assets, including the information required by this Item 1111. Present statistical information in tabular or graphical format, if such presentation will aid understanding. Present statistical information in appropriate distributional groups or incremental ranges in addition to presenting appropriate overall pool totals, averages and weighted averages, if such presentation will aid in the understanding of the data. In addition to presenting the number, amount and percentage of pool assets by distributional group or range, also provide statistical information for each group or range by variables, to the extent material, such as, average balance, weighted average coupon, average age and remaining term, average loan-to-value or similar ratio and weighted average standardized credit score or other applicable measure of obligor credit quality. These variables are just examples and should be tailored to the particular asset class backing the asset-backed securities. Consider providing minimums and maximums when presenting averages on an aggregate basis and within each group or range. In addition, provide historical data on the pool assets as appropriate (*e.g.*, the lesser of three years or the time such assets have existed) to allow material evaluation of the pool data. In making any calculations regarding overall pool balances, disregard any funds set aside for a prefunding account.

(a) *General information regarding pool asset types and selection criteria.* Provide the following information:

(1) A brief description of the type or types of pool assets to be securitized.

(2) A general description of the material terms of the pool assets.

(3) A description of the solicitation, credit-granting or underwriting criteria used to originate or purchase the pool assets, including, to the extent known, any changes in such criteria and the extent to which such policies and criteria are or could be overridden.

(4) The method and criteria by which the pool assets were selected for the transaction.

(5) The cut-off date or similar date for establishing the composition of the asset pool, if applicable.

(6) If legal or regulatory provisions (such as bankruptcy, consumer protection, predatory lending, privacy, property rights or foreclosure laws or regulations) may materially affect pool asset performance or payments or expected payments on the asset-backed securities, briefly identify these provisions and their effects on such items.

Instruction to Item 1111(a)(6). Unless a material concentration of assets exists, it is not necessary to provide details of the laws in each jurisdiction. Even in that case, a legalistic description or recitation of the laws or regulations in a particular jurisdiction is not required.

(b) *Pool characteristics.* Describe the material characteristics of the asset pool. Provide appropriate introductory and explanatory information to introduce the characteristics, the methodology used in determining or calculating the characteristics and any terms or abbreviations used. While the material characteristics will vary depending on the nature of the pool assets, such characteristics may include, among other things:

(1) Number of each type of pool assets.

(2) Asset size, such as original balance and outstanding balance as of a designated cut-off date.

(3) Interest rate or rate of return, including type of interest rate if the pool includes different types, such as fixed and floating rates.

(4) Capitalized or uncapitalized accrued interest.

(5) Age, maturity, remaining term, average life (based on different prepayment assumptions), current payment/prepayment speeds and pool factors, as applicable.

(6) Servicer distribution, if different servicers service different pool assets.

(7) If a loan or similar receivable:

(i) Amortization period.

(ii) Loan purpose (*e.g.*, whether a purchase or refinance) and status, if applicable (*e.g.*, repayment or deferment).

(iii) Loan-to-value (LTV) ratios and debt service coverage ratios (DSCR), as applicable.

(iv) Type and/or use of underlying property, product or collateral (*e.g.*, occupancy type for residential mortgages or industry sector for commercial mortgages).

(8) If a receivable or other financial asset that arises under a revolving account, such as a credit card receivable:

(i) Monthly payment rate.

(ii) Maximum credit lines.

(iii) Average account balance.

(iv) Yield percentages.

(v) Type of asset.

(vi) Finance charges, fees and other income earned.

(vii) Balance reductions granted for refunds, returns, fraudulent charges or other reasons.

(viii) Percentage of full-balance and minimum payments made.

(9) If the asset pool includes commercial mortgages, the following information, to the extent material:

(i) For all commercial mortgages:

(A) The location and present use of each mortgaged property.

(B) Net operating income and net cash flow information, as well as the components of net operating income and net cash flow, for each mortgaged property.

(C) Current occupancy rates for each mortgaged property.

(D) The identity, square feet occupied by and lease expiration dates for the three largest tenants at each mortgaged property.

(E) The nature and amount of all other material mortgages, liens or encumbrances against such properties and their priority.

(ii) For each commercial mortgage that represents, by dollar value, 10% or more of the asset pool, as measured as of the cut-off date:

(A) Any proposed program for the renovation, improvement or development of such properties, including the estimated cost thereof and the method of financing to be used.

(B) The general competitive conditions to which such properties are or may be subject.

(C) Management of such properties.

(D) Occupancy rate expressed as a percentage for each of the last five years.

(E) Principal business, occupations and professions carried on in, or from the properties.

(F) Number of tenants occupying 10% or more of the total rentable square footage of such properties and principal nature of business of such tenant, and the principal provisions of the leases with those tenants including, but not limited to: rental per annum, expiration date, and renewal options.

(G) The average effective annual rental per square foot or unit for each of the last three years prior to the date of filing.

(H) Schedule of the lease expirations for each of the ten years starting with the year in which the registration statement is filed (or the year in which the prospectus supplement is dated, as applicable), stating:

(1) The number of tenants whose leases will expire.

(2) The total area in square feet covered by such leases.

(3) The annual rental represented by such leases.

(4) The percentage of gross annual rental represented by such leases.

Instruction to Item 1111(b)(9). What is required is information material to an investor's understanding of the asset-backed securities. Detailed descriptions of the physical characteristics of individual properties or legal descriptions by metes and bounds are not required.

(10) Whether the pool asset is secured or unsecured, and if secured, the type(s) of collateral.

(11) Standardized credit scores of obligors and other information regarding obligor credit quality.

(12) Billing and payment procedures, including frequency of payment, payment options, fees, charges and origination or payment incentives.

(13) Information about the origination channel and origination process for the pool assets, such as originator information (and how acquired) and the level of origination documentation required, as applicable.

(14) Geographic distribution, such as by state or other material geographic region. If 10% or more of the pool assets are or will be located in any one state or other geographic region, describe any economic or other factors specific to such state or region that may materially impact the pool assets or pool asset cash flows.

Instruction to Item 1111(b)(14). For most assets, such as credit card accounts, motor vehicle leases, trade receivables and student loans, the location of the asset is the underlying obligor's billing address. For assets involving real estate, such as mortgages, the location of the asset is where the physical property underlying the asset is located.

(15) Other concentrations material to the asset type (*e.g.*, school type for student loans). If material, provide information required by paragraph (b)(14) of this section regarding such concentrations, as applicable.

(c) *Delinquency and loss information.* Provide delinquency and loss information for the asset pool, including statistical information regarding delinquencies and losses.

(d) *Sources of pool cash flow.* If the cash flows from the pool assets that are to be used to support the asset-backed securities are to come from more than one source (such as separate cash flows from lease payments and from the sale of the residual asset at the termination of the lease), provide the following information:

(1) Disclose the specific sources of funds that will be used to make the payments and distributions on the asset-backed securities, and, if applicable, provide information on the relative amount and percentage of funds that are to be derived from each source, including a description of any assumptions, data, models and methodology used to derive such amounts. If payments on different classes or different categories of payments on or related to the asset-backed securities (*e.g.*, principal, interest or expenses) are to come from different or segregated cash flows from the pool assets or other sources, disclose the source of funds that will be used for such payments.

(2) *Residual value information.* If the asset pool includes leases or other assets where a portion of the securitized pool balance is attributable to the residual value of the underlying physical property underlying the leases, disclose the following:

(i) How the residual values used to structure the transaction were estimated, including an explanation of any material discount rates, models or assumptions used and who selected such rates, models or assumptions.

(ii) Any material procedures or requirements incorporated to preserve residual values during the term of the lease, such as lessee responsibilities, prohibitions on subletting, indemnification or required insurance or guarantees.

(iii) The procedures by which the residual values will be realized and by whom those procedures will be carried out, including information on the experience of such party, any affiliations with a party described in Item 1119(a) of this Regulation AB and the compensation arrangements with such party.

(iv) Whether the pool assets are open-end leases (*e.g.*, where the lessee is required to cover the shortfall between the residual value of the leased property and the sale proceeds) or closed-end leases (*e.g.*, where the lessor is responsible for such shortfalls), and where both types of leases are included in the asset pool, the percentage of each.

(v) To the extent material, any lessor obligations that are required under the leases, and the effect or potential effect on the asset-backed securities from failure by the lessor to perform its obligations.

(vi) Statistical information regarding estimated residual values for the pool assets.

(vii) Summary historical statistics on turn-in rates, if applicable, and residual value realization rates by the party responsible for such process over the past three years, or such longer period as is material to an evaluation of the pool assets.

(viii) The effect on security holders if not enough cash flow is received from the realization of the residual values, whether there are any provisions to address this contingency, and how any cash flow greater than that necessary to pay security holders will be allocated.

(e) *Representations and warranties and repurchase obligations regarding pool assets.* Summarize any representations and warranties made concerning the pool assets by the sponsor, transferor, originator or other party to the transaction, and describe briefly the remedies available if those representations and warranties are breached, such as repurchase obligations.

(f) *Claims on pool assets.* Describe any material direct or contingent claim that parties other than the holders of the asset-backed securities have on any pool assets. Also, describe any material cross-collateralization or cross-default provisions relating to the pool assets.

(g) *Revolving periods, prefunding accounts and other changes to the asset pool.* If the transaction contemplates a prefunding or revolving period, provide the following information, as applicable. Provide similar information regarding any other circumstances where pool assets may be added, substituted or removed from the asset pool, such as in the event of additional issuances of asset-backed securities in a master trust or a breach of a pool asset representation or warranty:

(1) The term or duration of any prefunding or revolving period.

(2) For prefunding periods, the amount of proceeds to be deposited in the prefunding account.

(3) For revolving periods, the maximum amount of additional assets that may be acquired during the revolving period, if applicable.

(4) The percentage of the asset pool and any class or series of the asset-backed securities represented by the prefunding account or the revolving account, if applicable.

(5) Triggers or events that would trigger limits on or terminate the prefunding or revolving period and the effects of such triggers. In particular for a revolving period, describe the operation of the revolving period and the amortization period.

(6) When and how new pool assets may be acquired during the prefunding or revolving period, and if, when and how pool assets can be removed or substituted. Describe any limits on the amount, type or speed with which pool assets may be acquired, substituted or removed.

(7) The acquisition or underwriting criteria for additional pool assets to be acquired during the prefunding or revolving period, including a description of any differences from the criteria used to select the current asset pool.

(8) Which party has the authority to add, remove or substitute assets from the asset pool or determine if such pool assets meet the acquisition or underwriting criteria for additional pool assets. In addition, disclose whether or not there will be any independent verification of such person's exercise of authority or determinations.

(9) Any requirements to add or remove minimum amounts of pool assets and any effects of not meeting those requirements.

(10) If applicable, the procedures and standards for the temporary investment of funds in a prefunding or revolving account pending use (including the disposition of gains and losses on pending funds) and a description of the financial products or instruments eligible for such accounts.

(11) The circumstances under which funds in a prefunding or revolving account will be returned to investors or otherwise disposed of.

(12) A statement of whether, and if so, how, investors will be notified of changes to the asset pool.

[As adopted in Release No. 33-8518, effective March 8, 2005 (Compliance dates are triggered by initial bona fide offer date or registration statement filing date and extend out to March 31, 2006. Complete compliance date details can be found in the "Dates" section of the release.), 70 F.R. 1506.]

[¶ 13,375] Significant obligors of pool assets

Reg. § 229.1112 (Item 1112). (a) *Descriptive information.* Provide the following information for each significant obligor:

(1) The name of the obligor.

(2) The organizational form and general character of the business of the obligor.

(3) The nature of the concentration of the pool assets with the obligor.

(4) The material terms of the pool assets and the agreements with the obligor involving the pool assets.

(b) *Financial information.* (1) If the pool assets relating to a significant obligor represent 10% or more, but less than 20%, of the asset pool, provide selected financial data required by Item 301 of Regulation S-K (§ 229.301) for the significant obligor, provided, however, that for a significant obligor under Item 1101(k)(2) of this Regulation AB, only net operating income for the most recent fiscal year and interim period is required.

(2) If pool assets relating to a significant obligor represent 20% or more of the asset pool, provide financial statements meeting the requirements of Regulation S-X (§§ 210.1-01 through 210.12-29 of this chapter), except § 210.3-05 of this chapter and Article 11 of Regulation S-X (§§ 210.11-01 through 210.11-03 of this chapter), of the significant obligor. Financial statements of such obligor and its subsidiaries consolidated (as required by § 240.14a-3(b) of this chapter) shall be filed under this item.

Instructions to Item 1112(b).

1. No information need be provided pursuant to paragraph (b) of this section if the obligations of the significant obligor as they relate to the pool assets are backed by the full faith and credit of the United States.

2. No information need be provided pursuant to paragraph (b) of this section if the obligations of the significant obligor as they relate to the pool assets are backed by the full faith and credit of a foreign government (as defined in § 240.3b-4(a) of this chapter) if the pool assets are investment grade securities as defined in Item I.B.2 of Form S-3 (§ 239.13 of this chapter). If the pool assets are not investment grade securities, information required by paragraph (5) of Schedule B of the Securities Act (15 U.S.C. 77aa) regarding the foreign government may be incorporated by reference from a Commission filing in lieu of providing the financial information required pursuant to paragraph (b) of this section.

3. If the significant obligor is an asset-backed issuer and the pool assets relating to the significant obligor are asset-backed securities, provide the following information in lieu of the information required by paragraph (b) of this section:

a. For a registration statement under the Securities Act or the Exchange Act or a prospectus to be filed pursuant to §230.424 of this chapter, the information required by Items 1104 through 1115, 1117 and 1119 of this Regulation AB regarding such asset-backed securities; and

b. For an Exchange Act report on Form 10-K or Form 10-D (§249.310 or 249.312 of this chapter), the information required by General Instruction J. of Form 10-K regarding such asset-backed securities for the period for which the last Form 10-K of the asset-backed securities was due (or would have been due if such asset-backed securities are not required to file reports with the Commission pursuant to section 13(a) or 15(d) of the Exchange Act (15 U.S.C. 78m(a) or 78o(d)).

4. If the significant obligor is a foreign business (as defined §210.1-02 of this chapter):

a. Paragraph (b)(1) of this section may be complied with by providing the information required by Item 3.A. of Form 20-F (§249.220f of this chapter). If a reconciliation to U.S. generally accepted accounting principles called for by Instruction 2. to Item 3.A. of Form 20-F is unavailable or not obtainable without unreasonable cost or expense, at a minimum provide a narrative description of all material variations in accounting principles, practices and methods used in preparing the non-U.S. GAAP financial statements used as a basis for the selected financial data from those accepted in the U.S.

b. Paragraph (b)(2) of this section may be complied with by providing financial statements meeting the requirements of Item 17 of Form 20-F for the periods specified by Item 8.A. of Form 20-F.

[As adopted in Release No. 33-8518, effective March 8, 2005 (Compliance dates are triggered by initial bona fide offer date or registration statement filing date and extend out to March 31, 2006. Complete compliance date details can be found in the "Dates" section of the release.), 70 F.R. 1506.]

[¶ 13,390] Structure of the transaction

Reg. § 229.1113 (Item 1113). (a) *Description of the securities and transaction structure.* In providing the information required by Item 202 of Regulation S-K (§229.202), address the following specific factors relating to the asset-backed securities, as applicable:

(1) The types or categories of securities that may be offered, such as interest-weighted or principal-weighted classes (including IO (interest only) or PO (principal only) securities), planned amortization or companion classes or residual or subordinated interests.

(2) The flow of funds for the transaction, including the payment allocations, rights and distribution priorities among all classes of the issuing entity's securities, and within each class, with respect to cash flows, credit enhancement or other support and any other structural features designed to enhance credit, facilitate the timely payment of monies due on the pool assets or owing to security holders, adjust the rate of return on the asset-backed securities, or preserve monies that will or might be distributed to security holders. In addition to an appropriate narrative discussion of the allocation and priority structure of pool cash flows, present the flow of funds graphically if doing so will aid understanding. In the flow of funds discussion, provide information regarding any requirements directing cash flows from the pool assets (such as to reserve accounts, cash collateral accounts or expenses) and the purpose and operation of such requirements.

(3) In describing the interest rate or rate of return on the asset-backed securities and how such amounts are payable, explain how the rate is determined and how frequently it will be determined. If the rate to be paid can be a combination of two or more rates (such as the lesser of a variable rate or the actual weighted average net coupon on the pool assets), provide clear information regarding each rate and when each rate applies.

(4) How principal, if any, will be paid on the asset-backed securities, including maturity dates, amortization or principal distribution schedules, principal distribution dates, formulas for calculating principal distributions from the cash flows and other factors that will affect the timing or amount of principal payments for each class of securities.

(5) The denominations in which the asset-backed securities may be issued.

(6) Any specified changes to the transaction structure that would be triggered upon a default or event of default (such as a change in distribution priority among classes).

(7) Any liquidation, amortization, performance or similar triggers or events, and the rights of investors or changes to the transaction structure or flow of funds if such events were to occur.

(8) Whether the servicer or other party is required to provide periodic evidence of the absence of a default or of compliance with the terms of the transaction agreements.

(9) If applicable, the extent, expressed as a percentage, the transaction is overcollateralized or undercollateralized as measured by comparing the principal balance of the asset-backed securities to the asset pool.

(10) Any provisions contained in other securities that could result in a cross-default or cross-collateralization.

(11) Any minimum standards, restrictions or suitability requirements regarding potential investors in purchasing the securities or any restrictions on ownership or transfer of the securities.

(12) Security holder vote required to amend the transaction documents and allocation of voting rights among security holders.

(b) *Distribution frequency and cash maintenance.* (1) Disclose the frequency of distribution dates for the asset-backed securities and the collection periods for the pool assets.

(2) Describe how cash held pending distribution or other uses is held and invested. Also describe the length of time cash will be held pending distributions to security holders. Identify the party or parties with access to cash balances and the authority to invest cash balances. Specify who determines any decisions regarding the deposit, transfer or disbursement of pool asset cash flows and whether there will be any independent verification of the transaction accounts or account activity.

(c) *Fees and expenses.* Provide in a separate table an itemized list of all fees and expenses to be paid or payable out of the cash flows from the pool assets. In itemizing the fees and expenses, also indicate their general purpose, the party receiving such fees or expenses, the source of funds for such fees or expenses (if different from other fees or expenses or if such fees or expenses are to be paid from a specified portion of the cash flows) and the distribution priority of such expenses. If the amount of such fees or expenses is not fixed, provide the formula used to determine such fees or expenses. The tabular presentation should be accompanied by footnotes or other accompanying narrative disclosure to the extent necessary for an understanding of the timing or amount of such fees or expenses, such as any restrictions or limits on fees or whether the estimate may change in certain instances, such as in an event of default (and how the fees would change in such an instance or the factors that would affect the change). In addition, through footnote or other accompanying narrative disclosure, describe if any, and if so how, such fees or expenses can be changed without notice to, or approval by, security holders and any restrictions on the ability to change a fee or expense amount, such as due to a change in transaction party.

(d) *Excess cash flow.* (1) Describe the disposition of residual or excess cash flows. Identify who owns any residual or retained interests to the cash flows if such person is affiliated with the sponsor, depositor, issuing entity or any entity identified in Item 1119(a) of this Regulation AB or if such person has rights that may alter the transaction structure beyond receipt of residual or excess cash flows. Describe such rights, as material.

(2) Disclose any requirements in the transaction agreements to maintain a minimum amount of excess cash flow or spread from, or retained interest in, the transaction and any actions that would be required or changes to the transaction structure that would occur if such requirements were not met.

(3) To the extent material to an understanding of the asset-backed securities, disclose any features or arrangements to facilitate a securitization of the excess cash flow or retained interest from the transaction, including whether any material changes to the transaction structure may be made without the consent of asset-backed security holders in connection with these securitizations.

(e) *Master trusts.* If one or more additional series or classes have been or may be issued that are backed by the same asset pool, provide information regarding the additional securities to the extent material to an understanding of their effect on the securities being offered, including the following:

(1) Relative priority of such additional securities to the securities being offered and rights to the underlying pool assets and their cash flows.

(2) Allocation of cash flow from the asset pool and any expenses or losses among the various series or classes.

(3) Terms under which such additional series or classes may be issued and pool assets increased or changed.

(4) The terms of any security holder approval or notification of such additional securities.

(5) Which party has the authority to determine whether such additional securities may be issued. In addition, if there are conditions to such additional issuance, disclose whether or not there will be an independent verification of such person's exercise of authority or determinations.

(f) *Optional or mandatory redemption or termination.* (1) If any class of the asset-backed securities includes an optional or mandatory redemption or termination feature, provide the following information:

(i) Terms for triggering the redemption or termination.

(ii) The identity of the party that holds the redemption or termination option or obligation, as well as whether such party is an affiliate of the sponsor, depositor, issuing entity or any entity identified in Item 1119(a) of this Regulation AB.

(iii) The amount of the redemption or repurchase price or formula for determining such amount.

(iv) The procedures for redemption or termination, including any notices to security holders.

(v) If the amount allocated to security holders is reduced by losses, the policy regarding any amounts recovered after redemption or termination.

(2) The title of any class of securities with an optional redemption or termination feature that may be exercised when 25% or more of the original principal balance of the pool assets is still outstanding must include the word "callable," *provided, however*, that in the case of a master trust, a title of a class of securities must include the word "callable" when an optional redemption or termination feature may be exercised when 25% or more of the original principal balance of the particular series in which the class was issued is still outstanding.

(g) *Prepayment, maturity and yield considerations.* (1) Describe any models, including the related material assumptions and limitations, used as a means to identify cash flow patterns with respect to the pool assets.

(2) Describe to the extent material the degree to which each class of securities is sensitive to changes in the rate of payment on the pool assets (*e.g.*, prepayment or interest rate sensitivity), and describe the consequences of such changing rate of payment. Provide statistical information of such effects, such as the effect of prepayments on yield and weighted average life.

(3) Describe any special allocations of prepayment risks among the classes of securities, and whether any class protects other classes from the effects of the uncertain timing of cash flow.

[As adopted in Release No. 33-8518, effective March 8, 2005 (Compliance dates are triggered by initial bona fide offer date or registration statement filing date and extend out to March 31, 2006. Complete compliance date details can be found in the "Dates" section of the release.), 70 F.R. 1506.]

[¶ 13,401] Credit enhancement and other support, except for certain derivatives instruments

Reg. § 229.1114 (Item 1114). (a) *Descriptive information.* To the extent material, describe the following, including a clear discussion of the manner in which each potential item is designed to affect or ensure timely payment of the asset-backed securities:

(1) Any external credit enhancement designed to ensure that the asset-backed securities or pool assets will pay in accordance with their terms, such as bond insurance, letters of credit or guarantees.

(2) Any mechanisms to ensure that payments on the asset-backed securities are timely, such as liquidity facilities, lending facilities, guaranteed investment contracts and minimum principal payment agreements.

(3) Any derivatives whose primary purpose is to provide credit enhancement related to pool assets or the asset-backed securities.

(4) Any internal credit enhancement as a result of the structure of the transaction that increases the likelihood that payments will be made on one or more classes of the asset-backed securities in accordance with their terms, such as subordination provisions, overcollateralization, reserve accounts, cash collateral accounts or spread accounts.

Instructions to Item 1114(a).

1. Include a description of the material terms of any enhancement or support described, including any limits on the timing or amount of the enhancement or support or any conditions that must be met before the enhancement or support can be accessed. The enhancement or support agreement is to be filed as an exhibit. Also describe any provisions regarding the substitution of enhancement or support.

2. This Item should not be construed as allowing anything other than an asset-backed security whose payment is based primarily by reference to the performance of the receivables or other financial assets in the asset pool

(b) *Information regarding significant enhancement providers.*

(1) *Descriptive information.* If an entity or group of affiliated entities providing enhancement or other support described in paragraph (a) of this section is liable or contingently liable to provide payments representing 10% or more of the cash flow supporting any offered class of asset-backed securities, provide the following information:

(i) The name of such enhancement provider.

(ii) The organizational form of enhancement provider.

(iii) The general character of the business of such enhancement provider.

(2) *Financial information.* (i) If any entity or group of affiliated entities providing enhancement or other support described in paragraph (a) of this section is liable or contingently liable to provide payments representing 10% or more, but less than 20%, of the cash flow supporting any offered class of the asset-backed securities, provide financial data required by Item 301 of Regulation S-K (§ 229.301) for each such entity or group of affiliated entities.

(ii) If any entity or group of affiliated entities providing enhancement or other support described in paragraph (a) of this section is liable or contingently liable to provide payments representing 20% or more of the cash flow supporting any offered class of the asset-backed securities, provide financial statements meeting the requirements of Regulation S-X (§ § 210.1-01 through 210.12-29 of this chapter), except § 210.3-05 of this chapter and Article 11 of Regulation S-X (§ § 210.11-01 through 210.11-03 of this chapter), of such entity or group of affiliated entities. Financial statements of such enhancement provider and its subsidiaries consolidated (as required by § 240.14a-3(b) of this chapter) shall be filed under this item.

Instructions to Item 1114.

1. The requirements in paragraph (b) of this section apply to all providers of external credit enhancement or other support, other than those described in Item 1115 of this Regulation AB. Enhancement may support payment on the pool assets or payments on the asset-backed securities themselves.

2. No information need be provided pursuant to paragraph (b)(2) of this section if the obligations of the enhancement provider are backed by the full faith and credit of the United States.

3. No information need be provided pursuant to paragraph (b)(2) of this section if the obligations of the enhancement provider are backed by the full faith and credit of a foreign government (as defined in § 240.3b-4(a) of this chapter) if the enhancement provider has an investment grade credit rating, as the term investment grade is used in Item I.B.2 of Form S-3 (§ 239.13 of this chapter). If the enhancement provider does not have an investment grade credit rating, information required by paragraph (5) of Schedule B of the Securities Act (15 U.S.C. 77aa) regarding the foreign government may be incorporated by reference from a Commission filing in lieu of providing the financial information required pursuant to paragraph (b)(2) of this section.

4. If the pool assets are student loans originated under the Federal Family Education Loan Program of the Higher Education Act of 1965 (20 U.S.C. 1001 *et seq*.)) and the enhancement provider for the pool assets is a guarantee agency as defined under the Higher Education Act, then the following information may be provided in lieu of providing financial information required pursuant to paragraph (b)(2) of this section:

a. The number of pool assets and aggregate outstanding principal balance of pool assets guaranteed by the guarantee agency (both by number and percentage of the asset pool as of the cut-off date or other applicable date).

b. Disclosure of the following with respect to the guarantee agency, as applicable, including a brief description regarding the method of calculation, covering at least five federal fiscal years:

i. Aggregate principal amount of all student loans guaranteed.

ii. Reserve ratio.

iii. Recovery rate.

iv. Loss rate.

v. Claims rate.

5. If the enhancement provider is a foreign business (as defined § 210.1-02 of this chapter):

a. Paragraph (b)(2)(i) of this section may be complied with by providing the information required by Item 3.A. of Form 20-F (§ 249.220f of this chapter). If a reconciliation to U.S. generally accepted accounting principles called for by Instruction 2. to Item 3.A. of Form 20-F is unavailable or not obtainable without unreasonable cost or expense, at a minimum provide a narrative description of all material variations in accounting principles, practices and methods used in preparing the non-U.S. GAAP financial statements used as a basis for the selected financial data from those accepted in the U.S.

b. Paragraph (b)(2)(ii) of this section may be complied with by providing financial statements meeting the requirements of Item 17 of Form 20-F for the periods specified by Item 8.A. of Form 20-F.

[As adopted in Release No. 33-8518, effective March 8, 2005 (Compliance dates are triggered by initial bona fide offer date or registration statement filing date and extend out to March 31, 2006. Complete compliance date details can be found in the "Dates" section of the release.), 70 F.R. 1506.]

[¶ 13,415] Certain derivatives instruments

Reg. § 229.1115 (Item 1115). This item relates to derivative instruments, such as interest rate and currency swap agreements, that are used to alter the payment characteristics of the cashflows from the issuing entity and whose primary purpose is not to provide credit enhancement related to the pool assets or the asset-backed securities. For purposes of this section, the "significance estimate" of the derivative instrument is to be determined based on a reasonable good-faith estimate of maximum probable exposure, made in substantially the same manner as that used in the sponsor's internal risk management process in respect of similar instruments. The "significance percentage" is the percentage that the amount of the significance estimate represents of the aggregate principal balance of the pool assets, provided, that if the derivative instrument relates only to one or more classes of the asset-backed securities, the "significance percentage" is the percentage that the amount of the significance estimate represents of the aggregate principal balance of such classes.

(a) *Descriptive information.*

(1) Describe the following regarding the external counterparty:

(i) The name of the derivative counterparty.

(ii) The organizational form of the derivative counterparty.

(iii) The general character of the business of the derivative counterparty.

(2) Describe the operation and material terms of the derivative instrument, including any limits on the timing or amount of payments or any conditions to payments.

(3) Describe any material provisions regarding substitution of the derivative instrument.

(4) At a minimum, disclose whether the significance percentage, as calculated in accordance with this section, is less than 10%, at least 10% but less than 20%, or 20% or more.

(5) File the agreement relating to the derivative instrument as an exhibit.

(b) *Financial information.*

(1) If the aggregate significance percentage related to any entity or group of affiliated entities providing derivative instruments contemplated by this section is 10% or more, but less than 20%, provide financial data required by Item 301 of Regulation S-K (§ 229.301) for such entity or group of affiliated entities.

(2) If the aggregate significance percentage related to any entity or group of affiliated entities providing derivative instruments contemplated by this section is 20% or more, provide financial statements meeting the requirements of Regulation S-X (§§ 210.1-01 through 210.12-29 of this chapter), except § 210.3-05 of this chapter and Article 11 of Regulation S-X (§§ 210.11-01 through 210.11-03 of this chapter), of such entity or group of affiliated entities. Financial statements of such entity and its subsidiaries consolidated (as required by § 240.14a-3(b) of this chapter) shall be filed under this item.

Instructions to Item 1115.

1. Instructions 2, 3 and 5 to Item 1114 of this Regulation AB apply to the information contemplated by paragraph (b) of this item.

2. This Item should not be construed as allowing anything other than an asset-backed security whose payment is based primarily by reference to the performance of the receivables or other financial assets in the asset pool.

[As adopted in Release No. 33-8518, effective March 8, 2005 (Compliance dates are triggered by initial bona fide offer date or registration statement filing date and extend out to March 31, 2006. Complete compliance date details can be found in the "Dates" section of the release.), 70 F.R. 1506.]

[¶ 13,431] Tax matters

Reg. § 229.1116 (Item 1116). (a) The tax treatment of the asset-backed securities transaction under federal income tax laws.

(b) The material federal income tax consequences of purchasing, owning and selling the asset-backed securities. If any of the material federal income tax consequences are not expected to be the same for investors in all classes offered by the registration statement, describe the material differences.

(c) The substance of counsel's tax opinion, including identification of the material consequences upon which counsel has not been asked, or is unable, to opine.

[As adopted in Release No. 33-8518, effective March 8, 2005 (Compliance dates are triggered by initial bona fide offer date or registration statement filing date and extend out to March 31, 2006. Complete compliance date details can be found in the "Dates" section of the release.), 70 F.R. 1506.]

[¶ 13,445] Legal proceedings

Reg. § 229.1117 (Item 1117). Describe briefly any legal proceedings pending against the sponsor, depositor, trustee, issuing entity, servicer contemplated by Item 1108(a)(3) of this Regulation AB, originator contemplated by Item 1110(b) of this Regulation AB, or other party contemplated by Item 1100(d)(1) of this Regulation AB, or of which any property of the foregoing is the subject, that is material to security holders. Include similar information as to any such proceedings known to be contemplated by governmental authorities.

[As adopted in Release No. 33-8518, effective March 8, 2005 (Compliance dates are triggered by initial bona fide offer date or registration statement filing date and extend out to March 31, 2006. Complete compliance date details can be found in the "Dates" section of the release.), 70 F.R. 1506.]

[¶ 13,461] Reports and Additional Information

Reg. § 229.1118 (Item 1118). (a) *Reports required under the transaction documents.*

Describe the reports or other documents provided to security holders required under the transaction agreements, including information included, schedule and manner of distribution or other availability, and the entity or entities that will prepare and provide the reports.

(b) *Reports to be filed with the Commission.*

(1) Specify the names, and if available, the Commission file numbers of the entity or entities under which reports about the asset-backed securities will be filed with the Securities and Exchange Commission. Identify the reports and other information filed with the Commission.

(2) State that the public may read and copy any materials filed with the Commission at the Commission's Public Reference Room at 100 F Street, NE, Washington, DC 20549, on official business days between the hours of 10:00 am and 3:00 pm. State that the public may obtain information on the operation of the Public Reference Room by calling the Securities and Exchange Commission at 1-800-SEC-0330. State that the Commission maintains an Internet site that contains reports, proxy and information statements, and other information regarding issuers that file electronically with the Commission and state the address of that site (http://www.sec.gov).

(c) *Web site access to reports.*

(1) State whether the issuing entity's annual reports on Form 10-K (§ 249.310 of this chapter), distribution reports on Form 10-D (§ 249.312 of this chapter), current reports on Form 8-K (§ 249.308 of this chapter), and amendments to those reports filed or furnished pursuant to section 13(a) or 15(d) of the Exchange Act (15 U.S.C. 78m(a) or 78o(d)) will be made available on the Web site of a specified transaction party (*e.g.*, the sponsor, depositor, servicer, issuing entity or trustee) as soon as reasonably practicable after such material is electronically filed with, or furnished to, the Commission.

(2) Disclose whether other reports to security holders or information about the asset-backed securities will be made available in this manner.

(3) If filings and other reports will be made available in this manner, disclose the Web site address where such filings may be found.

(4) If filings and other reports will not be made available in this manner, describe the reasons why they will not and whether an identified transaction party voluntarily will provide electronic or paper copies of those filings and other reports free of charge upon request.

[As amended in Release No. 33-8876, effective February 4, 2008, 73 F.R. 934.]

[¶ 13,475] Affiliations and certain relationships and related transactions

Reg. § 229.1119 (Item 1119). (a) Describe if so, and how, the sponsor, depositor or issuing entity is an affiliate (as defined in § 230.405 of this chapter) of any of the following parties as well as, to the extent known and material, if so, and how, any of the following parties are affiliates of any of the other following parties:

(1) Servicer contemplated by Item 1108(a)(3) of this Regulation AB.

(2) Trustee.

(3) Originator contemplated by Item 1110 of this Regulation AB.

(4) Significant obligor contemplated by Item 1112 of this Regulation AB.

(5) Enhancement or support provider contemplated by Items 1114 or 1115 of this Regulation AB.

(6) Any other material parties related to the asset-backed securities contemplated by Item 1100(d)(1) of this Regulation AB.

(b) Describe whether there is, and if so the general character of, any business relationship, agreement, arrangement, transaction or understanding that is entered into outside the ordinary course of business or is on terms other than would be obtained in an arm's length transaction with an unrelated third party, apart from the asset-backed securities transaction, between the sponsor, depositor or issuing entity and any of the parties in paragraphs (a)(1) through (a)(6) of this section, or any affiliates of such parties, that currently exists or that existed during the past two years and that is material to an investor's understanding of the asset-backed securities.

Instruction to Item 1119(b). What is required is information material to an investor's understanding of the asset-backed securities. A detailed description or itemized listing of all commercial relationships among the parties is not required. Instead, the disclosure should indicate whether any relationships outside of the asset-backed securities transaction do exist that are outside the normal course and the general character of those relationships.

(c) Notwithstanding paragraph (b) of this section, describe, to the extent material, any specific relationships involving or relating to the asset-backed securities transaction or the pool assets, including the material terms and approximate dollar amount involved, between the sponsor, depositor or issuing entity and any of the parties in paragraphs (a)(1) through (a)(6) of this section, or any affiliates of such parties, that currently exists or that existed during the past two years.

Instruction to Item 1119. With respect to disclosure in an annual report on Form 10-K, information required by this Item 1119 may be omitted to the extent that substantially the same information had been provided previously in an annual report on Form 10-K (§ 249.310) for the asset-backed securities or in an effective registration statement under the Securities Act or a prospectus timely filed pursuant to

§ 230.424 of this chapter under the same Central Index Key (CIK) code as the current annual report on Form 10-K.

[As adopted in Release No. 33-8518, effective March 8, 2005 (Compliance dates are triggered by initial bona fide offer date or registration statement filing date and extend out to March 31, 2006. Complete compliance date details can be found in the "Dates" section of the release.), 70 F.R. 1506.]

[¶ 13,491] Ratings

Reg. § 229.1120 (Item 1120). Disclose whether the issuance or sale of any class of offered securities is conditioned on the assignment of a rating by one or more rating agencies, whether or not NRSROs. If so, identify each rating agency and the minimum rating that must be assigned. Describe any arrangements to have such rating monitored while the asset-backed securities are outstanding.

[As adopted in Release No. 33-8518, effective March 8, 2005 (Compliance dates are triggered by initial bona fide offer date or registration statement filing date and extend out to March 31, 2006. Complete compliance date details can be found in the "Dates" section of the release.), 70 F.R. 1506.]

[¶ 13,501] Distribution and pool performance information

Reg. § 229.1121 (Item 1121). (a) Describe the distribution for the related distribution period and the performance of the asset pool during the distribution period. Provide appropriate introductory and explanatory information to introduce any material terms, parties or abbreviations used (or a cross-reference to a Commission filing where such information may be found). Present statistical information in tabular or graphical format, if such presentation will aid understanding. While the material information regarding the related distribution and pool performance will vary depending on the nature of the transaction, such information may include, among other things:

(1) Any applicable record dates, accrual dates, determination dates for calculating distributions and actual distribution dates for the distribution period.

(2) Cash flows received and the sources thereof for distributions, fees and expenses (including portfolio yield, if applicable).

(3) Calculated amounts and distribution of the flow of funds for the period itemized by type and priority of payment, including:

(i) Fees or expenses accrued and paid, with an identification of the general purpose of such fees and the party receiving such fees or expenses.

(ii) Payments accrued or paid with respect to enhancement or other support identified in Item 1114 of this Regulation AB (such as insurance premiums or other enhancement maintenance fees), with an identification of the general purpose of such payments and the party receiving such payments.

(iii) Principal, interest and other distributions accrued and paid on the asset-backed securities by type and by class or series and any principal or interest shortfalls or carryovers.

(iv) The amount of excess cash flow or excess spread and the disposition of excess cash flow.

(4) Beginning and ending principal balances of the asset-backed securities.

(5) Interest rates applicable to the pool assets and the asset-backed securities, as applicable. Consider providing interest rate information for pool assets in appropriate distributional groups or incremental ranges.

(6) Beginning and ending balances of transaction accounts, such as reserve accounts, and material account activity during the period.

(7) Any amounts drawn on any credit enhancement or other support identified in Item 1114 of this Regulation AB, as applicable, and the amount of coverage remaining under any such enhancement, if known and applicable.

(8) Number and amount of pool assets at the beginning and ending of each period, and updated pool composition information, such as weighted average coupon, weighted average life, weighted average remaining term, pool factors and prepayment amounts. For asset-backed securities backed by leases where a portion of the securitized pool balance is attributable to residual values of the physical property underlying the leases, this information also would include turn-in rates and residual value realization rates.

(9) Delinquency and loss information for the period. In addition, describe any material changes to the information specified in Item 1100(b)(5) of this Regulation AB regarding the pool assets.

(10) Information on the amount, terms and general purpose of any advances made or reimbursed during the period, including the general use of funds advanced and the general source of funds for reimbursements.

(11) Any material modifications, extensions or waivers to pool asset terms, fees, penalties or payments during the distribution period or that have cumulatively become material over time.

(12) Material breaches of pool asset representations or warranties or transaction covenants.

(13) Information on ratio, coverage or other tests used for determining any early amortization, liquidation or other performance trigger and whether the trigger was met.

(14) Information regarding any new issuance of asset-backed securities backed by the same asset pool, any pool asset changes (other than in connection with a pool asset converting into cash in accordance with its terms), such as additions or removals in connection with a prefunding or revolving period and pool asset substitutions and repurchases (and purchase rates, if applicable), and cash flows available for future purchases, such as the balances of any prefunding or revolving accounts, if applicable. Disclose any material changes in the solicitation, credit-granting, underwriting, origination, acquisition or pool selection criteria or procedures, as applicable, used to originate, acquire or select the new pool assets.

(b) During a prefunding or revolving period, or if there has been a new issuance of asset-backed securities backed by the same pool under a master trust during the fiscal year of the issuing entity, provide the information required by Items 1110, 1111 and 1112 of this Regulation AB applied taking the revised pool composition into account in the Form 10-D report (§ 249.312 of this chapter) for the last required distribution of the fiscal year of the issuing entity. In addition, provide such updated information in the first Form 10-D report for the period in which the prefunding or revolving period ends (if applicable). However, no disclosure need be provided by this paragraph if the information has not materially changed from that previously provided in an Exchange Act report relating to the asset-backed securities or in an effective registration statement under the Securities Act or a prospectus timely filed pursuant to § 230.424 of this chapter under the same Central Index Key (CIK) code regarding a subsequent issuance of asset-backed securities backed by a pool of assets that includes the pool assets that are the subject of this paragraph.

[As adopted in Release No. 33-8518, effective March 8, 2005 (Compliance dates are triggered by initial bona fide offer date or registration statement filing date and extend out to March 31, 2006. Complete compliance date details can be found in the "Dates" section of the release.), 70 F.R. 1506.]

[¶ 13,515] Compliance with applicable servicing criteria

Reg. § 229.1122 (Item 1122). (a) *Reports on assessment of compliance with servicing criteria for asset-backed securities.* As required by paragraph (b) of § 240.13a-18 or 240.15d-18 of this chapter, provide as an exhibit from each party participating in the servicing function a report on an assessment of compliance with the servicing criteria set forth in paragraph (d) of this section that contains the following:

(1) A statement of the party's responsibility for assessing compliance with the servicing criteria applicable to it;

(2) A statement that the party used the criteria in paragraph (d) of this section to assess compliance with the applicable servicing criteria;

(3) The party's assessment of compliance with the applicable servicing criteria as of and for the period ending the end of the fiscal year covered by the Form 10-K report (§ 249.310 of this chapter). This discussion must include disclosure of any material instance of noncompliance identified by the party; and

(4) A statement that a registered public accounting firm has issued an attestation report on the party's assessment of compliance with the applicable servicing criteria as of and for the period ending the end of the fiscal year covered by the Form 10-K report.

(b) *Registered public accounting firm attestation reports.* Provide the registered public accounting firm's attestation report required by paragraph (c) of § 240.13a-18 or 240.15d-18 of this chapter on the party's assessment of compliance with the applicable servicing criteria as an exhibit.

(c) *Additional disclosure for the Form 10-K report.*

(1) If any party's report on assessment of compliance with servicing criteria required by paragraph (a) of this section, or related registered public accounting firm attestation report required by paragraph (b) of this section, identifies any material instance of noncompliance with the servicing criteria, identify the material instance of noncompliance in the report on Form 10-K.

(2) If any party's report on assessment of compliance with servicing criteria required by paragraph (a) of this section, or related registered public accounting firm attestation report required by paragraph (b) of this section, is not included as an exhibit to the Form 10-K report, disclosure that the report is not included and an associated explanation must be provided in the report on Form 10-K.

(d) *Servicing criteria.*

(1) *General servicing considerations.*

(i) Policies and procedures are instituted to monitor any performance or other triggers and events of default in accordance with the transaction agreements.

(ii) If any material servicing activities are outsourced to third parties, policies and procedures are instituted to monitor the third party's performance and compliance with such servicing activities.

(iii) Any requirements in the transaction agreements to maintain a back-up servicer for the pool assets are maintained.

(iv) A fidelity bond and errors and omissions policy is in effect on the party participating in the servicing function throughout the reporting period in the amount of coverage required by and otherwise in accordance with the terms of the transaction agreements.

(2) *Cash collection and administration.*

(i) Payments on pool assets are deposited into the appropriate custodial bank accounts and related bank clearing accounts no more than two business days of receipt, or such other number of days specified in the transaction agreements.

(ii) Disbursements made via wire transfer on behalf of an obligor or to an investor are made only by authorized personnel.

(iii) Advances of funds or guarantees regarding collections, cash flows or distributions, and any interest or other fees charged for such advances, are made, reviewed and approved as specified in the transaction agreements.

(iv) The related accounts for the transaction, such as cash reserve accounts or accounts established as a form of overcollateralization, are separately maintained (*e.g.*, with respect to commingling of cash) as set forth in the transaction agreements.

(v) Each custodial account is maintained at a federally insured depository institution as set forth in the transaction agreements. For purposes of this criterion, "federally insured depository institution" with respect to a foreign financial institution means a foreign financial institution that meets the requirements of § 240.13k-1(b)(1) of this chapter.

(vi) Unissued checks are safeguarded so as to prevent unauthorized access.

(vii) Reconciliations are prepared on a monthly basis for all asset-backed securities related bank accounts, including custodial accounts and related bank clearing accounts. These reconciliations:

(A) Are mathematically accurate;

(B) Are prepared within 30 calendar days after the bank statement cutoff date, or such other number of days specified in the transaction agreements;

(C) Are reviewed and approved by someone other than the person who prepared the reconciliation; and

(D) Contain explanations for reconciling items. These reconciling items are resolved within 90 calendar days of their original identification, or such other number of days specified in the transaction agreements.

(3) *Investor remittances and reporting.*

(i) Reports to investors, including those to be filed with the Commission, are maintained in accordance with the transaction agreements and applicable Commission requirements. Specifically, such reports:

(A) Are prepared in accordance with timeframes and other terms set forth in the transaction agreements;

(B) Provide information calculated in accordance with the terms specified in the transaction agreements;

(C) Are filed with the Commission as required by its rules and regulations; and

(D) Agree with investors' or the trustee's records as to the total unpaid principal balance and number of pool assets serviced by the servicer.

(ii) Amounts due to investors are allocated and remitted in accordance with timeframes, distribution priority and other terms set forth in the transaction agreements.

(iii) Disbursements made to an investor are posted within two business days to the servicer's investor records, or such other number of days specified in the transaction agreements.

(iv) Amounts remitted to investors per the investor reports agree with cancelled checks, or other form of payment, or custodial bank statements.

(4) *Pool asset administration.*

(i) Collateral or security on pool assets is maintained as required by the transaction agreements or related pool asset documents.

(ii) Pool assets and related documents are safeguarded as required by the transaction agreements.

(iii) Any additions, removals or substitutions to the asset pool are made, reviewed and approved in accordance with any conditions or requirements in the transaction agreements.

(iv) Payments on pool assets, including any payoffs, made in accordance with the related pool asset documents are posted to the applicable servicer's obligor records maintained no more than two business days after receipt, or such other number of days specified in the transaction agreements, and allocated to principal, interest or other items (*e.g.*, escrow) in accordance with the related pool asset documents.

(v) The servicer's records regarding the pool assets agree with the servicer's records with respect to an obligor's unpaid principal balance.

(vi) Changes with respect to the terms or status of an obligor's pool asset (*e.g.*, loan modifications or re-agings) are made, reviewed and approved by authorized personnel in accordance with the transaction agreements and related pool asset documents.

(vii) Loss mitigation or recovery actions (*e.g.*, forbearance plans, modifications and deeds in lieu of foreclosure, foreclosures and repossessions, as applicable) are initiated, conducted and concluded in accordance with the timeframes or other requirements established by the transaction agreements.

(viii) Records documenting collection efforts are maintained during the period a pool asset is delinquent in accordance with the transaction agreements. Such records are maintained on at least a monthly basis, or such other period specified in the transaction agreements, and describe the entity's activities in monitoring delinquent pool assets including, for example, phone calls, letters and payment rescheduling plans in cases where delinquency is deemed temporary (*e.g.*, illness or unemployment).

(ix) Adjustments to interest rates or rates of return for pool assets with variable rates are computed based on the related pool asset documents.

(x) Regarding any funds held in trust for an obligor (such as escrow accounts):

(A) Such funds are analyzed, in accordance with the obligor's pool asset documents, on at least an annual basis, or such other period specified in the transaction agreements;

(B) Interest on such funds is paid, or credited, to obligors in accordance with applicable pool asset documents and state laws; and

(C) Such funds are returned to the obligor within 30 calendar days of full repayment of the related pool asset, or such other number of days specified in the transaction agreements.

(xi) Payments made on behalf of an obligor (such as tax or insurance payments) are made on or before the related penalty or expiration dates, as indicated on the appropriate bills or notices for such payments, provided that such support has been received by the servicer at least 30 calendar days prior to these dates, or such other number of days specified in the transaction agreements.

(xii) Any late payment penalties in connection with any payment to be made on behalf of an obligor are paid from the servicer's funds and not charged to the obligor, unless the late payment was due to the obligor's error or omission.

(xiii) Disbursements made on behalf of an obligor are posted within two business days to the obligor's records maintained by the servicer, or such other number of days specified in the transaction agreements.

(xiv) Delinquencies, charge-offs and uncollectable accounts are recognized and recorded in accordance with the transaction agreements.

(xv) Any external enhancement or other support, identified in Item 1114(a)(1) through (3) or Item 1115 of this Regulation AB, is maintained as set forth in the transaction agreements.

Instructions to Item 1122.

1. If certain servicing criteria are not applicable to the asserting party based on the activities it performs with respect to asset-backed securities transactions taken as a whole involving such party and that are backed by the same asset type backing the class of asset-backed securities, the inapplicability of the criteria must be disclosed in that asserting party's and the related registered public accounting firm's reports.

2. If multiple parties are participating in the servicing function, a separate assessment report and attestation report must be included for each party participating in the servicing function. A party participating in the servicing function means any entity (*e.g.*, master servicer, primary servicers, trustees) that is performing activities that address the criteria in paragraph (d) of this section, unless such entity's activities relate only to 5% or less of the pool assets.

3. If the asset pool backing the asset-backed securities includes a pool asset representing an interest in or the right to the payments or cash flows of another asset pool and both the issuing entity for the asset-backed securities and the entity issuing the asset to be included in the issuing entity's asset pool were established under the direction of the same sponsor and depositor, see also Item 1100(d)(2) of this Regulation AB.

[As adopted in Release No. 33-8518, effective March 8, 2005 (Compliance dates are triggered by initial bona fide offer date or registration statement filing date and extend out to March 31, 2006. Complete compliance date details can be found in the "Dates" section of the release.), 70 F.R. 1506.]

[¶ 13,531] Servicer compliance statement

Reg. § 229.1123 (Item 1123). Provide as an exhibit a statement of compliance from the servicer, signed by an authorized officer of such servicer, to the effect that:

(a) A review of the servicer's activities during the reporting period and of its performance under the applicable servicing agreement has been made under such officer's supervision.

(b) To the best of such officer's knowledge, based on such review, the servicer has fulfilled all of its obligations under the agreement in all material respects throughout the reporting period or, if there has been a failure to fulfill any such obligation in any material respect, specifying each such failure known to such officer and the nature and status thereof.

Instruction to Item 1123. If multiple servicers are involved in servicing the pool assets, a separate servicer compliance statement is required from each servicer that meets the criteria in Item 1108(a)(2)(i) through (iii) of this Regulation AB.

[As adopted in Release No. 33-8518, effective March 8, 2005 (Compliance dates are triggered by initial bona fide offer date or registration statement filing date and extend out to March 31, 2006. Complete compliance date details can be found in the "Dates" section of the release.), 70 F.R. 1506.]

Subpart 229.1200—Disclosure by Registrants Engaged in Oil and Gas Producing Activities

[¶ 13,541] General Instructions to Oil and Gas Industry-Specific Disclosures

Reg. § 229.1201 (Item 1201). (a) If oil and gas producing activities are material to the registrant's or its subsidiaries' business operations or financial position, the disclosure specified in this Subpart 229.1200 should be included under appropriate captions (with cross references, where applicable, to related information disclosed in financial statements). However, limited partnerships and joint ventures that conduct, operate, manage, or report upon oil and gas drilling or income programs, that acquire properties either for drilling and production, or for production of oil, gas, or geothermal steam or water, need not include such disclosure.

(b) To the extent that Items 1202 through 1208 (§§ 229.1202 - 229.1208) call for disclosures in tabular format, as specified in the particular Item, a registrant may modify such format for ease of presentation, to add information or to combine two or more required tables.

(c) The definitions in Rule 4-10(a) of Regulation S-X (17 CFR 210.4-10(a)) shall apply for purposes of this Subpart 229.1200.

(d) For purposes of this Subpart 229.1200, the term by geographic area means, as appropriate for meaningful disclosure in the circumstances:

(1) By individual country;

(2) By groups of countries within a continent; or

(3) By continent.

[Added in Release No. 33-8995, effective January 1, 2010, 74 F.R. 2157.]

[¶ 13,542] Disclosure of Reserves

Reg. § 229.1202 (Item 1202). (a) *Summary of oil and gas reserves at fiscal year end.* (1) Provide the information specified in paragraph (a)(2) of this Item in tabular format as provided below:

Summary of Oil and Gas Reserves as of Fiscal-Year End Based on Average Fiscal-Year Prices

	Reserves				
	Oil	Natural Gas	Synthetic Oil	Synthetic Gas	Product A
Reserves category	(mbbls)	(mmcf)	(mbbls)	(mmcf)	(measure)
PROVED					
Developed					
Continent A					
Continent B					
Country A					
Country B					
Other Countries in Continent B					
Undeveloped					
Continent A					
Continent B					
Country A					
Country B					
Other Countries in Continent B					
TOTAL PROVED					

	Oil	Natural Gas	Synthetic Oil	Synthetic Gas	Product A
			Reserves		
PROBABLE					
Developed					
Undeveloped					
POSSIBLE					
Developed					
Undeveloped					

(2) Disclose, in the aggregate and by geographic area and for each country containing 15% or more of the registrant's proved reserves, expressed on an oil-equivalent-barrels basis, reserves estimated using prices and costs under existing economic conditions, for the product types listed in paragraph (a)(4) of this Item, in the following categories:

    (i) Proved developed reserves;

    (ii) Proved undeveloped reserves;

    (iii) Total proved reserves;

    (iv) Probable developed reserves (optional);

    (v) Probable undeveloped reserves (optional);

    (vi) Possible developed reserves (optional); and

    (vii) Possible undeveloped reserves (optional).

Instruction 1 to paragraph (a)(2): Disclose updated reserves tables as of the close of each fiscal year.

Instruction 2 to paragraph (a)(2): The registrant is permitted, but not required, to disclose probable or possible reserves pursuant to paragraphs (a)(2)(iv) through (a)(2)(vii) of this Item.

Instruction 3 to paragraph (a)(2): If the registrant discloses amounts of a product in barrels of oil equivalent, disclose the basis for such equivalency.

Instruction 4 to paragraph (a)(2): A registrant need not provide disclosure of the reserves in a country containing 15% or more of the registrant's proved reserves if that country's government prohibits disclosure of reserves in that country. In addition, a registrant need not provide disclosure of the reserves in a country containing 15% or more of the registrant's proved reserves if that country's government prohibits disclosure in a particular field and disclosure of reserves in that country would have the effect of disclosing reserves in particular fields.

(3) Reported total reserves shall be simple arithmetic sums of all estimates for individual properties or fields within each reserves category. When probabilistic methods are used, reserves should not be aggregated probabilistically beyond the field or property level; instead, they should be aggregated by simple arithmetic summation.

(4) Disclose separately material reserves of the following product types:

    (i) Oil;

    (ii) Natural gas;

    (iii) Synthetic oil;

    (iv) Synthetic gas; and

    (v) Sales products of other non-renewable natural resources that are intended to be upgraded into synthetic oil and gas.

(5) If the registrant discloses probable or possible reserves, discuss the uncertainty related to such reserves estimates.

(6) If the registrant has not previously disclosed reserves estimates in a filing with the Commission or is disclosing material additions to its reserves estimates, the registrant shall provide a general discussion of the technologies used to establish the appropriate level of certainty for reserves estimates from material properties included in the total reserves disclosed. The particular properties do not need to be identified.

(7) *Preparation of reserves estimates or reserves audit.* Disclose and describe the internal controls the registrant uses in its reserves estimation effort. In addition, disclose the qualifications of the technical person primarily responsible for overseeing the preparation of the reserves estimates and, if the registrant represents that a third party conducted a reserves audit, disclose the qualifications of the technical person primarily responsible for overseeing such reserves audit.

(8) *Third party reports.* If the registrant represents that a third party prepared, or conducted a reserves audit of, the registrant's reserves estimates, or any estimated valuation thereof, or conducted a process review, the registrant shall file a report of the third party as an exhibit to the relevant registration statement or other Commission filing. If the report relates to the preparation of, or a reserves audit of, the registrant's reserves estimates, it must include the following disclosure, if applicable to the type of filing:

(i) The purpose for which the report was prepared and for whom it was prepared;

(ii) The effective date of the report and the date on which the report was completed;

(iii) The proportion of the registrant's total reserves covered by the report and the geographic area in which the covered reserves are located;

(iv) The assumptions, data, methods, and procedures used, including the percentage of the registrant's total reserves reviewed in connection with the preparation of the report, and a statement that such assumptions, data, methods, and procedures are appropriate for the purpose served by the report;

(v) A discussion of primary economic assumptions;

(vi) A discussion of the possible effects of regulation on the ability of the registrant to recover the estimated reserves;

(vii) A discussion regarding the inherent uncertainties of reserves estimates;

(viii) A statement that the third party has used all methods and procedures as it considered necessary under the circumstances to prepare the report;

(ix) A brief summary of the third party's conclusions with respect to the reserves estimates; and

(x) The signature of the third party.

(9) For purposes of this Item 1202, the term *reserves audit* means the process of reviewing certain of the pertinent facts interpreted and assumptions underlying a reserves estimate prepared by another party and the rendering of an opinion about the appropriateness of the methodologies employed, the adequacy and quality of the data relied upon, the depth and thoroughness of the reserves estimation process, the classification of reserves appropriate to the relevant definitions used, and the reasonableness of the estimated reserves quantities.

(b) *Reserves sensitivity analysis (optional).* (1) The registrant may, but is not required to, provide the information specified in paragraph (b)(2) of this Item in tabular format as provided below:

Sensitivity of Reserves to Prices By Principal Product Type and Price Scenario

Price Case	Proved Reserves					Probable Reserves					Possible Reserves				
	Oil	Gas	Syn. Oil	Syn. Gas	Product A	Oil	Gas	Syn. Oil	Syn. Gas	Product A	Oil	Gas	Syn. Oil	Syn Gas	Product A
	mbbls	mmcf	mbbls	mmcf	measure	mbbls	mmcf	mbbls	mmcf	measure	mbbls	mmcf	mbbls	mmcf	measure
Scenario 1															
Scenario 2															

(2) The registrant may, but is not required to, disclose, in the aggregate, an estimate of reserves estimated for each product type based on different price and cost criteria, such as a range of prices and costs that may reasonably be achieved, including standardized futures prices or management's own forecasts.

(3) If the registrant provides disclosure under this paragraph (b), disclose the price and cost schedules and assumptions on which the disclosed values are based.

Instruction to Item 1202: Estimates of oil or gas resources other than reserves, and any estimated values of such resources, shall not be disclosed in any document publicly filed with the Commission, unless such information is required to be disclosed in the document by foreign or state law; provided, however, that where such estimates previously have been provided to a person (or any of its affiliates) that is offering to acquire, merge, or consolidate with the registrant or otherwise to acquire the registrant's securities, such estimate may be included in documents related to such acquisition.

[Added in Release No. 33-8995, effective January 1, 2010, 74 F.R. 2157.]

[¶ 13,543] Proved Undeveloped Reserves

Reg. § 229.1203 (Item 1203). (a) Disclose the total quantity of proved undeveloped reserves at year end.

(b) Disclose material changes in proved undeveloped reserves that occurred during the year, including proved undeveloped reserves converted into proved developed reserves.

(c) Discuss investments and progress made during the year to convert proved undeveloped reserves to proved developed reserves, including, but not limited to, capital expenditures.

(d) Explain the reasons why material amounts of proved undeveloped reserves in individual fields or countries remain undeveloped for five years or more after disclosure as proved undeveloped reserves.

[Added in Release No. 33-8995, effective January 1, 2010, 74 F.R. 2157.]

[¶ 13,544] Oil and Gas Production, Production Prices and Production Costs

Reg. § 229.1204 (Item 1204). (a) For each of the last three fiscal years disclose production, by final product sold, of oil, gas, and other products. Disclosure shall be made by geographical area and for each country and field that contains 15% or more of the registrant's total proved reserves expressed on an oil-equivalent-barrels basis unless prohibited by the country in which the reserves are located.

(b) For each of the last three fiscal years disclose, by geographical area:

(1) The average sales price (including transfers) per unit of oil, gas and other products produced; and

(2) The average production cost, not including ad valorem and severance taxes, per unit of production.

Instruction 1 to Item 1204: Generally, net production should include only production that is owned by the registrant and produced to its interest, less royalties and production due others. However, in special situations (*e.g.*, foreign production) net production before any royalties may be provided, if more appropriate. If "net before royalty" production figures are furnished, the change from the usage of "net production" should be noted.

Instruction 2 to Item 1204: Production of natural gas should include only marketable production of natural gas on an "as sold" basis. Production will include dry, residue, and wet gas, depending on whether liquids have been extracted before the registrant transfers title. Flared gas, injected gas, and gas consumed in operations should be omitted. Recovered gas-lift gas and reproduced gas should not be included until sold. Synthetic gas, when marketed as such, should be included in natural gas sales.

Instruction 3 to Item 1204: If any product, such as bitumen, is sold or custody is transferred prior to conversion to synthetic oil or gas, the product's production, transfer prices, and production costs should be disclosed separately from all other products.

Instruction 4 to Item 1204: The transfer price of oil and gas (natural and synthetic) produced should be determined in accordance with SFAS 69.

Instruction 5 to Item 1204: The average production cost, not including ad valorem and severance taxes, per unit of production should be computed using production costs disclosed pursuant to SFAS 69. Units of production should be expressed in common units of production with oil, gas, and other products converted to a common unit of measure on the basis used in computing amortization.

[Added in Release No. 33-8995, effective January 1, 2010, 74 F.R. 2157.]

[¶ 13,545] Drilling and Other Exploratory and Development Activities

Reg. § 229.1205 (Item 1205). (a) For each of the last three fiscal years, by geographical area, disclose:

(1) The number of net productive and dry exploratory wells drilled; and

(2) The number of net productive and dry development wells drilled.

(b) *Definitions.* For purposes of this Item 1205, the following terms shall be defined as follows:

(1) A *dry well* is an exploratory, development, or extension well that proves to be incapable of producing either oil or gas in sufficient quantities to justify completion as an oil or gas well.

(2) A *productive well* is an exploratory, development, or extension well that is not a dry well.

(3) *Completion* refers to installation of permanent equipment for production of oil or gas, or, in the case of a dry well, to reporting to the appropriate authority that the well has been abandoned.

(4) The *number of wells drilled* refers to the number of wells completed at any time during the fiscal year, regardless of when drilling was initiated.

(c) Disclose, by geographic area, for each of the last three years, any other exploratory or development activities conducted, including implementation of mining methods for purposes of oil and gas producing activities.

[Added in Release No. 33-8995, effective January 1, 2010, 74 F.R. 2157.]

[¶ 13,546] Present Activities

Reg. § 229.1206 (Item 1206). (a) Disclose, by geographical area, the registrant's present activities, such as the number of wells in the process of being drilled (including wells temporarily suspended), waterfloods in process of being installed, pressure maintenance operations, and any other related activities of material importance.

(b) Provide the description of present activities as of a date at the end of the most recent fiscal year or as close to the date that the registrant files the document as reasonably possible.

(c) Include only those wells in the process of being drilled at the "as of" date and express them in terms of both gross and net wells.

(d) Do not include wells that the registrant plans to drill, but has not commenced drilling unless there are factors that make such information material.

[Added in Release No. 33-8995, effective January 1, 2010, 74 F.R. 2157.]

[¶ 13,547] Delivery Commitments

Reg. § 229.1207 (Item 1207). (a) If the registrant is committed to provide a fixed and determinable quantity of oil or gas in the near future under existing contracts or agreements, disclose material information concerning the estimated availability of oil and gas from any principal sources, including the following:

(1) The principal sources of oil and gas that the registrant will rely upon and the total amounts that the registrant expects to receive from each principal source and from all sources combined;

(2) The total quantities of oil and gas that are subject to delivery commitments; and

(3) The steps that the registrant has taken to ensure that available reserves and supplies are sufficient to meet such commitments for the next one to three years.

(b) Disclose the information required by this Item:

(1) In a form understandable to investors; and

(2) Based upon the facts and circumstances of the particular situation, including, but not limited to:

(i) Disclosure by geographic area;

(ii) Significant supplies dedicated or contracted to the registrant;

(iii) Any significant reserves or supplies subject to priorities or curtailments which may affect quantities delivered to certain classes of customers, such as customers receiving services under low priority and interruptible contracts;

(iv) Any priority allocations or price limitations imposed by Federal or State regulatory agencies, as well as other factors beyond the registrant's control that may affect the registrant's ability to meet its contractual obligations (the registrant need not provide detailed discussions of price regulation);

(v) Any other factors beyond the registrant's control, such as other parties having control over drilling new wells, competition for the acquisition of reserves and supplies, and the availability of foreign reserves and supplies, which may affect the registrant's ability to acquire additional reserves and supplies or to maintain or increase the availability of reserves and supplies; and

(vi) Any impact on the registrant's earnings and financing needs resulting from its inability to meet short-term or long-term contractual obligations. (See Items 303 and 1209 of Regulation S-K (§§ 229.303 and 229.1209).)

(c) If the registrant has been unable to meet any significant delivery commitments in the last three years, describe the circumstances concerning such events and their impact on the registrant.

(d) For purposes of this Item, *available reserves* are estimates of the amounts of oil and gas which the registrant can produce from current proved developed reserves using presently installed equipment under existing economic and operating conditions and an estimate of amounts that others can deliver to the registrant under long-term contracts or agreements on a per-day, per-month, or per-year basis.

[Added in Release No. 33-8995, effective January 1, 2010, 74 F.R. 2157.]

[¶ 13,548] Oil and Gas Properties, Wells, Operations, and Acreage

Reg. § 229.1208 (Item 1208). (a) Disclose, as of a reasonably current date or as of the end of the fiscal year, the total gross and net productive wells, expressed separately for oil and gas (including synthetic oil and gas produced through wells) and the total gross and net developed acreage (*i.e.*, acreage assignable to productive wells) by geographic area.

(b) Disclose, as of a reasonably current date or as of the end of the fiscal year, the amount of undeveloped acreage, both leases and concessions, if any, expressed in both gross and net acres by geographic area, together with an indication of acreage concentrations, and, if material, the minimum remaining terms of leases and concessions.

(c) *Definitions.* For purposes of this Item 1208, the following terms shall be defined as indicated:

(1) A *gross well or acre* is a well or acre in which the registrant owns a working interest. The number of gross wells is the total number of wells in which the registrant owns a working interest. Count one or more completions in the same bore hole as one well. In a footnote, disclose the number of wells with multiple completions. If one of the multiple completions in a well is an oil completion, classify the well as an oil well.

(2) A *net well or acre* is deemed to exist when the sum of fractional ownership working interests in gross wells or acres equals one. The number of net wells or acres is the sum of the fractional working interests owned in gross wells or acres expressed as whole numbers and fractions of whole numbers.

(3) *Productive wells* include producing wells and wells mechanically capable of production.

(4) *Undeveloped acreage* encompasses those leased acres on which wells have not been drilled or completed to a point that would permit the production of economic quantities of oil or gas regardless of whether such acreage contains proved reserves. Do not confuse undeveloped acreage with undrilled acreage held by production under the terms of the lease.

[Added in Release No. 33-8995, effective January 1, 2010, 74 F.R. 2157.]

REGULATION S-T

REGULATION S-T

TABLE OF CONTENTS

Regulation S-T

PART 232—GENERAL RULES AND REGULATIONS FOR ELECTRONIC FILINGS

Subpart 232.1—General

[¶ 14,001] Application of Part 232

Reg. § 232.10. (a) This part, in conjunction with the EDGAR Filer Manual and the electronic filing provisions of applicable rules, regulations and forms, shall govern the electronic submission of documents filed or otherwise submitted to the Commission and shall be controlling for an electronic format document in the manner and respects provided herein.

(b) Each registrant, third party filer, or agent to whom the Commission previously has not assigned a Central Index Key (CIK) code, must, before filing on EDGAR:

(1) File electronically the information required by Form ID (§§ 239.63, 249.446, 269.7 and 274.402 of this chapter), the uniform application form for access codes to file on EDGAR, and

(2) File, by uploading as a Portable Document Format (PDF) attachment to the Form ID filing or by faxing to (202) 504-2474 or (703) 914-4240 within two business days before or after the electronic Form ID filing, a notarized document, manually signed by the applicant over the applicant's typed signature, that includes the information required to be included in the Form ID filing, confirms the authenticity of the Form ID filing and, if filed by fax after the electronic Form D filing, includes the accession number assigned to the electronic Form ID filing.

Note: The Commission strongly urges any person or entity about to become subject to the disclosure and filing requirements of the federal securities laws to submit a Form ID well in advance of the first required filing, including a registration statement relating to an initial public offering, in order to facilitate electronic filing on a timely basis.

[As last amended in Release No. 33-9013, effective March 16, 2009, 74 F.R. 10836.]

[¶ 14,002] Definition of Terms Used in Part 232

Reg. § 232.11. Unless otherwise specifically provided, the terms used in Regulation S-T (Part 232 of this chapter) have the same meanings as in the federal securities laws and the rules, regulations and forms promulgated thereunder. In addition, the following definitions of terms apply specifically to electronic format documents and shall apply wherever they appear in laws, rules, regulations and forms governing such documents, unless the context otherwise specifies:

Animated graphics. The term *animated graphics* means text or images that do not remain static but that may move when viewed in a browser.

ASCII document. The term *ASCII document* means an electronic text document with contents limited to American Standard Code for Information Interchange (ASCII) characters and that is tagged with Standard Generalized Mark Up Language (SGML) tags in the format required for ASCII/SGML documents by the EDGAR Filer Manual.

Business development company. The term *business development company* has the meaning set forth in Section 2(a)(48) of the Investment Company Act.

Direct transmission. The term *direct transmission* means the transmission of one or more electronic submissions via a telephonic communication session.

Disruptive code. The term *disruptive code* means any active content or other executable code, or any program or set of electronic computer instructions inserted into a computer, operating system, or program that replicates itself or that actually or potentially modifies or in any way alters, damages, destroys or disrupts the file content or the operation of any computer, computer file, computer database, computer system, computer network or software, and as otherwise set forth in the EDGAR Filer Manual.

EDGAR. The term *EDGAR* (Electronic Data Gathering, Analysis, and Retrieval) means the computer system for the receipt, acceptance, review and dissemination of documents submitted in electronic format.

EDGAR Filer Manual. The term *EDGAR Filer Manual* means the current version of the manual prepared by the Commission setting out the technical format requirements for an electronic submission.

Note: See Rule 301 of Regulation S-T (§ 232.301).

Electronic document. The term *electronic document* means the portion of an electronic submission separately tagged as an individual document in the format required by the EDGAR Filer Manual.

Electronic filer. The term *electronic filer* means a person or an entity that submits filings electronically pursuant to Rules 100 and 101 of Regulation S-T (§§ 232.100 and 232.101, respectively).

Electronic filing. The term *electronic filing* means one or more electronic documents filed under the federal securities laws that are transmitted or delivered to the Commission in electronic format.

Electronic format. The term *electronic format* means the computerized format of a document prepared in accordance with the EDGAR Filer Manual.

Electronic submission. The term *electronic submission* means any document, such as a filing, correspondence, or modular submission, or any discrete set of documents, transmitted or delivered to the Commission in electronic format.

Exchange Act. The term *Exchange Act* means the Securities Exchange Act of 1934.

Executable code. The term *executable code* means instructions to a computer to carry out operations that use features beyond the viewer's, reader's, or Internet browser's native ability to interpret and display HTML, PDF, and static graphic files. Such code may be in binary (machine language) or in script form. Executable code includes disruptive code.

HTML document. The term *HTML document* means an electronic text document tagged with HyperText Markup Language tags in the format required by the EDGAR Filer Manual.

Header information. The term *header information* means information designated by the EDGAR Filer Manual to precede the text of each electronic submission and document submitted therewith via EDGAR that identifies characteristics of the submission and documents in order to facilitate electronic processing by the EDGAR system.

Hypertext links or hyperlinks. The term *hypertext links or hyperlinks* means the representation of an Internet address in a form that an Internet browser application can recognize as an Internet address.

Interactive Data File. The term *Interactive Data File* means the machine-readable computer code that presents information in eXtensible Business Reporting Language (XBRL) electronic format pursuant to § 232.405.

Investment Company Act. The term *Investment Company Act* means the Investment Company Act of 1940.

Modular submission. The term *modular submission* means an electronic submission that contains one or more documents, or portions of a document, submitted for storage in the non-public EDGAR data storage area for purposes of subsequent inclusion in one or more electronic filings pursuant to Rule 501(a) of Regulation S-T (§ 232.501(a) of this chapter).

Official filing. The term *official filing* means any filing that is received and accepted by the Commission, regardless of filing medium and exclusive of header information, tags and any other technical information required in an electronic filing; except that electronic identification of investment company type and inclusion of identifiers for series and class (or contract, in the case of separate accounts of insurance companies) as required by rule 313 of Regulation S-T (§ 232.313) are deemed part of the official filing.

Original. The term *original*, when used or implied in the securities laws, rules, regulations or forms, includes the writing itself or any counterpart intended to have the same effect by a person executing or issuing it. If data are stored in a computer or similar device, any printout or other output readable by sight, shown to reflect the data accurately, is an original.

Paper format. The term *paper format* means a paper document.

Promptly. The term *Promptly* means as soon as reasonably practicable under the facts and circumstances at the time. An amendment to the Interactive Data File made by the later of 24 hours or 9:30 a.m. Eastern Standard Time or Eastern Daylight Saving Time, whichever is currently in effect, on the next business day after the electronic filer becomes aware of the need for such amendment shall be deemed to be "promptly" made.

Public Utility Act. The term *Public Utility Act* means the Public Utility Holding Company Act of 1935.

Registrant. The term *registrant* means an issuer of securities for which a Securities Act registration statement is required to be filed and/or an issuer of securities with respect to which an Exchange Act registration statement or report is required to be filed and/or an investment company required to file an Investment Company Act registration statement or report.

Related Official Filing. The term *Related Official Filing* means the ASCII or HTML format part of the official filing with which an Interactive Data File appears as an exhibit or, in the case of a filing on Form N-1A, the ASCII or HTML format part of an official filing that contains the information to which an Interactive Data File corresponds.

Securities Act. The term *Securities Act* means the Securities Act of 1933.

Segmented Filing. The term *segmented filing* means an electronic format document assembled from segments previously submitted to the non-public EDGAR data storage for one-time inclusion in an electronic filing pursuant to Rule 501(b) of Regulation S-T (§ 232.501(b) of this chapter).

Tag. The term *tag* means an identifier that highlights specific information to EDGAR that is in the format required by the EDGAR Filer Manual.

Third party filer. The term *third party filer* means any person or entity that files documents with the Commission with respect to another entity.

Trust Indenture Act. The term *Trust Indenture Act* means the Trust Indenture Act of 1939.

Unofficial PDF copy. The term *unofficial PDF copy* means an optional copy of an electronic document that may be included in an EDGAR submission tagged as a Portable Document Format document in the format required by the EDGAR Filer Manual and submitted in accordance with Rule 104 of Regulation S-T (§ 232.104).

XBRL-Related Documents. The term *XBRL-Related Documents* means documents related to presenting information in eXtensible Business Reporting Language that are part of a voluntary submission in electronic format in accordance with § 232.401.

[As last amended by Release No. 33-9002, effective April 13, 2009, 74 F.R. 6776 and further amended by Release No. 33-9006, effective July 15, 2009, 74 F.R. 7748 (see the release for more detailed compliance information).]

[¶ 14,003] Business Hours of the Commission

Reg. § 232.12. (a) *General.* The principal office of the Commission, at 100 F Street, NE, Washington, D.C. 20549, is open each day, except Saturdays, Sundays, and federal holidays, from 9:00 a.m. to 5:30 p.m., Eastern Standards Time or Eastern Daylight Saving Time, whichever is currently in effect, *provided that* hours for the filing of documents pursuant to the Acts or the rules and regulations thereunder are as set forth in paragraphs (b) and (c) of this section.

(b) *Submissions made in paper.* Filers may submit paper documents filed with or otherwise furnished to the Commission each day, except Saturdays, Sundays and federal holidays, from 8 a.m. to 5:30 p.m., Eastern Standard Time or Eastern Daylight Saving Time, whichever is currently in effect.

(c) *Submissions by direct transmission.* Electronic filings and other documents may be submitted by direct transmission, via dial-up modem or Internet, to the Commission each day, except Saturdays, Sundays and federal holidays, from 8 a.m. to 10 p.m., Eastern Standard Time or Eastern Daylight Saving Time, whichever is currently in effect.

[As last amended in Release No. 34-57877, effective June 5, 2008, 73 F.R. 32222 (technical amendment).]

⋙→ *CCH Note: The SEC has stayed the effectiveness of proxy rule amendments adopted in Release 33-9136 pending resolution of a challenge filed by the Business Roundtable and the U.S. Chamber of Commerce in the U.S. Court of Appeals for the District of Columbia Circuit. See Release No. 33-9149, October 4, 2010.*

⋙→ *Amended by Release No. 33-9136, effective November 15, 2010, 75 F.R. 56668.*

[¶ 14,004] Date of Filing; Adjustment of Filing date

Reg. § 232.13. (a) *General.* (1) Except as provided in paragraph (b) of this section, the business day on which a filing is received by the Commission shall be the date of filing thereof, if:

(i) all requirements of the Acts and rules applicable to such filing have been complied with;

(ii) the filing conforms to the applicable technical standards regarding electronic format in the EDGAR Filer Manual; and

(iii) with respect to Securities Act filings including filings under section 24(f) of the Investment Company Act (15 U.S.C. 80a-24(f)), the required fee payment has been confirmed, *provided that* the failure to pay an insignificant amount of the fee at the time of the filing, as a result of a *bona fide* error, shall not affect the date of filing.

(2) If the conditions of paragraph (a)(1) of this section are otherwise satisfied, all filings submitted by direct transmission commencing on or before 5:30 p.m. Eastern Standard Time or Eastern Daylight Saving Time, whichever is currently in effect, shall be deemed filed on the same business day, and all filings submitted by direct transmission commencing after 5:30 p.m. Eastern Standard Time or Eastern Daylight Saving Time, whichever is currently in effect, shall be deemed filed as of the next business day.

(3) Notwithstanding paragraph (a)(2) of this section, any registration statement or any post-effective amendment thereto filed pursuant to Rule 462(b) (§ 230.462(b) of this chapter) by direct transmission commencing on or before 10:00 p.m. Eastern Standard Time or Eastern Daylight Savings Time, whichever is currently in effect, shall be deemed filed on the same business day.

(4) Notwithstanding paragraph (a)(2) of this section, a Form 3, 4 or 5 (§§ 249.103, 249.104 and 249.105 of this chapter) submitted by direct transmission on or before 10 p.m. Eastern Standard Time or Eastern Daylight Saving Time, whichever is currently in effect, shall be deemed filed on the same business day.

Amendment

(4) Notwithstanding paragraph (a)(2) of this section, a Form 3, 4 or 5 (§§ 249.103, 249.104, and 249.105 of this chapter) or a Schedule 14N (§ 240.14n-101 of this chapter) submitted by direct

transmission on or before 10 p.m. Eastern Standard Time or Eastern Daylight Saving Time, whichever is currently in effect, shall be deemed filed on the same business day.

End of Amendment

    Note: Electronic filings that have an automatic or immediate effective date must be deemed filed, as provided in paragraph (a) of this section, before any waiting period for automatic effectiveness commences or before the filing becomes immediately effective, whichever applies.

    (b) *Adjustment of the filing date.* In an electronic filer in good faith attempts to file a document with the Commission in a timely manner but the filing is delayed due to technical difficulties beyond the electronic filer's control, the electronic filer may request an adjustment of the filing date of such document. The Commission, or other staff acting pursuant to the delegated authority, may grant the request if it appears that such adjustments is appropriate and consistent with the public interest and the protection of investors.

    (c) *Payment of fees.* Fees required with respect to a filing that is submitted electronically shall be paid in accordance with the procedures set forth in Instructions for Filing Fees—Rule 3a of the Commission's Informal and Other Procedures (§ 202.3a of this chapter).

    Note. All filing fees paid by electronic filers must be submitted to the lockbox depository, as provided in Rule 3a, including those pertaining to documents filed in paper pursuant to a hardship exemption.

    (d) Where the Commission's rules, schedules and forms provide that a document may be filed on the same day it is published, furnished, sent or given to security holders or others, an electronic filer may file the document with the Commission electronically before or on the date the document is published, furnished, sent or given, or if such publication or distribution does not occur during official business hours of the Commission, as soon as practicable on the next business day. Any associated time periods shall be calculated on the basis of the publication or distribution date (as applicable), and not on the basis of the date of filing.

    [As last amended in Release No. 33-9136, effective November 15, 2010, 75 F.R. 56668, stayed by Release No. 33-9149, October 4, 2010.]

[¶ 14,005] Paper Filings Not Accepted Without Exemption

    Reg. § 232.14. The Commission will not accept in paper format any filing required to be submitted electronically under Rules 100 and 101 of Regulation S-T (§ § 232.100 and 232.101 respectively), unless the filing satisfies the requirements for a temporary or continuing hardship exemption under Rule 201 or 202 of Regulation S-T (§ § 232.201 or 232.202 respectively).

    [As adopted in Release No. 33-7472, October 24, 1997, effective January 1, 1998, 62 F.R. 58647.]

Subpart 232.100—Electronic Filing Requirements

[¶ 14,010] Persons and Entities Subject to Mandated Electronic Filing

    Reg. § 232.100. The following persons or entities shall be subject to the electronic filing requirements of this Part 232:

    (a) Registrants and other entities whose filings are subject to review by the Division of Corporation Finance;

    (b) Registrants whose filings are subject to review by the Division of Investment Management;

    (c) Persons or entities whose filings are subject to review by the Division of Market Regulation; and

    (d) Any party (including natural persons) that files a document jointly with, or as a third party filer with respect to, a person or entity that is subject to mandated electronic filing requirements.

    [As last amended in Release No. 33-8891, effective September 15, 2008, 73 F.R. 10592.]

[¶ 14,011] Mandated Electronic Submissions and Exceptions

    Reg. § 232.101. (a) *Mandated electronic submissions.* (1) The following filings, including any related correspondence and supplemental information, except as otherwise provided, shall be submitted in electronic format:

    (a) *Mandated electronic submissions.* (1) The following filings, including any related correspondence and supplemental information, except as otherwise provided, shall be submitted in electronic format:

    (i) Registration statements and prospectuses filed pursuant to the Securities Act (15 U.S.C. 77a, *et seq.*) or registration statements filed pursuant to Sections 12(b) or 12(g) of the Exchange Act (15 U.S.C. 78*l*(b) or (g));

    (ii) Statements and applications filed with the Commission pursuant to the Trust Indenture Act (15 U.S.C. 77aaa, *et seq.*), other than applications for exemptive relief filed pursuant to Section 304 (15 U.S.C. 77ddd) and Section 310 (15 U.S.C. 77jjj) of that Act;

(iii) Statements, reports and schedules filed with the Commission pursuant to sections 13, 14, 15(d) or 16(a) of the Exchange Act (15 U.S.C. 78m, 78n, 78o(d) and 78p(a)), and proxy materials required to be furnished for the information of the Commission in connection with annual reports on Form 10-K (§ 249.310 of this chapter), or Form 10-KSB (§ 249.310b of this chapter) filed pursuant to section 15(d) of the Exchange Act.

Note 1. Electronic filers filing Schedules 13D and 13G with respect to foreign private issuers should include in the submission header all zeroes (i.e., 00-0000000) for the IRS tax identification number because the EDGAR system requires an IRS number tag to be inserted for the subject company as a prerequisite to acceptance of the filing.

Note 2. Foreign private issuers must file or submit their Form 6-K reports (249.306 of this chapter) in electronic format, except as otherwise permitted by paragraphs (b)(1) and (b)(7) of this section.

(iv) Documents filed with the Commission pursuant to sections 8, 17, 20, 23(c), 24(b), 24(e), 24(f), and 30 of the Investment Company Act (15 U.S.C. 80a-8, 80a-17, 80a-20, 80a-23(c), 80a-24(b), 80a-24(e), 80a-24(f), and 80a-29); *provided, however* that submissions under section 6(c) of that Act (15 U.S.C. 80a-6(c)) and documents related to applications for exemptive relief under any section of that Act, shall not be made in electronic format;

(v) Documents filed with the Commission pursuant to the Public Utility Act (15 U.S.C. 79a *et seq.*);

(iv) Documents filed with the Commission pursuant to sections 8, 17, 20, 23(c), 24(b), 24(e), 24(f), and 30 of the Investment Company Act (15 U.S.C. 80a-8, 80a-17, 80a-20, 80a-23(c), 80a-24(b), 80a-24(e), 80a-24(f), and 80a-29) and any application for an order under any section of the Investment Company Act (15 U.S. C. 80a-1 *et seq.)*;

(v) Documents relating to offerings exempt from registration under the Securities Act filed with the Commission pursuant to Regulation E (§ § 230.601 - 230.610a of this chapter);

(vi) Form CB (§ § 239.800 and 249.480 of this chapter) filed or submitted under § 230.801 or 230.802 of this chapter or § 240.13e-4(h)(8), 240.14d-1(c), or 240.14e-2(d) of this chapter;

(vii) Form F-X (§ 239.42 of this chapter) when filed in connection with a Form CB (§ § 239.800 and 249.480 of this chapter);

(viii) Form F-N (§ 239.43 of this chapter) filed by foreign banks and insurance companies and certain of their holding companies and finance subsidiaries under § 230.489 of this chapter;

(ix) Form ID (§ § 239.63, 249.446, 269.7 and 274.402 of this chapter), except that the authenticating document required by Rule 10(b) of Regulation S-T (§ 232.10(b)) may be filed either in electronic format as an uploaded Portable Document Format (PDF) attachment to the Form ID filing or by fax as provided in that rule, and other related correspondence and supplemental information submitted after the Form ID filing shall not be submitted in electronic format.

(x) Form 25 (§ 249.25 of this chapter);

(xi) Form TA-1 (§ 249.100 of this chapter), Form TA-2 (§ 249.102 of this chapter), and Form TA-W (§ 249.101 of this chapter);

(xii) Forms 15 and 15F (§ 249.323 and § 249.324 of this chapter); and

(xiii) Form D (§ 239.500 of this chapter).

(2) The following amendments to filings and applications, including any related correspondence and supplemental information except as otherwise provided, shall be submitted as follows:

(i) Any amendment to a filing or application submitted by or relating to a registrant or an applicant that is required to file electronically, including any amendment to a paper filing or application, shall be submitted in electronic format;

(ii) The first electronic amendment to a paper format Schedule 13D (§ 240.13d-101 of this chapter) or Schedule 13G (§ 240.13d-102 of this chapter), shall restate the entire text of the Schedule 13D or 13G, but previously filed paper exhibits to such Schedules are not required to be restated electronically. See Rule 102 (§ 232.102) regarding amendments to exhibits previously filed in paper format. Notwithstanding the foregoing, if the sole purpose of filing the first electronic Schedule 13D or 13G amendment is to report a change in beneficial ownership that would terminate the filer's obligation to report, the amendment need not include a restatement of the entire text of the Schedule being amended.

(3) Supplemental information, including documents related to applications under any section of the Investment Company Act, shall be submitted in electronic format except as provided in paragraph (c)(2) of this section. The information shall be stored in the non-public EDGAR date storage area as correspondence. Supplemental information that is submitted in electronic format shall not be returned.

Note: Failure to submit a required electronic filing pursuant to this paragraph (a), as well as any required confirming electronic copy of a paper filing made in reliance on a hardship exemption, as provided in Rules 201 and 202 of Regulation S-T (§ § 232.201 and 232.202), will result in ineligibility to use Forms S-2, S-3, S-8, F-2 and F-3 (*see* § 239.12, 239.13, 239.16b, 239.32 and 239.33 of this chapter, respectively), restrict incorporation by reference of the document submitted in paper (*see* Rule 303 of

Regulation S-T [§ 232.303]), or toll certain time periods associated with tender offers (*see* Rule 13e-4(f)(12) [§ 240.13e-4(f)(12) of this chapter] and Rule 14e-1(e) [§ 240.14e-1(e) of this chapter]).

(b) *Permitted electronic submissions.* The following documents may be submitted to the Commission in electronic format, at the option of the electronic filer:

(1) Annual reports to security holders furnished for the information of the Commission under § 240.14a-3(c) of this chapter or § 240.14c-3(b) of this chapter, under the requirements of Form 10-K or Form 10-KSB (§ § 249.310 or 249.310b of this chapter) filed by registrants under Exchange Act Section 15(d) (15 U.S.C. 78o(d)), or by foreign private issuers filed on Form 6-K (§ 249.306 of this chapter) under § 240.13a-16 of this chapter or § 240.15d-16 of this chapter;

(2) Notices of exempt solicitation furnished for the information of the Commission pursuant to Rule 14a-6(g) (§ 240.14a-6(g) of this chapter) and notices of exempt preliminary roll-up communications furnished for the information of the Commission pursuant to Rule 14a-6(n) (§ 240.14a-6(n) of this chapter);

(3) Form 11-K (§ 249.311 of this chapter). Registrants who satisfy their Form 11-K filing obligations by filing amendments to Forms 10-K or 10-KSB, as provided by Rule 15d-21 (§ 240.15d-21 of this chapter), also may choose to file such amendments in paper or electronic format:

(4) Form 144 (§ 239.144 of this chapter), where the issuer of the securities is subject to the reporting requirements of Section 13 or 15(d) of the Exchange Act (15 U.S.C. 78m or 78o(d), respectively);

(5) Periodic reports and reports with respect to distributions of primary obligations filed by:

(i) The International Bank for Reconstruction and Development under Section 15(a) of the Bretton Woods Agreements Act (22 U.S.C. 286k-1(a)) and Part 285 of this chapter;

(ii) The Inter-American Development Bank under Section 11(a) of the Inter-American Development Bank Act (22 U.S.C. 283h(a)) and Part 286 of this chapter;

(iii) The Asian Development Bank under Section 11(a) of the Asian Development Bank Act (22 U.S.C. 285h(a)) and Part 287 of this chapter;

(iv) The African Development Bank under Section 9(a) of the African Development Bank Act (22 U.S.C. 290i-9(a)) and Part 288 of this chapter;

(v) The International Finance Corporation under Section 13(a) of the International Finance Corporation Act (22 U.S.C. 282k(a)) and Part 289 of this chapter; and

(vi) The European Bank for Reconstruction and Development under Section 9(a) of the European Bank for Reconstruction and Development Act (22 U.S.C. 290*l*-7(a)) and Part 290 of this chapter;

(6) A report or other document submitted by a foreign private issuer under cover of Form 6-K (§ 249.306 of this chapter) that the issuer must furnish and make public under the laws of the jurisdiction in which the issuer is incorporated, domiciled or legally organized (the foreign private issuer's "home country"), or under the rules of the home country exchange on which the issuer's securities are traded, as long as the report or other document is not a press release, is not required to be and has not been distributed to the issuer's security holders, and, if discussing a material event, has already been the subject of a Form 6-K or other Commission filing or submission on EDGAR;

(7) [Removed and reserved.]

(8) Form F-X (§ 232.42 of this chapter) if filed by a Canadian issuer when qualifying an offering statement pursuant to the provisions of Regulation A (§ § 230.251 230.263 of this chapter); and

(9) Documents filed with the Commission pursuant to section 33 of the Investment Company Act (15 U.S.C. 80a-32).

(c) *Documents to be submitted in paper only.* The following shall not be submitted in electronic format:

(1)(i) Confidential treatment requests and the information with respect to which confidential treatment is requested;

(ii) Preliminary proxy materials and information statements with respect to a matter specified in Item 14 of Schedule 14A (§ 240.14a-101 of this chapter) for which confidential treatment has been requested in the manner prescribed by Rule 14a-6(e)(2) (§ 240.14a-6(e)(2) of this chapter) or Rule 14c-5(d)(2) (§ 240.14c-5(d)(2) of this chapter);

(2) Supplemental information, if the submitter requests that the information be protected from public disclosure under the Freedom of Information Act (5 U.S.C. 552) pursuant to a request for confidential treatment under Rule 83 (§ 200.83 of this chapter) or if the submitter requests that the information be returned after staff review and the information is of the type typically returned by the staff pursuant to Rule 418(b) of Regulation C [§ 230.418(b) of this chapter]or Rule 12b-4 of Regulation 12B (§ 240.12b-4 of this chapter);

(3) Shareholder proposals and all related correspondence submitted pursuant to Rule 14a-8 of the Exchange Act (§ 240.14a-8 of this chapter);

(4) No-action and interpretive letter requests (§ 200.81 of this chapter and 15 U.S.C. 78*l* (h));

(5) Applications for exemptive relief filed pursuant to Sections 304 and 310 of the Trust Indenture Act;

(6) Filings relating to offerings exempt from registration under the Securities Act, including filings made pursuant to Regulation A (§ § 230.251-230.263 of this chapter), as well as filings on Form 144 (§ 239.144 of this chapter) where the issuer of the securities is not subject to the reporting requirements of Section 13 or 15(d) of the Exchange Act (15 U.S.C. 78m or 78o(d), respectively);

(7) Promotional and sales material submitted pursuant to Securities Act Industry Guide 5 (§ 229.801(e) of this chapter) or otherwise supplementally furnished for review by the staff of the Division of Corporation Finance;

(8) Documents and symbols in a foreign language (*see* Rule 306 of Regulation S-T); and

(9) Exchange Act filings submitted to the Division of Market Regulation other than those that are submitted in electronic format as mandated or permitted electronic submissions under paragraph (a) and (b) of this section or that are submitted electronically in a filing system other than EDGAR.

(10) Documents relating to investigations and litigation submitted pursuant to Subpart D of Part 201 of this chapter.

(11) [Removed.]

(12) Annual Reports to Security Holders furnished by Public Utility Holding Companies under Exhibit A to Form U5S (§ 259.5s of this chapter) or under Rule 29 (§ 250.29 of this chapter);

(13) Reports to State Commissions, if furnished by Public Utility Holding Companies under Exhibit E to Form U5S (§ 259.5s of this chapter);

(14) Maps furnished by Public Utility Holding Companies under Exhibits E to Forms U5B and U-1 (§ 259.5b and 259.101 of this chapter);

(15) Annual reports filed with the Commission by indenture trustees pursuant to Section 313 of the Trust Indenture Act (15 U.S.C. 77mmm);

(16) Applications for an exemption from Exchange Act reporting obligations filed pursuant to Section 12(h) of the Exchange Act (15 U.S.C. 78*l*(h)).

[As last amended by Release No. 33-9013, effective March 16, 2009, 74 F.R. 10836.]

[¶ 14,012] Exhibits

Reg. § 232.102. (a) Exhibits to an electronic filing that have not previously been filed with the Commission shall be filed in electronic format, absent a hardship exemption. Previously filed exhibits, whether in paper or electronic format, may be incorporated by reference into an electronic filing to the extent permitted by § 228.10(f) and § 229.10(d) of this chapter, Rule 411 under the Securities Act (§ 230.411 of this chapter), Rule 12b-23 or 12b-32 under the Exchange Act (§ 240.12b-23 or § 240.12b-32 of this chapter), Rule 22 under the Public Utility Holding Company Act (§ 250.22 of this chapter), Rules 0-4, 8b-23, and 8b-32 under the Investment Company Act (§ 270.0-4, § 270.8b-23 and § 270.8b-32 of this chapter) and Rule 303 of Regulation S-T (§ 232.303). An electronic filer may, at its option, restate in electronic format an exhibit incorporated by reference that originally was filed in paper format.

Note to paragraph a: Exhibits to a Commission schedule filed pursuant to Section 13 or 14(d) of the Exchange Act may be filed in paper under cover of Form SE where such exhibits previously were filed in paper (prior to a registrant's becoming subject to mandated electronic filing or pursuant to a hardship exemption) and are required to be refiled pursuant to the schedule's general instructions. *See* Rule 311(b) of Regulation S-T (17 CFR 232.311(b)).

(b) Amendments to all exhibits shall be filed in electronic format, absent a hardship exemption.

(c) Notwithstanding any other provision of this section, an electronic filer shall, upon amendment, restate in electronic format its articles of incorporation, by-laws or investment advisory agreement (in the case of a registered investment company or a business development company).

(d) Each electronic filing requiring exhibits must include an exhibit index which must immediately precede the exhibits filed with the document. The index must list each exhibit filed, whether filed electronically or in paper. Whenever a filer files an exhibit in paper pursuant to a temporary or continuing hardship exemption (§ 232.201 or § 232.202) or pursuant to § 232.311, the filer must place the letter "P" next to the listed exhibit in the exhibit index of the electronic filing to reflect the fact that the filer filed the exhibit in paper. In addition, if the exhibit is filed in paper pursuant to § 232.311, the filer must place the designation "Rule 311" next to the letter "P" in the exhibit index. If the exhibit is filed in paper pursuant to a temporary or continuing hardship exemption, the filer must place the letters "TH" or "CH," respectively, next to the letter "P" in the exhibit index. Whenever an electronic confirming copy of an exhibit is filed pursuant to a hardship exemption (§ 232.201 or § 232.202(d)), the exhibit index should specify where the confirming electronic copy can be located; in addition, the designation "CE" (confirming electronic) should be placed next to the listed exhibit in the exhibit index.

(e) Notwithstanding the provisions of paragraphs (a) through (d) of this section, any incorporation by reference by a registered investment company or a business development company must relate only to documents that have been filed in electronic format on the EDGAR system, unless the document has been filed in paper under a hardship exemption (§ 232.201 or § 232.202) and any required confirming electronic copy has been submitted.

(1) The document has been filed in paper pursuant to a hardship exemption (§§ 232.201 and 232.202 of this chapter) and any required confirming copy has been submitted or

(2) The document is an exhibit, filed in paper in accordance with applicable rules, to Form N-SAR being incorporated by reference only into another Form N-SAR filing.

(f) Persons submitting filings electronically under the Public Utility Act shall not be subject to paragraph (c) of this section.

[As last amended in Release No. 33-8458, effective September 19, 2005, 70 F.R. 43558.]

[¶ 14,013] Liability for Transmission Errors or Omissions in Documents Filed Via EDGAR

Reg. § 232.103. An electronic filer shall not be subject to the liability and anti-fraud provisions of the federal securities laws with respect to an error or omission in an electronic filing resulting solely from electronic transmission errors beyond the control of the filer, where the filer corrects the error or omission by the filing of an amendment in electronic format as soon as reasonably practicable after the electronic filer becomes aware of the error or omission.

[As last amended in Release No. 33-7855, effective May 30, 2000, 65 F.R. 24788.]

[¶ 14,014] Unofficial PDF Copies Included in an Electronic Submission

Reg. § 232.104. (a) An electronic submission, other than a Form 3 (§ 249.103 of this chapter), a Form 4 (§ 249.104 of this chapter), a Form 5 (§ 249.105 of this chapter), a Form ID (§§ 239.63, 249.446, 269.7 and 274.402 of this chapter), a Form TA-1 (§ 249.100 of this chapter), a Form TA-2 (§ 249.102 of this chapter), a Form TA-W (§ 249.101 of this chapter) or a Form D (§ 239.500 of this chapter), may include one unofficial PDF copy of each electronic document contained within that submission, tagged in the format required by the EDGAR Filer Manual.

(b) Except as provided in paragraphs (c) and (f) of this section, each unofficial PDF copy must be substantively equivalent to its associated electronic document contained in the electronic submission. An unofficial PDF copy may contain graphic and image material (but not animated graphics, or audio or video material), notwithstanding the fact that its HTML or ASCII document counterpart may not contain such material but instead may contain a fair and accurate narrative description or tabular representation of any omitted graphic or image material.

(c) If a filer omits an unofficial PDF copy from, or submits one or more flawed unofficial PDF copies in, the electronic submission of an official filing, the filer may add or resubmit an unofficial PDF copy by electronically submitting an amendment to the filing to which it relates. The amendment must include an explanatory note that the purpose of the amendment is to add or to correct an unofficial PDF copy.

(1) If such an amendment is filed, the official amendment may consist solely of the cover page (or first page of the document), the explanatory note, and the signature page and exhibit index (where appropriate). The corresponding unofficial copy must include the complete text of the official filing document for which the amendment is being submitted.

(2) If the amendment is being filed to add or resubmit an unofficial PDF copy of one or more exhibits, the submission may consist of the following: the official filing—consisting of the cover page (or first page of the document), the explanatory note, the signature page (where appropriate), the exhibit index, and a separate electronic exhibit document for each exhibit for which an unofficial PDF copy is being submitted—and the corresponding unofficial PDF copy of each exhibit document. However, the text of the official exhibit document need not repeat the text of the exhibit; that document may contain only the following legend: RESUBMITTED TO ADD/REPLACE UNOFFICIAL PDF COPY OF EXHIBIT.

(d) An unofficial PDF copy is not filed for purposes of section 11 of the Securities Act (15 U.S.C. 77k), section 18 of the Exchange Act (15 U.S.C. 78r), section 16 of the Public Utility Act (15 U.S.C. 79p), section 323 of the Trust Indenture Act (15 U.S.C. 77www), or section 34(b) of the Investment Company Act (15 U.S.C. 80a-33(b)), or otherwise subject to the liabilities of such sections, and is not part of any registration statement to which it relates. An unofficial PDF copy is, however, subject to all other civil liability and anti-fraud provisions of the above Acts or other laws.

(e) Unofficial PDF copies that are prospectuses are subject to liability under Section 12 of the Securities Act (15 U.S.C. 77l).

(f) An unofficial PDF copy of a correspondence document contained in an electronic submission need not be substantively equivalent to that correspondence document.

[As last amended in Release No. 33-8891, effective September 15, 2008, 73 F.R. 10592.]

[¶ 14,015] Limitation on Use of HTML Documents and Hypertext Links

Reg. § 232.105. (a) Electronic filers must submit the following documents in ASCII: Form N-SAR (§ 274.101 of this chapter) and Form 13F (§ 249.325 of this chapter). Notwithstanding the provisions of this section, electronic filers may submit exhibits to Form N-SAR in HTML.

(b) Electronic filers may not include in any HTML document hypertext links to sites, locations, or documents outside the HTML document, except to links to officially filed documents within the current submission and to documents previously filed electronically and located in the EDGAR database on the Commission's public web site (www.sec.gov). Electronic filers also may include within an HTML document hypertext links to different sections within that single HTML document.

(c) If a filer includes an external hypertext link within a filed document, the information contained in the linked material will not be considered part of the document for determining compliance with reporting obligations, but the inclusion of the link will cause thefiler to be subject to the civil liability and antifraud provisions of the federal securities laws with reference to the information contained in the linked material.

[As last amended in Release No. 33-7855, effective May 30, 2000, and January 1, 2001, 65 F.R. 24788.]

[¶ 14,016] Prohibition Against Electronic Submissions Containing Executable Code

Reg. § 232.106. (a) Electronic submissions must not contain executable code. Attempted submissions identified as containing executable code will be suspended, unless the executable code is contained only in one or more PDF documents, in which case the submission will be accepted but the PDF document(s) containing executable code will be deleted and not disseminated.

(b) If an electronic submission has been accepted, and the Commission staff later determines that the accepted submission contains executable code, the staff may delete from the EDGAR system the entire accepted electronic submission or any document contained in the accepted electronic submission. The Commission staff may direct the electronic filer to resubmit electronically replacement document(s) or a replacement submission in its entirety, in compliance with this provision and the EDGAR Filer Manual.

Note to § 232.106: A violation of this section or the relevant EDGAR Filer Manual section also may be a violation of the Computer Fraud and Abuse Act of 1986, as amended, and other statutes and laws.

[As adopted in Release No. 33-7684, effective June 28, 1999, 64 F.R. 27888.]

Subpart 232.200—Hardship Exemptions

[¶ 14,021] Temporary Hardship Exemption

Reg. § 232.201 (a) If an electronic filer experiences unanticipated technical difficulties preventing the timely preparation and submission of an electronic filing, other than a Form 3 (§ 249.103 of this chapter), a Form 4 (§ 249.104 of this chapter), a Form 5 (§ 249.105 of this chapter), a Form ID (§§ 239.63, 249.446, 269.7 and 274.402 of this chapter), a Form TA-1 (§ 249.100 of this chapter), a Form TA-2 (§ 249.102 of this chapter), a Form TA-W (§ 249.101 of this chapter), a Form D (§ 239.500 of this chapter), an application for an order under any section of the Investment Company Act (15 U.S.C. 80a-1 *et. seq.*), or an Interactive Data File (§ 232.11 of this chapter), the electronic filer may file the subject filing, under cover of Form TH (§§ 239.65, 249.447, 269.10 and 274.404 of this chapter), in paper format no later than one business day after the date on which the filing was to be made.

(1) An electronic imaged copy of the paper format document shall be the official filing for purposes of the federal securities laws.

(2) The following legend shall be set forth in capital letters on the cover page of the paper format document:

IN ACCORDANCE WITH RULE 201 OF REGULATION S-T, THIS (SPECIFY DOCUMENT)
IS BEING FILED IN PAPER PURSUANT TO A TEMPORARY HARDSHIP EXEMPTION.

(3) Signatures to the paper format document may be in typed form rather than manual format. *See* Rule 302 of Regulation S-T (§ 232.302). All other requirements relating to paper format filings shall be satisfied.

(4) If the exemption pertains to a document filed pursuant to Section 13(a) or 15(d) of the Exchange Act (15 U.S.C. 78m and 78o(d)) or Section 30 of the Investment Company Act and the paper format document is filed in the manner specified in paragraph (a) of this section, the filing shall be deemed to have been filed by its required due date.

Notes : 1. Where a temporary hardship exemption relates to an exhibit only, the paper format exhibit shall be filed under cover of Form SE (§§ 239.64, 249.444, 259.603, 269.8, and 274.403 of this chapter).

2. Filers unable to submit a report within a prescribed time period because of electronic difficulties shall comply with the provisions of this section and shall not use Form 12b-25 (§ 249.322 of this chapter) as a notification of late filing.

Notes to paragraph (a):

1. Where a temporary hardship exemption relates to an exhibit only, the filer must file the paper format exhibit and a Form TH (§§ 239.65, 249.447, 259.604, 269.10, and 274.404 of this chapter) under cover of Form SE (§§ 239.64, 249.444, 259.601, 269.8, and 274.403 of this chapter).

2. Filers unable to submit a report within a prescribed time period because of electronic difficulties shall comply with the provisions of this section and shall not use Form 12b-25 (§ 249.322 of this chapter) as a notification of late filing.

(b) An electronic format copy of the filed paper format document shall be submitted to the Commission within six business days of filing the paper format document. The electronic format version shall contain the following statement in capital letters at the top of the first page of the document: THIS DOCUMENT IS A COPY OF THE (SPECIFY DOCUMENT) FILED ON (DATE) PURSUANT TO A RULE 201 TEMPORARY HARDSHIP EXEMPTION.

Note 1 to paragraph (b): Failure to submit the confirming electronic copy of a paper filing made in reliance on the temporary hardship exemption, as required in paragraph (b) of this section, will result in ineligibility to use Forms S-2, S-3, S-8, F-2 and F-3 (*see* §§ 239.12, 239.13, 239.16b, 239.32 and 239.33 of this section, respectively), restrict incorporation by reference of the document submitted in paper (*see* Rule 303 of Regulation S-T [§ 232.303]), and toll certain time periods associated with tender offers (*see* Rule 13e4(f)(12) [§ 240.13e-4(f)(12) of this chapter] and Rule 14e-1(e) [§ 240.14e-1(e) of this chapter]).

Note 2 to paragraph (b): If the exemption relates to an exhibit only, the requirement to submit a confirming electronic copy shall be satisfied by refiling the exhibit in electronic format in an amendment to the filing to which it relates. The confirming copy tag should not be used. The amendment should note that the purpose of the amendment is to add an electronic copy of an exhibit previously filed in paper pursuant to a temporary hardship exemption.

(c) If an electronic filer experiences unanticipated technical difficulties preventing the timely preparation and

(1) Submission of an Interactive Data File (§ 232.11) as an exhibit as required pursuant to Rule 405 of Regulation S-T (§ 232.405), the electronic filer still can timely satisfy the requirement to submit the Interactive Data File in the following manner:

(i) Substitute for the Interactive Data File in the required exhibit a document that sets forth the following legend:

IN ACCORDANCE WITH THE TEMPORARY HARDSHIP EXEMPTION PROVIDED BY RULE 201 OF REGULATION S-T, THE DATE BY WHICH THE INTERACTIVE DATA FILE IS REQUIRED TO BE SUBMITTED HAS BEEN EXTENDED BY SIX BUSINESS DAYS; and

(ii) Submit the required Interactive Data File no later than six business days after the Interactive Data File originally was required to be submitted.

(2) Posting on its corporate Web site of an Interactive Data File as required pursuant to Rule 405 of Regulation S-T, the electronic filer still can timely satisfy the requirement to post the Interactive Data File by so posting the Interactive Data File within six business days after the Interactive Data File was required to be submitted to the Commission.

Note to paragraph (c): Electronic filers unable to submit or post, as applicable, the Interactive Data File under the circumstances specified by paragraph (c), must comply with the provisions of this section and cannot use Form 12b-25 (§ 249.322 of this chapter) as a notification of late filing. Failure to submit or post, as applicable, the Interactive Data File as required by the end of the six-business-day period specified by paragraph (c) of this section will result in ineligibility to use Forms S-3, S-8 and F-3 (§§ 239.13, 239.16b and 239.33 of this chapter) and constitute a failure to have filed all required reports for purposes of the current public information requirements of Rule 144(c)(1) (§ 230.144(c)(1) of this chapter).

[As last amended in Release No. 33-9002, effective April 13, 2009, 74 F.R. 6776 and corrected in Release No. 33-9002A, 74 F.R. 15666.]

[¶ 14,022] Continuing Hardship Exemption

Reg. § 232.202. (a) An electronic filer may apply in writing for a continuing hardship exemption if all or part of a filing, group of filings or submission, other than a Form ID (§§ 239.63, 249.446, 269.7, and 274.402 of this chapter) or a Form D (§ 239.500 of this chapter), otherwise to be filed or submitted in electronic format or, in the case of an Interactive Data File (§ 232.11), to be posted on the electronic filer's corporate Web site, cannot be so filed, submitted or posted, as applicable, without undue burden or expense. Such written application shall be made at least ten business days before the required due date of the filing(s), submission(s) or posting or the proposed filing, submission or posting date, as appropriate, or within such shorter period as may be permitted. The written application shall contain the information set forth in paragraph (b) of this section.

(1) The application shall not be deemed granted until the applicant is notified by the Commission or the staff.

(2) If the Commission, or the staff acting pursuant to delegated authority, denies the application for a continuing hardship exemption, the electronic filer shall file or submit the required document or Interactive Data File in electronic format or post the Interactive Data File on its corporate Web site, as applicable, on the required due date or the proposed filing, submission, or posting date, or such other date as may be permitted.

(3) If the Commission, or the staff acting pursuant to delegated authority, determines that the grant of the exemption is appropriate and consistent with the public interest and the protection of investors and so notifies the applicant, the electronic filer shall follow the procedures set forth in paragraph (c) of this section.

(b) The request for the continuing hardship exemption shall include, but not be limited to, the following:

(1) the reason(s) that the necessary hardware and software is not available without unreasonable burden and expense;

(2) the burden and expense involved to employ alternative means to make the electronic submission; and/or

(2) The burden and expense involved to employ alternative means to make the electronic submission or posting, as applicable; and/or

(3) The reasons for not submitting electronically the document, group of documents or Interactive Data File or not posting the Interactive Data File, as well as the justification for the requested time period.

(c) If the request is granted with respect to:

(1) Electronic filing of a document or group of documents, not electronic submission or posting of an Interactive Data File, then the electronic filer shall submit the document or group of documents for which the continuing hardship exemption is granted in paper format on the required due date specified in the applicable form, rule or regulation, or the proposed filing date, as appropriate and the following legend shall be placed in capital letters at the top of the cover page of the paper format document(s):

IN ACCORDANCE WITH RULE 202 OF REGULATION S-T, THIS (specify document) IS BEING FILED IN PAPER PURSUANT TO A CONTINUING HARDSHIP EXEMPTION.

(2) Electronic submission of an Interactive Data File, then the electronic filer shall substitute for the Interactive Data File in the exhibit in which it was required a document that sets forth one of the following legends, as appropriate:

IN ACCORDANCE WITH A CONTINUING HARDSHIP EXEMPTION OBTAINED UNDER RULE 202 OF REGULATION S-T, THE DATE BY WHICH THE INTERACTIVE DATA FILE IS REQUIRED TO BE SUBMITTED HAS BEEN EXTENDED TO (specify date); or

IN ACCORDANCE WITH A CONTINUING HARDSHIP EXEMPTION OBTAINED UNDER RULE 202 OF REGULATION S-T, THE INTERACTIVE DATA FILE IS NOT REQUIRED TO BE SUBMITTED.

(3) Web site posting by an electronic filer of its Interactive Data File, the electronic filer need not post on its Web site any statement with regard to the grant of the request.

(d) If a continuing hardship exemption is granted for a limited period of time for:

(1) Electronic filing of a document or group of documents, not electronic submission or posting of an Interactive Data File, then the grant may be conditioned upon the filing of the document or group of documents that is the subject of the exemption in electronic format upon the expiration of the period for which the exemption is granted. The electronic format version shall contain the following statement in capital letters at the top of the first page of the document:

THIS DOCUMENT IS A COPY OF THE (specify document) FILED ON (DATE) PURSUANT TO A RULE 202(d) CONTINUING HARDSHIP EXEMPTION.

(2) Electronic submission or posting of an Interactive Data File, then the grant may be conditioned upon the electronic submission and posting, as applicable, of the Interactive Data File that is the subject of the exemption upon the expiration of the period for which the exemption is granted.

THIS DOCUMENT IS A COPY OF THE (SPECIFY DOCUMENT) FILED ON (DATE) PURSUANT TO A RULE 202(d) CONTINUING HARDSHIP EXEMPTION

Note 1 to § 232.202: Where a continuing hardship exemption is granted with respect to an exhibit only, the paper format exhibit shall be filed under cover of Form SE (§ § 239.64, 249.444, 259.603, 269.8 and 274.403 of this chapter).

Note 2 to §232.202: If the exemption relates to an exhibit only and a confirming electronic copy of the exhibit is required to be submitted, the exhibit should be refiled in electronic format in an amendment to the filing to which it relates. The confirming copy tag should not be used. The amendment should note that the purpose of the amendment is to add an electronic copy of an exhibit previously filed in paper pursuant to a continuing hardship exemption.

Note 3 to §232.202: Failure to submit a required confirming electronic copy of a paper filing made in reliance on a continuing hardship exemption granted pursuant to paragraph (d) of this section will result in ineligibility to use Forms S-2, S-3, S-8, F-2 and F-3 (see, §§239.12, 239.13, 239.16b, 239.32 and 239.33, respectively), restrict incorporation by reference of the document submitted in paper (see Rule 303 of Regulation S-T [§232.303], and toll certain time periods associated with tender offers (see Rule 13e-4(f)(12) [§240.13e-4(f)(12)] and Rule 14e-1(e) [§240.14e-1(e)]).

Note 4 to §232.202: Failure to submit or post, as applicable, the Interactive Data File as required by Rule 405 by the end of the continuing hardship exemption if granted for a limited period of time, will result in ineligibility to use Forms S-3, S-8, and F-3 (§§ 239.13, 239.16b and 239.33 of this chapter), constitute a failure to have filed all required reports for purposes of the current public information requirements of Rule 144(c)(1) (§ 230.144(c)(1) of this chapter), and, pursuant to Rule 485(c)(3), suspend the ability to file post-effective amendments under Rule 485(b) (§ 230.485 of this chapter).

[As last amended in Release No. 33-9006, effective July 15, 2009, 74 F.R. 7748 (see the release for detailed compliance information).]

Subpart 232.300—Preparation of Electronic Submissions

[¶ 14,031] EDGAR Filer Manual

Reg. § 232.301. Filers must prepare electronic filings in the manner prescribed by the EDGAR Filer Manual, promulgated by the Commission, which sets out the technical formatting requirements for electronic submissions. The requirements for becoming an EDGAR Filer and updating company data are set forth in the EDGAR Filer Manual, Volume I: "General Information," Version 8 (September 2009). The requirements for filing on EDGAR are set forth in the updated EDGAR Filer Manual, Volume II: "EDGAR Filing," Version 14 (April 2010). Additional provisions applicable to Form N-SAR filers are set forth in the EDGAR Filer Manual, Volume III: "N-SAR Supplement," Version 1 (September 2005). All of these provisions have been incorporated by reference into the Code of Federal Regulations, which action was approved by the Director of the Federal Register in accordance with 5 U.S.C. 552(a) and 1 CFR Part 51. You must comply with these requirements in order for documents to be timely received and accepted. You can obtain paper copies of the EDGAR Filer Manual from the following address: Public Reference Room, U.S. Securities and Exchange Commission, 100 F Street, NE, Room 1520, Washington, DC 20549, or call (202) 551-5850, on official business days between the hours of 10:00 am and 3:00 pm. Electronic copies are available on the Commission's Web site. The address for the Filer Manual is *http://www.sec.gov/info/edgar.shtml*. You can also inspect the document at the National Archives and Records Administration (NARA). For information on the availability of this material at NARA, call 202-741-6030, or go to: *http://www.archives.gov/federal_register/code_of_federal_regulations/ibr_locations.html*.

[As last amended in Release No. 33-9115, effective April 8, 2010, 75 FR 17853.]

[¶ 14,032] Signatures

Reg. § 232.302. (a) Required signatures to, or within, any electronic submission (including, without limitation, signatories within the certifications required by §§240.13a-14, 240.15d-14 and 270.30a-2 of this chapter) must be in typed form rather than manual format. Signatures in an HTML document that are not required may, but are not required to, be presented in an HTML graphic or image file within the electronic filing, in compliance with the formatting requirements of the EDGAR Filer Manual. When used in connection with an electronic filing, the term "signature" means an electronic entry in the form of a magnetic impulse or other form of computer data compilation of any letters or series of letters or characters comprising a name, executed, adopted or authorized as a signature. Signatures are not required in unofficial PDF copies submitted in accordance with §232.104.

(b) Each signatory to an electronic filing (including, without limitation, each signatory to the certifications required by §§240.13a-14, 240.15d-14 and 270.30a-2 of this chapter) shall manually sign a signature page or other document authenticating, acknowledging or otherwise adopting his or her signature that appears in typed form within the electronic filing. Such document shall be executed before or at the time the electronic filing is made and shall be retained by the filer for a period of five years. Upon request, an electronic filer shall furnish to the Commission or its staff a copy of any or all documents retained pursuant to this section.

(c) Where the Commission's rules require a registrant to furnish to a national securities exchange or national securities association paper copies of a document filed with the Commission in electronic format, signatures to such paper copies may be in typed form.

[As last amended in Release No. 33-8124, effective August 29, 2002, 67 F.R. 57276.]

[¶ 14,033] Incorporation by Reference

Reg. § 232.303. (a) The following documents shall not be incorporated by reference into an electronic filing:

(1) any document filed in paper in violation of mandated electronic filing requirements;

(2) Any document filed in paper pursuant to a hardship exemption for which a required confirming electronic copy has not been submitted.

(3) For a registered investment company or a business development company, documents that have not been filed in electronic format, unless the document has been filed in paper under a hardship exemption (§ 232.201 or 232.202 of this chapter) and any required confirming copy has been submitted.

(b) If a filer incorporates by reference into an electronic filing any portion of an annual or quarterly report to security holders, it must also file the portion of the annual or quarterly report to security holders in electronic format as an exhibit to the filing, as required by Regulation S-K Item 601(b)(13) (§ 229.601(b)(13) of this chapter) and Regulation S-B Item 601(b)(13) (§ 228.601(b)(13) of this chapter). If a foreign private issuer incorporates by reference into an electronic filing any portion of an annual or other report to security holders, or of a Form 6-K report (§ 249.306 of this chapter) filed or submitted in paper, it also must file the incorporated portion in electronic format as an exhibit to the filing. The requirements of this paragraph do not apply to incorporation by reference by an investment company from an annual or quarterly report to security holders.

[As last amended in Release No. 33-8099, effective November 4, 2002, 67 F.R. 36678.]

[¶ 14,034] Graphic, Image, Audio and Video Material

Reg. § 232.304. (a) If a filer includes graphic, image, audio or video material in a document delivered to investors and others that is not reproduced in an electronic filing, the electronically filed version of that document must include a fair and accurate narrative description, tabular representation or transcript of the omitted material. Such descriptions, representations or transcripts may be included in the text of the electronic filing at the point where the graphic, image, audio or video material is presented in the delivered version, or they may be listed in an appendix to the electronic filing. Immaterial differences between the delivered and electronically filed versions, such as pagination, color, type size or style, or corporate logo need not be described.

Note to paragraph (a): If the omitted graphic, image, audio or video material includes data, filers must include a tabular representation or other appropriate representation of that data in the electronically filed version of the document.

(b)(1) The graphic, image, audio and video material in the version of a document delivered to investors and others is deemed part of the electronic filing and subject to the civil liability and anti-fraud provisions of the federal securities laws.

(2) Narrative descriptions, tabular representations or transcripts of graphic, image, audio and video material included in an electronic filing or appendix thereto also are deemed part of the filing. However, to the extent such descriptions, representations or transcripts represent a good faith effort to fairly and accurately describe omitted graphic, image, audio or video material, they are not subject to the civil liability and anti-fraud provisions of the federal securities laws.

(c) An electronic filer must retain for a period of five years a copy of each publicly distributed document, in the format used, that contains graphic, image, audio or video material where such material is not included in the version filed with the Commission. The five-year period shall commence as of the filing date, or the date that appears on the document, whichever is later. Upon request, an electronic filer shall furnish to the Commission or its staff a copy of any or all of the documents contained in the file.

(d) For electronically filed ASCII documents, the performance graph that is to appear in registrant annual reports to security holders required by Exchange Act Rule 14a-3 (§ 240.14a-3 of this chapter) or Exchange Act Rule 14c-3 (§ 240.14c-3 of this chapter) to precede or accompany proxy statements or information statements relating to annual meetings of security holders at which directors are to be elected (or special meetings or written consents in lieu of such meetings), as required by Item 201(e) of Regulation S-K (§ 229.201(e) of this chapter), and the line graph that is to appear in registrant annual reports to security holders, as required by paragraph (b)(7)(ii) of Item 27 of Form N-1A (§ 274.11A of this chapter), must be furnished to the Commission by presenting the data in tabular or chart form within the electronic ASCII document, in compliance with paragraph (a) of this section and the formatting requirements of the EDGAR Filer Manual.

(e) Notwithstanding the provisions of paragraphs (a) through (d) of this section, electronically filed HTML documents must present the following information in an HTML graphic or image file within the electronic submission in compliance with the formatting requirements of the EDGAR Filer Manual: the performance graph that is to appear in registrant annual reports to security holders required by

Exchange Act Rule 14a-3 (§ 240.14a-3 of this chapter) or Exchange Act Rule 14c-3 (§ 240.14c-3 of this chapter) to precede or accompany registrant proxy statements or information statements relating to annual meetings of security holders at which directors are to be elected (or special meetings or written consents in lieu of such meetings), as required by Item 201(e) of Regulation S-K (§ 229.201(e) of this chapter); the line graph that is to appear in registrant annual reports to security holders, as required by paragraph (b)(7)(ii) of Item 27 of Form N-1A (§ 274.11A of this chapter); and any other graphic material required by rule or form to be filed with the Commission. Filers may, but are not required to, submit any other graphic material in a HTML document by presenting the data in an HTML graphic or image file within the electronic filing, in compliance with the formatting requirements of the EDGAR Filer Manual. However, filers may not present in a graphic or image file information such as text or tables that users must be able to search and/or download into spreadsheet form (*e.g.*, financial statements); filers must present such material as text in an ASCII document or as text or an HTML table in an HTML document.

(f) Electronic filers may not include animated graphics in any EDGAR document.

[As last amended in Release No. 33-8998, effective March 31, 2009, 74 F.R. 4546.]

[¶ 14,035] Number of Characters Per Line; Tabular and Columnar Information

Reg. § 232.305. (a) The narrative portion of a document shall not exceed 80 characters per line, including blank spaces, and shall not be presented in multi-column newspaper format. Non-narrative information (*e.g.*, financial statements) may be presented in tabular or columnar format and may exceed 80 positions only if it is tagged as specified in the EDGAR Filer Manual. In no event shall information presented in tabular or columnar format exceed 132 positions wide.

(b) Paragraph (a) of this section does not apply to HTML documents, Interactive Data Files (§ 232.11) or XBRL-Related Documents (§ 232.11).

[As last amended in Release No. 33-9002, effective April 13, 2009, 74 F.R. 6776.]

[¶ 14,036] Foreign Language Documents and Symbols

Reg. § 232.306. (a) All electronic filings and submissions must be in the English language, except as otherwise provided by paragraph (d) of this section. If a filing or submission requires the inclusion of a document that is in a foreign language, a party must submit instead a fair and accurate English translation of the foreign language document in accordance with § 230.403(c) or § 240.12b-12(d) of this chapter, except as otherwise provided by paragraph (c) of this section. Alternatively, if the foreign language document is an exhibit or attachment to a filing or submission subject to review by the Division of Corporation Finance, a party may provide a fair and accurate English summary of the foreign language document if permitted by § 230.403(c)(3) or § 240.12b-12(d)(3) of this chapter.

(b) When including an English summary or English translation of a foreign language document in an electronic filing or submission, a party may also submit a copy of the unabridged foreign language document in paper under cover of Form SE (§§ 239.64, 249.444, 259.603, 269.8, and 274.403 of this chapter) in accordance with § 232.311 of this chapter. A filer must provide a copy of any foreign language document upon the request of Commission staff.

(c) A foreign government or its political subdivision must electronically file a fair and accurate English translation, if available, of its latest annual budget as presented to its legislative body, as Exhibit B to Form 18 (§ 249.218 of this chapter) or Exhibit (c) to Form 18-K (§ 249.318 of this chapter). If no English translation is available, a foreign government or political subdivision must submit a copy of the foreign language version of its latest annual budget in paper under cover of Form SE (§§ 239.64, 249.444, 259.603, 269.8, and 274.403 of this chapter).

(d) A Canadian issuer may file an HTML document, as defined in § 232.11 of this chapter, that contains text in both French and English if the issuer included the French text to comply with the requirements of the Canadian securities administrator or other Canadian authority, and the French text is in an exhibit to or part of:

(1) A registration statement on Form F-7, F-8, F-9, F-10, or F-80 (§§ 239.37, 239.38, 239.39, 239.40, and 239.41 of this chapter);

(2) A registration statement or annual report on Form 40-F (§ 249.240f of this chapter); or

(3) A Schedule 13E-4F (§ 240.13e-102 of this chapter), Schedule 14D-1F (§ 240.14d-102), or Schedule 14D-9F (§ 240.14d-103).

(e) Foreign currency denominations must be expressed in words or letters in the English language rather than representative symbols, except that HTML documents may include any representative foreign currency symbols that the EDGAR Filer Manual specifies. The limitations of this paragraph do not apply to unofficial PDF copies submitted in accordance with Rule 104 of Regulation S-T (§ 232.104).

[As last amended in Release No. 33-8099, effective November 4, 2002, 67 F.R. 36678.]

[¶ 14,037] Bold Face Type

Reg. § 232.307. (a) Provisions requiring presentation of information in bold face type shall be satisfied in an electronic format document by presenting such information in capital letters.

(b) Paragraph (a) of this section does not apply to HTML documents.

[As last amended in Release No. 33-7684, effective June 28, 1999, 64 F.R. 27888.]

[¶ 14,038] Type Size and Font; Legibility

Reg. § 232.308. Provisions relating to type size, font and other legibility requirements shall not apply to electronic format documents.

[As adopted in Release No. 33-6977, February 23, 1993, 58 F.R. 14628.]

[¶ 14,039] Paper Size; Binding; Sequential Numbering; Number of Copies

Reg. § 232.309. (a) Requirements as to paper size, binding, and sequential page numbering shall not apply to electronic format documents.

(b) An electronic format document, submitted in the manner prescribed by the EDGAR Filer Manual, shall satisfy any requirement that more than one copy of such document be filed with or provided to the Commission.

[As adopted in Release No. 33-6977, February 23, 1993, 58 F.R. 14628.]

[¶ 14,040] Marking Changed Material

Reg. § 232.310. Provisions requiring the marking of changed materials are satisfied in ASCII and HTML documents by inserting the tag <R> before and the tag </R> following a paragraph containing changed material. HTML documents may be marked to show changed materials within paragraphs. Financial statements and notes thereto need not be marked for changed material.

[As last amended in Release No. 33-7684, effective June 28, 1999, 64 F.R. 27888.]

[¶ 14,041] Documents Submitted in Paper Under Cover of Form SE

Reg. § 232.311. Form SE (§§ 239.64, 249.444, 259.603, 269.8, and 274.403 of this chapter) shall be filed as a paper cover sheet to the following documents submitted to the Commission in paper:

(a) Exhibits filed in paper pursuant to a hardship exemption shall be filed under cover of Form SE. *See* Rules 201 and 202 of Regulation S-T (§§ 232.201 and 232.202).

(b) Exhibits to a Commission schedule filed pursuant to Section 13 or 14(d) of the Exchange Act may be filed in paper under cover of Form SE where such exhibits previously were filed in paper (prior to a registrant's becoming subject to mandated electronic filing or pursuant to a hardship exemption) and are required to be refiled pursuant to the schedule's general instructions.

(c) Annual Reports to Security Holders furnished by Public Utility Holding Companies as Exhibit A to Form U5S (§ 259.5s of this chapter) or under rule 29 (§ 250.29 of this chapter) shall be filed in paper under cover of Form SE.

(d) Reports to State Commissions, if furnished by Public Utility Holding Companies as Exhibit E to Form U5S (§ 259.5s of this chapter), shall be filed in paper under cover of Form SE.

(e) Maps furnished by Public Utility Holding Companies under Exhibits E to Forms U5B and U-1 (§ 259.5b and 259.101 of this chapter) shall be filed in paper under cover of Form SE.

(f) A party may submit a copy of an unabridged foreign language document in paper under cover of Form SE if the electronic filing or submission includes an English summary or English translation of the foreign language document in accordance with § 232.306(b) or if permitted by the applicable form.

(g) A foreign government or political subdivision that is not filing in electronic format an English translation of its latest annual budget submitted as Exhibit B to Form 18 (§ 249.218 of this chapter) or Exhibit (c) to Form 18-K (§ 249.318 of this chapter) must file a copy of the foreign language version of its latest annual budget in paper under cover of Form SE in accordance with § 232.306(c) of this chapter.

(h) The Form SE shall be submitted in the following manner:

(1) If the subject of a temporary hardship exemption is an exhibit only, the filer must file the exhibit and a Form TH (§§ 239.65, 249.447, 259.604, 269.10, and 274.404 of this chapter) under cover of Form SE (§§ 239.64, 249.444, 259.601, 269.8, and 274.403 of this chapter) no later than one business day after the date the exhibit was to be filed electronically.

(2) An exhibit filed pursuant to a continuing hardship exemption, or any other document filed in paper under cover of Form SE (other than an exhibit filed pursuant to a temporary hardship exemption), as allowed by paragraphs (a) through (g) of this section, may be filed up to six business days prior to, or on the date of filing of, the electronic format document to which it relates but shall not be filed after such filing date. If a paper document is submitted in this manner, requirements that the document be filed with, provided with or accompany the electronic filing shll be satisfied.

(i) Any requirements as to delivery or furnishing the information to persons other than the Commission shall not be affected by this section.

[As last amended in Release No. 33-8458, effective September 19, 2005, 70 F.R. 43558.]

[¶ 14,045] Accommodation for Certain Information in Filings with Respect to Asset-Backed Securities

Reg. § 232.312. (a) For filings with respect to asset-backed securities filed on or before December 31, 2010, the information provided in response to Item 1105 of Regulation AB (§ 229.1105 of this chapter) may be provided under the following conditions on an Internet Web site for inclusion in the prospectus for the asset-backed securities, and will be deemed to be included in the prospectus included in the registration statement, in lieu of reproducing the information in the electronically filed version of that document. Terms used in this section have the same meaning as in Item 1101 of Regulation AB (§ 229.1101 of this chapter).

(1) The prospectus in the registration statement at the time of effectiveness shall disclose the intention to provide such information through a Web site and the prospectus to be filed pursuant to § 230.424 of this chapter shall provide the specific Internet address where the information is posted.

(2) Such information shall be provided through the Web site unrestricted as to access and free of charge.

(3) Such information shall remain available on the Web site for a period of not less than five years. If a subsequent update or change is made to the information, the date of such update or change shall be clearly indicated on the Web site.

(4) The registrant shall retain all versions of such information provided through the Web site for a period of not less than five years in a form that permits delivery to an investor or the Commission. Upon request, the registrant shall furnish to the Commission or its staff a copy of any or all information retained pursuant to this requirement.

(5) The registration statement shall contain the undertakings required by Item 512(*l*) of Regulation S-K (§ 229.512(*l*) of this chapter) that:

(i) Except as otherwise provided by this section, such information provided through the specified Internet address is deemed to be a part of the prospectus included in the registration statement for the asset-backed securities.

(ii) The registrant shall provide to any person without charge, upon request, a copy of such information provided through the specified Internet address as of the date of the prospectus included in the registration statement if a subsequent update or change is made to that information.

Note to paragraph (a). With respect to paragraphs (a)(3) and (a)(4) of this section, the five-year period shall commence from the filing date of the prospectus filed pursuant to § 230.424 of this chapter, or the date of first use of the prospectus, whichever is earlier.

(b) This section does not affect any obligation to provide any other information in the filing electronically on EDGAR.

[As last amended in Release No. 33-9087, effective December 31, 2009, 74 F.R. 67812 (this rule will apply to filings with respect to asset-backed securities filed on or before December 31, 2010).]

[¶ 14,048] Identification of Investment Company Type and Series and/or Class (or Contract)

Reg. § 232.313. (a) Registered investment companies and business development companies must indicate their investment company type, based on whether the registrant's last effective registration statement or amendment (other than a merger/proxy filing on Form N-14 (§ 239.23 of this chapter) was filed on Form N-1 (§§ 239.15 and 274.11 of this chapter), Form N-1A (§§ 239.15A and 274.11A of this chapter), Form N-2 (§§ 239.14 and 274.11a-1 of this chapter), Form N-3 (§§ 239.17A and 274.11b of this chapter), Form N-4 (§§ 239.17b and 274.11c of this chapter), Form N-5 (§§ 239.24 and 274.5 of this chapter), Form N-6 (§§ 239.17c and 274.11d of this chapter), Form S-1 (§ 239.11 of this chapter), Form S-3 (§ 239.13 of this chapter), or Form S-6 (§ 239.16 of this chapter) in those EDGAR submissions identified in the EDGAR Filer Manual.

(b) Registered investment companies whose last effective registration statement or amendment (other than a merger/proxy filing on Form N-14 (§ 239.23 of this chapter) was filed on Form N-1A (§§ 239.15A and 274.11A of this chapter), Form N-3 (§§ 239.17A and 274.11b of this chapter), Form N-4 (§§ 239.17b and 274.11c of this chapter), or Form N-6 (§§ 239.17c and 274.11d of this chapter) must, under the procedures set forth in the EDGAR Filer Manual:

(1) Provide electronically, and keep current, information concerning their existing and new series and/or classes (or contracts, in the case of separate accounts), including series and/or class (contract) name and ticker symbol, if any, and be issued series and/or class (or contract) identification numbers;

(2) Deactivate for EDGAR purposes any series and/or class (or contract, in the case of separate accounts) that are no longer offered, go out of existence, or deregister following the last filing for that

series and/or class (or contract, in the case of separate accounts), but the registrant must not deactivate the last remaining series unless the registrant deregisters; and

(3) For those EDGAR submissions identified in the EDGAR Filer Manual, include all series and/or class (or contract) identifiers of each series and/or class (or contract) on behalf of which the filing is made.

(c) Registered investment companies whose last effective registration statement or amendment (other than a merger/proxy filing on Form N-14 (§ 239.23 of this chapter)) was filed on Form N-1A (§ § 239.15A and 274.11A of this chapter), Form N-3 (§ § 239.17A and 274.11b of this chapter), Form N-4 (§ § 239.17b and 274.11c of this chapter), or Form N-6 (§ § 239.17c and 274.11d of this chapter) must provide electronically, as specified in the EDGAR Filer Manual, in the EDGAR submission identifying information concerning the acquiring fund and the target fund (and the series and/or classes (contracts), if any, of each if in existence at the time of the filing) in connection with merger filings on Form N-14 (§ 239.23 of this chapter), under § 230.425 of this chapter, and in compliance with Regulation 14A (§ 240.14a-1 of this chapter), Schedule 14A (§ 240.14a-101 of this chapter), and all other applicable rules and regulations adopted pursuant to Section 14(a) of the Exchange Act, as referenced in Investment Company Act Rule 20a-1 (§ 270.20a-1 of this chapter).

(d) Non-registrant third party filers making proxy filings with respect to investment companies must designate in the EDGAR submission the type of investment company (as referenced in paragraph (a) of this section) and include series and/or class (or contract) identifiers in designated EDGAR proxy submission types, in accordance with the EDGAR Filer Manual.

[As adopted in Release No. 33-8458, effective February 6, 2006, 70 F.R. 43558.]

Subpart 232.400—XBRL Related Documents

[¶ 14,051] XBRL-Related Document Submissions

Reg. § 232.401. (a) Only an electronic filer that is an investment company registered under the Investment Company Act of 1940 (15 U.S.C. 80a-1 et seq.), a "business development company" as defined in section 2(a)(48) of that Act, or an entity that reports under the Exchange Act and prepares its financial statements in accordance with Article 6 of Regulation S-X (17 CFR 210.6-01 et seq.) is permitted to participate in the voluntary XBRL (eXtensible Business Reporting Language) program. An electronic filer that participates in the voluntary XBRL program may submit XBRL-Related Documents (§ 232.11) in electronic format as an exhibit to: the filing (other than a Form N-1A (§ 239.15A and § 274.11A of this chapter) to which the XBRL-Related Documents relate; an amendment to such filing, but, in the case of a Form N-1A filing, an amendment made only after the effective date of the Form N-1A filing to which the XBRL-Related Documents relate; or, if the electronic filer is eligible to file a Form 8-K (§ 249.308 of this chapter) or a Form 6-K (§ 249.306 of this chapter), a Form 8-K or a Form 6-K, as applicable, that references the filing to which the XBRL-Related Documents relate if such Form 8-K or Form 6-K is submitted no earlier than the date of that filing. The XBRL-Related Documents must comply with the content and format requirements of this section, be submitted as an exhibit to a form that contains the disclosure required by this section and be submitted in accordance with the EDGAR Filer Manual and, as applicable, one of Item 601(b)(100) of Regulation S-K (§ 229.601(b)(100) of this chapter), Item 601(b)(100) of Regulation S-B (§ 228.601(b)(100) of this chapter), Form 20-F (§ 249.220f of this chapter), Form 6-K or § 270.8b-33 of this chapter.

(b) XBRL-Related Documents must consist of mandatory content and may consist of optional content but only if the optional content accompanies the mandatory content in the same submission.

(1) Mandatory content consists of a complete set of information for all periods presented in the corresponding official EDGAR filing from one or more of the following categories (as filed in the corresponding official EDGAR filing):

(i) The complete set of financial statements (the only exceptions are that notes to the financial statements and schedules related to the financial statements may be omitted unless the electronic filer is a registered management investment company in which case it must include Schedule I - Investments in Securities of Unaffiliated Issuers (§ 210.12-12 of this chapter));

(ii) Earnings information set forth in Form 6-K or Items 2.02 or 8.01 of Form 8-K (whether contained in the body of the Form 6-K or Form 8-K or in an exhibit, and whether filed or furnished);

(iii) Financial highlights or condensed financial information set forth in Item 13(a) of Form N-1A, Item 4.1 of Form N-2 (§ 239.14 and § 274.11a-1 of this chapter) or Item 4(a) of Form N-3 (§ 239.17a and § 274.11b of this chapter);

(iv) The risk/return summary information set forth in Items 2, 3, and 4 of Form N-1A provided that the filing is submitted prior to January 1, 2011, and, in the case of a Form N-1A filing that includes more than one series (as that term is used in rule 18f-2(a) under the Investment Company Act (§ 270.18f-2(a) of this chapter), a filer may include in mandatory content complete risk/return summary information for any one or more of those series; or

(v) If the electronic filer is an investment company registered under the Investment Company Act of 1940 (15 U.S.C. 80a-1 *et seq.*), a "business development company" as defined in section 2(a)(48) of that Act, or an entity that reports under the Exchange Act and prepares its financial statements in accordance with Article 6 of Regulation S-X (17 CFR 210.6-01 *et seq.*), *Schedule I - Investments in Securities of Unaffiliated Issuers* (§ 210.12-12 of this chapter).

(2) Optional content can consist only of a complete set of information that is:

(i) For all periods presented in the corresponding official EDGAR filing;

(ii) Related to financial information in the corresponding official EDGAR filing that is simultaneously submitted as mandatory content (as specified in paragraph (b)(1) of this section); and

(iii) From one or more of the following categories (as filed in the corresponding official EDGAR filing):

(A) Audit opinions (as specified by Rule 2-02 of Regulation S-X (§ 210.2-02 of this chapter));

(B) Interim review reports (as specified by Rule 10-01(d) of Regulation S-X (§§ 10.10-01(d) of this chapter));

(C) Reports of management on the financial statements;

(D) Certifications;

(E) Management's discussion and analysis of financial condition and results of operations (as specified by Item 303 of Regulation S-K (§ 229.303 of this chapter));

(F) Management's discussion and analysis or plan of operation (as specified by Item 303 of Regulation S-B (§ 228.303 of this chapter));

(G) Operating and financial review and prospects (as specified by Item 5 of Form 20-F); or

(H) Management's discussion of fund performance (as specified by Item 22(b)(7) of Form N-1A).

(c) XBRL-Related Documents must appear in voluntary program format. XBRL-Related Documents appear in voluntary program format if:

(1) Each data element (*i.e.*, all text and all line item names and associated values, dates and other labels) contained in the XBRL-Related Documents reflects the same information in the corresponding official EDGAR filing (*i.e.*, the HTML or ASCII version);

(2) No data element contained in the corresponding official EDGAR filing is changed, deleted or summarized in the XBRL-Related Documents;

(3) The XBRL-Related Documents correlate to the appropriate version of a standard taxonomy, supplemented with extension taxonomies as specified in the EDGAR Filer Manual (§ 232.11);

(4) Each data element contained in the XBRL-Related Documents is matched with an appropriate tag in accordance with any applicable taxonomy; and

(5) The XBRL-Related Documents contain any additional mark-up related content (*e.g.*, the XBRL tags themselves, identification of the core XML documents used and other technology related content) not found in the corresponding official EDGAR filing that are necessary to comply with the EDGAR Filer Manual requirements.

(d) The filing with which XBRL-Related Documents are submitted as an exhibit must contain the disclosures specified in paragraph (d)(1) of this section in the location specified in paragraph (d)(2) of this section.

(1) The filing must disclose:

(i) That the financial information contained in the XBRL-Related Documents is "unaudited" or "unreviewed," as applicable (but only if the mandatory content contained in the XBRL-Related Documents contains information other than risk/return summary information submitted under paragraph (b)(1)(iv) of this section);

(ii) That the purpose of submitting the XBRL-Related Documents is to test the related format and technology and, as a result, investors should not rely on the XBRL-Related Documents in making investment decisions; and

(iii) The identity of the corresponding official EDGAR filing (but only if the filing is a Form 8-K or Form 6-K or an amendment to a Form 8-K or Form 6-K and a purpose of filing the form was to submit as an exhibit XBRL-Related Documents that present information related to financial information filed as part of a different form in the corresponding official EDGAR filing).

(2) The disclosures required by paragraph (d)(1) of this section must appear within the XBRL-Related Documents as a tagged data element and, as applicable, in:

(i) The exhibit index of a Form 10-K (§ 249.310 of this chapter), 10-Q (§ 249.308a of this chapter), 10 (§ 249.210 of this chapter), 10-SB (§ 249.210b of this chapter), 10-KSB (§ 249.310b of this chapter), 10-QSB (§ 249.308b of this chapter), 20-F or N-1A and, in the case of risk/return summary information submitted under paragraph (b)(1)(iv) of this section, within the XBRL-Related Documents as a tagged data element;

(ii) Item 2.02 or 8.01 of a Form 8-K; or

(iii) The body of a Form 6-K, N-CSR (§ 274.128 of this chapter) or N-Q (§ 274.130 of this chapter).

Note to § 232.401: Although XBRL-Related Documents are required by this section to comply with content and format requirements related to the corresponding official EDGAR filing, the purpose of submitting the XBRL-Related Documents is to test the related format and technology and, as a result, investors and others should continue to rely on the official version of the filing and not rely on the XBRL-Related Documents in making investment decisions.

[As last amended in Release No. 33-9006, effective July 15, 2009, 74 F.R. 7748 (see the release for detailed compliance information).]

[¶ 14,052] Liability for XBRL-Related Documents

Reg. § 232.402. (a) *Not deemed filed for liability purposes.* XBRL-Related Documents, regardless of whether they are exhibits to a document incorporated by reference into a filing::

(1) Are not deemed filed for purposes of section 11 of the Securities Act (15 U.S.C 77k), section 18 of the Exchange Act (15 U.S.C. 78r), or section 34(b) of the Investment Company Act (15 U.S.C. 80a-33(b)), or otherwise subject to the liabilities of these sections, and are not part of any registration statement to which they relate;

(2) Are not deemed incorporated by reference;

(3) Are subject to all other liability and anti-fraud provisions of these Acts; and

(4) Are deemed filed for purposes of Item 103 of Regulation S-T (§ 232.103).

(b) *Accurate reflection of underlying documents.* An electronic filer is not liable under the Securities Act, Exchange Act, Public Utility Act, Trust Indenture Act or Investment Company Act for information in its XBRL-Related Documents that complies with the requirements of Rule 401 of Regulation S-T (§ 232.401) to the extent that such information was not materially false or misleading in the corresponding official EDGAR filing. To the extent the information in an electronic filer's XBRL-Related Documents does not comply with the requirements of Rule 401, the information in the XBRL-Related Documents will be deemed to comply with Rule 401 for purposes of this paragraph if the electronic filer makes a good faith and reasonable attempt to comply with Rule 401 and, as soon as reasonably practicable after the electronic filer becomes aware that the information in the XBRL-Related Documents does not comply with Rule 401, the electronic filer amends the XBRL-Related Documents and, as a result, the information complies with Rule 401.

[As last amended in Release No. 33-8823, effective August 20, 2007, 72 F.R. 39290.]

[¶ 14,055] Interactive Data File Submissions and Postings

Reg. § 232.405. *Preliminary Note 1.* Sections 405 and 406T of Regulation S-T (§§ 232.405 and 232.406T) apply to electronic filers that submit or post Interactive Data Files. Item 601(b)(101) of Regulation S-K (§ 229.601(b)(101) of this chapter), paragraph (101) of Part II – Information Not Required to be Delivered to Offerees or Purchasers of both Form F-9 (§ 239.39 of this chapter) and Form F-10 (§ 239.40 of this chapter), paragraph 101 of the Instructions as to Exhibits of Form 20-F (§ 249.220f of this chapter), paragraph B.(15) of the General Instructions to Form 40-F (§ 249.240f of this chapter), paragraph C.(6) of the General Instructions to Form 6-K (§ 249.306 of this chapter), and General Instruction C.3.(g) of Form N-1A (§§ 239.15A and 274.11A of this chapter) specify when electronic filers are required or permitted to submit or post an Interactive Data File (§ 232.11), as further described in the Note to § 232.405.

Preliminary Note 2. Section 405 imposes content, format, submission and Web site posting requirements for an Interactive Data File, but does not change the substantive content requirements for the financial and other disclosures in the Related Official Filing (§ 232.11).

Preliminary Note 3. Section 406T addresses liability related to Interactive Data Files.

(a) *Content, format, submission and posting requirements - General.* An Interactive Data File must:

(1) Comply with the content, format, submission and Web site posting requirements of this section;

(2) Be submitted only by an electronic filer either required or permitted to submit an Interactive Data File as specified by Item 601(b)(101) of Regulation S-K, paragraph (101) of Part II – Information Not Required to be Delivered to Offerees or Purchasers of either Form F-9 or Form F-10, paragraph 101 of the Instructions as to Exhibits of Form 20-F, paragraph B.(15) of the General Instructions to Form 40-F, paragraph C.(6) of the General Instructions to Form 6-K, or General Instruction C.3.(g) of Form N-1A, as applicable, as an exhibit to:

(i) A form that contains the disclosure required by this section; or

(ii) If the electronic filer is not an open-end management investment company registered under the Investment Company Act, an amendment to a form that contains the disclosure required by this section if the amendment is filed no more than 30 days after the earlier of the due date or filing date of the form and the Interactive Data File is the first Interactive Data File the electronic filer submits or the first Interactive Data File the electronic filer submits that complies or is required to comply, whichever occurs first, with paragraphs (d)(1) through (d)(4), (e)(1), and (e)(2) of this section;

(3) Be submitted in accordance with the EDGAR Filer Manual and, as applicable, either Item 601(b)(101) of Regulation S-K, paragraph (101) of Part II – Information Not Required to be Delivered to Offerees or Purchasers of either Form F-9 or Form F-10, paragraph 101 of the Instructions as to Exhibits of Form 20-F, paragraph B.(15) of the General Instructions to Form 40-F, paragraph C.(6) of the General Instructions to Form 6-K, or General Instruction C.3.(g) of Form N-1A; and

(4) Be posted on the electronic filer's corporate Web site, if any, in accordance with, as applicable, either Item 601(b)(101) of Regulation S-K, paragraph (101) of Part II – Information Not Required to be Delivered to Offerees or Purchasers of either Form F-9 or Form F-10, paragraph 101 of the Instructions as to Exhibits of Form 20-F, paragraph B.(15) of the General Instructions to Form 40-F, paragraph C.(6) of the General Instructions to Form 6-K, or General Instruction C.3.(g) of Form N-1A.

(b)(1) *Content - categories of information presented.* If the electronic filer is not an open-end management investment company registered under the Investment Company Act of 1940, an Interactive Data File must consist of only a complete set of information for all periods required to be presented in the corresponding data in the Related Official Filing, no more and no less, from all of the following categories:

(i) The complete set of the electronic filer's financial statements (which includes the face of the financial statements and all footnotes); and

(ii) All schedules set forth in Article 12 of Regulation S-X (§§ 210.12-01 - 210.12-29) related to the electronic filer's financial statements.

Note to paragraph (b)(1): It is not permissible for the Interactive Data File to present only partial face financial statements, such as by excluding comparative financial information for prior periods.

(2) If the electronic filer is an open-end management investment company registered under the Investment Company Act of 1940, an Interactive Data File must consist of only a complete set of information for all periods required to be presented in the corresponding data in the Related Official Filing, no more and no less, from the risk/return summary information set forth in Items 2, 3, and 4 of Form N-1A.

(c) *Format - Generally.* An Interactive Data File must comply with the following requirements, except as modified by paragraph (d) or (e) of this section, as applicable, with respect to the corresponding data in the Related Official Filing consisting of footnotes to financial statements or financial statement schedules as set forth in Article 12 of Regulation S-X:

(1) *Data elements and labels.*

(i) *Element accuracy.* Each data element (*i.e.*, all text, line item names, monetary values, percentages, numbers, dates and other labels) contained in the Interactive Data File reflects the same information in the corresponding data in the Related Official Filing;

(ii) *Element specificity.* No data element contained in the corresponding data in the Related Official Filing is changed, deleted or summarized in the Interactive Data File;

(iii) *Standard and special labels and elements.* Each data element contained in the Interactive Data File is matched with an appropriate tag from the most recent version of the standard list of tags specified by the EDGAR Filer Manual. A tag is appropriate only when its standard definition, standard label and other attributes as and to the extent identified in the list of tags match the information to be tagged, except that:

(A) *Labels.* An electronic filer must create and use a new special label to modify a tag's existing standard label when that tag is an appropriate tag in all other respects (*i.e.*, in order to use a tag from the standard list of tags only its label needs to be changed); and

(B) *Elements.* An electronic filer must create and use a new special element if and only if an appropriate tag does not exist in the standard list of tags for reasons other than or in addition to an inappropriate standard label; and

(2) *Additional mark-up related content.* The Interactive Data File contains any additional mark-up related content (*e.g.*, the eXtensible Business Reporting Language tags themselves, identification of the core XML documents used and other technology related content) not found in the corresponding data in the Related Official Filing that is necessary to comply with the EDGAR Filer Manual requirements.

(d) *Format - Footnotes - Generally.* The part of the Interactive Data File for which the corresponding data in the Related Official Filing consists of footnotes to financial statements must comply with the requirements of paragraphs (c)(1) and (c)(2) of this section, as modified by this paragraph (d), unless the electronic filer is within one of the categories specified in paragraph (f) of this section. Footnotes to financial statements must be tagged as follows:

(1) Each complete footnote must be block-text tagged;

(2) Each significant accounting policy within the significant accounting policies footnote must be block-text tagged;

(3) Each table within each footnote must be block-text tagged; and

(4) Within each footnote,

(i) Each amount (*i.e.*, monetary value, percentage, and number) must be tagged separately; and

(ii) Each narrative disclosure may be tagged separately to the extent the electronic filer chooses.

(e) *Format - Schedules - Generally.* The part of the Interactive Data File for which the corresponding data in the Related Official Filing consists of financial statement schedules as set forth in Article 12 of Regulation S-X must comply with the requirements of paragraphs (c)(1) and (c)(2) of this section, as modified by this paragraph (e), unless the electronic filer is within one of the categories specified in paragraph (f) of this section. Financial statement schedules as set forth in Article 12 of Regulation S-X must be tagged as follows:

(1) Each complete financial statement schedule must be block-text tagged; and

(2) Within each financial statement schedule,

(i) Each amount (*i.e.*, monetary value, percentage and number) must be tagged separately; and

(ii) Each narrative disclosure may be tagged separately to the extent the electronic filer chooses.

(f) *Format - Footnotes and Schedules Eligible for Phased-In Detail.* The following electronic filers must comply with paragraphs (c)(1) and (c)(2) of this section as modified by paragraphs (d) and (e) of this section, except that they may choose to comply with paragraph (d)(1) of this section rather than paragraphs (d)(1) through (d)(4) of this section and may choose to comply with paragraph (e)(1) of this section rather than paragraphs (e)(1) and (e)(2) of this section:

(1) Any large accelerated filer (§ 240.12b-2 of this chapter) that had an aggregate worldwide market value of the voting and non-voting common equity held by non-affiliates of more than $5 billion as of the last business day of the second fiscal quarter of its most recently completed fiscal year that prepares its financial statements in accordance with generally accepted accounting principles as used in the United States, if none of the financial statements for which an Interactive Data File is required is for a fiscal period that ends on or after June 15, 2010;

(2) Any large accelerated filer not specified in paragraph (f)(1) of this section that prepares its financial statements in accordance with generally accepted accounting principles as used in the United States, if none of the financial statements for which an Interactive Data File is required is for a fiscal period that ends on or after June 15, 2011; and

(3) Any filer not specified in paragraph (f)(1) or (f)(2) of this section that prepares its financial statements in accordance with either generally accepted accounting principles as used in the United States or International Financial Reporting Standards as issued by the International Accounting Standards Board, if none of the financial statements for which an Interactive Data File is required is for a fiscal period that ends on or after June 15, 2012.

(g) *Posting.* Any electronic filer that maintains a corporate Web site and is required to submit an Interactive Data File must post that Interactive Data File on that Web site by the end of the calendar day on the earlier of the date the Interactive Data File is submitted or is required to be submitted, and, if the electronic filer is not an open-end management company registered under the Investment Company Act of 1940, the Interactive Data File must remain accessible on that Web site for at least a 12-month period. For an electronic filer that is an open-end management investment company registered under the Investment Company Act of 1940, General Instruction C.3.(g) of Form N-1A specifies the period of time for which an Interactive Data File must remain accessible on a company's Web site.

Note to § 232.405: Item 601(b)(101) of Regulation S-K specifies the circumstances under which an Interactive Data File must be submitted as an exhibit and be posted to the issuer's corporate Web site, if any, and the circumstances under which it is permitted to be submitted as an exhibit, with respect to Forms S-1 (§ 239.11 of this chapter), S-3 (§ 239.13 of this chapter), S-4 (§ 239.25 of this chapter), S-11 (§ 239.18 of this chapter), F-1 (§ 239.31 of this chapter), F-3 (§ 239.33 of this chapter), F-4 (§ 239.34 of this chapter), 10-K (§ 249.310 of this chapter), 10-Q (§ 249.308a of this chapter) and 8-K (§ 249.308 of this chapter). Paragraph 101 of the Information Not Required to be Delivered to Offerees or Purchasers of both Form F-9 and Form F-10 specifies the circumstances under which an Interactive Data File must be submitted as an exhibit and be posted to the issuer's corporate Web site, if any, and the circumstances under which it is permitted to be submitted as an exhibit, with respect to Form F-9 and Form F-10, respectively. Item 101 of the Instructions as to Exhibits of Form 20-F specifies the circumstances under which an Interactive Data File must be submitted as an exhibit and be posted to the issuer's corporate Web site, if any, and the circumstances under which it is permitted to be submitted as an exhibit, with respect to Form 20-F. Paragraph B.7 of the General Instructions to Form 40-F and Paragraph C.6 of the General Instructions to Form 6-K specify the circumstances under which an Interactive Data File must be submitted as an exhibit and be posted to the issuer's corporate Web site, if any, and the circumstances under which it is permitted to be submitted as an exhibit, with respect to Form 40-F and Form 6-K, respectively. Item 601(b)(101) of Regulation S-K, paragraph 101 of the Information Not Required to be Delivered to Offerees or Purchasers of both Form F-9 and Form F-10, Item 101 of the Instructions as to Exhibits of Form 20-F, paragraph B.7 of the General Instructions to Form 40-F and paragraph C.6 of the General Instructions to Form 6-K all prohibit submission of an Interactive Data File by an issuer that prepares its financial statements in accordance with Article 6 of Regulation S-X (17 CFR 210.6-01 *et. seq.*). For an issuer that is an open-end management investment company registered under the Investment Company Act of 1940, General Instruction C.3.(g) of Form N-1A specifies the circumstances under which an Interactive Data File must be submitted as an exhibit and be posted to the company's Web site, if any.

[Corrected in Release No. 33-9006A, 74 F.R. 21255, effective July 15, 2009 (see the release for detailed compliance information).]

⫸→ *Added by Release No. 33-9002, effective April 13, 2009 until October 31, 2014, 74 F.R. 6776.*

[¶ 14,057] Temporary Rule Related to Interactive Data Files

Reg. § 232.406T. (a) *Scope.* Section 232.406T addresses the liability for the Interactive Data File. An Interactive Data File is subject to the same liability provisions as the Related Official Filing except as provided in paragraphs (b) and (c) of this section.

(b) *In general.* The Interactive Data File, regardless of whether it is an exhibit to a document incorporated by reference into filings:

(1) Is subject to the anti-fraud provisions of section 17(a)(1) of the Securities Act, section 10(b) of the Exchange Act, § 240.10b-5 of this chapter, and section 206(1) of the Investment Advisers Act except as provided in paragraph (c) of this section;

(2) Is deemed not filed or part of a registration statement or prospectus for purposes of sections 11 or 12 of the Securities Act, is deemed not filed for purposes of section 18 of the Exchange Act or section 34(b) of the Investment Company Act, and otherwise is not subject to liability under these sections; and

(3) Is deemed filed for purposes of § 232.103.

(c) *Good faith attempts and prompt correction.* Subject to paragraph (b) of this section, the Interactive Data File shall be subject to liability for a failure to comply with § 232.405, but shall be deemed to have complied with § 232.405 and would not be subject to liability under the anti-fraud provisions set forth in paragraph (b)(1) of this section or under any other liability provision if the electronic filer:

(1) Makes a good faith attempt to comply with § 232.405; and

(2) After the electronic filer becomes aware that the Interactive Data File fails to comply with § 232.405, promptly amends the Interactive Data File to comply with § 232.405.

(d) *Temporary section.* Section 232.406T is a temporary section that applies to an Interactive Data File submitted to the Commission less than 24 months after the electronic filer first was required to submit an Interactive Data File to the Commission pursuant to § 232.405, not taking into account any grace period, but no later than October 31, 2014. After these dates, an Interactive Data File is subject to the same liability provisions as the Related Official Filing. This temporary section will expire on October 31, 2014.

[Added by Release No. 33-9002, effective April 13, 2009 until October 31, 2014, 74 F.R. 6776.]

Subpart 232.500—EDGAR Functions

[¶ 14,061] Modular Submissions and Segmented Filings

Reg. § 232.501. An electronic filer may use the following procedures to submit information to the EDGAR system for subsequent inclusion in an electronic filing:

(a) *Modular Submissions.*

(1) One or more electronic format documents may be submitted for storage in the non-public EDGAR data storage area as a modular submission for subsequent inclusion in one or more electronic submissions.

(2) An electronic filer shall be permitted a maximum of ten modular submissions in the non-public EDGAR data storage area at any time, not to exceed a total of one megabyte of digital information. If an electronic filer attempts to submit a modular filing which would cause either of these limits to be

exceeded, EDGAR will suspend the modular submission and notify the electronic filer by electronic mail. After six business days, the modular submission held in suspense will be deleted from the system.

(3) A modular submission may be corrected or amended only by resubmitting the entire modular submission.

(b) *Segmented Filings.*

(1) Segments of a document intended to become an electronic filing may be submitted to the non-public EDGAR data storage area for assembly as a segmented filing.

(2) Segments shall be submitted no more than six business days in advance of the anticipated filing date and are not limited in number or size. They may be submitted from several geographic locations by more than one filing entity. Segments may be included in only one electronic filing. Once used, segments will be removed from the non-public EDGAR data storage area. The assembly of segments into a segmented filing shall be effected pursuant to the applicable provisions of the EDGAR Filer Manual. If segments are not prepared in accordance with the EDGAR Filer Manual, the filing will not be constructed. The filing date of a segmented filing shall be the date upon which the filing is assembled and satisfies the requirements of Rule 13(a) of Regulation S-T (§ 232.13(a)).

(3) Segments may be corrected or amended only by resubmitting the entire segment.

(c) A modular submission or segment shall not:

(1) be publicly available;

(2) be deemed filed with the Commission for purposes of Securities Act Section 11 (15 U.S.C. 77k), Exchange Act Section 18 (15 U.S.C. 78r), Public Utility Act Section 16 (15 U.S.C. 79p), Trust Indenture Act Section 323 (15 U.S.C. 77www), or Investment Company Act Section 34(b) (15 U.S.C. 80a-33(b)) prior to its inclusion in a filing; or

(3) be deemed to constitute an official filing prior to its inclusion in a filing under the federal securities laws. Once a modular submission or segment has been included in an electronic filing, the liability and anti-fraud provisions of the Securities Act, the Exchange Act, the Trust Indenture Act, the Public Utility Act and the Investment Company Act shall apply to the electronic filing.

[As last amended in Release No. 33-7855, effective May 30, 2000, 65 F.R. 24788.]

Subpart 232.600—Foreign Private Issuers and Foreign Governments

[¶ 14,071] Foreign Private Issuers and Foreign Governments

Reg. § 232.601. Reserved.

[Removed and Reserved in Release No. 33-8099, effective November 4, 2002, 67 F.R. 36678.]

Subpart 232.700—[Reserved]

Subpart 232.800—[Reserved]

Subpart 232.900—Transition to Electronic Filing

[Removed and reserved in Release No. 33-7427, July 1, 1997, effective August 7, 1997, 62 F.R. 36450.]

[¶ 14,101] Division of Corporation Finance EDGAR Transition

Reg. § 232.901. [Removed and reserved in Release No. 33-7427, July 1, 1997, effective August 7, 1997, 62 F.R. 36450.]

[¶ 14,102] Division of Investment Management EDGAR Transition

Reg. § 232.902. [Removed and reserved in Release No. 33-7427, July 1,1997, effective August 7, 1997, 62 F.R. 36450.]

[¶ 14,103] Division of Investment Management Investment Management Electronic Submissions during Transition

Reg. § 232.903. [Removed and reserved in Release No. 33-7427, July 1, 1997, effective August 7, 1997, 62 F.R. 36450.]

EXCHANGE ACT RULES (selected)

EXCHANGE ACT RULES (SELECTED)

TABLE OF CONTENTS

EXCHANGE ACT

Regulations

ATTENTION ELECTRONIC FILERS
THIS REGULATION SHOULD BE READ IN CONJUNCTION WITH REGULATION S-T (PART 232 OF THIS CHAPTER), WHICH GOVERNS THE PREPARATION AND SUBMISSION OF DOCUMENTS IN ELECTRONIC FORMAT. MANY PROVISIONS RELATING TO THE PREPARATION AND SUBMIS-SION OF DOCUMENTS IN PAPER FORMAT CONTAINED IN THIS REGULATION ARE SUPER-SEDED BY THE PROVISIONS OF REGULATION S-T FOR DOCUMENTS REQUIRED TO BE FILED IN ELECTRONIC FORMAT.

RULES OF GENERAL APPLICATION

[¶ 20,001] Definitions

Reg. § 240.0-1. (a) As used in the Rules and Regulations prescribed by the Commission pursuant to Title I of the Securities Exchange Act of 1934, unless the context otherwise specifically requires—

(1) The term "Commission" means the Securities and Exchange Commission.

(2) The term "Act" means Title I of the Securities Exchange Act of 1934.

(3) The term "section" refers to a section of the Securities Exchange Act of 1934.

(4) The term "rules and regulations" refers to all rules and regulations adopted by the Commission pursuant to the Act, including the forms for registration and reports and the accompanying instructions thereto.

(5) The term "electronic filer" means a person or an entity that submits filings electronically pursuant to Rules 100 and 101 of Regulation S-T (§ § 232.100 and 232.101 of this chapter, respectively).

(6) The term "electronic filing" means a document under the federal securities laws that is transmitted or delivered to the Commission in electronic format.

(b) Unless otherwise specifically stated, the terms used in the Rules and Regulations shall have the meaning defined in the Act.

(c) A Rule or Regulation which defines a term without express reference to the Act or to the Rules and Regulations, or to a portion thereof, defines such term for all purposes as used both in the Act and in the Rules and Regulations, unless the context otherwise specifically requires.

(d) Unless otherwise specified or the context otherwise requires, the term "prospectus" means a prospectus meeting the requirements of Section 10(a) of the Securities Act of 1933 as amended.

[As last amended in Release No. 34-38798, July 1, 1997, effective August 7, 1997, 62 F.R. 36450.]

[¶ 20,011] Business Hours of the Commission

Reg. § 240.0-2. (a) The principal office of the Commission, at 100 F Street, NE, Washington, DC 20549, is open each day, except Saturdays, Sundays, and Federal holidays, from 9 a.m. to 5:30 p.m., Eastern Standard Time or Eastern Daylight Saving Time, whichever currently is in effect in Washington, DC, *provided that* hours for the filing of documents pursuant to the Act or the rules and regulations thereunder are as set forth in paragraphs (b) and (c) of this section.

(b) *Submissions made in paper.* Paper documents filed with or otherwise furnished to the Commission may be submitted to the Commission each day, except Saturdays, Sundays and federal holidays, from 8 a.m. to 5:30 p.m., Eastern Standard Time or Eastern Daylight Saving Time, whichever is currently in effect.

(c) *Filings by direct transmission.* Filings made by direct transmission may be submitted to the Commission each day, except Saturdays, Sundays and federal holidays, from 8:00 a.m. to 10:00 p.m., Eastern Standard Time or Eastern Daylight Saving Time, whichever is currently in effect.

[As last amended in Release No. 33-8876, effective February 4, 2008, 73 F.R. 934.]

[¶ 20,021] Filing of Material with the Commission

Reg. § 240.0-3. (a) All papers required to be filed with the Commission pursuant to the Act or the rules and regulations thereunder shall be filed at the principal office in Washington, D.C. Material may be filed by delivery to the Commission, through the mails or otherwise. The date on which papers are actually received by the Commission shall be the date of filing thereof if all of the requirements with respect to the filing have been complied with, except that if the last day on which papers can be accepted as timely filed falls on a Saturday, Sunday or holiday, such papers may be filed on the first business day following.

(b) The manually signed original (or in the case of duplicate originals, one duplicate original) of all registrations, applications, statements, reports, or other documents filed under the Securities Exchange Act of 1934, as amended, shall be numbered sequentially (in addition to any internal numbering which otherwise may be present) by handwritten, typed, printed, or other legible form of notation from the facing page of the document through the last page of that document and any exhibits or attachments thereto. Further, the total number of pages contained in a numbered original shall be set forth on the first page of the document.

(c) Each document filed shall contain an exhibit index, which should immediately precede the exhibits filed with such document. The index shall list each exhibit filed and identify by handwritten, typed, printed, or other legible form of notation in the manually signed original, the page number in the sequential numbering system described in paragraph (b) of this section where such exhibit can be found or where it is stated that the exhibit is incorporated by reference. Further, the first page of the manually signed document shall list the page in the filing where the exhibit index is located.

[As last amended in Release No. 34-17095, effective October 6, 1980, 45 F.R. 58822.]

[¶ 20,031] Non-disclosure of Information Obtained in the Course of Examinations and Investigations

Reg. § 240.0-4. Information or documents obtained by officers or employees of the Commission in the course of any examination or investigation pursuant to Section 17(a) or 21(a) shall, unless made a matter of public record, be deemed confidential. Except as provided by 17 CFR 203.2, officers and employees are hereby prohibited from making such confidential information or documents or any other non-public records of the Commission available to anyone other than a member, officer or employee of the Commission, unless the Commission or the General Counsel, pursuant to delegated authority, authorizes the disclosure of such information or the production of such documents as not being contrary to the public interest. Any officer or employee who is served with a subpoena requiring the disclosure of such information or the production of such documents shall appear in court and, unless the authorization described in the preceding sentence shall have been given, shall respectfully decline to disclose the information or produce the documents called for, basing his refusal upon this rule. Any officer or employee who is served with such a subpoena shall promptly advise the General Counsel of the service of such subpoena, the nature of the information or documents sought, and any circumstances which may bear upon the desirability of making available such information or documents.

[As last amended in Release No. 34-25683, May 10, 1988, 53 F.R. 17458.]

[¶ 20,041] Reference to Rule by Obsolete Designation

Reg. § 240.0-5. Wherever in any rule, form, or instruction book specific reference is made to a rule by number or other designation which is now obsolete, such reference shall be deemed to be made to the corresponding rule or rules in these existing General Rules and Regulations.

[As adopted in Release No. 34-1887, September 10, 1938, 13 F.R. 8177.]

[¶ 20,051] Disclosure Detrimental to the National Defense or Foreign Policy

Reg. § 240.0-6. (a) Any requirement to the contrary notwithstanding, no registration statement, report, proxy statement or other document filed with the Commission or any securities exchange shall contain any document or information which, pursuant to Executive order, has been classified by an appropriate department or agency of the United States for protection in the interests of national defense or foreign policy.

(b) Where a document or information is omitted pursuant to paragraph (a) of this section, there shall be filed, in lieu of such document or information, a statement from an appropriate department or agency of the United States to the effect that such document or information has been classified or that the status thereof is awaiting determination. Where a document is omitted pursuant to paragraph (a) of this section, but information relating to the subject matter of such document is nevertheless included in material filed with the Commission pursuant to a determination of an appropriate department or agency of the United States that disclosure of such information would not be contrary to the interests of national defense or foreign policy, a statement from such department or agency to that effect shall be submitted for the information of the Commission. A registrant may rely upon any such statement in filing or omitting any document or information to which the statement relates.

(c) The Commission may protect any information in its possession which may require classification in the interests of national defense or foreign policy pending determination by an appropriate department or agency as to whether such information should be classified.

(d) It shall be the duty of the registrant to submit the documents or information referred to in paragraph (a) of this section to the appropriate department or agency of the United States prior to filing them with the Commission and to obtain and submit to the Commission, at the time of filing such documents or information, or in lieu thereof, as the case may be, the statements from such department or agency required by paragraph (b) of this section. All such statements shall be in writing.

[As last amended in Release No. 34-8313, May 14, 1968, 33 F.R. 7682.]

[¶ 20,071] Application of Rules to Registered Broker-Dealers

Reg. § 240.0-8. Any provisions of any rule or regulation under the Act which prohibits any act, practice, or course of business by any person if the mails or any means or instrumentality of interstate commerce are used in connection therewith, shall also prohibit any such act, practice, or course of business by any broker or dealer registered pursuant to Section 15(b) of the Act, or any person acting on behalf of such a broker or dealer, irrespective of any use of the mails or by any means or instrumentality of interstate commerce.

[As adopted in Release No. 34-7406, September 3, 1964, 29 F.R. 12554.]

[¶ 20,081] Payment of Fees

Reg. § 240.0-9. All payment of fees shall be made by wire transfer, or by certified check, bank cashier's check, United States postal money order, or bank money order payable to the Securities and Exchange Commission, omitting the name or title of any official of the Commission. Payment of filing fees required by this section shall be made in accordance with the directions set forth in § 202.3a of this chapter.

[As last amended in Release No. 33-8885, effective February 1, 2008, 73 F.R. 6011.]

[¶ 20,091] Small Entities Under the Securities Exchange Act for Purposes of the Regulatory Flexibility Act

Reg. § 240.0-10. For purposes of Commission rulemaking in accordance with the provisions of Chapter Six of the Administrative Procedure Act [5 U.S.C. § 601 *et seq.*], and unless otherwise defined for purposes of a particular rulemaking proceeding, the term "small business" or "small organization" shall—

(a) When used with reference to an "issuer" or a "person," other than an investment company, mean an "issuer" or "person" that, on the last day of its most recent fiscal year, had total assets of $5 million or less;

(b) When used with reference to an "issuer" or "person" that is an investment company, have the meaning ascribed to those terms by § 270.0-10 of this chapter;

(c) When used with reference to a broker or dealer, mean a broker or dealer that:

(1) Had total capital (net worth plus subordinated liabilities) of less than $500,000 on the date in the prior fiscal year as of which its audited financial statements were prepared pursuant to § 240.17a-5(d) or, if not required to file such statements, a broker or dealer that had total capital (net worth plus subordinated liabilities) of less than $500,000 on the last business day of the preceding fiscal year (or in the time that it has been in business, if shorter); and

(2) Is not affiliated with any person (other than a natural person) that is not a small business or small organization as defined in this section;

(d) When used with reference to a clearing agency, mean a clearing agency that:

(1) Compared, cleared and settled less than $500 million in securities transactions during the preceding fiscal year (or in the time that it has been in business, if shorter);

(2) Had less than $200 million of funds and securities in its custody or control at all times during the preceding fiscal year (or in the time that it has been in business, if shorter); and

(3) Is not affiliated with any person (other than a natural person) that is not a small business or small organization as defined in this section;

(e) When used with reference to an exchange, mean any exchange that:

(1) Has been exempted from the reporting requirements of § 242.601 of this chapter; and

(2) Is not affiliated with any person (other than a natural person) that is not a small business or small organization as defined in this section;

(f) When used with reference to a municipal securities dealer that is a bank (including any separately identifiable department or division of a bank), mean any such municipal securities dealer that:

(1) Had, or is a department of a bank that had, total assets of less than $10 million dollars at all times during the preceding fiscal year (or in the time that it has been in business, if shorter);

(2) Had an average monthly volume of municipal securities transactions in the preceding fiscal year (or in the time it has been registered, if shorter) of less than $100,000; and

(3) Is not affiliated with any person (other than a natural person) that is not a small business or small organization as defined in this section;

(g) When used with reference to a securities information processor, mean a securities information processor that:

(1) Had gross revenues of less than $10 million during the preceding fiscal year (or in the time it has been in business, if shorter);

(2) Provided service to fewer than 100 interrogation devices or moving tickers at all times during the preceding fiscal year (or in the time that it has been in business, if shorter); and

(3) Is not affiliated with any person (other than a natural person) that is not a small business or small organization under this section; and

(h) When used with reference to a transfer agent, mean a transfer agent that:

(1) Received less than 500 items for transfer and less than 500 items for processing during the preceding six months (or in the time that it has been in business, if shorter);

(2) Transferred items only of issuers that would be deemed "small businesses" or "small organizations" as defined in this section; and

(3) Maintained master shareholder files that in the aggregate contained less than 1,000 shareholder accounts or was the named transfer agent for less than 1,000 shareholder accounts at all times during the preceding fiscal year (or in the time that it has been in business, if shorter); and

(4) Is not affiliated with any person (other than a natural person) that is not a small business or small organization under this section.

(i) For purposes of paragraph (c) of this section, a broker or dealer is affiliated with another person if:

(1) Such broker or dealer controls, is controlled by, or is under common control with such other person; a person shall be deemed to control another person if that person has the right to vote 25 percent or more of the voting securities of such other person or is entitled to receive 25 percent or more of the net profits of such other person or is otherwise able to direct or cause the direction of the management or policies of such other person; or

(2) Such broker or dealer introduces transactions in securities, other than registered investment company securities or interests or participations in insurance company separate accounts, to such other person, or introduces accounts of customers or other brokers or dealers, other than accounts that hold only registered investment company securities or interests or participations in insurance company separate accounts, to such other person that carries such accounts on a fully disclosed basis.

(j) For purposes of paragraphs (d) through (h) of this section, a person is affiliated with another person if that person controls, is controlled by, or is under common control with such other person; a person shall be deemed to control another person if that person has the right to vote 25 percent or more of the voting securities of such other person or is entitled to receive 25 percent or more of the net profits of such other person or is otherwise able to direct or cause the direction of the management or policies of such other person.

(k) For purposes of paragraph (g) of this section, "interrogation device" shall refer to any device that may be used to read or receive securities information, including quotations, indications of interest, last sale data and transaction reports, and shall include proprietary terminals or personal computers that receive securities information via computer-to-computer interfaces or gateway access.

[As last amended in Release No. 34-51808, effective August 29, 2005, 70 F.R. 37496.]

[¶ 20,092] Filing Fees for Certain Acquisitions, Dispositions and Similar Transactions

Reg. § 240.0-11. (a) *General.* (1) At the time of filing a disclosure document described in paragraphs (b) through (d) of this section relating to certain acquisitions, dispositions, business combinations, consolidations or similar transactions, the person filing the specified document shall pay a fee payable to the Commission to be calculated as set forth in paragraph (b) through (d) of this section.

(2) Only one fee per transaction is required to be paid. A required fee shall be reduced in an amount equal to any fee paid with respect to such transaction pursuant to either Section 6(b) of the Securities Act of 1933 or any applicable provision of this rule; the fee requirements under Section 6(b) shall be reduced in an amount equal to the fee paid the Commission with respect to a transaction under this regulation. No part of a filing fee is refundable.

(3) If at any time after the initial payment the aggregate consideration offered is increased, an additional filing fee based upon such increase shall be paid with the required amended filing.

(4) When the fee is based upon the market value of securities, such market value shall be established by either the average of the high and low prices reported in the consolidated reporting system (for exchange traded securities and last sale reported over-the-counter securities) or the average of the bid and asked price (for other over-the-counter securities) as of a specified date within 5 business days prior to the date of the filing. If there is no market for the securities, the value shall be based upon the book value of the securities computed as of the latest practicable date prior to the date of the filing,

unless the issuer of the securities is in bankruptcy or receivership or has an accumulated capital deficit, in which case one-third of the principal amount, par value or stated value of the securities shall be used.

(5) The cover page of the filing shall set forth the calculation of the fee in tabular format, as well as the amount offset by a previous filing and the identification of such filing, if applicable. [Amended in Release No. 34-31905, effective April 26, 1993, 58 FR 14628.]

(b) *Section 13(e)(1) Filings.* At the time of filing such statement as the Commission may require pursuant to section 13(e)(1) of the Exchange Act, a fee of one-fiftieth of one percent of the value of the securities proposed to be acquired by the acquiring person. The value of the securities proposed to be acquired shall be determined as follows:

(1) The value of the securities to be acquired solely for cash shall be the amount of cash to be paid for them;

(2) The value of the securities to be acquired with securities or other non-cash consideration, whether or not in combination with a cash payment for the same securities, shall be based upon the market value of the securities to be received by the acquiring person as established in accordance with paragraph (a)(4) of this section.

(c) *Proxy and information statement filings.* At the time of filing a preliminary proxy statement pursuant to Rule 14a-6(a) or preliminary information statement pursuant to Rule 14c-5(a) that concerns a merger, consolidation, acquisition of a company, or proposed sale or other disposition of substantially all the assets of the registrant (including a liquidation), the following fee:

(1) For preliminary material involving a vote upon a merger, consolidation or acquisition of a company, a fee of one-fiftieth of one percent of the proposed cash payment or of the value of the securities and other property to be transferred to security holders in the transaction. The fee is payable whether the registrant is acquiring another company or being acquired.

(i) The value of securities or other property to be transferred to security holders, whether or not in combination with a cash payment for the same securities, shall be based upon the market value of the securities to be received by the acquiring person as established in accordance with paragraph (a)(4) of this section.

(ii) Notwithstanding the above, where the acquisition, merger or consolidation is for the sole purpose of changing the registrant's domicile, no filing fee is required to be paid. [Amended in Release No. 34-37692, September 17, 1996, effective October 7, 1996, 61 F.R. 49957.]

(2) For preliminary material involving a vote upon a proposed sale or other disposition of substantially all the assets of the registrant, a fee of one-fiftieth of one percent of the aggregate of the cash and the value of the securities (other than its own) and other property to be received by the registrant. In the case of a disposition in which the registrant will not receive any property, such as a liquidation or spin-off, the fee shall be one-fiftieth of one percent of the aggregate of the cash and the value of the securities and other property to be distributed to security holders.

(i) The value of the securities to be received (or distributed in the case of a spin-off or liquidation) shall be based upon the market value of such securities as established in accordance with paragraph (a)(4) of this section.

(ii) The value of other property shall be a bona fide estimate of the fair market value of such property.

(3) Where two or more companies are involved in the transaction, each shall pay a proportionate share of such fee, determined by the persons involved.

(4) Notwithstanding the above, the fee required by this paragraph (c) shall not be payable for a proxy statement filed by a company registered under the Investment Company Act of 1940.

(d) *Section 14(d)(1) filings.* At the time of filing such statement as the Commission may require pursuant to section 14(d)(1) of the Act, a fee of one-fiftieth of one percent of the aggregate of the cash or of the value of the securities or other property offered by the bidder. Where the bidder is offering securities or other non-cash consideration for some or all of the securities to be acquired, whether or not in combination with a cash payment for the same securities, the value of the consideration to be offered for such securities shall be based upon the market value of the securities to be received by the bidder as established in accordance with paragraph (a)(4) of this section.

[As last amended in Release No. 34-55146A, effective April 1, 2008, 73 F.R. 17809 (technical correction).]

[¶ 20,093] Commission Procedures for Filing Applications for Orders For Exemptive Relief Pursuant to Section 36 of the Exchange Act

Reg. § 240.0-12. (a) The application shall be in writing in the form of a letter, must include any supporting documents necessary to make the application complete, and otherwise must comply with § 240.0-3. All applications must be submitted to the Office of the Secretary of the Commission.

Requestors may seek confidential treatment of their applications to the extent provided under § 200.81 of this chapter. If an application is incomplete, the Commission, through the Division handling the application, may request that the application be withdrawn unless the applicant can justify, based on all the facts and circumstances, why supporting materials have not been submitted and undertakes to submit the omitted materials promptly.

(b) An applicant may submit a request electronically in standard electronic mail text or ASCII format. The electronic mailbox to use for these applications is described on the Commission's website at www.sec.gov in the "Exchange Act Exemptive Applications" subsection located under the "Current SEC Rulemaking" section. In the event electronic mailboxes are revised in the future, applicants can find the appropriate mailbox by accessing the Commission's website directory of electronic mailboxes at http://www.sec.gov/asec/mailboxs.htm.

(c) An applicant also may submit a request in paper format. Five copies of every paper application and every amendment to such an application must be submitted to the Office of the Secretary at 100 F Street, NE, Washington, DC 20549-1090. Applications must be on white paper no larger than 8-1/2 by 11 inches in size. The left margin of applications must be at least 1-1/2 inches wide, and if the application is bound, it must be bound on the left side. All typewritten or printed material must be on one side of the paper only and must be set forth in black ink so as to permit photocopying.

(d) Every application (electronic or paper) must contain the name, address and telephone number of each applicant and the name, address, and telephone number of a person to whom any questions regarding the application should be directed. The Commission will not consider hypothetical or anonymous requests for exemptive relief. Each applicant shall state the basis for the relief sought, and identify the anticipated benefits for investors and any conditions or limitations the applicant believes would be appropriate for the protection of investors. Applicants should also cite to and discuss applicable precedent.

(e) Amendments to the application should be prepared and submitted as set forth in these procedures and should be marked to show what changes have been made.

(f) After the filing is complete, the applicable Division will review the application. Once all questions and issues have been answered to the satisfaction of the Division, the staff will make an appropriate recommendation to the Commission. After consideration of the recommendation by the Commission, the Commission's Office of the Secretary will issue an appropriate response and will notify the applicant. If the application pertains to a section of the Exchange Act pursuant to which the Commission has delegated its authority to the appropriate Division, the Division Director or his or her designee will issue an appropriate response and notify the applicant.

(g) The Commission, in its sole discretion, may choose to publish in the Federal Register a notice that the application has been submitted. The notice would provide that any person may, within the period specified therein, submit to the Commission any information that relates to the Commission action requested in the application. The notice also would indicate the earliest date on which the Commission would take final action on the application, but in no event would such action be taken earlier than 25 days following publication of the notice in the Federal Register.

(h) The Commission may, in its sole discretion, schedule a hearing on the matter addressed by the application.

[As last amended in Release No. 33-8876, effective February 4, 2008, 73 F.R. 934.]

[¶ 20,094] Exemption from the Definition of the "Exchange" under Section 3(a)(1) of the Act

Reg. § 240.3a1-1. (a) An organization, association, or group of persons shall be exempt from the definition of the term "exchange" under Section 3(a)(1) of the Act, (15 U.S.C. 78c(a)(1)), if such organization, association, or group of persons:

(1) Is operated by a national securities association;

(2) Is in compliance with Regulation ATS, 17 CFR 242.300 through 242.303; or

(3) Pursuant to paragraph (a) of § 242.301 of Regulation ATS, 17 CFR 242.301(a), is not required to comply with Regulation ATS, 17 CFR 242.300 through 242.303.

(b) Notwithstanding paragraph (a) of this section, an organization, association, or group of persons shall not be exempt under this section from the definition of "exchange," if:

(1) During three of the preceding four calendar quarters such organization, association, or group of persons had:

(i) Fifty percent or more of the average daily dollar trading volume in any security and five percent or more of the average daily dollar trading volume in any class of securities; or

(ii) Forty percent or more of the average daily dollar trading volume in any class of securities; and

(2) The Commission determines, after notice to the organization, association, or group of persons, and an opportunity for such organization, association, or group of persons to respond, that such an

exemption would not be necessary or appropriate in the public interest or consistent with the protection of investors taking into account the requirements for exchange registration under Section 6 of the Act, (15 U.S.C. 78f), and the objectives of the national market system under Section 11A of the Act, (15 U.S.C 78k-1).

(3) For purposes of paragraph (b) of this section, each of the following shall be considered a "class of securities":

(i) Equity securities, which shall have the same meaning as in § 240.3a11-1;

(ii) Listed options, which shall mean any options traded on a national securities exchange or automated facility of a national securities exchange;

(iii) Unlisted options, which shall mean any options other than those traded on a national securities exchange or automated facility of a national securities association;

(iv) Municipal securities, which shall have the same meaning as in Section 3(a)(29) of the Act, (15 U.S.C. 78c(a)(29));

(v) Corporate debt securities, which shall mean any securities that:

(A) Evidence a liability of the issuer of such securities;

(B) Have a fixed maturity date that is at least one year following the date of issuance; and

(C) Are not exempted securities, as defined in section 3(a)(12) of the Act, (15 U.S.C. 78c(a)(12));

(vi) Foreign corporate debt securities, which shall mean any securities that:

(A) Evidence a liability of the issuer of such debt securities;

(B) Are issued by a corporation or other organization incorporated or organized under the laws of any foreign country; and

(C) Have a fixed maturity date that is at least one year following the date of issuance; and

(vii) Foreign sovereign debt securities, which shall mean any securities that:

(A) Evidence a liability of the issuer of such debt securities;

(B) Are issued or guaranteed by the government of a foreign country, any political subdivision of a foreign country or any supranational entity; and

(C) Do not have a maturity date of a year or less following the date of issuance.

[As last amended by Release No. 34-60789, effective November 12, 2009, 74 F.R. 52358.]

[¶ 20,095] Associated Persons of an Issuer Deemed Not to Be Brokers

Reg. § 240.3a4-1. (a) An associated person of an issuer of securities shall not be deemed to be a broker solely by reason of his participation in the sale of the securities of such issuer if the associated person:

(1) Is not subject to a statutory disqualification, as that term is defined in Section 3(a)(39) of the Act, at the time of his participation; and

(2) Is not compensated in connection with his participation by the payment of commissions or other remuneration based either directly or indirectly on transactions in securities; and

(3) Is not at the time of his participation an associated person of a broker or dealer; and

(4) Meets the conditions of any one of paragraphs (a)(4)(i), (ii), or (iii) of this section.

(i) The association person restricts his participation to transactions involving offers and sales of securities:

(A) To a registered broker or dealer; a registered investment company (or registered separate account); an insurance company; a bank; a savings and loan association; a trust company or simliar institution supervised by a state or federal banking authority; or a trust for which a bank, a savings and loan association, a trust company, or a registered investment adviser either is the trustee or is authorized in writing to make investment decisions; or

(B) That are exempted by reason of Section 3(a)(7), 3(a)(9) or 3(a)(10) of the Securities Act of 1933 from the registration provisions of that Act; or

(C) That are made pursuant to a plan or agreement submitted for the vote or consent of the security holders who will receive securities of the issuer in connection with a reclassification of securities of the issuer, a merger or consolidation or a similar plan of acquisition involving an exchange of securities, or a transfer of assets of any other person to the issuer in exchange for securities of the issuer; or

(D) That are made pursuant to a bonus, profit-sharing, pension, retirement, thrift, savings, incentive, stock purchase, stock ownership, stock appreciation, stock option, dividend reinvestment or similar plan for employees of an issuer or a subsidiary of the issuer;

(ii) The associated person meets all of the following conditions:

(A) The associated person primarily performs, or is intended primarily to perform at the end of the offering, substantial duties for or on behalf of the issuer otherwise than in connection with transactions in securities; and

(B) The associated person was not a broker or dealer, or an associated person of a broker or dealer, within the preceding 12 months; and

(C) The associated person does not participate in selling an offering of securities for any issuer more than once every 12 months other than in reliance on paragraphs (a)(4)(i) or (a)(4)(iii) of this section, except that for securities issued pursuant to Rule 415 under the Securities Act of 1933, the 12 months shall begin with the last sale of any security included within one Rule 415 registration.

(iii) The associated person restricts his participation to any one or more of the following activities:

(A) Preparing any written communication or delivering such communication through the mails or other means that does not involve oral solicitation by the associated person of a potential purchaser; *provided, however,* that the content of such communication is approved by a partner, officer or director of the issuer;

(B) Responding to inquiries of a potential purchaser in a communication initiated by the potential purchaser; *provided, however,* that the content of such responses are limited to information contained in a registration statement filed under the Securities Act of 1933 or other offering document; or

(C) Performing ministerial and clerical work involved in effecting any transaction.

(b) No presumption shall arise that an associated person of an issuer has violated Section 15(a) of the Act solely by reason of his participation in the sale of securities of the issuer if he does not meet the conditions specified in paragraph (a) of this section.

(c) *Definitions.* When used in this section:

(1) The term "associated person of an issuer" means any natural person who is a partner, officer, director, or employee of:

(i) The issuer;

(ii) A corporate general partner of a limited partnership that is the issuer;

(iii) A company or partnership that controls, is controlled by, or is under common control with, the issuer; or

(iv) An investment adviser registered under the Investment Advisers Act of 1940 to an investment company registered under the Investment Company Act of 1940 which is the issuer.

(2) The term "associated person of a broker or dealer" means any partner, officer, director, or branch manager of such broker or dealer (or any person occupying a similar status or performing similar functions), any person directly or indirectly controlling, controlled by, or under common control with such broker or dealer, or any employee of such broker or dealer, except that any person associated with a broker or dealer whose functions are solely clerical or ministerial and any person who is required under the laws of any state to register as a broker or dealer in that state solely because such person is an issuer of securities or associated person of an issuer of securities shall not be included in the meaning of such term for purposes of this section.

[As adopted in Release No. 34-22172, June 27, 1985, 50 F.R. 26584.]

DEFINITIONS

[¶ 20,281] Definition of "Penny Stock"

Reg. § 240.3a51-1. For purposes of Section 3(a)(51) of the Act, the term "penny stock" shall mean any equity security other than a security:

(a) That is an NMS stock, as defined in § 242.600(b)(47), provided that:

(1) The security is registered, or approved for registration upon notice of issuance, on a national securities exchange that has been continuously registered as a national securities exchange since April 20, 1992 (the date of the adoption of Rule 3a51-1 (§ 240.3a51-1) by the Commission); and the national securities exchange has maintained quantitative listing standards that are substantially similar to or stricter than those listing standards that were in place on that exchange on January 8, 2004; or

(2) The security is registered, or approved for registration upon notice of issuance, on a national securities exchange, or is listed, or approved for listing upon notice of issuance on, an automated quotation system sponsored by a registered national securities association, that:

(i) Has established initial listing standards that meet or exceed the following criteria:

(A) The issuer shall have:

(1) Stockholders' equity of $5,000,000;

(2) Market value of listed securities of $50 million for 90 consecutive days prior to applying for the listing (market value means the closing bid price multiplied by the number of securities listed); or

(3) Net income of $750,000 (excluding extraordinary or non-recurring items) in the most recently completed fiscal year or in two of the last three most recently completed fiscal years;

(B) The issuer shall have an operating history of at least one year or a market value of listed securities of $50 million (market value means the closing bid price multiplied by the number of securities listed);

(C) The issuer's stock, common or preferred, shall have a minimum bid price of $4 per share;

(D) In the case of common stock, there shall be at least 300 round lot holders of the security (a round lot holder means a holder of a normal unit of trading);

(E) In the case of common stock, there shall be at least 1,000,000 publicly held shares and such shares shall have a market value of at least $5 million (market value means the closing bid price multiplied by number of publicly held shares, and shares held directly or indirectly by an officer or director of the issuer and by any person who is the beneficial owner of more than 10 percent of the total shares outstanding are not considered to be publicly held);

(F) In the case of a convertible debt security, there shall be a principal amount outstanding of at least $10 million;

(G) In the case of rights and warrants, there shall be at least 100,000 issued and the underlying security shall be registered on a national securities exchange or listed on an automated quotation system sponsored by a registered national securities association and shall satisfy the requirements of paragraph (a) or (e) of this section;

(H) In the case of put warrants (that is, instruments that grant the holder the right to sell to the issuing company a specified number of shares of the company's common stock, at a specified price until a specified period of time), there shall be at least 100,000 issued and the underlying security shall be registered on a national securities exchange or listed on an automated quotation system sponsored by a registered national securities association and shall satisfy the requirements of paragraph (a) or (e) of this section;

(I) In the case of units (that is, two or more securities traded together), all component parts shall be registered on a national securities exchange or listed on an automated quotation system sponsored by a registered national securities association and shall satisfy the requirements of paragraph (a) or (e) of this section; and

(J) In the case of equity securities (other than common and preferred stock, convertible debt securities, rights and warrants, put warrants, or units), including hybrid products and derivative securities products, the national securities exchange or registered national securities association shall establish quantitative listing standards that are substantially similar to those found in paragraphs (a)(2)(i)(A) through (a)(2)(i)(I) of this section; and

(ii) Has established quantitative continued listing standards that are reasonably related to the initial listing standards set forth in paragraph (a)(2)(i) of this section, and that are consistent with the maintenance of fair and orderly markets;

(b) that is issued by an investment company registered under the Investment Company Act of 1940;

(c) that is a put or call option issued by the Options Clearing Corporation;

(d) except for purposes of Section 7(b) of the Securities Act and Rule 419 (17 CFR 230.419), that has a price of five dollars or more;

(1) For purposes of paragraph (d) of this section:

(i) a security has a price of five dollars or more for a particular transaction if the security is purchased or sold in that transaction at a price of five dollars or more, excluding any broker or dealer commission, commission equivalent, mark-up, or mark-down; and

(ii) other than in connection with a particular transaction, a security has a price of five dollars or more at a given time if the inside bid quotation is five dollars or more; *provided, however,* that if there is no such inside bid quotation, a security has a price of five dollars or more at a given time if the average of three or more interdealer bid quotations at specified prices displayed at that time in an interdealer quotation system, as defined in 17 CFR 240.15c2-7(c)(1), by three or more market makers in the security, is five dollars or more.

(iii) The term "inside bid quotation" shall mean the highest bid quotation for the security displayed by a market maker in the security on an automated interdealer quotation system that has the characteristics set forth in Section 17B(b)(2) of the Act, or such other automated interdealer quotation system designated by the Commission for purposes of this section, at any time in which at least two market makers are contemporaneously displaying on such system bid and offer quotations for the security at specified prices.

(2) If a security is a unit composed of one or more securities, the unit price divided by the number of shares of the unit that are not warrants, options, rights, or similar securities must be five dollars or more, as determined in accordance with paragraph (d)(1) of this section, and any share of the unit that is a warrant, option, right, or similar security, or a convertible security, must have an exercise price or conversion price of five dollars or more;

(e)(1) That is registered, or approved for registration upon notice of issuance, on a national securities exchange that makes transaction reports available pursuant to § 242.601, provided that:

(i) Price and volume information with respect to transactions in that security is required to be reported on a current and continuing basis and is made available to vendors of market information pursuant to the rules of the national securities exchange;

(ii) The security is purchased or sold in a transaction that is effected on or through the facilities of the national securities exchange, or that is part of the distribution of the security; and

(iii) The security satisfies the requirements of paragraph (a)(1) or (a)(2) of this section;

(2) A security that satisfies the requirements of this paragraph (e), but does not otherwise satisfy the requirements of paragraph (a), (b), (c), (d), (f), or (g) of this section, shall be a penny stock for purposes of section 15(b)(6) of the Act (15 U.S.C. 78o(b)(6));

(f) That is a security futures product listed on a national securities exchange or an automated quotation system sponsored by a registered national securities association; or

(g) whose issuer has:

(1) net tangible assets (*i.e.*, total assets less intangible assets and liabilities) in excess of $2,000,000, if the issuer has been in continuous operation for at least three years, or $5,000,000, if the issuer has been in continuous operation for less than three years; or

(2) average revenue of at least $6,000,000 for the last three years.

(3) For purposes of paragraph (g) of this section, net tangible assets or average revenues must be demonstrated by financial statements dated less than fifteen months prior to the date of the transaction that the broker or dealer has reviewed and has a reasonable basis for believing are accurate in relation to the date of the transaction, and:

(i) if the issuer is other than a foreign private issuer, are the most recent financial statements for the issuer that have been audited and reported on by an independent public accountant in accordance with the provisions of 17 CFR 210.2-02; or

(ii) if the issuer is a foreign private issuer, are the most recent financial statements for the issuer that have been filed with the Commission or furnished to the Commission pursuant to 17 CFR 240.12g3-2(b) of this chapter; *provided, however,* that if financial statements for the issuer dated less than fifteen months prior to the date of the transaction have not been filed with or furnished to the Commission, financial statements dated within fifteen months prior to the transaction shall be prepared in accordance with generally accepted accounting principles in the country of incorporation, audited in compliance with the requirements of that jurisdiction, and reported on by an accountant duly registered and in good standing in accordance with the regulations of that jurisdiction;

(4) The broker or dealer shall preserve, as part of its records, copies of the financial statements required by paragraph (g)(3) of this section for the period specified in 17 CFR 240.17a-4(b) of this chapter.

[As last amended in Release No. 34-51983A, effective September 12, 2005, 70 F.R. 46089.]

[¶ 20,286] Method for Determining Market Capitalization and Dollar Value of Average Daily Trading Volume; Application of the Definition of Narrow-Based Security Index

Reg. § 240.3a55-1. (a) *Market capitalization.* For purposes of Section 3(a)(55)(C)(i)(III)(bb) of the Act (15 U.S.C. 78c(a)(55)(C)(i)(III)(bb)):

(1) On a particular day, a security shall be 1 of 750 securities with the largest market capitalization as of the preceding 6 full calendar months when it is included on a list of such securities designated by the Commission and the CFTC as applicable for that day.

(2) In the event that the Commission and the CFTC have not designated a list under paragraph (a)(1) of this section:

(i) The method to be used to determine market capitalization of a security as of the preceding 6 full calendar months is to sum the values of the market capitalization of such security for each U.S. trading day of the preceding 6 full calendar months, and to divide this sum by the total number of such trading days.

(ii) The 750 securities with the largest market capitalization shall be identified from the universe of all NMS securities as defined in § 242.600 of this chapter that are common stock or depositary shares.

(b) *Dollar value of ADTV.*

(1) For purposes of Section 3(a)(55)(B) of the Act (15 U.S.C. 78c(a)(55)(B)):

(i)(A) The method to be used to determine the dollar value of ADTV of a security is to sum the dollar value of ADTV of all reported transactions in such security in each jurisdiction as calculated pursuant to paragraphs (b)(1)(ii) and (iii).

(B) The dollar value of ADTV of a security shall include the value of all reported transactions for such security and for any depositary share that represents such security.

(C) The dollar value of ADTV of a depositary share shall include the value of all reported transactions for such depositary share and for the security that is represented by such depositary share.

(ii) For trading in a security in the United States, the method to be used to determine the dollar value of ADTV as of the preceding 6 full calendar months is to sum the value of all reported transactions in such security for each U.S. trading day during the preceding 6 full calendar months, and to divide this sum by the total number of such trading days.

(iii) (A) For trading in a security in a jurisdiction other than the United States, the method to be used to determine the dollar value of ADTV as of the preceding 6 full calendar months is to sum the value in U.S. dollars of all reported transactions in such security in such jurisdiction for each trading day during the preceding 6 full calendar months, and to divide this sum by the total number of trading days in such jurisdiction during the preceding 6 full calendar months.

(B) If the value of reported transactions used in calculating the ADTV of securities under paragraph (b)(1)(iii)(A) is reported in a currency other than U.S. dollars, the total value of each day's transactions in such currency shall be converted into U.S. dollars on the basis of a spot rate of exchange for that day obtained from at least one independent entity that provides or disseminates foreign exchange quotations in the ordinary course of its business.

(iv) The dollar value of ADTV of the lowest weighted 25% of an index is the sum of the dollar value of ADTV of each of the component securities comprising the lowest weighted 25% of such index.

(2) For purposes of Section 3(a)(55)(C)(i)(III)(cc) of the Act (15 U.S.C. 78c(a)(55)(C)(i)(III)(cc)):

(i) On a particular day, a security shall be 1 of 675 securities with the largest dollar value of ADTV as of the preceding 6 full calendar months when it is included on a list of such securities designated by the Commission and the CFTC as applicable for that day.

(ii) In the event that the Commission and the CFTC have not designated a list under paragraph (b)(2) of this section:

(A) The method to be used to determine the dollar value of ADTV of a security as of the preceding 6 full calendar months is to sum the value of all reported transactions in such security in the United States for each U.S. trading day during the preceding 6 full calendar months, and to divide this sum by the total number of such trading days.

(B) The 675 securities with the largest dollar value of ADTV shall be identified from the universe of all NMS securities as defined in § 242.600 of this chapter that are common stock or depositary shares.

(c) *Depositary Shares and Section 12 Registration.* For purposes of Section 3(a)(55)(C) of the Act (15 U.S.C. 78c(a)(55)(C)), the requirement that each component security of an index be registered pursuant to Section 12 of the Act (15 U.S.C. 78*l*) shall be satisfied with respect to any security that is a depositary share if the deposited securities underlying the depositary share are registered pursuant to Section 12 of the Act and the depositary share is registered under the Securities Act of 1933 (15 U.S.C. 77a *et seq.*) on Form F-6 (17 CFR 239.36).

(d) *Definitions.* For purposes of this section:

(1) *CFTC* means Commodity Futures Trading Commission.

(2) *Closing price* of a security means:

(i) If reported transactions in the security have taken place in the United States, the price at which the last transaction in such security took place in the regular trading session of the principal market for the security in the United States.

(ii) If no reported transactions in a security have taken place in the United States, the closing price of such security shall be the closing price of any depositary share representing such security divided by the number of shares represented by such depositary share.

(iii) If no reported transactions in a security or in a depositary share representing such security have taken place in the United States, the closing price of such security shall be the price at which the last transaction in such security took place in the regular trading session of the principal market for the security. If such price is reported in a currency other than U.S. dollars, such price shall be converted into U.S. dollars on the basis of a spot rate of exchange relevant for the time of the transaction obtained from at least one independent entity that provides or disseminates foreign exchange quotations in the ordinary course of its business.

(3) *Depositary share* has the same meaning as in § 240.12b-2.

(4) *Foreign financial regulatory authority* has the same meaning as in Section 3(a)(52) of the Act (15 U.S.C. 78c(a)(52)).

(5) *Lowest weighted 25% of an index.*

With respect to any particular day, the lowest weighted component securities comprising, in the aggregate, 25% of an index's weighting for purposes of Section 3(a)(55)(B)(iv) of the Act (15 U.S.C. 78c(a)(55)(B)(iv)) ("lowest weighted 25% of an index") means those securities:

(i) That are the lowest weighted securities when all the securities in such index are ranked from lowest to highest based on the index's weighting methodology; and

(ii) For which the sum of the weight of such securities is equal to, or less than, 25% of the index's total weighting.

(6) *Market capitalization* of a security on a particular day:

(i) If the security is not a depositary share, is the product of:

(A) The closing price of such security on that same day; and

(B) The number of outstanding shares of such security on that same day.

(ii) If the security is a depositary share, is the product of:

(A) The closing price of the depositary share on that same day divided by the number of deposited securities represented by such depositary share; and

(B) The number of outstanding shares of the security represented by the depositary share on that same day. (7) *Outstanding shares* of a security means the number of outstanding shares of such security as reported on the most recent Form10-K, Form10-Q, Form 10-KSB, Form 10-QSB, or Form 20-F (17 CFR 249.310, 249.308a, 249.310b, 249.308b, or 249.220f) filed with the Commission by the issuer of such security, including any change to such number of outstanding shares subsequently reported by the issuer on a Form 8-K (17 CFR 249.308).

(8) *Preceding 6 full calendar months* means, with respect to a particular day, the period of time beginning on the same day of the month 6 months before and ending on the day prior to such day. (9) *Principal market* for a security means the single securities market with the largest reported trading volume for the security during the preceding 6 full calendar months.

(10) *Reported transaction* means:

(i) With respect to securities transactions in the United States, any transaction for which a transaction report is collected, processed, and made available pursuant to an effective transaction reporting plan, or for which a transaction report, last sale data, or quotation information is disseminated through an automated quotation system as described in Section 3(a)(51)(A)(ii) of the Act (15 U.S.C. 78c(a)(51)(A)(ii); and

(ii) With respect to securities transactions outside the United States, any transaction that has been reported to a foreign financial regulatory authority in the jurisdiction where such transaction has taken place.

(11) *U.S. trading day* means any day on which a national securities exchange is open for trading.

(12) *Weighting* of a component security of an index means the percentage of such index's value represented, or accounted for, by such component security.

[As last amended in Release No. 33-52115, effective August 29, 2005, 70 F.R. 43748.]

[¶ 20,287] Indexes Underlying Futures Contracts Trading for Fewer Than 30 Days

Reg. § 240.3a55-2. (a) An index on which a contract of sale for future delivery is trading on a designated contract market, registered derivatives transaction execution facility, or foreign board of trade is not a narrow-based security index under Section 3(a)(55) of the Act (15 U.S.C. 78c(a)(55)) for the first 30 days of trading, if:

(1) Such index would not have been a narrow-based security index on each trading day of the preceding 6 full calendar months with respect to a date no earlier than 30 days prior to the commencement of trading of such contract;

(2) On each trading day of the preceding 6 full calendar months with respect to a date no earlier than 30 days prior to the commencement of trading such contract:

(i) Such index had more than 9 component securities;

(ii) No component security in such index comprised more than 30 percent of the index's weighting;

(iii) The 5 highest weighted component securities in such index did not comprise, in the aggregate, more than 60 percent of the index's weighting; and

(iv) The dollar value of the trading volume of the lowest weighted 25% of such index was not less than $50 million (or in the case of an index with 15 or more component securities, $30 million); or (3) On each trading day of the preceding 6 full calendar months, with respect to a date no earlier than 30 days prior to the commencement of trading such contract:

(i) Such index had at least 9 component securities;

(ii) No component security in such index comprised more than 30 percent of the index's weighting; and

(iii) Each component security in such index was:

(A) Registered pursuant to Section 12 of the Act (15 U.S.C. 78) or was a depositary share representing a security registered pursuant to Section 12 of the Act;

(B) 1 of 750 securities with the largest market capitalization that day; and

(C) 1 of 675 securities with the largest dollar value of trading volume that day.

(b) An index that is not a narrow-based security index for the first 30 days of trading pursuant to paragraph (a) of this section, shall become a narrow-based security index if such index has been a narrow-based security index for more than 45 business days over 3 consecutive calendar months.

(c) An index that becomes a narrow-based security index solely because it was a narrow-based security index for more than 45 business days over 3 consecutive calendar months pursuant to paragraph (b) of this section shall not be a narrow-based security index for the following 3 calendar months.

(d) *Definitions.* For purposes of this section:

(1) *Market capitalization* has the same meaning as in § 240.3a55-1(d)(6).

(2) *Dollar value of trading volume* of a security on a particular day is the value in U.S. dollars of all reported transactions in such security on that day. If the value of reported transactions used in calculating dollar value of trading volume is reported in a currency other than U.S. dollars, the total value of each day's transactions shall be converted into U.S. dollars on the basis of a spot rate of exchange for that day obtained from at least one independent entity that provides or disseminates foreign exchange quotations in the ordinary course of its business.

(3) *Lowest weighted 25% of an index* has the same meaning as in § 240.3a55-1(d)(5).

(4) *Preceding 6 full calendar months* has the same meaning as in § 240.3a55-1(d)(8).

(5) *Reported transaction* has the same meaning as in § 240.3a55-1(d)(10).

[As adopted in Release No. 34-44724, effective August 21, 2001, 66 F.R. 44490.]

[¶ 20,288] Futures Contracts on Security Indexes Trading on or Subject to the Rules of a Foreign Board of Trade

Reg. § 240.3a55-3. When a contract of sale for future delivery on a security index is traded on or subject to the rules of a foreign board of trade, such index shall not be a narrow-based security index if it would not be a narrow-based security index if a futures contract on such index were traded on a designated contract market or registered derivatives transaction execution facility.

[As adopted in Release No. 34-44724, effective August 21, 2001, 66 F.R. 44490.]

[¶ 20,301] Definition of "Listed"

Reg. § 240.3b-1. The term "listed" means admitted to full trading privileges upon application by the issuer or its fiscal agent or, in the case of the securities of a foreign corporation, upon application by a banker engaged in distributing them; and includes securities for which authority to add to the list on official notice of issuance has been granted.

[As last amended in Release No. 34-1887, September 10, 1938.]

[¶ 20,311] Definition of "Officer"

Reg. § 240.3b-2. The term "officer" means a president, vice president, secretary, treasurer or principal financial officer, comptroller or principal accounting officer, and any person routinely performing corresponding functions with respect to any organization whether incorporated or unincorporated.

[As last amended in Release No. 34-18524, effective for all documents filed on or after May 24, 1982, 47 F.R. 11380.]

[¶ 20,331] Definition of "foreign government", "foreign issuer" and "foreign private issuer"

Reg. § 240.3b-4. (a) The term "foreign government" means the government of any foreign country or of any political subdivision of a foreign country.

(b) The term "foreign issuer" means any issuer which is a foreign government, a national of any foreign country or a corporation or other organization incorporated or organized under the laws of any foreign country.

(c) The term *foreign private issuer* means any foreign issuer other than a foreign government except for an issuer meeting the following conditions as of the last business day of its most recently completed second fiscal quarter:

(1) More than 50 percent of the issuer's outstanding voting securities are directly or indirectly held of record by residents of the United States; and

(2) Any of the following:

(i) The majority of the executive officers or directors are United States citizens or residents;

(ii) More than 50 percent of the assets of the issuer are located in the United States; or

(iii) The business of the issuer is administered principally in the United States.

Instruction to paragraph (c)(1): To determine the percentage of outstanding voting securities held by U.S. residents:

A. Use the method of calculating record ownership in Rule 12g3-2(a) under the Act (§240.12g3-2(a)), except that your inquiry as to the amount of shares represented by accounts of customers resident in the United States may be limited to brokers, dealers, banks and other nominees located in (1) the United States, (2) your jurisdiction of incorporation, and (3) the jurisdiction that is the primary trading market for your voting securities, if different than your jurisdiction of incorporation.

B. If, after reasonable inquiry, you are unable to obtain information about the amount of shares represented by accounts of customers resident in the United States, you may assume, for purposes of this definition, that the customers are residents of the jurisdiction in which the nominee has its principal place of business.

C. Count shares of voting securities beneficially owned by residents of the United States as reported on reports of beneficial ownership provided to you or filed publicly and based on information otherwise provided to you.

(d) Notwithstanding paragraph (c) of this section, in the case of a new registrant with the Commission, the determination of whether an issuer is a foreign private issuer will be made as of a date within 30 days prior to the issuer's filing of an initial registration statement under either the Act or the Securities Act of 1933.

(e) Once an issuer qualifies as a foreign private issuer, it will immediately be able to use the forms and rules designated for foreign private issuers until it fails to qualify for this status at the end of its most recently completed second fiscal quarter. An issuer's determination that it fails to qualify as a foreign private issuer governs its eligibility to use the forms and rules designated for foreign private issuers beginning on the first day of the fiscal year following the determination date. Once an issuer fails to qualify for foreign private issuer status, it will remain unqualified unless it meets the requirements for foreign private issuer status as of the last business day of its second fiscal quarter.

[As last amended in Release No. 33-8959, effective December 5, 2008, 73 F.R. 58300.]

[¶ 20,341] Non-Exempt Securities Issued Under Governmental Obligations

Reg. § 240.3b-5. (a) Any part of an obligation evidenced by any bond, note, debenture, or other evidence of indebtedness issued by any governmental unit specified in Section 3(a)(12) of the Act which is payable from payments to be made in respect of property or money which is or will be used, under a lease, sale, or loan arrangement, by or for industrial or commercial enterprise, shall be deemed to be a separate "security" within the meaning of Section 3(a)(10) of the Act, issued by the lessee, or obligor under the lease, sale or loan arrangement.

(b) An obligation shall not be deemed a separate "security" as defined in paragraph (a) hereof if, (1) the obligation is payable from the general revenues of a governmental unit, specified in Section 3(a)(12) of the Act, having other resources which may be used for payment of the obligation, or (2) the obligation relates to a public project or facility owned and operated by or on behalf of and under the control of a governmental unit specified in such section, or (3) the obligation relates to a facility which is leased to and under the control of an industrial or commercial enterprise but is a part of a public project which, as a whole, is owned by and under the general control of a governmental unit specified in such section, or an instrumentality thereof.

(c) This rule shall apply to transactions of the character described in paragraph (a) only with respect to bonds, notes, debentures or other evidences of indebtedness sold after December 31, 1968.

[As last amended in Release No. 34-8850, March 31, 1970, 35 F.R. 6000.]

[¶ 20,351] Liability for Certain Statements by Issuers

Reg. § 240.3b-6. (a) A statement within the coverage of paragraph (b) of this section which is made by or on behalf of an issuer or by an outside reviewer retained by the issuer shall be deemed not to be a fraudulent statement (as defined in paragraph (d) of this section), unless it is shown that such statement was made or reaffirmed without a reasonable basis or was disclosed other than in good faith.

(b) This rule applies to the following statements:

(1) A forward-looking statement (as defined in paragraph (c) of this section) made in a document filed with the Commission, in Part I of a quarterly report on Form 10-Q, § 249.308a of this chapter, or in an annual report to security holders meeting the requirements of Rules 14a-3(b) and (c) or 14c-3(a) and (b) (§§ 240.14a-3(b) and (c) or 240.14c-3(a) and (b)), a statement reaffirming such forward-looking statement after the date the document was filed or the annual report was made publicly available, or a forward-looking statement made before the date the document was filed or the date the annual report was made publicly available if such statement is reaffirmed in a filed document, in Part I of a quarterly report on Form 10-Q, or in an annual report made publicly available within a reasonable time after the making of such forward-looking statement; *Provided,* that:

(i) At the time such statements are made or reaffirmed, either the issuer is subject to the reporting requirements of Section 13(a) or 15(d) of the Act and has complied with the requirements of Rule 13a-1 or 15d-1 thereunder, if applicable, to file its most recent annual report on Form 10-K, Form 20-F or Form 40-F; or if the issuer is not subject to the reporting requirements of Section 13(a) or 15(d) of the Act, the statements are made in a registration statement filed under the Securities Act of 1933 offering statement or solicitation of interest, written document or broadcast script under Regulation A or pursuant to Section 12 (b) or (g) of the Securities Exchange Act of 1934; and

(ii) The statements are not made by or on behalf of an issuer that is an investment company registered under the Investment Company Act of 1940; and

(2) Information that is disclosed in a document filed with the Commission in Part I of a quarterly report on Form 10-Q (§ 249.308a of this chapter) or in an annual report to security holders meeting the requirements of Rules 14a-3(b) and (c) or 14c-3(a) and (b) under the Act (§§ 240.14a-3(b) and (c) or 240.14c-3(a) and (b) of this chapter) and that relates to:

(i) The effects of changing prices on the business enterprise, presented voluntarily or pursuant to Item 303 of Regulation S-K (§ 229.303 of this chapter), "Management's Discussion and Analysis of Financial Condition and Results of Operations," Item 5 of Form 20-F (§ 240.220(f) of this chapter), "Operating and Financial Review and Prospects," Item 302 of Regulation S-K (§ 229.302 of this chapter) "Supplementary Financial Information," or Rule 3-20(c) of Regulation S-X (§ 210.3-20(c)) of this chapter); or

(ii) The value of proved oil and gas reserves (such as a standardized measure of discounted future net cash flows relating to proved oil and gas reserves as set forth in paragraphs 30-34 of Statement of Financial Accounting Standards No. 69), presented voluntarily or pursuant to Item 302 of Regulation S-K (§ 229.302 of this chapter).

(c) For the purpose of this rule, the term *forward-looking statement* shall mean and shall be limited to:

(1) A statement containing a projection of revenues, income (loss), earnings (loss) per share, capital expenditures, dividends, capital structure or other financial items;

(2) A statement of management's plans and objectives for future operations;

(3) A statement of future economic performance contained in management's discussion and analysis of financial condition and results of operations included pursuant to Item 303 of Regulation S-K (§ 229.303 of this chapter) or Item 5 of Form 20-F or

(4) Disclosed statements of the assumptions underlying or relating to any of the statements described in paragraphs (c) (1), (2), or (3) of this section.

(d) For the purpose of this rule the term *fraudulent statement* shall mean a statement which is an untrue statement of a material fact, a statement false or misleading with respect to any material fact, an omission to state a material fact necessary to make a statement not misleading, or which constitutes the employment of a manipulative, deceptive, or fraudulent device, contrivance, scheme, transaction, act, practice, course of business, or an artifice to defraud, as those terms are used in the Securities Exchange Act of 1934 or the rules or regulations promulgated thereunder.

[As last amended in Release No. 33-8876, effective February 4, 2008, 73 F.R. 934.]

[¶ 20,361] Definition of "Executive Officer"

Reg. § 240.3b-7. The term "executive officer," when used with reference to a registrant, means its president, any vice president of the registrant in charge of a principal business unit, division or function (such as sales, administration, or finance), any other officer who performs a policy making function or any other person who performs similar policy making functions for the registrant. Executive officers of subsidiaries may be deemed executive officers of the registrant if they perform such policy making functions for the registrant.

[As last amended in Release No. 34-28869, February 8, 1991, effective May 1, 1991, 56 F.R. 7242.]

[¶ 20,371] Definitions of "Qualified OTC Market Maker," "Qualified Third Market Maker" and "Qualified Block Positioner"

Reg. § 240.3b-8. For the purposes of Regulation U under the Act (12 CFR 221):

(a) The term "Qualified OTC Market Maker" in an over-the-counter ("OTC") margin security means a dealer in any "OTC Margin Security" [as that term is defined in Section 2(j) of Regulation U (12 CFR 221.2(j)] who (1) is a broker or dealer registered pursuant to Section 15 of the Act, (2) is subject to and is in compliance with Rule 15c3-1 (17 CFR 240.15c3-1), (3) has and maintains minimum net capital, as defined in Rule 15c3-1, of the lesser of (i) $250,000 or (ii) $25,000 plus $5,000 for each security in excess of five with regard to which the broker or dealer is, or is seeking to become a Qualified OTC Market Maker, and (4) except when such activity is unlawful, meets all of the following conditions with respect to such security: (i) he regularly publishes bona fide, competitive bid and offer quotations in a recognized inter-dealer quotation system, (ii) he furnishes bona fide, competitive bid and offer quotations to other brokers and dealers on request, (iii) he is ready, willing and able to effect transactions in reasonable amounts, and at his quoted prices, with other brokers and dealers, and (iv) he has a reasonable average rate of inventory turnover in such security.

(b) The term "Qualified Third Market Maker" means a dealer in any stock registered on a national securities exchange ("exchange") who (1) is a broker or dealer registered pursuant to Section 15 of the Act, (2) is subject to and is in compliance with Rule 15c3-1 (17 CFR 240.15c3-1), (3) has and maintains minimum net capital, as defined in Rule 15c3-1, of the lesser of (i) $500,000 or (ii) $100,000 plus $20,000 for each security in excess of five with regard to which the broker or dealer is, or is seeking to become, a Qualified Third Market Maker, and (4) except when such activity is unlawful, meets all of the following conditions with respect to such security: (i) he furnishes bona fide, competitive bid and offer quotations at all times to other brokers and dealers on request, (ii) he is ready, willing and able to effect transactions for his own account in reasonable amounts, and at his quoted prices with other brokers and dealers, and (iii) he has a reasonable average rate of inventory turnover in such security.

(c) The term "Qualified Block Positioner" means a dealer who (1) is a broker or dealer registered pursuant to Section 15 of the Act, (2) is subject to and in compliance with Rule 15c3-1 (17 CFR 240.15c3-1), (3) has and maintains minimum net capital, as defined in Rule 15c3-1 of $1,000,000 and (4) except when such activity is unlawful, meets all of the following conditions: (i) he engages in the activity of purchasing long or selling short from time to time, from or to a customer (other than a partner or a joint venture or other entity in which a partner, the dealer, or a person associated with such dealer, as defined in Section 3(a)(18) of the Act, participates) a block of stock with a current market value of $200,000 or more in a single transaction, or in several transactions at approximately the same time, from a single source to facilitate a sale or purchase by such customer, (ii) he has determined in the exercise of reasonable diligence that the block could not be sold to or purchased from others on equivalent or better terms, and (iii) he sells the shares comprising the block as rapidly as possible commensurate with the circumstances.

[As adopted in Release No. 34-20121, August 26, 1983, 48 F.R. 39604.]

[¶ 20,383] Definitions Relating to Limited Partnership Roll-Up Transactions for Purposes of Sections 6(b)(9), 14(h) and 15A(b)(12)—(13)

Reg. § 240.3b-11. For purposes of Sections 6(b)(9), 14(h) and 15A(b)(12)—(13) of the Act (15 U.S.C. 78f(b)(9), 78n(h) and 78o-3(b)(12)—(13)):

(a) The term *limited partnership roll-up transaction* does not include a transaction involving only entities that are not "finite-life" as defined in Item 901(b)(2) of Regulation S-K (§ 229.901(b)(2) of this chapter).

(b) The term *limited partnership roll-up transaction* does not include a transaction involving only entities registered under the Investment Company Act of 1940 (15 U.S.C. 80a-1 *et seq.*) or any Business Development Company as defined in § 2(a)(48) of that Act (15 U.S.C. 80a-2(a)(48)).

(c) The term "regularly traded" shall be defined as in Item 901(c)(2)(v)(C) of Regulation S-K (§ 229.901(c)(2)(v)(C) of this chapter).

[As adopted in Release No. 34-35036, December 1, 1994, 59 F.R. 63676.]

[¶ 20,384] Definition of OTC Derivatives Dealer

Reg. § 240.3b-12. The term *OTC derivatives dealer* means any dealer that is affiliated with a registered broker or dealer (other than an OTC derivatives dealer), and whose securities activities:

(a) Are limited to:

(1) Engaging in dealer activities in eligible OTC derivative instruments that are securities;

(2) Issuing and reacquiring securities that are issued by the dealer, including warrants on securities, hybrid securities, and structured notes;

(3) Engaging in cash management securities activities;

(4) Engaging in ancillary portfolio management securities activities; and

(5) Engaging in such other securities activities that the Commission designates by order pursuant to § 240.15a-1(b)(1); and

(b) Consist primarily of the activities described in paragraphs (a)(1), (a)(2), and (a)(3) of this section; and

(c) Do not consist of any other securities activities, including engaging in any transaction in any security that is not an eligible OTC derivative instrument, except as permitted under paragraphs (a)(3), (a)(4), and (a)(5) of this section.

(d) For purposes of this section, the term *hybrid security* means a security that incorporates payment features economically similar to options, forwards, futures, swap agreements, or collars involving currencies, interest or other rates, commodities, securities, indices, quantitative measures, or other financial or economic interests or property of any kind, or any payment or delivery that is dependent on the occurrence or nonoccurrence of any event associated with a potential financial, economic, or commercial consequence (or any combination, permutation, or derivative of such contract or underlying interest).

[As adopted in Release No. 34-40594, effective January 4, 1999, 63 F.R. 59361.]

[¶ 20,385] Definition of Eligible OTC Derivative Instrument

Reg. § 240.3b-13. (a) Except as otherwise provided in paragraph (b) of this section, the term *eligible OTC derivative instrument* means any contract, agreement, or transaction that:

(1) Provides, in whole or in part, on a firm or contingent basis, for the purchase or sale of, or is based on the value of, or any interest in, one or more commodities, securities, currencies, interest or other rates, indices, quantitative measures, or other financial or economic interests or property of any kind; or

(2) Involves any payment or delivery that is dependent on the occurrence or nonoccurrence of any event associated with a potential financial, economic, or commercial consequence; or

(3) Involves any combination or permutation of any contract, agreement, or transaction or underlying interest, property, or event described in paragraphs (a)(1) or (a)(2) of this section.

(b) The term *eligible OTC derivative instrument* does not include any contract, agreement, or transaction that:

(1) Provides for the purchase or sale of a security, on a firm basis, unless:

(i) The settlement date for such purchase or sale occurs at least one year following the trade date or, in the case of an eligible forward contract, at least four months following the trade date; or

(ii) The material economic features of the contract, agreement, or transaction consist primarily of features of a type described in paragraph (a) of this section other than the provision for the purchase or sale of a security on a firm basis; or

(2) Provides, in whole or in part, on a firm or contingent basis, for the purchase or sale of, or is based on the value of, or any interest in, any security (or group or index of securities), and is:

(i) Listed on, or traded on or through, a national securities exchange or registered national securities association, or facility or market thereof; or

(ii) Except as otherwise determined by the Commission by order pursuant to § 240.15a-1(b)(2), one of a class of fungible instruments that are standardized as to their material economic terms.

(c) The Commission may issue an order pursuant to § 240.15a-1(b)(3) clarifying whether certain contracts, agreements, or transactions are within the scope of eligible OTC derivative instrument.

(d) For purposes of this section, the term *eligible forward contract* means a forward contract that provides for the purchase or sale of a security other than a government security, provided that, if such contract provides for the purchase or sale of margin stock (as defined in Regulation U of the Regulations of the Board of Governors of the Federal Reserve System, 12 CFR Part 221), such contract either:

(1) Provides for the purchase or sale of such stock by the issuer thereof (or an affiliate that is not a bank or a broker or dealer); or

(2) Provides for the transfer of transaction collateral in an amount that would satisfy the requirements, if any, that would be applicable assuming the OTC derivatives dealer party to such transaction were not eligible for the exemption from Regulation T of the Regulations of the Board of Governors of the Federal Reserve System, 12 CFR Part 220, set forth in § 240.36a1-1.

[As adopted in Release No. 34-40594, effective January 4, 1999, 63 F.R. 59361.]

[¶ 20,386] Definition of Cash Management Securities Activities

Reg. § 240.3b-14. The term *cash management securities activities* means securities activities that are limited to transactions involving:

(a) Any taking possession of, and any subsequent sale or disposition of, collateral provided by a counterparty, or any acquisition of, and any subsequent sale or disposition of, collateral to be provided to a counterparty, in connection with any securities activities of the dealer permitted under § 240.15a-1 or any non-securities activities of the dealer that involve eligible OTC derivative instruments or other financial instruments;

(b) Cash management, in connection with any securities activities of the dealer permitted under § 240.15a-1 or any non-securities activities of the dealer that involve eligible OTC derivative instruments or other financial instruments; or

(c) Financing of positions of the dealer acquired in connection with any securities activities of the dealer permitted under § 240.15a-1 or any non-securities activities that involve eligible OTC derivative instruments or other financial instruments.

[As adopted in Release No. 34-40594, effective January 4, 1999, 63 F.R. 59361.]

[¶ 20,387] Definition of Ancillary Portfolio Management Securities Activities

Reg. § 240.3b-15. (a) The term *ancillary portfolio management securities activities* means securities activities that:

(1) Are limited to transactions in connection with:

(i) Dealer activities in eligible OTC derivative instruments;

(ii) The issuance of securities by the dealer; or

(iii) Such other securities activities that the Commission designates by order pursuant to § 240.15a1(b)(1); and

(2) Are conducted for the purpose of reducing the market or credit risk of the dealer or consist of incidental trading activities for portfolio management purposes; and

(3) Are limited to risk exposures within the market, credit, leverage, and liquidity risk parameters set forth in:

(i) The trading authorizations granted to the associated person (or to the supervisor of such associated person) who executes a particular transaction for, or on behalf of, the dealer; and

(ii) The written guidelines approved by the governing body of the dealer and included in the internal risk management control system for the dealer pursuant to § 240.15c3-4; and

(4) Are conducted solely by one or more associated persons of the dealer who perform substantial duties for, or on behalf of, the dealer in connection with its dealer activities in eligible OTC derivative instruments.

(b) The Commission may issue an order pursuant to § 240.15a-1(b)(4) clarifying whether certain securities activities are within the scope of ancillary portfolio management securities activities.

[As adopted in Release No. 34-40594, effective January 4, 1999, 63 F.R. 59361.]

[¶ 20,388] Definitions of Terms Used in Section 3(a)(1) of the Act

Reg. § 240.3b-16. (a) An organization, association, or group of persons shall be considered to constitute, maintain, or provide "a market place or facilities for bringing together purchasers and sellers of securities or for otherwise performing with respect to securities the functions commonly performed by a stock exchange," as those terms are used in Section 3(a)(1) of the Act, (15 U.S.C. 78c(a)(1)), if such organization, association, or group of persons:

(1) Brings together the orders for securities of multiple buyers and sellers; and

(2) Uses established, non-discretionary methods (whether by providing a trading facility or by setting rules) under which such orders interact with each other, and the buyers and sellers entering such orders agree to the terms of a trade.

(b) An organization, association, or group of persons shall not be considered to constitute, maintain, or provide "a market place or facilities for bringing together purchasers and sellers of securities or for otherwise performing with respect to securities the functions commonly performed by a stock exchange," solely because such organization, association, or group of persons engages in one or more of the following activities:

(1) Routes orders to a national securities exchange, a market operated by a national securities association, or a broker-dealer for execution; or

(2) Allows persons to enter orders for execution against the bids and offers of a single dealer; and

(i) As an incidental part of these activities, matches orders that are not displayed to any person other than the dealer and its employees; or

(ii) In the course of acting as a market maker registered with a self-regulatory organization, displays the limit orders of such market maker's, or other broker-dealer's, customers; and

(A) Matches customer orders with such displayed limit orders; and

(B) As an incidental part of its market making activities, crosses or matches orders that are not displayed to any person other than the market maker and its employees.

(c) For purposes of this section the term *order* means any firm indication of a willingness to buy or sell a security, as either principal or agent, including any bid or offer quotation, market order, limit order, or other priced order.

(d) For the purposes of this section, the terms *bid* and *offer* shall have the same meaning as under § 242.600 of this chapter.

(e) The Commission may conditionally or unconditionally exempt any organization, association, or group of persons from the definition in paragraph (a) of this section.

[As last amended in Release No. 34-51808, effective August 29, 2005, 70 F.R. 37496.]

[¶ 20,390] Definitions of Terms Used in Section 3(a)(5) of the Act

Reg. § 240.3b-18. For the purposes of section 3(a)(5)(C) of the Act (15 U.S.C. 78c(a)(5)(C):

(a) The term *affiliate* means any company that controls, is controlled by, or is under common control with another company.

(b) The term "consumer-related receivable" means any obligation incurred by any natural person to pay money arising out of a transaction in which the money, property, insurance, or services (being purchased) are primarily for personal, family, or household purposes.

(c) The term "member" as it relates to the term "syndicate of banks" means a bank that is a participant in a syndicate of banks and together with its affiliates, other than its broker or dealer affiliates, originates no less than 10% of the value of the obligations in a pool of obligations used to back the securities issued through a grantor trust or other separate entity.

(d) The term "obligation" means any note, draft, acceptance, loan, lease, receivable, or other evidence of indebtedness that is not a security issued by a person other than the bank.

(e) The term "originated" means:

(1) Funding an obligation at the time that the obligation is created; or

(2) Initially approving and underwriting the obligation, or initially agreeing to purchase the obligation, provided that:

(i) The obligation conforms to the underwriting standards or is evidenced by the loan documents of the bank or its affiliates, other than its broker or dealer affiliates; and

(ii) The bank or its affiliates, other than its broker or dealer affiliates, fund the obligation in a timely manner, not to exceed six months after the obligation is created.

(f) The term "pool" means more than one obligation or type of obligation grouped together to provide collateral for a securities offering.

(g) The term "predominantly originated" means that no less than 85% of the value of the obligations in any pool were originated by:

(1) The bank or its affiliates, other than its broker or dealer affiliates; or

(2) Banks that are members of a syndicate of banks and affiliates of such banks, other than their broker or dealer affiliates, if the obligations or pool of obligations consist of mortgage obligations or consumer-related receivables.

(3) For this purpose, the bank and its affiliates include any financial institution with which the bank or its affiliates have merged but does not include the purchase of a pool of obligations or the purchase of a line of business

(h) The term "syndicate of banks" means a group of banks that acts jointly, on a temporary basis, to issue through a grantor trust or other separate entity, securities backed by obligations originated by each of the individual banks or their affiliates, other than their broker or dealer affiliates.

[As last amended in Release No. Release No. 34-47364, effective March 26, 2003, (compliance September 30, 2003), 68 F.R. 8686; Release No. 34-47366, February 13, 2003, extended the exemption from the definition of "dealer" until September 30, 2003.]

[¶ 20,395] Definition of "Issuer" in Section 3(a)(8) of the Act in Relation to Asset-backed Securities

Reg. § 240.3b-19. The following applies with respect to asset-backed securities under the Act. Terms used in this section have the same meaning as in Item 1101 of Regulation AB (§ 229.1101 of this chapter).

(a) The depositor for the asset-backed securities acting solely in its capacity as depositor to the issuing entity is the "issuer for purposes of the asset-backed securities of that issuing entity."

(b) The person acting in the capacity as the depositor specified in paragraph (a) of this section is a different "issuer" from that same person acting as a depositor for another issuing entity or for purposes of that person's own securities.

[As adopted in Release No. 33-8518, effective March 8, 2005, 70 F.R. 1506.]

MANIPULATIVE AND DECEPTIVE DEVICES AND CONTRIVANCES

[¶ 20,701] Prohibition of Use of Manipulative or Deceptive Devices or Contrivances with Respect to Certain Securities Exempted from Registration

Reg. § 240.10b-1. The term manipulative or deceptive device or contrivance, as used in Section 10(b), is hereby defined to include any act or omission to act with respect to any security exempted from the operation of Section 12(a) pursuant to a rule which specifically provides that this rule shall be applicable to such security, if such act or omission to act would have been unlawful under Section 9(a), or any rule or regulation heretofore or hereafter prescribed thereunder, if done or omitted to be done with respect to a security registered on a national securities exchange, and the use of any means or instrumentality of interstate commerce or of the mails or of any facility of any national securities exchange to use or employ any such device or contrivance in connection with the purchase or sale of any such security is hereby prohibited.

[As last amended in Release No. 34-1887, September 10, 1938.]

[¶ 20,721] Employment of Manipulative and Deceptive Devices

Reg. § 240.10b-3. (a) It shall be unlawful for any broker or dealer, directly or indirectly, by the use of any means or instrumentality of interstate commerce, or of the mails, or any facility of any national securities exchange, to use or employ, in connection with the purchase or sale of any security otherwise than on a national securities exchange, any act, practice, or course of business defined by the Commission to be included within the term "manipulative, deceptive or other fraudulent device or contrivance", as such term is used in Section 15(c) of the Act.

(b) It shall be unlawful for any municipal securities dealer directly or indirectly, by the use of any means or instrumentality of interstate commerce, or of the mails, or of any facility of any national securities exchange, to use or employ, in connection with the purchase or sale of any municipal security, any act, practice, or course of business defined by the Commission to be included within the term "manipulative, deceptive, or other fraudulent device or contrivance," as such term is used in Section 15(c)(1) of the Act.

[As last amended in Release No. 34-12468, May 20, 1976, 41 F.R. 22824.]

[¶ 20,741] Employment of Manipulative and Deceptive Devices

Reg. § 240.10b-5. It shall be unlawful for any person, directly or indirectly, by the use of any means or instrumentality of interstate commerce, or of the mails, or of any facility of any national securities exchange,

(a) to employ any device, scheme, or artifice to defraud,

(b) to make any untrue statement of a material fact or to omit to state a material fact necessary in order to make the statements made, in the light of the circumstances under which they were made, not misleading, or

(c) to engage in any act, practice, or course of business which operates or would operate as a fraud or deceit upon any person, in connection with the purchase or sale of any security.

[As adopted in Release No. 34-3230, May 21, 1942, 13 F.R. 8177.]

[¶ 20,742] Trading "on the basis of" Material Nonpublic Information in Insider Trading Cases

Reg. § 240.10b5-1. Preliminary Note to § 240.10b5-1: This provision defines when a purchase or sale constitutes trading "on the basis of" material nonpublic information in insider trading cases brought under Section 10(b) of the Act and Rule 10b-5 thereunder. The law of insider trading is otherwise defined by judicial opinions construing Rule 10b-5, and Rule 10b5-1 does not modify the scope of insider trading law in any other respect.

(a) General. The "manipulative and deceptive devices" prohibited by Section 10(b) of the Act (15 U.S.C. 78j) and § 240.10b-5 thereunder include, among other things, the purchase or sale of a security of any issuer, on the basis of material nonpublic information about that security or issuer, in breach of a duty of trust or confidence that is owed directly, indirectly, or derivatively, to the issuer of that security or the shareholders of that issuer, or to any other person who is the source of the material nonpublic information.

(b) Definition of "on the basis of." Subject to the affirmative defenses in paragraph (c) of this section, a purchase or sale of a security of an issuer is "on the basis of" material nonpublic information about that security or issuer if the person making the purchase or sale was aware of the material nonpublic information when the person made the purchase or sale.

(c) Affirmative defenses. (1)(i) Subject to paragraph (c)(1)(ii) of this section, a person's purchase or sale is not "on the basis of" material nonpublic information if the person making the purchase or sale demonstrates that:

(A) Before becoming aware of the information, the person had:

(1) Entered into a binding contract to purchase or sell the security,

(2) Instructed another person to purchase or sell the security for the instructing person's account, or

(3) Adopted a written plan for trading securities;

(B) The contract, instruction, or plan described in paragraph (c) (1) (i) (A) of this Section:

(1) Specified the amount of securities to be purchased or sold and the price at which and the date on which the securities were to be purchased or sold;

(2) Included a written formula or algorithm, or computer program, for determining the amount of securities to be purchased or sold and the price at which and the date on which the securities were to be purchased or sold; or

(3) Did not permit the person to exercise any subsequent influence over how, when, or whether to effect purchases or sales; provided, in addition, that any other person who, pursuant to the contract, instruction, or plan, did exercise such influence must not have been aware of the material nonpublic information when doing so; and

(C) The purchase or sale that occurred was pursuant to the contract, instruction, or plan. A purchase or sale is not "pursuant to a contract, instruction, or plan" if, among other things, the person who entered into the contract, instruction, or plan altered or deviated from the contract, instruction, or plan to purchase or sell securities (whether by changing the amount, price, or timing of the purchase or sale), or entered into or altered a corresponding or hedging transaction or position with respect to those securities.

(ii) Paragraph (c) (1) (i) of this section is applicable only when the contract, instruction, or plan to purchase or sell securities was given or entered into in good faith and not as part of a plan or scheme to evade the prohibitions of this section.

(iii) This paragraph (c) (1) (iii) defines certain terms as used in paragraph (c) of this Section.

(A) Amount. "Amount" means either a specified number of shares or other securities or a specified dollar value of securities.

(B) Price. "Price" means the market price on a particular date or a limit price, or a particular dollar price.

(C) Date. "Date" means, in the case of a market order, the specific day of the year on which the order is to be executed (or as soon thereafter as is practicable under ordinary principles of best execution). "Date" means, in the case of a limit order, a day of the year on which the limit order is in force.

(2) A person other than a natural person also may demonstrate that a purchase or sale of securities is not "on the basis of" material nonpublic information if the person demonstrates that:

(i) The individual making the investment decision on behalf of the person to purchase or sell the securities was not aware of the information; and

(ii) The person had implemented reasonable policies and procedures, taking into consideration the nature of the person's business, to ensure that individuals making investment decisions would not violate the laws prohibiting trading on the basis of material nonpublic information. These policies and procedures may include those that restrict any purchase, sale, and causing any purchase or sale of any security as to which the person has material nonpublic information, or those that prevent such individuals from becoming aware of such information.

[As adopted in Release No. 33-7881, effective October 23, 2000, 65 F.R. 51715.]

[¶ 20,743] Duties of Trust or Confidence in Misappropriation Insider Trading Cases

Reg. § 240.10b5-2. Preliminary Note to § 240.10b5-2: This section provides a non-exclusive definition of circumstances in which a person has a duty of trust or confidence for purposes of the "misappropriation" theory of insider trading under Section 10(b) of the Act and Rule 10b-5. The law of insider trading is otherwise defined by judicial opinions construing Rule 10b-5, and Rule 10b5-2 does not modify the scope of insider trading law in any other respect.

(a) Scope of Rule. This section shall apply to any violation of Section 10(b) of the Act (15 U.S.C. 78j(b)) and § 240.10b-5 thereunder that is based on the purchase or sale of securities on the basis of, or the communication of, material nonpublic information misappropriated in breach of a duty of trust or confidence.

(b) Enumerated "duties of trust or confidence." For purposes of this section, a "duty of trust or confidence" exists in the following circumstances, among others:

(1) Whenever a person agrees to maintain information in confidence;

(2) Whenever the person communicating the material nonpublic information and the person to whom it is communicated have a history, pattern, or practice of sharing confidences, such that the

recipient of the information knows or reasonably should know that the person communicating the material nonpublic information expects that the recipient will maintain its confidentiality; or

(3) Whenever a person receives or obtains material nonpublic information from his or her spouse, parent, child, or sibling; provided, however, that the person receiving or obtaining the information may demonstrate that no duty of trust or confidence existed with respect to the information, by establishing that he or she neither knew nor reasonably should have known that the person who was the source of the information expected that the person would keep the information confidential, because of the parties' history, pattern, or practice of sharing and maintaining confidences, and because there was no agreement or understanding to maintain the confidentiality of the information.

[As adopted in Release No. 33-7881, effective October 23, 2000, 65 F.R. 51715.]

[¶ 20,781] Prohibited Representations in Connection with Certain Offerings

Reg. § 240.10b-9. (a) It shall constitute a "manipulative or deceptive device or contrivance," as used in Section 10(b) of the Act, for any person, directly or indirectly, in connection with the offer or sale of any security, to make any representation:

(1) To the effect that the security is being offered or sold on an "all-or-none" basis, unless the security is part of an offering or distribution being made on the condition that all or a specified amount of the consideration paid for such security will be promptly refunded to the purchaser unless (A) all of the securities being offered are sold at a specified price within a specified time, and (B) the total amount due to the seller is received by him by a specified date; or

(2) to the effect that the security is being offered or sold on any other basis whereby all or part of the consideration paid for any such security will be refunded to the purchaser if all or some of the securities are not sold unless the security is part of an offering or distribution being made on the condition that all or a specified part of the consideration paid for such security will be promptly refunded to the purchaser unless (A) a specified number of units of the security are sold at a specified price within a specified time, and (B) the total amount due to the seller is received by him by a specified date.

(b) This rule shall not apply to any offer or sale of securities as to which the seller has a firm commitment from underwriters or others (subject only to customary conditions precedent, including "market outs") for the purchase of all the securities being offered.

[As adopted in Release No. 34-6905, November 5, 1962, 27 F.R. 9943.]

[¶ 20,791] Confirmation of Transactions

Reg. § 240.10b-10. Preliminary Note. This section requires broker-dealers to disclose specified information in writing to customers at or before completion of a transaction. The requirements under this section that particular information be disclosed is not determinative of a broker-dealer's obligation under the general antifraud provisions of the federal securities laws to disclose additional information to a customer at the time of the customer's investment decision.

(a) *Disclosure Requirement.* It shall be unlawful for any broker or dealer to effect for or with an account of a customer any transaction in, or to induce the purchase or sale by such customer of, any security (other than U.S. Savings Bonds or municipal securities) unless such broker or dealer, at or before completion of such transaction, gives or sends to such customer written notification disclosing:

(1) The date and time of the transaction (or the fact that the time of the transaction will be furnished upon written request to such customer) and the identity, price, and number of shares or units (or principal amount) of such security purchased or sold by such customer; and

(2) Whether the broker or dealer is acting as agent for such customer, as agent for some other person, as agent for both such customer and some other person, or as principal for its own account; and if the broker or dealer is acting as principal, whether it is a market maker in the security (other than by reason of acting as a block positioner); and

(i) If the broker or dealer is acting as agent for such customer, for some other person, or for both such customer and some other person:

(A) The name of the person from whom the security was purchased, or to whom it was sold, for such customer or the fact that the information will be furnished upon written request of such customer; and

(B) The amount of any remuneration received or to be received by the broker from such customer in connection with the transaction unless remuneration paid by such customer is determined pursuant to written agreement with such customer, otherwise than on a transaction basis; and

(C) For a transaction in any NMS stock as defined in § 242.600 of this chapter or a security authorized for quotation on an automated interdealer quotation system that has the characteristics set forth in section 17B of the Act (15 U.S.C. 78q-2), a statement whether payment for order flow is received by the broker or dealer for transactions in such securities and the fact that the source and nature of the compensation received in connection with the particular transaction will be furnished upon written request of the customer; *provided, however,* that brokers or dealers that do not receive payment for order flow in connection with any transaction have no disclosure obligations under this paragraph; and

(D) The source and amount of any other remuneration received or to be received by the broker in connection with the transaction: *Provided, however,* that if, in the case of a purchase, the broker was not participating in a distribution, or in the case of a sale, was not participating in a tender offer, the written notification may state whether any other remuneration has been or will be received and the fact that the source and amount of such other remuneration will be furnished upon written request of such customer; or

(ii) If the broker or dealer is acting as principal for its own account:

(A) In the case where such broker or dealer is not a market maker in an equity security and, if, after having received an order to buy from a customer, the broker or dealer purchased the equity security from another person to offset a contemporaneous sale to such customer or, after having received an order to sell from a customer, the broker or dealer sold the security to another person to offset a contemporaneous purchase from such customer, the difference between the price to the customer and the dealer's contemporaneous purchase (for customer purchases) or sale price (for customer sales); or

(B) In the case of any other transaction in an NMS stock as defined by § 242.600 of this chapter, or an equity security that is traded on a national securities exchange and that is subject to last sale reporting, the reported trade price, the price to the customer in the transaction, and the difference, if any, between the reported trade price and the price to the customer.

(3) Whether any odd-lot differential or equivalent fee has been paid by such customer in connection with the execution of an order for an odd-lot number of shares or units (or principal amount) of a security and the fact that the amount of any such differential or fee will be furnished upon oral or written request: *Provided, however*, that such disclosure need not be made if the differential or fee is included in the remuneration disclosure, or exempted from disclosure, pursuant to paragraph (a)(2)(i)(B) of this section; and

(4) In the case of any transaction in a debt security subject to redemption before maturity, a statement to the effect that such debt security may be redeemed in whole or in part before maturity, that such a redemption could affect the yield represented and the fact that additional information is available upon request; and

(5) In the case of a transaction in a debt security effected exclusively on the basis of a dollar price:

(i) The dollar price at which the transaction was effected, and

(ii) The yield to maturity calculated from the dollar price: *Provided, however*, that this paragraph (a)(5)(ii) shall not apply to a transaction in a debt security that either:

(A) Has a maturity date that may be extended by the issuer thereof, with a variable interest payable thereon; or

(B) Is an asset-backed security, that represents an interest in or is secured by a pool of receivables or other financial assets that are subject continuously to prepayment; and

(6) In the case of a transaction in a debt security effected on the basis of yield:

(i) The yield at which the transaction was effected, including the percentage amount and its characterization (*e.g.*, current yield, yield to maturity, or yield to call) and if effected at yield to call, the type of call, the call date and call price; and

(ii) The dollar price calculated from the yield at which the transaction was effected; and

(iii) If effected on a basis other than yield to maturity and the yield to maturity is lower than the represented yield, the yield to maturity as well as the represented yield; *Provided, however*, that this paragraph (a)(6)(iii) shall not apply to a transaction in a debt security that either:

(A) Has a maturity date that may be extended by the issuer thereof, with a variable interest rate payable thereon; or

(B) Is an asset-backed security, that represents an interest in or is secured by a pool of receivables or other financial assets that are subject continuously to prepayment; and

(7) In the case of a transaction in a debt security that is an asset-backed security, which represents an interest in or is secured by a pool of receivables or other financial assets that are subject continuously to prepayment, a statement indicating that the actual yield of such asset-backed security may vary according to the rate at which the underlying receivables or other financial assets are prepaid and a statement of the fact that information concerning the factors that affect yield (including at a minimum estimated yield, weighted average life, and the prepayment assumptions underlying yield) will be furnished upon written request of such customer; and

(8) In the case of a transaction in a debt security, other than a government security, that the security is unrated by a nationally recognized statistical rating organization, if such is the case; and

(9) That the broker or dealer is not a member of the Securities Investor Protection Corporation (SIPC), or that the broker or dealer clearing or carrying the customer account is not a member of SIPC,

if such is the case: *Provided, however,* that this paragraph (a)(9) shall not apply in the case of a transaction in shares of a registered open-end investment company or unit investment trust if:

(i) The customer sends funds or securities directly to, or received funds or securities directly from, the registered open-end investment company or unit investment trust, its transfer agent, its custodian, or other designated agent, and such person is not an associated person of the broker or dealer required by paragraph (a) of this section to send written notification to the customer; and

(ii) The written notification required by paragraph (a) of this section is sent on behalf of the broker or dealer to the customer by a person described in paragraph (a)(9)(i) of this section.

(b) *Alternative Periodic Reporting.* A broker or dealer may effect transactions for or with the account of a customer without giving or sending to such customer the written notification described in paragraph (a) of this section if:

(1) Such transactions are effected pursuant to a periodic plan or an investment company plan, or effected in shares of any open-end management investment company registered under the Investment Company Act of 1940 that holds itself out as a money market fund and attempts to maintain a stable net asset value per share: *Provided, however,* that no sales load is deducted upon the purchase or redemption of shares in the money market fund; and

(2) Such broker or dealer gives or sends to such customer within five business days after the end of each *quarterly* period, for transactions involving investment company and periodic plans, and after the end of each *monthly* period, for other transactions described in paragraph (b)(1) of this section, a written statement disclosing each purchase or redemption, effected for or with, and each dividend or distribution credited to or reinvested for, the account of such customer during the month; the date of such transaction; the identity, number, and price of any securities purchased or redeemed by such customer in each such transaction; the total number of shares of such securities in such customer's account; any remuneration received or to be received by the broker or dealer in connection therewith; and that any other information required by paragraph (a) of this section will be furnished upon written request: *Provided, however,* that the written statement may be delivered to some other person designated by the customer for distribution to the customer; and

(3) Such customer is provided with prior notification in writing disclosing the intention to send the written information referred to in paragraph (b)(1) of this section in lieu of an immediate confirmation.

(c) A broker or dealer shall give or send to a customer information requested pursuant to this rule within 5 business days of receipt of the request; *Provided, however,* That in the case of information pertaining to a transaction effected more than 30 days prior to receipt of the request, the information shall be given or sent to the customer within 15 business days.

(d) *Definitions.* For the purposes of this section:

(1) *Customer* shall not include a broker or dealer;

(2) *Completion of the transaction* shall have the meaning provided in Rule 15c1-1 under the Act;

(3) *Time of the transaction* means the time of execution, to the extent feasible, of the customer's order;

(4) *Debt security* as used in paragraphs (a)(3), (4), and (5) only, means any security, such as a bond, debenture, note, or any other similar instrument which evidences a liability of the issuer (including any such security that is convertible into stock or a similar security) and fractional or participation interests in one or more of any of the foregoing; *Provided, however,* that securities issued by an investment company registered under the Investment Company Act of 1940 shall not be included in this definition;

(5) *Periodic plan* means any written authorization for a broker acting as agent to purchase or sell for a customer a specific security or securities (other than securities issued by an open end investment company or unit investment trust registered under the Investment Company Act of 1940), in specific amounts (calculated in security units or dollars), at specific time intervals and setting forth the commissions or charges to be paid by the customer in connection therewith (or the manner of calculating them); and

(6) *Investment company plan* means any plan under which securities issued by an open-end investment company or unit investment trust registered under the Investment Company Act of 1940 are purchased by a customer (the payments being made directly to, or made payable to, the registered investment company, or the principal underwriter, custodian, trustee, or other designated agent of the registered investment company), or sold by a customer pursuant to:

(i) An individual retirement or individual pension plan qualified under the Internal Revenue Code;

(ii) A contractual or systematic agreement under which the customer purchases at the applicable public offering price, or redeems at the applicable redemption price, such securities in specified amounts (calculated in security units or dollars) at specified time intervals and setting forth the commissions or charges to be paid by such customer in connection therewith (or the manner of calculating them); or

(iii) Any other arrangement involving a group of two or more customers and contemplating periodic purchases of such securities by each customer through a person designated by the group; *Provided,* That such arrangement requires the registered investment company or its agent—

(A) To give or send to the designated person, at or before the completion of the transaction for the purchase of such securities, a written notification of the receipt of the total amount paid by the group;

(B) To send to anyone in the group who was a customer in the prior quarter and on whose behalf payment has not been received in the current quarter a quarterly written statement reflecting that a payment was not received on his behalf; and

(C) To advise each customer in the group if a payment is not received from the designated person on behalf of the group within 10 days of a date certain specified in the arrangement for delivery of that payment by the designated person and thereafter to send to each such customer the written notification described in paragraph (a) of this section for the next three succeeding payments.

(7) *NMS stock* shall have the meaning provided in § 242.600 of this chapter.

(8) *Effective transaction reporting plan* shall have the meaning provided in Rule 11Aa3-1 under the Act.

(9) *Payment for order flow* shall mean any monetary payment, service, property, or other benefit that results in remuneration, compensation, or consideration to a broker or dealer from any broker or dealer, national securities exchange, registered securities association, or exchange member in return for the routing of customer orders by such broker or dealer to any broker or dealer, national securities exchange, registered securities association, or exchange member for execution, including but not limited to: research, clearance, custody, products or services; reciprocal agreements for the provision of order flow; adjustment of a broker or dealer's unfavorable trading errors; offers to participate as underwriter in public offerings; stock loans or shared interest accrued thereon; discounts, rebates, or any other reductions of or credits against any fee to, or expense or other financial obligation of, the broker or dealer routing a customer order that exceeds that fee, expense or financial obligation.

(10) *Asset-backed security* means a security that is primarily serviced by the cashflows of a discrete pool of receivables or other financial assets, either fixed or revolving, that by their terms convert into cash within a finite time period plus any rights or other assets designed to assure the servicing or timely distribution of proceeds to the security holders.

(e) *Security futures products.* The provisions of paragraphs (a) and (b) of this section shall not apply to a broker or dealer registered pursuant to section 15(b)(11)(A) of the Act (15 U.S.C. 78o(b)(11)(A)) to the extent that it effects transactions for customers in security futures products in a futures account (as that term is defined in §240.15c3-3(a)(15)) and a broker or dealer registered pursuant to section 15(b)(1) of the Act (15 U.S.C. 78o(b)(1)) that is also a futures commission merchant registered pursuant to section 4f(a)(1) of the Commodity Exchange Act (7 U.S.C. 6f(a)(1)), to the extent that it effects transactions for customers in security futures products in a futures account (as that term is defined in §240.15c3-3(a)(15)), *Provided* that:

(1) The broker or dealer that effects any transaction for a customer in security futures products in a futures account gives or sends to the customer no later than the next business day after execution of any futures securities product transaction, written notification disclosing:

(i) The date the transaction was executed, the identity of the single security or narrow-based security index underlying the contract for the security futures product, the number of contracts of such security futures product purchased or sold, the price, and the delivery month;

(ii) The source and amount of any remuneration received or to be received by the broker or dealer in connection with the transaction, including, but not limited to, markups, commissions, costs, fees, and other charges incurred in connection with the transaction, provided, however, that if no remuneration is to be paid for an initiating transaction until the occurrence of the corresponding liquidating transaction, that the broker or dealer may disclose the amount of remuneration only on the confirmation for the liquidating transaction;

(iii) The fact that information about the time of the execution of the transaction, the identity of the other party to the contract, and whether the broker or dealer is acting as agent for such customer, as agent for some other person, as agent for both such customer and some other person, or as principal for its own account, and if the broker or dealer is acting as principal, whether it is engaging in a block transaction or an exchange of security futures products for physical securities, will be available upon written request of the customer; and

(iv) Whether payment for order flow is received by the broker or dealer for such transactions, the amount of this payment and the fact that the source and nature of the compensation received in connection with the particular transaction will be furnished upon written request of the customer; provided, however, that brokers or dealers that do not receive payment for order flow have no disclosure obligation under this paragraph.

(2) *Transitional provision.*

(i) Broker-dealers are not required to comply with paragraph (e)(1)(iii) of this section until June 1, 2003, *Provided* that, if, not withstanding the absence of the disclosure required in that paragraph, the broker-dealer receives a written request from a customer for the information described in paragraph (e)(1)(iii) of this section, the broker-dealer must make the information available to the customer; and

(ii) Broker-dealers are not required to comply with paragraph (e)(1)(iv) of this section until June 1, 2003.

(f) The Commission may exempt any broker or dealer from the requirements of paragraphs (a) and (b) of this section with regard to specific transactions or specific classes of transactions for which the broker or dealer will provide alternative procedures to effect the purposes of this section; any such exemption may be granted subject to compliance with such alternative procedures and upon such other stated terms and conditions as the Commission may impose.

[As last amended in Release No. 34-51808, effective August 29, 2005, 70 F.R. 37496.]

[¶ 20,831] Disclosure of Credit Terms in Margin Transactions

Reg. § 240.10b-16. (a) It shall be unlawful for any broker or dealer to extend credit, directly or indirectly, to any customer in connection with any securities transaction unless such broker or dealer has established procedures to assure that each customer

(1) is given or sent at the time of opening the account, a written statement or statements disclosing (i) the conditions under which an interest charge will be imposed; (ii) the annual rate or rates of interest that can be imposed; (iii) the method of computing interest; (iv) if rates of interest are subject to change without prior notice, the specific conditions under which they can be changed; (v) the method of determining the debit balance or balances on which interest is to be charged and whether credit is to be given for credit balances in cash accounts; (vi) what other charges resulting from the extension of credit, if any, will be made and under what conditions; and (vii) the nature of any interest or lien retained by the broker or dealer in the security or other property held as collateral and the conditions under which additional collateral can be required; *provided, however,* that the requirements of this Paragraph (a)(1) will be met in any case where the account is opened by telephone if the information required to be disclosed is orally communicated to the customer at that time and the required written statement or statements are sent to the customer immediately thereafter; and *provided, further,* that in the case of customers to whom credit is already being extended on the effective date of this Rule, the written statement or statements required hereunder must be given or sent to said customers within 90 days after the effective date of this Rule; and

(2) is given or sent a written statement or statements, at least quarterly, for each account in which credit was extended, disclosing (i) the balance at the beginning of the period; the date, amount and a brief description of each debit and credit entered during such period; the closing balance; and, if interest is charged for a period different from the period covered by the statement, the balance as of the last day of the interest period; (ii) the total interest charge for the period during which interest is charged (or, if interest is charged separately for separate accounts, the total interest charge for each such account), itemized to show the dates on which the interest period began and ended; the annual rate or rates of interest charged and the interest charge for each such different annual rate of interest; and either each different debit balance on which an interest calculation was based or the average debit balance for the interest period, except that if an average debit balance is used, a separate average debit balance must be disclosed for each interest rate applied; and (iii) all other charges resulting from the extension of credit in that account; *provided, however,* that if the interest charge disclosed on a statement is for a period different from the period covered by the statement, there must be printed on the statement appropriate language to the effect that it should be retained for use in conjunction with the next statement containing the remainder of the required information; and *provided further,* that in the case of "equity funding programs" registered under the Securities Act of 1933, the requirements of this Paragraph (a)(2) will be met if the broker or dealer furnishes to the customer, within one month after each extension of credit, a written statement or statements containing the information required to be disclosed under this Paragraph (a)(2).

(b) It shall be unlawful for any broker or dealer to make any changes in the terms and conditions under which credit charges will be made (as described in the initial statement made under Paragraph (a) of this Rule), unless the customer shall have been given not less than thirty (30) days written notice of such changes, except that no such prior notice shall be necessary where such changes are required by law; *provided, however,* that if any change for which prior notice would otherwise be required under this paragraph results in a lower interest charge to the customer than would have been imposed before the change, notice of such change may be given within a reasonable time after the effective date of the change.

[As last amended in Release No. 34-8844, March 18, 1970, 35 F.R. 5542.]

[¶ 20,841] Untimely Announcements of Record Dates

Reg. § 240.10b-17. (a) It shall constitute a "manipulative or deceptive device or contrivance" as used in Section 10(b) of the Act for any issuer of a class of securities publicly traded by the use of any means or instrumentality of interstate commerce or of the mails or of any facility of any national securities exchange to fail to give notice in accordance with paragraph (b) hereof of the following actions relating to such class of securities:

(1) a dividend or other distribution in cash or in kind, except an ordinary interest payment on a debt security, but including a dividend or distribution of any security of the same or another issuer;

(2) a stock split or reverse split; or

(3) a rights or other subscription offering.

(b) Notice shall be deemed to have been given in accordance with this rule only if:

(1) given to the National Association of Securities Dealers, Inc. no later than ten days prior to the record date involved or, in case of a rights subscription or other offering if such 10 days advance notice is not practical, on or before the record date and in no event later than the effective date of the registration statement to which the offering relates, and such notice includes:

(i) title of the security to which the declaration relates;

(ii) date of declaration;

(iii) date of record for determining holders entitled to receive the dividend or other distribution or to participate in the stock or reverse split;

(iv) date of payment or distribution or, in the case of a stock or reverse split or rights or other subscription offering, the date of delivery;

(v) for a dividend or other distribution including a stock or reverse split or rights or other subscription offering;

(a) in cash, the amount of cash to be paid or distributed per share, except if exact per share cash distributions cannot be given because of existing conversion rights which may be exercised during the notice period and which may affect the per share cash distribution, then a reasonable approximation of the per share distribution may be provided so long as the actual per share distribution is subsequently provided on the record date;

(b) in the same security, the amount of the security outstanding immediately prior to and immediately following the dividend or distribution and the rate of the dividend or distribution;

(c) in any other security of the same issuer, the amount to be paid or distributed and the rate of the dividend or distribution;

(d) in any security of another issuer, the name of the issuer and title of that security, the amount to be paid or distributed, and the rate of the dividend or distribution and if that security is a right or a warrant, the subscription price;

(e) in any other property (including securities not covered under paragraphs (b)(l)(v)(b) through (d) of this section the identity of the property and its value and basis for assigning that value;

(vi) method of settlement of fractional interests;

(vii) details of any condition which must be satisfied or government approval which must be secured to enable payment or distribution; and in

(viii) the case of stock or reverse split in addition to the aforementioned information;

(a) the name and address of the transfer or exchange agent; or

(2) The Commission, upon written request or upon its own motion, exempts the issuer from compliance with paragraph (b)(1) of this section either unconditionally or on specified terms or conditions, as not constituting a manipulative or deceptive device or contrivance comprehended within the purpose of this rule or;

(3) given in accordance with procedures of the national securities exchange or exchanges upon which a security of such issuer is registered pursuant to Section 12 of the Act which contain requirements substantially comparable to those set forth in paragraph (b)(1) of this section.

(c) The provisions of this rule shall not apply, however, to redeemable securities issued by open-end investment companies and unit investment trusts registered with the Commission under the Investment Company Act of 1940.

[As last amended in Release No. 34-9503, February 29, 1972, 37 F.R. 4330.]

[¶ 20,851] Purchases of Certain Equity Securities by the Issuer and Others

Reg. § 240.10b-18. Preliminary Notes

1. Section 240.10b-18 provides an issuer (and its affiliated purchasers) with a "safe harbor" from liability for manipulation under sections 9(a)(2) of the Act and § 240.10b-5 under the Act *solely* by reason of the manner, timing, price, and volume of their repurchases when they repurchase the issuer's

common stock in the market in accordance with the section's manner, timing, price, and volume conditions. As a safe harbor, compliance with § 240.10b-18 is voluntary. To come within the safe harbor, however, an issuer's repurchases must satisfy (on a daily basis) each of the section's four conditions. Failure to meet any one of the four conditions will remove all of the issuer's repurchases from the safe harbor for that day. The safe harbor, moreover, is not available for repurchases that, although made in technical compliance with the section, are part of a plan or scheme to evade the federal securities laws.

2. Regardless of whether the repurchases are effected in accordance with § 240.10b-18, reporting issuers must report their repurchasing activity as required by Item 703 of Regulations S-K and S-B (17 CFR 229.703 and 228.703) and Item 15(e) of Form 20-F (17 CFR 249.220f) (regarding foreign private issuers), and closed-end management investment companies that are registered under the Investment Company Act of 1940 must report their repurchasing activity as required by Item 8 of Form N-CSR (17 CFR 249.331; 17 CFR 274.128).

(a) *Definitions.* Unless otherwise provided, all terms used in this section shall have the same meaning as in the Act. In addition, the following definitions shall apply:

(1) *ADTV* means the average daily trading volume reported for the security during the four calendar weeks preceding the week in which the Rule 10b-18 purchase is to be effected.

(2) *Affiliate* means any person that directly or indirectly controls, is controlled by, or is under common control with, the issuer.

(3) *Affiliated purchaser* means:

(i) A person acting, directly or indirectly, in concert with the issuer for the purpose of acquiring the issuer's securities; or

(ii) An affiliate who, directly or indirectly, controls the issuer's purchases of such securities, whose purchases are controlled by the issuer, or whose purchases are under common control with those of the issuer; *Provided, however,* that "affiliated purchaser" shall not include a broker, dealer, or other person solely by reason of such broker, dealer, or other person effecting Rule 10b-18 purchases on behalf of the issuer or for its account, and shall not include an officer or director of the issuer solely by reason of that officer or director's participation in the decision to authorize Rule 10b-18 purchases by or on behalf of the issuer.

(4) *Agent independent of the issuer* has the meaning contained in § 242.100 of this chapter.

(5) *Block* means a quantity of stock that either:

(i) Has a purchase price of $200,000 or more; or

(ii) Is at least 5,000 shares and has a purchase price of at least $50,000; or

(iii) Is at least 20 round lots of the security and totals 150 percent or more of the trading volume for that security or, in the event that trading volume data are unavailable, is at least 20 round lots of the security and totals at least one-tenth of one percent (.001) of the outstanding shares of the security, exclusive of any shares owned by any affiliate;

Provided, however, That a block under paragraph (a)(5)(i), (ii), and (iii) shall not include any amount a broker or dealer, acting as principal, has accumulated for the purpose of sale or resale to the issuer or to any affiliated purchaser of the issuer if the issuer or such affiliated purchaser knows or has reason to know that such amount was accumulated for such purpose, nor shall it include any amount that a broker or dealer has sold short to the issuer or to any affiliated purchaser of the issuer if the issuer or such affiliated purchaser knows or has reason to know that the sale was a short sale.

(6) *Consolidated system* means a consolidated transaction or quotation reporting system that collects and publicly disseminates on a current and continuous basis transaction or quotation information in common equity securities pursuant to an effective transaction reporting plan or an effective national market system plan (as those terms are defined in § 242.600 of this chapter).

(7) *Market-wide trading suspension* means a market-wide trading halt of 30 minutes or more that is:

(i) Imposed pursuant to the rules of a national securities exchange or a national securities association in response to a market-wide decline during a single trading session; or

(ii) Declared by the Commission pursuant to its authority under section 12(k) of the Act (15 U.S.C. 78l (k)).

(8) *Plan* has the meaning contained in § 242.100 of this chapter.

(9) *Principal market* for a security means the single securities market with the largest reported trading volume for the security during the six full calendar months preceding the week in which the Rule 10b-18 purchase is to be effected.

(10) *Public float value* has the meaning contained in § 242.100 of this chapter.

(11) *Purchase price* means the price paid per share as reported, exclusive of any commission paid to a broker acting as agent, or commission equivalent, mark-up, or differential paid to a dealer.

(12) *Riskless principal transaction* means a transaction in which a broker or dealer after having received an order from an issuer to buy its security, buys the security as principal in the market at the

same price to satisfy the issuer's buy order. The issuer's buy order must be effected at the same price per-share at which the broker or dealer bought the shares to satisfy the issuer's buy order, exclusive of any explicitly disclosed markup or markdown, commission equivalent, or other fee. In addition, only the first leg of the transaction, when the broker or dealer buys the security in the market as principal, is reported under the rules of a self-regulatory organization or under the Act. For purposes of this section, the broker or dealer must have written policies and procedures in place to assure that, at a minimum, the issuer's buy order was received prior to the offsetting transaction; the offsetting transaction is allocated to a riskless principal account or the issuer's account within 60 seconds of the execution; and the broker or dealer has supervisory systems in place to produce records that enable the broker or dealer to accurately and readily reconstruct, in a time-sequenced manner, all orders effected on a riskless principal basis.

(13) *Rule 10b-18 purchase* means a purchase (or any bid or limit order that would effect such purchase) of an issuer's common stock (or an equivalent interest, including a unit of beneficial interest in a trust or limited partnership or a depository share) by or for the issuer or any affiliated purchaser (including riskless principal transactions). However, it does *not* include any purchase of such security:

(i) Effected during the applicable restricted period of a distribution that is subject to § 242.102 of this chapter;

(ii) Effected by or for an issuer plan by an agent independent of the issuer;

(iii) Effected as a fractional share purchase (a fractional interest in a security) evidenced by a script certificate, order form, or similar document;

(iv) Effected during the period from the time of public announcement (as defined in § 230.165(f)) of a merger, acquisition, or similar transaction involving a recapitalization, until the earlier of the completion of such transaction or the completion of the vote by target shareholders. This exclusion does *not* apply to Rule 10b-18 purchases:

(A) Effected during such transaction in which the consideration is solely cash and there is no valuation period; or

(B) Where:

(*1*) The total volume of Rule 10b-18 purchases effected on any single day does not exceed the lesser of 25% of the security's four-week ADTV or the issuer's average daily Rule 10b-18 purchases during the three full calendar months preceding the date of the announcement of such transaction;

(*2*) The issuer's block purchases effected pursuant to paragraph (b)(4) of this section do not exceed the average size and frequency of the issuer's block purchases effected pursuant to paragraph (b)(4) of this section during the three full calendar months preceding the date of the announcement of such transaction; and

(*3*) Such purchases are not otherwise restricted or prohibited;

(v) Effected pursuant to § 240.13e-1;

(vi) Effected pursuant to a tender offer that is subject to § 240.13e-4 or specifically excepted from § 240.13e-4; or

(vii) Effected pursuant to a tender offer that is subject to section 14(d) of the Act (15 U.S.C. 78n(d)) and the rules and regulations thereunder.

(b) *Conditions to be met.* Rule 10b-18 purchases shall not be deemed to have violated the anti-manipulation provisions of sections 9(a)(2) or 10(b) of the Act (15 U.S.C. 78i(a)(2) or 78j(b)), or § 240.10b-5 under the Act, solely by reason of the time, price, or amount of the Rule 10b-18 purchases, or the number of brokers or dealers used in connection with such purchases, if the issuer or affiliated purchaser of the issuer effects the Rule 10b-18 purchases according to each of the following conditions:

(1) *One broker or dealer.* Rule 10b-18 purchases must be effected from or through only one broker or dealer on any single day; *Provided, however,* that:

(i) The "one broker or dealer" condition shall not apply to Rule 10b-18 purchases that are not solicited by or on behalf of the issuer or its affiliated purchaser(s);

(ii) Where Rule 10b-18 purchases are effected by or on behalf of more than one affiliated purchaser of the issuer (or the issuer and one or more of its affiliated purchasers) on a single day, the issuer and all affiliated purchasers must use the same broker or dealer; and

(iii) Where Rule 10b-18 purchases are effected on behalf of the issuer by a broker-dealer that is not an electronic communication network (ECN) or other alternative trading system (ATS), that broker-dealer can access ECN or other ATS liquidity in order to execute repurchases on behalf of the issuer (or any affiliated purchaser of the issuer) on that day.

(2) *Time of purchases.* Rule 10b-18 purchases must not be:

(i) The opening (regular way) purchase reported in the consolidated system;

(ii) Effected during the 10 minutes before the scheduled close of the primary trading session in the principal market for the security, and the 10 minutes before the scheduled close of the primary trading session in the market where the purchase is effected, for a security that has an ADTV value of $1 million or more and a public float value of $150 million or more; and

(iii) Effected during the 30 minutes before the scheduled close of the primary trading session in the principal market for the security, and the 30 minutes before the scheduled close of the primary trading session in the market where the purchase is effected, for all other securities;

(iv) However, for purposes of this section, Rule 10b-18 purchases may be effected following the close of the primary trading session until the termination of the period in which last sale prices are reported in the consolidated system so long as such purchases are effected at prices that do not exceed the lower of the closing price of the primary trading session in the principal market for the security and any lower bids or sale prices subsequently reported in the consolidated system, and all of this section's conditions are met. However, for purposes of this section, the issuer may use one broker or dealer to effect Rule 10b-18 purchases during this period that may be different from the broker or dealer that it used during the primary trading session. However, the issuer's Rule 10b-18 purchase may not be the opening transaction of the session following the close of the primary trading session.

(3) *Price of purchases.* Rule 10b-18 purchases must be effected at a purchase price that:

(i) Does not exceed the highest independent bid or the last independent transaction price, whichever is higher, quoted or reported in the consolidated system at the time the Rule 10b-18 purchase is effected;

(ii) For securities for which bids and transaction prices are not quoted or reported in the consolidated system, Rule 10b-18 purchases must be effected at a purchase price that does not exceed the highest independent bid or the last independent transaction price, whichever is higher, displayed and disseminated on any national securities exchange or on any inter-dealer quotation system (as defined in § 240.15c2-11) that displays at least two priced quotations for the security, at the time the Rule 10b-18 purchase is effected; and

(iii) For all other securities, Rule 10b-18 purchases must be effected at a price no higher than the highest independent bid obtained from three independent dealers.

(4) *Volume of purchases.* The total volume of Rule 10b-18 purchases effected by or for the issuer and any affiliated purchasers effected on any single day must not exceed 25 percent of the ADTV for that security; *However,* once each week, in lieu of purchasing under the 25 percent of ADTV limit for that day, the issuer or an affiliated purchaser of the issuer may effect one block purchase if:

(i) No other Rule 10b-18 purchases are effected that day, and

(ii) The block purchase is *not* included when calculating a security's four week ADTV under this section.

(c) *Alternative conditions.* The conditions of paragraph (b) of this section shall apply in connection with Rule 10b-18 purchases effected during a trading session following the imposition of a market-wide trading suspension, except:

(1) That the time of purchases condition in paragraph (b)(2) of this section shall not apply, either:

(i) From the reopening of trading until the scheduled close of trading on the day that the market-wide trading suspension is imposed; or

(ii) At the opening of trading on the next trading day until the scheduled close of trading that day, if a market-wide trading suspension was in effect at the close of trading on the preceding day; and

(2) The volume of purchases condition in paragraph (b)(4) of this section is modified so that the amount of Rule 10b-18 purchases must not exceed 100 percent of the ADTV for that security.

(d) *Other purchases.* No presumption shall arise that an issuer or an affiliated purchaser has violated the anti-manipulation provisions of sections 9(a)(2) or 10(b) of the Act (15 U.S.C. 78i(a)(2) or 78j(b)), or § 240.10b-5 under the Act, if the Rule 10b-18 purchases of such issuer or affiliated purchaser do not meet the conditions specified in paragraph (b) or (c) of this section.

[As last amended in Release No. 34-51808, effective August 29, 2005, 70 F.R. 37496.]

[¶ 20,871] Deception in Connection with a Seller's Ability or Intent to Deliver Securities on the Date Delivery Is Due

Reg. § 240.10b-21. *PRELIMINARY NOTE to § 240.10b-21: This rule is not intended to limit, or restrict, the applicability of the general antifraud provisions of the federal securities laws, such as section 10(b) of the Act and rule 10b-5 thereunder.*

(a) It shall also constitute a "manipulative or deceptive device or contrivance" as used in section 10(b) of this Act of any person to submit an order to sell an equity security if such person deceives a broker or dealer, a participant of a registered clearing agency, or a purchaser about its intention or ability to deliver the security on or before the settlement date, and such person fails to deliver the security on or before the settlement date.

(b) For purposes of this rule, the term settlement date shall mean the business day on which delivery of a security and payment of money is to be made through the facilities of a registered clearing agency in connection with the sale of a security.

[Added by Release No. 34-58774, effective Octover 17, 2008, 73 F.R. 61666.]

NOTICE PURSUANT TO SECTION 10A OF THE ACT

[¶ 20,875] Notice to the Commission Pursuant to Section 10A of the Act

Reg. § 240.10A-1. (a)(1) If any issuer with a reporting obligation under the Act receives a report requiring a notice to the Commission in accordance with section 10A(b)(3) of the Act, 15 U.S.C. 78j-1(b)(3), the issuer shall submit such notice to the Commission's Office of the Chief Accountant within the time period prescribed in that section. The notice may be provided by facsimile, telegraph, personal delivery, or any other means, provided it is received by the Office of the Chief Accountant within the required time period.

(2) The notice specified in paragraph (a)(1) of this section shall be in writing and:

(i) Shall identify the issuer (including the issuer's name, address, phone number, and file number assigned to the issuer's filings by the Commission) and the independent accountant (including the independent accountant's name and phone number, and the address of the independent accountant's principal office);

(ii) Shall state the date that the issuer received from the independent accountant the report specified in section 10A(b)(2) of the Act, 15 U.S.C. 78j-1(b)(2);

(iii) Shall provide, at the election of the issuer, either:

(A) A summary of the independent accountant's report, including a description of the act that the independent accountant has identified as a likely illegal act and the possible effect of that act on all affected financial statements of the issuer or those related to the most current three-year period, whichever is shorter; or

(B) A copy of the independent accountant's report; and

(iv) May provide additional information regarding the issuer's views of and response to the independent accountant's report.

(3) Reports of the independent accountant submitted by the issuer to the Commission's Office of the Chief Accountant in accordance with paragraph (a)(2)(iii)(B) of this section shall be deemed to have been made pursuant to section 10A(b)(3) or section 10A(b)(4) of the Act, 15 U.S.C. 78j-1(b)(3) or 78j-1(b)(4), for purposes of the safe harbor provided by section 10A(c) of the Act, 15 U.S.C. 78j-1(c).

(4) Submission of the notice in paragraphs (a)(1) and (a)(2) of this section shall not relieve the issuer from its obligations to comply fully with all other reporting requirements, including, without limitation:

(i) The filing requirements of Form 8-K, § 249.308 of this chapter, and Form N-SAR, § 274.101 of this chapter, regarding a change in the issuer's certifying accountant and

(ii) The disclosure requirements of Item 304 of Regulation S-K, § 229.304 of this chapter.

(b)(1) Any independent accountant furnishing to the Commission a copy of a report (or the documentation of any oral report) in accordance with section 10A(b)(3) or section 10A(b)(4) of the Act, 15 U.S.C. 78j-1(b)(3) or 78j-1(b)(4), shall submit that report (or documentation) to the Commission's Office of the Chief Accountant within the time period prescribed by the appropriate section of the Act. The report (or documentation) may be submitted to the Commission's Office of the Chief Accountant by facsimile, telegraph, personal delivery, or any other means, provided it is received by the Office of the Chief Accountant within the time period set forth in section 10A(b)(3) or 10A(b)(4) of the Act, 15 U.S.C. 78j-1(b)(3) or 78j-1(b)(4), whichever is applicable in the circumstances.

(2) If the report (or documentation) submitted to the Office of the Chief Accountant in accordance with paragraph (b)(1) of this section does not clearly identify both the issuer (including the issuer's name, address, phone number, and file number assigned to the issuer's filings with the Commission) and the independent accountant (including the independent accountant's name and phone number, and the address of the independent accountant's principal office), then the independent accountant shall place that information in a prominent attachment to the report (or documentation) and shall submit that attachment to the Office of the Chief Accountant at the same time and in the same manner as the report (or documentation) is submitted to that Office.

(3) Submission of the report (or documentation) by the independent accountant as described in paragraphs (b)(1) and (b)(2) of this section shall not replace, or otherwise satisfy the need for, the newly engaged and former accountants' letters under Items 304(a)(2)(D) and 304(a)(3) of Regulation S-K, §§ 229.304(a)(2)(D) and 229.304(a)(3) of this chapter, respectively, and shall not limit, reduce, or affect in any way the independent accountant's obligations to comply fully with all other legal and professional responsibilities, including, without limitation, those under generally accepted auditing standards and the rules or interpretations of the Commission that modify or supplement those auditing standards.

(c) A notice or report submitted to the Office of the Chief Accountant in accordance with paragraphs (a) and (b) of this section shall be deemed to be an investigative record and shall be non-public and exempt from disclosure pursuant to the Freedom of Information Act to the same extent and for the same periods of time that the Commission's investigative records are non-public and exempt from disclosure under, among other applicable provisions, 5 U.S.C. 552(b)(7) and § 200.80(b)(7) of this chapter. Nothing in this paragraph, however, shall relieve, limit, delay, or affect in any way, the obligation of any issuer or any independent accountant to make all public disclosures required by law, by any Commission disclosure item, rule, report, or form, or by any applicable accounting, auditing, or professional standard.

Instruction to paragraph (c).

Issuers and independent accountants may apply for additional bases for confidential treatment for a notice, report, or part thereof, in accordance with § 200.83 of this chapter. That section indicates, in part, that any person who, pursuant to any requirement of law, submits any information or causes or permits any information to be submitted to the Commission, may request that the Commission afford it confidential treatment by reason of personal privacy or business confidentiality, or for any other reason permitted by Federal law.

[As last amended in Release No. 33-8876, effective February 4, 2008, 73 F.R. 934.]

[¶ 20,876] Auditor Independence

Reg. § 240.10A-2. It shall be unlawful for an auditor not to be independent under § 210.2-01(c)(2)(iii)(B), (c)(4), (c)(6), (c)(7), and § 210.2-07.

[As added in Release No. 33-8183, effective May 6, 2003, 68 F.R. 6006.]

[¶ 20,877] Listing Standards Relating to Audit Committees

Reg. § 240.10A-3. (a) Pursuant to section 10A(m) of the Act (15 U.S.C. 78j-1(m)) and section 3 of the Sarbanes-Oxley Act of 2002 (15 U.S.C. 7202):

(1) *National securities exchanges.* The rules of each national securities exchange registered pursuant to section 6 of the Act (15 U.S.C. 78f) must, in accordance with the provisions of this section, prohibit the initial or continued listing of any security of an issuer that is not in compliance with the requirements of any portion of paragraph (b) or (c) of this section.

(2) *National securities associations.* The rules of each national securities association registered pursuant to section 15A of the Act (15 U.S.C. 78o-3) must, in accordance with the provisions of this section, prohibit the initial or continued listing in an automated inter-dealer quotation system of any security of an issuer that is not in compliance with the requirements of any portion of paragraph (b) or (c) of this section.

(3) *Opportunity to cure defects.* The rules required by paragraphs (a)(1) and (a)(2) of this section must provide for appropriate procedures for a listed issuer to have an opportunity to cure any defects that would be the basis for a prohibition under paragraph (a) of this section, before the imposition of such prohibition. Such rules also may provide that if a member of an audit committee ceases to be independent in accordance with the requirements of this section for reasons outside the member's reasonable control, that person, with notice by the issuer to the applicable national securities exchange or national securities association, may remain an audit committee member of the listed issuer until the earlier of the next annual shareholders meeting of the listed issuer or one year from the occurrence of the event that caused the member to be no longer independent.

(4) *Notification of noncompliance.* The rules required by paragraphs (a)(1) and (a)(2) of this section must include a requirement that a listed issuer must notify the applicable national securities exchange or national securities association promptly after an executive officer of the listed issuer becomes aware of any material noncompliance by the listed issuer with the requirements of this section.

(5) *Implementation.*

(i) The rules of each national securities exchange or national securities association meeting the requirements of this section must be operative, and listed issuers must be in compliance with those rules, by the following dates:

(A) July 31, 2005 for foreign private issuers and smaller reporting companies (as defined in § 240.12b-2); and

(B) For all other listed issuers, the earlier of the listed issuer's first annual shareholders meeting after January 15, 2004, or October 31, 2004.

(ii) Each national securities exchange and national securities association must provide to the Commission, no later than July 15, 2003, proposed rules or rule amendments that comply with this section.

(iii) Each national securities exchange and national securities association must have final rules or rule amendments that comply with this section approved by the Commission no later than December 1, 2003.

(b) *Required standards.*

(1) *Independence.*

(i) Each member of the audit committee must be a member of the board of directors of the listed issuer, and must otherwise be independent; provided that, where a listed issuer is one of two dual holding companies, those companies may designate one audit committee for both companies so long as each member of the audit committee is a member of the board of directors of at least one of such dual holding companies.

(ii) *Independence requirements for non-investment company issuers.* In order to be considered to be independent for purposes of this paragraph (b)(1), a member of an audit committee of a listed issuer that is not an investment company may not, other than in his or her capacity as a member of the audit committee, the board of directors, or any other board committee:

(A) Accept directly or indirectly any consulting, advisory, or other compensatory fee from the issuer or any subsidiary thereof, provided that, unless the rules of the national securities exchange or national securities association provide otherwise, compensatory fees do not include the receipt of fixed amounts of compensation under a retirement plan (including deferred compensation) for prior service with the listed issuer (provided that such compensation is not contingent in any way on continued service); or

(B) Be an affiliated person of the issuer or any subsidiary thereof.

(iii) *Independence requirements for investment company issuers.* In order to be considered to be independent for purposes of this paragraph (b)(1), a member of an audit committee of a listed issuer that is an investment company may not, other than in his or her capacity as a member of the audit committee, the board of directors, or any other board committee:

(A) Accept directly or indirectly any consulting, advisory, or other compensatory fee from the issuer or any subsidiary thereof, provided that, unless the rules of the national securities exchange or national securities association provide otherwise, compensatory fees do not include the receipt of fixed amounts of compensation under a retirement plan (including deferred compensation) for prior service with the listed issuer (provided that such compensation is not contingent in any way on continued service); or

(B) Be an "interested person" of the issuer as defined in section 2(a)(19) of the Investment Company Act of 1940 (15 U.S.C. 80a-2(a)(19)).

(iv) *Exemptions from the independence requirements.*

(A) For an issuer listing securities pursuant to a registration statement under section 12 of the Act (15 U.S.C. 78*l*), or for an issuer that has a registration statement under the Securities Act of 1933 (15 U.S.C. 77a *et seq.*) covering an initial public offering of securities to be listed by the issuer, where in each case the listed issuer was not, immediately prior to the effective date of such registration statement, required to file reports with the Commission pursuant to section 13(a) or 15(d) of the Act (15 U.S.C. 78m(a) or 78o(d)):

(*1*) All but one of the members of the listed issuer's audit committee may be exempt from the independence requirements of paragraph (b)(1)(ii) of this section for 90 days from the date of effectiveness of such registration statement; and

(*2*) A minority of the members of the listed issuer's audit committee may be exempt from the independence requirements of paragraph (b)(1)(ii) of this section for one year from the date of effectiveness of such registration statement.

(B) An audit committee member that sits on the board of directors of a listed issuer and an affiliate of the listed issuer is exempt from the requirements of paragraph (b)(1)(ii)(B) of this section if the member, except for being a director on each such board of directors, otherwise meets the independence requirements of paragraph (b)(1)(ii) of this section for each such entity, including the receipt of only ordinary-course compensation for serving as a member of the board of directors, audit committee or any other board committee of each such entity.

(C) An employee of a foreign private issuer who is not an executive officer of the foreign private issuer is exempt from the requirements of paragraph (b)(1)(ii) of this section if the employee is elected or named to the board of directors or audit committee of the foreign private issuer pursuant to the issuer's governing law or documents, an employee collective bargaining or similar agreement or other home country legal or listing requirements.

(D) An audit committee member of a foreign private issuer may be exempt from the requirements of paragraph (b)(1)(ii)(B) of this section if that member meets the following requirements:

(*1*) The member is an affiliate of the foreign private issuer or a representative of such an affiliate;

(*2*) The member has only observer status on, and is not a voting member or the chair of, the audit committee; and

(*3*) Neither the member nor the affiliate is an executive officer of the foreign private issuer.

(E) An audit committee member of a foreign private issuer may be exempt from the requirements of paragraph (b)(1)(ii)(B) of this section if that member meets the following requirements:

(*1*) The member is a representative or designee of a foreign government or foreign governmental entity that is an affiliate of the foreign private issuer; and

(*2*) The member is not an executive officer of the foreign private issuer.

(F) In addition to paragraphs (b)(1)(iv)(A) through (E) of this section, the Commission may exempt from the requirements of paragraphs (b)(1)(ii) or (b)(1)(iii) of this section a particular relationship with respect to audit committee members, as the Commission determines appropriate in light of the circumstances.

(2) *Responsibilities relating to registered public accounting firms.* The audit committee of each listed issuer, in its capacity as a committee of the board of directors, must be directly responsible for the appointment, compensation, retention and oversight of the work of any registered public accounting firm engaged (including resolution of disagreements between management and the auditor regarding financial reporting) for the purpose of preparing or issuing an audit report or performing other audit, review or attest services for the listed issuer, and each such registered public accounting firm must report directly to the audit committee.

(3) *Complaints.* Each audit committee must establish procedures for:

(i) The receipt, retention, and treatment of complaints received by the listed issuer regarding accounting, internal accounting controls, or auditing matters; and

(ii) The confidential, anonymous submission by employees of the listed issuer of concerns regarding questionable accounting or auditing matters.

(4) *Authority to engage advisers.* Each audit committee must have the authority to engage independent counsel and other advisers, as it determines necessary to carry out its duties.

(5) *Funding.* Each listed issuer must provide for appropriate funding, as determined by the audit committee, in its capacity as a committee of the board of directors, for payment of:

(i) Compensation to any registered public accounting firm engaged for the purpose of preparing or issuing an audit report or performing other audit, review or attest services for the listed issuer;

(ii) Compensation to any advisers employed by the audit committee under paragraph (b)(4) of this section; and

(iii) Ordinary administrative expenses of the audit committee that are necessary or appropriate in carrying out its duties.

(c) *General exemptions.*

(1) At any time when an issuer has a class of securities that is listed on a national securities exchange or national securities association subject to the requirements of this section, the listing of other classes of securities of the listed issuer on a national securities exchange or national securities association is not subject to the requirements of this section.

(2) At any time when an issuer has a class of common equity securities (or similar securities) that is listed on a national securities exchange or national securities association subject to the requirements of this section, the listing of classes of securities of a direct or indirect consolidated subsidiary or an at least 50% beneficially owned subsidiary of the issuer (except classes of equity securities, other than non-convertible, non-participating preferred securities, of such subsidiary) is not subject to the requirements of this section.

(3) The listing of securities of a foreign private issuer is not subject to the requirements of paragraphs (b)(1) through (b)(5) of this section if the foreign private issuer meets the following requirements:

(i) The foreign private issuer has a board of auditors (or similar body), or has statutory auditors, established and selected pursuant to home country legal or listing provisions expressly requiring or permitting such a board or similar body;

(ii) The board or body, or statutory auditors is required under home country legal or listing requirements to be either:

(A) Separate from the board of directors; or

(B) Composed of one or more members of the board of directors and one or more members that are not also members of the board of directors;

(iii) The board or body, or statutory auditors, are not elected by management of such issuer and no executive officer of the foreign private issuer is a member of such board or body, or statutory auditors;

(iv) Home country legal or listing provisions set forth or provide for standards for the independence of such board or body, or statutory auditors, from the foreign private issuer or the management of such issuer;

(v) Such board or body, or statutory auditors, in accordance with any applicable home country legal or listing requirements or the issuer's governing documents, are responsible, to the extent permitted by law, for the appointment, retention and oversight of the work of any registered public accounting firm engaged (including, to the extent permitted by law, the resolution of disagreements between management and the auditor regarding financial reporting) for the purpose of preparing or issuing an audit report or performing other audit, review or attest services for the issuer; and

(vi) The audit committee requirements of paragraphs (b)(3), (b)(4) and (b)(5) of this section apply to such board or body, or statutory auditors, to the extent permitted by law.

(4) The listing of a security futures product cleared by a clearing agency that is registered pursuant to section 17A of the Act (15 U.S.C. 78q-1) or that is exempt from the registration requirements of section 17A pursuant to paragraph (b)(7)(A) of such section is not subject to the requirements of this section.

(5) The listing of a standardized option, as defined in § 240.9b-1(a)(4), issued by a clearing agency that is registered pursuant to section 17A of the Act (15 U.S.C. 78q-1) is not subject to the requirements of this section.

(6) The listing of securities of the following listed issuers are not subject to the requirements of this section:

(i) Asset-Backed Issuers (as defined in § 229.1101 of this chapter);

(ii) Unit investment trusts (as defined in 15 U.S.C. 80a-4(2)); and

(iii) Foreign governments (as defined in § 240.3b-4(a)).

(7) The listing of securities of a listed issuer is not subject to the requirements of this section if:

(i) The listed issuer, as reflected in the applicable listing application, is organized as a trust or other unincorporated association that does not have a board of directors or persons acting in a similar capacity; and

(ii) The activities of the listed issuer that is described in paragraph (c)(7)(i) of this section are limited to passively owning or holding (as well as administering and distributing amounts in respect of) securities, rights, collateral or other assets on behalf of or for the benefit of the holders of the listed securities.

(d) *Disclosure.* Any listed issuer availing itself of an exemption from the independence standards contained in paragraph (b)(1)(iv) of this section (except paragraph (b)(1)(iv)(B) of this section), the general exemption contained in paragraph (c)(3) of this section or the last sentence of paragraph (a)(3) of this section, must:

(1) Disclose its reliance on the exemption and its assessment of whether, and if so, how, such reliance would materially adversely affect the ability of the audit committee to act independently and to satisfy the other requirements of this section in any proxy or information statement for a meeting of shareholders at which directors are elected that is filed with the Commission pursuant to the requirements of section 14 of the Act (15 U.S.C. 78n); and

(2) Disclose the information specified in paragraph (d)(1) of this section in, or incorporate such information by reference from such proxy or information statement filed with the Commission into, its annual report filed with the Commission pursuant to the requirements of section 13(a) or 15(d) of the Act (15 U.S.C. 78m(a) or 78o(d)).

(e) *Definitions.* Unless the context otherwise requires, all terms used in this section have the same meaning as in the Act. In addition, unless the context otherwise requires, the following definitions apply for purposes of this section:

(1)(i) The term *affiliate* of, or a person *affiliated* with, a specified person, means a person that directly, or indirectly through one or more intermediaries, controls, or is controlled by, or is under common control with, the person specified.

(ii)(A) A person will be deemed not to be in control of a specified person for purposes of this section if the person:

(*1*) Is not the beneficial owner, directly or indirectly, of more than 10% of any class of voting equity securities of the specified person; and

(*2*) Is not an executive officer of the specified person.

(B) Paragraph (e)(1)(ii)(A) of this section only creates a safe harbor position that a person does not control a specified person. The existence of the safe harbor does not create a presumption in any way that a person exceeding the ownership requirement in paragraph (e)(1)(ii)(A)(*1*) of this section controls or is otherwise an affiliate of a specified person.

(iii) The following will be deemed to be affiliates:

(A) An executive officer of an affiliate;

(B) A director who also is an employee of an affiliate;

(C) A general partner of an affiliate; and

(D) A managing member of an affiliate.

(iv) For purposes of paragraph (e)(1)(i) of this section, dual holding companies will not be deemed to be affiliates of or persons affiliated with each other by virtue of their dual holding company arrangements with each other, including where directors of one dual holding company are also directors of the other dual holding company, or where directors of one or both dual holding companies are also directors of the businesses jointly controlled, directly or indirectly, by the dual holding companies (and, in each case, receive only ordinary-course compensation for serving as a member of the board of directors, audit committee or any other board committee of the dual holding companies or any entity that is jointly controlled, directly or indirectly, by the dual holding companies).

(2) In the case of foreign private issuers with a two-tier board system, the term *board of directors* means the supervisory or non-management board.

(3) In the case of a listed issuer that is a limited partnership or limited liability company where such entity does not have a board of directors or equivalent body, the term board of directors means the board of directors of the managing general partner, managing member or equivalent body.

(4) The term *control* (including the terms *controlling, controlled by* and under *common control with*) means the possession, direct or indirect, of the power to direct or cause the direction of the management and policies of a person, whether through the ownership of voting securities, by contract, or otherwise.

(5) The term *dual holding companies* means two foreign private issuers that:

(i) Are organized in different national jurisdictions;

(ii) Collectively own and supervise the management of one or more businesses which are conducted as a single economic enterprise; and

(iii) Do not conduct any business other than collectively owning and supervising such businesses and activities reasonably incidental thereto.

(6) The term *executive officer* has the meaning set forth in §240.3b-7.

(7) The term *foreign private issuer* has the meaning set forth in §240.3b-4(c).

(8) The term *indirect* acceptance by a member of an audit committee of any consulting, advisory or other compensatory fee includes acceptance of such a fee by a spouse, a minor child or stepchild or a child or stepchild sharing a home with the member or by an entity in which such member is a partner, member, an officer such as a managing director occupying a comparable position or executive officer, or occupies a similar position (except limited partners, non-managing members and those occupying similar positions who, in each case, have no active role in providing services to the entity) and which provides accounting, consulting, legal, investment banking or financial advisory services to the issuer or any subsidiary of the issuer.

(9) The terms *listed* and *listing* refer to securities listed on a national securities exchange or listed in an automated inter-dealer quotation system of a national securities association or to issuers of such securities.

Instructions to §240.10A-3.

1. The requirements in paragraphs (b)(2) through (b)(5), (c)(3)(v) and (c)(3)(vi) of this section do not conflict with, and do not affect the application of, any requirement or ability under a listed issuer's governing law or documents or other home country legal or listing provisions that requires or permits shareholders to ultimately vote on, approve or ratify such requirements. The requirements instead relate to the assignment of responsibility as between the audit committee and management. In such an instance, however, if the listed issuer provides a recommendation or nomination regarding such responsibilities to shareholders, the audit committee of the listed issuer, or body performing similar functions, must be responsible for making the recommendation or nomination.

2. The requirements in paragraphs (b)(2) through (b)(5), (c)(3)(v), (c)(3)(vi) and Instruction 1 of this section do not conflict with any legal or listing requirement in a listed issuer's home jurisdiction that prohibits the full board of directors from delegating such responsibilities to the listed issuer's audit committee or limits the degree of such delegation. In that case, the audit committee, or body performing similar functions, must be granted such responsibilities, which can include advisory powers, with respect to such matters to the extent permitted by law, including submitting nominations or recommendations to the full board.

3. The requirements in paragraphs (b)(2) through (b)(5), (c)(3)(v) and (c)(3)(vi) of this section do not conflict with any legal or listing requirement in a listed issuer's home jurisdiction that vests such responsibilities with a government entity or tribunal. In that case, the audit committee, or body performing similar functions, must be granted such responsibilities, which can include advisory powers, with respect to such matters to the extent permitted by law.

4. For purposes of this section, the determination of a person's beneficial ownership must be made in accordance with §240.13d-3.

[As last amended in Release No. 33-8876, effective February 4, 2008, 73 F.R. 934.]

REGULATION 12B—REGISTRATION AND REPORTING

ATTENTION ELECTRONIC FILERS

THIS REGULATION SHOULD BE READ IN CONJUNCTION WITH REGULATION S-T (PART 232 OF THIS CHAPTER), WHICH GOVERNS THE PREPARATION AND SUBMISSION OF DOCUMENTS IN ELECTRONIC FORMAT. MANY PROVISIONS RELATING TO THE PREPARATION AND SUBMISSION OF DOCUMENTS IN PAPER FORMAT CONTAINED IN THIS REGULATION ARE SUPERSEDED BY THE PROVISIONS OF REGULATION S-T FOR DOCUMENTS REQUIRED TO BE FILED IN ELECTRONIC FORMAT.

General

[¶ 21,301] Scope of Regulation

Reg. § 240.12b-1. The rules contained in this regulation shall govern all registration statements pursuant to Sections 12(b) and 12(g) of the Act and all reports filed pursuant to Sections 13 and 15(d) of the Act, including all amendments to such statements and reports, except that any provision in a form covering the same subject matter as any such rule shall be controlling.

[As last amended in Release No. 34-18524, effective for all documents filed on or after May 24, 1982, 47 F.R. 11380.]

[¶ 21,311] Definitions

Reg. § 240.12b-2. Unless the context otherwise requires, the following terms, when used in the rules contained in this regulation or in Regulation 13A or 15D or in the forms for statements and reports filed pursuant to Sections 12, 13 or 15(d) of the Act, shall have the respective meanings indicated in this rule:

Accelerated filer and large accelerated filer. (1) *Accelerated filer.* The term accelerated filer means an issuer after it first meets the following conditions as of the end of its fiscal year:

(i) The issuer had an aggregate worldwide market value of the voting and non-voting common equity held by its non-affiliates of $75 million or more, but less than $700 million, as of the last business day of the issuer's most recently completed second fiscal quarter;

(ii) The issuer has been subject to the requirements of section 13(a) or 15(d) of the Act (15 U.S.C. 78m or 78o(d)) for a period of at least twelve calendar months;

(iii) The issuer has filed at least one annual report pursuant to section 13(a) or 15(d) of the Act; and

(iv) The issuer is not eligible to use the requirements for smaller reporting companies in Part 229 of this chapter for its annual and quarterly reports.

(2) *Large accelerated filer.* The term *large accelerated filer* means an issuer after it first meets the following conditions as of the end of its fiscal year:

(i) The issuer had an aggregate worldwide market value of the voting and non-voting common equity held by its non-affiliates of $700 million or more, as of the last business day of the issuer's most recently completed second fiscal quarter;

(ii) The issuer has been subject to the requirements of section 13(a) or 15(d) of the Act for a period of at least twelve calendar months;

(iii) The issuer has filed at least one annual report pursuant to section 13(a) or 15(d) of the Act; and

(iv) The issuer is not eligible to use the requirements for smaller reporting companies in Part 229 of this chapter for its annual and quarterly reports.

(3) Entering and exiting accelerated filer and large accelerated filer status.

(i) The determination at the end of the issuer's fiscal year for whether a non-accelerated filer becomes an accelerated filer, or whether a non-accelerated filer or accelerated filer becomes a large accelerated filer, governs the deadlines for the annual report to be filed for that fiscal year, the quarterly and annual reports to be filed for the subsequent fiscal year and all annual and quarterly reports to be filed thereafter while the issuer remains an accelerated filer or large accelerated filer.

(ii) Once an issuer becomes an accelerated filer, it will remain an accelerated filer unless the issuer determines at the end of a fiscal year that the aggregate worldwide market value of the voting and non-voting common equity held by non-affiliates of the issuer was less than $50 million, as of the last business day of the issuer's most recently completed second fiscal quarter. An issuer making this determination becomes a non-accelerated filer. The issuer will not become an accelerated filer again unless it subsequently meets the conditions in paragraph (1) of this definition.

(iii) Once an issuer becomes a large accelerated filer, it will remain a large accelerated filer unless the issuer determines at the end of a fiscal year that the aggregate worldwide market value of the voting and non-voting common equity held by non-affiliates of the issuer was less than $500 million, as of the last business day of the issuer's most recently completed second fiscal quarter. If the issuer's aggregate worldwide market value was $50 million or more, but less than $500 million, as of the last business day of the issuer's most recently completed second fiscal quarter, the issuer becomes an accelerated filer. If the issuer's aggregate worldwide market value was less than $50 million, as of the last business day of the issuer's most recently completed second fiscal quarter, the issuer becomes a non-accelerated filer. An issuer will not become a large accelerated filer again unless it subsequently meets the conditions in paragraph (2) of this definition.

(iv) The determination at the end of the issuer's fiscal year for whether an accelerated filer becomes a non-accelerated filer, or a large accelerated filer becomes an accelerated filer or a non-accelerated filer, governs the deadlines for the annual report to be filed for that fiscal year, the quarterly and annual reports to be filed for the subsequent fiscal year and all annual and quarterly reports to be filed thereafter while the issuer remains an accelerated filer or non-accelerated filer.

NOTE to paragraphs (1), (2) and (3): The aggregate worldwide market value of the issuer's outstanding voting and non-voting common equity shall be computed by use of the price at which the common equity was last sold, or the average of the bid and asked prices of such common equity, in the principal market for such common equity.

Affiliate. An "affiliate" of, or a person "affiliated" with, a specified person, is a person that directly, or indirectly through one or more intermediaries, controls, or is controlled by, or is under common control with, the person specified.

Amount. The term "amount," when used in regard to securities, means the principal amount if relating to evidences of indebtedness, the number of shares if relating to shares, and the number of units if relating to any other kind of security.

Associate. The term "associate" used to indicate a relationship with any person, means (1) any corporation or organization (other than the registrant or a majority-owned subsidiary of the registrant) of which such person is an officer or partner or is, directly or indirectly, the beneficial owner of 10 percent or more of any class of equity securities, (2) any trust or other estate in which such person has a substantial beneficial interest or as to which such person serves as trustee or in a similar fiduciary capacity, and (3) any relative or spouse of such person, or any relative of such spouse, who has the same home as such person or who is a director or officer of the registrant or any of its parents or subsidiaries.

Business combination related shell company. The term *business combination related shell company* means a shell company (as defined in § 240.12b-2) that is:

(1) Formed by an entity that is not a shell company solely for the purpose of changing the corporate domicile of that entity solely within the United States; or

(2) Formed by an entity that is not a shell company solely for the purpose of completing a business combination transaction (as defined in § 230.165(f) of this chapter) among one or more entities other than the shell company, none of which is a shell company.

Certified. The term "certified," when used in regard to financial statements, means examined and reported upon with an opinion expressed by an independent public or certified public accountant.

Charter. The term "charter" includes articles of incorporation, declarations of trust, articles of association or partnership, or any similar instrument, as amended, effecting (either with or without filing with any governmental agency) the organization or creation of an incorporated or unincorporated person.

Common equity. The term "common equity" means any class of common stock or an equivalent interest, including but not limited to a unit of beneficial interest in a trust or a limited partnership interest.

Control. The term "control" (including the terms "controlling," "controlled by" and "under common control with") means the possession, direct or indirect, of the power to direct or cause the direction of the management and policies of a person, whether through the ownership of voting securities, by contract, or otherwise.

Depositary share. The term "depositary share" means a security, evidenced by an American Depositary Receipt, that represents a foreign security or a multiple of or fraction thereof deposited with a depositary.

Employee. The term "employee" does not include a director, trustee, or officer.

Fiscal Year. The term "fiscal year" means the annual accounting period or, if no closing date has been adopted, the calendar year ending on December 31.

Majority-owned Subsidiary. The term "majority-owned subsidiary" means a subsidiary more than fifty percent of whose outstanding securities representing the right, other than as affected by events of default, to vote for the election of directors, is owned by the subsidiary's parent and/or one or more of the parent's other majority-owned subsidiaries.

Managing underwriter. The term "managing underwriter" includes an underwriter (or underwriters) who, by contract or otherwise, deals with the registrant; organizes the selling effort; receives some benefit directly or indirectly in which all other underwriters similarly situated do not share in proportion to their respective interests in the underwriting; or represents any other underwriters in such matters as maintaining the records of the distribution, arranging the allotments of securities offered or arranging for appropriate stabilization activities, if any.

Material. The term "material," when used to qualify a requirement for the furnishing of information as to any subject, limits the information required to those matters to which there is a substantial likelihood that a reasonable investor would attach importance in determining whether to buy or sell the securities registered.

Material weakness. The term *material weakness* is a deficiency, or a combination of deficiencies, in internal control over financial reporting such that there is a reasonable possibility that a material misstatement of the registrant's annual or interim financial statements will not be prevented or detected on a timely basis.

Parent. A "parent" of a specified person is an affiliate controlling such person directly, or indirectly through one or more intermediaries.

Predecessor. The term "predecessor" means a person the major portion of the business and assets of which another person acquired in a single succession or in a series of related successions in each of which the acquiring person acquired the major portion of the business and assets of the acquired person.

Previously Filed or Reported. The terms "previously filed" and "previously reported" mean previously filed with, or reported in, a statement under Section 12, a report under Section 13 or 15(d), a definitive proxy statement or information statement under Section 14 of the Act, or a registration statement under the Securities Act of 1933: *Provided,* That information contained in any such document shall be deemed to have been previously filed with, or reported to, an exchange only if such document is filed with such exchange.

Principal Underwriter. The term "principal underwriter" means an underwriter in privity of contract with the issuer of the securities as to which he is underwriter.

Promoter. (1) The term "promoter" includes:

(i) Any person who, acting alone or in conjunction with one or more other persons, directly or indirectly takes initiative in founding and organizing the business or enterprise of an issuer; or

(ii) Any person who, in connection with the founding and organizing of the business or enterprise of an issuer, directly or indirectly receives in consideration of services or property, or both services and property, 10 percent or more of any class of securities of the issuer or 10 percent or more of the proceeds from the sale of any class of such securities. However, a person who receives such securities or proceeds either solely as underwriting commissions or solely in consideration of property shall not be deemed a promoter within the meaning of this paragraph if such person does not otherwise take part in founding and organizing the enterprise.

(2) All persons coming within the definition of "promoter" in paragraph (o)(1) of this section may be referred to as "founders" or "organizers" or by another term provided that such term is reasonably descriptive of those persons' activities with respect to the issuer.

Prospectus. Unless otherwise specified or the context otherwise requires, the term "prospectus" means a prospectus meeting the requirements of Section 10(a) of the Securities Act of 1933 as amended.

Registrant. The term "registrant" means an issuer of securities with respect to which a registration statement or report is to be filed.

Registration Statement. The term "registration statement" or "statement", when used with reference to registration pursuant to Section 12 of the Act, includes both an application for registration of securities on a national securities exchange pursuant to Section 12(b) of the Act and a registration statement filed pursuant to Section 12(g) of the Act.

Share. The term "share" means a share of stock in a corporation or unit of interest in an unincorporated person.

Shell company. The term *shell company* means a registrant, other than an asset-backed issuer as defined in Item 1101(b) of Regulation AB (§ 229.1101(b) of this chapter), that has:

(1) No or nominal operations; and

(2) Either:

(i) No or nominal assets;

(ii) Assets consisting solely of cash and cash equivalents; or

(iii) Assets consisting of any amount of cash and cash equivalents and nominal other assets.

NOTE: For purposes of this definition, the determination of a registrant's assets (including cash and cash equivalents) is based solely on the amount of assets that would be reflected on the registrant's balance sheet prepared in accordance with generally accepted accounting principles on the date of that determination.

Significant deficiency. The term *significant deficiency* is a deficiency, or a combination of deficiencies, in internal control over financial reporting that is less severe than a material weakness, yet important enough to merit attention by those responsible for oversight of the registrant's financial reporting.

Significant subsidiary. The term *significant subsidiary* means a subsidiary, including its subsidiaries, which meets any of the following conditions:

(1) The registrant's and its other subsidiaries' investments in and advances to the subsidiary exceed 10 percent of the total assets of the registrant and its subsidiaries consolidated as of the end of the most recently completed fiscal year (for a proposed combination between entities under common control, this condition is also met when the number of common shares exchanged or to be exchanged by the registrant exceeds 10 percent of its total common shares outstanding at the date the combination is initiated); or

(2) The registrant's and its other subsidiaries' proportionate share of the total assets (after intercompany eliminations) of the subsidiary exceeds 10 percent of the total assets of the registrant and its subsidiaries consolidated as of the end of the most recently completed fiscal year; or

(3) The registrant's and its other subsidiaries' equity in the income from continuing operations before income taxes, extraordinary items and cumulative effect of a change in accounting principle of the subsidiary exclusive of amounts attributable to any noncontrolling interests exceeds 10 percent of such income of the registrant and its subsidiaries consolidated for the most recently completed fiscal year.

Computational note: For purposes of making the prescribed income test the following guidance should be applied:

1. When a loss exclusive of amounts attributable to any noncontrolling interests has been incurred by either the parent and its subsidiaries consolidated or the tested subsidiary, but not both, the equity in the income or loss of the tested subsidiary exclusive of amounts attributable to any noncontrolling interests should be excluded from such income of the registrant and its subsidiaries consolidated for purposes of the computation.

2. If income of the registrant and its subsidiaries consolidated exclusive of amounts attributable to any noncontrolling interests for the most recent fiscal year is at least 10 percent lower than the average of the income for the last five fiscal years, such average income should be substituted for purposes of the computation. Any loss years should be omitted for purposes of computing average income.

Smaller reporting company: As used in this part, the term *smaller reporting company* means an issuer that is not an investment company, an asset-backed issuer (as defined in § 229.1101 of this chapter), or a majority-owned subsidiary of a parent that is not a smaller reporting company and that:

(1) Had a public float of less than $75 million as of the last business day of its most recently completed second fiscal quarter, computed by multiplying the aggregate worldwide number of shares of its voting and non-voting common equity held by non-affiliates by the price at which the common equity was last sold, or the average of the bid and asked prices of common equity, in the principal market for the common equity; or

(2) In the case of an initial registration statement under the Securities Act or Exchange Act for shares of its common equity, had a public float of less than $75 million as of a date within 30 days of the date of the filing of the registration statement, computed by multiplying the aggregate worldwide number of such shares held by non-affiliates before the registration plus, in the case of a Securities Act registration statement, the number of such shares included in the registration statement by the estimated public offering price of the shares; or

(3) In the case of an issuer whose public float as calculated under paragraph (1) or (2) of this definition was zero, had annual revenues of less than $50 million during the most recently completed fiscal year for which audited financial statements are available. (4) *Determination*: Whether or not an issuer is a smaller reporting company is determined on an annual basis.

(i) For issuers that are required to file reports under section 13(a) or 15(d) of the Exchange Act, the determination is based on whether the issuer came within the definition of smaller reporting company using the amounts specified in paragraph (f)(2)(iii) of Item 10 of Regulation S-K (§ 229.10(f)(1)(i) of this chapter), as of the last business day of the second fiscal quarter of the issuer's previous fiscal year. An issuer in this category must reflect this determination in the information it provides in its quarterly report on Form 10-Q for the first fiscal quarter of the next year, indicating on the cover page of that filing, and in subsequent filings for that fiscal year, whether or not it is a smaller reporting company, except that, if a determination based on public float indicates that the issuer is newly eligible to be a smaller reporting company, the issuer may choose to reflect this determination beginning with its first quarterly report on Form 10-Q following the determination, rather than waiting until the first fiscal quarter of the next year.

(ii) For determinations based on an initial Securities Act or Exchange Act registration statement under paragraph (f)(1)(ii) of Item 10 of Regulation S-K (§ 229.10(f)(1)(ii) of this chapter), the issuer must reflect the determination in the information it provides in the registration statement and must appropriately indicate on the cover page of the filing, and subsequent filings for the fiscal year in which the filing is made, whether or not it is a smaller reporting company. The issuer must redetermine its status at the end of its second fiscal quarter and then reflect any change in status as provided in paragraph (4)(i) of this definition. In the case of a determination based on an initial Securities Act registration statement, an issuer that was not determined to be a smaller reporting company has the option to redetermine its status at the conclusion of the offering covered by the registration statement based on the actual offering price and number of shares sold.

(iii) Once an issuer fails to qualify for smaller reporting company status, it will remain unqualified unless it determines that its public float, as calculated in accordance with paragraph (f)(1) of this definition, was less than $50 million as of the last business day of its second fiscal quarter or, if that calculation results in zero because the issuer had no public equity outstanding or no market price for its equity existed, if the issuers had annual revenues of less than $40 million during its previous fiscal year.

Subsidiary. A "subsidiary" of a specified person is an affiliate controlled by such person directly, or indirectly through one or more intermediaries. (See also "majority-owned subsidiary," "significant subsidiary," and "totally-held subsidiary.")

Succession. The term *succession* means the direct acquisition of the assets comprising a going business, whether by merger, consolidation, purchase, or other direct transfer; or the acquisition of control of a shell company in a transaction required to be reported on Form 8-K (§ 249.308 of this chapter) in compliance with Item 5.01 of that Form or on Form 20-F (§ 249.220f of this chapter) in compliance with Rule 13a-19 (§ 240.13a-19) or Rule 15d-19 (§ 240.15d-19). Except for an acquisition of control of a shell company, the term does not include the acquisition of control of a business unless followed by the direct acquisition of its assets. The terms *succeed* and *successor* have meanings correlative to the foregoing.

Totally held subsidiary. The term "totally held subsidiary" means a subsidiary (1) substantially all of whose outstanding securities are owned by its parent and/or the parent's other totally held subsidiaries, and (2) which is not indebted to any person other than its parent and/or the parent's other totally held subsidiaries in an amount which is material in relation to the particular subsidiary, excepting indebtedness incurred in the ordinary course of business which is not overdue and which matures within one year from the date of its creation, whether evidenced by securities or not.

Voting Securities. The term "voting securities" means securities the holders of which are presently entitled to vote for the election of directors.

Wholly-owned Subsidiary. The term "wholly-owned subsidiary" means a subsidiary substantially all of whose outstanding voting securities are owned by its parent and/or the parent's other wholly-owned subsidiaries.

[As last amended in Release No. 33-9026, effective April 23, 2009, 74 F.R. 18612.]

[¶ 21,321] Title of Securities

Reg. § 240.12b-3. Wherever the title of securities is required to be stated there shall be given such information as will indicate the type and general character of the securities, including the following:

(a) In the case of shares, the par or stated value, if any; the rate of dividends, if fixed, and whether cumulative or non-cumulative; a brief indication of the preference, if any; and if convertible, a statement to that effect.

(b) In the case of funded debt, the rate of interest; the date of maturity, or if the issue matures serially, a brief indication of the serial maturities, such as "maturing serially from 1950 to 1960"; if the payment of principal or interest is contingent, an appropriate indication of such contingency; a brief indication of the priority of the issue; and if convertible, a statement to that effect.

(c) In the case of any other kind of security, appropriate information of comparable character.

[As adopted in Release No. 34-4194, January 17, 1949, 13 F.R. 9322.]

[¶ 21,331] Supplemental Information

Reg. § 240.12b-4. The Commission or its staff may, where it is deemed appropriate, request supplemental information concerning the registrant, a registration statement or a periodic or other report under the Act. This information shall not be required to be filed with or deemed part of the registration statement or report. The information shall be returned to the registrant upon request, provided that:

(a) Such request is made at the time such information is furnished to the staff;

(b) The return of such information is consistent with the protection of investors; and

(c) The return of such information is consistent with the provisions of the Freedom of Information Act [5 U.S.C. 552].

[As adopted in Release No. 34-18524, March 3, 1982, effective for all documents filed on or after May 24, 1982, 47 F.R. 11380.]

[¶ 21,341] Determination of Affiliates of Banks

Reg. § 240.12b-5. In determining whether a person is an "affiliate" or "parent" of a bank or whether a bank is a "subsidiary" or "majority-owned subsidiary" of a person, within the meaning of those terms as defined in § 240.12b-2, voting securities of the bank held by a corporation all of the stock of which is directly owned by the United States Government shall not be taken into consideration.

[As adopted in Release No. 34-4194, January 17, 1949, 13 F.R. 9322.]

[¶ 21,351] When Securities Are Deemed to Be Registered

Reg. § 240.12b-6. A class of securities with respect to which a registration statement has been filed pursuant to Section 12 of the Act shall be deemed to be registered for the purposes of Sections 13, 14, 15(d) and 16 of the Act and the rules and regulations thereunder only when such statement has become effective as provided in Section 12, and securities of said class shall not be subject to Sections 13, 14 and 16 of the Act until such statement has become effective as provided in Section 12.

[As adopted in Release No. 34-7500, January 5, 1965, 30 F.R. 482.]

Formal Requirements

[¶ 21,371] Requirements as to Proper Form

Reg. § 240.12b-10. Every statement or report shall be on the form prescribed therefor by the Commission, as in effect on the date of filing. Any statement or report shall be deemed to be filed on the proper form unless objection to the form is made by the Commission within thirty days after the date of filing.

[As last amended in Release No. 34-7525, February 5, 1965, 30 F.R. 2022.]

[¶ 21,381] Number of Copies—Signatures—Binding

Reg. § 240.12b-11. (a) Except as provided in a particular form, three complete copies of each statement or report, including exhibits and all other papers and documents filed as a part thereof, shall be filed with the Commission. At least one complete copy of each statement shall be filed with each exchange on which the securities covered thereby are to be registered. At least one complete copy of each report under section 13 of the Act shall be filed with each exchange on which the registrant has securities registered.

(b) At least one copy of each statement or report filed with the Commission and one copy thereof filed with each exchange shall be signed in the manner prescribed by the appropriate form.

(c) Each copy of a statement or report filed with the Commission or with an exchange shall be bound in one or more parts. Copies filed with the Commission shall be bound without stiff covers. The statement or report shall be bound on the left side in such a manner as to leave the reading matter legible.

(d) *Signatures.* Where the Act or the rules, forms, reports or schedules thereunder, including paragraph (b) of this section, require a document filed with or furnished to the Commission to be signed, such document shall be manually signed, or signed using either typed signatures or duplicated or facsimile versions of manual signatures. Where typed, duplicated or facsimile signatures are used, each signatory to the filing shall manually sign a signature page or other document authenticating, acknowledging or otherwise adopting his or her signature that appears in the filing. Such document shall be executed before or at the time the filing is made and shall be retained by the filer for a period of five years. Upon request, the filer shall furnish to the Commission or its staff a copy of any or all documents retained pursuant to this section.

[As last amended in Release No. 34-37262, May 31, 1996, effective July 15, 1996, 61 F.R. 30397.]

[¶ 21,391] Requirements as to Paper, Printing and Language

Reg. § 240.12b-12. (a) Statements and reports shall be filed on good quality, unglazed white paper, no longer than 8½ × 11 inches in size, insofar as practicable. To the extent that the reduction of larger documents would render them illegible, such documents may be filed on paper larger than 8½ × 11 inches in size.

(b) The statement or report and, insofar as practicable, all papers and documents filed as a part thereof, shall be printed, lithographed, mimeographed, or typewritten. However, the statement or report or any portion thereof may be prepared by any similar process which, in the opinion of the Commission, produces copies suitable for a permanent record and microfilming. Irrespective of the process used, all copies of any such material shall be clear, easily readable and suitable for repeated photocopying. Debits in credit categories and credits in debit categories shall be designated so as to be clearly distinguishable as such an photocopies.

(c) The body of all printed statements and reports and all notes to financial statements and other tabular data included therein shall be in roman type at least as large and as legible as 10-point modern type. However, to the extent necessary for convenient presentation, financial statements and other tabular data, including tabular data in notes, may be in roman type at least as large and as legible as 8-point modern type. All such type shall be leaded at least 2 points.

(d)(1) All Exchange Act filings and submissions must be in the English language, except as otherwise provided by this section. If a filing or submission requires the inclusion of a document that is in a foreign language, a party must submit instead a fair and accurate English translation of the entire foreign language document, except as provided by paragraph (d)(3) of this section.

(2) If a filing or submission subject to review by the Division of Corporation Finance requires the inclusion of a foreign language document as an exhibit or attachment, a party must submit a fair and accurate English translation of the foreign language document if consisting of any of the following, or an amendment of any of the following:

(i) Articles of incorporation, memoranda of association, bylaws, and other comparable documents, whether original or restated;

(ii) Instruments defining the rights of security holders, including indentures qualified or to be qualified under the Trust Indenture Act of 1939;

(iii) Voting agreements, including voting trust agreements;

(iv) Contracts to which directors, officers, promoters, voting trustees or security holders named in a registration statement, report or other document are parties;

(v) Contracts upon which a filer's business is substantially dependent;

(vi) Audited annual and interim consolidated financial information; and

(vii) Any document that is or will be the subject of a confidential treatment request under § 240.24b-2 or § 230.406 of this chapter.

(3)(i) A party may submit an English summary instead of an English translation of a foreign language document as an exhibit or attachment to a filing or submission subject to review by the Division of Corporation Finance, as long as:

(A) The foreign language document does not consist of any of the subject matter enumerated in paragraph (d)(2) of this section; or

(B) The applicable form permits the use of an English summary.

(ii) Any English summary submitted under paragraph (d)(3) of this section must:

(A) Fairly and accurately summarize the terms of each material provision of the foreign language document; and

(B) Fairly and accurately describe the terms that have been omitted or abridged.

(4) When submitting an English summary or English translation of a foreign language document under this section, a party must identify the submission as either an English summary or English translation. A party may submit a copy of the unabridged foreign language document when including an English summary or English translation of a foreign language document in a filing or submission. A party must provide a copy of any foreign language document upon the request of Commission staff.

(5) A foreign government or its political subdivision must provide a fair and accurate English translation of its latest annual budget submitted as Exhibit B to Form 18 (§ 249.218 of this chapter) or Exhibit (c) to Form 18-K (§ 249.318 of this chapter) only if one is available. If no English translation is available, a filer must provide a copy of the foreign language version of its latest annual budget as an exhibit.

(6) A Canadian issuer may file an exhibit, attachment or other part of a Form 40-F registration statement or annual report (§ 249.240f of this chapter), Schedule 13E-4F (§ 240.13e-102), Schedule 14D-1F (§ 240.14d-102), or Schedule 14D-9F (§ 240.14d-103), that contains text in both French and English if the issuer included the French text to comply with the requirements of the Canadian securities administrator or other Canadian authority and, for an electronic filing, if the filing is an HTML document, as defined in Regulation S-T Rule 11 (17 CFR 232.11)

(e) Where a statement or report is distributed to investors through an electronic medium, issuers may satisfy legibility requirements applicable to printed documents, such as paper size and type size and font, by presenting all required information in a format readily communicated to investors.

[As last amended in Release No. 33-8099, effective November 4, 2002, 67 F.R. 36678.]

[¶ 21,401] Preparation of Statement or Report

Reg. § 240.12b-13 The statement or report shall contain the numbers and captions of all items of the appropriate form, but the text of the items may be omitted provided the answers thereto are so prepared as to indicate to the reader the coverage of the items without the necessity of his referring to the text of the items or instructions thereto. However, where any item requires information to be given in tabular form, it shall be given in substantially the tabular form specified in the item. All instructions, whether appearing under the items of the form or elsewhere therein, are to be omitted. Unless expressly provided otherwise, if any item is inapplicable or the answer thereto is in the negative, an appropriate statement to that effect shall be made.

[As last amended in Release No. 34-7525, February 5, 1965, 30 F.R. 2023.]

[¶ 21,411] Riders—Inserts

Reg. § 240.12b-14 Riders shall not be used. If the statement or report is typed on a printed form, and the space provided for the answer to any given item is insufficient, reference shall be made in such space to a full insert page or pages on which the item number and caption and the complete answer are given.

[As last amended in Release No. 34-7525, February 5, 1965, 30 F.R. 2023.]

[¶ 21,421] Amendments

Reg. § 240.12b-15 All amendments must be filed under cover of the formamended, marked with the letter "A" to designate the document as an amendment, e.g., "10-K/A," and in compliance with pertinent requirements applicable to statements and reports. Amendments filed pursuant to this section must set forth the complete text of each item asamended. Amendments must be numbered sequentially and be filed separately for each statement or report amended. Amendments to a statement may be filed either before or after registration becomes effective. Amendments must be signed on behalf of the registrant by a duly authorized representative of the registrant. An amendment to any report required to include the certifications as specified in § 240.13a-14(a) or § 240.15d-14(a) must include new certifications by each principal executive and principal financial officer of the registrant, and an amendment to any report required to be accompanied by the certifications as specified in § 240.13a-14(b) or § 240.15d-14(b) must be accompanied by new certifications by each principal executive and principal financial officer of the registrant. An amendment to any report required to include the certifications as specified in § 240.13a-14(d) or § 240.15d-14(d) must include a new certificationby an individual specified in § 240.13a-14(e) or § 240.15d-14(e), as applicable. The requirements of the form being amended will govern the number of copies to be filed in connection with a paper format amendment. Electronic filers satisfy the provisions dictating the number of copies by filing one copy of the amendment in electronic format. See § 232.309 of this chapter (Rule 309 of Regulation S-T).

[As last amended in Release No. 33-8518, effective March 8, 2005, 70 F.R. 1506.]

General Requirements as to Contents

[¶ 21,451] Additional Information

Reg. § 240.12b-20 In addition to the information expressly required to be included in a statement or report, there shall be added such further material information, if any, as may be necessary to make the required statements, in the light of the circumstances under which they are made not misleading.

[As last amended in Release No. 34-7525, February 5, 1965, 30 F.R. 2023.]

[¶ 21,461] Information Unknown or Not Available

Reg. § 240.12b-21 Information required need be given only insofar as it is known or reasonably available to the registrant. If any required information is unknown and not reasonably available to the registrant, either because the obtaining thereof would involve unreasonable effort or expense, or because it rests peculiarly within the knowledge of another person not affiliated with the registrant, the information may be omitted, subject to the following conditions:

(a) The registrant shall give such information on the subject as it possesses or can acquire without unreasonable effort or expense, together with the sources thereof.

(b) The registrant shall include a statement either showing that unreasonable effort or expense would be involved or indicating the absence of any affiliation with the person within whose knowledge the information rests and stating the result of a request made to such person for the information.

[As adopted in Release No. 34-4194, January 17, 1949, 13 F.R. 9323.]

[¶ 21,471] Disclaimer of Control

Reg. § 240.12b-22 If the existence of control is open to reasonable doubt in any instance, the registrant may disclaim the existence of control and any admission thereof; in such case, however, the registrant shall state the material facts pertinent to the possible existence of control.

[As adopted in Release No. 34-4194, January 17, 1949, 13 F.R. 9323.]

[¶ 21,481] Incorporation by Reference

Reg. § 240.12b-23 (a) Except for information filed as an exhibit which is covered by Rule 12b-32 (17 CFR 240.12b-32), information may be incorporated by reference in answer, or partial answer, to any item of a registration statement or report subject to the following provisions:

(1) Financial statements incorporated by reference shall satisfy the requirements of the form or report in which they are incorporated. Financial statements or other financial data required to be given in comparative form for two or more fiscal years or periods shall not be incorporated by reference unless the material incorporated by reference includes the entire period for which the comparative data is given;

(2) Information in any part of the registration statement or report may be incorporated by reference in answer, or partial answer, to any other item of the registration statement or report; and

(3) Copies of any information or financial statement incorporated into a registration statement or report by reference, or copies of the pertinent pages of the document containing such information or statements, shall be filed as an exhibit to the statement or report, except that:

(i) A proxy or information statement incorporated by reference in response to Part III of Form 10-K (17 CFR 249.310);

(ii) A form of prospectus filed pursuant to 17 CFR 230.424(b) incorporated by reference in response to Item 1 of Form 8-A (17 CFR 249.208a); and

(iii) Information filed on Form 8-K (17 CFR 249.308) need not be filed as an exhibit.

(b) Any incorporation by reference of matter pursuant to this section shall be subject to the provisions of § 229.10(d) of this chapter restricting incorporation by reference of documents that incorporate by reference other information. Material incorporated by reference shall be clearly identified in the reference by page, paragraph, and caption or otherwise. Where only certain pages of a document are incorporated by reference and filed as an exhibit, the document from which the material is taken shall be clearly identified in the reference. An express statement that the specified matter is incorporated by reference shall be made at the particular place in the statement or report where the information is required. Matter shall not be incorporated by reference in any case where such incorporation would render the statement or report incomplete, unclear or confusing.

[As last amended in Release No. 33-8876, effective February 4, 2008, 73 F.R. 934.]

[¶ 21,501] Notification of Inability to Timely File All or Any Required Portion of a Form 10-K, 20-F, 11-K, N-SAR, N-CSR, 10-Q, or 10-D

Reg. § 240.12b-25. (a) If all or any required portion of an annual or transition report on Form 10-K, 20-F or 11-K (17 CFR 249.310, 249.220f or 249.311), a quarterly or transition report on Form 10-Q (17 CFR 249.308a), or a distribution report on Form 10-D (17 CFR 249.312) required to be filed pursuant to Section 13 or 15(d) of the Act (15 U.S.C. 78m or 78o(d)) and rules thereunder, or if all or any required portion of a semi-annual, annual or transition report on Form N-CSR (17 CFR 249.331; 17 CFR 274.128) or Form N-SAR (17 CFR 249.330; 17 CFR 274.101) required to be filed pursuant to Section 13 or 15(d) of the Act or section 30 of the Investment Company Act of 1940 (15 U.S.C. 80a-29) and the rules thereunder, is not filed within the time period prescribed for such report, the registrant, no later than one business day after the due date for such report, shall file a Form 12b-25 (17 CFR 249.322) with the Commission which shall contain disclosure of its inability to file the report timely and the reasons therefore in reasonable detail.

(b) With respect to any report or portion of any report described in paragraph (a) of this section which is not timely filed because the registrant is unable to do so without unreasonable effort or expense, such report shall be deemed to be filed on the prescribed due date for such report if:

(1) The registrant files the Form 12b-25 in compliance with paragraph (a) of this section and, when applicable, furnishes the exhibit required by paragraph (c) of this section;

(2) The registrant represents in the Form 12b-25 that:

(i) The reason(s) causing the inability to file timely could not be eliminated by the registrant without unreasonable effort or expense; and

(ii) The subject annual report, semi-annual report or transition report on Form 10-K, 20-F, 11-K, N-SAR, or N-CSR, or portion thereof, will be filed no later than the fifteenth calendar day following the prescribed due date; or the subject quarterly report or transition report on Form 10-Q or distribution report on Form 10-D, or portion thereof, will be filed no later than the fifth calendar day following the prescribed due date; and

(3) The report/portion thereof is actually filed within the period specified by paragraph (b)(2)(ii) of this section.

(c) If paragraph (b) of this section is applicable and the reason the subject report/portion thereof cannot be filed timely without unreasonable effort or expense relates to the inability of any person, other than the registrant, to furnish any required opinion, report or certification, the Form 12b-25 shall have attached as an exhibit a statement signed by such person stating the specific reasons why such person is unable to furnish the required opinion, report or certification on or before the date such report must be filed.

(d) Notwithstanding paragraph (b) of this section, a registrant will not be eligible to use any registration statement form under the Securities Act of 1933 the use of which is predicated on timely filed reports until the subject report is actually filed pursuant to paragraph (b)(3) of this section.

(e) If a Form 12b-25 filed pursuant to paragraph (a) of this section relates only to a portion of a subject report, the registrant shall:

(1) File the balance of such report and indicate on the cover page thereof which disclosure items are omitted; and

(2) Include, on the upper right corner of the amendment to the report which includes the previously omitted information, the following statement:

The following items were the subject of a Form 12b-25 and are included herein: *(List Item Numbers)*

(f) The provisions of this section shall not apply to financial statements to be filed by amendment to a form 10-K and 10-KSB as provided for by paragraph (a) of §210.3-09 or schedules to be filed by amendment in accordance with General Instruction A to form 10-K and 10-KSB.

(g) *Electronic filings.* The provisions of this section shall not apply to reports required to be filed in electronic format if the sole reason the report is not filed within the time period prescribed is that the filer is unable to file the report in electronic format. Filers unable to submit a report in electronic format within the time period prescribed solely due to difficulties with electronic filing should comply with either Rule 201 or 202 of Regulation S-T (§232.201 and §232.202 of this chapter), or apply for an adjustment of filing date pursuant to Rule 13(c) of Regulation S-T (232.13(c) of this chapter).

(h) *Interactive data submissions* . The provisions of this section shall not apply to the submission or posting of an Interactive Data File (§232.11 of this chapter). Filers unable to submit or post an Interactive Data File within the time period prescribed should comply with either Rule 201 or 202 of Regulation S-T (§232.201 and §232.202 of this chapter).

[As last amended in Release No. 33-9002, effective April 13, 2009, 74 F.R. 6776.]

Exhibits

[¶ 21,511] Additional Exhibits

Reg. §240.12b-30. The registrant may file such exhibits as it may desire, in addition to those required by the appropriate form. Such exhibits shall be so marked as to indicate clearly the subject matters to which they refer.

[As adopted in Release No. 34-4194, January 17, 1949, 13 F.R. 9323.]

[¶ 21,521] Omission of Substantially Identical Documents

Reg. §240.12b-31. In any case where two or more indentures, contracts, franchises, or other documents required to be filed as exhibits are substantially identical in all material respects except as to the parties thereto, the dates of execution, or other details, the registrant need file a copy of only one of such documents, with a schedule identifying the other documents omitted and setting forth the material details in which such documents differ from the document of which a copy is filed. The Commission may at any time in its discretion require the filing of copies of any documents so omitted.

[As adopted in Release No. 34-4194, January 17, 1949, 13 F.R. 9323.]

[¶ 21,531] Incorporation of Exhibits by Reference

Reg. § 240.12b-32. (a) Any document or part thereof filed with the Commission pursuant to any Act administered by the Commission may, subject to §228.10(f) and §229.10(d) of this chapter, be incorporated by reference as an exhibit to any statement or report filed with the Commission by the same or any other person. Any document or part thereof filed with an exchange pursuant to the Act may be incorporated by reference as an exhibit to any statement or report filed with the exchange by the same or any other person.

(b) If any modification has occurred in the text of any document incorporated by reference since the filing thereof, the registrant shall file with the reference a statement containing the text of any such modification and the date thereof.

[As last amended in Release No. 34-7525, February 5, 1965, 30 F.R. 2023.]

[¶ 21,541] Annual Reports to Other Federal Agencies

Reg. § 240.12b-33. Notwithstanding any rule or other requirement to the contrary, whenever copies of an annual report by a registrant to any other Federal agency are required or permitted to be filed as an exhibit to an application or report filed by such registrant with the Commission or with a securities exchange, only one copy of such annual report need be filed with the Commission and one copy thereof with each such exchange, provided appropriate reference to such copy is made in each copy of the application or report filed with the Commission or with such exchange.

[As adopted in Release No. 34-4808, March 5, 1953, 18 F.R. 1441.]

Special Provisions

[¶ 21,551] Use of Financial Statements Filed Under Other Acts

Reg. § 240.12b-36. Where copies of certified financial statements filed under other Acts administered by the Commission are filed with a statement or report, the accountant's certificate shall be manually signed or manually signed copies of the certificate shall be filed with the financial statements. Where such financial statements are incorporated by reference in a statement or report, the written consent of the accountant to such incorporation by reference shall be filed with the statement or report. Such consent shall be dated and signed manually.

[As last amended in Release No. 34-7525, February 5, 1965, 30 F.R. 2023.]

[¶ 21,552] Satisfaction of Filing Requirements

Reg. § 240.12b-37. With regard to issuers eligible to rely on Release No. 34-45589 (March 18, 2002) or Release No. IC-25463 (March 18, 2002) (each of which may be viewed on the Commission's website at www.sec.gov), filings made in accordance with the provisions of those Releases shall satisfy the issuer's requirement to make such a filing under Section 13(a), 14 or 15(d) of the Act (15 U.S.C. §§ 77m(a), 78n or 78o(d)), as applicable, and the Commission's rules and regulations thereunder.

[As adopted in Release No. 33-8070, effective March 18, 2002, 67 F.R. 13518.]

EXTENSIONS AND TEMPORARY EXEMPTIONS—DEFINITIONS

[¶ 21,851] Exemptions from Section 12(g)

Reg. § 240.12g-1. An issuer shall be exempt from the requirement to register any class of equity securities pursuant to section 12(g)(1) if on the last day of its most recent fiscal year the issuer had total assets not exceeding $10,000,000 and, with respect to a foreign private issuer, such securities were not quoted in an automated inter-dealer quotation system.

[As last amended in Release No. 34-37157, May 1, 1996, 61 F.R. 21354.]

[¶ 21,861] Securities Deemed to Be Registered Pursuant to Section 12(g)(1) upon Termination of Exemption Pursuant to Section 12(g)(2)(A) or (B)

Reg. § 240.12g-2. Any class of securities which would have been required to be registered pursuant to section 12(g)(1) of the Act except for the fact that it was exempt from such registration by section 12(g)(2)(A) because it was listed and registered on a national securities exchange, or by section 12(g)(2)(B) because it was issued by an investment company registered pursuant to section 8 of the Investment Company Act of 1940, shall upon the termination of the listing and registration of such class or the termination of the registration of such company and without the filing of an additional registration statement be deemed to be registered pursuant to said section 12(g)(1) if at the time of such termination (i) the issuer of such class of securities has elected to be regulated as a business development company pursuant to section 55 through 65 of the Investment Company Act of 1940 and such election has not been withdrawn, or (ii) securities of the class are not exempt from such registration pursuant to section 12 or rules thereunder and all securities of such class are held of record by 300 or more persons.

[As last amended in Release No. 34-18647, April 15, 1982, 47 F.R. 17046.]

[¶ 21,871] Registration of Securities of Successor Issuers Under Section 12(b) or 12(g)

Reg. § 240.12g-3. (a) Where in connection with a succession by merger, consolidation, exchange of securities, acquisition of assets or otherwise, securities of an issuer that are not already registered pursuant to section 12 of the Act (15 U.S.C. 78l) are issued to the holders of any class of securities of another issuer that is registered pursuant to either section 12(b) or (g) of the Act (15 U.S.C. 78l(b) or (g)), the class of securities so issued shall be deemed to be registered under the same paragraph of section 12 of the Act unless upon consummation of the succession:

(1) Such class is exempt from such registration other than by § 240.12g3-2;

(2) All securities of such class are held of record by less than 300 persons; or

(3) The securities issued in connection with the succession were registered on Form F-8 or Form F-80 (§ 239.38 or § 239.41 of this chapter) and following succession the successor would not be required to register such class of securities under section 12 of the Act (15 U.S.C. 78l) but for this section.

(b) Where in connection with a succession by merger, consolidation, exchange of securities, acquisition of assets or otherwise, securities of an issuer that are not already registered pursuant to section 12 of the Act (15 U.S.C. 78l) are issued to the holders of any class of securities of another issuer that is required to file a registration statement pursuant to either section 12(b) or (g) of the Act (15 U.S.C. 78l(b) or (g)) but has not yet done so, the duty to file such statement shall be deemed to have been assumed by the issuer of the class of securities so issued. The successor issuer shall file a registration statement pursuant to the same paragraph of section 12 of the Act with respect to such class within the period of time the predecessor issuer would have been required to file such a statement unless upon consummation of the succession:

(1) Such class is exempt from such registration other than by § 240.12g3-2;

(2) All securities of such class are held of record by less than 300 persons; or

(3) The securities issued in connection with the succession were registered on Form F-8 or Form F-80 (§ 239.38 or § 239.41 of this chapter) and following the succession the successor would not be required to register such class of securities under section 12 of the Act (15 U.S.C. 78l) but for this section.

(c) Where in connection with a succession by merger, consolidation, exchange of securities, acquisition of assets or otherwise, securities of an issuer that are not already registered pursuant to section 12 of the Act (15 U.S.C. 78l) are issued to the holders of classes of securities of two or more other issuers that are each registered pursuant to section 12 of the Act, the class of securities so issued shall be deemed to be registered under section 12 of the Act unless upon consummation of the succession:

(1) Such class is exempt from such registration other than by § 240.12g3-2;

(2) All securities of such class are held of record by less than 300 persons; or

(3) The securities issued in connection with the succession were registered on Form F-8 or Form F-80 (§ 239.38 or § 239.41 of this chapter) and following succession the successor would not be required to register such class of securities under section 12 of the Act (15 U.S.C. 78l) but for this section.

(d) If the classes of securities issued by two or more predecessor issuers (as described in paragraph (c) of this section) are registered under the same paragraph of section 12 of the Act (15 U.S.C. 78l), the class of securities issued by the successor issuer shall be deemed registered under the same paragraph of section 12 of the Act. If the classes of securities issued by the predecessor issuers are not registered under the same paragraph of section 12 of the Act, the class of securities issued by the successor issuer shall be deemed registered under section 12(g) of the Act (15 U.S.C. 78l(g)).

(e) An issuer that is deemed to have a class of securities registered pursuant to section 12 of the Act (15 U.S.C. 78l) according to paragraph (a), (b), (c) or (d) of this section shall file reports on the same forms and such class of securities shall be subject to the provisions of sections 14 and 16 of the Act (15 U.S.C. 78n and 78p) to the same extent as the predecessor issuers, except as follows:

(1) An issuer that is not a foreign issuer shall not be eligible to file on Form 20-F (§ 249.220f of this chapter) or to use the exemption in § 240.3a12-3.

(2) A foreign private issuer shall be eligible to file on Form 20-F (§ 249.220f of this chapter) and to use the exemption in § 240.3a12-3.

(f) An issuer that is deemed to have a class of securities registered pursuant to section 12 of the Act (15 U.S.C. 78l) according to paragraphs (a), (b), (c) or (d) of this section shall indicate in the Form 8-K (§ 249.308 of this chapter) report filed with the Commission in connection with the succession, pursuant to the requirements of Form 8-K, the paragraph of section 12 of the Act under which the class of securities issued by the successor issuer is deemed registered by operation of paragraphs (a), (b), (c) or (d) of this section. If a successor issuer that is deemed registered under section 12(g) of the Act (15 U.S.C. 78l(g)) by paragraph (d) of this section intends to list a class of securities on a national securities exchange, it must file a registration statement pursuant to section 12(b) of the Act (15 U.S.C. 78l(b)) with respect to that class of securities.

(g) An issuer that is deemed to have a class of securities registered pursuant to section 12 of the Act (15 U.S.C. 78l) according to paragraph (a), (b), (c) or (d) of this section shall file an annual report for each fiscal year beginning on or after the date as of which the succession occurred. Annual reports shall be filed within the period specified in the appropriate form. Each such issuer shall file an annual report for each of its predecessors that had securities registered pursuant to section 12 of the Act (15 U.S.C. 78l) covering the last full fiscal year of the predecessor before the registrant's succession, unless such report has been filed by the predecessor. Such annual report shall contain information that would be required if filed by the predecessor.

[As last amended in Release No. 34-38850, July 18, 1997, effective September 2, 1997, 62 F.R. 39755.]

[¶ 21,881] Exemptions for American Depositary Receipts and Certain Foreign Securities

Reg. § 240.12g3-2. (a) Securities of any class issued by any foreign private issuer shall be exempt from section 12(g) (15 U.S.C. 78l(g)) of the Act if the class has fewer than 300 holders resident in the United States. This exemption shall continue until the next fiscal year end at which the issuer has a class of equity securities held by 300 or more persons resident in the United States. For the purpose of determining whether a security is exempt pursuant to this paragraph:

(1) Securities held of record by persons resident in the United States shall be determined as provided in § 240.12g5-1 except that securities held of record by a broker, dealer, bank or nominee for any of them for the accounts of customers resident in the United States shall be counted as held in the United States by the number of separate accounts for which the securities are held. The issuer may rely in good faith on information as to the number of such separate accounts supplied by all owners of the class of its securities which are brokers, dealers, or banks or a nominee for any of them.

(2) Persons in the United States who hold the security only through a Canadian Retirement Account (as that term is defined in rule 237(a)(2) under the Securities Act of 1933 (§ 230.237(a) (2) of this chapter)), shall not be counted as holders resident in the United States.

(b)(1) A foreign private issuer shall be exempt from the requirement to register a class of equity securities under section 12(g) of the Act (15 U.S.C. 78l(g)) if:

(i) The issuer is not required to file or furnish reports under section 13(a) of the Act (15 U.S.C. 78m(a)) or section 15(d) of the Act (15 U.S.C. 78o(d));

(ii) The issuer currently maintains a listing of the subject class of securities on one or more exchanges in a foreign jurisdiction that, either singly or together with the trading of the same class of the issuer's securities in another foreign jurisdiction, constitutes the primary trading market for those securities; and

(iii) The issuer has published in English, on its Internet Web site or through an electronic information delivery system generally available to the public in its primary trading market, information that, since the first day of its most recently completed fiscal year, it:

(A) Has made public or been required to make public pursuant to the laws of the country of its incorporation, organization or domicile;

(B) Has filed or been required to file with the principal stock exchange in its primary trading market on which its securities are traded and which has been made public by that exchange; and

(C) Has distributed or been required to distribute to its security holders.

Note 1 to Paragraph (b)(1): For the purpose of paragraph (b) of this section, *primary trading market* means that at least 55 percent of the trading in the subject class of securities on a worldwide basis took place in, on or through the facilities of a securities market or markets in a single foreign jurisdiction or in no more than two foreign jurisdictions during the issuer's most recently completed fiscal year. If a foreign private issuer aggregates the trading of its subject class of securities in two foreign jurisdictions for the purpose of this paragraph, the trading for the issuer's securities in at least one of the two foreign jurisdictions must be larger than the trading in the United States for the same class of the issuer's securities. When determining an issuer's primary trading market under this paragraph, calculate average daily trading volume in the United States and on a worldwide basis as under Rule 12h-6 under the Act (§ 240.12h-6).

Note 2 to Paragraph (b)(1): Paragraph (b)(1)(iii) of this section does not apply to an issuer when claiming the exemption under paragraph (b) upon the effectiveness of the termination of its registration of a class of securities under section 12(g) of the Act, or the termination of its obligation to file or furnish reports under section 15(d) of the Act.

Note 3 to Paragraph (b)(1): Compensatory stock options for which the underlying securities are in a class exempt under paragraph (b) of this section are also exempt under that paragraph.

(2)(i) In order to maintain the exemption under paragraph (b) of this section, a foreign private issuer shall publish, on an ongoing basis and for each subsequent fiscal year, in English, on its Internet Web site or through an electronic information delivery system generally available to the public in its primary trading market, the information specified in paragraph (b)(1)(iii) of this section.

(ii) An issuer must electronically publish the information required by paragraph (b)(2) of this section promptly after the information has been made public.

(3)(i) The information required to be published electronically under paragraph (b) of this section is information that is material to an investment decision regarding the subject securities, such as information concerning:

(A) Results of operations or financial condition;

(B) Changes in business;

(C) Acquisitions or dispositions of assets;

(D) The issuance, redemption or acquisition of securities;

(E) Changes in management or control;

(F) The granting of options or the payment of other remuneration to directors or officers; and

(G) Transactions with directors, officers or principal security holders.

(ii) At a minimum, a foreign private issuer shall electronically publish English translations of the following documents required to be published under paragraph (b) of this section if in a foreign language:

(A) Its annual report, including or accompanied by annual financial statements;

(B) Interim reports that include financial statements;

(C) Press releases; and

(D) All other communications and documents distributed directly to security holders of each class of securities to which the exemption relates.

(c) The exemption under paragraph (b) of this section shall remain in effect until:

(1) The issuer no longer satisfies the electronic publication condition of paragraph (b)(2) of this section;

(2) The issuer no longer maintains a listing of the subject class of securities on one or more exchanges in a primary trading market, as defined under paragraph (b)(1) of this section; or

(3) The issuer registers a class of securities under section 12 of the Act or incurs reporting obligations under section 15(d) of the Act.

(d) Depositary shares registered on Form F-6 (§ 239.36 of this chapter), but not the underlying deposited securities, are exempt from section 12(g) of the Act under this paragraph.

[As last amended in Release No. 34-58465, effective October 10, 2008, 73 F.R. 52752.]

[¶ 21,891] Certifications of Termination of Registration under Section 12(g)

Reg. § 240.12g-4. (a) Termination of registration of a class of securities under section 12(g) of the Act (15 U.S.C. 78l(g)) shall take effect 90 days, or such shorter period as the Commission may determine, after the issuer certifies to the Commission on Form 15 (17 CFR 249.323) that the class of securities is held of record by:

(1) Less than 300 persons; or

(2) Less than 500 persons, where the total assets of the issuer have not exceeded $10 million on the last day of each of the issuer's most recent three fiscal years.

(b) The issuer's duty to file any reports required under section 13(a) shall be suspended immediately upon filing a certification on Form 15. *Provided, however,* That if the certification on Form 15 is subsequently withdrawn or denied, the issuer shall, within 60 days after the date of such withdrawal or denial, file with the Commission all reports which would have been required had the certification on Form 15 not been filed. If the suspension resulted from the issuer's merger into, or consolidation with, another issuer or issuers, the certification shall be filed by the successor issuer.

[As last amended in Release No. 34-55540, effective June 4, 2007, 72 F.R. 16934.]

[¶ 21,901] Definition of Securities "Held of Record"

Reg. § 240.12g5-1. (a) For the purpose of determining whether an issuer is subject to the provisions of Sections 12(g) and 15(d) of the Act, securities shall be deemed to be "held of record" by each person who is identified as the owner of such securities on records of security holders maintained by or on behalf of the issuer, subject to the following:

(1) In any case where the records of security holders have not been maintained in accordance with accepted practice, any additional person who would be identified as such an owner on such records if they had been maintained in accordance with accepted practice shall be included as a holder of record.

(2) Securities identified as held of record by a corporation, a partnership, a trust whether or not the trustees are named, or other organization shall be included as so held by one person.

(3) Securities identified as held of record by one or more persons as trustees, executors, guardians, custodians or in other fiduciary capacities with respect to a single trust, estate or account shall be included as held of record by one person.

(4) Securities held by two or more persons as co-owners shall be included as held by one person.

(5) Each outstanding unregistered or bearer certificate shall be included as held of record by a separate person, except to the extent that the issuer can establish that, if such securities were registered, they would be held of record, under the provisions of this rule, by a lesser number of persons.

(6) Securities registered in substantially similar names where the issuer has reason to believe because of the address or other indications that such names represent the same person, may be included as held of record by one person.

(b) Notwithstanding paragraph (a) of this section:

(1) Securities held, to the knowledge of the issuer, subject to a voting trust, deposit agreement or similar arrangement shall be included as held of record by the record holders of the voting trust certificates, certificates of deposit, receipts or similar evidences of interest in such securities; *Provided however,* That the issuer may rely in good faith on such information as is received in response to its request from a non-affiliated issuer of the certificates or evidences of interest.

(2) Whole or fractional securities issued by a savings and loan association, building and loan association, cooperative bank, homestead association, or similar institution for the sole purpose of qualifying a borrower for membership in the issuer, and which are to be redeemed or repurchased by the issuer when the borrower's loan is terminated, shall not be included as held of record by any person.

(3) If the issuer knows or has reason to know that the form of holding securities of record is used primarily to circumvent the provisions of Section 12(g) or 15(d) of the Act, the beneficial owners of such securities shall be deemed to be the record owners thereof.

[As adopted in Release No. 34-7492, January 5, 1965, 30 F.R. 483.]

[¶ 21,911] Definition of "Total Assets"

Reg. § 240.12g5-2. For the purpose of Section 12(g)(1) of the Act, the term "total assets" shall mean the total assets as shown on the issuer's balance sheet or the balance sheet of the issuer and its subsidiaries consolidated, whichever is larger, as required to be filed on the form prescribed for registration under this section and prepared in accordance with the pertinent provisions of Regulation S-X. Where the security is a certificate of deposit, voting trust certificate, or certificate or other evidence of interest in a similar trust or agreement, the "total assets" of the issuer of the security held under the trust or agreement shall be deemed to be the "total assets" of the issuer of such certificate or evidence of interest.

[As adopted in Release No. 34-7492, January 5, 1965, 30 F.R. 483.]

[¶ 21,931] Exemptions from Registration under Section 12(g) of the Act

Reg. § 240.12h-1. Issuers shall be exempt from the provisions of Section 12(g) of the Act with respect to the following securities:

Issuers shall be exempt from the provisions of Section 12(g) of the Act with respect to the following securities:

(a) Any interest or participation in an employee stock bonus, stock purchase, profit sharing, pension, retirement, incentive, thrift, savings or similar plan which is not transferable by the holder except in the event of death or mental incompetency, or any security issued solely to fund such plans;

(b) Any interest or participation in any common trust fund or similar fund maintained by a bank exclusively for the collective investment and reinvestment of monies contributed thereto by the bank in its capacity as a trustee, executor, administrator, or guardian. For purposes of this paragraph (b), the term "common trust fund" shall include a common trust fund which is maintained by a bank which is a member of an affiliated group, as defined in section 1504(a) of the Internal Revenue Code of 1954 [26 U.S.C. 1504(a)], and which is maintained exclusively for the investment and reinvestment of monies contributed thereto by one or more bank members of such affiliated group in the capacity of trustee, executor, administrator, or guardian, provided that:

(1) the common trust fund is operated in compliance with the same state and federal regulatory requirements as would apply if the bank maintaining such fund and any other contributing banks were the same entity; and

(2) the rights of persons for whose benefit a contributing bank acts as trustee, executor, administrator or guardian would not be diminished by reason of the maintenance of such common trust fund by another bank member of the affiliated group;

(c) Any class of equity security which would not be outstanding 60 days after a registration statement would be required to be filed with respect thereto;

(d) Any standardized option, as that term is defined in section 240.9b-1(a)(4), that is issued by a clearing agency registered under section 17A of the Act (15 U.S.C. 78q-1) and traded on a national securities exchange registered pursuant to section 6(a) of the Act (15 U.S.C. 78f(a)) or on a national securities association registered pursuant to section 15A(a) of the Act (15 U.S.C. 78o-3(a));

(e) Any security futures product that is traded on a national securities exchange registered pursuant to section 6 of the Act (15 U.S.C. 78f) or on a national securities association registered pursuant to section 15A(a) of the Act (15 U.S.C. 78o-3(a)) and cleared by a clearing agency that is registered pursuant to section 17A of the Act (15 U.S.C. 78q-1) or is exempt from registration under section 17A(b)(7) of the Act (15 U.S.C. 78q-1(b)(7)).

(f)(1) Stock options issued under written compensatory stock option plans under the following conditions:

(i) The issuer of the equity security underlying the stock options does not have a class of security registered under section 12 of the Act and is not required to file reports pursuant to section 15(d) of the Act;

(ii) The stock options have been issued pursuant to one or more written compensatory stock option plans established by the issuer, its parents, its majority-owned subsidiaries or majority-owned subsidiaries of the issuer's parents;

Note to paragraph (f)(1)(ii): All stock options issued under all written compensatory stock option plans on the same class of equity security of the issuer will be considered part of the same class of equity security for purposes of the provisions of paragraph (f) of this section.

(iii) The stock options are held only by those persons described in Rule 701(c) under the Securities Act (17 CFR 230.701(c)) or their permitted transferees as provided in paragraph (f)(1)(iv) of this section;

(iv) The stock options and, prior to exercise, the shares to be issued on exercise of the stock options are restricted as to transfer by the optionholder other than to persons who are family members (as defined in Rule 701(c)(3) under the Securities Act (17 CFR 230.701(c)(3)) through gifts or domestic relations orders, or to an executor or guardian of the optionholder upon the death or disability of the optionholder until the issuer becomes subject to the reporting requirements of section 13 or 15(d) of the Act or is no longer relying on the exemption pursuant to this section; provided that the optionholder may transfer the stock options to the issuer, or in connection with a change of control or other acquisition transaction involving the issuer, if after such transaction the stock options no longer will be outstanding and the issuer no longer will be relying on the exemption pursuant to this section;

Note to paragraph (f)(1)(iv): For purposes of this section, optionholders may include any permitted transferee under paragraph (f)(1)(iv) of this section; provided that such permitted transferees may not further transfer the stock options;

(v) The stock options and the shares issuable upon exercise of such stock options are restricted as to any pledge, hypothecation, or other transfer, including any short position, any "put equivalent position" (as defined in § 240.16a-1(h) of this chapter), or any "call equivalent position" (as defined in § 240.16a-1(b) of this chapter) by the optionholder prior to exercise of an option, except in the circumstances permitted in paragraph (f)(1)(iv) of this section, until the issuer becomes subject to the reporting requirements of section 13 or 15(d) of the Act or is no longer relying on the exemption pursuant paragraph (f)(1) of this section;

Note to paragraphs (f)(1)(iv) and (f)(1)(v): The transferability restrictions in paragraphs (f)(1)(iv) and (f)(1)(v) of this section must be contained in a written compensatory stock option plan, individual written compensatory stock option agreement, other stock purchase or stockholder agreement to which the issuer and the optionholder are a signatory or party, other enforceable agreement by or against the issuer and the optionholder, or in the issuer's by-laws or certificate or articles of incorporation; and

(vi) The issuer has agreed in the written compensatory stock option plan, the individual written compensatory stock option agreement, or another agreement enforceable against the issuer to provide the following information to optionholders once the issuer is relying on the exemption pursuant to paragraph (f)(1) of this section until the issuer becomes subject to the reporting requirements of section 13 or 15(d) of the Act or is no longer relying on the exemption pursuant paragraph (f)(1) of this section:

The information described in Rules 701(e)(3), (4), and (5) under the Securities Act (17 CFR 230.701(e)(3), (4), and (5)), every six months with the financial statements being not more than 180 days old and with such information provided either by physical or electronic delivery to the optionholders or by written notice to the optionholders of the availability of the information on an Internet site that may be password-protected and of any password needed to access the information.

Note to paragraph (f)(1)(vi): The issuer may request that the optionholder agree to keep the information to be provided pursuant to this section confidential. If an optionholder does not agree to keep the information to be provided pursuant to this section confidential, then the issuer is not required to provide the information.

(2) If the exemption provided by paragraph (f)(1) of this section ceases to be available, the issuer of the stock options that is relying on the exemption provided by this section must file a registration statement to register the class of stock options under section 12 of the Act within 120 calendar days after the exemption provided by paragraph (f)(1) of this section ceases to be available; and

(g)(1) Stock options issued under written compensatory stock option plans under the following conditions:

(i) The issuer of the equity security underlying the stock options has registered a class of security under section 12 of the Act or is required to file periodic reports pursuant to section 15(d) of the Act;

(ii) The stock options have been issued pursuant to one or more written compensatory stock option plans established by the issuer, its parents, its majority-owned subsidiaries or majority-owned subsidiaries of the issuer's parents;

Note to paragraph (g)(1)(ii): All stock options issued under all of the written compensatory stock option plans on the same class of equity security of the issuer will be considered part of the same class of equity security of the issuer for purposes of the provisions of paragraph (g) of this section; and

(iii) The stock options are held only by those persons described in Rule 701(c) under the Securities Act (17 CFR 230.701(c)) or those persons specified in General Instruction A.1(a) of Form S-8 (17 CFR 239.16b); provided that an issuer can still rely on this exemption if there is an insignificant deviation from satisfaction of the condition in this paragraph (g)(1)(iii) and after December 7, 2007 the issuer has made a good faith and reasonable attempt to comply with the conditions of this paragraph (g)(1)(iii). For purposes of this paragraph (g)(1)(iii), an insignificant deviation exists if the number of optionholders that do not meet the condition in this paragraph (g)(1)(iii) are insignificant both as to the aggregate number of optionholders and number of outstanding stock options.

(2) If the exemption provided by paragraph (g)(1) of this section ceases to be available, the issuer of the stock options that is relying on the exemption provided by this section must file a registration statement to register the class of stock options or a class of security under section 12 of the Act within 60 calendar days after the exemption provided in paragraph (g)(1) of this section ceases to be available.

(h)T any eligible credit default swap, as defined in Rule 239T of the Securities Act of 1933 (17 CFR 230.239T), issued or cleared by a clearing agency registered as a clearing agency under Section 17A of the Act (15 U.S.C. 78q-1) or exempt from registration under Section 17A of the Act pursuant to a rule, regulation, or order of the Commission that will be purchased by or sold to an eligible contract participant (as defined in Section 1a(12) of the Commodity Exchange Act (7 U.S.C. 1a(12)) as in effect on the date of adoption of this section, other than a person who is an eligible contract participant under

Section 1(a)(12)(C) of the Commodity Exchange Act). This temporary rule will expire on November 30, 2010.

[As last amended in Release No. 33-9063, effective January 22, 2009 to November 30, 2010, 74 F.R. 57719.]

[¶ 21,951] Suspension of Duty to File Reports under Section 15(d)

Reg. § 240.12h-3. (a) Subject to paragraphs (c) and (d) of this section, the duty under section 15(d) to file reports required by section 13(a) of the Act with respect to a class of securities specified in paragraph (b) of this section shall be suspended for such class of securities immediately upon filing with the Commission a certification on Form 15 [17 CFR 249.323] if the issuer of such class has filed all reports required by Section 13(a), without regard to Rule 12b-25 [17 CFR 249.322], for the shorter of its most recent three fiscal years and the portion of the current year preceding the date of filing Form 15, or the period since the issuer became subject to such reporting obligation. If the certification on Form 15 is subsequently withdrawn or denied, the issuer shall, within 60 days, file with the Commission all reports which would have been required if such certification had not been filed.

(b) The classes of securities eligible for the suspension provided in paragraph (a) of this section are:

(1) Any class of securities held of record by: (i) less than 300 persons; or (ii) by less than 500 persons, where the total assets of the issuer have not exceeded $10 million on the last day of each of the issuer's three most recent fiscal years; and

(2) Any class of securities deregistered pursuant to section 12(d) of the Act if such class would not thereupon be deemed registered under section 12(g) of the Act or the rules thereunder.

(c) This section shall not be available for any class of securities for a fiscal year in which a registration statement relating to that class becomes effective under the Securities Act of 1933, or is required to be updated pursuant to section 10(a)(3) of the Act, and, in the case of paragraph (b)(1)(ii), the two succeeding fiscal years. Provided, however, That this paragraph shall not apply to the duty to file reports which arises solely from a registration statement filed by an issuer with no significant assets, for the reorganization of a non-reporting issuer into a one subsidiary holding company in which equity security holders receive the same proportional interest in the holding company as they held in the non-reporting issuer, except for changes resulting from the exercise of dissenting shareholder rights under state law.

(d) The suspension provided by this rule relates only to the reporting obligation under section 15(d) with respect to a class of securities, does not affect any other duties imposed on that class of securities, and shall continue as long as either criteria (i) or (ii) of paragraph (b)(1) is met on the first day of any subsequent fiscal year. Provided, however, That such criteria need not be met if the duty to file reports arises solely from a registration statement filed by an issuer with no significant assets in a reorganization of a non-reporting company into a one subsidiary holding company in which equity security holders receive the same proportional interest in the holding company as they held in the non-reporting issuer except for changes resulting from the exercise of dissenting shareholder rights under state law.

(e) If the suspension provided by this section is discontinued because a class of securities does not meet the eligibility criteria of paragraph (b) of this section on the first day of an issuer's fiscal year, then the issuer shall resume periodic reporting pursuant to section 15(d) of the Act by filing an annual report on Form 10-K for its preceding fiscal year, not later than 120 days after the end of such fiscal year.

[As last amended in Release No. 33-8876, effective February 4, 2008, 73 F.R. 934.]

[¶ 21,952] Exemption From Duty to File Reports Under Section 15(d)

Reg. § 240.12h-4. An issuer shall be exempt from the duty under section 15(d) of the Act to file reports required by section 13(a) of the Act with respect to securities registered under the Securities Act of 1933 on Form F-7, Form F-8 or Form F-80, provided that the issuer is exempt from the obligations of Section 12(g) of the Act pursuant to Rule 12g3-2(b).

[As adopted in Release No. 34-29354, June 13, 1991, 56 F.R. 30036.]

[¶ 21,953] Exemption for Subsidiary Issuers of Guaranteed Securities and Subsidiary Guarantors

Reg. § 240.12h-5. (a) Any issuer of a guaranteed security, or guarantor of a security, that is permitted to omit financial statements by § 210.3-10 of Regulation S-X of this chapter is exempt from the requirements of Section 13(a) or 15(d) of the Act (15 U.S.C. 78m(a) or 78o(d)).

(b) Any issuer of a guaranteed security, or guarantor of a security, that would be permitted to omit financial statements by § 210.3-10 of Regulation S-X of this chapter, but is required to file financial statements in accordance with the operation of § 210.3-10(g) of Regulation S-X of this chapter, is exempt from the requirements of Section 13(a) or 15(d) of the Act (15 U.S.C. 78m(a) or 78o(d)).

[As adopted in Release No. 33-7878, effective September 25, 2000, 65 F.R. 51692.]

[¶ 21,954] Certification by a Foreign Private Issuer Regarding the Termination of Registration of a Class of Securities Under Section 12(g) or the Duty to File Reports Under Section 13(a) or Section 15(d)

Reg. § 240.12h-6. (a) A foreign private issuer may terminate the registration of a class of securities under section 12(g) of the Act (15 U.S.C. 78l(g)), or terminate the obligation under section 15(d) of the Act (15 U.S.C. 78o(d)) to file or furnish reports required by section 13(a) of the Act (15 U.S.C. 78m(a)) with respect to a class of equity securities, or both, after certifying to the Commission on Form 15F (17 CFR 249.324) that:

(1) The foreign private issuer has had reporting obligations under section 13(a) or section 15(d) of the Act for at least the 12 months preceding the filing of the Form 15F, has filed or furnished all reports required for this period, and has filed at least one annual report pursuant to section 13(a) of the Act;

(2) The foreign private issuer's securities have not been sold in the United States in a registered offering under the Securities Act of 1933 (15 U.S.C. 77a *et seq.*) during the 12 months preceding the filing of the Form 15F, other than securities issued:

(i) To the issuer's employees;

(ii) By selling security holders in non-underwritten offerings;

(iii) Upon the exercise of outstanding rights granted by the issuer if the rights are granted pro rata to all existing security holders of the class of the issuer's securities to which the rights attach;

(iv) Pursuant to a dividend or interest reinvestment plan; or

(v) Upon the conversion of outstanding convertible securities or upon the exercise of outstanding transferable warrants issued by the issuer;

Note to Paragraph (a)(2): The exceptions in paragraphs (a)(2)(iii)-(v) do not apply to securities issued pursuant to a standby underwritten offering or other similar arrangement in the United States;

(3) The foreign private issuer has maintained a listing of the subject class of securities for at least the 12 months preceding the filing of the Form 15F on one or more exchanges in a foreign jurisdiction that, either singly or together with the trading of the same class of the issuer's securities in another foreign jurisdiction, constitutes the primary trading market for those securities; and

(4)(i) The average daily trading volume of the subject class of securities in the United States for a recent 12-month period has been no greater than 5 percent of the average daily trading volume of that class of securities on a worldwide basis for the same period; or

(ii) On a date within 120 days before the filing date of the Form 15F, a foreign private issuer's subject class of equity securities is either held of record by:

(A) Less than 300 persons on a worldwide basis; or

(B) Less than 300 persons resident in the United States.

Note to Paragraph (a)(4): If an issuer's equity securities trade in the form of American Depositary Receipts in the United States, for purposes of paragraph (a)(4)(i), it must calculate the trading volume of its American Depositary Receipts in terms of the number of securities represented by those American Depositary Receipts.

(b) A foreign private issuer must wait at least 12 months before it may file a Form 15F to terminate its section 13(a) or 15(d) reporting obligations in reliance on paragraph (a)(4)(i) of this section if:

(1) The issuer has delisted a class of equity securities from a national securities exchange or inter-dealer quotation system in the United States, and at the time of delisting, the average daily trading volume of that class of securities in the United States exceeded 5 percent of the average daily trading volume of that class of securities on a worldwide basis for the preceding 12 months; or

(2) The issuer has terminated a sponsored American Depositary Receipts facility, and at the time of termination the average daily trading volume in the United States of the American Depositary Receipts exceeded 5 percent of the average daily trading volume of the underlying class of securities on a worldwide basis for the preceding 12 months.

(c) A foreign private issuer may terminate its duty to file or furnish reports pursuant to section 13(a) or section 15(d) of the Act with respect to a class of debt securities after certifying to the Commission on Form 15F that:

(1) The foreign private issuer has filed or furnished all reports required by section 13(a) or section 15(d) of the Act, including at least one annual report pursuant to section 13(a) of the Act; and

(2) On a date within 120 days before the filing date of the Form 15F, the class of debt securities is either held of record by:

(i) Less than 300 persons on a worldwide basis; or

(ii) Less than 300 persons resident in the United States.

(d) (1) Following a merger, consolidation, exchange of securities, acquisition of assets or otherwise, a foreign private issuer that has succeeded to the registration of a class of securities under section 12(g) of the Act of another issuer pursuant to §240.12g-3, or to the reporting obligations of another issuer under section 15(d) of the Act pursuant to §240.15d-5, may file a Form 15F to terminate that registration or those reporting obligations if:

(i) Regarding a class of equity securities, the successor issuer meets the conditions under paragraph (a) of this section; or

(ii) Regarding a class of debt securities, the successor issuer meets the conditions under paragraph (c) of this section.

(2) When determining whether it meets the prior reporting requirement under paragraph (a) (1) or paragraph (c) (1) of this section, a successor issuer may take into account the reporting history of the issuer whose reporting obligations it has assumed pursuant to §240.12g-3 or §240.15d-5.

(e) *Counting method.* When determining under this section the number of United States residents holding a foreign private issuer's equity or debt securities:

(1) (i) Use the method for calculating record ownership §240.12g3-2(a), except that you may limit your inquiry regarding the amount of securities represented by accounts of customers resident in the United States to brokers, dealers, banks and other nominees located in:

(A) The United States;

(B) The foreign private issuer's jurisdiction of incorporation, legal organization or establishment; and

(C) The foreign private issuer's primary trading market, if different from the issuer's jurisdiction of incorporation, legal organization or establishment.

(ii) If you aggregate the trading volume of the issuer's securities in two foreign jurisdictions for the purpose of complying with paragraph (a) (3) of this section, you must include both of those foreign jurisdictions when conducting your inquiry under paragraph (e) (1) (i) of this section.

(2) If, after reasonable inquiry, you are unable without unreasonable effort to obtain information about the amount of securities represented by accounts of customers resident in the United States, for purposes of this section, you may assume that the customers are the residents of the jurisdiction in which the nominee has its principal place of business.

(3) You must count securities as owned by United States holders when publicly filed reports of beneficial ownership or other reliable information that is provided to you indicates that the securities are held by United States residents.

(4) When calculating under this section the number of your United States resident security holders, you may rely in good faith on the assistance of an independent information services provider that in the regular course of its business assists issuers in determining the number of, and collecting other information concerning, their security holders.

(f) *Definitions.* For the purpose of this section:

(1) *Debt security* means any security other than an equity security as defined under §240.3a11-1, including:

(i) Non-participatory preferred stock, which is defined as non-convertible capital stock, the holders of which are entitled to a preference in payment of dividends and in distribution of assets on liquidation, dissolution, or winding up of the issuer, but are not entitled to participate in residual earnings or assets of the issuer; and

(ii) Notwithstanding §240.3a11-1, any debt security described in paragraph (f) (3) (i) and (ii) of this section;

(2) *Employee* has the same meaning as the definition of employee provided in Form S-8 (§239.16b).

(3) *Equity security* means the same as under §240.3a11-1, but, for purposes of paragraphs (a) (3) and (a) (4) (i) of this section, does not include:

(i) Any debt security that is convertible into an equity security, with or without consideration;

(ii) Any debt security that includes a warrant or right to subscribe to or purchase an equity security;

(iii) Any such warrant or right; or

(iv) Any put, call, straddle, or other option or privilege that gives the holder the option of buying or selling a security but does not require the holder to do so.

(4) *Foreign private issuer* has the same meaning as under §240.3b-4.

(5) *Primary trading market* means that:

(i) At least 55 percent of the trading in a foreign private issuer's class of securities that is the subject of Form 15F took place in, on or through the facilities of a securities market or markets in a single foreign jurisdiction or in no more than two foreign jurisdictions during a recent 12-month period; and

(ii) If a foreign private issuer aggregates the trading of its subject class of securities in two foreign jurisdictions for the purpose of paragraph (a)(3) of this section, the trading for the issuer's securities in at least one of the two foreign jurisdictions must be larger than the trading in the United States for the same class of the issuer's securities.

(6) *Recent 12-month period* means a 12-calendar-month period that ended no more than 60 days before the filing date of the Form 15F.

(g)(1) Suspension of a foreign private issuer's duty to file reports under section 13(a) or section 15(d) of the Act shall occur immediately upon filing the Form 15F with the Commission if filing pursuant to paragraph (a), (c) or (d) of this section. If there are no objections from the Commission, 90 days, or such shorter period as the Commission may determine, after the issuer has filed its Form 15F, the effectiveness of any of the following shall occur:

(i) The termination of registration of a class of securities under section 12(g); and

(ii) The termination of a foreign private issuer's duty to file reports under section 13(a) or section 15(d) of the Act.

(2) If the Form 15F is subsequently withdrawn or denied, the issuer shall, within 60 days after the date of the withdrawal or denial, file with or submit to the Commission all reports that would have been required had the issuer not filed the Form 15F.

(h) As a condition to termination of registration or reporting under paragraph (a), (c) or (d) of this section, a foreign private issuer must, either before or on the date that it files its Form 15F, publish a notice in the United States that discloses its intent to terminate its registration of a class of securities under section 12(g) of the Act, or its reporting obligations under section 13(a) or section 15(d) of the Act, or both. The issuer must publish the notice through a means reasonably designed to provide broad dissemination of the information to the public in the United States. The issuer must also submit a copy of the notice to the Commission, either under cover of a Form 6-K (17 CFR 249.306) before or at the time of filing of the Form 15F, or as an exhibit to the Form 15F.

(i)(1) A foreign private issuer that, before the effective date of this section, terminated the registration of a class of securities under section 12(g) of the Act or suspended its reporting obligations regarding a class of equity or debt securities under section 15(d) of the Act may file a Form 15F in order to:

(i) Terminate under this section the registration of a class of equity securities that was the subject of a Form 15 (§ 249.323 of this chapter) filed by the issuer pursuant to § 240.12g-4; or

(ii) Terminate its reporting obligations under section 15(d) of the Act, which had been suspended by the terms of that section or by the issuer's filing of a Form 15 pursuant to § 240.12h-3, regarding a class of equity or debt securities.

(2) In order to be eligible to file a Form 15F under this paragraph:

(i) If a foreign private issuer terminated the registration of a class of securities pursuant to § 240.12g-4 or suspended its reporting obligations pursuant to § 240.12h-3 or section 15(d) of the Act regarding a class of equity securities, the issuer must meet the requirements under paragraph (a)(3) and paragraph (a)(4)(i) or (a)(4)(ii) of this section; or

(ii) If a foreign private issuer suspended its reporting obligations pursuant to § 240.12h-3 or section 15(d) of the Act regarding a class of debt securities, the issuer must meet the requirements under paragraph (c)(2) of this section.

(3)(i) If the Commission does not object, 90 days after the filing of a Form 15F under this paragraph, or such shorter period as the Commission may determine, the effectiveness of any of the following shall occur:

(A) The termination under this section of the registration of a class of equity securities, which was the subject of a Form 15 filed pursuant to § 240.12g-4, and the duty to file reports required by section 13(a) of the Act regarding that class of securities; or

(B) The termination of a foreign private issuer's reporting obligations under section 15(d) of the Act, which had previously been suspended by the terms of that section or by the issuer's filing of a Form 15 pursuant to § 240.12h-3, regarding a class of equity or debt securities.

(ii) If the Form 15F is subsequently withdrawn or denied, the foreign private issuer shall, within 60 days after the date of the withdrawal or denial, file with or submit to the Commission all reports that would have been required had the issuer not filed the Form 15F.

[As adopted in Release No. 34-55540, effective June 4, 2007, 72 F.R. 16934.]

REGULATION 13A—REPORTS OF ISSUERS OF SECURITIES REGISTERED PURSUANT TO SECTION 12

Annual Reports

[¶ 22,001] Requirements of Annual Reports

Reg. § 240.13a-1. Every issuer having securities registered pursuant to section 12 of the Act (15 U.S.C. 78l) shall file an annual report on the appropriate form authorized or prescribed therefor for each fiscal year after the last full fiscal year for which financial statements were filed in its registration statement. Annual reports shall be filed within the period specified in the appropriate form.

[As last amended in Release No. 34-38850, July 18, 1997, effective September 2, 1997, 62 F.R. 39755.]

[¶ 22,012] Reporting by Form 40-F Registrant

Reg. § 240.13a-3. A registrant that is eligible to use Forms 40-F and 6-K and files reports in accordance therewith shall be deemed to satisfy the requirements of Regulation 13A (§ § 240.13a-1 through 240.13a-17 of this chapter).

[As adopted in Release No. 34-29354, June 13, 1991, 56 F.R. 30036.]

Other Reports

[¶ 22,021] Transition Reports

Reg. § 240.13a-10. (a) Every issuer that changes its fiscal closing date shall file a report covering the resulting transition period between the closing date of its most recent fiscal year end and the opening date of its new fiscal year; *Provided, however,* that an issuer shall file an annual report for any fiscal year that ended before the date on which the issuer determined to change its fiscal year end. In no event shall the transition report cover a period of 12 or more months.

(b) The report pursuant to this section shall be filed for the transition period not more than the number of days specified in paragraph (j) of this section after either the close of the transition period or the date of the determination to change the fiscal closing date, whichever is later. The report shall be filed on the form appropriate for annual reports of the issuer, shall cover the period from the close of the last fiscal year end and shall indicate clearly the period covered. The financial statements for the transition period filed therewith shall be audited. Financial statements, which may be unaudited, shall be filed for the comparable period of the prior year, or a footnote, which may be unaudited, shall state for the comparable period of the prior year, revenues, gross profits, income taxes, income or loss from continuing operations before extraordinary items and cumulative effect of a change in accounting principles and net income or loss. The effects of any discontinued operations and/or extraordinary items as classified under the provisions of generally accepted accounting principles also shall be shown, if applicable. Per share data based upon such income or loss and net income or loss shall be presented in conformity with applicable accounting standards. Where called for by the time span to be covered, the comparable period financial statements or footnote shall be included in subsequent filings.

(c) If the transition period covers a period of less than six months, in lieu of the report required by paragraph (b) of this section, a report may be filed for the transition period on Form 10-Q (§ 249.308a of this chapter) not more than the number of days specified in paragraph (j) of this section after either the close of the transition period or the date of the determination to change the fiscal closing date, whichever is later. The report on Form 10-Q shall cover the period from the close of the last fiscal year end and shall indicate clearly the period covered. The financial statements filed therewith need not be audited but, if they are not audited, the issuer shall file with the first annual report for the newly adopted fiscal year separate audited statements of income and cash flows covering the transition period. The notes to financial statements for the transition period included in such first annual report may be integrated with the notes to financial statements for the full fiscal period. A separate audited balance sheet as of the end of the transition period shall be filed in the annual report only if the audited balance sheet as of the end of the fiscal year prior to the transition period is not filed. Schedules need not be filed in transition reports on Form 10-Q.

(d) Notwithstanding the foregoing in paragraphs (a), (b), and (c) of this section, if the transition period covers a period of one month or less, the issuer need not file a separate transition report if either:

(1) the first report required to be filed by the issuer for the newly adopted fiscal year after the date of the determination to change the fiscal year end is an annual report, and that report covers the transition period as well as the fiscal year; or

(2) (i) the issuer files with the first annual report for the newly adopted fiscal year separate audited statements of income and cash flows covering the transition period; and

(ii) The first report required to be filed by the issuer for the newly adopted fiscal year after the date of the determination to change the fiscal year end is a quarterly report on Form 10-Q; and

(iii) Information on the transition period is included in the issuer's quarterly report on Form 10-Q for the first quarterly period (except the fourth quarter) of the newly adopted fiscal year that ends after the date of the determination to change the fiscal year. The information covering the transition period required by Part II and Item 2 of Part I may be combined with the information regarding the quarter. However, the financial statements required by Part I, which may be unaudited, shall be furnished separately for the transition period.

(e) Every issuer required to file quarterly reports on Form 10-Q pursuant to § 240.13a-13 of this chapter that changes its fiscal year end shall:

(1) File a quarterly report on Form 10-Q within the time period specified in General Instruction A.1. to that form for any quarterly period (except the fourth quarter) of the old fiscal year that ends before the date on which the issuer determined to change its fiscal year end, except that the issuer need not file such quarterly report if the date on which the quarterly period ends also is the date on which the transition period ends;

(2) File a quarterly report on Form 10-Q within the time specified in General Instruction A.1. to that form for each quarterly period of the old fiscal year within the transition period. In lieu of a quarterly report for any quarter of the old fiscal year within the transition period, the issuer may file a quarterly report on Form 10-Q for any period of three months within the transition period that coincides with a quarter of the newly adopted fiscal year if the quarterly report is filed within the number of days specified in paragraph (j) of this section after the end of such three month period, provided the issuer thereafter continues filing quarterly reports on the basis of the quarters of the newly adopted fiscal year;

(3) commence filing quarterly reports for the quarters of the new fiscal year no later than the quarterly report for the first quarter of the new fiscal year that ends after the date on which the issuer determined to change the fiscal year end; and

(4) Unless such information is or will be included in the transition report, or the first annual report on Form 10-K for the newly adopted fiscal year, include in the initial quarterly report on Form 10-Q for the newly adopted fiscal year information on any period beginning on the first day subsequent to the period covered by the issuer's final quarterly report on Form 10-Q or annual report on Form 10-K for the old fiscal year. The information covering such period required by Part II and Item 2 of Part I may be combined with the information regarding the quarter. However, the financial statements required by Part I, which may be unaudited, shall be furnished separately for such period.

Note to paragraphs (c) and (e): If it is not practicable or cannot be cost-justified to furnish in a transition report on Form 10-Q or a quarterly report for the newly adopted fiscal year financial statements for corresponding periods of the prior year where required, financial statements may be furnished for the quarters of the preceding fiscal year that most nearly are comparable if the issuer furnishes an adequate discussion of seasonal and other factors that could affect the comparability of information or trends reflected, an assessment of the comparability of the data, and a representation as to the reason recasting has not been undertaken.

(f) Every successor issuer with securities registered under Section 12 of this Act that has a different fiscal year from that of its predecessor(s) shall file a transition report pursuant to this section, containing the required information about each predecessor, for the transition period, if any, between the close of the fiscal year covered by the last annual report of each predecessor and the date of succession. The report shall be filed for the transition period on the form appropriate for annual reports of the issuer not more than the number of days specified in paragraph (j) of this section after the date of the succession, with financial statements in conformity with the requirements set forth in paragraph (b) of this section. If the transition period covers a period of less than six months, in lieu of a transition report on the form appropriate for the issuer's annual reports, the report may be filed for the transition period on Form 10-Q and Form 10-QSB not more than the number of days specified in paragraph (j) of this section after the date of the succession, with financial statements in conformity with the requirements set forth in paragraph (c) of this section. Notwithstanding the foregoing, if the transition period covers a period of one month or less, the successor issuer need not file a separate transition report if the information is reported by the successor issuer in conformity with the requirements set forth in paragraph (d) of this section.

(g)(1) Paragraphs (a) through (f) of this section shall not apply to foreign private issuers.

(2) Every foreign private issuer that changes its fiscal closing date shall file a report covering the resulting transition period between the closing date of its most recent fiscal year end and the opening date of its new fiscal year. In no event shall a transition report cover a period longer than 12 months.

(3) The report for the transition period shall be filed on Form 20-F responding to all items to which such issuer is required to respond when Form 20-F is used as an annual report. The financial statements

for the transition period filed therewith shall be audited. The report shall be filed within the following period:

(i) Within six months after either the close of the transition period or the date on which the issuer made the determination to change the fiscal closing date, whichever is later, for new fiscal years ending before December 15, 2011; and

(ii) Within four months after either the close of the transition period or the date on which the issuer made the determination to change the fiscal closing date, whichever is later, for new fiscal years ending on or after December 15, 2011.

(4) If the transition period covers a period of six or fewer months, in lieu of the report required by paragraph (g)(3) of this section, a report for the transition period shall be filed on Form 20-F responding to Items 5, 8.A.7., 13, 14, and 17 or 18 within three months after either the close of the transition period or the date on which the issuer made the determination to change the fiscal closing date, whichever is later. The financial statements required by either Item 17 or Item 18 shall be furnished for the transition period. Such financial statements may be unaudited and condensed as permitted in Article 10 of Regulation S-X (§ 210.10-01 of this chapter), but if the financial statements are unaudited and condensed, the issuer shall file with the first annual report for the newly adopted fiscal year separate audited statements of income and cash flow covering the transition period.

(5) Notwithstanding the foregoing in paragraphs (g)(2), (g)(3), and (g)(4) of this section, if the transition period covers a period of one month or less, a foreign private issuer need not file a separate transition report if the first annual report for the newly adopted fiscal year covers the transition period as well as the fiscal year.

(h) The provisions of this rule shall not apply to investment companies required to file reports pursuant to Rule 30b1-1 (§ 270.30b1-1 of this chapter) under the Investment Company Act of 1940 (15 U.S.C. 80a-1 *et seq.*).

(i) No filing fee shall be required for a transition report filed pursuant to this section.

(j)(1) For transition reports to be filed on the form appropriate for annual reports of the issuer, the number of days shall be:

(i) 60 days (75 days for fiscal years ending before December 15, 2006) for large accelerated filers (as defined in § 240.12b-2);

(ii) 75 days for accelerated filers (as defined in § 240.12b-2); and

(iii) 90 days for all other issuers; and

(2) For transition reports to be filed on Form 10-Q (§ 249.308a of this chapter) the number of days shall be:

(i) 40 days for large accelerated filers and accelerated filers (as defined in § 240.12b-2); and

(ii) 45 days for all other issuers.

(k)(1) Paragraphs (a) through (g) of this section shall not apply to asset-backed issuers.

(2) Every asset-backed issuer that changes its fiscal closing date shall file a report covering the resulting transition period between the closing date of its most recent fiscal year and the opening date of its new fiscal year. In no event shall a transition report cover a period longer than 12 months.

(3) The report for the transition period shall be filed on Form 10-K (§ 249.310 of this chapter) responding to all items to which such asset-backed issuer is required to respond pursuant to General Instruction J. of Form 10-K. Such report shall be filed within 90 days after the later of either the close of the transition period or the date on which the issuer made the determination to change the fiscal closing date.

(4) Notwithstanding the foregoing in paragraphs (k)(2) and (k)(3) of this section, if the transition period covers a period of one month or less, an asset-backed issuer need not file a separate transition report if the first annual report for the newly adopted fiscal year covers the transition period as well as the fiscal year.

(5) Any obligation of the asset-backed issuer to file distribution reports pursuant to § 240.13a-17 will continue to apply regardless of a change in the asset-backed issuer's fiscal closing date.

Note 1: In addition to the report or reports required to be filed pursuant to this section, every issuer, except a foreign private issuer or an investment company required to file reports pursuant to § 270.30b1-1 of this chapter, that changes its fiscal closing date is required to file a Form 8-K (§ 249.308 of this chapter) report that includes the information required by Item 5.03 of Form 8-K within the period specified in General Instruction B.1. to that form.

Additional Note: The report or reports to be filed pursuant to this section must include the certification required by § 240.13a-14.

[As last amended in Release No. 33-8959, effective December 5, 2008, 73 F.R. 58300.]

>>>→ *CCH Note: The SEC has stayed the effectiveness of proxy rule amendments adopted in Release 33-9136 pending resolution of a challenge filed by the Business Roundtable and the U.S. Chamber of Commerce in the U.S. Court of Appeals for the District of Columbia Circuit. See Release No. 33-9149, October 4, 2010.*

>>>→ *Amended by Release No. 33-9136, effective November 15, 2010, 75 F.R. 56668.*

[¶ 22,031] Current Reports on Form 8-K (§ 249.308 of this chapter)

Reg. § 240.13a-11. (a) Except as provided in paragraph (b) of this section, every registrant subject to § 240.13a-1 shall file a current report on Form 8-K within the period specified in that form, unless substantially the same information as that required by Form 8-K has been previously reported by the registrant.

(b) This section shall not apply to foreign governments, foreign private issuers required to make reports on Form 6-K (17 CFR 249.306) pursuant to § 240.13a-16, issuers of American Depositary Receipts for securities of any foreign issuer, or investment companies required to file reports pursuant to § 270.30b1-1 of this chapter under the Investment Company Act of 1940, except where such investment companies are required to file notice of a blackout period pursuant to § 245.104 of this chapter.

Amendment
_____

(b) This section shall not apply to foreign governments, foreign private issuers required to make reports on Form 6-K (17 CFR 249.306) pursuant to § 240.13a-16, issuers of American Depositary Receipts for securities of any foreign issuer, or investment companies required to file reports pursuant to § 270.30b1-1 of this chapter under the Investment Company Act of 1940, except where such an investment company is required to file:

(1) Notice of a blackout period pursuant to § 245.104 of this chapter;

(2) Disclosure pursuant to Instruction 2 to § 240.14a-11(b)(1) of information concerning outstanding shares and voting; or

(3) Disclosure pursuant to Instruction 2 to § 240.14a-11(b)(10) of the date by which a nominating shareholder or nominating shareholder group must submit the notice required pursuant to § 240.14a-11(b)(10).

End of Amendment
_____

(c) No failure to file a report on Form 8-K that is required solely pursuant to Item 1.01, 1.02, 2.03, 2.04, 2.05, 2.06, 4.02(a), 5.02(e) or 6.03 of Form 8-K shall be deemed to be a violation of 15 U.S.C. 78j(b) and § 240.10b-5.

[As last amended in Release No. 33-9136, effective November 15, 2010, 75 F.R. 56668, stayed by Release No. 33-9149, October 4, 2010.]

[¶ 22,051] Quarterly reports on Form 10-Q (§ 249.308a of this chapter)

Reg. § 240.13a-13. (a) Except as provided in paragraphs (b) and (c) of this section, every issuer that has securities registered pursuant to section 12 of the Act and is required to file annual reports pursuant to section 13 of the Act, and has filed or intends to file such reports on Form 10-K (§ 249.310 of this chapter), shall file a quarterly report on Form 10-Q (§ 249.308a of this chapter) within the period specified in General Instruction A.1. to that form for each of the first three quarters of each fiscal year of the issuer, commencing with the first fiscal quarter following the most recent fiscal year for which full financial statements were included in the registration statement, or, if the registration statement included financial statements for an interim period subsequent to the most recent fiscal year end meeting the requirements of Article 10 of Regulation S-X and Rule 8-03 of Regulation S-X for smaller reporting companies, for the first fiscal quarter subsequent to the quarter reported upon in the registration statement. The first quarterly report of the issuer shall be filed either within 45 days after the effective date of the registration statement or on or before the date on which such report would have been required to be filed if the issuer has been required to file reports on Form 10-Q as of its last fiscal quarter, whichever is later.

(b) The provisions of this rule shall not apply to the following issuers:

(1) Investment companies required to file reports pursuant to § 270.30b1-1;

(2) Foreign private issuers required to file reports pursuant to § 240.13a-16; and

(3) Asset-backed issuers required to file reports pursuant to § 240.13a-17.

(c) Part I of the quarterly reports on Form 10-Q need not be filed by:

(1) Mutual life insurance companies; or

(2) Mining companies not in the production stage but engaged primarily in the exploration for the development of mineral deposits other than oil, gas or coal, if all the following conditions are met:

(i) The registrant has not been in production during the current fiscal year or the two years immediately prior thereto; except that being in production for an aggregate period of not more than eight months over the three-year period shall not be a violation of this condition.

(ii) Receipts from the sale of mineral products or from the operations of mineral producing properties by the registrant and its subsidiaries combined have not exceeded $500,000 in any of the most recent six years and have not aggregated more than $1,500,000 in the most recent six fiscal years.

(d) Notwithstanding the foregoing provisions of this section, the financial information required by Part I of Form 10-Q shall not be deemed to be "filed" for the purpose of Section 18 of the Act or otherwise subject to the liabilities of that section of the Act, but shall be subject to all other provisions of the Act.

[As last amended in Release No. 33-8876, effective February 4, 2008, 73 F.R. 934.]

[¶ 22,053] Certification of Disclosure in Annual and Quarterly Reports

Reg. § 240.13a-14. (a) Each report, including transition reports, filed on Form 10-Q, Form 10-K, Form 20-F or Form 40-F (§§ 249.308a, 249.310, 249.220f or 249.240f of this chapter) under Section 13(a) of the Act (15 U.S.C. 78m(a)), other than a report filed by an Asset-Backed Issuer (as defined in § 229.1101 of this chapter) or a report on Form 20-F filed under § 240.13a-19, must include certifications in the form specified in the applicable exhibit filing requirements of such report and such certifications must be filed as an exhibit to such report. Each principal executive and principal financial officer of the issuer, or persons performing similar functions, at the time of filing of the report must sign a certification. The principal executive and principal financial officers of an issuer may omit the portion of the introductory language in paragraph 4 as well as language in paragraph 4(b) of the certification that refers to the certifying officers' responsibility for designing, establishing and maintaining internal control over financial reporting for the issuer until the issuer becomes subject to the internal control over financial reporting requirements in § 240.13a-15 or 240.15d-15..

(b) Each periodic report containing financial statements filed by an issuer pursuant to section 13(a) of the Act (15 U.S.C. 78m(a)) must be accompanied by the certifications required by Section 1350 of Chapter 63 of Title 18 of the United States Code (18 U.S.C. 1350) and such certifications must be furnished as an exhibit to such report as specified in the applicable exhibit requirements for such report. Each principal executive and principal financial officer of the issuer (or equivalent thereof) must sign a certification. This requirement may be satisfied by a single certification signed by an issuer's principal executive and principal financial officers.

(c) A person required to provide a certification specified in paragraph (a), (b) or (d) of this section may not have the certification signed on his or her behalf pursuant to a power of attorney or other form of confirming authority.

(d) Each annual report and transition report filed on Form 10-K (§ 249.310 of this chapter) by an asset-backed issuer under section 13(a) of the Act (15 U.S.C. 78m(a)) must include a certification in the form specified in the applicable exhibit filing requirements of such report and such certification must be filed as an exhibit to such report. Terms used in paragraphs (d) and (e) of this section have the same meaning as in Item 1101 of Regulation AB (§ 229.1101 of this chapter).

(e) With respect to asset-backed issuers, the certification required by paragraph (d) of this section must be signed by either:

(1) The senior officer in charge of securitization of the depositor if the depositor is signing the report; or

(2) The senior officer in charge of the servicing function of the servicer if the servicer is signing the report on behalf of the issuing entity. If multiple servicers are involved in servicing the pool assets, the senior officer in charge of the servicing function of the master servicer (or entity performing the equivalent function) must sign if a representative of the servicer is to sign the report on behalf of the issuing entity.

(f) The certification requirements of this section do not apply to:

(1) An Interactive Data File, as defined in Rule 11 of Regulation S-T (§ 232.11 of this chapter); or

(2) XBRL-Related Documents, as defined in Rule 11 of Regulation S-T.

[As last amended in Release No. 33-9002, effective April 13, 2009, 74 F.R. 6776.]

[¶ 22,055] Controls and Procedures

Reg. § 240.13a-15. (a) Every issuer that has a class of securities registered pursuant to section 12 of the Act (15 U.S.C. 78*l*), other than an Asset-Backed Issuer (as defined in § 229.1101 of this chapter), a small business investment company registered on Form N-5 (§§ 239.24 and 274.5 of this chapter), or a unit investment trust as defined in section 4(2) of the Investment Company Act of 1940 (15 U.S.C. 80a-4(2)), must maintain disclosure controls and procedures (as defined in paragraph (e) of this section) and, if the issuer either had been required to file an annual report pursuant to section 13(a) or 15(d) of the Act (15 U.S.C. 78m(a) or 78o(d)) for the prior fiscal year or had filed an annual report with the Commission for the prior fiscal year, internal control over financial reporting (as defined in paragraph (f) of this section).

(b) Each such issuer's management must evaluate, with the participation of the issuer's principal executive and principal financial officers, or persons performing similar functions, the effectiveness of the issuer's disclosure controls and procedures, as of the end of each fiscal quarter, except that management must perform this evaluation:

(1) In the case of a foreign private issuer (as defined in § 240.3b-4) as of the end of each fiscal year; and

(2) In the case of an investment company registered under section 8 of the Investment Company Act of 1940 (15 U.S.C. 80a-8), within the 90-day period prior to the filing date of each report requiring certification under § 270.30a-2 of this chapter.

(c) The management of each such issuer, that either had been required to file an annual report pursuant to section 13(a) or 15(d) of the Act (15 U.S.C. 78m(a) or 78o(d)) for the prior fiscal year or previously had filed an annual report with the Commission for the prior fiscal year, other than an investment company registered under section 8 of the Investment Company Act of 1940, must evaluate, with the participation of the issuer's principal executive and principal financial officers, or persons performing similar functions, the effectiveness, as of the end of each fiscal year, of the issuer's internal control over financial reporting. The framework on which management's evaluation of the issuer's internal control over financial reporting is based must be a suitable, recognized control framework that is established by a body or group that has followed due-process procedures, including the broad distribution of the framework for public comment. Although there are many different ways to conduct an evaluation of the effectiveness of internal control over financial reporting to meet the requirements of this paragraph, an evaluation that is conducted in accordance with the interpretive guidance issued by the Commission in Release No. 34-55929 will satisfy the evaluation required by this paragraph.

(d) The management of each such issuer that either had been required to file an annual report pursuant to section 13(a) or 15(d) of the Act (15 U.S.C. 78m(a) or 78o(d) for the prior fiscal year or had filed an annual report with the Commission for the prior fiscal year, other than an investment company registered under section 8 of the Investment Company Act of 1940 (15 U.S.C. 80a-8), must evaluate, with the participation of the issuer's principal executive and principal financial officers, or persons performing similar functions, any change in the issuer's internal control over financial reporting, that occurred during each of the issuer's fiscal quarters, or fiscal year in the case of a foreign private issuer, that has materially affected, or is reasonably likely to materially affect, the issuer's internal control over financial reporting.

(e) For purposes of this section, the term *disclosure controls and procedures* means controls and other procedures of an issuer that are designed to ensure that information required to be disclosed by the issuer in the reports that it files or submits under the Act (15 U.S.C. 78a et seq.) is recorded, processed, summarized and reported, within the time periods specified in the Commission's rules and forms. Disclosure controls and procedures include, without limitation, controls and procedures designed to ensure that information required to be disclosed by an issuer in the reports that it files or submits under the Act is accumulated and communicated to the issuer's management, including its principal executive and principal financial officers, or persons performing similar functions, as appropriate to allow timely decisions regarding required disclosure.

(f) The term *internal control over financial reporting* is defined as a process designed by, or under the supervision of, the issuer's principal executive and principal financial officers, or persons performing similar functions, and effected by the issuer's board of directors, management and other personnel, to provide reasonable assurance regarding the reliability of financial reporting and the preparation of financial statements for external purposes in accordance with generally accepted accounting principles and includes those policies and procedures that:

(1) Pertain to the maintenance of records that in reasonable detail accurately and fairly reflect the transactions and dispositions of the assets of the issuer;

(2) Provide reasonable assurance that transactions are recorded as necessary to permit preparation of financial statements in accordance with generally accepted accounting principles, and that receipts and expenditures of the issuer are being made only in accordance with authorizations of management and directors of the issuer; and

(3) Provide reasonable assurance regarding prevention or timely detection of unauthorized acquisition, use or disposition of the issuer's assets that could have a material effect on the financial statements.

[As last amended in Release No. 33-8809, effective August 27, 2007, 72 F.R. 35310.]

[¶ 22,061] Reports of Foreign Private Issuers on Form 6-K (17 CFR 249.306)

Reg. § 240.13a-16. (a) Every foreign private issuer which is subject to Rule 13a-1 (17 CFR 240.13a-1) shall make reports on Form 6-K, except that this rule shall not apply to:

(1) Investment companies required to file reports pursuant to Rule 30b1-1 (17 CFR 270.30b1-1);

(2) Issuers of American depositary receipts for securities of any foreign issuer;

(3) Issuers filing periodic reports on Forms 10-K, Form 10-Q, and Form 8-K; or

(4) Asset-backed issuers, as defined in § 229.1101 of this chapter.

(b) Such reports shall be transmitted promptly after the information required by Form 6-K is made public by the issuer, by the country of its domicile or under the laws of which it was incorporated or organized, or by a foreign securities exchange with which the issuer has filed the information.

(c) Reports furnished pursuant to this rule shall not be deemed to be "filed" for the purpose of section 18 of the Act or otherwise subject to the liabilities of that section.

[As last amended in Release No. 33-8876, effective February 4, 2008, 73 F.R. 934.]

[¶ 22,071] Reports of asset-backed issuers on Form 10-D (§ 249.312 of this chapter)

Reg. § 240.13a-17. Every asset-backed issuer subject to § 240.13a-1 shall make reports on Form 10-D (§ 249.312 of this chapter). Such reports shall be filed within the period specified in Form 10-D.

[As adopted in Release No. 33-8518, effective March 8, 2005 (Compliance dates are triggered by initial bona fide offer date or registration statement filing date and extend out to March 31, 2006. Complete compliance date details can be found in the "Dates" section of the release.), 70 F.R. 1506.]

[¶ 22,091] Compliance with servicing criteria for asset-backed securities

Reg. § 240.13a-18. (a) This section applies to every class of asset-backed securities subject to the reporting requirements of section 13(a) of the Act (15 U.S.C. 78m(a)). Terms used in this section have the same meaning as in Item 1101 of Regulation AB (§ 229.1101 of this chapter).

(b) *Reports on assessments of compliance with servicing criteria for asset-backed securities required.* With regard to a class of asset-backed securities subject to the reporting requirements of section 13(a) of the Act, the annual report on Form 10-K (§ 249.308 of this chapter) for such class must include from each party participating in the servicing function a report regarding its assessment of compliance with the servicing criteria specified in paragraph (d) of Item 1122 of Regulation AB (§ 229.1122(d) of this chapter), as of and for the period ending the end of each fiscal year, with respect to asset-backed securities transactions taken as a whole involving the party participating in the servicing function and that are backed by the same asset type backing the class of asset-backed securities (including the asset-backed securities transaction that is to be the subject of the report on Form 10-K for that fiscal year).

(c) *Attestation reports on assessments of compliance with servicing criteria for asset-backed securities required.* With respect to each report included pursuant to paragraph (b) of this section, the annual report on Form 10-K must also include a report by a registered public accounting firm that attests to, and reports on, the assessment made by the asserting party. The attestation report on assessment of compliance with servicing criteria for asset-backed securities must be made in accordance with standards for attestation engagements issued or adopted by the Public Company Accounting Oversight Board.

Note to § 240.13a-18. If multiple parties are participating in the servicing function, a separate assessment report and attestation report must be included for each party participating in the servicing function. A party participating in the servicing function means any entity (*e.g.,* master servicer, primary servicers, trustees) that is performing activities that address the criteria in paragraph (d) of Item 1122 of Regulation AB (§ 229.1122(d) of this chapter), unless such entity's activities relate only to 5% or less of the pool assets.

[As adopted in Release No. 33-8518, effective March 8, 2005 (Compliance dates are triggered by initial bona fide offer date or registration statement filing date and extend out to March 31, 2006. Complete compliance date details can be found in the "Dates" section of the release.), 70 F.R. 1506.]

[¶ 22,096] Reports by shell companies on Form 20-F

Reg. § 240.13a-19. Every foreign private issuer that was a shell company, other than a business combination related shell company, immediately before a transaction that causes it to cease to be a shell company shall, within four business days of completion of that transaction, file a report on Form 20-F (§ 249.220f of this chapter) containing the information that would be required if the issuer were filing a form for registration of securities on Form 20-F to register under the Act all classes of the issuer's securities subject to the reporting requirements of section 13 (15 U.S.C. 78m) or section 15(d) (15 U.S.C. 78o(d)) of the Act upon consummation of the transaction, with such information reflecting the registrant and its securities upon consummation of the transaction.

[As adopted in Release No. 33-8587, effective August 22, 2005, 70 F.R. 42234.]

[¶ 22,099] Plain English presentation of specified information

Reg. § 240.13a-20. (a) Any information included or incorporated by reference in a report filed under section 13(a) of the Act (15 U.S.C. 78m(a)) that is required to be disclosed pursuant to Item 402, 403, 404 or 407 of Regulation S-K (§ 229.402, 229.403, 229.404 or 229.407 of this chapter) must be presented in a clear, concise and understandable manner. You must prepare the disclosure using the following standards:

(1) Present information in clear, concise sections, paragraphs and sentences;

(2) Use short sentences;

(3) Use definite, concrete, everyday words;

(4) Use the active voice;

(5) Avoid multiple negatives;

(6) Use descriptive headings and subheadings;

(7) Use a tabular presentation or bullet lists for complex material, wherever possible;

(8) Avoid legal jargon and highly technical business and other terminology;

(9) Avoid frequent reliance on glossaries or defined terms as the primary means of explaining information. Define terms in a glossary or other section of the document only if the meaning is unclear from the context. Use a glossary only if it facilitates understanding of the disclosure; and

(10) In designing the presentation of the information you may include pictures, logos, charts, graphs and other design elements so long as the design is not misleading and the required information is clear. You are encouraged to use tables, schedules, charts and graphic illustrations that present relevant data in an understandable manner, so long as such presentations are consistent with applicable disclosure requirements and consistent with other information in the document. You must draw graphs and charts to scale. Any information you provide must not be misleading.

(b) Reserved.

Note to § 240.13a-20. In drafting the disclosure to comply with this section, you should avoid the following:

1. Legalistic or overly complex presentations that make the substance of the disclosure difficult to understand;

2. Vague "boilerplate" explanations that are imprecise and readily subject to different interpretations;

3. Complex information copied directly from legal documents without any clear and concise explanation of the provision(s); and

4. Disclosure repeated in different sections of the document that increases the size of the document but does not enhance the quality of the information.

[As last amended in Release No. 33-8876, effective February 4, 2008, 73 F.R. 934.]

REGULATION 13B-2: MAINTENANCE OF RECORDS AND PREPARATION OF REQUIRED REPORTS

[¶ 22,101] Falsification of Accounting Records

Reg. § 240.13b2-1. No person shall, directly or indirectly, falsify or cause to be falsified, any book, record or account subject to Section 13(b)(2)(A) of the Securities Exchange Act

[As adopted in Release No. 34-15570, February 15, 1979, 44 F.R. 10970.]

[¶ 22,111] Representations and conduct in connection with the preparation of required reports and documents

Reg. § 240.13b2-2. (a) No director or officer of an issuer shall, directly or indirectly:

(1) Make or cause to be made a materially false or misleading statement to an accountant in connection with; or

(2) Omit to state, or cause another person to omit to state, any material fact necessary in order to make statements made, in light of the circumstances under which such statements were made, not misleading, to an accountant in connection with:

(i) Any audit, review or examination of the financial statements of the issuer required to be made pursuant to this subpart; or

(ii) The preparation or filing of any document or report required to be filed with the Commission pursuant to this subpart or otherwise.

(b)(1) No officer or director of an issuer, or any other person acting under the direction thereof, shall directly or indirectly take any action to coerce, manipulate, mislead, or fraudulently influence any independent public or certified public accountant engaged in the performance of an audit or review of the financial statements of that issuer that are required to be filed with the Commission pursuant to this subpart or otherwise if that person knew or should have known that such action, if successful, could result in rendering the issuer's financial statements materially misleading.

(2) For purposes of paragraphs (b)(1) and (c)(2) of this section, actions that,"if successful, could result in rendering the issuer's financial statements materially misleading" include, but are not limited to, actions taken at any time with respect to the professional engagement period to coerce, manipulate, mislead, or fraudulently influence an auditor:

(i) To issue or reissue a report on an issuer's financial statements that is not warranted in the circumstances (due to material violations of generally accepted accounting principles, generally accepted auditing standards, or other professional or regulatory standards);

(ii) Not to perform audit, review or other procedures required by generally accepted auditing standards or other professional standards;

(iii) Not to withdraw an issued report; or

(iv) Not to communicate matters to an issuer's audit committee.

(c) In addition, in the case of an investment company registered under section 8 of the Investment Company Act of 1940 (15 U.S.C. 80a-8), or a business development company as defined in section 2(a)(48) of the Investment Company Act of 1940 (15 U.S.C. 80a-2(a)(48)), no officer or director of the company's investment adviser, sponsor, depositor, trustee, or administrator (or, in the case of paragraph (c)(2) of this section, any other person acting under the direction thereof) shall, directly or indirectly:

(1)(i) Make or cause to be made a materially false or misleading statement to an accountant in connection with; or

(ii) Omit to state, or cause another person to omit to state, any material fact necessary in order to make statements made, in light of the circumstances under which such statements were made, not misleading to an accountant in connection with:

(A) Any audit, review, or examination of the financial statements of the investment company required to be made pursuant to this subpart; or

(B) The preparation or filing of any document or report required to be filed with the Commission pursuant to this subpart or otherwise; or

(2) Take any action to coerce, manipulate, mislead, or fraudulently influence any independent public or certified public accountant engaged in the performance of an audit or review of the financial statements of that investment company that are required to be filed with the Commission pursuant to this subpart or otherwise if that person knew or should have known that such action, if successful, could result in rendering the investment company's financial statements materially misleading.

[As last amended by Release No. 34-47890, effective June 27, 2003, 68 F.R. 31820.]

REGULATION 13D

ATTENTION ELECTRONIC FILERS
THIS REGULATION SHOULD BE READ IN CONJUNCTION WITH REGULATION S- T (PART 232 OF THIS CHAPTER), WHICH GOVERNS THE PREPARATION AND SUBMISSION OF DOCU- MENTS IN ELECTRONIC FORMAT. MANY PROVISIONS RELATING TO THE PREPARATION AND SUBMISSION OF DOCUMENTS IN PAPER FORMAT CONTAINED IN THIS REGULATION ARE SUPERSEDED BY THE PROVISIONS OF REGULATION S-T FOR DOCUMENTS REQUIRED TO BE FILED IN ELECTRONIC FORMAT.

»»→ CCH Note: The SEC has stayed the effectiveness of proxy rule amendments adopted in Release 33-9136 pending resolution of a challenge filed by the Business Roundtable and the U.S. Chamber of Commerce in the U.S. Court of Appeals for the District of Columbia Circuit. See Release No. 33-9149, October 4, 2010.

»»→ Amended by Release No. 33-9136, effective November 15, 2010, 75 F.R. 56668.

[¶ 22,151] Filing of Schedules 13D and 13G

Reg. § 240.13d-1. (a) Any person who, after acquiring directly or indirectly the beneficial owner- ship of any equity security of a class which is specified in paragraph (i) of this section, is directly or indirectly the beneficial owner of more than five percent of the class shall, within 10 days after the acquisition, file with the Commission, a statement containing the information required by Schedule 13D (§ 240.13d-101).

(b)(1) A person who would otherwise be obligated under paragraph (a) of this section to file a statement on Schedule 13D (§ 240.13d-101) may, in lieu thereof, file with the Commission, a short-form statement on Schedule 13G (§ 240.13d-102), *Provided,* That:

(i) Such person has acquired such securities in the ordinary course of his business and not with the purpose nor with the effect of changing or influencing the control of the issuer, nor in connection with or as a participant in any transaction having such purpose or effect, including any transaction subject to Rule 13d-3(b) (§ 240.13d-3(b)); and

Amendment_____

(i) Such person has acquired such securities in the ordinary course of his business and not with the purpose nor with the effect of changing or influencing the control of the issuer, nor in connection with or as a participant in any transaction having such purpose or effect, including any transaction subject to § 240.13d-3(b), other than activities solely in connection with a nomination under § 240.14a-11; and

End of Amendment_____

(ii) Such person is:

(A) A broker or dealer registered under section 15 of the Act (15 U.S.C. 78o);

(B) A bank as defined in section 3(a)(6) of the Act (15 U.S.C. 78c);

(C) An insurance company as defined in section 3(a)(19) of the Act (15 U.S.C. 78c);

(D) An investment company registered under section 8 of the Investment Company Act of 1940 (15 U.S.C. 80a-8);

(E) Any person registered as an investment adviser under Section 203 of the Investment Advisers Act of 1940 (15 U.S.C. 80b-3) or under the laws of any state;

(F) An employee benefit plan as defined in Section 3(3) of the Employee Retirement Income Security Act of 1974, as amended, 29 U.S.C. 1001 et seq. ("ERISA") that is subject to the provisions of ERISA, or any such plan that is not subject to ERISA that is maintained primarily for the benefit of the employees of a state or local government or instrumentality, or an endowment fund;

(G) A parent holding company or control person, provided the aggregate amount held directly by the parent or control person, and directly and indirectly by their subsidiaries or affiliates that are not persons specified in § 240.13d-1(b)(1)(ii)(A) through (J), does not exceed one percent of the securities of the subject class;

(H) A savings association as defined in Section 3(b) of the Federal Deposit Insurance Act (12 U.S.C. 1813);

(I) A church plan that is excluded from the definition of an investment company under section 3(c)(14) of the Investment Company Act of 1940 (15 U.S.C. 80a-3);

(J) A non-U.S. institution that is the functional equivalent of any of the institutions listed in paragraphs (b)(1)(ii)(A) through (I) of this section, so long as the non-U.S. institution is subject to a regulatory scheme that is substantially comparable to the regulatory scheme applicable to the equivalent U.S. institution; and

(K) A group, provided that all the members are persons specified in § 240.13d1(b)(1)(ii)(A) through (J).

(iii) Such person has promptly notified any other person (or group within the meaning of Section 13(d)(3) of the Act) on whose behalf it holds, on a discretionary basis, securities exceeding five percent of the class, of any acquisition or transaction on behalf of such other person which might be reportable by that person under Section 13(d) of the Act. This paragraph only requires notice to the account owner of information which the filing person reasonably should be expected to know and which would advise the account owner of an obligation he may have to file a statement pursuant to Section 13(d) of the Act or an amendment thereto.

Amendment_____

Instruction 1 to paragraph (b)(1). For purposes of paragraph (b)(1)(i) of this section, the exception for activities solely in connection with a nomination under § 240.14a-11 will not be available after the election of directors.

End of Amendment_____

(2) The Schedule 13G filed pursuant to paragraph (b)(1) of this section shall be filed within 45 days after the end of the calendar year in which the person became obligated under paragraph (b)(1) of this section to report the person's beneficial ownership as of the last day of the calendar year, *Provided, That* it shall not be necessary to file a Schedule 13G unless the percentage of the class of equity security specified in paragraph (i) of this section beneficially owned as of the end of the calendar year is more than five percent; However, if the person's direct or indirect beneficial ownership exceeds 10 percent of the class of equity securities prior to the end of the calendar year, the initial Schedule 13G shall be filed within 10 days after the end of the first month in which the person's direct or indirect beneficial ownership exceeds 10 percent of the class of equity securities, computed as of the last day of the month.

(c) A person who would otherwise be obligated under paragraph (a) of this section to file a statement on Schedule 13D (§ 240.13d-101) may, in lieu thereof, file with the Commission, within 10 days after an acquisition described in paragraph (a) of this section, a short-form statement on Schedule 13G (§ 240.13d-102). *Provided,* That the person:

(1) Has not acquired the securities with any purpose, or with the effect of, changing or influencing the control of the issuer, or in connection with or as a participant in any transaction having that purpose or effect, including any transaction subject to § 240.13d-3(b);

Amendment_____

(1) Has not acquired the securities with any purpose, or with the effect, of changing or influencing the control of the issuer, or in connection with or as a participant in any transaction having that purpose or effect, including any transaction subject to § 240.13d-3(b), other than activities solely in connection with a nomination under § 240.14a-11;

End of Amendment_____

(2) Is not a person reporting pursuant to paragraph (b)(1) of this section; and

(3) Is not directly or indirectly the beneficial owner of 20 percent or more of the class.

Amendment_____

Instruction 1 to paragraph (c)(1). For purposes of paragraph (c)(1) of this section, the exception for activities solely in connection with a nomination under § 240.14a-11 will not be available after the election of directors.

End of Amendment_____

(d) Any person who, as of the end of any calendar year, is or becomes directly or indirectly the beneficial owner of more than five percent of any equity security of a class specified in paragraph (i) of this section and who is not required to file a statement under paragraph (a) of this section by virtue of the exemption provided by Section 13(d)(6)(A) or (B) of the Act (15 U.S.C. 78m(d)(6)(A) or 78m(d)(6)(B)), or because the beneficial ownership was acquired prior to December 22, 1970, or because the person otherwise (except for the exemption provided by Section 13(d)(6)(C) of the Act (15 U.S.C. 78m(d)(6)(C))) is not required to file a statement, shall file with the Commission, within 45 days after the end of the calendar year in which the person became obligated to report under this paragraph (d), a statement containing the information required by Schedule 13G (§ 240.13d-102).

(e)(1) Notwithstanding paragraphs (b) and (c) of this section and § 240.13d-2(b), a person that has reported that it is the beneficial owner of more than five percent of a class of equity securities in a statement on Schedule 13G (§ 240.13d-102) pursuant to paragraph (b) or (c) of this section, or is required to report the acquisition but has not yet filed the schedule, shall immediately become subject to §§ 240.13d-1(a) and 240.13d-2(a) and shall file a statement on Schedule 13D (§ 240.13d-101) within 10 days if, and shall remain subject to those requirements for so long as, the person:

(i) Has acquired or holds the securities with a purpose or effect of changing or influencing control of the issuer, or in connection with or as a participant in any transaction having that purpose or effect, including any transaction subject to § 240.13d-3(b); and

(ii) Is at that time the beneficial owner of more than five percent of a class of equity securities described in § 240.13d-1(i).

(2) From the time the person has acquired or holds the securities with a purpose or effect of changing or influencing control of the issuer, or in connection with or as a participant in any transaction having that purpose or effect until the expiration of the tenth day from the date of the filing of the Schedule 13D (§ 240.13d-101) pursuant to this section, that person shall not:

(i) Vote or direct the voting of the securities described therein; or

(ii) Acquire an additional beneficial ownership interest in any equity securities of the issuer of the securities, nor of any person controlling the issuer.

(f) (1) Notwithstanding paragraph (c) of this section and § 240.13d-2(b), persons reporting on Schedule 13G (§ 240.13d-102) pursuant to paragraph (c) of this section shall immediately become subject to § § 240.13d-1(a) and 240.13d-2(a) and shall remain subject to those requirements for so long as, and shall file a statement on Schedule 13D (§ 240.13d-101) within 10 days of the date on which, the person's beneficial ownership equals or exceeds 20 percent of the class of equity securities.

(2) From the time of the acquisition of 20 percent or more of the class of equity securities until the expiration of the tenth day from the date of the filing of the Schedule 13D (§ 240.13d-101) pursuant to this section, the person shall not:

(i) Vote or direct the voting of the securities described therein, or

(ii) Acquire an additional beneficial ownership interest in any equity securities of the issuer of the securities, nor of any person controlling the issuer.

(g) Any person who has reported an acquisition of securities in a statement on Schedule 13G (§ 240.13d-102) pursuant to paragraph (b) of this section, or has become obligated to report on the Schedule 13G (§ 240.13d-102) but has not yet filed the Schedule, and thereafter ceases to be a person specified in paragraph (b)(1)(ii) of this section or determines that it no longer has acquired or holds the securities in the ordinary course of business shall immediately become subject to § 240.13d-1(a) or § 240.13d-1(c) (if the person satisfies the requirements specified in § 240.13d-1(c)), and § § 240.13d-2(a), (b) or (d), and shall file, within 10 days thereafter, a statement on Schedule 13D (§ 240.13d-101) or amendment to Schedule 13G, as applicable, if the person is a beneficial owner at that time of more than five percent of the class of equity securities.

(h) Any person who has filed a Schedule 13D (§ 240.13d-101) pursuant to paragraph (e), (f) or (g) of this section may again report its beneficial ownership on Schedule 13G (§ 240.13d-102) pursuant to paragraphs (b) or (c) of this section provided the person qualifies thereunder, as applicable, by filing a Schedule 13G (§ 240.13d-102) once the person determines that the provisions of paragraph (e), (f) or (g) of this section no longer apply.

(i) For the purpose of this regulation, the term "equity security" means any equity security of a class which is registered pursuant to Section 12 of that Act, or any equity security of any insurance company which would have been required to be so registered except for the exemption contained in Section 12(g)(2)(G) of the Act, or any equity security issued by a closed-end investment company registered under the Investment Company Act of 1940; provided, such term shall not include securities of a class of non-voting securities.

(j) For the purposes of Sections 13(d) and 13(g), any person, in determining the amount of outstanding securities of a class of equity securities, may rely upon information set forth in the issuer's most recent quarterly or annual report, and any current report subsequent thereto, filed with the Commission pursuant to this Act, unless he knows or has reason to believe that the information contained therein is inaccurate.

(k)(1) Whenever two or more persons are required to file a statement containing the information required by Schedule 13D or Schedule 13G with respect to the same securities, only one statement need be filed, provided that:

(i) Each person on whose behalf the statement is filed is individually eligible to use the Schedule on which the information is filed;

(ii) Each person on whose behalf the statement is filed is responsible for the timely filing of such statement and any amendments thereto, and for the completeness and accuracy of the information concerning such person contained therein; such person is not responsible for the completeness or accuracy of the information concerning the other persons making the filing, unless such person knows or has reason to believe that such information is inaccurate; and

(iii) Such statement identifies all such persons, contains the required information with regard to each such person, indicates that such statement is filed on behalf of all such persons, and includes, as an exhibit, their agreement in writing that such a statement is filed on behalf of each of them.

(2) A group's filing obligation may be satisfied either by a single joint filing or by each of the group's members making an individual filing. If the group's members elect to make their own filings, each such filing should identify all members of the group but the information provided concerning the other persons making the filing need only reflect information which the filing person knows or has reason to know.

[As last amended in Release No. 33-9136, effective November 15, 2010, 75 F.R. 56668, stayed by Release No. 33-9149, October 4, 2010.]

[¶ 22,161] Filing of Amendments to Schedules 13D or 13G

Reg. § 240.13d-2. (a) If any material change occurs in the facts set forth in the Schedule 13D (§ 240.13d-101) required by § 240.13d-1(a), including, but not limited to, any material increase or decrease in the percentage of the class beneficially owned, the person or persons who were required to file the statement shall promptly file or cause to be filed with the Commission an amendment disclosing that change. An acquisition or disposition of beneficial ownership of securities in an amount equal to one percent or more of the class of securities shall be deemed "material" for purposes of this section; acquisitions or dispositions of less than those amounts may be material, depending upon the facts and circumstances.

(b) Notwithstanding paragraph (a) of this section, and provided that the person filing a Schedule 13G (§ 240.13d-102) pursuant to § 240.13d-1(b) or § 240.13d-1(c) continues to meet the requirements set forth therein, any person who has filed a Schedule 13G (§ 240.13d-102) pursuant to § 240.13d-1(b), § 240.13d-1(c) or § 240.13d-1(d) shall amend the statement within forty-five days after the end of each calendar year if, as of the end of the calendar year, there are any changes in the information reported in the previous filing on that Schedule; *Provided, however,* That an amendment need not be filed with respect to a change in the percent of class outstanding previously reported if the change results solely from a change in the aggregate number of securities outstanding. Once an amendment has been filed reflecting beneficial ownership of five percent or less of the class of securities, no additional filings are required unless the person thereafter becomes the beneficial owner of more than five percent of the class and is required to file pursuant to § 240.13d-1.

(c) Any person relying on § 240.13d-1(b) that has filed its initial Schedule 13G (§ 240.13d-102) pursuant to that paragraph shall, in addition to filing any amendments pursuant to § 240.13d-2(b), file an amendment on Schedule 13G (§ 240.13d-102) within 10 days after the end of the first month in which the person's direct or indirect beneficial ownership, computed as of the last day of the month, exceeds 10 percent of the class of equity securities. Thereafter, that person shall, in addition to filing any amendments pursuant to § 240.13d-2(b), file an amendment on Schedule 13G (§ 240.13d-102) within 10 days after the end of the first month in which the person's direct or indirect beneficial ownership, computed as of the last day of the month, increases or decreases by more than five percent of the class of equity securities. Once an amendment has been filed reflecting beneficial ownership of five percent or less of the class of securities, no additional filings are required by this paragraph (c).

(d) Any person relying on § 240.13d-1(c) and has filed its initial Schedule 13G (§ 240.13d-102) pursuant to that paragraph shall, in addition to filing any amendments pursuant to § 240.13d-2(b), file an amendment on Schedule 13G (§ 240.13d-102) promptly upon acquiring, directly or indirectly, greater than 10 percent of a class of equity securities specified in § 240.13d-1(d), and thereafter promptly upon increasing or decreasing its beneficial ownership by more than five percent of the class of equity securities. Once an amendment has been filed reflecting beneficial ownership of five percent or less of the class of securities, no additional filings are required by this paragraph (d).

(e) The first electronic amendment to a paper format Schedule 13D (§ 240.13d-101 of this chapter) or Schedule 13G (§ 240.13d-102 of this chapter) shall restate the entire text of the Schedule 13D or 13G, but previously filed paper exhibits to such Schedules are not required to be restated electronically. See Rule 102 of Regulation S-T (§ 232.102 of this chapter) regarding amendments to exhibits previously filed in paper format. Notwithstanding the foregoing, if the sole purpose of filing the first electronic Schedule 13D or 13G amendment is to report a change in beneficial ownership that would terminate the filer's obligation to report, the amendment need not include a restatement of the entire text of the Schedule being amended.

Note to § 240.13d-2: For persons filing a short-form statement pursuant to Rule 13d-1(b) or (c), see also Rules 13d-1(e), (f), and (g).

[As last amended in Release No. 34-39538, January 12, 1998, effective February 17, 1998, 63 F.R. 2854.]

[¶ 22,171] Determination of Beneficial Ownership

Reg. § 240.13d-3. (a) For the purposes of Sections 13(d) and 13(g) of the Act a beneficial owner of a security includes any person who, directly or indirectly, through any contract, arrangement, understanding, relationship, or otherwise has or shares:

(1) Voting power which includes the power to vote, or to direct the voting of, such security; and/or

(2) Investment power which includes the power to dispose, or to direct the disposition of, such security.

(b) Any person who, directly or indirectly, creates or uses a trust, proxy, power of attorney, pooling arrangement or any other contract, arrangement, or device with the purpose or effect of divesting such person of beneficial ownership of a security or preventing the vesting of such beneficial ownership as part of a plan or scheme to evade the reporting requirements of Section 13(d) or 13(g) of the Act shall be deemed for purposes of such sections to be the beneficial owner of such security.

(c) All securities of the same class beneficially owned by a person, regardless of the form which such beneficial ownership takes, shall be aggregated in calculating the number of shares beneficially owned by such person.

(d) Notwithstanding the provisions of paragraphs (a) and (c) of this rule:

(1)(i) A person shall be deemed to be the beneficial owner of a security, subject to the provisions of paragraph (b) of this rule, if that person has the right to acquire beneficial ownership of such security, as defined in Rule 13d-3(a) (§ 240.13d-3(a)) within sixty days, including but not limited to any right to acquired: (A) through the exercise of any option, warrant or right; (B) through the conversion of a security; (C) pursuant to the power to revoke a trust, discretionary account, or similar arrangement; or (D) pursuant to the automatic termination of a trust, discretionary account or similar arrangement; provided, however, any person who acquires a security or power specified in paragraphs (A), (B) or (C), above, with the purpose or effect of changing or influencing the control of the issuer, or in connection with or as a participant in any transaction having such purpose or effect, immediately upon such acquisition shall be deemed to be the beneficial owner of the securities which may be acquired through the exercise or conversion of such security or power. Any securities not outstanding which are subject to such options, warrants, rights or conversion privileges shall be deemed to be outstanding for the purpose of computing the percentage of outstanding securities of the class owned by such person but shall not be deemed to be outstanding for the purpose of computing the percentage of the class by any other person.

(ii) Paragraph (d)(1)(i) of this section remains applicable for the purpose of determining the obligation to file with respect to the underlying security even though the option, warrant, right or convertible security is of a class of equity security, as defined in § 240.13d-1(i), and may therefore give rise to a separate obligation to file.

(2) A member of a national securities exchange shall not be deemed to be a beneficial owner of securities held directly or indirectly by it on behalf of another person solely because such member is the record holder of such securities and, pursuant to the rules of such exchange, may direct the vote of such securities, without instruction, on other than contested matters or matters that may affect substantially the rights or privileges of the holders of the securities to be voted, but is otherwise precluded by the rules of such exchange from voting without instruction.

(3) A person who in the ordinary course of business is a pledgee of securities under a written pledge agreement shall not be deemed to be the beneficial owner of such pledged securities until the pledgee has taken all formal steps necessary which are required to declare a default and determines that the power to vote or to direct to vote or to dispose or to direct the disposition of such pledged securities will be exercised, provided that:

(i) The pledgee agreement is bona fide and was not entered into with the purpose nor with the effect of changing or influencing the control of the issuer, nor in connection with any transaction having such purpose or effect, including any transaction subject to Rule 13d-3(b);

(ii) The pledgee is a person specified in Rule 13d-1(b)(ii), including persons meeting the conditions set forth in paragraph (G) thereof; and

(iii) The pledgee agreement, prior to default, does not grant to the pledgee:

(A) The power to vote or to direct the vote of the pledged securities; or

(B) The power to dispose or direct the disposition of the pledged securities, other than the grant of such power(s) pursuant to a pledge agreement under which credit is extended subject to Regulation T (12 CFR 220.1 to 220.8) and in which the pledgee is a broker or dealer registered under section 15 of the Act.

(4) A person engaged in business as an underwriter of securities who acquires securities through his participation in good faith in a firm commitment underwriting registered under the Securities Act of

1933 shall not be deemed to be the beneficial owner of such securities until the expiration of forty days after the date of such acquisition.

[As last amended in Release No. 34-39538, January 12, 1998, effective February 17, 1998, 63 F.R. 2854.]

[¶ 22,181] Disclaimer of Beneficial Ownership

Reg. § 240.13d-4. Any person may expressly declare in any statement filed that the filing of such statement shall not be construed as an admission that such person is, for the purposes of section 13(d), or 13(g) of the Act, the beneficial owner of any securities covered by the statement.

[As last amended in Release No. 34-14692. April 21, 1978, 43 F.R. 18484.]

[¶ 22,191] Acquisition of Securities

Reg. § 240.13d-5. (a) A person who becomes a beneficial owner of securities shall be deemed to have acquired such securities for purposes of Section 13(d)(1) of the Act, whether such acquisition was through purchase or otherwise. However, executors or administrators of a decedent's estate generally will be presumed not to have acquired beneficial ownership of the securities in the decedent's estate until such time as such executors or administrators are qualified under local law to perform their duties.

(b)(1) When two or more persons agree to act together for the purpose of acquiring, holding, voting or disposing of equity securities of an issuer, the group formed thereby shall be deemed to have acquired beneficial ownership, for purposes of Sections 13(d) and 13(g) of the Act, as of the date of such agreement, of all equity securities of that issuer beneficially owned by any such persons.

(2) Notwithstanding the previous paragraph, a group shall be deemed not to have acquired any equity securities beneficially owned by the other members of the group solely by virtue of their concerted actions relating to the purchase of equity securities directly from an issuer in a transaction not involving a public offering, provided that:

(i) All the members of the group are persons specified in Rule 13d-1(b)(1)(ii);

(ii) The purchase is in the ordinary course of each member's business and not with the purpose nor with the effect of changing or influencing control of the issuer, nor in connection with or as a participant in any transaction having such purpose or effect, including any transaction subject to Rule 13d-3(b);

(iii) There is no agreement among, or between any members of the group to act together with respect to the issuer or its securities except for the purpose of facilitating the specific purchase involved; and

(iv) The only actions among or between any members of the group with respect to the issuer or its securities subsequent to the closing date of the non-public offering are those which are necessary to conclude ministerial matters directly related to the completion of the offer or sale of the securities.

[As last amended in Release No. 34-14692. April 21, 1978, 43 F.R. 18484.]

[¶ 22,201] Exemption of Certain Acquisitions

Reg. § 240.13d-6. The acquisition of securities of an issuer by a person who, prior to such acquisition, was a beneficial owner of more than five percent of the outstanding securities of the same class as those acquired shall be exempt from section 13(d) of the Act, provided that:

(a) The acquisition is made pursuant to preemptive subscription rights in an offering made to all holders of securities of the class to which the preemptive subscription rights pertain;

(b) Such person does not acquire additional securities except through the exercise of his pro rata share of the preemptive subscription rights; and

(c) The acquisition is duly reported, if required, pursuant to section 16(a) of the Act and the rules and regulations thereunder.

[As last amended in Release No. 34-14692, April 21, 1978, 43 F.R. 18484.]

[¶ 22,211] Dissemination

Reg. § 240.13d-7. One copy of the Schedule filed pursuant to §§ 240.13d-1 and 240.13d-2 shall be sent to the issuer of the security at its principal executive office, by registered or certified mail. A copy of Schedules filed pursuant to §§ 240.13d-1(a) and 240.13d-2(a) shall also be sent to each national securities exchange where the security is traded.

[Adopted in Release No. 34-39538, January 12, 1998, effective February 17, 1998, 63 F.R. 2854.]

SCHEDULE 13D

[¶ 22,221] Reg. § 240.13d-101 (Schedule 13D) Information to be Included in Statements Filed Pursuant to § 240.13d-1(a) and Amendments Thereto Filed Pursuant to § 240.13d-2(a).

SECURITIES AND EXCHANGE COMMISSION
Washington, D.C. 20549
SCHEDULE 13D
Under the Securities Exchange Act of 1934
(Amendment No . . .) *

. . . .
(Name of Issuer)

. . . .
(Title of Class of Securities)

. . . .
(CUSIP Number)

. . . .
(Name, Address and Telephone Number of Person Authorized to Receive Notices and Communications)

. . . .
(Date of Event which Requires Filing of this Statement)

If the filing person has previously filed a statement on Schedule 13G to report the acquisition that is the subject of this Schedule 13D, and is filing this schedule because of §§ 240.13d-1(e), 240.13d-1(f) or 240.13d-1(g), check the following box. [ ]

NOTE: Schedules filed in paper format shall include a signed original and five copies of the schedule, including all exhibits. See Rule 13d-7 for other parties to whom copies are to be sent.

* The remainder of this cover page shall be filled out for a reporting person's initial filing on this form with respect to the subject class of securities, and for any subsequent amendment containing information which would alter disclosures provided in a prior cover page.

The information required on the remainder of this cover page shall not be deemed to be "filed" for the purpose of Section 18 of the Securities Exchange Act of 1934 ("Act") or otherwise subject to the liabilities of that section of the Act but shall be subject to all other provisions of the Act (however, see the Notes).

CUSIP No. . . . .

1) Names of Reporting Persons.	
. . . .	
2) Check the Appropriate Box if a Member of a Group (See Instructions)	
(a)	
(b)	
3) SEC Use Only	
4) Source of Funds (See Instructions)	
5) Check if Disclosure of Legal Proceedings is Required Pursuant to Items 2(d) or 2(e)	
. . . .	
6) Citizenship or Place of Organization	

Number of Shares Bene-ficially Owned by Each Report-ing Person With	(7) Sole Voting Power . . . .
	(8) Shared Voting Power . . . .
	(9) Sole Dispositive Power . . . .
	(10) Shared Dispositive Power . . . .

11) Aggregate Amount Beneficially Owned by Each Reporting Person	
12) Check if the Aggregate Amount in Row (11) Excludes Certain Shares (See Instructions)	
. . . .	
13) Percent of Class Represented by Amount in Row (11)	
14) Type of Reporting Person (See Instructions)	
. . . .	

. . . .
. . . .
. . . .
. . . .
. . . .
. . . .
. . . .
. . . .

Instructions for Cover Page

(1) *Names of Reporting Persons* - Furnish the full legal name of each person for whom the report is filed - *i.e.*, each person required to sign the schedule itself - including each member of a group. Do not include the name of a person required to be identified in the report but who is not a reporting person.

(2) If any of the shares beneficially owned by a reporting person are held as a member of a group and the membership is expressly affirmed, please check row 2(a). If the reporting person disclaims membership in a group or describes a relationship with other person but does not affirm the existence of a group, please check row 2(b) [unless it is a joint filing pursuant to Rule 13d-1(k)(1) in which case it may not be necessary to check row 2 (b)].

(3) The 3rd row is for SEC internal use; please leave blank.

(4) Classify the source of funds or other consideration used or to be used in making the purchases as required to be disclosed pursuant to Item 3 of Schedule 13D and insert the appropriate symbol (or symbols if more than one is necessary in row (4):

Category of Source	Symbol
Subject Company (Company whose securities are being acquired)	SC
Bank	BK
Affiliate (of reporting person)	AF
Working Capital (of reporting person)	WC
Personal Funds (of reporting person)	PF
Other	OO

(5) If disclosure of legal proceedings or actions is required pursuant to either Items 2(d) or 2(e) of Schedule 13D, row 5 should be checked.

(6) *Citizenship or Place of Organization*—Furnish citizenship if the named reporting person is a natural person. Otherwise, furnish place of organization. (See Item 2 of Schedule 13D).

(7)-(11), (13) *Aggregate Amount Beneficially Owned by Each Reporting Person, etc.*—Rows (7) through (11), inclusive, and (13) are to be completed in accordance with the provisions of Item 5 of Schedule 13D. All percentages are to be rounded off to nearest tenth (one place after decimal point).

(12) Check if the aggregate amount reported as beneficially owned in row (11) does not include shares which the reporting person discloses in the report but as to which beneficial ownership is disclaimed pursuant to Rule 13d-4 under the Securities Exchange Act of 1934.

(14) *Type of Reporting Person*—Please classify each "reporting person" according to the following breakdown and place the appropriate symbol (or symbols, i.e., if more than one is applicable, insert all applicable symbols) on the form:

Category	Symbol
Broker Dealer	BD
Bank	BK
Insurance Company	IC
Investment Company	IV
Investment Adviser	IA
Employee Benefit Plan or Endowment Fund	EP
Parent Holding Company/Control Person	HC
Savings Association	SA
Church Plan	CP
Corporation	CO
Partnership	PN
Individual	IN
Other	OO

Note: Attach additional pages if needed.

Notes:

Attach as many copies of the second part of the cover page as are needed, one reporting person per page.

Filing persons may, in order to avoid unnecessary duplication, answer items on the schedules (Schedule 13D, 13G or TO) by appropriate cross references to an item or items on the cover page(s). This approach may only be used where the cover page item or items provide all the disclosure required by the schedule item. Moreover, such a use of a cover page item will result in the item becoming a part of the schedule and accordingly being considered as "filed" for purposes of Section 18 of the Securities Exchange Act or otherwise subject to the liabilities of that section of the Act.

Reporting persons may comply with their cover page filing requirements by filing either completed copies of the blank forms available from the Commission, printed or typed facsimiles, or computer printed facsimiles, provided the documents filed have identical formats to the forms prescribed in the Commission's regulations and meet existing Securities Exchange Act rules as to such matters as clarity and size (Securities Exchange Act Rule 12b-12).

SPECIAL INSTRUCTIONS FOR COMPLYING WITH SCHEDULE 13D

Under sections 13(d) and 23 of the Securities Exchange Act of 1934 and the rules and regulations thereunder, the Commission is authorized to solicit the information required to be supplied by this schedule by certain security holders of certain issuers.

Disclosure of the information specified in this schedule is mandatory. The information will be used for the primary purpose of determining and disclosing the holdings of certain beneficial owners of certain equity securities. This statement will be made a matter of public record. Therefore, any information given will be available for inspection by any member of the public.

Because of the public nature of the information, the Commission can use it for a variety of purposes, including referral to other governmental authorities or securities self-regulatory organizations for investigatory purposes or in connection with litigation involving the federal securities laws or other civil, criminal or regulatory statutes or provisions.

Failure to disclose the information requested by this schedule may result in civil or criminal action against the persons involved for violation of the federal securities laws and rules promulgated thereunder.

General Instructions

A. The item numbers and captions of the items shall be included but the text of the items is to be omitted. The answers to the items shall be so prepared as to indicate clearly the coverage of the items without referring to the text of the items. Answer every item. If an item is inapplicable or the answer is in the negative, so state.

B. Information contained in exhibits to the statement may be incorporated by reference in answer or partial answer to any item or sub-item of the statement unless it would render such answer misleading, incomplete, unclear or confusing. Matter incorporated by reference shall be clearly identified in the reference by page, paragraph, caption or otherwise. An express statement that the specified matter is incorporated by reference shall be made at the particular place in the statement where the information is required. A copy of any information or a copy of the pertinent pages of a document containing such information which is incorporated by reference shall be submitted with this statement as an exhibit and shall be deemed to be filed with the Commission for all purposes of the Act.

C. If the statement is filed by a general or limited partnership, syndicate, or other group, the information called for by Items 2-6, inclusive, shall be given with respect to (i) each partner of such general partnership; (ii) each partner who is denominated as a general partner or who functions as a general partner of such limited partnership; (iii) each member of such syndicate or group; and (iv) each person controlling such partner or member. If the statement is filed by a corporation or if a person referred to in (i), (ii), (iii) or (iv) of this Instruction is a corporation, the information called for by the above mentioned items shall be given with respect to (a) each executive officer and director of such corporation; (b) each person controlling such corporation; and (c) each executive officer and director of any corporation or other person ultimately in control of such corporation.

Item 1. Security and Issuer

State the title of the class of equity securities to which this statement relates and the name and address of the principal executive offices of the issuer of such securities.

Item 2. Identity and Background

If the person filing this statement or any person enumerated in Instruction C of this statement is a corporation, general partnership, limited partnership, syndicate or other group of persons, state its name, the state or other place of its organization, its principal business, the address of its principal business, the address of its principal office and the information required by (d) and (e) of this Item. If the person filing this statement or any person enumerated in Instruction C is a natural person, provide the information specified in (a) through (f) of this Item with respect to such person(s).

(a) Name;

(b) Residence or business address;

(c) Present principal occupation or employment and the name, principal business and address of any corporation or other organization in which such employment is conducted;

(d) Whether or not, during the last five years, such person has been convicted in a criminal proceeding (excluding traffic violations or similar misdemeanors) and, if so, give the dates, nature of conviction, name and location of court, any penalty imposed, or other disposition of the case;

(e) Whether or not, during the last five years, such person was a party to a civil proceeding of a judicial or administrative body of competent jurisdiction and as a result of such proceeding was or is subject to a judgment, decree or final order enjoining future violations of, or prohibiting or mandating activities subject to, federal or state securities laws or finding any violation with respect to such laws; and, if so, identify and describe such proceedings and summarize the terms of such judgment, decree or final order; and

(f) Citizenship.

Item 3. Source and Amount of Funds or Other Consideration

State the source and the amount of funds or other consideration used or to be used in making the purchases, and if any part of the purchase price is or will be represented by funds or other consideration borrowed or otherwise obtained for the purpose of acquiring, holding, trading or voting the securities, a description of the transaction and the names of the parties thereto. Where material, such information should also be provided with respect to prior acquisitions not previously reported pursuant to this regulation. If the source of all or any part of the funds is a loan made in the ordinary course of business by a bank, as defined in Section 3(a)(6) of the Act, the name of the bank shall not be made available to the public if the person at the time of filing the statement so requests in writing and files such request, naming such bank, with the Secretary of the Commission. If the securities were acquired other than by purchase, describe the method of acquisition.

Item 4. Purpose of Transaction

State the purpose or purposes of the acquisition of securities of the issuer. Describe any plans or proposals which the reporting persons may have which relate to or would result in:

(a) The acquisition by any person of additional securities of the issuer, or the disposition of securities of the issuer;

(b) An extraordinary corporate transaction, such as a merger, reorganization or liquidation, involving the issuer or any of its subsidiaries;

(c) A sale or transfer of a material amount of assets of the issuer or any of its subsidiaries;

(d) Any change in the present board of directors or management of the issuer, including any plans or proposals to change the number or term of directors or to fill any existing vacancies on the board;

(e) Any material change in the present capitalization or dividend policy of the issuer;

(f) Any other material change in the issuer's business or corporate structure, including but not limited to, if the issuer is a registered closed-end investment company, any plans or proposals to make any changes in its investment policy for which a vote is required by section 13 of the Investment Company Act of 1940;

(g) Changes in the issuer's charter, bylaws or instruments corresponding thereto or other actions which may impede the acquisition of control of the issuer by any person;

(h) Causing a class of securities of the issuer to be delisted from a national securities exchange or to cease to be authorized to be quoted in an inter-dealer quotation system of a registered national securities association;

(i) A class of equity securities of the issuer becoming eligible for termination of registration pursuant to Section 12(g)(4) of the Act; or

(j) Any action similar to any of those enumerated above.

Item 5. Interest in Securities of the Issuer

(a) State the aggregate number and percentage of the class of securities identified pursuant to Item 1 (which may be based on the number of securities outstanding as contained in the most recently available filing with the Commission by the issuer unless the filing person has reason to believe such information is not current) beneficially owned (identifying those shares which there is a right to acquire) by each person named in Item 2. The above mentioned information should also be furnished with respect to persons who, together with any of the persons named in Item 2, comprise a group within the meaning of Section 13(d)(3) of the Act;

(b) For each person named in response to paragraph (a), indicate the number of shares as to which there is sole power to vote or to direct the vote, shared power to vote or to direct the vote, sole power to dispose or to direct the disposition, or shared power to dispose or to direct the disposition. Provide the applicable information required by Item 2 with respect to each person with whom the power to vote or to direct the vote or to dispose or direct the disposition is shared;

(c) Describe any transactions in the class of securities reported on that were effected during the past sixty days or since the most recent filing on Schedule 13D (§ 240.13d-101), whichever is less, by the persons named in response to paragraph (a).

Instruction. The description of a transaction required by Item 5(c) shall include, but not necessarily be limited to: (1) the identity of the person covered by Item 5(c) who effected the transaction; (2) the date of the transaction; (3) the amount of securities involved; (4) the price per share or unit; and (5) where and how the transaction was effected.

(d) If any other person is known to have the right to receive or the power to direct the receipt of dividends from, or the proceeds from the sale of, such securities, a statement to that effect should be included in response to this item and, if such interest relates to more than five percent of the class, such person should be identified. A listing of the shareholders of an investment company registered under the Investment Company Act of 1940 or the beneficiaries of an employee benefit plan, pension fund or endowment fund is not required.

(e) If applicable, state the date on which the reporting person ceased to be the beneficial owner of more than five percent of the class of securities.

Instruction. For computations regarding securities which represent a right to acquire an underlying security, see Rule 13d-3(d)(1) and the note thereto.

Item 6. Contracts, Arrangements, Understandings or Relationships with Respect to Securities of the Issuer

Describe any contracts, arrangements, understandings or relationships (legal or otherwise) among the persons named in Item 2 and between such persons and any person with respect to any securities of the issuer, including but not limited to transfer or voting of any of the securities, finder's fees, joint ventures, loan or option arrangements, put or calls, guarantees of profits, division of profits or loss, or the giving or withholding of proxies, naming the persons with whom such contracts, arrangements, understandings or relationships have been entered into. Include such information for any of the securities that are pledged or otherwise subject to a contingency the occurrence of which would give another person voting power or investment power over such securities except that disclosure of standard default and similar provisions contained in loan agreements need not be included.

Item 7. Material to Be Filed as Exhibits

The following shall be filed as exhibits: copies of written agreements relating to the filing of joint acquisition statements as required by Rule 13d-1(k) and copies of all written agreements, contracts, arrangements, understandings, plans or proposals relating to (1) the borrowing of funds to finance the acquisition as disclosed in Item 3; (2) the acquisition of issuer control, liquidation, sale of assets, merger, or change in business or corporate structure or any other matter as disclosed in Item 4; and (3) the transfer or voting of the securities, finder's fees, joint ventures, options, puts, calls, guarantees of loans, guarantees against loss or of profit, or the giving or withholding of any proxy as disclosed in Item 6.

Signature.

After reasonable inquiry and to the best of my knowledge and belief, I certify that the information set forth in this statement is true, complete and correct.

. . . .

Date

. . . .

Signature

. . . .

Name/Title

The original statement shall be signed by each person on whose behalf the statement is filed or his authorized representative. If the statement is signed on behalf of a person by his authorized representative (other than an executive officer or general partner of this filing person), evidence of the representative's authority to sign on behalf of such person shall be filed with the statement, provided, however, that a power of attorney for this purpose which is already on file with the Commission may be incorporated by reference. The name and any title of each person who signs the statement shall be typed or printed beneath his signature.

Attention: Intentional misstatements or omissions of fact constitute Federal criminal violations (See 18 U. S. C. 1001).

[As last amended by Release No. 34-55146A, effective April 1, 2008, 73 F.R. 17809 (technical correction).]

REGULATION 13E

[¶ 22,251] Purchase of Securities by the Issuer During a Third-Party Tender Offer

Reg. § 240.13e-1. An issuer that has received notice that it is the subject of a tender offer made under Section 14(d) (1) of the Act (15 U.S.C. 78n), that has commenced under § 240.14d-2 must not purchase any of its equity securities during the tender offer unless the issuer first:

(a) Files a statement with the Commission containing the following information:

(1) The title and number of securities to be purchased;

(2) The names of the persons or classes of persons from whom the issuer will purchase the securities;

(3) The name of any exchange, inter-dealer quotation system or any other market on or through which the securities will be purchased;

(4) The purpose of the purchase;

(5) Whether the issuer will retire the securities, hold the securities in its treasury, or dispose of the securities. If the issuer intends to dispose of the securities, describe how it intends to do so; and

(6) The source and amount of funds or other consideration to be used to make the purchase. If the issuer borrows any funds or other consideration to make the purchase or enters any agreement for the purpose of acquiring, holding, or trading the securities, describe the transaction and agreement and identify the parties; and

(b) Pays the fee required by § 240.0-11 when it files the initial statement.

(c) This section does not apply to periodic repurchases in connection with an employee benefit plan or other similar plan of the issuer so long as the purchases are made in the ordinary course and not in response to the tender offer.

Instruction to § 240.13e-1:

File eight copies if paper filing is permitted.

[As last amended in Release No. 33-7760, effective January 24, 2000, 64 F.R. 61408.]

[¶ 22,261] Going Private Transactions by Certain Issuers or Their Affiliates

Reg. § 240.13e-3. (a) *Definitions.* Unless indicated otherwise or the context requires, all terms used in this section and in Schedule 13E-3 [§ 240.13e-100] shall have the same meaning as in the Act or elsewhere in the General Rules and Regulations thereunder. In addition, the following definitions apply:

(1) An "affiliate" of an issuer is a person that directly or indirectly through one or more intermediaries controls, is controlled by, or is under common control with such issuer. For the purposes of this section only, a person who is not an affiliate of an issuer at the commencement of such person's tender offer for a class of equity securities of such issuer will not be deemed an affiliate of such issuer prior to the stated termination of such tender offer and any extensions thereof;

(2) The term "purchase" means any acquisition for value including, but not limited to, (i) any acquisition pursuant to the dissolution of an issuer subsequent to the sale or other disposition of substantially all the assets of such issuer to its affiliate, (ii) any acquisition pursuant to a merger, (iii) any acquisition of fractional interests in connection with a reverse stock split, and (iv) any acquisition subject to the control of an issuer or an affiliate of such issuer;

(3) A "Rule 13e-3 transaction" is any transaction or series of transactions involving one or more of the transactions described in paragraph (a) (3) (i) of this section which has either a reasonable likelihood or a purpose of producing, either directly or indirectly, any of the effects described in paragraph (a) (3) (ii) of this section;

(i) The transactions referred to in paragraph (a) (3) of this section are:

(A) A purchase of any equity security by the issuer of such security or by an affiliate of such issuer;

(B) A tender offer for or request or invitation for tenders of any equity security made by the issuer of such class of securities or by an affiliate of such issuer; or

(C) A solicitation subject to Regulation 14A [§§ 240.14a-1 to 240.14b-1] of any proxy, consent or authorization of, or a distribution subject to Regulation 14C [§§ 240.14c-1 to 240.14c-101] of information statements to, any equity security holder by the issuer of the class of securities or by an affiliate of such issuer, in connection with: a merger, consolidation, reclassification, recapitalization, reorganization or similar corporate transaction of an issuer or between an issuer (or its subsidiaries) and its affiliate; a sale of substantially all the assets of an issuer to its affiliate or group of affiliates; or a reverse stock split of any class of equity securities of the issuer involving the purchase of fractional interests.

(ii) The effects referred to in paragraph (a) (3) of this section are:

(A) Causing any class of equity securities of the issuer which is subject to section 12(g) or section 15(d) of the Act to become eligible for termination of registration under Rule 12g-4 (§ 240.12g-4) or Rule 12h-6 (§ 240.12h-6), or causing the reporting obligations with respect to such class to become eligible for termination under Rule 12h-6 (§ 240.12h-6); or suspension under Rule 12h-3 (§ 240.12h-3) or section 15(d); or

(B) Causing any class of equity securities of the issuer which is either listed on a national securities exchange or authorized to be quoted in an inter-dealer quotation system of a registered national securities association to be neither listed on any national securities exchange nor authorized to be quoted on an inter-dealer quotation system of any registered national securities association.

(4) An "unaffiliated security holder" is any security holder of an equity security subject to a Rule 13e-3 transaction who is not an affiliate of the issuer of such security.

(b) *Application of section to an issuer (or an affiliate of such issuer) subject to section 12 of the Act.*

(1) It shall be a fraudulent, deceptive or manipulative act or practice, in connection with a Rule 13e-3 transaction, for an issuer which has a class of equity securities registered pursuant to Section 12 of the Act or which is a closed-end investment company registered under the Investment Company Act of 1940, or an affiliate of such issuer, directly or indirectly.

(i) To employ any device, scheme or artifice to defraud any person;

(ii) To make any untrue statement of a material fact or to omit to state a material fact necessary in order to make the statements made, in light of the circumstances under which they were made, not misleading; or

(iii) To engage in any act, practice or course of business which operates or would operate as a fraud or deceit upon any person.

(2) As a means reasonably designed to prevent fraudulent, deceptive or manipulative acts or practices in connection with any Rule 13e-3 transaction, it shall be unlawful for an issuer which has a class of equity securities registered pursuant to Section 12 of the Act, or an affiliate of such issuer, to engage, directly or indirectly, in a Rule 13e-3 transaction unless:

(i) Such issuer or affiliate complies with the requirements of paragraphs (d), (e) and (f) of this Section; and

(ii) The Rule 13e-3 transaction is not in violation of paragraph (b)(1) of this section.

(c) *Application of section to an issuer (or an affiliate of such issuer) subject to Section 15(d) of the Act.*

(1) It shall be unlawful as a fraudulent, deceptive or manipulative act or practice for an issuer which is required to file periodic reports pursuant to Section 15(d) of the Act, or an affiliate of such issuer, to engage, directly or indirectly, in a Rule 13e-3 transaction unless such issuer or affiliate complies with the requirements of paragraphs (d), (e) and (f) of this section.

(2) An issuer or affiliate which is subject to paragraph (c)(1) of this section and which is soliciting proxies or distributing information statements in connection with a transaction described in paragraph (a)(3)(i)(A) of this section may elect to use the timing procedures for conducting a solicitation subject to Regulation 14A (§§ 240.14a-1 to 240.14b-1) or a distribution subject to Regulation 14C (§§ 240.14c-1 to 240.14c-101) in complying with paragraphs (d), (e) and (f) of this section, provided that if an election is made, such solicitation or distribution is conducted in accordance with the requirements of the respective regulations, including the filing of preliminary copies of soliciting materials or an information statement at the time specified in Regulation 14A or 14C, respectively.

(d) *Material required to be filed.* The issuer or affiliate engaging in a Rule 13e-3 transaction must file with the Commission:

(1) A Schedule 13E-3 (§ 240.13e-100), including all exhibits;

(2) An amendment to Schedule 13E-3 reporting promptly any material changes in the information set forth in the schedule previously filed; and

(3) A final amendment to Schedule 13E-3 reporting promptly the results of the Rule 13e-3 transaction.

(e) *Disclosure of information to security holders.*

(1) In addition to disclosing the information required by any other applicable rule or regulation under the federal securities laws, the issuer or affiliate engaging in a § 240.13e-3 transaction must disclose to security holders of the class that is the subject of the transaction, as specified in paragraph (f) of this section, the following:

(i) The information required by Item 1 of Schedule 13E-3 (§ 240.13e-100) (Summary Term Sheet);

(ii) The information required by Items 7, 8 and 9 of Schedule 13E-3, which must be prominently disclosed in a "Special Factors" section in the front of the disclosure document;

(iii) A prominent legend on the outside front cover page that indicates that neither the Securities and Exchange Commission nor any state securities commission has: approved or disapproved of the transaction; passed upon the merits or fairness of the transaction; or passed upon the adequacy or accuracy of the disclosure in the document. The legend also must make it clear that any representation to the contrary is a criminal offense;

(iv) The information concerning appraisal rights required by § 229.1016(f) of this chapter; and

(v) The information required by the remaining items of Schedule 13E-3, except for § 229.1016 of this chapter (exhibits), or a fair and adequate summary of the information.

Instructions to paragraph (e)(1):

1. If the Rule 13e-3 transaction also is subject to Regulation 14A (§§ 240.14a-1 through 240.14b-2) or 14C (§§ 240.14c-1 through 240.14c-101), the registration provisions and rules of the Securities Act of 1933, Regulation 14D or § 240.13e-4, the information required by paragraph (e)(1) of this section must be combined with the proxy statement, information statement, prospectus or tender offer material sent or given to security holders.

2. If the Rule 13e-3 transaction involves a registered securities offering, the legend required by § 229.501(b)(7) of this chapter must be combined with the legend required by paragraph (e)(1)(iii) of this section.

3. The required legend must be written in clear, plain language.

(2) If there is any material change in the information previously disclosed to security holders, the issuer or affiliate must disclose the change promptly to security holders as specified in paragraph (f)(1)(iii) of this section.

(f) *Dissemination of information to security holders.* (1) If the Rule 13e-3 transaction involves a purchase as described in paragraph (a)(3)(i)(A) of this section or a vote, consent, authorization, or distribution of information statements as described in paragraph (a)(3)(i)(C) of this section, the issuer or affiliate engaging in the Rule 13e-3 transaction shall:

(i) Provide the information required by paragraph (e) of this section: (A) in accordance with the provisions of any applicable federal or state law, but in no event later than 20 days prior to: any such purchase; any such vote, consent or authorization; or with respect to the distribution of information statements, the meeting date, or if corporate action is to be taken by means of the written authorization or consent of security holders, the earliest date on which corporate action may be taken: *Provided, however,* That if the purchase subject to this section is pursuant to a tender offer excepted from Rule 13e-4 by paragraph (g)(5) of Rule 13e-4, the information required by paragraph (e) of this section shall be disseminated in accordance with paragraph (e) of Rule 13e-4 no later than 10 business days prior to any purchase pursuant to such tender offer, (B) to each person who is a record holder of a class of equity security subject to the Rule 13e-3 transaction as of a date not more than 20 days prior to the date of dissemination of such information.

(ii) If the issuer or affiliate knows that securities of the class of securities subject to the Rule 13e-3 transaction are held of record by a broker, dealer, bank or voting trustee or their nominees, such issuer or affiliate shall (unless Rule 14a-13(a) [§ 240-14a-13(a)]or 14c-7 [§ 240.14c-7] is applicable) furnish the number of copies of the information required by paragraph (e) of this section that are requested by such persons (pursuant to inquiries by or on behalf of the issuer or affiliate), instruct such persons to forward such information to the beneficial owners of such securities in a timely manner and undertake to pay the reasonable expenses incurred by such persons in forwarding such information; and

(iii) Promptly disseminate disclosure of material changes to the information required by paragraph (d) of this section in a manner reasonably calculated to inform security holders.

(2) If the Rule 13e-3 transaction is a tender offer or a request or invitation for tenders of equity securities which is subject to Regulation 14D [§§ 240.14d-1 to 240.14d-101] or Rule 13e-4 [§ 240.13e-4], the tender offer containing the information required by paragraph (e) of this section, and any material change with respect thereto, shall be published, sent or given in accordance with Regulation 14D or Rule 13e-4, respectively, to security holders of the class of securities being sought by the issuer or affiliate.

(g) *Exceptions.* This section shall not apply to:

(1) Any Rule 13e-3 transaction by or on behalf of a person which occurs within one year of the date of termination of a tender offer in which such person was the bidder and became an affiliate of the issuer as a result of such tender offer *provided* that the consideration offered to unaffiliated security holders in such Rule 13e-3 transaction is at least equal to the highest consideration offered during such tender offer and *provided further* that:

(i) If such tender offer was made for any or all securities of a class of the issuer;

(A) Such tender offer fully disclosed such person's intention to engage in a Rule 13e-3 transaction, the form and effect of such transaction and, to the extent known, the proposed terms thereof; and

(B) Such Rule 13e-3 transaction is substantially similar to that described in such tender offer; or

(ii) If such tender offer was made for less than all the securities of a class of the issuer:

(A) Such tender offer fully disclosed a plan of merger, a plan of liquidation or a similar binding agreement between such person and the issuer with respect to a Rule 13e-3 transaction; and

(B) Such Rule 13e-3 transaction occurs pursuant to the plan of merger, plan of liquidation or similar binding agreement disclosed in the bidder's tender offer.

(2) Any Rule 13e-3 transaction in which the security holders are offered or receive only an equity security *provided* That:

(i) such equity security has substantially the same rights as the equity security which is the subject of the Rule 13e-3 transaction including, but not limited to, voting, dividends, redemption and liquidation rights except that this requirement shall be deemed to be satisfied if unaffiliated security holders are offered common stock;

(ii) such equity security is registered pursuant to section 12 of the Act or reports are required to be filed by the issuer thereof pursuant to section 15(d) of the Act; and

(iii) if the security which is the subject of the Rule 13e-3 transaction was either listed on a national securities exchange or authorized to be quoted in an inter-dealer quotation system of a registered national securities association, such equity security is either listed on a national securities exchange or authorized to be quoted in an inter-dealer quotation system of a registered national securities association.

(3) [Removed and reserved.]

(4) Redemptions, calls or similar purchases of an equity security by an issuer pursuant to specific provisions set forth in the instrument(s) creating or governing that class of equity securities; or

(5) Any solicitation by an issuer with respect to a plan of reorganization under Chapter XI of the Bankruptcy Act, as amended, if made after the entry of an order approving such plan pursuant to section 1125(b) of that Act and after, or concurrently with, the transmittal of information concerning such plan as required by section 1125(b) of that Act.

(6) Any tender offer or business combination made in compliance with § 230.802 of this chapter, § 240.13e-4(h)(8) or § 240.14d-1(c) or any other kind of transaction that otherwise meets the conditions for reliance on the cross-border exemptions set forth in § 240.13e-4(h)(8), 240.14d-1(c) or 230.802 of this chapter except for the fact that it is not technically subject to those rules.

Instruction to § 240.13e-3(g)(6): To the extent applicable, the acquiror must comply with the conditions set forth in § 230.802 of this chapter, and §§ 240.13e-4(h)(8) and 14d-1(c). If the acquiror publishes or otherwise disseminates an informational document to the holders of the subject securities in connection with the transaction, the acquiror must furnish an English translation of that informational document, including any amendments thereto, to the Commission under cover of Form CB (§ 239.800 of this chapter) by the first business day after publication or dissemination. If the acquiror is a foreign entity, it must also file a Form F-X (§ 239.42 of this chapter) with the Commission at the same time as the submission of the Form CB to appoint an agent for service in the United States.

[As last amended in Release No. 33-8957, effective December 8, 2008, 73 F.R. 60050.]

[¶ 22,266] Tender Offers by Issuers

Reg. § 240.13e-4. (a) *Definitions.* Unless the context otherwise requires, all terms used in this section and in Schedule TO [§ 240.14d-100] shall have the same meaning as in the Act or elsewhere in the General Rules and Regulations thereunder. In addition, the following definitions shall apply:

(1) The term "issuer" means any issuer which has a class of equity security registered pursuant to section 12 of the Act, or which is required to file periodic reports pursuant to section 15(d) of the Act, or which is a closed-end investment company registered under the Investment Company Act of 1940.

(2) The term "issuer tender offer" refers to a tender offer for, or a request or invitation for tenders of, any class of equity security, made by the issuer of such class of equity security or by an affiliate of such issuer.

(3) As used in this section and in Schedule TO [§ 240.14d-100], the term "business day" means any day, other than Saturday, Sunday or a federal holiday, and shall consist of the time period from 12:01 a.m. through 12:00 midnight Eastern Time. In computing any time period under this Rule or Schedule TO, the date of the event that begins the running of such time period shall be included *except that* if such event occurs on other than a business day such period shall begin to run on and shall include the first business day thereafter.

(4) The term *commencement* means 12:01 a.m. on the date that the issuer or affiliate has first published, sent or given the means to tender to security holders. For purposes of this section, the means to tender includes the transmittal form or a statement regarding how the transmittal form may be obtained.

(5) The term "termination" means the date after which securities may not be tendered pursuant to an issuer tender offer.

(6) The term "security holders" means holders of record and beneficial owners of securities of the class of equity security which is the subject of an issuer tender offer.

(7) The term "security position listing" means, with respect to the securities of any issuer held by a registered clearing agency in the name of the clearing agency or its nominee, a list of those participants

in the clearing agency on whose behalf the clearing agency holds the issuer's securities and of the participants' respective positions in such securities as of a specified date.

(b) As soon as practicable on the date of commencement of the issuer tender offer, the issuer or affiliate making the issuer tender offer must comply with:

(1) The filing requirements of paragraph (c)(2) of this section;

(2) The disclosure requirements of paragraph (d)(1) of this section; and

(3) The dissemination requirements of paragraph (e) of this section.

(c) *Material required to be filed.* The issuer or affiliate making the issuer tender offer must file with the Commission:

(1) All written communications made by the issuer or affiliate relating to the issuer tender offer, from and including the first public announcement, as soon as practicable on the date of the communication;

(2) A Schedule TO (§ 240.14d-100), including all exhibits;

(3) An amendment to Schedule TO (§ 240.14d-100) reporting promptly any material changes in the information set forth in the schedule previously filed; and

(4) A final amendment to Schedule TO (§ 240.14d-100) reporting promptly the results of the issuer tender offer.

Instructions to § 240.13e-4(c):

1. Pre-commencement communications must be filed under cover of Schedule TO (§ 240.14d-100) and the box on the cover page of the schedule must be marked.

2. Any communications made in connection with an exchange offer registered under the Securities Act of 1933 need only be filed under § 230.425 of this chapter and will be deemed filed under this section.

3. Each pre-commencement written communication must include a prominent legend in clear, plain language advising security holders to read the tender offer statement when it is available because it contains important information. The legend also must advise investors that they can get the tender offer statement and other filed documents for free at the Commission's web site and explain which documents are free from the issuer.

4. See Sections 230.135, 230.165 and 230.166 of this chapter for pre-commencement communications made in connection with registered exchange offers.

5. "Public announcement" is any oral or written communication by the issuer, affiliate or any person authorized to act on their behalf that is reasonably designed to, or has the effect of, informing the public or security holders in general about the issuer tender offer.

(d) *Disclosure of tender offer information to security holders.*

(1) The issuer or affiliate making the issuer tender offer must disclose, in a manner prescribed by paragraph (e)(1) of this section, the following:

(i) The information required by Item 1 of Schedule TO (§ 240.14d-100) (summary term sheet); and

(ii) The information required by the remaining items of Schedule TO for issuer tender offers, except for Item 12 (exhibits), or a fair and adequate summary of the information.

(2) If there are any material changes in the information previously disclosed to security holders, the issuer or affiliate must disclose the changes promptly to security holders in a manner specified in paragraph (e)(3) of this section.

(3) If the issuer or affiliate disseminates the issuer tender offer by means of summary publication as described in paragraph (e)(1)(iii) of this section, the summary advertisement must not include a transmittal letter that would permit security holders to tender securities sought in the offer and must disclose at least the following information:

(i) The identity of the issuer or affiliate making the issuer tender offer;

(ii) The information required by § 229.1004(a)(1) and § 229.1006(a) of this chapter;

(iii) Instructions on how security holders can obtain promptly a copy of the statement required by paragraph (d)(1) of this section, at the issuer or affiliate's expense; and

(iv) A statement that the information contained in the statement required by paragraph (d)(1) of this section is incorporated by reference.

(e) *Dissemination of tender offers to security holders.* An issuer tender offer will be deemed to be published, sent or given to security holders if the issuer or affiliate making the issuer tender offer complies fully with one or more of the methods described in this section.

(1) For issuer tender offers in which the consideration offered consists solely of cash and/or securities exempt from registration under Section 3 of the Securities Act of 1933 (15 U.S.C. 77c):

(i) Dissemination of cash issuer tender offers by long-form publication: By making adequate publication of the information required by paragraph (d)(1) of this section in a newspaper or newspapers, on the date of commencement of the issuer tender offer.

(ii) Dissemination of any issuer tender offer by use of stockholder and other lists:

(A) By mailing or otherwise furnishing promptly a statement containing the information required by paragraph (d)(1) of this section to each security holder whose name appears on the most recent stockholder list of the issuer;

(B) By contacting each participant on the most recent security position listing of any clearing agency within the possession or access of the issuer or affiliate making the issuer tender offer, and making inquiry of each participant as to the approximate number of beneficial owners of the securities sought in the offer that are held by the participant;

(C) By furnishing to each participant a sufficient number of copies of the statement required by paragraph (d)(1) of this section for transmittal to the beneficial owners; and

(D) By agreeing to reimburse each participant promptly for its reasonable expenses incurred in forwarding the statement to beneficial owners.

(iii) Dissemination of certain cash issuer tender offers by summary publication:

(A) If the issuer tender offer is not subject to § 240.13e-3, by making adequate publication of a summary advertisement containing the information required by paragraph (d)(3) of this section in a newspaper or newspapers, on the date of commencement of the issuer tender offer; and

(B) By mailing or otherwise furnishing promptly the statement required by paragraph (d)(1) of this section and a transmittal letter to any security holder who requests a copy of the statement or transmittal letter.

Instruction to paragraph (e)(1): For purposes of paragraphs (e)(1)(i) and (e)(1)(iii) of this section, adequate publication of the issuer tender offer may require publication in a newspaper with a national circulation, a newspaper with metropolitan or regional circulation, or a combination of the two, depending upon the facts and circumstances involved.

(2) For tender offers in which the consideration consists solely or partially of securities registered under the Securities Act of 1933, a registration statement containing all of the required information, including pricing information, has been filed and a preliminary prospectus or a prospectus that meets the requirements of Section 10(a) of the Securities Act (15 U.S.C. 77j(a)), including a letter of transmittal, is delivered to security holders. However, for going-private transactions (as defined by § 240.13e-3) and roll-up transactions (as described by Item 901 of Regulation S-K (§ 229.901 of this chapter)), a registration statement registering the securities to be offered must have become effective and only a prospectus that meets the requirements of Section 10(a) of the Securities Act may be delivered to security holders on the date of commencement.

Instructions to paragraph (e)(2): 1. If the prospectus is being delivered by mail, mailing on the date of commencement is sufficient.

2. A preliminary prospectus used under this section may not omit information under § 230.430 or § 230.430A of this chapter.

3. If a preliminary prospectus is used under this section and the issuer must disseminate material changes, the tender offer must remain open for the period specified in paragraph (e)(3) of this section.

4. If a preliminary prospectus is used under this section, tenders may be requested in accordance with § 230.162(a) of this chapter.

(3) If a material change occurs in the information published, sent or given to security holders, the issuer or affiliate must disseminate promptly disclosure of the change in a manner reasonably calculated to inform security holders of the change. In a registered securities offer where the issuer or affiliate disseminates the preliminary prospectus as permitted by paragraph (e)(2) of this section, the offer must remain open from the date that material changes to the tender offer materials are disseminated to security holders, as follows:

(i) Five business days for a prospectus supplement containing a material change other than price or share levels;

(ii) Ten business days for a prospectus supplement containing a change in price, the amount of securities sought, the dealer's soliciting fee, or other similarly significant change;

(iii) Ten business days for a prospectus supplement included as part of a post-effective amendment; and

(iv) Twenty business days for a revised prospectus when the initial prospectus was materially deficient.

(f) *Manner of making tender offer.*

(1) The issuer tender offer, unless withdrawn, shall remain open until the expiration of:

(i) at least twenty business days from its commencement; and

(ii) At least ten business days from the date that notice of an increase or decrease in the percentage of the class of securities being sought or the consideration offered or the dealer's soliciting fee to be given is first published, sent or given to security holders.

Provided, however, That, for purposes of this paragraph, the acceptance for payment by the issuer or affiliate of an additional amount of securities not to exceed two percent of the class of securities that is the subject of the tender offer shall not be deemed to be an increase. For purposes of this paragraph, the percentage of a class of securities shall be calculated in accordance with section 14(d)(3) of the Act.

(2) The issuer or affiliate making the issuer tender offer shall permit securities tendered pursuant to the issuer tender offer to be withdrawn:

(i) At any time during the period such issuer tender offer remains open; and

(ii) If not yet accepted for payment, after the expiration of forty business days from the commencement of the issuer tender offer.

(3) If the issuer or affiliate makes a tender offer for less than all of the outstanding equity securities of a class, and if a greater number of securities is tendered pursuant thereto than the issuer or affiliate is bound or willing to take up and pay for, the securities taken up and paid for shall be taken up and paid for as nearly as may be pro rata, disregarding fractions, according to the number of securities tendered by each security holder during the period such offer remains open; *Provided, however,* That this provision shall not prohibit the issuer or affiliate making the issuer tender offer from:

(i) accepting all securities tendered by persons who own, beneficially or of record, an aggregate of not more than a specified number which is less than one hundred shares of such security and who tender all their securities, before prorating securities tendered by others; or

(ii) accepting by lot securities tendered by security holders who tender all securities held by them and who, when tendering their securities, elect to have either all or none or at least a minimum amount or none accepted, if the issuer or affiliate first accepts all securities tendered by security holders who do not so elect;

(4) In the event the issuer or affiliate making the issuer tender offer increases the consideration offered after the issuer tender offer has commenced, such issuer or affiliate shall pay such increased consideration to all security holders whose tendered securities are accepted for payment by such issuer or affiliate.

(5) The issuer or affiliate making the tender offer shall either pay the consideration offered, or return the tendered securities, promptly after the termination or withdrawal of the tender offer.

(6) Until the expiration of at least ten business days after the date of termination of the issuer tender offer, neither the issuer nor any affiliate shall make any purchases, otherwise than pursuant to the tender offer, of:

(i) any security which is the subject of the issuer tender offer, or any security of the same class and series, or any right to purchase any such securities; and

(ii) in the case of an issuer tender offer which is an exchange offer, any security being offered pursuant to such exchange offer, or any security of the same class and series, or any right to purchase any such security.

(7) The time periods for the minimum offering periods pursuant to this section shall be computed on a concurrent as opposed to a consecutive basis.

(8) No issuer or affiliate shall make a tender offer unless:

(i) The tender offer is open to all security holders of the class of securities subject to the tender offer; and

(ii) The consideration paid to any security holder for securities tendered in the tender offer is the highest consideration paid to any other security holder for securities tendered in the tender offer.

(9) Paragraph (f)(8)(i) of this section shall not:

(i) Affect dissemination under paragraph (e) of this section; or

(ii) Prohibit an issuer or affiliate from making a tender offer excluding all security holders in a state where the issuer or affiliate is prohibited from making the tender offer by administrative or judicial action pursuant to a state statute after a good faith effort by the issuer or affiliate to comply with such statute.

(10) Paragraph (f)(8)(ii) of this section shall not prohibit the offer of more than one type of consideration in a tender offer, provided that:

(i) Security holders are afforded equal right to elect among each of the types of consideration offered; and

(ii) The highest consideration of each type paid to any security holder is paid to any other security holder receiving that type of consideration.

(11) If the offer and sale of securities constituting consideration offered in an issuer tender offer is prohibited by the appropriate authority of a state after a good faith effort by the issuer or affiliate to register or qualify the offer and sale of such securities in such state:

(i) The issuer or affiliate may offer security holders in such state an alternative form of consideration; and

(ii) Paragraph (f)(10) of this section shall not operate to require the issuer or affiliate to offer or pay the alternative form of consideration to security holders in any other state.

(12)(i) Paragraph (f)(8)(ii) of this section shall not prohibit the negotiation, execution or amendment of an employment compensation, severance or other employee benefit arrangement, or payments made or to be made or benefits granted or to be granted according to such an arrangement, with respect to any security holder of the issuer, where the amount payable under the arrangement:

(A) Is being paid or granted as compensation for past services performed, future services to be performed, or future services to be refrained from performing, by the security holder (and matters incidental thereto); and

(B) Is not calculated based on the number of securities tendered or to be tendered in the tender offer by the security holder.

(ii) The provisions of paragraph (f)(12)(i) of this section shall be satisfied and, therefore, pursuant to this non-exclusive safe harbor, the negotiation, execution or amendment of an arrangement and any payments made or to be made or benefits granted or to be granted according to that arrangement shall not be prohibited by paragraph (f)(8)(ii) of this section, if the arrangement is approved as an employment compensation, severance or other employee benefit arrangement solely by independent directors as follows:

(A) The compensation committee or a committee of the board of directors that performs functions similar to a compensation committee of the issuer approves the arrangement, regardless of whether the issuer is a party to the arrangement, or, if an affiliate is a party to the arrangement, the compensation committee or a committee of the board of directors that performs functions similar to a compensation committee of the affiliate approves the arrangement; or

(B) If the issuer's or affiliate's board of directors, as applicable, does not have a compensation committee or a committee of the board of directors that performs functions similar to a compensation committee or if none of the members of the issuer's or affiliate's compensation committee or committee that performs functions similar to a compensation committee is independent, a special committee of the board of directors formed to consider and approve the arrangement approves the arrangement; or

(C) If the issuer or affiliate, as applicable, is a foreign private issuer, any or all members of the board of directors or any committee of the board of directors authorized to approve employment compensation, severance or other employee benefit arrangements under the laws or regulations of the home country approves the arrangement.

Instructions to paragraph (f)(12)(ii): For purposes of determining whether the members of the committee approving an arrangement in accordance with the provisions of paragraph (f)(12)(ii) of this section are independent, the following provisions shall apply:

1. If the issuer or affiliate, as applicable, is a listed issuer (as defined in §240.10A-3 of this chapter) whose securities are listed either on a national securities exchange registered pursuant to section 6(a) of the Exchange Act (15 U.S.C. 78f(a)) or in an inter-dealer quotation system of a national securities association registered pursuant to section 15A(a) of the Exchange Act (15 U.S.C. 78o-3(a)) that has independence requirements for compensation committee members that have been approved by the Commission (as those requirements may be modified or supplemented), apply the issuer's or affiliate's definition of independence that it uses for determining that the members of the compensation committee are independent in compliance with the listing standards applicable to compensation committee members of the listed issuer.

2. If the issuer or affiliate, as applicable, is not a listed issuer (as defined in §240.10A-3 of this chapter), apply the independence requirements for compensation committee members of a national securities exchange registered pursuant to section 6(a) of the Exchange Act (15 U.S.C. 78f(a)) or an inter-dealer quotation system of a national securities association registered pursuant to section 15A(a) of the Exchange Act (15 U.S.C. 78o-3(a)) that have been approved by the Commission (as those requirements may be modified or supplemented). Whatever definition the issuer or affiliate, as applicable, chooses, it must apply that definition consistently to all members of the committee approving the arrangement.

3. Notwithstanding Instructions 1 and 2 to paragraph (f)(12)(ii), if the issuer or affiliate, as applicable, is a closed-end investment company registered under the Investment Company Act of 1940, a director is considered to be independent if the director is not, other than in his or her capacity as a member of the board of directors or any board committee, an "interested person" of the investment company, as defined in section 2(a)(19) of the Investment Company Act of 1940 (15 U.S.C. 80a-2(a)(19)).

4. If the issuer or affiliate, as applicable, is a foreign private issuer, apply either the independence standards set forth in Instructions 1 and 2 to paragraph (f)(12)(ii) or the independence requirements of the laws, regulations, codes or standards of the home country of the issuer or affiliate, as applicable, for

members of the board of directors or the committee of the board of directors approving the arrangement.

5. A determination by the issuer's or affiliate's board of directors, as applicable, that the members of the board of directors or the committee of the board of directors, as applicable, approving an arrangement in accordance with the provisions of paragraph (f)(12)(ii) are independent in accordance with the provisions of this instruction to paragraph (f)(12)(ii) shall satisfy the independence requirements of paragraph (f)(12)(ii).

Instruction to paragraph (f)(12): The fact that the provisions of paragraph (f)(12) of this section extend only to employment compensation, severance and other employee benefit arrangements and not to other arrangements, such as commercial arrangements, does not raise any inference that a payment under any such other arrangement constitutes consideration paid for securities in a tender offer.

(13) *Electronic filings.* If the issuer or affiliate is an electronic filer, the minimum offering periods set forth in paragraph (f)(1) of this section shall be tolled for any period during which it fails to file in electronic format, absent a hardship exemption (§§ 232.201 and 232.202 of this chapter), the Schedule TO (§ 240.14d-100), the tender offer material specified in Item 1016(a)(1) of Regulation M-A (§ 229.1016(a)(1) of this chapter), and any amendments thereto. If such documents were filed in paper pursuant to a hardship exemption (see § 232.201 and § 232.202 of this chapter), the minimum offering periods shall be tolled for any period during which a required confirming electronic copy of such Schedule and tender offer material is delinquent.

(g) The requirements of section 13(e)(1) of the Act and Rule 13e-4 and Schedule TO (§ 240.14d-100) thereunder shall be deemed satisfied with respect to any issuer tender offer, including any exchange offer, where the issuer is incorporated or organized under the laws of Canada or any Canadian province or territory, is a foreign private issuer, and is not an investment company registered or required to be registered under the Investment Company Act of 1940, if less than 40 percent of the class of securities that is the subject of the tender offer is held by U.S. holders, and the tender offer is subject to, and the issuer complies with, the laws, regulations and policies of Canada and/or any of its provinces or territories governing the conduct of the offer (unless the issuer has received an exemption(s) from, and the issuer tender offer does not comply with, requirements that otherwise would be prescribed by this section), *provided that*:

(1) Where the consideration for an issuer tender offer subject to this paragraph consists solely of cash, the entire disclosure document or documents required to be furnished to holders of the class of securities to be acquired shall be filed with the Commission on Schedule 13E-4F (§ 240.13e-102) and disseminated to shareholders residing in the United States in accordance with such Canadian laws, regulations and policies; or

(2) Where the consideration for an issuer tender offer subject to this paragraph includes securities to be issued pursuant to the offer, any registration statement and/or prospectus relating thereto shall be filed with the Commission along with the Schedule 13E-4F referred to in paragraph (g)(1) of this section, and shall be disseminated, together with the home jurisdiction document(s) accompanying such Schedule, to shareholders of the issuer residing in the United States in accordance with such Canadian laws, regulations and policies.

NOTE: Notwithstanding the grant of an exemption from one or more of the applicable Canadian regulatory provisions imposing requirements that otherwise would be prescribed by this section, the issuer tender offer will be eligible to proceed in accordance with the requirements of this section if the Commission by order determines that the applicable Canadian regulatory provisions are adequate to protect the interest of investors.

(h) This section shall not apply to:

(1) Calls or redemptions of any security in accordance with the terms and conditions of its governing instruments;

(2) Offers to purchase securities evidenced by a scrip certificate, order form or similar document which represents a fractional interest in a share of stock or similar security;

(3) Offers to purchase securities pursuant to a statutory procedure for the purchase of dissenting security holders' securities;

(4) Any tender offer which is subject to section 14(d) of the Act;

(5) Offers to purchase from security holders who own an aggregate of not more than a specified number of shares that is less than one hundred: *Provided however,* That:

(i) the offer complies with paragraph (f)(8)(i) of this section with respect to security holders who own a number of shares equal to or less than the specified number of shares, except that an issuer can elect to exclude participants in a plan as that term is defined in § 242.100 of this chapter, or to exclude security holders who do not own their shares as of a specified date determined by the issuer; and

(ii) The offer complies with paragraph (f)(8)(ii) of this section or the consideration paid pursuant to the offer is determined on the basis of a uniformly applied formula based on the market price of the subject security;

(6) An issuer tender offer made solely to effect a rescission offer: *Provided, however,* That the offer is registered under the Securities Act of 1933 (15 U. S. C. 77a *et seq.*), and the consideration is equal to the price paid by each security holder, plus legal interest if the issuer elects to or is required to pay legal interest;

(7) Offers by closed-end management investment companies to repurchase equity securities pursuant to § 270.23c-3 of this chapter;

(8) *Cross-border tender offers (Tier I).* Any issuer tender offer (including any exchange offer) where the issuer is a foreign private issuer as defined in § 240.3b-4 if the following conditions are satisfied.

(i) Except in the case of an issuer tender offer that is commenced during the pendency of a tender offer made by a third party in reliance on § 240.14d-1(c), U.S. holders do not hold more than 10 percent of the subject class sought in the offer (as determined under Instructions 2 or 3 to paragraph (h)(8) and paragraph (i) of this section);

(ii) The issuer or affiliate must permit U.S. holders to participate in the offer on terms at least as favorable as those offered any other holder of the same class of securities that is the subject of the offer; however:

(A) *Registered exchange offers.* If the issuer or affiliate offers securities registered under the Securities Act of 1933 (15 U.S.C. 77a *et seq.*), the issuer or affiliate need not extend the offer to security holders in those states or jurisdictions that prohibit the offer or sale of the securities after the issuer or affiliate has made a good faith effort to register or qualify the offer and sale of securities in that state or jurisdiction, except that the issuer or affiliate must offer the same cash alternative to security holders in any such state or jurisdiction that it has offered to security holders in any other state or jurisdiction.

(B) *Exempt exchange offers.* If the issuer or affiliate offers securities exempt from registration under § 230.802 of this chapter, the issuer or affiliate need not extend the offer to security holders in those states or jurisdictions that require registration or qualification, except that the issuer or affiliate must offer the same cash alternative to security holders in any such state or jurisdiction that it has offered to security holders in any other state or jurisdiction.

(C) *Cash only consideration.* The issuer or affiliate may offer U.S. holders cash only consideration for the tender of the subject securities, notwithstanding the fact that the issuer or affiliate is offering security holders outside the United States a consideration that consists in whole or in part of securities of the issuer or affiliate, if the issuer or affiliate has a reasonable basis for believing that the amount of cash is substantially equivalent to the value of the consideration offered to non-U.S. holders, and either of the following conditions are satisfied:

(*1*) The offered security is a "margin security" within the meaning of Regulation T (12 CFR 220.2) and the issuer or affiliate undertakes to provide, upon the request of any U.S. holder or the Commission staff, the closing price and daily trading volume of the security on the principal trading market for the security as of the last trading day of each of the six months preceding the announcement of the offer and each of the trading days thereafter; or

(*2*) If the offered security is not a "margin security" within the meaning of Regulation T (12 CFR 220.2), the issuer or affiliate undertakes to provide, upon the request of any U.S. holder or the Commission staff, an opinion of an independent expert stating that the cash consideration offered to U.S. holders is substantially equivalent to the value of the consideration offered security holders outside the United States.

(D) *Disparate tax treatment.* If the issuer or affiliate offers "loan notes" solely to offer sellers tax advantages not available in the United States and these notes are neither listed on any organized securities market nor registered under the Securities Act of 1933 (15 U.S.C. 77a *et seq.*), the loan notes need not be offered to U.S. holders.

(iii) *Informational documents.* (A) If the issuer or affiliate publishes or otherwise disseminates an informational document to the holders of the securities in connection with the issuer tender offer (including any exchange offer), the issuer or affiliate must furnish that informational document, including any amendments thereto, in English, to the Commission on Form CB (§ 249.480 of this chapter) by the first business day after publication or dissemination. If the issuer or affiliate is a foreign company, it must also file a Form F-X (§ 239.42 of this chapter) with the Commission at the same time as the submission of Form CB to appoint an agent for service in the United States.

(B) The issuer or affiliate must disseminate any informational document to U.S. holders, including any amendments thereto, in English, on a comparable basis to that provided to security holders in the home jurisdiction.

(C) If the issuer or affiliate disseminates by publication in its home jurisdiction, the issuer or affiliate must publish the information in the United States in a manner reasonably calculated to inform U.S. holders of the offer.

(iv) An investment company registered or required to be registered under the Investment Company Act of 1940 (15 U.S.C. 80a-1 *et seq.*), other than a registered closed-end investment company, may not use this paragraph (h)(8); or

(9) Any other transaction or transactions, if the Commission, upon written request or upon its own motion, exempts such transaction or transactions, either unconditionally, or on specified terms and conditions, as not constituting a fraudulent, deceptive or manipulative act or practice comprehended within the purpose of this section.

(i) *Cross-border tender offers (Tier II)*. Any issuer tender offer (including any exchange offer) that meets the conditions in paragraph (i)(1) of this section shall be entitled to the exemptive relief specified in paragraph (i)(2) of this section, provided that such issuer tender offer complies with all the requirements of this section other than those for which an exemption has been specifically provided in paragraph (i)(2) of this section. In addition, any issuer tender offer (including any exchange offer) subject only to the requirements of section 14(e) of the Act and Regulation 14E (§§ 240.14e-1 through 240.14e-8) thereunder that meets the conditions in paragraph (i)(1) of this section also shall be entitled to the exemptive relief specified in paragraph (i)(2) of this section, to the extent needed under the requirements of Regulation 14E, so long as the tender offer complies with all requirements of Regulation 14E other than those for which an exemption has been specifically provided in paragraph (i)(2) of this section:

(1) *Conditions*. (i) The issuer is a foreign private issuer as defined in § 240.3b-4 and is not an investment company registered or required to be registered under the Investment Company Act of 1940 (15 U.S.C. 80a-1 *et seq.*), other than a registered closed-end investment company; and

(ii) Except in the case of an issuer tender offer commenced during the pendency of a tender offer made by a third party in reliance on § 240.14d-1(d), U.S. holders do not hold more than 40 percent of the class of securities sought in the offer (as determined in accordance with Instructions 2 or 3 to paragraphs (h)(8) and (i) of this section).

(2) *Exemptions*. The issuer tender offer shall comply with all requirements of this section other than the following:

(i) *Equal treatment - loan notes*. If the issuer or affiliate offers loan notes solely to offer sellers tax advantages not available in the United States and these notes are neither listed on any organized securities market nor registered under the Securities Act (15 U.S.C. 77a *et seq.*), the loan notes need not be offered to U.S. holders, notwithstanding paragraph (f)(8) and (h)(9) of this section.

(ii) *Equal treatment - separate U.S. and foreign offers*. Notwithstanding the provisions of paragraph (f)(8) of this section, an issuer or affiliate conducting an issuer tender offer meeting the conditions of paragraph (i)(1) of this section may separate the offer into multiple offers: one offer made to U.S. holders, which also may include all holders of American Depositary Shares representing interests in the subject securities, and one or more offers made to non-U.S. holders. The U.S. offer must be made on terms at least as favorable as those offered any other holder of the same class of securities that is the subject of the tender offers. U.S. holders may be included in the foreign offer(s) only where the laws of the jurisdiction governing such foreign offer(s) expressly preclude the exclusion of U.S. holders from the foreign offer(s) and where the offer materials distributed to U.S. holders fully and adequately disclose the risks of participating in the foreign offer(s).

(iii) *Notice of extensions*. Notice of extensions made in accordance with the requirements of the home jurisdiction law or practice will satisfy the requirements of § 240.14e-1(d).

(v) *Suspension of withdrawal rights during counting of tendered securities*. The issuer or affiliate may suspend withdrawal rights required under paragraph (f)(2) of this section at the end of the offer and during the period that securities tendered into the offer are being counted, provided that:

(A) The issuer or affiliate has provided an offer period, including withdrawal rights, for a period of at least 20 U.S. business days;

(B) At the time withdrawal rights are suspended, all offer conditions have been satisfied or waived, except to the extent that the issuer or affiliate is in the process of determining whether a minimum acceptance condition included in the terms of the offer has been satisfied by counting tendered securities; and

(C) Withdrawal rights are suspended only during the counting process and are reinstated immediately thereafter, except to the extent that they are terminated through the acceptance of tendered securities.

(vi) *Early termination of an initial offering period.* An issuer or affiliate conducting an issuer tender offer may terminate an initial offering period, including a voluntary extension of that period, if at the time the initial offering period and withdrawal rights terminate, the following conditions are met:

(A) The initial offering period has been open for at least 20 U.S. business days;

(B) The issuer or affiliate has adequately discussed the possibility of and the impact of the early termination in the original offer materials;

(C) The issuer or affiliate provides a subsequent offering period after the termination of the initial offering period;

(D) All offer conditions are satisfied as of the time when the initial offering period ends; and

(E) The issuer or affiliate does not terminate the initial offering period or any extension of that period during any mandatory extension required under U.S. tender offer rules.

Instructions to paragraph (h) (8) and (i) of this section:

1. Home jurisdiction means both the jurisdiction of the issuer's incorporation, organization or chartering and the principal foreign market where the issuer's securities are listed or quoted.

2. U.S. holder means any security holder resident in the United States. To determine the percentage of outstanding securities held by U.S. holders:

i. Calculate the U.S. ownership as of a date no more than 60 days before and no more than 30 days after the public announcement of the tender offer. If you are unable to calculate as of a date within these time frames, the calculation may be made as of the most recent practicable date before public announcement, but in no event earlier than 120 days before announcement;

ii. Include securities underlying American Depositary Shares convertible or exchangeable into the securities that are the subject of the tender offer when calculating the number of subject securities outstanding, as well as the number held by U.S. holders. Exclude from the calculations other types of securities that are convertible or exchangeable into the securities that are the subject of the tender offer, such as warrants, options and convertible securities;

iii. Use the method of calculating record ownership in § 240.12g3-2(a), except that your inquiry as to the amount of securities represented by accounts of customers resident in the United States may be limited to brokers, dealers, banks and other nominees located in the United States, your jurisdiction of incorporation, and the jurisdiction that is the primary trading market for the subject securities, if different than your jurisdiction of incorporation;

iv. If, after reasonable inquiry, you are unable to obtain information about the amount of securities represented by accounts of customers resident in the United States, you may assume, for purposes of this definition, that the customers are residents of the jurisdiction in which the nominee has its principal place of business; and

v. Count securities as beneficially owned by residents of the United States as reported on reports of beneficial ownership that are provided to you or publicly filed and based on information otherwise provided to you.

3. If you are unable to conduct the analysis of U.S. ownership set forth in Instruction 2 above, U.S. holders will be presumed to hold 10 percent or less of the outstanding subject securities (40 percent for Tier II) so long as there is a primary trading market outside the United States, as defined in Rule 12h-6(f)(5), unless:

i. Average daily trading volume of the subject securities in the United States for a recent twelve-month period ending on a date no more than 60 days before the public announcement of the tender offer exceeds 10 percent (or 40 percent) of the average daily trading volume of that class of securities on a worldwide basis for the same period; or

ii. The most recent annual report or annual information filed or submitted by the issuer with securities regulators of the home jurisdiction or with the Commission or any jurisdiction in which the subject securities trade before the public announcement of the offer indicates that U.S. holders hold more than 10 percent (or 40 percent) of the outstanding subject class of securities; or

iii. You know or have reason to know, before the public announcement of the offer, that the level of U.S. ownership of the subject securities exceeds 10 percent (or 40 percent) of such securities. As an example, you are deemed to know information about U.S. ownership of the subject class of securities that is publicly available and that appears in any filing with the Commission or any regulatory body in the home jurisdiction and, if different, the non-U.S. jurisdiction in which the primary trading market for the subject class of securities is located. You are also deemed to know information obtained or readily available from any other source that is reasonably reliable, including from persons you have retained to advise you about the transaction, as well as from third-party information providers. These examples are not intended to be exclusive.

4. *United States* means the United States of America, its territories and possessions, any State of the United States, and the District of Columbia.

5. The exemptions provided by paragraphs (h)(8) and (i) of this section are not available for any securities transaction or series of transactions that technically complies with paragraph (h)(8) and (i) of this section but are part of a plan or scheme to evade the provisions of this section.

(j)(1) It shall be a fraudulent, deceptive or manipulative act or practice, in connection with an issuer tender offer, for an issuer or an affiliate of such issuer, in connection with an issuer tender offer:

(i) to employ any device, scheme or artifice to defraud any person;

(ii) to make any untrue statement of a material fact or to omit to state a material fact necessary in order to make the statements made, in the light of the circumstances under which they were made, not misleading; or

(iii) to engage in any act, practice or course of business which operates or would operate as a fraud or deceit upon any person.

(2) As a means reasonably designed to prevent fraudulent, deceptive or manipulative acts or practices in connection with any issuer tender offer, it shall be unlawful for an issuer or an affiliate of such issuer to make an issuer tender offer unless:

(i) such issuer or affiliate complies with the requirements of paragraphs (b), (c), (d), (e) and (f) of this section; and

(ii) the issuer tender offer is not in violation of paragraph (j)(1) of this section.

[As last amended in Release No. 33-8957, effective December 8, 2008, 73 F.R. 60050.]

[¶ 22,271] Schedule 13E-3

§ 240.13e-100. Schedule 13E-3, Transaction Statement under Section 13(e) of the Securities Exchange Act of 1934 and Rule 13e-3 (§ 240.13e-3) thereunder.

SECURITIES AND EXCHANGE COMMISSION

Washington, D.C. 20549

Rule 13e-3 Transaction Statement under Section 13(e) of the Securities Exchange Act of 1934

[Amendment No. . . . .]

. . . .

(Name of the Issuer)

. . . .

(Name of Person(s) Filing Statement)

. . . .

(Title of Class of Securities)

. . . .

(CUSIP Number of Class of Securities)

. . . .

(Name, Address and Telephone Numbers of Person Authorized to Receive Notices and Communications on Behalf of Persons Filing Statement)

This statement is filed in connection with (check the appropriate box):

a. [ ] The filing of solicitation materials or an information statement subject to Regulation 14A (§§ 240.14a-1 through 240.14b-2), Regulation 14C (§§ 240.14c-1 through 240.14c-101) or Rule 13e-3(c) (§ 240.13e-3(c)) under the Securities Exchange Act of 1934 ("the Act").

b. [ ] The filing of a registration statement under the Securities Act of 1933.

c. [ ] A tender offer.

d. [ ] None of the above.

Check the following box if the soliciting materials or information statement referred to in checking box (a) are preliminary copies: [ ]

Check the following box if the filing is a final amendment reporting the results of the transaction: [ ]

Calculation of Filing Fee

Transaction valuation*	Amount of filing fee

*Set forth the amount on which the filing fee is calculated and state how it was determined.

[ ] Check the box if any part of the fee is offset as provided by § 240.0-11(a)(2) and identify the filing with which the offsetting fee was previously paid. Identify the previous filing by registration statement number, or the Form or Schedule and the date of its filing.

Amount Previously Paid:⎯⎯⎯⎯⎯⎯

Form or Registration No.:⎯⎯⎯⎯⎯⎯

Filing Party:⎯⎯⎯⎯⎯⎯

Date Filed:⎯⎯⎯⎯⎯⎯

General Instructions:

A. File eight copies of the statement, including all exhibits, with the Commission if paper filing is permitted.

B. This filing must be accompanied by a fee payable to the Commission as required by § 240.0-11(b)

C. If the statement is filed by a general or limited partnership, syndicate or other group, the information called for by Items 3, 5, 6, 10 and 11 must be given with respect to: (i) each partner of the general partnership; (ii) each partner who is, or functions as, a general partner of the limited partnership; (iii) each member of the syndicate or group; and (iv) each person controlling the partner or member. If the statement is filed by a corporation or if a person referred to in (i), (ii), (iii) or (iv) of this Instruction is a corporation, the information called for by the items specified above must be given with respect to: (a) each executive officer and director of the corporation; (b) each person controlling the corporation; and (c) each executive officer and director of any corporation or other person ultimately in control of the corporation.

D. Depending on the type of Rule 13e-3 transaction (§ 240.13e-3(a)(3)), this statement must be filed with the Commission:

1. At the same time as filing preliminary or definitive soliciting materials or an information statement under Regulations 14A or 14C of the Act;

2. At the same time as filing a registration statement under the Securities Act of 1933;

3. As soon as practicable on the date a tender offer is first published, sent or given to security holders; or

4. At least 30 days before any purchase of securities of the class of securities subject to the Rule 13e-3 transaction, if the transaction does not involve a solicitation, an information statement, the registration of securities or a tender offer, as described in paragraphs 1, 2 or 3 of this Instruction; and

5. If the Rule 13e-3 transaction involves a series of transactions, the issuer or affiliate must file this statement at the time indicated in paragraphs 1 through 4 of this Instruction for the first transaction and must amend the schedule promptly with respect to each subsequent transaction.

E. If an item is inapplicable or the answer is in the negative, so state. The statement published, sent or given to security holders may omit negative and not applicable responses, except that responses to Items 7, 8 and 9 of this schedule must be provided in full. If the schedule includes any information that is not published, sent or given to security holders, provide that information or specifically incorporate it by reference under the appropriate item number and heading in the schedule. Do not recite the text of disclosure requirements in the schedule or any document published, sent or given to security holders. Indicate clearly the coverage of the requirements without referring to the text of the items.

F. Information contained in exhibits to the statement may be incorporated by reference in answer or partial answer to any item unless it would render the answer misleading, incomplete, unclear or confusing. A copy of any information that is incorporated by reference or a copy of the pertinent pages of a document containing the information must be submitted with this statement as an exhibit, unless it was previously filed with the Commission electronically on EDGAR. If an exhibit contains information responding to more than one item in the schedule, all information in that exhibit may be incorporated by reference once in response to the several items in the schedule for which it provides an answer. Information incorporated by reference is deemed filed with the Commission for all purposes of the Act.

G. If the Rule 13e-3 transaction also involves a transaction subject to Regulation 14A (§§ 240.14a-1 through 240.14b-2) or 14C (§§ 240.14c-1 through 240.14c-101) of the Act, the registration of securities under the Securities Act of 1933 and the General Rules and Regulations of that Act, or a tender offer subject to Regulation 14D (§§ 240.14d-1 through 240.14d-101) or § 240.13e-4, this statement must incorporate by reference the information contained in the proxy, information, registration or tender offer statement in answer to the items of this statement.

H. The information required by the items of this statement is intended to be in addition to any disclosure requirements of any other form or schedule that may be filed with the Commission in connection with the Rule 13e-3 transaction. If those forms or schedules require less information on any topic than this statement, the requirements of this statement control.

I. If the Rule 13e-3 transaction involves a tender offer, then a combined statement on Schedules 13E-3 and TO may be filed with the Commission under cover of Schedule TO (§ 240.14d-100). See Instruction J of Schedule TO (§ 240.14d-100).

J. Amendments disclosing a material change in the information set forth in this statement may omit any information previously disclosed in this statement.

Item 1. *Summary Term Sheet*

Furnish the information required by Item 1001 of Regulation M-A (§ 229.1001 of this chapter) unless information is disclosed to security holders in a prospectus that meets the requirements of § 230.421(d) of this chapter.

Item 2. *Subject Company Information*

Furnish the information required by Item 1002 of Regulation M-A (§ 229.1002 of this chapter).

Item 3. *Identity and Background of Filing Person*

Furnish the information required by Item 1003(a) through (c) of Regulation M-A (§ 229.1003 of this chapter).

Item 4. *Terms of the Transaction*

Furnish the information required by Item 1004(a) and (c) through (f) of Regulation M-A (§ 229.1004 of this chapter).

Item 5. *Past Contacts, Transactions, Negotiations and Agreements*

Furnish the information required by Item 1005(a) through (c) and (e) of Regulation M-A (§ 229.1005 of this chapter).

Item 6. *Purposes of the Transaction and Plans or Proposals*

Furnish the information required by Item 1006(b) and (c)(1) through (8) of Regulation M-A (§ 229.1006 of this chapter).

Instruction to Item 6:

In providing the information specified in Item 1006(c) for this item, discuss any activities or transactions that would occur after the Rule 13e-3 transaction.

Item 7. *Purposes, Alternatives, Reasons and Effects*

Furnish the information required by Item 1013 of Regulation M-A (§ 229.1013 of this chapter).

Item 8. *Fairness of the Transaction*

Furnish the information required by Item 1014 of Regulation M-A (§ 229.1014 of this chapter).

Item 9. *Reports, Opinions, Appraisals and Negotiations*

Furnish the information required by Item 1015 of Regulation M-A (§ 229.1015 of this chapter).

Item 10. *Source and Amounts of Funds or Other Consideration*

Furnish the information required by Item 1007 of Regulation M-A (§ 229.1007 of this chapter).

Item 11. *Interest in Securities of the Subject Company*

Furnish the information required by Item 1008 of Regulation M-A (§ 229.1008 of this chapter).

Item 12. *The Solicitation or Recommendation*

Furnish the information required by Item 1012(d) and (e) of Regulation M-A (§ 229.1012 of this chapter).

Item 13. *Financial Statements*

Furnish the information required by Item 1010(a) through (b) of Regulation M-A (§ 229.1010 of this chapter) for the issuer of the subject class of securities.

Instructions to Item 13:

1. The disclosure materials disseminated to security holders may contain the summarized financial information required by Item 1010(c) of Regulation M-A (§ 229.1010 of this chapter) instead of the financial information required by Item 1010(a) and (b). In that case, the financial information required

by Item 1010(a) and (b) of Regulation M-A must be disclosed directly or incorporated by reference in the statement. If summarized financial information is disseminated to security holders, include appropriate instructions on how more complete financial information can be obtained. If the summarized financial information is prepared on the basis of a comprehensive body of accounting principles other than U.S. GAAP, the summarized financial information must be accompanied by a reconciliation as described in Instruction 2.

2. If the financial statements required by this Item are prepared on the basis of a comprehensive body of accounting principles other than U.S. GAAP, provide a reconciliation to U.S. GAAP in accordance with Item 17 of Form 20-F (§ 249.220f of this chapter).

3. The filing person may incorporate by reference financial statements contained in any document filed with the Commission, solely for the purposes of this schedule, if: (a) the financial statements substantially meet the requirements of this Item; (b) an express statement is made that the financial statements are incorporated by reference; (c) the matter incorporated by reference is clearly identified by page, paragraph, caption or otherwise; and (d) if the matter incorporated by reference is not filed with this Schedule, an indication is made where the information may be inspected and copies obtained. Financial statements that are required to be presented in comparative form for two or more fiscal years or periods may not be incorporated by reference unless the material incorporated by reference includes the entire period for which the comparative data is required to be given. *See* General Instruction F to this Schedule.

Item 14. *Persons/Assets, Retained, Employed, Compensated or Used*

Furnish the information required by Item 1009 of Regulation M-A (§ 229.1009 of this chapter).

Item 15. *Additional Information*

Furnish the information required by Item 1011(b) of Regulation M-A (§ 229.1011 of this chapter).

Item 16. *Exhibits*

File as an exhibit to the Schedule all documents specified in Item 1016(a) through (d), (f) and (g) of Regulation M-A (§ 229.1016 of this chapter).

Signature. After due inquiry and to the best of my knowledge and belief, I certify that the information set forth in this statement is true, complete and correct.

_____
(Signature)

_____
(Name and title)

_____
(Date)

Instruction to Signature:

The statement must be signed by the filing person or that person's authorized representative. If the statement is signed on behalf of a person by an authorized representative (other than an executive officer of a corporation or general partner of a partnership), evidence of the representative's authority to sign on behalf of the person must be filed with the statement. The name and any title of each person who signs the statement must be typed or printed beneath the signature. See § 240.12b-11 with respect to signature requirements.

[As last amended in Release No. 33-7760), effective January 24, 2000, 64 F.R. 61408.]

SCHEDULE 13E-4F

[¶ 22,297] Schedule 13E-4F

Reg. § 240.13e-102. Tender offer statement pursuant to section 13(e)(1) of the Securities Exchange Act of 1934 and § 240.13e-4 thereunder.

U.S. Securities and Exchange Commission Washington, D.C. 20549

Schedule 13E-4F

ISSUER TENDER OFFER STATEMENT PURSUANT TO SECTION 13(E)(1) OF THE SECURITIES EXCHANGE ACT OF 1934

(Amendment No. ___)

. . . .
(Exact number of Issuer as specified in its charter)

. . . .
(Translation of Issuer's Name into English (if applicable)

. . . .
(Jurisdiction of Issuer's Incorporation or Organization)

. . . .
(Name(s) of Person(s) Filing Statement)

. . . .

(Title of Class of Securities)   (CUSIP Number of Class of Securities) (if applicable)

. . . .
(Name, address (including zip code) and telephone number (including area code) of person authorized to receive notices and communications on behalf of the person(s) filing statement)

. . . .
(Date tender offer first published, sent or given to securityholders)

CALCULATION OF FILING FEE*

Transaction Valuation	Amount of Filing Fee

* Set forth the amount on which the filing fee is calculated and state how it was determined. See General Instruction II.C. for rules governing the calculation of the filing fee.

[] Check box if any part of the fee is offset as provided by Rule 0-11(a)(2) and identify the filing with which the offsetting fee was previously paid. Identify the previous filing by registration statement number, or the Form or Schedule and the date of its filing.

Amount Previously Paid: . . . . Registration No. . . . .

Filing Party: . . . .

Form: . . . . Date Filed: . . . .

GENERAL INSTRUCTIONS

I. Eligibility Requirements for Use of Schedule 13E-4F

A. Schedule 13E-4F may be used by any foreign private issuer if: (1) the issuer is incorporated or organized under the laws of Canada or any Canadian province or territory; (2) the issuer is making a cash tender or exchange offer for the issuer's own securities; and (3) less than 40 percent of the class of such issuer's securities outstanding that is the subject of the tender offer is held by U.S holders. The calculation of securities held by U.S. holders shall be made as of the end of the issuer's last quarter or, if such quarter terminated within 60 days of the filing date, as of the end of the issuer's preceding quarter.

Instructions

1. For purposes of this Schedule, "foreign private issuer" shall be construed in accordance with Rule 405 under the Securities Act.

2. For purposes of this Schedule, the term "U.S. holder" shall mean any person who address appears on the records of the issuer, any voting trustee, any depositary, any share transfer agent or any person acting in a similar capacity on behalf of the issuer as being located in the United States.

3. If this Schedule is filed during the pendency of one or more ongoing cash tender or exchange offers for securities of the class subject to this offer that was commenced or was eligible to be commenced on Schedule 14D-1F and/or Form F-8 or Form F-80, the date for calculation of U.S. ownership for purposes of this Schedule shall be the same as that date used by the initial bidder or issuer.

4. For purposes of this Schedule, the class of subject securities shall not include any securities that may be converted into or are exchangeable for the subject securities.

B. Any issuer using this Schedule must extend the cash tender or exchange offer to U.S. holders of the class of securities subject to the offer upon terms and conditions not less favorable than those extended to any other holder of the same class of such securities, and must comply with the requirements of any Canadian federal, provincial and/or territorial law, regulation or policy relating to the terms and conditions of the offer.

C. This Schedule shall not be used if the issuer is an investment company registered or required to be registered under the Investment Company Act of 1940.

II. Filing Instructions and Fees

A.(1) The issuer must file this Schedule and any amendment to the Schedule (see Part I, Item 1.(b)), including all exhibits and other documents filed as part of the Schedule or amendment, in electronic format via the Commission's Electronic Data Gathering, Analysis, and Retrieval (EDGAR) system in accordance with the EDGAR rules set forth in Regulation S-T (17 CFR Part 232). For assistance with technical questions about EDGAR or to request an access code, call the EDGAR Filer Support Office at (202) 551-8900. For assistance with the EDGAR rules, call the Office of EDGAR and Information Analysis at (202) 551-3610.

(2) If filing the Schedule in paper under a hardship exemption in or 232.202 of Regulation S-T, or as otherwise permitted, the issuer must file with the Commission at its principal office five copies of the complete Schedule and any amendment, including exhibits and all other documents filed as a part of the Schedule or amendment. The issuer must bind, staple or otherwise compile each copy in one or more parts without stiff covers. The issuer must further bind the Schedule or amendment on the side or stitching margin in a manner that leaves the reading matter legible. The issuer must provide three additional copies of the Schedule or amendment without exhibits to the Commission.

B. An electronic filer must provide the signatures required for the Schedule or amendment in accordance with of Regulation S-T. An issuer filing in paper must have the original and at least one copy of the Schedule and any amendment signed in accordance with Exchange Act Rule 12b-11(d) by the persons whose signatures are required for this Schedule or amendment. The issuer must also conform the unsigned copies.

C. At the time of filing this Schedule with the Commission, the issuer shall pay to the Commission in accordance with Rule 0-11 of the Exchange Act, a fee in U.S. dollars in the amount prescribed by Section 13(e)(3) of the Exchange Act. See also Rule 0-9 of the Exchange Act.

(1) The value of the securities to be acquired solely for cash shall be the amount of cash to be paid for them, calculated into U.S. dollars.

(2) The value of the securities to be acquired with securities or other non-cash consideration, whether or not in combination with a cash payment for the same securities, shall be based on the market value of the securities to be acquired by the issuer as established in accordance with paragraph (3) of this section.

(3) When the fee is based upon the market value of the securities, such market value shall be established by either the average of the high and low prices reported on the consolidated reporting system (for exchange-traded securities and last sale reported for over-the-counter securities) or the average of the bid and asked price (for other over-the-counter securities) as of a specified date within 5 business days prior to the date of filing the Schedule. If there is no market for the securities to be acquired by the issuer, the value shall be based upon the book value of such securities computed as of the latest practicable date prior to the date of filing of the Schedule, unless the issuer of the securities is in bankruptcy or receivership or has an accumulated capital deficit, in which case one-third of the principal amount, par value or stated value of such securities shall be used.

D. If at any time after the initial payment of the fee the aggregate consideration offered is increased, an additional filing fee based upon such increase shall be paid with the required amended filing.

E. The issuer must file the Schedule or amendment in electronic format in the English language in accordance with of Regulation S-T. The issuer may file part of the Schedule or amendment, or exhibit or other attachment to the Schedule or amendment, in both French and English if the issuer included the French text to comply with the requirements of the Canadian securities administrator or other Canadian authority and, for an electronic filing, if the filing is an HTML document, as defined in of Regulation S-T. For both an electronic filing and a paper filing, the issuer may provide an English translation or English summary of a foreign language document as an exhibit or other attachment to the Schedule or amendment as permitted by the rules of the applicable Canadian securities administrator.

F. A paper filer must number sequentially the signed original of the Schedule or amendment (in addition to any internal numbering that otherwise may be present) by handwritten, typed, printed or other legible form of notation from the first page through the last page of the Schedule or amendment, including any exhibits or attachments. A paper filer must disclose the total number of pages on the first page of the sequentially numbered Schedule or amendment.

III. Compliance with the Exchange Act

A. Pursuant to Rule 13e-4(g) under the Exchange Act, the issuer shall be deemed to comply with the requirements of Section 13(e)(1) of the Exchange Act and Rule 13e-4 and Schedule TO thereunder in connection with a cash tender or exchange offer for securities that may be made pursuant to this Schedule, *provided that*, if an exemption has been granted from the requirements of Canadian federal, provincial and/or territorial laws, regulations or policies, and the tender offer does not comply with requirements that otherwise would be prescribed by Rule 13e-4, the issuer (absent an order from the Commission) shall comply with the provisions of Section 13(e)(1) of the Exchange Act and Rule 13e-4 and Schedule TO thereunder.

B. Any cash tender or exchange offer made pursuant to this Schedule is not exempt from the antifraud provisions of Section 10(b) of the Exchange Act and Rule 10b-5 thereunder, Section 13(e)(1) of the Exchange Act and Rule 13e-4(b)(1) thereunder, and Section 14(e) of the Exchange Act and Rule 14e-3 thereunder, and this Schedule shall be deemed "filed" for purposes of Section 18 of the Exchange Act.

C. The issuer's attention is directed to Regulation M (§ § 242.100 through 242.105 of this chapter), in the case of an issuer exchange offer, and to Rule 14e-5 under the Exchange Act (§ 240.14e-5), in the case of an issuer cash tender offer or issuer exchange offer. [*See* Exchange Act Release No. 29355 (June 12, 1991) containing an exemption from Rule 10b-13, the predecessor to Rule 14e5.]

PART I INFORMATION REQUIRED TO BE SENT TO SHAREHOLDERS

Item 1. Home Jurisdiction Documents

(a) This Schedule shall be accompanied by the entire disclosure document or documents required to be delivered to holders of securities to be acquired by the issuer in the proposed transaction pursuant to the laws, regulations or policies of the Canadian jurisdiction in which the issuer is incorporated or organized, and any other Canadian federal, provincial and/or territorial law, regulation or policy relating to the terms and conditions of the offer. The Schedule need not include any documents incorporated by reference into such disclosure document(s) and not distributed to offerees pursuant to any such law, regulation or policy.

(b) Any amendment made by the issuer to a home jurisdiction document or documents shall be filed with the Commission under cover of this Schedule, which must indicate on the cover page the number of the amendment.

(c) In an exchange offer where securities of the issuer have been or are to be offered or cancelled in the transaction, such securities shall be registered on forms promulgated by the Commission under the Securities Act of 1933 including, where available, the Commission's Form F-8 or F-80 providing for inclusion in that registration statement of the home jurisdiction prospectus.

Item 2. Informational Legends

The following legends, to the extent applicable, shall appear on the outside front cover page of the home jurisdiction document(s) in bold-face roman type at least as high as ten-point modern type and at least two-points leaded:

"This tender offer is made by a foreign issuer for its own securities, and while the offer is subject to disclosure requirements of the country in which the issuer is incorporated or organized, investors should be aware that these requirements are different from those of the United States. Financial statements included herein, if any, have been prepared in accordance with foreign generally accepted accounting principles and thus may not be comparable to financial statements of United States companies.

"The enforcement by investors of civil liabilities under the federal securities laws may be affected adversely by the fact that the issuer is located in a foreign country, and that some or all of its officers and directors are residents of a foreign country.

"Investors should be aware that the issuer or its affiliates, directly or indirectly, may bid for or make purchases of the securities of the issuer subject to the offer, or of its related securities, during the period of the issuer tender offer, as permitted by applicable Canadian laws or provincial laws or regulations."

Note to Item 2. If the home jurisdiction document(s) are delivered through an electronic medium, the issuer may satisfy the legibility requirements for the required legends relating to type size and fonts by presenting the legend in any manner reasonably calculated to draw security holder attention to it.

PART II INFORMATION NOT REQUIRED TO BE SENT TO SHAREHOLDERS

The exhibits specified below shall be filed as part of the Schedule, but are not required to be sent to shareholders unless so required pursuant to the laws, regulations or policies of Canada and/or any of its provinces or territories. Exhibits shall be lettered or numbered appropriately for convenient reference.

(1) File any reports or information that, in accordance with the requirements of the home jurisdiction(s), must be made publicly available by the issuer in connection with the transaction, but need not be disseminated to shareholders.

(2) File copies of any documents incorporated by reference into the home jurisdiction document(s).

(3) If any name is signed to the Schedule pursuant to power of attorney, manually signed copies of any such power of attorney shall be filed. If the name of any officer signing on behalf of the issuer is signed pursuant to a power of attorney, certified copies of a resolution of the issuer's board of directors authorizing such signature also shall be filed.

PART III UNDERTAKINGS AND CONSENT TO SERVICE OF PROCESS

1. Undertakings

The Schedule shall set forth the following undertakings of the issue:

(a) The issuer undertakes to make available, in person or by telephone, representatives to respond to inquiries made by the Commission staff, and to furnish promptly, when requested to do so by the Commission staff, information relating to this Schedule or to transactions in said securities.

(b) The issuer also undertakes to disclose in the United States, on the same basis as it is required to make such disclosure pursuant to applicable Canadian federal and/or provincial or territorial laws, regulations or policies, or otherwise discloses, information regarding purchases of the issuer's securities in connection with the cash tender or exchange offer covered by this Schedule. Such information shall be set forth in amendments to this Schedule.

2. Consent to Service of Process

(a) At the time of filing this Schedule, the issuer shall file with the Commission a written irrevocable consent and power of attorney on Form F-X.

(b) Any change to the name or address of a registrant's agent for service shall be communicated promptly to the Commission by amendment to Form F-X referencing the file number of the registrant.

PART IV SIGNATURES

A. The Schedule shall be signed by each person on whose behalf the Schedule is filed or its authorized representative. If the Schedule is signed on behalf of a person by his authorized representative (other than an executive officer or general partner of the company), evidence of the representative's authority shall be filed with the Schedule.

B. The name of each person who signs the Schedule shall be typed or printed beneath his signature.

C. By signing this Schedule, the person(s) filing the Schedule consents without power of revocation that any administrative subpoena may be served, or any administrative proceeding, civil suit or civil action where the cause of action arises out of or relates to or concerns any offering made or purported to be made in connection with the filing on Schedule 13E-4F or any purchases or sales of any securities in connection therewith, may be commenced against it in any administrative tribunal or in any appropriate court in any place subject to the jurisdiction of any state or of the United States by service of said subpoena or process upon the registrant's designated agent.

After due inquiry and to the best of my knowledge and belief, I certify that the information set forth in this statement is true, complete and correct.

(Signature) . . . .

(Name and Title) . . . .

(Date) . . . .

[As last amended in Release No. 34-55146A, effective April 1, 2008, 73 F.R. 17809 (technical correction).]

[¶ 22,301] Reporting by Institutional Investment Managers of Information with Respect to Accounts Over Which They Exercise Investment Discretion

Reg. §240.13f-1. (a)(1) Every institutional investment manager which exercises investment discretion with respect to accounts holding section 13(f) securities, as defined in paragraph (c) of this section, having an aggregate fair market value on the last trading day of any month of any calendar year of at least $100,000,000 shall file a report on Form 13F [§249.325 of this Chapter] with the Commission within 45 days after the last day of such calendar year and within 45 days after the last day of each of the first three calendar quarters of the subsequent calendar year.

(2) An amendment to a Form 13F (§249.325 of this chapter) report, other than one reporting only holdings that were not previously reported in a public filing for the same period, must be set forth the complete text of the Form 13F. Amendments must be numbered sequentially.

(b) For the purposes of this rule, "investment discretion" has the meaning set forth in section 3(a)(35) of the Act [15 U.S.C. 78c(a)(35)]. An institutional investment manager shall also be deemed to exercise "investment discretion" with respect to all accounts over which any person under its control exercises investment discretion.

(c) For purposes of this rule "section 13(f) securities" shall mean equity securities of a class described in section 13(d)(1) of the Act that are admitted to trading on a national securities exchange or quoted on the automated quotation system of a registered securities association. In determining what classes of securities are section 13(f) securities, an institutional investment manager may rely on the most recent list of such securities published by the Commission pursuant to section 13(f)(3) of the Act [15 U.S.C. 78m(f)(3)]. Only securities of a class on such list shall be counted in determining whether an institutional investment manager must file a report under this rule [240.13f-1(a)] and only those securities shall be reported in such report. Where a person controls the issuer of a class of equity securities which are "section 13(f) securities" as defined in this rule, those securities shall not be deemed to be "section 13(f) securities" with respect to the controlling person, provided that such person does not otherwise exercise investment discretion with respect to accounts with fair market value of at least $100,000,000 within the meaning of paragraph (a) of this section.

[As last amended in Release No. 34-40934, effective February 18, 1999, 64 F.R. 2843.]

SCHEDULE 13G

»»→ CCH Note: The SEC has stayed the effectiveness of proxy rule amendments adopted in Release 33-9136 pending resolution of a challenge filed by the Business Roundtable and the U.S. Chamber of Commerce in the U.S. Court of Appeals for the District of Columbia Circuit. See Release No. 33-9149, October 4, 2010.

»»→ Amended by Release No. 33-9136, effective November 15, 2010, 75 F.R. 56668.

[¶ 22,311] Schedule 13G

Reg. § 240.13d-102 Information to be included in statements filed pursuant to § 240.13d(1) (b), (c) and (d) and amendments thereto filed pursuant to § 240.13d-2.

SECURITIES AND EXCHANGE COMMISSION
Washington, D.C. 20549
SCHEDULE 13G
Under the Securities Exchange Act of 1934
(Amendment No . . .)

. . . .
(Name of Issuer)

. . . .
(Title of Class of Securities)

. . . .
(CUSIP Number)

. . . .
(Date of Event Which Requires Filing of this Statement)

Check the appropriate box to designate the rule pursuant to which this Schedule is filed:

[ ] Rule 13d-1(b)
[ ]Rule 13d-1(c)
[ ] Rule 13d-1(d)

* The remainder of this cover page shall be filled out for a reporting person's initial filing on this form with respect to the subject class of securities, and for any subsequent amendment containing information which would alter the disclosures provided in a prior cover page.

The information required in the remainder of this cover page shall not be deemed to be "filed" for the purpose of Section 18 of the Securities Exchange Act of 1934 ("Act") or otherwise subject to the liabilities of that section of the Act but shall be subject to all other provisions of the Act (however, see the Notes).

CUSIP No. . . . .

1) Names of Reporting Persons.	
2) Check the Appropriate Box if a Member of a Group (See Instructions) (a) . . . . (b)	
3) SEC Use Only	
4) Citizenship or Place of Organization	

Number of Shares Bene- ficially Owned by Each Report-	(5) Sole Voting Power . . . .
	(6) Shared Voting Power . . . .
	(7) Sole Dispositive Power . . . .

ing Person With		
	(8) Shared Dispositive Power	

9) Aggregate Amount Beneficially Owned by Each Reporting Person ....

10) Check if the Aggregate Amount in Row (9) Excludes Certain Shares (See Instructions) ....

11) Percent of Class Represented by Amount in Row 9 ....

12) Type of Reporting Person (See Instructions) ....

Instructions for Cover Page

(1) *Names of Reporting Persons* - Furnish the full legal name of each person for whom the report is filed - *i.e.*, each person required to sign the schedule itself - including each member of a group. Do not include the name of a person required to be identified in the report but who is not a reporting person.

(2) If any of the shares beneficially owned by a reporting person are held as a member of a group and that membership is expressly affirmed, please check row 2(a). If the reporting person disclaims membership in a group or describes a relationship with other person but does not affirm the existence of a group, please check row 2(b) [unless it is a joint filing pursuant to Rule 13d-1(k)(1) in which case it may not be necessary to check row 2(b)].

(3) The third row is for SEC internal use: please leave blank.

(4) *Citizenship or Place of Organization*—Furnish citizenship if the named reporting person is a natural person. Otherwise, furnish place of organization.

(5)-(9), (11) *Aggregate Amount Beneficially Owned By Each Reporting Person, etc.*—Rows (5) through (9) inclusive, and (11) are to be completed in accordance with the provisions of Item 4 of Schedule 13G. All percentages are to be rounded off to the nearest tenth (one place after decimal point).

(10) Check if the aggregate amount reported as beneficially owned in row (9) does not include shares as to which beneficial ownership is disclaimed pursuant to Rule 13d-4 [17 CFR 240.13d-4] under the Securities Exchange Act of 1934.

Category	Symbol
Broker Dealer	BD
Bank	BK
Insurance Company	IC
Investment Company	IV
Investment Adviser	IA
Employee Benefit Plan or Endowment Fund	EP
Parent Holding Company/Control Person	HC
Savings Association	SA
Church Plan	CP
Corporation	CO
Partnership	PN
Individual	IN
Other	OO

(12) *Type of Reporting Person*—Please classify each "reporting person" according to the following breakdown (see Item 3 of Schedule 13G) and place the appropriate Symbol on the form:

Category	Symbol
Broker Dealer	BD
Bank	BK
Insurance Company	IC
Investment Company	IV
Investment Adviser	IA
Employee Benefit Plan or Endowment Fund	EP
Parent Holding Company/Control Person	HC
Savings Association	SA
Church Plan	CP
Corporation	CO
Partnership	PN

Category	Symbol
Individual	IN
Non-U.S. Institution	FI
Other	OO

Notes:

Attach as many copies of the second part of the cover page as are needed, one reporting person per page.

Filing persons may, in order to avoid unnecessary duplication, answer items on the schedules (Schedule 13D, 13G or TO) by appropriate cross references to an item or items on the cover page(s). This approach may only be used where the cover page item or items provide all the disclosure required by the schedule item. Moreover, such a use of a cover page item will result in the item becoming a part of the schedule and accordingly being considered as "filed" for purposes of Section 18 of the Securities Exchange Act or otherwise subject to the liabilities of that section of the Act.

Reporting persons may comply with their cover page filing requirements by filing either completed copies of the blank forms available from the Commission, printed or typed facsimiles, or computer printed facsimiles, provided the documents filed have identical formats to the forms prescribed in the Commission's regulations and meet existing Securities Exchange Act rules as to such matters as clarity and size (Securities Exchange Act Rule 12b-12).

SPECIAL INSTRUCTIONS FOR COMPLYING WITH SCHEDULE 13G

Under Sections 13(d), 13(g) and 23 of the Securities Exchange Act of 1934 and the rules and regulations thereunder, the Commission is authorized to solicit the information required to be supplied by this schedule by certain security holders of certain issuers.

Disclosure of the information specified in this schedule is mandatory. The information will be used for the primary purpose of determining and disclosing the holdings of certain beneficial owners of certain equity securities. This statement will be made a matter of public record. Therefore, any information given will be available for inspection by any member of the public.

Because of the public nature of the information, the Commission can use it for a variety of purposes, including referral to other governmental authorities or securities self-regulatory organizations for investigatory purposes or in connection with litigation involving the Federal securities laws or other civil, criminal or regulatory statutes or provisions.

Failure to disclose the information requested by this schedule may result in civil or criminal action against the persons involved for violation of the Federal securities laws and rules promulgated thereunder.

Instructions

A. Statements filed pursuant to Rule 13d-1(b) containing the information required by this schedule shall be filed not later than February 14 following the calendar year covered by the statement or within the time specified in Rules 13d-1(b)(2) and 13d-2(c). Statements filed pursuant to Rule 13d-1(d) shall be filed within the time specified in Rules 13d-1(c), 13d-2(b) and 13d-2(d). Statements filed pursuant to Rule 13d-1(d) shall be filed not later than February 14 following the calendar year covered by the statement pursuant to Rules 13d-1(d) and 13d-2(b).

B. Information contained in a form which is required to be filed by rules under section 13(f) (15 U.S.C. 78m(f)) for the same calendar year as that covered by a statement on this schedule may be incorporated by reference in response to any of the items of this schedule. If such information is incorporated by reference in this schedule, copies of the relevant pages of such form shall be filed as an exhibit to this schedule.

C. The item numbers and captions of the items shall be included but the text of the items is to be omitted. The answers to the items shall be so prepared as to indicate clearly the coverage of the items without referring to the text of the items. Answer every item. If an item is inapplicable or the answer is in the negative, so state.

      Item 1(a) Name of Issuer:

. . . .

      Item 1(b) Address of Issuer's Principal Executive Offices:

. . . .

      Item 2(a) Name of Person Filing:

. . . .

      Item 2(b) Address of Principal Business Office or, if none, Residence:

. . . .

Item 2(c) Citizenship:

. . . .

Item 2(d) Title of Class of Securities:

. . . .

Item 2(e) CUSIP Number:

. . . .

Item 3. If this statement is filed pursuant to §§ 240.13d-1(b) or 240.13d-2(b) or (c), check whether the person filing is a:

(a) [ ] Broker or dealer registered under section 15 of the Act (15 U.S.C. 78o);

(b) [ ] Bank as defined in section 3(a)(6) of the Act (15 U.S.C. 78c);

(c) [ ] Insurance company as defined in section 3(a)(19) of the Act (15 U.S.C. 78c);

(d) [ ] Investment company registered under section 8 of the Investment Company Act of 1940 (15 U.S.C 80a-8);

(e) [ ] An investment adviser in accordance with § 240.13d-1(b)(1)(ii)(E);

(f) [ ] An employee benefit plan or endowment fund in accordance with § 240.13d-1(b)(1)(ii)(F);

(g) [ ] A parent holding company or control person in accordance with § 240.13d-1(b)(1)(ii)(G);

(h) [ ] A savings associations as defined in Section 3(b) of the Federal Deposit Insurance Act (12 U.S.C. 1813);

(i) [ ] A church plan that is excluded from the definition of an investment company under section 3(c)(14) of the Investment Company Act of 1940 (15 U.S.C. 80a-3);

(j) [ ] A non-U.S. institution in accordance with § 240.13d-1(b)(1)(ii)(J);

(k) [ ]Group, in accordance with § 240.13d-1(b)(1)(ii)(K).

If filing as a non-U.S. institution in accordance with § 240.13d-1(b)(1)(ii)(J), please specify the type of institution: _____

Item 4. Ownership

Provide the following information regarding the aggregate number and percentage of the class of securities of the issuer identified in Item 1.

(a) Amount beneficially owned: . . . .

(b) Percent of class: . . . .

(c) Number of shares as to which the person has: . . . .

(a) Sole power to vote or to direct the vote . . . .

(b) Shared power to vote or to direct the vote . . . .

(c) Sole power to dispose or to direct the disposition of . . . .

(d) Shared power to dispose or to direct the disposition of . . . .

Instruction. For computations regarding securities which represent a right to acquire an underlying security see § 240.13d-3(d)(1).

Item 5. Ownership of Five Percent or Less of a Class

If this statement is being filed to report the fact that as of the date hereof the reporting person has ceased to be the beneficial owner of more than five percent of the class of securities, check the following [   ].

Instruction: Dissolution of a group requires a response to this item.

Item 6. Ownership of More than Five Percent on Behalf of Another Person.

If any other person is known to have the right to receive or the power to direct the receipt of dividends from, or the proceeds from the sale of, such securities, a statement to that effect should be included in response to this item and, if such interest relates to more than five percent of the class, such person should be identified. A listing of the shareholders of an investment company registered under the Investment Company Act of 1940 or the beneficiaries of employee benefit plan, pension fund or endowment fund is not required.

Item 7. Identification and Classification of the Subsidiary Which Acquired the Security Being Reported on By the Parent Holding Company or Control Person

If a parent holding company or control person has filed this schedule, pursuant to Rule 13d-1(b)(1)(ii)(G), so indicate under Item 3(g) and attach an exhibit stating the identity and the Item 3 classification of the relevant subsidiary. If a parent holding company or control person has filed this schedule pursuant to Rule 13d-1(c) or Rule 13d-1(d), attach an exhibit stating the identification of the relevant subsidiary.

Item 8. Identification and Classification of Members of the Group

If a group has filed this schedule pursuant to § 240.13d-1(b)(1)(ii)(J), so indicate under Item 3(j) and attach an exhibit stating the identity and Item 3 classification of each member of the group. If a group has filed this schedule pursuant to Rule 240.13d-1(c) or Rule 240.13d-1(d), attach an exhibit stating the identity of each member of the group.

Item 9. Notice of Dissolution of Group

Notice of dissolution of a group may be furnished as an exhibit stating the date of the dissolution and that all further filings with respect to transactions in the security reported on will be filed, if required, by members of the group, in their individual capacity. See Item 5.

Item 10. Certifications

(a) The following certification shall be included if the statement is filed pursuant to § 240.13d-1(b):

By signing below I certify that, to the best of my knowledge and belief, the securities referred to above were acquired and are held in the ordinary course of business and were not acquired and are not held for the purpose of or with the effect of changing or influencing the control of the issuer of the securities and were not acquired and are not held in connection with or as a participant in any transaction having that purpose or effect.

*Amendment*_____

By signing below I certify that, to the best of my knowledge and belief, the securities referred to above were acquired and are held in the ordinary course of business and were not acquired and are not held for the purpose of or with the effect of changing or influencing the control of the issuer of the securities and were not acquired and are not held in connection with or as a participant in any transaction having that purpose or effect, other than activities solely in connection with a nomination under § 240.14a-11.

*End of Amendment*_____

(b) The following certification shall be included if the statement is filed pursuant to § 240.13d-1(b)(1)(ii)(J), or if the statement is filed pursuant to § 240.13d-1(b)(1)(ii)(K) and a member of the group is a non-U.S. institution eligible to file pursuant to § 240.13d1(b)(1)(ii)(J):

By signing below I certify that, to the best of my knowledge and belief, the foreign regulatory scheme applicable to [insert particular category of institutional investor] is substantially comparable to the regulatory scheme applicable to the functionally equivalent U.S. institution(s). I also undertake to furnish to the Commission staff, upon request, information that would otherwise be disclosed in a Schedule 13D.

(c) The following certification shall be included if the statement is filed pursuant to § 240.13d-1(c):

By signing below I certify that, to the best of my knowledge and belief, the securities referred to above were not acquired and are not held for the purpose of or with the effect of changing or influencing the control of the issuer of the securities and were not acquired and are not held in connection with or as a participant in any transaction having that purpose or effect.

*Amendment*_____

By signing below I certify that, to the best of my knowledge and belief, the securities referred to above were not acquired and are not held for the purpose of or with the effect of changing or influencing the control of the issuer of the securities and were not acquired and are not held in connection with or as a participant in any transaction having that purpose or effect, other than activities solely in connection with a nomination under § 240.14a-11.

*End of Amendment*_____

SIGNATURE

After reasonable inquiry and to the best of my knowledge and belief, I certify that the information set forth in this statement is true, complete and correct.

. . . .

Date

. . . .

Signature

. . . .

Name/Title

The original statement shall be signed by each person on whose behalf the statement is filed or his authorized representative. If the statement is signed on behalf of a person by his authorized representative other than an executive officer or general partner of this filing person, evidence of the representative's authority to sign on behalf of such person shall be filed with the statement, provided, however, that a power of attorney for this purpose which is already on file with the Commission may be incorporated by reference. The name and any title of each person who signs the statement shall be typed or printed beneath his signature.

¶ 22,311   **Schedule 13G**

NOTE: Schedules filed in paper format shall include a signed original and five copies of the schedule, including all exhibits. See Rule 13d-7 for other parties for whom copies are to be sent.

Attention: Intentional misstatements or omissions of fact constitute Federal criminal violations (See 18 U.S.C. 1001).

[As last amended in Release No. 33-9136, effective November 15, 2010, 75 F.R. 56668, stayed by Release No. 33-9149, October 4, 2010.]

REGULATIONS UNDER SECTION 13(k)

[¶ 22,351] Foreign bank exemption from the insider lending prohibition under section 13(k)

Reg. § 240.13k-1. (a) For the purpose of this section:

(1) *Foreign bank* means an institution:

(i) The home jurisdiction of which is other than the United States;

(ii) That is regulated as a bank in its home jurisdiction; and

(iii) That engages directly in the business of banking.

(2) *Home jurisdiction* means the country, political subdivision or other place in which a foreign bank is incorporated or organized.

(3) *Engages directly in the business of banking* means that an institution engages directly in banking activities that are usual for the business of banking in its home jurisdiction.

(4) *Affiliate, parent* and *subsidiary* have the same meaning as under 17 CFR 240.12b-2.

(b) An issuer that is a foreign bank or the parent or other affiliate of a foreign bank is exempt from the prohibition of extending, maintaining, arranging for, or renewing credit in the form of a personal loan to or for any of its directors or executive officers under section 13(k) of the Act (15 U.S.C. 78m(k)) with respect to any such loan made by the foreign bank as long as:

(1) Either:

(i) The laws or regulations of the foreign bank's home jurisdiction require the bank to insure its deposits or be subject to a deposit guarantee or protection scheme; or

(ii) The Board of Governors of the Federal Reserve System has determined that the foreign bank or another bank organized in the foreign bank's home jurisdiction is subject to comprehensive supervision or regulation on a consolidated basis by the bank supervisor in its home jurisdiction under 12 CFR 211.24(c); and

(2) The loan by the foreign bank to any of its directors or executive officers or those of its parent or other affiliate:

(i) Is on substantially the same terms as those prevailing at the time for comparable transactions by the foreign bank with other persons who are not executive officers, directors or employees of the foreign bank, its parent or other affiliate; or

(ii) Is pursuant to a benefit or compensation program that is widely available to the employees of the foreign bank, its parent or other affiliate and does not give preference to any of the executive officers or directors of the foreign bank, its parent or other affiliate over any other employees of the foreign bank, its parent or other affiliate; or

(iii) Has received express approval by the bank supervisor in the foreign bank's home jurisdiction.

Notes to paragraph (b):

1. The exemption provided in paragraph (b) of this section applies to a loan by the subsidiary of a foreign bank to a director or executive officer of the foreign bank, its parent or other affiliate as long as the subsidiary is under the supervision or regulation of the bank supervisor in the foreign bank's home jurisdiction, the subsidiary's loan meets the requirements of paragraph (b)(2) of this section, and the foreign bank meets the requirements of paragraph (b)(1) of this section.

2. For the purpose of paragraph (b)(1)(ii) of this section, a foreign bank may rely on a determination by the Board of Governors of the Federal Reserve System that another bank in the foreign bank's home jurisdiction is subject to comprehensive supervision or regulation on a consolidated basis by the bank supervisor under 12 CFR 211.24(c) as long as the foreign bank is under substantially the same banking supervision or regulation as the other bank in their home jurisdiction.

(c) As used in paragraph (1) of section 13(k) of the Act (15 U.S.C. 78m(k)(1)), *issuer* does not include a foreign government, as defined under 17 CFR 230.405, that files a registration statement under the Securities Act of 1933 (15 U.S.C. 77a et seq.) on Schedule B.

[Adopted in Release No. 34-49616, effective April 30, 2004, 69 F.R. 24016.]

REGULATIONS 14A–14N

[¶ 22,371] Regulation 14A—Regulations 14A through 14N

Reg. § 240.14A. [The text of Regulations 14A–14N (17 CFR 240.14a-1 et seq.) is reproduced at ¶ 40,001 et seq.]

REGULATION 15D—REPORTS OF REGISTRANTS UNDER THE SECURITIES ACT OF 1933
Annual Reports

[¶ 23,401] Requirement of Annual Reports

Reg. § 240.15d-1. Every registrant under the Securities Act of 1933 shall file an annual report, on the appropriate form authorized or prescribed therefor, for the fiscal year in which the registration statement under the Securities Act of 1933 became effective and for each fiscal year thereafter, unless the registrant is exempt from such filing by section 15(d) of the Act or rules thereunder. Annual reports shall be filed within the period specified in the appropriate report form.

[As last amended in Release No. 34-37692, effective October 7, 1996, 61 F.R. 49957.]

[¶ 23,411] Special Financial Report

Reg. § 240.15d-2. (a) If the registration statement under the Securities Act of 1933 did not contain certified financial statements for the registrant's last full fiscal year (or for the life of the registrant if less than a full fiscal year) preceding the fiscal year in which the registration statement became effective, the registrant shall, within 90 days after the effective date of the registration statement, file a special report furnishing certified financial statements for such last full fiscal year or other period, as the case may be, meeting the requirements of the form appropriate for annual reports of the registrant. If the registrant is a foreign private issuer as defined in § 230.405 of this chapter, then the special financial report shall be filed on the appropriate form for annual reports of the registrant and shall be filed within the following period:

(i) By the later of 90 days after the date on which the registration statement became effective, or six months following the end of the registrant's full fiscal year, for fiscal years ending before December 15, 2011; and

(ii) By the later of 90 days after the date on which the registration statement became effective, or four months following the end of the registrant's latest full fiscal year, for fiscal years ending on or after December 15, 2011.

(b) The report shall be filed under cover of the facing sheet of the form appropriate for annual reports of the registrant, shall indicate on the facing sheet that it contains only financial statements for the fiscal year in question, and shall be signed in accordance with the requirements of the annual report form.

[As last amended in Release No. 33-8959, effective December 5, 2008, 73 F.R. 58300.]

[¶ 23,415] Reports for Depositary Shares Registered on Form F-6.

Reg. § 240.15d-3. Annual and other reports are not required with respect to Depositary Shares registered on Form F-6 (§ 230.36 of this chapter). The exemption in this section does not apply to any deposited securities registered on any other form under the Securities Act of 1933.

[As last amended in Release No. 34-38850, July 18, 1997, effective September 2, 1997, 62 F.R. 39755.]

[¶ 23,416] Reporting by Form 40-F Registrants

Reg. § 240.15d-4. A registrant that is eligible to use Forms 40-F and 6-K and files reports in accordance therewith shall be deemed to satisfy the requirements of Regulation 15D (§§ 240.15d-1 through 240.15d-21 of this chapter).

[As adopted in Release No. 34-29354, June 13, 1991, 56 F.R. 30036.]

[¶ 23,421] Reporting by Successor Issuers

Reg. § 240.15d-5. (a) Where in connection with a succession by merger, consolidation, exchange of securities, acquisition of assets or otherwise, securities of any issuer that is not required to file reports pursuant to section 15(d) (15 U.S.C. 78o(d)) of the Act are issued to the holders of any class of securities of another issuer that is required to file such reports, the duty to file reports pursuant to such section shall be deemed to have been assumed by the issuer of the class of securities so issued. The successor issuer shall, after the consummation of the succession, file reports in accordance with section 15(d) of the Act (15 U.S.C. 78o(d)) and the rules and regulations thereunder, unless that issuer is exempt from filing such reports or the duty to file such reports is suspended under section 15(d) of the Act (15 U.S.C. 78o(d)).

(b) An issuer that is deemed to be a successor issuer according to paragraph (a) of this section shall file reports on the same forms as the predecessor issuer except as follows:

(1) An issuer that is not a foreign issuer shall not be eligible to file on Form 20-F (§ 240.220f of this chapter).

(2) A foreign private issuer shall be eligible to file on Form 20-F.

(c) The provisions of paragraph (a) of this section shall not apply to an issuer of securities in connection with a succession that was registered on Form F-8 (§ 239.38 of this chapter), Form F-10 (§ 239.40 of this chapter) or Form F-80 (§ 239.41 of this chapter).

[As last amended in Release No. 34-38850, July 18, 1997, effective September 2, 1997, 62 F.R. 39755.]

[¶ 23,431] Suspension of Duty to File Reports

Reg. § 240.15d-6. If the duty of an issuer to file reports pursuant to section 15(d) of the Act as to any fiscal year is suspended as provided in section 15(d) of the Act, such issuer shall, within 30 days after the beginning of the first fiscal year, file a notice on Form 15 informing the Commission of such suspension unless Form 15 has already been filed pursuant to Rule 12h-3. If the suspension resulted from the issuer's merger into, or consolidation with, another issuer or issuers, the notice shall be filed by the successor issuer.

[As last amended in Release No. 34-20784, March 22, 1984, 49 F.R. 12688.]

Other Reports

[¶ 23,441] Transition Reports

Reg. § 240.15d-10. (a) Every issuer that changes its fiscal closing date shall file a report covering the resulting transition period between the closing date of its most recent fiscal year end and the opening date of its new fiscal year; *Provided, however,* that an issuer shall file an annual report for any fiscal year that ended before the date on which the issuer determined to change its fiscal year end. In no event shall the transition report cover a period of 12 or more months.

(b) The report pursuant to this section shall be filed for the transition period not more than the number of days specified in paragraph (j) of this section after either the close of the transition period or the date of the determination to change the fiscal closing date, whichever is later. The report shall be filed on the form appropriate for annual reports of the issuer, shall cover the period from the close of the last fiscal year end and shall indicate clearly the period covered. The financial statements for the transition period filed therewith shall be audited. Financial statements, which may be unaudited, shall be filed for the comparable period of the prior year, or a footnote, which may be unaudited, shall state for the comparable period of the prior year, revenues, gross profits, income taxes, income or loss from continuing operations before extraordinary items and cumulative effect of a change in accounting principles and net income or loss. The effects of any discontinued operations and/or extraordinary items as classified under the provisions of generally accepted accounting principles also shall be shown, if applicable. Per share data based upon such income or loss and net income or loss shall be presented in conformity with applicable accounting standards. Where called for by the time span to be covered, the comparable period financial statements or footnote shall be included in subsequent filings.

(c) If the transition period covers a period of less than six months, in lieu of the report required by paragraph (b) of this section, a report may be filed for the transition period on Form 10-Q (§ 249.308 of this chapter) not more than the number of days specified in paragraph (j) of this section after either the close of the transition period or the date of the determination to change the fiscal closing date, whichever is later. The report on Form 10-Q shall cover the period from the close of the last fiscal year end and shall indicate clearly the period covered. The financial statements filed therewith need not be audited but, if they are not audited, the issuer shall file with the first annual report for the newly adopted fiscal year separate audited statements of income and cash flows covering the transition period. The notes to financial statements for the transition period included in such first annual report may be integrated with the notes to financial statements for the full fiscal period. A separate audited balance sheet as of the end of the transition period shall be filed in the annual report only if the audited balance sheet as of the end of the fiscal year before the transition period is not filed. Schedules need not be filed in transition reports on Form 10-Q.

(d) Notwithstanding the foregoing in paragraphs (a), (b), and (c) of this section, if the transition period covers a period of one month or less, the issuer need not file a separate transition report if either:

(1) the first report required to be filed by the issuer for the newly adopted fiscal year after the date of the determination to change the fiscal year end is an annual report, and that report covers the transition period as well as the fiscal year; or

(2) (i) the issuer files with the first annual report for the newly adopted fiscal year separate audited statements of income and cash flows covering the transition period; and

(ii) The first report required to be filed by the issuer for the newly adopted fiscal year after the date of the determination to change the fiscal year end is a quarterly report on Form 10-Q; and

(iii) Information on the transition period is included in the issuer's quarterly report on Form 10-Q for the first quarterly period (except the fourth quarter) of the newly adopted fiscal year that ends after the date of the determination to change the fiscal year. The information covering the transition period required by Part II and Item 2 of Part I may be combined with the information regarding the quarter. However, the financial statements required by Part I, which may be unaudited, shall be furnished separately for the transition period.

(e) Every issuer required to file quarterly reports on Form 10-Q pursuant to § 240.15d-13 that changes its fiscal year end shall:

(1) File a quarterly report on Form 10-Q within the time period specified in General Instruction A.1. to that form for any quarterly period (except the fourth quarter) of the old fiscal year that ends before the date on which the issuer determined to change its fiscal year end, except that the issuer need not file such quarterly report if the date on which the quarterly period ends also is the date on which the transition period ends;

(2) File a quarterly report on Form 10-Q within the time specified in General Instruction A.1 to that form for each quarterly period of the old fiscal year within the transition period. In lieu of a quarterly report for any quarter of the old fiscal year within the transition period, the issuer may file a quarterly

report on Form 10-Q for any period of three months within the transition period that coincides with a quarter of the newly adopted fiscal year if the quarterly report is filed within the number of days specified in paragraph (j) of this section after the end of such three month period, provided the issuer thereafter continues filing quarterly reports on the basis of the quarters of the newly adopted fiscal year;

(3) commence filing quarterly reports for the quarters of the new fiscal year no later than the quarterly report for the first quarter of the new fiscal year that ends after the date on which the issuer determined to change the fiscal year end; and

(4) Unless such information is or will be included in the transition report, or the first annual report on Form 10-K for the newly adopted fiscal year, include in the initial quarterly report on Form 10-Q for the newly adopted fiscal year information on any period beginning on the first day after the period covered by the issuer's final quarterly report on Form 10-Q or annual report on Form 10-K for the old fiscal year. The information covering such period required by Part II and Item 2 of Part I may be combined with the information regarding the quarter. However, the financial statements required by Part I, which may be unaudited, shall be furnished separately for such period.

Note to Paragraphs (c) and (e): If it is not practicable or cannot be cost-justified to furnish in a transition report on Form 10-Q or a quarterly report for the newly adopted fiscal year financial statements for corresponding periods of the prior year where required, financial statements may be furnished for the quarters of the preceding fiscal year that most nearly are comparable if the issuer furnishes an adequate discussion of seasonal and other factors that could affect the comparability of information or trends reflected, an assessment of the comparability of the data, and a representation as to the reason recasting has not been undertaken.

(f) Every successor issuer that has a different fiscal year from that of its predecessor(s) shall file a transition report pursuant to this section, containing the required information about each predecessor, for the transition period, if any, between the close of the fiscal year covered by the last annual report of each predecessor and the date of succession. The report shall be filed for the transition period on the form appropriate for annual reports of the issuer not more than the number of days specified in paragraph (j) of this section after the date of the succession, with financial statements in conformity with the requirements set forth in paragraph (b) of this section. If the transition period covers a period of less than six months, in lieu of a transition report on the form appropriate for the issuer's annual reports, the report may be filed for the transition period on Form 10-Q not more than the number of days specified in paragraph (j) of this section after the date of the succession, with financial statements in conformity with the requirements set forth in paragraph (c) of this section. Notwithstanding the foregoing, if the transition period covers a period of one month or less, the successor issuer need not file a separate transition report if the information is reported by the successor issuer in conformity with the requirements set forth in paragraph (d) of this section.

(g)(1) Paragraphs (a) through (f) of this section shall not apply to foreign private issuers.

(2) Every foreign private issuer that changes its fiscal closing date shall file a report covering the resulting transition period between the closing date of its most recent fiscal year end and the opening date of its new fiscal year. In no event shall a transition report cover a period longer than 12 months.

(3) The report for the transition period shall be filed on Form 20-F responding to all items to which such issuer is required to respond when Form 20-F is used as an annual report. The financial statements for the transition period filed therewith shall be audited. The report shall be filed within the following period:

(i) Within six months after either the close of the transition period or the date on which the issuer made the determination to change the fiscal closing date, whichever is later, for new fiscal years ending before December 15, 2011; and

(ii) Within four months after either the close of the transition period or the date on which the issuer made the determination to change the fiscal closing date, whichever is later, for new fiscal years ending on or after December 15, 2011.

(4) If the transition period covers a period of six or fewer months, in lieu of the report required by paragraph (g)(3) of this section, a report for the transition period shall be filed on Form 20-F responding to Items 5, 8.A.7, 13, 14, and 17 or 18 within three months after either the close of the transition period or the date on which the issuer made the determination to change the fiscal closing date, whichever is later. The financial statements required by Item 17 or Item 18 shall be furnished for the transition period. Such financial statements may be unaudited and condensed as permitted in Article 10 of Regulation S-X (§ 210.10-01 of this chapter), but if the financial statements are unaudited and condensed, the issuer shall file with the first annual report for the newly adopted fiscal year separate audited statements of income and cash flow covering the transition period.

(5) Notwithstanding the foregoing in paragraphs (g)(2), (g)(3), and (g)(4) of this section, if the transition period covers a period of one month or less, a foreign private issuer need not file a separate

transition report if the first annual report for the newly adopted fiscal year covers the transition period as well as the fiscal year.

(h) The provisions of this rule shall not apply to investment companies required to file reports pursuant to Rule 30b-1 (§ 270.30b-1 of this chapter) under the Investment Company Act of 1940 (15 U.S.C. 80a-1 *et seq.*).

(i) No filing fee shall be required for a transition report filed pursuant to this section.

(j)(1) For transition reports to be filed on the form appropriate for annual reports of the issuer, the number of days shall be:

(i) 60 days (75 days for fiscal years ending before December 15, 2006) for large accelerated filers (as defined in § 240.12b-2);

(ii) 75 days for accelerated filers (as defined in § 240.12b-2); and

(iii) 90 days for all other issuers; and

(2) For transition reports to be filed on Form 10-Q (§ 249.308 of this chapter), the number of days shall be:

(i) 40 days for large accelerated filers and accelerated filers (as defined in § 240.12b-2); and

(ii) 45 days for all other issuers.

(k)(1) Paragraphs (a) through (g) of this section shall not apply to asset-backed issuers.

(2) Every asset-backed issuer that changes its fiscal closing date shall file a report covering the resulting transition period between the closing date of its most recent fiscal year and the opening date of its new fiscal year. In no event shall a transition report cover a period longer than 12 months.

(3) The report for the transition period shall be filed on Form 10-K (§ 249.310 of this chapter) responding to all items to which such asset-backed issuer is required to respond pursuant to General Instruction J. of Form 10-K. Such report shall be filed within 90 days after the later of either the close of the transition period or the date on which the issuer made the determination to change the fiscal closing date.

(4) Notwithstanding the foregoing in paragraphs (k)(2) and (k)(3) of this section, if the transition period covers a period of one month or less, an asset-backed issuer need not file a separate transition report if the first annual report for the newly adopted fiscal year covers the transition period as well as the fiscal year.

(5) Any obligation of the asset-backed issuer to file distribution reports pursuant to § 240.15d-17 will continue to apply regardless of a change in the asset-backed issuer's fiscal closing date.

Note 1: In addition to the report or reports required to be filed pursuant to this section, every issuer, except a foreign private issuer or an investment company required to file reports pursuant to § 270.30b1-1 of this chapter, that changes its fiscal closing date is required to file a Form 8-K (§ 249.308 of this chapter) report that includes the information required by Item 5.03 of Form 8-K within the period specified in General Instruction B.1. to that form.

Additional Note: The report or reports to be filed pursuant to this section must include the certification required by § 240.15d-14.

[As last amended in Release No. 33-8959, effective December 5, 2008, 73 F.R. 58300.]

    ⋙→ *CCH Note: **The SEC has stayed the effectiveness of proxy rule amendments adopted in Release 33-9136 pending resolution of a challenge filed by the Business Roundtable and the U.S. Chamber of Commerce in the U.S. Court of Appeals for the District of Columbia Circuit. See Release No. 33-9149, October 4, 2010.***

    ⋙→ *Amended by Release No. 33-9136, effective November 15, 2010, 75 F.R. 56668.*

[¶ 23,451] Current Reports on Form 8-K

Reg. § 240.15d-11. (a) Except as provided in paragraph (b) of this section, every registrant subject to § 240.15d-1 shall file a current report on Form 8-K within the period specified in that form unless substantially the same information as that required by Form 8-K has been previously reported by the registrant.

(b) This section shall not apply to foreign governments, foreign private issuers required to make reports on Form 6-K (17 CFR 249.306) pursuant to § 240.15d-16, issuers of American Depositary Receipts for securities of any foreign issuer, or investment companies required to file periodic reports pursuant to § 270.30b1-1 of this chapter under the Investment Company Act of 1940, except where such investment companies are required to file notice of a blackout period pursuant to § 245.104 of this chapter.

*Amendment*_____

(b) This section shall not apply to foreign governments, foreign private issuers required to make reports on Form 6-K (17 CFR 249.306) pursuant to § 240.15d-16, issuers of American Depositary Receipts for securities of any foreign issuer, or investment companies required to file reports pursuant to

§ 270.30b1-1 of this chapter under the Investment Company Act of 1940, except where such an investment company is required to file:

(1) Notice of a blackout period pursuant to § 245.104 of this chapter;

(2) Disclosure pursuant to Instruction 2 to § 240.14a-11(b)(1) of information concerning outstanding shares and voting; or

(3) Disclosure pursuant to Instruction 2 to § 240.14a-11(b)(10) of the date by which a nominating shareholder or nominating shareholder group must submit the notice required pursuant to § 240.14a-11(b)(10).

End of Amendment

(c) No failure to file a report on Form 8-K that is required solely pursuant to Item 1.01, 1.02, 2.03, 2.04, 2.05, 2.06, 4.02(a), 5.02(e) or 6.03 of Form 8-K shall be deemed to be a violation of 15 U.S.C. 78j(b) and § 240.10b-5.

[As last amended in Release No. 33-9136, effective November 15, 2010, 75 F.R. 56668, stayed by Release No. 33-9149, October 4, 2010.]

[¶ 23,471] Quarterly Reports on Form 10-Q (§ 249.308 of this chapter).

Reg. § 240.15d-13. (a) Except as provided in paragraphs (b) and (c) of this section, every issuer that has securities registered pursuant to the Securities Act and is required to file annual reports pursuant to section 15(d) of the Act on Form 10-K (§ 249.310 of this chapter) shall file a quarterly report on Form 10-Q (§ 249.308 of this chapter) within the period specified in General Instruction A.1 to that form for each of the first three quarters of each fiscal year of the issuer, commencing with the first fiscal quarter following the most recent fiscal year for which full financial statements were included in the registration statement, or, if the registration statement included financial statements for an interim period after the most recent fiscal year end meeting the requirements of Article 10 of Regulation S-X, or Rule 8-03 of Regulation S-X for smaller reporting companies, for the first fiscal quarter after the quarter reported upon in the registration statement. The first quarterly report of the issuer shall be filed either within 45 days after the effective date of the registration statement or on or before the date on which such report would have been required to be filed if the issuer had been required to file reports on Form 10-Q as of its last fiscal quarter, whichever is later.

(b) The provisions of this rule shall not apply to the following issuers:

(1) Investment companies required to file reports pursuant to § 270.30b1-1;

(2) Foreign private issuers required to file reports pursuant to § 240.15d-16; and

(3) Asset-backed issuers required to file reports pursuant to § 240.15d-17.

(c) Part I of the quarterly reports on Form 10-Q need not be filed by:

(1) Mutual life insurance companies; or

(2) Mining companies not in the production stage but engaged primarily in the exploration for the development of mineral deposits other than oil, gas or coal, if all the following conditions are met:

(i) The registrant has not been in production during the current fiscal year or the two years immediately prior thereto; except that being in production for an aggregate period of not more than eight months over the three-year period shall not be a violation of this condition.

(ii) Receipts from the sale of mineral products or from the operations of mineral producing properties by the registrant and its subsidiaries combined have not exceeded $500,000 in any of the most recent six years and have not aggregated more than $1,500,000 in the most recent six fiscal years.

(d) Notwithstanding the foregoing provisions of this section, the financial information required by Part I of Form 10-Q shall not be deemed to be "filed" for the purpose of section 18 of the Act or otherwise subject to the liabilities of that section of the Act, but shall be subject to all other provisions of the Act.

(e) Notwithstanding the foregoing provisions of this section, the financial information required by Part I of Form 10-Q, or financial information submitted in lieu thereof pursuant to paragraph (d) of this section, shall not be deemed to be "filed" for the purpose of section 18 of the Act or otherwise subject to the liabilities of that section of the Act, but shall be subject to all other provisions of the Act.

[As last amended in Release No. 33-8876, effective February 4, 2008, 73 F.R. 934.]

[¶ 23,473] Certification of Disclosure in Annual and Quarterly Reports

Reg. § 240.15d-14. (a) Each report, including transition reports, filed on Form 10-Q, Form 10-K, Form 20-F or Form 40-F (§ 249.308a, 249.310, 249.220f or 249.240f of this chapter) under section 15(d) of the Act (15 U.S.C. 78o(d)), other than a report filed by an Asset-Backed Issuer (as defined in § 229.1101 of this chapter) or a report on Form 20-F filed under § 240.15d-19, must include certifications in the form specified in the applicable exhibit filing requirements of such report, and such certifications must be filed as an exhibit to such report. Each principal executive and principal financial officer of the issuer, or persons performing similar functions, at the time of filing of the report must sign a certification. The principal executive and principal financial officers of an issuer may omit the portion of the introductory language in paragraph 4 as well as language in paragraph 4(b) of the certification that refers to the certifying officers' responsibility for designing, establishing and maintaining internal control over financial reporting for the issuer until the issuer becomes subject to the internal control over financial reporting requirements in § 240.13a-15 or 240.15d-15.

(b) Each periodic report containing financial statements filed by an issuer pursuant to section 15(d) of the Act (15 U.S.C. 78o(d)) must be accompanied by the certifications required by Section 1350 of Chapter 63 of Title 18 of the United States Code (18 U.S.C. 1350) and such certifications must be furnished as an exhibit to such report as specified in the applicable exhibit requirements for such report. Each principal executive and principal financial officer of the issuer (or equivalent thereof) must sign a certification. This requirement may be satisfied by a single certification signed by an issuer's principal executive and principal financial officers.

(c) A person required to provide a certification specified in paragraph (a), (b) or (d) of this section may not have the certification signed on his or her behalf pursuant to a power of attorney or other form of confirming authority.

(d) Each annual report and transition report filed on Form 10-K (§ 249.310 of this chapter) by an asset-backed issuer under section 15(d) of the Act (15 U.S.C. 78o(d)) must include a certification in the form specified in the applicable exhibit filing requirements of such report and such certification must be filed as an exhibit to such report. Terms used in paragraphs (d) and (e) of this section have the same meaning as in Item 1101 of Regulation AB (§ 229.1101 of this chapter).

(e) With respect to asset-backed issuers, the certification required by paragraph (d) of this section must be signed by either:

(1) The senior officer in charge of securitization of the depositor if the depositor is signing the report; or

(2) The senior officer in charge of the servicing function of the servicer if the servicer is signing the report on behalf of the issuing entity. If multiple servicers are involved in servicing the pool assets, the senior officer in charge of the servicing function of the master servicer (or entity performing the equivalent function) must sign if a representative of the servicer is to sign the report on behalf of the issuing entity.

(f) The certification requirements of this section do not apply to XBRL-Related Documents, as defined in § 232.11 of this chapter.

[As last amended in Release No. 33-8876, effective February 4, 2008, 73 F.R. 934.]

[¶ 23,475] Controls and Procedures

Reg. § 240.15d-15. (a) Every issuer that files reports under section 15(d) of the Act (15 U.S.C. 78o(d)), other than an Asset Backed Issuer (as defined in § 229.1101 of this chapter), a small business investment company registered on Form N-5 (§ § 239.24 and 274.5 of this chapter), or a unit investment trust as defined in section 4(2) of the Investment Company Act of 1940 (15 U.S.C. 80a-4(2)), must maintain disclosure controls and procedures (as defined in paragraph (e) of this section) and, if the issuer either had been required to file an annual report pursuant to section 13(a) or 15(d) of the Act (15 U.S.C. 78m(a) or 78o(d)) for the prior fiscal year or had filed an annual report with the Commission for the fiscal year, internal control over financial reporting (as defined in paragraph (f) of this section).

(b) Each such issuer's management must evaluate, with the participation of the issuer's principal executive and principal financial officers, or persons performing similar functions, the effectiveness of the issuer's disclosure controls and procedures, as of the end of each fiscal quarter, except that management must perform this evaluation:

(1) In the case of a foreign private issuer (as defined in § 240.3b-4) as of the end of each fiscal year; and

(2) In the case of an investment company registered under section 8 of the Investment Company Act of 1940 (15 U.S.C. 80a-8), within the 90-day period prior to the filing date of each report requiring certification under § 270.30a-2 of this chapter.

(c) The management of each such issuer, that either had been required to file an annual report pursuant to section 13(a) or 15(d) of the Act (15 U.S.C. 78m(a) or 78o(d)) for the prior fiscal year or previously had filed an annual report with the Commission for the prior fiscal year, other than an investment company registered under section 8 of the Investment Company Act of 1940, must evaluate, with the participation of the issuer's principal executive and principal financial officers, or persons performing similar functions, the effectiveness, as of the end of each fiscal year, of the issuer's internal control over financial reporting. The framework on which management's evaluation of the issuer's internal control over financial reporting is based must be a suitable, recognized control framework that is established by a body or group that has followed due-process procedures, including the broad distribution of the framework for public comment. Although there are many different ways to conduct an evaluation of the effectiveness of internal control over financial reporting to meet the requirements of this paragraph, an evaluation that is conducted in accordance with the interpretive guidance issued by the Commission in Release No. 34-55929 will satisfy the evaluation required by this paragraph.

(d) The management of each such issuer that previously either had been required to file an annual report pursuant to section 13(a) or 15(d) of the Act (15 U.S.C. 78m(a) or 78o(d)) for the prior fiscal year or previously had filed an annual report with the Commission for the prior fiscal year, other than an investment company registered under section 8 of the Investment Company Act of 1940 (15 U.S.C. 80a-8), must evaluate, with the participation of the issuer's principal executive and principal financial officers, or persons performing similar functions, any change in the issuer's internal control over financial reporting, that occurred during each of the issuer's fiscal quarters, or fiscal year in the case of a foreign private issuer, that has materially affected, or is reasonably likely to materially affect, the issuer's internal control over financial reporting.

(e) For purposes of this section, the term *disclosure controls and procedures* means controls and other procedures of an issuer that are designed to ensure that information required to be disclosed by the issuer in the reports that it files or submits under the Act (15 U.S.C. 78a *et seq.*) is recorded, processed, summarized and reported, within the time periods specified in the Commission's rules and forms. Disclosure controls and procedures include, without limitation, controls and procedures designed to ensure that information required to be disclosed by an issuer in the reports that it files or submits under the Act is accumulated and communicated to the issuer's management, including its principal executive and principal financial officers, or persons performing similar functions, as appropriate to allow timely decisions regarding required disclosure.

(f) The term *internal control over financial reporting* is defined as a process designed by, or under the supervision of, the issuer's principal executive and principal financial officers, or persons performing similar functions, and effected by the issuer's board of directors, management and other personnel, to provide reasonable assurance regarding the reliability of financial reporting and the preparation of financial statements for external purposes in accordance with generally accepted accounting principles and includes those policies and procedures that:

(1) Pertain to the maintenance of records that in reasonable detail accurately and fairly reflect the transactions and dispositions of the assets of the issuer;

(2) Provide reasonable assurance that transactions are recorded as necessary to permit preparation of financial statements in accordance with generally accepted accounting principles, and that receipts and expenditures of the issuer are being made only in accordance with authorizations of management and directors of the issuer; and

(3) Provide reasonable assurance regarding prevention or timely detection of unauthorized acquisition, use or disposition of the issuer's assets that could have a material effect on the financial statements.

[As last amended in Release No. 33-8809, effective August 27, 2007, 72 F.R. 35310.]

[¶ 23,491] Reports of Foreign Private Issuers on Form 6-K

Reg. § 240.15d-16. (a) Every foreign private issuer which is subject to Rule 15d-1 [17 CFR 240.15d-1] shall make reports on Form 6-K, except that this rule shall not apply to:

(1) Investment companies required to file reports pursuant to Rule 30b1-1 [17 CFR 270.30b1-1];

(2) Issuers of American depositary receipts for securities of any foreign issuer; or

(3) Asset-backed issuers, as defined in § 229.1101 of this chapter.

(b) Such reports shall be transmitted promptly after the information required by Form 6-K is made public by the issuer, by the country of its domicile or under the laws of which it was incorporated or organized or by a foreign securities exchange with which the issuer has filed the information.

(c) Reports furnished pursuant to this rule shall not be deemed to be "filed" for the purpose of section 18 of the Act or otherwise subject to the liabilities of that section.

[As last amended in Release No. 33-8518, effective March 8, 2005, 70 F.R. 1506.]

[¶ 23,501] Reports of asset-backed issuers on Form 10-D

Reg. § 240.15d-17. Every asset-backed issuer subject to § 240.15d-1 shall make reports on Form 10-D (§ 249.312 of this chapter). Such reports shall be filed within the period specified in Form 10-D.

[As adopted in Release No. 33-8518, effective March 8, 2005 (Compliance dates are triggered by initial bona fide offer date or registration statement filing date and extend out to March 31, 2006. Complete compliance date details can be found in the "Dates" section of the release.), 70 F.R. 1506.]

[¶ 23,505] Compliance with servicing criteria for asset-backed securities

Reg. § 240.15d-18. (a) This section applies to every class of asset-backed securities subject to the reporting requirements of section 15(d) of the Act (15 U.S.C. 78o(d)). Terms used in this section have the same meaning as in Item 1101 of Regulation AB (§ 229.1101 of this chapter).

(b) *Reports on assessments of compliance with servicing criteria for asset-backed securities required.* With regard to a class of asset-backed securities subject to the reporting requirements of section 15(d) of the Act, the annual report on Form 10-K (§ 249.308 of this chapter) for such class must include from each party participating in the servicing function a report regarding its assessment of compliance with the servicing criteria specified in paragraph (d) of Item 1122 of Regulation AB (§ 229.1122(d) of this chapter), as of and for the period ending the end of each fiscal year, with respect to asset-backed securities transactions taken as a whole involving the party participating in the servicing function and that are backed by the same asset type backing the class of asset-backed securities (including the asset-backed securities transaction that is to be the subject of the report on Form 10-K for that fiscal year).

(c) *Attestation reports on assessments of compliance with servicing criteria for asset-backed securities required.* With respect to each report included pursuant to paragraph (b) of this section, the annual report on Form 10-K must also include a report by a registered public accounting firm that attests to, and reports on, the assessment made by the asserting party. The attestation report on assessment of compliance with servicing criteria for asset-backed securities must be made in accordance with standards for attestation engagements issued or adopted by the Public Company Accounting Oversight Board.

Note to § 240.15d-18. If multiple parties are participating in the servicing function, a separate assessment report and attestation report must be included for each party participating in the servicing function. A party participating in the servicing function means any entity (*e.g.*, master servicer, primary servicers, trustees) that is performing activities that address the criteria in paragraph (d) of Item 1122 of Regulation AB (§ 229.1122(d) of this chapter), unless such entity's activities relate only to 5% or less of the pool assets.

[As adopted in Release No. 33-8518, effective March 8, 2005, 70 F.R. 1506.]

[¶ 23,508] Reports by shell companies on Form 20-F

Reg. § 240.15d-19. Every foreign private issuer that was a shell company, other than a business combination related shell company, immediately before a transaction that causes it to cease to be a shell company shall, within four business days of completion of that transaction, file a report on Form 20-F (§ 249.220f of this chapter) containing the information that would be required if the issuer were filing a form for registration of securities on Form 20-F to register under the Act all classes of the issuer's securities subject to the reporting requirements of section 13 (15 U.S.C. 78m) or section 15(d) (15 U.S.C. 78o(d)) of the Act upon consummation of the transaction, with such information reflecting the registrant and its securities upon consummation of the transaction.

[As adopted in Release No. 33-8587, effective August 22, 2005, 70 F.R. 42234.]

[¶ 23,510] Plain English presentation of specified information

Reg. § 240.15d-20. (a) Any information included or incorporated by reference in a report filed under section 15(d) of the Act (15 U.S.C. 78o(d)) that is required to be disclosed pursuant to Item 402, 403, 404 or 407 of Regulation S-K (§ 229.402, 229.403, 229.404 or 229.407 of this chapter) must be presented in a clear, concise and understandable manner. You must prepare the disclosure using the following standards:

(1) Present information in clear, concise sections, paragraphs and sentences;

(2) Use short sentences;

(3) Use definite, concrete, everyday words;

(4) Use the active voice;

(5) Avoid multiple negatives;

(6) Use descriptive headings and subheadings;

(7) Use a tabular presentation or bullet lists for complex material, wherever possible;

(8) Avoid legal jargon and highly technical business and other terminology;

(9) Avoid frequent reliance on glossaries or defined terms as the primary means of explaining information. Define terms in a glossary or other section of the document only if the meaning is unclear from the context. Use a glossary only if it facilitates understanding of the disclosure; and

(10) In designing the presentation of the information you may include pictures, logos, charts, graphs and other design elements so long as the design is not misleading and the required information is clear. You are encouraged to use tables, schedules, charts and graphic illustrations that present relevant data in an understandable manner, so long as such presentations are consistent with applicable

disclosure requirements and consistent with other information in the document. You must draw graphs and charts to scale. Any information you provide must not be misleading.

(b) Reserved.

Note to § 240.15d-20. In drafting the disclosure to comply with this section, you should avoid the following:

1. Legalistic or overly complex presentations that make the substance of the disclosure difficult to understand;

2. Vague "boilerplate" explanations that are imprecise and readily subject to different interpretations;

3. Complex information copied directly from legal documents without any clear and concise explanation of the provision(s); and

4. Disclosure repeated in different sections of the document that increases the size of the document but does not enhance the quality of the information.

[As adopted in Release No. 33-8876, effective February 4, 2008, 73 F.R. 934.]

Exemption of Certain Issuers from Section 15(d) of the Act

[¶ 23,511] Reports for Employee Stock Purchase, Savings and Similar Plans

Reg. § 240.15d-21. (a) Separate annual and other reports need not be filed pursuant to Section 15(d) of the Act with respect to any employee stock purchase, savings or similar plan, provided—

(1) The issuer of the stock or other securities offered to employees through their participation in the plan files annual reports on Form 10-K (§ 249.310 of this chapter); and

(2) such issuer furnishes, as a part of its annual report on such form or as an amendment thereto, the financial statements required by Form 11-K (§ 249.311 of this chapter) with respect to the plan.

(b) If the procedure permitted by this Rule is followed, the financial statements required by Form 11-K with respect to the plan shall be filed within 120 days after the end of the fiscal year of the plan, either as a part of or as an amendment to the annual report of the issuer for its last fiscal year, *provided that* if the fiscal year of the plan ends within 62 days prior to the end of the fiscal year of the issuer, such information, financial statements and exhibits may be furnished as a part of the issuer's next annual report. If a plan subject to the Employee Retirement Income Security Act of 1974 uses the procedure permitted by this Rule, the financial statements required by Form 11-K shall be filed within 180 days after the plan's fiscal year end.

[As last amended in Release No. 33-8876, effective February 4, 2008, 73 F.R. 934.]

[¶ 23,514] Reporting regarding asset-backed securities under section 15(d) of the Act

Reg. § 240.15d-22. (a) With respect to an offering of asset-backed securities registered pursuant to § 230.415(a)(1)(x) of this chapter, annual and other reports need not be filed pursuant to section 15(d) of the Act (15 U.S.C. 78o(d)) regarding any class of securities to which such registration statement relates until the first bona fide sale in a takedown of securities under the registration statement.

(b) Regarding any class of asset-backed securities in a takedown off of a registration statement pursuant to § 230.415(a)(1)(x) of this chapter, no annual and other reports need be filed pursuant to section 15(d) of the Act regarding such class of securities as to any fiscal year, other than the fiscal year within which the takedown occurred, if at the beginning of such fiscal year the securities of each class in the takedown are held of record by less than three hundred persons.

(c) Paragraph (a) or (b) of this section does not affect any other reporting obligation applicable with respect to any classes of securities from additional takedowns under the same or different registration statements or any reporting obligation that may be applicable pursuant to section 12 of the Act (15 U.S.C. 78*l*).

[As adopted in Release No. 33-8518, effective March 8, 2005, 70 F.R. 1506.]

[¶ 23,518] Reporting regarding certain securities underlying asset-backed securities under section 15(d) of the Act

Reg. § 240.15d-23. (a) Regarding a class of asset-backed securities, if the asset pool for the asset-backed securities includes a pool asset representing an interest in or the right to the payments or cash flows of another asset pool, then no separate annual and other reports need be filed pursuant to section 15(d) of the Act (15 U.S.C. 78o(d)) because of the separate registration of the distribution of the pool asset under the Securities Act (15 U.S.C. 77a *et seq.*), if the following conditions are met:

(1) Both the issuing entity for the asset-backed securities and the entity that issued the pool asset were established under the direction of the same sponsor and depositor;

(2) The pool asset was created solely to satisfy legal requirements or otherwise facilitate the structuring of the asset-backed securities transaction;

(3) The pool asset is not part of a scheme to avoid the registration or reporting requirements of the Act;

(4) The pool asset is held by the issuing entity and is a part of the asset pool for the asset-backed securities; and

(5) The offering of the asset-backed securities and the offering of the pool asset were both registered under the Securities Act (15 U.S.C. 77a *et seq.*).

(b) Paragraph (a) of this section does not affect any reporting obligation applicable with respect to the asset-backed securities or any other reporting obligation that may be applicable with respect to the pool asset or any other securities by the issuer of that pool asset pursuant to section 12 or 15(d) of the Act (15 U.S.C. 78*l* or 78o(d)).

(c) This section does not affect any obligation to provide information regarding the pool asset or the asset pool underlying the pool asset in a filing with respect to the asset-backed securities. See Item 1100(d) of Regulation AB (§ 229.1100(d) of this chapter).

(d) Terms used in this section have the same meaning as in Item 1101 of Regulation AB (§ 229.1101 of this chapter).

[As adopted in Release No. 33-8518, effective March 8, 2005, 70 F.R. 1506.]

REPORTS OF DIRECTORS, OFFICERS, AND PRINCIPAL STOCKHOLDERS

[¶ 23,701] Definition of Terms

Reg. § 240.16a-1. Terms defined in this Rule shall apply solely to Section 16 of the Act and the rules thereunder. These terms shall not be limited to Section 16(a) of the Act but also shall apply to all other subsections under Section 16 of the Act.

(a) The term "beneficial owner" shall have the following applications:

(1) Solely for purposes of determining whether a person is a beneficial owner of more than 10 percent of any class of equity securities registered pursuant to Section 12 of the Act, the term "beneficial owner" shall mean any person who is deemed a beneficial owner pursuant to Section 13(d) of the Act and the rules thereunder; *provided, however,* that the following institutions or persons shall not be deemed the beneficial owner of securities of such class held for the benefit of third parties or in customer or fiduciary accounts in the ordinary course of business (or in the case of an employee benefit plan specified in subparagraph (vi) below, of securities of such class allocated to plan participants where participants have voting power) as long as such shares are acquired by such institutions or persons without the purpose or effect of changing or influencing control of the issuer or engaging in any arrangement subject to Rule 13d-3(b) (§ 240.13d-3(b)):

(i) A broker or dealer registered under section 15 of the Act (15 U.S.C. 78o);

(ii) A bank as defined in section 3(a)(6) of the Act (15 U.S.C. 78c);

(iii) An insurance company as defined in section 3(a)(19) of the Act (15 U.S.C. 78c);

(iv) An investment company registered under section 8 of the Investment Company Act of 1940 (15 U.S.C. 80a-8);

(v) Any person registered as an investment adviser under Section 203 of the Investment Advisers Act of 1940 (15 U.S.C. 80b-3) or under the laws of any state;

(vi) An employee benefit plan as defined in Section 3(3) of the Employee Retirement Income Security Act of 1974, as amended, 29 U.S.C. 1001 et seq. ("ERISA") that is subject to the provisions of ERISA, or any such plan that is not subject to ERISA that is maintained primarily for the benefit of the employees of a state or local government or instrumentality, or an endowment fund;

(vii) A parent holding company or control person, provided the aggregate amount held directly by the parent or control person, and directly and indirectly by their subsidiaries or affiliates that are not persons specified in paragraphs (a)(1)(i) through (x), does not exceed one percent of the securities of the subject class;

(viii) A savings association as defined in Section 3(b) of the Federal Deposit Insurance Act (12 U.S.C. 1813);

(ix) A church plan that is excluded from the definition of an investment company under section 3(c)(14) of the Investment Company Act of 1940 (15 U.S.C. 80a-3);

(x) A non-U.S. institution that is the functional equivalent of any of the institutions listed in paragraphs (a)(1)(i) through (ix) of this section, so long as the non-U.S. institution is subject to a regulatory scheme that is substantially comparable to the regulatory scheme applicable to the equivalent U.S. institution and the non-U.S. institution is eligible to file a Schedule 13G pursuant to § 240.13d-1(b)(1)(ii)(J); and

(xi) A group, provided that all the members are persons specified in § 240.16a-1(a)(1)(i) through (x).

(x) A group, provided that all the members are persons specified in § 240.16a-1(a)(1)(i) through (ix).

(xi) A group, provided that all the members are persons specified in § 240.16a-1(a)(1)(i) through (vii).

Note to paragraph (a). Pursuant to this section, a person deemed a beneficial owner of more than 10 percent of any class of equity securities registered under Section 12 of the Act would file a Form 3 (§ 249.103), but the securities holdings disclosed on Form 3, and changes in beneficial ownership reported on subsequent Forms 4 (§ 249.104) or 5 (§ 249.105), would be determined by the definition of "beneficial owner" in paragraph (a)(2) of this section.

(2) Other than for purposes of determining whether a person is a beneficial owner of more than 10 percent of any class of equity securities registered under Section 12 of the Act, the term "beneficial owner" shall mean any person who, directly or indirectly, through any contract, arrangement, understanding, relationship or otherwise, has or shares a direct or indirect pecuniary interest in the equity securities, subject to the following:

(i) The term "pecuniary interest" in any class of equity securities shall mean the opportunity, directly or indirectly, to profit or share in any profit derived from a transaction in the subject securities.

(ii) The term "indirect pecuniary interest" in any class of equity securities shall include, but not be limited to:

(A) securities held by members of a person's immediate family sharing the same household; *provided, however,* that the presumption of such beneficial ownership may be rebutted; *see* also § 240.16a-1(a)(4);

(B) a general partner's proportionate interest in the portfolio securities held by a general or limited partnership. The general partner's proportionate interest, as evidenced by the partnership agreement in effect at the time of the transaction and the partnership's most recent financial statements, shall be the greater of:

(*1*) the general partner's share of the partnership's profits, including profits attributed to any limited partnership interests held by the general partner and any other interests in profits that arise from the purchase and sale of the partnership's portfolio securities; or

(*2*) the general partner's share of the partnership capital account, including the share attributable to any limited partnership interest held by the general partner.

(C) a performance-related fee, other than an asset-based fee, received by any broker, dealer, bank, insurance company, investment company, investment adviser, investment manager, trustee or person or entity performing a similar function; *provided, however,* that no pecuniary interest shall be present where:

(*1*) the performance-related fee, regardless of when payable, is calculated based upon net capital gains and/or net capital appreciation generated from the portfolio or from the fiduciary's overall performance over a period of one year or more; and

(*2*) equity securities of the issuer do not account for more than 10 percent of the market value of the portfolio. A right to a nonperformance-related fee alone shall not represent a pecuniary interest in the securities;

(D) A person's right to dividends that is separated or separable from the underlying securities. Otherwise, a right to dividends alone shall not represent a pecuniary interest in the securities;

(E) A person's interest in securities held by a trust, as specified in § 240.16a-8(b); and

(F) A person's right to acquire equity securities through the exercise or conversion of any derivative security, whether or not presently exercisable.

(iii) A shareholder shall not be deemed to have a pecuniary interest in the portfolio securities held by a corporation or similar entity in which the person owns securities if the shareholder is not a controlling shareholder of the entity and does not have or share investment control over the entity's portfolio.

(3) Where more than one person subject to section 16 of the Act is deemed to be a beneficial owner of the same equity securities, all such persons must report as beneficial owners of the securities, either separately or jointly, as provided in § 240.16a-3(j). In such cases, the amount of short-swing profit recoverable shall not be increased above the amount recoverable if there were only one beneficial owner.

(4) Any person filing a statement pursuant to Section 16(a) of the Act may state that the filing shall not be deemed an admission that such person is, for purposes of Section 16 of the Act or otherwise, the beneficial owner of any equity securities covered by the statement.

(5) The following interests are deemed not to confer beneficial ownership for purposes of Section 16 of the Act:

(i) Interests in portfolio securities held by any holding company registered under the Public Utility Holding Company Act of 1935 (15 U.S.C. § 79a *et seq.*);

(ii) Interests in portfolio securities held by any investment company registered under the Investment Company Act of 1940 (15 U.S.C. § 80a-1 *et seq.*); and

(iii) Interests in securities comprising part of a broad-based, publicly traded market basket or index of stocks, approved for trading by the appropriate federal governmental authority.

(b) The term "call equivalent position" shall mean a derivative security position that increases in value as the value of the underlying equity increases, including, but not limited to, a long convertible security, a long call option, and a short put option position.

(c) The term "derivative securities" shall mean any option, warrant, convertible security, stock appreciation right, or similar right with an exercise or conversion privilege at a price related to an equity security, or similar securities with a value derived from the value of an equity security, but shall not include:

(1) rights of a pledgee of securities to sell the pledged securities;

(2) rights of all holders of a class of securities of an issuer to receive securities pro rata, or obligations to dispose of securities, as a result of a merger, exchange offer, or consolidation involving the issuer of the securities;

Reg. § 240.16a-1 ¶ 23,701

(3) Rights or obligations to surrender a security, or have a security withheld, upon the receipt or exercise of a derivative security or the receipt or vesting of equity securities, in order to satisfy the exercise price or the tax withholding consequences of receipt, exercise or vesting;

(4) interests in broad-based index options, broad-based index futures, and broad-based publicly traded market baskets of stocks approved for trading by the appropriate federal governmental authority;

(5) Interests or rights to participate in employee benefit plans of the issuer;

(6) Rights with an exercise or conversion privilege at a price that is not fixed; or

(7) Options granted to an underwriter in a registered public offering for the purpose of satisfying over-allotments in such offering.

(d) The term "equity security of such issuer" shall mean any equity security or derivative security relating to an issuer, whether or not issued by that issuer.

(e) The term "immediate family" shall mean any child, stepchild, grandchild, parent, stepparent, grandparent, spouse, sibling, mother-in-law, father-in-law, son-in-law, daughter-in-law, brother-in-law, or sister-in-law, and shall include adoptive relationships.

(f) The term "officer" shall mean an issuer's president, principal financial officer, principal accounting officer (or, if there is no such accounting officer, the controller), any vice-president of the issuer in charge of a principal business unit, division or function (such as sales, administration or finance), any other officer who performs a policy-making function, or any other person who performs similar policy-making functions for the issuer. Officers of the issuer's parent(s) or subsidiaries shall be deemed officers of the issuer if they perform such policy-making functions for the issuer. In addition, when the issuer is a limited partnership, officers or employees of the general partner(s) who perform policy-making functions for the limited partnership are deemed officers of the limited partnership. When the issuer is a trust, officers or employees of the trustee(s) who perform policy-making functions for the trust are deemed officers of the trust.

Note: "Policy-making function" is not intended to include policy-making functions that are not significant. If pursuant to Item 401(b) of Regulation S-K (§ 229.401(b)) the issuer identifies a person as an "executive officer," it is presumed that the Board of Directors has made that judgment and that the persons so identified are the officers for purposes of Section 16 of the Act, as are such other persons enumerated in this paragraph (f) but not in Item 401(b).

(g) The term "portfolio securities" shall mean all securities owned by an entity, other than securities issued by the entity.

(h) The term "put equivalent position" shall mean a derivative security position that increases in value as the value of the underlying equity decreases, including, but not limited to, a long put option and a short call option position.

[As last amended in Release No. 33-8957, effective December 8, 2008, 73 F.R. 60049.]

[¶ 23,711] Persons and Transactions Subject to Section 16

Reg. § 240.16a-2. Any person who is the beneficial owner, directly or indirectly, of more than ten percent of any class of equity securities ("ten percent beneficial owner") registered pursuant to section 12 of the Act (15 U.S.C. 78*l*), any director or officer of the issuer of such securities, and any person specified in section 17(a) of the Public Utility Holding Company Act of 1935 (15 U.S.C. 79q(a)) or section 30(h) of the Investment Company Act of 1940 (15 U.S.C. 80a-29(h)), including any person specified in § 240.16a-8, shall be subject to the provisions of section 16 of the Act (15 U.S.C. 78p). The rules under Section 16 of the Act apply to any class of equity securities of an issuer whether or not registered under Section 12 of the Act. The rules under Section 16 of the Act also apply to non-equity securities as provided by the Public Utility Holding Company Act of 1935 and the Investment Company Act of 1940. With respect to transactions by persons subject to Section 16 of the Act:

(a) A transaction(s) carried out by a director or officer in the six months prior to the director or officer becoming subject to Section 16 of the Act shall be subject to Section 16 of the Act and reported on the first required Form 4 only if the transaction(s) occurred within six months of the transaction giving rise to the Form 4 filing obligation and the director or officer became subject to Section 16 of the Act solely as a result of the issuer registering a class of equity securities pursuant to Section 12 of the Act.

(b) A transaction(s) following the cessation of director or officer status shall be subject to section 16 of the Act only if:

(1) Executed within a period of less than six months of an opposite transaction subject to section 16(b) of the Act that occurred while that person was a director or officer; and

(2) Not otherwise exempted from section 16(b) of the Act pursuant to the provisions of this chapter.

Note to paragraph (b): For purposes of this paragraph, an acquisition and a disposition each shall be an opposite transaction with respect to the other.

(c) The transaction that results in a person becoming a ten percent beneficial owner is not subject to Section 16 of the Act unless the person otherwise is subject to Section 16 of the Act. A ten percent beneficial owner not otherwise subject to Section 16 of the Act must report only those transactions conducted while the beneficial owner of more than ten percent of a class of equity securities of the issuer registered pursuant to Section 12 of the Act.

(d)(1) Transactions by a person or entity shall be exempt from the provisions of Section 16 of the Act for the 12 months following appointment and qualification, to the extent such person or entity is acting as:

(i) Executor or administrator of the estate of a decedent;

(ii) Guardian or member of a committee for an incompetent;

(iii) Receiver, trustee in bankruptcy, assignee for the benefit of creditors, conservator, liquidating agent, or other similar person duly authorized by law to administer the estate or assets of another person; or

(iv) Fiduciary in a similar capacity.

(2) Transactions by such person or entity acting in a capacity specified in paragraph (d)(1) of this section after the period specified in that paragraph shall be subject to section 16 of the Act only where the estate, trust or other entity is a beneficial owner of more than ten percent of any class of equity security registered pursuant to section 12 of the Act.

[As last amended in Release No. 34-46106, effective July 8, 2002, 67 F.R. 43534.]

[¶ 23,721] Reporting Transactions and Holdings

Reg. § 240.16a-3. (a) Initial statements of beneficial ownership of equity securities required by Section 16(a) of the Act shall be filed on Form 3. Statements of changes in beneficial ownership required by that Section shall be filed on Form 4. Annual statements shall be filed on Form 5. At the election of the reporting person, any transaction required to be reported on Form 5 may be reported on an earlier filed Form 4. All such statements shall be prepared and filed in accordance with the requirements of the applicable form.

(b) A person filing statements pursuant to Section 16(a) of the Act with respect to any class of equity securities registered pursuant to Section 12 of the Act need not file an additional statement on Form 3:

(1) When an additional class of equity securities of the same issuer becomes registered pursuant to Section 12 of the Act; or

(2) When such person assumes a different or an additional relationship to the same issuer (for example, when an officer becomes a director).

(c) Any issuer that has equity securities listed on more than one national securities exchange may designate one exchange as the only exchange with which reports pursuant to Section 16(a) of the Act need be filed. Such designation shall be made in writing and shall be filed with the Commission and with each national securities exchange on which any equity security of the issuer is listed at the time of such election. The reporting person's obligation to file reports with each national securities exchange on which any equity security of the issuer is listed shall be satisfied by filing with the exchange so designated.

(d) Any person required to file a statement with respect to securities of a single issuer under both section 16(a) of the Act (15 U.S.C. 78p(a)) and either section 17(a) of the Public Utility Holding Company Act of 1935 (15 U.S.C. 79q(a)) or section 30(h) of the Investment Company Act of 1940 (15 U.S.C. 80a-29(h)) may file a single statement containing the required information, which will be deemed to be filed under both Acts.

(e) Any person required to file a statement under Section 16(a) of the Act shall, not later than the time the statement is transmitted for filing with the Commission, send or deliver a duplicate to the person designated by the issuer to receive such statements, or, in the absence of such a designation, to the issuer's corporate secretary or person performing equivalent functions.

(f)(1) A Form 5 shall be filed by every person who at any time during the issuer's fiscal year was subject to Section 16 of the Act with respect to such issuer, except as provided in paragraph (2) below. The Form shall be filed within 45 days after the issuer's fiscal year end, and shall disclose the following holdings and transactions not reported previously on Forms 3, 4 or 5:

(i) All transactions during the most recent fiscal year that were exempt from section 16(b) of the Act, except:

(A) Exercises and conversions of derivative securities exempt under either § 240.16b-3 or § 240.16b-6(b), and any transaction exempt under § 240.16b-3(d), § 240.16b-3(e), or § 240.16b-3(f) (these are required to be reported on Form 4);

(B) Transactions exempt from section 16(b) of the Act pursuant to § 240.16b-3(c), which shall be exempt from section 16(a) of the Act; and

(C) Transactions exempt from section 16(a) of the Act pursuant to another rule;

(ii) Transactions that constituted small acquisitions pursuant to § 240.16a-6(a);

(iii) all holdings and transactions that should have been reported during the most recent fiscal year, but were not; and

(iv) with respect to the first Form 5 requirement for a reporting person, all holdings and transactions that should have been reported in each of the issuer's last two fiscal years but were not, based on the reporting person's reasonable belief in good faith in the completeness and accuracy of the information.

(2) Notwithstanding the above, no Form 5 shall be required where all transactions otherwise required to be reported on the Form 5 have been reported before the due date of the Form 5.

Note: Persons no longer subject to Section 16 of the Act, but who were subject to the Section at any time during the issuer's fiscal year, must file a Form 5 unless paragraph (f)(2) is satisfied. *See also* § 240.16a-2(b) regarding the reporting obligations of persons ceasing to be officers or directors.

(g)(1) A Form 4 must be filed to report: all transactions not exempt from section 16(b) of the Act; all transactions exempt from section 16(b) of the Act pursuant to § 240.16b-3(d), § 240.16b-3(e), or § 240.16b-3(f); and all exercises and conversions of derivative securities, regardless of whether exempt from section 16(b) of the Act. Form 4 must be filed before the end of the second business day following the day on which the subject transaction has been executed.

(2) Solely for purposes of section 16(a)(2)(C) of the Act and paragraph (g)(1) of this section, the date on which the executing broker, dealer or plan administrator notifies the reporting person of the execution of the transaction is deemed the date of execution for a transaction where the following conditions are satisfied:

(i) the transaction is pursuant to a contract, instruction or written plan for the purchase or sale of equity securities of the issuer (as defined in § 16a-1(d)) that satisfies the affirmative defense conditions of § 240.10b5-1(c) of this chapter; and

(ii) the reporting person does not select the date of execution.

(3) Solely for purposes of section 16(a)(2)(C) of the Act and paragraph (g)(1) of this section, the date on which the plan administrator notifies the reporting person that the transaction has been executed is deemed the date of execution for a discretionary transaction (as defined in § 16b-3(b)(1)) for which the reporting person does not select the date of execution.

(4) In the case of the transactions described in paragraphs (g)(2) and (g)(3) of this section, if the notification date is later than the third business day following the trade date of the transaction, the date of execution is deemed to be the third business day following the trade date of the transaction.

(5) At the option of the reporting person, transactions that are reportable on Form 5 may be reported on Form 4, so long as the Form 4 is filed no later than the due date of the Form 5 on which the transaction is otherwise required to be reported.

(h) The date of filing with the Commission shall be the date of receipt by the Commission.

(i) *Signatures.* Where Section 16 of the Act, or the rules or forms thereunder, require a document filed with or furnished to the Commission to be signed, such document shall be manually signed, or signed using either typed signatures or duplicated or facsimile versions of manual signatures. Where typed, duplicated or facsimile signatures are used, each signatory to the filing shall manually sign a signature page or other document authenticating, acknowledging or otherwise adopting his or her signature that appears in the filing. Such document shall be executed before or at the time the filing is made and shall be retained by the filer for a period of five years. Upon request, the filer shall furnish to the Commission or its staff a copy of any or all documents retained pursuant to this section.

(j) Where more than one person subject to section 16 of the Act is deemed to be a beneficial owner of the same equity securities, all such persons must report as beneficial owners of the securities, either separately or jointly. Where persons in a group are deemed to be beneficial owners of equity securities pursuant to § 240.16a-1(a)(1) due to the aggregation of holdings, a single Form 3, 4 or 5 may be filed on behalf of all persons in the group. Joint and group filings must include all required information for each beneficial owner, and such filings must be signed by each beneficial owner, or on behalf of such owner by an authorized person.

(k) Any issuer that maintains a corporate website shall post on that website by the end of the business day after filing any Form 3, 4 or 5 filed under section 16(a) of the Act as to the equity securities of that issuer. Each such form shall remain accessible on such issuer's website for at least a 12-month period. In the case of an issuer that is an investment company and that does not maintain its own website, if any of the issuer's investment adviser, sponsor, depositor, trustee, administrator, principal underwriter, or any affiliated person of the investment company maintains a website that includes the name of the issuer, the issuer shall comply with the posting requirements by posting the forms on one such website.

[As last amended in Release No. 33-8230, effective June 30, 2003, 68 F.R. 25788.]

[¶ 23,731] Derivative Securities

Reg. § 240.16a-4. (a) For purposes of Section 16 of the Act, both derivative securities and the underlying securities to which they relate shall be deemed to be the same class of equity securities, *except that* the acquisition or disposition of any derivative security shall be separately reported.

(b) The exercise or conversion of a call equivalent position shall be reported on Form 4 and treated for reporting purposes as:

(1) A purchase of the underlying security; and

(2) A closing of the derivative security position.

(c) The exercise or conversion of a put equivalent position shall be reported on Form 4 and treated for reporting purposes as:

(1) A sale of the underlying security; and

(2) A closing of the derivative security position.

(d) The disposition or closing of a long derivative security position, as a result of cancellation or expiration, shall be exempt from section 16(a) of the Act if exempt from section 16(b) of the Act pursuant to § 240.16b-6(d).

Note to § 240.16a-4: A purchase or sale resulting from an exercise or conversion of a derivative security may be exempt from section 16(b) of the Act pursuant to § 240.16b-3 or § 240.16b6(b).

[As last amended in Release No. 34-37260, May 31, 1996, effective August 15, 1996, 61 F.R. 30376.]

[¶ 23,741] Odd-Lot Dealers

Reg. § 240.16a-5. Transactions by an odd-lot dealer (a) in odd-lots as reasonably necessary to carry on odd-lot transactions, or (b) in round lots to offset odd-lot transactions previously or simultaneously executed or reasonably anticipated in the usual course of business, shall be exempt from the provisions of Section 16(a) of the Act with respect to participation by such odd-lot dealer in such transaction.

[As last amended in Release No. 34-28869, February 8, 1991, effective May 1, 1991, 56 F.R. 7242.]

[¶ 23,751] Small Acquisitions

Reg. § 240.16a-6. (a) Any acquisition of an equity security or the right to acquire such securities, other than an acquisition from the issuer (including an employee benefit plan sponsored by the issuer), not exceeding $10,000 in market value shall be reported on Form 5, subject to the following conditions:

(1) Such acquisition, when aggregated with other acquisitions of securities of the same class (including securities underlying derivative securities, but excluding acquisitions exempted by rule from section 16(b) or previously reported on Form 4 or Form 5) within the prior six months, does not exceed a total of $10,000 in market value; and

(2) The person making the acquisition does not within six months thereafter make any disposition, other than by a transaction exempt from section 16(b) of the Act.

(b) If an acquisition no longer qualifies for the reporting deferral in paragraph (a) of this section, all such acquisitions that have not yet been reported must be reported on Form 4 before the end of the second business day following the day on which the conditions of paragraph (a) of this section are no longer met.

[As last amended in Release No. 34-46421, effective August 29, 2002, 67 F.R. 56462.]

[¶ 23,761] Transactions Effected in Connection With a Distribution

Reg. § 240.16a-7. (a) Any purchase and sale, or sale and purchase, of a security that is made in connection with the distribution of a substantial block of securities shall be exempt from the provisions of Section 16(a) of the Act, to the extent specified in this Rule, subject to the following conditions:

(1) The person effecting the transaction is engaged in the business of distributing securities and is participating in good faith, in the ordinary course of such business, in the distribution of such block of securities; and

(2) The security involved in the transaction is:

(i) part of such block of securities and is acquired by the person effecting the transaction, with a view to distribution thereof, from the issuer or other person on whose behalf such securities are being distributed or from a person who is participating in good faith in the distribution of such block of securities; or

(ii) a security purchased in good faith by or for the account of the person effecting the transaction for the purpose of stabilizing the market price of securities of the class being distributed or to cover an over-allotment or other short position created in connection with such distribution.

(b) Each person participating in the transaction must qualify on an individual basis for an exemption pursuant to this section.

[As last amended in Release No. 34-28869, February 8, 1991, effective May 1, 1991, 56 F.R. 7242.]

[¶ 23,771] Trusts

Reg. § 240.16a-8. (a) *Persons Subject to Section 16.*

(1) *Trusts.* A trust shall be subject to section 16 of the Act with respect to securities of the issuer if the trust is a beneficial owner, pursuant to § 240.16a-1(a)(1), of more than ten percent of any class of equity securities of the issuer registered pursuant to section 12 of the Act ("ten percent beneficial owner").

(2) *Trustees, Beneficiaries, and Settlors.* In determining whether a trustee, beneficiary, or settlor is a ten percent beneficial owner with respect to the issuer:

(i) such persons shall be deemed the beneficial owner of the issuer's securities held by the trust, to the extent specified by § 240.16a-1(a)(1); and

(ii) settlors shall be deemed the beneficial owner of the issuer's securities held by the trust where they have the power to revoke the trust without the consent of another person.

(b) *Trust Holdings and Transactions.* Holdings and transactions in the issuer's securities held by a trust shall be reported by the trustee on behalf of the trust, if the trust is subject to Section 16 of the Act, except as provided below. Holdings and transactions in the issuer's securities held by a trust (whether or not subject to Section 16 of the Act) may be reportable by other parties as follows:

(1) *Trusts.* The trust need not report holdings and transactions in the issuer's securities held by the trust in an employee benefit plan subject to the Employee Retirement Income Security Act over which no trustee exercises investment control.

(2) *Trustees.* If, as provided by § 240.16a-1(a)(2), a trustee subject to Section 16 of the Act has a pecuniary interest in any holding or transaction in the issuer's securities held by the trust, such holding or transaction shall be attributed to the trustee and shall be reported by the trustee in the trustee's individual capacity, as well as on behalf of the trust. With respect to performance fees and holdings of the trustee's immediate family, trustees shall be deemed to have a pecuniary interest in the trust holdings and transactions in the following circumstances:

(i) a performance fee is received that does not meet the proviso of § 240.16a-1(a)(2)(ii) (C); or

(ii) at least one beneficiary of the trust is a member of the trustee's immediate family. The pecuniary interest of the immediate family member(s) shall be attributed to and reported by the trustee.

(3) *Beneficiaries.* A beneficiary subject to Section 16 of the Act shall have or share reporting obligations with respect to transactions in the issuer's securities held by the trust, if the beneficiary is a beneficial owner of the securities pursuant to § 240.16a-1(a)(2), as follows:

(i) If a beneficiary shares investment control with the trustee with respect to a trust transaction, the transaction shall be attributed to and reported by both the beneficiary and the trust;

(ii) If a beneficiary has investment control with respect to a trust transaction without consultation with the trustee, the transaction shall be attributed to and reported by the beneficiary only; and

(iii) In making a determination as to whether a beneficiary is the beneficial owner of the securities pursuant to § 240.16a-1(a)(2), beneficiaries shall be deemed to have a pecuniary interest in the issuer's securities held by the trust to the extent of their pro rata interest in the trust where the trustee does not exercise exclusive investment control.

Note to paragraph (b)(3): Transactions and holdings attributed to a trust beneficiary may be reported by the trustee on behalf of the beneficiary, provided that the report is signed by the beneficiary or other authorized person. Where the transactions and holdings are attributed both to the trustee and trust beneficiary, a joint report may be filed in accordance with § 240.16a-3(j).

(4) *Settlors.* If a settlor subject to Section 16 of the Act reserves the right to revoke the trust without the consent of another person, the trust holdings and transactions shall be attributed to and reported by the settlor instead of the trust; *provided, however,* that if the settlor does not exercise or share investment control over the issuer's securities held by the trust, the trust holdings and transactions shall be attributed to and reported by the trust instead of the settlor.

(c) *Remainder interests.* Remainder interests in a trust are deemed not to confer beneficial ownership for purposes of Section 16 of the Act, provided that the persons with the remainder interests have no power, directly or indirectly, to exercise or share investment control over the trust.

(d) A trust, trustee, beneficiary or settlor becoming subject to Section 16(a) of the Act pursuant to this Rule also shall be subject to Sections 16(b) and 16(c) of the Act.

[As last amended in Release No. 34-46421, effective August 29, 2002, 67 F.R. 56462.]

[¶ 23,781] Stock Splits, Stock Dividends, and Pro Rata Rights

Reg. § 240.16a-9. The following shall be exempt from Section 16 of the Act:

(a) The increase or decrease in the number of securities held as a result of a stock split or stock dividend applying equally to all securities of a class, including a stock dividend in which equity securities of a different issuer are distributed; and

(b) the acquisition of rights, such as shareholder or pre-emptive rights, pursuant to a pro rata grant to all holders of the same class of equity securities registered under Section 12 of the Act.

Note: The exercise or sale of a pro rata right shall be reported pursuant to § 240.16a-4 and the exercise shall be eligible for exemption from Section 16(b) of the Act pursuant to § 240.16b-6(b).

[As last amended in Release No. 34-37260, May 31, 1996, effective August 15, 1996, 61 F.R. 30376.]

[¶ 23,791] Exemptions Under Section 16(a)

Reg. § 240.16a-10. Except as provided in § 240.16a-6, any transaction exempted from the requirements of Section 16(a) of the Act, insofar as it is otherwise subject to the provisions of Section 16(b), shall be likewise exempt from Section 16(b) of the Act.

[As last amended in Release No. 34-28869, February 8, 1991, effective May 1, 1991, 56 F.R. 7242.]

[¶ 23,792] Dividend or Interest Reinvestment Plans

Reg. § 240.16a-11. Any acquisition of securities resulting from the reinvestment of dividends or interest on securities of the same issuer shall be exempt from section 16 of the Act if the acquisition is made pursuant to a plan providing for the regular reinvestment of dividends or interest and the plan provides for broad-based participation, does not discriminate in favor of employees of the issuer, and operates on substantially the same terms for all plan participants.

[As adopted in Release No. 34-37260, May 31, 1996, effective August 15, 1996, 61 F.R. 30376.]

[¶ 23,793] Domestic Relations Orders

Reg. § 240.16a-12. The acquisition or disposition of equity securities pursuant to a domestic relations order, as defined in the Internal Revenue Code or Title I of the Employee Retirement Income Security Act, or the rules thereunder, shall be exempt from section 16 of the Act.

[As adopted in Release No. 34-37260, May 31, 1996, effective August 15, 1996, 61 F.R. 30376.]

[¶ 23,794] Change in Form of Beneficial Ownership

Reg. § 240.16a-13. A transaction, other than the exercise or conversion of a derivative security or deposit into or withdrawal from a voting trust, that effects only a change in the form of beneficial ownership without changing a person's pecuniary interest in the subject equity securities shall be exempt from section 16 of the Act.

[As adopted in Release No. 34-37260, May 31, 1996, effective August 15, 1996, 61 F.R. 30376.]

EXEMPTION OF CERTAIN TRANSACTIONS FROM SECTION 16(b)

[¶ 23,801] Transactions Approved by a Regulatory Authority

Reg. § 240.16b-1. (a) Any purchase and sale, or sale and purchase, of a security shall be exempt from Section 16(b) of the Act, if the transaction is effected by an investment company registered under the Investment Company Act of 1940 (15 U.S.C. § 80a-1 *et seq.*) and both the purchase and sale of such security have been exempted from the provisions of Section 17(a)(15 U.S.C. § 80a-17(a)) of the Investment Company Act of 1940, by rule or order of the Commission.

(b) Any purchase and sale, or sale and purchase, of a security shall be exempt from the provisions of Section 16(b) of the Act if:

(1) the person effecting the transaction is either a holding company registered under the Public Utility Holding Company Act of 1935 (15 U.S.C. § 79a *et seq.*) or a subsidiary thereof; and

(2) both the purchase and the sale of the security have been approved or permitted by the Commission pursuant to the applicable provisions of that Act and the rules and regulations thereunder.

[As last amended in Release No. 34-37262, May 31, 1996, effective July 15, 1996, 61 F.R. 30397.]

[¶ 23,821] Transactions between an issuer and its officers or directors

Reg. § 240.16b-3. (a) *General.* A transaction between the issuer (including an employee benefit plan sponsored by the issuer) and an officer or director of the issuer that involves issuer equity securities shall be exempt from section 16(b) of the Act if the transaction satisfies the applicable conditions set forth in this section.

(b) *Definitions.* (1) A Discretionary Transaction shall mean a transaction pursuant to an employee benefit plan that:

(i) Is at the volition of a plan participant;

(ii) Is not made in connection with the participant's death, disability, retirement or termination of employment;

(iii) Is not required to be made available to a plan participant pursuant to a provision of the Internal Revenue Code; and

(iv) Results in either an intra-plan transfer involving an issuer equity securities fund, or a cash distribution funded by a volitional disposition of an issuer equity security.

(2) An Excess Benefit Plan shall mean an employee benefit plan that is operated in conjunction with a Qualified Plan, and provides only the benefits or contributions that would be provided under a Qualified Plan but for any benefit or contribution limitations set forth in the Internal Revenue Code of 1986, or any successor provisions thereof.

(3) (i) A Non-Employee Director shall mean a director who:

(A) Is not currently an officer (as defined in § 240.16a-1(f)) of the issuer or a parent or subsidiary of the issuer, or otherwise currently employed by the issuer or a parent or subsidiary of the issuer;

(B) Does not receive compensation, either directly or indirectly, from the issuer or a parent or subsidiary of the issuer, for services rendered as a consultant or in any capacity other than as a director, except for an amount that does not exceed the dollar amount for which disclosure would be required pursuant to § 229.404(a) of this chapter; and

(C) Does not possess an interest in any other transaction for which disclosure would be required pursuant to § 229.404(a) of this chapter.

(ii) Notwithstanding paragraph (b)(3)(i) of this section, a Non-Employee Director of a closedend investment company shall mean a director who is not an "interested person" of the issuer, as that term is defined in Section 2(a)(19) of the Investment Company Act of 1940.

(4) A Qualified Plan shall mean an employee benefit plan that satisfies the coverage and participation requirements of sections 410 and 401(a)(26) of the Internal Revenue Code of 1986, or any successor provisions thereof.

(5) A Stock Purchase Plan shall mean an employee benefit plan that satisfies the coverage and participation requirements of sections 423(b)(3) and 423(b)(5), or section 410, of the Internal Revenue Code of 1986, or any successor provisions thereof.

(c) *Tax-conditioned plans.* Any transaction (other than a Discretionary Transaction) pursuant to a Qualified Plan, an Excess Benefit Plan, or a Stock Purchase Plan shall be exempt without condition.

(d) *Acquisitions from the issuer.* Any transaction, other than a Discretionary Transaction, involving an acquisition from the issuer (including without limitation a grant or award), whether or not intended for a compensatory or other particular purpose, shall be exempt if:

(1) The transaction is approved by the board of directors of the issuer, or a committee of the board of directors that is composed solely of two or more Non-Employee Directors;

(2) The transaction is approved or ratified, in compliance with section 14 of the Act, by either: the affirmative votes of the holders of a majority of the securities of the issuer present, or represented, and entitled to vote at a meeting duly held in accordance with the applicable laws of the state or other jurisdiction in which the issuer is incorporated; or the written consent of the holders of a majority of the securities of the issuer entitled to vote; provided that such ratification occurs no later than the date of the next annual meeting of shareholders; or

(3) The issuer equity securities so acquired are held by the officer or director for a period of six months following the date of such acquisition, provided that this condition shall be satisfied with respect to a derivative security if at least six months elapse from the date of acquisition of the derivative security to the date of disposition of the derivative security (other than upon exercise or conversion) or its underlying equity security.

(e) *Dispositions to the issuer.* Any transaction, other than a Discretionary Transaction, involving the disposition to the issuer of issuer equity securities, whether or not intended for a compensatory or other particular purpose, shall be exempt, provided that the terms of such disposition are approved in advance in the manner prescribed by either paragraph (d)(1) or paragraph (d)(2) of this section.

(f) *Discretionary Transactions.* A Discretionary Transaction shall be exempt only if effected pursuant to an election made at least six months following the date of the most recent election, with respect to any plan of the issuer, that effected a Discretionary Transaction that was:

(i) An acquisition, if the transaction to be exempted would be a disposition; or

(ii) A disposition, if the transaction to be exempted would be an acquisition.

Notes to § 240.16b-3:

Note (1): The exercise or conversion of a derivative security that does not satisfy the conditions of this section is eligible for exemption from section 16(b) of the Act to the extent that the conditions of § 240.16b-6(b) are satisfied.

Note (2): Section 16(a) reporting requirements applicable to transactions exempt pursuant to this section are set forth in § 240.16a-3(f) and (g) and § 240.16a-4.

Note (3): The approval conditions of paragraphs (d)(1), (d)(2) and (e) of this section require the approval of each specific transaction, and are not satisfied by approval of a plan in its entirety except for the approval of a plan pursuant to which the terms and conditions of each transaction are fixed in advance, such as a formula plan. Where the terms of a subsequent transaction (such as the exercise price of an option, or the provision of an exercise or tax with-holding right) are provided for in a transaction as initially approved pursuant to paragraphs (d)(1), (d)(2) or (e), such subsequent transaction shall not require further specific approval.

Note (4): For purposes of determining a director's status under those portions of paragraph (b)(3)(i) that reference § 229.404(a) of this chapter, an issuer may rely on the disclosure provided under § 229.404(a) of this chapter for the issuer's most recent fiscal year contained in the most recent filing in which disclosure required under § 229.404(a) is presented. Where a transaction disclosed in that filing was terminated before the director's proposed service as a Non-Employee Director, that transaction will not bar such service. The issuer must believe in good faith that any current or contemplated transaction in which the director participates will not be required to be disclosed under § 229.404(a) of this chapter, based on information readily available to the issuer and the director at the time such director proposes to act as a Non-Employee Director. At such time as the issuer believes in good faith, based on readily available information, that a current or contemplated transaction with a director will be required to be disclosed under § 229.404(a) in a future filing, the director no longer is eligible to serve as a Non-Employee Director; *provided, however,* that this determination does not result in retroactive loss of a Rule 16b-3 exemption for a transaction previously approved by the director while serving as a Non-Employee Director consistent with this note. In making the determinations specified in this Note, the issuer may rely on information it obtains from the director, for example, pursuant to a response to an inquiry.

[As last amended in Release No. 33-8732, effective November 7, 2006, 71 F.R. 53158.]

[¶ 23,841] Bona Fide Gifts and Inheritance

Reg. § 240.16b-5. Both the acquisition and the disposition of equity securities shall be exempt from the operation of Section 16(b) of the Act if they are: (a) bona fide gifts; or (b) transfers of securities by will or the laws of descent and distribution.

[As last amended in Release No. 34-28869, February 8, 1991, effective May 1, 1991, 56 F.R. 7242.]

[¶ 23,851] Derivative Securities

Reg. § 240.16b-6. (a) The establishment of or increase in a call equivalent position or liquidation of or decrease in a put equivalent position shall be deemed a purchase of the underlying security for purposes of Section 16(b) of the Act, and the establishment of or increase in a put equivalent position or liquidation of or decrease in a call equivalent position shall be deemed a sale of the underlying securities for purposes of Section 16(b) of the Act; *provided, however,*that if the increase or decrease occurs as a result of the fixing of the exercise price of a right initially issued without a fixed price, where the date the price is fixed is not known in advance and is outside the control of the recipient, the increase or decrease shall be exempt from Section 16(b) of the Act with respect to any offsetting transaction within the six months prior to the date the price is fixed.

(b) The closing of a derivative security position as a result of its exercise or conversion shall be exempt from the operation of Section 16(b) of the Act, and the acquisition of underlying securities at a fixed exercise price due to the exercise or conversion of a call equivalent position or the disposition of underlying securities at a fixed exercise price due to the exercise of a put equivalent position shall be exempt from the operation of Section 16(b) of the Act; *provided, however,* that the acquisition of underlying securities from the exercise of an out-of-the-money option, warrant, or right shall not be exempt unless the exercise is necessary to comport with the sequential exercise provisions of the Internal Revenue Code (26 U.S.C. § 422A).

Note to Paragraph (b): The exercise or conversion of a derivative security that does not satisfy the conditions of this section is eligible for exemption from section 16(b) of the Act to the extent that the conditions of § 240.16b-3 are satisfied.

(c) In determining the short-swing profit recoverable pursuant to Section 16(b) of the Act from transactions involving the purchase and sale or sale and purchase of derivative and other securities, the following rules apply:

(1) Short-swing profits in transactions involving the purchase and sale or sale and purchase of derivative securities that have identical characteristics (*e.g.*, purchases and sales of call options of the same strike price and expiration date, or purchases and sales of the same series of convertible debentures) shall be measured by the actual prices paid or received in the short-swing transactions.

(2) Short-swing profits in transactions involving the purchase and sale or sale and purchase of derivative securities having different characteristics but related to the same underlying security (*e.g.*, the purchase of a call option and the sale of a convertible debenture) or derivative securities and underlying securities shall not exceed the difference in price of the underlying security on the date of purchase or sale and the date of sale or purchase. Such profits may be measured by calculating the short-swing profits that would have been realized had the subject transactions involved purchases and sales solely of the derivative security that was purchased or solely of the derivative security that was sold, valued as of the time of the matching purchase or sale, and calculated for the lesser of the number of underlying securities actually purchased or sold.

(d) Upon cancellation or expiration of an option within six months of the writing of the option, any profit derived from writing the option shall be recoverable under Section 16(b) of the Act. The profit shall not exceed the premium received for writing the option. The disposition or closing of a long derivative security position, as a result of cancellation or expiration, shall be exempt from Section 16(b) of the Act where no value is received from the cancellation or expiration.

[As last amended in Release No. 34-37260, May 31, 1996, effective August 15, 1996, 61 F.R. 30376.]

[¶ 23,861] Mergers, Reclassifications, and Consolidations

Reg. § 240.16b-7. (a) The following transactions shall be exempt from the provisions of Section 16(b) of the Act:

(1) The acquisition of a security of a company, pursuant to a merger, reclassification or consolidation, in exchange for a security of a company that before the merger, reclassification or consolidation, owned 85 percent or more of either:

(i) The equity securities of all other companies involved in the merger, reclassification or consolidation, or in the case of a consolidation, the resulting company; or

(ii) The combined assets of all the companies involved in the merger, reclassification or consolidation, computed according to their book values before the merger, reclassification or consolidation as determined by reference to their most recent available financial statements for a 12 month period before the merger, reclassification or consolidation, or such shorter time as the company has been in existence.

(2) The disposition of a security, pursuant to a merger, reclassification or consolidation, of a company that before the merger, reclassification or consolidation, owned 85 percent or more of either:

(i) The equity securities of all other companies involved in the merger, reclassification or consolidation or, in the case of a consolidation, the resulting company; or

(ii) The combined assets of all the companies undergoing merger, reclassification or consolidation, computed according to their book values before the merger, reclassification or consolidation as determined by reference to their most recent available financial statements for a 12 month period before the merger, reclassification or consolidation.

(b) A merger within the meaning of this section shall include the sale or purchase of substantially all the assets of one company by another in exchange for equity securities which are then distributed to the security holders of the company that sold its assets.

(c) The exemption provided by this section applies to any securities transaction that satisfies the conditions specified in this section and is not conditioned on the transaction satisfying any other conditions.

(d) Notwithstanding the foregoing, if a person subject to section 16 of the Act makes any non-exempt purchase of a security in any company involved in the merger, reclassification or consolidation and any non-exempt sale of a security in any company involved in the merger, reclassification or consolidation within any period of less than six months during which the merger, reclassification or consolidation took place, the exemption provided by this section shall be unavailable to the extent of such purchase and sale.

[As last amended in amended by Release No. 33-8600, effective August 9, 2005, 70 F.R. 46080.]

[¶ 23,871] Voting Trusts

Reg. § 240.16b-8. Any acquisition or disposition of an equity security or certificate representing equity securities involved in the deposit or withdrawal from a voting trust or deposit agreement shall be exempt from Section 16(b) of the Act if substantially all of the assets held under the voting trust or deposit agreement immediately after the deposit or immediately prior to the withdrawal consisted of equity securities of the same class as the security deposited or withdrawn; *provided, however,* that this exemption shall not apply if there is a non-exempt purchase or sale of an equity security of the class deposited within six months (including the date of withdrawal or deposit) of a nonexempt sale or purchase, respectively, of any certificate representing such equity security (other than the actual deposit or withdrawal).

[As last amended in Release No. 34-28869, February 8, 1991, effective May 1, 1991, 56 F.R. 7242.]

REGULATION FD—Fair Disclosure

⟫→ *Amended by Release No. 33-9146, effective October 4, 2010, 75 F.R. 61050.*

[¶ 25,151] General Rule Regarding Selective Disclosure

Reg. § 243.100. (a) Whenever an issuer, or any person acting on its behalf, discloses any material nonpublic information regarding that issuer or its securities to any person described in paragraph (b)(1) of this section, the issuer shall make public disclosure of that information as provided in § 243.101(e):

(1) Simultaneously, in the case of an intentional disclosure; and

(2) Promptly, in the case of a non-intentional disclosure.

(b)(1) Except as provided in paragraph (b)(2) of this section, paragraph (a) of this section shall apply to a disclosure made to any person outside the issuer:

(i) Who is a broker or dealer, or a person associated with a broker or dealer, as those terms are defined in Section 3(a) of the Securities Exchange Act of 1934 (15 U.S.C. 78c(a));

(ii) Who is an investment adviser, as that term is defined in Section 202(a)(11) of the Investment Advisers Act of 1940 (15 U.S.C. 80b-2(a)(11)); an institutional investment manager, as that term is defined in Section 13(f)(5) of the Securities Exchange Act of 1934 (15 U.S.C. 78m(f)(5)), that filed a report on Form 13F (17 CFR 249.325) with the Commission for the most recent quarter ended prior to the date of the disclosure; or a person associated with either of the foregoing. For purposes of this paragraph, a "person associated with an investment adviser or institutional investment manager" has the meaning set forth in Section 202(a)(17) of the Investment Advisers Act of 1940 (15 U.S.C. 80b-2(a)(17)), assuming for these purposes that an institutional investment manager is an investment adviser;

(iii) Who is an investment company, as defined in Section 3 of the Investment Company Act of 1940 (15 U.S.C. 80a-3), or who would be an investment company but for Section 3(c)(1) (15 U.S.C. 80a-3(c)(1)) or Section 3(c)(7) (15 U.S.C. 80a-3(c)(7)) thereof, or an affiliated person of either of the foregoing. For purposes of this paragraph, "affiliated person" means only those persons described in Section 2(a)(3)(C), (D), (E), and (F) of the Investment Company Act of 1940 (15 U.S.C. 80a-2(a)(3)(C), (D), (E), and (F)), assuming for these purposes that a person who would be an investment company but for Section 3(c)(1) (15 U.S.C. 80a-3(c)(1)) or Section 3(c)(7) (15 U.S.C. 80a-3(c)(7)) of the Investment Company Act of 1940 is an investment company; or

(iv) Who is a holder of the issuer's securities, under circumstances in which it is reasonably foreseeable that the person will purchase or sell the issuer's securities on the basis of the information.

(2) Paragraph (a) of this section shall not apply to a disclosure made:

(i) To a person who owes a duty of trust or confidence to the issuer (such as an attorney, investment banker, or accountant);

(ii) To a person who expressly agrees to maintain the disclosed information in confidence;

⟫→ *Paragraph (b)(2)(iii) removed and paragraph (b)(2)(iv) redesignated (b)(2)(iii) in Release No. 33-9146.*

(iii) To the following entities solely for the purpose of determining or monitoring a credit rating:

(A) any nationally recognized statistical rating organization, as that term is defined in Section 3(a)(62) of the Securities Exchange Act of 1934 (15 U.S.C. 78c(a)(62)), pursuant to § 240.17g-5(a)(3) of this chapter; or

(B) any credit rating agency, as that term is defined in Section 3(a)(61) of the Securities Exchange Act of 1934 (15 U.S.C. 78c(a)(61)), that makes its credit ratings publicly available; or

(iv) In connection with a securities offering registered under the Securities Act, other than an offering of the type described in any of Rule 415(a)(1)(i) through (vi) under the Securities Act (§ 230.415(a)(1)(i) through (vi) of this chapter) (except an offering of the type described in Rule 415(a)(1)(i) under the Securities Act (§ 230.415(a)(1)(i) of this chapter) also involving a registered offering, whether or not underwritten, for capital formation purposes for the account of the issuer (unless the issuer's offering is being registered for the purpose of evading the requirements of this section)), if the disclosure is by any of the following means:

(A) A registration statement filed under the Securities Act, including a prospectus contained therein;

(B) A free writing prospectus used after filing of the registration statement for the offering or a communication falling within the exception to the definition of prospectus contained in clause (a) of section 2(a)(10) of the Securities Act;

(C) Any other Section 10(b) prospectus;

(D) A notice permitted by Rule 135 under the Securities Act (§ 230.135 of this chapter);

(E) A communication permitted by Rule 134 under the Securities Act (§ 230.134 of this chapter); or

(F) An oral communication made in connection with the registered securities offering after filing of the registration statement for the offering under the Securities Act.

Amendment

>>>→ *Paragraph (b)(2)(iii) removed and paragraph (b)(2)(iv) redesignated (b)(2)(iii) in Release No. 33-9146.*

(iii) In connection with a securities offering registered under the Securities Act, other than an offering of the type described in any of Rule 415(a)(1)(i) through (vi) under the Securities Act (§ 230.415(a)(1)(i) through (vi) of this chapter) (except an offering of the type described in Rule 415(a)(1)(i) under the Securities Act (§ 230.415(a)(1)(i) of this chapter) also involving a registered offering, whether or not underwritten, for capital formation purposes for the account of the issuer (unless the issuer's offering is being registered for the purpose of evading the requirements of this section)), if the disclosure is by any of the following means:

(A) A registration statement filed under the Securities Act, including a prospectus contained therein;

(B) A free writing prospectus used after filing of the registration statement for the offering or a communication falling within the exception to the definition of prospectus contained in clause (a) of section 2(a)(10) of the Securities Act;

(C) Any other Section 10(b) prospectus;

(D) A notice permitted by Rule 135 under the Securities Act (§ 230.135 of this chapter);

(E) A communication permitted by Rule 134 under the Securities Act (§ 230.134 of this chapter); or

(F) An oral communication made in connection with the registered securities offering after filing of the registration statement for the offering under the Securities Act.

End of Amendment

[As last amended in Release No. 33-9146, effective October 4, 2010, 75 F.R. 61050.]

[¶ 25,152] Definitions

Reg. § 243.101. This section defines certain terms as used in Regulation FD (§§ 243.100 -243.103).

(a) Intentional. A selective disclosure of material nonpublic information is "intentional" when the person making the disclosure either knows, or is reckless in not knowing, that the information he or she is communicating is both material and nonpublic.

(b) Issuer. An "issuer" subject to this regulation is one that has a class of securities registered under Section 12 of the Securities Exchange Act of 1934 (15 U.S.C. 78l), or is required to file reports under Section 15(d) of the Securities Exchange Act of 1934 (15 U.S.C. 78o(d)), including any closed-end investment company (as defined in Section 5(a)(2) of the Investment Company Act of 1940) (15 U.S.C. 80a-5(a)(2)), but not including any other investment company or any foreign government or foreign private issuer, as those terms are defined in Rule 405 under the Securities Act (§ 230.405 of this chapter).

(c) Person acting on behalf of an issuer. "Person acting on behalf of an issuer" means any senior official of the issuer (or, in the case of a closed-end investment company, a senior official of the issuer's investment adviser), or any other officer, employee, or agent of an issuer who regularly communicates with any person described in § 243.100(b)(1)(i), (ii), or (iii), or with holders of the issuer's securities. An officer, director, employee, or agent of an issuer who discloses material nonpublic information in breach of a duty of trust or confidence to the issuer shall not be considered to be acting on behalf of the issuer.

(d) Promptly. "Promptly" means as soon as reasonably practicable (but in no event after the later of 24 hours or the commencement of the next day's trading on the New York Stock Exchange) after a senior official of the issuer (or, in the case of a closed-end investment company, a senior official of the issuer's investment adviser) learns that there has been a non-intentional disclosure by the issuer or person acting on behalf of the issuer of information that the senior official knows, or is reckless in not knowing, is both material and nonpublic.

(e) Public disclosure. (1) Except as provided in paragraph (e)(2) of this section, an issuer shall make the "public disclosure" of information required by § 243.100(a) by furnishing to or filing with the Commission a Form 8-K (17 CFR 249.308) disclosing that information.

(2) An issuer shall be exempt from the requirement to furnish or file a Form 8-K if it instead disseminates the information through another method (or combination of methods) of disclosure that is reasonably designed to provide broad, non-exclusionary distribution of the information to the public.

(f) Senior official. "Senior official" means any director, executive officer (as defined in § 240.3b-7 of this chapter), investor relations or public relations officer, or other person with similar functions.

(g) Securities offering. For purposes of § 243.100(b)(2)(iv):

(1) Underwritten offerings. A securities offering that is underwritten commences when the issuer reaches an understanding with the broker-dealer that is to act as managing underwriter and continues

until the later of the end of the period during which a dealer must deliver a prospectus or the sale of the securities (unless the offering is sooner terminated);

(2) *Non-underwritten offerings.* A securities offering that is not underwritten:

(i) If covered by Rule 415(a)(1)(x) (§ 230.415(a)(1)(x) of this chapter), commences when the issuer makes its first bona fide offer in a takedown of securities and continues until the later of the end of the period during which each dealer must deliver a prospectus or the sale of the securities in that takedown (unless the takedown is sooner terminated);

(ii) If a business combination as defined in Rule 165(f)(1) (§ 230.165(f)(1) of this chapter), commences when the first public announcement of the transaction is made and continues until the completion of the vote or the expiration of the tender offer, as applicable (unless the transaction is sooner terminated);

(iii) If an offering other than those specified in paragraphs (a) and (b) of this section, commences when the issuer files a registration statement and continues until the later of the end of the period during which each dealer must deliver a prospectus or the sale of the securities (unless the offering is sooner terminated).

[As adopted in Release No. 33-7881, effective October 23, 2000, 65 F.R. 51715.]

[¶ 25,153] No Effect on Antifraud Liability

Reg. § 243.102. No failure to make a public disclosure required solely by § 243.100 shall be deemed to be a violation of Rule 10b-5 (17 CFR 240.10b-5) under the Securities Exchange Act.

[As adopted in Release No. 33-7881, effective October 23, 2000, 65 F.R. 51715.]

[¶ 25,154] No Effect on Exchange Act Reporting Status

Reg. § 243.103. A failure to make a public disclosure required solely by § 243.100 shall not affect whether:

(a) For purposes of Forms S-2 (17 CFR 239.12), S-3 (17 CFR 239.13) and S-8 (17 CFR 239.16b) under the Securities Act, an issuer is deemed to have filed all the material required to be filed pursuant to Section 13 or 15(d) of the Securities Exchange Act of 1934 (15 U.S.C. 78m or 78o(d)) or, where applicable, has made those filings in a timely manner; or

(b) There is adequate current public information about the issuer for purposes of § 230.144(c) of this chapter (Rule 144(c)).

[As adopted in Release No. 33-7881, effective October 23, 2000, 65 F.R. 51715.]

REGULATION G

Part 244—DISCLOSURE OF NON-GAAP FINANCIAL MEASURES

[¶ 25,201] General Rules Regarding Disclosure of Non-GAAP Financial Measures

Reg. § 244.100. (a) Whenever a registrant, or person acting on its behalf, publicly discloses material information that includes a non-GAAP financial measure, the registrant must accompany that non-GAAP financial measure with:

(1) A presentation of the most directly comparable financial measure calculated and presented in accordance with Generally Accepted Accounting Principles (GAAP); and

(2) A reconciliation (by schedule or other clearly understandable method), which shall be quantitative for historical non-GAAP measures presented, and quantitative, to the extent available without unreasonable efforts, for forward-looking information, of the differences between the non-GAAP financial measure disclosed or released with the most comparable financial measure or measures calculated and presented in accordance with GAAP identified in paragraph (a)(1) of this section.

(b) A registrant, or a person acting on its behalf, shall not make public a non-GAAP financial measure that, taken together with the information accompanying that measure and any other accompanying discussion of that measure, contains an untrue statement of a material fact or omits to state a material fact necessary in order to make the presentation of the non-GAAP financial measure, in light of the circumstances under which it is presented, not misleading.

(c) This section shall not apply to a disclosure of a non-GAAP financial measure that is made by or on behalf of a registrant that is a foreign private issuer if the following conditions are satisfied:

(1) The securities of the registrant are listed or quoted on a securities exchange or inter-dealer quotation system outside the United States;

(2) The non-GAAP financial measure is not derived from or based on a measure calculated and presented in accordance with generally accepted accounting principles in the United States; and

(3) The disclosure is made by or on behalf of the registrant outside the United States, or is included in a written communication that is released by or on behalf of the registrant outside the United States.

(d) This section shall not apply to a non-GAAP financial measure included in disclosure relating to a proposed business combination, the entity resulting therefrom or an entity that is a party thereto, if the disclosure is contained in a communication that is subject to § 230.425 of this chapter, § 240.14a-12 or § 240.14d-2(b)(2) of this chapter or § 229.1015 of this chapter.

Notes to § 244.100:

1. If a non-GAAP financial measure is made public orally, telephonically, by webcast, by broadcast, or by similar means, the requirements of paragraphs (a)(1)(i) and (a)(1)(ii) of this section will be satisfied if:

(i) The required information in those paragraphs is provided on the registrant's web site at the time the non-GAAP financial measure is made public; and

(ii) The location of the web site is made public in the same presentation in which the non-GAAP financial measure is made public.

2. The provisions of paragraph (c) of this section shall apply notwithstanding the existence of one or more of the following circumstances:

(i) A written communication is released in the United States as well as outside the United States, so long as the communication is released in the United States contemporaneously with or after the release outside the United States and is not otherwise targeted at persons located in the United States;

(ii) Foreign journalists, U.S. journalists or other third parties have access to the information;

(iii) The information appears on one or more web sites maintained by the registrant, so long as the web sites, taken together, are not available exclusively to, or targeted at, persons located in the United States; or

(iv) Following the disclosure or release of the information outside the United States, the information is included in a submission by the registrant to the Commission made under cover of a Form 6-K.

[Added by Release No. 33-8176, effective March 28, 2003, 68 F.R. 4820.]

[¶ 25,205] Definitions

Reg. § 244.101. This section defines certain terms as used in Regulation G (§§ 244.100 through 244.102).

(a)(1) *Non-GAAP financial measure.* A non-GAAP financial measure is a numerical measure of a registrant's historical or future financial performance, financial position or cash flows that:

(i) Excludes amounts, or is subject to adjustments that have the effect of excluding amounts, that are included in the most directly comparable measure calculated and presented in accordance with

GAAP in the statement of income, balance sheet or statement of cash flows (or equivalent statements) of the issuer; or

(ii) Includes amounts, or is subject to adjustments that have the effect of including amounts, that are excluded from the most directly comparable measure so calculated and presented.

(2) A non-GAAP financial measure does not include operating and other financial measures and ratios or statistical measures calculated using exclusively one or both of:

(i) Financial measures calculated in accordance with GAAP; and

(ii) Operating measures or other measures that are not non-GAAP financial measures.

(3) A non-GAAP financial measure does not include financial measures required to be disclosed by GAAP, Commission rules, or a system of regulation of a government or governmental authority or self-regulatory organization that is applicable to the registrant.

(b) *GAAP.* GAAP refers to generally accepted accounting principles in the United States, except that (1) in the case of foreign private issuers whose primary financial statements are prepared in accordance with non-U.S. generally accepted accounting principles, GAAP refers to the principles under which those primary financial statements are prepared; and (2) in the case of foreign private issuers that include a non-GAAP financial measure derived from a measure calculated in accordance with U.S. generally accepted accounting principles, GAAP refers to U.S. generally accepted accounting principles for purposes of the application of the requirements of Regulation G to the disclosure of that measure.

(c) *Registrant.* A registrant subject to this regulation is one that has a class of securities registered under Section 12 of the Securities Exchange Act of 1934 (15 U.S.C. 78*l*), or is required to file reports under Section 15(d) of the Securities Exchange Act of 1934 (15 U.S.C. 78o(d)), excluding any investment company registered under Section 8 of the Investment Company Act of 1940 (15 U.S.C. 80a-8).

(d) *United States.* United States means the United States of America, its territories and possessions, any State of the United States, and the District of Columbia.

[Added by Release No. 33-8176, effective March 28, 2003, 68 F.R. 4820.]

[¶ 25,211] No Effect on Antifraud Liability

Reg. § 244.102. Neither the requirements of this Regulation G (17 CFR § 244.100 through 244.102) nor a person's compliance or non-compliance with the requirements of this Regulation shall in itself affect any person's liability under Section 10(b) (15 U.S.C. 78j(b)) of the Securities Exchange Act of 1934 or § 240.10b-5 of this chapter.

[Added by Release No. 33-8176, effective March 28, 2003, 68 F.R. 4820.]

EXCHANGE ACT FORMS (selected)

EXCHANGE ACT FORMS (SELECTED)

TABLE OF CONTENTS

[¶ 33,021] FORM 10

[As last amended in Release No. 33-8876, effective February 4, 2008, 73 F.R. 934.]

SECURITIES AND EXCHANGE COMMISSION

Washington, D.C. 20549

FORM 10

GENERAL FORM FOR REGISTRATION OF SECURITIES PURSUANT TO SECTION 12(b) or (g) OF THE SECURITIES EXCHANGE ACT OF 1934

GENERAL INSTRUCTIONS

A. Rule as to Use of Form 10

Form 10 shall be used for registration pursuant to Section 12(b) or (g) of the Securities Exchange Act of 1934 of classes of securities of issuers for which no other form is prescribed.

B. Application of General Rules and Regulations

(a) The General Rules and Regulations under the Act contain certain general requirements which are applicable to registration on any form. These general requirements should be carefully read and observed in the preparation and filing of registration statements on this form.

(b) Particular attention is directed to Regulation 12B [17 CFR 240.12b-1—240.12b-36] which contains general requirements regarding matters such as the kind and size of paper to be used, the legibility of the registration statement, the information to be given whenever the title of securities is required to be stated, and the filing of the registration statement. The definitions contained in Rule 12b-2 [17 CFR 240.12b-2] should be especially noted.

C. Preparation of Registration Statement

(a) This form is not to be used as a blank form to be filled in, but only as a guide in the preparation of the registration statement on paper meeting the requirements of Rule 12b-12 [17 CFR 240.12b-12]. The registration statement shall contain the item numbers and captions, but the text of the items may be omitted. The answers to the items shall be prepared in the manner specified in Rule 12b-13 [17 CFR 240.12b-13].

(b) Unless otherwise stated, the information required shall be given as of a date reasonably close to the date of filing the registration statement.

(c) Attention is directed to Rule 12b-20 [17 CFR 240.12b-20]which states: "In addition to the information expressly required to be included in a statement or report, there shall be added such further material information, if any, as may be necessary to make the required statements, in light of the circumstances under which they are made, not misleading."

D. Signature and Filing of Registration Statement

Three complete copies of the registration statement, including financial statements, exhibits and all other papers and documents filed as a part thereof, and five additional copies which need not include exhibits, shall be filed with the Commission. At least one complete copy of the registration statement, including financial statements, exhibits and all other papers and documents filed as a part thereof, shall be filed with each exchange on which any class of securities is to be registered. At least one complete copy of the registration statement filed with the Commission and one such copy filed with each exchange shall be manually signed. Copies not manually signed shall bear typed or printed signatures.

E. Omission of Information Regarding Foreign Subsidiaries

Information required by any item or other requirement of this form with respect to any foreign subsidiary may be omitted to the extent that the required disclosure would be detrimental to the registrant. However, financial statements, otherwise required, shall not be omitted pursuant to this instruction. Where information is omitted pursuant to this instruction, a statement shall be made that such information has been omitted and the names of the subsidiaries involved shall be separately furnished to the Commission. The Commission may, in its discretion, call for justification that the required disclosure would be detrimental.

F. Incorporation by Reference

Attention is directed to Rule 12b-23 [17 CFR 240.12b-23] which provides for the incorporation by reference of information contained in certain documents in answer or partial answer to any item of a registration statement.

SECURITIES AND EXCHANGE COMMISSION
Washington, D.C. 20549

FORM 10

GENERAL FORM FOR REGISTRATION OF SECURITIES

Pursuant to Section 12(b) or (g) of The Securities Exchange Act of 1934

SECURITIES AND EXCHANGE COMMISSION

Washington, D.C. 20549

FORM 10

GENERAL FORM FOR REGISTRATION OF SECURITIES

Pursuant to Section 12(b) or (g) of The Securities Exchange Act of 1934

. . . .

(Exact name of registrant as specified in its charter)

. . . .

(State or other jurisdiction of incorporation or organization)	(I.R.S. Employer Identification No.)

. . . .

(Address of principal executive offices)	(Zip Code)

Registrant's telephone number, including area code . . . .

Securities to be registered pursuant to Section 12(b) of the Act:

Title of each class to be so registered	Name of each exchange on which each class is to be registered

. . . .

. . . .

Securities to be registered pursuant to Section 12(g) of the Act:

. . . .

(Title of class)

. . . .

Indicate by check mark whether the registrant is a large accelerated filer, an accelerated filer, a non-accelerated filer, or a smaller reporting company. See the definitions of "large accelerated filer," "accelerated filer" and "smaller reporting company" in Rule 12b-2 of the Exchange Act. (Check one):

[ ] Large accelerated filer

[ ] Accelerated filer

[ ] Non-accelerated filer (do not check if a smaller reporting company)

[ ] Smaller reporting company

INFORMATION REQUIRED IN REGISTRATION STATEMENT

Item 1. Business

Furnish the information required by Item 101 of Regulation S-K (§ 229.101 of this chapter).

Item 1A. Risk Factors.

Set forth, under the caption "Risk Factors," where appropriate, the risk factors described in Item 503(c) of Regulation S-K (§ 229.503(c) of this chapter) applicable to the registrant. Provide any discussion of risk factors in plain English in accordance with Rule 421(d) of the Securities Act of 1933 (§ 230.421(d) of this chapter). Smaller reporting companies are not required to provide the information required by this item.

Item 2. Financial Information

Furnish the information required by Items 301, 303, and 305 of Regulation S-K (§§ 229.301, 229.303, and 229.305 of this chapter).

Item 3. Properties

Furnish the information required by Item 102 of Regulation S-K (§ 229.102 of this chapter).

Item 4. Security Ownership of Certain Beneficial Owners and Management

Furnish the information required by Item 403 of Regulation S-K (§ 229.403 of this chapter).

Item 5. Directors and Executive Officers

Furnish the information required by Item 401 of Regulation S-K (§ 229.401 of this chapter).

Item 6. Executive Compensation.

Furnish the information required by Item 402 of Regulation S-K (§ 229.402 of this chapter) and paragraph (e)(4) of Item 407 of Regulation S-K (§ 229.407 of this chapter).

Item 7. Certain Relationships and Related Transactions, and Director Independence.

Furnish the information required by Item 404 of Regulation S-K (§ 229.404 of this chapter) and Item 407(a) of Regulation S-K (§ 229.407(a) of this chapter).

Item 8. Legal Proceedings

Furnish the information required by Item 103 of Regulation S-K (§ 229.103 of this chapter).

Item 9. Market Price of and Dividends on the Registrant's Common Equity and Related Stockholder Matters

Furnish the information required by Item 201 of Regulation S-K (§ 229.201 of this chapter).

Item 10. Recent Sales of Unregistered Securities

Furnish the information required by Item 701 of Regulation S-K (§ 229.701 of this chapter).

Item 11. Description of Registrant's Securities to be Registered

Furnish the information required by Item 202 of Regulation S-K (§ 229.202 of this chapter). If the class of securities to be registered will trade in the form of American Depositary Receipts, furnish Item 202(f) disclosure for such American Depositary Receipts as well.

Item 12. Indemnification of Directors and Officers

Furnish the information required by Item 702 of Regulation S-K (§ 229.702 of this chapter).

Item 13. Financial Statements and Supplementary Data

Furnish all financial statements required by Regulation S-X and supplementary financial information required by Item 302 of Regulation S-K (§ 229.302 of this chapter). Smaller reporting companies may provide the financial information required by Article 8 of Regulation S-X in lieu of the information required by in other parts of Regulation S-X.

Item 14. Changes in and Disagreements with Accountants on Accounting and Financial Disclosure

Furnish the information required by Item 304 of Regulation S-K (§ 229.304 of this chapter).

Item 15. Financial Statements and Exhibits

(a) List separately all financial statements filed as part of the registration statement.

(b) Furnish the exhibits required by Item 601 of Regulation S-K (§ 229.601 of this chapter).

SIGNATURES

Pursuant to the requirements of Section 12 of the Securities Exchange Act of 1934, the registrant has duly caused this registration statement to be signed on its behalf by the undersigned, thereunto duly authorized.

. . . .

(Registrant)

. . . .

Date ....

By ....

(Signature)*

---

* Print name and title of the signing officer under his signature.

[¶ 33,061] # FORM 18

[As last amended in Release No. 34-31905, February 23, 1993, 58 F.R. 14628.]

FORM 18

For Foreign Governments and Political Subdivisions Thereof

Published 7/5/35   File No. . . . .

(Leave Blank)

APPLICATION FOR REGISTRATION PURSUANT TO SECTION 12(b) AND (c) OF THE SECURITIES EXCHANGE ACT OF 1934

SECURITIES AND EXCHANGE COMMISSION

Washington, D.C.

. . . .

(Name of Registrant)

Securities to be Registered		Names of Exchanges on which Registration
Title of Issue or Issues	Amount to be Registered	Applied for

Name and Address of Person Authorized to Receive Notices and Communications from the Securities and Exchange Commission:

RULE AS TO THE USE OF FORM 18

This form shall be used for applications for the permanent registration of securities of foreign governments and political subdivisions thereof, filed on or after July 1, 1935; provided, however, that any public corporation or other autonomous entity in the nature of a political subdivision, except a state, province, county or municipality or similar body politic, may, at its option, use Form 21 in lieu of this Form.

INSTRUCTIONS

1. The application, including exhibits, is to be filed with the exchange upon which registration is being sought and in triplicate with the Commission. At least one application filed with the Commission and one filed with the exchange is to be signed. If application is made for the registration of securities of the registrant on more than one exchange, the registrant may prepare one application covering all securities to be registered on any of the exchanges and, in such case, should file such application with each exchange and in triplicate with the Commission. A registrant may, however, at its option prepare separate applications for each exchange upon which registration of any of its securities is being sought, and, in such case, should file each such application in triplicate with the Commission.

2. All applications should be typed or printed on paper 8½ by 13 inches in size. Tables and financial data, however, may be on larger paper but should be folded to such size. Typed or printed matter should leave a margin of at least 1½ inches on the left. Applications should be securely bound and on the left only. The regis-trant's typewritten or printed application should contain both the items in the form and the answers thereto.

3. Where "brief" answers are indicated, the answer may incorporate by reference particular items, sections or paragraphs of any Exhibit, and may be qualified in its entirety by such reference.

4. If there are several principle parties obligor of the securities being registered, the financial information required may be presented in a consolidated form, if that is desired.

5. Where information is asked as of the close of the last fiscal year, if such information is not yet available for such date, it may be furnished as of the close of the latest fiscal year for which it is available.

6. The application is to be made in the English language.

7. *Privilege of Filing Prospectus*

If the registrant has filed a registration statement under the Securities Act of 1933 which has become effective within the current fiscal year of the registrant or becomes effective within the current fiscal year of the registrant on or prior to the effective date of the registration of the securities covered by the application herein and is not subject to any proceeding under Section 8(d) of the Act or to an order entered thereunder, the registrant may substitute for the information required by Items 1 to 12 inclusive (1) a copy of the registrant's prospectus filed with the registration statement under the Securities Act of 1933 and (2) a description of the securities being registered as required by Item 3 herein unless such description is contained in such prospectus. If this procedure is followed the prospectus and the description shall be physically substituted for the items of this form and the answers thereto, and the text of the items shall be omitted from the application.

DEFINITIONS

Unless the context clearly indicates the contrary, all terms used in these instructions and in the Form have the same meaning as in the Securities Exchange Act of 1934 and in the general Rules and Regulations of the Commission thereunder.

1. Name of registrant.

2. If the registrant is a governmental unit other than a national government, give the name of the national government of which the registrant is a unit and a brief description of the relationship of the registrant to such national government.

3. For each issue of securities to be registered hereunder:

(a) Give the title and full designation of the issue, and if not included therein, the rate of interest and the date of maturity. If due serially, a brief indication should be given of the serial maturities, for example, "maturing serially from 1936 to 1940."

(b) State the currency or currencies in which payable, and give the basis of determination for the currency conversion and at whose option, if payable in two or more currencies.

(c) Outline briefly the amortization, sinking fund, redemption and retirement provisions.

(d) State whether secured by any lien, the kind thereof, and briefly describe the property or revenues subjected to such lien.

(e) If by law, decree, or other administrative action, the security is not being serviced according to its original terms, outline briefly the provisions of such law, decree, or other administrative action.

(f) State briefly the circumstances of any other failure to pay principal, interest or any sinking fund or amortization installment.

(g) If guaranteed, state by whom guaranteed, and outline briefly the terms of the guarantee.

4. Give the date of the close of the last fiscal year of the registrant.

5. State as of the close of the last fiscal year of the registrant the total outstanding of:

(a) Internal Funded Debt of the registrant. (Total to be stated in the currency of the registrant. If any internal funded debt is payable in a foreign currency it should not be included under this item, but under 5 (b).)

(b) External Funded Debt of the registrant. (Totals to be stated in the respective currencies in which payable.)

6. Give the title and amount outstanding, together with the currency or currencies in which payable, of each issue of Funded Debt of the registrant outstanding as of the close of the last fiscal year of the registrant.

7. State as of the close of the last fiscal year of the registrant to the estimated total of:

(a) Internal floating indebtedness of the registrant. (Total to be stated in the currency of the registrant.)

(b) External floating indebtedness of the registrant. (Total to be stated in the respective currencies in which payable.)

8. A statement of the receipts, classified by source, and of the expenditures, classified by purpose, of the registrant for the last fiscal year of the registrant. This statement should be so itemized as to be reasonably informative and should cover both ordinary and extraordinary receipts and expenditures.

9. If any exchange control has been established by the registrant, or, if the registrant is other than a national government, by its national government, briefly describe such exchange control.

(Note: If the registrant is a governmental unit other than a national government, it need not answer the following items.)

10. A brief statement regarding the note issue and gold reserves of the central bank of issue of the registrant, and of any further gold stocks held by the registrant, as of a date reasonably close to the date of filing the application with the exchange.

11. A statement, in terms of weight and value, of imports and exports of merchandise for the last fiscal year of the registrant. If the statistics have been established only in terms of value, such will suffice.

12. Set forth the balance of international payments of the registrant for the last fiscal year of the registrant, conforming, if possible, to the nomenclature and form used in the "Statistical Handbook of the League of Nations." (This statement need be furnished only if the registrant has published a balance of international payments.)

EXHIBITS

The following Exhibits should be attached as part of the application. The registrant may file such other Exhibits as it may desire, marking them so as to indicate clearly the items to which they refer.

Exhibit "A"—A copy of the General Bond, Fiscal Agency Agreement, Loan Contract, or any other agreement defining the rights of the holders of the securities registered hereunder. If not in English, submit in addition, a translation into English.

Exhibit "B"—A copy of the last annual budget of the registrant as presented to its legislative body. This document need not be translated.

Exhibit "C"—A copy of any law, decree, or administrative document outlined in answer to Item 3(e). If not in English, submit in addition, a translation into English.

Upon the basis of the statements and documents comprising this application the undersigned hereby applies for registration pursuant to Section 12(b) and (c) of the Securities Exchange Act of 1934 of the securities specified on the facing sheet of this application on the respective exchanges there specified.

For . . . .

                                 (Name of Registrant)

By . . . .

                (Name)   (Title)

[¶ 33,081]   Form 20-F

[As last amended in Release No. 33-9142, effective September 21, 2010, 75 F.R. 57385.]

UNITED STATES

SECURITIES AND EXCHANGE COMMISSION

Washington, D.C. 20549

FORM 20-F

[ ]   **REGISTRATION STATEMENT PURSUANT TO SECTION 12(b) OR (g) OF THE SECURITIES EXCHANGE ACT OF 1934**

OR

[ ]   **ANNUAL REPORT PURSUANT TO SECTION 13 OR 15(d) OF THE SECURITIES EXCHANGE ACT OF 1934**

For the fiscal year ended . . . .

OR

[ ]   **TRANSITION REPORT PURSUANT TO SECTION 13 or 15(d) OF THE SECURITIES EXCHANGE ACT OF 1934**

For the transition period from _____ to . . . .

OR

[ ]   **SHELL COMPANY REPORT PURSUANT TO SECTION 13 OR 15(d) OF THE SECURITIES EXCHANGE ACT OF 1934**

Date of event requiring this shell company report . . . .

Commission file number . . . .

. . . .

(Exact name of Registrant as specified in its charter)

. . . .

(Translation of Registrant's name into English)

. . . .

(Jurisdiction of incorporation or organization)

. . . .

(Address of principal executive offices)

(Name, Telephone, E-mail and/or Facsimile number and Address of Company Contact Person)

Securities registered or to be registered pursuant to Section 12(b) of the Act.

Title of each class	Name of each exchange on which registered
. . . .	. . . .
. . . .	. . . .

Securities registered or to be registered pursuant to Section 12(g) of the Act.

. . . .

(Title of Class)

. . . .

(Title of Class)

Securities for which there is a reporting obligation pursuant to Section 15(d) of the Act.

. . . .

(Title of Class)

Indicate the number of outstanding shares of each of the issuer's classes of capital or common stock as of the close of the period covered by the annual report.

. . . .
. . . .

Indicate by check mark if the registrant is a well-known seasoned issuer, as defined in Rule 405 of the Securities Act.

Yes. . . . No. . . . .

If this report is an annual or transition report, indicate by check mark if the registrant is not required to file reports pursuant to Section 13 or 15(d) of the Securities Exchange Act of 1934.

Yes. . . . No. . . . .

Note – Checking the box above will not relieve any registrant required to file reports pursuant to Section 13 or 15(d) of the Securities Exchange Act of 1934 from their obligations under those Sections.

Indicate by check mark whether the registrant (1) has filed all reports required to be filed by Section 13 or 15(d) of the Securities Exchange Act of 1934 during the preceding 12 months (or for such shorter period that the registrant was required to file such reports), and (2) has been subject to such filing requirements for the past 90 days.

Yes. . . . No. . . . .

Indicate by check mark whether the registrant has submitted electronically and posted on its corporate Web site, if any, every Interactive Data File required to be submitted and posted pursuant to Rule 405 of Regulation S-T (§ 232.405 of this chapter) during the preceding 12 months (or for such shorter period that the registrant was required to submit and post such files).

Yes___
No___

Indicate by check mark whether the registrant is a large accelerated filer, an accelerated filer, or a non-accelerated filer. See definition of accelerated filer and large accelerated filer in Rule 12b-2 of the Exchange Act. (Check one):

Large accelerated filer___Accelerated filer ___Non-accelerated filer___

Indicate by check mark which basis of accounting the
registrant has used to prepare the financial statements
included in this filing:
[] U.S. GAAP
[] International Financial Reporting Standards as issued
by the International Accounting Standards Board
[] Other
If "Other" has been checked in response to the previous
question, indicate by check mark which financial
statement item the registrant has elected to follow.
[] Item 17
[] Item 18

If this is an annual report, indicate by check mark whether the registrant is a shell company (as defined in Rule 12b-2 of the Exchange Act).

Yes. . . . No. . . . .

(APPLICABLE ONLY TO ISSUERS INVOLVED IN BANKRUPTCY PROCEEDINGS DURING THE PAST FIVE YEARS)

Indicate by check mark whether the registrant has filed all documents and reports required to be filed by Sections 12, 13 or 15(d) of the Securities Exchange Act of 1934 subsequent to the distribution of securities under a plan confirmed by a court.

Yes. . . . No. . . . .

GENERAL INSTRUCTIONS

A. Who May Use Form 20-F and When It Must be Filed.

(a) Any foreign private issuer, other than an asset-backed issuer (as defined in 17 CFR 229.1101), may use this form as a registration statement under Section 12 of the Securities Ex-change Act of 1934 (referred to as the Exchange Act) or as an annual or transition report filed under Section 13(a) or 15(d) of the Exchange Act. A transition report is filed when an issuer changes its fiscal year end. The term "foreign private is-suer" is defined in Rule 3b-4 under the Exchange Act.

(b) A foreign private issuer must file its annual report on this Form within the following period:

(1) Within six months after the end of the fiscal year covered by the report for fiscal years ending before December 15, 2011; and

(2) Within four months after the end of the fiscal year covered by the report for fiscal years ending on or after December 15, 2011.

(c) A foreign private issuer filing a transition report on this Form must file its report in accordance with the requirements set forth in Rule 13a-10 or Rule 15d-10 under the Exchange Act that apply when an issuer changes its fiscal year end.

(d) A foreign private issuer that was a shell company, other than a business combination related shell company, as those terms are defined in Rule 12b-2 under the Exchange Act (17 CFR 240.12b-2), immediately before a transaction that causes it to cease to be a shell company must file a report on this form in accordance with the requirements set forth in Rule 13a-19 or Rule 15d-19 under the Exchange Act (17 CFR 240.13a-19 and 240.15d-19). Issuers filing such reports shall provide all information required in, and follow all instructions of, Form 20-F relating to an Exchange Act registration statement of all classes of the registrant's securities subject to the reporting requirements of Section 13 (15 U.S.C. 78m) or Section 15(d) (15 U.S.C. 78o(d)) of such Act upon consummation of the transaction, with such information reflecting the registrant and its securities upon consummation of the transaction. Rule 12b-25 under the Exchange Act (17 CFR 240.12b-25) is not available to extend the due date of the report required under this subparagraph (d).

B. General Rules and Regulations That Apply to this Form.

(a) The General Rules and Regulations under the Securities Act of 1933 (referred to as the Securities Act) contain general requirements that apply to registration on any form. Read these general requirements carefully and follow them when preparing and filing registration statements and reports on this Form.

(b) Pay particular attention to Regulation 12B under the Exchange Act. Regulation 12B contains general requirements about matters such as the kind and size of paper to be used, the legibility of the registration statement or report, the information to give in response to a requirement to state the title of securities, the language to be used and the filing of the registration statement or report.

(c) In addition to the definitions in the General Rules and Regulations under the Securities Act and the definitions in Rule 12b-2 under the Exchange Act, General Instruction F defines certain terms for purposes of this Form.

(d) Note Regulation S-X, which applies to the presentation of financial information in a registration statement or report.

(e) Where the Form is being used as an annual report filed under Section 13(a) or 15(d) of the Exchange Act, provide the certifications required by Rule 13a-14 (17 CFR 240.13a-14) or Rule 15d-14 (17 CFR 240.15d-14).

(f) A foreign private issuer that is a smaller reporting company, as defined in Rule 12b-2 under the Exchange Act (17 CFR 240.12b-2), may not use the scaled disclosure requirements in Regulation S-X and Regulation S-K available to smaller reporting companies for the purposes of preparing this form.

C. How to Prepare Registration Statements and Reports on this Form.

(a) Do not use this Form as a blank form to be filled in; use it only as a guide in the preparation of the registration statement or annual report. General Instruction E states which items must be responded to in a registration statement and which items must be responded to in an annual report. The registration statement or report must contain the numbers and captions of all items. You may omit the text following each caption in this Form, which describes what must be disclosed under each item. Omit the text of all instructions in this Form. If an item is inapplicable or the answer to the item is in the negative, respond to the item by making a statement to that effect.

(b) Unless an item directs you to provide information as of a specific date or for a specific period, give the information in a registration statement as of a date reasonably close to the date of filing the registration statement and give the information in an annual report as of the latest practicable date.

(c) Note Exchange Act Rule 12b-20, which states: "In addition to the information expressly required to be included in a statement or report, there shall be added such further material information, if any, as may be necessary to make the required statements, in light of the circumstances under which they are made, not misleading."

(d) If the same information required by this Form also is required by the body of accounting principles used in preparing the financial statements, you may respond to an item of this Form by providing a cross-reference to the location of the information in the financial statements, in lieu of repeating the information.

(e) Note Item 10 of Regulation S-K which explains the Commission policy on projections of future economic performance, the Commission's policy on securities ratings, and the Commission's policy on use of non-GAAP financial measures in Commission filings.

(f) If you are providing the information required by this Form in connection with a registration statement under the Securities Act, note that Rule 421 requires you to follow plain English drafting principles. You can find helpful information in "A Plain English Handbook - How to create clear SEC disclosure documents" and in staff legal bulletins supplementing the Handbook. These documents are available on our Internet website, at www.sec.gov.

D. How to File Registration Statements and Reports on this Form.

(a) You must file the Form 20-F registration statement or annual report in electronic format via our Electronic Data Gathering and Retrieval System (EDGAR) in accordance with the EDGAR rules set forth in Regulation S-T (17 CFR Part 232). The Form 20-F registration statement or annual report must be in the English language as required by Regulation S-T Rule 306 (17 CFR 232.306). You must provide the signatures required for the Form 20-F registration statement or annual report in accordance with Regulation S-T Rule 302 (17 CFR 232.302). If you have technical questions about EDGAR or want to request an access code, call the EDGAR Filer Support Office at (202) 551-8900. If you have questions about the EDGAR rules, call the Office of EDGAR and Information Analysis at (202) 551-3610.

(b) If you are filing the Form 20-F registration statement or annual report in paper under a hardship exemption in Rule 201 or 202 of Regulation S-T (17 CFR 232.201 or 232.202), or as otherwise permitted, you must file with the Commission (i) three complete copies of the registration statement or report, including financial statements, exhibits and all other papers and documents filed as part of the registration statement or report, and (ii) five additional copies of the registration statement or report, which need not contain exhibits. Whether filing electronically or in paper, you must also file at least one complete copy of the registration statement or report, including financial statements, exhibits and all other papers and documents filed as part of the registration statement or report, with each exchange on which any class of securities is or will be registered. When submitting the Form 20-F in paper, you must sign at least one complete copy of the registration statement or report filed with the Commission and one copy filed with each exchange in accordance with Exchange Act Rule 12b-11(d) (17 CFR 12b-11(d)). You must conform the unsigned copies when submitting the Form 20-F registration statement or report in paper. When submitting the Form 20-F in electronic format to the Commission, you may submit a paper copy containing typed signatures to each United States stock exchange

in accordance with Regulation S-T Rule 302(c) (17 CFR 302(c)). See also Exchange Act Rule 12b-12(d) and Form 20-F's Instructions as to Exhibits for requirements concerning use of the English language and treatment of foreign language documents.

(c) When registration statements and reports are permitted to be filed in paper, they are filed with the Commission by sending or delivering them to our File Desk between the hours of 9:00 a.m. and 5:30 p.m., Washington, D.C. time. The File Desk is closed on weekends and federal holidays. If you file a paper registration statement or report by mail or by any means other than hand delivery, the address is U.S. Securities and Exchange Commission, Attention: File Desk, 100 F Street, N.E., Washington, D.C. 20549. We consider documents to be filed on the date our File Desk receives them.

E. Which Items to Respond to in Registration Statements and Annual Reports.

(a) *Exchange Act Registration Statements.* A registration statement filed under the Exchange Act on this Form must include the information specified in Part I and Part III. Read the instructions to each item carefully before responding to the item. In some cases, the instructions may permit you to omit some of the information specified in certain items in Part I.

(b) *Annual Reports.* An annual report on this Form must include the information specified in Parts I, II and III. Read the instructions to each item carefully before responding to the item. In some cases, the instructions may permit you to omit some of the information specified in certain items in Part I. The instructions also may permit you to omit certain information if it was previously reported to us and has not changed. If that is the case, you do not have to file copies of the previous report with the report being filed on this Form.

(c) *Financial Statements.*

(1) For an issuer's fiscal years ending before December 15, 2011, an Exchange Act registration statement or annual report filed on this Form must contain the financial statements and related information specified in Item 17 of this Form. We encourage you to provide the financial statements and related information specified in Item 18 of this Form in lieu of Item 17, but the Item 18 statements and information are not required. In certain circumstances, Forms F-1, F-3 or F-4 for the registration of securities under the Securities Act require that you provide the financial statements and related information specified in Item 18 in your annual report on Form 20-F. Consult those Securities Act forms for the specific requirements and consider the potential advantages of complying with Item 18 instead of Item 17 of this Form. Note that Items 17 and 18 may require you to file

financial statements of other entities in certain circumstances. These circumstances are described in Regulation S-X.

(2) For the issuer's fiscal years ending on or after December 15, 2011, an Exchange Act registration statement or annual report filed on this Form must contain the financial statements and related information specified in Item 18 of this Form. Note that Items 17 and 18 may require you to file the financial statements of other entities in certain circumstances. These circumstances are described in Regulation S-X.

(3) The financial statements must be audited in accordance with U.S. generally accepted auditing standards, and the auditor must comply with the U.S. standards for auditor independence. If you have any questions about these requirements, contact the Office of Chief Accountant in the Division of Corporation Finance at (202) 551-3400.

(d) *Securities Act Registration Statements.* The registration statement forms under the Securities Act direct you to provide information required by specific items of Form 20-F. Some items of Form 20-F only apply to Securities Act registration statements, and you do not have to respond to those items if you are using Form 20-F to file an Exchange Act registration statement or an annual report. The instructions to the items of Form 20-F identify which information is required only in Securities Act registration statements.

F. Definitions

The following definitions apply to various terms used in this Form, unless the context indicates otherwise.

Affiliate -An "affiliate" of a specified person or entity refers to one who, directly or indirectly, either controls, is controlled by or is under common control with, the specified person or entity.

Beneficial owner - The term "beneficial owner" of securities refers to any person who, even if not the record owner of the securities, has or shares the underlying benefits of ownership. These benefits include the power to direct the voting or the disposition of the securities or to receive the economic benefit of ownership of the securities. A person also is considered to be the "beneficial owner" of securities that the person has the right to acquire within 60 days by option or other agreement. Beneficial owners include persons who hold their securities through one or more trustees, brokers, agents, legal representatives or other intermediaries, or through companies in which they have a "controlling interest," which means the direct or indirect power to direct the management and policies of the entity.

Company - References to the "company" mean the company whose securities are being offered or listed, and refer to the company on a consolidated basis unless the context indicates otherwise.

Directors and senior management -This term includes (a) the company's directors, (b) members of its administrative, supervisory or management bodies, (c) partners with unlimited liability, in the case of a limited partnership with share capital, (d) nominees to serve in any of the aforementioned positions, and (e) founders, if the company has been established for fewer than five years. The persons covered by the term "administrative, supervisory or management bodies" vary in different countries and, for purposes of complying with the disclosure standards, will be determined by the host country.

Document - This term covers prospectuses and offering documents used in connection with a public offering of securities and registration statements or prospectuses used in connection with the initial listing of securities.

Instruction: *References to the "document" mean whatever type of document is being prepared using Form 20-F disclosure requirements, including, as applicable, a prospectus, an Exchange Act registration statement, and an annual report.*

Equity securities - The term "equity securities" includes common or ordinary shares, preferred or preference shares, options or warrants to subscribe for equity securities, and any securities, other than debt securities, which are convertible into or exercisable or redeemable for equity securities of the same company or another company. If the equity securities available upon conversion, exercise or redemption are those of another company, the disclosure standards also apply to the other company.

Group - A "group" is a parent and all its subsidiaries. References to a company's group mean the group of which it is a member.

Home country -This term refers to the jurisdiction in which the company is legally organized, incorporated or established and, if different, the jurisdiction where it has its principal listing.

Host country - This term refers to jurisdictions, other than the home country, in which the company is seeking to offer, register or list its securities.

Instruction: *Note that, as used in this Form, the term "host country" means the United States and its territories.*

Pre-emptive issue - The term "pre-emptive issue" and references to "pre-emptive purchase rights" refer to offerings made to the company's existing shareholders in order to permit them to maintain their pro rata ownership in the company.

G. First-Time Application of International Financial Reporting Standards.

(a) *Omission of Certain Required Financial Statements.* An issuer that changes the body of accounting principles used in preparing its financial statements presented pursuant to Item 8.A.2 ("Item 8.A.2") to International Financial Reporting Standards ("IFRS") issued by the International Accounting Standards Board ("IASB") may omit the earliest of three years of audited financial statements required by Item 8.A.2 if the issuer satisfies the conditions set forth in this Instruction G. For purposes of this instruction, the term "financial year" refers to the first financial year beginning on or after January 1 of the same calendar year.

(b) *Applicable Documents.* This General Instruction G shall be available only for the following registration statements and annual reports:

(1) *Registration Statements.* This instruction shall be available for registration statements if:

(A) The issuer adopts IFRS for the first time by an explicit and unreserved statement of compliance with IFRS; and

(B) The audited financial statements for the issuer's most recent financial year for which audited financial statements are required by Item 8.A.2 are prepared in accordance with IFRS.

(2) *Annual Reports.* This instruction shall be available for annual reports if:

(A) The issuer adopts IFRS for the first time by an explicit and unreserved statement of compliance with IFRS; and

(B) The audited financial statements for the issuer's financial year to which the annual report relates are prepared in accordance with IFRS.

(c) *Selected Financial Data.* The selected historical financial data required pursuant to Item 3.A shall be based on financial statements prepared in accordance with IFRS and shall be presented for the two most recent financial years. The issuer shall present selected historical financial data in accordance with U.S. GAAP for the five most recent financial years, except as the issuer is otherwise permitted to omit U.S. GAAP information for any of the earliest of the five years pursuant to Item 3.A.1.

(d) *Information on the Company.* The reference in Item 4.B to the "body of accounting principles used in preparing the financial statements," means IFRS as issued by the IASB and not the basis of accounting that was previously used ("Previous GAAP") or accounting principles used only to prepare a U.S. GAAP reconciliation.

(e) *Operating and Financial Review and Prospects.* The issuer shall present the information provided pursuant to Item 5. The discussion should focus on the financial statements for the two most recent financial years prepared in accordance with IFRS as issued by the IASB. No part of the discussion should relate to financial statements prepared in accordance with Previous GAAP.

(f) *Financial Information.*

(1) *General.* With respect to the financial information required by Item 8.A, all instructions contained in Item 8, including the instruction requiring audits in accordance with U.S. generally accepted auditing standards, shall apply.

(2) *Interim Period Financial Information in a Registration Statement or Prospectus.* This instruction shall apply when an issuer is changing the body of accounting principles used in preparing its financial statements presented pursuant to Item 8.A.2 to IFRS. This instruction shall be available during the financial year in which the issuer is changing its accounting principles to IFRS and during the financial year thereafter until the date as of which the issuer is required to comply with Item 8.A.4.

(A) Instruction 3 of the Instructions to Item 8.A.5 shall not apply to published financial information that is prepared with reference to IFRS. This General Instruction G(f)(2)(A) shall be available for any financial information for any interim or annual financial period that the issuer publishes that is prepared with reference to IFRS.

(B) An issuer that is required to provide interim financial statements under the first sentence of Item 8.A.5 may satisfy the requirements of that item by providing one of the following:

(i) Three financial years of audited financial statements and interim financial statements (which may be unaudited) for the current and comparable prior year period, prepared in accordance with Previous GAAP and reconciled to U.S. GAAP as required by Item 17(c) or 18, as applicable;

(ii) Two financial years of audited financial statements and interim financial statements (which may be unaudited) for the current and comparable prior year period, prepared in accordance with IFRS as issued by the IASB;

(iii) Three financial years of audited financial statements prepared in accordance with Previous GAAP; interim statements (which may be unaudited) for the current and comparable prior year period prepared in accordance with IFRS as issued by the IASB; and condensed financial information prepared in accordance with U.S. GAAP for the most recent financial year and the current and comparable prior year interim period (the form and content of this financial information shall be in a level of detail substantially similar to that required by Article 10 of Regulation S-X).

Instruction:

An issuer that is unable to provide information that complies with Instruction G.(f)(2)(B) but has available comparable financial information based on a combination of Previous GAAP, IFRS and U.S. GAAP should contact the Office of International Corporate Finance in the Division of Corporation Finance, in writing and well in advance of any filing deadlines, to discuss its interim period financial information.

(g) *Quantitative and Qualitative Disclosures about Market Risk.* Information in the document that responds to Item 11 shall be presented on the basis of IFRS.

(h) *Financial Statements.* A document to which this Instruction G applies shall include financial statements that comply with Item 17 or 18 as follows:

(1) *Financial Statements in Accordance with IFRS.* The issuer may omit the earliest of the three years of financial statements required by Item 8.A.2.

(2) *U.S. GAAP Information.* The U.S. GAAP reconciliation referenced in Item 17(c) or 18 shall not be required for periods presented in accordance with IFRS as issued by the IASB.

Instructions:

1. An eligible issuer relying on this General Instruction G may elect to include, refer to, or incorporate by reference financial data prepared in accordance with Previous GAAP. An issuer electing to include, refer to, or incorporate by reference Previous GAAP financial information shall prominently disclose, at an appropriate location in the document, that the document includes, refers to, or incorporates by reference, as applicable, financial statements and other financial information based on both IFRS and Previous GAAP, and that the information based on Previous GAAP is not comparable to information prepared in accordance with IFRS.

2. Companies electing to include or incorporate by reference Previous GAAP financial information shall:

a. Present or incorporate by reference selected historical financial data prepared in accordance with Previous GAAP for the four financial years prior to the most recent financial year.

b. Present or incorporate by reference operating and financial review and prospects information pursuant to Item 5 that focuses on the financial statements for the two most recent financial years prior to the most recent financial year that were prepared in accordance with Previous GAAP. The discussion should not refer to a reconciliation to U.S. GAAP. No part of the discussion should relate to financial statements prepared in accordance with IFRS.

c. Include or incorporate by reference comparative financial statements prepared in accordance with Previous GAAP that cover the two financial years prior to the most recent financial year.

3. Companies electing to include or incorporate by reference Previous GAAP financial information shall not present that information side-by-side with IFRS financial information.

4. An issuer that has published audited financial statements prepared in accordance with IFRS for each of the three latest financial years shall include all three years of audited IFRS financial statements in its SEC filings.

PART I

Item 1. Identity of Directors, Senior Management and Advisers

The purpose of this standard is to identify the company representatives and other individuals involved in the company's listing or registration.

A. ***Directors and senior management.*** Provide the names, business addresses and functions of the company's directors and senior management.

B. ***Advisers.*** Provide the names and addresses of the company's principal bankers and legal advisers to the extent the company has a continuing relationship with such entities, the sponsor for listing (where required by the host country regulations), and the legal advisers to the issue.

C. ***Auditors.*** Provide the names and addresses of the company's auditors for the preceding three years (together with their membership in a professional body).

Instructions to Item 1:

If you are filing Form 20-F as an annual report under the Exchange Act, you do not have to provide the information called for by Item 1. You must provide this information, to the extent applicable, if you are filing a registration statement under either the Securities Act or the Exchange Act.

Instructions to Item 1.B:

You only have to provide the information called for by Item 1.B if you are required to disclose the information in a jurisdiction outside the United States. These persons will not be considered "experts" or "sellers" under the Securities Act solely due to the fact that they are named in response to Item 1.B.

Item 2. Offer Statistics and Expected Timetable

The purpose of this standard is to provide key information regarding the conduct of any offering and the identification of important dates relating to that offering.

A. ***Offer statistics.*** For each method of offering, e.g., rights offering, general offering, etc., state the total expected amount of the issue, including the expected issue price or the method of determining the price and the number of securities expected to be issued.

B. ***Method and expected timetable.*** For all offerings, and separately for each group of targeted potential investors, the document shall state the following information to the extent applicable to the offering procedure:

1. The time period during which the offer will be open, and where and to whom purchase or subscription applications shall be addressed. Describe whether the purchase period may be extended or shortened, and the manner and duration of possible extensions or possible early closure or shortening of this period. Describe the manner in which the latter shall be made public. If the exact dates are not known when the document is first filed or distributed to the public, describe arrangements for announcing the final or definitive date or period.

2. Method and time limits for paying up securities; where payment is partial, the manner and dates on which amounts due are to be paid.

3. Method and time limits for delivery of equity securities (including provisional certificates, if applicable) to subscribers or purchasers.

4. In the case of pre-emptive purchase rights, the procedure for the exercise of any right of pre-emption, the negotiability of subscription rights and the treatment of subscription rights not exercised.

5. A full description of the manner in which results of the distribution of securities are to be made public, and when appropriate, the manner for refunding excess amounts paid by applicants (including whether interest will be paid).

Instructions to Item 2:

If you are filing Form 20-F as a registration statement or annual report under the Exchange Act, you do not have to provide the information called for by Item 2. You must provide this information if you are filing a registration statement under the Securities Act.

Item 3. Key Information

The purpose of this standard is to summarize key information about the company's financial condition, capitalization and risk factors. If the financial statements included in the document are restated to reflect material changes in the company's group structure or accounting policies, the selected financial data also must be restated. See Item 8.

A. *Selected financial data.*

1. The company shall provide selected historical financial data regarding the company, which shall be presented for the five most recent financial years (or such shorter period that the company has been in operation), in the same currency as the financial statements. Selected financial data for either or both of the earliest two years of the five-year period may be omitted, however, if the company represents to the host country regulator that such information cannot be provided, or cannot be provided on a restated basis, without unreasonable effort or expense. If interim period financial statements are included, the selected financial data should be updated for that interim period, which may be unaudited, provided that fact is stated. If selected financial data for interim periods is provided, comparative data from the same period in the prior financial year shall also be provided, except that the requirement for comparative balance sheet data is satisfied by presenting the year end balance sheet information.

2. The selected financial data presented shall include items generally corresponding to the following, except that the specific line items presented should be expressed in the same manner as the corresponding line items in the company's financial statements. Such data shall include, at a minimum, net sales or operating revenues; income (loss) from operations; income (loss) from continuing operations; net income (loss); net income (loss) from operations per share; income (loss) from continuing operations per share; total assets; net assets; capital stock (excluding long term debt and redeemable preferred stock); number of shares as adjusted to reflect changes in capital; dividends declared per share in both the currency of the financial statements and the host country currency, including the formula used for any adjustments to dividends declared; and diluted net income per share. Per share amounts must be determined in accordance with the body of accounting principles used in preparing the financial statements.

3. Where the financial statements provided in response to Item 8 are prepared in a currency other than the currency of the host country, disclosure of the exchange rate between the financial reporting currency and the currency of the host country should be provided, using the exchange rate designated by the host country for this purpose, if any:

(a) at the latest practicable date;

(b) the high and low exchange rates for each month during the previous six months; and

(c) for the five most recent financial years and any subsequent interim period for which financial statements are presented, the average rates for each period, calculated by using the average of the exchange rates on the last day of each month during the period.

B. ***Capitalization and indebtedness.*** A statement of capitalization and indebtedness (distinguishing between guaranteed and unguaranteed, and secured and unsecured, indebtedness) as of a date no earlier than 60 days prior to the date of the document shall be provided showing the company's capitalization on an actual basis and, if applicable, as adjusted to reflect the sale of new securities being issued and the intended application of the net proceeds therefrom. Indebtedness also includes indirect and contingent indebtedness.

C. *Reasons for the offer and use of proceeds.*

1. The document shall disclose the estimated net amount of the proceeds broken down into each principal intended use thereof. If the anticipated proceeds will not be sufficient to fund all the proposed purposes, the order of priority of such purposes should be given, as well as the amount and sources of other funds needed. If the company has no specific plans for the proceeds, it should discuss the principal reasons for the offering.

2. If the proceeds are being used directly or indirectly to acquire assets, other than in the ordinary course of business, briefly describe the assets and their cost. If the assets will be acquired from affiliates of the company or their associates, disclose the persons from whom they will be acquired and how the cost to the company will be determined.

3. If the proceeds may or will be used to finance acquisitions of other businesses, give a brief description of such businesses and information on the status of the acquisitions.

4. If any material part of the proceeds is to be used to discharge, reduce or retire indebtedness, describe the interest rate and maturity of such indebtedness and, for indebtedness incurred within the past year, the uses to which the proceeds of such indebtedness were put.

D. *Risk factors.* The document shall prominently disclose risk factors that are specific to the company or its industry and make an offering speculative or one of high risk, in a section headed "Risk Factors." Companies are encouraged, but not required, to list the risk factors in the order of their priority to the company. Among other things, such factors may include, for example: the nature of the business in which it is engaged or proposes to engage; factors relating to the countries in which it operates; the absence of profitable operations in recent periods; the financial position of the company; the possible absence of a liquid trading market for the company's securities; reliance on the expertise of management; potential dilution; unusual competitive conditions; pending expiration of material patents, trademarks or contracts; or dependence on a limited number of customers or suppliers. The Risk Factors section is intended to be a summary of more detailed discussion contained elsewhere in the document.

Instructions to Item 3:

1. If you are filing Form 20-F as an annual report under the Exchange Act, you do not have to provide the information called for by Item 3.B or 3.C. If you are filing Form 20-F as a registration statement under the Exchange Act, you do not have to provide the information called for by Item 3.C. You must provide the information called for by Item 3 if you are filing a registration statement under the Securities Act.

2. Throughout Form 20-F, the terms "financial year" and "fiscal year" have the same meaning. The term "fiscal year" is defined in Rule 405 under the Securities Act and Rule 12b-2 under the Exchange Act.

Instructions to Item 3.A:

1. This item refers to the company, but note that in some cases, you may have to provide selected financial data for a predecessor. See the definition of predecessor in Exchange Act Rule 12b-2 and Securities Act Rule 405.

2. You may present the selected financial data on the basis of the accounting principles used in your primary financial statements. If you use a basis of accounting other than IFRS as issued by the IASB, however, you also must include in this summary any reconciliations of the data to U.S. generally accepted accounting principles and Regulation S-X, pursuant to Item 17 or 18 of this Form. For financial statements prepared using a basis of accounting other than IFRS as issued by the IASB, you only have to provide selected financial data on a basis reconciled to U.S. generally accepted accounting principles for (i) those periods for which you were required to reconcile the primary annual financial statements in a filing under the Securities Act or the Exchange Act, and (ii) any interim periods.

If you are unable to provide selected financial data for the earliest two years of the five-year period, submit the required representation to us before or at the time you file the document. Disclose in the document that data for the earliest two years have been omitted and explain the reasons for the omission.

Instructions to Item 3.B:

1. If you are including the capitalization table called for by Item 3.B in a prospectus supplement for a shelf offering registered on Form F-3, the amounts shown in the table may be as of the date of the most recent balance sheet filed as part of the registration statement, if the information in the table is updated to reflect securities issued up to 60 days prior to the date of the supplement.

2. If you are not selling new securities in a firm commitment underwritten offering or an "all or none" best efforts offering, reflect the capitalization "as adjusted" for the net proceeds of the offering only in the following ways:

a. In a best efforts "minimum/maximum" offering, reflect both the minimum and maximum proceeds; and

b. In a rights offering or an offering of securities upon the exercise of outstanding warrants, reflect the proceeds only to the extent exercise is likely in view of the current market price.

Instructions to Item 3.D:

Risk factors should be concise and explain clearly how the risk affects the issuer or the securities.

Item 4. Information on the Company

The purpose of this standard is to provide information about the company's business operations, the products it makes or the services it provides, and the factors that affect the business. The standard also is intended to provide information regarding the adequacy and suitability of the company's properties, plants and equipment, as well as its plans for future increases or decreases in such capacity.

A. *History and development of the company.* The following information shall be provided:

1. The legal and commercial name of the company.

2. The date of incorporation and the length of life of the company, except where indefinite.

3. The domicile and legal form of the company, the legislation under which the company operates, its country of incorporation and the address and telephone number of its registered office (or principal place of business if different from its registered office). Provide the name and address of the company's agent in the host country, if any.

4. The important events in the development of the company's business, e.g. information concerning the nature and results of any material reclassification, merger or consolidation of the company or any of its significant subsidiaries; acquisitions or dispositions of material assets other than in the ordinary course of business; any material changes in the mode of conducting the business; material changes in the types of products produced or services rendered; name changes; or the nature and results of any bankruptcy, receivership or similar proceedings with respect to company or significant subsidiaries.

5. A description, including the amount invested, of the company's principal capital expenditures and divestitures (including interests in other companies), since the beginning of the company's last three financial years to the date of the offering or listing document.

6. Information concerning the principal capital expenditures and divestitures currently in progress, including the distribution of these investments geographically (home and abroad) and the method of financing (internal or external).

7. An indication of any public takeover offers by third parties in respect of the company's shares or by the company in respect of other companies' shares which have occurred during the last and current financial year. The price or exchange terms attaching to such offers and the outcome thereof are to be stated.

B. *Business overview.* The information required by this item may be presented on the same basis as that used to determine the company's business segments under the body of accounting principles used in preparing the financial statements. The following information shall be provided:

1. A description of the nature of the company's operations and its principal activities, stating the main categories of products sold and/or services performed for each of the last three financial years. Indicate any significant new products and/or services that have been introduced and, to the extent the development of new products or services has been publicly disclosed, give the status of development.

2. A description of the principal markets in which the company competes, including a breakdown of total revenues by category of activity and geographic market for each of the last three financial years.

3. A description of the seasonality of the company's main business.

4. A description of the sources and availability of raw materials, including a description of whether prices of principal raw materials are volatile.

5. A description of the marketing channels used by the company, including an explanation of any special sales methods, such as installment sales.

6. Summary information regarding the extent to which the company is dependent, if at all, on patents or licenses, industrial, commercial or financial contracts (including contracts with customers or suppliers) or new manufacturing processes, where such factors are material to the company's business or profitability.

7. The basis for any statements made by the company regarding its competitive position shall be disclosed.

8. A description of the material effects of government regulations on the company's business, identifying the regulatory body.

C. *Organizational structure.* If the company is part of a group, include a brief description of the group and the company's position within the group. Provide a listing of the company's significant subsidiaries, including name, country of incorporation or residence, proportion of ownership interest and, if different, proportion of voting power held.

D. **Property, plants and equipment.** The company shall provide information regarding any material tangible fixed assets, including leased properties, and any major encumbrances thereon, including a description of the size and uses of the property; productive capacity and extent of utilization of the company's facilities; how the assets are held; the products produced; and the location. Also describe any environmental issues that may affect the company's utilization of the assets. With regard to any material plans to construct, expand or improve facilities, describe the nature of and reason for the plan, an estimate of the amount of expenditures including the amount of expenditures already paid, a description of the method of financing the activity, the estimated dates of start and completion of the activity, and the increase of production capacity anticipated after completion.

Instruction to Item 4:

1. Furnish the information specified in any industry guide listed in Subpart 229.800 of Regulation S-K (§ 229.801 et seq. of this chapter) that applies to you.

2. If oil and gas operations are material to you or your subsidiaries' business operations or financial position, provide the information specified in Subpart 1200 of Regulation S-K (§ 229.1200 et seq. of this chapter).

Instructions to Item 4.A.4:

1. If you are providing the information called for by Item 4.A.4 in an annual report, you only have to provide the required information for the period from the beginning of your last full financial year up to the latest practicable date.

2. If you are filing a report under Rule 13a-19 or Rule 15d-19 under the Exchange Act (17 CFR 240.13a-19 or 240.15d-19), you must disclose the material terms of the transaction as a result of which you ceased to be a shell company and you should file as an exhibit under Item 4(a) of the Exhibits to Form 20-F any contracts relating to the transaction.

Instructions to Item 4.B:

1. The reference in Item 4.B to "the body of accounting principles used in preparing the financial statements" means the accounting principles used in preparing the primary financial statements, not to accounting principles used only to prepare the U.S. GAAP reconciliation.

2. If you:

(a) are filing a registration statement on Form F-1 under the Securities Act or on Form 20-F under the Exchange Act,

(b) were not required to file reports under Section 13(a) or 15(d) of the Exchange Act immediately prior to filing that registration statement, and

(c) have not received (or your predecessor has not received) revenue from operations during each of the three fiscal years immediately prior to filing the registration statement,

you must provide information about your plan of operations. Provide information comparable to the information required by Item 101(a)(2) of Regulation S-K.

Instructions to Item 4.D:

1. In the case of an extractive enterprise, other than an oil and gas producing activity:

(a) Provide material information about production, reserves, locations, developments and the nature of your interest. If individual properties are of major significance to you, provide more detailed information about those properties and use maps to disclose information about their location.

(b) In documents that you file publicly with the Commission, do not disclose estimates of reserves unless the reserves are proven or probable and do not give estimated values of those reserves, unless foreign law requires you to disclose the information. If these types of estimates have already been provided to any person that is offering to acquire you, however, you may include the estimates in documents relating to the acquisition.

(i) consult the staff of the Office of International Corporate Finance of the Division of Corporation Finance. That office may request that you provide supplementally a copy of the full report of the engineer or other expert who estimated the reserves. See Rule 418 of Regulation C (§ 230.418 of this chapter) and Rule 12b-4 of Regulation 12B (§ 240.12b-4 of this chapter) for information about submitting supplemental information to the Commission and requesting its return.

(ii) in documents you file publicly with the Commission, do not disclose estimates of oil or gas reserves unless the reserves are proved (or in the case of other extractive industries, proved or probable) and do not give estimated values of those reserves, unless foreign law requires you to disclose the information. If these types of estimates have already been provided to any person that is offering to acquire you, however, you may include the estimates in documents relating to the acquisition.

(iii) if you represent that the estimates of reserves you provide, or any estimated valuation of those reserves, are based on estimates prepared or reviewed by independent consultants, you must name those consultants in the document.

(c) [Removed.]

Item 4A. Unresolved Staff Comments

If the registrant is an accelerated filer or a large accelerated filer, as defined in Rule 12b-2 of the Exchange Act (§ 240.12b-2 of this chapter), or is a well-known seasoned issuer as defined in Rule 405 of the Securities Act (§ 230.405 of this chapter) and has received written comments from the Commission staff regarding its periodic reports under the Exchange Act not less than 180 days before the end of its fiscal year to which the annual report relates, and such comments remain unresolved, disclose the substance of any such unresolved comments that the registrant believes are material. Such disclosure may provide other information including the position of the registrant with respect to any such comment.

Item 5. Operating and Financial Review and Prospects

The purpose of this standard is to provide management's explanation of factors that have affected the company's financial condition and results of operations for the historical periods covered by the financial statements, and management's assessment of factors and trends which are anticipated to have a material effect on the company's financial condition and results of operations in future periods.

Discuss the company's financial condition, changes in financial condition and results of operations for each year and interim period for which financial statements are required, including the causes of material changes from year to year in financial statement line items, to the extent necessary for an understanding of the company's business as a whole. Information provided also shall relate to all separate segments of the company. Provide the information specified below as well as such other information that is necessary for an investor's understanding of the company's financial condition, changes in financial condition and results of operations.

A. *Operating results.* Provide information regarding significant factors, including unusual or infrequent events or new developments, materially affecting the company's income from operations, indicating the extent to which income was so affected. Describe any other significant component of revenue or expenses necessary to understand the company's results of operations.

1. To the extent that the financial statements disclose material changes in net sales or revenues, provide a narrative discussion of the extent to which such changes are attributable to changes in prices or to changes in the volume or amount of products or services being sold or to the introduction of new products or services.

2. Describe the impact of inflation, if material. If the currency in which financial statements are presented is of a country that has experienced hyperinflation, the existence of such inflation, a five year history of the annual rate of inflation and a discussion of the impact of hyperinflation on the company's business shall be disclosed.

3. Provide information regarding the impact of foreign currency fluctuations on the company, if material, and the extent to which foreign currency net investments are hedged by currency borrowings and other hedging instruments.

4. Provide information regarding any governmental economic, fiscal, monetary or political policies or factors that have materially affected, or could materially affect, directly or indirectly, the company's operations or investments by host country shareholders.

B. *Liquidity and capital resources.* The following information shall be provided:

1. Information regarding the company's liquidity (both short and long term), including:

(a) a description of the internal and external sources of liquidity and a brief discussion of any material unused sources of liquidity. Include a statement by the company that, in its opinion, the working capital is sufficient for the company's present requirements, or, if not, how it proposes to provide the additional working capital needed.

(b) an evaluation of the sources and amounts of the company's cash flows, including the nature and extent of any legal or economic restrictions on the ability of subsidiaries to transfer funds to the company in the form of cash dividends, loans or advances and the impact such restrictions have had or are expected to have on the ability of the company to meet its cash obligations.

(c) information on the level of borrowings at the end of the period under review, the seasonality of borrowing requirements and the maturity profile of borrowings and committed borrowing facilities, with a description of any restrictions on their use.

2. Information regarding the type of financial instruments used, the maturity profile of debt, currency and interest rate structure. The discussion also should include funding and treasury policies and objectives in terms of the manner in which treasury activities are controlled, the currencies in which cash and cash equivalents are held, the extent to which borrowings are at fixed rates, and the use of financial instruments for hedging purposes.

3. Information regarding the company's material commitments for capital expenditures as of the end of the latest financial year and any subsequent interim period and an indication of the general purpose of such commitments and the anticipated sources of funds needed to fulfill such commitments.

C. *Research and development, patents and licenses, etc.* Provide a description of the company's research and development policies for the last three years, where it is significant, including the amount spent during each of the last three financial years on company-sponsored research and development activities.

D. *Trend information.* The company should identify the most significant recent trends in production, sales and inventory, the state of the order book and costs and selling prices since the latest financial year. The company also should discuss, for at least the current financial year, any known trends, uncertainties, demands, commitments or events that are reasonably likely to have a material effect on the company's net sales or revenues, income from continuing operations, profitability, liquidity or capital resources, or that would cause reported financial information not necessarily to be indicative of future operating results or financial condition.

E. Off-balance sheet arrangements.

1. In a separately-captioned section, discuss the company's off-balance sheet arrangements that have or are reasonably likely to have a current or future effect on the company's financial condition, changes in financial condition, revenues or expenses, results of operations, liquidity, capital expenditures or capital resources that is material to investors. The disclosure shall include the items specified in Items 5.E.1(a), (b), (c) and (d) of this Item to the extent necessary to an understanding of such arrangements and effect, and shall also include such other information that the company believes is necessary for such an understanding.

(a) The nature and business purpose to the company of such off-balance sheet arrangements;

(b) The importance to the company of such off-balance sheet arrangements in respect of its liquidity, capital resources, market risk support, credit risk support or other benefits;

(c) The amounts of revenues, expenses and cash flows of the company arising from such arrangements; the nature and amounts of any interests retained, securities issued and other indebtedness incurred by the company in connection with such arrangements; and the nature and amounts of any other obligations or liabilities (including contingent obligations or liabilities) of the company arising from such arrangements that are or are reasonably likely to become material and the triggering events or circumstances that could cause them to arise; and

(d) Any known event, demand, commitment, trend or uncertainty that will result in or is reasonably likely to result in the termination, or material reduction in availability to the company, of its off-balance sheet arrangements that provide material benefits to it, and the course of action that the company has taken or proposes to take in response to any such circumstances.

2. As used in this Item 5.E., the term *off-balance sheet arrangement* means any transaction, agreement or other contractual arrangement to which an entity unconsolidated with the company is a party, under which the company has:

(a) Any obligation under a guarantee contract that has any of the characteristics identified in paragraph 3 of FASB Interpretation No. 45, *Guarantor's Accounting and Disclosure Requirements for Guarantees, Including Indirect Guarantees of Indebtedness of Others* (November 2002) ("FIN 45"), as may be modified or supplemented, excluding the types of guarantee contracts described in paragraphs 6 and 7 of FIN 45;

(b) A retained or contingent interest in assets transferred to an unconsolidated entity or similar arrangement that serves as credit, liquidity or market risk support to such entity for such assets;

(c) Any obligation under a derivative instrument that is both indexed to the company's own stock and classified in stockholders' equity, or not reflected, in the company's statement of financial position; or

(d) Any obligation, including a contingent obligation, arising out of a variable interest (as referenced in FASB Interpretation No. 46, *Consolidation of Variable Interest Entities* (January 2003), as may be modified or supplemented) in an unconsolidated entity that is held by, and material to, the company, where such entity provides financing, liquidity, market risk or credit risk support to, or engages in leasing, hedging or research and development services with, the company.

F. Tabular disclosure of contractual obligations.

1. In a tabular format, provide the information specified in this Item 5.F.1 as of the latest fiscal year end balance sheet date with respect to the company's known contractual obligations specified in the table that follows this Item 5.F.1. The company shall provide amounts, aggregated by type of contractual obligation. The company may disaggregate the specified categories of contractual obligations using other categories suitable to its business, but the presentation must include all of the obligations of the company that fall within the specified categories. A presentation covering at least the periods specified shall be included. The tabular presentation may be accompanied by footnotes to describe provisions that create, increase or accelerate obligations, or other pertinent data to the extent necessary for an understanding of the timing and amount of the company's specified contractual obligations.

	Payments due by period			
Contractual Obligations	Total	Less than 1 year	1-3 years	3-5 years	More than 5 years
[Long-Term Debt Obligations]					
[Capital (Finance) Lease Obligations]					
[Operating Lease Obligations]					
[Purchase Obligations]					
[Other Long-Term Liabilities Reflected on the Company's Balance Sheet under the GAAP of the primary financial statements]					
Total					

2. As used in this Item 5.F.1, the term purchase obligation means an agreement to purchase goods or services that is enforceable and legally binding on the company that specifies all significant terms, including: fixed or minimum quantities to be purchased; fixed, minimum or variable price provisions; and the approximate timing of the transaction.

G. Safe harbor.

1. The safe harbor provided in Section 27A of the Securities Act and Section 21E of the Exchange Act ("statutory safe harbors") shall apply to forward-looking information provided pursuant to Item 5.E and F, provided that the disclosure is made by: an issuer; a person acting on behalf of the issuer; an outside reviewer retained by the issuer making a statement on behalf of the issuer; or an underwriter, with respect to information provided by the issuer or information derived from information provided by the issuer.

2. For purposes of Item 5.G.1 of this Item only, all information required by Item 5.E.1 and 5.E.2 of this Item is deemed to be a "forward looking statement" as that term is defined in the statutory safe harbors, except for historical facts.

3. With respect to Item 5.E, the meaningful cautionary statements element of the statutory safe harbors will be satisfied if a company satisfies all requirements of that same Item 5.E.

Instructions to Item 5:

1. Refer to the Commission's interpretive release (No. 33-6835) dated May 18, 1989 for guidance in preparing this discussion and analysis by management of the company's financial condition and results of operations.

2. The discussion should focus on the primary financial statements presented in the document. You should refer to the reconciliation to U.S. GAAP, if any, and discuss any aspects of the differences between foreign and U.S. GAAP, not otherwise discussed in the reconciliation, that you believe are necessary for an understanding of the financial statements as a whole.

3. We encourage you to supply forward-looking information, but that type of information is not required. Forward-looking information is covered expressly by the safe harbor provisions of Section 27A of the Securities Act and Section 27A of the Exchange Act. Forward-looking information is different than presently known data which will have an impact on future operating results, such as known future increases in costs of labor or materials. You are required to disclose this latter type of data if it is material.

4. To the extent the primary financial statements reflect the use of exceptions permitted or required by IFRS 1, the issuer shall:

a. Provide detailed information as to the exceptions used, including:

i. An indication of the items or class of items to which the exception was applied; and

ii. A description of what accounting principle was used and how it was applied;

b. Include, where material, qualitative disclosure of the impact on financial condition, changes in financial condition and results of operations that the treatment specified by IFRS would have had absent the election to rely on the exception.

5. An issuer filing financial statements that comply with IFRS as issued by the IASB should, in providing information in response to paragraphs of this Item 5 that refer to pronouncements of the FASB, provide disclosure that satisfies the objective of the Item 5 disclosure requirements. In responding to this Item 5, an issuer need not repeat information contained in financial statements that comply with IFRS as issued by the IASB.

Instruction to Item 5.A:

1. You must provide the information required by Item 5.A.2 with respect to hyperinflation if hyperinflation has occurred in any of the periods for which you are required to provide audited financial statements or unaudited interim financial statements in the document. See Rule 3-20(c) of Regulation S-X for a discussion of cumulative inflation rates that trigger this requirement.

Instructions to Item 5.E:

1. No obligation to make disclosure under Item 5.E shall arise in respect of an off-balance sheet arrangement until a definitive agreement that is unconditionally binding or subject only to customary closing conditions exists or, if there is no such agreement, when settlement of the transaction occurs.

2. Companies should aggregate off-balance sheet arrangements in groups or categories that provide material information in an efficient and understandable manner and should avoid repetition and disclosure of immaterial information. Effects that are common or similar with respect to a number of off-balance sheet arrangements must be analyzed in the aggregate to the extent the aggregation increases understanding. Distinctions in arrangements and their effects must be discussed to the extent the information is material, but the discussion should avoid repetition and disclosure of immaterial information.

3. For purposes of paragraph Item 5.E only, contingent liabilities arising out of litigation, arbitration or regulatory actions are not considered to be off-balance sheet arrangements.

4. Generally, the disclosure required by Item 5.E shall cover the most recent fiscal year. However, the discussion should address changes from the previous year where such discussion is necessary to an understanding of the disclosure.

5. In satisfying the requirements of Item 5.E, the discussion of off-balance sheet arrangements need not repeat information provided in the footnotes to the financial statements, provided that such discussion clearly cross-references to specific information in the relevant footnotes and integrates the substance of the footnotes into such discussion in a manner designed to inform readers of the significance of the information that is not included within the body of such discussion.

Instructions to Item 5.F:

1. The company is not required to include the table required by Item 5.F.1 for interim periods. Instead, the company should disclose material changes outside the ordinary course of the company's business in the specified contractual obligations during the interim period.

2. Except for "purchase obligations," the contractual obligations in the table required by Item 5.F.1 should be based on the classifications used in the generally accepted accounting principles under which the company prepares its primary financial statements. If the generally accepted accounting principles under which the company prepares its primary financial statements do not distinguish between capital (finance) leases and operating leases, then present all leases under one category.

Item 6. Directors, Senior Management and Employees

The purpose of this standard is to provide information concerning the company's directors and managers that will allow investors to assess such individuals' experience, qualifications and levels of compensation, as well as their relationship with the company. Information concerning the company's employees is also required.

A. *Directors and senior management.* The following information shall be disclosed with respect to the company's directors and senior management, and any employees such as scientists or designers upon whose work the company is dependent:

1. Name, business experience, functions and areas of experience in the company.

2. Principal business activities performed outside the issuing company (including, in the case of directors, other principal directorships).

3. Date of birth or age (if required to be reported in the home country or otherwise publicly disclosed by the company).

4. The nature of any family relationship between any of the persons named above.

5. Any arrangement or understanding with major shareholders, customers, suppliers or others, pursuant to which any person referred to above was selected as a director or member of senior management.

B. *Compensation.* Provide the following information for the last full financial year for the company's directors and members of its administrative, supervisory or management bodies:

1. The amount of compensation paid, and benefits in kind granted, to such persons by the company and its subsidiaries for services in all capacities to the company and its subsidiaries by any person. Disclosure of compensation is required on an individual basis unless individual disclosure is not required in the company's home country and is not otherwise publicly disclosed by the company. The standard also covers contingent or deferred compensation accrued for the year, even if the compensation is payable at a later date. If any portion of the compensation was paid (a) pursuant to a bonus or profit-sharing plan, provide a brief description of the plan and the basis upon which such persons participate in the plan; or (b) in the form of stock options, provide the title and amount of securities covered by the options, the exercise price, the purchase price (if any), and the expiration date of the options.

2. The total amounts set aside or accrued by the company or its subsidiaries to provide pension, retirement or similar benefits.

C. **Board practices.** The following information for the company's last completed financial year shall be given with respect to, unless otherwise specified, the company's directors, and members of its administrative, supervisory or management bodies.

1. Date of expiration of the current term of office, if applicable, and the period during which the person has served in that office.

2. Details of directors' service contracts with the company or any of its subsidiaries providing for benefits upon termination of employment, or an appropriate negative statement.

3. Details relating to the company's audit committee and remuneration committee, including the names of committee members and a summary of the terms of reference under which the committee operates.

D. **Employees.** Provide either the number of employees at the end of the period or the average for the period for each of the past three financial years (and changes in such numbers, if material) and, if possible, a breakdown of persons employed by main category of activity and geographic location. Also disclose any significant change in the number of employees, and information regarding the relationship between management and labor unions. If the company employs a significant number of temporary employees, include disclosure of the number of temporary employees on an average during the most recent financial year.

E. **Share ownership.**

1. With respect to the persons listed in subsection 6.B, above, provide information as to their share ownership in the company as of the most recent practicable date (including disclosure on an individual basis of the number of shares and percent of shares outstanding of that class, and whether they have different voting rights) held by the persons listed in subsection 6.B and options granted to them on the company's shares. Information regarding options shall include: the title and amount of securities called for by the options; the exercise price; the purchase price, if any; and the expiration date of the options.

2. Describe any arrangements for involving the employees in the capital of the company, including any arrangement that involves the issue or grant of options or shares or securities of the company.

Instructions to Item 6.C:

1. The term "plan" is used very broadly and includes any type of arrangement for compensation, *even if the terms of the plan are not contained in a formal document.*

2. If the company is a listed issuer as defined in Exchange Act Rule 10A-3 (17 CFR 240.10A-3) and its entire board of directors is acting as the company's audit committee as specified in section 3(a)(58)(B) of the Exchange Act (15 U.S.C. 78c(a)(58)(B)), so state.

3. If the company has a board of auditors or similar body, as described in Exchange Act Rule 10A-3(c)(3) (17 CFR 240.10A-3(c)(3)), the disclosure required by this Item 6.C. with regard to the company's audit committee can be provided with respect to the company's board of auditors, or similar body.

Instruction to Item 6.E:

If (a) any of the persons listed in subsection 6.B beneficially owns less than one percent of the class of shares and (b) that person's individual share ownership previously has not been disclosed to shareholders or otherwise made public, you may indicate, by an asterisk and explanatory footnote or similar means, that the person beneficially owns less than one percent of the class, instead of providing that person's individual share ownership.

Item 7. Major Shareholders and Related Party Transactions

The purpose of this standard is to provide information regarding the major shareholders and others that control or may control the company. The standard also provides information regarding transactions the company has entered into with persons affiliated with the company and whether the terms of such transactions are fair to the company. These standards may require disclosure of related party transactions not required to be disclosed under the body of accounting principles used in preparing the financial statements. This standard is not intended to address the thresholds at which shareholders are required, on a continuing basis, to disclose their beneficial ownership of securities.

A. **Major shareholders.** To the extent that the following information is known to the company or can be ascertained from public filings, it should be provided as of the most recent practicable date, with references to the number of shares held in the company including shares beneficially owned.

1. The following information shall be provided regarding the company's major shareholders, which means shareholders that are the beneficial owners of 5% or more of each class of the company's voting securities (unless the company is required to disclose a lesser percentage in its home country, in which case that lesser percentage applies):

(a) Provide the names of the major shareholders, and the number of shares and the percentage of outstanding shares of each class owned by each of them as of the most recent practicable date, or an appropriate negative statement if there are no major shareholders.

(b) Disclose any significant change in the percentage ownership held by any major shareholders during the past three years.

(c) Indicate whether the company's major shareholders have different voting rights, or an appropriate negative statement.

2. Information shall be provided as to the portion of each class of securities held in the host country and the number of record holders in the host country.

3. To the extent known to the company, state whether the company is directly or indirectly owned or controlled by another corporation(s), by any foreign government or by any other natural or legal person(s) severally or jointly, and, if so, give the name(s) of such controlling corporation(s), government or other person(s), and briefly describe the nature of such control, including the amount and proportion of capital held giving a right to vote.

4. Describe any arrangements, known to the company, the operation of which may at a subsequent date result in a change in control of the company.

B. *Related party transactions.* Provide the information required below for the period since the beginning of the company's preceding three financial years up to the date of the document, with respect to transactions or loans between the company and (a) enterprises that directly or indirectly through one or more intermediaries, control or are controlled by, or are under common control with, the company; (b) associates; (c) individuals owning, directly or indirectly, an interest in the voting power of the company that gives them significant influence over the company, and close members of any such individual's family; (d) key management personnel, that is, those persons having authority and responsibility for planning, directing and controlling the activities of the company, including directors and senior management of companies and close members of such individuals' families; and (e) enterprises in which a substantial interest in the voting power is owned, directly or indirectly, by any person described in (c) or (d) or over which such a person is able to exercise significant influence. This includes enterprises owned by directors or major shareholders of the company and enterprises that have a member of key management in common with the company. Close members of an individual's family are those that may be expected to influence, or be influenced by, that person in their dealings with the company. An associate is an unconsolidated enterprise in which the company has a significant

influence or which has significant influence over the company. Significant influence over an enterprise is the power to participate in the financial and operating policy decisions of the enterprise but is less than control over those policies. Shareholders beneficially owning a 10% interest in the voting power of the company are presumed to have a significant influence on the company.

1. The nature and extent of any transactions or presently proposed transactions which are material to the company or the related party, or any transactions that are unusual in their nature or conditions, involving goods, services, or tangible or intangible assets, to which the company or any of its parent or subsidiaries was a party.

2. The amount of outstanding loans (including guarantees of any kind) made by the company, its parent or any of its subsidiaries to or for the benefit of any of the persons listed above. The information given should include the largest amount outstanding during the period covered, the amount outstanding as of the latest practicable date, the nature of the loan and the transaction in which it was incurred, and the interest rate on the loan. In addition, if the company, its parent or any of its subsidiaries is a foreign bank (as defined in 17 CFR 240.13k-1) that has made a loan to which Instruction 2 of this Item does not apply, identify the director, senior management member, or other related party required to be described by this Item who received the loan, and describe the nature of the loan recipient's relationship to the foreign bank.

C. *Interests of experts and counsel.* If any of the named experts or counselors was employed on a contingent basis, owns an amount of shares in the company or its subsidiaries which is material to that person, or has a material, direct or indirect economic interest in the company or that depends on the success of the offering, provide a brief description of the nature and terms of such contingency or interest.

Instructions to Item 7.B:

1. If you are providing the information called for by Item 7.B in an annual report, you only have to provide the required information for the period from the beginning of your last full fiscal year up to the latest practicable date.

2. In response to Item 7.B.2, if the lender is a bank, savings and loan association, or broker dealer extending credit under Federal Reserve Regulation T, and the loans are not disclosed as nonaccrual, past due, restructured or potential problems under Industry Guide 3, your response may consist of a statement, if true, that the loans in question (A) were made in the ordinary course of business, (B) were made on substantially the same terms, including interest rates and collateral, as those prevailing at the time for comparable transactions with other persons, and (C) did not involve more than the normal risk of collectibility or present other unfavorable features.

3. In response to Item 7.B.2, if you are unable to identify the recipient of a foreign bank loan to which Instruction 2 of this Item does not apply because you have concluded that such disclosure would conflict with privacy laws, such as customer confidentiality and data protection laws, of your home jurisdiction, you must provide a legal opinion attesting to that conclusion as an exhibit. You must also disclose that:

(A) an unnamed director, senior management member, or other related party for which disclosure is required by this Item, has been the recipient of a loan to which Instruction 2 of this Item does not apply;

(B) your home jurisdiction's privacy laws prevent the disclosure of the name of this loan recipient; and

(C) this loan recipient is unable to waive or has otherwise not waived application of these privacy laws.

Instruction to Item 7.C:

If you are filing Form 20-F as a registration statement or annual report under the Exchange Act, you do not have to provide the information called for by Item 7.C. You must provide this information if you are filing a registration statement under the Securities Act. Accountants who provide a report on financial statements that are presented or incorporated by reference in a registration statement should note Article 2 of Regulation S-X. That Article contains the Commission's requirements for qualifications and reports of accountants.

Item 8. Financial Information

The purpose of this standard is to specify which financial statements must be included in the document, as well as the periods to be covered, the age of the financial statements and other information of a financial nature.

A. Consolidated Statements and Other Financial Information.

1. The document must contain consolidated financial statements, audited by an independent auditor and accompanied by an audit report, comprised of:

(a) balance sheet;

(b) income statement;

(c) statement showing either (i) changes in equity other than those arising from capital transactions with owners and distributions to owners; or (ii) all changes in equity (including a subtotal of all non-owner items recognized directly in equity);

(d) cash flow statement;

(e) related notes and schedules required by the comprehensive body of accounting standards pursuant to which the financial statements are prepared; and

(f) if not included in the primary financial statements, a note analyzing the changes in each caption of shareholders' equity presented in the balance sheet.

2. The document should include comparative financial statements that cover the latest three financial years, audited in accordance with a comprehensive body of auditing standards.

3. The audit report(s) must cover each of the periods for which these international disclosure standards require audited financial statements. If the auditors have refused to provide a report on the annual accounts or if the report(s) contain qualifications or disclaimers, such refusal or such qualifications or disclaimers shall be reproduced in full and the reasons given, so the host country securities regulator can determine whether or not to accept the financial statements. Include an indication of any other information in the document which has been audited by the auditors.

4. The last year of audited financial statements may not be older than 15 months at the time of the offering or listing; provided, however, that in the case of the company's initial public offering, the audited financial statements also shall be as of a date not older than 12 months at the time the document is filed. In such cases, the audited financial statements may cover a period of less than a full year.

5. If the document is dated more than nine months after the end of the last audited financial year, it should contain consolidated interim financial statements, which may be unaudited (in which case that fact should be stated), covering at least the first six months of the financial year. The interim financial statements should include a balance sheet, income statement, cash flow statement, and a statement showing either (i) changes in equity other than those arising from capital transactions with owners and distributions to owners, or (ii) all changes in equity (including a subtotal of all non-owner items recognized directly in equity). Each of these statements may be in condensed form as long as it contains the major line items from the latest audited financial statements and includes the major components of assets, liabilities and equity (in the case of the balance sheet); income and expenses (in the case of the income statement) and the major subtotals of cash flows (in the case of the cash flow statement). The interim financial statements should include comparative statements for the same period in the prior financial year, except that the requirement for comparative balance sheet information may be satisfied by presenting the year end balance sheet. If not included in the primary financial statements,

a note should be provided analyzing the changes in each caption of shareholders' equity presented in the balance sheet. The interim financial statements should include selected note disclosures that will provide an explanation of events and changes that are significant to an understanding of the changes in financial position and performance of the enterprise since the last annual reporting date. If, at the date of the document, the company has published interim financial information that covers a more current period than those otherwise required by this standard, the more current interim financial information must be included in the document. Companies are encouraged, but not required, to have any interim financial statements in the document reviewed by an independent auditor. If such a review has been performed and is referred to in the document, a copy of the auditor's interim review report must be provided in the document.

6. If the amount of export sales constitutes a significant portion of the company's total sales volume, provide the total amount of export sales and the percent and amount of export sales in the total amount of sales volume.

7. Provide information on any legal or arbitration proceedings, including those relating to bankruptcy, receivership or similar proceedings and those involving any third party, which may have, or have had in the recent past, significant effects on the company's financial position or profitability. This includes governmental proceedings pending or known to be contemplated.

8. Describe the company's policy on dividend distributions.

B. **Significant Changes.** Disclose whether or not any significant change has occurred since the date of the annual financial statements, and/or since the date of the most recent interim financial statements, if any, included in the document.

Instructions to Item 8:

1. This item refers to the company, but note that under Rules 3-05, 3-09, 3-10, 3-14 and 3-16 of Regulation S-X, you also may have to provide financial statements or financial information for entities other than the issuer. In some cases, you may have to provide financial statements for a predecessor. See the definition of "predecessor" in Exchange Act Rule 12b-2 and Securities Act Rule 405.

2. For offerings of securities (a) upon the exercise of outstanding rights granted by the issuer of the securities to be offered, if the rights are granted pro rata to all existing securityholders of the class of securities to which the rights attach; or (b) pursuant to a dividend or interest reinvestment plan; or (c) upon the conversion of outstanding convertible securities or upon the exercise of outstanding transferable warrants issued by the issuer of the securities to

be offered, or by an affiliate of that issuer, the 15-month period referred to in Item 8.A.4 is extended to 18 months and the interim financial statements referred to in Item 8.A.5 shall be as of a date within 12 months of the date of the document. The provisions of this paragraph are not applicable if securities are to be offered or sold in a standby underwriting in the United States or similar arrangement.

3. If the primary financial statements included in the document represent the first filing by the issuer with the SEC of consolidated financial statements prepared in accordance with IFRS, the notes to the financial statements prepared in accordance with IFRS shall disclose the following:

a. The reconciliation from Previous GAAP to IFRS required by IFRS 1 shall be presented in a form and level of information sufficient to explain all material adjustments to the balance sheet and income statement and, if presented under Previous GAAP, to the cash flow statement; and

b. To the extent the primary financial statements reflect the use of exceptions permitted or required by IFRS 1, the issuer shall identify each exception used, including:

i. An indication of the items or class of items to which the exception was applied; and

ii. A description of what accounting principle was used and how it was applied.

Instructions to Item 8.A.2:

1. You do not have to provide a balance sheet for the earliest of the three-year periods specified in Item 8.A.2 if that balance sheet is not required by a jurisdiction outside the United States.

2. The financial statements must be audited in accordance with U.S. generally accepted auditing standards, and the auditor must comply with the U.S. and Commission standards for auditor independence. Note Article 2 of Regulation S-X, which contains requirements for qualifications and reports of accountants.

3. In initial registration statements, if the financial statements presented pursuant to Item 8.A.2 are prepared in accordance with U.S. generally accepted accounting principles, the earliest of the three years may be omitted if that information has not previously been included in a filing made under the Securities Act of 1933 or the Securities Exchange Act of 1934. Selected financial data presented pursuant to Item 3.A of Form 20-F for the full five fiscal years is still required.

Instruction to Item 8.A.3:

The circumstances in which we would accept an audit report containing a disclaimer or qualification are extremely limited. If you plan to submit this type of report, we recommend that you contact the staff of the Office of Chief Accountant in the Division of Corporation Finance well in advance of filing the document, to discuss thereport.

Instructions to Item 8.A.4:

1. In calculating the 15-month requirement for the age of financial statements, determine the age based on the period of time that has elapsed between the date of the balance sheet and "the time of the offering or listing," which means the time the registration statement is declared effective.

2. The additional requirement that financial statements be no older than 12 months at the date of filing applies only in those limited cases where a nonpublic company is registering its initial public offering of securities. We will waive this requirement in cases where the company is able to represent adequately to us that it is not required to comply with this requirement in any other jurisdiction outside the United States and that complying with the requirement is impracticable or involves undue hardship. File this representation as an exhibit to the registration statement. If we waive the 12-month requirement, you must comply with the 15-month requirement in this item.

Instructions to Item 8.A.5:

1. Item 8.A.5 does not apply to annual reports on Form 20-F.

2. The third sentence of Item 8.A.5 explains that the required interim financial statements may be in condensed form using major line items from the latest audited financial statements. To determine which major line items must be included in condensed interim information, see Rules 10-01(a)(1) through (7).

3. The third sentence from the end of Item 8.A.5 requires you to include in the document interim financial information that has been published by the company if that information covers a more current period than the statements otherwise required by Item 8. This requirement does not apply to annual reports filed on Form 20-F. The requirement covers any publication of financial information that includes, at a minimum, revenue and income information, even if that information is not published as part of a complete set of financial statements. Whenever you provide more current interim financial information in response to this requirement:

(a) Describe any ways in which the accounting principles, practices and methods used in preparing that interim financial information vary materially from the principles, practices and methods accepted in the United States, and

(b) Quantify any material variations, unless they already are quantified because they occur in other financial statements included in the document.

A registrant filing financial information that complies with IFRS as issued by the IASB is not required to provide the information described in paragraphs 3(a) and (b) to this Instruction to Item 8.A.5. if that registrant prepares its annual financial statements in accordance with IFRS as issued by the IASB.

4. A registrant that files interim period financial statements pursuant to Item 8.A.5 is not required to comply with Article 10 of Regulation S-X if that registrant prepares its annual financial statements in accordance with IFRS as issued by the IASB, prepares its interim period financial statements in compliance with IAS 34 "Interim Financial Reporting," and explicitly states its compliance with IAS 34 in the notes to the interim financial statements.

Instructions to Item 8.A.7:

1. This Item also requires disclosure of any material proceeding in which any director, any member of senior management, or any of your affiliates is either a party adverse to you or your subsidiaries or has a material interest adverse to your or your subsidiaries.

2. If you are providing the information called for by Item 8.A.7 in an annual report, also describe the disposition of any previously reported litigation that occurred during the last fiscal year.

Item 9. The Offer and Listing.

The purpose of this standard is to provide information regarding the offer or listing of securities, the plan for distribution of the securities and related matters.

A. *Offer and listing details.*

1. Indicate the expected price at which the securities will be offered or the method of determining the price, and the amount of any expenses specifically charged to the subscriber or purchaser.

2. If there is not an established market for the securities, the document shall contain information regarding the manner of determination of the offering price as well as of the exercise price of warrants and the conversion price of convertible securities, including who established the price or who is formally responsible for the determination of the price, the various factors considered in such determination and the parameters or elements used as a basis for establishing the price.

3. If the company's shareholders have preemptive purchase rights and where the exercise of the right of pre-emption of shareholders is restricted or withdrawn, the company shall indicate the basis for the issue price if the issue is for cash, together with the reasons for such restriction or withdrawal and the beneficiaries of such restriction or withdrawal if intended to benefit specific persons.

4. Information regarding the price history of the stock to be offered or listed shall be disclosed as follows:

(a) for the five most recent full financial years: the annual high and low market prices;

(b) for the two most recent full financial years and any subsequent period: the high and low market prices for each full financial quarter;

(c) for the most recent six months: the high and low market prices for each month;

(d) for pre-emptive issues, the market prices for the first trading day in the most recent six months, for the last trading day before the announcement of the offering and (if different) for the latest practicable date prior to publication of the document.

Information shall be given with respect to the market price in the host market and the principal trading market outside the host market. If significant trading suspensions occurred in the prior three years, they shall be disclosed. If the securities are not regularly traded in an organized market, information shall be given about any lack of liquidity.

5. State the type and class of the securities being offered or listed and furnish the following information:

(a) Indicate whether the shares are registered shares or bearer shares and provide the number of shares to be issued and to be made available to the market for each kind of share. The nominal par or equivalent value should be given on a per share basis and, where applicable, a statement of the minimum offer price. Describe the coupons attached, if applicable.

(b) Describe arrangements for transfer and any restrictions on the free transferability of the shares.

6. If the rights evidenced by the securities being offered or listed are or may be materially limited or qualified by the rights evidenced by any other class of securities or by the provisions of any contract or other documents, include information regarding such limitation or qualification and its effect on the rights evidenced by the securities to be listed or offered.

7. With respect to securities other than common or ordinary shares to be listed or offered, outline briefly the rights evidenced thereby.

(a) If subscription warrants or rights are to be listed or offered, state: the title and amount of securities called for; the amount of warrants or rights outstanding; provisions for changes to or adjustments in the exercise price; the period during which and the price at which the warrants or rights are exercisable; and any other material terms of such warrants or rights.

(b) Where convertible securities or stock purchase warrants to be listed or offered are subject to redemption or call, the description of the conversion terms of the securities or material terms of the warrants shall include whether the right to convert or purchase the securities will be forfeited unless it is exercised before the date specified in the notice of redemption or call; the expiration or termination date of the warrants; the kind, frequency and timing of notice of the redemption or call, including where the notice will be published; and, in the case of bearer securities, that investors are responsible for making arrangements to prevent loss of the right to convert or purchase in the event of redemption or call.

B. *Plan of distribution.*

1. The names and addresses of the entities underwriting or guaranteeing the offering shall be listed.

2. To the extent known to the company, indicate whether major shareholders, directors or members of the company's management, supervisory or administrative bodies intend to subscribe in the offering, or whether any person intends to subscribe for more than 5% of the offering.

3. Identify any group of targeted potential investors to whom the securities are offered. If the offering is being made simultaneously in the markets of two or more countries and if a tranche has been or is being reserved for certain of these, indicate any such tranche.

4. If securities are reserved for allocation to any group of targeted investors, including, for example, offerings to existing shareholders, directors, or employees and past employees of the company or its subsidiaries, provide details of these and any other preferential allocation arrangements.

5. Indicate whether the amount of the offering could be increased, such as by the exercise of an underwriter's over-allotment option or "greenshoe," and by how much.

6. Indicate the amount, and outline briefly the plan of distribution, of any securities that are to be offered otherwise than through underwriters. If the securities are to be offered through the selling efforts of brokers or dealers, describe the plan of distribution and the terms of any agreement or understanding with such entities. If known, identify the broker(s) or dealer(s) that will participate in the offering and state the amount to be offered through each.

7. If the securities are to be offered in connection with the writing of exchange-traded call options, describe briefly such transactions.

8. If simultaneously or almost simultaneously with the creation of shares for which admission to official listing is being sought, shares of the same

class are subscribed for or placed privately or if shares of other classes are created for public or private placing, details are to be given of the nature of such operations and of the number and characteristics of the shares to which they relate.

9. Unless otherwise described under the response to Item 10.C (Material Contracts), describe the features of the underwriting relationship together with the amount of securities being underwritten by each underwriter in privity of contract with the company or selling shareholders. The foregoing information should include a statement as to whether the underwriters are or will be committed to take and to pay for all of the securities if any are taken, or whether it is an agency or the type of "best efforts" arrangement under which the underwriters are required to take and to pay for only such securities as they may sell to the public.

10. If any underwriter or other financial adviser has a material relationship with the company, describe the nature and terms of such relationship.

C. **Markets.** The company shall disclose all stock exchanges and other regulated markets on which the securities to be offered or listed are traded. When an application for admission to any exchange and/or regulated market is being or will be sought, this must be mentioned, without creating the impression that the listing necessarily will be approved. If known, the dates on which the shares will be listed and dealt in should be given.

D. **Selling shareholders.** The following information shall be provided:

1. The name and address of the person or entity offering to sell the shares, the nature of any position, office or other material relationship that the selling shareholder has had within the past three years with the company or any of its predecessors or affiliates.

2. The number and class of securities being offered by each of the selling shareholders, and the percentage of the existing equity capital. The amount and percentage of the securities for each particular type of securities beneficially held by the selling shareholder before and immediately after the offering shall be specified.

E. **Dilution.** The following information shall be provided:

1. Where there is a substantial disparity between the public offering price and the effective cash cost to directors or senior management, or affiliated persons, of equity securities acquired by them in transactions during the past five years, or which they have the right to acquire, include a comparison of the public contribution in the proposed public offering and the effective cash contributions of such persons.

2. Disclose the amount and percentage of immediate dilution resulting from the offering, computed as the difference between the offering price per share and the net book value per share for the equivalent class of security, as of the latest balance sheet date.

3. In the case of a subscription offering to existing shareholders, disclose the amount and percentage of immediate dilution if they do not subscribe to the new offering.

F. **Expenses of the issue.** The following information shall be provided:

1. The total amount of the discounts or commissions agreed upon by the underwriters or other placement or selling agents and the company or offeror shall be disclosed, as well as the percentage such commissions represent of the total amount of the offering and the amount of discounts or commissions per share.

2. A reasonably itemized statement of the major categories of expenses incurred in connection with the issuance and distribution of the securities to be listed or offered and by whom the expenses are payable, if other than the company. If any of the securities are to be offered for the account of a selling shareholder, indicate the portion of such expenses to be borne by such shareholder. The information may be given subject to future contingencies. If the amounts of any items are not known, estimates (identified as such) shall be given.

Instruction to Item 9:

If you are using this Form as a registration statement under the Exchange Act, provide only the information called for by Items 9.A.4-7 and 9.C. If you are using this Form as an annual report, provide only the information called for by Items 9.A.4 and 9.C. If you are providing this information in a Securities Act registration statement, provide the information called for by the entire Item.

Instruction to Item 9.A:

When you are required to state the title of the securities, the title must indicate the type and general character of the securities, such as whether they are callable, convertible or redeemable and whether there is any preference or fixed rate of dividends.

Instructions to Item 9.B:

1. You may satisfy the requirement in Item 9.B.1 to provide the underwriters' addresses by giving the addresses of the lead underwriters for the offering.

2. If previously you have not been required to file reports under section 13(a) or 15(d) of the Exchange Act and any of the managing underwriters (or a majority of the principal underwriters) has been organized, reactivated or first registered as a broker-dealer within the past three years, disclose that fact. Also disclose, if true, that the principal business function of this underwriter will be to sell the securities being registered or that your promoters or founders have a material relationship with this underwriter. Give enough details to provide a clear picture of the underwriter's experience and its relationship with you, your promoters or founders, and their controlling persons.

Instruction to Item 9.F:

Major categories of expenses include at least the following: registration fees, federal taxes, state taxes and fees, trustees' and transfer agents' fees, printing and engraving costs, legal fees, accounting fees, engineering fees, and any premiums paid to insure directors or officers for liabilities in connection with the registration, offer or sale of the securities you are registering.

Item 10. Additional Information.

The purpose of this standard is to provide information, most of which is of a statutory nature, that is not covered elsewhere in the document.

A. **Share capital.** The following information shall be given as of the date of the most recent balance sheet included in the financial statements and as of the latest practicable date:

1. The amount of issued capital and, for each class of share capital: (a) the number of shares authorized; (b) the number of shares issued and fully paid and issued but not fully paid; (c) the par value per share, or that the shares have no par value; and (d) a reconciliation of the number of shares outstanding at the beginning and end of the year. If more than 10% of capital has been paid for with assets other than cash within the past five years, that fact should be stated.

2. If there are shares not representing capital, the number and main characteristics of such shares shall be stated.

3. Indicate the number, book value and face value of shares in the company held by or on behalf of the company itself or by subsidiaries of the company.

4. Where there is authorized but unissued capital or an undertaking to increase the capital, for example, in connection with warrants, convertible obligations or other outstanding equity-linked securities, or subscription rights granted, indicate: (i) the amount of outstanding equity-linked securities and of such authorized capital or capital increase and, where appropriate, the duration of the authorization; (ii) the categories of persons having preferential subscription rights for such additional portions of capital; and (iii) the terms, arrangements and procedures for the share issue corresponding to such portions.

5. The persons to whom any capital of any member of the group is under option or agreed conditionally or unconditionally to be put under option, including the title and amount of securities covered by the options; the exercise price; the purchase price, if any; and the expiration date of the options, or an appropriate negative statement. Where options have been granted or agreed to be granted to all the holders of shares or debt securities, or of any class thereof, or to employees under an employees' share scheme, it will be sufficient so far as the names are concerned, to record that fact without giving names.

6. A history of share capital for the last three years identifying the events during such period which have changed the amount of the issued capital and/or the number and classes of shares of which it composed, together with a description of changes in voting rights attached to the various classes of shares during that time. Details should be given of the price and terms of any issue including particulars of consideration where this was other than cash (including information regarding discounts, special terms or installment payments). If there are no such issues, an appropriate negative statement must be made. The reason for any reduction of the amount of capital and the ratio of capital reductions also shall be given.

7. An indication of the resolutions, authorizations and approvals by virtue of which the shares have been or will be created and/or issued, the nature of the issue and amount thereof and the number of shares which have been or will be created and/or issued, if predetermined.

B. **Memorandum and articles of association.** The following information shall be provided:

1. Indicate the registor and the entry number therein, if applicable, and describe the company's objects and purposes and where they can be found in the memorandum and articles.

2. With respect to directors, provide a summary of any provisions of the company's articles of association or charter and bylaws with respect to: (a) a director's power to vote on a proposal, arrangement or contract in which the director is materially interested; (b) the directors' power, in the absence of an independent quorum, to vote compensation to themselves or any members of their body; (c) borrowing powers exercisable by the directors and how such borrowing powers can be varied; (d) retirement or non-retirement of directors under an age limit requirement; and (e) number of shares, if any, required for director's qualification.

3. Describe the rights, preferences and restrictions attaching to each class of the shares, including: (a) dividend rights, including the time limit after which dividend entitlement lapses and an indication of the party in whose favor this entitlement operates; (b) voting rights, including whether directors stand for reelection at stag-

gered intervals and the impact of that arrangement where cumulative voting is permitted or required; (c) rights to share in the company's profits; (d) rights to share in any surplus in the event of liquidation; (e) redemption provisions; (f) sinking fund provisions; (g) liability to further capital calls by the company; and (h) any provision discriminating against any existing or prospective holder of such securities as a result of such shareholder owning a substantial number of shares.

4. Describe what action is necessary to change the rights of holders of the stock, indicating where the conditions are more significant than is required by law.

5. Describe the conditions governing the manner in which annual general meetings and extraordinary general meetings of shareholders are convoked, including the conditions of admission.

6. Describe any limitations on the rights to own securities, including the rights of non-resident or foreign shareholders to hold or exercise voting rights on the securities imposed by foreign law or by the charter or other constituent document of the company or state that there are no such limitations if that is the case.

7. Describe briefly any provision of the company's articles of association, charter or bylaws that would have an effect of delaying, deferring or preventing a change in control of the company and that would operate only with respect to a merger, acquisition or corporate restructuring involving the company (or any of its subsidiaries).

8. Indicate the bylaw provisions, if any, governing the ownership threshold above which shareholder ownership must be disclosed.

9. With respect to items 2 through 8 above, if the law applicable to the company in these areas is significantly different from that in the host country, the effect of the law in these areas should be explained.

10. Describe the conditions imposed by the memorandum and articles of association governing changes in the capital, where such conditions are more stringent than is required by law.

C. *Material contracts.* Provide a summary of each material contract, other than contracts entered into in the ordinary course of business, to which the company or any member of the group is a party, for the two years immediately preceding publication of the document, including dates, parties, general nature of the contracts, terms and conditions, and amount of any consideration passing to or from the company or any other member of the group.

D. *Exchange controls.* Describe any governmental laws, decrees, regulations or other legisla-

tion of the home country of the company which may affect:

1. the import or export of capital, including the availability of cash and cash equivalents for use by the company's group.

2. the remittance of dividends, interest or other payments to nonresident holders of the company's securities.

E. *Taxation.* The company shall provide information regarding taxes (including withholding provisions) to which shareholders in the host country may be subject. Information should be included as to whether the company assumes responsibility for the withholding of tax at the source and regarding applicable provisions of any reciprocal tax treaties between the home and host countries, or a statement, if applicable, that there are no such treaties.

F. *Dividends and paying agents.* Disclose any dividend restrictions, the date on which the entitlement to dividends arises, if known, and any procedures for nonresident holders to claim dividends. Identify the financial organizations which, at the time of admission of shares to official listing, are the paying agents of the company in the countries where admission has taken place or is expected to take place.

G. *Statement by experts.* Where a statement or report attributed to a person as an expert is included in the document, provide such person's name, address and qualifications and a statement to the effect that such statement or report is included, in the form and context in which it is included, with the consent of that person, who has authorized the contents of that part of the document.

H. *Documents on display.* The company shall provide an indication of where the documents concerning the company which are referred to in the document may be inspected. Exhibits and documents on display generally should be translated into the language of the host country, or a summary in the host country language should be provided.

I. *Subsidiary Information.* Certain information relating to the company's subsidiaries must be provided in some countries, if the information is not otherwise called for by the body of generally accepted accounting principles used in preparing the financial statements.

Instructions to Item 10:

1. In annual reports filed on Form 20-F:

(a) You do not have to provide the information called for by Items 10.A, 10.F and 10.G; and

(b) If the information called for by Item 10.B has been reported previously in a registration statement on Form 20-F or a registration statement filed under the Securities Act and has not changed, you may incorporate that information by a specific reference in the annual report to the previous registration statement.

2. In registration statements filed under the Securities Act or the Exchange Act that relate to securities other than common equity, you do not have to provide the information called for by Items 10.A or 10.F.

3. The information referred to in Item 10.I is not required for registration statements and reports filed in the United States.

Item 11. Quantitative and Qualitative Disclosures About Market Risk.

(a) *Quantitative information about market risk.*

(1) Registrants shall provide, in their reporting currency, quantitative information about market risk as of the end of the latest fiscal year, in accordance with one of the following three disclosure alternatives. In preparing this quantitative information, registrants shall categorize market risk sensitive instruments into instruments entered into for trading purposes and instruments entered into for purposes other than trading purposes. Within both the trading and other than trading portfolios, separate quantitative information shall be presented, to the extent material, for each market risk exposure category (i.e., interest rate risk, foreign currency exchange rate risk, commodity price risk, and other relevant market risks, such as equity price risk). A registrant may use one of the three alternatives set forth below for all of the required quantitative disclosures about market risk. A registrant also may choose, from among the three alternatives, one disclosure alternative for market risk sensitive instruments entered into for trading purposes and another disclosure alternative for market risk sensitive instruments entered into for other than trading purposes. Alternatively, a registrant may choose any disclosure alternative, from among the three alternatives, for each risk exposure category within the trading and other than trading portfolios. The three disclosure alternatives are:

(i) (A) (*1*) Tabular presentation of information related to market risk sensitive instruments; such information shall include fair values of the market risk sensitive instruments and contract terms sufficient to determine future cash flows from those instruments, categorized by expected maturity dates.

(*2*) Tabular information relating to contract terms shall allow readers of the table to determine expected cash flows from the market risk sensitive instruments for each of the next five years. Comparable tabular information for any remaining years shall be displayed as an aggregate amount.

(*3*) Within each risk exposure category, the market risk sensitive instruments shall be grouped based on common characteristics. Within the foreign currency exchange rate risk category, the market risk sensitive instruments shall be grouped by functional currency and within the commodity price risk category, the market risk sensitive instruments shall be grouped by type of commodity.

(*4*) See the Appendix to this Item for a suggested format for presentation of this information; and

(B) Registrants shall provide a description of the contents of the table and any related assumptions necessary to understand the disclosures required under paragraph (a) (1) (i) (A) of this Item 11; or

(ii) (A) Sensitivity analysis disclosures that express the potential loss in future earnings, fair values, or cash flows of market risk sensitive instruments resulting from one or more selected hypothetical changes in interest rates, foreign currency exchange rates, commodity prices, and other relevant market rates or prices over a selected period of time. The magnitude of selected hypothetical changes in rates or prices may differ among and within market risk exposure categories; and

(B) Registrants shall provide a description of the model, assumptions, and parameters, which are necessary to understand the disclosures required under paragraph (a) (1) (ii) (A) of this Item 11; or

(iii) (A) Value at risk disclosures that express the potential loss in future earnings, fair values, or cash flows of market risk sensitive instruments over a selected period of time, with a selected likelihood of occurrence, from changes in interest rates, foreign currency exchange rates, commodity prices, and other relevant market rates or prices;

(B) (*1*) For each category for which value at risk disclosures are required under paragraph (a) (1) (iii) (A) of this Item 11, provide either:

(*i*) The average, high and low amounts, or the distribution of the value at risk amounts for the reporting period; or

(*ii*) The average, high and low amounts, or the distribution of actual changes in fair values, earnings, or cash flows from the market risk sensitive instruments occurring during the reporting period; or

(*iii*) The percentage or number of times the actual changes in fair values, earnings, or cash flows from the market risk sensitive instruments exceeded the value at risk amounts during the reporting period;

(2) Information required under paragraph (a)(1)(iii)(B)(1) of this Item 11 is not required for the first fiscal year end in which a registrant must present Item 11 information; and

(C) Registrants shall provide a description of the model, assumptions, and parameters, which are necessary to understand the disclosures required under paragraphs (a)(1)(iii)(A) and (B) of this Item 11.

(2) Registrants shall discuss material limitations that cause the information required under paragraph (a)(1) of this Item 11 not to reflect fully the net market risk exposures of the entity. This discussion shall include summarized descriptions of instruments, positions, and transactions omitted from the quantitative market risk disclosure information or the features of instruments, positions, and transactions that are included, but not reflected fully in the quantitative market risk disclosure information.

(3) Registrants shall present summarized market risk information for the preceding fiscal year. In addition, registrants shall discuss the reasons for material quantitative changes in market risk exposures between the current and preceding fiscal years. Information required by this paragraph(a)(3), however, is not required if disclosure is not required under paragraph (a)(1) of this Item 11 for the current fiscal year. Information required by this paragraph (a)(3) is not required for the first fiscal year end in which a registrant must present Item 11 information.

(4) If registrants change disclosure alternatives or key model characteristics, assumptions, and parameters used in providing quantitative information about market risk (e.g., changing from tabular presentation to value at risk, changing the scope of instruments included in the model, or changing the definition of loss from fair values to earnings), and if the effects of any such change is material, the registrant shall:

(i) Explain the reasons for the change; and

(ii) Either provide summarized comparable information, under the new disclosure method, for the year preceding the current year or, in addition to providing disclosure for the current year under the new method, provide disclosures for the current year and preceding fiscal year under the method used in the preceding year.

Instruction to Item 11: An issuer filing financial statements that comply with IFRS as issued by the IASB should, in providing information in response to paragraphs of this Item 11 that refer to pronouncements of the FASB, provide disclosure that satisfies the objective of the Item 11 disclosure requirements. In responding to this Item 11, an issuer need not repeat information contained in financial statements that comply with IFRS as issued by the IASB.

Instructions to Item 11(a).

1. Under Item 11(a)(1):

A. For each market risk exposure category within the trading and other than trading portfolios, registrants may report the average, high, and low sensitivity analysis or value at risk amounts for the reporting period, as an alternative to reporting year-end amounts.

B. In determining the average, high, and low amounts for the fiscal year under instruction 1.A. of the Instructions to Item 11(a), registrants should use sensitivity analysis or value at risk amounts relating to at least four equal time periods throughout the reporting period (e.g., four quarter-end amounts, 12 month-end amounts, or 52 week-end amounts).

C. Functional currency means functional currency as defined by generally accepted accounting principles (see, e.g., FASB, Statement of Financial Accounting Standards No. 52, "Foreign Currency Translation", ("FAS 52") paragraph 20 (December 1981)).

D. Registrants using the sensitivity analysis and value at risk disclosure alternatives are encouraged, but not required, to provide quantitative amounts that reflect the aggregate market risk inherent in the trading and other than trading portfolios.

2. Under Item 11(a)(1)(i):

A. Examples of contract terms sufficient to determine future cash flows from market risk sensitive instruments include, but are not limited to:

i. Debt instruments - principal amounts and weighted average effective interest rates;

ii. Forwards and futures - contract amounts and weighted average settlement prices;

iii. Options - contract amounts and weighted average strike prices;

iv. Swaps - notional amounts, weighted average pay rates or prices, and weighted average receive rates or prices; and

v. Complex instruments - likely to be a combination of the contract terms presented in 2.A.i. through iv. of this Instruction;

B. When grouping based on common characteristics, instruments should be categorized, at a minimum, by the following characteristics, when material:

i. Fixed rate or variable rate assets or liabilities;

ii. Long or short forwards and futures;

iii. Written or purchased put or call options with similar strike prices;

iv. *Receive fixed and pay variable swaps, receive variable and pay fixed swaps, and receive variable and pay variable swaps;*

v. *The currency in which the instruments' cash flows are denominated;*

vi. *Financial instruments for which foreign currency transaction gains and losses are reported in the same manner as translation adjustments under generally accepted accounting principles (see, e.g., FAS 52 paragraph 20 (December 1981)); and*

vii. *Derivatives used to manage risks inherent in anticipated transactions;*

C. *Registrants may aggregate information regarding functional currencies that are economically related, managed together for internal risk management purposes, and have statistical correlations of greater than 75% over each of the past three years;*

D. *Market risk sensitive instruments that are exposed to rate or price changes in more than one market risk exposure category should be presented within the tabular information for each of the risk exposure categories to which those instruments are exposed;*

E. *If a currency swap (see, e.g., FAS 52 Appendix E for a definition of currency swap) eliminates all foreign currency exposures in the cash flows of a foreign currency denominated debt instrument, neither the currency swap nor the foreign currency denominated debt instrument are required to be disclosed in the foreign currency risk exposure category. However, both the currency swap and the foreign currency denominated debt instrument should be disclosed in the interest rate risk exposure category; and*

F. *The contents of the table and related assumptions that should be described include, but are not limited to:*

i. *The different amounts reported in the table for various categories of the market risk sensitive instruments (e.g., principal amounts for debt, notional amounts for swaps, and contract amounts for options and futures);*

ii. *The different types of reported market rates or prices (e.g., contractual rates or prices, spot rates or prices, forward rates or prices); and*

iii. *Key prepayment or reinvestment assumptions relating to the timing of reported amounts.*

3. *Under Item 11(a)(1)(ii):*

A. *Registrants should select hypothetical changes in market rates or prices that are expected to reflect reasonably possible near-term changes in those rates and prices. In this regard, absent economic justification for the selection of a different amount, registrants should use changes that are not less than 10 percent of end of period market rates or prices;*

B. *For purposes of instruction 3.A. of the Instructions to Item 11(a), the term reasonably possible has the same meaning as defined by generally accepted accounting principles (see, e.g., FASB, Statement of Financial Accounting Standards No. 5, "Accounting for Contingencies," ("FAS 5") paragraph 3 (March 1975));*

C. *For purposes of instruction 3.A. of the Instructions to Item 11(a), the term near term means a period of time going forward up to one year from the date of the financial statements (see generally AICPA, Statement of Position 946,"Disclosure of Certain Significant Risks and Uncertainties," ("SOP 94-6") at paragraph 7 (December 30, 1994));*

D. *Market risk sensitive instruments that are exposed to rate or price changes in more than one market risk exposure category should be included in the sensitivity analysis disclosures for each market risk category to which those instruments are exposed;*

E. *Registrants with multiple foreign currency exchange rate exposures should prepare foreign currency sensitivity analysis disclosures that measure the aggregate sensitivity to changes in all foreign currency exchange rate exposures, including the effects of changes in both transactional currency/functional currency exchange rate exposures and functional currency/reporting currency exchange rate exposures. For example, assume a French division of a registrant presenting its financial statements in U.S. dollars ($US) invests in a deutschmark (DM)-denominated debt security. In these circumstances, the $US is the reporting currency and the DM is the transactional currency. In addition, assume this division determines that the French franc (FF) is its functional currency according to FAS 52. In preparing the foreign currency sensitivity analysis disclosures, this registrant should report the aggregate potential loss from hypothetical changes in both the DM/FF exchange rate exposure and the FF/$US exchange rate exposure; and*

F. *Model, assumptions, and parameters that should be described include, but are not limited to, how loss is defined by the model (e.g., loss in earnings, fair values, or cash flows), a general description of the modeling technique (e.g., duration modeling, modeling that measures the change in net present values arising from selected hypothetical changes in market rates or prices, and a description as to how optionality is addressed by the model), the types of instruments covered by the model (e.g., derivative financial instruments, other financial instruments, derivative commodity instruments, and whether other instruments are included voluntarily, such as certain commodity instruments and positions, cash flows from anticipated transactions, and certain financial instruments excluded under instruction 3.C.ii.of the General Instructions to Items 11(a) and 11(b)), and other relevant information about the model's assumptions and parameters, (e.g., the magnitude and timing of selected hypothet-*

ical changes in market rates or prices used, the method by which discount rates are determined, and key prepayment or reinvestment assumptions).

4. Under Item 11(a)(1)(iii):

A. The confidence intervals selected should reflect reasonably possible near-term changes in market rates and prices. In this regard, absent economic justification for the selection of different confidence intervals, registrants should use intervals that are 95 percent or higher;

B. For purposes of instruction 4.A. of the Instructions to Item 11(a), the term reasonably possible has the same meaning as defined by generally accepted accounting principles (see, e.g., FAS 5, paragraph 3 (March 1975));

C. For purposes of instruction 4.A. of the Instructions to Item 11(a), the term near term means a period of time going forward up to one year from the date of the financial statements (see generally SOP 94-6, at paragraph 7 (December 30, 1994));

D. Registrants with multiple foreign currency exchange rate exposures should prepare foreign currency value at risk analysis disclosures that measure the aggregate sensitivity to changes in all foreign currency exchange rate exposures, including the aggregate effects of changes in both transactional currency/functional currency exchange rate exposures and functional currency/reporting currency exchange rate exposures. For example, assume a French division of a registrant presenting its financial statements in U.S. dollars ($US) invests in a deutschmark (DM)-denominated debt security. In these circumstances, the $US is the reporting currency and the DM is the transactional currency. In addition, assume this division determines that the French franc (FF) is its functional currency according to FAS 52. In preparing the foreign currency value at risk disclosures, this registrant should report the aggregate potential loss from hypothetical changes in both the DM/FF exchange rate exposure and the FF/$US exchange rate exposure; and

E. Model, assumptions, and parameters that should be described include, but are not limited to, how loss is defined by the model (e.g., loss in earnings, fair values, or cash flows), the type of model used (e.g., variance/covariance, historical simulation, or Monte Carlo simulation and a description as to how optionality is addressed by the model), the types of instruments covered by the model (e.g., derivative financial instruments, other financial instruments, derivative commodity instruments, and whether other instruments are included voluntarily, such ascertain commodity instruments and positions, cash flows from anticipated transactions, and certain financial instruments excluded under instruction 3.C.ii. of the General Instructions to Items 11(a) and 11(b)), and other relevant information about the model's assumptions and parameters, (e.g., holding periods, confidence intervals, and,

when appropriate, the methods used for aggregating value at risk amounts across market risk exposure categories, such as by assuming perfect positive correlation, independence, or actual observed correlation).

5. Under Item 11(a)(2), limitations that should be considered include, but are not limited to:

A. The exclusion of certain market risk sensitive instruments, positions, and transactions from the disclosures required under Item 11(a)(1) (e.g., derivative commodity instruments not permitted by contract or business custom to be settled in cash or with another financial instrument, commodity positions, cash flows from anticipated transactions, and certain financial instruments excluded under instruction 3.C.ii. of the General Instructions to Items 11(a) and 11(b)). Failure to include such instruments, positions, and transactions in preparing the disclosures under Item 11(a)(1) may be a limitation because the resulting disclosures may not fully reflect the net market risk of a registrant; and

B. The ability of disclosures required under Item 11(a)(1) to reflect fully the market risk that may be inherent in instruments with leverage, option, or prepayment features (e.g., options, including written options, structured notes, collateralized mortgage obligations, leveraged swaps, and options embedded in swaps).

[end of Instructions to Item 11(a)]

(b) Qualitative information about market risk.

(1) To the extent material, describe:

(i) The registrant's primary market risk exposures;

(ii) How those exposures are managed. Such descriptions shall include, but not be limited to, a discussion of the objectives, general strategies, and instruments, if any, used to manage those exposures; and

(iii) Changes in either the registrant's primary market risk exposures or how those exposures are managed, when compared to what was in effect during the most recently completed fiscal year and what is known or expected to be in effect in future reporting periods.

(2) Qualitative information about market risk shall be presented separately for market risk sensitive instruments entered into for trading purposes and those entered into for purposes other than trading.

Instructions to Item 11(b).

1. For purposes of disclosure under Item 11(b), primary market risk exposures means:

A. The following categories of market risk: interest rate risk, foreign currency exchange rate risk, commodity price risk, and other relevant market rate or price risks (e.g., equity price risk); and

B. Within each of these categories, the particular markets that present the primary risk of loss to the registrant. For example, if a registrant has a material exposure to foreign currency exchange rate risk and, within this category of market risk, is most vulnerable to changes in dollar/yen, dollar/pound, and dollar/peso exchange rates, the registrant should disclose those exposures. Similarly, if a registrant has a material exposure to interest rate risk and, within this category of market risk, is most vulnerable to changes in short-term U.S.prime interest rates, it should disclose the existence of that exposure.

2. For purposes of disclosure under Item 11(b), registrants should describe primary market risk exposures that exist as of the end of the latest fiscal year, and how those exposures are managed.

General Instructions to Items 11(a) and 11(b).

1. The disclosures called for by Items 11(a) and 11(b) are intended to clarify the registrant's exposures to market risk associated with activities in derivative financial instruments, other financial instruments, and derivative commodity instruments.

2. In preparing the disclosures under Items 11(a) and 11(b), registrants are required to include derivative financial instruments, other financial instruments, and derivative commodity instruments.

3. For purposes of Items 11(a) and 11(b), derivative financial instruments, other financial instruments, and derivative commodity instruments (collectively referred to as "market risk sensitive instruments") are defined as follows:

A. Derivative financial instruments has the same meaning as defined by generally accepted accounting principles (see, e.g., FASB, Statement of Financial Accounting Standards No. 119, "Disclosure about Derivative Financial Instruments and Fair Value of Financial Instruments," ("FAS 119") paragraphs 5-7 (October 1994)), and includes futures, forwards, swaps, options, and other financial instruments with similar characteristics;

B. Other financial instruments means all financial instruments as defined by generally accepted accounting principles for which fair value disclosures are required (see, e.g., FASB, Statement of Financial Accounting Standards No. 107, "Disclosures about Fair Value of Financial Instruments," ("FAS 107") paragraphs 3 and 8 (December 1991)), except for derivative financial instruments, as defined above;

C.

i. Other financial instruments include, but are not limited to, trade accounts receivable, investments, loans, structured notes, mortgagebacked securities, trade accounts payable, indexed debt instruments, interest-only and principal-only obligations, deposits, and other debt obligations;

ii. Other financial instruments exclude employers and plans obligations for pension and other postretirement benefits, substantively extinguished debt, insurance contracts, lease contracts, warranty obligations and rights, unconditional purchase obligations, investments accounted for under the equity method, noncontrolling interests in consolidated enterprises, and equity instruments issued by the registrant and classified in stockholders' equity in the statement of financial position (see, e.g., FAS 107, paragraph 8 (December 1991)). For purposes of this item, trade accounts receivable and trade accounts payable need not be considered other financial instruments when their carrying amounts approximate fair value; and

D. Derivative commodity instruments include, to the extent such instruments are not derivative financial instruments, commodity futures, commodity forwards, commodity swaps, commodity options, and other commodity instruments with similar characteristics that are permitted by contract or business custom to be settled in cash or with another financial instrument. For purposes of this paragraph, settlement in cash includes settlement in cash of the net change in value of the derivative commodity instrument (e.g., net cash settlement based on changes in the price of the underlying commodity).

4.

A. In addition to providing required disclosures for the market risk sensitive instruments defined in instruction 2. of the General Instructions to Items 11(a) and 11(b), registrants are encouraged to include other market risk sensitive instruments, positions, and transactions within the disclosures required under Items 11(a) and 11(b). Such instruments, positions, and transactions might include commodity positions, derivative commodity instruments that are not permitted by contract or business custom to be settled in cash or with another financial instrument, cash flows from anticipated transactions, and certain financial instruments excluded under instruction 3.C.ii. of the General Instructions to Items 11(a) and 11(b).

B. Registrants that voluntarily include other market risk sensitive instruments, positions and transactions within their quantitative disclosures about market risk under the sensitivity analysis or value at risk disclosure alternatives are not required to provide separate market risk disclosures for any voluntarily selected instruments, positions, or transactions. Instead, registrants selecting the sensitivity analysis and value at risk disclosure alternatives are permitted to present comprehensive market risk disclosures, which reflect the combined market risk exposures inherent in both the required and any voluntarily selected instruments, position, or transactions. Registrants that choose the tabular presentation disclosure alternative should present voluntarily selected instruments, positions, or transactions in a manner consistent with the requirements in Item 11(a) for market risk sensitive instruments.

C. If a registrant elects to include voluntarily a particular type of instrument, position, or transaction in their quantitative disclosures about market risk, that registrant should include all, rather than some, of those instruments, positions, or transactions within those disclosures. For example, if a registrant holds in inventory a particular type of commodity position and elects to include that commodity position within their market risk disclosures, the registrant should include the entire commodity position, rather than only a portion thereof, in their quantitative disclosures about market risk.

5.

A. Under Items 11(a) and 11(b), a materiality assessment should be made for each market risk exposure category within the trading and other than trading portfolios.

B. For purposes of making the materiality assessment under instruction 5.A. of the General Instructions to Items 11(a) and 11(b), registrants should evaluate both:

i. The materiality of the fair values of derivative financial instruments, other financial instruments, and derivative commodity instruments outstanding as of the end of the latest fiscal year; and

ii. The materiality of potential, near-term losses in future earnings, fair values, and cash flows from reasonably possible near-term changes in market rates or prices.

iii. If either paragraphs B.i. or B.ii. in this instruction of the General Instructions to Items 11(a) and 11(b) are material, the registrant should disclose quantitative and qualitative information about market risk, if such market risk for the particular market risk exposure category is material.

C. For purposes of instruction 5.B.i. of the General Instructions to Items 11(a) and 11(b), registrants generally should not net fair values, except to the extent allowed under generally accepted accounting principles (see, e.g., FASB Interpretation No. 39, "Offsetting of Amounts Related to Certain Contracts" (March 1992)). For example, under this instruction, the fair value of assets generally should not be netted with the fair value of liabilities.

D. For purposes of instruction 5.B.ii. of the General Instructions to Items 11(a) and 11(b), registrants should consider, among other things, the magnitude of:

i. Past market movements;

ii. Reasonably possible, near-term market movements; and

iii. Potential losses that may arise from leverage, option, and multiplier features.

E. For purposes of instructions 5.B.ii. and 5.D.ii. of the General Instructions to Items 11(a) and 11(b), the term near term means a period of time going forward up to one year from the date of the financial statements (see generally SOP 946, at paragraph 7 (December 30, 1994)).

F. For the purpose of instructions 5.B.ii. and 5.D.ii. of the General Instructions to Items 11(a) and 11(b), the term reasonably possible has the same meaning as defined by generally accepted accounting principles (see, e.g., FAS 5, paragraph 3 (March 1975)).

6. For purposes of Items 11(a) and 11(b), registrants should present the information outside of, and not incorporate the information into, the financial statements (including the footnotes to the financial statements). In addition, registrants are encouraged to provide the required information in one location. However, alternative presentation, such as inclusion of all or part of the information in Management's Discussion and Analysis, may be used at the discretion of the registrant. If information is disclosed in more than one location, registrants should provide cross-references to the locations of the related disclosures.

7. For purposes of the instructions to Items 11(a) and 11(b), trading purposes has the same meaning as defined by generally accepted accounting principles (see, e.g., FAS 119, paragraph 9a (October 1994)). In addition, anticipated transactions means transactions (other than transactions involving existing assets or liabilities or transactions necessitated by existing firm commitments) an enterprise expects, but is not obligated, to carry out in the normal course of business (see, e.g., FASB, Statement of Financial Accounting Standards No. 80, "Accounting for Futures Contracts," paragraph 9, (August 1984)).

[end of General Instructions to Items 11(a) and 11(b)]

(c) Interim periods. If interim period financial statements are included or are required to be included by Article 3 of Regulation S-X (17 CFR 210), discussion and analysis shall be provided so as to enable the reader to assess the sources and effects of material changes in information that would be provided under Item 11 of Form 20-F from the end of the preceding fiscal year to the date of the most recent interim balance sheet.

Instructions to Item 11(c).

1. Information required by paragraph (c) of this Item 11 is not required until after the first fiscal year end in which this Item 11 is applicable.

(d) Safe Harbor.

(1) The safe harbor provided in Section 27A of the Securities Act of 1933 (15 U.S.C. 77z-2) and Section 21E of the Securities Exchange Act of 1934 (15 U.S.C. 78u-5) ("statutory safe harbors")

shall apply, with respect to all types of issuers and transactions, to information provided pursuant to paragraphs (a), (b), and (c) of this Item 11, provided that the disclosure is made by an issuer; a person acting on behalf of the issuer; an outside reviewer retained by the issuer making a statement on behalf of the issuer; or an underwriter, with respect to information provided by the issuer or information derived from information provided by the issuer.

(2) For purposes of this paragraph (d) of this Item 11 only:

(i) All information required by paragraphs (a), (b)(1)(i), (b)(1)(iii), and (c) of this Item 11 is considered forward looking statements for purposes of the statutory safe harbors, except for historical facts such as the terms of particular contracts and the number of market risk sensitive instruments held during or at the end of the reporting period; and

(ii) With respect to paragraph (a) of this Item 11, the meaningful cautionary statements prong of the statutory safe harbors will be satisfied if a registrant satisfies all requirements of that same paragraph (a) of this Item 11.

(e) *Small business issuers.* Small business issuers, as defined in § 230.405 of this chapter and § 240.12b-2 of this chapter, need not provide the information required by this Item 11, whether or not they file on forms specially designated as small business issuer forms.

General Instructions to Items 11(a), 11(b), 11(c), 11(d), and 11(e).

1. Bank registrants, thrift registrants, and non-bank and non-thrift registrants with market capitalizations on January 28, 1997 in excess of $2.5 billion should provide Item 11 disclosures in filings with the Commission that include annual financial statements for fiscal years ending after June 15, 1997. Non-bank and non-thrift registrants with market capitalizations on January 28, 1997 of $2.5 billion or less should provide Item 11 disclosures in filings with the Commission that include annual financial statements for fiscal years ending after June 15, 1998.

2.

A. For purposes of instruction 1. of the General Instructions to Items 11(a), 11(b), 11(c), 11(d), and 11(e), bank registrants and thrift registrants include any registrant which has control over a depository institution.

B. For purposes of instruction 2.A. of the General Instructions to Items 11(a), 11(b), 11(c), 11(d), and 11(e), a registrant has control over a depository institution if:

i. The registrant directly or indirectly or acting through one or more other persons owns, controls, or has power to vote 25% or more of any class of voting securities of the depository institution;

ii. The registrant controls in any manner the election of a majority of the directors or trustees of the depository institution; or

iii. The Federal Reserve Board or Office of Thrift Supervision determines, after notice and opportunity for hearing, that the registrant directly or indirectly exercises a controlling influence over the management or policies of the depository institution;

C. For purposes of instruction 2.B. of the General Instructions to Items 11(a), 11(b), 11(c), 11(d), and 11(e), a depository institution means any of the following:

i. An insured depository institution as defined in section 3(c)(2) of the Federal Deposit Insurance Act (12 U.S.C.A. Sec. 1813(c));

ii. An institution organized under the laws of the United States, any State of the United States, the District of Columbia, any territory of the United States, Puerto Rico, Guam, American Samoa, or the Virgin Islands, which both accepts demand deposits or deposits that the depositor may withdraw by check or similar means for payment to third parties or others and is engaged in the business of making commercial loans.

D. For purposes of instruction 1. of the General Instructions to Items 11(a), 11(b), 11(c), 11(d), and 11(e), market capitalization is the aggregate market value of common equity as set forth in General Instruction I.B.1. of Form S-3; provided however, that common equity held by affiliates is included in the calculation of market capitalization; and provided further that instead of using the 60 day period prior to filing referenced in General Instruction I.B.1. of Form S-3, the measurement date is January 28, 1997.

Appendix to Item 11—Tabular Disclosures

The tables set forth below are illustrative of the format that might be used when a registrant elects to present the information required by paragraph (a)(1)(i)(A) of Item 11 regarding terms and information about derivative financial instruments, other financial instruments, and derivative commodity instruments. These examples are for illustrative purposes only. Registrants are not required

to display the information in the specific format illustrated below. Alternative methods of display are permissible as long as the disclosure requirements of the section are satisfied. Furthermore, these examples were designed primarily to illustrate possible formats for presentation of the information required by the disclosure item and do not purport to illustrate the broad range of derivative financial instruments, other financial instruments, and derivative commodity instruments utilized by registrants.

Interest Rate Sensitivity

The table below provides information about the Company's derivative financial instruments and other financial instruments that are sensitive to changes in interest rates, including interest rate swaps and debt obligations. For debt obligations, the table presents principal cash flows and related weighted average interest rates by expected maturity dates. For interest rate swaps, the table presents notional amounts and weighted average interest rates by expected (contractual) maturity dates. Notional amounts are used to calculate the contractual payments to be exchanged under the contract. Weighted average variable rates are based on implied forward rates in the yield curve at the reporting date. The information is presented in U.S. dollar equivalents, which is the Company's reporting currency. The instrument's actual cash flows are denominated in both U.S. dollars ($US) and German deutschmarks (DM), as indicated in parentheses.

December 31, 19x1

| | Expected Maturity Date | | | | | | | |
	19x2	19x3	19x4	19x5	19x6	There-after	Total	Fair Value
							(US$ Equivalent in millions)	
Liabilities Long-Term Debt								
Fixed Rate ($US)	$XXX	$XXX	$XXX	$XXX	$XXX	$XXX	$XXX	$XXX
Average interest rate	X.X%	X.X%	X.X%	X.X%	X.X%	X.X%	X.X%	
Fixed Rate (DM)	XXX	XXX	XXX	XXX	XXX	XXX	XXX	XXX
Average interest rate	X.X%	X.X%	X.X%	X.X%	X.X%	X.X%	X.X%	
Variable Rate ($US)	XXX	XXX	XXX	XXX	XXX	XXX	XXX	XXX
Average interest rate	X.X%	X.X%	X.X%	X.X%	X.X%	X.X%	X.X%	

| | Expected Maturity Date | | | | | | | |
Interest Rate Derivatives	19x2	19x3	19x4	19x5	19x6	There-after	Total	Fair Value
							(in millions)	
Interest Rate Swaps								
Variable to Fixed ($US)	$XXX	$XXX	$XXX	$XXX	$XXX	$XXX	$XXX	$XXX
Average pay rate	X.X%	X.X%	X.X%	X.X%	X.X%	X.X%	X.X%	
Average receive rate	X.X%	X.X%	X.X%	X.X%	X.X%	X.X%	X.X%	
Fixed to Variable ($US)	XXX	XXX	XXX	XXX	XXX	XXX	XXX	XXX
Average pay rate	X.X%	X.X%	X.X%	X.X%	X.X%	X.X%	X.X%	
Average receive rate	X.X%	X.X%	X.X%	X.X%	X.X%	X.X%	X.X%	

Exchange Rate Sensitivity

The table below provides information about the Company's derivative financial instruments, other financial instruments, and firmly committed sales transactions by functional currency and presents such information in U.S. dollar equivalents.[1] The table summarizes information on instruments and transactions that are sensitive to foreign currency exchange rates, including foreign currency forward exchange agreements, deutschmark (DM)-denominated debt obligations, and firmly committed DM sales transactions. For debt obligations, the table presents principal cash flows and related weighted average interest rates by expected maturity dates. For firmly committed DM-sales transactions, sales amounts are presented by the expected transaction date, which are not expected to exceed two years. For foreign currency forward exchange agreements, the table presents the notional amounts and weighted average exchange rates by expected (contractual) maturity dates. These notional amounts generally are used to calculate the contractual payments to be exchanged under the contract.

December 31, 19x1

| | Expected Maturity Date | | | | | | | |
	19x2	19x3	19x4	19x5	19x6	There-after	Total	Fair Value
On-Balance Sheet Financial Instruments								
				(US$ Equivalent in millions)				
$US Functional Currency[2]								

---

[1] The information is presented in U.S. dollars because that is the registrant's reporting currency.

[2] Similar tabular information would be provided for other functional currencies.

	Expected Maturity Date							
	19x2	19x3	19x4	19x5	19x6	There-after	Total	Fair Value
Liabilities Long-Term Debt Fixed Rate (DM)	$XXX	$XXX	$XXX	$XXX	$XXX	$XXX	$XXX	$XXX
Average interest rate	X.X	X.X	X.X	X.X	X.X	X.X	X.X	

	Expected Maturity or Transaction Date							
	19x2	19x3	19x4	19x5	19x6	There-after	Total	Fair Value
Anticipated Transactions and Related Derivatives[3]				(US$ Equivalent in millions)				
$US Functional Currency: Firmly committed transactions: Sales Contracts (DM)	$XXX	$XXX	-	-	-		$XXX	$XXX
Forward Exchange Agreements (Receive $US/Pay DM) Contract Amount	XXX	XXX	-	-	-		XXX	XXX
Average Contractual Exchange Rate	X.X	X.X	-	-	-	-	X.X	

Commodity Price Sensitivity

The table below provides information about the Company's corn inventory and futures contracts that are sensitive to changes in commodity prices, specifically corn prices. For inventory, the table presents the carrying amount and fair value at December 31, 19x1. For the futures contracts the table presents the notional amounts in bushels, the weighted average contract prices, and the total dollar contract amount by expected maturity dates, the latest of which occurs one year from the reporting date. Contract amounts are used to calculate the contractual payments and quantity of corn to be exchanged under the futures contracts.

December 31, 19x1

On Balance Sheet Commodity Position and Related Derivatives		
	Carrying Amount	Fair Value
	(In millions)	
Corn Inventory	$XXX	$XXX[4]

Related Derivatives		
	Expected Maturity 1992	Fair Value
Futures Contracts (Short) Contract Volumes (100,000 bushels)	XXX	
Weighted Average Price (Per 100,000 bushels)	$X.XX	
Contract Amount ($US in millions)	$XXX	$XXX

Item 12. Description of Securities Other than Equity Securities.

A. Debt Securities. If you are registering debt securities, provide the following information if it is relevant to the securities you are registering.

1. Information about interest, conversions, maturity, redemption, amortization, sinking funds or retirement.

2. The kind and priority of any lien securing the issue, as well as a brief identification of the principal properties subject to each lien.

3. Subordination of the rights of holders of the securities to other security holders or creditors. If the securities are designated in their title as subordinated, give the aggregate amount of outstanding indebtedness as of the most recent practicable date that is senior to the subordinated debt and briefly describe any limitations on the issuance of additional senior indebtedness, or state that there is no limitation.

4. Information about provisions restricting the declaration of dividends or requiring the creation or maintenance of any reserves or of any ratio

---

[3] Pursuant to General Instruction 4 to Items 11(a) and 11(b) of Form 20-F, registrants may include cash flows from anticipated transactions and operating cash flows resulting from non-financial and non-commodity instruments.

[4] Pursuant to General Instruction 4 to Items 305(a) and 305(b) of Regulation S-K, registrants may include information on commodity positions, such as corn inventory.

of assets or requiring the maintenance of properties.

5. Information about provisions permitting or restricting the issuance of additional securities, the withdrawal of cash deposited against the issuance of additional securities, the incurring of additional debt, the release or substitution of assets securing the issue, the modification of the terms of the security and similar provisions. You do not need to describe provisions permitting the release of assets upon the deposit of equivalent funds or the pledge of equivalent property, the release of property no longer required in the business, obsolete property or property taken by eminent domain, the application of insurance monies, and similar provisions.

6. The general type of event that constitutes a default and whether or not you are required to provide periodic evidence of the absence of a default or of compliance with the terms of the indenture.

7. Modification of the terms of the security or the rights of security holders.

8. If the rights evidenced by the securities you are registering are or may be materially limited or qualified by the rights of any other authorized class of securities, provide enough information about the other class of securities so investors will understand the rights evidenced by the securities you are registering. You do not need to provide information about the other class of securities if all of it will be retired, as long as you have taken appropriate steps to ensure that retirement will be completed on or before the time you deliver the securities you are registering.

9. The tax effects of any "original issue discount" as that term is defined in Section 1232 of the Internal Revenue Code (26 U.S.C. 1232), including cases where the debt security is being sold in a package with another security and the allocation of the offering price between the two securities may have the effect of offering the debt security at an original issue discount.

10. The name and address of the trustee and the nature of any material relationship between the trustee and you or any of your affiliates, the percentage of the class of securities that is needed to require the trustee to take action, and what indemnification the trustee may require before proceeding to enforce the lien.

11. The names and addresses of the paying agents.

12. The currency or currencies in which the debt is payable. If the debt may be paid in two or more currencies, state who has the option to determine the currency conversion and what the basis will be for that determination.

13. Any law or decree determining the extent to which the securities may be serviced.

14. The consequences of any failure to pay principal, interest, or any sinking or amortization installment.

15. If the securities are guaranteed, the name of the guarantor and a brief outline of the contract of guarantee.

B. *Warrants and Rights.* If the securities you are registering are being offered pursuant to warrants or rights, provide the following information, in addition to the description of the securities the warrants or rights represent.

1. The amount of securities called for by the warrants or rights.

2. The period during and the price at which the warrants or rights are exercisable.

3. The amount of warrants or rights outstanding.

4. Provisions for changes or adjustments in the exercise price.

5. Any other material terms of the warrants or rights.

C. Other Securities. If you are registering securities other than equity, debt, warrants or rights, briefly describe the rights evidenced by the securities you are registering. The description should be comparable in detail to the description you would be required to provide for equity, debt, warrants or rights.

D. American Depositary Shares. If you are registering securities represented by American Depositary Receipts in a sponsored facility, provide the following information.

1. Give the name of the depositary and the address of its principal executive office.

2. Give the title of the American Depositary Receipts and identify the deposited security. Briefly describe the American depositary shares, including provisions, if any, regarding:

(a) the amount of deposited securities represented by one unit of American Depositary Receipts;

(b) any procedure for voting the deposited securities;

(c) the procedure for collecting and distributing dividends;

(d) the procedures for transmitting notices, reports and proxy soliciting material;

(e) the sale or exercise of rights;

(f) the deposit or sale of securities resulting from dividends, splits or plans of reorganization;

(g) amendment, extension or termination of the deposit arrangements;

(h) the rights that holders of American Depositary Receipts have to inspect the books of the depositary and the list of receipt holders;

(i) any restrictions on the right to transfer or withdraw the underlying securities; and

(j) any limitation on the depositary's liability.

3. Describe all fees and charges that a holder of American Depositary Receipts may have to pay, either directly or indirectly. Indicate the type of service, the amount of the fees or charges and to whom the fees or charges are paid. In particular, provide information about any fees or charges in connection with (a) depositing or substituting the underlying shares; (b) receiving or distributing dividends; (c) selling or exercising rights; (d) withdrawing an underlying security; (e) transferring, splitting or grouping receipts; and (f) general depositary services, particularly those charged on an annual basis. Provide information about the depositary's right, if any, to collect fees and charges by offsetting them against dividends received and deposited securities.

4. In addition, describe all fees and other direct and indirect payments made by the depositary to the foreign issuer of the deposited securities.

Instructions to Item 12:

1. You do not need to provide the information called for by this Item if you are using the form as an annual report for your fiscal years ending before December 15, 2009. For your fiscal years ending on or after December 15, 2009, except for Item 12.D.3. and Item 12.D.4, you do not need to provide the information called for by this Item if you are using this form as an annual report.

2. You do not need to include any information in a registration statement or prospectus in response to Item 305(a)(2) of the Trust Indenture Act of 1939, 15 U.S.C. 77aaa et seq., as amended, if the information is not otherwise required by this Item.

3. If you are registering convertible securities or stock purchase warrants that are subject to redemption or call, include the following information in your description of the securities.

a. Whether holders will forfeit the right to convert or purchase the securities unless they exercise that right before the date specified in the notice of redemption or call;

b. The expiration or termination date of the warrants;

c. The kinds, frequency and timing of the redemption or call notice, including the cities or newspapers in which you will publish the notice; and

d. In the case of bearer securities, that investors are responsible for making arrangements to avoid losing the right to convert or purchase if there is a

redemption or call, such as by reading the newspapers in which you will publish the redemption or call notice.

4. When you are required to state the title of the securities, the title must indicate the type and general character of the securities.

Item 13. Defaults, Dividend Arrearages and Delinquencies.

A. If there has been:

1. a material default in the payment of principal, interest, a sinking or purchase fund installment, or

2. any other material default not cured within 30 days, relating to indebtedness of you or any of your significant subsidiaries, and if the amount of the indebtedness exceeds 5% of your total assets on a consolidated basis, identify the indebtedness and state the nature of the default. If the default falls under paragraph A.1 above, state the amount of the default and the total arrearage on the date you file this report.

B. If the payment of dividends is in arrears or there has been any other material delinquency not cured within 30 days, relating to:

1. any class of your preferred stock which is registered or ranks prior to any class of registered securities, or

2. any class of preferred stock of your significant subsidiaries, state the title of the class and the nature of the arrearage or delinquency. If the payment of dividends is in arrears, state the amount of this arrearage and the total arrearage on the date you file this report.

Instructions to Item 13:

1. If you previously have reported information called for by this item in a report on Form 6-K, you may incorporate the information by specifically referring in this report to the previous report.

2. You do not have to provide the information called for by this Item if the default or arrearage relates to a class of securities held entirely by or for the account of you or any of your wholly owned subsidiaries.

Instructions to Item 13.A:

This requirement only applies to events that have become defaults under the governing instruments, i.e., after any grace period has expired and any notice requirements have been satisfied.

Item 14. Material Modifications to the Rights of Security Holders and Use of Proceeds.

A. If you or anyone else has modified materially the instruments defining the rights of holders of any class of registered securities, identify that class of securities and briefly describe the general effect of the modification on the rights of those security holders.

B. If you or anyone else has modified materially or qualified the rights evidenced by any class of registered securities by issuing or modifying any other class of securities, briefly describe the general effect of the issuance or modification on the rights of holders of the registered securities.

C. If you or anyone else has withdrawn or substituted a material amount of the assets securing any class of your registered securities, provide the following information.

1. Give the title of the securities.

2. Identify and describe briefly the assets withdrawn or substituted.

3. Indicate the provisions in the underlying indenture, if any, that authorize the withdrawal or substitution.

D. If the trustees or paying agents for any registered securities have changed during the last financial year, give the names and addresses of the new trustees or paying agents.

E. *Use of proceeds.* If required pursuant to Rule 463 under the Securities Act, report the use of proceeds after the effective date of the first Securities Act registration statement filed by you or your predecessor. You must report the use of proceeds:

(i) on the first Form 20-F annual report you file pursuant to sections 13(a) and 15(d) of the Exchange Act after the Securities Act registration statement is effective, and

(ii) on each of your subsequent Form 20-F annual reports filed pursuant to sections 13(a) and 15(d) of the Exchange Act.

You may cease reporting the use of proceeds on the later of the date you disclose application of all the offering proceeds, or the date you disclose termination of the offering. If a required report on the use of proceeds relates to the first effective registration statement of your predecessor, you must provide the report.

Provide the information required by paragraphs E.1 through E.4 below in the first Form 20-F annual report you file pursuant to sections 13(a) and 15 (d) of the Exchange Act. In subsequent Form 20-F annual reports, you only need to provide the information required by paragraphs E.2 through E.4 if that information has changed since the last Form 20-F annual report you filed.

1. The effective date of the Securities Act registration statement for which the use of proceeds information is being disclosed and the Commission file number assigned to that registration statement;

2. The offering date, if the offering has commenced, or an explanation of why it has not commenced;

3. If the offering terminated before any securities were sold, an explanation for the termination; and

4. If the offering did not terminate before any securities were sold, disclose:

(a) Whether the offering has terminated and, if so, whether it terminated before all of the registered securities were sold;

(b) The name(s) of the managing underwriter(s), if any;

(c) The title of each class of securities registered and, if a class of convertible securities is being registered, the title of any class of securities into which the convertible securities may be converted;

(d) For each class of securities (other than a class into which a class of registered convertible securities may be converted without additional payment to the issuer) the following information, provided for both the account of the issuer and the account(s) of any selling shareholder (s): the amount registered, the aggregate price of the offering amount registered, the amount sold and the aggregate offering price of the amount sold to date;

(e) From the effective date of the Securities Act registration statement to the ending date of the reporting period, the amount of expenses incurred for the issuer's account in connection with the issuance and distribution of the registered securities for underwriting discounts and commissions, finders' fees, expenses paid to or for underwriters, other expenses and total expenses. Indicate if a reasonable estimate for the amount of expenses is provided instead of the actual amount of the expense. Indicate whether the payments were:

(i) Direct or indirect payments to directors, officers, general partners of the issuer or their associates; to persons owning 10% or more of any class of the issuer's equity securities; and to affiliates of the issuer; or

(ii) Direct or indirect payments to others;

(f) The net offering proceeds to the issuer after deducting the total expenses described in paragraph E.4(e) of this Item;

(g) From the effective date of the Securities Act registration statement to the ending date of the reporting period, the amount of net offering proceeds to the issuer used for construction of plant, building and facilities; purchase and installation of machinery and equipment; purchases of real estate; acquisition of other business(es); repayment of indebtedness; working capital; temporary investments (which should be specified); and any other purposes for which at least 5% of the issuer's total offering proceeds or $100,000 (whichever is less) has been used (which should be specified). Indicate if a reasonable estimate for the amount of net offering proceeds applied instead of the actual amount of net offering proceeds used. Indicate whether such payments were:

(i) Direct or indirect payments to directors, officers, general partners of the issuer or their associates; to persons owning 10% or more of any class of the issuer's equity securities; and to affiliates of the issuer; or

(ii) Direct or indirect payments to others; and

(h) If the use of proceeds in paragraph E.4(g) of this Item represents a material change in the use of proceeds described in the prospectus, the issuer should describe briefly the material change.

Instruction to Item 14:

If you previously have reported information called for by this item in a report on Form 6-K, you may incorporate the information by specifically referring in this report to the previous report.

Instruction to Item 14.B:

You should report any working capital restrictions or other limitations on the payment of dividends.

Instruction to Item 14.C:

You do not have to provide the information called for by Item 14.C. if the withdrawal or substitution is made pursuant to the terms of an indenture qualified under the Trust Indenture Act of 1939.

Item 15. Controls and Procedures.

(a) *Disclosure Controls and Procedures.* Where the Form is being used as an annual report filed under Section 13(a) or 15(d) of the Exchange Act, disclose the conclusions of the issuer's principal executive and principal financial officers, or persons performing similar functions, regarding the effectiveness of the issuer's disclosure controls and procedures (as defined in 17 CFR 240.13a-15(e) or 240.15d-15(e)) as of the end of the period covered by the report, based on the evaluation of these controls and procedures required by paragraph (b) of 17 CFR 240.13a-15 or 240.15d-15.

(b) *Management's annual report on internal control over financial reporting.* Where the Form is being used as an annual report filed under Section 13(a) or 15(d) of the Exchange Act, provide a report of management on the issuer's internal control over financial reporting (as defined in 17 CFR 240.13a-15(f) or 240.15d-15(f)) that contains:

(1) A statement of management's responsibility for establishing and maintaining adequate internal control over financial reporting for the issuer;

(2) A statement identifying the framework used by management to evaluate the effectiveness of the issuer's internal control over financial reporting as required by paragraph (c) of 17 CFR 240.13a-15 or 240.15d-15;

(3) Management's assessment of the effectiveness of the issuer's internal control over financial reporting as of the end of the issuer's most recent fiscal year, including a statement as to whether or not internal control over financial reporting is effective. This discussion must include disclosure of any material weakness in the issuer's internal control over financial reporting identified by management. Management is not permitted to conclude that the issuer's internal control over financial reporting is effective if there are one or more material weaknesses in the issuer's internal control over financial reporting; and

(4) If an issuer is an accelerated filer or a large accelerated filer (as defined in § 240.12b-2 of this chapter), or otherwise includes in its annual report a registered public accounting firm's attestation report on internal control over financial reporting, a statement that the registered public accounting firm that audited the financial statements included in the annual report containing the disclosure required by this Item has issued an attestation report on management's assessment of the issuer's internal control over financial reporting.

(c) *Attestation report of the registered public accounting firm.* If an issuer is an accelerated filer or a large accelerated filer (as defined in § 240.12b-2 of this chapter), and where the Form is being used as an annual report filed under Section 13(a) or 15(d) of the Exchange Act, provide the registered public accounting firm's attestation report on management's assessment of the issuer's internal control over financial reporting in the issuer's annual report containing the disclosure required by this Item.

(d) *Changes in internal control over financial reporting.* Disclose any change in the issuer's internal control over financial reporting identified in connection with the evaluation required by paragraph (d) of 17 CFR 240.13a-15 or 240.15d-15 that occurred during the period covered by the annual report that has materially affected, or is reasonably likely to materially affect, the issuer's internal control over financial reporting.

Instructions to Item 15.

1. An issuer need not comply with paragraphs (b) and (c) of this Item until it either had been required to file an annual report pursuant to Section 13(a) or 15(d) of the Exchange Act (15 U.S.C.

78m(a) or 78o(d)) for the prior fiscal year or had filed an annual report with the Commission for the prior fiscal year. An issuer that does not comply shall include a statement in the first annual report that it files in substantially the following form: "This annual report does not include a report of management's assessment regarding internal control over financial reporting or an attestation report of the company's registered public accounting firm due to a transition period established by rules of the Securities and Exchange Commission for newly public companies."

2. The issuer must maintain evidential matter, including documentation, to provide reasonable support for management's assessment of the effectiveness of the issuer's internal control over financial reporting.

⋙→ Compliance date extended to June 15, 2010 by Release No. 33-9072, effective December 18, 2009, 74 F.R. 53628.

Item 15T. Controls and Procedures.

Note to Item 15T : This is a special temporary section that applies instead of Item 15 only to:

(1) an issuer that is an "accelerated filer," but not a "large accelerated filer," as those terms are defined in § 240.12b-2 of this chapter and only with respect to an annual report that the issuer is required to file for a fiscal year ending on or after July 15, 2006 but before July 15, 2007; or

(2) an issuer that is neither a "large accelerated filer" nor an "accelerated filer" as those terms are defined in § 240.12b-2 of this chapter and only with respect to an annual report that the issuer is required to file for a fiscal year ending on or after December 15, 2007 but before June 15, 2010.

(a) *Disclosure Controls and Procedures.* Where the Form is being used as an annual report filed under section 13(a) or 15(d) of the Exchange Act, disclose the conclusions of the issuer's principal executive and principal financial officers, or persons performing similar functions, regarding the effectiveness of the issuer's disclosure controls and procedures (as defined in 17 CFR 240.13a-15(e) or 240.15d-15(e)) as of the end of the period covered by the report, based on the evaluation of these controls and procedures required by paragraph (b) of 17 CFR 240.13a-15 or 240.15d-15.

(b) *Management's annual report on internal control over financial reporting.* Where the Form is being used as an annual report filed under section 13(a) or 15(d) of the Exchange Act, provide a report of management on the issuer's internal control over financial reporting (as defined in § 240.13a-15(f) or 240.15d-15(f) of this chapter). The report shall not be deemed to be filed for purposes of section 18 of the Exchange Act or otherwise subject to the liabilities of that section,

unless the issuer specifically states that the report is to be considered "filed" under the Exchange Act or incorporates it by reference into a filing under the Securities Act or the Exchange Act. The report must contain:

(1) A statement of management's responsibility for establishing and maintaining adequate internal control over financial reporting for the issuer;

(2) A statement identifying the framework used by management to evaluate the effectiveness of the issuer's internal control over financial reporting as required by paragraph (c) of § 240.13a-15 or 240.15d-15 of this chapter;

(3) Management's assessment of the effectiveness of the issuer's internal control over financial reporting as of the end of the issuer's most recent fiscal year, including a statement as to whether or not internal control over financial reporting is effective. This discussion must include disclosure of any material weakness in the issuer's internal control over financial reporting identified by management. Management is not permitted to conclude that the issuer's internal control over financial reporting is effective if there are one or more material weaknesses in the issuer's internal control over financial reporting; and

(4) A statement in substantially the following form: "This annual report does not include an attestation report of the company's registered public accounting firm regarding internal control over financial reporting. Management's report was not subject to attestation by the company's registered public accounting firm pursuant to temporary rules of the Securities and Exchange Commission that permit the company to provide only management's report in this annual report."

(c) *Changes in internal control over financial reporting.* Disclose any change in the issuer's internal control over financial reporting identified in connection with the evaluation required by paragraph (d) of § 240.13a-15 or 240.15d-15 of this chapter that occurred during the period covered by the annual report that has materially affected, or is reasonably likely to materially affect, the issuer's internal control over financial reporting.

(d) This temporary Item 15T, and accompanying note and instructions, will expire on December 15, 2010.

Instructions to Item 15T

1. An issuer need only comply with paragraph (b) of this Item until it either had been required to file an annual report pursuant to section 13(a) or 15(d) of the Exchange Act (15 U.S.C. 78m(a) or 78o(d)) for the prior fiscal year or had filed an annual report with the Commission for the prior fiscal year. An issuer that does not comply shall include a statement in the first annual report that

it files in substantially the following form: "This annual report does not include a report of management's assessment regarding internal control over financial reporting or an attestation report of the company's registered public accounting firm due to a transition period established by rules of the Securities and Exchange Commission for newly public companies."

2. The registrant must maintain evidential matter, including documentation, to provide reasonable support for management's assessment of the effectiveness of the issuer's internal control over financial reporting.

Item 16. [Reserved]

Item 16A. Audit committee financial expert.

(a)(1) Disclose that the registrant's board of directors has determined that the registrant either:

(i) Has at least one audit committee financial expert serving on its audit committee; or

(ii) Does not have an audit committee financial expert serving on its audit committee.

(2) If the registrant provides the disclosure required by paragraph (a)(1)(i) of this Item, it must disclose the name of the audit committee financial expert and whether that person is *independent*, as that term is defined in the listing standards applicable to the registrant if the registrant is a listed issuer, as defined in 17 CFR 240.10A-3. If the registrant is not a listed issuer, it must use a definition of audit committee member independence of a national securities exchange registered pursuant to section 6(a) of the Exchange Act (15 U.S.C. 78f(a)) or a national securities association registered pursuant to section 15A(a) of the Exchange Act (15 U.S.C. 78o-3(a)) that has been approved by the Commission (as such definition may be modified or supplemented) in determining whether its audit committee financial expert is independent, and state which definition was used.

(3) If the registrant provides the disclosure required by paragraph (a)(1)(ii) of this Item, it must explain why it does not have an audit committee financial expert.

Instruction to paragraph (a) of Item 16A:

If the registrant's board of directors has determined that the registrant has more than one audit committee financial expert serving on its audit committee, the registrant may, but is not required to, disclose the names of those additional persons.

(b) For purposes of this Item, an "audit committee financial expert" means a person who has the following attributes:

(1) An understanding of generally accepted accounting principles and financial statements;

(2) The ability to assess the general application of such principles in connection with the accounting for estimates, accruals and reserves;

(3) Experience preparing, auditing, analyzing or evaluating financial statements that present a breadth and level of complexity of accounting issues that are generally comparable to the breadth and complexity of issues that can reasonably be expected to be raised by the registrant's financial statements, or experience actively supervising one or more persons engaged in such activities;

(4) An understanding of internal controls over financial reporting; and

(5) An understanding of audit committee functions.

(c) A person shall have acquired such attributes through:

(1) Education and experience as a principal financial officer, principal accounting officer, controller, public accountant or auditor or experience in one or more positions that involve the performance of similar functions;

(2) Experience actively supervising a principal financial officer, principal accounting officer, controller, public accountant, auditor or person performing similar functions;

(3) Experience overseeing or assessing the performance of companies or public accountants with respect to the preparation, auditing or evaluation of financial statements; or

(4) Other relevant experience.

(d) *Safe Harbor*

(1) A person who is determined to be an audit committee financial expert will not be deemed an "expert" for any purpose, including without limitation for purposes of section 11 of the Securities Act of 1933 (15 U.S.C. 77k), as a result of being designated or identified as an audit committee financial expert pursuant to this Item 16A.

(2) The designation or identification of a person as an audit committee financial expert pursuant to this Item 16A does not impose on such person any duties, obligations or liability that are greater than the duties, obligations and liability imposed on such person as a member of the audit committee and board of directors in the absence of such designation or identification.

(3) The designation or identification of a person as an audit committee financial expert pursuant to this Item 16A does not affect the duties, obligations or liability of any other member of the audit committee or board of directors.

Instructions to Item 16A:

1. Item 16A applies only to annual reports, and does not apply to registration statements, on Form 20-F.

2. If a person qualifies as an audit committee financial expert by means of having held a position described in paragraph (c)(4) of this Item, the registrant shall provide a brief listing of that person's relevant experience. Such disclosure may be made by reference to disclosures required under Item 6.A.

3. In the case of a foreign private issuer with a two-tier board of directors, for purposes of this Item 16A, the term *board of directors* means the supervisory or non-management board. In the case of a foreign private issuer meeting the requirements of 17 CFR 240.10A-3(c)(3), for purposes of this Item 16A, the term *board of directors* means the issuer's board of auditors (or similar body) or statutory auditors, as applicable. Also, in the case of a foreign private issuer, the term *generally accepted accounting principles* in paragraph (b)(1) of this Item means the body of generally accepted accounting principles used by that issuer in its primary financial statements filed with the Commission.

Item 16B. Code of Ethics.

(a) Disclose whether the registrant has adopted a code of ethics that applies to the registrant's principal executive officer, principal financial officer, principal accounting officer or controller, or persons performing similar functions. If the registrant has not adopted such a code of ethics, explain why it has not done so.

(b) For purposes of this Item 16B, the term "code of ethics" means written standards that are reasonably designed to deter wrongdoing and to promote:

(1) Honest and ethical conduct, including the ethical handling of actual or apparent conflicts of interest between personal and professional relationships;

(2) Full, fair, accurate, timely, and understandable disclosure in reports and documents that a registrant files with, or submits to, the Commission and in other public communications made by the registrant;

(3) Compliance with applicable governmental laws, rules and regulations;

(4) The prompt internal reporting of violations of the code to an appropriate person or persons identified in the code; and

(5) Accountability for adherence to the code.

(c) The registrant must:

(1) File with the Commission a copy of its code of ethics that applies to the registrant's principal executive officer, principal financial officer, principal accounting officer or controller, or persons performing similar functions, as an exhibit to its annual report;

(2) Post the text of such code of ethics on its Internet website and disclose, in its annual report, its Internet address and the fact that it has posted such code of ethics on its Internet website; or

(3) Undertake in its annual report filed with the Commission to provide to any person without charge, upon request, a copy of such code of ethics and explain the manner in which such request may be made.

(d) The registrant must briefly describe the nature of any amendment to a provision of its code of ethics that applies to the registrant's principal executive officer, principal financial officer, principal accounting officer or controller, or persons performing similar functions and that relates to any element of the code of ethics definition enumerated in Item 16B(b), which has occurred during the registrant's most recently completed fiscal year.

(e) If the registrant has granted a waiver, including an implicit waiver, from a provision of the code of ethics to one of the officers or persons described in Item 16B(a) that relates to one or more of the items set forth in Item 16B(b) during the registrant's most recently completed fiscal year, the registrant must briefly describe the nature of the waiver, the name of the person to whom the waiver was granted, and the date of the waiver.

Instructions to Item 16B:

1. Item 16B applies only to annual reports, and does not apply to registration statements, on Form 20-F.

2. A registrant may have separate codes of ethics for different types of officers. Furthermore, a "code of ethics" within the meaning of paragraph (b) of this Item may be a portion of a broader document that addresses additional topics or that applies to more persons than those specified in paragraph (a). In satisfying the requirements of paragraph (c), a registrant need only file, post or provide the portions of a broader document that constitutes a "code of ethics" as defined in paragraph (b) and that apply to the persons specified in paragraph (a).

3. If a registrant elects to satisfy paragraph (c) of this Item by posting its code of ethics on its website pursuant to paragraph (c)(2), the code of ethics must remain accessible on its website for as long as the registrant remains subject to the requirements of this Item and chooses to comply with this Item by posting its code on its website pursuant to paragraph (c)(2).

4. The registrant does not need to provide any information pursuant to paragraphs (d) and (e) of this Item if it discloses the required information on its Internet website within five business days following the date of the amendment or

waiver and the registrant has disclosed in its most recently filed annual report its Internet address and intention to provide disclosure in this manner. If the registrant elects to disclose the information required by paragraphs (d) and (e) through its website, such information must remain available on the website for at least a 12-month period. Following the 12-month period, the registrant must retain the information for a period of not less than five years. Upon request, the registrant must furnish to the Commission or its staff a copy of any or all information retained pursuant to this requirement.

5. The registrant does not need to disclose technical, administrative or other non-substantive amendments to its code of ethics.

6. For purposes of this Item 16B:

a. The term "waiver" means the approval by the registrant of a material departure from a provision of the code of ethics; and

b. The term "implicit waiver" means the registrant's failure to take action within a reasonable period of time regarding a material departure from a provision of the code of ethics that has been made known to an executive officer, as defined in Rule 3b-7 (§ 240.3b-7 of this chapter), of the registrant.

Item 16C. Principal Accountant Fees and Services.

(a) Disclose, under the caption *Audit Fees,* the aggregate fees billed for each of the last two fiscal years for professional services rendered by the principal accountant for the audit of the registrant's annual financial statements or services that are normally provided by the accountant in connection with statutory and regulatory filings or engagements for those fiscal years.

(b) Disclose, under the caption *Audit-Related Fees,* the aggregate fees billed in each of the last two fiscal years for assurance and related services by the principal accountant that are reasonably related to the performance of the audit or review of the registrant's financial statements and are not reported under paragraph (a) of this Item. Registrants shall describe the nature of the services comprising the fees disclosed under this category.

(c) Disclose, under the caption *Tax Fees,* the aggregate fees billed in each of the last two fiscal years for professional services rendered by the principal accountant for tax compliance, tax advice, and tax planning. Registrants shall describe the nature of the services comprising the fees disclosed under this category.

(d) Disclose, under the caption *All Other Fees,* the aggregate fees billed in each of the last two fiscal years for products and services provided by the principal accountant, other than the ser-

vices reported in paragraphs (a) through (c) of this Item. Registrants shall describe the nature of the services comprising the fees disclosed under this category.

(e)(1) Disclose the audit committee's pre-approval policies and procedures described in paragraph (c)(7)(i) of Rule 2-01 of Regulation S-X.

(2) Disclose the percentage of services described in each of paragraphs (b) through (d) of this Item that were approved by the audit committee pursuant to paragraph (c)(7)(i)(C) of Rule 2-01 of Regulation S-X.

(f) If greater than 50 percent, disclose the percentage of hours expended on the principal accountant's engagement to audit the registrant's financial statements for the most recent fiscal year that were attributed to work performed by persons other than the principal accountant's full-time, permanent employees.

Instruction to Item 16C.

1. You do not need to provide the information called for by this Item 16C unless you are using this form as an annual report.

Item 16D. Exemptions from the Listing Standards for Audit Committees.

If applicable, provide the disclosure required by Exchange Act Rule 10A-3(d) (17 CFR 240.10A-3(d)) regarding an exemption from the listing standards for audit committees. You do not need to provide the information called for by this Item 16D unless you are using this form as an annual report.

Item 16E. Purchases of Equity Securities by the Issuer and Affiliated Purchasers.

(a) In the following tabular format, provide the information specified in paragraph (b) of this Item with respect to any purchase made by or on behalf of the issuer or any "affiliated purchaser," as defined in § 240.10b-18(a)(3), of shares or other units of any class of the issuer's equity securities that is registered by the issuer pursuant to section 12 of the Exchange Act (15 U.S.C. 78*l*).

Item 16F. Change in Registrant's Certifying Accountant.

(a)(1) If during the registrant's two most recent fiscal years or any subsequent interim period, an independent accountant who was previously engaged as the principal accountant to audit the registrant's financial statements, or an independent accountant who was previously engaged to audit a significant subsidiary and on whom the principal accountant expressed reliance in its report, has resigned (or indicated it has declined to stand for re-election after the completion of the current audit) or was dismissed, then the registrant shall:

(i) State whether the former accountant resigned, declined to stand for re-election or was dismissed and the date thereof.

(ii) State whether the principal accountant's report on the financial statements for either of the past two years contained an adverse opinion or a disclaimer of opinion, or was qualified or modified as to uncertainty, audit scope, or accounting principles; and also describe the nature of each such adverse opinion, disclaimer of opinion, modification, or qualification.

(iii) State whether the decision to change accountants was recommended or approved by:

(A) Any audit or similar committee of the board of directors, if the issuer has such a committee; or

(B) The board of directors, if the issuer has no such committee.

(iv) State whether during the registrant's two most recent fiscal years and any subsequent interim period preceding such resignation, declination or dismissal there were any disagreements with the former accountant on any matter of accounting principles or practices, financial statement disclosure, or auditing scope or procedure, which disagreement(s), if not resolved to the satisfaction of the former accountant, would have caused it to make reference to the subject matter of the disagreement(s) in connection with its report. The disagreements required to be reported in response to this Item include both those resolved to the former accountant's satisfaction and those not resolved to the former accountant's satisfaction. Disagreements contemplated by this Item are those that occur at the decision-making level, *i.e.*, between personnel of the registrant responsible for presentation of its financial statements and personnel of the accounting firm responsible for rendering its report. Also:

(A) Describe each such disagreement;

(B) State whether any audit or similar committee of the board of directors, or the board of directors, discussed the subject matter of each of such disagreements with the former accountant; and

(C) State whether the registrant has authorized the former accountant to respond fully to the inquiries of the successor accountant concerning the subject matter of each of such disagreements and, if not, describe the nature of any limitation thereon and the reason therefore.

(v) Provide the information required by paragraph (a)(1)(iv) of this Item for each of the kinds of events (even though the registrant and the former accountant did not express a difference of opinion regarding the event) listed in paragraphs (a)(1)(v) (A) through (D) of this Item, that occurred within the registrant's two most recent

fiscal years and any subsequent interim period preceding the former accountant's resignation, declination to stand for re-election, or dismissal ("reportable events"). If the event led to a disagreement or difference of opinion, then the event should be reported as a disagreement under paragraph (a)(1)(iv) of this Item and need not be repeated under this paragraph.

(A) The accountant's having advised the registrant that the internal controls necessary for the registrant to develop reliable financial statements do not exist;

(B) The accountant's having advised the registrant that information has come to the accountant's attention that has led it to no longer be able to rely on management's representations, or that has made it unwilling to be associated with the financial statements prepared by management;

(C)(*1*) The accountant's having advised the registrant of the need to expand significantly the scope of its audit, or that information has come to the accountant's attention during the time period covered by Item 16F(a)(1)(iv), that if further investigated may:

(*i*) Materially impact the fairness or reliability of either: a previously issued audit report or the underlying financial statements; or the financial statements issued or to be issued covering the fiscal period(s) subsequent to the date of the most recent financial statements covered by an audit report (including information that may prevent it from rendering an unqualified audit report on those financial statements); or

(*ii*) Cause it to be unwilling to rely on management's representations or be associated with the registrant's financial statements; and

(*2*) Due to the accountant's resignation (due to audit scope limitations or otherwise) or dismissal, or for any other reason, the accountant did not so expand the scope of its audit or conduct such further investigation; or

(D)(*1*) The accountant's having advised the registrant that information has come to the accountant's attention that it has concluded materially impacts the fairness or reliability of either (i) a previously issued audit report or the underlying financial statements, or (ii) the financial statements issued or to be issued covering the fiscal period(s) subsequent to the date of the most recent financial statements covered by an audit report (including information that, unless resolved to the accountant's satisfaction, would prevent it from rendering an unqualified audit report on those financial statements); and

(*2*) Due to the accountant's resignation, dismissal or declination to stand for reelection, or for any other reason, the issue has not been resolved to the accountant's satisfaction prior to its resignation, dismissal or declination to stand for re-election.

(2) If during the registrant's two most recent fiscal years or any subsequent interim period, a new independent accountant has been engaged as either the principal accountant to audit the registrant's financial statements, or as an independent accountant to audit a significant subsidiary and on whom the principal accountant is expected to express reliance in its report, then the registrant shall identify the newly engaged accountant and indicate the date of such accountant's engagement. In addition, if during the registrant's two most recent fiscal years, and any subsequent interim period prior to engaging that accountant, the registrant (or someone on its behalf) consulted the newly engaged accountant regarding:

(i) Either: The application of accounting principles to a specified transaction, either completed or proposed; or the type of audit opinion that might be rendered on the registrant's financial statements, and either a written report was provided to the registrant or oral advice was provided that the new accountant concluded was an important factor considered by the registrant in reaching a decision as to the accounting, auditing or financial reporting issue; or

(ii) Any matter that was either the subject of a disagreement (as defined in Item 16F(a)(1)(iv) and the related instructions to this Item) or a reportable event (as described in Item 16F(a)(1)(v), then the registrant shall:

(A) So state and identify the issues that were the subjects of those consultations;

(B) Briefly describe the views of the newly engaged accountant as expressed orally or in writing to the registrant on each such issue and, if written views were received by the registrant, file them as an exhibit to the annual report requiring compliance with this Item 16F(a);

(C) State whether the former accountant was consulted by the registrant regarding any such issues, and if so, provide a summary of the former accountant's views; and

(D) Request the newly engaged accountant to review the disclosure required by this Item 16F(a) before it is filed with the Commission and provide the new accountant the opportunity to furnish the registrant with a letter addressed to the Commission containing any new information, clarification of the registrant's expression of its views, or the respects in which it does not agree with the statements made by the registrant in response to Item 16F(a). The registrant shall file any such letter as an exhibit to the annual report containing the disclosure required by this Item.

(3) The registrant shall provide the former accountant with a copy of the disclosures it is making in response to this Item 16F(a). The registrant shall request the former accountant to furnish the registrant with a letter addressed to the Commission stating whether it agrees with the statements made by the registrant in response to this Item 16F(a) and, if not, stating the respects in which it does not agree. The registrant shall file the former accountant's letter as an exhibit to the annual report or registration statement containing this disclosure. If the change in accountants occurred less than 30 days prior to the filing of the annual report or registration statement and the former accountant's letter is unavailable at the time of the filing, then the registrant shall request the former accountant to provide the letter as promptly as possible so that the registrant can file the letter with the Commission within ten business days after the filing of the annual report or registration statement. In either case, the former accountant may provide the registrant with an interim letter highlighting specific areas of concern and indicating that a more detailed letter will be forthcoming. If not filed with the annual report or registration statement containing the registrant's disclosure under this Item 16F(a), then the interim letter, if any, shall be filed by the registrant by amendment promptly.

(b) If: (1) In connection with a change in accountants subject to paragraph (a) of this Item 16F, there was any disagreement of the type described in paragraph (a)(1)(iv) or any reportable event as described in paragraph (a)(1)(v) of this Item;

(2) During the fiscal year in which the change in accountants took place or during the subsequent fiscal year, there have been any transactions or events similar to those which involved such disagreement or reportable event; and

(3) Such transactions or events were material and were accounted for or disclosed in a manner different from that which the former accountants apparently would have concluded was required, the registrant shall state the existence and nature of the disagreement or reportable event and also state the effect on the financial statements if the method had been followed which the former accountants apparently would have concluded was required. These disclosures need not be made if the method asserted by the former accountants ceases to be generally accepted because of authoritative standards or interpretations subsequently issued.

Instructions to Item 16F:

1. Item 16F applies to all annual reports and registration statements filed on Form 20-F for the issuer's fiscal years ending on or after December 15, 2009.

2. The disclosure called for by paragraph (a) of this Item need not be provided if it has been

previously reported, as that term is defined in Rule 12b-2 under the Exchange Act (§ 240.12b-2 of this chapter). The disclosure called for by paragraph (b) of this Item must be furnished, where required, notwithstanding any prior disclosure about accountant changes or disagreements.

3. The information required by paragraph (a) of this Item need not be provided for a company being acquired by the registrant in a transaction being registered on Form F-4 that is not subject to the filing requirements of either Section 13(a) or 15(d) of the Exchange Act.

4. The term "disagreements" as used in this Item shall be interpreted broadly to include any difference of opinion concerning any matter of accounting principles or practices, financial statement disclosure, or auditing scope or procedure which (if not resolved to the satisfaction of the former accountant) would have caused it to make reference to the subject matter of the disagreement in connection with its report. It is not necessary for there to have been an argument to have had a disagreement, merely a difference of opinion. For purposes of this Item, however, the term "disagreements" does not include initial differences of opinion based on incomplete facts or preliminary information that were later resolved to the former accountant's satisfaction by, and providing the registrant and the accountant do not continue to have a difference of opinion upon, obtaining additional relevant facts or information.

5. In determining whether any disagreement or reportable event has occurred, an oral communication from the engagement partner or another person responsible for rendering the accounting firm's opinion (or his/her designee) will generally suffice as the accountant advising the registrant of a reportable event or as a statement of a disagreement at the "decision-making level" within the accounting firm and require disclosure under this Item.

6. The term "board of directors" as used in this Item 16F has the meaning set forth in § 240.10A-3(e)(2).

Item 16G. Corporate Governance.:

If the registrant's securities are listed on a national securities exchange, provide a concise summary of any significant ways in which its corporate governance practices differ from those followed by domestic companies under the listing standards of that exchange.

Instructions to Item 16G:

A registrant must provide the information required in Item 16G beginning with the annual report that its files for its first fiscal year ending on or after December 15, 2008. Item 16G only applies to annual reports, and not to registration statements on Form 20-F. Registrants should provide a brief and general discussion, rather than a detailed, item-by-item analysis.

ISSUER PURCHASES OF EQUITY SECURITIES

Period	(a) Total Number of Shares (or Units) Purchased	(b) Average Price Paid per Share (or Units)	(c) Total Number of Shares (or Units) Purchased as Part of Publicly Announced Plans or Programs	(d) Maximum Number (or Approximate Dollar Value) of Shares (or Units) that May Yet Be Purchased Under the Plans or Programs
Month #1 (identify beginning and ending dates)				
Month #2 (identify beginning and ending dates)				
Month #3 (identify beginning and ending dates)				
Month #4 (identify beginning and ending dates)				
Month #5 (identify beginning and ending dates)				
Month #6 (identify beginning and ending dates)				
Month #7 (identify beginning and ending dates)				
Month #8 (identify beginning and ending dates)				
Month #9 (identify beginning and ending dates)				
Month #10 (identify beginning and ending dates)				

Period	(a) Total Number of Shares (or Units) Purchased	(b) Average Price Paid per Share (or Units)	(c) Total Number of Shares (or Units) Purchased as Part of Publicly Announced Plans or Programs	(d) Maximum Number (or Approximate Dollar Value) of Shares (or Units) that May Yet Be Purchased Under the Plans or Programs
Month #11 (identify beginning and ending dates)				
Month #12 (identify beginning and ending dates)				
Total				

(b) The table shall include the following information for each class or series of securities for each month included in the period covered by the report:

(1) The total number of shares (or units) purchased (column (a)).

Instruction to paragraph (b)(1) of Item 16E

Include in this column all issuer repurchases, including those made pursuant to publicly announced plans or programs and those not made pursuant to publicly announced plans or programs. Briefly disclose, by footnote to the table, the number of shares purchased other than through a publicly announced plan or program and the nature of the transaction (e.g., whether the purchases were made in open-market transactions, tender offers, in satisfaction of the company's obligations upon exercise of outstanding put options issued by the company, or other transactions).

(2) The average price paid per share (or unit) (column (b)).

(3) The number of shares (or units) purchased as part of a publicly announced repurchase plan or program (column (c)).

(4) The maximum number (or approximate dollar value) of shares (or units) that may yet be purchased under the plans or programs (column (d)).

Instructions to paragraphs (b)(3) and (b)(4) of Item 16E

1. In the table, disclose this information in the aggregate for all plans or programs publicly announced.

2. By footnote to the table, indicate:

a. The date each plan or program was announced;

b. The dollar amount (or share or unit amount) approved;

c. The expiration date (if any) of each plan or program;

d. Each plan or program that has expired during the period covered by the table; and

e. Each plan or program the issuer has determined to terminate prior to expiration, or under which the issuer does not intend to make further purchases.

Instruction to Item 16E

Disclose all purchases covered by this item, including purchases that do not satisfy the conditions of the safe harbor of §240.10b-18. Price data and other data should be stated in the same currency used in the issuer's primary financial statements provided in Item 8 of this Form.

PART III

[See General Instruction E(c)]

Item 17. Financial Statements.

(a) The registrant shall furnish financial statements for the same fiscal years and accountants' certificates that would be required to be furnished if the registration statement were on Form 10 or the annual report on *Form 10-K*. Schedules designated by §§ *210.12-04, 210.12-09, 210.12-15, 210.12-16, 210.12-17, 210.12-18, 210.12-28,* and *210.12-29* of this chapter shall be furnished if applicable to the registrant.

(b) The financial statements shall disclose an information content substantially similar to financial statements that comply with U.S. generally accepted accounting principles and *Regulation S-X*.

(c) The financial statements and schedules required by paragraph (a) above may be prepared according to U.S. generally accepted accounting principles or IFRS as issued by the IASB. If the financial statements comply with IFRS as issued by the IASB, such compliance must be unreservedly and explicitly stated in the notes to the financial statements and the auditor's report must include an opinion on whether the financial statements comply with IFRS as issued by the IASB. If the notes and auditor's report of an issuer do not contain the information in the preceding sentence, then the U.S. GAAP reconciliation information described in paragraphs (c)(1) and (c)(2) must be provided. Alternatively, such financial statements and schedules may be prepared according to a comprehensive body of accounting principles other than those generally accepted in the United States or IFRS as issued by the IASB if the following are disclosed:

(1) An indication, in the accountant's report or in a reasonably prominent headnote before the financial statements, of the comprehensive body of accounting principles used to prepare the financial statements.

(2) A discussion of the material variations in the accounting principles, practices, and methods used in preparing the financial statements from the principles, practices, and methods generally accepted in the United States and in Regulation S-X. Such material variations shall be quantified in the following format:

(i) For each year and any interim periods for which an income statement is presented, net income shall be reconciled in a tabular format, substantially similar to the one shown below, on the face of the income statement or in a note thereto. Each material variation shall be described and quantified as a separate reconciling item, but several material variations may be combined on the face of the income statement if shown separately in a note. However, reconciliation of net income of the earliest of the three years may be omitted if that information has not previously been included in a filing made under the Securities Act or Exchange Act.

Net income as shown in the financial statements XXX

Description of items having the effect of increasing reported income

     Item 1 XXX

     Item 2, etc. XXX

Description of items having the effect of decreasing reported income

     Item 1 . . . . (XXX)

     Item 2, etc. . . . . (XXX)

Net income according to generally accepted accounting principles in the United States   XXX

(ii) For each balance sheet presented, indicate the amount of each material variation between an amount of a line item appearing in a balance sheet and the amount determined using U.S. generally accepted accounting principles and *Regulation S-X*. Such amounts may be shown in parentheses, in columns, as a reconciliation of the equity section, as a restated balance sheet, or in any similar format that clearly presents the differences in the amounts.

(iii) For each period for which an income statement is presented and required to be reconciled to generally accepted accounting principles in the United States, provide either a statement of cash flows prepared in accordance with generally accepted accounting principles in the United States or with International Accounting Standard No. 7, as amended in October 1992; or furnish in a note to the financial statements a quantified description of the material differences between cash or funds flows reported in the primary financial statements and cash flows that would be reported in a statement of cash flows prepared in accordance with accounting principles generally accepted in the United States.

(iv) (A) Issuers that prepare their financial statements on a basis of accounting other than U.S. generally accepted accounting principles in a

reporting currency that comprehensively includes the effects of price level changes in its primary financial statements using the historical cost/constant currency or current cost approach, may omit the disclosures specified by paragraphs (c)(2)(i), (c)(2)(ii), and (c)(2)(iii) of this Item relating to effects of price level changes. The financial statements should describe the basis of presentation, and that such effects have not been included in the reconciliation.

(B) Issuers that prepare their financial statements on a basis of accounting other than U.S. generally accepted accounting principles that translates amounts in financial statements stated in a currency of a hyperinflationary economy into the issuer's reporting currency in accordance with International Accounting Standards No. 21, "The Effects of Changes in Foreign Exchange Rates," as amended in 1993, using the historical cost/constant currency approach, may omit the disclosures specified by paragraphs (c)(2)(i), (c)(2)(ii), and (c)(2)(iii) of this Item relating to the effects of the different method of accounting for an entity in a hyperinflationary environment.

(C) If the method of accounting for an operation in a hyperinflationary economy complies with IAS 21, a statement to that effect must be included in the financial statements. The reconciliation shall state that such amounts presented comply with Item 17 of *Form 20-F* and are different from that required by U.S. generally accepted accounting principles.

(v) Issuers that prepare financial statements on a basis of accounting other than U.S. generally accepted accounting principles that are furnished for a business acquired or to be acquired pursuant to § 210.3-05 of this chapter may omit the disclosures specified by paragraphs (c)(2)(i), (c)(2)(ii) and (c)(2)(iii) of this Item if the conditions specified in the definition of a significant subsidiary in § 210.1-02(v) of this chapter do not exceed 30 percent. Issuers that prepare financial statements using IFRS as issued by the IASB that are furnished pursuant to § 210.3-05 may omit the disclosures specified by paragraphs (c)(2)(i), (c)(2)(ii), and (c)(2)(iii) of this Item regardless of the size of the business acquired or to be acquired.

(vi) Issuers that prepare financial statements on a basis of accounting other than U.S. generally accepted accounting principles that are furnished for a less-than-majority-owned investee pursuant to § 210.3-09 of this chapter may omit the disclosures specified by paragraphs (c)(2)(i), (c)(2)(ii) and (c)(2)(iii) of this Item if the first and third conditions specified in the definition of a significant subsidiary in § 210.1-02(v) of this chapter do not exceed 30 percent. Issuers that prepare financial statements using IFRS as issued by the IASB that are furnished pursuant to § 210.3-09 may omit the disclosures specified by paragraphs (c)(2)(i), (c)(2)(ii), and (c)(2)(iii) of this Item regardless of the size of the investee.

(vii) Issuers that prepare financial statements on a basis of accounting other than U.S. generally accepted accounting principles that allows proportionate consolidation for investments in joint ventures that would be accounted for under the equity method pursuant to U.S. generally accepted accounting principles may omit differences in classification or display that result from using proportionate consolidation in the reconciliation to U.S. generally accepted accounting principles specified by paragraphs (c)(2)(i), (c)(2)(ii) and (c)(2)(iii) of this Item; Provided, the joint venture is an operating entity, the significant financial operating policies of which are, by contractual arrangement, jointly controlled by all parties having an equity interest in the entity. Financial statements that are presented using proportionate consolidation must provide summarized balance sheet and income statement information using the captions specified in § 210.1-02(aa) of this chapter and summarized cash flow information resulting from operating, financing and investing activities relating to its pro rata interest in the joint venture.

Instructions:

1. If the variations quantified pursuant to paragraph (c) are significant, the registrant should consider presenting them on the face of the financial statements.

2. Earnings per share computed according to generally accepted accounting principles in the United States shall be presented if materially different from the earnings per share otherwise presented.

3. For its fiscal years ending before December 15, 2009, if the registrant presents its financial statements according to generally accepted accounting principles in the United States except for SFAS No. 131 and if it furnishes the information relating to categories of activity required by Items 4.B.1. and 4.B.2. of this Form, then such financial statements will be considered to comply with this Item, even if the auditor's report is qualified for noncompliance with SFAS No. 131. Such report and financial statements, however, must comply with all other applicable requirements.

4. If the cash flows statement prepared under the basis of accounting used in the primary financial statements complies with International Accounting Standard No. 7 or U.S. generally accepted accounting principles, a statement to this effect must be included in the financial statements or the accountant's report. If the cash flows statement in the primary financial statements is prepared in accordance with either U.S. generally accepted accounting principles or International Accounting Standard No. 7 but such presentation departs from the comprehensive body of accounting principles otherwise followed in the financial statements, the reference to the departure in the accountant's report must identify the body of accounting standards used in preparing the cash flow statement. If a supplemental cash flows statement that complies with either International Accounting Standards or U.S. generally accepted accounting principles is furnished in a note to the financial statements, the body of accounting standards used in preparing the statement must be indicated. The basis of presentation must be consistent for all periods.

5. For purposes of this Item, a hyperinflationary economy is one that has cumulative inflation of approximately 100% or more over the most recent three year period.

Special Instruction for Certain European Issuers:

An issuer incorporated in a Member State of the European Union that has complied with the carve out to IAS 39 "Financial Instruments: Recognition and Measurement," as adopted by the European Union, in financial statements previously filed with the Commission, may file financial statements for its first two financial years that end after November 15, 2007 without reconciling to U.S. GAAP if that issuer's financial statements otherwise comply with IFRS as issued by the IASB and the issuer provides an audited reconciliation to IFRS as issued by the IASB. This reconciliation to

IFRS as issued by the IASB is to contain information relating to financial statement line items and footnote disclosure based on full compliance with IFRS as issued by the IASB, and is to be prepared and disclosed in the same manner that an issuer would provide a reconciliation to U.S. GAAP, following the requirements in Item 17(c)(2). All financial statements of such an issuer for periods prior to the financial year that ends after November 15, 2007 must continue to be reconciled to U.S. GAAP. For financial years following the two financial years ending after November 15, 2007, such an issuer will be required to include reconciliations to U.S. GAAP unless the issuer complies with the requirements in Item 17(c).

Item 18. Financial Statements.

Provide the following information:

(a) All of the information required by Item 17 of this Form, and

(b) If the financial statements are prepared using a basis of accounting other than IFRS as issued by the IASB, all other information required by U.S. generally accepted accounting principles and Regulation S-X unless such requirements specifically do not apply to the registrant as a foreign issuer. However, information may be omitted (i) for any period in which net income has not been presented on a basis reconciled to United States generally accepted accounting principles, or (ii) if the financial statements are furnished pursuant to §210.3-05 or less-than-majority owned investee pursuant to §210.3-09 of this chapter.

Instructions to Item 18:

1. For fiscal years ending before December 15, 2009, all of the instructions to Item 17 also apply to this Item, except Instruction 3 to Item 17, which does not apply. For all fiscal years ending on or after December 15, 2009, *all of the instructions to Item 17 also apply to this Item.*

2. An issuer that is required to provide disclosure under FASB Statement of Accounting Standards No. 69, "Disclosures about Oil and Gas Producing Activities," shall do so regardless of the basis of accounting on which it prepares its financial statements.

Special Instruction for Certain European Issuers:

An issuer incorporated in a Member State of the European Union that has complied with the carve out to IAS 39 "Financial Instruments: Recognition and Measurement," as adopted by the European Union, in financial statements previously filed with the Commission, may file financial statements for its first two financial years that end after November 15, 2007 without reconciling to U.S. GAAP if that issuer's financial statements otherwise comply with IFRS as issued by the IASB and the issuer provides an audited reconciliation to

IFRS as issued by the IASB. This reconciliation to IFRS as issued by the IASB is to contain information relating to financial statement line items and footnote disclosure based on full compliance with IFRS as issued by the IASB, and is to be prepared and disclosed in the same manner that an issuer would provide a reconciliation to U.S. GAAP, following the requirements in Item 18. All financial statements of such an issuer for periods prior to the financial year that ends after November 15, 2007 must continue to be reconciled to U.S. GAAP. For financial years following the two financial years ending after November 15, 2007, such an issuer will be required to include reconciliations to U.S. GAAP unless the issuer complies with the requirements in Item 18(a).

Item 19. Exhibits.

List all exhibits filed as part of the registration statement or annual report, including exhibits incorporated by reference.

Instruction to Item 19:

If you incorporate any financial statement or exhibit by reference, include the incorporation by reference in the list required by this Item. Note Rule 12b-23 regarding incorporation by reference. Note also the Instructions to Exhibits at the end of this Form.

SIGNATURES*

The registrant hereby certifies that it meets all of the requirements for filing on Form 20-F and that it has duly caused and authorized the undersigned to sign this registration statement [annual report]on its behalf.

(Registrant)

(Signature)

Date:

*Print the name and title of the signing officer under this signature.

INSTRUCTIONS AS TO EXHIBITS

File the exhibits listed below as part of an Exchange Act registration statement or report. Exchange Act Rule 12b-32 explains the circumstances in which you may incorporate exhibits by reference. Exchange Act Rule 24b-2 explains the procedure to be followed in requesting confidential treatment of information required to be filed.

Previously filed exhibits may be incorporated by reference. If any previously filed exhibits have been amended or modified, file copies of the amendment or modification or copies of the entire exhibit as amended or modified.

If the Form 20-F registration statement or annual report requires the inclusion, as an exhibit or attachment, of a document that is in a foreign language, you must provide instead either an English translation or an English summary of the foreign language document in accordance with Exchange Act Rule 12b-12(d) (17 CFR 240.12b-12(d)) for both electronic and paper filings. You may submit a copy of the unabridged foreign language document along with the English translation or summary as permitted by Regulation S-T Rule 306(b) (17 CFR 232.306(b)) for electronic filings or by Exchange Act Rule 12b-12(d)(4) (17 CFR 240.12b-12(d) (4)) for paper filings.

Include an exhibit index in each registration statement or report you file, immediately preceding the exhibits you are filing. The exhibit index must list each exhibit according to the number assigned to it below. If an exhibit is incorporated by reference, note that fact in the exhibit index. For paper filings, the pages of the manually signed original registration statement should be numbered in sequence, and the exhibit index should give the page number in the sequential numbering system where each exhibit can be found.

1. The articles of incorporation or association and bylaws, or comparable instruments, as currently in effect and any amendments to those documents. If you are filing an amendment, file a complete copy of the document as amended.

2. (a) All instruments defining the rights of holders of the securities being registered. You do not have to file instruments that define the rights of participants, rather than security holders, in an employee benefit plan.

(b) All instruments defining the rights of holders of long-term debt issued by you or any subsidiary for which you are required to file consolidated or unconsolidated financial statements, except that you do not have to file:

(i) Any instrument relating to long-term debt that is not being registered on this registration statement, if the total amount of securities authorized under that instrument does not exceed 10% of the total assets of you and your subsidiaries on a consolidated basis and you have filed an agreement to furnish us a copy of the instrument if we request it;

(ii) Any instrument relating to a class of securities if, on or before the date you deliver the securities being registered, you take appropriate steps to assure that class of securities will be redeemed or retired; or

(iii) Copies of instruments evidencing script certificates for fractions of shares.

(c) A copy of the indenture, if the securities being registered are or will be issued under an indenture qualified under the Trust Indenture Act of 1939. Include a reasonably itemized and informative table of contents and a cross-reference sheet showing the location in the indenture of the provisions inserted pursuant to sections 310 through 318 (a) inclusive of the Trust Indenture Act.

3. Any voting trust agreements and any amendments to those agreements.

4. (a) Every contract that is material to you and (i) is to be performed in whole or in part on or after the date you file the registration statement or (ii) was entered into not more than two years before the filing date. Only file a contract if you or your subsidiary is a party or has succeeded to a party by assumption or assignment or if you or your subsidiary has a beneficial interest.

(b) If a contract is the type that ordinarily accompanies the kind of business you and your subsidiaries conduct, we will consider it have been made in the ordinary course of business and will not require you to file it, unless it falls within one or more of the following categories. Even if it falls into one of these categories, you do not have to file the contract if it is immaterial in amount or significance.

(i) Any contract to which (A) directors, (B) officers, (C) promoters, (D) voting trustees or (E) security holders named in the registration statement are parties, unless the contract involves only the purchase or sale of current assets that have a determinable market price and the assets are purchased or sold at that price;

(ii) Any contract upon which your business is substantially dependent. Examples of these types of contracts might be (a) continuing contracts to sell the major part of your products or services or to purchase the major part of your requirement of goods, services or raw materials, or (b) any franchise or license or other agreement to use a patent, formula, trade secret, process or trade name if your business depends to a material extent on that patent, formula, trade secret processor trade name;

(iii) Any contract for the acquisition or sale of any property, plant or equipment if the consideration exceeds 15% of your fixed assets on a consolidated basis; or

(iv) Any material lease under which you hold part of the property described in the registration statement.

(c) We will consider any management contract or compensatory plan, contract or arrangement in which your directors or members of your administrative, supervisory or management bodies participate to be material. File these management contracts or compensatory plans, contracts or arrangements unless they fall into one of the following categories:

(i) Ordinary purchase and sale agency agreements;

(ii) Agreements with managers of stores in a chain or similar organization;

(iii) Contracts providing for labor or salesmen's bonuses or for payments to a class of security holders in their capacity as security holders;

(iv) Any compensatory plan, contract or arrangement that is available by its terms to employees, officers or directors generally, if the operation of the plan, contract or arrangement uses the same method to allocate benefits to management and nonmanagment participants; and

(v) Public filing of the management contract or compensatory plan, contract or arrangement, or portion thereof, is not required in the company's home country and is not otherwise publicly disclosed by the company.

If you are filing compensatory plans, contracts or arrangements, only file copies of the plans and not copies of each individual's personal agreement under the plans, unless there are particular provisions in a personal agreement that should be filed as an exhibit so investors will understand that individual's compensation under the plan.

5. A list showing the number and a brief identification of each material foreign patent for an invention not covered by a United States patent, but only if we request you to file the list.

6. A statement explaining in reasonable detail how earnings per share information was calculated, unless the computation is clear from material contained in the registration statement or report.

7. A statement explaining in reasonable detail how any ratio of earning to fixed charges, any ratio of earnings to combined fixed charges and preferred stock dividends or any other ratios in the registration statement or report were calculated.

8. A list of all your subsidiaries, their jurisdiction of incorporation and the names under which they do business. You may omit the names of subsidiaries that, in the aggregate, would not be a

"significant subsidiary" as defined in rule 1-02(w) of Regulation S-X as of the end of the year covered by the report. You may omit the names of multiple wholly owned subsidiaries carrying on the same line of business, such as chain stores or service stations, if you give the name of the immediate parent company, the line of business and the number of omitted subsidiaries broken down by U.S. and foreign operations.

9. Statement pursuant to the instructions to Item 8.A.4, regarding the financial statements filed in registration statements for initial public offerings of securities.

10. Any notice required by Rule 104 of Regulation BTR (17 CFR 245.104 of this chapter) that you sent during the past fiscal year to directors and executive officers (as defined in 17 CFR 245.100(d) and (h) of this chapter) concerning any equity security subject to a blackout period (as defined in 17 CFR 245.100(c) of this chapter) under Rule 101 of Regulation BTR (17 CFR 245.101 of this chapter). Each notice must have included the information specified in 17 CFR 245.104(b) of this chapter.

Note: The exhibit requirement in paragraph (10) applies only to an annual report, and not to a registration statement, on Form 20-F. The Commission will consider the attachment of any Rule 104 notice as an exhibit to a timely filed Form 20-F annual report to satisfy an issuer's duty to notify the Commission of a blackout period in a timely manner. Although an issuer need not submit a Rule 104 notice under cover of a Form 6-K, if an issuer has already submitted this notice under cover of Form 6-K, it need not attach the notice as an exhibit to a Form 20-F annual report.

11. Any code of ethics, or amendment thereto, that is the subject of the disclosure required by Item 16B of Form 20-F, to the extent that the registrant intends to satisfy the Item 16B requirements through filing of an exhibit.

12. The certifications required by Rule 13a-14(a) (17 CFR 240.13a-14(a)) or Rule 15d-14(a) (17 CFR 240.15d-14(a)) exactly as set forth below:

CERTIFICATIONS*

I, [identify the certifying individual], certify that:

1. I have reviewed this annual report on Form 20-F of [identify company];

2. Based on my knowledge, this report does not contain any untrue statement of a material fact or omit to state a material fact necessary to make the statements made, in light of the circumstances under which such statements were made, not misleading with respect to the period covered by this report;

3. Based on my knowledge, the financial statements, and other financial information included in this report, fairly present in all material respects the financial condition, results of operations and cash flows of the company as of, and for, the periods presented in this report;

4. The company's other certifying officer(s) and I are responsible for establishing and maintaining disclosure controls and procedures (as defined in Exchange Act Rules 13a-15(e) and 15d-15(e)) and

internal control over financial reporting (as defined in Exchange Act Rules 13a-15(f) and 15d-15(f)) for the company and have:

(a) Designed such disclosure controls and procedures, or caused such disclosure controls and procedures to be designed under our supervision, to ensure that material information relating to the company, including its consolidated subsidiaries, is made known to us by others within those entities, particularly during the period in which this report is being prepared;

(b) Designed such internal control over financial reporting, or caused such internal control over financial reporting to be designed under our supervision, to provide reasonable assurance regarding the reliability of financial reporting and the preparation of financial statements for external purposes in accordance with generally accepted accounting principles;

(c) Evaluated the effectiveness of the company's disclosure controls and procedures and presented in this report our conclusions about the effectiveness of the disclosure controls and procedures, as of the end of the period covered by this report based on such evaluation; and

(d) Disclosed in this report any change in the company's internal control over financial reporting that occurred during the period covered by the annual report that has materially affected, or is reasonably likely to materially affect, the company's internal control over financial reporting; and

5. The company's other certifying officer(s) and I have disclosed, based on our most recent evaluation of internal control over financial reporting, to the company's auditors and the audit committee of the company's board of directors (or persons performing the equivalent functions):

(a) All significant deficiencies and material weaknesses in the design or operation of internal control over financial reporting which are reasonably likely to adversely affect the company's ability to record, process, summarize and report financial information; and

(b) Any fraud, whether or not material, that involves management or other employees who have a significant role in the company's internal control over financial reporting.

Date:. . . . .

[Signature]

[Title]

* Provide a separate certification for each principal executive officer and principal financial officer of the company. See Rules 13a-14(a) and 15d-14(a).

13. (a) The certifications required by Rule 13a-14(b) (17 CFR 240.13a-14(b)) or Rule 15d-14(b) (17 CFR 240.15d-14(b)) and Section 1350 of Chapter 63 of Title 18 of the United States Code (18 U.S.C. 1350).

(b) A certification furnished pursuant to Rule 13a-14(b) (17 CFR 240.13a-14(b)) or Rule 15d-14(b) (17 CFR 240.15d-14(b)) and Section 1350 of Chapter 63 of Title 18 of the United States Code (18 U.S.C. 1350) will not be deemed "filed" for purposes of Section 18 of the Exchange Act [15 U.S.C. 78r], or otherwise subject to the liability of that section. Such certification will not be deemed to be incorporated by reference into any filing under the Securities Act or the Exchange Act, except to the extent that the company specifically incorporates it by reference.

14. The legal opinion required by Instruction 3 of Item 7.B of this Form.

15. (a) Any additional exhibits you wish to file as part of the registration statement or report, clearly marked to indicate their subject matter, and

(b) any document or part of a document incorporated by reference in this filing if it is not otherwise required to be filed or is not a Commis-

sion filed document incorporated in a Securities Act registration statement.

16 through 99

[Reserved]

100. *XBRL-Related Documents.* Only a registrant that prepares its financial statements in accordance with Article 6 of Regulation S-X (17 CFR 210.6-01 *et. seq.*) is permitted to participate in the voluntary XBRL (eXtensible Business Reporting Language) program and, as a result, may submit XBRL-Related Documents (§ 232.11 of this chapter). Rule 401 of Regulation S-T (§ 232.401 of this chapter) sets forth further details regarding eligibility to participate in the voluntary XBRL program.

101. *Interactive Data File.* An Interactive Data File (§ 232.11 of this chapter) is:

(a) *Required to be submitted and posted.* Required to be submitted to the Commission and posted on the registrant's corporate Web site, if any, in the manner provided by Rule 405 of Regulation S-T (§ 232.405 of this chapter) if the Form 20-F is an annual report and the registrant does not prepare its financial statements in accordance with Article 6 of Regulation S-X (17 CFR 210.6-01 *et. seq.*) and is:

(i) a large accelerated filer (§ 240.12b-2 of this chapter) that had an aggregate worldwide market value of the voting and non-voting common equity held by non-affiliates of more than $5 billion as of the last business day of the second fiscal quarter of its most recently completed fiscal year that prepares its financial statements in accordance with generally accepted accounting principles as used in the United States and the filing contains financial statements of the registrant for a fiscal period that ends on or after June 15, 2009;

(ii) A large accelerated filer not specified in subparagraph (a)(i) of this paragraph 101 that prepares its financial statements in accordance with generally accepted accounting principles as used in the United States and the filing contains financial statements of the registrant for a fiscal period that ends on or after June 15, 2010; or

(iii) A filer not specified in subparagraph (a)(i) or (a)(ii) of this paragraph 101 that prepares its financial statements in accordance with either generally accepted accounting principles as used in the United States or International Financial Reporting Standards as issued by the International Accounting Standards Board, and the filing contains financial statements of the registrant for a fiscal period that ends on or after June 15, 2011.

(b) *Permitted to be submitted.* Permitted to be submitted to the Commission in the manner provided by Rule 405 of Regulation S-T (§ 232.405 of this chapter) if the:

(i) Registrant prepares its financial statements:

(A) In accordance with either:

(1) Generally accepted accounting principles as used in the United States; or

(2) International Financial Reporting Standards as issued by the International Accounting Standards Board; and

(B) Not in accordance with Article 6 of Regulation S-X (17 CFR 210.6-01 *et. seq.*); and

(ii) Interactive Data File is not required to be submitted to the Commission under subparagraph (a) of this paragraph 101.

(c) *Not permitted to be submitted.* Not permitted to be submitted to the Commission if the registrant prepares its financial statements in accordance with Article 6 of Regulation S-X (17 CFR 210.6-01 *et. seq.*).

⋙→ *Appendix A to Item 4.D—Oil and Gas was removed by Release No. 33-8995, effective January 1, 2010, 74 F.R. 2157.*

APPENDIX A TO ITEM 4.D—OIL AND GAS

Reserve and Production Disclosure.

Registrants specified in Item 4.D shall furnish the following information under appropriate captions (in tabular form if practicable, and with cross reference, where applicable, to related information disclosed in financial statements):

(a) *Reserves.* As of the end of each of the last three fiscal years (but not for fiscal years ending prior to December 31, 1979), estimated net quantities of: (i) proved oil and gas reserves; (ii) proved developed oil and gas reserves; and (iii) oil and gas applicable to long-term supply or similar agreements with foreign governments or authorities in which the registrant acts as producer.

Instructions.

1. The following definitions shall apply to this Appendix:

(i) Proved oil and gas reserves. Proved oil and gas reserves are the estimated quantities of crude oil, natural gas, and natural gas liquids which geological and engineering data demonstrate with reasonable certainty to be recoverable in future years from known reservoirs under existing economic and operating conditions, i.e., prices and costs as of the date the estimate is made. Prices include consideration of changes in existing prices provided only by contractual arrangements, but not on escalations based upon future conditions.

(A) Reservoirs are considered proved if economic producibility is supported by either actual production or conclusive formation test. The area of a reservoir considered proved includes (1) that portion delineated by drilling and defined by gas-oil and/or oil-water contacts, if any, and (2) the immediately adjoining portions not yet drilled, but which can be reasonably judged as economically productive on the basis of available geological and engineering data. In the absence of information on fluid contacts, the lowest known structural occurrence of hydrocarbons controls the lower proved limit of the reservoir.

(B) Reserves which can be produced economically through application of improved recovery techniques (such as fluid injection) are included in the "proved" classification when successful testing by a pilot project, or the operation of an installed program in the reservoir, provides support for the engineering analysis on which the project or program was based.

(C) Estimates of proved reserves do not include the following: (1) oil that may become available from known reservoirs but is classified separately as "indicated additional reserves;" (2) crude oil, natural gas, and natural gas liquids, the recovery of which is subject to reasonable doubt because of uncertainty as to geology, reservoir characteristics, or economic factors; (3) crude oil, natural gas, and natural gas liquids, that may occur in undrilled prospects; and (4) crude oil, natural gas, and natural gas liquids, that may be recovered from oil shales, coal, gilsonite and other such sources.

(ii) Proved developed oil and gas reserves. Proved developed oil and gas reserves are reserves that can be expected to be recovered through existing wells with existing equipment and operating methods. Additional oil and gas expected to be obtained through the application of fluid injection or other improved recovery techniques for supplementing the natural forces and mechanisms of primary recovery should be included as "proved developed reserves" only after testing by a pilot project or after the operation of an installed program has confirmed through production response that increased recovery will be achieved.

(iii) Other definitions. The definitions in Rule 210.4-10(a) of Regulation S-X (§ 210.4-10 (a) of this chapter) shall apply to this Appendix.

2. If any foreign government restricts the disclosure of estimated reserves for properties under its governmental authority, or amounts under long-term supply, purchase, or similar agreements, or if the foreign government requires the disclosure of reserves other than proved, the registrant should notify the Office of Engineering, Division of Corporation Finance, of the Commission. If the required information is not disclosed or if categories of reserves other than proved are disclosed for these reasons, the document should identify the country, cite the law or regulation which restricts or requires such disclosure, and indicate that the reported reserve estimates or amounts do not include figures for the named country or that the reserve estimates include reserves other than proved.

3. If these reserves are located entirely within the registrant's home country, that fact shall be disclosed. If some or all of the reserves are located in foreign countries, the disclosure of net quantities of reserves of oil and gas shall be separately reported for the entity's home country (if significant reserves are located there) and each foreign geographic area in which significant reserves are located. Foreign geographic areas are individual countries or groups of countries, as appropriate, for meaningful disclosure in the circumstances.

4. Disclosure shall be given of the effect on ownership of reserves of any takover or nationalization within the most recent fiscal year by foreign governments of properties owned by the registrant, including any change of a property interest into a long-term supply, purchase, or similar agreement.

[end of Instructions to paragraph (a)].

(b) *Production.* Net quantities of oil (including condensate and natural gas liquids) and of gas produced for each of the last three fiscal years (but not for fiscal years ending prior to December 31, 1979) and the net quantities of each received during each of these years applicable to long-term supply or similar agreements with foreign governments or authorities in which the registrant acts as producer, by areas no larger than the geographic areas used for estimated reserves in paragraph (a) above.

Instructions.

1. Generally, net production should include only production that is owned by the registrant and produced to its interest, less royalties and production due others. However, in special situations (e.g., foreign production) net production before royalties may be provided if more appropriate. If "net before royalty" production figures are furnished, the change from the common usage of "net production" shall be noted.

2. Any part of natural gas liquids production obtained through or from plant ownership rather than through leasehold ownership should be reported separately, if material.

[¶ 33,085]   **FORM 40-F**

U.S. Securities and Exchange Commission

Washington, D.C. 20549

[As last amended in Release 33-9142, effective September 21, 2010, 75 F.R. 57385.]

Form 40-F

U.S. Securities and Exchange Commission

Washington, D.C. 20549

Form 40-F

[Check one]

REGISTRATION STATEMENT PURSUANT TO SECTION 12 OF THE SECURITIES
[ ]   EXCHANGE ACT OF 1934

OR

ANNUAL REPORT PURSUANT TO SECTION 13(a) OR 15(d) OF THE SECURITIES
[ ]   EXCHANGE ACT OF 1934

For the fiscal year ended . . . .   Commission File Number . . . .

. . . .

(Exact name of Registrant as specified in its charter)

. . . .

(Translation of Registrant's name into English (if applicable))

. . . .

(Province or other jurisdiction of incorporation or organization)

. . . .

(Primary Standard Industrial Classification Code Number (if applicable))

. . . .

(I.R.S. Employer Identification Number (if applicable))

. . . .

(Address and telephone number of Registrant's principal executive offices)

. . . .

(Name, address (including zip code) and telephone number (including area code) of
agent for service in the United States)

Securities registered or to be registered pursuant to Section 12(b) of the Act.

Title of each class   Name of each exchange on which registered

. . . .

. . . .

Securities registered or to be registered pursuant to Section 12(g) of the Act.

. . . .

(Title of Class)

. . . .

(Title of Class)

Securities for which there is a reporting obligation pursuant to Section 15(d) of the Act.

. . . .

(Title of Class)

For annual reports, indicate by check mark the information filed with this Form:

        [ ] Annual information form   [ ] Audited annual financial statements

Indicate the number of outstanding shares of each of the issuer's classes of capital or common stock as of the close of the period covered by the annual report.

. . . .

Yes —   No —

Indicate by check mark whether the Registrant (1) has filed all reports required to be filed by Section 13 or 15(d) of the Exchange Act during the preceding 12 months (or for such shorter period that the Registrant was required to file such reports) and (2) has been subject to such filing requirements for the past 90 days.

Yes —   No —

Indicate by check mark whether the registrant has submitted electronically and posted on its corporate Web site, if any, every Interactive Data File required to be submitted and posted pursuant to Rule 405 of Regulation S-T (§ 232.405 of this chapter) during the preceding 12 months (or for such shorter period that the registrant was required to submit and post such files).

Yes___ No___

GENERAL INSTRUCTIONS

A. Rules As To Use of Form 40-F

(1) Form 40-F may be used to file reports with the Commission pursuant to Section 15(d) of the Exchange Act and Rule 15d-4 thereunder by Registrants that are subject to the reporting requirements of that Section solely by reason of their having filed a registration statement on Form F-7, F-8, F-9, F-10 or F-80 under the Securities Act of 1933 (the "Securities Act").

NOTE: No reporting obligation arises under Section 15(d) of the Securities Act from the registration of securities on Form F-7, F-8 or F-80 if the issuer, at the time of filing such Form, is exempt from the requirements of Section 12(g) of the Exchange Act pursuant to Rule 12g3-2(b). *See* Rule 12h-4 under the Exchange Act.

(2) Form 40-F may be used to register securities with the Commission pursuant to Section 12(b) or 12(g) of the Exchange Act, to file reports with the Commission pursuant to Section 13(a) of the Exchange Act and Rule 13a-3 thereunder, and to file reports with the Commission pursuant to Section 15(d) of the Exchange Act if: (i) the Registrant is incorporated or organized under the laws of Canada or any Canadian province or territory; (ii) the Registrant is a foreign private issuer or a crown corporation; (iii) the Registrant has been subject to the periodic reporting requirements of any securities commission or equivalent regulatory authority in Canada for a period of at least 12 calendar months immediately proceding the filing of this Form and is currently in compliance with such obligations; and (iv) the aggregate market value of the public float of the Registrant's outstanding equity shares is $75 million or more; *provided, however,* that no market value threshold need be satisfied in connection with non-convertible securities eligible for registration on Form F-9.

Instructions

1. For purposes of this Form, "foreign private issuer" shall be construed in accordance with Rule 405 under the Securities Act.

2. For purposes of this Form, the term "crown corporation" shall mean a corporation all of whose common shares or comparable equity is owned directly or indirectly by the Government of Canada or a Province or Territory of Canada.

3. For purposes of this Form, the "public float" of specified securities shall mean only such securities held by persons other than affiliates of the issuer.

4. For purposes of this Form, an "affiliate" of a person is anyone who beneficially owns, directly or indirectly, or exercises control or direction over, more than 10 percent of the outstanding equity shares of such person. The determination of a person's affiliates shall be made as of the end of such person's most recently completed fiscal year.

5. For purposes of this Form, "equity shares" shall mean common shares, non-voting equity shares and subordinate or restricted voting equity shares, but shall not include preferred shares.

6. For purposes of this Form, the market value of outstanding equity shares (whether or not held by affiliates) shall be computed by use of the price at which the shares were last sold, or the average of the bid and asked prices of such shares, in the principal market for such shares as of a date within 60 days prior to the date of filing. If there is no market for any of such securities, the book value of such securities computed as of the latest practicable date prior to the filing of this Form shall be used for purposes of calculating the market value, unless the issuer of such securities is in bankruptcy or receivership or has an accumulated capital deficit, in which case one-third of the prin-

cipal amount, par value or stated value of such securities shall be used.

(3) If the Registrant is a successor Registrant subsisting after a business combination, it shall be deemed to meet the 12-month reporting requirement of A.(2)(iii) above if: (1) the time the successor registrant has been subject to the continuous disclosure requirements of any securities commission or equivalent regulatory authority in Canada, when added separately to the time each predecessor had been subject to such requirements at the time of the business combination, in each case equals at least 12 calendar months, *provided, however,* that any predecessor need not be considered for purposes of the reporting history calculation if the reporting histories of predecessors whose assets and gross revenues, respectively, would contribute at least 80 percent of the total assets and gross revenues from continuing operations of the successor Registrant, as measured based on pro forma combination of such participating companies' most recently completed fiscal years immediately prior to the business combination, when combined with the reporting history of the successor Registrant in each case satisfy such 12-month reporting requirement and (2) the successor Registrant has been subject to such continuous disclosure requirements since the business combination, and is currently in compliance with its obligations thereunder.

(4) This Form shall not be used if the Registrant is an investment company registered or required to be registered under the Investment Company Act of 1940.

B. Information To Be Filed on this Form

(1) Except as hereinafter noted, Registrants registering securities under Section 12 shall file with the Commission on this Form all information material to an investment decision that the Registrant, since the beginning of its last full fiscal year: (1) made or was required to make public pursuant to the law of any Canadian jurisdiction, (ii) filed or was required to file with a stock exchange on which its securities are traded and which was made public by such exchange, or (iii) distributed or was required to distribute to its securityholders. A list of all documents filed with the Commission as a part of the registration statement shall be set forth in or attached as an exhibit to the Form.

(2) Unless otherwise furnished in information provided pursuant to General Instruction B.(1), all registration statements on this Form shall include that portion of its home jurisdiction reports, forms or listing applications containing a description of the securities to be registered.

(3) Registrant reporting pursuant to Section 13(a) or 15(d) of the Exchange Act should file under cover of this Form the annual information form required under Canadian law and the Registrant's audited annual financial statements and accompanying management's discussion and analysis. All other information material to an investment decision that a Registrant (i) makes or is required to make public pursuant to the law of the jurisdiction of its domicile, (ii) files or is required to file with a stock exchange on which its securities are traded or (iii) distributes or is required to distribute to its securityholders shall be furnished by Registrants under cover of Form 6-K.

(4) A filer must file the Form 40-F registration statement or annual report in electronic format in the English language in accordance with Regulation S-T Rule 306 (17 CFR 232.306). A filer may file part of an exhibit or other attachment to the Form 40-F registration statement or annual report in both French and English if it included the French text to comply with the requirements of the Canadian securities administrator or other Canadian authority and, for an electronic filing, if the filing is an HTML document, as defined in Regulation S-T Rule 11 (17 CFR 232.11). For both an electronic filing and a paper filing, a filer may provide an English translation or English summary of a foreign language document as an exhibit or other attachment to the registration statement or amendment as permitted by the rules of the applicable Canadian securities administrator.

(5) If a report filed on this Form incorporates by reference any information not previously filed with the Commission, such information must be attached as an exhibit and filed with this Form.

(6) Where the Form is being used as an annual report filed under Section 13(a) or 15(d) of the Exchange Act:

(a) (1) Provide the certifications required by Rule 13a-14(a) (17 CFR 240.13a-14(a)) or Rule 15d-14(a) (17 CFR 240.15d-14(a)) as an exhibit to this report exactly as set forth below.

CERTIFICATIONS*

I, [identify the certifying individual], certify that:

1. I have reviewed this annual report on Form 40-F of [identify issuer]

2. Based on my knowledge, this report does not contain any untrue statement of a material fact or omit to state a material fact necessary to make the statements made, in light of the circumstances under which such statements were made, not misleading with respect to the period covered by this report;

3. Based on my knowledge, the financial statements, and other financial information included in this report, fairly present in all material respects the financial condition, results of operations and cash flows of the issuer as of, and for, the periods presented in this report;

4. The issuer's other certifying officer(s) and I are responsible for establishing and maintaining disclosure controls and procedures (as defined in Exchange Act Rules 13a-15(e) and 15d-15(e)) and internal control over financial reporting (as defined in Exchange Act Rules 13a-15(f) and 15d-15(f)) for the issuer and have:

(a) Designed such disclosure controls and procedures, or caused such disclosure controls and procedures to be designed under our supervision, to ensure that material information relating to the issuer, including its consolidated subsidiaries, is made known to us by others within those entities, particularly during the period in which this report is being prepared;

(b) Designed such internal control over financial reporting, or caused such internal control over financial reporting to be designed under our supervision, to provide reasonable assurance regarding the reliability of financial reporting and the preparation of financial statements for external purposes in accordance with generally accepted accounting principles;

(c) Evaluated the effectiveness of the issuer's disclosure controls and procedures and presented in this report our conclusions about the effectiveness of the disclosure controls and procedures, as of the end of the period covered by this report based on such evaluation; and

(d) Disclosed in this report any change in the issuer's internal control over financial reporting that occurred during the period covered by the annual report that has materially affected, or is reasonably likely to materially affect, the issuer's internal control over financial reporting; and

5. The issuer's other certifying officer(s) and I have disclosed, based on our most recent evaluation of internal control over financial reporting, to the issuer's auditors and the audit committee of the issuer's board of directors (or persons performing the equivalent functions):

(a) All significant deficiencies and material weaknesses in the design or operation of internal control over financial reporting which are reasonably likely to adversely affect the issuer's ability to record, process, summarize and report financial information; and

(b) Any fraud, whether or not material, that involves management or other employees who have a significant role in the issuer's internal control over financial reporting.

Date:. . . . .

. . . .
[Signature]
[Title]

*Provide a separate certification for each principal executive officer and principal financial officer of the issuer. See Rules 13a-14(a) and 15d-14(a).

(2) (i) Provide the certifications required by Rule 13a-14(b) (17 CFR 240.13a-14(b)) or Rule 15d-14(b) (17 CFR 240.15d-14(b)) and Section 1350 of Chapter 63 of Title 18 of the United States Code (18 U.S.C. 1350) as an exhibit to this report.

(ii) A certification furnished pursuant to Rule 13a-14(b) (17 CFR 240.13a-14(b)) or Rule 15d-14(b) (17 CFR 240.15d-14(b)) and Section 1350 of Chapter 63 of Title 18 of the United States Code (18 U.S.C. 1350) will not be deemed "filed" for purposes of Section 18 of the Exchange Act [15 U.S.C. 78r], or otherwise subject to the liability of that section. Such certification will not be deemed to be incorporated by reference into any filing under the Securities Act or the Exchange Act, except to the extent that the issuer specifically incorporates it by reference.

(b) *Disclosure Controls and Procedures.* Where the Form is being used as an annual report filed under Section 13(a) or 15(d) of the Exchange Act, disclose the conclusions of the issuer's principal executive and principal financial officers, or persons performing similar functions, regarding the effectiveness of the issuer's disclosure controls and procedures (as defined in 17 CFR 240.13a-15(e) or 240.15d-15(e)) as of the end of the period covered by the report, based on the evaluation of these controls and procedures required by paragraph (b) of 17 CFR 240.13a-15 or 240.15d-15.

(c) *Management's annual report on internal control over financial reporting.* Where the Form is being used as an annual report filed under Section 13(a) or 15(d) of the Exchange Act, provide a report of management on the issuer's internal control over financial reporting (as defined in 17 CFR 240.13a-15(f) or 240.15d-15(f)) that contains:

(1) A statement of management's responsibility for establishing and maintaining adequate internal control over financial reporting for the issuer;

(2) A statement identifying the framework used by management to evaluate the effectiveness of the issuer's internal control over financial reporting as required by paragraph (c) of 17 CFR 240.13a-15 or 240.15d-15;

(3) Management's assessment of the effectiveness of the issuer's internal control over financial reporting as of the end of the issuer's most recent fiscal year, including a statement as to whether or not internal control over financial reporting is effective. This discussion must include disclosure of any material weakness in the issuer's internal control over financial reporting identified by management. Management is not permitted to conclude that the issuer's internal control over financial reporting is effective if there are one or more material weaknesses in the issuer's internal control over financial reporting; and

(4) If an issuer is an accelerated filer or a large accelerated filer (as defined in 17 CFR 240.12b-2), or otherwise includes in its annual report a registered public accounting firm's attestation report on internal control over financial reporting, a statement that the registered public accounting firm that audited the financial statements included in the annual report containing the disclosure required by this Item has issued an attestation report on management's assessment of the issuer's internal control over financial reporting.

(d) *Attestation report of the registered public accounting firm.* If an issuer is an accelerated filer or a large accelerated filer (as defined in § 240.12b-2 of this chapter), and where the Form is being used as an annual report filed under Section 13(a) or 15(d) of the Exchange Act, provide the registered public accounting firm's attestation report on management's assessment of the issuer's internal control over financial reporting in the issuer's annual report containing the disclosure required by this Item.

(e) *Changes in internal control over financial reporting.* Disclose any change in the issuer's internal control over financial reporting identified in connection with the evaluation required by paragraph (d) of 17 CFR 240.13a-15 or 240.15d-15 that occurred during the period covered by the annual report that has materially affected, or is reasonably likely to materially affect, the issuer's internal control over financial reporting.

Instructions to paragraphs (b), (c), (d) and (e) of General Instruction B.(6).

1. An issuer need not comply with paragraphs (c) and (d) of this Instruction until it either had been required to file an annual report pursuant to

the requirements of section 13(a) or 15(d) of the Exchange Act (15 U.S.C. 78m(a) or 78o(d)) for the prior fiscal year or had filed an annual report with the Commission for the prior fiscal year. An issuer that does not comply shall include a statement in the first annual report that it files in substantially the following form: "This annual report does not include a report of management's assessment regarding internal control over financial reporting or an attestation report of the company's registered public accounting firm due to a transition period established by rules of the Securities and Exchange Commission for newly public companies."

2. The issuer must maintain evidential matter, including documentation, to provide reasonable support for management's assessment of the effectiveness of the issuer's internal control over financial reporting.3T. Paragraphs (c)(4) and (d) of this General Instruction B.6 do not apply to:

(1) an issuer that is an "accelerated filer," but not a "large accelerated filer," as those terms are defined in § 240.12b-2 of this chapter and only with respect to an annual report that the issuer is required to file for a fiscal year ending on or after July 15, 2006 but before July 15, 2007; or

(2) an issuer that is neither a "large accelerated filer" nor an "accelerated filer," as those terms are defined in § 240.12b-2 of this chapter, with respect to an annual report that the issuer is required to file for a fiscal year ending on or after December 15, 2007 but before June 15, 2010. Management's report on internal control over financial reporting that is included in an annual report filed by the type of issuer and within the period set forth in (1) or (2) above in this Instruction 3T shall not be deemed to be filed for purposes of Section 18 of the Exchange Act or otherwise subject to the liabilities of that section, unless the issuer specifically states that the report is to be considered "filed" under the Exchange Act or incorporates it by reference into a filing under the Securities Act or the Exchange Act. An issuer to which this instruction applies should provide a statement in substantially the following form: "This annual report does not include an attestation report of the company's registered public accounting firm regarding internal control over financial reporting. Management's report was not subject to attestation by the company's registered public accounting firm pursuant to temporary rules of the Securities and Exchange Commission that permit the company to provide only management's report in this annual report."

This temporary Instruction 3T will expire on December 15, 2010.

(7) An issuer must attach as an exhibit to an annual report filed on Form 40-F a copy of any notice required by Rule 104 of Regulation BTR (17 CFR 245.104 of this chapter) that it sent during

the past fiscal year to directors and executive officers (as defined in 17 CFR 245.100(d) and (h) of this chapter) concerning any equity security subject to a blackout period (as defined in 17 CFR 245.100(c) of this chapter) under Rule 101 of Regulation BTR (17 CFR 245.101 of this chapter). Each notice must have included the information specified in 17 CFR 245.104(b) of this chapter.

Note: The Commission will consider the attachment of any Rule 104 notice as an exhibit to a timely filed Form 40-F annual report to satisfy an issuer's duty to notify the Commission of a blackout period in a timely manner. Although an issuer need not submit a Rule 104 notice under cover of a Form 6-K, if an issuer has already submitted this notice under cover of Form 6-K, it need not attach the notice as an exhibit to a Form 40-F annual report.

(8)(a)(1) Disclose that the registrant's board of directors has determined that the registrant either:

(i) Has at least one audit committee financial expert serving on its audit committee; or

(ii) Does not have an audit committee financial expert serving on its audit committee.

(2) If the registrant provides the disclosure required by paragraph (8)(a)(1)(i) of this General Instruction B, it must disclose the name of the audit committee financial expert and whether that person is *independent,* as that term is defined in the listing standards applicable to the registrant if the registrant is a listed issuer, as defined in 17 CFR 240.10A-3. If the registrant is not a listed issuer, it must use a definition of audit committee member independence of a national securities exchange registered pursuant to section 6(a) of the Exchange Act (15 U.S.C. 78f(a)) or a national securities association registered pursuant to section 15A(a) of the Exchange Act (15 U.S.C. 78o-3(a)) that has been approved by the Commission (as such definition may be modified or supplemented) in determining whether its audit committee financial expert is independent, and state which definition was used.

(3) If the registrant provides the disclosure required by paragraph (8)(a)(1)(ii) of this General Instruction B, it must explain why it does not have an audit committee financial expert.

Note to paragraph (8)(a) of General Instruction B:

If the registrant's board of directors has determined that the registrant has more than one audit committee financial expert serving on its audit committee, the registrant may, but is not required to, disclose the names of those additional persons.

(b) For purposes of paragraph (8) of General Instruction B, an "audit committee financial expert" means a person who has the following attributes:

(1) An understanding of generally accepted accounting principles and financial statements;

(2) The ability to assess the general application of such principles in connection with the accounting for estimates, accruals and reserves;

(3) Experience preparing, auditing, analyzing or evaluating financial statements that present a breadth and level of complexity of accounting issues that are generally comparable to the breadth and complexity of issues that can reasonably be expected to be raised by the registrant's financial statements, or experience actively supervising one or more persons engaged in such activities;

(4) An understanding of internal control over financial reporting; and

(5) An understanding of audit committee functions.

(c) A person shall have acquired such attributes through:

(1) Education and experience as a principal financial officer, principal accounting officer, controller, public accountant or auditor or experience in one or more positions that involve the performance of similar functions;

(2) Experience actively supervising a principal financial officer, principal accounting officer, controller, public accountant, auditor or person performing similar functions;

(3) Experience overseeing or assessing the performance of companies or public accountants with respect to the preparation, auditing or evaluation of financial statements; or

(4) Other relevant experience.

(d) *Safe Harbor*

(1) A person who is determined to be an audit committee financial expert will not be deemed an "expert" for any purpose, including without limitation for purposes of section 11 of the Securities Act of 1933 (15 U.S.C. 77k), as a result of being designated or identified as an audit committee financial expert pursuant to this paragraph (8) of General Instruction B.

(2) The designation or identification of a person as an audit committee financial expert pursuant to this paragraph (8) of General Instruction B does not impose on such person any duties, obligations or liability that are greater than the duties, obligations and liability imposed on such person as a member of the audit committee and board of directors in the absence of such designation or identification.

(3) The designation or identification of a person as an audit committee financial expert pursuant to this paragraph (8) of General Instruction B

does not affect the duties, obligations or liability of any other member of the audit committee or board of directors.

Notes to Paragraph (8) of General Instruction B:

1. Paragraph (8) of General Instruction B applies only to annual reports, and does not apply to registration statements, on Form 40-F.

2. If a person qualifies as an audit committee financial expert by means of having held a position described in paragraph (8)(c)(4) of General Instruction B, the registrant shall provide a brief listing of that person's relevant experience. Such disclosure may be made by reference to disclosures in the annual report relating to the business experience of that director.

3. In the case of a foreign private issuer with a two-tier board of directors, for purposes of this paragraph (8) of General Instruction B, the term "board of directors" means the supervisory or non-management board. Also, the term "generally accepted accounting principles" in paragraph (8)(b)(1) of General Instruction B means the body of generally accepted accounting principles used by the foreign private issuer in its primary financial statements filed with the Commission.

(9)(a) Disclose whether the registrant has adopted a code of ethics that applies to the registrant's principal executive officer, principal financial officer, principal accounting officer or controller, or persons performing similar functions. If the registrant has not adopted such a code of ethics, explain why it has not done so.

(b) For purposes of this paragraph (9) of General Instruction B, the term "code of ethics" means written standards that are reasonably designed to deter wrongdoing and to promote:

(1) Honest and ethical conduct, including the ethical handling of actual or apparent conflicts of interest between personal and professional relationships;

(2) Full, fair, accurate, timely, and understandable disclosure in reports and documents that a registrant files with, or submits to, the Commission and in other public communications made by the registrant;

(3) Compliance with applicable governmental laws, rules and regulations;

(4) The prompt internal reporting of violations of the code to an appropriate person or persons identified in the code; and

(5) Accountability for adherence to the code.

(c) The registrant must:

(1) File with the Commission a copy of its code of ethics that applies to the registrant's principal executive officer, principal financial officer, principal accounting officer or controller, or persons performing similar functions, as an exhibit to its annual report;

(2) Post the text of such code of ethics on its Internet website and disclose, in its annual report, its Internet address and the fact that it has posted such code of ethics on its Internet website; or

(3) Undertake in its annual report filed with the Commission to provide to any person without charge, upon request, a copy of such code of ethics and explain the manner in which such request may be made.

(d) The registrant must briefly describe the nature of any amendment to a provision of its code of ethics that applies to the registrant's principal executive officer, principal financial officer, principal accounting officer or controller, or persons performing similar functions and that relates to any element of the code of ethics definition enumerated in paragraph (9)(b) of General Instruction B, which has occurred during the registrant's most recently completed fiscal year. File a copy of the amendment as an exhibit to the annual statement.

(e) If the registrant has granted a waiver, including an implicit waiver, from a provision of the code of ethics to one of the officers or persons described in paragraph (9)(a) that relates to one or more of the items set forth in paragraph (9)(b) of General Instruction B during the registrant's most recently completed fiscal year, the registrant must briefly describe the nature of the waiver, the name of the person to whom the waiver was granted, and the date of the waiver.

Notes to paragraph (9) of General Instruction B:

1. Paragraph (9) of General Instruction B applies only to annual reports, and does not apply to registration statements, on Form 40-F.

2. A registrant may have separate codes of ethics for different types of officers. Furthermore, a "code of ethics" within the meaning of paragraph (9)(b) of this General Instruction may be a portion of a broader document that addresses additional topics or that applies to more persons than those specified in paragraph (9)(a). In satisfying the requirements of paragraph (9)(c), a registrant need only file, post or provide the portions of a broader document that constitutes a "code of ethics" as defined in paragraph (9)(b) and that apply to the persons specified in paragraph (9)(a).

3. If a registrant elects to satisfy paragraph (9)(c) of this General Instruction by posting its code of ethics on its website pursuant to paragraph (9)(c)(2), the code of ethics must remain accessible on its website for as long as the registrant remains subject to the requirements of this paragraph (9) of General Instruction B and

chooses to comply with this paragraph (9) of General Instruction B by posting its code on its website pursuant to paragraph (9)(c)(2).

4. The registrant does not need to provide any information pursuant to paragraphs (9)(d) and (9)(e) of General Instruction B if it discloses the required information on its Internet website within five business days following the date of the amendment or waiver and the registrant has disclosed in its most recently filed annual report its Internet address and intention to provide disclosure in this manner. If the registrant elects to disclose the information required by paragraphs (9)(d) and (9)(e) of General Instruction B through its website, such information must remain available on the website for at least a 12-month period. Following the 12-month period, the registrant must retain the information for a period of not less than five years. Upon request, the registrant must furnish to the Commission or its staff a copy of any or all information retained pursuant to this requirement.

5. The registrant does not need to disclose technical, administrative or other non-substantive amendments to its code of ethics.

6. For purposes of this paragraph (9) of General Instruction B:

a. The term "waiver" means the approval by the registrant of a material departure from a provision of the code of ethics; and

b. The term "implicit waiver" means the registrant's failure to take action within a reasonable period of time regarding a material departure from a provision of the code of ethics that has been made known to an executive officer, as defined in Rule 3b-7 (§ 240.3b-7 of this chapter), of the registrant.

(10)*Principal Accountant Fees and Services.*

(1) Disclose, under the caption *Audit Fees*, the aggregate fees billed for each of the last two fiscal years for professional services rendered by the principal accountant for the audit of the registrant's annual financial statements or services that are normally provided by the accountant in connection with statutory and regulatory filings or engagements for those fiscal years.

(2) Disclose, under the caption *Audit-Related Fees*, the aggregate fees billed in each of the last two fiscal years for assurance and related services by the principal accountant that are reasonably related to the performance of the audit or review of the registrant's financial statements and are not reported under paragraph B.(10)(1) of this Instruction. Registrants shall describe the nature of the services comprising the fees disclosed under this category.

(3) Disclose, under the caption *Tax Fees*, the aggregate fees billed in each of the last two fiscal years for professional services rendered by the principal accountant for tax compliance, tax advice, and tax planning. Registrants shall describe the nature of the services comprising the fees disclosed under this category.

(4) Disclose, under the caption *All Other Fees*, the aggregate fees billed in each of the last two fiscal years for products and services provided by the principal accountant, other than the services reported in paragraphs B.(10)(1) through B.(10)(3) of this Instruction. Registrants shall describe the nature of the services comprising the fees disclosed under this category.

(5)(i) Disclose the audit committee's pre-approval policies and procedures described in paragraph (c)(7)(i) of Rule 2-01 of Regulation S-X.

(ii) Disclose the percentage of services described in each of paragraphs B.(10)(2) through B.(10)(4) of this Instruction that were approved by the audit committee pursuant to paragraph (c)(7)(i)(C) of Rule 2-01 of Regulation S-X.

(6) If greater than 50 percent, disclose the percentage of hours expended on the principal accountant's engagement to audit the registrant's financial statements for the most recent fiscal year that were attributed to work performed by persons other than the principal accountant's full-time, permanent employees.

Notes to Instruction B.(10)

1. You do not need to provide the information called for by this Instruction B.(10) unless you are using this form as an annual report.

(11) *Off-balance sheet arrangements.* (i) In a separately-captioned section, discuss the registrant's off-balance sheet arrangements that have or are reasonably likely to have a current or future effect on the registrant's financial condition, changes in financial condition, revenues or expenses, results of operations, liquidity, capital expenditures or capital resources that is material to investors. The disclosure shall include the items specified in this General Instruction B.(11)(i)(A), (B), (C) and (D) to the extent necessary to an understanding of such arrangements and effect and shall also include such other information that the registrant believes is necessary for such an understanding.

(A) The nature and business purpose to the registrant of such off-balance sheet arrangements;

(B) The importance to the registrant of such off-balance sheet arrangements in respect of its liquidity, capital resources, market risk support, credit risk support or other benefits; and

(C) The amounts of revenues, expenses and cash flows of the registrant arising from such arrangements; the nature and amounts of any interests retained, securities issued and other indebtedness incurred by the registrant in connection with such arrangements; and the nature and amounts of any other obligations or liabilities (including contingent obligations or liabilities) of the registrant arising from such arrangements that are or are reasonably likely to become material and the triggering events or circumstances that could cause them to arise.

(D) Any known event, demand, commitment, trend or uncertainty that will result in or is reasonably likely to result in the termination, or material reduction in availability to the registrant, of its off-balance sheet arrangements that provide material benefits to it, and the course of action that the registrant has taken or proposes to take in response to any such circumstances.

(ii) As used in this General Instruction B.(11), the term *off-balance sheet arrangement* means any transaction, agreement or other contractual arrangement to which an entity unconsolidated with the registrant is a party, under which the registrant has:

(A) Any obligation under a guarantee contract that has any of the characteristics identified in paragraph 3 of FASB Interpretation No. 45, *Guarantor's Accounting and Disclosure Requirements for Guarantees, Including Indirect Guarantees of Indebtedness of Others* (November 2002) ("FIN 45"), as may be modified or supplemented, excluding the types of guarantee contracts described in paragraphs 6 and 7 of FIN 45;

(B) A retained or contingent interest in assets transferred to an unconsolidated entity or similar arrangement that serves as credit, liquidity or market risk support to such entity for such assets;

(C) Any obligation under a derivative instrument that is both indexed to the registrant's own stock and classified in stockholders' equity, or not reflected, in the company's statement of financial position; or

(D) Any obligation, including a contingent obligation, arising out of a variable interest (as referenced in FASB Interpretation No. 46, *Consolidation of Variable Interest Entities* (January 2003), as may be modified or supplemented) in an unconsolidated entity that is held by, and material to, the registrant, where such entity provides financing, liquidity, market risk or credit risk support to, or engages in leasing, hedging or research and development services with, the registrant.

(12) *Tabular disclosure of contractual obligations.* (i) In a tabular format, provide the information specified in this General Instruction B.(12) as of the latest fiscal year end balance sheet date with respect to the registrant's known contractual obligations specified in the table that follows this General Instruction B.(12). The registrant shall provide amounts, aggregated by type of contractual obligation. The registrant may disaggregate the specified categories of contractual obligations using other categories suitable to its business, but the presentation must include all of the obligations of the registrant that fall within the specified categories. A presentation covering at least the periods specified shall be included. The tabular presentation may be accompanied by footnotes to describe provisions that create, increase or accelerate obligations, or other pertinent data to the extent necessary for an understanding of the timing and amount of the registrant's specified contractual obligations.

Contractual Obligations	Total	Less than 1 year	1-3 years	3-5 years	More than 5 years
			Payments due by period		
[Long-Term Debt Obligations]					
[Capital (Finance) Lease Obligations]					
[Operating Lease Obligations]					
[Purchase Obligations]					
[Other Long-Term Liabilities Reflected on the Registrant's Balance Sheet under the GAAP of the primary financial statements]					
Total					

(ii) As used in this General Instruction B.(12), the term *purchase obligation* means an agreement to purchase goods or services that is enforceable and legally binding on the registrant that specifies all significant terms, including: fixed or minimum quantities to be purchased; fixed, minimum or variable price provisions; and the approximate timing of the transaction.

(13) *Safe harbor.* (i) The safe harbor provided in Section 27A of the Securities Act and Section 21E of the Exchange Act ("statutory safe harbors") shall apply to forward-looking information provided pursuant to General Instruction B.(11) and (12) of this Form 40-F, provided that the disclosure is made by: an issuer; a person acting on behalf of the issuer; an outside reviewer

retained by the issuer making a statement on behalf of the issuer; or an underwriter, with respect to information provided by the issuer or information derived from information provided by the issuer.

(ii) For purposes of paragraph (i) of this General Instruction B.(13) only, all information required by General Instruction B.(11) and (12) of this Form 40-F is deemed to be a "forward looking statement" as that term is defined in the statutory safe harbors, except for historical facts.

(iii) With respect to General Instruction B.(11), the meaningful cautionary statements element of the statutory safe harbors will be satisfied if a registrant satisfies all requirements of that same General Instruction B.(11).

Instructions

1. No obligation to make disclosure under General Instruction B.(11) shall arise in respect of an off-balance sheet arrangement until a definitive agreement that is unconditionally binding or subject only to customary closing conditions exists or, if there is no such agreement, when settlement of the transaction occurs.

2. Registrants should aggregate off-balance sheet arrangements in groups or categories that provide material information in an efficient and understandable manner and should avoid repetition and disclosure of immaterial information. Effects that are common or similar with respect to a number of off-balance sheet arrangements must be analyzed in the aggregate to the extent the aggregation increases understanding. Distinctions in arrangements and their effects must be discussed to the extent the information is material, but the discussion should avoid repetition and disclosure of immaterial information.

3. For purposes of paragraph General Instruction B.(11) only, contingent liabilities arising out of litigation, arbitration or regulatory actions are not considered to be off-balance sheet arrangements.

4. Generally, the disclosure required by General Instruction B.(11) shall cover the most recent fiscal year. However, the discussion should address changes from the previous year where such discussion is necessary to an understanding of the disclosure.

5. In satisfying the requirements of General Instruction B.(11), the discussion of off-balance sheet arrangements need not repeat information provided in the footnotes to the financial statements, provided that such discussion clearly cross-references to specific information in the relevant footnotes and integrates the substance of the footnotes into such discussion in a manner designed to inform readers of the significance of the information that is not included within the body of such discussion.

6. The registrant is not required to include the table required by General Instruction B.(12) for interim periods. Instead, the registrant should disclose material changes outside the ordinary course of the registrant's business in the specified contractual obligations during the interim period.

7. Except for "purchase obligations," the contractual obligations in the table required by General Instruction B.(12) should be based on the classifications used in the generally accepted accounting principles under which the registrant prepares its primary financial statements. If the generally accepted accounting principles under which the registrant prepares its primary financial statements do not distinguish between capital (finance) leases and operating leases, then present all leases under one category.

(14) *Identification of the Audit Committee.* (a) If you meet the following requirements, provide the disclosure in paragraph (b) of this section:

(1) You are a listed issuer, as defined in Exchange Act Rule 10A-3 (17 CFR 240.10A-3) of this chapter;

(2) You are using this form as an annual report; and

(3) You are neither:

(i) A subsidiary of another listed issuer that is relying on the exemption in Exchange Act Rule 10A-3(c)(2) (17 CFR 240.10A-3(c)(2)); nor

(ii) Relying on any of the exemptions in Exchange Act Rule 10A-3(c)(4) through (c)(7) (17 CFR 240.10A-3(c)(4) through (c)(7)).

(b)(1) State whether or not the registrant has a separately-designated standing audit committee established in accordance with section 3(a)(58)(A) of the Exchange Act (15 U.S.C. 78c(a)(58)(A)), or a committee performing similar functions. If the registrant has such a committee, however designated, identify each committee member. If the entire board of directors is acting as the registrant's audit committee as specified in section 3(a)(58)(B) of the Exchange Act (15 U.S.C. 78c(a)(58)(B)), so state.

(2) If applicable, provide the disclosure required by Exchange Act Rule 10A-3(d) (17 CFR 240.10A-3(d)) regarding an exemption from the listing standards for audit committees.

(15) An Interactive Data File (§ 232.11 of this chapter) is:

(a) *Required to be submitted and posted.* Required to be submitted to the Commission and posted on the registrant's corporate Web site, if any, in the manner provided by Rule 405 of Regulation S-T (§ 232.405 of this chapter), and, as submitted, listed as exhibit 101, if the Form 40-F is an annual report and the registrant does not prepare its financial statements in accordance with Article 6 of Regulation S-X (17 CFR 210.6-01 *et. seq.*) and is:

(i) a large accelerated filer (§ 240.12b-2 of this chapter) that had an aggregate worldwide market value of the voting and non-voting common equity held by non-affiliates of more than $5 billion as of the last business day of the second fiscal quarter of its most recently completed fiscal year that prepares its financial statements in accordance with generally accepted accounting principles as used in the United States and the filing contains financial statements of the registrant for a fiscal period that ends on or after June 15, 2009;

(ii) A large accelerated filer not specified in subparagraph (a)(i) of this paragraph (15) that prepares its financial statements in accordance with generally accepted accounting principles as used in the United States and the filing contains financial statements of the registrant for a fiscal period that ends on or after June 15, 2010; or

(iii) A filer not specified in subparagraph (a)(i) or (a)(ii) of this paragraph (15) that prepares its financial statements in accordance with either generally accepted accounting principles as used in the United States or International Financial Reporting Standards as issued by the International Accounting Standards Board, and

the filing contains financial statements of the registrant for a fiscal period that ends on or after June 15, 2011.

(b) *Permitted to be submitted.* Permitted to be submitted to the Commission in the manner provided by Rule 405 of Regulation S-T (§ 232.405 of this chapter) if the registrant lists it as exhibit 101 and the:

(i) Registrant prepares its financial statements:

(A) In accordance with either:

(1) Generally accepted accounting principles as used in the United States; or

(2) International Financial Reporting Standards as issued by the International Accounting Standards Board; and

(B) Not in accordance with Article 6 of Regulation S-X (17 CFR 210.6-01 *et. seq.*); and

(ii) Interactive Data File is not required to be submitted to the Commission under subparagraph (a) of this paragraph (15).

(c) *Not permitted to be submitted.* Not permitted to be submitted to the Commission if the registrant prepares its financial statements in accordance with Article 6 of Regulation S-X (17 CFR 210.6-01 *et. seq.*).

C. Compliance with Auditor Independence and Reconciliation Requirements

(1) The Commission's rules on auditor independence, as codified in Section 600 of the Codification of Financial Reporting Policies, apply to auditor reports on all financial statements that are included in this registration statement or annual report, except that such rules do not apply with respect to periods prior to the most recent fiscal year for which financial statements are included in a registration statement under the Securities Act filed by the issuer on Form F-8, Form F-9, Form F-10 or Form F-80 or under the Exchange Act filed by the issuer on Form 40-F. Notwithstanding the exception in the previous sentence, such rules do apply with respect to any periods prior to the most recent fiscal year if the issuer previously was required to file with the Commission a report or registration statement containing an audit report on financial statements for such periods as to

which the Commission's rules on auditor independence applied.

(2) Any financial statements, other than interim financial statements, included in this Form by registrants registering securities pursuant to Section 12 of the Exchange Act or reporting pursuant to the provisions of Section 13(a) or 15(d) of the Exchange Act must be reconciled to U.S. GAAP as required by Item 17 of Form 20-F under the Exchange Act, unless this Form is filed with respect to securities that would be eligible for registration under the Securities Act on Form F-9, in which case no such reconciliation is required, or unless this Form is filed with respect to a reporting obligation under Section 15(d) that arose solely as a result of a filing made on Form F-7, F-8, F-9 or F-80, in which case no such reconciliation is required.

D. Application of General Rules and Regulations

(1) Rules 12b-2, 12b-5, 12b-10, 12b-11, 12b-12, 12b-13, 12b-14, 12b-21, 12b-22, 12b-23, 12b-25, 12b-33 and 12b-37 under the Exchange Act shall not apply to filings on this Form. The rules and regulations applicable in the home jurisdiction regarding the form and method of preparation of disclosure documents shall apply to filings on this Form. Exchange Act rules and regulations other

than Rules 12b-2, 12b-5, 12b-10, 12b-11, 12b-12, 12b-13, 12b-14, 12b-21, 12b-22, 12b-25, 12b-33 and 12b-37 shall apply to filings on this Form unless specifically excluded in this Form. Pursuant to Rule 13a-3, an eligible registrant that files reports on Form 40-F and Form 6-K is deemed to satisfy the requirements of Regulation 13A under the Exchange Act.

(2) A registration statement on this Form shall be deemed to be filed on the proper form unless objection to the Form is made by the Commission prior to the effective date.

(3) An annual report on this Form or any amendment thereto shall be filed the same day the information therein is due to be filed with any securities commission or equivalent regulatory authority in Canada.

(4) A registration statement filed pursuant to Section 12 of the Exchange Act on this Form shall become effective in accordance with Section 12(d) and Rule 12b-6 or Section 12(g)(1) of such Act, an applicable.

(5) Rule 12b-20, which provides that in addition to the information expressly required to be included in a statement or report, there shall be added such further material information, if any, as may be necessary to make the required statements, in light of the circumstances under which they are made, not misleading, shall apply to filing on this Form.

(6) Pursuant to Rule 12b-15, all amendments to this Form shall be filed under cover of Form 8.

(7) A filer must file the Form 40-F registration statement or annual report in electronic format via the Commission's Electronic Data Gathering, Analysis, and Retrieval (EDGAR) system in accordance with the EDGAR rules set forth in Regulation S-T (17 CFR Part 232). For assistance with technical questions about EDGAR or to request an access code, call the EDGAR Filer Support Office at (202) 942-8900. For assistance with the EDGAR rules, call the Office of EDGAR and Information Analysis at (202) 942-2940.

If filing the Form 40-F registration statement or annual report in paper under a hardship exemption in Rule 201 or 202 of Regulation S-T (17 CFR 232.201 or 232.202), or as otherwise permitted, a filer must file with the Commission at its principal office five copies of the complete registration statement or annual report, including exhibits and all other documents filed as a part of the registration statement or annual report. The filer must bind, staple or otherwise compile each copy in one or more parts without stiff covers. The filer must further bind the registration statement or annual

report on the side or stitching margin in a manner that leaves the reading matter legible. The filer must provide three additional copies of the registration statement or annual report without exhibits to the Commission.

(8) An electronic filer must provide the signatures required for the Form 40-F registration statement or annual report in accordance with Regulation S-T Rule 302 (17 CFR 232.302). A paper filer must have at least one copy of the Form 40-F registration statement or annual report signed by an officer authorized to sign the registration statement or annual report. A paper filer must also conform the unsigned copies.

(9) If any accountant, engineer or appraiser, or any person whose profession gives authority to a statement made by him, is named as having prepared or certified any part of the registration statement or annual report, or is named as having prepared or certified a report or valuation for use in connection with the registration statement or annual report, the manually signed, written consent of such person shall be filed.

If any person is named as having prepared or certified any other report or valuation (other than a public official document or statement) which is used in connection with the registration statement or annual report, but is not named as having prepared or certified such report or valuation for use in connection with the registration statement or annual report, the manually signed, written consent of such person also shall be filed unless the Commission dispenses with such filing as impracticable or as involving undue hardship.

Any other consent required by rule 12b-36 also shall be filed. Every amendment relating to a certified financial statement shall include the manually signed, written consent of the certifying accountant to the use of such accountant's certificate in connection with the amended financial statements in the registration statement or annual report and to being named as having certified such financial statements.

NOTE: The consents required by this item shall specifically indicate consent regarding use of the report or valuation in the registration statement filed in the United States.

A. Undertaking

This Form shall set forth the following undertaking of the Registrant:

Registrant undertakes to make available, in person or by telephone, representatives to respond to inquiries made by the Commission staff, and to furnish promptly, when requested to do so by the Commission staff, information relating to: the securities registered pursuant to Form 40-F; the securities in relation to which the obligation to

file an annual report on Form 40-F arises; or transactions in said securities.

B. Consent to Service of Process

(1) Registrants registering securities on this Form, and Registrants filing annual reports on this Form who have not previously filed a Form F-X in connection with the class of securities in relation to which the obligation to file this report arises, shall file a Form F-X with the Commission together with this Form.

(2) Any change to the name or address of a Registrant's agent for service shall be communicated promptly to the Commission by amendment to Form F-X referencing the file number of the Registrant.

Registrant ....

By (Signature and Title) ....

Date ....

Instructions

A. The name and title of the officer who signs the registration statement or annual report shall be typed or printed beneath such person's signature. Any such person who occupies more than one position shall indicate each capacity in which the registration statement is signed.

B. By signing this Form, the Registrant consents without power of revocation that any administrative subpoena may be served, or any administrative proceeding, civil suit or civil action where the

Date........

     [Signature]

     [Title]

SIGNATURES

Pursuant to the requirements of the Exchange Act, the Registrant certifies that it meets all of the requirements for filing on Form 40-F and has duly caused this registration statement [annual report]to be signed on its behalf by the undersigned, thereto duly authorized.

cause of action arises out of or relates to or concerns any purchases or sales of any security registered pursuant to Form 40-F on the securities in relation to which the obligation to file an annual report on Form 40-F arises, or transactions in said securities, may be commenced against it in any administrative tribunal or in any appropriate court in any place subject to the jurisdiction of any state or of the United States or of the District of Columbia or Puerto Rico by service of said subpoena or process upon the Registrant's designated agent.

[¶ 33,111]   FORM 8-A

[As last amended in Release No. 33-8876, effective February 4, 2008, 73 F.R. 934.]

SECURITIES AND EXCHANGE COMMISSION

Washington, D.C. 20549

FORM 8-A

FOR REGISTRATION OF CERTAIN CLASSES OF SECURITIES

PURSUANT TO SECTION 12(b) OR (g) OF THE

SECURITIES EXCHANGE ACT OF 1934

GENERAL INSTRUCTIONS

A. Rule as to Use of Form 8-A

(a) Subject to paragraph (b) below, this form may be used for registration pursuant to Section 12(b) or (g) of the Securities Exchange Act of 1934 of any class of securities of any issuer which is required to file reports pursuant to Section 13 or 15(d) of that Act or pursuant to an order exempting the exchange on which the issuer has securities listed from registration as a national securities exchange.

(b) If the registrant would be required to file an annual report pursuant to Section 15(d) of the Act for its last fiscal year, except for the fact that the registration statement on this form will become effective before such report is required to be filed, an annual report for such fiscal year shall nevertheless be filed within the period specified in the appropriate annual report form.

(c) If this form is used for the registration of a class of securities under Section 12(b), it shall become effective:

(1) If a class of securities is not concurrently being registered under the Securities Act of 1933 (15 U.S.C. 77a et seq.) ("Securities Act"), upon the later of receipt by the Commission of certification from the national securities exchange listed on this form or the filing of the Form 8-A with the Commission; or

(2) If a class of securities is concurrently being registered under the Securities Act, upon the later of the filing of the Form 8-A with the Commission, receipt by the Commission of certification from the national securities exchange listed on this form or effectiveness of the Securities Act registration statement relating to the class of securities.

(d) If this form is used for the registration of a class of securities under Section 12(g), it shall become effective:

(1) If a class of securities is not concurrently being registered under the Securities Act, upon the filing of the Form 8-A with the Commission; or

(2) If class of securities is concurrently being registered under the Securities Act, upon the later of the filing of the Form 8-A with the Commission or the effectiveness of the Securities Act registration statement relating to the class of securities.

B. Application of General Rules and Regulations

(a) The General Rules and Regulations under the Act contain certain general requirements which are applicable to registration on any form. These general requirements should be carefully read and observed in the preparation and filing of registration statements on this form.

(b) Particular attention is directed to Regulation 12B which contains general requirements regarding matters such as the kind and size of paper to be used, legibility, information to be given whenever the title of securities is required to be stated, incorporation by reference and the filing of the registration statement. The definitions contained in Rule 12b-2 should be especially noted.

C. Preparation of Registration Statement

This form is not to be used as a blank form to be filled in, but only as a guide in the preparation of the registration statement on paper meeting the requirements of Rule 12b-12. The registration statement shall contain the item numbers and captions, but the text of the items may be omitted. The answers to the items shall be prepared in the manner specified in Rule 12b-13.

D. Signature and Filing of Registration Statement

Eight complete copies of the registration statement, including all papers and documents filed as a part thereof (other than exhibits) shall be filed with the Commission and at least one such copy shall be filed with each exchange on which the securities are to be registered. Exhibits shall be filed with the Commission and with any exchange in accordance with the Instructions as to Exhibits. At least one copy of the registration statement filed with the Commission and one filed with each exchange shall be manually signed. Unsigned copies shall be conformed.

UNITED STATES

SECURITIES AND EXCHANGE COMMISSION

Washington, D.C. 20549

FOR REGISTRATION OF CERTAIN CLASSES OF SECURITIES PURSUANT TO SECTION 12(b) OR (g) OF THE SECURITIES EXCHANGE ACT OF 1934

. . . .

(Exact name of registrant as specified in its charter)

. . . .

(State of incorporation or organization)   (I.R.S. Employer Identification No.)

. . . .

(Address of principal executive offices)   (Zip Code)

Securities to be registered pursuant to Section 12(b) of the Act:

Title of each class to be so registered	Name of each exchange on which each class is to be registered
. . . .	. . . .
. . . .	. . . .
. . . .	. . . .

If this form relates to the registration of a class of securities pursuant to Section 12(b) of the Exchange Act and is effective pursuant to General Instruction A.(c), check the following box. [ ]

If this form relates to the registration of a class of securities pursuant to Section 12(g) of the Exchange Act and is effective pursuant to General Instruction A.(d), check the following box. [ ]

Securities Act registration statement file number to which this form relates:

. . . . (if applicable)

Securities to be registered pursuant to Section 12(g) of the Act:

. . . .

(Title of class)

. . . .

(Title of class)

INFORMATION REQUIRED IN REGISTRATION STATEMENT

Item 1. Description of Registrant's Securities to be Registered

Furnish the information required by Item 202 of Regulation S-K (§ 229.202 of this chapter), as applicable.

Instruction. If a description of the securities comparable to that required here is contained in any prior filing with the Commission, such description may be incorporated by reference to such other filing in answer to this item. If such description will be included in a form of prospectus subsequently filed by the registrant pursuant to Rule 424(b) under the Securities Act [§ 230.424(b) of this chapter] this registration statement shall state that such prospectus shall be deemed to be incorporated by reference into the registration statement. If the securities are to be registered on a national securities exchange and the description has not previously been filed with such exchange, copies of the description shall be filed with copies of the application filed with the exchange.

Item 2. Exhibits

List below all exhibits filed as a part of the registration statement:

Instruction. See the instructions as to exhibits, set forth below.

SIGNATURE

Pursuant to the requirements of Section 12 of the Securities Exchange Act of 1934, the registrant has duly caused this registration statement to be signed on its behalf by the undersigned, thereto duly authorized.

(Registrant) ....

Date ....

By ....

* Print the name and title of the signing officer
under his signature.

INSTRUCTIONS AS TO EXHIBITS

If the securities to be registered on this form
are to be registered on an exchange on which
other securities of the registrant are registered, or
are to be registered pursuant to Section 12(g) of
the Act, copies of all constituent instruments defining the rights of the holders of each class of such
securities, including any contracts or other documents which limit or qualify the rights of such
holders, shall be filed as exhibits with each copy
of the registration statement filed with the Commission or with an exchange, subject to Rule
12b-32 regarding incorporation of exhibits by
reference.

FORM 6-K

[As last amended in Release No. 33-9002, effective April 13, 2009, 74 F.R. 6776 and corrected in Release No. 33-9002A, 74 F.R. 15666.]

UNITED STATES

SECURITIES AND EXCHANGE COMMISSION

Washington, D.C. 20549

FORM 6-K

GENERAL INSTRUCTIONS

A. Rule as to Use of Form 6-K

This form shall be used by foreign private issuers which are required to furnish reports pursuant to Rule 13a-16 or 15d-16 under the Securities Exchange Act of 1934.

B. Information and Document Required to be Furnished

Subject to General Instruction D herein, an issuer furnishing a report on this form shall furnish whatever information, not required to be furnished on Form 40-F or previously furnished, such issuer (i) makes or is required to make public pursuant to the law of the jurisdiction of its domicile or in which it is incorporated or organized, or (ii) files or is required to file with a stock exchange on which its securities are traded and which was made public by that exchange, or (iii) distributes or is required to distribute to its securityholders.

The information required to be furnished pursuant to (i), (ii) or (iii) above is that which is material with respect to the issuer and its subsidiaries concerning; changes in business; changes in management or control; acquisitions or dispositions of assets; bankruptcy or receivership; changes in registrant's certifying accountants; the financial condition and results of operations; material legal proceedings; changes in securities or in the security for registered securities; defaults upon senior securities; material increases or decreases in the amount outstanding of securities or indebtedness; the results of the submission of matters to a vote of securityholders; transactions with directors, officers or principal securityholders; the granting of options or payment of other compensation to directors or officers; and any other information which the registrant deems of material importance to securityholders.

This report is required to be furnished promptly after the material contained in the report is made public as described above. The information and documents furnished in this report shall not be deemed to be "filed" for the purposes of

Section 18 of the Act or otherwise subject to the liabilities of that section.

If a report furnished on this form incorporates by reference any information not previously filed with the Commission, such information must be attached as an exhibit and furnished with the form.

C. Preparation and Filing of Report

(1) The Form 6-K report shall consist of a cover page, the report or document furnished by the issuer, and a signature page. An issuer must submit the Form 6-K report in electronic format via the Commission's Electronic Data Gathering, Analysis, and Retrieval (EDGAR) system in accordance with the EDGAR rules set forth in Regulation S-T (17 CFR Part 232) except as discussed below. An issuer submitting the Form 6-K in electronic format must provide the signatures required for the Form 6-K report in accordance with Regulation S-T Rule 302 (17 CFR 232.302). For assistance with technical questions about EDGAR or to request an access code, call the EDGAR Filer Support Office at (202) 942-8900. For assistance with the EDGAR rules, call the Office of EDGAR and Information Analysis at (202) 942-2940.

(2) An issuer may submit a Form 6-K in paper under:

• Regulation S-T Rule 101(b)(1) (17 CFR 232.101(b)(1)) if the sole purpose of the Form 6-K is to furnish an annual report to security holders;

• Regulation S-T Rule 101(b)(7) to provide a report or other document that the issuer must furnish and make public under the laws of the jurisdiction in which it is incorporated, domiciled or legally organized (the issuer's "home country"), or under the rules of the home country exchange on which the issuer's securities are traded, as long as the report or other document is not a press release, is not required to be and has not been distributed to the issuer's security holders, and, if discussing a material event, including the disclosure of annual audited or interim consolidated financial results, has already been the subject of a

Form 6-K submission or other Commission filing on EDGAR; or

• a hardship exemption provided by Regulation S-T Rule 201 or 202 (17 CFR 232.201 or 232.202).

Note to paragraph (2): An issuer that is or will be incorporating by reference all or part of an annual or other report to security holders, or of any part of a paper Form 6-K, into an electronic filing must file the incorporated portion in electronic format as an exhibit to the filing in accordance with Regulation S-T Rule 303(b) (17 CFR 232.303(b)).

(3) When submitting a Form 6-K in paper under one of the above rules, an issuer must check the appropriate box on the cover page of the Form 6-K. When submitting a Form 6-K in paper under a hardship exemption, an issuer must provide the legend required by Regulation S-T Rule 201(a)(2) or 202(c) (17 CFR 232.201(a)(2) or 232.202(c)) on the cover page of the Form 6-K.

(4) An issuer furnishing the Form 6-K in paper under one of the above rules, or as otherwise permitted by the Commission, must deposit with the Commission eight complete copies of the Form 6-K report. An issuer must also file at least one complete copy of the Form 6-K with each United States stock exchange on which any security of the issuer is listed and registered under Section 12(b) of the Exchange Act. The issuer must have signed at least one of the paper copies deposited with the Commission and one filed with each United States stock exchange in accordance with Exchange Act Rule 12b-11(d) (17 CFR 240.12b-11(d)) when submitting the Form 6-K in paper to the Commission. An issuer submitting the Form 6-K in paper must also conform the unsigned copies. When submitting the Form 6-K in electronic format to the Commission, an issuer may submit a paper copy containing typed signatures to each United States stock exchange in accordance with Regulation S-T Rule 302(c) (17 CFR 232.302(c)).

(5) *XBRL-Related Documents.* Only a registrant that prepares its financial statements in accordance with Article 6 of Regulation S-X (17 CFR 210.6-01 et. seq.) is permitted to participate in the voluntary XBRL (eXtensible Business Reporting Language) program and, as a result, may submit XBRL-Related Documents (§ 232.11 of this chapter). XBRL-Related Documents submitted as an exhibit to a Form 6-K must be listed as exhibit 100. Rule 401 of Regulation S -T (§ 232.401 of this chapter) sets forth further details regarding eligibility to participate in the voluntary XBRL program.

(6) *Interactive Data File.* An Interactive Data File (§ 232.11 of this chapter) is:

(a) *Required to be submitted and posted.* Required to be submitted to the Commission and posted on the registrant's corporate Web site, if any, in the manner provided by Rule 405 of Regulation S-T (§ 232.405 of this chapter) and, as submitted, listed as exhibit 101, if the registrant does not prepare its financial statements in accordance with Article 6 of Regulation S-X (17 CFR 210.6-01 et. seq.) and is described in subparagraph (a)(i), (ii), or (iii) of this paragraph (6), except that an Interactive Data File: first is required for a periodic report on Form 10-Q (§ 249.308a of this chapter), Form 20-F (§ 249.220f of this chapter) or Form 40-F (§ 249.240f of this chapter), as applicable; and is required for a Form 6-K (§ 249.306 of this chapter) only when the Form 6-K contains either of the following: audited annual financial statements that are a revised version of financial statements that previously were filed with the Commission that have been revised pursuant to applicable accounting standards to reflect the effects of certain subsequent events, including a discontinued operation, a change in reportable segments or a change in accounting principle; or current interim financial statements included pursuant to the nine-month updating requirement of Item 8.A.5 of Form 20-F, and, in either such case, the Interactive Data File would be required only as to such revised financial statements or current interim financial statements regardless of whether the Form 6-K contains other financial statements:

(i) A large accelerated filer (§ 240.12b-2 of this chapter) that had an aggregate worldwide market value of the voting and non-voting common equity held by non-affiliates of more than $5 billion as of the last business day of the second fiscal quarter of its most recently completed fiscal year that prepares its financial statements in accordance with generally accepted accounting principles as used in the United States and the filing contains financial statements of the registrant for a fiscal period that ends on or after June 15, 2009;

(ii) A large accelerated filer not specified in subparagraph (a)(i) of this paragraph (6) that prepares its financial statements in accordance with generally accepted accounting principles as used in the United States and the filing contains financial statements of the registrant for a fiscal period that ends on or after June 15, 2010; or

(iii) A filer not specified in subparagraph (a)(i) or (ii) of this paragraph (6) that prepares its financial statements in accordance with either generally accepted accounting principles as used in the United States or International Financial Reporting Standards as issued by the International Accounting Standards Board, and the filing contains financial statements of the registrant for a fiscal period that ends on or after June 15, 2011.

(b) *Permitted to be submitted.* Permitted to be submitted to the Commission in the manner provided by Rule 405 of Regulation S-T (§ 232.405 of this chapter) if the:

(i) Registrant prepares its financial statements:

(A) In accordance with either:

(1) Generally accepted accounting principles as used in the United States; or

(2) International Financial Reporting Standards as issued by the International Accounting Standards Board; and

(B) Not in accordance with Article 6 of Regulation S-X (17 CFR 210.6-01 *et. seq.*); and

(ii) Interactive Data File is not required to be submitted to the Commission under subparagraph (a)(i) of this paragraph (6).

(c) *Not permitted to be submitted.* Not permitted to be submitted to the Commission if the registrant prepares its financial statements in accordance with Article 6 of Regulation S-X (17 CFR 210.6-01 *et. seq.*).

D. Treatment of Foreign Language Documents.

(1) An issuer must submit the Form 6-K report in electronic format in the English language in accordance with Regulation S-T Rule 306 (17 CFR 232.306) and Exchange Act Rule 12b-12(d) (17 CFR 240.12b-12(d)), as referenced in Regulation S-T Rule 306(a) (17 CFR 232.306(a)), except as otherwise provided by this Form. An issuer submitting the Form 6-K in paper must meet the requirements of Exchange Act Rule 12b-12(d) (17 CFR 240.12b-12(d)). In accordance with, or in addition to, the list of documents specified in Exchange Act Rule 12b-12(d)(2) (17 CFR 240.12b-12(d)(2)), an issuer must provide a full English translation of the following documents furnished under cover of Form 6-K whether submitted electronically or in paper:

• press releases;

• communications and other documents distributed directly to security holders for each class of securities to which a reporting obligation under Exchange Act Section 13(a) or 15(d) pertains,

except for offering circulars and prospectuses that relate entirely to securities offerings outside the United States ("foreign offerings"); and

• documents disclosing annual audited or interim consolidated financial information.

(2) In addition to the documents specified in Exchange Act Rule 12b-12(d)(3) (17 CFR 240.12b-12(d)(3)), an issuer may furnish under cover of Form 6-K, whether submitted electronically or in paper, an English summary instead of a full English translation of a report required to be furnished and made public under the laws of the issuer's home country or the rules of the issuer's home country stock exchange, as long as it is not a press release and is not required to be and has not been distributed to the issuer's security holders. Such a document may include a report disclosing unconsolidated financial information about a parent company.

(3) An issuer is not required to submit under cover of Form 6-K an offering circular or prospectus that pertains solely to a foreign offering, even when an English translation or English summary is available, if the issuer has already submitted a Form 6-K or filed a Form 20-F or other Commission filing on EDGAR that reported material information disclosed in the offering circular or prospectus. If an issuer has not previously disclosed this material information to the Commission, it may submit in electronic format under cover of Form 6-K an English translation or English summary of the portion of the foreign offering circular or prospectus that discusses the new material information.

(4) Any submitted English summary must meet the requirements of Exchange Act Rule 12b-12(d)(3)(ii) (17 CFR 240.12b-12(d)(3)(ii)). An issuer may submit the unabridged foreign language report or other document along with the English summary or English translation as permitted by Regulation S-T Rule 306(b) (17 CFR 232.306(b)) for electronic filings and Exchange Act Rule 12b-12(d)(4) (17 CFR 240.12b-12(d)(4)) for paper filings.

(5) *XBRL-Related Documents.* XBRL-Related Documents (§ 232.11 of this chapter) can be submitted if listed as exhibit 100.

FORM 6-K

SECURITIES AND EXCHANGE COMMISSION

Washington, D.C. 20549

Report of Foreign Private Issuer

Pursuant to Rule 13a-16 or 15d-16

under the Securities Exchange Act of 1934

For the month of . . . . , 20 . .

Commission File Number . . . .

. . . .

(Translation of registrant's name into English)

. . . .

(Address of principal executive offices)

Indicate by check mark whether the registrant files or will file annual reports under cover of Form 20-F or Form 40-F:

Form 20-F . . . . Form 40-F . . . .

Indicate by check mark if the registrant is submitting the Form 6-K in paper as permitted by Regulation S-T Rule 101(b)(1): . . . .

Note: Regulation S-T Rule 101(b)(1) only permits the submission in paper of a Form 6-K if submitted solely to provide an attached annual report to security holders.

Indicate by check mark if the registrant is submitting the Form 6-K in paper as permitted by Regulation S-T Rule 101(b)(7): . . . .

Note: Regulation S-T Rule 101(b)(7) only permits the submission in paper of a Form 6-K if submitted to furnish a report or other document that the registrant foreign private issuer must furnish and make public under the laws of the jurisdiction in which the registrant is incorporated, domiciled or legally organized (the registrant's "home country"), or under the rules of the home country exchange on which the registrant's securities are traded, as long as the report or other document is not a press release, is not required to be and has not been distributed to the registrant's security holders, and, if discussing a material event, has already been the subject of a Form 6-K submission or other Commission filing on EDGAR.

Yes . . . . No . . . .

SIGNATURES

Pursuant to the requirements of the Securities Exchange Act of 1934, the registrant has duly caused this report to be signed on its behalf by the undersigned, thereunto duly authorized.

. . . .

(Registrant)

Date . . . .   By . . . .

(Signature)*

* Print the name and title of the signing officer under his signature.

>>>→ *CCH Note: The SEC has stayed the effectiveness of proxy rule amendments adopted in Release 33-9136 pending resolution of a challenge filed by the Business Roundtable and the U.S. Chamber of Commerce in the U.S. Court of Appeals for the District of Columbia Circuit. See Release No. 33-9149, October 4, 2010.*

>>>→ *Amended by Release No. 33-9136, effective November 15, 2010, 75 F.R. 56668.*

[¶ 33,211] FORM 8-K

[As last amended in Release No. 33-9136, effective November 15, 2010, 75 F.R. 56668, stayed by Release No. 33-9149, October 4, 2010.]

UNITED STATES

SECURITIES AND EXCHANGE COMMISSION

Washington, D.C. 20549

FORM 8-K

CURRENT REPORT

Pursuant to Section 13 or 15(d) of the Securities Exchange Act of 1934

UNITED STATES

SECURITIES AND EXCHANGE COMMISSION

Washington, D.C. 20549

FORM 8-K

CURRENT REPORT

Pursuant to Section 13 or 15(d) of the Securities Exchange Act of 1934

Date of Report (Date of earliest event reported) . . . .

(Exact name of registrant as specified in its charter)

. . . .

(State or other jurisdiction of incorporation)   (Commission File Number)   (IRS Employer Identification No.)

. . . .

(Address of principal executive offices)   (Zip Code)

Registrant's telephone number, including area code . . . .

. . . .

(Former name or former address, if changed since last report.)

Check the appropriate box below if the Form 8-K filing is intended to simultaneously satisfy the filing obligation of the registrant under any of the following provisions (see General Instruction A.2. below):

[ ] Written communications pursuant to Rule 425 under the Securities Act (17 CFR 230.425)

[ ] Soliciting material pursuant to Rule 14a-12 under the Exchange Act (17 CFR 240.14a-12)

[ ] Pre-commencement communications pursuant to Rule 14d-2(b) under the Exchange Act (17 CFR 240.14d-2(b))

[ ]Pre-commencement communications pursuant to Rule 13e-4(c) under the Exchange Act (17 CFR 240.13e-4(c))

GENERAL INSTRUCTIONS

A. Rule as to Use of Form 8-K

1. Form 8-K shall be used for current reports under Section 13 or 15(d) of the Securities Exchange Act of 1934, filed pursuant to Rule 13a-11 or Rule 15d-11, and for reports of nonpublic infor-

mation required to be disclosed by Regulation FD (17 CFR 243.100 and 243.101).

2. Form 8-K may be used by a registrant to satisfy its filing obligations pursuant to Rule 425 under the Securities Act, regarding written com-

munications related to business combination transactions, or Rules 14a-12(b) or Rule 14d-2(b) under the Exchange Act, relating to soliciting materials and pre-commencement communications pursuant to tender offers, respectively, provided that the Form 8-K filing satisfies all the substantive requirements of those rules (other than the Rule 425(c) requirement to include certain specified information in any prospectus filed pursuant to such rule). Such filing is also deemed to be filed pursuant to any rule for which the box is checked. A registrant is not required to check the box in connection with Rule 14a-12(b) or Rule 14d-2(b) if the communication is filed pursuant to Rule 425. Communications filed pursuant to Rule 425 are deemed filed under the other applicable sections. See Note 2 to Rule 425, Rule 14a-12(b) and Instruction 2 to Rule 14d-2(b)(2).

B. Events to be Reported and Time for Filing of Reports

1. A report on this form is required to be filed or furnished, as applicable, upon the occurrence of any one or more of the events specified in the items in Sections 1 - 6 and 9 of this form. Unless otherwise specified, a report is to be filed or furnished within four business days after occurrence of the event. If the event occurs on a Saturday, Sunday or holiday on which the Commission is not open for business, then the four business day period shall begin to run on, and include, the first business day thereafter. A registrant either furnishing a report on this form under Item 7.01 (Regulation FD Disclosure) or electing to file a report on this form under Item 8.01 (Other Events) solely to satisfy its obligations under Regulation FD (17 CFR 243.100 and 243.101) must furnish such report or make such filing, as applicable, in accordance with the requirements of Rule 100(a) of Regulation FD (17 CFR 243.100(a)), including the deadline for furnishing or filing such report.

*Amendment*_____

1. A report on this form is required to be filed or furnished, as applicable, upon the occurrence of any one or more of the events specified in the items in Sections 1 - 6 and 9 of this form. Unless otherwise specified, a report is to be filed or furnished within four business days after occurrence of the event. If the event occurs on a Saturday, Sunday or holiday on which the Commission is not open for business, then the four business day period shall begin to run on, and include, the first business day thereafter. A registrant either furnishing a report on this form under Item 7.01 (Regulation FD Disclosure) or electing to file a report on this form under Item 8.01 (Other Events) solely to satisfy its obligations under Regulation FD (17 CFR 243.100 and 243.101) must furnish such report or make such filing, as applicable, in accordance with the requirements of Rule

100(a) of Regulation FD (17 CFR 243.100(a)), including the deadline for furnishing or filing such report. A report pursuant to Item 5.08 is to be filed within four business days after the registrant determines the anticipated meeting date.

*End of Amendment*_____

2. The information in a report furnished pursuant to Item 2.02 (Results of Operations and Financial Condition) or Item 7.01 (Regulation FD Disclosure) shall not be deemed to be "filed" for purposes of Section 18 of the Exchange Act or otherwise subject to the liabilities of that section, unless the registrant specifically states that the information is to be considered "filed" under the Exchange Act or incorporates it by reference into a filing under the Securities Act or the Exchange Act. If a report on Form 8-K contains disclosures under Item 2.02 or Item 7.01, whether or not the report contains disclosures regarding other items, all exhibits to such report relating to Item 2.02 or Item 7.01 will be deemed furnished, and not filed, unless the registrant specifies, under Item 9.01 (Financial Statements and Exhibits), which exhibits, or portions of exhibits, are intended to be deemed filed rather than furnished pursuant to this instruction.

3. If the registrant previously has reported substantially the same information as required by this form, the registrant need not make an additional report of the information on this form. To the extent that an item calls for disclosure of developments concerning a previously reported event or transaction, any information required in the new report or amendment about the previously reported event or transaction may be provided by incorporation by reference to the previously filed report. The term *previously reported* is defined in Rule 12b-2 (17 CFR 240.12b-2).

4. Copies of agreements, amendments or other documents or instruments required to be filed pursuant to Form 8-K are not required to be filed or furnished as exhibits to the Form 8-K unless specifically required to be filed or furnished by the applicable Item. This instruction does not affect the requirement to otherwise file such agreements, amendments or other documents or instruments, including as exhibits to registration statements and periodic reports pursuant to the requirements of Item 601 of Regulation S-K.

5. When considering current reporting on this form, particularly of other events of material importance pursuant to Item 7.01 (Regulation FD Disclosure) and Item 8.01(Other Events), registrants should have due regard for the accuracy, completeness and currency of the information in registration statements filed under the Securities Act which incorporate by reference information in reports filed pursuant to the Exchange Act, including reports on this form.

6. A registrant's report under Item 7.01 (Regulation FD Disclosure) or Item 8.01 (Other Events) will not be deemed an admission as to the materiality of any information in the report that is required to be disclosed solely by Regulation FD.

C. Application of General Rules and Regulations

1. The General Rules and Regulations under the Act (17 CFR Part 240) contain certain general requirements which are applicable to reports on any form. These general requirements should be carefully read and observed in the preparation and filing of reports on this form.

2. Particular attention is directed to Regulation 12B (17 CFR 240.12b-1 et seq.) which contains general requirements regarding matters such as the kind and size of paper to be used, the legibility of the report, the information to be given whenever the title of securities is required to be stated, and the filing of the report. The definitions contained in Rule 12b-2 should be especially noted. See also Regulations 13A (17 CFR 240.13a-1 et seq.) and 15D (17 CFR 240.15d-1 et seq.).

D. Preparation of Report.

This form is not to be used as a blank form to be filled in, but only as a guide in the preparation of the report on paper meeting the requirements of Rule 12b-12 (17 CFR 240.12b-12). The report shall contain the number and caption of the applicable item, but the text of such item may be omitted, provided the answers thereto are prepared in the manner specified in Rule 12b-13 (17 CFR 240.12b-13). To the extent that Item 1.01 and one or more other items of the form are applicable, registrants need not provide the number and caption of Item 1.01 so long as the substantive disclosure required by Item 1.01 is disclosed in the report and the number and caption of the other applicable item(s) are provided. All items that are not required to be answered in a particular report may be omitted and no reference thereto need be made in the report. All instructions should also be omitted.

E. Signature and Filing of Report

Three complete copies of the report, including any financial statements, exhibits or other papers or documents filed as a part thereof, and five additional copies which need not include exhibits, shall be filed with the Commission. At least one complete copy of the report, including any financial statements, exhibits or other papers or documents filed as a part thereof, shall be filed, with each exchange on which any class of securities of the registrant is registered. At least one complete copy of the report filed with the Commission and one such copy filed with each exchange shall be manually signed. Copies not manually signed shall bear typed or printed signatures.

F. Incorporation by Reference

If the registrant makes available to its stockholders or otherwise publishes, within the period prescribed for filing the report, a press release or other document or statement containing information meeting some or all of the requirements of this form, the information called for may be incorporated by reference to such published document or statement, in answer or partial answer to any item or items of this form, provided copies thereof are filed as an exhibit to the report on this form.

G. Use of this Form by Asset-Backed Issuers.

The following applies to registrants that are asset-backed issuers. Terms used in this General Instruction G. have the same meaning as in Item 1101 of Regulation AB (17 CFR 229.1101).

1. *Reportable Events That May Be Omitted.*

The registrant need not file a report on this Form upon the occurrence of any one or more of the events specified in the following:

(a) Item 2.01, Completion of Acquisition or Disposition of Assets;

(b) Item 2.02, Results of Operations and Financial Condition;

(c) Item 2.03, Creation of a Direct Financial Obligation or an Obligation under an Off-Balance Sheet Arrangement of a Registrant;

(d) Item 2.05, Costs Associated with Exit or Disposal Activities;

(e) Item 2.06, Material Impairments;

(f) Item 3.01, Notice of Delisting or Failure to Satisfy a Continued Listing Rule or Standard; Transfer of Listing;

(g) Item 3.02, Unregistered Sales of Equity Securities;

(h) Item 4.01, Changes in Registrant's Certifying Accountant;

(i) Item 4.02, Non-Reliance on Previously Issued Financial Statements or a Related Audit Report or Completed Interim Review;

(j) Item 5.01, Changes in Control of Registrant;

(k) Item 5.02, Departure of Directors or Principal Officers; Election of Directors; Appointment of Principal Officers;

(l) Item 5.04, Temporary Suspension of Trading Under Registrant's Employee Benefit Plans; and

(m) Item 5.05, Amendments to the Registrant's Code of Ethics, or Waiver of a Provision of the Code of Ethics.

2. *Additional Disclosure for the Form 8-K Cover Page.*

Immediately after the name of the issuing entity on the cover page of the Form 8-K, as separate line items, identify the exact name of the depositor as specified in its charter and the exact name of the sponsor as specified in its charter.

3. *Signatures.*

The Form 8-K must be signed by the depositor. In the alternative, the Form 8-K may be signed on behalf of the issuing entity by a duly authorized representative of the servicer. If multiple servicers are involved in servicing the pool assets, a duly authorized representative of the master servicer (or entity performing the equivalent function) must sign if a representative of the servicer is to sign the report on behalf of the issuing entity.

INFORMATION TO BE INCLUDED IN THE REPORT

Section 1 - Registrant's Business and Operations

Item 1.01 Entry into a Material Definitive Agreement.

(a) If the registrant has entered into a material definitive agreement not made in the ordinary course of business of the registrant, or into any amendment of such agreement that is material to the registrant, disclose the following information:

(1) the date on which the agreement was entered into or amended, the identity of the parties to the agreement or amendment and a brief description of any material relationship between the registrant or its affiliates and any of the parties, other than in respect of the material definitive agreement or amendment; and

(2) a brief description of the terms and conditions of the agreement or amendment that are material to the registrant.

(b) For purposes of this Item 1.01, a *material definitive agreement* means an agreement that provides for obligations that are material to and enforceable against the registrant, or rights that are material to the registrant and enforceable by the registrant against one or more other parties to the agreement, in each case whether or not subject to conditions.

Instructions.

1. Any material definitive agreement of the registrant not made in the ordinary course of the registrant's business must be disclosed under this Item 1.01. An agreement is deemed to be not made in the ordinary course of a registrant's business even if the agreement is such as ordinarily accompanies the kind of business conducted by the registrant if it involves the subject matter identified in Item 601(b)(10)(ii)(A) - (D) of Regulation S-K (17 CFR 229.601(b)(10)(ii)(A) - (D)). An agreement involving the subject matter identified in Item 601(b)(10)(iii)(A) or (B) need not be disclosed under this Item.

2. A registrant must provide disclosure under this Item 1.01 if the registrant succeeds as a party to the agreement or amendment to the agreement by assumption or assignment (other than in connection with a merger or acquisition or similar transaction).

3. With respect to asset-backed securities, as defined in Item 1101 of Regulation AB (17 CFR 229.1101), disclosure is required under this Item 1.01 regarding the entry into or an amendment to a definitive agreement that is material to the asset-backed securities transaction, even if the registrant is not a party to such agreement (*e.g.*, a servicing agreement with a servicer contemplated by Item 1108(a)(3) of Regulation AB (17 CFR 229.1108(a)(3)).

Item 1.02 Termination of a Material Definitive Agreement.

(a) If a material definitive agreement which was not made in the ordinary course of business of the registrant and to which the registrant is a party is terminated otherwise than by expiration of the agreement on its stated termination date, or as a result of all parties completing their obligations under such agreement, and such termination of the agreement is material to the registrant, disclose the following information:

(1) the date of the termination of the material definitive agreement, the identity of the parties to the agreement and a brief description of any material relationship between the registrant or its affiliates and any of the parties other than in respect of the material definitive agreement;

(2) a brief description of the terms and conditions of the agreement that are material to the registrant;

(3) a brief description of the material circumstances surrounding the termination; and

(4) any material early termination penalties incurred by the registrant.

(b) For purposes of this Item 1.02, the term *material definitive agreement* shall have the same meaning as set forth in Item 1.01(b).

Instructions.

1. No disclosure is required solely by reason of this Item 1.02 during negotiations or discussions regarding termination of a material definitive

agreement unless and until the agreement has been terminated.

2. No disclosure is required solely by reason of this Item 1.02 if the registrant believes in good faith that the material definitive agreement has not been terminated, unless the registrant has received a notice of termination pursuant to the terms of agreement.

3. With respect to asset-backed securities, as defined in Item 1101 of Regulation AB (17 CFR 229.1101), disclosure is required under this Item 1.02 regarding the termination of a definitive agreement that is material to the asset-backed securities transaction (otherwise than by expiration of the agreement on its stated termination date or as a result of all parties completing their obligations under such agreement), even if the registrant is not a party to such agreement (*e.g.*, a servicing agreement with a servicer contemplated by Item 1108(a)(3) of Regulation AB (17 CFR 229.1108(a)(3)).

Item 1.03 Bankruptcy or Receivership.

(a) If a receiver, fiscal agent or similar officer has been appointed for a registrant or its parent, in a proceeding under the U.S. Bankruptcy Code or in any other proceeding under state or federal law in which a court or governmental authority has assumed jurisdiction over substantially all of the assets or business of the registrant or its parent, or if such jurisdiction has been assumed by leaving the existing directors and officers in possession but subject to the supervision and orders of a court or governmental authority, disclose the following information:

(1) the name or other identification of the proceeding;

(2) the identity of the court or governmental authority;

(3) the date that jurisdiction was assumed; and

(4) the identity of the receiver, fiscal agent or similar officer and the date of his or her appointment.

(b) If an order confirming a plan of reorganization, arrangement or liquidation has been entered by a court or governmental authority having supervision or jurisdiction over substantially all of the assets or business of the registrant or its parent, disclose the following:

(1) the identity of the court or governmental authority;

(2) the date that the order confirming the plan was entered by the court or governmental authority;

(3) a summary of the material features of the plan and, pursuant to Item 9.01 (Financial State-

ments and Exhibits), a copy of the plan as confirmed;

(4) the number of shares or other units of the registrant or its parent issued and outstanding, the number reserved for future issuance in respect of claims and interests filed and allowed under the plan, and the aggregate total of such numbers; and

(5) information as to the assets and liabilities of the registrant or its parent as of the date that the order confirming the plan was entered, or a date as close thereto as practicable.

Instructions.

1. The information called for in paragraph (b)(5) of this Item 1.03 may be presented in the form in which it was furnished to the court or governmental authority.

2. With respect to asset-backed securities, disclosure also is required under this Item 1.03 if the depositor (or servicer if the servicer signs the report on Form 10-K (17 CFR 249.310) of the issuing entity) becomes aware of any instances described in paragraph (a) or (b) of this Item with respect to the sponsor, depositor, servicer contemplated by Item 1108(a)(3) of Regulation AB (17 CFR 229.1108(a)(3)), trustee, significant obligor, enhancement or support provider contemplated by Items 1114(b) or 1115 of Regulation AB (17 CFR 229.1114(b) or 229.1115) or other material party contemplated by Item 1101(d)(1) of Regulation AB (17 CFR 1101(d)(1)). Terms used in this Instruction 2 have the same meaning as in Item 1101 of Regulation AB (17 CFR 229.1101).

Section 2 - Financial Information

Item 2.01 Completion of Acquisition or Disposition of Assets.

If the registrant or any of its majority-owned subsidiaries has completed the acquisition or disposition of a significant amount of assets, otherwise than in the ordinary course of business, disclose the following information:

(a) the date of completion of the transaction;

(b) a brief description of the assets involved;

(c) the identity of the person(s) from whom the assets were acquired or to whom they were sold and the nature of any material relationship, other than in respect of the transaction, between such person(s) and the registrant or any of its affiliates, or any director or officer of the registrant, or any associate of any such director or officer;

(d) the nature and amount of consideration given or received for the assets and, if any material relationship is disclosed pursuant to paragraph (c) of this Item 2.01, the formula or principle followed in determining the amount of such consideration; and

(e) if the transaction being reported is an acquisition and if a material relationship exists between the registrant or any of its affiliates and the source(s) of the funds used in the acquisition, the identity of the source(s) of the funds unless all or any part of the consideration used is a loan made in the ordinary course of business by a bank as defined by Section 3(a)(6) of the Act, in which case the identity of such bank may be omitted provided the registrant:

(1) has made a request for confidentiality pursuant to Section 13(d)(1)(B) of the Act; and

(2) states in the report that the identity of the bank has been so omitted and filed separately with the Commission; and

(f) If the registrant was a shell company, other than a business combination related shell company, as those terms are defined in Rule 12b-2 under the Exchange Act (17 CFR 240.12b-2), immediately before the transaction, the information that would be required if the registrant were filing a general form for registration of securities on Form 10 under the Exchange Act reflecting all classes of the registrant's securities subject to the reporting requirements of Section 13 (15 U.S.C. 78m) or Section 15(d) (15 U.S.C. 78o(d)) of such Act upon consummation of the transaction, with such information reflecting the registrant and its securities upon consummation of the transaction. Notwithstanding General Instruction B.3 to Form 8-K, if any disclosure required by this Item 2.01(f) is previously reported, as that term is defined in Rule 12b-2 under the Exchange Act (17 CFR 240.12b-2), the registrant may identify the filing in which that disclosure is included instead of including that disclosure in this report.

Instructions.

1. No information need be given as to:

(i) any transaction between any person and any wholly-owned subsidiary of such person;

(ii) any transaction between two or more wholly-owned subsidiaries of any person; or

(iii) the redemption or other acquisition of securities from the public, or the sale or other disposition of securities to the public, by the issuer of such securities or by a wholly-owned subsidiary of that issuer.

2. The term *acquisition* includes every purchase, acquisition by lease, exchange, merger, consolidation, succession or other acquisition, except that the term does not include the construction or development of property by or for the registrant or its subsidiaries or the acquisition of materials for such purpose. The term *disposition* includes every sale, disposition by lease, exchange, merger, consolidation, mortgage, assignment or hypothecation of assets, whether for the

benefit of creditors or otherwise, abandonment, destruction, or other disposition.

3. The information called for by this Item 2.01 is to be given as to each transaction or series of related transactions of the size indicated. The acquisition or disposition of securities is deemed the indirect acquisition or disposition of the assets represented by such securities if it results in the acquisition or disposition of control of such assets.

4. An acquisition or disposition shall be deemed to involve a significant amount of assets:

(i) if the registrant's and its other subsidiaries' equity in the net book value of such assets or the amount paid or received for the assets upon such acquisition or disposition exceeded 10% of the total assets of the registrant and its consolidated subsidiaries; or

(ii) if it involved a business (see 17 CFR 210.11-01(d)) that is significant (see 17 CFR 210.11-01(b)).

Acquisitions of individually insignificant businesses are not required to be reported pursuant to this Item 2.01 unless they are related businesses (see 17 CFR 210.3-05(a)(3)) and are significant in the aggregate.

5. Attention is directed to the requirements in Item 9.01 (Financial Statements and Exhibits) with respect to the filing of:

(i) financial statements of businesses acquired;

(ii) *pro forma* financial information; and

(iii) copies of the plans of acquisition or disposition as exhibits to the report.

Item 2.02 Results of Operations and Financial Condition.

(a) If a registrant, or any person acting on its behalf, makes any public announcement or release (including any update of an earlier announcement or release) disclosing material non-public information regarding the registrant's results of operations or financial condition for a completed quarterly or annual fiscal period, the registrant shall disclose the date of the announcement or release, briefly identify the announcement or release and include the text of that announcement or release as an exhibit.

(b) A Form 8-K is not required to be furnished to the Commission under this Item 2.02 in the case of disclosure of material non-public information that is disclosed orally, telephonically, by webcast, by broadcast, or by similar means if:

(1) the information is provided as part of a presentation that is complementary to, and initially occurs within 48 hours after, a related, written announcement or release that has been furnished on Form 8-K pursuant to this Item 2.02 prior to the presentation;

(2) the presentation is broadly accessible to the public by dial-in conference call, by webcast, by broadcast or by similar means;

(3) the financial and other statistical information contained in the presentation is provided on the registrant's website, together with any information that would be required under 17 CFR 244.100; and

(4) the presentation was announced by a widely disseminated press release, that included instructions as to when and how to access the presentation and the location on the registrant's website where the information would be available.

Instructions.

1. The requirements of this Item 2.02 are triggered by the disclosure of material non-public information regarding a completed fiscal year or quarter. Release of additional or updated material non-public information regarding a completed fiscal year or quarter would trigger an additional Item 2.02 requirement.

2. The requirements of paragraph (e)(1)(i) of Item 10 of Regulation S-K (17 CFR 229.10(e)(1)(i)) shall apply to disclosures under this Item 2.02.

3. Issuers that make earnings announcements or other disclosures of material non-public information regarding a completed fiscal year or quarter in an interim or annual report to shareholders are permitted to specify which portion of the report contains the information required to be furnished under this Item 2.02.

4. This Item 2.02 does not apply in the case of a disclosure that is made in a quarterly report filed with the Commission on Form 10-Q (17 CFR 249.308a) or an annual report filed with the Commission on Form 10-K (17 CFR 249.310).

Item 2.03 Creation of a Direct Financial Obligation or an Obligation under an Off-Balance Sheet Arrangement of a Registrant.

(a) If the registrant becomes obligated on a direct financial obligation that is material to the registrant, disclose the following information:

(1) the date on which the registrant becomes obligated on the direct financial obligation and a brief description of the transaction or agreement creating the obligation;

(2) the amount of the obligation, including the terms of its payment and, if applicable, a brief description of the material terms under which it may be accelerated or increased and the nature of any recourse provisions that would enable the registrant to recover from third parties; and

(3) a brief description of the other terms and conditions of the transaction or agreement that are material to the registrant.

(b) If the registrant becomes directly or contingently liable for an obligation that is material to the registrant arising out of an off-balance sheet arrangement, disclose the following information:

(1) the date on which the registrant becomes directly or contingently liable on the obligation and a brief description of the transaction or agreement creating the arrangement and obligation;

(2) a brief description of the nature and amount of the obligation of the registrant under the arrangement, including the material terms whereby it may become a direct obligation, if applicable, or may be accelerated or increased and the nature of any recourse provisions that would enable the registrant to recover from third parties;

(3) the maximum potential amount of future payments (undiscounted) that the registrant may be required to make, if different; and

(4) a brief description of the other terms and conditions of the obligation or arrangement that are material to the registrant.

(c) For purposes of this Item 2.03, *direct financial obligation* means any of the following:

(1) a long-term debt obligation, as defined in Item 303(a)(5)(ii)(A) of Regulation S-K (17 CFR 229.303(a)(5)(ii)(A));

(2) a capital lease obligation, as defined in Item 303(a)(5)(ii)(B) of Regulation S-K (17 CFR 229.303(a)(5)(ii)(B));

(3) an operating lease obligation, as defined in Item 303(a)(5)(ii)(C) of Regulation S-K (17 CFR 229.303(a)(5)(ii)(C)); or

(4) a short-term debt obligation that arises other than in the ordinary course of business.

(d) For purposes of this Item 2.03, *off-balance sheet arrangement* has the meaning set forth in Item 303(a)(4)(ii) of Regulation S-K (17 CFR 229.303(a)(4)(ii)).

(e) For purposes of this Item 2.03, *short-term debt obligation* means a payment obligation under a borrowing arrangement that is scheduled to mature within one year, or, for those registrants that use the operating cycle concept of working capital, within a registrant's operating cycle that is longer than one year, as discussed in Accounting Research Bulletin No. 43, Chapter 3A, *Working Capital.*

Instructions.

1. A registrant has no obligation to disclose information under this Item 2.03 until the registrant enters into an agreement enforceable against the registrant, whether or not subject to conditions, under which the direct financial obligation will arise or be created or issued. If there is no such agreement, the registrant must provide the disclosure within four business days after the oc-

currence of the closing or settlement of the transaction or arrangement under which the direct financial obligation arises or is created.

2. A registrant must provide the disclosure required by paragraph (b) of this Item 2.03 whether or not the registrant is also a party to the transaction or agreement creating the contingent obligation arising under the off-balance sheet arrangement. In the event that neither the registrant nor any affiliate of the registrant is also a party to the transaction or agreement creating the contingent obligation arising under the off-balance sheet arrangement in question, the four business day period for reporting the event under this Item 2.03 shall begin on the earlier of (i) the fourth business day after the contingent obligation is created or arises, and (ii) the day on which an executive officer, as defined in 17 CFR 240.3b-7, of the registrant becomes aware of the contingent obligation.

3. In the event that an agreement, transaction or arrangement requiring disclosure under this Item 2.03 comprises a facility, program or similar arrangement that creates or may give rise to direct financial obligations of the registrant in connection with multiple transactions, the registrant shall:

(i) disclose the entering into of the facility, program or similar arrangement if the entering into of the facility is material to the registrant; and

(ii) as direct financial obligations arise or are created under the facility or program, disclose the required information under this Item 2.03 to the extent that the obligations are material to the registrant (including when a series of previously undisclosed individually immaterial obligations become material in the aggregate).

4. For purposes of Item 2.03(b)(3), the maximum amount of future payments shall not be reduced by the effect of any amounts that may possibly be recovered by the registrant under recourse or collateralization provisions in any guarantee agreement, transaction or arrangement.

5. If the obligation required to be disclosed under this Item 2.03 is a security, or a term of a security, that has been or will be sold pursuant to an effective registration statement of the registrant, the registrant is not required to file a Form 8-K pursuant to this Item 2.03, *provided* that the prospectus relating to that sale contains the information required by this Item 2.03 and is filed within the required time period under Securities Act Rule 424 (§ 230.424 of this chapter).

Item 2.04 Triggering Events That Accelerate or Increase a Direct Financial Obligation or an Obligation under an Off-Balance Sheet Arrangement.

(a) If a triggering event causing the increase or acceleration of a direct financial obligation of the registrant occurs and the consequences of the event, taking into account those described in paragraph (a)(4) of this Item 2.04, are material to the registrant, disclose the following information:

(1) the date of the triggering event and a brief description of the agreement or transaction under which the direct financial obligation was created and is increased or accelerated;

(2) a brief description of the triggering event;

(3) the amount of the direct financial obligation, as increased if applicable, and the terms of payment or acceleration that apply; and

(4) any other material obligations of the registrant that may arise, increase, be accelerated or become direct financial obligations as a result of the triggering event or the increase or acceleration of the direct financial obligation.

(b) If a triggering event occurs causing an obligation of the registrant under an off-balance sheet arrangement to increase or be accelerated, or causing a contingent obligation of the registrant under an off-balance sheet arrangement to become a direct financial obligation of the registrant, and the consequences of the event, taking into account those described in paragraph (b)(4) of this Item 2.04, are material to the registrant, disclose the following information:

(1) the date of the triggering event and a brief description of the off-balance sheet arrangement;

(2) a brief description of the triggering event;

(3) the nature and amount of the obligation, as increased if applicable, and the terms of payment or acceleration that apply; and

(4) any other material obligations of the registrant that may arise, increase, be accelerated or become direct financial obligations as a result of the triggering event or the increase or acceleration of the obligation under the off-balance sheet arrangement or its becoming a direct financial obligation of the registrant.

(c) For purposes of this Item 2.04, the term *direct financial obligation* has the meaning provided in Item 2.03 of this form, but shall also include an obligation arising out of an off-balance sheet arrangement that is accrued under FASB Statement of Financial Accounting Standards No. 5 *Accounting for Contingencies* (SFAS No. 5) as a probable loss contingency.

(d) For purposes of this Item 2.04, the term *off-balance sheet arrangement* has the meaning provided in Item 2.03 of this form.

(e) For purposes of this Item 2.04, a *triggering event* is an event, including an event of default, event of acceleration or similar event, as a result of which a direct financial obligation of the registrant or an obligation of the registrant arising under an off-balance sheet arrangement is increased or becomes accelerated or as a result of which a contingent obligation of the registrant arising out of an off-balance sheet arrangement becomes a direct financial obligation of the registrant.

Instructions.

1. Disclosure is required if a triggering event occurs in respect of an obligation of the registrant under an off-balance sheet arrangement and the consequences are material to the registrant, whether or not the registrant is also a party to the transaction or agreement under which the triggering event occurs.

2. No disclosure is required under this Item 2.04 unless and until a triggering event has occurred in accordance with the terms of the relevant agreement, transaction or arrangement, including, if required, the sending to the registrant of notice of the occurrence of a triggering event pursuant to the terms of the agreement, transaction or arrangement and the satisfaction of all conditions to such occurrence, except the passage of time.

3. No disclosure is required solely by reason of this Item 2.04 if the registrant believes in good faith that no triggering event has occurred, unless the registrant has received a notice described in Instruction 2 to this Item 2.04.

4. Where a registrant is subject to an obligation arising out of an off-balance sheet arrangement, whether or not disclosed pursuant to Item 2.03 of this form, if a triggering event occurs as a result of which under that obligation an accrual for a probable loss is required under SFAS No. 5, the obligation arising out of the off-balance sheet arrangement becomes a direct financial obligation as defined in this Item 2.04. In that situation, if the consequences as determined under Item 2.04(b) are material to the registrant, disclosure is required under this Item 2.04.

5. With respect to asset-backed securities, as defined in 17 CFR 229.1101, disclosure also is required under this Item 2.04 if an early amortization, performance trigger or other event, including an event of default, has occurred under the transaction agreements for the asset-backed securities that would materially alter the payment priority or distribution of cash flows regarding the asset-backed securities or the amortization schedule for the asset-backed securities. In providing the disclosure required by this Item, identify the changes to the payment priorities, flow of funds or asset-backed securities as a result. Disclosure is required under this Item whether or not the registrant is a party to the transaction agreement that results in the occurrence identified.

Item 2.05 Costs Associated with Exit or Disposal Activities.

If the registrant's board of directors, a committee of the board of directors or the officer or officers of the registrant authorized to take such action if board action is not required, commits the registrant to an exit or disposal plan, or otherwise disposes of a long-lived asset or terminates employees under a plan of termination described in paragraph 8 of FASB Statement of Financial Accounting Standards No. 146 *Accounting for Costs Associated with Exit or Disposal Activities* (SFAS No. 146), under which material charges will be incurred under generally accepted accounting principles applicable to the registrant, disclose the following information:

(a) the date of the commitment to the course of action and a description of the course of action, including the facts and circumstances leading to the expected action and the expected completion date;

(b) for each major type of cost associated with the course of action (for example, one-time termination benefits, contract termination costs and other associated costs), an estimate of the total amount or range of amounts expected to be incurred in connection with the action;

(c) an estimate of the total amount or range of amounts expected to be incurred in connection with the action; and

(d) the registrant's estimate of the amount or range of amounts of the charge that will result in future cash expenditures, *provided, however,* that if the registrant determines that at the time of filing it is unable in good faith to make a determination of an estimate required by paragraphs (b), (c) or (d) of this Item 2.05, no disclosure of such estimate shall be required; *provided further, however,* that in any such event, the registrant shall file an amended report on Form 8-K under this Item 2.05 within four business days after it makes a determination of such an estimate or range of estimates.

Item 2.06 Material Impairments.

If the registrant's board of directors, a committee of the board of directors or the officer or officers of the registrant authorized to take such action if board action is not required, concludes that a material charge for impairment to one or more of its assets, including, without limitation, impairments of securities or goodwill, is required under generally accepted accounting principles applicable to the registrant, disclose the following information:

(a) the date of the conclusion that a material charge is required and a description of the impaired asset or assets and the facts and circumstances leading to the conclusion that the charge for impairment is required;

(b) the registrant's estimate of the amount or range of amounts of the impairment charge; and

(c) the registrant's estimate of the amount or range of amounts of the impairment charge that will result in future cash expenditures, *provided, however,* that if the registrant determines that at the time of filing it is unable in good faith to make a determination of an estimate required by paragraphs (b) or (c) of this Item 2.06, no disclosure of such estimate shall be required; *provided further, however,* that in any such event, the registrant shall file an amended report on Form 8-K under this Item 2.06 within four business days after it makes a determination of such an estimate or range of estimates.

Instruction.

No filing is required under this Item 2.06 if the conclusion is made in connection with the preparation, review or audit of financial statements required to be included in the next periodic report due to be filed under the Exchange Act, the periodic report is filed on a timely basis and such conclusion is disclosed in the report.

Section 3 - Securities and Trading Markets

Item 3.01 Notice of Delisting or Failure to Satisfy a Continued Listing Rule or Standard; Transfer of Listing.

(a) If the registrant has received notice from the national securities exchange or national securities association (or a facility thereof) that maintains the principal listing for any class of the registrant's common equity (as defined in Exchange Act Rule 12b-2 (17 CFR 240.12b-2)) that:

- the registrant or such class of the registrant's securities does not satisfy a rule or standard for continued listing on the exchange or association;

- the exchange has submitted an application under Exchange Act Rule 12d2-2 (17 CFR 240.12d2-2) to the Commission to delist such class of the registrant's securities; or

- the association has taken all necessary steps under its rules to delist the security from its automated inter-dealer quotation system,

the registrant must disclose:

(i) the date that the registrant received the notice;

(ii) the a rule or standard for continued listing on the national securities exchange or national securities association that the registrant fails, or has failed to, satisfy; and

(iii) any action or response that, at the time of filing, the registrant has determined to take in response to the notice.

(b) If the registrant has notified the national securities exchange or national securities association (or a facility thereof) that maintains the principal listing for any class of the registrant's common equity (as defined in Exchange Act Rule 12b-2 (17

CFR 240.12b-2) that the registrant is aware of any material noncompliance with a rule or standard for continued listing on the exchange or association, the registrant must disclose:

(i) the date that the registrant provided such notice to the exchange or association;

(ii) the rule or standard for continued listing on the exchange or association that the registrant fails, or has failed, to satisfy; and

(iii) any action or response that, at the time of filing, the registrant has determined to take regarding its noncompliance.

(c) If the national securities exchange or national securities association (or a facility thereof) that maintains the principal listing for any class of the registrant's common equity (as defined in Exchange Act Rule 12b-2 (17 CFR 240.12b-2)), in lieu of suspending trading in or delisting such class of the registrant's securities, issues a public reprimand letter or similar communication indicating that the registrant has violated a rule or standard for continued listing on the exchange or association, the registrant must state the date, and summarize the contents of the letter or communication.

(d) If the registrant's board of directors, a committee of the board of directors or the officer or officers of the registrant authorized to take such action if board action is not required, has taken definitive action to cause the listing of a class of its common equity to be withdrawn from the national securities exchange, or terminated from the automated inter-dealer quotation system of a registered national securities association, where such exchange or association maintains the principal listing for such class of securities, including by reason of a transfer of the listing or quotation to another securities exchange or quotation system, describe the action taken and state the date of the action.

Instructions.

1. The registrant is not required to disclose any information required by paragraph (a) of this Item 3.01 where the delisting is a result of one of the following:

- the entire class of the security has been called for redemption, maturity or retirement; appropriate notice thereof has been given; if required by the terms of the securities, funds sufficient for the payment of all such securities have been deposited with an agency authorized to make such payments; and such funds have been made available to security holders;

- the entire class of the security has been redeemed or paid at maturity or retirement;

- the instruments representing the entire class of securities have come to evidence, by operation of law or otherwise, other securities in substitution therefor and represent no other right, except, if true, the right to receive an immediate cash payment (the right of dissenters to receive the appraised or fair value of their holdings shall not prevent the application of this provision); or

• all rights pertaining to the entire class of the security have been extinguished; *provided, however,* that where such an event occurs as the result of an order of a court or other governmental authority, the order shall be final, all applicable appeal periods shall have expired and no appeals shall be pending.

2. A registrant must provide the disclosure required by paragraph (a) or (b) of this Item 3.01, as applicable, regarding any failure to satisfy a rule or standard for continued listing on the national securities exchange or national securities association (or a facility thereof) that maintains the principal listing for any class of the registrant's common equity (as defined in Exchange Act Rule 12b-2 (17 CFR 240.12b-2)) even if the registrant has the benefit of a grace period or similar extension period during which it may cure the deficiency that triggers the disclosure requirement.

3. Notices or other communications subsequent to an initial notice sent to, or by, a registrant under Item 3.01(a), (b) or (c) that continue to indicate that the registrant does not comply with the same rule or standard for continued listing that was the subject of the initial notice are not required to be filed, but may be filed voluntarily.

4. Registrants whose securities are quoted exclusively (i.e., the securities are not otherwise listed on an exchange or association) on automated inter-dealer quotation systems are not subject to this Item 3.01 and such registrants are thus not required to file a Form 8-K pursuant to this Item 3.01 if the securities are no longer quoted on such quotation system. If a security is listed on an exchange or association and is also quoted on an automated inter-dealer quotation system, the registrant is subject to the disclosure obligations of Item 3.01 if any of the events specified in Item 3.01 occur.

Item 3.02 Unregistered Sales of Equity Securities.

(a) If a registrant sells equity securities in a transaction that is not registered under the Securities Act, furnish the information set forth in paragraphs (a) and (c) through (e) of Item 701 of Regulation S-K (17 CFR 229.701(a) and (c) through (e)). For purposes of determining the required filing date for the Form 8-K under this Item 3.02(a), the registrant has no obligation to disclose information under this Item 3.02 until the registrant enters into an agreement enforceable against the registrant, whether or not subject to conditions, under which the equity securities are

to be sold. If there is no such agreement, the registrant must provide the disclosure within four business days after the occurrence of the closing or settlement of the transaction or arrangement under which the equity securities are to be sold.

(b) No report need be filed under this Item 3.02 if the equity securities sold, in the aggregate since its last report filed under this Item 3.02 or its last periodic report, whichever is more recent, constitute less than 1% of the number of shares outstanding of the class of equity securities sold. In the case of a smaller reporting company, no report need be filed if the equity securities sold, in the aggregate since its last report filed under this Item 3.02 or its last periodic report, whichever is more recent, constitute less than 5% of the number of shares outstanding of the class of equity securities sold.

Instructions.

1. For purposes of this Item 3.02, "the number of shares outstanding" refers to the actual number of shares of equity securities of the class outstanding and does not include outstanding securities convertible into or exchangeable for such equity securities.

2. A smaller reporting company is defined in Item 10(f)(1) of Regulation S-K (17 CFR 229.10(f)(1)).

Item 3.03 Material Modification to Rights of Security Holders.

(a) If the constituent instruments defining the rights of the holders of any class of registered securities of the registrant have been materially modified, disclose the date of the modification, the title of the class of securities involved and briefly describe the general effect of such modification upon the rights of holders of such securities.

(b) If the rights evidenced by any class of registered securities have been materially limited or qualified by the issuance or modification of any other class of securities by the registrant, briefly disclose the date of the issuance or modification, the general effect of the issuance or modification of such other class of securities upon the rights of the holders of the registered securities.

Instruction.

Working capital restrictions and other limitations upon the payment of dividends must be reported pursuant to this Item 3.03.

Section 4 - Matters Related to Accountants and Financial Statements

Item 4.01 Changes in Registrant's Certifying Accountant.

(a) If an independent accountant who was previously engaged as the principal accountant to audit the registrant's financial statements, or an independent accountant upon whom the principal accountant expressed reliance in its report regarding a significant subsidiary, resigns (or indicates that it declines to stand for re-appointment after completion of the current audit) or is dismissed, disclose the information required by Item 304(a)(1) of Regulation S-K (§ 229.304(a)(1) of this chapter), including compliance with Item 304(a)(3) of Regulation S-K (§ 229.304(a)(3) of this chapter).

(b) If a new independent accountant has been engaged as either the principal accountant to audit the registrant's financial statements or as an independent accountant on whom the principal accountant is expected to express reliance in its report regarding a significant subsidiary, the registrant must disclose the information required by Item 304(a)(2) of Regulation S-K (17 CFR 229.302(a)(2)).

Instruction.

The resignation or dismissal of an independent accountant, or its refusal to stand for re-appointment, is a reportable event separate from the engagement of a new independent accountant. On some occasions, two reports on Form 8-K are required for a single change in accountants, the first on the resignation (or refusal to stand for re-appointment) or dismissal of the former accountant and the second when the new accountant is engaged. Information required in the second Form 8-K in such situations need not be provided to the extent that it has been reported previously in the first Form 8-K.

Item 4.02 Non-Reliance on Previously Issued Financial Statements or a Related Audit Report or Completed Interim Review.

(a) If the registrant's board of directors, a committee of the board of directors or the officer or officers of the registrant authorized to take such action if board action is not required, concludes that any previously issued financial statements, covering one or more years or interim periods for which the registrant is required to provide financial statements under Regulation S-X (17 CFR 210) should no longer be relied upon because of an error in such financial statements as addressed in Accounting Principles Board Opinion No. 20, as may be modified, supplemented or succeeded, disclose the following information:

(1) the date of the conclusion regarding the non-reliance and an identification of the financial statements and years or periods covered that should no longer be relied upon;

(2) a brief description of the facts underlying the conclusion to the extent known to the registrant at the time of filing; and

(3) a statement of whether the audit committee, or the board of directors in the absence of an audit committee, or authorized officer or officers,

discussed with the registrant's independent accountant the matters disclosed in the filing pursuant to this Item 4.02(a).

(b) If the registrant is advised by, or receives notice from, its independent accountant that disclosure should be made or action should be taken to prevent future reliance on a previously issued audit report or completed interim review related to previously issued financial statements, disclose the following information:

(1) the date on which the registrant was so advised or notified;

(2) identification of the financial statements that should no longer be relied upon;

(3) a brief description of the information provided by the accountant; and

(4) a statement of whether the audit committee, or the board of directors in the absence of an audit committee, or authorized officer or officers, discussed with the independent accountant the matters disclosed in the filing pursuant to this Item 4.02(b).

(c) If the registrant receives advisement or notice from its independent accountant requiring disclosure under paragraph (b) of this Item 4.02, the registrant must:

(1) provide the independent accountant with a copy of the disclosures it is making in response to this Item 4.02 that the independent accountant shall receive no later than the day that the disclosures are filed with the Commission;

(2) request the independent accountant to furnish to the registrant as promptly as possible a letter addressed to the Commission stating whether the independent accountant agrees with the statements made by the registrant in response to this Item 4.02 and, if not, stating the respects in which it does not agree; and

(3) amend the registrant's previously filed Form 8-K by filing the independent accountant's letter as an exhibit to the filed Form 8-K no later than two business days after the registrant's receipt of the letter.

Section 5 - Corporate Governance and Management

Item 5.01 Changes in Control of Registrant.

(a) If, to the knowledge of the registrant's board of directors, a committee of the board of directors or authorized officer or officers of the registrant, a change in control of the registrant has occurred, furnish the following information:

(1) the identity of the person(s) who acquired such control;

(2) the date and a description of the transaction(s) which resulted in the change in control;

(3) the basis of the control, including the percentage of voting securities of the registrant now beneficially owned directly or indirectly by the person(s) who acquired control;

(4) the amount of the consideration used by such person(s);

(5) the source(s) of funds used by the person(s), *unless* all or any part of the consideration used is a loan made in the ordinary course of business by a bank as defined by Section 3(a)(6) of the Act, in which case the identity of such bank may be omitted provided the person who acquired control:

(i) has made a request for confidentiality pursuant to Section 13(d)(1)(B) of the Act; and

(ii) states in the report that the identity of the bank has been so omitted and filed separately with the Commission.

(6) the identity of the person(s) from whom control was assumed; and

(7) any arrangements or understandings among members of both the former and new control groups and their associates with respect to election of directors or other matters.

(8) if the registrant was a shell company, other than a business combination related shell company, as those terms are defined in Rule 12b-2 under the Exchange Act (17 CFR 240.12b-2), immediately before the change in control, the information that would be required if the registrant were filing a general form for registration of securities on Form 10 under the Exchange Act reflecting all classes of the registrant's securities subject to the reporting requirements of Section 13 (15 U.S.C. 78m) or Section 15(d) (15 U.S.C. 78o(d)) of such Act upon consummation of the change in control, with such information reflecting the registrant and its securities upon consummation of the transaction. Notwithstanding General Instruction B.3. to Form 8-K, if any disclosure required by this Item 5.01(a)(8) is previously reported, as that term is defined in Rule 12b-2 under the Exchange Act (17 CFR 240.12b-2), the registrant may identify the filing in which that disclosure is included instead of including that disclosure in this report.

(b) Furnish the information required by Item 403(c) of Regulation S-K (17 CFR 229.403(c)).

Item 5.02 Departure of Directors or Certain Officers; Election of Directors; Appointment of Certain Officers; Compensatory Arrangements of Certain Officers.

(a)(1) If a director has resigned or refuses to stand for re-election to the board of directors since the date of the last annual meeting of shareholders because of a disagreement with the registrant, known to an executive officer of the registrant, as defined in 17 CFR 240.3b-7, on any matter relating to the registrant's operations, policies or practices, or if a director has been removed for cause from the board of directors, disclose the following information:

(i) the date of such resignation, refusal to stand for re-election or removal;

(ii) any positions held by the director on any committee of the board of directors at the time of the director's resignation, refusal to stand for re-election or removal; and

(iii) a brief description of the circumstances representing the disagreement that the registrant believes caused, in whole or in part, the director's resignation, refusal to stand for re-election or removal.

(2) If the director has furnished the registrant with any written correspondence concerning the circumstances surrounding his or her resignation, refusal or removal, the registrant shall file a copy of the document as an exhibit to the report on Form 8-K.

(3) The registrant also must:

(i) provide the director with a copy of the disclosures it is making in response to this Item 5.02 no later than the day the registrant file the disclosures with the Commission;

(ii) provide the director with the opportunity to furnish the registrant as promptly as possible with a letter addressed to the registrant stating whether he or she agrees with the statements made by the registrant in response to this Item 5.02 and, if not, stating the respects in which he or she does not agree; and

(iii) file any letter received by the registrant from the director with the Commission as an exhibit by an amendment to the previously filed Form 8-K within two business days after receipt by the registrant.

(b) If the registrant's principal executive officer, president, principal financial officer, principal accounting officer, principal operating officer, or any person performing similar functions, or any named executive officer, retires, resigns or is terminated from that position, or if a director retires, resigns, is removed, or refuses to stand for re-election (except in circumstances described in paragraph (a) of this Item 5.02), disclose the fact that the event has occurred and the date of the event.

(c) If the registrant appoints a new principal executive officer, president, principal financial officer, principal accounting officer, principal operating officer, or person performing similar functions, disclose the following information with respect to the newly appointed officer:

(1) the name and position of the newly appointed officer and the date of the appointment;

(2) the information required by Items 401(b), (d), (e) and Item 404(a) of Regulation S-K (17 CFR 229.401(b), (d), (e) and 229.404(a)); and

(3) a brief description of any material plan, contract or arrangement (whether or not written) to which a covered officer is a party or in which he or she participates that is entered into or material amendment in connection with the triggering event or any grant or award to any such covered person or modification thereto, under any such plan, contract or arrangement in connection with any such event.

Instruction to paragraph (c).

If the registrant intends to make a public announcement of the appointment other than by means of a report on Form 8-K, the registrant may delay filing the Form 8-K containing the disclosures required by this Item 5.02(c) until the day on which the registrant otherwise makes public announcement of the appointment of such officer.

(d) If the registrant elects a new director, except by a vote of security holders at an annual meeting or special meeting convened for such purpose, disclose the following information:

(1) the name of the newly elected director and the date of election;

(2) a brief description of any arrangement or understanding between the new director and any other persons, naming such persons, pursuant to which such director was selected as a director;

(3) the committees of the board of directors to which the new director has been, or at the time of this disclosure is expected to be, named; and

(4) the information required by Item 404(a) of Regulation S-K (17 CFR 229.404(a)).

(5) a brief description of any material plan, contract or arrangement (whether or not written) to which the director is a party or in which he or she participates that is entered into or material amendment in connection with the triggering event or any grant or award to any such covered person or modification thereto, under any such plan, contract or arrangement in connection with any such event.

(e) If the registrant enters into, adopts, or otherwise commences a material compensatory plan, contract or arrangement (whether or not written), as to which the registrant's principal executive officer, principal financial officer, or a named executive officer participates or is a party, or such compensatory plan, contract or arrangement is materially amended or modified, or a material grant or award under any such plan, contract or arrangement to any such person is made or materially modified, then the registrant shall provide a brief description of the terms and conditions of the plan, contract or arrangement and the amounts payable to the officer thereunder.

Instructions to paragraph (e).

1. Disclosure under this Item 5.02(e) shall be required whether or not the specified event is in connection with events otherwise triggering disclosure pursuant to this Item 5.02.

2. Grants or awards (or modifications thereto) made pursuant to a plan, contract or arrangement (whether involving cash or equity), that are materially consistent with the previously disclosed terms of such plan, contract or arrangement, need not be disclosed under this Item 5.02(e), provided the registrant has previously disclosed such terms and the grant, award or modification is disclosed when Item 402 of Regulation SK (17 CFR 229.402) requires such disclosure.

(f) If the salary or bonus of a named executive officer cannot be calculated as of the most recent practicable date and is omitted from the Summary Compensation Table as specified in Instruction 1 to Item 402(c)(2)(iii) and (iv) of Regulation S-K, disclose the appropriate information under this Item 5.02(f) when there is a payment, grant, award, decision or other occurrence as a result of which such amounts become calculable in whole or in part. Disclosure under this Item 5.02(f) shall include a new total compensation figure for the named executive officer, using the new salary or bonus information to recalculate the information that was previously provided with respect to the named executive officer in the registrant's Summary Compensation Table for which the salary and bonus information was omitted in reliance on Instruction 1 to Item 402(c)(2)(iii) and (iv) of Regulation S-K (17 CFR 229.402(c)(2)(iii) and (iv)).

Instructions to Item 5.02.

1. The disclosure requirements of this Item 5.02 do not apply to a registrant that is a wholly-owned subsidiary of an issuer with a class of securities registered under Section 12 of the Exchange Act (15 U.S.C. 78l), or that is required to file reports under Section 15(d) of the Exchange Act (15 U.S.C. 78o(d)).

2. To the extent that any information called for in Item 5.02(c)(3) or Item 5.02(d)(3) or Item 5.02(d)(4) is not determined or is unavailable at the time of the required filing, the registrant shall include a statement to this effect in the filing and then must file an amendment to its Form 8-K filing under this Item 5.02 containing such information within four business days after the information is determined or becomes available.

3. The registrant need not provide information with respect to plans, contracts, and arrangements to the extent they do not discriminate in scope, terms or operation, in favor of executive officers or directors of the registrant and that are available generally to all salaried employees.

(4) For purposes of this Item, the term "named executive officer" shall refer to those executive officers for whom disclosure was required in the registrant's most recent filing with the Commission under the Securities Act (15 U.S.C. 77a *et seq.*) or Exchange Act (15 U.S.C. 78a *et seq.*) that required disclosure pursuant to Item 402(c) of Regulation S-K (17 CFR 229.402(c)).

Item 5.03 Amendments to Articles of Incorporation or Bylaws; Change in Fiscal Year.

(a) If a registrant with a class of equity securities registered under Section 12 of the Exchange Act (15 U.S.C. 78l) amends its articles of incorporation or bylaws and a proposal for the amendment was not disclosed in a proxy statement or information statement filed by the registrant, disclose the following information:

(1) the effective date of the amendment; and

(2) a description of the provision adopted or changed by amendment and, if applicable, the previous provision.

(b) If the registrant determines to change the fiscal year from that used in its most recent filing with the Commission other than by means of:

(1) a submission to a vote of security holders through the solicitation of proxies or otherwise; or

(2) an amendment to its articles of incorporation or bylaws,

disclose the date of such determination, the date of the new fiscal year end and the form (for example, Form 10-K or Form 10-Q) on which the report covering the transition period will be filed.

Instructions to Item 5.03.

1. Refer to Item 601(b)(3) of Regulation S-K (17 CFR 229.601(b)(3)) regarding the filing of exhibits to this Item 5.03.

2. With respect to asset-backed securities, as defined in 17 CFR 229.1101, disclosure is required under this Item 5.03 regarding any amendment to the governing documents of the issuing entity, regardless of whether the class of asset-backed securities is reporting under Section 13 or 15(d) of the Exchange Act.

Item 5.04 Temporary Suspension of Trading Under Registrant's Employee Benefit Plans.

(a) No later than the fourth business day after which the registrant receives the notice required by section 101(i)(2)(E) of the Employment Retirement Income Security Act of 1974 (29 U.S.C. 1021(i)(2)(E)), or, if such notice is not received by the registrant, on the same date by which the registrant transmits a timely notice to an affected officer or director within the time period prescribed by Rule 104(b)(2)(i)(B) or 104(b)(2)(ii) of Regulation BTR (17 CFR 245.104(b)(2)(i)(B) or 17

CFR 245.104(b)(2)(ii)), provide the information specified in Rule 104(b) (17 CFR 245.104(b)) and the date the registrant received the notice required by section 101(i)(2)(E) of the Employment Retirement Income Security Act of 1974 (29 U.S.C. 1021(i)(2)(E)), if applicable.

(b) On the same date by which the registrant transmits a timely updated notice to an affected officer or director, as required by the time period under Rule 104(b)(2)(iii) of Regulation BTR (17 CFR 245.104(b)(2)(iii)), provide the information specified in Rule 104(b)(3)(iii) (17 CFR 245.104(b)(2)(iii)).

Item 5.05 Amendments to the Registrant's Code of Ethics, or Waiver of a Provision of the Code of Ethics.

(a) Briefly describe the date and nature of any amendment to a provision of the registrant's code of ethics that applies to the registrant's principal executive officer, principal financial officer, principal accounting officer or controller or persons performing similar functions and that relates to any element of the code of ethics definition enumerated in Item 406(b) of Regulation S-K (17 CFR 229.406(b)).

(b) If the registrant has granted a waiver, including an implicit waiver, from a provision of the code of ethics to an officer or person described in paragraph (a) of this Item 5.05, and the waiver relates to one or more of the elements of the code of ethics definition referred to in paragraph (a) of this Item 5.05, briefly describe the nature of the waiver, the name of the person to whom the waiver was granted, and the date of the waiver.

(c) The registrant does not need to provide any information pursuant to this Item 5.05 if it discloses the required information on its Internet website within four business days following the date of the amendment or waiver and the registrant has disclosed in its most recently filed annual report its Internet address and intention to provide disclosure in this manner. If the registrant elects to disclose the information required by this Item 5.05 through its website, such information must remain available on the website for at least a 12-month period. Following the 12-month period, the registrant must retain the information for a period of not less than five years. Upon request, the registrant must furnish to the Commission or its staff a copy of any or all information retained pursuant to this requirement.

Instructions.

1. The registrant does not need to disclose technical, administrative or other non-substantive amendments to its code of ethics.

2. For purposes of this Item 5.05:

(i) The term *waiver* means the approval by the registrant of a material departure from a provision of the code of ethics; and

(ii) The term *implicit waiver* means the registrant's failure to take action within a reasonable period of time regarding a material departure from a provision of the code of ethics that has been made known to an executive officer, as defined in Rule 3b-7 (17 CFR 240.3b-7) of the registrant.

Item 5.06 Change in Shell Company Status.

If a registrant that was a shell company, other than a business combination related shell company, as those terms are defined in Rule 12b-2 under the Exchange Act (17 CFR 240.12b-2), has completed a transaction that has the effect of causing it to cease being a shell company, as defined in Rule 12b-2, disclose the material terms of the transaction. Notwithstanding General Instruction B.3. to Form 8-K, if any disclosure required by this Item 5.06 is previously reported, as that term is defined in Rule 12b-2 under the Exchange Act (17 CFR 240.12b-2), the registrant may identify the filing in which that disclosure is included instead of including that disclosure in this report.

Item 5.07 Submission of Matters to a Vote of Security Holders.

If any matter was submitted to a vote of security holders, through the solicitation of proxies or otherwise, provide the following information:

(a) The date of the meeting and whether it was an annual or special meeting. This information must be provided only if a meeting of security holders was held.

(b) If the meeting involved the election of directors, the name of each director elected at the meeting, as well as a brief description of each other matter voted upon at the meeting; and state the number of votes cast for, against or withheld, as well as the number of abstentions and broker non-votes as to each such matter, including a separate tabulation with respect to each nominee for office.

(c) A description of the terms of any settlement between the registrant and any other participant (as defined in Instruction 3 to Item 4 of Schedule 14A (17 CFR 240.14a-101)) terminating any solicitation subject to Rule 14a-12(c), including the cost or anticipated cost to the registrant.

Instruction 1 to Item 5.07. The four business day period for reporting the event under this Item 5.07 shall begin to run on the day on which the meeting ended. The registrant shall disclose on Form 8-K under this Item 5.07 the preliminary voting results. The registrant shall file an amended report on Form 8-K under this Item 5.07 to disclose the final voting results within four business days after the final voting results are known. *However*, no preliminary voting results

need be disclosed under this Item 5.07 if the registrant has disclosed final voting results on Form 8-K under this Item.

Instruction 2 to Item 5.07. If any matter has been submitted to a vote of security holders otherwise than at a meeting of such security holders, corresponding information with respect to such submission shall be provided. The solicitation of any authorization or consent (other than a proxy to vote at a stockholders' meeting) with respect to any matter shall be deemed a submission of such matter to a vote of security holders within the meaning of this item.

Instruction 3 to Item 5.07. If the registrant did not solicit proxies and the board of directors as previously reported to the Commission was re-elected in its entirety, a statement to that effect in answer to paragraph (b) will suffice as an answer thereto regarding the election of directors.

Instruction 4 to Item 5.07. If the registrant has furnished to its security holders proxy soliciting material containing the information called for by paragraph (c), the paragraph may be answered by reference to the information contained in such material.

Instruction 5 to Item 5.07. A registrant may omit the information called for by this Item 5.07 if, on the date of the filing of its report on Form 8-K, the registrant meets the following conditions:

1. All of the registrant's equity securities are owned, either directly or indirectly, by a single person which is a reporting company under the Exchange Act and which has filed all the material required to be filed pursuant to Section 13, 14 or 15(d) thereof, as applicable; and

2. During the preceding thirty-six calendar months and any subsequent period of days, there has not been any material default in the payment of principal, interest, a sinking or purchase fund installment, or any other material default not cured within thirty days, with respect to any indebtedness of the registrant or its subsidiaries, and there has not been any material default in the payment of rentals under material long-term leases.

Amendment

Item 5.08 Shareholder Director Nominations

(a) If the registrant did not hold an annual meeting the previous year, or if the date of this year's annual meeting has been changed by more than 30 calendar days from the date of the previous year's meeting, then the registrant is required to disclose the date by which a nominating shareholder or nominating shareholder group must submit the notice on Schedule 14N (§ 240.14n-101) required pursuant to § 240.14a-11(b)(10), which date shall be a reasonable time before the registrant mails its proxy materials for the meeting. Where a registrant is required to include shareholder director nominees in the registrant's proxy materials pursuant to either an applicable state or foreign law provision, or a provision in the registrant's governing documents, then the registrant is required to disclose the date by which a nominating shareholder or nominating shareholder group must submit the notice on Schedule 14N required pursuant to § 240.14a-18.

(b) If the registrant is a series company as defined in Rule 18f-2(a) under the Investment Company Act of 1940 (§ 270.18f-2 of this chapter), then the registrant is required to disclose in connection with the election of directors at an annual meeting of shareholders (or, in lieu of such an annual meeting, a special meeting of shareholders) the total number of shares of the registrant outstanding and entitled to be voted (or if the votes are to be cast on a basis other than one vote per share, then the total number of votes entitled to be voted and the basis for allocating such votes) on the election of directors at such meeting of shareholders as of the end of the most recent calendar quarter.

*End of Amendment*_____

Section 6—Asset-Backed Securities

The Items in this Section 6 apply only to asset-backed securities. Terms used in this Section 6 have the same meaning as in Item 1101 of Regulation AB (17 CFR 229.1101).

Item 6.01 ABS Informational and Computational Material.

Report under this Item any ABS informational and computational material filed in, or as an exhibit to, this report.

Item 6.02 Change of Servicer or Trustee.

If a servicer contemplated by Item 1108(a)(2) of Regulation AB (17 CFR 229.1108(a)(2)) or a trustee has resigned or has been removed, replaced or substituted, or if a new servicer contemplated by Item 1108(a)(2) of Regulation AB or trustee has been appointed, state the date the event occurred and the circumstances surrounding the change. In addition, provide the disclosure required by Item 1108(d) of Regulation AB (17 CFR 229.1108(c)), as applicable, regarding the servicer or trustee change. If a new servicer contemplated by Item 1108(a)(3) of this Regulation AB or a new trustee has been appointed, provide the information required by Item 1108(b) through (d) of Regulation AB regarding such servicer or Item 1109 of Regulation AB (17 CFR 229.1109) regarding such trustee, as applicable.

Instruction.

To the extent that any information called for by this Item regarding such servicer or trustee is not determined or is unavailable at the time of the required filing, the registrant shall include a statement to this effect in the filing and then must file an amendment to its Form 8-K filing under this Item 6.02 containing such information within four business days after the information is determined or becomes available.

Item 6.03 Change in Credit Enhancement or Other External Support.

(a) *Loss of existing enhancement or support.* If the depositor (or servicer if the servicer signs the report on Form 10-K (17 CFR 249.310) of the issuing entity) becomes aware that any material enhancement or support specified in Item 1114(a)(1) through (3) of Regulation AB (17 CFR 229.1114(a)(1) through (3)) or Item 1115 of Regulation AB (17 CFR 229.1115) that was previously applicable regarding one or more classes of the asset-backed securities has terminated other than by expiration of the contract on its stated termination date or as a result of all parties completing their obligations under such agreement, then disclose:

(1) the date of the termination of the enhancement;

(2) the identity of the parties to the agreement relating to the enhancement or support;

(3) a brief description of the terms and conditions of the enhancement or support that are material to security holders;

(4) a brief description of the material circumstances surrounding the termination; and

(5) any material early termination penalties paid or to be paid out of the cash flows backing the asset-backed securities.

(b) *Addition of new enhancement or support.* If the depositor (or servicer if the servicer signs the report on Form 10-K (17 CFR 249.310) of the issuing entity) becomes aware that any material enhancement specified in Item 1114(a)(1) through (3) of Regulation AB (17 CFR 229.1114(a)(1) through (3)) or Item 1115 of Regulation AB (17 CFR 229.1115) has been added with respect to one or more classes of the asset-backed securities, then provide the date of addition of the new enhancement or support and the disclosure required by Items 1114 or 1115 of Regulation AB, as applicable, with respect to such new enhancement or support.

(c) *Material change to enhancement or support.* If the depositor (or servicer if the servicer signs the report on Form 10-K (17 CFR 249.310) of the issuing entity) becomes aware that any existing material enhancement or support specified in Item 1114(a)(1) through (3) of Regulation AB or Item 1115 of Regulation AB with respect to one or more classes of the asset-backed securities has been materially amended or modified, disclose:

(1) the date on which the agreement or agreements relating to the enhancement or support was amended or modified;

(2) the identity of the parties to the agreement or agreements relating to the amendment or modification; and

(3) a brief description of the material terms and conditions of the amendment or modification.

Instructions.

1. Disclosure is required under this Item whether or not the registrant is a party to any agreement regarding the enhancement or support if the loss, addition or modification of such enhancement or support materially affects, directly or indirectly, the asset-backed securities, the pool assets or the cash flow underlying the asset-backed securities.

2. To the extent that any information called for by this Item regarding the enhancement or support is not determined or is unavailable at the time of the required filing, the registrant shall include a statement to this effect in the filing and then must file an amendment to its Form 8-K filing under this Item 6.03 containing such information within four business days after the information is determined or becomes available.

3. The instructions to Items 1.01 and 1.02 of this Form apply to this Item.

4. Notwithstanding Items 1.01 and 1.02 of this Form, disclosure regarding changes to material enhancement or support is to be reported under this Item 6.03 in lieu of those Items.

Item 6.04 Failure to Make a Required Distribution.

If a required distribution to holders of the asset-backed securities is not made as of the required distribution date under the transaction documents, and such failure is material, identify the failure and state the nature of the failure to make the timely distribution.

Item 6.05 Securities Act Updating Disclosure.

Regarding an offering of asset-backed securities registered on Form S-3 (17 CFR 239.13), if any material pool characteristic of the actual asset pool at the time of issuance of the asset-backed securities differs by 5% or more (other than as a result of the pool assets converting into cash in accordance with their terms) from the description of the asset pool in the prospectus filed for the offering pursuant to Securities Act Rule 424 (17 CFR 230.424), disclose the information required by Items 1111 and 1112 of Regulation AB (17 CFR 229.1111 and 17 CFR 229.1112) regarding the characteristics of the actual asset pool. If applicable, also provide information required by Items 1108 and 1110 of Regulation AB (17 CFR 229.1108 and 17 CFR 229.1110) regarding any new servicers or originators that would be required to be disclosed under those items regarding the pool assets.

Instruction.

No report is required under this Item if substantially the same information is provided in a post-effective amendment to the Securities Act registration statement or in a subsequent prospectus filed pursuant to Securities Act Rule 424 (17 CFR 230.424).

Section 7 - Regulation FD

Item 7.01 Regulation FD Disclosure.

Unless filed under Item 8.01, disclose under this item only information that the registrant elects to disclose through Form 8-K pursuant to Regulation FD (17 CFR 243.100 through 243.103).

Section 8 - Other Events

Item 8.01 Other Events.

The registrant may, at its option, disclose under this Item 8.01 any events, with respect to which information is not otherwise called for by this form, that the registrant deems of importance to security holders. The registrant may, at its option, file a report under this Item 8.01 disclosing the nonpublic information required to be disclosed by Regulation FD (17 CFR 243.100 through 243.103).

Section 9 - Financial Statements and Exhibits

Item 9.01 Financial Statements and Exhibits.

List below the financial statements, pro forma financial information and exhibits, if any, filed as a part of this report.

(a) *Financial statements of businesses acquired.*

(1) For any business acquisition required to be described in answer to Item 2.01 of this form, financial statements of the business acquired shall be filed for the periods specified in Rule 3-05(b) of Regulation S-X (17 CFR 210.3-05(b)) or Rule 8-04(b) of Regulation S-X (17 CFR 210.8-04(b)) for smaller reporting companies.

(2) The financial statements shall be prepared pursuant to Regulation S-X except that supporting schedules need not be filed. A manually signed accountant's report should be provided pursuant to Rule 2-02 of Regulation S-X (17 CFR 210.2-02).

(3) With regard to the acquisition of one or more real estate properties, the financial statements and any additional information specified by Rules 3-14 (17 CFR 210.3-14) or Rule 8-06 of Regulation S-X (17 CFR 210.8-06) for smaller reporting companies.

(4) Financial statements required by this item may be filed with the initial report, or by amendment not later than 71 calendar days after the date that the initial report on Form 8-K must be filed. If the financial statements are not included in the initial report, the registrant should so indicate in the Form 8-K report and state when the required financial statements will be filed. The registrant may, at its option, include unaudited financial statements in the initial report on Form 8-K.

(b) *Pro forma financial information.*

(1) For any transaction required to be described in answer to Item 2.01 of this form, furnish any pro forma financial information that would be required pursuant to Article 11 of Regulation S-X (§ 210.11 of this chapter) or Rule 8-05 of Regulation S-X (§ 210.8-05 of this chapter) for smaller reporting companies.

(2) The provisions of paragraph (a)(4) of this Item 9.01 shall also apply to pro forma financial information relative to the acquired business.

(c) *Shell company transactions.* The provisions of paragraph (a)(4) and (b)(2) of this Item shall not apply to the financial statements or *pro forma* financial information required to be filed under this Item with regard to any transaction required to be described in answer to Item 2.01 of this Form by a registrant that was a shell company, other than a business combination related shell company, as those terms are defined in Rule 12b-2 under the Exchange Act (17 CFR 240.12b-2), immediately before that transaction. Accordingly, with regard to any transaction required to be described in answer to Item 2.01 of this Form by a registrant that was a shell company, other than a business combination related shell company, immediately before that transaction, the financial statements and *pro forma* financial information required by this Item must be filed in the initial report. Notwithstanding General Instruction B.3. to Form 8-K, if any financial statement or any financial information required to be filed in the initial report by this Item 9.01(c) is previously reported, as that term is defined in Rule 12b-2 under the Exchange Act (17 CFR 240.12b-2), the registrant may identify the filing in which that disclosure is included instead of including that disclosure in the initial report.

(d) *Exhibits.* The exhibits will be deemed to be filed or furnished, depending upon the relevant item requiring such exhibit, in accordance with the provisions of Item 601 of Regulation S-K (17 CFR 229.601) and Instruction B.2 of this form.

Instruction.

During the period after a registrant has reported a business combination pursuant to Item 2.01 of this form, until the date on which the financial statements specified by this Item 9.01 must be filed, the registrant will be deemed current for purposes of its reporting obligations under Section 13(a) or 15(d) of the Exchange Act (15 U.S.C. 78m or 78o(d)). With respect to filings under the Securities Act, however, registration statements will not be declared effective and post-effective amendments to registrations statements will not be declared effective unless financial statements meeting the requirements of Rule 3-05 of Regulation S-X (17 CFR 210.3-05) are provided. In addition, offerings should not be made pursuant to effective registration statements, or pursuant to Rules 505 and 506 of Regulation D (17 CFR 230.505 and 230.506) where any purchasers are not accredited investors under Rule 501(a) of that Regulation, until the audited financial statements required by Rule 3-05 of Regulation S-X (17 CFR 210.3-05) are filed; *provided, however,* that the following offerings or sales of securities may proceed notwithstanding that financial statements of the acquired business have not been filed:

(a) offerings or sales of securities upon the conversion of outstanding convertible securities or upon the exercise of outstanding warrants or rights;

(b) dividend or interest reinvestment plans;

(c) employee benefit plans;

(d) transactions involving secondary offerings; or

(e) sales of securities pursuant to Rule 144 (17 CFR 230.144).

SIGNATURES

Pursuant to the requirements of the Securities Exchange Act of 1934, the registrant has duly caused this report to be signed on its behalf by the undersigned hereunto duly authorized.

. . . .

(Registrant)

Date . . . .

(Signature)*

_____

* Print name and title of the signing officer under his signature.

[¶ 33,221]   **FORM 10-Q**

[As last amended in Release No. 33-9089, effective February 28, 2010, 74 F.R. 68334
and corrected in Release No. 33-9089A, effective February 28, 2010, 75 F.R. 9100.]

UNITED STATES
SECURITIES AND EXCHANGE COMMISSION
Washington, D.C. 20549

FORM 10-Q

GENERAL INSTRUCTIONS

A. Rule as to Use of Form 10-Q.

1. Form 10-Q shall be used for quarterly reports under Section 13 or 15(d) of the Securities Exchange Act of 1934 (15 U.S.C. 78m or 78o(d)), filed pursuant to Rule 13a-13 (17 CFR 240.13a-13) or Rule 15d-13 (17 CFR 240.15d-13). A quarterly report on this form pursuant to Rule 13a-13 or Rule 15d-13 shall be filed within the following period after the end of each of the first three fiscal quarters of each fiscal year, but no report need be filed for the fourth quarter of any fiscal year:

a. 40 days after the end of the fiscal quarter for large accelerated filers and accelerated filers (as defined in 17 CFR 240.12b-2); and

b. 45 days after the end of the fiscal quarter for all other registrants.

B. Application of General Rules and Regulations.

1. The General Rules and Regulations under the Act contain certain general requirements which are applicable to reports on any form. These general requirements should be carefully read and observed in the preparation and filing of reports on this form.

2. Particular attention is directed to Regulation 12B which contains general requirements regarding matters such as the kind and size of paper to be used, the legibility of the report, the information to be given whenever the title of securities is required to be stated, and the filing of the report. The definitions contained in Rule 12b-2 (17 CFR 240.12b-2) should be especially noted. See also Regulations 13A and 15D.

C. Preparation of Report.

1. This is not a blank form to be filled in. It is a guide copy to be used in preparing the report in accordance with Rules 12b-11 (17 CFR 240.12b-11) and 12b-12 (17 CFR 240.12b-2). The Commission does not furnish blank copies of this form to be filled in for filing.

2. These general instructions are not to be filed with the report. The instructions to the various captions of the form are also to be omitted from the report as filed.

D. Incorporation by Reference.

1. If the registrant makes available to its stockholders or otherwise publishes, within the period prescribed for filing the report, a document or statement containing information meeting some or all of the requirements of Part I of this form, the information called for may be incorporated by reference from such published document or statement, in answer or partial answer to any item or items of Part I of this form, provided copies thereof are filed as an exhibit to Part I of the report on this form.

2. Other information may be incorporated by reference in answer or partial answer to any item or items of Part II of this form in accordance with the provisions of Rule 12b-23 (17 CFR 240.12b-23).

3. If any information required by Part I or Part II is incorporated by reference into an electronic format document from the quarterly report to security holders as provided in General Instruction D, any portion of the quarterly report to security holders incorporated by reference shall be filed as an exhibit in electronic format, as required by Item 601(b)(13) of Regulation S-K.

E. Integrated Reports to Security Holders.

Quarterly reports to security holders may be combined with the required information of Form 10-Q and will be suitable for filing with the Commission if the following conditions are satisfied:

1. The combined report contains full and complete answers to all items required by Part I of this form. When responses to a certain item of required disclosure are separated within the combined report, an appropriate cross-reference should be made.

2. If not included in the combined report, the cover page, appropriate responses to Part II, and the required signatures shall be included in the Form 10-Q. Additionally, as appropriate, a cross-reference sheet should be filed indicating the loca-

tion of information required by the items of the form.

3. If an electronic filer files any portion of a quarterly report to security holders in combination with the required information of Form 10-Q, as provided in this instruction, only such portions filed in satisfaction of the Form 10-Q requirements shall be filed in electronic format.

F. Filed Status of Information Presented.

1. Pursuant to Rule 13a-13(d) and Rule 15d-13(d), the information presented in satisfaction of the requirements of Items 1, 2, and 3 of Part I of this form, whether included directly in a report on this form, incorporated therein by reference from a report, document or statement filed as an exhibit to Part I of this form pursuant to Instruction D(1) above, included in an integrated report pursuant to Instruction E above, or contained in a statement regarding computation of per share earnings or a letter regarding a change in accounting principles filed as an exhibit to Part I pursuant to Item 601 of Regulation S-K (§ 229.601 of this chapter), except as provided by Instruction F(2) below, shall not be deemed filed for the purpose of Section 18 of the Act or otherwise subject to the liabilities of that section of the Act but shall be subject to the other provisions of the Act.

2. Information presented in satisfaction of the requirements of this form other than those of Items 1, 2, and 3 of Part I of this form shall be deemed filed for the purpose of Section 18 of the Act; except that, where information presented in response to Items 1, 2, and 3 of Part I of this form (or as an exhibit thereto) is also used to satisfy Part II requirements through incorporation by reference, only that portion of Part I (or exhibit thereto) consisting of the information required by Part II shall be deemed so filed.

G. Signature and Filing of Report.

If the report is filed in paper pursuant to a hardship exemption from electronic filing (see Item 201 *et seq.* of Regulation S-T (17 CFR 232.201 *et seq.*), three complete copies of the report, including any financial statements, exhibits or other papers or documents filed as a part thereof, and five additional copies which need not include exhibits must be filed with the Commission. At least one complete copy of the report, including any financial statements, exhibits or other papers or documents filed as a part thereof, must be filed with each exchange on which any class of securities of the registrant is registered. At least one complete copy of the report filed with the Commission and one such copy filed with each exchange must be manually signed on the registrant's behalf by a duly authorized officer of the registrant and by the principal financial or

chief accounting officer of the registrant. (See Rule 12b-11(d) (17 CFR 240.12b-11(d).) Copies not manually signed must bear typed or printed signatures. In the case where the principal executive officer, principal financial officer or chief accounting officer is also duly authorized to sign on behalf of the registrant, one signature is acceptable provided that the registrant clearly indicates the dual responsibilities of the signatory.

H. Omission of Information by Certain Wholly-Owned Subsidiaries.

If on the date of the filing of its report on Form 10-Q, the registrant meets the conditions specified in paragraph (1) below, then such registrant may omit the information called for in the items specified in paragraph (2) below.

1. Conditions for availability of the relief specified in paragraph (2) below:

a. All of the registrant's equity securities are owned, either directly or indirectly, by a single person which is a reporting company under the Act and which has filed all the material required to be filed pursuant to section 13, 14 or 15(d) thereof, as applicable;

b. During the preceding thirty-six calendar months and any subsequent period of days, there has not been any material default in the payment of principal, interest, a sinking or purchase fund installment, or any other material default not cured within thirty days, with respect to any indebtedness of the registrant or its subsidiaries, and there has not been any material default in the payment of rentals under material long-term leases; and

c. There is prominently set forth, on the cover page of the Form 10-Q, a statement that the registrant meets the conditions set forth in General Instruction H(1)(a) and (b) of Form 10-Q and is therefore filing this form with the reduced disclosure format.

2. Registrants meeting the conditions specified in paragraph (1) above are entitled to the following relief:

a. Such registrants may omit the information called for by Item 2 of Part I, Management's Discussion and Analysis of Financial Condition and Results of Operations, provided that the registrant includes in the Form 10-Q a management's narrative analysis of the results of operations explaining the reasons for material changes in the amount of revenue and expense items between the most recent fiscal year-to-date period presented and the corresponding year-to-date period in the preceding fiscal year. Explanations of material changes should include, but not be limited to, changes in the various elements which determine revenue and expense levels such as unit sales volume, prices charged and paid, production levels, production cost variances, labor costs and discretionary spending programs. In addition, the analysis should include an explanation of the effect of any changes in accounting principles and practices or method of application that have a material effect on net income as reported.

b. Such registrants may omit the information called for in the following Part II Items: Item 2,

Changes in Securities; Item 3, Defaults Upon Senior Securities; and Item 4, Submission of Matters to a Vote of Security Holders.

c. Such registrants may omit the information called for by Item 3 of Part I, Quantitative and Qualitative Disclosures About Market Risk.

UNITED STATES

SECURITIES AND EXCHANGE COMMISSION

Washington, D.C. 20549

FORM 10-Q

FORM 10-Q

SECURITIES AND EXCHANGE COMMISSION

Washington, D.C. 20549

(Mark One)

[ ]   QUARTERLY REPORT PURSUANT TO SECTION 13 OR 15(d) OF THE SECURITIES EXCHANGE ACT OF 1934

For the quarterly period ended _____

OR

[ ]   TRANSITION REPORT PURSUANT TO SECTION 13 OR 15(d) OF THE SECURITIES EXCHANGE ACT OF 1934

For the transition period from _____ to _____

Commission file number _____

_____

(Exact name of registrant as specified in its charter)

_____   _____

(State or other jurisdiction of incorporation   (I.R.S. Employer

or organization)   Identification No.)

_____

(Address of principal executive offices)

(Zip Code)

_____

(Registrant's telephone number, including area code)

_____

(Former name, former address and former fiscal year, if changed since last report)

Indicate by check mark whether the registrant (1) has filed all reports required to be filed by Section 13 or 15(d) of the Securities Exchange Act of 1934 during the preceding 12 months (or for such shorter period that the registrant was required to file such reports), and (2) has been subject to such filing requirements for the past 90 days.

Yes___ No___

Indicate by check mark whether the registrant has submitted electronically and posted on its corporate Web site, if any, every Interactive Data File required to be submitted and posted pursuant to Rule 405 of Regulation S-T (§ 232.405 of this chapter) during the preceding 12 months (or for such shorter period that the registrant was required to submit and post such files).

Yes___ No___

Indicate by check mark whether the registrant is a large accelerated filer, an accelerated filer, a non-accelerated filer, or a smaller reporting company. See the definitions of "large accelerated filer," "accelerated filer" and "smaller reporting company" in Rule 12b-2 of the Exchange Act. (Check one):

Large accelerated filer ☐   Accelerated filer ☐

Non-accelerated filer (Do not check if a smaller reporting company) ☐   Smaller reporting company ☐

Indicate by check mark whether the registrant is a shell company (as defined in Rule 12b-2 of the Exchange Act).

Yes___ No___

APPLICABLE ONLY TO ISSUERS INVOLVED IN BANKRUPTCY PROCEEDINGS DURING THE PRECEDING FIVE YEARS:

Indicate by check mark whether the registrant has filed all documents and reports required to be filed by Sections 12, 13 or 15(d) of the Securities Exchange Act of 1934 subsequent to the distribution of securities under a plan confirmed by a court.

Yes___ No___

APPLICABLE ONLY TO CORPORATE ISSUERS:

Indicate the number of shares outstanding of each of the issuer's classes of common stock, as of the latest practicable date.

PART I—FINANCIAL INFORMATION

Item 1. Financial Statements.

Provide the information required by Rule 10-01 of Regulation S-X (17 CFR 210). A smaller reporting company, defined in Rule 12b-2 (§ 240.12b-2 of this chapter) may provide the information required by Article 8-03 of Regulation S-X (§ 210.8-03 of this chapter).

Item 2. Management's Discussion and Analysis of Financial Condition and Results of Operations.

Furnish the information required by Item 303 of Regulation S-K (§ 229.303 of this chapter).

Item 3. Quantitative and Qualitative Disclosures About Market Risk.

Furnish the information required by Item 305 of Regulation S-K (§ 229.305 of this chapter).

Item 4. Controls and Procedures.

Furnish the information required by Items 307 of Regulation S-K (17 CFR 229.307) and 308(c) of Regulation S-K (17 CFR 229.308(c)).

Item 4T. Controls and Procedures.

(a) If the registrant is neither a large accelerated filer nor an accelerated filer as those terms are defined in § 240.12b-2 of this chapter, furnish the information required by Items 307 and 308T(b) of Regulation S-K (17 CFR 229.307 and 229.308T(b)) with respect to a quarterly report that the registrant is required to file for a fiscal year ending on or after December 15, 2007 but before June 15, 2010.

(b) This temporary Item 4T will expire on December 15, 2010.

PART II—OTHER INFORMATION

Instruction. The report shall contain the item numbers and captions of all applicable items of Part II, but the text of such items may be omitted provided the responses clearly indicate the coverage of the item. Any item which is inapplicable or to which the answer is negative may be omitted and no reference thereto need be made in the report. If substantially the same information has been previously reported by the registrant, an additional report of the information on this form need not be made. The term "previously reported" is defined in Rule 12b-2 (17 CFR 240.12b-2). A separate response need not be presented in Part II where information called for is already disclosed in the financial information provided in Part I and is incorporated by reference into Part II of the report by means of a statement to that effect in Part II which specifically identifies the incorporated information.

Item 1. Legal Proceedings.

Furnish the information required by Item 103 of Regulation S-K (§ 229.103 of this chapter). As to such proceedings which have been terminated during the period covered by the report, provide similar information, including the date of termination and a description of the disposition thereof with respect to the registrant and its subsidiaries.

Instruction. A legal proceeding need only be reported in the 10-Q filed for the quarter in which it first became a reportable event and in subsequent quarters in which there have been material developments. Subsequent Form 10-Q filings in the same fiscal year in which a legal proceeding or a material development is reported should reference any previous reports in that year.

Item 1A. Risk Factors

Set forth any material changes from risk factors as previously disclosed in the registrant's Form 10-K (§ 249.310) in response to Item 1A. to Part 1 of Form 10-K. Smaller reporting companies are not required to provide the information required by this item.

Item 2. Unregistered Sales of Equity Securities and Use of Proceeds.

(a) Furnish the information required by Item 701 of Regulation S-K (17 CFR 229.701) as to all equity securities of the registrant sold by the registrant during the period covered by the report that were not registered under the Securities Act. If the Item 701 information previously has been included in a Current Report on Form 8-K (17 CFR 249.308), however, it need not be furnished.

(b) If required pursuant to Rule 463 (17 CFR 230.463) of the Securities Act of 1933, furnish the information required by Item 701(f) of Regulation S-K (229.701(f) of this chapter).

(c) Furnish the information required by Item 703 of Regulation S-K (§ 229.703 of this chapter) for any repurchase made in the quarter covered by the report. Provide disclosures covering repurchases made on a monthly basis. For example, if the quarter began on January 16 and ended on April 15, the chart would show repurchases for the months from January 16 through February 15, February 16 through March 15, and March 16 through April 15. February 15, February 16 through March 15, and March 16 through April 15.

Instruction. Working capital restrictions and other limitations upon the payment of dividends are to be reported hereunder.

Item 3. Defaults Upon Senior Securities.

(a) If there has been any material default in the payment of principal, interest, a sinking or purchase fund installment, or any other material default not cured within 30 days, with respect to any indebtedness of the registrant or any of its significant subsidiaries exceeding 5 percent of the total assets of the registrant and its consolidated subsidiaries, identify the indebtedness and state the nature of the default. In the case of such a default in the payment of principal, interest, or a sinking or purchase fund installment, state the amount of the default and the total arrearage on the date of filing this report.

Instruction. This paragraph refers only to events which have become defaults under the governing instruments, i.e., after the expiration of any period of grace and compliance with any notice requirements.

(b) If any material arrearage in the payment of dividends has occurred or if there has been any other material delinquency not cured within 30 days, with respect to any class of preferred stock of the registrant which is registered or which ranks prior to any class of registered securities, or with respect to any class of preferred stock of any significant subsidiary of the registrant, give the title of the class and state the nature of the arrearage or delinquency. In the case of an arrearage in the payment of dividends, state the amount and the total arrearage on the date of filing this report.

Instructions to Item 3

1. Item 3 need not be answered as to any default or arrearage with respect to any class of securities all of which is held by or for the account of the registrant or its totally held subsidiaries.

2. The information required by Item 3 need not be made if previously disclosed on a report on Form 8-K (17 CFR 249.308).

Item 4. Submission of Matters to a Vote of Security Holders.

[Removed and reserved.]

Item 5. Other Information.

(a) The registrant must disclose under this item any information required to be disclosed in a report on Form 8-K during the period covered by this Form 10-Q, but not reported, whether or not otherwise required by this Form 10-Q. If disclosure of such information is made under this item, it need not be repeated in a report on Form 8-K which would otherwise be required to be filed with respect to such information or in a subsequent report on Form 10-Q.

(b) Furnish the information required by Item 407(c)(3) of Regulation S-K (§ 229.407 of this chapter).

Item 6. Exhibits.

Furnish the exhibits required by Item 601 of Regulation S-K (§ 229.601 of this chapter).

SIGNATURES*

Pursuant to the requirements of the Securities Exchange Act of 1934, the registrant has duly caused this report to be signed on its behalf by the undersigned thereunto duly authorized.

(Registrant)_____

Date
_____

(Signature)**_____

Date
_____

(Signature)**_____

* See General Instruction E.

** Print name and title of the signing officer under his signature.

[¶ 33,251] **FORM 10-K**

[As last amended in Release No. 33-9089, effective February 28, 2010, 74 F.R. 68334 and corrected in Release No. 33-9089A, effective February 28, 2010, 75 F.R. 9100.]

SECURITIES AND EXCHANGE COMMISSION
Washington, D.C. 20549

FORM 10-K
Annual Report Pursuant to Section 13 or 15(d) of the Securities Exchange Act of 1934

GENERAL INSTRUCTIONS

A. Rule as to Use of Form 10-K.

(1) This Form shall be used for annual reports pursuant to Section 13 or 15(d) of the Securities Exchange Act of 1934 (15 U.S.C. 78m or 78o(d)) (the "Act") for which no other form is prescribed. This Form also shall be used for transition reports filed pursuant to Section 13 or 15(d) of the Act.

(2) Annual reports on this Form shall be filed within the following period:

(a) 60 days after the end of the fiscal year covered by the report (75 days for fiscal years ending before December 15, 2006) for large accelerated filers (as defined in 17 CFR 240.12b-2);

(b) 75 days after the end of the fiscal year covered by the report for accelerated filers (as defined in 17 CFR 240.12b-2); and

(c) 90 days after the end of the fiscal year covered by the report for all other registrants.

(3) Transition reports on this Form shall be filed in accordance with the requirements set forth in Rule 13a-10 (17 CFR 240.13a-10) or Rule 15d-10 (17 CFR 240.15d-10) applicable when the registrant changes its fiscal year end.

(4) Notwithstanding paragraphs (2) and (3) of this General Instruction A., all schedules required by Article 12 of Regulation S-X (17 CFR 210.12-01 – 210.12-29) may, at the option of the registrant, be filed as an amendment to the report not later than 30 days after the applicable due date of the report.

B. Application of General Rules and Regulations.

(1) The General Rules and Regulations under the Act (17 CFR 240) contain certain general requirements which are applicable to reports on any form. These general requirements should be carefully read and observed in the preparation and filing of reports on this Form.

(2) Particular attention is directed to Regulation 12B which contains general requirements regarding matters such as the kind and size of paper to be used, the legibility of the report, the information to be given whenever the title of securities is required to be stated, and the filing of the report. The definitions contained in Rule 12b-2 should be especially noted. *See also* Regulations 13A and 15D.

C. Preparation of Report.

(1) This Form is not to be used as a blank form to be filled in, but only as a guide in the preparation of the report on paper meeting the requirements of Rule 12b-12. Except as provided in General Instruction G, the answers to the items shall be prepared in the manner specified in Rule 12b-13.

(2) Except where information is required to be given for the fiscal year or as of a specified date, it shall be given as of the latest practicable date.

(3) Attention is directed to Rule 12b-20, which states: "In addition to the information expressly required to be included in a statement or report, there shall be added such further material information, if any, as may be necessary to make the required statements, in the light of the circumstances under which they are made, not misleading."

D. Signature and Filing of Report.

(1) Three complete copies of the report, including financial statements, financial statement schedules, exhibits, and all other papers and documents filed as a part thereof, and five additional copies which need not include exhibits, shall be filed with the Commission. At least one complete copy of the report, including financial statements, financial statement schedules, exhibits, and all other papers and documents filed as a part thereof, shall be filed with each exchange on which any class of securities of the registrant is registered. At least one complete copy of the report filed with the Commission and one such copy filed with each exchange shall be manually

signed. Copies not manually signed shall bear typed or printed signatures.

(2)(a) The report must be signed by the registrant, and on behalf of the registrant by its principal executive officer or officers, its principal financial officer or officers, its controller or principal accounting officer, and by at least the majority of the board of directors or persons performing similar functions. Where the registrant is a limited partnership, the report must be signed by the majority of the board of directors of any corporate general partner who signs the report.

(b) The name of each person who signs the report shall be typed or printed beneath his signature. Any person who occupies more than one of the specified positions shall indicate each capacity in which he signs the report. Attention is directed to Rule 12b-11 (17 CFR 240.12b-11) concerning manual signatures and signatures pursuant to powers of attorney.

(3) Registrants are requested to indicate in a transmittal letter with the Form 10-K whether the financial statements in the report reflect a change from the preceding year in any accounting principles or practices, or in the method of applying any such principles or practices.

E. Disclosure With Respect to Foreign Subsidiaries.

Information required by any item or other requirement of this form with respect to any foreign subsidiary may be omitted to the extent that the required disclosure would be detrimental to the registrant. However, financial statements and financial statement schedules, otherwise required, shall not be omitted pursuant to this Instruction. Where information is omitted pursuant to this Instruction, a statement shall be made that such information has been omitted and the names of the subsidiaries involved shall be separately furnished to the Commission. The Commission may, in its discretion, call for justification that the required disclosure would be detrimental.

F. Information as to Employee Stock Purchase, Savings and Similar Plans.

Attention is directed to Rule 15d-21 which provides that separate annual and other reports need not be filed pursuant to Section 15(d) of the Act with respect to any employee stock purchase, savings or similar plan if the issuer of the stock or other securities offered to employees pursuant to the plan furnishes to the Commission the information and documents specified in the Rule.

G. Information to be Incorporated by Reference.

(1) Attention is directed to Rule 12b-23 which provides for the incorporation by reference of information contained in certain documents in answer or partial answer to any item of a report.

(2) The information called for by Parts I and II of this Form (Items 1 through 9A or any portion thereof) may, at the registrant's option, be incorporated by reference from the registrant's annual report to security holders furnished to the Commission pursuant to Rule 14a-3(b) or Rule 14c-3(a) or from the registrant's annual report to security holders, even if not furnished to the Commission pursuant to Rule 14a-3(b) or Rule 14c-3(a), provided such annual report contains the information required by Rule 14a-3.

Note 1.—In order to fulfill the requirements of Part 1 of Form 10-K, the incorporated portion of the annual report to security holders must contain the information required by Items 1-3 of Form 10-K, to the extent applicable.

Note 2.—If any information required by Part I or Part II is incorporated by reference into an electronic format document from the annual report to security holders as provided in General Instruction G, any portion of the annual report to security holders incorporated by reference shall be filed as en exhibit in electronic format, as required by Item 601(b)(13) of Regulation S-K.

(3) The information required by Part III (Items 10, 11, 12, 13 and 14) may be incorporated by reference from the registrant's definitive proxy statement (filed or to be filed pursuant to Regulation 14A) or definitive information statement (filed or to be filed pursuant to Regulation 14C) which involves the election of directors, if such definitive proxy statement or information statement is filed with the Commission not later than 120 days after the end of the fiscal year covered by the Form 10-K. However, if such definitive proxy statement or information statement is not filed with the Commission in the 120-day period or is not required to be filed with the Commission by virtue of Rule 3a12-3(b) under the Exchange Act, the Items comprising the Part III information must be filed as part of the Form 10-K, or as an amendment to the Form 10-K, not later than the end of the 120-day period. It should be noted that the information regarding executive officers required by Item 401 of Regulation S-K (§ 229.401 of this chapter) may be included in Part I of Form 10-K under an appropriate caption. See Instruction 3 to Item 401(b) of Regulation S-K (§ 229.401(b) of this chapter).

(4) No item numbers of captions of items need be contained in the material incorporated by reference into the report. However, the registrant's attention is directed to Rule 12b-23(e) (17 CFR 240.12b-23(e)) regarding the specific disclosure required in the report concerning information incorporated by reference. When the registrant combines all of the information in Parts I and II of this Form (Items 1 through 9A) by

incorporation by reference from the registrant's annual report to security holders and all of the information in Part III of this Form (Items 10 through 14) by incorporating by reference from a definitive proxy statement or information statement involving the election of directors, then, notwithstanding General Instruction C(1), this Form shall consist of the facing or cover page, those sections incorporated from the annual report to security holders, the proxy or information statement, and the information, if any, required by Part IV of this Form, signatures, and a cross-reference sheet setting forth the item numbers and captions in Parts I, II and III of this Form and the page and/or pages in the referenced materials where the corresponding information appears.

H. Integrated Reports to Security Holders.

Annual reports to security holders may be combined with the required information of Form 10-K and will be suitable for filing with the Commission if the following conditions are satisfied:

(1) The combined report contains full and complete answers to all items required by Form 10-K. When responses to a certain item of required disclosure are separated within the combined report, an appropriate cross-reference should be made. If the information required by Part III of Form 10-K is omitted by virtue of General Instruction G, a definitive proxy or information statement shall be filed.

(2) The cover page and the required signatures are included. As appropriate, a cross-reference sheet should be filed indicating the location of information required by the items of the Form.

(3) If an electronic filer files any portion of an annual report to security holders in combination with the required information of Form 10-K, as provided in this instruction, only such portions filed in satisfaction of the Form 10-K requirements shall be filed in electronic format.

I. Omission of Information by Certain Wholly-Owned Subsidiaries.

If, on the date of the filing of its report on Form 10-K, the registrant meets the conditions specified in paragraph (1) below, then such registrant may furnish the abbreviated narrative disclosure specified in paragraph (2) below.

(1) Conditions for availability of the relief specified in paragraph (2) below.

(a) All of the registrant's equity securities are owned, either directly or indirectly, by a single person which is a reporting company under the Act and which has filed all the material required to be filed pursuant to section 13, 14, or 15(d) thereof, as applicable, and which is named in conjunction with the registrant's description of its business;

(b) During the preceding thirty-six calendar months and any subsequent period of days, there has not been any material default in the payment of principal, interest, a sinking or purchase fund installment, or any other material default not cured within thirty days, with respect to any indebtedness of the registrant or its subsidiaries, and there has not been any material default in the payment of rentals under material long-term leases;

(c) There is prominently set forth, on the cover page of the Form 10-K, a statement that the registrant meets the conditions set forth in General Instruction (I)(1)(a) and (b) of Form 10-K and is therefore filing this Form with the reduced disclosure format; and

(d) The registrant is not an asset-backed issuer, as defined in Item 1101 of Regulation AB (17 CFR 229.1101).

(2) Registrants meeting the conditions specified in paragraph (1) above are entitled to the following relief:

(a) Such registrants may omit the information called for by Item 6, Selected Financial Data, and Item 7, Management's Discussion and Analysis of Financial Condition and Results of Operations provided that the registrant includes in the Form 10-K a management's narrative analysis of the results of operations explaining the reasons for material changes in the amount of revenue and expense items between the most recent fiscal year presented and the fiscal year immediately preceding it. Explanations of material changes should include, but not be limited to, changes in the various elements which determine revenue and expense levels such as unit sales volume, prices charged and paid, production levels, production cost variances, labor costs and discretionary spending programs. In addition, the analysis should include an explanation of the effect of any changes in accounting principles and practices or method of application that have a material effect on net income as reported.

(b) Such registrants may omit the list of subsidiaries exhibit required by Item 601 of Regulation S-K (§ 229.601 of this chapter).

(c) Such registrants may omit the information called for by the following otherwise required Items: Item 4, Submission of Matters to a Vote of Security Holders; Item 10, Directors and Executive Officers of the Registrant; Item 11, Executive Compensation; Item 12, Security Ownership of Certain Beneficial Owners and Management; and Item 13, Certain Relationships and Related Transactions.

(d) In response to Item 1, Business, such registrant only need furnish a brief description of the business done by the registrant and its subsidiaries during the most recent fiscal year which will, in the opinion of management, indicate the general nature and scope of the business of the registrant and its subsidiaries, and in response to Item 2, Properties, such registrant only need furnish a brief description of the material properties of the registrant and its subsidiaries to the extent, in the opinion of the management, necessary to an understanding of the business done by the registrant and its subsidiaries.

J. Use of this Form by Asset-Backed Issuers.

The following applies to registrants that are asset-backed issuers. Terms used in this General Instruction J. have the same meaning as in Item 1101 of Regulation AB (17 CFR 229.1101).

(1) *Items that May be Omitted.* Such registrants may omit the information called for by the following otherwise required Items:

(a) Item 1, Business;

(b) Item 1A. Risk Factors;

(c) Item 2, Properties;

(d) Item 3, Legal Proceedings;

(e) Item 4, Submission of Matters to a Vote of Security Holders;

(f) Item 5, Market for Registrant's Common Equity and Related Stockholder Matters;

(g) Item 6, Selected Financial Data;

(h) Item 7, Management's Discussion and Analysis of Financial Condition and Results of Operations;

(i) Item 7A, Quantitative and Qualitative Disclosures About Market Risk;

(j) Item 8, Financial Statements and Supplementary Data;

(k) Item 9, Changes in and Disagreements With Accountants on Accounting and Financial Disclosure;

(l) Item 9A, Controls and Procedures;

(m) If the issuing entity does not have any executive officers or directors, Item 10, Directors and Executive Officers of the Registrant, Item 11, Executive Compensation, Item 12, Security Ownership of Certain Beneficial Owners and Management, and Item 13, Certain Relationships and Related Transactions; and

(n) Item 14, Principal Accountant Fees and Services.

(2) *Substitute Information to be Included.* In addition to the Items that are otherwise required by this Form, the registrant must furnish in the Form 10-K the following information:

(a) Immediately after the name of the issuing entity on the cover page of the Form 10-K, as separate line items, the exact name of the depositor as specified in its charter and the exact name of the sponsor as specified in its charter.

(b) Item 1112(b) of Regulation AB;

(c) Items 1114(b)(2) and 1115(b) of Regulation AB;

(d) Item 1117 of Regulation AB;

(e) Item 1119 of Regulation AB;

(f) Item 1122 of Regulation AB; and

(g) Item 1123 of Regulation AB.

(3) *Signatures.*

The Form 10-K must be signed either:

(a) On behalf of the depositor by the senior officer in charge of securitization of the depositor; or

(b) On behalf of the issuing entity by the senior officer in charge of the servicing function of the servicer. If multiple servicers are involved in servicing the pool assets, the senior officer in charge of the servicing function of the master servicer (or entity performing the equivalent function) must sign if a representative of the servicer is to sign the report on behalf of the issuing entity.

UNITED STATES

SECURITIES AND EXCHANGE COMMISSION

Washington, D.C. 20549

FORM 10-K

UNITED STATES

SECURITIES AND EXCHANGE COMMISSION

Washington, D.C. 20549

FORM 10-K

(Mark One)

[ ]   **ANNUAL REPORT PURSUANT TO SECTION 13 OR 15(d) OF THE SECURITIES EXCHANGE ACT OF 1934**

For the fiscal year ended . . . .

OR

[ ]   **TRANSITION REPORT PURSUANT TO SECTION 13 OR 15(d) OF THE SECURITIES EXCHANGE ACT OF 1934**

For the transition period from . . . . to . . . .

Commission file number . . . .

. . . .

(Exact name of registrant as specified in its charter)

. . . .

. . . . . . State or other jurisdiction of   (I.R.S. Employer .

. . . . incorporation or organization   Identification No.) .

. . . .

(Address of principal executive offices)   (Zip Code) . .

Registrant's telephone number, including area code . . . .

Securities registered pursuant to Section 12(b) of the Act:

Title of each class	Name of each exchange on which registered

. . . .

. . . .

Securities registered pursuant to section 12(g) of the Act:

. . . .

(Title of class)

. . . .

(Title of class)

Indicate by check mark if the registrant is a well-known seasoned issuer, as defined in Rule 405 of the Securities Act. Yes . . . No . . .

Indicate by check mark if the registrant is not required to file reports pursuant to Section 13 or Section 15(d) of the Act. Yes . . . No . . .

Indicate by check mark whether the registrant (1) has filed all reports required to be filed by Section 13 or 15(d) of the Securities Exchange Act of 1934 during the preceding 12 months (or for such shorter period that the registrant was required to file such reports), and (2) has been subject to such filing requirements for the past 90 days. Yes . . . No . . .

Indicate by check mark whether the registrant has submitted electronically and posted on its corporate Web site, if any, every Interactive Data File required to be submitted and posted pursuant to

Rule 405 of Regulation S-T (§ 232.405 of this chapter) during the preceding 12 months (or for such shorter period that the registrant was required to submit and post such files).

Yes [ ] No [ ]

Indicate by check mark if disclosure of delinquent filers pursuant to Item 405 of Regulation S-K (§ 229.405 of this chapter) is not contained herein, and will not be contained, to the best of registrant's knowledge, in definitive proxy or information statements incorporated by reference in Part III of this Form 10-K or any amendment to this Form 10-K. [ ]

Indicate by check mark whether the registrant is a large accelerated filer, an accelerated filer, a non-accelerated filer, or a smaller reporting company. See the definitions of "large accelerated filer," "accelerated filer" and "smaller reporting company" in Rule 12b-2 of the Exchange Act. (Check one):

       Large accelerated filer ☐   Accelerated filer ☐

       Non-accelerated filer ☐   Smaller reporting company ☐

(Do not check if a smaller reporting company)

Indicate by check mark whether the registrant is a shell company (as defined in Rule 12b-2 of the Exchange Act). Yes___ No___

State the aggregate market value of the voting and non-voting common equity held by non-affiliates computed by reference to the price at which the common equity was last sold, or the average bid and asked price of such common equity, as of the last business day of the registrant's most recently completed second fiscal quarter.

Note.—If a determination as to whether a particular person or entity is an affiliate cannot be made without involving unreasonable effort and expense, the aggregate market value of the common stock held by non-affiliates may be calculated on the basis of assumptions reasonable under the circumstances, provided that the assumptions are set forth in this Form.

APPLICABLE ONLY TO REGISTRANTS INVOLVED IN BANKRUPTCY

PROCEEDINGS DURING THE PRECEDING FIVE YEARS:

Indicate by check mark whether the registrant has filed all documents and reports required to be filed by Section 12, 13 or 15(d) of the Securities Exchange Act of 1934 subsequent to the distribution of securities under a plan confirmed by a court.

YES . . . NO . . .

(APPLICABLE ONLY TO CORPORATE REGISTRANTS)

Indicate the number of shares outstanding of each of the registrant's classes of common stock, as of the latest practicable date.

DOCUMENTS INCORPORATED BY REFERENCE

List hereunder the following documents if incorporated by reference and the Part of the Form 10-K (e.g., Part I, Part II, etc.) into which the document is incorporated: (1) Any annual report to security holders; (2) Any proxy or information statement; and (3) Any prospectus filed pursuant to Rule 424(b) or (c) under the Securities Act of 1933. The listed documents should be clearly described for identification purposes (e.g., annual report to security holders for fiscal year ended December 24, 1980).

PART I

[See General Instruction G(2)]

Item 1. Business.

Furnish the information required by Item 101 of Regulation S-K (§ 229.101 of this chapter) except that the discussion of the development of the registrant's business need only include developments since the beginning of the fiscal year for which this report is filed.

Set forth, under the caption "Risk Factors," where appropriate, the risk factors described in Item 503(c) of Regulation S-K (§ 229.503(c) of this chapter) applicable to the registrant. Provide any discussion of risk factors in plain English in accordance with Rule 421(d) of the Securities Act of 1933 (§ 230.421(d) of this chapter). Smaller reporting companies are not required to provide the information required by this item.

Item 1A. Risk Factors   **Item 1B. Unresolved Staff Comments.**

If the registrant is an accelerated filer or a large accelerated filer, as defined in Rule 12b-2 of the Exchange Act (§ 240.12b-2 of this chapter), or is a well-known seasoned issuer as defined in Rule 405 of the Securities Act (§ 230.405 of this chapter) and has received written comments from the Commission staff regarding its periodic or current reports under the Act not less than 180 days before the end of its fiscal year to which the annual report relates, and such comments remain unresolved, disclose the substance of any such unresolved comments that the registrant believes are material. Such disclosure may provide other information including the position of the registrant with respect to any such comment.

Item 2. Properties.

Furnish the information required by Item 102 of Regulation S-K (§ 229.102 of this chapter).

Item 3. Legal Proceedings.

(a) Furnish the information required by Item 103 of Regulation S-K (§ 229.103 of this chapter).

(b) As to any proceeding that was terminated during the fourth quarter of the fiscal year covered by this report, furnish information similar to that required by Item 103 of Regulation S-K (§ 229.103 of this chapter), including the date of termination and a description of the disposition thereof with respect to the registrant and its subsidiaries.

Item 4. [Removed and reserved.]

PART II

[See General Instruction G(2)]

Item 5. Market for Registrant's Common Equity, Related Stockholder Matters and Issuer Purchases of Equity Securities.

(a) Furnish the information required by Item 201 of Regulation S-K (17 CFR 229.201) and Item 701 of Regulation S-K (17 CFR 229.701) as to all equity securities of the registrant sold by the registrant during the period covered by the report that were not registered under the Securities Act. If the Item 701 information previously has been included in a Quarterly Report on Form 10-Q (17 CFR 249.308a) or in a Current Report on Form 8-K (17 CFR 249.308), it need not be furnished.

(b) If required pursuant to Rule 463 (17 CFR 230.463) of the Securities Act of 1933, furnish the information required by Item 701(f) of Regulation S-K (229.701(f) of this chapter).

(c) Furnish the information required by Item 703 of Regulation S-K (§ 229.703 of this chapter) for any repurchase made in a month within the fourth quarter of the fiscal year covered by the report. Provide disclosures covering repurchases made on a monthly basis. For example, if the fourth quarter began on January 16 and ended on April 15, the chart would show repurchases for the months from January 16 through February 15, February 16 through March 15, and March 16 through April 15.

Item 6. Selected Financial Data.

Furnish the information required by Item 301 of Regulation S-K (§ 229.301 of this chapter).

Item 7. Management's Discussion and Analysis of Financial Condition and Results of Operation.

Furnish the information required by Item 303 of Regulation S-K (§ 229.303 of this chapter).

Item 7A. Quantitative and Qualitative Disclosures About Market Risk.

Furnish the information required by Item 305 of Regulation S-K (§ 229.305 of this chapter).

Item 8. Financial Statements and Supplementary Data.

(a) Furnish financial statements meeting the requirements of Regulation S-X (§ 210 of this chapter), except § 210.3-05 and Article 11 thereof, and the supplementary financial information required by Item 302 of Regulation S-K (§ 229.302 of this chapter). Financial statements of the registrant and its subsidiaries consolidated (as required by Rule 14a-3(b)) shall be filed under this item. Other financial statements and schedules required under Regulation S-X may be filed as "Financial Statement Schedules" pursuant to Item 15, Exhibits, Financial Statement Schedules, and Reports on Form 8-K, of this Form.

(b) A smaller reporting company may provide the information required by Article 8 of Regulation S-X in lieu of any financial statements required by Item 8 of this Form.

Item 9. Changes in and Disagreements With Accountants on Accounting and Financial Disclosure.

Furnish the information required by Item 304(b) of Regulation S-K (17 CFR 229.304(b) of this chapter).

Item 9A. Controls and Procedures.

Furnish the information required by Items 307 and 308 of Regulation S-K (17 CFR 229.307 and 229.308).

Item 9A(T). Controls and Procedures.

(a) If the registrant is neither a large accelerated filer nor an accelerated filer as those terms are defined in § 240.12b-2 of this chapter, furnish the information required by Items 307 and 308T of Regulation S-K (17 CFR 229.307 and 229.308T) with respect to an annual report that the registrant is required to file for a fiscal year ending on or after December 15, 2007 but before June 15, 2010.

(b) This temporary Item 9A(T) will expire on December 15, 2010.

Item 9B. Other Information.

The registrant must disclose under this item any information required to be disclosed in a report on Form 8-K during the fourth quarter of the year covered by this Form 10-K, but not reported, whether or not otherwise required by this Form 10-K. If disclosure of such information is made under this item, it need not be repeated in a report on Form 8-K which would otherwise be required to be filed with respect to such information or in a subsequent report on Form 10-K.

Instruction.

With respect to a report on this Form regarding a class of asset-backed securities, the relevant period where disclosure is required is the period since the last required distribution report on Form 10-D (17 CFR 249.312).

PART III

[See General Instruction G(3)]

Item 10. Directors, Executive Officers and Corporate Governance.

Furnish the information required by Items 401, 405, 406, and 407(c)(3), (d)(4) and (d)(5) of Regulation S-K (§§ 229.401, 229.405, 229.406, and 229.407(c)(3), (d)(4) and (d)(5) of this chapter).

Instruction

Checking the box provided on the cover page of this Form to indicate that Item 405 disclosure of delinquent Form 3, 4, or 5 filers is not contained herein is intended to facilitate Form processing and review. Failure to provide such indication will not create liability for violation of the federal securities laws. The space should be checked only if there is no disclosure in this Form of reporting person delinquencies in response to Item 405 and the registrant, at the time of filing the Form 10-K, has reviewed the information necessary to ascertain, and has determined that, Item 405 disclosure is not expected to be contained in Part III of the Form 10-K or incorporated by reference.

Item 11. Executive Compensation.

Furnish the information required by Item 402 of Regulation S-K (§ 229.402 of this chapter) and paragraphs (e)(4) and (e)(5) of Item 407 of Regulation S-K (§ 229.407(e)(4) and (e)(5) of this chapter).

Item 12. Security Ownership of Certain Beneficial Owners and Management and Related Stockholder Matters.

Furnish the information required by Item 201(d) of Regulation S-K (§ 229.201(d) of this chapter) and by Item 403 of Regulation S-K (§ 229.403 of this chapter).

Item 13. Certain Relationships and Related Transactions, and Director Independence.

Furnish the information required by Item 404 of Regulation S-K (§ 229.404 of this chapter) and Item 407(a) of Regulation S-K (§ 229.407(a) of this chapter).

Item 14. Principal Accountant Fees and Services.

Furnish the information required by Item 9(e) of Schedule 14A (§ 240.14a-101 of this chapter).

(1) Disclose, under the caption *Audit Fees*, the aggregate fees billed for each of the last two fiscal years for professional services rendered by the principal accountant for the audit of the registrant's annual financial statements and review of financial statements included in the registrant's Form 10-Q (17 CFR 249.308a) or services that are normally provided by the accountant in connection with statutory and regulatory filings or engagements for those fiscal years.

(2) Disclose, under the caption *Audit-Related Fees*, the aggregate fees billed in each of the last two fiscal years for assurance and related services by the principal accountant that are reasonably related to the performance of the audit or review of the registrant's financial statements and are not reported under Item 9(e)(1) of Schedule 14A. Registrants shall describe the nature of the services comprising the fees disclosed under this category.

(3) Disclose, under the caption *Tax Fees*, the aggregate fees billed in each of the last two fiscal years for professional services rendered by the principal accountant for tax compliance, tax advice, and tax planning. Registrants shall describe

the nature of the services comprising the fees disclosed under this category.

(4) Disclose, under the caption *All Other Fees*, the aggregate fees billed in each of the last two fiscal years for products and services provided by the principal accountant, other than the services reported in Items 9(e)(1) through 9(e)(3) of Schedule 14A. Registrants shall describe the nature of the services comprising the fees disclosed under this category.

(5)(i) Disclose the audit committee's pre-approval policies and procedures described in paragraph (c)(7)(i) of Rule 2-01 of Regulation S-X.

(ii) Disclose the percentage of services described in each of Items 9(e)(2) through 9(e)(4) of Schedule 14A that were approved by the audit committee pursuant to paragraph (c)(7)(i)(C) of Rule 2-01 of Regulation S-X.

(6) If greater than 50 percent, disclose the percentage of hours expended on the principal accountant's engagement to audit the registrant's financial statements for the most recent fiscal year that were attributed to work performed by persons other than the principal accountant's full-time, permanent employees.

PART IV

Item 15. Exhibits and Financial Statement Schedules.

(a) List the following documents filed as a part of the report:

1. All financial statements;

2. Those financial statement schedules required to be filed by Item 8 of this form, and by paragraph (b) below.

3. Those exhibits required by Item 601 of Regulation S-K (17 CFR 229.601 of this chapter) and by paragraph (b) below. Identify in the list each management contract or compensatory plan or arrangement required to be filed as an exhibit to this form pursuant to Item 15(b) of this report.

(b) Registrants shall file, as exhibits to this Form, the exhibits required by Item 601 of Regulation S-K (§ 229.601 of this chapter).

(c) Registrants shall file, as financial statement schedules to this Form, the financial statements required by Regulation S-X (17 CFR 210) which are excluded from the annual report to shareholders by Rule 14a-3(b) including (1) separate financial statements of subsidiaries not consolidated and fifty percent or less owned persons; (2) separate financial statements of affiliates whose securities are pledged as collateral; and (3) schedules.

SIGNATURES

[See General Instruction D]

Pursuant to the requirements of Section 13 or 15(d) of the Securities Exchange Act of 1934, the registrant has duly caused this report to be signed on its behalf by the undersigned, thereunto duly authorized.

(Registrant) . . . .

By (Signature and Title)* . . . .

Date . . . .

Pursuant to the requirements of the Securities Exchange Act of 1934, this report has been

signed below by the following persons on behalf of the registrant and in the capacities and on the dates indicated.

By (Signature and Title)* . . . .

Date . . . .

By (Signature and Title)* . . . .

Date . . . .

* Print the name and title of each signing officer under his signature.

Supplemental Information to be Furnished With Reports Filed Pursuant to Section 15(d) of the Act by Registrants Which Have Not Registered Securities Pursuant to Section 12 of the Act

(a) Except to the extent that the materials enumerated in (1) and/or (2) below are specifically incorporated into this Form by reference (in which case *see* Rule 12b-23(d)), every registrant which files an annual report on this Form pursuant to Section 15(d) of the Act shall furnish to the Commission for its information, at the time of filing its report on this Form, four copies of the following:

(1) Any annual report to security holders covering the registrant's last fiscal year; and

(2) Every proxy statement, form of proxy or other proxy soliciting material sent to more than ten of the registrant's security holders with respect to any annual or other meeting of security holders.

(b) The foregoing material shall not be deemed to be "filed" with the Commission or otherwise subject to the liabilities of Section 18 of the Act, except to the extent that the registrant specifically incorporates it in its annual report on this Form by reference.

(c) If no such annual report or proxy material has been sent to security holders, a statement to that effect shall be included under this caption. If such report or proxy material is to be furnished to security holders subsequent to the filing of the annual report of this Form, the registrant shall so state under this caption and shall furnish copies of such material to the Commission when it is sent to security holders.

[¶ 33,261]   **FORM 11-K**

[As last amended in Release No. 33-8876, effective February 4, 2008, 73 F.R. 934.]

SECURITIES AND EXCHANGE COMMISSION

Washington, D.C. 20549

FORM 11-K

FOR ANNUAL REPORTS OF EMPLOYEE STOCK PURCHASE, SAVINGS AND SIMILAR PLANS PURSUANT TO SECTION 15(d) OF THE SECURITIES EXCHANGE ACT OF 1934

GENERAL INSTRUCTIONS

A. Rule as to Use of Form 11-K

This form shall be used for annual reports pursuant to Section 15(d) of the Securities Exchange Act of 1934 ("Exchange Act") with respect to employee stock purchase, savings and similar plans, interests in which constitute securities registered under the Securities Act of 1933. This form also shall be used for transition reports filed pursuant to Section 15(d) of the Act. Such a report is required to be filed even though the issuer of the securities offered to employees pursuant to the plan also files annual reports pursuant to Section 13(a) or 15(d) of the Exchange Act. However, attention is directed to Rule 15d-21 (§ 240.15d-21), which provides that in certain cases the information required by this form may be furnished with respect to the plan as a part of the annual report of such issuer. Reports on this form shall be filed within 90 days after the end of the fiscal year of the plan, *provided that* plans subject to the Employee Retirement Income Security Act of 1974 ("ERISA") shall file the plan financial statements within 180 days after the plan's fiscal year end.

B. Application of General Rules and Regulations

(a) The General Rules and Regulations under the Exchange Act contain requirements applicable to reports on any form. These general requirements should be carefully read and observed in the preparation and filing of reports on this form.

(b) Particular attention is directed to Regulation 12B, which contains general requirements regarding matters such as the kind and size of paper to be used, the legibility of the report, and the filing of the report. The definitions contained in Rule 12b-2 (§ 240.12b-2) should be especially noted. See also Regulation 15D.

(c) Four complete copies of each report on this form, including exhibits and all papers and documents filed as a part thereof, shall be filed with the Commission. At least one of the copies filed shall be manually signed. Copies not manually signed shall bear typed or printed signatures.

C. Preparation of Report

This form is not to be used as a blank form to be filled in, but only as a guide in the preparation of the report on paper meeting the requirements of Rule 12b-12 (§ 240.12b-12). The report may omit the text of Form 11-K specifying the information required provided the answers thereto are prepared in the manner specified in Rule 12b-13 (§ 240.12b-13).

D. Incorporation of Information in Report to Employees

Any financial statements contained in any plan annual report to employees covering the latest fiscal year of the plan may be incorporated by reference from such document in response to part or all of the requirements of this form, provided such financial statements substantially meet the requirements of this form and provided that such document is filed as an exhibit to this report on Form 11-K.

E. Electronic Filers

Reports on this Form may be filed either in paper or in electronic format, at the filer's option. *See* Rule 101(b)(3) of Regulation S-T (§ 232.101(b)(3) of this chapter).

SECURITIES AND EXCHANGE COMMISSION

Washington, D.C. 20549

FORM 11-K

(Mark One)

[ ]   ANNUAL REPORT PURSUANT TO SECTION 15(d) OF THE SECURITIES EXCHANGE ACT OF 1934 [FEE REQUIRED]

For the fiscal year ended . . . .

OR

[ ]   TRANSITION REPORT PURSUANT TO SECTION 15(d) OF THE SECURITIES EXCHANGE ACT OF 1934 [NO FEE REQUIRED]

For the transition period from . . . . to . . . .

Commission file number . . . .

A. Full title of the plan and the address of the plan, if different from that of the issuer named below:

B. Name of issuer of the securities held pursuant to the plan and the address of its principal executive office:

REQUIRED INFORMATION

The following financial statements shall be furnished for the plan:

1. An audited statement of financial condition as of the end of the latest two fiscal years of the plan (or such lesser period as the plan has been in existence).

2. An audited statement of income and changes in plan equity for each of the latest three fiscal years of the plan (or such lesser period as the plan has been in existence).

3. The statements required by Items 1 and 2 shall be prepared in accordance with the applicable provisions of Article 6A of Regulation S-X (17 CFR 210.6A-01-.6A-05).

4. In lieu of the requirements of Items 1-3 above, plans subject to ERISA may file plan financial statements and schedules prepared in accordance with the financial reporting requirements of ERISA. To the extent required by ERISA, the plan financial statements shall be examined by an independent accountant, except that the "limited scope exemption" contained in Section 103(a)(3)(C) of ERISA shall not be available.

Note: A written consent of the accountant is required with respect to the plan annual financial statements which have been incorporated by reference in a registration statement on Form S-8 under the Securities Act of 1933. The consent should be filed as an exhibit to this annual report. Such consent shall be currently dated and manually signed.

SIGNATURES

The Plan. Pursuant to the requirements of the Securities Exchange Act of 1934, the trustees (or other persons who administer the employee benefit plan) have duly caused this annual report to be signed on its behalf by the undersigned hereunto duly authorized.

. . . .

. . . . . .

(Name of Plan) . . . .

Date . . . .

. . . . . .

(Signature)* . . . .

_____

* Print name and title of the signing official under the signature.

[¶ 33,291] FORM 18-K

For Foreign Governments and Political Subdivisions Thereof

SECURITIES AND EXCHANGE COMMISSION

Washington, D.C. 20549

FORM 18-K

ANNUAL REPORT

of . . . .

Name of registrant

Date of end of last fiscal year . . . .

SECURITIES REGISTERED

As of the close of the fiscal year)

Title of issue	Amount as to which registration is effective	Names of exchanges on which registered

Name and address of person authorized to receive notices and communications from the Securities and Exchange Commission:

The information set forth below is to be furnished:

1. In respect of each issue of securities of the registrant registered, a brief statement as to:

(a) The general effect of any material modifications, not previously reported, of the rights of the holders of such securities.

(b) The title and the material provisions of any law, decree or administrative action, not previously reported, by reason of which the security is not being serviced in accordance with the terms thereof.

(c) The circumstances of any other failure, not previously reported, to pay principal, interest, or any sinking fund or amortization installment.

2. A statement as of the close of the last fiscal year of the registrant giving the total outstanding of:

(a) Internal funded debt of the registrant. (Total to be stated in the currency of the registrant. If any internal funded debt is payable in a foreign currency it should not be included under this paragraph (a), but under paragraph (b) of this item.)

(b) External funded debt of the registrant. (Totals to be stated in the respective currencies in which payable. No statement need be furnished as to intergovernmental debt).

3. A statement giving the title, date of issue, date of maturity, interest rate and amount outstanding, together with the currency or currencies in which payable, of each issue of funded debt of the registrant outstanding as of the close of the last fiscal year of the registrant.

4. (a) As to each issue of securities of the registrant which is registered, there should be furnished a break-down of the total amount outstanding, as shown in Item 3, into the following:

(1) Total amount held by or for the amount of the registrant.

(2) Total estimated amount held by nationals of the registrant (or if registrant is other than a national government by the nationals of its national government); this estimate need be furnished only if it is practicable to do so.

(3) Total amount otherwise outstanding.

(b) If a substantial amount is set forth in answer to paragraph (a)(1) above, describe briefly the method employed by the registrant to reacquire such securities.

5. A statement as of the close of the last fiscal year of the registrant giving the estimated total of:

(a) Internal floating indebtedness of the registrant. (Total to be stated in the currency of the registrant.)

(b) External floating indebtedness of the registrant. (Total to be stated in the respective currencies in which payable.)

6. Statements of the receipts, classified by source, and of the expenditures, classified by purpose, of the registrant for each fiscal year of the registrant ended since the close of the latest fiscal year for which such information was previously reported. These statements should be so itemized as to be reasonably informative and should cover both ordinary and extraordinary receipts and expenditures; there should be indicated separately, if practicable, the amount of receipts pledged or otherwise specifically allocated to any issue registered, indicating the issue.

7. (a) If any foreign exchange control, not previously reported, has been established by the registrant (or if the registrant is other than a national government, by its national government), briefly describe such foreign exchange control.

(b) If any foreign exchange control previously reported has been discontinued or materially modified, briefly describe the effect of any such action, not previously reported.

IF THE REGISTRANT IS A GOVERNMENTAL UNIT OTHER THAN A NATIONAL GOVERNMENT, IT NEED NOT ANSWER ITEMS 8, 9, AND 10.

8. Brief statements as of a date reasonably close to the date of the filing of this report, (indicating such date) in respect of the note issue and gold reserves of the central bank of issue of the registrant, and of any further gold stocks held by the registrant.

9. Statements of imports and exports of merchandise for each year ended since the close of the latest year for which such information was previously reported. Such statements should be reasonably itemized so far as practicable as to commodities and as to countries. They should be set forth in terms of value and of weight or quantity; if statistics have been established only in terms of value, such will suffice.

10. The balances of international payments of the registrant for each year ended since the close of the latest year for which such information was previously reported. The statements of such balances should conform, if possible, to the nomenclature and form used in the "Statistical Handbook of the League of Nations." (These statements need be furnished only if the registrant has published balances of international payments.)

EXHIBITS

The following exhibits should be filed as part of the annual report:

(a) Copies of any amendments or modifications, other than such as have been previously filed, to all exhibits previously filed other than annual budgets. If such amendments or modifications are not in the English language, there should be furnished in addition a translation into English if the original exhibit was translated into English.

(b) A copy of any law, decree, or administrative document outlined in answer to Item 1(b). If such law, decree, or document is not in the English language, there should be furnished in addition thereto a translation thereof into English.

(c) A copy of the latest annual budget of the registrant, if not previously filed, as presented to its legislative body. This document need not be translated into English.

The registrant may file such other exhibits as it may desire, marking them so as to indicate clearly the items to which they refer.

This annual report comprises:

(a) Pages numbered . . . . to . . . . consecutively, and insert pages numbered . . . .

(b) The following exhibits:

This annual report is filed subject to the Instructions for Form 18-K for Foreign Governments and Political Subdivisions Thereof, and the amendments to such Instructions numbered:

SIGNATURE

Pursuant to the requirements of the Securities Exchange Act of 1934, the registrant has duly caused this annual report to be signed on its behalf by the undersigned, thereunto duly authorized, at . . . ., on the . . . . day of . . . ., 20 . . . .

. . . .
(Name of registrant)

By . . . .
(Name and title)

INSTRUCTION BOOK FOR FORM 18-K

For Foreign Governments and Political Subdivisions Thereof

ANNUAL REPORT

Rule as to Use of Form 18-K

This form is to be used for the annual reports of foreign governments or political subdivisions thereof, except any public corporations or other autonomous entity in the nature of a political sub-division, other than a state, province, county or municipality or similar body politic, which, at its option, has registered securities on Form 21 in lieu of Form 18.

Instructions as to the Preparation and Filing of the Report

1. An annual report on this form is to be filed by each issuer for which this form is appropriate:

(a) On or before September 30, 1937; and, thereafter,

(b) Within nine months after the close of each fiscal year of such issuer ending after March 31, 1937.

2. The report, including exhibits, is to be filed with the exchange upon which the securities are registered and in triplicate with the Commission. At least one copy of the report filed with the Commission and one filed with the exchange are to be signed. If securities are registered on more than one exchange the registrant may prepare one annual report covering all securities registered on any of the exchanges and, in such case, should file originals of such annual report with each exchange and a duplicate original and two copies, as above, of such annual report with the Commission. A registrant may, however, at its option prepare separate annual reports for each exchange upon which its securities are registered and, in such case, should file a duplicate original and two copies, as above, of each such report with the Commission.

3. (a) The report should be typed or printed on paper 8½ by 13 inches in size. Tables and financial data, however, may be on larger paper if folded to such size. Typed or printed matter should leave a margin of at least 1½ inches on the left. The report should be securely bound on the left.

(b) The report should contain both the items in the form and the answers thereto.

4. Where a "brief" answer is indicated the answer may incorporate by reference particular items, sections or paragraphs of any exhibit in the English language and may be qualified in its entirety by such reference.

5. If information is asked as of the close of, or for, a specified year, and if such information is not yet available for such date or period, it may be furnished as of the close of, or for, the latest year for which it is available. In each case the date or period for which information is given should be indicated.

6. The answers are to be made in the English language.

Instructions as to the Facing Sheet

Table of "Securities Registered." (a) In the column entitled "amount as to which registration is effective" there should be shown the total, by classes, of securities which had become registered and were outstanding at the close of the last fiscal year of the registrant.

(b) If the registrant has filed more than one application with a particular exchange, all issues presently registered pursuant to such applications should be included.

[¶ 33,321] Form 12b-25

[As last amended in Release No. 33-9002, effective April 13, 2009, 74 F.R. 6776.]

UNITED STATES

SECURITIES AND EXCHANGE COMMISSION

Washington, D.C. 20549

FORM 12b-25

NOTIFICATION OF LATE FILING

UNITED STATES
SECURITIES AND EXCHANGE COMMISSION
Washington, D.C. 20549
FORM 12b-25
NOTIFICATION OF LATE FILING

SEC FILE NUMBER
CUSIP NUMBER

(Check One) ☐ Form 10-K ☐ Form 20-F ☐ Form 11-K ☐ Form 10-Q ☐ Form 10-D ☐ Form N-SAR ☐ Form N-CSR

For Period Ended: ———

[ ] Transition Report on Form 10-K

[ ] Transition Report on Form 20-F

[ ] Transition Report on Form 11-K

[ ] Transition Report on Form 10-Q

[ ] Transition Report on Form N-SAR

For the Transition Period Ended: ———

Read Instruction (on back page) Before Preparing Form. Please Print or Type.

Nothing in this form shall be construed to imply that the Commission has verified any information contained herein.

If the notification relates to a portion of the filing checked above, identify the Item(s) to which the notification relates:

———

PART I—REGISTRANT INFORMATION

———

Full Name of Registrant

———

Former Name if Applicable

———

Address of Principal Executive Office *(Street and Number)*

———

City, State and Zip Code

PART II—RULES 12b-25(b) AND (c)

If the subject report could not be filed without unreasonable effort or expense and the registrant seeks relief pursuant to Rule 12b-25(b), the following should be completed. (Check box if appropriate) ☐

(a) The reasons described in reasonable detail in Part III of this form could not be eliminated without unreasonable effort or expense;

(b) The subject annual report, semi-annual report, transition report on Form 10-K, Form 20-F, Form 11-K, Form N-SAR or Form N-CSR, or portion thereof, will be filed on or before the fifteenth calendar day following the prescribed due date; or the subject quarterly report or transition report on Form 10-Q or subject distribution report on Form 10-D, or portion thereof, will be filed on or before the fifth calendar day following the prescribed due date; and

(c) The accountant's statement or other exhibit required by Rule 12b-25(c) has been attached if applicable.

PART III—NARRATIVE

State below in reasonable detail why Forms 10-K, 20-F, 11-K, 10-Q, 10-D, N-SAR, N-CSR, or the transition report or portion thereof, could not be filed within the prescribed time period.

(Attach Extra Sheets if Needed)

PART IV—OTHER INFORMATION

(1) Name and telephone number of person to contact in regard to this notification

———————————

(Name)

———————————

(Area Code) (Telephone Number)

(2) Have all other periodic reports required under Section 13 or 15(d) of the Securities Exchange Act of 1934 or Section 30 of the Investment Company Act of 1940 during the preceeding 12 months or for such shorter period that the registrant was required to file such report(s) been filed? If answer is no, identify report(s). ☐ Yes ☐ No

———————————

(3) Is it anticipated that any significant change in results of operations from the corresponding period for the last fiscal year will be reflected by the earnings statements to be included in the subject report or portion thereof? ☐ Yes ☐ No

If so, attach an explanation of the anticipated change, both narratively and quantitatively, and, if appropriate, state the reasons why a reasonable estimate of the results cannot be made.

———————————

———————————

(Name of Registrant as Specified in Charter)

has caused this notification to be signed on its behalf by the undersigned hereunto duly authorized.

Date ——————— By ———————————

INSTRUCTION: The form may be signed by an executive officer of the registrant or by any other duly authorized representative. The name and title of the person signing the form shall be typed or printed beneath the signature. If the statement is signed on behalf of the registrant by an authorized representative (other than an executive officer), evidence of the representative's authority to sign on behalf of the registrant shall be filed with the form.

ATTENTION

Intentional misstatements or omissions of fact constitute Federal Criminal Violations (See 18 U.S.C. 1001).

GENERAL INSTRUCTIONS

1. This form is required by Rule 12b-25 (17 CFR 240.12b-25) of the General Rules and Regulations under the Securities Exchange Act of 1934.

2. One signed original and four conformed copies of this form and amendments thereto must be completed and filed with the Securities and Exchange Commission, Washington, D.C. 20549, in accordance with Rule0-3 of the General Rules and Regulations under the Act. The information contained in or filed with the form will be made a matter of public record in the Commission files.

3. A manually signed copy of the form and amendments thereto shall be filed with each national securities exchange on which any class of securities of the registrant is registered.

4. Amendments to the notifications must also be filed on form 12b-25 but need not restate information that has been correctly furnished. The form shall be clearly identified as an amended notification.

5. Electronic filers. This form shall not be used by electronic filers unable to timely file a report solely due to electronic difficulties. Filers unable to submit a report within the time period prescribed due to difficulties in electronic filing should comply with either Rule 201 or Rule 202 of Regulation S-T (§ 232.201 or § 232.202 of this chapter) or apply for an adjustment in filing date pursuant to Rule 13(b) of Regulation S-T (§ 232.13(b) of this Chapter).

6. *Interactive data submissions.* This form shall not be used by electronic filers with respect to the submission or posting of an Interactive Data File (§ 232.11 of this chapter). Electronic filers unable to submit or post an Interactive Data File within the time period prescribed should comply with either Rule 201 or 202 of Regulation S-T (§ 232.201 and § 232.202 of this chapter).

[¶ 33,331] FORM 15

[As adopted in Release No. 34-20784, March 22, 1984, 49 F.R. 12688.]

UNITED STATES

SECURITIES AND EXCHANGE COMMISSION

Washington, D.C. 20549

FORM 15

CERTIFICATION AND NOTICE OF TERMINATION OF REGISTRATION UNDER SECTION 12(g) OF THE SECURITIES EXCHANGE ACT OF 1934 OR SUSPENSION OF DUTY TO FILE REPORTS UNDER SECTIONS 13 AND 15(d) OF THE SECURITIES EXCHANGE ACT OF 1934

Commission File Number _____

....

(Exact name of registrant as specified in its charter)

....

(Address, including zip code, and telephone number, including area code, of registrant's principal executive offices)

....

(Title of each class of securities covered by this Form)

....

(Titles of all other classes of securities for which a duty to file reports under section 13(a) or 15(d) remains)

Please place an X in the box(es) to designate the appropriate rule provisions(s) relied upon to terminate or suspend the duty to file reports:

Rule 12g-4(a)(1)(i) ☐

Rule 12g-4(a)(1)(ii) ☐

Rule 12g-4(a)(2)(i) ☒

Rule 12g-4(a)(2)(ii) ☐

Rule 12h-3(b)(1)(i) ☐

Rule 12h-3(b)(1)(ii) ☐

Rule 12h-3(b)(2)(i) ☐

Rule 12h-3(b)(2)(ii) ☐

Rule 15d-6 ☐

Approximate number of holders of record as of the certification or notice date: _____

Pursuant to the requirements of the Securities Exchange Act of 1934 (*Name of registrant as specified in charter*) has caused this certification/notice to be signed on its behalf by the undersigned duly authorized person.

Date ——— By ——————————

Instruction: This form is required by Rules 12g-4, 12h-3 and 15d-6 of the General Rules and Regulations under the Securities Exchange Act of 1934. The registrant shall file with the Commission three copies of Form 15, one of which shall be manually signed. It may be signed by an officer of the registrant, by counsel or by any other duly authorized person. The name and title of the person signing the form shall be typed or printed under the signature.

[¶ 33,335]   **FORM 15F**

[As last amended in Release No. 34-58465, effective October 10, 2008, 73 F.R. 52752.]

CERTIFICATION OF A FOREIGN PRIVATE ISSUER'S TERMINATION OF REGISTRATION OF A CLASS OF SECURITIES UNDER SECTION 12(g) OF THE SECURITIES EXCHANGE ACT OF 1934 OR ITS TERMINATION OF THE DUTY TO FILE REPORTS UNDER SECTION 13(a) OR SECTION 15(d) OF THE SECURITIES EXCHANGE ACT OF 1934

Commission File Number _____

_____
(Exact name of registrant as specified in its charter)

_____
(Address, including zip code, and telephone number, including area code, of registrant's principal executive offices)

_____
(Title of each class of securities covered by this Form)

Place an X in the appropriate box(es) to indicate the provision(s) relied upon to terminate the duty to file reports under the Securities Exchange Act of 1934:

Rule 12g-6(a) ☐   Rule 12g-6(d) ☐
(for equity securites)   (for successor registrants)

Rule 12g-6(c) ☐   Rule 12g-6(i) ☐
(for debt securites)   (for prior Form 15 filers)

GENERAL INSTRUCTIONS

A. Who May Use Form 15F and When

1. A foreign private issuer may file Form 15F, pursuant to Rule 12h-6(a) (17 CFR 240.12h-6(a)) under the Securities Exchange Act of 1934 ("Exchange Act"), when seeking to terminate:

- *the registration of a class of securities under section 12(g) of the Exchange Act and the corresponding duty to file or furnish reports required by section 13(a) of the Exchange Act; or*
- *the obligation under section 15(d) of the Exchange Act to file or furnish reports required by section 13(a) of the Act regarding a class of equity securities; or*
- *both.*

2. A foreign private issuer may file Form 15F, pursuant to Rule 12h-6(c) (17 CFR 240.12h-6(c)), when seeking to terminate its reporting obligations under section 13(a) or section 15(d) of the Exchange Act regarding a class of debt securities.

3. A foreign private issuer may file Form 15F, pursuant to Rule 12h-6(d) (17 CFR 240.12h-6(d)), when seeking to terminate the registration of a class of securities under section 12(g), or reporting obligations under section 13(a) or section 15(d) of the Exchange Act, to which it has succeeded pursuant to Rule 12g-3 (17 CFR 240.12g-3) or Rule 15d-5 (17 CFR 240.15d-5).

4. A foreign private issuer may file Form 15F, pursuant to Rule 12h-6(i) (17 CFR 240.12h-6(i)), if, before the effective date of Rule 12h-6, it terminated the registration of a class of securities under section 12(g) of the Act, or suspended its reporting obligations regarding a class of equity or debt securities under section 15(d) of the Act, in order to:

- *terminate under Rule 12h-6 the registration of a class of equity securities that was the subject of a Form 15 (§ 249.323 of this chapter) filed by the issuer pursuant to § 240.12g-4; or*
- *terminate its reporting obligations under section 15(d) of the Act, which had been suspended by the terms of that section or by the issuer's filing of a Form 15 pursuant to § 240.12h-3, regarding a class of equity or debt securities.*

B. Certification Effected by Filing Form 15F

By completing and signing this Form, the issuer certifies that:

- *it meets all of the conditions for termination of Exchange Act reporting specified in Rule 12h-6 (17 CFR 240.12h-6); and*
- *there are no classes of securities other than those that are the subject of this Form 15F regarding which the issuer has Exchange Act reporting obligations.*

C. Effective Date

For an issuer filing Form 15F under Rule 12h-6(a), (c) or (d), the duty to file any reports required under section 13(a) or 15(d) of the Exchange Act will be suspended immediately upon filing the Form 15F. If there are no objections from the Commission, 90 days, or within a shorter period as the Commission may determine, after the issuer has filed its Form 15F, there shall take effect:

- *the termination of registration of a class of securities under section 12(g) of the Act;*
- *the termination of the issuer's duty to file or submit reports under section 13(a) or section 15(d) of the Act; or*
- *both.*

For an issuer that has already terminated its registration of a class of equity securities pursuant to Rule 12g-4 or suspended its reporting obligations under section 15(d) or Rule 12h-3, the effectiveness of its termination of section 12(g) registration under Rule 12h-6 and the corresponding duty to file reports required by section 13(a) of the Act, or the termination of its previously suspended reporting obligations under section 15(d) of the Act, shall also occur 90 days after the issuer has filed its Form 15F under Rule 12h-6(i), or within a shorter period as the Commission may determine, if there are no objections from the Commission.

D. Other Filing Requirements

You must file Form 15F and related materials, including correspondence, in electronic format via our Electronic Data Gathering, Analysis, and Retrieval (EDGAR) system in accordance with the EDGAR rules set forth in Regulation S-T (17 CFR Part 232). The Form 15F and related materials must be in the English language as required by Regulation S-T Rule 306 (17 CFR 232.306). You must provide the signature required for Form 15F in accordance with Regulation S-T Rule 302 (17 CFR 232.302). If you have technical questions about EDGAR, call the EDGAR Filer Support Office at (202) 551-8900. If you have questions about the EDGAR rules, call the Office of EDGAR and Information Analysis at (202) 551-3610.

If the Form 15F is subsequently withdrawn or denied, you must, within 60 days after the date of the withdrawal or denial, file with or submit to the Commission all reports that would have been required had you not filed the Form 15F. See Rule 12h-6(g)(2) (17 CFR 240.12h-6(g)(2)) and Rule 12h-6(i)(3)(ii) (17 CFR 240.12h-6(i)(3)(ii)).

E. Rule 12g3-2(b) Exemption

Regardless of the particular Rule 12h-6 provision under which it is proceeding, a foreign private issuer that has filed a Form 15F regarding a class of equity securities shall receive the exemption under Rule 12g3-2(b) (17 CFR 240.12g3-2(b)) for the subject class of equity securities immediately upon the effective date of its termination of registration and reporting under Rule 12h-6. Refer to Rules 12g3-2(b)(2) and (b)(3) (17 CFR 240.12g3-2(b)(2) and (b)(3)) and Rule 12g3-2(c) (17 CFR 240.12g3-2(c)) for the conditions that a foreign private issuer must meet in order to maintain the Rule 12g3-2(b) exemption following its termination of Exchange Act registration and reporting.

PART I

The purpose of this part is to provide information to investors and to assist the Commission in assessing whether you meet the requirements for terminating your Exchange Act reporting under Rule 12h-6. If, pursuant to Rule 12h-6, there is an item that does not apply to you, mark that item as inapplicable.

Item 1. Exchange Act Reporting History

A. State when you first incurred the duty to file reports under section 13(a) or section 15(d) of the Exchange Act.

B. State whether you have filed or submitted all reports required under Exchange Act section 13(a) or section 15(d) and corresponding Commission rules for the 12 months preceding the filing of this form, and whether you have filed at least one annual report under section 13(a).

Instruction to Item 1.

If you are a successor issuer that has filed this Form 15F pursuant to Rule 12h-6(d), and are relying on the reporting history of the issuer to which you have succeeded under Rule 12g-3 (17 CFR 12g-3) or Rule 15d-5 (17 CFR 240.15d-5), identify that issuer and provide the information required by this section for that issuer.

Item 2. Recent United States Market Activity

State when your securities were last sold in the United States in a registered offering under the Securities Act of 1933 (15 U.S.C. 77a *et seq.*) ("Securities Act").

Instructions to Item 2.

1. Do not include registered offerings involving the issuance of securities:

a. to your employees, as that term is defined in Form S-8 (17 CFR 239.16b);

b. by selling security holders in non-underwritten offerings;

c. upon the exercise of outstanding rights granted by the issuer if the rights are granted pro rata to all existing security holders of the class of the issuer's securities to which the rights attach;

d. pursuant to a dividend or interest reinvestment plan; or

e. upon the conversion of outstanding convertible securities or upon the exercise of outstanding transferable warrants issued by the issuer.

However, you must include registered offerings described in paragraphs (c) through (e) of this instruction if undertaken pursuant to a standby underwritten offering or other similar arrangement in the United States.

2. If you have registered equity securities on a shelf or other Securities Act registration statement under which securities remain unsold, disclose the last sale of securities under that registration statement. If no sale has occurred during the preceding 12 months, disclose whether you have filed a post-effective amendment to terminate the registration of unsold securities under that registration statement.

Item 3. Foreign Listing and Primary Trading Market

A. Identify the exchange or exchanges outside the United States, and the foreign jurisdiction in which the exchange or exchanges are located, on which you have maintained a listing of the class of securities that is the subject of this Form, and which, either singly or together with the trading of the same class of the issuer's securities in another foreign jurisdiction, constitutes the primary trading market for those securities.

B. Provide the date of initial listing on the foreign exchange or exchanges identified in response to Item 3.A. In addition, disclose whether you have maintained a listing of the subject class of securities on one or more of those foreign exchanges for at least the 12 months preceding the filing of this Form.

C. Disclose the percentage of trading in the subject class of securities that occurred in the identified jurisdiction or jurisdictions of your foreign listing as of a recent 12-month period.

Instructions to Item 3.

1. When responding to this item, refer to the definition of "primary trading market" in Rule 12h-6(f) (17 CFR 240.12h-6(f)). In accordance with that definition, if your primary trading market consists of two foreign jurisdictions, provide the information required by this section for both foreign jurisdictions. In addition, disclose whether the trading market for your securities in at least one of those two foreign jurisdictions is larger than the trading market for your securities in the United States as of the same recent 12-month period. Disclose the first and last days of that recent 12-month period.

2. For the purpose of the primary trading market determination, you must measure the average daily trading volume of on-exchange transactions in the subject securities aggregated over one or two foreign jurisdictions against your worldwide trading volume. You may include in this measure off-exchange transactions in those jurisdictions comprising the numerator only if you include those off-exchange transactions when calculating worldwide trading volume in the denominator. This denominator should be the same as the denominator used for the trading volume benchmark under Rule 12h-6(a)(4)(i) (17 CFR 240.12h-6(a)(4)(i)) and Item 4 of this Form.

Item 4. Comparative Trading Volume Data

If relying on Rule 12h-6(a)(4)(i), provide the following information:

A. Identify the first and last days of the recent 12-month period used to meet the requirements of that rule provision.

B. For the same recent 12-month period, disclose the average daily trading volume of the class of securities that is the subject of this Form both in the United States and on a worldwide basis.

C. For the same recent 12-month period, disclose the average daily trading volume of the subject class of securities in the United States as a percentage of the average daily trading volume for that class of securities on a worldwide basis.

D. Disclose whether you have delisted the subject class of securities from a national securities exchange or inter-dealer quotation system in the United States. If so, provide the date of delisting, and, as of that date, disclose the average daily trading volume of the subject class of securities in the United States as a percentage of the average daily trading volume for that class of securities on a worldwide basis for the preceding 12-month period.

E. Disclose whether you have terminated a sponsored American depositary receipt (ADR) facility regarding the subject class of securities. If so, provide the date of the ADR facility termination, and, as of that date, disclose the average daily trading volume of the subject class of securities in the United States as a percentage of the average daily trading volume for that class of securities on a worldwide basis for the preceding 12-month period.

F. Identify the sources of the trading volume information used for determining whether you meet the requirements of Rule 12h-6. If you used more than one source, disclose the reasons why you used each source.

Instructions to Item 4.

1. "Recent 12-month period" means a 12-calendar-month period that ended no more than 60

days before the filing date of this form, as defined under Rule 12h-6(f). You may disclose the comparative trading volume data in response to this item in tabular format and attached as an exhibit to this Form.

2. An issuer is ineligible to rely on paragraph (a)(4)(i) of Rule 12h-6 if, as of the date of delisting or termination of an ADR facility, the average daily trading volume of the subject class of securities in the United States exceeded 5 percent of the average daily trading volume of that class of securities on a worldwide basis, as measured over the preceding 12 months, and 12 months has not elapsed from the date of delisting or termination of the ADR facility. See Rule 12h-6(b) (17 CFR 240.12h-6(b)).

3. For purposes of paragraph (a)(4)(i) of Rule 12h-6:

a. when determining your U.S. average daily trading volume, you must include all transactions, whether on-exchange or off-exchange;

b. when determining your worldwide average daily trading volume, in addition to on-exchange transactions, which you must include, you may include off-exchange transactions; and

c. the sources of your trading volume information may include publicly available sources, market data vendors or other commercial information service providers upon which you have reasonably relied in good faith, and as long as the information does not duplicate any other trading volume information obtained from exchanges or other sources.

Item 5. Alternative Record Holder Information

If relying on Rule 12h-6(a)(4)(ii) (17 CFR 240.12h-6(a)(4)(ii)):

Disclose the number of record holders of the subject class of equity securities on a worldwide basis or who are United States residents at a date within 120 days before filing this Form. Disclose the date used for the purpose of Item 5.

Item 6. Debt Securities

If relying on Rule 12h-6(c) (17 CFR 240.12h-6(c)):

Disclose the number of record holders of your debt securities either on a worldwide basis or who are United States residents at a date within 120 days before the date of filing of this Form. Disclose the date used for the purpose of Item 6.

Instructions to Items 5 and 6.

1. When determining the number of record holders of your equity or debt securities who are United States residents, refer to Rule 12h-6(e) (17 CFR 240.12h-6(e)) for the appropriate counting method.

2. If you have relied upon the assistance of an independent information services provider to determine the number of your United States equity or debt securities holders, identify this party in your response.

Item 7. Notice Requirement

If filing Form 15F pursuant to Rule 12h-6(a), (c) or (d):

A. Disclose the date of publication of the notice, required by Rule 12h-6(h) (17 CFR 240.12h-6(h)), disclosing your intent to terminate your duty to file reports under section 13(a) or 15(d) of the Exchange Act or both.

B. Identify the means, such as publication in a particular newspaper or transmission by a particular wire service, used to disseminate the notice in the United States.

Instruction to Item 7.

If you have submitted a copy of the notice under cover of a Form 6-K (17 CFR 249.306), disclose the submission date of the Form 6-K. If not, attach a copy of the notice as an exhibit to this Form. See Rule 12h-6(h).

Item 8. Prior Form 15 Filers

If relying on Rule 12h-6(i):

A. Disclose whether, before the effective date of Rule 12h-6, you filed a Form 15 (17 CFR 249.323) to terminate the registration of a class of equity securities pursuant to Rule 12g-4 (17 CFR 240.12g-4) or to suspend your reporting obligations under section 15(d) of the Act regarding a class of equity or debt securities pursuant to Rule 12h-3 (17 CFR 240.12h-3). If so, disclose the date that you filed the Form 15. If you suspended your reporting obligations by the terms of section 15(d), disclose the effective date of that suspension as well as the date that you filed a Form 15 to notify the Commission of that suspension pursuant to Rule 15d-6 (17 CFR 240.15d-6).

B. If you terminated the registration of a class of securities pursuant to Rule 12g-4 or suspended your reporting obligations pursuant to Rule 12h-3 or by the terms of section 15(d) of the Act regarding a class of equity securities, provide the disclosure required by Item 3 of this Form, "Primary Trading Market." Further provide the disclosure required by Item 4 of this Form, "Comparative Trading Volume Data," or the disclosure required by Item 5 of the Form, "Alternative Record Holder Information."

C. If you suspended your reporting obligations pursuant to Rule 12h-3 or by the terms of section 15(d) of the Act regarding a class of debt securities, provide the disclosure required by Item 6 of this Form, "Debt Securities."

PART II

Item 9. Rule 12g3-2(b) Exemption

Disclose the address of your Internet Web site or of the electronic information delivery system in your primary trading market on which you will publish the information required to maintain the exemption under Rule 12g3-2(b).

Instruction to Item 9.

Refer to Rule 12g3-2(b)(3)(ii) (17 CFR 240.12g3-2(b)(3)(ii)) for instructions regarding providing English translations of documents required to maintain the Rule 12g3-2(b) exemption.

PART III

Item 10. Exhibits

List the exhibits attached to this Form.

Instruction to Item 10.

In addition to exhibits specifically mentioned on this Form, you may attach as an exhibit any document providing information that is material to your eligibility to terminate your reporting obligations under Exchange Act Rule 12h-6. You should refer to any relevant exhibit when responding to the items on this Form.

Item 11. Undertakings

Furnish the following undertaking:

The undersigned issuer hereby undertakes to withdraw this Form 15F if, at any time before the effectiveness of its termination of reporting under Rule 12h-6, it has actual knowledge of information that causes it reasonably to believe that, at the time of filing the Form 15F:

a. The average daily trading volume of its subject class of securities in the United States exceeded 5 percent of the average daily trading volume of that class of securities on a worldwide basis for the same recent 12-month period that the issuer used for purposes of Rule 12h-6(a)(4)(i);

b. Its subject class of securities was held of record by 300 or more United States residents or 300 or more persons worldwide, if proceeding under Rule 12h-6(a)(4)(ii) or Rule 12h-6(c); or

c. It otherwise did not qualify for termination of its Exchange Act reporting obligations under Rule 12h-6.

Instruction to Item 11.

After filing this Form, an issuer has no continuing obligation to make inquiries or perform other work concerning the information contained in this Form, including its assessment of trading volume or ownership of its securities in the United States.

Signature

Pursuant to the requirements of the Securities Exchange Act of 1934, [name of registrant as specified in charter] has duly authorized the undersigned person to sign on its behalf this certification on Form 15F. In so doing, [name of registrant as specified in charter] certifies that, as represented on this Form, it has complied with all of the conditions set forth in Rule 12h-6 for terminating its registration under section 12(g) of the Exchange Act, or its duty to file reports under section 13(a) or section 15(d) of the Exchange Act, or both.

[¶ 33,601]   **FORM 3**

[As last amended in Release No. 33-8830, effective August 10, 2007, 72 F.R. 45110.]

SECURITIES AND EXCHANGE COMMISSION
Washington, D.C. 20549

FORM 3

INITIAL STATEMENT OF BENEFICIAL OWNERSHIP OF SECURITIES

The Commission is authorized to solicit the information required by this form pursuant to sections 16(a) and 23(a) of the Securities Exchange Act of 1934, and Sections 30(h) and 38 of the Investment Company Act of 1940, and the rules and regulations thereunder.

Disclosure of information specified on this form is mandatory. The information will be used for the primary purpose of disclosing the holdings of directors, officers, and beneficial owners of registered companies. Information disclosed will be a matter of public record and available for inspection by members of the public. The Commission can use it in investigations or litigation involving the federal securities laws or other civil, criminal, or regulatory statutes or provisions, as well as for referral to other governmental authorities and self-regulatory organizations. Failure to disclose required information may result in civil or criminal action against persons involved for violations of the federal securities laws and rules.

GENERAL INSTRUCTIONS

1. Who Must File

(a) This Form must be filed by the following persons ("reporting person"):

(i) any director or officer of an issuer with a class of equity securities registered pursuant to Section 12 of the Securities Exchange Act of 1934 ("Exchange Act"); (*Note*: Title is not determinative for purposes of determining "officer" status. *See* Rule 16a-1(f) for the definition of "officer");

(ii) any beneficial owner of greater than 10% of a class of equity securities registered under Section 12 of the Exchange Act, as determined by voting or investment control over the securities pursuant to Rule 16a-1(a)(1) ("ten percent holder");

(iii) any officer or director of a registered holding company pursuant to Section 17(a) of the Public Utility Holding Company Act of 1935;

(iv) any officer, director, member of an advisory board, investment adviser, affiliated person of an investment adviser, or beneficial owner of more than 10% of any class of outstanding securities (other than short-term paper) of a registered closed-end investment company, under Section 30(h) of the Investment Company Act; and

(v) any trust, trustee, beneficiary or settlor required to report pursuant to Rule 16a-8.

(b) If a reporting person is not an officer, director, or 10% holder, the person should check "other" in Item 5 (Relationship of Reporting Person to Issuer) and describe the reason for reporting status in the space provided.

(c) If a person described above does not beneficially own any securities required to be reported (*see* Rule 16a-1 and Instruction 5), the person is required to file this Form and state that no securities are beneficially owned.

2. When Form Must be Filed

(a) This Form must be filed within 10 days after the event by which the person becomes a reporting person (*i.e.*, officer, director, ten percent holder or other person). This Form and any amendment is deemed filed with the Commission or the Exchange on the date it is received by the Commission or the Exchange, respectively. *See*, however, Rule 16a-3(h) regarding delivery to a third party business that guarantees delivery of the filing no later than the specified due date.

(b) A reporting person of an issuer that is registering securities for the first time under Section 12 of the Exchange Act must file this Form no later than the effective date of the registration statement.

(c) A separate Form shall be filed to reflect beneficial ownership of securities of each issuer, except that a single statement shall be filed with respect to the securities of a registered public utility holding company and all of its subsidiary companies.

3. Where Form Must be Filed

(a) A reporting person must file this Form in electronic format via the Commission's Electronic Data Gathering Analysis and Retrieval System

(EDGAR) in accordance with EDGAR rules set forth in Regulation S-T (17 CFR Part 232), except that a filing person that has obtained a hardship exception under Regulation S-T Rule 202 (17 CFR 232.202) may file the Form in paper. For assistance with technical questions about EDGAR or to request an access code, call the EDGAR Filer Support Office at (202) 942-8900. For assistance with questions about the EDGAR rules, call the Office of EDGAR and Information Analysis at (202) 942-2940.

(b) At the time this Form or any amendment is filed with the Commission, file one copy with each Exchange on which any class of securities of the issuer is registered. If the issuer has designated a single Exchange to receive Section 16 filings, the copy shall be filed with that Exchange only.

(c) Any person required to file this Form or amendment shall, not later than the time the Form is transmitted for filing with the Commission, send or deliver a copy to the person designated by the issuer to receive the copy or, if no person is so designated, the issuer's corporate secretary (or person performing similar functions) in accordance with Rule 16a-3(e).

NOTE: If filing pursuant to a hardship exception under Regulation S-T Rule 202 (17 CFR 232.202), file three copies of this Form or any amendment, at least one of which is signed, with the Securities and Exchange Commission, 450 5th Street, NW, Washington, DC 20549. (Acknowledgement of receipt by the Commission may be obtained by enclosing a self-addressed stamped postcard identifying the Form or amendment filed.)

4. Class of Securities Reported

(a) (i) Persons reporting pursuant to Section 16(a) of the Exchange Act shall include information as to their beneficial ownership of any class of equity securities of the issuer, even though one or more of such classes may not be registered pursuant to Section 12 of the Exchange Act.

(ii) Persons reporting pursuant to section 17(a) of the Public Utility Holding Company Act of 1935 shall include information as to their beneficial ownership of any class of securities (equity or debt) of the registered holding company and of all of its subsidiary companies and specify the name of the parent or subsidiary issuing the securities.

(iii) Persons reporting pursuant to Section 30(h) of the Investment Company Act shall include information as to their beneficial ownership of any class of securities (equity or debt) of the registered closed-end investment company (other than "short-term paper" as defined in Section 2(a)(38) of the Investment Company Act).

(b) The title of the security should clearly identify the class, even if the issuer has only one class of securities outstanding; for example, "Common Stock," "Class A Common Stock," "Class B Convertible Preferred Stock," etc.

(c) The amount of securities beneficially owned should state the face amount of debt securities (U.S. Dollars) or the number of equity securities, whichever is appropriate.

5. Holdings Required to be Reported

(a) *General Requirements*

Report holdings of each class of securities of the issuer beneficially owned as of the date of the event requiring the filing of this Form. See Instruction 4 as to securities required to be reported.

(b) *Beneficial Ownership Reported (Pecuniary Interest)*

(i) Although, for purposes of determining status as a ten percent holder, a person is deemed to beneficially own securities over which that person has voting or investment control (*see* Rule 16a-1(a)(1)), for reporting purposes, a person is deemed to be the beneficial owner of securities if that person has or shares the opportunity, directly or indirectly, to profit or share in any profit derived from a transaction in the securities ("pecuniary interest"). *See* Rule 16a-1(a)(2). *See also* Rule 16a-8 for application of the beneficial ownership definition to trust holdings and transactions.

(ii) Both direct and indirect beneficial ownership of securities shall be reported. Securities beneficially owned directly are those held in the reporting person's name or in the name of a bank, broker or nominee for the account of the reporting person. In addition, securities held as joint tenants, tenants in common, tenants by the entirety, or as community property are to be reported as held directly. If a person has a pecuniary interest, by reason of any contract, understanding or relationship (including a family relationship or arrangement), in securities held in the name of another person, that person is an indirect beneficial owner of those securities. *See* Rule 16a-1(a)(2)(ii) for certain indirect beneficial ownerships.

(iii) Report securities beneficially owned directly on a separate line from those beneficially owned indirectly. Report different forms of indirect ownership on separate lines. The nature of indirect ownership shall be stated as specifically as possible; for example, "By Self as Trustee for X," "By Spouse," "By X Trust," "By Y Corporation," etc.

(iv) In stating the amount of securities owned indirectly through a partnership, corporation, trust, or other entity, report the number of securities representing the reporting person's proportionate interest in securities beneficially owned by that entity. Alternatively, at the option of the reporting person, the entire amount of the entity's interest may be reported. *See* Rule 16a-1(a)(2)(ii) (B) and Rule 16a-1(a)(2)(iii).

(v) Where more than one person beneficially owns the same equity securities, such owners may file Form 3 individually or jointly. Joint and group filings may be made by any designated beneficial owner. Holdings of securities owned separately by any joint or group filer are permitted to be included in the joint filing. Indicate only the name and address of the designated filer in Item 1 of Form 3 and attach a list of the names and addresses of each other reporting person. Joint and group filings must include all required information for each beneficial owner, and such filings must be signed by each beneficial owner, or on behalf of such owner by an authorized person.

If this Form is being filed in paper pursuant to a hardship exemption and the space provided for signatures is insufficient, attach a signature page. If this Form is being filed in paper, submit any attached listing of names or signatures on another Form 3, copy of Form 3 or separate page of 8 1/2 by 11 inch white paper, indicate the number of pages comprising the report (Form plus attachments) at the bottom of each report page (*e.g.*, 1 of 3, 2 of 3, 3 of 3), and include the name of the designated filer and information required by Items 2 and 3 of the Form on the attachment.

(c) *Non-Derivative and Derivative Securities*

(i) Report non-derivative securities beneficially owned in Table I and derivative securities (*e.g.*, puts, calls, options, warrants, convertible securities, or other rights or obligations to buy or sell securities) beneficially owned in Table II. Derivative securities beneficially owned that are both equity securities and convertible or exchangeable for other equity securities (*e.g.*, convertible preferred securities) should be reported only on Table II.

(ii) The title of a derivative security and the title of the equity security underlying the derivative security should be shown separately in the appropriate columns in Table II. The "puts" and "calls" reported in Table II include, in addition to separate puts and calls, any combination of the two, such as spreads and straddles. In reporting an option in Table II, state whether it represents a right to buy, a right to sell, an obligation to buy, or an obligation to sell the equity securities subject to the option.

(iii) Describe in the appropriate columns in Table II characteristics of derivative securities, including title, exercise or conversion price, date exercisable, expiration date, and the title and amount of securities underlying the derivative security.

(iv) Securities constituting components of a unit shall be reported separately on the applicable table (*e.g.*, if a unit has a non-derivative security component and a derivative security component, the non-derivative security component shall be reported in Table I and the derivative security component shall be reported in Table II). The relationship between individual securities comprising the unit shall be indicated in the space provided for explanation of responses.

6. Additional Information

(a) If the space provided in the line items on the electronic Form is insufficient, use the space provided for footnotes. If the space provided for footnotes is insufficient, create a footnote that refers to an exhibit to the form that contains the additional information.

(b) If the space provided in the line items on the paper Form or space provided for additional comments is insufficient, attach another Form 3, copy of Form 3 or separate 8 1/2 by 11 inch white paper to Form 3, completed as appropriate to include the additional comments. Each attached page must include information required in Items 1, 2 and 3 of the Form. The number of pages comprising the report (Form plus attachments) shall be indicated at the bottom of each report page (*e.g.*, 1 of 3, 2 of 3, 3 of 3).

(c) If one or more exhibits are included, whether due to a lack of space or because the exhibit is, by nature, a separate document (*e.g.*, a power of attorney), provide a sequentially numbered list of the exhibits in the Form. Use the number "24"for any power of attorney and the number "99" for any other exhibit. If there is more than one of either such exhibit, then use numerical subparts. If the exhibit is being filed as a confirming electronic copy under Regulation S-T Rule 202(d) (17 CFR 232.202(d)), then place the designation "CE" (confirming exhibit) next to the name of the exhibit in the exhibit list. If the exhibit is being filed in paper pursuant to a hardship exception under Regulation S-T Rule 202 (17 CFR 232.202), then place the designation "P'"(paper) next to the name of the exhibit in the exhibit list.

(d) If additional information is not reported as provided in paragraph (a), (b) or (c) of this instruction, whichever apply, it will be assumed that no additional information was provided

7. Signature

(a) If the Form is filed for an individual, it shall be signed by that person or specifically on behalf of the individual by a person authorized to sign for the individual. If signed on behalf of the individual by another person, the authority of such person to sign the Form shall be confirmed to the Commission in writing in an attachment to the Form or as soon as practicable in an amendment by the individual for whom the Form is filed, unless such a confirmation still in effect is on file with the Commission. The confirming statement need only indicate that the reporting person authorizes and designates the named person or persons to file the Form on the reporting person's behalf, and state the duration of the authorization.

(b) If the Form is filed for a corporation, partnership, trust, or other entity, the capacity in which the individual signed shall be set forth. (*e.g.*, John Smith, Secretary, on behalf of X Corporation).

8. Amendments

(a) If this Form is filed as an amendment in order to add one or more lines of ownership information to Table I or Table II of the Form being amended, provide each line being added, together with one or more footnotes, as necessary, to explain the addition of the line or lines. Do not repeat lines of ownership information that were disclosed in the original Form and are not being amended.

(b) If this Form is filed as an amendment in order to amend one or more lines of ownership information that already were disclosed in Table I or Table II of the Form being amended, provide the complete line or lines being amended, as amended, together with one or more footnotes, as necessary, to explain the amendment of the line or lines. Do not repeat lines of ownership information that were disclosed in the original Form and are not being amended.

(c) If this Form is filed as an amendment for any purpose other than or in addition to the purposes described in paragraphs (a) and (b) of this General Instruction 8, provide one or more footnotes, as necessary, to explain the amendment.

FORM 3

UNITED STATES SECURITIES AND EXCHANGE COMMISSION
Washington, D.C. 20549

INITIAL STATEMENT OF BENEFICIAL OWNERSHIP OF SECURITIES

Filed pursuant to Section 16(a) of the Securities Exchange Act of 1934, Section 17(a) of the Public Utility Holding Company Act of 1935 or Section 30(h) of the Investment Company Act

(Print or Type Responses)

1. Name and Address of Reporting Person*	2. Date of Event Requiring Statement (Month/Day/Year)	3. Issuer Name and Ticker or Trading Symbol	
(Last) (First) (Middle)		4. Relationship of Reporting Person(s) to Issuer (Check all applicable)	5. If Amendment, Date Original Filed (Month/Day/Year)
(Street)		___ Director ___ 10% Owner ___ Officer (give title below) ___ Other (specify below)	6. Individual or Joint/Group Filing (Check Applicable Line) ___ Form filed by One Reporting Person ___ Form filed by More than One Reporting Person
(City) (State) (Zip)			

Table I — Non-Derivative Securities Beneficially Owned

1. Title of Security (Instr. 4)	2. Amount of Securities Beneficially Owned (Instr. 4)	3. Ownership Form: Direct (D) or Indirect (I) (Instr. 5)	4. Nature of Indirect Beneficial Ownership (Instr. 5)

Reminder: Report on a separate line for each class of securities beneficially owned directly or indirectly.

* If the form is filed by more than one reporting person, see Instruction 5(b)(v).

FORM 3 (continued)   **Table II — Derivative Securities Beneficially Owned (*e.g.*, puts, calls, warrants, options, convertible securities)**

1. Title of Derivative Security (Instr. 4)	2. Date Exercisable and Expiration Date (Month/Day/Year)		3. Title and Amount of Securities Underlying Derivative Security (Instr. 4)		4. Conversion or Exercise Price of Derivative Security	5. Ownership Form of Derivative Security: Direct (D) or Indirect (I) (Instr. 5)	6. Nature of Indirect Beneficial Ownership (Instr. 5)
	Date Exercisable	Expiration Date	Title	Amount or Number of Shares			

Explanation of Responses:

_____ _____

Signature of Reporting Person   **Date

** Intentional misstatements or omissions of facts constitute Federal Criminal Violations. *See* 18 U.S.C. 1001 and 15 U.S.C. 78ff(a).

Note: File three copies of this Form, one of which must be manually signed. If space is insufficient, *See* Instruction 6 for procedure.

Potential persons who are to respond to the collection of information contained in this form are not required to respond unless the form displays a currently valid OMB Number.

FORM 4

[As last amended in Release No. 33-8830, effective August 10, 2007, 72 F.R. 45110.]

U.S. SECURITIES AND EXCHANGE COMMISSION

Washington, D.C. 20549

FORM 4

STATEMENT OF CHANGES IN BENEFICIAL OWNERSHIP OF SECURITIES

The Commission is authorized to solicit the information required by this form pursuant to Sections 16(a) and 23(a) of the Securities Exchange Act of 1934, and Sections 30(h) and 38 of the Investment Company Act of 1940, and the rules and regulations thereunder.

Disclosure of information specified on this form is mandatory. The information will be used for the primary purpose of disclosing the transactions and holdings of directors, officers, and beneficial owners of registered companies. Information disclosed will be a matter of public record and available for inspection by members of the public. The Commission can use it in investigations or litigation involving the federal securities laws or other civil, criminal, or regulatory statutes or provisions, as well as for referral to other governmental authorities and self-regulatory organizations. Failure to disclose required information may result in civil or criminal action against persons involved for violations of the federal securities laws and rules.

GENERAL INSTRUCTIONS

1. When Form Must be Filed

(a) This Form must be filed before the end of the second business day following the day on which a transaction resulting in a change in beneficial ownership has been executed (see Rule 16a-1(a)(2) and Instruction 4 regarding the meaning of "beneficial owner," and Rule 16a-3(g) regarding determination of the date of execution for specified transactions). This Form and any amendment is deemed filed with the Commission or the Exchange on the date it is received by the Commission or the Exchange, respectively. See, however, Rule 16a-3(h) regarding delivery to a third party business that guarantees delivery of the filing no later than the specified due date.

(b) A reporting person no longer subject to section 16 of the Securities Exchange Act of 1934 ("Exchange Act") must check the exit box appearing on this Form. However, Form 4 and Form 5 obligations may continue to be applicable. *See* Rules 16a-3(f) and 16a-2(b). Form 5 transactions to date may be included on this Form and subsequent Form 5 transactions may be reported on a later Form 4 or Form 5, provided all transactions are reported by the required date.

(c) A separate Form shall be filed to reflect beneficial ownership of securities of each issuer, except that a single statement shall be filed with respect to the securities of a registered public utility holding company and all of its subsidiary companies.

(d) If a reporting person is not an officer, director, or 10% holder, the person should check "other" in Item 6 (Relationship of Reporting Person to Issuer) and describe the reason for reporting status in the space provided.

2. Where Form Must be Filed

(a) A reporting person must file this Form in electronic format via the Commission's Electronic Data Gathering Analysis and Retrieval System (EDGAR) in accordance with EDGAR rules set forth in Regulation S-T (17 CFR Part 232), except that a filing person that has obtained a hardship exception under Regulation S-T Rule 202 (17 CFR 232.202) may file the Form in paper. For assistance with technical questions about EDGAR or to request an access code, call the EDGAR Filer Support Office at (202) 942-8900. For assistance with questions about the EDGAR rules, call the Office of EDGAR and Information Analysis at (202) 942-2940.

(b) At the time this Form or any amendment is filed with the Commission, file one copy with each Exchange on which any class of securities of the issuer is registered. If the issuer has designated a single Exchange to receive Section 16 filings, the copy shall be filed with that Exchange only.

(c) Any person required to file this Form or amendment shall, not later than the time the Form or amendment is transmitted for filing with the Commission, send or deliver a copy to the person designated by the issuer to receive the copy or, if no person is so designated, the issuer's corporate secretary (or person performing similar functions) in accordance with Rule 16a-3(e).

NOTE: If filing pursuant to a hardship exception under Regulation S-T Rule 202 (17 CFR 232.202), file three copies of this Form or any amendment, at least one of which is signed, with the Securities and Exchange Commission, 450 5th Street, NW, Washington, DC 20549. (Acknowledgement of receipt by the Commission may be obtained by enclosing a self-addressed stamped postcard identifying the Form or amendment filed.)

3. Class of Securities Reported

(a) (i) Persons reporting pursuant to Section 16(a) of the Exchange Act must report each transaction resulting in a change in beneficial ownership of any class of equity securities of the issuer and the beneficial ownership of that class of securities following the reported transaction(s), even though one or more of such classes may not be registered pursuant to Section 12 of the Exchange Act.

(ii) Persons reporting pursuant to Section 17(a) of the Public Utility Holding Company Act of 1935 must report each transaction resulting in a change in beneficial ownership of any class of securities (equity or debt) of the registered holding company and all of its subsidiary companies and the beneficial ownership of that class of securities following the reported transaction(s). Specify the name of the parent or subsidiary issuing the securities.

(iii) Persons reporting pursuant to Section 30(h) of the Investment Company Act of 1940 must report each transaction resulting in a change in beneficial ownership of any class of securities (equity or debt) of the registered closed-end investment company (other than "short-term paper" as defined in Section 2(a)(38) of the Investment Company Act) and the beneficial ownership of that class of securities following the reported transaction(s).

(b) The title of the security should clearly identify the class, even if the issuer has only one class of securities outstanding; for example, "Common Stock," "Class A Common Stock," "Class B Convertible Preferred Stock," etc.

(c) The amount of securities beneficially owned should state the face amount of debt securities (U.S. Dollars) or the number of equity securities, whichever is appropriate.

4. Transactions and Holdings Required to be Reported

(a) *General Requirements*

(i) Report, in accordance with Rule 16a-3(g): (1) all transactions not exempt from Section 16(b);

(2) all transactions exempt from Section 16(b) pursuant to §240.16b-3(d), §240.16b-3(e), or §240.16b-3(f); and (3) all exercises and conversions of derivative securities, regardless of whether exempt from Section 16(b) of the Act. Every transaction must be reported even though acquisitions and dispositions are equal. Report total beneficial ownership following the reported transaction(s) for each class of securities in which a transaction was reported.

Note: The amount of securities beneficially owned following the reported transaction(s) specified in Column 5 of Table I and Column 9 of Table II should reflect holdings reported or required to be reported by the date of the Form. Transactions and holdings eligible for deferred reporting on Form 5 need not be reflected in the month end total unless the transactions were reported earlier or are included on this Form.

(ii) Each transaction should be reported on a separate line. Transaction codes specified in Instruction 8 should be used to identify the nature of the transaction resulting in an acquisition or disposition of a security. A deemed execution date must be reported in Column 2A of Table I or Column 3A of Table II only if the execution date for the transaction is calculated pursuant to §240.16a-3(g)(2) or §240.16a-3(g)(3).

Note: Transactions reportable on Form 5 may, at the option of the reporting person, be reported on a Form 4 filed before the due date of the Form 5. (*See* Instruction 8 for the code for voluntarily reported transactions.)

(b) *Beneficial Ownership Reported (Pecuniary Interest)*

(i) Although for purposes of determining status as a ten percent holder, a person is deemed to beneficially own securities over which that person has voting or investment control (*see* Rule 16a-1(a)(1)), for reporting transactions and holdings, a person is deemed to be the beneficial owner of securities if that person has or shares the opportunity, directly or indirectly, to profit or share in any profit derived from a transaction in the securities ("pecuniary interest"). *See* Rule 16a-1(a)(2). *See also* Rule 16a-8 for the application of the beneficial ownership definition to trust holdings and transactions.

(ii) Both direct and indirect beneficial ownership of securities shall be reported. Securities beneficially owned directly are those held in the reporting person's name or in the name of a bank, broker or nominee for the account of the reporting person. In addition, securities held as joint tenants, tenants in common, tenants by the entirety, or as community property are to be reported as held directly. If a person has a pecuniary interest, by reason of any contract, understanding, or relationship (including a family relationship or arrangement), in securities held in the name of another person, that person is an indirect beneficial owner of the securities. *See* Rule 16a-1(a)(2)(ii) for certain indirect beneficial ownerships.

(iii) Report transactions in securities beneficially owned directly on separate lines from those beneficially owned indirectly. Report different forms of indirect ownership on separate lines. The nature of indirect ownership shall be stated as specifically as possible; for example, "By Self as Trustee for X," "By Spouse," "By X Trust," "By Y Corporation," etc.

(iv) In stating the amount of securities acquired, disposed of, or beneficially owned indirectly through a partnership, corporation, trust, or other entity, report the number of securities representing the reporting person's proportionate interest in transactions conducted by that entity or holdings of that entity. Alternatively, at the option of the reporting person, the entire amount of the entity's interest may be reported. *See* Rule 16a-1(a)(2)(ii)(B) and Rule 16a-1(a)(2)(iii).

(v) Where more than one beneficial owner of the same equity securities must report the same transaction on Form 4, such owners may file Form 4 individually or jointly. Joint and group filings may be made by any designated beneficial owner. Transactions with respect to securities owned separately by any joint or group filer are permitted to be included in the joint filing. Indicate only the name and address of the designated filer in Item 1 of Form 4 and attach a list of the names and addresses of each other reporting person. Joint and group filings must include all required information for each beneficial owner, and such filings must be signed by each beneficial owner, or on behalf of such owner by an authorized person.

If this Form is being filed in paper pursuant to a hardship exemption and the space provided for signatures is insufficient, attach a signature page. If this Form is being filed in paper, submit any attached listing of names or signatures on another Form 4, copy of Form 4 or separate page of 8 1/2 by 11 inch white paper, indicate the number of pages comprising the report (Form plus attachments) at the bottom of each report page (*e.g.*, 1 of 3, 2 of 3, 3 of 3), and include the name of the designated filer and information required by Items 2 and 3 of the Form on the attachment.

See Rule 16a-3(i) regarding signatures.

(c) *Non-Derivative and Derivative Securities*

(i) Report acquisitions or dispositions and holdings of non-derivative securities in Table I. Report acquisitions or dispositions and holdings of derivative securities (*e.g.*, puts, calls, options, warrants, convertible securities, or other rights or obligations to buy or sell securities) in Table II. Report the exercise or conversion of a derivative

security in Table II (as a disposition of the derivative security) and report in Table I the holdings of the underlying security. Report acquisitions or dispositions and holdings of derivative securities that are both equity securities and convertible or exchangeable for other equity securities (*e.g.*, convertible preferred securities) only on Table II.

(ii) The title of a derivative security and the title of the equity security underlying the derivative security should be shown separately in the appropriate columns in Table II. The "puts" and "calls" reported in Table II include, in addition to separate puts and calls, any combination of the two, such as spreads and straddles. In reporting an option in Table II, state whether it represents a right to buy, a right to sell, an obligation to buy, or an obligation to sell the equity securities subject to the option.

(iii) Describe in the appropriate columns in Table II characteristics of derivative securities, including title, exercise or conversion price, date exercisable, expiration date, and the title and amount of securities underlying the derivative security. If the transaction reported is a purchase or sale of a derivative security, the purchase or sale price of that derivative security shall be reported in column 8. If the transaction is the exercise or conversion of a derivative security, leave column 8 blank and report the exercise or conversion price of the derivative security in column 2.

(iv) Securities constituting components of a unit shall be reported separately on the applicable table (*e.g.*, if a unit has a non-derivative security component and a derivative security component, the non-derivative security component shall be reported in Table I and the derivative security component shall be reported in Table II). The relationship between individual securities comprising the unit shall be indicated in the space provided for explanation of responses. When securities are purchased or sold as a unit, state the purchase or sale price per unit and other required information regarding the unit securities.

5. Price of Securities

(a) Prices of securities shall be reported in U.S. dollars on a per share basis, not an aggregate basis, except that the aggregate price of debt shall be stated. Amounts reported shall exclude brokerage commissions and other costs of execution.

(b) If consideration other than cash was paid for the security, describe the consideration, including the value of the consideration, in the space provided for explanation of responses.

6. Additional Information

(a) If the space provided in the line items on the electronic Form is insufficient, use the space provided for footnotes. If the space provided for footnotes is insufficient, create a footnote that refers to an exhibit to the form that contains the additional information

(b) If the space provided in the line items on the paper Form or space provided for additional comments is insufficient, attach another Form 4, copy of Form 4 or separate 8 1/2 by 11 inch white paper to Form 4, completed as appropriate to include the additional comments. Each attached page must include information required in Items 1, 2 and 3 of the Form. The number of pages comprising the report (Form plus attachments) shall be indicated at the bottom of each report page (*e.g.* 1 of 3, 2 of 3, 3 of 3).

(c) If one or more exhibits are included, whether due to a lack of space or because the exhibit is, by nature, a separate document (*e.g.*, a power of attorney), provide a sequentially numbered list of the exhibits in the Form. Use the number ``24'' for any power of attorney and the number "99" for any other exhibit. If there is more than one of either such exhibit, then use numerical subparts. If the exhibit is being filed as a confirming electronic copy under Regulation S-T Rule 202(d) (17 CFR 232.202(d)), then place the designation ``CE'' (confirming exhibit) next to the name of the exhibit in the exhibit list. If the exhibit is being filed in paper pursuant to a hardship exception under Regulation S-T Rule 202 (17 CFR 232.202), then place the designation ``P'' (paper) next to the name of the exhibit in the exhibit list.

(d) If additional information is not reported as provided in paragraph (a), (b) or (c) of this instruction, whichever apply, it will be assumed that no additional information was provided.

7. Signature

(a) If the Form is filed for an individual, it shall be signed by that person or specifically on behalf of the individual by a person authorized to sign for the individual. If signed on behalf of the individual by another person, the authority of such person to sign the Form shall be confirmed to the Commission in writing in an attachment to the Form or as soon as practicable in an amendment by the individual for whom the Form is filed, unless such a confirmation still in effect is on file with the Commission. The confirming statement need only indicate that the reporting person authorizes and designates the named person or persons to file the Form on the reporting person's behalf, and state the duration of the authorization.

(b) If the Form is filed for a corporation, partnership, trust, or other entity, the capacity in which the individual signed shall be set forth (*e.g.*, John Smith, Secretary, on behalf of X Corporation).

8. Transaction Codes

Use the codes listed below to indicate in Table I, Column 3 and Table II, Column 4 the character of the transaction reported. Use the code that most appropriately describes the transaction. If the transaction is not specifically listed, use transaction Code "J" and describe the nature of the transaction in the space for explanation of responses. If a transaction is voluntarily reported earlier than required, place "V" in the appropriate column to so indicate; otherwise, the column should be left blank. If a transaction involves an equity swap or instrument with similar characteristics, use transaction Code "K" in addition to the code(s) that most appropriately describes the transaction, *e.g.*, "S/K" or "P/K."

General Transaction Codes

P - Open market or private purchase of non-derivative or derivative security

S - Open market or private sale of non-derivative or derivative security

V - Transaction voluntarily reported earlier than required

Rule 16b-3 Transaction Codes

A - Grant, award or other acquisition pursuant to Rule 16b3(d)

D - Disposition to the issuer of issuer equity securities pursuant to Rule 16b-3(e)

F - Payment of exercise price or tax liability by delivering or withholding securities incident to the receipt, exercise, or vesting of a security issued in accordance with Rule 16b-3

I - Discretionary transaction in accordance with Rule 16b3(f) resulting in acquisition or disposition of issuer securities

M - Exercise or conversion of derivative security exempted pursuant to Rule 16b-3

Derivative Securities Codes (Except for transactions exempted pursuant to Rule 16b-3)

C - Conversion of derivative security

E - Expiration of short derivative position

H - Expiration (or cancellation) of long derivative position with value received

O - Exercise of out-of-the-money derivative security

X - Exercise of in-the-money or at-the-money derivative security

Other Section 16(b) Exempt Transactions and Small Acquisition Codes (except for Rule 16b-3 codes above)

G - Bona fide gift

L - Small acquisition under Rule 16a-6

W - Acquisition or disposition by will or laws of descent and distribution

Z - Deposit into or withdrawal from voting trust

Other Transaction Codes

J - Other acquisition or disposition (describe transaction)

K - Transaction in equity swap or instrument with similar characteristics

U - Disposition pursuant to a tender of shares in a change of control transaction

9. Amendments

(a) If this Form is filed as an amendment in order to add one or more lines of transaction information to Table I or Table II of the Form being amended, provide each line being added, together with one or more footnotes, as neces-sary, to explain the addition of the line or lines. Do not repeat lines of transaction information that were disclosed in the original Form and are not being amended.

(b) If this Form is filed as an amendment in order to amend one or more lines of transaction information that already were disclosed in Table I or Table II of the Form being amended, provide the complete line or lines being amended, as amended, together with one or more footnotes, as necessary, to explain the amendment of the line or lines. Do not repeat lines of transaction informa-tion that were disclosed in the original Form and are not being amended.

(c) If this Form is filed as an amendment for any purpose other than or in addition to the pur-poses described in paragraphs (a) and (b) of this General Instruction 9, provide one or more foot-notes, as necessary, to explain the amendment.

Form 4

FORM 4

☐ Check this box if no longer subject to Section 16. Form 4 or Form 5 obligations may continue. *See* Instruction 1(b).

UNITED STATES SECURITIES AND EXCHANGE COMMISSION
Washington, D.C. 20549

STATEMENT OF CHANGES IN BENEFICIAL OWNERSHIP OF SECURITIES

Filed pursuant to Section 16(a) of the Securities Exchange Act of 1934, Section 17(a) of the Public Utility Holding Company Act of 1935 or Section 30(h) of the Investment Company Act of 1940

Print or Type Responses

1. Name and Address of Reporting Person*		2. Issuer Name and Ticker or Trading Symbol	5. Relationship of Reporting Person(s) to Issuer (Check all applicable)
(Last)	(First)		____ Director ____ 10% Owner
	(Middle)	3. Date of Earliest Transaction Required to be Reported (Month/Year)	____ Officer (give title below) ____ Other (specify below)
(Street)			
(City)	(State)	(Zip)	4. If Amendment, Date Original Filed (Month/Day/Year)	6. Individual or Joint/Group Filing (Check Applicable Line) ____ Form filed by One Reporting Person ____ Form filed by More than One Reporting Person

Table I — Non-Derivative Securities Acquired, Disposed of, or Beneficially Owned

1. Title of Security (Instr. 3)	2. Transaction Date (Month/Day/Year)	2A. Deemed Execution Date, if any (Month/Day/Year)	3. Transaction Code (Instr. 8)		4. Securities Acquired (A) or Disposed of (D) (Instr. 3, 4 and 5)			5. Amount of Securities Beneficially Owned Following Reported Transaction(s) (Instr. 3 and 4)	6. Ownership Form: Direct (D) or Indirect (I) (Instr. 4)	7. Nature of Indirect Beneficial Ownership (Instr. 4)
			Code	V	Amount	(A) or (D)	Price			

Reminder: Report on a separate line for each class of securities beneficially owned directly or indirectly.

* If the form is filed by more than one reporting person, *see* Instruction 4(b)(v).

(Over)

FORM 4 (continued)

Table II — Derivative Securities Acquired, Disposed of, or Beneficially Owned
(e.g. puts, calls, warrants, options, convertible securities)

1. Title of Derivative Security (Instr. 3)	2. Conversion or Exercise Price of Derivative Security	3. Transaction Date (Month/Day/Year)	3A. Deemed Execution Date, if any (Month/Day/Year)	4. Transaction Code (Instr. 8)		5. Number of Derivative Securities Acquired (A) or Disposed of (D) (Instr. 3, 4, and 5)		6. Date Exercisable and Expiration Date (Month/Day/Year)		7. Title and Amount of Underlying Securities (Instr. 3 and 4)		8. Price of Derivative Security (Instr. 5)	9. Number of derivative Securities Beneficially Owned Following Reported Transaction(s) (Instr. 4)	10. Ownership Form of Derivative Security Direct (D) or Indirect (I) (Instr. 4)	11. Nature of Indirect Beneficial Ownership (Instr. 4)
				Code	V	(A)	(D)	Date Exercisable	Expiration Date	Title	Amount or Number of Shares				

Explanation of Responses:

_____
**Signature of Reporting Person   Date

*** Intentional misstatements or omissions of facts constitute Federal Criminal Violations. See 18 U.S.C. 1001 and 15 U.S.C. 78ff(a).

Note: File three copies of this Form, one of which must be manually signed. If space is insufficient, see Instruction 6 for procedure.

Potential persons who are to respond to the collection of information contained in this form are not required to respond unless the form displays a currently valid OMB Number.

[¶ 33,621]   **FORM 5**

[As last amended in Release No. 33-8830, effective August 10, 2007, 72 F.R. 45110.]

U.S. SECURITIES AND EXCHANGE COMMISSION
Washington, D.C. 20549

FORM 5

ANNUAL STATEMENT OF BENEFICIAL OWNERSHIP OF SECURITIES

The Commission is authorized to solicit the information required by this form pursuant to Sections 16(a) and 23(a) of the Securities Exchange Act of 1934, and Sections 30(h) and 38 of the Investment Company Act of 1940, and the rules and regulations thereunder.

Disclosure of information specified on this form is mandatory. The information will be used for the primary purpose of disclosing the transactions and holdings of directors, officers, and beneficial owners of registered companies. Information disclosed will be a matter of public record and available for inspection by members of the public. The Commission can use it in investigations or litigation involving the federal securities laws or other civil, criminal, or regulatory statutes or provisions, as well as for referral to other governmental authorities and self-regulatory organizations. Failure to disclose required information may result in civil or criminal action against persons involved for violations of the federal securities laws and rules.

GENERAL INSTRUCTIONS

1. When Form Must be Filed

(a) This Form must be filed on or before the 45th day after the end of the issuer's fiscal year in accordance with Rule 16a-3(f). This Form and any amendment is deemed filed with the Commission or the Exchange on the date it is received by the Commission or the Exchange, respectively. *See*, however, Rule 16a-3(h) regarding delivery to a third party business that guarantees delivery of the filing no later than the specified due date.

(b) A reporting person no longer subject to Section 16 of the Securities Exchange Act of 1934 ("Exchange Act") must check the exit box appearing on this Form. Transactions and holdings previously reported are not required to be included on this Form. Form 4 or Form 5 obligations may continue to be applicable. *See* Rules 16a-3(f) and 16a-2(b).

(c) A separate Form shall be filed to reflect beneficial ownership of securities of each issuer, except that a single statement shall be filed with respect to the securities of a registered public utility holding company and all of its subsidiary companies.

(d) If a reporting person is not an officer, director, or 10% holder, the person should check "other" in Item 6 (Relationship of Reporting Person to Issuer) and describe the reason for reporting status in the space provided.

2. Where Form Must be Filed

(a) A reporting person must file this Form in electronic format via the Commission's Electronic Data Gathering Analysis and Retrieval System (EDGAR) in accordance with EDGAR rules set forth in Regulation S-T (17 CFR Part 232), except that a filing person that has obtained a hardship exception under Regulation S-T Rule 202 (17 CFR 232.202) may file the Form in paper. For assistance with technical questions about EDGAR or to request an access code, call the EDGAR Filer Support Office at (202) 942-8900. For assistance with questions about the EDGAR rules, call the Office of EDGAR and Information Analysis at (202) 942-2940.

(b) At the time this Form or any amendment is filed with the Commission, file one copy with each Exchange on which any class of securities of the issuer is registered. If the issuer has designated a single Exchange to receive Section 16 filings, the copy shall be filed with that Exchange only.

(c) Any person required to file this Form or amendment shall, not later than the time the Form or amendment is transmitted for filing with the Commission, send or deliver a copy to the person designated by the issuer to receive the copy or, if no person is so designated, the issuer's corporate secretary (or person performing similar functions) in accordance with Rule 16a-3(e).

NOTE: If filing pursuant to a hardship exception under Regulation S-T Rule 202 (17 CFR 232.202), file three copies of this Form or any amendment, at least one of which is signed, with the Securities and Exchange Commission, 450 5th Street, NW, Washington, DC 20549. (Acknowledgement of receipt by the Commission may be obtained by enclosing a self-addressed stamped postcard identifying the Form or amendment filed.)

3. Class of Securities Reported

(a)(i) Persons reporting pursuant to Section 16(a) of the Exchange Act shall include information as to transactions and holdings required to be reported in any class of equity securities of the issuer and the beneficial ownership at the end of the year of that class of equity securities, even though one or more of such classes may not be registered pursuant to Section 12 of the Exchange Act.

(ii) Persons reporting pursuant to Section 17(a) of the Public Utility Holding Company Act of 1935 shall include transactions and holdings required to be reported in any class of securities (equity or debt) of the registered holding company and any of its subsidiary companies and the beneficial ownership at the end of the issuer's fiscal year of that class of securities. Specify the name of the parent or subsidiary issuing the securities.

(iii) Persons reporting pursuant to Section 30(h) of the Investment Company Act shall include transactions and holdings required to be reported in any class of securities (equity or debt) of the registered closed-end investment company (other than "short-term paper" as defined in Section 2(a)(38) of the Act) and the beneficial ownership at the end of the year of that class of securities.

(b) The title of the security should clearly identify the class, even if the issuer has only one class of securities outstanding; for example, "Common Stock," "Class A Common Stock," "Class a Convertible Preferred Stock," etc.

(c) The amount of securities beneficially owned should state the face amount of debt securities (U.S. Dollars) or the number of equity securities, whichever is appropriate.

4. Transactions and Holdings Required to Be Reported

(a) *General Requirements*

(i) Pursuant to Rule 16a-3(f), if not previously reported, the following transactions, and total beneficial ownership as of the end of the issuer's fiscal year (or the earlier date applicable to a person ceasing to be an insider during the fiscal year) for any class of securities for which a transaction is reported, shall be reported:

(A) any transaction during the issuer's most recent fiscal year that was exempt from Section

16(b) of the Act, except: (1) any transaction exempt from Section 16(b) pursuant to § 240.16b-3(d), § 240.16b-3(e), or § 240.16b-3(f) (these are required to be reported on Form 4); (2) any exercise or conversion of derivative securities exempt under either § 240.16b-3 or § 240.16b-6(b) (these are required to be reported on Form 4); (3) any transaction exempt from Section 16(b) of the Act pursuant to § 240.16b-3(c), which is exempt from Section 16(a) of the Act; and (4) any transaction exempt from Section 16 of the Act pursuant to another Section 16(a) rule;

(B) any small acquisition or series of acquisitions in a six month period during the issuer's fiscal year not exceeding $10,000 in market value (*see* Rule 16a-6); and

(C) any transactions or holdings that should have been reported during the issuer's fiscal year on a Form 3 or Form 4, but were not reported. The first Form 5 filing obligation shall include all holdings and transactions that should have been reported in each of the issuer's last two fiscal years but were not. *See* Instruction 8 for the code to identify delinquent Form 3 holdings or Form 4 transactions reported on this Form 5.

Note: A required Form 3 or Form 4 must be filed within the time specified by the Form. Form 3 holdings or Form 4 transactions reported on Form 5 represent delinquent Form 3 and Form 4 filings.

(ii) Each transaction should be reported on a separate line. Transaction codes specified in Instruction 8 should be used to identify the nature of the transaction resulting in an acquisition or disposition of a security. A deemed execution date must be reported in Column 2A of Table I or Column 3A of Table II only if the execution date for the transaction is calculated pursuant to § 240.16a-3(g)(2) or § 240.16a-3(g)(3).

(iii) Every transaction shall be reported even though acquisitions and dispositions with respect to a class of securities are equal. Report total beneficial ownership as of the end of the issuer's fiscal year for all classes of securities in which a transaction was reported.

(b) *Beneficial Ownership Reported (Pecuniary Interest)*

(i) Although, for purposes of determining status as a ten percent holder, a person is deemed to beneficially own securities over which that person has voting or investment control (*see* Rule 16a-1(a)(1)), for reporting transactions and holdings, a person is deemed to be the beneficial owner of securities if that person has or shares the opportunity, directly or indirectly, to profit or share in any profit derived from a transaction in the securities ("pecuniary interest"). *See* Rule 16a-1(a)(2). *See also* Rule 16a-8 for the application of the beneficial ownership definition to trust holdings and transactions.

(ii) Both direct and indirect beneficial ownership of securities shall be reported. securities beneficially owned directly are those held in the reporting person's name or in the name of a bank, broker or nominee for the account of the reporting person. In addition, securities held as joint tenants, tenants in common, tenants by the entirety, or as community property are to be reported as held directly. If a person has a pecuniary interest, by reason of any contract, understanding, or relationship (including a family relationship or arrangement), in securities held in the name of another person, that person is an indirect beneficial owner of the securities. *See* Rule 16a-1(a)(2)(ii) for certain indirect beneficial ownerships.

(iii) Report transactions in securities beneficially owned directly on separate lines from those beneficially owned indirectly. Report different forms of indirect ownership on separate lines. The nature of indirect ownership shall be stated as specifically as possible; for example, "By Self as Trustee for X," "By Spouse," "By X Trust," "By Y Corporation," etc.

(iv) In stating the amount of securities acquired, disposed of, or beneficially owned indirectly through a partnership, corporation, trust, or other entity, report the number of securities representing the reporting person's proportionate interest in transactions conducted by that entity or holdings of that entity. Alternatively, at the option of the reporting person, the entire amount of the entity's interest may be reported. *See* Rule 16a-1(a)(2)(ii)(B) and Rule 16a-1(a)(2)(iii).

(v) Where more than one beneficial owner of the same equity securities must report the same transaction or holding on Form 5, such owners may file Form 5 individually or jointly. Joint and group filings may be made by any designated beneficial owner. Transactions and holdings with respect to securities owned separately by any joint or group filer are permitted to be included in the joint filing. Indicate only the name and address of the designated filer in Item 1 of Form 5 and attach a list of the names and addresses of each other reporting person. Joint and group filings must include all required information for each beneficial owner, and such filings must be signed by each beneficial owner, or on behalf of such owner by an authorized person.

If this Form is being filed in paper pursuant to a hardship exemption and the space provided for signatures is insufficient, attach a signature page. If this Form is being filed in paper, submit any attached listing of names or signatures on another Form 5, copy of Form 5 or separate page of 8 1/2 by 11 inch white paper, indicate the number of pages comprising the report (Form plus attachments) at the bottom of each report page (*e.g.*, 1 of 3, 2 of 3, 3 of 3), and include the name of the designated filer and information required by Items 2 and 3 of the Form on the attachment.

See Rule 16a-3(i) regarding signatures.

(c) *Non-Derivative and Derivative Securities*

(i) Report acquisitions or dispositions and holdings of non-derivative securities in Table I. Report acquisitions or dispositions and holdings of derivative securities (*e.g.*, puts, calls, options, warrants, convertible securities, or other rights or obligations to buy or sell securities) in Table II. Report the exercise or conversion of a derivative security in Table II (as a disposition of the derivative security) and report in Table I the holdings of the underlying security. Report acquisitions or dispositions and holdings of derivative securities that are both equity securities and convertible or exchangeable for other equity securities (*e.g.*, convertible preferred securities) only on Table II.

(ii) The title of a derivative security and the title of the equity security underlying the derivative security should be shown separately in the appropriate columns in Table II. The "puts" and "calls" reported in Table II include, in addition to separate puts and calls, any combination of the two, such as spreads and straddles. In reporting an option in Table II, state whether it represents a right to buy, a right to sell, an obligation to buy, or an obligation to sell the equity securities subject to the option.

(iii) Describe in the appropriate columns in Table II characteristics of derivative securities, including title, exercise or conversion price, date exercisable, expiration date, and the title and amount of securities underlying the derivative security. If the transaction reported is a purchase or sale of a derivative security, the purchase or sale price of the derivative security shall be reported in column 8. If the transaction is the exercise or conversion of a derivative security, leave column 8 blank and report the exercise or conversion price of the derivative security in column 2.

(iv) Securities constituting components of a unit shall be reported separately on the applicable table (*e.g.*, if a unit has a non-derivative security component and a derivative security component, the non-derivative security component shall be reported in Table I and the derivative security component shall be reported in Table II). The relationship between individual securities comprising the unit shall be indicated in the space provided for explanation of responses. When securities are purchased or sold as a unit, state the purchase or sale price per unit and other required information regarding the unit securities.

5. Price of Securities

(a) Prices of securities shall be reported in U.S. dollars and on a per share basis, not an aggregate basis, except that the aggregate price of debt shall be stated. Amounts reported shall exclude brokerage commissions and other costs of execution.

(b) If consideration other than cash was paid for the security, describe the consideration, including the value of the consideration in the space provided for explanation of responses.

6. Additional Information

(a) If the space provided in the line items on the electronic Form is insufficient, use the space provided for footnotes. If the space provided for footnotes is insufficient, create a footnote that refers to an exhibit to the form that contains the additional information.

(b) If the space provided in the line items on the paper Form or space provided for additional comments is insufficient, attach another Form 5, copy of Form 5 or separate 8 1/2 by 11 inch white paper to Form 5, completed as appropriate to include the additional comments. Each attached page must include information required in Items 1, 2 and 3 of the Form. The number of pages comprising the report (Form plus attachments) shall be indicated at the bottom of each report page (*e.g.*, 1 of 3, 2 of 3, 3 of 3).

(c) If one or more exhibits are included, whether due to a lack of space or because the exhibit is, by nature, a separate document (*e.g.*, a power of attorney), provide a sequentially numbered list of the exhibits in the Form. Use the number "24" for any power of attorney and the number "99" for any other exhibit. If there is more than one of either such exhibit, then use numerical subparts. If the exhibit is being filed as a confirming electronic copy under Regulation S-T Rule 202(d) (17 CFR 232.202(d)), then place the designation "CE"(confirming exhibit) next to the name of the exhibit in the exhibit list. If the exhibit is being filed in paper pursuant to a hardship exception under Regulation S-T Rule 202 (17 CFR 232.202), then place the designation "P" (paper) next to the name of the exhibit in the exhibit list.

(d) If additional information is not reported as provided in paragraph (a), (b) or (c) of this instruction, whichever apply, it will be assumed that no additional information was provided.

7. Signature

(a) If the Form is filed for an individual, it shall be signed by that person or specifically on behalf of the individual by a person authorized to sign for the individual. If signed on behalf of the individual by another person, the authority of such person to sign the Form shall be confirmed to the Commission in writing in an attachment to the Form or as soon as practicable in an amendment by the individual for whom the Form is filed, unless such a confirmation still in effect is on file with the Commission. The confirming statement need only yindicate that the reporting person authorizes and designates the named person or persons to file the Form on the reporting person's behalf, and state the duration of the authorization.

(b) If the Form is filed for a corporation, partnership, trust, or other entity, the capacity in which the individual signed shall be set forth (*e.g.*, John Smith, Secretary, on behalf of X Corporation).

8. Transaction Codes

Use the codes listed below to indicate in Table I, Column 3 and Table II, Column 4 the character of the transaction reported. Use the code that most appropriately describes the transaction. If the transaction is not specifically listed, use transaction Code "J" and describe the nature of the transaction in the space for explanation of responses. If a transaction involves an equity swap or instrument with similar characteristics, use transaction Code "K" in addition to the code(s) that most appropriately describes the transaction, e.g., "S/K" or "P/K."

General Transaction Codes

P—Open market or private purchase of non-derivative or derivative security

S—Open market or private sale of non-derivative or derivative security

Rule 16b-3 Transaction Codes

A—Grant, award or other acquisition transaction pursuant to Rule 16b-3(d)

D—Disposition to the issuer of issuer equity securities pursuant to Rule 16b-3(e)

F—Payment of exercise price or tax liability by delivering or withholding securities incident to the receipt, exercise or vesting of a security issued in accordance with Rule 16b-3

I—Discretionary transaction in accordance with Rule 16b3(f) resulting in acquisition or disposition of issuer securities

M—Exercise or conversion of derivative security exempted pursuant to Rule 16b-3

Derivative Securities Codes (Except for transactions exempted pursuant to Rule 16b-3)

C—Conversion of derivative security

E—Expiration of short derivative position

H—Expiration (or cancellation) of long derivative position with value received

O—Exercise of out-of-the-money derivative security

X—Exercise of in-the-money or at-the-money derivative security

Other Section 16(b) Exempt Transactions and Small Acquisition Codes (except for Rule 16b-3 codes above)

G—Bona fide gift

L—Small acquisition under Rule 16a-6

W—Acquisition or disposition by will or the laws of descent and distribution

Z—Deposit into or withdrawal from voting trust

Other Transaction Codes

J—Other acquisition or disposition (describe transaction)

K—Transaction in equity swap or instrument with similar characteristics

U—Disposition pursuant to a tender of shares in a change of control transaction

Form 3 or Form 4 Holdings or transactions Not Previously Reported

To indicate that a holding should have been reported previously on Form 3, place a "3" in Table I, column 3 or Table II, column 4, as appropriate. Indicate in the space provided for explanation of responses the event triggering the Form 3 filing obligation. To indicate that a transaction should have been reported previously on Form 4, place a "4" next to the transaction code reported in Table I, column 3 or Table II, column 4 (*e.g.*, an open market purchase of a non-derivative security

that should have been reported previously on Form 4 should be designated as "P4"). To indicate that a transaction should have been reported on a previous Form 5, place a "5" in Table I, column 3 or Table II, column 4, as appropriate. In addition, the appropriate box on the front page of the Form should be checked.

9. Amendments

(a) If this Form is filed as an amendment in order to add one or more lines of transaction or ownership information to Table I or Table II of the Form being amended, provide each line being added, together with one or more footnotes, as necessary, to explain the addition of the line or lines. Do not repeat lines of transaction or ownership information that were disclosed in the original Form and are not being amended.

(b) If this Form is filed as an amendment in order to amend one or more lines of transaction or ownership information that already were disclosed in Table I or Table II of the Form being amended, provide the complete line or lines being amended, as amended, together with one or more footnotes, as necessary, to explain the amendment of the line or lines. Do not repeat lines of transaction or ownership information that were disclosed in the original Form and are not being amended.

(c) If this Form is filed as an amendment for any purpose other than or in addition to the purposes described in paragraphs (a) and (b) of this General Instruction 9, provide one or more footnotes, as necessary, to explain the amendment.

FORM 5

☐ Check box if no longer subject to Section 16. Form 4 or Form 5 obligations may continue. *See* Instruction 1(b).
☐ Form 3 Holdings Reported
☐ Form 4 Transactions Reported

UNITED STATES SECURITIES AND EXCHANGE COMMISSION
Washington, D.C. 20549

ANNUAL STATEMENT OF BENEFICIAL OWNERSHIP OF SECURITIES

Filed pursuant to Section 16(a) of the Securities Exchange Act of 1934, Section 17(a) of the Public Utility Holding Company Act of 1935 or Section 30(h) of the Investment Company Act of 1940

1. Name and Address of Reporting Person*

(Last)   (First)   (Middle)

(Street)

(City)   (State)   (Zip)

2. Issuer Name **and** Ticker or Trading Symbol

3. Statement for Issuer's Fiscal Year Ended (Month/Day/Year)

4. If Amendment, Date Original Filed (Month/Day/Year)

5. Relationship of Reporting Person(s) to Issuer
(Check all applicable)
___ Director   ___ 10% Owner
___ Officer (give   ___ Other (specify
     title   below)
     below)

6. Individual or Joint/Group Reporting
(check applicable line)
___ Form Filed by One Reporting Person
___ Form Filed by More than One Reporting Person

Table 1 — Non-Derivative Securities Acquired, Disposed of, or Beneficially Owned

1. Title of Security (Instr. 3)	2. Transaction Date (Month/Day/Year)	2A. Deemed Execution Date, if any (Month/Day/Year)	3. Transaction Code (Instr. 8)	4. Securities Acquired (A) or Disposed of (D) (Instr. 3, 4 and 5) Amount	(A) or (D)	Price	5. Amount of Securities Beneficially Owned at end of Issuer's Fiscal Year (Instr. 3 and 4)	6. Ownership Form: Direct (D) or Indirect (I) (Instr. 4)	7. Nature of Indirect Beneficial Ownership (Instr. 4)

Reminder: Report on a separate line for each class of securities beneficially owned directly or indirectly.
* If the form is filed by more than one reporting person, see instruction 4(b)(v).

(Over)

FORM 5 (continued)

Table II — Derivative Securities Acquired, Disposed of, or Beneficially Owned
(*e.g.*, puts, calls, warrants, options, convertible securities)

1. Title of Derivative Security (Instr. 3)	2. Conversion or Exercise Price of Derivative Security	3. Transaction Date (Month/Day/Year)	3A. Deemed Execution Date, if any (Month/Day/Year)	4. Transaction Code (Instr. 8)	5. Number of Derivative Securities Acquired (A) or Disposed of (D) (Instr. 3, 4, and 5)		6. Date Exercisable and Expiration Date (Month/Day/Year)		7. Title and Amount of Underlying Securities (Instr. 3 and 4)		8. Price of Derivative Security (Instr. 5)	9. Number of Derivative Securities Beneficially Owned at End of Issuer's Fiscal Year (Instr. 4)	10. Ownership Form of Derivative Securities: Direct (D) or Indirect (I) (Instr. 4)	11. Nature of Indirect Beneficial Ownership (Instr. 4)
					(A)	(D)	Date Exercisable	Expiration Date	Title	Amount or Number of Shares				

Explanation of Responses:

** Intentional misstatements or omissions of facts constitute Federal Criminal Violations. *See* 18 U.S.C. 1001 and 15 U.S.C. 78ff(a).

Note: File three copies of this Form, one of which must be manually signed. If space provided is insufficient, *see* Instruction 6 for procedure.

_____   _____
** Signature of Reporting Person   Date

Page 2

REGULATION S-X

REGULATION S-X

TABLE OF CONTENTS

ACCOUNTING RULES

Regulation S-X

(Title 17, Code of Federal Regulations)

PART 210—FORM AND CONTENT OF AND REQUIREMENTS FOR FINANCIAL STATEMENTS, SECURITIES ACT OF 1933, SECURITIES EXCHANGE ACT OF 1934, PUBLIC UTILITY HOLDING COMPANY ACT OF 1935, INVESTMENT COMPANY ACT OF 1940, AND ENERGY POLICY AND CONSERVATION ACT OF 1975

ATTENTION ELECTRONIC FILERS
THIS REGULATION SHOULD BE READ IN CONJUNCTION WITH REGULATION S- T (PART 232 OF THIS CHAPTER), WHICH GOVERNS THE PREPARATION AND SUBMISSION OF DOCU-MENTS IN ELECTRONIC FORMAT. MANY PROVISIONS RELATING TO THE PREPARATION AND SUBMISSION OF DOCUMENTS IN PAPER FORMAT CONTAINED IN THIS REGULATION ARE SUPERSEDED BY THE PROVISIONS OF REGULATION S-T FOR DOCUMENTS REQUIRED TO BE FILED IN ELECTRONIC FORMAT.

Article 1—Application or Regulation S-X (17 CFR Part 210)

[¶ 35,001] Application of Regulation S-X (17 CFR Part 210)

Reg. § 210.1-01. (a) This part (together with the Financial Reporting Releases (Part 211 of this chapter)) [listed on page 161] sets forth the form and content of and requirements for financial statements required to be filed as a part of:

(1) Registration statements under the Securities Act of 1933 [Part 239 of this chapter], except as otherwise specifically provided in the forms which are to be used for registration under this Act;

(2) Registration statements under section 12 [Subpart C of Part 249 of this chapter], annual or other reports under sections 13 and 15(d) [Subparts D and E of Part 249 of this chapter], and proxy and information statements under section 14 of the Securities Exchange Act of 1934 except as otherwise specifically provided in the forms which are to be used for registration and reporting under these sections of this Act;

(3) Registration statements and annual reports filed under the Public Utility Holding Company Act of 1935 [Part 259 of this chapter]by public utility holding companies registered under such Act; and

(4) Registration statements and shareholder reports under the Investment Company Act of 1940 (Part 274 of this chapter), except as otherwise specifically provided in the forms which are to be used for registration under this Act.

(b) The term "financial statements" as used in this Part shall be deemed to include all notes to the statements and all related schedules.

(c) In addition to filings pursuant to the federal securities laws, § 210.4-10 applies to the preparation of accounts by persons engaged, in whole or in part, in the production of crude oil or natural gas in the United States pursuant to Section 503 of the Energy Policy and Conservation Act of 1975 [42 U.S.C. 6383] ("EPCA") and Section 1(c) of the Energy Supply and Environmental Coordination Act of 1974 [15 U.S.C. 796], as amended by Section 505 of EPCA.

[As last amended in Release No. FR-21, June 6, 1985, 50 F.R. 25214.]

[¶ 35,011] Definitions of Terms Used in Regulation S-X (17 CFR Part 210)

Reg. § 210.1-02. Unless the context otherwise requires, terms defined in the general rules and regulations or in the instructions to the applicable form, when used in Regulation S-X (this Part 210), shall have the respective meanings given in such instructions or rules. In addition, the following terms shall have the meanings indicated in this section unless the context otherwise requires.

(a)(1) *Accountant's report.* The term "accountant's report," when used in regard to financial statements, means a document in which an independent public or certified public accountant indicates the scope of the audit (or examination) which he has made and sets forth his opinion regarding the financial statements taken as a whole, or an assertion to the effect that an overall opinion cannot be expressed. When an overall opinion cannot be expressed, the reasons therefor shall be stated.

(2) *Attestation report on internal control over financial reporting.* The term *attestation report on internal control over financial reporting* means a report in which a registered public accounting firm expresses an opinion, either unqualified or adverse, as to whether the registrant maintained, in all

material respects, effective internal control over financial reporting (as defined in § 240.13a-15(f) or 240.15d-15(f) of this chapter), except in the rare circumstance of a scope limitation that cannot be overcome by the registrant or the registered public accounting firm which would result in the accounting firm disclaiming an opinion.

(3) *Attestation report on assessment of compliance with servicing criteria for asset-backed securities.* The term *attestation report on assessment of compliance with servicing criteria for asset-backed securities* means a report in which a registered public accounting firm, as required by § 240.13a-18(c) or 240.15d-18(c) of this chapter, expresses an opinion, or states that an opinion cannot be expressed, concerning an asserting party's assessment of compliance with servicing criteria, as required by § 240.13a-18(b) or 240.15d-18(b) of this chapter, in accordance with standards on attestation engagements. When an overall opinion cannot be expressed, the registered public accounting firm must state why it is unable to express such an opinion.

(4) *Definitions of terms related to internal control over financial reporting.*

The term *material weakness* means a deficiency, or a combination of deficiencies, in internal control over financial reporting (as defined in § 240.13a-15(f) or 240.15d-15(f) of this chapter) such that there is a reasonable possibility that a material misstatement of the registrant's annual or interim financial statements will not be prevented or detected on a timely basis.

The term *significant deficiency* means a deficiency, or a combination of deficiencies, in internal control over financial reporting that is less severe than a material weakness, yet important enough to merit attention by those responsible for oversight of the registrant's financial reporting.

(b) *Affiliate.* An "affiliate" of, or a person "affiliated" with, a specific person is a person that directly, or indirectly through one or more intermediaries, controls, or is controlled by, or is under common control with, the person specified.

(c) *Amount.* The term "amount," when used in regard to securities, means the principal amount if relating to evidences of indebtedness, the number of shares if relating to shares, and the number of units if relating to any other kind of security.

(d) *Audit (or examination).* The term audit (or examination), when used in regard to financial statements, means an examination of the financial statements by an independent accountant in accordance with generally accepted auditing standards, as may be modified or supplemented by the Commission, for the purpose of expressing an opinion thereon.

(e) *Bank holding company.* The term "bank holding company" means a person who is engaged, either directly or indirectly, primarily in the business of owning securities of one or more banks for the purpose, and with the effect, of exercising control.

(f) *Certified.* The term "certified," when used in regard to financial statements, means examined and reported upon with an opinion expressed by an independent public or certified public accountant.

(g) *Control.* The term "control" (including the terms "controlling," "controlled by" and "under common control with") means the possession, direct or indirect, of the power to direct or cause the direction of the management and policies of a person, whether through the ownership of voting shares, by contract, or otherwise.

(h) *Development stage company.* A company shall be considered to be in the development stage if it is devoting substantially all of its efforts to establishing a new business and either of the following conditions exists: (1) Planned principal operations have not commenced. (2) Planned principal operations have commenced, but there has been no significant revenue therefrom.

(i) *Equity security.* The term "equity security" means any stock or similar security; or any security convertible, with or without consideration, into such a security, or carrying any warrant or right to subscribe to or purchase such a security; or any such warrant or right.

(j) *Fifty-percent-owned person.* The term "50-percent-owned person," in relation to a specified person, means a person approximately 50 percent of whose outstanding voting shares is owned by the specified person either directly, or indirectly through one or more intermediaries.

(k) *Fiscal year.* The term "fiscal year" means the annual accounting period or, if no closing date has been adopted, the calendar year ending on December 31.

(l) *Foreign business.* A business that is majority owned by persons who are not citizens or residents of the United States and is not organized under the laws of the United States or any state thereof, and either:

(1) More than 50 percent of its assets are located outside the United States; or

(2) The majority of its executive officers and directors are not United States citizens or residents.

(m) *Insurance holding company.* The term "insurance holding company" means a person which is engaged, either directly or indirectly, primarily in the business of owning securities of one or more insurance companies for the purpose, and with the effect, of exercising control.

(n) *Majority-owned subsidiary.* The term "majority-owned subsidiary" means a subsidiary more than 50 percent of whose outstanding voting shares is owned by its parent and/or the parent's other majority-owned subsidiaries.

(o) *Material.* The term "material," when used to qualify a requirement for the furnishing of information as to any subject, limits the information required to those matters about which an average prudent investor ought reasonably to be informed.

(p) *Parent.* A "parent" of a specified person is an affiliate controlling such person directly, or indirectly through one or more intermediaries.

(q) *Person.* The term "person" means an individual, a corporation, a partnership, an association, a joint-stock company, a business trust, or an unincorporated organization.

(r) *Principal holder of equity securities.* The term "principal holder of equity securities," used in respect of a registrant or other person named in a particular statement or report, means a holder of record or a known beneficial owner of more than 10 percent of any class of equity securities of the registrant or other person, respectively, as of the date of the related balance sheet filed.

(s) *Promoter.* The term "promoter" includes—

(1) Any person who, acting alone or in conjunction with one or more other persons, directly or indirectly takes initiative in founding and organizing the business or enterprise of an issuer;

(2) Any person who, in connection with the founding and organizing of the business or enterprise of an issuer, directly or indirectly receives in consideration of services or property, or both services and property, 10 percent or more of any class of securities of the issuer or 10 percent or more of the proceeds from the sale of any class of securities. However, a person who receives such securities or proceeds either solely as underwriting commissions or solely in consideration of property shall not be deemed a promoter within the meaning of this paragraph if such person does not otherwise take part in founding and organizing the enterprise.

(t) *Registrant.* The term "registrant" means the issuer of the securities for which an application, a registration statement, or a report is filed.

(u) *Related parties.* The term "related parties" is used as that term is defined in the Glossary to Statement of Financial Accounting Standards No. 57, "Related Party Disclosures."

(v) *Share.* The term "share" means a share of stock in a corporation or unit of interest in an unincorporated person.

(w) *Significant subsidiary.* The term "significant subsidiary" means a subsidiary, including its subsidiaries, which meets any of the following conditions:

(1) The registrant's and its other subsidiaries' investments in and advances to the subsidiary exceed 10 percent of the total assets of the registrant and its subsidiaries consolidated as of the end of the most recently completed fiscal year (for a proposed combination between entities under common control, this condition is also met when the number of common shares exchanged or to be exchanged by the registrant exceeds 10 percent of its total common shares outstanding at the date the combination is initiated); or

(2) The registrant's and its other subsidiaries' proportionate share of the total assets (after intercompany eliminations) of the subsidiary exceeds 10 percent of the total assets of the registrant and its subsidiaries consolidated as of the end of the most recently completed fiscal year; or

(3) The registrant's and its other subsidiaries' equity in the income from continuing operations before income taxes, extraordinary items and cumulative effect of a change in accounting principle of the subsidiary exclusive of amounts attributable to any noncontrolling interests exceeds 10 percent of such income of the registrant and its subsidiaries consolidated for the most recently completed fiscal year.

Note to paragraph (w): A registrant that files its financial statements in accordance with or provides a reconciliation to U.S. Generally Accepted Accounting Principles shall make the prescribed tests using amounts determined under U.S. Generally Accepted Accounting Principles. A foreign private issuer that files its financial statements in accordance with IFRS as issued by the IASB shall make the prescribed tests using amounts determined under IFRS as issued by the IASB.

Computational note: For purposes of making the prescribed income test the following guidance should be applied:

1. When a loss exclusive of amounts attributable to any noncontrolling interests has been incurred by either the parent and its subsidiaries consolidated or the tested subsidiary, but not both, the equity in the income or loss of the tested subsidiary exclusive of amounts attributable to any noncontrolling interests should be excluded from such income of the registrant and its subsidiaries consolidated for purposes of the computation.

2. If income of the registrant and its subsidiaries consolidated exclusive of amounts attributable to any noncontrolling interests for the most recent fiscal year is at least 10 percent lower than the average

of the income for the last five fiscal years, such average income should be submitted for purposes of the computation. Any loss years should be omitted for purposes of computing average income.

3. Where the test involves combined entities, as in the case of determining whether summarized financial data should be presented, entities reporting losses shall not be aggregated with entities reporting income.

(x) *Subsidiary.* A "subsidiary" of a specified person is an affiliate controlled by such person directly, or indirectly through one or more intermediaries.

(y) *Totally held subsidiary.* The term "totally held subsidiary" means a subsidiary (1) substantially all of whose outstanding equity securities are owned by its parent and/or the parent's other totally held subsidiaries, and (2) which is not indebted to any person other than its parent and/or the parent's other totally held subsidiaries, in an amount which is material in relation to the particular subsidiary, excepting indebtedness incurred in the ordinary course of business which is not overdue and which matures within 1 year from the date of its creation, whether evidenced by securities or not, Indebtedness of a subsidiary which is secured by its parent by guarantee, pledge, assignment, or otherwise is to be excluded for purposes of (2) herein.

(z) *Voting shares.* The term "voting shares" means the sum of all rights, other than as affected by events of default, to vote for election of directors and/or the sum of all interests in an unincorporated person.

(aa) *Wholly owned subsidiary.* The term "wholly owned subsidiary" means a subsidiary substantially all of whose outstanding voting shares are owned by its parent and/or the parent's other wholly owned subsidiaries.

(bb) *Summarized financial information.* (1) Except as provided in paragraph (bb)(2), "summarized financial information" referred to in this regulation shall mean the presentation of summarized information as to the assets, liabilities and results of operations of the entity for which the information is required. Summarized financial information shall include the following disclosures:

(i) Current assets, noncurrent assets, current liabilities, noncurrent liabilities, and, when applicable, redeemable preferred stocks (see § 210.5-02.27) and noncontrolling interests (for specialized industries in which classified balance sheets are normally not presented, information shall be provided as to the nature and amount of the majority components of assets and liabilities);

(ii) Net sales or gross revenues, gross profit (or, alternatively, costs and expenses applicable to net sales or gross revenues), income or loss from continuing operations before extraordinary items and cumulative effect of a change in accounting principle, net income or loss, and net income or loss attributable to the entity (for specialized industries, other information may be substituted for sales and related costs and expenses if necessary for a more meaningful presentation); and

(2) Summarized financial information for unconsolidated subsidiaries and 50 percent or less owned persons referred to in and required by § 210.10-01(b) for interim periods shall include the information required by paragraph (bb)(1)(ii) of this section.

[As last amended in Release No. 33-9026, effective April 23, 2009, 74 F.R. 18612.]

Article 2—Qualifications and Reports of Accountants

[¶ 35,051] Qualifications of Accountants

Reg. § 210.2-01. *Preliminary Note.*

1. Rule 2-01 is designed to ensure that auditors are qualified and independent of their audit clients both in fact and in appearance. Accordingly, the rule sets forth restrictions on financial, employment, and business relationships between an accountant and an audit client and restrictions on an accountant providing certain non-audit services to an audit client.

2. Rule 2-01(b) sets forth the general standard of auditor independence. Paragraphs (c)(1) to (c)(5) reflect the application of the general standard to particular circumstances. The rule does not purport to, and the Commission could not, consider all circumstances that raise independence concerns, and these are subject to the general standard in paragraph 2-01(b). In considering this standard, the Commission looks in the first instance to whether a relationship or the provision of a service: (a) creates a mutual or conflicting interest between the accountant and the audit client; (b) places the accountant in the position of auditing his or her own work; (c) results in the accountant acting as management or an employee of the audit client; or (d) places the accountant in a position of being an advocate for the audit client.

3. These factors are general guidance only and their application may depend on particular facts and circumstances. For that reason, Rule 2-01 provides that, in determining whether an accountant is independent, the Commission will consider all relevant facts and circumstances. For the same reason, registrants and accountants are encouraged to consult with the Commission's Office of the Chief Accountant before entering into relationships, including relationships involving the provision of services, that are not explicitly described in the Rule.

(a) The Commission will not recognize any person as a certified public accountant who is not duly registered and in good standing as such under the laws of the place of his residence or principal office. The Commission will not recognize any person as a public accountant who is not in good standing and entitled to practice as such under the laws of the place of his residence or principal office.

(b) The Commission will not recognize an accountant as independent, with respect to an audit client, if the accountant is not, or a reasonable investor with knowledge of all relevant facts and circumstances would conclude that the accountant is not, capable of exercising objective and impartial judgment on all issues encompassed within the accountant's engagement. In determining whether an accountant is independent, the Commission will consider all relevant circumstances, including all relationships between the accountant and the audit client, and not just those relating to reports filed with the Commission.

(c) This paragraph sets forth a non-exclusive specification of circumstances inconsistent with paragraph (b) of this section.

(1) *Financial relationships.* An accountant is not independent if, at any point during the audit and professional engagement period, the accountant has a direct financial interest or a material indirect financial interest in the accountant's audit client, such as:

(i) *Investments in audit clients.* An accountant is not independent when:

(A) The accounting firm, any covered person in the firm, or any of his or her immediate family members, has any direct investment in an audit client, such as stocks, bonds, notes, options, or other securities. The term *direct investment* includes an investment in an audit client through an intermediary if:

(*1*) The accounting firm, covered person, or immediate family member, alone or together with other persons, supervises or participates in the intermediary's investment decisions or has control over the intermediary; or

(*2*) The intermediary is not a diversified management investment company, as defined by Section 5(b)(1) of the Investment Company Act of 1940, 15 U.S.C. 80a-5(b)(1), and has an investment in the audit client that amounts to 20% or more of the value of the intermediary's total investments.

(B) Any partner, principal, shareholder, or professional employee of the accounting firm, any of his or her immediate family members, any close family member of a covered person in the firm, or any group of the above persons has filed a Schedule 13D or 13G (17 CFR 240.13d-101 or 240.13d-102) with the Commission indicating beneficial ownership of more than five percent of an audit client's equity securities or controls an audit client, or a close family member of a partner, principal, or shareholder of the accounting firm controls an audit client.

(C) The accounting firm, any covered person in the firm, or any of his or her immediate family members, serves as voting trustee of a trust, or executor of an estate, containing the securities of an audit client, unless the accounting firm, covered person in the firm, or immediate family member has no authority to make investment decisions for the trust or estate.

(D) The accounting firm, any covered person in the firm, any of his or her immediate family members, or any group of the above persons has any material indirect investment in an audit client. For purposes of this paragraph, the term *material indirect investment* does not include ownership by any covered person in the firm, any of his or her immediate family members, or any group of the above persons of 5% or less of the outstanding shares of a diversified management investment company, as defined by Section 5(b)(1) of the Investment Company Act of 1940, 15 U.S.C. 80a-5(b)(1), that invests in an audit client.

(E) The accounting firm, any covered person in the firm, or any of his or her immediate family members:

(*1*) Has any direct or material indirect investment in an entity where:

(*i*) An audit client has an investment in that entity that is material to the audit client and has the ability to exercise significant influence over that entity; or

(*ii*) The entity has an investment in an audit client that is material to that entity and has the ability to exercise significant influence over that audit client;

(*2*) Has any material investment in an entity over which an audit client has the ability to exercise significant influence; or

(*3*) Has the ability to exercise significant influence over an entity that has the ability to exercise significant influence over an audit client.

(ii) *Other financial interests in audit client.* An accountant is not independent when the accounting firm, any covered person in the firm, or any of his or her immediate family members has:

(A) *Loans/debtor-creditor relationship.* Any loan (including any margin loan) to or from an audit client, or an audit client's officers, directors, or record or beneficial owners of more than ten percent of the audit client's equity securities, except for the following loans obtained from a financial institution under its normal lending procedures, terms, and requirements:

(*1*) Automobile loans and leases collateralized by the automobile;

(*2*) Loans fully collateralized by the cash surrender value of an insurance policy;

(*3*) Loans fully collateralized by cash deposits at the same financial institution; and

(*4*) A mortgage loan collateralized by the borrower's primary residence provided the loan was not obtained while the covered person in the firm was a covered person.

(B) *Savings and checking accounts.* Any savings, checking, or similar account at a bank, savings and loan, or similar institution that is an audit client, if the account has a balance that exceeds the amount insured by the Federal Deposit Insurance Corporation or any similar insurer, except that an accounting firm account may have an uninsured balance provided that the likelihood of the bank, savings and loan, or similar institution experiencing financial difficulties is remote.

(C) *Broker-dealer accounts.* Brokerage or similar accounts maintained with a broker-dealer that is an audit client, if:

(*1*) Any such account includes any asset other than cash or securities (within the meaning of "security" provided in the Securities Investor Protection Act of 1970 ("SIPA") (15 U.S.C. 78aaa *et seq.*));

(*2*) The value of assets in the accounts exceeds the amount that is subject to a Securities Investor Protection Corporation advance, for those accounts, under Section 9 of SIPA (15 U.S.C. 78fff-3); or

(*3*) With respect to non-U.S. accounts not subject to SIPA protection, the value of assets in the accounts exceeds the amount insured or protected by a program similar to SIPA.

(D) *Futures commission merchant accounts.* Any futures, commodity, or similar account maintained with a futures commission merchant that is an audit client.

(E) *Credit cards.* Any aggregate outstanding credit card balance owed to a lender that is an audit client that is not reduced to $10,000 or less on a current basis taking into consideration the payment due date and any available grace period.

(F) *Insurance products.* Any individual policy issued by an insurer that is an audit client unless:

(*1*) The policy was obtained at a time when the covered person in the firm was not a covered person in the firm; and

(*2*) The likelihood of the insurer becoming insolvent is remote.

(G) *Investment companies.* Any financial interest in an entity that is part of an investment company complex that includes an audit client.

(iii) *Exceptions.* Notwithstanding paragraphs (c)(1)(i) and (c)(1)(ii) of this section, an accountant will not be deemed not independent if:

(A) *Inheritance and gift.* Any person acquires an unsolicited financial interest, such as through an unsolicited gift or inheritance, that would cause an accountant to be not independent under paragraph (c)(1)(i) or (c)(1)(ii) of this section, and the financial interest is disposed of as soon as practicable, but no later than 30 days after the person has knowledge of and the right to dispose of the financial interest.

(B) *New audit engagement.* Any person has a financial interest that would cause an accountant to be not independent under paragraph (c)(1)(i) or (c)(1)(ii) of this section, and:

(*1*) The accountant did not audit the client's financial statements for the immediately preceding fiscal year; and

(*2*) The accountant is independent under paragraph (c)(1)(i) and (c)(1)(ii) of this section before the earlier of:

(*i*) Signing an initial engagement letter or other agreement to provide audit, review, or attest services to the audit client; or

(*ii*) Commencing any audit, review, or attest procedures (including planning the audit of the client's financial statements).

(C) *Employee compensation and benefit plans.* An immediate family member of a person who is a covered person in the firm only by virtue of paragraphs (f)(11)(iii) or (f)(11)(iv) of this section has a financial interest that would cause an accountant to be not independent under paragraph (c)(1)(i) or (c)(1)(ii) of this section, and the acquisition of the financial interest was an unavoidable consequence of participation in his or her employer's employee compensation or benefits program, provided that the financial interest, other than unexercised employee stock options, is disposed of as soon as practicable, but no later than 30 days after the person has the right to dispose of the financial interest.

(iv) *Audit clients' financial relationships.* An accountant is not independent when:

(A) *Investments by the audit client in the accounting firm.* An audit client has, or has agreed to acquire, any direct investment in the accounting firm, such as stocks, bonds, notes, options, or other securities, or the audit client's officers or directors are record or beneficial owners of more than 5% of the equity securities of the accounting firm.

(B) *Underwriting.* An accounting firm engages an audit client to act as an underwriter, broker-dealer, market-maker, promoter, or analyst with respect to securities issued by the accounting firm.

(2) *Employment relationships.* An accountant is not independent if, at any point during the audit and professional engagement period, the accountant has an employment relationship with an audit client, such as:

(i) *Employment at audit client of accountant.* A current partner, principal, shareholder, or professional employee of the accounting firm is employed by the audit client or serves as a member of the board of directors or similar management or governing body of the audit client.

(ii) *Employment at audit client of certain relatives of accountant.* A close family member of a covered person in the firm is in an accounting role or financial reporting oversight role at an audit client, or was in such a role during any period covered by an audit for which the covered person in the firm is a covered person.

(iii) *Employment at audit client of former employee of accounting firm.*

(A) A former partner, principal, shareholder, or professional employee of an accounting firm is in an accounting role or financial reporting oversight role at an audit client, unless the individual:

(*1*) Does not influence the accounting firm's operations or financial policies;

(*2*) Has no capital balances in the accounting firm; and

(*3*) Has no financial arrangement with the accounting firm other than one providing for regular payment of a fixed dollar amount (which is not dependent on the revenues, profits, or earnings of the accounting firm):

(*i*) Pursuant to a fully funded retirement plan, rabbi trust, or, in jurisdictions in which a rabbi trust does not exist, a similar vehicle; or

(*ii*) In the case of a former professional employee who was not a partner, principal, or shareholder of the accounting firm and who has been disassociated from the accounting firm for more than five years, that is immaterial to the former professional employee; and

(B) A former partner, principal, shareholder, or professional employee of an accounting firm is in a financial reporting oversight role at an issuer (as defined in section 10A(f) of the Securities Exchange Act of 1934 (15 U.S.C. 78j-1(f)), except an issuer that is an investment company registered under section 8 of the Investment Company Act of 1940 (15 U.S.C. 80a-8), unless the individual:

(*1*) Employed by the issuer was not a member of the audit engagement team of the issuer during the one year period preceding the date that audit procedures commenced for the fiscal period that included the date of initial employment of the audit engagement team member by the issuer;

(*2*) For purposes of paragraph (c)(2)(iii)(B)(*1*) of this section, the following individuals are not considered to be members of the audit engagement team:

(*i*) Persons, other than the lead partner and the concurring partner, who provided ten or fewer hours of audit, review, or attest services during the period covered by paragraph (c)(2)(iii)(B)(*1*) of this section;

(*ii*) Individuals employed by the issuer as a result of a business combination between an issuer that is an audit client and the employing entity, provided employment was not in contemplation of the business combination and the audit committee of the successor issuer is aware of the prior employment relationship; and

(*iii*) Individuals that are employed by the issuer due to an emergency or other unusual situation provided that the audit committee determines that the relationship is in the interest of investors;

(*3*) For purposes of paragraph (c)(2)(iii)(B)(*1*) of this section, audit procedures are deemed to have commenced for a fiscal period the day following the filing of the issuer's periodic annual report with the Commission covering the previous fiscal period; or

(C) A former partner, principal, shareholder, or professional employee of an accounting firm is in a financial reporting oversight role with respect to an investment company registered under section 8 of the Investment Company Act of 1940 (15 U.S.C. 80a-8), if:

(*1*) The former partner, principal, shareholder, or professional employee of an accounting firm is employed in a financial reporting oversight role related to the operations and financial reporting of the registered investment company at an entity in the investment company complex, as defined in (f)(14) of this section, that includes the registered investment company; and

(*2*) The former partner, principal, shareholder, or professional employee of an accounting firm employed by the registered investment company or any entity in the investment company complex was a member of the audit engagement team of the registered investment company or any other registered investment company in the investment company complex during the one year period preceding the date that audit procedures commenced that included the date of initial employment of the audit engagement team member by the registered investment company or any entity in the investment company complex.

(*3*) For purposes of paragraph (c)(2)(iii)(C)(*2*) of this section, the following individuals are not considered to be members of the audit engagement team:

(*i*) Persons, other than the lead partner and concurring partner, who provided ten or fewer hours of audit, review or attest services during the period covered by paragraph (c)(2)(iii)(C)(*2*) of this section;

(*ii*) Individuals employed by the registered investment company or any entity in the investment company complex as a result of a business combination between a registered investment company or any entity in the investment company complex that is an audit client and the employing entity, provided employment was not in contemplation of the business combination and the audit committee of the registered investment company is aware of the prior employment relationship; and

(*iii*) Individuals that are employed by the registered investment company or any entity in the investment company complex due to an emergency or other unusual situation provided that the audit committee determines that the relationship is in the interest of investors.

(*4*) For purposes of paragraph (c)(2)(iii)(C)(*2*) of this section, audit procedures are deemed to have commenced the day following the filing of the registered investment company's periodic annual report with the Commission.

(iv) *Employment at accounting firm of former employee of audit client.* A former officer, director, or employee of an audit client becomes a partner, principal, shareholder, or professional employee of the accounting firm, unless the individual does not participate in, and is not in a position to influence, the audit of the financial statements of the audit client covering any period during which he or she was employed by or associated with that audit client.

(3) *Business relationships.* An accountant is not independent if, at any point during the audit and professional engagement period, the accounting firm or any covered person in the firm has any direct or material indirect business relationship with an audit client, or with persons associated with the audit client in a decision-making capacity, such as an audit client's officers, directors, or substantial stockholders. The relationships described in this paragraph do not include a relationship in which the accounting firm or covered person in the firm provides professional services to an audit client or is a consumer in the ordinary course of business.

(4) *Non-audit services.* An accountant is not independent if, at any point during the audit and professional engagement period, the accountant provides the following non-audit services to an audit client:

(i) *Bookkeeping or other services related to the accounting records or financial statements of the audit client.* Any service, unless it is reasonable to conclude that the results of these services will not be subject to audit procedures during an audit of the audit client's financial statements, including:

(A) Maintaining or preparing the audit client's accounting records;

(B) Preparing the audit client's financial statements that are filed with the Commission or that form the basis of financial statements filed with the Commission; or

(C) Preparing or originating source data underlying the audit client's financial statements.

(ii) *Financial information systems design and implementation.* Any service, unless it is reasonable to conclude that the results of these services will not be subject to audit procedures during an audit of the audit client's financial statements, including:

(A) Directly or indirectly operating, or supervising the operation of, the audit client's information system or managing the audit client's local area network; or

(B) Designing or implementing a hardware or software system that aggregates source data underlying the financial statements or generates information that is significant to the audit client's financial statements or other financial information systems taken as a whole.

(iii) *Appraisal or valuation services, fairness opinions, or contribution-in-kind reports.* Any appraisal service, valuation service, or any service involving a fairness opinion or contribution-in-kind report for an audit client, unless it is reasonable to conclude that the results of these services will not be subject to audit procedures during an audit of the audit client's financial statements.

(iv) *Actuarial services.* Any actuarially-oriented advisory service involving the determination of amounts recorded in the financial statements and related accounts for the audit client other than assisting a client in understanding the methods, models, assumptions, and inputs used in computing an amount, unless it is reasonable to conclude that the results of these services will not be subject to audit procedures during an audit of the audit client's financial statements.

(v) *Internal audit outsourcing services.* Any internal audit service that has been outsourced by the audit client that relates to the audit client's internal accounting controls, financial systems, or financial statements, for an audit client unless it is reasonable to conclude that the results of these services will not be subject to audit procedures during an audit of the audit client's financial statements.

(vi) *Management functions.* Acting, temporarily or permanently, as a director, officer, or employee of an audit client, or performing any decision-making, supervisory, or ongoing monitoring function for the audit client.

(vii) *Human resources.* (A) Searching for or seeking out prospective candidates for managerial, executive, or director positions;

(B) Engaging in psychological testing, or other formal testing or evaluation programs;

(C) Undertaking reference checks of prospective candidates for an executive or director position;

(D) Acting as a negotiator on the audit client's behalf, such as determining position, status or title, compensation, fringe benefits, or other conditions of employment; or

(E) Recommending, or advising the audit client to hire, a specific candidate for a specific job (except that an accounting firm may, upon request by the audit client, interview candidates and advise the audit client on the candidate's competence for financial accounting, administrative, or control positions).

(viii) *Broker-dealer, investment adviser, or investment banking services.* Acting as a broker-dealer (registered or unregistered), promoter, or underwriter, on behalf of an audit client, making investment decisions on behalf of the audit client or otherwise having discretionary authority over an audit client's investments, executing a transaction to buy or sell an audit client's investment, or having custody of assets of the audit client, such as taking temporary possession of securities purchased by the audit client.

(ix) *Legal services.* Providing any service to an audit client that, under circumstances in which the service is provided, could be provided only by someone licensed, admitted, or otherwise qualified to practice law in the jurisdiction in which the service is provided.

(x) *Expert services unrelated to the audit.* Providing an expert opinion or other expert service for an audit client, or an audit client's legal representative, for the purpose of advocating an audit client's interests in litigation or in a regulatory or administrative proceeding or investigation. In any litigation or regulatory or administrative proceeding or investigation, an accountant's independence shall not be deemed to be impaired if the accountant provides factual accounts, including in testimony, of work performed or explains the positions taken or conclusions reached during the performance of any service provided by the accountant for the audit client.

(5) *Contingent fees.* An accountant is not independent if, at any point during the audit and professional engagement period, the accountant provides any service or product to an audit client for a contingent fee or a commission, or receives a contingent fee or commission from an audit client.

(6) *Partner rotation.* (i) Except as provided in paragraph (c) (6) (ii) of this section, an accountant is not independent of an audit client when:

(A) Any audit partner as defined in paragraph (f) (7) (ii) of this section performs:

(1) The services of a lead partner, as defined in paragraph (f) (7) (ii) (A) of this section, or concurring partner, as defined in paragraph (f) (7) (ii) (B) of this section, for more than five consecutive years; or

(2) One or more of the services defined in paragraphs (f) (7) (ii) (C) and (D) of this section for more than seven consecutive years;

(B) Any audit partner:

(*1*) Within the five consecutive year period following the performance of services for the maximum period permitted under paragraph (c)(6)(i)(A)(*1*) of this section, performs for that audit client the services of a lead partner, as defined in paragraph (f)(7)(ii)(A) of this section, or concurring partner, as defined in paragraph (f)(7)(ii)(B) of this section, or a combination of those services, or

(*2*) Within the two consecutive year period following the performance of services for the maximum period permitted under paragraph (c)(6)(i)(A)(*2*) of this section, performs one or more of the services defined in paragraph (f)(7)(ii) of this section.

(ii) Any accounting firm with less than five audit clients that are issuers (as defined in section 10A(f) of the Securities Exchange Act of 1934 (15 U.S.C. 78j-1(f))) and less than ten partners shall be exempt from paragraph (c)(6)(i) of this section *provided* the Public Company Accounting Oversight Board conducts a review at least once every three years of each of the audit client engagements that would result in a lack of auditor independence under this paragraph.

(iii) For purposes of paragraph (c)(6)(i) of this section, an audit client that is an investment company registered under section 8 of the Investment Company Act of 1940 (15 U.S.C. 80a-8), does not include an affiliate of the audit client that is an entity in the same investment company complex, as defined in paragraph (f)(14) of this section, except for another registered investment company in the same investment company complex. For purposes of calculating consecutive years of service under paragraph (c)(6)(i) of this section with respect to investment companies in an investment company complex, audits of registered investment companies with different fiscal year-ends that are performed in a continuous 12-month period count as a single consecutive year.

(7) *Audit committee administration of the engagement.* An accountant is not independent of an issuer (as defined in section 10A(f) of the Securities Exchange Act of 1934 (15 U.S.C. 78j-1(f))), other than an issuer that is an Asset-Backed Issuer as defined in § 229.1101 of this chapter, or an investment company registered under section 8 of the Investment Company Act of 1940 (15 U.S.C. 80a-8), other than a unit investment trust as defined by section 4(2) of the Investment Company Act of 1940 (15 U.S.C. 80a-4(2)), unless:

(i) In accordance with Section 10A(i) of the Securities Exchange Act of 1934 (15 U.S.C. 78j-1(i)) either:

(A) Before the accountant is engaged by the issuer or its subsidiaries, or the registered investment company or its subsidiaries, to render audit or non-audit services, the engagement is approved by the issuer's or registered investment company's audit committee; or

(B) The engagement to render the service is entered into pursuant to pre-approval policies and procedures established by the audit committee of the issuer or registered investment company, *provided* the policies and procedures are detailed as to the particular service and the audit committee is informed of each service and such policies and procedures do not include delegation of the audit committees responsibilities under the Securities Exchange Act of 1934 to management; or

(C) With respect to the provision of services other than audit, review or attest services the pre-approval requirement is waived if:

(*1*) The aggregate amount of all such services provided constitutes no more than five percent of the total amount of revenues paid by the audit client to its accountant during the fiscal year in which the services are provided;

(*2*) Such services were not recognized by the issuer or registered investment company at the time of the engagement to be non-audit services; and

(*3*) Such services are promptly brought to the attention of the audit committee of the issuer or registered investment company and approved prior to the completion of the audit by the audit committee or by one or more members of the audit committee who are members of the board of directors to whom authority to grant such approvals has been delegated by the audit committee.

(ii) A registered investment company's audit committee also must pre-approve its accountant's engagements for non-audit services with the registered investment company's investment adviser (not including a sub-adviser whose role is primarily portfolio management and is sub-contracted or overseen by another investment adviser) and any entity controlling, controlled by, or under common control with the investment adviser that provides ongoing services to the registered investment company in accordance with paragraph (c)(7)(i) of this section, if the engagement relates directly to the operations and financial reporting of the registered investment company, except that with respect to the waiver of the pre-approval requirement under paragraph (c)(7)(i)(C) of this section, the aggregate amount of all services provided constitutes no more than five percent of the total amount of revenues paid to the registered investment company's accountant by the registered investment company, its investment adviser and any entity controlling, controlled by, or under common control with the investment adviser that provides ongoing services to the registered investment company during the fiscal year in which the services are provided that would have to be pre-approved by the registered investment company's audit committee pursuant to this section.

(8) *Compensation.* An accountant is not independent of an audit client if, at any point during the audit and professional engagement period, any audit partner earns or receives compensation based on the audit partner procuring engagements with that audit client to provide any products or services other than audit, review or attest services. Any accounting firm with fewer than ten partners and fewer than five audit clients that are issuers (as defined in section 10A(f) of the Securities Exchange Act of 1934 (15 U.S.C. 78j-1(f))) shall be exempt from the requirement stated in the previous sentence.

(d) *Quality controls.* An accounting firm's independence will not be impaired solely because a covered person in the firm is not independent of an audit client provided:

(1) The covered person did not know of the circumstances giving rise to the lack of independence;

(2) The covered person's lack of independence was corrected as promptly as possible under the relevant circumstances after the covered person or accounting firm became aware of it; and

(3) The accounting firm has a quality control system in place that provides reasonable assurance, taking into account the size and nature of the accounting firm's practice, that the accounting firm and its employees do not lack independence, and that covers at least all employees and associated entities of the accounting firm participating in the engagement, including employees and associated entities located outside of the United States.

(4) For an accounting firm that annually provides audit, review, or attest services to more than 500 companies with a class of securities registered with the Commission under Section 12 of the Securities Exchange Act of 1934 (15 U.S.C. 78*l*), a quality control system will not provide such reasonable assurance unless it has at least the following features:

(i) Written independence policies and procedures;

(ii) With respect to partners and managerial employees, an automated system to identify their investments in securities that might impair the accountant's independence;

(iii) With respect to all professionals, a system that provides timely information about entities from which the accountant is required to maintain independence;

(iv) An annual or on-going firm-wide training program about auditor independence;

(v) An annual internal inspection and testing program to monitor adherence to independence requirements;

(vi) Notification to all accounting firm members, officers, directors, and employees of the name and title of the member of senior management responsible for compliance with auditor independence requirements;

(vii) Written policies and procedures requiring all partners and covered persons to report promptly to the accounting firm when they are engaged in employment negotiations with an audit client, and requiring the firm to remove immediately any such professional from that audit client's engagement and to review promptly all work the professional performed related to that audit client's engagement; and

(viii) A disciplinary mechanism to ensure compliance with this section.

(e)(1) *Transition and grandfathering.* Provided the following relationships did not impair the accountant's independence under pre-existing requirements of the Commission, the Independence Standards, Board, or the accounting profession in the United States, the existence of the relationship on May 6, 2003, will not be deemed to impair an accountant's independence:

(i) Employment relationships that commenced at the issuer prior to May 6, 2003, as described in paragraph (c)(2)(iii)(B) of this section.

(ii) Compensation earned or received, as described in paragraph (c)(8) of this section during the fiscal year of the accounting firm that includes the effective date of this section.

(iii) Until May 6, 2004, the provision of services described in paragraph (c)(4) of this section provided those services are pursuant to contracts in existence on May 6, 2003.

(iv) The provision of services by the accountant under contracts in existence on May 6, 2003, that have not been pre-approved by the audit committee as described in paragraph (c)(7) of this section.

(v) Until the first day of the issuer's fiscal year beginning after May 6, 2003, by a "lead" partner and other audit partner (other than the "concurring" partner) providing services in excess of those permitted under paragraph (c)(6) of this section. An accountant's independence will not be deemed to be impaired until the first day of the issuer's fiscal year beginning after May 6, 2004, by a "concurring" partner providing services in excess of those permitted under paragraph (c)(6) of this section. For the purposes of calculating periods of service under paragraph (c)(6) of this section:

(A) For the "lead" and "concurring" partner, the period of service includes time served as the "lead" or "concurring" partner prior to May 6, 2003,; and

(B) For audit partners other than the "lead" partner or "concurring" partner, and for audit partners in foreign firms, the period of service does not include time served on the audit engagement team prior to the first day of issuer's fiscal year beginning on or after May 6, 2003.

(2) *Settling financial arrangements with former professionals.* To the extent not required by pre-existing requirements of the Commission, the Independence Standards Board, or the accounting profession in the United States, the requirement in paragraph (c)(2)(iii) of this section to settle financial arrangements with former professionals applies to situations that arise after the effective date of this section.

(f) *Definitions of terms.* For purposes of this section:

(1) *Accountant,* as used in paragraphs (b) through (e) of this section, means a registered public accounting firm, certified public accountant or public accountant performing services in connection with an engagement for which independence is required. References to the accountant include any accounting firm with which the certified public accountant or public accountant is affiliated.

(2) *Accounting firm* means an organization (whether it is a sole proprietorship, incorporated association, partnership, corporation, limited liability company, limited liability partnership, or other legal entity) that is engaged in the practice of public accounting and furnishes reports or other documents filed with the Commission or otherwise prepared under the securities laws, and all of the organization's departments, divisions, parents, subsidiaries, and associated entities, including those located outside of the United States. Accounting firm also includes the organization's pension, retirement, investment, or similar plans.

(3)(i) *Accounting role* means a role in which a person is in a position to or does exercise more than minimal influence over the contents of the accounting records or anyone who prepares them.

(ii) *Financial reporting oversight role* means a role in which a person is in a position to or does exercise influence over the contents of the financial statements or anyone who prepares them, such as when the person is a member of the board of directors or similar management or governing body, chief executive officer, president, chief financial officer, chief operating officer, general counsel, chief accounting officer, controller, director of internal audit, director of financial reporting, treasurer, or any equivalent position.

(4) *Affiliate of the audit client* means:

(i) An entity that has control over the audit client, or over which the audit client has control, or which is under common control with the audit client, including the audit client's parents and subsidiaries;

(ii) An entity over which the audit client has significant influence, unless the entity is not material to the audit client;

(iii) An entity that has significant influence over the audit client, unless the audit client is not material to the entity; and

(iv) Each entity in the investment company complex when the audit client is an entity that is part of an investment company complex.

(5) *Audit and professional engagement period* includes both:

(i) The period covered by any financial statements being audited or reviewed (the "audit period"); and

(ii) The period of the engagement to audit or review the audit client's financial statements or to prepare a report filed with the Commission (the "professional engagement period"):

(A) The professional engagement period begins when the accountant either signs an initial engagement letter (or other agreement to review or audit a client's financial statements) or begins audit, review, or attest procedures, whichever is earlier; and

(B) The professional engagement period ends when the audit client or the accountant notifies the Commission that the client is no longer that accountant's audit client.

(iii) For audits of the financial statements of foreign private issuers, the "audit and professional engagement period" does not include periods ended prior to the first day of the last fiscal year before the foreign private issuer first filed, or was required to file, a registration statement or report with the Commission, provided there has been full compliance with home country independence standards in all prior periods covered by any registration statement or report filed with the Commission.

(6) *Audit client* means the entity whose financial statements or other information is being audited, reviewed, or attested and any affiliates of the audit client, other than, for purposes of paragraph (c)(1)(i) of this section, entities that are affiliates of the audit client only by virtue of paragraph (f)(4)(ii) or (f)(4)(iii) of this section.

(7)(i) *Audit engagement team* means all partners, principals, shareholders and professional employees participating in an audit, review, or attestation engagement of an audit client, including audit partners and all persons who consult with others on the audit engagement team during the audit, review, or attestation engagement regarding technical or industry-specific issues, transactions, or events.

(ii) *Audit partner* means a partner or persons in an equivalent position, other than a partner who consults with others on the audit engagement team during the audit, review, or attestation engagement regarding technical or industry-specific issues, transactions, or events, who is a member of the audit engagement team who has responsibility for decision-making on significant auditing, accounting, and reporting matters that affect the financial statements, or who maintains regular contact with management and the audit committee and includes the following:

(A) The lead or coordinating audit partner having primary responsibility for the audit or review (the "lead partner");

(B) The partner performing a second level of review to provide additional assurance that the financial statements subject to the audit or review are in conformity with generally accepted accounting principles and the audit or review and any associated report are in accordance with generally accepted auditing standards and rules promulgated by the Commission or the Public Company Accounting Oversight Board (the "concurring or reviewing partner");

(C) Other audit engagement team partners who provide more than ten hours of audit, review, or attest services in connection with the annual or interim consolidated financial statements of the issuer or an investment company registered under section 8 of the Investment Company Act of 1940 (15 U.S.C. 80a-8); and

(D) Other audit engagement team partners who serve as the "lead partner" in connection with any audit or review related to the annual or interim financial statements of a subsidiary of the issuer whose assets or revenues constitute 20% or more of the assets or revenues of the issuer's respective consolidated assets or revenues.

(8) *Chain of command* means all persons who:

(i) Supervise or have direct management responsibility for the audit, including at all successively senior levels through the accounting firm's chief executive;

(ii) Evaluate the performance or recommend the compensation of the audit engagement partner; or

(iii) Provide quality control or other oversight of the audit.

(9) *Close family members* means a person's spouse, spousal equivalent, parent, dependent, nondependent child, and sibling.

(10) *Contingent fee* means, except as stated in the next sentence, any fee established for the sale of a product or the performance of any service pursuant to an arrangement in which no fee will be charged unless a specified finding or result is attained, or in which the amount of the fee is otherwise dependent upon the finding or result of such product or service. Solely for the purposes of this section, a fee is not a "contingent fee" if it is fixed by courts or other public authorities, or, in tax matters, if determined based on the results of judicial proceedings or the findings of governmental agencies. Fees may vary depending, for example, on the complexity of services rendered.

(11) *Covered persons in the firm* means the following partners, principals, shareholders, and employees of an accounting firm:

(i) The "audit engagement team";

(ii) The "chain of command";

(iii) Any other partner, principal, shareholder, or managerial employee of the accounting firm who has provided ten or more hours of non-audit services to the audit client for the period beginning on the date such services are provided and ending on the date the accounting firm signs the report on the financial statements for the fiscal year during which those services are provided, or who expects to provide ten or more hours of non-audit services to the audit client on a recurring basis; and

(iv) Any other partner, principal, or shareholder from an "office" of the accounting firm in which the lead audit engagement partner primarily practices in connection with the audit.

(12) *Group* means two or more persons who act together for the purposes of acquiring, holding, voting, or disposing of securities of a registrant.

(13) *Immediate family members* means a person's spouse, spousal equivalent, and dependents.

(14) *Investment company complex.*

(i) "Investment company complex" includes:

(A) An investment company and its investment adviser or sponsor;

(B) Any entity controlled by or controlling an investment adviser or sponsor in paragraph (f)(14)(i)(A) of this section, or any entity under common control with an investment adviser or sponsor in paragraph (f)(14)(i)(A) of this section if the entity:

(*1*) Is an investment adviser or sponsor; or

(2) Is engaged in the business of providing administrative, custodian, underwriting, or transfer agent services to any investment company, investment adviser, or sponsor; and

(C) Any investment company or entity that would be an investment company but for the exclusions provided by Section 3(c) of the Investment Company Act of 1940 (15 U.S.C. 80a-3(c)) that has an investment adviser or sponsor included in this definition by either paragraph (f)(14)(i)(A) or (f)(14)(i)(B) of this section.

(ii) An investment adviser, for purposes of this definition, does not include a sub-adviser whose role is primarily portfolio management and is subcontracted with or overseen by another investment adviser.

(iii) Sponsor, for purposes of this definition, is an entity that establishes a unit investment trust.

(15) *Office* means a distinct sub-group within an accounting firm, whether distinguished along geographic or practice lines.

(16) *Rabbi trust* means an irrevocable trust whose assets are not accessible to the accounting firm until all benefit obligations have been met, but are subject to the claims of creditors in bankruptcy or insolvency.

(17) *Audit committee* means a committee (or equivalent body) as defined in section 3(a)(58) of the Securities Exchange Act of 1934 (15 U.S.C. 78c(a)(58)).

[As last amended in Release No. 33-8518, effective March 8, 2005, 70 F.R. 1506.]

[¶ 35,061] Accountants' Reports and Attestation Reports

Reg. § 210.2-02. (a) *Technical requirements for accountants' reports.* The accountant's report (1) shall be dated; (2) shall be signed manually; (3) shall indicate the city and State where issued; and (4) shall identify without detailed enumeration the financial statements covered by the report.

(b) *Representations as to the audit included in accountants' reports.* The accountant's report (1) shall state whether the audit was made in accordance with generally accepted auditing standards; and (2) shall designate any auditing procedures deemed necessary by the accountant under the circumstances of the particular case, which have been omitted, and the reasons for their omission. Nothing in this rule shall be construed to imply authority for the omission of any procedure which independent accountants would ordinarily employ in the course of an audit made for the purpose of expressing the opinions required by paragraph (c) of this section.

(c) *Opinions to be expressed in accountants' reports.* The accountant's report shall state clearly: (1) The opinion of the accountant in respect of the financial statements covered by the report and the accounting principles and practices reflected therein; and (2) the opinion of the accountant as to the consistency of the application of the accounting principles, or as to any changes in such principles which have a material effect on the financial statements.

(d) *Exceptions identified in accountants' reports.* Any matters to which the accountant takes exception shall be clearly identified, the exception thereto specifically and clearly stated, and, to the extent practicable, the effect of each such exception on the related financial statements given. (See § 101 of the Codification of Financial Reporting Policies.)

(e) Paragraph (e) of this section applies only to registrants that are providing financial statements in a filing for a period with respect to which Arthur Andersen LLP or a foreign affiliate of Arthur Andersen LLP ("Andersen") issued an accountants' report. Notwithstanding any other Commission rule or regulation, a registrant that cannot obtain an accountants' report that meets the technical requirements of paragraph (a) of this section after reasonable efforts may include in the document a copy of the latest signed and dated accountants' report issued by Andersen for such period in satisfaction of that requirement, if prominent disclosure that the report is a copy of the previously issued Andersen accountants' report and that the report has not been reissued by Andersen is set forth on such copy.

(f) *Attestation report on internal control over financial reporting.* (1) Every registered public accounting firm that issues or prepares an accountant's report for a registrant, other than a registrant that is neither an accelerated filer nor a large accelerated filer (as defined in § 240.12b-2 of this chapter) or an investment company registered under section 8 of the Investment Company Act of 1940 (15 U.S.C. 80a-8), that is included in an annual report required by section 13(a) or 15(d) of the Securities Exchange Act of 1934 (15 U.S.C. 78a et seq.) containing an assessment by management of the effectiveness of the registrant's internal control over financial reporting must include an attestation report on internal control over financial reporting.

(2) If an attestation report on internal control over financial reporting is included in an annual report required by section 13(a) or 15(d) of the Securities Exchange Act of 1934 (15 U.S.C. 78a et seq.), it shall clearly state the opinion of the accountant, either unqualified or adverse, as to whether the registrant maintained, in all material respects, effective internal control over financial reporting, except in the rare circumstance of a scope limitation that cannot be overcome by the registrant or the registered public accounting firm which would result in the accounting firm disclaiming an opinion. The attestation report on internal control over financial reporting shall be dated, signed manually, identify the period covered

by the report and indicate that the accountant has audited the effectiveness of internal control over financial reporting. The attestation report on internal control over financial reporting may be separate from the accountant's report.

(g) *Attestation report on assessment of compliance with servicing criteria for asset-backed securities.* The attestation report on assessment of compliance with servicing criteria for asset-backed securities, as required by § 240.13a-18(c) or 240.15d-18(c) of this chapter, shall be dated, signed manually, identify the period covered by the report and clearly state the opinion of the registered public accounting firm as to whether the asserting party's assessment of compliance with the servicing criteria is fairly stated in all material respects, or must include an opinion to the effect that an overall opinion cannot be expressed. If an overall opinion cannot be expressed, explain why.

[As last amended in Release No. 33-9142, effective September 21, 2010, 75 F.R. 57385.]

[¶ 35,063] Accountants' Reports and Attestation Reports on Internal Control over Financial Reporting.

Reg. § 210.2-02T. (a) The requirements of § 210.2-02(f) shall not apply to a registered public accounting firm that issues or prepares an accountant's report that is included in an annual report filed by a registrant that is neither a "large accelerated filer" nor an "accelerated filer,"; as those terms are defined in § 240.12b-2 of this chapter, for a fiscal year ending on or after December 15, 2007 but before June 15, 2010.

(b) This section expires on December 15, 2010.

[As last amended in Release No. 33-9072, effective December 18, 2009, 74 F.R. 53628.]

[¶ 35,071] Examination of Financial Statements by Foreign Government Auditors

Reg. § 210.2-03. Notwithstanding any requirements as to examination by independent account-ants, the financial statements of any foreign governmental agency may be examined by the regular and customary auditing staff of the respective government if public financial statements of such governmen-tal agency are customarily examined by such auditing staff.

[As adopted in Release No. 34-9648, June 23, 1972, 37 F.R. 14591.]

[¶ 35,081] Examination of Financial Statements of Persons Other Than the Registrant

Reg. § 210.2-04. If a registrant is required to file financial statements of any other person, such statements need not be examined if examination of such statements would not be required if such person were itself a registrant.

[As adopted in Release No. 34-9648, June 23, 1972, 37 F.R. 14591.]

[¶ 35,091] Examination of Financial Statements by More Than One Accountant

Reg. § 210.2-05. If, with respect to the examination of the financial statements, part of the examination is made by an independent accountant other than the principal accountant and the principal accountant elects to place reliance on the work of the other accountant and makes reference to that effect in his report, the separate report of the other accountant shall be filed. However, notwithstanding the provisions of this section, reports of other accountants which may otherwise be required in filings need not be presented in annual reports to security holders furnished pursuant to the proxy and information statement rules under the Securities Exchange Act of 1934 [§§ 240.14a-3 and 240.14c-3].

[As last amended in Release No. AS-295, August 5, 1981, 46 F.R. 40872.]

[¶ 35,092] Retention of Audit and Review Records

Reg. § 210.2-06. (a) For a period of seven years after an accountant concludes an audit or review of an issuer's financial statements to which section 10A(a) of the Securities Exchange Act of 1934 (15 U.S.C. 78j-1(a)) applies, or of the financial statements of any investment company registered under section 8 of the Investment Company Act of 1940 (15 U.S.C. 80a-8), the accountant shall retain records relevant to the audit or review, including workpapers and other documents that form the basis of the audit or review, and memoranda, correspondence, communications, other documents, and records (including electronic records), which:

(1) Are created, sent or received in connection with the audit or review, and

(2) Contain conclusions, opinions, analyses, or financial data related to the audit or review.

(b) For the purposes of paragraph (a) of this section, *workpapers* means documentation of auditing or review procedures applied, evidence obtained, and conclusions reached by the accountant in the audit or review engagement, as required by standards established or adopted by the Commission or by the Public Company Accounting Oversight Board.

(c) Memoranda, correspondence, communications, other documents, and records (including elec-tronic records) described in paragraph (a) of this section shall be retained whether they support the auditor's final conclusions regarding the audit or review, or contain information or data, relating to a significant matter, that is inconsistent with the auditor's final conclusions regarding that matter or the audit or review. Significance of a matter shall be determined based on an objective analysis of the facts and circumstances. Such documents and records include, but are not limited to, those documenting a consultation on or resolution of differences in professional judgment.

(d) For the purposes of paragraph (a) of this section, the term *issuer* means an issuer as defined in section 10A(f) of the Securities Exchange Act of 1934 (15 U.S.C. 78j-1(f)).

[As added in Release No. 33-8180, effective March 3, 2003 (compliance required for audits and reviews completed on or after October 31, 2003), 68 F.R. 4862.]

[¶ 35,093] Communicaton with Audit Committees

Reg. § 210.2-07. (a) Each registered public accounting firm that performs for an audit client that is an issuer (as defined in section 10A(f) of the Securities Exchange Act of 1934 (15 U.S.C. 78j-1(f))), other than an issuer that is an Asset-Backed Issuer as defined in § 229.1101 of this chapter, or an investment company registered under section 8 of the Investment Company Act of 1940 (15 U.S.C. 80a-8), other than a unit investment trust as defined by section 4(2) of the Investment Company Act of 1940 (15 U.S.C. 80a-4(2)), any audit required under the securities laws shall report, prior to the filing of such audit report with the Commission (or in the case of a registered investment company, annually, and if the annual communication is not within 90 days prior to the filing, provide an update, in the 90 day period prior to the filing, of any changes to the previously reported information), to the audit committee of the issuer or registered investment company:

(1) All critical accounting policies and practices to be used;

(2) All alternative treatments within Generally Accepted Accounting Principles for policies and practices related to material items that have been discussed with management of the issuer or registered investment company, including:

(i) Ramifications of the use of such alternative disclosures and treatments; and

(ii) The treatment preferred by the registered public accounting firm;

(3) Other material written communications between the registered public accounting firm and the management of the issuer or registered investment company, such as any management letter or schedule of unadjusted differences;

(4) If the audit client is an investment company, all non-audit services provided to any entity in an investment company complex, as defined in 210.2-01(f)(14) of this section, that were not pre-approved by the registered investment company's audit committee pursuant to 210.2-01(c)(7) of this section.

(b) [Reserved]

[As last amended in Release No. 33-8518, effective March 8, 2005, 70 F.R. 1506.]

Article 3—General Instructions as to Financial Statements

Note.—These instructions specify the balance sheets and statements of income and cash flows to be included in disclosure documents prepared in accordance with Regulaton S-X. Other portions of Regulation S-X govern the examination, form and content of such financial statements, including the basis of consolidation and the schedules to be filed. The financial statements described below shall be audited unless otherwise indicated.

For filings under the Securities Act of 1933, attention is directed to § 230.411(b) regarding incorporation by reference to financial statements and to section 10(a)(3) of the Act regarding information required in the prospectus.

For filings under the Securities Exchange Act of 1934, attention is directed to § 240.12b-23 regarding incorporation by reference and § 240.12b-36 regarding use of financial statements filed under other acts.

[Amended in Release No. FR-40A, effective November 2, 1992, 57 F.R. 45287.]

[¶ 35,111] Consolidated Balance Sheets

Reg. § 210.3-01. (a) There shall be filed, for the registrant and its subsidiaries consolidated, audited balance sheets as of the end of each of the two most recent fiscal years. If the registrant has been in existence for less than one fiscal year, there shall be filed an audited balance sheet as of a date within 135 days of the date of filing the registration statement.

(b) If the filing, other than a filing on Form 10-K or Form 10, is made within 45 days after the end of the registrant's fiscal year and audited financial statements for the most recent fiscal year are not available, the balance sheets may be as of the end of the two preceding fiscal years and the filing shall include an additional balance sheet as of an interim date at least as current as the end of the registrant's third fiscal quarter of the most recently completed fiscal year.

(c) The instruction in paragraph (b) of this section is also applicable to filings, other than on Form 10-K or Form 10, made after 45 days but within the number of days of the end of the registrant's fiscal year specified in paragraph (i) of this section: *Provided*, that the following conditions are met:

(1) The registrant files annual, quarterly and other reports pursuant to section 13 or 15(d) of the Securities Exchange Act of 1934 and all reports due have been filed;

(2) For the most recent fiscal year for which audited financial statements are not yet available the registrant reasonably and in good faith expects to report income attributable to the registrant, after taxes but before extraordinary items and cumulative effect of a change in accounting principle; and

(3) For at least one of the two fiscal years immediately preceding the most recent fiscal year the registrant reported income attributable to the registrant, after taxes but before extraordinary items and cumulative effect of a change in accounting principle.

(d) For filings made after 45 days but within the number of days of the end of the registrant's fiscal year specified in paragraph (i) of this section where the above conditions are not met, the filing must include the audited balance sheets required by the first paragraph of this rule.

(e) For filings made after the number of days specified in paragraph (i)(2) of this section, the filing shall also include a balance sheet as of an interim date within the following number of days of the date of filing:

(1) 130 days for large accelerated filers and accelerated filers (as defined in § 240.12b-2 of this chapter); and

(2) 135 days for all other registrants.

(f) Any interim balance sheet provided in accordance with the requirements of this section may be unaudited and need not be presented in greater detail than is required by § 210.10-01. Notwithstanding the requirements of this section, the most recent interim balance sheet included in a filing shall be at least as current as the most recent balance sheet filed with the Commission on Form 10-Q.

(g) For filings by registered management investment companies, the requirements of § 210.3-18 shall apply in lieu of the requirements of this section.

(h) Any foreign private issuer, other than a registered management investment company or an employee plan, may file the financial statements required by Item 8.A of Form 20-F (§ 249.220 of this chapter) in lieu of the financial statements specified in this rule.

(i)(1) For purposes of paragraphs (c) and (d) of this section, the number of days shall be:

(i) 60 days (75 days for fiscal years ending before December 15, 2006) for large accelerated filers (as defined in § 240.12b-2 of this chapter);

(ii) 75 days for accelerated filers (as defined in § 240.12b-2 of this chapter); and

(iii) 90 days for all other registrants.

(2) For purposes of paragraph (e) of this section, the number of days shall be:

(i) 129 days subsequent to the end of the registrant's most recent fiscal year for large accelerated filers and accelerated filers (as defined in §240.12b-2 of this chapter); and

(ii) 134 days subsequent to the end of the registrant's most recent fiscal year for all other registrants.

[As last amended in Release No. 33-9026, effective April 23, 2009, 74 F.R. 18612.]

[¶ 35,121] Consolidated Statements of Income and Changes in Financial Position

Reg. § 210.3-02. (a) There shall be filed, for the registrant and its subsidiaries consolidated and for its predecessors, audited statements of income and cash flows for each of the three fiscal years preceding the date of the most recent audited balance sheet being filed or such shorter period as the registrant (including predecessors) has been in existence.

(b) In addition, for any interim period between the latest audited balance sheet and the date of the most recent interim balance sheet being filed, and for the corresponding period of the preceding fiscal year, statements of income and cash flows shall be provided. Such interim financial statements may be unaudited and need not be presented in greater detail than is required by §210.10-01.

(c) For filings by registered management investment companies, the requirements of §210.3-18 shall apply in lieu of the requirements of this section.

(d) Any foreign private issuer, other than a registered management investment company or an employee plan, may file the financial statements required by Item 8.A of Form 20-F (§249.220 of this chapter) in lieu of the financial statements specified in this rule.

[As last amended in Release No. 33-7745, September 30, 2000, 64 F.R. 53900 and 64 F.R. 61962.]

[¶ 35,131] Instructions to Income Statement Requirements

Reg. § 210.3-03. (a) The statements required shall be prepared in compliance with the applicable requirements of this Regulation.

(b) If the registrant is engaged primarily (1) in the generation, transmission or distribution of electricity, the manufacture, mixing, transmission or distribution of gas, the supplying or distribution of water, or the furnishing of telephone or telegraph service; or (2) in holding securities of companies engaged in such businesses, it may at its option include statements of income and cash flows (which may be unaudited) for the twelve-month period ending on the date of the most recent balance sheet being filed, in lieu of the statements of income and cash flows for the interim periods specified.

(c) If a period or periods reported on include operations of a business prior to the date of acquisition, or for other reasons differ from reports previously issued for any period, the statements shall be reconciled as to sales or revenues and net income in the statement or in a note thereto with the amounts previously reported: *Provided, however,* That such reconciliations need not be made (1) if they have been made in filings with the Commission in prior years or (2) the financial statements which are being retroactively adjusted have not previously been filed with the Commission or otherwise made public.

(d) Any unaudited interim financial statements furnished shall reflect all adjustments which are, in the opinion of management, necessary to a fair statement of the results for the interim periods presented. A statement to that effect shall be included. Such adjustments shall include, for example, appropriate estimated provisions for bonus and profit sharing arrangements normally determined or settled at year-end. If all such adjustments are of a normal recurring nature, a statement to that effect shall be made; otherwise, there shall be furnished information describing in appropriate detail the nature and amount of any adjustments other than normal recurring adjustments entering into the determination of the results shown.

(e) Disclosures regarding segments required by generally accepted accounting principles shall be provided for each year for which an audited statement of income is provided. To the extent that the segment information presented pursuant to this instruction complies with the provisions of Item 101 of Regulation S-K, the disclosures may be combined by cross referencing to or from the financial statements.

[As last amended in Release No. 33-7620, effective February 11, 1999, 64 F.R. 1728.]

[¶ 35,141] Changes in Other Stockholders' Equity

Reg. § 210.3-04. An analysis of the changes in each caption of stockholders' equity and noncontrolling interests presented in the balance sheets shall be given in a note or separate statement. This analysis shall be presented in the form of a reconciliation of the beginning balance to the ending balance for each period for which an income statement is required to be filed with all significant reconciling items described by appropriate captions with contributions from and distribution to owners shown separately. Also, state separately the adjustments to the balance at the beginning of the earliest period presented for items which were retroactively applied to periods prior to that period. With respect to any dividends, state the amount per share and in the aggregate for each class of shares. Provide a separate schedule in the notes to the financial statements that shows the effects of any changes in the registrant's ownership interest in a subsidiary on the equity attributable to the registrant.

[As last amended in Release No. 33-9026, effective April 23, 2009, 74 F.R. 18612.]

[¶ 35,151] Financial Statements of Businesses Acquired or to be Acquired

Reg. § 210.3-05. (a) Financial statements required.

(1) Financial statements prepared and audited in accordance with this regulation should be furnished for the periods specified in (b) below if any of the following conditions exist:

(i) (i) A business combination has occurred or is probable (for purposes of this section, this encompasses the acquisition of an interest in a business accounted for by the equity method); or

(ii) Consummation of a combination between entities under common control is probable.

(2) For purposes of determining whether the provisions of this rule apply, the determination of whether a "business" has been acquired should be made in accordance with the guidance set forth in § 210.11-01(d).

(3) Acquisitions of a group of related businesses that are probable or that have occurred subsequent to the latest fiscal year-end for which audited financial statements of the registrant have been filed shall be treated under this section as if they are a single business combination. The required financial statements of related businesses may be presented on a combined basis for any periods they are under common control or management. For purposes of this section, businesses shall be deemed to be related if:

(i) They are under common control or management;

(ii) The acquisition of one business is conditional on the acquisition of each other business; or

(iii) Each acquisition is conditioned on a single common event.

(4) This rule shall not apply to a business which is totally held by the registrant prior to consummation of the transaction.

(b) Periods to be presented. (1) If securities are being registered to be offered to the security holders of the business to be acquired, the financial statements specified in § § 210.3-01 and 210.3-02 shall be furnished for the business to be acquired, except as provided otherwise for filings on Form N-14, S-4 or F-4 (§ § 239.23, 239.25 or 239.34 of this chapter). The financial statements covering fiscal years shall be audited except as provided in Item 14 of Schedule 14A (§ 240.14a-101 of this chapter) with respect to certain proxy statements or in registration statements filed on Forms N-14, S-4 or F-4 (§ § 239.23, 239.25 or 239.34 of this chapter).

(2) In all cases not specified in paragraph (b)(1) of this section, financial statements of the business acquired or to be acquired shall be filed for the periods specified in this paragraph (b)(2) or such shorter period as the business has been in existence. The periods for which such financial statements are to be filed shall be determined using the conditions specified in the definition of significant subsidiary in § 210.1-02(w) as follows:

(i) If none of the conditions exceeds 20 percent, financial statements are not required. However, if the aggregate impact of the individually insignificant businesses acquired since the date of the most recent audited balance sheet filed for the registrant exceeds 50%, financial statements covering at least the substantial majority of the businesses acquired shall be furnished. Such financial statements shall be for at least the most recent fiscal year and any interim periods specified in § § 210.3-01 and 210.3-02.

(ii) If any of the conditions exceeds 20 percent, but none exceed 40 percent, financial statements shall be furnished for at least the most recent fiscal year and any interim periods specified in § § 210.3-01 and 210.3-02.

(iii) If any of the conditions exceeds 40 percent, but none exceed 50 percent, financial statements shall be furnished for at least the two most recent fiscal years and any interim periods specified in § § 210.3-01 and 210.3-02.

(iv) If any of the conditions exceed 50 percent, the full financial statements specified in § § 210.3-01 and 210.3-02 shall be furnished. However, financial statements for the earliest of the three fiscal years required may be omitted if net revenues reported by the acquired business in its most recent fiscal year are less than $50 million

(3) The determination shall be made by comparing the most recent annual financial statements of each such business, or group of related businesses on a combined basis, to the registrant's most recent annual consolidated financial statements filed at or prior to the date of acquisition. However, if the registrant made a significant acquisition subsequent to the latest fiscal year-end and filed a report on Form 8-K (§ 249.308 of this chapter) which included audited financial statements of such acquired

business for the periods required by this section and the pro forma financial information required by § 210.11, such determination may be made by using pro forma amounts for the latest fiscal year in the report on Form 8-K (§ 249.308 of this chapter) rather than by using the historical amounts of the registrant. The tests may not be made by "annualizing" data.

(4) Financial statements required for the periods specified in paragraph (b)(2) of this section may be omitted to the extent specified as follows:

(i) Registration statements not subject to the provisions of § 230.419 of this chapter (Regulation C) and proxy statements need not include separate financial statements of the acquired or to be acquired business if it does not exceed any of the conditions of significance in the definition of significant subsidiary in § 210.1-02 at the 50 percent level, and either:

(A) The consummation of the acquisition has not yet occurred; or

(B) The date of the final prospectus or prospectus supplement relating to an offering as filed with the Commission pursuant to § 230.424(b) of this chapter, or mailing date in the case of a proxy statement, is no more than 74 days after consummation of the business combination, and the financial statements have not previously been filed by the registrant.

(ii) An issuer, other than a foreign private issuer required to file reports on Form 6-K, that omits from its initial registration statement financial statements of a recently consummated business combination pursuant to paragraph (b)(4)(i) of this section shall furnish those financial statements and any pro forma information specified by Article 11 of this chapter under cover of Form 8-K (§ 249.308 of this chapter) no later than 75 days after consummation of the acquisition.

(iii) Separate financial statements of the acquired business need not be presented once the operating results of the acquired business have been reflected in the audited consolidated financial statements of the registrant for a complete fiscal year unless such financial statements have not been previously filed or unless the acquired business is of such significance to the registrant that omission of such financial statements would materially impair an investor's ability to understand the historical financial results of the registrant. For example, if,at the date of acquisition, the acquired business met at least one of the conditions in the definition of significant subsidiary in § 210.1-02 at the 80 percent level, the income statements of the acquired business should normally continue to be furnished for such periods prior to the purchase as may be necessary when added to the time for which audited income statements after the purchase are filed to cover the equivalent of the period specified in § 210.3-02.

(iv) A separate audited balance sheet of the acquired business is not required when the registrant's most recent audited balance sheet required by § 210.3-01 is for a date after the date the acquisition was consummated.

(c) *Financial statements of foreign businesses.*

If the business acquired or to be acquired is a foreign business, financial statements of the business meeting the requirements of Item 17 of Form 20-F (§ 249.220f of this chapter) will satisfy this section.

[As last amended in Release No. 33-9026, effective April 23, 2009, 74 F.R. 18612.]

[¶ 35,161] Financial Statements Covering a Period of Nine to Twelve Months

Reg. § 210.3-06. Except with respect to registered investment companies, the filing of financial statements covering a period of nine to 12 months shall be deemed to satisfy a requirement for filing financial statements for a period of one year where:

(a) the issuer has changed its fiscal year;

(b) the issuer has made a significant business acquisition for which financial statements are required under § 210.3-05 of this chapter and the financial statements covering the interim period pertain to the business being acquired; or

(c) the Commission so permits pursuant to § 210.3-13 of this chapter. Where there is a requirement for filing financial statements for a time period exceeding one year but not exceeding three consecutive years (with not more than 12 months included in any period reported upon), the filing of financial statements covering a period of nine to 12 months shall satisfy a filing requirement of financial statements for one year of that time period only if the conditions described in either paragraph (a), (b), or (c) of this section exist and financial statements are filed that cover the full fiscal year or years for all other years in the time period.

[Adopted in Release No. FR-35, effective April 12, 1989, 54 F.R. 10306.]

[¶ 35,191] Separate Financial Statements of Subsidiaries Not Consolidated and 50 Percent or Less Owned Persons

Reg. § 210.3-09. (a) If any of the conditions set forth in 210.1-02(w), substituting 20 percent for 10 percent in the tests used therein to determine a significant subsidiary, are met for a majority-owned subsidiary not consolidated by the registrant or by a subsidiary of the registrant, separate financial statements of such subsidiary shall be filed. Similarly, if either the first or third condition set forth in 210.1-02(w), substituting 20 percent for 10 percent, is met by a 50 percent or less owned person accounted for by the equity method either by the registrant or a subsidiary of the registrant, separate financial statements of such 50 percent or less owned person shall be filed.

(b) Insofar as practicable, the separate financial statements required by this section shall be as of the same dates and for the same periods as the audited consolidated financial statements required by §§ 210.3-01 and 3-02. However, these separate financial statements are required to be audited only for those fiscal years in which either the first or third condition set forth in § 210.1-02(w), substituting 20 percent for 10 percent, is met. For purposes of a filing on Form 10-K (§ 249.310 of this chapter):

(1) If the registrant is an accelerated filer (as defined in § 240.12b-2 of this chapter) but the 50 percent or less owned person is not an accelerated filer, the required financial statements may be filed as an amendment to the report within 90 days, or within six months if the 50 percent or less owned person is a foreign business, after the end of the registrant's fiscal year.

(2) If the fiscal year of any 50 percent or less owned person ends within the *registrant's number of filing days* before the date of the filing, or if the fiscal year ends after the date of the filing, the required financial statements may be filed as an amendment to the report within the *subsidiary's number of filing days*, or within six months if the 50 percent or less owned person is a foreign business, after the end of such subsidiary's or person's fiscal year.

(3) The term *registrant's number of filing days* means:

(i) 60 days (75 days for fiscal years ending before December 15, 2006) if the registrant is a large accelerated filer;

(ii) 75 days if the registrant is an accelerated filer; and

(iii) 90 days for all other registrants.

(4) The term *subsidiary's number of filing days* means:

(i) 60 days (75 days for fiscal years ending before December 15, 2006) if the 50 percent or less owned person is a large accelerated filer;

(ii) 75 days if the 50 percent or less owned person is an accelerated filer; and

(iii) 90 days for all other 50 percent or less owned persons.

(c) Notwithstanding the requirements for separate financial statements in paragraph (a) of this section, where financial statements of two or more majority-owned subsidiaries not consolidated are required, combined or consolidated statements of such subsidiaries may be filed subject to principles of inclusion and exclusion which clearly exhibit the financial position, cash flows and results of operations of the combined or consolidated group. Similarly, where financial statements of two or more 50 percent or less owned persons are required, combined or consolidated statements of such persons may be filed subject to the same principles of inclusion or exclusion referred to above.

(d) If the 50 percent or less owned person is a foreign business, financial statements of the business meeting the requirements of Item 17 of Form 20-F (§ 249.220f of this chapter) will satisfy this section.

[As last amended Release No. 33-8644, effective December 27, 2005, 70 F.R. 76626.]

[¶ 35,201] Financial Statements of Guarantors and Issuers of Guaranteed Securities Registered or Being Registered

Reg. § 210.3-10. (a)(1) *General rule.* Every issuer of a registered security that is guaranteed and every guarantor of a registered security must file the financial statements required for a registrant by Regulation S-X.

(2) *Operation of this rule.* Paragraphs (b), (c), (d), (e) and (f) of this section are exceptions to the general rule of paragraph (a)(1) of this section. Only one of these paragraphs can apply to a single issuer or guarantor. Paragraph (g) of this section is a special rule for recently acquired issuers or guarantors that overrides each of these exceptions for a specific issuer or guarantor. Paragraph (h) of this section defines the following terms used in this section: 100% owned, full and unconditional, annual report, quarterly report, no independent assets or operations, minor, finance subsidiary and operating subsidiary. Paragraph (i) of this section states the requirements for preparing the condensed consolidating financial information required by paragraphs (c), (d), (e) and (f) of this section.

Note to paragraph (a)(2).

Where paragraphs (b), (c), (d), (e) and (f) of this section specify the filing of financial statements of the parent company, the financial statements of an entity that is not an issuer or guarantor of the registered security cannot be substituted for those of the parent company.

(3) *Foreign private issuers.* Where any provision of this section requires compliance with §§ 210.301 and 3-02, a foreign private issuer may comply by providing financial statements for the periods specified by Item 8.A of Form 20-F (§ 249.220f of this chapter).

(b) *Finance subsidiary issuer of securities guaranteed by its parent company.* When a finance subsidiary issues securities and its parent company guarantees those securities, the registration statement, parent company annual report, or parent company quarterly report need not include financial statements of the issuer if:

(1) The issuer is 100% owned by the parent company guarantor;

(2) The guarantee is full and unconditional;

(3) No other subsidiary of the parent company guarantees the securities; and

(4) The parent company's financial statements are filed for the periods specified by §§ 210.3-01 and 210.302 and include a footnote stating that the issuer is a 100%owned finance subsidiary of the parent company and the parent company has fully and unconditionally guaranteed the securities. The footnote also must include the narrative disclosures specified in paragraphs (i)(9) and (i)(10) of this section.

Note to paragraph (b).

Paragraph (b) is available if a subsidiary issuer satisfies the requirements of this paragraph but for the fact that, instead of the parent company guaranteeing the security, the subsidiary issuer co-issued the security, jointly and severally, with the parent company. In this situation, the narrative information required by paragraph (b)(4) must be modified accordingly.

(c) *Operating subsidiary issuer of securities guaranteed by its parent company.* When an operating subsidiary issues securities and its parent company guarantees those securities, the registration statement, parent company annual report, or parent company quarterly report need not include financial statements of the issuer if:

(1) The issuer is 100% owned by the parent company guarantor;

(2) The guarantee is full and unconditional;

(3) No other subsidiary of the parent company guarantees the securities; and

(4) The parent company's financial statements are filed for the periods specified by §§ 210.3-01 and 210.302 and include, in a footnote, condensed consolidating financial information for the same periods with a separate column for:

(i) The parent company;

(ii) The subsidiary issuer;

(iii) Any other subsidiaries of the parent company on a combined basis;

(iv) Consolidating adjustments; and

(v) The total consolidated amounts.

Notes to paragraph (c).

1. Instead of the condensed consolidating financial information required by paragraph (c)(4), the parent company's financial statements may include a footnote stating, if true, that the parent company has no independent assets or operations, the guarantee is full and unconditional, and any subsidiaries of the parent company other than the subsidiary issuer are minor. The footnote also must include the narrative disclosures specified in paragraphs (i)(9) and (i)(10) of this section.

2. If the alternative disclosure permitted by Note 1 to this paragraph is not applicable because the parent company has independent assets or operations, the condensed consolidating financial information described in paragraph (c)(4) may omit the column for "any other subsidiaries of the parent company on a combined basis" if those other subsidiaries are minor.

3. Paragraph (c) is available if a subsidiary issuer satisfies the requirements of this paragraph but for the fact that, instead of the parent company guaranteeing the security, the subsidiary issuer co-issued the security, jointly and severally, with the parent company. In this situation, the narrative information required by paragraph (i)(8) of this section must be modified accordingly.

(d) *Subsidiary issuer of securities guaranteed by its parent company and one or more other subsidiaries of that parent company.* When a subsidiary issues securities and both its parent company and one or more other subsidiaries of that parent company guarantee those securities, the registration statement, parent company annual report, or parent company quarterly report need not include financial statements of the issuer or any subsidiary guarantor if:

(1) The issuer and all subsidiary guarantors are 100% owned by the parent company guarantor;

(2) The guarantees are full and unconditional;

(3) The guarantees are joint and several; and

(4) The parent company's financial statements are filed for the periods specified by §§ 210.3-01 and 210.302 and include, in a footnote, condensed consolidating financial information for the same periods with a separate column for:

(i) The parent company;

(ii) The subsidiary issuer;

(iii) The guarantor subsidiaries of the parent company on a combined basis;

(iv) Any other subsidiaries of the parent company on a combined basis;

(v) Consolidating adjustments; and

(vi) The total consolidated amounts.

Notes to paragraph (d).

1. Paragraph (d) applies in the same manner whether the issuer is a finance subsidiary or an operating subsidiary.

2. The condensed consolidating financial information described in paragraph (d)(4) may omit the column for "any other subsidiaries of the parent company on a combined basis" if those other subsidiaries are minor.

3. Paragraph (d) is available if a subsidiary issuer satisfies the requirements of this paragraph but for the fact that, instead of the parent company guaranteeing the security, the subsidiary issuer co-issued the security, jointly and severally, with the parent company. In this situation, the narrative information required by paragraph (i)(8) of this section must be modified accordingly.

4. If all of the requirements in paragraph (d) are satisfied except that the guarantee of a subsidiary is not joint and several with, as applicable, the parent company's guarantee or the guarantees of the parent company and the other subsidiaries, then each subsidiary guarantor whose guarantee is not joint and several need not include separate financial statements, but the condensed consolidating financial information should include a separate column for each guarantor whose guarantee is not joint and several.

5. Instead of the condensed consolidating financial information required by paragraph (d)(4), the parent company's financial statements may include a footnote stating, if true, that the parent company has no independent assets or operations, the subsidiary issuer is a 100% owned finance subsidiary of the parent company, the parent company has guaranteed the securities, all of the parent company's subsidiaries other than the subsidiary issuer have guaranteed the securities, all of the guarantees are full and unconditional, and all of the guarantees are joint and several. The footnote also must include the narrative disclosures specified in paragraphs (i)(9) and (i)(10) of this section.

(e) *Single subsidiary guarantor of securities issued by the parent company of that subsidiary.* When a parent company issues securities and one of its subsidiaries guarantees those securities, the registration statement, parent company annual report, or parent company quarterly report need not include financial statements of the subsidiary guarantor if:

(1) The subsidiary guarantor is 100% owned by the parent company issuer;

(2) The guarantee is full and unconditional;

(3) No other subsidiary of that parent guarantees the securities; and

(4) The parent company's financial statements are filed for the periods specified by §§ 210.3-01 and 210.302 and include, in a footnote, condensed consolidating financial information for the same periods with a separate column for:

(i) The parent company;

(ii) The subsidiary guarantor;

(iii) Any other subsidiaries of the parent company on a combined basis;

(iv) Consolidating adjustments; and

(v) The total consolidated amounts.

Notes to paragraph (e).

1. Paragraph (e) applies in the same manner whether the guarantor is a finance subsidiary or an operating subsidiary.

2. Instead of the condensed consolidating financial information required by paragraph (e)(4), the parent company's financial statements may include a footnote stating, if true, that the parent company has no independent assets or operations, the guarantee is full and unconditional, and any subsidiaries of the parent company other than the subsidiary guarantor are minor. The footnote also must include the narrative disclosures specified in paragraphs (i)(9) and (i)(10) of this section.

3. If the alternative disclosure permitted by Note 2 to this paragraph is not applicable because the parent company has independent assets or operations, the condensed consolidating financial information described in paragraph (e)(4) may omit the column for "any other subsidiaries of the parent company on a combined basis" if those other subsidiaries are minor.

4. If, instead of guaranteeing the subject security, a subsidiary co-issues the security jointly and severally with its parent company, this paragraph (e) does not apply. Instead, the appropriate financial information requirement would depend on whether the subsidiary is a finance subsidiary or an operating subsidiary. If the subsidiary is a finance subsidiary, paragraph (b) applies. If the subsidiary is an operating company, paragraph (c) applies.

(f) *Multiple subsidiary guarantors of securities issued by the parent company of those subsidiaries.* When a parent company issues securities and more than one of its subsidiaries guarantee those securities, the registration statement, parent company annual report, or parent company quarterly report need not include financial statements of the subsidiary guarantors if:

(1) Each of the subsidiary guarantors is 100% owned by the parent company issuer;

(2) The guarantees are full and unconditional;

(3) The guarantees are joint and several; and

(4) The parent company's financial statements are filed for the periods specified by §§ 210.3-01 and 210.302 and include, in a footnote, condensed consolidating financial information for the same periods with a separate column for:

(i) The parent company;

(ii) The subsidiary guarantors on a combined basis;

(iii) Any other subsidiaries of the parent company on a combined basis;

(iv) Consolidating adjustments; and

(v) The total consolidated amounts.

Notes to paragraph (f).

1. Instead of the condensed consolidating financial information required by paragraph (f) (4), the parent company's financial statements may include a footnote stating, if true, that the parent company has no independent assets or operations, the guarantees are full and unconditional and joint and several, and any subsidiaries of the parent company other than the subsidiary guarantors are minor. The footnote also must include the narrative disclosures specified in paragraphs (i) (9) and (i) (10) of this section.

2. If the alternative disclosure permitted by Note 1 to this paragraph is not applicable because the parent company has independent assets or operations, the condensed consolidating financial information described in paragraph (f) (4) may omit the column for "any other subsidiaries of the parent company on a combined basis" if those other subsidiaries are minor.

3. If any of the subsidiary guarantees is not joint and several with the guarantees of the other subsidiaries, then each subsidiary guarantor whose guarantee is not joint and several need not include separate financial statements, but the condensed consolidating financial information must include a separate column for each subsidiary guarantor whose guarantee is not joint and several.

(g) *Recently acquired subsidiary issuers or subsidiary guarantors.*

(1) The Securities Act registration statement of the parent company must include the financial statements specified in paragraph (g) (2) of this section for any subsidiary that otherwise meets the conditions in paragraph (c), (d), (e) or (f) of this section for omission of separate financial statements if:

(i) The subsidiary has not been included in the audited consolidated results of the parent company for at least nine months of the most recent fiscal year; and

(ii) The net book value or purchase price, whichever is greater, of the subsidiary is 20% or more of the principal amount of the securities being registered.

Instructions to paragraph (g) (1):

1. The significance test of paragraph (g) (1) (ii) of this section should be computed using net book value of the subsidiary as of the most recent fiscal year end preceding the acquisition.

2. Information required by this paragraph (g) is not required to be included in an annual report or quarterly report.

3. Acquisitions of a group of subsidiary issuers or subsidiary guarantors that are related prior to their acquisition shall be aggregated for purposes of applying the 20% test in paragraph (g) (1) (ii) of this section. Subsidiaries shall be deemed to be related prior to their acquisition if:

(a) They are under common control or management;

(b) The acquisition of one subsidiary is conditioned on the acquisition of each subsidiary; or

(c) The acquisition of each subsidiary is conditioned on a single common event.

(2) Financial statements required.

(i) Audited financial statements for a subsidiary described in paragraph (g) (1) of this section must be filed for the subsidiary's most recent fiscal year preceding the acquisition. In addition, unaudited financial statements must be filed for any interim periods specified in §§ 210.3-01 and 210.3-02.

(ii) The financial statements must conform to the requirements of Regulation S-X (§§ 210.1-01 through 12-29), except that supporting schedules need not be filed. If the subsidiary is a foreign business, financial statements of the subsidiary meeting the requirements of Item 17 of Form 20-F (§ 249.220f) will satisfy this item.

(h) *Definitions.* For the purposes of this section:

(1) A subsidiary is *100% owned* if all of its outstanding voting shares are owned, either directly or indirectly, by its parent company. A subsidiary not in corporate form is 100% owned if the sum of all interests are owned, either directly or indirectly, by its parent company other than:

(i) Securities that are guaranteed by its parent and, if applicable, other 100%-owned subsidiaries of its parent; and

(ii) Securities that guarantee securities issued by its parent and, if applicable, other 100%-owned subsidiaries of its parent.

(2) A guarantee is *full and unconditional*, if, when an issuer of a guaranteed security has failed to make a scheduled payment, the guarantor is obligated to make the scheduled payment immediately and, if it doesn't, any holder of the guaranteed security may immediately bring suit directly against the guarantor for payment of all amounts due and payable.

(3) *Annual report* refers to an annual report on Form 10-K or Form 20-F (§ 249.310 or 249.220f of this chapter).

(4) *Quarterly report* refers to a quarterly report on Form 10-Q (§ 249.308a of this chapter).

(5) A parent company has *no independent assets or operations* if each of its total assets, revenues, income from continuing operations before income taxes, and cash flows from operating activities (excluding amounts related to its investment in its consolidated subsidiaries) is less than 3% of the corresponding consolidated amount.

(6) A subsidiary is *minor* if each of its total assets, stockholders' equity, revenues, income from continuing operations before income taxes, and cash flows from operating activities is less than 3% of the parent company's corresponding consolidated amount.

Note to paragraph (h)(6).

When considering a group of subsidiaries, the definition applies to each subsidiary in that group individually and to all subsidiaries in that group in the aggregate.

(7) A subsidiary is a *finance subsidiary* if it has no assets, operations, revenues or cash flows other than those related to the issuance, administration and repayment of the security being registered and any other securities guaranteed by its parent company.

(8) A subsidiary is an *operating subsidiary* if it is not a finance subsidiary.

(i) Instructions for preparation of condensed consolidating financial information required by paragraphs (c), (d), (e) and (f) of this section.

(1) Follow the general guidance in § 210.10-01 for the form and content for condensed financial statements and present the financial information in sufficient detail to allow investors to determine the assets, results of operations and cash flows of each of the consolidating groups;

(2) The financial information should be audited for the same periods that the parent company financial statements are required to be audited;

(3) The parent company column should present investments in all subsidiaries based upon their proportionate share of the subsidiary's net assets;

(4) The parent company's basis shall be "pushed down" to the applicable subsidiary columns to the extent that push down would be required or permitted in separate financial statements of the subsidiary;

(5) All subsidiary issuer or subsidiary guarantor columns should present the following investments in subsidiaries under the equity method:

(i) Non-guarantor subsidiaries;

(ii) Subsidiary issuers or subsidiary guarantors that are not 100% owned or whose guarantee is not full and unconditional;

(iii) Subsidiary guarantors whose guarantee is not joint and several with the guarantees of the other subsidiaries; and

(iv) Subsidiary guarantors with differences in domestic or foreign laws that affect the enforceability of the guarantees;

(6) Provide a separate column for each subsidiary issuer or subsidiary guarantor that is not 100% owned, whose guarantee is not full and unconditional, or whose guarantee is not joint and several with the guarantees of other subsidiaries. Inclusion of a separate column does not relieve that issuer or guarantor from the requirement to file separate financial statements under paragraph (a) of this section. However, paragraphs (b) through (f) of this section will provide this relief if the particular paragraph is satisfied except that the guarantee is not joint and several;

(7) Provide separate columns for each guarantor by legal jurisdiction if differences in domestic or foreign laws affect the enforceability of the guarantees;

(8) Include the following disclosure, if true:

(i) Each subsidiary issuer or subsidiary guarantor is 100% owned by the parent company;

(ii) All guarantees are full and unconditional; and

(iii) Where there is more than one guarantor, all guarantees are joint and several;

(9) Disclose any significant restrictions on the ability of the parent company or any guarantor to obtain funds from its subsidiaries by dividend or loan;

(10) Provide the disclosures prescribed by § 210.408(e)(3) with respect to the subsidiary issuers and subsidiary guarantors;

(11) The disclosure:

(i) May not omit any financial and narrative information about each guarantor if the information would be material for investors to evaluate the sufficiency of the guarantee;

(ii) Shall include sufficient information so as to make the financial information presented not misleading; and

(iii) Need not repeat information that would substantially duplicate disclosure elsewhere in the parent company's consolidated financial statements; and

(12) Where the parent company's consolidated financial statements are prepared on a comprehensive basis other than U.S. Generally Accepted Accounting Principles or International Financial Reporting Standards as issued by the International Accounting Standards Board, reconcile the information in each column to U.S. Generally Accepted Accounting Principles to the extent necessary to allow investors to evaluate the sufficiency of the guarantees. The reconciliation may be limited to the information specified by Item 17 of Form 20-F (§ 249.220f of this chapter). The reconciling information need not duplicate information included elsewhere in the reconciliation of the consolidated financial statements.

[As last amended in Release No. 33-9026, effective April 23, 2009, 74 F.R. 18612.]

[¶ 35,211] Financial Statements of an Inactive Registrant

Reg. § 210.3-11. If a registrant is an inactive entity as defined below, the financial statements required by this regulation for purposes of reports pursuant to the Securities Exchange Act of 1934 may be unaudited. An inactive entity is one meeting all of the following conditions:

(a) Gross receipts from all sources for the fiscal year are not in excess of $100,000;

(b) The registrant has not purchased or sold any of its own stock, granted options therefor, or levied assessments upon outstanding stock;

(c) Expenditures for all purposes for the fiscal year are not in excess of $100,000;

(d) No material change in the business has occurred during the fiscal year, including any bankruptcy, reorganization, readjustment or succession or any material acquisition or disposition of plants, mines, mining equipment, mine rights or leases; and

(e) No exchange upon which the shares are listed, or governmental authority having jurisdiction, requires the furnishing to it or the publication of audited financial statements.

[As adopted by Release No. AS-281, September 2, 1980, 45 F.R. 63682.]

[¶ 35,221] Age of Financial Statements at Effective Date of Registration Statement or at Mailing Date of Proxy Statement

Reg. § 210.3-12. (a) If the financial statements in a filing are as of a date the number of days specified in paragraph (g) of this section or more before the date the filing is expected to become effective, or proposed mailing date in the case of a proxy statement, the financial statements shall be updated, except as specified in the following paragraphs, with a balance sheet as of an interim date within the number of days specified in paragraph (g) of this section and with statements of income and cash flows for the interim period between the end of the most recent fiscal year and the date of the interim balance sheet provided and for the corresponding period of the preceding fiscal year. Such interim financial statements may be unaudited and need not be presented in greater detail than is required by § 210.10-01. Notwithstanding the above requirements, the most recent interim financial statements shall be at least as current as the most recent financial statements filed with the Commission on Form 10-Q.

(b) Where the anticipated effective date of a filing, or in the case of a proxy statement the proposed mailing date, falls within the number of days subsequent to the end of the fiscal year specified in paragraph (g) of this section, the filing need not include financial statements more current than as of the end of the third fiscal quarter of the most recently completed fiscal year unless the audited financial statements for such fisccal year are available or unless the anticipated effective date or proposed mailing date falls after 45 days subsequent to the end of the fiscal year and the registrant does not meet the conditions prescribed under paragraph (c) of § 210.3-01. If the anticipated effective date or proposed mailing date falls after 45 days subsequent to the end of the fiscal year and the registrant does not meet the conditions prescribed under paragraph (c) of § 210.3-01, the filing must include audited financial statements for the most recently completed fiscal year.

(c) Where a filing is made near the end of a fiscal year and audited financial statements for that fiscal year are not included in the filing, the filing shall be updated with such audited financial statements if they become available prior to the anticipated effective date, or proposed mailing date in the case of a proxy statement.

(d) The age of the registrant's most recent audited financial statements included in a registration statement filed under the Securities Act of 1933 or filed on Form 10 (17 CFR 249.210) under the Securities Exchange Act of 1934 shall not be more than one year and 45 days old at the date the registration statement becomes effective if the registration statement relates to the security of an issuer that was not subject, immediately before the time of filing the registration statement, to the reporting requirements of section 13 or 15(d) of the Securities Exchange Act of 1934.

(e) For filings by registered management investment companies, the requirements of § 210.3-18 shall apply in lieu of the requirements of this section.

(f) Any foreign private issuer may file financial statements whose age is specified in Item 8.A of Form 20-F (§ 249.220f of this chapter). Financial statements of a foreign business which are furnished pursuant to §§ 210.3-05 or 210.3-09 because it is an acquired business or a 50 percent or less owned person may be of the age specified in Item 8.A of Form 20-F.

(g)(1) For purposes of paragraph (a) of this section, the number of days shall be:

(i) 130 days for large accelerated filers and accelerated filers (as defined in § 240.12b-2 of this chapter); and

(ii) 135 days for all other registrants.

(2) For purposes of paragraph (b) of this section, the number of days shall be:

(i) 60 days (75 days for fiscal years ending before December 15, 2006) for large accelerated filers (as defined in § 240.12b-2 of this chapter);

(ii) 75 days for accelerated filers (as defined in § 240.12b-2 of this chapter); and

(iii) 90 days for all other registrants.

[As last amended in Release No. 33-8876, effective February 4, 2008, 73 F.R. 934.]

[¶ 35,231] Filing of Other Financial Statements in Certain Cases

Reg. § 210.3-13. The Commission may, upon the informal written request of the registrant, and where consistent with the protection of investors, permit the omission of one or more of the financial statements herein required or the filing in substitution therefor of appropriate statements of comparable character. The Commission may also by informal written notice require the filing of other financial statements in addition to, or in substitution for, the statements herein required in any case where such statements are necessary or appropriate for an adequate presentation of the financial condition of any person whose financial statements are required, or whose statements are otherwise necessary for the protection of investors.

[As adopted by Release No. AS-281, September 2, 1980, 45 F.R. 63682.]

[¶ 35,241] Special Instructions for Real Estate Operations to Be Acquired

Reg. § 210.3-14. (a) If, during the period for which income statements are required the registrant (a) has acquired one or more properties which in the aggregate are significant, or (b) since the date of the latest balance sheet required has acquired or proposes to acquire one or more properties which in the aggregate are significant, the following shall be furnished with respect to such properties:

(1) Audited income statements (not including earnings per unit, for the three most recent fiscal years, which shall exclude items not comparable to the proposed future operations of the property such as mortgage interest, leasehold rental, depreciation, corporate expenses and Federal and state income taxes: *Provided however,* That such audited statements need be presented for only the most recent fiscal year if (i) the property is not acquired from a related party; (ii) material factors considered by the registrant in assessing the property are described with specificity in the filing with regard to the property, including sources of revenue (including, but not limited to, competition in the rental market, comparative rents, occupancy rates) and expense (including, but not limited to, utility rates, ad valorem tax rates, maintenance expenses, capital improvements anticipated); and (iii) the registrant indicates in the appropriate filing that, after reasonable inquiry, the registrant is not aware of any material factors relating to that specific property other than those discussed in response to paragraph (a)(1)(ii) of this section that would cause the reported financial information not to be necessarily indicative of future operating results.

NOTE: The discussion of material factors considered should be combined with that required by Item 15 of Form S-11.

(2) If the property is to be operated by the registrant, there shall be furnished a statement showing the estimated taxable operating results of the registrant based on the most recent twelve month period including such adjustments as can be factually supported. If the property is to be acquired subject to a net lease the estimated taxable operating results shall be based on the rent to be paid for the first year of the lease. In either case, the estimated amount of cash to be made available by operations shall be shown. There shall be stated in an introductory paragraph the principal assumptions which have been made in preparing the statements of estimated taxable operating results and cash to be made available by operations.

(3) If appropriate under the circumstances, there shall be given in tabular form for a limited number of years the estimated cash distribution per unit showing the portion thereof reportable as taxable income and the portion representing a return of capital together with an explanation of annual variations, if any. If taxable net income per unit will become greater than the cash available for distribution per unit, that fact and approximate year of occurrence shall be stated, if significant.

(b) Information required by this section is not required to be included in a filing on Form 10-K.

[As last amended in Release No. 33-8876, effective February 4, 2008, 73 F.R. 934.]

[¶ 35,251] Special Provisions as to Real Estate Investment Trusts

Reg. § 210.3-15. (a) (1) The income statement prepared pursuant to § 210.5-03 shall include the following additional captions between those required by § 210.5-03.15 and 16: (i) Income or loss before gain or loss on sale of properties, extraordinary items and cumulative effects of accounting changes, and (ii) gain or loss on sale of properties, less applicable income tax. (2) The balance sheet required by § 210.5-02 shall set forth in lieu of the captions required by § 210.5-02.31(a)(3): (i) The balance of undistributed income from other than gain or loss on sale of properties and (ii) accumulated undistributed net realized gain or loss on sale of properties. The information specified in § 210.3-04 shall be modified similarly.

(b) The trust's status as a "real estate investment trust" under applicable provisions of the Internal Revenue Code as amended shall be stated in a note referred to in the appropriate statements. Such note shall also indicate briefly the principal present assumptions on which the trust has relied in making or not making provisions for Federal income taxes.

(c) The tax status of distributions per unit shall be stated (e.g., ordinary income, capital gain, return of capital).

[As last amended in Release No. FR-22, November 21, 1985, 50 F.R. 49529.]

[¶ 35,261] Financial Statements of Affiliates Whose Securities Collateralize an Issue Registered or Being Registered

Reg. § 210.3-16. (a) For each of the registrant's affiliates whose securities constitute a substantial portion of the collateral for any class of securities registered or being registered, there shall be filed the financial statements that would be required if the affiliate were a registrant and required to file financial statements. However, financial statements need not be filed pursuant to this section for any person whose statements are otherwise separately included in the filing on an individual basis or on a basis consolidated with its subsidiaries.

(b) For the purposes of this section, securities of a person shall be deemed to constitute a substantial portion of collateral if the aggregate principal amount, par value, or book value of the securities as carried by the registrant, or the market value of such securities, whichever is the greatest, equals 20 percent or more of the principal amount of the secured class of securities.

[As adopted in Release No. 33-7878, effective September 25, 2000, 65 F.R. 51692.]

[¶ 35,265] Financial Statements of Natural Persons

Reg. § 210.3-17. (a) In lieu of the financial statements otherwise required, a natural person may file an unaudited balance sheet as of a date within 90 days of date of filing and unaudited statements of income for each of the three most recent fiscal years.

(b) Financial statements conforming with the instructions as to financial statements of subsidiaries not consolidated and 50 percent or less owned persons under § 210.3-09(a) shall be separately presented for: (1) Each business owned as a sole proprietor, (2) each partnership, business trust, unincorporated association, or similar business organization of which the person holds a controlling interest and (3) each corporation of which the person, directly or indirectly, owns securities representing more than 50 percent of the voting power.

(c) Separate financial statements may be omitted, however, for each corporation, business trust, unincorporated association, or similar business organization if the person's total investment in such entity does not exceed 5 percent of his total assets *and* the person's total income from such entity does not exceed 5 percent of his gross income; *Provided,* that the person's aggregate investment in and income from all such omitted entities shall not exceed 15 percent of his total assets and gross income, respectively.

[As last amended in Release No. FR-21, June 6, 1985, 50 F.R. 25214.]

[¶ 35,266] Special Provisions as to Registered Management Investment Companies and Companies Required to be Registered as Management Investment Companies

Reg. § 210.3-18. (a) For filings by registered management investment companies, the following financial statements shall be filed:

(1) An audited balance sheet or statement of assets and liabilities as of the end of the most recent fiscal year;

(2) An audited statement of operations for the most recent fiscal year conforming to the requirements of § 210.6-07.

(3) An audited statement of cash flows for the most recent fiscal year if necessary to comply with generally accepted accounting principles. (Further references in this rule to the requirement for such statement are likewise applciable only to the extent that they are consistent with the requirements of generally accepted accounting principles.)

(4) Audited statements of changes in net assets conforming to the requirements of § 210.6-08 for the two most recent fiscal years.

(b) If the filing is made within 60 days after the end of the registrant's fiscal year and audited financial statements for the most recent fiscal year are not available, the balance sheet or statement of assets and liabilities may be as of the end of the preceding fiscal year and the filing shall include an additional balance sheet or statement of assets and liabilities as of an interim date within 245 days of the date of filing. In addition, the statements of operations and cash flows (if required by generally accepted accounting principles) shall be provided for the preceding fiscal year and the statement of changes in net assets shall be provided for the two preceding fiscal years and each of the statements shall be provided for the interim period between the end of the preceding fiscal year and the date of the most recent balance sheet or statement of assets and liabilities being filed. Financial statements for the corresponding period of the preceding fiscal year need not be provided.

(c) If the most current balance sheet or statement of assets and liabilities in a filing is as of a date 245 days or more prior to the date the filing is expected to become effective, the financial statements shall be updated with a balance sheet or statement of assets and liabilities as of an interim date within 245 days. In addition, the statements of operations, cash flows, and changes in net assets shall be provided for the interim period between the end of the most recent fiscal year for which a balance sheet or statement of assets and liabilities is presented and the date of the most recent interim balance sheet or statement of assets and liabilities filed.

(d) Interim financial statements provided in accordance with these requirements may be unaudited but shall be presented in the same detail as required by § § 210.6-01 to 6-10. When unaudited financial statements are presented in a registration statement, they shall include the statement required by § 210.3-03(d).

[As last amended in Release No. FR-40A, September 24, 1992, 57 F.R. 45287.]

[¶ 35,267] Special Provisions as to Financial Statements for Foreign Private Issuers

Reg. § 210.3-19. [Removed and Reserved in Release No. 33-7745, effective September 30, 2000, 64 F.R. 53900 and 64 F.R. 61962.]

[¶ 35,268] Currency for Financial Statements of Foreign Private Issuers

Reg. § 210.3-20. (a) A foreign private issuer, as defined in § 230.405 of this chapter, shall state amounts in its primary financial statements in the currency which it deems appropriate.

(b) The currency in which amounts in the financial statements are stated shall be disclosed prominently on the face of the financial statements. If dividends on publicly-held equity securities will be declared in a currency other than the reporting currency, a note to the financial statements shall identify that currency. If there are material exchange restrictions or controls relating to the issuer's reporting currency, the currency of the issuer's domicile, or the currency in which the issuer will pay dividends, prominent disclosure of this fact shall be made in the financial statements. If the reporting currency is not the U.S. dollar, dollar-equivalent financial statements or convenience translations shall not be presented, except a translation may be presented of the most recent fiscal year and any subsequent interim period presented using the exchange rate as of the most recent balance sheet included in the filing, except that a rate as of the most recent practicable date shall be used if materially different.

(c) If the financial statements of a foreign private issuer are stated in a currency of a country that has experienced cumulative inflationary effects exceeding a total of 100 percent over the most recent three year period, and have not been recast or otherwise supplemented to include information on a historical cost/constant currency or current cost basis prescribed or permitted by appropriate authoritative standards, the issuer shall present supplementary information to quantify the effects of changing prices upon its financial position and results of operations.

(d) Notwithstanding the currency selected for reporting purposes, the issuer shall measure separately its own transactions, and those of each of its material operations (*e.g.*, branches, divisions, subsidiaries, joint ventures, and similar entities) that is included in the issuer's consolidated financial statements and not located in a hyperinflationary environment, using the particular currency of the primary economic environment in which the issuer or the operation conducts its business. Assets and liabilities so determined shall be translated into the reporting currency at the exchange rate at the balance sheet date; all revenues, expenses, gains, and losses shall be translated at the exchange rate existing at the time of the transaction or, if appropriate, a weighted average of the exchange rates during the period; and all translation effects of exchange rate changes shall be included as a separate component ("cumulative translation adjustment") of shareholders' equity. For purposes of this paragraph, the currency of an operation's primary economic environment is normally the currency in which cash is primarily generated and expended; a hyperinflationary environment is one that has cumulative inflation of approximately 100% or more over the most recent three year period. Departures from the methodology presented in this paragraph shall be quantified pursuant to Item 17(c)(2) of Form 20-F (§ 249.220f of this chapter).

(e) The issuer shall state its primary financial statements in the same currency for all periods for which financial information is presented. If the financial statements are stated in a currency that is different from that used in financial statements previously filed with the Commission, the issuer shall recast its financial statements as if the newly adopted currency had been used since at least the earliest period presented in the filing. The decision to change and the reason for the change in the reporting currency shall be disclosed in a note to the financial statements in the period in which the change occurs.

[As last amended in Release No. 33-7745, effective September 30, 2000, 64 F.R. 53900 and 64 F.R. 61962.]

Article 3A—Consolidated and Combined Financial Statements

[¶ 35,271] Application of §§ 210.3A-01 to 210.3A-05

Reg. § 210.3A-01. Sections 210.3A-01 to 210.3A-05 shall govern the presentation of consolidated and combined financial statements.

[As last amended in Release No. FR-21, June 6, 1985, 50 F.R. 25214.]

[¶ 35,281] Consolidated Financial Statements of the Registrant and its Subsidiaries

Reg. § 210.3A-02. In deciding upon consolidation policy, the registrant must consider what financial presentation is most meaningful in the circumstances and should follow in the consolidated financial statements principles of inclusion or exclusion which will clearly exhibit the financial position and results of operations of the registrant. There is a presumption that consolidated statements are more meaningful than separate statements and that they are usually necessary for a fair presentation when one entity directly or indirectly has a controlling financial interest in another entity. Other particular facts and circumstances may require combined financial statements, an equity method of accounting, or valuation allowances in order to achieve a fair presentation. In any case, the disclosures required by § 210.3A-03 should clearly explain the accounting policies followed by the registrant in this area, including the circumstances involved in any departure from the normal practice of consolidating majority owned subsidiaries and not consolidating entities that are less than majority owned. Among the factors that the registrant should consider in determining the most meaningful presentation are the following:

(a) *Majority ownership:* Generally, registrants shall consolidate entities that are majority owned and shall not consolidate entities that are not majority owned. The determination of "majority ownership" requires a careful analysis of the facts and circumstances of a particular relationship among entities. In rare situations, consolidation of a majority owned subsidiary may not result in a fair presentation, because the registrant, in substance, does not have a controlling financial interest (for example, when the subsidiary is in legal reorganization or in bankruptcy). In other situations, consolidation of an entity, notwithstanding the lack of technical majority ownership, is necessary to present fairly the financial position and results of operations of the registrant, because of the existence of a parent-subsidiary relationship by means other than record ownership of voting stock.

(b) *Different fiscal periods:* Generally, registrants shall not consolidate any entity whose financial statements are as of a date or for periods substantially different from those of the registrant. Rather, the earnings or losses of such entities should be reflected in the registrant's financial statements on the equity method of accounting. However:

(1) A difference in fiscal periods does not of itself justify the exclusion of an entity from consolidation. It ordinarily is feasible for such entity to prepare, for consolidation purposes, statements for a period which corresponds with or closely approaches the fiscal year of the registrant. Where the difference is not more than 93 days, it is usually acceptable to use, for consolidation purposes, such entity's statements for its fiscal period. Such difference, when it exists, should be disclosed as follows: the closing date of the entity should be expressly indicated, and the necessity for the use of different closing dates should be briefly explained. Furthermore, recognition should be given by disclosure or otherwise to the effect of intervening events which materially affect the financial position or results of operations.

(2) Notwithstanding the 93-day provision specified in (b)(1) above, in connection with the retroactive combination of financial statements of entities following a combination between entities of common control, the financial statements of the constituents may be combined even if their respective fiscal periods do not end within 93 days, except that the financial statements for the latest fiscal year shall be recast to dates which do not differ by more than 93 days, if practicable. Disclosure shall be made of the periods combined and of the sales or revenues, net income before extraordinary items and net income of any interim periods excluded from or included more than once in results of operations as a result of such recasting.

(c) *Bank Holding Company Act:* Registrants shall not consolidate any subsidiary or group of subsidiaries of a registrant subject to the Bank Holding Company Act of 1956 as amended as to which (1) a decision requiring divestiture has been made, or (2) there is substantial likelihood that divestiture will be necessary in order to comply with provisions of the Bank Holding Company Act.

(d) *Foreign subsidiaries:* Due consideration shall be given to the propriety of consolidating with domestic corporations foreign subsidiaries which are operated under political, economic or currency restrictions. If consolidated, disclosure should be made as to the effect, insofar as this can reasonably be determined, of foreign exchange restrictions upon the consolidated financial position and operating results of the registrant and its subsidiaries.

[As last amended in Release No. 33-9026, effective April 23, 2009, 74 F.R. 18612.]

[¶ 35,291] Statement as to Principles of Consolidation or Combination Followed

Reg. § 210.3A-03. (a) A brief description of the principles followed in consolidating or combining the separate financial statements, including the principles followed in determining the inclusion or exclusion of (1) subsidiaries in consolidated or combined financial statements and (2) companies in consolidated or combined financial statements, shall be stated in the notes to the respective financial statements.

(b) As to each consolidated financial statement and as to each combined financial statement, if there has been a change in the persons included or excluded in the corresponding statement for the preceding fiscal period filed with the Commission which has a material effect on the financial statements, the persons included and the persons excluded shall be disclosed. If there have been any changes in the respective fiscal periods of the persons included made during the periods of the report which have a material effect on the financial statements, indicate clearly such changes and the manner of treatment.

[As last amended in Release No. AS-302, effective for companies with fiscal years ending after March 15, 1982, 46 F.R. 56171.]

[¶ 35,301] Intercompany Items and Transactions

Reg. § 210.3A-04. In general, there shall be eliminated intercompany items and transactions between persons included in the (a) consolidated financial statements being filed and, as appropriate, (b) unrealized intercompany profits and losses on transactions between persons for which financial statements are being filed and persons the investment in which is presented in such statements by the equity method. If such eliminations are not made, a statement of the reasons and the methods of treatment shall be made.

[As last amended in Release No. AS-302, effective for companies with fiscal years ending after March 15, 1982, 46 F.R. 56171.]

[¶ 35,311] Special Requirements as to Public Utility Holding Companies

Reg. § 210.3A-05. There shall be shown in the consolidated balance sheet of a public utility holding company the difference between the amount at which the parent's investment is carried and the underlying book equity of subsidiaries as at the respective dates of acquisition.

[As last amended in Release No. AS-302, 46 F.R. 56171.]

Article 4—Rules of General Application

[¶ 35,341] Form, Order, and Terminology

Reg. § 210.4-01. (a) Financial statements should be filed in such form and order, and should use such generally accepted terminology, as will best indicate their significance and character in the light of the provisions applicable thereto. The information required with respect to any statement shall be furnished as a minimum requirement to which shall be added such further material information as is necessary to make the required statements, in the light of the circumstances under which they are made, not misleading.

(1) Financial statements filed with the Commission which are not prepared in accordance with generally accepted accounting principles will be presumed to be misleading or inaccurate, despite footnote of other disclosures, unless the Commission has otherwise provided. This article and other articles of Regulation S-X provide clarification of certain disclosures which must be included in any event, in financial statements filed with the Commission.

(2) In all filings of foreign private issuers (see § 230.405 of this chapter), except as stated otherwise in the applicable form, the financial statements may be prepared according to a comprehensive set of accounting principles, other than those generally accepted in the United States or International Financial Reporting Standards as issued by the International Accounting Standards Board, if a reconciliation to U. S. Generally Accepted Accounting Principles and the provisions of Regulation S-X of the type specified in Item 18 of Form 20-F (§ 249.220f of this chapter) is also filed as part of the financial statements. Alternatively, the financial statements may be prepared according to U.S. Generally Accepted Accounting Principles or International Financial Reporting Standards as issued by the International Accounting Standards Board.

(3)(i) Notwithstanding the effective dates set forth in Statement of Financial Accounting Standards No. 123 (revised 2004), *Share-Based Payment* ("Statement No. 123R"), financial statements shall be prepared in accordance with Statement No. 123R beginning with:

(A) The first interim or annual reporting period of the registrant's first fiscal year beginning on or after June 15, 2005, provided the registrant does not file as a small business issuer; and

(B) The first interim or annual reporting period of the registrant's first fiscal year beginning on or after December 15, 2005, provided the registrant files as a small business issuer.

(ii) For periods prior to the effective dates set forth in this paragraph, both Statement No. 123R and Statement of Financial Accounting Standards No. 123, *Accounting for Stock-Based Compensation* (October 1995), shall be considered to be generally accepted accounting principles.

(b) All money amounts required to be shown in financial statements may be expressed in whole dollars or multiples thereof, as appropriate: *Provided,* That, when stated in other than whole dollars, an indication to that effect is inserted immediately beneath the caption of the statement or schedule, at the top of the money columns, or at an appropriate point in narrative material.

(c) Negative amounts (red figures) shall be shown in a manner which clearly distinguishes the negative attribute. When determining methods of display, consideration should be given to the limitations of reproduction and microfilming processes.

[As last amended in Release No. 33-8879, effective March 4, 2008, 73 F.R. 986.]

[¶ 35,351] Items Not Material

Reg. § 210.4-02. If the amount which would otherwise be required to be shown with respect to any item is not material, it need not be separately set forth. The combination of insignificant amounts is permitted.

[As last amended in Release No. AS-280, September 2, 1980, 45 F.R. 63660.]

[¶ 35,361] Inapplicable Captions and Omission of Unrequired or Inapplicable Financial Statements

Reg. § 210.4-03. (a) No caption should be shown in any financial statement as to which the items and conditions are not present.

(b) Financial statements not required or inapplicable because the required matter is not present need not be filed.

(c) The reasons for the omission of any required financial statements shall be indicated.

[As last amended in Release No. AS-280, September 2, 1980, 45 F.R. 63660.]

[¶ 35,371] Omission of Substantially Identical Notes

Reg. § 210.4-04. If a note covering substantially the same subject matter is required with respect to two or more financial statements relating to the same or affiliated persons, for which separate sets of notes are presented, the required information may be shown in a note to only one of such statements: *Provided,* That a clear and specific reference thereto is made in each of the other statements with respect to which the note is required.

[As last amended in Release No. AS-280, September 2, 1980, 45 F.R. 63660.]

[¶ 35,381] Current Assets and Current Liabilities

Reg. § 210.4-05. [Removed and reserved in Release No. 33-7300, May 31, 1996, effective July 15, 1996, 61 F.R. 30397.]

[¶ 35,391] Reacquired Evidences of Indebtedness

Reg. § 210.4-06. [Removed and reserved in Release No. 33-7300, May 31, 1996, effective July 15, 1996, 61 F.R. 30397.]

[¶ 35,401] Discount on Shares

Reg. § 210.4-07. Discount on shares, or any unamortized balance thereof, shall be shown separately as a deduction from the applicable account(s) as circumstances require.

[As last amended in Release No. AS-280, September 2, 1980, 45 F.R. 63660.]

[¶ 35,411] General Notes to Financial Statements

Reg. § 210.4-08. If applicable to the person for which the financial statements are filed, the following shall be set forth on the face of the appropriate statement or in appropriately captioned notes. The information shall be provided for each statement required to be filed, except that the information required by items (b), (c), (d), (e), and (f) shall be provided as of the most recent audited balance sheet being filed and for item (j) as specified therein. When specific statements are presented separately, the pertinent notes shall accompany such statements unless cross-referencing is appropriate.

(a) *Principles of consolidation or combination.* With regard to consolidated or combined financial statements, refer to § § 210.3A-01 to 3A-08 for requirements for supplemental information in notes to the financial statements.

(b) *Assets subject to lien.* Assets mortgaged pledged, or otherwise subject to lien, and the approximate amounts thereof, shall be designated and the obligations collateralized briefly identified.

(c) *Defaults.* The facts and amounts concerning any default in principal, interest, sinking fund, or redemption provisions with respect to any issue of securities or credit agreements, or any breach of covenant of a related indenture or agreement, which default or breach existed at the date of the most recent balance sheet being filed and which has not been subsequently cured, shall be stated in the notes to the financial statements. If a default or breach exists but acceleration of the obligation has been waived for a stated period of time beyond the date of the most recent balance sheet being filed, state the amount of the obligation and the period of the waiver.

(d) *Preferred shares.* (1) Aggregate preferences on involuntary liquidation, if other than par or stated value, shall be shown parenthetically in the equity section of the balance sheet.

(2) Disclosure shall be made of any restriction upon retained earnings that arises from the fact that upon involuntary liquidation the aggregate preferences of the preferred shares exceeds the par or stated value of such shares.

(e) *Restrictions which limit the payment of dividends by the registrant.* (1) Describe the most significant restrictions, other than as reported under paragraph (d) of this section, on the payment of dividends by the registrant, indicating their sources, their pertinent provisions, and the amount of retained earnings or net income restricted or free of restrictions.

(2) Disclose the amount of consolidated retained earnings which represents undistributed earnings of 50 percent or less owned persons accounted for by the equity method.

(3) The disclosures in paragraph (3)(i) and (ii) in this section shall be provided when the restricted net assets of consolidated and unconsolidated subsidiaries and the parent's equity in the undistributed earnings of 50 percent or less owned persons accounted for by the equity method together exceed 25 percent of consolidated net assets as of the end of the most recently completed fiscal year. For purposes of this test, restricted net assets of subsidiaries shall mean that amount of the registrant's proportionate share of net assets (after intercompany eliminations) reflected in the balance sheets of its consolidated and unconsolidated subsidiaries as of the end of the most recent fiscal year which may not be transferred to the parent company in the form of loans, advances or cash dividends by the subsidiaries

without the consent of a third party (i.e., lender, regulatory agency, foreign government, etc.). Not all limitations on transferability of assets are considered to be restrictions for purposes of this test, which considers only specific third party restrictions on the ability of subsidiaries to transfer funds outside of the entity. For example, the presence of subsidiary debt which is secured by certain of the subsidiary's assets does not constitute a restriction under this rule. However, if there are any loan provisions prohibiting dividend payments, loans or advances to the parent by a subsidiary, these are considered restrictions for purposes of computing restricted net assets. When a loan agreement requires that a subsidiary maintain certain working capital, net tangible asset, or net asset levels, or where formal compensating arrangements exist, there is considered to be a restriction under the rule because the lender's intent is normally to preclude the transfer by dividend or otherwise of funds to the parent company. Similarly, a provision which requires that a subsidiary reinvest all of its earnings is a restriction, since this precludes loans, advances or dividends in the amount of such undistributed earnings by the entity. Where restrictions on the amount of funds which may be loaned or advanced differ from the amount restricted as to transfer in the form of cash dividends, the amount least restrictive to the subsidiary shall be used. Redeemable preferred stocks (§ 210.5-02.27) and noncontrolling interests shall be deducted in computing net assets for purposes of this test.

(i) Describe the nature of any restrictions on the ability of consolidated subsidiaries and unconsolidated subsidiaries to transfer funds to the registrant in the form of cash dividends, loans or advances (i.e., borrowing arrangements, regulatory restraints, foreign government, etc.)

(ii) Disclose separately the amounts of such restricted net assets for unconsolidated subsidiaries and consolidated subsidiaries as of the end of the most recently completed fiscal year.

(f) *Significant changes in bonds, mortgages and similar debt.* Any significant changes in the authorized or issued amounts of bonds, mortgages and similar debt since the date of the latest balance sheet being filed for a particular person or group shall be stated.

(g) *Summarized financial information of subsidiaries not consolidated and 50 percent or less owned persons.* (1) The summarized information as to assets, liabilities and results of operations as detailed in § 210.1-02(bb) shall be presented in notes to the financial statements on an individual or group basis for:

(i) Subsidiaries not consolidated; or

(ii) For 50 percent or less owned persons accounted for by the equity method by the registrant or by a subsidiary of the registrant, if the criteria in § 210.1-02(w) for a significant subsidiary are met:

(A) Individually by any subsidiary not consolidated or any 50% or less owned person; or

(B) On an aggregated basis by any combination of such subsidiaries and persons.

(2) Summarized financial information shall be presented insofar as is practicable as of the same dates and for the same periods as the audited consolidated financial statements provided and shall include the disclosures prescribed by § 210.1-02(bb). Summarized information of subsidiaries not consolidated shall not be combined for disclosure purposes with the summarized information of 50 percent or less owned persons.

(h) *Income tax expense.* (1) Disclosure shall be made in the income statement or a note thereto, of (i) the components of income (loss) before income tax expense (benefit) as either domestic or foreign; (ii) the components of income tax expense, including (A) taxes currently payable and (B) the net tax effects, as applicable, of timing differences (indicate separately the amount of the estimated tax effect of each of the various types of timing differences, such as depreciation, warranty costs, etc., where the amount of each such tax effect exceeds five percent of the amount computed by multiplying the income before tax by the applicable statutory Federal income tax rate; other differences may be combined.)

Note: Amounts applicable to United States Federal income taxes, to foreign income taxes and the other income taxes shall be stated separately for each major component. Amounts applicable to foreign income (loss) and amounts applicable to foreign or other income taxes which are less than five percent of the total of income before taxes or the component of tax expense, respectively, need not be separately disclosed. For purposes of this rule, foreign income (loss) is defined as income (loss) generated from a registrant's foreign operations, i.e., operations that are *located outside* of the registrant's home country.

(2) Provide a reconciliation between the amount of reported total income tax expense (benefit) and the amount computed by multiplying the income (loss) before tax by the applicable statutory Federal income tax rate, showing the estimated dollar amount of each of the underlying causes for the difference. If no individual reconciling item amounts to more than five percent of the amount computed by multiplying the income before tax by the applicable statutory Federal income tax rate, and the total difference to be reconciled is less than five percent of such computed amount, no reconciliation need be provided unless it would be significant in appraising the trend of earnings. Reconciling items that are individually less than five percent of the computed amount may be aggregated in the reconciliation. The reconciliation may be presented in percentages rather than in dollar amounts. Where the reporting person is a foreign entity, the income tax rate in that person's country of domicile should normally be

used in making the above computation, but different rates should not be used for subsidiaries or other segments of a reporting entity. When the rate used by a reporting person is other than the United States Federal corporate income tax rate, the rate used and the basis for using such rate shall be disclosed.

(3) Paragraphs (h)(1) and (2) of this section shall be applied in the following manner to financial statements which reflect the adoption of Statement of Financial Accounting Standards No. 109, *Accounting for Income Taxes.*

(i) The disclosures required by paragraph (h)(1)(ii) and by the parenthetical instruction at the end of paragraph (h)(1) and by the introductory sentence of paragraph (h)(2) of this section shall not apply.

(ii) The instructional note between paragraphs (h)(1) and (2) and the balance of the requirements of paragraphs (h)(1) and (2) shall continue to apply.

[Paragraph (h)(3) added in Release No. FR-40A, effective November 2, 1992, 57 F.R. 45287.]

(i) *Warrants or rights outstanding.* Information with respect to warrants or rights outstanding at the date of the related balance sheet shall be set forth as follows:

(1) Title of issue of securities called for by warrants or rights.

(2) Aggregate amount of securities called for by warrants or rights outstanding.

(3) Date from which warrants or rights are exercisable.

(4) Price at which warrant or right is exercisable.

(j) [Reserved]

(k) *Related party transactions which affect the financial statements.* (1) Related party transactions should be identified and the amounts stated on the face of the balance sheet, income statement, or statement of cash flows. [Redesignated as paragraph (k) and amended in Release No. FR-22, effective December 3, 1985, F.R. 49529; amended in Release No. FR-40A, effective November 2, 1992, 57 F.R. 45287.]

(2) In cases where separate financial statements are presented for the registrant, certain investees, or subsidiaries, separate disclosure shall be made in such statements of the amounts in the related consolidated financial statements which are (i) eliminated and (ii) not eliminated. Also, any intercompany profits or losses resulting from transactions with related parties and not eliminated and the effects thereof shall be disclosed.

(l) [Reserved.]

(m) *Repurchase and reverse repurchase agreements.* (1) *Repurchase agreements (assets sold under agreements to repurchase).* (i) If, as of the most recent balance sheet date, the carrying amount (or market value, if higher than the carrying amount or if there is no carrying amount) of the securities or other assets sold under agreements to repurchase ("repurchase agreements") exceeds 10% of total assets, disclose separately in the balance sheet the aggregate amount of liabilities incurred pursuant to repurchase agreements including accrued interest payable thereon.

(ii) (A) If, as of the most recent balance sheet date, the carrying amount (or market value, if higher than the carrying amount) of securities or other assets sold under repurchase agreements, other than securities or assets specified in (1)(ii)(B) of this section, exceeds 10% of total assets, disclose in an appropriately captioned footnote containing a tabular presentation, segregated as to type of such securities or assets sold under agreements to repurchase (e.g., U.S. Treasury obligations, U.S. Government agency obligations and loans), the following information as of the balance sheet date for each such agreement or group of agreements (other than agreements involving securities or assets specified in (1)(ii)(B) of this section) maturing *(1)* overnight; *(2)* term up to 30 days; *(3)* term of 30 to 90 days; *(4)* term over 90 days and *(5)* demand:

(i) carrying amount and market value of the assets sold under agreement to repurchase, including accrued interest plus any cash or other assets on deposit under the repurchase agreements; and

(ii) the repurchase liability associated with such transaction or group of transactions and the interest rate(s) thereon.

(B) For purposes of (1)(ii)(A) of this section only, do not include securities or other assets for which unrealized changes in market value are reported in current income or which have been obtained under reverse repurchase agreements.

(iii) If, as of the most recent balance sheet date, the amount at risk under repurchase agreements with any individual counterparty or group of related counterparties exceeds 10% of stockholders' equity (or in the case of investment companies, net asset value), disclose the name of each such counterparty or group of related counterparties, the amount at risk with each, and the weighted average maturity of the repurchase agreements with each. The amount at risk under repurchase agreements is defined as the excess of carrying amount (or market value, if higher than the carrying amount or if there is no carrying amount) of the securities or other assets sold under agreement to repurchase, including accrued interest plus any cash or other assets on deposit to secure the repurchase obligation, over the amount of the repurchase liability (adjusted for accrued interest). (Cash deposits in connection with repurchase agreements shall not be reported as unrestricted cash pursuant to rule 5-02.1.)

(2) *Reverse repurchase agreements (assets purchased under agreements to resell)*. (i) If, as of the most recent balance sheet date, the aggregate carrying amount of "reverse repurchase agreements" (securities or other assets purchased under agreements to resell) exceeds 10% of total assets: (A) disclose separately such amount in the balance sheet; and (B) disclose in an appropriately captioned footnote: *(1)* the registrant's policy with regard to taking possession of securities or other assets purchased under agreements to resell; and *(2)* whether or not there are any provisions to ensure that the market value of the underlying assets remains sufficient to protect the registrant in the event of default by the counterparty and if so, the nature of those provisions.

(ii) If, as of the most recent balance sheet date, the amount of risk under reverse repurchase agreements with any individual counterparty or group of related counterparties exceeds 10% of stockholders' equity (or in the case of investment companies, net asset value), disclose the name of each such counterparty or group of related counterparties, the amount at risk with each, and the weighted average maturity of the reverse repurchase agreements with each. The amount at risk under reverse repurchase agreements is defined as the excess of the carrying amount of the reverse repurchase agreements over the market value of assets delivered pursuant to the agreements by the counterparty to the registrant (or to a third party agent that has affirmatively agreed to act on behalf of the registrant) and not returned to the counterparty, except in exchange for their approximate market value in a separate transaction. [Added in Release No. FR-24, effective for financial statements covering fiscal years ending on or after February 28, 1986, 51 F.R. 3031.]

(n) *Accounting policies for certain derivative instruments.* Disclosures regarding accounting policies shall include descriptions of the accounting policies used for derivative financial instruments and derivative commodity instruments and the methods of applying those policies that materially affect the determination of financial position, cash flows, or results of operation. This description shall include, to the extent material, each of the following items:

(1) A discussion of each method used to account for derivative financial instruments and derivative commodity instruments;

(2) The types of derivative financial instruments and derivative commodity instruments accounted for under each method;

(3) The criteria required to be met for each accounting method used, including a discussion of the criteria required to be met for hedge or deferral accounting and accrual or settlement accounting (e.g., whether and how risk reduction, correlation, designation, and effectiveness tests are applied);

(4) The accounting method used if the criteria specified in paragraph (n)(3) of this section are not met;

(5) The method used to account for terminations of derivatives designated as hedges or derivatives used to affect directly or indirectly the terms, fair values, or cash flows of a designated item;

(6) The method used to account for derivatives when the designated item matures, is sold, is extinguished, or is terminated. In addition, the method used to account for derivatives designated to an anticipated transaction, when the anticipated transaction is no longer likely to occur; and

(7) Where and when derivative financial instruments and derivative commodity instruments, and their related gains and losses, are reported in the statements of financial position, cash flows, and results of operations.

Instructions to Paragraph 4-08(n)

1. For purposes of this paragraph 4-08(n), derivative financial instruments and derivative commodity instruments (collectively referred to as "derivatives") are defined as follows:

(i) Derivative financial instruments have the same meaning as defined by generally accepted accounting principles (see, e.g., Financial Accounting Standards Board ("FASB"), Statement of Financial Accounting Standards No. 119, "Disclosure about Derivative Financial Instruments and Fair Value of Financial Instruments," ("FAS 119") paragraphs 5-7, (October 1994)), and include futures, forwards, swaps, options, and other financial instruments with similar characteristics.

(ii) Derivative commodity instruments include, to the extent such instruments are not derivative financial instruments, commodity futures, commodity forwards, commodity swaps, commodity options, and other commodity instruments with similar characteristics that are permitted by contract or business custom to be settled in cash or with another financial instrument. For purposes of this paragraph, settlement in cash includes settlement in cash of the net change in value of the derivative commodity instrument (e.g., net cash settlement based on changes in the price of the underlying commodity).

2. For purposes of paragraphs 4-08(n)(2), 4-08(n)(3), 4-08(n)(4), and 4-08(n)(7), the required disclosures should address separately derivatives entered into for trading purposes and derivatives entered into for purposes other than trading. For purposes of this paragraph, trading purposes has the same meaning as defined by generally accepted accounting principles (see, e.g., FAS 119, paragraph 9a (October 1994)).

3. For purposes of paragraph 4-08(n)(6), anticipated transactions means transactions (other than transactions involving existing assets or liabilities or transactions necessitated by existing firm commitments) an enterprise expects, but is not obligated, to carry out in the normal course of business (see, e.g., FASB, Statement of Financial Accounting Standards No. 80, "Accounting for Futures Contracts," paragraph 9, (August 1984)).

4. Registrants should provide disclosures required under paragraph 4-08(n) in filings with the Commission that include financial statements of fiscal periods ending after June 15, 1997.

[As last amended in Release No. 33-9026, effective April 23, 2009, 74 F.R. 18612.]

[¶ 35,431] Financial Accounting and Reporting for Oil and Gas Producing Activities Pursuant to the Federal Securities Laws and the Energy Policy and Conservation Act of 1975

Reg. § 210.4-10. This section prescribes financial accounting and reporting standards for registrants with the Commission engaged in oil and gas producing activities in filings under the federal securities laws and for the preparation of accounts by persons engaged, in whole or in part, in the production of crude oil or natural gas in the United States, pursuant to Section 503 of the Energy Policy and Conservation Act of 1975 [42 U.S.C. 6383] ("EPCA") and section 11(c) of the Energy Supply and Environmental Coordination Act of 1974 [15 U.S.C. 796]("ESECA"), as amended by section 505 of EPCA. The application of this section to those oil and gas producing operations of companies regulated for rate-making purposes on an individual-company-cost-of-service basis may, however, give appropriate recognition to differences arising because of the effect of the rate-making process.

> *Exemption.* Any person exempted by the Department of Energy from any record-keeping or reporting requirements pursuant to Section 11(c) of ESECA, as amended, is similarly exempted from the related provisions of this section in the preparation of accounts pursuant to EPCA. This exemption does not affect the applicability of this section to filings pursuant to the federal securities laws.

Definitions

(a) *Definitions.* The following definitions apply to the terms listed below as they are used in this section:

(1) *Oil and gas producing activities.* (i) Such activities include:

(A) The search for crude oil, including condensate and natural gas liquids, or natural gas ("oil and gas") in their natural states and original locations.

(B) The acquisition of property rights or properties for the purpose of further exploration and/or for the purpose of removing the oil or gas from existing reservoirs on those properties.

(C) The construction, drilling and production activities necessary to retrieve oil and gas from its natural reservoirs, and the acquisition, construction, installation, and maintenance of field gathering and storage systems—including lifting the oil and gas to the surface and gathering, treating, field processing (as in the case of processing gas to extract liquid hydrocarbons) and field storage. For purposes of this section, the oil and gas production function shall normally be regarded as terminating at the outlet valve on the lease or field storage tank; if unusual physical or operational circumstances exist, it may be appropriate to regard the production functions as terminating at the first point at which oil, gas, or gas liquids are delivered to a main pipeline, a common carrier, a refinery, or a marine terminal.

(ii) Oil and gas producing activities do not include:

(A) The transporting, refining and marketing of oil and gas.

(B) Activities relating to the production of natural resources other than oil and gas.

(C) The production of geothermal steam or the extraction of hydrocarbons as a by-product of the production of geothermal steam or associated geothermal resources as defined in the Geothermal Steam Act of 1970.

(D) The extraction of hydrocarbons from shale, tar sands, or coal.

(2) *Analogous reservoir.* Analogous reservoirs, as used in resources assessments, have similar rock and fluid properties, reservoir conditions (depth, temperature, and pressure) and drive mechanisms, but are typically at a more advanced stage of development than the reservoir of interest and thus may provide concepts to assist in the interpretation of more limited data and estimation of recovery. When used to support proved reserves, an "analogous reservoir" refers to a reservoir that shares the following characteristics with the reservoir of interest:

(i) Same geological formation (but not necessarily in pressure communication with the reservoir of interest);

(ii) Same environment of deposition;

(iii) Similar geological structure; and

(iv) Same drive mechanism.

Instruction to paragraph (a)(2): Reservoir properties must, in the aggregate, be no more favorable in the analog than in the reservoir of interest.

(3) *Bitumen.* Bitumen, sometimes referred to as natural bitumen, is petroleum in a solid or semi-solid state in natural deposits with a viscosity greater than 10,000 centipoise measured at original temperature in the deposit and atmospheric pressure, on a gas free basis. In its natural state it usually contains sulfur, metals, and other nonhydrocarbons.

(4) *Condensate.* Condensate is a mixture of hydrocarbons that exists in the gaseous phase at original reservoir temperature and pressure, but that, when produced, is in the liquid phase at surface pressure and temperature.

(5) *Deterministic estimate.* The method of estimating reserves or resources is called deterministic when a single value for each parameter (from the geoscience, engineering, or economic data) in the reserves calculation is used in the reserves estimation procedure.

(6) *Developed oil and gas reserves.* Developed oil and gas reserves are reserves of any category that can be expected to be recovered:

(i) Through existing wells with existing equipment and operating methods or in which the cost of the required equipment is relatively minor compared to the cost of a new well; and

(ii) Through installed extraction equipment and infrastructure operational at the time of the reserves estimate if the extraction is by means not involving a well.

(7) *Development costs.* Costs incurred to obtain access to proved reserves and to provide facilities for extracting, treating, gathering and storing the oil and gas. More specifically, development costs, including depreciation and applicable operating costs of support equipment and facilities and other costs of development activities, are costs incurred to:

(i) Gain access to and prepare well locations for drilling, including surveying well locations for the purpose of determining specific development drilling sites, clearing ground, draining, road building, and relocating public roads, gas lines, and power lines, to the extent necessary in developing the proved reserves.

(ii) Drill and equip development wells, development-type stratigraphic test wells, and service wells, including the costs of platforms and of well equipment such as casing, tubing, pumping equipment, and the wellhead assembly.

(iii) Acquire, construct, and install production facilities such as lease flow lines, separators, treaters, heaters, manifolds, measuring devices, and production storage tanks, natural gas cycling and processing plants, and central utility and waste disposal systems.

(iv) Provide improved recovery systems.

(8) *Development project.* A development project is the means by which petroleum resources are brought to the status of economically producible. As examples, the development of a single reservoir or field, an incremental development in a producing field, or the integrated development of a group of several fields and associated facilities with a common ownership may constitute a development project.

(9) *Development well.* A well drilled within the proved area of an oil or gas reservoir to the depth of a stratigraphic horizon known to be productive.

(10) *Economically producible.* The term economically producible, as it relates to a resource, means a resource which generates revenue that exceeds, or is reasonably expected to exceed, the costs of the operation. The value of the products that generate revenue shall be determined at the terminal point of oil and gas producing activities as defined in paragraph (a)(16) of this section.

(11) *Estimated ultimate recovery (EUR).* Estimated ultimate recovery is the sum of reserves remaining as of a given date and cumulative production as of that date.

(12) *Exploration costs.* Costs incurred in identifying areas that may warrant examination and in examining specific areas that are considered to have prospects of containing oil and gas reserves, including costs of drilling exploratory wells and exploratory-type stratigraphic test wells. Exploration costs may be incurred both before acquiring the related property (sometimes referred to in part as prospecting costs) and after acquiring the property. Principal types of exploration costs, which include depreciation and applicable operating costs of support equipment and facilities and other costs of exploration activities, are:

(i) Costs of topographical, geographical and geophysical studies, rights of access to properties to conduct those studies, and salaries and other expenses of geologists, geophysical crews, and others conducting those studies. Collectively, these are sometimes referred to as geological and geophysical or "G&G" costs.

(ii) Costs of carrying and retaining undeveloped properties, such as delay rentals, ad valorem taxes on properties, legal costs for title defense, and the maintenance of land and lease records.

(iii) Dry hole contributions and bottom hole contributions.

(iv) Costs of drilling and equipping exploratory wells.

(v) Costs of drilling exploratory-type stratigraphic test wells.

(13) *Exploratory well.* An exploratory well is a well drilled to find a new field or to find a new reservoir in a field previously found to be productive of oil or gas in another reservoir. Generally, an exploratory well is any well that is not a development well, an extension well, a service well, or a stratigraphic test well as those items are defined in this section.

(14) *Extension well.* An extension well is a well drilled to extend the limits of a known reservoir.

(15) *Field.* An area consisting of a single reservoir or multiple reservoirs all grouped on or related to the same individual geological structural feature and/or stratigraphic condition. There may be two or more reservoirs in a field which are separated vertically by intervening impervious strata, or laterally by local geologic barriers, or by both. Reservoirs that are associated by being in overlapping or adjacent fields may be treated as a single or common operational field. The geological terms "structural feature" and "stratigraphic condition" are intended to identify localized geological features as opposed to the broader terms of basins, trends, provinces, plays, areas-of-interest, etc.

(16) *Oil and gas producing activities.* (i) Oil and gas producing activities include:

(A) The search for crude oil, including condensate and natural gas liquids, or natural gas ("oil and gas") in their natural states and original locations;

(B) The acquisition of property rights or properties for the purpose of further exploration or for the purpose of removing the oil or gas from such properties;

(C) The construction, drilling, and production activities necessary to retrieve oil and gas from their natural reservoirs, including the acquisition, construction, installation, and maintenance of field gathering and storage systems, such as:

(*1*) Lifting the oil and gas to the surface; and

(*2*) Gathering, treating, and field processing (as in the case of processing gas to extract liquid hydrocarbons); and

(D) Extraction of saleable hydrocarbons, in the solid, liquid, or gaseous state, from oil sands, shale, coalbeds, or other nonrenewable natural resources which are intended to be upgraded into synthetic oil or gas, and activities undertaken with a view to such extraction.

Instruction 1 to paragraph (a)(16)(i): The oil and gas production function shall be regarded as ending at a "terminal point", which is the outlet valve on the lease or field storage tank. If unusual physical or operational circumstances exist, it may be appropriate to regard the terminal point for the production function as:

a. The first point at which oil, gas, or gas liquids, natural or synthetic, are delivered to a main pipeline, a common carrier, a refinery, or a marine terminal; and

b. In the case of natural resources that are intended to be upgraded into synthetic oil or gas, if those natural resources are delivered to a purchaser prior to upgrading, the first point at which the natural resources are delivered to a main pipeline, a common carrier, a refinery, a marine terminal, or a facility which upgrades such natural resources into synthetic oil or gas.

Instruction 2 to paragraph (a)(16)(i): For purposes of this paragraph (a)(16), the term *saleable hydrocarbons* means hydrocarbons that are saleable in the state in which the hydrocarbons are delivered.

(ii) Oil and gas producing activities do not include:

(A) Transporting, refining, or marketing oil and gas;

(B) Processing of produced oil, gas or natural resources that can be upgraded into synthetic oil or gas by a registrant that does not have the legal right to produce or a revenue interest in such production;

(C) Activities relating to the production of natural resources other than oil, gas, or natural resources from which synthetic oil and gas can be extracted; or

(D) Production of geothermal steam.

(17) *Possible reserves.* Possible reserves are those additional reserves that are less certain to be recovered than probable reserves.

(i) When deterministic methods are used, the total quantities ultimately recovered from a project have a low probability of exceeding proved plus probable plus possible reserves. When probabilistic methods are used, there should be at least a 10% probability that the total quantities ultimately recovered will equal or exceed the proved plus probable plus possible reserves estimates.

(ii) Possible reserves may be assigned to areas of a reservoir adjacent to probable reserves where data control and interpretations of available data are progressively less certain. Frequently, this will be in areas where geoscience and engineering data are unable to define clearly the area and vertical limits of commercial production from the reservoir by a defined project.

(iii) Possible reserves also include incremental quantities associated with a greater percentage recovery of the hydrocarbons in place than the recovery quantities assumed for probable reserves.

(iv) The proved plus probable and proved plus probable plus possible reserves estimates must be based on reasonable alternative technical and commercial interpretations within the reservoir or subject project that are clearly documented, including comparisons to results in successful similar projects.

(v) Possible reserves may be assigned where geoscience and engineering data identify directly adjacent portions of a reservoir within the same accumulation that may be separated from proved areas by faults with displacement less than formation thickness or other geological discontinuities and that have not been penetrated by a wellbore, and the registrant believes that such adjacent portions are in communication with the known (proved) reservoir. Possible reserves may be assigned to areas that are structurally higher or lower than the proved area if these areas are in communication with the proved reservoir.

(vi) Pursuant to paragraph (a)(22)(iii) of this section, where direct observation has defined a highest known oil (HKO) elevation and the potential exists for an associated gas cap, proved oil reserves should be assigned in the structurally higher portions of the reservoir above the HKO only if the higher contact can be established with reasonable certainty through reliable technology. Portions of the reservoir that do not meet this reasonable certainty criterion may be assigned as probable and possible oil or gas based on reservoir fluid properties and pressure gradient interpretations.

(18) *Probable reserves.* Probable reserves are those additional reserves that are less certain to be recovered than proved reserves but which, together with proved reserves, are as likely as not to be recovered.

(i) When deterministic methods are used, it is as likely as not that actual remaining quantities recovered will exceed the sum of estimated proved plus probable reserves. When probabilistic methods are used, there should be at least a 50% probability that the actual quantities recovered will equal or exceed the proved plus probable reserves estimates.

(ii) Probable reserves may be assigned to areas of a reservoir adjacent to proved reserves where data control or interpretations of available data are less certain, even if the interpreted reservoir continuity of structure or productivity does not meet the reasonable certainty criterion. Probable reserves may be assigned to areas that are structurally higher than the proved area if these areas are in communication with the proved reservoir.

(iii) Probable reserves estimates also include potential incremental quantities associated with a greater percentage recovery of the hydrocarbons in place than assumed for proved reserves.

(iv) See also guidelines in paragraphs (a)(17)(iv) and (a)(17)(vi) of this section.

(19) *Probabilistic estimate.* The method of estimation of reserves or resources is called probabilistic when the full range of values that could reasonably occur for each unknown parameter (from the geoscience and engineering data) is used to generate a full range of possible outcomes and their associated probabilities of occurrence.

(20) *Production costs.* (i) Costs incurred to operate and maintain wells and related equipment and facilities, including depreciation and applicable operating costs of support equipment and facilities and other costs of operating and maintaining those wells and related equipment and facilities. They become part of the cost of oil and gas produced. Examples of production costs (sometimes called lifting costs) are:

(A) Costs of labor to operate the wells and related equipment and facilities.

(B) Repairs and maintenance.

(C) Materials, supplies, and fuel consumed and supplies utilized in operating the wells and related equipment and facilities.

(D) Property taxes and insurance applicable to proved properties and wells and related equipment and facilities.

(E) Severance taxes.

(21) *Proved area.* The part of a property to which proved reserves have been specifically attributed.

(22) *Proved oil and gas reserves.* Proved oil and gas reserves are those quantities of oil and gas, which, by analysis of geoscience and engineering data, can be estimated with reasonable certainty to be economically producible—from a given date forward, from known reservoirs, and under existing

economic conditions, operating methods, and government regulations—prior to the time at which contracts providing the right to operate expire, unless evidence indicates that renewal is reasonably certain, regardless of whether deterministic or probabilistic methods are used for the estimation. The project to extract the hydrocarbons must have commenced or the operator must be reasonably certain that it will commence the project within a reasonable time.

(i) The area of the reservoir considered as proved includes:

(A) The area identified by drilling and limited by fluid contacts, if any, and

(B) Adjacent undrilled portions of the reservoir that can, with reasonable certainty, be judged to be continuous with it and to contain economically producible oil or gas on the basis of available geoscience and engineering data.

(ii) In the absence of data on fluid contacts, proved quantities in a reservoir are limited by the lowest known hydrocarbons (LKH) as seen in a well penetration unless geoscience, engineering, or performance data and reliable technology establishes a lower contact with reasonable certainty.

(iii) Where direct observation from well penetrations has defined a highest known oil (HKO) elevation and the potential exists for an associated gas cap, proved oil reserves may be assigned in the structurally higher portions of the reservoir only if geoscience, engineering, or performance data and reliable technology establish the higher contact with reasonable certainty.

(iv) Reserves which can be produced economically through application of improved recovery techniques (including, but not limited to, fluid injection) are included in the proved classification when:

(A) Successful testing by a pilot project in an area of the reservoir with properties no more favorable than in the reservoir as a whole, the operation of an installed program in the reservoir or an analogous reservoir, or other evidence using reliable technology establishes the reasonable certainty of the engineering analysis on which the project or program was based; and

(B) The project has been approved for development by all necessary parties and entities, including governmental entities.

(v) Existing economic conditions include prices and costs at which economic producibility from a reservoir is to be determined. The price shall be the average price during the 12-month period prior to the ending date of the period covered by the report, determined as an unweighted arithmetic average of the first-day-of-the-month price for each month within such period, unless prices are defined by contractual arrangements, excluding escalations based upon future conditions.

(23) *Proved properties.* Properties with proved reserves.

(24) *Reasonable certainty.* If deterministic methods are used, reasonable certainty means a high degree of confidence that the quantities will be recovered. If probabilistic methods are used, there should be at least a 90% probability that the quantities actually recovered will equal or exceed the estimate. A high degree of confidence exists if the quantity is much more likely to be achieved than not, and, as changes due to increased availability of geoscience (geological, geophysical, and geochemical), engineering, and economic data are made to estimated ultimate recovery (EUR) with time, reasonably certain EUR is much more likely to increase or remain constant than to decrease.

(25) *Reliable technology.* Reliable technology is a grouping of one or more technologies (including computational methods) that has been field tested and has been demonstrated to provide reasonably certain results with consistency and repeatability in the formation being evaluated or in an analogous formation.

(26) *Reserves.* Reserves are estimated remaining quantities of oil and gas and related substances anticipated to be economically producible, as of a given date, by application of development projects to known accumulations. In addition, there must exist, or there must be a reasonable expectation that there will exist, the legal right to produce or a revenue interest in the production, installed means of delivering oil and gas or related substances to market, and all permits and financing required to implement the project.

Note to paragraph (a)(26): Reserves should not be assigned to adjacent reservoirs isolated by major, potentially sealing, faults until those reservoirs are penetrated and evaluated as economically producible. Reserves should not be assigned to areas that are clearly separated from a known accumulation by a non-productive reservoir (*i.e.*, absence of reservoir, structurally low reservoir, or negative test results). Such areas may contain prospective resources (*i.e.*, potentially recoverable resources from undiscovered accumulations).

(27) *Reservoir.* A porous and permeable underground formation containing a natural accumulation of producible oil and/or gas that is confined by impermeable rock or water barriers and is individual and separate from other reservoirs.

(28) *Resources.* Resources are quantities of oil and gas estimated to exist in naturally occurring accumulations. A portion of the resources may be estimated to be recoverable, and another portion may be considered to be unrecoverable. Resources include both discovered and undiscovered accumulations.

(29) *Service well.* A well drilled or completed for the purpose of supporting production in an existing field. Specific purposes of service wells include gas injection, water injection, steam injection, air injection, salt-water disposal, water supply for injection, observation, or injection for in-situ combustion.

(30) *Stratigraphic test well.* A stratigraphic test well is a drilling effort, geologically directed, to obtain information pertaining to a specific geologic condition. Such wells customarily are drilled without the intent of being completed for hydrocarbon production. The classification also includes tests identified as core tests and all types of expendable holes related to hydrocarbon exploration. Stratigraphic tests are classified as "exploratory type" if not drilled in a known area or "development type" if drilled in a known area.

(31) *Undeveloped oil and gas reserves.* Undeveloped oil and gas reserves are reserves of any category that are expected to be recovered from new wells on undrilled acreage, or from existing wells where a relatively major expenditure is required for recompletion.

(i) Reserves on undrilled acreage shall be limited to those directly offsetting development spacing areas that are reasonably certain of production when drilled, unless evidence using reliable technology exists that establishes reasonable certainty of economic producibility at greater distances.

(ii) Undrilled locations can be classified as having undeveloped reserves only if a development plan has been adopted indicating that they are scheduled to be drilled within five years, unless the specific circumstances, justify a longer time.

(iii) Under no circumstances shall estimates for undeveloped reserves be attributable to any acreage for which an application of fluid injection or other improved recovery technique is contemplated, unless such techniques have been proved effective by actual projects in the same reservoir or an analogous reservoir, as defined in paragraph (a)(2) of this section, or by other evidence using reliable technology establishing reasonable certainty.

Successful Efforts Method

(b) A reporting entity that follows the successful efforts method shall comply with the accounting and financial reporting disclosure requirements of Statement of Financial Accounting Standards No. 19, as amended.

Full Cost Method

(c) *Application of the full cost method of accounting.* A reporting entity that follows the full cost method shall apply that method to all of its operations and to the operations of its subsidiaries, as follows:

(1) *Determination of cost centers.* Cost centers shall be established on a country-by-country basis.

(2) *Costs to be capitalized.* All costs associated with property acquisition, exploration, and development activities (as defined in paragraph (a) of this section) shall be capitalized within the appropriate cost center. Any internal costs that are capitalized shall be limited to those costs that can be directly identified with acquisition, exploration, and development activities undertaken by the reporting entity for its own account, and shall not include any costs related to production, general corporate overhead, or similar activities.

(3) *Amortization of capitalized costs.* Capitalized costs within a cost center shall be amortized on the unit-of-production basis using proved oil and gas reserves, as follows:

(i) Costs to be amortized shall include (A) all capitalized costs, less accumulated amortization, other than the cost of properties described in paragraph (ii) below; (B) the estimated future expenditures (based on current costs) to be incurred in developing proved reserves; and (C) estimated dismantlement and abandonment costs, net of estimated salvage values.

(ii) The cost of investments in unproved properties and major development projects may be excluded from capitalized costs to be amortized, subject to the following:

(A) All costs directly associated with the acquisition and evaluation of unproved properties may be excluded from the amortization computation until it is determined whether or not proved reserves can be assigned to the properties, subject to the following conditions: (*1*) Until such a determination is made, the properties shall be assessed at least annually to ascertain whether impairment has occurred. Unevaluated properties whose costs are individually significant shall be assessed individually. Where it is not practicable to individually assess the amount of impairment of properties for which costs are not individually significant, such properties may be grouped for purposes of assessing impairment. Impairment may be estimated by applying factors based on historical experience and other data such as primary lease terms of the properties, average holding periods of unproved properties, and geographic and geologic data to groupings of individually insignificant properties and projects. The amount of impairment assessed under either of these methods shall be added to the costs to be amortized. (*2*) The costs of drilling exploratory dry holes shall be included in the amortization base immediately upon determination that the well is dry. (*3*) If geological and geophysical costs cannot be directly associated with specific unevaluated properties, they shall be included in the amortization base as incurred. Upon complete evaluation of a property, the total remaining excluded cost (net of any impairment) shall be included in the full cost amortization base.

(B) Certain costs may be excluded from amortization when incurred in connection with major development projects expected to entail significant costs to ascertain the quantities of proved reserves attributable to the properties under development (e.g., the installation of an offshore drilling platform from which development wells are to be drilled, the installation of improved recovery programs, and similar major projects undertaken in the expectation of significant additions to proved reserves). The amounts which may be excluded are applicable portions of (*1*) the costs that relate to the major development project and have not previously been included in the amortization base, and (*2*) the estimated future expenditures associated with the development project. The excluded portion of any common costs associated with the development project should be based, as is most appropriate in the circumstances, on a comparison of either (i) existing proved reserves to total proved reserves expected to be established upon completion of the project, or (ii) the number of wells to which proved reserves have been assigned and total number of wells expected to be drilled. Such costs may be excluded from costs to be amortized until the earlier determination of whether additional reserves are proved or impairment occurs.

(C) Excluded costs and the proved reserves related to such costs shall be transferred into the amortization base on an ongoing (well-by-well or property-by-property) basis as the project is evaluated and proved reserves established or impairment determined. Once proved reserves are established, there is no further justification for continued exclusion from the full cost amortization base even if other factors prevent immediate production or marketing.

(iii) Amortization shall be computed on the basis of physical units, with oil and gas converted to a common unit of measure on the basis of their approximate relative energy content, unless economic circumstances (related to the effects of regulated prices) indicate that use of units of revenue is a more appropriate basis of computing amortization. In the latter case, amortization shall be computed on the basis of current gross revenues (excluding royalty payments and net profits disbursements) from production in relation to future gross revenues, based on current prices (including consideration of changes in existing prices provided only by contractual arrangements), from estimated production of proved oil and gas reserves. The effect of a significant price increase during the year on estimated future gross revenues shall be reflected in the amortization provision only for the period after the price increase occurs.

(iv) In some cases it may be more appropriate to depreciate natural gas cycling and processing plants by a method other than the unit-of-production method.

(v) Amortization computations shall be made on a consolidated basis, including investees accounted for on a proportionate consolidation basis. Investees accounted for on the equity method shall be treated separately.

(4) *Limitation on capitalized costs.* (i) For each cost center, capitalized costs, less accumulated amortization and related deferred income taxes, shall not exceed an amount (the cost center ceiling) equal to the sum of:

(A) The present value of estimated future net revenues computed by applying current prices of oil and gas reserves (with consideration of price changes only to the extent provided by contractual arrangements) to estimated future production of proved oil and gas reserves as of the date of the latest balance sheet presented, less estimated future expenditures (based on current costs) to be incurred in developing and producing the proved reserves computed using a discount factor of ten percent and assuming continuation of existing economic conditions; plus

(B) the cost of properties not being amortized pursuant to paragraph (i)(3)(ii) of this section; plus

(C) the lower of cost or estimated fair value of unproven properties included in the costs being amortized; less

(D) income tax effects related to differences between the book and tax basis of the properties referred to in paragraphs (i)(4)(i)(B) and (C) of this section.

(ii) If unamortized costs capitalized within a cost center, less related deferred income taxes, exceed the cost center ceiling, the excess shall be charged to expense and separately disclosed during the period in which the excess occurs. Amounts thus required to be written off shall not be reinstated for any subsequent increase in the cost center ceiling.

(5) *Production costs.* All costs relating to production activities, including workover costs incurred solely to maintain or increase levels of production from an existing completion interval, shall be charged to expense as incurred.

(6) *Other transactions.* The provisions of paragraph (h) of this section, "Mineral property conveyances and related transactions if the successful efforts method of accounting is followed," shall apply also to those reporting entities following the full cost method except as follows:

(i) *Sales and abandonments of oil and gas properties.* Sales of oil and gas properties, whether or not being amortized currently, shall be accounted for as adjustments of capitalized costs, with no gain or loss recognized, unless such adjustments would significantly alter the relationship between capitalized costs and proved reserves of oil and gas attributable to a cost center. For instance, a significant alteration would not ordinarily be expected to occur for sales involving less than 25 percent of the reserve quantities of a given cost center. If gain or loss is recognized on such a sale, total capitalization costs within the cost center shall be allocated between the reserves sold and reserves retained on the same basis used to compute amortization, unless there are substantial economic differences between the properties sold and those retained, in which case capitalized costs shall be allocated on the basis of the relative fair values of the properties. Abandonments of oil and gas properties shall be accounted for as adjustments of capitalized costs; that is, the cost of abandoned properties shall be charged to the full cost center and amortized (subject to the limitation on capitalized costs in paragraph (b) of this section). [Amended in Release No. 33-6483, effective for costs incurred in fiscal years beginning after December 15, 1983, 48 F. R. 44198.]

(ii) *Purchases of reserves.* Purchases of oil and gas reserves in place ordinarily shall be accounted for as additional capitalized costs within the applicable cost center; however, significant purchases of production payments or properties with lives substantially shorter than the composite productive life of the cost center shall be accounted for separately.

(iii) *Partnerships, joint ventures and drilling arrangements.* (A) Except as provided in subparagraph (i)(6)(i) of this section, all consideration received from sales or transfers of properties in connection with partnerships, joint venture operations, or various other forms of drilling arrangements involving oil and gas exploration and development activities (e.g., carried interest, turnkey wells, management fees, etc.) shall be credited to the full cost account, except to the extent of amounts that represent reimbursement of organization, offering, general and administrative expenses, etc., that are identifiable with the transaction, if such amounts are currently incurred and charged to expense.

(B) Where a registrant organizes and manages a limited partnership involved only in the purchase of proved developed properties and subsequent distribution of income from such properties, management fee income may be recognized provided the properties involved do not require aggregate development expenditures in connection with production of existing proved reserves in excess of 10% of the partnership's recorded cost of such properties. Any income not recognized as a result of this limitation would be credited to the full cost account and recognized through a lower amortization provision as reserves are produced.

(iv) *Other services.* No income shall be recognized in connection with contractual services performed (e.g. drilling, well service, or equipment supply services, etc.) in connection with properties in which the registrant or an affiliate (as defined in §210.1-02(b)) holds an ownership or other economic interest, except as follows:

(A) Where the registrant acquires an interest in the properties in connection with the service contract, income may be recognized to the extent the cash consideration received exceeds the related contract costs plus the registrant's share of costs incurred and estimated to be incurred in connection with the properties. Ownership interests acquired within one year of the date of such a contract are considered to be acquired in connection with the service for purposes of applying this rule. The amount of any guarantees or similar arrangements undertaken as part of this contract should be considered as part of the costs related to the properties for purposes of applying this rule.

(B) Where the registrant acquired an interest in the properties at least one year before the date of the service contract through transactions unrelated to the service contract, and that interest is unaffected by the service contract, income from such contract may be recognized subject to the general provisions for elimination of intercompany profit under generally accepted accounting principles.

(C) Notwithstanding the provisions of (A) and (B) above, no income may be recognized for contractual services performed on behalf of investors in oil and gas producing activities managed by the registrant or an affiliate. Furthermore, no income may be recognized for contractual services to the extent that the consideration received for such services represents an interest in the underlying property.

(D) Any income not recognized as a result of these rules would be credited to the full cost account and recognized through a lower amortization provision as reserves are produced.

(7) *Disclosures.* Reporting entities that follow the full cost method of accounting shall disclose all of the information required by paragraph (k) of this section, with each cost center considered as a separate

geographic area, except that reasonable groupings may be made of cost centers that are not significant in the aggregate. In addition:

(i) For each cost center for each year that an income statement is required, disclose the total amount of amortization expense (per equivalent physical unit of production if amortization is computed on the basis of physical units or per dollar of gross revenue from production if amortization is computed on the basis of gross revenue).

(ii) State separately on the face of the balance sheet the aggregate of the capitalized costs of unproved properties and major development projects that are excluded, in accordance with paragraph (i)(3) of this section, from the capitalized costs being amortized. Provide a description in the notes to the financial statements of the current status of the significant properties or projects involved, including the anticipated timing of the inclusion of the costs in the amortization computation. Present a table that shows, by category of cost, (A) the total costs excluded as of the most recent fiscal year; and (B) the amounts of such excluded costs, incurred (1) in each of the three most recent fiscal years and (2) in the aggregate for any earlier fiscal years in which the costs were incurred. Categories of cost to be disclosed include acquisition costs, exploration costs, development costs in the case of significant development projects and capitalized interest.

(8) For purposes of this paragraph (c), the term "current price" shall mean the average price during the 12-month period prior to the ending date of the period covered by the report, determined as an unweighted arithmetic average of the first-day-of-the-month price for each month within such period, unless prices are defined by contractual arrangements, excluding escalations based upon future conditions.

Income Taxes

(d) *Income taxes.* Comprehensive interperiod income tax allocation by a method which complies with generally accepted accounting principles shall be followed for intangible drilling and development costs and other costs incurred that enter into the determination of taxable income and pretax accounting income in different periods.

[As last amended in Release No. 33-8995, effective January 1, 2010, 74 F.R. 2158.]

Article 5—Commercial and Industrial Companies

[¶ 35,441] Application of §§ 210.5-01 to 210.5-04

Reg. § 210.5-01. Sections 210.5-01 to 210.5-04 shall be applicable to financial statements filed for all persons except—

(a) Registered investment companies (see §§ 210.6-01 to 210.6-10).

(b) Employee stock purchase, savings and similar plans (see §§ 210.6A-01 to 210.6A-05).

(c) Insurance companies (see §§ 210.7-01 to 210.7-05).

(d) Bank holding companies and banks (see §§ 210.9-01 to 210.9-07).

(e) Brokers and dealers when filing Form X-17A-5 [249.617] (see §§ 240.17a-5 and 240.17a-10 under the Securities Exchange Act of 1934).

[As last amended in Release No. FR-22, November 21, 1985, 50 F.R. 49529.]

[¶ 35,451] Balance Sheets

Reg. § 210.5-02. The purpose of this rule is to indicate the various line items and certain additional disclosures which, if applicable, and except as otherwise permitted by the Commission, should appear on the face of the balance sheets or related notes filed for the persons to whom this article pertains (see § 210.4-01(a)).

Assets and Other Debits

Current Assets, When Appropriate [See § 210.4-05]

1. *Cash and cash items.* Separate disclosure shall be made of the cash and cash items which are restricted as to withdrawal or usage. The provisions of any restrictions shall be described in a note to the financial statements. Restrictions may include legally restricted deposits held as compensating balances against short-term borrowing arrangements, contracts entered into with others, or company statements of intention with regard to particular deposits; however, time deposits and short-term certificates of deposit are not generally included in legally restricted deposits. In cases where compensating balance arrangements exist but are not agreements which legally restrict the use of cash amounts shown on the balance sheet, describe in the notes to the financial statements these arrangements and the amount involved, if determinable, for the most recent audited balance sheet required and for any subsequent unaudited balance sheet required in the notes to the financial statements. Compensating balances that are maintained under an agreement to assure future credit availability shall be disclosed in the notes to the financial statements along with the amount and terms of such agreement.

2. *Marketable securities.* The accounting and disclosure requirements for current marketable equity securities are specified by generally accepted accounting principles. With respect to all other current marketable securities, state, parenthetically or otherwise, the basis of determining the aggregate amount shown in the balance sheet, along with the alternatives of the aggregate cost or the aggregate market value at the balance sheet date.

3. *Accounts and notes receivable.* (a) State separately amounts receivable from: (1) customers (trade); (2) related parties (see § 210.4-08(k)); (3) underwriters, promoters, and employees (other than related parties) which arose in other than the ordinary course of business; and (4) others.

(b) If the aggregate amount of notes receivable exceeds 10 percent of the aggregate amount of receivables, the above information shall be set forth separately, in the balance sheet or in a note thereto, for accounts receivable and notes receivable.

(c) If receivables include amounts due under long-term contracts (see § 210.5-02.6(d)), state separately in the balance sheet or in a note to the financial statements the following amounts:

(1) Balances billed but not paid by customers under retainage provisions in contracts.

(2) Amounts representing the recognized sales value of performance and such amounts that had not been billed and were not billable to customers at the date of the balance sheet. Include a general description of the prerequisites for billing.

(3) Billed or unbilled amounts representing claims or other similar items subject to uncertainty concerning their determination or ultimate realization. Include a description of the nature and status of the principal items comprising such amount.

(4) With respect to (1) through (3) above, also state the amounts included in each item which are expected to be collected after one year. Also state, by year, if practicable, when the amounts of retainage (see (1) above) are expected to be collected.

4. *Allowances for doubtful accounts and notes receivable.* The amount is to be set forth separately in the balance sheet or in a note thereto.

5. *Unearned income.*

6. *Inventories.* (a) State separately in the balance sheet or in a note thereto, if practicable, the amounts of major classes of inventory such as: (1) finished goods; (2) inventoried costs relating to long-term contracts or programs (see (d) below and § 210.4-05); (3) work in process (see § 210.4-05); (4) raw materials; and (5) supplies. If the method of calculating a LIFO inventory does not allow for the practical determination of amounts assigned to major classes of inventory, the amounts of those classes may be stated under cost flow assumptions other than LIFO with the excess of such total amount over the aggregate LIFO amount shown as a deduction to arrive at the amount of the LIFO inventory. [Amended in Release No. FR-22, effective December 3, 1985, 50 F. R. 49529.]

(b) The basis of determining the amounts shall be stated.

If "cost" is used to determine any portion of the inventory amounts, the description of this method shall include the nature of the cost elements included in inventory. Elements of "cost" include, among other items, retained costs representing the excess of manufacturing or production costs over the amounts charged to cost of sales or delivered or in-process units, initial tooling or other deferred startup costs, or general and administrative costs.

The method by which amounts are removed from inventory (e.g., "average cost," "first-in, first-out," "last-in, first-out," "estimated average cost per unit") shall be described. If the estimated average cost per unit is used as a basis to determine amounts removed from inventory under a total program or similar basis of accounting, the principal assumptions (including, where meaningful, the aggregate number of units expected to be delivered under the program, the number of units delivered to date and the number of units on order) shall be disclosed.

If any general and administrative costs are charged to inventory, state in a note to the financial statements the aggregate amount of the general and administrative costs incurred in each period and the actual or estimated amount remaining in inventory at the date of each balance sheet.

(c) If the LIFO inventory method is used, the excess of replacement or current cost over stated LIFO value shall, if material, be stated parenthetically or in a note to the financial statements.

(d) For purposes of §§ 210.5-02-3 and 210.5-02-6, long-term contracts or programs include (1) all contracts or programs for which gross profits are recognized on a percentage-of-completion method of accounting or any variant thereof (e.g., delivered unit, cost to cost, physical completion), and (2) any contracts or programs accounted for on a completed contract basis of accounting where, in either case, the contracts or programs have associated with them material amounts of inventories or unbilled receivables and where such contracts or programs have been or are expected to be performed over a period of more than twelve months. Contracts or programs of shorter duration may also be included, if deemed appropriate.

For all long-term contracts or programs, the following information, if applicable, shall be stated in a note to the financial statements:

(i) The aggregate amount of manufacturing or production costs and any related deferred costs (e.g., initial tooling costs) which exceeds the aggregate estimated cost of all in-process and delivered units on the basis of the estimated average cost of all units expected to be produced under long-term contracts and programs not yet complete, as well as that portion of such amount which would not be absorbed in cost of sales based on existing firm orders at the latest balance sheet date. In addition, if practicable, disclose the amount of deferred costs by type of cost (e.g., initial tooling, deferred production, etc.).

(ii) The aggregate amount representing claims or other similar items subject to uncertainty concerning their determination or ultimate realization, and include a description of the nature and status of the principal items comprising such aggregate amount.

(iii) The amount of progress payments netted against inventory at the date of the balance sheet.

7. *Prepaid expenses.*

8. *Other current assets.* State separately, in a balance sheet or in a note thereto, any amounts in excess of five percent of total current assets.

9. *Total current assets, when appropriate.*

10. *Securities of related parties.* (See § 210.4-08(k).)

11. *Indebtedness of related parties—not current.* (See § 210.4-08(k).)

12. *Other investments.* The accounting and disclosure requirements for non-current marketable equity securities are specified by generally accepted accounting principles. With respect to other security investments and any other investment, state, parenthetically or otherwise, the basis of determining the aggregate amounts shown in the balance sheet, along with the alternate of the aggregate cost or aggregate market value at the balance sheet date.

13. *Property, plant and equipment.* (a) State the basis of determining the amounts.

(b) Tangible and intangible utility plant of a public utility company shall be segregated so as to show separately the original cost, plant acquisition adjustments, and plant adjustments, as required by the system of accounts prescribed by the applicable regulatory authorities. This rule shall not be applicable in respect to companies which are not required to make such a classification.

14. *Accumulated depreciation, depletion, and amortization of property, plant and equipment.* The amount is to be set forth separately in the balance sheet or in a note thereto.

15. *Intangible assets.* State separately each class of such assets which is in excess of five percent of the total assets, along with the basis of determining the respective amounts. Any significant addition or deletion shall be explained in a note.

16. *Accumulated depreciation and amortization of intangible assets.* The amount is to be set forth separately in the balance sheet or in a note thereto.

17. *Other assets.* State separately, in the balance sheet or in a note thereto, any other item not properly classed in one of the preceding asset captions which is in excess of five percent of total assets. Any significant addition or deletion should be explained in a note. With respect to any significant deferred charge, state the policy for deferral and amortization.

18. *Total assets.*

Liabilities and Stockholders' Equity
Current Liabilities, When Appropriate (See § 210.4-05)

19. *Accounts and notes payable.* (a) State separately amounts payable to (1) banks for borrowings; (2) factors or other financial institutions for borrowings; (3) holders of commercial paper; (4) trade creditors; (5) related parties (see § 210.4-08(k)); (6) underwriters, promoters, and employees (other than related parties); and (7) others. Amounts applicable to (1), (2) and (3) may be stated separately in the balance sheet or in a note thereto.

(b) The amount and terms (including commitment fees and the conditions under which lines may be withdrawn) of unused lines of credit for short-term financing shall be disclosed, if significant, in the notes to the financial statements. The weighted average interest rate on short term borrowings outstanding as of the date of each balance sheet presented shall be furnished in a note. The amount of these lines of credit which support a commercial paper borrowing arrangement or similar arrangements shall be separately identified. [Amended in Release No. FR-44, effective December 20, 1994, 59 F.R. 65632.]

20. *Other current liabilities.* State separately, in the balance sheet or in a note thereto, any item in excess of 5 percent of total current liabilities. Such items may include, but are not limited to, accrued payrolls, accrued interest, taxes, indicating the current portion of deferred income taxes, and the current portion of long-term debt. Remaining items may be shown in one amount.

21. *Total current liabilities, when appropriate.*

Long-Term Debt

22. *Bonds, mortgages and other long-term debt, including capitalized leases.* (a) State separately, in the balance sheet or in a note thereto, each issue or type of obligation and such information as will indicate (see § 210.4-06):

(1) The general character of each type of debt including the rate of interest; (2) the date of maturity, or, if maturing serially, a brief indication of the serial maturities, such as "maturing serially from 1980 to 1990"; (3) if the payment of principal or interest is contingent, an appropriate indication of such contingency; (4) a brief indication of priority; and (5) if convertible, the basis. For amounts owed to related parties, see § 210.4-08(k). [Amended in Release No. AS-297, effective for fiscal years ending after June 15, 1981, 46 F. R. 43411.]

(b) The amount and terms (including commitment fees and the conditions under which commitments may be withdrawn) of unused commitments for long-term financing arrangements that would be disclosed under this rule if used shall be disclosed in the notes to the financial statements if significant.

23. *Indebtedness to related parties—noncurrent.* Include under this caption indebtedness to related parties as required under § 210.4-08(k).

24. *Other liabilities.* State separately, in the balance sheet or in a note thereto, any item not properly classified in one of the preceding liability captions which is in excess of 5 percent of total liabilities.

25. *Commitments and contingent liabilities.*

26. *Deferred credits.* State separately in the balance sheet amounts for (a) deferred income taxes, (b) deferred tax credits, and (c) material items of deferred income.

27. *Preferred stocks subject to mandatory redemption requirements or whose redemption is outside the control of the issuer.* (a) Include under this caption amounts applicable to any class of stock which has any of the following characteristics: (1) it is redeemable at a fixed or determinable price on a fixed or determinable date or dates, whether by operation of a sinking fund or otherwise; (2) it is redeemable at the option of the holder; or (3) it has conditions for redemption which are not solely within the control of the issuer, such as stocks which must be redeemed out of future earnings. Amounts attributable to preferred stock which is not redeemable or is redeemable solely at the option of the issuer shall be included under § 210.5-02.28 unless it meets one or more of the above criteria.

(b) State on the face of the balance sheet the title of each issue, the carrying amount, and redemption amount. (If there is more than one issue, these amounts may be aggregated on the face of the balance sheet and details concerning each issue may be presented in the note required by paragraph (c) below.) Show also the dollar amount of any shares subscribed but unissued, and show the deduction of subscriptions receivable therefrom. If the carrying value is different from the redemption amount, describe the accounting treatment for such difference in the note required by paragraph (c) below. Also state in this note or on the face of the balance sheet, for each issue, the number of shares authorized and the number of shares issued or outstanding, as appropriate [See § 210.4-07].

(c) State in a separate note captioned "Redeemable Preferred Stocks" (1) a general description of each issue, including its redemption features (e.g. sinking fund, at option of holders, out of future earnings) and the rights, if any, of holders in the event of default, including the effect, if any, on junior securities in the event a required dividend, sinking fund, or other redemption payment(s) is not made; (2) the combined aggregate amount of redemption requirements for all issues each year for the five years following the date of the latest balance sheet; and (3) the changes in each issue for each period for which an income statement is required to be filed. [See also § 210.4-08(d).]

(d) Securities reported under this caption are not to be included under a general heading "stockholders' equity" or combined in a total with items described in captions 29, 30 or 31 which follow.

Non-Redeemable Preferred Stocks

28. *Preferred stocks which are not redeemable or are redeemable solely at the option of the issuer.* State on the face of the balance sheet, or if more than one issue is outstanding state in a note, the title of each issue and the dollar amount thereof. Show also the dollar amount of any shares subscribed but unissued, and show the deduction of subscriptions receivable therefrom. State on the face of the balance sheet or in a note, for each issue, the number of shares authorized and the number of shares issued or outstanding, as appropriate [See § 210.4-07]. Show in a note or separate statement the changes in each class of preferred shares reported under this caption for each period for which an income statement is required to be filed. [See also § 210.4-08(d).]

Common Stocks

29. *Common stocks.* For each class of common shares state, on the face of the balance sheet, the number of shares issued or outstanding, as appropriate [see § 210.4-07] and the dollar amount thereof. If convertible, this fact should be indicated on the face of the balance sheet. For each class of common shares state, on the face of the balance sheet or in a note, the title of the issue, the number of shares

authorized, and, if convertible, the basis of conversion [see also § 210.4-08(d)]. Show also the dollar amount of any common shares subscribed but unissued, and show the deduction of subscriptions receivable therefrom. Show in a note or statement the changes in each class of common shares for each period for which an income statement is required to be filed.

Other Stockholders' Equity

30. *Other stockholders' equity.* (a) Separate captions shall be shown for (1) additional paid-in capital, (2) other additional capital and (3) retained earnings (i) appropriated and (ii) unappropriated. [See § 210.4-08(e).] Additional paid-in capital and other additional capital may be combined with the stock caption to which it applies, if appropriate.

(b) For a period of at least 10 years subsequent to the effective date of a quasi-reorganization, any description of retained earnings shall indicate the point in time from which the new retained earnings dates and for a period of at least three years shall indicate, on the face of the balance sheet, the total amount of the deficit eliminated.

Noncontrolling Interests

31. *Noncontrolling interests in consolidated subsidiaries.* State separately in a note the amounts represented by preferred stock and the applicable dividend requirements if the preferred stock is material in relation to the consolidated equity.

32. *Total liabilities and equity.*

[As last amended in Release No. 33-9026, effective April 23, 2009, 74 F.R. 18612.]

[¶ 35,461] Income Statements

Reg. § 210.5-03. (a) The purpose of this rule is to indicate the various line items which, if applicable, and except as otherwise permitted by the Commission, should appear on the face of the income statements filed for the persons to whom this article pertains (See § 210.4-01(a)).

(b) If income is derived from more than one of the subcaptions described under § 210.5-03.1, each class which is not more than 10 percent of the sum of the items may be combined with another class. If these items are combined, related costs and expenses as described under § 210.5-03.2 shall be combined in the same manner.

1. *Net sales and gross revenues.* State separately:

(a) Net sales of tangible products (gross sales less discounts, returns and allowances), (b) operating revenues of public utilities or others; (c) income from rentals; (d) revenues from services; and (e) other revenues. Amounts earned from transactions with related parties shall be disclosed as required under § 210.4-08(k). A public utility company using a uniform system of accounts or a form for annual report prescribed by federal or state authorities, or a similar system or report, shall follow the general segregation of operating revenues and operating expenses reported under § 210.5-03.2 prescribed by such system or report. If the total of sales and revenues reported under this caption includes excise taxes in an amount equal to 1 percent or more of such total, the amount of such excise taxes shall be shown on the face of the statement parenthetically or otherwise.

2. *Costs and expenses applicable to sales and revenues.* State separately the amount of (a) cost of tangible goods sold, (b) operating expenses of public utilities or others, (c) expenses applicable to rental income, (d) cost of services, and (e) expenses applicable to other revenues. Merchandising organizations, both wholesale and retail, may include occupancy and buying costs under caption 2(a). Amounts of costs and expenses incurred from transactions with related parties shall be disclosed as required under § 210.4-08(k).

3. *Other operating costs and expenses.* State separately any material amounts not included under caption 2 above.

4. *Selling, general and administrative expenses.*

5. *Provision for doubtful accounts and notes.*

6. *Other general expenses.* Include items not normally included in caption 4 above. State separately any material item.

7. *Non-operating income.* State separately in the income statement or in a note thereto amounts earned from (a) dividends, (b) interest on securities, (c) profits on securities (net of losses), and (d) miscellaneous other income. Amounts earned from transactions in securities of related parties shall be disclosed as required under § 210.4-08(k). Material amounts included under miscellaneous other income shall be separately stated in the income statement or in a note thereto, indicating clearly the nature of the transactions out of which the items arose. [Amended in Release No. AS-284, effective November 21, 1980, 45 F. R. 76974.]

8. *Interest and amortization of debt discount and expense.*

9. *Non-operating expenses.* State separately in the income statement or in a note thereto amounts of (a) losses on securities (net of profits) and (b) miscellaneous income deductions. Material amounts

included under miscellaneous income deductions shall be separately stated in the income statement or in a note thereto, indicating clearly the nature of the transactions out of which the items arose.

10. *Income or loss before income tax expense and appropriate items below.*

11. *Income tax expense.* Include under this caption only taxes based on income. (See § 210.4-08(h)). [Amended in Release No. FR-2, effective June 18, 1985, 50 F. R. 25214.]

12. *Equity in earnings of unconsolidated subsidiaries and 50 percent or less owned persons.* State, parenthetically or in a note, the amount of dividends received from such persons. If justified by the circumstances, this item may be presented in a different position and a different manner. (See § 210.4-01(a).)

13. *Income or loss from continuing operations.*

14. *Discontinued operations.*

15. *Income or loss before extraordinary items and cumulative effects of changes in accounting principles.*

16. *Extraordinary items, less applicable tax.*

17. *Cumulative effects of changes in accounting principles.*

18. *Net income or loss.*

19. *Net income attributable to the noncontrolling interest.*

20. *Net income attributable to the controlling interest.*

21. *Earnings per share data.*

[As last amended in Release No. 33-9026, effective April 23, 2009, 74 F.R. 18612.]

[¶ 35,471] What Schedules are to be Filed

Reg. § 210.5-04. (a) Except as expressly provided otherwise in the applicable form:

(1) The schedules specified below in this Section as Schedules II and III shall be filed as of the date of the most recent audited balance sheet for each person or group.

(2) Schedule II shall be filed for each period for which an audited income statement is required to be filed for each person or group.

(3) Schedules I and IV shall be filed as of the date and for periods specified in the schedule.

(b) When information is required in schedules for both the registrant and the registrant and its subsidiaries consolidated it may be presented in the form of a single schedule: *Provided,* That items pertaining to the registrant are separately shown and that such single schedule affords a properly summarized presentation of the facts. If the information required by any schedule (including the notes thereto) may be shown in the related financial statement or in a note thereto without making such statement unclear or confusing, that procedure may be followed and the schedule omitted.

(c) The schedules shall be examined by the independent accountant if the related financial statements are so examined.

Schedule I—Condensed financial information of registrant. The schedule prescribed by § 210.12-04 shall be filed when the restricted net assets (§ 210.4-08(e)(3)) of consolidated subsidiaries exceed 25 percent of consolidated net assets as of the end of the most recently completed fiscal year. For purposes of the above test, restricted net assets of consolidated subsidiaries shall mean that amount of the registrant's proportionate share of net assets of consolidated subsidiaries (after intercompany elimina-tions) which as of the end of the most recent fiscal year may not be transferred to the parent company by subsidiaries in the form of loans, advances or cash dividends without the consent of a third party (i.e., lender, regulatory agency, foreign government, etc.). Where restrictions on the amount of funds which may be loaned or advanced differ from the amount restricted as to transfer in the form of cash dividends, the amount least restrictive to the subsidiary shall be used. Redeemable preferred stocks (§ 210.5-02.27) and noncontrolling interests shall be deducted in computing net assets for purposes of this test.

Schedule II—Valuation and qualifying accounts. The schedule prescribed by § 210.12-09 shall be filed in support of valuation and qualifying accounts included in each balance sheet but not included in Schedule VI. (See § 210.4-02.)

Schedule III—Real estate and accumulated depreciation. The schedule prescribed by § 210.12-28 shall be filed for real estate (and the related accumulated depreciation) held by persons a substantial portion of whose business is that of acquiring and holding for investment real estate or interests in real estate, or interests in other persons a substantial portion of whose business is that of acquiring and holding real estate or interests in real estate for investment. Real estate used in the business shall be excluded from the schedule.

Schedule IV—Mortgage loans on real estate. The schedule prescribed by § 210.12-29 shall be filed by persons specified under Schedule XI for investments in mortgage loans on real estate.

Schedule V—Supplemental information concerning property-casualty insurance operations. The sched-ule prescribed by § 210.12-18 shall be filed when a registrant, its subsidiaries or 50%-or-less-owned equity basis investees, have liabilities for property-casualty ("P/C") insurance claims. The required information shall be presented as of the same dates and for the same periods for which the information is reflected in the audited consolidated financial statements required by §§ 210.3-01 and 3-02. The schedule may be omitted if reserves for unpaid P/C claims and claims adjustment expenses of the registrant and its consolidated subsidiaries, its unconsolidated subsidiaries and its 50%-or-less-owned equity basis investees did not, in the aggregate, exceed one-half of common stockholders' equity of the registrant and its consolidated subsidiaries as of the beginning of the fiscal year. For purposes of this test only the proportionate share of the registrant and its other subsidiaries in the reserves for unpaid claims and claim adjustment expenses of 50%-or-less-owned equity basis investees taken in the aggregate after intercompany eliminations shall be taken into account.

[As last amended in Release No. 33-9026, effective April 23, 2009, 74 F.R. 18612.]

Article 6—Registered Investment Companies

[¶ 35,702] Application of §§ 210.6-01 to 210.6-10

Reg. § 210.6-01. Sections 210.6-01 to 210.6-10 shall be applicable to financial statements filed for registered investment companies.

[Adopted in Release No. FR-8, December 6, 1982, 47 F.R. 56835.]

[¶ 35,703] Definition of Certain Terms

Reg. § 210.6-02. The following terms shall have the meaning indicated in this rule unless the context otherwise requires. (Also see § 210.1-02 of this part.)

(a) *Affiliate.* The term "affiliate" means an "affiliated person" as defined in section 2(a)(3) of the Investment Company Act of 1940 unless otherwise indicated. The term "control" has the meaning [given] in section 2(a)(9) of that Act.

(b) *Value.* As used in §§ 210.6-01 to 210.6-10, the term "value" shall have the meaning given in section 2(a)(41)(B) of the Investment Company Act of 1940.

(c) *Balance sheets; statements of net assets.* As used in §§ 210.6-01 to 210.6-10, the term "balance sheets" shall include statements of assets and liabilities as well as statements of net assets unless the context clearly indicates the contrary.

(d) *Qualified assets.* (1) For companies issuing face-amount certificates subsequent to December 31, 1940 under the provisions of section 28 of the Investment Company Act of 1940, the term "qualified assets" means qualified investments as that term is defined in section 28(b) of the Act. A statement to that effect shall be made in the balance sheet.

(2) For other companies, the term "qualified assets" means cash and investments which such companies do maintain or are required, by applicable governing legal instruments, to maintain in respect of outstanding face-amount certificates.

(3) Loans to certificate holders may be included as qualified assets in an amount not in excess of certificate reserves carried on the books of account in respect of each individual certificate upon which the loans were made.

[Adopted in Release No. FR-8, December 6, 1982, 47 F.R. 56835.]

[¶ 35,704] Special Rules of General Application to Registered Investment Companies

Reg. § 210.6-03. The financial statements filed for persons to which §§ 210.6-01 to 210.6-10 are applicable shall be prepared in accordance with the following special rules in addition to the general rules in §§ 210.1-01 to 210.4-10 (Articles 1, 2, 3, and 4). Where the requirements of a special rule differ from those prescribed in a general rule, the requirements of the special rule shall be met.

(a) *Content of financial statements.* The financial statements shall be prepared in accordance with the requirements of this part (Regulation S-X) notwithstanding any provision of the articles of incorporation, trust indenture or other governing legal instruments specifying certain accounting procedures inconsistent with those required in §§ 210.6-01 to 210.6-10.

(b) *Audited financial statements.* Where, under Article 3 of this part, financial statements are required to be audited, the independent accountant shall have been selected and ratified in accordance with section 32 of the Investment Company Act of 1940.

(c) *Consolidated and combined statements.*

(1) Consolidated and combined statements filed for registered investment companies shall be prepared in accordance with §§ 210.3A-01 to 210.3A-05 (Article 3A), except that (i) statements of the registrant may be consolidated only with the statements of subsidiaries which are investment companies; (ii) a consolidated statement of the registrant and any of its investment company subsidiaries shall not be filed unless accompanied by a consolidating statement which sets forth the individual statements of each significant subsidiary included in the consolidated statement: *Provided, however,* That a consoli-

dating statement need not be filed if all included subsidiaries are totally held; and (iii) consolidated or combined statements filed for subsidiaries not consolidated with the registrant shall not include any investment companies unless accompanied by consolidating or combining statements which set forth the individual statements of each included investment company which is a significant subsidiary.

(2) If consolidating or combining statements are filed, the amounts included under each caption in which financial data pertaining to affiliates is required to be furnished shall be subdivided to show separately the amounts (i) eliminated in consolidation and (ii) not eliminated in consolidation.

(d) *Valuation of assets.* The balance sheets of registered investment companies, other than issuers of face-amount certificates, shall reflect all investments at value, with the aggregate cost of each category of investment reported under §§ 210.6-04.1, 6-04.2 and 6-04.3 and of the total investments reported under § 210.6-04.4 or § 210.6-05.1 shown parenthetically. State in a note the methods used in determining value of investments. As required by section 28(b) of the Investment Company Act of 1940, "qualified" assets of face-amount certificate companies shall be valued in accordance with certain provisions of the Code of the District of Columbia. For guidance as to valuation of securities, see §§ 404.03 to 404.05 of the Codification of Financial Reporting Policies.

(e) *Qualified assets.* State in a note the nature of any investments and other assets maintained or required to be maintained, by applicable legal instruments, in respect of outstanding face-amount certificates. If the nature of the qualifying assets and amount thereof are not subject to the provisions of section 28 of the Investment Company Act of 1940, a statement to that effect shall be made.

(f) *Restricted securities.* State in a note unless disclosed elsewhere the following information as to investment securities which cannot be offered for public sale without first being registered under the Securities Act of 1933 (restricted securities):

(1) The policy of the person with regard to acquisition of restricted securities.

(2) The policy of the person with regard to valuation of restricted securities. Specific comments shall be given as to the valuation of an investment in one or more issues of securities of a company or group of affiliated companies if any part of such investment is restricted and the aggregate value of the investment in all issues of such company or affiliated group exceeds five percent of the value of total assets. (As used in this paragraph, the term "affiliated" shall have the meaning given in § 210.6-02(a) of this part.)

(3) A description of the person's rights with regard to demanding registration of any restricted securities held at the date of the latest balance sheet.

(g) *Income recognition.* Dividends shall be included in income on the ex-dividend date; interest shall be accrued on a daily basis. Dividends declared on short positions existing on the record date shall be recorded on the ex-dividend date and included as an expense of the period.

(h) *Federal income taxes.* The company's status as a "regulated investment company" as defined in Subtitle A, Chapter 1, Subchapter M of the Internal Revenue Code, as amended, shall be stated in a note referred to in the appropriate statements. Such note shall also indicate briefly the principal assumptions on which the company relied in making or not making provisions for income taxes. However, a company which retains realized capital gains and designates such gains as a distribution to shareholders in accordance with section 852(b)(3)(D) of the Internal Revenue Code shall, on the last day of its taxable year (and not earlier), make provision for taxes on such undistributed capital gains realized during such year.

(i) *Issuance and repurchase by a registered investment company of its own securities.* Disclose for each class of the company's securities:

(1) The number of shares, units, or principal amount of bonds sold during the period of report, the amount received therefor, and, in the case of shares sold by closed-end management investment companies, the difference, if any, between the amount received and the net asset value or preference in involuntary liquidation (whichever is appropriate) of securities of the same class prior to such sale; and

(2) The number of shares, units, or principal amount of bonds repurchased during the period of report and the cost thereof. Closed-end management investment companies shall furnish the following additional information as to securities repurchased during the period of report:

(i) As to bonds and preferred shares, the aggregate difference between cost and the face amount or preference in involuntary liquidation and, if applicable net assets taken at value as of the date of repurchase were less than such face amount or preference, the aggregate difference between cost and such net asset value;

(ii) As to common shares, the weighted average discount per share, expressed as a percentage, between cost of repurchase and the net asset value applicable to such shares at the date of repurchases.

The information required by paragraphs (i)(2)(i) and (ii) may be based on reasonable estimates if it is impracticable to determine the exact amounts involved.

(j) *Series companies.* The information required by this part shall, in the case of a person which in essence is comprised of more than one separate investment company, be given as if each class or series of such investment company were a separate investment company; this shall not prevent the inclusion, at the option of such person, of information applicable to other classes or series of such person on a comparative basis, except as to footnotes which need not be comparative.

If the particular class or series for which information is provided may be affected by other classes or series of such investment company, such as by the offset of realized gains in one series with realized losses in another, or through contingent liabilities, such situation shall be disclosed.

(k) *Certificate reserves.* (1) For companies issuing face-amount certificates subsequent to December 31, 1940 under the provisions of section 28 of the Investment Company Act of 1940, balance sheets shall reflect reserves for outstanding certificates computed in accordance with the provisions of section 28(a) of the Act.

(2) For other companies, balance sheets shall reflect reserves for outstanding certificates determined as follows:

(i) For certificates of the installment type, such amount which, together with the lesser of future payments by certificate holders as and when accumulated at a rate not to exceed 3½ per centum per annum (or such other rate as may be appropriate under the circumstances of a particular case) compounded annually, shall provide the minimum maturity or face amount of the certificate when due.

(ii) For certificates of the fully-paid type, such amount which, as and when accumulated at a rate not to exceed 3½ per centum per annum (or such other rate as may be appropriate under the circumstances of a particular case) compounded annually, shall provide the amount or amounts payable when due.

(iii) Such amount or accrual therefor, as shall have been credited to the account of any certificate holder in the form of any credit, or any dividend, or any interest in addition to the minimum maturity or face amount specified in the certificate, plus any accumulations on any amount so credited or accrued at rates required under the terms of the certificate.

(iv) An amount equal to all advance payments made by certificate holders, plus any accumulations thereon at rates required under the terms of the certificate.

(v) Amounts for other appropriate contingency reserves, for death and disability benefits or for reinstatement rights on any certificate providing for such benefits or rights.

(l) *Inapplicable captions.* Attention is directed to the provisions of §§ 210.4-02 and 210.4-03 which permit the omission of separate captions in financial statements as to which the items and conditions are not present, or the amounts involved not significant. However, amounts involving directors, officers, and affiliates shall nevertheless be separately set forth except as otherwise specifically permitted under a particular caption.

[Adopted in Release No. FR-8, December 6, 1982, 47 F.R. 56835.]

[¶ 35,705] Balance Sheets

Reg. § 210.6-04. This rule is applicable to balance sheets filed by registered investment companies except for persons who substitute a statement of net assets in accordance with the requirements specified in § 210.6-05, and issuers of face-amount certificates which are subject to the special provisions of § 210.6-06 of this part. Balance sheets filed under this rule shall comply with the following provisions:

Assets

1. *Investments in securities of unaffiliated issuers.*

2. *Investments in and advances to affiliates.* State separately investments in and advances to (a) controlled companies and (b) other affiliates.

3. *Investments—other than securities.* State separately each major category.

4. *Total investments.*

5. *Cash.* Include under this caption cash on hand and demand deposits. Provide in a note to the financial statements the information required under § 210.5-02.1 regarding restrictions and compensating balances.

6. *Receivables.* (a) State separately amounts receivable from (1) sales of investments; (2) subscriptions to capital shares; (3) dividends and interest; (4) directors and officers; and (5) others.

(b) If the aggregate amount of notes receivable exceeds 10 percent of the aggregate amount of receivables, the above information shall be set forth separately, in the balance sheet or in a note thereto, for accounts receivable and notes receivable.

7. *Deposits for securities sold short and open option contracts.* State separately amounts held by others in connection with (a) short sales and (b) open option contracts.

8. *Other assets.* State separately (a) prepaid and deferred expenses; (b) pension and other special funds; (c) organization expenses; and (d) any other significant item not properly classified in another asset caption.

9. *Total assets.*

Liabilities

10. *Accounts payable and accrued liabilities.* State separately amounts payable for (a) securities sold short; (b) open option contracts written; (c) other purchases of securities; (d) capital shares redeemed; (e) dividends or other distributions on capital shares; and (f) others. State separately the amount of any other liabilities which are material. Securities sold short and open option contracts written shall be stated at value.

11. *Deposits for securities loaned.* State the value of securities loaned and indicate the nature of the collateral received as security for the loan, including the amount of any cash received.

12. *Other liabilities.* State separately (a) amounts payable for investment advisory, management and service fees; and (b) the total amount payable to (1) officers and directors; (2) controlled companies; and (3) other affiliates, excluding any amounts owing to noncontrolled affiliates which arose in the ordinary course of business and which are subject to usual trade terms.

13. *Notes payable, bonds and similar debt.* (a) State separately amounts payable to (1) banks or other financial institutions for borrowings; (2) controlled companies; (3) other affiliates; and (4) others, showing for each category amounts payable within one year and amounts payable after one year.

(b) Provide in a note the information required under § 210.5-02.19(b) regarding unused lines of credit for short-term financing and § 210.5-02.22(b) regarding unused commitments for long-term financing arrangements.

14. *Total liabilities.*

15. *Commitments and contingent liabilities.*

Net Assets

16. *Units of capital.* (a) Disclose the title of each class of capital shares or other capital units, the number authorized, the number outstanding, and the dollar amount thereof.

(b) Unit investment trusts, including those which are issuers of periodic payment plan certificates, also shall state in a note to the financial statements (a) the total cost to the investors of each class of units or shares; (b) the adjustment for market depreciation or appreciation; (c) other deductions from the total cost to the investors for fees, loads and other charges, including an explanation of such deductions; and (d) that the net amount applicable to the investors.

17. *Accumulated undistributed income (loss).* Disclose (a) the accumulated undistributed investment income-net, (b) accumulated undistributed net realized gains (losses) on investment transactions, and (c) net unrealized appreciation (depreciation) in value of investments at the balance sheet date.

18. *Other elements of capital.* Disclose any other elements of capital or residual interests appropriate to the capital structure of the reporting entity.

19. *Net assets applicable to outstanding units of capital.* State the net asset value per share.

[Adopted in Release No. FR-8, December 6, 1982, 47 F.R. 56835.]

[¶ 35,706] Statement of Net Assets

Reg. § 210.6-05. In lieu of the balance sheet otherwise required by § 210.6-04 of this part, persons may substitute a statement of net assets if at least 95 percent of the amount of the person's total assets are represented by investments in securities of unaffiliated issuers. If presented in such instances, a statement of net assets shall consist of the following:

1. A schedule of investments in securities of unaffiliated issuers as prescribed in § 210.12-12.

2. The excess (or deficiency) of other assets over (under) total liabilities stated in one amount, except that any amounts due from or to officers, directors, controlled persons, or other affiliates, excluding any amounts owing to noncontrolled affiliates which arose in the ordinary course of business and which are subject to usual trade terms, shall be stated separately.

3. Disclosure shall be provided in the notes to the financial statements for any item required under §§ 210.6-04.10 to 210.6-04.13.

4. The balance of the amounts captioned as *net assets.* The number of outstanding shares and net asset value per share shall be shown parenthetically.

5. The information required by (i) § 210.6-04.16, (ii) § 210.6-04.17 and (iii) § 210.6-04.18 shall be furnished in a note to the financial statements.

[Adopted in Release No. FR-8, December 6, 1982, 47 F.R. 56835.]

[¶ 35,707] Special Provisions Applicable to the Balance Sheets of Issuers of Face-Amount Certificates

Reg. § 210.6-06. Balance sheets filed by issuers of face-amount certificates shall comply with the following provisions:

Assets

1. *Investments.* State separately each major category: such as, real estate owned, first mortgage loans on real estate, other mortgage loans on real estate, investments in securities of unaffiliated issuers, and investments in and advances to affiliates.

2. *Cash.* Include under this caption cash on hand and demand deposits. Provide in a note to the financial statements the information required under § 210.5-02.1 regarding restrictions and compensating balances.

3. *Receivables.* (a) State separately amounts receivable from (1) sales of investments; (2) dividends and interest; (3) directors and officers; and (4) others.

(b) If the aggregate amount of notes receivable exceeds 10 percent of the aggregate amount of receivables, the above information shall be set forth separately, in the balance sheet or in a note thereto, for accounts receivable and notes receivable.

4. *Total qualified assets.* State in a note to the financial statements the amount of qualified assets on deposit classified as to general categories of assets and as to general types of depositories, such as banks and states, together with a statement as to the purpose of the deposits.

5. *Other assets.* State separately (a) investments in securities of unaffiliated issuers not included in qualifying assets in item 1 above; (b) investments in and advances to affiliates not included in qualifying assets in item 1 above; and (c) any other significant item not properly classified in another asset caption.

6. *Total assets.*

Liabilities

7. *Certificate reserves.* Issuers of face-amount certificates shall state separately reserves for (a) certificates of the installment type; (b) certificates of the fully-paid type; (c) advance payments; (d) additional amounts accrued for or credited to the account of certificate holders in the form of any credit, dividend, or interest in addition to the minimum amount specified in the certificate; and (e) other certificate reserves. State in an appropriate manner the basis used in determining the reserves, including the rates of interest of accumulation.

8. *Notes payable, bonds and similar debt.* (a) State separately amounts payable to (1) banks or other financial institutions for borrowings; (2) controlled companies; (3) other affilates; and (4) others, showing for each category amounts payable within one year and amounts payable after one year.

(b) Provide in a note the information required under § 210.5-02.19(b) regarding unused lines of credit for short-term financing and § 210.5-02.22(b) regarding unused commitments for long-term financing arrangements.

9. *Accounts payable and accrued liabilities.* State separately (a) amounts payable for investment advisory, management and service fees; and (b) the total amount payable to (1) officers and directors; (2) controlled companies; and (3) other affiliates, excluding any amounts owing to noncontrolled affiliates which arose in the ordinary course of business and which are subject to usual trade terms. State separately the amount of any other liabilities which are material.

10. *Total liabilities.*

11. *Commitments and contingent liabilities.*

Stockholders' Equity

12. *Capital shares.* Disclose the title of each class of capital shares or other capital units, the number authorized, the number outstanding and the dollar amount thereof. Show also the dollar amount of any capital shares subscribed but unissued, and show the deduction for subscriptions receivable therefrom.

13. *Other elements of capital.* (a) Disclose any other elements of capital or residual interests appropriate to the capital structure of the reporting entity.

(b) A summary of each account under this caption setting forth the information prescribed in § 210.3-04 shall be given in a note or separate statement for each period in which a statement of operations is presented.

14. *Total liabilities and stockholders' equity.*

[Adopted in Release No. FR-8, December 6, 1982, 47 F.R. 56835.]

[¶ 35,708] Statements of Operations

Reg. § 210.6-07. Statements of operations filed by registered investment companies, other than issuers of face-amount certificates subject to the special provisions of § 210.6-08 of this part, shall comply with the following provisions:

1. *Investment income.* State separately income from (a) dividends; (b) interest on securities; and (c) other income. If income from investments in or indebtedness of affiliates is included hereunder, such income shall be segregated under an appropriate caption subdivided to show separately income from (1) controlled companies; and (2) other affiliates. If non-cash dividends are included in income, the bases of recognition and measurement used in respect to such amounts shall be disclosed. Any other category of income which exceeds five percent of the total shown under this caption shall be stated separately.

2. *Expenses.* (a) State separately the total amount of investment advisory, management and service fees, and expenses in connection with research, selection, supervision, and custody of investments. Amounts of expenses incurred from transactions with affiliated persons shall be disclosed together with the identity of the related amount applicable to each such person accounting for five percent or more of the total expenses shown under this caption together with a description of the nature of the affiliation. Expenses incurred within the person's own organization in connection with research, selection and supervision of investments shall be stated separately. Reductions or reimbursements of management or service fees shall be shown as a negative amount or as a reduction of total expenses shown under this caption.

(b) State separately any other expense item the amount of which exceeds five percent of the total expenses shown under this caption.

(c) A note to the financial statements shall include information concerning management and service fees, the rate of fee, and the base and method of computation. State separately the amount and a description of any fee reductions or reimbursements representing (1) expense limitation agreements or commitments; and (2) offsets received from broker-dealers showing separately for each amount received or due from (i) unaffiliated persons; and (ii) affiliated persons. If no management or service fees were incurred for a period, state the reason therefor.

(d) If any expenses were paid otherwise than in cash, state the details in a note.

(e) State in a note to the financial statements the amount of brokerage commissions (including dealer markups) paid to affiliated broker-dealers in connection with purchase and sale of investment securities. Open-end management companies shall state in a note the net amounts of sales charges deducted from the proceeds of sale of capital shares which were retained by any affiliated principal underwriter or other affiliated broker-dealer.

(f) State separately all amounts paid in accordance with a plan adopted under rule 12b-1 of the Investment Company Act of 1940 [17 CFR 270.12b-1]. Reimbursement to the fund of expenses incurred under such plan (12b-1 expense reimbursement) shall be shown as a negative amount and deducted from current 12b-1 expenses. If 12b-1 expense reimbursements exceed current 12b-1 costs, such excess shall be shown as a negative amount used in the calculation of total expenses under this caption.

(g) (1) *Brokerage/Service Arrangements.* If a broker-dealer or an affiliate of the broker-dealer has, in connection with directing the person's brokerage transactions to the broker-dealer, provided, agreed to provide, paid for, or agreed to pay for, in whole or in part, services provided to the person (other than brokerage and research services as those terms are used in Section 28(e) of the Securities Exchange Act of 1934 [15 U.S.C. 78bb(e)]), include in the expense items set forth under this caption the amount that would have been incurred by the person for the services had it paid for the services directly in an arms-length transaction.

(2) *Expense Offset Arrangements.* If the person has entered into an agreement with any other person pursuant to which such other person reduces, or pays a third party which reduces, by a specified or reasonably ascertainable amount, its fees for services provided to the person in exchange for use of the person's assets, include in the expense items set forth under this caption the amount of fees that would have been incurred by the person if the person had not entered into the agreement.

(3) *Financial Statement Presentation.* Show the total amount by which expenses are increased pursuant to paragraphs (1) and (2) of this paragraph 2.(g) as a corresponding reduction in total expenses under this caption. In a note to the financial statements, state separately the total amounts by which expenses are increased pursuant to paragraphs (1) and (2) of this paragraph 2.(g), and list each category of expense that is increased by an amount equal to at least 5 percent of total expenses. If applicable, the note should state that the person could have employed the assets used by another person to produce income if it had not entered into an arrangement described in paragraph 2.(g)(2) of this section.

3. *Interest and amortization of debt discount and expense.* Provide in the body of the statements or in the footnotes, the average dollar amount of borrowings and the average interest rate.

4. *Investment income before income tax expense.*

5. *Income tax expense.* Include under this caption only taxes based on income.

6. *Investment income—net.*

7. *Realized and unrealized gain (loss) on investments—net.* (a) State separately the net realized gain or loss on transactions in (1) investment securities of unaffiliated issuers, (2) investment securities of affiliated issuers, and (3) investments other than securities.

(b) Distributions of realized gains by other investment companies shall be shown separately under this caption.

(c) State separately (1) the gain or loss from expiration or closing of option contracts written, (2) the gain or loss on closed short positions in securities, and (3) other realized gain or loss. Disclose in a note to the financial statements the number and associated dollar amounts as to option contracts written: (a) at the beginning of the period; (b) during the period; (c) expired during the period; (d) closed during the period; (e) exercised during the period; (f) balance at end of the period.

(d) State separately the amount of the net increase or decrease during the period in the unrealized appreciation or depreciation in the value of investment securities and other investments held at the end of the period.

(e) State separately any (1) Federal income taxes and (2) other income taxes applicable to realized and unrealized gain (loss) on investments, distinguishing taxes payable currently from deferred income taxes.

8. *Net gain (loss) on investments.*

9. *Net increase (decrease) in net assets resulting from operations.*

[As last amended in Release No. FR-46, July 21, 1995, 60 F.R. 38918.]

[¶ 35,709] Special Provisions Applicable to the Statements of Operations of Issuers of Face-Amount Certificates

Reg. § 210.6-08. Statements of operations filed by issuers of face-amount certificates shall comply with the following provisions:

1. *Investment income.* State separately income from (a) interest on mortgages; (b) interest on securities; (c) dividends; (d) rental income; and (e) other investment income. If income from investments in or indebtedness of affiliates is included hereunder, such income shall be segregated under an appropriate caption subdivided to show separately income from (1) controlled companies; and (2) other affiliates. If non-cash dividends are included in income, the bases of recognition and measurement used in respect to such amounts shall be disclosed. Any other category of income which exceeds five percent of the total shown under this caption shall be stated separately.

2. *Investment expenses.* (a) State separately the total amount of investment advisory, management and service fees, and expenses in connection with research, selection, supervision, and custody of investments. Amounts of expenses incurred from transactions with affiliated persons shall be disclosed together with the identity of and related amount applicable to each such person accounting for five percent or more of the total expenses shown under this caption together with a description of the nature of the affiliation. Expenses incurred within the person's own organization in connection with research, selection and supervision of investments shall be stated separately. Reductions or reimbursements of management or service fees shall be shown as a negative amount or as a reduction of total expenses shown under this caption.

(b) State separately any other expense item the amount of which exceeds five percent of the total expenses shown under this caption.

(c) A note to the financial statements shall include information concerning management and service fees, the rate of fee, and the base and method of computation. State separately the amount and a description of any fee reductions or reimbursements representing (1) expense limitation agreements or commitments; and (2) offsets received from broker-dealers showing separately for each amount received or due from (i) unaffiliated persons; and (ii) affiliated persons. If no management or service fees were incurred for a period, state the reason therefor.

(d) If any expenses were paid otherwise than in cash, state the details in a note.

(e) State in a note to the financial statements the amount of brokerage commissions (including dealer markups) paid to affiliated broker-dealers in connection with purchase and sale of investment securities.

3. *Interest and amortization of debt discount and expense.*

4. *Provision for certificate reserves.* State separately any provision for additional credits, or dividends, or interests, in addition to the minimum maturity or face amount specified in the certificates. State also in an appropriate manner reserve recoveries from surrenders or other causes.

5. *Investment income before income tax expense.*

6. *Income tax expense.* Include under this caption only taxes based on income.

7. *Investment income—net.*

8. *Realized gain (loss) on investments—net.* (a) State separately the net realized gain or loss on transactions in (1) investment securities of unaffiliated issuers, (2) investment securities of affiliated issuers, and (3) other investments.

(b) Distributions of capital gains by other investment companies shall be shown separately under this caption.

(c) State separately any (1) Federal income taxes and (2) other income taxes applicable to realized gain (loss) on investments, distinguishing taxes payable currently from deferred income taxes.

9. *Net income or loss.*

[Adopted in Release No. FR-8, December 6, 1982, 47 F.R. 56835.]

[¶ 35,710] Statements of Changes in Net Assets

Reg. § 210.6-09. Statements of changes in net assets filed for persons to whom this article is applicable shall comply with the following provisions:

1. *Operations.* State separately (a) investment income-net as shown by § 210.6-07.6; (b) realized gain (loss) on investments-net of any Federal or other income taxes applicable to such amounts; (c) increase (decrease) in unrealized appreciation or depreciation-net of any Federal or other income taxes applicable to such amounts; and (d) net increase (decrease) in net assets resulting from operations as shown by § 210.6-07.9.

2. *Net equalization charges and credits.* State the net amount of accrued undivided earnings separately identified in the price of capital shares issued and repurchased.

3. *Distributions to shareholders.* State separately distributions to shareholders from (a) investment income-net; (b) realized gain from investment transactions-net; and (c) other sources.

4. *Capital share transactions.* (a) State the increase or decrease in net assets derived from the net change in the number of outstanding shares or units.

(b) Disclose in the body of the statements or in the notes, for each class of the person's shares, the number and value of shares issued in reinvestment of dividends as well as the number and dollar amounts received for shares sold and paid for shares redeemed.

5. *Total increase (decrease).*

6. *Net assets at the beginning of the period.*

7. *Net assets at the end of the period.* Disclose parenthetically the balance of undistributed net investment income included in net assets at the end of the period.

[Adopted in Release No. FR-8, December 6, 1982, 47 F.R. 56835.]

[¶ 35,711] What Schedules Are to be Filed

Reg. § 210.6-10. (a) When information is required in schedules for both the person and the person and its subsidiaries consolidated, it may be presented in the form of a single schedule, provided that items pertaining to the registrant are separately shown and that such single schedule affords a properly summarized presentation of the facts. If the information required by any schedule (including the notes thereto) is shown in the related financial statement or in a note thereto without making such statement unclear or confusing, that procedure may be followed and the schedule omitted.

(b) The schedules shall be examined by an independent accountant if the related financial statements are so examined.

(c) *Management investment companies.*

(1) Except as otherwise provided in the applicable form, the schedules specified in this paragraph shall be filed for management investment companies as of the dates of the most recent audited balance sheet and any subsequent unaudited statement being filed for each person or group.

Schedule I - Investments in securities of unaffiliated issuers. The schedule prescribed by § 210.12-12 shall be filed in support of caption 1 of each balance sheet.

Schedule II - Investments - other than securities. The schedule prescribed by § 210.12-13 shall be filed in support of caption 3 of each balance sheet. This schedule may be omitted if the investments, other than securities, at both the beginning and end of the period amount to less than one percent of the value of total investments (§ 210.6-04.4).

Schedule III - Investments in and advances to affiliates. The schedule prescribed by § 210.12-14 shall be filed in support of caption 2 of each balance sheet.

Schedule IV - Investments - securities sold short. The schedule prescribed by § 210.12-12A shall be filed in support of caption 10(a) of each balance sheet.

Schedule V - Open option contracts written. The schedule prescribed by § 210.12-12B shall be filed in support of caption 10(b) of each balance sheet.

(2) When permitted by the applicable form, the schedule specified in this paragraph may be filed for management investment companies as of the dates of the most recent audited balance sheet and any subsequent unaudited statement being filed for each person or group.

Schedule VI - Summary schedule of investments in securities of unaffiliated issuers. The schedule prescribed by § 210.12-12C may be filed in support of caption 1 of each balance sheet.

(d) *Unit investment trusts.* Except as otherwise provided in the applicable form:

(1) Schedules I and II, specified below in this section, shall be filed for unit investment trusts as of the dates of the most recent audited balance sheet and any subsequent unaudited statement being filed for each person or group.

(2) Schedule III, specified below in this section, shall be filed for unit investment trusts for each period for which a statement of operations is required to be filed for each person or group.

Schedule I—Investment in securities. The schedule prescribed by § 210.12-12 shall be filed in support of caption 1 of each balance sheet (§ 210.6-04).

Schedule II—Allocation of trust assets to series of trust shares. If the trust assets are specifically allocated to different series of trust shares, and if such allocation is not shown in the balance sheet in columnar form or by the filing of separate statements for each series of trust shares, a schedule shall be filed showing the amount of trust assets, indicated by each balance sheet filed, which is applicable to each series of trust shares.

Schedule III—Allocation of trust income and distributable funds to series of trust shares. If the trust income and distributable funds are specifically allocated to different series of trust shares and if such allocation is not shown in the statement of operations in columnar form or by the filing of separate statements for each series of trust shares, a schedule shall be submitted showing the amount of income and distributable funds, indicated by each statement of operations filed, which is applicable to each series of trust shares.

(e) *Face-amount certificate investment companies.* Except as otherwise provided in the applicable form:

(1) Schedules I, V and X, specified below, shall be filed for face-amount certificate investment companies as of the dates of the most recent audited balance sheet and any subsequent unaudited statement being filed for each person or group.

(2) All other schedules specified below in this section shall be filed for face-amount certificate investment companies for each period for which a statement of operations is filed, except as indicated for Schedules III and IV.

Schedule I—Investment in securities of unaffiliated issuers. The schedule prescribed by § 210.12-21 shall be filed in support of caption 1 and, if applicable, caption 5(a) of each balance sheet. Separate schedules shall be furnished in support of each caption, if applicable.

Schedule II—Investments in and advances to affiliates and income thereon. The schedule prescribed by § 210.12-22 shall be filed in support of captions 1 and 5(b) of each balance sheet and caption 1 of each statement of operations. Separate schedules shall be furnished in support of each caption, if applicable.

Schedule III—Mortgage loans on real estate and interest earned on mortgages. The schedule prescribed by § 210.12-23 shall be filed in support of captions 1 and 5(c) of each balance sheet and caption 1 of each statement of operations, except that only the information required by column G and note 8 of the schedule need be furnished in support of statements of operations for years for which related balance sheets are not required.

Schedule IV—Real estate owned and rental income. The schedule prescribed by § 210.12-24 shall be filed in support of captions 1 and 5(a) of each balance sheet and caption 1 of each statement of operations for rental income included therein, except that only the information required by columns H, I and J, and item "Rent from properties sold during the period" and note 4 of the schedule need be furnished in support of statements of operations for years for which related balance sheets are not required.

Schedule V—Qualified assets on deposit. The schedule prescribed by § 210.12-27 shall be filed in support of the information required by caption 4 of § 210.6-06 as to total amount of qualified assets on deposit.

Schedule VI—Certificate reserves. The schedule prescribed by § 210.12-26 shall be filed in support of caption 7 of each balance sheet.

Schedule VII—Valuation and qualifying accounts. The schedule prescribed by § 210.12-09 shall be filed in support of all other reserves included in the balance sheet.

[As last amended in Release No. 33-8393, effective May 10, 2004, 69 F.R. 11244.]

Article 6A—Employee Stock Purchase, Savings and Similar Plans

[¶ 35,781] Application of §§ 210.6A-01 to 210.6A-05

Reg. § 210.6A-01. (a) Sections 210.6A-01 to 210.6A-05 shall be applicable to financial statements filed for employee stock purchase, savings and similar plans.

[As last amended in Release No. FR-8, December 6, 1982, 47 F.R. 56835.]

[¶ 35,791] Special Rules Applicable to Employee Stock Purchase, Savings and Similar Plans

Reg. § 210.6A-02. The financial statements filed for persons to which this article is applicable shall be prepared in accordance with the following special rules in addition to the general rules in §§ 210.1-01 to 210.4-10. Where the requirements of a special rule differ from those prescribed in a general rule, the requirements of the special rule shall be met.

(a) *Investment programs.* If the participating employees have an option as to the manner in which their deposits and contributions may be invested, a description of each investment program shall be given in a footnote or otherwise. The number of employees under each investment program shall be stated.

(b) *Net asset value per unit.* Where appropriate, the number of units and the net asset value per unit shall be given by footnote or otherwise.

(c) *Federal income taxes.* (1) If the plan is not subject to Federal income taxes, a note shall so state indicating briefly the principal assumptions on which the plan relied in not making provision for such taxes.

(2) State the Federal income tax status of the employee with respect to the plan.

(d) *Valuation of assets.* The statement of financial condition shall reflect all investments at value, showing cost parenthetically. For purposes of this rule, the term "value" shall mean (1) market value for those securities having readily available market quotations and (2) fair value as determined in good faith by the trustee(s) for the plan (or by the person or persons who exercise similar responsibilities) with respect to other securities and assets.

[As last amended in Release No. FR-8, December 6, 1982, 47 F.R. 56835.]

[¶ 35,801] Statements of Financial Condition

Reg. § 210.6A-03. Statements of financial condition filed under this rule shall comply with the following provisions:

Plan Assets

1. *Investments in securities of participating employers.* State separately each class of securities of the participating employer or employers.

2. *Investments in securities of unaffiliated issuers.*

(a) *United States Government bonds and other obligations.* Include only direct obligations of the United States Government.

(b) *Other securities.* State separately (1) marketable securities and (2) other securities.

3. *Investments. Other than securities.* State separately each major class.

4. *Dividends and interest receivable.*

5. *Cash.*

6. *Other assets.* State separately (a) total of amounts due from participating employers or any of their directors, officers and principal holders of equity securities; (b) total of amounts due from trustees or managers of the plan; and (c) any other significant amounts.

Liabilities and Plan Equity

7. *Liabilities.* State separately (a) total of amounts payable to participating employers; (b) total of amounts payable to participating employees; and (c) any other significant amounts.

8. *Reserves and other credits.* State separately each significant item and describe each such item by using an appropriate caption or by a footnote referred to in the caption.

9. *Plan equity at close of period.*

[As last amended in Release No. FR-8, December 6, 1982, 47 F.R. 56835.]

[¶ 35,811] Statements of Income and Changes in Plan Equity

Reg. § 210.6A-04. Statements of income and changes in plan equity filed under this rule shall comply with the following provisions:

1. *Net investment income.*

(a) *Income.* State separately income from (1) cash dividends, (2) interest, and (3) other sources. Income from investments in or indebtedness of participating employers shall be segregated under the appropriate subcaption.

(b) *Expenses.* State separately any significant amounts.

(c) *Net investment income.*

2. *Realized gain or loss on investments.* (a) State separately the net of gains or losses arising from transactions in (1) investments in securities of the participating employer or employers; (2) other investments in securities; and (3) other investments.

(b) State in a footnote or otherwise for each category of investment in paragraph (a) above the aggregate cost, the aggregate proceeds and the net gain or loss. State the principle followed in determining the cost of securities sold, e.g., "average cost" or "first-in, first-out."

3. *Unrealized appreciation or depreciation of investments.* (a) State the amount of increase or decrease in unrealized appreciation or depreciation of investments during the period.

(b) State in a footnote or otherwise the amount of unrealized appreciation or depreciation of investments at the beginning of the period of report, at the end of the period of report, and the increase or decrease during the period.

4. *Contributions and deposits.* (a) State separately (1) total of amounts deposited by participating employees, and (2) total of amounts contributed by the participating employer or employers.

(b) If employees of more than one employer participate in the plan, state in tabular form in a footnote or otherwise the amount contributed by each employer and the deposits of the employees of each such employer.

5. *Withdrawals, lapses and forfeitures.* State separately (a) balances of employees' accounts withdrawn, lapsed or forfeited during the period; (b) amounts disbursed in settlement of such accounts; and (c) disposition of balances remaining after settlement specified in (b).

6. *Plan equity at beginning of period.*

7. *Plan equity at end of period.*

[As last amended in Release No. FR-8, December 6, 1982, 47 F.R. 56835.]

[¶ 35,821] What Schedules Are to be Filed

Reg. § 210.6A-05. (a) Schedule I, specified below, shall be filed as of the most recent audited statement of financial condition and any subsequent unaudited statement of financial condition being filed. Schedule II shall be filed as of the date of each statement of financial condition being filed. Schedule III shall be filed for each period for which a statement of income and changes in plan equity is filed. All schedules shall be audited if the related statements are audited.

Schedule I—Investments. A schedule substantially in form prescribed by § 210.12-12 shall be filed in support of captions 1, 2 and 3 of each statement of financial condition unless substantially all of the information is given in the statement of financial condition by footnote or otherwise.

Schedule II—Allocation of plan assets and liabilities to investment program. If the plan provides for separate investment programs with separate funds, and if the allocation of assets and liabilities to the several funds is not shown in the statement of financial condition in columnar form or by the submission of separate statements for each fund, a schedule shall be submitted showing the allocation of each caption of each statement of financial condition filed to the applicable fund.

Schedule III—Allocation of plan income and changes in plan equity to investment programs. If the plan provides for separate investment programs with separate funds, and if the allocation of income and changes in plan equity to the several funds is not shown in the statement of income and changes in plan equity in columnar form or by the submission of separate statements for each fund, a schedule shall be submitted showing the allocation of each caption of each statement of income and changes in plan equity filed to the applicable fund.

[As last amended in Release No. FR-21, June 6, 1985, 50 F.R. 25214.]

Article 7—Insurance Companies

[¶ 35,851] Application of §§ 210.7-01 to 210.7-05

Reg. § 210.7-01. This article shall be applicable to financial statements filed for insurance companies.

[As last amended in Release No. AS-301, effective for companies with fiscal years ending after December 15, 1981, 46 F.R. 54332.]

[¶ 35,861] General Requirement

Reg. § 210.7-02. (a) The requirements of the general rules in §§ 210.1-01 to 210.4-10 (Articles 1, 2, 3, 3A and 4) shall be applicable except where they differ from requirements of §§ 210.7-01 to 210.7-05.

(b) Financial statements filed for mutual life insurance companies and wholly-owned stock insurance company subsidiaries of mutual life insurance companies may be prepared in accordance with statutory accounting requirements. Financial statements prepared in accordance with statutory accounting requirements may be condensed as appropriate, but the amounts to be reported for net gain from operations (or net income or loss) and total capital and surplus (or surplus as regards policyholders) shall be the same as those reported on the corresponding Annual Statement.

[As last amended in Release No. AS-301, 46 F.R. 54332.]

[¶ 35,871] Balance Sheets

Reg. § 210.7-03. (a) The purpose of this rule is to indicate the various items which, if applicable, and except as otherwise permitted by the Commission, should appear on the face of the balance sheets and in the notes thereto filed for persons to whom this article pertains. (See § 210.4-01(a).)

Assets

1. *Investments—other than investments in related parties.*
   (a) *Fixed maturities.*
   (b) *Equity securities.*
   (c) *Mortgage loans on real estate.*
   (d) *Investment real estate.*
   (e) *Policy loans.*
   (f) *Other long-term investments*
   (g) *Short-term investments.*
   (h) *Total investments.*

Notes: (1) State parenthetically or otherwise in the balance sheet (a) the basis of determining the amounts shown in the balance sheet and (b) as to fixed maturities and equity securities either aggregate cost or aggregate value at the balance sheet date, whichever is the alternate amount of the carrying value in the balance sheet. Consideration shall be given to the discussion of "Valuation of Securities" in § 404.03 of the Codification of Financial Reporting Policies.

(2) Include under fixed maturities: bonds, notes, marketable certificates of deposit with maturities beyond one year, and redeemable preferred stocks. Include under equity securities: common stocks and nonredeemable preferred stocks.

(3) State separately in the balance sheet or in a note thereto the amount of accumulated depreciation and amortization deducted from investment real estate. Subcaption (d) shall not include real estate acquired in settling title claims, mortgage guaranty claims, and similar insurance claims. Real estate acquired in settling claims shall be included in caption 10, "Other Assets," or shown separately, if material. [Amended in Release No. FR-21, effective June 18, 1985, 50 F.R. 30917.]

(4) Include under subcaption (g) investments maturing within one year, such as commercial paper maturing within one year, marketable certificates of deposit maturing within one year, savings accounts, time deposits and other cash accounts and cash equivalents earning interest. State in a note any amounts subject to withdrawal or usage restrictions. (See § 210.5-02.1.)

(5) State separately in a note the amount of any class of investments included in subcaption (f) if such amount exceeds ten percent of stockholders' equity.

(6) State in a note the name of any person in which the total amount invested in the person and its affiliates, included in the above subcaptions, exceeds ten percent of total stockholders' equity. For this disclosure, include in the amount invested in a person and its affiliates the aggregate of indebtedness and stocks issued by such person and its affiliates that is included in the several subcaptions above, and the amount of any real estate included in subcaption (d) that was purchased or acquired from such person and its affiliates. Indicate the amount

included in each subcaption. An investment in bonds and notes of the United States Government or of a United States Government agency or authority which exceeds ten percent of total stockholders' equity need not be reported.

(7) State in a note the amount of investments included under each subcaption (a), (c), (d) and (f) which have been non-income producing for the twelve months preceding the balance sheet date.

2. *Cash.* Cash on hand or on deposit that is restricted as to withdrawal or usage shall be disclosed separately on the balance sheet. The provisions of any restrictions shall be described in a note to the financial statements. Restrictions may include legally restricted deposits held as compensating balances against short-term borrowing arrangements, contracts entered into with others, or company statements of intention with regard to particular deposits. In cases where compensating balance arrangements exist but are not agreements which legally restrict the use of cash amounts shown on the balance sheet, describe in the notes to the financial statements these arrangements and the amount involved, if determinable, for the most recent audited balance sheet required. Compensating balances that are maintained under an agreement to assure future credit availability shall be disclosed in the notes to the financial statements along with the amount and terms of the agreement.

3. *Securities and indebtedness of related parties.* State separately (a) investments in related parties and (b) indebtedness from such related parties. [See § 210.4-08(k).]

4. *Accrued investment income.*

5. *Accounts and notes receivable.* Include under this caption (a) amounts receivable from agents and insureds, (b) uncollected premiums and (c) other receivables. State separately in the balance sheet or in a note thereto any category of other receivable which is in excess of five percent of total assets. State separately in the balance sheet or in a note thereto the amount of allowance for doubtful accounts that was deducted.

6. *Reinsurance recoverable on paid losses.*

7. *Deferred policy acquisition costs.*

8. *Property and equipment.* (a) State the basis of determining the amounts.

(b) State separately in the balance sheet or in a note thereto the amount of accumulated depreciation and amortization of property and equipment.

9. *Title plant.*

10. *Other assets.* State separately in the balance sheet or in a note thereto any other asset the amount of which exceeds five percent of total assets.

11. *Assets held in separate accounts.* Include under this caption the aggregate amount of assets used to fund liabilities related to variable annuities, pension funds and similar activities. The aggregate liability shall be included under caption 18. Describe in a note to the financial statements the general nature of the activities being reported on in the separate accounts.

12. *Total assets.*

Liabilities and Stockholders' Equity

13. *Policy liabilities and accruals.* (a) State separately in the balance sheet the amounts of (1) future policy benefits and losses, claims and loss expenses, (2) unearned premiums and (3) other policy claims and benefits payable.

(b) State in a note to the financial statements the basis of assumptions (interest rates, mortality, withdrawals) for future policy benefits and claims and settlements which are stated at present value.

(c) Information shall be given in a note concerning the general nature of reinsurance transactions, including a description of the significant types of reinsurance agreements executed. The information provided shall include (1) the nature of the contingent liability in connection with insurance ceded and (2) the nature and effect of material nonrecurring reinsurance transactions.

14. *Other policyholders' funds.* (a) Include amounts of supplementary contracts without life contingencies, policyholders' dividend accumulations, undistributed earnings on participating business, dividends to policyholders and retrospective return premiums (not included elsewhere) and any similar items. State separately in the balance sheet or in a note thereto any item the amount of which is in excess of five percent of total liabilities.

(b) State in a note to the financial statements the relative significance of participating insurance expressed as percentages of (1) insurance in force and (2) premium income; and the method by which earnings and dividends allocable to such insurance is determined.

15. *Other liabilities.* (a) Include under this caption such items as accrued payrolls, accrued interest and taxes. State separately in the balance sheet or in a note thereto any item included in other liabilities the amount of which exceeds five percent of total liabilities.

(b) State separately in the balance sheet or in a note thereto the amount of (1) income taxes payable and (2) deferred income taxes. Disclose separately the amount of deferred income taxes applicable to unrealized appreciation of equity securities.

16. *Notes payable, bonds, mortgages and similar obligations, including capitalized leases.* (a) State separately in the balance sheet the amounts of (1) short-term debt and (2) long-term debt including capitalized leases.

(b) The disclosure required by § 210.5-02.19(b) shall be given if the aggregate of short-term borrowings from banks, factors and other financial institutions and commercial paper issued exceeds five percent of total liabilities.

(c) The disclosure requirements of § 210.5-02.22 shall be followed for long-term debt.

17. *Indebtedness to related parties.* [See § 210.4-08(k).]

18. *Liabilities related to separate accounts.* [See caption 11.]

19. *Commitments and contingent liabilities.*

Redeemable Preferred Stocks

20. *Preferred stocks subject to mandatory redemption requirements or whose redemption is outside the control of the issuer.* The classification and disclosure requirements of § 210.5-02.27 shall be followed.

Nonredeemable Preferred Stocks

21. *Preferred stocks which are not redeemable or are redeemable solely at the option of the issuer.* The classification and disclosure requirements of § 210.5-02.28 shall be followed.

Common Stocks

22. *Common stocks.* The classification and disclosure requirements of § 210.5-02.29 shall be followed.

Other Stockholders' Equity

23. *Other stockholders' equity.*

(a) Separate captions shall be shown for (1) additional paid-in capital, (2) other additional capital, (3) unrealized appreciation or depreciation of equity securities less applicable deferred income taxes, (4) retained earnings (i) appropriated and (ii) unappropriated. [See § 210.4-08(e).] Additional paid-in capital and other additional capital may be combined with the stock caption to which they apply, if appropriate.

(b) The classification and disclosure requirements of § 210.5-02.30(b) shall be followed for dating and effect of a quasi-reorganization.

(c) State in a note the following information separately for (1) life insurance legal entities, and (2) property and liability insurance legal entities: the amount of statutory stockholders' equity as of the date of each balance sheet presented and the amount of statutory net income or loss for each period for which an income statement is presented.

Noncontrolling Interests

24. *Noncontrolling interests in consolidated subsidiaries.* The disclosure requirements of § 210.5-02.31 shall be followed.

25. *Total liabilities and equity.*

[As last amended in Release No. 33-9026, effective April 23, 2009, 74 F.R. 18612.]

[¶ 35,881] Income Statements

Reg. § 210.7-04. The purpose of this rule is to indicate the various items which, if applicable, should appear on the face of the income statements and in the notes thereto filed for persons to whom this article pertains. [See § 210.4-01(a).]

Revenues

1. *Premiums.* Include premiums from reinsurance assumed and deduct premiums on reinsurance ceded. Where applicable, the amounts included in this caption should represent premiums earned.

2. *Net investment income.* State in a note to the financial statements, in tabular form, the amounts of (a) investment income from each category of investments listed in the subcaptions of § 210.7-03.1 that exceeds five percent of total investment income, (b) total investment income, (c) applicable expenses, and (d) net investment income.

3. *Realized investment gains and losses.* Disclose the following amounts:

(a) Net realized investment gains and losses, which shall be shown separately regardless of size.

(b) Indicate in a footnote the registrant's policy with respect to whether investment income and realized gains and losses allocable to policyholders and separate accounts are included in the investment income and realized gain and loss amounts reported in the income statement. If the income statement includes investment income and realized gains and losses allocable to policyholders and separate accounts, indicate the amounts of such allocable investment income and realized gains and losses and the manner in which the insurance enterprise's obligation with respect to allocation of such investment income and realized gains and losses is otherwise accounted for in the financial statements.

(c) The method followed in determining the cost of investments sold (e.g., "average cost," "first-in, first-out," or "identified certificate") shall be disclosed.

(d) For each period for which an income statement is filed, include in a note an analysis of realized and unrealized investment gains and losses on fixed maturities and equity securities. For each period, state separately for fixed maturities [see §210.7-03.1(a)]and for equity securities [see §210.7-03.1(b)] the following amounts: (1) realized investment gains and losses, and (2) the change during the period in the difference between value and cost.

The change in the difference between value and cost shall be given for both categories of investments even though they may be shown on the related balance sheet on a basis other than value.

4. *Other income.* Include all revenues not included in captions 1 and 2 above. State separately in the statement any amounts in excess of five percent of total revenue, and disclose the nature of the transactions from which the items arose.

Benefits, Losses and Expenses

5. *Benefits, claims, losses and settlement expenses.*

6. *Policyholders' share of earnings on participating policies, dividends and similar items.* [See §210.7-03.14(b).]

7. *Underwriting, acquisition and insurance expenses.* State separately in the income statement or in a note thereto (a) the amount included in this caption representing deferred policy acquisition costs amortized to income during the period, and (b) the amount of other operating expenses. State separately in the income statement any material amount included in all other operating expenses.

8. *Income or loss before income tax expense and appropriate items below.*

9. *Income tax expense.* Include under this caption only taxes based on income. [See §210.4-08(g).]

10. *Equity in earnings of unconsolidated subsidiaries and 50% or less owned persons.* State, parenthetically or in a note, the amount of dividends received from such persons. If justified by the circumstances, this item may be presented in a different position and a different manner. (See §210.4-01(a).)

11. *Income or loss from continuing operations.*

12. *Discontinued operations.*

13. *Income or loss before extraordinary items and cumulative effects of changes in accounting principles.*

14. *Extraordinary items, less applicable tax.*

15. *Cumulative effects of changes in accounting principles*

16. *Net income or loss.*

17. *Net income attributable to the noncontrolling interest.*

18. *Net income attributable to the controlling interest.*

19. *Earnings per share data.*

[As last amended in Release No. 33-9026, effective April 23, 2009, 74 F.R. 18612.]

[¶ 35,891] What Schedules Are to Be Filed

Reg. § 210.7-05. (a) Except as expressly provided otherwise in the applicable form:

(1) The schedule specified below in this section as Schedules I shall be as of the date of the most recent audited balance sheet for each person or group.

(2) The schedules specified below in this section as Schedule IV and V shall be filed for each period for which an audited income statement is required to be filed for each person or group.

(3) Schedules II, III and V shall be filed as of the date and for periods specified in the schedule.

(b) When information is required in schedules for both the registrant and the registrant and its subsidiaries consolidated it may be presented in the form of a single schedule: *Provided,* That items pertaining to the registrant are shown separately and that such single schedule affords a properly summarized presentation of the facts. If the information required by any schedule (including the notes thereto) may be shown in the related financial statement or in a note thereto without making such statement unclear or confusing, that procedure may be followed and the schedule omitted.

(c) The schedules shall be examined by the independent accountant.

Schedule I—Summary of investments—other than investments in related parties. The schedule prescribed by § 210.12-15 shall be filed in support of caption 1 of the most recent audited balance sheet.

Schedule II—Condensed financial information of registrant. The schedule prescribed by § 210.12-04 shall be filed when the restricted net assets (§ 210.4-08(e)(3)) of consolidated subsidiaries exceed 25 percent of consolidated net assets as of the end of the most recently completed fiscal year. For purposes of the above test, restricted net assets of consolidated subsidiaries shall mean that amount of the registrant's proportionate share of net assets of consolidated subsidiaries (after intercompany eliminations) which as of the end of the most recent fiscal year may not be transferred to the parent company by subsidiaries in the form of loans, advances or cash dividends without the consent of a third party (i.e., lender, regulatory agency, foreign government, etc.). Where restrictions on the amount of funds which may be loaned or advanced differ from the amount restricted as to transfer in the form of cash dividends, the amount least restrictive to the subsidiary shall be used. Redeemable preferred stocks (§ 210.7-03.20) and noncontrolling interests shall be deducted in computing net assets for purposes of this test.

Schedule III—Supplementary insurance information. The schedule prescribed by § 210.12-16 shall be filed giving segment detail in support of various balance sheet and income statement captions. The required balance sheet information shall be presented as of the date of each audited balance sheet filed, and the income statement information shall be presented for each period for which an audited income statement is required to be filed, for each person or group.

Schedule IV—Reinsurance. The schedule prescribed by § 210.12-17 shall be filed for reinsurance ceded and assumed.

Schedule V—Valuation and qualifying accounts. The schedule prescribed by § 210.12-09 shall be filed in support of valuation and qualifying accounts included in the balance sheet [see § 210.4-02].

Schedule VI—Supplemental information concerning property-casualty insurance operations. The information required by § 210.12-18 shall be presented as of the same dates and for the same periods for which the information is reflected in the audited consolidated financial statements required by § 210.3-01 and 3-02. The schedule may be omitted if reserves for unpaid property-casualty claims and claim adjustment expenses of the registrant and its consolidated subsidiaries, its unconsolidated subsidiaries and its 50%-or-less-owned equity basis investees did not in the aggregate, exceed one-half of common stockholders' equity of the registrant and its consolidated subsidiaries as of the beginning of the fiscal year. For purposes of this test, only the proportionate share of the registrant and its other subsidiaries in the reserves for unpaid claims and claim adjustment expenses of 50%-or-less-owned equity investees taken in the aggregate after intercompany elimination shall be taken into account.

[As last amended in Release No. 33-9026, effective April 23, 2009, 74 F.R. 18612.]

Article 8—Financial Statements of Smaller Reporting Companies

[¶ 35,901] Preliminary Notes to Article 8

Reg. § 210.8-01. Sections 210.8-01 to 210.8-08 shall be applicable to financial statements filed for smaller reporting companies. These section are not applicable to financial statements prepared for the purposes of Item 17 or Item 18 of Form 20-F.

Note 1 to § 210.8: Financial statements of a smaller reporting company, as defined by § 229.10(f)(1) of this chapter, its predecessors or any businesses to which the smaller reporting company is a successor shall be prepared in accordance with generally accepted accounting principles in the United States.

Note 2 to § 210.8: Smaller reporting companies electing to prepare their financial statements with the form and content required in this article need not apply the other form and content requirements in Regulation S-X with the exception of the following:

a. The report and qualifications of the independent accountant shall comply with the requirements of Article 2 of this part;

b. The description of accounting policies shall comply with Article 4-08(n) of this part; and

c. Smaller reporting companies engaged in oil and gas producing activities shall follow the financial accounting and reporting standards specified in Article 4-10 of this part with respect to such activities.

To the extent that Article 11-01 of this part (Pro Forma Presentation Requirements) offers enhanced guidelines for the preparation, presentation and disclosure of pro forma financial information, smaller reporting companies may wish to consider these items.

Note 3 to § 210.8: Financial statements for a subsidiary of a smaller reporting company that issues securities guaranteed by the smaller reporting company or guarantees securities issued by the smaller reporting company must be presented as required by § 210.3-10, except that the periods presented are those required by § 210.8-02.

Note 4 to § 210.8: Financial statements for a smaller reporting company's affiliates whose securities constitute a substantial portion of the collateral for any class of securities registered or being registered must be presented as required by § 210.3-16, except that the periods presented are those required by § 210.8-02.

Note 5 to § 210.8: The Commission, where consistent with the protection of investors, may permit the omission of one or more of the financial statements or the substitution of appropriate statements of comparable character. The Commission by informal written notice may require the filing of other financial statements where necessary or appropriate.

Note 6 to § 210.8: Section 210.4-01(a)(3) shall apply to the preparation of financial statements of smaller reporting companies.

[Added by Release No. 33-8876, effective February 4, 2008, 73 F.R. 934.]

[¶ 35,902] Annual Financial Statements

Reg. § 210.8-02. Smaller reporting companies shall file an audited balance sheet as of the end of each of the most recent two fiscal years, or as of a date within 135 days if the issuer has existed for a period of less than one fiscal year, and audited statements of income, cash flows and changes in stockholders' equity for each of the two fiscal years preceding the date of the most recent audited balance sheet (or such shorter period as the registrant has been in business).

[Added by Release No. 33-8876, effective February 4, 2008, 73 F.R. 934.]

[¶ 35,903] Interim Financial Statements

Reg. § 210.8-03. Interim financial statements may be unaudited; however, before filing, interim financial statements included in quarterly reports on Form 10-Q (§ 249.308(a) of this chapter) must be reviewed by an independent public accountant using professional standards and procedures for conducting such reviews, as established by generally accepted auditing standards, as may be modified or supplemented by the Commission. If, in any filing, the issuer states that interim financial statements have been reviewed by an independent public accountant, a report of the accountant on the review must be filed with the interim financial statements. Interim financial statements shall include a balance sheet as of the end of the issuer's most recent fiscal quarter, a balance sheet as of the end of the preceding fiscal year, and income statements and statements of cash flows for the interim period up to the date of such balance sheet and the comparable period of the preceding fiscal year.

(a) *Condensed format.* Interim financial statements may be condensed as follows:

(1) Balance sheets should include separate captions for each balance sheet component presented in the annual financial statements that represents 10% or more of total assets. Cash and retained earnings should be presented regardless of relative significance to total assets. Registrants that present a

classified balance sheet in their annual financial statements should present totals for current assets and current liabilities.

(2) Income statements should include net sales or gross revenue, each cost and expense category presented in the annual financial statements that exceeds 20% of sales or gross revenues, provision for income taxes, discontinued operations, extraordinary items and cumulative effects of changes in accounting principles or practices. (Financial institutions should substitute net interest income for sales for purposes of determining items to be disclosed.) Dividends per share should be presented.

(3) Cash flow statements should include cash flows from operating, investing and financing activities as well as cash at the beginning and end of each period and the increase or decrease in such balance.

(4) Additional line items may be presented to facilitate the usefulness of the interim financial statements, including their comparability with annual financial statements.

(b) *Disclosure required and additional instructions as to content.*

(1) *Footnotes.* Footnote and other disclosures should be provided as needed for fair presentation and to ensure that the financial statements are not misleading.

(2) *Material subsequent events and contingencies.* Disclosure must be provided of material subsequent events and material contingencies notwithstanding disclosure in the annual financial statements.

(3) *Significant equity investees.* Sales, gross profit, net income (loss) from continuing operations, net income, and net income attributable to the investee must be disclosed for equity investees that constitute 20 percent or more of a registrant's consolidated assets, equity or income from continuing operations attributable to the registrant.

(4) *Significant dispositions and business combinations.* If a significant disposition or business combination has occurred during the most recent interim period and the transaction required the filing of a Form 8-K (§ 249.308 of this chapter), pro forma data must be presented that reflects revenue, income from continuing operations, net income, net income attributable to the registrant and income per share for the current interim period and the corresponding interim period of the preceding fiscal year as though the transaction occurred at the beginning of the periods.

(5) *Material accounting changes.* Disclosure must be provided of the date and reasons for any material accounting change. The registrant's independent accountant must provide a letter in the first Form 10-Q (§ 249.308a of this chapter) filed after the change indicating whether or not the change is to a preferable method. Disclosure must be provided of any retroactive change to prior period financial statements, including the effect of any such change on income and income per share.

(6) *Development stage companies.* A registrant in the development stage must provide cumulative financial information from inception.

Instruction 1 to § 210.8-03: Where Article 8 is applicable to a Form 10-Q and the interim period is more than one quarter, income statements must also be provided for the most recent interim quarter and the comparable quarter of the preceding fiscal year.

Instruction 2 to § 210.8-03: Interim financial statements must include all adjustments that, in the opinion of management, are necessary in order to make the financial statements not misleading. An affirmative statement that the financial statements have been so adjusted must be included with the interim financial statements.

[As last amended in Release No. 33-9026, effective April 23, 2009, 74 F.R. 18612.]

[¶ 35,904] Financial Statements of Businesses Acquired or to Be Acquired

Reg. § 210.8-04. (a) If a business combination has occurred or is probable, financial statements of the business acquired or to be acquired shall be furnished for the periods specified in paragraph (c) of this section:

(1) This encompasses the purchase of an interest in a business accounted for by the equity method.

(2) Acquisitions of a group of related businesses that are probable or that have occurred subsequent to the latest fiscal year end for which audited financial statements of the issuer have been filed shall be treated as if they are a single business combination for purposes of this section. The required financial statements of related businesses may be presented on a combined basis for any periods they are under common control or management. A group of businesses is deemed to be related if:

(i) They are under common control or management;

(ii) The acquisition of one business is conditioned on the acquisition of each other business; or

(iii) Each acquisition is conditioned on a single common event.

(3) Annual financial statements required by this rule shall be audited. The form and content of the financial statements shall be in accordance with §§ 210.8-02 and 8-03.

(b) The periods for which financial statements are to be presented are determined by comparison of the most recent annual financial statements of the business acquired or to be acquired and the smaller reporting company's most recent annual financial statements filed at or before the date of acquisition to evaluate each of the following conditions:

(1) Compare the smaller reporting company's investments in and advances to the acquiree to the total consolidated assets of the smaller reporting company as of the end of the most recently completed fiscal year.

(2) Compare the smaller reporting company's proportionate share of the total assets (after intercompany eliminations) of the acquiree to the total consolidated assets of the smaller reporting company as of the end of the most recently completed fiscal year.

(3) Compare the smaller reporting company's equity in the income from continuing operations before income taxes, extraordinary items and cumulative effect of a change in accounting principles of the acquiree exclusive of amounts attributable to any noncontrolling interests to such consolidated income of the smaller reporting company for the most recently completed fiscal year.

Computational note to § 210.8-04(b): For purposes of making the prescribed income test the following guidance should be applied: If income of the smaller reporting company and its subsidiaries consolidated exclusive of amounts attributable to any noncontrolling interests for the most recent fiscal year is at least 10 percent lower than the average of the income for the last five fiscal years, such average income should be substituted for purposes of the computation. Any loss years should be omitted for purposes of computing average income.

(c)(1) If none of the conditions specified in paragraph (b) of this section exceeds 20%, financial statements are not required. If any of the conditions exceed 20%, but none exceeds 40%, financial statements shall be furnished for the most recent fiscal year and any interim periods specified in § 210.8-03. If any of the conditions exceed 40%, financial statements shall be furnished for the two most recent fiscal years and any interim periods specified in § 210.8-03.

(2) The separate audited balance sheet of the acquired business is not required when the smaller reporting company's most recent audited balance sheet filed is for a date after the acquisition was consummated.

(3) If the aggregate impact of individually insignificant businesses acquired since the date of the most recent audited balance sheet filed for the registrant exceeds 50%, financial statements covering at least the substantial majority of the businesses acquired shall be furnished. Such financial statements shall be for the most recent fiscal year and any interim periods specified in § 210.8-03.

(4) Registration statements not subject to the provisions of § 230.419 of this chapter (Regulation C) and proxy statements need not include separate financial statements of the acquired or to be acquired business if it does not meet or exceed any of the conditions specified in paragraph (b) of this section at the 50 percent level, and either:

(i) The consummation of the acquisition has not yet occurred; or

(ii) The effective date of the registration statement, or mailing date in the case of a proxy statement, is no more than 74 days after consummation of the business combination, and the financial statements have not been filed previously by the registrant.

(5) An issuer that omits from its initial registration statement financial statements of a recently consummated business combination pursuant to paragraph (c)(4) of this section shall furnish those financial statements and any pro forma information specified by § 210.8-05 under cover of Form 8-K (§ 249.308 of this chapter) no later than 75 days after consummation of the acquisition.

(d) If the smaller reporting company made a significant business acquisition after the latest fiscal year end and filed a report on Form 8-K, which included audited financial statements of such acquired business for the periods required by paragraph (c) of this section and the pro forma financial information required by § 210.8-05, the determination of significance may be made by using pro forma amounts for the latest fiscal year in the report on Form 8-K rather than by using the historical amounts of the registrant. The tests may not be made by "annualizing" data.

(e) If the business acquired or to be acquired is a foreign business, financial statements of the business meeting the requirements of Item 17 of Form 20-F (§ 249.220f of this chapter) will satisfy this section.

[As last amended in Release No. 33-9026, effective April 23, 2009, 74 F.R. 18612.]

[¶ 35,905] Pro forma Financial Information

Reg. § 210.8-05. (a) Pro forma information showing the effects of the acquisition shall be furnished if financial statements of a business acquired or to be acquired are presented.

(b) Pro forma statements should be condensed, in columnar form showing pro forma adjustments and results, and should include the following:

(1) If the transaction was consummated during the most recent fiscal year or subsequent interim period, pro forma statements of income reflecting the combined operations of the entities for the latest fiscal year and interim period, if any; or

(2) If consummation of the transaction has occurred or is probable after the date of the most recent balance sheet required by § 210.8-02 or §210.8-03, a pro forma balance sheet giving effect to the combination as of the date of the most recent balance sheet. For a purchase, pro forma statements of income reflecting the combined operations of the entities for the latest fiscal year and interim period, if any, are required.

[Added by Release No. 33-8876, effective February 4, 2008, 73 F.R. 934.]

[¶ 35,906] Real Estate Operations Acquired or to Be Acquired

Reg. § 210.8-06. If, during the period for which income statements are required, the smaller reporting company has acquired one or more properties that in the aggregate are significant, or since the date of the latest balance sheet required by § 210.8-02 or § 210.8-03, has acquired or proposes to acquire one or more properties that in the aggregate are significant, the following shall be furnished with respect to such properties:

(a) Audited income statements (not including earnings per unit) for the two most recent years, which shall exclude items not comparable to the proposed future operations of the property such as mortgage interest, leasehold rental, depreciation, corporate expenses and federal and state income taxes; *Provided, however,* that such audited statements need be presented for only the most recent fiscal year if:

(1) The property is not acquired from a related party;

(2) Material factors considered by the smaller reporting company in assessing the property are described with specificity in the registration statement with regard to the property, including source of revenue (including, but not limited to, competition in the rental market, comparative rents, occupancy rates) and expenses (including but not limited to, utilities, *ad valorem* tax rates, maintenance expenses, and capital improvements anticipated); and

(3) The smaller reporting company indicates that, after reasonable inquiry, it is not aware of any material factors relating to the specific property other than those discussed in response to paragraph (a)(2) of this section that would cause the reported financial information not to be necessarily indicative of future operating results.

(b) If the property will be operated by the smaller reporting company, a statement shall be furnished showing the estimated taxable operating results of the smaller reporting company based on the most recent twelve-month period, including such adjustments as can be factually supported. If the property will be acquired subject to a net lease, the estimated taxable operating results shall be based on the rent to be paid for the first year of the lease. In either case, the estimated amount of cash to be made available by operations shall be shown. Disclosure must be provided of the principal assumptions that have been made in preparing the statements of estimated taxable operating results and cash to be made available by operations.

(c) If appropriate under the circumstances, a table should be provided that shows, for a limited number of years, the estimated cash distribution per unit, indicating the portion reportable as taxable income and the portion representing a return of capital with an explanation of annual variations, if any. If taxable net income per unit will be greater than the cash available for distribution per unit, that fact and the approximate year of occurrence shall be stated, if significant.

[Added by Release No. 33-8876, effective February 4, 2008, 73 F.R. 934.]

[¶ 35,907] Limited Partnerships

Reg. § 210.8-07. (a) Smaller reporting companies that are limited partnerships must provide the balance sheets of the general partners as described in paragraphs (b) through (d) of this section.

(b) Where a general partner is a corporation, the audited balance sheet of the corporation as of the end of its most recently completed fiscal year must be filed. Receivables, other than trade receivables, from affiliates of the general partner should be deducted from shareholders' equity of the general partner. Where an affiliate has committed itself to increase or maintain the general partner's capital, the audited balance sheet of such affiliate must also be presented.

(c) Where a general partner is a partnership, there shall be filed an audited balance sheet of such partnership as of the end of its most recently completed fiscal year.

(d) Where the general partner is a natural person, there shall be filed, as supplemental information, a balance sheet of such natural person as of a recent date. Such balance sheet need not be audited. The assets and liabilities should be carried at estimated fair market value, with provisions for estimated income taxes on unrealized gains. The net worth of such general partner(s), based on such balance sheet(s), singly or in the aggregate, shall be disclosed in the registration statement.

[Added by Release No. 33-8876, effective February 4, 2008, 73 F.R. 934.]

[¶ 35,908] Age of Financial Statements

Reg. § 210.8-08. At the date of filing, financial statements included in filings other than filings on Form 10-K must be not less current than the financial statements that would be required in Forms 10-K and 10-Q if such reports were required to be filed. If required financial statements are as of a date 135 days or more before the date a registration statement becomes effective or proxy material is expected to be mailed, the financial statements shall be updated to include financial statements for an interim period ending within 135 days of the effective or expected mailing date. Interim financial statements must be prepared and presented in accordance with paragraph (b) of this section.

(a) When the anticipated effective or mailing date falls within 45 days after the end of the fiscal year, the filing may include financial statements only as current as of the end of the third fiscal quarter; *Provided, however,* that if the audited financial statements for the recently completed fiscal year are available or become available before effectiveness or mailing, they must be included in the filing; and

(b) If the effective date or anticipated mailing date falls after 45 days but within 90 days of the end of the smaller reporting company's fiscal year, the smaller reporting company is not required to provide the audited financial statements for such year end provided that the following conditions are met:

(1) If the smaller reporting company is a reporting company, all reports due must have been filed;

(2) For the most recent fiscal year for which audited financial statements are not yet available, the smaller reporting company reasonably and in good faith expects to report income from continuing operations attributable to the registrant before taxes; and

(3) For at least one of the two fiscal years immediately preceding the most recent fiscal year the smaller reporting company reported income from continuing operations attributable to the registrant before taxes.

[As last amended in Release No. 33-9026, effective April 23, 2009, 74 F.R. 18612.]

Article 9—Bank Holding Companies

[¶ 35,981] Application of §§ 210.9-01 to 210.9-07

Reg. § 210.9-01. This article is applicable to consolidated financial statements filed for bank holding companies and to any financial statements of banks that are included in filings with the Commission.

[As adopted in Release No. FR-11, March 7, 1983, 48 F.R. 11104.]

[¶ 35,982] General Requirement

Reg. § 210.9-02. The requirements of the general rules in §§ 210.1 to 210.4 (Articles 1, 2, 3, 3A and 4) should be complied with where applicable.

[As adopted in Release No. FR-11, March 7, 1983, 48 F.R. 11104.]

[¶ 35,983] Balance Sheets

Reg. § 210.9-03. The purpose of this rule is to indicate the various items which, if applicable, should appear on the face of the balance sheets or in the notes thereto.

Assets

1. *Cash and due from banks.* The amounts in this caption should include all noninterest bearing deposits with other banks.

(a) Any withdrawal and usage restrictions (including requirements of the Federal Reserve to maintain certain average reserve balances) or compensating balance requirements should be disclosed (see § 210.5-02-1).

2. *Interest-bearing deposits in other banks.*

3. *Federal funds sold and securities purchased under resale agreements or similar arrangements.* These amounts should be presented gross and not netted against Federal funds purchased and securities sold under agreement to repurchase as reported in Caption 13.

4. *Trading account assets.* Include securities or any other investments held for trading purposes only.

5. *Other short-term investments.*

6. *Investment securities.* Include securities held for investment only. Disclose the aggregate book value of investment securities; show on the balance sheet the aggregate market value at the balance sheet date. The aggregate amounts should include securities pledged, loaned or sold under repurchase agreements and similar arrangements; borrowed securities and securities purchased under resale agreements or similar arrangements should be excluded.

(a) Disclose in a note the carrying value and market value of securities of (1) the U.S. Treasury and other U.S. Government agencies and corporations; (2) states of the U.S. and political subdivisions; and (3) other securities.

7. *Loans.* Disclose separately (1) total loans, (2) the related allowance for losses and (3) unearned income.

(a) Disclose on the balance sheet or in a note the amount of total loans in each of the following categories:

(1) Commercial, financial and agricultural

(2) Real estate—construction

(3) Real estate—mortgage

(4) Installment loans to individuals

(5) Lease financing

(6) Foreign

(7) Other (State separately any other loan category regardless of relative size if necessary to reflect any unusual risk concentration).

(b) A series of categories other than those specified in (a) above may be used to present details of loans if considered a more appropriate presentation.

(c) The amount of foreign loans must be presented if the disclosures provided by § 210.9-05 are required.

(d) For each period for which an income statement is required, furnish in a note a statement of changes in the allowance for loan losses showing the balances at beginning and end of the period, provision charged to income, recoveries of amounts charged off and losses charged to the allowance.

(e)(1)(i) As of each balance sheet date, disclose in a note the aggregate dollar amount of loans (exclusive of loans to any such persons which in the aggregate do not exceed $60,000 during the latest year) made by the registrant or any of its subsidiaries to directors, executive officers, or principal holders of equity securities (§ 210.1-02) of the registrant or any of its significant subsidiaries (§ 210.1-02), or to any associate of such persons. For the latest fiscal year, an analysis of activity with respect to such aggregate loans to related parties should be provided. The analysis should include the aggregate amount at the beginning of the period, new loans, repayments, and other changes. (Other changes, if significant, should be explained.)

(ii) This disclosure need not be furnished when the aggregate amount of such loans at the balance sheet date (or with respect to the latest fiscal year, the maximum amount outstanding during the period) does not exceed 5 percent of stockholders' equity at the balance sheet date.

(2) If a significant portion of the aggregate amount of loans outstanding at the end of the fiscal year disclosed pursuant to (e)(1)(i) above relates to loans which are disclosed as nonaccrual, past due, restructured or potential problems (see Item III.C.1. or 2. of Industry Guide 3, Statistical Disclosure by Bank Holding Companies), so state and disclose the aggregate amounts of such loans along with such other information necessary to an understanding of the effects of the transactions on the financial statements. [Amended in Release No. FR-13, effective for filings after December 30, 1983, 48 F.R. 37609.]

(3) Notwithstanding the aggregate disclosure called for by (e)(1) above, if any loans were not made in the ordinary course of business during any period for which an income statement is required to be filed, provide an appropriate description of each such loan (See § 210.4-08(L)(3)).

(4) Definition of terms. For purposes of this rule, the following definitions shall apply:

"Associate" means (i) a corporation, venture or organization of which such person is a general partner or is, directly or indirectly, the beneficial owner of 10 percent or more of any class of equity securities; (ii) any trust or other estate in which such person has a substantial beneficial interest or for which such person serves as trustee or in a similar capacity and (iii) any member of the immediate family of any of the foregoing persons. [Amended in Release No. FR-21, effective June 18, 1985, 50 F.R. 25214.]

"Executive officers" means the president, any vice president in charge of a principal business unit, division or function (such as loans, investments, operations, administration or finance), and any other officer or person who performs similar policymaking functions.

"Immediate family" means such person's spouse; parents; children; siblings; mothers- and fathers-in-law; sons and daughters-in-law; and brothers and sisters-in-law.

"Ordinary course of business" means those loans which were made on substantially the same terms, including interest rate and collateral, as those prevailing at the same time for comparable transactions with unrelated persons and did not involve more than the normal risk of collectibility or present other unfavorable features.

8. *Premises and equipment.*

9. *Due from customers on acceptances.* Include amounts receivable from customers on unmatured drafts and bills of exchange that have been accepted by a bank subsidiary or by other banks for the account of a subsidiary and that are outstanding—that is, not held by a subsidiary bank, on the reporting date. (If held by a bank subsidiary, they should be reported as "loans" under § 210.9-03.7.)

10. *Other assets.* Disclose separately on the balance sheet or in a note thereto any of the following assets or any other asset the amount of which exceeds 30 percent of stockholders' equity. The remaining assets may be shown as one amount.

(1) Excess of cost over tangible and identifiable intangible assets acquired (net of amortization).

(2) Other intangible assets (net of amortization).

(3) Investments in and indebtedness of affiliates and other persons.

(4) Other real estates.

(a) Disclose in a note the basis at which other real estate is carried. Any reduction to fair market value from the carrying value of the related loan at the time of acquisition shall be accounted for as a loan loss. Any allowance for losses on other real estate which has been established subsequent to acquisition should be deducted from other real estate. For each period for which an income statement is required, disclosures should be made in a note as to the changes in the allowances, including balance at beginning and end of period, provision charged to income, and losses charged to the allowance.

11. *Total assets.*

Liabilities And Stockholders' Equity
Liabilities

12. *Deposits.* Disclose separately the amounts of noninterest bearing deposits and interest bearing deposits.

(a) The amount of noninterest bearing deposits and interest bearing deposits in foreign banking offices must be presented if the disclosure provided by § 210.9-05 are required.

13. *Short-term borrowing.* Disclose separately on the balance sheet or in a note, amounts payable for (1) Federal funds purchased and securities sold under agreements to repurchase; (2) commercial paper; and (3) other short-term borrowings.

(a) Disclose any unused lines of credit for short-term financing (§ 210.5-02.19(b)).

14. *Bank acceptances outstanding.* Disclose the aggregate of unmatured drafts and bills of exchange accepted by a bank subsidiary, or by some other bank as its agent, less the amount of such acceptances acquired by the bank subsidiary through discount or purchase.

15. *Other liabilities.* Disclose separately on the balance sheet or in a note any of the following liabilities or any other items which are individually in excess of 30 percent of stockholders' equity (except that amounts in excess of 5 percent of stockholders' equity should be disclosed with respect to item (4)). The remaining items may be shown as one amount.

(1) Income taxes payable.

(2) Deferred income taxes.

(3) Indebtedness to affiliates and other persons the investments in which are accounted for by the equity method.

(4) Indebtedness to directors, executive officers, and principal holders of equity securities of the registrant or any of its significant subsidiaries (the guidance in § 210.9-03.7(e) shall be used to identify related parties for purposes of this disclosure).

(5) Accounts payable and accrued expenses.

16. *Long-term debt.* Disclose in a note the information required by § 210.5-02.22.

17. *Commitments and contingent liabilities.*

Redeemable Preferred Stocks

18. *Preferred stocks subject to mandatory redemption requirements or whose redemption is outside the control of the issuer.* See § 210.5-02.27.

Non-redeemable Preferred Stocks

19. *Preferred stocks which are not redeemable or are redeemable solely at the option of the issuer.* See § 210.5-02.28.

Common Stocks

20. *Common stocks.* See § 210.5-02.29.

Other Stockholders' Equity

21. *Other stockholders' equity.* See § 210.5-02.30.

Noncontrolling Interests

22. *Noncontrolling interests in consolidated subsidiaries.* The disclosure requirements of § 210.5-02.31 shall be followed.

23. *Total liabilities and equity.*

[As last amended in Release No. 33-9026, effective April 23, 2009, 74 F.R. 18612.]

[¶ 35,984] Income Statements

Reg. § 210.9-04. The purpose of this rule is to indicate the various items which, if applicable, should appear on the face of the income statement or in the notes thereto.

1. *Interest and fees on loans.* Include commitment and origination fees, late charges and current amortization of premium and accretion of discount on loans which are related to or are an adjustment of the loan interest rate.

2. *Interest and dividends on investment securities.* Disclose separately (1) taxable interest income, (2) nontaxable interest income, and (3) dividends.

3. *Trading account interest.*

4. *Other interest income.*

5. *Total interest income (total of lines 1 through 4).*

6. *Interest on deposits.*

7. *Interest on short-term borrowings.*

8. *Interest on long-term debt.*

9. *Total interest expense (total of lines 6 through 8).*

10. *Net interest income (line 5 minus line 9).*

11. *Provision for loan losses.*

12. *Net interest income after provision for loan losses.*

13. *Other income.* Disclose separately any of the following amounts, or any other item of other income, which exceed one percent of the aggregate of total interest income and other income. The

remaining amounts may be shown as one amount, except for investment securities gains or losses which shall be shown separately regardless of size.

(a) Commissions and fees from fiduciary activities.

(b) Commissions, broker's fees and markups on securities underwriting and other securities activities.

(c) Insurance commissions, fees and premiums.

(d) Fees for other customer services.

(e) Profit or loss on transactions in securities in dealer trading account.

(f) Equity in earnings of unconsolidated subsidiaries and 50 percent or less owned persons.

(g) Gains or losses on disposition of equity in securities of subsidiaries or 50 percent or less owned persons.

(h) Investment securities gains or losses. The method followed in determining the cost of investments sold (e.g., "average cost," "first-in, first-out," or "identified certificate") and related income taxes shall be disclosed.

14. *Other expenses.* Disclose separately any of the following amounts, or any other item of other expense, which exceed one percent of the aggregate of total interest income and other income. The remaining amounts may be shown as one amount.

(a) Salaries and employee benefits.

(b) Net occupancy expense of premises.

(c) Goodwill amortization.

(d) Net cost of operation of other real estate (including provisions for real estate losses, rental income and gains and losses on sales of real estate).

15. *Income or loss before income tax expense.*

16. *Income tax expense.* The information required by § 210.4-08(h) should be disclosed.

17. *Income or loss before extraordinary items and cumulative effects of changes in accounting principles.*

18. *Extraordinary items, less applicable tax.*

19. *Cumulative effects of changes in accounting principles.*

20. *Net income or loss.*

21. *Earnings per share data.*

21. *Net income attributable to the noncontrolling interest.*

22. *Net income attributable to the controlling interest.*

23. *Earnings per share data.*

[As last amended in Release No. 33-9026, effective April 23, 2009, 74 F.R. 18612.]

[¶ 35,985] Foreign Activities

Reg. § 210.9-05. (a) *General requirement.* Separate disclosure concerning foreign activities shall be made for each period in which either (1) assets, or (2) revenue, or (3) income (loss) before income tax expense, or (4) net income (loss), each as associated with foreign activities, exceeded ten percent of the corresponding amount in the related financial statements.

(b) *Disclosures.* (1) Disclose total identifiable assets (net of valuation allowances) associated with foreign activities.

(2) For each period for which an income statement is filed, state the amount of revenue, income (loss) before taxes, and net income (loss) associated with foreign activities. Disclose significant estimates and assumptions (including those related to the cost of capital) used in allocating revenue and expenses to foreign activities; describe the nature and effects of any changes in such estimates and assumptions which have a significant impact on interperiod comparability.

(3) The information in paragraph (b)(1) and (2) of this section shall be presented separately for each significant geographic area and in the aggregate for all other geographic areas not deemed significant.

(c) *Definitions.* (1) "Foreign activities" include loans and other revenues producing assets and transactions in which the debtor or customer, whether an affiliated or unaffiliated person, is domiciled outside the United States.

(2) The term "revenue" includes the total of the amount reported at §§ 210.9-04.5 and 210.9-04.13.

(3) A "significant geographic area" is one in which assets or revenue or income before income tax or net income exceed 10 percent of the comparable amount as reported in the financial statements.

[As adopted in Release No. FR-11, March 7, 1983, 48 F.R. 11104.]

[¶ 35,986] Condensed Financial Information of Registrant

Reg. § 210.9-06. The information prescribed by § 210.12-04 shall be presented in a note to the financial statements when the restricted net assets (§ 210.4-08(e)(3)) of consolidated subsidiaries exceed 25 percent of consolidated net assets as of the end of the most recently completed fiscal year. The investment in and indebtedness of and to bank subsidiaries shall be stated separately in the condensed balance sheet from amounts for other subsidiaries; the amount of cash dividends paid to the registrant for each of the last three years by bank subsidiaries shall be stated separately in the condensed income statement from amounts for other subsidiaries. For purposes of the above test, restricted net assets of consolidated subsidiaries shall mean that amount of the registrant's proportionate share of net assets of consolidated subsidiaries (after intercompany eliminations) which as of the end of the most recent fiscal year may not be transferred to the parent company by subsidiaries in the form of loans, advances or cash dividends without the consent of a third party (i.e., lender, regulatory agency, foreign government, etc.). Where restrictions on the amount of funds which may be loaned or advanced differ from the amount restricted as to transfer in the form of cash dividends, the amount least restrictive to the subsidiary shall be used. Redeemable preferred stocks (§ 210.5-02.27) and noncontrolling interests shall be deducted in computing net assets for purposes of this test.

[As last amended in Release No. 33-9026, effective April 23, 2009, 74 F.R. 18612.]

[¶ 35,987] Reg. § 210.9-07. [Removed and reserved in Release No. FR-44, December 13, 1994, 59 F.R. 65632.]

Article 10—Interim Financial Statements

[¶ 35,991] Interim Financial Statements

Reg. § 210.10-01. (a) *Condensed statements.* Interim financial statements shall follow the general form and content of presentation prescribed by the other sections of this Regulation with the following exceptions:

(1) Interim financial statements required by this rule need only be provided as to the registrant and its subsidiaries consolidated and may be unaudited. Separate statements of other entities which may otherwise be required by this regulation may be omitted.

(2) Interim balance sheets shall include only major captions (i.e., numbered captions) prescribed by the applicable sections of this Regulation with the exception of inventories. Data as to raw materials, work in process and finished goods inventories shall be included either on the face of the balance sheet or in the notes to the financial statements, if applicable. Where any major balance sheet caption is less than 10% of total assets, and the amount in the caption has not increased or decreased by more than 25% since the end of the preceding fiscal year, the caption may be combined with others.

(3) Interim statements of income shall also include major captions prescribed by the applicable sections of this Regulation. When any major income statement caption is less than 15% of average net income for the most recent three fiscal years and the amount in the caption has not increased or decreased by more than 20% as compared to the corresponding interim period of the preceding fiscal year, the caption may be combined with others. In calculating average net income, loss years should be excluded. If losses were incurred in each of the most recent three years, the average loss shall be used for purposes of this test. Notwithstanding these tests, § 210.4-02 applies and de minimis amounts therefore need not be shown separately, except that registrants reporting under § 210.9 shall show investment securities gains or losses separately regardless of size.

(4) The statement of cash flows may be abbreviated starting with a single figure of net cash flows from operating activities and showing cash changes from investing and financing activities individually only when they exceed 10% of the average of net cash flows from operating activities for the most recent three years. Notwithstanding this test, § 210.4-02 applies and *de minimis* amounts therefore need not be shown separately.

(5) The interim financial information shall include disclosures either on the face of the financial statements or in accompanying footnotes sufficient so as to make the interim information presented not misleading. Registrants may presume that users of the interim financial information have read or have access to the audited financial statements for the preceding fiscal year and that the adequacy of additional disclosure needed for a fair presentation, except in regard to material contingencies may be determined in that context. Accordingly, footnote disclosure which would substantially duplicate the disclosure contained in the most recent annual report to security holders or latest audited financial statements, such as a statement of significant accounting policies and practices, details of accounts which have not changed significantly in amount or composition since the end of the most recently completed fiscal year, and detailed disclosures prescribed by Rule 4-08 of this Regulation, may be omitted. However, disclosure shall be provided where events subsequent to the end of the most recent fiscal year have occurred which have a material impact on the registrant. Disclosures should encompass for example, significant changes since the end of the most recently completed fiscal year in such items as: accounting principles and practices; estimates inherent in the preparation of financial statements; status of long-term contracts; capitalization including significant new borrowings or modification of existing financing arrangements; and the reporting entity resulting from business combinations or dispositions. Notwithstanding the above, where material contingencies exist, disclosure of such matters shall be provided even though a significant change since year end may not have occurred.

(6) Detailed schedules otherwise required by this Regulation may be omitted for purposes of preparing interim financial statements.

(7) In addition to the financial statements required by paragraphs (a)(2), (3) and (4) of this section, registrants in the development stage shall provide the cumulative financial statements (condensed to the same degree as allowed in this paragraph) and disclosures required by Statement of Financial Accounting Standards No. 7, "Accounting and Reporting by Development Stage Enterprises" to the date of the latest balance sheet presented.

(b) *Other instructions as to content.* The following additional instructions shall be applicable for purposes of preparing interim financial statements:

(1) Summarized income statement information shall be given separately as to each subsidiary not consolidated or 50 percent or less owned persons or as to each group of such subsidiaries or fifty percent or less owned persons for which separate individual or group statements would otherwise be required for annual periods. Such summarized information, however, need not be furnished for any such

unconsolidated subsidiary or person which would not be required pursuant to Rule 13a-13 or 15d-13 to file quarterly financial information with the Commission if it were a registrant.

(2) If appropriate, the income statement shall show earnings per share and dividends declared per share applicable to common stock. The basis of the earnings per share computation shall be stated together with the number of shares used in the computation. In addition, see Item 601(b)(11) of Regulation S-K (17 CFR 229.601(b)(11)).

(3) If, during the most recent interim period presented, the registrant or any of its consolidated subsidiaries entered into a combination between entities under common control, the interim financial statements for both the current year and the preceding year shall reflect the combined results of the combined businesses. Supplemental disclosure of the separate results of the combined entities for periods prior to the combination shall be given, with appropriate explanations.

(4) Where a material business combination has occurred during the current fiscal year, pro forma disclosure shall be made of the results of operations for the current year up to the date of the most recent interim balance sheet provided (and for the corresponding period in the preceding year) as though the companies had combined at the beginning of the period being reported on. This pro forma information shall, at a minimum, show revenue, income before extraordinary items and the cumulative effect of accounting changes, including such income on a per share basis, net income, net income attributable to the registrant, and net income per share.

(5) Where the registrant has disposed of any significant segment of its business (as defined in paragraph 13 of Accounting Principles Board Opinion No. 30) during any of the periods covered by the interim financial statements, the effect thereof on revenues and net income—total and per share—for all periods shall be disclosed.

(6) In addition to meeting the reporting requirements specified by existing standards for accounting changes, the registrant shall state the date of any material accounting change and the reasons for making it. In addition, for filings on Form 10-Q, a letter from the registrant's independent accountant shall be filed as an exhibit (in accordance with the provisions of Item 601 of Regulation S-K, 17 CFR 229.601) in the first Form 10-Q after the date of an accounting change indicating whether or not the change is to an alternative principle which, in the accountant's judgment, is preferable under the circumstances; except that no letter from the accountant need be filed when the change is made in response to a standard adopted by the Financial Accounting Standards Board that requires such change.

(7) Any material retroactive prior period adjustment made during any period covered by the interim financial statements shall be disclosed, together with the effect thereof upon net income—total and per share—of any prior period included and upon the balance of retained earnings. If results of operations for any period presented have been adjusted retroactively by such an item subsequent to the initial reporting of such period, similar disclosure of the effect of the change shall be made.

(8) Any unaudited interim financial statements furnished shall reflect all adjustments which are, in the opinion of management, necessary to a fair statement of the results for the interim periods presented. A statement to that effect shall be included. Such adjustments shall include, for example, appropriate estimated provisions for bonus and profit sharing arrangements normally determined or settled at year-end. If all such adjustments are of a normal recurring nature, a statement to that effect shall be made; otherwise, there shall be furnished information describing in appropriate detail the nature and amount of any adjustments other than normal recurring adjustments entering into the determination of the results shown.

(c) *Periods to be covered.* The periods for which interim financial statements are to be provided in registration statements are prescribed elsewhere in this Regulation (see §§ 210.3-01 and 3-02). For filings on Form 10-Q, financial statements shall be provided as set forth in this paragraph (c):

(1) An interim balance sheet as of the end of the most recent fiscal quarter and a balance sheet as of the end of the preceding fiscal year shall be provided. The balance sheet as of the end of the preceding fiscal year may be condensed to the same degree as the interim balance sheet provided. An interim balance sheet as of the end of the corresponding fiscal quarter of the preceding fiscal year need not be provided unless necessary for an understanding of the impact of seasonal fluctuations on the registrant's financial condition.

(2) Interim statements of income shall be provided for the most recent fiscal quarter, for the period between the end of the preceding fiscal year and the end of the most recent fiscal quarter, and for the corresponding periods of the preceding fiscal year. Such statements may also be presented for the cumulative twelve month period ended during the most recent fiscal quarter and for the corresponding preceding period.

(3) Interim statements of cash flows shall be provided for the period between the end of the preceding fiscal year and the end of the most recent fiscal quarter, and for the corresponding period of the preceding fiscal year. Such statements may also be presented for the cumulative twelve month period ended during the most recent fiscal quarter and for the corresponding preceding period.

(4) Registrants engaged in seasonal production and sale of a single-crop agricultural commodity may provide interim statements of income and cash flows for the twelve month period ended during the most recent fiscal quarter and for the corresponding preceding period in lieu of the year-to-date statements specified in (2) and (3) above.

(d) *Interim review by independent public accountant.* Prior to filing, interim financial statements included in quarterly reports on Form 10-Q (17 CFR 249.308(a)) must be reviewed by an independent public accountant using professional standards and procedures for conducting such reviews, as established by generally accepted auditing standards, as may be modified or supplemented by the Commission. If, in any filing, the company states that interim financial statements have been reviewed by an independent public accountant, a report of the accountant on the review must be filed with the interim financial statements.

(e) *Filing of other interim financial information in certain cases.* The Commission may, upon the informal written request of the registrant, and where consistent with the protection of investors, permit the omission of any of the interim financial information herein required or the filing in substitution thereof of appropriate information of comparable character. The Commission may also by informal written notice require the filing of other information in addition to, or in substitution for, the interim information herein required in any case where such information is necessary or appropriate for an adequate presentation of the financial condition of any person for which interim financial information is required, or whose financial information is otherwise necessary for the protection of investors.

[As last amended in Release No. 33-9026, effective April 23, 2009, 74 F.R. 18612.]

Article 11—Pro Forma Financial Information

[¶ 35,993] Presentation Requirements

Reg. § 210.11-01. (a) Pro forma financial information shall be furnished when any of the following conditions exists:

(1) (1) During the most recent fiscal year or subsequent interim period for which a balance sheet is required by § 210.3-01, a significant business combination has occurred (for purposes of these rules, this encompasses the acquisition of an interest in a business accounted for by the equity method);;

(2) (2) After the date of the most recent balance sheet filed pursuant to § 210.3-01, consummation of a significant business combination or a combination of entities under common control has occurred or is probable;

(3) Securities being registered by the registrant are to be offered to the security holders of a significant business to be acquired or the proceeds from the offered securities will be applied directly or indirectly to the purchase of a specific significant business;

(4) The disposition of a significant portion of a business either by sale, abandonment or distribution to shareholders by means of a spin-off, split-up or split-off has occurred or is probable and such disposition is not fully reflected in the financial statements of the registrant included in the filing;

(5) During the most recent fiscal year or subsequent interim period for which a balance sheet is required by § 210.3-01, the registrant has acquired one or more real estate operations or properties which in the aggregate are significant, or since the date of the most recent balance sheet filed pursuant to that section the registrant has acquired or proposes to acquire one or more operations or properties which in the aggregate are significant.

(6) Pro forma financial information required by § 229.914 is required to be provided in connection with a roll-up transaction as defined in § 229.901(c).

(7) The registrant previously was a part of another entity and such presentation is necessary to reflect operations and financial position of the registrant as an autonomous entity; or

(8) Consummation of other events or transactions has occurred or is probable for which disclosure of pro forma financial information would be material to investors.

(b) A business combination or disposition of a business shall be considered significant if:

(1) A comparison of the most recent annual financial statements of the business acquired or to be acquired and the registrant's most recent annual consolidated financial statements filed at or prior to the date of acquisition indicates that the business would be a significant subsidiary pursuant to the conditions specified in 210.1-02(w), substituting 20 percent for 10 percent each place it appears therein; or

(2) The business to be disposed of meets the conditions of a significant subsidiary in 210.1-02(w).

(c) The pro forma effects of a business combination need not be presented pursuant to this section if separate financial statements of the acquired business are not included in the filing.

(d) For purposes of this rule, the term business should be evaluated in light of the facts and circumstances involved and whether there is sufficient continuity of the acquired entity's operations prior to and after the transactions so that disclosure of prior financial information is material to an understanding of future operations. A presumption exists that a separate entity, a subsidiary, or a division is a business. However, a lesser component of an entity may also constitute a business. Among the facts and circumstances which should be considered in evaluating whether an acquisition of a lesser component of an entity constitutes a business are the following:

(1) Whether the nature of the revenue-producing activity of the component will remain generally the same as before the transaction; or

(2) Whether any of the following attributes remain with the component after the transaction:

    (i) Physical facilities,

    (ii) Employee base,

    (iii) Market distribution system,

    (iv) Sales force,

    (v) Customer base,

    (vi) Operating rights,

    (vii) Production techniques, or

(viii) Trade names.

(e) This rule does not apply to transactions between a parent company and its totally held subsidiary.

[As last amended in Release No. 33-9026, effective April 23, 2009, 74 F.R. 18612.]

[¶ 35,995] Preparation Requirements

Reg. § 210.11-02. (a) *Objective.* Pro forma financial information should provide investors with information about the continuing impact of a particular transaction by showing how it might have affected historical financial statements if the transaction had been consummated at an earlier time. Such statements should assist investors in analyzing the future prospects of the registrant because they illustrate the possible scope of the change in the registrant's historical financial position and results of operations caused by the transaction.

(b) *Form and content.* (1) Pro forma financial information shall consist of a pro forma condensed balance sheet, pro forma condensed statements of income, and accompanying explanatory notes. In certain circumstances (i.e., where a limited number of pro forma adjustments are required and those adjustments are easily understood), a narrative description of the pro forma effects of the transaction may be furnished in lieu of the statements described herein.

(2) The pro forma financial information shall be accompanied by an introductory paragraph which briefly sets forth a description of (i) the transaction, (ii) the entities involved, and (iii) the periods for which the pro forma information is presented. In addition, an explanation of what the pro forma presentation shows shall be set forth.

(3) The pro forma condensed financial information need only include major captions (*i.e.*, the numbered captions) prescribed by the applicable sections of this Regulation. Where any major balance sheet caption is less than 10 percent of total assets, the caption may be combined with others. When any major income statement caption is less than 15 percent of average net income attributable to the registrant for the most recent three fiscal years, the caption may be combined with others. In calculating average net income attributable to the registrant, loss years should be excluded unless losses were incurred in each of the most recent three years, in which case the average loss shall be used for purposes of this test. Notwithstanding these tests, *de minimis* amounts need not be shown separately.

(4) Pro forma statements shall ordinarily be in columnar form showing condensed historical statements, pro forma adjustment, and the pro forma results.

(5) The pro forma condensed income statement shall disclose income (loss) from continuing operations before nonrecurring charges or credits directly attributable to the transaction. Material nonrecurring charges or credits and related tax effects which result directly from the transaction and which will be included in the income of the registrant within the 12 months succeeding the transaction shall be disclosed separately. It should be clearly indicated that such charges or credits were not considered in the pro forma condensed income statement. If the transaction for which pro forma financial information is presented relates to the disposition of a business, the pro forma results should give effect to the disposition and be presented under an appropriate caption.

(6) Pro forma adjustments related to the pro forma condensed income statement shall be computed assuming the transaction was consummated at the beginning of the fiscal year presented and shall include adjustments which give effect to events that are (i) directly attributable to the transaction, (ii) expected to have a continuing impact on the registrant, and (iii) factually supportable. Pro forma adjustments related to the pro forma condensed balance sheet shall be computed assuming the transaction was consummated at the end of the most recent period for which a balance sheet is required by § 210.3-01 and shall include adjustments which give effect to events that are directly attributable to the transaction and factually supportable regardless of whether they have a continuing impact or are nonrecurring. All adjustments should be referenced to notes which clearly explain the assumptions involved.

(7) Historical primary and fully diluted per share data based on continuing operations (or net income if the registrant does not report either discontinued operations, extraordinary items, or the cumulative effects of accounting changes) for the registrant, and primary and fully diluted pro forma per share data based on continuing operations before nonrecurring charges or credits directly attributable to the transaction shall be presented on the face of the pro forma condensed income statement together with the number of shares used to compute such per share data. For transactions involving the issuance of securities, the number of shares used in the calculation of the pro forma per share data should be based on the weighted average number of shares outstanding during the period adjusted to give effect to shares subsequently issued or assumed to be issued had the particular transaction or event taken place at the beginning of the period presented. If a convertible security is being issued in the transaction, consideration should be given to the possible dilution of the pro forma per share data.

(8) If the transaction is structured in such a manner that significantly different results may occur, additional pro forma presentations shall be made which give effect to the range of possible results.

Instructions. 1. The historical statement of income used in the pro forma financial information shall not report operations of a segment that has been discontinued, extraordinary items, or the cumulative effects of accounting changes. If the historical statement of income includes such items, only the portion of the income statement through "income from continuing operations" (or the appropriate modification thereof) should be used in preparing pro forma results.

2. For a business combination, pro forma adjustments for the income statement shall include amortization, depreciation and other adjustments based on the allocated purchase price of net assets acquired. In some transactions, such as in financial institution acquisitions, the purchase adjustments may include significant discounts of the historical cost of the acquired assets to their fair value at the acquisition date. When such adjustments will result in a significant effect on earnings (losses) in periods immediately subsequent to the acquisition which will be progressively eliminated over a relatively short period, the effect of the purchase adjustments on reported results of operations for each of the next five years should be disclosed in a note.

3. For a disposition transaction, the pro forma financial information shall begin with the historical financial statements of the existing entity and show the deletion of the business to be divested along with the pro forma adjustments necessary to arrive at the remainder of the existing entity. For example, pro forma adjustments would include adjustments of interest expense arising from revised debt structures and expenses which will be or have been incurred on behalf of the business to be divested such as advertising costs, executive salaries and other costs.

4. For entities which were previously a component of another entity, pro forma adjustments should include adjustments similar in nature to those referred to in Instruction 3 above. Adjustments may also be necessary when charges for corporate overhead, interest, or income taxes have been allocated to the entity on a basis other than one deemed reasonable by management.

5. Adjustments to reflect the acquisition of real estate operations or properties for the pro forma income statement shall include a depreciation charge based on the new accounting basis for the assets, interest financing on any additional or refinanced debt, and other appropriate adjustments that can be factually supported. See also Instruction 4 above.

6. When consummation of more than one transaction has occurred or is probable during a fiscal year, the pro forma financial information may be presented on a combined basis; however, in some circumstances (e.g., depending upon the combination of probable and consummated transactions, and the nature of the filing) it may be more useful to present the pro forma financial information on a disaggregated basis even though some or all of the transactions would not meet the tests of significance individually. For combined presentations, a note should explain the various transactions and disclose the maximum variances in the pro forma financial information which would occur for any of the possible combinations. If the pro forma financial information is presented in a proxy or information statement for purposes of obtaining shareholder approval of one of the transactions, the effects of that transaction must be clearly set forth.

7. Tax effects, if any, of pro forma adjustments normally should be calculated at the statutory rate in effect during the periods for which pro forma condensed income statements are presented and should be reflected as a separate pro forma adjustment.

(c) *Periods to be presented.* (1) A pro forma condensed balance sheet as of the end of the most recent period for which a consolidated balance sheet of the registrant is required by § 210.3-01 shall be filed unless the transaction is already reflected in such balance sheet.

(2) (i) Pro forma condensed statements of income shall be filed for only the most recent fiscal year and for the period from the most recent fiscal year end to the most recent interim date for which a balance sheet is required. A pro forma condensed statement of income may be filed for the corresponding interim period of the preceding fiscal year. A pro forma condensed statement of income shall not be filed when the historical income statement reflects the transaction for the entire period.

(ii) For a business combination accounted for as a pooling of interests, the pro forma income statements (which are in effect a restatement of the historical income statements as if the combination had been consummated) shall be filed for all periods for which historical statements of the registrant are required.

(3) Pro forma condensed statements of income shall be presented using the registrant's fiscal year end. If the most recent fiscal year end of any other entity involved in the transaction differs from the registrant's most recent fiscal year end by more than 93 days, the other entity's income statement shall be brought up to within 93 days of the registrant's most recent fiscal year end, if practicable. This updating could be accomplished by adding subsequent interim period results to the most recent fiscal year-end information and deducting the comparable preceding year interim period results. Disclosure shall be made of the periods combined and of the sales or revenues and income for any periods which

were excluded from or included more than once in the condensed pro forma income statements (e.g., an interim period that is included both as part of the fiscal year and the subsequent interim period). For investment companies subject to § § 210.6-01 to 210.6-10, the periods covered by the pro forma statements must be the same.

(4) Whenever unusual events enter into the determination of the results shown for the most recently completed fiscal year, the effect of such unusual events should be disclosed and consideration should be given to presenting a pro forma condensed income statement for the most recent twelve-month period in addition to those required in paragraph (c)(2)(i) above if the most recent twelve-month period is more representative of normal operations.

[As last amended in Release No. 33-9026, effective April 23, 2009, 74 F.R. 18612.]

[¶ 35,997] Presentation of Financial Forecast

Reg. § 210.11-03. (a) A financial forecast may be filed in lieu of the pro forma condensed statements of income required by § 210.11-02(b)(1).

(1) The financial forecast shall cover a period of at least 12 months from the latest of (i) the most recent balance sheet included in the filing or (ii) the consummation date or estimated consummation date of the transaction.

(2) The forecasted statement of income shall be presented in the same degree of detail as the pro forma condensed statement of income required by § 210.11-02(b)(3).

(3) Assumptions particularly relevant to the transaction and effects thereof should be clearly set forth.

(4) Historical condensed financial information of the registrant and the business acquired or to be acquired, if any, shall be presented for at least a recent 12 month period in parallel columns with the financial forecast.

(b) Such financial forecast shall be presented in accordance with the guidelines established by the American Institute of Certified Public Accountants.

(c) Forecasted earnings per share data shall be substituted for pro forma per share data.

(d) This rule does not permit the filing of a financial forecast in lieu of pro forma information required by generally accepted accounting principles.

[As last amended in Release No. FR-2, June 24, 1982, 47 F.R. 29832.]

Article 12—Form and Content of Schedules

General

[¶ 36,001] Application of §§ 210.12-01 to 210.12-29

Reg. § 210.12-01. These sections prescribe the form and content of the schedules required by §§ 210.5-04, 210.6-10, 210.6A-05 and 210.7-05.

[As last amended in Release No. FR-44, December 13, 1994, 59 F.R. 65632.]

[¶ 36,011] Reg. 210.12-02. [Removed and reserved in Release No. FR-44, December 13, 1994, 59 F.R. 65632.]

[¶ 36,021] Reg. § 210.12-03. [Removed and reserved in Release No. FR-44, December 13, 1994, 59 F.R. 65632.]

[¶ 36,031] Condensed Financial Information of Registrant

Reg. § 210.12-04. (a) Provide condensed financial information as to financial position, changes in financial position and results of operations of the registrant as of the same dates and for the same periods for which audited consolidated financial statements are required. The financial information required need not be presented in greater detail than is required for condensed statements by § 210.10-01(a)(2), (3) and (4). Detailed footnote disclosure which would normally be included with complete financial statements may be omitted with the exception of disclosures regarding material contingencies, long-term obligations and guarantees. Descriptions of significant provisions of the registrant's long-term obligations, mandatory dividend or redemption requirements of redeemable stocks, and guarantees of the registrant shall be provided along with a five-year schedule of maturities of debt. If the material contingencies, long-term obligations, redeemable stock requirements and guarantees of the registrant have been separately disclosed in the consolidated statements, they need not be repeated in this schedule.

(b) Disclose separately the amounts of cash dividends paid to the registrant for each of the last three fiscal years by consolidated subsidiaries, unconsolidated subsidiaries and 50 percent or less owned persons accounted for by the equity method, respectively.

[As last amended in Release No. FR-40A, effective November 2, 1992, 57 F.R. 45287.]

[¶ 36,041] Reg. § 210.12-05. [Removed and reserved in Release No. FR-44, December 13, 1994, 59 F.R. 65632.]

[¶ 36,051] Reg. § 210.12-06. [Removed and reserved in Release No. FR-44, December 13, 1994, 59 F.R. 65632.]

[¶ 36,061] Reg. § 210.12-07. [Removed and reserved in Release No. FR-44, December 13, 1994, 59 F.R. 65632.]

[¶ 36,071] Reg. § 210.12-08. [Removed and reserved in Release No. FR-44, December 13, 1994, 59 F.R. 65632.]

[¶ 36,081] Reg. § 210.12-09. **Valuation and Qualifying Accounts**

Column A—Description[1]	Column B—Balance at beginning of period	Column C—Additions		Column D—Deductions—describe	Column E—Balance at end of period
		(1)—Charged to costs and expenses	(2)—Charged to other accounts—describe		

[1] List, by major classes, all valuation and qualifying accounts and reserves not included in specific schedules. Identify each class of valuation and qualifying accounts and reserves by descriptive title. Group (a) those valuation and qualifying accounts which are deducted in the balance sheet from the assets to which they apply and (b) those reserves which support the balance sheet caption, Reserves. Valuation and qualifying accounts and reserves as to which the additions, deductions, and balances were not individually significant may be grouped in one total and in such case the information called for under columns C and D need not be given.

[As last amended in Release No. AS-280, September 2, 1980, 45 F.R. 63660.]

[¶ 36,091] Reg. § 210.12-10. [Removed and reserved in Release No. FR-44, December 13, 1994, 59 F.R. 65632.]

[¶ 36,101] Reg. § 210.12-11. [Removed and reserved in Release No. FR-44, December 13, 1994, 59 F.R. 65632.]

FOR MANAGEMENT INVESTMENT COMPANIES

[¶ 36,111] Reg. § 210.12-12. Investments in Securities of Unaffiliated Issuers

Column A	Column B	Column C
Name of issuer and title of issue[1, 2]	Balance held at close of period. Number of shares—principal amount of bonds and notes[5]	Value of each item at close of period[3,4,6,7,8]

[1] Each issue shall be listed separately: *Provided,* however, that an amount not exceeding five percent of the total of Column C may be listed in one amount as "Miscellaneous securities," provided the securities so listed are not restricted, have been held for not more than one year prior to the date of the related balance sheet, and have not previously been reported by name to the shareholders of the person for which the schedule is filed or to any exchange, or set forth in any registration statement, application, or annual report or otherwise made available to the public. If any securities are listed as "Miscellaneous securities," briefly explain in a footnote what the term represents.

[2] Categorize the schedule by (i) the type of investment (such as common stocks, preferred stocks, convertible securities, fixed income securities, government securities, options purchased, warrants, loan participations and assignments, commercial paper, bankers' acceptances, certificates of deposit, short-term securities, repurchase agreements, other investment companies, and so forth); and (ii) the related industry, country, or geographic region of the investment. Short-term debt instruments (*i.e.*, debt instruments whose maturities or expiration dates at the time of acquisition are one year or less) of the same issuer may be aggregated, in which case the range of interest rates and maturity dates shall be indicated. For issuers of periodic payment plan certificates and unit investment trusts, list separately: (i) Trust shares in trusts created or serviced by the depositor or sponsor of this trust; (ii) trust shares in other trusts; and (iii) securities of other investment companies. Restricted securities shall not be combined with unrestricted securities of the same issuer. Repurchase agreements shall be stated separately showing for each the name of the party or parties to the agreement, the date of the agreement, the total amount to be received upon repurchase, the repurchase date and description of securities subject to the repurchase agreements.

[3] The subtotals for each category of investments, subdivided by business grouping or instrument type, shall be shown together with their percentage value compared to net assets (§§ 210.6-04.19 or 210.6-05.4).

[4] Column C shall be totaled. The total of column C shall agree with the correlative amounts shown on the related balance sheet.

[5] Indicate by an appropriate symbol each issue of securities which is non-income producing. Evidences of indebtedness and preferred shares may be deemed to be income producing if, on the respective last interest payment date or date for the declaration of dividends prior to the date of the related balance sheet, there was only a partial payment of interest or a declaration of only a partial amount of the dividends payable; in such case, however, each such issue shall be indicated by an appropriate symbol referring to a note to the effect that, on the last interest or dividend date, only partial interest was paid or partial dividends declared. If, on such respective last interest or dividend date, no interest was paid or no cash or in kind dividends declared, the issue shall not be deemed to be income producing. Common shares shall not be deemed to be income producing unless, during the last year preceding the date of the related balance sheet, there was at least one dividend paid upon such common shares.

[6] Indicate by an appropriate symbol each issue of restricted securities. State the following in a footnote: (a) As to each such issue: (1) Acquisition date, (2) carrying value per unit of investment at date of related balance sheet, e.g., a percentage of current market value of unrestricted securities of the same issuer, etc., and (3) the cost of such securities; (b) as to each issue acquired during the year preceding the date of the related balance sheet, the carrying value per unit of investment of unrestricted securities of the same issuer at: (1) The day the purchase price was agreed to; and (2) the day on which an enforceable right to acquire such securities was obtained; and (c) the aggregate value of all restricted securities and the percentage which the aggregate value bears to net assets.

[7] Indicate by an appropriate symbol each issue of securities held in connection with open put or call option contracts or loans for short sales.

[8] State in a footnote the following amounts based on cost for Federal income tax purposes: (a) Aggregate gross unrealized appreciation for all securities in which there is an excess of value over tax cost, (b) the aggregate gross unrealized depreciation for all securities in which there is an excess of tax cost over value, (c) the net unrealized appreciation or depreciation, and (d) the aggregate cost of securities for Federal income tax purposes.

[As last amended in Release No. 33-8393, effective May 10, 2004, (the amendments in this release have a complex transition period and a variety of compliance dates extending through July 8, 2005; Subscribers should consult the text of the release at release section II.D. "Compliance Date" to determine how and when to comply with amendments) 69 F.R. 11244.]

[¶ 36,112] Reg. § 210.12-12A. Investments—Securities Sold Short

[For management investment companies only]

Column A	Column B	Column C
Name of issuer and title of issue[1]	Balance of short position at close of period. (Number of shares)	Value of each open short position[2]

[1] Each issue shall be listed separately.
[2] Column C shall be totaled. The total of column C shall agree with the correlative amounts shown on the related balance sheet.

[As adopted in Release No. FR-8, December 6, 1982, 47 F.R. 56835.]

[¶ 36,113] Reg. § 210.12-12B. Open Option Contracts Written

Column A	Column B	Column C	Column D	Column E
Name of Issuer[1,2]	Number of contracts[3]	Exercise price	Expiration date	Value[4]

[For management investment companies only]

[1] Information as to put options shall be shown separately from information as to call options.
[2] Options of an issuer where exercise prices or expiration dates differ shall be listed separately.
[3] If the number of shares subject to option is substituted for number of contracts, the column name shall reflect that change.
[4] Column E shall be totalled and shall agree with the correlative amount shown on the related balance sheet.

[As adopted in Release No. FR-8, December 6, 1982, 47 F.R. 56835.]

[¶ 36,119] Reg. § 210.12-12C. Summary Schedule of Investments in Securities of Unaffiliated Issuers

Column A	Column B	Column C	Column D
Name of issuer and title of issue[1,3,4,5,6]	Balance held at close of period. Number of shares—principal amount of bonds and notes[8]	Value of each item at close of period[2,7,9,10,11]	Percentage value compared to net assets

1. Categorize the schedule by (a) the type of investment (such as common stocks, preferred stocks, convertible securities, fixed income securities, government securities, options purchased, warrants, loan participations and assignments, commercial paper, bankers' acceptances, certificates of deposit, short-term securities, repurchase agreements, other investment companies, and so forth); and (b) the related industry, country, or geographic region of the investment.

2. The subtotals for each category of investments, subdivided by industry, country, or geographic region, shall be shown together with their percentage value compared to net assets.

3. Except as provided in note 5, list separately the 50 largest issues and any other issue the value of which exceeded one percent of net asset value of the registrant as of the close of the period. For purposes of the list (including, in the case of short-term debt instruments, the first sentence of note 4), aggregate and treat as a single issue, respectively, (a) short-term debt instruments (*i.e.*, debt instruments whose maturities or expiration dates at the time of acquisition are one year or less) of the same issuer (indicating the range of interest rates and maturity dates); and (b) fully collateralized repurchase agreements (indicate in a footnote the range of dates of the repurchase agreements, the total purchase price of the securities, the total amount to be received upon repurchase, the range of repurchase dates, and description of securities subject to the repurchase agreements). Restricted and unrestricted securities of the same issue should be aggregated for purposes of determining whether the issue is among the 50 largest issues, but should not be combined in the schedule. For purposes of determining whether the value of an issue exceeds one percent of net asset value, aggregate and treat as a single issue all securities of any one issuer, except that all fully collateralized repurchase agreements shall be aggregated and treated as a single issue. The U.S. Treasury and each agency, instrumental-

ity, or corporation, including each government-sponsored entity, that issues U.S. government securities is a separate issuer.

4. If multiple securities of an issuer aggregate to greater than one percent of net asset value, list each issue of the issuer separately (including separate listing of restricted and unrestricted securities of the same issue) except that the following may be aggregated and listed as a single issue: (a) fixed-income securities of the same issuer which are not among the 50 largest issues and whose value does not exceed one percent of net asset value of the registrant as of the close of the period (indicating the range of interest rates and maturity dates); and (b) U.S. government securities of a single agency, instrumentality, or corporation, which are not among the 50 largest issues and whose value does not exceed one percent of net asset value of the registrant as of the close of the period (indicating the range of interest rates and maturity dates). For each category identified pursuant to note 1, group all issues that are neither separately listed nor included in a group of securities that is listed in the aggregate as a single issue in a sub-category labeled "Other securities," and provide the information for Columns C and D.

5. Any securities that would be required to be listed separately or included in a group of securities that is listed in the aggregate as a single issue may be listed in one amount as "Miscellaneous securities," provided the securities so listed are eligible to be, and are, categorized as "Miscellaneous securities" in the registrant's Schedule of Investments in Securities of Unaffiliated Issuers required under § 210.12-12. However, if any security that is included in "Miscellaneous securities" would otherwise be required to be included in a group of securities that is listed in the aggregate as a single issue, the remaining securities of that group must nonetheless be listed as required by notes 3 and 4 even if the remaining securities alone would not otherwise be required to be listed in this manner (*e.g.*, because the combined value of the security listed in "Miscellaneous securities" and the remaining securities of the same issuer exceeds one percent of net asset value, but the value of the remaining securities alone does not exceed one percent of net asset value).

6. If any securities are listed as "Miscellaneous securities" pursuant to note 5 or "Other securities" pursuant to note 4, briefly explain in a footnote what those terms represent.

7. Total Column C. The total of column C should equal the total shown on the related balance sheet for investments in securities of unaffiliated issuers.

8. Indicate by an appropriate symbol each issue of securities which is non-income producing. Evidences of indebtedness and preferred shares may be deemed to be income producing if, on the respective last interest payment date or date for the declaration of dividends prior to the date of the related balance sheet, there was only a partial payment of interest or a declaration of only a partial amount of the dividends payable; in such case, however, each such issue shall be indicated by an appropriate symbol referring to a note to the effect that, on the last interest or dividend date, only partial interest was paid or partial dividends declared. If, on such respective last interest or dividend date, no interest was paid or no cash or in kind dividends declared, the issue shall not be deemed to be income producing. Common shares shall not be deemed to be income producing unless, during the last year preceding the date of the related balance sheet, there was at least one dividend paid upon such common shares.

9. Indicate by an appropriate symbol each issue of restricted securities. State the following in a footnote: (a) as to each such issue: (1) acquisition date, (2) carrying value per unit of investment at date of related balance sheet, *e.g.*, a percentage of current market value of unrestricted securities of the same issuer, etc., and (3) the cost of such securities; (b) as to each issue acquired during the year preceding the date of the related balance sheet, the carrying value per unit of investment of unrestricted securities of the same issuer at: (1) the day the purchase price was agreed to; and (2) the day on which an enforceable right to acquire such securities was obtained; and (c) the aggregate value of all restricted securities and the percentage which the aggregate value bears to net assets.

10. Indicate by an appropriate symbol each issue of securities held in connection with open put or call option contracts or loans for short sales.

11. State in a footnote the following amounts based on cost for Federal income tax purposes: (a) Aggregate gross unrealized appreciation for all securities in which there is an excess of value over tax cost, (b) the aggregate gross unrealized depreciation for all securities in which there is an excess of tax cost over value, (c) the net unrealized appreciation or depreciation, and (d) the aggregate cost of securities for Federal income tax purposes.

[As added by Release No. 33-8393, effective May 10, 2004, (the amendments in this release have a complex transition period and a variety of compliance dates extending through July 8, 2005; Subscribers should consult the text of the release at release section II.D. "Compliance Date" to determine how and when to comply with amendments) 69 F.R. 11244.]

[¶ 36,121] Reg. § 210.12-13. Investments Other than Securities

[For management investment companies only]

Column A	Column B	Column C
Description[1]	Balance held at close of period—quanity[235]	Value of each item at close of period[467]

[1] List each major category of investments by descriptive title.

[2] If practicable, indicate the quantity or measure in appropriate units.

[3] Indicate by an appropriate symbol each investment which is non-income producing.

[4] Indicate by an appropriate symbol each investment not readily marketable. The term "investment not readily marketable" shall include investments for which there is no independent publicly quoted market and investments which cannot be sold because of restrictions or conditions applicable to the investment or the company.

[5] Indicate by an appropriate symbol each investment subject to option. State in a footnote: (a) The quantity subject to option, (b) nature of option contract, (c) option price, and (d) dates within which options may be exercised.

[6] Column C shall be totalled and shall agree with the correlative amount shown on the related balance sheet.

[7] State in a footnote the following amounts based on cost for Federal income tax purposes: (a) Aggregate gross unrealized appreciation for all investments in which there is an excess of value over tax cost, (b) the aggregate gross unrealized depreciation for all investments in which there is an excess of tax cost over value, (c) the net unrealized appreciation or depreciation, and (d) the aggregate cost of investments for Federal income tax purposes.

[As last amended in Release No. FR-8, December 6, 1982, 47 F.R. 56835.]

[¶ 36,131] Reg. § 210.12-14. Investments in and Advances to Affiliates

[For management investment companies only]

Column A	Column B	Column C	Column D	Column E
Name of issuer and title of issue or nature of indebtedness[1]	Number of shares—principal amount of bonds, notes and other indebtedness held at close of period	Amount of equity in net profit and loss for the period[26]	Amount of dividends or interest[25]	Value of each item at close of period[2345]
			(1) Credited to income	
			(2) Other	

[1] (a) List each issue separately and group (1) Investments in majority-owned subsidiaries, segregating subsidiaries consolidated; (2) other controlled companies; and (3) other affiliates.

(b) If during the period there has been any increase or decrease in the amount of investment in and advance to any affiliate, state in a footnote (or if there have been changes to numerous affiliates, in a supplementary schedule) (1) name of each issuer and title of issue or nature of indebtedness; (2) balance at beginning of period; (3) gross additions; (4) gross reductions; (5) balance at close of period as shown in Column E. Include in the footnote or schedule comparable information as to affiliates in which there was an investment at any time during the period even though there was no investment at the close of the period of report.

[2] Give totals for each group. If operations of any controlled companies are different in character from those of the company, group such affiliates (1) within divisions and (2) by type of activities.

[3] Columns C, D and E shall be totaled. The totals of Column E shall agree with the correlative amount shown on the related balance sheet.

[4] (a) Indicate by an appropriate symbol each issue of restricted securities. The information required by instruction 5 of § 210.12-12 shall be given in a footnote.

(b) Indicate by an appropriate symbol each issue of securities subject to option. The information required by instruction 5 of § 210.12-13 shall be given in a footnote.

[5] (a) Include in Column D (1) as to each issue held at the close of the period, the dividends or interest included in caption 1 of the statement of operations. In addition, show as the final item in Column D (1) the aggregate of dividends and interest included in the statement of operations in respect of investments in affiliates not held at the close of the period. The total of this column shall agree with the correlative amount shown on the related statement of operations.

(b) Include in Column D (2) all other dividends and interest. Explain in an appropriate footnote the treatment accorded each item.

(c) Indicate by an appropriate symbol all non-cash dividends and explain the circumstances in a footnote.

(d) Indicate by an appropriate symbol each issue of securities which is non-income producing.

[6] The information required by Column C shall be furnished only as to controlled companies.

[As last amended in Release No. FR-8, December 6, 1982, 47 FR. 56835.]

[¶ 36,141] Reg. § 210.12-15. Summary of Investments—Other than Investments in Related Parties

[For insurance companies]

Column A	Column B	Column C	Column D
			Amount at which shown in the balance sheet[2]
Type of investment	Cost[1]	Value	
Fixed maturities:			
Bonds:			
United States Government and government agencies and authorities			
States, municipalities and political subdivisions			
Foreign governments			
Public utilities			
Convertibles and bonds with warrants attached[3]			
All other corporate bonds			
Certificates of deposit			
Redeemable preferred stock	_____	_____	_____
Total fixed maturities	_____	_____	_____
Equity securities:			
Common stocks			
Public utilities			
Banks, trust and insurance companies			
Industrial, miscellaneous and all other			
Nonredeemable preferred stocks	_____	_____	_____
Total equity securities	_____	_____	_____
Mortgage loans on real estate		xxxxxxx	
Real estate[4]		xxxxxxx	
Policy loans		xxxxxxx	
Other long-term investments		xxxxxxx	
Short-term investments	_____	xxxxxxx	_____
Total investments	_____	xxxxxxx	_____

[1] Original cost of equity securities and, as to fixed maturities, original cost reduced by repayments and adjusted for amortization of premiums or accrual of discounts.

[2] If the amount at which shown in the balance sheet is different from the amount shown in either column B or C, state the reason for such difference. The total of this column should agree with the balance sheet.

[3] All convertibles and bonds with warrants shall be included in this caption, regardless of issuer.

[4] State separately any real estate acquired in satisfaction of debt.

[As last amended in Release No. AS-301, 46 F. R. 54332.]

[¶ 36,151] Reg. § 210.12-16. Supplementary Insurance Information

Column A Segments [1]	Column B Deferred policy acquisition cost (caption 7)	Column C Future policy benefits, losses, claims and loss expenses (caption 13-a-1)	Column D Unearned premiums (caption 13-a-2)	Column E Other policy claims and benefits payable (caption 13-a-3)	Column F Premium revenue (caption 1)	Column G Net investment income (caption 2) [3]	Column H Benefits, claims, losses and settlement expenses (caption 4)	Column I Amortization of deferred policy acquisition costs [4]	Column J Other operating expenses [3,4]	Column K Premiums written [2]
Total [5]										

[1] Segments shown should be the same as those presented in the footnote disclosures called for by Statement of Financial Accounting Standards No. 14.

[2] Does not apply to life insurance or title insurance. This amount should include premiums from reinsurance assumed, and be net premiums on reinsurance ceded.

[3] State the basis for allocation of net investment income and, where applicable, other operating expenses.

[4] The total of columns I and J should agree with the amount shown for income statement caption 6.

[5] Totals should agree with the indicated balance sheet and income statement caption amounts, where a caption number is shown.

[As last amended in Release No. AS-301, 46 F. R. 54332.]

[¶ 36,161] Reg. § 210.12-17. Reinsurance

[For insurance companies]

Column A	Column B	Column C	Column D	Column E	Column F
	Gross amount	Ceded to other companies[1]	Assumed from other companies	Net amount[2]	Percentage of amount assumed to net[3]
Life insurance in force					
Premiums					
Life insurance					
Accident and health insurance					
Property and liability insurance					
Title insurance					
Total premiums					

[1] Indicate in a note any amounts of reinsurance or coinsurance income netted against premiums ceded.

[2] This Column represents the total of column B less column C plus column D. The total premiums in this column should represent the amount of premium revenue on the income statement.

[3] Calculated as the amount in column D divided by amount in column E.

[As last amended in Release No. AS-301, 46 F. R. 54332.]

[¶ 36,171] Reg. §210.12-18. Supplemental Information

Affiliation with Registrant Column A	Deferred Policy Acquisition Costs Column B	Reserves for Unpaid Claims and Claim Adjustment Expenses Column C	Discount, if any, deducted in Column C [4] Column D	Unearned Premiums Column E	Earned Premiums Column F	Net Investment Income Column G	Claims and Claim Adjustment Expenses Incurred Related to (1) Current Year Column H	(2) Prior Years Column H	Amortization of Deferred Policy Acquisition Costs Column I	Paid Claims and Claim Adjustment Expenses Column J	Premiums Written Column K
(a) Consolidated property casualty entities [3]											
(b) Unconsolidated property casualty subsidiaries [2][3]											
(c) Proportionate share of registrant and its subsidiaries' 50%-or-less-owned property-casualty equity investees [2][3]											

[1] Information included in audited financial statements, including other schedules, need not be repeated in this schedule. Columns B, C, D and E are as of the balance sheet dates, columns F, G, H, I, J and K are for the same periods for which income statements are presented in the registrant's audited consolidated financial statements.

[2] Present combined or consolidated amounts, as appropriate for each category, after intercompany eliminations.

[3] Information is not required here for 50%-or-less-owned equity investees that file similar information with the Commission as registrants in their own right, if that fact and the name of the affiliated registrant is stated. If ending reserves in any category (a), (b), or (c) above is less than 5% of the total reserves otherwise required to be reported in this schedule, that category may be omitted and that fact so noted. If the amount of the reserves attributable to 50%-or-less-owned equity investors that file this information as registrants in their own right exceeds 95% of the total category (c) reserves, information for the other 50%-or-less-owned equity investees need not be provided.

[4] Disclose in a footnote to this schedule the rate, or range of rates, estimated if necessary, at which the discount was computed for each category.

[Adopted in Release No. FR-20, November 27, 1984, 49 F.R. 47594.]

FOR FACE-AMOUNT CERTIFICATE INVESTMENT COMPANIES

[¶ 36,201] Reg. § 210.12-21. Investments in Securities of Unaffiliated Issuers

Column A	Column B	Column C	Column D
Name of issuer and title of issue[1]	Balance held at close of period. Number of shares—principal amount of bonds and notes[2]	Cost of each item[3,4]	Value of each item at close of period[3,5]

[1] (a) The required information is to be given as to all securities held as of the close of the period of report. Each issue shall be listed separately.

(b) Indicate by an appropriate symbol those securities which are non-income-producing securities. Evidences of indebtedness and preferred shares may be deemed to be income-producing if, on the respective last interest payment date or dates for the declaration of dividends prior to the date of the related balance sheet, there was only a partial payment of interest or a declaration of only a partial amount of the dividends payable; in such case, however, each such issue shall be indicated by an appropriate symbol referring to a note to the effect that, on the last interest or dividend date, only partial interest was paid or partial dividends declared. If, on such respective last interest or dividend date, no interest was paid or no dividends declared, the issue shall not be deemed to be income-producing. Common shares shall not be deemed to be income-producing unless, during the last year preceding the date of the related balance sheet, there was at least one dividend paid upon such common shares. List separately (1) bonds; (2) preferred shares; (3) common shares. Within each of these subdivisions classify according to type of business, insofar as practicable: e.g., investment companies, railroads, utilities, banks, insurance companies, or industrials. Give totals for each group, subdivision, and class.

[2] Indicate any securities subject to option at the end of the most recent period and state in a note the amount subject to option, the option prices, and the dates within which such options may be exercised.

[3] Columns C and D shall be totaled. The totals of columns C and D should agree with the correlative amounts required to be shown by the related balance sheet captions. State in a footnote to column C the aggregate cost for Federal income tax purposes.

[4] If any investments have been written down or reserved against by such companies pursuant to § 210.6-21(f), indicate each such item by means of an appropriate symbol and explain in a footnote.

[5] Where value is determined on any other basis than closing prices reported on any national securities exchange, explain such other basis in a footnote.

[As last amended in Release No. AS-280, September 2, 1980, 45 F.R. 63660.]

[¶ 36,211] Reg. § 210.12-22. Investments in and Advances to Affiliates and Income Thereon

Column A	Column B	Column C	Column D	Column E		Column F
				Amount of dividends or interest[4,6]		
Name of issuer and title of issue or amount of indebtedness[1]	Balance held at close of period. Number of shares—principal amount of bonds, notes and other indebtedness[2]	Cost of each item[3,4]	Amount at which carried at close of period[4,5]	(1) Credited to income	(2) Other	Amount of equity in net profit and loss for the period[7]

[1] (a) The required information is to be given as to all investments in affiliates as of the close of the period. See captions 10, 13 and 20 of § 210.6-22. List each issue and group separately (1) investments in majority-owned subsidiaries, segregating subsidiaries consolidated; (2) other controlled companies; and (3) other affiliates. Give totals for each group. If operations of any controlled companies are different in character from those of the registrant, group such affiliates within divisions (1) and (2) by type of activities.

(b) *Changes during the period.* If during the period there has been any increase or decrease in the amount of investment in any affiliate, state in a footnote (or if there have been changes as to numerous affiliates, in a supplementary schedule) (1) name of each issuer and title of issue; (2) balance at beginning of period; (3) gross purchases and additions; (4) gross sales and reductions; (5) balance at close of period as shown in column C. Include in such footnote or schedule comparable information as to affiliates in which there was an investment at any time during the period even though there was no investment in such affiliate as of the close of such period.

[2] Indicate any securities subject to option at the end of the most recent period and state in a footnote the amount subject to option, the option prices, and the dates within which such options may be exercised.

[3] If the cost in column C represents other than cash expenditure, explain.

[4] (a) Columns C, D and E shall be totaled. The totals of columns C and D should agree with correlative amounts required to be shown by the related balance sheet captions. State in a footnote the aggregate cost for Federal income tax purposes.

(b) If any investments have been written down or reserved against by such companies pursuant to § 210.6-21(f), indicate each such item by means of an appropriate symbol and explain in a footnote.

[5] State the basis of determining the amounts shown in column D.

[6] Shown in column E (1) as to each issue held at close of period, the dividends or interest included in caption 1 of the profit and loss or income statement. In addition, show as the final item in column E (1) the aggregate dividends and interest included in the profit and loss or income statement in respect of investments in affiliates not held at the close of the period. The total of this column should agree with the amounts shown under such caption. Include in column E (2) all other dividends and interest. Explain briefly in an appropriate footnote the treatment accorded each item. Identify by an appropriate symbol all non-cash dividends and explain the circumstances in a footnote. See §§ 210.6-22(b) and 210.6-23(a).

[7] The information required by column F need be furnished only as to controlled companies. The equity in the net profit and loss of each person required to be listed separately shall be computed on an individual basis. In addition, there may be submitted the information required as computed on the basis of the statements of each such person and its subsidiaries consolidated.

[As last amended in Release No. AS-280, September 2, 1980, 45 F.R. 63660.]

[¶ 36,221] Reg. § 210.12-23. Mortgage Loans on Real Estate and Interest Earned on Mortgages[1]

			Part 1—Mortgage loans on real estate at close of period			Part 2—Interest earned on mortgages	
Column A—List by classification indicated below[237]	Column B—Prior liens [2]	Column C— Carrying amount of mortgage[891011]	Column D—Amount of principal unpaid at close of period		Column E—Amount of mortgage being foreclosed	Column F— Interest due and accrued at end of period[6]	Column G— Interest income earned applicable to period[5]
			(1)— Total	(2)— Subject to delinquent interest[4]			
Liens on:							
Farms (total)							
Residential (total)							
Apartments and business (total)							
Unimproved (total)							
Total [1][2]							

[1] All money columns shall be totaled.

[2] If mortgages represent other than first liens, list separately in a schedule in a like manner, indicating briefly the nature of the lien. Information need not be furnished as to such liens which are fully insured or wholly guaranteed by an agency of the United States Government.

[3] In a separate schedule classify by states in which the mortgaged property is located the total amounts in support of columns B, C, D and E.

[4] (a) Interest in arrears for less than 3 months may be disregarded in computing the total amount of principal subject to delinquent interest.

(b) Of the total principal amount, state the amount acquired from controlled and other affiliates.

[5] In order to reconcile the total of column G with the amount shown in the profit and loss or income statement, interest income earned applicable to period from mortgages sold or canceled during period should be added to the total of this column.

[6] If the information required by columns F and G is not reasonably available because the obtaining thereof would involve unreasonable effort or expense, such information may be omitted if the registrant shall include a statement showing that unreasonable effort or expense would be involved. In such an event, state in column G for each of the above classes of mortgage loans the average gross rate of interest on mortgage loans held at the end of the fiscal period.

[7] Each mortgage loan included in column C in an amount in excess of $500,000 shall be listed separately. Loans from $100,000 to $500,000 shall be grouped by $50,000 groups, indicating the number of loans in each group.

[8] In a footnote to this schedule, furnish a reconciliation, in the following form, of the carrying amount of mortgage loans at the beginning of the period with the total amount shown in column C:

Balance at beginning of period. . . . . $ . . . .

Additions during period:

New mortgage loans. . . . . $ . . . .

Other (describe). . . . .

$ . . . . Deductions during period:

Collections of principal. . . . . $ . . . .

Foreclosures. . . . .

Cost of mortgages sold. . . . .

Amortization of premium. . . . .

Other (describe). . . . .

Balance at close of period. . . . . $ . . . .

If additions represent other than cash expenditures, explain. If any of the changes during the period result from transactions, directly or indirectly with affiliates, explain the bases of such transactions, and amounts involved. State the aggregate amount of mortgages (a) renewed and (b) extended. If the carrying amount of the new mortgages is in excess of the unpaid amount (not including interest) of prior mortgages, explain.

---

[9] If any item of mortgage loans on real estate investments has been written down or reserved against pursuant to §210.6-21 describe the item and explain the basis for the write-down or reserve.

[10] State in a footnote to column C the aggregate cost for Federal income tax purposes.

[11] If the total amount shown in column C includes intercompany profits, state the bases of the transactions resulting in such profits and, if practicable, state the amounts thereof.

[12] Summarize the aggregate amounts for each column applicable to —captions 6(b), 6(c) and 12 of §210.6-22.

[As last amended in Release No. September 2, 1980, 45 F.R. 63660.]

[¶ 36,231] Reg. § 210.12-24. Real Estate Owned and Rental Income[1]

| | Part 1—Real Estate owned at end period | | | | | | Part 2—Rental income | | |
Column A	Column B	Column C	Column D	Column E	Column F	Column G	Column H	Column I	Column J
List classification of property as indicated below[23]	Amount of incumbrances	Initial cost to company	Cost of improvements, etc.	Amount at which carried at close of period[4567]	Reserve for depreciation	Rents due and accrued at end of period	Total rental income applicable to period	Expended for interest, taxes, repairs and expenses	Net income applicable to period
Farms	. . . . .	. . . .	. . . .	. . . .	. . . .	. . . . . .	. . . . .	. . . . .	. . . . .
Residential	. . . . .	. . . .	. . . .	. . . .	. . . .	. . . . . .	. . . . .	. . . . .	. . . . .
Apartments and business	. . . . .	. . . .	. . . .	. . . .	. . . .	. . . . . .	. . . . .	. . . . .	. . . . .
Unimproved	. . . . .	. . . .	. . . .	. . . .	. . . .	. . . . . .	. . . . .	. . . . .	. . . . .
Total[8]	. . . .	. . . .	. . . .	. . . .	. . . .	. . . . . .	. . . . .	. . . . .	. . . . .
Rent from properties sold during period	XXXX	XXXX	XXXX	XXXX	XXXX	XXXX	. . . . .	. . . . .	. . . . .
Total	XXXX	XXXX	XXXX	XXXX	XXXX	XXXX	. . . . .	. . . . .	. . . . .

[1] All money columns shall be totaled.

[2] Each item of property included in column E in an amount in excess of $100,000 shall be listed separately.

[3] In a separate schedule classify by states in which the real estate owned is located the total amounts in support of columns E and F.

[4] In a footnote to this schedule, furnish a reconciliation, in the following form, of the total amount at which real estate was carried at the beginning of the period with the total amount shown in column E:

Balance at beginning of period . . . . $_____

    Additions during period:

      Aquisitions through foreclosure . . . . $_____

      Other acquisitions. . . . . _____

      Improvements, etc. . . . . _____

Other (describe). . . . . _____

Deductions during period:

Cost of real estate sold. . . . . $_____

Other (describe) . . . . _____

Balance at close of period. . . . . $_____

If additions, except acquisitions through foreclosure, represent other than cash expenditures, explain. If any of the changes during the period result from transactions, directly or indirectly, with affiliatesm explain and state the amount of any intercompany gain or loss.

_____

[5] If any item of real estate investments has been written down or reserved against pursuant to §210.6-21(f), describe the item and explain the basis for the write-down or reserve.

[6] State in a footnote to column E the aggregate cost for Federal income tax purposes.

[7] The amount of all intercompany profits included in the total of column E shall be stated if material.

[8] Summarize the aggregate amounts for each column applicable to captions 7 and 12 of §210.6-22.

[As last amended in Release No. AS-280, September 2, 1980, 45 F.R. 63660.]

[¶ 36,241] Reg. § 210.12-25. Supplementary Profit and Loss Information

Column A	Column B	Column C		Column D
		Charged to other accounts		
Item[1]	Charged to investment expense	(1) Account	(2) Amount	Total
1. Legal expenses (including those in connection with any matter, measure or proceeding before legislative bodies, officers or government departments)	. . . .	. . . .	. . . .	. . . .
2. Advertising and publicity	. . . .	. . . .	. . . .	. . . .
3. Sales promotion[2].	. . . .	. . . .	. . . .	. . . .
4. Payments directly and indirectly to trade associations and service organizations, and contributions to other organizations	. . . .	. . . .	. . . .	. . . .

_____

[1] Amounts resulting from transactions with affiliates shall be stated separately.

[2] State separately each category of expense representing more than 5 percent of the total expense shown under this item.

[As last amended in Release No. AS-280, September 2, 1980, 45 F.R. 63660.]

[¶ 36,251] Reg. § 210.12-26. Certificate Reserves

Column A—Description[1]	Column B—Balance at beginning of period			Column C—Additions		
	(1)— Number of accounts with security bidders	(2)— Amount of maturity value	(3)— Amount of reserved[2]	(1)— Charged to profit and loss or income	(2)— Reserve payments by certificate holders	(3)— Charged to other accounts describe

Column D—Deductions			Column E—Balance at close of period		
(1)— Maturities	(2)— Cash surrenders prior to maturity	(3)— Other— describe	(1)— Number of accounts with security holders	(2)— Amount of maturity value	(3)— Amount of reserves[2]

[1] (a) Each series of certificates shall be stated separately. The description shall include the yield to maturity on an annual payment basis.

(b) For certificates of the installment type, information required by columns B, D (2) and (3) and E shall be given by age groupings, according to the number of months paid by security holders, grouped to show those upon which 1—12 monthly payments have been made, 13—24 payments, etc.

[2] (a) If the total of the reserves shown in these columns differs from the total of the reserves per the accounts, there should be stated (i) the aggregate difference and (ii) the difference on a $1,000 face-amount certificate basis.

(b) There shall be shown by footnote or by supplemental schedule (i) the amounts periodically credited to each class of security holders' accounts from installment payments and (ii) such other amounts periodically credited to accumulate the maturity amount of the certificate. Such information shall be stated on a $1,000 face-amount certificate basis for the term of the certificate.

[As last amended in Release No. AS-280, September 2, 1980, 45 F.R. 63660.]

[¶ 36,261] Reg. § 210.12-27. Qualified Assets on Deposit

Column A	Column B	Column C	Column D	Column E	Column F
Name of depositary[2]	Cash	Investments in securities	First mortgages and other first liens on real estate	Other	Total[3]

[1] All money columns shall be totaled.
[2] Classify names of individual depositaries under group headings, such as banks and states.
[3] Total of column F shall agree with note required by caption 11 of § 210.6-22 as to total amount of qualified Assets on Deposit.

[As last amended in Release No. AS-280, September 2, 1980, 45 F.R. 63660.]

[¶ 36,271] Reg. § 210.12-28. Real Estate and Accumulated Depreciation [1]

(For certain real estate companies)

Column A	Column B	Column C	Column D	Column E	Column F	Column G	Column H	Column I
Descrip-tion[2]	Encum-brances	Initial cost to company	Cost capitalized subsequent to acquisition	Gross amount at which carried at close of period[3456 7]	Accumulated depreciation	Date of construction	Date acquired	Life on which depreciation in latest income statements is computed
		Buildings and Land improvements	Improvements Car- rying costs	Buildings and Land improvements Total				

[1] All money columns shall be totaled.
[2] The description for each property should include type of property (e.g., unimproved land, shopping center, garden apartments, etc.) and the geographical location.
[3] The required information is to be given as to each individual investment included in column E except that an amount not exceeding 5 percent of the total of column E may be listed in one amount as "miscellaneous investments."
[4] In a note to this schedule, furnish a reconciliation, in the following form, of the total amount at which real estate was carried at the beginning of each period for which income statements are required, with the total amount shown in column E:

Balance at beginning of period . . . . $ . . . . .

Additions during period:

Acquisitions through foreclosure . . . . . $ . . . . .

Other acquisitions . . . .

Improvements etc. . . . .

Other (describe) . . . .

$ . . . . .

Deductions during period:

Cost of real estate sold . . . . $ . . . . .

Other (describe) . . . .

$ . . . . .

Balance at close of period . . . . $ . . . . .

If additions, except acquisitions through foreclosure, represent other than cash expenditures, explain. If any of the changes during the period result from transactions, directly or indirectly with affiliates, explain the basis of such transactions and state the amounts involved.

A similar reconciliation shall be furnished for the accumulated depreciation.

[5] If any item of real estate investments has been written down or reserved against, describe the item and explain the basis for the write-down or reserve.

[6] State in a note to column E the aggregate cost for Federal income tax purposes.

[7] The amount of all intercompany profits included in the total of column E shall be stated if material.

[As last amended in Release No. AS-280, September 2, 1980, 45 F.R. 63660.]

[¶ 36,281] Reg. § 210.12-29. Mortgage Loans on Real Estate[1]

(For certain real estate companies)

Column A	Column B	Column C	Column D	Column E	Column F	Column G	Column H
Description[234]	Interest rate	Final maturity date	Periodic payment term[5]	Prior liens	Face amount of mortgages	Carrying amount of mortgages [26789]	Principal amount of loans subject to delinquent principal or interest[1] [4]

[1] All money columns shall be totaled.

[2] The required information is to be given for each individual mortgage loan which exceeds three percent of the total of column G.

[3] If the portfolio includes large numbers of mortgages most of which are less than three percent of column G, the mortgages not required to be reported separately should be grouped by classifications that will indicate the dispersion of the portfolio, i.e., for a portfolio of mortgages on single family residential housing. The description should also include number of loans by original loan amounts (e.g., over $100,000, $50,000-99,999, $20,000-$49,000, under $20,000) and type loan (e.g., VA, FHA, Conventional). Interest rates and maturity dates may be stated in terms of ranges. Data required by columns D, E and F may be omitted for mortgages not required to be reported individually.

[4] Loans should be grouped by categories, e.g., first mortgage, second mortgage, construction loans, etc., and for each loan the type of property, e.g., shopping center, high rise apartments, etc., and its geographic location should be stated.

[5] State whether principal and interest is payable at level amount over life to maturity or at varying amounts over life to maturity. State amount of balloon payment at maturity, if any. Also state prepayment penalty terms, if any.

[6] In a note to this schedule, furnish a reconciliation, in the following form, of the carrying amount of mortgage loans at the beginning of each period for which income statements are required, with the total amount shown in column G:

Balance at beginning of period . . . . $ . . . . .

Additions during period:

New mortgage loans . . . . $ . . . . .

Other (describe) . . . .

. . . . $_____

Deductions during period:

Collections of principal . . . . $ . . . . .

Foreclosures . . . .

Cost of mortgages sold . . . .

Amortization of premium . . . .

Other (describe) . . . .

Balance at close of period . . . . $_____

If additions represent other than cash expenditures, explain. If any of the changes during the period result from transactions, directly or indirectly with affiliates, explain the bases of such transactions, and state the amounts involved. State the aggregate mortgages (a) renewed and (b) extended. If the carrying amount of new mortgages is in excess of the unpaid amount of the extended mortgages, explain.

---

[7] If any item of mortgage loans on real estate investments has been written down or reserved against, describe the item and explain the basis for the write-down or reserve.

[8] State in a note to column G the aggregate cost for Federal income tax purposes.

[9] The amount of all intercompany profits in the total of column G shall be stated, if material.

[10] (a) Interest in arrears for less than 3 months may be disregarded in computing the total amount of principal subject to delinquent interest.

(b) Of the total principal amount, state the amount acquired from controlled and other affiliates.

[As last amended in Release No. AS-280, September 2, 1980, 45 F.R. 63660.]

FINANCIAL REPORTING CODIFICATION

CODIFICATION OF FINANCIAL REPORTING POLICIES

Table of Contents

Section	Subject	Paragraph

CODIFICATION OF FINANCIAL REPORTING POLICIES

SECTION 100—GENERAL

[¶ 38,021] Sec. 101. Statement of Policy on the Establishment and Improvement of Accounting Principles and Standards

ASR 4:

[On April 25, 1938, the Commission issued the following statement of its administrative policy with respect to financial statements.]

In cases where financial statements filed with the Commission pursuant to its rules and regulations under the Securities Act or the Exchange Act are prepared in accordance with accounting principles for which there is no substantial authoritative support, such financial statements will be presumed to be misleading or inaccurate despite disclosures contained in the certificate of the accountant or in footnotes to the statements provided the matters involved are material. In cases where there is a difference of opinion between the Commission and the registrant as to the proper principles of accounting to be followed, disclosure will be accepted in lieu of correction of the financial statements themselves only if the points involved are such that there is substantial authoritative support for the practices followed by the registrant and the position of the Commission has not previously been expressed in rules, regulations or other official releases of the Commission, including the published opinions of its Chief Accountant.

ASR 150:

[On December 20, 1973, the 1938 policy statement was updated to recognize the establishment of the FASB as follows.]

Various Acts of Congress administered by the Securities and Exchange Commission clearly state the authority of the Commission to prescribe the methods to be followed in the preparation of accounts and the form and content of financial statements to be filed under the Acts and the responsibility to assure that investors are furnished with information necessary for informed investment decisions. In meeting this statutory responsibility effectively, in recognition of the expertise, energy and resources of the accounting profession, and without abdicating its responsibilities, the Commission has historically looked to the standard-setting bodies designated by the profession to provide leadership in establishing and improving the accounting principles. The determinations by these bodies have been re-garded by the Commission, with minor exceptions, as being responsive to the needs of investors.

The body presently designated by the Council of the AICPA to establish accounting principles is the FASB. This designation by the AICPA followed the issuance of a report in March 1972 recommending the formation of the FASB, after a study of the matter by a broadly based study group. The recommendations contained in that report were widely endorsed by industry, financial analysts, accounting educators, and practicing accountants. The Commission endorsed the establishment of the FASB in the belief that the Board would provide an institutional framework which will permit prompt and responsible actions flowing from research and consideration of varying viewpoints. The collective experience and expertise of the members of the FASB and the individuals and professional organizations supporting it are substantial. Equally important, the commitment of resources to the FASB is impressive evidence of the willingness and intention of the private sector to support the FASB in accomplishing its task. In view of these considerations, the Commission intends to continue its policy of looking to the private sector for leadership in establishing and improving accounting principles and standards through the FASB with the expectation that the body's conclusions will promote the interests of investors.

In ASR 4, the Commission stated its policy that financial statements prepared in accordance with accounting practices for which there was no substantial authoritative support were presumed to be misleading and that footnote or other disclosure would not avoid this presumption. It also stated that, where there was a difference of opinion between the Commission and a registrant as to the proper accounting to be followed in a particular case, disclosure would be accepted in lieu of correction of the financial statements themselves only if substantial authoritative support existed for the accounting practices followed by the registrant and the position of the Commission had not been expressed in rules, regulations or other official releases. For purposes of this policy, principles, standards and practices promulgated by the FASB in its Statements and Interpretations* will be considered by the Commission as having substantial authoritative support, and those contrary to such

---

* ARBs of the Committee on Accounting Procedure of the AICPA and effective opinions of the APB should be considered as continuing in force with the same degree of authority

except to the extent altered, amended, supplemented, revoked or superseded by one or more SFAS issued by the FASB.

FASB promulgations will be considered** to have no such support.

In the exercise of its statutory authority with respect to the form and content of filings under the Acts, the Commission has the responsibility to assure that investors are provided with adequate information. A significant portion of the necessary information is provided by a set of basic financial statements (including the notes thereto) which conform to generally accepted accounting principles. Information in addition to that included in financial statements conforming to generally accepted accounting principles is also necessary. Such additional disclosures are required to be made in various fashions, such as in financial statements and schedules reported on by independent public accountants or as textual statements required by items in the applicable forms and reports filed with the Commission. The Commission will continue to identify areas where investor information needs exist and will determine the appropriate methods of disclosure to meet these needs.

It must be recognized that in its administration of the Federal Securities Acts and in its review of filings under such Acts, the Commission staff will continue as it has in the past to take action on a day-to-day basis as may be appropriate to resolve specific problems of accounting and reporting under the particular factual circumstances involved in filings and reports of individual registrants.

The Commission believes that the foregoing statement of policy provides a sound basis for the Commission and the FASB to make significant contributions to meeting the needs of the registrants and investors.

ASR 280:

[On September 2, 1980, the Commission again commented on the role of the FASB in establishing and improving accounting principles.]

The Commission does not believe that any decision to require particular disclosures or, less likely, a decision to require a particular method of accounting through rule-making in Regulation S-X, conflicts with the basic policy of relying on the FASB for leadership in establishing financial accounting and reporting standards. Furthermore, it believes that the requirements of Regulation S-X address those areas where GAAP standards are not explicit and there is a need for an authoritative source for such requirements. While there is, of course, always the possibility that the Commission may conclude it cannot accept an FASB standard

in a particular area, such events have been rare. The Commission intends to continue its present policy of carefully re-evaluating its rules as the FASB effectuates changes in financial accounting and reporting standards and will eliminate those rules which become unnecessary. For example, as standards are issued by the FASB regarding "Funds Flows and Liquidity," "Reporting Earnings" and other phases of the conceptual framework project, the Commission expects it will be able to defer to the requirements to the private sector.

FR-70

[The SEC added the following text in Financial Reporting Release No. 70, April 25, 2003.]

I. Background

On July 30, 2002, President Bush signed the Sarbanes-Oxley Act of 2002. Section 108 of that Act amends section 19 of the Securities Act of 1933[1] to establish criteria that must be met in order for the work product of an accounting standard-setting body to be recognized as "generally accepted." A new subsection 19(b) indicates that in carrying out its authority under section 19 and under section 13(b) of the Securities Exchange Act of 1934[2] the Commission may recognize as "generally accepted" for purposes of the federal securities laws any accounting principles established by a standard setting body that:

• is organized as a private entity;

• has, for administrative and operational purposes, a board of trustees serving in the public interest, the majority of whom are not, concurrent with their service on such board, and have not been during the two-year period preceding such service, associated persons of any registered public accounting firm;

• is funded as provided in Section 109 of the Sarbanes-Oxley Act;

• has adopted procedures to ensure prompt consideration, by majority vote of its members, of changes to accounting principles necessary to reflect emerging accounting issues and changing business practices; and

• considers, in adopting accounting principles, the need to keep standards current in order to reflect changes in the business environment, the extent to which international convergence on high quality accounting standards is necessary or appropriate in the public interest and for the protection of investors.

Representatives of the FASB and FAF have requested that "[t]he FASB . . . continue to be the designated organization in the private sector for

---

** It should be noted that Rule 203 of the Rules of Conduct of the Code of Ethics of the AICPA provides that it is necessary to depart from accounting principles promulgated by the body designated by the Council of the AICPA if, due to unusual circumstances, failure to do so would result in mis-

leading financial statements. In such a case, the use of other principles may be accepted or required by the Commission.

[1] 15 U.S.C. 77s.

[2] 15 U.S.C. 78m.

establishing standards of financial accounting and reporting."[3]

II. Qualification and Recognition of the FASB

A. *Structure of the FASB*

In assessing compliance with the provisions of Section 108, the Commission has evaluated the organizational structure, operations, and procedures of both the FAF and the FASB. The FAF is comprised of independent trustees and is responsible for overseeing, funding,[4] and appointing members of the Board, as well as selecting members of an advisory body.[5] The Commission has been informed that the majority of the FAF trustees are not, and have not been during the two-year period preceding their service on the FAF, associated with a public accounting firm. Based on our past relationship with the FAF, we believe that the FAF serves the public interest. Accordingly, the FAF meets the applicable criteria in section 108 of the Sarbanes-Oxley Act for the board of trustees of a recognized private sector accounting standard setter.

The Board is responsible for promulgating financial accounting and reporting standards. It currently has seven members who have expertise in accounting and financial reporting. Members generally are appointed for five-year terms and can be reappointed to one additional term. Board members are full time employees of the FAF.

B. *Commission Oversight of FASB Activities*

While the Commission consistently has looked to the private sector in the past to set accounting standards, the securities laws, including the Sarbanes-Oxley Act, clearly provide the Commission with authority to set accounting standards for public companies and other entities that file financial statements with the Commission.[6] In addition, recognition of standards set by a private sector standard-setting body as "generally accepted" is only appropriate under section 108 of the Sarbanes-Oxley Act if, among other things, the Commission determines that the private sector body "has the capacity to assist the Commission in fulfilling the requirements of . . . the Securities Exchange Act . . . because, at a minimum, the standard setting body is capable of improving the accuracy and effectiveness of financial reporting and the protection of investors under the securities laws."[7] As noted above, section 108 also emphasizes the Commission's responsibility to determine that the standard setting body:

- has "procedures to ensure prompt consideration . . . of changes to accounting principles necessary to reflect emerging accounting issues and changing business practices";
- considers the need to amend standards "to reflect changes in the business environment"; and
- considers, to the extent necessary or appropriate, international convergence of accounting standards.

Given the Commission's responsibilities under the securities laws and our specific responsibilities under the Sarbanes-Oxley Act to make findings regarding the procedures, capabilities, activities, and results of any designated accounting standards-setting body, we believe that:

- The FAF and FASB should give the Commission timely notice of, and discuss with the Commission, the FAF's intention to appoint a new member of the FAF or FASB.[8] While the FAF makes the final determinations regarding the selection of FASB and FAF members, we believe that to fulfill our statutory responsibilities we should provide the FAF with our views and that the FAF should consider those views in making its final selection. The Commission, FAF, and FASB share the belief that the qualifications and appropriateness of each member of the FAF and the

---

[3] Letter dated August 16, 2002 to SEC Chairman Harvey L. Pitt from Robert H. Herz, Chairman, FASB and Manuel H. Johnson, Chairman and President, FAF. The Act does not restrict the Commission's ability to develop accounting principles on its own, and does not limit the number of private-sector bodies the Commission may recognize.

[4] The funding provisions under Section 109 of the Sarbanes-Oxley Act replace the FAF's funding responsibilities; the FAF will continue to be responsible for the fee requests, including establishing the FASB's budget for review by the Commission each year.

[5] The FASB receives input from, among other sources, a standing advisory body, the Financial Accounting Standards Advisory Council (FASAC), which is comprised of members from the accounting and business communities, academia, and professional organizations, all of whom share an interest in fostering quality financial reporting and disclosure. FASAC's primary mission is to advise the FASB on its projects and agenda. In addition, the FASB has established a User Advisory Council (UAC) to assist the FASB in raising awareness of how investors and investment professionals, equity and credit analysts, and rating agencies use financial information. The FASB has recruited more than 40 professionals,

representing a variety of investment and analytical disciplines, to participate on the UAC.

[6] Section 108(c) of the Sarbanes-Oxley Act states, "Nothing in this Act, including this section . . . shall be construed to impair or limit the authority of the Commission to establish accounting principles or standards for purposes of enforcement of the securities laws."

[7] *See* Securities Act of 1933, section 19(b)(1)(B), as added by the Sarbanes-Oxley Act.

[8] Such consultations have occurred in the past. *See, e.g.*, SEC Press Release No. 96-87, "FAF and SEC Reach Agreement on Changes in Composition of Accounting Foundation: Appointing Three New Trustees to Serve," dated July 8, 1996, which states, "The FAF selected the new At-Large Trustees in consultation with the SEC"; SEC Annual Report 1996, at 90-91, which states, "The change in composition of the FAF's Board was made in consultation with the SEC to include a greater representation by those who do not have a special interest in the outcome of accounting standards setting,"; and FAF, *1996 Annual Report of the Financial Accounting Foundation*," at 5, which states, "In consultation with the chairman of the Securities and Exchange Commission, the FAF agreed in July to change the composition of the Foundation's Board."

FASB are critical if the FASB is to continue to be a premier private-sector standards-setting body.

• The FASB, in its role of "assist(ing) the Commission in fulfilling the requirements of the Securities Exchange Act,"[9] should provide timely guidance to public companies, accounting firms, regulators and others on accounting issues that the Commission considers to be of immediate significance to investors. The Commission and its staff, however, do not prohibit the FASB from also addressing other topics, and do not dictate the direction or outcome of specific FASB projects so long as the conclusions reached by the FASB are in the interest of investor protection. We expect that the Commission staff[10] will refer issues to the FASB or one of its affiliated organizations[11] when those issues may warrant new, amendments to, or formal interpretations of, accounting standards. We also expect that the FASB will address such issues in a timely manner. On those occasions when the FASB may determine that consideration of the issue is not advisable or that the issue cannot be resolved within the time frame acceptable to the Commission,[12] we expect that the FASB promptly will notify the Commission or its staff, provide us with its views regarding an appropriate resolution of the issue, and diligently work with us and our staff to ensure the protection of investors from misleading or inadequate accounting or disclosures.

• Because the Commission and FASB share the common goal of providing investors with the disclosure of meaningful financial information, we anticipate continuation of our collegial working relationship with the FASB. To that end, we expect that, when requested to do so, the FASB will make information and staff reasonably available to facilitate our, or our staff's, understanding and implementation of a FASB standard. The Commission and its staff intend to work with the FAF and the Board to ensure that proper oversight procedures and policies are in place to allow the Com-

mission to assess whether the FASB continues to meet the characteristics of an accounting-standard setter that are discussed in the Sarbanes-Oxley Act.

C. *Key FASB Initiatives*

As noted earlier, the Commission has treated FASB accounting standards as "authoritative" since 1973. In order for U.S. accounting standards to remain relevant and to continue to improve, however, the Commission expects the FASB to:

• Consider, in adopting accounting principles, the extent to which international convergence on high quality accounting standards is necessary or appropriate in the public interest and for the protection of investors,[13] including consideration of moving towards greater reliance on principles-based accounting standards whenever it is reasonable to do so;

• Take reasonable steps to continue to improve the timeliness with which it completes its projects, while satisfying appropriate public notice and comment requirements[14] ; and

• Continue to be objective in its decision-making and to weigh carefully the views of its constituents and the expected benefits and perceived costs of each standard.[15] CDC. *FASB's Independence*

While effective oversight of the FASB's activities is necessary in order for the Commission to carry out its responsibilities under the securities laws, we recognize the importance of the FASB's independence. By virtue of today's Commission determination, the FASB will continue its role as the preeminent accounting standard setter in the private sector. In performing this role, the FASB must use independent judgment in setting standards and should not be constrained in its exploration and discussion of issues. This is necessary to ensure that the standards developed are free from bias and have the maximum credibility in the business and investing communities.[16]

---

[9] Section 19(b)(1)(B) of the Securities Act of 1933, as added by section 108 of the Sarbanes-Oxley Act of 2002.

[10] The Commission staff will continue to take such action on a day-to-day basis as may be appropriate to resolve specific accounting and reporting issues under the particular factual circumstances involved in filings and reports of individual registrants.

[11] For example, the issue may be referred to the FASB's Emerging Issues Task Force (EITF). The EITF is comprised of approximately 13 members who serve, generally without compensation, on a part-time basis. EITF members are partners in large, medium and small accounting firms, business executives, financial analysts and other users of financial statements, and academics. Upon ratification of an EITF consensus by the FASB, the consensus is published as part of the EITF's minutes and may be relied on by Commission registrants and others in the preparation of financial statements that purport to conform to generally accepted accounting principles.

[12] We expect such occasions will be infrequent because the Commission and the FASB share the goal of providing timely

guidance to public companies and accounting firms on matters that are significant to investors.

[13] We expect that during its deliberations of an accounting issue the FASB will consider, among other things, international accounting standards addressing that issue.

[14] These ideas, among others, are embodied in the FASB's current Rules of Procedure. To the extent that the FAF or FASB determines that inadequate staffing or resources hampers the timeliness of the FASB's processes, the Commission will review requests for increases in the FASB's budget in accordance with the procedures in section 109(e) of the Sarbanes-Oxley Act.

[15] *Id.*

[16] The occasions where the Commission has not accepted a particular FASB standard have been rare due, in part, to our recognition and support of FASB's independence. As noted elsewhere in this release, the Commission and its staff do not prohibit the FASB from addressing a particular topic and do not dictate the direction or outcome of specific FASB projects provided that the conclusions reached by the FASB are in the interest of investor protection.

E. *Conclusion*

Based on available information, the organizational structure, operating activities, and procedures of the FAF and FASB meet the criteria in section 108 the Sarbanes-Oxley Act.[17] In addition, the Commission has determined that the FASB has the capacity to assist the Commission in fulfilling the requirements of subsection 19(a) of the Securities Act of 1933 and section 13(b) of the Securities Exchange Act of 1934 and is capable of improving both the accuracy and effectiveness of financial reporting and the protection of investors under the securities laws.[18] Accordingly, the standards set by the FASB are recognized as "generally accepted" under section 108 of the Sarbanes-Oxley Act.

As required under the securities laws, including the Sarbanes-Oxley Act, the Commission will monitor the FASB's procedures, qualifications, capabilities, activities, and results, as well as the FAF's and FASB's ongoing compliance with the expectations and views expressed in this policy statement. We will issue an appropriate revision of this policy statement if we determine that the FAF or FASB no longer meets the statutory criteria or expectations discussed in this policy statement, or if we consider it otherwise necessary or appropriate to do so.

FR-80A: Commission Guidance Regarding FASB's Accounting Standards Codification

[The SEC added the following text in Financial Reporting Release No. 80A, August 18, 2009.]

I. Background

Section 108 of the Sarbanes-Oxley Act of 2002[1] amended Section 19(b) of the Securities Act of 1933[2] to provide that the Commission may recognize, as generally accepted for purposes of the securities laws, any accounting principles established by a standard setting body that meets specified criteria. On April 25, 2003, the Commission issued a policy statement concluding that the FASB and its parent organization, the Financial Accounting Foundation, satisfied the criteria for an accounting standard setting body under the Act, and recognizing the FASB's financial accounting and reporting standards as "generally accepted" for purposes of the federal securities laws.[3]

On June 30, 2009, the FASB issued FASB Statement of Financial Accounting Standards No. 168, *The FASB Accounting Standards Codification(TM) and the Hierarchy of Generally Accepted Accounting Principles - a replacement of FASB Statement No. 162* (Statement No. 168), to establish the FASB Codification as the source of authoritative non-Commission accounting principles recognized by the FASB to be applied by nongovernmental entities in the preparation of financial statements in conformity with U.S. generally accepted accounting principles ("U.S. GAAP"). Statement No. 168 is effective for financial statements issued for interim and annual periods ending after September 15, 2009. The FASB Codification reorganizes existing U.S. accounting and reporting standards issued by the FASB and other related private-sector standard setters, and all guidance contained in the FASB Codification carries an equal level of authority.[4]

The FASB Codification directly impacts certain of the Commission's rules, regulations, releases and staff bulletins (collectively referred to in this release as "Commission's rules and staff guidance"), which refer to specific FASB standards or other private sector standard-setter literature under U.S. GAAP, because such references are now superseded by the FASB Codification. The Commission is therefore issuing interpretive guidance to avoid confusion on the part of issuers, auditors, investors, and other users of financial statements and Commission rules and staff guidance.

II. Discussion

Many parts of the Commission's rules and staff guidance include direct references to specific standards under U.S. GAAP. For example, Regulation S-X, which, together with the Commission's Financial Reporting Releases, sets forth the form and content of and requirements for financial statements required to be filed with the Commission,[5] includes specific references to specific standards under U.S. GAAP.[6] In addition, some parts of the Commission's rules and staff guidance outside of the financial statement context include specific references to specific standards under U.S. GAAP, such as in Item 402 of Regulation S-K regarding disclosure of executive compensation.[7]

---

[17] As noted above, one of the statutory criteria is that the recognized accounting body is funded as provided in section 109 of the Sarbanes-Oxley Act. We are providing an endorsement of the FASB so that it may begin to work with the Public Company Accounting Oversight Board to implement the funding mechanisms in section 109. Our recognition of the FASB is in anticipation of and with the expectation that this funding will be forthcoming in the near term.

[18] *See*, section 108(a) of the Sarbanes-Oxley Act; section 19(b)(1)(B) of the Securities Act of 1933, 15 U.S.C. 77s(b)(1)(B).

[1] Pub. L. 107-204, 116 Stat. 745 (2002).

[2] 15 U.S.C. 77s(b).

[3] See Commission Statement of Policy Reaffirming the Status of the FASB as a Designated Private-Sector Standard Setter, Release Nos. 33-8221; 34-47743; IC-26028; FR-70 (April 25, 2003) [68 FR 23333 (May 1, 2003)].

[4] The FASB Codification is available at *http://asc.fasb.org/home.*

[5] 17 CFR 210.1-01.

[6] See, *e.g.*, Rule 1-02(u) of Regulation S-X [17 CFR 210.1-02(u)], which defines the term "related parties" by reference to FASB Statement of Financial Accounting Standards No. 57, *Related Party Disclosures.*

[7] 17 CFR 229.402.

Given the possible confusion between the Commission's rules and staff guidance, on the one hand, and the FASB Codification, on the other hand, the Commission believes it is necessary to publish the guidance in this release. Concurrent with the effective date of the FASB Codification, references in the Commission's rules and staff guidance to specific standards under U.S. GAAP should be understood to mean the corresponding reference in the FASB Codification. We note that the FASB Codification includes a cross-reference finding tool that can assist users in identifying where previous accounting literature resides in the FASB Codification. The Commission and its staff also intend to embark on a longer term rulemaking and updating initiative to revise comprehensively specific references to specific standards under U.S. GAAP in the Commission's rules and staff guidance.

It should be noted that although the FASB has stated that the FASB Codification supersedes existing references in U.S. GAAP, the FASB Codification does not supersede Commission rules or regulations. We understand that the FASB Codification, as a service to users, includes references to some Commission rules and staff guidance. However, the FASB Codification is not the authoritative source for such content, nor does its inclusion in the FASB Codification affect how such content may be updated in the future.

[¶ 38,025] Sec. 102. Integrated Disclosure System

[On September 2, 1980, the Commission announced the first of a series of revisions and proposals intended to improve disclosure, reduce disclosure burdens and to facilitate the integration of the disclosure systems under the Securities Act and the Exchange Act.These initiatives included, among other things, final rules relating to: (1) amendment to the annual report form required to be filed by most publicly-owned companies, Form 10-K, and to related forms, rules, and regulations and guides under the Securities Acts; (2) amendments to Regulation S-X designed to eliminate, to the extent possible, the differences between the requirements of generally accepted accounting principles and Regulation S-X; and (3) uniform financial statement instructions for certain forms and reports required pursuant to the Securities Acts. In March 1982 (ASR 306), the Commission announced the adoption of a comprehensive revision to the rules and forms governing the registration of securities under the Securities Act. This action represented the final stage of the Commission's program to integrate the disclosure systems under the various Federal securities laws and to simplify and improve the disclosure requirements imposed under these systems.]

.01. Form 10-K

.a. General

ASR 279:

The Commission adopted** major changes in the Securities Act and Exchange Act disclosure systems. These changes were designed to improve the disclosure made to investors and other users of financial information, to facilitate the integration of the two disclosure systems into the single disclosure system long advocated by many commentators*, and to reduce impediments to combining informal security holder communications, such as annual reports to security holders, with official Commission filings.

This release deals with format and content changes in the Form 10-K and in the annual report to security holders. Under the system in effect as a result of these changes, minimum disclosure requirements have been developed by the Commission for the Form 10-K and the annual report to security holders. To the extent these disclosure requirements have common elements, the Commission has made it easier now to simply incorporate from the annual report to security holders to the Form 10-K, if registrants so choose.

The Commission has determined to require only portions of the Form 10-K and the annual report to security holders to have equivalent disclosure because these documents are not necessarily used in an identical manner. Disclosure requirements in annual reports evolved in the context of shareholders making voting decisions. The Form 10-K has traditionally confirmed information previously delivered to investors and other users making economic decisions about the company

---

** [In ASR 306, March 1982, the Commission adopted the final components of the Integrated Disclosure System. These included (1) the adoption of three registration forms which serve as the basic framework for the registration of securities under the Securities Act; (2) the expansion and reorganization of Regulation S-K, the central repository of uniform disclosure requirements under the Securities Act and the Exchange Act; (3) the revision of Regulation C which contains the procedural requirements for the registration of securities under the Securities Act and the registration and reports of certain issuers under the Exchange Act; (4) the adoption of a temporary rule governing the registration of securities to be sold in delayed or continuous offerings; (5) the adoption of a rule identifying certain circumstances bearing upon the reasonableness of the investigation to discharge one's obligation under Section 11(b) of the Securities Act and upon what constitutes reasonable grounds for belief under that Section; (6) the adoption of rules permitting the voluntary disclosure of security ratings in registration statements under the Securities Act; (7) the revision of various rules, forms and schedules under the Securities Act and the Exchange Act to implement and to reflect other changes and the rescission of obsolete and rarely used forms under the Securities Act and the Exchange Act.]

* *See generally* Cohen, "Truth in Securities" Revisited, 79 Harv. L. Rev. 1340 (1968); SEC, *Disclosure to Investors* (Wheat Report) (1969); R eport of the Advisory Committee on Corporate Disclosure to the Securities and Exchange Commission, Committee Print 95-29, House Committee on Interstate and Foreign Commerce, 95th Cong., 1st Sess., November 3, 1977 ("Advisory Committee").

and, as a result, has been more detailed. The Commission recognizes that the information content in Form 10-K not only was originally formulated for a specialized use, but that within those groups which have utilized the Form there are different constituencies. Those constituencies which have been the most frequent users of Form 10-K information are institutional investors, professional security analysts and sophisticated individual investors. The Commission believes that it continues to be appropriate to focus primarily on these frequent user constituencies in formulating Form 10-K requirements, but that such a focus would not be appropriate in formulating requirements for the annual report to security holders.

With regard to the content of the restructured Form 10-K, several items in the present Form have been deleted and others have been simplified or have been moved to schedules or exhibits. The prime focus of this effort has been to eliminate unnecessary or duplicative disclosure throughout Commission filings through the further expansion of Regulation S-K and to relegate disclosures of a technical or supplementary nature to schedules or exhibits which are available to users upon request.

Insofar as the annual report to security holders is concerned, the principal effort has been to standardize disclosure items to make them consistent with similar requirements in Commission filings. In particular, the focus has been primarily upon financial disclosure to provide uniformity in form, content and timing of the required information.

102.01.b. Background and Development
ASR 279:

The Commission's review of the purpose and utility of the Form 10-K led it to believe that there is a basic information package which most, if not all, investors expect to be furnished. Further, it has become apparent that this basic information package, which in the context of Form 10-K developed to support the current information requirements of an active trading market, is virtually identical to the similar information package independently developed in connection with the registration and sale of newly issued shares under the Securities Act. The essential content of these Form 10-K and registration statement information packages includes audited financial statements, a summary of selected financial data appropriate for trend analysis, and a meaningful description of the registrant's business and financial condition.

The restructured Form 10-K which the Commission adopted is specifically designed to segre-gate the basic information package contained in that Form from proxy related or supplemental information. In this regard, the new Form 10-K is structured in four parts. The first part retains the detailed disclosure requirements relating to business, properties, legal proceedings and beneficial ownership. The second part consists of the basic disclosure package which is common to both Securities Act and Exchange Act filings. The third part consists of the traditional proxy disclosure information relating to directors and executive officers and management remuneration. Finally, the fourth part contains requirements for financial statement schedules and exhibits.

Although the revised Form 10-K is designed to promote the integration of the Securities Act and Exchange Act disclosure systems, which was the basic goal set forth in the report of the Advisory Committee, the restructured format of the new form does not precisely follow that suggested by the Advisory Committee. That Committee recommended a relatively unstructured document which would encourage registrants to combine informal annual and quarterly reports to security holders into single documents to be filed as Form 10-Ks and 10-Qs. The new Form 10-K continues to encourage the combination of formal and informal reports. However, the new form changes the emphasis from the Form 10-K (which the Advisory Committee emphasized) to the basic disclosure package, wherever it appears. As a result, where the Advisory Committee envisioned the Form 10-K as the document to be integrated with the Securities Act filing, the new Form 10-K permits registrants to utilize the minimum disclosure package from the annual report to security holders sent with the proxy statement, from the Form 10-K, or to completely restate it.

Furthermore, the Commission does not believe it would be appropriate at this time to adopt the Advisory Committee approach and to mandate a totally combined Form 10-K and annual report to security holders in order to produce the readable Form 10-K which would be needed to form the basis for integration. Such a mandate might be overly burdensome on some registrants and could adversely affect the annual report to security holders.[*] Under these circumstances, the Commission believes that it would be wise to encourage combination on a voluntary basis. In the meantime, the detailed disclosure will remain available in the filed Form 10-K in order to supplement the more abbreviated presentation in the annual report to security holders.

102.01.c. Annual Report to Security Holders

---

[*] The inability to assure in all cases that there will be a single document which will be usable as a combined report to security holders and Form 10-K arises primarily because of the Business, Properties and Legal Proceedings disclosures called for under Items 1, 2 and 5 of Regulation S-K and because of certain parent and subsidiary financial statements required by Regulation S-X. Although it is hoped that most registrants will have little difficulty in presenting these items in a combined document, there is considerable evidence that in some cases the sheer volume of the disclosure called for by these items would adversely impact the readability of the registrant's annual reports to security holders.

ASR 279:

In a release issued on January 10, 1974,[**] the Commission amended Rules 14a-3 and 14c-3 to require that annual reports to security holders contain a variety of information, including certified financial statements, a summary of operations, a management analysis, a brief description of the issuer's business, a lines of business breakdown, an identification of the issuer's directors and executive officers, and an identification of the principal market in which securities entitled to vote were traded. These requirements were based on substantially similar requirements in the then existing Form 10-K. In requiring this new information, the Commission made the following statement:

> The annual report to security holders has long been recognized as the most effective means of communication between management and security holders. Such reports are readable because they generally avoid legalistic and technical terminology and present information in an understandable, and often innovative, form. . . . The Commission believes it is in the public interest that all security holders be provided with meaningful information regarding the business, management, operations and financial position of the issuer and that the annual report to security holders is the most suitable vehicle presently available for providing this information.

The Commission continues to believe that all security holders should be provided with meaningful information and that the changes in the Form 10-K requirements on which the annual report to security holder requirements were based should also be made in the annual report because of the importance of the disclosure. This results in a uniformity of the minimum disclosure package in the annual report to security holders and in Form 10-K. The equivalency of the minimum disclosure package in both documents not only satisfies shareholder and investor needs, it also should avoid duplication by allowing issuers to use the disclosure in the annual report to security holders to satisfy some of the requirements of Form 10-K and, if they choose, when selling securities to the public. The changes made in the annual report to security holders do not mean, however, that any further changes in Form 10-K will be reflected automatically in the annual report to security holders.

The Commission is aware that increasing the amount of required disclosure in annual security holder reports involves a risk that readability may be impaired. Although it is difficult to predict with certainty what the effect may be, the Commission does not believe that the changes implemented should or will have general adverse conse-

quences. The Commission staff, however, will continue to monitor the situation and, if adverse effects do occur, the new disclosure requirements will be revisited promptly.

With the same information appearing in the annual report to security holders and in Part II of the Form 10-K, the Commission is hopeful that most, if not all, registrants will incorporate that portion of the annual report to security holders into the Form 10-K. The four-part Form 10-K system has been designed to encourage, but not to require, the combination of annual reports and Form 10-K's into one document. For example, the revised financial statement requirements have been designed to require that only the financial statements of the registrant and its subsidiaries consolidated must appear in the annual report and in the financial statements section of the Form 10-K, Part II. The other financial statements and schedules have been designated "financial statement schedules" and have been placed in Part IV of the Form 10-K. This permits a less detailed minimum disclosure package, which is more compatible with a combined presentation, while nonetheless preserving in a separate information package the more detailed financial data for those who want it.

It should be emphasized that the minimal content changes adopted by the Commission are not intended to change the basic structure or quality of existing security holder reports. Indeed, the Commission continues to believe that the communicative style of these reports is generally excellent and that, by and large, these reports do not include the type of boilerplate disclosure and disclaimers which frequently do appear in formal Commission filings. It is hoped that the type of attention to style which is evidenced by better examples of security holder reports will continue to have a salutary effect on all of the report content, whether or not the particular information is also a part of the Form 10-K.

102.01.d. Signatures and Filing of Report

ASR 279:

The Commission concluded that a requirement for the signatures of a majority of a registrant's directors—in addition to those of its principal executive officer, its principal financial officer, and its controller or principal accounting officer—is an appropriate one under the circumstances. The Commission believes that just as its rules and the administrative focus of the Division of Corporation Finance are being realigned to reflect the shift in emphasis toward relying on periodic disclosure under the Exchange Act, so too the attention of the private sector, including management, directors, accountants, and attorneys, must also be refocused towards Exchange Act filings if a suffi-

---

[**] Exchange Act Release 10591 (January 10, 1974) [39 FR 3820].

cient degree of discipline is to be instilled in the system to make it work. With an expanded signature requirement, the Commission anticipates that directors will be encouraged to devote the needed attention to reviewing the Form 10-K and to seek the involvement of other professionals to the degree necessary to give themselves sufficient comfort. In the Commission's view, this added measure of discipline is vital to the disclosure objectives of the Federal securities laws and outweighs the potential impact, if any, of the signature on legal liability. The Commission has given attention to the concerns of commentators over the expense and logistics of obtaining the requisite signatures but believes they do not constitute an undue obstacle to the imposition of this requirement.

The Commission recognizes, however, that this requirement may result in certain hardships and inconveniences. It has therefore instructed the staff to report to it on the results of imposing the requirement after an appropriate time has passed, and the Commission will revisit the question if such action appears necessary or appropriate at that time.

102.01.e. Considerations for the Future
ASR 279:

The system will be carefully monitored for effectiveness, and future alternative systems will not be foreclosed. For example, consideration is still being given to approaches which might differentiate between user constituencies and which might give a security holder the option of receiving a simplified annual report containing summary indicators and other data in lieu of the traditional annual report or in lieu of the financial statement section of such report. This type of approach would be based upon an as yet unproven hypothesis that some users, particularly certain individual investors, either rely on financial advisers and therefore do not use detailed disclosure, or are overwhelmed by the technical nature or volume of presently required disclosure.* The Commission expects that these as well as other issues relating to concepts of differential disclosure will be pursued and studied as the integrated disclosure system evolves.

102.02. General Revision of Regulation S-X
.a. Overview
ASR 280:

The Commission adopted a general revision of Articles 3 and 5 and the related sections of Article 12 of Regulation S-X. The changes in the content of Regulation S-X (i) eliminated rules which were duplicative of GAAP, (ii) effected changes to recognize predominant current practice and changes in circumstances, (iii) clarified and modified re-

quirements which were subject to differing interpretations, and (iv) expanded certain requirements to improve financial reporting. These changes were structured in a manner to facilitate the integration of the Securities Act and the Exchange Act by attaining uniformity between financial statements included in annual reports to shareholders and those prepared in accordance with Regulation S-X.

102.02.b. Background
ASR 280:

In 1940, the Commission announced the adoption of Regulation S-X in ASR 12. Regulation S-X codified the existing instructions as to the form and content of financial statements included as a part of each of the registration and reporting forms. The regulation did not prescribe accounting methods, but rather stated requirements which were intended to elicit informative disclosures. In 1940, there was little available authoritative accounting literature. Indeed, the predecessor of the AICPA only two years earlier had instituted a research program resulting in the publication of accounting principles in the form of ARBs. This was the first attempt by the accounting profession to formally promulgate standards. Consequently, the Commission considered it beneficial that Regulation S-X included condensed requirements contained in one authoritative source.

Since the development of Regulation S-X, however, the private sector has established and improved accounting and reporting standards through various organized bodies—the APB, other units of the AICPA and, most recently, the FASB. The Commission indicated support for the FASB in ASR 150, which stated that financial statements conforming to standards set by the FASB will be presumed to have substantial authoritative support. Additionally, the Commission has indicated in its reports to Congress on its oversight of the accounting profession that it continues to believe that the initiative for establishing and improving accounting standards should remain in the private sector, subject to Commission oversight.

Similarly, the Advisory Committee on Corporate Disclosure supported private sector standard setting in its report to the Commission, issued in November 1977, in which it recommended among other things, that:

> A continuing goal of the Commission should be the elimination of rules of general applicability which cause differences between financial statements prepared in accordance with Regulation S-X and those prepared in accordance with GAAP. When the Commission requires an extension of disclosures beyond those required by GAAP because of an

---

* It is interesting to note, however, that studies such as that conducted by Professors Lucia S. Chang and Kenneth S. Most at Florida International University indicate that the typical

"unsophisticated small investor" often is quite sophisticated. L. Chang and K. Most, Financial Statements and Investment Decisions (1979).

emerging problem, the reasons for the extension and the underlying accounting issues involved should be stated. The Commission should then ask the FASB to consider the issue . . . the Commission should undertake the following:

1. Eliminate all financial statement disclosures required by Regulation S-X which duplicate those required in financial statements prepared in accordance with codified GAAP.

2. Critically review all disclosures of general applicability which are supplementary to those required by GAAP with the objective of eliminating disclosures which may not be necessary to users in making investment decisions.

The most recent comprehensive revision of Regulation S-X was in 1972, which was prior to the issuance by the APB of its last seven opinions and the establishment of the FASB. During the ensuing eight year period, the authoritative accounting literature has expanded dramatically and some of the requirements of Regulation S-X are now outdated. Accordingly, this revision was undertaken to respond to that situation.

102.03. Uniform Instructions as to Financial Statements

ASR 281:

The Commission adopted amendments to rules establishing uniform instructions as to the periods to be covered by financial statements included in most registration and reporting forms filed with the Commission under the Securities Act and the Exchange Act and in annual reports to security holders furnished pursuant to the proxy rules. Further, amendments were adopted which modify requirements as to the form and content of interim financial information included in registration statements, conforming for most registrants previous requirements under the Securities Act with current requirements for quarterly data under the Exchange Act. [See Section 300] The amendments removed substantially all present instructions as to financial statements from the various registration and reporting forms and established a centralized set of revised instructions in Regulation S-X.

As registration and reporting requirements have evolved, differences have been created in the rules covering the periods for which financial disclosures are required. These differences have resulted to some extent from a piecemeal approach, covering many years, in developing the disclosure system. Also, these differences have resulted from continuous attempts to tailor disclosure requirements to the particular circumstances surrounding the use of each of the respective forms. Such differences in requirements have contributed to the complexity of the disclosure rules and frequently have been a source of confusion to those attempting to understand filing requirements.

The Commission, in connection with its reassessment of the reporting and disclosure requirements, has questioned the necessity for these differences among forms. Common to all investment decisions involving securities is the need for sufficient information to assess the financial health of the underlying issuer. Whether a potential investor is considering investing in a security traded on the open market or in one being registered for the first time, his method of analysis and evaluation is most likely very similar and his basic informational needs the same.

It is difficult, therefore, to draw meaningful distinctions among the various registration and reporting forms to support the need for the financial statements to encompass differing periods of time. Although the nature of securities and the purpose of registration may differ in many respects and thus require certain disclosures tailored to the specific circumstances of the filing, the Commission believes that such varying circumstances do not warrant a variation among forms as to the periods to which primary financial statements relate.

Accordingly, the Commission in conjunction with the adoption of a uniform financial disclosure package, adopted uniform instructions as to periods to be covered by financial statements. These instructions require registrants to, among other things, provide audited statements of income and cash flows for three fiscal years and audited balance sheets as of the end of two fiscal years in most disclosure documents prepared under the securities acts. The Commission believes that the adoption of this uniform requirement will improve overall disclosure and simplify existing rules.

In response to comments questioning the benefits accruing from the third year's information and suggesting that such data is already available in previously filed documents, the Commission has reviewed its stated objectives for developing a uniform financial disclosure package. A principal objective of the uniform package is to provide enough data to satisfy the needs of most users desiring to make an informed judgment as to the financial well-being of an underlying issuer. It has been designed with the intention of providing users with easy access to sufficient data for an informed decision while refraining from requiring data in excess of the amount necessary to satisfy most users or data for which the costs of preparation cannot be justified by the benefits.

The decision to require statements of income and cash flows for three years is premised on the view that investors should be provided sufficient detail to analyze and understand a company's results of operations for at least the most recent two fiscal years. Since information for the immediately preceding year is needed to understand changes in operations for one year, comparative information for three years is necessary for an understanding of changes in operations for two years.

One of the Commission's principal intentions in developing the uniform financial disclosure package was to refocus the concentration of users to the financial statements as a whole. In the past, the results of operations was given greater emphasis than financial condition by separate display in a detailed summary of operations, which, in turn, was the exclusive focus of management's discussion and analysis. The Commission believes that, by eliminating the summary of operations, requiring the financial statements to cover results of operations for three years, and by refocusing management's discussion and analysis on the financial statements, users will concentrate more on the financial statements as a whole and be provided a more effective presentation.

102.04. Foreign Private Issuers

[*Sec. 102.04 added by FR-7.*]

The Commission is adopting various rules and forms relating to filings by foreign private issuers under the Securities Act of 1933 (the "Securities Act") [15 U.S.C. 77a et seq. (1976 and Supp. III 1979), and the Securities Exchange Act of 1934 (the "Exchange Act") [15 U.S.C. 78a et seq. (1976 and Supp. III 1979)]. This action constitutes the development of an integrated disclosure system for foreign private issuers. Recently, the Commission adopted an integrated disclosure system for United States ("U.S.") issuers.[1] These two systems are designed and intended to operate separately.

Specifically, the Commission has adopted: (1) three new registration forms, Forms F-1, F-2, and F-3 (17 CFR 239.31, 239.32 and 239.33) that will serve as the basic framework for the registration of securities by non-Canadian foreign private issuers under the Securities Act; (2) Rule 3-19 of Regulation S-X [17 CFR 210.3-19] relating to the age of financial statements included in filings of foreign private issuers; (3) Rule 3-20 of Regulation S-X [17 CFR 210.3-20] relating to the currency in which the financial statements of foreign private issuers should be presented; (4) various other rules and revisions to existing rules that are necessitated by the adoption of the forms and rules mentioned above or that clarify the requirements applicable to foreign private issuers.

The Commission solicited public comments on proposed rules and forms in Release Nos. 33-6360 (November 30, 1981), 33-6361 (November 20, 1981), and 33-6362 (November 20, 1981) [46 FR 58505]. Those releases contained detailed discussions of rules and forms and their development, including the Commission's rationale and objectives regarding various aspects of the integrated

disclosure system for foreign private issuers that such issuers may find relevant to an understanding of the Commission's requirements.[2] Rather than repeat those discussions, this release explains the differences from the proposals. Attention is directed to the discussion in the proposing releases and to the text of the rules and forms for a more complete understanding.

102.05 Issuer's Change of Fiscal Year

[Amended in Release No. 33-8644, effective December 27, 2005, 70 F.R. 76626. See section III.D of the release for compliance date information.]

Prior to the amendments, Rules 13a-10 and 15d-10 required an issuer changing its fiscal year end to file an "interim report" with the Commission containing financial and other information about the "interim period" from the end of the most recently concluded fiscal year to the opening date of the new fiscal year if that period covered three or more months. Such reports were required to be filed on the form used for the issuer's annual report.

To avoid confusion with other reports, such as quarterly reports, which commonly are referred to as interim reports, under the amendments, interim reports are referred to as "transition reports" and interim periods called "transition periods." The amendments also include the following substantive revisions:

(1) *Transition Reporting on Forms 10-Q and 10-K*

Separate transition reports are required for all transition periods, except those of one month or less. Issuers will continue to file a transition report on the annual reporting form, usually Form 10-K, including audited financial statements, for transition periods of six or more months. For a transition period shorter than six months, issuers are given an option to file a transition report on either Form 10-Q, including unaudited financial statements, or Form 10-K, including audited financial statements. Information for a transition period of one month or less may be included in the issuer's report on Form 10-Q for the first quarter of the newly adopted fiscal year that ends after the date on which the issuer determined to change its fiscal year, if separate audited statements of income and cash flows covering the transition period are filed with the first annual report for the newly adopted fiscal year. If the issuer's next report is the first annual report for the newly adopted fiscal year, instead of a quarterly report, a transition period of one month or less may be covered in that annual report.

---

[1] *See* Release Nos. 33-6383 (March 3, 1982), 33-6384 (March 3, 1982), 33-6385 (March 3, 1982), and 33-6386 (March 3, 1982) [47 FR 11380].

[2] See generally: Barbara S. Thomas, *Internationalization of the Securities Markets: An Empirical Analysis,* 50 Geo. Wash. L. Rev. 155 (1982) and an address by Thomas, *The Integrated Disclosure System for Foreign Issuers: An Introduction for Foreign Lawyers,* NYU School of Law (July 1981).

(2) Conforming the Filing Requirements of Transition Reports to the Current Requirements for Forms 10-Q and 10-K

To conform to the current filing periods for reports on Forms 10-K and 10-Q, the filing period for transition reports on Form 10-K is 60 days for large accelerated filers (75 days for fiscal years ending before December 15, 2006), 75 days for accelerated filers, and 90 days for other issuers after the close of the transition period or the date of the determination to change the fiscal year, whichever is later, and for transition reports on Form 10-Q, the filing period is 40 days for large accelerated filers and accelerated filers or 45 days for other issuers after the later of these two events.

(3) Codification of Staff Rule Interpretation of the Quarterly Reporting Requirements When an Issuer Changes Its Fiscal Year End

Consistent with staff practice, issuers will continue to have the option of filing quarterly reports for the transition period on the basis of either the old or new fiscal year. Also, consistent with staff rule interpretations, issuers, in most cases, will continue to be required to file a quarterly report for any quarter of the old fiscal year that ended before the date of the issuer's determination to change its year end. The amendments specify that the requirement to file quarterly reports on the new basis begins with the first quarter in the new fiscal year that ends after the issuer determined to change its year end.

(4) Clarification of Transition Reporting for Successor Issuers

Amendments to Rules 13a-10 and 15d-10 require transition reporting for all successor issuers, but only where they have a different fiscal year end from that of the predecessor. Successor issuers are required to file a transition report concerning the predecessor for any transition period between the close of the fiscal year covered by the last annual report of the predecessor and the date of succession. For a transition period of six or more months, the successor issuer must file the transition report on Form 10-K, including audited financial statements. For a transition period of less than six months, the successor issuer may opt instead to file the transition report on Form 10-Q, including unaudited financial statements. Just as for changes in fiscal year, where the transition period is one month or less, the successor issuer need not file a separate transition report, provided that the required information for the transition period is contained in a subsequent quarterly report, or if the next report is an annual report, in that annual report.

(5) Separate Transition Reporting Rules for Foreign Private Issuers

Separate provisions require a foreign private issuer with a transition period longer than six months to file a Form 20-F containing responses to all items required when the Form is used as an annual report, and including audited financial statements. For a transition period of six or fewer months, a foreign private issuer may opt instead to file a transition report on Form 20-F that includes responses to only a limited number of specified items and unaudited financial statements. Where the transition period is one month or less, a foreign private issuer is not required to file a separate transition report if the first annual report for the newly adopted fiscal year covers the transition period as well as the fiscal year.

(6) Reporting a Change in Fiscal Year on Form 8-K

New Item 8 of Form 8-K requires an issuer to report its new fiscal year end, the Form (10-K or 10-Q) on which the report covering the transition period will be filed, and the date of the determination to change its fiscal year end. The Form 8-K must be filed within 15 days after that date.

(7) Specific Provisions Regarding Filing Fees and Extensions of Time

No filing fee is required for transition reports. Amended Rule 12b-25 and amended Form 12b-25 add transition reports to those reports for which an extension of time for filing is available.

(8) Separate Rule for Transition Reporting of Investment Companies

New Investment Company Act Rule 30b1-3 provides transition reporting requirements specifically tailored to the semi-annual and annual reporting obligations of investment companies. The new Rule codifies the staff practice of requiring investment companies that change their fiscal year end to file a report on Form N-SAR within 60 days of either the close of the resulting transition period or the date of the determination to change the fiscal year end, whichever is later.

(9) Codification of Staff Practice of Permitting Reliance on Nine Months Statements

New accounting Rule 3-06 and a parallel note to Rule 14a-3(b)(1)[22] of the proxy rules codify the staff practice of accepting, under specified circumstances such as a change in fiscal year, financial statements covering a nine to 12 month period in satisfaction of a requirement for financial statements for either one year or one year of a multiple year period.

(10) Codification of Staff Practice on Age of Audited Financial Statements in a First-Time Registrant's Registration Statement

To assure that timely financial statements for first-time registrants are available, amended accounting Rule 3-12 codifies the staff practice of requiring that the most recent audited financial

---

[22] 17 CFR 240.14a-3(b)(1).

statements in a registration statement under the Securities Act of 1933 ("Securities Act")[23] or on Form 10[24] filed by a non-reporting company be no more than one year and 45 days old.

(11) *Period to be Covered by First Report on Form 10-Q for First-Time Registrants*

To avoid reporting gaps, amended Rule 13a-13 and 15d-13 governing quarterly reporting require a new registrant to file its first report on Form 10-Q for the first fiscal quarter following the most recent fiscal year or full quarter for which financial statements were included in its registration statement.

Examples illustrating the application of the amendments to typical reporting situations are contained in the Appendix in Part V of this Release. The example have been modified where appropriate to reflect changes from the proposals.

Appendix

Preliminary Note: The following examples are applicable if the issuer is neither a large accelerated filer nor an accelerated filer. If the issuer is a large accelerated filer, substitute 60 days (75 days for fiscal years ending before December 15, 2006) for 90 days in the examples for transition reports on Form 10-K, and substitute 40 days for 45 days in the examples for transition reports on Form 10-Q. If the issuer is an accelerated filer, substitute 75 days for 90 days in the examples for transition reports on Form 10-K, and substitute 40 days for 45 days in the examples for transition reports on Form 10-Q.

1. *Examples of Reporting Under the Amendments for a Domestic Issuer with a Dec. 31 year End that Files Periodic Reports Pursuant to Section 13 or 15(d) of the Exchange Act*

a. *Decision made early in year to change year end to date already past with resulting transition period of one month or less:*

On March 1, 1990 the issuer decides to change year end to Jan. 31, 1990

—15 days after March 1, 1990 files an 8-K

—90 days after Dec. 31, 1989 files a 10-K covering full year from Jan. 1, 1989 through Dec. 31, 1989

—At the option of the issuer, it may file a separate transition report on Form 10-Q 45 days after March 1, 1990 covering the transition period from Jan. 1, 1990 through Jan. 31, 1990

—At the option of the issuer, it may file a separate transition report on Form 10-K 90 days after March 1, 1990 covering the transition period from Jan. 1, 1990 through Jan. 31, 1990

—45 days after April 30, 1990 files a 10-Q covering the first quarter ending April 30, 1990 of the new fiscal year; if the issuer has not opted to file a separate transition report on either Form 10-Q or 10-K, the 10-Q for the quarter ending April 30,

1990 must cover the transition period from Jan. 1, 1990 through Jan. 31, 1990 and include separate financial statements, which may be unaudited, for the transition period from Jan. 1, 1990 through Jan. 31, 1990

—45 days after July 31, 1990 and Oct. 31, 1990 files 10-Qs covering the quarters ending July 31, 1990 and Oct. 31, 1990 of the new fiscal year, respectively

—90 days after Jan. 31, 1991 files a 10-K covering the full year from Feb. 1, 1990 through Jan. 31, 1991, with regular timing of quarterly and annual reporting continuing thereafter; if the issuer filed a separate transition report on Form 10-Q or the transition period information was included in the 10-Q for the quarter ending April 30, 1990, the 10-K must include separated audited financial statements covering the transition period from Jan. 1, 1990 through Jan. 31, 1990

b. *Decision made early in year to change year end to date already past with resulting transition period shorter than six months but longer than one month:*

On March 1, 1990 the issuer decides to change year end to Feb. 28, 1990

—15 days after March 1, 1990 files an 8-K

—90 days after Dec. 31, 1989 files a 10-K covering full year from Jan. 1, 1989 through Dec. 31, 1989

—Either 45 days after March 1, 1990 files a transition report on Form 10-Q or 90 days after March 1, 1990 files a transition report on Form 10-K covering the transition period from Jan. 1, 1990 through Feb. 28, 1990

—45 days after May 31, 1990 files a 10-Q covering the first quarter ending May 31, 1990 of the new fiscal year, with regular timing of quarterly and annual reporting continuing thereafter; if the transition report was filed on Form 10-Q, the 10-K covering the full year from March 1, 1990 through Feb. 28, 1991 must include separate audited financial statements covering the transition period from Jan. 1, 1990 through Feb. 28, 1990

c. *Decision made early in year to change year end to future date with resulting transition period shorter than six months but longer than one month:*

On Feb. 1, 1990 the issuer decides to change year end to May 31, 1990

—15 days after Feb. 1, 1990 files an 8-K

—90 days after Dec. 31, 1989 files a 10-K covering full year from Jan. 1, 1989 through Dec. 31, 1989

—Either 45 days after Feb. 28, 1990 files a 10-Q covering the period ending Feb. 28, 1990 coinciding with a quarter of the new fiscal year or 45 days after March 31, 1990 files a 10-Q covering the quarter ending March 31, 1990 of the old fiscal year.

---

[23] 15 U.S.C. 77a *et seq.*

[24] 17 CFR 249.210.

—Either 45 days after May 31, 1990 files a transition report on Form 10-Q or 90 days after May 31, 1990 files a transition report on Form 10-K covering the transition period from Jan. 1, 1990 through May 31, 1990

—45 days after Aug. 31, 1990 files a 10-Q covering the first quarter ending Aug. 31, 1990 of the new fiscal year, with regular timing of quarterly and annual reporting continuing thereafter; if the transition report was filed on Form 10-Q, the 10-K covering the full year from June 1, 1990 the 10-K covering the full year from June 1, 1990 through May 31, 1991 would include separate audited financial statements covering the transition period from Jan. 1, 1990 through May 31, 1990

d. *Decision made early in year to change year end to future date with resulting transition period six months or longer:*

On Feb. 1, 1990 the issuer decides to change year end to Sept. 30, 1990

—15 days after Feb. 1, 1990 files an 8-K

—90 days after Dec. 31, 1989 files a 10-K covering the full year from Jan. 1, 1989 Dec. 31, 1989

—45 days after March 31, 1990 and June 30, 1990 files 10-Qs covering the quarters ending March 31, 1990 and June 30, 1990, respectively

90 days after Sept. 30, 1990 files a transition report on Form 10-K covering the transition period from Jan. 1, 1990 through Sept. 30, 1990

—45 days after Dec. 31, 1990 files a 10-Q covering the first quarter ending Dec. 31, 1990 of the new fiscal year, with regular timing of quarterly and annual reporting continuing thereafter

e. *Decision made late in year to change year end to date already past with resulting transition period of one month or less:*

On Sept. 1, 1990 the issuer decides to change year end to Jan. 31, 1990

—15 days after Sept. 1, 1990 files an 8-K

—At the option of the issuer, it may file a separate transition report on Form 10-Q 45 days after Sept. 1, 1990 covering the transition period from Jan. 1, 1990 through Jan. 31, 1990

—at the option of the issuer, it may file a separate transition report on Form 10-K 90 days after Sept. 1, 1990 covering the transition period from Jan. 1, 1990 through Jan. 31, 1990

—45 days after Oct. 31, 1990 files a 10-Q covering the quarter ending Oct. 31, 1990 of the new fiscal year; if the issuer has not opted to file a separate transition report on either Form 10-Q or 10-K, the 10-Q for the quarter ending Oct. 31, 1990 must cover the transition period from Jan. 1, 1990 and include separate financial statements, which may be unaudited, covering the transition period from Jan. 1, 1990 through Jan. 31, 1990; the 10-Q for the quarter ending Oct. 31, 1990 also must cover and include separate financial statements for the period from July 1, 1990 through July 31, 1990

—90 days after Jan. 31, 1991 files a 10-K covering the full year from Feb. 1, 1990 through Jan. 31, 1991, with regular timing of quarterly and annual reporting continuing thereafter; if the issuer filed a separate transition report on Form 10-Q or the transition period information was included in the 10-Q for the quarter ending Oct. 31, 1990, the 10-K must include audited financial statement covering the transition period from Jan. 1, 1990 through Jan. 31, 1990

f. *Decision made late in year to change year end to date already past with resulting transition period shorter than six months but longer than one month:*

On Nov. 1, 1990 the issuer decides to change year end to Feb. 28, 1990

—45 days after Sept. 30, 1990 files a 10-Q covering the quarter ending Sept. 30, 1990 of the old fiscal year

—15 days after Nov. 1, 1990 files an 8-K

—Either 45 days after Nov. 1, 1990 files a transition report on Form 10-Q or 90 days after Nov. 1, 1990 files a transition report on Form 10-K covering the transition period from Jan. 1, 1990 through Feb. 28, 1990

—45 days after Nov. 30, 1990 files a 10-Q covering the quarter ending Nov. 30, 1990 of the new fiscal year

—90 days after Feb. 28 1991 files a 10-K covering the full year from March 1, 1990 through Feb. 28, 1991, with regular timing of quarterly and annual reporting continuing thereafter; if the transition report was filed on Form 10-Q, the 10-K must include separate audited financial statements covering the transition period from Jan. 1, 1990 through Feb. 28, 1990

g. *Decision made late in year to change year end to date already past with resulting transition period six months or longer:*

On Nov. 1, 1990 the issuer decides to change year end to Sept. 30, 1990

—15 days after Nov. 1, 1990 files an 8-K

—90 days after Nov. 1, 1990 files a transition report on Form 10-K covering the transition period from Jan. 1, 1990 through Sept. 30, 1990

—45 days after Dec. 31, 1990 files a 10-Q covering the first quarter ending Dec. 31, 1990 of the new fiscal year, with regular timing of quarterly and annual reporting continuing thereafter

h. *Decision made late in year to change year end to date already past with resulting transition period six months or longer where fiscal quarters of newly adopted year do not coincide with those of old fiscal year:*

On Nov. 20, 1990 the issuer decides to change year end to Aug. 31, 1990

—15 days after Nov. 20, 1990 files an 8-K

—45 days after Nov. 30, 1990 files a 10-Q covering the first quarter ending Nov. 30, 1990 of the new fiscal year

—90 days after Nov. 20, 1990 files a transition report on Form 10-K covering the transition period from Jan. 1, 1990 through Aug. 31, 1990, with regular timing of quarterly and annual reporting continuing thereafter

2. Examples of Reporting Under the Amendments for the Successor Issuer that has a Fiscal Year Different from the December 31 Year End of the Predecessor

a. Succession with resulting transition period shorter than six months but longer than one month:

The date of succession is April 30, 1990

—15 days after April 30, 1990 files an 8-K

—Either 45 days after April 30, 1990 files a transition report regarding the predecessor on Form 10-Q or 90 days after April 30, 1990 files a transition report regarding the predecessor on Form 10-K covering the transition period from Jan. 1, 1990 through April 30, 1990

—If the transition report was filed on Form 10-Q, the next annual report of the successor issuer must include audited statements of income and cash flows for the transition period

b. Succession with resulting transition period six months or longer:

The date of succession is July 31, 1990

—15 days after July 31, 1990 files an 8-K

—90 days after July 31, 1990 files a transition report regarding the predecessor on Form 10-K covering the transition period from Jan. 1, 1990 through July 31, 1990

3. Examples of Reporting Under the Amendments for a Management Investment Company Issuer With a December 31 Year End that Changes is Fiscal Year

a. On Feb. 1, 1990 decides to change the year end to April 30

—60 days after April 30 files Form N-SAR covering the period from Jan. 1 to April 30

b. On Feb. 1, 1990 decides to change the year end to Sept. 30

—60 days after March 31 files Form N-SAR covering the period from Jan. 1 to March 31

b. On Feb. 1, 1990 decides to change the year end to Sept. 30

—60 days after March 31 files Form N-SAR covering the period from Jan. 1 to March 31

c. On April 1, 1990 decides to change the year end to Jan. 31

—60 days after April 1 files Form N-SAR covering the period from Jan. 1 to Jan. 31

d. On Oct 1, 1990 decides to change the year end to Nov. 30

—60 days after Nov. 30 files Form N-SAR covering the period from July 1 to Nov. 30

e. On Nov. 1, 1990 decides to change the year end to Jan. 31

—60 days after Nov. 1 files Form N-SAR covering the period from July 1 to July 31

f. On Nov. 1, 1990 decides to change the year end to Sept. 30

—60 days after Nov. 1 files Form N-SAR covering the period from July 1 to Sept. 30

[¶ 38,035] Sec. 103. Staff Accounting Bulletins
ASR 180:

In November 1975, the Commission announced the institution of a series of SABs intended to achieve a wider dissemination of the administrative interpretations and practices utilized by the Commission's staff in reviewing financial statements. The Division of Corporation Finance and the Office of the Chief Accountant began the series with the publication of Bulletin No. 1. The statements in the Bulletin are not rules or interpretations of the Commission nor are they published as bearing the Commission's official approval; they represent interpretations and practices followed by the Division and the Chief Accountant in administering the disclosure requirements of the Federal securities laws.

The process of financial reporting is dynamic and evolutionary. Consequently, new or revised administrative interpretations and practices must be implemented in response to changes in the reporting process. While large accounting firms who practice before the Commission have many opportunities to exchange information and views with the staff, the Commission has been concerned about comments that small accounting firms have fewer such opportunities and may be at an unfair competitive disadvantage because there has been no formal dissemination of staff positions.

The announced series of bulletins attempts to curtail these problems by making available to the public a compilation of certain existing staff interpretations and practices and by providing a means by which new or revised interpretations and practices can be quickly and easily communicated to registrants and their advisors. Thus, this series should not only reduce the staff's workload by eliminating repetitive comments and inquiries but also save registrants both time and money in the registration and reporting process.

All interested persons are invited to submit their views and comments on the administration of these interpretations and practices to the Chief Accountant of the Division of Corporation Finance; and on the policies reflected therein to the Chief Accountant of the Commission.

[On January 23, 1981, the Commission's staff issued SAB 40 which updated and codified the material included in Bulletins 1-38.]

[¶ 38,036] Sec. 104. The Significance of Oral Guarantees to the Financial Reporting Process
[Sec. 104 added by FRR-23.]
a. Background.

During the course of a private investigation, the Commission learned that an issuer engaged in schemes to manipulate and materially overstate its earnings and financial position. As a result of these schemes, the issuer materially overstated its income and net assets. These material misstatements were not discovered by the issuer's independent auditor, in part, because a bank responding to an audit confirmation request from the issuer's independent auditors failed to report a material oral guarantee.

One of the schemes to defraud in this matter involved the improper removal of a substantial amount of assets from the balance sheet of a foreign subsidiary of the issuer by means of a purported sale of such assets to an unrelated foreign company. The scheme was effected in order to raise cash to improve the subsidiary's debt-to-equity ratio. However, no sale occurred under generally accepted accounting principles ("GAAP") because the risks of ownership never passed to the unrelated foreign company. The issuer's subsidiary was obligated, by side letters and oral agreements, to repurchase an amount of assets sufficient to enable the unrelated foreign company to pay its debt incurred in purchasing the "sold" assets.

In order to obtain financing for the transaction, the unrelated foreign company sought standby letters of credit from several banks. In an effort to assist the unrelated foreign company in obtaining the standby letters of credit, the issuer told the banks it would issue comfort letters stating that the issuer had full knowledge of the obligations of its subsidiary arising from its agreement with the unrelated foreign company. A senior financial executive, with the approval of his superior, assured a representative of one bank that the issuer viewed its comfort letter as a guarantee. In making the decision to extend credit, the bank relied upon, among other things, the issuer's oral guarantee. However, the bank did not report the existence of the guarantee to the issuer's independent auditor in response to an audit confirmation request for information regarding guarantees, liabilities or other third party obligations. The bank's failure to respond accurately to the audit confirmation request caused, in part, the filing of financial statements with the Commission which were materially false and misleading.

b. Discussion.

As a result of this private investigation, the Commission believes that the conduct and procedures of certain banks in responding to audit confirmation requests may impair the integrity of the financial reporting process, insofar as certain banks may be failing to report the existence of oral guarantees that may affect an issuer's financial statements.

The audit process generally involves the issuer's independent auditor confirming, with banks and other lending institutions ("financial institutions"), the existence and amount of account balances, loans and contingent liabilities, including guarantees, among other items. Additionally, auditors routinely confirm financial information with other entities that have business relationships with the issuer. The Commission is concerned that financial institutions and other entities which respond to such audit confirmation requests may fail to include information concerning contingent liabilities created by oral guarantees. These failures may be due to, among other things, lack of an adequate system for recording such contingent liabilities, a failure to understand that oral guarantees may create contingent liabilities, or an agreement to honor a borrower's request for confidential treatment.

In particular, the above-referenced Commission investigation revealed that a senior financial executive of the issuer told representatives of a large New York bank that the issuer viewed its comfort letter, provided in connection with the bank's extension of credit to an unrelated foreign company, as a guarantee. The executive further informed the bank, in substance, that in the event of a default by the unrelated foreign company, the issuer would make sure that the bank was paid and did not lose money on the transaction. The executive made it clear that his oral guarantee to the bank was a representation made on behalf of the issuer's senior management. In making the decision to extend credit, the bank relied upon the issuer's oral guarantee. However, the bank did not report the existence of the oral guarantee to the issuer's independent auditor in the bank's response to a subsequent audit confirmation request. The fact that an oral guarantee was given to the bank was not disclosed for at least two reasons. First, bank officers failed to consider whether the oral guarantee was an item which required disclosure on the audit confirmation request. Additionally, information of material significance concerning the issuance of the oral guarantee was routinely retained by the loan officers responsible for the issuer's account and was not placed in the central credit files. Such information was not accessible to the department that had primary responsibility for answering audit confirmation requests. As a result of the failure to report that an oral guarantee had been provided to the bank, the bank returned a false and misleading response to the audit confirmation request. The false and misleading response contributed to the issuer's failure to properly account for this transaction, the failure of the issuer's independent auditor to discover the improprieties in the issuer's financial statements, and therefore to the issuer's filing with the Commission materially false and misleading financial statements.

The Commission believes that it is critical that financial institutions and other entities which receive audit confirmation requests maintain a system by which information of material significance concerning guarantees and other contingent liabilities is available to those persons responding to audit confirmation requests and employ reasonable procedures to keep such information current, accurate and complete. Failure to maintain such a system may prevent auditors from receiving all information of material significance to the audit of the issuer's financial statements.

Even though representatives of the bank conceded that, in deciding to extend credit, the bank relied upon, among other things, the issuer's guarantees, representatives of both the issuer and the bank argued, as a matter of contract law, that oral guarantees were not legally binding under applicable state law and that only legally binding guarantees should be reported in reponse to an audit confirmation request. However, the Commission, is of the view that, depending upon the facts and circumstances, oral guarantees, even if legally unenforceable, may have the same financial reporting significance as written guarantees. Statement of Financial Accounting Standards No. 5, paragraph 12, states that material undertakings which in substance have the characteristics of a guarantee should be disclosed in financial statements.

Thus, whether oral or written, a material commitment which is in substance a guarantee should be reported. One factor, among others, in determining whether statements made by an issuer constitute an oral guarantee which should be reported is whether the financial institution relied upon the statements in making the decision to extend credit.

Guarantees and guarantees-in-substance can affect the accounting treatment for transactions. For example, Statement of Financial Accounting Standards No. 49 includes guarantees as indicia that a product financing arrangement is a borrowing rather than a sale. Therefore, financial institutions and other entities should report those oral arrangements which constitute guarantees-in-substance in response to an audit confirmation request.

Summary.

Based upon the applicable accounting literature, the Commission believes that oral statements, which are in substance guarantees, are contingent liabilities which may, under certain circumstances, require disclosure. They may also have material significance in accounting for transactions. The Commission emphasizes that the substance of oral agreements should be considered by financial institutions and others in completing audit confirmations. Agreements which in substance constitute guarantees should be reported in response to an audit confirmation request.

The audit process is central to the Commission's financial reporting requirements and to the full and fair disclosure policy underlying the federal securities laws. The inability of an independent auditor to obtain material audit evidence interferes with the audit of the issuer's financial statements. Financial institutions and other entities which provide information to auditors, such as audit confirmations, should provide accurate and complete information. Additionally, auditors should take steps to ensure that audit confirmations clearly request information necessary to the proper conduct of their audit responsibilities.

[¶ 38,037] Sec. 105. Consolidated Financial Statements of the Registrant and its Subsidiaries

[Sec. 105 added by FR-25.]

a. FASB Consolidations Projects.

The FASB presently has a major project on its agenda on Consolidations and the Equity Method which is dealing with a host of issues in the consolidations area. The amendment of Rule 3A-02 is consistent with present GAAP and does not impact the FASB's major project. The Commission is supportive of the FASB's efforts to address these important issues.

b. Definitive Guidance

Several commentators stated the belief that registrants should be given additional guidance to aid in determination of when an entity should be consolidated with a registrant. They believed this could be done by setting forth criteria that may be indicative of the need to consolidate or alternatively, by including examples from recent enforcement actions in the adopting release. Some commentators also suggested a companion staff accounting bulletin to provide implementation guidance.

Rule 3A-02, as amended, does not list specific criteria that need to be considered in determining whether an entity should be consolidated. Rather, it emphasizes the need to consider substance over form to determine appropriate consolidation policy. Such determination requires the use of judgment by registrants and their independent accountants.

The Commission believes it would be difficult to develop an all-inclusive list of criteria because of the variety of possible facts and circumstances encountered in practice. Additionally, development by the Commission of definitive factors would represent a major rulemaking initiative that could directly compete with the FASB's efforts in this area.

The amendment of Rule 3A-02 is being made to bring the language of the rule in line with the way it has been applied by the Commission and by registrants generally. Notwithstanding releases which have indicated the Commission's view that the overriding requirement of the rule is to clearly exhibit the financial position and operating results of a company and its subsidiaries, the wording of the rule prior to amendment was an impediment to an understanding of the Commission's position on consolidations. The intent and scope of this amendment is to remove this impediment and to capture the Commission's position in Regulation S-X. Any further guidance is not deemed necessary at this time.

c. Rescission of Rule 3A-02

Several commentators suggested rescission of Rule 3A-02 on the theory that the Rule, as amended, is duplicative of GAAP. The Commission, however, believes it is preferable to amend the rule. The language of the Rule, while consistent with ARB No. 51, is more explicit than GAAP because it specifically addresses the possible need to consolidate a less than majority owned subsidiary, and it states the possible need to employ the equity method or a valuation allowance to achieve a fair presentation.

SECTION 200—ANNUAL FINANCIAL STATEMENTS

[¶ 38,041] 201. Business Combinations

»»→ *Section 201.01 removed and reserved in FR-79, effective April 23, 2009, 74 F.R. 18612.*

.01. Risk-Sharing in Business Combinations Accounted for as Pooling-of-Interests

ASR 130:

The Commission noted an increasing number of business combinations which appeared to meet the individual requirements for pooling-of-interests accounting set forth in APBO 16 but which did not conform with the overriding thrust of that Opinion which requires that a combination represent a sharing of rights and risks among constituent stockholder groups if it is to be a pooling of interests. Paragraphs 28, 45 and 47 of that Opinion clearly provide that such a sharing of risk is an essential element in poolings, and the specific requirements set forth in paragraphs 46, 47 and 48 should certainly not be construed as a formula which, if followed with precision, may be used to overcome an essential concept which underlies the entire Opinion. Despite the clarity of the Opinion in articulating the need for a sharing of risk, a number of registrants and their auditors proposed to account for combinations which did not meet this basic requirement as poolings.

Accordingly, the Commission concluded that any confusion regarding this matter should be laid to rest. It is the Commission's understanding that the APB authorized its staff to issue an interpretation [Interpretation No. 37 of APBO 16, issued November, 1972] providing that a business combination should be accounted for as a purchase if its consummation is contingent upon the purchase by a third party of any of the common stocks to be issued. Including such a contingency in the arrangement of the combination, either explicitly or by intent, would be considered a financial arrangement which is precluded in a pooling under APBO 16. The Commission endorses this interpretation.

As a matter of policy, the Commission believes that it is unwise to set forth absolute rules in such an accounting matter which will be followed regardless of all other factual situations which may surround a particular transaction. To do so would be to encourage the application of form over substance. Nevertheless, it appears reasonable for the Commission to establish guidelines which it will use in making determinations as to disposition of various individual cases brought before it and to make these guidelines known to registrants and independent public accountants.

ASR 135:

The Commission will henceforth consider that the risk sharing required for the applicability of pooling-of-interests accounting will have occurred if no affiliate of either company in the business combination sells or in any other way reduces his risk relative to any common shares received in the business combination until such time as financial results covering at least 30 days of post-merger combined operations have been published. This would include all sales whether private or public. Publication of combined financial results can take the form of a post-effective amendment, a Form 10-Q or 8-K filing, the issuance of a quarterly earnings report, or any other public issuance which includes combined sales and net income.

ASR 130:

This policy is not intended to restrict sale of stock at the option of the stockholders subsequent to the pooling as long as a sharing of risks for the period of time indicated above has taken place. An arrangement to register shares subsequent to the combination would therefore not bar pooling. However, an agreement which requires sale of shares after such a period would preclude pooling treatment as would any agreement to reduce the risk borne by the stockholders subsequent to the transaction.

201.02. Effect of Treasury Stock Transactions

»»→ *Section 201.02 removed and reserved in FR-79, effective April 23, 2009, 74 F.R. 18612.*

.a General

ASR 146:

APBO 16 identifies certain conditions which must be present (or in some cases absent) if a business combination is to be accounted for as a pooling of interests. Two of these conditions, which are set forth in paragraphs 47-c and 47-d, include provisions related to the reacquisition of voting common stock within two years prior to initiation and between initiation and consummation of a business combination which is planned to be accounted for by the pooling-of-interests method. The Commission observed that these provisions were subject to varying interpretations in practice, and concluded that certain of these interpretations are not compatible with concepts underlying the Opinion. Accordingly, the Commission set forth its conclusions as to certain problems relating to the effect of treasury stock transactions on accounting for business combinations.

When cash or other assets are used or liabilities are incurred to effect a business combination, APBO 16 concludes that the combination should be accounted for as a purchase. This concept might be circumvented if cash or other assets were used or liabilities were incurred to reacquire common shares and common shares were then exchanged to consummate the combination. Therefore, for the pooling-of-interests method to apply, paragraph 47-c of the Opinion requires that "none on the combining companies changes the equity interest of the voting common stock in contemplation of effecting the combination either within two years before the plan of combination is initiated or between the dates the combination is initiated and consummated; . . . ." Further, paragraph 47-d stipulates that "each of the combining companies [may reacquire] shares of voting common stock only for purposes other than business combinations . . . ."

In some cases, it is difficult to determine the purposes of treasury stock acquisitions. An AICPA Accounting Interpretation of APBO 16 (No. 20 issued September 1971) states: "In the absence of persuasive evidence to the contrary, however, it should be presumed that all acquisitions of treasury stock during the two years preceding the date a plan of combination is initiated . . . and between initiation and consummation were made in contemplation of effecting business combinations to be accounted for as a pooling of interests. Thus, lacking such evidence, this combination would be accounted for by the purchase method regardless of whether treasury stock or unissued shares or both are issued in the combination." The Commission believes that this presumption and conclusion should be followed.

In determining the purposes of treasury stock acquisitions, it is ordinarily appropriate to focus on the intended subsequent distribution of common shares rather than on the business reasons for acquiring treasury shares. For example, shares may be reacquired because management believes the company is overcapitalized or considers that "the price is right," but such reasons do not overcome the presumption that they were acquired in contemplation of effecting business combinations to be accounted for as poolings of interests. On the other hand, the presumption may be overcome when shares are acquired for a specific use unrelated to business combinations, such as stock option or purchase plans or stock dividends, are associated with a combination accounted for as a

purchase, or are acquired to resolve an existing contingent share agreement. However, the mere assertion that common shares are reacquired for such purposes, even where the assertion is formalized by action of the board of directors reserving the treasury shares, does not provide persuasive evidence that they were not reacquired in contemplation of pooling-of-interests combinations. If a resolution of the board of directors or other statement of intent were sufficient to provide persuasive contrary evidence, the restrictions on treasury stock acquisitions would be totally ineffective. Accordingly, while a board resolution made prior to acquisition of treasury shares may be useful evidence as to corporate intent, reference also must be made to the actual or probable issuance of shares for purposes unrelated to pooling-of-interests business combinations.

When treasury shares are acquired during a period beginning two years prior to initiation and ending at the date of consummation of a business combination to be accounted for as a pooling of interests (hereinafter referred to as the "restricted period"), the issuance of an equivalent number of shares prior to the date of consummation would generally provide persuasive evidence that the treasury shares were not acquired in contemplation of the combination. The shares issued may be treasury shares or previously unissued shares since, with regard to the equity interests of the common shareholders, there is no substantive difference between the two. Thus, a company might "cure" a condition which would preclude pooling-of-interests accounting by selling common shares prior to consummation of the combination. The "cure" could not be effected by merely retiring treasury shares.

Paragraph 47-d of APBO 16 includes the statement that "treasury stock acquired for purposes other than business combinations includes shares for stock option and compensation plans and other recurring distributions provided a systematic pattern of reacquisitions is established at least two years before the plan of combination is initiated." Further, "a systematic pattern of reacquisitions may be established for less than two years if it coincides with the adoption of a new stock option or compensation plan." In AICPA Accounting Interpretation No. 20 of APBO 16, no reference is made to a systematic pattern of reacquisition, and some accountants have asserted that this test has been effectively superseded. The Commission does not accept this assertion. Accordingly, the Commission concludes that treasury shares acquired in the restricted period for recurring distributions should be considered "tainted" unless they are acquired in a systematic pattern of reacquisitions established at least two years before the plan of combination is initiated (or coincidentally with the adoption of a new stock option or compensation plan) and there is reasonable expectation that shares will be issued for such purposes.

A systematic pattern of reacquisitions might be demonstrated by the reacquisition of a specified number of shares in successive time periods, e.g., 1,000 shares per month. A systematic pattern might also be demonstrated where, pursuant to a formal reacquisition plan, shares are acquired based on specified criteria such as the market price of the stock and cash availability. The criteria of the reacquisition plan must be sufficiently explicit so that the pattern of reacquisitions may be objectively compared to the plan. Unanticipated interruptions caused by legal constraints on a company's ability to reacquire shares would not upset an otherwise systematic pattern of reacquisition.

The determinations of whether there is reasonable expectation that shares will be issued for the stated purposes of acquiring the shares is a matter of judgment. Generally, there would appear to be such reasonable expectation where the following circumstances exist at the time a reacquisition plan is adopted or shares are reacquired:

1. As to stock option plans, warrants or convertible securities, the quoted price of the common shares is not less than 75 percent of the exercise or conversion price.

2. As to stock purchase or bonus plans or stock dividends, either (a) shares are reacquired to fulfill existing commitments or dividends declared or (b) based on a pattern of issuing shares for such purposes in the prior two years, the shares are reacquired to fulfill anticipated requirements in the succeeding year.

A systematic pattern of reacquisitions test would not apply to treasury shares acquired for issuance in a specific "purchase" business combination or to resolve an existing contingent share agreement from a prior business combination, as these issuances would not be regarded as recurring distributions. Thus, shares acquired and reserved for these purposes at the date a pooling-of-interests business combination is consummated would not be regarded as "tainted" when, based on current negotiations, presently existing earnings levels or market price of shares, etc., there is reasonable expectation that shares will be issued for the stated purposes.

APBO 16 does not discuss treasury share acquisitions subsequent to consummation of a business combination. In specific fact situations, subsequent reacquisitions may be so closely related to the prior combination that they should be considered part of the combination plan. Thus, significant reacquisitions closely following a combination which otherwise qualifies as a pooling of interests may invalidate the applicability of that method. Conversely, significant reacquisitions following a combination accounted for as a purchase might be associated with that purchase

and would not adversely affect subsequent pooling combinations.

ASR 146-A:

On October 5, 1973, in Securities Act Release 5429, the Commission requested comments on the substance of ASR 146 and stated that until these comments were considered the Commission would accept filings from registrants using principles of accounting for business combinations in accordance with practice deemed acceptable by public accountants prior to ASR 146. Comments were received from numerous individuals, companies and groups.

After considering these comments, the Commission concluded that the statement of policy set forth in ASR 146 represents a proper interpretation of APBO 16 which deals with accounting for business combinations.

A number of comment letters indicated a need for the clarification of certain aspects of ASR 146. The following interpretive comments are designed to guide registrants and their independent public accountants.

201.02.b. Purpose of Acquisition of Shares

⟫→ Section 201.02 removed and reserved in FR-79, effective April 23, 2009, 74 F.R. 18612.

ASR 146-A:

In determining the purposes of treasury stock acquisitions, it is *ordinarily* appropriate to focus on the intended subsequent distribution of shares, e.g., exercise of options, conversion of preferred stock, etc. APBO 16, AICPA Accounting Interpretation No. 20 thereof, and ASR 146 all discuss and emphasize subsequent distribution in assessing purpose of acquisition. It must be recognized, however, that circumstances may exist where a company is obliged by contract to reacquire specific shares or must reacquire specific shares to settle outstanding claims. For example, reacquisition might be made to (1) comply with an agreement to purchase stock upon the death of a stockholder, (2) settle a claim or lawsuit involving alleged misrepresentation or other acts relating to the original issuance of stock, (3) repossess stock pledged as collateral for a receivable or other contractual obligation, and (4) repurchase stock from employees pursuant to contractual rights or obligations. Such contracts or claims provide persuasive evidence that resulting reacquisitions were not made in contemplation of a business combination to be treated as a pooling of interests. Accordingly, unless it appears that such rights or obligations are contrived to skirt the requirements of APBO 16, resulting reacquisitions would not result in "tainted" shares.

201.02.c. Reasonable Expectation of Reissuance

⟫→ Section 201.02 removed and reserved in FR-79, effective April 23, 2009, 74 F.R. 18612.

ASR 146-A:

Many of those commenting on ASR 146 expressed concern that the guidelines relating to reasonable expectation of issuance of shares for stock option plans, warrants or convertible securities, i.e., the quoted price of common shares is not less than 75 percent of the exercise or conversion price, would be applied as an immutable rule. The Commission does not intend that this guideline be a rule. Reasonable expectation is a matter of judgment. Some of the other factors which may affect that judgment are the volatility of quoted prices, the remaining time period before conversion or exercise rights expire, and price and earnings trends. The Commission intends that the 75 percent guideline be viewed as a presumption which may be rebutted by relevant, probative evidence.

201.02.d. Acquisitions Subsequent to Consummation

»»→ Section 201.02 removed and reserved in FR-79, effective April 23, 2009, 74 F.R. 18612.

ASR 146-A:

Several of those commenting on ASR 146 were concerned about the lack of specific guidelines for determining when there are "significant reacquisitions closely following a combination." The Commission does not intend to establish an additional criterion for determining the accounting treatment of a business combination. Rather, it intended simply to caution registrants and auditors that the substance of reacquisitions closely following consummation of a combination should not be ignored. For example, if a company wished to replace untainted shares issued in a purchase by acquiring an equivalent number of shares closely following its consummation, such shares would not be tainted. Conversely, if an enterprise were to complete a pooling and very short time thereafter repurchase an equivalent number of shares, such a purchase could affect the status of the combination and bar pooling accounting.

201.02.e. Materiality

»»→ Section 201.02 removed and reserved in FR-79, effective April 23, 2009, 74 F.R. 18612.

ASR 146-A:

AICPA Interpretation No. 20 of APBO 16 indicates that the presence of "tainted" treasury shares will not preclude pooling-of-interests accounting if the number of shares is not material in relation to the total number of shares issued to effect the combination. In practice, "tainted" shares are apparently being considered together with other items under paragraph 47-b. This would limit "tainted" shares to a maximum of 10% of the total number of shares issued to effect the combination. ASR 146 does not address this matter because practice appears reasonable and reasonably uniform.

[¶ 38,051] 202. Reporting Cash Flow

.01. Introduction

ASR 142:

The Commission received preliminary registration statements which included "cash flow per share" data in the narrative section of the prospectus. Use of such data had also been noted in annual reports to shareholders, particularly in the "Financial Highlights" or "President's Letter" section. These and other means of presenting financial data appear designed to decrease the credibility of conventional financial statements as a measure of business activity.

The variation in form and purposes of such data creates confusion. The term "Cash Flow" and similar formulations such as "Earnings Before Non-Cash Charges," "Adjusted Net Income," "Net Operating Income" and "Operating Funds Generated" do not have precise definitions and may mean different things to different people. In addition to this definitional problem, there are different purposes for presenting these data. One is to present an apparent alternative to net income as a measure of performance. A second is to present information about liquid or near-liquid assets provided by operations which may be available for reinvestment or distribution to shareholders.

While differing definitions and purposes are basic sources of the confusion investors and registrants are experiencing with "cash flow" data, the presentation of such data on a per share basis compounds this confusion.

202.02. "Cash Flow" as a Proxy for Income Measurement

ASR 142:

One of the principal reasons given for presenting "cash flow" is that the income measurement model currently prescribed by generally accepted accounting principles does not accurately reflect the economic performance of certain types of companies, typically those with substantial assets which arguably do not depreciate or require replacement. While the Commission recognizes that there are problems of income measurement for some industries, the unilateral development and presentation on an unaudited basis of various measures of performance by different companies which constitute departures from the generally understood accounting model has led to conflicting results and confusion for investors. Additionally, it is not clear that the simple omission of depreciation and other non-cash charges deducted in the computation of net income provides an appropriate alternative measure of performance for any industry either in theory or in practice. This problem was recognized by the APB in APBO 19 where it was noted that "the amount of working capital or cash provided from operations is not a substitute for or an improvement upon properly determined net income as a measure of results of operations . . . ."

If accounting net income computed in conformity with generally accepted accounting principles is not an accurate reflection of economic performance for a company or an industry, it is not an appropriate solution to have each company independently decide what the best measure of its performance should be and present that figure to its shareholders as Truth. This would result in many different concepts and numbers which could not be used meaningfully by investors to compare different candidates for their investment dollars.

Where the measurement of economic performance is an industry-wide problem, representatives of the industry and the accounting profession should present the problem and suggested solutions to the FASB which is the body charged with responsibility for researching and defining principles of financial measurements. Until new and uniform measurement principles are developed and approved for an industry, the presentation of measures of performance other than net income should be approached with extreme caution. Such measures should not be presented in a manner which gives them greater authority or prominence than conventionally computed earnings.

Where management believes that the existing conventional income model does not present the results of operations realistically or fully, an explanation of the reasons and a description of possible alternatives which might be used to measure results may be presented to shareholders and potential investors to supplement conventional financial data. The presentation of additional data in tabular form is also acceptable. Such tables should be accompanied by a careful explanation of the data presented. The adding together of figures derived by different measurement techniques (such as net income and cash flow) should be avoided as should per share data relating to measures other than net income (see discussion below). In addition, when various measurement models are used for different lines of business, there should be a consistent application of such models to all similar segments of the firm's operations. Also, results for all segments included in consolidated statements of net income should be included in any tabular or summary presentation.

Annual reports to shareholders as well as filings with the Commission should include explanations and data as discussed above whenever measurement models other than conventionally computed income are used. Such additional information and data would typically be presented in the "Financial Highlights," the "President's Letter," or the text of the report and should not be presented without also presenting net income.* Terms such as "Net Operating Income" which leave the impression

that a figure other than net income is really income should not be used.

In cases where a measurement problem exists for an individual company rather than in an entire industry, a solution already exists in the procedures of the accounting profession. Under the Code of Ethics of the AICPA, an auditor is permitted to render an opinion approving statements prepared even though they deviate from the principles adopted by the FASB, if he believes and can support the assertion that due to unusual circumstances the financial statements would otherwise be misleading. Under such circumstances, full disclosure must be made by both company and auditor, and the basic statements must be prepared in accordance with the principles determined to present operating results most meaningfully. In such cases, the staff of the Commission will naturally consider the circumstances which gave rise to the situation, but it will normally give great weight to the judgment of the registrants and their independent accountants.

The above discussion is designed to assist companies which believe the conventional income measurement model is unsatisfactory in providing disclosure which is useful and not misleading. This discussion is not intended to support or reject any particular new measurement model and the Commission strongly urges the accounting profession and other interested parties to consider the development of new techniques for the measurement of results in industries where the current model seems deficient.

202.03. "Cash Flow" as a Measurement of Funds Generated from Operations[2]

ASR 142:

A second basic reason for highlighting cash flows from operations data in financial summaries is to show the liquid or near-liquid resources generated from operations which may be available for the discretionary use of management. Analysts have suggested that this is a useful measure of the ability of the entity to accept new investment opportunities, to maintain its current productive capacity by replacement of fixed assets and to make distributions to shareholders without drawing on new external sources of capital.

While presentation of cash flows from operating activities is useful, these data should be considered in the framework of a statement of cash flows which reflects management's decisions as to the use of these cash flows and the external sources of capital used. The implication of a presentation which shows only the cash flows generated from operations portion of a cash flows statement is that the use of such cash flows is entirely at the discretion of management. In fact, certain obliga-

---

* [See Section 501 for a discussion of the requirements of management's discussion and analysis.]

[2] [See also Section 501 for a discussion of the requirements to discuss "liquidity" in Management's Discussion and Analysis of Financial Condition and Results of Operations.]

tions (e.g., mortgage payments) may exist even if replacement of nondepreciating assets is considered unnecessary. Therefore, presentation of one part of a cash flows statement should be avoided.

The Commission has also noted situations where investors were misled by cash distributions which were in excess of net income and were not accompanied by disclosure indicating clearly that part of the distribution represented a return of capital.

Cash flow presentations designed to reflect the liquid assets or working capital generated by the firm should be consistent with the principles outlined in this section.

202.04. Per Share Information
ASR 142:

Many of the problems outlined above are accentuated when cash flow data is presented on a per share basis. Most importantly, such a presentation emphasizes the implication that cash flow is more meaningful than net income as a measure of performance, particularly when a per share figure is included in the "Financial Highlights" section of a report.

The first major problem in the presentation of cash flow per share data is that of investor understanding. Investors over many years have grown accustomed to seeing operating per share data computed only in the case of net income. Accounting authorities have considered and largely settled the measurement problems associated with the presentation of net income on a per share basis. If other data are presented in this way, there is a danger that the investor will think that what he is seeing is the conventional accounting measure of earning power when in fact this is not the case. In a number of reports, cash flow per share data have been presented in such a manner as to lead to this inference despite the strong recommendation of the APB in APBO 19 that "isolated statistics of working capital or cash provided from operations, especially per share amounts, not be presented in annual reports to shareholders." Such presentations run a high risk of materially misleading investors, and companies are urged to avoid this type of disclosure.

Beyond the problem of understandability is the question of relevance. The investment community generally recognizes the relevance of "earnings per share" as a measure of the historically achieved earning power of an economic entity in terms of a unit which is being bought, sold and quoted in the market place, the share of common stock. The earning power represented by that share has generally been considered a significant element in the determination of its worth. Net income, as a measure of ultimate result, may reasonably be interpreted on a per share basis since no significant claims stand between it and the common stock owner. Where there are senior equity claims, these are deducted before comput-

ing the per share figure. Dividends are similarly logically presented in terms of the individual share, as are net assets.

Significant questions as to relevance arise, however, when other data are presented on a per share basis. Sales, current assets, cash flow, total assets, cash and other similar figures cannot logically be related to the common shareholder without adjustment. These are aggregate data which are of great importance to analysts and management alike in understanding the operations of the total economic entity, but they are not items which accrue directly to the benefit of the owner of a part of the common equity. Charges and claims must be considered before the owner is benefited. To reflect such items on a per share basis may mislead the unsophisticated, since there is an implication that the shareholder is directly affected. In fact, such data are only meaningful from an operating viewpoint and not from that of an external investment unit.

Accordingly, per share data other than that relating to net income, net assets and dividends should be avoided in reporting financial results.

[¶ 38,055] 203. Disclosure of Compensating Balances and Short-Term Borrowing Arrangements

[In ASR 148, the Commission amended Article 5 of Regulation S-X to require the disclosure of compensating balances and information about short-term debt and unused lines of credit. In addition, ASR 148 provided interpretations and guidelines to assist registrants in implementing the disclosure rules adopted therein. Subsequently, in ASR 280, the disclosure requirements relating to short-term borrowings were modified to permit the disclosures either in a schedule to the financial statements or in MD&A if that results in a more meaningful presentation of the information.]

.01. Reasons for Requirements
ASR 148:

The management of liquidity is an important part of the financial management of a business entity. The maintenance of short-term borrowing capacity and the ability to obtain such funds at reasonable cost are major elements of such a management responsibility. If investors are to understand the financial policies of management, disclosure relative to these elements is necessary.

It is generally recognized in the financial community that one of the major elements in short-term financing policy is the maintenance of compensating balances supporting present and future credit from financial institutions. Such balances affect liquidity and the effective cost of borrowing. Nevertheless, disclosure of the essential details of such arrangements had been infrequent. When disclosure had occurred, the information supplied was generally insufficient to permit statement users to deal analytically with the subject. Lack of disclosure of amounts affecting liquidity such as compensating balances has been justified on the grounds that such arrangements were generally unwritten, informal and not subject to precise quantification. None of these reasons are sufficient to support a policy of nondisclosure of situations which are recognized to be both real and significant. They do, however, support the need for rule changes and disclosure guidelines so that reasonably uniform and understood standards for disclosure can be applied. They also indicate that disclosure must be based in many circumstances on reasonable estimates and that precision of measurement cannot be expected.

The interest rate paid for short-term borrowings is also of significance in appraising the financial policies and operating results of business entities. Changes in this rate over time may have a significant impact on profitability. The relationship of the rate paid at year end to short-term rates generally being charged at that date to corporate borrowers may be indicative of the future level of interest costs to be incurred by the corporation under varying conditions in the credit markets. In addition, information as to the magnitude of such borrowings during a fiscal period should further assist investors in determining the impact of changing credit conditions on business operations.

203.02. Compensating Balances
ASR 148:

Rule 5-02.1 of Regulation S-X requires disclosure of compensating balances in order to avoid undisclosed commingling of such balances with other funds having different liquidity characteristics and bearing no determinable relationship to borrowing arrangements. Rule 5-02.1 also requires footnote disclosure distinguishing the amounts of such balances maintained under a formal agreement to assure future credit availability.

203.02.a. Definition
ASR 148:

A compensating balance is defined as that portion of any demand deposit (or any time deposit or certificate of deposit) maintained by a corporation (or by any other person on behalf of the corporation) which constitutes support for existing borrowing arrangements of the corporation (or any other person) with a lending institution. Such arrangements would include both outstanding borrowings and the assurance of future credit availability.

203.02.b. Form of Disclosure
ASR 148:

The manner of disclosure cannot be specified with precision since it will vary according to the factual situation involved. These rules call for disclosure of compensating balance arrangements. Such disclosure will involve segregation on the face of the balance sheet whenever such balances

are maintained under an agreement which legally restricts the use of such funds. Examples of such arrangements would include situations where a certificate of deposit must be held while a loan is outstanding or where a minimum balance must be maintained at all times while credit is extended or available. Footnote disclosure will be appropriate in other circumstances where such balances are determinable amounts although not legally restricted as to withdrawal. Footnote disclosure would be required even though the arrangement is not reduced to writing if determinable amounts (e.g., a percentage of short-term borrowings, a percentage of unused lines of credit, an agreed average balance) have been agreed upon by both parties involved. An arrangement where the balance required is expressed as an average over time would ordinarily lead to additional footnote disclosure of the average amount required to be maintained for arrangements in existence at the reporting date since the amount held at the close of the reporting period might vary significantly from the average balance held during the period and bear little relationship to the amount required to be maintained over time. If arrangements requiring maintenance of compensating balances during the year were materially greater than those at year end, that fact should be disclosed. Disclosure may also include a statement, if appropriate, that the amounts are legally subject to withdrawal with or without sanctions, as applicable. If many banks are involved, the disclosure should summarize the most common arrangements and aggregate the compensating balances involved.

Restrictions on the use of funds may include contracts entered into with others or company statements of intention with regard to particular deposits. Examples of the former might be letters of credit and escrow accounts. Examples of the latter are cash balances set aside for use in a capital expenditure program or to meet a particular debt obligation when it comes due. Cash balances related to statements of intention should only be segregated when particular deposits or balances have been earmarked for such special purposes. Board approval of a capital budget calling for the expenditure of certain amounts would not be the basis for segregation unless the specific amounts of cash to be spent are identified and set aside.

Where a company is not in compliance with a compensating balance requirement, that fact generally should be disclosed along with stated or possible sanctions whenever such possible sanctions may be immediate (not vague or unpredictable) and material.

In determining whether compensating balance arrangements are sufficiently material to require segregation or disclosure, various factors should be considered. Among these may be the relationship of the amount of the balances to total cash, total liquid assets and net working capital, and the impact of the balances on the effective cost of financing. In the usual case, reportable compensating balances which in the aggregate amount to more than 15 percent of liquid assets (current cash balances, restricted and unrestricted, plus marketable securities) would be considered to be material. Lesser amounts may be material if they have a significant impact on the cost of financing. Compensating balances maintained by the company for the benefit of affiliates, officers, directors, principal stockholders or other similar parties may be of particular significance to investors. Separate disclosure of such balances may be required under other Commission rules and regulations even if they are not of magnitude such that they would meet the materiality guidelines set forth above.

203.02.c. Measurement Problems

ASR 148:

A number of problems arise in the process of determining the amount of compensating balances. It is recognized that precision of measurement may not be practicable, but that fact should not limit the disclosure of material arrangements since reasonable estimates can be made. Since several of the problems of measurement occur frequently, and since it is desirable that they be similarly solved to assure uniformity of practice among companies, the following guidelines have been developed to assist registrants. It is recognized that every situation cannot be anticipated, and the need for judgment on the part of registrants and their auditors cannot and should not be avoided.

203.02.c.i. Minimum Operating Balance

ASR 148:

All corporations require some minimum amount of cash on which to operate. The amount will depend upon the extent of seasonal and random fluctuations in short-term cash demand as well as management judgment regarding necessary safety factors. It has been argued that, in those cases where part of the compensating balance reflects funds that would be held anyway as a minimum operating balance, such funds should be subtracted from compensating balances since the maintenance of such a compensating balance has no incremental cost to the borrower. For purposes of these disclosure requirements, such a subtraction is not appropriate. The concept of subtraction implies that the compensating balance is of secondary importance, and this is by no means apparent. It would be equally reasonable to contend that operating funds are free of cost because compensating balances must be maintained. In any event, the utilization of such amounts for compensating balances precludes the sound cash management alternative of investing available cash in highly liquid interest bearing securities. It may be desirable, however, for companies to supplement disclosure with statements regarding the dual purpose of such amounts.

203.02.c.ii. Float

ASR 148:

The balance shown on the bank's ledgers and the company's books will differ due to delays in presentment of checks and deposits in transit. In addition, some amounts included in the bank ledger figure may include funds subject to collection which may not be considered as meeting compensating balance requirements. These factors complicate the calculation of the amount of compensating balance to be disclosed both conceptually and empirically. The compensating balance arrangements negotiated between a company and its bank are normally expressed in terms of the collected bank ledger balance, but the financial statements are presented on the basis of the company's books. In order to make the disclosure of compensating balance amounts segregated on the balance sheet consistent with the cash amounts reflected in the financial statements, the balance figure agreed upon by the bank and the company should be adjusted, if possible, by the estimated "float" so that such an adjusted amount shown on the balance sheet will properly relate to company book amounts for total cash. Both the agreed upon collected balance at the bank and the adjusted balance relating to the corporation's books should be disclosed along with a brief description of the criteria used to make the adjustment. Similar adjustments and disclosure should be made for arrangements disclosed only in the footnotes if practicable and relevant to the arrangements described. A reasonable estimate of "float" based on the information management uses to manage its bank relationships will be satisfactory.

203.02.c.iii. Compensation for Other Bank Services

ASR 148:

Balances are maintained not only in connection with financial arrangements but also to compensate the bank for its account handling function, and in some cases, to pay for other services such as lock boxes and account reconcilement. Balances maintained for these purposes should not be included in the disclosed compensating balances and would not be construed as special funds per Rule 5-02.1 since such funds are available for use upon payment of a service charge and would not affect the cost of borrowing. If a bank allows balances to serve both purposes, the balances should be considered as a compensating balance and should be disclosed in accordance with Rule 5-02.1. Supplemental disclosure by companies of the dual purpose of such amounts may be desirable.

203.02.c.iv. Reporting Periods

ASR 148:

In general, compensating balance arrangements should only be disclosed for the latest fiscal year and later interim period for which statements are presented. If the terms of the arrangements require balance sheet segregation, however, this should be reflected in all balance sheets presented. In addition, if the change in the arrangements from one period to the next is so great as to constitute a fact of unusual significance to the investor in appraising the company, the change should be disclosed.

203.03. Funds Maintained for Future Credit Availability

ASR 148:

Rule 5-02.1 requires disclosure of funds maintained under an agreement for the purpose of assuring future credit availability. These funds would be included as part of compensating balances disclosed separately on the balance sheet or in the footnotes in accordance with Rule 5-02.1. This requirement contemplates separate disclosure of such amounts and the related terms for both long- and short-term future credit availability in the notes to the financial statements. Separate disclosure provides important and useful information to the investor about policies regarding cash management and future financing.

203.04. Unused Lines of Credit or Commitments

ASR 148:

Rules 5-02.19 and 5-02.22 of Regulation S-X also call for the disclosure of the amount and terms of unused lines of credit and commitments if significant. Various factors should be considered in determining significance such as total debt by term of such debt, total capital, total cash requirements, and the like.

The disclosure of unused lines and commitments supplies the investor with information regarding borrowing potential and future liquidity under varying money market conditions. It is recognized that lines of credit or commitments are frequently extended to a borrower subject to the condition that the borrower maintain certain standards of credit worthiness, and that the existence of such lines or commitments therefore does not assure the availability of credit under conditions of deteriorating financial position. Accordingly, the rule provides that disclosure be made of the conditions under which lines or commitments may be withdrawn. It is also recognized that such lines and commitments are occasionally offered by financial institutions as a marketing device and accepted by corporations without any intention of use and not as part of their financing plan. Disclosure of such lines is not contemplated by this rule.

Unused lines disclosed as supporting commercial paper or other debt arrangements should include only usable lines. For this purpose usable lines are construed to be total lines used to support commercial paper less lines needed to meet "clean-up" provisions of a borrowing arrangement. Such provisions require borrowers to retire credit extended at a bank or banks at some specified interval for a specified period. Total lines outstanding are therefore not necessarily a measure of the total credit available on a continuing basis. Similarly, if a corporation has lines arranged with several banks which in total exceed borrowing levels permitted under existing lending agreements, disclosure should be limited to usable amounts.

Rule 5-02.22 would include disclosure of commitments such as standby commitments, commitments for future disbursements, and unused revolving credits maturing after one year.

203.05. Responsibilities

ASR 148:

The registrant is responsible for preparing financial statement disclosure of short-term interest rates, compensating balances, unused confirmed lines of credit, commercial paper and other disclosures as specified in these rules and guidelines. The independent accountant has the responsibility of satisfying himself that the disclosure is adequate. When arrangements such as compensating balances and unused confirmed lines of credit exist, their determination and verification would be facilitated and more readily substantiated if the borrower set forth the bases of the mutual understanding in a letter submitted to the lender (or potential lender) with a request for confirmation.

[¶ 38,071] 204. Disclosures Regarding Income Taxes

[In ASR 149, the Commission adopted rules which require disclosure of the components of income tax expense, the reasons for and tax effects of timing differences between book and tax reporting resulting in deferred income taxes, and a reconciliation between the effective income tax rate indicated by the income statement and the statutory Federal income tax rate. In ASR 280, a requirement was added to disclose separately domestic and foreign pretax income.]

.01. Reasons for Disclosure

ASR 149:

The objectives of these disclosure requirements (Rule 4-08(g) of Regulation S-X) are to enable users of financial statements to understand better the basis for the registrant's tax accounting and the degree to which, and the reasons why it is able to, operate at a different level of tax expense than that which would be incurred at the statutory tax rate. By developing such an understanding, users will be able to distinguish more easily between one-time and continuing tax advantages enjoyed by a company and to appraise the significance of changing effective tax rates. In addition, users will be able to gain additional insights into the current and prospective cash drain associated with payment of income taxes.

The Commission notes that financial statements prepared in conformity with generally accepted accounting principles as set forth in APBO 11 require disclosure of the "reasons for significant variations in the customary relationships between income tax expense and pretax accounting income if they are not otherwise apparent from the financial statements or from the nature of the entity's business," and it believes that many of the disclosures required by Rule 4-08(g) may be necessary in order to reflect the spirit of APBO 11.

Comments indicated that the rule would require disclosure of information which would be valuable to competitors since it would reveal tax strategy or which would lead taxing authorities to question tax deductions or assess claims based on amounts provided in computing tax expense where items subject to varying tax interpretations were treated in a manner favorable to the taxpayer. Those who made such comments did not provide specific examples of items and amounts involved, but the Commission believes that most items of this sort would be of a size such that disclosure would not be required under the significance criteria set forth in the rule. In those cases, if any, where the amounts involved are sufficiently large to require disclosure, the needs of present and potential investors in public corporations are best served by providing such significant information even though there may be an increased risk of adverse consequences at the hands of competitors.

In order to clarify the rules, an example of disclosure and associated assumptions and computations was provided. (See following paragraph.)

204.02. Example*

ASR 149:

Assumptions

The following facts apply to a hypothetical business corporation for the calendar year 19×3 (all figures in thousands).

Book income before tax $15,000

(1) Assets purchased at the beginning of 19×3 at a cost of $10,000, eight year life, double declining balance depreciation for tax purposes, straight line on books, eligible for 7% investment credit.

(2) Research costs of $3,000 deducted on tax return but amortized over following years for book purposes.

(3) Warranty reserve of $1,400 provided for book purposes is not deductible for tax purposes until warranty costs are incurred.

(4) Income before taxes includes $2,000 related to construction-type contracts still in process which are accounted for on the percentage of completion method for book purposes and on the completed contract method for tax purposes.

(5) Amortization of goodwill of $800 is not deductible for tax purposes.

(6) Book income before taxes includes $2,400 which represents the net income of wholly-owned foreign subsidiaries that are expected to indefinitely invest their undistributed earnings. Foreign Subsidiary A is permitted under its local tax laws to deduct a provision for an inventory reserve related to increased inventory decline. For consolidated financial statement purposes, no such accrual is made and the associated deferred tax expense is $420. The subsidiaries have reportable taxes in their respective foreign jurisdictions as follows:

	Foreign Subsidiary A	Foreign Subsidiary B	Total
Foreign Book Income before Taxes	$2,100	$300	$2,400
Foreign Jurisdiction Tax Rate	30 %	50 %	
Currently Taxable Income	$ 700	$300	$1,000
Current Tax Expense	210	150	360
Deferred Tax Expense	420	-0-	420
Total Foreign Income Tax Expense	$ 630	$150	$ 780

(7) Investments sold during the year resulted in a gain of $1,000, which is taxed at capital gain rates of 30%.

(8) Included in income is $1,500 of interest on tax exempt municipal bonds.

(9) State and local income taxes amounted to $400.

Current Tax Expense			
Deferred Tax Expense			

Illustrative Note

Note—Income tax expense (all data in thousands).

Income tax expense is made up of the following components:

	U.S. Federal	Foreign	State & Local	Total
Current Tax Expense	$2,312	$360	$400	$3,072
Deferred Tax Expense	2,328	420	-0-	2,748

* [This example was originally published prior to adoption in ASR 280 of the requirement for separate disclosure of domestic and foreign pre-tax income. Therefore, it does NOT illustrate disclosures under that requirement. Also this example was published before the adoption of the Accelerated Cost Recovery System and certain other changes in the Internal Revenue Code and before the FASB issued SFAS 2 on accounting for research and development costs. Although the example does not reflect current tax law and accounting literature, it does illustrate the type of data required.]

	U.S. Federal $4,640	Foreign $780	State & Local $400	Total $5,820

Deferred tax expense results from timing differences in the recognition of revenue and expense for tax and financial statement purposes. The sources of these differences in 19×3 and the tax effect of each were as follows:

Excess of tax over book depreciation	$ 600
Research and development costs expensed on tax return and deferred on books	1,440
Revenue recognized on completed contract basis on tax return and on percentage of completion basis on books	960
Tax deductible inventory reserve provided in foreign tax jurisdiction	420
Warranty cost charged to expense on books but not deductible until paid	(672)
	$2,748

Total tax expense amounted to $5,820 (an effective rate of 38.8%), a total less than the amount of $7,200 computed by applying the U.S. Federal income tax rate of 48% to income before tax. The reasons for this difference are as follows:

	$ Amount	% of pretax income
Computed "expected" tax expense	$7,200	48.0%
Increases (reductions) in taxes resulting from:		
Foreign income subject to foreign income tax but not expected to be subject to U.S. tax in foreseeable future ($2,000 × 48%) – $780=$372	$(372)	(2.5)
Tax exempt municipal bond income	(720)	(4.8)
Investment tax credit on assets purchased in 19×3	(700)	(4.7)
Goodwill amortization not deductible for tax purposes	384	2.6
State and local income taxes, net of Federal income tax benefit*	208	1.4
Benefit from income taxed at capital gains rate (1,000 × 48%)–(1,000 × 30%) = $180*	(180)	(1.2)
Actual tax expense	$5,820	38.8 %

---

* Since these amounts are less than 5% of the computed "expected" tax expense, they could be combined with any other items less than $360 into an aggregate total. For example, these items could be disclosed as follows: "Miscellaneous items . . . $28 . . . 0.2%."

  If no single item had exceeded $360 in this case and the total net difference of all items was also less than $360, this reconciliation would not have been required.

Computational Guide

(Furnished only to enable interested parties to determine source of numbers shown in above illustrative note; not to be required of registrants in filings.)

Tax Computations		
Book income before tax		$15,000
State income tax		(400)
Permanent differences:		
Goodwill amortization	800	
Municipal bond income	(1,500)	
Foreign income, no domestic income tax	(2,400)	
Capital gain	(1,000)	(4,100)
		$10,500
Timing differences:		
Excess depreciation		(1,250)
R & D deduction on tax return		(3,000)
Warranty cost not deductible until paid		1,400
Percentage of completion income		(2,000)
Taxable income (excl. cap. gain)		$ 5,650
Tax to be paid		
Tax on ordinary income .48 × 5,650		$ 2,712
Plus capital gain tax .30 × 1,000		300
Less investment credit		(700)
Actual tax paid		$ 2,312
Tax expense per books		
Tax expense on ordinary income .48 × 10,500		$ 5,040
Plus capital gain tax		300
Less investment credit		(700)
Tax expense—Federal		$ 4,640
Foreign tax		$ 780
State and local income tax		$ 400

Computation of Disclosure Limit

Computed amount	15,000 × .48 = 7,200
5% of computed amount	.05 × 7,200 = 360

204.03. Disclosure About Future Cash Outlays

ASR 280:

The Commission specifically invited commentators to address whether the Commission should retain the requirement concerning disclosure about future cash outlays for income taxes that are anticipated to substantially exceed income tax expense. Most registrants suggested that the rule be deleted, notwithstanding the importance of the disclosure it requires, because it is difficult to predict. The Commission understands that it is difficult to accurately predict this information; however, it believes that in situations where future cash outlays are anticipated to substantially exceed income tax expense, disclosure should be made. Since this disclosure may be more useful in relation to the liquidity section of the revised MD&A*, the Commission has determined to delete this portion of the income tax rule. It should be pointed out that although this disclosure has not been explicitly required in the MD&A, when applicable, this is the type of information which should be provided.

[¶ 38,075] 205. LIFO Method of Accounting for Inventories

[In July 1981, the Commission issued ASR 293 which announced that several enforcement cases and amendments to the IRS regulations in January 1981 concerning the LIFO book/tax conformity statute caused the Commission to focus on certain LIFO practices and disclosures.]

205.01. Background

ASR 293:

LIFO is an inventory pricing method based on a flow-of-cost assumption that the last item purchased is the first item sold. In times of rising prices, LIFO generally results in higher current costs being charged against income, while older, lower costs are retained in inventory. Of the two fundamental reasons for using LIFO, one is oriented toward financial accounting and the other is income tax oriented. From the standpoint of financial accounting, proponents of LIFO argue that, by charging to expense those costs which more closely reflect the replacement cost of inventory, LIFO tends to reduce the illusionary profits obtained from merely holding inventories and thereby reflects more accurately the "true" income of a company.* Most companies that have changed to the LIFO method from other methods in the past decade have indicated that LIFO is a preferable method because of its ability to match current costs with current revenues during periods of rising prices. For income tax purposes many companies prefer LIFO because, during periods of rising prices, it generally reduces taxable income and thereby results in reduced income tax expense.

When LIFO became an acceptable tax method as announced in the Revenue Act of 1938, its application was limited to the specific identification method for raw materials in the inventories of leather tanners and producers and processors of certain nonferrous metals. Since then, the IRS regulations have been amended a number of times and today dollar value LIFO[1] is an acceptable method that can be used for almost all types of inventory goods. While allowing broad usage of the LIFO method, the statute was structured in a unique manner permitting only those taxpayers who use LIFO for financial accounting to use LIFO for tax purposes.

On January 13, 1981, the IRS published amended regulations[2] concerning the LIFO conformity rule. For many years, the IRS strictly enforced the conformity rule and required companies to apply LIFO in most cases identically for book and tax purposes and did not permit companies to disclose supplemental information about alternative methods of inventory pricing.[3] The Commission considers two aspects of the IRS amendments to be significant: (1) companies may apply LIFO differently for book purposes than for tax purposes as long as they use some acceptable form of LIFO; and (2) companies may provide supplemental non-LIFO disclosures if they are not presented on the face of the income statement.

205.02. Applying LIFO for Book and Tax Purposes

ASR 293:

The Commission believes that the conceptual basis for the LIFO method is the proper matching of current costs with current revenues. However, based on matters which the Commission and its staff have dealt with, we have concluded that when the dollar value method is used, changes in product mix, product prices and inventory pool liquidations can sometimes prevent a proper matching of

---

* [See Section 501 (¶ 38,271).]

* The Commission, in ASR 151, January 3, 1974, stated, "[s]uch [inventory] profits do not reflect an increase in the economic earning power of a business and they are not normally repeatable in the absence of continued price level increase."

[1] The dollar value method, in contrast to the specific identification method, values dollar rather than quantity increases in ending inventory and the dollar, rather than the physical item, is the unit of measure. There are four major dollar value methods: double extension, index, link chain and retail.

[2] Treasury Decision 7756, Title 26 CFR 1.472-2(e).

[3] There have been exceptions to this rule, e.g., the IRS issued annual waivers to permit companies to comply with ASR 190, involving replacement cost, without violating the conformity rule.

cost and revenues. Accordingly, the Commission believes that the amended regulations which permit companies to compute LIFO differently for book and tax purposes are very positive. For too long, the application of the LIFO method for financial accounting and reporting has been unduly influenced by the tax application. Most explanations or analyses of LIFO in textbooks and articles have been oriented toward tax implications, rather than financial accounting and reporting. With few exceptions, the accounting profession has deferred to the IRS in this area; indeed, many accountants appear to view IRS LIFO regulations as if they were GAAP. The Commission disagrees with this approach and believes that since LIFO may now be applied differently for book accounting and tax accounting, it is appropriate for the current practices used in the application of LIFO to be examined.**

Activities of the Commission and its staff concerning LIFO include the following: (1) a requirement to disclose the excess of replacement or current cost over LIFO value stated on the balance sheet, if material (Rule 5-02.6 of Regulation S-X); (2) an SAB which explicitly identifies the need to disclose the amount of income, if material, that has been recorded because a LIFO inventory liquidation has taken place*** ; (3) enforcement actions for improper reporting; and (4) meetings and communications with registrants on matters of application and disclosure. This release describes some of the particular facts and conclusions concerning LIFO issues, that the Commission and its staff have considered, in order to enhance the examination of LIFO practices. The examples which follow are limited by the issues which the Commission and its staff have addressed and are not intended to be a complete consideration of concerns about the LIFO method.

205.02.a. Enforcement Issues
ASR 293:

The Commission has instituted enforcement actions against a number of registrants that used the LIFO method to report a desired but fallacious result. These enforcement actions involve two distinct topics: new product designations and inventory levels.

205.02a.i. New Product Designations
ASR 293:

The accounting treatment given products entering an inventory pool for the first time ("new products") can affect financial statement results when they are reported at current cost. This has been noted particularly when the double extension approach to the dollar-value LIFO method is

used. When the effects of inflation on the cost of new products are measured by making a comparison with current cost as the base-year cost rather than a reconstructed base-year cost,* income tends to be increased.

The Commission has noted instances in which companies incorrectly designated pre-existing inventory items as new products and recorded them at current cost. They attempted to justify this treatment by distinguishing between the so-called new product and the same item already contained in the inventory based on insignificant and sometimes arbitrary differences in attributes. For example, new products have been designated because of slight differences in chemical composition, changes in manufacturing or production line location, and differences in supply sources.

The following examples illustrate instances where the Commission took exception to a registrant's new product policies.

    (1) Company A treated an item as new product merely because the production of that item was shifted from one plant to another. The change in manufacturing location and the changes in costs associated with the manufacture of that item were given as the major justifications for the new product treatment.

    (2) Company B designated part of its nickel inventory as a "new product" because it contained cobalt. Although cobalt did not preclude the use of the nickel in the manufacture of stainless steel, the presence of the cobalt content caused modification in the manufacturing process and resulted in a lower quality steel. The Commission focused on the apparent contradiction inherent in income being increased (by several million dollars) simply because a particular inventory commodity contained a physical property making it less valuable.

    (3) Company C's policy was to treat iron ore obtained from different mine locations as distinct inventory products, arguably because of differences in chemical composition. The Commission objected, however, when Company C increased pre-tax earnings by $4.9 million simply by designating the mixture of three different kinds of iron ore as a new product and recording it at current cost.

205.02.a.ii. Inventory Levels
ASR 293:

The Commission has noted where registrants have manipulated the reported level of their inventory or parts of their inventory in order to affect reported earnings. In the following illustrative cases the Commission initiated enforcement ac-

---

** The Commission is aware of a task force which has been established by AcSEC to accumulate information about application problems. This type of effort, in addition to self-examination by individual registrants, is appropriate and should assist the FASB in considering these matters.

*** Topic 11F of SAB 40 (46 FR 11513).

* Reconstructed base-year costs are "reasonable" estimates of what a particular inventory item would have cost had it been in the inventory in the base year.

tions against registrants because it considered the transactions to be improper.

(1) Company D as part of a plan to shift income from 1974, a high income year, to 1975, an expected low income year, recorded the transfer of 1,088 tons of stainless steel from its FIFO to its LIFO inventory. The transfer was recorded on the company's books but the stainless steel was not physically moved. The LIFO effect of the transfer substantially lowered 1974 reported income. In 1975, a book entry was made to transfer the stainless steel back to the FIFO valued inventory, increasing reported earnings for that year.

(2) Company E misclassified some of the raw material in its inventory records. Although this misclassification did not affect the overall inventory quantity, the differences in the LIFO base cost of the misclassified raw materials resulted in reported increases in inventory and earnings.

Transactions such as those described above represent a perversion of the reporting process. Accordingly, financial statements prepared using these devices will be considered to be misleading.

205.02.b. LIFO Applications
ASR 293:

Because of the nature of LIFO, transactions which would have no financial accounting impact if another method were used can significantly change reported income under LIFO. The following is an example of a recent registrant inquiry that was considered by the staff which illustrates this situation.

Company F, a company using LIFO, found itself with raw material commitments which were greater than it could utilize and decided to sell the excess. There was excess supply on the market and the sale was not anticipated to be accomplished by year end. The Company inquired whether the staff would object if a new non-LIFO subsidiary were established to hold and eventually sell the inventory. (This transaction would have occurred at an interim period during the Company's fiscal year and would have involved a bookkeeping transfer without physical movement of the inventory.) Since, for other reasons, the Company's inventory had decreased, the net effect of the transfer would have been to further decrease LIFO inventory causing a further decrement of LIFO layers and a substantial infusion of income. Although the staff did not assert any devious intent, it was concerned about the precedent of a bookkeeping transaction that did not involve a physical event but resulted in reporting considerable income. The Company stated that the IRS had approved of the transaction and that it did not expect the Commission staff to object. The staff informed the Company that it could not consider the transaction acceptable because its reported effect contradicted the economic substance of the situation.

205.02.c. Supplemental Disclosures
ASR 293:

The other matter which the recent amendments affect is supplemental income disclosures based on non-LIFO inventory methods. Because there appears to be a tendency by some companies using LIFO to infer that FIFO earnings are the "real" earnings, the Commission reminds registrants that disclosures must be considered carefully so as not to result in misleading reporting for financial statement purposes. Those disclosures which previously were prohibited by the conformity rule should not be present in financial reports without consideration of their desirability or effect.

The most troublesome disclosures relate to proforma income information usually assuming the FIFO method is used. The asserted reason for these disclosures is usually that they are necessary to permit comparison of companies using LIFO and those using FIFO. The Commission does not believe that FIFO-based supplemental income disclosures by companies using the LIFO method for inventory determination are necessarily the best way to obtain comparable information. A better method would be to use the disclosures prescribed by SFAS 33, "Financial Reporting and Changing Prices." However, when such supplemental disclosures are properly formed and located, the Commission has not objected to them.

The Commission's primary concern, the risk of user misinterpretation, is mitigated when registrants providing these disclosures (1) state clearly that the use of LIFO results in a better matching of costs and revenues (i.e., supporting the preferability of this method for their purposes), (2) indicate the reason why supplemental income disclosures are being provided and (3) present essential information about the supplemental income calculation to enable users to appreciate the quality of the information. Also, registrants should be careful of the terminology that they use since terms such as "LIFO reserve" or "LIFO adjustment" may be misunderstood by readers.

The purpose of presenting supplemental FIFO income information will have an impact on the location of the information. If companies present FIFO-based disclosures because they believe users want to have information available for comparison to operating results of companies not on LIFO, the Commission believes such disclosures should not be made in financial highlights, press releases or president's letters, since such analytical data, in the required detail, usually is not included in those places. These disclosures would be better placed in footnotes to financial statements or management's discussion and analysis of financial condition and results of operations.

ASR 141:

In the determination of replacement or current cost for the purpose of disclosing the excess of that amount over the stated LIFO value [required by Rule 5-02 of Regulation S-X], any inventory method may be used (such as FIFO or average cost) which derives a figure approximating current cost.

[¶ 38,085] 206. Disclosures Related to Defense and Other Long-Term Contract Activities

.01. Introduction

ASR 164:

The Commission has long been concerned about the quality of disclosures made by registrants engaged in defense and other long-term contract activities because these activities involve inventories and receivables with unique risk and liquidity characteristics. The Commission believes that it is necessary and appropriate to require disclosure of greater detail in certain critical areas of long-term contract activity, particularly with respect to the nature of costs accumulated in inventories, the effect of cost accumulation policies on cost of sales, and the effect of revenue recognition practices on receivables and inventories.

206.02. Disclosures in Financial Statements

.a. Disclosure Regarding Receivables

.i. Retainage

ASR 164:

Due to the unique liquidity characteristics of retainage, the Commission believes that any material amount of retainage should be disclosed no matter when such amount is expected to be collected. However, the Commission also believes that the significant uncertainties which often affect the determination of a mutually satisfactory contract completion may cause the estimates of amounts to be collected within specific years to become progressively less reliable. Consequently, Rule 5-02.3(c)(1) of Regulation S-X requires the isolation of only the aggregate amount of retainage expected to be collected after one year. However, registrants are encouraged to provide estimated collections by year if their experience or other factors enable them to do so with reasonable accuracy.

The Commission believes that it is unnecessary for the rule to provide specifically for amounts retained by contractors pursuant to the provisions of subcontracts because Rule 5-02.25 can be interpreted to require separate disclosure of significant amounts of retentions payable to subcontractors.

206.02.a.ii. Unbilled Amounts

ASR 164:

Rule 5-02.3(c)(2) calls for disclosure of the amounts of receivables not billed or billable that are expected to be collected after one year. The Commission believes that disclosure of the timing of expected collections provides investors with meaningful liquidity and risk information.

It should be noted that the rule is not directed at items which are "unbilled" at the balance sheet date merely because the necessary paperwork has not been processed in accordance with the normal operation of a billing system. Such items would generally be considered "billable" for purposes of this rule.

206.02.a.iii. Claims and Similar Items

ASR 164:

The Commission believes that amounts due under routine change orders and escalation features commonly found in the terms of contracts are typically not subject to such uncertainty that separate disclosure is required. On the other hand, it believes that disclosure is necessary when amounts are recorded which are not reasonably determinable under the specific terms of existing contracts. Accordingly, Rule 5-02.3(c)(3) requires disclosure where the amounts included in receivables whether billed or unbilled, are either claims or other similar items subject to uncertainty concerning their determination or ultimate realization.

206.02.b. Disclosure Regarding Inventories

ASR 164:

The Commission expects that the description of the cost elements included in inventory will appropriately disclose the existence of items not typically included in inventoried costs in a usual manufacturing operation. In general, the Commission believes that the accounting treatment of such costs is sufficiently unique to warrant the disclosure of their existence and, to the extent noted below, their magnitude.

206.02.b.i. Cost Elements Included in Inventories

ASR 164:

The Commission recognizes that some registrants may find it impracticable to determine the actual amount of general and administrative costs remaining in inventory at the balance sheet dates. However, the Commission believes that registrants can provide reasonable estimates of such remaining costs determined, for example, on the assumption that costs related to a particular contract or program have been removed from inventory on a basis proportional to the totals of the various cost elements expected to be charged to cost of sales for that contract or program. The assumptions used to develop these estimates should be described in a note to the financial statements. (Rule 5-02.6(b)).

206.02.b.ii. Claims and Similar Items

ASR 164:

Rule 5-02.6(d)(2)(ii) recognizes that certain registrants classify amounts representing claims or other similar items subject to uncertainties as inventories rather than as receivables reportable under Rule 5-02.3(c). Regardless of where such amounts are classified, the Commission believes that material amounts must be disclosed together with an appropriate description of the nature and status of the principal items comprising such amounts.

206.03. Example

ASR 164:

The following hypothetical example is furnished to illustrate the character and detail of the disclosures which might be furnished in response to Rules 5-02.3 and 5-02.6 of Regulation S-X. The illustration is provided to assist in understanding and evaluating the rules.

XYZ Company and Subsidiaries Consolidated Balance Sheets At December 31,

	19×4	19×3
	(000 omitted)	
ASSETS		
CURRENT ASSETS:		
Cash	$ 438	$ 627
Accounts receivable:		
Trade and other receivables, net of allowance for uncollectible accounts of $38,000 in 19×4 and $36,000 in 19×3	2,846	2,396
Long-term contracts and programs (notes 1 and 2)	18,985	19,036
Total accounts receivable	21,831	21,432
Inventories and costs relating to long-term contracts and programs in process, net of progress payments (notes 1 and 3)	6,278	6,257
Prepaid expenses	46	27
Total current assets	$28,593	$28,343

Note 1. Summary of Significant Accounting Policies

Revenue Recognition. Sales of commercial products under long-term contracts and programs are recognized in the accounts as deliveries are made. The estimated sales value of performance under Government fixed-price and fixed-price incentive contracts in process is recognized under the percentage of completion method of accounting whereunder the estimated sales value is determined on the basis of physical completion to date (the total contract amount multiplied by percent of performance to date less sales value recognized in previous periods) and cost (including general and administrative, except as described below) are expensed as incurred. Sales under cost-reimbursement contracts are recorded as costs are incurred and include estimated earned fees in the proportion that costs incurred to date bear to total estimated costs. The fees under certain Government contracts may be increased or decreased in accordance with cost or performance incentive provisions which measure actual performance against established targets or other criteria. Such incentive fee awards or penalties are included in sales at the time the amounts can be determined reasonably.

Inventories. Inventories, other than inventoried costs relating to long-term contracts and programs, are stated at the lower of cost (prinicpally

first-in, first-out) or market. Inventoried costs relating to long-term contracts and programs are stated at the actual production cost, including factory overhead, initial tooling and other related non-recurring costs, incurred to date reduced by amounts identified with revenue recognized on units delivered or progress completed. General and administrative costs applicable to cost-plus Government contracts are also included inventories. Inventoried costs relating to long-term contracts and programs are reduced by charging any amounts in excess of estimated realizable value to cost of sales. The costs attributed to units delivered under long-term commercial contracts and programs are based on the estimated average cost of all units expected to be produced and are determined under the learning curve concept which anticipates a predictable decrease in unit costs as tasks and production techniques become more efficient through repetition.

In accordance with industry practice, inventories include amounts relating to contracts and programs having production cycles longer than one year and a portion thereof will not be realized within one year.

Note 2. Accounts Receivable

The following tabulation shows the component elements of accounts receivable from long-term contracts and programs:

	19×4	19×3
	(000 omitted)	
U.S. Government:		
Amounts billed	$ 7,136	$ 6,532
Recoverable costs and accrued profit on progress completed—not billed	4,173	3,791

	19×4	19×3
	(000 omitted)	
Unrecovered costs and estimated profits subject to future negotiation— not billed	1,468	1,735
	12,777	12,058
Commercial Customers:		
Amounts billed	1,937	3,442
Recoverable costs and accrued profit on units delivered—not billed . .	1,293	364
Retainage, due upon completion of contracts	2,441	2,279
Unrecovered costs and estimated profits subject to future negotiation— not billed	537	893
	$18,985	$19,036

The balances billed but not paid by customers pursuant to retainage provisions in construction contracts will be due upon completion of the contracts and acceptance by the owner. Based on the Company's experience with similar contracts in recent years, the retention balances at December 31, 19×4 are expected to be collected as follows: $270,000 in 19×5, $845,000 in 19×6 and the balance in 19×7.

Recoverable costs and accrued profit not billed comprise principally amounts of revenue recognized on contracts for which billings had not been presented to the contract owners because the amounts were not billable at balance sheet date. It is anticipated such unbilled amounts receivable from the U.S. Government at December 31, 19×4 will be billed over the next 60 days as units are delivered. The unbilled accounts receivable applicable to commercial customers are billable upon completion of performance tests which are expected to be completed in September 19×5.

Unrecovered costs and estimated profits subject to future negotiation, the principal amount of which is expected to be billed and collected within one year, consist of the following elements:

	19×4	19×3
	(000 omitted)	
U.S. Government Contracts:		
Excess of estimated or proposed over provisional price	$ 190	$ 157
Amounts claimed for incremental costs arising from customer-occasioned contract delays	1,278	1,578
	1,468	1,735
Commercial Contracts:		
Unrecovered costs and estimated profit relating to work not specified in express contract provisions	537	893
	$2,005	$2,628

Note 3. Inventories

Inventories and inventoried costs relating to long-term contracts and programs are classified as follows:

	December 31,	
	19×4	19×3
	(000 omitted)	
Finished goods	$3,562	$3,435
Inventories costs relating to long-term contracts and programs, net of amounts attributed to revenues recognized to date	2,552	2,638
Work in process	738	947
Raw materials	453	383
Supplies	112	71
	7,417	7,474
Deduct progress payments related to long-term contracts and programs	1,139	1,217
	$6,278	$6,257

The following tabulation shows the cost elements included in inventoried costs related to long-term contracts:

	December 31,	
	19×4	19×3
	(000 omitted)	
Production costs of goods currently in process	$1,184	$960
Excess of production cost of delivered units over the estimated average cost of all units expected to be produced	647	893
Unrecovered costs subject to future negotiation	280	310
General and administrative costs	260	270
Initial tooling and other non-recurring costs	181	205
	$2,552	$2,638

The inventoried costs relating to long-term contracts and programs includes unrecovered costs of $280,000 and $310,000 at December 31, 19×4 and 19×3, respectively, which are subject to future determination through negotiation or other procedures not complete at balance sheet dates. Of such amounts, $260,000 and $280,000 are in respect to contracts under which all goods have been delivered at December 31, 19×4 and 19×3, respectively. The unrecovered amount at December 31, 19×3 consisted of three items, one of which was settled during 19×4. The amount remaining at December 31, 19×4 is represented principally by a claim asserted against a customer for amounts incurred as a result of faulty materials furnished by the customer which in turn caused delays in performance under the contract. In the opinion of management, these costs will be recovered by contract modification or litigation. It is expected that the negotiations which are being conducted currently with the customer will be successfully concluded during the next twelve months. If this expectation is not realized, the matter will be referred to the Armed Services Board of Contract Appeals, with the consequence that settlement could be delayed for an indeterminate period.

The actual per unit production cost of the NX-4C aircraft produced during the most recent fiscal year was less than the estimated average per unit cost of all units expected to be produced under the program. Prior to 19×4, the Company's NX-4C commercial aircraft program was in the early high cost period. During the initial years of the program, the cost of units produced exceeded the sales price of the delivered units and the estimated average unit cost of all units to be produced under the program. At December 31, 19×4, inventories included costs of $647,000 representing the excess of costs incurred over estimated average costs per aircraft for the 117 aircraft delivered through the year end. The estimated average unit cost is predicated on the assumption that 250 planes will be produced and that production costs (principally labor and materials) will decrease as the project matures and efficiencies associated with increased volume, improved production techniques and the performance of repetitive tasks (the learning curve concept) are realized. (Note: The amount by which the production costs of the equivalent finished units in process at the date of the latest balance sheet exceeds the cost of such units on the basis of the estimated average unit cost of all units expected to be produced under the program should be stated. Since, as stated above, the actual per unit production cost is currently less than the estimated average per unit cost of all units expected to be produced under the program, no such excess is assumed in this example.)

Recovery of the deferred production, initial tooling and related non-recurring costs is dependent on the number of aircraft ultimately sold and actual selling prices and production costs associated with future transactions. Sales significantly under estimates or costs significantly over estimates could result in the realization of substantial losses on the program in future years. Realization of

approximately $421,000 of the gross commercial aircraft inventories at December 31, 19×4 is dependent on receipt of future firm orders.

Based on studies by and on behalf of the Company, management believes there exists for this aircraft a market for over 250 units, including deliveries to date, with production and deliveries continuing at a normal rate to at least 19y0. At December 31, 19×4, 117 aircraft had been delivered under the program, and the backlog included 64 firm unfilled orders and options for 43 units.

The aggregate amounts of general and administrative costs incurred during 19×4 and 19×3 were $2,251,000 and $2,238,000, respectively. As stated in Note 1, the Company allocates general and administrative costs to certain types of Government contracts. The amounts of general and administrative costs remaining in inventories at December 31, 19×4 and 19×3 are estimated at $260,000 and $270,000, respectively. Such estimates assume that costs have been removed from inventories on a basis proportional to the amounts of each cost element expected to be charged to cost of sales.

[¶ 38,095] 207. Disclosure of Concentrations of Investments in Marketable Securities and Other Investments

[In ASR 226, the Commission revised the disclosure requirements for commercial and industrial companies regarding investments in marketable securities and other security investments. In ASR 237, the Commission clarified the revised rules in response to inquiries.]

ASR 237:

Clarification was requested for the term "agency" as used in Instruction 1 of the schedule under Rule 12-02 of Regulation S-X, e.g., the U.S. Government and its agencies are to be classed as one issuer of securities, in regard to whether a corporation in the private sector whose securities are guaranteed in whole or in part by a governmental unit could be considered an agency of that government unit for purposes of this instruction. For this purpose, a corporation would not be considered an agency of the governmental unit unless it is wholly or partially owned by the governmental unit.

[¶ 38,101] 208. General Notes to Financial Statements

ASR 280:

Article 4 of Regulation S-X specifies the required general notes to the financial statements and requires disclosure of certain applicable information which is not explicitly required by generally accepted accounting principles. It requires presentation of the information either on the face of the appropriate financial statements or in appropriately captioned notes. The Commission believes note references can be valuable to users of financial statements if properly utilized by preparers but it does not desire to impede preparer efforts to develop more effective means of communicating financial information. Accordingly, cross-references to the applicable notes should appear on the face of the financial statements when appropriate for the effective presentation of financial information to the user of the financial statements.

[¶ 38,105] 209. Property, Plant and Equipment Disclosure Requirements

209.01. Introduction

ASR 298:

The Commission adopted amendments to the disclosure requirements for the detailed property, plant and equipment schedule and the related schedule of accumulated depreciation, depletion and amortization. The amendments limit the presentation of these schedules to instances where property, plant and equipment is at a high level of significance.

209.02. Background

ASR 298:

The Commission initially proposed amendments which would have revised its schedule requirements for property, plant and equipment (PP&E) and accumulated depreciation, depletion and amortization. This proposal was later withdrawn for further study. A second proposal would have required the PP&E information to be organized by business segments and would have modified the exemption rules to reduce the number of registrants required to file the schedules. Disclosures of fully depreciated assets still in use and idle capacity were retained in the second proposal but would have been required only if significant to the business segment to which they related.

209.03. Conclusion

ASR 298:

The Commission concluded that the proposed expanded disclosures would not be a cost-beneficial addition to the existing segment data. The Commission continues to believe that information about the idle facilities may be important to an analysis of an enterprise. However, generally accepted accounting principles require disclosure of the existence of significant idle facilities; and Instruction 1 to Item 102 of Regulation S-K (Description of Property) calls for information on the extent of utilization of facilities. In addition, where current year changes in idle facilities have a material impact on the results of operations, it would also be necessary to address such matters in Management's Discussion and Analysis of Financial Condition and Results of Operations.

The Commission understands that the supplemental PP&E disclosures are primarily of benefit to investors and potential investors analyzing companies in capital intensive industries. Accordingly, the Commission concluded that the PP&E sched-

ules should be required only of relatively capital intensive registrants. Therefore, the rules exempt those registrants whose PP&E, net of accumulated depreciation, depletion and amortization, is less than 25 percent of total assets at both the beginning and end of the latest fiscal year. The test is to be applied at both the beginning and end of the year in order to offset unusual fluctuations in total assets. Schedules will not be necessary for prior years if not required currently. However, the schedules will be required for previous years if they are required for the current year.

[¶ 38,111] 210. Quasi-Reorganization

ASR 25:

Inquiry has been made from time to time as to the conditions under which a quasi-reorganization has come to be applied in accounting to the corporate procedures in the course of which a company, without the creation of new corporate entity and without the intervention of formal court proceedings, is enabled to eliminate a deficit whether resulting from operations or the recognition of other losses or both and to establish a new earned surplus account for the accumulation of earnings subsequent to the date selected as the effective date of the quasi-reorganization.

It has been the Commission's view for some time that a quasi-reorganization may not be considered to have been effected unless at least all of the following conditions exist:

(1) Earned surplus, as of the date selected, is exhausted;

(2) Upon consummation of the quasi-reorganization, no deficit exists in any surplus account;

(3) The entire procedure is made known to all persons entitled to vote on matters of general corporate policy and the appropriate consents to the particular transactions are obtained in advance in accordance with the applicable law and charter provisions;

(4) The procedure accomplishes, with respect to the accounts, substantially what might be accomplished in a reorganization by legal proceedings—namely, the restatement of assets in terms of present conditions as well as appropriate modifications of capital and capital surplus, in order to obviate so far as possible the necessity of future reorganizations of like nature.

It is implicit in such a procedure that reductions in the carrying value of assets at the effective date may not be made beyond a point which gives appropriate recognition to conditions which appear to have resulted in relatively permanent reductions in asset values; as for example, complete or partial obsolescence, lessened utility value, reduction in investment value due to changed economic conditions, or, in the case of current assets, declines in indicated realization value. It is also implicit in a procedure of this kind that it is not to be employed recurrently but only under circumstances which would justify an actual reorganization or formation of a new corporation, particularly if the sole or principal purpose of the quasi-reorganization is the elimination of a deficit in earned surplus resulting from operating losses.

In the case of the quasi-reorganization of a parent company, it is an implicit result of such procedure that the effective date should be recognized as having the significance of a date of acquisition of control of subsidiaries. Likewise, in consolidated statements, earned surplus of subsidiaries at the effective date should be excluded from earned surplus on the consolidated balance sheet.

[¶ 38,115] 211. Redeemable Preferred Stocks

.01. General

ASR 268:

On July 27, 1979, the Commission amended Regulation S-X to modify the financial statement presentation of preferred stocks subject to mandatory redemption requirements or whose redemption is outside the control of the issuer. The rules adopted do not impact reporting practices of registrants not having such securities outstanding. Registrants having such securities outstanding are required to present separately, in balance sheets, amounts applicable to the following three general classes of securities: (i) preferred stocks subject to mandatory redemption requirements or whose redemption is outside the control of the issuer; (ii) preferred stocks which are not redeemable or are redeemable solely at the option of the issuer; and (iii) common stocks. A general heading, "Stockholders' Equity," is not to be used and presentation of a combined total for equity securities, inclusive of redeemable preferred stocks, is prohibited. In addition, the rules require disclosure of redemption terms, five-year maturity data, and changes in redeemable preferred stocks in a separate note to the financial statements captioned "Redeemable Preferred Stocks."

There is a significant difference between a security with mandatory redemption requirements or whose redemption is outside the control of the issuer and conventional equity capital. The Commission believes that it is necessary to highlight the future cash obligations attached to this type of security so as to distinguish it from permanent capital. It is expected that the rules will provide more meaningful presentation of the financial obligations of those companies which finance operations through the use of such securities.

The Commission noted an increase in the issuance, by registrants, of preferred stocks to finance operations, consummate mergers and acquisitions, or to restructure existing debt arrangements. Many of the preferred stock issues included terms which required the issuer to redeem the stock at a fixed or determinable price on a fixed or determinable date. Other issues required the issuer to redeem the stock at the option of the holder at the time certain prescribed conditions are met which are not necessarily within the control of the issuer, such as attainment of a specified level of earnings.

The Commission believes that redeemable preferred stocks are significantly different from conventional equity capital. Such securities have characteristics similar to debt and should, in the opinion of the Commission, be distinguished from permanent capital. The Commission believes that traditional financial reporting practices do not provide the most meaningful presentation of the financial obligations attached to these types of securities and that improvement in the financial statement presentation of redeemable preferred stocks is necessary.

The rules are intended to highlight the future cash obligations attached to redeemable preferred stock through appropriate balance sheet presentation and footnote disclosure. They do not attempt to deal with the conceptual question of whether such a security is a liability. Further, the rules do not attempt to deal with the income statement treatment of payments to holders of such a security or with any related income statement matters, including accounting for its extinguishment. The Commission is cognizant of these conceptual problems in determining the appropriate accounting for and reporting of redeemable preferred stock and believes that these matters can best be addressed by the FASB. As an interim measure, the rules require that the amounts applicable to redeemable preferred stock be presented in financial statements as a separate item—and not combined with equity investments not having similar redemption requirements. The Commission believes the presentation required by the rules will highlight the redemption obligation and the fact that amounts attributable to these securities are not part of permanent capital.

211.02. Definitions

ASR 268:

The following definitions apply to the terms listed below as they are used in this section:

Preferred Stocks Subject to Mandatory Redemption Requirements or Whose Redemption is Outside the Control of the Issuer ("Redeemable Preferred Stock"). The term means any stock which (i) the issuer undertakes to redeem at a fixed or determinable price on a fixed or determinable date or dates, whether by operation of a sinking fund or otherwise; (ii) is redeemable at the option of the holder, or (iii) has conditions for redemption which are not solely within the control of the issuer, such as stocks which must be redeemed out of future earnings.*

Preferred Stocks Which Are Not Redeemable or Are Redeemable Solely at the Option of the Issuer ("Non-Redeemable Preferred Stock"). The term means any preferred stock which does not meet the criteria for classification as a "redeemable preferred stock."

211.03. Exemption

ASR 268:

The Commission has concluded that the necessary refinements concerning the presentation in financial statements of amounts applicable to redeemable preferred stocks should not impact the present reporting practices of registrants who do not use such securities to finance their operations. Therefore, registrants not having such securities may continue to use the general heading "Stockholders' Equity" and show a combined total. Where redeemable preferred stocks are outstanding, the Commission will not prohibit the combining of non-redeemable preferred stocks, common stocks and other equity accounts under an appropriately designated caption (e.g., "Non-Redeemable Preferred Stocks, Common Stocks, and Other Stockholders' Equity") provided that any combinations be exclusive of redeemable preferred stocks.

211.04. Footnote Disclosure of Future Cash Obligations

ASR 268:

In the interest of clear and prominent disclosure of the future cash obligations attendant with these types of securities, the rules require disclosure of the terms of redemption, five-year maturity data, and changes in these securities in a separate note to the financial statements captioned "Redeemable Preferred Stocks." It should be noted that although in the past a registrant may have disclosed changes in redeemable preferred stocks in a statement of stockholders' equity, such changes are now required to be disclosed in a separate note as described above.

211.05. Existing Loan Agreements

ASR 268:

It is not the Commission's present intention to establish whether redeemable preferred stocks are liabilities or components of equity. Therefore, the rules should not require any change in the calculation of debt-equity ratios under existing loan agreements. Further, the Commission believes that creditors already consider the distinctive characteristics of the types of securities which comprise a company's capital structure when evaluating a potential loan.

211.06. Ratios and Materiality Tests

ASR 268:

Where certain ratios or other data involving amounts attributable to stockholders' equity are presented as required or are optionally presented in filings with the Commission, such ratios or other data should be accompanied by an explanation as to their basis of calculation. If material amounts of redeemable preferred stock are combined with amounts applicable to non-redeemable preferred and common stocks for purposes of computing a ratio, there should also be presented a similar ratio which excludes amounts applicable to redeemable preferred stock from equity and includes such amounts as debt. This would also apply to any financial information such as tables, charts, graphic illustrations and ratios presented in annual reports to shareholders if such reports are to meet the requirements of Rule 14a-3 of the General Rules and Regulations under the Exchange Act.

In addition, the Commission did not amend its rules, regulations and releases to the extent that they provide for various materiality tests for disclosure purposes using a percentage of total stockholders' equity. In making these tests, registrants may use amounts applicable to all classes of capital stock.

[*Sec. 212 deleted by Release No. FR-22. CCH.*]

[¶ 38,125] 213. Separate Financial Statements

.01. Introduction

ASR 302:

The Commission modified requirements in Regulation S-X for including in filings with the Commission separate financial statements of the parent company only and of unconsolidated subsidiaries and 50 percent or less owned persons accounted for by the equity method. In addition, certain related amendments were adopted to revise the definition of a significant subsidiary. Also, the requirement to provide separate financial statements of consolidated subsidiaries engaged in diverse financial-type businesses was eliminated. These rules reduced the number of instances where separate financial statements are required and are designed to place greater reliance on summarized and condensed financial information.

The Commission believes that the amended rules improve the disclosure system and continue to provide for necessary and meaningful disclosures. It is interested, however, in hearing further from users of financial information, if after observing the results of application of the new rules, they believe that the results do not meet their needs. Specific areas of interest include the following:

(1) Is the need for parent company and unconsolidated subsidiary information satisfactorily met by the summarized and condensed financial infor-

---

* Under this definition, preferred stocks which meet one or more of the above criteria would be classified as redeemable preferred stock regardless of their other attributes such as voting rights, dividend rights or conversion features.

mation furnished in the 10-K filings with the Commission?

(2) Does the segment information required by SFAS 14 provide sufficient information about the activities of regulated industries?

(3) Are there additional criteria which should require the furnishing of parent company information, such as when the parent has outstanding public debt but the net asset restriction test is not met?

If the Commission's monitoring efforts or public comment on these or other matters indicate a need for further action, the related issues will be revisited at that time.

213.02. Parent Company Only Disclosures

.a. General

ASR 302:

The rules adopted for parent company disclosures require certain disclosure in footnotes to consolidated financial statements and the presentation of condensed financial information in a schedule when certain restrictions exist on the ability of subsidiary companies to transfer funds to the parent through intercompany loans, advances or cash dividends. Complete separate financial statements of the parent are no longer required.

The rules require, among other things, that registrants identify and quantify restrictions on the ability of subsidiary companies to transfer funds to the parent through intercompany loans, advances and cash dividends. To determine whether additional footnote disclosure is required, registrants must compute the total net assets of subsidiary companies (including unconsolidated subsidiaries) which are restricted from transfer to the parent company in the form of loans, advances, or cash dividends. This amount is then added to the parent's equity in undistributed earnings of 50 percent or less owned persons accounted for by the equity method and the resulting total compared to total consolidated net assets as of the end of the most recent fiscal year. If the restricted net assets of subsidiaries and the parent's equity in the undistributed earnings of 50 percent or less owned persons exceed 25 percent of total consolidated net assets, additional footnote disclosure regarding funds flow restrictions is required. Since a parent may be unable to control the payment of dividends, loans or advances from a 50 percent or less owned person, the net assets of such persons are relevant and need be considered, if significant, along with restricted net assets of both consolidated and unconsolidated subsidiaries to evaluate the need for footnote discussion of restrictions on the parent's control.

The computation of restricted net assets focuses on formal restrictions which have an impact on the flow of funds from subsidiaries to the parent. For this purpose, the restricted net assets of subsidiaries would be the amount of the parent's proportionate share of net assets (after intercompany eliminations) which, as of the end of the most recent fiscal year, may not be transferred to the parent by subsidiaries in the form of loans, advances or cash dividends without the consent of a third party (i.e., lender, regulatory agency, foreign government, etc.). Not all limitations on transferability of assets are considered to be restrictions for purposes of this test, which considers only specific third party restrictions on the ability of subsidiaries to transfer funds outside of the entity. For example, the presence of subsidiary debt which is secured by certain of the subsidiary's assets does not constitute a restriction under this rule. However, if there are any loan provisions prohibiting dividend payments, loan or advances to the parent by a subsidiary, these are considered restrictions for purposes of computing restricted net assets. When a loan agreement requires that a subsidiary maintain certain working capital, net tangible asset, or net asset levels, or where formal compensating balance arrangements exist, there is considered to be a restriction under the rule because the lender's intent is normally to preclude the transfer by dividend or otherwise of funds to the parent company. Similarly, a provision which requires that a subsidiary reinvest all of its earnings is a restriction, since this precludes loans, advances or dividends in the amount of such undistributed earnings by the entity. Where restrictions on the amount of funds which may be loaned or advanced differ from the amount restricted as to transfer in the form of cash dividends, the amount least restrictive to the subsidiary should be used in computing restricted net assets.

To determine whether condensed parent company financial information is required to be provided in a schedule, the above computation is modified by excluding the parent's equity in undistributed earnings of 50 percent or less owned persons and the restricted net assets of unconsolidated subsidiaries from the test. If the total amount of restricted net assets of consolidated subsidiaries exceeds 25 percent of total consolidated net assets, disclosures regarding the financial condition of the parent company must be provided in a schedule to the financial statements.

An instruction to Management's Discussion and Analysis of Financial Condition and Results of Operations provides that where footnote disclosure of restrictions on the ability of subsidiaries to transfer funds to the parent in the form of cash dividends, loans or advances is required by Regulation S-X, management's discussion of liquidity should include the nature and extent of the restrictions and the impact they have had or are expected to have on the ability of the parent company to meet its cash obligations.

213.02.b. Basis for Disclosure Requirements

ASR 302:

Basic premises of consolidated financial statements are that the parent company controls the affairs of its constituent companies, that there is a relatively free flow of funds among the various companies combined in the consolidated entity, and that the parent has the ability to manage their resources in the best interests of shareholders and creditors. The Commission concluded that parent company disclosures were needed in circumstances where the parent company may not exercise the level of control which consolidated statements lead users to presume. The operations of subsidiaries engaged in banking or insurance, for example, are in most cases subject to the strict government regulation. The financial flexibility of these entities and the nature of their relationships with affiliated persons, including the parent company, are subject to regulatory restraints. In addition, subsidiaries often have financing agreements which may restrict the transfer of funds to a parent or other affiliated party or other types of transactions with affiliates. Also, where subsidiaries have significant noncontrolling equity interests, their operations may be influenced by these equity holders.

Where a parent company's ability to control may be restricted to the extent that substantial control over the flow of funds within an enterprise may be impaired, the Commission believes investors should be provided the information necessary to evaluate the impact of such restrictions on the strength of the enterprise as a whole and on the security of their investments.

The Commission believes that adequate disclosure is not provided in consolidated financial statements where significant restrictions exist on the ability of a parent company to control the flow of funds of its consolidated group. Where parent company financial information is considered necessary, the Commission concluded that complete separate statements of the parent were not necessary to meet the needs of investors.

Since the rules are intended to provide information as to the ability of a parent company to meet its financial obligations, appropriate consideration should be given to the impact on a parent company of future cash obligations associated with redeemable preferred stocks. Similarly, it would be inappropriate to include noncontrolling interests in criteria used to evaluate the parent's control over consolidated resources. Therefore, the rules provide that redeemable preferred stocks and minority interests shall be deducted in computing net assets for purposes of this test.

[*As amended in FR-79, effective April 23, 2009, 74 F.R. 18612.*]

213.03. Unconsolidated Subsidiaries and 50 Percent or Less Owned Persons

.a. General

ASR 302:

The rules require the presentation of summarized financial information for unconsolidated subsidiaries and 50 percent or less owned persons accounted for by the equity method in a footnote when either asset or income tests based on certain 10 percent measurements are met. In addition, audited separate financial statements are required in filings with the Commission if either of the tests are met at a higher level of 20 percent. These tests are referred to in Regulation S-X as the significant subsidiary test (Rule 1-02(v)).

By raising the level of the percentage tests for providing audited separate financial statements in Commission filings from 10 to 20 percent, greater reliance is being placed on summarized financial information. To improve consistency in reporting this information, rules were adopted to establish standards for the content of summarized financial information.

Since separate financial statements of unconsolidated subsidiaries and 50 percent or less owned persons are only considered necessary to satisfy the informational needs of sophisticated users, they are required in registration and reporting forms filed with the Commission, but not in annual reports to security holders. These separate statements should comply with all provisions of Regulation S-X, including the schedule requirements.

213.03.b. Discussion of Rules

ASR 302:

These rules are based on the Commission's view that summarized financial information may be adequate for disclosure purposes up to the point when the financial impact of a subsidiary or person becomes so significant that more detailed disclosure becomes necessary to an evaluation of the overall financial condition of a reporting entity. While recognizing that quantifying that level of significance may be an arbitrary determination, the Commission concluded that the 20 percent level is a reasonable standard for determining when the more detailed disclosures provided by complete financial statements are necessary in filings with the Commission.

While the Commission recognizes that GAAP (APPO 18) calls for the presentation of either separate financial statements or summarized financial information, guidance is not provided as to when either of these alternatives may be more appropriate. The rules establish uniform standards to determine the degree of detailed information to be included in filings with the Commission. The Commission recognizes that many registrants often elect to include full separate financial statements for significant unconsolidated subsidiaries or 50 percent or less owned persons in their annual reports to security holders. The rules do not eliminate this option, and registrants may continue to provide either separate financial statements or summarized financial information in their annual reports as they deem to be appropriate.

The rules require the presentation of summarized financial information when any of the significant subsidiary tests is met on an aggregate basis by any combination of unconsolidated subsidiaries and 50 percent or less owned persons. The Commission emphasizes that the required additional financial information is warranted whether "significance" is attributable to the contribution of an individual subsidiary or person or from a combination of such subsidiaries or persons. Since the Commission believes that the summarized information should be complete, requests for permission to omit some entities from the summarized financial information will not be granted in a routine manner.

213.03.c. Summarized Financial Information

ASR 302:

An integral part of the rules concerned the establishment of standards for the content of summarized financial information. Such information is required for those entities which meet the revised significant subsidiary rules. The Commission believes that standards for summarized information are necessary in order for it to adopt these reduced requirements and to provide consistency in reporting this financial information. Should the FASB establish such standards, the Commission will re-evaluate the necessity for its own standards.

The items to be included in the summarized results of operations are based on existing requirements for footnote disclosure of certain selected quarterly financial data. For specialized industries, information may be substituted which is more meaningful to an entity's operations. A bank, for example, could present total interest income, total interest expense, provision for loan losses, and security gains or losses in lieu of sales and related costs and expenses. Similarly, an insurance company could present information as to net premiums earned, net investment income, underwriting costs and expenses, and realized gains or losses or investments.

The rules for summarized financial information as to assets and liabilities recognize that differences exist in balance sheet presentations among different industries. In industries in which classified balance sheets are presented, disclosure is required of the amounts of current and noncurrent assets and liabilities. For industries in which classified balance sheets are not presented, information is required as to the nature and amount of the major components of an entity's assets and liabilities. A finance company, for example, should disclose the portion of its total assets represented by net loan receivables when that item represents one of that company's largest assets. Long-term liabilities and redeemable preferred stock should be disclosed regardless of the type of balance sheet presented.

213.04. Consolidated Subsidiaries Engaged in Diverse Financial Activities

ASR 302:

Consolidated financial statements comprised of a variety of specialized financial-type businesses are often complex and difficult to analyze and the disaggregated disclosure provided by separate financial statements has been considered necessary to perform a detailed analysis of the enterprise. A matter which frequently contributes to the complexity of a consolidated presentation is the fact that certain of the consolidated entities operate in highly regulated environments. The portion of the consolidated entity to which regulatory restraints relate and the impact such restraints have on the enterprise as a whole are often difficult to ascertain from the consolidated statements. Disclosures can provide sophisticated investors with a better understanding of the relative strengths and weaknesses of the various businesses which the enterprise operates and generally provide a better basis upon which to evaluate trends.

SFAS 14 requires public companies to provide certain disaggregated disclosures regarding operations in different industries, foreign operations, export sales and major customers. The Commission reiterates its view that the disclosures required by SFAS 14 provide meaningful information regarding the principal segments of a business in which an enterprise operates and that the degree of disclosure provided is adequate for purposes of annual reports to shareholders. The Commission's decision to delete all requirements for additional financial information for consolidated finance-type subsidiaries in Commission filings was significantly influenced by its conclusion that the disclosures required by SFAS 14 provide adequate information on these activities to most investors and by the views of commentators that the marginal utility of additional information may not be cost-justified, considering the burdens associated with the presentation of such information.

213.05. Affiliates Whose Securities Are Pledged as Collateral

ASR 302:

Financial statements of affiliates are required in filings with the Commission when the securities of the affiliate constitute a substantial portion of the collateral of any class of securities registered or being registered. For purposes of compliance with these requirements, an affiliate's securities are deemed to constitute a substantial portion of collateral if the aggregate principal amount, par value, book value as carried by the registrant, or market value of such securities, whichever is greatest, equals 20 percent or more of the principal amount of the secured class of securities.

In addition to situations involving collateralized securities of affiliates, separate financial statements of the guarantors of indebtedness of a registrant are required to be filed under the Commission's rules. The basis for requiring separate financial statements of both guarantors and affiliates whose securities collateralize an offering are the same. In both instances, separate financial statements are considered necessary for an assessment of the ability of an entity to satisfy its commitment in the event of default by the registrant.

[¶ 38,135] 214. Pro Rata Stock Distributions to Shareholders

ASR 124:

Several instances had come to the attention of the Commission in which registrants made pro rata stock distributions which were misleading. These situations arise particularly when a registrant makes distributions at a time when its retained earnings or its current earnings are substantially less than the fair value of the shares distributed. Under present GAAP, if the ratio of distribution is less than 25 percent of shares of the same class outstanding, the fair value of the shares issued must be transferred from retained earnings to other capital accounts. Failure to make this transfer in connection with a distribution or making a distribution in the absence of retained or current earnings is evidence of a misleading practice. Distributions of over 25 percent (which do not normally call for transfers of fair value) may also lend themselves to such an interpretation if they appear to be part of a program of recurring distributions designed to mislead shareholders.

It has long been recognized that no income accrues to the shareholder as a result of such stock distributions or dividends, nor is there any change in either the corporate assets or the shareholders' interests therein. However, it is also recognized that many recipients of such stock distributions, which are called or otherwise characterized as dividends, consider them to be distributions of corporate earnings equivalent to the fair value of the additional shares received. In recognition of these circumstances, the AICPA has specified in ARB 43, Chapter 7, paragraph 10, that ". . . the corporation should in the public interest account for the transaction by transferring from earned surplus to the category of permanent capitalization (represented by the capital stock and capital surplus accounts) an amount equal to the fair value of the additional shares issued. Unless this is done, the amount of earnings which the shareholder may believe to have been distributed will be left, except to the extent otherwise dictated by legal requirements, in earned surplus subject

to possible further similar stock issuances or cash distributions."

The Commission also considers that if such stock distributions are not accounted for in this manner, the shareholders may be misled. In a stop order proceeding,[*] the Commission found that a registration statement was materially misleading because a series of four stock distributions made between 1966 and 1968 ". . . were 'part of a frequent recurrence of issuances of shares' . . . [and] . . . under generally accepted accounting principles they should have been accounted for as stock dividends."

If, in addition to failing to account for the distribution properly, the registrant does not have sufficient retained earnings or current income to cover the appropriate transfer to permanent capital, a question immediately arises whether these factors may be part of a manipulative or fraudulent scheme, and as such are proscribed under Rule 10b-5 of the Exchange Act. The Commission has stated in published opinions,[**] in situations where companies did not have retained or current earnings, that the declaration of a dividend not warranted by the business condition of a company is characteristic of a manipulative scheme.

The Commission emphasizes that it will deem the types of transactions noted above to be misleading if the accounting is improper or disclosure is inadequate, and if there is a question of whether the condition of the business warrants the distribution, a further investigation will be considered to determine whether such distribution may be part of a manipulative or fraudulent scheme.

[¶ 38,141] 215. Creation of Surplus by Appraisal

ASR 8:

The Commission issued the following statement relating to the creation of surplus by appraisal in balance sheets representing the accounts of promotional companies:

In connection with a registration statement, an industrial company in its promotional stages with no record of business or earning capacity, filed a balance sheet in which Property, Plant and Equipment, acquired in an arms-length transaction at a cost of $200,000, was carried at $720,042.81 which represented its "sound value" derived from an independent appraisal of the estimated "replacement value new less (observed) depreciation". Thus, the balance sheet figure exceeded cost by $520,042.81, which excess was carried as "surplus arising from revaluation of property".

In the appraisal report filed, the term "sound value" was qualified by the appraiser as being "the value for use by a going concern having prospects

---

[*] *Monmouth Capital Corporation,* Securities Act Release No. 5169 (July 14, 1971).

[**] *Gob Shops of America, Inc.,* 39 S.E.C. 92 (1959); *Mac Robbins & Co., Inc.* 41 S.E.C. 116 (1962).

for the profitable use, at normal plant capacity, of the properties appraised".

The registrant was required to amend its balance sheet to eliminate the surplus and to show the fixed assets at cost.

[¶ 38,145] 216. Disclosure of Unusual Charges and Credits to Income

[The Commission adopted amendments to certain forms requiring increased disclosure of unusual charges and credits to income. The requirements were later deleted when, in March 1975, the FASB issued SFAS 5, "Accounting for Contingencies." The following comments were made in the release which adopted the disclosure requirements in January 1973.]

ASR 138:

The Commission noted that it had observed an increasing number of large charges to income which often appeared without warning and were not generally understood by investors. While many of such charges result from an identifiable event, many also appear to be made on the basis of a discretionary decision to dispose of marginal facilities or operations or to write off deferred development or excess production costs. In the latter situations, where facilities or operations gradually deteriorate or the outlook for a contract or program gradually worsens to the point where a write-off is deemed necessary, registrants have an obligation to forewarn public investors of the deteriorating conditions which, unless reversed, may result in a subsequent write-off. This includes an obligation to provide information regarding the magnitude of exposure to loss.

The Commission, therefore, reiterates its view that registrants should make special efforts to recognize incipient problems that might lead to such charges and to identify them clearly at the earliest possible time in financial statements and other forms of public disclosure, including public reports filed with the Commission, so that public investors may recognize the risks involved. In this connection, registrants should consider disclosure of the investment involved in divisions operating at a loss; the undepreciated cost of plant and equipment currently considered to be obsolete or of marginal utility; and other similar items where significant uncertainties exist as to realization.

In addition to disclosure of incipient problems, the Commission believes that substantial additional disclosure in regard to extraordinary items and material unusual charges and credits to income or major provisions for loss is necessary to enable public investors to assess the impact of

such items. This would include transactions that are classified as extraordinary items under GAAP and other unusual or nonrecurring material transactions or provisions for loss, such as (but not restricted to) material write-downs of inventories, receivables, provisions for loss on major long-term contracts or purchase commitments, and losses on disposition of assets or business segments.

[¶ 38,146] Sec. 217. Accounting for Extinguishment of Debt

[*Sec. 217 added by* FRR-15.]

Sec. 217.01. Background

FRR-15:

In Financial Reporting Release (FRR) No. 3, issued in August 1982 (47 FR 38868), the Commission announced its support of the tentative view of the FASB that, except in certain limited circumstances, debt should not be accounted for as extinguished unless the debtor has no further legal obligation. The Commission indicated that, to avoid inconsistent accounting, registrants should follow that tentative position while the FASB was considering the issue. Recently, after study and deliberation, the FASB issued Statement of Financial Accounting Standards (SFAS) No. 76, "Extinguishment of Debt", which clarifies the accounting for such "quasi-defeasance" or "in-substance defeasance" arrangements. Accordingly, the Commission has determined to rescind FRR No. 3.

Sec. 217.02. Requirements for Extinguishment of Debt

FRR-15:

SFAS No. 76 provides that a debtor shall consider debt to be extinguished under three circumstances. The first two are the traditional criteria for extinguishment of debt (payment of the debt and legal release as primary obligor). The third, described in paragraph 3(c), is new and provides for extinguishment under certain conditions when eligible assets are irrevocably placed in a trust to be used solely for satisfying scheduled payments on the debt.

SFAS No. 76 does not have any specific eligibility requirements for the trustee of the trust created pursuant to paragraph 3(c) of that standard. The Commission believes, however, that paragraph 3(c) of the standard contemplates that the trustee should be independent with respect to the company.[1]

Paragraph 4 of SFAS No. 76 provides that the assets used to effect an extinguishment of debt under paragraph 3(c) must be monetary assets

---

[1] Trustees that meet the eligibility requirements for trustees under Sections 310(a)(1) and 310(a)(2) of the Trust Indenture Act of 1939 (the "1939 Act"), for example, will be presumed by the staff of the Commission to be appropriate trustees. Those sections of the 1939 Act provide that a trustee must be a corporation organized and doing business under

the laws of the United States or of any State or Territory or of the District of Columbia, which (a) is authorized under such laws to exercise corporate trust powers, (b) is subject to supervision or examination by Federal, State, Territorial or District of Columbia authority, and (c) has combined capital and surplus of at least $150,000.

essentially risk free as to the amount, timing, and collection of interest and principal. These requirements are designed to assure that all interest and principal payments are made on time. Accordingly, they are very important and must be strictly interpreted.

Paragraph 4 lists the three types of assets in U.S. dollars that might meet those requirements: (1) direct obligations of the U.S. government, (2) obligations guaranteed by the U.S. government, and (3) securities that are backed by U.S. government obligations as collateral under an arrangement by which the interest and principal payments on the collateral generally flow immediately through to the holder of the security (for example, as in a closed trust). The Commission believes that very few securities of the types listed in (2) and (3) above can satisfy the essentially risk free requirements, particularly because the requirement for the assets to be risk free as to timing of collection applies to the risk of late as well as early payments. For example, if a guarantee provides only for the ultimate collection, but not for the collection of interest and principal in sufficient time to ensure payments on the defeased debt as they become due, the security would not qualify.

The Commission notes that the determination whether debt can be considered to be extinguished requires an assessment as to the likelihood of the debtor being required to make future payments with respect to the debt, not only because of an inadequacy of trust assets attributable to a failure to realize scheduled cash flows, but also because of an acceleration of the debt's maturity. An acceleration might occur because of a violation of a covenant of the debt issue being extinguished, or, under cross-default provisions, because of a violation of a covenant of another debt issue.

The determination whether debt can be considered to be extinguished is also affected by the irrevocable nature of the trust. The trust must be designed so that neither the corporation nor its creditors or others can rescind or revoke it, or obtain access to the assets.

The Commission emphasizes that the qualifications of the trustee and nature of the trust and of the assets in the trust are areas of concern and that it expects registrants which extinguish debt under paragraph 3(c) to carefully evaluate those areas.

[¶ 38,147]   Sec. 218.   Costs of Internally Developing Computer Software for Sale or Lease to Others

[Sec. 218 added by FRR-12.]

Sec. 218.01. Background

FRR-12:

As a result of its concern about the increasing number of registrants capitalizing costs of internal development of computer software, on April 14, 1983 the Commission authorized the publication of proposed Rule 3-21 of Regulation S-X and Item 21(j) of Form S-18 for public comment.[1] The Commission's concerns resulted from the fact that this trend created a source of incomparability in financial reporting between those registrants that are capitalizing such costs and those that are following the predominant practice of expensing them as incurred. The existing accounting literature in this area is unclear[2] and has not been interpreted consistently. Therefore, similar factual situations are being accounted for differently. This inhibits meaningful comparison of the financial position and results of operations of registrants engaged in these activities. Further, while acknowledging that the computer software industry and the accounting profession have begun activities intended to result in clarification of the accounting literature, the Commission expressed its concern about continuation of the trend towards capitalization in the intervening period, not only because it would exacerbate the problems of financial comparison, but also because of the potential for inappropriate capitalization in the absence of clear guidance.

Therefore, the proposed rules were intended to accomplish two purposes. The first was to maintain present practice in place during the time the private sector develops clear guidance for the classification of the costs of these activities. Guidance is needed regarding both the relationship of internal development of computer software to research and development and the proper accounting for the costs of any such activities which are not research and development activities. The latter issue is not explicitly addressed by the existing accounting literature. The second purpose of the proposal was to facilitate comparison of financial information of companies engaged in these activities by requiring disclosure of the effect of not expensing all such costs as incurred which the Commission understands to be the predominant accounting practice in the industry.

---

[1] Securities Act Release No. 6461 [48 FR 17107]. The proposing release specified that the proposed rules would provide that companies which had not disclosed the practice of capitalizing internal software development costs either in audited financial statements issued prior to the date of the proposing release (i.e., April 14, 1983) or in a report or registration statement filed with the Commission prior to that date shall not follow such a practice in financial statements filed with the Commission after that date.

[2] The Financial Accounting Standards Board's ("FASB") pronouncements in this area address accounting for noncontractual internal software development costs, in the context of their relationship to research and development costs, which are required to be expensed as incurred. *See,* Release No. 33-6461 for a description of these pronouncements and certain recent developments in the interpretation thereof.

Sec. 218.02. Views of Commentators and Final Rules

FRR-12:

The Commission received a total of 49 letters during the comment period which expired May 31, 1983.[3] The principal comments and the Commission's response to them are discussed below.

Sec. 218.02.a. Prohibition of Adoption of Practice of Capitalization

FRR-12:

The proposed prohibition on adoption of the practice of capitalizing internal software development costs was supported by financial analysts, as well as by several other commentators.

The analysts indicated that their major concern is comparability of financial information. The analysts' letter referred to in footnote 3 also stated that the committee and a substantial majority of the aforementioned 40 industry specialists believe that internal software development costs should never be capitalized. This belief is based on the following:

1. Such costs are very similar to research and development expenditures, which must be expensed.

2. The substantial degree of competition in the industry as well as the very rapid pace of change makes capitalized software development costs a highly questionable asset.

3. There is potential for abuse in this area because of the subjectivity involved.

The letter also states that a significant minority of the industry specialists believe that the costs are different from research and development and that capitalization of such costs may be appropriate in some circumstances. This latter group would like to see the FASB establish guidelines governing capitalization.

Most of the commentators from industry and public accounting expressed the view that adoption of such a prohibition by the Commission would be undesirable and unnecessary. Many of them acknowledged the existence of diverse accounting practices in this area, but emphasized that they believed that a prohibition would be inequitable because companies that had previously disclosed a capitalization practice would be allowed to continue it, while others who, for various reasons, had not made such a disclosure would be precluded from adopting an accounting practice that would be appropriate for their software development activities. Included in this latter group would be those companies that have not disclosed capitalized internal software development costs because they had not incurred any such costs in the past (or had not incurred material amounts thereof), nonpublic companies desirous of registering with the Commission that had not previously issued audited financial statements, and companies that had capitalized material amounts of such costs but had not disclosed that fact because it was not believed to be required by either Regulation S-X or generally accepted accounting principles ("GAAP").[4] Thus, it was argued, the Commission's proposal would have the effect of prohibiting the practice of capitalization for certain companies in the absence of clear evidence that capitalization is always inappropriate for those companies. Most of these commentators also expressed concerns that such an action by the Commission conveyed a bias against the practice of capitalization and thus would prejudge the outcome of the private sector standards-setting activities which had already begun prior to the Commission's proposal, and unfavorably impact the credibility of private sector standards-setting in general. Finally, many of the critical commentators expressed views about the competitive impact of adoption of the proposed rules. They maintained that those companies prevented from adopting the practice of capitalization (and especially smaller companies) would not be able to effectively compete in the capital markets for funds necessary for growth due to the fact that their financial statements would suffer in comparison with others in the industry permitted to continue capitalizing. As an alternative that would prevent these consequences, it was suggested that the Commission limit its activities in this area to a requirement for disclosure of the practice being followed.

The Commission, after careful consideration of the views of all commentators on the proposed rules, has determined that it should issue final rules prohibiting the adoption of the practice of capitalizing costs of internal development of computer software to be sold or leased to others. The Commission recognized at the time of issuance of its proposal that such rules would permit the continuation of diverse accounting practices during the period necessary to develop specific accounting guidance in this area. As a result, the final rules (as did the proposed rules) contain a disclosure requirement to facilitate comparison of financial information among companies following different practices. However, disclosure requirements alone would not alleviate the Commission's concerns that in the absence of clear accounting guidance (which is not expected before 1984),

---

[3] Representation among the commentators was as follows: industry and related groups (38); accounting firms and groups (8); others (3).

The latter group includes a letter prepared by the Financial Accounting Policy Committee of the Financial Analysts Federation which stated that it encompassed the views of approximately 40 analysts who specialize in the securities of registrants in the computer services industry.

[4] It is important to note that no specific instances of nondisclosure of material amounts of such costs were brought to the Commission's attention as a result of the comment process.

continuation of the recent trend towards increased use of capitalization, including inconsistencies in the application of that practice, will result in increasing disparity among companies engaged in these activities notwithstanding the fact that they have essentially the same facts and circumstances. Further, it may result in inappropriate capitalization by some registrants. The only alternative action that would alleviate those concerns would be development by the Commission of definitive accounting guidelines in this area which, as stated in the proposing release, the Commission determined not to undertake in view of the current and expected private sector activities. Additionally, the Commission has determined that its rules will terminate when an FASB pronouncement which provides specific accounting guidance in this area becomes effective. Thus, the Commission views its action as consistent with its previous expressions of its policy of relying on the FASB for leadership in establishing financial accounting and reporting standards.[5] Further, the Commission believes that concerns about the effect of its action on competition and access to capital markets must be evaluated in the context of its understanding, disputed by none of the commentators, that the predominant practice in accounting for such costs is to charge them all to expense as incurred. The Commission believes that it would be preferable for a change from such predominant practice to occur only after deliberation of the issues in the context of standards-setting.

The final rules predicate the ability to continue a previously adopted practice of capitalization on prior disclosure of that practice. The Commission does not anticipate that its action will require companies that have capitalized material amounts of internal software development costs to change their accounting practice.[6] With respect to existing registrants, the Commission believes that the requirements of Regulation S-X in Rules 5-02.15 and .16 (Intangible Assets) or, alternatively, 5-02.17 (Other Assets) and GAAP[7] would require disclosure of amounts of software costs capitalized and related amortization, together with the method and period of amortization, as well as the bases therefor. Not all of the disclosures are

specifically required by GAAP, but the APB 22 disclosures would permit formerly nonpublic companies to meet the test of having previously disclosed the practice of capitalizing software costs.[8]

Sec. 218.02.b. Disclosure of Effect of Capitalization

FRR-12:

As noted above many commentators agreed that diverse accounting practices for internal software development costs exist. Some stated that the proposed requirement to disclose the effect on net income and earnings per share of not following the predominant practice of expensing such costs as incurred would provide an adequate basis for comparison of financial information during the time specific accounting guidance is being developed. Several commentators, however, expressed the view that disclosure of these amounts would be potentially confusing and may imply that the financial statements are not prepared in conformity with GAAP.

In response to these latter comments, the final rules have been modified to require disclosure, for each period for which an income statement is required to be presented, only of the amount of internal software development costs capitalized during the period, less amortization. These disclosures will enable financial statement users to ascertain the impact of capitalization on the financial statements.

Sec. 218.02.c. Other Matters

FRR-12:

The final rules have been modified in several other respects in response to comments.

It was pointed out by one commentator that the text of the proposed rules would literally require their application to development activities undertaken pursuant to contractual arrangements. This was not the Commission's intent and the final rules clarify their applicability only to costs of internal development of software not subject to accounting for contracts.

Several commentators addressed the applicability of the proposed rules to development of computer software to be used as part of a product or process to be sold or leased to others. Since the

---

[5] *See* Accounting Series Release Nos. 150 and 280, reproduced in pertinent part in Section 101 of the Commission's Codification of Financial Reporting Policies, announced in Financial Reporting Release No. 1 (April 15, 1982) [47 FR 21028].

[6] Obviously this conclusion would not apply to companies whose capitalization practices are clearly inconsistent with the existing accounting literature (e.g., costs associated with the "conceptual formulation or translation of knowledge into a design" phase of a software development project).

[7] Paragraph 12b of Accounting Principles Board Opinion No. 22, "Disclosure of Accounting Policies," ("APB 22") provides that disclosure of accounting policies should encompass

"principles and methods peculiar to the industry in which the reporting entity operates, even if such principles and methods are predominantly followed in that industry." Paragraph 13 of APB 22 cites policies with respect to amortization of intangibles as an example of a disclosure that would commonly be required.

[8] After consideration of the comments received, the Commission has amended the final rules to permit disclosure in a document for an offering of securities by the issuer, other than a registration statement, which document was used in such offering prior to April 14, 1983 (e.g., offering documents prepared under Regulation D under the Securities Act [17 CFR 230.501-.506]), as an additional exception to the prohibition of the practice of capitalization.

existing accounting literature[9] discusses the relationship of such activities to research and development activities in the same context as it does software developed solely as a product or process to be sold or leased, the Commission intended that the new rules apply to such development costs. The text of the rules has been modified to make this clear.

There were several comments about the Commission's views on appropriate amortization periods for capitalized software costs. While not incorporated in the final rules, the Commission deems it appropriate to reaffirm the views expressed in Release No. 33-6461. GAAP requires that the determination of an appropriate amortization period for such amounts be based on careful consideration of the relevant facts. The Commission believes that computer software (whether internally developed or purchased) is an area characterized by both rapid technological development and increased industry competition and growth. Therefore, the use of very short amortization periods is indicated. Further, the Commission reminds registrants that have capitalized such costs that careful periodic evaluation of the recoverability thereof is necessary.

[¶ 38,148] 219. Disclosure of Accounting Policies for Derivative Financial Instruments and Derivative Commodity Instruments

[Added by FR-48]

219.01. Background

During the last several years, a significant number of issues relating to the accounting for derivatives have been raised. The FASB is working on a project that will address comprehensively the accounting for derivatives. However, currently there is little authoritative literature on the accounting for options and complex derivatives.[35]

In the absence of comprehensive accounting literature, registrants have developed accounting practices for options and complex derivatives by analogy to the limited amount of literature that does exist. Those analogies are complicated because, under existing accounting literature, there are at least three distinctly different methods of accounting for derivatives (e.g., fair value accounting, deferral accounting, and accrual accounting).[36] Further, the underlying concepts and criteria used in determining the applicability of those accounting methods are not consistent.[37] As a result, during its 1994 and 1995 reviews of annual reports, the SEC staff observed that registrants with similar risk management objectives often accounted for derivatives with similar economic characteristics in different ways.[38] Thus, it was difficult to ascertain and compare the financial statement effects of derivatives among registrants.

To provide a better understanding of the accounting for derivative financial instruments, paragraph 8 of FAS 119 requires disclosure of the policies used to account for those instruments, pursuant to the requirements of APB 22.[39] Specifically, FAS 119 emphasizes the disclosure of "policies for recognizing (or not recognizing) and

---

[9] FASB Interpretation No. 6, "Applicability of FASB Statement No. 2 to Computer Software," paragraph 9.

[35] The authoritative accounting literature for options and complex derivatives generally is limited to a few consensuses from the FASB Emerging Issues Task Force ("EITF"), which by their nature address the accounting for specific transactions. See, e.g., EITF Issues 88-8, "Mortgage Swaps," and 90-17, "Hedging Foreign Currency Risks with Purchased Options."

[36] Under the fair value method, derivatives are carried on the balance sheet at fair value with changes in that value recognized in earnings or stockholders' equity (see, e.g., FASB, Statement of Financial Accounting Standards No. 52, "Foreign Currency Translation," ("FAS 52") (December 1981), and FAS 80. Under the deferral method, gains and losses from derivatives are deferred on the balance sheet and recognized in earnings in conjunction with earnings of designated items (see, e.g., FAS 52 and FAS 80). Under the accrual method, each net payment/receipt due or owed under the derivative is recognized in earnings during the period to which the payment/receipt relates; there is no recognition on the balance sheet for changes in the derivative's fair value (see, e.g., EITF Issue 84-36, "Interest Rate Swap Transactions").

[37] For example, the risk reduction criterion in FAS 52 is different from the risk reduction criterion in FAS 80. FAS 52 specifies risk reduction on a transaction basis, while FAS 80 specifies risk reduction on an enterprise basis. In addition, FAS 80 permits the use of deferral accounting for futures contracts used to hedge probable, but not firmly committed, anticipated transactions, while FAS 52 prohibits deferral ac-

counting for foreign currency forward exchange contracts used to hedge thos e same types of anticipated transactions.

[38] The Commission does not mean to imply by this statement that registrants may justify the use of any method of accounting for derivatives. Registrants must select appropriate accounting methods that are consistent with generally accepted accounting principles. In particular, generally accepted accounting principles require registrants using derivatives for trading, dealing, or speculative purposes to recognize those instruments on the balance sheet at fair value and to recognize changes in that value immediately in earnings (see, e.g., FAS 80 3).

[39] APB 22 12 states:

Disclosure of accounting policies should identify and describe the accounting policies followed by the reporting entity and the methods of applying those principles that materially affect the determination of financial position, cash flows or results of operations. In general, the disclosure should encompass important judgments as to the appropriateness of principles relating to recognition of revenue and allocation of asset costs to current and future periods; in particular, it should encompass those accounting principles and methods that involve ... a selection from existing acceptable alternatives.

The Accounting Principles Board was the predecessor to the FASB. Unless superseded by FASB Statements, APB Opinions continue to be regarded as the highest level of generally accepted accounting principles followed by the accounting profession. See generally AICPA, Statements on Auditing Standards No. 69, "The Meaning of Present Fairly in Conformity With Generally Accepted Accounting Principles in the Independent Auditor's Report," 5 (March 1992); AU § 411.05.

---

measuring derivative financial instruments . . . and when recognized, where those instruments and related gains and losses are reported in the statements of financial position and income."[40] Notwithstanding its helpful guidance, FAS 119 does not explicitly indicate the type of information that should be included in the accounting policies footnote to help investors understand the effects of derivatives on the statements of financial position, cash flows, and results of operations. FAS 119 also does not address disclosure of accounting policies for derivative commodity instruments.

.02. Rule 4-08(n) of Regulation S-X and Item 310 of Regulation S-B

To facilitate a more informed assessment of the effects of derivatives on financial statements, Rule 4-08(n) and Item 310 explicitly require that seven items be disclosed in the derivatives accounting policies footnote, when material. For example, Rule 4-08(n) and Item 310 require a description of the methods used to account for derivatives, the types of derivatives accounted for under each method, and the criteria required to be met for each accounting method used. See Rule 4-08(n) and Item 310 for further requirements.

When assessing materiality under Rule 4-08(n) and Item 310, the Commission expects registrants to consider (i) the financial statement effects of all derivatives, including those not recognized in the statement of financial position and (ii) the relative effects of using the accounting method selected as compared to the other methods available (e.g., accrual, deferral, or fair value methods of accounting).

In essence, Rule 4-08(n) and Item 310 clarify how the accounting policy disclosure requirements in FAS 119 should be applied to derivative financial instruments. They also extend those requirements to derivative commodity instruments. The Commission expects to reconsider the effectiveness of and the need for the accounting policy disclosures, prescribed under Rule 4-08(n) and Item 310, when a new accounting standard for derivatives is issued by the FASB.

SECTION 300—INTERIM REPORTING

[¶ 38,151] 301. Form 10-Q

[Most publicly owned companies are required to file a quarterly report on Form 10-Q under the Exchange Act. In ASR 286, the Commission revised requirements for interim financial information in quarterly reports and registration statements to make them consistent with the requirements for annual reporting.]*

.01. Adequacy of Disclosure

ASR 286:

Interim financial information is to include disclosure, either on the face of the financial statements or in accompanying footnotes, sufficient so as to make the interim information presented not misleading. The need for and adequacy of additional disclosure is to be determined, except in regard to material contingencies, in the context of a presumption that users of interim financial information have either read or have access to the audited financial statements for the latest fiscal year. Footnote disclosure which would substantially duplicate the disclosure contained in the audited financial statements for the most recent fiscal year, such as a statement of significant accounting policies and practices, details of accounts which have not changed significantly in amount or composition since the end of the most recent fiscal year, and detailed disclosures prescribed by Rule 4-08 of Regulation S-X (note requirements for complete financial statements) may be omitted.

Disclosure is required to be provided, however, where events having a material impact on the registrant have occurred since the end of the most fiscal year. Disclosure will encompass, for example, significant changes since the end of the most recent fiscal year in such items as: accounting principles and practices; estimates inherent in the preparation of financial statements; status of long-term contracts; capitalization including significant new borrowings or modification of existing financing arrangements; and the reporting entity resulting from business combinations or dispositions. Where material contingencies exist, disclosure of these contingencies must be included even though a material change in such contingencies may not have occurred since the end of the prior fiscal year.

The Commission believes that even for interim reporting it is important to distinguish between disclosures necessary for fair presentation of financial condition and disclosures which are supplemental in nature. Accordingly, the rule does not allow registrants to provide the disclosures necessary for fair presentation in MD&A.

301.02. Disclosure of Material Contingencies

ASR 286:

The requirement to repeat the disclosure of material contingencies in interim reports was proposed by the Commission because of its understanding of the disclosure requirements already existing under GAAP.** The Commission contin-

---

[40] See FAS 119 60.

* [In Securities Act Releases 6360, 6361 and 6362, an integrated disclosure system for foreign private issuers was proposed. That project will address, among other things, interim reporting for foreign private issuers.]

** Paragraph 22 of APBO 28, "Interim Financial Reporting," states:

ues to believe that APBO 28 requires material contingencies to be disclosed in interim reports regardless of whether a material change in the status of the contingencies has occurred. Accordingly, the rules specify that "when material contingencies exist, disclosure of such matters shall be provided even though a significant change since year end may not have occurred."

301.03. Status of Information Disclosed
ASR 286:

Form 10-Q contains Instruction E (Filed Status of Information Presented) which makes explicit whether various information provided in response to the requirements of the form will be deemed filed for the purpose of liability under Section 18 of the Exchange Act. The instruction contains a statement that financial information provided in response to Item 1 and Item 2 of Part I will not be deemed filed, pursuant to Rule 13a-13(d) and Rule 15d-13(d). The instruction goes on to state that this is the case regardless of whether the information is presented directly in the Form 10-Q, is incorporated by reference from an informal report containing the required information, or is in an exhibit to Part I. In addition, the instruction also provides that information provided to satisfy all requirements of Form 10-Q will be deemed filed for the purpose of Section 18 of the Exchange Act.

The Commission adopted an amendment to the safe harbor rule for forward-looking information, Rule 175 under the Securities Act, which makes clear that a projection of the type enumerated by that rule is protected if included or properly reaffirmed in Part I of Form 10-Q. This action codifies the staff position which deems Part I "filed" for purposes of the safe harbor rule even though it is not filed for purposes of Section 18 of the Exchange Act.

301.04. Management's Discussion and Analysis
ASR 286:

Requirements governing the scope and content of management's discussion and analysis of interim financial statements are contained in Item 303 of Regulation S-K. These provisions are intended to complement the requirements established for discussions of annual periods by requiring interim period discussions to focus on the same information discussed for annual periods in order to provide an update of the annual discus-

sion. The interim discussion is not required to reiterate all of the information presented in the full year discussion. Rather, only material changes in financial condition and results of operations occurring during the periods covered by the interim financial statements need be discussed.

The discussion of material changes in financial condition must cover the period from the end of the preceding fiscal year to the date of the most recent interim balance sheet provided and must focus on items required for annual discussions such as liquidity and capital resources. A discussion of changes in financial condition from the corresponding interim balance sheet date of the preceding fiscal year is only required if the interim balance sheet as of that date is included in the interim financial statements. Thus, only when the registrant believes the discussion is necessary for an understanding of the impact of seasonal fluctuations on financial condition as of an interim date will that period be required in the discussion of financial condition.

The rules for management's discussion and analysis of interim financial statements also require registrants to discuss any material changes with respect to results of operations for the most recent interim year-to-date period for which an income statement is provided and the corresponding year-to-date period of the preceding fiscal year. If interim financial statements are required or are otherwise provided in a filing for the most recent fiscal quarter,* the registrant must also discuss the material changes in the results of operations with respect to that quarter and the corresponding quarter of the preceding fiscal year. In addition, if a registrant chooses to provide financial statements for a cumulative twelve-month period preceding the date of the most recent interim balance sheet provided, material changes in results of operations must also be discussed with respect to that period and the preceding cumulative twelve-month period. However, if a registrant provides a cumulative twelve-month income statement in a registration statement in place of the interim statements of income otherwise required, as provided for by paragraph (b) of Rule 3-06 of Regulation S-X, the discussion of material changes in results of operations for that period shall be in respect to the preceding fiscal year as opposed to the corresponding preceding period.[1]

(Footnote Continued)

Contingencies and other uncertainties that could be expected to affect the fairness of presentation of financial data at an interim date should be disclosed in interim reports in the same manner required for annual reports. Such disclosures should be repeated in interim and annual reports until the contingencies have been removed, resolved, or have become immaterial.

* Only Form 10-Q requires income statements for the most recent fiscal quarter and for the corresponding quarter of the

preceding fiscal year in addition to comparative statements for year-to-date periods.

[1] Rule 3-06 of Regulation S-X contains instructions to income statement requirements and applies to interim statements in certain registration statements. Paragraph (b) provides that:

If the registrant is engaged primarily (1) in the generation, transmission or distribution of electricity, the manufacture, mixing, transmission or distribution of gas, the supplying or distribution of water, or the furnishing of telephone or tele-

The same items required to be addressed in annual discussions of results of operations must, with the exception of the impact of inflation, also be addressed in discussions of interim periods. Although the Commission believes registrants should strive to provide users of interim reports with information regarding the impact of inflation and changing prices, it also believes that it would be premature to require all registrants to address inflation for interim reporting purposes, particularly in light of the experimental nature of this type of disclosure. Once registrants have had the opportunity to experiment with alternative methods of disclosing the impact of changing prices and once improved reporting standards are developed by the accounting profession, the Commission will reconsider disclosure obligations for reporting interim results. In the meantime, the Commission encourages registrants to experiment with this type of disclosure.

The Commission has determined to make the same relief from certain of the MD&A disclosure requirements which is granted to qualified wholly-owned subsidiaries for reporting on Form 10-K[2] also available for quarterly reporting on Form 10-Q.[3] The Commission believes that it is appropriate at this time to grant consistent treatment to these registrants with respect to discussions of capital resources and liquidity for annual and interim periods.[4]

301.05. Incorporation by Reference

ASR 286:

Where an informal report to shareholders contains some or all of the required information, appropriate portions of that report may be incorporated by reference into the Form 10-Q in lieu of repetitive disclosure, just as the annual report to security holders may be used to satisfy some of the requirements of Form 10-K.

The interim financial information and MD&A called for by Part I of the Form could be satisfied, in whole or in part, through incorporation by reference from an informal quarterly report to shareholders containing the required information. The Commission intends to facilitate the practice of sending quarterly reports to shareholders by emphasizing that issuers have the option of incorporating their informal communications into the Form 10-Q. It should be noted that Rule 12b-23(b) already operates to provide that non-financial statement disclosure contained in informal reports

to security holders may be incorporated by reference in answer or partial answer to any item of Part II of Form 10-Q.

The Commission believes that it is appropriate at this time to reiterate its support for the recommendation of the Advisory Committee on Corporate Disclosure that companies be encouraged to publish readable, understandable quarterly reports to shareholders which include the information content of a Form 10-Q, and to file these documents with the Commission in satisfaction of Form 10-Q reporting obligations.* The Commission believes that companies can reduce their reporting burden by taking advantage of the option to incorporate by reference to their informal quarterly report in partial or full satisfaction of the requirements of Parts I and II of Form 10-Q. More importantly, use of this option could effect a significant enhancement of the corporate communications system.

301.06. Duplication of Generally Accepted Accounting Principles

ASR 286:

The Commission at this time does not believe that generally accepted accounting principles for interim reporting purposes are as well defined as the principles for annual reporting purposes, especially in regard to financial statements which constitute less than a complete set of financial statements but which are more comprehensive than summarized data of operations. Consequently, the Commission has elected to retain, and in some cases add to, the level of guidance offered applicable to the interim data it requires.

301.07. Use of Form 10-Q in Lieu of Form 8-K

ASR 286:

Item 5 may be used to fulfill any or all of the reporting requirements under Form 8-K. Item 5 permits registrants to reduce reporting burdens by including in a report on Form 10-Q information which would otherwise be required to be reported on Form 8-K. Of course, all Form 8-K timing and substantive disclosure requirements would have to be met by the filing on Form 10-Q in order to avoid the obligation to file a Form 8-K.

301.08. Signature Requirements

ASR 177:

Form 10-Q must be signed by either the chief financial officer or the chief accounting officer of

---

(Footnote Continued)

graph service; or (2) in holding securities in companies engaged in such businesses, it may at its option include statements of income and changes in financial position (which may be unaudited) for the twelve-month period ending on the date of the most recent balance sheet being filed, in lieu of the statements of income and changes in financial position for the interim periods specified.

[2] See General Instruction I to Form 10-K.

[3] Instruction G(2)(a) reflects this conforming change.

[4] It should be noted that, in light of the changed focus of MD&A from the former summary of operations onto the financial statements themselves, the Commission may reconsider this area, both for annual and interim periods, as it gains experience with the new MD&A.

* Report of the Advisory Committee on Corporate Disclosure to the Securities and Exchange Commission, House Committee on Interstate and Foreign Commerce, 95th Cong., 1st Sess. (1977), Committee Print 95-29, 470-5.

the corporation. This requirement is included in recognition of the fact that the data in the form is primarily financial, and that is appropriate to emphasize the responsibility of the chief financial or accounting officer for the representations explicit and implicit in the filing. This signature will not relieve other corporate officers of their responsibilities.

[¶ 38,161] 302. Registration Statement Requirements

.01 Age of Financial Statements

ASR 281:

In general, the rules regarding the inclusion of interim financial information in registration statements parallel requirements for interim financial data under Form 10-Q. The rules do not require registrants to provide in registration statements interim financial data any more current than interim data required for most registrants in quarterly reports on Form 10-Q. A discussion of the rules, which specify the interim data to be included both as of the date of filing and as of the expected effective date of the filing, or proposed mailing date in the case of a proxy statement, and a description of the exceptions to the general rule are set forth below.

302.01.a. Filings Within 90 Days of Year-End

[Amended in Release No. 33-8644, effective December 27, 2005, 70 F.R. 76626. See section III.D of the release for compliance date information.]

ASR 281:

The uniform financial statement requirement requires audited balance sheets as of the end of the two most recent fiscal years and audited statements of income and cash flows for each of the most recent three fiscal years. Exceptions to this rule occur when filings, other than on Form 10-K or Form 10, are made within 45 days after the end of the registrant's fiscal year and audited financial statements for the most recent fiscal year are not yet available. In these circumstances, the rules provide that the audited balance sheets may be as of the end of the two preceding fiscal years and audited statements of income and cash flows may be presented for each of the three fiscal years preceding the most recent audited balance sheet presented. Under these circumstances, however, an additional balance sheet (which may be unaudited) is required as of an interim date at least as current as the end of the registrant's third fiscal quarter of the most recently completed fiscal year and unaudited statements of income and cash flows are required on a comparative basis for the interim period between the date of the most recent audited balance sheet presented and the date of the most recent interim balance sheet.

This same provision for filing interim financial data is applicable to filings, other than on Form 10-K or Form 10, made after 45 days but within 60 days of the end of the registrant's fiscal year (75

days for fiscal years ending before December 15, 2006) for large accelerated filers or after 45 days but within 75 days of the end of the registrant's fiscal year for accelerated filers (or after 45 days but within 90 days of the end of the registrant's fiscal year for other registrants) provided the registrant meets certain prescribed conditions.

To this extent, the rules parallel interim reporting requirements under the Exchange Act. A potential investor of securities already registered and traded in the open market, for instance, wishing to make an investment decision on March 1, may only have available to him for a calendar year company the audited financial statements for the two years preceding the fiscal year most recently completed and unaudited interim data on a condensed basis through the end of the third fiscal quarter of the most recent fiscal year (as filed on Form 10-Q). This same level of disclosure will be available to the investor considering an investment in shares being registered on March 1.

However, where a company files a registration statement or plans to become effective with a registration after 45 days but within 60 days (75 days for fiscal years ending before December 15, 2006) of the end of its fiscal year if the registrant is a large accelerated filer (*i.e.*, February 16 to March 1 (or March 15 for fiscal years ending before December 15, 2006) for calendar year companies), after 45 days but within 75 days of the end of its fiscal year if the registrant is an accelerated filer (*i.e.*, February 16 to March 15 for calendar year companies), or after 45 days but within 90 days of the end of its fiscal year for other registrants (*i.e.*, February 16 to March 31 for calendar year companies) and does not meet the conditions prescribed by the rules described below, the Commission requires that audited financial statements for the most recently completed fiscal year be included in the registration statement. To avoid the possibility of having to accelerate the preparation and audit of the financial statements for the most recently completed fiscal year, a company filing in the "45 day window" specified above must: (a) be a registrant who files annual, quarterly and other reports pursuant to section 13 or 15(d) of the Exchange Act; (b) have filed all reports due; (c) reasonably and in good faith expect income, after taxes but before extraordinary items and cumulative effect of a change in accounting principle, for the most recent fiscal year for which audited financial statements are not yet available; and (d) for at least one of the two immediately preceding fiscal years for which audited financial statements are available, have reported income, after taxes but before extraordinary items and cumulative effect of a change in accounting principle.

The Commission recognizes that for some short period of time certain registrants may be prevented from going to the market. However, the Commission has concluded that, when a company is either a new registrant or is a registrant with unprofitable operations and is attempting to raise capital in the marketplace during the 45 days before audited financial statements for the most recent fiscal year would otherwise be required, it is reasonable to delay registration until such financial statements become available. The Commission believes that companies which do not meet the conditions described above will be cognizant of applicable registration requirements and will plan to accelerate the preparation and audit of their financial statements when planning to file or become effective in this 45 day period.

The Commission believes that this exception in the rules is in the best interest of the investing public and will not create any burden on the large majority of registrants. Also, it should be understood that, as in the past, the Commission will offer waivers to the rules where unusual circumstances dictate the need for them.

302.01.b. Filings After 134 Days of Year-End

[Amended in Release No. 33-8644, effective December 27, 2005, 70 F.R. 76626. See section III.D of the release for compliance date information.]

ASR 281:

The rules also provide for interim financial information in registration statements filed after 129 days subsequent to the end of a registrant's fiscal year if the registrant is a large accelerated filer or an accelerated filer (or 134 days subsequent to the end of a registrant's fiscal year for other registrants) —the period after audited financial statements for the most recently completed fiscal year are already required to be filed by most registrants on Form 10-K and on or after the date most registrants are required to have filed interim financial statements for the first fiscal quarter. When a registration statement is filed during this period, an additional balance sheet is required as of an interim date within 130 days of the date of the filing if the registrant is a large accelerated filer or an accelerated filer (or 135 days of the date of the filing for other registrants) but as of a date at least as current as the date of the most recent quarterly data filed with the Commission on Form 10-Q. Also, statements of income and cash flows are required, on a comparative basis, for the interim period between the date of the most recent audited balance sheet and the date of the most recent interim balance sheet being filed. Here again, the rules parallel the requirements for interim information under the Exchange Act but also provide some flexibility for those registrants who may not be required to file quarterly data on Form 10-Q.*

302.01.c. Age at Effective Date of Filing

[Amended in Release No. 33-8644, effective December 27, 2005, 70 F.R. 76626. See section III.D of the release for compliance date information.]

ASR 281:

Where financial statements in a filing are as of a date 130 days or more, if the registrant is a large accelerated filer or an accelerated filer (or 135 days or more for other registrants) prior to the date the filing is expected to become effective or proposed mailing date in the case of a proxy statement, the rules require the financial statements to be updated with a balance sheet as of an interim date within 130 days, if the registrant is a large accelerated filer or an accelerated filer (or 135 days for other registrants) and with statements of income and cash flows on a comparative basis, for the interim period between the end of the most recent fiscal year and the date of the interim balance sheet provided.

Two exceptions to this rule have been provided. First, where the registrant meets the four conditions described in the previous section and the anticipated effective date or proposed mailing date in the case of a proxy statement falls after 45 days but within 60 days (75 days for fiscal years ending before December 15, 2006) of the end of the fiscal year if the registrant is a large accelerated filer, after 45 days but within 75 days if the registrant is an accelerated filer (or after 45 days but within 90 days of the end of the fiscal year for other registrants), the filing need not be updated with financial statements more current than as of the end of the third fiscal quarter of the most recently completed fiscal year provided audited financial statements for such fiscal year are not available. Second, where the registrant does not meet the prescribed conditions referred to above and the anticipated effective date or proposed mailing date falls after 45 days but within 60 days (75 days for fiscal years ending before December 15, 2006) of the end of the fiscal year if the registrant is a large accelerated filer, after 45 days but within 75 days if the registrant is an accelerated filer (or after 45 days but within 90 days of the end of the fiscal year for other registrants), the filing must include audited financial statements for the most recent fiscal year. Both of these exceptions are consistent with the rules governing financial statements as of the date of filing and have been included for the same reasons described in the previous sections.

In addition, the updating rules include a general provision that, if a filing is made near the end of a fiscal year and the audited financial statements for that fiscal year are not included in the original

---

* For instance, a calendar year company not subject to quarterly reporting requirements under the Exchange Act and therefore not required to file a Form 10-Q may, in a filing on May 30, include interim financial statements as of, say, the end of January or February as opposed to the end of the first fiscal quarter (March 31). For some companies not accus-tomed to reporting as of an interim date, a requirement for data as of the end of the most recent fiscal quarter imposes a significant burden in preparing a registration statement. Data less current than as of the end of the most recent fiscal quarter will be acceptable as long as it is within the prescribed 135 day period prior to the date of filing.

filing, the filing shall be updated with such audited financial statements if they become available prior to the anticipated effective date, or proposed mailing date in the case of a proxy statement.

302.02. Form and Content

ASR 281:

As an additional step toward attaining consistency between the disclosures required under the Securities Act and those required under the Exchange Act, the Commission adopted amendments which conform the requirements as to form and content of interim financial data under the Securities Act with requirements as to form and content under Form 10-Q under the Exchange Act.

[¶ 38,171] 303. Reporting in Conjunction with Historical Financial Statements

[The Commission originally required disclosure of selected quarterly financial data in notes to annual financial statements of certain registrants as announced in ASR 177. Subsequently, the requirement for such disclosure was moved from Regulation S-X to Item 302.(a) of Regulation S-K thereby permitting such disclosure outside of the financial statements as announced in ASR 280. These disclosures are required in annual reports filed with the Commission and annual reports to security holders furnished pursuant to the proxy rules. A certain level of auditor involvement with this unaudited information is required.]

ASR 177:

The Commission determined that disclosure of selected quarterly financial data (net sales, gross profit, income before extraordinary items and cumulative effect of a change in accounting, per share data based upon such income, and net income for each quarter within the two most recent fiscal years and any subsequent fiscal period for which income statements are required) is appropriate for the protection of investors in the case of large companies whose shares are actively traded. The Commission believes that the greatest investor need for these data exists in the case of such companies whose activities are most closely followed by analysts and investors. Accordingly, registrants whose shares are not actively traded or whose size is below certain limits have been exempted from this rule. In making this judgment, the Commission also recognized that the costs of such disclosure would be relatively a greater burden to smaller companies. Nevertheless, the Commission urges registrants who are exempt from the rule to consider the desirability of including such data in their annual reports.

The Commission believes that such disclosure will materially assist investors in understanding the pattern of corporate activities throughout a fiscal period and it feels that such an understanding is important if financial statements are to serve their objective of allowing investors to develop reasonable expectations about the future prospects of enterprises in which they are investing or considering investment. Presentation of such quarterly data will supply information about the trend of business operations over segments of time which are sufficiently short to reflect business turning points. Annual periods may obscure such turning points and may reflect a pattern of stability and growth which is not consistent with business reality. In addition, quarterly data will reflect seasonal patterns which are of significance to an investor's understanding of the business operations of a reporting entity.

While the Commission recognizes that random events can materially affect quarterly results, it believes that its rule which requires disclosure of any unusual or infrequently occurring items recognized in any quarter disclosed, will enable investors to ascertain the effect of such items and hence not be misled. It also recognizes that short period estimates are imprecise, and did not propose any change in the traditional accounting practice of making the best estimate practicable at the time the estimate must be made, and then reflecting subsequent adjustments in the estimate in subsequent periods as the need became apparent. Estimates are a necessary part of all financial reporting, and since registrants have had many years experience in making the estimates required in quarterly reporting and investors have had equivalent experience in using the reports encompassing these estimates, the Commission is not prepared to conclude that including quarterly data in an annual report will create an impression of reliability which will mislead investors. In addition, the rule requires the disclosure of the aggregate effect and the nature of year end or other adjustments which are material to the results of each quarter presented. This disclosure will permit investors to determine the nature and effect of substantial changes in estimates.

[¶ 38,175] 304. Involvement of Independent Public Accountants

.01. Review of Interim Data

[In ASR 177, the Commission announced a requirement that auditors review interim financial information filed with annual financial statements.]

ASR 177:

The Commission believes that all registrants would find it useful and prudent to have independent public accountants review quarterly financial data on a timely basis during the year prior to the filing of Form 10-Q and it encourages registrants to have such a review made. While such a review does not represent an audit and cannot be relied upon to detect all errors and omissions that might be discovered in a full audit of quarterly data, it will bring the reporting, accounting and analytical expertise of independent professional accountants to bear on financial reports included in Form 10-Q and, therefore, should increase the quality and the reliability of the data therein in a cost-effective way. The Commission believes that an accountant's report on a limited review may provide significant and useful information to investors and that such reports should be encouraged. However, the Commission does not require such reports in connection with Form 10-Q filings.

The Commission believes that as reviews of quarterly information become a regular part of the audit examination of public companies, auditors will revise the timing of their audit examinations so that they will perform procedures related to the testing of internal controls and the analytical review of internal financial reports on a regular basis throughout the year. In addition, programs encompassing regular analytical review should increase the efficiency of auditors in finding and focusing promptly on potentially troublesome areas in the audit. The Commission believes, therefore, that many of the costs included in the studies reported to the Commission will not prove to be incremental costs but will reduce the cost of the year-end audit examination. In addition, it is the Commission's view that many of the costs will be of a one time rather than a continuing nature since audit programs and corporate control systems will be improved promptly to keep costs at a minimum. The Commission does not suggest that the cost of auditor involvement in quarterly data will be trivial, but it does believe that some of the higher estimates supplied to it will not prove to be correct.

The benefits resulting from such increased costs cannot be quantified, but the Commission is satisfied that they will be substantial. While the rules do not mandate the timely involvement of the independent accountant with quarterly reports, the Commission believes that it is likely that such involvement will occur so that management will be less likely to face the necessity of revising quarterly data at the time year-end statements are published. Either timely or retrospective involvement should increase the care and attention devoted to quarterly reports which will increase the likelihood that management will discover needed adjustments on a timely basis. In addition, management may be able to identify problem areas more promptly so that unusual charges and credits are not made so frequently in the last month of a fiscal year. Finally, the involvement of independent accountants will add the expertise of professional accountants with wide experience in reporting problems to the quarterly reporting process. This should improve individual company reporting and direct greater professional attention to the general problems of interim reporting.

The Commission has brought a number of enforcement actions involving quarterly reports and it has observed other cases where quarterly reports have required correction. In addition, it has noted the preponderance of Form 8-K filings covering unusual charges and credits to income being made late in the year. While these are not suggested to be evidence of systematic abuse in quarterly reporting, they do indicate that deficiencies exist. Although auditor involvement will not prevent all deficiencies, the Commission does believe that it will enhance the reliability of interim reports and reduce the likelihood of abuse. In the final analysis, however, the benefits of auditor involvement in quarterly data are expected primarily to result from improvement in the quality of interim reporting and the annual auditing process and only secondarily from the prevention of specific abuses currently perceived.

After appraising the costs and benefits, the Commission determined that the benefits of mandatory involvement of independent accountants in quarterly data on the basis set forth in the rules substantially outweigh the costs thereof, and that such involvement is required in the interests of investors.

In exempting certain registrants from these rules, the Commission has noted that the cost of auditor involvement will fall with the greatest relative severity on smaller registrants in which public investor interest is not of great magnitude. In these cases, the Commission believes that it is less clear that the benefits of auditor involvement with interim data outweigh the costs. Accordingly, it has not required such involvement for such registrants at the present time, although it will continue to study the question as it evaluates the experience gained from the rules adopted.

304.02. Preferability Letters
ASR 177:

In connection with accounting changes, a letter from the registrant's independent public accountant is required to be filed in which the accountant states whether or not the change is to an alternative principle which in his judgment is preferable under the circumstances. The Commission believes that professional accounting judgment can be applied to determine whether an alternative accounting principle is preferable in a particular set of circumstances. Since a substantial burden of proof falls upon management to justify a change, the Commission believes that the burden has not been met unless the justification is sufficiently persuasive to convince an independent professional accounting expert that in his judgment the new method represents an improved method of measuring business operations in the particular circumstances involved.

[¶ 38,181] 305. Form 8-K
ASR 306:

Form 8-K plays a critical role in the periodic reporting system, which is intended to provide investors with a continuous stream of corporate information. Reports on Form 8-K are used to provide material information concerning certain specified events that may have occurred since the latest annual report on Form 10-K or quarterly report on Form 10-Q was filed. In addition, registrants may, and in fact are encouraged to, file voluntary reports on Form 8-K pursuant to Item 5 describing any other events that may be of interest to investors. Item 5 makes clear that registrants may file voluntary reports not only to report material events, but also to inform their security holders of other matters that may be of interest. This provision is intended to encourage further voluntary reports on Form 8-K and to remove any reluctance that registrants may have to file voluntary reports pursuant to Item 5 on the basis that they will be deemed to have admitted the materiality of the event reported.

ASR 206:

Registrants are reminded of the obligations of publicly held companies to make full and prompt announcements of material facts regarding the company's financial condition, notwithstanding their compliance with the reporting requirements of the Exchange Act. The failure of companies to make prompt and accurate disclosure of both favorable and unfavorable information to security holders and the investing public may violate the Exchange Act and, in the case of an issuer making a continuous offering of its shares, may also violate the Securities Act if the prospectus is not appropriately updated. Therefore, corporate managements are urged to review their policies with respect to corporate disclosure and endeavor to set up procedures which will insure that prompt disclosure be made of all material corporate developments.[*]

SECTION 400—SPECIALIZED INDUSTRIES

[¶ 38,191] 401. Banks and Bank Holding Companies

[In ASR 254, the Commission adopted a comprehensive revision of Article 9 of Regulation S-X relating to bank holding companies and banks. In ASR 276, the Commission adopted revisions to certain sections of those rules. In FRR 11, the Commission adopted further revisions to Article 9 to (1) eliminate rules which are duplicative of GAAP, (2) integrate and simplify the rules, (3) reflect current financial reporting practices, and (4) improve financial reporting generally. In addition, certain related amendments to the Guides for Statistical Disclosure by Bank Holding Companies (Industry Guide 3) were adopted in order to incorporate a number of disclosures which were eliminated from the requirements of Article 9. The Commission also amended the proxy rules to require bank holding companies to include in annual reports to shareholders financial statements prepared in accordance with Regulation S-X.]

.01. Income Statement Format

ASR 254:

The Commission believes that the net interest income format presents valuable information for analysis by investors even when it is not on a tax equivalent basis. The tax equivalency adjustment is not in accordance with generally accepted accounting principles but reflects theoretical income never actually realized by a company. Although such an adjustment may be appropriate for statistical analytical purposes, it is not appropriate for inclusion in financial statements.

401.02. Disclosure of Loans to Nonofficer Directors

ASR 276:

In view of commentator requests and the limitations in the Financial Institutions Regulatory and Interest Rate Control Act of 1978 on when banks can make loans to executive officers, directors and certain stockholders, the Commission considered whether detailed disclosure of loans to nonofficer directors in a schedule to the financial statements was useful in evaluating the financial condition and future prospects of bank holding companies and banks. The Commission believes, that an investor should be aware of the extent, at least in the aggregate, to which a bank makes loans to insiders as against loans to the general public.

FR 11:

A significant number of commentators suggested that the Commission eliminate all requirements for disclosure of related party loans because banks engage in lending transactions in the ordinary course of business. Many of these commentators suggested that no distinction is necessary for loans to related parties since such transactions are highly regulated and subject to certain legal requirements. Other commentators suggested that specific Commission requirements are unnecessary since GAAP adequately addresses this area under the Financial Accounting Standards Board's Statement of Financial Accounting Standards No. 57, "Related Party Disclosures" ("SFAS 57"). The Commission has considered the views of these commentators and continues to believe specific information about loans to related parties is material information for investors and shareholders. Furthermore, analysis of commentator letters indicates some confusion about the applicability of SFAS 57 to bank holding companies, since SFAS 57 contains an exception for certain related party transactions in the ordinary

---

[*] See Securities Act Release 5092 (October 15, 1970), 35 FR 16733 (October 29, 1970).

course of business. Therefore, the Commission has determined to retain its specific disclosure requirements to ensure consistent minimum disclosure in this important area.

401.03. Foreign Activities
ASR 254:

The definition of foreign activities recognizes the ability of banks at times to place loans in a foreign or domestic office depending on the availability of funds. Although the definitions and details of items to be reported for foreign activities in Article 9 differ in certain respects from those in the reports of condition and income (call report) of the Federal bank regulatory agencies because of differences in the purposes for which the reports are required, the Commission believes that there is no difference in details and totals of corresponding assets, liabilities, revenue and income which are to be reported. The provisions of Article 9 have also been designed to reflect the application of the general provisions of SFAS 14 to the special nature of banking.

The general requirement for disclosure of foreign activities and the requirement that disclosure be made if income before income tax expense or net income exceeds 10 percent of the corresponding amount in the related financial statement are appropriate for bank holding companies and other financial type companies because their leveraged nature creates different relationships between assets, revenue and income as against the relationships existing in commercial and industrial companies.

401.04. Investment Securities
ASR 254:

The Commission believes that disclosure of market value of investment securities on the balance sheet is valuable in the evaluation of this asset specifically and in relation to the balance sheet in its entirety. The significance of market value of investments is such that it should not be completely relegated to a note to the financial statements.

FR 11:

Investment Securities Gains or Losses. The proposed rules called for a change in the income statement format to report gains or losses on investment securities as a separate component of income before income tax expense, rather than as a separate item (less applicable taxes) after the caption entitled "income before securities gains or losses." This proposed elimination of the so-called two-step format of reporting income both before and after investment security transactions was commented on by approximately three-fourths of the respondents. A majority of those commentators opposed the proposed change. Objection to the proposed one-step approach was based primarily on the view that the two-step reporting format is a customary presentation which banks have used for many years, and that the inclusion

of the effect of investment securities transactions as a part of income from banking operations is inappropriate and will result in a less useful presentation. A few commentators objected for other reasons, indicating that banks should have the ability to restructure their investment portfolio without penalizing current "operating" income with the related losses, or that the proposed change would increase the potential to manage or smooth reported earnings through the timing and selection of securities transactions.

Although the rule met with considerable opposition, a significant number of commentators strongly endorsed the change. Proponents indicated that a uniform net income approach was long overdue and that conforming the reporting format used by bank holding companies to that used by virtually all other entities would eliminate much of the confusion surrounding a bank holding company's actual earnings. These commentators generally agreed with the Commission that there is no conceptual basis for reporting investment transactions in a manner that implies that the gains or losses thereon represent something other than operating earnings. Further, the present reporting was viewed as being inconsistent in that security losses are excluded from operations, while the interest on the replacement security, which generally exceeds the interest on the previous security, is included in operating income. On this point, it was mentioned that the sale of securities generally has the same objective as the sale of mortgage loans and should be classified similarly.

Careful consideration has been given to the comments of respondents, particularly those of users, and the needs of investors. While the Commission understands that some persons believe that income before securities gains or losses provides a better basis upon which to evaluate trends, the Commission continues to believe that the two-step income format promotes the misconception that securities transactions are not part of normal banking operations, and that this format detracts from the importance of net income, which should be of primary importance to investors. Furthermore, there are many other discretionary items (similar to securities transactions) which are included in income before securities gains and losses.

For these reasons, and because of the potential for inappropriate reporting of certain transactions as security gains or losses, the Commission is adopting the one-step income statement format for bank holding companies as proposed, with one change. In response to commentator suggestions that the proposed presentation of securities gains or losses as a separate caption after other income and other expenses retains some of the complexity of the present two-step format, the final rules call for the presentation of investment securities gains and losses as a separate subcategory of other income.

In response to certain commentator suggestions that the one-step format will somehow influence investment policies regarding the content of the investment portfolio and the restructuring thereof (including the potential for registrants to manage earnings through the timing and selection of securities transactions), the Commission wishes to emphasize its belief that the revised reporting format should not have a bearing on prudent decision making. Furthermore, the Commission's existing disclosure requirements require specific disclosures about the content of the investment securities portfolio and the yields thereon. Such disclosures should provide users with the necessary information to evaluate management's investment policies and strategies.

In response to certain commentator suggestions that the one-step format will increase the potential for registrants to manage earnings, the Commission emphasizes the responsibility of bank holding companies, as well as all other registrants, to clearly identify and explain in the Management's Discussion and Analysis the nature and impact of all special, discretionary, or nonrecurring items (such as investment securities gains or losses) having a material effect on reported financial condition, changes in financial condition and results of operations.

The Commission is aware of certain private-sector initiatives to promote the adoption of the one-step income statement for the entire banking industry. This action would complement the Commission's action, which is only applicable to bank holding companies required to file with the Commission.

In addition, the FASB has a project on its agenda as part of its conceptual framework to explore display issues in reporting earnings.[2] This project will deal with, among other things, the purpose of the income statement, the concept of operating performance and how information should be displayed in the income statement (i.e., the reporting of details, subtotals, and which kind of items should be presented separately within the statement). The Commission expects that the outcome of this project (which has been under consideration for some time and is not yet near completion) should result in more useful financial reports for companies in all industries. Thus, the Commission encourages the FASB to aggressively pursue this project and stands ready to reconsider the provisions of Article 9 being adopted today, as well as other provisions of S-X governing the form and content of financial statements, based on its evaluation of the results of the FASB project.

401.05. Reporting of Large Certificates of Deposit and Time Deposits
ASR 276:

Informative disclosure of the aggregate amount of time certificates of deposit (CD) and other time deposits (TD) in denominations of $100,000 or more in both domestic and foreign categories appears necessary to show the increasing significance of large CD's and TD's and in some banks the increasing reliance on large interest bearing deposits in foreign offices. Separate disclosure of large foreign CD's and TD's would not be necessary if the aggregate of such deposits is a majority of total foreign deposit liabilities. In such cases, a note should explain that the aggregate amount of deposits in excess of $100,000 is a majority of total foreign deposits.

401.06. Bankers' Acceptances
FR 11:

In the proposing release, the Commission requested comments on the balance sheet presentation of banker's acceptance transactions. Although no changes were proposed to the present requirement to disclose on the balance sheet amounts due from customers on acceptances and banks' acceptances outstanding as assets and liabilities, the Commission noted that some have indicated that the current presentation should be reevaluated to determine whether these transactions should be reported as contingent liabilities.

Response to the inquiry was diverse. Some commentators maintained that acceptances are best characterized as contingent liabilities, while others stated their belief that the present practice is appropriate. A significant number of commentators suggested that this issue should be left to the private sector for resolution.

In the absence of a consensus as to the most appropriate accounting in this area, and considering the complexity of the issues, the Commission has determined that it will not take any further action at this time. Rather, the Commission encourages industry and accounting groups to continue to consider this issue, and if deemed necessary, to refer the matter to the Financial Accounting Standards Board for resolution.

401.07. Parent Company Financial Information
FR 11:

In the proposing release, the Commission requested comments on the need for parent company financial information when consolidated financial statements are presented for bank holding companies. The response to this inquiry indicates that many users and preparers of bank

---

[2] FASB Exposure Draft, Proposed Statement of Financial Accounting Concepts, "Reporting Income, Cash Flows and Financial Position of Business Enterprises," (November 16, 1981). The comment period on this exposure draft expired May 3, 1982. After reviewing the comments received, the

FASB decided that further development of concepts for reporting earnings should be delayed so as to be concurrent with the development of concepts for measurement and recognition criteria.

holding company financial statements strongly believe that information provided by separate financial statements of the parent company are necessary for informed decisions since inter-company loans, advances and cash dividends by bank subsidiaries are subject to substantial regulatory restrictions. The Commission believes that these views are valid and that the parent company information should be widely available to assist in making informed investment decisions. Accordingly, the final rules provide that the condensed parent only financial information currently provided in Schedule III (modified to prescribe certain separate disclosures about bank and non-bank subsidiaries which was previously required in a schedule)[4] be [presented in the notes to the consolidated financial statements. The effect of the change will be to require parent company financial information in the annual reports to shareholders of bank holding companies.

Other. In addition to various editorial revisions, certain other substantive changes have been made in the final rules:

—The instructions in Article 9 concerning disclosure of the valuation of trading account assets have been deleted since GAAP calls for such assets to be carried at market value.

—A provision was added to Rule 9-03(7) allowing the registrant to use different loan categories than those specified if it results in a more meaningful presentation; this provision currently exists in Article 9 but was not included in the proposal.

—The requirements of Section V-A of Guide 3 regarding the types of deposits have been amended to provide for disclosures of the average rates paid thereon. Also, an instruction was added to allow the use of captions other than those specified for domestic deposits if appropriate. These changes were made in light of the impact of deregulation on the costs and sources of funds, and should provide additional useful information about these funding sources and provide flexibility to appropriately describe the nature of the deposits.[5]

Sec. 401.08. Risk Elements Involved in Lending Activities

[*Sec. 401.08 added by FRR-13.*]

Sec. 401.08a. Executive Summary

FRR 13:

This release amends the existing Item III.C., "Nonperforming Loans," of the Industry Disclo-

sure Guides for Bank Holding Companies ("Guide 3") to establish a new section—"Risk Elements."[1] The terminology "nonperforming loans" is no longer utilized in Guide 3. This risk elements section calls for four categories of disclosure:

- Nonaccrual, past due and restructured loans
- Potential problem loans
- Foreign outstandings
- Loan concentrations

The above information does not have to be set forth in a single table.

The first of the four risk categories contains three of the four classifications of loans which are designated as nonperforming loans in the current Item III.C. of Guide 3, except that the Commission's existing criterion for determining a restructured loan is being replaced by the criteria of Statement of Financial Accounting Standards No. 15 ("FAS 15")[2] for troubled debt restructurings. A significant change in the amended guidelines for disclosure of nonaccrual, past due and restructured loans is the exclusion of certain instructions present in the current Guide which allowed for the use of different criteria, and permitted exclusion of certain loans. This change has the effect of enhancing comparability of disclosures among registrants. Users of this information, particularly financial analysts, have stressed the importance of comparability in this area.

The second category, potential problem loans, is currently the fourth existing criterion for classification of loans as nonperforming (i.e., "serious doubts" loans). These are loans which are not disclosed as part of the first category described above, but where information known by management indicates that the borrower may not be able to comply with present payment terms.

The third category calls for "foreign outstandings" disclosures. This new category is a codification of the substance of the alternative table disclosures of Staff Accounting Bulletin No. 49 ("SAB 49"), *"Disclosures by Bank Holding Companies about Certain Foreign Loans"* [47 FR 49627, November 2, 1982]. The threshold for disclosure provided in SAB 49, however, has been changed and certain additional disclosures are called for. Certain implementation guidance has also been provided.

The fourth category calls for disclosure of "loan concentrations" which are defined as amounts loaned to a multiple number of borrowers en-

---

[4] The requirement to provide information in a schedule about investments in and indebtedness of and to bank subsidiaries, and cash dividends paid by bank subsidiaries was rescinded by Accounting Series Release No. 302 in Securities Act Release No. 6359 (November 6, 1981) [46 FR 56171].

[5] As provided for in General Instruction No. 5 of Industry Guide 3, if information as to average rates paid on domestic deposits or the average balances of the categories of foreign deposits is not reasonably available on an historical basis, a

waiver may be granted and thus these disclosures may be provided prospectively.

[1] The Commission solicited public comments on the proposed revision of Guide 3 in Release No. 33-6462 (April 15, 1983) [48 FR 18826, April 26, 1983]. Forty-nine comment letters were received in response to this proposal.

[2] Financial Accounting Standards Board Statement of Financial Accounting Standards No. 15 "Accounting by Debtors and Creditors for Troubled Debt Restructurings" (June 1977).

gaged in similar activities which would cause them to be similarly impacted by economic or other conditions. A disclosure threshold of 10% of total loans has been provided.

The Commission believes that these revised guidelines will improve the utility of disclosures by bank holding companies by focusing more broadly on the various risk elements involved in lending activities. Since they require more uniformity in the preparation of the disclosures, the revisions should improve comparability of disclosures among registrants, a factor important to analysts and other users of the data in assessing risk.

As a result of a coordinated effort by the Commission and the Federal banking agencies, the amended guidelines pertaining to "nonaccrual, past due and restructured loans" as well as "foreign outstandings" are consistent with the present and planned disclosure requirements of the Federal banking agencies. Uniformity in the bases for presenting information by bank holding companies in Commission filings and by banks in supplementary disclosures for bank regulatory purposes will reduce compliance burdens and enhance the usefulness of the disclosure reports by investors and the public.

Sec. 401.08b. Risk Elements Disclosure

FRR 13:

The final guidelines contain a revised format for "Risk Element" disclosures which includes four categories: (1) nonaccrual, past due and restructured loans; (2) potential problem loans; (3) foreign outstandings; and (4) loan concentrations.

A majority of the commentators expressed concerns about the perceived requirement for a tabular format. They were concerned that investors might add all of the amounts disclosed in such a presentation and equate the total to the previously reported "nonperforming loan" amount, and conclude that the risk had increased. The Commission did not intend that the proposed disclosures necessarily be presented in a single tabular format. Registrants may present this data in a manner deemed appropriate to their facts and circumstances provided that such presentation is not misleading.

Rather than adopting the proposal that would have required a breakdown of each of the risk element disclosures by type of loan as set forth in Item III.A. of Guide 3 (loan categories), the final guidelines call for separate disclosure of aggregate foreign and domestic loan amounts only. The proposed display was intended to provide information for assessing relative risks based on the classification of the loan and on the nature of the borrower. This change was made in response to commentators' concerns that such detailed disclosure would be burdensome and complex. However, as discussed later under "Foreign Outstandings," the final amendments call for disclosure of foreign outstandings by type of borrower.

The Commission has adopted a provision for disclosure of potential problem loans which are not reported as "nonaccrual, past due or restructured," but where known information causes management to have serious doubts as to the ability of the borrowers to comply with the present loan repayment terms. "Potential problem loan" information is only required to be presented for the latest reported period. Some commentators asserted that this provision was unnecessary because many such loans may already be reported as nonaccrual in accordance with the registrant's policies. While the Commission understands that the amounts of potential problem loans may not be significant for most registrants because they may place such loans on nonaccrual status, it recognizes there may be difficult judgments as to classification of certain loans and believes that potential problem loans represent material information to investors.

These final amendments add the "foreign outstandings" disclosures to the matters encompassed in the risk elements section in the proposing release. The Commission determined that it is appropriate to include foreign outstandings in the risk elements section in order to embody all risk related disclosure guidelines in one section of the Guide and to emphasize the risks present in cross-border lending activities.

In response to commentators' concerns, the final amendments include a disclosure provision, as an instruction to the "foreign outstandings" category, concerning foreign borrowers whose economic and political conditions are expected to have a material impact on the timely payment of interest or principal. The proposal would have required that "any loans to private and public sector borrowers in foreign countries experiencing economic and political conditions which have created liquidity problems which may have a material impact on the timing of interest or principal payments" be included in the "serious doubts" category. The majority of respondents to the proposal expressed concern that including liquidity-impaired foreign loans in a category of loans which typically comprises credit-impaired loans may be misleading because of the dissimilarity of respective risks. These respondents asserted that any discussion of foreign loans where borrowers may be adversely affected by liquidity problems are best made in the context of disclosures about foreign lending activities.

Many respondents did not concur with the Commission's characterization of industry loan concentrations as a "risk element" because they believed it was inappropriate to present loan concentrations with nonaccrual, past due and restructured loans and other loans as to which there are serious doubts about the ability of the borrower to comply with loan repayment terms. As noted above, loan concentration data would not necessarily have to be presented together with data called for by the other categories of risk elements. The Commission recognizes that the nature of the risks associated with each of the four categories may vary but believes that this can be effectively communicated in registrant filings.

Sec. 401.08c. Determination of Certain Risk Elements

FRR 13:

The final amendments do not include the substance of certain instructions in the existing Item III.C. which allowed registrants to use different criteria and exclude certain loans in the classification of loans as "nonperforming." The Commission has determined that uniformity in the presentation of this data, and thus comparability among registrants, is important to investors.

Many respondents urged the Commission to retain the substance of the existing Instruction 5 to Item III.C. which provides that "the registrant may use different criteria and may present quantitative information in a different manner than described above if such presentation more effectively identifies and communicates the present risk elements in the loan portfolio."[3] Some respondents urged the Commission to include a similar instruction to provide necessary flexibility in communicating the diversity of lending risks.

Many respondents also urged the Commission to retain the current Instruction 1 to Item III.C. for presentation of past due, nonaccrual and restructured loans. That instruction provided that installment loans to individuals and lease financing amounts may be excluded if the total amount of such loans does not exceed 10% of total loans. These respondents contended that the specific 10% materiality threshold for exclusion should be retained and that data on delinquent consumer loans, if material, should be presented and analyzed separately from data on troubled commercial loans. These persons asserted that consumer delinquencies are not indicative of the same sort of risks as commercial loans because of the nature of the loans and the fact that the accounting convention of automatic charge-off when installment loans reach a certain delinquency mitigates much of the uncertainty, and therefore risk, normally associated with commercial loans.

The Commission is concerned that there has been disparity of practice among registrants in disclosing nonperforming loans thereby impacting the comparability of that data. Users who responded to the proposal indicated that risk elements were important indicators and that comparability among registrants is essential. Be-

cause the Commission agrees that consistency will enhance the utility of this information to investors, analysts and other users, the substance of Instruction 5 has not been included in the final amendments, and an instruction has been added to the revised Item III.C.1. to specifically prohibit any exclusions. Varying risk elements associated with the types of loans included in the past due, nonaccrual and restructured loan categories may be described in narrative discussions setting forth the reasons for and impact of such factors.

Sec. 401.08d. Forgone Interest on Certain Loans

FRR 13:

The final guidelines reflect the proposed amendment to include disclosure of interest income that would have been earned under the original loan terms for nonaccrual and restructured loans, and the amounts actually recognized. The proposing release indicated that the amount of interest earned and the amount actually recognized on troubled debt restructurings is an existing financial statement disclosure requirement of FAS 15. The additional disclosure of such amounts related to nonaccrual loans should supplement the disclosures required under generally accepted accounting principles ("GAAP").

Over half of the respondents addressing this point agreed with the proposed disclosures and financial analysts stated that this disclosure was particularly important. Other commentators raised various conceptual objections to any presentation of information representing hypothetical interest that would have been earned by the registrant if the loan had been current. This amendment was adopted because it communicates an element of the cost of carrying certain problem loans, provides supplemental data for nonaccrual loans similar to information already required under GAAP and is an important factor in the estimation of current and potential earning power. Registrants may supplement these disclosures by appropriate textual discussions to the extent they believe necessary to explain the impact of such loans on their operations.

Sec. 401.08e. Foreign Outstandings

FRR 13:

The Commission has codified the substance of SAB 49's alternative table disclosure for foreign outstandings. Information about foreign outstandings is required for a three-year period rather than the proposed five-year period.

A majority of the commentators responding to the proposal to disclose outstandings to foreign countries in excess of 1% of consolidated outstandings urged retention of the alternatives provided

---

[3] The genesis of Instruction 5 to Section III.C. was the initial adoption in 1976 of Guide 3. The intent of this instruction was to provide flexibility in reporting what was the new information about risk elements in the loan portfolio. This

instruction was provided since there were varying opinions as to the most appropriate method of determining such elements and the disclosures were in a sense experimental.

by SAB 49. SAB 49 allows either a tabular presentation of foreign outstandings exceeding 1% or identification of outstandings to foreign countries in excess of 1% where economic or political conditions may impact the timely payment of principal or interest. Many commentators believed that it is not appropriate to require disclosure of outstandings in each country where outstandings exceed 1% of total outstandings because the reader of financial statements could inappropriately interpret this total amount as an unusual risk. Although these commentators generally agreed that there is an additional risk that a foreign government may impose restrictions on funds leaving the country or that foreign exchange may not be available to make timely payments of interest or principal, they did not believe that these risks warranted the type of disclosure proposed by the Commission.

The Commission has carefully considered the views of commentators and has concluded that the proposed table disclosure approach is preferable to one that focuses only on certain countries that are currently experiencing liquidity problems. The amendments adopted herein identify the registrant's significant cross-border exposures in foreign countries and allow investors to arrive at their own conclusions as to any potential or actual transfer risks involved.

The final guidelines call for certain additional disclosures when a foreign country is experiencing liquidity problems because of economic or political conditions which *are expected to have* a material impact on timely payment. This standard implies a greater degree of certainty in determining the impact of such conditions than that of the proposal, viz. when such conditions *may have* an impact on timely payment. The adopted standard should result in greater consistency of disclosures among registrants.

The revised guidelines utilize a disclosure threshold based on total assets. In response to the Commission's inquiry with respect to the propriety of the proposed disclosure threshold of 1% of outstandings, approximately half the respondents stated that the Commission should retain the "consolidated outstandings" threshold measurement for disclosure; slightly less than half of the respondents felt the measurement should be based on consolidated assets; and the remainder believed that the threshold should be based on a percentage of registrants' equity.

The Commission has determined that the use of a threshold based on 1% of total assets has the merit of simplicity of calculation since the total assets amount is readily obtainable from a registrant's balance sheet. In contrast, outstandings typically can not be computed unless supplemental data is furnished. Also, disclosures using a 1% of total assets threshold will be similar to disclosures made pursuant to SAB 49. Finally, in addition to disclosures about individual countries whose outstandings exceed 1% of total assets, the final guidelines (Instruction 7 to Item III.C.3.) call for aggregate disclosures for countries where outstandings are between .75% and 1% of total assets. This disclosure format is consistent with that proposed in the Federal banking agencies' Country Exposure Report.[4]

The proposed separate disclosure of private and public-sector cross-border outstandings has been revised to call for disclosure of outstandings by the types of borrowers specified in Item III.A., i.e., governments and official institutions, banks and other financial institutions, commercial and industrial, and other. Registrants have presented breakdowns similar to that adopted, and users have commented that this level of disclosure is important in assessing a registrant's exposure in certain countries.

The final amendments call for disclosure of outstandings which are repayable in dollars or other non-local currency; they do not require that gross amounts repayable in *local* currency be disclosed. Many commentators asserted that most loans repayable in local currency are substantially funded by local operations and that any net unfunded amounts normally do not reflect significant transfer risk since they generally are not material. The revised guide provides that any material amounts of local currency outstandings which are not hedged or are not funded by local currency borrowings should be reflected in cross-border outstandings.

An instruction to Item III.C.3. allows any legally enforceable written guarantees of principal or interest by domestic or other non-local third parties to be netted against the amounts of foreign outstandings presented. The Commission agrees with those respondents who asserted that, when the source of repayment of outstandings is assured by third parties, and the registrant is clearly not exposed to transfer risk because of this recourse, presentation of amounts net of such guarantees more appropriately reflects the registrant's exposure to transfer risks. The amendments also allow collateral values to be netted against the cross-border outstandings of a foreign country in certain limited circumstances.

Several commentators queried whether commitments to lend additional dollar amounts, such as through irrevocable letter of credit agreements, should be included in the determination of "outstandings." Under the revised guide, such com-

---

[4] The Federal banking agencies have announced their intention to provide for increased and more timely disclosures about banks' country exposures. These disclosures would be based on the information called for by the revised Item III.C. of Guide 3 and would be available to the public upon request.

mitments would not be included in outstandings, but they would be separately disclosed if material.

In the proposing release, the Commission requested specific comment as to whether a loan to a foreign branch of a foreign bank was or should be reflected as a loan to the foreign country in which the parent bank is located. A substantial majority of those commenting stated that such interbank loans should be reflected as a loan of the parent of the foreign branch. Accordingly, the final amendments include an instruction which indicates that loans made to a branch of a foreign bank located outside the foreign bank's home country should be classified based on the parent's geographic location.

Sec. 401.08.e.i. Outstandings to Countries Experiencing Liquidity Problems

[*Sec. 401.08.e.i. added by FR-28.*]

.i.a. Executive Summary

The Commission has authorized amendments ("the amendments") to the Industry Guides for Statistical Disclosure by Bank Holding Companies ("Guide 3"), regarding disclosure of outstandings[1] to borrowers in certain foreign countries experiencing liquidity problems that are expected to have a material impact on timely repayment of principal or interest ("liquidity problems"),[2] and certain restructurings of outstandings to those countries.

The amendments call for a tabular analysis of changes in aggregate outstandings to each country experiencing liquidity problems, if the aggregate amount exceeds one percent of the registrant's total assets. The analyses are to include amounts of new outstandings, collections of principal and interest, interest income accrued, and other changes. If material amounts of outstandings to such countries are restructured (or if an agreement in principle for restructuring has been reached), the amendments call for tabular presentations of pre- and post-restructuring maturities and interest rates on the restructured amounts, disclosure of commitments arising in connection with the restructurings, and disclosure of amounts removed or expected to be removed from nonaccrual status as a result of the restructurings. The amendments are intended to enable users of bank holding company ("BHC") financial reports ("users") to better assess BHCs' exposures to certain foreign countries, the nature of

changes in those exposures, and the impact of significant restructurings of those exposures. The amendments are based largely on views of the Commission staff previously expressed in interpretive letters regarding disclosures of significant foreign debt restructurings.

.i.b. Description of "Other Changes"

The proposed amendments called for descriptions of significant changes in outstandings other than the changes reported as new outstandings, collections, and accruals of interest. Several respondents suggested that specific descriptions of reductions in BHCs' reported exposures to particular countries, resulting from sales, swaps or charge-offs of outstandings, could disadvantage BHC's efforts to collect what is legally due from debtors in those countries.

In consideration of these comments, the final amendments do not include a specific requirement for inclusion of a description of "other changes". However, a description of the components of amounts reported as "other changes" would be required to the extent that such information is material to an understanding of results of operations or financial condition, or is necessary to make information otherwise included in the filing not misleading.

.i.c. Troubled Debt Restructurings

The proposed amendments called for disclosures regarding restructurings of foreign outstandings irrespective of whether they are troubled debt restructurings ("TDRs") as defined in Statement of Financial Accounting Standards No. 15 ("FAS 15").[5] On that basis, it was proposed that restructurings disclosed pursuant to the proposed amendments and which occurred for reasons unrelated to concerns as to ultimate collectibility need not be reported as TDRs pursuant to Item III.C.1.(c) of Guide 3. Item III.C.1. calls for reporting of aggregate amounts of what are commonly referred to as "nonperforming" loans which include, among other categories, loans that are TDRs.

Several respondents requested clarification as to whether the proposed amendments were intended to supercede or modify the accounting and/or disclosure requirements of FAS 15 for purposes of complying with generally accepted accounting principles ("GAAP"). Others suggested that the need to determine whether a foreign debt

---

[1] Outstandings to a foreign country (or "cross-border outstandings") are defined by Instruction (1) to Item III.C.3. of Guide 3 to include those loans, accrued interest, acceptances, interest-bearing deposits or investments, and other monetary assets which are denominated in U.S. dollars or other non-local currency, and those which are denominated in local currency if not hedged or funded by local borrowings.

[2] The provisions of Guide 3 distinguish liquidity problems from credit problems in countries that are currently unable to fully service their debts. Unlike credit problems, liquidity problems (i.e., current inability to raise sufficient amounts of

the requisite currency to meet principal or interest repayment obligations to U.S. banks) do not necessarily affect the assessment of whether loans will ultimately be uncollectible. The amendments do not affect current guidance regarding disclosure of loans beset by credit problems.

[5] FAS 15, *Accounting by Debtors and Creditors for Troubled Debt Restructurings* (Financial Accounting Standards Board, 1977), states that a TDR occurs if a creditor, for economic or legal reasons related to a debtor's financial difficulties, grants a concession to the debtor that it would not otherwise consider.

restructuring is a TDR should not depend on whether the restructuring occurred due to credit problems or liquidity problems.

The proposal was not intended to suggest that FAS 15 should be interpreted as not applicable to foreign debt restructurings that occur due to liquidity problems, nor was it intended to supercede or modify the accounting and/or disclosure requirements of GAAP with respect to TDRs. Thus, BHCs and their auditors would still need to assess whether a foreign debt restructuring is a TDR for purposes of complying with GAAP requirements.

As stated in the proposing release, (a) there may be practical difficulties in determining whether certain foreign debt restructurings are TDRs and what disclosures should be provided if they are deemed TDRs,[6] and (b) the proposed disclosures were intended to enable users to assess for themselves whether restructured foreign outstandings are "nonperforming" loans. On that basis, the separate disclosure regarding foreign restructurings was proposed to avoid the possibility of having particular restructurings of foreign outstandings reported twice within the Guide 3 disclosure (i.e., pursuant to both the new instruction (6)(d) to Item III.C.3. and, if TDRs, Item III.C.1.(c)). The final amendments retain the provision that restructurings disclosed pursuant to the new instruction, and which occurred for reasons unrelated to concerns about ultimate collectibility, need not be disclosed pursuant to Item III.C.1.(c).

.i.d. Updating of Disclosures

Several respondents suggested that applicability of General Instruction 3 of Guide 3 should be clarified in regard to the need for providing the disclosures called for by the amendments in quarterly reports and for updating the disclosures in subsequent periodic reports. Others suggested that the status of Staff Accounting Bulletin ("SAB") No. 49A should be clarified. SAB No. 49A provided guidance for disclosures regarding developments, such as restructurings and implementation of deposit/relending mechanisms, occurring subsequent to the initial disclosures of outstandings to countries experiencing liquidity problems.

Disclosures regarding aggregate outstandings to an individual country experiencing liquidity problems (i.e., those called for by Instructions (6)(b) and (6)(c) to Item III.C.3. of Guide 3) should initially be made in the first periodic report

(quarterly or annual) covering a period during which the disclosure threshold specified in Instruction (6)(b) is met. Subsequent to the initial disclosure, those disclosures should be provided in each annual report as long as the disclosure threshold continues to be met with respect to that country as of the end of the annual period. The disclosures need not be provided in subsequent quarterly reports unless (a) they had not been provided in the most recent annual report, (b) there have been material changes in outstandings to that country, or (c) updated disclosure is necessary to keep information previously disclosed from being misleading.

Disclosures regarding restructurings (i.e., those called for by Instruction (6)(d) to Item III.C.3. of Guide 3) should initially be provided in the first quarterly and annual reports filed after an agreement in principle for restructuring is reached. The disclosures should be updated in the first quarterly and annual reports filed after the agreement in principle is either significantly modified or finally executed.

Concurrently with the issuance of this release, the Commission's staff is rescinding the portions of SAB Nos. 49[7] and 49A which have been codified in Guide 3.

Sec. 401.08f. Loan Concentrations

FRR 13:

The Commission believes that information about loan concentrations is material information to investors. Accordingly, the final amendments include a requirement to disclose, as of the most recent reported period, any concentration of loans exceeding 10% of total loans. The substance of the concentration disclosure requirement was transferred from the instructions to Item III.A. which calls for disclosure of the categories of loans in the registrant's portfolio. However, concentration disclosures do not have to be made pursuant to the amended Item III.C. if the substance of such disclosures is otherwise made pursuant to Item III.A.

While not intended to indicate levels of prudent lending, the 10% threshold for disclosure of concentrations is intended to provide useful information to investors in evaluating lending portfolios. A 10% threshold has been utilized in other areas in Guide 3 and in Article 9 of Regulation S-X [17 CFR 210.9] for purposes of specifying materiality levels for disclosure purposes.[5]

General guidance is provided in a definition of loan concentrations which states that concentrations are considered to exist when there are

---

[6] For example, it may be difficult to assess whether the post-restructuring interest rate is below market rates for similar loans, because there may no sources of significant amounts of new loans to the country, other than the lenders participating in the restructuring. FAS 15 calls for disclosures regarding TDRs that are effected through modifications of

terms (e.g., interest rates and/or maturities) only if the post-restructuring interest rates are below market rates.

[7] The substance of SAB 49, regarding disclosure of loans to countries experiencing liquidity problems, had been codified in Guide 3 with the issuance of Financial Reporting Release No. 13 in August 1983.

[5] E.g., *see* 210.9-05(c)(3), Items III.C. and V.A. of Guide 3.

amounts loaned to a multiple number of borrowers engaged in similar activities which would cause them to be similarly impacted by economic or other conditions. The definition reflects the objective of this category, i.e., to highlight potential risks when economic or other conditions may result in an adverse impact on the financial condition of the registrant due to concentrated levels of lending activities to borrowers with common characteristics.

As with the other revised guidelines, the Commission staff will monitor disclosures in this area and assess whether additional guidance or a different threshold is appropriate.

Sec. 401.09. Accounting for Loan Losses by Registrants Engaged in Lending Activities

.a. Background

[*Sec. 401.09 added by FR-27.*]

The Commission has determined that certain financial reporting practices of some registrants engaged in lending activities may result in misstatement of their loan losses. The Commission is publishing its views on these practices so that they may be appropriately considered by registrants and auditors in meeting their responsibilities under the Federal securities laws. The practices regarding substantive repossessions of collateral and valuation of formally or substantively repossessed collateral are described in the context of circumstances illustrative of actual circumstances noted in investigative and other activities of the Commission's staff.

Sec. 401.09.b. Procedural Discipline in Determining the Allowance and Provision for Loan Losses to be Reported

Certain registrants have appeared to lack adequate documentation of procedures for: (a) performing periodic detailed reviews to identify risks inherent in their loan portfolios (e.g., problem loans, potential problem loans, loans to be charged off) and assessing the overall quality (i.e., collectibility) of their portfolios; and (b) determining amounts of allowances and provisions for loan losses to be reported based on the results of the detailed reviews. Neither the detailed reviews nor the determinations of amounts to be reported as loan losses appeared to have been conducted in an appropriately systematic manner by those registrants. Periodic fluctuations in their reported loan losses appeared, generally, to have no logical relationship to the results of their periodic detailed loan reviews.

Arriving at an appropriate reported allowance for loan losses necessarily involves a high degree of management judgment. Because the allowance and the related provision for loan losses are key elements of financial statements of registrants engaged in lending activities, it is critical that those judgments be exercised in a disciplined manner that is based on and reflective of adequate detailed analyses of the loan portfolio.

Accordingly, in conducting an investigation, the Commission's staff normally would expect to find that the books and records of registrants engaged in lending activities include documentation of: (a) systematic methodology to be employed each period in determining the amount of loan losses to be reported, and (b) rationale supporting each period's determination that the amounts reported were adequate. The systematic methodology to be employed each period would be documented not so that reported amounts will be the result of routine mathematical exercise, but to help ensure that all relevant matters affecting loan collectibility will consistently be identified in the detailed review process, and that the findings of the detailed review will be considered in an appropriately disciplined manner by persons exercising judgment in determining the amounts to be reported. The specific rationale upon which the amount actually reported in each individual period is based—i.e., the bridge between the findings of the detailed review and the amount actually reported in each period—would be documented to help ensure the adequacy of the reported amount, to improve auditability, and to serve as a benchmark for exercise of prudent judgment in future periods.

Sec. 401.09.c. Substantive Repossessions of Collateral

Assume that a registrant had extended loans to oil and gas producers, who had pledged certain producing properties as collateral for those loans. The fair value of the collateral was in excess of the loan balances at the time the loans were extended. However, as energy prices declined, the borrowers determined that their further exploitation of the collateral would not be sufficiently rewarding and defaulted on the loans. The registrant sought negotiations to restructure the loans by extending the repayment schedule (knowing, of course, that a restructuring would not affect the amount or timing of cash flow that could be generated by operation of the collateral) while the borrowers retained legal title to the collateral.

Further assume that, at the time of default, the properties were still thought to be capable of generating positive cash flow, but at a rate much lower than originally anticipated for various reasons (e.g., the energy price decline and/or downward revisions of reserve quantity estimates). Engineering estimates prepared at the time of default, based on long-term assumptions regarding energy prices, projected that the undiscounted net cash flow from continued operation of the collateral would recover the carrying amount of the loans over a period much longer than originally anticipated (e.g., thirty to forty years). The present value of that projected cash flow and, thus, the fair value of the collateral, was significantly less than the carrying value of the loans.

The Commission has become aware that, in circumstances such as those described above, some registrants may believe that no loss need be recognized on the loans, on the basis that there is always the option of modifying the terms of the loans to call for repayments which, on an undiscounted basis, would eventually recover the carrying value of the loans. Should that option be exercised, some have argued, no loss recognition would be required under the provisions of paragraphs 30 and 31 of Statement of Financial Accounting Standards No. 15 ("FAS 15").[1] Essentially, this argument is founded on the premise that if collateral is not formally repossessed, there is no requirement to recognize losses based on the collateral's fair value.

Reliance upon accounting standards applicable to restructurings of debt through modification of terms (e.g., changes in maturities and/or interest rates) will often be inappropriate in these circumstances. The lenders may be more exposed to the risks of ownership of the collateral and more in a position to benefit from any recovery in its fair value than the borrowers. Thus, even if the maturity and/or interest rate terms of the loans would be formally modified to allow for repayment over many years, such a troubled debt restructuring may, in substance, constitute a repossession of the collateral. Paragraph 34 of FAS 15 states that a troubled debt restructuring that is in substance a repossession requires loss recognition based on the excess of the recorded investment in the loan over the fair value of the collateral that is, in substance, respossessed.

A registrant cannot avoid the fair value accounting required by FAS 15 when collateral is repossessed, simply by avoiding a formal repossession. That concept is clearly expressed in paragraphs 34 and 84 of FAS 15, although it is expressed there in the context of a formal debt restructuring. Collateral that has substantively been repossessed should be accounted for in the same manner as collateral that has been formally repossessed, irrespective of whether the related loan is formally restructured. To encourage more consistent applications of accounting principles in this area, the following discussion sets forth criteria which generally should be considered in determining whether substantive repossession accounting is appropriate, and the rationale for those criteria.

A. *Applicability*

The criteria listed below should be applied to any collateralized loan[2] which, because of the surrounding facts and circumstances, represents a loss contingency for the creditor and is being

evaluated for possible accrual of the loss contingency,[3] irrespective of whether it has been restructured formally by modification of terms.

B. *Criteria*

Collateral generally should be considered repossessed in substance and accounted for at its fair value, consistent with repossession accounting as described in paragraphs 28 and 29 of FAS 15, when:

    1. The debtor has little or no equity in the collateral, considering the current fair value of the collateral; *and*

    2. Proceeds for repayment of the loan can be expected to come only from the operation or sale of the collateral; *and*

    3. The debtor has either:

        (a) formally or effectively abandoned control of the collateral to the creditor, *or*

        (b) retained control of the collateral but, because of the current financial condition of the debtor, or the economic prospects for the debtor and/or the collateral in the foreseeable future, it is doubtful that the debtor will be able to rebuild equity in the collateral or otherwise repay the loan in the foreseeable future.

C. *Discussion of Criteria*

The first two criteria are analogous to certain criteria contained in the February 1986 AICPA Notice to Practitioners ("the Notice") regarding accounting for real estate acquisition, development and construction ("ADC") arrangements,[4] and are intended to be used here in the same spirit as used in the Notice. Pursuant to the Notice, those criteria are used by a financial institution in determining, at the time it finances an ADC project, whether the financing is in substance an investment rather than a loan based on whether the risks and rewards of the project rest first and foremost with the financial institution. In assessing whether substantive repossession accounting is appropriate, these criteria should be used to identify situations where the primary risks and rewards of collateral ownership have passed from the debtor to the lender.

The third criterion recognizes that ongoing debtor commitment is a factor in assessing whether collateral has in substance been repossessed. It is intended to allow that repossession accounting may not be necessary when the debtor

---

[1] Statement of Financial Accounting Standards No. 15: *Accounting by Debtors and Creditors for Troubled Debt Restructurings* (Stamford, CT: FASB, 1977).

[2] A collateralized loan, for this purpose, is any loan extended by a creditor in whole or in part on the basis of a security interest in assets or other property (tangible or intangible) of the debtor or a third-party guarantor. It would not include, for example, unsecured loans or loans to governmental agencies secured by tax-supported revenue streams.

[3] The accounting requirements for accrual of loss contingencies are specified in paragraphs 8 (generally) and 22-23 (specifically in the context of receivables) of Statement of Financial Accounting Standards No. 5, *Accounting for Contingencies* (Stamford, CT: FASB, 1975).

[4] *Notice to Practitioners—ADC Arrangements* (New York: AICPA, 1986).

continues good faith efforts toward successful operation of the collateral and eventual repayment of the loan; provided, however, that the creditor can demonstrate a reasonable basis for concluding that the loan will be ultimately collectible.

The spirit of each of the above criteria should be carefully applied in the context of the facts and circumstances surrounding specific loans being evaluated. This is of particular importance with respect to criterion 3(b). For example, when using forecasts to assess a debtor's ability to improve its financial condition or future economic prospects for collateral, registrants and their auditors should be mindful that it is difficult to establish reasonable reliability of assumptions as to future events for purposes of overcoming doubts. Because assumptions underlying forecasts become less reliable as they look farther into the future, the word "foreseeable" in criterion 3(b) establishes that any relied-upon assumptions must be expected to be attainable within a reasonably manageable future period.

Sec. 401.09.c.i. Amendment of Interpretation Regarding Substantive Repossession of Collateral

In 1993, the FASB issued SFAS 114, which addresses, among other things, the accounting for substantive repossessions of collateral. SFAS 114 amends SFAS 15 to clarify that substantive repossession accounting applies in the circumstances in which the debtor surrenders the collateral to the creditor and the creditor receives physical possession of the debtor's assets (the collateral).[1] Consequently, the accounting guidance relating to the accounting for substantive repossessions of collateral in FR 28 is not consistent with the accounting requirements for substantive repossession accounting in SFAS 114.

Because SFAS 114 clarifies the accounting literature that addresses the accounting for substantive repossessions of collateral, the portion of FR 28 that addresses substantive repossession accounting no longer is necessary once a registrant adopts SFAS 114.[2] Accordingly, registrants that have adopted SFAS 114 should not apply the portion of FR 28 that addresses the accounting for substantive repossessions of collateral. Registrants that have not adopted SFAS 114 should continue to apply all portions of FR 28, including the portion that addresses the accounting for substantive repossessions of collateral.

Sec. 401.09.d. Valuation of Formally or Substantively Repossessed Collateral

Assume that a registrant had extended loans to oil and gas drilling companies, with the borrowers'

drilling rigs serving as collateral. The fair value of the rigs was in excess of the amounts loaned at the time the loans were granted. However, as energy prices declined, the borrowers were unable to profitably operate the rigs and defaulted on the loans. The registrant repossessed the rigs and placed them in storage while considering whether to sell them immediately or to hold them in anticipation of a future recovery in energy prices.

Assume further that the only active market in which rigs similar to those repossessed by the registrant were then being sold was an auction market where rigs were being purchased for speculative purposes (i.e., by persons who hoped to profit by holding rigs in anticipation of a future recovery in energy prices) or for parts, at prices substantially lower than the rigs' historical prices. The registrant elected to hold the rigs rather than sell them at their then-current market values. The registrant requested and obtained from a petroleum engineering company a projection of energy price and rig utilization levels several years hence and an estimate of the cost to store and maintain the rigs for that number of years, and derived from that data an estimate of the rigs' value which was substantially higher than their then-current market value.

The Commission has become aware that some registrants, in circumstances such as these, may believe that it would be acceptable to value the repossessed rigs at the derived amount, rather than at current market value, for financial reporting purposes.

FAS 15 requires that the accounting for collateral that is formally or substantively repossessed in satisfaction of a loan receivable is to be based on the collateral's fair value, and that fair value for this purpose is equal to market value if an active market for the collateral exists.[5] Registrants will, of course, opt for the strategies they expect will maximize returns or minimize losses. However, where fair value accounting is required by generally accepted accounting principles ("GAAP"), the mere adoption of strategies (such as a hold-for-the-future strategy that is based on expectations of future price increases, or a strategy of operating the repossessed collateral for one's own behalf) cannot justify use of derived accounting valuations that portray results of operations more favorably than would use of current values in active markets.

The Commission will presume that active markets reflect objective measures of current fair values, determined by the beliefs of reasonably informed persons regarding the present and fu-

---

[1] See SFAS 114, paragraphs 22d, 70, 71.

[2] SFAS 114 applies to financial statements for fiscal years beginning after December 15, 1994. Earlier application is encouraged.

[5] If no active market exists for a particular item, FAS 15 requires the fair value of the item to be estimated based on selling prices of similar items in active markets or, if there are no active markets for similar items, by discounting the cash flows expected to be generated by the item at a rate commensurate with the risk involved.

ture economic utility of the items being traded and the risks associated therewith. Thus, without independent and objective support for derived valuations that can be demonstrated to more appropriately reflect fair value in particular sets of circumstances, derived valuations exceeding current values in active markets should not be used in cases where fair value accounting is required by GAAP.[6]

[¶ 38,201] 402. Broker-Dealers

[The Commission, through various requirements, specifies the books and records that must be maintained and kept current by a broker-dealer, and in some instances, specifies the period of time over which certain books and records must be preserved. In connection with these requirements, the Commission has periodically expressed its view as to the appropriate recordkeeping responsibilities of a broker-dealer.]

.01. Recordkeeping Responsibilities
ASR 98:

It came to the attention of the Commission that some broker-dealers who act as underwriters of investment company shares did not record on their books and records transactions arising from the sale and redemption by them of such shares. Such transactions should be recorded in a separate account for each customer including each investment company and each broker-dealer distributing or redeeming such shares. Such transactions may not properly be recorded in the "fail" records in lieu of maintaining separate accounts for each customer as the customary arrangement that payment shall be against delivery on a traditional settlement date is not present in the sale of investment company shares.

Failure by an underwriter to record such assets and liabilities in its accounts would result in violation of Rule 17a-3 under Section 17(a) of the Exchange Act which prescribes that every member of a national securities exchange who transacts a business in securities directly with other than members of a national securities exchange, and every broker and dealer who transacts a business in securities through the medium of any such member, and every broker or dealer registered pursuant to Section 15 of the Exchange Act, as amended, shall make and keep current, among other records relating to his business, ledgers (or other records) reflecting all assets and liabilities, income and expense and capital accounts including ledger accounts as to each customer. As the Commission has held on repeated occasions, the requirement that records be maintained carries with it the implicit further requirement that such records must be true and correct.

402.02. Maintenance of Current Books and Records
.a. Purpose
ASR 156:

Rule 17a-3(a) requires that registered broker-dealers prepare records of transactions and dealings in securities for the accounts of the firm's customers as well as for its own risk and account, and to prepare records of other financial transactions related to the business of the broker-dealer. These requirements are intended to serve three basic regulatory purposes. First, it is expected that the broker-dealer maintain current books and records for the protection and convenience of customers; that is, customers are entitled to prompt responses to inquiries and resolution of claims relating to their accounts. Secondly, these requirements are intended to enable a broker-dealer to be aware of the extent of its compliance with the various rules and requirements, particularly the net capital and other customer protection rules,[*] and be able to demonstrate compliance to the Commission and the self-regulatory authorities without the burden of bringing books and records up-to-date being placed upon the regulatory authorities. Third, a broker-dealer should have current books and records to enable it to fulfill its obligations and responsibilities to other broker-dealers with whom business is transacted. Additionally, good business practice requires timely information for effective management decisions. In order to serve these purposes, the Commission provided general guidelines for the maintenance of current books and records with respect to the requirements of Rules 17a-3(a) and 17a-11.

402.02.b. Order Tickets and Confirmations
ASR 156:

Subparagraphs (6) and (7) of Rule 17a-3(a) require the preparation of a memorandum of each brokerage order and each principal transaction and subparagraph (8) requires maintenance of copies of confirmations of transactions for the accounts of customers and partners. These are the basic source documents and transaction records of a broker-dealer. By their nature, the memoranda of brokerage and principal transactions should be prepared at the time of the transactions, and the confirmations, which are prepared from the memoranda, should be prepared and mailed on the day of the transaction or the following business day.

402.02.c. Records of Original Entry
ASR 156:

The blotters or other records of original entry described in subparagraph (1) of Rule 17a-3 itemize each day's transactions in a format that facili-

---

[6] Computations of gain or loss on repossession of collateral must consider not only the collateral's fair value, but also whether the registrant's security interest in the collateral is perfected and, if so, the priority of the registrant's claim.

[*] Including Rule 15c3-1 or comparable requirements of a national securities exchange of which the broker-dealer is a member and Rule 15c3-3.

tates posting to the general and subsidiary ledgers. Blotter records relating to securities transactions—e.g., daily purchase and sale blotters—should reflect all transactions as of the trade date and should be prepared no later than the following business day. Similarly, blotter records relating to securities movements and the receipt and disbursement of cash should reflect such transactions on the date they occur and should be prepared no later than the following business day.

402.02.d. General Ledgers

ASR 156:

The ledgers prescribed in subparagraph (2) of Rule 17a-3 are the general records reflecting all asset, liability and capital accounts and all income and expense accounts and include control accounts for subsidiary ledgers. The blotters and other records of original entry should be maintained not only on a daily basis, as discussed above, but in a form which will facilitate posting of the general ledger as frequently as necessary to enable the broker-dealer to make the computations necessary to ascertain his compliance with the net capital rule and the customers' reserve requirement rule.** For many broker-dealers, compliance with the customers' reserve requirement entails a weekly computation based on updated general ledger account balances.

A broker-dealer is required to be in compliance with the net capital rule at all times and the general ledger must be posted as frequently as may be necessary to make that determination. Compliance with this rule and the concern for frequent computations becomes particularly important in periods of sharp changes in securities prices and increases in trading volume. Firms which are frequent participants in underwriting syndicates or which effect transactions in large blocks of stock may also find it necessary to post their ledger on a daily basis because of the need for making frequent net capital computations. If a broker-dealer effects only a limited number of transactions during an accounting period and it is clear from the nature of the business conducted that such transactions would have no material adverse effect on the broker-dealer's financial and operational condition, net capital or customer's protection requirements during the period, it may be appropriate to post the general ledger on a monthly basis.*

402.02.e. Customer's Ledger Accounts

ASR 156:

Transactions involving the purchase and sale of securities should be posted to the customer's ledger accounts described in subparagraph (3) of Rule 17a-3 no later than settlement date. Other customer transactions relating to securities movements and cash receipts and disbursements should be reflected as of the transaction date and should be posted to the accounts no later than the first business day following the transaction.

402.02.f. Subsidiary Ledgers

ASR 156:

The subsidiary ledgers and other records** relating to securities in transfer, dividends and interest received, securities borrowed and securities loaned, and monies loaned required under subparagraphs (4)(A)-(D) should be posted no later than two business days subsequent to the date of the securities or money movements. Transactions between brokers not completed on settlement date should be posted to the appropriate fail to deliver or fail to receive ledger (or other record) no later than the first business day following settlement date; resolution of fail transactions should be recorded no later than the first business day following resolution. A broker-dealer who maintains his accounts on the trade date basis of accounting and uses "fail" accounts to reflect transactions with other brokers should post transactions to the accounts no later than two business days subsequent to the transaction date. In accordance with the provisions of Rule 17a-13(b)(5), long and short stock record differences shall be entered in an appropriate ledger account (subparagraph (4)(F)) no later than seven business days after the date of a required quarterly securities examination and verification.***

402.02.g. Securities Position Record

ASR 156:

The securities record required by subparagraph (5) of Rule 17a-3(a) shall reflect the changes resulting from purchase and sale transactions either as broker or dealer as of clearance date, or settlement date, and should be recorded no later than the following business day.† In addition, other changes in securities positions should be reflected on the date of the security movement or on the following business day as of the date of the move-

---

** Rule 15c3-3(e).

* In the course of posting the books at interim dates during a month, it may not be necessary to make adjustments for accruals and deferrals, such as for depreciation or prepaid expenses, if they would not materially affect the financial condition of the broker-dealer.

** As used in subparagraph (4) and elsewhere in Rule 17a-3, the term "other records" should be construed to include, where appropriate, copies of vouchers, confirmations, or similar documents which reflect the information required by the applicable subparagraph arranged in appropriate sequence and in permanent form, including similar records

developed by the use of automatic data processing systems and produced or reproduced on microfilm.

*** If counts are made on a cyclical basis in accordance with Rule 17a-13(c), any stock record difference shall be recorded within seven business days subsequent to examination and verification of a particular security.

† The requirement for current maintenance of the securities record can be met by broker-dealers through preparation of a full securities record weekly, supplemented by a daily "takeoff" sheet summarizing and balancing each day's securities movements.

ment. Long and short securities record differences shall be entered concurrently with their recording in the subsidiary ledger required by subparagraph (4)(F).

402.02.h. Transactions in Options
ASR 156:

The record of puts, calls, spreads, straddles, and other options described in subparagraph (10) should reflect transactions as of the date an option is written, guaranteed, traded or exercised and should be prepared no later than the business day following the transaction.

402.02.i. Trial Balances and Capital Computation
ASR 156:

Subparagraph (11) requires the monthly preparation of a trial balance of all ledger accounts and a computation of aggregate indebtedness and net capital as of the trial balance date. These records should be prepared no later than 10 business days after the end of the accounting period, except in those instances where the records must be prepared in a lesser period to satisfy any reporting requirements established by any self-regulatory authority of which the broker-dealer is a member.††

402.02.j. Other Records
ASR 156:

The record of beneficial ownership of each cash or margin account (subparagraph (9) of Rule 17a-3) should be prepared before transactions are effected in an account. The employment questionnaire or application (subparagraph (12) of Rule 17a-3) should be prepared at or prior to the commencement of employment.

402.02.k. Time Lag in Transmission of Data
ASR 156:

Under certain limited circumstances the accounting department of a broker-dealer may not be aware of a transaction until a few days after it occurs. Transactions such as receipts and disbursements in out-of-town branches or by correspondents should be recorded no later than the day after the transaction is reported to the accounting department, and dividend and interest claims from other brokers should be recorded no later than the day after the validity of the claim is established.

402.02.l. Service Bureaus
ASR 156:

If a broker-dealer hires or engages an outside service bureau or other recordkeeping service to handle its records, the requirement to make and keep current the broker-dealer's books and records is in no way diminished and under such circumstances the broker-dealer is responsible to the same degree for maintaining current books and records as if he were maintaining them himself. Where a broker-dealer undertakes to have his books and records prepared and maintained by a service bureau or recordkeeping service, he should assure himself that the service will be provided in conformity with the Commission recordkeeping rules.

[¶ 38,215] 403. Insurance Companies
.01. Consolidation and Supplementary Segment Disclosures

[The Commission originally required that separate financial statements be filed for property and liability insurance companies and for life insurance companies. In ASR 301, the Commission issued revised rules allowing a consolidated presentation by multi-line insurance companies, including title insurance as well as life insurance and property and liability insurance.]

ASR 301:

These revisions are in recognition of the growing trend among multi-line insurance entities to give a consolidated presentation in their financial statements. Companies which prefer not to consolidate may simply ignore the inapplicable captions in the revised Article 7.

At the same time that Article 7 specifies a format for consolidated presentations, it has been structured to preserve detailed information disclosure. Article 7 requires disclosure in a schedule of the breakdown of the key financial statement captions among the company's various business segments as they are defined for purposes of the segment disclosures under SFAS 14. The Commission concluded that, although this level of information is needed to assist sophisticated users in understanding and evaluating the fundamental economic differences between life and property/liability insurance operations, it can most appropriately be presented in a schedule on a segment basis.

403.02. Statutory Accounting and Applicability to Mutual Life Insurance Companies
ASR 152:

Filings by mutual companies with the Commission are generally in the capacity of co-issuers of variable annuity contracts and are included in prospectuses because of the guarantee of certain liabilities of the related variable annuity account. In consideration of the nature of the filings by mutual companies and the absence of a body of established generally accepted accounting principles for them, an exemption from the requirement for GAAP financial statements has been provided. In

---

†† Although not specifically referred to in Rule 17a-3, the weekly or monthly computation of the amount to be on deposit under the customers' reserve requirement rule must be made in sufficient time to enable the broker-dealer to make the required deposit not later than one hour after the opening of banking business on the second business day following the date on which the computation is based, as required by Rule 15c3-3(e).

addition, a similar exemption has been provided for wholly owned stock life insurance subsidiaries of mutual life insurance companies.

ASR 301:

Article 7 of Regulation S-X requires disclosure of the amounts of statutory net income and stockholders' equity as well as disclosure of significant statutory restrictions on dividends. The Commission believes that GAAP earnings and stockholders' equity are the relevant amounts for investor financial reporting and by definition should stand on their own.

Although the Commission deleted the requirement for a reconciliation of stockholders' equity and net income as determined under statutory accounting requirements with the corresponding GAAP amounts, registrants are free to continue to present them, or any other supplemental information they consider necessary to a fair presentation of their financial condition or results of operations. Care should, of course, be taken not to misrepresent the nature of such information.

403.03. Investment Disclosures

ASR 301:

Rule 7-03(1) and Rule 12-15 of Regulation S-X require that bonds and notes, preferred stocks and common stocks be reported, both on the balance sheet and in the investment summary schedule, in two categories—fixed maturities and equity securities. This two-category presentation reflects the consideration given redeemable preferred stocks in ASR 268.* It also reflects the assumptions underlying the carrying value for the various types of investments. GAAP provides that bonds and redeemable preferred stocks generally be carried at amortized cost, while nonredeemable preferred stocks and common stocks are carried at market.

The analysis of realized and unrealized gains and losses on securities has been retained as a note disclosure and is included with the requirement for the income statement under the "Realized gains or losses . . . ." caption. The Commission decided to retain the footnote analysis because it believes information on both realized and unrealized gains and losses is necessary to a full evaluation of total portfolio activity for the period. During periods of overall market decline, selected realized gains may mask heavy unrealized losses, and although a registrant may fully intend to carry such investments to maturity, investors should be informed of the possible impact of near-term sales. The footnote analysis of both realized and unrealized gains and losses provides quantitative information on this impact. In addition, the implications of significant unrealized losses in a company's investment portfolio would be discussed in the MD&A.

The Commission determined to maintain the requirement to disclose the name of any person in which the total amount invested in the person and affiliates exceeds 2% of total investments as relevant to the analysis of investment risk. However, the Commission revised the disclosure threshold from 2% of total investments to 10% of total stockholders' equity. This threshold is consistent with that used in Article 9 for banks and relates more directly to investor risk than the old test. Based on the dollar magnitude and diversity of most investment portfolios, the Commission believes that this disclosure is not a burdensome requirement and that, in fact, it will elicit disclosure only in a relatively limited number of cases.

Article 7 also requires the disclosure requirements for nonincome producing investments in fixed maturities, mortgage loans on real estate, real estate, and other long-term investments; however, the test period triggering such disclosure has been increased to twelve months. Notwithstanding GAAP requirements to evaluate asset realizability, the Commission believes this information is necessary to the ongoing evaluation of a company's financial strength.

Sec. 403.04. Disclosures Concerning Reserves for Unpaid Claims and Claim Adjustment Expenses of Property-Casualty Underwriters

Sec. 403.04.a. Disclosure Threshold Criteria

[Sec. 403.04.a added by FRR-20.]

An issue that generated significant comment was the absence of separate tests for determining the need for presentation of separate information for unconsolidated subsidiaries and 50%-or-less-owned equity investees. Commentators considered it impracticable to provide detailed disclosures for what may be insignificant groups of subsidiaries or investees. Some also stated that many 50%-or-less-owned equity investees are public companies that would be required to include claim reserve disclosures in their own filings with the Commission.

The final rules and guidelines include criteria that are responsive to the concerns of commentators. First, to the extent possible, the criteria have been conformed in each requirement. Disclosure requirements are triggered when P/C reserves exceed one-half of consolidated common stockholders' equity. Second, exemptions have been provided for certain quantitative data of 50%-or-less-owned equity investees if those entities provide disclosures to the Commission as registrants in their own right. Third, if ending reserves of (a) the registrant and its consolidated subsidiaries, (b) unconsolidated subsidiaries or (c) the proportionate share of the registrant and its other subsidiaries in the reserves of its 50%-or-less owned equity investees are less than 5% of the total

---

* Section 211 of this codification.

reserves of categories (a), (b) and (c), that category has been omitted from the disclosure requirements.

Sec. 403.04.b. Reconciliation of Beginning and Ending Claims Reserves and Exhibit of Deficiencies (Redundancies)

[Sec. 403.04.b added by FRR-20.]

The proposal called for a reconciliation of beginning and ending GAAP reserves for unpaid claims and claim adjustment expenses in the aggregate, for each of the latest three years. Disclosure of the portion of incurred losses for each year attributable to the current year and to each of the two preceding years separately was also proposed, as well as the amount of discount reflected in the provision for losses for the current year and the amortization of discounts provided in prior years.

The principal opposition to the proposed reconciliation concerned the requirement to disaggregate incurred losses attributable to prior years. Some commentators indicated that the breakdown of losses into specific prior years was difficult. Others were concerned that less sophisticated investors might simply recalculate net income of prior years, without recognizing that the prior years already include the same type of adjustments for previous years. Other commentators opposed the proposal to disclose the effects of discounting on each year's reconciliation. Many believed it would be difficult, if not impossible, to quantify discount amortization. Supportive commentators indicated that the reconciliations were effective in illustrating the impact of provisions for prior years' losses on current income.

The Commission continues to believe that investors may be able to better evaluate reserves if they can review subsequent adjustments to historical reserve estimates, and that, together with management's comments, a reconciliation of reserves is appropriate. The proposal has been modified to eliminate the provision to show separately in this table the amount of the adjustment to income in the current year applicable to each of the two prior years. However, the reconciliation still calls for the amount of the adjustment to income in the current year applicable to all prior years. The development table discussed below provides information about adjustments to the liability for unpaid claims and claim adjustment expenses, as originally reported, on a year by year basis for the ten prior years.[6]

The proposed rules would also have required disclosure by statutory line of business, of deficiencies (redundancies) in GAAP claims reserves in increments of one year, five years and ten years. The disclosure would have been provided separately for the parent and its consolidated subsidiaries, for the unconsolidated subsidiaries and for the 50%-or-less-owned equity investees. The proposal also required disclosure of the amount of whether claims reserves were ceded during any of the years during each development period, and, if so, a statement of the reserves eliminated and the related premiums paid.

Comment letters from all groups suggested that the information was too detailed (particularly with respect to the disclosures by line of business), and that it represented only one of many formats in which someone might want to consider the basic data. A significant number of commentators suggested alternative approaches to reduce the cost and complexity of the proposed disclosure, the principal focus being on providing information on an aggregate basis. In this connection, commentators generally agreed that a discussion by management of the registrant's reserving experience presented in reasonable proximity to the aggregate development information could provide understandable information to most readers.

The Commission continues to believe that disclosure of the development of incurred claims, paid claims and claim reserves is necessary for an evaluation of a P/C underwriter's reserving practices. However, it agrees with commentators that it may not be necessary to provide this information by line of business to meet the Commission's disclosure objectives.

Therefore, the provisions of item 2B of Guide 6 have been changed to include a table which reflects reserve development information on an aggregate basis. This table is intended to inform investors of the materiality of adjustments required during periods following the dates as of which its original reserves were established by showing the historical pattern of changes in reserve estimates and claim payments. The Commission believes that disclosure of the historical patterns and management's explanation of such changes will provide investors with greater understanding of the factors that may affect future earnings. An example of the table follows.

	CONSOLIDATED ($MILLION)								
YEAR ENDED	1976	1977	1978	1979	1980	1981	1982	1983	1984
LIABILITY FOR UNPAID CLAIMS AND CLAIM ADJ. EXP.	484	602	775	952	1154	1380	1626	1703	1749
PAID (CUMULATIVE) AS OF:									
End of year	—	—	—	—	—	—	—	—	—
One year later	241	262	305	343	369	458	504	554	—

---

[6] Only eight years coverage would be expected to be provided for calendar year 1984 and only nine years coverage is required for calendar year 1985. The phased-in requirement is consistent with changes in reporting requirements of state regulatory authorities.

YEAR ENDED	CONSOLIDATED ($MILLION)								
	1976	1977	1978	1979	1980	1981	1982	1983	1984
Two years later	358	411	488	518	644	724	805	—	—
Three years later	451	525	612	643	818	915	—	—	—
Four years later	521	606	727	813	942	—	—	—	—
Five years later	569	683	801	891	—	—	—	—	—
Six years later	619	731	939	—	—	—	—	—	—
Seven years later	650	764	—	—	—	—	—	—	—
Eight years later[7]	672	—	—	—	—	—	—	—	—
LIABILITY REESTIMATED AS OF:									
End of year	484	602	775	952	1154	1380	1626	1703	1749
One year later	562	662	793	886	1025	1197	1308	1475	—
Two years later	625	753	885	996	1182	1306	1472	—	—
Three years later	678	806	954	1088	1243	1386	—	—	—
Four years later	707	846	1013	1117	1286	—	—	—	—
Five years later	731	889	1032	1144	—	—	—	—	—
Six years later	761	904	1050	—	—	—	—	—	—
Seven years later	770	918	—	—	—	—	—	—	—
Eight years later	782	—	—	—	—	—	—	—	—
REDUNDANCY (DEFICIENCY)	(298)	(316)	(275)	(192)	(132)	(6)	154	228	—

The table is intended to illustrate the manner in which reserve estimates change as time passes. Each column reflects the underwriter's experience with the reserve it estimated at the end of the stated fiscal year. The first line shows the reserve as originally reported. The middle portion shows the cumulative amounts paid as of the end of successive years with respect to that reserve liability. The lower portion shows retroactive reestimates of the reserve as of the end of successive years resulting from management's awareness of additional facts and circumstances. To examine the pattern of payments or changes with respect to a particular reserve estimate investors would simply read down the column under that estimate.

Sec. 403.04.c. Provision for Inflation

[Sec. 403.04.c added by FRR-20.]

Although inclusion of a provision for inflation in estimated reserves is required by Statement of Financial Accounting Standards No. 60, no specific method is prescribed for calculating that provision. The proposal requested disclosure of the registrant's method of estimating the amount of any explicit provisions for inflation and for the circumstances relied upon by management in accepting the adequacy of implicit provisions for the effects of inflation.

A number of commentators indicated that the provision for inflation is included in overall projections of expected claim costs without being specifically identified. These commentators asserted that many factors are considered when providing for reserves; inflation is just one of those factors; and it is not feasible or meaningful to separate out the inflation factor individually.

The Commission believes that a general description of each registrant's practice in arriving at a provision for inflation may be useful in evaluating currently reported reserves. Provisions for inflation for this purpose may be taken to mean

provision for future changes in average claim severities, if this permits more meaningful disclosure.

Under the guide, registrants would disclose whether they make provisions for inflation implicitly or explicitly. Those whose provision is implicit would disclose how they satisfy themselves that the provision is appropriate. Those who make explicit provision would describe their procedures briefly.

Sec. 403.04.d. Disclosures Related to Discounting

[Sec. 403.04.d added by FRR-20.]

The proposal asked for a statement of the difference (estimated, if necessary) between GAAP basis claims reserves on a discounted basis, in total and by statutory line of business. In general, commentators agreed that disclosure of the effects of discounting is appropriate. They did not believe, however, that disclosure of discounts deducted from reserves by line of business is necessary unless the discount of a particular line is material. Some expressed concerns that "grossing up" reserves to undiscounted amounts would be difficult for registrants who use discounted tables required by regulatory authorities.

Proposed Rule 12-19 of Regulation S-X would have required disaggregation of P/C reserve balances and the discounts deducted for the latest two year-ends by the lines of business used in reports to state regulators. This breakdown was considered a cost effective method to provide investors with an indication of the relative risks of the reserve portfolios of different P/C insurers. Commentators pointed out that foreign subsidiaries have no need to prepare reserve information on the basis of the lines of business used by insurance regulators in the United States. Other commentators mentioned that line of business classification is not strictly uniform from company

---

[7] The example only covers eight years. See footnote 6 infra. The general format of this table was suggested by several

commentators as a cost effective way to meet the Commission's objectives as stated in the proposal.

to company. A number suggested that disaggregation by segment rather than by line of business should be permitted.

The Commission has, therefore, amended the proposal to take into account commentators concerns in several ways. The disclosures by statutory line of business are no longer required. Proposed Rule 12-19 has been eliminated. A column has been added to Rule 12-18 to provide for the disclosure of the aggregate discounts deducted from the reserves for the registrant and consolidated subsidiaries, for unconsolidated subsidiaries, and for 50%-or-less-owned equity investees. A footnote to the schedule requires disclosure of the rate, or range of rates, estimated if necessary, at which the discount was computed for each category. A provision calling for disclosure of the effects of discounting in the aggregate has been retained in Part 2(B)(5) of the Guide.

Sec. 403.04.e. Disclosures About Differences Between GAAP and Regulatory Reserves

The proposal asked for a statement of the nature and amount of differences, if any, between GAAP basis claim reserves and statutory claim reserves, in total and by applicable statutory lines of business. Most commentators recommended omission of all proposed requirements to present information by statutory line of business, but believed a reconciliation of aggregate reserves would be appropriate. A few suggested a reconciliation by major lines of business. Some objected to the presentation of a reconciliation from statutory to GAAP even on an aggregate basis. They argued that the principal difference was salvage and subrogation and that the amounts were not material. An analyst commented that the proposed requirement would provide useful information that is unavailable elsewhere.

The Commission had been advised that the aggregate amount of the differences between reserves reported in GAAP basis financial statements and those in reports to state regulatory authorities using regulatory accounting principles is usually small and that they usually occur in only one or a few statutory line of business. In order to permit users to judge when such differences indicate a possible need for further analysis, the Commission has determined to retain the provision for disclosure of the nature and aggregate amount of such differences for the parent and consolidated subsidiaries, for unconsolidated subsidiaries and for 50%-or-less-owned equity investees in the Guide. Disclosure of amounts which may be small in relation to aggregate reserve amounts is believed necessary because of the material effect on reported earnings which may result from a small change in reserve amounts.

Details of reconciliation may differ from one registrant to another depending on such factors as the need to make eliminations related to consolidation with life companies or other P/C companies and currency fluctuations among others. Each reconciling amount should be explained briefly.

Sec. 403.04.f. Summary Financial Disclosures About P/C Activities

[Sec. 403.04.f added by FRR-20.]

Proposed Rule 12-18 would have required disclosure of certain balance sheet and income statement items related to P/C operations (on a GAAP basis), by statutory line of business, for the parent and consolidated subsidiaries, for unconsolidated subsidiaries, and for 50%-or-less-owned equity investees.

Some commentators suggested elimination of statutory line of business disclosures and use of the same alignment of headings used in Rule 12-16 (which requires certain supplementary insurance information by segment). Others suggested that Rule 12-16 and proposed Rule 12-18 are redundant. These commentators may not have recognized that the schedule required in Rule 12-16 applies only to companies filing under Article 7 (Insurance Companies) of Regulation S-X: commercial and industrial companies that have insurance subsidiaries but file under Article 5 do not file that schedule. Some may not have realized that grouping data by segment could result in inclusion of non-property-casualty information.

The Commission continues to believe that when P/C loss reserves are significant (as defined in the rule), it is appropriate to require more detailed disclosure of certain P/C financial statement amounts in order to permit inter-enterprise comparison of trends and ratios. Therefore, when P/C related amounts are not stated separately in the financial statements of registrants engaged in diverse activities, certain summary disclosures will be required in new Schedule 12-18. Those disclosures would be presented separately for the registrant and its consolidated subsidiaries, the registrant's unconsolidated subsidiaries, and the registrant's 50%-or-less-owned equity investees. A footnote has been added to the schedule to allow the omission of certain immaterial items as discussed in "Disclosure Threshold Criteria" above, and an exemption has been provided for certain entities which file with the Commission themselves.

Sec. 403.04.g. Information from Reports Furnished to State Insurance Regulatory Authorities

[Sec. 403.04.g added by FRR-20.]

Proposed Exhibit 29 of Item 601 of Regulation S-K would require registrants to present Schedules O and P[8] on a consolidated or combined basis for (a) the registrant and its consolidated subsidiaries, (b) unconsolidated subsidiaries and (c) 50%-or-less-owned equity basis investees (proportionate share only).

Commentators generally agreed that Schedules O and P could provide useful information to certain investors and analysts and they should be provided as an exhibit. The industry commentators indicated a few difficulties in providing the information if certain immaterial entities did not have to be included. Accordingly, exemptions have been provided for immaterial entities and for certain entities which file with the Commission themselves (as discussed in "Disclosure Threshold Criteria" above).

[¶ 38,221] 404. Registered Investment Companies

.01. Nature of Examination and Report by Independent Public Accountants

[Under provisions of the Investment Company Act, an examination and report by an independent public accountant is required where registered management investment companies retain custody of their portfolio investments, or place them in the custody of a member of a national securities exchange. In addition, provisions of the Advisers Act require that an independent public accountant examine and report on all funds and securities of clients held by an investment adviser. The Commission has periodically issued interpretations describing the nature of the examination and content of the accountant's certificate.]

.a. Management Investment Companies

ASR 27:

Rule 17f-2 under the Investment Company Act sets certain standards to be followed by management investment companies registered under the Investment Company Act which maintain in their own custody their portfolio securities and similar investments. Paragraph (f) of that rule is as follows:

Such securities and similar investments shall be verified by complete examination by an independent public accountant retained by the investment company at least three times during the fiscal year, at least two of which shall be chosen by such accountant without prior notice to such company. A certificate of such accountant, stating that he has made an examination of such securities and investments and describing the nature and extent of the examination shall be transmitted to the Commission by the accountant promptly after each such examination.

The securities and similar investments referred to in the quoted paragraph include (a) securities on deposit in a vault or other depository maintained by a bank or other company whose function and physical facilities are supervised by federal or state authority; (b) securities which are collateralized to the extent of their full market value; (c) securities hypothecated, pledged, or placed in escrow for the account of such registered company; and (d) securities in transit. The examination and certificate required by the quoted paragraph should therefore cover all of the securities listed above.

In order to make a complete examination of the securities, it is necessary for the accountant not only to make a physical examination of the securities themselves, or in certain cases to obtain confirmation, but also to reconcile the physical count or confirmation with the book records. Furthermore, it is a necessary prerequisite to such a reconciliation that there have been made an appropriate examination of the investment accounts and supporting records, including an adequate check or analysis of the security transactions since the last examination and the entries pertaining thereto. While the certificate filed must describe the nature and extent of the examinations made, it is not necessary that each step taken be set out; instead, there should be included in the certificate in general terms an appropriate description of the scope of the examination of the accounts and the physical examination or confirmation of the securities.

Finally, in order to meet the requirements of Rule 17f-2(f) the certificate should comply with the usual technical requirements as to dating, salutation and manual signature and, in addition to the description of the examination made, should set forth:

(a) the date of the physical count and verification, and the period for which the investment accounts and transactions were examined;

(b) a clear designation of the depository;

(c) whether the examination was made without prior notice to the company; and

(d) the results of the examination.

Rule 17f-1 specifies the conditions under which a registered management investment company may place or maintain its securities and investments in the custody of a company which is a member of a national securities exchange. Paragraph (b)(4) of that rule calls for periodic examinations of the securities and investments so placed or maintained and for certificates as to the verification thereof. The requirements of such par-

---

[8] Schedules O and P are two of the schedules required in reports to state regulatory authorities by P/C insurance companies.

agraph (b)(4) involve substantially the same considerations as those of Rule 17f-2(f) and the above discussion is therefore likewise applicable to the examination and certificate required by such paragraph (b)(4).

404.01.b. Investment Advisers

I. Background

Rule 206(4)-2(a) under the Investment Advisers Act of 1940 (the "Act") provides, among other things, that it is a fraudulent, deceptive or manipulative act, practice, or course of business within the meaning of Section 206(4) of the Act for any investment adviser registered (or required to be registered) under Section 203 of the Act (herein "investment adviser") to have custody of client funds or securities unless:

(1) a qualified custodian maintains those funds and securities in a separate account for each client under that client's name; or in accounts that contain only clients' funds and securities, under the investment adviser's name as agent or trustee for the clients;

(2) clients are notified promptly in writing of the qualified custodian's name, address, and the manner in which the funds or securities are maintained, when an account is opened by an investment adviser on a client's behalf and following any changes to this information; and

(3) the investment adviser has a reasonable basis, after due inquiry, for believing that the qualified custodian sends an account statement, at least quarterly, to each of its clients for which it maintains funds or securities, identifying the amount of funds and of each security in the account at the end of the period and setting forth all transactions in the account during that period.

Rule 206(4)-2(a) generally requires that client funds and securities of which an investment adviser has custody under the rule be verified by actual examination at least once during each calendar year by an independent public accountant[1] ("accountant"), pursuant to a written agreement, between the investment adviser and the accountant, at a time that is chosen by the accountant without prior notice or announcement to the investment adviser and that is irregular from year to year.

II. Independent Verification of Funds and Securities

The objective of the accountant's examination[2] is to verify that client funds and securities of which an investment adviser has custody are held by a qualified custodian in a separate account for each client under that client's name, or in accounts that contain only clients' funds and securities, under the investment adviser's name as agent or trustee for the clients. The accountant should obtain from the investment adviser records that detail client funds and securities of which the investment adviser has custody and the identification of the qualified custodian(s) of those funds and securities.[3] The accountant should also obtain records of accounts that were closed during the period or that have a zero balance as of the date of the examination.

For a sample of client accounts, the accountant should obtain records of the purchases, sales, contributions, withdrawals and any other debits or credits to each selected client's account occurring since the date of the last examination. The accountant's procedures to meet the objective of the examination should normally include, but are not limited to, the following with respect to each selected client account:

• confirmation with the qualified custodian(s) of client funds and securities as of the date of the examination and that the client's funds and securities are held in either a separate account under the client's name or in accounts under the name of the investment adviser as agent or trustee for clients;

• confirmation with the client of funds and securities held in the account as of the date of the examination and contributions and withdrawals of funds and securities to and from the account since the date of the last examination; where confirmation replies are not received, the accountant should perform alternative procedures; and

• reconciliation of confirmations received and other evidence obtained to the investment adviser's records.

Privately offered securities

Rule 206(4)-(2)(b)(2) generally exempts privately offered securities from the qualified custodian requirements established under Rule 206(4)-(2)(a)(1).[4] Under the rule, a privately offered security is a security that is:

---

[1] If the investment adviser itself or a related person maintains clients' funds and securities as qualified custodian, the independent public accountant must be registered with, and subject to inspection by, the Public Company Accounting Oversight Board ("PCAOB"). *See* Rule 206(4)-2(a)(6)(i).

[2] The examination is a compliance examination to be conducted in accordance with American Institute of Certified Public Accountants' ("AICPA") attestation standards. *See* AT Section 601, *Compliance Attestation* ("AT 601").

[3] Rule 204-2(b) under the Act requires that an investment adviser who has custody or possession of funds and securities of any client must record all transactions for such client in a

journal and in separate ledger accounts for each client and must maintain copies of confirmations of all transactions in such accounts and a position record for each security in which a client has an interest. Rule 204-2(h) of the Act indicates that records maintained and preserved in compliance with Rules 17a-3 and 17a-4 under the Securities Exchange Act of 1934 (i.e., records maintained by a broker-dealer) can be deemed to satisfy the requirements of Rule 204-2(b), provided that they are substantially the same types of records. *See* Rule 204-2(b) and Rule 204-2(h) under the Act.

[4] The exemption provided by the rule is available with respect to securities held for the account of a limited partner-

(1) acquired from the issuer in a transaction or chain of transactions not involving any public offering;

(2) uncertificated, and ownership thereof is recorded only on the books of the issuer or its transfer agent in the name of the client; and

(3) transferable only with prior consent of the issuer or holders of the outstanding securities of the issuer.

The accountant's verification procedures with respect to any privately offered security selected for testing should include confirmation with the issuer of or counterparty to the security, or, where replies are not received, alternative procedures.

Reporting - Independent Verification

The accountant's examination report should include an opinion as to whether, with respect to the rules under the Act, the investment adviser was in compliance, in all material respects, with paragraph (a)(1) of Rule 206(4)-2 as of the examination date and had been complying with Rule 204-2(b) during the period since the prior examination date. The accountant should identify the date as of which the examination was made within the report.

Pursuant to the written agreement required under Rule 206(4)-2(a)(4), upon finding any material discrepancy during the course of the examination, the accountant should notify the Commission within one business day of the finding, by means of a facsimile transmission or electronic mail, followed by first class mail, directed to the attention of the Director of the Office of Compliance Inspections and Examinations. For purposes of this examination, a material discrepancy is material non-compliance with the provisions of either Rule 206(4)-2 or Rule 204-2(b) under the Act.[5]

Pursuant to the written agreement required under Rule 206(4)-2(a)(4), the examination should be completed and the resulting examination report should be filed on Form ADV-E by the accountant within 120 days of the time chosen by the accountant. The accountant should also file Form ADV-E with the Commission upon resignation or dismissal from, or other termination of, the engagement, or upon removing itself or being removed from consideration for being reappointed within four business days. Such filing should be accompanied by a statement that includes:

(1) the date of such resignation, dismissal, removal, or other termination, and the name, address, and contact information of the accountant; and

(2) an explanation of any problems relating to examination scope or procedure that contributed to such resignation, dismissal, removal, or other termination.

III. Internal Control Report

Rule 206(4)-2(a)(6) establishes additional requirements for an investment adviser that itself, or its related person, maintains client funds or securities as a qualified custodian in connection with advisory services provided to clients. Such an investment adviser must at least once each calendar year obtain or receive from its related person an internal control report related to its or its affiliates' custody services, including the safeguarding of funds and securities, prepared by an independent public accountant that is registered with, and subject to inspection by, the PCAOB.[6]

The objective of the examination supporting the internal control report is to obtain reasonable assurance that the qualified custodian's controls have been placed in operation as of a specific date, and are suitably designed and are operating effectively to meet control objectives related to custody of funds and securities during the period specified. The internal control report should address control objectives and associated controls related to the areas of client account setup and maintenance, authorization and processing of client transactions, security maintenance and setup, processing of income and corporate action transactions, reconciliation of funds and securities to depositories and other unaffiliated custodians, and client reporting. Control objectives addressing these areas should include -

• Documentation for the opening and modification of client accounts is received, authenticated, and established completely, accurately, and timely on the applicable system.

• Client transactions, including contributions and withdrawals, are authorized and processed in a complete, accurate, and timely manner.

• Trades are properly authorized, settled, and recorded completely, accurately, and timely in the client account.

• New securities and changes to securities are authorized and established in a complete, accurate and timely manner.

• Securities income and corporate action transactions are processed to client accounts in a complete, accurate, and timely manner.

• Physical securities are safeguarded from loss or misappropriation.

(Footnote Continued)

ship (or a limited liability company, or other type of pooled investment vehicle) only if the limited partnership is audited, and the audited financial statements are distributed, as described in paragraph (b)(4) of the rule.

[5] Reporting on material non-compliance is discussed within AT 601 of the AICPA attestation standards. *See* AT 601.

[6] A Type II SAS 70 Report conducted in accordance with AU Section 324, *Service Organizations* ("AU 324") of the AICPA auditing standards would be sufficient to satisfy the requirements of the internal control report. In addition to the Type II SAS 70 Report, an examination on internal control conducted in accordance with AT 601 would also be sufficient.

• Cash and security positions are reconciled completely, accurately and on a timely basis between the custodian and depositories.

• Account statements reflecting cash and security positions are provided to clients in a complete, accurate and timely manner.

Rule 206(4)-2(a)(6)(ii)(B) states that, as part of the internal control report, the independent public accountant must verify that funds and securities are reconciled to a custodian other than the adviser or its related person (for example, the Depository Trust Corporation). The accountant's tests of the custodian's reconciliation(s) should include either direct confirmation, on a test basis, with unaffiliated custodians or other procedures designed to verify that the data used in reconciliations performed by the qualified custodian is obtained from unaffiliated custodians and is unaltered.

Reporting - Internal Control Report

The accountant's internal control report should identify the control objectives included within the scope of the examination and include the accountant's opinion as to whether controls have been placed in operation as of the specific date, and are suitably designed and are operating effectively to meet the identified control objectives during the specified period. The report should also describe the nature, timing, extent and results of the accountant's procedures performed to verify that funds and securities are reconciled to depositories and other unaffiliated custodians.[7]

IV. Relationship between Independent Verification and Internal Control Report

When performing an independent verification of client funds and securities for an investment adviser that itself, or its related person, maintains custody as a qualified custodian, the accountant should obtain a copy of the most recently issued internal control report and determine whether there are any findings in the internal control report that would affect the nature and extent of his or her procedures. If findings within the internal control report indicate information provided by the qualified custodian may not be reliable, the accountant should consider whether the circumstances warrant the issuance of a qualified or adverse opinion, or a disclaimer of opinion.

If a significant period of time has elapsed since the issuance of the internal control report, the accountant should perform appropriate procedures to determine whether there have been significant changes to the procedures and controls related to custody at the qualified custodian since the date of the report. If significant changes have occurred, the accountant should perform procedures to update his or her understanding of whether the controls at the qualified custodian

have been placed in operation, are suitably designed, and are operating effectively to meet the identified control objectives, as appropriate in the circumstances. The accountant can perform these procedures directly or can request that the accountant that prepared the internal control report perform such procedures.

[Revised in FR-81.]

404.02. Accounting for Interest Collected on Defaulted Bonds

ASR 36:

A question has been raised as to the treatment by an investment company of interest collected on defaulted bonds applicable to a period prior to the date on which such bonds and defaulted interest were acquired. In the particular case an investment company purchased, at a "flat" price of $260,000, $1,000,000 principal amount of bonds with attached defaulted interest coupons amounting to $250,000. The company subsequent to the purchase received an interest payment of $40,000 on account of defaulted interest coupons for periods prior to the purchase.

Where a purchase is made of defaulted bonds with defaulted interest coupons attached, it is clear that the purchase price covers not only the right to receive the principal of the bond itself, but also the right to receive any payments made on the defaulted interest coupons purchased. Under these circumstances, the price paid cannot be deemed to reflect only the cost of acquisition of the issuer's obligation to pay the principal sum, but must instead be considered to reflect as well the cost of acquisition of the issuer's existing obligation to pay the interest coupons already matured. In the usual case, moreover, there is no satisfactory basis on which to allocate the total price between the bond on the one hand and the defaulted interest coupons on the other. Under such circumstances, the bond and defaulted coupons should be treated as a unit for accounting purposes and collections on account of the defaulted interest coupons should be treated not as interest on the sum invested but rather as repayments thereof. Moreover, in view of the uncertainty of eventually receiving payments in excess of the purchase price, ordinarily no part of any payment, whether on account of principal or the defaulted interest, should be considered as profit until the full purchase price has been recovered.

In the instant case, therefore, the receipt of the $40,000 interest payment should be treated as a reduction of the cost of the investment and not as interest income, or as a profit on the investment. After payments are received on account of the principal and defaulted interest in an amount equal to the purchase price, any further collections thereon should be treated not as interest, but

---

[7] Paragraph .62 of AU 324 discusses reporting on substantive procedures as part of a Type II SAS 70 report. *See* AU 324.

as profit on securities purchased. On the other hand, it seems clear that collection of interest coupons covering periods subsequent to the purchase may be treated as interest income unless the circumstances of a particular case are such as to indicate that, despite the apparent nature of the payment, recovery of the cost of the investment through sale or redemption is so uncertain as to make it necessary to treat the payment as a reduction of the investment.

404.03. Accounting, Valuation and Disclosure of Investment Securities

[The Commission has periodically published its views as to the appropriate method of accounting for and valuation of investment securities of registered investment companies. In addition, the Commission's views have also been published regarding the appropriate disclosure of certain types of investment securities.]

.a. General

ASR 118:

The statement of assets and liabilities of a registered investment company comprises, for the most part, not only investments in securities which are held by a custodian or are on hand, but also frequently includes securities as to which contracts to purchase have been entered into but which have not been received. Securities held by a custodian or on hand that have been contracted to be sold are excluded from the investments in such statement. In the ordinary transaction through a broker, recording the transaction on the date the broker advises the investment company that the securities have been purchased or sold (the "trade date"), rather than when delivery is made or due (the "settlement date"), is the established and acceptable practice in investment company accounting.

In the case of purchases or sales of securities other than in the usual brokerage transactions, the date on which the investment company obtains an enforceable right to demand the securities or the payment therefor—the date the transaction should be recorded—is sometimes difficult to determine. When a question arises as to the date an enforceable right is obtained by the investment company, an opinion of legal counsel as to when the right occurred should normally be obtained by the company's management and made available to the independent accountant. Such an opinion should be in writing, and a copy should be included in the accountant's working papers.

Where the propriety or validity of an investment in a security by an investment company is questionable because of particular provisions of the Investment Company Act, or state law, or the company's investment policy or other representations as stated in its filings with the Commission, or legal obligations in respect of a contract or transaction, a written opinion of legal counsel should also be obtained by the company's management, made available to the independent accountant, and a copy included in the working papers. If the questions of propriety or validity are not satisfactorily resolved, the circumstances of the investment should be disclosed in the financial statements or notes thereto.

Securities held by the company or its custodian should be substantiated by the company's independent accountant in the course of an audit by inspection of such securities in custody pursuant to Section 17(f) of the Investment Company Act. When securities contracted to be purchased but not yet received are included in the statement of assets and liabilities, confirmation of the contract to purchase should be obtained from the bank, broker, or other person responsible for the delivery of such securities. Where satisfactory confirmation has been received, audit procedures normally need not be extended to obtain evidence of subsequent receipt of the securities by the company or its custodian unless additional substantiation is considered necessary by the independent accountant under the circumstances. Where satisfactory confirmation has not been received, subsequent receipt of such securities should be substantiated by other appropriate procedures.

In accordance with Section 30(e) of the Investment Company Act, the certificate of the company's independent accountant should include a brief statement concerning the substantiation of securities owned. Except for securities contracted to be purchased but not received, the certificate should state that the securities were either inspected by the independent accountant or, where the company's securities were maintained in custody pursuant to Section 17(f) of the Investment Company Act, were confirmed to him by the custodian. In the case of securities contracted to be purchased but not received by the company or its custodian, reference should be made to confirmation by banks, brokers, or others or to alternative procedures, as appropriate in the circumstances.

404.03.b. Valuation of Securities

.i. Introduction

ASR 118:

Under Article 6 of Regulation S-X, the statements of assets and liabilities of open-end investment companies must reflect all assets at value, showing cost parenthetically, while closed-end companies may elect to use either this basis or to reflect all assets at cost, showing value parenthetically.

"Value" is defined in Section 2(a)(41) of the Investment Company Act. For purposes of determining the amounts at which securities and other assets are carried in the statements of assets and liabilities included in annual and other reports and in registration statements filed by investment companies, "value" is defined in pertinent part as: "(i) with respect to securities for which market quotations are readily available, the market value of such securities; and (ii) with respect to other securities and assets, fair value as determined in good faith by the board of directors . . . ." This definition is also used in Rule 2a-4 under the Investment Company Act as the required basis for computing periodically the current net asset value of redeemable securities of investment companies for the purpose of pricing their shares.

In some circumstances value can be determined fairly in more than one way. Hence, the standards set forth below should be considered as guidelines, one or more of which may be appropriate in the circumstances of a particular case. These standards should be followed, and a company's stated valuation policies should be consistent with them. Any variation from the standards should be disclosed in the financial statements or notes thereto even though the variation is in accordance with the company's stated valuation policy. In addition, any deviation from a stated valuation policy, whether or not in conformity with the standards, should be disclosed in the financial statements or notes thereto.

404.03.b.ii. Securities Listed or Traded on a National Securities Exchange

ASR 118:

Ordinarily, little difficulty should be experienced in valuing securities listed or traded on one or more national securities exchanges, since quotations of completed transactions are published daily. If a security is traded on the valuation date, the last quoted sale price generally is used. In the case of securities listed on more than one national securities exchange the last quoted sale, up to the time of valuation, on the exchange on which the security is principally traded should be used or, if there were no sales on that exchange on the valuation date, the last quoted sale, up to the time of valuation, on the other exchanges should be used. With respect to the time of valuation, Rule 22c-1 under the Investment Company Act specifies the frequency with which current net asset value shall be computed.

If there was no sale on the valuation date but published closing bid and asked prices are available, the valuation in such circumstances should be within the range of these quoted prices. Some companies as a matter of general policy use the bid price, others use the mean of the bid and asked prices, and still others use a valuation within the range considered best to represent value in the circumstances; each of these policies is acceptable if consistently applied. Normally, it is not acceptable to use the asked price alone. Where, on the valuation date, only a bid price or an asked price is quoted or the spread between bid and asked prices is substantial, quotations for several days should be reviewed. If sales have been infrequent or there is a thin market in the

security, further consideration should be given to whether "market quotations are readily available." If it is decided that they are not readily available, the alternative method of valuation prescribed by Section 2(a)(41)—"fair value as determined in good faith by the board of directors"—should be used.

404.03.b.iii. Over-the-Counter Securities

ASR 118:

Quotations are available from various sources for most unlisted securities traded regularly in the over-the-counter market. These sources include tabulations in the financial press, publications of the National Quotation Bureau and the "Blue List" of municipal bond offerings, several financial reporting services, and individual broker-dealers. These quotations generally are in the form of inter-dealer bid and asked prices. Because of the availability of multiple sources, a company frequently has a greater number of options open to it in valuing securities traded in the over-the-counter market than it does in valuing listed securities. A company may adopt a policy of using a mean of the bid prices, or of the bid and asked prices, or of the prices of a representative selection of broker-dealers quoting on a particular security; or it may use a valuation within the range of bid and asked prices considered best to represent value in the circumstances. Any of these policies is acceptable if consistently applied. Normally, the use of asked prices alone is not acceptable.

Ordinarily, quotations for a security should be obtained from more than one broker-dealer, particularly if quotations are available only from broker-dealers not known to be established market-makers for that security, and quotations for several days should be reviewed. If the validity of the quotations appears to be questionable, or if the number of quotations is such as to indicate that there is a thin market in the security, further consideration should be given to whether "market quotations are readily available." If it is decided that they are not readily available, the security should be considered one required to be valued at "fair value as determined in good faith by the board of directors."

404.03.b.iv. Securities Valued "in Good Faith"

ASR 118:

To comply with Section 2(a)(41) of the Investment Company Act and Rule 2a-4 under the Investment Company Act, it is incumbent upon the board of directors to satisfy themselves that all appropriate factors relevant to the value of securities for which market quotations are not readily available have been considered and to determine the method of arriving at the fair value of each such security. To the extent considered necessary, the board may appoint persons to assist them in the determination of such value, and to make the actual calculations pursuant to the board's direction. The board must also, consistent with this responsibility, continuously review the appropriateness of the method used in valuing each issue of security in the company's portfolio. The directors must recognize their responsibilities in this matter and whenever technical assistance is requested from individuals who are not directors, the findings of such individuals must be carefully reviewed by the directors in order to satisfy themselves that the resulting valuations are fair.

No single standard for determining "fair value . . . in good faith" can be laid down, since fair value depends upon the circumstances of each individual case. As a general principle, the current "fair value" of an issue of securities being valued by the board of directors would appear to be the amount which the owner might reasonably expect to receive for them upon their current sale. Methods which are in accord with this principle may, for example, be based on a multiple of earnings, or a discount from market of a similar freely traded security, or yield to maturity with respect to debt issues, or a combination of these and other methods. Some of the general factors which the directors should consider in determining a valuation method for an individual issue of securities include: 1) the fundamental analytical data relating to the investment, 2) the nature and duration of restrictions on disposition of the securities, and 3) an evaluation of the forces which influence the market in which these securities are purchased and sold. Among the more specific factors which are to be considered are: type of security, financial statements, cost at date of purchase, size of holding, discount from market value of unrestricted securities of the same class at time of purchase, special reports prepared by analysts, information as to any transactions or offers with respect to the security, existence of merger proposals or tender offers affecting the securities, price and extent of public trading in similar securities of the issuer or comparable companies, and other relevant matters.

The above guidance does not purport to delineate all factors which may be considered. The directors should take into consideration all indications of value available to them in determining the "fair value" assigned to a particular security. The information so considered together with, to the extent practicable, judgment factors considered by the board of directors in reaching its decisions should be documented in the minutes of the directors' meeting and the supporting data retained for the inspection of the company's independent accountant.

404.03.c. Auditing Security Valuations
ASR 118:

In the case of securities for which market quotations are readily available, the independent accountant should independently verify all the quotations used by the company at the balance sheet date and satisfy himself that such quotations may properly be used under the standards stated above.

In the case of securities carried at "fair value" as determined by the board of directors in "good faith," the accountant does not function as an appraiser and is not expected to substitute his judgment for that of the company's directors; rather, he should review all information considered by the board or by analysts reporting to it, read relevant minutes of directors' meetings, and ascertain the procedures followed by the directors. If the accountant is unable to express an unqualified opinion because of the uncertainty inherent in the valuations of the securities based on the directors' subjective judgment, he should nevertheless make appropriate mention in his certificate whether in the circumstances the procedures appear to be reasonable and the underlying documentation appropriate.

When considering values assigned to securities by the company, the independent accountant should consider any investment limitations or conditions on the acquisition or holding of such securities which may be imposed on the company by the Act, by its certificate or by-laws, by contract, or by its filings with the Commission. If such restrictions are met by a narrow margin, the independent accountant may need to exercise extra care in satisfying himself that the evidence indicates that the security valuation determinations were not biased to meet those restrictions.

404.03.d. Investments in Affiliates or Affiliated Persons
ASR 118:

Various rules of Regulation S-X require that the financial statements of an investment company state separately investments in, investment income from, gain or loss on sales of securities of, and management or other service fees payable to, (a) controlled companies and (b) other "affiliates." As stated in Rule 6-02(d) of Regulation S-X, the term "affiliate" means an affiliated person as defined in Section 2(a)(3) of the Investment Company Act, and the term "control" has the meaning given in Section 2(a)(9) of the Investment Company Act. The term "affiliated person" is defined in Section 2(a)(3) of the Investment Company Act in such a manner as to encompass such control relationships and also the direct or indirect ownership of five percent or more of the outstanding voting securities of any issuer. An affiliated person as there defined also includes any officer, director, partner, co-partner, or employee or, with respect to an investment company, any investment adviser or member of an advisory board thereof.

In ascertaining the existence of any such affiliations, the independent accountant should consider the facts obtained during the course of an audit and also make inquiries of the company's management; and his working papers should include written representations from the management as evidence of such inquiries. The representations should be in the form of a statement that the company, except to the extent indicated, (i) does not own any securities either of persons who are directly affiliated, or, to the best information and belief of management, of persons who are indirectly affiliated, (ii) has not received income from or realized gain or loss on sales of investments in or indebtedness of such persons, (iii) has not incurred expenses for management or other service fees payable to such persons, and (iv) has not otherwise engaged in transactions with such persons. Where there is a question as to the existence of an affiliation, a written opinion of legal counsel should be obtained by the company's management, made available to the independent accountant, and a copy included in the working papers. Regulation S-X requires disclosure in the financial statements or notes thereto of details of such investments and transactions.

404.03.e. Exhibit

[The following language in a "subject to" accountant's opinion was deemed to be acceptable to the Commission in the circumstances indicated below. A letter from the Chief Accountant to the Chairman of the Committee on Investment Companies of the AICPA acknowledging the acceptance of such language was communicated in ASR 118.]

ASR 118:

The Commission has considered the suggestions of the Committee on Investment Companies of the AICPA with particular reference to the circumstances in which a "subject to" opinion would be appropriate. This will advise you that the "subject to" form of qualified opinion may be used when an investment company's portfolio includes *a significant amount* represented by securities for which market quotations are not readily available *and* when the auditor is satisfied that the procedures followed and the information obtained are adequate to enable the board of directors to value the securities but is unable to form an opinion as to the fairness of the specific values determined in good faith by the board of directors. As developed in our conversations, an opinion in the following form, introduced by the standard scope paragraph, in the interests of uniformity of language should be used:

As discussed more fully in Note 1 to the financial statements, securities amounting to $____ (__% of net assets) have been valued at fair value as determined by the Board of Directors. We have reviewed the procedures applied by the directors in valuing such securities and have inspected underlying documentation; while in the circumstances the procedures appear to be reasonable and the documentation appropriate, determination of

fair values involves subjective judgment which is not susceptible to substantiation by auditing procedures.

In our opinion, subject to the effect on the financial statements of the valuation of securities determined by the Board of Directors as described in the preceding paragraph, the (financial statements) present fairly . . . .

404.04. "Restricted" Securities

ASR 113:

Section 4(2) of the Securities Act exempts from the registration requirements of that Act "transactions by an issuer not involving any public offering." This is the so-called "private offering" provision in the Securities Act. The securities involved in transactions effected pursuant to this exemption are referred to as restricted securities because they cannot be resold to the public without prior registration. They are also sometimes referred to as "investment letter securities" because of the practice frequently followed by the seller in such a transaction, in order to substantiate the claim that the transaction does not involve a public offering, of requiring that the buyer furnish a so-called "investment letter" representing that the purchase is for investment and not for resale to the general public.

The private offering exemption of Section 4(2) of the Securities Act is available only where the offerees do not need the protections afforded by the registration procedure. As the Court of Appeals for the Second Circuit stated in *Katz* v. *Amos Treat & Co.,* CCH Fed'l. Sec. Law Rep. ¶ 92,409 (1969):

The Supreme Court has instructed that the applicability of the exemption should turn on whether the particular class of persons affected need the protection of the Act. *SEC* v. *Ralston Purina Co.,* 346 U.S. 119, 125 (1953).

The test of the availability of the Section 4(2) exemption is whether the offerees are in such a position with respect to the issuer as to have access to the kind of information that would be made available in a registration statement filed pursuant to the Securities Act. This test is no different when the offeree is an investment company.

404.04.a. The Problem of the Valuation

ASR 113:

It is critically important that an investment company properly value its portfolio securities. It is obvious, for example, that any distortion in the valuation of a restricted security held by an investment company will distort the price at which the shares of the investment company are sold or redeemed. It is also clear that investment managers who are compensated on the basis of net asset value or performance may be unduly compensated if a restricted security, purchased at a discount from the market quotation for unrestricted securities of the same class, is overvalued. In such a case, investors may also be misled by the reported performance of the investment company.

The acquisition of restricted securities by both open-end and closed-end investment companies creates serious problems of valuation. Section 2(a)(41) of the Investment Company Act and Rule 2a-4 thereunder requires that in determining net asset value, "securities for which market quotations are readily available" must be valued at current market value while other securities and assets must be valued at "fair value as determined in good faith by the board of directors."

Readily available market quotations refers to reports of current public quotations for securities similar in all respects to the securities in question. No such current public quotations can exist in the case of restricted securities. For valuation purposes, therefore, restricted securities constitute securities for which market quotations are *not* readily available. Accordingly, their fair values must be determined in good faith by the board of directors and this obligation necessarily continues throughout the period these securities are retained in the company's portfolio.

Restricted securities should be included in the portfolio of a company and valued to determine current net asset value on the date that the investment company has an enforceable right to demand the securities from the seller.

Where the investment company negotiates the acquisition of the restricted securities directly with the owner of the securities, there are three significant dates. The first occurs when the investment company and the seller orally agree upon the price and the amount of the securities (the "handshake date"). At this point, there would not seem to be any enforceable right of the investment company to demand the securities from the seller since, in most states, particularly those which have adopted the Uniform Commercial Code, there is no enforceable right unless there exists some writing "sufficient to indicate that a contract has been made for sale of a stated quantity of described securities at a defined or stated price" (Section 8-319(a) of the Uniform Commercial Code). If the terms of the oral understanding do not contemplate compliance with any condition by the seller, it is suggested that the investment company procure, from the seller, a signed memorandum setting forth the price and quantity of securities to be sold. Upon receipt of that memorandum, an enforceable right would be obtained. The securities should be valued as of that date.

In those situations where the oral understanding contemplates the execution of a formal contract of purchase and sale, no enforceable right exists until the time the formal contract is signed (the "contract date"). If the formal contract does not require compliance with any conditions by the seller, an enforceable right is then obtained, and the securities should be valued as of that date.

Where the formal contract requires compliance with stated conditions which the investment company believes should not be waived, no enforceable right is obtained until the stated conditions are satisfied. In that situation, the valuation date should be the date upon which the conditions are satisfied (the "closing date").

Restricted securities are often purchased at a discount, frequently substantial, from the market price of outstanding unrestricted securities of the same class. This reflects the fact that securities which cannot be readily sold in the public market place are less valuable than securities which can be sold, and also the fact that, by the direct sale of restricted securities, sellers avoid the expense, time and public disclosure which registration entails.

As a general principle, the current fair value of restricted securities would appear to be the amount which the owner might reasonably expect to receive for them upon their current sale. This depends upon their inherent worth, without regard to the restrictive feature, adjusted for any diminution in value resulting from the restrictive feature. Consequently, the valuation of restricted securities at the market quotations for unrestricted securities of the same class would, except for most unusual situations, be improper. Further, the continued valuation of such securities at cost would be improper if, as a result of the operations of the issuer, change in general market conditions or otherwise, cost has ceased to represent fair value. In such circumstances, maintaining the value of the restricted securities at cost would mislead investors as to the value of the portfolio of the investment company which holds restricted securities.

Instead of valuing restricted securities at cost or at the market value of unrestricted securities of the same class, some investment companies value restricted securities held in their portfolio by applying either a constant percentage or an absolute dollar discount to the market quotation for unrestricted securities of the same class. The automatic valuation of restricted securities by such a method, however, would also not appear to satisfy the requirement of the Investment Company Act that each security, for which a market quotation is not readily available, be valued at fair value as determined in good faith by the board of directors.

Thus, it would be improper in valuing restricted securities automatically to maintain the same percentage discount (from the market quotation for unrestricted securities of the same class) that was received when the restricted securities were purchased, without regard to other relevant factors such as, for example, the extent to which the inherent value of the securities may have changed.

Furthermore, the valuation of restricted securities by reference to the market price for unrestricted securities of the same class assumes that the market price for unrestricted securities of the same class is representative of the fair value of the securities. This may not be the case when the market for the unrestricted securities is very thin, i.e., only a limited volume of shares are available for trading. With a thin market, the news of the investment company's purchase of the restricted securities may, by itself, have the effect of stimulating a public demand for the unrestricted securities, the supply of which has not been increased, and thus lead to a spiralling increase in the valuation of both the restricted and unrestricted securities.

Moreover, if in valuing restricted securities, the diminution in value attributable to the restrictive feature is itself affected by factors subject to change, such as the length of time which must elapse before the investment company may require the issuer to cause the securities to be registered for public sale, the valuation should reflect any such changes.

Some companies value restricted securities, acquired at prices below the market quotations for unrestricted securities of the same class, by automatically amortizing the difference over some chosen period on the assumption that it will be possible to sell them at the market price for unrestricted securities at the expiration of the time period. Under prevailing conditions, however, it cannot always be determined either that the securities will, in fact, be effectively registered at the expiration of that period or that their public sale will otherwise be possible. For example, the issuer may be unable or unwilling to register at the expiration of the estimated period, and public sale at the end of that period without registration may not be lawful. Consequently, the practice of automatically amortizing the discount over an arbitrarily chosen period creates the appearance of an appreciation in the value of the securities which has not, in fact, occurred, and, accordingly, is improper.

An undertaking by the issuer to register the securities within a specified time period would not dictate a different result. In view of the many factors that may alter the date of the proposed public offering, it is at best speculative to use such an undertaking alone as the basis for amortizing the discount.

In summary, there can be no automatic formula by which an investment company can value restricted securities in its portfolio to comply with Section 2(a)(41) and Rule 2a-4. It is the responsibility of the board of directors to determine the fair value of each issue of restricted securities in good faith; and the data and information considered and the analysis thereof should be retained for inspection by the company's independent auditors. While the board may, consistent with this responsibility, determine the method of valuing each issue of restricted security in the company's

portfolio, it must continuously review the appropriateness of any method so determined. The actual calculations may be made by persons acting pursuant to the direction of the board.

404.04.b. The Problems of Portfolio Management

ASR 113:

In addition to valuation, restricted securities present special problems of portfolio management.

The concept of the Securities Act exemption of a private placement of securities is premised on the belief that in such a situation the investor has such information concerning the issuer that he is able to fend for himself without need for the disclosures that would be provided by an effective registration statement. Correlatively, where the investor is a registered investment company, it would seem to be the fiduciary duty of the persons responsible for the investment decisions of the investment company to obtain, prior to purchase, the necessary information to make an independent analysis of the investment merits of the particular restricted securities. Also, in order to enable the continuing valuation of such securities, the investment company should require the seller to undertake to provide, to the extent known to the seller, information on a continuing basis as to any subsequent private sales of the issuer's securities. The investment company should also assure itself that it is in the position to obtain the appropriate financial information at appropriate times. It is assumed that any public disclosures, such as that made in periodic reports filed pursuant to the Exchange Act, are carefully considered by the investment company portfolio manager.

There is also the paradox of too much success to consider. For example, if restricted securities rapidly appreciate in value, perhaps because of an improvement in the business of the issuer, an investment company may find instead of having, for example, 5 percent of its assets invested in a particular company, it has instead, 25 percent of its assets in that company. The investment company to which this happens suffers a loss in diversification and may find that it has become overly sensitive to any adverse developments in the affairs of that particular portfolio company.

The foregoing factors in portfolio management relate to both open-end and closed-end management companies. There are additional special factors that relate only to open-end companies.

Section 2(a)(32), when read together with Section 5(a), of the Investment Company Act requires that the holders of redeemable shares issued by an open-end investment company be entitled to receive approximately their proportionate share of the issuer's current net assets, or the cash equivalent thereof, upon presentation of the security to the issuer or to a person designated by the issuer. Section 22(e) of the Investment Company

Act provides that, absent specified unusual conditions, payment of the redemption price must be made within seven days after the tender of a redeemable security to an investment company or its agent designated for that purpose.

It is desirable that on open-end company retain maximum flexibility in the choice of portfolio securities which, on the basis of their relative investment merits, could best be sold where necessary to meet redemptions. To the extent that the portfolio consists of restricted securities, this flexibility is reduced.

Restricted securities may not be publicly sold— nor can they be distributed to redeeming shareholders as an in-kind redemption. While they may be sold privately, there may not be sufficient time to obtain the best price since the date of payment or satisfaction may not be postponed more than seven days after the tender of the company's redeemable securities for redemption. A private sale within that period may result in the investment company receiving less than its carrying value of the restricted securities. This would result in a preference in favor of the redeeming shareholders and a diminution of the net asset value per share of shareholders who have not redeemed. Therefore, instead of arranging a private sale of restricted securities, an open-end company that is faced with redemptions may decide to sell unrestricted securities which it would otherwise have retained on the basis of comparative investment merit.

Significant holdings of restricted securities not only magnify the valuation difficulties but may also present serious liquidity questions. Because open-end companies hold themselves out at all times as being prepared to meet redemptions within seven days, it is essential that such companies maintain a portfolio of investments that enable them to fulfill that obligation. This requires a high degree of liquidity in the assets of open-end companies because the extent of redemption demands or other exigencies are not always predictable. The Commission is of the view that a prudent limit on any open-end company's acquisition of restricted securities, or other assets not having readily available market quotations, would be 10 percent. When as a result of either the increase in the value of some or all of the restricted securities held, or the diminution in the value of unrestricted securities in the portfolios, the restricted securities come to represent a larger percentage of the value of the company's net assets, the same valuation and liquidity questions occur. Accordingly, if the fair value of restricted holdings increases beyond 10 percent, it would be desirable for the open-end company to consider appropriate steps to protect maximum flexibility. The Commission will re-examine appropriate limitations in this area in light of all the policy objectives of the Investment Company Act.

404.04.c. The Problem of Disclosure

ASR 113:

Section 8(b)(1)(D) of the Investment Company Act requires that an investment company include, in its registration statement filed with the Commission under the Investment Company Act, information as to its policy with respect to "engaging in the business of underwriting securities issued by other persons." Item 5(b)(4) of Form N-1 and Item 7(b)(4) of Form N-2 require that a registrant under the Act describe its policy or proposed policy with respect to "the underwriting of securities of other issuers." In response to this item, registrant's policy with respect to the acquisition of restricted securities should be disclosed. In view of the fact that policies listed under these items are fundamental policies which cannot be changed without prior shareholder approval, the importance of adopting a clear policy with regard to such investments is apparent.

The prospectus of a registered investment company should also fully disclose the company's policy with respect to restricted securities. It is also clear that an investment company which has a policy of acquiring restricted securities is responsible for full and adequate disclosure with respect to all matters relating to the valuation of such securities. Specifically, there should be included, in a note to the financial statements, (1) identification of any restricted securities and the date of acquisition, (2) disclosure of the methods used in valuing such securities both at the date of acquisition and the date of the financial statements, (3) disclosure of the cost of such securities and the market quotation for unrestricted securities of the same class both on the day the purchase price was agreed to (the so-called "handshake date"), and on the day the investment company first obtained an enforceable right to acquire such securities, and (4) a statement as to whether the issuer of the registrant will bear costs, including those involved in registration under the Securities Act, in connection with the disposition of such securities.

Section 10(b) of the Exchange Act and Rule 10b-5 thereunder makes it unlawful, among other things, for any person, in connection with the purchase or sale of securities, to employ any device, scheme, or artifice to defraud or to make any untrue statement of a material fact or to omit to state a material fact necessary in order to make the statements made not misleading, or engage in any act, practice, or course of business which operates or would operate as a fraud or deceit upon any persons.

The offering price of securities issued by a management investment company is premised upon the net asset value of such shares as determined pursuant to Section 2(a)(41) of the Investment Company Act and Rule 2a-4 thereunder and is so represented in its prospectus. The improper valuation of restricted securities held by such a company would distort the net asset value of the shares being offered or, in the case of an open-end company, redeemed, and would therefore constitute a fraud and deceit within the meaning of Section 10(b) and Rule 10b-5.

An open-end company, of course, represents to investors, in its prospectus, that it will, as required by Section 22(e) of the Investment Company Act, redeem its securities at approximate net asset value within seven days after tender. To the extent a material percentage of the assets of an open-end company consist of restricted securities which cannot publicly be sold without registration under the Securities Act, the ability of the company to comply with the provisions of the Investment Company Act relating to redemption, and to fulfill the implicit representations made in its prospectus with respect thereto, may be adversely affected. In any such situation, the investment company concerned and the persons responsible for the sale of its securities should give careful consideration to the possible application of the provisions of Section 10(b) of the Exchange Act and Rule 10b-5 thereunder.

404.05. Money Market Funds
.a. Introduction
ASR 219:

The Commission issued an interpretation of a rule adopted under the Investment Company Act indicating, generally, that it shall be considered inappropriate under the provisions of the rule for "money market" funds and certain other open-end investment companies to determine the fair value of debt portfolio securities on an amortized cost basis, except in the case of securities with remaining maturities of 60 days or less.

The Commission recognized that there had been considerable confusion and uncertainty as to the appropriate methods to be utilized by "money market" funds in valuing their portfolio securities. This interpretation should help remove the uncertainty and further the objectives of enabling investors in such funds to: (1) Purchase and redeem their shares at prices appropriately reflecting the current value of fund portfolio securities; (2) be properly credited for any unrealized appreciation or depreciation in such portfolio securities; and (3) be provided with meaningful and comparable information with which to appraise investment returns and the current earning ability of "money market" funds.

404.05.b. Interpretation with Respect to Valuation of Debt Instruments by Money Market Funds and Certain Other Open-End Investment Companies[*]
ASR 219:

The Commission is aware that many investment companies, including some "money market" funds, value short-term debt instruments in their portfolios on an amortized cost basis. Under this method of valuation, investment companies initially value such instruments at their cost on the date of purchase and, if the instrument was purchased at a discount, thereafter assume a constant proportional increase in value until maturity.[1]

However, during the period a debt security is held, changes in the market rate of interest and other factors may affect the price at which that security could be sold. As a general principle, the longer the remaining maturity of an outstanding debt security, the more that price will be affected by such interest rate changes.

The Commission is concerned that the use of the amortized cost method in valuing portfolio securities of registered investment companies may result in overvaluation or undervaluation of the portfolios of such companies, relative to the value of the portfolios determined with reference to current market factors. In the case of registered open-end management investment companies ("mutual funds" or "funds"), this would mean investors purchasing or redeeming shares could pay or receive more or less than the actual value of their proportionate shares of the funds' current net assets. The effect of such sales or redemptions may therefore result in inappropriate dilution of the assets and returns of existing shareholders.[2]

Although inappropriate valuation of securities could cause these effects in various types of funds, the position taken herein is addressed specifically to the case of: (1) "Money market" funds, and (2) other open-end investment companies that hold a significant amount of debt securities, such that the use of the amortized cost method in valuing any portion or type of these debt securities could have a material impact on such funds' net asset values per share. Generally, the Commission would consider the use of a particular valuation method to have a material impact if the use of that method, as opposed to another method, might cause a

---

[*] [In Investment Company Release 12206, February 1982, the Commission published for public comment proposed Rule 2a-7 under the Investment Company Act which would permit, under certain conditions, the use of the amortized cost method of asset valuation for purposes of calculating current net asset value per share or the "penny-rounding" method of computing current price per share. If adopted, the rule would generally supplement rather than supersede this interpretive guidance.]

[1] In simplified terms, for instruments purchased at a discount, the difference between the cost of such an instrument at purchase and its maturity value is divided by the number of days to maturity and that amount is accrued daily as an

increase in the value of the instrument each day. More precisely, amortized cost valuation may be described as cost, adjusted for amortization of premium, or for accretion of discount.

[2] For example, redemptions of shares in a fund which has overvalued its portfolio or sales of shares in a fund which has undervalued its portfolio could result in the dilution of the assets and returns of other investors in the fund. The extent of such dilutive effects would be dependent upon several factors, including the extent of the overvaluation or undervaluation, and the proportion of fund shares sold or redeemed at such times.

change of at least one cent in a net asset value per share of $10.00.[3] The interpretation explained below will be applicable to both "money market" funds and these other open-end investment companies.

Generally, "money market" funds are open-end investment companies which invest primarily in short-term debt instruments. They provide a vehicle to permit investors to take advantage of what at times may be the higher short-term interest rates earned on large investments. Through a pooling of money these funds enable the purchase of larger denomination instruments than could normally be bought by the individual small investor. These funds have also attracted investments from corporations, bank trust departments, and other institutional investors. Another characteristic of money market funds is the short-term investment perspective of many shareholders. Although the portfolio composition of "money market" funds is variable both in terms of the types of securities purchased and their maturities, the portfolios of such funds typically include U.S. Government and government agency issues, certificates of deposit, banker's acceptances, and commercial paper.

Section 22(c) of the Investment Company Act by reference to section 22(a) of the Investment Company Act, authorizes the Commission to adopt rules prescribing, inter alia, methods for computing the minimum purchase price and maximum redemption price of redeemable securities issued by a registered investment company:

* * * for the purpose of eliminating or reducing so far as reasonably practicable any dilution of the value of other outstanding securities of such company or any other result of * * * purchase, redemption, or sale which is unfair to holders of such other outstanding securities. * * *

Section 2(a)(41) of the Investment Company Act defines "value", as here relevant, to mean:

(B) * * * (i) with respect to securities for which market quotations are readily available, the market value of such securities; and

(ii) with respect to other securities and assets, fair value as determined in good faith by the [registered investment company's] board of directors * * *

Rule 2a-4 promulgated under the Investment Company Act provides, in part, that the "current net asset value" of a redeemable security issued by a registered investment company used in computing its price, for the purposes of distribution and redemption, means:

* * * an amount which reflects calculation * * * made substantially in accordance with the following, with estimates used where necessary or appropriate:

(1) Portfolio securities with respect to which market quotations are readily available shall be valued at current market value, and other securities * * * shall be valued at fair value as determined in good faith by the board of directors * * *

Now that both the Commission and the money market fund industry have had the benefit of experience with this relatively new investment product, and to help insure that shares of such funds are sold and redeemed at prices reflecting the current market or fair value of such funds' portfolio securities, the Commission has concluded that it is inconsistent with the provisions of Rule 2a-4 for a money market fund to determine the fair value of debt securities which mature at a date more than 60 days subsequent to the valuation date on an amortized cost basis.

Although debt securities with remaining maturities in excess of 60 days should not be valued at amortized cost, the Commission will not object if the board of directors of a money market fund, in good faith, determines that the fair value of debt securities originally purchased with remaining maturities of 60 days or less shall be their amortized cost value, unless the particular circumstances dictate otherwise.[4] Nor will the Commission object if, under similar circumstances, the fair value of debt securities originally purchased with maturities in excess of 60 days, but which currently have maturities of 60 days or less, is determined by using amortized cost valuation for the 60 days prior to maturity, such amortization being based upon the market or fair value of the securities on the 61st day prior to maturity.[5]

The Commission believes that money market funds and those other companies to which this interpretation is applicable should value debt securities with greater than 60 days remaining to

---

[3] Although one cent differences in net asset values per share of $10.00 might appear to be insignificant, the effects of such differences can be material to the decisions of investors when translated into differences in rates of return. Moreover, the inequitable effects of amortized cost valuation can occur in the case of any openend investment company where a significant proportion of a company's portfolio consists of debt securities valued at amortized cost. The extent of such inequitable effects will, of course, depend upon changes in interest rates and the level of a company's sales and redemptions of shares.

[4] The fair value of securities with remaining maturities of 60 days or less may not always be accurately reflected through the use of amortized cost valuation, due to an impairment of the creditworthiness of an issuer, or other factors. In such situations, it would appear to be incumbent upon the directors of a fund to recognize such factors and take them into account in determining "fair value."

[5] A fund also may use amortized cost valuation for a period less than 60 days prior to maturity, in which case the principles indicated above would also be applicable.

maturity based upon current market quotations if readily available or, if such quotations are not readily available, in such a manner as to take into account any unrealized appreciation or depreciation due to changes in interest rates and other factors which would influence the current fair values of such securities.[6] These methods are sometimes referred to as "marking to market." In determining "fair value" by reference to current interest rates and other factors, the board of directors of money market fund may, of course, utilize whatever method it determines in good faith to be most appropriate. The method utilized could be based in part, for example, upon quotations by dealers or issuers for securities of similar type, quality and maturity.

Except in the circumstances delineated above, the Commission believes that, in view of the experience which has been gained with respect to the characteristics of money market funds, the use of the amortized cost method of valuation by a money market fund cannot in the future represent a "good faith" effort to determine the "fair value" of portfolio securities for purposes of Rule 2a-4; such valuation fails to consider the impact of market factors subsequent to the date a debt security is purchased on the value of such security. Moreover, the probability that amortized cost valuation will not approximate "fair value" is progressively greater for securities of increasingly longer maturities. The Commission believes that the use of amortized cost valuation by money market funds in valuing securities with remaining maturities in excess of 60 days is not an appropriate estimate of market value or "fair value" and further that, because alternative valuation procedures which consider market factors are available, use of amortized cost valuation under such circumstances as an estimate is not necessary. This standard should help insure that fund shares are sold and redeemed at prices reflecting the appropriate proportionate share of funds' current net assets, and minimize the potential for dilution of the assets and returns of existing shareholders.

The Commission is also of the view that money market fund shareholders should be accurately credited with the effects of any unrealized appreciation or depreciation that may occur when the value of a fund's portfolio fluctuates. If such effects are not reflected in either a fund's net asset value or its distributions to shareholders, as a practical matter the result would be a situation analogous to that which would exist if amortized cost valuation

were used, and similar dilutive effects could occur. Such may be the case, for example, where a money market fund "marks to market," but declares a daily dividend of accrued interest income and reflects any remaining unrealized appreciation or depreciation in a "floating" net asset value of $1.00 nominal value per share, rounded to the nearest cent. Under these circumstances, unrealized capital changes, which could materially affect the value of such fund's portfolio, would ordinarily not be of sufficient magnitude to cause the net asset value to change by one cent. The effects of unrealized appreciation and depreciation, in the case of a fund with a "floating" $1.00 net asset value per share, would generally appear in the third and fourth decimal places, and when rounded to the third decimal place (i.e., tenths of one cent) would still not have a one cent impact on the net asset value. Moreover, if such a one cent change should occur, dilution may also result, since a relatively small change in net asset value would cause a larger change in the computed net asset value per share due to rounding. For example, if in the type of fund described above the net asset value was calculated accurately to three decimal places and a change in net asset value from $1.004 to $1.006 occurred, such change of $.002 would cause the net asset value, when rounded to the nearest cent, to change by one full cent.

To alleviate these results and insure that shareholders are more properly credited for capital appreciation or depreciation, the Commission believes that any money market fund which reflects capital changes in its net asset value per share should calculate, and utilize for purposes of sales and redemptions, a current net asset value per share with an accuracy of one-tenth of one percent (equivalent to the nearest one cent on a net asset value of $10.00). Any less precise calculation by such a fund might have the effect of masking the impact of changing values of portfolio securities and therefore might not "reflect" the fund's calculations pertaining to its portfolio valuation as required by Rule 2a-4.

404.06. Article 6 of Regulation S-X—Special Rules Applicable to Registered Investment Companies[*]

.a. The Definition of "Affiliates"

ASR 57:

This rule defines the term "affiliate" to mean an "affiliated person" as defined in Section 2(a)(3) of the Investment Company Act. Thus the term as used in Article 6 of Regulation S-X includes a

---

[6] In ASR 118 [see Section 404.03], the Commission stated that: As a general principle, the current "fair value" of an issue of securities being valued by the board of directors would appear to be the amount which the owner might reasonably expect to receive for them upon their current sale. In that release, the Commission noted various factors that might be considered in arriving at "fair value", which factors included: Yield to maturity with respect to debt issues * * * an evalua-

tion of the forces which influence the market in which these securities are purchased and sold * * * (and the) price and extent of public trading in similar securities of the issuer or comparable companies, and other relevant matters.

[*] [A proposed revision to Article 6 was announced in Securities Act Release 6374, January 1982. However, the interpretive guidance provided in this section would be unchanged by the adoption of the proposals.]

company of which the registrant owns directly or indirectly 5% to 25% of the outstanding voting securities. Under this definition data as to such companies is required by several of the amended rules to be shown separately in financial statements filed with the Commission.

Thus, where the rule requires investments in affiliates to be segregated in the balance sheet, a company can describe each category of investment for exactly what it is; namely, majority owned (over 50%), other controlled affiliates (over 25%, but not more than 50% owned), and companies in which over 5% but not more than 25% is owned and as to which control is denied. The manner of describing the latter category should be sufficient to avoid any misconception as to its relationship with the reporting company.

404.06.b. Provision for Federal Income Tax

ASR 114:

Article 6 requires that appropriate provision shall be made in the financial statements of registered investment companies for Federal income taxes.

Rule 2a-4 under the Investment Company Act defines the term "current net asset value" of redeemable securities issued by registered investment companies used in computing periodically the current price of such securities for the purpose of distribution, redemption, and repurchase. Subparagraph (a)(4) of Rule 2a-4 provides that in computing such current net asset value expenses shall be included to the date of calculation.

Article 6 specifically provides that a company which retains realized capital gains and designates such gains as a distribution to shareholders in accordance with Section 852(b)(3)(D) of the Internal Revenue Code (Code) shall, on the last day of its taxable year (and not earlier), make provision for taxes on such undistributed capital gains realized during such year. Rule 2a-4 under the Investment Company Act requires that appropriate provision shall be made for Federal income taxes in accordance with Article 6.

The primary purpose of the rule is to assure that regulated investment companies excepted by provisions of the Code from payment of Federal income taxes on net income and realized gains distributed to shareholders will make appropriate provision for taxes on any realized undistributed capital gains designated as distributions to shareholders under the provisions of the Code. Most regulated investment companies follow the practice of distributing realized capital gains to shareholders, thereby relieving such companies of the payment of Federal income taxes on such gains. However, under the provisions of Section 852(b)(3)(D) of the Code, a regulated investment company which elects to do so may retain realized long-term capital gains and, in effect, pay the tax on those gains on behalf of the shareholders. Every such shareholder at the close of the com-

pany's taxable year shall include in his tax return his pro rata portion of the company's realized capital gains as if it had been distributed to him, accrue his capital gains tax thereon, and elsewhere in his tax return is allowed credit or refund for his pro rata share of the capital gains tax which has been paid for his benefit by the company but which is deemed to have been paid by him. At the same time, such shareholder shall increase the tax basis of his shares by the excess of his pro rata portion of the realized gains over the tax credit or refund allowed to him.

Under the provisions of the Code, the taxes on realized capital gains retained by the company are payable by the company only on behalf of those persons who are shareholders on the last day of the taxable year in which the gains were realized. It is only those persons who are shareholders on the last day of the taxable year who are deemed under the provisions of the Code to have paid the tax imposed on the designated capital gains retained by the company and who, accordingly, are allowed credit or refund for the tax so deemed to have been paid by them and are entitled to increase the tax basis of their shares by the excess of their pro rata portion of the realized gains over the tax credit or refund allowed to them. Accrual of the tax by the company at any time prior to the last day of its taxable year therefore reduces the net asset value of the shares of holders who redeem or sell their shares during the year and who consequently receive no credit for the tax so accrued.

[¶ 38,245] 405. Limited Partnerships

ASR 162:

Registration statements have been filed with the Commission under the Securities Act for the sale to the public of interests in limited partnerships which were formed in connection with activities involving income tax shelter or deferral opportunities, as well as the opportunity for investment gain in one form or another. Pursuant to Rule 15d-1 under the Exchange Act registrants under the Securities Act are required to file an annual report on Form 10-K for the fiscal year in which a registration statement becomes effective and for each subsequent fiscal year thereafter unless the registrant is exempt under Section 15(d) of the Exchange Act from such subsequent filings. Many of these limited partnership registrants qualify for the exemption from filing 10-K reports in subsequent fiscal years provided in Section 15(d) when securities to which the registration statement relates are held of record by less than 300 persons at the beginning of a fiscal year.

Some registrants, particularly those of the type which develop and sell a single asset, have filed Form 10-K reports presenting the required audited financial statements of the limited partnership on a tax basis of accounting rather than on the basis of GAAP. Historically, presentation of financial statements of commercial and industrial companies on a GAAP basis has been considered the only acceptable basis for investors and potential investors in a public company. The independent accountants' reports accompanying the financial statements presented on a tax basis acknowledge that the financial statements do not purport to be in conformity with GAAP, and an opinion is expressed on the fairness of presentation of the financial statements on the tax basis.

One of the basic purposes of both the Securities Act and the Exchange Act is to require registrants to provide full and fair disclosure regarding all significant aspects and activities of the business for the benefit of the investing public. The requirements for financial statements under the Acts implement this objective by causing disclosures regarding the stewardship of financial resources of the company with respect to their utilization and their condition. Since financial statements prepared on a tax basis do not necessarily give a complete presentation of the stewardship of the resources, they do not in general meet the requirements for full and fair disclosure as envisioned in the Acts.

Complete data relating to many aspects of financial position and operations are frequently not included in financial statements prepared on a tax basis and the scope of the independent audit of such tax basis statements also may not be the equivalent of the usual audit of financial statements prepared on a GAAP basis. In addition, some problem areas arising out of relationships between a general partner in the limited partnership and other related parties may cause particular accounting and auditing difficulties. If audits of the financial statements of these limited partnerships are performed on a GAAP basis, it is likely that these factors would receive more attention and have an important bearing on the determination of the scope of the audit.

While it is contended that, in some instances, investors in these limited partnerships are primarily interested in the tax status of their investments and thus tax basis financial statements are of more value to them, the ultimate recovery of the investment through sale of the project depends on the proper utilization and stewardship of the resources of the enterprise. Independent verification of the reporting on these matters can best be obtained from audited financial statements presented on a GAAP basis. Presentation of the financial data on a tax basis may also be desirable but the presentation should be in addition to the presentation on a GAAP basis and should not supplant it.[*] It is common practice for companies to make adjustments to their GAAP based accounts for income tax reporting purposes, and it is

considered that these limited partnerships can provide the tax basis financial statements in addition to the GAAP basis statements without undue difficulty. In the rare instances where the sole 10-K report required for the limited partnerships covers a period near the start of the venture, the GAAP basis financial statements serve a useful purpose by providing important information to the original investors on the custody of the funds received and whether plans and commitments are being made in conformity with the proposed schedule of development of the project.

The Commission has concluded that exemptions should not be granted to these limited partnership registrants from the general requirement that financial statements should be presented in conformity with GAAP with the audit opinion rendered thereon on that basis in filings with the Commission. Financial data presented on a tax basis may be necessary in footnotes or supporting schedules to provide disclosures regarding tax aspects of the investments.

»»→ *The seven introductory paragraphs to Section 406 were removed in Release No. 33-8995, effective January 1, 2010, 74 F.R. 2158.*

[¶ 38,251] 406. Oil and Gas Producing Activities

[The Energy Policy and Conservation Act of 1975 (EPCA) directed the Commission to assure the development and observance of accounting practices that would enable the Department of Energy to obtain the information necessary for a reliable energy data base. The Commission was permitted by EPCA to rely on accounting practices developed by the FASB only if assured that these practices would be observed to the same extent as would rules of the Commission and only after an opportunity had been given for public comment on the FASB's conclusions. The FASB effort, which commenced in 1975, to promulgate accounting and reporting standards for oil and gas producers resulted in the issuance of SFAS 19, "Financial Accounting and Reporting by Oil and Gas Producing Companies," in December 1977. SFAS 19 prescribes a form of the "successful efforts" method of accounting to the exclusion of the "full cost" method.

Following extensive public hearings in 1978, the Commission determined that the two traditional methods of accounting for oil and gas producers— successful efforts and full cost—are inherently limited because of their failure to provide timely recognition of oil and gas reserves in the assets and earnings reported in the primary financial statements. In August 1978, (ASR 253) the Commission announced its conclusion that significant

---

[*] [In March 1982, the Commission adopted Regulation D which permits, in certain circumstances, financial statements on the tax basis to be presented in lieu of those on a GAAP basis.]

improvement in the measurement of assets and earnings in the primary financial statements of oil and gas producing companies could best be achieved through the development and implementation of an accounting method that reflects provided oil and gas reserves as assets in the balance sheet; additions to proved reserves and changes in valuations of proved reserves in the income statement; and all costs associated with finding and developing additions to proved oil and gas reserves, together with all costs determined to be nonproductive during the current period, in the income statement. The Commission called the accounting method to be developed on this basis "reserve recognition accounting" or RRA. Because of the difficulties involved in the development of sufficiently reliable measures of proved reserves, a minimum period of three years was indicated as being necessary to provide experience with supplemental disclosures of reserve valuations and with the proposed RRA. During the period, the Commission permitted registrants to follow the successful efforts method of accounting (as defined by SFAS 19) or the full cost method as set forth in rules adopted by the Commission (ASR 258).

In September 1979, in ASR 269, the Commission adopted rules for the supplemental disclosure of a summary of changes in the present value of estimated future net revenues from the production of proved reserves. Also, adopted was a requirement for a summary of oil and gas producing activities prepared on the basis of RRA.

The Commission anticipated that these supplemental disclosures, and previously adopted requirements for the reporting of reserve quantities, estimated future net revenues, and present value of future net revenues, would provide the basis for evaluating the feasibility of requiring RRA as a uniform accounting method in the primary financial statements.

The Commission noted significant revisions to estimated proved reserves quantities in the supplemental disclosures included in various required filings, and received comments from oil and gas reservoir engineers that a significant range of reserve estimates is considered reasonable by that profession. Also, the published results of several studies suggested a substantial degree of uncertainty of oil and gas reserve estimates.

After assessing the development of RRA since September 1978, the Commission determined that, because of the inherent uncertainty of recoverable quantities of proved oil and gas reserves, RRA does not presently possess the requisite degree of certainty to be useful as a primary method of accounting. Therefore, in February 1981 (ASR 289), the Commission announced that it no longer considered RRA to be a potential method of accounting for use in the primary financial statements.

At that time, the Commission also announced its support for an FASB project to develop a comprehensive set of disclosures for oil and gas producers. This project comprehends all aspects of financial reporting by oil and gas producers except the issue of a uniform method of accounting since it believes that concepts developed by the FASB in its standard-setting role may have an impact on the ultimate resolution of the uniform method question.]

406.01.a. [Removed and reserved.]

406.01.b. Successful Efforts Method

The rules in Rule 4-10(b) specify that the application of successful efforts shall comply with SFAS 19. In 2008, the Commission published amendments to the definitions in Rule 4-10(a) that may not align completely with SFAS 19's existing terminology and application. Further, paragraph 7 of SFAS 25 states: "For purposes of applying this Statement and Statement 19, the definition of proved reserves, proved developed reserves, and proved undeveloped reserves shall be the definitions adopted by the SEC for its reporting purposes that are in effect on the date(s) as of which the reserve disclosures are to be made. Previous reported quantities shall not be revised retroactively if the SEC definitions are changed." In any case, the Commission expects the practical application of SFAS 19 will remain unchanged other than incorporating the effects of the new definitions.

[Revised in FR-78.]

406.01.c. Full Cost Method
i. Exclusion of Capitalized Costs
FRR 14:

In adopting final rules on this issue, the Commission agrees with the majority of commentators that it is appropriate to permit the exclusion of substantially all unevaluated costs from current amortization. The Commission concurs with the majority of the commentators that this approach is objective and conducive to consistent, comparable application. The Commission also believes that it properly associates evaluated costs with proved (or evaluated) reserves. Moreover, since unevaluated properties are required to be assessed periodically for impairment and to have value at least equal to their carrying costs (including any capitalized interest), exclusion from immediate amortization should not distort future income statements by postponing the recognition of nonproductive costs.

In view of the importance of timely assessment of impairment, the Commission is modifying its original proposals in several respects suggested by the commentators. First, the Commission finds convincing the arguments that drilling a dry hole on an unevaluated property provides evidence of impairment of the lease carrying cost at least to the extent of the dry hole costs. Accordingly, the final rules specify that dry hole costs should be included in the amortization base immediately upon determination that the well is dry. The Commission believes that drilling a dry hole also may be an indication that part or all of the other related leasehold carrying costs (property acquisition costs, related geological and geophysical costs, and other costs) have been impaired. Accordingly, the Commission cautions registrants to assess such leasehold costs particularly closely.

With respect to the assessment of impairment generally, the Commission also sees merit in the suggestion that an aggregate assessment of impairment be permitted on individually insignificant properties, and the final rules have been revised to permit, but not require, that approach. The rules do not include any specific guidance on the determination of "significance." However, the Commission believes that in general individual properties or projects would be expected to be individually significant if their costs exceed 10% of the net capitalized costs of the cost center. Where individual properties or projects with costs representing less than 10% of the cost center are involved, the Commission believes it is still appropriate to test impairment on an individual basis but will permit companies to aggregate such properties for purposes of this assessment.

In addition, the final rules revise the proposed guidance for allocation of costs on major development projects for purposes of transfers to the amortization base. On this issue, the Commission has concluded, as suggested by commentators, that it is appropriate to allow allocation, either on the basis of the radio of wells to which proved reserves have been assigned to the total expected number of wells or on the basis of the ratio of proved reserves already established to total proved reserves ultimately expected, whichever is more appropriate in the particular facts and circumstances.

Finally, the Commission is revising its disclosure requirements to provide for more specific information as to the category and age of capitalized costs excluded from current amortization. Because the rules being adopted in this release will have a significant effect on the financial condition and operating results of full cost oil and gas producers, the Commission believes it appropriate to provide for specific information as to the nature of these costs. Consequently, the Commission's existing requirements for disclosure of the nature of costs by category and approximate date such costs were first incurred are also being expanded to require footnote disclosure in tabular form as to the age and category of costs excluded from current amortization.

The revised rules call for an aging of excluded costs as of a registrant's most recent fiscal year end both by category and by date incurred. Disclosure is required of the amounts of each category of excluded costs (1) in total as of the end of the most recent fiscal year, (2) separately by year for amounts incurred in each of the three most recent fiscal years, and (3) in the aggregate for costs incurred in any earlier fiscal years. Categories of cost are to include acquisition costs, exploration costs, development costs in the case of significant development projects, and interest capitalized.

In addition, existing requirements for balance sheet disclosure of the aggregate amount of excluded costs and footnote description of the current status of the projects or properties involved, including information as to the timing of the inclusion of the costs in the amortization computation, have been carried forward in the revised rules. However, the existing requirement to disclose the potential future impact on the amortization rate of excluded costs has been deleted based on experience which has shown that many companies are unable to calculate this information. In complying with the requirements to describe the current status of properties or projects excluded from amortization, registrants may find it appropriate to provide the information as to the age and category of excluded costs in a format which distinguishes offshore and onshore properties.

In taking final action on this issue, the Commission is rejecting the normal inventory method as a basis for final rules in this area. The Commission finds persuasive the arguments of various commentators that the normal inventory method should not be adopted because it is conceptually inferior to full exclusion and, due to its arbitrary and complex nature, not sufficiently representative of an individual company's situation. The Commission appreciates the arguments of certain commentators that some level of nonproductive costs is unavoidable and shares the concern that unrecoverable costs should not be excluded from amortization. However, the Commission does not find that these arguments provide compelling support for the normal inventory method. Rather, the Commission believes these concerns underscore the need for the modifications to the original proposal to require the immediate inclusion of dry hole costs in the amortization base and to permit an aggregate assessment of impairment for individually insignificant properties.

While the final rules permit the general exclusion of all unevaluated costs from immediate amortization, the Commission emphasizes that as soon as it can be determined whether or not proved reserves can be assigned, the related costs should be included in the amortization base. Once these costs are included in the amortization base, they lose their identity for all future accounting purposes. Consequently, individual cost elements cannot subsequently be removed from this base.

406.01.c.ii. Basis of Amortization

ASR 258:

The Commission believes that there should be consistency in the methods used by companies following the full cost method of accounting. Further, the Commission believes that the use of physical units in terms of energy content (BTU's) as the amortization basis has the greatest conceptual merit in a market environment in which the relative prices of oil and gas approximate their relative energy content. However, the fact that substantial production is currently subject to pricing regulations may result in significant differences in amortization under the BTU method as compared to amortization based on sales values. Accordingly, the rules prescribe the use of the physical units method unless the use of such method, because of existing pricing regulations, would cause an amortization provision that would be inconsistent with the current prices being received. In those instances, the gross revenue method may be used as the basis for computing amortization rates.

406.01.c.iii. Limitation on Capitalized Costs

ASR 258:

The Commission believes that the aggregate of (1) the present value of proved reserves and (2) the lower of cost or fair market value of unproved properties is an appropriate basis for determining the limitation on capitalized costs. However, the rules specify that the costs of significant investments in unproved properties and development projects are to be considered separately for purposes of the ceiling computation.

If application of the rules, as a result of an unusual event or transaction such as a major purchase of proved properties, would require a writedown when the fair value of the properties in a cost center clearly exceeds the unamortized costs, the registrant may request an exemption from the general rule. In such cases, the registrant should be prepared to demonstrate that the additional value clearly exists beyond reasonable doubt.

The rules specify that the cost center ceiling is to be computed giving consideration to income tax effects. The Commission believes that unusual tax relationships may exist in certain instances, as a result of the expiration of operating loss carryforwards, changes in tax rates, etc. In these circumstances, it will be necessary to consider tax effects in computing the ceiling limitation.

Sec. 406.01.c.iv. Mineral Property Conveyances

[Sec. 406.01.c.iv amended by FRR-17.]

ASR 258:

The rules dealing with mineral property conveyances specify that a sale of oil and gas reserves shall be accounted for as an adjustment of capitalized costs, unless the adjustment causes a significant alteration of the relationship between remaining capitalized costs and proved reserves attributable to the cost center. A significant alteration would not normally be expected to result

from a sale involving less than 25 percent of the total reserve quantities of the cost center.

The rules provide that costs should be allocated between cost center assets sold and retained except where estimated relative fair values should be used in order to reflect other substantial economic differences between the properties sold and those retained.

FRR 17:

The final rules prohibit recognition of income on sales or other transfers of oil and gas properties in connection with partnerships, joint venture operations, or various other forms of drilling arrangements, except when there is a significant alteration of the relationship between costs and proved reserves pursuant to existing Rule 4-10(i)(6)(i) of Regulation S-X. The Commission concluded that the lease brokerage concept is not workable, and that the approach adopted is objective and will lead to more consistent and comparable application than the lease brokerage concept.

The revised rules also provide, as proposed, that income may be recognized for those amounts which represent reimbursement of organization, offering, general and administrative expenses, etc., that are identifiable with the transaction, if such amounts are currently incurred and charged to expense.

With respect to the recognition as income of management fees, the revised rules make a distinction between arrangements involving proved developed properties and those involving other properties because the Commission understands that the risk of realization of an investment in an income fund is substantially less than that related to properties requiring significant further exploration and development. Accordingly, the Commission's revised rules provide that management fees received in connection with income funds may be recognized as income provided that any estimated development expenditures required in connection with the production of the existing proved reserves are less than 10% of the partnership's recorded cost of the properties.

Any fees not recognized as income under this rule would be credited to the full cost pool and recognized through a lower amortization provision as reserves are produced. Any management fees received in connection with unproved properties or proved undeveloped properties would be credited to the full cost account.

The revised rules with respect to drilling and other contractual services on properties in which the registrant has or acquires an economic interest permit income recognition under specified circumstances. Commentators argued that a general prohibition against income recognition for contractual services would be unduly restrictive, particularly where a minor interest is required to be acquired in order to obtain the service contract.

The Commission is persuaded by the comments that the mere existence of an economic interest in properties upon which services are performed pursuant to a contract should not result in a prohibition of recognition of any income from such services. It believes, however, that income should only be recognized to the extent it exceeds a company's costs in connection with the contract and the properties. The identification of the costs of the properties may be difficult once the registrant has held an economic interest in the properties for more than one year, however. Under full cost accounting, costs of properties lose their specific identity once transferred into a full cost pool. To determine the cost of a specific property, it would be necessary to allocate certain adjustments, such as amortization, made to the properties as a group. Accordingly, the final rules differentiate between services performed on properties as to which the registrant has held an economic interest for at least a year from those performed on properties as to which the registrant acquires or acquired the interest within a year of the date of the service contract. If the interest is acquired within a year of the date of the service contract income may be recognized to the extent that cash consideration received exceeds the registrant's costs. These costs include the registrant's costs of acquiring the properties and performing the services as well as its share of other costs incurred and estimated to be incurred in connection with the properties. Registrants that acquired the economic interest in the properties more than a year before the date of the service contract are permitted to recognize income from the contract pursuant to generally accepted accounting principles. Accordingly, a company may recognize income for compensation received relating to contractual services under the following conditions:

(1) Where an interest in the properties is acquired in connection with a service contract, income may be recognized to the extent the cash consideration received, net of the cost associated with such contract, exceeds the company's share of costs incurred and estimated to be incurred in connection with such properties. Ownership interests acquired within one year of the date of such a contract are considered to be acquired in connection with the service for purposes of applying this rule. The amount of any guarantees or similar arrangements undertaken as part of this contract should be considered as part of such costs for purposes of applying this rule.[5]

(2) Where an interest in the properties has been held for at least one year through transactions unrelated to the service contract, and that interest is unaffected by the service contract, income may be recognized subject to the general provisions for elimination of intercompany profit under generally accepted accounting principles.

(3) If the company performs contractual services on behalf of investors in oil and gas producing activities managed by the company or an affiliate, no income from those contractual services should be recognized.

Any income not recognized as a result of these rules would be credited to the full cost account and recognized through a lower amortization provision as reserves are produced.

406.01.c.v. Consolidated Financial Statements

ASR 258:

The rules specify that a registrant must apply its accounting method to the operations of its subsidiaries. Rule 4-10(i)(3)(v) requires that amortization rates be determined on a consolidated basis even though this may result in a consolidated amortization provision that is not equal to the sum of the expenses for the individual members of the consolidated group. This same concept applies to the determination of the limitation on capitalized costs within cost centers.

406.01.c.vi. Other Matters

ASR 258:

An order to conform to comparable rules for the successful efforts method, Rule 4-10(i)(3)(iv) provides that, in some cases, depreciation of natural gas cycling and processing plants may appropriately be computed by a method other than unit-of-production.

The introduction to Rule 4-10 provides that appropriate recognition may be given to differences in capitalized costs and in the basis for amortization arising because of the effect of the rate-making process. This provision applies to both the successful efforts and the full cost rules.

406.01.d. Accounting Changes

ASR 300:

The Commission expects registrants to comply with GAAP in making an accounting change to or

---

[5] For example, assume that a company drills a well on a property in which it acquires a 2% working interest and receives $500,000 for these services. Assume also that the costs of drilling are $400,000. The company is required to pay $12,000 for its working interest in the property, and is obligated to pay an additional $15,000 for its share of estimated future exploration and development costs. In addition, the company guarantees $10,000 of the indebtedness incurred to acquire the leasehold. Under these rules, income from drilling would be recognized in the amount which the consideration received ($500,000) net of related costs ($400,000) exceeds the company's share of total costs, incurred and to be incurred ($27,000), and its guarantee of the indebtedness ($10,000), or $63,000. If the acquired interest is in addition to an existing interest held at least one year as a result of unrelated transactions, the company should base this computation on the costs incurred and to be incurred associated with the additional interest acquired.

from successful efforts or full costs. Since GAAP expresses a preference for successful efforts, no justification for the change to successful efforts is necessary nor is a preferability letter required by Rule 10-01(b)(6) of Regulation S-X. However, in view of SFAS 25, any change to full cost must be justified as being preferable in the registrant's circumstances and a preferability letter describing those circumstances must be filed with the Commission.

ASR 258:

Retroactive application of the provisions of Rule 4-10 require the use of estimates and approximations. A provision that would not have a significant effect on prior years' financial statements need not be retroactively applied. Further, retroactive application of some provisions of these rules may require the use of estimates of a type not previously made; information that may have become available some time after the year being restated may be taken into account in making those estimates, except that estimates of quantities of oil and gas reserves that had been made in prior years shall not currently be revised in retrospect.

For reporting entities following the full cost method of accounting, retroactive application of Rule 4-10(i)(4), "Limitations on capitalized costs," shall be applied as follows:

(a) If unamortized costs capitalized within a cost center do not exceed the cost center ceiling as of the beginning of the fiscal period in which the rules are initially adopted, then no provisions shall be made for past periods when application of the rules based on information known during those periods might have resulted in unamortized capitalized costs being in excess of the cost center ceiling.

(b) If unamortized costs capitalized within a cost center exceed the cost center ceiling as of the beginning of the fiscal year in which the rules are initially adopted, then this excess shall be recognized retroactively through a charge to expense in the periods in which the excess initially arose.

406.02. Supplemental Disclosures

⫸→ *Section 406.02.a removed and reserved in FR-78, effective January 1, 2010, 74 F.R. 2158.*

a. [Removed and reserved.]

b. [Removed and reserved.]

406.02.c. Separate Disclosure of Undiscounted Future Net Revenues

The Commission continues to believe that information to assess the impact of oil and gas producing activities on near term cash flows and liquidity may in some circumstances be essential to an understanding of a company's financial position and results of operations. Accordingly, the Commission reminds registrants that disclosures of undiscounted future cash flows from oil and gas operations may be necessary in the Management's Discussion and Analysis of the financial

statements. Such disclosures would ordinarily be expected where near-term cash flows are likely to be negative or only at a break-even level, and may be appropriate in other circumstances.

[Revised in FR-78.]

406.02.d. Discussion of Final Rules

The Commission has evaluated the differences between the FASB exposure draft and the final SFAS 69 and believes they are not sufficiently material to require re-exposure of the Commission's proposed rule changes. Overall, they reduce the compliance burden for detailed disclosure (by deleting the geographic breakdown of changes in the standardized measure) while making minor additions (e.g., information on affiliated sales and minority interests) only where necessary to a full understanding of the information presented.

406.02.d.i. Significance Criteria

The Commission has evaluated the differences between the FASB exposure draft and the final SFAS 69 and believes they are not sufficiently material to require re-exposure of the Commission's proposed rule changes. Overall, they reduce the compliance burden for detailed disclosure (by deleting the geographic breakdown of changes in the standardized measure) while making minor additions (e.g., information on affiliated sales and minority interests) only where necessary to a full understanding of the information presented.

406.02.d.ii. Applicability of Commission Requirements

The final rules also specify that the subject supplemental disclosures shall be presented whenever required by the terms of the applicable Federal securities form. The SFAS 69 requirements apply to enterprises which are "publicly traded" as defined by the standard. This FASB definition is both broader and narrower than the class of enterprises currently required to provide supplemental oil and gas disclosures in Commission filings. The FASB definition includes certain small enterprises which although "traded" may not be required to file reports under either the Securities Act or the Securities Exchange Act. However, the FASB definition would not apply to other enterprises filing reports with the Commission such as certain limited partnerships, nor would it apply to companies providing information to investors under the Regulation D exemptions. The Commission recognizes that it has a different constituency and must retain the specific requirements of its various filing forms.

406.02.d.iii. [Removed and reserved.]

406.02.e. [Removed and reserved.]

406.03. Transition

We believe that any accounting change resulting from the changes in definitions and required pricing assumptions in Rule 4-10, should be treated as a change in accounting principle that is inseparable from a change in accounting estimate, which does not require retroactive revision. We note that pursuant to AU 420.13, such a change requires recognition in the independent auditor's report through the addition of an explanatory paragraph.

With respect to resources formerly considered mining activities, we view the change from mining treatment to oil and gas treatment as a change in accounting principle that is inseparable from a change in accounting estimate, which does not require retroactive revision.

406.04. MD&A Guidance

However, we believe that added guidance would be beneficial to companies regarding the issues that the Commission's staff commented upon in its review of the MD&A section of filings made by oil and gas companies.

To begin, a fundamental premise of MD&A is that the information provided should be related to issues that are material to a company. Although we discuss a list of topics that a company might need to discuss, a company need only discuss a topic if it constitutes, involves, or indicates known trends, demands, commitments, uncertainties, and events that are reasonably likely to have a material effect on the company. These topics include:

—Changes in proved reserves and, if disclosed, probable and possible reserves, and the sources to which such changes are attributable, including changes made due to:

——Changes in prices;

—— Technical revisions; and

—— Changes in the status of any concessions held (such as terminations, renewals, or changes in provisions);

—Technologies used to establish the appropriate level of certainty for any material additions to, or increases in, reserves estimates, including any material additions or increases to reserves estimates that are the result of any of the final rules adopted in this release;

—Prices and costs, including the impact on depreciation, depletion and amortization as well as the full cost ceiling test;

—Performance of currently producing wells, including water production from such wells and the need to use enhanced recovery techniques to maintain production from such wells;

—Performance of any mining-type activities for the production of hydrocarbons;

—The company's recent ability to convert proved undeveloped reserves to proved developed reserves, and, if disclosed, probable reserves to proved reserves and possible reserves to probable or proved reserves;

—The minimum remaining terms of leases and concessions;

—Material changes to any line item in the tables described in Items 1202 through 1208 of Regulation S-K;

—Potential effects of different forms of rights to resources, such as production sharing contracts, on operations; and

—Geopolitical risks that apply to material concentrations of reserves.

The MD&A is typically presented in a self-contained section of the registration statement or report. However, the disclosure requirements that comprise new Subpart 1200 of Regulation S-K will cause a substantial amount of an oil and gas company's disclosure to appear in tabular format, providing an outline of much of a company's operations. Because the tables will present many of the types of changes that management often discusses in its MD&A, we believe it may be more helpful to investors to locate such discussion close to the tables themselves. Thus, to the extent that any discussion or analysis of known trends, demands, commitments, uncertainties, and events that are reasonably likely to have a material effect on the company is directly relevant to a particular disclosure required by Subpart 1200, the company may include that discussion or analysis with the relevant table, with appropriate cross-references, rather than including it in its general MD&A section.

SECTION 500—INFORMATION OUTSIDE OF FINANCIAL STATEMENTS

[¶ 38,271] 501. Management's Discussion and Analysis

[In ASR 159, the Commission adopted Securities Act Guide 22 and Exchange Act Guide 1 which required that registration statements and annual reports filed with the Commission include a narrative explanation of the summary of earnings. In ASR 279, adopted September 2, 1980, the Guides were rescinded and the discussion requirements were moved to Regulation S-K (currently Item 303) and were substantially revised and expanded to address the financial statements

as a whole. In September 1981, the Commission issued ASR 299, which was an interpretive release giving staff commentary and examples to assist registrants in preparing the MD&A. In 1988, a project was undertaken to evaluate current compliance with MD&A requirements. This project followed the issuance of a concept release in 1987 requesting public comment on, among other things, the adequacy of the existing MD&A requirements. In 1989, the Commission published Financial Reporting Release No. 36, which summarized the results of the project, included examples of disclosure and set forth the Commission's views regarding several disclosure matters under MD&A. The following excerpts from that release are presented to assist registrants in preparing MD&As. Registrants may wish to refer to the release for a discussion of the results of the project.

501.01. Evaluation of Disclosure—Interpretive Guidance

The MD&A requirements are intended to provide, in one section of a filing,[1] material historical and prospective textual disclosure enabling investors and other users to assess the financial condition and results of operations of the registrant, with particular emphasis on the registrant's prospects for the future. As the Concept Release states:

> The Commission has long recognized the need for a narrative explanation of the financial statements, because a numerical presentation and brief accompanying footnotes alone may be insufficient for an investor to judge the quality of earnings and the likelihood that past performance is indicative of future performance. MD&A is intended to give the investor an opportunity to look at the company through the eyes of management by providing both a short and long-term analysis of the business of the company. The Item asks management to discuss the dynamics of the business and to analyze the financials.[2]

As the Commission has stated, "[i]t is the responsibility of management to identify and address those key variables and other qualitative and quantitative factors which are peculiar to and necessary for an understanding and evaluation of the individual company."[3]

The Commission has determined that interpretive guidance is needed regarding the following matters: prospective information required in MD&A; long and short-term liquidity and capital resources analysis; material changes in financial statement line items; required interim period disclosure; MD&A analysis on a segment basis; participation in high yield financings, highly leveraged transactions or non-investment grade loans and investments; the effects of federal financial assistance upon the operations of financial institutions; and preliminary merger negotiations.

501.02. Prospective Information

Several specific provisions in Item 303 require disclosure of forward-looking information. MD&A requires discussions of "known trends or any known demands, commitments, events or uncertainties that will result in or that are reasonably likely to result in the registrant's liquidity increasing or decreasing in any material way."[4] Further, descriptions of known material trends in the registrant's capital resources and expected changes in the mix and cost of such resources are required.[5] Disclosure of known trends or uncertainties that the registrant reasonably expects will have a material impact on net sales, revenues, or income from continuing operations is also required.[6] Finally, the Instructions to Item 303 state that MD&A "shall focus specifically on material events and uncertainties known to management that would cause reported financial information not to be necessarily indicative of future operating results or of future financial condition."[7]

The Project results confirm that the distinction between prospective information that is required to be discussed and voluntary forward-looking disclosure is an area requiring additional attention. This critical distinction is explained in the Concept Release:

> Both required disclosure regarding the future impact of presently known trends, events or uncertainties and optional forward-looking information may involve some prediction or projection. The distinction between the two rests with the nature of the prediction required. Required disclosure is based on *currently known trends, events, and uncertainties that are reasonably expected to have material effects*, such as: A reduction in the registrant's product prices; erosion in the registrant's market share; changes in insurance coverage; or the likely non-renewal of a material contract. In contrast, optional forward-looking disclosure involves *anticipating a future trend or event or anticipating a less predictable impact of a known event, trend or uncertainty.*[8]

The rules establishing a safe harbor for disclosure of "forward-looking statements" define such statements to include statements of "future economic performance contained in" MD&A. These safe harbors apply to required statements concerning the future effect of known trends, de-

---

[1] The MD&A should contain a discussion of all the material impacts upon the registrant's financial condition or results of operations, including those arising from disclosure provided elsewhere in the filing.

[2] Securities Act Release No. 6711, (April 24, 1987) [52 FR 13715], at 13717.

[3] Securities Act Release No. 6349, (September 28, 1981), 23 SEC Docket 962 [not published in the Federal Register], at 964.

[4] 17 CFR 229.303(a)(1).

[5] 17 CFR 229.303(a)(2)(ii).

[6] 17 CFR 229.303(a)(3)(ii).

[7] 17 CFR 229.303(a), Instruction 3. The data known to management which may trigger required forward-looking disclosure is hereinafter referred to as "known trends, demands, commitments, events, or uncertainties."

[8] Securities Act Release No. 6711, *supra* n. 2 , at 13717 (emphasis added).

mands, commitments, events or uncertainties, as well as to optional forward-looking statements.[9]

A disclosure duty exists where a trend, demand, commitment, event or uncertainty is both presently known to management and reasonably likely to have material effects on the registrant's financial condition or results of operation.[10] Registrants preparing their MD&A disclosure should determine and carefully review what trends, demands, commitments, events or uncertainties are known to management. In the following example,[11] the registrant discloses the reasonably likely material effects on operating results of a known trend in the form of an expected further decline in unit sales of mature products.

> While market conditions in general remained relatively unchanged in 1987, unit volumes declined 10% as the Company's older products, representing 40% of overall revenues, continue to approach the end of their life cycle. Unit volumes of the older products are expected to continue to decrease at an accelerated pace in the future and materially adversely affect revenues and operating profits.

In preparing the MD&A disclosure, registrants should focus on each of the specific categories of known data. For example, Item 303(a)(2)(i) requires a description of the registrant's material "commitments" for capital expenditures as of the end of the latest fiscal period. However, even where no legal commitments, contractual or otherwise, have been made, disclosure is required if material planned capital expenditures result from a known demand, as where the expenditures are necessary to a continuation of the registrant's current growth trend. Similarly, if the same registrant determines not to incur such expenditures, a known uncertainty would exist regarding continuation of the current growth trend. If the adverse effect on the registrant from discontinuation of the growth trend is reasonably likely to be material, disclosure is required. Disclosure of planned material expenditures is also required, for example, when such expenditures are necessary to support a new, publicly announced product or line of business.[12]

In the following example, the registrant discusses planned capital expenditures, and related financing sources, necessary to maintain sales growth.

> The Company plans to open 20 to 25 new stores in fiscal 1988. As a result, the Company expects the trend of higher sales in fiscal 1988 to continue at approximately the same rate as in recent years. Management estimates that approximately $50 to $60 million will be required to finance the Company's cost of opening such stores. In addition, the Company's expansion program will require increases in inventory of about $1 million per store, which are anticipated to be financed principally by trade credit. Funds required to finance the Company's store expansion program are expected to come primarily from new credit facilities with the remainder provided by funds generated from operations and increased lease financings. The Company recently entered into a new borrowing agreement with its primary bank, which provides for additional borrowings of up to $50 million for future expansion. The Company intends to seek additional credit facilities during fiscal 1988.

Often a matter which had a material impact on past operating results also involves prospective effects which should be discussed.[13] In identifying the reason for a material change in income from continuing operations and quantifying its effects, the registrant in the following example also de-

---

[9] Rule 175(c) under the Securities Act of 1933 ("Securities Act"), 17 CFR 230.175(c), and Rule 3b-6(c) under the Exchange Act, 17 CFR 240.3b-6.

[10] Cf. *In re American Savings and Loan Association of Florida*, Exchange Act Release No. 25788 (June 8, 1988), 41 SEC Docket 78. In this administrative proceeding jointly conducted by the Commission and the Federal Home Loan Bank Board (the "FHLBB"), it was determined that the MD&As in a Form 10-K and two Forms 10-Q were inadequate under the FHLBB's disclosure requirements, which are substantially similar to the Commission's, for failing to disclose, among other matters, required forward-looking information regarding the potential exposure and risks associated with repurchase transactions between American Savings and Loan and E.S.M. Government Securities. Cf. also *In re Burroughs Corporation*, Exchange Act Release No. 21872 (March 20, 1985), 32 SEC Docket (CCH) 935 (failure to discuss the impact of inventory obsolescence); *In re Marsh & McClennan Companies, Inc.*, Exchange Act Release No. 24023 (January 22, 1987), 37 SEC Docket (CCH) 634 (failure adequately to disclose, in a Form 10-K, the effects of a principal subsidiary's investing and financing activities).

[11] The examples used herein, while modeled in large part upon Project registrants' original or revised MD&As, have

been changed so that the registrants are not identified and particular points are emphasized. Of course, each example has been removed from its context as part of a larger document. The examples are provided for purposes of illustration only.

[12] *See* Item 101(c)(1)(ii) of Regulation S-K.

[13] *See, e.g., In re Charter Company*, Exchange Act Release No. 21647 (January 10, 1985), 32 SEC Docket (CCH) 289, in which the MD&A in the registrant's Form 10-K failed to disclose the favorable effect on earnings of the accounting method used, and the anticipated substantial reduction in future profits that would result from use of such method. Cf. *SEC v. Baldwin-United Corporation*, Litigation Release No. 10878 (September 26, 1985) and *In re Robert S. Harrison*, Exchange Act Release No. 22466 (September 26, 1985), 34 SEC Docket (CCH) 141 (both involving a different means of accounting for the same insurance product as in *Charter*, and Baldwin-United Corporation's failure to disclose, in the MD&A of its Form 10-K, its failure to meet the earnings assumptions of the accounting model used, and internal estimates of insufficient taxable income to use tax benefits inherent in the earnings assumptions).

scribes the reasonably likely effect of a known event: completion of an important contract.

The Company produced operating income of $22 million during 1987 as compared to $15 million during 1986, a 47 percent increase. Substantially all of the 47 percent increase can be attributed to the Company's completion of a major contract at a cost less than anticipated. It is expected that operating income during the current year will be significantly less, as only a portion of the profit generated by the completed contract is expected to be replaced by new contracts as a result of a slowdown within the Company's principal industry.

Events that have already occurred or are anticipated often give rise to known uncertainties. For example, a registrant may know that a material government contract is about to expire. The registrant may be uncertain as to whether the contract will be renewed, but nevertheless would be able to assess facts relating to whether it will be renewed. More particularly, the registrant may know that a competitor has found a way to provide the same service or product at a price less than that charged by the registrant, or may have been advised by the government that the contract may not be renewed. The registrant also would have factual information relevant to the financial impact of nonrenewal upon the registrant. In situations such as these, a registrant would have identified a known uncertainty reasonably likely to have material future effects on its financial condition or results of operations, and disclosure would be required.

In the following example, the registrant discloses the reasonably likely material effect of a known uncertainty regarding implementation of recently adopted legislation.

The Company had no firm cash commitments as of December 31, 1987 for capital expenditures. However, in 1987, legislation was enacted which may require that certain vehicles used in the Company's business be equipped with specified safety equipment by the end of 1991. Pursuant to this legislation, regulations have been proposed which, if promulgated, would require the expenditure by the Company of approximately $30 million over a three-year period.

Where a trend, demand, commitment, event or uncertainty is known, management must make two assessments:

(1) Is the known trend, demand, commitment, event or uncertainty likely to come to fruition? If management determines that it is not reasonably likely to occur, no disclosure is required.

(2) If management cannot make that determination, it must evaluate objectively the consequences of the known trend, demand, commitment, event or uncertainty, on the assumption that it will come to fruition. Disclosure is then required unless management determines that a material effect on the registrant's financial condition or results of operations is not reasonably likely to occur.[14]

Each final determination resulting from the assessments made by management must be objectively reasonable, viewed as of the time the determination is made.[15]

Application of these principles may be illustrated using a common disclosure issue which was considered in the review of a number of Project registrants: designation as a potentially responsible party ("PRP") by the Environmental Protection Agency (the "EPA") under The Comprehensive Environmental Response, Compensation, and Liability Act of 1980 ("Superfund").[16]

FACTS: A registrant has been correctly designated a PRP by the EPA with respect to cleanup of hazardous waste at three sites. No statutory defenses are available. The registrant is in the process of preliminary investigations of the sites to determine the nature of its potential liability and the amount of remedial costs necessary to clean up the sites. Other PRPs also have been designated, but the ability to obtain contribution is unclear, as is the extent of insurance coverage, if any. Management is unable to determine that a material effect on future financial condition or results of operations is not reasonably likely to occur.

Based upon the facts of this hypothetical case, MD&A disclosure of the effects of the PRP status, quantified to the extent reasonably practicable, would be required.[17] For MD&A purposes, aggre-

---

[14] MD&A mandates disclosure of specified forward-looking information, and specifies its own standard for disclosure—*i.e.*, reasonably likely to have material effect. This specific standard governs the circumstances in which Item 303 requires disclosure. The probability/magnitude test for materiality approved by the Supreme Court in *Basic, Inc., v. Levinson*, 108 S.Ct. 978 (1988), is inapposite to Item 303 disclosure.

[15] Where a material change in a registrant's financial condition (such as a material increase or decrease in cash flows) or results of operations appears in a reporting period and the likelihood of such change was not discussed in prior reports, the Commission staff as part of its review of the current filing will inquire as to the circumstances existing at the time of the earlier filings to determine whether the registrant failed to discuss a known trend, demand, commitment, event or uncertainty as required by Item 303.

[16] 42 U.S.C. Sections 9601, *et seq.* (1983 & Supp. 1988).

[17] Designation as a PRP does not in and of itself trigger disclosure under Item 103 of Regulation S-K and Instruction 5 thereto, 17 CFR 229.103, regarding "Legal Proceedings," because PRP status alone does not provide knowledge that a governmental agency is contemplating a proceeding. Nonetheless, a registrant's particular circumstances, when coupled with PRP status, may provide that knowledge. While there are many ways a PRP can become subject to potential monetary sanctions, including triggering the stipulated penalty clause in

gate potential cleanup costs must be considered in light of the joint and several liability to which a PRP is subject. Facts regarding whether insurance coverage may be contested, and whether and to what extent potential sources of contribution or indemnification constitute reliable sources of recovery may be factored into the determination of whether a material future effect is not reasonably likely to occur.

501.03.a. Liquidity—Capital Resources

Instruction 2 to Item 303(a) calls for an evaluation of "amounts and certainty of cash flows." "Except where it is otherwise clear from the discussion," Item 303(a)(1) and Instructions 2 and 5 to Item 303(a) together also mandate indication of which balance sheet conditions or income or cash flow items should be considered in assessing liquidity, and a discussion of prospective information regarding the registrant's short and long-term sources of, and needs for, capital. Disclosure of material commitments for capital expenditures as of the end of the latest fiscal period is required by Item 303(a)(2). Trend analysis and a description of "any expected material changes in the mix and relative cost" of the registrant's capital resources must also be provided.[18]

Generally, short-term liquidity and short-term capital resources cover cash needs up to 12 months into the future. These cash needs and the sources of funds to meet such needs relate to the day-to-day operating expenses of the registrant and material commitments coming due during that 12-month period.

The discussion of long-term liquidity and long-term capital resources must address material capital expenditures, significant balloon payments or other payments due on long-term obligations, and other demands or commitments, including any off-balance sheet items, to be incurred beyond the

next 12 months, as well as the proposed sources of funding required to satisfy such obligations.[19]

Where a material deficiency in short or long-term liquidity has been identified, the registrant should disclose the deficiency, as well as disclosing either its proposed remedy, that it has not decided on a remedy, or that it is currently unable to address the deficiency.[20] In the following example, a financially troubled registrant discusses the material effects of its cash flow problems on its business, and its efforts to remedy those problems.

The Company has violated certain requirements of its debt agreements relating to failure to maintain certain minimum ratios and levels of working capital and stockholders' equity. The Company's lenders have not declared the Company in default and have allowed the Company to remain in violation of these agreements. Were a default to be declared, the Company would not be able to continue to operate. A capital infusion of $4,000,000 is necessary to cure these defaults. The Company has engaged an investment banker and is considering various alternatives, including the sale of certain assets or the sale of common shares, to raise these funds.

The Company frequently has not been able to make timely payments to its trade and other creditors. As of year-end and as of February 29, 1988, the Company had past due payables in the amount of $525,000 and $705,000, respectively. Deferred payment terms have been negotiated with most of these vendors. However, certain vendors have suspended parts deliveries to the Company. As a result, the Company was not always able to make all shipments on time, although no orders have been cancelled to date. Were significant volumes of orders to be cancelled, the Company's ability to continue to operate would be jeopardized. The Company is currently seeking sources of working

---

(Footnote Continued)

a remedial agreement, the costs anticipated agreement entered into in the normal course of negotiation with the EPA, generally are not "sanctions" within either Instruction 5(B) or (c) to Item 103. Such remedial costs normally would ocnstitute charges to income or in some cases capital expenditures. The availability of insurance, indemnification or contribution may be relevant under Instruction 5(A) or (B) in determining whether the criteria for disclosure have been met. *Thomas A. Cole, Esq.*, (January 17, 1989).

[18] Most registrants combine discussions of capital resources and liquidity as permitted by Item 303(a).

When viewed to encompass capital resources, the Commission's concept of liquidity is comparable to the Financial Accounting Standards Board's ("FASB") concept of financial flexibility or the ability of an enterprise to adjust its future cash flows to meet needs and opportunities, both expected and unexpected. Financial flexibility is broader than the FASB's concept of liquidity (defined as short-term nearness of assets and liabilities to cash) because it includes potential internal and external sources of cash not directly associated with items shown on the balance sheet.

Securities Act Release No. 6349, *supra* n. 3, at 972; *see also* Statement of Financial Accounting Concepts No. 5, *Recogni-*

tion and Measurement in Financial Statements of Business Enterprises, ¶ 24a.

[19] *See, e.g., In re Hiex Development USA, Inc.,* Exchange Act Release No. 26722 (April 13, 1989), 43 SEC Docket (CCH) 1041 (involving in part the registrant's failure to discuss in the MD&A of a Form 10, a material contractual commitment to purchase equipment from an affiliate over a ten year period).

[20] *See, e.g., SEC v. The Charter Company,* Exchange Act Release No. 23350 (June 20, 1986), 35 SEC Docket (CCH) 1232, and *In re Ray M. Van Landingham and Wallace A. Patzke, Jr.,* Exchange Act Release No. 23349 (June 20, 1986), 35 SEC Docket (CCH) 1227, both involving Charter Company's liquidity disclosure concerning losses of trade credit, demands by its banks for a series of materially restrictive loan covenants and discussions with Charter's banks regarding asset sales, dividend restrictions and operational changes.

In a filing which includes an independent accountant's repot that is modified as a result of uncertainty about a registrant's continued existence, Section 607.02 of the Codification of Financial Reporting Policies requires "appropriate and prominent disclosure of the registrant's financial difficulties and viable plans to overcome such difficulties."

---

capital financing sufficient to fund delinquent balances and meet ongoing trade obligations.

Short and long-term liquidity and capital resources analysis should become more comparable from registrant to registrant as a result of the Financial Accounting Standards Board's recent issuance of SFAS 95,[21] which requires the statement of changes in financial position to be replaced by a statement of cash flows as part of a full set of financial statements. This new statement reports net cash provided or used by each of operating, investing and financing activities, as defined, and the net effect of those flows on cash and cash equivalents.

Registrants are expected to use the statement of cash flows, and other appropriate indicators, in analyzing their liquidity, and to present a balanced discussion dealing with cash flows from investing and financing activities as well as from operations. This discussion should address those matters that have materially affected the most recent period presented but are not expected to have short or long-term implications, and those matters that have not materially affected the most recent period presented but are expected materially to affect future periods.[22] Examples of such matters include: a) discretionary operating expenses such as expenses relating to advertising, research and development or maintenance of equipment; b) debt refinancings or redemptions; or 3) levels of financing provided by suppliers or to customers. Liquidity analysis premised upon the new statement of cash flows and prepared in accordance with this guidance should enhance the utility to investors of MD&A disclosure by improving comparability from registrant to registrant and providing information more directly relevant to liquidity than that previously premised upon the statement of changes in financial position.

501.03.a.i. Additional Guidance on Presentation of Liquidity and Capital Resources Disclosures

[Added by FR-83.]

A. Liquidity Disclosure

As discussed in the Proposing Release, companies have expanded the types of funding methods and cash management tools they use. We remind registrants that Item 303(a)(1) of Regulation S-K requires them to "identify and separately describe internal and external sources of liquidity, and briefly discuss any material unused sources of liquidity." Accordingly, as the financing activities undertaken by registrants become more diverse and complex, it is increasingly important that the discussion and analysis of liquidity and capital resources provided by registrants meet the objectives of MD&A disclosure.

In 2003, the Commission issued interpretive guidance relating to MD&A disclosures of liquidity and capital resources, as well as MD&A generally.[23] We encourage registrants to review that guidance when preparing their MD&A, as it covers topics relating to the discussion of cash requirements, cash management, sources and uses of cash, as well as a registrant's debt instruments, guarantees and related covenants, that continue to be relevant to investors.

As we have stated in the past, MD&A requires companies to provide investors with disclosure that facilitates an appreciation of the known trends and uncertainties that have impacted historical results or are reasonably likely to shape future periods.[24] This disclosure should both discuss and analyze the company's business from the perspective of management.[25] In the context of liquidity, Item 303(a)(1) of Regulation S-K requires disclosure of known trends or any known demands, commitments, events or uncertainties that will result in, or that are reasonably likely to result in, the registrant's liquidity increasing or decreasing in any material way.[26] In past guidance, the Commission has highlighted a number of issues for management to consider when identifying trends, demands, commitments, events and uncertainties

---

[21] Statement of Financial Accounting Standards No. 95, *Statement of Cash Flows.* While the new statement is required for annual financial statements for fiscal years ending after July 15, 1988, financial statements for prior years are not required to be restated, and interim financial statements in the initial year of application are not required to use the new statement. Such interim period statements must be restated when presented as comparative prior periods with future interim financial statements.

[22] *See* 17 CFR 229.303(a), Instruction 3; *supra* n. 4-17 and accompanying text.

[23] *See* Commission Guidance Regarding Management's Discussion and Analysis of Financial Condition and Results of Operations, Release No. 33-8350 (Dec. 19, 2003) [68 FR 75056] (the "2003 Interpretive Release").

[24] *See* Disclosure in Management's Discussion and Analysis About Off Balance Sheet Arrangements, Contractual Obligations and Contingent Liabilities and Commitments, Release No. 33-8182 (Jan. 28, 2003) [68 FR 5982] (the "OBS Adopting Release"), at 5982 ("MD&A also provides a unique opportu-

nity for management to provide investors with an understanding of its view of the financial performance and condition of the company, an appreciation of what the financial statements show and do not show, as well as important trends and risks that have shaped the past and are reasonably likely to shape the future.").

[25] "MD&A should be a discussion and analysis of a company's business as seen through the eyes of those who manage that business. Management has a unique perspective on its business that only it can present. As such, MD&A should not be a recitation of financial statements in narrative form, or an otherwise uninformative series of technical responses to MD&A requirements, neither of which provides this important management perspective." *See* 2003 Interpretive Release, *supra* note 3, at 75056.

[26] "The scope of the discussion should thus address liquidity in the broadest sense, encompassing internal as well as external sources, current conditions as well as future commitments and known trends, changes in circumstances and uncertainties." *See* Commission Statement About Management's Discussion and Analysis of Financial Condition and Results of

that require disclosure in MD&A.[27] Some additional important trends and uncertainties relating to liquidity might include, for example, difficulties accessing the debt markets, reliance on commercial paper or other short-term financing arrangements, maturity mismatches between borrowing sources and the assets funded by those sources, changes in terms requested by counterparties, changes in the valuation of collateral, and counterparty risk.

In addition, in the context of liquidity and capital resources, if the registrant's financial statements do not adequately convey the registrant's financing arrangements during the period, or the impact of those arrangements on liquidity, because of a known trend, demand, commitment, event or uncertainty, additional narrative disclosure should be considered and may be required to enable an understanding of the amounts depicted in the financial statements. For example, depending on the registrant's circumstances, if borrowings during the reporting period are materially different than the period-end amounts recorded in the financial statements, disclosure about the intra-period variations is required under current rules to facilitate investor understanding of the registrant's liquidity position.

Moreover, the Commission's staff has noted that there may be confusion on the part of registrants about how to address disclosure of certain repurchase agreements that are accounted for as sales, as well as other types of short-term financings that are not otherwise fully captured in period-end balance sheets.[28] Again, disclosure is required in MD&A where a known commitment, event or uncertainty will result in (or is reasonably likely to result in) the registrant's liquidity increasing or decreasing in a material way.[29] The absence of specific references in existing disclosure requirements for off-balance sheet arrangements or contractual obligations to repurchase transactions that are accounted for as sales, or to any other

transfers of financial assets that are accounted for as sales, does not relieve registrants from the disclosure requirements of Item 303(a)(1).[30] Further, as stated in the 2002 Interpretive Release, legal opinions regarding "true sale" issues do not obviate the need for registrants to consider whether disclosure is required.[31] In evaluating whether disclosure in MD&A may be required in connection with a repurchase transaction, securities lending transaction, or any other transaction involving the transfer of financial assets with an obligation to repurchase financial assets, that has been accounted for as a sale under applicable accounting standards, the registrant should consider whether the transaction is reasonably likely to result in the use of a material amount of cash or other liquid assets. Disclosure may be required in the discussion of liquidity and capital resources, particularly where the registrant does not otherwise include such information in its off-balance sheet arrangements or its contractual obligations table. A registrant may determine where in its MD&A this information would be most informative based on the type of obligation and potential exposure involved, with an emphasis on providing disclosure that is clear and not misleading.

To provide context for the exposures identified in MD&A, companies should also consider describing cash management and risk management policies that are relevant to an assessment of their financial condition. Banks, in particular, should consider discussing their policies and practices in meeting applicable banking agency guidance on funding and liquidity risk management, or any policies and practices that differ from applicable agency guidance. In addition, a company that maintains or has access to a portfolio of cash and other investments that is a material source of liquidity should consider providing information about the nature and composition of that portfolio, including a description of the assets held and any related market risk, settlement risk or other risk

---

(Footnote Continued)

Operations, Release No. 33-8056 (Jan. 22, 2002) [67 FR 3746] (the "2002 Interpretive Release"), at 3748 n.11.

[27] See 2002 Interpretive Release, *supra* note 5, at 3748.

[28] In its 2005 OBS Report, the Commission's staff identified transfers of assets with continuing involvement as one of the principal areas in need of improvement in disclosure of off-balance sheet arrangements. *See* Staff of the U.S. Securities and Exchange Commission, Report and Recommendations Pursuant to Section 401(c) of the Sarbanes-Oxley Act of 2002 On Arrangements with Off-Balance Sheet Implications, Special Purpose Entities and Transparency of Filings by Issuers (June 2005), *available at* http://www.sec.gov/news/studies/soxoffbalancerpt.pdf. *See also*, the Division of Corporation Finance, Sample Letter Sent to Public Companies Asking for Information Related to Repurchase Agreements, Securities Lending Transactions, or Other Transactions Involving the Transfer of Financial Assets (Mar. 2010), *available at* http://www.sec.gov/divisions/corpfin/guidance/cforepurchase0310.htm., and the Division of Corporation Finance, Sample Letter Sent to Public Companies That Have

Identified Investments in Structured Investment Vehicles, Conduits or Collateralized Debt Obligations (Off-balance Sheet Entities) (Dec. 2007) *available at* http://www.sec.gov/divisions/corpfin/guidance/cfoffbalanceltr1207.htm.

[29] See Item 303(a)(1) [17 CFR 229.303(a)(1)].

[30] We also note that, in 1986, the Commission adopted changes to Rule 4-08 of Regulation S-X to require financial statement footnote disclosure of the nature and extent of a registrant's repurchase and reverse repurchase transactions and the degree of risk involved. *See* Disclosure Amendments to Regulation S-X Regarding Repurchase and Reverse Repurchase Agreements, Release No. 33-6621 (Jan. 22, 1986) [51 FR 3765]. These requirements focus on disclosure of risk of loss due to counter-party default. *See* Rule 4-08(m) of Regulation S-X [17 CFR § 210.4-08m]. However, the adopting release indicates that the requirements do not affect obligations under MD&A requirements to discuss "any material impact on liquidity or operations and risk resulting from involvement with repurchase and reverse repurchase agreements."

[31] See 2002 Interpretive Release, *supra* note 5, at 3749.

---

exposure. This could include information about the nature of any limits or restrictions and their effect on the company's ability to use or to access those assets to fund its business operations.

Transparent financial reporting that conveys a complete and understandable picture of a company's financial position reduces uncertainty in our markets. Surprises to investors can be reduced or avoided when a company provides clear and understandable information about known trends, events, demands, commitments and uncertainties, particularly where they are reasonably likely to have a current or future material impact on that company. The economic environment is not static. Circumstances and risks change and, as a result, disclosure about those circumstances and risks must also evolve. As we stated in the 2003 Interpretive Release, if prior disclosure "does not adequately foreshadow subsequent events, or if new information that impacts known trends and uncertainties becomes apparent . . . additional disclosure should be considered and may be required."[32] This principle is equally applicable in the context of liquidity and capital resources disclosure.

B. Leverage Ratio Disclosures

Where a registrant includes capital or leverage ratio disclosure in its filings with the Commission, and there are no regulatory requirements prescribing the calculation of that ratio, or where a registrant includes capital or leverage ratios that are calculated using a methodology that is modified from its prescribed form, we remind registrants of our longstanding approach to disclosure of financial measures and non-financial measures in MD&A. First, the registrant should determine whether the measure is a financial measure. If the measure is not a financial measure, registrants should refer to the guidance we provided in 2003 for disclosures relating to non-financial measures, such as industry metrics or value metrics.[33] If the measure is a financial measure, the registrant should next determine whether the measure falls within the scope of our requirements for non-GAAP financial measures, and if it is, the registrant would need to follow our rules and guidance governing the inclusion of non-GAAP financial measures in filings with the Commission.[34]

In any event, any ratio or measure included in a filing should be accompanied by a clear explana-

tion of the calculation methodology. The explanation would need to clearly articulate the treatment of any inputs that are unusual, infrequent or non-recurring, or that are otherwise adjusted so that the ratio is calculated differently from directly comparable measures. Similar to our guidance for the disclosure of non-financial measures, if the financial measure presented differs from other measures commonly used in the registrant's industry, the registrant would need to consider whether a discussion of those differences or presentation of those measures would be necessary to make the disclosures not misleading. Finally, a registrant would need to consider its reasons for presenting the particular financial measure, and should include disclosure clearly stating why the measure is useful to understanding its financial condition. Where the ratio is being presented in connection with disclosure on debt instruments and related covenants, registrants should also consult our past guidance on disclosure of debt instruments, guarantees and related covenants.[35]

C. Contractual Obligations Table Disclosures

As an aid to understanding other liquidity and capital resources disclosures in MD&A, the contractual obligations tabular disclosure should be prepared with the goal of presenting a meaningful snapshot of cash requirements arising from contractual payment obligations. The Commission's staff has observed that divergent practices have developed in connection with the contractual obligations table disclosure, with registrants drawing different conclusions about the information to be included and the manner of presentation. The requirement itself permits flexibility so that the presentation can reflect company-specific information in a way that is suitable to a registrant's business. Accordingly, registrants are encouraged to develop a presentation method that is clear, understandable and appropriately reflects the categories of obligations that are meaningful in light of its capital structure and business. Registrants should highlight any changes in presentation that are made, so that investors are able to use the information to make comparisons from period to period.

Since the adoption of Item 303(a)(5), registrants and industry groups have raised questions to our staff about how to treat a number of items under the contractual obligations requirement, includ-

---

[32] See 2003 Interpretive Release, *supra* note 3, at 75061, and Management's Discussion and Analysis of Financial Condition and Results of Operations; Certain Investment Company Disclosures, Release No. 33-6835 (May 18, 1989) [54 FR 22427] (the "1989 Interpretive Release"). The 1989 Interpretive Release clarifies that material changes to items disclosed in MD&A in annual reports should be discussed in the quarter in which they occur. The 2003 Interpretive Release states that "there may also be circumstances where an item may not be material in the context of a discussion of annual results of operations but is material in the context of interim results."

[33] See 2003 Interpretive Release, *supra* note 3, at 75060.

[34] See Conditions for Use of Non-GAAP Financial Measures, Release No. 33-8176 (Jan. 22, 2003) [68 FR 4820] and Item 10(e) of Regulation S-K [17 CFR 229.10(e)(5)]. We note that existing rules and guidance governing the inclusion of non-GAAP financial measures in filings with the Commission do not apply to financial measures that are "required to be disclosed by GAAP, Commission rules, or a system of regulation of a government or governmental authority or self-regulatory organization that is applicable to the registrant.

[35] See 2003 Interpretive Release, *supra* note 3, at 75064.

ing: interest payments, repurchase agreements, tax liabilities, synthetic leases, and obligations that arise under off-balance sheet arrangements. In addition, a variety of questions has been raised with our staff in the context of purchase obligations. Because the questions that arise tend to be fact-specific and closely related to a registrant's particular business and circumstances, we have not issued general guidance as to how to treat these items or other questions regarding the presentation of the contractual obligations table. The purpose of the contractual obligations table is to provide aggregated information about contractual obligations and contingent liabilities and commitments in a single location so as to improve transparency of a registrant's short-term and long-term liquidity and capital resources needs and to provide context for investors to assess the relative role of off-balance sheet arrangements;[36] registrants should prepare the disclosure consistent with that objective. Uncertainties about what to include or how to allocate amounts over the periods required in the table should be resolved consistent with the purpose of the disclosure. To that end, footnotes should be used to provide information necessary for an understanding of the timing and amount of the specified contractual obligations, as indicated in the instructions contained in Item 303(a)(5)(i), or, where necessary to promote understanding of the tabular data, additional narrative discussion outside of the table should be considered. Registrants should determine how best to present the information that is relevant to their own business in a manner that is clear, consistent with the purpose of the disclosure and not misleading, and should provide additional disclosure where necessary to explain what the tabular data includes and does not include.[37]

501.03.b. General Concept

ASR 299:

Liquidity requirements vary among industries but include demands such as capital expenditures (including any off-balance sheet commitments), expanded working capital needs, or scheduled debt repayments. Throughout the discussion of liquidity, it is also necessary to identify those balance sheet, income and cash flow items believed to be indicators of liquidity. The discussion will be enhanced by an explanation of the reasons why particular indicators are appropriate for the individual registrant. In this sense, unused credit lines, debt-equity ratios, bond ratings, and restrictions under existing debt agreements may be indicators of liquidity.

The staff also encourages registrants to identify and discuss those factors relevant to an understanding of the company's future objectives, plans and its ability to complete those plans. Anticipated sources of financing are particularly important to capital enterprises where *planned* expenditures also are many times more meaningful than legal commitments. Similarly, the anticipated cost of capital as well as its expected availability may be a key consideration for highly leveraged companies.

501.04. Material Changes

Some Project registrants did not provide adequate disclosure of the reasons for material year-to-year changes in line items, or discussion and quantification of the contribution of two or more factors to such material changes. Instruction 4 to Item 303(a) requires a discussion of the causes of material changes from year-to-year in financial statement line items "to the extent necessary to an understanding of the registrant's businesses as a whole." An analysis of changes in line items is required where material and where the changes diverge from changes in related line items of the financial statements, where identification and quantification of the extent of contribution of each of two or more factors is necessary to an understanding of a material change, or where there are material increases or decreases in net sales or revenue.[38]

Discussion of the impact of discounted operations and of extraordinary gains and losses is also required where these items have had or are reasonably likely to have a material effect on reported or future financial condition or results of operations. Other non-recurring items should be discussed as "unusual or infrequent" events or transactions "that materially affected the amount of reported income from continuing operations."[39]

As Instruction 4 to Item 303(a) states, repetition and line-by-line analysis is not required or generally appropriate when the causes for a change in one line item also relate to other line items. The same Instruction also states that the discussion need not recite amounts of changes readily com-

---

[36] *See* OBS Adopting Release, *supra* note 4, at 5990.

[37] As an example, if useful to a clear understanding of the information presented, a registrant might consider separating amounts in the table into those that are reflected on the balance sheet and those arising from off-balance sheet arrangements, particularly where such a distinction helps to tie the information to financial statement disclosure and other MD&A discussion.

[38] *See SEC v. The E.F. Hutton Group, Inc.*, Exchange Act Release No. 22579 (October 29, 1985), 34 SEC Docket (CCH) 538, involving Hutton's failure to disclose that its bank overdrafting practices were the cause for material changes in interest income from year-to-year, and the risks and uncertainties associated with such practices.

Although Item 303(a)(3)(iii) speaks only to material increases, not decreases, in net sales or revenues, the Commission interprets Item 303(a)(3)(i) and Instruction 4 as seeking similar disclosure for material decreases in net sales or revenues.

[39] 17 CFR 229.303(a)(3)(i); *see SEC v. Allegheny International, Inc.*, Litigation Release No. 11533 (September 9, 1987), 39 SEC Docket (CCH) 196 (failure to disclose a sale of realty that constituted an unusual and infrequent event which had a material impact on pre-tax income); *see generally* Accounting Principles Board Opinion No. 30.

putable from the financial statements and "shall not merely repeat numerical data contained in" such statements. However, quantification should otherwise be as precise, including use of dollar amounts or percentages, as reasonably practicable.

In the following example, the registrant analyzes the reasons for a material change in revenues and in so doing describes the effects of offsetting developments.

Revenue from sales of single-family homes for 1987 increased 6% from 1986. The increase resulted from a 14% increase in the average sales price per home, partially offset by a 6% decrease in the number of homes delivered. Revenues from sales of single-family homes for 1986 increased 2% from 1985. The average sales price per home in 1986 increased 6%, which was offset by a 4% decrease in the number of homes delivered.

The increase in the average sales prices in 1987 and 1986 is primarily the result of the Company's increased emphasis on higher priced single-family homes. The decrease in homes delivered in 1987 and 1986 was attributable to a decline in sales in Texas. The significant decline in oil prices and its resulting effect on energy-related business has further impacted the already depressed Texas area housing market and is expected to do so for the foreseeable future. The Company curtailed housing operations during 1987 in certain areas in Texas in response to this change in the housing market. Although the number of homes sold is expected to continue during the current year as a result of this action, this decline is expected to be offset by increases in average sales prices.

501.05. Interim Period Reporting

The second sentence of Item 303(b) states that MD&A relating to interim period financial statements "shall include a discussion of material changes in those items specifically listed in paragraph (a) of this Item, except that the impact of inflation and changing prices on operations for

interim periods need not be addressed."[40] As this sentence indicates, material changes to each and every specific disclosure requirement contained in paragraph (a), with the noted exception, should be discussed. This would include, for example, internal and external sources of liquidity, expected material changes in the mix and relative cost of such resources, and unusual or infrequent events or transactions that materially affected the amount of reported income from continuing operations.[41]

In light of the obligation to update MD&A disclosure periodically, the impact of known trends, demands, commitments, events or uncertainties arising during the interim period which are reasonably likely to have material effects on financial condition or results of oeprations constitutes required disclosure in MD&A.[42] For example, a calendar year end registrant describes, in its June 30 Form 10-Q, a recent event which is reasonably likely to have a material future effect on its financial condition or results of operations.

The Company was advised in late June that Company A, its principal customer, which accounted for 28% and 30% of revenues for the last six months and prior fiscal year, respectively, intends to terminate all purchases effective during the third quarter, due to in-house capabilities recently developed by this customer. The Company is materially dependent on its business with this customer and anticipates upon such termination a material adverse effect on revenues and income. Efforts are being made to replace revenues attributable to such customer by developing new customers. The Company expects it will take at least 6 months to generate such replacement revenues.

501.06. Other Observations
.a. Segment Analysis

In formulating a judgment as to whether a discussion of segment information is necessary to an understanding of the business, a multi-segment registrant preparing a full fiscal year MD&A should analyze revenues, profitability, and the cash needs of its significant segments.[43] To the

---

[40] 17 CFR 229.303(b).

[41] See, e.g., In re American Express Company, Exchange Act Release No. 23332 (June 17, 1986), 35 SEC Docket (CCH) 1163 (failure to discuss the impact, in several Forms 10-Q and a Form 10-K, of two reinsurance transactions by an insurance subsidiary which were treated by the registrant as materially increasing net income, but which lacked economic substance); In re Michael R. Maury, Exchange Act Release No. 23067 (March 26, 1986), 35 SEC Docket (CCH) 435 (the MD&A in a Form 10-Q was found deficient for its failure to disclose the effects on net income of the reversal of previously established reserves).

[42] See SEC v. Ronson Corporation, Litigation Release No. 10093 (August 15, 1983), 28 SEC Docket (CCH) 841, where the MD&As in a Form 10-K and two Forms 10-Q were found to be inadequate in their failure to state that Ronson's largest customer had shut down its operations which required

purchases from Ronson, that it was unlikely that this customer would resume purchases in the short term and that, due to technological changes being made at this customer's facilities, once purchases were resumed, an indefinite reduction in necessary purchases of 30-50% was likely.

[43] Where consistent with the registrant's internal management reports, SFAS No. 131 permits measures of segment profitability that differ from consolidated operating profit as defined by GAAP, or that exclude items included in the determination of the registrant's net income. Under SFAS No. 131, a registrant also must reconcile key segment amounts to the corresponding items reported in the consolidated financial statements in a note to the financial statements. Similarly, the Commission expects that the discussion of a segment whose profitability is determined on a basis that differs from consolidated operating profit as defined by GAAP or that excludes the effects of items attributable to the segment also will address the applicable reconciling items in Management's

extent any segment contributes in a materially disproportionate way to those items, or where discussion on a consolidated basis would present an incomplete and misleading picture of the enterprise, segment discussion should be included. This may occur, for example, when there are legal or other restrictions upon the free flow of funds from one segment, subsidiary, or division of the registrant to others; when known trends, demands, commitments, event, or uncertainties within a segment are reasonably likely to have a material effect on the business as a whole; when the ability to dispose of identified assets of a segment may be relevant to the financial flexibility of the registrant; and in other circumstances in which the registrant concludes that segment analysis is appropriate to an understanding of its business.

The following example illustrates segment disclosure for a manufacturer with two segments. The two segments contributed to segment profit amounts that were disproportionate to their respective revenues. The registrant discusses sales and segment profit trends, factors explaining such trends, and where applicable, known events that will impact future results of operations of the segment.

Net Sales by Segment

Segments	Year 3 ($ million)	Year 3 Percent of Total	Year 2 ($ million)	Year 2 Percent of Total	Year 1 ($ million)	Year 1 Percent of Total
Segment I	585	55	479	53	420	48
Segment II	472	45	433	47	457	52
Total Sales	1057	100	912	100	877	100

Year 3 vs. Year 2

Segment I sales increased 22% in Year 3 over the Year 2 period. The increase included the effect of the acquisition of Corporation T. Excluding this acquisition, sales would have increased by 16% over Year 2. Product Line A sales increased by 18% due to a 24% increase in selling prices, partially offset by lower shipments. Product Line B sales increased by 35% due to a 17% increase in selling prices and a 15% increase in shipment volume.

Segment II sales increased 9% due to a 12% increase in selling prices partly offset by a 3% reduction in shipment volume.

Year 2 vs. Year 1

Segment I sales increased 14% in Year 2. Product Line A sales increased 22%, in spite of a slight reduction in shipments, because of a 23% increase in selling prices.

Product Line B sales declined 5% due mainly to a 7% decrease in selling prices, partially offset by higher shipments.

The 5% decline in Segment II sales reflected a 3% reduction in selling prices and a 2% decline in shipments.

The substantial increases in selling prices of Product Line A during Year 3 and Year 2 occurred primarily because of heightened worldwide demand which exceeded the industry's production capacity. The Company expects these conditions to continue for the next several years. The Company anticipates that shipment volumes of Product Line A will increase as its new production facility reaches commercial production levels in Year 4.

Segment II shipment volumes have declined during the past two years primarily because of the discontinuation of certain products that were marginally profitable and did not have significant growth potential.

Profit by Segment

Segments	Year 3 ($ million)	Year 3 Percent of Total	Year 2 ($ million)	Year 2 Percent of Total	Year 1 ($ million)	Year 1 Percent of Total
Segment I	126	75	108	68	67	55
Segment II	42	25	51	32	54	45
Segment Profit	168	100	159	100	121	100

Year 3 vs. Year 2

Segment I profit was $18 million (17%) higher in Year 3 than in Year 2. This increase includes the effects of higher sales prices and slightly improved margins on Product Line A, higher shipments of Product Line B and the acquisition of Corporation T. Excluding this acquisition, Segment I profit would have been 11% higher than in Year 2. Partially offsetting these increases are costs and expenses of $11 million related to new plant start-up, slightly reduced margins on Product Line B and a $9 million increase in research and development expenses.

(Footnote Continued)

Discussion and Analysis. For example, if a material charge for restructuring or impairment relates to a specific segment, but is not included in management's measure of the segment's operating profit or loss, registrants would be expected to discuss in Management's Discussion and Analysis the applicable portion of the charge, the segment to which it relates and the circumstances of its incurrence. Likewise, the Commission expects that the effects of management's use of non-GAAP measures, either on a consolidated or segment basis, will be explained in a balanced and informative manner, and the disclosure will include a discussion of how that segment's performance has affected the registrant's GAAP financial statements.

Segment II profit declined $9 million (18%) due mainly to substantially higher costs in Year 3 resulting from a 23% increase in average raw material costs which could not be fully recovered through sales prices increases. The Company expects that Segment II margins will continue to decline, although at a lesser rate than in Year 3 as competitive factors limit the Company's ability to recover cost increases.

Year 2 vs. Year 1

Segment I profit was $41 million (61%) higher in Year 2 than in Year 1. After excluding the effect of the $34 million nonrecurring charge for the early retirement program in Year 1, Segment I profit in Year 2 was $18 million (27%) higher than in Year 1. This increase reflected higher prices and a corresponding 21% increase in margins on Product Line A, and a 17% increase in margins on Product Line B due primarily to costs reductions resulting from the early retirement program.

Segment II profit declined about $3 million (6%) due mainly to lower selling prices and slightly reduced margins in Year 2. 2. Replace paragraphs .01, .02 and .03 of Section 503 with new paragraph .01, to include the text of Section I of this release captioned "Background" and with new paragraph .02 to include the text of Section II.B.2 of this release captioned "Major Customers."

501.06.b. Participation in High Yield Financings, Highly Leveraged Transactions or Non-Investment Grade Loans and Investments

A registrant, whether a financial institution (such as a bank, thrift, insurance company or finance company), broker-dealer or one its affiliates, or any other public company, may participate in several ways, directly or indirectly, in high yield financings, or highly leveraged transactions or make noninvestment grade loans or investments relating to corporate restructurings such as leveraged buyouts, recapitalizations including significant stock buybacks and cash dividends, and acquisitions or mergers.[44] A registrant may participate in the financing of such a transaction either as originator, syndicator, lender, purchaser of secured senior debt, or as an investor in other debt instruments (often unsecured or subordinated), redeemable preferred stock or other equity securities. Participation in high yield or highly leveraged transactions, as well as investment in non-investment grade securities, generally involves greater returns, in the form of higher fees and higher average yields or potential market gains. Participation in such transactions may involve greater risks, often related to credit worthiness, solvency, relative liquidity of the secondary trading market, potential market losses, and vulnerability to rising interest rates and economic downturns.[45]

Similar risk-reward exposure appears to exist with the growing practice by certain registrants of originating low down-payment mortgages without obtaining mortgage insurance. Other registrants have substantial participations in venture capital financings.

In view of these potentially greater returns and potentially greater risks, disclosure of the nature and extent of a registrant's involvement with high yield or highly leveraged transactions and non-investment grade loans and investments may be required under one or more of several MD&A items, and registrants should consider carefully the extent of disclosure required.[46] MD&A analysis is required if such participation has had or is reasonably likely to have a material effect on financial condition or results of operations.

---

[44] On February 16, 1989 the Federal Reserve Board issued bank examination guidelines regarding highly leveraged transactions. Letter from William Taylor, Director, Division of Banking Supervision and Regulation, to the Officer in Charge of Supervision at each Federal Reserve Bank (February 16, 1989). The guidelines are intended to assist bank examiners in identifying exposure that may warrant closer scrutiny and are not intended to imply criticism of any particular transaction, nor to suggest what is deemed to be an appropriate degree of leverage in any particular industry. In these guidelines, criteria to define a highly leveraged financing include identification of borrowers whose debt to total assets ratio exceeds 75%. Registrants may refer to this guidance or to other recognized criteria that may be developed in defining highly leveraged transactions. In any event, registrants should indicate how highly leveraged transactions are defined for disclosure purposes. In this regard, the Commission recognizes that leverage characteristics may vary from industry to industry, and that debt ratios that are appropriate for some industries may be unusually high or low in other industries. Similarly, the Commission does not intend to imply criticism of any particular transaction or to suggest an appropriate degree of leverage in any particular industry or for any particular firm.

[45] See, e.g., P. Asquith, D. Mullins, Jr., and E. Wolff, Original Issue High Yield Bonds: Aging Analyses of Defaults, Exchanges, and Calls (March, 1989).

[46] Other related disclosure includes Schedule 1 of Rule 12-02 of Regulation S-X, 17 CFR 210.12-02, which requires separate disclosure for each particular issue of corporate securities carried on the balance sheet at greater than 2% of total assets, and allows reasonable groupings, e.g., by similar investment risk, of all other securities. Also, for securities with significantly greater investment risk factors than are typical for that class of issuer, such as securities where interest is in default or the issuer is in bankruptcy, separate listing or grouping is required to be accompanied by a brief description of the relevant risk factors. Guide 3, Item III(c)(4) requires bank holding companies to disclose concentrations of loans exceeding 10% of total loans, and defines "concentration" to exist where a number of borrowers are engaged in similar activities that would cause them to be similarly impacted by economic or other conditions. Item II of Guide 3 instructs that considerations should be given to disclosure of the risk characteristics of securities held as investments. Savings and loan holding companies should provide similar disclosures pursuant to Staff Accounting Bulletin Topic 11:K. Insurance companies are also subject to similar requirements under Article 7 of Regulation S-X, Rule 7-03(a)(1), Notes 5-6, 17 CFR 210.7-03(a)(1).

In determining the adequacy of disclosure concerning participation in high yield, highly leveraged and non-investment grade loans and investments, registrants should consider the need to disclose:

1. relevant lending and investing policies, including credit and risk management policies;

2. the amounts of holdings, stated separately by type if individually material, including guarantees and repurchase or other commitments to lend or acquire such loans and investments, and the potential risks inherent in such holdings;

3. information regarding the level of activity during the period, *e.g.,* organizations and retentions;

4. amounts of holdings, if any, giving rise to significantly greater risks (that may have material effects on financial condition or results of operations) than are present in other similar transactions and instruments; for example, where the issuer is bankrupt or has issued securities on which interest payments are in default, or where there are significant concentrations (e.g., in an individual borrower, industry or geographic area), particularly where those concentrations are in securities with relatively low trading market liquidity (such as those that depend upon a single market maker for their liquidity); and

5. analysis of the actual and reasonably likely material effects of the above matters on income and operations, *e.g. ,* the amounts of fees recognized and deferred, yields, amounts of realized and unrealized market gains or losses, and credit losses.

Such disclosure may appear in the business discussion, or other appropriate location, but the effects resulting from participation should be analyzed in MD&A.

Similar concerns are raised with regard to investment companies that invest, or are permitted to invest, all or a portion of their portfolios in high-yield or non-investment grade securities. An investment company that seeks high income by investing in other than high-grade bonds (or is permitted to do so, even if it does not currently include such securities in its portfolio) should disclose in its prospectus the risks involved in such investments.[47] These risks include, but are not limited to, the risks described above, such as market price volatility based upon interest rate sensitivity, creditworthiness and relative liquidity of the secondary trading market, as well as the effects such risks may have on the net asset value of the fund. In addition, the board of directors of a fund that invests in such securities should carefully consider factors affecting the secondary market for such securities in determining whether or not any particular security is liquid or illiquid, and whether market quotations are "readily available" for purposes of valuing portfolio securities.[48]

The nature of disclosure required by non-investment companies will vary depending on the type of participation. In the following example the registrant is a bank holding company that participates in highly leveraged transactions as a lender and not as an investor.

The Company is active in originating and syndicating loans in highly leveraged corporate transactions. The Company generally includes in this category domestic and international loans and commitments made by the Banks in recapitalizations, acquisitions, and leveraged buyouts which result in the borrower's debt to total assets ratio exceeding 75%. As of December 31, 1988, the Company had loans outstanding in approximately 61 highly leveraged transactions in an aggregate principal amount of approximately $900 million, was committed under definitive loan agreements relating to approximately 23 highly leveraged transactions to lend an additional amount of approximately $650 million, and had other highly leveraged transactions at various stages of discussion or preliminary commitment. The Company's equity investments in highly leveraged transactions are not material.

In recent years the Company has not made a loan in excess of $175 million in any individual highly leveraged transaction, and the Company has typically retained, after syndication and sales of loan participations, a principal amount not exceeding approximately $35 million in any such transaction. At December 31, 1988, only two loans had outstanding balances exceeding $35 million ($51 million and $47 million, respectively) and no industry represented more than 15% of the Company's total highly leveraged loan portfolio. Should an economic downturn or sustained period of rising interest rates occur, highly leveraged transaction borrowers may experience financial stress. As a result, risks associated with these transactions may be higher than for more traditional financing.

The Company estimates that its fees for lending and corporate finance activities relating to highly leveraged transactions were approximately $64 million during 1988, of which approximately $48 million was recognized as income and $16 million was deferred, compared with $40 million during 1987 of which approximately $32 million was recognized as income and $8 million was deferred. The deferred portion of such fees will be recognized over the terms of the related loans in accor-

---

[47] *See* Guide 20 to Form N-1A.

[48] *See* Guide 28 to Form N-1A.

dance with Statement of Financial Accounting Standards Number 91.

In recent years, the Company has had no significant charge-offs of loans made in highly leveraged transactions. At December 31, 1988, approximately $25 million (3%) of such outstanding loans were on nonaccrual status, which was not materially greater than that for the Company's other lending activities.

A reduction in the Company's activities relating to highly leveraged transactions could have some negative impact on the Company's results of operations. The size of such impact would depend on the magnitude of the reduction and on the profitability of the activities to which the Company might redirect its resources. Although any estimate of the impact of a total discontinuation of all new highly leveraged transactions depends on various factors that cannot now be determined, the Company believes that such a discontinuation would reduce its gross revenues approximately 6% and net income by approximately 12%.

In the following example, the registrant is an investor in non-investment grade debt securities.

At December 31, 1988, the Company held in its portfolio, net of reserves, $81 million of high yield, unrated or less than investment grade corporate debt securities with an aggregate market value of $75 million. Investments in unrated or less than investment grade corporate debt securities have different risks than other investments in corporate debt securities rated investment grade and held by the Company. Risk of loss upon default by the borrower is significantly greater with respect to such corporate debt securities than with other corporate debt securities because these securities are generally unsecured and are often subordinated to other creditors of the issuer, and because these issuers usually have high levels of indebtedness and are more sensitive to adverse economic conditions, such as recession or increasing interest rates, than are investment grade issuers. In addition, investments by the Company in corporate debt securities of any given issuer are generally larger than its investments in most other securities, thus resulting in a greater impact in the event of default. There is only a thinly traded market for such securities and recent market quotations are not available for some of these securities. Market quotes are generally available only from a limited number of dealers and may not represent firm bids of such dealers or prices for actual sales. As of De-

cember 31, 1988, the Company's five largest investments in corporate debt securities aggregated $35 million, none of which individually exceeded $10 million, and had an approximate market value of $31 million.

501.06.c. Effects of Federal Financial Assistance Upon Operations

Many financial institutions, such as thrifts and banks, are receiving financial assistance in connection with federally assisted acquisitions or restructurings. Such assistance may take various forms and is intended to make the surviving financial institution a viable entity. Examples of such methods of assistance include: a) yield maintenance assistance (which guarantees additional interest on specified interest bearing assets, a level of return on specified noninterest-bearing assets, reimbursement if covered assets are ultimately collected or sold for amounts that are less than a specified amount, or any combination thereof); b) indemnification against certain loss contingencies; c) the purchase of equity securities issued by the institution for cash or a note receivable from the federal agency; and d) arrangements designed to insulate the surviving entity from the economic effects of problem assets acquired from the predecessor financial institution (such as a "put agreement" whereby the surviving institution may "put" troubled loans directly or indirectly to the federal agency at higher than their fair value).

If these or any other types of federal financial assistance have materially affected, or are reasonably likely to have a material future effect upon, financial condition or results of operations, the MD&A should provide disclosure of the nature, amounts, and effects of such assistance.[49]

In the following example, a financial institution discloses the material effects of a federally assisted corporate reorganization. Such disclosure was in addition to various disclosures of the existence and effect of such federal assistance in the description of business portions of the filing (pursuant to Industry Guide 3) and in the registrant's financial statements.

During 1988, earnings for the Company included $60 million of assistance income, including (a) $10 million in indemnity from the Federal Agency in respect of litigation costs associated with the Company's predecessor and (b) $50 million related to the 1988 puts of troubled loans to the Federal Agency under the Company's Put Agreement. The assistance income arises from provisions in the Reorganization agreements that are intended to relieve the Company from the adverse economic effects of litigation and problem assets held by its predecessor. These provisions are intended to place the Company in substan-

---

[49] For a related discussion of the accounting treatment and financial statement disclosure of federal assistance associated with regulatory-assisted acquisitions of banking and thrift institutions, see *EITF Abstracts*, Issue No. 88-19.

tially the same position as if such litigation and problem assets had been assumed by the Federal Agency at the time of the reorganization. Based on existing ecomomic circumstances, management believes that the expiration of the Put Agreement in June 1989 may adversely affect future operations including an increased level of nonperforming loans and loan loss provisions which cannot be recovered pursuant to the Put Agreement.

501.06.d. Preliminary Merger Negotiations

While Item 303 could be read to impose a duty to disclose otherwise undisclosed preliminary merger negotiations, as known events or uncertainties reasonably likely to have material effects on future financial condition or results of operations, the Commission did not intend to apply, and has not applied, Item 303 in this manner.[50] As reflected in the various disclosure requirements under the Securities Act and Exchange Act that specifically address merger transactions, the Commission historically has balanced the informational need of investors against the risk that premature disclosure[51] of negotiations may jeopardize completion of the transaction.[52] In general, the Commission's recognition that registrants have an interest in preserving the confidentiality of such negotiations is clearest in the context of a registrant's continuous reporting obligations under the Exchange Act, where disclosure on Form 8-K of acquisitions or dispositions of assets not in the orindary course of business is triggered by completion of the transaction.[53]

In contrast, where a registrant registers securities for sale under the Securities Act, the Commission requires disclosure of material probable acquisitions and dispositions of businesses, including the financial statements of the business to be acquired or sold.[54] Where the proceeds from the sale of the securities being registered are to be used to finance an acquisition of a business, the registration statement must disclose the intended use of proceeds. Again, accommodating the need for confidentiality of negotiations, registrants are specifically permitted not to disclose in registration statements the identity of the parties and the nature of the business sought if the acquisition is not yet probable and the board of directors determines that the acquisition would be jeopardized.[55]

The Commission's interpretation of Item 303, as applied to preliminary merger negotiations, incorporates the same policy determinations. Accordingly, where disclosure is not otherwise required, and has not otherwise been made, the MD&A need not contain a discussion of the impact of such negotiations where, in the registrant's view, inclusion of such information would jeopardize completion of the transaction. Where disclosure is otherwise required or has otherwise been made by or on behalf of the registrant, the interests in avoiding premature disclosure no longer exist. In such case, the negotiations would be subject to the same disclosure standards under Item 303 as any other known trend, demand, commitment, event or uncertainty. These policy determinations also would extend to preliminary negotiations for the acquisition or disposition of assets not in the ordinary course of business.

501.07. Conclusion

In preparing MD&A disclosure, registrants should be guided by the general purpose of the MD&A requirements: to give investors an opportunity to look at the registrant through the eyes of management by providing a historical and pro-

---

[50] *See, e.g.* Brief for the Securities and Exchange Commission as Amicus Curiae at 7 and note 3, *Basic, Inc. v. Levinson,* supra n. 14; *In the Matter of Carnation Company,* Exchange Act Release No. 22214 (July 8, 1985), 33 SEC Docket (CCH) 874.

[51] *See Basic, Inc. v. Levinson,* supra n. 14, at 985 ("Arguments based on the premise that some disclosure would be 'premature' in a sense are more properly considered under the rubric of an issuer's duty to disclose. The 'secrecy' rationale is simply inapposite to the definition of materiality.").

[52] *See, e.g.,* Securities Exchange Act Release No. 16384 (November 20, 1979) [44 FR 70326, 70336] (considering these conflicting interests in adopting Item 7 of Schedule 14D-9, 17 CFR 240.101, which requires that the subject company of a public tender offer provide two levels of disclosure: (a) a statement as to whether or not "any negotiation [which would result in certain transactions or fundamental changes] is being undertaken or is underway . . . in response to the tender offer," which disclosure need not include "the possible terms of the transaction or the parties thereto" if in the registrant's view such disclosure would jeopardize the negotiations; and (b) a description of "any transaction, board resolution, agreement in principle, or a signed contract" relating to such transactions or changes).

[53] Item 2 of Form 8-K, 17 CFR 249.308. *See also* Item 8 of Form 10-K, 17 CFR 249.31 (excluding pro forma financial

information otherwise called for by Article 11 of Regulation S-K from the financial information required); Item 1 of Form 10-Q, 17 CFR 249.308a, and Rule 10-01 of Regulation S-X, 17 CFR 210.10-01.

With respect to the disposal of a segment of a business, however, Accounting Principles Board Opinion 30 requires that results of operations of the segment be reclassified as discontinued operations, and any estimated loss on disposal be recorded, as of the date management commits itself to a formal plan to dispose of the segment (*i.e.,* the "measurement date"). Filings, including periodic reports under the Exchange Act that contain annual or interim financial statements are required to reflect the prescribed accounting treatment as of the measurement date.

[54] Article 11 of Regulation S-X, 17 CFR 210.11-01 *et seq.* (generally requiring the provision of pro forma financial information where a significant acquisition or disposition "has occurred or is probable"). Entry int o the continuous reporting system by registration under the Exchange Act also requires the provision of such pro forma financial information. Item 13 of Form 10, 17 CFR 249.210. *See also* Item 14 of Schedule 14A, 17 CFR 240.14a-101 (requiring Article 11 pro forma financial information and extensive other information about certain extraordinary transactions if shareholder action is to be taken with respect to such a transaction).

[55] Item 504 of Regulation S-K, 17 CFR 229.504, Instruction 6.

spective analysis of the registrant's financial condition and results of operations, with particular emphasis on the registrant's prospectus for the future. The MD&A requirements are intentionally flexible and general. Because no two registrants are identical, good MD&A disclosure for one registrant is not necessarily good MD&A disclosure for another. The same is true for MD&A disclosure of the same registrant in different years. The flexibility of MD&A creates a framework for providing the marketplace with appropriate information concerning the registrant's financial condition, changes in financial condition and results of operations.

501.08. Inflation Disclosures

The Commission believes that, where material, management for all registered companies should translate inflation into a meaningful discussion of the effects of changing prices on the registrant's business. Consequently, Item 303(a)(3)(iv) requires that registrants include at least a narrative discussion of any material effects of inflation and other changing prices on net sales and revenues and on income from continuing operations. The Commission believes it is important to emphasize that the impact of inflation should be considered significant for discussion based on its materiality using its cumulative impact from the date assets were acquired or obligations incurred. Such determinations should not be based solely on the current year impact of inflation. The Commission's objective is to elicit useful disclosures concerning the impact of inflation without imposing an undue computational burden. Registrants may elect to provide supplemental disclosure on the effects of inflation and other changing prices as provided for in SFAS No. 89, "Financial Reporting and Changing Prices," or otherwise. Registrants that elect to include these supplemental disclosures may provide a cross reference to the location of such information.

501.09. Disclosure Considerations Related to Foreign Operations and Foreign Currency Translation Effects

.a. Background and Discussion

As a result of considerable controversy and criticism related to its Statement of Financial Accounting Standards ("SFAS") No. 8, "Accounting for the Translation of Foreign Currency Transactions and Foreign Currency Financial Statements," the FASB, in January 1979, added a project to its

agenda to reconsider accounting for foreign currency translation. That project turned out to be the most complex and controversial issue faced by the FASB to date. In December 1981, after almost three years of extensive proceedings, the FASB issued SFAS No. 52, "Foreign Currency Translation," which replaces SFAS No. 8. The new standard is effective for fiscal years beginning on or after December 15, 1982, although earlier application is encouraged. In fact, many companies adopted the standard for their 1981 financial statements and many more are expected to do so in 1982.

SFAS No. 52 embraces a methodology different from that of the previous standard and may significantly impact multinational corporations. SFAS No. 52 is also significant in that it represents a very broad, rather than a prescriptive, standard. It sets forth objectives and provides guidelines to be used by managements in meeting those objectives. The standard is designed to (1) provide information that is generally compatible with the expected economic effects of a rate change on an enterprise's cash flows and equity and (2) reflect in consolidated statements the financial results and relationships as measured in the primary currencies in which the individual entities conduct their businesses (i.e., the "functional currencies").[1]

The standard requires the exercise of management judgment in assessing the facts and circumstances of particular situations and applying the guidelines to those facts and circumstances. The principal determination involves the selection of the appropriate functional currency for each of a company's foreign operations.[2] The functional currency guidelines provided by the standard address indicators of the foreign operations' cash flows, sales prices and markets, expenses, financing, and inter-company transactions and arrangements. While application of these guidelines may result in a relatively clear determination in many cases, others will be more difficult. In such cases, the FASB stated that the economic facts and circumstances pertaining to a particular foreign operation shall be assessed in relation to the FASB's stated objectives for foreign currency translation.

Although a broad standard of this type carries with it the risk of decreasing the comparability of reported financial information, it is clear that there may be significant differences in the nature of

---

[1] An entity's functional currency is the currency of the primary economic environment in which the entity operates; normally that is the currency in which an entity primarily generates and expends cash. (Para. 5, SFAS 52)

[2] This determination can have a significant impact on reported financial results. The functional currency approach which SFAS No. 52 imposes differentiates between those operations that are relatively self-contained and integrated within a foreign country and those that are an extension of the parent's domestic operations. It concludes that "translation

adjustments" (which result from consolidating the former) are related to the parent company's net investment in those operations and have no immediate, direct impact on the parent's cash flows. Therefore, those adjustments are not included in determining net income for the period but are presented as part of consolidated stockholders' equity until the parent's investment in that operation is sold or liquidated. "Transaction gains and losses" (which result from the consolidation of all other foreign operations, as well as most other foreign currency transactions) are accounted for and reported in net income, as was the case under SFAS No. 8.

foreign operations both within a particular company and among companies, even those within the same industry.[3] The new standard gives managements the necessary flexibility to appropriately match reported accounting results with economic facts and circumstances. Ultimately, however, the success of SFAS No. 52 (and the usefulness of the concept of broad standards of financial reporting in general) depends on the confidence of the investment community in its application which in turn is heavily dependent on the quality of related disclosures.

SFAS No. 52 requires disclosure of the aggregate transaction gain or loss included in determining net income and an analysis of the changes during the period in the separate component of equity for cumulative translation adjustments. SFAS No. 52 also states that it may be necessary to disclose significant rate changes occurring after the date of the enterprise's financial statements or after the date of the foreign currency statements of a foreign entity (if different), and their effect on unsettled balances pertaining to foreign currency transactions. In addition, the FASB encouraged management to supplement the disclosures required by SFAS No. 52 with an analysis and discussion of the effects of rate changes on the reported results of operations. The FASB stated that the purpose of such supplemental disclosures is to assist financial report users in understanding the broader economic implications of rate changes and to compare recent results with those of prior periods.[4] The FASB considered requiring disclosure that would describe and possibly quantify the effects of rate changes on reported revenues and earnings, but decided not to, primarily because of the wide variety of potential effects, the perceived difficulties of developing the information, and the impracticality of providing meaningful guidelines.[5]

501.09.b. Disclosure Considerations

In review of a sample of annual reports of registrants who adopted SFAS No. 52 for their 1981 financial statements, the Commission's staff observed compliance with the specific disclosure requirements as well as certain voluntary supplemental disclosures of the type encouraged by the Board.[6] While SFAS No. 52 does not require disclosure as to a company's functional currencies or the extent to which foreign operations are measured in a currency other than the reporting currency, most companies disclosed (either explicitly or by implication) that either "all" or "most" of their foreign operations were measured in the local currency. Frequently, it was disclosed that exceptions were made for operations in high inflation countries (in some cases specific countries were named). A significant number of companies; however, only stated that "certain" operations were measured in a local currency or provided no disclosure as to the extent of foreign operations so measured. Some companies disclosed that the related translation adjustments did not impact cash flow or were unrealized.

The Commission believes that information as to the nature of a registrant's foreign operations gained as a result of implementing SFAS No. 52[7] could be used to develop improved disclosures relating to foreign operations and foreign currency translation effects, including information as to functional currencies. Such disclosures could provide meaningful information to investors and others who are attempting to understand the impact of a registrant's foreign operations on the financial statements. Segment disclosures provide information about the nature and extent of a company's foreign operations, but the standards inherent in SFAS No. 52 are premised on the fact that there may be significant differences in economic substance among various foreign operations—i.e., different exposure to exchange rate risk and different impact on cash flow, with resulting different accounting treatment. The Commission recognizes that this is a complex area and, thus, is not specifying the location[8] or nature of the particular

---

[3] Because of the nature of the standard and the complexity of the issues involved, the FASB has formed an implementation group to advise its staff of possible implementation problems. The Commission believes that it is important to identify and deal with implementation problems by providing timely guidance where necessary or appropriate.

[4] Paragraph 144, SFAS No. 52.

[5] Ibid.

[6] In 1981, the dollar significantly strengthened against many major foreign currencies and thus frequently had a depressing effect on reported sales and operations. Many companies in the staff's sample referred to the effect of the strong dollar. A significant number quantified the effect on sales; some also provided a quantification of the effect on operating results. A few companies discussed their foreign operating results as reflected in the local currency, with the effects of translation noted. Other disclosures included the effects of exchange rate changes on backlog, interest expense, wages, cost of raw material purchased from the parent, transactions between subsidiaries, inventory levels, debt to equity ratio, working capital, effective tax rate, and cost of

sales. The Commission encourages continuing experimentation by individual registrants in an effort to achieve meaningful disclosures in this area.

[7] Successful implementation of SFAS No. 52 requires a fundamental evaluation of the nature of each of a company's foreign operations. Often, this will require input from management personnel involved in various activities within the company. Also, investment objectives with respect to individual foreign operations will need to be reevaluated (e.g., amounts of intercompany accounts considered to be "permanent" advances).

[8] The management's discussion and analysis section may be used for these additional disclosures. The Commission's requirements for Management's Discussion and Analysis of Financial Condition and Results of Operations in Item 303 of Regulation S-K (17 CFR Part 229) are designed to elicit information necessary to an understanding of a registrant's financial statements. This is to be accomplished by providing information enabling an evaluation of the amounts and certainty of cash flows from operations and a registrant's ability to generate adequate amounts of cash to meet its needs for

---

disclosures to be made. Indeed, information such as a display of net investments by major functional currency or an analysis of the translation component of equity (either by significant functional currency or by geographical areas used for segment disclosure purposes) will not always be practicable. Nevertheless, the Commission encourages experimentation with narrative information, such as disclosure about the functional currencies used to measure significant foreign operations or the degree of exposure to exchange rate risks (which exists for all companies engaged in foreign operations, regardless of their functional currencies), in order to enable investors to assess the impact of exchange rate changes on the reporting entity.[9]

There follows a discussion of two specific situations which registrants may wish to explain to investors. When a registrant determines that the financial data of significant foreign operations should be measured in other than the reporting currency, there may be an indication that all or some of those operations' cash flows are generally not available to meet the company's other short-term needs for cash. Thus, it may be appropriate that such a registrant discuss those operations in a disaggregated manner in order to meaningfully address liquidity and capital resource considerations.[10] A discussion of the company's intracompany financing practices may also be meaningful in this regard. Of course, if those foreign cash flows are generally available to meet the parent's cash needs and the local functional currency determinations result from a preponderance of the other evaluative factors specified by SFAS No. 52, discussion of that fact would facilitate understanding of the registrant's operations.

Another example relates to significant foreign operations in highly inflationary economies. In SFAS No. 52, the FASB adopted a pragmatic solution to the problems resulting from the lack of a stable measuring unit (i.e., those operations' financial data must be measured in the reporting currency). As a result, the translation effects of rate changes are included in net income even though the operations may be relatively self-contained or have other environmental characteristics such that remittances to the parent are unlikely.[11] In

such cases, discussion only of consolidated, or even reporting currency, liquidity and capital resources may not be sufficient.

501.09.c. Disclosures During the Transition Period

Adoption of SFAS No. 52 is mandatory for fiscal years beginning on or after December 15, 1982, with earlier application encouraged. The financial statements for prior years *may* be restated to conform to the new standard and, if not restated, companies *may* present disclosure of earnings data for the prior year computed on a pro forma basis. Companies that adopted the standard for fiscal years ending *on or before March 31, 1982* were required to disclose the effect of adopting the new standard on earnings data for the year of the change in order to provide comparability with companies still using SFAS No. 8; that disclosure is not required for fiscal years ending after that date.

The Board determined that the extended mandatory effective date was appropriate to provide sufficient time for companies to make any desired changes in financial policies that might be prompted by the new standard and to prepare internally for the implementation of the standard. The Board did not require restatement because it recognized that the accounting exposure determined in accordance with SFAS No. 8 had been hedged by the management of some companies and that different management actions might have been taken if SFAS No. 8 had not been in effect. Finally, the Board did not extend the requirement to disclose the effect of adopting the standard to years ending after March 31, 1982 because it believed that many companies will have terminated some or all hedges of the SFAS No. 8 accounting exposure, thereby making any meaningful determination of the effect virtually impossible. In addition, the Board believed that the cost of requiring two systems of translation beyond early 1982 was not justified.

The Commission understands the rationale for the transition provisions outlined above. Nonetheless, the Commission is concerned about the adequacy of disclosure about the effects of accounting changes.[12] Financial statement users have a natu-

---

(Footnote Continued)

cash (liquidity) as well as an assessment of the impact of events that have had, or may have, a material effect on trends of operating results.

[9] The Commission also believes that a discussion as to the nature of the translation component of equity may assist investors in understanding the reported financial condition. This may be particularly important due to the fact that the Commission's staff has been advised that some analysts and others may be arbitrarily adjusting reported earnings for the translation adjustments. Meaningful disclosure about a company's foreign operations may help to overcome this tendency.

[10] Item 303(a) of Regulation S-K states in part that "where in the registrant's judgment a discussion of segment informa-

tion or of other subdivisions of the registrant's business would be appropriate to an understanding of such business, the discussion shall focus on each relevant reportable segment or other subdivision of the business and on the registrant as a whole."

[11] Similarly, the functional currency for foreign operations which are experiencing financial difficulties such that additional capital investments may be necessary may also be determined to be the reporting currency.

[12] In several of the annual reports included in the staff's sample, a substantial portion of record (or otherwise increased) earnings was attributable to the adoption of SFAS No. 52. While the 1981 effect of the accounting change was disclosed in the financial statements, information outside the

ral tendency to assume that accounting results are prepared using a consistent methodology throughout the reporting period and from year to year. Indeed, users have a right to make that assumption and the trends in reported financial results are a particularly useful indicator of a company's progress. Where accounting results and the trends therein are materially impacted by accounting changes, it is incumbent upon the registrant to clearly bring this fact to the attention of users, together with such other information which may be necessary to enable investors to adequately assess reported results.[13]

For those registrants that adopt SFAS No. 52 in 1982 or thereafter, the Commission believes that, where appropriate, useful information as to comparability can be best provided by restating prior years' financial statements (or making appropriate pro forma disclosures) and by disclosing the effect of the change on results of operations for the current year. However, the Commission understands that, for the reasons considered by the FASB in adopting the transition provisions included in SFAS No. 52, presentation of such information may not always be meaningful (or computation thereof may not be practicable). In such instances, the Commission expects registrants to discuss this fact and the reasons therefor. In this regard, registrants should consider discussing any modifications of operating, financing, or hedging practices which have been effected.

The Commission also believes that registrants that have not yet adopted SFAS No. 52 should discuss the potential effects of adoption in registration statements and reports filed with the Commission.

501.10. Disclosures Relating to Use of Repurchase and Reverse Repurchase Agreements

Under Item 303 of Regulation S-K, registrants have an obligation to include in the management's discussion and analysis ("MD&A") appropriate disclosure of any material impact on liquidity and operations, or risk due to significant exposure as a result of repurchase and reverse repurchase agreements. In addressing the impact on operations for any given period, registrants would, of course, have to consider all transactions during the period—not only those existing at the balance sheet date.

Repurchase and reverse repurchase agreements can be timed to close at particular points in time. This fact does not affect the obligations to include in the MD&A appropriate disclosure of any material impact on liquidity and operations, or risk due to significant exposure as a result of repurchase and reverse repurchase agreements.

Material deviations from a stated policy regarding taking possession of assets under reverse repurchase agreements are required to be disclosed. Also, the disclosure of provisions to ensure that the market value of the underlying assets remain sufficient to protect the registrant in the event of a counterparty default must be sufficiently detailed to accurately reflect registrant's positions.

501.11. Disclosure of the Effects of the Tax Reform Act of 1986

[*Sec. 501.08 added by FRR-26.*]

a. Background

On October 22, 1986, the President signed the Act, which significantly changes the federal income taxation of corporations. Its provisions include an overall reduction in corporate income tax rates, the elimination of the investment tax credit and reduction of investment tax credit carryforwards, changes in depreciation rates and lives and various provisions which affect specific industries. For many registrants, the reduction in corporate tax rates will cause future payments of deferred tax amounts to be at rates which are significantly lower than those used to determine the deferred income tax provision under Accounting Principles Board Opinion (APB) No. 11.

On September 2, 1986, the Financial Accounting Standards Board (FASB) requested public comment on the ED, which would supersede APB No. 11 as the authoritative literature on accounting for income taxes in financial statements prepared in accordance with generally accepted accounting principles (GAAP). The principles proposed in the ED would significantly change the manner in which income taxes are accounted for under GAAP. APB No. 11 presently utilizes a deferred credit approach under which deferred taxes are provided based on the tax rates during the current year without consideration of, or adjustment for, subsequent changes in future tax rates. In contrast, the ED proposes a liability approach under which deferred taxes would be provided based on enacted tax rates which would apply during the period the taxes become payable. Deferred tax liabilities would then be subsequently adjusted for changes in future tax rates. The ED would also require companies to provide deferred taxes on certain differences between financial and income

---

(Footnote Continued)

financial statements focused a high level of attention on the strength of the reported results without providing adequate information to permit an evaluation of the comparability of those results particularly since, in each of these cases, companies did not restate or provide pro forma disclosures.

[13] Item 301 of Regulation S-K [17 CFR 229.301] requires the presentation of certain selected financial data, the purpose

of which is to supply in a convenient and readable format data which highlight certain significant trends in the registrant's financial condition and results of operations. The instructions to that item require a description of factors, such as accounting changes, that materially affect the comparability of the information reflected.

tax reporting which are not currently required under APB No. 11 and would be more restrictive than APB No. 11 with respect to the recognition of deferred tax debits (assets).

501.11.b. Types of Disclosure

The provisions of the Act will impact the timing and amount of taxes payable upon the reversal of book/tax differences for which deferred tax amounts have previously been provided. They may also affect future financial position, liquidity and results of operations for certain registrants.

501.11.b.i. Effects on Existing Deferred Tax Amounts

The reductions in corporate tax rates may result in actual tax payments, when book/tax differences reverse, which are lower than the related deferred tax amounts which were previously established. This savings of liquid assets may, however, be partially offset by the reduction of investment tax credit carryforwards. Additionally, the timing of the payments of deferred tax amounts for some registrants may be accelerated by the amended alternative minimum tax. The interaction of these provisions of the Act and the liability approach in the ED would, for many registrants, produce a significant reduction in recorded deferred taxes when a final standard is applied in the preparation of registrants' financial statements.

Quantification by registrants of the potential effects of FASB exposure drafts is not generally required since any final standards may differ from those proposed in the exposure draft. However, some registrants may desire to present disclosures which quantify the effects of the Act on their existing deferred tax liabilities through the application of the liability method of accounting for income taxes because they believe such disclosures are practicable and informative. Disclosures quantifying those effects may be made as discussed below under "Quantification of Effects on Existing Deferred Tax Amounts."

Regulation S-K, Item 303 "Management's Discussion and Analysis of Financial Condition and Results of Operations" ("MD&A") (17 C.F.R. 229.303) calls for the discussion of any known trends or events or uncertainties that a registrant reasonably expects will have a material impact on liquidity or income from continuing operations.[1]

As previously indicated, certain provisions of the Act will affect registrant's future liquidity through their effect on the amount and timing of future tax payments upon the reversal of book/tax differences for which deferred tax amounts were

previously established. Registrants which do not elect to present disclosures which quantify the effects of the Tax Reform Act on existing deferred tax amounts should, nonetheless, discuss these potential effects on future liquidity, if material, as required by the MD&A rules. Such discussions should include both the potential effects upon reversal of book/tax differences for which deferred taxes have been provided and the potential effects upon the reversal of book/tax differences for which deferred taxes have not been provided pursuant to APB No. 23.[2]

501.11.b.ii. Other Effects

The provisions of the Act will also have potential effects on the results of operations and sources and uses of capital resources in future periods. For example, the repeal of the investment tax credit and the changes in the depreciation rules may affect a registrant's capital expenditure plans, and the changes in the foreign tax credit may affect the structure of foreign operations. While the impact of these provisions may not be quantifiable, the nature of the potential effects should be discussed, if material. This discussion should be presented in addition to the disclosure of the effects of the Tax Reform Act on existing deferred tax amounts and regardless of whether or not a registrant elects to present quantified disclosures of those effects.

501.11.c. Quantification of Effects on Existing Deferred Tax Amounts

Any quantified disclosures of the effects of the Act on existing deferred tax amounts should be based on the application of the ED to the registrant's historical financial statements for the most recent fiscal year.[3] This approach will adjust deferred tax amounts for the changes in the corporate tax rates, reduction of investment tax credit carryforwards and other provisions of the Act and give effect to the provisions of the ED which require the establishment of deferred taxes for items presently not so treated under APB No. 11 or which limit the recognition of deferred tax debits (assets).

The ED includes a proposed delayed effective date of 1991 for its application to the book/tax differences covered by APB No. 23.[4] In preparing quantified disclosure registrants may either (i) apply the provision of ED without regard to the delayed effective date, thus including the deferred tax effects of these differences or (ii) consider the delayed effective date and therefore omit the deferred tax effects of these items.[5] Registrants not

---

[1] Regulation S-K. Items 303(a)(1) and (a)(3)(ii).

[2] APB No. 23 provides that deferred taxes need not be provided for certain timing differences that may not reverse until indefinite future periods. Those timing differences are the undistributed earnings of subsidiaries and corporate joint ventures which will be indefinitely reinvested, certain bad debt reserves of savings and loan associations and policy holder surpluses of stock life insurance companies.

[3] The limitation of pro forma information to the most recent year is consistent with the Commission's rules regarding the disclosure of pro forma financial information in other circumstances.

[4] *See* Footnote 2.

[5] In general, the Commission believes that any disclosures by registrants which discuss and/or quantify the potential

reflecting the deferred tax effects on these book/tax differences in their quantified disclosures should, separately in a note thereto, disclose those book/tax differences and the amount of related deferred taxes[6] not reflected by reason of the proposed delayed effective date. Registrants may also separately discuss the effect on the pro forma amounts of any other provisions of the ED which are of special significance in their circumstances.

The provision for taxes currently payable should be based on the tax rate of 46 percent for 1986 and should not be adjusted to reflect the retroactive application to 1986 of the reduction in tax rates scheduled to take effect in 1987 and 1988. Those reductions in future tax rates are considered only in the calculation of the pro forma deferred tax provision.

Registrants should not use an approach which merely adjusts historical deferred tax provisions based on the difference between historical and future tax rates. For example, an approach that recognizes the reduction in deferred taxes resulting from the lowering of corporate tax rates but fails to give effect to other provisions of the Act and the ED could be misleading.

Registrants electing to present quantified disclosures may display them in narrative form, by the presentation of appropriate pro forma selected financial information, or by the presentation of a complete (condensed or full) pro forma balance sheet and statement of income.

Whichever method is selected, the disclosure should include a discussion of the purpose of the disclosure, the basis of presentation and any significant assumptions utilized in their preparation. The disclosures should also indicate that they were prepared on the basis of the provisions of the ED which could be changed in the issuance of a final statement and that, as a result, the pro forma information could differ from the eventual results of the actual application of a final FASB standard in the preparation of the registrant's historical financial statements.

501.12. Overall Approach to MD&A
[Added by FR-72.]

501.12.a. The Presentation of MD&A

Since the introduction of our MD&A requirements, many companies have become larger, more global and more complex. At the same time, the combination of our rules and investors' demands have led to an increase in the number of subjects and matters addressed in MD&A. For these and other reasons, many companies' MD&A have become necessarily lengthy and complex. Unfortunately, the presentation of the MD&A of too many companies also may have become unnecessarily lengthy, difficult to understand and confusing.

MD&A, like other disclosure, should be presented in clear and understandable language. We understand that complex companies and situations require disclosure of complex matters and we are not in any way seeking over-simplification or "dumbing down" of MD&A. However, we believe that companies can improve the clarity and understandability of their MD&A by using language that is clearer and less convoluted. We believe that efforts by companies to provide clearer and better organized presentations of MD&A can result in more understandable disclosure that does not sacrifice the appropriate level of complexity or nuance. In order to engender better understanding, companies should prepare MD&A with a strong focus on the most important information, provided in a manner intended to address the objectives of MD&A. In particular:

- Companies should consider whether a tabular presentation of relevant financial or other information may help a reader's understanding of MD&A. For example, a company's MD&A might be clearer and more concise if it provides a tabular comparison of its results in different periods, which could include line items and percentage changes as well as other information determined by a company to be useful, followed by a narrative discussion and analysis of known changes, events, trends, uncertainties and other matters. A reader's understanding of a company's fair value calculations or discounted cash flow figures also could, in some situations, be enhanced by providing a tabular summary of the company's various material interest and discount rate assumptions in one location.

- Companies should consider whether the headings they use assist readers in following the flow of, or otherwise assist in understanding, MD&A, and whether additional headings would be helpful in this regard.

- Many companies' MD&A could benefit from adding an introductory section or overview that would facilitate a reader's understanding. As with all disclosure, what companies would

---

(Footnote Continued)

effects of proposed accounting standards should be based on the proposed standards in their entirety. This exception is considered appropriate solely due to the potential significance of the proposed delayed effective date.

[6] The Commission understands that in some instance the precise quantification of those deferred tax effects may be difficult. In particular, the computation of the taxes payable upon the repatriation of foreign earnings can be complex, and the related deferred tax effect may vary dependent on numerous factors including the method by which foreign earnings will be repatriated. Reasonable estimates may be used in the calculation of these effects. Additionally, if the deferred tax effect of applying the ED to the APB No. 23 items could vary significantly depending on certain assumptions (i.e., the method of repatriation), registrants may present the upper and lower limits of the effects together with a discussion of the factors affecting the estimates and the assumptions inherent in each limit, if material.

appropriately include in an introduction or overview will depend on the circumstances of the particular company. As a general matter, an introduction or overview should include the most important matters on which a company's executives focus in evaluating financial condition and operating performance and provide the context for the discussion and analysis of the financial statements. Therefore, an introduction or overview should not be a duplicative layer of disclosure that merely repeats the more detailed discussion and analysis that follows.

• While all required information must of course be disclosed, companies should consider using a "layered" approach. Such an approach would present information in a manner that emphasizes, within the universe of material information that is disclosed, the information and analysis that is most important. This presentation would assist readers in identifying more readily the most important information. Using an overview or introduction is one example of a layered approach. Another is to begin a section containing detailed analysis, such as an analysis of period-to-period information, with a statement of the principal factors, trends or other matters that are the principal subjects covered in more detail in the section.

We would expect a good introduction or overview to provide a balanced, executive-level discussion that identifies the most important themes or other significant matters with which management is concerned primarily in evaluating the company's financial condition and operating results. A good introduction or overview would:

• include economic or industry-wide factors relevant to the company;

• serve to inform the reader about how the company earns revenues and income and generates cash;

• to the extent necessary or useful to convey this information, discuss the company's lines of business, location or locations of operations, and principal products and services (but an introduction should not merely duplicate disclosure in the Description of Business section); and

• provide insight into material opportunities, challenges and risks, such as those presented by known material trends and uncertainties, on which the company's executives are most focused for both the short and long term, as well as the actions they are taking to address these opportunities, challenges and risks.

Because these matters do not generally remain static from period to period, we would expect the

introduction to change over time to remain current. As is true with all sections of MD&A, boilerplate disclaimers and other generic language generally are not helpful in providing useful information or achieving balance, and would detract from the purpose of the introduction or overview.

An introduction or overview, by its very nature, cannot disclose everything and should not be considered by itself in determining whether a company has made full disclosure. Further, the failure to include disclosure of every material item in an introduction or overview should not trigger automatically the application of the "buried facts" doctrine, in which a court would consider disclosure to be false and misleading if its overall significance is obscured because material is "buried," such as in a footnote or an appendix.[1]

Throughout MD&A, including in an introduction or overview, discussion and analysis of financial condition and operating performance includes both past and prospective matters. In addressing prospective financial condition and operating performance, there are circumstances, particularly regarding known material trends and uncertainties, where forward-looking information is required to be disclosed. We also encourage companies to discuss prospective matters and include forward-looking information in circumstances where that information may not be required, but will provide useful material information for investors that promotes understanding.

501.12.b. The Content and Focus of MD&A

In addition to enhancing MD&A through the use of clearer language and presentation, many companies could improve their MD&A by focusing on the most important information disclosed in MD&A. Disclosure should emphasize material information that is required or promotes understanding and de-emphasize (or, if appropriate, delete) immaterial information that is not required and does not promote understanding.

Our MD&A requirements call for companies to provide investors and other users with material information that is necessary to an understanding of the company's financial condition and operating performance, as well as its prospects for the future.[2] While the desired focus of MD&A for a particular company will depend on the facts and circumstances of the company, some guidance about the content and focus of MD&A is generally applicable.

501.12.b.1. Focus on Key Indicators of Financial Condition and Operating Performance

As discussed, one of the principal objectives of MD&A is to give readers a view of the company through the eyes of management by providing both a short and long-term analysis of the busi-

[1] *See, e.g.,* Final Rule: Plain English Disclosure, Release No. 33-7497 (Jan. 28, 1998) [63 FR 6370 at 6375] (*citing Gould v. American Hawaiian Steamship Company,* 331 F. Supp. 981 (D. Del. 1971); *Kohn v. American Metal Climax, Inc.,* 322 F. Supp. 1331 (E.D. Pa. 1970), *modified,* 458 F.2d 255 (3d Cir. 1972).)

[2] *See* 1989 Release, Part III.A.

ness.[3] To do this, companies should "identify and address those key variables and other qualitative and quantitative factors which are peculiar to and necessary for an understanding and evaluation of the individual company."[4]

Financial measures generally are the starting point in ascertaining these key variables and other factors. However, financial measures often tell only part of how a company manages its business. Therefore, when preparing MD&A, companies should consider whether disclosure of all key variables and other factors that management uses to manage the business would be material to investors, and therefore required.[5] These key variables and other factors may be non-financial, and companies should consider whether that non-financial information should be disclosed.

Many companies currently disclose non-financial business and operational data.[6] Academics, authors, and consultants also have researched the types of information, outside of financial statement measures, that would be helpful to investors and other users.[7] Such information may relate to external or macro-economic matters as well as those specific to a company or industry. For example, interest rates or economic growth rates and their anticipated trends can be important variables for many companies. Industry-specific measures can also be important for analysis, although common standards for the measures also are important. Some industries commonly use non-financial data, such as industry metrics and value drivers.[8] Where a company discloses such information, and there is no commonly accepted method of calculating a particular non-financial metric, it should provide an explanation of its calculation to promote comparability across companies within the industry. Finally, companies may use non-financial performance measures that are company-specific.

In addition, if companies disclose material information (historical or forward-looking) other than in their filed documents (such as in earnings releases or publicly accessible analysts' calls or companion website postings) they also should evaluate that material information to determine whether it is required to be included in MD&A, either because it falls within a specific disclosure requirement or because its omission would render misleading the filed document in which the MD&A appears. We are not seeking to sweep into MD&A all the information that a company communicates. Rather, companies should consider their communications and determine what information is material and is required in, or would promote understanding of, MD&A.

Since we adopted the MD&A requirements, and even since the last comprehensive guidance on MD&A we released in 1989, there have been significant advancements in the ability to develop and access information quickly and effectively. Changes in business enterprise systems, communications and other aspects of information technology have significantly increased the amount of information available to management, as well as the speed with which they receive and are able to use information.[9] There is therefore a larger and more up-to-date universe of information, financial and non-financial alike, that companies have and should evaluate in determining whether disclosure is required. This situation presents companies with the challenge of identifying information that is required to be disclosed or that promotes understanding, while avoiding unnecessary information overload for readers by not disclosing a greater body of information, just because it is available, where disclosure is not required and does not promote understanding. Further, with advances in technology contributing to increasing amounts and currency of information, the factors relied upon by companies to operate and analyze the business may change. As this occurs, the discussion in MD&A should change over time to maintain an appropriate focus on material factors.

---

[3] *See, e.g.*, Release No. 33-6711 (Apr. 24, 1987) [52 FR 13715 at 13717] ("an opportunity to look at the company through the eyes of management by providing both a short and long-term analysis of the business of the company.").

[4] 1989 Release, Part III.A (*citing* Release No. 33-6349 (Sept. 28, 1981) 23 SEC Docket 962 at 964 [Release not published in the Federal Register]).

[5] Examples of such other factors, depending on the circumstances of a particular company, can include manufacturing plant capacity and utilization, backlog, trends in bookings and employee turnover rates. *See, e.g., Quality, Transparency, Accountability*, Lynn E. Turner, Chief Accountant, Securities and Exchange Commission, Remarks before Financial Executives Institute (Apr. 26, 2001), available at www.sec.gov/news/speech/spch485.htm.

Companies should also consider disclosing information that may be peripheral to the accounting function, but is integral to the business or operating activity. Examples of such measures, depending on the circumstances of a particular company, can include those based on units or volume, customer satisfaction, time-to-market, interest rates, product develop-

ment, service offerings, throughput capacity, affiliations/joint undertakings, market demand, customer/vendor relations, employee retention, business strategy, changes in the managerial approach or structure, regulatory actions or regulatory environment, and any other pertinent macroeconomic measures. Because these measures are generally non-financial in nature, we do not believe that their disclosure generally will raise issues under Item 10(e) of Regulation S-K [17 CFR 229.10(e)] or Item 10(h) of Regulation S-B [17 CFR 228.10(h)].

[6] *See Improving Business Reporting: Insights into Enhancing Voluntary Disclosures*, Steering Committee Report of the Business Reporting Research Project of the FASB (2001) available at www.fasb.org; the Jenkins Report; Financial Accounting Series Special Report, *Business and Financial Reporting, Challenges from the New Economy* (FASB) (2001) ("Special Report on Improving Business Reporting").

[7] *See* Special Report on Improving Business Reporting.

[8] *See, e.g.*, the Jenkins Report; the Special Report on Improving Business Reporting.

[9] *See* the Jenkins Report.

The focus on key performance indicators can be enhanced not only through the language and content of the discussion, but also through a format that will enhance the understanding of the discussion and analysis. The order of the information need not follow the order presented in Item 303 of Regulation S-K if another order of presentation would better facilitate readers' understanding. MD&A should provide a frame of reference that allows readers to understand the effects of material changes and events and known material trends and uncertainties arising during the periods being discussed, as well as their relative importance. To satisfy the objectives of MD&A, companies also should provide a balanced view of the underlying dynamics of the business, including not only a description of a company's successes, but also of instances when it failed to realize goals, if material. Good MD&A will focus readers' attention on these key matters.

501.12.b.2. Focus on Materiality

Companies must provide specified material information in their MD&A,[10] and they also must provide other material information that is necessary to make the required statements, in light of the circumstances in which they are made, not misleading.[11] MD&A must specifically focus on known material events and uncertainties that would cause reported financial information not to be necessarily indicative of future operating performance or of future financial condition.[12] Companies must determine, based on their own particular facts and circumstances, whether disclosure of a particular matter is required in MD&A. However, the effectiveness of MD&A decreases with the accumulation of unnecessary detail or duplicative or uninformative disclosure that obscures material information.[13] Companies should view this guidance as an opportunity to evaluate whether there is information in their MD&A that is no longer material or useful, and therefore

should be deleted, for example where there has been a change in their business or the information has become stale.

As the complexity of business structures and financial transactions increase, and as the activities undertaken by companies become more diverse, it is increasingly important for companies to focus their MD&A on material information. In preparing MD&A, companies should evaluate issues presented in previous periods and consider reducing or omitting discussion of those that may no longer be material or helpful, or revise discussions where a revision would make the continuing relevance of an issue more apparent.

Companies also should focus on an analysis of the consolidated financial condition and operating performance, with segment data provided where material to an understanding of consolidated information. Segment discussion and analysis should be designed to avoid unnecessary duplication and immaterial detail that is not required and does not promote understanding of a company's overall financial condition and operating performance.

Both Instruction 4 to Item 303 of Regulation S-K and the 1989 Release address the requirement of discussion and analysis of changes in line items. A review of current MD&A provided by some companies, however, reveals that this is a portion of MD&A that can include an excessive amount of duplicative disclosure, as well as disclosure of immaterial items that do not promote understanding. The 1989 Release explicitly provides for the grouping of line items for purposes of discussion and analysis in a manner that avoids duplicative disclosure. In addition, Instruction 4 and the guidance in the 1989 Release do not require a discussion of every line item and its changes without regard to materiality. Discussion of a line item and its changes should be avoided where the information that would be disclosed is not material and would not promote understanding of MD&A.

---

[10] See, e.g., Item 303(a)(1) of Regulation S-K [17 CFR 229.303(a)(1)] (requiring the identification of "known trends or known demands, commitments, events or uncertainties that will result in or that are reasonably likely to result in the registrant's liquidity increasing or decreasing in any material way"). See also Item 303(a)(2)(i) of Regulation S-K [17 CFR 229.303(a)(2)(i)] (requiring a description of registrant's material commitments for capital expenditures).

[11] See Securities Act Rule 408 [17 CFR 230.408], Securities Exchange Act of 1934 Section 10(b) [15 U.S.C. §78j(b)], Exchange Act Rule 10b-5 [17 CFR 240.10b-5], and Exchange Act Rule 12b-20 [17 CFR 240.12b-20]. See also, In the Matter of Edison Schools, Inc., Release No. 34-45925 (May 14, 2002) (finding, among other things, that the company failed to provide accurate and complete disclosure about its reported revenues); In the Matter of Sony Corporation and Sumio Sano, Release No. 34-40305 (Aug. 5, 1998) (finding that the company violated Section 13(a) of the Exchange Act by making inadequate disclosures about the nature and the extent of Sony Pictures' net losses and their impact on the consolidated results Sony was reporting); In the Matter of Caterpillar Inc., Release No. 34-30532 (Mar. 31, 1992) (finding failure to dis-

close the impact of a subsidiary's foreign operations on the company's results of operations violated Section 13(a) of the Exchange Act).

[12] Instruction 3 to Item 303(a) of Regulation S-K [17 CFR 229.303(a)].

[13] See, e.g., Instruction 4 to Item 303(a) of Regulation S-K (indicating that repetition and line-by-line analysis is not required nor is it appropriate when the causes for a change in one line item also relate to other line items and indicating that, to the extent the changes from year to year are readily computable from the financial statements, the changes need not be recited in the discussion). The 1989 Release also addressed these points directly. See 1989 Release, Part III.D.

Where companies believe that information from the face of financial statements is helpful to readers in MD&A, they should consider using a tabular presentation that shows the decimal percentages of components or year-over-year percentage changes of the financial statement line items. An appropriate analysis of this data, to the extent that it is material, should accompany the tabular presentation consistent with the guidance in Section III.B.3 of this Release.

Companies also must assess the materiality of items in preparing disclosure in their quarterly reports. There may be different quantitative and qualitative factors to consider when deciding whether to include certain information in a specific quarterly or annual report. The 1989 Release addresses some aspects of MD&A disclosure in the context of quarterly filings. That release clarifies that material changes to items disclosed in MD&A in annual reports should be discussed in the quarter in which they occur.[14] There also may be circumstances where an item may not be material in the context of a discussion of annual results of operations but is material in the context of interim results.

Disclosure in MD&A in quarterly reports is complementary to that made in the most recent annual report and in any intervening quarterly reports. Therefore, there may be cases, particularly where adequate disclosure is included in the MD&A in those earlier reports, where further disclosure in a quarterly report is not necessary. If, however, disclosure in those earlier reports does not adequately foreshadow subsequent events, or if new information that impacts known trends and uncertainties becomes apparent in a quarterly period, additional disclosure should be considered and may be required.

501.12.b.3. Focus on Material Trends and Uncertainties

One of the most important elements necessary to an understanding of a company's performance, and the extent to which reported financial information is indicative of future results, is the discussion and analysis of known trends, demands, commitments, events and uncertainties. Disclosure decisions concerning trends, demands, commitments, events, and uncertainties generally should involve the:

- consideration of financial, operational and other information known to the company;

- identification, based on this information, of known trends and uncertainties; and

- assessment of whether these trends and uncertainties will have, or are reasonably likely to have, a material impact on the company's liquidity, capital resources or results of operations.

As we have explained in prior guidance, disclosure of a trend, demand, commitment, event or

uncertainty is required unless a company is able to conclude either that it is not reasonably likely that the trend, uncertainty or other event will occur or come to fruition, or that a material effect on the company's liquidity, capital resources or results of operations is not reasonably likely to occur.[15] (In this release we sometimes use the term "known material trends and uncertainties" to describe trends, demands, commitments, events or uncertainties as to which disclosure is required.)

In identifying known material trends and uncertainties, companies should consider the substantial amount of financial and non-financial information available to them, and whether or not the available information itself is required to be disclosed. This information, over time, may reveal a trend or general pattern in activity, a departure or isolated variance from an established trend, an uncertainty, or a reasonable likelihood of the occurrence of such an event that should be disclosed.

One of the principal objectives of MD&A is to provide information about the quality and potential variability of a company's earnings and cash flow, so that readers can ascertain the likelihood that past performance is indicative of future performance. Ascertaining this indicative value depends to a significant degree on the quality of disclosure about the facts and circumstances surrounding known material trends and uncertainties in MD&A. Quantification of the material effects of known material trends and uncertainties can promote understanding. Quantitative disclosure should be considered and may be required to the extent material if quantitative information is reasonably available.

As discussed in the 1989 Release, the disclosures required to address known material trends and uncertainties in the discussion and analysis should not be confused with optional forward-looking information. Not all forward-looking information falls within the realm of optional disclosure. In particular, material forward-looking information regarding known material trends and uncertainties is required to be disclosed as part of the required discussion of those matters and the analysis of their effects.[16] In addition, forward-looking information is required in connection with the disclosure in MD&A regarding off-balance sheet arrangements.[17]

---

[14] *See* 1989 Release, Part III.E.

[15] *See* January 2002 Release at 3748 ("two assessments management must make where a trend, demand, commitment, event or uncertainty is known: 1. Is the known trend, demand, commitment, event or uncertainty likely to come to fruition? If management determines that it is not reasonably likely to occur, no disclosure is required. 2. If management cannot make that determination, it must evaluate objectively the consequences of the known trend, demand, commitment, event or uncertainty, on the assumption that it will come to

fruition. Disclosure is then required unless management determines that a material effect on the registrant's financial condition or results of operations is not reasonably likely to occur" (*citing* the 1989 Release)).

[16] *See* 1989 Release, Part III.B.

[17] In connection with our adoption of the off-balance sheet arrangements disclosure requirements, we eliminated a portion of the instructions in Item 303 of Regulation S-K that stated that registrants were not required to provide forward-looking information. Deleting that portion of the instructions

501.12.b.4. Focus on Analysis

MD&A requires not only a "discussion" but also an "analysis" of known material trends, events, demands, commitments and uncertainties. MD&A should not be merely a restatement of financial statement information in a narrative form. When a description of known material trends, events, demands, commitments and uncertainties is set forth, companies should consider including, and may be required to include, an analysis explaining the underlying reasons or implications, interrelationships between constituent elements, or the relative significance of those matters.

Identifying the intermediate effects of trends, events, demands, commitments and uncertainties alone, without describing the reasons underlying these effects, may not provide sufficient insight for a reader to see the business through the eyes of management. A thorough analysis often will involve discussing both the intermediate effects of those matters and the reasons underlying those intermediate effects. For example, if a company's financial statements reflect materially lower revenues resulting from a decline in the volume of products sold when compared to a prior period, MD&A should not only identify the decline in sales volume, but also should analyze the reasons underlying the decline in sales when the reasons are also material and determinable. The analysis should reveal underlying material causes of the matters described, including for example, if applicable, difficulties in the manufacturing process, a decline in the quality of a product, loss in competitive position and market share, or a combination of conditions.

Similarly, where a company's financial statements reflect material restructuring or impairment charges, or a decline in the profitability of a plant or other business activity, MD&A should also, where material, analyze the reasons underlying these matters, such as an inability to realize previously projected economies of scale, a failure to renew or secure key customer contracts, or a failure to keep downtime at acceptable levels due to aging equipment. Whether favorable or unfavorable conditions constitute or give rise to the material trends, demands, commitments, events or uncertainties being discussed, the analysis should consist of material substantive information and present a balanced view of the underlying dynamics of the business.

If there is a reasonable likelihood that reported financial information is not indicative of a company's future financial condition or future operating performance due, for example, to the levels of subjectivity and judgment necessary to account for highly uncertain matters and the susceptibility of such matters to change, appropriate disclosure in MD&A should be considered and may be required. For example, if a change in an estimate has a material favorable impact on earnings, the change and the underlying reasons should be disclosed so that readers do not incorrectly attribute the effect to operational improvements. In addition, if events and transactions reported in the financial statements reflect material unusual or non-recurring items, aberrations, or other significant fluctuations, companies should consider the extent of variability in earnings and cash flow, and provide disclosure where necessary for investors to ascertain the likelihood that past performance is indicative of future performance. Companies also should consider whether the economic characteristics of any of their business arrangements, or the methods used to account for them, materially impact their results of operations or liquidity in a structured or unusual fashion, where disclosure would be necessary to understand the amounts depicted in their financial statements.

501.13. Liquidity and Capital Resources

[Added by FR-72.]

Our rules require companies to provide disclosure in the related categories of liquidity and capital resources.[18] This information is critical to an assessment of a company's prospects for the future and even the likelihood of its survival.[19] A company is required to include in MD&A the following information, to the extent material:

- historical information regarding sources of cash and capital expenditures;

- an evaluation of the amounts and certainty of cash flows;

- the existence and timing of commitments for capital expenditures and other known and reasonably likely cash requirements;

- discussion and analysis of known trends and uncertainties;

- a description of expected changes in the mix and relative cost of capital resources;

- indications of which balance sheet or income or cash flow items should be considered in assessing liquidity; and

- a discussion of prospective information regarding companies' sources of and needs for

---

(Footnote Continued)

did not affect requirements to provide forward-looking information in other circumstances where required or reduce the availability of any safe harbor for forward-looking information. *See also* 2003 Off-Balance Sheet Release. *See* Securities Act Section 27A [15 U.S.C. §77z-2], Securities Act Rule 175 [17

CFR 230.175], Exchange Act Section 21E [17 U.S.C. §78u-5], and Exchange Act Rule 3b-6 [17 CFR 240.3b-6].

[18] *See* Item 303(a)(1) and (2) of Regulation S-K [17 CFR 229.303(a)(1) and (2)].

[19] *See* January 2002 Release; 2003 Off-Balance Sheet Release.

capital, except where otherwise clear from the discussion.[20]

Discussion and analysis of this information should be considered and may be required to provide a clear picture of the company's ability to generate cash and to meet existing and known or reasonably likely future cash requirements.

In determining required or appropriate disclosure, companies should evaluate separately their ability to meet upcoming cash requirements over both the short and long term.[21] Merely stating that a company has adequate resources to meet its short-term and/or long-term cash requirements is insufficient unless no additional more detailed or nuanced information is material. In particular, such a statement would be insufficient if there are any known material trends or uncertainties related to cash flow, capital resources, capital requirements, or liquidity.

501.13.a. Cash Requirements

In order to identify known material cash requirements, companies should consider whether the following information would have a material impact on liquidity (discussion of immaterial matters, and especially generic disclosure or boilerplate, should be avoided):

- funds necessary to maintain current operations, complete projects underway and achieve stated objectives or plans;

- commitments for capital or other expenditures;[22] and

- the reasonably likely exposure to future cash requirements associated with known trends or uncertainties, and an indication of the time periods in which resolution of the uncertainties is anticipated.

One starting point for a company's discussion and analysis of cash requirements is the tabular disclosure of contractual obligations,[23] supplemented with additional information that is material to an understanding of the company's cash requirements.[24]

For example, if a company has incurred debt in material amounts, it should explain the reasons for incurring that debt and the use of the proceeds, and analyze how the incurrence of that debt fits into the overall business plan, in each case to the extent material.[25] Where debt has been incurred for general working capital purposes, the anticipated amount and timing of working capital needs should be discussed, to the extent material.[26]

Companies should address, where material, the difficulties involved in assessing the effect of the amount and timing of uncertain events, such as loss contingencies, on cash requirements and liquidity. Any such discussion should be specific to the circumstances and informative, and companies should avoid generic or boilerplate disclosure. In addition, because of these difficulties and uncertainties, companies should consider whether they need to make or change disclosure in connection with quarterly as well as annual reports.

501.13.b. Sources and Uses of Cash

As with the discussion and analysis of the results of operations, a company's discussion and analysis of cash flows should not be a mere recitation of changes and other information evident to readers from the financial statements. Rather, MD&A should focus on the primary drivers of and other material factors necessary to an understanding of the company's cash flows and the indicative value of historical cash flows.

In addition to explaining how the cash requirements identified in MD&A fit into a company's overall business plan, the company should focus on the resources available to satisfy those cash requirements. Where there has been material variability in historical cash flows, MD&A should focus on the underlying reasons for the changes, as well as on their reasonably likely impact on future cash flows and cash management decisions. Even where reported amounts of cash provided and used by operations, investing activities or financing have been consistent, if the underlying sources of those cash flows have materially varied, analysis of that variability should be provided. The discussion and analysis of liquidity should focus on material changes in operating, investing and financing cash flows, as depicted in the statement of cash flows, and the reasons underlying those changes.

---

[20] *See* 1989 Release, Part III.C. *See also* Item 303(a)(1) and (2) of Regulation S-K [17 CFR 229.303(a)(1) and (2)], and Instructions 2 and 5 thereto.

[21] Short-term liquidity is defined as a period of twelve months or less and long-term is defined as a period in excess of twelve months. *See* 1989 Release, Part III.C. Note that the period of time over which a long-term discussion of liquidity is relevant is dependent upon the timing of the cash requirements of a company, as well as the period of time over which cash flows are managed. A vague reference to periods in excess of twelve months may not be sufficient.

[22] *See* Item 303(a)(2)(i) of Regulation S-K [17 CFR 229.303(a)(2)(i)].

[23] *See* Item 303(a)(5) of Regulation S-K [17 CFR 229.303(a)(5)].

[24] For example, the cash requirements for items such as interest, taxes or amounts to be funded to cover post-employment (including retirement) benefits may not be included in the tabular disclosure, but should be discussed if material.

[25] For example, debt may have been issued to fund the construction of a new plant, which will allow the company to expand its operations into a specific geographic area. Understanding that relationship and the expected commencement date of plant operations puts the cash requirement for the debt into an appropriate context to understand liquidity.

[26] Companies are reminded of their related disclosure obligations under Item 504 (Use of Proceeds) of Regulation S-K [17 CFR 229.504] and the requirement to update this disclosure in Item 701(f) (Use of Proceeds) of Regulation S-K [17 CFR 229.701(f)].

501.13.b.1. Operations

The discussion and analysis of operating cash flows should not be limited by the manner of presentation in the statement of cash flows.[27] Alternate accounting methods of deriving and presenting cash flows exist, and while they generally yield the same numeric result in the major captions, they involve the disclosure of different types of information. When preparing the discussion and analysis of operating cash flows, companies should address material changes in the underlying drivers (*e.g.* cash receipts from the sale of goods and services and cash payments to acquire materials for manufacture or goods for resale), rather than merely describe items identified on the face of the statement of cash flows, such as the reconciling items used in the indirect method of presenting cash flows.[28]

For example, consider a company that reports an overall increase in the components of its working capital other than cash[29] with the effect of having a material decrease in net cash provided by operations in the current period. If the increase in working capital was driven principally by an increase in accounts receivable that is attributable not to an increase in sales, but rather to a revised credit policy resulting in an extended payment period for customers, these facts would need to be addressed in MD&A to the extent material, along with the resulting decrease in cash provided by operations, if not otherwise apparent. In addition, if there is a material trend or uncertainty, the impact of the new credit policy on cash flows from operations should be disclosed.[30] While a cash flow statement prepared using the indirect method would report that various individual components of working capital increased or decreased during the period by a specified amount, it would not provide a sufficient basis for a reader to analyze the change. If the company reports negative cash flows from operations, the disclosure provided in MD&A should identify clearly this condition, discuss the operational reasons for the condition if material, and explain how the company intends to meet its cash requirements and maintain operations. If the company relies on external financing in these situations, disclosure of that fact and the company's assessment of whether this financing will continue to be available, and on what terms, should be considered and may be required.

A company should consider whether, in order to make required disclosures, it is necessary to expand MD&A to address the cash requirements of and the cash provided by its reportable segments or other subdivisions of the business, including issues related to foreign subsidiaries, as well as the indicative nature of those results.[31] A company also should discuss the effect of an inability to access the cash flow and financial assets of any consolidated entities. For example, an entity may be consolidated but, because the company lacks sufficient voting interests or the assets are legally isolated, the company may be unable to utilize the entity's cash flow, cash on hand, or other assets to satisfy its own liquidity needs.

501.13.b.2. Financing

To the extent material, a company must provide disclosure regarding its historical financing arrangements and their importance to cash flows, including, to the extent material, information that is not included in the financial statements. A company should discuss and analyze, to the extent material:

- its external debt financing;
- its use of off-balance sheet financing arrangements;
- its issuance or purchase of derivative instruments linked to its stock;
- its use of stock as a form of liquidity; and
- the potential impact of known or reasonably likely changes in credit ratings or ratings outlook (or inability to achieve changes).

In addition to these historical items, discussion and analysis of the types of financing that are, or that are reasonably likely to be, available (or of the types of financing that a company would want to use but that are, or are reasonably likely to be, unavailable) and the impact on the company's cash position and liquidity, should be considered and may be required. For example, where a company has decided to raise or seeks to raise material external equity or debt financing, or if it is reasonably likely to do so in the future, discussion and analysis of the amounts or ranges involved, the nature and the terms of the financing, other features of the financing and plans, and the impact on the company's cash position and liquidity (as well as results of operations in the case of matters such as interest payments) should be considered and may be required.[32]

---

[27] *See* Instruction 4 to Item 303(a) of Regulation S-K [17 CFR 229.303(a)].

[28] *See* SFAS No. 95.

[29] Working capital is defined as current assets less current liabilities. *See* Chapter 3, AICPA Accounting Research Bulletin (ARB) No. 43, *Restatement and Revision of Accounting Research Bulletins* (June 1953).

[30] To the extent that this change also materially impacts results of operations, discussion and analysis would also be required in that section, but companies should attempt to avoid unnecessary or confusing duplication.

[31] *See* Item 303(a) of Regulation S-K [17 CFR 229.303(a)].

[32] We believe that disclosure satisfying the requirements of MD&A can be made consistently with the restrictions of Section 5 of the Securities Act. *See, e.g.*, Securities Act Rules 135c [17 CFR 230.135c].

501.13.c. Debt Instruments, Guarantees and Related Covenants

There are at least two scenarios in which companies should consider whether discussion and analysis of material covenants related to their outstanding debt (or covenants applicable to the companies or third parties in respect of guarantees or other contingent obligations)[33] may be required.[34]

First, companies that are, or are reasonably likely to be, in breach of such covenants[35] must disclose material information about that breach and analyze the impact on the company if material. That analysis should include, as applicable and to the extent material:

- the steps that the company is taking to avoid the breach;

- the steps that the company intends to take to cure, obtain a waiver of or otherwise address the breach;

- the impact or reasonably likely impact of the breach (including the effects of any cross-default or cross-acceleration or similar provisions) on financial condition or operating performance; and

- alternate sources of funding to pay off resulting obligations or replace funding.

Second, companies should consider the impact of debt covenants on their ability to undertake additional debt or equity financing. Examples of these covenants include, but are not limited to, debt incurrence restrictions, limitations on interest payments, restrictions on dividend payments and various debt ratio limits. If these covenants limit, or are reasonably likely to limit, a company's ability to undertake financing to a material extent, the company is required to discuss the covenants in question and the consequences of the limitation to the company's financial condition and operating performance. Disclosure of alternate sources of funding and, to the extent material, the consequences (including but not limited to the cost) of accessing them should also be considered and may be required.

501.13.d. Cash Management

Companies generally have some degree of flexibility in determining when and how to use their cash resources to satisfy obligations and make other capital expenditures. MD&A should describe known material trends or uncertainties relating to such determinations. For example, a decision by a company in a highly capital-intensive business to spend significantly less on plant and equipment than it has historically may result in long-term effects that should be disclosed if material. Material effects could include more cash, less interest expense and lower depreciation, but higher future repair and maintenance expenses or a higher cost base than the company would otherwise have.

501.14. Critical Accounting Estimates

[Added by FR-72.]

Many estimates and assumptions involved in the application of GAAP have a material impact on reported financial condition and operating performance and on the comparability of such reported information over different reporting periods. Our December 2001 Release reminded companies that, under the existing MD&A disclosure requirements, a company should address material implications of uncertainties associated with the methods, assumptions and estimates underlying the company's critical accounting measurements.[36] In May 2002 we proposed rules, which remain under consideration, that would broaden the scope of disclosures beyond those currently required.[37]

When preparing disclosure under the current requirements, companies should consider whether they have made accounting estimates or assumptions where:

- the nature of the estimates or assumptions is material due to the levels of subjectivity and judgment necessary to account for highly uncertain matters or the susceptibility of such matters to change; and

- the impact of the estimates and assumptions on financial condition or operating performance is material.

If so, companies should provide disclosure about those critical accounting estimates or assumptions in their MD&A.

Such disclosure should supplement, not duplicate, the description of accounting policies that are already disclosed in the notes to the financial statements. The disclosure should provide greater insight into the quality and variability of information regarding financial condition and operating performance. While accounting policy notes in the financial statements generally describe the method used to apply an accounting principle, the discussion in MD&A should present a company's analysis of the uncertainties involved in applying a principle at a given time or the variability that is

---

[33] *See* FASB Interpretation No. (FIN) 45, *Guarantor's Accounting and Disclosure Requirements for Guarantees, Including Indirect Guarantees of Indebtedness of Others* (Nov. 2002); 2003 Off-Balance Sheet Release; and the discussion *infra*, regarding off-balance sheet arrangements.

[34] *See In the Matter of America West Airlines, Inc.*, Release No. 34-34047 (May 12, 1994) (finding that the company failed

to discuss uncertainties regarding its ability to comply with covenants).

[35] Companies also must take a similar approach to discussion and analysis with respect to mandatory prepayment provisions, "put" rights and other similar provisions.

[36] December 2001 Release.

[37] *See* 2002 Critical Accounting Policies Proposal.

reasonably likely to result from its application over time.

A company should address specifically why its accounting estimates or assumptions bear the risk of change. The reason may be that there is an uncertainty attached to the estimate or assumption, or it just may be difficult to measure or value. Equally important, companies should address the questions that arise once the critical accounting estimate or assumption has been identified, by analyzing, to the extent material, such factors as how they arrived at the estimate, how accurate the estimate/assumption has been in the past, how much the estimate/assumption has changed in the past, and whether the estimate/assumption is reasonably likely to change in the future. Since critical accounting estimates and assumptions are based on matters that are highly uncertain, a company should analyze their specific sensitivity to change, based on other outcomes that are reasonably likely to occur and would have a material effect. Companies should provide quantitative as well as qualitative disclosure when quantitative information is reasonably available and will provide material information for investors.

For example, if reasonably likely changes in the long-term rate of return used in accounting for a company's pension plan would have a material effect on the financial condition or operating performance of the company, the impact that could result given the range of reasonably likely outcomes should be disclosed and, because of the nature of estimates of long-term rates of return, quantified.

501.15. Climate Change Related Disclosures

[Added by FR-82.]

Overview of rules requiring disclosure of climate change issues

When a registrant is required to file a disclosure document with the Commission, the requisite form will largely refer to the disclosure requirements of Regulation S-K[37] and Regulation S-X.[38] Securities Act Rule 408 and Exchange Act Rule 12b-20 require a registrant to disclose, in addition to the information expressly required by Commission regulation, "such further material information, if any, as may be necessary to make the required statements, in light of the circumstances under which they are made, not misleading."[39] In this section, we briefly describe the most pertinent non-financial statement disclosure rules that

may require disclosure related to climate change; in the following section, we discuss their application to disclosure of certain specific climate change related matters.

A. Description of business.

Item 101 of Regulation S-K requires a registrant to describe its business and that of its subsidiaries. The Item lists a variety of topics that a registrant must address in its disclosure documents, including disclosure about its form of organization, principal products and services, major customers, and competitive conditions. The disclosure requirements cover the registrant and, in many cases, each reportable segment about which financial information is presented in the financial statements. If the information is material to individual segments of the business, a registrant must identify the affected segments.

Item 101 expressly requires disclosure regarding certain costs of complying with environmental laws.[40] In particular, Item 101(c)(1)(xii) states:

Appropriate disclosure also shall be made as to the material effects that compliance with Federal, State and local provisions which have been enacted or adopted regulating the discharge of materials into the environment, or otherwise relating to the protection of the environment, may have upon the capital expenditures, earnings and competitive position of the registrant and its subsidiaries. The registrant shall disclose any material estimated capital expenditures for environmental control facilities for the remainder of its current fiscal year and its succeeding fiscal year and for such further periods as the registrant may deem material.[41]

A registrant meeting the definition of "smaller reporting company" may satisfy its disclosure obligation by providing information called for by Item 101(h). Item 101(h)(4)(xi) requires disclosure of the "costs and effects of compliance with environmental laws (federal, state and local)."[42]

B. Legal proceedings.

Item 103 of Regulation S-K[43] requires a registrant to briefly describe any material pending legal proceeding to which it or any of its subsidiaries is a party. A registrant also must describe material pending legal actions in which its property is the subject of the litigation.[44] If a registrant is aware of similar actions contemplated by governmental authorities, Item 103 requires disclosure of those proceedings as well. A registrant need not dis-

---

[37] 17 CFR Part 229.

[38] 17 CFR Part 210.

[39] 17 CFR 230.408 and 17 CFR 240.12b-20.

[40] The Commission first addressed disclosure of material costs and other effects on business resulting from compliance with existing environmental law in its first environmental disclosure interpretive release in 1971. *See* Release 33-5170 (July 19, 1971) [36 FR 13989]. The Commission codified that interpretive position in the disclosure forms two years later. *See* Release 33-5386 (April 20, 1973) [38 FR 12100]. The

Commission provided additional interpretive guidance in the 1979 Release. With some adjustments to reflect experience with the subject matter, the requirements were moved to Item 101 in 1982, and they have not changed since that time. *See* Release No. 33-6383 (March 3, 1982) [47 FR 11380].

[41] 17 CFR 229.101(c)(1)(xii).

[42] 17 CFR 229.101(h)(4)(xi).

[43] 17 CFR 229.103.

[44] *Id.*

close ordinary routine litigation incidental to its business or other types of proceedings when the amount in controversy is below thresholds designated in this Item.

Instruction 5 to Item 103 provides some specific requirements that apply to disclosure of certain environmental litigation.[45] Instruction 5 states:

Notwithstanding the foregoing, an administrative or judicial proceeding (including, for purposes of A and B of this Instruction, proceedings which present in large degree the same issues) arising under any Federal, State or local provisions that have been enacted or adopted regulating the discharge of materials into the environment or primary for the purpose of protecting the environment shall not be deemed "ordinary routine litigation incidental to the business" and shall be described if:

(A) Such proceeding is material to the business or financial condition of the registrant;

(B) Such proceeding involves primarily a claim for damages, or involves potential monetary sanctions, capital expenditures, deferred charges or charges to income and the amount involved, exclusive of interest and costs, exceeds 10 percent of the current assets of the registrant and its subsidiaries on a consolidated basis; or

(C) A governmental authority is a party to such proceeding and such proceeding involves potential monetary sanctions, unless the registrant reasonably believes that such proceeding will result in no monetary sanctions, or in monetary sanctions, exclusive of interest and costs, of less than $100,000; provided, however, that such proceedings which are similar in nature may be grouped and described generically.

C. Risk factors.

Item 503(c) of Regulation S-K[46] requires a registrant to provide where appropriate, under the heading "Risk Factors," a discussion of the most significant factors that make an investment in the registrant speculative or risky. Item 503(c) specifies that risk factor disclosure should clearly state the risk and specify how the particular risk affects the particular registrant; registrants should not present risks that could apply to any issuer or any offering.[47]

D. Management's discussion and analysis.

Item 303 of Regulation S-K[48] requires disclosure known as the Management's Discussion and Analysis of Financial Condition and Results of Operations, or MD&A. The MD&A requirements are intended to satisfy three principal objectives:

• to provide a narrative explanation of a registrant's financial statements that enables investors to see the registrant through the eyes of management;

• to enhance the overall financial disclosure and provide the context within which financial information should be analyzed; and

• to provide information about the quality of, and potential variability of, a registrant's earnings and cash flow, so that investors can ascertain the likelihood that past performance is indicative of future performance.[49]

MD&A disclosure should provide material historical and prospective textual disclosure enabling investors to assess the financial condition and results of operations of the registrant, with particular emphasis on the registrant's prospects for the future.[50] Some of this information is itself nonfinancial in nature, but bears on registrants' financial condition and operating performance.

The Commission has issued several releases providing guidance on MD&A disclosure, including on the general requirements of the item and its application to specific disclosure matters.[51] Over the years, the flexible nature of this requirement has resulted in disclosures that keep pace with the evolving nature of business trends without the need to continuously amend the text of the rule. Nevertheless, we and our staff continue to have to remind registrants, through comments issued in the filing review process, public statements by staff and Commissioners and otherwise, that the disclosure provided in response to this requirement should be clear and communicate to

---

[45] Instruction 5 in its current form was the product of the Commission's experience with environmental litigation disclosure. In 1973, we added provisions to the legal proceedings requirements of various disclosure forms singling out legal actions involving environmental matters. *See* Release No. 33-5386 (Apr. 20, 1973) [38 FR 12100]. The new rules required disclosure of any pending legal proceeding arising under environmental laws if a governmental entity was involved in the proceeding, and any other legal proceeding arising under environmental laws unless it was not material, or if in a civil suit for damages, unless it involved less than 10% of the current assets of the registrant on a consolidated basis. The Commission provided additional interpretive guidance regarding environmental litigation in the 1979 Release. When the Commission, in connection with its development of the integrated disclosure system, moved these rules out of various forms and into Item 103 of Regulation S-K, the Commission modified the requirements related to actions involving gov-

ernmental authorities to allow registrants to omit disclosure of a proceeding if they reasonably believed the action would result in a monetary sanction of less than $100,000. *See* Release No. 33-6383 (Mar. 3, 1982) [47 FR 11380]. At the time, the Commission noted that the reason for the revision was to address the problem that disclosure documents were being filled with descriptions of minor infractions that distracted from the other material disclosures included in the document.

[46] 17 CFR 229.503(c).

[47] *Id.*

[48] 17 CFR 229.303.

[49] 2003 Release.

[50] 1989 Release.

[51] *See, e.g.,* the 2003 Release; Release No. 33-8182 (Jan. 28, 2003) [68 FR 5982]; Release No. 33-8056 (Jan. 22, 2002) [67 FR 3746]; Release. No. 33-7558 (Jul. 29, 1998) [63 FR 41394]; and 1989 Release.

shareholders management's view of the company's financial condition and prospects.[52]

Item 303 includes a broad range of disclosure items that address the registrant's liquidity, capital resources and results of operations. Some of these provisions, such as the requirement to provide tabular disclosure of contractual obligations,[53] clearly specify the disclosure required for compliance. But others instead identify principles and require management to apply the principles in the context of the registrant's particular circumstances. For example, registrants must identify and disclose known trends, events, demands, commitments and uncertainties that are reasonably likely[54] to have a material effect on financial condition or operating performance. This disclosure should highlight issues that are reasonably likely to cause reported financial information not to be necessarily indicative of future operating performance or of future financial condition.[55] Disclosure decisions concerning trends, demands, commitments, events, and uncertainties generally should involve the:

- consideration of financial, operational and other information known to the registrant;

- identification, based on this information, of known trends and uncertainties; and

- assessment of whether these trends and uncertainties will have, or are reasonably likely to have, a material impact on the registrant's liquidity, capital resources or results of operations.[56]

The Commission has not quantified, in Item 303 or otherwise, a specific future time period that must be considered in assessing the impact of a known trend, event or uncertainty that is reasonably likely to occur. As with any other judgment required by Item 303, the necessary time period will depend on a registrant's particular circumstances and the particular trend, event or uncertainty under consideration. For example, a registrant considering its disclosure obligation with respect to its liquidity needs would have to consider the duration of its known capital requirements and the periods over which cash flows are managed in determining the time period of its

disclosure regarding future capital sources.[57] In addition, the time horizon of a known trend, event or uncertainty may be relevant to a registrant's assessment of the materiality of the matter and whether or not the impact is reasonably likely. As with respect to other subjects of disclosure, materiality "with respect to contingent or speculative information or events . . . 'will depend at any given time upon a balancing of both the indicated probability that the event will occur and the anticipated magnitude of the event in light of the totality of the company activity.'"[58]

The nature of certain MD&A disclosure requirements places particular importance on a registrant's materiality determinations. The Commission has recognized that the effectiveness of MD&A decreases with the accumulation of unnecessary detail or duplicative or uninformative disclosure that obscures material information.[59] Registrants drafting MD&A disclosure should focus on material information and eliminate immaterial information that does not promote understanding of registrants' financial condition, liquidity and capital resources, changes in financial condition and results of operations.[60] While these materiality determinations may limit what is actually disclosed, they should not limit the information that management considers in making its determinations. Improvements in technology and communications in the last two decades have significantly increased the amount of financial and non-financial information that management has and should evaluate, as well as the speed with which management receives and is able to use information. While this should not necessarily result in increased MD&A disclosure, it does provide more information that may need to be considered in drafting MD&A disclosure. In identifying, discussing and analyzing known material trends and uncertainties, registrants are expected to consider all relevant information even if that information is not required to be disclosed,[61] and, as with any other disclosure judgments, they should consider whether they have sufficient disclosure controls and procedures to process this information.[62]

---

[52] *See, e.g.,* speech by Commissioner Cynthia A. Glassman to the Corporate Counsel Institute (Mar. 9, 2006) available at www.sec.gov/news/speech/spch030906cag.htm; and speech by Commissioner Elisse B. Walter to the Corporate Counsel Institute (Oct. 2, 2009) available at www.sec.gov/news/speech/2009/spch100209ebw.htm.

[53] 17 CFR 229.303(a)(5).

[54] "Reasonably likely" is a lower disclosure standard than "more likely than not." Release No. 33-8056 (Jan. 22, 2002) [67 FR 3746].

[55] 2003 Release.

[56] *Id.*

[57] *Id.* at n.43.

[58] *Basic* at 238, quoting *Texas Gulf Sulfur Co.*, 401 F. 2d 833 (2d Cir. 1968) at 849.

[59] 2003 Release.

[60] *Id.*

[61] *Id.*

[62] Pursuant to Exchange Act Rules 13a-15 and 15d-15, a company's principal executive officer and principal financial officer must make certifications regarding the maintenance and effectiveness of disclosure controls and procedures. These rules define "disclosure controls and procedures" as those controls and procedures designed to ensure that information required to be disclosed by the company in the reports that it files or submits under the Exchange Act is (1) "recorded, processed, summarized and reported, within the time periods specified in the Commission's rules and forms," and (2) "accumulated and communicated to the company's management . . . as appropriate to allow timely decisions regarding required disclosure." As we have stated before, a

Analyzing the materiality of known trends, events or uncertainties may be particularly challenging for registrants preparing MD&A disclosure. As the Commission explained in the 1989 Release, when a trend, demand, commitment, event or uncertainty is known, "management must make two assessments:

- Is the known trend, demand, commitment, event or uncertainty likely to come to fruition? If management determines that it is not reasonably likely to occur, no disclosure is required.

- If management cannot make that determination, it must evaluate objectively the consequences of the known trend, demand, commitment, event or uncertainty, on the assumption that it will come to fruition. Disclosure is then required unless management determines that a material effect on the registrant's financial condition or results of operations is not reasonably likely to occur."[63]

Identifying and assessing known material trends and uncertainties generally will require registrants to consider a substantial amount of financial and non-financial information available to them, including information that itself may not be required to be disclosed.[64]

Registrants should address, when material, the difficulties involved in assessing the effect of the amount and timing of uncertain events, and provide an indication of the time periods in which resolution of the uncertainties is anticipated.[65] In accordance with Item 303(a), registrants must also disclose any other information a registrant believes is necessary to an understanding of its financial condition, changes in financial condition and results of operations.

E. Foreign private issuers.

The Securities Act and Exchange Act disclosure obligations of foreign private issuers are governed principally by Form 20-F's[66] disclosure requirements and not those under Regulation S-K. However, most of the disclosure requirements applicable to domestic issuers under Regulation S-K that are most likely to require disclosure related to climate change have parallels under Form 20-F, although some of the requirements are not as prescriptive as the provisions applicable to domestic issuers. For example, the following provisions of Form 20-F may require a foreign private issuer

to provide disclosure concerning climate change matters that are material to its business:

- Item 3.D, which requires a foreign private issuer to disclose its material risks;

- Item 4.B.8, which requires a foreign private issuer to describe the material effects of government regulation on its business and to identify the particular regulatory body;

- Item 4.D, which requires a foreign private issuer to describe any environmental issues that may affect the company's utilization of its assets;

- Item 5, which requires management's explanation of factors that have affected the company's financial condition and results of operations for the historical periods covered by the financial statements, and management's assessment of factors and trends that are anticipated to have a material effect on the company's financial condition and results of operations in future periods; and

- Item 8.A.7, which requires a foreign private issuer to provide information on any legal or arbitration proceedings, including governmental proceedings, which may have, or have had in the recent past, significant effects on the company's financial position or profitability.

Forms F-1[67] and F-3,[68] Securities Act registration statement forms for foreign private issuers, also require a foreign private issuer to provide the information, including risk factor disclosure, required under Regulation S-K Item 503.

Climate change related disclosures

In the previous section we summarized a number of Commission rules and regulations that may be the source of a disclosure obligation for registrants under the federal securities laws. Depending on the facts and circumstances of a particular registrant, each of the items discussed above may require disclosure regarding the impact of climate change. The following topics are some of the ways climate change may trigger disclosure required by these rules and regulations.[69] These topics are examples of climate change related issues that a registrant may need to consider.

A. Impact of legislation and regulation.

As discussed above, there have been significant developments in federal and state legislation and regulation regarding climate change. These devel-

---

(Footnote Continued)

company's disclosure controls and procedures should not be limited to disclosure specifically required, but should also ensure timely collection and evaluation of "information potentially subject to [required] disclosure," "information that is relevant to an assessment of the need to disclose developments and risks that pertain to the [company's] businesses," and "information that must be evaluated in the context of the disclosure requirement of Exchange Act Rule 12b-20." Release No. 33-8124 (Aug. 28, 2002) [67 FR 57276].

[63] 1989 Release.

[64] 2003 Release

[65] Id.

[66] 17 CFR 249.220f.

[67] 17 CFR 239.31.

[68] 17 CFR 239.33.

[69] In addition to the Regulation S-K items discussed in this section, registrants must also consider any financial statement implications of climate change issues in accordance with applicable accounting standards, including Financial Accounting Standards Board ("FASB") Accounting Standards Codification Topic 450, Contingencies, and FASB Accounting Standards Codification Topic 275, Risks and Uncertainties.

opments may trigger disclosure obligations under Commission rules and regulations, such as pursuant to Items 101, 103, 503(c) and 303 of Regulation S-K. With respect to existing federal, state and local provisions which relate to greenhouse gas emissions, Item 101 requires disclosure of any material estimated capital expenditures for environmental control facilities for the remainder of a registrant's current fiscal year and its succeeding fiscal year and for such further periods as the registrant may deem material. Depending on a registrant's particular circumstances, Item 503(c) may require risk factor disclosure regarding existing or pending legislation or regulation that relates to climate change. Registrants should consider specific risks they face as a result of climate change legislation or regulation and avoid generic risk factor disclosure that could apply to any company. For example, registrants that are particularly sensitive to greenhouse gas legislation or regulation, such as registrants in the energy sector, may face significantly different risks from climate change legislation or regulation compared to registrants that currently are reliant on products that emit greenhouse gases, such as registrants in the transportation sector.

Item 303 requires registrants to assess whether any enacted climate change legislation or regulation is reasonably likely to have a material effect on the registrant's financial condition or results of operation.[70] In the case of a known uncertainty, such as pending legislation or regulation, the analysis of whether disclosure is required in MD&A consists of two steps. First, management must evaluate whether the pending legislation or regulation is reasonably likely to be enacted. Unless management determines that it is not reasonably likely to be enacted, it must proceed on the assumption that the legislation or regulation will be enacted. Second, management must determine whether the legislation or regulation, if enacted, is reasonably likely to have a material effect on the registrant, its financial condition or results of operations. Unless management determines that a material effect is not reasonably likely,[71] MD&A disclosure is required.[72] In addition to disclosing the potential effect of pending legislation or regulation, the registrant would also have to consider disclosure, if material, of the difficulties involved in assessing the timing and effect of the pending legislation or regulation.[73]

A registrant should not limit its evaluation of disclosure of a proposed law only to negative consequences. Changes in the law or in the business practices of some registrants in response to the law may provide new opportunities for registrants. For example, if a "cap and trade" type system is put in place, registrants may be able to profit from the sale of allowances if their emissions levels end up being below their emissions allotment. Likewise, those who are not covered by statutory emissions caps may be able to profit by selling offset credits they may qualify for under new legislation.

Examples of possible consequences of pending legislation and regulation related to climate change include:

- Costs to purchase, or profits from sales of, allowances or credits under a "cap and trade" system;

- Costs required to improve facilities and equipment to reduce emissions in order to comply with regulatory limits or to mitigate the financial consequences of a "cap and trade" regime; and

- Changes to profit or loss arising from increased or decreased demand for goods and services produced by the registrant arising directly from legislation or regulation, and indirectly from changes in costs of goods sold.

We reiterate that climate change regulation is a rapidly developing area. Registrants need to regularly assess their potential disclosure obligations given new developments.

B. International accords.

Registrants also should consider, and disclose when material, the impact on their business of treaties or international accords relating to climate change. We already have noted the Kyoto Protocol, the EU ETS and other international activities in connection with climate change remediation. The potential sources of disclosure obligations related to international accords are the same as those discussed above for U.S. climate change regulation. Registrants whose businesses are reasonably likely to be affected by such agreements should monitor the progress of any potential agreements and consider the possible impact in satisfying their disclosure obligations based on the MD&A and materiality principles previously outlined.

C. Indirect consequences of regulation or business trends.

Legal, technological, political and scientific developments regarding climate change may create new opportunities or risks for registrants. These developments may create demand for new prod-

---

[70] *See* 1989 Release.

[71] Management should ensure that it has sufficient information regarding the registrant's greenhouse gas emissions and other operational matters to evaluate the likelihood of a material effect arising from the subject legislation or regulation. *See* n. 62, *supra.*

[72] In 2003 we issued additional guidance with respect to how registrants could improve MD&A disclosure, including

ideas about how to focus on material issues and how to present information in a more effective manner to be of more value to investors. *See* 2003 Release.

[73] *See* 2003 Release for a discussion of how companies should address, where material, the difficulties involved in assessing the effect of the amount and timing of uncertain events.

ucts or services, or decrease demand for existing products or services. For example, possible indirect consequences or opportunities may include:

- Decreased demand for goods that produce significant greenhouse gas emissions;
- Increased demand for goods that result in lower emissions than competing products;[74]
- Increased competition to develop innovative new products;
- Increased demand for generation and transmission of energy from alternative energy sources; and
- Decreased demand for services related to carbon based energy sources, such as drilling services or equipment maintenance services.

These business trends or risks may be required to be disclosed as risk factors or in MD&A. In some cases, these developments could have a significant enough impact on a registrant's business that disclosure may be required in its business description under Item 101. For example, a registrant that plans to reposition itself to take advantage of potential opportunities, such as through material acquisitions of plants or equipment, may be required by Item 101(a)(1) to disclose this shift in plan of operation. Registrants should consider their own particular facts and circumstances in evaluating the materiality of these opportunities and obligations.

Another example of a potential indirect risk from climate change that would need to be considered for risk factor disclosure is the impact on a registrant's reputation. Depending on the nature of a registrant's business and its sensitivity to public opinion, a registrant may have to consider whether the public's perception of any publicly available data relating to its greenhouse gas emissions could expose it to potential adverse consequences to its business operations or financial condition resulting from reputational damage.

D. Physical impacts of climate change.

Significant physical effects of climate change, such as effects on the severity of weather (for example, floods or hurricanes), sea levels, the arability of farmland, and water availability and quality,[75] have the potential to affect a registrant's operations and results. For example, severe weather can cause catastrophic harm to physical plants and facilities and can disrupt manufacturing and distribution processes. A 2007 Government Accountability Office report states that 88% of all property losses paid by insurers between 1980 and

2005 were weatherrelated.[76] As noted in the GAO report, severe weather can have a devastating effect on the financial condition of affected businesses. The GAO report cites a number of sources to support the view that severe weather scenarios will increase as a result of climate change brought on by an overabundance of greenhouse gases.

Possible consequences of severe weather could include:

- For registrants with operations concentrated on coastlines, property damage and disruptions to operations, including manufacturing operations or the transport of manufactured products;
- Indirect financial and operational impacts from disruptions to the operations of major customers or suppliers from severe weather, such as hurricanes or floods;
- Increased insurance claims and liabilities for insurance and reinsurance companies[77];
- Decreased agricultural production capacity in areas affected by drought or other weather-related changes; and
- Increased insurance premiums and deductibles, or a decrease in the availability of coverage, for registrants with plants or operations in areas subject to severe weather.

Registrants whose businesses may be vulnerable to severe weather or climate related events should consider disclosing material risks of, or consequences from, such events in their publicly filed disclosure documents.

[¶ 38,285] 502. Management Reports

[In April 1979, the Commission proposed rules which would have required certain disclosures about a registrant's system of internal accounting control in certain Commission filings and in annual reports to security holders. In ASR 278, June 1980, the Commission withdrew those rule proposals and announced its intention to monitor private-sector activities in this area. In ASR 305, January 1982, the Commission announced that it is no longer considering further action to require such disclosures.]

.01. Background

ASR 305:

On June 6, 1980, the Commission issued ASR 278 that announced the withdrawal of rule proposals which, if adopted, would have required inclusion of a statement of management on internal accounting control in annual reports on Form 10-K filed with the Commission under the Exchange

---

[74] For example, recent legislation will ultimately phase out most traditional incandescent light bulbs. This has resulted in the acceleration of the development and marketing of compact fluorescent light bulbs. *See* Energy Independence and Security Act of 2007, Pub. L. No. 110-140, 121 Stat. 1492 (2007).

[75] *See* "Climate Change: Financial Risks to Federal and Private Insurers in Coming Decades Are Potentially Significant: U.S. Government Accountability Office Report to the

Committee on Homeland Security and Governmental Affairs, U.S. Senate," GAO-07-285 (March 2007).

[76] *Id.* at p.17.

[77] Many insurers already have plans in place to address the increased risks that may arise as a result of climate change, with many reducing their near-term catastrophic exposure in both reinsurance and primary insurance coverage along the Gulf Coast and the eastern seaboard. *Id.* at 32.

Act and in annual reports to security holders furnished pursuant to the proxy rules. The rule proposals would also have required that the management statement be examined and reported on by an independent accountant.

The Commission's decision to withdraw the rule proposals was based, in part, on a determination that the private-sector initiatives for public reporting on internal accounting control had been significant and should be allowed to continue. The Commission stated its belief that this action would encourage further voluntary initiatives and permit public companies a maximum of flexibility in experimenting with various approaches to public reporting on internal accounting control. The Commission urged similar experimentation concerning auditor association with such statements.

In conjunction with the withdrawal of the rule proposals, the Commission announced its intention to monitor registrants' voluntary disclosure of management statements on internal accounting control and reports of independent accountants on such statements and implementation of the broader recommendations of the Commission on Auditors' Responsibilities (Cohen Commission) concerning comprehensive management reports.

502.02. Activities After ASR 278
ASR 305:

Since ASR 278 was issued, the Commission's staff has reviewed a sample of annual reports to security holders. The results of the review indicate a significant increase, particularly in larger companies, in the number of annual reports which include a management report. Several surveys conducted by private-sector organizations indicate similar results.

In addition to comments about the system of internal accounting control, many reports have included comments on topics recommended by the Cohen Commission, the FEI and the Special Advisory Committee on Reports by Management of the AICPA. The variety of reports demonstrates the willingness of public companies to experiment with a new form of reporting and to avoid boilerplate reporting.

Certain private-sector groups have taken actions which indicate that the private sector continues to be generally supportive of the development of the concept of management reports and is seeking to improve internal accounting control systems. As noted in ASR 278, the AICPA and FEI have encouraged the development of management statements. In August 1981, the American Bar Association Section of Corporation, Banking and Business Law approved a Discussion Paper which encourages the use of company reports. In addition, the FEI has sponsored extensive research in the area of internal controls. This research resulted in the publication in 1980 of a research study and report titled "Internal Control in U.S. Corporations: The State of the Art" and in 1981 a

report on "Criteria for Management Systems." An additional research project is exploring criteria for management use and control of data processing systems. The Commission is encouraged by this kind of private-sector research effort which should lead to continued improvements in corporate internal control systems.

The experimentation with public reporting by independent accountants on internal accounting control systems has not yet had time to develop. In July 1980, the ASB issued SAS 30, "Reporting on Internal Accounting Control," which sets forth guidance for auditors on how to review and report on a system of internal accounting control. As companies and their auditors become more familiar with the provisions of SAS 30 they may be able to integrate SAS 30 review procedures into annual audit procedures. Such integration may facilitate the conduct of these reviews and could result in increased reporting pursuant to SAS 30.

502.03. Conclusion
ASR 305:

Although the importance to companies of effective systems of internal accounting control has not diminished, the Commission now believes that there is no need for a regulatory requirement for disclosures about such systems. In the light of developments since the issuance of ASR 278, the Commission now believes that the private sector should determine the need for and nature of such disclosure. In reaching this conclusion, the Commission has considered the significant private-sector initiatives in this area, including the increased number of management reports to security holders of large companies.

[¶ 38,291] 503. Industry Segment Reporting
.01. Background
[Amended by FR-54 (Jan. 5, 1999).]

In 1976, the FASB issued SFAS No. 14, "Financial Reporting for Segments of a Business Enterprise." SFAS No. 14 required corporations to disclose certain financial information by "industry segment" as defined in the statement and by geographic area. In December 1977, we adopted amendments to our rules to integrate the information to be furnished under SFAS No. 14 with the narrative and financial disclosures required in various disclosure forms."

After extensive deliberations, including solicitation of public comments, the FASB adopted a number of fundamental changes to its standards for segment reporting by publishing SFAS No. 131 in June of 1997. SFAS No. 131 superseded SFAS No. 14 and established standards for reporting information about "operating segments" of an enterprise rather than following the "industry segment" standards that were in place previously.

On June 25, 1998, the Commission proposed for comment a number of technical changes to its reporting requirements to accommodate these modifications. Twelve commenters responded to the solicitation for public views on the proposed approach. Generally, the commenters were supportive of our efforts to conform our rules with the FASB standards. We have determined to adopt the rules essentially as proposed. We believe that this action is in keeping with our long-standing policy to look to the private sector for the promulgation of generally accepted accounting principles ("GAAP"). It also furthers our goal of integrating existing accounting information into the narrative disclosure in documents mandated by the federal securities laws. This release explains the new reporting requirements.

503.02. Major Customers

[Amended by FR-54 (Jan. 5, 1999).]

Since the adoption of SFAS No. 14, GAAP has required disclosure of revenues from major customers. SFAS No. 131 now requires issuers to disclose the amount of revenues from each external customer that amounts to 10 percent or more of an enterprise's revenue as well as the identity of the segment(s) reporting the revenues. The accounting standards, however, have never required issuers to identify major customers. On the other hand, Regulation S-K Item 101 historically has required naming a major customer if sales to that customer equal 10 percent or more of the issuer's consolidated revenues and if the loss of the customer would have a material adverse effect on the issuer and its subsidiaries. We continue to believe that the identity of major customers is material information to investors. This disclosure allows a reader to better assess risks associated with a particular customer, as well as material concentrations of revenues related to that customer. Consequently, we retain this Regulation S-K requirement, as we proposed.

.a. Class of Products

[FR-54 (Jan. 5, 1999) replaced paragraphs .01, .02 and .03 of Section 503 with new paragraph .01, to include the text of Section I of the release captioned "Background" and with new paragraph .02 to include the text of Section II.B.2 of the release captioned "Major Customers."]

503.02.b. Major Customers

[FR-54 (Jan. 5, 1999) replaced paragraphs .01, .02 and .03 of Section 503 with new paragraph .01, to include the text of Section I of the release captioned "Background" and with new paragraph .02 to include the text of Section II.B.2 of the release captioned "Major Customers."]

503.02.c. Foreign Operations and Export Sales

[FR-54 (Jan. 5, 1999) replaced paragraphs .01, .02 and .03 of Section 503 with new paragraph .01, to include the text of Section I of the release captioned "Background" and with new paragraph .02 to include the text of Section II.B.2 of the release captioned "Major Customers."]

503.02.d. Sample Disclosure

[FR-54 (Jan. 5, 1999) replaced paragraphs .01, .02 and .03 of Section 503 with new paragraph .01, to include the text of Section I of the release captioned "Background" and with new paragraph .02 to include the text of Section II.B.2 of the release captioned "Major Customers."]

503.03. Implementation of Segment Reporting Requirements

[FR-54 (Jan. 5, 1999) replaced paragraphs .01, .02 and .03 of Section 503 with new paragraph .01, to include the text of Section I of the release captioned "Background" and with new paragraph .02 to include the text of Section II.B.2 of the release captioned "Major Customers."]

.a. Determination of Industry Segments

[FR-54 (Jan. 5, 1999) replaced paragraphs .01, .02 and .03 of Section 503 with new paragraph .01, to include the text of Section I of the release captioned "Background" and with new paragraph .02 to include the text of Section II.B.2 of the release captioned "Major Customers."]

503.03.b. Discussion of Acceptable Segmentation

[FR-54 (Jan. 5, 1999) replaced paragraphs .01, .02 and .03 of Section 503 with new paragraph .01, to include the text of Section I of the release captioned "Background" and with new paragraph .02 to include the text of Section II.B.2 of the release captioned "Major Customers."]

503.03.b.i. Electrical and Electronic Products

[FR-54 (Jan. 5, 1999) replaced paragraphs .01, .02 and .03 of Section 503 with new paragraph .01, to include the text of Section I of the release captioned "Background" and with new paragraph .02 to include the text of Section II.B.2 of the release captioned "Major Customers."]

503.03.b.ii. Forest Products

[FR-54 (Jan. 5, 1999) replaced paragraphs .01, .02 and .03 of Section 503 with new paragraph .01, to include the text of Section I of the release captioned "Background" and with new paragraph .02 to include the text of Section II.B.2 of the release captioned "Major Customers."]

503.03.b.iii. Chemicals

[FR-54 (Jan. 5, 1999) replaced paragraphs .01, .02 and .03 of Section 503 with new paragraph .01, to include the text of Section I of the release captioned "Background" and with new paragraph .02 to include the text of Section II.B.2 of the release captioned "Major Customers."]

503.03.b.iv. Drugs

[FR-54 (Jan. 5, 1999) replaced paragraphs .01, .02 and .03 of Section 503 with new paragraph .01, to include the text of Section I of the release captioned "Background" and with new paragraph .02 to include the text of Section II.B.2 of the release captioned "Major Customers."]

503.03.b.v. Property/Casualty Insurance

[FR-54 (Jan. 5, 1999) replaced paragraphs .01, .02 and .03 of Section 503 with new paragraph .01, to include the text of Section I of the release captioned "Background" and with new paragraph .02 to include the text of Section II.B.2 of the release captioned "Major Customers."]

[¶ 38,305] 504. Selected Financial Data

[The Commission originally required that the Form 10-K include a Summary of Operations. Similarly, various registration statement forms required a Summary of Earnings. In ASR 279, these requirements were replaced by a new requirement in Item 301 of Regulation S-K for a Summary of Selected Financial Data.]

ASR 279:

The Selected Financial Data requirement is designed to present significant five-year trend data relating to a registrant's financial condition and results of continuing operations. Although a registrant is permitted to include other financial information in addition to that specified, it is expected that any presentation of additional information would not unnecessarily emphasize income or revenues as opposed to other components of financial condition.

The deletion of summary of operations and the substitution of Selected Financial Data reflected the Commission's concern that operations summaries duplicated information otherwise available in income statements and may have unduly emphasized income over other enterprise performance measures. The Commission recognizes that a detailed specification of the contents or format of a summary might not cure the perceived deficiencies. Accordingly, the revisions strike a reasonable balance between specified content and a flexible approach which permits registrants to select the data which best indicates performance. For example, those registrants who present voluntary disclosures on the impact of inflation and current prices on their business as specified by SFAS No. 89, "Financial Reporting and Changing Prices," are encouraged to combine this information with the information required by Item 301 of Regulation S-K.

[¶ 38,311] 505. Information on the Effects of Changing Prices

The Commission provides a safe harbor rule for information on the effects of changing prices disclosed by registrants pursuant to Item 303 of Regulation S-K relating to the management's discussion and analysis. This safe harbor was provided by amendment of the previously existing safe harbor rule for projections (*see* Rule 175 under the Securities Act of 1933, 17 CFR 230.175, and Rule 3b-6 under the Securities Exchange Act of 1934, 17 CFR 240.3b-6) to extend its coverage to information on the effects of changing prices.

[¶ 38,315] 506. Pro Forma Financial Information and Financial Statements of Businesses Acquired or to Be Acquired

[*Sec. 506 added by FRR-1.*]

506.01. Background

Pro forma financial information is principally used to show the effect of certain significant transactions which (a) occur or become probable after the date of the historical financial statements or (b) have occurred during the year and are not fully reflected in the historical financial statements. Pro forma disclosures are specifically required in a number of circumstances under generally accepted accounting principles (GAAP) and are also required in certain filings with the Commission to facilitate investor understanding of certain significant transactions. Notwithstanding this frequent use, guidance about the presentation and preparation of pro forma financial information is limited, and as a result, the form and content of these disclosures can vary significantly.

Problems encountered with pro forma disclosures in specific filings have been resolved by the Commission staff on a case-by-case basis. As a consequence, informal policies and practices have developed. The Commission believes that its administrative policies and practices should be set forth as formal regulations so that registrants know when and what pro forma financial information is required. Thus, the Commission has amended S-X to establish uniform instructions for the presentation and preparation of pro forma financial information.

As a part of the development of these new guidelines and in response to commentators' concerns, the Commission has reexamined its rules relating to the presentation of historical financial statements of businesses acquired or to be acquired. As a result of this review, the Commission has adopted amendments which significantly modify the requirements for presentation of these financial statements.

506.02. Discussion of Rules

.a. Pro Forma Financial Information

.i. Presentation Requirements

New Rule 11-01 lists various situations for which pro forma financial information is required. In addition to business combinations and dispositions, entities sometimes enter into other types of significant transactions for which pro forma financial information should be presented. Such transactions might include reorganizations, unusual asset exchanges and restructuring of existing indebtedness. It is not possible to anticipate all of the situations for which pro forma financial information should be presented, so a comprehensive listing of situations has not been incorporated in the rules. Registrants must exercise judgment in determining whether pro forma financial information will be meaningful in light of the particular facts and circumstances of the transaction.[2]

Rule 11-01 establishes criteria for determining the significance of a business combination or disposition of a business for purposes of furnishing pro forma financial information. As with new Rule 3-05, the criteria are those used in the definition of significant subsidiary.

506.02.a.ii. Preparation Requirements

Rule 11-02 contains rules and instructions for the preparation of pro forma financial information. These rules have been drafted in a broad fashion since flexibility is necessary to tailor pro forma disclosures to particular events and circumstances.

The presentation requirements for the pro forma condensed statement of income are designed to elicit disclosures that clearly distinguish between the one-time impact and the on-going impact of the transaction and thereby assist investors in focusing on the transaction at hand. Therefore, the rules call for the pro forma condensed income statement to show the impact of the transaction on income from continuing operations of the registrant; any discontinued operations, extraordinary items and the cumulative effects of accounting changes would not be reflected in the condensed historical financial statements used as the starting point for the pro forma presentation.

The rules provide that the only adjustments that are appropriate in the preparation of the pro forma condensed statement of income are those which give effect to events that are (i) directly attributable to the transaction, (ii) expected to have a continuing impact on the registrant, and (iii) factually supportable. Material nonrecurring charges or credits which result directly from the transaction and which will impact the income statement during the next 12 months should not be reflected in the pro forma condensed income statement, but should be separately disclosed (although not necessarily in a table, as proposed) with a clear indication that such charges or credits were not considered in the pro forma condensed income statement. Thus, the "bottom line" of the pro forma column of the condensed income statement will be "income (loss) from continuing operations before nonrecurring charges or credits directly attributable to the transaction." If, of course, the transaction for which the pro forma financial information is presented relates to a disposition of a business segment, the "bottom line" caption(s) in the pro forma condensed income statement

should be revised accordingly, e.g., "income (loss) from continuing operations before nonrecurring charges or credits directly attributable to the transaction adjusted to give effect to the proposed disposition of company A."

The pro forma condensed balance sheet, on the other hand, should reflect pro forma adjustments for all events which are directly attributable to the transaction and factually supportable regardless of whether the impact is expected to be continuing or nonrecurring since the objective of the pro forma balance sheet is to reflect the impact of the transaction on the financial position of the registrant.

506.02.a.iii. Financial Forecasts

Rule 11-03 permits registrants to file a financial forecast in lieu of the pro forma condensed statements of income. This provision is consistent with the Commission's goal of encouraging the disclosure of future oriented information when appropriate. The Commission believes that in certain circumstances the use of a forecast to reflect the impact of a transaction may be more relevant than a pro forma condensed income statement. Thus, the rules provide that this alternative may be used at the option of the registrant.

The Commission understands that there are many factors, in addition to those which are related to the transaction at hand, which must be considered in developing a forecast. The rules provide that when the forecast option is used, the assumptions particularly relevant to the transaction and effects thereof should be clearly set forth so that the effect of the transaction will not be obscured by the other date included in the forecast.

506.02.b. Financial Statements of Businesses Acquired or to Be Acquired

The Commission's requirements for financial statements of businesses acquired or to be acquired have been consolidated in new Rule 3-05 of S-X.[3] The reporting process should be simplified by the Commission's revision of these requirements which (1) base the number of periods for which financial statements are required on the significance of the acquisition and (2) limit the presentation of financial statements of businesses acquired in the past. The Commission recognizes that certain acquisitions have a greater impact on a registrant than others and, accordingly, has adopted a sliding scale type of requirement which determines the periods for which such financial statements are required.[4] The sliding scale test is

---

[2] The Commission may study the provisions of Rule 170 of the Securities Act as part of its merger proxy project. This rule currently precludes presentation of pro forma data when there is no guarantee that all securities offered will be taken.

[3] New Rule 3-05(b)(1) relating to the periods for which financial statements are required refers to Forms S-14 and S-15 for specific requirements applicable to those forms. The Commission has initiated a comprehensive program to ex-

amine proxy regulation and disclosure. The financial statement requirements of Forms S-14 and S-15 may be reviewed in the course of the merger proxy project which is part of that program.

[4] The sliding scale approach to the evaluation of the significance of a business acquisition is generally based on the principles applicable to requests for waiver of certain audited financial statement requirements set forth in Securities Act

based on the conditions specified in the definition of significant subsidiary[5] and although the percentages used are arbitrary, the Commission believes that they meet the objectives of providing adequate financial information to investors, shareholders and other users while at the same time reduci ng the reporting burdens of registrants involved in acquisitions.

The revised requirements adopted herein make the waiver procedures set forth in Securities Act Release No. 4950 obsolete. Therefore, the Commission is rescinding that release and the corresponding instruction in Form 8-K at this time.

The Commission has also reexamined the need for furnishing financial statements for businesses acquired in the past and has determined to codify the present staff practice of generally not insisting on the presentation of separate financial statements of an acquired business once the operating results of the acquired business have been reflected in the audited consolidated financial statements of the registrant for a complete fiscal year. The one exception to this general rule is when the acquired business is of such significance to the registrant that omission of its financial statements would materially impair an investor's ability to understand the historical financial results of the registrant. Codification of this practice will mean that registrants will be required to present separate financial statements of an acquired business when (1) the acquisition of the business is probable, (2) the business has been acquired during the latest fiscal year for which audited financial statements of the registrant are required or during the period between the end of the latest fiscal year and the filing date or (3) the business acquired was extremely significant to the registrant.

The Commission considered reducing the required disclosures to a condensed or summarized financial information level, but concluded that this level of disclosure would not be adequate for two reasons. First, there is important information contained in the notes to the financial statements which would not be reflected in condensed or summarized financial information. Second, there is currently no provision in the existing auditing literature which permits an independent auditor to issue a report on condensed or summarized financial information of nonpublic companies, and the Commission believes that certification of this financial information is essential in acquisition situations.

506.02.c. Requirements Applicable to Both Pro Forma Financial Statements of Businesses Acquired or to Be Acquired

.i. Guidance About What Is a "Business"

A recurring problem in deciding whether separate historical financial statements and pro forma financial information is required for business combinations is the determination of whether a "business" has been acquired. In order to assist registrants, the Commission has included in new Rule 11-01 guidelines which are relevant to that determination; however, the Commission cautions registrants that these guidelines may not be all inclusive or determinative. Registrants must continue to exercise judgment in this area.

506.02.c.ii. Businesses to be Acquired and Other Transactions Not Yet Consummated

Frequently, a registration statement is filed at a time when management is considering a transaction (e.g., a business combination) which is unrelated to the reason for which the registration statement is being filed. In these situations, a question arises about whether historical financial statements of the business to be acquired and pro forma financial information reflecting the unrelated transaction should be included in the filing. The rules provide that these disclosures are required when it is probable that the transaction will be consummated. Guidance as to when consummation of a transaction is probable cannot be given because such a determination is dependent upon the facts and circumstances. In essence, however, consummation of a transaction is considered to be probable whenever the registrants' financial statements alone would not provide investors with adequate financial information with which to make an investment decision.

506.03. Form 8-K

Form 8-K plays a critical role in the integrated disclosure system which is intended to provide investors with a continuous stream of corporate information. Reports on Form 8-K are used to disclose material information concerning certain specified events that have occurred since the latest annual report on Form 10-K or quarterly report on Form 10-Q was filed.

In light of the enhanced role this Exchange Act report plays in the integrated disclosure system, the Commission has amended this form to require reporting of pro forma financial information pursuant to Article 11 of Regulation SX whenever a significant business combination or disposition of a business is consummated. The Commission believes that investors should be informed of the potential financial statement impact in these circumstances. The Commission has also amended Form 8-K to be consistent with the new requirements for filing financial statements of a business acquired or to be acquired. Thus, when reporting business acquisitions on Form 8-K or in certain

---

(Footnote Continued)

Release No. 4950 (February 20, 1969) [34 FR 4886], "General Requirements for Certified Financial Statements of Companies Acquired or to be Acquired."

[5] Rule 1-02(v) of Regulation S-X.

registration statements, registrants need only look to one test to determine the need for and periods to be covered by financial statements of a business acquired or to be acquired.

In addition, the Commission has amended Form 8-K to make clear that the required financial statements and pro forma financial information should be included, if practicable, in the Form 8-K report filed within 15 days of the occurrence of the acquisition or disposition.[6] Thus, the Form provides that the required financial statements and information shall be presented in the report on Form 8-K, but also provides that, if it is impracticable to file the required statements or information at the time the Form 8-K is filed, the Commission may, upon written request, grant an extension of time. While some commentators expressed concern about time constraints imposed by a requirement for pro forma financial information in Form 8-K, the Commission believes that, once required historical financial statements are available, preparation of pro forma financial information does not involve significantly more preparation time. Moreover, any time constraints which do exist should be ameliorated, where necessary and appropriate, by the granting of specific extensions.

[¶ 38,316] 507. Disclosure of Quantitative and Qualitative Information About Market Risk Inherent in Derivative Financial Instruments, Other Financial Instruments, and Derivative Commodity Instruments

[*Added by FR-48*]

507.01. Initiatives Regarding Disclosures About Derivatives.

Certain private sector organizations expressed concerns that users of financial reports are dissatisfied with current disclosures about market risk sensitive instruments. For example, the Association for Investment Management and Research ("AIMR"), an organization of financial analysts, noted that users of financial information "are confounded by the . . . complexity of financial instruments."[22] In addition, after considerable investigation into the needs of investors and creditors, the American Institute of Certified Public Accountants' ("AICPA") Special Committee on Financial Reporting stated:

Users are confused. They complain that business reporting is not answering important questions, such as: . . . What [innovative financial] instruments has the company entered into, and what are their terms? How has the company accounted for those instruments, and how has that accounting affected the financial statements? What risks has the company transferred or taken on?[23]

In addition to identifying disclosure shortcomings, other organizations recommended improvements to disclosures about market risk sensitive instruments. These organizations include regulators, such as the General Accounting Office,[24] Group of 10 Central Bankers,[25] the Federal Reserve Bank of New York,[26] the Basle Committee and the Technical Committee of IOSCO,[27] and private sector bodies, such as the Group of Thirty[28] and a task force of the Financial Executives Institute ("FEI").[29]

In general, those organizations stressed the need to make the risks inherent in market risk sensitive instruments more understandable. To that end, many recommended additional quantita-

---

[6] The adoption of the integrated disclosure system included a revision to Form 8-K which provided that required financial statements for an acquired business, if not available at the time the Form 8-K is filed, could be filed up to 60 days after the report is filed and that any extension of time for filing beyond 60 days would have to be granted by the Division of Corporation Finance upon the registrant's written request. Securities Act Release No. 6383 (March 3, 1982) [47 FR 11380]. At the same time, however, the Commission noted that there were outstanding proposals relating to pro forma financial information in which comment had been solicited as to whether Form 8-K should be revised to require pro forma financial information and that it would reconsider revisions to Form 8-K as part of its final action with respect to the pro forma proposals. Upon reconsideration, particularly in light of the adoption of the sliding scale test for determining financial statement requirements and the rescission of Securities Act Release No. 4950, the Commission has determined to return to the requirement for financial statements to be filed with the Form 8-K filed with 15 days of the occurrence of the acquisition or disposition unless it is impracticable to do so and the Division of Corporation Finance grants a request for an extension of time to file.

[22] See AIMR, Financial Reporting in the 1990s and Beyond, page 30, (1993).

[23] See AICPA Special Committee on Financial Reporting, Improving Business Reporting —A Customer Focus: Meeting

the Information Needs of Investors and Creditors, at 76 (1994).

[24] See General Accounting Office, Financial Derivatives: Actions Taken or Proposed Since May 1994 (November 1996).

[25] See Bank for International Settlements, A Discussion Paper on Public Disclosure of Market and Credit Risks by Financial Intermediaries, prepared by working group of the Euro-currency Standing Committee of the Central Banks of the Group of Ten Countries (September 1994).

[26] See Federal Reserve Bank of New York, Public Disclosure of Risks Related to Market Activity; A Discussion Paper (November 1994).

[27] See Basle Committee and the Technical Committee of IOSCO, Framework for Supervisory Information about the Derivatives Activities of Banks and Securities Firms (May 1995). See also Basle Committee and the Technical Committee of IOSCO, Public Disclosure of the Trading and Derivatives Activities of Banks and Securities Firms (November 1995).

[28] See Group of Thirty, Derivatives: Practices and Principles (July 1993).

[29] See FEI, Derivative Financial Instruments Accounting and Disclosure Issues, ("FEI Report") prepared by FEI CCF/ CCR Derivatives Disclosure Task Force (August 1994).

tive and qualitative disclosures about market risk. For example, the Federal Reserve Bank of New York recommended a new financial statement providing quantitative information about the overall market risk of an entity.[30] In addition, the FEI task force recommended that companies "disclose some type of information which conveys overall exposure to market risk."[31] The FEI task force specifically suggested two distinct approaches. One approach is to provide a high-level summary of relevant statistics about outstanding activity in market risk sensitive instruments at period end. The second approach is to communicate the potential loss that could occur under specified conditions using either value at risk or another comprehensive model for measuring market risk.[32]

In October 1994, the FASB, responding in part to calls for improved disclosure, issued FAS 119 (October 1994).[33] Among other things, FAS 119 prescribes disclosures in the financial statements about the policies used to account for derivative financial instruments and a discussion of the nature, terms, and cash requirements of derivative financial instruments. FAS 119 also encourages, but does not require, disclosure of quantitative information about an entity's market risk exposures.[34]

During 1994, in response, in part, to the concerns of investors, regulators, and private sector entities, the SEC staff reviewed the annual reports of approximately 500 registrants. In addition, during 1995 the SEC staff reviewed more recent annual reports to assess the effect of FAS 119 on disclosures about market risk sensitive instruments. In comparing the 1994 and 1995 annual reports, the SEC staff observed that FAS 119 had a positive effect on the quality of disclosures about derivative financial instruments. However, the staff concluded that investors still needed improved disclosures about market risk sensitive instruments. In particular, the SEC staff identified three primary disclosure issues:

1. Footnote disclosures of accounting policies for derivatives often were too general to convey adequately the diversity in accounting that exists for derivatives. Thus, it often was difficult to determine the impact of derivatives on registrants' statements of financial position, cash flows, and results of operations.

2. Disclosures about different types of market risk sensitive instruments often were reported separately. Thus, it was difficult to assess the aggregate market risk exposures inherent in these instruments.

3. Disclosure about reported items in the footnotes to the financial statements, MD&A, schedules, and selected financial data may not have reflected adequately the effect of derivatives on such reported items. Thus, information about the reported items may have been incomplete and could be misleading.

The Commission designed Rule 4-08(n), Item 310, Item 305, and Item 9A to address these issues. In forming these requirements, the Commission used the following guiding principles:

• Disclosures should make transparent the impact of derivatives on a registrant's statements of financial position, cash flows, and results of operations;

• Disclosures should provide information about a registrant's exposures to market risk;

• Disclosures should explain how market risk sensitive instruments are used in the context of the registrant's business;

• Disclosures about market risk exposures should not focus on derivatives in isolation, but rather should reflect the risk of loss inherent in all market risk sensitive instruments;

• Market risk disclosure requirements should be flexible enough to accommodate different types of registrants, different degrees of market risk exposure, and alternative ways of measuring market risk;

• Disclosures about market risk should address, where appropriate, special risks relating to leverage, option, or prepayment features; and

• New disclosure requirements should build on existing requirements, where possible, to minimize compliance costs.

507.02. Disclosures of Quantitative and Qualitative Information About Market Risk.

1. Quantitative Information About Market Risk

a. Nature of Disclosures

A primary objective of the quantitative disclosure requirements is to provide investors with forward looking information about a registrant's potential exposures to market risk. These quantitative disclosures are dependent on several choices about key model characteristics and assumptions (e.g., hypothetical changes in future market rates or prices).[41] By their nature, these forward looking choices are only estimates and

---

[30] See note 26, supra.

[31] See Attachment A, page 1 of FEI Report.

[32] See Attachment B, pages 5 and 6 of FEI Report.

[33] Similar standards were recently adopted by the International Accounting Standards Committee, the Canadian Institute of Chartered Accountants, and the Australian Accounting Standards Board. See International Accounting Standards No. 32, "Financial Instruments: Disclosure and Presentation,"

("IAS 32") (March 1995), Section 3860 of the Handbook of the Canadian Institute of Chartered Accountants, and the Australian Accounting Standards Board's accounting standard entitled, "Presentation and Disclosure of Financial Instruments," (December 1996), respectively.

[34] See FAS 119 12.

[41] The Commission believes that the exercise of discretion in making such choices by registrants should not subject registrants to liability with respect to private rights of action.

will be different from what actually occurs in the future. As a result, actual future gains or losses will differ from those reported in the quantitative disclosures. For example, differences between actual and reported gains and losses will arise when (i) actual market rate or price changes differ from those estimated or (ii) the portfolio of market risk sensitive instruments held during the year differs from the portfolio held at the prior year-end.

Notwithstanding this limitation, the Commission believes that the reported market risk information should provide benefits to both investors and registrants. The quantitative disclosures should help investors better understand specific market risk exposures of different registrants, thereby allowing them to better manage market risks in their investment portfolios. Those disclosures also should provide a mechanism, where applicable, for registrants to disclose that their use of derivatives represents risk management, rather than speculation. Those disclosures are not precise indicators of expected future reported losses. Instead, depending on the modeling technique and assumptions used, they are indicators of remote or reasonably possible losses. Nevertheless, those disclosures should provide investors with important indicators of how a particular registrant views and manages its market risk.

The Commission has provided flexibility in the quantitative and qualitative disclosure requirements to accommodate different types of registrants, different degrees of market risk exposure, and alternative ways of measuring market risk. The Commission believes, at this time, that such flexibility is necessary and important to allow risk management and reporting practices to evolve, even though such flexibility is likely to reduce the comparability of disclosures. To address this comparability issue, registrants are required to disclose the key model characteristics and assumptions used in preparing the quantitative market risk disclosures. These disclosures are designed to allow investors to evaluate the potential impact of variations in those model characteristics and assumptions on the reported information. In addition, as more standard risk management practices and methods of reporting market risk are developed, the Commission anticipates reviewing the disclosure requirements with the view to enhancing comparability.

b. Background

Market risk is inherent in derivative and non-derivative instruments, including:

- derivative financial instruments - futures, forwards, swaps, options, and other financial instruments with similar characteristics;

- other financial instruments - non-derivative financial instruments, such as investments, loans, structured notes, mortgage-backed securities, indexed debt instruments, interest-only and principal-only obligations, deposits, and other debt obligations;

- derivative commodity instruments that are permitted by contract or business custom to be settled in cash or with another financial instrument - commodity futures, commodity forwards, commodity swaps, commodity options, and other commodity instruments with similar characteristics, to the extent such instruments are not derivative financial instruments.

Generally accepted accounting principles and prior Commission rules already require disclosure of certain quantitative information pertaining to some of these instruments. For example, registrants are required to disclose notional amounts of derivative financial instruments and the nature and terms of debt obligations.[42] However, this information (i) often is abbreviated, (ii) is presented piecemeal in different parts of the financial statements, and (iii) does not apply to all market risk sensitive instruments. Thus, investors often have been unable to assess the net market risk exposures inherent in these instruments.

FAS 119 encourages, but does not require, disclosure of quantitative information about the market risk exposures inherent in market risk sensitive instruments.[43] However, without an explicit requirement, the Commission observed that registrants often were not making these disclosures.

c. Item 305(a) of Regulation S-K and Item 9A(a) of Form 20-F

In essence, Items 305(a) and 9A(a)[44] are designed to make disclosures about market risk more comprehensive by requiring disclosures of quantitative information about market risk, similar to those encouraged by FAS 119. Items 305(a) and 9A(a) apply to market risk sensitive instruments.

Under these Items, registrants should furnish quantitative information about market risk using one or more of three prescribed alternative methods.[45] The three alternative methods, described in

---

[42] See, e.g., FAS 119 8b and Rule 5-02 of Regulation S-X, 17 CFR 210.5-02, respectively.

[43] In particular, FAS 119 12 lists five possible quantitative methods of measuring and disclosing market risk. They are: (i) details about current positions and perhaps activity during the period, (ii) the hypothetical effects on equity, or on annual income, of several possible changes in market price, (iii) a gap analysis of interest rate repricing or maturity dates, (iv) the duration of the financial instruments, and (v) the entity's value at risk from derivative financial instruments and from

other positions at the end of the reporting period and the average value at risk during the year.

[44] Item 9A(a) of Form 20-F, like the other portions of Item 9A, is substantively identical to related sections in Item 305.

[45] At the current time, the Commission is not prescribing standardized methods and procedures specifying how to comply with each of these disclosure alternatives. To facilitate comparison across registrants, however, Item 305(a) requires that registrants describe the model and assumptions used to prepare quantitative market risk disclosures.

detail below, are a tabular presentation, sensitivity analysis, and value at risk.

In preparing this quantitative information, registrants should categorize market risk sensitive instruments into instruments entered into for trading purposes and instruments entered into for purposes other than trading. Within both the trading and other than trading portfolios, separate quantitative information should be presented for each market risk exposure category (i.e., interest rate risk, foreign currency exchange rate risk, commodity price risk, and other relevant market risks, such as equity price risk), when material.

A registrant may use (i) the same alternative for all market risk disclosures, (ii) one alternative, such as value at risk, for all disclosures related to instruments entered into for trading purposes, and another alternative, such as sensitivity analysis, for all disclosures related to instruments entered into for other than trading purposes, or (iii) different or the same alternatives for each category of market risk within the trading and other than trading portfolios.

(i) Tabular Presentation

The tabular presentation alternative permits registrants to provide quantitative information about market risk sensitive instruments in a tabular format. The required information includes the fair values of market risk sensitive instruments and contract terms sufficient to determine the future cash flows from those instruments, categorized by expected maturity dates. These tabular disclosures should present information sufficient to allow readers of the table to determine expected cash flows from market risk sensitive instruments for each of the next five years and the aggregate cash flows expected for the remaining years thereafter.[46] These tabular disclosure requirements were selected because expected cash flows are common inputs to market risk measurement methods and, therefore, are expected to help investors make estimates of a registrant's market risk exposures.

To facilitate an investor's ability to make such estimates, Items 305(a) and 9A(a) require that tabular information be grouped based on common market risk characteristics. In particular, those Items require separate presentation of tabular information for instruments: (i) entered into for trading and other than trading purposes, (ii) subject to different categories of market risk exposure

(e.g, interest rate risk, foreign currency exchange rate risk, etc.), and (iii) subject to different market risk characteristics within a particular exposure category (e.g., different functional currencies,[47] different underlying commodity exposures, different instrument types, and different contractual rates or prices). See Items 305(a)(1)(i) and 9A(a)(1)(i) for further requirements.

In particular, when preparing the tabular disclosures registrants should consider whether differences in market risk would be reflected better by separately presenting tabular information for a particular instrument or group of instruments. For example, Items 305(a)(1)(i) and 9A(a)(1)(i) require the grouping of options with similar strike prices. This grouping is required because option payouts can differ significantly depending how far the option is in or out of the money. Thus, the separate presentation of tabular information for options with dissimilar strike prices should enhance an investor's ability to determine the potential market risk inherent in those instruments. Registrants should make similar evaluations when determining which instruments should be grouped together within the tabular disclosures.

Items 305(a) and 9A(a) also require disclosure of information regarding the contents of the table and related assumptions necessary to understand a registrant's market risk disclosures. In this regard, registrants should describe, for example, the different amounts reported in the table for the various categories of the market sensitive instruments (e.g., principal amounts for debt, notional amounts for swaps, and the different types of reported market rates or prices) and key prepayment or reinvestment assumptions relating to the timing of reported amounts. See Items 305(a)(1)(i) and 9A(a)(1)(i) for further details.

The Appendix to each of these Items provides a sample disclosure format.

(ii) Sensitivity Analysis

The sensitivity analysis disclosure alternative permits registrants to express the potential loss in future earnings, fair values, or cash flows of market risk sensitive instruments resulting from one or more selected hypothetical changes in interest rates, foreign currency exchange rates, commodity prices, and other relevant market rate or price changes (e.g., equity prices) over a selected time period.[48] Items 305(a) and 9A(a) require that registrants select hypothetical changes in market

---

[46] In some instances, the tabular presentation alternative is similar to the gap analysis commonly provided by financial institutions. Thus, with minor modifications, if any, those registrants could report a gap analysis and comply with the tabular information requirements.

[47] For purpose of Item 305 and Item 9A, functional currency means the currency of the primary economic environment in which the entity operates; normally, that is the currency of the environment in which an entity primarily

generates and expends cash. This definition is the same as the definition of functional currency in FAS 52, Appendix E.

[48] The term "sensitivity analysis," as used in Items 305(a) and 9A(a), describes a general class of models that assesses the risk of loss in market risk sensitive instruments based on hypothetical changes in market rates or prices. The term sensitivity analysis is not meant to refer to any one model for quantifying market risk. Sensitivity analysis models include, for example, duration analysis or other "sensitivity" measures already required to be calculated for regulatory purposes for

rates and prices that are expected to reflect reasonably possible[49] near-term[50] changes in those rates and prices. Absent economic justification for the selection of a different amount, registrants should use changes that are not less than 10 percent of end of period market rates or prices.

Items 305(a) and 9A(a) also require a description of the model, assumptions, and parameters underlying the registrant's sensitivity analysis that are necessary to understand the registrant's market risk disclosure. In this regard, registrants are required to specify, for example, (i) how "loss" is defined by the model (e.g., loss in earnings, fair values, or cash flows), (ii) a general description of the modeling technique (e.g., the change in net present values arising from selected shifts in market rates or prices), (iii) the types of instruments covered by the model, and (iv) other relevant information about the model's assumptions and parameters (e.g., the magnitude and timing of selected hypothetical changes in market rates or prices used). See Items 305(a)(1)(ii) and 9A(a)(1)(ii) for further requirements.

(iii) Value at Risk

The value at risk disclosure alternative permits registrants to express the potential loss in future earnings, fair values, or cash flows of market risk sensitive instruments over a selected period of time, with a selected likelihood of occurrence, from changes in interest rates, foreign currency exchange rates, commodity prices, and other relevant market rates or prices.[51] Items 305(a) and 9A(a) state that when preparing value at risk disclosures, registrants should select confidence intervals that reflect reasonably possible near-term changes in market rates and prices. In this regard, absent economic justification for the selection of different confidence intervals, registrants should use intervals that are 95 percent or higher.

For each category for which value at risk disclosures are presented, Items 305(a) and 9A(a) require registrants to provide either (i) the average, high and low amounts, or the distribution of value at risk amounts for the reporting period, (ii) the average, high and low amounts, or the distribution of actual changes in fair values, earnings, or cash flows from market risk sensitive instruments occurring during the reporting period, or (iii) the percentage or number of times the actual changes in fair values, earnings, or cash flows from market risk sensitive instruments exceeded the value at risk amounts during the reporting period.

Items 305(a) and 9A(a) also require a description of the model, assumptions, and parameters underlying the registrant's value at risk model that are necessary to understand the registrant's market risk disclosure. In this regard, registrants should specify, for example, (i) how "loss" is defined by the model (e.g., loss in earnings, fair values, or cash flows), (ii) the type of model used (e.g., variance/covariance, historical simulation, or Monte Carlo simulation and a description as to how optionality is addressed by the model), (iii) the types of instruments covered by the model, and (iv) other relevant information about the model's assumptions and parameters (e.g., holding periods and confidence intervals).[52] See Items 305(a)(1)(iii) and 9A(a)(1)(iii) for further requirements.

(iv) An Alternative to Reporting Year-End Information

Items 305(a) and 9A(a) require disclosure of quantitative information about market risk as of the end of the latest fiscal year. Alternatively, registrants, such as those with proprietary concerns about reporting year-end information under the sensitivity analysis and value at risk disclosure alternatives, may report the average, high, and low amounts for the reporting period. In determining those average, high, and low amounts for the fiscal year, registrants should use sensitivity analysis or value at risk amounts relating to at least four equal time periods throughout the reporting period (e.g., four quarter-end amounts, 12-month-end amounts, or 52 week-end amounts).

(v) Other Disclosure Requirements

Items 305(a) and 9A(a) require registrants to provide summarized quantitative information about market risk for the preceding fiscal year. In addition, registrants should discuss the reasons for material quantitative changes in market risk exposures between the current and preceding fiscal years.[53] In determining the amount and type of summarized information to be provided for the

---

(Footnote Continued)

thrift institutions (see Office of Thrift Supervision, Regulatory Capital: Interest Rate Risk Component, 12 CFR 567.5(c)(4) (August 1993)).

[49] See note 67, infra, for a definition of the term "reasonably possible."

[50] See note 66, infra, for a definition of the term "near-term."

[51] The term "value at risk," as used in Items 305(a) and 9A(a), describes a general class of models that provides a probabilistic assessment of the risk of loss in market risk sensitive instruments. The term value at risk is not meant to refer to any one model for quantifying market risk. Value at risk models can be adapted to non-trading activities as well as trading activities and to non-financial institutions as well as

financial institutions, depending on the model and assumptions selected by the registrant.

[52] The primary differences between the value at risk and sensitivity analysis disclosure alternatives are (i) value at risk analysis reports the potential loss arising from equally likely market movements across instruments, while sensitivity analysis reports the potential loss arising from hypothetical market movements with differing likelihoods of occurrence across instruments and (ii) value at risk explicitly adjusts the potential loss to reflect correlations between market movements, while sensitivity analysis is not designed explicitly to make such adjustments.

[53] For transition purposes, quantitative disclosures about market risk provided in the initial year in which a registrant

preceding fiscal year, registrants should evaluate whether sufficient information is disclosed to enable investors to assess material trends in quantitative market risk information. This summary should include information relating to each market risk exposure category disclosed in the preceding or latest fiscal year.

In addition, Items 305(a) and 9A(a) permit registrants to change disclosure alternatives or key model characteristics, assumptions, and parameters used in providing quantitative information about market risk (e.g., changing from tabular presentation to value at risk, changing the scope of instruments included in the model, changing the definition of loss from fair values to earnings). However, if the effects of such a change are material,[54] registrants should (i) explain the reasons for the change and (ii) either provide summarized comparable information, under the new disclosure method, for the year preceding the current reporting period or, in addition to providing disclosure for the current year under the new method, provide disclosure for the current year and preceding fiscal year under the method used in the preceding year.

(vi) Encouraged Disclosures

The Commission recognizes that market risk exposures may exist in instruments, positions, and transactions other than in the market risk sensitive instruments specifically covered by Items 305 and 9A. In particular, market risk, in its broadest view, also may be inherent in the following items:

- derivative commodity instruments that are not permitted by contract or business custom to be settled in cash or with another financial instrument - such as a commodity forward contract that must be settled in the commodity;

- commodity positions - such as investments in corn, wheat, oil, gas, lumber, silver, gold, and other commodity inventory positions;

- cash flows from anticipated transactions[55] - such as cash flows from anticipated purchases and sales of inventory, and operating cash flows from non-financial and non-commodity instruments (e.g., cash flows generated by manufacturing activities); and

- certain financial instruments not included among the required disclosure items - such as insurance contracts, lease contracts, and employers' and plans' obligations for pension and other post-retirement benefits.

The Commission also recognizes, however, that the amount and timing of the cash flows inherent in such instruments, positions, and transactions sometimes may be difficult to estimate. In addition, it has been represented to the staff that many risk measurement systems currently do not include such instruments, positions, and transactions in their quantitative assessments of market risk. For these practical reasons, the Commission is not requiring, at this time, that these items be included in the quantitative disclosures about market risk. Registrants, however, are encouraged to include such items within their quantitative market risk disclosures.

Registrants that choose the tabular presentation disclosure alternative should present voluntarily selected instruments, positions, or transactions in a manner consistent with the requirements in Items 305 and 9A for market risk sensitive instruments. Registrants selecting the sensitivity analysis or value at risk disclosure alternatives are not required to provide separate market risk disclosures for any voluntarily selected instruments, positions, or transactions. Instead, registrants selecting those disclosure alternatives are permitted to present comprehensive market risk disclosures, which reflect the combined market risk exposures inherent in both the required and any voluntarily selected instruments, position, or transactions.

If a registrant elects to include voluntarily a particular type of instrument, position, or transaction in their quantitative disclosures about market risk, that registrant should include all, rather than some, of those instruments, positions, or transactions within their disclosures. For example, if a registrant holds in inventory a particular type of commodity position and elects to include that commodity position within their market risk disclosures, the registrant should include the entire commodity position, rather than only a portion thereof, in their quantitative disclosures about market risk.

Finally, if instruments, positions, or transactions are not included voluntarily in the market risk disclosures and, as a result, the disclosures do not fully reflect the net market risk exposures of the registrant, the registrant should discuss the absence of those items as a limitation of the quantitative information, as discussed below.[56]

(vii) Limitations

(Footnote Continued)

must present information under Item 305 is not required to contain comparable summarized information for the preceding year. Similarly, in the first fiscal year in which a registrant must present information under Item 305, a discussion of the reasons for material changes in reported amounts as compared to the preceding year is not necessary.

[54] In this regard, the Commission believes that all changes from one disclosure alternative to another are material; how-

ever, other changes discussed in this section require judgment as to whether the effects of such changes are material.

[55] See note 19, supra.

[56] In addition, registrants should review the requirements of Item 303 of Regulation S-K, 17 CFR 229.303, to ensure their disclosures are sufficient to inform readers of material risks to which a registrant is exposed.

Items 305(a) and 9A(a) require registrants to discuss limitations that cause the quantitative information about market risk not to reflect fully the net market risk exposures of the entity. This discussion is to include a description of instruments, positions, and transactions omitted from the quantitative market risk disclosure information, or the features of instruments, positions, and transactions that are included, but not reflected fully in the quantitative information disclosed.

Two illustrative examples are provided. First, as just stated, certain instruments, positions, and transactions are excluded from the required quantitative disclosures about market risk, but may be included on a voluntary basis. The failure of a registrant to include voluntarily those instruments, positions, or transactions in the quantitative disclosures is a limitation of the quantitative information provided. This limitation should be discussed, if material, and a summarized description of the instruments, positions, or transactions not reflected fully within the quantitative market risk disclosures should be disclosed.

Second, the prescribed quantitative disclosures may not inform investors of the degree of market risk inherent in instruments with leverage, option, or prepayment features (e.g., options, including written options, structured notes, collateralized mortgage obligations, leveraged swaps, and options embedded in swaps). Tabular information on fair values and contract terms may not necessarily indicate that instruments have such features. Similarly, if leverage, option, or prepayment features are triggered by changes in market rates or prices outside those reflected in the value at risk and sensitivity analysis disclosures, the potential loss from such market rate or price changes may be significantly larger than would be implied by a simple linear extrapolation of the reported numbers. Thus, to make investors fully aware of the market risk inherent in instruments with such features, Item 305(a) and Item 9A(a) require a discussion of this limitation, including a summarized description of the features of the instruments causing the limitation.

2. Qualitative Information about Market Risk

a. Background

The Commission believes that quantitative information about market risk is more meaningful when accompanied by qualitative disclosures about a registrant's market risk exposures and how those exposures are managed. Such qualitative disclosures help investors understand a registrant's market risk management activities and help place those activities in the context of the business.

FAS 119 requires qualitative disclosures about market risk management activities associated with certain derivative financial instruments. In particular, FAS 119 requires disclosure of "the entity's objectives for holding or issuing the derivative financial instruments, the context needed to understand those objectives, and its general strategies for achieving those objectives."[57] However, the qualitative disclosure requirements of FAS 119 only apply to derivative financial instruments held or issued for purposes other than trading.

b. Item 305(b) and Item 9A(b)

Items 305(b) and 9A(b) expand the qualitative market risk disclosure requirements of FAS 119 to (i) encompass derivative commodity instruments, other financial instruments, and derivative financial instruments entered into for trading purposes and (ii) require registrants to evaluate and describe material changes in their primary risk exposures and in how those exposures are managed. In particular, Items 305(b) and 9A(b) require a description of (i) a registrant's primary market risk exposures[58] as of the end of the latest fiscal year, (ii) how those exposures are managed (such descriptions should include, but not be limited to, a discussion of the objectives, general strategies, and instruments, if any, used to manage those exposures), and (iii) changes in either the registrant's primary market risk exposures or in how those exposures are managed, when compared to what was in effect during the most recently completed fiscal year and what is known or expected to be in effect in future reporting periods.

Items 305(b) and 9A(b) apply to market risk sensitive instruments. In addition, the qualitative disclosures required by these items should be presented separately for market risk sensitive instruments entered into for trading purposes and those entered into for purposes other than trading.

Finally, to help make disclosures about market risk more comprehensive, the Commission encourages registrants to include within their qualitative disclosures about market risk, certain instruments, positions, and transactions not required under Items 305(b) and 9A(b). Those in-

---

[57] See FAS 119 11a. Footnote 4 of FAS 119 illustrates the qualitative disclosures required by 11a. That footnote states:

If an entity's objective for a derivative position is to keep a risk from the entity's non-derivative assets below a specified level, the context would be a description of those assets and their risks, and a strategy might be purchasing put options in a specified proportion to the assets at risk.

[58] For purposes of Items 305(b) and 9A(b), primary market risk exposures mean (i) the following categories of market

risk: interest rate risk, foreign currency exchange rate risk, commodity price risk, and other relevant market rate or price risks (e.g., equity price risk) and (ii) within each of these categories, the particular markets that present the primary risks of loss to the registrant. For example, if a registrant (i) has a material exposure to foreign currency exchange rate risk and, within this category of market risk, (ii) is most vulnerable to changes in dollar/yen, dollar/pound, and dollar/peso exchange rates, the registrant should disclose those exposures.

struments, positions, and transactions include derivative commodity instruments not permitted by contract or business custom to be settled in cash or with another financial instrument, commodity positions, cash flows from anticipated transactions, and certain financial instruments not included among the required disclosure items. See Items 305(b) and 9A(b) for further requirements.[59]

If a registrant elects not to include those instruments, positions, and transactions in its qualitative disclosures about market risk, the Commission reminds registrants to consider whether qualitative disclosures about the market risk inherent in those items would be required under (i) Items 101 or 303 of Regulation S-K[60] or (ii) Rules 12b-20 under the Securities Exchange Act of 1934 ("Exchange Act") or 408 under the Securities Act of 1933 ("Securities Act").[61] Item 101 of Regulation S-K requires disclosures relating to a "Description of the Business." Item 303 requires discussion of known risks and uncertainties within "Management's Discussion and Analysis." Rule 12b-20 under the Exchange Act and Rule 408 under the Securities Act state that registrants should include in any filings or reports any material information necessary to make statements made, in light of the circumstances, not misleading.

3. Safe Harbor for Forward Looking Information

In the release proposing Item 305 and Item 9A, the Commission noted its intention to consider the application of an appropriate safe harbor to the forward looking aspects of the disclosures. Such a safe harbor subsequently was proposed for public comment,[62] and the Commission is adopting that provision substantially as proposed.

As adopted, the safe harbors for forward looking statements provided in Section 27A of the Securities Act and Section 21E of the Exchange Act apply to quantitative information about market risk provided outside the financial statements and related notes thereto, all of which, as described further below, is deemed to be a forward looking statement for purposes of the safe harbor, pursuant to Item 305(a) or Item 9A(a); qualitative information about market risk provided outside the financial statements and related notes thereto, pursuant to Item 305(b) or Item 9A(b); and interim information provided pursuant to Item 305(c) and Item 9A(c).

As proposed, the safe harbor would have applied to information disclosed pursuant to Items 305 and 9A regardless of whether the information was set forth in the notes to the financial statements or elsewhere in a registrant's required filings. As discussed below,[63] the Commission has determined that information required by Items 305 and 9A should be disclosed outside of the financial statements and related notes thereto. Similarly, as adopted, the safe harbor applies only to information located in accordance with the revised rule.

The safe harbors are available with respect to the specified information, regardless of whether the issuer providing it or the type of transaction otherwise is excluded from the statutory safe harbors. For example, first-time Commission registrants and those making initial public offerings are covered by the safe harbors with respect to this specific information if all other conditions are satisfied.

As is the case with the statutory safe harbors, however, the safe harbors adopted pursuant to this release apply only to a forward looking statement made by: (i) an issuer, (ii) a person acting on behalf of the issuer, (iii) an outside reviewer retained by the issuer making a statement on behalf of the issuer, or (iv) an underwriter, with respect to information provided by the issuer or information derived from information provided by the issuer.

The Commission recognizes that, due to the difficult nature of the disclosures, some registrants may require assistance in preparing the information required by Items 305 and 9A. For example, registrants may need assistance from third parties with respect to compiling the required information, assessing the reasonableness of management's assumptions, or testing the mathematical computations that translate the assumptions into the required disclosures. Moreover, some registrants may wish to have outside third parties review the information prior to its disclosure. The Commission considers such assistance and reviews relating to forward looking disclosure required by Items 305 and 9A to be "made by an outside reviewer retained by the issuer making a statement on behalf of the issuer" under the safe harbor rule.

The rule now clarifies two additional points about the application of the new safe harbor rules. First, the Commission deems all information required by paragraphs (a), (b)(1)(i), (b)(1)(iii) and (c) of Items 305 and 9A to be "forward looking statements" for purposes of the new safe harbor rules, except for historical facts such as the terms of particular contracts and number of market risk sensitive instruments held during or at the end of the reporting period. To the extent that information provided pursuant to paragraph (b)(1)(ii) of

---

[59] See section III B.1.c.(vi), supra, for a discussion as to why these instruments are encouraged, but not required, to be included in disclosures about market risk.

[60] See 17 CFR 228.101 and 17 CFR 228.303, respectively.

[61] See 17 CFR 240.12b-20 and 17 CFR 230.408, respectively.

[62] Securities Act Release No. 7280; Exchange Act Release No. 37086; File No. S7-10-96 (April 9, 1996) [61 FR 16672].

[63] See section III B.4.b., infra, for a discussion about where these disclosures should appear.

Items 305 and 9A includes forward looking statements, those statements would be eligible for safe harbor protection.

Second, the "meaningful cautionary statements" prong of the safe harbors will be satisfied with respect to the Items 305(a) and 9A(a) disclosures if a registrant satisfies the requirements of those Items. In this regard, the Commission notes that Items 305(a) and 9A(a) require disclosure of both the assumptions underlying, and the limitations of, the disclosure provided. For the remainder of the information required by the new items, registrants desiring to qualify for the "meaningful cautionary statements" prong of the safe harbor will need to consider what information should be given to alert investors to important factors that could cause actual results to differ materially from the information given in the forward looking statements.[64]

Finally, although Item 305 and Item 9A information is not required of small business issuers (as defined by Commission rule),[65] the safe harbors are available to those small issuers that voluntarily choose to disclose such information. Similarly, the safe harbors are available to non-small business issuers who voluntarily disclose information under Item 305(a) and Item 9A(a) prior to the June 15, 1997 and June 15, 1998 effective dates.

4. Implementation Issues Relating to Quantitative and Qualitative Disclosures about Market Risk

a. Disclosure Threshold

Under Items 305 and 9A, quantitative and qualitative disclosures about market risk are required, when material, for each market risk exposure category within the trading and other than trading portfolios. For purposes of assessing materiality, registrants should evaluate both (i) the materiality of the fair values of market risk sensitive instruments outstanding as of the end of the latest fiscal year and (ii) the materiality of potential near-term[66] losses in future earnings, fair values, and cash flows from reasonably possible[67] near-term changes in market rates or prices.

If either (i) or (ii) in the previous paragraph are material, the registrant should disclose quantitative and qualitative information about market risk, if such market risk for the particular market risk exposure category is material. However, the

choice of methods, model characteristics, assumptions, and parameters used to comply with the quantitative market risk disclosures remain at the election of the registrant, provided disclosure is made regarding a material risk of loss in either earnings, fair values, or cash flows.

For example, if a registrant expects a material near-term loss in fair values only, that registrant should not report quantitative market risk information in terms of earnings or cash flows, rather than fair values. In these circumstances, the registrant could, of course, make additional quantitative disclosures about the loss in earnings or cash flows, but should disclose the risk of loss in fair values. In contrast, if a registrant is required to disclose market risk information because near-term losses in future earnings, fair values, and cash flows all are material, it may report quantitative information in terms of either earnings, fair values, or cash flows.

In assessing the materiality of the fair values of market risk sensitive instruments, those fair values generally should not be netted, except to the extent allowed under FASB Interpretation No. 39, "Offsetting of Amounts Related to Certain Contracts" ("Interpretation 39") (March 1992).[68] For example, the fair value of assets generally should not be netted with the fair value of liabilities. Instead, the fair values of such instruments should be aggregated, without netting, for purposes of assessing materiality.

In assessing the materiality of potential near-term losses in future earnings, fair values, or cash flows from reasonably possible near-term changes in market rates or prices, registrants should consider (i) the magnitude of past market movements, (ii) the magnitude of reasonably possible, near-term market movements, and (iii) potential losses that may arise from leverage, option, and multiplier features.

b. Location of Quantitative and Qualitative Disclosures

As adopted, Items 305 and 9A require that the quantitative and qualitative market risk disclosures be placed outside the financial statements and related notes thereto. As proposed, registrants would have been permitted to disclose such information in the notes to the financial statements. Because of the evolving nature of the dis-

---

[64] Registrants are reminded that the safe harbor requires that forward looking statements be identified as such.

[65] 17 CFR 228, et seq.

[66] For the purposes of Item 305 and Item 9A, the term "near-term" means a period of time going forward up to one year from the date of the financial statements. See generally AICPA, Statement of Position 94-6, Disclosure of Certain Significant Risks and Uncertainties, at paragraph 7 (December 30, 1994).

[67] For purposes of Item 305 and Item 9A, the term "reasonably possible" is defined by 3 of FASB, Statement of Financial Accounting Standards No. 5, "Accounting for Contingencies"

("FAS 5") (March 1975), which states that "reasonably possible" means the chance of a future transaction or event occurring is more than remote but less than likely.

[68] Interpretation 39 states that it is a general principle of accounting that the offsetting of assets and liabilities in the balance sheet is improper except where a right of set off exists. Interpretation 39 defines right of set off and specifies what conditions must be met to have that right. FAS 119 15(d) in disclosing the fair values of instruments also prohibits the netting of fair values, except to the extent that the offsetting of carrying amounts in the statement of financial position is permitted under Interpretation 39.

closures and the FASB's pending project on accounting for derivatives, which also will address disclosures about derivatives within the financial statements, the Commission has determined that the better course, at this time, is to require that the disclosures mandated by Items 305 and 9A be located outside of the financial statements and related notes.

The Commission believes that the information required by Items 305 and 9A should be included in the annual report delivered to shareholders; consequently Rule 14a-3 of the proxy rules has been amended to include this requirement. For other documents delivered to investors, the information should be included or incorporated by reference from other Commission filings.

c. Cross-Referencing of Disclosures

The Commission believes it is most meaningful to disclose together, in one location, quantitative and qualitative information relating to the same market risk exposure category. However, because market risk sensitive instruments often are used to manage known risks and uncertainties in market rates and prices, the disclosures provided under Items 305 and 9A may overlap with disclosures provided under Item 303 of Regulation S-K. To the extent that the disclosures in a registrant's MD&A satisfy the requirements of Items 305 or 9A, registrants need not repeat this information elsewhere in their filings. If this information is disclosed in more than one location, however, registrants should ensure that the resulting disclosures are meaningful to investors and provide cross-references to the locations of the related disclosures.

d. Application to Registrants

Items 305 and 9A are required to be followed by many different types of registrants, including, for example, commercial and industrial companies, financial institutions, broker-dealers, service companies, business development companies, and companies registering insurance contracts, such as market-value adjusted annuities and real estate funds underlying annuity contracts. Items 305 and 9A do not apply to registered investment companies and, as described further in Section IV, small business issuers.

e. Reporting Frequency

Items 305 and 9A apply to all registration statements filed under the Securities Act and all reports, proxy statements, and information statements filed under the Exchange Act that are required to include or incorporate financial state-

ments. However, for reports that include only interim financial statements (e.g., Form 10-Qs), registrants need only present market risk information if there have been material changes in reported market risks faced by the registrant since the end of the most recent fiscal year. In these circumstances, registrants should provide a discussion and analysis that enables investors to assess the sources and effects of those material changes in market risks.

507.03. Applicability of Amendments.

A. Application to Small Business Issuers

The Commission believes that because of (i) the evolving nature of these disclosures and (ii) the relative costs of complying with these disclosures for small business issuers,[69] it is appropriate, at this time, to exempt small business issuers from disclosing quantitative and qualitative information about market risk.[70]

Accordingly, at this time, the Commission is not adopting amendments to Regulation S-B to incorporate an item similar to Item 305. Small business issuers, however, are required (i) to comply with the amendment regarding accounting policies disclosures for derivatives, (ii) to comply with Rule 12b-20 under the Exchange Act and Rule 408 under the Securities Act, which require registrants to provide additional information about the material effects of derivatives on other information expressly required to be filed with the Commission, and (iii) to the extent market risk represents a known trend, event, or uncertainty, to discuss the impact of market risk on past and future financial condition and results of operations, pursuant to Item 303 of Regulation S-B.

B. Application to Foreign Private Issuers

Item 9A of Form 20-F requires disclosure by all foreign private issuers of quantitative and qualitative information about market risk. In addition, foreign private issuers that prepare financial statements in accordance with Item 18 of Form 20-F are required to provide all information required by U.S. generally accepted accounting principles and Regulation S-X, including descriptions in the footnotes to the financial statements of the policies used to account for derivatives. Foreign private issuers that prepare financial statements in accordance with Item 17 of Form 20-F are not required to provide financial statement disclosures required by U.S. generally accepted accounting principles and Regulation S-X. The amendments requiring disclosures of accounting policies in Rule 4-08(n) of Regulation S-X do not apply to

---

[69] "Small business issuer" is defined to mean any entity that (1) has revenues of less than $25,000,000, (2) is a United States or Canadian issuer, (3) is not an investment company, and (4) if a majority owned subsidiary, the parent corporation is also a small business issuer. An entity is not a small business issuer, however, if it has a public float (the aggregate market value of the outstanding securities held by non-affiliates) of $25,000,000 or more. See 17 CFR 230.405.

[70] Small business issuers will not be required to provide these market risk disclosures whether or not they file on specially designated small business forms.

In addition, as noted elsewhere in this release, the Commission has extended the safe harbor for forward looking information to Item 305 disclosures that are made voluntarily by small business issuers.

foreign private issuers filing under Item 17 of Form 20-F. However, foreign private issuers filing under Item 17 of Form 20-F should consider the guidance presented in Staff Accounting Bulletin Topic 1:D ("SAB Topic 1:D") to determine if information regarding accounting policies for derivatives should be provided in MD&A.[71]

C. Scope and Definition of Instruments

The instructions to Rule 4-08(n), Item 305, and Item 9A define financial instruments, derivative financial instruments, other financial instruments, and derivative commodity instruments as follows. "Financial instruments" have the same meaning as defined by generally accepted accounting principles (see, e.g., FASB, Statement of Financial Accounting Standards No. 107, "Disclosures about Fair Value of Financial Instruments," ("FAS 107") paragraphs 3 and 8 (December 1991)). "Derivative financial instruments" are a subset of financial instruments and include futures, forwards, swaps, options, and other financial instruments with similar characteristics, as defined by generally accepted accounting principles (see, e.g., FAS 119 paragraphs 5-7 (October 1994)). See, the General Instructions to Paragraphs 305(a) and 305(b) of Item 305 or the General Instructions to Paragraphs 9A(a) and 9A(b) of Item 9A for further details.

Other financial instruments include all financial instruments that must be disclosed at fair value under FAS 107, except for derivative financial instruments, as defined above. For example, other financial instruments include trade accounts receivable, investments, loans, structured notes, mortgage-backed securities, trade accounts payable, indexed debt instruments, interest-only and principal-only obligations, deposits, and other debt obligations. However, for purposes of this release, trade accounts receivable and trade accounts payable need not be considered other financial instruments when their carrying amounts approximate fair value. Other financial instruments exclude employers' and plans' obligations for pension and other post-retirement benefits, substantively extinguished debt, insurance contracts, lease contracts, warranty obligations and rights, unconditional purchase obligations, investments accounted for under the equity method, noncontrolling interests in consolidated enterprises, and equity instruments issued by the registrant and classified in stockholders' equity in the statement of financial position.

Derivative commodity instruments include, to the extent such instruments are not derivative financial instruments, commodity futures, commodity forwards, commodity swaps, commodity options, and other commodity instruments with similar characteristics, that are permitted by contract or business custom to be settled in cash or with another financial instrument.

Thus, the instrument definitions described above do not encompass (i) commodity positions, (ii) derivative commodity instruments that are not permitted by contract or business custom to be settled in cash or with another financial instrument (e.g., a commodity forward contract that must be settled in the commodity), (iii) cash flows from anticipated transactions, (e.g., operating cash flows from non-financial and non-commodity instruments), and/or (iv) certain financial instruments not included among the required disclosure items.[72]

[As amended in FR-79, effective April 23, 2009, 74 F.R. 18612.]

507.04. Disclosure of the Effects of Derivative Instruments on Reporting Financial Instruments, Commodity Positions, Firm Commitments, and Anticipated Transactions.

In conjunction with the adoption of Items 305 and 9A, the Commission reminds registrants that other reporting obligations also require certain disclosures about derivatives. The staff's 1994 and 1995 reviews of registrant filings suggested that some registrants are not providing sufficient disclosure about how derivatives directly or indirectly affect reported items. As a result, those disclosures may not have reflected as well as they otherwise might have such matters as the effective terms or expected cash flows of the derivatives and reported items.

It is fundamental that registrants include in any filings or reports any material information necessary to make statements made, in light of the circumstances, not misleading.[73] That is, registrants should provide disclosure about derivatives that affect, directly or indirectly, the terms, fair values, or cash flows of the reported items. This includes derivative transactions that are designated to reported items under generally accepted accounting principles.[74]

Thus, for example, information required to be disclosed in the footnotes to the financial statements about the interest rates and repricing characteristics of debt obligations should include, when material, information about the effects of derivatives. Similarly, summary information and disclosures in MD&A about the interest costs of debt obligations should include, when material,

---

[71] SAB Topic 1:D provides several examples of disclosures in MD&A that might be necessary to enable readers to understand the financial statements as a whole. One of those example disclosures includes significant accounting policies and measurement assumptions which may bear upon an understanding of operating trends or financial condition.

[72] See section III B.1.c.(vi), supra, for a further description of the instruments, positions, and transactions described in this paragraph.

[73] See, e.g., Rule 12b-20 under the Exchange Act and Rule 408 under the Securities Act.

[74] See, e.g., FAS 52 21a and FAS 80 4a.

disclosure of the effects of derivatives. Likewise, when derivatives directly or indirectly affect the terms and cash flows of items such as securities held as assets, servicing rights, oil and gas reserves, loan receivables, deposit liabilities, and leases, disclosure about the terms and cash flows

of those items should include, when material, disclosure of the effects of derivatives to the extent such disclosure is necessary to prevent the disclosure about the reported item from being misleading.

SECTION 600—MATTERS RELATING TO INDEPENDENT ACCOUNTANTS

[¶ 38,331] 601. Role of Independence in the Auditing Process

.01. Background

ASR 296:

The Commission has historically considered the independence of the auditors who examine financial statements filed with the Commission as central to the effective implementation of the federal securities laws. Indeed, the federal securities laws underscore the crucial function of independent auditors in protecting public investors by requiring that "independent" accountants certify financial statements filed with the Commission.* In keeping with these statutory mandates, Rule 2-01 of Regulation S-X provides that "[t]he Commission will not recognize any certified public accountant or public accountant as independent who is not in fact independent."

The accounting profession itself has traditionally recognized the importance of maintaining the public's confidence in the independence of accountants. As early as 1947, the Council of the American Institute of Accountants stated that "[i]n the field of auditing, the certified public accountant is under a responsibility peculiar to his profession and that is to maintain strict independence of attitude and judgment in planning and conducting his examinations and in expressing his opinion on financial statements."[1] In keeping with this philosophy of "strict independence," SAS 1 provides:

It is of utmost importance to the profession that the general public maintain confidence in the independence of independent auditors. Public confidence would be impaired by evidence that independence was actually lacking and it might also be impaired by the existence of circumstances which reasonable people might believe likely to influence independence.[2]

In a similar vein, the second general standard of generally accepted auditing standards indicates that "[i]n all matters relating to the assignment, an independence in mental attitude is to be maintained by the auditor or auditors."[3] The *Code of Professional Ethics* of the AICPA also states that "the public expects a number of character traits in a certified public accountant, but primarily integrity and objectivity and, in the practice of public accounting, independence."[4]

Independence has traditionally been defined by the profession as the ability to act with integrity and objectivity. An auditor is deemed to be independent if he is independent in fact and if he appears to be independent. He must act in an unbiased and objective manner and he must be free of any financial or other interest which would create the perception that he may not be independent. In the words of SAS 1:

To be independent, the auditor must be intellectually honest; to be recognized as independent, he must be free from any obligation to or interest in the client, its management, or its owners. . . . Independent auditors should not only be independent in fact; they should avoid situations that may lead outsiders to doubt their independence.[5]

The Commission continues to endorse and require scrupulous adherence to these principles. The Commission views both the fact and appearance of independence as essential in order that the public may justifiably view the audit process as a wholly unbiased review of management's presentation of the corporate financial picture. Through his audit and certification, the auditor provides the means for independently checking and confirming the information reported by corporations. Independence is thus of vital importance to investors, creditors, agencies of government and others who rely on the public accountant's opinion that financial statements fairly reflect the

---

* Thus Schedule A of the Securities Act, 15 U.S.C. 77aa, requires that balance sheets and profit and loss statements be "certified by an *independent* public or certified public accountant. . . ." Similarly, Section 12 of the Exchange Act, 15 U.S.C. 78*l*, gives the Commission the authority to require that applications for the registration of a security contain financial statements which have been "certified . . . by *independent* public accountants." And Section 13(a)(2) of that Act, 15 U.S.C. 78m(a)(2), likewise authorizes the Commission to specify that annual reports filed with the Commission contain

financial statements which have been "certified . . . by *independent* public accountants" (emphasis added).

[1] The Council of the American Institute of Accountants adopted an official statement on independence which was published in *The Journal of Accountancy* in July 1947.

[2] AICPA Professional Standards Vol. 1 AU Section 220.03.

[3] AICPA Professional Standards Vol. 1 AU Section 150.02.

[4] AICPA Professional Standards Vol. 2 ET Section 5201.

[5] AICPA Professional Standards Vol. 1 AU Section 220.03.

financial position and results of operations of the enterprise which he has audited. Absent independence, in fact and appearance, investors will have little confidence in public companies as investment vehicles.

Moreover, the capital formation process depends in large part on the confidence of investors in financial reporting. An investor's willingness to commit his capital to an impersonal market is dependent on the availability of accurate, material and timely information regarding the corporations in which he has invested or proposes to invest. The quality of information disseminated in the securities markets and the continuing conviction of individual investors that such information is reliable are thus key to the formation and effective allocation of capital. Accordingly, the audit function must be meaningfully performed and the accountants' independence not compromised. The auditor must be free to decide questions against his client's interests if his independent professional judgment compels that result. If the auditor is predisposed, or even appears predisposed, to blindly validate management's work rather than subjecting it to careful scrutiny, the ultimate result will be a diminution of public confidence in the profession and the integrity of the securities markets.

ASR 247:

The role of the independent accountant as an outside expert has expanded. Auditors now perform limited reviews of interim financial information and, on occasion, report the results of such reviews in Commission filings. In addition, generally accepted auditing standards require auditors to report to their clients material weaknesses in internal accounting controls that come to their attention during an examination of financial statements in accordance with such standards.[6]

The increased participation by the independent accountant in the financial reporting process makes it even more important that this relationship be fully understood and appreciated by investors and other users of financial information. To sustain confidence in financial statements by their users, the Commission and the accounting profession require that auditors remain independent, both in fact and appearance, of the companies they audit.

601.02. Commission's Efforts to Enhance Accountants' Independence

ASR 165:

One of the underpinnings of the Commission's administration of the disclosure requirements of the federal securities laws is its reliance on the reports of independent public accountants on the financial statements of registrants. These reports provide the assurance of an outside expert's exam-

ination and opinion, thereby substantially increasing the reliability of financial statements.

The decision that the Commission and investors should rely on independent public accountants for the audit of financial statements was made by Congress when it enacted the Securities Acts in the 1930's and in the judgment of the Commission this system has worked effectively in the interests of investors. The independence of these professionals both in fact and appearance is an essential ingredient in the system, and the Commission has taken a number of steps to strengthen this independence.

The Commission has described in various releases situations in which it concluded that the necessary independence did not exist due to economic or personal relationships between accountant and client. In this way, it assisted the accounting profession's own standard-setting bodies in the creation of credible and useful standards of independence for the profession as a whole. This process is a continuing one.

In addition, the Commission requires specific disclosure in a timely Form 8-K filing of any change in principal accountants made by the registrant, including disclosure of any disagreement between the registrant and its principal accountant in the eighteen months prior to the change which could have required or did require mention in the accountants' report. This is designed to strengthen accountants' independence by discouraging the practice of changing accountants in order to obtain more favorable accounting treatment.

In 1972, in ASR 123, the Commission urged registrants to create an audit committee of the outside members of the board of directors in order to provide for more effective communication between independent accountants and outside directors. It was believed that such a committee would lessen the accountants' direct reliance on management and would put them directly in touch with outside members of the board whose performance was less specifically being reported on in financial statements, thus increasing the accountants' independence.

Finally, the Commission and its staff have for many years offered support to accountants in numerous conferences and in informal administrative determinations of what reporting procedures should be followed in particular factual circumstances. The Commission's general refusal to accept opinions qualified in regard to audit scope or accounting principle as satisfying the Acts' requirements for certified financial statements has also strengthened the accountants' independence.

The Commission believes that the necessary independence of accountants does exist. It has

---

[6] SAS 20, "Required Communication of Material Weaknesses in Internal Accounting Control," AICPA, August 1977.

noted with approval reports in which the accountants have evidenced their independence by bringing significant information to the attention of investors. For example, in one case an independent accountant reported that its client's accounting procedures, while acceptable under GAAP, were not those which the firm believed best reported financial results under the particular factual circumstances. In another case, an independent accountant, while reporting on a five-year summary of earnings, noted in its report that the accounting principles used to account for a transaction in an unaudited interim period subsequent to the five-year period were such that had the firm been required to report on this period an adverse opinion would have been required. After discussions with the staff in this case, the registrant ultimately revised the interim statements.

601.03. Audit Committees and Independence

ASR 123:

As far back as 1917 it was urged that auditors in the United States should be appointed or selected by the shareholders in accordance with the practice in Great Britain and in Canada, and that state laws or company by-laws "should contain a provision for an independent report on the affairs of the company by an auditor appointed by the stockholders."*

Following the McKesson-Robbins investigation, in 1940 the Commission advocated the adoption of a program for: (1) current election of auditors at the annual meeting of stockholders; (2) nomination of auditors and arranging the details of the audit by a committee of nonofficer members of the board of directors; (3) addressing of the auditors' certificate, report or opinion to the stockholders; (4) mandatory attendance by auditors at the annual meetings of stockholders at which the audit report is presented; and (5) mandatory submission by auditors of a report on the amount of work done and of the reasons for noncompletion in situations where audit engagements are not completed. The stress of the program was on the responsibility of auditors to public investors.[1]

In 1967, the executive committee of the AICPA recommended that standing audit committees of outside directors should nominate auditors for the annual audits of publicly owned companies and should discuss the audit work with the auditors appointed to perform the audit. The AICPA considered that such standing audit committees " . . . can be a constructive force in the overall review of internal controls and financial structure, and give added assurance to stockholders as to the objectivity of corporate financial statements."[2]

A 1970 study has concluded that "[t]he potential for usefulness of corporate audit committees . . . sufficiently exceeds the possibilities for disturbance that we strongly recommend that all companies with significant nonmanagement shareholder interests consider carefully the desirability of establishing an audit committee . . . ."[3]

The Commission has a statutory duty to satisfy itself that the consolidated financial statements filed with it by publicly held companies of increasingly sophisticated and interlocking affiliations satisfy the requirements of Article 2 of Regulation S-X. To this end, the Commission, in the light of the foregoing historical recital, endorses the establishment by all publicly held companies of audit committees composed of outside directors and urges the business and financial communities and all shareholders of such publicly held companies to lend their full and continuing support to the effective implementation of the above-cited recommendations in order to assist in affording the greatest possible protection to investors who rely upon such financial statements.

[Added by FR-56]:

Issuers and other registrants have strong incentives to promote auditor independence. It is their financial statements that an auditor examines. They have the legal responsibility to file the financial information with the Commission, as a condition to accessing the public securities markets, and it is their filings that are legally deficient if auditors who are not independent certify their financial statements.

For most public companies, audit committees have become an essential means through which corporate boards of directors oversee the integrity of the company's financial reporting process, system of internal accounting control, and the financial statements themselves. Among other things, an audit committee serves as the board's principal interface with the company's auditors and facilitates communications between the company's board, its management, and its internal and independent auditors on significant accounting issues and policies.

The Commission is an advocate of effective and independent audit committees. Most recently, the Commission and three major exchanges adopted important audit committee rules. The New York Stock Exchange, the National Association of Securities Dealers, Inc., and the American Stock Exchange changed their listing standards. These

---

* John Thomas Madden, *Accounting Practice and Auditing: Modern Business Texts,* Vol. 21 (New York: Alexander Hamilton Institute, 1917, pp. 248-9).

[1] ASR 19 (December 5, 1940).

[2] "AICPA Executive Committee Statement on Audit Committees of Boards of Directors," *Journal of Accountancy,* Vol. 124 (September 1967), p. 10.

[3] R.K. Mautz and F.L. Neumann, *Corporate Audit Committees* (Urbana, Ill.: Bureau of Economic and Business Research, University of Illinois, 1970), p. 96.

changes require listed companies to have independent audit committees, and require audit committees to play a significant role in overseeing the company's auditors.[4]

Also, we adopted new disclosure rules regarding audit committees and auditor reviews of interim financial information[5] in response to recommendations of the Blue Ribbon Committee.[6] Those rules require that companies include in their proxy statements reports of their audit committees that state whether, among other things, the audit committees received the written disclosures and the letter from the independent auditors required by ISB Standard No. 1,[7] and discussed with the auditors the auditors' independence. ISB Standard No. 1 requires each auditor to disclose in writing to its client's audit committee all relationships between the auditor and the company that, in the auditor's judgment, reasonably may be thought to bear on independence and to discuss the auditor's independence with the audit committee.[8]

The final rule supplements those required disclosures with an additional disclosure as to whether the issuer's audit committee "has considered whether the provision of non-audit services] is compatible with maintaining the principal accountant's independence." The disclosure focuses particularly on non-audit services and requires disclosure of whether the audit committee itself has focused on the issue. We believe that our final rule, our new audit committee disclosure rules, and the new requirements of the NYSE, AMEX,

NASD, and ISB should encourage auditors, audit committees, and management to conduct robust and probing discussion on all issues that might affect the auditor's independence. According to the Blue Ribbon Report, "If the audit committee is to effectively accomplish its task of overseeing the financial reporting process, it must rely, in part, on the work, guidance and judgment of the outside auditor. Integral to this reliance is the requirement that the outside auditors perform their service without being affected by economic or other interests that would call into question their objectivity and, accordingly, the reliability of their attestation."[9]

Our final rule does not impose any new legal requirements on audit committees.[10] While the rule may serve to direct the attention of audit committees to the potential for independence issues arising from non-audit services, any action taken by audit committees will be business judgments. Nonetheless, the rule should help audit committees carry out their existing responsibilities by codifying the key legal requirements that may bear on audit committees' exercise of their business judgment.[11] We believe that audit committees, as well as management, should engage in active discussions of independence-related issues with the outside auditors.[12] As with discussions over the quality and acceptability of management's judgments, audit committees can be useful in considering whether assertions of independence rest on conservative or aggressive readings of the independence rules. Similarly, audit committees

---

[4] The New York Stock Exchange ("NYSE"), National Association of Securities Dealers, Inc. ("NASD"), and the American Stock Exchange ("AMEX") also changed their company listing standards to make it clear that the auditor is ultimately accountable to the board of directors and the audit committee, as opposed to management, and that the audit committee and the board of directors have the ultimate authority and responsibility to select, evaluate and, when appropriate, replace the auditor. *See* Order Approving Proposed Rule Change by the NASD, Exchange Act Rel. No. 42231, File No. SR-NASD-99-48 (Dec. 14, 1999); Order Approving Proposed Rule Change by the NYSE, Exchange Act Rel. No. 42233, File No. SR-NYSE-99-39 (Dec. 14, 1999); and Order Approving Proposed Rule Change by the AMEX, Exchange Act Rel. No. 42232, File No. SR-Amex-99-38 (Dec. 14, 1999).

[5] "Audit Committee Disclosure," Exchange Act Rel. No. 42266 (Dec. 22, 1999).

[6] In its report, the Blue Ribbon Committee noted that with respect to independent directors, even absent objective verification, "common sense dictates that a director without any financial, family, or other material personal ties to management is more likely to be able to evaluate objectively the propriety of management's accounting, internal control and reporting practices." Blue Ribbon Report, supra note 101, at 22.

[7] ISB Standard No. 1, "Independence Discussions with Audit Committees" (Jan. 1999). Copies of standards issued by the ISB are available on the ISB's website at www.cpaindependence.org.

[8] In a letter to the SECPS, ISB Chairman William Allen clarified the use of the auditor's judgment under the standard.

He stated:__p46_[I]n asking itself whether a fact or relationship is material in this setting the auditor may not rely on its professional judgment that such fact or relationship does not constitute an impairment of independence. Rather the auditor is to ask, in its informed good faith view, whether the members of the audit committee who represent reasonable investors, would regard the fact in question as bearing upon the board's judgment of auditor independence.__

p46_Letter from William T. Allen, Chairman, ISB, to Michael A. Conway, Chairman, Executive Committee, SECPS (Feb. 8, 1999). We believe that Chairman Allen's interpretation is appropriate.

[9] Blue Ribbon Report, *supra* note 101, at 40.

[10] *See* Testimony of Barry Melancon, President and Chief Executive Officer, AICPA (Sept. 21, 2000) ("[I]t's the audit firm's responsibility to determine that they are independent . . . . [T]he obligation is clearly on the auditor. The auditor cannot put that obligation off solely to the audit committee in any form or fashion. And even if the audit committee were to determine things were okay, the firm is still responsible to make an independent judgment that they are in fact independent.").

[11] *See* Testimony of John Whitehead, former Chairman, Goldman Sachs & Co. (Sept. 13, 2000).

[12] *See, e.g.,* Testimony of Robert L. Ryan, Chief Financial Officer, Medtronic, Inc. (Sept. 20, 2000) ("We believe that we should continue to require our audit committees, who are in the best position to evaluate independence, to play an active role in this assessment process as the proposed rule changes outline.").

---

may wish to consider whether to adopt formal or informal policies concerning when or whether to engage the company's auditing firm to provide non-audit services.[13]

In this latter connection, we note that recently the O'Malley Panel recommended certain guiding factors for audit committees to consider in making business judgments about particular non-audit services. According to the O'Malley Panel, one guiding principle should be whether the "service facilitates the performance of the audit, improves the client's financial reporting process, or is otherwise in the public interest."[14] Other matters to be considered are:

• Whether the service is being performed principally for the audit committee

• The effects of the service, if any, on audit effectiveness or on the quality and timeliness of the entity's financial reporting process

• Whether the service would be performed by specialists (e.g., technology specialists) who ordinarily also provide recurring audit support

• Whether the service would be performed by audit personnel and, if so, whether it will enhance their knowledge of the entity's business and operations

• Whether the role of those performing the service (e.g., a role where neutrality, impartiality and auditor skepticism are likely to be subverted) would be inconsistent with the auditor's role

• Whether the audit firm's personnel would be assuming a management role or creating a mutuality of interest with management

• Whether the auditors, in effect, would be auditing their own numbers

• Whether the project must be started and completed very quickly

• Whether the audit firm has unique expertise in the service

• The size of the fee(s) for the non-audit service(s)[15]

These factors expand upon the four factors in the Preliminary Note to Rule 2-01. Additionally,

the O'Malley Panel recommends that audit committees pre-approve non-audit services that exceed a threshold determined by the committee. We believe that the O'Malley Panel recommendations represent a thoughtful and appropriate approach to these issues by audit committees, and we encourage audit committees to consider the Panel's recommendations.

Some commenters suggested that the Commission and investors rely primarily on corporate audit committees to monitor and ensure auditor independence.[16] Other commenters, however, including investor representatives, indicated that this approach, without more, was inadequate.[17] While we welcome active oversight by audit committees with respect to auditor independence, we do not believe that this oversight obviates the need for the rule we adopt today. Audit committees bring business judgment to bear on the financial matters within their purview. Their purpose is not to set the independence standards for the profession, and we are not attempting to saddle them with that responsibility. On the other hand, we believe that the final rule facilitates the work of audit committees by establishing clear legal standards that audit committees can use as benchmarks against which to exercise business judgment.

601.04 Statement of Policy on the Establishment and Improvement of Standards Related to Auditor Independence

[Added by FR-50]:

I. *Background*

The various securities laws enacted by Congress and administered by the Securities and Exchange Commission underscore the crucial function of independent auditors in protecting public investors by requiring, or permitting the Commission to require, that financial statements filed with the Commission by public companies, investment companies, broker-dealers, public utilities, investment advisers, and others be certified (or audited) by "independent" public account-

---

[13] Companies have differing approaches to hiring their auditors to provide non-audit services. For example, John H. Biggs testified that TIAA-CREF does not hire its auditors to provide non-audit services (Testimony of John H. Biggs (July 26, 2000)), while Judy Lewent, Senior Vice President and CFO, Merck & Co., Inc., testified that her company employs a set of principles and practices for determining whether to hire their auditors to provide non-audit services, such as rotating its lead auditor every five years and requiring the audit committee to approve each request to use the outside audit firm for non-audit services. She noted that the company's process for such determinations has resulted in the use of their audit

firm for non-audit services only in limited circumstances (Testimony of Judy Lewent (Sept. 13, 2000)).

[14] O'Malley Panel Report, *supra* note 20, at ¶ 5.29.

[15] *Id.* at 116-17.

[16] *See, e.g.,* Testimony of Philip D. Ameen, Chair, Committee on Corporate Reporting, FEI-CRR (Sept. 20, 2000); Letter of Caroline Rook, Acxiom Corp. (Sept. 7, 2000); Letter of Allen J. Krowe, retired Vice Chairman, Texaco, Inc. (Sept. 5, 2000).

[17] *See, e.g.,* Testimony of Bill Patterson, Director of the Office of Investment, AFL-CIO (Sept. 20, 2000).

ants.[1] They also give the Commission the authority to define the term "independent."[2]

Since the Commission's creation in 1934, it consistently has emphasized the need for auditors to remain independent. The Commission's regulations are set forth in Rule 2-01 of Regulation S-X[3] and in the extensive interpretations, guidelines, and examples for registrants and auditors to use in evaluating specific independence questions that are collected in Section 600 of the Codification of Financial Reporting Policies ("Codification"), entitled "Matters Relating to Independent Accountants."[4] The Commission also makes publicly available the staff's written responses to requests for informal advice on its independence requirements. Pursuant to the Commission's regulations, the basic test for auditor independence is whether a reasonable investor, knowing all relevant facts and circumstances, would perceive an auditor as having neither mutual nor conflicting interests with its audit client and as exercising objective and impartial judgment on all issues brought to the auditor's attention.[5] In determining whether an auditor is independent, the Commission considers all relevant facts and circumstances, and its consideration is not confined to the relationships existing in connection with the filing of reports with the Commission.[6]

In certain matters, the Commission also has referred registrants and their auditors to independence requirements adopted by the American Institute of Certified Public Accountants ("AICPA"), to the extent those standards do not conflict with those of the Commission.[7]

Day-to-day, the Commission's staff receives inquiries regarding the application of the Commission's independence regulations to specific situations confronting registrants and their auditors. In recent years, these situations have be-come more complex as auditors have entered into new service areas for their clients, auditing firms have merged and restructured their operations, and business practices and technology have become more sophisticated and, increasingly, more global in scope. Some of the Commission's auditor independence regulations, written years ago, do not provide obvious guidance in today's business environment. The Commission recognizes, therefore, that an update of the Commission's regulations may be in order.

II. *The Independence Standards Board*

After careful consideration, and without abdicating its statutory responsibilities, the Commission intends to look to a standard-setting body designated by the accounting profession—known as the Independence Standards Board ("ISB")—to provide leadership not only in improving current auditor independence requirements, but also in establishing and maintaining a body of independence standards applicable to the auditors of all Commission registrants.[8] The Commission has taken a similar course in developing its relationship with the Financial Accounting Standards Board ("FASB"), a standard-setting body designated by the accounting profession that provides leadership in establishing and improving accounting principles.[9] Although the Commission expects to look to the ISB as the private sector body responsible for establishing independence standards and interpretations for auditors of public entities, the Commission's existing authority regarding auditor independence is not affected. This includes the Commission's authority to institute such enforcement actions as it deems appropriate, such as actions or proceedings instituted pursuant to Rule 102(e), 17 CFR 102(e). The Commission also retains ultimate authority to not accept, or to modify or supplement, ISB independence stan-

---

[1] Certain provisions of the Securities Act of 1933 ("Securities Act") and Securities Exchange Act of 1934 ("Exchange Act") expressly require that financial statements be audited by independent public or certified accountants. Securities Act Schedule A, items 25 and 26, 15 U.S.C. §§ 77aa(25) and (26); Exchange Act § 17(e), 15 U.S.C. § 78q. Various provisions of the securities laws authorize the Commission to require the filing of financial statements audited by independent accountants. Exchange Act §§ 12(b)(1)(J) and (K) and 13(a)(2), 15 U.S.C. §§ 78l and 78m; Public Utility Holding Company Act of 1935 ("PUHCA"), §§ 5(b)(H) and (I), 10(a)(1)(G), and 14, 15 U.S.C. § 79e(b), 79j, and 79n; Investment Company Act of 1940, §§ 8(b)(5) and 30(e), 15 U.S.C. § 80a-8 and 80a-29; Investment Advisers Act of 1940, § 203(c)(1)(D), 15 U.S.C. § 80b-3(c)(1). In accordance with these provisions, the Commission has required that certain financial statements be audited by independent accountants. See, e.g., Article 3 of Regulation S-X, 17 CFR 210.3-01 et seq. (1996).

[2] Various provisions of the securities laws grant the Commission the authority to define accounting, technical, and trade terms. Securities Act § 19(a), 15 U.S.C. § 77s(a); Exchange Ac t § 3(b), 15 U.S.C. § 78c(b); PUHCA § 20(a), 15 U.S.C. § 79t(a); and Investment Company Act § 38(a), 15 U.S.C. § 80a-37(a).

[3] 17 CFR 210.2-01 (1996).

[4] Financial Reporting Codification, Section 600-Matters Relating to Independent Accountants, reprinted in SEC Accounting Rules (CCH) ¶ 3,851, at 3,781.

[5] This test encompasses an evaluation of an auditor's independence in both fact and appearance. See Codification § 601.01 (quoting Accounting Series Release No. 296).

[6] Rule 2-01(c), 17 CFR 210.2-01(c) (1996).

[7] See, e.g., Office of the Chief Accountant, Staff Report on Auditor Independence, Appendix II at 5-7 (1994) (discussing AICPA requirements regarding loans to or from an audit client or its officers, directors, or stockholders; and stating that Commission has not adopted additional requirements in this area).

[8] The Commission generally has required foreign issuers and the auditors of their financial statements to comply with United States independence requirements when foreign issuers' audited financial statements are filed with the Commission. Accordingly, the ISB's pronouncements would apply to foreign as well as domestic audit reports that are filed with the Commission.

[9] See Accounting Series Release No. 150 (Dec. 20, 1973) (recognizing establishment of FASB); Accounting Series Release No. 280 (Sept. 2, 1980) (commenting on FASB's role in establishing and improving accounting principles).

dard s and interpretations in the same manner that the Commission can modify or supplement accounting standards and interpretations issued by the FASB. Moreover, the functioning of the ISB does not affect the authority of state licensing or disciplinary authorities regarding auditor independence.

The Commission expects that the public interest will be served by having the ISB take the lead in establishing, maintaining, and improving auditor independence requirements; and that operation of the ISB will promote efficiency, competition, and capital formation. The ISB, which is composed equally of public members (from which the ISB chairman must be elected) and practicing accountants, has undertaken to develop an institutional framework that will permit prompt and responsible actions by the ISB and its staff flowing from research and objective consideration of the issues. Collectively, the ISB members bring substantial experience and expertise to the process. In addition, the accounting profession's commitment of financial resources to the ISB is evidence of the private sector's willingness and intention to support the ISB. Under these circumstances, the Commission expects that determinations of the ISB will preserve and enhance the independence of public accountants, and thereby promote the interests of investors.

The central mission of the ISB will be to establish independence standards applicable to auditors of public entities that serve the public interest by promoting investor confidence in the securities markets. To further that goal, ISB standard-setting meetings will be open to the public, and proposed standards will be exposed for public comment before they are issued, in a process similar to that used by the FASB. In addition, the Commission will provide timely oversight of the ISB consistent with the Commission's statutory mandate to protect investors and safeguard the integrity of the capital markets.[10]

As noted, in the exercise of its statutory authority the Commission has the responsibility to ensure that independent audits of registrants' financial statements protect the interests of investors. In reviewing questions related to the fact or appearance of an auditor's independence from an audit client, the Commission will consider an auditor to be not independent unless the auditor has substantial authoritative support for the position

that the questioned transaction, event, or other circumstance, does not impair the auditor's independence. In this regard, the Commission will consider principles, standards, interpretations, and practices established or issued by the ISB as having substantial authoritative support for the resolution of auditor independence issues.[11] Conversely, the Commission will consider principles, standards, interpretations, and practices contrary to such ISB promulgations as having no such support.[12]

III. Review of ISB Operations

Since the formation of the ISB, there have been public announcements of mergers of several of the "Big 6" accounting firms. The impact of these mergers, and the accelerating trend toward consolidation of auditing firms generally, on foreign and domestic self-regulatory programs is being discussed within the United States, other countries, and international organizations. These events will be monitored closely and may prompt the Commission to reconsider certain of the accounting profession's self-regulatory programs, including the ISB.

In view of the significance of auditor independence to investor confidence in the securities markets, the Commission also will review the operations of the ISB as necessary or appropriate and, within five years from the date the ISB was established, will evaluate whether this new independence framework serves the public interest and protects investors.

[Amended by FR-56; FR-66].

[¶ 38,335] 602. Requirements and Interpretations Relating to Independence

602.01 Discussion of Rule 2-01.

[Added by FR-56]:

A. The Preliminary Note

We have included a Preliminary Note to Rule 2-01 that explains the Commission's approach to independence issues. Rule 2-01 does not purport to, and the Commission could not, consider all circumstances that raise independence concerns. The Preliminary Note makes clear that, in applying the standard in Rule 2-01(b), the Commission looks in the first instance to whether a relationship or the provision of a service:

(a) creates a mutual or conflicting interest between the accountant and the audit client;[1]

---

[10] The Commission and its staff will consult with the ISB during the course of ISB consideration of standards or interpretations, including those dealing with matters addressed by existing SEC guidance. As the ISB reconsiders and effectuates changes in independence standards and practices that involve existing SEC guidance, the Commission will consider modifying or withdrawing its conflicting guidance unless the Commission determines that it should not accept the ISB position in a particular area.

[11] Positions of the ISB staff and consensuses of a permanent task force that will assist the ISB, the Independence Issues Committee, will not be considered authoritative unless or until ratified by the ISB. Positions issued by the ISB staff to a particular party, however, may be relied upon by that party in accordance with the ISB Operating Policies.

[12] Entities that may issue such principles, standards, or interpretations include the AICPAs Professional Ethics Executive Committee.

[1] See, e.g., Codification § § 601.01 and 601.04.

(b) places the accountant in the position of auditing his or her own work;[2]

(c) results in the accountant acting as management or an employee of the audit client; or[3]

(d) places the accountant in a position of being an advocate for the audit client.[4]

These factors are general guidance and their application may depend on particular facts and circumstances. Nonetheless, we believe that these four factors provide an appropriate framework for analyzing auditor independence issues. We had proposed to include these four factors in the general standard of Rule 2-01(b). While some commenters agreed with including the four principles in the rule,[5] others did not. Some commenters believed that the principles were too general and difficult to apply to particular situations.[6] Others suggested that the principles should more appropriately be used as "guide posts" and included in a preamble instead of in the rule text.[7]

While the principles were derived from current independence requirements, because of these concerns, we are including them in the Preliminary Note. In the context of this Preliminary Note, the four factors play a role comparable to that of the Ethical Considerations in the American Bar Association's Model Code of Professional Responsibility. The Model Code contains three separate but interrelated parts.[8] Ethical Considerations "represent the objectives toward which every member of the profession should strive. They constitute a body of principles upon which the lawyer can rely for guidance in many specific situations."[9] Like those Ethical Considerations, the four principles constitute a body of principles to which accountants and audit committees can look for guidance when an independence issue is raised that is not explicitly addressed by the final rule.

The Preliminary Note states that "these factors are general guidance only and their application may depend on particular facts and circumstances." The Preliminary Note also reflects the notion that the influences on auditors may vary with the circumstances and, as a result, Rule 2-01 provides that the Commission will consider all relevant facts and circumstances in determining whether an accountant is independent.

B. *Qualifications of Accountants*

Rule 2-01(a) remains unchanged and requires that in order to practice before the Commission an auditor must be in good standing and entitled to practice in the state of the auditor's residence or principal office. This requirement has existed since the Federal Trade Commission first adopted rules under the Securities Act.[10] It acknowledges our deference to the states for the licensing of public and certified public accountants.

C. *The General Standard For Auditor Independence*

Our rule provides a general standard of auditor independence as well as specifying circumstances in which an auditor's independence is impaired. As to circumstances specifically set forth in our rule, we have set forth a bright-line test: an auditor is not independent if he or she maintains the relationships, acquires the interests, or engages in the transactions specified in the rule. In identifying particular circumstances in which an auditor's independence is impaired, we have taken into account the policy goals of promoting both auditor objectivity and public confidence that auditors are unbiased when addressing all issues encompassed within the audit engagement. We have also taken into account the value of specificity, and we have tried to give registrants and accountants substantial guidance and predictability. The particular circumstances that are set forth in our rule as impairing independence are those in which, in our judgment, it is sufficiently likely that an auditor's capacity for objective judgment will be impaired or that the investing public will believe that there has been an impairment of independence.

Circumstances that are not specifically set forth in our rule are measured by the general standard set forth in final Rule 2-01(b). Under that standard, we will not recognize an accountant as independent with respect to an audit client if the accountant is not, or if a reasonable investor knowing all relevant facts and circumstances would conclude that the accountant is not, capable of exercising

---

[2] *See, e.g.*, Codification § 602.02.c.i.

[3] *See* Rule 2-01(b), 17 CFR 210.2-01(b) (accountant cannot act as "director, officer or employee" of audit client and remain independent for purposes of Regulation S-X); Codification § 602.02.d.

[4] *See, e.g., Arthur Young*, 465 U.S. at 819 n.15; Codification §§ 602.02.e.i and ii.

[5] *See supra* note 15.

[6] *See supra* note 16; *see also* Written Testimony of Dan L. Goldwasser, Vedder, Price, Kaufman & Kammholz (July 26, 2000) (while acknowledging that "these concepts are not novel and can be found throughout the audit literature," stating that they "should not be adopted as guiding principles to be invoked each time a novel situation is encountered.").

[7] *See, e.g.*, Testimony of K. Michael Conaway, Presiding Officer, Texas State Board of Accountancy (Sept. 20, 2000) ("[W]e would ask that [the four principles] be better placed in a preamble or a guidance document."); Testimony of Clarence E. Lockett, Vice President and Corporate Controller, Johnson & Johnson (Sept. 20, 2000) ("[W]e do not believe the four governing principles should be stated as firm rules [but rather] be part of the framework and serve [as] guiding principles.").

[8] Thomas D. Morgan and Ronald D. Rotunda, eds., The Model Code of Professional Responsibility (1995).

[9] *Id.* at Preliminary Statement (citing "Professional Responsibility: Report of the Joint Conference," 44 A.B.A.J., at 1159 (1958)).

[10] Federal Trade Commission, *Rules and Regulations Under the Securities Act of 1933*, art. 14 (July 6, 1933).

objective and impartial judgment on all issues encompassed within the accountant's engagement.[11]

The general standard in paragraph (b) recognizes that an auditor must be independent in fact and appearance. Some commenters suggested that the use of an appearance-related standard departs from current rules.[12] As discussed above and in the Proposing Release, the Commission, courts, and the profession have long recognized the importance of the appearance of independence.[13]

Moreover, the general standard we are adopting merely reflects the different means of demonstrating a lack of objectivity. Objectivity is a state of mind,[14] and except in unusual circumstances, a state of mind is not subject to direct proof.[15] Usually, it is demonstrated by reference to circumstantial evidence. Accordingly, the final rule is formulated to indicate that an auditor's independence is impaired either when there is direct evidence of subjective bias, such as through a confession or some way of recording the auditor's thoughts, or when, as in the ordinary case, the facts and circumstances as externally observed demonstrate, under an objective standard, that an auditor would not be capable of acting without bias.

The appearance standard incorporated in the general standard is an objective one. Appearance is measured by reference to a reasonable investor. The "reasonable person" standard is embedded in the law generally. In particular, the "reasonable investor" standard is reflected in the concept of materiality under the federal securities laws.[16]

Commenters expressed concern that a general standard based on the conclusion of a "reasonable investor" may have some imprecision. They urged that the general standard require only independence "in fact." We believe, however, that we have reduced imprecision substantially by describing in some detail particular circumstances that give rise to an impairment of independence. Moreover, reliance solely on independence "in fact" would increase the imprecision beyond a "reasonable investor" test, because independence "in fact" is essentially an inquiry into the subjective workings of the accountant's mind, whereas a "reasonable investor" test relies on observable circumstances and is thus better suited to uniform and consistent application.

We recognize that there is an irreducible degree of imprecision in the notion of independence. We will be mindful of this imprecision, and the range of reasonable views that it engenders, in applying the auditor independence rules. We do not, for example, seek to discourage the development of non-audit services that do not raise independence issues. In considering our response to services not explicitly covered by these rules, we will take into account the nature of the service, prior contacts with the staff, relevant public statements by the Commission or staff, and any related professional literature.

Paragraphs (c)(1) through (5) require the accountant to be independent during the "audit and professional engagement period."[17] This term is defined in Rule 2-01(f)(5) to mean the period covered by any financial statements being audited or reviewed, and the period during which the auditor is engaged either to review or audit financial statements or to prepare a report filed with us, including at the date of the audit report.[18] The use of the word "during" in paragraphs (c)(1) through (5) is intended to make clear that an accountant will lack independence if, for example, he or she is independent at the outset of the engagement but acquires a financial interest in the audit client during the engagement.

We have further confined the legal standard by including the explicit reference to "all relevant facts and circumstances." To make this explicit, we have included the language in the rule text. We have also modified the language to refer to whether a reasonable investor would "conclude" as opposed to "perceive" that the accountant was not capable of exercising objective and impartial

---

[11] *Cf. Staff Report, supra* note 74, at 12-16. *See also* SEC, *Tenth Annual Report of the Securities and Exchange Commission,* at 205-207 (1944), which states:_p46_[T]he Commission has found an accountant to be lacking in independence with respect to a particular registrant if the relationships which exist between the accountant and the client are such as to create a reasonable doubt as to whether the accountant will or can have an impartial and objective judgment on the questions confronting him.

[12] *See, e.g.,* KPMG Letter.

[13] *See supra* note 38-40; Proposing Release, Section II.B.

[14] *See supra* note 39.

[15] *See United States v. Gamache,* 156 F.3d 1, 8 (1st Cir. 1998) ("Now, undoubtedly, establishing intent, short of a situation in which it is admitted, is difficult and usually depends on the use of circumstantial evidence.").

[16] *See TSC Industries, Inc. v. Northway, Inc.,* 426 U.S. 438, 449 (1976) (information is material if it would be "viewed by the reasonable investor as having significantly altered the 'total mix' of information made available"); *Basic, Inc. v. Levinson,* 485 U.S. 224, 234-236 (1988).

[17] *See also* AICPA Code of Professional Conduct, ET § 101.02 (revised Feb. 28, 1998).

[18] Rule 2-01(f)(5) states that the engagement period ends when the registrant or accountant notifies the Commission that the registrant is no longer the accountant's audit client. This notice typically would occur when the registrant files with the Commission a Form 8-K with disclosures under Item 4 "Changes in Registrant's Certifying Accountant." In some cases, however, a Form 8-K is not required, such as when the registrant is a foreign private issuer or when the audited financial statements of a non-reporting company are filed upon its acquisition by a public company. Notification to the Commission in these cases would occur by the filing of the next audited financial statements of the foreign private issuer or the successor corporation. Registrants or auditors in these situations, however, may provide earlier notice to the Commission on Form 6-K or by other appropriate means.

judgment. While this is not a substantive change, it makes clear that independence is an objective standard measured from the perspective of the reasonable investor.

Current Rule 2-01(c) provides that we will look to all relevant circumstances, including all relationships between the accountant and the audit client and not just those relating to reports filed with the Commission. We proposed to include this language in Rule 2-01(e). Under the adopted rule, however, the language appears in Rule 2-01(b) in order to highlight that in applying the general standard in Rule 2-01(b), we will consider "all relevant circumstances."

We remind registrants and accountants that auditor independence is not just a legal requirement. It is also a professional and ethical duty. That duty requires auditors to remain independent of audit clients,[19] and includes an obligation to "avoid situations that may lead outsiders to doubt [the auditor's]independence."[20]

In certain situations, whether or not legally required, the best course may be for the accountant to recuse himself or herself from an audit engagement. On occasion, there may be a relationship, apart from those contemplated by any standard or rule, that has an important meaning to an individual accountant and could create, or be viewed by a reasonable investor with knowledge of all relevant facts and circumstances as creating, a conflict with the accountant's duty to investors.[21] In this and any similar situation, we encourage accountants to seek to recuse themselves from any review, audit, or attest engagement, whether or not specifically required by the Commission's, the ISB's, or the profession's rules.

D. *Specific Applications of The Independence Standard*

Rule 2-01(c) ties the general standard of paragraph (b) to specific applications. Paragraphs (c)(1) through (c)(5) address separately situations in which an accountant is not independent of an audit client because of certain: (1) financial relationships, (2) employment relationships, (3) business relationships, (4) transactions or situations involving the provision of non-audit services, or (5) transactions or situations involving the receipt of contingent fees.[22]

The proposed rule included a provision under which an accountant's independence would have been impaired if the accountant had any of the relationships or provided any of the services described by proposed Rule 2-01(c), or "otherwise [did] not comply with the standard" of paragraph (b). We have eliminated from the text of the rule the language regarding the accountant's failure "otherwise" to comply with the standard. Instead, we have modified the structure of paragraph (c) to make clear that the paragraph sets forth a "non-exclusive specification of circumstances" that are inconsistent with the standard of paragraph (b).

1. Financial Relationships

Rule 2-01(c)(1) sets forth the general rule regarding financial relationships that impair independence. It addresses, among other things, direct or material indirect investments, trustee positions involving investment decision-making authority, investments in common with audit clients, debtor-creditor relationships, deposit accounts, brokerage accounts, commodity accounts, and insurance policies.

Rule 2-01(c)(1) contains the general standard that "[a]n accountant is not independent if, at any point during the audit and professional engagement period, the accountant has a direct financial interest or a material indirect financial interest in the accountant's audit client." The rule then specifies certain financial interests that constitute a direct or material indirect financial interest in an audit client. As the rule indicates, the list of specified interests is not intended to be exclusive. The specified interests represent common types of financial interests that impair independence, but the effect of other types of financial interests on auditor independence will be determined under the general standards of paragraphs (b) and (c)(1).

In applying the financial relationship provisions of the rule, it is important to bear in mind the definition of "audit client." "Audit client," when used in the rule, includes some "affiliate[s]of the audit client," as that term is defined in the rule.[23] Accordingly, financial relationships with certain affiliates of audit clients are subject to the provisions of Rule 2-01(c)(1). In this discussion, as well as in the rule, references to "audit client" should be understood to include the appropriate affiliates of the audit client.

For the most part, the specified financial interests described in this section of the rule impair

---

[19] *See* AICPA SAS No. 1, AU §220.03; AICPA Code of Professional Conduct, ET §101. Of course, accountants also have to comply with applicable state law on independence. *Id.*

[20] AICPA SAS No. 1, AU §220.03.

[21] *Cf. AUSA Life Ins. Co. v. Ernst & Young,* 206 F.3d 202, 205 (2d Cir. 2000) (noting "E&Y's failure lay in the seeming spinelessness" of the audit engagement partner and that "[p]art of the problem was undoubtedly the close personal relationship between" that partner and the company's chief executive officer, a former co-partner in the firm) (quoting 991 F. Supp. 234, 248 (S.D.N.Y. 1997) (district court opinion)).

[22] A number of the specified situations are based on examples in the Codification and the AICPA and SECPS membership rules.

[23] *See infra* Sections IV.H.3 and IV.H.5, for detailed discussions of the definitions of "audit client" and "affiliate of the audit client." As explained below, the affiliates of the audit client that are deemed to be included in the term "audit client" for purposes of the financial relationship provisions in paragraph (c)(1)(i) are more limited than the group included in other parts of the rule.

independence only if they are financial interests of the accounting firm, covered persons in the firm, or immediate family members of covered persons. (The exception concerns situations involving beneficial ownership of more than five percent of an entity, or control of an entity.) This represents a liberalization from prior restrictions that generally reached all partners in the firm regardless of whether they had any relationship to the audit of the particular client.

While the comments we received reflected widespread (although not universal) agreement with our goal of modernizing the financial relationships restrictions, some commenters urged us not to liberalize these restrictions to the extent we proposed. Generally, these commenters argued in favor of the prophylactic value of a rule precluding a broader scope of persons from having a financial interest in an audit client of the firm.[24] Several of these commenters also spoke of the importance of a firm culture that treats all clients as clients of the firm, and in which the firm can call on any partner to assist with the audit of any client on short notice without having to consider whether the partner's personal financial interests preclude it.[25]

On the other hand, some commenters, while agreeing generally with our proposal to scale back the scope of persons whose financial interests are restricted, advocated that we further narrow the group of persons who are included in the restrictions. These commenters generally expressed a preference for a "tiered" approach that would restrict even fewer people with respect to some types of financial interests.[26]

The balance we struck between these two sets of concerns was viewed favorably by many commenters.[27] We believe that fair, meaningful, and relevant independence rules concerning financial relationships should reflect a calibrated approach to determining what specific relationships realistically give rise to independence concerns. After considering the comments we received, we have drawn the lines essentially where we proposed— "covered persons in the firm" and their immediate family members—though we have modified slightly the definition of "covered persons" in the firm.[28] The final rule, like the proposed rule,

would attribute all investments by a covered person's "immediate family members," that is, the covered person's spouse, spousal equivalent, and dependents, to the covered person.

a. *Investments in Audit Clients*

Rule 2-01(c)(1)(i) describes investments that impair an accountant's independence as to a particular audit client. Paragraph (A) provides that an accountant is not independent of an audit client if the accounting firm, any covered person in the firm, or any immediate family member of any covered person has a "direct investment" — such as stocks, bonds, notes, options, or other securities—in the audit client. As the language of the rule makes clear, this is not an exclusive list of all ownership interests subject to the rule. Other than with respect to the scope of persons encompassed by the rule, paragraph (A) does not represent any substantive change to our rules on direct investments.

We noted in the Proposing Release that "as under current law, the rule cannot be avoided through indirect means."[29] We stated, as an example, that an accountant precluded from having a direct investment in an audit client could not evade that restriction by investing in the client through a corporation or as a member of an investment club.[30] Some commenters proposed that we address that issue with specific rule text, and they proposed language.[31] While not adopting the language proposed by commenters, we have, in the interest of increased clarity, included in the final rule language addressing that issue.

Specifically, we have added the proviso that an investment through an intermediary shall constitute a "direct investment" in the audit client if either of two conditions is satisfied: "(1) The accounting firm, covered person, or immediate family member, alone or together with other persons, supervises or participates in the intermediary's investment decisions or has control over the intermediary; or (2) The intermediary is not a diversified management investment company . . . and has an investment in the audit client that amounts to 20% or more of the value of the intermediary's total investments." If either of these criteria is

---

[24] *See, e.g.*, Written Testimony of Thomas M. Rowland, Senior Vice President, Fund Business Management Group, Capital Research and Management Company (Sept. 20, 2000) (restrictions should extend to persons in the firm beyond the scope of "covered persons"); Letter of John Spadafora (June 28, 2000) (narrowing the scope of persons whose investments are restricted "is another step backwards creating temptations to pass inside information to those whose investments are not restricted.").

[25] *See generally* Written Testimony of J. Michael Cook, former Chairman and Chief Executive Officer, Deloitte & Touche (July 26, 2000); Testimony of Ray J. Groves, former Chairman and Chief Executive Officer of Ernst & Young (July 26, 2000).

[26] *See, e.g.*, Ernst & Young Letter.

[27] *See, e.g.*, Written Testimony of William R. Kinney, Jr., Professor, University of Texas at Austin (Sept. 20, 2000) (proposed changes will "reduce aggregate regulatory compliance without affecting audit quality or increasing independence impairment risk for investors"); Testimony of Robert L. Ryan, Chief Financial Officer, Medtronic, Inc. (Sept. 20, 2000) (proposed financial relationship rules are "logical, less bureaucratic, and we're completely in agreement").

[28] *See infra* Section IV.H.9 for a detailed discussion of the definition of "covered persons in the firm."

[29] Proposing Release, Section III.C.1(a) citing Codification § 602.02.b.ii (Example 1).

[30] Proposing Release, Section III.C.1(a).

[31] *See* Ernst & Young Letter; PricewaterhouseCoopers Letter.

satisfied, the investment is treated as a direct investment in the audit client and, therefore, impairs independence. If an investment through an intermediary does not satisfy either of these two criteria, however, the investment is considered "indirect," and it impairs independence only if it crosses one of the thresholds set out in Rule 2-01(c)(1)(i)(D) or (E).

Rule 2-01(c)(1)(i)(B) provides that an accountant is not independent when "[a]ny partner, principal, shareholder, or professional employee of the accounting firm, any of his or her immediate family members, any close family member of a covered person in the firm, or any group of the above persons has filed a Schedule 13D or 13G[32] []with the Commission indicating beneficial ownership of more than five percent of an audit client's equity securities, or controls an audit client, or a close family member of a partner, principal, or shareholder of the accounting firm controls an audit client." Paragraph (B) is the only one of the financial relationship provisions that specifically encompasses a range of persons beyond covered persons and their immediate family members. The broader scope of coverage under paragraph (B) is based on the view that when a financial interest in an audit client of the firm becomes particularly large, the fact that the person holding that interest is distanced from the audit engagement no longer sufficiently mitigates the potential for a conflict.

We have made one substantive addition to the proposed paragraph (B). We have added at the end of the paragraph the clause "or a close family member of a partner, principal, or shareholder of the accounting firm controls an audit client." This provision identifies additional circumstances that impair independence, beyond the circumstances in our proposed rule.[33] For instance, this provision would provide that independence is impaired when the sister or parent of a partner in the firm who is not a covered person controls an audit client. We agree that the circumstances described by this provision would result in an impairment of independence. In addition, we note that this provision is consistent with existing rules.[34]

Rule 2-01(c)(1)(i)(C) provides that an accountant is not independent when "[t]he accounting firm, any covered person in the firm, or any of his or her immediate family members, serves as voting trustee of a trust or executor of an estate containing the securities of an audit client, unless the accounting firm, covered person in the firm or immediate family member has no authority to make investment decisions for the trust or estate."

Because a trustee or executor typically has a fiduciary duty to preserve or maximize the value of the trust's or estate's assets, we believe it is appropriate to treat the trustee's or executor's interest as a direct financial interest in the audit client and to deem the auditor's independence impaired. We understand, however, that a person might serve as a trustee or executor without having any authority to make investment decisions for the trust or estate. Because we see no reason to consider an auditor's independence impaired in those circumstances, we have added the proviso at the end of paragraph (C) to include an exception for those circumstances.

Rule 2-01(c)(1)(i)(D) covers material indirect investments in an audit client. The basic rule provides that an accountant is not independent when "[t]he accounting firm, any covered person in the firm, any of his or her immediate family members, or any group of the above persons has any material indirect investment in an audit client." This provision carries over the existing proscription on material indirect investments in audit clients.[35]

At the proposing stage, paragraph (D) included two examples of what would constitute a material indirect investment: (1) ownership of more than five percent of an entity that has an ownership interest in the audit client, and (2) ownership of more than five percent of an entity in which the audit client has an ownership interest. A number of commenters, however, proposed eliminating those examples as unnecessarily restrictive and burdensome. We agree that the examples would have consequences beyond what we intended. Accounting firms may, through their pension plans or otherwise, acquire more than five percent stakes in other entities. In these situations, it may well be impracticable for an accounting firm regularly to monitor whether that entity has *any* financial interest in an audit client or whether an audit client has *any* financial interest in the entity.[36] Accordingly, we have omitted those examples in the final rule.

Because the material indirect investment rule is a general standard, we have also decided to include one additional provision to clarify the meaning of "material indirect investment" in the context of mutual fund investments. Specifically, the rule makes explicit that the term "material indirect investment" does not include ownership by any covered person in the firm, any of his or her immediate family members, or any group of the above persons, of five percent or less of the outstanding shares of a diversified management in-

---

[32] 17 CFR 240.13d-101, 13d-102.

[33] *Cf.* Ernst & Young Letter; PricewaterhouseCoopers Letter (suggesting a similar provision for immediate family members of all partners in the firm).

[34] *See* Codification § 602.02.h (Examples 1 and 5).

[35] *See* former Rule 2-01(b).

[36] The analysis is different with respect to situations where the entity has a material investment in the audit client, or the audit client has a material investment in the entity. We address those situations in Rule 2-01(c)(1)(i)(E), discussed below.

vestment company that invests in an audit client.[37] Consequently, the material indirect investment rules, as adopted, allow auditors to invest in management investment companies, provided that the company is diversified as defined under the Investment Company Act of 1940.[38] If an investment company is non-diversified under the Investment Company Act of 1940,[39] the company must disclose that fact in its prospectus. As a result, an accountant can easily determine by reviewing the prospectus whether the company is diversified for purposes of the rule. In addition, this provision does not constitute any substantive change from the proposed rule, because the general categories of examples in the proposed rule would have covered this situation. This provision is intended to ensure that all firm personnel and their family members can freely invest (up to the five percent cap) in diversified mutual funds that are not audit clients and are not part of an investment company complex that includes an audit client, without bearing the burden of constantly monitoring whether, and to what degree, those funds invest in an audit client's securities.[40]

We have not included accounting firms within this provision for two reasons. First, in contrast to most individual investors, accounting firms through their pension funds may invest large sums and, therefore, better access diversified investment vehicles, such as managed accounts that do not invest in their audit clients. At the same time, the large amounts that may be invested by an accounting firm, through its pension plan or otherwise, increase the chances that the indirect investment may be material to the audit client. This should not be understood, however, to prevent accounting firms from investing in diversified mutual funds. Rather, when they invest in such funds, they must comply with the general "material indirect investment" standard.

Second, at the suggestion of commenters,[41] we have included a new paragraph (E) that governs (1) investments in entities that invest in audit clients ("intermediary investors") and (2) investment in entities in which audit clients invest ("common investees"). We have decided to codify in our rule the substance of the existing AICPA restrictions applicable to those situations.[42] We have codified those restrictions in paragraph (c)(1)(i)(E).

Paragraph (E), like the AICPA rule, is framed in terms of material investments and the ability to exercise significant influence over an entity.[43] In the case of an intermediary investor, paragraph (E) provides that an accountant is not independent if the firm, a covered person, or an immediate family member of a covered person has either (1) a direct or material indirect investment in an entity that has both an investment in an audit client that is material to that entity and the ability to exercise significant influence over the audit client,[44] or (2) the ability to exercise significant influence over an

---

[37] The term "diversified management investment company" refers to those entities meeting the definitions of "management company" and "diversified company" in Sections 4(3) and 5(b)(1) of the Investment Company Act, 15 U.S.C. §§ 80a-4(3) and 80a-5(b)(1).

[38] Under the Investment Company Act, a "diversified" management company must meet the following requirements: at least 75% of the value of its total assets is in cash, cash items, Government securities, securities of other investment companies, and other securities limited in respect of any one issuer to an amount not greater in value than five percent of the value of the total assets of such management company and not more than ten percent of the outstanding voting securities of such issuer. 15 U.S.C. § 80a-5(b)(1).

[39] One commenter recommended that diversification be measured under Subchapter M of the Internal Revenue Code rather than the Investment Compan y Act of 1940. See Letter of Investment Company Institute (Sept. 25, 2000) ("ICI Letter"). Under Subchapter M, at the end of each calendar quarter of the taxable year, at least 50% of the value of the fund's total assets must be represented by cash, cash items, U.S. Government securities, securities of other investment companies, and investments in other securities, which, with respect to any one issuer, do not represent more than five percent of the value of total assets of the fund or more than ten percent of the voting securities of the issuer. In addition, no more than 25% of the value of the fund's total assets may be invested in securities of any one issuer. The Commission determined not to adopt the tax code diversification test because an investment company could concentrate its investments in a smaller number of issues and requires diversification only at the close of each quarter.

[40] See Written Testimony of Thomas C. Rowland, Senior Vice President, Fund Business Management Group, Capital Research and Management Company (Sept. 20, 2000) (suggesting a similar rule).

[41] See Ernst & Young Letter; PricewaterhouseCoopers Letter.

[42] See AICPA Code of Professional Conduct, ET § 101-8.

[43] Here, as elsewhere in the rule, we use the term "significant influence" as it is used in Accounting Principles Board Opinion No. 18, "The Equity Method of Accounting for Investments in Common Stock" (Mar. 1971) ("APB No. 18"). See infra Section IV.H.3. Because we have included a specific rule on investments in non-clients, as well as the material indirect investment rule of paragraph (D), we have decided that a more limited definition of "affiliate of an audit client" is warranted for purposes of the investment rules in paragraph (c)(1)(i). The definition of "audit client" provides that, for purposes of paragraph (c)(1)(i), audit client does not include "entities that are affiliates of the audit client only by virtue of paragraph (f)(4)(ii) or (f)(4)(iii) of the section." In other words, the only "affiliates of the audit client" that are included in the term "audit client" in section (c)(1)(i) are those that are in a control relationship with the audit client or that are part of the same investment company complex as the audit client. The rules on investments specifically state that an investment in certain entities that significantly influence, or are significantly influenced by, the audit client, impair the auditor's independence. Accordingly, there is no need to include those entities within the more general definition of an "affiliate of the audit client."

[44] See Rule 2-01(c)(1)(i)(E)(1)(ii).

entity that has the ability to exercise significant influence over an audit client.[45]

In the case of a common investee, paragraph (E) provides that an accountant is not independent if the firm, a covered person, or an immediate family member of a covered person has either (1) a direct or material indirect investment in an entity in which an audit client has a material (to the audit client) investment and over which the audit client has the ability to exercise significant influence,[46] or (2) any material investment in an entity over which an audit client has the ability to exercise significant influence.[47]

With respect to paragraph (c) (1) (i) (E) (2), which turns in part on whether a covered person's or immediate family member's investment in an entity is material to that person, we do not anticipate that compliance requires a firm constantly to monitor the net worth of all covered persons and their immediate family members in order to know at all times whether any particular investment is material to them. We anticipate that monitoring for compliance with this paragraph will involve routine monitoring of the investments of all covered persons and their immediate family members, combined with monitoring of the identity of entities over which the firm's audit clients have the ability to exercise significant influence. When overlap between those categories appears, the firm can take additional steps to determine whether the relevant investment is material to the covered persons or immediate family members holding the investment.

If an "intermediary investor" or a "common investee" becomes an affiliate of the audit client under paragraph (f) (4) (i) or (iv), then paragraph (E) no longer governs the question of independence. Rather, paragraph (A)'s provision concerning direct investments in audit clients will apply to that intermediary investor or common investee, and *any* investment in that entity by the firm, a covered person, or an immediate family member of a covered person would impair independence.

b. *Other Financial Interests*

Rule 2-01 (c) (1) (ii) describes other financial interests of an auditor that would impair an auditor's independence with respect to an audit client because they create a debtor-creditor relationship or other commingling of the financial interests of the auditor and the audit client. In some situations, the continued viability of the audit client may be necessary for protection of the auditor's own as-

sets (*e.g.*, bank deposits or insurance) or for the auditor to receive a benefit (*e.g.*, insurance claim). These situations reasonably may be viewed as creating a self-interest that competes with the auditor's obligation to serve only investors' interests. We have adopted Rule 2-01 (c) (1) (ii) largely as proposed, though we have made some modifications, described below.

(i) *Loans/Debtor-Creditor Relationships*

Rule 2-01 (c) (1) (ii) (A) provides that an accountant will not be independent when the accounting firm, any covered person in the accounting firm, or any of the covered person's immediate family members has any loan (including any margin loan) to or from an audit client, or an audit client's officers, directors, or record or beneficial owners of more than ten percent of the audit client's equity securities. As proposed, we have also adopted exceptions for four types of loans:[48] (1) automobile loans and leases collateralized by the automobile; (2) loans fully collateralized by the cash surrender value of an insurance policy; (3) loans fully collateralized by cash deposits at the same financial institution; and (4) a mortgage loan collateralized by the borrower's primary residence provided the loan was not obtained while the covered person in the firm was a covered person.

As adopted, paragraph (A) varies from the proposed rule in two respects, one representing a substantive change and one a clarifying change. The substantive change involves increasing to ten percent (up from the proposed five percent) the percentage of an audit client's securities that a lender may own without posing an independence impairment for an accountant who borrows from that lender. We have made this change because we believe that doing so will not make the rule significantly less effective, and may significantly increase the ease with which one can obtain the information necessary to assure compliance with this rule. The ten percent threshold corresponds to the definitions in the Commission's Regulation S-X of a "principal holder of equity securities,"[49] as well as a "promoter."[50] In addition, other aspects of the securities laws attach significance to an equity interest in excess of ten percent.[51] These definitions and substantive legal provisions clearly classify ten percent shareholders as having a special and influential role with the issuer. Accordingly, a lender owning more than ten percent of an audit client's securities would be considered to be in a position to influence the policies and management of that client.

---

[45] Rule 2-01 (c) (1) (i) (E) (3). The operation of paragraphs (E) (*1*) (*ii*) and (E) (3) is illustrated in the chart attached as *Appendix A*.

[46] Rule 2-01 (c) (1) (i) (E) (*1*) (*i*).

[47] Rule 2-01 (c) (1) (i) (E) (2). The operation of paragraphs (E) (*1*) (*i*) and (E) (2) is illustrated in the chart attached as *Appendix B*.

[48] Consistent with the Proposing Release, we have treated credit card debt as a separate category. *See* discussion of paragraph (c) (1) (ii) (E) below.

[49] Regulation S-X, Rule 1-02 (r), 17 CFR 210.1-02 (r).

[50] Regulation S-X, Rule 1-02 (s) (2), 17 CFR 210.1-02 (s) (2).

[51] *See, e.g.*, Section 16 of the Securities Exchange Act of 1934, 15 U.S.C. § 78p.

The clarifying change involves the wording of paragraph (A)(4), which describes the mortgage loan exception. The proposed rule referred to a mortgage loan "collateralized by the accountant's primary residence." In the final rule, we have changed "accountant" to "borrower," because we intend for the exception to apply also to mortgage loans obtained by an immediate family member of a covered person. The proposed rule also specified that this exception was limited to loans "not obtained while the borrower was a covered person in the firm or an immediate family member of a covered person in the firm." In the final rule, we have changed this language to "not obtained while the covered person in the firm was a covered person." This change is intended only as a way of clarifying that the test focuses on the status of the relevant covered person at the time of the mortgage loan.

(ii) *Savings and Checking Accounts*

Rule 2-01(c)(1)(ii)(B) concerns savings and checking accounts. It provides that an accountant is not independent when the firm, a covered person, or an immediate family member of a covered person "has any savings, checking, or similar account at a bank, savings and loan, or similar institution that is an audit client, if the account has a balance that exceeds the amount insured by the Federal Deposit Insurance Corporation or any similar insurer, except that an accounting firm account may have an uninsured account balance provided that the likelihood of the bank, savings and loan, or similar institution experiencing financial difficulties is remote."

At the suggestion of commenters, we have modified this provision from the proposed rule by adding the exception for accounting firm accounts with institutions that have no more than a remote likelihood of experiencing financial difficulties.[52] Large firms often maintain account balances well in excess of FDIC limits, and the heavy daily volume of large transactions imposes such demands on a financial institution that there is, as a practical matter, a very limited universe of banks capable of servicing those accounts. Under the circumstances, we are persuaded that it is necessary to provide an exception that would allow accounting firms (but not individuals who are covered persons) to maintain balances above insured limits even if the financial institution is an audit client. We emphasize that this is a narrow exception mandated by practical necessity, and that, even so, the exception only applies as long as there is no more than a remote likelihood of the institution experiencing financial difficulties. If there is more than a remote likelihood of the institution experiencing financial difficulties, then

an uninsured balance will impair independence because the auditor would be placed in the situation of having to decide whether to express an opinion about the institution as a going concern when the auditor's own assets may be at risk.

(iii) *Broker-Dealer Accounts*

Rule 2-01(c)(1)(ii)(C) provides that an accountant will not be independent when the accounting firm, any covered person in the firm, or any of the covered person's immediate family members, has any brokerage or similar accounts maintained with a broker-dealer that is an audit client if any such accounts include any asset other than cash or securities (within the meaning of "security" provided in the Securities Investor Protection Act ("SIPA")), or where the value of the assets in the accounts exceeds the amount that is subject to a Securities Investor Protection Corporation ("SIPC") advance for those accounts, under Section 9 of SIPA. Those final provisions are as we proposed.

In addition, we have added to paragraph (C) a provision intended to ensure that brokerage accounts maintained outside of the U.S. not covered by SIPA will nonetheless not impair independence so long as the value of the assets in those accounts is insured or protected pursuant to a program similar to SIPA. Some commenters noted that SIPC insurance is not available in jurisdictions outside the U.S. and suggested that we add this provision.[53] We believe that this addition represents a logical extension of our purpose in originally proposing the SIPA exception. Again, however, the insurance must be similar to SIPA for the exception to apply.

(iv) *Futures Commission Merchant Accounts*

Rule 2-01(c)(1)(ii)(D) provides that the accountant will not be independent when the accounting firm, any covered person in the firm, or any covered person's immediate family member has any futures, commodity, or similar account maintained with a futures commission merchant that is an audit client. Few commenters commented on this provision,[54] and we have adopted it exactly as proposed.

(v) *Credit Cards*

Rule 2-01(c)(1)(ii)(E) provides that an accountant is not independent when the accounting firm, any covered person in the firm, or any covered person's immediate family member has "[a]ny aggregate outstanding credit card balance owed to a lender that is an audit client that is not reduced to $10,000 or less on a current basis taking into consideration the payment due date and any available grace period." This represents a slight modification from the rule as proposed. Under the proposed rule, independence would have been im-

---

[52] *See* Ernst & Young Letter; PricewaterhouseCoopers Letter.

[53] *See generally,* Deloitte & Touche Letter.

[54] *See* Deloitte & Touche Letter (agreeing that such accounts "might, in certain circumstances, create a perception that an accounting firm's independence has been impaired").

paired the moment that a relevant credit card balance exceeded $10,000. Commenters, noting the occasional use of credit cards for large consumer purchases, college tuition, and tax payments, asked that we modify the rule so that the $10,000 limit applies only as of the due date.[55] We agree that the issue we seek to address in this paragraph (E) is equally well addressed with a more flexible approach, taking account of the realities of day-to-day life, that allows a credit card balance to exceed $10,000 so long as the balance is brought back down below $10,000 within the immediate credit card payment cycle.

(vi) *Insurance Products*

Rule 2-01(c)(1)(ii)(F) provides that an auditor's independence is impaired whenever any covered person in the firm or any immediate family member of a covered person holds any individual insurance policy issued by an insurer that is an audit client unless: (1) the policy was obtained at a time when the person in the firm was not a covered person; or (2) the likelihood of the insurer becoming insolvent is remote. The final rule reflects two modifications from the proposed rule.

First, the rule that we proposed would have provided that an accounting firm's independence was impaired by having a professional liability policy originally issued by an audit client. We have reconsidered this issue in light of comments pointing out that professional liability insurance for accountants is provided by relatively few insurers and, moreover, complex syndication relationships among those insurers make it unreasonable to expect that any given professional liability insurer will ever be completely absent from the coverage scheme that insures its auditor.[56] The final rule, therefore, does not provide that a professional liability policy gives rise to an independence impairment. In addition, by leaving the word "individual" in our final rule, we intend to make clear that the rule does not apply to professional liability or any other type of insurance policy held by an accounting firm.

Second, the rule that we proposed would have provided that independence was impaired by a covered person or immediate family member having any individual policy originally issued by an insurer that is an audit client. Commenters pointed out how this provision could work a hardship where, for example, an accountant obtains a life insurance policy from an audit client of the firm, but obtains the policy when he or she is not a covered person with respect to the client. If that accountant later becomes a covered person with respect to that insurer, our proposed rule effectively would have required that accountant to obtain that insurance from another carrier. Changing

life insurers, however, could prove to be very difficult and expensive depending on many other factors that could have changed since the accountant first obtained the insurance.

We believe that the goal of this paragraph (F) can be served equally well by a provision that largely averts that potential hardship. The final rule, therefore, provides that, so long as the likelihood of the insurer becoming insolvent is remote, independence is not impaired if a covered person or immediate family member obtains a policy from an audit client when the covered person is not a covered person with respect to that audit client.[57] If, however, the likelihood of the insurer becoming insolvent is not remote, then independence is impaired regardless of the lack of "covered person" status at the time the policy was obtained. In any event, when the likelihood of insolvency is remote, and the policy was obtained when the covered person was not a covered person, it is our intention that the covered person be able to renew the policy and increase the coverage if done pursuant to the pre-existing contractual terms of the policy.

Finally, as discussed in more detail below, recusal remains an option in some circumstances. If a person or a member of that person's immediate family wished to obtain insurance from an audit client, the person may be able to recuse himself or herself from being a covered person for that audit client. For instance, depending on a firm's organization, persons that are covered persons only because they are within the definition of the "chain of command" may be able to re-structure their supervisory role with respect to a particular audit client so as to fall outside that definition with respect to the audit client.

(vii) *Investment Companies*

Rule 2-01(c)(1)(ii)(G) addresses investments in an entity that is part of an investment company complex. The rule provides that, when an audit client is part of an investment company complex, an accountant is not independent if the accounting firm, a covered person, or an immediate family member of a covered person has any financial interest in an entity in the investment company complex. Technically, this provision represents an explicit statement of a concept that otherwise necessarily follows from other aspects of the rule. Specifically, because the definition of "affiliate of the audit client" includes any entity that is part of an investment company complex (as defined in Rule 2-01(f)(14)) that includes an audit client,[58] the restrictions included in paragraphs (c)(1)(i) and (c)(1)(ii) necessarily apply to any such entity. We have singled out these entities in paragraph (G) to minimize the possibility that a reader fo-

---

[55] *See, e.g.,* AICPA Letter.

[56] Letter of XL Capital Limited (Sept. 25, 2000); AICPA Letter; Letter of Swiss Re (Sept. 22, 2000).

[57] *See* AICPA Letter (suggesting this approach).

[58] *See* Rule 2-01(f)(4)(iv).

cused on the financial relationship provisions might overlook those entities' inclusion as "an affiliate of the audit client." We solicited comment on whether we should follow ISB Standard No. 2,[59] and our intent, as stated in the Proposing Release, was to codify the substance of ISB Standard No. 2. Commenters generally did not object to this concept, although several expressed concerns about the definition of "investment company complex" as discussed below.[60] We have reworded paragraph (G) from the Proposing Release solely for the purpose of clarity. No substantive change is intended.

c. *Exceptions*

We are adopting Rule 2-01(c)(1)(iii) regarding limited exceptions to the financial relationship rules substantially as proposed, with slight modifications, and we are adding one additional exception. These exceptions recognize that there are situations in which an accountant, by virtue of being given a gift or receiving an inheritance, or because the accounting firm has taken on a new audit client, may lack independence solely because of events beyond the accountant's control. In these circumstances, independence is not deemed to be impaired if the financial interest is promptly disposed of or the financial relationship is promptly terminated. These exceptions operate to avert an independence impairment only with respect to the financial interests referenced in the exceptions. These exceptions do not have the effect of averting an independence impairment caused by any other factors, such as employment relationships or non-audit services.

(i) *Inheritance and Gift*

Rule 2-01(c)(1)(iii)(A) provides that an accountant's independence will not be impaired by virtue of an unsolicited financial interest, such as a gift or inheritance, so long as the recipient disposes of the interest as soon as practicable, but in no event later than thirty days after the recipient has knowledge of, and the right to dispose of, that interest. Our proposed version of this provision required that the interest be disposed of no later than thirty days after the recipient has a right to dispose of it. We have added the phrase "has knowledge of" to avoid the unfairness that could result in a case where the recipient of a financial interest does not learn of that interest immediately upon acquiring it. In addition, several commenters from foreign jurisdictions noted that there are situations abroad in which an accounting firm may be appointed executor of an estate without its advance knowledge.[61] We have modified the rule to address these situations. Specifically, we have expanded it

to cover "unsolicited financial interests" even if not acquired through inheritance or gift.

(ii) *New Audit Engagement*

We are adopting Rule 2-01(c)(1)(iii)(B) substantially as proposed. It is designed to allow accounting firms to bid for and accept new audit engagements, even if a person has a financial interest that would cause the accountant to be not independent under the financial relationship rules. This exception is available to an accountant so long as the accountant did not audit the client's financial statements for the immediately preceding fiscal year, and the accountant was independent before the earlier of (1) signing an initial engagement letter or other agreement to provide audit, review, or attest services to the audit client, or (2) commencing any audit, review, or attest procedures (including planning the audit of the client's financial statements).

The new audit engagement exception of Rule 2-01(c)(1)(iii)(B) is necessary because an auditor must be independent, not only during the period of the auditor's engagement, but also during the period covered by any financial statements being audited or reviewed. Because of an existing financial relationship between an accounting firm or one of its employees and a company (that is not an audit client), an accounting firm may not be able to bid for or accept an audit engagement from the company without this exception. This exception allows firms to bid for and accept engagements in these circumstances, provided they are otherwise independent of the audit client and they become independent of the audit client under the financial relationship rules before the earlier of the two events specified in paragraphs (B)(2)(i) and (ii).

We have modified the audit engagement exception slightly from the proposed rule. As proposed, the exception would have applied only if the firm was independent under the financial relationship rules before the earlier of beginning work on the audit or accepting the engagement to provide audit, review, or attest services. Commenters have pointed out that it would be reasonable to allow for some grace period to divest of financial interests after the audit client and the accountant first agree to an audit relationship. Otherwise, an accountant would have little choice but to come into compliance with the financial interest rules before even bidding to become the auditor for a particular client.

Accordingly, we have revised paragraph (B)(2)(i) to focus on the "signing of an initial engagement letter or other agreement," rather than "accepting the engagement." By this change, we mean to afford accountants a divestiture win-

---

[59] ISB Standard No. 2, "Certain Independence Implications of Audits of Mutual Funds and Related Entities," at ¶ 3 (Dec. 1999).

[60] *See infra* Section IV.H.11.

[61] *See* Letter of KPMG Europe (Sept. 22, 2000); Written Testimony of Institute of the Chartered Accountants in England & Whales ("ICAEW") (Sept. 13, 2000).

dow between the time they first understand that a new client has selected them to perform audit, review, or attest services—or there has been an oral agreement to that effect—and the time that an initial engagement letter or other written agreement is actually signed, or audit procedures commence. If an accountant is in compliance with the financial relationship rules before the earlier of that signing or the commencement of audit, review, or attest services, the accountant's independence is not impaired by the operation of the financial relationship rules of paragraphs (c) (1) (i) and (c) (1) (ii).

(iii) *Employee Compensation and Benefit Plans*

We are adopting an additional exception to the financial interest rules in response to concerns expressed by several commenters. These commenters encouraged us as part of this modernization to allow for broader participation by immediate family members of auditors in employee compensation and benefit plans.[62] This additional exception is consistent with our goal of updating the independence rules in ways that recognize the realities of the modern economy (and dual income households) and continue to protect the public interest.

The exception is necessary because our employment rules will allow an immediate family member of a covered person (most typically a spouse) to be employed by an audit client in a position other than an "accounting role or financial reporting oversight role" without impairing the auditor's independence. In these situations, the immediate family member would remain subject to our financial interest rules and therefore could not have a direct financial interest in the audit client. Accordingly, an employee in this situation could be prevented from participating in a stock-based compensation program.

We are adopting an additional exception to the financial interest rules to provide some relief in these situations. The exception will apply to investments in audit clients by immediate family members of covered persons who are covered persons only by virtue of being a partner in the same office as the lead audit engagement partner of, or a partner or manager performing ten or more hours of non-audit services for, an audit client. This exception will allow the immediate family members of these covered persons to acquire an interest in an audit client, if the immediate family member works for the audit client and acquires the interest as an "unavoidable consequence" of participating in an employee compensation program in which employees are granted, for example, stock options in the employer as part of their total compensation package, without im-

pairing the audit firm's independence. The phrase "unavoidable consequence" in this paragraph means that, to the extent the employee has the ability to participate in the program but has the option to select investments in entities that would not make him or her an investor in an audit client, the employee must choose other investments to avoid an impairment of independence.

Immediate family members of this subset of covered persons must dispose of the financial interest as soon as practicable once they have the right to do so, however, and they may not otherwise invest in the audit client without impairing the firm's independence. Where there are legal or other similar restrictions on a person's right to dispose of a financial interest at a particular time, the person need not dispose of the interest until the restrictions have lapsed. For example, a person will not have to dispose of an investment in an audit client if doing so would violate an employer's policies on insider trading. On the other hand, waiting for more advantageous market conditions to dispose of the interest would not fall within the exception.

This exception is similarly available to immediate family members of the same subset of covered persons who must invest in one or more audit clients in order to participate in their employer's 401(k) or similar retirement plan. Accordingly, under the exception, the spouse or another immediate family member of this subset of covered persons can participate in a 401(k) plan, even if his or her only investment option within the plan is, for example, a mutual fund that is in the same investment company complex as a mutual fund that is an audit client. If, however, the immediate family member has an alternative in the 401(k) plan that does not involve investing in a fund complex for which the person's relative is a covered person, then the family member may not invest in the audit client without impairing the auditor's independence. We highlight that the exception in paragraph (c) (1) (iii) (C) is available only to immediate family members of covered persons who are covered persons by virtue of being in the same office as the lead audit engagement partner of an audit client (paragraph (f) (11) (iv)) or because they perform ten or more hours of non-audit services for an audit client (paragraph (f) (11) (iii)).

The Investment Company Institute proposed that the exception apply to the immediate family members of all covered persons in the firm.[63] We believe, however, that the exception we are adopting is sufficiently broad. As discussed elsewhere in this release, even absent this exception, the rules we are adopting significantly shrink the cir-

---

[62] *See, e.g.*, ICI Letter; Deloitte & Touche Letter; *see also* Letter of the Association of Private Pension and Welfare Plans (Aug. 7, 2000).

[63] ICI Letter.

cle of firm personnel to whom the financial interest rules apply.

d. *Audit Clients' Financial Relationships*

Rule 2-01(c)(1)(iv) specifies two sets of circumstances in which an audit client's financial interests in the accounting firm cause an accountant to be not independent of that audit client. We have modified the proposed rule as discussed below.

(i) *Investments by the Audit Client in the Auditor*

As discussed in the Proposing Release, when an audit client invests in its auditor, the auditor may be placed in the position of auditing the value of any of its securities that are reflected as an asset in the financial statements of the audit client. In addition, the accountant may reasonably be presumed to have a mutuality of financial interest with the owners of the firm, including an audit client-shareholder.[64]

Under Rule 2-01(c)(1)(iv)(A), an accountant is not independent with respect to an audit client when the audit client has, or has agreed to acquire, any direct investment in the accounting firm, such as stocks, bonds, notes, options, or other securities, or the audit client's officers or directors are record or beneficial owners of more than five percent of the equity securities of the accounting firm. In applying this provision, it is important to remember that the definition of accounting firm includes "associated entities" of the accounting firm, including any that are public companies. Paragraph (A) seeks to prevent a situation in which an accountant, in order to audit asset valuations of a client that holds securities of the accounting firm, must value the accounting firm's own securities. Paragraph (A) also seeks to prevent a situation in which the audit client, or in some circumstances its officers and directors, can exercise any degree of influence over the accounting firm, whether by virtue of the accounting firm's fiduciary obligation to its investors or by nominating and voting for directors.

The AICPA noted in its comment letter that its current rules also do not permit an audit client to hold any investment in its auditor.[65] The AICPA was critical of the application of our proposed provision, at least without a materiality threshold, to subsidiaries and other entities related to the accounting firm. Consistent with our general approach, we have decided to apply this rule to not only the corporate entity performing the audit, but also its subsidiaries and associated entities. We note that we have eliminated the definition of "affiliate of the accounting firm," which many com-

menters argued captured more entities with some relation to the accounting firm than necessary.[66]

The proposed rule did not include any provision restricting audit client officers and directors from owning the accounting firm's securities. In that respect, our proposed approach was more liberal than existing law, which deems independence impaired if an audit client's officers or directors own any equity securities of the accounting firm. We sought comment, however, on whether the rule's prohibitions should also apply to other situations in which the audit client has a financial interest, such as when the audit client's CEO invests in the accounting firm. Although some commenters opposed the addition of this notion,[67] we have determined that the final rule should liberalize existing law, simply not to the extent we proposed. Accordingly, the final rule provides that independence is impaired if an officer or director of the audit client owns more than five percent of the equity securities of the accounting firm. We believe that investments in the accounting firm by audit client officers and directors do not routinely give rise to independence concerns, but that concerns arise when an officer or director of the audit client accumulates a significant stake in the accounting firm. Because record or beneficial ownership interests exceeding five percent will be reflected in Schedule 13D filings relating to the accounting firm, the firm will be able to monitor for compliance with this provision, without having to rely solely on an intrusive investigation or audit client monitoring of its officers' and directors' investments.

(ii) *Underwriting*

Rule 2-01(c)(1)(iv)(B) provides that an accountant is not independent of an audit client when the accounting firm "engages an audit client to act as an underwriter, broker-dealer, market maker, promoter, or analyst with respect to securities issued by the accounting firm." Few transactions are as significant to the financial health of a company, including an accounting firm, as the sale of its securities, whether in private or public offerings. In an offering, an underwriter either buys and then resells a company's securities or receives a commission for selling the securities. In either circumstance, were an audit client to act as underwriter of an accounting firm's or its associated entity's securities, the audit client would assume the role of advocate or seller of the accounting firm's securities. Moreover, depending on the terms of the underwriting, the underwriter could for a time become a significant shareholder of the

---

[64] *See* Letter from POB to ISB (Jan. 12, 2000) ("Public ownership in an audit firm or in its parent or in an entity that effectively has control of the audit firm would add another form of allegiance and accountability to those identified by the Supreme Court - a form of allegiance that in our opinion will

be viewed as detracting from, if not conflicting with, the auditor's 'public responsibility'").

[65] *See* AICPA Letter.

[66] *See infra* Section IV.H.2.

[67] *See* Written Testimony of William Travis, McGladrey & Pullen LLP (Sept. 20, 2000).

accounting firm. There also may be indemnification agreements that place the underwriter and auditor in adversarial positions.

In addition, the accounting firm would have a direct interest in ensuring the underwriter's viability and credibility, either of which could be damaged as the result of an audit. Moreover, the auditor would have a clear incentive not to displease an audit client to which it had entrusted a critical financial transaction. Similar conflicts of interest may arise if an audit client or an affiliate of an audit client is engaged to perform other financial services for an accounting firm, such as making a market in the accounting firm's securities or issuing an analyst report concerning the securities of the accounting firm.

We have reworded paragraph (B) from the proposed wording to avert an unintended consequence. The proposed rule provided that independence would be impaired if an audit client "performs any service for the accounting firm related to underwriting, offering, making a market in, marketing, promoting, or selling securities issued by the accounting firm, or issues an analyst report concerning the securities of the accounting firm." Worded that way, the provision could be read to impair independence any time, for example, a broker-dealer issues an analyst's report making a favorable recommendation concerning the securities of any associated entity of an accounting firm, because, in a broad sense, that report could benefit the accounting firm and could be seen as a "service for" the accounting firm. To avoid any possibility of that construction, we have reworded paragraph (B) to make clear that independence is impaired only if the accounting firm actually "engages" the audit client for the purpose of obtaining those services.

2. Employment Relationships

We are adopting, substantially as proposed, Rule 2-01(c)(2), which sets forth the employment relationships that impair an auditor's independence. As discussed in the Proposing Release, independence requirements related to employment relationships between accountants or their family members and audit clients are based on the premise that when an accountant is employed by an audit client, or has a close relative or former colleague employed in certain positions at an audit client, there is a significant risk that the accountant would not be capable of exercising the objective and impartial judgment that is the hallmark of independence.

We are modernizing the employment relationship rules in a manner consistent with the public interest and investor protection. We are keenly aware of the changes in traditional family structures, the increased mobility of professional employees, the recent globalization of accounting firms, and similar changes in society at large. We have determined that, in this environment, existing restrictions on employment relationships between accountants or their family members and audit clients are more restrictive than necessary to protect investors. Accordingly, we are narrowing those restrictions.

We received a number of comments on our proposals to modernize the employment relationship rules. The vast majority of commenters who spoke to this issue supported modernization in general, even if they did not support all aspects of our proposals.[68] For example, some commenters who agreed with the objectives of our proposals questioned if the ISB rather than the Commission should prescribe requirements in this area.[69] Some commenters expressed a preference for the language used in ISB proposals and ISB Standard No. 3.[70] IS Standard No. 3, "Employment with Audit Clients," states, "An audit firm's independence is impaired with respect to an audit client that employs a former firm professional who could, by reason of his or her knowledge of and relationships with the audit firm, adversely influence the quality or effectiveness of the audit, unless the firm has taken steps that effectively eliminate such risk." The standard also describes the types of safeguards that the ISB believes would effectively eliminate the risk of an impairment of independence.

We appreciate the concepts underlying ISB Standard No. 3 and strongly support firms' use of quality controls and "safeguards" to encourage their partners and employees to be aware of and adhere to auditor independence standards. We are concerned, however, that a "safeguards" approach, which is dependent on a firm's self-analysis and self-reviews, will not provide a definitive standard. In our view, independence is better assured by consistent and uniform rules, rather than by rules that rely on the auditor's assessment of the extent of its own self-interest. Furthermore, it has been our experience that the existence of safeguards or quality controls alone does not ensure compliance with even the most basic independence regulations.[71] Accordingly, we have chosen a more objective standard for employment

---

[68] *See* PricewaterhouseCoopers Letter ("We endorse and applaud the SEC's initiatives to modernize the archaic financial interest and employment rules in order to reflect today's social and business realities. We support, for the most part, the treatment of these topics in the Release.").

[69] *See, e.g.,* Deloitte & Touche Letter; Letter of Steven Ryan, Chair, Financial Accounting Standards Committee, American Accounting Association (Oct. 12, 2000); Written

Testimony of John C. Bogle, Public Member, ISB (July 26, 2000).

[70] *See, e.g.,* AICPA Letter; Written Testimony of William T. Allen, Chair, ISB (July 26, 2000).

[71] *See, e.g.,* Letter from Lynn E. Turner, Chief Accountant, SEC, to Charles A. Bowsher, Chairman, Public Oversight Board (Dec. 9, 1999); Letters from Lynn E. Turner, Chief Accountant, SEC, to Michael A. Conway, Chair, SECPS (Nov.

relationships, which is described in paragraph (c) (2).[72]

Like the financial interest rules we are adopting, the employment relationship rules greatly reduce the pool of people within audit firms whose families are affected by the independence requirements. Paragraph (c) (2) sets forth the general rule that an auditor is not independent of an audit client if the accountant or a family member has an employment relationship with an audit client. The provision includes a non-exclusive list of employment relationships that are inconsistent with the general standard of paragraphs (b) and (c) (2). Employment relationships not specifically described in paragraphs (c) (2) (i) through (c) (2) (iv) are subject to the general test of paragraphs (b) and (c) (2).

The following are examples of employment relationships that impair an auditor's independence under the final rule.[73]

• A current partner of an accounting firm serves as a member of the board of directors of the audit client;

• A sibling of a covered person is employed by an audit client as the director of internal audit;

• A former professional employee of an accounting firm who resigned from the accounting firm two years ago is employed by an audit client in an accounting role and the former employee receives a pension from the firm tied to the firm's revenues or profits;

• A former partner of an accounting firm accepts the position of chief accounting officer at an audit client, and the former partner continues to maintain a capital balance with the accounting firm; or,

• A former director of an audit client becomes a partner of the accounting firm, and that individual participates in the audit of the financial statements of the audit client for a period during which he or she was a director of the audit client.

We discuss each of the rules giving rise to these examples in turn.

a. *Employment at Audit Client of Accountant*

Rule 2-01 (c) (2) (i) continues the principle set forth in current Rule 2-01 (b) that to be independent, neither the accountant nor any member of his or her firm can be a director, officer, or employee of an audit client. Paragraph (2) (i) provides that an accountant is not independent if any current partner, principal, shareholder, or professional employee of the accounting firm is employed by the audit client, or serves as a member of the board of directors or similar management or governing body of the audit client. In the most basic sense, the accountant cannot be employed by his or her audit client and be independent.

b. *Employment at Audit Client of Certain Relatives of Accountant*

Rule 2-01 (c) (2) (ii) provides that certain employment relationships between covered persons' close family members and an audit client will impair the auditor's independence. As discussed below, close family members include the covered person's spouse, spousal equivalent, dependents, parents, nondependent children, and siblings. The application of the rule to close family members stands in contrast to the financial interest rules, where only the interests of the covered person's immediate family members (*i.e.*, spouse, spousal equivalent, and dependents) are attributed to the covered person. As we explained in the Proposing Release, we believe this distinction is appropriate because, while some close family members' investments may not be known to a covered person, the place and nature of such family members' employment should be obvious.

Like the proposed rule, final Rule 2-01 (c) (2) (ii) limits the employment relationships that impair auditor independence when held by a close family member of a covered person to those involving an "accounting role or financial reporting oversight role." As a result, an audit client's employment of even an immediate family member will not necessarily impair an auditor's independence, unless that family member is in an "accounting role or financial reporting oversight role."

Not all commenters agreed with the scope of the rule, some arguing that our proposal was too generous and others arguing that the proposal was too restrictive.[74] In this regard, we note that the ISB has taken a more restrictive approach in suggesting that independence is impaired if an immediate family member of a person on the audit

---

30, 1998; Dec. 9, 1999). These letters are available on our website.

[72] Nevertheless, we encourage, and we expect, firms to follow the steps described in ISB Standard No. 3, including the steps to be taken in the period after the firm's professional reports an intention to join an audit client and the steps to be taken after the professional actually joins the audit client. We also anticipate that peer reviews conducted by the POB will cover firms' compliance with these steps.

[73] These examples are illustrative only and should not be relied upon as a complete list of employment relationships that impair an accountant's independence under paragraphs (b) and (c) (2).

[74] *Compare* Letter of Paula Morris, MPA, CPA, Assistant Professor, Kennesaw State University (Sept. 25, 2000) (expressing her concerns about loosening the rules regarding spouses' and dependents' employment relationships) *with* Deloitte & Touche Letter (suggesting that an audit client's employment of a close family member of a covered person who is not on the audit engagement team or in the chain of command, should not be deemed to impair the auditor's independence, even if the person holds an accounting or financial reporting oversight role because there is only a "remote likelihood" that such a person could influence the audit).

engagement team is employed by the audit client in any position.[75] We continue to believe, however, that we need only apply our restriction to family members in an "accounting role or financial reporting oversight role" at an audit client. Some commenters, on the other hand, argued for a rule that did not impose restrictions on close family members of all covered persons. While we acknowledge that individuals who are covered persons because they provide ten or more hours of non-audit services to the audit client or work in the same office as the lead audit engagement partner are less likely to be able to influence an audit than covered persons who are on the audit engagement team or in the "chain of command," we do not agr ee that the likelihood is so remote as to warrant carving their close family members out of the rule.

We define "accounting role or financial reporting oversight role" in Rule 2-01(f)(3). The definition includes two categories of persons. One category includes those with more than minimal influence over the contents of the accounting records or anyone who prepares them. This typically would include certain persons working in the accounting department or who perform accounting functions. We have not chosen to reach as many persons in the audit client's accounting department as are covered by the "audit sensitive" category in the AICPA's employment rules.[76] The definition also may include certain individuals, such as an accounts receivable supervisor or manager, who are relied upon by management to calculate amounts that are placed directly into the company's financial statements.

The second category includes those who influence the preparers or the contents of the financial statements of the audit client. The definition lists positions in which we believe a person generally wields the type of influence over the financial statements that causes independence concerns, such as a member of the audit client's board of directors (or similar management or governing body), chief executive officer, president, chief financial officer, chief operating officer, general counsel, chief accounting officer, controller, director of internal audit, director of financial reporting, treasurer, vice president of marketing, or any equivalent position.

Several commenters expressed support for the concept of "accounting role or financial reporting oversight role," but recommended that we modify the definition in various ways, for example, by eliminating vice president of marketing from the scope of the rule or making the list an exhaustive

list of covered positions.[77] We believe that the vice president of marketing makes important determinations that affect the company's financial results.[78] These include, for example, supervising sales that result in the revenues reported in financial statements, shaping sales policies and procedures, and participating at a high level in the formulation of the company's budget. For these reasons, we consider a vice president of marketing to be involved in a financial reporting oversight role. We have declined to make the list of positions exhaustive because titles alone do not always accurately describe a person's duties and functions.

Other modifications to the definition make explicit our concerns about positions in which the employee would exercise more than minimal influence over the contents of the accounting records or anyone who prepares them, or would exercise influence over the contents of the financial statements or anyone who prepares them. As noted above, the final rule also incorporates the proposed list of examples of positions in which we consider a person to exercise influence over the contents of the financial statements or people who prepare the financial statements. We have singled out these two categories of positions because persons in these positions can influence the financial reporting of the company.

As noted in the Proposing Release, the so-called "five hundred mile rule" has been eliminated under Rule 2-01(c)(2)(ii). Whether a covered person lives near a close family member who is employed by the audit client no longer seems relevant in today's world of instantaneous international communications and global securities markets. Accordingly, we have dispensed with this test of auditor independence.

c. *Employment at Audit Client of Former Employee of Accounting Firm*

We are adopting Rule 2-01(c)(2)(iii) substantially as proposed, with the minor modifications discussed below. Rule 2-01(c)(2)(iii) describes the circumstances under which an auditor's independence will be impaired by an audit client's employment of a former partner, principal, shareholder, or professional employee of the accounting firm in an accounting role or financial reporting oversight role. As we noted in the Proposing Release, when these persons retire or resign from accounting firms, it is not unusual for them to join the management of former audit clients or to become members of their boards of directors. Registrants and their shareholders may benefit from the for-

---

[75] ISB, "Invitation to Comment 99-1: Family Relationships Between the Auditor and the Audit Client" (July 1999).

[76] AICPA Code of Professional Conduct, ET § 101.11.

[77] AICPA Letter ("For the most part, the specific positions listed in the definition . . . are appropriate and provide helpful advice to practitioners . . . . however . . . we do not believe

the vice president of marketing should be included in this list."); Ernst & Young Letter.

[78] *See, e.g., In the Matter of Jimmy L. Duckworth*, CPA, AAER No. 1205 (Nov. 10, 1999); *In the Matter of Pinnacle Micro, Inc., Scott A. Blum, and Lilia Craig*, AAER No. 975 (Oct. 3, 1997).

mer partner's accounting and financial reporting expertise. Investors and the public in general also may benefit when individuals on the board or in management can work effectively with the auditors, members of the audit committee, and management to provide informative financial statements and reports.

When these persons, however, assume positions with the firm's audit client and also remain linked in some fashion to the accounting firm, they may well be in a position to influence the content of the audit client's accounting records and financial statements on the one hand, and the conduct of the audit, on the other. This is particularly true when the individual, while at the accounting firm, was in some way associated with the audit of the client. A close association between a member of the board of directors or of senior management with his or her former firm creates an impression of a mutuality of interest and may well affect the auditor's judgment.[79]

In addition, even under the usual circumstances, there is some possibility that accounting firm partners may compromise their independence in order to secure management positions with the audit clients.[80] That risk is heightened where there is a "revolving door" between the auditor and the client.[81] Finally, there is the risk that the former partner's familiarity with the firm's audit process and the audit partners and employees of the firm will enable him or her to affect the

audit as it progresses.[82] Accordingly, under the final rule, as under current requirements, an auditor's independence with respect to an audit client is deemed to be impaired when former partners, shareholders, principals, or professional employees of the firm are employed in an accounting or financial reporting oversight role at an audit client, unless certain conditions are met.

Consistent with our proposal, the final rule provides that independence will not be impaired if certain steps are taken to ensure the individual's separation from the accounting firm. Under the final rule, the former partner, principal, shareholder, or professional employee must not: (i) influence the firm's operations or financial policies, (ii) have a capital balance in the firm, or (iii) have a financial arrangement, other than one providing for regular payment of a fixed dollar amount, as described in paragraphs 2-01(c)(2)(iii)(C)(1) and (2). Any payment of a fixed dollar amount must be made pursuant to a fully funded retirement plan, rabbi trust or similar vehicle. Or, in the case of a former professional employee who was not a partner, principal, or shareholder of the firm and has been disassociated from the accounting firm for more than five years, the fixed payments made to the former employee must be immaterial to him or her.

As proposed, the rule contemplated only fixed payments made pursuant to a fully funded retirement plan or rabbi trust.[83] Several commenters

---

[79] *See* AICPA, Auditing Standards Division, "Audit Risk Alert - 1994, General Update on Economic, Accounting, and Auditing Matters," at 35 (1994). _p46_A few litigation cases suggest auditors need to be more cautious in dealing with former coworkers employed by a client. None of these cases involved collusion or an intentional lack of objectivity. Nevertheless, if a close relationship previously existed between the auditor and a former colleague now employed by a client, the auditor must guard against being too trusting in his or her acceptance of representations about the entity's financial statements. Otherwise, the auditor may rely too heavily on the word of a former associate, overlooking that a common interest no longer exists.

[80] *See* Paul M. Clikeman, "Close revolving door between auditors, clients," *Accounting Today*, at 20 1996); *Cf. In the Matter of Richard A. Knight*, AAER No. 764 (Feb. 27, 1996) (individual allegedly learned of accounting misstatements while he was engagement partner for firm conducting audit and resigned to become registrant's executive vice president and chief financial officer).

[81] *See, e.g., AUSA Life Ins. Co. v. Ernst & Young*, 206 F.3d 202 (2d Cir. 2000); AICPA Board of Directors, *Meeting the Financial Reporting Needs of the Future: A Public Commitment From the Public Accounting Profession*, at 4 (June 1993) ("AICPA Board Report"); *see also Staff Report, supra* note 74, at 51-52; In addressing an example of this problem, the court in *Lincoln S&L v. Wall*, 743 F. Supp. 901, 917 n.23 (D.D.C. 1990) wrote:_p46_Atchison, who was in charge of the Arthur Young audit of Lincoln, left Arthur Young to assume a high paying position with Lincoln. This certainly raises questions about Arthur Young's independence. Here a person in charge of the Lincoln audit resigned from the accounting firm and immediately became an employee of Lincoln. This practice of "changing sides" should certainly be examined by the ac-

counting profession's standard setting authorities as to the impact such a practice has on an accountant's independenc e. It would seem that some "cooling off period" perhaps, one to two years, would not be unreasonable before a senior official on an audit can be employed by the client.

[82] In response to these and other concerns, the AICPA Board of Directors suggested in 1993 that we prohibit a public company from hiring the partner responsible for the audits of that company's financial statements for a minimum of one year after the partner ceases to serve that company. *See* AICPA Board Report, *supra* note 322, at 4. Our staff has indicated, however, that, if implemented, this suggestion would take the form of the firm's independence being impaired for a period of time from the date the individual left the audit engagement, rather than as a prohibition on hiring the former partner. *Staff Report, supra* note 74, at 52 n.146. *See also* Committee of Sponsoring Organizations of the Treadway Commission ("COSO"), "Fraudulent Financial Reporting: 1987-1997: An Analysis of U.S. Public Companies," at 21 (1999) (finding, with respect to companies where there was fraudulent financial reporting, that among 44 companies for which there was information available on their CFO's background, 11% of the companies' CFOs had previous experience with the companies' audit firms just before joining the company).

[83] As noted in the Proposing Release, to avoid adverse tax consequences to the individual, accounting firms often settle their retirement obligations to former partners by fully funding a "rabbi trust" from which payments will be made to the individual. Under Rule 2-01(f)(16), a "rabbi trust" is an irrevocable trust whose assets are not accessible to the firm until all benefit obligations have been met but are subject to claims of the firm's creditors in bankruptcy or insolvency. We are adopting the definition of "rabbi trust" as proposed.

expressed concern about the rule's application in foreign jurisdictions in which rabbi trusts are not recognized.[84] In response to these comments, we have modified the rule to indicate that using a similar payment vehicle will satisfy the rule. If a rabbi trust is available in the jurisdiction, however, the accounting firm and the former professional must use a rabbi trust, rather than some other vehicle.

As noted, to satisfy the conditions of paragraph (C)(1), the retirement plan or rabbi trust must be fully funded.[85] We believe that full funding is critical to breaking the link between the firm and the individual. Any situation that requires the individual to be dependent on the firm to fund his or her retirement payments weds the financial interests of the former employee and the firm, and creates the potential for the firm to exert influence over the individual, or vice versa.

The proposed rule did not contain a "cooling off" period. We solicited comment on whether we should require a mandatory cooling off period for former partners and professional staff of an audit firm who join an audit client.[86] Several commenters supported the notion of a cooling off period,[87] but others disagreed.[88] We have determined that a cooling off period unnecessarily restricts the employment opportunities of former professionals, and we have decided not to adopt a cooling off provision.[89]

We also solicited comment on whether application of the rule should depend on whether the professional leaving the accounting firm was a partner at the firm or non-managerial audit staff. We considered whether to provide a sunset provision so that accounting firms need not track all former professional employees indefinitely to determine, for purposes of this provision, whether they become employed in an accounting role or financial reporting oversight role at an audit client. While we believe that it is usual for accounting firms to know whether their former partners, principals, or shareholders are employed in these roles at an audit client, we understand the practical difficulties firms might have tracking all for-

mer professionals who left the firm while at a managerial or staff level. Accordingly, we are adopting a rule under which the accountant's independence will not be impaired when a former professional, who was not a partner, joins an audit client in an accounting role or financial reporting oversight role position after five years, provided the retirement benefits of the former employee are immaterial to him or her.

The materiality provision is necessary because, to satisfy the conditions in paragraph (C)(2), the retirement plan does not have to be fully funded. In the absence of such funding, we believe that the receipt by the former employee of more than an immaterial amount would create the unification of financial interests discussed above.

d. *Employment at Accounting Firm of Former Employee of Audit Client*

We are adopting Rule 2-01(c)(2)(iv) substantially as proposed. The rule specifies that individuals who were formerly officers, directors, or employees of an audit client and who later become partners, principals, or shareholders of the accounting firm will impair the independence of the firm with respect to that audit client, unless they do not participate in, and are not in a position to influence, the audit of the financial statements of the audit client covering a period during which the individuals were employed by or associated with the audit client. When a former employee of an audit client joins the accounting firm, the independence rules ensure that the employee is not in a position to influence the audit of his or her former employer.[90] Because participating in the audit of the former employer could easily require former employees to audit their own work, the rule provides that independence is impaired unless the former employees do not participate in and are not in a position to influence the audit of the financial statements of the audit client for any period during which they were employed by or associated with that audit client.

The final rule applies to all former employees of the audit client, not only those who were in accounting or financial reporting oversight roles. It

---

[84] *See, e.g.*, Written Testimony of ICAEW (Sept. 13, 2000).

[85] We would not consider an individual's 401(k) account to constitute a financial arrangement with the accounting firm to be fully funded for these purposes because, although the investment remains subject to market risk, the account balance is not dependent on the accounting firm's financial performance even if the firm continues to administer the account for the former firm personnel.

[86] With regard to cooling off periods, *see* AICPA Board Report, *supra* note 322, at 4 (June 1993) (suggesting that the Commission prohibit a public company from hiring the partner responsible for the audits of that company's financial statements for a minimum of one year after the partner ceases to serve that company) and *Lincoln S&L v. Wall*, 743 F. Supp. at 917 n.23 ("It would seem that some 'cooling off period,' perhaps one to two years, would not be unreasonable before a senior official on an audit can be employed by the client.").

[87] *See, e.g.*, Letter of Pamela Roush, Ph.D., CMA (undated).

[88] *See, e.g.*, Written Testimony of Mauricio Kohn, CFA, CMA, CFM, AIMR (Sept. 20, 2000) ("We do not believe it is necessary to impose a mandatory 'cooling-off period,' prohibit clients from hiring audit firm professionals, or stipulate that an audit firm's independence is impaired when its professionals accept key positions with current clients.").

[89] Nonetheless, we encourage firms to maintain adequate controls to ensure that former employees are not unduly influencing the audit engagement team.

[90] Of course, once an employee of an accounting firm, the person would also be subject to all other independence requirements applicable to other firm members. For example, if the former audit client employee becomes a covered person, he or she could have no financial interest in the audit client. *See* Rule 2-01(c)(1).

also applies to former audit client employees whether they become partners, principals, or shareholders of the accounting firm or professional employees of the firm.[91]

3. *Business Relationships*

We proposed Rule 2-01(c)(3) to describe the business relationships that impair an auditor's independence from an audit client. We are adopting the rule substantially as proposed with two minor modifications. The rule continues the Codification's current standard that an auditor's independence with respect to an audit client is impaired when the accounting firm, or a covered person in the firm, has a direct or material indirect business relationship with an audit client, or any person associated with the audit client in a decision-making capacity, such as an audit client's officers, directors, or substantial stockholders.

Commenters were generally supportive of the approach we took in the proposal, with the exception of one provision.[92] We proposed that independence was also impaired if the accounting firm or any covered person had a direct or material indirect business relationship with "record or beneficial owners of more than five percent of the [audit client's] equity securities." This formulation was intended to provide a more precise definition of the subset of associated persons who constitute "substantial stockholders" in the existing restrictions on business relationships in the Codification.[93] Commenters, however, expressed concerns with this threshold.[94] Similarly, one large accounting firm expressed concern with the proposed language, asserting that our proposal would "greatly expand[] the universe of venture capital firms with which we could not have any business relationships."[95]

In response to these comments, we are adopting instead the language used in the Codification, which refers to an associated person "in a decision-making capacity, such as an audit client's officers, directors or substantial stockholders." Because our rule, as adopted, conforms more closely to the Codification, we anticipate that it will provide greater clarity to the profession in interpreting Rule 2-01(c)(3) and address the concerns

about the proposal that were articulated by several commenters.

We are also clarifying the rule by adding the words "to the audit client" after "provides professional services" in the last sentence of the rule. As discussed in the Proposing Release, the exception for providing professional services is meant only to make clear that Rule 2-01(c)(3) does not address the provision of professional services by the auditor to the audit client. The addition of these four words is intended to make clear that joint business ventures or prime/subcontractor arrangements in which audit clients and auditors jointly provide "professional services" would continue to impair the auditor's independence.[96]

We also proposed defining the phrase "consumer in the ordinary course of business" as part of the definitions explicitly set forth in Rule 2-01(f). Commenters, however, expressed concern that, as defined, this phrase could have unintended consequences.[97] Accordingly, we omit the definition of "consumer in the ordinary course of business" in the rules we are adopting and will continue to apply the term consistent with its use in the Codification.

As we noted in the Proposing Release, we are retaining a number of the examples currently found in the Codification to provide guidance on permissible and impermissible business relationships.[98] We expect that the interpretations and examples that have evolved under the Codification with respect to this rule will continue to provide useful guidance to the profession.

We also solicited comment as to whether we should retain the "direct or material indirect business relationship" formulation or if there was another formulation that could provide additional or more precise guidance. The AICPA asserted that "not all business relationships with audit clients should be proscribed if they are immaterial. . . . The inclusion of a materiality standard in the context both of [sic] all business relationships (direct and indirect) sufficiently mitigates whatever independence risk would be posed."[99] For the same reasons we have explained before, we do not believe that auditors should be allowed to have any

---

[91] The AICPA recommended that the rule apply to all professional employees of the accounting firm, not just to partners, shareholders, and principals. *See* AICPA Letter. We agree and, therefore, have modified the final rule to encompass this situation.

[92] *See, e.g.*, Deloitte & Touche Letter; Written Testimony of Dennis Paul Spackman, Chairman, National Association of State Boards of Accountancy (Sept. 13, 2000) ("I am in full agreement with the provisions of the Commission's proposal [regarding] Business Relationships.").

[93] *See* Codification § 602.02.g.

[94] *See* Deloitte & Touche Letter ("Although we agree with the direction of [Rule 2-01(c)(3)], it provides no basis for prohibiting business relationships with beneficial owners of

more than five percent of the equity securities of the audit client or any of its affiliates.").

[95] Ernst & Young Letter; *see also* AICPA Letter ("Such sweeping new restrictions would dramatically constrict the parties with which accounting firms could engage, even though many such parties a t most have only very attenuated ties to audit clients. . . . We view independence risks as extremely remote in such circumstances and, therefore, consider the reach of such provisions unnecessarily broad.").

[96] *See* Codification § 602.02.g; Letter from Jonathan G. Katz, Secretary, SEC, to Duane R. Kulberg, Arthur Andersen & Co. (Feb. 14, 1989).

[97] *See, e.g.*, Deloitte & Touche Letter.

[98] *See infra* Section IX; Codification § 602.02(g).

[99] *See* AICPA Letter.

direct business relationships with their audit clients other than as a consumer in the ordinary course of business.[100] We have carefully considered the comments we have received and believe that the rule we are adopting constitutes a fair and balanced approach that protects independence without unduly restricting business opportunities for auditors or their clients.

4. Non-Audit Services

a. General Rule

We are adopting a rule that provides that an accountant is not independent if the accountant provides the non-audit services identified in paragraph (c)(4). The rule is derived from current Rule 2-01, our releases that have been incorporated into the Codification, and existing AICPA rules.

The proposed rule identified certain services that could not be provided by the auditor without impairing the auditor's independence with respect to the audit client "[e]ven if the audit client accept[ed] ultimate responsibility for the work that is performed or decisions that are made . . . ." In the final non-audit services rule, Rule 2-01(c)(4), we have eliminated that language. As described below, we have added certain exceptions to the non-audit services that impair an auditor's independence. These exceptions are appropriate only where management takes certain actions and accepts certain responsibilities. For example, we have set forth certain circumstances where an auditor does not lose his or her independence by providing certain actuarial services to insurance company audit clients. The exception, however, is available only where management accepts responsibility for significant actuarial methods and assumptions.

The final amendments identify nine non-audit services that, when provided by the auditor to an audit client, impair the auditor's independence. In the proposed rule, we identified ten such services. For many of the non-audit services that we proposed to include in the rule, we aimed to codify existing restrictions.[101] Commenters expressed concerns, however, that certain of our proposed rules were written more broadly than existing independence rules.[102] In addition, commenters indicated that, to the extent our proposals differed

from current standards, they believed current standards more appropriately circumscribed auditors' non-audit activities.[103] In response to these comments, we made several modifications to the rules, including eliminating altogether the provision on expert services.[104]

b. Particular Non-Audit Services that Impair Independence

(i) Bookkeeping or Other Services Related to the Audit Client's Accounting Records or Financial Statements

We proposed and are adopting paragraph (c)(4)(i), which, with limited exceptions, would deem an auditor's independence to be impaired when the auditor performs bookkeeping services for an audit client. Even prior to our proposals, auditors were restricted by AICPA Ethics Rules and the Codification from providing certain bookkeeping services.[105] As explained in the Codification and reiterated in the Proposing Release,[106] providing bookkeeping services for an audit client impairs the auditor's independence because the auditor will be placed in the position of auditing the firm's work when auditing the client's financial statements. It is hard to maintain the requisite objectivity about one's or one's firm's own work. This is especially true where finding an error would raise questions about the adequacy of the bookkeeping services provided by the firm. In addition, keeping the books is a management function, the performance of which leads to an inappropriate mutuality of interests between the auditor and the audit client.

We have modified our final rule in response to several comments.[107] First, commenters believed that the proposed definition should not cover all financial statements, including those not filed with the Commission. For example, auditors sometimes prepare statutory financial statements for foreign companies, and these are not filed with us. At least one commenter requested that we therefore exclude those financial statements from the rule's coverage.[108] Focusing solely on whether the financial statements are filed with us would not be appropriate in all circumstances, since in some instances statutory financial statements form the basis of the U.S. GAAP financial statements that are filed with us. Under these circumstances, an

---

[100] See Letter from Jonathan G. Katz, Secretary, SEC, to Duane R. Kulberg, Arthur Andersen & Co. (Feb. 14, 1989).

[101] See, e.g., Proposing Release, Section III.D.1.(b)(i), (iv) (regarding bookkeeping and actuarial services, respectively). But see Proposing Release, Section III.D.1.(b)(ii) (regarding financial information systems).

[102] See, e.g., Testimony of Barry Melancon, President and Chief Executive Officer, AICPA (Sept. 21, 2000).

[103] See Testimony of Joseph F. Berardino, Managing Partner, Assurance and Business Advisory Services, Arthur Andersen LLP (Sept. 20, 2000) and Testimony of James E. Copeland, Chief Executive Officer, Deloitte & Touche LLP (Sept. 20, 2000) (responding to questions from Chairman

Arthur Levitt, SEC, about whether they would be comfortable if our final rules on non-audit services paralleled the profession's own rules); see also Testimony of K. Michael Conaway, Presiding Officer, Texas State Board of Accountancy (Sept. 20, 2000).

[104] See infra Section IV.D.4.b(x).

[105] AICPA Code of Professional Conduct, ET § 101.05; Codification § 602.02.c.i.

[106] Proposing Release, Section III.D.1(b)(i); Codification § 602.02.c.

[107] See, e.g., Deloitte & Touche Letter; AICPA Letter.

[108] See Ernst & Young Letter.

auditor who has prepared the statutory financial statements of an audit client is put in the position of auditing its own work when auditing the resultant U.S. GAAP-converted financial statements. Accordingly, the final rule amendments cover not only financial statements that are filed with us, but also financial statements that form the basis of financial statements that are filed with us. As proposed, the final amendments also cover any service involving maintaining or preparing the audit client's accounting records.

Second, although we proposed to cover services that resulted in the accountant generating financial information that would be disclosed to investors, commenters believed that this language was too broad. As part of the audit process, auditors may generate data in connection with evaluating financial information that eventually may be disclosed to investors.[109] We believe that they should continue to be able to do so. Accordingly, we narrowed the definition to eliminate this language and instead are incorporating wording from the AICPA Ethics Rules to the effect that an accountant cannot prepare source documents or originate data underlying the client's financial statements without impairing independence.[110]

Third, several commenters requested that we provide an exception to the rule so that auditors could perform bookkeeping services in emergency or other unusual situations.[111] The Codification provides such an exception. Example 6 of Section 602.02.c.ii of the Codification states that when, due to the unexpected resignation of a company's comptroller at the end of the year, the accountant was called upon to provide assistance in closing the books and the accountant did not make decisions on a managerial level, the accountant's independence was not impaired.[112] We recognize that there may be emergency or other unusual situations, such as the one described above, in which the auditor will need to provide bookkeeping services that are otherwise prohibited. Accordingly, we are adopting an exception from the bookkeeping restriction for emergency or other unusual situations, provided that the accountant does not act as a manager or make any managerial decisions. We expect that such situations will be rare. We encourage registrants and

auditors to contact the staff with any questions about the application of this provision to particular circumstances.

Finally, the final rule contains a limited exception related to bookkeeping for foreign subsidiaries or divisions of audit clients. The Codification provides this type of exception.[113] The Proposing Release noted that the Commission recognized the need for relief in this area, and that therefore we had proposed to retain this section of the Codification.[114] In response to commenters' concerns,[115] however, we are incorporating the exception into the rule. Accountants therefore may provide these services for foreign divisions or subsidiaries of a domestic audit client under certain conditions. First, the services must be limited, routine, or ministerial. Second, it must be impractical for the entity receiving the services to obtain them from another provider.[116] Third, under the adopted rule as under the Codification, the foreign entity for which the accountant is performing these services cannot be material to the consolidated financial statements. Fourth, as under the Codification, the entity must not have employees capable or competent to perform the services. Fifth, the services performed must be consistent with local professional ethics rules.[117] Last, as explained in the Codification, "the Commission believes that a comparison of the fees for the bookkeeping services and the audit should provide a fair test for determining the significance of the work to the registrant and the accountant, and indirectly, the possible effect on the firm's independence," and that therefore a limit on the services can be "based on the relationship of the fee charged for the service to the total audit fee charged to the registrant."[118] Accordingly, the final rule provides that the total fees for the bookkeeping services provided by the auditor to a company's foreign entities collectively (for the entire group of companies) cannot exceed the greater of one percent of the consolidated audit fee or $10,000.[119]

(ii) *Financial Information Systems Design and Implementation*

Paragraph (c)(4)(ii) identifies certain information technology services that, if provided to an audit client, impair the accountant's indepen-

---

[109] For example, as part of the audit process, the auditor might propose adjustments that eventually are incorporated into the audit client's financial statements. *See* Deloitte & Touche Letter.

[110] AICPA Code of Professional Conduct, ET § 101.05.

[111] *See, e.g.,* Deloitte & Touche Letter.

[112] Codification § 602.02.c.ii, Example 6.

[113] Codification § 602.02.c.iii.

[114] Proposing Release, note 160.

[115] Deloitte & Touche Letter; Ernst & Young Letter; PricewaterhouseCoopers Letter.

[116] There may be entities that are not large enough to maintain the capability in-house, yet there may not be reputa-

ble providers of these services where domestic companies' foreign affiliates are located or a reputable firm may not want to provide the services because they will generate only minimal fees. *See* Codification § 602.02.e.iii.

[117] Codification § 602.02.c.iii (requiring compliance with this condition, "so that an informed observer in the foreign location would have no cause to question the fact or appearance of independence").

[118] Codification § 602.02.c.iii.

[119] The Commission has determined to raise to $10,000 from $1,000 the dollar threshold in the Codification in light of the inflation since the provisions in the Codification were adopted.

dence. Paragraph (c)(4)(ii) also identifies other information technology services that may be provided to an audit client without impairing independence so long as certain conditions are satisfied.

The rule we adopt today on information technology services represents a change from the rule we proposed. Some commenters objected to our proposed rule. This provision lay at the heart of some of the largest accounting firms' arguments that our proposed rules would hinder their access to technology, limit their understanding of their clients' operations, and hurt their recruiting efforts.[120] These arguments compete with the widespread and persistent perceptions that large, lucrative information technology consulting relationships with an audit client may give rise to conflicts of interest, may result in auditors functioning as management, or may result in an auditor auditing his or her own work.

The final rule reflects a pragmatic approach to a difficult issue. The rule singles out certain information technology services as independence impairments under any circumstances, and identifies other categories of information technology services that will not impair independence if certain conditions are fulfilled. Those conditions are designed to minimize the potential for an auditor to end up making management decisions or auditing his or her own work.

The rule also takes a pragmatic approach to the potential independence problem posed by the economic incentives that accompany large consulting contracts. Rather than effectively ban those relationships, we are amending the proxy disclosure rules to require public companies to make specific disclosure of fees paid to their auditor for information technology services. In addition, public companies must disclose that their audit committee (or, if there is no audit committee, the board of directors) considered whether the provision of the information technology services, as well as all other non-audit services, is compatible with maintaining the auditor's independence.

As discussed in greater detail below, we anticipate that audit committees will consider the independence implications of the engagements that are subject to the disclosure requirements. More-

over, the disclosure will provide information to enable investors themselves to evaluate auditor independence, and will enable future study of whether large information technology consulting relationships have an effect on audit quality and auditors' independence.

Paragraph (c)(4)(ii)(A) provides that an accountant is not independent of an audit client if the accountant is "[d]irectly or indirectly operating, or supervising the operation of, the audit client's information system or managing the audit client's local area network." These services impair an accountant's independence under existing AICPA rules,[121] and, under the rules we adopt today, will impair independence under any circumstances.

Under paragraph (c)(4)(ii)(B), "[d]esigning or implementing a hardware or software system that aggregates source data underlying the financial statements or generates information that is significant to the audit client's financial statements, taken as a whole," will impair an accountant's independence unless certain conditions are met.[122] This section of the final rule differs from the proposed rule in that we have modified the description of the hardware and software systems that the rule reaches by adding the phrase "that aggregates source data underlying the financial statements." This change was suggested by commenters.[123] We have adopted this change because, to the extent that the design and implementation activities concern hardware and software systems that aggregate source data, they are likely to be the types of systems that raise independence concerns.

The conditions that the rule imposes are intended to reduce the likelihood that the auditor will be placed in a position of making, and then auditing, managerial decisions. They are also intended to ensure that management will make all significant decisions during the process and, at its conclusion, will be fully responsible for the results of the project including the proper functioning of the company's internal accounting controls.

The first condition, set out in paragraph (c)(4)(ii)(B)(*1*), is that "the audit client's management has acknowledged in writing to the account-

---

[120] See generally, Arthur Andersen Letter; Deloitte & Touche Letter.

[121] See AICPA Code of Professional Conduct, ET § 101.05.

[122] Although we anticipate that accountants and their audit clients will usually seek to meet these conditions, we note certain points about paragraph (c)(4)(ii)(B) relevant to situations where these conditions are not met. First, by "significant," we refer to information that is reasonably likely to be material to the financial statements of the audit client. Since materiality determinations may not be final before financial statements are generated, an accounting firm may need to evaluate the general nature of the information rather than wait to evaluate system output during the period of the audit engagement. For example, without satisfying the conditions of paragraphs (c)(4)(ii)(B)(1)-(5), an accountant would not be

independent of an audit client for which it designed an integrated Enterprise Resource Planning ("ERP") system. (An ERP system is designed to integrate all functions and departments in a company into one computer system that can serve the needs of each department.) In addition, without satisfying the conditions, a firm's independence would be impaired if it designed and implemented an accounts receivable/order management system that recorded and summarized sales that were material to the financial statements of the audit client. A firm's independence would not be impaired, however, if the accounting firm designed and implemented a system for a foreign subsidiary whose financial condition and results of operations were not material to the financial statements of the audit client.

[123] Ernst & Young Letter; PricewaterhouseCoopers Letter.

---

ing firm and the audit client's audit committee, or if there is no such committee then the board of directors, the audit client's responsibility to establish and maintain a system of internal accounting controls in compliance with Section 13(b)(2) of the Securities Exchange Act of 1934, 15 U.S.C. § 78m(b)(2)." This condition makes clear that this statutory responsibility cannot be shifted to the accounting firm.

Paragraphs   (c)(4)(ii)(B)(2)   and (c)(4)(ii)(B)(3), setting out the second and third conditions, complement each other. Paragraph (B)(2) articulates the condition that "the audit client's management designates a competent employee or employees, preferably within senior management, with the responsibility to make all management decisions with respect to the design and implementation of the hardware or software system." Paragraph (B)(3) articulates the condition that "the audit client's management makes all management decisions with respect to the design and implementation of the hardware or software system including, but not limited to, decisions concerning the systems to be evaluated and selected, the controls and system procedures to be implemented, the scope and timetable of system implementation, and the testing, training and conversion plans." These conditions are intended to ensure that an audit client that receives information technology services from its auditor does not delegate to its auditor responsibility for "management decisions" relating to the design and implementation of the system.

The fourth condition, set out in paragraph (c)(4)(ii)(B)(4), is that "the audit client's management evaluates the adequacy and results of the design and implementation of the hardware or software system." Paragraph (c)(4)(ii)(B)(5) sets out the fifth condition, that "the audit client's management does not rely on the accountant's work as the primary basis for determining the adequacy of its internal controls and financial reporting systems." These conditions reiterate the principles that management is to make all substantive decisions, that the auditor should not have a mutual interest in the successful operation of the systems, and that the auditor should not be placed in the position of auditing his or her firm's decisions about the system.

The rule expressly does not limit services in connection with the assessment, design, and implementation of internal accounting and risk management controls, provided the auditor does not act as an employee or perform management functions. During the audit, accountants generally obtain an understanding of their audit clients'

systems of internal accounting controls and may recommend ways in which those controls can be improved or strengthened. This service can be valuable to companies and their audit committees, and may also enhance audit quality, without raising independence concerns. In addition, we do not see any significant reason for concern about an audit firm's work on hardware or software systems that are unrelated to the audit client's financial statements or accounting records.

(iii) *Appraisal or Valuation Services and Fairness Opinions*

We are adopting a rule that, with some exceptions, provides that an accountant is not independent if the accountant provides appraisal or valuation services or any service involving a fairness opinion.[124] Appraisal and valuation services include any process of valuing assets, both tangible and intangible, or liabilities. Fairness opinions are opinions that an accounting firm provides on the adequacy of consideration in a transaction. As explained more thoroughly in the Proposing Release, if an audit firm provides these services to an audit client, when it is time to audit the financial statements the accountant could well end up reviewing his or her own work, including key assumptions or variables suggested by his or her firm that underlie an entry in the financial statements.[125] Where the service involves the preparation of projections of future results or future cash flows, the accountant may develop a mutuality of interest with the audit client in attaining the forecasted results.

We solicited comment on whether we should provide an exception from the rule when the amounts involved are likely to be immaterial to the financial statements that later would be reviewed by the auditor. Several commenters stated that such an exception is warranted.[126] In response, we are limiting application of the rule to the provision of appraisals, valuations, or services involving a fairness opinion where it is reasonably likely that the results, individually or in the aggregate, would be material to the audit client's financial statements[127] or where the results would be audited by the auditor. As a general matter, auditors would be auditing the results when they perform a GAAS audit.

The rule also contains an exception for appraisal or valuation services where the accounting firm reviews and reports on work done by the audit client itself or an independent, third-party specialist employed by the audit client, and the audit client or specialist provides the primary support for the balance recorded in the client's financial

---

[124] The ISB has identified threats to the independence of firms that perform appraisal and valuation services for audit clients. *See* ISB, Discussion Memorandum 99-3 "Appraisal and Valuation Services," at 7-9.

[125] *See generally* Codification § 602.02.c.

[126] *See, e.g.,* Arthur Andersen Letter; Deloitte & Touche Letter; PricewaterhouseCoopers Letter.

[127] Of course, reference to financial statements includes results of operations, financial conditions and cash flows.

statements. In those instances, because a third party or the audit client is the source of the financial information subject to the review or audit, the accountant will not be reviewing or auditing his or her own work.

Another exception allows accountants to continue to value an audit client's pension, other post-employment benefit, or similar liabilities, so long as the audit client has determined and taken responsibility for all significant assumptions and data underlying the valuation.[128] Accountants historically have provided pension assistance to their audit clients, and if appropriate persons at the audit client determine the underlying assumptions and data, we believe that independence is not impaired.

Commenters also stated that an accountant's independence should not be deemed impaired when the accountant performs appraisal or valuation services as a necessary part of permitted tax services. As the rule text and this Release make clear, accountants will continue to be able to provide tax services to audit clients. A few commenters pointed out, however, that unless accountants can perform appraisal and valuation services that are part of a tax planning strategy or for tax compliance purposes, the client would not hire the accountant to provide tax services.[129] The final rule makes clear that accountants can perform appraisal and valuation services for those purposes without impairing independence.

Commenters requested an exception for appraisal and valuation services where the services are for non-financial purposes. Because our principal concern about appraisal and valuation services is that they lead auditors to audit their own work, so long as the results do not affect the financial statements, appraisal or valuation services performed for non-financial purposes do not impair an auditor's independence.

At least one commenter suggested that we include an exception for purchase price allocations.[130] An exception is not appropriate here because these allocation decisions, particularly those regarding the valuation of intangible assets, can have a direct, significant, and immediate impact on companies' financial statements. For example, where a company acquires another company with large, on-going in-process research and development projects, the acquiring company will need to decide how much of the purchase price to allocate to those projects. This may affect in turn the amount charged against earnings in the current year as in-process research and development expense, and the amount to be classified as goodwill and amortized against future years' earnings. Any such allocations later will be reviewed in the course of the audit, leading the firm to audit its own work.[131]

Finally, commenters raised concerns about the restriction on the provision of contribution-in-kind reports.[132] We have removed the language in the rule referring to contribution-in-kind reports because we view such reports to be akin to fairness opinions, which are restricted under the final rules. We understand from commenters that certain foreign jurisdictions require auditors to issue contribution-in-kind reports for their audit clients[133] and that, in some European jurisdictions, auditors may be appointed or approved by an administrative or judicial authority to act as an independent expert and issue a contribution-in-kind report for the audit client.[134] The Commission is sensitive to those issues and in the past has worked with foreign regulators and companies to reach an acceptable resolution.[135] We will continue our practice of determining whether to accept a contribution-in-kind report on a case-by-case basis. In this regard, we encourage registrants and their auditors to contact the staff to discuss particular situations where a foreign jurisdiction requires a contribution-in-kind report to enable the staff to work with the registrant and the foreign jurisdiction in reaching an appropriate resolution.

(iv) *Actuarial Services*

SECPS rules currently prohibit member accounting firms from providing certain actuarially oriented advisory services to insurance companies.[136] Accountants providing these services assume a key management task. In addition, because actuarially oriented advisory services may affect amounts reflected in an insurance com-

---

[128] AICPA Code of Professional Conduct, ET § 101.05 states that an auditor's independence would not be impaired in connection with appraisal and valuation services "when all significant matters of judgment are determined or approved by the client and the client is in a position to have an informed judgment on the results of the valuation."

[129] *See, e.g.,* Arthur Andersen Letter.

[130] Deloitte & Touche Letter.

[131] We note in this regard, that if an acquisition individually, and when aggregated with other acquisitions reflected in the financial statements, is immaterial to the audit client's financial statements, then assisting in the allocation of the purchase price would not fall within the conditions of the rule and therefore would not be deemed to impair the auditor's independence.

[132] *See, e.g.,* Deloitte & Touche Letter; Ernst & Young Letter; Letter of KPMG Europe (Sept. 22, 2000).

[133] Ernst & Young Letter.

[134] *See e.g.,* Deloitte & Touche Letter; Letter of KPMG Europe (Sept. 22, 2000).

[135] *See* Letter from Lynn Turner, Chief Accountant, SEC, to Antonio Rosati, CONSOB (Aug. 24, 2000). In that letter, our Chief Accountant did not deem the auditor's independence to be impaired where there were certain agreed-upon procedures for the contribution-in-kind report and the accountant represented in the report that the report did not express an opinion on the fairness of the transaction, the value of the security, or the adequacy of consideration to shareholders. This letter is available on our website.

[136] SECPS Reference Manual ("SECPS Manual") § 1000.35.

pany's financial statements, providing these services may cause an accountant later to audit his or her own work. Rule 2-01 (c) (4) (iv) addresses these issues.

Commenters expressed concern that the proposal was broader than a similar SECPS rule, in that the restrictions in the proposal applied to services provided to all public companies, not just insurance companies, and the proposal did not include the four examples of appropriate services that are included in the SECPS rule.[137] We have modified our final rule with respect to actuarial services to parallel closely the SECPS rule, including the four exceptions. The final rule limits only actuarially oriented advisory services involving the determination of insurance company policy reserves and related accounts. We are narrowing the prohibition to services for insurance companies because, as explained in the SECPS rule, it is primarily in these companies that the actuarial function is "basic to the operation and management" of the company.[138]

The final rule states that an auditor's independence is impaired if the audit firm provides certain actuarially oriented advisory services involving the determination of insurance company policy reserves and related accounts, unless three conditions are met. First, the audit client must use its own actuaries or third-party actuaries to provide management with the primary actuarial capabilities. Second, management must accept responsibility for any significant actuarial methods and assumptions employed by the accountant in performing or providing the actuarial services. Third, the accountant cannot render the actuarial services to the audit client on a continuous basis. All of these conditions are designed to ensure that the accountant does not assume a management function for the audit client.

Assuming these conditions are met, the accountant can perform four types of actuarial services for an insurance company audit client without impairing the accountant's independence. The four types of actuarial services are: (i) assisting management to develop appropriate methods, assumptions, and amounts for policy and loss reserves and other actuarial items presented in financial reports, based on the company's historical experience, current practice, and future plans;[139] (ii) assisting management in the conver-

sion of financial statements from a statutory basis to one conforming with GAAP; (iii) analyzing actuarial considerations and alternatives in federal income tax planning; and (iv) assisting management in the financial analyses of various matters, such as proposed new policies, new markets, business acquisitions, and reinsurance needs. Allowing accountants to provide these four types of actuarially oriented advisory services under the three conditions is consistent with the SECPS rule.[140] We believe that if the conditions are met, in the context of state-regulated insurance companies, the four services would not constitute an assumption of the insurance company management's role or responsibilities, and would not impair the auditor's independence.

(v) Internal Audit Services

Although companies are not required to do so, they may, as part of their internal controls, form internal audit departments that are used to make sure that control systems are adequate and working. According to the Committee of Sponsoring Organizations ("COSO"), internal auditors play an important role in evaluating and monitoring a company's internal control system.[141] As explained by Robert Denham, a member of the ISB, at our public hearings, "Good internal auditing . . . requires the internal auditor to be very closely integrated with management. The internal auditor is part of the management team. He or she is identifying problems and providing reports that help management correct those problems."[142] In sum, "the internal audit function is, basically, an arm of management,"[143] and internal auditors are, in effect, part of a company's internal accounting control system.

Although a company may prefer to outsource its internal audit function, management must continue to be responsible for the function.[144] When a company outsources the function to a third-party provider, there may be a concern that management has ceded this responsibility. While this is a concern in any internal audit outsourcing arrangement, there are additional concerns when a company outsources the work to its external auditor. As Comptroller of the Currency John D. Hawke, Jr. testified, "When a bank out-sources its internal audit function to the same firm that performs the bank's external financial audit . . . the possibility for inherent conflicts and impairments of auditor

---

[137] PricewaterhouseCooopers Letter; Ernst & Young Letter; see also Deloitte & Touche Letter.

[138] SECPS Manual § 1000.35, at ¶ 5.

[139] Although it addresses a different topic, accountants and registrants may refer to ISB, "Interpretation No. 99:1: Impact on Auditor Independence of Assisting Clients in the Implementation of FAS 133 (Derivatives)" for general guidance on what constitutes "assistance" as opposed to "performing" certain functions or services.

[140] See SECPS Manual § 1000.35.

[141] See Committee of Sponsoring Organizations of the Treadway Commission, Internal Control - Integrated Framework, at 7 (1992) (the "COSO Report").

[142] Testimony of Robert E. Denham (July 26, 2000); see also Testimony of John Whitehead, retired Chairman, Goldman Sachs & Co. (Sept. 13, 2000) ("internal auditing is the function of management").

[143] Testimony of Manuel H. Johnson, Public Member, ISB (July 26, 2000).

[144] See AICPA Code of Professional Conduct, ET § 101.15 (Interpretation 101-13).

independence and auditor integrity is greatest."[145] Although Mr. Hawke discussed the conflicts in the bank context, his comments are equally applicable to any registrant.

Research commissioned by the Institute of Internal Auditors indicates that the internal auditors surveyed perceive an independence problem where internal audit work is outsourced to the external auditor.[146] In particular, in auditing the company's financial statements, the accountant will consider the extent to which he or she may rely on the internal control system in designing its audit procedures.[147] When the auditor has performed the internal audit work, the auditor will need to consider or examine its own work.

Final Rule 2-01(c)(4)(v) seeks to curb these conflicting interests without precluding companies, particularly small companies, from obtaining internal audit services from their auditors where the auditor's independence would not be compromised. Under the final rule, an auditor's independence is impaired by performing more than forty percent of the audit client's internal audit work related to the internal accounting controls, financial systems, or financial statements, unless the audit client has $200 million or less in assets.

The final rule provides an exception for businesses with $200 million or less in assets. Specifically, the rule provides that audit clients who have less than $200 million in total assets may receive more than forty percent of their internal audit functions from their auditor without giving rise to an impairment of independence. We provide this exception after carefully considering the potential impact of our rules on small businesses. At the proposing stage, we requested comment on whether we should provide an exception for smaller businesses. We adopt this exception in response to comments that we received,[148] and in recognition of the fact that smaller businesses, many of which may be located away from major business centers, could suffer particular hardships if we do not provide some exception.[149]

We chose a $200 million threshold for various reasons. From the available data, the $200 million threshold appears to provide a line below which not only are the companies themselves smaller, but the accounting firms that audit them also tend to be smaller.[150]

Commenters distinguished the situation in which the auditor supplements an audit client's internal audit function from the situation in which the auditor supplants the client's internal audit function. They suggested that an auditor should not be permitted to provide all of the internal audit services required by an audit client but should be allowed to provide a limited amount of internal audit services without impairing the auditor's independence.[151] For example, Ray J. Groves, former Chairman and Chief Executive Officer of Ernst & Young, said that "limited amounts in specific areas of internal out-sourcing make a lot of sense, as opposed to complete out-sourcing, as long as the audit client maintains their own independent internal audit function with capable management and people within it."[152] These comments in large part reflect the current AICPA

---

[145] Testimony of John D. Hawke, Jr. (July 26, 2000). He also reported a trend among banks in favor of outsourcing internal audit work to the external auditor. He testified that "[o]f [the] 50 largest banks" within the jurisdiction of the OCC, "8 out-source their internal audit, and 7 of those 8 out-source to the same firm that does their external audit. That's a pretty good chunk of the largest banks." *Id.* In addition, Mr. Hawke reported that in a survey of the OCC banks in the Northeast region, one-third outsource their internal audit work and half of those banks outsource to their external auditor. *Id.*

[146] In this study, companies with small, "mean-sized," and large internal audit departments were asked to indicate their level of agreement (on a scale of zero to five, with five being the strongest) with the following statement: "There is an independence problem if the external audit firm performs extended audit services (internal audit services) for the same firm for which it performs the annual financial statement audit." The level of agreement among respondents was between 3.7 and 4.0, "indicating a perception of an independence problem." Larry E. Rittenberg and Mark A Covaleski, *The Outsourcing Dilemma: What's Best for Internal Auditing,* at 68 and Exh. 4-4 (Institute of Internal Auditors Research Foundation 1997).

[147] AICPA SAS No. 55, AU § 319 (effective for audits on or after Jan. 1, 1990).

[148] *See, e.g.,* Testimony of John D. Hawke, Jr., Comptroller of the Currency (July 26, 2000) (noting concerns about the effect of the proposed rule on small banks); Testimony of Wayne A. Kolins, National Director of Assurance, BDO Seidman, LLP (Sept. 20, 2000).

[149] These hardships could include, for example, difficulty in obtaining suitable professional services at a cost appropriate to the size of the business, or, for a small accounting firm, the loss of a substantial portion of its client base for either its audit or internal audit services.

[150] Using the $200 million threshold reasonably isolates companies that are relatively small themselves - approximately 54% of the 9,414 public reporting companies in the Standard & Poors Research Insight Compustat Database ("Compustat Database") - and has the effect of almost completely excepting smaller accounting firms. Approximately 85% of the public company audit clients (other than bank holding companies) of non-Big Five accounting firms have less than $200 million in assets. Of public company audit clients with more than $200 million in assets - the companies that would *not* trigger the exception - no more than 6.1% (again, excluding bank holding companies) are audited by non-Big Five firms. The source for these data is the Compustat Database, October 31, 2000. For further analysis, *see infra* Section V.B. (cost-benefit analysis).

[151] *See, e.g.,* Testimony of Jacquelyn Wagner (Sept. 13, 2000) (testifying for the Institute of Internal Auditors) ("The IIA believes that the total outsourcing of the internal auditing function to the organization's external auditing firm impairs that firm's independence."); Testimony of Dominick Esposito, Chief Executive Officer, Grant Thornton LLP (Sept. 13, 2000) ("I think if there is the entire internal audit department outsourced, it can present a conflict.").

[152] Testimony of Ray J. Groves (July 26, 2000).

rule on internal audit outsourcing,[153] which, as explained by a senior official of the AICPA, "prohibit[s] the complete outsourcing."[154] In response to these comments and in recognition of the AICPA rule, our final rule, with respect to registrants with $200 million or more in assets, allows auditors to perform up to forty percent of an audit client's internal audit work.[155]

Several commenters expressed concern about the effect of the proposed rule on small businesses that have no internal audit department or staff. They noted that smaller firms may not have sufficient need for full-time internal auditors but nonetheless, may need some services that internal auditors typically provide, which they obtain from their external auditors. According to these commenters, we should encourage this practice. Unless these companies can turn to their external auditors, they state, the work will not be done at all. Because we agree that small businesses should be encouraged to use internal audit services, the final rule allows auditors to provide an unlimited amount of internal audit services to clients with less than $200 million in assets, provided certain conditions are met.

In addition, the final rule does not restrict internal audit services regarding operational internal audits unrelated to the internal accounting controls, financial systems, or financial statements. This is because our focus is on services that affect the integrity of financial statements and reported financial information.[156]

Under all circumstances in which an auditor performs any internal audit services for an audit client, including with respect to companies with assets under $200 million, the auditor must comply with the six conditions listed in paragraph (B) to avoid an impairment of independence. Four of the six conditions are drawn from a ruling published in 1996 by the Ethics Committee of the AICPA.[157] It states that AICPA members may provide certain internal audit outsourcing services to audit clients without impairing their independence, so long as, among other things, (i) the client designates a competent member of manage-

ment to be responsible for the internal audit function, (ii) management determines the scope, risk, and frequency of internal audit activities, including those to be performed by the auditor, (iii) management evaluates the findings and results arising from the internal audit activities, including those performed by the auditor, and (iv) management evaluates the adequacy of the audit procedures performed and the findings resulting from performance of those procedures. In addition, consistent with a later ruling by the AICPA, the final rule requires that (v) the audit client acknowledges its responsibility to establish and maintain a system of internal accounting controls in compliance with Section 13(b)(2) of the Securities Exchange Act, and (vi) that management not rely on the auditor's work as the primary basis for determining the adequacy of its internal controls.[158]

In the Proposing Release we noted that we were inclined not to follow the AICPA rule on internal audit outsourcing because we believed that, in providing such services, the auditor assumed a management function and, in the course of the audit, would have to review his or her own work. As discussed above, however, we have been persuaded that the auditor can perform a limited amount of an audit client's internal audit function without supplanting management's role or auditing its own work. In addition, we have been persuaded that encouraging internal audit outsourcing at small businesses is wise public policy. We have, accordingly, determined to allow the limited relationships described above under the conditions recommended and used at this time by the AICPA.

(vi) *Management Functions*

Current Rule 2-01 of Regulation S-X and the AICPA's rules preclude accountants from acting as management.[159] We are adopting Rule 2-01(c)(4)(vi) as proposed, which provides that an accountant's independence is impaired with respect to an audit client for which the accountant acts, temporarily or permanently, as a director, officer, or employee or performs any decision-

---

[153] *See* AICPA Code of Professional Conduct, ET § 101.15 (Interpretation 101-13).

[154] Testimony of Barry Melancon, President and Chief Executive Officer (Sept. 13, 2000). Mr. Melancon also noted that "[t]h ere still has to be management responsibility for the overall internal audit function . . . we certainly agree that the ultimate responsibility for internal auditing, the management decision making, must [lie] with management, not with the auditor."

[155] When providing internal audit services to an audit client with $200 million or more in assets, the auditor must measure the internal audit services provided to the audit client in full-time employee hours. In order to remain independent, the auditor must ensure that it provides 40% or less of the total hours expended by the audit client, the auditor and anyone else on internal audit matters related to internal accounting controls, financial systems, and financial statements, and matters that impact the financial statements.

[156] In addition, performing procedures that generally are considered to be within the scope of the engagement for the audit of the audit client's financial statements, such as confirming accounts receivable and analyzing fluctuations in account balances, would not impair the accountant's independence, even if the extent of testing exceeds that required by GAAS. For example, if an accountant in normal circumstances would plan to observe ten percent of an audit client's inventory, but at the audit client's request the accountant observes 50% of inventory on hand, the accountant's independence would not be impaired.

[157] AICPA Code of Professional Conduct, ET § 101.15 (Interpretation 101-13).

[158] AICPA Code of Professional Conduct, ET § 191.206-207 (Interpretation 101-103).

[159] Former Rule 2-01(b), 17 C.F.R. 210.2-01(b); AICPA Code of Professional Conduct, ET § 101.02.

making, supervisory, or ongoing monitoring functions.

(vii) *Human Resources*

Under current SECPS rules, accountants cannot perform certain executive recruiting and human resource services for audit clients.[160] Specifically, under those rules, an accountant's independence would be impaired if the accountant: (a) searches for or seeks out prospective candidates for managerial, executive or director positions with audit clients;[161] (b) engages in psychological testing, or other formal testing or evaluation programs;[162] (c) undertakes reference checks of prospective candidates for executive or director positions with audit clients;[163] (d) acts as a negotiator on the audit client's behalf, such as in determining position, status or title, compensation, fringe benefits, or other conditions of employment;[164] or (e) recommends, or advises an audit client to hire, a specific candidate for a specific job.[165] Those rules do not, however, preclude an accountant from, upon request of the audit client, interviewing candidates and advising an audit client on the candidate's competence for financial, accounting, administrative or control positions.[166]

Excessive involvement in human resource selection or development places the auditor in the position of having an interest in the success of the employees that the auditor has selected, tested, or evaluated. Accordingly, an auditor may be reluctant to suggest that those employees failed to perform their jobs appropriately because doing so would require the auditor to acknowledge shortcomings in its human resource service.

Commenters were concerned that our proposed language expanded upon the limitations in the AICPA and SECPS rules.[167] For example, commenters expressed concern that the proposed rule would prohibit an accountant from advising an audit committee on the competence of a prospective controller or CFO.[168] Commenters also were concerned that the proposed rule limited accountants from providing tax-related services related to structuring compensation packages.[169] We agree

that an objective evaluation by the accountant of a candidate's competency for an accounting or financial position may be useful to some, particularly smaller, companies and that the impact of this evaluation is reduced by the proscription that the accountant may not recommend that the audit client hire a particular candidate. We also believe that an accountant should not negotiate regarding the contents of a compensation package the accountant has designed. Accordingly, in light of the comments received, we have modified the final rule, and final Rule 2-01(c)(4)(vii) more closely parallels the SECPS rules.

(viii) *Broker-Dealer Services*

Current Rule 2-01 states that an accountant's independence is impaired if the accountant is connected with the audit client as an underwriter or promoter.[170] The Codification further states that concurrent engagement as a broker-dealer is incompatible with the practice of public accounting.[171] Rule 2-01(c)(4)(viii) combines these provisions with certain provisions from the AICPA rules.[172] As adopted, the amendments state that an accountant's independence will be impaired if the accountant acts as a broker-dealer, promoter, or underwriter on behalf of an audit client, makes investment decisions on behalf of the audit client or otherwise has discretionary authority over an audit client's investments, executes a transaction to buy or sell an audit client's investment, or has custody of assets of the audit client, such as taking temporary possession of securities purchased by the audit client. As noted in our existing standards, activities such as recommending securities, soliciting customers, and executing orders create a mutuality of interest and the potential for self-review.

Although our intention was to codify current restrictions, commenters believed that our proposal went further.[173] In particular, commenters were concerned that by including the term "investment adviser", we were precluding accountants from providing certain investment advisory or personal financial planning services that they currently provide.[174] In response to these concerns,

---

[160] *See* SECPS Manual § 1000.35 App. A; *see also* AICPA Code of Professional Conduct, ET § 101.05 (Interpretation 101-3) (deeming an auditor's independence impaired when the auditor negotiates employee compensation or benefits, or hires or terminates client employees).

[161] SECPS Manual § 1000.35 App. A.

[162] *Id.*

[163] *Id.*

[164] *Id.*; AICPA Code of Professional Conduct, ET § 101.05.

[165] *Id.*

[166] SECPS Manual § 1000.35 App. A

[167] *See, e.g.*, Deloitte & Touche Letter; KPMG Letter; PricewaterhouseCoopers Letter; Ernst & Young Letter.

[168] *See, e.g.*, KPMG Letter; Ernst & Young Letter.

[169] *See, e.g.*, Deloitte & Touche Letter; Ernst & Young Letter.

[170] Former Rule 2-01(b), 17 CFR 210.2-01(b).

[171] Codification § 602.02.e.iii.

[172] *See* AICPA Code of Professional Conduct ET § 101.05.

[173] *See, e.g.*, Ernst & Young Letter; PricewaterhouseCoopers Letter.

[174] *See* Arthur Andersen & Co., 1994 SEC No Act. LEXIS 617 (July 8, 1994) ("Andersen No-Action Letter") in which the staff stated it would not recommend enforcement action under the Investment Advisers Act where an accounting firm did not register as an investment adviser but an affiliated registered investment adviser provided investment advisory services. The staff permitted the affiliate to publish a newsletter with financial planning information, provided the newsletter does not recommend any specific industry sectors or securities, to identify categories of mutual funds that satisfy an advisory client's investment objectives, and to recommend two or more mutual funds in each category. When an advisory client wants

---

we have removed the term "investment adviser" from the rule t ext.

Current AICPA rules specify investment advisory services that accountants may provide to audit clients without impairing their independence. Under these rules, accountants can recommend the allocation of funds that an audit client should invest in various asset classes, based on the client's risk tolerance and other factors; provide a comparative analysis of the client's investments to third-party benchmarks; review the manner in which the audit client's portfolio is being managed by investment account managers; and transmit a client's investment selection to a broker-dealer, provided that the client has made the investment decision and has authorized the broker-dealer to execute the transaction.[175] Accountants may continue to provide those services without impairing their independence.

Current AICPA rules also specify investment advisory services accountants may not provide to audit clients without impairing their independence. The final rule incorporates these restrictions. Accordingly, as under the AICPA's rules,[176] auditors cannot make investment decisions for audit clients or exercise discretionary trading authority over an audit client's account, cannot execute transactions for audit clients, and cannot take custody of an audit client's assets. Providing such services creates a mutuality of interest and may result in the auditor having to audit the value of investments that the auditor made for the client.

The Codification states that "[t]he functions customarily performed [by a broker-dealer] include the recommendation of securities, the solicitation of customers and the execution of orders, any one of which could involve securities transactions of clients either as issuer or investor and provide third parties with sufficient reason to question the accountant's ability to be impartial and objective."[177] Because these activities continue to be encompassed within the meaning of "broker-dealer" under the rule we are adopting, and therefore, when performed on behalf of an audit client, impair an auditor's independence, we

have eliminated the language "in any capacity recommending the purchase or sale of an audit client's securities" from the rule text.

By restricting broker-dealer services to those provided "on behalf of the audit client," we do not mean to suggest that an auditor can recommend an audit client's securities to either another audit client or a non-audit client.[178] The language "on behalf of" the audit client encompasses all situations in which the auditor is directly or indirectly compensated for the recommendation.

The final rule, however, will not alter current guidance as to the corporate finance consulting services auditors provide to audit and non-audit clients.[179] For example, accountants, without impairing their independence, may advise audit clients in need of capital that one alternative is to do a public offering of their securities. Also, the staff has indicated that limited activities on the part of the auditor by way of general explanatory work and limited fact finding (such as identifying and introducing an audit client to potential merger partners that meet specified criteria) would not impair an auditor's independence. An auditor's independence would be impaired, however, by entering into preliminary or other negotiations on behalf of an audit client, by promoting the client to potential buyers, or "with respect to subsequent audits of a client if the accountant renders advice as to whether, or at what price a transaction should be entered into."[180] These interpretations of former Rule 2-01(b) apply equally to the amended rule we adopt today. To the extent an auditor is otherwise permitted to provide services to a non-audit client conc erning corporate financing transactions to which an audit client is a party, the permissibility of those services does not turn on whether the advice involves transactions in which the consideration provided by an audit client to the non-audit client is in the form of an audit client's securities, as opposed to cash or other assets.

Commenters expressed concern that, because the terms "securities professional" and "analyst" are not defined in the securities laws, they would

---

(Footnote Continued)

more specific advice, the investment advisory affiliate accountant will provide a client with a list of two or more investment advisers or broker-dealers that meet certain predetermined criteria, provided that the accountant does not receive any fee or other economic benefit from the mutual funds, investment advisers or broker-dealers recommended. The advisory affiliate will disclose to advisory clients that the recommended mutual funds, investment advisers, or broker dealers may include audit clients. *See also* Ernst & Young Letter (citing Andersen No-Action Letter).

[175] AICPA Code of Professional Conduct, ET § 101.05 (Interpretation 101-3).

[176] *Id.*

[177] Codification § 602.02.e.iii.

[178] *See* Arthur Andersen Letter (acknowledging that it is appropriate to prohibit accountants from recommending any

specific securities to audit clients and from recommending audit clients' securities to non-audit clients).

[179] *See* AICPA Code of Professional Conduct, ET § 101.05, Interpretation 101-3, which states that an accountant's independence would not be impaired if that accountant assists in developing corporate strategies, assists in identifying or introducing the client to possible sources of capital that meet the client's specifications or criteria, assists in analyzing the effects of proposed transactions, assists in drafting an offering document or memorandum, or participates in transaction negotiations in an advisory capacity.

[180] Letter from Edmund Coulson, Chief Accountant, SEC, to Edward McGowen, Pannell Kerr Forster, at 2 (July 11, 1988) (discussing mergers and acquisition services, among others).

cause confusion.[181] To avoid any such confusion and to limit concerns about overbroad application of those terms, we have eliminated those terms from the rule text. We note, however, that broker-dealers provide an array of services that may include analyst activities.

Finally, we have not included in the final rule the prohibition relating to designing broker-dealer or investment adviser compliance systems. We have eliminated this provision to conform the rule to current law.

(ix) *Legal Services*

For the reasons set forth in the Proposing Release, we believe that there is a fundamental conflict between the role of an independent auditor and that of an attorney. The auditor's charge is to examine objectively and report, regardless of the impact on the client, while the attorney's fundamental duty is to advance the client's interests.[182] As discussed in the Proposing Release at greater length,[183] existing regulations,[184] the U.S. Supreme Court,[185] and professional legal organizations[186] have deemed it inconsistent with the concept of auditor independence for an accountant to provide legal services to an audit client. Accordingly, we are adopting the proposed rule as to legal services with a few modifications. Final Rule 2-01(c)(4)(ix) provides that an accountant is not independent of an audit client if the accountant provides any service to an audit client under circumstances in which the person providing the service must be admitted to practice before the courts of a U. S. jurisdiction.

We understand that some firms, largely through their foreign affiliates, are providing legal services outside of the United States. Moreover, we understand[187] that lawyers affiliated with foreign affiliates of U. S. accounting firms on occasion provide legal services in the United States where they are not required to be admitted to a bar in the United States. The final rule does not address these practices, where local law does not preclude such services and the services relate to matters that are not material to the consolidated financial statements of an SEC registrant or are routine and ministerial. We note, however, that it is clear to us that legal services provided outside the United States raise serious independence concerns under circumstances other than those meeting at least those minimum criteria.

We solicited comment on whether our proposed rule on legal services created uncertainty or complexity since the prohibition focused on the jurisdiction in which the legal services were provided. Commenters stated that indeed the rule should be revised because U.S. attorneys can, under various circumstances, render legal services in jurisdictions where they are not licensed to practice law. For example, when an attorney is not licensed to practice law in a particular jurisdiction, he or she can apply to a court *pro hac vice* to be able to appear before the court for purposes of the case.[188] Accordingly, we modified the rule so that an accountant's ability to render legal services no longer depends on his or her being licensed in the jurisdiction where the services are rendered, but rather on whether, under the circumstances, the provider of the services must be admitted to practice before the courts of a U.S. jurisdiction.

Some commenters suggested that safeguards, such as firewalls, could prevent or cure any independence problem that might arise by virtue of an accountant providing legal services to an audit client.[189] Recently, the Commission on Multidisciplinary Practice of the ABA considered whether firewalls would address sufficiently issues that might arise if a law firm were to provide both legal and other services.[190] That Commission rejected the firewall approach, stating "[We] explicitly recognize[] the[] incompatibility [of legal and audit services]. [We] do not believe that a single entity should be allowed to provide legal and audit services to the same client."[191] In light of current regulations and the ABA Report, we have determined not to adopt a firewall approach.

(x) *Expert Services*

We are not adopting the proposal to restrict the provision of expert services. The proposed rule would have provided that an accountant's independence is impaired as to an audit client if the accountant renders or supports expert opinions for the audit client or an affiliate of the audit client in legal, administrative, or regulatory filings or proceedings ("expert services"). Commenters said that our proposals went beyond current rules.[192] For example, AICPA Ethics Standards permit accountants to serve as expert witnesses.[193]

Commenters argued that accountants may need to act as experts in defending work they have done for audit clients before such bodies as the

---

[181] *See* Ernst & Young Letter; PricewaterhouseCoopers Letter.

[182] *See also* ISB, "Discussion Memorandum 99-4: Legal Services" (Dec. 1999).

[183] *See* Proposing Release, Section III.D.1(b)(ix).

[184] Codification § 602.02.e.ii.

[185] *Arthur Young*, 465 U.S. at 819-20 n.15.

[186] American Bar Association Commission on Multidisciplinary Practice, Report to the House of Delegates, at 5 (July 2000) ("ABA Report") (available at www.ABAnet.org/cpr/mdpfinalrep2000.html).

[187] *See* Ernst & Young Letter; PricewaterhouseCoopers Letter; Arthur Andersen Letter.

[188] *See, e.g.*, Va. Sup. Ct. R. 1A:4 (2000).

[189] *See, e.g.*, Arthur Andersen Letter.

[190] *See* ABA Report, *supra* note 427.

[191] *Id.* at 5 (footnote omitted).

[192] *See, e.g.*, PricewaterhouseCoopers Letter; Deloitte & Touche Letter.

[193] AICPA Code of Professional Conduct, ET § 101.202-101.203.

Internal Revenue Service, and indeed, this Commission.[194] As stated in the Proposing Release, we did not intend for our proposals to prohibit an auditor from testifying as a fact witness to its audit work for a particular client. In those instances, the auditor is merely providing a factual account of what he or she observed and the judgments he or she made. Nevertheless, to avoid confusion and any uncertainty that might be created by permitting the accountant to testify in one capacity but not another, we have determined not to adopt a restriction on expert services. When an accountant performs such services, however, he or she should be particularly mindful of his or her duty to maintain objectivity and integrity, as discussed in the AICPA Ethics Regulations.[195]

c. *Alternative Approaches to Scope of Services Restrictions*

As discussed in the Proposing Release, we considered a number of alternatives concerning scope of services. We solicited public comment on each alternative. After considering the comments received, we have determined not to adopt any of the alternatives proposed.

For the reasons discussed above, we have not adopted a disclosure-only approach or a complete ban on auditors' provision to audit clients of non-audit services. In addition, as discussed above, we welcome and encourage active oversight by audit committees with respect to auditor independence, but do not believe that such oversight obviates the need for the rule we adopt today. In this regard, it is our statutory responsibility to protect the public interest.

We are persuaded that relying on a firewalls approach is also unworkable. Under a firewalls approach, there would be a strict separation between those professionals in the accounting firm who perform audit work for an audit client and those who provide non-audit services for the client. GAAS, however, under certain circumstances requires that auditors seek out a registrant's consultants in the course of an audit to discuss work performed by the consultant.[196] Accordingly, a strict firewalls approach would conflict with GAAS requirements.

5. *Contingent Fees*

We proposed to restrict the receipt of contingent fees from audit clients, and we continue to believe that contingent fee arrangements result in

the auditor having a mutual interest with the client. For example, if an accounting firm arranged to receive an audit fee of $200,000, but half of that fee was contingent on the audit client successfully completing an initial public offering within the following year, the auditor would have a mutual interest with the audit client in the success of the planned IPO and in the continuing viability of the audit client. Consequently, we are adopting a restriction on contingent fees. In response to comments,[197] however, we modified the rules to parallel more closely the existing restrictions.[198]

Final Rule 2-01(c)(5) defines a contingent fee as any fee established for the performance of any service pursuant to an arrangement in which no fee will be charged unless a specified finding or result is attained, or in which the amount of the fee is otherwise dependent upon the finding or result of such service. Contingent fees include commissions and similar payments. Consistent with the AICPA rules, our definition of "contingent fees" contains an exception for fees fixed by courts or other public authorities, or, in tax matters, fees determined based on the results of judicial proceedings or the findings of governmental agencies. We have added the AICPA's exception for fees, in tax matters, determined based on the results of judicial proceedings or the findings of governmental agencies. This exception is based, in part, on the position that when the fee is determined not by the parties but by courts or government agencies acting in the public interest, it is less likely that such fees will be used to create a mutual financial interest between the auditor and audit client. This exception also acknowledges that, as explained above, tax services generally do not create the same independence risks as other non-audit services.

In response to comments, we have eliminated from the rule text the language regarding "value added" fees. Some commenters represented that accounting firms sometimes receive fees where the client determines at the end of the engagement whether the services rendered warrant an additional fee, but there is no agreement (written or otherwise) for the audit client to pay the additional fee. In these situations, the client, at its complete discretion, determines at the end of the performance period that the accountant provided services that had greater value than the amount

---

[194] *See, e.g.,* Arthur Andersen Letter.

[195] AICPA Code of Professional Conduct, ET § 102.07 ("[I]n the performance of any professional service, a member shall comply with rule 102 [ET § 102.01], which requires maintaining objectivity and integrity and prohibits subordination of judgment to others .... Moreover, there is a possibility that some requested professional services involving client advocacy may appear to stretch the bounds of performance standards, may go beyond sound and reasonable professional practice, or may compromise credibility, and thereby pose an

unacceptable risk of impairing the reputation of the member and his or her firm with respect to independence, integrity, and objectivity. In such circumstances, the member and the member's firm should consider whether it is appropriate to perform the services.").

[196] AICPA SAS No. 22, AU § 311.04b; AU § 9311.03.

[197] *See, e.g.,* PricewaterhouseCoopers Letter; Deloitte & Touche Letter.

[198] AICPA Code of Professional Conduct, ET § 302.01.

due under the contract. That type of "value added" fee is not within the scope of the prohibition.[199]

On the other hand, the staff will look closely to determine whether a fee labeled a "value added" fee is in fact a contingent fee, such as where there are side letters or other evidence that ties the fee to the success of the services rendered. For example, as discussed in the Proposing Release, an auditor might undertake a study of certain types of a client's expenditures in order to identify greater amounts of qualifying expenses that would result in greater income tax credits. Fees for such services might be based on a percentage of the tax credits generated, a base fee plus a percentage of tax credits generated over a predetermined base amount, or a base fee plus a "value added" amount to be added to the base fee. In that case, the accounting firm's economic benefit will be greater if the tax credits are maximized. Because this interest (in the economic benefit) is inconsistent with acting independently in assessing the accuracy of the impact on the income tax accounts and financial statements of the tax credits, those kinds of fee arrangements are prohibited under the final rule.

E. *Quality Control Provisions*

We recognize that situations may arise where an accountant's independence becomes impaired inadvertently, such as where a family member makes an investment of which the covered person is not aware. Paragraph (d) addresses those situations. We are adopting a limited exception pursuant to which inadvertent violations of these rules by covered persons will not make the accounting firm not independent if the accounting firm maintains certain quality controls and satisfies other conditions. The effect of this provision is that an accounting firm that has appropriate quality controls will not be deemed to lack independence when an accountant did not know of the circumstances giving rise to the impairment and, upon discovery, the impairment is quickly resolved.

As we explained in the Proposing Release, strong quality controls deter, detect, and provide a means to address impairments of an auditor's independence. Our staff has stated repeatedly that it is concerned that firms, particularly larger firms, may lack appropriate worldwide quality controls.[200] The staff has urged certain firms to review and modernize existing procedures.[201]

Many firms have designed and implemented quality controls or are doing so now. In that regard, several commenters wrote that because firms already have quality control procedures in place, there is no need for this provision.[202] Other commenters supported the provision and asked us to adopt it.[203] We are adopting this limited exception to the general principle that attributes to an entire firm independence impairments of individual accountants. We proposed such a limited exception in the belief that adequate quality controls would limit the occasions in which the exception would come into play. Without such a requirement, we fear that the incidence of individual violations would be much greater.

Paragraph (d) provides that an accounting firm's independence will not be impaired solely because a covered person in the firm is not independent, as long as three conditions are met. First, the covered person must not have known of the circumstances giving rise to the lack of independence. The proposed rule provided that to take advantage of the exception, the firm must show that the covered person did not know, and was "reasonable in not knowing," of the circumstances giving rise to the impairment. One commenter suggested eliminating this language because, once a firm implements a quality control system envisioned in the rule (with automated tracking of investments, ongoing training, and inspections and monitoring programs), a person may never be deemed to be "reasonable" in not knowing the circumstances giving rise to an impairment, and the exception would never be available.[204] Accordingly, we have revised the first condition to apply when the covered person did not know of the circumstances giving rise to the impairment.

The second condition is that the covered person's lack of independence was corrected as promptly as possible under the relevant circumstances after the covered person, or the firm, became aware of it. Several commenters suggested adding the phrase "under the relevant circumstances."[205] We agree that this change is appropriate because whether an action is "prompt" depends, at least in part, on the surrounding circumstances. In light of this change, however, we also have revised this provision so that the lack of

---

[199] As Ray J. Groves, former Chairman and CEO, Ernst & Young testified, "It does not impair independence to reward a professional who excels in his or her performance, or who exceeds reasonable expectations." Written Testimony of Ray J Groves (July 26, 2000).

[200] *See* Letter from Lynn Turner, Chief Accountant, SEC, to Charles Bowsher, Chairman, POB (Dec. 9, 1999); *see, e.g., In the Matter of PricewaterhouseCoopers, LLP*, AAER No. 1098 (Jan. 14, 1999).

[201] *See* Letters from Lynn Turner, Chief Accountant, SEC, to Michael Conway, Chairman, SECPS Executive Committee (Nov. 30, 1998; Dec. 8, 1999; May 1, 2000).

[202] AICPA Letter; Deloitte & Touche Letter; KPMG Letter; Letter of Jodi L. McFall, CPA (Sept. 1, 2000); Letter of Electronic Data Systems (Sept. 11, 2000); Letter of William Tourville, CPA (Sept. 14, 2000); Letter of Gary Whitsell (Sept. 19, 2000).

[203] Letter of Thomas Graves (July 18, 2000); Letter of the FEE (Sept. 25, 2000).

[204] *See* Ernst & Young Letter.

[205] *See, e.g.,* Ernst & Young Letter.

---

independence must be corrected as promptly as possible under the relevant circumstances.

The third condition is that the accounting firm must have a quality control system in place that provides "reasonable assurance" that the firm and its employees do not lack independence. As we stated in the Proposing Release, we believe that a quality control system is the first line of defense to guard against independence impairments. We understand that accounting firms vary greatly. The rule we are adopting, as proposed, explicitly states that the quality control provisions may take into account the size and nature of the firm's practice.

In the Proposing Release, we stated that a firm's quality controls should apply to the firm and its affiliates worldwide,[206] and we solicited comment about whether a firm's quality controls should be this comprehensive. We received useful comments about the applicability of this provision to foreign affiliates.[207] Because we have eliminated the definition of affiliate of the accounting firm, however, we have modified the third provision to state that the quality controls must cover at least all employees and associated entities of the accounting firm participating in the engagement, including employees and associated entities located abroad. While we do not necessarily expect a firm making use of the limited exception to demonstrate that it has implemented appropriate quality control systems in each of its offices worldwide, the rule requires that, to avail itself of the limited exception, the firm must have quality control systems that cover each employee and associated entity participating in the engagement for which independence was impaired.

Several commenters stated that while it is appropriate for the Commission to examine whether a firm or a covered person is independent, we should not prescribe quality controls.[208] The rule does not require any firm to adopt quality controls.[209] Rather, for the reasons stated above, it makes adequate quality controls a prerequisite for a limited exception where the firm otherwise would be deemed not independent.

Rule 2-01(d)(4) describes the elements of a quality control system that large accounting firms - those with more than 500 SEC registrants as audit, review, or attest clients - must have in place to qualify for the limited exception.[210] Many of the

elements are set forth in a 1999 letter from the staff to the SECPS.[211] While the rule as adopted requires only the larger firms to implement these elements to qualify for the limited exception, we note that some of these elements may be suitable for other firms as well. We discuss the elements below.

1. *Written Independence Policies and Procedures*

The largest firms' independence policies and procedures must be reduced to writing. As we stated in the Proposing Release, we expect the policies and procedures to be comprehensive, to cover all professionals in the accounting firm, and to address all aspects of independence, including financial, employment, and business relationships, as well as fee arrangements.

2. *Automated Systems*

Large firms must have automated systems to identify investments that may impair independence. In our proposal, this provision applied to all employees in the firm. Commenters stated, however, that it may not be necessary for the automated quality control system to include the financial investments of persons below the managerial level. Commenters also stated that it may be difficult to establish a system to identify all financial relationships that might impair independence.[212] These commenters suggested revising the provision for an automated tracking system to apply only to partners and managerial employees, while adding a provision providing for timely dissemination of information about its current list of audit clients to all professionals.[213] We agree with these commenters that non-managerial employees have less control over the audit process and, therefore, need not be included in the automated system. However, to meet this limited exception, a firm's quality control system must provide reasonable assurance that nonpartners and managerial employees are complying with the applicable independence rules. We also have clarified the scope of the required automated system, by changing the words "financial relationships" to "investments in securities." Accordingly, an automated system would not need to track covered persons' "other financial interests," such as brokerage and credit card accounts, to qualify for this limited exception. We also note that, for purposes of monitoring compliance with our rule on "material" indirect

---

[206] Proposing Release, n.192.

[207] *See* Ernst & Young Letter (acknowledging that the requirement applies worldwide).

[208] *See* KPMG Letter; Letter of KPMG Europe (Sept. 22, 2000).

[209] GAAS already requires firms to have quality controls for their audit practices and refers auditors to the "Statements on Quality Control Standards" ("SQCS") for guidance regarding the elements of those systems. AICPA SAS No. 25; AU § 161.

[210] We considered whether to use the number of firm professionals, instead of the number of SEC registrants, to determine which firms are required to implement the quality

controls in Rule 2-01(d)(4) to qualify for the limited exception. *See* SECPS Manual § 1000.46. We use number of SEC registrants because we are particularly concerned with those firms that audit a large number of SEC registrants, regardless of the number of professionals, and because we can more easily verify the number of SEC registrants audited by a firm.

[211] Letter from Lynn Turner, Chief Accountant, SEC, to Michael Conway, Chairman, SECPS Executive Committee (Dec. 9, 1999).

[212] *See, e.g.*, Letter of KPMG Europe (Sept. 22, 2000).

[213] *See* Ernst & Young Letter; PricewaterhouseCoopers Letter.

investments, an automated system need not track covered persons' net worth to determine if an indirect investment is material to that person. Nonetheless, such a system must provide some means of identifying indirect investments that might impair independence under the material indirect investment rule.

3. *Timely Information*

In light of the changes made to the requirement for automated systems, we added a provision that applies to all professionals. The quality controls of a large firm taking advantage of the limited exception must include a system that provides timely information about the entities from which the accountant must be independent. We expect that this system, for example, would contain current and accurate information about audit, review, and attest clients of the accounting firm and the affiliates of those audit clients. All professionals should be able quickly to determine whether an investment they are about to make may cause the independence of the firm to be impaired.

4. *Training*

Large firm quality controls also must include annual or ongoing firm-wide training about auditor independence, and we are adopting this provision as proposed. Each professional in a large accounting firm should be able to demonstrate competence with respect to professional standards, legal requirements, and firm policies and procedures.

5. *Internal Inspection and Testing*

For a large firm to qualify for the limited exception, its quality controls must include an internal inspection and testing program to monitor adherence to the independence requirements of the profession, standard setters, and other regulatory bodies. This would entail procedures to audit, on a test basis, information submitted by employees and partners and information in a client investment database. Firms also should monitor the investments of the firms themselves and their pension and retirement plans, and any business arrangements with their audit clients.

6. *Notice of Names of Senior Management Responsible for Independence*

We also proposed to require, with respect to large firms, that all firm members, officers, directors, and employees be notified of the name and title of the member of senior management responsible for compliance with the independence requirements. We are adopting this provision as proposed.

7. *Prompt Reporting of Employment Negotiations*

The quality control system of a large firm must contain written policies and procedures to require firm professionals to report promptly to the firm as soon as they begin employment negotiations with an audit client. The firm also should have appropriate procedures to remove immediately such a professional from an audit client's engagement and review the professional's work related to that audit client. In addition, we believe such engagements should be selected for peer review. As proposed, this provision would have applied to all firm professionals. Commenters, however, suggested that the provision should apply only to partners and covered persons.[214] Because of the number of professionals employed by the larger firms, and because we are most concerned with individuals who may affect the audit, we have revised this provision to apply only to partners and covered persons.

8. *Disciplinary Mechanism*

As we proposed, the quality control system of a large firm also must have a disciplinary mechanism to ensure compliance. One commenter stated that a disciplinary mechanism may only promote compliance, but cannot ensure it.[215] Although no system can guarantee 100% compliance in all circumstances, a firm's quality controls should be designed and implemented to ensure compliance, not merely to promote it. We are, therefore, adopting this language as proposed.

Several commenters noted that firms operating overseas may be prohibited from requesting certain information based on local restrictions on information gathering, or they may be required to amend an employee's employment contract before doing so.[216] We are sensitive to these concerns and we have responded, in part, by providing for a long transition period for accountants operating abroad, as discussed below. In any event, the SECPS has required member firms to implement quality controls, including many of these provisions.[217] If a firm is unable to apply its quality controls to offices outside the U.S., it may be unable to take advantage of the limited exception we are adopting.

F. *Transition and Grandfathering*

1. *Transition*

a. *Appraisal or Valuation Services or Fairness Opinions, and Internal Audit Services*

We proposed that, for the two years following the effective date of Rule 2-01, providing to an audit client certain non-audit services identified in the rule would not impair the accountant's independence if the services were provided under an

---

[214] *See* Ernst & Young Letter; PricewaterhouseCoopers Letter.

[215] Letter of KPMG Europe (Sept. 22, 2000).

[216] *See* Ernst & Young Letter; Letter of Ernst & Young, U.K. (Sept. 7, 2000); Letter of KPMG Europe (Sept. 22, 2000); Deloitte & Touche Letter.

[217] *See* Letter from Michael A. Conway, Chairman, SECPS Executive Committee, to the Managing Partners of the SECPS Member Firms (April 2000).

existing contract and performing the services would not impair the accountant's independence under existing requirements. As discussed above, we modified eight of the non-audit service provisions proposed to parallel or draw from current independence requirements regarding these services. Because the restrictions embodied in these provisions now more closely parallel current restrictions, we assume that accountants currently comply with them.

With respect to appraisal or valuation services or fairness opinions and internal audit services, however, we are providing for a longer transition because the new rule extends beyond current restrictions. Final Rule 2-01(e)(1)(i) provides that an accountant's independence will not be impaired if the accountant continues to provide to an audit client these services, so long as the services did not impair the accountant's independence under pre-existing independence requirements.

We recognize that adoption of these and other provisions might require a registrant to decide between continuing to engage its auditing firm to audit its financial statements and continuing to engage that firm to provide certain non-audit services. It may not be feasible for the registrant and the auditor to cease all ongoing or scheduled non-audit engagements immediately. The company may need time to find a new provider of those services, to complete works in progress, and to provide for a smooth transition from one provider of services to another. Consequently, with respect to the two identified non-audit services, the final rule provides for an eighteen-month transition.

Under the transition provision proposed, accounting firms could not have entered into any new non-audit service contracts with their audit clients without impairing their independence. In response to commenters' concerns that the viability of these lines of business could be called into question if they were prohibited from entering into new contracts, we modified the provision to allow firms the flexibility to make business decisions over the next eighteen months that, in light of the new rule, are appropriate for their firms.

Final Rule 2-01(e)(1)(i), however, requires performance on any contracts inconsistent with the non-audit service provisions to be completed within eighteen months of the effective date of the final rule. To the extent that work on current contracts and contracts entered into within eighteen months of the effective date cannot be completed before the non-audit service provisions of the final rule take effect, accountants must take whatever steps are necessary to ensure that, at the end of the eighteen-month transition period, they

are not providing any non-audit services inconsistent with final Rule 2-01.

b. *Other Financial Interests and Employment Relationships*

Rule 2-01(e)(1)(ii) provides for a three-month transition for certain of the financial interest rules (paragraph (c)(1)(ii)) and all of the employment provisions (paragraph (c)(2)) in the final rule. We are providing a transition period for these provisions because Rule 2-01 modestly expands current restrictions on certain accounting firm personnel in these areas. Because accounting firms may, therefore, need time to educate their employees and provide guidance on the new rule, we are providing a transition period of three months after the effective date of the rule.

c. *Quality Control Systems*

As discussed at length above, accounting firms can take advantage of the limited exception to the independence requirements provided by paragraph (d) of the rule, if they have in place a quality control system that, based on several factors, "provides reasonable assurance" that the firm and its employees do not lack independence. Under Rule 2-01(d)(4), the quality control systems of accounting firms that provide audit, review or attest services to more than 500 SEC registrants will not be considered to provide reasonable assurance of independence, unless the systems have certain characteristics. We are providing a transition provision that applies to the implementation date for the specific elements of a quality control system as described in paragraph (d)(4) of the rule.

Recently adopted SECPS provisions require quality controls substantially similar to those described in paragraph (d)(4).[218] Because these SECPS requirements are effective December 31, 2000, which precedes the effective date for the Commission's final rule, no transition date for paragraph (d)(4) is necessary for domestic accounting firms. By the date that this rule becomes effective, SECPS member firms should have appropriate quality control systems in place.

In the Proposing Release, however, we noted that foreign offices, or foreign "associated" or "sister" firms, of domestic firms may require additional time to develop and implement quality control systems that satisfy the requirements of paragraph (d)(4). We solicited comment on whether foreign offices, accordingly, should be afforded a transition period to phase in the quality control systems necessary to take advantage of the limited exception provided by the rule. Some commenters suggested that because establishing and implementing quality controls to apply worldwide would be difficult, we should provide for a long transition period.[219] In response to these comments, we determined to give accounting

---

[218] SECPS Manual § 1000.46 (April 2000).

[219] Ernst & Young Letter (suggesting a three-year transition period); Letter of Ernst & Young U.K. (Sept. 7, 2000).

firms' foreign offices until December 31, 2002 to implement the quality controls described by the final rule.

We believe that investors in our capital markets should have the right to expect that the same quality controls over a firm's adherence to the independence requirements apply irrespective of where the audit, or where parts of the audit, take place. The two-year transition period strikes a reasonable balance between the need for improved quality control systems by all offices participating in an audit and the practical problems inherent in implementing these controls abroad.

As a result of this transition provision, before January 1, 2003, if a domestic firm with more than 500 SEC registrants as audit clients seeks to avail itself of the limited exception in paragraph (d), it must have a quality control system that complies with paragraph (d)(4) and any foreign office of the firm (or foreign associated or sister firm) participating in the audit of that company must have a system that provides reasonable assurance of independence, as required by paragraph (d)(3). After December 31, 2002, the foreign office (or foreign associated or sister firm) also must comply with the requirements in paragraph (d)(4).

2. *Grandfathering*

The rule provisions related to loans, insurance products, and employment relationships take effect three months after the effective date of the rule. Under the new rule, absent a grandfathering provision, a limited number of accountants or their family members might have been required, for example, to refinance a mortgage loan with an audit client or to leave their current employment with an audit client, in order for the auditor to remain independent. Because we would expect it to be more problematic in some cases for auditors and their family members to refinance a loan or to obtain a replacement insurance policy than, for example, for them to obtain a new credit card (from a non-audit client), we have grandfathered these relationships in Rule 2-01(e)(2), provided that these relationships do not impair independence under existing requirements. The AICPA similarly grandfathered certain loans that auditors and their family members had with audit clients when it revised its independence requirements related to loans in November 1991.[220] Accordingly, under the final rule, auditors and their relatives should not have to alter their loan agreements, change insurance policy providers, or require family members to find different employment for the accountant to maintain his or her independence.

Likewise, we have grandfathered contracts for the provision of financial information systems de-

sign and implementation in existence on the effective date of the rule. The information technology rule we adopt today imposes five conditions on these services, but we believe it would be unfair to require auditors providing these services to their audit clients under existing contracts to satisfy these conditions. We do not, however, believe that the conditions are so onerous as to warrant a transition period for new contracts. Accordingly, we are grandfathering contracts that are in place on the effective date of the rule, but requiring all contracts entered after the effective date of the rule to meet the conditions imposed by Rule 2-01(c)(4)(ii)(B).

3. *Settling Financial Arrangements with Former Professionals*

As discussed above, under Rule 2-01(c)(2)(iii), an accounting firm will not be considered independent of an audit client if a former employee of the firm has an "accounting role or financial reporting oversight role" at the audit client and the firm and the former employee have a financial arrangement that does not satisfy the requirements set forth by Rule 2-01(c)(2)(iii). Rule 2-01(e)(3) provides that, notwithstanding Rule 2-01(c)(2)(iii), an accounting firm will not lose its independence with respect to an audit client if the former employee with whom it maintains a financial arrangement inconsistent with Rule 2-01(c)(2)(iii) assumed an accounting or financial reporting oversight role at the audit client prior to the effective date of this rule. With respect to former employees who join an audit client in such a role after the effective date of this rule, however, the firm must ensure that the requirements of paragraph (c)(2)(iii) are met in order to maintain its independence with respect to the audit client. We are including this provision, which essentially grandfathers existing employment relationships between former audit firm employees and audit clients, because our intention was not to require former firm employees who are currently in accounting or financial reporting oversight roles at audit clients to leave their positions to preserve the accounting firm's independence.

G. *Proxy Disclosure Requirement*

We proposed to require disclosure of certain information regarding, among other things, non-audit services provided by the registrant's auditor to the registrant. We solicited comment on whether the proposed disclosures would be useful to investors. As noted above, most commenters addressing the issue supported a disclosure requirement, though several raised concerns with elements of the proposal.[221] We believe that with the disclosures we are adopting, investors will be better able to evaluate the independence of the

---

[220] AICPA Ethical Standard ET § 101.07 (grandfathering certain loans that existed as of January 1, 1992).

[221] *See supra* note 25.

auditors of the companies in which they invest.[222] Accordingly, we are requiring companies to provide certain disclosures, but we have modified the proposed disclosure requirement as discussed below.[223] Our disclosure requirement has three components: (1) disclosure regarding fees billed for services rendered by the principal accountant; (2) disclosure regarding whether the aud it committee considered the compatibility of the non-audit services the company received from its auditor and the independence of the auditor; and (3) disclosure regarding the employment of leased personnel in connection with the audit.

1. *Disclosure of Fees*

The final proxy disclosure rule, like the proposal, requires registrants to aggregate and disclose the fee paid for the annual audit and for the review of the company's financial statements included in the company's Forms 10-Q or 10-QSB for the most recent fiscal year.[224] In light of the other modifications described below, we are requiring this fee disclosure under a caption entitled "Audit Fees."

We proposed to require registrants to describe each professional service, other than audit services, provided by their principal accountants during the most recent fiscal year, and to disclose the fee for each of these professional services; however, under the proposed disclosures, a registrant would not have had to describe the service or disclose the fee if the fee for the service was less than the lesser of $50,000 or ten percent of its audit fee. We solicited comment on the scope of this proposed disclosure. Several commenters believed that this proposed disclosure was too detailed. At least one commenter worried that the detailed disclosure requirement could place registrants at a competitive disadvantage when, for example, they disclose that the audit firm was retained to conduct due diligence in connection with a possible acquisition.[225] Other commenters

suggested that a simpler disclosure, focused on the aggregate amount of non-audit and audit services provided to a company by its auditor, would be more useful to investors.[226] We were persuaded by these arguments and, accordingly, we are adopting a more limited disclosure requirement.

Under the final rule, we are not requiring registrants to describe each professional service or to disclose the fee for each service. Instead, we are requiring that registrants disclose under the caption, "Financial Information Systems Design and Implementation Fees," the aggregate fees billed for services of the type described in final Rule 2-01(c)(4)(ii)(B)(information technology services)[227] rendered by the registrant's principal accountant during the most recent year, and, under the caption "All Other Fees," the fees billed for all other non-audit services, including fees for tax-related services, rendered by the principal accountant during the most recent year.

Although some commenters suggested that we require disclosure only of the aggregate fees billed by the principal accountant for audit and for non-audit services, we are, in essence, requiring registrants to break non-audit services into two categories - one category focused on information technology services and one category encompassing all other non-audit services. As discussed above, our concern with information technology services relates both to the relative size of non-audit fees to audit fees and the value of the services themselves.[228] Our two-pronged approach responds to both of these concerns.

We are also requiring disclosure of fees billed for non-audit services, other than information technology services, rendered by the principal accountant in the last fiscal year. While we proposed to require disclosure of fees for each service as discussed above, we have determined to require

---

[222] See Earnscliffe II, *supra* note 38, at 45, which states, "Most people sensed that the relationship between the auditor and auditee was appropriate, typically neither too close nor tension-ridden. The one area of greater concern had to do with the provision of non-audit services to audit clients, where participants felt unsettled and discomfited. Avoidance of this practice seemed preferred, but disclosure was seen as a helpful alternative step as well."

[223] The disclosure requirement pertains to the accounting firm that is the registrant's principal accountant. The principal accountant generally is the accounting firm that takes responsibility for the report on the financial statements of the registrant for each year presented. *See* SEC Division of Corporation Finance, "Accounting Disclosure Rules and Practices: An Overview," Topic Four, I.D. (Mar. 31, 2000).

[224] *See* proposed Rule 14a-101 Item 9(e)(4); Rule 10-01(d) of Regulation S-X and Item 310 of Regulation S-B, 17 C.F.R. 210.10-01, 228.310(b).

[225] Ernst & Young Letter.

[226] PricewaterhouseCoopers Letter; Ernst & Young Letter; Testimony of J. Michael Cook, former Chairman and Chief Executive Officer, Deloitte & Touche (July 26, 2000); Testi-

mony of Philip D. Ameen, Chair, Committee on Corporate Reporting, FEI-CRR (Sept. 20, 2000).

[227] *See supra* Section IV.D.4.b(ii). The services described in Rule 2-01(c)(4)(ii)(B) relate to systems that aggregate source data underlying, or generate information significant to, the financial statements, which may be a particular concern to investors. *See* Earnscliffe I, *supra* note 65, at 24, which states, "Some felt that installing computer systems was not a problem . . . others argued that if the computer system had anything to do with the financial reporting systems . . . then the auditor would be in serious conflict." The required disclosure will permit investors to decide whether such services create independence concerns.

[228] *See* Earnscliffe I, *supra* note 65, at 26, which describes responses to a scenario when the annual audit fee was $1 million and the auditor performed computer system work for $10 million, which was 1% of the auditor's annual revenues, and states, "First off, the sheer size of the contract was seen as a potential perception challenge. Even though $10 million might be good value for the client, and only a tiny fraction of the audit firm's business, there was a sense of doubt that the firm would be willing to walk away from such a relationship, if that were necessary to protect the independence of the audit."

only disclosure of aggregate fees billed for non-audit services, excluding information technology services. As noted above, commenters generally favored more simple disclosure, believing it is more useful to investors. In requiring disclosure of aggregate fees, we are adopting a disclosure requirement that is similar to the disclosure that the United Kingdom has required since 1989. As discussed in the Proposing Release, since 1989, the British government has required companies to disclose their annual audit fee and fees paid to their auditor for non-audit services.[229] "The [British] government believes that the publication of the existence of, and extent of, non-audit consultancy services provided to audit clients will enable shareholders, investors, and other parties to judge for themselves whether auditor independence is likely to be jeopardized."[230]

Some have argued that disclosure should be our sole response to auditor independence issues and that we should adopt no additional rules, noting that this is the regulatory scheme in the U.K.[231] As we discussed above, we have determined to adopt a two-pronged approach—disclosure plus restrictions on the provision of certain non-audit services. The U.K. disclosure rules are just one piece of a larger regime in the U.K. to address auditor independence issues. The self-regulatory authority in the U.K. has a majority of public members and generally exercises broad examination authority.[232] An "independent practice inspection unit" sends inspectors to the 20 largest accounting firms (who audit ninety percent of the companies listed on the London FTSE) every year to examine the accounting firms for independence issues.[233] The differences in the U.K. and U.S. regulatory schemes and self-regulatory approaches highlight the need for our two-pronged approach—disclosure plus restrictions on the provision of certain non-audit services.

We requested comment on whether, in the case of investment companies, the rule should extend beyond the registrant to require the disclosures as to all entities in the investment company complex. One commenter suggested that applying the proxy disclosure requirements to the investment company complex would be of limited utility to investors, particularly where the adviser's parent company is an entity, such as a bank, broker-dealer or insurance company whose operations are completely separate from the investment adviser and the registrant. The commenter suggested requiring disclosure only of the aggregate fees billed for information technology services and other non-audit services provided to certain other service providers in the investment company complex.[234]

We recognize that it could be confusing to provide investors with disclosure concerning audit and non-audit services for all entities (including all the funds) within the investment company complex. We believe, however, that the ability to compare the registrant's audit fee with the aggregate fees billed for non-audit services provided to all the entities that operate an investment company would be useful for investors in evaluating the independence of the investment company's auditor. Because the adviser plays an integral role in managing and overseeing the investment company, we believe the fees billed for non-audit services provided to a fund's adviser are relevant and should be disclosed. In addition, various service providers to the investment company are in a control relationship with the adviser. We believe that investors should be informed of the aggregate amount of the registrant's audit fee and the fees billed for information technology services and other non-audit services provided by the independent principal accountant to these service providers.

As a result, the proxy rules require investment companies to disclose a fund's audit fee and the aggregate fees billed for information technology and other non-audit services provided by the registrant's auditors to the registrant, its adviser, and entities in a control relationship with the adviser that provide services to the registrant. This approach will provide investors with pertinent information about the relationship between the fund's auditor and other entities in the investment company complex.

2. *Audit Committee Disclosure*

As discussed above, audit committees play an important role in overseeing the financial reporting process and the auditor's independence. We proposed to require that companies disclose in their proxy statements whether, before each disclosed non-audit service was rendered, the company's audit committee approved, and considered the effect on independence of, such service pro-

---

[229] Companies Act 1985, Part XI, Chapter V, Auditors, §390B, "Remuneration of Auditors and Their Associates for Non-audit Work," and Regulations 1991, §5, "Disclosure of Remuneration for Non-Audit Work." *See generally* Written Testimony of Graham Ward, Institute of Chartered Accountants of England and Wales ("ICAEW") (Sept. 13, 2000).

[230] Michael Firth, "The Provision of Nonaudit Services by Accounting Firms to their Audit Clients," *Contemporary Accounting Research*, at 6 (Summer 1997). Firth hypothesized that companies with potentially high agency costs (*i.e.*, companies in which directors do not control management or which have a large amount of debt) would limit the non-audit

services provided by their auditors because the appearance of a lack of auditor independence would increase their cost of capital. Firth's sample data came from the 500 largest British industrial, listed companies. Firth's findings were consistent with his hypothesis.

[231] *See* Arthur Andersen Letter.

[232] *See* Department of Trade and Industry, "A Framework of Independent Regulation for the Accounting Profession," ¶ 29, 35, 39, 44, and 46 (Nov. 1998).

[233] Testimony of Graham Ward, ICAEW (Sept. 13, 2000).

[234] ICI Letter.

vided by the company's principal accountant. Several commenters encouraged us to wait until the full effects of recently enacted audit committee reforms are known, in particular the effects of ISB Standard No. 1, the new exchange listing rules, and our recent audit committee disclosure rules. However, we think that the disclosure requirements that we are adopting will complement those initiatives by encouraging audit committees to focus particular attention on scope of services issues.

We have modified the proposed disclosure to require disclosure only of whether the audit committee considered whether the principal accountant's provision of the information technology services and other non-audit services to the registrant is compatible with maintaining the principal accountant's independence.[235] In light of the recommendations adopted by the O'Malley Panel and the other audit committee reforms,[236] we believe that companies will be providing useful information to investors under the modified requirement. Investors will be aided by knowing whether the company's audit committee considered whether the provision of non-audit services by the company's principal accountant is compatible with maintaining the accountant's independence. We are requiring issuers to disclose only whether the audit committee considered whether the principal accountant's provision of non-audit services is compatible with maintaining the principal accountant's independence. We are not requiring issuers to disclose the conclusions of the audit committee deliberations. Accordingly, we see little possibility of private liability arising from these disclosures.

3. Leased Employees

Under the final amendments, a company will have to disclose, if greater than fifty percent of the hours expended on the audit engagement, the percentage of hours expended by personnel the principal auditor leased or otherwise acquired from another entity. This disclosure requirement responds to a recent trend by some accounting firms to sell their non-audit practices to financial services companies. Often in these transactions, the partners and employees become employees of the financial services firm. The accounting firm then leases assets, namely professional auditors, back from those companies to complete audit engagements. In such an arrangement, audit professionals become full- or part-time employees of the financial services company, but work on audit engagements for their former accounting firm. They receive compensation from the financial services firm and, in some situations, from the accounting firm, as well.[237] We believe that investors should be informed of arrangements whereby most of the auditors who work on an audit are employed elsewhere.[238]

4. Proxy Statement

Finally, under the final rules, companies must provide the disclosures we are requiring in their proxy and information statements. We solicited comment on whether the disclosure should instead be required in the Form 10-K. Some commenters said that the disclosure should be made in the Form 10-K,[239] with some commenters expressing concern that the proxy statement will become overloaded with information. Other commenters expressed a preference for the disclosure to be in proxy statements.[240] We have determined that the proxy statement is the appropriate place for the disclosure since shareholders often vote on whether to select or ratify the selection of the auditors.[241] Companies must provide the disclosure only in the proxy statement relating to an annual meeting of shareholders at which directors are to be elected (or special meeting or written consents in lieu of such meeting). This disclosure is not required for companies reporting solely under Section 15(d) of the Exchange Act[242] since they are not subject to our proxy rules. Similarly, this disclosure will not be required to be provided by foreign private issuers[243] since they have different corporate governance regimes and are not subject to our proxy rules.

---

[235] We note that audit committees currently receive information about the auditor's provision of non-audit services under ISB Standard No. 1 and SECPS Manual § 1000.08. *See* ISB Standard No. 1, *supra* note 167; SECPS Manual § 1000.08 (requiring the auditor to report annually to the audit committee or board of directors (or its equivalent in a partnership) of SEC registered audit clients on the "total fees received from the client for management advisory services during the year under audit and a description of the types of such services rendered").

[236] The O'Malley Panel has recommended that audit committees pre-approve non-audit services that exceed a threshold determined by the committee. This recommendation is consistent with the recommendations of the Blue Ribbon Committee regarding auditors' services. The Panel set forth factors for audit committees to consider in determining the appropriateness of a service. *See* O'Malley Panel Report, *supra* note 20, at ¶ 5.30.

[237] The ISB cites threats to independence arising from these structures and identifies quality controls to ensure the

independence of the auditors in these situations. *See* ISB, "Discussion Memorandum 99-2: Evolving Forms of Firm Structure and Organization," at 20 (Oct. 1999).

[238] AICPA SAS No. 1, AU § 543 also sets forth guidance on when a principal auditor discloses and makes reference to another auditor who performs an audit of a component of the entity.

[239] *See, e.g.*, Testimony of Robert E. Denham, Member, ISB (July 26, 2000) (recommending that disclosure be put in footnotes to the financial statements or in the Form 10-K).

[240] *See, e.g.*, Letter of Peter C. Clapman, Senior Vice President and Chief Counsel, Investments, TIAA-CREF (Sept. 21, 2000).

[241] *See* Item 9 of Schedule 14A. 17 CFR 240.14a-101.

[242] 15 U.S.C. § 78(d).

[243] "Foreign private issuer" is defined in Securities Act Rule 405 (17 CFR 230.405) and Exchange Act Rule 3b-4 (17 CFR 240.3b-4).

Companies must comply with the new proxy and information statement disclosure requirements for all proxy and information statements filed with us after the effective date.

H. *Definitions*

As we proposed, we are including definitions of some of the key terms used in Rule 2-01 in paragraph (f) of the Rule. In this section of the release, we provide a more detailed explanation of those defined terms not discussed in the preceding sections. We have made clear in the rule we adopt that paragraph (f) provides definitions only for the purposes of Rule 2-01 and not for other sections of Regulation S-X.

1. *"Accountant"*

We are adopting, as proposed, Rule 2-01(f)(1) that defines the term "accountant." The rules are written in terms of an accountant's independence from the audit client. The definition of "accountant" includes the accounting firm in which the auditor practices. The definition makes clear that an individual accountant's lack of independence may be attributed to the firm.

2. *"Accounting Firm"*

We are adopting the definition of "accounting firm" in Rule 2-01(f)(2) with two modifications from the version proposed. As adopted, "accounting firm" means "an organization (whether it is a sole proprietorship, incorporated association, partnership, corporation, limited liability company, limited liability partnership, or other legal entity) that is engaged in the practice of public accounting and furnishes reports or other documents filed with the Commission or otherwise prepared under the securities laws, and all of the organization's departments, divisions, parents, subsidiaries, and associated entities, including those located outside of the United States." The definition also expressly includes "the organization's pension, retirement, investment or similar plans."

The first modification is solely to clarify the definition. We have simplified the description of what public accounting firms are covered under our rule by referring only to those that "furnish reports or other documents filed with the Commission or otherwise prepared under the securities laws." We believe that this description captures the accounting firms subject to our independence requirements. No substantive change from the rule as proposed is intended.

The second change is more significant. As proposed, the definition of "accounting firm" included "affiliate of the accounting firm." The term "affiliate of the accounting firm" was separately defined to include a broad group of entities that are either financially tied to or otherwise associated with the accounting firm enough to warrant being treated like the accounting firm for purposes of our independence requirements. Specifically, we defined as an "affiliate of the accounting firm" any person

controlling, controlled by, or under common control with the firm, shareholders of more than five percent of the firm's voting securities, and entities five percent or more of whose securities are owned by the firm. The proposed rule also included any officer, director, partner, or co-partner of any of the foregoing.

We also proposed defining as affiliates of the accounting firm certain entities that are business partners of the accounting firm. In general, these included certain (i) joint ventures in which the accounting firm participates, (ii) entities that provide non-audit services to the accounting firm's audit clients and with which the accounting firm has certain financial interests or relationships, and (iii) entities involved in "leasing" professional services to the accounting firm for their audits. The proposed definition also included all other entities with which the accounting firm is publicly associated in certain ways.

The definition we proposed also attributed to the auditor actions and interests of certain entities involved in joint ventures or partnerships with the accounting firm in which the parties agree to share revenues, ownership interests, appreciation, or certain other economic benefits. It also expressly included any entity that provides non-audit services to an audit client, if the accounting firm has an equity interest in, shares revenues with, loans money to, or if any covered person has certain direct business relationships with, the consulting entity, as well as persons "co-branding" or using the same (or substantially the same) name or logo as the accounting firm, cross-selling services with the accounting firm, or co-managing with the accounting firm.

Finally, the proposed definition of "affiliate of the accounting firm" addressed the situation where full- or part-time employees of an entity other than the firm signing the audit report perform a majority of the audit engagement. The proposal provided that if an auditor "leases" personnel from an entity to perform audit procedures or prepare reports to be filed with the Commission, and the "leased" personnel perform a majority of the hours worked on the engagement, then the actions and interests of the "lessor," and certain persons at the lessor are attributed to the audit firm.

Our proposed definition of "affiliate of the accounting firm" proved to be one of the most controversial aspects of our proposed rule. Many commenters believed that the definition was overbroad and expressed concern over the application of the proposed definition to their business arrangements. The largest accounting firms were concerned that the definition, as a practical matter, would inappropriately restrict their ability to enter into certain types of business relationships, including joint ventures and co-branding arrangements.[244] One of the so-called "middle tier" accounting firms expressed concern that the proposed definition would reach the "alliance" it has arranged with other accounting firms and service providers across the country.[245] Many commenters repeated the AICPA's comment that the definition was "overbroad."[246] Some commenters suggested an alternative, much narrower definition that defined affiliates of the accounting firm as entities that control, are controlled by, or are under common control with the accounting firm.[247] Some firms acknowledged that, at least with respect to the provision of non-audit services, a test based on significant influence may be appropriate.

In light of these comments and after careful consideration, we have decided not to adopt the definition of "affiliate of the accounting firm" we proposed. The issue of what entities other than the legal entity issuing reports or other documents filed with the Commission should be treated as the accounting firm is of relatively recent origin. In recent years, accounting firms have explored new "alternative practice structures" and increasingly entered into new business arrangements with entities not engaged in public accounting. To date, our staff has dealt with these questions by interpreting the existing rules. Our staff's approach has been to analyze these situations in light of all relevant facts and circumstances.[248] We proposed a comprehensive

definition that described all the relevant facts and circumstances that might lead us to conclude that a separate legal entity was sufficiently associated with the accounting firm to warrant applying the Commission's independence requirements to that entity. In light of the comments received, we are persuaded that the rule as proposed could have unintended consequences, and that varying criteria of affiliation could be appropriate depending on the regulatory context in which the issue of attribution arises.

Accordingly, we have eliminated the proposed definition of "affiliate of the accounting firm" from the rule we adopt and replaced the phrase "and affiliates of the accounting firm" in the proposed definition of "accounting firm" with "and associated entities, including those located outside of the United States."[249] We intend this phrase to reflect our staff's current practice of addressing these questions in light of all relevant facts and circumstances, looking to the factors identified in our staff's previous guidance on this subject.[250] While the rules we adopt do not provide accounting firms with the certainty of our proposed rule, we are convinced that a more flexible approach is warranted as the types and nature of accounting firms' business arrangements continue to develop.

3. *"Affiliate of the Audit Client"*

We are adopting a modified definition of "affiliate of the audit client." As proposed, Rule 2-01(f)(4) defined "affiliate of the audit client" as

---

[244] *See, e.g.,* KPMG Letter; Arthur Andersen Letter.

[245] *See* Written Testimony of Wayne Kolins, National Director of Assurance, BDO Seidman, LLP (Sept. 20, 2000).

[246] *See, e.g.,* Letter of Fred M. Rock, CPA (Sept. 20, 2000); Letter of Centerprise Advisors, Inc. (Sept. 25, 2000).

[247] *See, e.g.,* Deloitte & Touche Letter; Testimony of Wayne A. Kolins, BDO Seidman, LLP (Sept. 20, 2000).

[248] *See* Letter of Edmund Coulson, Chief Accountant, SEC, to Robert Mednick, Arthur Andersen (June 20, 1990).

[249] Questions of attribution in this context have not been analyzed on the basis of "affiliation" in the past. Indeed, the term "affiliate of the accounting firm" is not used in our current Rule 2-01 or in the Codification. The term was used in our proposed rule, along with the proposed definition of the term, to attempt to bring certainty to this issue. Since "affiliate" is defined in Rule 1-02 of Regulation S-X and we are eliminating the definition of "affiliate of the accounting firm," we have used the term "associated" instead of "affiliated" in our final rules to make clear that, consistent with the status quo, the entities treated as if they were the accounting firm will not be determined by reference to the definition of "affiliate" in Rule 1-02 of Regulation S-X. While the "control" relationships of Rule 1-02 may be adequate to warrant treating an entity as the accounting firm for independence purposes, Rule 1-02 does not set forth the exclusive circumstances in which an entity's interests will be imputed to the accounting firm in this context. In addition, we do not intend for the definition of "associated" used in any other context in the federal securities laws to apply to this term.

[250] *See, e.g.,* Letter of Edmund Coulson, Chief Accountant, SEC, to Robert Mednick, Arthur Andersen (June 20, 1990); Letter of W. Scott Bayless, Assistant Chief Accountant, SEC, to Larry Edgerton, Elms, Faris & Co. (June 7, 1996); Letter of

Lynn E. Turner, Chief Accountant, SEC, to Jeff Yabuki, American Express Financial Advisors (Nov. 2, 1998); Letter of Lynn E. Turner, Chief Accountant, SEC to Michael Gleespen, Century Business Services (Nov. 2, 1998); Letter of Lynn E. Turner, Chief Accountant, SEC, to Terry Putney, H&R Block Business Services (Nov. 2, 1998); Letter of Lynn E. Turner, Chief Accountant, SEC, to Michael Conway, KPMG Peat Marwick LLP (Jan. 7, 1999); Letter of Lynn E. Turner, Chief Accountant, SEC, to Nigel Buchanan, PricewaterhouseCoopers (July 26, 1999); Letter of Lynn E. Turner, Chief Accountant, SEC, to Kathryn A. Oberly, Esq., Ernst & Young (May 25, 2000); Letter of Lynn E. Turner, Chief Accountant, SEC, to Antonio Rosati, Director of Issuers Division, Commissione Nazionale per le Societa e la Borsa (August 24, 2000); Letter of Lynn E. Turner, Chief Accountant, SEC, to J. Terry Strange, KPMG (October 16, 2000); *see also* Codification § 602.02.b.ii, Ex. 8; 602.02.b.iv; 602.02.c.iii; 602.02.g, Ex. 5. *Cf.* SECPS Manual § 1000.45 (discussing application of SECPS rules to "foreign associated firm[s]"); AICPA Code of Professional Conduct, ET § 101.16 (Interpretation 101-14) (application of independence rules to alternative practice structures); AICPA Code of Professional Conduct, ET § 505.03 (application of independence rules to entities controlled by an accounting firm or its members). In addition, accounting firms entering into business transactions in which they acquire equity stakes in other companies will need to continue to consider whether they will have a direct or material indirect business relationship with, or a direct financial interest or material indirect financial interest in, any of their audit clients that are also clients of or enter into business relationships with or invest in or are invested in by that other company. *See* Letter of Lynn E. Turner, Chief Accountant, SEC, to Kathryn A. Oberly, Esq., Ernst & Young (May 25, 2000); Letter of Lynn E. Turner, Chief Accountant, SEC, to J. Terry Strange, KPMG (October 16, 2000).

any entity that has "significant influence" over the audit client, or any entity over which the audit client has significant influence. The definition was intended to cover both "upstream" and "downstream" affiliates of the audit client, including the audit client's corporate parent and subsidiary.

We received a number of comments expressing concern about our proposed definition of "affiliate of the audit client." Some members of the accounting profession felt that our proposed definition was overbroad and would require the auditor to maintain independence from entities far removed from the audit client.[251] Some commenters suggested that we should use the "control" test currently found in Rule 1-02 of Regulation S-X to define an affiliate of an audit client. At least one commenter suggested that our proposed definition should be limited to only those affiliates that are "material" to the audit client.[252]

After considering these comments, we have decided to modify substantially our proposed rule. Under the rule we adopt today, entities, if not part of an investment company complex, will be considered affiliates of the audit client if they satisfy the criteria of one of three paragraphs of Rule 2-01(f)(4). First, under paragraph (4)(i), which is based on the control definition currently in Rule 1-02 of Regulation S-X, an entity is an affiliate of the audit client when the entity controls, is controlled by, or is under common control with the audit client. Second, paragraph (4)(ii) defines as an affiliate of the audit client any entity over which the audit client has significant influence, unless that entity is not material to the audit client. Third, paragraph (4)(iii) includes those entities that have significant influence over the audit client, unless the audit client is not material to that entity.

Paragraph (4)(i) now makes clear that entities in a control relationship with the audit client, regardless of materiality considerations, are affiliates of the audit client for independence purposes. This includes the audit client's parent and subsidiaries and is consistent with current Rule 2-01(b). We are not convinced, however, that a control test alone captures all situations in which an entity is sufficiently related to the audit client to require it to be treated as the audit client's affiliate for independence purposes. Our Codification currently considers entities affiliates of the audit client in a number of situations in which control is not present.[253] As under our proposal, we continue to believe that a significant influence test sets a proper baseline threshold for audit client affiliation because, under the equity method of accounting,[254] it results in the marriage of financial information between the audit client and the entity influenced by, or influencing, the financial or operating policies of the audit client. As urged by commenters, however, the addition of the materiality threshold to the significant influence test should avoid undue hardships to accounting firms in situations where their audit clients have numerous affiliates that are immaterial to them.

As in our proposed rule, we continue to use the term "significant influence" in the definition to refer to the principles in APB No. 18. Some commenters suggested that, since the term "significant influence" is not defined in the rules, it would be difficult to apply.[255] Many other commenters, however, did not object to the term or express any uncertainty as to the term's meaning. Given the concept's familiarity to the accounting profession and its use in the profession's independence requirements, we have decided to retain its use without providing an explicit definition in the rules we adopt.

We use the term "significant influence" as it is used in APB No. 18. It recognizes that "significant influence" can be exercised in several ways: representation on the board of directors; participation in key policy decisions; material inter-company transactions; interchange of personnel; or other means. APB No. 18 also recognizes that an important consideration is the extent of the equity investment, particularly in relation to the concentration of other investments. In order to provide a reasonable degree of uniformity in application of this standard, the Board concluded that, *****

[A]n investment (direct or indirect) of 20% or more of the voting stock of an investee should lead to a presumption that in the absence of evidence to the contrary an investor has the ability to exercise significant influence over an investee. Conversely, an investment of less than 20% of the voting stock of an investee should lead to a presumption that an investor does not have the ability to exercise significant influence unless such ability can be demonstrated.[256]

In addition, we have added a new section to the definition of "affiliate of an audit client" to deal specifically with affiliation questions in mutual fund complexes. Paragraph (4)(iv) provides that when the audit client is part of an investment company complex, each entity in the investment company complex is an "affiliate of the audit client." In this respect, we are following the ISB's Standard No. 2, "Certain Independence Implica-

---

[251] *See* AICPA Letter; Arthur Andersen Letter.

[252] *See* Deloitte & Touche Letter.

[253] *See* Codification § 602.02.b.iii (Ex. 1); 602.02.b.iv; 602.02.c.iii; 602.02.h (Ex. 9).

[254] *See* APB No. 18.

[255] *See* Letter of Stanley Keller, Esq., and Richard Rowe, Esq., ABA Committees on Federal Regulation of Securities Law and Accounting (Sept. 27, 2000).

[256] *See* APB No. 18, at ¶ 17. Paragraph 17 of APB No. 18 also discusses a number of considerations that may affect the ability of an entity to have significant influence over an investee.

tions of Audits of Mutual Funds and Related Entities."[257]

While this provision was not in our proposed definition of "affiliate of the audit client," it was clearly embodied in our proposed Rule 2-01(c)(1)(ii)(G), which provided, "When the audit client is an entity that is part of an investment company complex, the accountant must be independent of each entity in the investment company complex." As we explained in the Proposing Release, this provision was meant to reflect the standard of ISB Standard No. 2. We pointed out in the Proposing Release that this provision applied to auditor-audit client relationships other than financial interests, and sought comment on whether it should be limited in any context other than financial interests. At least one commenter analyzed our proposed Rule 2-01(c)(1)(ii)(G) as an extension of the definition of "affiliate of the audit client."[258]

While some commenters suggested that we limit this principle through a restriction on the scope of the "investment company complex" definition, few commenters disagreed with the ISB's basic conclusion that the unique structure of mutual fund complexes warrants special rules of affiliation. After considering the comments on this issue, we have decided to adopt this provision substantively as proposed, but to move it to the definition of "affiliate of the audit client" to make its purpose and effect clearer.

4. "Audit and Professional Engagement Period"

We have adopted the definition of "audit and professional engagement period" in Rule 2-01(f)(5), as proposed, with one modification. As defined, the "audit and professional engagement period" is "[t]he period covered by any financial statements being audited or reviewed (the 'audit period'); and the period of the engagement to audit or review the audit client's financial statements or to prepare a report filed with the Commission (the 'professional engagement period')."

The definition specifies that the professional engagement period begins when the accountant either signs an initial engagement letter (or other agreement to review or audit a client's financial statements) or begins review, audit, or attest procedures, whichever is earlier,[259] and that the professional engagement period ends when the client or accountant notifies the Commission that the client is no longer that accountant's audit client.[260] Some commenters asserted that the professional

engagement period should begin when the accountant begins its procedures.[261] Commenters expressed concern that "time will be needed for covered persons and their family members to unwind financial interests or employment relationships."[262] We believe that our rule, as adopted, provides an appropriate amount of flexibility and certainty to the auditor because both signing the initial engagement letter and beginning the audit procedures are entirely within the control of the accountant. An accountant may orally agree to an engagement and then simply delay signing an engagement letter or beginning procedures so as to toll the start of its professional engagement period.

With regard to the termination of the professional engagement period, we note that the current rules of the SECPS require an auditor to notify the Commission in writing that an SEC registrant who was a former client is no longer a client.[263] Similarly, a domestic registrant has an obligation to report changes in its independent auditor on Form 8-K. While no corollary requirement applies to foreign private issuers, there is certainly no prohibition against either such an issuer or its auditor providing us with a private notification that would suffice to end the professional engagement period for purposes of our independence assessment, should this be an issue for the accountant or the registrant.

In response to concerns of commenters,[264] we are providing a limited exception in the definition that applies to foreign private issuers who are offering or listing securities in the United States for the first time. For auditors of those foreign private issuers who previously were not required to, and did not, file any registration statement or report with the Commission, the "audit and professional engagement period" does not include periods ended prior to the beginning of the last fiscal year ended before the issuer first filed or was required to file a registration statement or report with us, provided that the company has fully complied with home country independence standards in those prior periods.

5. "Audit Client"

Rule 2-01(f)(6) defines "audit client." We have defined this term as the entity whose financial statements or other information is being audited, reviewed, or attested. We believe this is how "audit client" commonly is used, and we are adopting this as part of the definition. Use of this definition,

---

[257] We have, however, narrowed the definition of "investment company complex" from the definition used in ISB Standard No. 2. *See infra* Section IV.H.11.

[258] *See* Arthur Andersen Letter.

[259] Rule 2-01(f)(5)(ii)(A).

[260] Rule 2-01(f)(5)(ii)(B).

[261] *See, e.g.,* Deloitte & Touche Letter.

[262] *See, e.g.,* Deloitte & Touche Letter.

[263] SECPS Manual §1000.08; *cf.* AICPA Code of Professional Conduct, ET §101.02.

[264] *See, e.g.,* Ernst & Young Letter ("We also would revise the definition of 'audit and professional engagement period' in the Release . . . to codify the Commission staff's practice of only requiring the latest audited period in initial filings by foreign private issuers to be fully compliant with SEC independence rules.").

of course, in no way changes our position that the auditor "owes ultimate allegiance to the corporation's creditors and stockholders, as well as to the investing public."[265]

We have made one change to the definition. Commenters suggested adding affiliate of the audit client, defined above, to the definition of audit client for the sake of simplicity, and we have done so.[266] The definition of audit client, for purposes of paragraph (c)(1)(i) (investments in audit clients), however, does not include entities that are affiliates of the audit client by virtue of paragraph (f)(4)(ii) or paragraph (f)(4)(iii), which define an affiliate in terms of significant influence. As discussed more fully above, if an entity is an affiliate of the audit client because of a "significant influence" relationship, it is covered by the rules relating to material indirect investments and investments in non-client entities under (c)(1)(i)(D) and (c)(1)(i)(E), and it is not necessary, therefore, to include it in the definition of audit client.

6. "Audit Engagement Team"

Rule 2-01(f)(7) defines the term "audit engagement team." The "audit engagement team" includes the people in the accounting firm who are most directly in a position to influence the audit. Members of the "audit engagement team" are included within the category of "covered persons in the firm," which is the term used to indicate the persons in the firm subject to a number of the specific provisions of paragraph (c) of Rule 2-01.

The "audit engagement team" includes "all partners, principals, shareholders, and professional employees participating in an audit, review, or attestation engagement of an audit client, including those conducting concurring or second partner reviews, and all persons who consult with others on the audit engagement team during the audit, review, or attestation engagement regarding technical or industry-specific issues, transactions, or events."

Commenters who addressed this definition generally agreed that persons in a position to influence the audit, such as the audit engagement team, should be covered persons for purposes of the rule's restrictions on certain relationships with audit clients.[267] We have adopted the definition with only one variation from the proposed definition. The proposed definition included the phrase "all persons who consult, *formally or informally*, with others . . . ." In the final rule, we have deleted the phrase "formally or informally," to avoid unintended overbreadth. Rather, we use the term "consult" to refer to meaningful discussions related to the audit.

7. "Chain of Command"

Rule 2-01(f)(8) defines the term "chain of command." This term is defined to refer to the group of people in the accounting firm who, while not directly on the audit engagement team, are capable of influencing the audit process either through their oversight of the audit itself or through their influence over the members of the audit engagement team. Like the "audit engagement team," persons in the "chain of command" are included as "covered persons in the firm," and therefore are subject to a number of the provisions in paragraph (c) of Rule 2-01.

Based on the input of commenters, we have modified this definition somewhat from the proposed definition. Commenters stated that our definition included too broad a range of persons, capturing people, such as managers who could "influence the . . . compensation of any member of the audit engagement team," whose connection to the audit is too tenuous to reasonably conclude that they have the ability to influence the audit.[268]

We are persuaded that the proposed definition was broader than necessary, and we have accordingly sharpened its focus and tried to eliminate any ambiguity. As defined in the final rule, "chain of command" includes all persons who (i) supervise or have direct management responsibility for the audit, including at all successively senior levels through the accounting firm's chief executive; (ii) evaluate the performance or recommend the compensation of the audit engagement partner; or (iii) provide quality control or other oversight of the audit.

8. "Close Family Members"

We are adopting, as proposed, Rule 2-01(f)(9) that defines "close family members." Close family members is defined to mean a person's spouse, spousal equivalent, parent, dependent, nondependent child, and sibling. These terms should be understood in terms of contemporary family relationships. Accordingly, "spouse" means a husband or wife, whether by marriage or under common law; "spousal equivalent" means a cohabitant occupying a relationship generally equivalent to that of a spouse; "parent" means any biological, adoptive, or step-parent; "dependent" means any person who received more than half of his or her support for the most recent calendar year from the relevant covered person; "child" means any person recognized by law as a child or step-child; and "sibling" means any person who has the same mother or father.

"Close family members" includes the persons separately defined as "immediate family members" (spouse, spousal equivalent, and dependent), and adds certain family members who may, as a general matter, be thought to have less regular, but not necessarily less close, contact with the

---

[265] *Arthur Young*, 465 U.S. at 818.

[266] *See, e.g.*, PricewaterhouseCoopers Letter.

[267] *See, e.g.*, Deloitte & Touche Letter.

[268] *See* Deloitte & Touche Letter.

covered person in question (parent, nondependent child, and sibling). We distinguish the two groups, in part, because the less immediate the family relationship to the covered person, the more substantial that family member's relationship to the audit client should be before we deem it to impair the auditor's independence. Commenters, in general, raised few issues with the proposed definition of "close family members" and, therefore, we are adopting this definition as proposed.

9. *"Covered Persons in the Firm"*

Rule 2-01(f)(11) defines the term "covered persons in the firm." The term includes four basic groups. The first two groups, the "audit engagement team" and the "chain of command," are described above. Their inclusion in the category of "covered persons in the firm" is unchanged from the proposed rule.

We have modified the description of the third category of covered persons from our proposal. The proposed rule referred to "any other partner, principal, shareholder, or professional employee of the accounting firm who is, or during the audit client's most recent fiscal year was, involved in providing any professional service to the audit client or an affiliate of the audit client." We included this category because the auditing literature, quite appropriately, directs the audit engagement team to discuss certain matters with the firm personnel responsible for providing such services to that client.[269]

In response to concerns raised by commenters,[270] we have modified the definition of this category of covered persons in two respects. First, we have changed the term "professional employee" to "managerial employee," to encompass a somewhat narrower scope of persons. Second, we have set a minimum hour threshold that must be crossed before an individual becomes a covered person by virtue of providing a non-audit service to an audit client. This subpart of the definition now includes only those individuals who have "provided ten or more hours of non-audit services to the audit client for the period beginning on the date such services are provided and ending on the date the accounting firm signs the report on the financial statements for the fiscal year during which those services are provided, or who expects to provide ten or more hours of non-audit services to the audit client on a recurring basis."

In this definition, the phrase "beginning on the date such services are provided" refers to the date on which the individual provides his or her tenth hour of non-audit service to a particular audit client within the space of a single fiscal year of that client. For example, if the client's fiscal year runs from January 1 to December 31, and an individual provides eight hours of non-audit services on February 1 and two hours of non-audit services on June 1, then the period described above would commence following the provision of the services on June 1. From that date through the date that the accounting firm signs the report on the financial statements for that fiscal year, that individual is a "covered person in the firm." We reiterate: the individual's status as a covered person does *not* end at the conclusion of the fiscal year in question, but continues until the firm has signed the report for the financial statements for that fiscal year.

The proposed rule described the fourth category of covered persons as "any other partner, principal, or shareholder from an 'office' of the accounting firm that participates in a significant portion of the audit." We included these people on the theory that they are the ones most likely to interact with the audit engagement team on substantive matters and may exert influence over the audit engagement team by virtue of their physical proximity to, or relatively frequent contact with, the audit engagement team.

In response to concerns raised by commenters about the breadth of the category, particularly the inclusion of every "office" that participates in a "significant portion" of the audit,[271] we have modified this definition. The final rule narrows the scope of the definition to "any other partner, principal, or shareholder from an 'office' of the accounting firm in which the lead audit engagement partner primarily practices in connection with the audit." We are persuaded that it is reasonable to draw the line at partners, principals, and shareholders, rather than at all "professional employees," and that it is also more reasonable and more practicable to draw a clear line at the "office"[272] of the firm in which the lead engagement partner primarily practices.

A person who is not a covered person at the time an audit engagement begins might nonetheless become a covered person at any time during the audit engagement. As soon as events or circumstances bring a person within any category of covered person defined above, that person is a "covered person in the firm." An individual must be independent of the audit client, pursuant to the provisions of the rule, before becoming a covered person in the firm. That means, for example, that an individual must dispose of any financial interest in the audit client completely and irrevocably before being consulted by another covered person concerning the audit engagement. For example, the rule does not allow the person consulted to participate in a discussion about the audit engage-

---

[269] AICPA SAS No. 22, AU § 311.046 and AUI 9311.03.

[270] *See, e.g.,* Deloitte & Touche Letter; Ernst & Young Letter.

[271] *See, e.g.,* Deloitte & Touche Letter; Ernst & Young Letter.

[272] For a discussion of the definition of "office," *see infra* Section IV.H.12.

ment and then "cure" an independence impairment by later disposing of an investment. Likewise, a person who becomes a covered person by rotating onto an engagement or being promoted into the chain of command must be independent pursuant to the provisions of the rule prior to becoming a covered person.

One commenter suggested that the definition of "covered persons in the firm" should include leased accounting personnel.[273] We note that to the extent leased personnel otherwise fall within any category of "covered persons in the firm," such as by being on the audit engagement team, they will be covered persons in the firm.[274]

Because the rule narrows the scope of firm personnel to whom investment and employment restrictions apply, an accounting firm employee in a distant part of the world, or even down the street, might own an audit client's securities, have a family member in a financial position at the client, or enter into a business relationship with a client without necessarily impairing the firm's independence from the audit client. We expect that many partners and employees who previously could not own securities issued by an audit client will be able to do so under the rule.

It should be noted that insider trading restrictions prohibit any partner, principal, shareholder, or employee of the firm, whether or not he or she performs any service for the client, from trading on the basis of any material nonpublic information about that client.

10. *"Immediate Family Members"*

We are adopting, as proposed, final Rule 2-01(f)(13), which defines "immediate family members" to mean a person's spouse, spousal equivalent, and dependents. These terms have the same meaning as they do in the definition of "close family members."

"Immediate family members" is a narrower group than "close family members." Again, we believe that the less immediate the family relationship to the covered person, the more substantial that family member's relationship to the audit client should be before we deem it to impair independence. By identifying "immediate family members," we are identifying those persons who have such regular and close contact with a "covered person" that it is fair, for independence purposes, to attribute to the covered person any financial and employment relationships that family member has with the audit client.

We received a few comments on the definition of "immediate family members." Some commenters agreed that the definition should not include emancipated adult children, while others expressed concern that non-dependent children were not included in this group.[275] On balance, we believe that, for purposes of these rules, emancipated children are sufficiently independent of their parents to warrant not imputing their financial interests to their parents. We are, therefore, adopting the definition as proposed.

11. *"Investment Company Complex"*

As proposed, the definition of "investment company complex" focused on investment advisers and entities in a control relationship with the adviser, including entities under common control with the adviser. The proposed definition was loosely based on ISB Standard No. 2, which defines "mutual fund complex" to mean "[t]he mutual fund operation in its entirety, including all the funds, plus the sponsor, its ultimate parent company, and their subsidiaries."[276]

We solicited comment on the definition proposed, and, in particular, on whether an alternative definition, focusing on the fund's principal underwriter and administrator would be more appropriate. Some commenters expressed concern about the scope of the investment company complex definition, particularly that it included entities that have no direct relationship to investment company operations.[277] These commenters' concern was that all subsidiaries of an adviser's parent company would also be included in the investment company complex. Therefore, an accounting firm could not provide certain non-audit services to, or invest in, subsidiaries of the parent of the adviser, even if those subsidiaries operated businesses unrelated to the investment company business. Under the proposed definition, for example, if a parent company owned an adviser and a manufacturing company, the accountant that audited the adviser (or a fund advised by the adviser) could not invest in the manufacturing company, even though its operations would not be affected by the audit of the adviser (or the fund).

In response to these comments, we have adopted in Rule 2-01(f)(14) a definition of investment company complex that is more limited than the one proposed. As adopted, the rule only includes an entity under common control with the adviser if the entity provides services to an investment company in the investment company complex. More specifically, if a sister entity of the investment adviser, other than another investment adviser, does not provide administrative, custodian, underwriting, or transfer agent services to the adviser or a fund, it is not part of the investment company complex.

---

[273] *See* Deloitte & Touche Letter.

[274] For example, leased accounting personnel might consult with a professional employee participating in an audit and thereby become a member of the audit engagement team.

[275] *See* Written Testimony of Ronald Nielsen and Kathleen Chapman, Iowa Accountancy Examining Board (Sept. 20, 2000).

[276] ISB Standard No. 2, *supra* note 226.

[277] *See, e.g.,* Deloitte & Touche Letter; AICPA Letter.

As proposed, an entity that would be an investment company but for the exclusions provided by section 3(c) of the Investment Company Act and that is advised by the investment adviser or sponsored by the sponsor is part of the investment company complex. Also, as proposed, the definition does not include sub-advisers whose role is primarily portfolio management and who provide services pursuant to a subcontract with, or are overseen by, an adviser in the complex. There was some support for excluding sub-advisers from the definition of investment company complex.[278] We have determined to exclude sub-advisers from the definition because a fund, or even its adviser, may not be able to know whether the sub-adviser obtained any non-audit services from the fund's or the adviser's auditor. Moreover, considering a sub-adviser or the funds it advises to be part of the investment company complex presents practical difficulties where the sub-adviser is itself an adviser in a separate investment company complex.

12. "Office"

Rule 2-01(f)(15) defines "office" to mean a distinct sub-group within an accounting firm, whether distinguished along geographic or practice lines. The term "office" is an integral part of the description of one category of "covered persons" and, thereby, helps identify firm personnel who cannot have financial or employment relationships with a particular audit client without impairing the firm's independence. The definition has not changed from the proposed definition.

We give "office" a meaning that does more than merely refer to a distinct physical location where the firm's personnel work. By "office" we mean to encompass any reasonably distinct sub-group within an accounting firm, whether constituted by formal organization or informal practice, where the personnel who make up the sub-group generally serve the same clients, work on the same matters, or work on the same categories of matters. In this sense, "office" may transcend physical boundaries, and it is possible that a firm may have a sub-group that constitutes an "office" even though the personnel making up that sub-group are stationed at various places around the country or the world.

At the same time, we intend for "office" also to include reference to a physical location. For this reason, "office" will generally include a distinct physical location where the firm's personnel work. We recognize, however, that in some cases thousands of firm personnel may work at a single, large physical location, but physical divisions may nonetheless effectively isolate different sub-groups of personnel from each other in ways that will warrant treating each sub-group as a separate "office" under the proposed definition.

Some commenters raised concerns about the definition of office.[279] One commenter asserted that the proposed definition is unworkable and does not provide helpful guidance.[280] This commenter expressed a preference for the ISB's approach to the concept of "office or practice unit," in the ISB's Exposure Draft on Financial Interests and Family Relationships.[281]

In some respects, the definition that we adopt overlaps with the ISB approach. Like the ISB approach, our definition will necessarily involve the application of judgment, governed by substance. And under our definition, as under the ISB approach, expected regular personnel interactions and assigned reporting channels may well be more important than an individual's physical location. We have determined to adopt the definition that we proposed, because it is unclear to us that the ISB approach would necessarily encompass each distinct sub-group that, in particular circumstances, should be encompassed.

I. *Codification*

As previously discussed, the Commission's current auditor independence requirements are found in various rules and interpretations. Section 600 of the Codification provides interpretations and guidance not otherwise available in Rule 2-01. The final rule articulates a number of situations and circumstances, such as financial relationships, employment relationships, and non-audit services that impair auditor independence. Accordingly, we are deleting some interpretations included in the Codification, either because they are reflected in the revised Rule 2-01 or they have been superseded, in whole or in part, by the rule. Because examples have been deleted both because they are no longer necessary and because they are inconsistent with the final rule, inferences should not be drawn from the deletion of a particular example. The revised Codification contains the

---

[278] *See, e.g.,* Arthur Andersen Letter.

[279] *See, e.g.,* Deloitte & Touche Letter; AICPA Letter.

[280] *See* AICPA Letter.

[281] The ISB Exposure Draft, cited in the AICPA Letter, states the following:__p46_the identification of the relevant 'office' or practice unit is based on the facts and circumstances, including the firm's operating structure, and requires judgment. In a traditional geographic practice office (one city location with one managing partner in charge of all operations - audit, tax, and consulting), that location should be considered to be the office. In addition, if there are smaller, nearby 'satellite' offices managed under the primary city office,

broadly sharing staff, etc., those locations should also be considered part of the primary office. On the other hand, many firms are now structured more on an industry specialization or line-of-service basis, and manage offices on that basis. For example, if a financial services group were a separate practice unit, and were operated that way with limited contact with personnel of other local units, that may represent a separate office for purposes of this standard. Substance should govern the office classification, and the expected regular personnel interactions and assigned reporting channels of an individual may well be more important than his or her physical location.

discussion of the final rule from this release, as well as the background information and interpretations that may continue to be useful in situations not specifically or definitively addressed in paragraph (c). Examples of these items include business relationships, unpaid prior professional fees, indemnification by clients, and litigation.

602.02. Interpretations Relating to Independence

.a. Introduction

The Commission's authority and responsibility for determining that accountants are independent is found in the statutory language of the Acts it administers. These Acts, and the rules adopted pursuant to them, principally provide for the adequate and accurate disclosure of all material facts to the public. The concept of independence, as it relates to the accountant, is fundamental to this purpose because it implies an objective analysis of the situation by a disinterested third party. In order to assure public confidence in the objective reporting of these material facts, certain rules, particularly Rule 2(e) of the Commission's Rules of Practice and Rule 2-01 of Regulation S-X, were adopted. Under Rule 2(e), the Commission may deny, temporarily or permanently, the privilege of appearing or practicing in any way before it to any person who is found by the Commission after notice of and opportunity for hearing in the matter (i) not to possess the requisite qualifications to represent others, or (ii) to be lacking in character or integrity or to have engaged in unethical or improper professional conduct, or (iii) to have willfully violated, or willfully aided and abetted the violation of any provision of the federal securities laws, or the rules and regulations thereunder. Contrasted with Rule 2(e), under which the Commission may impose sanctions once improper professional conduct (such as the lack of independence) has been determined, Rule 2-01 deals with the qualifications of accountants and broadly illustrates how the qualification of independence may be impaired. Audited financial statements which are used in connection with an offering of securities within the Commission's jurisdiction, including those offerings which are exempted from certification under the Securities Act, and those included in certain filings under the Exchange Act, must be audited by an accountant who satisfies the independence requirements of this Rule.

The critical distinction which must be recognized at the outset is that the concept of independence is more easily defined than applied. As a result, the guidelines and illustrations presented in this section cannot be, nor are they intended to be, definitive answers on any aspect of this subject. Rather, they are designed to apprise the practitioners of typical situations which have involved loss of independence, whether in appearance or in fact, and by so doing to place them on notice of these and similar potential threats to their independence.

The Commission has said that a question of independence is to be determined in the light of all the pertinent circumstances in the particular case. No set of rules or compilation of representative situations can embrace all the circumstances which could affect such a determination. But what they can do, and what they are intended to do, is act as a general notification which simultaneously educates practitioners and places on them the responsibility for recognizing these general areas of potential loss of independence. The Commission is aware of the fact that situations arise which require judgment in determining whether the Commission's standards of independence have been met and that a company or its accountants may wish assurance that no question as to independence will be raised if the company files financial statements with the Commission. Where this is the case, the Commission urges the parties concerned to bring the problem to the attention of the Commission's staff so that a timely and informed decision on the matter may be made.

The remainder of this section is subdivided into topics dealing with particular relationships, direct and indirect, which may affect adversely the fact or appearance of an accountant's independence.

602.02.b. Financial Interest

.i. General

The ownership of a financial interest in an audit client or its affiliates is one of the principal factors having an adverse effect on the independence of accountants.

The following compilation sets forth representative cases in which informal determinations were issued in response to inquiries based on particular fact situations bearing on the independence of an accountant.

602.02.b.ii. Financial Interest in Client Company

Example 1

Facts: An accountant took an option for shares of his client's common stock in settlement of his fee.

Conclusion: The option creates an interest in the client which impairs the independence of the accountant.

Example 2

Facts: Partners and staff members of a small accounting firm which had certified the financial statements included in a registration statement subsequently acquired shares of stock of the registrant.

Conclusion: The firm was not allowed to certify subsequent financial statements included in a post-effective amendment to the registration statement.

602.02.b.iii. Interests in Nonclient Affiliates and Investee Companies

With the advent of the use by investor companies of the equity method of accounting for less-than-fifty-percent investments in investees, questions have been raised regarding the provisions of Rule 2-01 with respect to the independence of accountants in relation to a financial interest in nonclient parents, subsidiaries, less-than-fifty-percent-owned investees, or other affiliates of audit clients where the investor company's interests in the investee are not material.

In general, an immaterial financial interest in a nonclient investee of a client company would not have an adverse effect on the independence of the auditor of the client/investor where the investor's investment in the investee does not exceed five percent of the investor's consolidated total assets and the investor's equity in the investee's income from continuing operations before income taxes does not exceed five percent of the investor's consolidated income from continuing operations before income taxes. In situations involving foreign accountants who examine the financial statements of nonmaterial segments of an international business (see 602.02.b.iv. below), materiality is determined in accordance with the definition of a "significant subsidiary" in Rule 1-02 in lieu of the five percent tests immediately above.

Example 1

Facts: A registrant owned a small percentage of the stock of a sales company that sold some of the registrant's products. The accountant who certified the financial statements of the registrant was the treasurer and one of the stockholders of the sales company.

Conclusion: If the shares held by the registrant and the nature of the sales relationship were such as to give the registrant a significant element of indirect control over the sales company, the accountant could not be considered independent for the purpose of certifying the financial statements of the registrant.

602.02.b.iv. Unpaid Prior Professional Fees

If fees for audit and other professional services are owed to an accountant for an extended period of time and become material in relation to the fee expected to be charged for a current audit, there may be a question concerning the accountant's independence with regard to the current audit because the accountant may appear to have a direct interest in the results of operations of the client. Generally, prior year audit and other unpaid fees should be paid before a current audit engagement is commenced in order for the accountant to be deemed independent with respect to the current audit.

When an unpaid fee problem exists in connection with the required audits of financial statements to be included in *annual reports* filed with the Commission, sometimes these guidelines are modified. Normally, a question would not be raised in such situations if, at the time the current audit engagement is commenced, a definite commitment is made by the client to pay the prior year fees before the current year audit report is issued, or an arrangement is agreed upon for periodic payments to settle the delinquent fee and there is reasonable assurance that the current audit fee will be paid before commencement of the audit for the ensuing year. Determinations on unpaid, prior year fee problems are illustrated in the following cases.

Example 1

Facts: An accounting firm had performed the 19x3 annual audit of the financial statements of a parent company, a partially owned insurance subsidiary and certain wholly owned subsidiaries. When the accounting firm was engaged to perform the 19x4 audit of the insurance subsidiary, the 19x3 audit fees for the parent and the other subsidiaries had not been settled because those entities were experiencing financial difficulties. As a means of resolving the financial difficulties, the parent had agreed to a divestiture of its interest in the insurance subsidiary. The accounting firm requested an opinion regarding its independence with respect to the audit of the insurance subsidiary's 19x4 financial statements to be filed with the Commission.

Conclusion: The accounting firm's independence was not questioned with respect to the 19x4 annual audit of the financial statements of the insurance subsidiary, since no prior audit fees for that subsidiary were outstanding at the time of engagement, the subsidiary had a favorable profit record, was precluded from involvement in the financial difficulties of the parent by the state insurance regulatory authority, and the subsidiary would soon cease to be related to the parent and the other subsidiaries.

Example 2

Facts: When an accounting firm was auditing a company's December 31, 19x3 consolidated balance sheet to be included in a proxy statement to be used in soliciting stockholders' consent to a Consolidated Plan of Arrangement under Chapter XI of the Bankruptcy Act, it was engaged to audit certain financial statements for an interim period ending July 31, 19x4, which were also to be included in the proxy statement. The letter of engagement for the 19x3 audit was signed by the Debtor in Possession and provided for compensation at normal hourly rates plus expenses in accordance with usual professional practice. Because of changes in the Rules of Bankruptcy Procedure, compensation for the 19x4 interim period audit work would be determined by the court, giving due consideration to the nature, extent and value of the services rendered. An opinion was requested regarding whether independence would be impaired by the fact that the 19x3 audit fees, which were material, were unpaid at the start of the 19x4 interim period audit, and whether the compensation for the 19x4 interim audit, determined as specified by the Rules of Bankruptcy Procedure, would be construed as a contingent fee and thus impair independence.

Conclusion: Independence would not be deemed to be impaired in either of these circumstances, since (1) the unpaid fees for the first audit would be outstanding a relatively short time at the start of the second audit and the Debtor in Possession and the court would be responsible for settling both audit fees; and (2) the compensation for the second audit determined by the court in accordance with the Rules of Bankruptcy Procedure would not represent a contingent fee.

Example 3

Facts: Recent operations of a client company have not been profitable and in order to improve its current working capital ratio, it has invited unsecured creditors to extend their settlement dates and subordinate their interests in exchange for receiving the first proceeds from a proposed offering. The accounting firm's fee was one of the debts to be subordinated.

Conclusion: If the accounting firm subordinates the amount due it, independence would be impaired.

602.02.c Bookkeeping and Related Professional Services

.i. General

Financial statements filed for the registrant and its subsidiaries have been recognized by the Commission and by public accountants generally as representations of management upon whom rests the primary responsibility for their propriety and accuracy. A part of the rationale which underlies any rule on independence is that managerial and decision-making functions are the responsibility of the client and not of the independent accountant. If the independent accountant were to perform functions of this nature, he would develop, or appear to develop, a mutuality of interest with his client which would differ only in degree, but not in kind, from that of an employee. And where this relationship appears to exist, it may be logically inferred that the accountant's professional judgment toward the particular client might be prejudiced in that he would, in effect, be auditing the results of his own work, thereby destroying the objectivity sought by users of financial statements. Consequently, the performance of such functions is fundamentally inconsistent with an impartial examination. However, independent accountants often advise management and offer professional advice on matters dealing with financial operations. Therefore, the problem posed by this dilemma is to ascertain the point where advice ends and managerial responsibility begins.

In this context, managerial responsibility begins when the accountant becomes, or appears to become, so identified with the client's management as to be indistinguishable from it. In making a determination of whether this degree of identification has been reached, the basic consideration is whether, to a third party, the client appears to be (i) substantially dependent upon the accountant's skill and judgment in its financial operations, or (ii) reliant only to the extent of the customary type of consultation or advice.

It is the Commission's position that an accounting firm cannot be deemed independent with regard to auditing financial statements of a client if it has participated closely, either manually or through its computer services, in maintenance of the basic accounting records and preparation of the financial statements, or if the firm performs other accounting services through which it participates with management in operational decisions.

A major value of an audit of financial statements by an independent accountant is derived from the fact that the accounting records and financial statements of management are reviewed and examined from an independent or outside viewpoint by knowledgeable professional accountants who are not connected with management. The application of an independent viewpoint is particularly important with respect to judgments exercised in the determination of appropriate principles and methods applicable to the recording, classification and presentation of financial data. By their nature such judgments cannot subsequently be evaluated on an impartial and objective basis by the same accountant who made them.

Where source data are provided by the client and the accountant's work is limited to processing and production of listings and reports, independence will be adversely affected if the listings and reports become part of the basic accounting records on which, at least in part, the accountant would base his opinion. In this situation the accountant, by preparing basic accounting records, has placed himself in a position where he would be reviewing his own recordkeeping and could therefore appear to a reasonable third party to lack the objectivity and impartiality with respect to that client which an independent audit requires. On the other hand, if the processing results in the production of statistical summaries and analyses which do not become part of the basic accounting records, independence would not be adversely affected because the accountant, in the course of his audit, would not be put in the position, actual or apparent, of evaluating and attesting to the accuracy of his own recordkeeping.

Conclusion: Neither the individual accountant nor his firm could be considered independent for the purpose of certifying the financial statements of the registrant.

602.02.d. Occupational Conflicting Interests

d.i. General

Certain concurrent occupations of accountants engaged in the practice of public accounting involve relationships with clients which may jeopardize the accountant's objectivity and, therefore, his independence. In general, this situation arises because the relationships and activities customarily associated with this occupation are not compatible with the auditor's appearance of complete objectivity or because the primary objectives of such occupations are fundamentally different from those of a public accountant. Acting as counsel or as a broker-dealer, or actively engaging in direct competition in a commercial enterprise are examples of occupations so classified. The following discussion relating thereto is intended to be illustrative only. The principles involved are equally applicable to any other similar undertaking.

602.02.d.ii. Accountant-Commercial Competitor

Occasionally, accountants engage in a commercial business concurrently with the practice of public accounting. Where such commercial business is directly competitive with that of a client, there would appear to third parties to be a conflict of interests which might influence the firm's objectivity since the public accounting firm would have access to the records, policies and practices of a business competitor.

602.02.e. Business Relationships

Direct and material indirect business relationships, other than as a consumer in the normal course of business, with a client or with persons associated with the client in a decision-making capacity, such as officers, directors or substantial stockholders, will adversely affect the accountant's independence with respect to that client. Such a mutuality or identity of interests with the client would cause the accountant to lose the appearance of objectivity and impartiality in the performance of his audit because the advancement of his interest would, to some extent, be dependent upon the client. In addition to the relationships specifically prohibited by Rule 2-01, joint business ventures, limited partnership agreements, investments in supplier or customer companies, leasing interests, (except for immaterial landlord-tenant relationships) and sales by the accountant of items other than professional services are examples of other connections which are also included within this classification.

The following cases illustrate the types of inquiries received by the staff in this area:

Example 1

Facts: A computer firm was engaged exclusively in computer processing income tax return data for professional tax return preparers, including various local offices of many national accounting firms. When the computer company was contemplating making a public offering of its stock, an inquiry was made regarding whether an accounting firm which utilized this computer service could be deemed independent with respect to the audits of the financial statements of the computer

firm required for the purpose of the public offering.

Conclusion: An accounting firm's independence would be adversely affected if billings for this service from the computer firm to the accounting firm or to the local office which would perform the audit were significant to the accounting firm, its local office, or to the computer firm. Since these computer services are a direct part of the professional tax service rendered by the accounting firm, any material amount of such computer services would create a mutuality of interests that would impair the appearance of objectivity of the accounting firm necessary for the performance of the audit.

Example 2

Facts: Five covered persons of an accounting firm owned ten percent of the voting interests in a small business investment company which planned to participate with another small business investment company in a loan to a client of the accounting firm. In conjunction with the loan, the lending companies would receive warrants for five percent of the common stock of the audit client.

Conclusion: Independence of the accounting firm would be adversely affected with respect to the audit of the client's financial statements if the covered persons retained their interests in the small business investment company, which would have a creditor relationship with the client and a right to acquire an equity interest as a result of the loan.

Example 3

Facts: An accounting firm inquired whether its independence would be adversely affected with respect to a client if the controlling shareholder became a limited partner in a partnership which is controlled by covered persons of the accounting firm in their capacity as general partner.

Conclusion: The accounting firm's independence would be questioned in these circumstances inasmuch as the joint business venture would impair the appearance of independence of the accounting firm.

Example 4

Facts: An accounting firm's client, a realtor corporation, was the general partner and ten percent owner in a limited partnership which owned unimproved land held for appreciation in value. The accounting firm also owned a five percent interest in this limited partnership and a covered person in the firm had a two percent interest.

Conclusion: The joint investment with the client was viewed as incompatible with the appearance of independence.

Example 5

Facts: A covered person in a foreign accounting firm that performed the audit of financial statements of a client in the foreign country which was a subsidiary of a company registered with the Commission also owned an industrial equipment company from which the client had ordered an expensive piece of equipment. A large deposit on the purchase commitment was held by the partner's company during the audit engagement. Engaging in commercial transactions with a client does not conflict with the professional standards for independence of accountants in the foreign country.

Conclusion: The accounting firm's independence was adversely affected since the partner's commercial company was dependent on the client for a profit on the commercial transaction and was in a debtor position in relation to the client as a result of the large deposit. These factors created a question regarding the objectivity of the firm in conducting the audit.

Example 6

Facts: Client of an accounting firm was engaged in the business of selling franchises. Two covered persons of this firm had invested approximately five percent of their personal fortunes to buy one-half of the stock of a corporation which held a franchise granted by this client. Except for the payment of a percentage of sales to the franchisor, the franchisee operated independently.

Conclusion: The firm could not be considered independent because the covered persons had a material investment in the franchisee which had a close identity in fact and in appearance with the client.

Example 7

Facts: Covered person in accounting firm was also a financial vice president and stockholder of a real estate investment trust. In addition, he was a limited partner in a company which manages the trust. A client of his firm had asked him to help them get a loan from the investment trust.

Conclusion: Independence for future periods would be adversely affected if the company were to obtain the loan from the real estate investment trust. However, no question would be raised as to periods prior to the commencement of negotiations for the loan.

Example 8

Facts: Covered persons in the accounting firm had a common investment with stockholders of a prospective client. These covered persons owned approximately 11 percent of Company A and the other investors, who owned approximately 78.5 percent of Company A, also owned 22 percent of the prospective client.

Conclusion: Independence was adversely affected because the common investment which the covered persons of the firm had with the substantial minority shareholders of the prospective client was such a circumstance as could lead a third party to question the firm's objectivity.

Example 9

Facts: An accounting firm planned to construct office buildings in which it would occupy a relatively small portion of the space and would rent the remainder to other tenants, some of whom might be clients of the firm.

Conclusion: The activity of owning and managing real property is more in the nature of a commercial business activity than of a professional service. Rental of a material amount of space to a client would raise a question of independence since the accounting firm would appear to have a material business relationship with the client. Some reasonable tests which would be applied in determining what constitutes a rental of material amount might be the relationship of a single lease to the fees earned in the office located in the building concerned, total lease rentals from all clients to the firm's total fees, and lease rentals from a particular client to the auditing fee paid by that client for the same period.

Example 10

Facts: Several covered persons of an accounting firm formed a general partnership to build two office buildings which would then be leased to third parties. Would leases entered into between the partnership and present or future clients of the accounting firm impair the firm's independence?

Conclusion: The activities conducted by the covered persons through the general partnership would be attributed to the accounting firm for purposes of independence determinations. Therefore, any material business relationship arising between the general partnership and a client of the accounting firm would impair the independence of the accounting firm as auditors for that client and its affiliates.

Example 11

Facts: An accounting firm had its office in a building which was owned by a client. The accounting firm, which occupied approximately 25 percent of the available office space in the building, was the only tenant other than the client.

Conclusion: The fact that the accounting firm was the only other tenant in the client's building and leased a substantial portion of the available office space are circumstances that would lead a reasonable third party to question the firm's objectivity. Therefore, independence was adversely affected.

Example 12

Facts: Accounting firm planned to rent block time on its computer to a client if the client's computer becomes overburdened.

Conclusion: Renting excess computer time to a client, except in emergency or temporary situations, is a business transaction with a client beyond the customary professional relationship and would therefore adversely affect independence.

Example 13

Facts: A covered person in an accounting firm acquired, and assigned to his minor daughter, a ten percent voting interest in a corporation which owned a retail store franchised from a proposed client that also operated similar stores directly.

Conclusion: Independence of the accounting firm would be adversely affected with respect to the audit of the client's financial statements because the covered person was deemed to have a direct interest in a company over which the client may exercise control through the franchise agreement for operation of the retail store. In addition, the company had a close identity in fact and appearance with the client through the operation of similar retail stores.

Example 14

Facts: An accountant and five persons who were the sole stockholders of the proposed registrant acquired a parcel of real estate for the purpose of selling or leasing it to the company. The total purchase price was $85,000, of which $26,000 was paid in cash and the balance by a note secured by a mortgage. In addition to providing his portion of the cash payment, the accountant loaned the others $21,000 on interest bearing notes to cover their share of the down payment. It was also provided that the accountant would receive 25 percent of any profit arising from sale of the property to an outsider.

Conclusion: Independence was impaired.

Example 15

Facts: A covered person, together with certain officers of the registrant, organized a corporation which purchased property from the registrant for $100,000 giving the registrant $25,000 cash and a purchase money mortgage for $75,000.

Conclusion: Independence was impaired.

Example 16

Facts: Certain covered persons of an accounting firm were to become principals in a finance company whose wholly owned insurance agency would place with an insurance company client of the firm all or a substantial part of the insurance on the chattels financed.

Conclusion: If the insurance were so placed, the accounting firm would not be considered independent with respect to its insurance company client.

Example 17

Facts: The wife of a covered person had a 47.5 percent interest in one of the three principal underwriters of a proposed issue by the registrant.

Conclusion: Not independent.

Example 18

Facts: A consultant to an accounting firm was also a director and member of the audit committee of a client served by the accounting firm. The consultant's compensation from each of these two involvements was significant in relation to his total earnings.

Conclusion: The apparent conflict of interest which arose from the dual roles of the consultant caused the appearance of the accounting firm's independence to be affected adversely.

Example 19

Facts: A covered person certifying the financial statements of a registered broker-dealer was a co-signer on the broker's indemnity bond.

Conclusion: Independence impaired.

Example 22

Facts: An accounting firm audited the brokerage operations of a financial concern and planned to perform what it considered to be consultative or advisory work for another branch of the business which marketed an estate planning service. This additional work would consist chiefly of developing individual estate planning packages for customers and making recommendations jointly with management to the customers.

Conclusion: The accounting firm's independence would be adversely affected with respect to the audit of the brokerage operations if it performed the additional services for another branch of the business, because it would be participating with management in the development and the sale of a product to be marketed by the company.

602.02.f. Other

f.i. Indemnification by Client

Inquiry was made as to whether an accountant who certifies financial statements included in a registration statement or annual report filed with the Commission under the Securities Act or the Exchange Act would be considered independent if he had entered into an indemnity agreement with the registrant. In the particular illustration cited, the board of directors of the registrant formally approved the filing of a registration statement with the Commission and agreed to indemnify and save harmless each and every accountant who certified any part of such statement, "from any and all losses, claims, damages or liabilities arising out of such act or acts to which they or any of them may become subject under the Securities Act, as amended, or at 'common law,' other than for their willful misstatements or omissions."

When an accountant and his client, directly or through an affiliate, have entered into an agreement of indemnity which seeks to assure to the accountant immunity from liability for his own negligent acts, whether of omission or commission, one of the major stimuli to objective and unbiased consideration of the problems encountered in a particular engagement is removed or greatly weakened. Such condition must frequently induce a departure from the standards of objectivity and impartiality which the concept of independence implies. In such difficult matters, for example, as the determination of the scope of audit necessary, existence of such an agreement may easily lead to the use of less extensive or thorough procedures than would otherwise be followed. In other cases it may result in a failure to appraise with professional acumen the information disclosed by the examination. Consequently, the accountant cannot be recognized as independent for the purpose of certifying the financial statements of the corporation.

602.02.f.ii. Litigation

When an adversary position between an client and its accountant with respect to the audit services rendered is created as a result of litigation, the accountant cannot be considered impartial or capable of exercising objective judgments in the performance of the audit work and could not be deemed to meet the Commission's requirements for independence. Other situations involving litigation or the possibility of litigation require careful consideration by the accountant to determine whether an adversary position is created which impairs his independence with respect to the audit work performed or to be performed.

In general, litigation would impair independence whenever it might be expected to alter substantially the normal relationship between client and public accountant. Such a relationship must be characterized by complete candor and full communication between client and auditor regarding all aspects of the client's business operations. In addition, the relationship must be marked by an absence of bias on the part of the auditor so that he may be in a position to exercise detached professional judgment on financial reporting decisions made by his client.

When the management of a client commences or threatens to commence legal action against a public accountant, or the accountant commences litigation against the client, in connection with audit work performed in serving that client, it is presumed that the auditor and the client management are placed in an adversary situation in which normal audit communication will be affected by legal considerations or behavioral reactions related to the lawsuit. Accordingly, the existence or expressed threat of such litigation would adversely affect the independence of the accountant.

Even the likelihood of litigation may have such an effect if the auditor concludes that there is a strong probability that a suit will be brought. In such cases both parties may be taking actions primarily designed to protect their legal positions which would prejudice effective communication between them.

Where an auditor is sued by a stockholder acting individually or on behalf of a class of stockholders, the situation may be different. Such an action would not necessarily affect independence, if the relationship between the auditor and the officers and directors is not affected. All the circumstances must be examined, however, both with respect to the complaint and the answer made by the charged parties. If officers and directors are sued at the same time as the auditors, for example, and it becomes apparent that one such defendant is likely to assert that any alleged deficiencies were those of the auditor, the fundamental relationship between auditor and client would

be changed. Similarly, if an auditor defends himself in such a suit by asserting management deceit or fraud, the same result would ensue.

Third party suits against public accountants must be similarly analyzed. In most cases, a suit by a third party would not alter fundamental relationships between auditor and client and hence would not have an unfavorable impact on independence. The facts alleged in complaints, however, and the responses to such allegations by all charged parties must be considered.

In regard to other situations where litigation or an expressed intention to commence litigation involving the accountant exists, the Commission will also consider whether the particular circumstances of the situation may impair the independence of the accountant. These situations include, but are not limited to, those in which the accountant and the person or its affiliates are or may be co-defendants; litigation between the accountant and former directors or officers of the person or its affiliates; claims against an accountant relating to the audit work performed for a third party whose financial statements are also examined by the accountant; and derivative or similar litigation assertedly brought on behalf of a person but not adopted by such person (including class action litigation where the person is a member of a class but not a named plaintiff). In evaluating particular litigation situations, the Commission will also consider the nature of the claims being asserted and the defenses made.

Finally, independence could also be adversely affected by litigation in situations where management and auditor are bound so closely together that the appearance of independence might be impaired. For example, in one situation, management and auditors were charged with agreeing together to withhold certain information from stockholders and from the staff of the Commission. Under such circumstances, it is doubtful whether auditors could be considered independent since they have commonality of legal interest with the client. Similarly, in a case where conspiracy between auditor and client is charged, further inquiry would be needed into the problems of appearance. The naming of auditors and client as co-defendants in a civil suit would not in and of itself have this effect, however.

The Commission's staff has also been asked whether, once conditions giving rise to a lack of independence are eliminated, it is possible for the independent auditor to report on a client's financial statements that cover a period during which litigation was taking place. While the facts of the particular circumstances must always govern, in general it appears that a report can be independently rendered for such a period as long as no audit field work was done while the circumstances which would have prejudiced independence existed. In addition, if an accountant was independent when his report was initially rendered, generally he may again sign this report or consent to its use at a later date while his independence is impaired, as long as no post-audit work is performed during the period when he is not independent. The term "post-audit work" in this context, does not include inquiries of subsequent auditors, reading of subsequent financial statements, or such procedures as may be necessary to assess the effect of subsequently discovered facts on the financial statements covered by the previously issued report.

The following cases are illustrative of the problems in these situations.

Example 1

Facts: An accounting firm and its client were named as co-defendants in litigation by a third party which alleged that the audited financial statements of the client were incorrect and misleading. The accounting firm filed a cross-claim suit against the client.

Conclusion: Since a direct adversary relationship that would preclude complete candor between the accounting firm and its client was created by the filing of the cross-claim suit, the accounting firm would not be deemed independent with respect to audits of the client's financial statements to be filed with the Commission while the suit is pending.

Example 2

Facts: After an accounting firm issued an audit report on the financial statements of a client, the client considered legal action against the firm, either directly or through subrogation of a claim to its bonding company, because the client believed that the firm should have detected a significant defalcation which had occurred.

Conclusion: When there is litigation by a client pending against an auditor (or litigation is being considered) relating to the audit services performed by the auditor for the client, an adversary relationship is created which would impair the appearance of independence of the auditor with regard to any work performed while the litigation is pending or being considered, whether the claim is asserted directly by the client or by the bonding company.

Example 3

Facts: During the annual audit of the financial statements of a client, an accounting firm became aware that the Internal Revenue Service had disallowed substantial losses claimed in the tax returns of the chairman of the board and substantial shareholder of the client that had been prepared by the accounting firm. It was expected that substantial damages would be assessed against the chairman. The accounting firm received assurance from the chairman that, based on the facts known at the time, the accounting firm would not be named as a defendant in any litigation regarding the damages. Prior to completing the audit, the firm requested an opinion regarding its independence in light of these circumstances.

Conclusion: The firm's independence was not deemed to be adversely affected with respect to the audit because no adversary relationship existed during the period of the audit, and the chairman of the board had given assurance that no claim against the accounting firm was contemplated at that time.

Example 4

Facts: An accounting firm received a letter from an officer of client company stating a claim against the accounting firm in connection with a prior acquisition audit. At the time the letter was received, the audit field work related to an examination of the annual financial statements of the multinational enterprise was approximately one-half complete. The claim was not material to the capital of the international accounting firm, and the firm believed it had valid defenses against the allegations.

Conclusion: The asserted claim placed the accounting firm in a defensive position adverse to that of its client and thus caused the firm's independence to be impaired.

602.03 Retention of Records Relevant to Audits and Review

[Added by FR-66]

Section 802 of the Sarbanes-Oxley Act[1] is intended to address the destruction or fabrication of evidence and the preservation of "financial and

---

[1] Section 802 of the Sarbanes-Oxley Act, among other things, adds sections 1519 and 1520 to Chapter 73 of Title 18 of the United States Code. Section 1519 states, among other things, that anyone who knowingly alters, destroys, mutilates, conceals, covers up, falsifies, or makes a false entry in any record, document, or tangible object with the intent to impede, obstruct, or influence an investigation or proper administration of any matter within the jurisdiction of any department or agency of the United States or any case filed under the bankruptcy code, or in relation to or contemplation of any such matter or case, may be fined, imprisoned for not more than 20 years, or both.

Section 1520(a)(1) specifies that: "Any accountant who conducts an audit of an issuer of securities to which section 10A(a) of the Securities Exchange Act of 1934 applies, shall maintain all audit or review workpapers for a period of 5 years

from the end of the fiscal period in which the audit or review was concluded." Section 1520(a)(2) directs the Commission to promulgate by January 26, 2003:

. . . such rules and regulations, as are reasonably necessary, relating to the retention of relevant records such as workpapers, documents that form the basis of an audit or review, memoranda, correspondence, communications, other documents, and records (including electronic records) which are created, sent, or received in connection with an audit or review and contain conclusions, opinions, analyses, or financial data relating to such an audit or review, which is conducted by an accountant who conducts an audit of an issuer of securities to which section 10A(a) of the Securities Exchange Act of 1934 (15 U.S.C. 78j-1(a)) applies. The Commission may, from time to time, amend or supplement the rules and regulations that it is required to promulgate under this section, after audit records."[2] We are directed under that section to promulgate rules related to the retention of records relevant to the audits and reviews of financial statements that issuers file with the Commission.

Section 802 states that the record retention requirements should apply to audits of issuers of securities to which section 10A(a) of the Securities Exchange Act of 1934 ("Exchange Act") applies. The term "issuer" in this context is defined in section 10A(f) of the Exchange Act to include certain entities filing reports under that Act and entities that have filed and not withdrawn registration statements to sell securities under the Securities Act of 1933.[3] As adopted, the record retention requirements also apply to any audit or review of the financial statements of any registered investment company.[4] We believe that it is important for these record retention requirements, like our other record retention requirements, to apply consistently with respect to all registered investment companies, regardless of whether they fall within the periodic reporting requirements of the Exchange Act.[5]

Neither section 802 nor the final rule exempts auditors of foreign issuers' financial statements. Commenters, including the European Commission, noted that application of the rule to foreign auditors would place additional and differing layers of retention requirements on those firms.[6] However, none of the commenters identified any direct conflicts with foreign requirements.

The availability of documents under this rule will assist in the oversight and quality of audits of an issuer's financial statements. Increased retention of identified records also may provide critical evidence of financial reporting impropriety or deficiencies in the audit process. In light of these benefits, and absent a direct conflict with foreign requirements, the retention requirements are to apply equally to domestic and foreign accounting firms auditing the financial statements of foreign issuers. Issues raised by commenters regarding Public Company Accounting Oversight Board ("the Oversight Board") oversight of foreign accounting firms and access by the SEC and the Oversight Board to the records retained by foreign accounting firms, as provided by Section 106 of the Sarbanes-Oxley Act, will be the subject of further discussion among staff, the Commission and the Oversight Board.[7]

In restricting the application of the rule to the audits and reviews of the financial statements of issuers and registered investment companies, we are not condoning more liberal document destruction policies for the audits and reviews of financial statements of other entities. For example, we would expect that auditors of the financial statements of those investment advisers, broker-dealers, and entities subject to Municipal Securities Rulemaking Board regulations that are not subject to the rule would retain relevant audit and review records consistent with applicable laws, regulations, and professional standards.

(Footnote Continued)

adequate notice and an opportunity for comment, in order to ensure that such rules and regulations adequately comport with the purposes of this section.

Section 1520 also provides that any person who knowingly and willfully violates subsection (a)(1), or any rule or regulation promulgated by the Securities and Exchange Commission under subsection (a)(2), may be fined, imprisoned for not more than 10 years, or both. It further provides that nothing in section 1520 shall be deemed to diminish or relieve any person of any other duty or obligation imposed by Federal or State law or regulation to maintain, or refrain from destroying, any document.

[2] Floor statement by Senator Leahy, 148 Cong. Rec. S7418 (July 26, 2002).

[3] Section 802 states that the record retention requirement applies to "an audit of an issuer of securities to which section 10A(a) of the Securities Exchange Act of 1934 (15 U.S.C. 78j-1(a)) applies." Section 10A(a) of the Securities Exchange Act of 1934 ("Exchange Act") states, "Each audit required pursuant to this title of the financial statements of an issuer by an independent public accountant shall include" designated procedures. Section 10A(f), which has been added to the Exchange Act by section 205(d) of the Sarbanes-Oxley Act, states: "As used in this section the term 'issuer' means an issuer (as defined in section 3 [of the Exchange Act]), the securities of which are registered under section 12, or that is required to file reports pursuant to section 15(d), or that files or has filed a registration statement that has not yet become effective under the Securities Act of 1933 (15 U.S.C. 77a et seq.), and that it has not withdrawn." Section 3(a)(8) of the Exchange Act, 15 U.S.C. 78c(a)(8), states that, with certain exceptions, an "issuer" is "any person who issues or proposes

to issue any security . . . ." Accordingly, the definition of "issuer" includes entities that have filed and not withdrawn a registration statement for an initial public offering.

Because investment advisers and broker-dealers are not necessarily issuers, audits of their financial statements required for regulatory purposes are not subject to the rule. In other words, only the audits of the financial statements of investment advisers and broker-dealers meeting the definition of "issuer" in section 10A(f) are subject to the retention requirements in rule 2-06. One commenter suggested that investment advisers and broker-dealers be included within the scope of the rule. Letter from Lynette Downing, HLB Tautges Redpath, Ltd., dated December 27, 2002. Another commenter noted, however, that broadening some but not all rules under the Sarbanes-Oxley Act beyond "issuers" as defined in the Act would be confusing. Letter from Grant Thornton LLP dated December 27, 2002.

[4] *See* section 8 of the Investment Company Act of 1940, 15 U.S.C. 80a-8.

[5] *Cf.* rules 31a-1 and 31a-2 under the Investment Company Act of 1940, 17 CFR 270.31a-1 and 31a-2 (record-keeping and record-retention requirements for registered investment companies).

[6] Letter from the European Commission dated December 20, 2002; letter from PricewaterhouseCoopers dated December 27, 2002; letter from KPMG LLP dated December 27, 2002; letter from the American Institute of Certified Public Accountants dated December 27, 2002.

[7] We also note that this rule is not intended to expand or restrict the Commission exisiting authority to investigate cross-border violations of the federal securities laws.

Documents to be Retained

Paragraph (a) of rule 2-06 identifies the documents that must be retained and the time period for retaining those documents.[8] The final rule requires that the auditor[9] retain records relevant to the audit or review, including workpapers and other documents that form the basis of the audit or review of an issuer's financial statements, and memoranda, correspondence, communications, other documents, and records (including electronic records) that meet two criteria. The two criteria are that the materials (1) are created, sent or received in connection with the audit or review, and (2) contain conclusions, opinions, analyses, or financial data related to the audit or review.

Paragraph (a) of the proposed rule did not contain the phrase, "records relevant to the audit or review." The proposal listed the records to be retained without a reference to the general notion of relevance to the audit or review. In response to commenters,[10] and to track more closely the wording in section 802,[11] we have added those words to the final rule.

In the Proposing Release, we stated that non-substantive materials that are not part of the workpapers, such as administrative records, and other documents that do not contain relevant financial data or the auditor's conclusions, opinions or analyses would not meet the second of the criteria in rule 2-06(a) and would not have to be retained. Commentators questioned whether the following documents would be considered substantive and have to be retained:

- Superseded drafts of memoranda, financial statements or regulatory filings,[12]

- Notes on superseded drafts of memoranda, financial statements or regulatory filings that reflect incomplete or preliminary thinking,[13]

- Previous copies of workpapers that have been corrected for typographical errors or errors due to training of new employees,[14]

- Duplicates of documents,[15] or

- Voice-mail messages.[16]

These records generally would not fall within the scope of new rule 2-06 provided they do not contain information or data, relating to a significant matter, that is inconsistent with the auditor's final conclusions, opinions or analyses on that matter or the audit or review.[17] For example, rule 2-06 would require the retention of an item in this list if that item documented a consultation or resolution of differences of professional judgment.

Commenters also questioned whether all of the issuer's financial information, records, databases, and reports that the auditor examines on the issuer's premises, but are not made part of the auditor's workpapers or otherwise currently retained by the auditor, would be deemed to be "received" by the auditor under rule 2-06(a)(1) and have to be retained by the auditor.[18] We do not believe that Congress intended for accounting firms to duplicate and retain all of the issuer's financial information, records, databases, and reports that might be read, examined, or reviewed by the auditor. Accordingly, we do not believe that the "received" criterion in rule 2-06(a)(1) requires that such records be retained.

Some commentators suggested that paragraph (a) of the proposed rule was overly broad and that the language in the rule, rather than following section 802 of the Sarbanes-Oxley Act, should conform to current auditing standards.[19] It would appear, however, that by requiring the retention of documents in addition to audit workpapers required by generally accepted auditing standards ("GAAS") Congress has rejected this approach. Congress intended that accounting firms retain

---

[8] Rule 2-06 is not intended to pre-empt or supersede any other federal or state record retention requirements.

[9] Rule 2-06 uses the term "accountant," which is defined in rule 2-01(f)(1) of the Commission's auditor independence rules, 17 CFR 210.2-01(f)(1), to mean "a certified public accountant or public accountant performing services in connection with an engagement for which independence is required. References to the accountant include any accounting firm with which the certified public or public accountant is affiliated." In a companion release, the Commission proposed to amend this definition to include the term "registered public accounting firm." We will apply the definition in rule 2-01(f)(1), as amended, to rule 2-06.

[10] See, e.g., letter from Deloitte & Touche dated December 27, 2002, and letter from McGladrey & Pullen dated December 31, 2002, which states, in part, "The key to promulgating record retention rules that enhance audit quality lies in the word 'relevant'."

[11] See note 3, supra.

[12] See, e.g., letter from BDO Seidman, LLP, dated December 27, 2002; letter from Ernst & Young LLP, dated December 27, 2002; letter from PricewaterhouseCoopers dated December 27, 2002.

[13] See letter from BDO Seidman, LLP, dated December 27, 2002.

[14] See letter from Gelfond Hochstadt Pangburn, P.C. dated November 26, 2002.

[15] See letter from Ernst & Young LLP, dated December 27, 2002, and letter from Gelfond Hochstadt Pangburn, P.C. dated November 26, 2002.

[16] Letter from Sullivan & Cromwell dated December 26, 2002.

[17] Senator Leahy stated on the Senate floor, "Non-substantive materials, however, which are not relevant to the conclusions or opinions expressed (or not expressed), need not be included in such retention regulations." 148 Cong. Rec. S7419 (July 26, 2002).

[18] See, e.g., letter from PricewaterhouseCoopers dated December 27, 2002.

[19] See, e.g., letter from BDO Seidman, LLP, dated December 27, 2002; letter from Deloitte & Touche dated December 27, 2002; letter from Ernst & Young LLP, dated December 27, 2002; letter from Grant Thornton LLP dated December 27, 2002; letter from KPMG LLP dated December 27, 2002. See the discussion of Statement on Auditing Standards No. 96, "Audit Documentation," infra.

substantive materials that are relevant to the review or audit of financial statements filed with the Commission and enumerated the records described in the rule as being relevant to audits and reviews. Narrowing the scope of the rule to conform to the current auditing literature would be contrary to the apparent congressional purpose embodied in section 802.

Time of Retention

The final rule states that records must be retained for seven years. We proposed that these materials be retained for five years after the end of the fiscal period in which an accountant audits or reviews an issuer's financial statements,[20] which is the period prescribed by section 802.[21] We also noted in the Proposing Release, however, that section 103 of the Sarbanes-Oxley Act directs the Oversight Board to require auditors to retain for seven years audit workpapers and other materials that support the auditor's conclusions in any audit report.[22] There may be fewer documents retained pursuant to section 103, which focuses more on workpapers that support the auditor's conclusions, than under section 802, which includes not only workpapers but also other documents that meet the criteria noted in this release. Many documents, however, may be covered by both retention requirements.[23]

Some commenters suggested that we adopt a uniform seven-year retention period,[24] while others indicated that the longer period would increase audit costs without any commensurate benefit.[25] We anticipate that most accounting firms, for administrative convenience, would retain all relevant materials for the longer of the two periods prescribed by the Commission and by the Oversight Board.[26] Incremental costs associated with requiring a seven-year retention period, therefore, should not be significant. We also believe that adopting a seven-year retention period would reduce inconsistencies between the forthcoming Oversight Board rules and the Commission's rules and lessen any potential confusion related to the calculation of retention periods.[27] Accordingly, the final rule requires that auditors retain the required documents for seven years from the conclusion of the audit or review.

Workpapers Defined

Section 802 is intended to require the retention of more than what traditionally has been thought of as auditor's "workpapers."[28] To clarify the distinction between workpapers and other materials that would be retained, paragraph (b) of the final rule defines the term "workpapers." The legislative history to section 802 states that the term is to be used as it is "widely understood" by the Commission and by the accounting profession.[29] We believe that the term is understood to refer to the documents required to be retained by GAAS. GAAS does not use the specific term "workpapers,"[30] but Statement on Auditing Standards No. 96, "Audit Documentation," states, in part:

The auditor should prepare and maintain audit documentation, the content of which should be designed to meet the circumstances of the particular audit engagement. Audit documentation is the principal record of the auditing procedures ap-

---

[20] The proposed retention period was not based on the fiscal period covered by the financial statements being audited or reviewed, but when the audit or review would occur. For example, if a company has a calendar year-end fiscal year, for an audit of year 2002 financial statements that concludes in February or March 2003, under the proposal, the records would have been required to be retained until January 1, 2009.

[21] *See* Statement of Senator Leahy on the Senate floor: "[I]t is intended that the SEC promulgate rules and regulations that require the retention of such substantive material . . . for such a period as is reasonable and necessary for effective enforcement of the securities laws and the criminal laws, most of which have a five-year statute of limitations." 148 Cong. Rec. S7419 (July 26, 2002).

[22] The Oversight Board is required under section 103(a)(2)(A)(i) of the Sarbanes-Oxley Act to adopt an auditing standard that requires accounting firms registered with the Oversight Board to " . . . prepare, and maintain for a period of not less than 7 years, audit work papers, and other information related to any audit report, in sufficient detail to support the conclusions reached in such report." The standard to be adopted by the Oversight Board, therefore, is to be both a documentation and retention standard.

[23] *See, e.g.*, letter from KPMG LLP, dated December 27, 2002, which states, in part: "Clearly, the documents to be retained under both Sections [103 and 802] overlap to a large extent."

[24] *See, e.g.*, letter from Wendy Perez, President of California Board of Accountancy dated December 23, 2002; letter from

Grant Thornton LLP dated December 27, 2002; letter from Lynette Downing, HLB Tautges Redpath, Ltd., dated December 27, 2002.

[25] *See, e.g.*, letter form Donald G. DeBuck, Controller, Computer Sciences Corporation dated December 26, 2002; letter from PricewaterhouseCoopers dated December 27, 2002; letter from the American Institute of Certified Public Accountants dated December 27, 2002.

[26] *See e.g.*, letter from Grant Thornton LLP dated December 27, 2002, which states, "We believe that most firms will adopt a policy of retaining all audit documentation for the longer period of seven years."

[27] *Id.*

[28] Senator Leahy stated on the Senate floor that section 802 "requires the SEC to promulgate reasonable and necessary regulations . . . regarding the retention of categories of electronic and non-electronic audit records, which contain opinions, conclusions, analysis or financial data, in addition to the actual work papers." 148 Cong. Rec. S7418 (July 26, 2002).

[29] Statement by Senator Leahy on the Senate floor, 148 Cong. Rec. S7418 (July 26, 2002).

[30] American Institute of Certified Public Accountants ("AICPA"), Statement on Auditing Standards No. ("SAS") 96, "Audit Documentation," at footnote 1, however, acknowledges that: "*Audit Documentation* also may be referred to as *working papers*"; Codification of Statements on Auditing Standards ("AU") § 339.

plied, evidence obtained, and conclusions reached by the auditor in the engagement.[31]

We have placed the body of this provision into paragraph (b) and stated that "workpapers" means "documentation of auditing or review procedures applied, evidence obtained, and conclusions reached by the accountant in the audit or review engagement, as required by standards established or adopted by the Commission or by the Public Company Accounting Oversight Board."[32] The proposed rule, therefore, recognizes that the Oversight Board, subject to Commission oversight, has the ability to review and change the nature and scope of the required documentation of procedures, evidence, and conclusions related to audits and reviews of financial statements.[33]

As noted by several commenters, there may be significant overlap of the documents falling within the definition of "workpapers" and the documents that would be retained pursuant to the description in paragraph (a) of the rule of "other documents that form the basis of the audit or review, and memoranda, correspondence, communications, other documents, and records (including electronic records), which (1) are created, sent or received in connection with the audit or review, and (2) contain conclusions, opinions, analyses, or financial data related to the audit or review."[34]

Differences of Opinion

SAS 96 states that audit documentation serves mainly to provide the principal support for the auditor's report and to aid the auditor in the conduct and supervision of the audit.[35] Section 802, however, is intended to facilitate effective enforcement of the securities laws and criminal laws,[36] which requires the retention of not only records that *support* the auditor's report (as required by SAS 96) but also records that would be inconsistent with, or otherwise challenge, the conclusions in the auditor's report. In order to ensure that the purposes of the Act are fulfilled, we proposed that paragraph (c) of the rule include the specific requirement that the materials retained under paragraph (a) would include not only those that

support an auditor's conclusions about the financial statements but also those materials that may "cast doubt" on those conclusions.[37] We stated in the Proposing Release that paragraph (c) was intended to ensure the preservation of those records that reflect differing professional judgments and views (both within the accounting firm and between the firm and the issuer) and how those differences were resolved. To better communicate what we intended by "cast doubt" on the auditor's conclusions, we included in the proposed rule the example of documentation of differences of opinion concerning accounting and auditing issues.

The auditor in a variety of contexts may create materials related to differences of opinion. For example, SAS No. 22, "Planning and Supervision," states in part:

The auditor with final responsibility for the audit and assistants should be aware of the procedures to be followed when differences of opinion concerning accounting and auditing issues exist among firm personnel involved in the audit. Such procedures should enable an assistant to document his disagreement with the conclusions reached if, after appropriate consultation, he believes it necessary to disassociate himself from the resolution of the matter. In this situation, the basis for the final resolution should also be documented.[38]

An interpretation of this section issued by the AICPA's Auditing Standards Board emphasizes the professional obligation on each person involved in an audit engagement to bring his or her concerns to the attention of others in the firm and, as appropriate, to document those concerns. This interpretation states:

Accordingly, each assistant has a professional responsibility to bring to the attention of appropriate individuals in the firm, disagreements or concerns the assistant might have with respect to accounting and auditing issues that he believes are of significance to the financial statements or auditor's report, however those disagreements or concerns may have arisen. In addition, each assis-

---

[31] SAS 96, at ¶ 1; AU § 339.01. This paragraph also states: "The quality, type, and content of audit documentation are matters of the auditor's professional judgment." The rule does not include this sentence, but instead notes that the Commission or the Oversight Board may reexamine these requirements in the auditing standards.

[32] Prior to the establishment or adoption of auditing standards by the Oversight Board, "workpapers" would continue to mean the documentation of auditing or review procedures applied, evidence obtained, and conclusions reached by the accountant in the audit or review engagement as required by GAAS.

[33] *See* section 103(a) of the Sarbanes-Oxley Act.

[34] *See, e.g.,* letter from PricewaterhouseCoopers dated December 27, 2002.

[35] SAS 96, at ¶ 3; AU § 339.03.

[36] *See* Statement of Senator Leahy on the Senate floor, 148 Cong. Rec. S7419 (July 26, 2002).

[37] Senator Leahy stated on the

Senate floor:

In light of the apparent massive document destruction by Andersen, and the company's apparently misleading document retention policy, even in light of its prior SEC violations, it is intended that the SEC promulgate rules and regulations that require the retention of such substantive material, including material that casts doubt on the views expressed in the audit or review, for such a period as is reasonable and necessary for effective enforcement of the securities laws and the criminal laws, most of which have a five-year statute of limitations.

148 Cong. Rec. S7419 (July 26, 2002).

[38] SAS 22, ¶ 22 (as amended by SAS 47, 48 and 77); AU § 311.22. "Assistants," in the context of the first sentence of the quoted paragraph, is intended to include other partners who are on the audit engagement team.

tant should have a right to document his disagreement if he believes it is necessary to disassociate himself from the resolution of the matter.[39]

In addition, SAS 96 states that the documentation for an audit should include the findings or issues that in the auditor's judgment are significant, the actions taken to address them (including any additional evidence obtained), and the basis for the final conclusions reached.[40] For example, if a memorandum is prepared by a member of a large accounting firm's national office that is critical of the accounting used by an audit client, or of a position taken by the partner in charge of the audit of those financial statements, that memorandum should be retained.[41] Another example would be documentation related to an auditor's communications with an issuer's audit committee about alternative disclosures and accounting methods used by the issuer that are not the disclosures or accounting preferred by the auditor.[42]

We continue to believe that retaining any materials that might cast doubt on the final conclusions reflected in the auditor's report, including those created under SAS 22 and SAS 96, would be consistent with the letter and spirit of the Sarbanes-Oxley Act. One commenter, the National Association of State Boards of Accountancy ("NASBA"), endorsed requiring the retention of documents that "cast doubt" on an auditor's audit or review because "state attorneys' general staff members assigned to accountancy boards often have complained of receiving only those documents that support the final report." NASBA also noted, however, that the Commission promptly should revise the rule if it becomes too burdensome or otherwise unworkable.[43]

Several commentators stated that the proposed "cast doubt" language was unworkable. They indicated that the phrase was pejorative,[44] vague and unnecessary, and might be used to attribute doubt to virtually any remark made during an audit, regardless of its relevance or materiality.[45] One accounting firm stated that the proposed rule "could be read to require retention of every document reflecting an error however temporary - even typographical or addition errors made in preparing a workpaper . . . . It also could be read to require preservation of each and every exchange of differing views on any topic, however fleeting and trivial the differences."[46] Another accounting firm stated that on many occasions correcting or redoing workpapers is not the result of differences of opinion but from on-the-job training and a normal learning process.[47] One commenter stated that the "cast doubt" language in the proposed rule might deter auditors from asking legitimate questions.[48]

Some commenters suggested language to replace the provision in subparagraph (c) that documents be retained if they "cast doubt on the final conclusions reached by the auditor." For example, commenters suggested that records be retained only if they would constitute a reportable "disagreement" under Item 304 of Regulation S-K.[49] Item 304 indicates that a disagreement is reportable upon a change in an entity's principal accountant if, among other things, the disagreement occurs at the decision-making level on any matter of accounting principles or practices, financial statement disclosure, or auditing scope or procedure, which, if not resolved to the accountant's satisfaction, would cause the auditor to make ref-

---

[39] "Planning and Supervision: Auditing Interpretations of Section 311," AU § 9311.37. "Assistants," in the context of this interpretation, includes other partners who are on the audit engagement team.

[40] SAS 96, ¶ 9; AU § 339.09, which states:

In addition, the auditor should document findings or issues that in his or her judgment are significant, actions taken to address them (including any additional evidence obtained), and the basis for the final conclusions reached. *See also*, SAS 96, ¶ 6; AU § 339.06, which states:

Audit documentation should be sufficient to (a) enable members of the engagement team with supervision and review responsibilities to understand the nature, timing, extent, and results of auditing procedures performed, and the evidence obtained; (b) indicate the engagement team member(s) who performed and reviewed the work; and (c) show that the accounting records agree or reconcile with the financial statements or other information being reported on.

[41] Such a memorandum might be prepared in connection with the consultation process that is part of an accounting firm's quality controls. *See, e.g.*, Section 103(a)(2)(B)(ii) of the Sarbanes-Oxley Act.

[42] Section 204 of the Sarbanes-Oxley Act adds section 10A(k) to the Exchange Act and requires auditors to report certain matters to audit committees, including: "(a) all critical accounting policies and practices to be used, (2) all alternative treatments of financial information within generally accepted

accounting principles that have been discussed with management officials of the issuer, ramifications of the use of such alternative disclosures and treatments, and the treatment preferred by the registered public accounting firm; and (3) other material written communications between the registered public accounting firm and the management of the issuer, such as the management letter or schedule of unadjusted differences."

[43] Letter from K. Michael Conaway, Chair, NASBA, and David A. Costello, President and CEO, NASBA, dated December 23, 2002.

[44] Letter from Donald G. DeBuck, Computer Sciences Corporation, dated December 26, 2002.

[45] *See, e.g.*, letter from BDO Seidman, LLP, dated December 27, 2002; letter from Grant Thornton LLP dated December 27, 2002; letter from KPMG LLP dated December 27, 2002; letter from Deloitte & Touche LLP dated December 27, 2002.

[46] Letter from Ernst & Young LLP, dated December 27, 2002.

[47] Letter from Donald D. Pangburn, Director, Gelfond Hochstadt Pangburn, P.C., dated November 26, 2002.

[48] Letter from Sullivan & Cromwell dated December 26, 2002.

[49] *See, e.g.*, letter from Ernst & Young LLP, dated December 27, 2002; letter from PricewaterhouseCoopers dated December 27, 2002; letter from Deloitte & Touche dated December 27, 2002.

erence to the matter in connection with his or her audit report.[50]

We are reluctant, however, to follow Item 304 of Regulation S-K, which has a different purpose than the rule being adopted in this release. Item 304 requires disclosure to investors of potential "opinion shopping" situations and provides a forum for the registrant, the newly engaged auditor, and the former auditor to provide their views of "disagreements" and other "reportable events." New rule 2-06, on the other hand, addresses the retention of documents relevant to enforcement of the securities laws, Commission rules, and criminal laws. In the proposing release we asked if, in place of the "cast doubt" language, a different test for retention of documents would be appropriate. We specifically asked if such a test should be documentation of "significant differences in professional judgment" or "differences of opinion on issues that are material to the issuer's financial statements or to the auditor's final conclusions regarding any audit or review." Several commenters supported using one or a combination of these tests.[51]

In consideration of the comments received, we have revised paragraph (c) of the rule. We have removed the phrase "cast doubt" to reduce the possibility that the rule mistakenly would be interpreted to reach typographical errors, trivial or "fleeting" matters, or errors due to "on-the-job" training. We continue to believe, however, that records that either support or contain significant information that is inconsistent with the auditor's final conclusions would be relevant to an investigation of possible violations of the securities laws, Commission rules, or criminal laws and should be retained. Paragraph (c), therefore, now provides that the materials described in paragraph (a) shall be retained whether they support the auditor's final conclusions or contain information or data, relating to a significant matter, that is inconsistent with the final conclusions of the auditor on that matter or on the audit or review. Paragraph (c)

also states that the documents and records to be retained include, but are not limited to, those documenting consultations on or resolutions of differences in professional judgment.

The reference in paragraph (c) to "significant" matters is intended to refer to the documentation of substantive matters that are important to the audit or review process or to the financial statements of the issuer or registered investment company.[52] Rule 2-06(c) requires that the documentation of such matters, once prepared, must be retained even if it does not "support" the auditor's final conclusions, because it may be relevant to an investigation.[53] Similarly, the retention of records regarding a consultation about, and resolution of, differences in professional judgment would be relevant to such an investigation and must be retained. We intend for Rule 2-06 to be incremental to, and not to supersede or otherwise affect, any other legal or procedural requirement related to the retention of records or potential evidence in a legal, administrative, disciplinary, or regulatory proceeding.

Finally, we recognize that audits and reviews of financial statements are interactive processes and views within an accounting firm on accounting, auditing or disclosure issues may evolve as new information or data comes to light during the audit or review. We do not view "differences in professional judgment" within subparagraph (c) to include such changes in preliminary views when those preliminary views are based on what is recognized to be incomplete information or data.

Response to Other Significant Comments

In response to our request in the Proposing Release, commenters addressed whether issuers and registered investment companies should be required to retain documents that the auditor examines, reviews or otherwise considers during the audit or review but are not made part of the auditor's records. Commenters generally opposed

---

[50] Item 304 of Regulation S-K, 17 CFR 229.304.

[51] *See, e.g.,* letter from Sullivan & Cromwell dated December 26, 2002; letter from Lynette Downing, HLB Tautges Redpath, Ltd. dated December 27, 2002; letter from Grant Thornton LLP dated December 27, 2002; letter from KPMG LLP dated December 27, 2002; letter from the American Institute of Certified Public Accountants dated December 27, 2002.

[52] SAS 96 requires the auditor to document findings or issues that in his or her judgment are significant. It states that "significant audit findings or issues" include:

• "Matters that both (a) are significant and (b) involve issues regarding the appropriate selection, application, and consistency of accounting principles with regard to the financial statements, including related disclosures. Such matters often relate to (a) accounting for complex or unusual transactions or (b) estimates and uncertainties and, if applicable, the related management assumptions.

• "Results of auditing procedures that indicate that (a) the financial statements or disclosures could be materially mis-

stated or (b) auditing procedures need to be significantly modified.

• "Circumstances that cause significant difficulty in applying auditing procedures that the auditor considered necessary.

• "Other findings that could result in modification of the auditor's report." SAS 96, ¶ 9, AU § 339.09 (Footnote omitted.) This literature may provide helpful guidance as to the scope of the term "significant." However, the term significant as used in this rule is not limited to items identified in SAS 96. Moreover, we do not intend for the auditor's subjective judgment of whether a matter is significant to be determinative. Instead, we believe that the more objective test of what may be significant to a reasonable investor should be applied in evaluating whether information is "significant."

[53] *See* letter from Deloitte & Touche dated December 27, 2002, *quoting* Statement of Senator Orrin Hatch before the Senate Judiciary Committee (April 25, 2002): "I anticipate that the SEC will exercise its discretion to promulgate only those rules and regulations that are necessary to ensure that documents material to an audit or review, as well as any future investigation, are retained."

such a requirement.[54] One commenter indicated that it was unclear whether section 802 of the Sarbanes-Oxley Act applies to such records and that, if such a requirement was imposed, it would go beyond those documents that are relevant to the audit or review or that contain the auditor's conclusions, opinions, or analyses.[55] An accounting firm similarly stated that it was not practical for an issuer to keep track of the documents examined by the auditor and then apply the retention requirements to those documents.[56] An issuer commented that, due to the host of documents, databases, and other material provided to an auditor, it is impossible for an issuer to determine what, if any, documents provided to the auditor were relevant to the auditor or provided the basis for the auditor's conclusions.[57] Accordingly, we are not instituting such a requirement at this time.

We also requested comments on whether a transition period was necessary or appropriate in implementing the rule. Accounting firms[58] and a law firm[59] noted that time may be required to develop systems related to the retention of documents (particularly electronic documents) and to train people to use them. Accordingly, we have indicated in the beginning of this release that accounting firms should comply with the rule no later than October 31, 2003.

Several items were raised in the comment letters that may be addressed more appropriately by the Public Company Accounting Oversight Board. For example, one commenter suggested that the Commission adopt the standard promulgated by the General Accounting Office, or a previously proposed draft auditing standard, related to the form and content of audit workpapers.[60] This commenter also suggested that the Commission adopt standards requiring accounting firms to: document differences of opinion on issues that are material to the audit; have written documentation and destruction policies; document significant relationships regarding the auditor and issuer; and have auditors performing audit or review work related to the issuer's subsidiaries or foreign affiliates document all work performed and certify in writing that such documentation is complete and available for inspection.[61] These matters are more appropriately within the purview of setting auditing standards and should be addressed, in the first instance, by the Oversight Board.[62]

The same commenter suggested that the Commission provide that if audit work is not documented in the workpapers then the burden of proof shifts to the auditor to prove by a preponderance of evidence that the work in fact was performed.[63] We note that the retention requirements under SAS 96, as discussed above, and new rule 2-06 should provide documentation of all significant matters considered during the audit. If such work is performed but not documented, the auditor generally would violate GAAS or new rule 2-06.

Another commenter suggested that the Commission require that all accounting firms registered with the Public Company Accounting Oversight Board comply with consultation requirements, and related documentation requirements, currently prescribed by the SEC Practice Section of the American Institute of Certified Public Accountants for large accounting firms.[64] We believe these matters relate to quality control standards within the scope of the Oversight Board's standard setting authority and we encourage the Oversight Board to consider adoption of such requirements. This commenter also suggested that the Commission address the application of rule 2-06 to documents prepared for a firm's internal inspection or outside peer review.[65] Such documents generally would not be considered to be created, sent or received in connection with an audit or review engagement and, therefore, would not be within the new rule. We would encourage the Oversight Board to consider, however, whether there are circumstances in which certain of the records prepared for inspection purposes may be considered part of the audit or review workpapers.

602.04 Strengthening the Commission's Requirements Regarding Auditor Independence

[Added by FR-68]

---

[54] One commenter supported such a requirement. Letter from Lynette Downing, HLB Tautges Redpath, Ltd. dated December 27, 2002.

[55] Letter from Sullivan & Cromwell dated December 26, 2002.

[56] Letter from BDO Seidman, LLP dated December 27, 2002. *See also* letter from the American Institute of Certified Public Accountants dated December 27, 2002.

[57] Letter from Mr. Donald G. DeBuck, Computer Sciences Corporation, dated December 26, 2002.

[58] *See, e.g.*, letter from BDO Seidman, LLP dated December 27, 2002 and letter from KPMG LLP dated December 27, 2002.

[59] Letter from Sullivan & Cromwell dated December 26, 2002.

[60] Letter from Wendy S. Perez, President, California Board of Accountancy, dated December 23, 2002.

[61] *Id.*

[62] Sections 103(a) and 103(c) of the Sarbanes-Oxley Act empower the Oversight Board to establish auditing standards, including, to the extent it determines appropriate, adopting standards proposed by professional groups of accountants or by expert advisory groups convened by the Oversight Board.

[63] *Id.*

[64] Letter from BDO Seidman, LLP dated December 27, 2002. *See* Section 1000.08(q) of the SECPS membership requirements. This section requires large firms to have policies on internal consultations and to document: the matter, the action taken to address the matter, and the basis for the final conclusion reached. Under this provision, the auditor must either follow the position taken by the person consulted or appeal any disagreement to a higher level of authority within the firm for ultimate resolution.

[65] *Id.*

⫸→ *Amended effective May 6, 2003, Release No. 33-8183, 68 F.R. 6006.*

A. Conflicts of Interest Resulting from Employment Relationships

The Commission's previous rules deem an accounting firm to be not independent with respect to an audit client if a former partner, principal, shareholder, or professional employee of an accounting firm[1] accepts employment with a client if he or she has a continuing financial interest in the accounting firm or is in a position to influence the firm's operations or financial policies. These rules renumber, but do not otherwise change, that existing requirement.

Consistent with Section 206 of the Sarbanes-Oxley Act, we are adding a restriction on employment with audit clients by former employees of the accounting firm. The Act specifies that an accounting firm cannot perform an audit for a registrant:

[i]f a chief executive officer, controller, chief financial officer, chief accounting officer, or any person serving in an equivalent position for the issuer, was employed by that registered independent public accounting firm and *participated in any capacity in the audit* of that issuer during the 1-year period preceding the date of the initiation of the audit.[2]

(emphasis added)

Thus, the Act requires a "cooling off" period of one year before a member of the audit engagement team can begin working for the registrant in certain key positions. Based on the provisions of the Act, we proposed that the employment of former audit engagement team[3] members of an accounting firm in a financial reporting oversight role[4] at an audit client would cause the accounting firm not to be independent with respect to that registrant if they were members of the audit engagement team within one year prior to the commencement of procedures for the current audit engagement. The rules that we proposed would have applied to employment relationships entered into between "audit engagement team" members and their "audit clients."[5]

The concept of a "cooling-off" period before an auditor can take a position at the audit client was previously considered by the Independence Standards Board.[6] In considering a cooling-off period, the Independence Standards Board noted that a mandated cooling-off period for partners and professional staff might create a greater appearance of independence between the accounting firm and the registrant.[7] Ultimately, however, the Independence Standards Board provided for an alternative to a cooling-off period. The Independence Standards Board concluded that:

An audit firm's independence is impaired with respect to an audit client that employs a former firm professional who could, by reason of his or her knowledge of and relationships with the audit firm, adversely influence the quality or effectiveness of the audit, unless the firm has taken steps that effectively eliminate such risk.[8]

Independence Standards Board's Standard No. 3 specifically notes that additional caution is warranted when it has been less than one year since the professional disassociated him or herself from the firm.[9] The provisions of the Sarbanes-Oxley Act reflect the view that the passage of time is an additional safeguard to reduce the perceived loss of independence for the audit firm caused by the acceptance of employment by a member of the engagement team with an audit client.

Some commenters[10] stated that the rule should apply only to partners on the audit engagement team. However, we believe that the Act is clear that the cooling off period should apply more broadly. Additionally, our proposal would have applied to relationships between members of the audit engagement team and the audit client. Some commenters[11] believe that extending the requirement to the audit client was too broad. In some situations (such as certain affiliate companies), it could be difficult for the accounting firm and its audit clients to monitor and, in some cases, control the employment relationship.

Our proposed rule did not make a distinction based on the number of hours of audit, review, or attest services provided in determining who would be subject to this rule. The Act refers to individuals who "participated in any capacity in the audit."

---

[1] Consistent with our existing rules, the terms accounting firm and accountant are used interchangeably in this release. The term "accountant" is defined in § 210.2-01(f)(1) below.

[2] *See*, Section 206 of the Sarbanes-Oxley Act.

[3] *See*, Rule 2-01(f)(7).

[4] *See*, Rule 2-01(f)(3)(ii).

[5] *See*, Rule 2-01(f)(6).

[6] The Independence Standards Board was a private sector body that, from 1997 to 2001, was charged with the responsibility to set auditor independence standards for auditors of the financial statements of SEC registrants. See Financial Reporting Release Nos. 50 (February 18, 1998) and 50A (July 17, 2001).

[7] Independence Standards Board, "Employment with Audit Clients," *Discussion Memorandum 99-1* (March 12, 1999).

[8] Independence Standards Board, "Employment with Audit Clients," *Standard No. 3* (July 2000).

[9] *Id.*, ¶ 2(b)(iii).

[10] *See, e.g.,* letter from Asahi & Co., dated January 10, 2003; letter from CPA Associates, dated January 3, 2003; letter from International Group of Accounting Firms, dated December 24, 2002.

[11] *See, e.g.,* letter from Eli Lilly and Company, dated January 9, 2003; letter from KPMG, dated January 9, 2003; letter from PricewaterhouseCoopers, dated January 8, 2003; letter from Roland G. Ley, dated January 9, 2003.

Commenters[12] noted that not all members of the audit engagement team, as that term is currently defined, necessarily participate in a meaningful audit capacity.

As discussed both in our proposing release and in this release, the term "financial reporting oversight role" refers to any individual who has direct responsibility for oversight over those who prepare the registrant's financial statements and related information (e.g., management's discussion and analysis) that are included in filings with the Commission. Some commenters[13] stated that the final rule only should apply to the four named positions in the Act (e.g., chief executive officer, controller, chief financial officer, chief accounting officer). Other commenters,[14] however, agreed with the Commission's approach of using the concept of financial reporting oversight role.

In response to the issues raised by commenters,[15] we are requiring that when the lead partner, the concurring partner, or any other member of the audit engagement team[16] who provides more than ten hours of audit, review or attest services for the issuer accepts a position with the issuer in a financial reporting oversight role within the one year period preceding the commencement of audit procedures for the year that included employment by the issuer of the former member of the audit engagement team, the accounting firm is not independent with respect to that registrant. Our rule applies to all members of the audit engagement team unless specifically exempted, as discussed later in this section of the release.

We agree with the commenters[17] who noted that extending the requirement to the "audit client" might be difficult to monitor because of the potentially broad scope of that defined term—particularly in situations where a member of the audit engagement team begins employment with an affiliate of the audit client.[18] Accordingly, the rules that we are adopting apply to employment relationships entered into between members of the audit engagement team and the "issuer."[19]

The Commission recognizes that, in certain instances, there are individuals who meet the defini-

tion of engagement team members while spending a relatively small amount of time on audit-related matters of the issuer. For example, a staff member may be asked to spend one day of time to observe inventory. While the input may have been important to resolving specific aspects of the audit, the staff member likely has not had significant interaction with the audit engagement team or management of the issuer. However, it is likely that those who spent more than a de minimis amount of time on the engagement team did participate in a meaningful audit capacity. Because of their roles in the engagement, the lead and concurring partner always should participate in a meaningful audit capacity, regardless of the number of hours spent on the engagement.

In order to provide useful guidance, our rule on conflicts of interest resulting from employment relationships specifies that, other than the lead and concurring partner, an individual[20] must provide more than ten hours of service during the annual audit period[21] as a member of the engagement team to have participated in an audit capacity. The Commission previously has considered a threshold based on the number of hours of service and, based on our experience, concluded that use of ten hours of service to the client constitutes a reasonable basis for distinguishing whether there has been participation on the audit.[22]

The Commission has determined that using the "financial reporting oversight role" is a better test for the scope of the provision than the four particular officers named in the Act. As discussed in the definitions section of this release, the term financial reporting oversight role is not a new concept. Furthermore, in addition to naming four specific positions, the Act also states that the cooling off period applies to "any person serving in an equivalent position for the issuer." Because issuers do not use uniform titles nor do all named positions (e.g., controller) have uniform duties among all issuers, we believe that a more complete definition of the applicable positions is needed. Furthermore, the term financial reporting oversight role captures other key positions, such as members of the board of directors, who may

---

[12] See, e.g., letter from American Institute of Certified Public Accountants, dated January 9, 2003; letter from KPMG, dated January 9, 2003; letter from Instituted of Chartered Accountants of Scotland, dated January 8, 2003.

[13] See, e.g., letter from Eli Lilly and Company, dated January 9, 2003; letter from McGladrey & Pullen LLP, dated January 9, 2003; letter from PricewaterhouseCoopers, dated January 8, 2003; letter from Computer Sciences Corporation, dated January 13, 2003.

[14] See, e.g., letter from Consumer Federation of America, dated January 13, 2003.

[15] See, e.g., letter from Deloitte & Touche, dated January 10, 2003; letter from KPMG, dated January 9, 2003; letter from PricewaterhouseCoopers, dated January 8, 2003.

[16] See, Rule 2-01(f)(7).

[17] See, e.g., letter from KPMG, dated January 9, 2003; letter from PricewaterhouseCoopers, dated January 8, 2003.

[18] See, Rule 2-01(f)(4).

[19] See, Section 3(a)(8) of the Securities Exchange Act of 1934 (15 U.S.C. 78c(a)(8)).

[20] It should be noted that the ten hour threshold does not apply to the lead or concurring review partner. Such individuals are always subject to these rules, regardless of the number of hours of audit, review or attest services provided.

[21] This includes hours of service provided in reviewing the issuer's quarterly filing or in providing attest services for the issuer related to the audit.

[22] Use of ten hours as a threshold is consistent with the determination of a "covered person" as specified by § 210.2-01(f).

have significant interaction with the audit engagement team.

While the rule is intended to apply broadly to members of the audit engagement team, we recognize the need to provide accommodations for certain unique situations. In addition to the exemption discussed previously for those who provided ten or fewer hours of audit, review, or attest services, the final rule provides an exception for conflicts that are created through merger or acquisition. Some commenters[23] noted that an individual may have complied fully with the rule and, subsequent to his or her beginning employment with an issuer, the issuer merged with or was acquired by another entity resulting in he or she becoming a person in a financial reporting oversight role of the combined entity and the combined entity being audited by the individual's previous employer. In such a situation, unless the employment was taken in contemplation of the combination, the individual or the issuer could not be expected to know that his or her employment decision would result in a conflict. Thus, as long as the audit committee is aware of this conflict, the audit firm would continue to be independent under these rules.

Further, we recognize that other unusual situations that may arise. For example, some commenters[24] have stated that in certain foreign jurisdiction it may be extremely difficult or costly to comply with these requirements. Accordingly, we have provided an additional exemption for emergency or unusual circumstances which we anticipate being invoked very rarely. However, in order for a company to avail itself of this exemption, the audit committee[25] must determine that doing so is in the best interests of investors.

Some commenters[26] stated that determining the time period of the prohibition would be difficult to apply as proposed. We recognize the difficulties when there is, potentially, a different applicable date for each member of the engagement team. For that reason, our final rule adopts a uniform date for all members of the engagement team.

For purposes of this rule, audit procedures are deemed to have commenced for the current audit engagement period the day after the prior year's periodic annual report (*e.g.*, Form 10-K, 10-KSB, 20-F or 40-F) is filed with the Commission. The audit engagement period for the current year is deemed to conclude the day the current year's periodic annual report (for example, Form 10-K,

10-KSB, 20-F or 40-F) is filed with the Commission.

To illustrate the application of this rule, assume that Issuer A's Forms 10-K are filed on March 15, 2003, April 5, 2004, March 10, 2005, and March 30, 2006. Issuer A is a calendar-year reporting entity. The audit engagement periods would be deemed to commence and end:

Annual Period	Engagement Period Commences	Engagement Period Ends
2003	March 16, 2003	April 5, 2004
2004	April 6, 2004	March 10, 2005
2005	March 11, 2005	March 30, 2006

If audit engagement person B provided audit, review or attest services for Issuer A *at any time* during the 2003 engagement period (March 16, 2003 - April 5, 2004), and he or she begins employment with Issuer A in a financial reporting oversight role prior to March 11, 2005, the accounting firm would be deemed to be not independent with respect to Issuer A. For example, if person B last performed audit, review or attest services for Issue A on March 24, 2003 and he or she began employment with Issuer A in a financial reporting oversight role prior to March 11, 2005, the accounting firm would be deemed to be not independent with respect to Issuer A. Likewise, if person B provided audit, review or attest services for Issuer A at any time during the 2004 engagement period (April 6, 2004 - March 10, 2005) and he or she began employment with Issuer A in a financial reporting oversight role prior to March 31, 2006, the accounting firm would be deemed to be not independent with respect to Issuer A.

The Act specifies that the cooling off period must be one year. Under our rules, the prohibition would require that the accounting firm has completed one annual audit[27] subsequent to when an individual was a member of the audit engagement team. As previously discussed, the measurement period is based upon the dates the issuer filed its annual financial information with the Commission.

With respect to investment companies, we proposed that the employment of a former audit engagement team member in a financial reporting

---

[23] *See, e.g.*, letter from Deloitte & Touche, dated January 10, 2003; letter from KPMG, dated January 9, 2003; letter from PricewaterhouseCoopers, dated January 8, 2003.

[24] *See, e.g.*, letter from Deloitte & Touche, dated January 10, 2003; letter from European Commission, dated January 13, 2003.

[25] These rules do not require the company to have an independent audit committee. *See,* discussion of definitions in this release.

[26] *See, e.g.*, letter from Ernst & Young, dated January 6, 2003; letter from KPMG, dated January 9, 2003; letter from Sullivan & Cromwell LLP, dated January 10, 2003; letter from California Public Employees' Retirement System, dated January 10, 2003.

[27] As used here, the term annual audit also includes procedures needed to conduct timely review of interim periods as well as procedures needed to attest to the registrant's internal controls.

oversight role at any entity in the same investment company complex during the one year period after the completion of the last audit would impair the independence of the accounting firm with respect to the audit client. The proposed rule was designed to prevent a former audit engagement team member from taking a position in an investment company complex where they could influence the preparation of the financial statements or the conduct of the audit.

Several commenters[28] suggested this requirement was too broad and could have unintended consequences, such as preventing a former audit engagement team member on an investment company audit engagement from taking a financial reporting position at an entity in the investment company complex whose operations are unrelated to the investment company. Some commenters[29] acknowledged, however, that it was in investors' interests to prevent audit engagement team members from leaving the firm and assuming a financial reporting oversight role at an entity in the investment company complex that had responsibility for the financial reporting or operations of the investment company audit client. One commenter[30] suggested the rule should not apply to positions at service providers solely because they are in the investment company complex.

Due to the unique structure of investment companies, where the normal operating activities, including activities related to the preparation of financial statements, are provided by outside service providers, we believe the rules need to extend beyond the investment company itself. After considering the comments, we agree, however, that the reach of the rule as proposed was too broad and have determined to tailor the scope of the rule with respect to investment companies to those situations where independence could be impaired. As adopted, an accounting firm would not be independent if a former audit engagement team member is employed in a financial reporting oversight role with not only the registered investment company, but also with any entity in the same investment company complex that is responsible for the financial reporting or operations of the registered investment company or any other registered investment company in the same investment company complex. The adopted rule prohibits employment in positions at an investment company complex that would allow a former audit engagement team member to bring undue influence over the audit process of an investment company. The rule recognizes that certain positions

exist at an entity in the investment company complex that would be considered financial reporting or oversight positions but those positions have no direct influence in the financial reporting or operations of an investment company in the investment company complex. In these instances, we believe tailoring the focus of this rule will not harm investor interests.

We recognize the need to provide for orderly transition. We believe it would be unfair to expect those who began employment before the effective date of these rules to be asked to sever those employment relationships. Accordingly, these rules are effective for employment relationships with the issuer that commence after the effective date of these rules.

B. Scope of Services Provided by Auditors

Section 201(a) of the Sarbanes-Oxley Act adds new Section 10A(g) to the Securities Exchange Act of 1934. Except as discussed below, this section states that it shall be unlawful for a registered public accounting firm that performs an audit of an issuer's financial statements (and any person associated with such a firm) to provide to that issuer, contemporaneously with the audit, any non-audit services, including the nine categories of services set forth in the Act. Additionally, the Act provides that the provision of "any non-audit service, including tax services, that is not described" as a prohibited service, can be provided by the auditor without impairing the auditor's independence "only if" the service has been pre-approved by the issuer's audit committee. The nine categories of prohibited non-audit services included in the Act are:

- Bookkeeping or other services related to the accounting records or financial statements of the audit client;
- Financial information systems design and implementation;
- Appraisal or valuation services, fairness opinions, or contribution-in-kind reports;
- Actuarial services;
- Internal audit outsourcing services;
- Management functions or human resources;
- Broker or dealer, investment adviser, or investment banking services;
- Legal services and expert services unrelated to the audit; and
- Any other service that the Board[31] determines, by regulation, is impermissible.

The Commission's principles of independence with respect to services provided by auditors are

---

[28] *See,* letter from Deloitte & Touche, dated January 10, 2003; letter from PricewaterhouseCoopers, dated January 8, 2003; letter from Investment Company Institute, dated January 13, 2003.

[29] *See,* letter from Investment Company Institute, dated January 13, 2003; letter from Deloitte & Touche, dated January 10, 2003.

[30] *See,* letter from PricewaterhouseCoopers dated January 8, 2003.

[31] As used in this section of the Act, the term Board refers to the Public Company Accounting Oversight Board.

largely predicated on three basic principles, violations of which would impair the auditor's independence: (1) an auditor cannot function in the role of management, (2) an auditor cannot audit his or her own work, and (3) an auditor cannot serve in an advocacy role for his or her client.[32]

Some commenters[33] stated that the Commission should prohibit the audit firm from performing most, if not all, non-audit services. Others commenters[34] supported a less strict approach. Consistent with our proposing release,[35] we are adopting rules related to the scope of services that independent accountants can provide to their audit clients. In adopting these rules, the Commission is clarifying the scope of the prohibited services. The prohibited services contained in these rules only apply to non-audit services provided by independent accountants to their audit clients. These rules do not limit the scope of non-audit services provided by an accounting firm to a non-audit client. Under the Act, the responsibility falls on the audit committee to pre-approve all audit and non-audit services provided by the accountant.

Recognizing that audit clients may need a period of time to exit existing contracts our rules provide that until May 6, 2004, the provision of services described in § 210.2-01(c)(4) will not impair an accountant's independence *provided* those services are pursuant to contracts in existence on May 6, 2003.[36]

1. Bookkeeping or Other Services Related Accounting Records or Financial Statements of the Audit Client

Previously, an auditor's independence was impaired if the auditor provided bookkeeping services to an audit client, except in limited situations, such as in an emergency or where the services are provided in a foreign jurisdiction and certain conditions were met. The current Rule 2-01(c)(4)(i) continues the prohibition on bookkeeping, but we have eliminated the limited situations where bookkeeping services could have been provided under the previous rules.

Some commenters[37] suggested that bookkeeping services should be permitted, especially under the previous exceptions. However, our independence rules are predicated on the three basic principles enumerated earlier. One of those principles is that an auditor cannot audit his or her own work and maintain his or her independence. When an accounting firm provides bookkeeping services for an audit client, the firm may be put in the position of later auditing the accounting firm's own work. If, during an audit, an accountant must audit the bookkeeping work performed by his or her accounting firm, it is questionable that the accountant could, or that a reasonable investor would believe that the accountant could, remain objective and impartial. If the accountant found an error in the bookkeeping, the accountant could well be under pressure not to raise the issue with the client if raising the issue could jeopardize the firm's contract with the client for bookkeeping services or result in heightened litigation risk for the firm. In addition, keeping the books is a management function, which also is prohibited.[38]

Accordingly, we are adopting rules stating that all bookkeeping services would cause the auditor to lack independence unless it is reasonable to conclude that the results will not be subject to audit procedures. We proposed to prohibit bookkeeping services unless it was "reasonably likely that such services would not be subject to audit procedures." Our final rules make clear the presumption to emphasize the responsibility the accounting firm has in making a determination that the bookkeeping services will not be subject to audit procedures.

The rules utilize the previous definition of bookkeeping or other services, which focuses on the provision of services involving: (1) maintaining or preparing the audit client's accounting records, (2) preparing financial statements that are filed with the Commission or the information that forms the basis of financial statements filed with the Commission, or (3) preparing or originating source data underlying the audit client's financial statements. Our experience with this definition demonstrates that the concept of bookkeeping and other services is well understood in practice.

We understand that accountants sometimes are asked to prepare statutory financial statements for foreign companies, and these are not filed with us. Consistent with the Commission's previous rules,

---

[32] *See,* Preliminary note to Rule 2-01 of Regulation S-X, 17 CFR 210.2-01.

[33] *See, e.g.,* letter from California Public Employees' Retirement System, dated January 10, 2003; letter from William E. Fraser, dated November 26, 2002; letter from Ellen Sweet, dated November 26, 2002; letter from Council on Institutional Investors, dated January 10, 2003.

[34] *See, e.g.,* letter from Chamber of Commerce of the United States of America, dated January 9, 2003; letter from America's Community Bankers, dated January 13, 2003; letter from Deloitte & Touche LLP, dated January 10, 2003; letter from American Society of Corporate Secretaries, dated January 13, 2003.

[35] 17 CFR PARTS 210, 240, 249 and 274.

[36] Additionally, in the unusual instance where additional time is needed to exit and existing contract, the staff in the Office of the Chief Accountant or the Public Company Accounting Oversight Board may be consulted on a case by case basis.

[37] *See, e.g.,* letter from American Institute of Certified Public Accountants, dated January 9, 2003; letter from Radin, Gloss & Co., dated December 31, 2002; letter from Grant Thornton LLP, dated January 13, 2003; letter from International Federation of Accountants, dated January 10, 2003.

[38] Letter of Samuel L. Burke, Associate Chief Accountant, SEC, to Florida Institute of Certified Public Accountants re: bookkeeping (March 4, 2002).

an accountant's independence would be impaired where the accountant prepared the statutory financial statements if those statements form the basis of the financial statements that are filed with us. Under these circumstances, an accountant or accounting firm who has prepared the statutory financial statements of an audit client is put in the position of auditing its own work when auditing the resultant U.S. GAAP financial statements.

With respect to the prohibitions on (1) bookkeeping; (2) financial information systems design and implementation; (3) appraisal, valuation, fairness opinions, or contribution-in-kind reports; (4) actuarial; and (5) internal audit outsourcing, the rules state that the service may not be provided "unless it is reasonable to conclude that the results of these services will not be subject to audit procedures during an audit of the audit client's financial statements."[39] As proposed, for bookkeeping, appraisal or valuation, and actuarial services, the provision was "where it is reasonably likely that the results of these services will be subject to audit procedures during an audit of the audit client's financial statements" while for the other two services, there was no such wording. We have added the new wording to all five services to provide consistency in application. Additionally, the change from "reasonably likely . . ." to "unless it is reasonable to conclude" is intended to narrow the circumstances in which that condition can be invoked to justify the provision of such services.[40]

2. Financial Information Systems Design and Implementation

Currently, Paragraph (c)(4)(ii) identifies certain information technology services that, if provided to an audit client, impair the accountant's independence. The proposed rules identified information technology services that would impair the auditor's independence. Under Paragraph (c)(4)(ii)(A) of the proposed rule, an accountant would not be independent if the accountant directly or indirectly operates or supervises the operation of the audit client's information system or manages the audit client's local area network or information system. Further, Paragraph (c)(4)(ii)(B) of the proposed rule provided that an accountant is *not* deemed independent if the accountant designs or implements a hardware or software system that aggregates source data underlying the financial statements or generates information that is signifi-

cant to the audit client's financial statements taken as a whole. These services were deemed to impair an accountant's independence under our previous rules.

Some commenters[41] suggested that the Commission's rules should include a dollar threshold limit or other qualifying language. Others[42] suggested that the Commission should clarify that the prohibition on designing and implementing systems would include selecting and testing a client's financial information system. Commenters[43] also believe that the Commission should clarify that recommendations for improvements in the systems should be permitted.

The Commission is adopting rules, consistent with our previous rules, that prohibited the accounting firm from providing any service related to the audit client's information system, unless it is reasonable to conclude that the results of these services will not be subject to audit procedures during an audit of the audit client's financial statements. These rules do not preclude an accounting firm from working on hardware or software systems that are unrelated to the audit client's financial statements or accounting records as long as those services are pre-approved by the audit committee.

As noted above, the rule prohibits the accountant from designing or implementing a hardware or software system that aggregates source data or generates information that is "significant" to the financial statements taken as a whole. In this context, information would be "significant" if it is reasonably likely to be material to the financial statements of the audit client. Since materiality determinations may not be complete before financial statements are generated, the audit client and accounting firm by necessity will need to evaluate the general nature of the information as well as system output during the period of the audit engagement. An accountant, for example, would not be independent of an audit client for which it designed an integrated Enterprise Resource Planning ("ERP") or similar system since the system would serve as the basis for the audit client's financial reporting system.

Designing, implementing, or operating systems affecting the financial statements may place the accountant in a management role, or result in the accountant auditing his or her own work or attesting to the effectiveness of internal control systems

---

[39] An example of a situation where it would be reasonable to conclude that the results would not be subject to audit procedures would be where an accounting firm provides a prohibited service to an affiliate of the client, as defined in Rule 2-01(f)(4), but the accounting firm is not the auditor of the entity or entities that controls the accounting firm's audit client or its affiliate.

[40] As such, there is a rebuttable presumption that the services are subject to audit procedures.

[41] *See, e.g.*, letter from Radin, Glass & Co., dated December 31, 2002; letter from Institute of Chartered Accountants in England & Wales, dated December 24, 2002; letter from Deloitte & Touche LLP, dated January 10, 2003.

[42] *See, e.g.*, letter from HarborView Partners LLC, dated December 4, 2002; letter from California Public Employees' Retirement System, dated January 10, 2003; letter from Center for Investor Trust, dated January 13, 2003.

[43] *See, e.g.*, letter from Sullivan & Cromwell LLP, dated January 10, 2003.

designed or implemented by that accountant.[44] For example, if an auditor designs or installs a computer system that generates the financial records, and that system generates incorrect data, the accountant is placed in a position of having to report on his or her firms' own work. Investors may perceive that the accountant would be unwilling to challenge the integrity and efficacy of the client's financial or accounting information collection systems that the accountant designed or installed.

However, this prohibition does not preclude the accountant from evaluating the internal controls of a system as it is being designed, implemented or operated either as part of an audit or attest service and making recommendations to management. Likewise, the accountant would not be precluded from making recommendations on internal control matters to management or other service providers in conjunction with the design and installation of a system by another service provider.

3. Appraisal or Valuation Services, Fairness Opinions, or Contribution-in-Kind Reports

The Commission's previous independence rules stated that an accountant is deemed to lack independence when providing appraisal or valuation services, fairness opinions, or contribution-in-kind reports for audit clients. However, the previous rules contained certain exemptions that we proposed to eliminate.[45] The proposals provided that the auditor is not independent if the auditor provides appraisal or valuation services, or contribution-in-kind reports,[46] where it is reasonably likely that the results of the service will not be subject to audit procedures by the auditor because the auditor is in a position of auditing his or her own work. Additionally, an accountant was not independent under the proposal if he or she provided a fairness opinion because to do so requires the accountant to function as a part of management and may require the accountant to audit the results of his or her own work.

Appraisal and valuation services include any process of valuing assets, both tangible and intangible, or liabilities. They include valuing, among other things, in-process research and development, financial instruments, assets and liabilities

acquired in a merger, and real estate. Fairness opinions and contribution-in-kind reports are opinions and reports in which the firm provides its opinion on the adequacy of consideration in a transaction.

Some commenters[47] believe that our proposed prohibitions were appropriate and others would be even more restrictive.[48] Other commenters,[49] however, believe that certain valuation services should be permissible.

We continue to believe that providing these services to audit clients raises several independence concerns. When it is time to audit the financial statements, it is likely that the accountant would review his or her own work, including key assumptions or variables that underlie an entry in the financial statements. Also, if the appraisal methodology involves a projection of future results of operations and cash flows, some[50] believe that the accountant that prepares the projection may be unable to evaluate skeptically and without bias the accuracy of that valuation or appraisal. Accordingly, the rules we are adopting prohibit the accountant from providing any appraisal service, valuation service or any service involving a fairness opinion or contribution-in-kind report for an audit client, unless it is reasonable to conclude that the results of these services will not be subject to audit procedures during an audit of the audit client's financial statements.

Our rules do not prohibit an accounting firm from providing such services for non-financial reporting (e.g., transfer pricing studies, cost segregation studies, and other tax-only valuations) purposes. Also, the rule does not prohibit an accounting firm from utilizing its own valuation specialist to review the work performed by the audit client itself or an independent, third-party specialist employed by the audit client, provided the audit client or the client's specialist (and not the specialist used by the accounting firm) provides the technical expertise that the client uses in determining the required amounts recorded in the client financial statements. In those instances the accountant will not be auditing his or her own work because a third party or the audit client is the source of the financial information subject to

---

[44] *See*, Section 404(b) of the Sarbanes-Oxley Act.

[45] Exemptions proposed to be eliminated included: (1) firm's valuation expert can review the work of a client's specialist; (2) firm's actuaries can value a client's pension or other post-retirement benefit obligation provided that the client assumes responsibility for significant assumptions; (3) valuations performed for planning and implementing tax-planning strategies; and (4) valuations for non-financial purposes which do not affect the financial statements.

[46] Laws or regulations in certain foreign countries require the auditor in connection with designated transac tions of its audit clients, to provide contribution-in-kind reports that express an opinion on the fairness of the transaction, the value of a security, or the adequacy of consideration to shareholders.

[47] *See, e.g.,* letter from Piercy, Bowler, Taylor & Kern, dated January 7, 2003; letter from Robert G. Beard, undated; letter from BDO Seidman LLP, dated January 13, 2003.

[48] *See, e.g.,* letter from Stikeman Elliot, dated January 13, 2003; letter from California Public Employees' Retirement System, dated January 10, 2003.

[49] *See, e.g.,* letter from American Institute of Certified Public Accountants, dated January 9, 2003; letter from HSBC, dated January 1, 2003; letter from PricewaterhouseCoopers, dated January 8, 2003.

[50] *See, e.g.,* letter from Aurora Group, dated January 13, 2003; letter from Cowhey, Girard Consulting, dated December 30, 2002.

the audit. Additionally, the quality of the audit may be improved where specialists are utilized in such situations.

Some commenters[51] believe that a strict application of these rules related to contribution-in-kind reports may create conflicts in certain foreign jurisdictions. We are sensitive to these issues and, as we have done in the past,[52] we will continue to work with other regulatory agencies.

4. Actuarial Services

The previous rules generally bar auditors only from providing actuarial services related to insurance company policy reserves and related accounts. Our proposal provided that the accountant is not independent if the auditor provides any actuarial service involving the amounts recorded in the financial statements and related accounts for the audit client where it is reasonably likely that the results of these services will be subject to audit procedures during an audit of the audit client's financial statements because providing these services may cause an accountant later to audit his or her own work. Additionally, accountants providing these services assume a key management task. In addition, actuarially-oriented advisory services may affect amounts reflected in some company's financial statements.

Some commenters[53] agreed with our proposed prohibition of actuarial services. Others,[54] however, believe that some types of actuarial services should be permitted.

Consistent with our proposal, we continue to believe that when the accountant provides actuarial services for the client, he or she is placed in a position of auditing his or her own work. Accordingly, the rules we are adopting prohibit an accountant from providing to an audit client any actuarially-oriented advisory service involving the determination of amounts recorded in the financial statements and related accounts for the audit client other than assisting a client in understanding the methods, models, assumptions, and inputs used in computing an amount, unless it is reasonable to conclude that the results of these services will not be subject to audit procedures during an audit of the audit client's financial statements.

As can be seen, however, we believe that it is appropriate to advise the client on the appropriate actuarial methods and assumptions that will be used in the actuarial valuations. It is not appropriate for the accountant to provide the actuarial valuations for the audit client.

The rules also provide that the accountant may utilize his or her own actuaries to assist in conducting the audit provided the audit client uses its own actuaries or third-party actuaries to provide management with its actuarial capabilities.

5. Internal Audit Outsourcing

Our previous rules on internal audit outsourcing allowed a company to outsource part of its internal audit function to the independent audit firm subject to certain exemptions. For example, smaller businesses were exempt from the internal audit outsourcing prohibition because there had been concerns about the potentially disproportionate impact on such companies.

Some companies "outsource" internal audit functions by contracting with an outside source to perform, among other things, all or part of their audits of internal controls. As emphasized by the Committee of Sponsoring Organizations ("COSO"), internal auditors play an important role in evaluating and monitoring a company's internal control system.[55] As a result, some argue that internal auditors are, in effect, part of a company's system of internal accounting control.[56]

Since the external auditor typically will rely, at least to some extent, on the existence of an internal audit function and consider its impact on the internal control system when conducting the audit of the financial statements,[57] the accountant may be placed in the position of auditing his or her firm as part of the internal control system. In other words, if the internal audit function is outsourced to an accountant, the accountant assumes a management responsibility and becomes part of the company's control system. Our proposed rule provided that an accountant is not independent when the accountant performs internal audit services related to the internal accounting controls, financial systems, or financial statements, for an audit client.

---

[51] *See, e.g.*, letter from Japanese Institute of Certified Public Accountants, dated January 13, 2003; letter from The Hundred Group of Finance Directors, dated January 13, 2003; letter from European Commission, dated January 13, 2003.

[52] Letter of Lynn Turner, Chief Accountant, SEC, to Commissione Nazionale per le Societa e la Borsa re: auditor independence (August 24, 2000). In that letter, the Chief Accountant did not deem the auditor's independence to be impaired where there were certain agreed-upon procedures for the contribution-in-kind report and the accountant represented in the report that the report did not express an opinion on the fairness of the transaction, the value of the security, or the adequacy of consideration to shareholders. This letter is available on our website.

[53] *See, e.g.*, letter from California Public Employees' Retirement System, dated January 10, 2003; letter from Aon Consulting, dated January 13, 2003.

[54] *See, e.g.*, letter from PricewaterhouseCoopers, dated January 8, 2003; letter from Deloitte & Touche LLP, dated January 10, 2003; letter from General Electric Company, dated January 9, 2003.

[55] *See*, Committee of Sponsoring Organizations of the Treadway Commission (COSO), *Internal Control - Integrated Framework*, at 7 (1992) (the "COSO Report").

[56] *See*, SAS No. 65, "The Auditor's Consideration of the Internal Audit Function in an Audit of Financial Statements," AU § 322.

[57] SAS No. 55, "Consideration of Internal Control in a Financial Audit," AU § 319.

Some commenters[58] agreed with the proposed rule. While some commenters[59] believed that our rule should contain exemptions for smaller companies, others[60] did not. Some commenters[61] believed that the final rule should include a "reasonably likely to be subject to audit procedures" provision similar to other prohibited services (*e.g.*, bookkeeping). Still other commenters[62] suggested that the Commission should clarify that services provided in conjunction with an audit or attest service are permissible.

The rules we are adopting prohibit the accountant from providing to the audit client internal audit outsourcing services. This prohibition would include any internal audit service that has been outsourced by the audit client that relates to the audit client's internal accounting controls, financial systems, or financial statements unless it is reasonable to conclude that the results of these services will not be subject to audit procedures during an audit of the audit client's financial statements.

During the conduct of the audit in accordance with generally accepted auditing standards ("GAAS") or when providing attest services related to internal controls, the auditor evaluates the company's internal controls and, as a result, may make recommendations for improvements to the controls. Doing so is a part of the accountant's responsibilities under GAAS or applicable attestation standards and, therefore, does not constitute an internal audit outsourcing engagement.

Along those lines, this prohibition on "outsourcing" does not preclude engaging the accountant to perform nonrecurring evaluations of discrete items or other programs that are not in substance the outsourcing of the internal audit function. For example, the company may engage the accountant, subject to the audit committee pre-approval requirements, to conduct "agreed-upon procedures" engagements[63] related to the company's internal controls, since management takes responsibility for the scope and assertions in those engagements. The prohibition also does not preclude the accountant from performing operational internal audits unrelated to the internal accounting controls, financial systems, or financial statements.

6. Management Functions.

In our proposal, we did not propose any significant change to our previous rule on management functions. Some commenters[64] suggested that we clarify that evaluations of and recommendations for improvements in a company's systems or controls does not constitute a management function.

Consistent with our proposal, the final rules prohibit the accountant from acting, temporarily or permanently, as a director, officer, or employee of an audit client, or performing any decision-making, supervisory, or ongoing monitoring function for the audit client.

We believe, however, that services in connection with the assessment of internal accounting and risk management controls, as well as providing recommendations for improvements, do not impair an accountant's independence. Accountants must gain an understanding of their audit clients' systems of internal controls when conducting an audit in accordance with GAAS.[65] With this insight, accountants often become involved in diagnosing, assessing, and recommending to audit committees and management ways in which their audit client's internal controls can be improved or strengthened.[66] The resulting improvements in the audit client's controls not only result in improved financial reporting to investors but also can facilitate the performance of high quality audits. For these reasons, we are continuing to allow accountants to assess the effectiveness of an audit client's internal controls and to recommend improvements in the design and implementation of internal controls and risk management controls.

As discussed in the previous section on financial information systems design and implementation, when an accountant designs and implements its audit client's internal accounting and risk management control systems, some believe that the accountant will lack objectivity if called upon to audit financial statements that are derived, at least in part, from data from those systems or to report on

---

[58] *See, e.g.*, letter from Perry Adkins, dated December 24, 2002; letter from The Center for Investor Trust, dated January 13, 2003.

[59] *See, e.g.*, letter from James L. Crites, dated December 28, 2002; letter from Cranmore, FitzGerald & Meaney, dated December 27, 2002; letter from America's Community Bankers, dated January 13, 2003; letter from Dixon Odom LLC, dated December 20, 2002.

[60] *See, e.g.*, letter from California Public Employees' Retirement System, dated January 10, 2003; letter from Institute of Internal Auditors, dated January 13, 2003.

[61] *See, e.g.*, letter from Deloitte & Touche, dated January 10, 2003; letter from Ernst & Young LLP, dated January 6, 2003.

[62] *See, e.g.*, letter from Hansen, Barnett & Maxwell, dated January 13, 2003; letter from Deloitte & Touche LLP, dated January 10, 2003; letter from PricewaterhouseCoopers, dated January 8, 2003; letter from American Institute of Certified Public Accountants, dated January 9, 2003.

[63] *See*, AT § 201, "Agreed-Upon Procedures."

[64] *See, e.g.*, letter from American Institute of Certified Public Accountants, dated January 9, 2003; letter from Grant Thornton, LLP dated January 13, 2003; letter from Sullivan & Cromwell LLP, dated January 10, 2003; letter from Computer Sciences Corporation, dated January 13, 2003.

[65] AU § 319, "Consideration of Internal Control in a Financial Statement Audit." In addition, Section 404(b) of the Act requires a company's audit to attest to the internal control report provided annually by management.

[66] AU § 325, "Communication of Internal Control Related Matters Noted in an Audit," requires the auditor to communicate reportable conditions and material weaknesses in internal control to the company's audit committee or equivalent.

those controls or on management's assessment of those controls. As such, we believe that designing and implementing internal accounting and risk management controls is fundamentally different from obtaining an understanding of the controls and testing the operation of the controls which is an integral part of any audit of the financial statements of a company. Likewise, design and implementation of these controls involves decision-making and, therefore, is different from recommending improvements in the internal accounting and risk management controls of an audit client (which is permissible, if pre-approved by the audit committee).

For example, management could engage a third-party service provider to design and implement an inventory control system. In the course of that engagement, the third-party service provider might ask the accountant to make recommendations on internal control and accounting system components that have been included in the system being designed. Providing such recommendations to the third-party service provider would not place the independent accountant in the role of management.

Because of this fundamental difference, we believe that designing and implementing internal accounting and risk management controls impairs the accountant's independence because it places the accountant in the role of management. Conversely, obtaining an understanding of, assessing effectiveness of, and recommending improvements to the internal accounting and risk management controls is fundamental to the audit process and does not impair the accountant's independence. Furthermore, the accountant may be engaged by the company, subject to the audit committee pre-approval requirements, to conduct an agreed-upon procedures engagement[67] related to the company's internal controls or to provide attest services related to the company's internal controls without impairing his or her independence.

7. Human Resources

Our previous rules deem an accountant to lack independence when performing certain human re-

sources functions, and we did not propose any significant change to those rules. Many commenters[68] agreed that the accountant should be prohibited from providing certain human resources functions for audit clients.

Consistent with our proposal, these rules provide that an accountant's independence is impaired with respect to an audit client when the accountant searches for or seeks out prospective candidates for managerial, executive or director positions; acts as negotiator on the audit client's behalf, such as determining position, status, compensation, fringe benefits, or other conditions of employment; or undertakes reference checks of prospective candidates. Under the rule, an accountant's independence also is impaired when the accountant engages in psychological testing, or other formal testing or evaluation programs, or recommends or advises the audit client to hire a specific candidate for a specific job.

Assisting management in human resource selection or development places the accountant in the position of having an interest in the success of the employees that the accountant has selected, tested, or evaluated. Accordingly, observers may perceive that an accountant would be reluctant to suggest the possibility that those employees failed to perform their jobs appropriately, or at least reasonable investors might perceive the accountant to be reluctant, because doing so would require the accountant to acknowledge shortcomings in its human resource service. The accountant also might have other incentives not to report such employees' ineffectiveness, including that the accountant would identify and be identified with the recruited employees.

8. Broker-Dealer, Investment Adviser Or Investment Banking Services

Our previous rules deem an accountant to lack independence when performing brokerage or investment advising services for an audit client.[69] We are adopting rules that add serving as an unregistered broker-dealer[70] to our rules that prohibit serving as a promoter or underwriter, making investment decisions on behalf of the audit client or otherwise having discretionary authority

---

[67] *See*, AT § 201, "Agreed-Upon Procedures."

[68] *See, e.g.*, letter from California Public Employees' Retirement System, dated January 10, 2003; letter from Aon Consulting, dated January 13, 2003.

[69] These rules are not meant to change the Commission's previous position that an audit firm's broker-dealer division can cover an industry (including industry surveys and analyses) which includes an audit client when performing analyst functions. However, analysis of a specific audit client's stock places the auditor in the position of acting as an advocate for the client and would cause the auditor to lack independence.

[70] Accountants and the companies that retain them should recognize that the key determination required here is a functional one (*i.e.*, Is the accounting firm or its employee acting as a broker-dealer?). The failure to register as a broker-dealer does not necessarily mean that the accounting firm is not a

broker-dealer. In relevant part, the statutory definition of "broker" captures persons "engaged in the business of effecting transactions in securities for the account of others." Securities Exchange Act of 1934 § 3(a)(4). Unregistered persons who provide services related to mergers and acquisitions or other securities-related transactions should limit their activities so they remain outside of that statutory definition. A person may "effect transactions," among other ways, by assisting an issuer to structure prospective securities transactions, by helping an issuer to identify potential purchasers of securities, or by soliciting securities transactions. A person may be "engaged in the business," among other ways, by receiving transaction-related compensation or by holding itself out as a broker-dealer. Involvement of accounting personnel as unregistered broker-dealers not only can impair auditor independence, but also would violate Section 15(a) of the Exchange Act.

over an audit client's investments, or executing a transaction to buy or sell an audit client's investment, or having custody of assets of the audit client. The rule is substantially the same as the Commission's previous rule related to the provision of these types of services to audit clients. We are including unregistered broker-dealers within the rules because the nature of the threat to independence is unchanged whether the entity is or is not a registered broker-dealer.

Selling - directly or indirectly - an audit client's securities is incompatible with the accountant's responsibility of assuring the public that the company's financial condition is fairly presented. When an accountant, in any capacity, recommends to anyone (including non-audit clients) that they buy or sell the securities of an audit client or an affiliate of the audit client, the accountant has an interest in whether those recommendations were correct. That interest could affect the audit of the client whose securities, or whose affiliate's securities, were recommended. These concepts are echoed in the "simple principles" included in the legislative history to the Sarbanes-Oxley Act.[71] In such a situation, if an accountant uncovers an accounting error in a client's financial statements, and the accountant, in an investment adviser capacity, had recommended that client's securities to investment clients, the accountant performing the audit may be reluctant to recommend changes to the client's financial statements if the changes could negatively affect the value of the securities recommended by the accountant to its investment adviser clients.

Broker-dealers[72] often give advice and recommendations on investments and investment strategies. The value of that advice is measured principally by the performance of a customer's securities portfolio. When the customer is an audit client, the accountant has an interest in the value of the audit client's securities portfolio, even as the accountant must determine whether management has properly valued the portfolio as part of an audit. Thus, the accountant would be placed in a position of auditing his or her own work. Further-

more, the accountant is placed in a position of acting as an advocate on behalf of the client.

9. Legal Services

Our previous rule stated that an accountant is deemed to lack independence when he or she provides legal services to an audit client. The proposed rule provided that an accountant was not independent of an audit client if the accountant provides any service to the audit client that, under circumstances in which the service is provided, could be provided only by someone licensed, admitted or otherwise qualified to practice law in the jurisdiction in which the service is provided.

We believe that a lawyer's core professional obligation is to advance clients' interests. Rules of professional conduct in the U.S. require the lawyer to "represent a client zealously and diligently within the bounds of the law."[73] The lawyer must "take whatever lawful and ethical measures are required to vindicate a client's cause or endeavor . . . . In the exercise of professional judgment, a lawyer should always act in a manner consistent with the best interests of the client."[74] We have long maintained that an individual cannot be both a zealous legal advocate for management or the client company, and maintain the objectivity and impartiality that are necessary for an audit.[75] The Supreme Court has agreed with our view. In *United States v. Arthur Young*, the Supreme Court emphasized, "If investors were to view the accountant as an advocate for the corporate client, the value of the audit function itself might well be lost."[76]

Some commenters[77] believed that the prohibition on legal services should apply to all registrants, regardless of their jurisdiction. Others believed that certain accommodations should be made for foreign jurisdictions[78] or for routine or ministerial duties.[79]

The rules we are adopting are consistent with our proposal. Accordingly, an accountant is prohibited from providing to an audit client any service that, under circumstances in which the service is provided, could be provided only by someone licensed, admitted, or otherwise quali-

---

[71] Floor Statement of Senator Sarbanes, 148 Cong. Rec. S7364 (July 25, 2002) " . . . A public company auditor should not be a promoter of the company's stock or other financial interest (as it would be if it served as broker-dealer, investment adviser, or investment banker for the company)." To do so places the auditor in a position of serving as an advocate for his or her audit client.

[72] In the past, some have expressed concern that terms such as "securities professional" and "analyst" are not defined in the securities laws and use of the terms could cause confusion. Because of that concern, we have not used those terms in these rules. We note, however, that broker-dealers provide an array of services that may include certain analyst activities.

[73] *See, e.g.*, D.C. Rules of Professional Conduct, Rule 1.3(a).

[74] *Id.* at Rule 1.5.

[75] In the Matter of Charles Falk, AAER No. 1134 (May 19, 1999) (formally disciplining an attorney/accountant who gave legal advice to an audit client of another partner in his accounting firm).

[76] *United States v. Arthur Young*, 465 U.S 805 (1984) at 819-20 n.15.

[77] *See, e.g.*, letter of Lynn E. Turner, dated January 13, 2003; letter from California Public Employees' Retirement System, dated January 10, 2003.

[78] *See, e.g.*, letter from HSBC, dated January 10, 2003; letter from Institute of Chartered Accountants in England and Wales, dated December 24, 2002; letter from Institut der Wirtschaftsprufer, dated December 27, 2002; letter from Federation des Experts Comptables Europeens, dated January 13, 2003.

[79] *See, e.g.*, letter from KPMG, dated January 9, 2003.

fied to practice law in the jurisdiction in which the service is provided.

We recognize that there may be implications for some foreign registrants from this rule. For example, we understand that in some jurisdictions it is mandatory that someone licensed to practice law perform tax work, and that an accounting firm providing such services, therefore, would be deemed to be providing legal services. As a general matter, our rules are not intended to prohibit foreign accounting firms from providing services that an accounting firm in the United States may provide. In determining whether or not a service would impair the accountant's independence solely because the service is labeled a legal service in a foreign jurisdiction, the Commission will consider whether the provision of the service would be prohibited in the United States as well as in the foreign jurisdiction.

Evaluating and determining whether services are permissible may require a comprehensive analysis of the facts and circumstances. We are, however, sensitive to these issues and, as we have done in the past,[80] we encourage accounting firms and foreign regulators to consult with the staff to address these issues.

10. Expert Services

The Sarbanes-Oxley Act includes expert services in the list of non-audit services an accountant is prohibited from performing for an audit client. As discussed earlier, the legislative history related to expert services is focused on the accountant's role when serving in an advocacy capacity.

Some commenters[81] believed that the prohibition on expert services should be limited to instances of public advocacy or public adversarial proceedings and should not extend to situations where the accountant is advising a client or its counsel on technical matters apart from a public proceeding. Other commenters[82] believed a distinction exists between serving as an expert witness and serving as a fact witness in a proceeding. Additionally, many commenters[83] simply raised concerns over the lack of clarity of the term "expert" indicating that, as proposed, the meaning of the term is unclear.

Clients retain experts to lend authority to their contentions in various proceedings by virtue of the expert's specialized knowledge and experience. In situations involving advocacy, the provision of expert services by the accountant makes the accountant part of the "team" that has been assembled to advance or defend the client's interests.[84] The appearance of advocacy created by providing such expert services is sufficient to deem the accountant's independence impaired. The prohibition on providing "expert" services included in this rule covers engagements that are intended to result in the accounting firm's specialized knowledge, experience and expertise being used to support the audit client's positions in various adversarial proceedings.[85]

The rules we are adopting prohibit an accountant from providing expert opinions or other services to an audit client, or a legal representative of an audit client, for the purpose of advocating that audit client's interests in litigation or regulatory, or administrative investigations or proceedings. For example, under this rule an auditor's independence would be impaired if the auditor were engaged to provide forensic accounting services to the audit client's legal representative in connection with the defense of an investigation by the Commission's Division of Enforcement. Additionally, an accountant's independence would be impaired if the audit client's legal counsel, in order to acquire the requisite expertise, engaged the accountant to provide such services in connection with a litigation, proceeding or investigation.[86]

Our rules do not, however, preclude an audit committee or, at its direction, its legal counsel, from engaging the accountant to perform internal investigations or fact finding engagements. These types of engagements may include, among others, forensic or other fact-finding work that results in the issuance of a report to the audit client. The involvement by the accountant in this capacity generally requires performing procedures that are consistent with, but more detailed or more comprehensive than, those required by GAAS. Performing such procedures is consistent with the role of the independent auditor and should improve audit quality. If, subsequent to the comple-

---

[80] Letter of Lynn Turner, Chief Accountant, SEC, to Commissione Nazionale per le Sonieta e la Borsa re: statutory procedures (August 24, 2000).

[81] See, e.g., letter from Sullivan & Cromwell LLP, letter from Deloitte & Touche LLP, dated January 10, 2003; letter from American Institute of Certified Public Accountants, dated January 9, 2003; letter from Federation des Experts Comptables Europeens, dated January 13, 2003.

[82] See, e.g., letter from Sullivan & Cromwell LLP, dated January 10, 2003; letter from California Public Employees' Retirement System, dated January 10, 2003; letter from Grant Thornton LLP, dated January 13, 2003; letter from American Academy of Actuaries, dated January 6, 2003.

[83] See, e.g., letter from Eli Lily and Co., dated January 9, 2003; letter from Federation des Experts Comptables

Europeens, dated January 13, 2003; letter from PG&E Corporation, dated January 10, 2003; letter from America's Community Bankers, dated January 13, 2003.

[84] The accountant becomes an advocate under such circumstances even if the accountant is working behind the scenes to advance the client's interests.

[85] As we discussed in our proposing release, virtually all services provided by an accountant may be perceived to be expert services. This prohibition, however, only applies to those services that involve advocacy in proceedings and investigations (as discussed in this section of the release) and does not apply to other permitted non-audit services, such as tax services.

[86] For purposes of this release, an investigation is an inquiry by a regulatory body, including by its staff.

tion of such an engagement,[87] a proceeding or investigation is initiated, the accountant may allow its work product to be utilized by the audit client and its legal counsel without impairing the accountant's independence. The accountant, however, may not then provide additional services, but may provide factual accounts or testimony about the work performed.

Accordingly, our rules would not prohibit an accountant from assisting the audit committee[88] in fulfilling its responsibilities to conduct its own investigation of a potential accounting impropriety.[89] For example, if the audit committee is concerned about the accuracy of the inventory accounts at a subsidiary, it may engage the auditor to conduct a thorough inspection and analysis of those accounts, the physical inventory at the subsidiary, and related matters without impairing the auditor's independence.

We recognize that auditors have obligations under Section 10A of the Exchange Act and GAAS[90] to search for fraud that is material to an issuer's financial statements and to make sure the audit committee and others are informed of their findings. Auditors should conduct these procedures whether they become aware of a potential illegal act as a result of audit, review or attestation procedures they have performed or as a result of the audit committee expressing concerns about a part of the company's operations or compliance with the company's financial reporting system. In these situations, we believe that the auditor may conduct the procedures, with the approval of the audit committee, and provide the reports that the auditor deems appropriate. Should litigation arise or an investigation commence during the time period that the auditors are conducting such procedures, we would not deem the completion of these procedures to be prohibited expert services so long as the auditor remains in control of his or

her work and that work does not become subject to the direction or influence of legal counsel for the issuer.

Furthermore, under this rule, an accountant's independence will not be deemed to be impaired if, in an investigation or proceeding, an accountant provides factual accounts or testimony describing work it performed. Further, an accountant's independence will not be deemed to be impaired if an accountant explains the positions taken or conclusions reached during the performance of any service provided by the accountant for the audit client.

11. Tax Services

Since the Commission issued its auditor independence proposal, there has been considerable debate regarding whether an accountant's provision of tax services for an audit client can impair the accountant's independence. Tax services are unique among non-audit services for a variety of reasons. Detailed tax laws must be consistently applied, and the Internal Revenue Service has discretion to audit any tax return. Additionally, accounting firms have historically provided a broad range of tax services to their audit clients.[91]

In the proposing release, we suggested that in determining whether a given tax service should be allowed, the audit committee should be mindful of the three basic principles. In response, some commenters[92] indicated that asking audit committees to evaluate the provision of tax services by the accountant in light of the three basic principles would significantly alter the Commission's historic position related to tax services. Other commenters raised significant clarity and certainty issues. Some commenters[93] that urged clarity would, for example, prohibit accountants from providing any tax services to audit clients. Other commenters[94] believed that accountants should be permitted to provide only certain types of tax

---

[87] See, infra, discussion stating that if litigation arises or an investigation commences during the auditor's performance of such procedures, completion of the procedures is not prohibited provided the auditor remains in control of his or her work and that work does not become subject to the direction or influence of legal counsel for the issuer.

[88] For example, Section 301 of the Act stipulates that each audit committee shall have the authority to engage independent counsel and other advisers, as it determines necessary to carry out its duties.

[89] An auditor's independence would, however, be impaired if its assistance to the audit committee included defending, or helping to defend, the audit committee or the company generally in a shareholder class action or derivative lawsuit, other than as a fact witness.

[90] See, SAS No. 99, "Consideration of Fraud in a Financial Statement Audit," AU § 316.

[91] The provision of tax services by accountants to their audit clients existed and continued without change when Congress formulated the securities laws in the 1930s. The Sarbanes-Oxley Act also recognized that accountants may engage in certain non-audit services "including tax services

. . . only if the activity is approved in advance by the audit committee."

[92] Some commenters (see, e.g., letter from Ernst & Young, dated January 6, 2003; letter from Deloitte & Touche, dated January 10, 2003; letter from KPMG, dated January 9, 2003; letter from the Chamber of Commerce of the United States of America, dated January 9, 2003; letter from SafeCo Corporation, dated January 7, 2003; letter from Pfizer, dated January 13, 2003; letter from The Business Roundtable, dated January 14, 2003) believe that asking audit committees to evaluate tax services in light of the three principles in its pre-approval process creates an unnecessary degree of uncertainty in the marketplace.

[93] See, e.g., letter from Norman Marks, dated December 9, 2002; letter from Harbor View Partners, dated December 4, 2002; letter from Douglas Estes, dated November 30, 2002; letter from William Fraser, dated November 26, 3002; letter from M.E. Saunders, dated November 26, 2002.

[94] See, e.g., letter from Robert T. Bossart, dated January 2, 2003; letter from FedEx Corporation, dated December 31, 2002; letter from the American Bar Association Section of Taxation, dated January 6, 2003; letter from California Public Employees' Retirement System, dated January 10, 2003.

services to their audit clients.[95] Some commenters[96] believed that allowing the accountant to perform tax services both enhances the quality of the audit and provides greater independent oversight over the provision of tax services than would occur if a non-audit firm were engaged to provide these services. Additionally, one commenter's research suggests that higher levels of tax services fees are associated with substantially lower instances of financial restatements.[97]

The Commission reiterates its long-standing position that an accounting firm can provide tax services to its audit clients without impairing the firm's independence. Accordingly, accountants may continue to provide tax services such as tax compliance, tax planning, and tax advice to audit clients, subject to the normal audit committee pre-approval requirements under 2-01(c)(7). Additionally, the rules we are adopting require registrants to disclose the amount of fees paid to the accounting firm for tax services. The rules are consistent with the Act which states that:

A registered public accounting firm may engage in any non-audit service, *including tax services*, that is not described in any of paragraphs (1) through (9) of subsection (g) for an audit client, only if the activity is approved in advance by the audit committee of the issuer.[98] (Emphasis added)

Nonetheless, merely labeling a service as a "tax service" will not necessarily eliminate its potential to impair independence under Rule 2-01(b).[99] Audit committees and accountants should understand that providing certain tax services to an audit client would, as described below, or could, in certain circumstances, impair the independence of the accountant. Specifically, accountants would impair their independence by representing an audit client before a tax court, district court, or federal court of claims. In addition, audit committees also should scrutinize carefully the retention

of an accountant in a transaction initially recommended by the accountant, the sole business purpose of which may be tax avoidance and the tax treatment of which may be not supported in the Internal Revenue Code and related regulations.[100]

C. Partner Rotation

For 25 years, partner rotation has been a component of quality control processes for a vast majority of the accounting firms that audit SEC registrants.[101] The judgment about who should be subject to rotation and how long the partner(s) should remain on the engagement prior to rotating involves balancing the need to bring a "fresh look" to the audit engagement with the need to maintain continuity and audit quality.

The Sarbanes-Oxley Act requires rotation of certain audit partners on a five-year basis in order to continue to provide audit services for a registrant. Section 203 of the Sarbanes-Oxley Act of 2002 specifies that:

It shall be unlawful for a registered public accounting firm to provide audit services to an issuer if the lead (or coordinating) audit partner (having primary responsibility for the audit), or the audit partner responsible for reviewing the audit, has performed audit services for that issuer in each of the 5 previous fiscal years of that issuer.

Section 301 of the Sarbanes-Oxley Act specifies that the Commission is to direct the national securities exchanges and associations to adopt company listing standards stating that the company's audit committee has the responsibility for appointment, compensation, and oversight of the work of the company's audit firm.[102] In that capacity, the audit committee has the responsibility for evaluating and determining that the audit engagement team has the competence necessary to conduct the audit engagement in accordance with GAAS. Additionally, the accountant is required to conduct the audit in accordance with GAAS.[103]

---

[95] Commenters identified a variety of tax services they believe should be prohibited. However, there was no "consensus" view on what tax services should be prohibited.

[96] *See, e.g.*, letter from Philip A. Laskawy, dated January 2, 2003; letter from FedEx Corporation, dated December 31, 2002; letter from The Business Roundtable, dated January 14, 2003.

[97] *See*, comment letter of William Kinney, University of Texas, Zoe-Vonna Palmrose, University of Southern California, and Susan Scholz, University of Kansas.

[98] Sarbanes-Oxley Act of 2002, Section 201.

[99] It would not be appropriate to provide a prohibited service, label it a "tax service," and argue that it is, therefore, permissible. For example, an accountant seeking to provide a broker-dealer service and arguing that, because there are tax implications of certain brokerage activities, the service is permissible would constitute an attempt to improperly circumvent the list of prohibited services. *See,* letter of Ernst & Young dated January 6, 2003 (p. 16).

[100] The Commission on Public Trust and Private Enterprise recently concluded as a "best practice" that an accounting firm should not be providing "novel and debatable tax strate-

gies and products that involve income tax shelters and extensive off-shore partnerships or affiliates" to audit clients. *See* The Conference Board Commission on Public Trust and Private Enterprise, *Findings and Recommendations*, January 9, 2003, p. 37.

[101] American Institute of Certified Public Accountants (AICPA), *Division for CPA Firms SEC Practice Section Peer Review Manual*, 1978.

[102] *See*, Release No. 33-8173 (Jan 8, 2003).

[103] In addition to the audit, registrants are required to have their quarterly financial information subjected to a timely review by the accounting firm. Such review is typically conducted according to the provisions required by GAAS—*see*, AU §722. Furthermore, Section 404 of the Sarbanes-Oxley Act, as well as the Commission's proposed rules—*see*, Release No. 33-8138, Oct. 22, 2002, (67 FR 66208)—would require the accounting firm to attest to management's report on the registrant's internal controls. Both a timely review engagement and an attestation engagement require the accounting firm to be independent with respect to the registrant. Accordingly, the Commission's rules for partner rotation extend to partners who serve on the engagement team that conducts the timely review of the registrant's interim financial information as well

In particular, the third general standard requires that the accountant exercise due professional care in the conduct of the audit.[104] In order to exercise due professional care, it is necessary to ensure that the engagement is properly staffed with individuals competent to understand the unique issues relevant to that audit. Additionally, the accounting profession's quality control standards require that the firm have processes in place to ensure that appropriate personnel are assigned to each audit engagement.[105]

In our proposing release, we proposed that all partners on the audit engagement team, with the exception of certain "technical services" or "national office" partners and those serving on significant subsidiaries as defined in 1-02(w) of Regulation S-X, be subject to rotation after five years and that after rotation, they would be subject to a five year time-out before they could return to that engagement. Furthermore, the proposed rules would have applied the partner rotation requirements at the audit client[106] level.

Some commenters[107] have suggested that the fresh look can only be accomplished by requiring mandatory rotation of audit firms. In contrast, others[108] expressed the concern that the loss of continuity and audit competence created by mandatory firm rotation creates an even greater risk to audit quality. The issue of mandatory audit firm rotation as an effective means of safeguarding auditor independence has been debated for many years. Several different groups, including appointed commissions, professional organizations, and academics, have researched and analyzed the issue of audit firm rotation.[109] The results of those

efforts have raised many of the same concerns as our commenters which the Commission considered in this rule-making. This issue will continue to be monitored by the Commission and others. As directed by Section 207 of the Sarbanes-Oxley Act, the issue of mandatory firm rotation is a matter requiring further study.[110]

1. Rotation of the Lead and Concurring Partner

Under the current requirements of the profession, the balance between the need for a fresh look with concerns about loss of continuity and competence is accomplished by requiring the lead partner to rotate off the audit engagement of SEC registrants after seven years with a two year time out period.[111] However, some commenters[112] believed that extending the partner rotation requirements to other audit partners would be a better balance of the need for a fresh look with concerns about continuity and competence.

These commenters' views are consistent with the provisions of the Sarbanes-Oxley Act, which clearly specify that, at a minimum, two partners be subject to rotation: the lead audit partner and the concurring partner. Furthermore, the Act specifies a five-year period prior to rotation rather than the current seven-year period specified in the membership requirements of the SECPS.[113] While the Act specified that these two partners were subject to rotation after five years, the Act is silent with regard to the time out period. One approach to the partner rotation rules could have been to preclude the partner from returning to the audit client after he or she rotates off to that engagement. Many commenters,[114] however, believed

---

(Footnote Continued)

as the engagement team that conducts the attest engagement on management's report on the registrant's internal controls.

[104] *See*, AU § 150.02.

[105] *See*, QC § 20.13.

[106] As defined in Rule 2-01(f).

[107] *See, e.g.*, letter from Jason Zahner, dated December 23, 2002; letter from Hugh Higgins, dated November 20, 2002.

[108] *See, e.g.*, letter from American Institute of Certified Public Accountants, dated January 9, 2003.

[109] *See*, The Commission on Auditors' Responsibilities, "Report, Conclusions, and Recommendations," 1978, p. 109; Report of the National Commission on Fraudulent Financial Reporting, 1987, p. 54; research commissioned by the Committee of Sponsoring Organizations of the Treadway Commission, "Report of the National Commission on Fraudulent Financial Reporting," 1987, p. 113; Committee of Sponsoring Organizations of the Treadway Commission, "Fraudulent Financial Reporting: 1987-1997 An Analysis of U.S. Public Companies," 1999, p. 28; United States General Accounting Office, Report to the Ranking Minority Member, Committee on Commerce, House of Representatives, "The Accounting Profession, Major Issues: Progress and Concerns," 1996, p. 56; Arrunada, Benito, "Mandatory Rotation of Company Auditors: A Critical Examination," *International Review of Law And Economics*, March 1997; St. Pierre, K. and J. Anderson, "An Analysis of Factors Associated with Lawsuits Against Public Accountants," *Accounting Review* (1984), p. 256; and Dal-

locchio, M. and A. Viganò, "The Impact Of Mandatory Audit Rotation On Audit Quality And On Audit Pricing: The Case Of Italy," SDA Università Bocconi, 2003.

[110] Section 207 of the Act directs the Comptroller General of the United States to conduct a study and review of the potential effects of mandatory rotation of firms.

[111] AICPA, SEC Practice Section, Requirements of Members, at item e. The membership requirements are available online at www.aicpa.org/members/div/secps/require.htm. Audit firms which are members of the SEC Practice Section must comply with its rules (e.g., partner rotation) and undergo periodic peer review to ensure that the firms' audit practice is consistent with both the rules of the AICPA and those of the Commission.

[112] *See, e.g.*, letter from California Public Employees' Retirement System, dated January 10, 2003; letter from Denzil Dias, dated December 11, 2002; letter from HSBC, dated January 11, 2003.

[113] While the current lead partner rotation requirements specify a seven-year period prior to rotation, the original rotation requirements developed by the SECPS specified a five-year rotation period. *See*, AICPA, *Division for CPA Firms SEC Practice Section Peer Review Manual*, 1978, p.1-5.

[114] *See, e.g.*, letter from The Putnam Funds, not dated; letter from Commercial Federal Bank, dated January 13, 2003; letter from Dixon Odom, dated December 20, 2002; letter from American Instituted of Certified Public Accountants, dated January 9, 2003.

that the time out should be shorter than in our proposal. Other commenters[115] did not object to or even agreed with the five-year time out period for the lead and concurring partners.

The Commission is adopting rules to require the lead and concurring partners to rotate after five years and, upon rotation, be subject to a five-year "time out" period. Because of the importance of achieving a fresh look to the independence of the audit function, we believe that a five-year time out period is appropriate for these two partners.

2. Additional Partner Rotation

Clearly, the lead partner and the concurring partner perform critical functions that affect the conduct and effectiveness of the engagement. However, in many larger engagements, the engagement team will include more than just the lead partner and the concurring partner. Often, those other partners on the engagement team play a significant role in the conduct of the audit and maintaining ongoing relationships with the audit client.

Our proposal would have applied the same rotation requirements to all partners on the audit engagement team with the exception of certain "national office" technical partners and those who did not work on significant subsidiaries as defined in Rule 1-02(w) of Regulation S-X. Some commenters[116] believed that the rotation requirements should be at or extend beyond our proposal level to include, for example, "national office" or "technical" partners[117] or other audit engagement team members below the level of partner.[118] Other commenters,[119] however, believed that extending the rotation requirements beyond the two partners named in the Act could potentially harm audit quality and could impose additional costs on registrants. For example, one commenter[120] indicated that the proposed rotation requirements would cause the firm to have to rotate 181 partners in 88 countries for one large multi-national

client. Another commenter[121] estimated that more than 250 partners in 80 countries would be subject to the rotation requirements under the proposed rules. Additionally, some commenters stated that the additional costs that accounting firms would incur to rotate and, in many cases, relocate audit partners would have to be passed on to registrants.

While other commenters[122] agreed with the concept of extending the partner rotation requirements beyond the two partners named in the Act, they suggested that the final rules should not apply as broadly as the Commission had proposed. One commenter suggested that assessing the "right cut" in identifying partners for rotation was a balance between the responsibility for final decisions on accounting and financial reporting issues affecting the financial statements and the level of the relationship with management.[123]

Commenters[124] noted that applying the rotation requirements too deeply could threaten the quality of the audit in certain situations. For example, in certain countries there may be a limited pool of audit partners who are familiar with U.S. GAAP and GAAS. In certain "specialty" areas, there may be a limited number of "specialty" partners available to service the client.[125] In certain industries there may be limited industry expertise. Also, by applying the rotation requirements more deeply, firms might have a difficult time grooming another partner to both have sufficient knowledge of the industry and the client and have sufficient time remaining prior to rotation when the lead partner or concurring partner must rotate. Also, some commenters[126] noted that applying the proposed rotation requirements to specialty partners could impact audit quality.

We believe that the partner rotation requirements must strike a balance between the need to achieve a fresh look on the engagement and a need for the audit engagement team to be com-

---

[115] See, e.g., letter from Aetna, Inc., dated January 13, 2003; letter from Royal Philips Electronics, dated January 9, 2003; letter from Lynn Turner, dated January 13, 2003; letter from Medtronic, Inc., dated January 13, 2003.

[116] See, e.g., letter from Denzil Dias, dated December 11, 2002.

[117] See, e.g., letter from California Public Employees' Retirement System dated January 10, 2003.

[118] See, e.g., letter from Lynn E. Turner dated January 13, 2003.

[119] See, e.g., letter from Aramark Corporation, dated December 26, 2002; letter from Aetna, Inc., dated January 13, 2003; letter from PricewaterhouseCoopers, dated January 8, 2003; letter from Mellon Financial Corporation, dated January 10, 2003; letter from SAP AG, undated; letter from Chamber of Commerce of the United States of America, dated January 9, 2003; letter from The Business Roundtable, dated January 14, 2003.

[120] See, letter from PricewaterhouseCoopers dated January 8, 2003.

[121] See, letter from HSBC dated January 10, 2003.

[122] See, e.g., letter from Ernst & Young LLP, dated January 6, 2003; letter from Robert G. Beard, undated; letter from Institute of Chartered Accountants in England and Wales, dated January 10, 2003.

[123] See, letter from Deloitte & Touche LLP, dated January 10, 2003.

[124] See, e.g., letter from The Business Roundtable, dated January 14, 2003; PricewaterhouseCoopers, dated January 8, 2003; letter from KPMG, dated January 9, 2003; letter from Philip A. Laskawy, dated January 9, 2003; letter from Pfizer, dated January 13, 2003; letter from Aetna, Inc., dated January 13, 2003.

[125] Specialty partners are, among others, those partners who consult with others on the audit engagement team during the audit, review or attestation engagement regarding technical or industry-specific issues. For example, such partners would include tax specialist and valuation specialist.

[126] See, e.g., letter from Ernst & Young LLP, dated January 6, 2003; letter from Deloitte & Touche, dated January 10, 2003.

posed of competent accountants. We believe that a proper balance is one that weighs the responsibility for decisions on accounting and financial reporting issues impacting the financial statements with the level of the relationship with senior management of the client. Such a balancing clearly would include the lead (high on both dimensions) and concurring partners (high on responsibility for final decisions, somewhat lower on level of relationship with management). In addition to that, the lead partner at significant operating units has a high involvement with senior management and, for significant operations, responsibility for decisions on accounting matters that affect the financial statements. Likewise, other audit partners at the parent or issuer have a high involvement with senior management and some responsibility for accounting matters to be included in the financial statements.

In contrast, partners at smaller operating units and "specialty" partners typically have a low level of involvement with senior management and the responsibility for the overall presentation in the financial statements is relatively low.

Nonetheless, the Commission is sensitive to the impact that its proposed rotation requirements would have on audit competence in certain instances as well as costs to registrants. Consistent with this approach, we believe that the proper balance is achieved by extending the partner rotation requirements beyond the lead and concurring partner but less deeply than we proposed. In response to the concerns of commenters that our proposed rules went too deep, thus imposing significant costs on registrants and accountants as well as creating potential concerns of audit quality, the rules we are adopting will subject a smaller number of partners to the rotation requirement. Accordingly, we are adopting rules that apply the partner rotation requirements to "audit partners" which is a new term defined in these rules.

In addition to the lead and concurring partners, "audit partners" include partners on the audit engagement team who have responsibility for decision-making on significant auditing, accounting, and reporting matters that affect the financial statements or who maintain regular contact with management and the audit committee. In particular, audit partners would include all those who serve the client at the issuer or parent level, other than specialty partners. Further, the lead partner on subsidiaries of the issuer whose assets or revenues constitute 20% or more of the consolidated assets or revenues are included within the definition of "audit partner."

Thus, the term audit partner does not extend to all partners on the audit engagement team. For example, partners serving on subsidiaries which constitute less than 20% of the assets and revenues of the issuer would not be audit partners as we have defined that term and, thus, would not be subject to rotation. Likewise, partners on subsidiaries above the 20% threshold, other than the lead partner on those subsidiaries, are not subject to rotation.[127]

Audit partners also would exclude "specialty" partners because they typically do not have significant interaction with management on an ongoing basis regarding significant audit, accounting, and reporting matters. It is the lead partner (who is subject to rotation) who has the ultimate responsibility for the audit. We believe that this addresses the concern that many commenters expressed regarding certain "specialty" partners.

We believe that defining the term "audit partners" as the basis for defining those partners who are subject to the rotation requirements is responsive to the concerns expressed by some commenters of the problems that would be created by applying the rotation requirements deeper in the firm. Accordingly, we believe that this requirement establishes an appropriate balance between the need for a fresh look with the difficulties encountered in certain locations where the pool of available talent is limited.

In many cases, registrants have complex business transactions and other situations which may require that the engagement team consult with the accounting firm's national office or others on technical issues. Consistent with our proposal, partners assigned to "national office" duties (which can include technical accounting and auditing—whether at a local or national level—as well as centralized quality control functions) who may be consulted on specific accounting issues related to a client are not audit partners even though they may periodically consult on client matters.[128] While these partners play an important role in the audit process, they serve, primarily, as a technical resource for members of the audit team. Because these partners are not involved in the audit *per se* and do not routinely interact or develop relationships with the audit client, we do not believe that it is necessary to rotate the involvement of these personnel.

3. Rotation Period for Partners Other Than The Lead and Concurring Partners

Some commenters[129] believed that a different rotation period should be provided to partners other than the lead and concurring partners. In

---

[127] A threshold of 20% often has been used in the accounting literature as a basis for "significance" tests. *See, e.g.*, APB Opinion No. 18, "The Equity Method of Accounting for Investments in Common Stock, and ARB No. 43, Chapter 7, "Capital Accounts."

[128] 17 CFR 210.2-01(f)(7).

[129] *See, e.g.*, letter from Ernst & Young, dated January 6, 2003; letter from Deloitte & Touche, dated January 10, 2003; letter from KPMG, dated January 9, 2003; letter from Dixon Odom, dated December 20, 2002; letter from The Business Roundtable, dated January 14, 2003.

particular, if other partners subject to the rotation requirements had a longer period before they were required to rotate, firms would be better able to establish appropriate transition plans from one lead or concurring partner to the next. The longer rotation period for the other partners would allow them to spend time on the engagement team to learn about the business and the industry before having the ultimate responsibility for the engagement.

In response to these concerns, the rules we are adopting require partners subject to the rotation requirements, other than the lead and concurring partner, to rotate after no more than seven years and to be subject to a two-year time-out. In this way, a partner could serve either as the lead partner on a significant subsidiary or as an "audit partner" at the parent or issuer level for a period of time (e.g., two years) prior to becoming the lead or concurring partner on the engagement and still be able to serve in that lead or concurring role for five years.[130]

In conducting its oversight review of registered public accounting firms, we expect that the Public Company Accounting Oversight Board ("the Board") will monitor the impact of these rules on audit quality and independence.

4. Small Business/Small Firm Considerations

Many commenters[131] stated that if the rotation requirements were applied to smaller firms, many smaller firms would be unable to provide audit services to their public clients and would be forced to give up their public clients. Many commenters[132] suggested that this would result in those clients incurring greater costs such as from having to identify a new accounting firm, from the need to familiarize accountants with the client firm's industry and business practices and from the resulting reduction in competition among firms.[133] As we noted in the proposal, we are sensitive to the impact of our rules on smaller business and smaller firms.

Commenters[134] made a number of suggestions about how to accommodate the needs of smaller issuers and smaller firms including: (1) exempting the firms based on criteria such as number of partners, number of SEC clients, firm revenue, or number of professional personnel and (2) exempting accountants of smaller issuers as measured by revenue, assets, market capitalization, or profitability.

The existing professional standards on partner rotation contain an exemption for firms with fewer than five audit clients and fewer than ten partners.[135] We recognize the need to consider the impact of our rules on smaller businesses and smaller firms. While we believe it is appropriate to codify that exemption, we remain concerned about the quality of audits of all registrants. Accordingly, in order for audit firms with fewer than five audit clients that are issuers[136] and fewer than ten partners to qualify for the exemption from partner rotation, the Board must conduct a review of all of the firm's engagements subject to the rule at least once every three years. This special review should focus on the overall quality of the audit and, in particular, the independence and competence of the key personnel on the audit engagement teams.

5. Investment Companies

Under the proposed rule, a partner performing audit, review, or attestation services for any entity in the investment company complex could only do so if they had not served five consecutive years on any entity in the same investment company complex. The rotation requirement would have extended not only to the audit partners, but also those specialized partners, such as tax partners, that work on significant aspects of the audit. Those partners affected by the rotation requirement would have had to remain completely off any engagements in the investment company complex for a period of five years before they could again audit the investment company.

---

[130] An audit partner who starts in a position other than the lead or concurring partner and subsequently moves to the lead or concurring partner cannot serve the client in an audit partner capacity for more than seven consecutive years. For example, a person serving as the lead partner on a significant subsidiary for a period of four years who then becomes the lead partner on the issuer would be able to serve in that capacity for three additional years before reaching a total of seven years as an audit partner on that client.

[131] *See, e.g.*, letter from Piercy, Bowler, Taylor & Kern, dated January 7, 2003; letter from Witt, Mares & Company PLC, dated January 11, 2003; letter from Burton, McCumber & Cortez LLP, dated January 2, 2003; letter from American Institute of Certified Public Accountants, dated January 9, 2003; letter from Spence, Marston, Bunch, Morris & Co., dated January 13, 2003; letter from The Business Roundtable, dated January 14, 2003.

[132] *See, e.g.*, letter from Weaver & Martin LLC, dated December 31, 2002; letter from CPA Associates, dated January 3,

2003; letter from Symonds, Evans & Company PC, dated December 19, 2002.

[133] *See, e.g.*, letter from U.S. Small Business Administration's Office of Advocacy, January 13, 2003. We note that the GAO also is conducting a study on the consolidation in the accounting industry as directed by Section 701 of the Sarbanes-Oxley Act.

[134] *See, e.g.*, letter from Castaing, Hussey & Lolan LLC, dated January 10, 2003; letter from Piercy, Bowler, Taylor & Kern, dated January 7, 2003; letter from Trice, Geary & Myers LLC, dated January 13, 2003; letter from Smith, Carney & Co., dated January 7, 2003; letter from Cranmore, FitzGerald & Meaney, dated December 27, 2002.

[135] AICPA, SEC Practice Section, Requirements of Members, at item e.

[136] As defined in section 10A(f) of the Securities Exchange Act of 1934 (15 U.S.C. 78j-1(f)).

Commenters[137] raised significant concerns in the application of the proposed rule to investment companies. Two commenters[138] were concerned with the prohibition of partners who had served five consecutive years at a service provider or other non-investment company entity in the investment company complex from serving on the audit of a registered investment company in the same investment company complex without first observing the five year "time out" period.[139] One commenter[140] was concerned with the prohibition against partners who had served five consecutive years at an unregistered fund from serving on the audit of a registered investment company in the same investment company complex without first observing the five year "time out" period. One commenter[141] emphasized the financial reporting personnel and accounting control systems used by investment companies are different from those used for other entities in the investment company complex. As a result, the rotation of an audit partner from a non-registered investment company entity in the investment company complex to a registered investment company would provide a "fresh look" at the accounting control systems and the financial reporting process. In addition, due to the structure of the investment company complex organizations, the rotated partner typically would not be dealing with the same individuals in management or on the audit committee that they might have dealt with previously as the audit partner on an entity in the investment company complex.

We believe that the rotation requirements with regard to investment companies should prohibit the rotation of partners between different investment companies in the same investment company complex. We do not believe, however, that it is necessary for the rule to prohibit accountants from rotating to other entities in the investment company complex. Consequently, the rule, as adopted, will not allow audit partners to satisfy the partner rotation requirements by rotating between investment companies in the same investment company complex. The individual required to rotate and the applicable periods for rotation and

"time-out" from the audit client will be applied in the same manner to investment companies as to other issuers. Lead and concurring partners will be required to rotate after a total of five consecutive years in either role. At a minimum, all audit partners that audit investment companies will be required to rotate after a total of seven years of consecutive service on any of the investment companies in the same investment company complex. Lead and concurring partners will be required to observe a "time out" period for five years before returning to the investment company and all other audit partners are be subject to a two year "time out" period.

The unique structure of investment company complexes allows for many different fiscal year-ends within the same investment company complex. In order to allow a partner to serve the total number of allowable periods on any one investment company audit in the complex, while still requiring partners to rotate off an investment company complex at the end of their specific periods, we have defined consecutive years of service for investment companies. A consecutive year of service for audit partners includes all fiscal year-end audits of investment companies in the same investment company complex that are performed in a continuous 12-month period. This would allow audit partners auditing multiple investment companies in the same investment company complex to audit each investment company for five or seven complete fiscal years, as appropriate.

6. Effective Date and Transition

In order to allow firms to establish an orderly transition of their audit engagement teams, the Commission is establishing transition provisions related to the partner rotation requirements. Since the lead partner was previously subject to rotation requirements, these rotation requirements should not impose a significant incremental burden on accounting firms. Accordingly, the rotation requirements applicable to the lead partner are effective for the first fiscal year ending after the effective date of these rules. Furthermore, in determining when the lead partner must rotate, time served in the capacity of lead partner prior to the

---

[137] *See, e.g.,* letter from Deloitte & Touche, dated January 10, 2003; letter from Putnam Mutual Funds, not dated; letter from The Vanguard Group, dated January 13, 2003; letter from PricewaterhouseCoopers, dated January 8, 2003.

[138] *See,* letter from PricewaterhouseCoopers, dated January 8, 2003; letter from Investment Company Institute, dated January 13, 2003.

[139] Commenters also were concerned with the availability of competent audit, tax and other specialized partners to effectively rotate between the investment company audits. One commenter indicated tax partners typically served a far greater number of investment company audit clients per partner than their counterparts in the other industry practices (*see,* letter from Investment Company Institute, dated January 13, 2003). Commenters were concerned that lack of depth in this industry would ultimately reduce audit quality and harm

investors (*see, e.g.,* letter from Putnam Mutual Funds, not dated). Commenters also were concerned with the depth of audit resources in certain markets (*see, e.g.,* letter from Oppenheimer Funds, Inc., dated January 13, 2003). One commenter indicated the proposed rule would effectively bar them from performing audits of investment companies (*see,* letter from McCurdy & Associates, CPAs, Inc., dated December 12, 2002). We have addressed these concerns by the changes to the partner rotation requirements that impact all issuers in addition to registered investment companies.

[140] *See,* letter from PricewaterhouseCoopers, dated January 8, 2003.

[141] *See,* letter from PricewaterhouseCoopers, dated January 8, 2003. *See, also,* letter from Investment Company Institute, dated January 6, 2003.

effective date of these rules is included. For example, for a lead partner serving a calendar year audit client, if 2003 was that partner's fifth, sixth or seventh year as lead partner for that audit client, he or she would be able to complete the current year's audit and he or she must rotate off for the 2004 engagement.

The other partners subject to these rotation requirements were not previously subject to rotation. Accordingly, we believe that some additional transition is needed for these partners. In order to maintain continuity on the engagement, firms will need to stagger the rotation of partners. This is especially critical for the lead and concurring partners. As a consequence, to facilitate the process of staggering the rotation of the lead and concurring partners, the rotation requirements for the concurring partner are effective as of the end of the second fiscal year after the effective date of the rules. Therefore, a concurring partner for a calendar year audit client for which 2003 was his or her fourth or greater year in that role,[142] he or she would be able to serve in that capacity for the 2004 audit before being subject to rotation.

Since the other partners covered by these rules were neither identified in the Act nor previously subject to rotation requirements, we believe, consistent with many commenters, that a longer transition period is warranted. Accordingly, for other partners, the rules are effective as of the beginning of the first fiscal year after the effective date of these rules. However, in determining the time served, that first fiscal year will constitute the first year of service for such partners. For example, for a lead partner on a significant subsidiary with a calendar year reporting period, 2004 would constitute the first year in the seven year rotation period, regardless of how many years he or she had previously served in that capacity.

Finally, we recognize that in many foreign jurisdictions partners previously were not subject to rotation requirements. Accordingly, for all partners with foreign accounting firms who are subject to rotation requirements, the rules are effective as of the beginning of the first fiscal year after the effective date of these rules. Likewise, in determining the time served, that first fiscal year will constitute the first year of service for such partners. Thus, for a partner from a foreign firm who is serving as the lead partner for an issuer with a calendar year, 2004 would constitute the first year of the five year rotation period for that partner, without regard to the number of years he or she had previously served in that capacity.

D. Audit Committee Administration of the Engagement

Historically, management has retained the accounting firm, negotiated the audit fee, and contracted with the accounting firm for other services. Our proposed rules, however, recognized the critical role that audit committees can play in the financial reporting process and in helping accountants maintain their independence from audit clients. An effective audit committee may enhance the accountant's independence by, among other things, providing a forum apart from management where the accountants may discuss their concerns. It may facilitate communications among the board of directors, management, internal auditors and independent accountants. An audit committee also may enhance auditor independence from management by appointing, compensating and overseeing the work of the independent accountants.

In that light, Section 202 of the Sarbanes-Oxley Act requires that audit committees pre-approve the services—both audit and permitted non-audit—of the accounting firm.

Specifically, our proposed rules would have required the audit committee to approve the engagement of the independent accountant to audit the issuer and its subsidiary's financial statements and have ongoing communications with the accountant. The proposals also would have required that the audit committee pre-approve all permissible non-audit services and all audit, review or attest engagements required under the securities laws either:

- before the accountant is engaged by the audit client to provide services other than audit, review or attest services, the audit client's audit committee expressly approve the particular engagement; or

- any such engagement be entered into pursuant to detailed pre-approval policies and procedures established by the audit committee and the audit committee be informed on a timely basis of each service.

Finally, consistent with the provisions of the Act, under our proposals, audit committees could apply a de minimis exception to the pre-approval requirements in certain circumstances.

Some commenters[143] believed that the pre-approval alternatives stated above, coupled with the disclosure of fees based on the pre-approval practices conveyed an impression that one method of pre-approval was preferable. Other commenters[144]

---

[142] Since concurring partners were not previously subject to rotation requirements, it is quite likely that many partners will have served in significantly more than five years in that capacity at the time of transition.

[143] *See, e.g.,* letter from The Business Roundtable, dated January 13, 2003; letter from Chamber of Commerce of the United States of America, dated January 9, 2003; letter from

Investment Company Institute, dated January 13, 2003; letter from Pfizer, dated January 13, 2003; letter from Sullivan & Cromwell LLP, dated January 10, 2003; letter from Wells Fargo & Company, dated January 13, 2003.

[144] *See, e.g.,* letter from America's Community Bankers, dated January 13, 2003; letter from American Society of Cor-

stated that it was uncertain whether audit committees could use policies and procedures as the basis for pre-approving audit services.

The rules we are adopting are intended to clarify that, to the extent permitted by the Sarbanes-Oxley Act,[145] the audit committee may pre-approve audit and non-audit services based on policies and procedures and that explicit approval and approval based on policies and procedures are equally acceptable. As discussed later in this release, we have revised the proposed disclosures to match our conclusions about pre-approval processes.

Accordingly, the final rules require that the audit committee pre-approve all permissible non-audit services and all audit, review or attest engagements required under the securities laws. The rules require that before the accountant is engaged by the issuer or its subsidiaries, or the registered investment company or its subsidiaries, to render the service, the engagement is:

• approved by the issuer's or registered investment company's audit committee; or

• entered into pursuant to pre-approval policies and procedures established by the audit committee of the issuer or registered investment company, provided the policies and procedures are detailed as to the particular service, the audit committee is informed of each service, and such policies and procedures do not include delegation of the audit committee's responsibilities to management.

As provided in the Sarbanes-Oxley Act, the rules recognize audit services to be broader than those services required to perform an audit pursuant to GAAS. For example, the Act identifies services related to the issuance of comfort letters and services related to statutory audits required for insurance companies for purposes of state law as audit services.[146] We recognize that domestically and internationally there are various requirements for statutory audits. These rules recognize this fact; accordingly, such engagements are viewed as audit services in the context of these rules.

Furthermore, audit services also would include services performed to fulfill the accountant's responsibility under GAAS. For example, in some situations, a tax partner may be involved in reviewing the tax accrual that appears in the company's financial statements. Since that is a necessary part of the audit process, that activity constitutes an audit service. Likewise, complex accounting is-

sues may require that the firm engage in consultation with "national office" or other technical reviewers to reach an audit judgment. Whether or not the firm separately charges for that consultation, the activity constitutes an audit service since it is a necessary procedure used by the accountant in reaching an opinion on the financial statements.

This would contrast with a situation where a registrant is evaluating a proposed transaction and asks the independent accountant to evaluate the accounting for the proposed transaction. After research and consultation, the accounting firm provides an answer to the registrant and bills for those services. In considering the nature of the services, these services would not be considered to be audit services.

These rules require that the audit committee pre-approve all services. In doing so, the Act permits the audit committee to establish policies and procedures for pre-approval provided they are detailed as to the particular service and designed to safeguard the continued independence of the accountant. For example, the Sarbanes-Oxley Act allows for one or more audit committee members who are independent board directors to pre-approve the service. Decisions made by the designated audit committee members must be reported to the full audit committee at each of its scheduled meetings.[147]

Consistent with the Sarbanes-Oxley Act, our rules also reflect a de minimis exception solely related to the provision of non-audit services for an issuer. This exception waives the pre-approval requirements for non-audit services provided that: (1) all such services do not aggregate to more than five percent of total revenues paid by the audit client to its accountant in the fiscal year when services are provided, (2) were not recognized as non-audit services at the time of the engagement, and (3) are promptly brought to the attention of audit committee and approved prior to the completion of the audit by the audit committee or one or more designated representatives. Lastly, as further discussed later in this release, the audit committee's policies for pre-approvals of services should be disclosed by registrants in periodic annual reports.

As noted earlier, the proposed rules provided two alternatives related to pre-approval of permissible non-audit services as well as all audit, review, or attest engagements required under the securities laws: either pre-approval before the account-

---

(Footnote Continued)

porate Secretaries, dated January 13, 2003; letter from Ernst & Young, dated January 6, 2003.

[145] Section 202 of the Sarbanes-Oxley Act.

[146] Section 202 of the Sarbanes-Oxley Act; 15 U.S.C 78j-1(i)(1)(A).

[147] The Act permits the audit committee to pre-approve a service at any time in advance of the activity. We expect that

audit committees will establish policies for the maximum period in advance of the activity the approval may be granted. *See* "Report of the Senate Committee on Banking, Housing and Urban Affairs, Public Company Accounting Reform and Investor Protection Act of 2002," 107th Cong., 2nd Sess., at 20 (Report 107-205. July 3, 2002).

ant is engaged to provide the services or the engagement is entered into pursuant to detailed pre-approval policies and procedures established by the audit committee, with the audit committee informed on a timely basis of each service. In response to issues raised by commenters, the final rule has been modified to remove the appearance of an implicit preference of one alternative over another.

With respect to investment companies, the proposed rule would have required pre-approval not only of the non-auditing services provided to the investment company, but also require pre-approval by the investment company's audit committee of the non-auditing services provided to the investment company's investment adviser and any entity controlling, controlled by, or under common control with the investment adviser that provides services to the investment company.

Commenters[148] expressed concern over the breadth of this proposed rule and the unintended consequences of the pre-approval process. Commenters[149] observed that an auditor could provide a non-audit service to an entity in an investment company complex that would require the pre-approval of multiple audit committees. Some commenters[150] indicated investment company complexes often have more than one audit committee for the various investment companies in the complex. Additionally, the other entities in the complex, themselves, will often have their own audit committees. As proposed, the rule would require not only the audit committee of the entity engaging the auditor to provide the non-audit service to pre-approve the use of the accountant, but also would require each audit committee of an investment company registrant in the complex to pre-approve the use of the accountant. This would ultimately result in each investment company audit committee having veto power over all non-audit services provided to the complex even if those services did not relate directly to the financial reporting or operations of the investment company. One commenter[151] expressed concern over the burden this would place on the investment company's audit committee. Other commenters[152] expressed concern with whether the members of the audit committee would be capable of evaluating the appropriateness of services provided to

entities unrelated to the investment company's operations or financial reporting.

Commenters[153] suggested the rule should require the audit committee of the investment company to only pre-approve those audit and non-audit services provided directly to the investment company. One commenter[154] suggested the rule should require the audit committee of the investment company to pre-approve those audit and non-audit services that relate to the operations of the investment company.

After considering the comments, we believe modifying the approach by requiring the pre-approval of non-audit services to only those provided to the investment company directly, as suggested by several of the commenters, would not be consistent with the spirit or intent of the Sarbanes-Oxley Act. To address the commenters' concerns, but preserve the intent of the legislation, the rules as adopted would limit the investment company's audit committee pre-approval responsibility to those services provided directly to the investment company and those services provided to an entity in the investment company complex where the nature of the services provided have a direct impact on the operations or financial reporting of the investment company. The final rules would allow the investment company's audit committee to assess and determine before the work is conducted the impact that the services might reasonably have on the investment company accountant's independence as it relates to the audits of the investment company's financial statements. In addition, in response to one commenter's[155] suggestion concerning the non-audit services that should be disclosed, we have clarified the entities that provide services to the investment company that must be pre-approved. As adopted only the service providers that provide "ongoing" services to the investment company must have their non-audit services pre-approved. Thus, the final rules would limit the number of instances where pre-approval would be sought from multiple audit committees in the complex.

Although it may not be practical or feasible for the investment company audit committee to pre-approve all services provided to the investment company complex, we continue to believe the audit committee should be aware of all services the

---

[148] *See, e.g.,* letter from Deloitte & Touche, dated January 10, 2003; letter from Ernst & Young, dated January 6, 2003; letter from Investment Company Institute, dated January 13, 2003.

[149] *See, e.g.,* letter from Ernst & Young, dated January 6, 2003; letter from Deloitte & Touche, dated January 10, 2003; letter from PricewaterhouseCoopers, dated January 8, 2003.

[150] *See,* letter from PricewaterhouseCoopers, dated January 8, 2003; letter from Investment Company Institute, dated January 13, 2003.

[151] *See,* letter from Investment Company Institute, dated January 13, 2003.

[152] *See,* letter from PricewaterhouseCoopers, dated January 8, 2003; letter from Deloitte & Touche, LLP, dated January 10, 2003.

[153] *See,* letter from Ernst & Young, LLP, dated January 6, 2003; letter from Investment Company Institute, dated January 13, 2003.

[154] *See,* letter from PricewaterhouseCoopers, dated January 8, 2003.

[155] *See,* letter from PricewaterhouseCoopers, dated January 8, 2003.

accountant is providing to entities in the investment company complex. One commenter[156] agreed with this position suggesting non-audit services be disclosed quarterly. As a result, we are adopting a requirement in the rule that the accountant disclose to the audit committee all services provided to the investment company complex, including the fees associated with those services.

The de minimis exception that was proposed would have calculated the percentage threshold based on the total revenues paid to the investment company's accountant by the investment company, its investment adviser and any entity controlling, controlled by, or under common control with the investment adviser that provided services to the investment company. We asked for comment on the appropriate methodology for calculating the de minimis exception. One commenter[157] suggested it would be unfair to determine the calculation of the de minimis exception based on the total fees paid to the accountant by the investment company because the resulting threshold would be so low; the practical effect would be no de minimis exception for investment companies. Therefore, the commenter suggested the threshold should coincide with the scope of the pre-approval requirement. We agree with the commenter and believe that the calculation of the de minimis exception should not relate solely to the level of services provided to the investment company. We have modified the proposed rule to determine the threshold based on the services provided to the investment company complex that were subject to the pre-approval requirements for the investment company's audit committee.

The proposed rules would require the audit committee to pre-approve all audit, review, and attest reports required under the securities laws. Section 32(a) of the Investment Company Act requires that a majority of the directors who are not interested persons appoint the independent accountant of the investment company. We requested comment on who should approve the selection of the accountant of the investment company, for example, the independent directors, the audit committee or both. One commenter[158] stated that the audit committee should select the accountant and the independent directors should ratify the selection, thereby retaining the independent directors as the ultimate decision making authority with respect to accountant selection. After consideration of these matters, we have determined to adopt the rules as proposed.

Also, as discussed later in this release, these provisions are supplemented as a result of the proxy disclosure requirements. We believe that disclosure of the procedures the audit committee uses to pre-approve audit services, as well as the disclosure of all non-audit services by category, including those meeting the de minimis exception stated above, will provide investors valuable information that may be used to evaluate the relationships that exist between the accountant and the audit client.

These rules apply to all audit, review, and attest services and non-audit services that are entered into after the effective date of these rules. For arrangements for non-audit services entered into prior to the effective date of these rules—regardless of whether or not they were pre-approved by the audit committee—the accounting firm will have 12 months from the effective date of these rules to complete these services. For example, an engagement to provide non-audit services that was entered into in December 2002, which may or may not be complete by the effective date of these rules, is not subject to these rules, but must be completed within 12 months of the effective date of these rules. We believe these transition provisions will permit an orderly completion of existing engagements and permit accountants and audit committees adequate time to prepare to implement the new rules.

E. Compensation

We understand that some accounting firms offer their professionals cash bonuses and other financial incentives to sell products or services, other than audit, review, or attest services, to their audit clients. Such compensation arrangements may create a financial or other self-interest that could constitute a threat to the accountant's objectivity.[159] These arrangements also may detract from audit quality by incentivizing the audit partner to focus on selling non-audit services rather than providing high quality audit services.

We also question whether a reasonable investor with full knowledge of such incentive programs would believe that the accountant could function with the independence and objectivity that is necessary for him or her to maintain, both in fact and in appearance. We are concerned that an accountant might be viewed as compromising accounting judgments in order not to jeopardize the potential for increased income from the act of selling non-audit services to the audit client. Because of this concern, we proposed that an accountant's independence would be deemed to have been impaired when he or she is compensated for selling or performing non-audit services for an audit client. Our proposed rule limited such compensa-

---

[156] See, letter from KPMG, LLP, dated January 9, 2003.

[157] See, letter from PricewaterhouseCoopers, dated January 8, 2003.

[158] See, letter from Investment Company Institute, dated January 13, 2003.

[159] See, e.g., AICPA, Practice Alert 99-1, Guidance for Independence Discussions with Audit Committees, (May 1999).

tion, direct or otherwise, that could be provided to any audit engagement team partner.

Commenters expressed two primary concerns with the proposals. First,[160] because the compensation was not directly related to sales activities, the operation of the rule would have been difficult given the size and nature of some firms' national and global operations. For example, read literally as proposed, a partner's compensation could not include a proportionate share of the accounting firm's overall profits, because some of those profits would be derived from the provision of non-audit services by other firm personnel. Second, some commenters[161] observed that the provisions were perceived to be overly broad because, as proposed, they would have applied to partners who provide specialized services and would have prevented them from being rewarded for selling or performing services in their area of expertise. For example, under the proposal an audit partner could be rewarded for selling audit, review or attest services; however, tax partners could not be rewarded for selling additional tax services to audit clients if they were members of the audit engagement team. That is, audit partners could be rewarded for selling within their own discipline, but tax partners could not.

We are addressing these concerns by clarifying that the compensation concerns exist where the audit partner's compensation is based on the act of selling non-audit services and specifying that the rule applies to audit partners. As described more fully in our discussion of definitions, the term audit partner refers to the lead and concurring partners and other partners on the audit engagement team who have responsibility for decision-making on significant auditing, accounting, and reporting matters that affect the financial state-

ments or who maintain regular contact with management or the audit committee. In particular, audit partners, other than specialty partners, would include all audit partners serving the client at the issuer or parent.[162] Further, the lead partner on subsidiaries of the issuer whose assets or revenues constitute 20% or more of the consolidated assets or revenues are included within the definition of audit partner. Conceivably, "compensation" could include any form of cash or other assets distributed to the audit partner, including any income or benefit based on an evaluation of the partner's performance.

This rule prohibits accounting firms from establishing an audit partner's compensation or allocation of partnership "units" based on the sale[163] of non-audit services to the partner's audit clients.[164] This provision also reinforces the position that accountants at the partner level should be viewed as skilled professionals and not as conduits for the sale of non-audit services to the audit partner's individual clients. This provision recognizes and focuses on the need for independence of the most senior members of the engagement team. However, this rule does not preclude an audit partner from sharing in the profits of the audit practice and those of the overall firm.[165] And, an audit partner's evaluation could take into account a number of factors directly or indirectly related to selling services to an audit client.[166]

Accordingly, we are amending the auditor independence rules to address the practice of accountants being compensated by their firms for selling non-audit products and services to their audit clients.[167] The new rule would provide that an accountant is not independent if, at any point during the audit and professional engagement period,[168] any audit partner,[169] other than specialty part-

---

[160] *See, e.g.*, letter from American Institute of Certified Public Accountants, dated January 9, 2003; letter from Deloitte & Touche, LLP, dated January 10, 2003; letter from Ernst & Young, LLP, dated January 6, 2003; letter from Federation des Experts Comptables Europeens, dated January 13, 2003; letter from Institute of Chartered Accountants in England and Wales, dated December 24, 2002; letter from KPMG, LLP, dated January 9, 2003; letter from PricewaterhouseCoopers, dated January 8, 2003.

[161] *See, e.g.*, letter from Ernst & Young, LLP, dated January 6, 2003; letter from Deloitte & Touche, LLP, dated January 10, 2003; letter from KPMG, LLP, dated January 9, 2003; letter from McGladrey & Pullen, LLP, dated January 9, 2003.

[162] As discussed previously, partners who provided ten or fewer hours of service are excluded from the definition of audit partner.

[163] For purposes of this rule, the term "sale" is meant to encompass any revenue, fees, or compensation related to non-audit services provided over the period of the evaluation, regardless when contracted.

[164] *Id.*

[165] Consistent with the idea that an audit partner cannot be directly compensated for selling non-audit services, no part of that partner's distribution or other form of compensation should be directly received from selling of non-audit services

(for example, from a "pool" of profits generated by a valuation services business unit). In contrast, that partner may receive distributions or other compensation from the "pool" attributable to the audit practice, a geographic unit comprised of several services or offices, or the entire firm.

[166] For example, an audit partner could be evaluated on the complexity of his or her engagements, the overall management of the relationship with an audit client including the provision of non-audit services, and/or the attainment of explicit sales goals.

[167] An audit partner could be compensated for selling audit or audit-related services to an audit client. Additionally, an audit partner could be compensated for selling either audit or non-audit services to a non-audit client.

[168] "Audit and professional engagement period" includes both the period covered by the financial statements being audited or reviewed and the period of engagement to audit or review the client's financial statements or to prepare a report filed with the Commission. The period of engagement begins when the auditor signs an initial engagement letter or begins audit, review or attest procedures, and ends when the client or the auditor notifies the Commission that the client is no longer the auditor's audit client. *See* Rule 2-01(f)(5) of Regulation S-X, 17 CFR 210.2-01(f)(5).

[169] 17 CFR 210.2-01(f)(7)(ii).

---

ners,[170] earns or receives compensation[171] based on selling engagements to that audit client, to provide any services,[172] other than audit, review, or attest services.

The lead partner is responsible for managing not only the audit engagement but also the client relationship. The lead partner is in a position to identify potential services that could benefit the audit client. Furthermore, because of the lead partner's frequent interaction with management, he or she has the opportunity to "pitch" those services to management. Thus, the lead partner relationship with management has been used by some as a conduit to sell non-audit services to the audit client.[173]

In contrast, partners at smaller operating units and "specialty" partners typically have a low level of involvement with senior management and the responsibility for the overall presentation in the financial statements is relatively low.

The application of these rules allows partners to be compensated for selling services with their discipline. Thus, just as an audit partner can be compensated for selling audit and audit-related services, so, too, can a tax partner be compensated for selling tax services. A specialty partner receiving compensation for selling within his or her discipline does not create the same threat to independence as when an audit partner is compensated for selling those non-audit services because the lead partner retains overall responsibility for the conduct of the audit. Additionally, there is a concurring partner who reviews the work on the audit engagement team. Finally, specialty partners have limited relationships with management in the context of their activities as a member of the audit engagement team.

The rules that we are adopting mitigate the concerns that an audit partner might be viewed as compromising audit judgments in order not to jeopardize the potential for selling non-audit services. These rules do not specifically address the provision of compensation to other audit engagement team members for directly selling non-audit services. We believe that, however, the other audit engagement team members will perform in a fashion that is consistent with the direction and tone set by the audit partners. Nonetheless, as it pre-approves non-audit services an audit committee may wish to consider whether, in the company's particular circumstances, compensating a senior

staff member on the audit engagement team based on his or her success in selling the service to the company compromises that individual's or the firm's independence.

Further, in conducting its oversight review of registered public accounting firms, we expect that the Board will monitor the impact of these rules on audit quality and independence.

With respect to investment companies, the proposed rule on compensation would have prohibited all partners, principals and shareholders of an accounting firm that are members of the audit engagement team from being compensated for selling non-audit services to a registered investment company audit client or any other entity in the investment company complex. One commenter[174] suggested the rule on partner compensation for investment companies should apply only to the selling of non-audit services to the investment company itself and not to other entities in the investment company complex. We disagree and continue to believe a partner on a registered investment company audit should not be directly compensated for selling non-audit services to other entities in the investment company complex, for example, the investment company's investment adviser. Thus, we have not made changes to this aspect of the rule.

We understand that because of the seasonal nature of accounting firms that many firms have fiscal periods that end in the April to September time frame. In recognition of this fact and understanding that individuals may be operating in the current period under an established set of performance goals, the provisions of this paragraph will be effective in the fiscal periods of the accounting firm that commence after the effective date of these rules. Further, recognizing that the application of this rule could have a disproportionate economic impact on small firms, we are exempting firms with fewer than five audit clients that are issuers[175] and fewer than ten partners from the provisions of this requirement.

F. Definitions

The rules that the Commission is adopting impact various parties involved in the audit and financial reporting process of issuers. To more clearly identify those parties, we have revised and added to the definitions in Rule 2-01(f) of Regulation S-X. This section discusses those definitions.

1. Accountant

---

[170] Specialty partners are, among others, those partners who consults with others on the audit engagement team during the audit, review or attestation engagement regarding technical or industry-specific issues. For example, such partners would include tax specialist and valuation specialist.

[171] Nothing in these rules is meant to limit the ability of an accounting firm from distributing profits in a manner that is consistent with the operation of a partnership or service organization.

[172] For purposes of this discussion, services include tangible products as well as professional services.

[173] See e.g., In the Matter of Arthur Andersen LLP, Accounting and Auditing Enforcement Release No. 1405 (June 19, 2001), at notes 15-17.

[174] See, letter from Investment Company Institute, dated January 13, 2003.

[175] As defined in section 10A(f) of the Securities Exchange Act of 1934 (15 U.S.C. 78j-1(f)).

The term "accountant" previously was defined under the rules of the Commission as a "certified public accountant or public accountant performing services in connection with an engagement for which independence is required."[176] We have added to the definition the phrase, "registered public accounting firm." Under the provisions of the Sarbanes-Oxley Act, public accounting firms must register with the Board in order to prepare or issue, or to participate in the preparation or issuance of, any audit report with respect to any issuer.[177] Thus, the term "registered public accounting firm" refers to a firm that has registered with the Board in accordance with the requirements of the Sarbanes-Oxley Act.

2. Accounting Role

Under the previous rules of the Commission, "accounting role or financial reporting oversight role" was a defined term. However, because the rules requiring a cooling-off period for employment at the issuer relate only to those performing a financial reporting oversight role, the Commission has separated the definition of "accounting role" from that of "financial reporting oversight role." The term "accounting role" refers to a role where a person can or does exercise more than minimal influence over the contents of the accounting records or over any person who prepares the accounting records. All persons in a "financial reporting oversight role" (defined below) also are in an "accounting role." Persons in an accounting role include individuals in clerical positions responsible for accounting records (e.g., payroll, accounts payable, accounts receivable, purchasing, sales) as well as those who report to individuals in financial reporting oversight roles (e.g., assistant controller, assistant treasurer, manager of internal audit, manager of financial reporting).

3. Financial Reporting Oversight Role

The term "financial reporting oversight role" refers to a role in which an individual has direct responsibility for or oversight of those who prepare the registrant's financial statements and related information (e.g., management discussion and analysis), which will be included in a registrant's document filed with the Commission. As noted above, "accounting role and financial reporting oversight role" previously was one definition. In order to subject the appropriate individuals to certain portions of these rules, we have bifurcated the definitions.

4. Audit Committee

Section 205 of the Sarbanes-Oxley Act defines an audit committee as:

A committee (or equivalent body) established by and amongst the board of directors of an issuer for the purpose of overseeing the accounting and financial reporting processes of the issuer and audits of the financial statements of the issuer.

The Act further stipulates that if no such committee exists, then the audit committee is the entire board of directors. For purposes of these independence rules, the Commission is adopting the same meaning for audit committee as used in the Act.

The audit committee serves as an important body, serving the interests of investors, to help ensure that the registrant and its accountants fulfill their responsibilities under the securities laws. Because the definition of an audit committee can include the entire board of directors if no such committee of the board exists, these rules do not require registrants to establish audit committees. Likewise, the auditor independence rules do not require that the committee be composed of independent members of the board.[178]

Some entities do not have boards of directors and therefore do not have audit committees. For example, some limited liability companies and limited partnerships that do not have a corporate general partner may not have an oversight body that is the equivalent of an audit committee. We are not exempting these entities from the requirements. Rather, such issuers should look through each general partner of the successive limited partnerships until a corporate general partner or an individual general partner is reached. With respect to a corporate general partner, the registrant should look to the audit committee of the corporate general partner or to the full board of directors as fulfilling the role of the audit committee. With respect to an individual general partner, the registrant should look to the individual as fulfilling the role of the audit committee.

We are, however, exempting asset-backed issuers[179] and unit investment trusts[180] from this requirement. Because of the nature of these entities, such issuers are subject to substantially different reporting requirements. Most significantly, asset-backed issuers are not required to file financial statements like other companies. Similarly, unit investment trusts are not required to provide shareholder reports containing audited financial statements. Also, such entities typically are passively managed pools of assets. Therefore, we are not applying the requirements related to audit committees in this release to such entities.

5. Audit Engagement Team

As discussed earlier in this release, the cooling off period applies to members of the audit engagement team. As used in this release, the term audit engagement team means all partners (or person in an equivalent position) and professional employees participating in an audit, review, or attestation

---

[176] 17 CFR 2-01(f)(1).

[177] *See*, Section 102(a) of the Sarbanes-Oxley Act.

[178] *See*, Release No. 33-8173 (Jan. 8, 2003).

[179] As defined in 17 CFR 240.13a-14(g) and 240.15d-14(g).

[180] As defined by Section 4(2) of the Investment Company Act [15 U.S.C. 80a-4(2)].

engagement of an audit client. Included within the audit engagement team would be partners and all other persons who consult with other members of the engagement team during the audit, review, or attestation engagement regarding technical or industry-specific issues, transactions, or events.

6. Audit Partner

The term audit partner is an integral part of the rules we are adopting related to partner compensation and partner rotation. In each case, the affected parties are audit partners. As used in this rule, the term audit partner means a partner (or person in an equivalent position) who is a member of the audit engagement team (as defined above) who has responsibility for decision-making on significant auditing, accounting, and reporting matters that affect the financial statements or who maintains regular contact with management and the audit committee.

The term audit partner would include the lead and concurring partners, partners such as relationship partners who serve the client at the issuer or parent level, other than a partner who consults with others on the audit engagement team during the audit, review, or attestation engagement regarding technical or industry-specific issues, transactions, or events, and the lead partner on subsidiaries of the issuer whose assets or revenues constitute 20% or more of the consolidated assets or revenues of the issuer.[181]

G. Communication with Audit Committees

Auditors are required by GAAS to communicate certain matters to the audit committee. In particular, GAAS require that the accountant should determine that the audit committee is informed about matters such as:

- Auditor's responsibility under GAAS,
- Significant accounting policies,
- Methods used to account for significant unusual transactions,
- Effects of significant accounting policies in controversial or emerging areas for which there is a lack of authoritative guidance or consensus,
- Process used by management in formulating particularly sensitive accounting estimates and the basis for the auditor's conclusions regarding the reasonableness of those estimates,
- Material audit adjustments proposed and immaterial adjustments not recorded by management,

- Auditor's judgments about the quality of the company's accounting principles,
- Auditor's responsibility for other information in documents containing audited financial statements,
- Auditor's views about significant matters that were the subject of consultation between management and other accountants,
- Major issues discussed with management prior to retention,
- Difficulties with management encountered in performing the audit, and
- Disagreements with management over the application of accounting principles, the basis for management's accounting estimates, and the disclosures in the financial statements.[182]

Accountants are required under GAAS to provide these communications in a timely manner but not necessarily before the issuance of the audit report.[183] Accountants also may communicate with audit committees on matters in addition to those specifically required by GAAS, including auditing issues, engagement letters, management representation letters, internal controls, auditor independence, and others.

Section 204 of the Sarbanes-Oxley Act directs the Commission to issue rules requiring timely reporting of specific information by accountants to audit committees. In response to the Act, we proposed amending Regulation S-X to require each public accounting firm registered with the Board that audits an issuer's financial statements to report, prior to the filing of such report with the Commission, to the issuer or registered investment company's audit committee: (1) all critical accounting policies and practices used by the issuer or registered investment company, (2) all alternative accounting treatments of financial information within generally accepted accounting principles ("GAAP") that have been discussed with management, including the ramifications of the use of such alternative treatments and disclosures and the treatment preferred by the accounting firm, and (3) other material written communications between the accounting firm and management of the issuer or registered investment company.

Some commenters[184] believe that these communications should be the responsibility of manage-

---

[181] The term "audit partner" also would include any audit partner on a registered investment company whether or not the investment company issues consolidated financial statements.

[182] See, AU §380, "Communication with Audit Committees." There are additional GAAS requirements related to auditor communications that are not included in this rule, such as the auditor's responsibilities under GAAS, the auditor's responsibilities related to documents containing audited financial statements, and disagreements with management,

consultations with other accountants, major issues discussed with management prior to retention, and difficulties encountered in performing the audit, to the extent that those matters do not relate to accounting policies and practices.

[183] Id.

[184] See, e.g., letter from The Institute of Chartered Accountants of Scotland, dated January 8, 2003; letter from Battelle & Battelle, LLP, dated December 20, 2002; letter from Grant Thornton LLP, dated January 13, 2003.

ment alone. Others,[185] however, believe that both the accountant and management should share the responsibility for informing the audit committee about such matters. While we understand that management has the primary responsibility for the information contained in the financial statements, since the accounting firm is retained by the audit committee, we share the view reflected in Section 205 of the Sarbanes-Oxley Act and current auditing standards, that the accounting firm has a responsibility to communicate certain information to the audit committee. As discussed below, we are adopting rules requiring that certain information be communicated by the independent accountant to the audit committee. Some commenters[186] believe that the Commission should require that these communications be in writing. Others,[187] however, disagree. We have not required that the communication be in writing. We would expect, however, that such communications would be documented by the accountant and the audit committee. We believe that many of these communications currently are being made as accountants fulfill their responsibilities under GAAS and the securities laws.[188]

In describing the role and responsibilities of the audit committee, Warren Buffett has stated that:

Their function . . . is to hold the auditor's feet to the fire. And, I suggest . . . the audit committee ask [questions]of the auditors [including]: if the auditor were solely responsible for preparation of the company's financial statements, would they have been prepared in any way differently than the manner selected by management? They should inquire as to both material and non-material differences. If the auditor would have done anything differently than management, then explanations should be made of management's argument and the auditor's response.[189]

Requiring that the accountants communicate information to the audit committee will aid the audit committee in fulfilling its responsibilities.

1. Critical Accounting Policies and Practices

Consistent with our proposal, we are establishing rules requiring communication by accountants to audit committees of all critical accounting policies and practices.[190] In December 2001, we issued cautionary advice regarding each issuer disclosing in the Management's Discussion and Analysis[191] section of its annual report those accounting policies that management believes are most critical to the preparation of the issuer's financial statements.[192] The cautionary advice indicated that "critical" accounting policies are those that are both most important to the portrayal of the company's financial condition and results and require management's most difficult, subjective or complex judgments, often as a result of the need to make estimates about the effect of matters that are inherently uncertain.[193] As part of that cautionary advice, we stated:

Prior to finalizing and filing annual reports, audit committees should review the selection, application and disclosure of critical accounting policies. Consistent with auditing standards, audit committees should be apprised of the evaluative criteria used by management in their selection of the accounting principles and methods. Proactive discussions between the audit committee and the company's senior management and auditor about critical accounting policies are appropriate.[194]

In May 2002, the Commission proposed rules to require disclosures that would enhance investors' understanding of the application of companies' critical accounting policies.[195] The May 2002 proposed rules cover (1) accounting estimates a company makes in applying its accounting policies and (2) the initial adoption by a company of an accounting policy that has a material impact on its financial presentation. Under the first part of those proposed rules, a "critical accounting estimate" is defined as an accounting estimate recognized in the financial statements (1) that requires the registrant to make assumptions about matters that are highly uncertain at the time the accounting estimate is made and (2) for which different estimates that the company reasonably could have used in the current period, or changes in the accounting estimate that are reasonably likely to occur from period to period, would have a material impact on the presentation of the registrant's fi-

[185] *See, e.g.,* letter from Gelford Hochstadt Pangburn, PC, dated January 3, 2003; letter from Ernst & Young LLP, dated January 6, 2003.

[186] *See, e.g.,* letter from Piercy Bowler Taylor & Kern, dated January 7, 2003; letter from Robert G. Beard, undated; letter from Eide Bailly LLP, dated January 8, 2003; letter from California Public Employees' Retirement System, dated January 10, 2003; letter from Lynn E. Turner, dated January 13, 2003.

[187] *See, e.g.,* letter from Computer Sciences Corporation, dated January 13, 2003; letter from Sullivan & Cromwell LLP, dated January 10, 2003; letter from America's Community Bankers, dated January 13, 2003; letter from Deloitte & Touche LLP, dated January 10, 2003.

[188] *See,* "Audit Committee Disclosures," Release No. 34-42266, Dec. 22, 1999.

[189] Warren Buffett, Comments during SEC "Roundtable Discussion on Financial Disclosure and Auditor Oversight," March 4, 2002.

[190] In this release, the terms "critical accounting policies and practices" and "critical accounting policies" are used interchangeably.

[191] Item 303 of Regulation S-K, (17 CFR 229.303), which requires disclosure about, among other things, trends, events or uncertainties known to management that would have a material impact on reported financial information.

[192] Release No. 33-8040, Dec. 12, 2001, (66 FR 65013).

[193] *Id.*

[194] *Id.* (footnotes omitted).

[195] Release No. 33-8090, May 10, 2002, (67 FR 35620).

nancial condition, changes in financial condition or results of operations. The May 2002 proposed rules outline certain disclosures that a company would be required to make about its critical accounting estimates. In addition, under the second part of the May 2002 proposed rules, a company would be required to make certain disclosures about its initial adoption of accounting policies, including the choices the company had among accounting principles.

Accountants and issuers should read and refer to the December 2001 Cautionary Guidance to determine the types of matters that should be communicated to the audit committee under this rule. We are not requiring that those discussions follow a specific form or manner, but we expect, at a minimum, that the discussion of critical accounting estimates and the selection of initial accounting policies will include the reasons why estimates or policies meeting the criteria in the Guidance are or are not considered critical and how current and anticipated future events impact those determinations. In addition, we anticipate that the communications regarding critical accounting policies will include an assessment of management's disclosures along with any significant proposed modifications by the accountants that were not included.

2. Alternative Accounting Treatments

We recognize that the complexity of financial transactions results in accounting answers that are often the subject of significant debate between management and the accountants. Some commenters[196] to the proposed rules suggested that this rule be restricted to material accounting alternatives. These commenters indicated that restricting these communications will assist audit committee members by focusing their attention on important accounting alternatives. One commenter[197] believes that only alternative treatments under GAAP that were the subject of serious consideration and debate by the accountant and management should be communicated to the audit committee.

We understand the concerns expressed and, accordingly, we have clarified the final rule. Providing audit committees with information on material accounting alternatives is consistent with the objectives of the Act and will minimize the risk that audit committee members will be distracted from material accounting policy matters by the numerous discussions between the accountant and management on the application of accounting principles to relatively small transaction or events. Therefore, these rules require communication, ei-

ther orally or in writing, by accountants to audit committees of all alternative treatments within GAAP for policies and practices related to material items that have been discussed with management, including the ramifications of the use of such alternative treatments and disclosures and the treatment preferred by the accounting firm. This rule is intended to cover recognition, measurement, and disclosure considerations related to the accounting for specific transactions as well as general accounting policies.

We believe that communications regarding specific transactions should identify, at a minimum, the underlying facts, financial statement accounts impacted, and applicability of existing corporate accounting policies to the transaction. In addition, if the accounting treatment proposed does not comply with existing corporate accounting policies, or if an existing corporate accounting policy is not applicable, then an explanation of why the existing policy was not appropriate or applicable and the basis for the selection of the alternative policy should be discussed. Regardless of whether the accounting policy selected preexists or is new, the entire range of alternatives available under GAAP that were discussed by management and the accountants should be communicated along with the reasons for not selecting those alternatives. If the accounting treatment selected is not, in the accountant's view, the preferred method, we expect that the reasons why the accountant's preferred method was not selected by management also will be discussed.

Communications regarding general accounting policies should focus on the initial selection of and changes in significant accounting policies, as required by GAAS,[198] and should include the impact of management's judgments and accounting estimates, as well as the accountant's judgments about the quality of the entity's accounting principles. The discussion of general accounting policies should include the range of alternatives available under GAAP that were discussed by management and the accountants along with the reasons for selecting the chosen policy. If an existing accounting policy is being modified, then the reasons for the change also should be communicated. If the accounting policy selected is not the accountant's preferred policy, then we expect the discussions to include the reasons why the accountant considered one policy to be preferred but that policy was not selected by management.

The separate discussion of critical accounting policies and practices is not considered a substitute for communications regarding general ac-

---

[196] *See, e.g.,* letter from Chamber of Commerce of the United States of America, dated January 9,2003; letter from Battelle & Battelle LLP, dated December 20, 2002; letter from Eli Lilly and Company, dated January 9, 2003; letter from

Computer Sciences Corporation, dated January 13, 2003; letter from PricewaterhouseCoopers, dated January 8, 2003.

[197] *See, e.g.,* letter from Deloitte & Touche LLP, dated January 10, 2003.

[198] *See,* AU § 380.

counting policies, since the discussion about critical accounting policies and practices might not encompass any new or changed general accounting policies and practices. Likewise, this discussion of general accounting policies and practices is not intended to dilute the communications related to critical accounting policies and practices, since the issues affecting critical accounting policies and practices, such as sensitivities of assumptions and others, may be tailored specifically to events in the current year, and the selection of general accounting policies and practices should consider a broad range of transactions over time.

3. Other Material Written Communications

We understand written communications between accountants and management range from formal documents, such as engagement letters, to informal correspondence, such as administrative items. We also acknowledge that historically not all forms of written communications provided to management have been provided to the audit committee. Our rule is intended to implement Section 205 of the Sarbanes-Oxley Act, which clarified the substance of information that should be provided by accountants to audit committees to facilitate accountant and management oversight by those committees.

The Sarbanes-Oxley Act specifically cites the management letter and schedules of unadjusted differences as examples of material written communications to be provided to audit committees. Examples of additional written communications that we expect will be considered material to an issuer include:

- Management representation letter;[199]

- Reports on observations and recommendations on internal controls;[200]

- Schedule of unadjusted audit differences,[201] and a listing of adjustments and reclassifications not recorded, if any;

- Engagement letter;[202] and

- Independence letter.[203]

These examples are not exhaustive, and accountants are encouraged to critically consider what additional written communications should be provided to audit committees.

4. Timing of Communications

Commenters[204] generally agreed with our proposal that the communications should occur prior to the filing of the issuer's periodic annual report, although a commenter[205] suggested that the communications should occur throughout the period. The Act requires that the communications be timely reported to the audit committee. For purposes of the requirements of this provision, our rule specifies that the communications between the accountant and the audit committee occur prior to the filing of the audit report with the Commission pursuant to applicable securities laws. As a result, these discussions will occur, at a minimum, during the annual audit, but we expect that they could occur as frequently as quarterly or more often on a real-time basis.

The timing of these communications is intended to occur before any audit report is filed with the Commission pursuant to the securities laws. We believe that this rule will ensure that these communications occur prior to filing of annual reports and proxy statements, as well as prior to filing registration statements and other periodic or current reports when audit reports are included.

5. Investment Companies

The proposed rules would have required accountants to communicate with an audit committee of an investment company all critical accounting policies, alternative methodologies and other material information before filing an audit report with the Commission. Although commenters[206] generally agreed that the information required to be communicated was appropriate, the timing of such communications would be problematic for investment companies. Commenters[207] stated that investment companies within an investment company complex frequently have a common board of directors, but have staggered fiscal-year ends. As a result, the proposed rules could require accountants to communicate with audit committees as frequently as monthly. To eliminate this burden, some commenters[208] suggested these discussions occur as infrequently as annu-

---

[199] See, SAS No. 85, "Management Representations," AU § 333.

[200] See, SAS 60, "Communication of Internal Control Related Matters Noted in an Audit," AU § 325.

[201] See, SAS No. 89, "Audit Adjustments," AU § 333.

[202] See, SAS No. 83, "Establishing an Understanding With the Client," AU § 310.

[203] See, SQCS No. 2, "System of Quality Control for a CPA Firm's Accounting and Auditing Practice," QC § 20.

[204] See, e.g., letter from California Public Employees' Retirement System, dated January 10, 2003; letter from Computer Sciences Corporation, dated January 13, 2003; letter from American Institute of Certified Public Accountants, dated January 9, 2003; letter from PricewaterhouseCoopers, dated January 8, 2003.

[205] See, e.g., letter from Lynn E. Turner, dated January 13, 2003.

[206] See, letter from The Vanguard Group, dated January 13, 2003; letter from Investment Company Institute, dated January 13, 2003; letter from PricewaterhouseCoopers, dated January 8, 2003.

[207] See, e.g., letter from The Vanguard Group, dated January 13, 2003; letter from Investment Company Institute, dated January 13, 2003; letter from Ernst & Young, dated January 6, 2003.

[208] See, letter from The Vanguard Group, dated January 13, 2003; letter from Investment Company Institute, dated January 13, 2003; letter from PricewaterhouseCoopers, dated January 8, 2003.

ally, with two commenters[209] suggesting updates for material changes. Another commenter[210] suggested that we leave communication of these matters up to the discretion of the investment company's audit committee and the accountant.

We believe it is important to discuss critical accounting policies, alternative methodologies, and other material information close to the time when the audit report is filed. It is not our intention, however, to have accountants communicate the same information to the audit committee multiple times during the year. As adopted, the final rules require the accountant to communicate to the audit committee of an investment company annually, and if the annual communication is not within 90 days prior to the filing, provide an update in the 90 day period prior to the filing, of any changes to the previously reported information.[211]

The adopted rules, in effect, would require an accountant of an investment company complex where the individual funds have different fiscal year ends to communicate the required information no more frequently than four times during a calendar year. We believe this should not place an undue burden on investment company audit committees because many of the boards of directors for investment companies meet on a quarterly basis.[212]

H. Expanded Disclosure

To allow the issuer's investors to be better able to evaluate the independence of the accountant, we believe that disclosures should be made by issuers of the scope of services provided by its independent public accountants. Section 202 of the Sarbanes-Oxley Act requires pre-approval of all audit and non-audit services, with exceptions provided for de minimis amounts under certain circumstances, as described in the Act and in rules discussed previously in this release. The Sarbanes-Oxley Act further requires disclosure in periodic reports of non-audit services approved by the audit committee.

Current proxy disclosure rules require that a registrant disclose, in the most recent fiscal year,

the professional fees paid for both audit and non-audit services to its principal independent accountant. As a result of the requirements of Sarbanes-Oxley and partly in response to public comment on the current proxy disclosures requirements since their adoption in 2000, we proposed rules to change both the types of fees that must be described and the number of years for which the disclosures must be provided.[213] The proposed rules would have increased the disclosed categories of professional fees paid for audit and non-audit services from three to four. The categories of reportable fees proposed were: (1) Audit Fees, (2) Audit-Related Fees, (3) Tax Fees, and (4) All Other Fees.[214] The proposed disclosure called for information to be provided for each of the two most recent fiscal years, rather than just the most recent fiscal year. In addition, we proposed that registrants be required to describe in subcategories the nature of the services provided that are categorized as audit-related fees and all other fees.

Our proposed changes to the proxy disclosure rules were intended to clarify the categorization of services provided by the audit firm in order to provide increased transparency for investors. Many commenters[215] favored the approach of our proposals, however, some commenters[216] requested clarification relating to the categorization of certain types of services. For example, the discussion accompanying the proposed rules stated that the "tax fees" category would capture all services performed by professional staff in the independent accountant's tax division. Thus, the proposed rules would have required that the fees associated with the review by the tax partner of the tax accrual during the audit be included within the "tax services category." However, as stated elsewhere in the proposing release, the "audit services" category should include services performed to fulfill the accountant's responsibility under GAAS. Likewise, complex accounting issues may require that the firm engage in consultation with national office or other technical reviewers to reach an audit judgment.

---

[209] *See,* letter from Investment Company Institute, dated January 13, 2003; letter from The Vanguard Group, dated January 13, 2003.

[210] *See,* letter from Ernst & Young, dated January 6, 2003.

[211] The rule also would require communication of a description of all non-audit services provided, including fees associated with the services, to the investment company complex that were not subject to the pre-approval requirements for investment companies as discussed in Section II.D of this release.

[212] Similarly, the accountant only would need to disclose those non-audit services provided to the investment company complex that they were engaged to perform during the intervening period since their last communication, but for which pre-approval by the investment company's audit committee was not required.

[213] *See,* proposed Item 9(e), Schedule 14A.

[214] Previously, registrants were required to disclose only "Audit Fees," "Financial Systems Design and Implementation Fees" and "All Other Fees."

[215] *See, e.g.,* letter from California Public Employees' Retirement System, dated January 10, 2003; letter from The Business Roundtable, dated January 13, 2003; letter from America' Community Bankers, dated January 13, 2003; letter from American Institute of Certified Public Accountants, dated January 9, 2003; letter from Financial Executives International's Committee on Corporate Reporting, dated January 14,2003.

[216] *See, e.g.,* letter from Eli Lilly and Company, dated January 9, 2003; letter from KPMG, dated January 9, 2003; letter from Deloitte & Touche, LLP, dated January 10, 2003.

Some commenters[217] generally agreed with the proposed categories of services. Some,[218] however, suggested modifications or clarifications to the categories or reductions in the number of categories. Additionally, some commenters suggested that the disclosures should be provided for three years[219] and others suggested that they be provided for only one year.[220]

Our final rules retain the basic provisions of our proposals. In response to the requests by commenters for clarification of the categorization of services, we expect that all services performed to comply with GAAS should be classified as "audit services" in providing the disclosures. Certain services, such as tax services and accounting consultations, may not be billed as audit services. However, to the extent that such services are necessary to comply with GAAS, an appropriate allocation of those fees may be included in the audit fee category. We recognize, however, that some services may be difficult to classify and we encourage issuers and their accountants to contact our staff to discuss the appropriate classifications.

Consistent with our proposal, we are adopting rules requiring issuers to provide disclosures of fees paid to the independent accountant segregated into the four previously-identified categories. Additionally, other than for the audit category, the issuer is required to describe, in qualitative terms, the types of services provided under the remaining three categories. Also, consistent with our proposal, this information is required for the two most recent years. Finally, consistent with our proposal, this information must be provided either in the issuer's proxy statement, or its periodic annual filing.

While the rules we are adopting continue to require issuers to disclose fees paid to the principal accountant for audit services, we are expanding the types of fees that should be included in this category to include fees for services that normally would be provided by the accountant in connection with statutory and regulatory filings or engagements. In addition to including fees for services necessary to perform an audit or review in accordance with GAAS,[221] this category also may include services that generally only the independent accountant reasonably can provide, such as comfort letters, statutory audits, attest services,

consents and assistance with and review of documents filed with the Commission.

We believe that the addition of a new category, "Audit-Related Fees," will enable registrants to present the audit fee relationship with the principal accountant in a more transparent fashion. In general, "Audit-Related Fees" are assurance and related services (*e.g.*, due diligence services) that traditionally are performed by the independent accountant. More specifically, these services would include, among others: employee benefit plan audits, due diligence related to mergers and acquisitions, accounting consultations and audits in connection with acquisitions, internal control reviews, attest services that are not required by statue or regulation and consultation concerning financial accounting and reporting standards.

We also believe it is appropriate to add transparency regarding a second category of fees: "Tax Fees." The review of a registrant's tax returns and reserves is a task that often requires extensive knowledge about the audit client. In many public companies, the fee for tax services is substantial in relation to other services. We believe that investors will benefit from being able to consider those fees separately from the "All Other Fees" category. The "Tax Fees" category would capture all services performed by professional staff in the independent accountant's tax division except those services related to the audit as discussed previously. Typically, it would include fees for tax compliance, tax planning, and tax advice. Tax compliance generally involves preparation of original and amended tax returns, claims for refund and tax payment-planning services. Tax planning and tax advice encompass a diverse range of services, including assistance with tax audits and appeals,[222] tax advice related to mergers and acquisitions, employee benefit plans and requests for rulings or technical advice from taxing authorities.

The category of "All Other Fees" would remain unchanged from the existing rule, except that to the extent that financial information systems implementation and design exist they would be disclosed as a component of "All Other Fees."

Consistent with our proposal, we also are requiring that the information be provided for two periods so that investors will have comparative

---

[217] *See, e.g.*, letter from Ralph S. Saul, dated December 23,2002; letter from Ernst & Young, dated January 6, 2003; letter from Commercial Federal Corporation, dated January 13, 2003.

[218] *See, e.g.*, letter from Lynn E. Turner, dated January 13, 2003; letter from California Public Employees' Retirement System, dated January 10, 2003; letter from Eli Lily and Company, dated January 9, 2003; letter from American Bar Association, Sector of Business Law, dated January 14, 2003.

[219] *See, e.g.*, letter from California Public Employees' Retirement System, dated January 10, 2003; letter from Califor-

nia Board of Accountancy, dated January 13, 2003; letter from Lynn E. Turner, dated January 13, 2003.

[220] *See, e.g.*, letter from American Institute of Certified Public Accountants, dated January 9, 2003; letter from Wells Fargo & Company, dated January 13, 2003.

[221] *See also*, Section 2(a)(2) the Sarbanes-Oxley Act which defines the term "audit."

[222] As discussed previously in this release an accountant's independence is deemed to be impaired when representing the audit client before a tax court, district court and U.S. federal court of claims.

information about the fees paid to the independent accountant by the issuer.

As noted in our previous discussion about audit committee pre-approval requirements, we have clarified the guidance on audit committee pre-approval of services provided by the independent accountant. Accordingly, the issuer must provide disclosure of the audit committee's pre-approval policies and procedures. Additionally, to the extent that the audit committee has applied the de minimis exception discussed previously, the issuer must disclose the percentage of the total fees paid to the independent accountant where the de minimis exception was used. This information should be provided by category.

We expect registrants to provide clear, concise and understandable descriptions of the policies and procedures. Alternatively, registrants could include a copy of those policies and procedures with the information delivered to investors and filed with the Commission. Either method should allow shareholders to obtain a complete and accurate understanding of the audit committee's policies and procedures. We expect the policies and procedures would address auditor independence oversight functions in a prudent and responsible manner. Additionally, these procedures would describe, if applicable, the specific processes in place that monitor activities where the de minimis exception is invoked.

Consistent with our proposal, we are requiring that the disclosures be included in a company's annual report. However, because we believe that this information is relevant to a decision to vote for a particular director or to elect, approve or ratify the choice of an independent public accountant, we are requiring that this disclosure be included in a company's proxy statement on Schedule 14A or information statement on Schedule 14C. Since the information is included in Part III of annual reports on Forms 10-K and 10-KSB, domestic companies are able to incorporate the required disclosures from the proxy or information statement into the annual report.

Our intent is that this information be made available to investors of all registrants. However, not all registrants are required to file proxy statements. Thus, consistent with the provisions in the Act, registrants that do not issue proxy statements are required to include appropriate disclosures in their annual filing included in Form 10-K, Form 10-KSB, 20-F, Form 40-F and Form N-CSR[223] as

appropriate. For the reasons noted previously in this release, we are exempting asset-backed issuers and unit investment trusts from these disclosure requirements.

With respect to investment companies, we proposed to require investment companies to make disclosure that is similar to the disclosure proposed for operating companies filing with the Commission. The proposed rule required an investment company to disclose the audit fees paid by the investment company to its accountant and the aggregate fees paid for audit related, tax services, and other services to the investment company's accountant by the investment company and its investment adviser and any entity controlling, controlled by or under common control with the adviser, that provides services to the investment company. The proposed rule also required the disclosure of the percentage, for each category presented, of fees which were subject to: (1) direct pre-approval; (2) pre-approval pursuant to policies and procedures; and (3) pre-approval pursuant to the de minimis exception. Lastly, the proposed rule would require these disclosures in the annual report on proposed Form N-CSR and proxy and information statements.

Commenters[224] generally raised several significant issues related to the disclosure that would be required for investment companies. Many commenters[225] believed the fee disclosures should only be required to be made for the services provided by the accountant to the investment company registrant. One commenter[226] suggested the fees presented should be disclosed separately for those services provided to the investment company directly and those provided to the other entities in the investment company complex. Some commenters[227] believed that only those fees required to be pre-approved by the investment company's audit committee should be disclosed. Lastly, one commenter[228] expressed concern that providing percentage disclosure by type of pre-approval method (*i.e.*, direct, pursuant to policy and procedures, or the de minimis exception) would imply that some of these methodologies were improper.

After considering the comments, we do not believe that the fee disclosures should be limited to only those fees paid directly by the investment company registrant. We believe the fees paid by other entities in the investment company complex can have a bearing on the investment company

---

[223] We recently adopted Form N-CSR to be used by registered management investment companies to file certified shareholder reports with the Commission under the Sarbanes-Oxley Act of 2002.

[224] *See, e.g.,* letter from Investment Company Institute, dated January 13, 2003; letter from PricewaterhouseCoopers, dated January 8, 2003.

[225] *See, e.g.,* letter from KPMG, dated January 9, 2003; letter from PricewaterhouseCoopers, dated January 8, 2003; letter from Ernst & Young, dated January 6, 2003.

[226] *See,* letter from Ernst & Young, dated January 6, 2003.

[227] *See,* letter from PricewaterhouseCoopers, dated January 8, 2003; letter from Deloitte & Touche, dated January 10, 2003.

[228] *See,* letter from Investment Company Institute, dated January 13, 2003.

accountant's independence. However, we are concerned that the disclosures provide meaningful information to investors. Consequently, we have determined to modify the proposed requirements.

Our final rule requires the investment company to disclose separately those audit and non-audit fees from services provided directly to the investment company and those non-audit fees from services provided to all other entities in the investment company complex where the services were subject to pre-approval by the investment company's audit committee. Like an operating company, the investment company would be required to disclose the percentage of fees for each category of fees that were pre-approved pursuant to the deexception. The final rules require disclosure of the total non-audit fees paid to the accountant, regardless of whether those fees were pre-approved by the investment company's audit committee, by the investment company, its adviser, and any entity controlling, controlled by, or under common control with the investment adviser that provides ongoing services to the fund. The final rule also will require the investment company to disclose if the audit committee has considered whether the provision of non-audit services provided to the investment company's adviser and its related parties that were not subject to the investment company audit committee's pre-approval is compatible with maintaining the principal accountant's independence.

These disclosure provisions are effective for periodic annual filings for the first fiscal year ending after December 15, 2003. We encourage issuers who have not previously issued their periodic annual filings to adopt these disclosure provisions earlier.

I. International Impact

The Commission realizes that these rules will have an international impact. It will affect foreign accounting firms that conduct audits of both foreign private issuers and foreign subsidiaries and affiliates of U.S. issuers. Through its participation in the International Organization of Securities Commissions and bilateral meetings, and through a roundtable held in Washington in December, the Commission has made a concerted effort to obtain the views of the international community of regulators, market participants and practitioners. Through this process and public consultation, the Commission has received valuable insight into various foreign regulatory regimes relating to auditor independence, and detailed and specific comments on the proposed rule.

The partner rotation requirements set forth in the proposed rule were of particular concern to the international community. The proposal, as mandated by the Act, called for the rotation of the lead and concurring partners on a five-year basis. In addition, it precluded these partners from returning to an audit of the same registrant for five years. The proposal also applied the same rotation requirement to all partners on the audit engagement team. Commentators noted that the proposed requirements could have a particularly adverse impact in foreign countries, especially in emerging countries, where there may be a more limited pool of accountants and experts conversant in U.S. GAAP and U.S. GAAS. Other commentators indicated that the proposed rotation requirements would cause firms to rotate hundreds of partners in scores of countries. The resulting widespread rotation would affect audit quality adversely, and would be hard, if not impossible, to achieve practically.

We are extending the partner rotation requirements beyond the lead and concurring partners. However, taking into account these and other comments, the rotation will not be applied as broadly as proposed. We believe that partner rotation should be a function of the level of responsibility for decisions on accounting and financial reporting issues, and the level of interaction with senior management of an issuer. Accordingly, under the final rule, the rotation requirement will apply to partners that serve the client at the issuer or parent level. It also will apply to the lead partner serving an issuer's subsidiary whose revenues constitute 20% or more of the consolidated assets or revenues of the parent. Partners serving subsidiaries whose assets and revenues fall below the threshold are not subject to rotation. The same is true for partners, other than lead partners, serving subsidiaries above the threshold.

The international community also requested that the Commission modify its approach to conflicts of interest resulting from employment relationships. The Act requires a "cooling off" period of one year before a member of the audit engagement team can work for a registrant in certain key positions. Under the proposed rule, the restriction applied with regard to employment by the issuer and its affiliates. Some commentators stated that the rule should only apply to partners on the audit engagement team. Commentators also indicated that extending the requirement to apply with regard to key positions at the issuer and its affiliates was overbroad, difficult to monitor, and possibly impossible to control. Moreover, we have become aware that in certain jurisdictions the labor law or jurisprudence would prohibit foreign accounting firms from imposing restrictions on the future employment opportunities of their personnel.

We agree that extending the requirement to the audit client might be difficult to monitor particularly in situations where a member of the audit engagement team begins employment with an affiliate of the issuer. Further, we recognize that in certain foreign jurisdiction it may be extremely difficult to comply with these requirements. In response to the concerns raised, the cooling-off period will apply to the lead, concurring partner or any other member of the audit engagement team, unless exempted, who provides more than ten hours of audit, review or attest services. The restriction on employment will apply only with regard to key positions at the issuer. Members of the audit engagement team, including those employed by a foreign accounting firm, will be able to take positions with the subsidiaries or affiliates of an issuer. They also may take key positions at the issuer in certain circumstances and upon the approval of the audit committee (or a similar body).

The Commission also has given consideration to comments regarding foreign requirements with respect to the provision of appraisal and valuation services. The Commission believes that the extension of these services to audit clients raises concerns with respect to the auditor's independence. The Commission is, therefore, eliminating some exemptions previously provided in this area. However, we understand that laws and regulations in certain foreign countries require auditors to provide contribution-in-kind reports or valuation services. The Commission has historically addressed conflicts between US and foreign requirements regarding non-audit services on an *ad hoc* basis. Commission staff has previously afforded relief from proscriptions against appraisal and valuation services where, among other things, the auditor and issuer were able to demonstrate that the auditor was not providing an opinion on the fairness of a given transaction. The Commission will continue to take this *ad hoc* approach, and will continue to consider requests for exemptive relief from foreign auditors.

Finally, several foreign commentators noted that a prohibition on legal services could amount to a prohibition on the provision of tax services by foreign accounting firms from particular jurisdictions. It would appear that in certain jurisdictions tax services are defined as legal services and can only be rendered by persons licensed to practice law. The Commission is making clear that foreign accounting firms can provide tax services, as appropriate, despite their local definition and local licensing requirements.

The Commission is mindful of the fact that this rule may overlap with foreign requirements designed to achieve auditor independence. The Commission has taken foreign requirements into account, and afforded accommodations to foreign accounting firms in a manner and to the extent consistent with the spirit and intent of the Act. As the rule is implemented, the Commission, as well as the PCAOB, will monitor its international impact and continue to dialogue with its foreign counterparts.

[¶ 38,361] 603. Disclosures About Independent Accountants

.01. Purpose of Disclosures

ASR 165:

It is essential that both the fact and the appearance of independence be sustained so that the confidence of the investing public in the reliability of audited financial statements and the integrity of the public accounting profession will be maintained and enhanced. The level of disclosure regarding relationships between independent accountants and their clients required by the Commission is intended to enhance the accountant's independence by the disclosure of auditor-client relationships.

603.02. Reports on Form 8-K

.a. Changes in Accountants

.i. Resignation and Dismissal

ASR 165:

The resignation (or declination to stand for re-election after completion of the current audit) and dismissal of accountants are reportable events as well as the engagement of a new accountant. Before 1974, when only the engagement of a new accountant triggered the reporting requirement, there was sometimes considerable delay in bringing significant disagreements to the attention of investors. Under the current rule, timely disclosure is required. This may mean on some occasions that two reports on Form 8-K will be required for a single change of accountants, the first on the resignation (or declination to stand for re-election after completion of the current audit) or dismissal of the previous accountant and the second where a new accountant is selected.

A special variant of resignation, declination to stand for re-election after completion of the current audit, is specified as a trigger for reporting because of a recognition that, where an auditor declines to stand for re-election after completion of his current audit, such action is the substantive act of resignation, rather than the later time when his current engagement is terminated.

Changes in the independent accountant for a significant subsidiary on whom the principal accountant expressed reliance are also reportable events. For these purposes, significant subsidiary is as defined in Rule 1-02 of Regulation S-X except that a non-incorporated segment such as a division which meets the size tests of the definition would be included.

In some circumstances, a report would be required regarding an accountant who did not report on financial statements of the registrant. For example, where Accountant A reported on the financial statements of the prior year, Accountant B was engaged for the current year but was replaced by Accountant C before he completed any examination, reports on Form 8-K would be required with respect to the change from Accountant A to Accountant B and from Accountant B to Accountant C.

603.02.a.ii. Qualified, Disclaimed, or Adverse Opinion

ASR 165:

Form 8-K requires disclosure as to whether the principal accountants' reports for either of the past two years contained an adverse opinion or a disclaimer of opinion or was qualified as to uncertainty, audit scope or accounting principles. "Consistency" exceptions need not be reported in this item.

This disclosure should assist users of Form 8-K to determine whether there were any items in the previous two years which were of such an unusual and material nature that disclosure was required in the accountants' report. Although such data are on file elsewhere in most cases, including them in the 8-K report brings together in one place information which is relevant in the evaluation of auditor-client relationships.

603.02.a.iii. Replaced Accountants' Responsibility

ASR 165:

When a change in independent accountants occurs so that the accountant being replaced is aware that a Form 8-K should be filed reporting the event, he might well bring that reporting responsibility to the attention of the registrant. If he becomes aware that the required reporting has not been made, e.g., because he has not been requested to furnish a letter as required by the Form 8-K item, he should consider advising the registrant in writing of that reporting responsibility with a copy to the Commission.

603.02.b. Reasons for Change in Independent Accountants

ASR 247:

The Commission has determined not to require disclosure of the reasons for all changes in independent accountants. The Commission, however, encourages disclosure of these reasons on a voluntary basis. People argued in the past that such disclosure was probably not useful and, in their view, meaningful information would not be presented for a variety of reasons. Most often cited were the disclosures would take the form of "boiler plate" (e.g, "audit rotation policy," "need a fresh look," etc.); that accountants would be unable to make meaningful comments on subjective reasons (e.g., "poor service," "high fees"); that disclosure of reasons for all changes might downgrade or obscure the disclosures of disagreements now required; that candid disclosures would not be made for fear of litigation involving libel or other allegations; and that disclosure might inhibit changes in accountants (i.e., that it might tend to lead to a continuation of unsatisfactory situations in an effort to avoid disclosure).

While the Commission does not endorse all of the arguments against required disclosure, it nevertheless believes that disclosure of reasons for all changes should not be required at this time. However, the Commission encourages registrants to include in the Form 8-K filing, on a voluntary

basis, information beyond the minimum required concerning changes in accountants. Accountants are encouraged to include such additional information in the former accountant's letter which is required to be filed with Form 8-K.

It is particularly appropriate to include such additional information in filings with the Commission when such matters are discussed in a public forum, to assure the widest public dissemination of such information. For example, in a Form 8-K filing regarding a change in independent accountants the registrant indicated that there were no reportable disagreements with their former accountants and the departing accountants concurred. No additional disclosures relative to the change were made in the filing. Accounts in the financial press, however, reflected substantial additional information provided by the registrant and the accountant regarding the change. In the Commission's view, it would have been appropriate to include such information in filings with the Commission.

603.02.c. Disagreements with Accountants

ASR 165:

Form 8-K was amended in 1974 to clarify the intent to require a description of all disagreements, including those where the disagreement was resolved to the satisfaction of the accountant. This clarification was necessary as a result of the experience gained from analyzing 8-Ks filed in which no description was given of disagreements or in which a simple statement was made that there were no unresolved disagreements and staff follow-up was required to obtain the necessary information. Disagreements contemplated by this rule occur at the decision-making level; i.e., between personnel of the registrant responsible for presentation of its financial statements and personnel of the accounting firm responsible for rendering its report.

The term "disagreements" should be interpreted broadly in responding to this item. For example, if an accountant resigned or was dismissed after advising the registrant that he had concluded that internal controls necessary to develop reliable statements did not exist, this would constitute a reportable disagreement in the event of a change of accountants. Similarly, if an accountant were to resign or be dismissed after informing the registrant that he had discovered facts which led him no longer to be able to rely on management representations or which made him unwilling to be associated with statements prepared by management, such situations would constitute reportable disagreements.

The item requires that the registrant's statement as to whether any disagreements existed be included in the Form 8-K filing rather than in a separate letter attached to the filing and that copies of the accountant's letter be filed as an exhibit with all 8-K copies filed. The full disclosure of any disagreement should be readily available to the public.

ASR 247:

In 1978, the Commission stated its concern that the practice of reporting disagreements in Form 8-K filings had deteriorated. Filings had been made in which the registrant indicated no disagreements, while the former accountant's letter concluded that reportable disagreements did occur. Thus, the Commission again reminded registrants and accountants to consider very carefully the requirements regarding the disclosure of disagreements, and reiterated that the term "disagreements" should be interpreted broadly in responding to these requirements.

603.02.d. A Registrant's Filing on Form 8-K Regarding a Change in Certifying Accountants

The Commission has accelerated the timing for filing an initial Form 8-K regarding a change in certifying accountants from 15 calendar days to five business days.[18]

In proposing a five *calendar* day period, the Commission noted that documentation regarding disagreements and reportable events should be readily available to both the registrant and the former accountant.[19] While 14 of the 19 commentators generally supported reduction of the filing period, only one agreed with the five calendar day proposal. Others stated that the proposed periods may be too short for the preparation of complete and informative disclosures.[20] They indicated that the individuals who prepare and review the Form 8-K filing may not be available during a period as short as five calendar days. They also noted that with intervening weekends and holidays the filing period effectively could be reduced to as few as two business days if the change occurred immediately preceding a "three-day weekend." Several commentators, therefore, suggested that the filing period be either extended or expressed in business rather than calendar days. Four commentators specifically suggested a ten calendar day period, four others suggested a ten business day period, and five specifically recommended a five business day period.

In recognition of the commentators' concerns, the Commission has adopted a five business day period. In calculating the five business day period, the day on which the change in accountants occurs would not be counted. For example, assuming there are no intervening federal holidays, if

the accountant resigns[21] on a Monday, the Form 8-K must be filed no later than the close of the Commission's business[22] on the following Monday. If the Item 4, Form 8-K event occurs on other than a business day, the filing period begins to run on and includes the first business day thereafter.

603.03. Proxy Statement

.a. Identity of Principal Accountants

ASR 165:

The proxy rules require certain disclosures in the proxy statement of the relationships between issuers and independent public accountants. Since this disclosure is unlikely to be relevant to other solicitations, it is required only for annual meetings of securities holders or where financial statements are required pursuant to Item 15 of the proxy rules.

Disclosure is required of the name of the principal accountant for the previous year if different from that selected or recommended for the current year or if no accountant has been selected for the current year. This disclosure is designed to inform the stockholder when a change in accountants has occurred and who the independent accountant of record is in cases where no action has been taken to select an accountant for the current year.

Disclosure of the principal accountant selected or to be recommended to shareholders for election, approval or ratification for the current year is designed to make stockholders aware of the identity of the independent accountant of record for the current year, even in cases when the shareholders are not asked to take formal action to approve his selection. The Commission believes that such knowledge will enhance the stockholders' recognition of the role of the independent accountant.

603.03.b. Disagreements with Accountants

ASR 247:

Proxy statement disclosure of disagreements required to be reported on Form 8-K is required whether or not such reports were filed.

ASR 165:

The disclosure is designed to call disagreements to stockholders' attention so that they may be more fully informed of the relationships between accountant and issuer. Since any disagreement must by its nature have two sides, it seems desirable that both sides have an opportunity to

---

[18] The term "business day" means any day other than a Saturday, Sunday, or federal holiday on which the Commission is not opened for business.

[19] Securities Act Release No. 6767, *supra*, note 11.

[20] Copies of the letters from commentators are available to the public in File No. S7-6-88 in the Commission's Public Reference Room, 450 Fifth Street, N.W., Washington, D.C. 20549.

[21] In contrast to the dismissal of an accountant through the mail, which occurs when the registrant sends the notice of

dismissal, when the accountant resigns by mailing a letter of resignation to the registrant the resignation is deemed to occur for the purpose of this requirement when the registrant receives the letter.

[22] The business hours of the principal office of the Commission in Washington D.C. are from 9:00 a.m. to 5:30 p.m. Eastern Standard Time or Eastern Daylight Savings Time, whichever is currently in effect in Washington, each day except Saturdays, Sundays and holidays. Rule 0-2 under the Securities Exchange Act of 1934, 17 CFR 240.0-2.

review its description in the interests of obtaining a balanced and complete presentation. Accordingly, the issuer is required to submit the description included in the preliminary proxy material to the accountant, and if the accountant believes that the description is incorrect or incomplete he may include a brief statement, ordinarily expected not to exceed 200 words, in the proxy statement presenting his view of the disagreement. [See also Section 603.02.c]

603.03.c. Attendance at Stockholders' Meeting

ASR 165:

Disclosure is required of whether or not representatives of the principal accountants for the current year and the most recently completed fiscal year are expected to be present at the stockholders' meeting with the opportunity to make a statement and available to respond to appropriate questions. The Commission believes that it is desirable for communication between stockholders and their independent accountants to be encouraged. While the principal communication is the accountants' report on financial statements, there may be some matters which the accountants wish to bring to the attention of stockholders and there may be questions which stockholders wish to address to the accountants. This disclosure will emphasize the existence of this opportunity for communication when it is available.

603.04. Approval by Audit Committee

ASR 247:

To enhance the independence of the outside auditor, the Commission has encouraged the formation of audit committees. Such committees can serve as links between independent accountants and shareholders and give auditors a knowledgeable level of authority higher than management for the discussion of controversial matters. In furtherance of these objectives, the Commission believes that one of the principal responsibilities of an audit committee should be that of recommending or approving the engagement or discharge of the company's independent accountants.

The Commission requires disclosure [in proxy statements and reports on Form 8-K] of whether changes in accountants were considered, recommended or approved by the board of directors or an audit or similar committee thereof. Registrants which have audit or similar committees are required to state affirmatively whether the committee reviewed the change. These disclosures should be useful to investors in better understanding and evaluating the company's relationship with its independent accountants.

603.05. Disclosure Accompanying Financial Statements

ASR 280:

Disclosure about disagreements between registrants and their predecessor accountant involving certain accounting and financial disclosure matters is required in certain filings with the Commission that contain audited financial statements. This disclosure, however, can be made outside of the financial statements. The Commission continues to believe that this disclosure is necessary to put readers of financial statements on notice that such a disagreement existed which could have significantly affected the statements.

ASR 165:

This disclosure will make investors aware of situations where alternative accounting approaches may be followed and are favored by at least one professional accountant, and the effect of such alternative approaches. In addition, it is believed that such disclosure requirements may have the effect of discouraging shifts in accountants simply to obtain approval of an alternative accounting approach. If registrants and their present independent accountants believe that the disclosure of the effect of applying the alternative accounting approach favored by the predecessor accountant would not be significant to investors in the circumstances, they may submit a statement to that effect to the staff which will consider a waiver of the rule.

603.06. Clarification of the Term "Disagreements"

Disclosure of "disagreements" between the registrant and its former auditor over accounting, auditing or financial reporting issues acts as an "early warning" of potentially troublesome areas, provides the accountant with a forum to disclose its concerns on these issues, and triggers additional disclosures under Item 304(b) of Regulation S-K.[1]

The Commission has historically stated that the term "disagreements" should be interpreted broadly.[2] Despite this position, some maintain that confusion exists concerning the scope of the term. In order to reduce the potential for such confusion an instruction to Item 304 has been adopted specifically to state that "disagreements" include any differences of opinion concerning any matter of accounting principles or practices, financial statement disclosure or auditing scope or procedure, which if not resolved to the satisfaction of the former accountant would have caused it to make reference in connection with its report to the subject of the disagreement. Commentators, however, indicated that the definition, as proposed, may

---

[1] 17 CFR 229.304(b). Item 304(b) requires disclosure of what the accounting for a particular transaction or event that was the subject of a disagreement would have been under the former accountant's opinion, if the former accountant's view

was different than the accounting treatment being accepted by the newly engaged accountant.

[2] *See, e.g.,* Accounting Series Releas No. ("ASR") 165 (December 20, 1974).

have required disclosure of preliminary disagreements or differences of opinion based on incomplete information. The Commission has responded to this concern by adding a sentence in the instruction to state that initial differences of opinion based on incomplete facts or preliminary information are not considered to be "disagreements" if those differences are later resolved by obtaining additional, relevant facts or information. If the auditor is dismissed or resigns before initial differences of opinion are resolved, they would be reportable as "disagreements". This modification uses the language in the Statement on Auditing Standards recently adopted by the Auditing Standards Board concerning the auditor's communications with audit committees or equivalent representatives of the board of directors.[3] The effect of using this language, therefore, is that if the difference of opinion does not have to be communicated by the auditor to the audit committee under this standard because it is based on preliminary information or incomplete facts (but there is no difference of opinion when the registrant and the auditor obtain the relevant factual information), then it is not required to be disclosed as a "disagreement" under Item 304 of Regulation S-K.

Reportable Events

In the proposing release the Commission identified certain events that may not be literal "disagreements" because management may not have expressed a difference of opinion with the auditor's concern, but nontheless should be disclosed.[4] These reportable events involve situations where the accountant has advised the registrant that it questions the accuracy or reliability of the registrant's financial statements, management's representations, the registrant's internal controls, or prior audits.

"Disagreements" and "reportable events" are similar in that they involve situations where the position of management may be considered to be generally at odds with that of the auditor. With a reportable "disagreement" the differing positions of management and the auditor have been expressed, either orally or in writing. A reportable event, however, requires only that the accountant advise the registrant of its concerns. If, therefore, the auditor is dismissed, resigns or declines to stand for re-election before the registrant responds (to either agree or disagree) to the auditor's concern, the event must be reported. The auditor may not therefore merely advise the registrant of its concern and then resign (or be dismissed) prior to receiving a response from management and walk away without disclosure of its concerns.

In order to clarify the significance of these "reportable events," they have been moved from the instruction to the body of Item 304. The new paragraph addressing "reportable events" incorporates the detailed disclosure requirements for "disagreements". The disclosure required for a "reportable event" is therefore the same as that required for a "disagreement".

In response to commentators' concerns, the Commission has clarified the list of reportable events in several respects. These events are now listed in paragraphs (A) through (D) of Item 304(a)(1)(v).

Paragraphs (A) and (B) are a codification of existing Commission positions announced in Accounting Series Release No. 165 (December 20, 1974). In that release, the Commission stated that a reportable disagreement exists if the accountant has advised the registrant that (1) the registrant did not have the internal controls necessary to develop reliable financial statements, (2) the accountant has discovered information that has led it to no longer be able to rely on management's reprseentations, or (3) the accountant has discovered information that has made it unwilling to be associated with the financial statements prepared by management. Paragraph (B) has been amended to change the phrase, "the accountant has discovered information" to "information has come to the accountant's attention," to clarify the Commission's position that the manner in which the information was acquired by the accountant is irrelevant. A similar change has been made in paragraphs (C) and (D).

An additional clarification to paragraph (C) has been made from the proposal. This paragraph now requires disclosure where (1) the former accountant has adrvised the registrant that it must either significantly expand the scope of its audit or have an investigation conducted that may result in the auditor (A) determining that there are issues that materially impact current or past financial statements or audit reports or (B) being unwilling to rely on management's representations or be associated with the registrant's financial statements, and (2) the auditor resigns, declines to stand for re-election, or is dismissed before the expanded audit steps have been performed or the investigation has been completed. If, therefore, prior to the auditor leaving the engagement, the expanded audit procedures have been performed or the investigation has been completed to the former accountant's satisfaction, no disclosure is required

---

[3] Statement on Auditing Standards No. 61, *Communication with Audit Committees or Others with Equivalent Authority and Responsibility.* This document has been approved for issuance as a final statement on auditing standard s and will be available from the Auditing Standards Board, May 1, 1988.

[4] If management and the auditor had a difference of opinion regarding the auditor's concern, that difference of opinion would have been reportable as a disagreement. For example, a difference of opinion over whether an allegation regarding management's integrity should be investigated would constitute a disagreement regarding audit scope.

under paragraph (C). It should be noted, however, that disclosure will be required pursuant to the reportable events listed in paragraphs (A), (B) or (D) if as a result of the expanded audit steps or investigation the former accountant advises the registrant that: the registrant lacks necessary internal controls, the accountant is no longer able to rely on management or be associated with its financial statements, or there are issues that materially impact current or past financial statements or audit reports that were not resolved to the former accountant's satisfaction prior to its resignation, dismissal or declination to stand for re-election. The change was made to avoid the implication that disclosures under paragraph (C) would be required only when the information that came to the accountant's attention may impact current or future financial statements and that information which may impact previously issued financial statements for either annual or interim periods would not have to be disclosed.

Paragraph (D) has been significantly revised in response to commentators' concerns. As proposed, paragraph (D) would have required disclosure of each time during approximately the past two years the accountant advised the registrant that the accountant had discovered information that may impact the fairness or reliability of audit reports or the underlying financial statements. Commentators were concerned with the breadth of this disclosure. The Commission has amended this paragraph to narrow the required disclosures. First, rather than disclosing information that "may impact" the fairness or reliability of financial statements or reports, disclosure will be required only if the former accountant has concluded that the information that has come to its attention does materially impact the financial statements or audit reports. Second, disclosure will not be required of those issues that have been resolved to the former accountant's satisfaction prior to its resignation, dismissal or declination to stand for re-election. Accordingly, paragraph (D) requires disclosure of those situations where information had come to the former accountant's attention, the former accountant concluded that the information materially impacts financial statements or audit reports (either previously issued or to be issued), and the matter was not resolved to the former accountant's satisfaction prior to its resignation, dismissal or declination to stand for re-election. In order not to be disclosed, however, the matter must be completely resolved to the auditor's satisfaction. If the matter is unresolved or not resolved to the auditor's satisfaction at the time it resigns, declines to stand for re-election or is dismissed, it must be disclosed notwithstanding management's concurrence with the auditor's concern. Further, if management addresses the auditor's concern by

expressing a difference of opinion over the issue, then the matter would be disclosed a s a "disagreement" (rather than as a "reportable event") whether or not eventually resolved to the auditor's satisfaction.

Paragraph (D) also has been clarified in several respects. First, the proposed paragraph (D) contained parenthetical language stating that disclosure would be required "(whether or not . . . [an] audit has been completed)." The purpose of this language was to indicate that the scope of the required disclosures would include not only prior audits and previously issued financial statements, but also information concerning audits currently in progress or contemplated, and the underlying annual and quarterly financial statements. In order to further clarify this position, the proposed parenthetical has been deleted and the paragraph has been revised to state that disclosure would be required if the information materially impacts, "(i) a previously issued audit report or the underlying financial statements, or (ii) the financial statements issued or to be issued covering the fiscal period(s) subsequent to the date of the most recent financial statements covered by an audit report." Second, several commentators noted that paragraph (D) would require disclosure of situations that would prevent, or should have prevented, the auditor from rendering an unqualified report on the registrant's current or prior financial statements. Parenthetical language therefore has been added to paragraph (D) to emphasize this point. Finally, the Commission believes that the revision changing the proposed requirement to disclose information that "may impact" the fairness or reliability of financial statements or reports to a requirement to disclose information that the former accountant concluded "materially impacts" those items clarifies the distinction between paragraphs (C) and (D). Paragraph (C) is meant to encompass those situations where information came to the former accountant's attention that it was unable to thoroughly explore and thus reach a conclusion as to its implications prior to its resignation, dismissal or declination to stand for re-election. Paragraph (D) is meant to encompass those situations where the accountant has reached the conclusion that the information does have a material impact.

Letter From the American Institute of Certified Public Accountants ("AICPA")

By letter dated August 20, 1986, the AICPA proposed that the Commission amend the disclosure requirements concerning changes in accountants to include, among other things, disclosure of: whether the audit or similar committee of the board of directors and the former accountant discussed the subject matter of reportable disagreements and events;[5] whether the registrant authorized the former accountant to respond fully to the inquiries of the successor auditor concerning such issues; and whether the former accountant resigned, declined to stand for re-election or was dismissed. Commentators were generally supportive of these proposals, and they have been adopted as proposed.

603.07. Disclosure of Potential Opinion Shopping Situations

SEC registrants may, of course, change auditors at their discretion. It is imperative, however, that when a new auditor is engaged that auditor possess the integrity, objectivity and independence required by professional and Commission standards.[1] The auditor must, at all times, maintain a "healthy skepticism" to ensure that a review of a client's accounting treatment is fair and impartial.[2] The willingness of an auditor to support a proposed accounting treatment that is intended to accomplish the registrant's reporting objectives even though that treatment might frustrate reliable reporting, indicates that there may be a lack of such skepticism and independence on the part of the auditor.[3] The search for such an auditor by management may indicate an effort by management to avoid the requirement for an independent examination of the registrant's financial statements. Engaging an accountant under such circumstances is generally referred to as "opinion shopping." Should this practice result in false or misleading financial disclosures the registrant and the accountant would be subject to enforcement and/or disciplinary action by the Commission.[4]

The National Commission on Fraudulent Financial Reporting,[5] the heads of seven major accounting firms,[6] and others have recommended expanded disclosures in this area.[7]

In order to provide increased public disclosure of possible opinion shopping situations, the Commission has adopted new disclosure requirements concerning consultations between the registrant and the newly engaged auditor that occurred within approximately two years prior to the engagement, if those discussions (1) were or should have been subject to SAS 50[8] or (2) concerned the

---

[5] The AICPA's letter suggested that disclosure be provided when the former auditor provides a written communication to the audit committee or the board of directors that "specifically communicated concerns or conclusions regarding the integrity of management or the presence or materiality of possible irregularities or illegal acts that were not resolved to the former accountant's satisfaction." As discussed in the proposing release, such a letter would be encompassed by the broad term "disagreements," and the Commission's proposal, therefore, substituted language referring to the written communication with the term "disagreements." *See* Securities Act Release No. 6719 (June 18, 1987) [52 FR 24018].

[1] See, e.g., Rule 2-01(c), Regulation S-X, 17 CFR 210.2-01(c); Statement on Auditing Standards No. 1, AU Section 220. As recognized by the Commission and the courts, not only the fact but also the appearance of independence by the auditor is essential to the integrity of the securities markets. *U.S. v. Arthur Young*, 465 U.S. 805, 819 n.15 (1984); Securities Act Release No, 33-6594 [July 1, 1985] [50 FR 28219]. Opinion shopping has an obvious and negative impact on the general public's perception of the professionalism exhibited by accountants and their firms.

[2] *See, In the Matter of Touche Ross & Co.,* Accounting and Auditing Enforcement Release ("AAER") No. 16 (November 13, 1983).

[3] As previously discussed, a disclosure requirement is being adopted as part of Item 304(a)(1)(iv) that pertains to limitations on discussions between successor and predecessor auditors concerning matters that were the subject of reportable events or disagreements. It should be noted, however, that Statement on Auditing Standards No. 7 states, "Inquiry of the predecessor is a necessary procedure . . . ," and stresse s that such inquiries or consultations should include all matters that may "assist him in determining whether to accept the engagement." While this standard does not directly prohibit the accountant from accepting an engagement where limitations have been imposed on discussions between the new and former accountants; the new accountant should inquire as to the reasons and consider the implications of such limitations in deciding whether to accept the engagement. In the Commission's view, the imposition of limitations on such communication may materially impact the conduct of audits. Therefore, accountants accepting such engagements

should ensure appropriate work paper documentation as to the nature of, and the reasons for, any such limitations and their responses thereto.

[4] For example, if the registrant's financial statements are materially misleading, the registrant may be in violation of Section 13(a) or 15(d) of the Securities Exchange Act of 1934 ("the Exchange Act"), 15 U.S.C. 78a et seq. If fraudulent activity has occurred, the registrant may have violated Section 17(a) et seq., or Section 10(b) of the Exchange Act. Among other areas of potential liability, the accountant may directly violate several sections of the federal securities laws, including Section 10(b) above, and may be subject to disciplinary action under Rule 2(e) of the Commission's Rules of Practice and Investigations, 17 CFR 201.2(e). *See, e.g., In the Matter of Frantz, Warrick, Strack & Associates,* AAER No. 86 (February 10, 1986); *In the Matter of Broadview Financial Corporation,* AAER No. 54 (April 17, 1985); *In the Matter of Stephen O. Wade; Ralph H. Newton, Jr.; Clark C. Burritt, Jr.,* AAER No. 32 (June 25, 1984); *In the Matter of Accounting for Gains and Losses Incurred in Connection With Certain Securities Transactions,* AAER No. 14 (October 6, 1983).

[5] See note 3 *supra.*

[6] See the April 1986 paper entitled "Recommendations to the AICPA Board of Directors: The Future Relevance, Reliability and Credibility of Financial Information" signed by the managing partners of seven major accounting firms.

[7] For a discussion of these recommendations, see the proposing release, Securities Act Release No. 6719, *supra.*

[8] See note 2 *supra.* Paragraph 2 of SAS 50 states:

2. This statement provides guidance that an accountant in public practice ("reporting accountant"), either in connection with a proposal to obtain a new client or otherwise, should apply—

a. When preparing a written report on the application of accounting principles to specified transactions, either completed or proposed ("specific transactions").

b. When requested to provide a written report on the type of opinion that may be rendered on a specific entity's financial statements.

c. When preparing a written report to intermediaries on the application of accounting principles not involving facts or circumstances of a particular principal ("hypothetical transactions").

subject matter of a disagreement or reportable event with the former auditor. The information to be disclosed includes: (1) an identification of the issues that were the subject of those consultations; (2) a brief description of the newly engaged accountant's oral or written views on those issues as expressed to the registrant, with any written views received by the registrant filed as an exhibit to the document containing this disclosure; and (3) a statement by the registrant whether it consulted the former accountant on those issues, and if so, a summary of the former accountant's views. The new accountant will have the opportunity to review the registrant's summary of its views and furnish a letter (to be filed as an exhibit to the filing or report containing this disclosure) to proide additional information or clarify the registrant's summary of its views and comment on other disclosures under this item. The registrant also must request that the former accountant review the disclosure and provide a statement as to whether it agrees with the registrant's summary of its views, and if not, the respects in which it does not agree.

The adopted disclosure item is narrower than the proposal in two respects. First, the proposal would have required disclosure of any issue material to or expected in the future to be material to the registrant's financial statements that the registrant discussed with the newly engaged auditor during approximately two years prior to its engagement. The adopted disclosure item narrows the range of discloseable issues to those that were the subject of SAS 50 requirements or those that were the subject of reportable events or disagreements with the former auditors. Commentators were concerned with the breadth of the proposed disclosure requirement. These commentators indicated that the proposal could result in voluminous disclosures that would not highlight the areas most important to investors, shareholders and the public. The Commission has therefore narrowed the disclosure requirement to those consultations that would be most likely to be relied on by registrants due to the auditor's compliance with the SAS 50 reporting, performance and documentation standards,[9] and those areas that have been the subject of contention between the registrant and the former auditor.

Second, the Commission has determined not to adopt the proposed disclosure requirement calling for the names of other accountants consulted on the listed issues and an indication of the extent the views of such other accountants materially differed from the views of the new accountant. After a review of the comments, it has been determined that effective disclosure would necessitate disclosing each consulted accountant's individual views on each issue. Further, commentators argued that the views of other accountants not subsequently engaged as the registrant's auditor may not be relevant. The Commission has therefore determined to adopt, at this time, only those disclosure requirements focusing on the registrant's relationship with its new and former auditors. The Commission staff monitors changes in accountants disclosures closely, however, and if necessary will readdress this area.

603.08. Filing Period Related to the Former Accountant's Letter

The Commission is amending Item 304(a)(3) of Regulation S-K to state that the former accountant's letter should be provided to the registrant as promptly as possible to permit the letter to be filed by the registrant with the Commission within ten business days[23] after the filing of the Form 8-K or other report or registration statement announcing the change in accountants. In order to facilitate the preparation of the accountant's letter, the Commission also has adopted, as proposed,[24] a requirement that the registrant provide the former accountant with a copy of the disclosures it has made concerning the change in accountants no later than the day those disclosures are filed with the Commission.

Fifteen of 17 commentators addressing the issue supported a reduction in the 30 day period for filing the former accountant's letter. Four of these commentators supported the proposed ten calendar day period, but others suggested longer periods citing the unavailability of personnel and the impact of weekends, among other factors, on promptly preparing and reviewing a complete and informative letter. Nine commentators suggested

---

(Footnote Continued)

This statement also applies to oral advice on the application of accounting principles to a specific transaction, or the type of opinion that may be rendered on an entity's financial statements, when the reporting accountant concludes the advice is intended to be used by a principal to the transaction as an important factor considered in reaching a decision.

[9] The Commission is aware that there may be valid reasons for obtaining the views of an independent accountant other than the registrant's current accountant, and that some registrants have a practice of routinely using a separate accountant for additional advice on complex issues. The Commission does not wish to interfere with such practices. When a registrant changes auditors, however, it is important for investors to be aware of any pre-existing relationships or understand-ings between the registrant and the new auditor and how the engagement of the new auditor may impact the registrant's accounting and reporting policies.

[23] The term "business day" means any day other than a Saturday, Sunday, or federal holiday on which the Commission is not opened for business.

[24] Securities Act Release No. 6767, *supra* note 11. The proposal stated that the accountant should be provided with a copy of these disclosures no later than the "time" they are filed with the Commission. To avoid controversy over the specific time that the disclosures were filed and the time they were received by the accountant, this provision has been revised to require that the accountant receive the disclosures on the same day they are filed with the Commission.

a ten business day period, four suggested a ten calendar day period, two recommended 21 calendar days, one suggested 15 business days, and one suggested a period of 21 business days.[25] After considering these comments, the Commission has revised the proposed ten calendar day period to ten business days. Calculation of this period should begin on and include the first business day after the initial filing with the Commission.

The new rules, as amended, contain the proposed language that the registrant shall request that the former accountant provide the letter "as promptly as possible." One commentator objected to this language, stating that it would be impossible to demonstrate compliance with that request.[26] This language has been added to the disclosure requirement to focus the accountant's attention on the need to address the issue in a timely manner, that is, with the diligence that may be expected under the circumstances.

The accountant's letter, therefore, may be received by the registrant prior to the expiration of the ten business day period. In order that such a letter may be made available to the public on a timely basis, the Commission proposed that the registrant file the letter within two calendar days of receipt. Three of the 11 commentators addressing this issue supported the proposed two calendar day period, while seven commentators suggested a two business day period and cited the adverse impact of weekends and holidays on their ability to meet the two calendar day requirement. One commentator noted that the proposed period may cause timing problems but did not offer a specific recommendation as to the appropriate time period. In response to the commentators' concerns, the Commission has adopted a two *business* day period.[27]

The newly adopted filing requirements for Form 8-K concerning a change in accountants result in a reduction in the overall time period for filing both the Form 8-K and the former accountant's letter from 45 calendar days to 15 business days.[28] The new time periods reflect an appropri-

ate balance between the need for prompt disclosure and the time required to research, prepare and review the disclosures called for when a change in accountants occurs.[29]

603.08.a. Interim Letter from the Former Accountant

The amendments to Item 304(a)(3) of Regulation S-K include the proposed provision specifying that the former accountant, at its discretion, may provide the registrant with an interim letter highlighting specific areas of concern and indicating a more detailed letter will follow. If such an interim letter is provided it must be filed by the registrant within two business days of receipt.[30]

Ten of 11 commentators addressing the interim letter provision generally opposed the provision because: the statements in the interim letter may be based on incomplete information; the provision could create a de facto reporting obligation; or the need for such a provision is diminished by the reduction of the filing period relating to the accountant's letter. The Commission recognizes these concerns. However, it believes it is important explicitly to provide former accountants with the opportunity to provide expedited notice to the public of situations where former accountants have concluded that registrants' Forms 8-K contain patently false disclosures. The Commission does not intend to establish a de facto reporting obligation and, to the contrary, believes that such interim letters will generally pertain to cases where there is no reasonable uncertainty regarding the former accountant's objection to the registrant's disclosures. An example of a case where the accountant may file such an interim letter is when the accountant is dismissed after having an obvious disagreement with the registrant and the registrant's initial Form 8-K states that there were no disagreements.

[¶ 38,375] 604. Relation of the Performance of Nonaudit Services to Auditor Independence

.01. Background

ASR 296:

---

[25] Some commentators suggested more than one time period.

[26] Letter to Jonathan G. Katz from Peat Marwick Main & Co. dated May 16, 1988, available in File No. S7-6-88. *See* note 16, *supra.*

[27] The requirement to file the former accountant's letter within two business days of receipt is independent of the ten business day period discussed above and is not intended to result in an extension of that ten business day period.

[28] It should be noted that in current practice the accountant's letter often is filed with the initial Form 8-K.

[29] *See generally* Item 4 of Form 8-K, 17 CFR 249.308, and Item 304 of Regulation S-K, 17 CFR 229.304.

[30] A two calendar day period was proposed for comment. The Commission, however, has adopted a two business day period due to the impact of weekends and holidays on the registrant's ability to comply with the requirement. The requirement to file the former accountant's letter within two business days of receipt is independent of the ten business day period discussed above and is not intended to result in an extension of that ten business day period.

During the mid 1970's, Congress,[*] the accounting profession[1] and the Commission[2] reexamined the role and responsibilities of independent accountants. This interest in the accounting profession was stimulated by a decline in public confidence in the business community and the accounting profession resulting from several significant unexpected corporate failures and various questionable payments made by certain publicly held corporations.[3] Each of these bodies focused attention on the independence of accountants because of its critical importance to public confidence in the profession and in business generally.[4] Among other things, they considered the performance of management advisory services by independent accountants for their audit clients because the increase, particularly during the last decade, in the performance of such services heightened concern that accountants who performed such services could, or could appear to, have a conflict of interest which would impair their independence.

Several witnesses at Congressional hearings on the accounting profession were critical of the expansion of accounting firms' business into management advisory services. Members of Congress considered various recommendations relating to curtailment of management advisory services to be performed by independent accountants for their publicly owned audit clients.[5] The Cohen Commission, however, only recommended the prohibition of executive search and placement services. Outside of these areas, the Cohen Commission cited a lack of evidence that nonaudit services compromised independence. The Cohen Commission did, however, urge the accounting profession to take steps to diminish the concerns of a "significant minority" that the performance of such nonaudit services impaired the independence of accountants and recommended, among other

things, that audit committees or boards of directors evaluate all of the services performed by independent accountants, and that registrants or accountants appropriately disclose other services to dispel the concerns of users.[6]

The Commission responded to the concerns about nonaudit services by proposing a rule to require disclosure about such services and requesting comments on the effect of nonaudit services on accountants' independence and the advisability of prohibiting certain services.[7] After reviewing the comments received, the Commission issued ASR 250 announcing the adoption of the disclosure rule concerning nonaudit services. This rule was adopted to permit security holders to better evaluate registrants' relationships with independent accountants. In addition, the Commission intended to use the disclosures to monitor the nature and extent of nonaudit services performed by accountants to assist in developing an empirical basis from which to determine the need for any further action in this area. The Commission did not propose rules to proscribe particular services, however, because the POB was considering the issue of management advisory services performed by independent accountants.

The POB conducted an extensive study of the question of the scope of services provided by CPA firms. In March 1979, the POB published its report[8] in which it endorsed public disclosure about nonaudit services rather than proscription of specific management advisory services but admonished "members of the SEC Practice Section to exercise self-restraint and judgment before venturing into new areas of [management advisory services]."[9] The POB did concur, however, in the SEC Practice Section's previously announced proscription of executive recruiting services and urged certain limitations on actuarial services. Although the POB found that available empirical

---

[*] E.g., Senate Subcommittee on Reports, Accounting and Management of the Committee on Governmental Affairs, "Improving the Accountability of Publicly Owned Corporations and their Auditors," 95th Cong., 1st Sess. (1977) [hereinafter cited as Metcalf Report]. In addition, the Subcommittee on Oversight and Investigations of the House Committee on Interstate and Foreign Commerce examined and held hearings on the nature and structure of the accounting profession. *See Securities and Exchange Commission Report to Congress on the Accounting Profession and the Commission's Oversight Role* 1-2 (July 1978) [hereinafter cited as 1978 Report to Congress].

[1] E.g., "The Commission on Auditors' Responsibilities: Report, Conclusions, and Recommendations" (1978) [hereinafter cited as Cohen Commission]. This independent Commission was established by the AICPA in 1974 to study the role and responsibilities of independent accountants.

[2] *See* 1978 Report to Congress.

[3] *Id.* at 3.

[4] The Metcalf Report also conveyed the need for urgent action to achieve public confidence in the profession's resolve and ability to regulate and discipline accountants and in the processes by which accounting and auditing standards are promulgated.

[5] The Senate Subcommittee on Reports, Accounting and Management stated that independent accountants should only perform for their audit clients services directly related to accounting. Metcalf Report at 16-17. In 1978, the then chairman and certain members of the House Subcommittee on Oversight and Investigations of the Committee on Interstate and Foreign Commerce introduced legislation which, among other things, would have required the Commission to formulate standards relating to divestiture by independent accountants of all services which would prejudice their audit independence and to require that the "appropriate organization" study this issue. H.R. 13175, 95th Cong., 2d Sess. (1978) (the proposed "Public Accounting Regulatory Act"). *See also Securities and Exchange Commission Report to Congress on the Accounting Profession and the Commission's Oversight Role* 320 (July 1979).

[6] Cohen Commission at 103-104.

[7] Securities Act Release No. 5869 (September 26, 1977) (42 FR 53635).

[8] POB Report, *Scope of Services by CPA Firms* (1979) [hereinafter cited as POB Services Report].

[9] *Id.* at 4-5.

evidence did not reveal any impairment of independence stemming from accountants providing such services,[10] it stated that the disclosures required by ASR 250 "should either allay suspicion or cause clients and auditors to alter their relationships . . . and . . . should serve to provide a stronger data base for monitoring of this area."[11] To further enhance an understanding of management advisory services, the POB recommended that the SEC Practice Section's membership requirements be revised to require additional disclosure regarding fees for management advisory and tax services performed for audit clients. The POB also recommended that the Section specifically require compliance with the AICPA professional standards relating to management advisory services and that the impact of management advisory services on independence be considered during peer reviews conducted pursuant to SEC Practice Sectio n requirements.

The Commission issued ASR 264 in response to the POB's report. The Commission stated that the POB's report did "not adequately sensitize the profession and its clients to the potential effects on the independence of accountants of performance of nonaudit services for audit clients." ASR 264 discussed certain factors that the Commission identified as relevant to an evaluation by accountants, audit committees, boards of directors and managements of whether performance by independent accountants of specific services could impair their independence, either in fact or appearance. The Commission invited comments on the factors discussed in the release.

604.02. Reactions to ASRs 250 and 264
ASR 296:

Both the proxy rule requiring disclosure about nonaudit services and ASR 264 caused confusion.* In addition, ASRs 250 and 264 together were claimed to have resulted in unwarranted curtailment of nonaudit services.[1] Three aspects of these releases proved especially confusing, particularly to accountants. First, some commentators perceived the Commission to be deprecating the benefits that may accrue to registrants from certain management advisory services performed by the independent accountants. Second, some expressed concern that the Commission might ques-

tion the independence of an accountant, after the fact, based solely on the percentage relationships disclosed in proxy statements. And third, some were concerned about the suggestion that independence was a function, not only of accountants' relationships with individual clients, but also of the relationship of all nonaudit services, or even all management advisory services, to firms' aggregate revenues; and they were confused as to whether the Commission was concerned about all nonaudit services, which includes tax work and accounting and review services, or just management advisory services.

The Commission addressed these concerns in its August 1980 *Report to Congress on the Accounting Profession and the Commission's Oversight Role.*[2] That report stated that ASR 264 was issued to encourage accountants, audit committees, boards of directors, and managements to assess carefully the potential impact of nonaudit services on auditor independence. The Commission also stated that it did not intend to deprecate the benefits that may accrue to registrants from certain management advisory services performed by their independent accountants and, on the contrary, had expressly recognized that such benefits could be significant in many cases. The Commission did not expect, and certainly did not intend, that registrants would, as apparently some have, set arbitrary maximum percentage limits on the amount of nonaudit services for which they will engage their independent accountants and not even consider the possible impact of proposed services on the accountants' independence. Nor did the Commission intend to question the independence of an accountant in subsequent Commission filings based solely on the percentage relationships between audit and nonaudit services disclosed in proxy statements. Finally, although the Commission acknowledged that it had used the terms "nonaudit services" and "management advisory services" somewhat interchangeably in ASR 264, it noted that its primary concern was with the impact on accountants' independence of management advisory services performed for individual audit clients.

604.03. Review of Proxy Disclosures
ASR 296:

---

[10] *Id.* at 35.

[11] *Id.* at 5-6.

* Forty-nine letters of comment were received in response to the Commission's invitation to comment in ASR 264. A majority of those commentators were accountants who expressed strong opposition to ASR 264 and the disclosures called for by ASR 250. The POB also criticized ASR 264 in its letter of comment and in its 1979-80 Annual Report [hereinafter cited as POB 1980 Report]. Many of the consultants and actuaries who commented, however, urged that accounting firms be prohibited from providing certain management advisory services.

[1] *E.g.,* one accounting firm that commented on ASR 264 described four examples that it characterized as representa-

tive of 10 to 15 situations in which clients did not engage it to perform a nonaudit service either historically performed by that firm or discussed prior to the issuance of ASR 264. In the commentator's opinion, it was not hired because these companies were afraid of Commission questions or criticisms or disclosure of "too high" a percentage or were confused by ASRs 250 and 264.

[2] Former Chairman Williams had previously responded to these concerns in a January 1980 speech to the AICPA's Seventh National Conference on Current SEC Developments. An address by Harold M. Williams, Chairman, SEC, "The 1980's: The Future of the Accounting Profession," January 3, 1980.

The Commission's staff monitored the disclosures in proxy statements about nonaudit services performed by accountants to obtain a better understanding of the nature and magnitude of such nonaudit services. Approximately 1,200 proxy statements filed by registrants in 1979 and 1980 were reviewed. A substantial majority of the registrants in the survey (approximately 91% in 1979 and 92% in 1980) disclosed that they had engaged their accountants for some type of nonaudit service and the most frequently disclosed services were in tax related areas. Few of the registrants

reported that their independent accountants had performed the services which had been mentioned by the Commission or others as being particularly sensitive, such as consumer surveys, plant layout and actuarial services.[*]

The staff also reviewed the magnitude of the nonaudit services performed by independent accountants. This review showed that the following percentages of the registrants in the survey disclosed the listed categories of percentage relationships of fees for nonaudit services to audit fees:

Percentage relationship of fees for nonaudit services to audit fees	Percentage of companies in the sample	
	1979	1980
0-25%	68 %	74 %
26-50%	22	15
51-100%	7	8
Over 100%	3	3

Based on the staff's review of these disclosures, the Commission obtained a better understanding of the nature and extent of nonaudit services provided by accountants to their audit clients. Although the Commission continues to believe that information about nonaudit services performed by independent accountants is important for monitoring the relationships between accountants and their clients, it is not clear that routine disclosure of such detailed information in proxy statements is material to security holders.

The staff also reviewed the information in proxy statements about audit committees disclosed pursuant to Items 6(d) and 8(g). Item 6(d) requires a registrant to state whether or not it has standing audit, nominating and compensation committees, and if so, to describe the functions performed by each committee.[1] A significant percentage of the surveyed registrants had audit committees and many of these registrants reported that the audit committee considered the nonaudit professional services.[2]

604.04. Private-Sector Initiatives

ASR 296:

The private sector took steps to maintain and strengthen accountants' independence through review of management advisory services by audit

committees and others, and disclosure about such services.

As noted above, many publicly held companies have audit committees and many of these committees review the nonaudit services performed by accountants. Audit committee or board of director review of nonaudit functions is encouraged by the requirement of the AICPA's SEC Practice Section that member firms report to the audit committee, or board of directors, of each client registered with the Commission the total fees received from the client for management advisory services during the audit year and to describe the types of such services rendered.[*] The Commission believes that audit committees can be effective forces in helping to assure that management advisory services performed by accountants do not impair their independence.

In addition, the SEC Practice Section is monitoring management advisory services through its peer review program.[1] In its 1979-1980 Annual Report, the POB also stated that it would monitor the area of management advisory services and "comment if the facts suggest that the self-restraint [they] urged . . . is ignored by the profession or if the magnitude of [management advisory services]appears to increase to an extent that it

---

[*] In ASR 264, the Commission noted that the performance of such services might be difficult to justify in many cases. The Metcalf Report states that these and other nonaccounting management services are incompatible with the public responsibilities of independent accountants.

[1] The adoption of this rule and other amendments to the proxy rules designed to improve the information available to shareholders regarding boards of directors was announced in Exchange Act Release 15384 (December 6, 1978) [43 FR 58522]. Beginning with the 1979 proxy season, the proxy disclosures required by Item 6(b), (d), and (e) and Item 8(g) were monitored.

[2] The results of the 1979 proxy statement disclosure monitoring program were reported in Division of Corporation

Finance, Securities and Exchange Commission, "Staff Report on Corporate Accountability," 96th Cong., 2d Sess., Printed for use of the Senate Comm. on Banking, Housing and Urban Affairs (1980) at 589-624. The results of the 1980 monitoring program were reported in Exchange Act Release 17518 (Feb. 5, 1981) [46 FR 11954]. 84% of the registrants in the 1980 survey had audit committees. 50% of these registrants reported that the audit committee approved each professional service and 38% reported that the audit committee considered the range of audit and nonaudit fees.

[*] "Organizational Structure and Functions of the SEC Practice Section of the AICPA Division for CPA Firms," Section IV, 3(j) [hereinafter cited as Organizational Document].

[1] *Id.* at Section VIII, 3(c).

threatens professional image generally."[2] The Commission believes that these efforts, together with the interpretation and enforcement by the AICPA of its professional standards relating to management advisory services, constitute significant safeguards against impairment of accountants' independence.

Finally, information about nonaudit services is otherwise publicly available. The SEC Practice Section requires its member firms to file annual reports that are available for public inspection[3] and state, among other things, firms' gross fees for accounting and auditing, tax, and management advisory services expressed as a percentage of the total gross fees, and their gross fees for management advisory services and tax services performed for audit clients registered with the Commission expressed as a percentage of total fees charged to such clients.[4] This information alone, however, does not provide sufficient information to enable appropriate monitoring of nonaudit services performed by independent accountants. Both the Cohen Commission[5] and the POB[6] endorsed the concept of disaggregated disclosure about services to dispel the concerns about potential conflicts of interest resulting from the performance by accountants of nonaudit services. Moreover, the POB recognized that it would "have to reconsider its views and consider whether there are other devices that it can recommend to achieve the same results" if ASR 250 were withdrawn or the disclosure rule adopted therein was substantially modified.[7] Accordingly, the Commission noted that in taking final action on the proposal to rescind Item 8(g) of the proxy rules, it would consider what action the POB and the SEC Practice Section had taken to ensure that the nonaudit services performed by accountants can be adequately monitored.

604.05. Withdrawal of ASR 250

ASR 304:

The Commission determined to rescind Item 8(g) for the reasons more fully discussed in ASR 296. It concluded that the detailed nonaudit service disclosure required by that provision was not generally of sufficient utility to investors to justify continuation of the disclosure requirement.

Notwithstanding this action, the Commission believes it should continue to monitor the nonaudit service activity by accountants as a part of its oversight of the accounting profession. Other people may also want to monitor this activity. The Commission is satisfied with the informa-

tion that will be available because of a revision of the membership requirements of the SEC Practice Section of the Division for Firms of the AICPA. The SEC Practice Section responded promptly to the Commission's comment in ASR 296 that the accounting profession's self-regulatory mechanism should be able to generate sufficient information about nonaudit services performed by accountants to enable the Commission, the POB and other interested persons to continue to monitor the nonaudit services performed by accountants. The SEC Practice Section revised its membership provisions to require member accounting firms to disclose additional information about their nonaudit service activity for clients that file with the Commission. In annual reports filed with the Section for years ending on or after January 1, 1982, member firms will be required to report the number of such clients from which they receive fees for management advisory services that, when expressed as a percentage of the audit fees for such clients, are in the range of 1 to 25%, 26 to 50%, 51 to 100% and over 100%. In addition, they will be required to state how many of the audit clients in the "over 100%" category fall into that category for three consecutive years, including the current year. The Commission is satisfied that the additional disclosure required by the SEC Practice Section will enable it to adequately monitor trends in aggregate levels of nonaudit services performed by accountants for their registrant clients.

604.06. Withdrawal of ASR 264

ASR 296:

The Commission withdrew ASR 264. Although the Commission's views expressed in ASR 264 are unchanged and registrants and accountants must continue to carefully evaluate their relationships to ensure that the public maintains confidence in the integrity of financial reporting, the Commission withdrew that release because it might confuse independent accountants, audit committees and others who evaluate services performed or to be performed by the accountants. Moreover, the Commission believes it has achieved its objective in issuing ASR 264. Accountants and their self-regulatory structure, audit committees, boards of directors and managements are aware of the Commission's views on accountants' independence and should be sensitive to the possible impact on independence of nonaudit services performed by accountants. The Commission believes it should be able to rely on these persons to ensure adequate

---

[2] POB 1980 Report at 22.

[3] Organizational Document at Section IV, 3(g)(12) and (13).

[4] An AICPA review of annual reports filed with the SEC Practice Section indicates that over 90% of the 223 member firms that audit registrants reported that their firm-wide gross fees charged to such clients for management advisory ser-

vices constituted 10% or less of the total fees charged to those clients. Less than 1% of such firms reported that management advisory service fees amounted to more than 20% of total fees charged to registrant audit clients.

[5] Cohen Commission at 104.

[6] POB Services Report at 43.

[7] *Id.* at fn. 133.

consideration of the impact on accountants' independence of nonaudit services because they share the responsibility to assure that the public maintains confidence in the independence of accountants.

604.07. Conclusion
ASR 296:

The independence of the public accountant—both in fact and in appearance—is critical to his role as auditor because, absent independence, the auditor's skills and services are of little value. The Commission has the responsibility and authority under the securities laws to assure that accountants who practice before it are independent and, therefore, is prepared to take further action if either the fact or appearance of accountants' independence is questioned seriously in the future. The Commission rejected the recommendations that it prohibit accounting firms from providing nonaudit services to their audit clients, conduct hearings or sponsor an investigation of the nonaudit service activity of accountants, reinstate ASR 264 or repeat the substance of that release. The Commission's view on accountants' independence are clearly articulated in ASR 296 and registrants and accountants understand and appreciate that accountants independence must be carefully evaluated and preserved. Moreover, the Commission is satisfied that the self-regulatory mechanism established by the accounting profession, accountants, audit committees and managements should ensure that adequate consideration is given to the impact of nonaudit services on accountants' independence.

[¶ 38,385] 605. Accountants' Liability for Reports on Unaudited Interim Financial Information Under Securities Act of 1933

.01. Summary
ASR 274:

In December 1979, the Commission adopted amendments to Rule 436 which provides that a report prepared or certified by an accountant within the meaning of Sections 7 and 11 of the Securities Act shall not include a report by an independent accountant on a review of unaudited interim financial information,* thereby having the effect of excluding accountants issuing such reports from Section 11(a) liability. The rule was adopted, in part, to further the Commission's goals of encouraging increased auditor involvement with interim financial information and greater usage of reports containing a limited statement of assurance by accountants concerning unaudited financial information or other matters for which a full audit has not been undertaken. The Commission emphasized that it will closely monitor the rule as well as other matters relating to excluding accountants from liability under Section 11 for similar reports on unaudited data and that the rule adopted is not necessarily a final resolution of this matter.

The rule has the effect of excluding accountants from potential liability under Section 11(a) of the Securities Act for SAS 36 reports included in Securities Act filings.

605.02. Background
.a. Review of Interim Financial Information
ASR 274:

SAS 36 delineates procedures to be followed by accountants with respect to reviews of unaudited interim financial information and sets forth standards for reports based on such reviews. The prescribed procedures are limited to inquiries and review procedures which are substantially less than an audit.

The Commission has encouraged increased auditor involvement with interim financial information and greater usage of reports containing a limited statement of assurance by accountants concerning unaudited financial information or other matters for which a full audit has not been undertaken.* Reports on unaudited interim financial information represented the first type of public reporting, applicable to public companies, by independent accountants containing such limited assurances based on procedures less than an audit.

605.02.b. Statutory Framework
ASR 274:

Section 11(a)(4) of the Securities Act imposes civil liability for material misstatements or omissions in registration statements upon every accountant . . . who has, with his consent, been named as having prepared or certified any part of the registration statement, or as having prepared or certified any report or valuation which is used in connection with the registration statement . . . .** Section 7 of the Securities Act deals with the matter of consent by requiring the filing of a written consent with the registration statement by

---

* [In March 1979, the ASB issued SAS 24, "Review of Interim Financial Information." In April 1981, the ASB issued SAS 36 of the same title, which superseded the previous statement. All references in this Section have been updated to refer to SAS 36.]

* *See, e.g., Securities and Exchange Commission Report to Congress on the Accounting Profession and the Commission's Oversight Role,* U.S. Government Printing Office, July 1979, pages 241-243.

** Section 11(a) in imposing civil liability for material misstatements or omissions in registration statements applies to:

(4) every accountant, engineer, or appraiser, or any person whose profession gives authority to a statement made by him, who has with his consent been named as having prepared or certified any part of the registration statement, or as having prepared or certified any report or valuation which is used in connection with the registration statement, with respect to the statement in such registration statement, report, or valuation, which purports to have been prepared or certified by him . . . .

any accountant who is named as having prepared or certified a report for use in connection with the registration statement. Section 7 establishes a separate requirement for reports which are used in a registration statement but which were prepared by the accountant for some other purpose; here, written consent is required "unless the Commission dispenses with such filings as impracticable or as involving undue hardship on the person filing the registration statement."[1]

An important consequence of Section 11(a) liability is that a plaintiff who makes a showing of a material misstatement or omission in a registration statement will have met his burden of proof. The burden will then shift to the defendant under Section 11(b)(3)(B)(i) to demonstrate that he believed the statement was true and not misleading after conducting a "reasonable investigation" and that he had reasonable ground for this belief.[2]

Accountants have heretofore considered their duty to conduct a "reasonable investigation" under Section 11 to have been met when they performed a full audit and not when only limited procedures are involved as in SAS 36 reviews.

As a consequence of the interrelationship between Sections 7 and 11, concern had been expressed that accountants issuing SAS 36 reports, who subsequently consent under Section 7 to being named in a registration statement which incorporates their report by reference, could be held subject to Section 11(a) which imposes liability on every accountant "who has with his consent been named as having prepared . . . and report . . . ."

The question of whether accountants could be held liable under Section 11(a) for SAS 36 reports included with the consent of the accountants pursuant to Section 7 in Securities Act filings has not yet been tested in the courts. Under existing case law, Section 11(a) liability of an accountant who has consented to being named in a registration statement has been limited to audited financial statements which have been certified by him. *See Escott* v. *Bar Chris Construction Corp.*, 283 F. Supp. 643 (S.D.N.Y. 1968), and *Grimm* v. *Whitney-Fidalgo Seafoods, Inc.*, (1977-78 Transfer Binder) CCH

Fed. Sec. L. Rep. ¶ 96,029 (S.D.N.Y. 1973). These cases arose, however, before the issuance of reports on unaudited interim financial information and their inclusion in Securities Act filings with the accountant's consent to being named as having prepared them. As a result of the different facts presented by issuance of SAS 36 reports, absent the rule adopted, the accountant's consent and issuance of such a report may have been found to come within the language of Section 11(a)(4) which imposes liability on an accountant "who has with his consent been named as having prepared or certified . . . any report or valuation which is used in connection with the registration statement . . . ." Therefore, absent the rule adopted, additional uncertainty would exist, if Section 11(a)(4) were applicable to accountants for SAS 36 reports, as to whether SAS 36 limited procedures would constitute a reasonable investigation defense in the circumstances under Section 11(b)(3)(B)(i).

605.03. Purpose

ASR 274:

An impetus for the rule was concern that, if SAS 36 reports are used by registrants in connection with Securities Act registration statements, there may be reluctance on the part of accountants to issue reports on the basis of the limited review procedures specified in SAS 36 because of their potential liability under Section 11(a) of the Securities Act; and that, alternatively, if accountants perform significantly expanded procedures, much closer to a complete audit, in order to meet potential liability concerns under Section 11(a), substantial increased costs to issuers could result.

The Commission expects that directors and underwriters will continue to exercise due diligence in a vigorous manner with respect to SAS 36 reports. In any suit for damages under Section 11(a), the directors and underwriters in defense should not be able to rely on reports on interim financial data included in a registration statement as statements "purporting to be made on the authority of an expert . . . which they had no ground to believe . . . were untrue . . . ." under

---

[1] The pertinent language of Section 7 is:

If any accountant, engineer, or appraiser, or any person whose profession gives authority to a statement made by him, is named as having prepared or certified any part of the registration statement, or is named as having prepared or certified a report or valuation for use in connection with the registration statement, the written consent of such person shall be filed with the registration statement. If any such person is named as having prepared or certified a report or valuation (other than a public official document or statement) which is used in connection with the registration statement, but is not named as having prepared or certified such report or valuation for use in connection with the registration statement, the written consent of such person shall be filed with the registration statement unless the Commission dispenses with such filing as impractical or as involving undue hardship on the person filing the registration statement.

[2] Section 11(b)(3) provides a defense to Section 11(a) liability for every person named in Section 11(a), other than an issuer, if such person sustains the burden of proof that:

(B) as regards any part of the registration statement purporting to be made upon his authority as an expert or purporting to be a copy of or extract from a report or valuation of himself as an expert, (i) he had, after reasonable investigation, reasonable ground to believe and did believe, at the time such part of the registration statement became effective, that the statements therein were true and that there was no omission to state a material fact required to be stated therein or necessary to make the statements therein not misleading, or (ii) such part of the registration statement did not fairly represent his statement as an expert or was not a fair copy of or extract from his report or valuation as an expert.

Section 11(b)(3)(C).[*] Rather, directors and underwriters should be required, as has previously been the case whenever unaudited financials are included in a registration statement, to demonstrate affirmatively under Section 11(b)(3)(A) that, after conducting a reasonable investigation, they had reasonable ground to believe, and did believe, that the interim financial data was true.[1]

It should be emphasized that accountants nevertheless remain subject to liability under Section 17(a) of the Securities Act for SAS 36 reports used in connection with registration statements.[2] This section provides a vehicle for securing many of the protections afforded under Section 11 of the Securities Act,[3] although there are significant differences between the two sections.

605.04. Other Considerations
.a. Other Remedies Available to Shareholders
ASR 274:

The Commission recognizes that, although, as a result of this rule, accountants will not be liable to shareholders in actions under Section 11, there are other remedies available to aggrieved shareholders including those under common law, state statutes, and the general anti-fraud provisions of the federal securities statutes. For example, a shareholder may bring an action under Section 10(b) of the Exchange Act and Rule 10b-5 thereunder, although the plaintiff will have the burden of proving scienter in that case.[*] As to directors and underwriters who rely on the accountant's report on interim financial information, they also can bring actions under other applicable laws.

605.04.b. Control of Use of Reports
ASR 274:

An independent accountant should have the ability to control the use of his SAS 36 report in a registration statement, and the Commission's staff should have a vehicle to determine that the SAS 36 report has not been included in a registration statement without the accountant's knowledge. While the rule eliminates the requirement of Section 7 of the Securities Act that accountants consent to use of SAS 36 reports, the Commission believes that independent accountants should acknowledge their awareness that their SAS 36 reports are being included in a registration statement. [Issuers are required by Item 601(b)(15) in Regulation S-K to file as an exhibit to a registration statement a letter from the independent accountants which acknowledges their awareness of the use in a registration statement of their report on unaudited interim financial information which is not subject to the consent requirement of Section 7.]

Disclosure which clarifies the distinction between the role of accountants in preparing SAS 36 reports as opposed to their role in certifying financial statements is needed in order to fully inform investors. Such disclosure would correct any misleading implication about the extent of accountants' involvement which might otherwise arise from the inclusion of both an SAS 36 report and a certification in a registration statement and thus satisfy the requirements of Rule 408 of Regulation C under the Securities Act. Accordingly, a pro-

---

[*] Section 11(b)(3) provides a defense to Section 11(a) liability to every person named in Section 11(a), other than an issuer, if such person sustains the burden of proof that:

(C) as regards any part of the registration statement purporting to be made on the authority of an expert (other than himself) or purporting to be a copy or extract from a report or valuation of an expert (other than himself), he had no reasonable ground to believe, and did not believe, at the time such part of the registration statement became effective, that the statements therein were untrue or that there was an omission to state a material fact required to be stated therein or necessary to make the statements therein not misleading, or that such part of the registration statement did not fairly represent the statement of the expert or was not a fair copy of or extract from the report or valuation of the expert . . . .

[1] Section 11(b)(3) provides a defense to Section 11(a) liability to every person named in Section 11(a), other than an issuer, if such person shall sustain the burden of proof that:

(A) as regards any part of the registration statement not purporting to be made on the authority of any expert and not purporting to be a copy of or extract from a report or valuation of an expert, and not purporting to be made on the authority of a public official document or statement, he had, after reasonable investigation, reasonable ground to believe and did believe, at the time such part of the registration statement became effective, that the statements therein were true and that there was no omission to state a material fact required to be stated therein or necessary to make the statements therein not misleading . . . .

[2] Section 17(a) of the Securities Act provides in its entirety:

It shall be unlawful for any person in the offer or sale of any securities by the use of any means or instruments of transportation or communication in interstate commerce or by the use of the mails, directly or indirectly—

(1) to employ any device, scheme, or artifice to defraud, or

(2) to obtain money or property by means of any untrue statement of a material fact or any omission to state a material fact necessary in order to make the statements made, in the light of the circumstances under which they were made, not misleading, or

(3) to engage in any transaction, practice, or course of business which operates or would operate as a fraud or deceit upon the purchaser.

[3] [With respect to Commission enforcement actions, the Supreme Court held that proof of scienter is not necessary in an action to enjoin further violations of paragraphs (2) and (3) of Section 17(a), but that scienter is a prerequisite for an injunction restraining further violations of Sections 17(a)(1), Section 10(b) and Rule 10b-5. *Aaron* v. *Securities and Exchange Commission,* 446 U.S. 680 (1980). Therefore, insofar as material misstatements or omissions are made by accountants in SAS 36 reports used in registration statements, the Commission may take appropriate enforcement action against such accountants under Section 17(a)(2) and (3). Of course, where an accountant's report is found to be fraudulent, and the fraud has occurred in connection with the purchase or sale of a security, civil liability would also arise pursuant to Sections 10(b) and 17(a)(1) of the Exchange Act, 15 U.S.C. 78j(b), and Rule 10b-5 thereunder, 17 CFR 240, 10b-5. *See,* e.g., *Blue Chip Stamps* v. *Manor Drug Stores,* 421 U.S. 723 (1975).]

[*] *See Ernst & Ernst* v. *Hochfelder,* 425 U.S. 185 (1976).

spectus which includes a discussion about the independent accountants' involvement in a registration statement should clarify that a SAS 36 report included in such registration statement is not a "report" or "part" of the registration statement within the meaning of Sections 7 and 11 of the Securities Act. The fact that the independent accountants' Section 11 liability does not extend to such SAS 36 reports should be specifically stated.

[¶ 38,391] 606. Requirements for Signatures and Accountants' Consents with Regard to Form S-8

ASR 303:

In an effort to reduce reporting burdens on registrants without reducing the quality of disclosure made to investors, and to reduce staff workload, the Commission in 1980 adopted two series of amendments to Form S-8, the form for registration under the Securities Act of securities to be offered to employees pursuant to certain plans. The first of these series of amendments was adopted on February 22, 1980** and provided a means whereby all filings on Form S-8 would become effective automatically without affirmative action on the part of the Commission or its staff. While this release did not alter the existing signature requirements of Form S-8,[1] it did add the requirement for a certification by all signatories concerning the issuer's eligibility to use the form. On April 2, 1980, the Commission adopted the second series of amendments to Form S-8[2] which made the disclosure and updating features of Form S-16 available to many issuers using Form S-8. More specifically, the amendments allowed updating of the Form S-8 to be accomplished by means of periodic reports, such as Forms 10-K, 11-K, 8-K and 10-Q filed under the Exchange Act thereby eliminating, in many instances, the necessity of filing a post-effective amendment. A critical element to a registrant's ability to use Exchange Act reports is contained in Item 12 of Form S-8 (Incorporation of Certain Documents by Reference). If any accountant, engineer or other "expert" is named as having prepared or certified any part of the material incorporated by reference, Item 12 requires the written consent of such person to be included in the registration statement (or amendment thereto) unless an express consent to the incorporation by reference is contained in the material incorporated by reference.

In the February 1980 Release, the Commission announced that, while regular staff review of Form S-8's was being eliminated, there would be monitoring of compliance with disclosure requirements, on an audit basis, both prior to and after such filings become effective.

The staff of the Division of Corporation Finance completed its first such monitoring effort. The results of such review show a failure of a significant number of registrants filing Form S-8's to comply with the requirements of the form in three distinct areas:

(1) failure to supply the requisite signatures, such as those of officers and a majority of the board of directors; (2) failure to include, as part of the signature sections, the required certifications that the issuer meets all of the requirements for filing on Form S-8; and (3) failure, in subsequent years, to include the requisite written accountants' consent in either an amendment to the registration statement or in the filing being incorporated by reference, such as in the Form 10-K. The Commission considers these to be serious deficiencies and reminds registrants of their statutory obligation to fully comply with the requirements of any form they utilize, whether or not staff review is accorded such forms. Moreover, the Commission notes that the viability of many of its new programs designed to reduce the burdens on registrants depends upon the careful and complete preparation of filed documents by such registrants and their counsel.

[¶ 38,395] 607. Certification of Financial Statements

.01. First Time Audit
.a. Background

ASR 90:

It came to the attention of the Commission that wide variations had developed in certificates of independent accountants contained in registration statements filed under the Securities Act with respect to representations concerning the verification of inventories of prior years in first audits. This development had been noted particularly in situations involving the offering of securities of closely held corporations which had failed to maintain and preserve accounting records and data necessary to permit verification of financial statements. In some cases a question arose about whether the certifying accountant intended to limit his opinion as to the fairness of presentation of the income statements.

The following is the pertinent part of an example of this type of certificate:

"* * * Except as noted in the succeeding paragraph, our examination was made in accordance with generally accepted auditing

---

** Securities Act Release 6190 (February 22, 1980) [45 FR 13438] (hereinafter the "February 1980 Release").

[1] The instruction presently provides, as it did prior to February 22, 1980, that the registration statement shall be signed by the issuer (and where interests in the plan are

being registered, by the plan), their respective principal executive officers, and by at least the majority of the respective boards of directors or persons performing similar functions.

[2] Securities Act Release 6202 (April 2, 1980) [45 FR 23653].

standards and accordingly included such tests of the accounting records and such other auditing procedures as we considered necessary in the circumstances.

"Since this was our initial examination of the financial statements of the Company, September 30, 19x1, was the only date at which we observed the taking of physical inventories. However, based on other tests we applied, including tests of gross profits and review of physical inventory records, we have no reason to believe that inventories at September 30, 19y8, 19y9, and 19x0, were not also fairly stated.

"In our opinion, with the foregoing comment regarding inventories * * *"

The Commission reminded the financial community that the Securities Act requires that registration statements contain a certificate of an independent account based on an audit conducted in accordance with generally accepted auditing standards and meeting the reporting requirements of the Commission.

607.01.b. Conclusion

ASR 90:

If an accountant reports that his examination was made in accordance with generally accepted auditing standards, and accordingly included such tests of the accounting records and such other auditing procedures as he considered necessary in the circumstances, an exception as to failure to observe beginning inventories is contradictory and should be omitted. A middle paragraph explaining that the certificate covers a first audit is informative and in some cases is essential to describe the alternative procedures applied. A negative type conclusion to this paragraph is not acceptable. Lost and inadequate records may give rise to questions as to the reliability of the results shown in the financial statements and may make it impracticable to apply alternative audit procedures. Alternative procedures must be adequate to support an unqualified opinion as to the fairness of presentation of the income statements by years.

If, as a result of the examination and the conclusions reached, the accountant is not in a position to express an affirmative opinion as to the fairness of the presentation of earnings year by year, the registration statement is defective because the certificate does not meet the requirements of Rule 2-02 of Regulation S-X. If the accountant is not satisfied with the results of his examination he should not issue an affirmative opinion. If he is satisfied, any reference from the opinion paragraph to an explanatory paragraph devoted solely to the scope of the audit is inconsistent and unnec-

essary. Accordingly, phrases such as "with the foregoing explanation as to inventories" raise questions as to whether the certifying accountant intended to limit his opinion as to the fairness of the presentation of the results shown and should be omitted.

A "subject to" or "except for" opinion paragraph in which these phrases refer to the scope of the audit, indicating that the accountant has not been able to satisfy himself on some significant element in the financial statements, is not acceptable in certificates filed with the Commission in connection with the public offering of securities. The "subject to" qualification is appropriate when the reference is to a middle paragraph or to footnotes explaining the status of matters which cannot be resolved at statement date.

607.02. Uncertainty About an Entity's Continued Existence

[Amended by FRR-16.]

Financial statements will be considered false and misleading if those statements are prepared on the assumption of a going concern but should more appropriately be based on the assumption of liquidation or if the classification and amounts of assets and liabilities should be otherwise adjusted. Moreover, filings containing accountant's reports that are qualified as a result of questions about the entity's continued existence must contain appropriate and prominent disclosure of the registrant's financial difficulties and viable plans to overcome these difficulties. Such disclosure is required by existing rules and by the antifraud provisions of the federal securities law.[*]

For example, the requirements of Item 303 of Regulation S-K, Management's Discussion and Analysis, insofar as they relate to disclosure of any known demands, commitments or uncertainties that will result in (or that are reasonably likely to result in) the registrant's liquidity increasing or decreasing in any material way, are intended to and should elicit detailed cash flow discussions from any registrant whose dependent accountant's report is qualified because of doubt about the entity's continued existence. In responding to these requirements, any registrant with such pressing financial problems should include a reasonably detailed discussion of its ability or inability to generate sufficient cash to support its operation during the twelve month period following the date of the financial statements being reported upon. Thereafter, this discussion would be updated as necessary on a quarterly basis.

The Commission notes that generally accepted auditing standards provide in Statement on Auditing Standards No. 34 ("SAS 34")[4] that the auditor

---

[*] See, *e.g.,* Items 101, 303, 503 and 504 of Regulation S-K [17 CFR 229], Description of Business, Management's Discussion and Analysis, Summary Information and Risk Factors,

and Use of Proceeds, respectively, and Rule 408 [17 CFR 230.408], Additional Information.

[4] SAS 34, "The Auditors Considerations When a Question Arises About an Entity's Continued Existence", issued in

who issues a report that is qualified as a result of questions about the entity's continued existence must evaluate the disclosure about the financial problems giving rise to the accountant's qualification. The Commission believes that in such cases Paragraph 10 of SAS 34 requires the auditor to include in his report, if not otherwise disclosed in the financial statements, appropriate "disclosure of the principal conditions that raise [the] question about [the] entity's ability to continue in existence, the possible effects of such conditions, and management's evaluation of the significance of those conditions and any mitigating factors". The Commission also believes that paragraph 10 of SAS 34 requires auditors to assure the adequacy of disclosure about plans to resolve the doubts about the entity's continued existence.[5]

(Footnote Continued)

1981, provides guidance regarding the auditor's responsibilities when there are questions about an

[5] Paragraph 10 of SAS 34 concludes by stating ". . . [i]f disclosure is necessary and a satisfactory resolution of the question [about an entity's ability to continue in existence] depends primarily on the realization of particular plans of management, the disclosure should deal with that fact and such plans."

[¶ 38,501]
APPENDIX A

ASR Codification—Glossary of Terms

The following abbreviations are used in the codification.

AcSEC—Accounting Standards Executive Committee of the American Institute of Certified Public Accountants

Advisers Act—Investment Advisers Act of 1940

AICPA—American Institute of Certified Public Accountants

APB—Accounting Principles Board

APBO—Accounting Principles Board Opinion

ARB—Accounting Research Bulletin

ASB—Auditing Standards Board of the AICPA

ASR—Accounting Series Release

AudSEC—Auditing Standards Executive Committee of the AICPA

Exchange Act—Securities Exchange Act of 1934

FASB—Financial Accounting Standards Board

FEI—Financial Executives Institute

FIFO—First-In, First-Out Method of Inventory Valuation

GAAP—Generally Accepted Accounting Principles

Investment Company Act—Investment Company Act of 1940

IRS—Internal Revenue Service

LIFO—Last-In, First-Out Method of Inventory Valuation

MD&A—Management's Discussion and Analysis of Financial Condition and Results of Operations

POB—Public Oversight Board of the SEC Practice Section of the Division for CPA Firms of the AICPA

SAB—Staff Accounting Bulletin

SAS—Statement on Auditing Standards

Securities Act—Securities Act of 1933

SFAC—Statement of Financial Accounting Concepts

SFAS—Statement of Financial Accounting Standards

[¶ 38,511]
APPENDIX B

Disposition of Accounting Series Releases

This appendix lists each ASR and identifies the disposition of the material in that ASR. Where material from an ASR has been included in the codification, a reference to the codification topic is noted in the right hand column. If no material from the ASR has been codified, the reason why the material has been excluded is noted in accordance with the legend below.

Legend

R—The ASR had previously been formally rescinded.

O—The ASR has been omitted because the material is obsolete or otherwise unnecessary.

E—This release announces the results of an enforcement-related action and enforcement-related releases have not been codified.

ASR No.	Title	Status or Cross Ref.
1	Treatment of Losses from Reevaluation of Assets. (4-1-37)	R
2	Independence of Accountants—Relationship to Registrant. (5-6-37)	R
3	Treatment of Investments in Subsidiaries in Consolidated Statements. (9-13-37)	R
4	Administrative Policy on Financial Statements. (4-25-38)	101
5	Treatment of Dividends on Corporation's Own Capital Stock Held in Sinking-Fund. (5-10-38)	R
6	Treatment of Excess of Proceeds from Sale of Treasury Stock Over Cost Thereof. (5-10-38)	R
7	Commonly Cited Deficiencies in Financial Statements Filed Under the Securities Act of 1933 and the Securities Exchange Act of 1934. (5-16-38)	R
8	Creation by Promotional Companies of Surplus by Appraisal. (5-20-38)	215
9	Presentation of Stock Having Preferences on Involuntary Liquidation in Excess of Par or Stated Value. (12-23-38)	R
10	Treatment of Unamortized Bond Discount and Expense Applicable to Bonds Retired Prior to Maturity with Proceeds from Sale of Capital Stock. (12-23-38)	R
11	Consolidation of Foreign Subsidiaries of Domestic Corporation. (1-4-40)	R
12	Adoption of Regulation S-X—Amendments to Form 15 and Form 17. (2-21-40)	O
13	Form of Accountants' Certificate. (2-20-40)	R
14	Amendment of Rule Adopting Regulation S-X. (2-29-40)	R
15	Description of Surplus Accruing Subsequent to Effective Date of Quasi-Reorganization. (3-16-40)	R
16	Disclosure of Charge of Deficit to Capital Surplus Without Approval of Stockholders. (3-16-40)	R
17	Use of Natural Business Year as Basis for Corporate Reporting. (3-18-40)	R
18	Amendment of Rule 4-09 of Regulation S-X. (11-19-40)	O
19	In the Matter of McKesson & Robbins, Inc.—Summary of Findings and Conclusions—File No. 1-1435—Securities Exchange Act of 1934, Section 21(a). (12-5-40)	E
20	Amendment of Rule 12-16 of Regulation S-X. (12-20-40)	O
21	Amendment of Rules 2-02 and 3-07 of Regulation S-X. (2-5-41)	O
22	Independence of Accountants—Indemnification by Registrant. (3-14-41)	602
23	Treatment of Federal Income and Excess Profits Taxes. (4-9-41)	R
24	Amendment to Articles 1, 6 and 12 of Regulation S-X. (5-23-41)	O
25	Procedure in Quasi-Reorganization. (5-29-41)	210
26	Interpretation of Rule 5-02 of Regulation S-X Regarding the Omission of an Analysis of Registrant's Surplus Accounts. (7-1-41)	R
27	The Nature of the Examination and Certificate Required by Paragraph (4) of Rule N-17F-1 and Paragraph (7) of Rule N-17F-2 Under the Investment Company Act of 1940. (12-11-41)	404
28	Findings and Opinion of the Commission in the Matter of Proceedings Under Rule 2(e) of the Rules of Practice, to Determine Whether the Privilege of Kenneth N. Logan to Practice as an Accountant Before the Securities and Exchange Commission Should be Denied, Temporarily or Permanently. (1-8-42)	E
29	Amendment of Rule 1-01 of Regulation S-X and Adoption of Article 6A and the Related Rules of Article 12 of Regulation S-X Pertaining to Unit Investment Trusts. (1-9-42)	O
30	Auditing of Inventories Under Wartime Conditions. (1-22-42)	R
31	Amendment to Articles 5, 6 and 12 of Regulation S-X. (2-5-42)	O

ASR No.	Title	Status or Cross Ref.
61	Notice of Proposal to Issue a Release in the Accounting Series Regarding the Use of Public Accountants' Names in Connection With Summary Earnings Tables Included in Registration Statements Filed Under the Securities Act of 1933. (5-15-47)	R
62	Circumstances Under Which Independent Public Accountants May Properly Express an Opinion, and the Form of Such Opinion With Respect to Summary Earnings Tables to be Included in Registration Statements Filed Under the Securities Act of 1933. (6-27-47)	R
63	Notice of Proposals to Amend Rule N-8B-2 and to Adopt Form N-8B-4 and Rule N-8C-4 Under the Investment Company Act of 1940—Notice of Proposal to Adopt a New Article 6B in Regulation S-X. (8-5-47)	R
64	In the Matter of Drayer-Hanson, Incorporated—Report of Investigation Pursuant to Section 8(e) of the Securities Act of 1933 File No. 2-6670. (3-15-48)	E
65	Notice of Proposal to Amend Regulation S-X. (6/21/48)	R
66	Amendment of Regulation S-X by Adoption of Article 5A; Amendment to Article 1, Rule 1-01; Article 4, Rule 4-14; Article 5, Rule 5-01; Article 12, Rule 12-06, Rule 12-06A, and Rule 12-07; Amendments to Form 10 and Form 10-K. (10/19/48)	O
67	Findings and Opinion of the Commission in the Matter of Proceedings Under Rule 2(e) of the Rules of Practice, to Determine Whether the Privilege of Barrow, Wade, Guthrie & Co., Henry H. Dalton and Everett L. Mangam to Practice as Accountants Before the Securities and Exchange Commission Should be Denied, Temporarily or Permanently. (4/18/49)	E
68	Findings and Opinion of the Commission in the Matter of Proceedings Under Rule 2(e) of the Rules of Practice to Determine Whether the Privilege of F.G. Masquelette & Co. and J.E. Cassel to Practice as Accountants Before the Securities and Exchange Commission Should be Denied, Temporarily or Permanently. (7/5/49).	E
69	Notice of Proposal to Amend Regulation S-X; A General Revision of Articles 1, 2, 3, 4, 5 and 11 of that Regulation. (7/12/50)	R
70	Amendment of Regulation S-X; Adoption of Comprehensive Amendments to Articles 1, 2, 3, 4, 5 and 11. (12/20/50)	O
71	Amendment of Rule N-8B-2; Adoption of Form N-8B-4 and Rule N-8C-4; Adoption of 6B of Regulation S-X. (12/29/50)	O
72	Adoption of Revised Form U5S. (3/12/51)	O
73	Findings and Opinion of the Commission in the Matter of Haskins & Sells and Andrew Stewart File No. 4-66, (Rules of Practice—Rule 2(e). (10/30/52)	E
74	Adoption of Amendments to Certain Rules of Article 6 of Regulation S-X. (5/29/53)	O
75	Adoption of Amendments to Certain Rules of Article 6 of Regulation S-X. (5/29/53)	O
76	Adoption of Rule 3-20(d) of Article 3 of Regulation S-X. (11/3/53)	O
77	Disposition of Rule 2(e) Proceedings Against Certifying Accountant Alleged to Have Failed to Observe Appropriate Audit Requirements as to Financial Statements of Broker-Dealer Under Rule X-17A-5 Under the Securities Exchange Act of 1934. (2/19/54)	E
78	Findings and Opinion of the Commission in the Matter of Touche, Niven, Bailey & Smart, et. al., Proceeding Pursuant to Rule 2(e), Rules of Practice. (3/25/57)	E
79	Amendment of Rule 2-01 of Regulation S-X. (4/8/58)	602
80	Amendment to Rule 1-01 of Article 1 and Rule 5A-01 of Article 5A of Regulation S-X. (8/19/58)	O
81	Independence of Certifying Accountants—Compilation of Representative Administrative Rulings in Cases Involving the Independence of Accountants. (12/11/58)	602
82	Findings and Opinion of the Commission in the Matter of Bollt and Shapiro, Theodore Bollt and Bernard L. Shapiro, Proceeding Pursuant to Rule 2(e), Rules of Practice. (1/28/59)	E
83	Amendment to Minimum Audit Requirements Prescribed in Form X-17A-5 Under the Securities Exchange Act of 1934. (10/28/59)	O
84	Revision to Uniform System of Accounts for Public Utility Holding Companies. (11/24/59)	O
85	Statement of Administrative Policy Regarding Balance Sheet Treatment of Credit Equivalent to Reduction in Income Taxes. (2/29/60)	R
86	Response to Comment on Statement of Administrative Policy Regarding Balance Sheet Treatment of Credit Equivalent to Reduction in Income Taxes. (4/12/60)	R
87	In the Matter of Bollt and Shapiro, Theodore Bollt and Bernard L. Shapiro. (1/17/61)	E
88	Findings and Opinion of the Commission In the Matter of Myron Swartz Pursuant to Rule 2(e), Rules of Practice. (5/24/61)	E
89	Revision of Articles 7 and 12 of Regulation S-X. (7/26/61)	O
90	Certification of Income Statements. (3/1/62)	607
91	Findings and Opinion of the Commission In the Matter of Arthur Levison and Levison and Company, Pursuant to Rule 2(e), Rules of Practice. (7/20/62)	E
92	Findings and Opinion of the Commission In the Matter of Morton I. Myers, Pursuant to Rule 2(e), Rules of Practice. (7/20/62)	E
93	Adoption of Form 11-K and Rule 15d-21 and Amendments to Form 10-K and Regulation S-X. (7/23/62)	O
94	Order In the Matter of Nathan Wechsler, Pursuant to Rule 2(e), Rules of Practice. (11/5/62)	E

ASR No.	Title	Status or Cross Ref.
95	Accounting for Real Estate Transactions Where Circumstances Indicate that Profits Were Not Earned at the Time the Transactions Were Recorded. (12/28/62)	R
96	Accounting for the "Investment Credit." (1/10/63)	R
97	Findings and Opinion of the Commission In the Matter of Harmon R. Stone, Pursuant to Rule 2(e), Rules of Practice. (5/21/63)	E
98	Maintenance of Records of Transactions by Broker-Dealer as Underwriters of Investment Companies Shares. (11/13/63)	402
99	Order Dismissing Proceedings In the Matter of Roberts & Morrow, Pursuant to Rule 2(e), Rules of Practice. (2/28/64)	E
100	Adoption of Article 7A and Rule 12-31 of Regulation S-X. (10/6/64)	O
101	Order Readmitting Accountant to Practice Before Commission In the Matter of Morton I. Myers, Pursuant to Rule 2(e), Rules of Practice. (4/26/65)	E
102	Balance Sheet Classification of Deferred Income Taxes Arising from Installment Sales. (12/7/65)	R
103	The Nature of the Examination and Certificate Required by Paragraph (a)(5) of Rule 206(4)-2 Under the Investment Advisers Act of 1940. (5/26/66)	404
104	Order In the Matter of John C. Hurdman, Doing Business as Hurdman and Company. (6/1/66)	E
105	Order Accepting Withdrawal from Practice and Dismissing Proceedings—In the Matter of Homer E. Kerlin, Pursuant to Rule 2(e), Rules of Practice. (7/29/66)	E
106	Adoption of Revisions of the Uniform Systems of Accounts for Mutual Service Companies and Subsidiary Service Companies, Under the Public Utility Holding Company Act of 1935, to Permit Orderly Destruction of Certain Records of Service Companies. (8/12/66)	O
107	Net Capital Requirements for Broker and Dealers—Interpretation and Guide. (1-18-67)	R
108	Order In the Matter of Nicolas J. Raftery, a Certified Public Accountant. (2/9/67)	E
109	Order In the Matter of Edwin Aronowitz, a Public Accountant. (9/25/67)	E
110	Order In the Matter of Meyer Weiner, a Certified Public Accountant. (1/18/68)	E
111	Amendment to Rule 1-01 of Article I of Regulation S-X. (3/20/68)	O
112	Independence of Accountants Examining a Nonmaterial Segment of an International Business. (8/12/68)	602
113	Statement Regarding "Restricted Securities." (10/21/69)	404
114	Adoption of Amendments to Rule 6-02-9 of Article 6 of Regulation S-X and Rule 2a-4 Under the Investment Company Act of 1940 with Respect to Provision by Registered Investment Companies for Federal Income Taxes. (12/31/69)	404
115	Certification of Financial Statements. (2/19/70)	607
116	Disclosure Concerning "Restricted Securities." (4/13/70)	O
117	Adoption of Article 11A of Regulation S-X. (10/14/70)	O
118	Accounting for Investment Securities by Registered Investment Companies. 12-23-70	404
119	Computation of Ratio of Earnings to Fixed Charges. (6/15/71)	R
120	Notice of Revision of Annual Report Form N-1R for Management Investment Companies and Withdrawal of Proposal to Amend Rule 30a-1. (7/15/71)	O
121	Adoption of Amendments to Regulation S-X and to Forms 10 and 10-K to Revise the Exemption from Certification of Financial Statements of Banks Filed Under the Securities Act of 1933 and the Securities Exchange Act of 1934. (7/19/71)	O
122	Coverage of Fixed Charges. (8/10/71)	R
123	Standing Audit Committees Composed of Outside Directors. (3/23/72)	601
124	Pro Rata Stock Distributions to Shareholders. (6/1/72)	214
125	Notice of Adoption of Amendments to Regulation S-X. (6/23/72)	O
126	Independence of Accountants—Guidelines and Examples of Situations Involving the Independence of Accountants. (7/5/72)	602
127	Notice that Initial Decision Has Become Final In the Matter of Martin L. Sanchez (Rule 2(3) of the Rules of Practice). (9/11/72)	E
128	Notice of Adoption of Revision of Article 9 of Regulation S-X. (9/20/72)	O
129	Order Accepting Resignation from Commission Practice In the Matter of Barry L. Kessler (Rule 2(e) of the Rules of Practice). (9/26/72)	E
130	Pooling-of-Interests Accounting. (9/29/72)	201
131	Order Accepting Resignation from Commission Practice In the Matter of Robert Trivison (Rule 2(e) of the Rules of Practice). (10/19/72)	E
132	Reporting of Leases in Financial Statements of Lessees. (11/17/72)	R
133	Disclosure of Contingent Liabilities Arising Under the Economic Stabilization Act of 1970. (12/14/72)	R
134	Accounting for Catastrophe Reserves. (1/3/73)	R
135	Revised Guidelines for the Application of Accounting Series Release No. 130. (1/5/73)	201
136	Notice of Adoption of Amendment to Regulation S-X Deferring Effective Date of Rule 5-02-1 As It Relates to Disclosure of Compensating Balances. (1/11/73)	O
137	Financial Statements of Life Insurance Companies. (1/11/73)	R
138	Notice of Adoption of Amendments to Forms 8-K, 10-K, 12-K, S-1, S-7, S-8, S-9, S-11, 10 and 12 Requiring Increased Disclosure of Unusual Charges and Credits to Income. (1/12/73)	216

ASR No.	Title	Status or Cross Ref.
201	Order Accepting Resignation from Commission Practice as Accountant In the Matter of Paul D. Klinger. (11/23/76)	E
202	Notice of Permanent Disqualification from Appearance or Practice Before the Commission In the Matter of Phillip Shelby Merkatz. (11/24/76)	E
203	Disclosure of Certain Replacement Cost Data; Amendment to Regulation S-X. 12-9-76	R
204	Notice of Permanent Disqualification from Appearance or Practice Before the Commission In the Matter of E. Veon Scott. (1/7/77)	E
205	Notice that Initial Decision Has Become Final In the Matter of Robert N. Campbell. (1/7/77)	E
206	Adoption of Amendments of Certain Forms and Related Rules. (1/13/77)	305
207	Order Instituting Proceeding and Permanently Barring from Practice Before the Commission In the Matter of Joseph Scansaroli. (1/21/77)	E
208	Order Accepting Resignation from Commission Practice as Accountant In the Matter of Bernard C. Zipern, 321 Richmond Avenue, Massapequa, New York. (2/10/77)	E
209	Opinion and Order Pursuant to Rule 2(e) of the Commission's Rules of Practice In the Matter of S.D. Leidesdorf & Co., Kenneth Larsen, Joseph Grendi. (2/16/77)	E
210	Opinion and Order Pursuant to Rule 2(e) of the Commission's Rules of Practice In the Matter of Reich, Weiner & Co. (2/25/77)	E
211	Accounting Series Release No. 132; Rescission. (3/2/77)	O
212	Order Instituting Proceedings and Imposing Remedial Sanctions In the Matter of Eugene Testa and W.A. Stebbins. (4/18/77)	E
213	Order Pursuant to Rule 2(e) of the Commission's Rules of Practice In the Matter of Maurice Rosen. (5/2/77)	E
214	Notice of Permanent Disqualification from Appearance or Practice Before the Commission In the Matter of Marvin F. Rosenbaum. (5/2/77)	E
215	Opinion and Order Pursuant to Rule 2(e) of the Commission's Rules of Practice In the Matter of Phillip J. Wolfson. (5/9/77)	E
216	Order Accepting Resignation from Commission Practice as an Accountant In the Matter of John W. Hosford, d/b/a John W. Hosford & Co. (5/16/77)	E
217	Order Accepting Resignation from Commission Practice as an Accountant In the Matter of Wilbert S. Fox. (5/16/77)	E
218	Quarterly Reporting Requirements for Life Insurance Companies. (5/23/77)	O
219	Valuation of Debt Instruments by Money Market Funds and Certain Other Open-End Investment Companies. (5/31/77)	404
220	Rescission of Certain Accounting Series Releases. (6/15/77)	O
221	Notice of Permanent Disqualification from Appearance or Practice Before the Commission In the Matter of C. Wayne Litchfield. (6/24/77)	E
222	Notice of Permanent Disqualification from Appearance or Practice Before the Commission In the Matter of Ernest C. Neuman. (6/24/77)	E
223	Opinion and Order Pursuant to the Commission's Rules of Practice In the Matter of Thomas Leger & Co. and Thomas Leger. (6/28/77)	E
224	Notice of Permanent Disqualification from Appearance or Practice Before the Commission In the Matter of Allen M. Lindenberg. (7/18/77)	E
225	Lease Accounting and Disclosure Rules. (8/31/77)	O
226	Marketable Securities and Other Security Investments. (9/8/77)	O
227	Other Instituting Proceedings and Opinion and Order Pursuant to Rule 2(e) of the Commission's Rules of Practice In the Matter of Laventhol & Horwath, Louis Goldfine, Jeffrey Lipschutz and Jack E. Klein. (9/21/77)	E
228	Quarterly Reporting Requirements for Life Insurance Companies. (9/28/77)	O
229	Opinion and Order Pursuant to Rule 2(e) of the Commission's Rules of Practice In the Matter of Luke J. LaLande, John F. Swart, Jr. and William A. Owens. (10/27/77)	E
230	Order Accepting Resignation from Commission Practice as an Accountant In the Matter of Bruce Flamm. (10/28/77)	E
231	Order Accepting Resignation from Commission Practice as an Accountant In the Matter of Harvey Fein. (10/28/77)	E
232	Order Accepting Resignation from Commission Practice as an Accountant In the Matter of Stephen Kneapler. (10/28/77)	E
233	Opinion for Proceedings and Opinion and Order Pursuant to Rule 2(e) of the Commission's Rules of Practice In the Matter of Norman A. Weiner, C.P.A. (12/12/77)	E
234	Independence of Accountants. (12/13/77)	602
235	Lease Accounting and Disclosure Rules. (12/22/77)	O
236	Industry Segment Reporting. (12/23/77)	503
237	Marketable Securities and Other Security Investments. (12/29/77)	207
238	Litigation Involving Price Waterhouse & Co. (1/16/78)	E
239	Opinion and Order Pursuant to Rule 2(e)(1) of the Commission's Rules of Practice In the Matter of Paul N. Conner. (1/16/78)	E
240	Order Granting Accountant's Application for Reinstatement to Practice Before the Commission In the Matter of Thomas R. Mathews. (1/18/78)	E

¶38,511

STAFF ACCOUNTING BULLETINS

STAFF ACCOUNTING BULLETINS

CONTENTS

Codification—Table of Contents

STAFF ACCOUNTING BULLETINS

RELEASES

RELEASE Nos. 1—38 [Superseded by SAB No. 40]

RELEASE No. 39 [No longer pertinent]

[¶ 39,001]　　　　RELEASE NO. 40, January 23, 1981, 46 F.R. 11513

Codification of SAB Nos. 1-38

AGENCY: Securities and Exchange Commission.

ACTION: Publication of Staff Accounting Bulletin.

SUMMARY: This staff accounting bulletin represents a codification of the material included in staff accounting bulletin nos. 1-38. It deletes these bulletins and replaces them with an integrated package which has been updated and indexed. The principal revisions relate to deletion of material no longer necessary because of private sector developments in generally accepted accounting principles and recent Commission actions. This material has been updated to give effect to recent Commission revisions of rules and forms as part of the integration of the disclosure system under the various securities acts. The purpose of this publication is to make the staff accounting bulletins more useful to issuers, accountants and others.

DATE: January 23, 1981.

FOR FURTHER INFORMATION CONTACT: Edmund Coulson or John W. Albert, Office of the Chief Accountant (202-272-2130) or Howard P. Hodges, Jr., Chief Accountant, Division of Corporation Finance (202-272-2553), Securities and Exchange Commission, Washington, D.C. 20549.

SUPPLEMENTARY INFORMATION: On November 4, 1975, the Commission's Division of Corporation Finance and the Office of the Chief Accountant instituted a series of Staff Accounting Bulletins ("SABs") with the publication of SAB No. 1. Since that time, a total of 39 SABs[1] have been issued covering a wide range of topics including financial statement matters, business combinations, senior securities, equity accounts, miscellaneous accounting, interpretations of accounting series releases, real estate companies, retail companies, finance companies, and miscellaneous disclosure matters.

SABs represent interpretations and practices followed by the Division of Corporation Finance and the Office of the Chief Accountant in administering the disclosure requirements of the Federal securities laws; they are not rules or interpretations of the Commission, nor do they bear official Commission approval. The Commission's staff issues SABs as a means of informing the financial community of its views on certain matters relating to accounting and disclosure practices. In general, SABs are considered to be an effective and expeditious means of communication and contribute to consistency in the implementation of the Federal securities laws.

In an effort to improve the usefulness of the SABs, the Commission's staff has conducted a comprehensive review of the material included in SAB Nos. 1-38. As a result, the staff has determined that it is necessary to revise and update certain of these materials. In addition, the staff has determined that re-issuing the revised and updated materials in a codified form would significantly improve their readability, and thus their usefulness. Therefore, this SAB supersedes SAB Nos. 1 through 38.

The principal revisions incorporated in the codified version relate to the deletion of material no longer necessary because of recent Commission actions and developments in generally accepted accounting principles—largely attributed to the activities of the Financial Accounting Standards Board ("FASB"). For example, due to the issuance of the FASB's Statement of Financial Accounting Standards No. 33, "Financial Reporting and Changing Prices," and the Commission's subsequent rescission[2] of its replacement cost rule, the interpretations of Accounting Series Release ("ASR") No 190 (previously Topic 6.I) are no longer necessary, and therefore have been deleted. Similarly, since ASR No. 163, "Capitalization of Interest by Companies Other than Public Utilities," was rescinded[3] in response to the establishment by the

---

[1] The codification does not include the material in SAB No. 39 which was issued on October 6, 1980. SAB No. 39 interprets certain accounting series releases dealing with independence of accountants. The staff is presently studing the issues covered in SAB No. 39 and expects to either clarify its views, or recommend that the Commission address this area in the form of an accounting series release, in the near future.

[2] See Accounting Series Release No. 271, "Deletion of Requirement to Disclose Replacement Cost Information" (October 23, 1979). Under ASR 271, the requirements for disclosure of replacement cost data will no longer apply for fiscal years ending on or after December 25, 1980—the date that the FASB's Statement No.

33 becomes fully effective. For registrants with fiscal years ending prior to December 25, 1980, an automatic waiver of the replacement cost rule is provided when the current cost disclosures called for by Statement No. 33 are included in their financial reports. Thus, it is possible that after the date of this SAB, some companies who choose not to take advantage of the automatic waiver will be required to include replacement cost data in filing with the Commission. In these cases, it should be noted that notwithstanding the deletive action in this SAB, registrants would be expected to follow the guidance previously given in the SABs.

[3] See Accounting Series Release No. 272, "Rescission of Moratorium on Capitalization of Interest Cost" (November 6, 1979).

FASB of a financial accounting and reporting standard for capitalization of interest cost (Statement of Financial Accounting Standards No. 34, "Capitalization of Interest Cost"), the interpretations of ASR No. 163 (previously Topic 6.D) have been deleted. Other examples of deletions to the SABs made possible by private sector standard-setting initiatives relate to accounting for leases, prior period adjustments and involuntary conversions.

The SABs have been revised to take into account the recent Commission initiatives designed to facilitate the integration of the disclosure system under the various securities acts. In August 1980, the Commission adopted a group of rulemaking initiatives[4] which, taken together, constitute by far the single most important advance toward achieving the Commission's longstanding goals of an integrated and simplified disclosure system. Among the releases adopted were amendments to the present annual report Form 10-K required to be filed by most publicly owned companies, uniform instructions to govern the periods covered by financial statements included in most registration and reporting forms filed under the 1933 and 1934 Acts, as well as in annual reports to shareholders (this release also substantially conforms

requirements for interim financial information under the 1933 Act with those under the 1934 Act), and revisions to certain articles of Regulation S-X to give recognition to the accounting standard-setting efforts of the private sector and to react to the ever changing needs of users of financial statements.

The previous SABs contained numerous references to various articles in Regulation S-X which have changed—these references have been revised in the codification. In addition, various changes and deletions have been made to reflect other aspects of the integration program, including the deletion of the five-year summary of operations, the revised management's discussion and analysis, the content of the annual report to shareholders, updating of financial statements, incorporation by reference, and various specific changes to Regulation S-X such as in the areas of disclosure of compensating balances and short term debt, and income tax expense.

Following is a reference table of changes which shows the old topic and subsection (as they existed prior to this SAB), the source of the material (SABs 1-38), the disposition of the material (either no change, updating, or deletion as per this SAB), and the new topic and subsection as codified in this SAB.

STAFF ACCOUNTING BULLETINS (SABs)
Reference Table of Changes

Legend: N/C No Substantive Change
            (1) Updated for Integrated Disclosure Program Releases
            (2) Deleted

Old Reference Topic Paragraph			Source	Disposition	New Reference Topic Paragraph
	General Principles Intended as Guidance for Events and Transactions with Similar Accounting Implications		SAB 27	Substance included in note to table of contents	
1	FINANCIAL STATEMENTS				1
A	Target Companies				A
		Question 1	SAB 1	N/C	
		Question 2	SAB 1	(1)	
B	Parent Only Financial Statements		SAB 1	(1)	B
C	Unaudited Financial Statements for a Full Year		SAB 1	(1)	C
D	Filings on Form S-14		SAB 1	(2)	—
E	Headnote to Summary of Operations		SAB 1	(2)	—
F	Foreign Companies				D
1	Convenience Statements		SAB 1, amended by SAB 8	N/C	1
2			SAB 1, amended by SAB 8		
	"Free Distributions" by Japanese Companies		SAB 8	N/C	2
G	Requirements for Audited or Certified Financial Statements				E
1	Meaning of the Word "Audited"		SAB 1	N/C	1

---

[4] See Securities Act Release Nos. 6231, 6232, 6233, 6234 (September 25, 1980).

Old Reference Topic Paragraph		Source	Disposition	New Reference Topic Paragraph
2	Qualified Auditors' Opinions	SAB 1	N/C	2
H	Incorporation by Reference			
	Question 1	SAB 1	(2)	—
	Question 2	SAB 1	(2)	—
	Question 3	SAB 1	(2)	—
I	Tax Loss Carryforward—Form 8-K	SAB 1	(2)	—
J	Summary of Operations—Capsule Updating	SAB 26	(2)	—
2	BUSINESS COMBINATIONS			2
A	Purchase Method			A
1	Cash Contingencies	SAB 1	N/C	1
2	Determination of the Acquiring Corporation	SAB 24	N/C	2
B		SAB 1, amended by		
	Merger Expenses	SAB 8	N/C	B
3	SENIOR SECURITIES			3
A	Convertible Securities	SAB 1	(1)	A
B	Fixed Charge Coverage Ratios for Debt and Preferred Stocks	SAB 1	N/C	B
C	Balance Sheet Presentation for Preferred Stock with Sinking Funds or Mandatory Redemption Features	SAB 1	(1)*	C
4	EQUITY ACCOUNTS			4
A	Subordinated Debt	SAB 1	N/C	A
B	Subchapter S Corporations	SAB 1	N/C	B
C	Change in Capital Structure	SAB 1	N/C	C
D	Quasi-Reorganizations	SAB 1	(2)	—
E	Cheap Stock	SAB 1	N/C	D
F	[Previously deleted]			
G	Receivables From Sale of Stock			E
	Question 1	SAB 1 SAB 2, deleted by	(1)	
	Question 2	SAB 31	—	—
H	Limited Partnerships	SAB 8	N/C	F
I	Limitation on Payment of Dividends by Subsidiary Banks to Parent Holding Company	SAB 26	(2)	—
J		SABs 31,		
	Notes and Other Receivables from Affiliates	31A	(1)	G
5	MISCELLANEOUS ACCOUNTING			5
A	Expenses of Offering	SAB 1	N/C	A
B	Gain or Loss from Disposition of Equipment	SAB 1	N/C	B
C	Accrued Vacation Pay	SAB 1	(2)**	—
D	Reclassification of Self-Insurance Reserves	SAB 1	(2)	—
E	Tax Benefit of Loss Carryforwards			C
1	Current Recognition of Tax Benefit			1
		SAB 8, amended by		
	Question 1	SAB 17	N/C	
		SAB 8, amended by		
	Question 2	SAB 17	N/C	
2	Realization of Tax Benefit			2
		SAB 8, amended by		
	Question 1	SAB 17	N/C	

Old Reference Topic Paragraph			Source	Disposition	New Reference Topic Paragraph
			SAB 8, amended by		
		Question 2	SAB 17	N/C	
			SAB 8, amended by		
		Question 3	SAB 17	N/C	
			SAB 8, amended by		
		Question 4	SAB 17	N/C	
F	[Previously deleted]				
G	Employee Stock Ownership Trust (ESOT)		SAB 8	(2)	—
H	Prior Period Adjustments		SAB 8	(2)	—
I	Real Estate Acquired in Foreclosure, Settlement, etc.		SAB 13	(2)	—
J	Involuntary Conversions		SAB 21	(2)	—
K	Organization and Offering Expenses and Selling Commissions—Limited Partnerships Trading in Commodity Futures				D
		Question 1	SAB 22	N/C	
		Question 2	SAB 22	N/C	
		Question 3	SAB 22	N/C	
		Question 4	SAB 22	N/C	
L	Financing by Electric Utility Companies Through Use of Construction Intermediaries		SAB 28	(1)	10A
M	Accounting for Divestiture of a Subsidiary or Other Business Operation				
		Question 1	SAB 30	N/C	5E
		Question 2	SAB 30	N/C	
		Question 3	SAB 30	N/C	
		Question 4	SAB 30	N/C	
N	Accounting Changes Not Retroactively Applied Due to Immateriality		SAB 32	N/C	F
6	INTERPRETATIONS OF ACCOUNTING SERIES RELEASES				6
A	*Accounting Series Release No. 147*—Improved Disclosure of Leases [delete Subsections A1-A4]		SAB 1	(2)	—
B	*Accounting Series Release No. 148*—Disclosure of Compensating Balances and Short-Term Borrowing Arrangements				H
1	Applicability				1
a	Annual Reports to Shareholders		SAB 1	(2)	—
b	Arrangements with Other Lending Institutions		SAB 1	(1)	a
c	Bank Holding Companies and Brokerage Firms		SAB 1	(1)	b
d	Financial Statements of Parent Company and Unconsolidated Subsidiaries		SAB 1	(1)	c
e	Foreign Lenders		SAB 1	(1)	d
2	Classification of Short-Term Obligations				2
a	Financial Accounting Standards Board Statement No. 6				—
		Question 1	SAB 1	(2)	—
		Question 2	SAB 1	(2)	—
b	Other Classifications of Debt Due Within One Year				—
		Question 1	SAB 1	(2)	—
		Question 2	SAB 1	(2)	—
c	Debt Related to Long-Term Projects		SAB 1	N/C	a
3	Compensating Balances				3
a	Compensating Balances for Future Credit Availability		SAB 1	(1)	a
b	Changes in Compensating Balances		SAB 1	N/C	b
c	Float		SAB 1	N/C	c
4	Miscellaneous				4
a	Periods Required		SAB 1	(1)	a

Old Reference Topic Paragraph			Source	Disposition	New Reference Topic Paragraph
b	10-Q Disclosures		SAB 1	N/C	b
c	Determining Average Interest Rate		SAB 1	(1)	c
C	*Accounting Series Release No. 149—Improved Disclosure of*		SAB 1, amended	SABs 8,	
	Income Tax Expense		by SABs	17	I
1	Inclusion in Annual Report		1, 8	(2)	—
2	Tax Rate	Question 1	SAB 1	N/C	1
		Question 2	SAB 1	N/C	
3	Taxes of Investee Company		SAB 1	(1)	2
4	Net of Tax Presentation		SAB 1	N/C	3
5	Loss Years		SAB 1	N/C	4
6	Foreign Registrants	Question 1	SAB 1	(1)	5
		Question 2	SAB 1	N/C	
7	Securities Gains and Losses		SAB 1	N/C	6
			SABs		
8	Tax Expense Components v. "Overall" Presentation		8, 17	(1)	7
D	*Accounting Series Release No. 163 —/Capitalization of Interest by Companies Other than Public Utilities [Delete Subsections D1-D3]*		SAB 1	(2)	—
E	*Accounting Series Release No. 166—Disclosure of Unusual Risks and Uncertainties in Financial Reporting*				A
1	Market Value Changes	Question 1	SAB 1	N/C	1
		Question 2	SAB 1	N/C	
2	Insurance Companies		SAB 1	(2)	—
F	*Accounting Series Release No. 175—Rule 3A-02(e) Relating to Consolidated Financial Statements*		SAB 2	(1)	B
1	Definitions				1
a	Engaged in the Business				a
		Question 1	SAB 2	(1)	
		Question 2	SAB 2	(1)	
b	All Nonsignificant Consolidated Subsidiaries not Otherwise Included		SAB 2	N/C	b
c	Registrant's Investment		SAB 2	(1)	c
d	Registrant's Total Assets				d
		Question 1	SAB 2	(1)	
		Question 2	SAB 2	(1)	
e	Income (or Loss) Before Income Taxes and Extraordinary Items		SAB 2	(1)	e
f	Proportionate Share		SAB 2	(1)	f
g	Average Income		SAB 2	(1)	g
h	Sales and Revenues Derived from Registrant		SAB 2	(1)	h
2	Tests Under Rule 3A-02(e)				2
a	Financial Statements Used		SAB 2	(1)	a
b	Additional Statements/Omission of Statements		SAB 2	(1)	b
c	Tests Apply to Subsidiary as a Whole		SAB 2	(1)	c
d	Application of Tests		SAB 2	N/C	d
3	Financial Statements to be Presented				3
a	Subsidiaries		SAB 2	(1)	a
b	Subsidiaries of Subsidiaries				b
		Question 1	SAB 2	(1)	
		Question 2	SAB 2	(1)	
c	Number of Financial Statements		SAB 2	(1)	c
4	Presentation of Financial Statements				4
a	Significant Subsidiaries		SAB 2	(1)	a
b	Nonsignificant Subsidiaries		SAB 2	(1)	b
c	General Form and Content		SAB 2	N/C	c
5	Miscellaneous				
a	Separate Financial Statements in Form 10-Q		SAB 2	(1)	5
b	Retroactive Application		SAB 2	(2)	—
c	Annual Report to Shareholders		SAB 2	(2)	—
G	*Accounting Series Release No. 159—Management's Discussion*				

Old Reference Topic Paragraph			Source	Disposition	New Reference Topic Paragraph
	and Analysis of the Summary of Earnings or Operations		SABs		
	[subsection 1-6]		3, 29	(2)	—
H	Accounting Series Release No. 177—Relating to Amendments to Form 10-Q and Regulation S-X Regarding Interim Financial Statements				G
1	Amendments to Regulation S-X [new Item 12 of Regulation S-K]			(1)	1
a	Effective Date of Amendments				
		Question 1	SAB 6	(2)	—
		Question 2	SAB 6	(1)	a
b	Disclosure of Selected Quarterly Financial Data in Notes to Financial Statements				b
		Question 1	SAB 6	(1)	
		Question 2	SAB 6	(1)	
		Question 3	SAB 6	(1)	
		Question 4	SAB 6	(1)	
		Question 5	SAB 6	(1)	
		Question 6	SAB 6	N/C	
		Question 7	SAB 6	N/C	
		Question 8	SAB 6	N/C	
c	Financial Statements Presented on Other Than a Quarterly Basis				c
		Question 1	SAB 6	(1)	
		Question 2	SAB 6	N/C	
		Question 3	SAB 6	N/C	
d	Exemption from Item 12 Requirements				d
		Question 1	SAB 6	(1)	
		Question 2	SAB 6	(1)	
		Question 3	SAB 6	(1)	
		Question 4	SABs 6, 13	(2)	
		Question 5	SABs 6, 13	(1)	
		Question 6	SABs 6, 13	(1)	
e	Incorporation by Reference in Annual Reports to Shareholders		SAB 6	(2)	—
2	Amendments to Form 10-Q				2
a	Effective Date of Amendments		SAB 6	(2)	
b	Form of Condensed Financial Statements				a
		Question 1	SAB 6	(1)	
		Question 2	SAB 6	N/C	
		Question 3	SAB 6	N/C	
		Question 4	SAB 6	N/C	
		Question 5	SAB 6	N/C	
		Question 6	SAB 6	N/C	
c	Need for Supplemental Financial Statements				
		Question 1	SAB 6	(2)	—
		Question 2	SAB 6	(2)	—
d	Disclosure with Respect to the Dispositions of Business		SAB 6	(1)	b
e	Disclosure of Form 8-K Filed During the Most Recent Quarter		SAB 6	(2)	—
f	Reporting Requirements for Accounting Changes				c
	[First set of facts]	Question 1	SAB 14	N/C	1
		Question 2	SAB 14	N/C	
		Question 3	SAB 14	N/C	
		Question 4	SAB 14	N/C	
		Question 5	SAB 14	N/C	
		Question 6	SAB 14	N/C	
		Question 7	SABs 6, 14	N/C	
	[Second set of facts]	Question 1	SAB 13	N/C	2
g	Signatures		SAB 13	(2)	—

Old Reference Topic Paragraph			Source	Disposition	New Reference Topic Paragraph
			SABs		
			7, 9,		
I			10, 11,		
	Accounting Series Release No. 190—Relating to Amendments		12,		
			13, 17,		
	to Regulation S-X Requiring Disclosure of Replacement Cost		18,		
	Data (Rule 3-17) [Delete Subsection II-III]		20, 23	(2)	—
J	*Accounting Series Release No. 125—Adoption of Amendments*				
	to Regulation S-X		SAB 8	N/C	F
K	*Accounting Series Release No. 188—Interpretive Statements*				
	by the Commission on Disclosure by Registrants of Holdings				
	of Securities of New York City and Accounting for Securities				
	Subject to Exchange Offer and Moratorium		SAB 13	(2)	—
L	*Accounting Series Release No. 250—Disclosure of*				
	Relationships with Independent Accountants				C
			SABs		
		Question 1	25, 38	N/C	1
			SABs		
		Question 2	25, 33	N/C	
		Question 3	SAB 25	N/C	
		Question 4	SAB 25	N/C	2
		Question 5	SAB 25	N/C	
		Question 6	SAB 25	N/C	
		Question 7	SAB 25	N/C	
		Question 8	SAB 25	N/C	
		Question 9	SAB 25	N/C	
		Question 10	SAB 25	N/C	
		Question 11	SAB 25	N/C	
		Question 12	SAB 25	N/C	3
		Question 13	SAB 25	(2)	—
		Question 14	SAB 25	N/C	4
		Question 15	SAB 25	N/C	
M	*Accounting Series Release No. 257—Requirements for*				
	Financial Accounting and Reporting Practices for Oil and				
	Gas Producing Activities				D
1	Estimates of Quantities of Proved Reserves				1
		Question 1	SAB 35	(1)	
		Question 2	SAB 35	(1)	
		Question 3	SAB 35	N/C	
		Question 4	SAB 35	N/C	
2	Estimates of Future Net Revenues				2
		Question 1	SAB 35	(1)	
		Question 2	SAB 35	N/C	
		Question 3	SAB 35	N/C	
		Question 4	SAB 35	N/C	
		Question 5	SAB 35	(1)	
		Question 6	SAB 35	N/C	
		Question 7	SAB 35	N/C***	
		Question 8	SAB 35	N/C	
3	Disclosure of Reserve Information				3
a	Income Tax Effects		SAB 35	(1)	a
b	Unproved Properties		SAB 35	N/C	b
c	Limited Partnership 10-K Reports		SAB 36	(1)	c
d	Limited Partnership Registration Statements		SAB 36	(1)	d
4	Filings by Canadian Registrants		SAB 36	(1)	4
N	*Accounting Series Release No. 269—Supplemental Disclosures*				
	on the Basis of Reserve Recognition Accounting				E
1	Provision for Income Taxes		SAB 35	N/C	1
7	REAL ESTATE COMPANIES				7
A	Reporting Requirements		SAB 1	N/C	A
B	Gains or Losses on Investments in Real Estate		SAB 1	(2)	—

Old Reference Topic Paragraph		Source	Disposition	New Reference Topic Paragraph
C	Land Development Companies	SAB 1	N/C	B
D	Schedules of Real Estate and Accumulated Depreciation, and of Mortgage Loans on Real Estate	SAB 1	(1)	C
E	Income Before Depreciation	SAB 1	N/C	D
F	Disclosure and Reporting by Real Estate Investment Trusts	SAB 4	(2)	—
8	RETAIL COMPANIES			8
A	Sales of Leased or Licensed Departments	SAB 1	N/C	A
B	Finance Charges	SAB 1	N/C	B
9	FINANCE COMPANIES			9
A	Points	SAB 1	N/C	A
B	Ratio of Earnings to Fixed Charges	SAB 1	(1)	B
10	MISCELLANEOUS DISCLOSURE			11
A	Consumer Excise Taxes	SAB 1	(2)	—
B	Operating-Differential Subsidies	SAB 1	(1)	A
C	Depreciation and Depletion Excluded from Cost of Sales	SAB 1	N/C	B
D	Tax Holidays	SAB 1	N/C	C
E	Offsetting Assets and Liabilities	SAB 1	N/C	D
F	Allowance for Funds Used During Construction	SABs 1, 15	(2)	—
G	Chronological Ordering of Data	SAB 1	N/C	E
H	LIFO Liquidations	SAB 1	N/C	F
I	[Previously deleted]			
J	Estimated Future Costs Related to Spent Nuclear Fuel and Nuclear Electric Generating Plants	SAB 19	N/C	10B
K	Tax Equivalent Adjustment in Financial Statements of Bank Holding Companies			11G
	Question 1	SAB 26	(1)	
	Question 2	SAB 26	(1)	
	Question 3	SAB 26	(1)	
	Question 4	SAB 26	(2)	—
	Question 5	SAB 26	(1)	
L	Jointly Owned Electric Utility Plants	SAB 28	N/C	10C
M	Long-Term Contracts for Purchase of Electric Power	SAB 28	N/C	D

* Also revised to clarify SAB 1 which allowed presentation of redeemable preferred stock at other than fair value at date of issue.

** Deleted as a result of the issuance in November 1980 of FASB Statement No. 43, "Accounting for Compensated Absences." It should be noted that although Statement No. 43 is not effective until fiscal years beginning after December 15, 1980, the staff will expect its principles, as they relate to vacation pay, to be applied in filings with the Commission prior to that time.

*** Updated to reflect enactment of "windfall profits" tax.

STAFF ACCOUNTING BULLETIN NO. 40

NOTE: Staff Accounting Bulletins may be written narrowly in describing the individual facts and circumstances which resulted in the expression of the staff's views. However, registrants and their accountants should be aware that the purpose of the Staff Accounting Bulletins is to disseminate staff views on particular matters for guidance in other situations where events and transactions have similar accounting implications.

Where a registrant and its accountant believe that because of its peculiar circumstances the appropriate accounting should be different than would result from following the practice expressed in a Staff Accounting Bulletin, the registrant is encouraged to discuss the specifics with the staff.

[For text of Topics 1-11, see ¶ 39,101—39,201.—CCH.]

[¶ 39,002]   RELEASE No. 41, February 6, 1981, 46 F.R. 12698

Interpretation Relating to the Application of Financial Accounting and Disclosure Rules for Oil and Gas Producers

AGENCY: Securities and Exchange Commission.   ACTION: Publication of Staff Accounting Bulletin.

SUMMARY: These interpretations of the staff deal with matters relating to the application of the financial accounting and disclosure rules for oil and gas producers adopted in Accounting Series Release Nos. 257 and 261. In particular, the interpretations set forth the staff's views on questions pertaining to the effect of the recently announced, accelerated decontrol of oil prices on the computation of future net revenues, the phaseout period for windfall profit tax, and accounting changes by first-time registrants engaged in oil and gas producing activities.

DATE: February 6, 1981.

FOR FURTHER INFORMATION CONTACT: James D. Hall or Rita J. Gunter, Office of the Chief Accountant, Securities and Exchange Commission, 500 N. Capitol Street, Washington, D.C. 20549 (202-272-2133).

SUPPLEMENTARY INFORMATION: The statements in Staff Accounting Bulletins are not rules or interpretations of the Commission nor are they published as bearing the Commission's official approval; they represent interpretations and practices followed by the Division of Corporation Finance and the Office of the Chief Accountant in administering the disclosure requirements of the Federal securities laws.

STAFF ACCOUNTING BULLETIN NO. 41

The staff hereby adds questions 9 and 10 to Topic 6-D-2 and adds a new Topic 6-J, setting forth the staff's views on questions pertaining to the effect of the recently announced, accelerated decontrol of oil prices on the computation of future net revenues, the phaseout period for windfall profit tax, and accounting changes by first-time registrants engaged in oil and gas producing activities.

[Topic 6-D redesignated as Topic 12-A by SAB-47 at ¶ 39,211. Topic 6-J deleted by SAB-47.—CCH.]

[¶ 39,003]   RELEASE No. 42, December 23, 1981, 46 F.R. 63252

Interpretation Relating to Acquisitions Involving Financial Institutions

AGENCY: Securities and Exchange Commission.

ACTION: Publication of Staff Accounting Bulletin.

SUMMARY: The interpretations in this Staff Accounting Bulletin express the staff's views concerning the application of existing financial accounting standards to business combinations accounted for by the purchase method involving financial institutions, including the allocation of purchase price to tangible and intangible assets acquired and amortization periods for intangible assets.

EFFECTIVE DATE: December 23, 1981.

FOR FURTHER INFORMATION CONTACT: Marc D. Oken, Office of the Chief Accountant, Securities and Exchange Commission, 500 N. Capitol Street, Washington, D.C. 20549, (202/272-2131).

SUPPLEMENTARY INFORMATION: The statements in Staff Accounting Bulletins are not rules or interpretations of the Commission nor are they published as bearing the Commission's official approval. They represent interpretations and practices followed by the Division of Corporation Finance and the Office of the Chief Accountant in administering the disclosure requirements of the Federal securities laws.

STAFF ACCOUNTING BULLETIN NO. 42

The staff hereby adds new topic, 2-A-3, setting forth the staff's views on questions pertaining to the application of existing accounting standards to business combinations accounted for by the purchase method involving financial institutions.

[For text of Topic 2-A-3, see ¶ 39,111.—CCH.]

[¶ 39,003A]   RELEASE No. 42A, December 31, 1986

Amortization of Goodwill by Financial Institutions Upon Becoming SEC Registrants

AGENCY: Securities and Exchange Commission

ACTION: Publication of Staff Accounting Bulletin

SUMMARY: This staff accounting bulletin expresses the staff's views regarding goodwill amortization periods for financial institutions which become SEC registrants in a period after a business combination. It amends Section A of Topic 2 relating to the purchase method for business combinations.

DATE: December 31, 1985.

FOR FURTHER INFORMATION CONTACT: Laurel R. Bond or Robert J. Kueppers, Office of the Chief Accountant (202-272-2130) or Howard P. Hodges, Jr., Division of Corporation Finance (202-272-2553), Securities and Exchange Commission, 450 Fifth Street, N.W., Washington, D.C. 20549.

SUPPLEMENTARY INFORMATION: The statements in Staff Accounting Bulletins are not rules or interpretations of the Commission nor are they published as bearing the Commission's official approval. They represent interpretations and practices followed by the Division of Corporation Finance and the Office of the Chief Accountant in administering the disclosure requirements of the Federal securities laws.

Part 211—(AMENDED)

Accordingly, Part 211 of Title 17 of the Code of Federal Regulations is amended by adding Staff Accounting Bulletin No. 42A to the table found in Subpart B.

STAFF ACCOUNTING BULLETIN No. 42A

The staff hereby adds Section A-4 to Topic 2 setting forth the staff's views on the selection of goodwill amortization periods for financial institutions which become SEC registrants in a period after a business combination.

[For text of Topic 2-A-4, see ¶ 39,111.—CCH.]

[¶ 39,004]   RELEASE No. 43, January 5, 1982, 47 F.R. 1266

Interpretation Regarding Early Adoption of ASR No. 302

AGENCY: Securities and Exchange Commission.

ACTION: Publication of Staff Accounting Bulletin.

SUMMARY: The interpretation in this Staff Accounting Bulletin indicates the staff's views on early adoption of the new rules for parent company and other financial disclosures announced in Accounting Series Release No. 302.

DATE: January 5, 1982.

FOR FURTHER INFORMATION CONTACT: Marc D. Oken (202-272-2130) or John W. Albert (202-272-2133), Office of the Chief Accountant, Securities and Exchange Commission, Washington, D.C. 20549.

SUPPLEMENTARY INFORMATION: The statements in Staff Accounting Bulletins are not rules or interpretations of the Commission nor are they published as bearing the Commission's official approval. They represent interpretations and practices followed by the Division of Corporation Finance and the Office of the Chief Accountant in administering the disclosure requirements of the Federal securities laws.

STAFF ACCOUNTING BULLETIN NO. 43

The staff hereby adds new topic, 6-K, which provides the staff's views on early adoption of the new rules for parent company and other financial disclosures announced in Accounting Series Release No. 302.

[For text of Topic 6-K, see ¶ 39,151.—CCH.]

[¶ 39,005]   RELEASE No. 44, March 3, 1982, 47 F.R. 10789

Interpretation Regarding Implementation of ASR No. 302

AGENCY: Securities and Exchange Commission.

ACTION: Publication of Staff Accounting Bulletin.

SUMMARY: The interpretations in this Staff Accounting Bulletin indicate the staff's views on certain matters involved in the implementation of Accounting Series Release No. 302, Separate Financial Statements Required by Regulation S-X. It also deletes certain topics published in Staff Accounting Bulletin No. 40, the codification of Staff Accounting Bulletins Nos. 1-38, which are no longer relevant because of amendments to the proxy rules and to Regulation S-X which covers form and content of financial statements filed with the Commission.

EFFECTIVE DATE: March 3, 1982

FOR FURTHER INFORMATION CONTACT: Marc D. Oken (202-272-2130) or John W. Albert (202-272-2133), Office of the Chief Accountant, Securities and Exchange Commission, 500 North Capitol Street, Washington, D.C. 20549.

SUPPLEMENTARY INFORMATION: The statements in Staff Accounting Bulletins are not rules or interpretations of the Commission nor are they published as bearing the Commission's official approval. They represent interpretations and practices followed by the Division of Corporation Finance and the Office of the Chief Accountant in administering the disclosure requirements of the Federal securities laws.

STAFF ACCOUNTING BULLETIN NO. 44

The staff hereby deletes topics 1-B, 6-B and 6-C of Staff Accounting Bulletin No. 40. Topics 1-B and 6-B relate to the financial statement requirements for parent company only and for consolidated subsidiaries engaged in diverse financial-type activities which were amended by Accounting Series Release No. 302. Topic 6-C relates to the requirements for disclosures of certain relationships with independent accountants which were eliminated by Accounting Series Release No. 304. In addition, Topic 6-K is expanded to provide the staff's interpretation of certain matters involved in the implementation of the requirements of Accounting Series Release No. 302.

[For text of Topics 6-K-2—6-K-4, see ¶ 39,151.—CCH.]

[¶ 39,006]   RELEASE No. 45, May 20, 1982, 47 F.R. 23915

Interpretation Relating to Presentation of Pro Forma Information

AGENCY: Securities and Exchange Commission.

ACTION: Publication of Staff Accounting Bulletin.

SUMMARY: This Staff Accounting Bulletin presents the staff's view concerning the presentation of pro forma information under certain narrow circumstances. When a planned or consummated business combination to be accounted for as a pooling of interests involves a closely owned and managed enterprise and the salary of an owner-manager will be substantially changed resulting from a new employment contract, the registrant may include a —supplemental pro forma presentation to reflect changes in salary expense following the merger. Although this interpretation focuses on the owner-manager's salary in particular, the staff believes that the general principles are relevant to other types of expenses related to owner-managers that might be substantially increased or reduced as a result of contractual agreements.

DATE: May 20, 1982.

FOR FURTHER INFORMATION CONTACT: Eugene W. Green, Office of the Chief Accountant (202/272-2130), or Howard P. Hodges, Jr., Chief Accountant, Division of Corporation Finance (202/272-2554), Securities and Exchange Commission, Washington, D.C. 20549.

SUPPLEMENTARY INFORMATION: The statements in Staff Accounting Bulletins are not rules or interpretations of the Commission nor are they published as bearing the Commission's official approval; they represent interpretations and practices followed by the Division of Corporation Finance and the Office of the Chief Accountant in administering the disclosure requirements of the Federal securities laws.

STAFF ACCOUNTING BULLETIN NO. 45

The staff hereby adds Topic 2-C, regarding disclosure of pro forma financial information.

[For text of Topic 2-C, see ¶ 39,111.—CCH.]

[¶ 39,007]   RELEASE No. 46, May 20, 1982, 47 F.R. 23916

Revision of Interpretations on Interim Financial Reporting

AGENCY: Securities and Exchange Commission.

ACTION: Publication of Staff Accounting Bulletin.

SUMMARY: The interpretations in this Staff Accounting Bulletin revise existing staff interpretations of requirements for interim financial reporting resulting from the adoption of Accounting Series Release Nos. 286, 302 and 306. In addition, a revised topical index is being published to reflect the impact of all actions to date on the Staff Accounting Bulletin series.

DATE: May 20, 1982.

FOR FURTHER INFORMATION CONTACT: John W. Albert, Office of the Chief Accountant (202-272-2133) or Howard P. Hodges, Jr., Chief Accountant, Division of Corporation Finance (202-272-2554), Securities and Exchange Commission, Washington, D.C. 20549.

SUPPLEMENTARY INFORMATION: The statements in Staff Accounting Bulletins are not rules or interpretations of the Commission nor are they published as bearing the Commission's official approval; they represent interpretations and practices followed by the Division of Corporation Finance and the Office of the Chief Accountant administering the disclosure requirements of the Federal securities laws.

STAFF ACCOUNTING BULLETIN NO. 46

The staff hereby deletes subsections 1, 2(a) and 2(b) of topic 6-G of Staff Accounting Bulletin No. 40

and replaces them with the following revised interpretations. The staff is also redesignating and amending subsection 2(c) as 2(b) of this same topic. These interpretations do not reflect any substantive changes in staff position. Rather, they simply reflect adoption of revised disclosure requirements for interim financial reporting announced in Accounting Series Release No. ("ASR") 286, the elimination of requirements for the presentation of separate financial statements of the parent company only and of consolidated subsidiaries engaged in diverse financial-type activities announced in ASR 302, and revisions to the disclosure requirements of Form S-K announced in ASR 306.

[For text of Topic 6-G, see ¶ 39,151.—CCH.]

STAFF ACCOUNTING BULLETIN SERIES

REVISED TOPICAL INDEX THRU STAFF ACCOUNTING BULLETIN NO. 46

NOTE: The topical index has been revised to reflect the impact of all actions affecting the Staff Accounting Bulletin series up through the issuance of Staff Accounting Bulletin No. ("SAB") 46. This index updates the index previously published in SAB 40 (January 23, 1981). For the convenience of users, the sources of any changes to the index published in SAB 40 are identified parenthetically.

⋙→ *Interpretive guidance in Topic 12-D-4 superseded by FRR-17, effective 6-1-84.*

[¶ 39,008]   RELEASE No. 47, September 16, 1982, 47 F.R. 41727

Interpretations Relating to Oil and Gas Accounting

AGENCY: Securities and Exchange Commission.

ACTION: Publication of Staff Accounting Bulletin.

SUMMARY: The interpretations in this Staff Accounting Bulletin express certain views of the staff concerning (i) the preparation of financial statements of oil

and gas exchange offers included in filings with the Commission and (ii) the application of the Commission's rules for oil and gas producing activities, particularly with respect to the determination of future net revenues and various full cost accounting matters.

DATE: September 16, 1982.

FOR FURTHER INFORMATION CONTACT: M. Elizabeth Rader or John W. Albert (202-272-2130), Office of the Chief Accountant, or James W. Ford, Jr., (202-272-2553), Division of Corporation Finance, Securities and Exchange Commission, Washington, D.C. 20549.

SUPPLEMENTARY INFORMATION: The statements in Staff Accounting Bulletins are not rules or interpretations of the Commission nor are they published as bearing the Commission's official approval. They represent interpretations and practices followed by the Division of Corporation Finance and the Office of the Chief Accountant in administering the disclosure requirements of the Federal securities laws.

List of Subjects in 17 CFR 211

Accounting, Reporting requirements, Securities.

STAFF ACCOUNTING BULLETIN NO. 47

The staff hereby adds new major Topic 12 "Oil and Gas Producing Activities" and Topic 2-D "Financial Statements of Oil and Gas Exchange Offers" to the staff accounting bulletin series. In addition, the staff hereby deletes Topic 6-J, redesignates Topics 6-D and 6-E as Topics 12-A and 12-B,. respectively, adds Question 11 to redesignated Topic 12-A-2, adds Subsection 3-e to Topic 12-A and adds Topics 12-C, 12-D and 12-E.

Topic 2-D describes the staff's administrative policies with respect to the financial statements of oil and gas exchange offers included in filings with the Commission. Question 11 of Topic 12-A-2 sets forth the staff's view on the impact of natural gas deregulation on the determination of estimates of future net revenues. Topic 12-C updates the guidance previously provided in Topic 6-J concerning the selection of accounting methods for oil and gas producing activities. Topic 12-D sets forth the staff's views on questions pertaining to the application of the Commission's rules for the full cost method of accounting for oil and gas producing activities. Topic 12-E discusses financial statements of royalty trusts. The purpose of the redesignation under Topic 12 is to centralize the staff's interpretations of matters involving oil and gas producing activities within one topic of the staff accounting bulletin series.

[For text of Topic 2-D, see ¶ 39,111, and ¶ 39,211 for text of Topics 12-A—E.—CCH.]

[¶ 39,009]   **RELEASE No. 47A, September 29, 1982**

Correction of SAB No. 47

AGENCY: Securities and Exchange Commission.

ACTION: Publication of Staff Accounting Bulletin.

SUMMARY: This Staff Accounting Bulletin corrects a numerical error in previously issued Staff Accounting Bulletin No. 47 concerning the application of the Commission's rules on accounting for mineral property conveyances by companies using the full cost method of accounting for oil and gas producing activities.

DATE: September 29, 1982.

FOR FURTHER INFORMATION CONTACT: M. Elizabeth Rader of John W. Albert (202-272-2130), Office of the Chief Accountant, or James W. Ford, Jr., (202-272-2553), Division of Corporation Finance, Securities and Exchange Commission, Washington, D.C. 20549.

SUPPLEMENTARY INFORMATION: The statements in Staff Accounting Bulletins are not rules or interpretations of the Commission nor are they published as bearing the Commission's official approval. They represent interpretations and practices followed by the Division of Corporation Finance and the Office of the Chief Accountant in administering the disclosure requirements of the Federal securities laws.

STAFF ACCOUNTING BULLETIN NO. 47A

The staff hereby revises Question 7 of topic 12-D-4 to replace Case V as presented in Staff Accounting Bulletin No. 47 with a new Case V example.

[For text of corrected Question 7, see Topic 12-D-4 at ¶ 39,211.—CCH.]

[¶ 39,010]   **RELEASE No. 48, September 27, 1982, 47 F.R. 43673**

Staff Position on Transfer of Assets by Promoters and Shareholders

AGENCY: Securities and Exchange Commission.

ACTION: Publication of Staff Accounting Bulletin.

SUMMARY: This staff accounting bulletin reflects the staff's long-standing position that when a company acquires assets from promoters and shareholders in exchange for stock prior to or at the time of its initial public offering such assets should generally be recorded at the cost to the promoter or shareholder.

DATE: September 27, 1982.

FOR FURTHER INFORMATION CONTACT: Eugene W. Green, Office of the Chief Accountant (202/272-2161); Joseph Cribbin, Office of Small Business Policy, Division of Corporation Finance (202/272-2644); or Howard P. Hodges, Jr., Chief Accountant, Division of Corporation Finance (202/272-2554), Securities and Exchange Commission, Washington, D.C. 20549.

SUPPLEMENTARY INFORMATION: The statements in Staff Accounting Bulletins are not rules or interpretations of the Commission nor are they published as bearing the Commission's official approval.

They represent interpretations and practices followed by the Division of Corporation Finance and the Office of the Chief Accountant in administering the disclosure requirements of the Federal securities laws.

List of Subjects in 17 CFR 211

Accounting, Reporting requirements, Securities.

STAFF ACCOUNTING BULLETIN NO. 48

The staff herein adds Section G to Topic 5 regarding the valuation of assets acquired from promoters and shareholders. The staff believes that if nonmonetary assets are received by a newly formed or closely held company from promoters or shareholders in exchange for stock, such assets should normally be recorded at the historical cost basis of the promoters, or shareholders.

[For text at Topic 5-G, see ¶ 39,141.—CCH.]

[¶ 39,011]   RELEASE No. 49, October 26, 1982, 47 F.R. 49627

Views on Loans to Borrowers in Countries with Liquidity Problems

AGENCY: Securities and Exchange Commission.

ACTION: Publication of Staff Accounting Bulletin.

SUMMARY: This staff accounting bulletin expresses the staff's views regarding disclosures by bank holding companies about loans to public and private sector borrowers located in countries that are experiencing liquidity problems.

DATE: October 26, 1982.

FOR FURTHER INFORMATION CONTACT: Marc D. Oken or Edmund Coulson, Office of the Chief Accountant (202/272-2130); or Howard P. Hodges, Jr. or Charles A. Oglebay, Jr., Division of Corporation Finance (202/272-2553), Securities and Exchange Commission, Washington, D.C. 20549.

SUPPLEMENTARY INFORMATION: The statements in Staff Accounting Bulletins are not rules or interpretations of the Commission nor are they published as bearing the Commission's official approval. They represent interpretations and practices followed by the Division of Corporation Finance and the Office of the Chief Accountant in administering the disclosure requirements of the Federal securities laws.

STAFF ACCOUNTING BULLETIN NO. 49

The staff herein adds Section H to Topic 11 of the Staff Accounting Bulletin Series. This section discusses the disclosures by bank holding companies about loans to foreign countries that are experiencing liquidity problems.

[For text of Topic 11-H, see ¶ 39,201.—CCH.]

[¶ 39,012]   RELEASE No. 49A, January 18, 1983, 48 F.R. 3585

Addition to SAB No. 49

AGENCY: Securities and Exchange Commission.

ACTION: Publication of Staff Accounting Bulletin.

SUMMARY: Staff Accounting Bulletin No. 49 (SAB 49), which was released on October 26, 1982 (47 FR 49627, Nov. 2, 1982), expressed the staff's views regarding disclosures by bank holding companies about loans to public and private sector borrowers located in countries that are experiencing liquidity problems. Since the issuance of SAB 49, the staff has received inquiries about its views with respect to the necessity to provide additional disclosures about restructurings of existing debt in these countries, funding of additional borrowings and other related matters. This staff accounting bulletin addresses these issues.

DATE: January 18, 1983.

FOR FURTHER INFORMATION CONTACT: Marc D. Oken or Edmund Coulson, Office of the Chief Accountant (202/272-2130); or Howard P. Hodges,

Jr., Division of Corporation Finance (202/272-2553), Securities and Exchange Commission, Washington, D.C. 20549.

SUPPLEMENTARY INFORMATION: The statements in Staff Accounting Bulletins are not rules or interpretations of the Commission nor are they published as bearing the Commission's official approval. They represent interpretations and practices followed by the Division of Corporation Finance and the Office of the Chief Accountant in administering the disclosure requirements of the Federal securities laws.

STAFF ACCOUNTING BULLETIN NO. 49A

The staff herein adds Question 2 to Section H of Topic 11 of the Staff Accounting Bulletin Series. Section H discusses the appropriate disclosures by bank holding companies about loans to foreign countries that are experiencing liquidity problems.

[For text of Topic 11-H, see ¶ 39,201.—CCH.]

[¶ 39,013]   RELEASE No. 50, March 3, 1983, 48 F.R. 10043

Financial Statements and Industry Guide Disclosures in Filings Involving Formation of One-Bank Holding Company

AGENCY: Securities and Exchange Commission.   ACTION: Publication of Staff Accounting Bulletin.

SUMMARY: This Staff Accounting Bulletin expresses the staff's views with respect to financial statement and industry guide disclosures required in a filing involving the formation of a bank holding company structure over a bank when the only substantial asset of the holding company is its investment in the bank. It also discusses requirements for subsequently filed reports on Form 10-K for such registrants.

DATE: March 3, 1983.

FOR FURTHER INFORMATION CONTACT: Howard P. Hodges, Jr. or Henry J. Velsor, Division of Corporation Finance (202-272-2553), or Marc D. Oken or Eugene W. Green, Office of the Chief Accountant (202-272-2130), Securities and Exchange Commission, Washington, D.C. 20549.

SUPPLEMENTARY INFORMATION: The statements in Staff Accounting Bulletins are not rules or interpretations of the Commission nor are they published as bearing the Commission's official approval. They represent interpretations and practices followed by the Division of Corporation Finance and the Office of the Chief Accountant in administering the disclosure requirements of the Federal securities laws.

STAFF ACCOUNTING BULLETIN NO. 50

The staff herein adds Section F to Topic 1 of the Staff Accounting Bulletin Series. This section discusses the requirements for financial statements and industry guide disclosures in filings involving the formation of a bank holding company structure over a bank and requirements for subsequent filings on Form 10-K.

[For text of Topic 1-F, see ¶ 39,101.—CCH.]

[¶ 39,014]   **RELEASE No. 51, March 29, 1983, 48 F.R. 14595**

Accounting for Sales of Stock by Subsidiary

AGENCY: Securities and Exchange Commission.

ACTION: Publication of Staff Accounting Bulletin.

SUMMARY: This staff accounting bulletin expresses the staff's views regarding accounting in consolidation for issuances of a subsidiary's stock that cause changes in the parent's ownership percentage in the subsidiary.

DATE: March 29, 1983.

FOR FURTHER INFORMATION CONTACT: Marc D. Oken, Office of the Chief Accountant (202/272-2130); or Howard P. Hodges, Jr., Division of Corporation Finance (202/272-2553), Securities and Exchange Commission, Washington, D.C. 20549.

SUPPLEMENTARY INFORMATION: The statements in Staff Accounting Bulletins are not rules or interpretations of the Commission nor are they published as bearing the Commission's official approval. They represent interpretations and practices followed by the Division of Corporation Finance and the Office of the Chief Accountant in administering the disclosure requirements of the Federal securities laws.

STAFF ACCOUNTING BULLETIN NO. 51

The staff herein adds Section H to Topic 5 of the Staff Accounting Bulletin Series. This section discusses the staff's position on accounting in consolidation for issuances of a subsidiary's stock that cause changes in the parent's ownership percentage in the subsidiary.

[For text of Topic 5-H, see ¶ 39,141.—CCH.]

[¶ 39,015]   **RELEASE No. 52, May 16, 1983, 48 F.R. 23172**

Accounting for Terminations of Overfunded Defined Benefit Pension Plans

AGENCY: Securities and Exchange Commission.

ACTION: Publication of Staff Accounting Bulletin.

SUMMARY: This staff accounting bulletin expresses the staff's views regarding accounting for terminations of overfunded defined benefit pension plans.

DATE: May 16, 1983

FOR FURTHER INFORMATION CONTACT: Lawrence S. Jones, Office of the Chief Accountant (202/272-2158); or Howard P. Hodges, Jr., Division of Corporation Finance (202/272-2553), Securities and Exchange Commission, Washington, D.C. 20549.

SUPPLEMENTARY INFORMATION: The statements in Staff Accounting Bulletins are not rules or interpretations of the Commission nor are they published as bearing the Commission's official approval. They represent interpretations and practices followed by the Division of Corporation Finance and the Office of the Chief Accountant in administering the disclosure requirements of the Federal securities laws.

List of Subjects in 17 CFR Part 211

Accounting, Reporting and recordkeeping requirements, Securities.

Part 211—[Amended]

Accordingly, Part 211 of title 17 of the Code of Federal Regulations is amended by adding Staff Accounting Bulletin No. 52 to the table found in Subpart B.

STAFF ACCOUNTING BULLETIN NO. 52

The staff herein adds Section I to Topic 5 of the Staff Accounting Bulletin Series. This section discusses the staff's position on the recognition of gains on termination of overfunded defined benefit pension plans.

[For text of Topic 5-I, see ¶ 39,141.—CCH.]

⋙→ *Rescinded in Release No. 33-7878, effective September 25, 2000, 65 F.R. 51692.*

[¶ 39,016]   RELEASE No. 53, June 13, 1983, 48 F.R. 28230

Financial Statement Requirements Where Securities Are Guaranteed by Parent or Subsidiary

AGENCY: Securities and Exchange Commission.

ACTION: Publication of Staff Accounting Bulletin.

SUMMARY: This Staff Accounting Bulletin expresses the staff's views with respect to certain disclosure and reporting requirements relating to the issuance of securities guaranteed by affiliates of the issuer and to Rule 3-10 of Regulation S-X (17 CFR 210.3-10).

DATE: June 13, 1983.

FOR FURTHER INFORMATION CONTACT: David Martin, (202) 272-2573, or, regarding, Rule 3-10, Howard Hodges, (202) 272-2553, Division of Corporation Finance, or Robert K. Herdman, (202) 272-2141, Office of the Chief Accountant, Securities and Exchange Commission, Washington, D.C. 20549.

SUPPLEMENTARY INFORMATION: The statements in Staff Accounting Bulletins are not rules or interpretations of the Commission nor are they published as bearing the Commission's official approval. They represent interpretations and practices followed by the Division of Corporation Finance and the Office of the Chief Accountant in administering the disclosure requirements of the Federal securities laws.

List of Subjects in 17 CFR Part 210

Accounting, Reporting and recordkeeping requirements, Securities.

Part 211—[Amended]

Accordingly, Part 211 of Title 17 of the Code of Federal Regulations is amended by adding Staff Accounting Bulletin No. 53 to the table found in Subpart B.

STAFF ACCOUNTING BULLETIN NO. 53

The staff herein adds Sections G and H to Topic 1 of the Staff Accounting Bulletin Series. Section G discusses the requirements for financial statements of an issuer of securities guaranteed by its parent to be included in registration statements and reports. Section H interprets the financial statement requirements of Rule 3-10 of Regulation S-X for a subsidiary that guarantees securities of its parent.

[For text of Topics 1-G and H, see ¶ 39,101.—CCH.]

[¶ 39,017]   RELEASE No. 54, November 3, 1983, 48 F.R. 51769

Application of "Push Down" Basis of Accounting in Financial Statements of Subsidiaries Acquired by Purchase

AGENCY: Securities and Exchange Commission.

ACTION: Publication of Staff Accounting Bulletin.

SUMMARY: This staff accounting bulletin expresses the staff's views regarding the application of the "push down" basis of accounting in the separate financial statements of subsidiaries acquired in purchase transactions.

DATE: November 3, 1983

FOR FURTHER INFORMATION CONTACT: Michael P. McLaughlin, Office of the Chief Accountant (202/272-2130); or Howard P. Hodges, Jr., Division of Corporation Finance (202/272-2553), Securities and Exchange Commission, Washington, D.C. 20549.

SUPPLEMENTARY INFORMATION: The statements in Staff Accounting Bulletins are not rules or interpretations of the Commission nor are they published as bearing the Commission's official approval. They represent interpretations and practices followed by the Division of Corporation Finance and the Office of the Chief Accountant in administering the disclosure requirements of the Federal securities laws.

STAFF ACCOUNTING BULLETIN NO. 54

The staff herein adds Section J to Topic 5 of the Staff Accounting Bulletin Series. This section discusses the staff's position on the appropriateness of applying the "push down" basis of accounting in the separate financial statements of subsidiaries acquired in purchase transactions.

[For text of Topic 5-J, see ¶ 39,141.—CCH.]

[¶ 39,018]   RELEASE No. 55, November 30, 1983, 48 F.R. 54810

Allocation of Expenses and Related Disclosure in Subsidiaries' Financial Statements

AGENCY: Securities and Exchange Commission.

ACTION: Publication of Staff Accounting Bulletin.

SUMMARY: This Staff Accounting Bulletin expresses the staff's views concerning the allocation of expenses and related disclosure in financial statements of subsidiaries, divisions, or lesser business components of another entity. This Bulletin also amends Section D of Topic 4 relating to the issuance of shares prior to an initial public offering.

DATE: November 30, 1983.

FOR FURTHER INFORMATION CONTACT: Robert Lavery or Michael P. McLaughlin, Office of the Chief Accountant (202-272-2130) or Howard P. Hodges, Jr. or James O'Brien, Division of Corporation Finance (202-272-2553), Securities and Exchange Commission, Washington, D.C. 20549.

SUPPLEMENTARY INFORMATION: The statements in Staff Accounting Bulletins are not rules or interpretations of the Commission nor are they published as bearing the Commission's official approval; they represent interpretations and practices followed by the Division of Corporation Finance and the Office of the Chief Accountant in administering the disclosure requirements of the Federal securities laws.

Part 211—[Amended]

Accordingly, Part 211 of Title 17 of the Code of Federal Regulations is amended by adding Staff Accounting Bulletin No. 55 to the table found in Subpart B.

STAFF ACCOUNTING BULLETIN NO. 55

The staff hereby adds Section B to Topic 1 of the Staff Accounting Bulletin Series. Section B discusses the staff's approach in particular situations to the allocation of expenses and related disclosure in financial statements of subsidiaries, divisions, or lesser business components of another entity.

The staff also hereby amends the Facts and the Question in Section D of Topic 4 of the Staff Accounting Bulletin Series, and adds a second question to that Section. Section D relates to the issuance of shares to selected persons prior to an initial public offering.

[For text of Topic 4-D, see ¶ 39,131.—CCH.]

[¶ 39,019]   RELEASE No. 56, February 6, 1984, 49 F.R. 4936

Interpretation Regarding Disclosure of Allocated Transfer Risk Reserves Mandated by Federal Banking Agencies

AGENCY: Securities and Exchange Commission.

ACTION: Publication of Staff Accounting Bulletin.

SUMMARY: This Staff Accounting Bulletin expresses the staff's views concerning disclosures under the Federal securities laws about certain reserves mandated by the Federal banking agencies for purposes of the regulatory and supervisory functions of those agencies.

DATE: January 31, 1984

FOR FURTHER INFORMATION CONTACT: Michael P. McLaughlin, Office of the Chief Accountant (202-272-2130) or Howard P. Hodges, Jr. Division of Corporation Finance (202-272-2553), Securities and Exchange Commission, Washington, D.C. 20549.

SUPPLEMENTARY INFORMATION: The statements in Staff Accounting Bulletins are not rules or interpretations of the Commission nor are they published as bearing the Commission's official approval; they represent interpretations and practices followed

by the Division of Corporation Finance and the Office of the Chief Accountant in administering the disclosure requirements of the Federal securities laws.

By the Commission.

Part 211—[Amended]

Accordingly, Part 211 of Title 17 of the Code of Federal Regulations is amended by adding Staff Accounting Bulletin No. 56 to the table found in Subpart B.

STAFF ACCOUNTING BULLETIN NO. 56

The staff hereby adds Section I to Topic 11 of the Staff Accounting Bulletin Series. Section I discusses the staff's views concerning disclosures under the Federal securities laws about certain reserves mandated by the Federal banking agencies for purposes of the regulatory and supervisory functions of those agencies.

[For text of Topic 11-I, see ¶ 39,201.—CCH.]

[¶ 39,020]   RELEASE No. 57, July 18, 1984

[Rescinded by SAB-95]

[¶ 39,021]   RELEASE No. 58, March 19, 1985

LIFO Inventory Accounting Practices

AGENCY: Securities and Exchange Commission.

ACTION: Publication of Staff Accounting Bulletin.

SUMMARY: This staff accounting bulletin expresses the staff's views regarding last-in, first-out (LIFO)

inventory accounting practices for financial statement purposes.

DATE: March 19, 1985.

FOR FURTHER INFORMATION CONTACT: Leland E. Graul, Office of the Chief Accountant

(202-272-2130), or Howard P. Hodges, Jr., Division of Corporation Finance (202-272-2553), Securities and Exchange Commission, 450 Fifth Street, N.W., Washington, D.C. 20549.

SUPPLEMENTARY INFORMATION: The statements in Staff Accounting Bulletins are not rules or interpretations of the Commission nor are they published as bearing the Commission's official approval. They represent interpretations and practices followed by the Division of Corporation Finance and the Office of the Chief Accountant in administering the disclosure requirements of the Federal securities laws.

Part 211—(Amended)

Accordingly, Part 211 of Title 17 of the Code of Federal Regulations is amended by adding Staff Accounting Bulletin No. 58 to the table found in Subpart B.

STAFF ACCOUNTING BULLETIN NO. 58

The staff hereby adds Section L to Topic 5 of the staff accounting bulletin series. Section L discusses the staff's views regarding last-in, first-out (LIFO) inventory accounting practices for financial reporting purposes.

[For text of Topic 5-L, see ¶ 39,141.—CCH.]

[¶ 39,022]   RELEASE No. 59, September 5, 1985

Accounting for Noncurrent Marketable Equity Securities

ACTION: Publication of Staff Accounting Bulletin.

SUMMARY: This staff accounting bulletin expresses the staff's views regarding accounting for noncurrent marketable equity securities.

DATE: September 5, 1985

FOR FURTHER INFORMATION CONTACT: Leland E. Graul, Office of the Chief Accountant (202-272-2130), or Howard P. Hodges, Jr., Division of Corporation Finance (202-272-2553), Securities and Exchange Commission, 450 Fifth Street, N.W., Washington, D.C. 20549.

SUPPLEMENTARY INFORMATION: The statements in Staff Accounting Bulletins are not rules or interpretations of the Commission nor are they published as bearing the Commission's official approval. They represent interpretations and practices followed

by the Division of Corporation Finance and the Office of the Chief Accountant in administering the disclosure requirements of the Federal securities laws.

Part 211—(AMENDED)

Accordingly, Part 211 of Title 17 of the Code of Federal Regulations is amended by adding Staff Accounting Bulletin No. 59 to the table found in Subpart B.

STAFF ACCOUNTING BULLETIN NO. 59

The staff hereby adds Section M to Topic 5 of the staff accounting bulletin series. Section M discusses the staff's views regarding accounting for noncurrent marketable equity securities.

[For text of Topic 5-M, see ¶ 39,141.—CCH.]

[¶ 39,023]   RELEASE No. 60, December 20, 1985, 50 F.R. 52916

Accounting for and Disclosure of Financial Guarantees

ACTION: Publication of Staff Accounting Bulletin.

SUMMARY: The interpretations in this Staff Accounting Bulletin express certain views of the staff regarding accounting for and disclosure of certain financial guarantees.

DATE: December 20, 1985.

FOR FURTHER INFORMATION CONTACT: Lawrence Salva or Jeremiah J. Harrington, Office of the Chief Accountant (202-272-2130), or Howard P. Hodges, Jr., Division of Corporation Finance (202-272-2553), Securities and Exchange Commission, 450 Fifth Street, N.W., Washington, D.C. 20549.

SUPPLEMENTARY INFORMATION: The statements in staff accounting bulletins are not rules or interpretations of the Commission nor are they published as bearing the Commission's official approval.

They represent interpretations and practices followed by the Division of Corporation Finance and the Office of the Chief Accountant in administering the disclosure requirements of the Federal Securities laws.

Part 211—(AMENDED)

Accordingly, Part 211 of Title 17 of the Code of Federal Regulations is amended by adding Staff Accounting Bulletin No. 60 to the table found in Subpart B.

STAFF ACCOUNTING BULLETIN NO. 60

The staff hereby adds Section J to Topic 11 of the staff accounting bulletin series. Section J discusses the staff's views regarding disclosures by issuers of certain financial guarantees.

[For text of Topic 11-J, see ¶ 39,201.—CCH.]

[¶ 39,024]   RELEASE No. 61, May 6, 1986

Adjustments of Allowances For Loan Losses in Connection With Business Combinations Accounted For by the Purchase Method

AGENCY: Securities and Exchange Commission.

ACTION: Publication of Staff Accounting Bulletin

SUMMARY: This Staff Accounting Bulletin expresses the staff's views regarding adjustments of allowances for loan losses in connection with business combinations accounted for by the purchase method.

DATE: May 6, 1986

FOR FURTHER INFORMATION CONTACT: Wayne G. Pentrack, Office of the Chief Accountant (202-272-2130) or Howard P. Hodges, Jr., Division of Corporation Finance (202-272-2553), Securities and Exchange Commission, 450 Fifth Street, N.W., Washington, D.C. 20549.

SUPPLEMENTARY INFORMATION: The statements in Staff Accounting Bulletins are not rules or interpretations of the Commission nor are they published as bearing the Commission's official approval.

They represent interpretations and practices followed by the Division of Corporation Finance and the Office of the Chief Accountant in administering the disclosure requirements of the Federal securities laws.

Part 211—(AMENDED)

Accordingly, Part 211 of Title 17 of the Code of Federal Regulations is amended by adding Staff Accounting Bulletin No. 61 to the Table found in Subpart B.

STAFF ACCOUNTING BULLETIN NO. 61

The staff hereby adds Section A-5 to Topic 2 expressing the staff's views regarding adjustments of allowances for loan losses in connection with business combinations accounted for by the purchase method.

[For text of Topic 2-A-5, see ¶ 39,111.—CCH.]

[¶ 39,025]   RELEASE No. 62, July 7, 1986

Discounting by Property-Casualty Insurance Companies

ACTION: Publication of Staff Accounting Bulletin.

SUMMARY: This staff accounting bulletin expresses the staff's views regarding the appropriate accounting and financial reporting when a registrant adopts or changes its policy with respect to discounting certain unpaid claims liabilities related to short-duration insurance contracts.

DATE: July 7, 1986.

FOR FURTHER INFORMATION CONTACT: Lawrence Salva or Jeremiah J. Harrington, Office of the Chief Accountant (202-272-2130), or Howard P. Hodges, Jr. Division of Corporation Finance (202-272-2553), Securities and Exchange Commission, 450 Fifth Street, N.W., Washington, D.C. 20549.

SUPPLEMENTARY INFORMATION: The statements in staff accounting bulletins are not rules or interpretations of the Commission nor are they published as bearing the Commission's official approval.

They represent interpretations and practices followed by the Division of Corporation Finance and the Office of the Chief Accountant in administering the disclosure requirements of the Federal Securities laws.

PART 211—(AMENDED)

Part 211 of Title 17 of the Code of Federal Regulations is amended by adding Staff Accounting Bulletin No. 62 to the table found in Subpart B.

STAFF ACCOUNTING BULLETIN NO. 62

The staff hereby adds Section N to Topic 5 of the staff accounting bulletin series. Section N discusses the staff's views regarding the appropriate accounting and financial reporting when a registrant adopts or changes its policy with respect to discounting certain unpaid claims liabilities related to short-duration insurance contracts.

[For text of Topic 5-N, see ¶ 39,141.—CCH.]

[¶ 39,026]   RELEASE No. 63, September 11, 1986

Research and Development Arrangements

ACTION: Publication of Staff Accounting Bulletin.

SUMMARY: The interpretations in this staff accounting bulletin express certain views of the staff regarding accounting for research and development arrangements.

DATE: September 11, 1986.

FOR FURTHER INFORMATION CONTACT: John A. Heyman, Office of the Chief Accountant (202-272-2130), or Howard P. Hodges, Jr., Division of Corporation Finance (202-272-2553), Securities and Exchange Commission, 450 Fifth Street, N.W., Washington, D.C. 20549.

SUPPLEMENTARY INFORMATION: The statements in staff accounting bulletins are not rules or interpretations of the Commission nor are they published as bearing the Commission's official approval. They represent interpretations and practices followed by the Division of Corporation Finance and the Office of the Chief Accountant in administering the disclosure requirements of the Federal Securities laws.

Part 211—(AMENDED)

Accordingly, Part 211 of Title 17 of the Code of Federal Regulations is amended by adding Staff Accounting Bulletin No. 63 to the table found in Subpart B.

STAFF ACCOUNTING BULLETIN NO. 63

The staff herein adds Section O to Topic 5 of the staff accounting bulletin Series. This section discusses the staff's position regarding the application of

the provisions of Statement of Financial Accounting Standards No. 68, "Research and Development Arrangements," when the parties that fund an enterprise's research and development activities are affiliated or related to the enterprise performing those activities.

[For text of Topic 5-O, see ¶ 39,141.—CCH.]

[¶ 39,027]   RELEASE No. 64, October 2, 1986

Applicability of Guidance in Staff Accounting Bulletins; Reporting of Income or Loss Applicable to Common Stock; Accounting for Redeemable Preferred Stock; Issuances of Shares Prior to an Initial Public Offering

ACTION: Publication of Staff Accounting Bulletin.

SUMMARY: This Staff Accounting Bulletin expresses the staff's views regarding: (a) applicability of guidance contained in Staff Accounting Bulletins, (b) reporting of income or loss applicable to common stock, (c) accounting for redeemable preferred stock (amending Topic 3.C.), and (d) issuances of shares prior to an initial public offering (amending Topic 4.D.).

DATE: October 2, 1986.

FOR FURTHER INFORMATION CONTACT: Wayne G. Pentrack, Office of the Chief Accountant (202-272-2130) or Howard P. Hodges, Jr., Division of Corporation Finance (202-272-2553), Securities and Exchange Commission, 450 Fifth Street, N.W., Washington, D.C. 20549.

SUPPLEMENTARY INFORMATION: The statements in Staff Accounting Bulletins are not rules or interpretations of the Commission nor are they published as bearing the Commission's official approval. They represent interpretations and practices followed by the Division of Corporation Finance and the Office of the Chief Accountant in administering the disclosure requirements of the Federal securities laws.

Part 211—(AMENDED)

Accordingly, Part 211 of Title 17 of the Code of Federal Regulations is amended by adding Staff Accounting Bulletin No. 64 to the Table found in Subpart B.

STAFF ACCOUNTING BULLETIN NO. 64

The staff hereby adds the following to the Staff Accounting Bulletin Series:

(a) Topic 6.B.1., regarding the reporting of income or loss applicable to common stock; and

(b) Topic 6.C.1., regarding applicability of guidance contained in Staff Accounting Bulletins.[1]

Also, the staff hereby amends the following in the Staff Accounting Bulletin Series:

(a) Topic 3.C., regarding accounting for redeemable preferred stock; and

(b) Topic 4.D., regarding issuances of shares prior to an initial public offering.

[For text of Topics 3-C, 4-D, 6-B-1 and 6-C-1, see ¶ 39,121, 39,131 and 39,151.—CCH.]

[¶ 39,028]   RELEASE No. 65, November 5, 1986

Risk Sharing in Business Combinations Accounted for as Pooling of Interests

ACTION: Publication of Staff Accounting Bulletin.

SUMMARY: The interpretations in this staff accounting bulletin indicate the staff's views on certain matters involved in the application of Accounting Series Release Nos. 130 and 135 regarding risk sharing in business combinations accounted for as pooling of interests.

DATE: November 5, 1986.

FOR FURTHER INFORMATION CONTACT: Lawrence Salva, Office of the Chief Accountant (202-272-2130), or Howard P. Hodges, Jr. Division of Corporation Finance (202-272-2553), Securities and Exchange Commission, 450 Fifth Street, N.W., Washington, D.C. 20549.

SUPPLEMENTARY INFORMATION: The statements in staff accounting bulletins are not rules or interpretations of the Commission nor are they published as bearing the Commission's official approval. They represent interpretations and practices followed by the Division of Corporation Finance and the Office of the Chief Accountant in administering the disclosure requirements of the Federal Securities laws.

PART 211—(AMENDED)

Part 211 of Title 17 of the Code of Federal Regulations is amended by adding Staff Accounting Bulletin No. 65 to the table found in Subpart B.

---

[1] Previous staff publications (most recently, SAB No. 40) have expressed the staff's intent regarding applicability of guidance contained in SABs, although not within the codification of SAB

topics. The staff is hereby adding Topic 6.C.1. to emphasize this intent.

STAFF ACCOUNTING BULLETIN NO. 65

The staff hereby adds Section E to Topic 2 of the staff accounting bulletin series. Section E discusses the staff's views on certain matters involved in the application of Accounting Series Release Nos. 130 and 135 regarding risk sharing in business combinations accounted for as pooling of interests.

[For text of Topic 2-E, see ¶ 39,111.—CCH.]

[¶ 39,029]   **RELEASE No. 66, November 25, 1986**

Deposit/Relending Arrangements Between U.S. Banks and Debtors in Foreign Countries

ACTION: Publication of Staff Accounting Bulletin.

SUMMARY: This Staff Accounting Bulletin (SAB) amends Topic 11.H. with respect to deposit/relending arrangements between U.S. banks and debtors in certain foreign countries, and rescinds other portions of Topic 11.H. that were originally published in SAB Nos. 49 and 49A. The rescinded portions are no longer needed because the substance of that guidance has been codified in Industry Guide 3, "Statistical Disclosure by Bank Holding Companies".

DATE: November 25, 1986.

FOR FURTHER INFORMATION CONTACT: Wayne G. Pentrack or Edmund Coulson, Office of the Chief Accountant (202-272-2130) or Howard P. Hodges, Jr., Division of Corporation Finance (202-272-2553), Securities and Exchange Commission, 450 Fifth Street, N.W., Washington, DC 20549. SUPPLEMENTARY INFORMATION: The statements in Staff Accounting Bulletins are not rules or interpretations of the Commission nor are they published as bearing the Commission's official approval. They represent interpretations and practices followed by the Division of Corporation Finance and the Office of the Chief Accountant in administering the disclosure requirements of the Federal Securities laws.

Part 211—(AMENDED)

Accordingly, Part 211 of Title 17 of the Code of Federal Regulations is amended by adding Staff Accounting Bulletin No. 66 to the Table found in Subpart B.

STAFF ACCOUNTING BULLETIN NO.65

The staff hereby amends Topic 11.H. in the Staff Accounting Bulletin Series, "Disclosures by Bank Holding Companies Regarding Certain Foreign Loans".

[For text of Topic 11-H, see ¶ 39,201.—CCH.]

[¶ 39,030]   **RELEASE No. 67, December 8, 1986**

Income Statement Presentation of Restructuring Charges

ACTION: Publication of Staff Accounting Bulletin.

SUMMARY: The interpretations in this staff accounting bulletin express certain views of the staff regarding the appropriate income statement presentation of restructuring charges.

DATE: December 8, 1986.

FOR FURTHER INFORMATION CONTACT: John A. Heyman, Office of the Chief Accountant (202-272-2130), or Howard P. Hodges, Jr., Division of Corporation Finance (202-272-2553), Securities and Exchange Commission, 450 Fifth Street, N.W., Washington, D.C. 20549.

SUPPLEMENTARY INFORMATION: The statements in staff accounting bulletins are not rules or interpretations of the Commission nor are they published as bearing the Commission's official approval. They represent interpretations and practices followed by the Division of Corporation Finance and the Office of the Chief Accountant in administering the disclosure requirements of the Federal Securities laws.

PART 211—(AMENDED)

Accordingly, Part 211 of Title 17 of the Code of Federal Regulations is amended by adding Staff Accounting Bulletin No. 67 to the table found in Subpart B.

STAFF ACCOUNTING BULLETIN NO. 67

The staff hereby adds Section P to Topic 5 of the staff accounting bulletin series. Section P discusses the staff's views on the appropriate income statement presentation of what are commonly referred to as "restructuring charges."

[For text of Topic 5-P, see ¶ 39,141.]

[¶ 39,031]   **RELEASE No. 68, May 4, 1987**

Accounting for Increasing Rate Preferred Stock

ACTION: Publication of Staff Accounting Bulletin.

SUMMARY: This staff accounting bulletin expresses the staff's views regarding accounting for increasing rate preferred stock.

DATE: May 4, 1987.

FOR FURTHER INFORMATION CONTACT: Wayne G. Pentrack, Office of the Chief Accountant, or Howard P. Hodges, Jr., Division of Corporation Finance, Securities and Exchange Commission, 450 Fifth Street, N.W., Washington, D.C. 20549.

SUPPLEMENTARY INFORMATION: The statements in staff accounting bulletins are not rules or interpretations of the Commission nor are they published as bearing the Commission's official approval. They represent interpretations and practices followed by the Division of Corporation Finance and the Office of the Chief Accountant in administering the disclosure requirements of the Federal securities laws.

Part 211—(AMENDED)

Accordingly, Part 211 of Title 17 of the Code of Federal Regulations is amended by adding Staff Accounting Bulletin No. 68 to the Table found in Subpart B.

The staff hereby adds Section Q to Topic 5 of the staff accounting bulletin series. Section Q discusses the staff's views regarding accounting for increasing rate preferred stock.

[For text of Topic 5-Q, See ¶ 39,141.]

[¶ 39,032] RELEASE No. 69, May 8, 1987

Application of Article 9 of Regulation S-X and Industry Guide 3 for Certain Disclosures by Registrants Which Are Not Bank Holding Companies But Are Engaged in Similar Lending and Deposit Activities

ACTION: Publication of Staff Accounting Bulletin.

SUMMARY: The interpretations in this staff accounting bulletin express certain views of the staff regarding: (a) the use of Article 9 of Regulation S-X and Industry Guide 3 as guidance for certain disclosures of registrants which are not bank holding companies, but which are engaged in similar lending and deposit activities; and (b) income statement presentation for casino-hotel activities.

DATE: May 8, 1987

FOR FURTHER INFORMATION CONTACT: John M. Riley or John W. Albert, Office of the Chief Accountant (202-272-2130), or Howard P. Hodges, Jr. Division of Corporation Finance (202-272-2553), Securities and Exchange Commission, 450 Fifth Street, N. W., Washington, D. C. 20549.

SUPPLEMENTATY INFORMATION: The statements in staff accounting bulletins are not rules or interpretations of the Commission nor are they published as bearing the Commission's official approval. They represent interpretations and practices followed by the Division of Corporation Finance and the Office of the Chief Accountant in administering the disclosure requirements of the Federal Securities laws.

Part 211—(AMENDED)

Accordingly, Part 211 of Title 17 of the Code of Federal Regulations is amended by adding Staff Accounting Bulletin No. 69 to the table found in Subpart B.

STAFF ACCOUNTING BULLETIN NO. 69

The staff hereby adds Sections K and L to Topic 11 of the staff accounting bulletin series. Section K discusses the staff's views on the use of Article 9 of Regulation S-X ("Bank Holding Companies") and Industry Guide 3 ("Statistical disclosure by bank holding companies") as guidance for certain disclosures of registrants which are not bank holding companies, but which are engaged in similar lending and deposit activities. Section L discusses appropriate income statement presentation by casinos with hotel and restaurant operations.

[For text of Topic 11-K and L, see ¶ 39,201.]

[¶ 39,033] RELEASE No. 70, June 5, 1987

Accounting and Balance Sheet Presentation for Non-Recourse Debt that is Collateralized by Lease Receivable and/or the Related Lease Assets

ACTION: Publication of Staff Accounting Bulletin.

SUMMARY: This staff accounting bulletin expresses the staff's views relative to the accounting and balance sheet presentation for non-recourse debt that is collateralized by lease receivables and/or the related leased assets. It also deletes certain interpretations published in Staff Accounting Bulletin No. 52 that are no longer relevant because of accounting standards adopted by the Financial Accounting Standards Board.

DATE: June 5, 1987

FOR FURTHER INFORMATION CONTACT: James R. Bradow, Office of the Chief Accountant (202/272-2130); or Howard P. Hodges, Jr., Division of

Corporation Finance (202/272-2553), Securities and Exchange Commission, Washington, D.C. 20549.

SUPPLEMENTARY INFORMATION: The statements in Staff Accounting Bulletins are not rules or interpretations of the Commission nor are they published as bearing the Commission's official approval. They represent interpretations and practices followed by the Division of Corporation Finance and the Office of the Chief Accountant in administering the disclosure requirements of the Federal securities laws.

Part 211—(AMENDED)

Part 211 of Title 17 of the Code of Federal Regulations is amended by adding Staff Accounting Bulletin No. 70 to the table found in Subpart B.

STAFF ACCOUNTING BULLETIN NO. 70

The staff hereby adds Section R to Topic 5 and deletes Topic 5-I of the staff accounting bulletin series. Topic 5-R discusses the staff's views relative to the accounting and balance sheet presentation for non-recourse debt that is collateralized by lease receivables and/or the related leased assets. Topic 5-I relates to recognition of gains on terminations of overfunded defined benefit pension plans, the accounting for which is now addressed by FASB Statement No. 88.

[For text of Topic 5-R, see ¶ 39,141.]

[¶ 39,034]   RELEASE No. 71, August 12, 1987

Financial Statement of Properties Securing Mortgage Loans

ACTION: Publication of Staff Accounting Bulletin.

SUMMARY: This staff accounting bulletin expresses the staff's views regarding the requirements for financial statements of properties securing mortgage loans.

DATE: August 12, 1987.

FOR FURTHER INFORMATION CONTACT: Jeffrey C. Jones or John M. Riley, Office of the Chief Accountant (202-272-2130), or Howard P. Hodges, Jr. or Joseph S. Aleknavage, Division of Corporation Finance (202-272-2553), Securities and Exchange Commission, 450 Fifth Street, N. W., Washington, D.C. 20549.

SUPPLEMENTARY INFORMATION: The statements in staff accounting bulletins are not rules or interpretations of the Commission nor are they published as bearing the Commission's official approval. They represent interpretations and practices followed by the Division of Corporation Finance and the Office of the Chief Accountant in administering the disclosure requirements of the Federal securities laws.

Part 211—(AMENDED)

Accordingly, Part 211 of Title 17 of the Code of Federal Regulations is amended by adding Staff Accounting Bulletin No. 71 to the table found in Subpart B.

The staff hereby adds Section I to Topic 1 of the staff accounting bulletin series. Section I discusses the staff's views regarding the requirements for financial statements of properties securing mortgage loans.

[For the text of Topic 1-I, see ¶ 39,101.]

[¶ 39,034A]   RELEASE No. 71A, December 15, 1987

Determining Adequacy of Borrower's Equity in Underlying Property

ACTION: Publication of Staff Accounting Bulletin.

SUMMARY: Staff Accounting Bulletin No. 71 ("SAB 71"), which was released on August 12, 1987, expressed the staff's views regarding the requirements for financial statements of properties securing mortgage loans. Since the issuance of SAB 71, the staff has received inquiries about its position concerning (1) determining the adequacy of the borrower's equity in the underlying property; (2) the financial statements to be included for loan arrangements reported as investments in real estate ("investment-type arrangements") in filings under the Securities Act of 1933 ("Securities Act"), and the Securities Exchange Act of 1934 ("Exchange Act"); and (3) the application of SAB 71 to loans entered into prior to the date of its issuance. This staff accounting bulletin addresses these issues.

DATE: December 15, 1987

FOR FURTHER INFORMATION CONTACT: Jeffrey C. Jones or John M. Riley, Office of the Chief Accountant (202/272-2130); or Howard P. Hodges, Jr., Joseph S. Aleknavage (202/272-2553), or Lester J. Shapiro (202/272-3322), Division of Corporation Finance, Securities and Exchange Commission, 450 Fifth Street, N.W., Washington, D.C. 20549.

SUPPLEMENTARY INFORMATION: The statements in Staff Accounting Bulletins are not rules or interpretations of the Commission nor are they published as bearing the Commission's official approval. They represent interpretations and practices followed by the Division of Corporation Finance and the Office of the Chief Accountant in administering the disclosure requirements of the Federal securities laws.

PART 211—(AMENDED)

Accordingly, Part 211 of Title 17 of the Code of Federal Regulations is amended by adding Staff Account Bulletin No. 71A to the table found in Subpart B.

STAFF ACCOUNTING BULLETIN NO. 71A

The staff herein adds questions 3, 4, 5, 6, 7, and 8 to Section I of Tipic 1 of the Staff Accounting Bulletin Series. The staff also herein rescinds the last two sentences of the fifth paragraph of the interpretive response in question 1 of Section I of Topic 1. Section I discusses financial statement requirements.

[For the text of Topic 1-I, see ¶ 39,101.]

[¶ 39,035]   RELEASE No. 72, November 10, 1987

Income Statement Classification of Charges by Utilities for Disallowed Costs or the Costs of Abandoned Plants

ACTION: Publication of Staff Accounting Bulletin.

SUMMARY: This staff accounting bulletin expresses the staff's views concerning the appropriate income statement classification of charges by utilities for disallowed costs or the costs of abandoned plants.

DATE: November 10, 1987.

FOR FURTHER INFORMATION CONTACT: John A. Heyman, Office of the Chief Accountant (202/272-2130); or Howard P. Hodges, Jr., Division of Corporation Finance (202/272-2553), Securities and Exchange Commission, Washington, D. C. 20549.

SUPPLEMENTARY INFORMATION: The statements in staff accounting bulletins are not rules or interpretations of the Commission nor are they published as bearing the Commission's official approval. They represent interpretations and practices followed by the Division of Corporation Finance and the Office of the Chief Accountant in administering the disclosure requirements of the Federal securities laws.

Part 211—(AMENDED)

Part 211 of Title 17 of the Code of Federal Regulations is amended by adding Staff Accounting Bulletin No. 72 to the table found in Subpart B.

STAFF ACCOUNTING BULLETIN NO. 72

The staff hereby adds Section E to Topic 10. Topic 10-E discusses the staff's view concerning the appropriate income statement classification of charges by utilities for disallowed costs or the costs of abandoned plants.

[For the text of Topic 10-E, see ¶ 39,191.]

[¶ 39,036]   RELEASE No. 73, December 30, 1987

Application of "Push down" Accounting in Separate Financial Statements of Subsidiaries Acquired in Purchase Transactions

ACTION: Publication of Staff Accounting Bulletin.

SUMMARY: Staff Accounting Bulletin No. 54 (SAB 54), which was released on November 3, 1983, expressed the staff's views regarding the application of the "push down" basis of accounting in the separate financial statements of subsidiaries acquired in purchase transactions. Since the issuance of SAB 54, the staff has received inquiries about its views with respect to recording (or "pushing down") parent company debt in the separate financial statements of the subsidiary when such debt is incurred in connection with or otherwise related to the acquisition of the subsidiary in a purchase transaction. This staff accounting bulletin addresses these issues.

DATE: December 30, 1987

FOR FURTHER INFORMATION CONTACT: James R. Bradow, Office of the Chief Accountant (202/272-2130) or Howard P. Hodges, Jr., Division of Corporation Finance (202/272-2553), Securities and Exchange Commission, Washington, D.C. 20549.

SUPPLEMENTARY INFORMATION: The statements in Staff Accounting Bulletins are not rules or interpretations of the Commission nor are they published as bearing the Commission's official approval. They represent interpretations and practices followed by the Division of Corporation Finance and the Office of the Chief Accountant in administering the disclosure requirements of the Federal securities laws.

Part 211—(AMENDED)

Part 211 of Title 17 of the Code of Federal Regulations is amended by adding Staff Accounting Bulletin No. 73 to the table found in Subpart B.

STAFF ACCOUNTING BULLETIN NO. 73

The staff hereby adds Question 3 to Topic 5.J. of the Staff Accounting Bulletin Series. Topic 5.J. discusses the staff's position on the appropriateness of applying the "push down" method of accounting in the separate financial statements of subsidiaries acquired in purchase transactions.

[For the text of Topic 5-J, see ¶ 39,141.]

[¶ 39,037]   RELEASE No. 74, December 30, 1987

Disclosures by Registrant When an Accounting Standard Has Been Issued But Not Yet Adopted

ACTION: Publication of Staff Accounting Bulletin.

SUMMARY: This staff accounting bulletin expresses the staff's views concerning disclosures that generally should be provided by a registrant when an accounting standard has been issued but not yet adopted.

DATE: December 30, 1987.

FOR FURTHER INFORMATION CONTACT: Jack C. Parsons, Office of the Chief Accountant (202/272-2130); or Howard P. Hodges, Jr., Division of Corporation Finance (202/272-2553), Securities and Exchange Commission, Washington, D.C. 20549.

SUPPLEMENTARY INFORMATION: The statements in staff accounting bulletins are not rules or interpretations of the Commission nor are they published as bearing the Commission's official approval. They represent interpretations and practices followed by the Division of Corporation Finance and the Office of the Chief Accountant in administering the disclosure requirements of the Federal securities laws.

Part 211—(AMENDED)

Part 211 of Title 17 of the Code of Federal Regulations is amended by adding Staff Accounting Bulletin No. 74 to the table found in Subpart B.

STAFF ACCOUNTING BULLETIN NO. 74

The staff hereby adds Section M to Topic 11. Topic 11-M expresses the staff's views concerning disclosure of the impact that recently issued accounting standards will have on the financial statements of the registrant when adopted in a future period.

[For the text of Topic 11-M, see ¶ 39,201.]

[¶ 39,038]   RELEASE No. 75, January 4, 1988

Certain Accounting and Disclosure Issues Relevant to a Proposed Mexican Debt Exchange Transaction

ACTION: Publication of Staff Accounting Bulletin.

SUMMARY: This staff accounting bulletin expresses the staff's views regarding certain accounting and disclosure issues relevant to a proposed Mexican Debt Exchange transaction.

DATE: January 4, 1988.

FOR FURTHER INFORMATION CONTACT: Jeffrey C. Jones, Office of the Chief Accountant (202/272-2130); or Howard P. Hodges, Jr., Division of Corporation Finance (202/272-2553), Securities and Exchange Commission, 450 Fifth Street, N.W., Washington, D.C. 20549.

SUPPLEMENTARY INFORMATION: The statements in staff accounting bulletins are not rules or interpretations of the Commission nor are they published as bearing the Commission's official approval.

They represent interpretations and practices followed by the Division of Corporation Finance and the Office of the Chief Accountant in administering the disclosure requirements of the Federal securities laws.

Part 211—(AMENDED)

Part 211 of Title 17 of the Code of Federal Regulations is amended by adding Staff Accounting Bulletin No. 75 to the table found in Subpart B.

STAFF ACCOUNTING BULLETIN NO. 75

The staff hereby adds Sub-Section 2 to Topic 11.H of the staff accounting bulletin series. Topic 11.H.2 discusses the staff's views regarding certain accounting and disclosure issues relevant to a proposed Mexican Debt Exchange transaction.

[For the text of Topic 11-H, see ¶ 39,201.]

[¶ 39,039]   RELEASE No. 76, January 12, 1988

Effect of Certain *De Minimis* Sales by Affiliates on Compliance With ASRs 130 and 135 Regarding Risk Sharing in Business Combinations Accounted For as Pooling of Interests

ACTION: Publication of Staff Accounting Bulletin.

SUMMARY: This staff accounting bulletin amends Topic 2-E of the staff accounting bulletin series to express the staff's views on the effect of certain *de minimis* sales by affiliates on compliance with the requirement of Accounting Series Release Nos. 130 and 135 regarding risk sharing in business combinations accounted for as pooling of interests.

FOR FURTHER INFORMATION CONTACT: John A. Heyman, Office of the Chief Accountant (202-272-2130), or Howard P. Hodges, Jr., Division of Corporation Finance (202-272-2553), Securities and Exchange Commission, 450 Fifth Street, N.W., Washington, D.C. 20549.

SUPPLEMENTARY INFORMATION: The statements in staff accounting bulletins are not rules or interpretations of the Commission nor are they published as bearing the Commission's official approval. They represent interpretations and practices followed by the Division of Corporation Finance and the Office of the Chief Accountant in administering the disclosure requirements of the Federal securities laws.

STAFF ACCOUNTING BULLETIN NO. 76

In Staff Accounting Bulletin ("SAB") No. 65 (Topic 2-E), the staff indicated that it will generally not question whether there is a lack of the risk sharing requisite for the use of pooling of interests accounting as the result of sales by affiliates which occur prior to 30 days before the consummation of the combination. After the issuance of SAB No. 65, the staff was asked whether the use of pooling of interests accounting would be precluded by sales by affiliates, after a date 30 days prior to the consummation of the combination and prior to the publication of financial results covering at least 30 days of post-merger combined operations, if those sales were *de minimis* in amount.

The staff hereby amends Question 2 of Section E of Topic 2 to include its view on what constitutes a *de minimis* sale, and the effects of such sales during the aforementioned period on the applicability of pooling of interests accounting.

[For the text of Topic 2-E, see ¶ 39,111.]

[¶ 39,040]   RELEASE No. 77, March 4, 1988

Allocation of Debt Issue Costs in a Business Combination Accounted For as a Purchase

ACTION: Publication of Staff Accounting Bulletin.

SUMMARY: This staff accounting bulletin expresses the staff's views regarding the allocation of debt issue costs in a business combination accounted for as a purchase.

FOR FURTHER INFORMATION CONTACT: John A. Heyman or John M. Riley, Office of the Chief Accountant (202-272-2130), or Howard P. Hodges, Jr., Division of Corporation Finance (202-272-2553), Securities and Exchange Commission, 450 Fifth Street, N.W., Washington, D.C. 20549.

SUPPLEMENTARY INFORMATION: The statements in staff accounting bulletins are not rules or interpretations of the Commission nor are they published as bearing the Commission's official approval.

They represent interpretations and practices followed by the Division of Corporation Finance and the Office of the Chief Accountant in administering the disclosure requirements of the Federal securities laws.

Part 211—(AMENDED)

Accordingly, Part 211 of Title 17 of the Code of Federal Regulations is amended by adding Staff Accounting Bulletin No. 77 to the table found in Subpart B.

The staff hereby adds Sub-Section 6 to Topic 2.A of the staff accounting bulletin series. Topic 2.A.6 discusses the staff's views regarding the allocation of debt issue costs in a business combination accounted for as a purchase.

[For the text of Topic 2-A, see ¶ 39,111.]

[¶ 39,041]   **RELEASE No. 78, August 25, 1988**

Certain Matters Relating to Quasi-Organizations, Including Deficit Eliminations

ACTION: Publication of Staff Accounting Bulletin

SUMMARY: This staff accounting bulletin expresses the staff's views regarding certain matters relating to quasi-reorganizations, including deficit eliminations.

FOR FURTHER INFORMATION CONTACT: Kenneth V. Moreland, Office of the Chief Accountant (202/272-2130) or Howard P. Hodges, Jr., or Nathan Cheney, Division of Corporation Finance (202/272-2553), Securities and Exchange Commission, Washington, D.C. 20549.

SUPPLEMENTARY INFORMATION: The statements in staff accounting bulletins are not rules or interpretations of the Commission nor are they published as bearing the Commission's official approval. They represent interpretations and practice followed

by the Division of Corporation Finance and the Office of the Chief Accountant in administering the disclosure requirements of the Federal securities laws.

Part 211—(AMENDED)

Part 211 of Title 17 of the Code of Federal Regulations is amended by adding Staff Accounting Bulletin No. 78 to the table found in Subpart B.

STAFF ACCOUNTING BULLETIN NO. 78

The staff hereby adds Section S to Topic 5 of the Staff Accounting Bulletin Series. Section S discusses the staff's views regarding certain matters relating to quasi-reorganizations, including deficit eliminations.

[For the text of Topic 5-S, see ¶ 39,141.]

[¶ 39,042]   **RELEASE No. 79, September 2, 1988**

Accounting for Transactions Undertaken by a Company's Principal Stockholder(s) For the Benefit of the Company

ACTION: Publication of Staff Accounting Bulletin.

SUMMARY: This staff accounting bulletin expresses the staff's views regarding the accounting for transactions undertaken by a company's principal stockholder(s) for the benefit of the company.

FOR FURTHER INFORMATION CONTACT: Kenneth V. Moreland, Office of the Chief Accountant (202-272-2130), or Howard P. Hodges, Jr. or Robert A. Bayless, Division of Corporation Finance (202-272-2553), Securities and Exchange Commission, 450 Fifth Street, N.W., Washington, D.C. 20549.

SUPPLEMENTARY INFORMATION: The statements in staff accounting bulletins are not rules or interpretations of the Commission nor are they published as bearing the Commission's official approval. They represent interpretations and practices followed

by the Division of Corporation Finance and the Office of the Chief Accountant in administering the disclosure requirements of the Federal securities laws.

PART 211—(AMENDED)

Part 211 of Title 17 of the Code of Federal Regulations is amended by adding Staff Accounting Bulletin No. 79 to the table found in Subpart B.

STAFF ACCOUNTING BULLETIN NO. 79

The staff hereby adds Section T to Topic 5 of the staff accounting bulletin series. Section T discusses the staff's views regarding the accounting for transactions undertaken by a company's principal stockholder(s) for the benefit of the company.

[For the text of Topic 5-T, see ¶ 39,141.]

PART 211—(AMENDED)

Part 211 of Title 17 of the Code of Federal Regulations is hereby amended by adding Staff Accounting Bulletin No. 76 to the table found in Subpart B.

[¶ 39,043]   **RELEASE No. 80, November 21, 1988**

Financial Statements of Businesses Acquired or To Be Acquired

ACTION: Publication of Staff Accounting Bulletin.

SUMMARY: the interpretations in this staff accounting bulletin express certain views of the staff regarding the application of Rules 3-05 and 1-02(v) of Regulation S-X in determining the financial statements of businesses acquired or to be acquired that are required to be included in registration statements for initial public offerings.

DATE: November 21, 1988.

FOR FURTHER INFORMATION CONTACT: Teresa Iannaconi, Office of the Chief Accountant (202-272-2130), or Robert Bayless, Division of Corporation Finance (202-272-2553), Securities and Exchange Commission, 450 Fifth Street, N. W., Washington, D. C. 20549.

SUPPLEMENTARY INFORMATION: The statements in staff accounting bulletins are not rules or interpretations of the Commission nor are they published as bearing the Commission's official approval. They represent interpretations and practices followed by the Division of Corporation Finance and the Office of the Chief Accountant in administering the disclosure requirements of the Federal Securities laws.

Part 211—(AMENDED)

Accordingly, Part 211 of Title 17 of the Code of Federal Regulations is amended by adding Staff Accounting Bulletin No. 80 to the table found in Subpart B.

STAFF ACCOUNTING BULLETIN NO. 80

The staff hereby adds Section J to Topic 1 of the staff accounting bulletin series. Topic 1-J sets forth the administrative policy of the Division of Corporation Finance and the Office of the Chief Accountant as to the method of application of Rules 3-05 and 1-02(v) of Regulation S-X to the requirements for financial statements of businesses acquired and to be acquired to registration statements for certain types of initial public offerings.

[For the text of Topic 1-J, see ¶ 39,101.]

[¶ 39,044]   **RELEASE No. 81, April 4, 1989**

Gain Recognition on the Sale of a Business or Operating Assets to a Highly Leveraged Entity

ACTION: Publication of Staff Accounting Bulletin.

SUMMARY: This staff accounting bulletin expresses the staff's views regarding the appropriateness of gain recognition on the sale of a business or operating assets to a highly leveraged entity.

FOR FURTHER INFORMATION CONTACT: Jack C. Parsons or John M. Riley, Office of the Chief Accountant (202-272-2130), or Howard P. Hodges, Jr., Division of Corporation Finance (202-272-2553), Securities and Exchange Commission, 450 Fifth Street, N.W., Washington, D.C. 20549.

SUPPLEMENTARY INFORMATION: The statements in staff accounting bulletins are not rules or interpretations of the Commission nor are they published as bearing the Commission's official approval. They represent interpretations and practices followed by the Division of Corporation Finance and the Office of the Chief Accountant in administering the disclosure requirements of the Federal securities laws.

STAFF ACCOUNTING BULLETIN NO. 81

The staff herein adds Section U to Topic 5 of the Staff Accounting Bulletin Series. Topic 5-U discusses the staff's position on the appropriateness of gain recognition on the sale of a business or operating assets to a highly leveraged entity.

[For the text of Topic 5-U, see ¶ 39,141.]

[¶ 39,045]   **RELEASE No. 82, July 5, 1989**

Transfers of Nonperforming Assets; Disclosure of the Impact of Financial Assistance From Regulators

ACTION; Publication of Staff Accounting Bulletin.

SUMMARY: This staff accounting bulletin expresses the staff's view regarding the accounting for transfers of nonperforming assets by financial institutions, and disclosure of the impact of financial assistance from regulators.

FOR FURTHER INFORMATION CONTACT: Teresa Iannaconi, Office of the Chief Accountant (202-272-2130), or Robert A. Bayless, Division of Corporation Finance (202-272-2553), Securities and Exchange Commission, 450 Fifth Street, N.W., Washington, D.C. 20549.

SUPPLEMENTARY INFORMATION: The statements in staff accounting bulletins are not rules or interpretations of the Commission nor are they published as bearing the Commission's official approval. They represent interpretations and practices followed by the Division of Corporation Finance and the Office of the Chief Accountant in administering the disclosure requirements of the Federal securities laws.

Part 211—(AMENDED)

Accordingly, Part 211 of Title 17 of the Code of Federal Regulations is amended by adding Staff Accounting Bulletin No. 82 to the table found in Subpart B.

STAFF ACCOUNTING BULLETIN NO. 82

The staff hereby adds Section V to Topic 5 and Section N to Topic 11 of the staff accounting bulletin series. Section V of Topic 5 discusses the staff's views regarding the accounting for transfers of nonperforming assets by financial institutions, and Section N of Topic 11 discusses the staff's views regarding the disclosure of the impact of regulatory assistance received in transfers or other regulatory assisted reorganizations or combinations.

[For the text of Topics 5-V and 11-n, See ¶ 39,141 and 39,201.]

[¶ 39,046]   RELEASE No. 83, July 31, 1989

Earnings Per Share Computations in an Initial Public Offering

ACTION: Publication of Staff Accounting Bulletin.

SUMMARY: This staff accounting bulletin revises the staff's existing guidance set forth in Topic 4-D regarding the computation of earnings per share and expresses the staff's position regarding the responsibility of the registrant to determine whether compensation expense must be recognized when common stock or other dilutive securities are issued during the period covered by income statements included in a registration statement or in subsequent periods prior to the filing of the registration statement for an initial public offering. This bulletin amends Topic 4-D based upon the experience of the staff in addressing registrant matters during the review process.

FOR FURTHER INFORMATION CONTACT: John W. Albert, Office of the Chief Accountant (202-272-2130) or Robert A. Bayless, Division of Corporation Finance (202-272-2553), Securities and Exchange Commission, 450 Fifth Street, N.W., Washington, D.C. 20549.

SUPPLEMENTARY INFORMATION: The statements in staff accounting bulletins are not rules or interpretations of the Commission nor are they published as bearing the Commission's official approval. They represent interpretations and practices followed by the Division of Corporation Finance and the Office of the Chief Accountant in administering the disclosure requirements of the Federal Securities Laws.

Part 211—(AMENDED)

Part 211 of Title 17 of the Code of Federal Regulations is amended by adding Staff Accounting Bulletin No. 83 to the table found in Subpart B.

STAFF ACCOUNTING BULLETIN NO. 83

The staff herein amends Section D of Topic 4 of the Staff Accounting Bulletin series. Topic 4-D discusses the staff's position regarding the computation of earnings per share and the responsibility of the registrant to determine whether compensation expense must be recognized when common stock or other dilutive securities are issued during the period covered by income statements included in a registration statement or in subsequent periods prior to the filing of the registration statement for an initial public offering.

[For the text of Topic 4-D, see ¶ 39,131.]

[¶ 39,047]   RELEASE No. 84, July 31, 1989

Accounting for Sales of Stock by a Subsidiary

ACTION: Publication of Staff Accounting Bulletin.

SUMMARY: Staff Accounting Bulletin No. 51, released March 29, 1983, expresses the staff's views regarding accounting in consolidation for issuances of a subsidiary's stock that cause changes in the parent's ownership percentage in the subsidiary. The purpose of this staff accounting bulletin is to address a number of issues that have arisen regarding the application of that SAB.

FOR FURTHER INFORMATION CONTACT: John M. Riley, Office of the Chief Accountant (202-272-2130), or Robert A. Bayless, Division of Corporation Finance (202-272-2553), Securities and Ex-

change Commission, 450 Fifth Street, N.W., Washington, D.C. 20549.

SUPPLEMENTARY INFORMATION: The statements in staff accounting bulletins are not rules or interpretations of the Commission nor are they published as bearing the Commission's official approval. They represent interpretations and practices followed by the Division of Corporation Finance and the Office of the Chief Accountant in administering the disclosure requirements of the Federal Securities laws.

Part 211—(AMENDED)

Part 211 of Title 17 of the Code of Federal Regulations is hereby amended by adding Staff Accounting Bulletin No. 84 to the table found in Subpart B.

STAFF ACCOUNTING BULLETIN NO. 84

The staff hereby adds questions 2 through 6 to Section H of Topic 5 of the Staff Accounting Bulletin Series and deletes the last paragraph of the Interpretive Response to existing Question 1, the substance of which is now included in Question 6. Section H discusses accounting for sales of stock by a subsidiary. The Facts, Question and remaining portion of the Interpretive Response presently appearing as Topic 5-H are reprinted herein for reference purposes.

[For the text of Topic 5-H, see ¶ 39,141.]

[¶ 39,048]   RELEASE No. 85, September 18, 1989

Amortizing Capitalized Cost of Oil and Gas Properties; Inclusion of Methane Gas within Proved Reserves

ACTION: Publication of Staff Accounting Bulletin.

SUMMARY: This staff accounting bulletin expresses the staff's views relating to (i) use of the gross revenue method of amortizing capitalized costs of oil and gas properties by entities using the full cost method of accounting, and (ii) the inclusion of methane gas within the definition of proved oil and gas reserves.

FOR FURTHER INFORMATION CONTACT: Robert F. Lavery or John W. Albert (202-272-2130), Office of the Chief Accountant, or Robert Bayless (202-272-2553), Division of Corporation Finance, Securities and Exchange Commission, Washington, D.C. 20549.

SUPPLEMENTARY INFORMATION: The statements in staff accounting bulletins are not rules or interpretations of the Commission nor are they published as bearing the Commission's official approval. They represent interpretations and practices followed by the Division of Corporate Finance and the Office of the Chief Accountant in administering the disclosure requirements of the Federal securities laws.

PART 211—(AMENDED)

Part 211 of Title 17 of the Code of Federal Regulations is amended by adding Staff Accounting Bulletin No. 85 to the table found in Subpart B.

STAFF ACCOUNTING BULLETIN NO.85

The staff hereby adds Sections F and G to Topic 12 of the staff accounting bulletin series. Section F discusses the staff's views regarding use of the gross revenue method of amortizing capitalized costs of oil and gas properties, and Section G discusses the inclusion of methane gas within proved reserves for purposes of presenting the standardized measure of discounted future net cash flows and applying the full cost ceiling test.

[For the text of Topic 12-F and G, see ¶ 39,211.]

[¶ 39,049]   RELEASE No. 86, September 28, 1989

Quasi-Reorganizations

ACTION: Publication of Staff Accounting Bulletin.

SUMMARY: Staff Accounting Bulletin No. 78 ("SAB 78"), which was released on August 25, 1988, expressed the staff's views regarding certain matters relating to quasi-reorganizations, including deficit eliminations. Since the issuance of SAB 78, the staff has received inquiries about its position concerning the accounting for the tax benefits of operating loss carryforwards that existed as of the date of a quasi-reorganization that are subsequently recognized in the financial statements. This staff accounting bulletin addresses this issue.

FOR FURTHER INFORMATION CONTACT: Kenneth V. Moreland, Office of the Chief Accountant (202/272-2130); or Robert A. Bayless (202/272-2553), Division of Corporation Finance, Securities and Exchange Commission, 450 Fifth Avenue, N.W., Washington, D.C. 20549.

SUPPLEMENTARY INFORMATION: The statements in Staff Accounting Bulletins are not rules or interpretations of the Commission nor are they published as bearing the Commission's official approval. They represent interpretations and practices followed by the Division of Corporation Finance and the Office of the Chief Accountant in administering the disclosure requirements of the Federal securities laws.

STAFF ACCOUNTING BULLETIN NO. 86

The staff herein adds questions 4 and 5 to Section S of Topic 5 of the Staff Accounting Bulletin Series. Section S discusses certain matters related to quasi-reorganizations, including deficit eliminations.

[For the text of Topic 5-S, see ¶ 39,141.]

[¶ 39,050]   RELEASE No. 87, December 12, 1989

Contingency Disclosures Regarding Property-Casualty Insurance Reserves for Unpaid Claim Costs

ACTION: Publication of Staff Accounting Bulletin.

SUMMARY: This staff accounting bulletin expresses the staff's views regarding contingency disclosures on property-casualty insurance reserves for unpaid claim costs.

FOR FURTHER INFORMATION CONTACT: James W. Barge Office of the Chief Accountant (202-272-2130), Robert A. Bayless, Division of Corporation Finance (202-272-2553), or Michael L. Hund, Division of Corporation Finance (202-272-3233), Securities and Exchange Commission, 450 Fifth Street, N.W., Washington, D.C. 20549.

SUPPLEMENTARY INFORMATION: The statements in staff accounting bulletins are not rules or interpretations of the Commission nor are they published as bearing the Commission's official approval. They represent interpretations and practices followed by the Division of Corporation Finance and the Office of the Chief Accountant in administering the disclosure requirements of the Federal securities laws.

Part 211 of Title 17 of the Code of Federal Regulations is amended by adding Staff Accounting Bulletin No. 87 to the table found in Subpart B.

STAFF ACCOUNTING BULLETIN NO. 87

The staff hereby adds Section W to Topic 5 of the Staff Accounting Bulletin Series. Topic 5-W discusses contingency disclosures related to property-casualty insurance reserves for unpaid claim costs.

[For the text of Topic 5-W, see ¶ 39,141.]

[¶ 39,051]   RELEASE No. 88, August 10, 1990

Views Regarding the Requirements of Item 17 of Form 20-F which Relate to Reconciliation of Financial Measurements and Disclosures in Financial Statements Prepared on a Comprehensive Basis of Accounting other than U.S. Generally Accepted Accounting Principles

ACTION: Publication of Staff Accounting Bulletin.

SUMMARY: This staff accounting bulletin expresses certain views of the staff regarding the requirements of Item 17 of Form 20-F which relate to reconciliation of financial measurements and disclosures in financial statements prepared on a comprehensive basis of accounting other than U.S. generally accepted accounting principles.

FOR FURTHER INFORMATION CONTACT: Richard J. Reinhard, Office of the Chief Accountant (202-272-2130), or Robert A. Bayless or Teresa E. Iannaconi, Division of Corporation Finance (202-272-2553), Securities and Exchange Commission, 450 Fifth Street, N.W., Washington, D.C. 20549.

SUPPLEMENTARY INFORMATION: The statements in staff accounting bulletins are not rules or interpretations of the Commission nor are they published as bearing the Commission's official approval. They represent interpretations and practices followed by the Division of Corporation Finance and the Office of the Chief Accountant in administering the disclosure requirements of the Federal Securities laws.

Part 211—(AMENDED)

Accordingly, Part 211 of Title 17 of the Code of Federal Regulations is amended by adding Staff Accounting Bulletin No. 88 to the table found in Subpart B.

STAFF ACCOUNTING BULLETIN NO. 88

The staff hereby adds Section D.1. to Topic 1 of the staff accounting bulletin series. Section D.1 of Topic 1 sets forth the interpretive position of the Division of Corporation Finance and the Office of the Chief Accountant with respect to the requirements of Item 17 of Form 20-F to provide reconciliation of financial measurements and disclosures in financial statements prepared on a basis other than U.S. generally accepted accounting principles.

[For the text of Topic 1-D-1, see ¶ 39,101.]

[¶ 39,052]   RELEASE No. 89, January 7, 1991

Views Regarding the Application of Rules 3-05 and 11-01 of Regulation S-X and the Availability of Waivers of Certain Financial Institutions Acquired or to be Acquired that Are Required to Be Included in Filings With the Commission

ACTION: Publication of Staff Accounting Bulletin.

SUMMARY: The interpretations in this staff accounting bulletin express certain views of the staff regarding the application of Rules 3-05 and 11-01 of Regulation S-X and the availability of waivers of certain financial statement requirements with respect to troubled financial institutions acquired or to be acquired that are required to be included in filings with the Commission.

FOR FURTHER INFORMATION CONTACT: Gregory W. Norwood, Office of the Chief Accountant (202-272-2130), or Robert Bayless, Division of Corporation Finance (202-272-2553), Securities and Exchange Commission, 450 Fifth Street, N.W., Washington, D.C. 20549.

SUPPLEMENTARY INFORMATION: The statements in staff accounting bulletins are not rules or interpretations of the Commission nor are they published as bearing the Commission's official approval. They represent interpretations and practices followed by the Division of Corporation Finance and the Office of the Chief Accountant in administering the disclosure requirements of the Federal Securities laws.

Part 211—(AMEND)

Accordingly, Part 211 of Title 17 of the Code of Federal Regulations is amended by adding Staff Accounting Bulletin No. 89 to the table found in Subpart B.

STAFF ACCOUNTING BULLETIN NO. 89

The staff hereby adds Section K to Topic 1 of the staff accounting bulletin series. Topic 1-K sets forth the administrative policy of the Division of Corpora-

tion Finance and the Office of the Chief Accountant as to the application of Rules 3-05 and 11-01 of Regulation S-X to the requirements for financial statements of troubled financial institutions acquired or to be acquired which are required to be included in filings with the Commission.

[For the text of Topic 1-K, see ¶ 39,101.]

[¶ 39,053] RELEASE No. 90, January 31, 1991

Views Regarding the Bankruptcy of an Accounting Firm that had Public Company Clients

ACTION: Publication of Staff Accounting Bulleting.

SUMMARY: The Commission has authorized the staff to publish this staff accounting bulletin which sets forth staff intepretations on various matters relating to Laventhol & Horwath ("L&H"), a public accounting firm which filed for bankruptcy on November 21, 1990 and ceased to performe audit and accounting services. These interpretations are intended to provide guidance as to the disclosure to be provided by, and the relief to be granted to, registrants who are former clients of L&H. As a result of L&H's actions, a number of public reporting audit clients will be unable to file a manually signed audit report pursuant to Rule 2-02 of Regulation S-X and, in connection with registered public securities offerings, a manually signed accountants' consent pursuant to Section 7 of the Securities Act of 1933 and Rule 436 of Regulation C thereunder.

FOR FURTHER INFORMATION CONTACT: Teresa E. Iannaconi, Division of Corporation Finance, (202-272-2553); John M. Riley, Office of the Chief Accountant, (202-272-2130); or Lawrence A. Friend, Division of Investment Management, (202-272-7716), Securities and Exchange Commission, 450 Fifth Street, N.W., Washington, D.C. 20549.

SUPPLEMENTARY INFORMATION: The Commission has authorized the staff to issue this staff ac-

counting bulletin setting forth interpretations and practices to be followed by the Division of Corporation Finance, the Office of the Chief Accountant and, the Division of Investment Management in administering the disclosure requirements of the Federal Securities laws with respect to registrants who are former clients of Laventhol & Horwath, a public accounting firm that filed a bankruptcy petition on November 21, 1990, and ceased to perform audit and accounting services.

Part 211—(AMEND)

Accordingly, Part 211 of Title 17 of the Code of Federal Regulations is amended by adding Staff Accounting Bulletin No. 90 to the table found in Subpart B.

STAFF ACCOUNTING BULLETIN NO. 90

The staff hereby adds Section L to Topic 1 of the staff accounting bulletin series. Topic 1-L indicates the disclosure to be made and relief that may be sought by registrants who are former clients of Laventhol & Horwath, a public accounting firm, which filed a bankruptcy petition on November 21, 1990.

[For the text of Topic 1-L, see ¶ 74,101.]

[¶ 39,054] RELEASE No. 91, July 17, 1991

Accounting for Income Tax Benefits of Bad Debts of Thrifts

ACTION: Publication of Staff Accounting Bulletin.

SUMMARY: Staff Accounting Bulletin No. 91 ("SAB 91"), which was release on July 17, 1991, expresses the staff's views regarding the accounting for income tax benefits of thrift bad debt losses. This staff accounting bulletin is intended to serve as interim guidance until a new standard on accounting for income taxes is adopted.

FOR FURTHER INFORMATION CONTACT: Margaret Ruffin Horvath, Office of the Chief Accountant (202-272-2130); or Robert A. Bayless, Division of Corporation Finance (202-272-2553); Securities and Exchange Commission, 450 Fifth Street, N.W., Washington, D.C. 20549.

SUPPLEMENTARY INFORMATION: The statements in staff accounting bulletins are not rules or

interpretations of the Commission nor are they published as bearing the Commission's official approval. They represent interpretations and practices followed by the Division of Corporation Finance and the Office of the Chief Accountant in administering the disclosure requirements of the Federal securities laws.

Part 211 (AMEND)

Accordingly, Part 211 of Title 17 of the Code of Federal Regulations is amended by adding Staff Accounting Bulletin No. 91 to the table found in Subpart B.

STAFF ACCOUNTING BULLETIN NO. 91

The staff hereby adds Section X to Topic 5 of the Staff Accounting Bulletin Series. Topic 5-X discusses accounting for the income tax benefits associated with bad debts of thrifts.

[For the text of Topic 5-X, see ¶ 39,141.]

[¶ 39,055]   RELEASE No. 92, June 8, 1993

Accounting and Disclosures Relating to Loss Contingencies

ACTION: Publication of Staff Accounting Bulletin.

SUMMARY: The interpretations in this staff accounting bulletin express certain views of the staff regarding accounting and disclosures relating to loss contingencies.

FOR FURTHER INFORMATION CONTACT: Randall Larson, Office of the Chief Accountant (202-272-2130), or Kurt Hohl, Division of Corporation Finance (202-272-2553), Securities and Exchange Commission, 450 Fifth Street, N.W., Washington, D.C. 20549.

SUPPLEMENTARY INFORMATION: The statements in staff accounting bulletins are not rules or interpretations of the Commission nor are they published as bearing the Commission's official approval. They represent interpretations and practices followed by the Division of Corporation Finance and the Office of the Chief Accountant in administering the disclosure requirements of the Federal securities laws.

Part 211—(AMENDED)

Accordingly, Part 211 of Title 17 of the Code of Federal Regulations is amended by adding Staff Accounting Bulletin No. 92 to the table found in Subpart B.

STAFF ACCOUNTING BULLETIN NO. 92

The staff hereby adds Section Y to Topic 5 of the Staff Accounting Bulletin Series. Topic 5-Y provides guidance regarding the accounting and disclosures relating to loss contingencies. In addition, the staff hereby adds Question 7 to Topic 2-A and adds Section F to Topic 10. Question 7 of Topic 2-A discusses loss contingencies assumed in a business combination accounted for as a purchase. Topic 10-F discusses the presentation by utility companies of liabilities for environmental costs.

[For the text of Topics 2-A, 5-Y and 10-F, see ¶ 39,111; 39,141 and 39,191.]

[¶ 39,056]   RELEASE No. 93, November 4, 1993

Accounting and Disclosures Relating to Discontinued Operations

ACTION: Publication of Staff Accounting Bulletin.

SUMMARY: The interpretations in this staff accounting bulletin express certain views of the staff regarding accounting and disclosures relating to discontinued operations.

FOR FURTHER INFORMATION CONTACT: Jeffrey Swormstedt, Office of the Chief Accountant (202-272-2130), or Craig Olinger, Division of Corporation Finance (202-272-2553), Securities and Exchange Commission, 450 Fifth Street, N.W., Washington, D.C. 20549.

SUPPLEMENTARY INFORMATION: The statements in staff accounting bulletins are not rules or interpretations of the Commission nor are they published as bearing the Commission's official approval. They represent interpretations and practices followed

by the Division of Corporation Finance and the Office of the Chief Accountant in administering the disclosure requirements of the Federal securities laws.

Part 211—(AMEND)

Accordingly, Part 211 of Title 17 of the Code of Federal Regulations is amended by adding Staff Accounting Bulletin No. 93 to the table found in Subpart B.

STAFF ACCOUNTING BULLETIN NO. 93

The staff hereby adds Section Z to Topic 5 of the Staff Accounting Bulletin Series. Topic 5-Z provides guidance regarding the accounting and disclosures relating to discontinued operations.

[For the text of Topic 5-Z, see ¶ 39,141.]

[¶ 39,057]   RELEASE No. 94, April 18, 1995

Recognition of a Gain or Loss on Early Extinguishment of Debt

ACTION: Publication of Staff Accounting Bulletin.

SUMMARY: The interpretations in this staff accounting bulletin express the views of the staff regarding the period n which a gain or loss is recognized on the early extinguishment of debt.

FOR FURTHER INFORMATION CONTACT: Tracy Barber, Office of Chief Accountant (202) 942-4400, or Douglas Tanner, Division of Corporation Finance

(202) 942-2960, Securities and Exchange Commission, 450 Fifth Street N.W., Washington, D.C. 20549.

SUPPLEMENTARY INFORMATION: The statements in staff accounting bulletins are not rules or interpretations of the Commission nor are they published as bearing the Commission's official approval. They represent interpretations and practices followed by the Division of Corporation Finance and the Office of the Chief Accountant in administering the disclosure requirements of the Federal securities laws.

Part 211—(AMEND)

Accordingly, Part 211 of Title 17 of the Code of Federal Regulations is amended by adding Staff Accounting Bulletin No. 94 to the table found in Subpart B.

STAFF ACCOUNTING BULLETIN NO. 94

The staff hereby adds Section AA to Topic 5 of the Staff Accounting Bulletin Series. Topic 5-AA provides guidance regarding the period in which a gain or loss is recognized on the early extinguishment of debt.

[For the text of Topic 5-AA, see ¶ 39,141.]

[¶ 39,058]   RELEASE No. 95, December 15, 1995

Rescission of SAB No. 57 (Topic 5-K—Contingent Stock Purchase Warrants)

ACTION: Publication of Staff Accounting Bulletin.

SUMMARY: This staff accounting bulletin rescinds the views of the staff contained in Staff Accounting Bulletin No. 57 (Topic 5-K—Contingent Stock Purchase Warrants).

FOR FURTHER INFORMATION CONTACT: Michael Morrissey, Office of the Chief Accountant (202) 942-4400, or Douglas Tanner, Division of Corporation Finance (202) 942-2960, Securities and Exchange Commission, 450 Fifth Street N.W., Washington, D.C. 20549.

SUPPLEMENTARY INFORMATION: The statements in staff accounting bulletins are not rules or interpretations of the Commission nor are they published as bearing the Commission's official approval. They represent interpretations and practices followed by the Division of Corporation Finance and the Office of the Chief Accountant in administering the disclosure requirements of the Federal securities laws.

Part 211—(AMEND)

Accordingly, Part 211 of Title 17 of the Code of Federal Regulations is amended by adding Staff Accounting Bulletin No. 95 to the table found in Subpart B.

STAFF ACCOUNTING BULLETIN NO. 95

The staff hereby deletes Staff Accounting Bulletin No. 57 (Section K to Topic of the Staff Accounting Bulletin Series). Staff Accounting Bulletin No. 57 pro-

vided interpretative guidance on the accounting for contingent stock purchase warrants. Footnote 2 to Staff Accounting Bulletin No. 57 notes that in March 1984, the Financial Accounting Standards Board (FASB) added a project to its agenda to reconsider Accounting Principles Board Opinion No. 25, *Accounting for Stock Issued to Employees* (APB 25). Footnote 2 indicates that when this project is completed, the staff will consider whether the accounting articulated in this staff accounting bulletin is still appropriate.

The FASB's reconsideration of APB 25 is now complete with the issuance of Statement of Financial Accounting Standards No. 123, *Accounting for Stock-Based Compensation* (FAS 123). Consistent with our stated intention, the staff has reconsidered the guidance in Staff Accounting Bulletin No. 57 and concludes that the interpretative guidance providing for an intrinsic value measurement is no longer necessary due to the general guidance in FAS 123 that provides for fair value measurement for transactions with other than employees.

FAS 123 does not provide specific guidance on the methodology for determining fair value for such an arrangement or the measurement date on which the fair value of the equity instrument is determined. The staff intends to request that the Emerging Issues Task Force consider the need to issue additional guidance that would address those issues.

[Rescission of SAB-57 and Topic 5-K, at ¶ 39,020 and 39,141.]

[¶ 39,059]   RELEASE No. 96, March 19, 1996

Treasury Stock Acquisition Following Consummation of a Business Combination Accounted for as a Pooling-of-Interests

ACTION: Publication of Staff Accounting Bulletin.

SUMMARY: The interpretations in this staff accounting bulletin express certain views of the staff regarding treasury stock acquisitions following a business combination accounted for as a pooling-of-interests.

FOR FURTHER INFORMATION CONTACT: Mary Tokar or Brian Heckler, Office of the Chief Accountant (202-942-4400), or Kurt Hohl, Division of Corporation Finance (202-942-2960), Securities and Exchange Commission, 450 Fifth Street, N.W., Washington, D.C. 20549.

SUPPLEMENTARY INFORMATION: The statements in staff accounting bulletins are not rules or interpretations of the Commission nor are they published as bearing the Commission's official approval. They represent interpretations and practices followed by the Division of Corporation Finance and the Office of the Chief Accountant in administering the disclosure requirements of the Federal securities laws.

PART 211—(AMEND)

Accordingly, Part 211 of Title 17 of the Code of Federal Regulations is amended by adding Staff Accounting Bulletin No. 96 to the table found in Subpart B.

STAFF ACCOUNTING BULLETIN NO. 96

The staff hereby adds Section F to Topic 2 of the Staff Accounting Bulletin Series. Topic 2-F provides guidance regarding the effect of treasury stock acqui-

sitions following consummation of a business combination accounted for as a pooling-of-interests.

[For the text of Topic 2-F, see ¶ 39,111.]

[¶ 39,060]

RELEASE No. 97, July 31, 1996

The Inappropriate Application of Staff Accounting Bulletin No. 48, *Transfers of Nonmonetary Assets by Promoters or Shareholders,* to Purchase Business Combinations Consummated Just Prior to or Concurrent With an Initial Public Offering, and the Identification of an Accounting Acquirer in Accordance With APB Opinion No. 16, *Business Combinations,* for Purchase Business Combinations Involving More Than Two Entities

ACTION: Publication of Staff Accounting Bulletin.

SUMMARY: The interpretations in this staff accounting bulletin express the views of the staff regarding 1) the inappropriate application of Staff Accounting Bulletin No. 48, Transfers of Nonmonetary Assets by Promoters or Shareholders, to purchase business combinations consummated just prior to or concurrent with an initial public offering, and 2) the identification of an accounting acquirer in accordance with APB Opinion No. 16, Business Combinations, for purchase business combinations involving more than two entities.

FOR FURTHER INFORMATION CONTACT: Brian Heckler, Office of the Chief Accountant (202-942-4400), or Douglas Tanner, Division of Corporation Finance (202-942-2960), Securities and Exchange Commission, 450 Fifth Street, N.W., Washington, D.C. 20549.

SUPPLEMENTARY INFORMATION: The statements in staff accounting bulletins are not rules or interpretations of the Commission, nor are they published as bearing the Commission's official approval.

They represent interpretations and practices followed by the Division of Corporation Finance and the Office of the Chief Accountant in administering the disclosure requirements of the Federal securities laws.

Part 211—(AMEND)

Accordingly, Part 211 of Title 17 of the Code of Federal Regulations is amended by adding Staff Accounting Bulletin No. 97 to the table found in Subpart B.

STAFF ACCOUNTING BULLETIN NO. 97

The staff hereby adds Item 8 and Question 2 to Item 2 to Section A of Topic 2 of the Staff Accounting Bulletin Series. Item 8 of Topic 2:A provides guidance regarding the applicability of SAB No. 48 to purchase business combinations just prior to or concurrent with an initial public offering. Question 2 of Topic 2:A(2) provides the staff's views regarding the identification of an accounting acquirer in a business combination involving more than two entities.

[For the text of Topic 2-A, see ¶ 39,111.]

[¶ 39,061]

RELEASE No. 98, February 3, 1998

Revision of Certain SAB Topics to Reflect the Provisions of Statement of Financial Accounting Standards (SFAS) No. 128, *Earnings Per Share* and SFAS No. 130, *Reporting Comprehensive Income*

ACTION: Publication of Staff Accounting Bulletin.

SUMMARY: This staff accounting bulletin revises the views of the staff contained in certain topics of the staff accounting bulletin series to be consistent with the provisions of certain accounting standards recently adopted by the Financial Accounting Standards Board. Topics include: Topic 1.B—Allocation of Expenses and Related Disclosure in Financial Statements of Subsidiaries, Divisions or Lesser Business Components of Another Entity; Topic 3.A—Convertible Securities; Topic 4.D—Earnings per Share Computations in an Initial Public Offering; Topic 6.B.1—Income or Loss Applicable to Common Stock; and, Topic 6.G.1—Selected Quarterly Financial Data (Item 302(a) of Regulation S-K).

EFFECTIVE DATE: February 3, 1998.

FOR FURTHER INFORMATION CONTACT: Cody L. Smith, Office of the Chief Accountant

(202-942-4400), Kenneth T. Marceron, Division of Corporation Finance (202-942-2960), Securities and Exchange Commission, 450 Fifth Street, N.W., Washington, D.C. 20549.

SUPPLEMENTARY INFORMATION: The statements in staff accounting bulletins are not rules or interpretations of the Commission, nor are they published as bearing the Commission's official approval. They represent interpretations and practices followed by the Division of Corporation Finance and the Office of the Chief Accountant in administering the disclosure requirements of the Federal securities laws.

Part 211—(AMEND)

Accordingly, Part 211 of Title 17 of the Code of Federal Regulations is amended by adding Staff Accounting Bulletin No. 98 to the table found in Subpart B.

STAFF ACCOUNTING BULLETIN NO. 98

The staff hereby amends the following in the Staff Accounting Bulletin Series:

(a) Topics 1.B.2 and 1.B.3, regarding the allocation of expenses and related disclosure in financial statements of subsidiaries, divisions or lesser business components of another entity to eliminate instructions to delete historical EPS in the entity's financial statements;

(b) Topic 3.A, regarding the presentation of supplemental earnings per share in a convertible security registration to remove the reference to APB Opinion No. 15, Earnings per Share, and remind registrants of the pro forma requirements of Regulation S-X;

(c) Topic 4.D, regarding the computation of earnings per share in an initial public offering (IPO) to revise instructions regarding the dilutive effects of stock issued for consideration below the IPO price or op-

tions and warrants to purchase common stock with exercise prices below the IPO price. New guidance highlights the treatment that should be given to the dilutive effect of common stock or options and warrants to purchase common stock issued for nominal consideration (referred to as nominal issuances);

(d) Topic 6.B.1, regarding the presentation of income or loss applicable to common stock to clarify the Topic's continuing applicability to all registrants and to suggest a presentation format for registrants that elect to present a single statement of income and comprehensive income; and

(e) Topic 6.G.1, regarding selected quarterly financial data to replace the terms "primary" and "fully diluted" with "basic" and "diluted."

[For the text of Topic 1-B-2 and 1-B-3, see ¶ 39,101; text of Topic 3-A, see ¶ 39,121; text of Topic 4-D, see ¶ 39,131; text of Topic 6-B-1 and Topic 6-G-1, see ¶ 39,151.]

[¶ 39,062]   RELEASE No. 99, August 12, 1999

Materiality

ACTION: Publication of Staff Accounting Bulletin

SUMMARY: This staff accounting bulletin expresses the views of the staff that exclusive reliance on certain quantitative benchmarks to assess materiality in preparing financial statements and performing audits of those financial statements is inappropriate; misstatements are not immaterial simply because they fall beneath a numerical threshold.

DATE: August 12, 1999

FOR FURTHER INFORMATION CONTACT: W. Scott Bayless, Associate Chief Accountant, or Robert E. Burns, Chief Counsel, Office of the Chief Accountant (202-942-4400), or David R. Fredrickson, Office of General Counsel (202-942-0900), Securities and Exchange Commission, 450 Fifth Street, N.W., Washington, D.C. 20549-1103; electronic addresses: BaylessWS@sec.gov; BurnsR@sec.gov; FredricksonD@sec.gov.

SUPPLEMENTARY INFORMATION: The statements in the staff accounting bulletins are not rules or

interpretations of the Commission, nor are they published as bearing the Commission's official approval. They represent interpretations and practices followed by the Division of Corporation Finance and the Office of the Chief Accountant in administering the disclosure requirements of the Federal securities laws.

Part 211—(AMEND)

Accordingly, Part 211 of Title 17 of the Code of Federal Regulations is amended by adding Staff Accounting Bulletin No. 99 to the table found in Subpart B.

STAFF ACCOUNTING BULLETIN NO. 99

The staff hereby adds Section M to Topic 1 of the Staff Accounting Bulletin Series. Section M, entitled "Materiality," provides guidance in applying materiality thresholds to the preparation of financial statements filed with the Commission and the performance of audits of those financial statements.

[For the text of Topic 1-M, see ¶ 39,101.]

[¶ 39,063]   RELEASE No. 100, November 24, 1999

Restructuring and Impairment Charges

ACTION: Publication of Staff Accounting Bulletin

SUMMARY: This staff accounting bulletin expresses views of the staff regarding the accounting for and disclosure of certain expenses commonly reported in connection with exit activities and business combinations. This includes accrual of exit and employee termination costs pursuant to Emerging Issues Task Force (EITF) Issues No. 94-3, *Liability Recognition for Certain Employee Termination Benefits and Other Costs to Exit an Activity (Including Certain Costs Incurred in a Restructuring)*, and No. 95-3, *Recognition of Liabilities in Connection with a Purchase Business*

Combination, and the recognition of impairment charges pursuant to Accounting Principles Board (APB) Opinion No. 17, *Intangible Assets*, and Statement of Financial Accounting Standards (SFAS) No. 121, *Accounting for the Impairment of Long-Lived Assets and for Long-Lived Assets to be Disposed Of*.

DATE: Effective November 24, 1999

FOR FURTHER INFORMATION CONTACT: Eric Jacobsen, Paul Kepple, or Eric Casey, Office of the Chief Accountant (202-942-4400), Robert Bayless, Division of Corporation Finance (202-942-2960), Securities and Exchange Commission, 450 Fifth Street,

N.W., Washington, D.C., 20549; electronic addresses: jacobsene@sec.gov; kepplep@sec.gov; caseye@sec.gov; baylessr@sec.gov.

SUPPLEMENTARY INFORMATION: The statements in staff accounting bulletins are not rules or interpretations of the Commission, nor are they published as bearing the Commission's official approval. They represent interpretations and practices followed by the Division of Corporation Finance and the Office of the Chief Accountant in administering the disclosure requirements of the Federal securities laws.

Part 211 - (AMEND)

Accordingly, Part 211 of Title 17 of the Code of Federal Regulations is amended by adding Staff Accounting Bulletin No. 100 to the table found in Subpart B.

STAFF ACCOUNTING BULLETIN NO. 100

1. Amend Section A of Topic 2 of the Staff Accounting Bulletin Series to add new subsection 9. *Liabilities Assumed in a Purchase Business Combination.* Revise the title of Section P of Topic 5 to *Restructuring Charges,* designate the current section P as subsection 3 of Section P of Topic 5, *Income Statement Presentation of Restructuring Charges,* deleting the first paragraph under that subsection, and renumbering Questions 1, 2, and 3 in that subsection to be Questions 13, 14, and 15. Add new subsection 1. *Characteristics of an Exit Plan* to Section P of Topic 5. Add new subsection 2. *Characteristics of an Exit Cost* to Section P of Topic 5. Add new subsection 4. *Disclosures.* to Section P of Topic 5 Furthermore, add new Sections BB. *Inventory Valuation Allowances* and CC. *Impairments* to Topic 5.

[For the text of Topic 2A, see ¶ 39,111. For the text of Topic 5-P, 5-BB, and 5-CC, see ¶ 39,141. CCH.]

⸽→ Caution: See also frequently asked questions and answers at ¶ 39,067.

[¶ 39,064]   **RELEASE No. 101, December 3, 1999**

Revenue Recognition in Financial Statements

ACTION: Publication of Staff Accounting Bulletin

SUMMARY: This staff accounting bulletin summarizes certain of the staff's views in applying generally accepted accounting principles to revenue recognition in financial statements. The staff is providing this guidance due, in part, to the large number of revenue recognition issues that registrants encounter. For example, a March 1999 report entitled *Fraudulent Financial Reporting: 1987-1997 An Analysis of U. S. Public Companies,* sponsored by the Committee of Sponsoring Organizations (COSO) of the Treadway Commission, indicated that over half of financial reporting frauds in the study involved overstating revenue.

DATE: Effective December 3, 1999

FOR FURTHER INFORMATION CONTACT: Richard Rodgers, Scott Taub, or Eric Jacobsen, Professional Accounting Fellows (202/942-4400) or Robert Bayless, Division of Corporation Finance (202/942-2960), Securities and Exchange Commission, 450 Fifth Street, NW, Washington, DC 20549; electronic addresses: RodgersR@sec.gov; TaubS@sec.gov; JacobsenE@sec.gov; BaylessR@sec.gov.

SUPPLEMENTARY INFORMATION: The statements in the staff accounting bulletins are not rules or interpretations of the Commission, nor are they published as bearing the Commission's official approval. They represent interpretations and practices followed by the Division of Corporation Finance and the Office of the Chief Accountant in administering the disclosure requirements of the Federal securities laws.

Part 211 - (AMEND)

Accordingly, Part 211 of Title 17 of the Code of Federal Regulations is amended by adding Staff Accounting Bulletin No. 101 to the table found in Subpart B.

STAFF ACCOUNTING BULLETIN NO. 101

The staff hereby adds new major Topic 13, "Revenue Recognition," and Topic 13-A, "Views on Selected Revenue Recognition Issues," to the Staff Accounting Bulletin Series. Topic 13-A provides the staff's views in applying generally accepted accounting principles to selected revenue recognition issues. In addition, the staff hereby revises Topic 8-A to conform to FASB Statement No. 13, *Accounting for Leases.*

[For the text of Topic 8, See ¶ 39,171. For the text of Topic 13 and 13-A, see ¶ 39,221. CCH.]

[¶ 39,065]   **RELEASE No. 101A, March 24, 2000**

Amendment: Revenue Recognition in Financial Statements (delay of SAB 101 implementation)

ACTION: Publication of Staff Accounting Bulletin

SUMMARY: Staff Accounting Bulletin No. 101 ("SAB 101") was released on December 3, 1999 (64FR68936 December 9, 1999) and provides the staff's views in

applying generally accepted accounting principles to selected revenue recognition issues. Since the issuance of SAB 101, the staff received requests from a number of groups asking for additional time to study the guidance. Many registrants have calendar year-ends and may need more time to perform a detailed review of the SAB since its issuance on December 3, 1999. This staff accounting bulletin delays the implementation date of SAB 101 for registrants with fiscal years that begin between December 16, 1999 and March 15, 2000.

DATE: March 24, 2000

FOR FURTHER INFORMATION CONTACT: Richard Rodgers, Scott Taub, or Eric Jacobsen, Professional Accounting Fellows, Office of the Chief Accountant (202/942-4400) or Robert Bayless, Division of Corporation Finance (202/942-2960), Securities and Exchange Commission, 450 Fifth Street, NW, Washington, DC 20549; electronic addresses: RodgersR@sec.gov; TaubS@sec.gov; JacobsenE@sec.gov; or BaylessR@sec.gov.

SUPPLEMENTARY INFORMATION: The statements in the staff accounting bulletins are not rules or interpretations of the Commission, nor are they published as bearing the Commission's official approval. They represent interpretations and practices followed by the Division of Corporation Finance and the Office of the Chief Accountant in administering the disclosure requirements of the Federal securities laws.

Part 211 - (AMEND)

Accordingly, Part 211 of Title 17 of the Code of Federal Regulations is amended by adding Staff Accounting Bulletin No. 101A to the table found in Subpart B.

STAFF ACCOUNTING BULLETIN NO. 101A

The staff hereby amends Question 2 of Section B of Topic 13 of the Staff Accounting Bulletin Series.

[For the text of Topic 13-B, see ¶ 39,221. CCH]

[¶ 39,066]   RELEASE No. 101B, June 26, 2000

Second Amendment: Revenue Recognition in Financial Statements (Delay of SAB 101 Implementation)

Action: Publication of Staff Accounting Bulletin

Summary: Staff Accounting Bulletin No. 101 ("SAB 101") was released on December 3, 1999 (64 FR 68936 December 9, 1999) and provides the staff's views in applying generally accepted accounting principles to selected revenue recognition issues. SAB 101A was released on March 24, 2000 (65 FR 16811 March 30, 2000) and delayed for one fiscal quarter the implementation date of SAB 101 for registrants with fiscal years beginning between December 16, 1999 and March 15, 2000. Since the issuance of SAB 101 and SAB 101A, the staff has continued to receive requests from a number of groups asking for additional time to determine the effect, if any, on registrant's revenue recognition practices. This staff accounting bulletin delays the implementation date of SAB 101 until no later than the fourth fiscal quarter of fiscal years beginning after December 15, 1999.

Date: June 26, 2000

For Further Information Contact: Richard Rodgers, Scott Taub, or Eric Jacobsen, Professional Accounting Fellows, Office of the Chief Accountant (202/942-4400) or Robert Bayless, Division of Corporation Finance (202/942-2960), Securities and Exchange Commission, 450 Fifth Street, NW, Washington, DC 20549; electronic addresses: RodgersR@sec.gov; TaubS@sec.gov; JacobsenE@sec.gov; or BaylessR@sec.gov.

Supplementary Information: The statements in the staff accounting bulletins are not rules or interpretations of the Commission, nor are they published as bearing the Commission's official approval. They represent interpretations and practices followed by the Division of Corporation Finance and the Office of the Chief Accountant in administering the disclosure requirements of the Federal securities laws.

Jonathan G. Katz Secretary

Date: June 26, 2000

Part 211 - (AMEND)

Accordingly, Part 211 of Title 17 of the Code of Federal Regulations is amended by adding Staff Accounting Bulletin No. 101B to the table found in Subpart B.

STAFF ACCOUNTING BULLETIN NO. 101B

The staff hereby amends Question 2 of Section B of Topic 13 of the Staff Accounting Bulletin Series.

[For the text of Topic 13-B, see ¶ 39,221. CCH.]

[¶ 39,067] Frequently Asked Questions and Answers about Staff Accounting Bulletin No. 101— Revenue Recognition in Financial Statements (Office of the Chief Accountant October 12, 2000)

On December 3, 1999, the Securities and Exchange Commission staff issued Staff Accounting Bulletin No. 101 (SAB 101). Staff Accounting Bulletins do not represent rules or interpretations of the Commission but rather represent the interpretations and practices followed by the Division of Corporation Finance and the Office of the Chief Accountant in administering the disclosure requirements of the Federal securities laws. SAB 101 reflects the basic principles of revenue recognition in existing generally accepted accounting principles (GAAP). SAB 101 does not supersede any existing authoritative literature.

Studies on financial reporting, such as the Committee of Sponsoring Organizations (COSO) Report issued in early 1999, indicate that a significant portion of fraudulent financial reporting involves improper revenue recognition. In recent years improper revenue recognition has been the single largest category of financial statement restatements.

One of the goals of SAB 101 is to summarize in one location the existing guidance on revenue recognition and make that guidance more accessible to registrants and their auditors.

Since the issuance of SAB 101, the staff has received inquiries from auditors, preparers, and analysts about how the guidance in accounting standards and SAB 101 would apply to particular transactions. This document responds to those inquiries. The staff worked with accounting firms and preparers to identify the recurring questions and develop answers to those questions.

The staff has deferred the implementation date of SAB 101 until no later than the fourth quarter of fiscal years beginning after December 15, 1999. Prior to implementing SAB 101, the staff reminds registrants and their auditors that certain disclosures are required by SAB Topic 11-M, *Disclosure of the Impact that Recently Issued Accounting Standards will have on the Financial Statements of the Registrant when Adopted in a Future Period*; American Institute of Certified Public Accountants (AICPA) Professional Standards AU section 9410, Item 3, *The Impact on an Auditor's Report of an FASB Statement Prior to the Statement's Effective Date*; and Regulation S-K, Item 303, *Management's Discussion and Analysis of Financial Condition and Results of Operations*.

For further information contact: Scott Taub (*taubs@sec.gov*) or Scott Blackley (*blackleys@sec.gov*) in the Office of the Chief Accountant at (202) 942-4400 or Robert Bayless (*baylessr@sec.gov*) in the Division of Corporation Finance at (202) 942-2960.

Contents

Exhibit A: Effects of Customer Acceptance and Unfulfilled Obligations on Revenue Recognition

I. Topic 13.A. 2 and 13.A.3 – Transfer of Title

SAB 101 summarizes the staff's views on selected revenue recognition issues based upon existing generally accepted accounting principles. SAB 101 identifies four essential criteria that should be met before product revenue can be recognized. One of the criteria is that delivery has occurred. The staff's responses to Questions 2 and 3 in SAB 101 emphasize that a necessary element of the delivery of a tangible product is the transfer of its title. The staff has responded to questions concerning that guidance, as discussed below.

Question 1

Q: The laws of some countries do not provide for a seller's retention of a security interest in goods in the same manner as established in the U.S. Uniform Commercial Code (UCC). In these countries, it is common for a seller to retain a form of title to goods delivered to customers until the customer makes payment so that the seller can recover the goods in the event of customer default on payment. Is it acceptable to recognize revenue in these transactions before payment is made and title has transferred?

A: Presuming all other revenue recognition criteria have been met, the staff would not object to revenue recognition at delivery if the only rights that a seller retains with the title are those enabling recovery of the goods in the event of customer default on payment. This limited form of ownership may exist in some foreign jurisdictions where, despite technically holding title, the seller is not entitled to direct the disposition of the goods, cannot rescind the transaction, cannot prohibit its customer from moving, selling, or otherwise using the goods in the ordinary course of business, and has no other rights that rest with a titleholder of property that is subject to a lien under the U.S. UCC. On the other hand, if retaining title results in the seller retaining rights normally held by an owner of goods, the situation is not sufficiently different from a delivery of goods on consignment. In this particular case, revenue should not be recognized until payment is received. Registrants and their auditors may wish to consult legal counsel knowledgeable of the local law and customs outside the U.S. to determine the seller's rights.

II. Topic 13.A.3. – Substantial Performance and Acceptance

The guidance in Question 3 of SAB 101 applies to the delivery of products and performance of services not directly addressed by authoritative literature. For example, a transaction within the scope of AICPA Statement of Position (SOP) 81-1, *Accounting for Performance of Construction-Type and Certain Production-Type Contracts*, is not subject to the staff's views expressed in SAB 101. The staff's response to Question 3 in SAB 101 discusses accounting literature that should be considered in a registrant's evaluation of whether delivery of products or performance of services has occurred. The staff's response reiterates accounting literature that states:

(a) a seller should substantially complete or fulfill the terms specified in the sales arrangement,[1] and

(b) after delivery or performance, if uncertainty exists about customer acceptance, revenue should not be recognized until acceptance occurs.[2]

The staff has responded to questions concerning that guidance, as discussed below.

Question 2

Q: When accounting for sales of products and/or services in accordance with SAB 101, does the failure to deliver one item or perform one service specified by the sales arrangement *always* preclude immediate recognition of any revenue for the sales arrangement?

A: No. Assuming all other recognition criteria are met, the following circumstances exist under which revenue may be recognized for a sales arrangement, notwithstanding the seller's remaining obligation for additional performance or delivery.

(a) Revenue from the sales arrangement may be recognized in its entirety if the seller's remaining obligation is inconsequential or perfunctory. In this case, costs expected to be incurred upon fulfillment of the remaining obligation must be reliably[3] estimable and accrued when the revenue is recognized.[4] Question 3 below discusses how the staff evaluates whether the remaining obligation is inconsequential or perfunctory.

(b) A portion of the contract revenue may be recognized when the seller has substantially completed[5] or fulfilled the terms of a separate element of a multiple-element arrangement. Question 4 below discusses the accounting for multiple-element arrangements.

Question 3

Q: When applying SAB 101, what factors should be considered in the evaluation of whether a remaining obligation is inconsequential or perfunctory?

A: A remaining performance obligation is not inconsequential or perfunctory if it is essential to the functionality of the delivered products or services (see Question 7 below). In addition, remaining activities are not inconsequential or perfunctory if failure to complete the activities would result in the customer receiving a full or partial refund or rejecting (or a right to a refund or to reject) the products delivered or services performed to date. The terms of the sales contract regarding both the right to a full or partial refund and the right of return or rejection should be considered when evaluating whether a portion of the purchase price would be refundable. If the company

has a historical pattern of granting such rights, that historical pattern should also be considered even if the current contract expressly precludes such rights. Further, other factors should be considered in assessing whether remaining obligations are inconsequential or perfunctory. For example, the staff also considers the following factors, which are not all-inclusive, in evaluating whether a remaining performance obligation is substantive rather than inconsequential or perfunctory:

- The seller does not have a demonstrated history of completing the remaining tasks in a timely manner and reliably estimating their costs.

- The cost or time to perform the remaining obligations for similar contracts historically has varied significantly from one instance to another.

- The skills or equipment required to complete the remaining activity are specialized or are not readily available in the marketplace.

- The cost of completing the obligation, or the fair value of that obligation, is more than insignificant in relation to such items as the contract fee, gross profit, and operating income.

- The period before the remaining obligation will be extinguished is lengthy. Registrants should consider whether reasonably possible variations in the period to complete performance affect the certainty that the remaining obligations will be completed successfully and on budget.

- The timing of payment of a portion of the sales price is coincident with completing performance of the remaining activity.

Registrants' determinations of whether remaining obligations are inconsequential or perfunctory should be consistently applied.

Question 4

Q: Although SAB 101 does not establish a framework for accounting for multiple-element arrangements, what factors would the staff consider in assessing whether an arrangement is accounted for as a multiple-element arrangement?

A: SAB 101 does not modify existing practice in accounting for multiple-element arrangements. Recognizing the diversity in practice in the accounting for multiple-element arrangements and the complexity of these arrangements, the staff asked the Emerging Issues Task Force (EITF) *and* the Auditing Standards Board (ASB) to provide additional accounting and auditing guidance on those transactions. The EITF has added Issue No. 00-21, *Accounting for Multiple Element Revenue Arrangements*, to its agenda to address the accounting issues. Pending additional guid-

---

[1] Financial Accounting Standards Board (FASB) Statement of Financial Accounting Concepts (SFAC) No. 5, *Recognition and Measurement in Financial Statements of Business Enterprises*, paragraph 83(b).

[2] SOP 97-2, *Software Revenue Recognition*, paragraph 20.

[3] Reliability is defined in SFAC No. 2, *Qualitative Characteristics of Accounting Information*, as "the quality of information that assures that information is reasonably free from error and bias and

faithfully represents what it purports to represent." Paragraph 63 of SFAC No. 5 reiterates the definition of reliability, requiring that "the information is representationally faithful, verifiable, and neutral."

[4] This view is consistent with Statement of Financial Accounting Standards (SFAS) No. 45, *Accounting for Franchise Fee Revenue*, paragraph 17.

[5] SFAC No. 5, paragraph 83(b).

ance, registrants should use a reasoned method of accounting for multiple-element arrangements that is applied consistently and disclosed appropriately. In response to questions, the staff has stated that it will not object to a method that includes the following conditions.

1. *To be considered a separate element, the product or service in question represents a separate earnings process.* The staff notes that determining whether an obligation represents a separate element requires significant judgment. The staff also notes that the best indicator that a separate element exists is that a vendor sells or could readily sell that element unaccompanied by other elements.

2. *Revenue is allocated among the elements based on the fair value of the elements.* The fair values used for the allocations should be reliable, verifiable and objectively determinable. The staff does not believe that allocating revenue among the elements based solely on cost plus a profit margin that is not specific to the particular product or service is acceptable because, in the absence of other evidence of fair value, there is no objective means to verify what a profit margin should be for the particular element(s). Additional guidance on allocating among elements may be found in SOP 81-1, paragraphs 35 through 42; SOP 97-2, paragraphs 9 through 14; and SOP 98-9, *Modification of SOP 97-2, Software Revenue Recognition, With Respect to Certain Transactions.* All of the methods of allocating revenue in those SOPs, including the residual method discussed in SOP 98-9, are acceptable. If sufficient evidence of the fair values of the individual elements does not exist, revenue would not be allocated among them until that evidence exists. Instead, the revenue would be recognized as earned using revenue recognition principles applicable to the entire arrangement as if it were a single element arrangement. Prices listed in a multiple-element arrangement with a customer may not be representative of fair value of those elements because the prices of the different components of the arrangement can be altered in negotiations and still result in the same aggregate consideration.

3. *If an undelivered element is essential to the functionality of a delivered element, no revenue allocated to the delivered element is recognized until that undelivered element is delivered.* See Question 7 below.

Question 5

Q: SAB 101 states that, "the staff presumes that such contractual customer acceptance provisions are substantive, bargained-for terms of an arrangement. Accordingly, when such contractual customer acceptance provisions exist, the staff generally believes that the seller should not recognize revenue until customer acceptance occurs or the acceptance provisions lapse." When applying SAB 101, do circumstances exist in which formal customer sign-off (that a contractual customer acceptance provision is met) is unnecessary to meet the delivery criterion?

A: Yes. Formal customer sign-off is not always necessary to recognize revenue provided that the seller objectively demonstrates that the criteria specified in the acceptance provisions are satisfied. Customer acceptance provisions generally allow the customer to cancel the arrangement when a seller delivers a product that the customer has not yet agreed to purchase or delivers a product that does not meet the specifications of the customer's order. In those cases, revenue should not be recognized because a sale has not occurred. In applying this concept, the staff observes that customer acceptance provisions normally take one of four general forms. Those forms, and how the staff generally assesses whether customer acceptance provisions should result in revenue deferral, are described below:

(a) *Acceptance provisions in arrangements that purport to be for trial or evaluation purposes.*[6] In these arrangements, the seller delivers a product to a customer, and the customer agrees to receive the product, solely to give the customer the ability to evaluate the delivered product prior to acceptance.

The customer does not agree to purchase the delivered product until it accepts the product. In some cases, the acceptance provisions lapse by the passage of time without the customer rejecting the delivered product, and in other cases affirmative acceptance from the customer is necessary to trigger a sales transaction. Frequently, the title to the product does not transfer and payment terms are not established prior to customer acceptance.

These arrangements are, in substance, consignment arrangements until the customer accepts the product as set forth in the contract with the seller.

Accordingly, in arrangements where products are delivered for trial or evaluation purposes, revenue should not be recognized until the earlier of when acceptance occurs or the acceptance provisions lapse.

In contrast, other arrangements do not purport to be for trial or evaluation purposes. In these instances, the seller delivers a specified product pursuant to a customer's order, establishes payment terms, and transfers title to the delivered product to the customer. However, customer acceptance provisions may be included in the arrangement to give the purchaser the ability to ensure the delivered product meets the criteria set forth in its order. The staff evaluates these provisions as follows:

(b) *Acceptance provisions that grant a right of return or exchange on the basis of subjective matters.* An example of such a provision is one that allows the customer to return a product if the customer is dissatisfied with the product.[7] The staff believes these provisions are not different from general rights of return and should be accounted for in accordance with SFAS No. 48. SFAS No. 48 requires that the amount of future returns must be reasonably estimable in order for revenue to be recognized prior to the expiration of return

---

[6] See, for example, SOP 97-2, paragraph 25.

[7] SFAS No. 48, *Revenue Recognition When Right of Return Exists,* paragraph 13.

rights.[8] That estimate may not be made in the absence of a large volume of homogeneous transactions or if customer acceptance is likely to depend on conditions for which sufficient historical experience is absent.[9] Satisfaction of these requirements may vary from product-to-product, location-to-location, customer-to-customer, and vendor-to-vendor.

(c) *Acceptance provisions that grant a right of replacement on the basis of seller-specified objective criteria.* An example of such a provision is one that gives the customer a right of return or replacement if the delivered product is defective or fails to meet the vendor's published specifications for the product.[10]

Such rights are generally identical to those granted to all others within the same class of customer and for which satisfaction can be generally assured without consideration of conditions specific to the customer. Provided the seller has previously demonstrated that the product meets the specified criteria, the staff believes that these provisions are not different from general or specific warranties and should be accounted for as warranties in accordance with SFAS No. 5. In this case, the cost of potentially defective goods must be reliably estimable based on a demonstrated history of substantially similar transactions.[11] However, if the seller has not previously demonstrated that the delivered product meets the seller's specifications, the staff believes that revenue should be deferred until the specifications have been objectively achieved.

(d) *Acceptance provisions based on customer-specified objective criteria.* These provisions are referred to in this document as "customer-specific acceptance provisions" against which substantial completion and contract fulfillment must be evaluated. While formal customer sign-off provides the best evidence that these acceptance criteria have been met, revenue recognition also would be appropriate, presuming all other revenue recognition criteria have been met, if the seller reliably demonstrates that the delivered products or services meet all of the specified criteria prior to customer acceptance. For example, if a seller reliably demonstrates that a delivered product meets the customer-specified objective criteria set forth in the arrangement, the delivery criterion would generally be satisfied when title and the risks and rewards of ownership transfers unless product performance may reasonably be different under the customer's testing conditions specified by the acceptance provisions. Further, the seller should consider whether it would be successful in enforcing a claim for payment even in the absence of formal sign-off. Whether the vendor has fulfilled the terms of the contract before customer acceptance is a matter of contract law, and depending on the facts and circumstances, an opinion of counsel may be necessary to reach a conclusion. See Question 6 below.

Question 6

Q: Some arrangements that call for the transfer of title to equipment upon delivery to a customer's site include customer-specific acceptance provisions that permit the customer to return the equipment unless the equipment satisfies certain performance tests. If SAB 101 is applicable to that transaction, must revenue allocable to the equipment *always* be deferred until installation and on-site testing are successfully completed?

A: No. The staff would not object to revenue recognition for the equipment upon delivery (presuming all other revenue recognition criteria, including those appropriate for a multiple-element arrangement, have been met) if the seller demonstrates that, at the time of delivery, the equipment already meets all of the criteria and specifications in the customer-specific acceptance provisions. This may be demonstrated if conditions under which the customer intends to operate the equipment are replicated in pre-shipment testing unless the performance of the equipment, once installed and operated at the customer's facility, may reasonably be different from that tested prior to shipment.

Determining whether the delivered equipment meets all of a product's criteria and specifications is a matter of judgment that must be evaluated in light of the facts and circumstances of a particular transaction. Consultation with knowledgeable project managers or engineers may be necessary in such circumstances.

For example, if the customer acceptance provisions were based on meeting certain size and weight characteristics, it should be possible to determine whether those criteria have been met before shipment. Historical experience with the same specifications and functionality of a particular machine that demonstrates that the equipment meets the customer's specifications also may provide sufficient evidence that the currently shipped equipment satisfies the customer-specific acceptance provisions.

If an arrangement includes customer acceptance criteria or specifications that cannot be effectively tested before delivery or installation at the customer's site, the staff believes that revenue recognition should be deferred until it can be demonstrated that the criteria are met. This situation usually will exist when equipment performance can vary based on how the equipment works in combination with the customer's other equipment, software, or environmental conditions. In these situations, testing to determine whether the criteria are met cannot be reasonably performed until the products are installed or integrated at the customer's facility.

Some have requested us to provide examples applying the guidance in SAB 101 to a variety of circumstances that involve customer acceptance. The exhibit to this document provides a few examples.

---

[8] SFAS No. 48, paragraph 6(f).
[9] SFAS No. 48, paragraphs 8(c) and 8(d).

[10] SFAS No. 5, *Accounting for Contingencies*, paragraph 24 and SFAS No. 48, paragraph 4(c).
[11] SFAS No. 5, paragraph 25.

However, the determination of when customer-specific acceptance provisions of an arrangement are met in the absence of the customer's formal notification of acceptance depends on the weight of the evidence in the particular circumstances.

Different conclusions could be reached in similar circumstances that vary only with respect to a single variable, such as complexity of the equipment, nature of the interface with the customer's environment, extent of the seller's experience with the same type of transactions, or a particular clause in the agreement. The staff believes management and auditors are uniquely positioned to evaluate the facts and arrive at a reasoned conclusion. The staff will not object to a determination that is well reasoned on the basis of this guidance.

In light of the integral nature of installation services to equipment sold on an installed basis, a registrant may elect a policy of not recognizing any revenue on equipment sold on an installed basis until installation is complete. Registrants' accounting policies for these types of transactions should be consistently applied and appropriately disclosed. The staff expects that the EITF will provide further guidance on these arrangements as part of its project on accounting for multiple-element arrangements.

Question 7

Q: When applying SAB 101, if a customer is not obligated to pay a portion of the contract price allocable to delivered equipment until installation or similar service has been completed, must recognition of revenue on the delivered equipment *always* be deferred until that service has been performed?

A: No. Registrants should evaluate first whether the undelivered service is essential to the functionality of the delivered equipment.[12] Examples of indicators that installation is essential to the functionality of equipment include:

• The installation involves significant changes to the features or capabilities of the equipment or building complex interfaces or connections;

• The installation services are unavailable from other vendors.[13]

Conversely, examples of indicators that installation is not be essential to the functionality of the equipment include:

• The equipment is a standard product;

• Installation does not significantly alter the equipment's capabilities;

• Other companies are available to perform that job.[14]

If the undelivered service is essential to the functionality of the delivered equipment, revenue recognition

should be deferred until that service has been performed.[15]

If it is determined that the undelivered service is not essential to the functionality of the delivered product but a portion of the contract fee is not payable until the undelivered element is delivered, the staff would not consider that obligation to be inconsequential or perfunctory. Generally, the portion of the contract price that is withheld or refundable should be deferred until the outstanding element is delivered because that portion would not be realized or realizable.[16]

However, if the registrant has an enforceable claim at the balance sheet date through which it can realize some or all of the withheld or refundable amount even if it failed to fulfill the remaining obligation, deferral of a lesser amount, but not less than the fair value of the undelivered product or service, would be appropriate. The exhibit to this document includes a few examples demonstrating the analysis of revenue recognition issues in circumstances of undelivered products or services.

As noted in Question 6 above, due to the integral nature of installation services to equipment sold on an installed basis, a registrant may elect a policy of not recognizing any revenue on equipment sold on an installed basis until installation is complete. The staff expects that the EITF will provide further guidance on these arrangements as part of its project on accounting for multiple-element arrangements.

Question 8

Q: If a company (the seller) has a patent to its intellectual property which it licenses to customers, the seller may represent and warrant to its licensees that it has a valid patent, and will defend and maintain that patent. When applying SAB 101, does that obligation to maintain and defend patent rights, in and of itself, constitute an element for which revenue should be allocated and initially deferred?

A: No. Provided the seller has legal and valid patents upon entering the license arrangement, existing GAAP on licenses of intellectual property (e.g., SOP 97-2, SOP 00-2, *Accounting by Producers or Distributors of Films*, and SFAS No. 50, *Financial Reporting in the Record and Music Industry*) does not indicate that an obligation to defend valid patents represents an additional deliverable to which a portion of an arrangement fee should be allocated in an arrangement that otherwise qualifies for sales-type accounting.

While this clause may obligate the licenser to incur costs in the defense and maintenance of the patent, that obligation does not involve an additional deliverable to the customer. Defending the patent is generally consistent with the seller's representation in the license that such patent is legal and valid. Therefore, the staff would not consider a clause like this to require revenue deferral.

---

[12] See SOP 97-2, paragraph 13.
[13] See SOP 97-2, paragraphs 68-71 for analogous guidance.
[14] Ibid.

[15] See SOP 97-2, paragraph 13.
[16] SFAC No. 5, paragraph 83(a) and SFAS No. 48, paragraph 6(b).

Question 9

Q: Assume that intellectual property is physically delivered and payment is received on December 20, upon the registrant's consummation of an agreement granting its customer a license to use the intellectual property for a term beginning on the following January 1. Should the license fee be recognized in the period ending December 31?

A: No. Revenue should not be recognized before the inception of the license term.[17]

Until the beginning of the license term, the customer does not yet have the legal right to use the intellectual property. Effective delivery has not occurred in these situations until the license term begins.

III. Topic 13.A.3. – Nonrefundable Payments

The staff's response to Question 5 in SAB 101 highlights the requirement under GAAP to defer revenue recognition in certain circumstances, notwithstanding the receipt of a nonrefundable upfront payment from the customer.[18] The discussion in SAB 101 demonstrates the need to consider two related questions in the assessment of when a nonrefundable upfront payment may be recognized as revenue:

• What is the earnings process, and when does it culminate?

• Is the undelivered or unperformed obligation essential to the functionality of the performance or product for which the upfront payment is ostensibly received?

The staff indicated in SAB 101 that a registrant's analysis of these questions should consider the customer's perspective on the transaction. The staff has responded to questions concerning that guidance, as discussed below.

Question 10

Q: In each of the following situations, when should the company receiving the fee recognize the related revenue?

Example 1: A company charges users a fee for non-exclusive access to its web site that contains proprietary databases. The fee allows access to the web site for a one-year period. After the customer is provided with an identification number and trained in the use of the database, there are no incremental costs that will be incurred in serving this customer.

Example 2: An internet company charges a fee to users for advertising a product for sale or auction on certain pages of its web site. The company agrees to maintain the listing for a period of time. The cost of maintaining the advertisement on the web site for the stated period is minimal.

Example 3: A company charges a fee for hosting another company's web site for one year.

The arrangement does not involve exclusive use of any of the hosting company's servers or other equipment. Almost all of the projected costs to be incurred will be incurred in the initial loading of information on the host company's internet server and setting up appropriate links and network connections.

A: Some propose that revenue should be recognized when the initial set-up is completed in these cases because the on-going obligation involves minimal or no cost or effort and should be considered perfunctory or inconsequential. However, the staff believes that the substance of each of these transactions indicates that the purchaser is paying for a service that is delivered over time.

Therefore, revenue recognition should occur over time, reflecting the provision of service.[19] In certain cases, the arrangement with the customer may be a multiple-element arrangement, with separate revenue recognition for those initial services. Question 4 of this document discusses multiple-element arrangements.

Question 11

Q: Question 5 of SAB 101 addresses a telecommunications company's accounting for nonrefundable upfront activation fees. How should the activation fee for telephone service be accounted for in the following situation?

Facts: To provide basic local service to a customer, the registrant must activate the customer's service at the central office. The registrant charges $50 to activate basic local service. On-going fees related to basic local service consist of a flat monthly fee and usage-related charges. There is no contract between the customer and the registrant. The costs associated with activation are $40 and consist primarily of the technician's salary and related benefits.

A: The staff believes that the revenue from the fee should be deferred and recognized over the expected term of the customer relationship. The customer can be expected to view activation as a necessary and inseparable part of buying ongoing telephone service, and not as a separate service.

Question 5 of SAB 101 describes a situation in which the activation costs are nominal. The staff has been asked whether the incurrence of more than nominal costs for activation would permit revenue recognition when activation was performed. Question 5 of SAB 101 cited nominal costs solely to make it clear that there was not a separate earnings event in the situation described in that question.

However, incurrence of substantive costs does not necessarily indicate that there is a separate earnings event.[20] Whether there is a separate earnings event should be evaluated on a case-by-case basis.

Some have questioned whether revenue may be recognized in these transactions to the extent of the incremental direct costs incurred in the activation.

---

[17] See SOP 00-2, paragraphs 7(c), 14, and 76.

[18] SFAC No. 5, paragraph 83(b).

[19] SFAC No. 5, paragraph 84(d).

[20] See footnote 51 of SFAC No. 5 for a description of the "earnings process."

Because there is no separable element or earnings event, the staff would generally object to that approach, except where it is provided for in the authoritative literature (e.g., SFAS No. 51, *Financial Reporting by Cable Television Companies*). However, the staff believes that capitalization of certain contract acquisition and origination costs may be appropriate in these circumstances, as addressed below in Questions 14 through 17.

Question 12

Q: How should a registrant account for a fee received for installation of an additional telephone jack in the following situation?

Facts: Assume the registrant is a provider of wireline telecommunications services. To install a phone jack for a customer, the registrant must dispatch a field technician to a customer's residence. This service may be performed at the same time as activation of phone service or at a different time. The registrant charges the customer $65 to install the additional phone jack. The costs of performing this service are $55 and consist primarily of the field technician's hourly wage, related benefits, materials (e.g., jack and wiring) and transportation costs (e.g., gas). Although rare, the registrant does provide this installation service in situations where it is not also providing basic local service. In addition, customers could choose other vendors to install the additional phone jack in their residence or they could do it themselves.

A: The staff believes that revenue should be recognized when the additional jack is installed. In this case, installation of the additional phone jack represents a separate and distinct earnings process, as indicated by the following factors:

- The functionality of the on-going basic local service is unaffected by the number of phone jacks that exist at a customer location, as evidenced by the fact that the timing of the installation of the jack need not coincide with the activation of basic service. The functionality of the jack is unaffected by the extent of future phone service.

- The registrant provides these installation services in situations where it is not also activating basic local service.

- The registrant provides telecommunications services without installation of a phone jack (e.g., when the customer does not want an additional jack).

- Customers may choose other vendors to install the phone jack in their residence.

- Customers may install additional phone jacks themselves.

- The installation of the jack provides an enhancement to the value of the customer's residence, even if no local telephone service is contracted for.

If the installation of the additional phone jack is one element in a multiple-element arrangement, there should be sufficient reliable, objective and verifiable evidence of fair value for the various elements in order to allocate the related fee among the elements. The staff expects that the EITF will provide further guidance on these types of arrangements as part of its project on accounting for multiple element arrangements.

Question 13

Q: Research and development arrangements may have terms that include up-front payments upon contract signing, scheduled payments during the term of the arrangement, and additional payments if and when certain milestones in the product's development are reached. The arrangements often include provisions for ongoing product manufacturing and distribution rights. How should a registrant account for the up-front payment and the other payments?

A: The answer depends on the facts and circumstances. Question 5 of SAB 101 specifically addresses only the circumstance when a nonrefundable fee is received at the outset of an arrangement or at another specified date without a corresponding performance or delivery by the registrant that is the culmination of a separate earnings process. In that situation, the ongoing research and development services are essential for the customer to receive any benefit from the technology or access to other assets. In addition, a basis does not exist to objectively determine the fair value of technology access separate from the ongoing research activities.

Many research and development arrangements in the pharmaceutical and biotechnology industries are more complicated and contain multiple elements. As discussed in Question 4 of this document, the staff has requested that the EITF address the accounting for multiple-element contracts.

While an outright sale of technology by the registrant may qualify for separate revenue recognition if sufficient verifiable and objective evidence of fair value exists, research and development arrangements commonly involve granting access to facilities, technology, and other properties along with an agreement to perform research and development activities.[21] In the latter circumstances, immediate recognition of the fee generally is inappropriate because the registrant has continuing involvement with the technology through its provision of research and development services that precludes the ability to objectively measure the fair value of the any of the elements individually. Similarly, a nonrefundable fee received without any corresponding performance or delivery should be treated as a nonrefundable advance from the customer and recognized as performance occurs. The accounting for other payments specifically related to the achievement of milestones or for any manufactur-

---

[21] The arrangements may fall within the scope of SFAS No. 68, *Research and Development Arrangements*. Provided that the conditions that require accounting for proceeds received as a liability to repay the funding party are not met, SFAS No. 68, paragraph 10, requires that the arrangement be accounted for as an obligation to perform contractual research and development services. If the research and development arrangement is with the Federal Government, then the arrangement may be within the scope of the AICPA Audit and Accounting Guide, *Audits of Federal Government Contractors*, paragraphs 3.49 through 3.56.

ing or distribution arrangements should be evaluated based on the specific facts of the arrangements between the parties.

IV. Topic 13.A.3. – Accounting for Certain Costs of Revenues

Footnote 29 of SAB 101 refers to contract acquisition and origination costs and indicates that certain incremental and direct "set-up costs" may be deferred and accounted for by analogy to SFAS No. 91, *Accounting for Nonrefundable Fees and Costs Associated with Originating or Acquiring Loans and Initial Direct Costs of Leases*, and FASB Technical Bulletin ("FTB") No. 90-1, *Accounting for Separately Priced Extended Warranty and Product Maintenance Contracts*. The staff has responded to questions concerning that guidance, as discussed below.

Question 14

Q: In SAB 101, what is the intended scope of the guidance on incremental direct contract acquisition and origination costs?

A: Our comments in footnote 29 of SAB 101 and in this document should be read to apply only to the deferral of incremental direct costs of transactions for which revenue has been deferred. Those comments do not address the accounting for costs of contract acquisition and origination in transactions that do not involve deferred revenue.

Question 15

Q: When applying SAB 101, what is the staff's view of the pool of contract acquisition and origination costs that are eligible for capitalization?

A: As noted in footnote 29 of SAB 101, SFAS No. 91 includes a definition of incremental direct costs in its glossary. Paragraph 6 of SFAS No. 91 provides further guidance on the types of costs eligible for capitalization as customer acquisition costs indicating that only costs that result from successful loan origination efforts are capitalized. The FASB staff has published an Implementation Guide on SFAS No. 91 that provides additional guidance on the costs that qualify for capitalization as customer acquisition costs.

Further, FTB 90-1 also requires capitalization of incremental direct customer acquisition costs and requires that those costs be "identified consistent with the guidance in paragraph 6 of Statement 91."

Although the facts of a particular situation should be analyzed closely to capture those costs that are truly direct and incremental, the staff generally would not object to an accounting policy that results in the capitalization of costs in accordance with paragraph 6(a) and (b) of SFAS No. 91 or FTB 90-1. Registrants should disclose their policies for determining which costs to capitalize as contract acquisition and origination costs.

Question 16

Q: When applying SAB 101, over what period should the seller amortize deferred costs associated with deferred revenue?

A: When both costs and revenue (in an amount equal to or greater than the costs) are deferred, the staff believes that the deferred costs should be charged to expense proportionally and over the same period that deferred revenue is recognized as revenue.[22]

Question 17

Q: Is the deferral of contract acquisition and origination costs in the transactions addressed in SAB 101 required or is it merely permitted?

A: Such deferral is permitted. In recognition of diversity in practice in accounting for contract acquisition and origination costs, the Accounting Standards Executive Committee (AcSEC) has added a project on the subject to its agenda. Until new guidance is adopted, the staff would not object to either expensing or capitalizing incremental direct costs of contract acquisition and origination, except in situations where the accounting literature specifically requires one treatment or the other. The accounting policy for these costs should be disclosed and applied consistently.

V. Topic 13.A.4. – Refundable Fees for Services

Question 7 of SAB 101 discusses the appropriate timing of recognizing revenue for fees received for services that remain refundable even after the services are provided. While the staff indicated that the preferable method is to account for refundable amounts received as deposits in accordance with SFAS No. 125, *Accounting for Transfers and Servicing of Financial Assets and* Extinguishments of Liabilities, paragraph 16, the SAB also indicates that the staff would not object to accounting for those fees by analogy to SFAS No. 48 if certain criteria are met. The staff has responded to questions concerning that guidance, as discussed below.

Question 18

Q: Will the staff accept an analogy to SFAS No. 48 for service transactions subject to customer cancellation privileges other than those specifically addressed in Question 7 of SAB 101, so long as the criteria specified in Question 7 of SAB 101 are met?

A: The staff has accepted the analogy in limited circumstances due to the existence of a large pool of homogeneous transactions and satisfaction of the criteria in Question 7 of SAB 101. Examples of other arrangements involving customer cancellation privileges and refundable service fees that the staff has addressed include the following:

• a leasing broker whose commission from the lessor upon a commercial tenant's signing of a lease agreement is refundable (or in some cases, is not due) under lessor cancellation privileges if the tenant

---

[22] FTB 90-1, paragraph 4.

fails to move into the leased premises by a specified date.

- a talent agent whose fee receivable from its principal (i.e., a celebrity) for arranging a celebrity endorsement for a five-year term is cancelable by the celebrity if the celebrity breaches the endorsement contract with its customer.

- an insurance agent whose commission received from the insurer upon selling an insurance policy is refundable in whole for the 30-day period that state law permits the consumer to repudiate the contract and then refundable on a declining pro rata basis until the consumer has made six monthly payments.

In the first two of these cases, the staff advised the registrants that the portion of revenue subject to customer cancellation and refund must be deferred until no longer subject to that contingency because the registrants did not have an ability to make reliable estimates of customer cancellations due to the lack of a large pool of homogeneous transactions. In the case of the insurance agent, however, the particular registrant demonstrated that it had a sufficient history of homogeneous transactions with the same characteristics from which to reliably estimate contract cancellations and satisfy all the criteria specified in Question 7 of SAB 101. Accordingly, the staff did not object to that registrant's policy of recognizing its sales commission as revenue when its performance was complete, with an appropriate allowance for estimated cancellations.

Question 19

Q: If a registrant meets the criteria in Question 7 of SAB 101 regarding reliable estimates of cancellations, in the staff's view, must it analogize to SFAS No. 48, or may it defer all revenue until the refund period lapses as suggested by SFAS No. 125?

A: The analogy to SFAS No. 48 is presented as an alternative that would be acceptable to the staff when the listed conditions are met. However, a registrant may choose to defer all revenue until the refund period lapses. The policy chosen should be disclosed and applied consistently.

Question 20

Q: May a registrant that meets the criteria in Question 7 of SAB 101 for reliable estimates of cancellations choose at some point in the future to change from the SFAS No. 48 method to the SFAS No. 125 method of accounting for these refundable fees? May a registrant in that situation change from the SFAS No. 125 method to the SFAS No. 48 method?

A: As noted in SAB 101, the staff believes that SFAS No. 125 provides a preferable accounting model for service transactions subject to potential refunds. Therefore, the staff would not object to a change from the SFAS No. 48 method to the SFAS No. 125 method. However, if a registrant had previously cho-

sen the SFAS No. 125 method when it could otherwise have qualified to use the SFAS No. 48 method, the staff would object to a subsequent change from the SFAS No. 125 method to the SFAS No. 48 method.

Question 21

Q: Question 7 of SAB 101 indicates that refundable membership fees can be recognized over the membership term so long as certain criteria are met (i.e., homogeneous pool, ability to reliably estimate refunds, etc.). Is there a minimum level of customers that must be projected not to cancel before use of SFAS No. 48 type accounting is appropriate?

A: SFAS No. 48 does not include any such minimum. Therefore, the staff does not believe that a minimum must apply in service transactions either. However, as the refund rate increases, it may be increasingly difficult to make reasonable and reliable estimates of cancellation rates.

Question 22

Q: When a registrant first determines that reliable estimates of cancellations of service contracts can be made (e.g., two years of historical evidence becomes available), how should the change from the complete deferral method to the method of recognizing revenue, net of estimated cancellations, over time be reflected?

A: Changes in the ability to meet the criteria set forth in Question 7 of SAB 101 should be accounted for in the manner described in paragraph 6 of SFAS No. 48, which addresses the accounting when a company experiences a change in the ability to make reasonable estimates of future product returns.

Question 23

Q: When the "retrospective approach" to account for changes in estimates of deferred revenue is used in connection with a service transaction that meets the criteria in Question 7 of SAB 101, in the staff's view should related deferred costs being amortized on a basis consistent with the deferred revenue be similarly adjusted?

A: Yes.[23]

VI. Topic 13.A.4. – Estimates and Changes in Estimates

Accounting for revenues and costs of revenues requires estimates in many cases; those estimates sometimes change. Registrants should ensure that they have appropriate internal controls and adequate books and records that will result in timely identification of necessary changes in estimates that should be reflected in the financial statements and notes thereto. The staff has responded to questions concerning the reporting of estimates and changes in estimates when applying SAB 101, which are discussed below.

---

[23] Such an approach is generally consistent with the amortization methodology in SFAS No. 91, paragraph 19.

Question 24

Q: Is the requirement cited in Question 9 of SAB 101 for "reliable" estimates meant to imply a new, higher requirement than the "reasonable" estimates discussed in SFAS No. 48?

A: No. "Reliability" of financial information is one of the qualities of accounting information discussed in SFAC No. 2. The staff's expectation that estimates be reliable does not change the existing requirement of SFAS No. 48. If management cannot develop an estimate that is sufficiently reliable for use by investors, the staff believes it cannot make a reasonable estimate meeting the requirements of that standard.

Question 25

Q: Question 7 of SAB 101 identifies specific criteria that should be met if the guidance in SFAS No. 48 is applied by analogy to refundable revenues from service transactions. Does the staff expect registrants to apply the guidance in Question 7 of SAB 101 to sales of tangible goods and other transactions specifically within the scope of SFAS No. 48?

A: The specific guidance in Question 7 of SAB 101 does not apply to transactions covered by SFAS No. 48. The views set forth in Question 7 of SAB 101 are applicable to the service transactions discussed in that Question. Service transactions are explicitly outside the scope of SFAS No. 48.

As noted in Question 7 of SAB 101, the staff has not objected to analogies to SFAS No. 48 for service transactions, provided that all of the criteria discussed in that question are satisfied. This guidance is intended to ensure that revenue is recognized based on estimates of cancellation when those estimates are consistent, comparable, reliable, and appropriately disclosed.

Question 26

Q: Question 7 of SAB 101 states that the staff would expect a two-year history of selling a new service in order to be able to make reliable estimates of cancellations. How long a history does the staff believe is necessary to estimate returns in a product sale transaction that is within the scope of SFAS No. 48?

A: The staff does not believe there is any specific length of time necessary in a product transaction. However, SFAS No. 48 states that returns must be subject to reasonable estimation. Preparers and auditors should be skeptical of estimates of product returns when little history with a particular product line exists, when there is inadequate verifiable evidence of historical experience, or when there are inadequate internal controls that ensure the reliability and timeliness of the reporting of the appropriate historical information. Start-up companies and companies selling new or significantly modified products are frequently unable to develop the requisite historical data on which to base estimates of returns.

Question 27

Q: If a company selling products subject to a right of return concludes that it cannot reasonably estimate the actual return rate due to its limited history, but it can conservatively estimate the maximum possible returns, does the staff believe that the company may recognize revenue for the portion of the sales that exceeds the maximum estimated return rate?

A: No. If a reasonable estimate of future returns cannot be made, SFAS No. 48 requires that revenue not be recognized until the return period lapses or a reasonable estimate can be made.[24] Deferring revenue recognition based on the upper end of a wide range of potential return rates is inconsistent with the provisions of SFAS No. 48.

VII. Topic 13.A.4. – Fixed or Determinable Fees

Question 28

Q: Company M performs claims processing and medical billing services for healthcare providers. In this role, Company M is responsible for preparing and submitting claims to third-party payers, tracking outstanding billings, and collecting amounts billed. Company M's fee is a fixed percentage (e.g., five percent) of the amount collected. If no collections are made, no fee is due to Company M. Company M has historical evidence indicating that the third-party payers pay 85 percent of the billings submitted with no further effort by Company M. May Company M recognize as revenue its five percent fee on 85 percent of the gross billings at the time it prepares and submits billings, or should it wait until collections occur to recognize any revenue?

A: The staff believes that Company M must wait until collections occur before recognizing revenue.

Before the third-party payer has remitted payment to Company M's customers for the services billed, Company M is not entitled to any revenue. That is, its revenue is not yet realized or realizable.[25] Until Company M's customers collect on the billings, Company M has not performed the requisite activity under its contract to be entitled to a fee.[26] Further, no amount of the fee is fixed or determinable or collectible until Company Ms' customers collect on the billings.

VIII. Topic 13.B.2. – Implementing the Guidance in SAB 101

The staff has responded to questions concerning how registrants should implement the guidance in SAB 101, as discussed below.

Question 29

Q: SAB 101 indicates that the staff will not object to cumulative effect-type transition so long as the prior accounting does not represent an error. Could a company whose prior accounting does not represent an error voluntarily adopt a new method consistent with

---

[24] SFAS No. 48, paragraph 6(f).

[25] SFAC No. 5, paragraph 83(a).

[26] SFAC No. 5, paragraph 83(b).

SAB 101 by restatement of prior periods, rather than through a cumulative catch-up adjustment?

A: In most instances, no. APB Opinion No. 20 does not permit restatement of financial statements for a change in accounting principle that does not represent correction of an error, except in very rare circumstances.[27] An exception is a company that is filing publicly for the first time. As stated in paragraph 29 of APB Opinion No. 20, those companies are permitted to reflect the adoption of the new policy via a restatement, and the staff believes that approach is usually necessary to avoid confusing investors in an initial public offering.

Question 30

Q: Should a registrant reporting a change in accounting principle as a result of SAB 101 file a preferability letter?

A: No preferability letter is required if an accounting change is made in response to a newly issued Staff Accounting Bulletin.

Question 31

Q: If a company had not previously adjusted sales revenues, but deferred recognition of the gross margin of estimated returns for a transaction subject to SFAS No. 48, how should it present a current change in accounting to reduce revenue and cost of sales for estimated returns?

A: Paragraph 7 of SFAS No. 48 states that "sales revenue and cost of sales reported in the income statement *shall be reduced* to reflect estimated returns." SFAS No. 48 does not provide for recognition of sales and costs of sales while deferring gross margin under any circumstance. SAB 101 provided no new guidance on this point. If a registrant has failed to comply with GAAP, the registrant should retroactively revise prior financial statements in the manner set forth in Accounting Principles Board (APB) Opinion No. 20, *Accounting Changes* and SFAS No. 16, *Prior Period Adjustments*.

Exhibit A: Effects of Customer Acceptance and Unfulfilled Obligations on Revenue Recognition

Example 1

Company E is an equipment manufacturer whose main product is generally sold in a standard model. The contracts for sale of that model provide for customer acceptance to occur after the equipment is received and tested by the customer. The acceptance provisions state that if the equipment does not perform to Company E's published specifications, the customer may return the equipment for a full refund or a replacement unit, or may require Company E to repair the equipment so that it performs up to published specifications. Customer acceptance is indicated by either a formal sign-off by the customer or by the passage of 90 days without a claim under the acceptance provisions.

Title to the equipment passes upon delivery to the customer. Company E does not perform any installation or other services on the equipment it sells and tests each piece of equipment against its specifications before shipment. Payment is due under Company E's normal payment terms for that product which is 30 days after customer acceptance.

For each response below, all of the above facts apply, in addition to any others specifically stated in the "Additional Facts" section.

Scenario A:

Additional Facts: Company E receives an order from a new customer for a standard model of its main product. Based on the customer's intended use of the product, location and other factors, there is no reason that the equipment would operate differently in a customer's environment than it does in Company E's facility.

Assuming all other revenue recognition criteria are met (other than the issue raised with respect to the acceptance provision), when should Company E recognize revenue from the sale of this piece of equipment?

Response: While the staff presumes that customer acceptance provisions are substantive provisions that generally result in revenue deferral, that presumption can be overcome as discussed in Question 5 of this document. Although the contract includes a customer acceptance clause, acceptance is based on meeting Company E's published specifications for a standard model.

Company E demonstrates that the equipment shipped meets the specifications before shipment, and the equipment is expected to operate the same in the customer's environment as it does in Company E's.

In this situation, Company E should evaluate the customer acceptance provision as a warranty under SFAS No. 5. If Company E can reasonably and reliably estimate the amount of warranty obligations, the staff believes that it should recognize revenue upon delivery of the equipment, with an appropriate liability for probable warranty obligations.

Scenario B:

Additional Facts: Company E enters into an arrangement with a new customer to deliver a version of its standard product modified as necessary to fit into a space of specific dimensions while still meeting all of the published vendor specifications with regard to performance.

In addition to the customer acceptance provisions relating to the standard performance specifications, the customer may reject the equipment if it does not conform to the specified dimensions. Company E creates a testing chamber of the exact same dimensions as specified by the customer and makes simple design changes to the product so that it fits into the testing chamber.

---

[27] See, for example, APB Opinion No. 20, paragraph 27.

The equipment still meets all of the standard performance specifications.

Assuming all other revenue recognition criteria are met (other than the issue raised with respect to the acceptance provision), when should Company E recognize revenue from the sale of this piece of equipment?

Response: Although the contract includes a customer acceptance clause that is based, in part, on a customer specific criterion, Company E demonstrates that the equipment shipped meets that objective criterion, as well as the published specifications, before shipment. Therefore, the staff believes that Company E should evaluate the customer acceptance provision as a warranty under SFAS No. 5. If Company E can reasonably and reliably estimate the amount of warranty obligations, it should recognize revenue upon delivery of the equipment, with an appropriate liability for probable warranty obligations.

Scenario C:

Additional Facts: Company E enters into an arrangement with a new customer to deliver a version of its standard product modified as necessary to be integrated into the customer's new assembly line while still meeting all of the standard published vendor specifications with regard to performance. The customer may reject the equipment if it fails to meet the standard published performance specifications or cannot be satisfactorily integrated into the new line.

Company E has never modified its equipment to work on an integrated basis in the type of assembly line the customer has proposed. In response to the request, Company E designs a version of its standard equipment that is modified as believed necessary to operate in the new assembly line. The modified equipment still meets all of the standard published performance specifications, and Company E believes the equipment will meet the requested specifications when integrated into the new assembly line. However, Company E is unable to replicate the new assembly line conditions in its testing.

Assuming all other revenue recognition criteria are met (other than the issue raised with respect to the acceptance provision), when should Company E recognize revenue from the sale of this piece of equipment?

Response: This contract includes a customer acceptance clause that is based, in part, on a customer specific criterion, and Company E cannot demonstrate that the equipment shipped meets that criterion before shipment. Accordingly, the staff believes that the contractual customer acceptance provision is substantive and is not overcome upon shipment. Therefore, the staff believes that Company E should wait until the product is successfully integrated at its customer's location and meets the customer-specific criteria before recognizing revenue. While this is best evidenced by formal customer acceptance, other objective evidence that the equipment has met the customer-specific criteria may also exist (e.g., confirmation from the customer that the specifications were met).

Example 2

Company A develops, manufactures, and sells complex manufacturing equipment. Company A enters into a sales contract with Customer B to sell and install a specific piece of equipment for $20 million.

Company A is experienced in the production and installation of this type of equipment and has a history of successfully installing the equipment.

Company A concludes that installation is neither (a) inconsequential or perfunctory nor (b) essential to the functionality of the equipment.

Company A has developed its own internal specifications for the model of equipment Customer B ordered and has previously demonstrated that the equipment meets those specifications. Company A provides a warranty on all equipment sales that guarantees the delivered equipment will meet Company A's published specifications and be free of defects in materials and workmanship. Title to the equipment passes to the customer upon delivery. Company A sells the equipment separately to some customers, without installation, for $19,500,000.

In those cases, a general contractor installs the equipment. Company A routinely sells separately its services of the type required for equipment installation on a time and materials basis. Based on the extent of effort expected in an installation of this equipment, Company A determines that the fair value of the installation services approximates $500,000.

For each response below, all of the above facts apply, in addition to any others specifically stated in the "Additional Facts" section.

Scenario A:

Additional Facts: The equipment must be integrated into a larger production line that includes other manufacturer's equipment. At Customer B's request, the contract includes a number of customer-specific technical and performance criteria regarding speed, quality, interaction with other equipment, and reliability.

Because of the nature of the equipment, Company A is unable to demonstrate that the equipment will meet the customer-specific specifications before installation. The contract includes a customer acceptance provision that obligates Company A to demonstrate that the installed equipment meets all specified criteria before customer acceptance. If customer acceptance is not achieved within 120 days of installation, Customer B can require Company A to remove the equipment and refund all payments. Payment terms are 80% due 30 days after delivery and 20% due 30 days after customer acceptance.

Assuming all other revenue recognition criteria are met (other than the issues raised with respect to the acceptance provision), when should Company A recognize revenue on this transaction?

Response: While Company A believes that its equipment can be made to meet the customer's specifications, it is unable to demonstrate that it has delivered what Customer B ordered until installation and testing occurs. Accordingly, the staff believes that it would be inappropriate for Company A to recognize any revenue until it has demonstrated that it has delivered equipment meeting the specifications set forth in the contract. This would normally occur upon customer acceptance.

Scenario B:

Additional Facts: The equipment must be integrated into a larger production line. At Customer B's request, the contract includes a number of customer-specific technical and performance criteria regarding speed, quality, and reliability. However, the integration of the product into Customer B's factory and production line is not complex. Because of this, the product is tested in Company A's facility before shipment and is shipped only after all specifications are met. The contract includes a customer acceptance provision that obligates Company A to demonstrate that the installed equipment meets all specified criteria before customer acceptance. Because the integration is not complex, there is virtually no uncertainty as to whether the product will continue to meet those specifications, without further modification, once installed in the customer's facility. However, the customer is obligated to pay the fee only upon completed installation. The contract specifies that if Company A does not complete the installation to Customer B's satisfaction, Customer B can require Company A to remove the equipment with no payment becoming due.

Assuming all other revenue recognition criteria are met (other than the issues raised with respect to the acceptance provision), when should Company A recognize revenue on this transaction?

Response: Upon delivery, Company A has completed the earnings process and met the delivery criterion with respect to the equipment because it has demonstrated that the equipment delivered to the customer meets the requirements of the customer's order. However, because the customer is not obligated to pay Company A if installation of the equipment is not completed, the staff believes that no revenue may be recognized until installation is complete and the customer becomes obligated to pay. Conversely, if Company A has an enforceable claim at the balance sheet date through which it can realize some or all of the $20 million fee even if it failed to fulfill the installation obligation, deferral of a lesser amount, but not less than the estimated fair value of the installation (i.e., $500,000), would be appropriate.

Alternatively, if Company A's policy is to defer all revenue until installation is complete, recognition of the $20,000,000 fee upon completion of installation would be appropriate. Company A's policy should be appropriately disclosed and consistently applied.

Scenario C:

Additional Facts: The equipment must be integrated into a larger production line. At Customer B's request, the contract includes a number of customer-specific technical and performance criteria regarding speed, quality, and reliability. However, the integration of the product into Customer B's factory and production line is not complex. Because of this, the product is tested in Company A's facility before shipment and is shipped only after all specifications are met. The contract includes a customer acceptance provision that obligates Company A to demonstrate that the installed equipment meets all specified criteria before customer acceptance. Because the integration is not complex, there is virtually no uncertainty as to whether the product will continue to meet those specifications, without further modification once installed in Customer B's facility. Customer B is obligated to pay one hundred percent of the fee no later than 90 days after delivery regardless of whether installation has occurred.

Assuming all other revenue recognition criteria are met (other than the issues raised with respect to the acceptance provision), when should Company A recognize revenue on this transaction?

Response: Upon delivery, Company A has completed the earnings process and met the delivery criterion with respect to the equipment because it has demonstrated that the equipment delivered to the customer meets the requirements of the customer's order. In addition, Company B's obligation to pay the fee is not contingent upon completion of installation. Therefore, Company A should recognize the revenue allocable to the equipment, $19,500,000, as revenue upon delivery.

The staff believes that the remaining $500,000 of the arrangement fee should be recognized when installation is performed.

Alternatively, if Company A's policy is to defer all revenue until installation is complete, recognition of the $20,000,000 fee upon completion of installation would be appropriate. Company A's policy should be appropriately disclosed and consistently applied.

As published by the SEC staff on 10/12/2000.

http://www.sec.gov/offices/account/sab101fq.htm

[¶ 39,068] RELEASE No. 102, July 6, 2001

Selected Loan Loss Allowance Methodology and Documentation Issues

Action: Publication of Staff Accounting Bulletin

Summary: This staff accounting bulletin expresses certain of the staff's views on the development, documentation, and application of a systematic methodology as required by Financial Reporting Release No. 28 for determining allowances for loan and lease losses in accordance with generally accepted accounting principles. In particular, the guidance focuses on the documentation the staff normally would expect registrants to prepare and maintain in support of their allowances for loan losses. The guidance in this staff accounting bulletin is being issued in light of the

March 10, 1999 Joint Interagency Letter to Financial Institutions in which the staff agreed to provide, in parallel with guidance provided by the federal banking agencies, guidance on loan loss allowance methodologies and supporting documentation. On July 6, 2001, the federal banking agencies issued their guidance through the Federal Financial Institutions Examination Council (FFIEC) as interagency guidance, "Policy Statement on Allowance for Loan and Lease Losses Methodologies and Documentation for Banks and Savings Institutions."

Date: July 6, 2001

For Further Information Contact: Jenifer Minke-Girard, Office of the Chief Accountant (202-942-4400), or Donald A.Walker, Jr., Division of Corporation Finance (202-942-1799), Securities and Exchange Commission, 450 Fifth Street, N.W., Washington, D.C. 20549; electronic addresses: Minke-GirardJ@sec.gov; WalkerDo@sec.gov.

Supplementary Information

Background

In December 1986, the Commission issued Financial Reporting Release No. 28, which added subsection (b), *Procedural Discipline in Determining the Allowance and Provision for Loan Losses to be Reported*, of Section 401.09, *Accounting for Loan Losses by Registrants Engaged in Lending Activities*, to the Codification of Financial Reporting Policies (hereafter referred to as FRR No. 28). In FRR No. 28, the Commission noted that certain registrants had appeared to lack adequate documentation of procedures for performing detailed reviews of loan portfolios and for determining amounts of allowances and provisions for loan losses. The Commission indicated that the staff normally would expect to find "that the books and records of registrants engaged in lending activities include documentation of: (a) systematic methodology to be employed each period in determining the amount of loan losses to be reported, and (b) rationale supporting each period's determination that the amounts reported were adequate."

Since the issuance of FRR No. 28, the Commission's staff has continued to observe, in some cases, insufficient documentation of allowances for loan losses. In the ordinary course of its reviews of filings, the staff asked a number of registrants why significant favorable or unfavorable trends in the quality of the loan portfolio, as evidenced by statistical data presented in Management's Discussion and Analysis and/or in the notes to the financial statements, did not correspond with decreases or increases in the allowance for loan losses reported in the financial statements. Explanations offered by some registrants have indicated a lack of reasoned analysis or discipline in the establishment of the loss allowance. Some registrants assured the staff that they had assessed significant loans individually for impairment, but

could not produce documentation demonstrating how the loans were evaluated or how any loan impairment was measured. In other cases, registrants' internal documentation indicating that a particular loan was impaired could not be reconciled with management's ultimate decision not to provide for any loss on that loan. Several registrants that recorded loan loss allowances for pools of loans did not maintain documentation indicating how the amounts of the loan loss allowances were determined or how the amounts related to the composition of the loan pool at any particular balance sheet date.

The staff's observations were similar to those of the General Accounting Office (GAO). In its October 1994 Report to Congressional Committees, *Depository Institutions: Divergent Loan Loss Methods Undermine Usefulness of Financial Reports*(GAO Report), the GAO reported its findings resulting from its review of the loan loss reserving practices of 12 depository institutions. One of the GAO's principal findings was that most of the reviewed institutions' loan loss allowances included large supplemental reserves that generally were not linked to an analysis of loss exposure or supported by evidence.[1] The GAO noted: "Such use of unjustified supplemental reserves can conceal critical changes in the quality of an institution's loan portfolio and undermine the credibility of financial reports."[2]

In recognition of these concerns, the Federal Deposit Insurance Corporation, the Federal Reserve Board, the Office of the Comptroller of the Currency, the Office of Thrift Supervision, and the Commission (together, the Agencies) issued a joint letter to financial institutions on the allowance for loan and lease losses (ALLL) on March 10, 1999 (the Joint Letter).

In the Joint Letter, the Agencies announced the establishment of a Joint Working Group to study ALLL issues and to assist financial institutions by providing them with improved guidance on this topic.[3]

On September 7, 2000, the federal banking agencies, working through the FFIEC, sought public comment on a proposed policy statement on ALLL methodologies and documentation practices for banks and savings institutions. After considering the 31 comment letters received on the proposed guidance, the FFIEC issued its final interagency guidance, "Policy Statement on Allowance for Loan and Lease Losses Methodologies and Documentation for Banks and Savings Institutions," on July 6, 2001. This Staff Accounting Bulletin represents the SEC staff's views relating to methodologies and supporting documentation for the ALLL that should be observed by all public companies in complying with the federal securities laws and the Commission's interpretations. It is also generally consistent with the guidance published by the FFIEC on July 6, 2001.

Loan loss estimates developed without a disciplined methodology or adequate documentation (of both a

---

[1] Page 5 of GAO Report.

[2] *Ibid.*

[3] The Accounting Standards Executive Committee (AcSEC) of the American Institute of Certified Public Accountants (AICPA) is

in the process of developing guidance on the accounting for loan losses and the techniques for measuring probable incurred losses in a loan portfolio.

disciplined methodology and the resulting amounts of loan loss provisions and allowances) can undermine the credibility of an institution's financial statements. A critical function of the independent accountant's examination of the financial statements is to evaluate the reasonableness of accounting estimates made by management, including its estimates of loan impairments and the associated allowance for loan losses.[4] To perform that duty, an auditor must obtain an understanding of how management developed the estimate, and must apply that understanding to the review and testing of the estimation process or its results.[5] The auditor must obtain sufficient competent evidential matter supporting the financial statements, and must give adequate attention to the propriety and accuracy of the data underlying material assumptions and estimates. Chapter 7 of the AICPA Audit and Accounting Guide, Banks and Savings Institutions (Audit Guide), states that "[a]n institution's method of estimating credit losses should be well documented, with clear explanations of the supporting analyses and rationale."[6] Additionally, the Audit Guide states that "the institution's conclusions about the appropriate amount [of the loan loss allowance]should be well documented."[7] Chapter 7[8] provides details of audit procedures to be performed, including procedures that relate to documentary evidence supporting the loan loss allowance. The staff believes that the documentation described in this Staff Accounting Bulletin regarding a registrant's loan loss allowance methodologies, policies, procedures, and decisions is likely to be necessary for most regis-

trants with material loan portfolios in order to provide sufficient competent evidential matter that auditors must consider in accordance with GAAS.[9]

The statements in staff accounting bulletins are not rules or interpretations of the Commission, nor are they published as bearing the Commission's official approval. They represent interpretations and practices followed by the Division of Corporation Finance and the Office of the Chief Accountant in administering the disclosure requirements of the Federal securities laws.

Jonathan G. Katz

Secretary

Date: July 6, 2001

Part 211 - (AMEND)

Accordingly, Part 211 of Title 17 of the Code of Federal Regulations is amended by adding Staff Accounting Bulletin No. 102 to the table found in Subpart B.

STAFF ACCOUNTING BULLETIN NO. 102

The staff hereby revises the title of Topic 6 of the Staff Accounting Bulletin Series to be "Interpretations of Accounting Series Releases and Financial Reporting Releases" and adds Section L entitled "Financial Reporting Release No. 28 - Accounting for Loan Losses by Registrants Engaged in Lending Activities" to Topic 6.

[For the text of Topic 6, See ¶ 39,151. CCH]

[¶ 39,069] RELEASE NO. 103, May 9, 2003

Update of Codification of Staff Accounting Bulletins.

Action: Publication of Staff Accounting Bulletins.

Summary: This staff accounting bulletin revises or rescinds portions of the interpretive guidance included in the codification of staff accounting bulletins in order to make this interpretive guidance consistent with current authoritative accounting and auditing guidance and SEC rules and regulations. The principal revisions relate to the rescission of material no longer necessary because of private sector developments in U.S. generally accepted accounting principles, as well as Commission rulemaking.

Date: May 9, 2003

For Further Information Contact: Paul Munter or Jack Albert, Office of the Chief Accountant (202-942-4400), or Craig Olinger, Division of Corpora-

tion Finance (202-942-2960), Securities and Exhange Commission, 450 Fifth Street, N.W., Washington, DC 20549

Supplementary Information

Background

The last comprehensive review of the staff accounting bulletins was completed by the staff in 1981, which culminated in issuance of Staff Accounting Bulletin No. 40. At that time, the staff completed a comprehensive review of the material included in staff accounting bulletin numbers 1 through 38 to revise and update such materials, and to codify those staff accounting bulletins in order to make the interpretive guidance contained therein more useful to regis-

---

[4] See Auditing Accounting Estimates, AU Section 342.04.

[5] See AU Section 342.10.

[6] See paragraph 7.05, item j, in the Audit Guide.

[7] See paragraph 7.14 in the Audit Guide.

[8] See, in particular, the section on Auditing in paragraphs 7.34 to 7.74.

[9] In responding to requests for comment on the interagency guidance published by the FFIEC, AcSEC stated:

"Although AcSEC agrees that documentation is needed to support loss recognition, AcSEC believes the Policy Statement

should make clear that financial institutions may not avoid recognizing losses by deliberately failing to comply with the Policy Statement's documentation requirements."

The Commission's staff agrees with the statement made by AcSEC and reiterates that the statements made herein represent interpretations and examples of documentation that are likely to be necessary for sufficient competent evidential matter in the course of an audit in accordance with GAAS. Failure to adequately document the loan loss allowance is not in accordance with GAAP (see paragraphs 7.05 and 7.14 in the Audit Guide) and can also demonstrate a lack of adequate internal accounting controls.

trants, accountants and others (Staff Accounting Bulletin No. 39 was separately considered by the staff).

Since that time, the staff has issued 62 additional staff accounting bulletins (through number 102) and occasional amendments (*e.g.*, SAB No. 71A), and has, on a sporadic basis, revised or rescinded the guidance in individual staff accounting bulletins based on subsequent Commission rulemaking activities or developments by private sector accounting and auditing standards-setters. However, a comprehensive review of the guidance contained in the staff accounting bulletin codification has not been undertaken since 1981.

Recent guidance issued by the Financial Accounting Standards Board (FASB), specifically Statements of Financial Accounting Standards (Statements) 141, *Business Combinations*, 142, *Goodwill and Other Intangible Assets*, 143, *Accounting for Asset Retirement Obligations*, 144, *Accounting for the Impairment or Disposal of Long-Lived Assets*, 146, *Accounting for Costs Associated with Exit or Disposal Activities*, 147 *Acquisitions of Certain Financial Institutions - an Amendment of FASB Statements No. 72 and 144 and FASB Interpretation No. 9*, and Interpretations 45, *Guarantor's Accounting and Disclosure Requirements for Guarantees, Including Indirect Guarantees of Indebtedness of Others - an Interpretation of FASB Statements No. 5, 57, and 107 and Rescission of FASB Interpretation No. 34* and 46, *Consolidation of Variable Interest Entities*, revise or supersede certain guidance contained in Accounting Principles Board (APB) Opinions 16, *Business Combinations*, 17, *Intangible Assets*, and 30, *Reporting the Results of Operations - Reporting the Effects of Disposal of a Segment of a Business, and Extraordinary, Unusual and Infrequently Occurring Events and Transactions*, Statements 5, *Accounting for Contingencies*, and 121, *Accounting for the Impairment of Long-Lived Assets and for Long-Lived Assets to Be Disposed Of*, as well as several issues addressed by the FASB's Emerging Issues Task Force (EITF) and other authoritative guidance. Provisions of the accounting standards identified above that have been revised or superseded were the subject of several staff interpretations included in the staff accounting bulletins. Furthermore, certain guidance contained in many of the staff accounting bulletins either is no longer useful or relevant due to the passage of time, or has been made obsolete by subsequent Commission rulemaking activities.

Therefore, the purpose of this staff accounting bulletin is to comprehensively update the existing codification to enhance the integrity and usefulness of this guidance.

The statements in staff accounting bulletins are not rules or interpretations of the Commission, nor are they published as bearing the Commission's official approval. They represent interpretations and practices followed by the Division of Corporation Finance and the Office of the Chief Accountant in administering the disclosure requirements of the Federal securities laws.

Margaret H. McFarland

Deputy Secretary

Date: May 9, 2003.

Part 211 - (AMEND)

Accordingly, Part 211 of Title 17 of the Code of Federal Regulations is amended by adding Staff Accounting Bulletin No. 103 to the table found in Subpart B.

STAFF ACCOUNTING BULLETIN NO. 103

The staff hereby revises the Staff Accounting Bulletin Series as follows:

1. TOPIC 1: FINANCIAL STATEMENTS

a. Topic 1.A is modified to delete the reference to previously-deleted Rules 3-07 and 3-08 of Regulation S-X.

b. Topic 1.B.1 is modified to reflect the provisions of FASB Statement 109, *Accounting for Income Taxes*.

c. Topic 1.D.1 is modified to conform such guidance with the revised disclosure requirements for foreign private issuers required under Form 20-F as a result of the Commission's International Disclosure Standards rule (Exchange Act Release No. 34-41936) which became effective September 30, 2000. The modifications primarily relate to changes in the former reference in this guidance to Item 9 (Management's Discussion and Analysis) of Form 20-F to make the reference consistent with the new non-financial disclosure requirements of this Form.

d. Topic 1.E.1 is deleted. A definition of the term "audit (or examination)," which was the subject of this interpretive guidance, is now provided in Rule 1-02 of Regulation S-X, thus making the guidance contained in this staff accounting bulletin unnecessary.

e. Topic 1.F is modified to change the references in this guidance from Form S-14 to Form S-4, since Form S-4 subsequently replaced Form S-14. This topic is also modified to delete question 3 and the related interpretive response. The guidance contained in this interpretive response, related to the appropriate accounting treatment for costs incurred to register securities issued for the formation of one-bank holding companies, has been superseded by American Institute of Certified Public Accountants' (AICPA) Statement of Position (SOP) 98-5, *Reporting on the Costs of Start-Up Activities*.

f. Topic 1.I is modified to update the former reference in this guidance to the American Institute of Certified Public Accountants' February 1986 Notice to Practitioners, *ADC Arrangements*. *ADC Arrangements* was originally issued as a notice to practitioners, published in the April 1986 issue of *The Journal of Accountancy*. This notice was subsequently reprinted without modification as Exhibit I to the AICPA's Practice Bulletin 1 dated November 1987. Furthermore, question 8 of this topic is deleted because the guidance contained in this question and interpretive response, which related to transition to the guidance in Topic 1.I, is no longer relevant due to the passage of time. Furthermore, the reference in the interpretive response to question 1 to Rule 1-02(v) of Regulation S-X has been changed to Rule 1-02(w) of Regulation

S-X, since this Rule was redesignated in Exchange Act Release No. 34-35094.

g. Topic 1.J, the first paragraph of the interpretative response is modified to remove the reference to specific percentages and refer to the significance tests in Rule 3-05.

h. Topic 1.L is deleted since it refers to the bankruptcy of a specific accounting firm (Laventhol & Horwath) which occurred in 1990.

i. Topic 1.M is modified to update references to authoritative literature such as SAS 99, *Consideration of Fraud in a Financial Statement Audit*, which superseded SAS 82, *Consideration of Fraud in a Financial Statement Audit*.

2. TOPIC 2: BUSINESS COMBINATIONS-Note: In June 2001, the FASB issued Statement 141, which superseded APB Opinion 16, and Statement 142 which superseded APB Opinion 17. Paragraph 13 of Statement 141 requires all business combinations within the scope of that statement to be accounted for using the purchase method as described in that statement. The provisions of Statement 141 are applicable to all business combinations initiated after June 30, 2001. The pooling-of-interests method of accounting for business combinations, as provided for in APB Opinion 16, is no longer permitted for business combinations initiated after June 30, 2001. Several of the interpretive questions in this topic relate to the conditions that must be met in order for a business combination to be appropriately accounted for under the pooling-of-interests method. Accordingly, these interpretive questions are no longer needed.

a. Topic 2.A.1 is deleted. This topic addresses the impact of cash contingencies on classifying a combination as a pooling-of-interests. Since business combinations cannot be accounted for using the pooling-of-interests method, the guidance is no longer relevant.

b. Topic 2.A.2 is deleted. This topic contained two interpretive questions regarding how the acquiring corporation should be determined in a purchase business combination, following the guidance in APB Opinion 16. These interpretations were premised on the language contained in paragraph 70 of APB Opinion 16, which indicated that ". . . presumptive evidence of the acquiring corporation in combinations effected by an exchange of stock is obtained by identifying the former common stockholder interests of a combining company which either retain or receive the larger portion of the voting rights in the combined corporation. That corporation should be treated as the acquirer unless other evidence clearly indicates that another corporation is the acquirer." Guidance on identifying the acquiring entity is now provided in paragraphs 15 through 19 of Statement 141. This guidance provides several factors to be considered in determining the acquiring entity, one of which is the relative voting rights in the combined entity after the combination. The presumptive language contained in APB Opinion 16 was not retained in Statement 141. Therefore, the guidance in Topic 2.A.2 is no longer relevant.

c. Topic 2.A.3 is deleted. This topic provided interpretive guidance regarding the application of the purchase method of accounting for business combinations to acquisitions of financial institutions during a period of unusual economic conditions (i.e., a period of abnormally high interest rates). This guidance focused on: 1) unique considerations in the allocation of purchase price to acquired tangible and intangible assets in financial institution acquisitions (such as the determination of the fair values of assets acquired, and the identification and valuation of identifiable intangible assets), 2) the appropriate measure of the fair value of deposit liabilities assumed in acquisitions of financial institutions, and 3) the appropriate amortization periods and methods for intangible assets acquired and goodwill arising from financial institution acquisitions. Statements 141 and 147 provide new guidance as to the criteria for recognizing an intangible asset apart from goodwill in a purchase business combination. Statement 142 provides new guidance on the initial recognition and measurement of intangible assets, and the determination of the useful lives and amortization methods for intangible assets subject to amortization. Statement 142 also provides new guidance on accounting for goodwill. Consequently, the guidance contained in this topic is no longer relevant.

d. Topic 2.A.4 is deleted. This topic provided guidance on the determination of the appropriate amortization period for goodwill arising from financial institution acquisitions which occurred after December 23, 1981 at the time an entity participating in such an acquisition became an SEC registrant. Under the provisions of Statement 142, goodwill is not amortized, but instead must be tested for impairment at least annually following the methodology provided in that statement. Therefore, the guidance in this topic is no longer relevant.

e. Topic 2.A.5 is modified to update the former references to APB Opinion 16 contained therein to the relevant portions of Statement 141, and to otherwise make the language in this guidance consistent with the provisions of Statement 141.

f. Topic 2.A.6 is modified to update the former references to APB Opinion 16 contained therein to the relevant portions of Statement 141, and to otherwise make the language in this guidance consistent with the provisions of Statement 141.

g. Topic 2.A.7 is modified to update the former references to APB Opinion 16 contained therein to the relevant portions of Statement 141, and to otherwise make the language in this guidance consistent with the provisions of Statement 141.

h. Topic 2.A.8 is modified to update the former references to APB Opinion 16 contained therein to the relevant portions of Statement 141, and to otherwise make the language in this guidance consistent with the provisions of Statement 141. Furthermore, footnote 2 is deleted, since this footnote provided transition guidance which is no longer necessary due to the passage of time.

i. Topic 2.A.9 is modified to update the former references to APB Opinion 16 contained therein to the relevant portions of Statement 141, and to otherwise make the language in this guidance consistent with the provisions of Statement 141.

j. Topic 2.B is deleted. It addressed the treatment of merger expenses in a pooling-of-interests combination. Since, under Statement 141, all combinations are treated as purchases, this guidance is no longer necessary.

k. Topic 2.C is deleted. It addressed certain pro forma disclosures required for a pooling-of-interests combination. Since, under Statement 141, all combinations are treated as purchases, this guidance is no longer necessary.

l. Topic 2.D is modified to update the former references to APB Opinion 16 contained therein to the relevant portions of Statement 141, and to otherwise make the language in this guidance consistent with the provisions of Statement 141 and to delete portions of the guidance related to pooling-of-interests accounting.

m. Topic 2.E is deleted. The topic addressed the implications of risk sharing provisions on the classification of a combination as a pooling-of-interests. Since, under Statement 141, all combinations are treated as purchases, this guidance is no longer necessary.

n. Topic 2.F is deleted. This topic addressed the implications of treasury stock transactions following the consummation of a business combination on the classification of a combination as a pooling-of-interest. Since, under Statement 141, all combinations are treated as purchases, this guidance is no longer necessary.

3. TOPIC 3: SENIOR SECURITIES

a. Topic 3.C is modified to include a reference to EIT Topic D-98 in the interpretive response to Question 1.

4. TOPIC 4: EQUITY ACCOUNTS

a. Topic 4.B is retitled. It previously referred to Subchapter S Corporations. Such entities are now referred to as S Corporations.

b. Topic 4.E is modified to revise the interpretive response to be consistent with revisions subsequently made in Rule 5-02.30 of Regulation S-X.

5. TOPIC 5: MISCELLANEOUS ACCOUNTING

a. Topics 5.C.1 and 5.C.2 are deleted. These topics provided interpretive guidance related to the current recognition of tax loss carryforwards under APB Opinion 11, *Accounting for Income Taxes*. APB Opinion 11 has since been superseded by Statement 109 and the guidance contained in these topics is no longer relevant.

b. Topic 5.E, question 1 is modified to add an appropriate reference to FASB Interpretation 46.

c. Topic 5.E, question 2 is modified to remove, in the interpretive response, the reference to APB Opinion 30, since the relevant authoritative guidance that this response was referring to (accounting for the

disposal of a segment of a business) has been superseded by Statement 144. Additionally, that interpretive response is modified to remove the reference to ASR 95, *Accounting for Real Estate Transactions Where Circumstances Indicate that Profits Were Not Earned at the Time the Transactions Were Recorded*, which previously was rescinded.

d. Topic 5.F is modified to delete the reference in the interpretive response to Statement 8, *Accounting for the Translation of Foreign Currency Transactions and Foreign Currency Financial Statements*, which has since been superseded.

e. Topic 5.J, footnote 1 has been modified to reflect the fact that the FASB has not determined when or whether it will address push down accounting. Additionally, the interpretive response to question 3 has been modified to include reference to the guidance provided in Interpretation 45.

f. Topic 5.M is modified in order to conform this guidance with the provisions of Statement 115, *Accounting for Certain Investments in Debt and Equity Securities*, which superseded Statement 12, *Accounting for Certain Marketable Securities*. The guidance contained in question 1 of this interpretation continues to be relevant, because Statement 115, like Statement 12, requires a determination of whether a decline in the fair value of debt or equity securities is other than temporary. References to the applicable authoritative literature in the interpretive response to this question are changed, and the language in the interpretive response to question 1 is modified, to be consistent with the new authoritative guidance. Question 2 and the related interpretive response are deleted since Statement 115, paragraph 16 now provides relevant guidance on determining the amount of the write down when a decline in fair value is judged to be other than temporary.

g. Topics 5.P.1 and 5.P.2 are deleted. These topics provided interpretive guidance related to APB Opinion 30 and EITF Issues 94-3, *Liability Recognition for Certain Employee Termination Benefits and Other Costs to Exit an Activity (Including Certain Costs Incurred in a Restructuring)*, and 95-3, *Recognition of Liabilities in Connection with a Purchase Business Combination*, as they applied to restructuring provisions. Statement 146 establishes standards for accruing liabilities related to exiting activities and requires that the liability be recorded when it has been incurred and that it be recorded at its fair value. Accordingly, the previous guidance provided in these topics is no longer needed.

h. Topic 5.P.3 is modified to delete the language that referred to the requirements of APB Opinion 30 regarding the reporting of discontinued operations, which has since been superseded by Statement 144. Footnote 13 of this guidance also has been modified and renumbered to make reference to Statement 131, *Disclosures about Segments of an Enterprise and Related Information*, which superseded Statement 14, *Financial Reporting for Segments of a Business Enterprise*. The guidance in this footnote continues to be relevant, considering the revisions hereby made, under Statement 131.

¶39,069 **Release No. 103**

i. Topic 5.P.4 is modified to change the reference in former footnote 16 from Statement 38, *Accounting for Preacquisition Contingencies of Purchased Enterprises*, to Statement 141. Statement 141 superseded Statement 38, although the guidance in Statement 38 was carried forward into the new standard without reconsideration. Therefore, the guidance in this footnote remains relevant. Additionally, the topic is modified to reflect the disclosure requirements of Statement 146.

j. Topic 5.R is deleted. With the issuance of Statement 140, *Accounting for Transfers and Servicing of Financial Assets and Extinguishments of Liabilities*, and Interpretation 39, *Offsetting of Amounts Related to Certain Contracts*, this guidance is no longer needed.

k. Topic 5.S, question 4 is modified to change the references in the interpretive response from Statement 96, *Accounting for Income Taxes*, to the relevant provisions in Statement 109. Although Statement 109 superseded Statement 96, the guidance in this interpretive response remains relevant, considering the revisions hereby made, because Statement 109 carried forward the same guidance contained in Statement 96 with respect to quasi-reorganizations.

l. Topic 5.T, footnote 2 is modified to remove reference to APB Opinion 16, which was superseded, and Topic 2.B, which is being deleted.

m. Topic 5.U is modified to add new footnotes 4 and 5 to clarify the guidance applicable to gain deferral situations.

n. Topic 5.V is modified to note that the interpretive guidance therein does not apply to sales of the residual equity in an entity holding nonperforming loans to an unrelated party. Instead, the provisions of Statement 140 apply to such transactions. Also, it is modified to add an appropriate reference to FASB Interpretation 46 and to delete the reference to EITF Topic D-14, *Transactions involving Special-Purpose Entities*. In addition, footnote 5 has been modified to note that EITF Issue 87-17, *Spinoffs or Other Distributions of Loans Receivable to Shareholders*, was subsequently codified as issue 11 of EITF Issue 01-02, *Interpretations of APB Opinion No. 29*.

o. Topic 5.W is modified to incorporate the guidance of SOP 94-6, *Disclosure of Certain Significant Risks and Uncertainties*.

p. Topic 5.X is deleted. This interpretive guidance expressed the staff's views regarding the accounting for income tax benefits of thrift bad-debt losses. This guidance was intended to serve as interim guidance until a new standard on accounting for income taxes was adopted. The FASB subsequently issued Statement 109 which provides guidance on this issue.

q. Topic 5.Y is modified as follows:

i. The *Facts* section, questions 1, 2, and 3 are deleted. The remaining questions are renumbered. This information is no longer needed because the issues are addressed in SOP 96-1, *Environmental Remediation Liabilities*.

ii. Previously-numbered question 4 is modified to replace the reference to EITF Issue No. 93-5, *Accounting For Environmental Liabilities*, with SOP 96-1 (SOP

96-1 carried forward the guidance previously contained in EITF Issue 93-5). In addition, previously-numbered footnote 3, included in the interpretive response to question 4, is modified to provide the relevant language from Concepts Statement 7, *Using Cash Flow Information and Present Value in Accounting Measurements*.

iii. Previously-numbered question 5 is modified to incorporate guidance from and reference to SOP 96-1.

iv. The interpretive response to previously-numbered question 7 is modified to refer registrants to the disclosure requirements of Statement 143 for legal obligations associated with the retirement of tangible long-lived assets within the scope of that statement and to Interpretation 45 for guarantees.

v. Previously-numbered question 8 and the related interpretive response are deleted. This guidance, related to the appropriate accounting for site restoration costs, post-closure and monitoring costs, or other environmental costs incurred at the end of the useful life of an asset, is no longer relevant due to the issuance of Statement 143, which establishes accounting standards for recognition and measurement of liabilities for asset retirement obligations and associated asset retirement costs.

r. Topic 5.Z.1 is deleted. The guidance in this interpretive response provided the staff's views as to whether the criteria under APB Opinion 30 for presentation as discontinued operations had been met under certain facts and circumstances. Statement 144 provides new guidance on reporting discontinued operations that supersedes the portions of APB Opinion 30 that addressed this issue. Therefore, this interpretative guidance is no longer relevant.

s. Topic 5.Z.2 is deleted. The guidance in these interpretive responses provided the staff's views as to whether the criteria under APB Opinion 30 for presentation as discontinued operations had been met under certain facts and circumstances. Statement 144 provides new guidance on reporting discontinued operations that supersedes the portions of APB Opinion 30 that addressed this issue. Therefore, this interpretative guidance is no longer relevant.

t. Topic 5.Z.3 is deleted. The guidance in these interpretive responses provided the staff's views as to whether the criteria under APB Opinion 30 for presentation as discontinued operations had been met under certain facts and circumstances. Statement 144 provides new guidance on reporting discontinued operations that supersedes the portions of APB Opinion 30 that addressed this issue. Therefore, this interpretative guidance is no longer relevant.

u. Topic 5.Z.4 is modified to be consistent with the guidance of Statement 144, which superseded the previous guidance of APB Opinion 30.

v. Topic 5.Z.5 is modified to reflect the appropriate terminology from Statement 144 (separate component) rather than that previously provided by APB Opinion 30 (segment of a business), to make other changes related to the accounting provisions of Statement 144, and to remind registrants of the disclosure requirements of Interpretation 45.

w. Topic 5.Z.6 is deleted. This topic provided the staff's views as to whether subsidiaries that a company intends to sell, which cannot be reported as discontinued operations under APB Opinion 30, must be consolidated in the company's financial statements. This interpretive question arose as a result of the "temporary control" exception to consolidation in ARB 51, *Consolidated Financial Statements*, as amended by Statement 94, *Consolidation of all Majority-Owned Subsidiaries*. Statement 144 provides guidance which supersedes the guidance in APB Opinion 30 related to the reporting of discontinued operations. Statement 144 also amended ARB 51 to eliminate the exception to consolidation for a subsidiary for which control is likely to be temporary. Therefore, the interpretive guidance in this topic is no longer relevant.

x. Topic 5.Z.7 is modified to change the reference therein from APB Opinion 30 to Statement 144. Furthermore, the interpretive response is also amended to add language clarifying the staff's interpretation of the term "dissimilar" based on long-standing staff practice.

y. Topic 5.AA is deleted. Statement 140 superseded the previous guidance on extinguishments of debt. Accordingly, the guidance is no longer needed.

z. Topic 5.CC is modified. Topic 5.CC provides interpretive guidance on certain questions related to the recognition and measurement of impairment of the carrying amount of long-lived assets, certain identifiable intangible assets, and goodwill pursuant to the provisions of Statement 121 and APB Opinion 17. A portion of this guidance has since been superseded by Statements 142 and 144 and is now deleted. The remaining relevant guidance is rewritten so that it is consistent with the requirements of Statements 142 and 144.

6. TOPIC 6: INTERPRETATIONS OF ACCOUNTING SERIES RELEASES

a. Topic 6.A.1 is deleted. ASR 166, *Disclosure of Unusual Risks and Uncertainties in Financial Reporting*, has been rescinded. Therefore, the guidance contained in this topic is no longer relevant.

b. Topic 6.F.1 is deleted. This interpretation provided interpretive guidance on the requirements of Rule 12-03 of Regulation S-X. The schedule previously required under Rule 12-03 was eliminated by Exchange Act Release No. 34-35094. Therefore, the guidance contained in this topic is no longer necessary.

c. Topic 6.G.1 is modified as follows:

i. The interpretive response to Question 5 is modified to incorporate the terminology used in Statement 144.

ii. Question 7 and the related interpretive response under sub-section a. to this topic are modified to remove the reference to Form 8, which was rescinded by Exchange Act Release No. 34-31905.

iii. Sub-section c. and the related questions and interpretive responses thereunder are deleted. Item 302(a)(5) of Regulation S-K was amended by Exchange Act Release No. 34-42266 which made the requirements of Item 302(a) of Regulation S-K applicable to any registrant, except a foreign private issuer, that has securities registered pursuant to sections 12(b) or 12(g) of the Exchange Act. Therefore, the guidance contained in these questions and interpretive responses, which related to the former requirements of Item 302(a) of Regulation S-K, no longer applies.

d. Topic 6.G.2.a is modified as follows:

i. Question 4 is modified to refer to cash and cash equivalents rather than to funds. APB Opinion 19, *Reporting Changes in Financial Position*, referred to flow of funds. Statement 95, *Statement of Cash Flows*, superseded APB Opinion 19 and refers to flow of cash and cash equivalents.

ii. Question 5 is deleted. Question 5 refers to an analysis of changes in each element of working capital, which is consistent with a "funds" model. However, with the provisions of Statement 95, which uses "cash and cash equivalents," this guidance is no longer relevant.

e. Topic 6.G.2.b.1 is modified to add a footnote reference to APB Opinion 20, *Accounting Changes*, which requires disclosure of the nature and justification of a change in accounting principle.

f. Topic 6.H is modified as follows:

i. The *Facts* section is modified to delete item (3), since the related supplemental schedule that this item was referring to (Rule 12-10 of Regulation S-X) was eliminated by Exchange Act Release No. 34-35094.

ii. Topic 6.H.1.b is modified to refer to Rule 17a-5 as currently numbered.

iii. Topic 6.H.2.a is modified to remove the reference to ASR 172, *Notice of Rescission of Guidelines Set Forth in Accounting Series Release No. 148 Pertaining to Classification of Short-Term Obligations Expected to be Refinanced*.

iv. Topic 6.H.4.c and the related question and interpretive response thereunder are deleted. The schedule formerly required pursuant to Rule 12-10 of Regulation S-X was eliminated by Exchange Act Release No. 34-35094. Therefore, this guidance, which related to the disclosures previously required under Rule 12-10, is no longer relevant.

g. Topic 6.I.3 is modified to refer to discontinued operations rather than discontinuance or disposals of business segments so that it is consistent with Statement 144.

h. Topic 6.I.7 is modified to refer to Rule 4-08(h) rather than Rule 4-08(g) to reflect current numbering.

i. Topic 6.K.1 is deleted. This topic provided interpretive guidance related to the early adoption of ASR 302, *Separate Financial Statements Required by Regulation S-X*. This guidance is no longer necessary due to the passage of time.

j. Topic 6.4.b is modified to refer to Rule 1-02(w). The rules for determining significant subsidiaries were previously renumbered and moved to subsection (w).

7. TOPIC 7: REAL ESTATE COMPANIES

a. Topic 7.A is deleted. This topic provided guidance on the presentation of funds data in quarterly reports on Form 10-Q for real estate companies. This guidance is no longer relevant due to the issuance Statement 95.

b. Topic 7.B is deleted. This topic provided guidance on the appropriate format for the statement of changes in financial position for registrants engaged in retail land development and sale activities. This guidance is no longer relevant due to the issuance of Statement 95.

8. TOPIC 8: RETAIL COMPANIES

a. The *Facts* to Topic 8.A are rewritten to make them more generically applicable to retail companies.

9. TOPIC 9: FINANCE COMPANIES

a. Topic 9.A is deleted. This topic provided interpretive guidance on the appropriate accounting for nonrefundable "points" charged by finance companies at the time a loan transaction is closed. Related guidance is now provided in Statement 91, *Accounting for Nonrefundable Fees and Costs Associated with Originating or Acquiring Loans and Initial Direct Costs of Leases*, making the continued need for the guidance in this topic unnecessary.

10. TOPIC 10: UTILITY COMPANIES

a. In the interpretive response to Topic 10.A, reference to Rule 4-08(j) is deleted since that rule no longer exists.

b. Topic 10.B is deleted. This topic provided interpretive guidance on disclosures that should be made concerning the estimated future costs of storing spent nuclear fuel and decommissioning nuclear generating plants. Statement 143 establishes accounting standards for recognition and measurement of a liability for an asset retirement obligation and the associated asset retirement cost, including required disclosures. Therefore, the guidance in this topic is no longer relevant.

c. Topic 10.C is modified to add a footnote reminding registrants to consider the guidance provided in Interpretation 46.

d. In the interpretive response to Topic 10.D, the second, third and fourth sentences of the final paragraph are deleted. These sentences referred to ASR 122, *Coverage of Fixed Charges*, which has been rescinded. Additionally, a footnote is added to remind registrants of the need to consider the guidance provided in Interpretations 45 and 46 and Statement 133, *Accounting for Derivative Instruments and Hedging Activities* and related literature.

e. Topic 10.E, question 2 and related interpretive response dealing with transition to the requirements of Statement 90, *Regulated Enterprises - Accounting for Abandonments and Disallowances of Plant Costs* is deleted as no longer necessary due to the passage of time.

f. Topic 10.F is modified to incorporate a footnote to the interpretive response to relate the response to the requirements of SOP 96-1.

11. TOPIC 11: MISCELLANEOUS DISCLOSURE

a. Topic 11.D is deleted. This topic provided interpretive guidance on the offsetting of related assets and liabilities. This guidance is no longer necessary due to the issuance of Interpretation 39.

b. Question 1 of Topic 11.H.2 is deleted with Questions 2 and 3 being renumbered as Questions 1 and 2. Question 1 and the Interpretive Response are no longer needed in light of the provisions of Statements 15 and 114.

c. Topic 11.J is deleted. This topic provided interpretive guidance on reporting information related to financial guarantees. This guidance is no longer necessary due to the issuance of Interpretation 45.

d. Topic 11.K, footnote one is modified to remove reference to activities of the FASB's financial instruments project which subsequently have been completed.

e. Topic 11.N, footnote 2 is modified to remove reference to Statement 72, *Accounting for Certain Acquisitions of Banking or Thrift Institutions (an Amendment of APB Opinion No. 17, an Interpretation of APB Opinions 16 and 17, and an Amendment of FASB Interpretation No. 9)*. With the issuance of Statement 147, the provisions of Statement 72 are no longer relevant to the accounting for such transactions.

12. TOPIC 12: OIL AND GAS PRODUCING ACTIVITIES

a. Topic 12.A.1 is revised to delete, in the interpretive response to question 3, the reference to Item 2(b)(3) of Regulation S-K, which has been redesignated within Industry Guide 2.

b. Topic 12.A.2 is revised to update the references to the required disclosures of the standardized measure of discounted future net cash flows to the provisions of Statement 69, *Disclosures about Oil and Gas Producing Activities*. Consistent with this change, reference to "standardized measure of discounted future net cash flows" is substituted for "estimated future net revenues" and "year end prices" substituted for "current prices" for consistency with the terminology used in Statement 69. Furthermore, questions 4-11, and the related interpretive responses to those questions which deal with the reporting implications of the Windfall Profits Tax and the 1985 natural gas price decontrol and disclosure of reserve information are deleted as no longer being relevant.

c. Topic 12 A.3.a is deleted. The required disclosures of the standardized measure of discounted future net cash flows is provided by Statement 69 and the guidance is no longer necessary.

d. Topic 12.A.3.c is revised to update the references to the required disclosures of the standardized measure of discounted future net cash flows to the provisions of Statement 69.

e. Topic 12.A.3.d is revised to update the references to the required disclosures of the standardized measure of discounted future net cash flows to the provisions of Statement 69.

f. Topic 12.A.4, regarding filings by Canadian registrants, is deleted as no longer being relevant.

g. Topic 12.B regarding supplemental disclosures on the basis of reserve recognition accounting is deleted as no longer being relevant.

h. Topic 12.C.2 is revised to update the references currently included in Regulation S-X.

i. Topic 12.D.1 is revised to update the references currently included in Regulation S-X.

j. Topic 12.D.2 is revised to update the references to the required disclosures of the standardized measure of discounted future net cash flows to the provisions of Statement 69.

k. Topic 12.D.3.a is revised to update the references currently included in Regulation S-X.

l. Topic 12.D.3.b is redesignated as Topic 12.D.3.c and revised to provide updated guidance consistent with Statement 133.

m. Topic 12.D.3.b is rewritten to reflect the changes in the computation as a result of changes in the authoritative literature related to derivatives accounted for in accordance with Statement 133.

n. Topic 12.F is revised to substitute the reference to Rule 4-10(c)(3)(iii) of Regulation S-X for outdated Rule 4-10(i)(3)(iii) of Regulation S-X.

o. Topic 12.G is revised to update the references to the required disclosures of the standardized measure of discounted future net cash flows to the provisions of Statement 69 and to substitute the reference to Rule 4-10(c)(4) of Regulation S-X for Rule 4-10(k)(4) of Regulation S-X.

13. TOPIC 13: REVENUE RECOGNITION

a. Topic 13.A.3, the following changes are made:

i. The interpretive response to question 3 is modified to incorporate the guidance on separate elements of an arrangement from EITF Issue 00-21. Additionally, footnote 24 is modified to remove the reference to Statement 53, *Financial Reporting by Producers and Distributors of Motion Picture Films*, which has been superseded and to add a reference to SOP 00-2, *Accounting by Producers or Distributors of Films*.

ii. The interpretive response to question 7 is modified to refer to Statement 140 which replaced Statement 125, *Accounting for Transfers and Servicing of Financial Assets and Extinguishments of Liabilities*.

b. Topic 13.B, footnote 6 is modified to refer to SAS 99 which superseded SAS 82.

[For the text of Topics 1—13, See ¶ 39,101—39,221. CCH]

[¶ 39,070]   RELEASE NO. 104, December 17, 2003

Revision of Topic 13.

ACTION: Publication of Staff Accounting Bulletin.

SUMMARY: This staff accounting bulletin revises or rescinds portions of the interpretative guidance included in Topic 13 of the codification of staff accounting bulletins in order to make this interpretive guidance consistent with current authoritative accounting and auditing guidance and SEC rules and regulations. The principal revisions relate to the rescission of material no longer necessary because of private sector developments in U.S. generally accepted accounting principles.

This staff accounting bulletin also rescinds the Revenue Recognition in Financial Statements Frequently Asked Questions and Answers document issued in conjunction with Topic 13. Selected portions of that document have been incorporated into Topic 13.

DATE: December 17, 2003

FOR FURTHER INFORMATION CONTACT: Chad Kokenge or Shelly Luisi in the Office of the Chief Accountant (202) 942-4400, Securities and Exchange Commission, 450 Fifth Street, NW, Washington, DC 20549-1103.

SUPPLEMENTARY INFORMATION: The statements in staff accounting bulletins are not rules or interpretations of the Commission, nor are they published as bearing the Commission's approval. They represent interpretations and practices followed by the Division of Corporation Finance and the Office of

Chief Accountant in administering the disclosure requirements of the Federal securities laws.

Margaret H. McFarland

Deputy Secretary

Date: December 17, 2003

Part 211 - (AMEND)

Accordingly, Part 211 of Title 17 of the Code of Federal Regulations is amended by adding Staff Accounting Bulletin No. 104 to the table found in Subpart B.

STAFF ACCOUNTING BULLETIN NO. 104

[*Note*: The text of SAB 104 will not appear in the Code of Federal Regulations.]

The staff hereby revises Topic 13 of the Staff Accounting Bulletin Series as follows:

1. Topic 13.A.1 is modified as follows:

a. The examples of existing literature referenced in the first paragraph are deleted.

b. The last paragraph, including footnote 7, is added to make reference to EITF Issue 00-21, "*Revenue Arrangements with Multiple Deliverables*," which governs how to determine if revenue arrangements contain more than one unit of accounting.

2. Topic 13.A.2 is modified as follows:

a. Question 3 (formerly Question 1 of the staff's Revenue Recognition in Financial Statements Frequently Asked Questions and Answers document (FAQ)) is added.

3. Topic 13.A.3 is modified as follows:

a. The subheading *Bill and hold arrangements* is added.

b. Topic 13.A.3(a) Question is formerly Question 3.

c. The subheading *Customer acceptance* is added.

d. Topic 13.A.3(b) Question 1 (formerly Question 5 of the FAQ) is added. The question format is conformed.

e. Topic 13.A.3(b) Question 2 (formerly Question 6 of the FAQ) is added. The facts, question and interpretive response are modified to reflect the evaluation of the arrangement in the context of separate units of accounting. In addition, the last paragraph of the interpretive response is deleted due to the issuance of EITF Issue 00-21.

f. Footnote 29 is added to highlight that the changes to Topic 13.A.3(b) Question 2 are to facilitate an analysis of revenue recognition, not interpret EITF Issue 00-21.

g. Topic 13.A.3(b) Question 3 (formerly Exhibit A Example 1 Scenario A of the FAQ) is added.

h. Topic 13.A.3(b) Question 4 (formerly Exhibit A Example 1 Scenario B of the FAQ) is added.

i. Topic 13.A.3(b) Question 5 (formerly Exhibit A Example 1 Scenario C of the FAQ) is added.

j. The subheading *Inconsequential or perfunctory performance obligations* is added.

k. Topic 13.A.3(c) Question 1 (formerly Question 2 of the FAQ) is added. The question and interpretive response are modified from the FAQ to reflect the evaluation of the arrangement in the context of a single unit of accounting. The question format is conformed.

l. Topic 13.A.3(c) Question 2 (formerly Question 3 of the FAQ) is added. The question and interpretive response are modified from the FAQ to reflect the evaluation in the context of a single unit of accounting.

m. Topic 13.A.3(c) Question 3 (formerly Question 7 of the FAQ) is added. The facts, question and interpretive response are modified to reflect the evaluation of the arrangement in the context of combined deliverables, which result in a single unit of accounting. In addition, the interpretive response is modified to delete the last four sentences as this guidance is no longer necessary due to the issuance of EITF 00-21.

n. The segue sentence and related footnote discussing delivery or performance of multiple deliverables is deleted to eliminate redundancy.

o. The subheading *License fee revenue* is added.

p. Topic 13.A.3(d) Question (formerly Question 9 of the FAQ) is added. The interpretive response is modified to eliminate redundancy.

q. The subheading *Layaway sales arrangements* is added.

r. Topic 13.A.3(e) Question is formerly Question 4.

s. The subheading *Nonrefundable up-front fees* is added.

t. The examples in Topic 13.A.3(f) Question 1 (formerly Question 5) are modified to include the examples from what was formerly Question 10 of the FAQ. Guidance in the interpretive response is added and conformed from Question 10 of the FAQ which clarifies the incurrence of substantive costs does not necessarily indicate there is a separate earnings event, and that the determination of a separate earnings event should be evaluated on a case-by-case basis.

u. Footnote 36 is added to clarify the staff's view regarding the vendor activities associated with up-front fees.

v. Topic 13.A.3(f) Question 2 (formerly Question 6) is modified to reflect the evaluation in the context of a single unit of accounting.

w. Footnote 14 is deleted. The subject matter of footnote 14 is conformed and included in Topic 13.A.3(f) Question 3; accordingly, Topic 13.A.3(f) Question 3 reflects the guidance formerly located in footnote 14.

x. Topic 13.A.3(f) Question 4 (formerly Question 15 of the FAQ) is added. The question format is conformed.

y. Topic 13.A.3(f) Question 5 (formerly Question 16 of the FAQ) is added. The question format is conformed.

z. The subheading *Deliverables within an arrangement* is added.

aa. Topic 13.A.3(g) Question (formerly Question 8 of the FAQ) is added and is modified to reflect the evaluation of the question under EITF Issue 00-21.

bb. Footnote 45 is added to clarify the staff's view of the obligation described in Topic 13.A.3(g) Question under FIN 45.

4. Topic 13.A.4 is modified as follows:

a. The subheading *Refundable fees for services* is added.

b. Topic 13.A.4(a) Question 1 is formerly Question 7.

c. Footnote 56 is added to include guidance from Question 23 of the FAQ.

d. Topic 13.A.4(a) Question 2 (formerly Question 18 of the FAQ) is added.

e. Topic 13.A.4(a) Question 3 (formerly Question 19 of the FAQ) is added. The question format is conformed.

f. Topic 13.A.4(a) Question 4 (formerly Question 20 of the FAQ) is added.

g. Topic 13.A.4(a) Question 5 (formerly Question 21 of the FAQ) is added. The question format is conformed.

h. Topic 13.A.4(a) Question 6 (formerly Question 22 of the FAQ) is added.

i. The subheading *Estimates and changes in estimates* is added.

j. Topic 13.A.4(b) Question 1 is formerly Question 9.

k. Topic 13.A.4(b) Question 2 (formerly Question 24 of the FAQ) is added.

l. Topic 13.A.4(b) Question 3 (formerly Question 25 of the FAQ) is added. The question format is conformed. The last two sentences of the interpretive response are deleted to eliminate redundancy.

m. Topic 13.A.4(b) Question 4 (formerly Question 26 of the FAQ) is added.

n. Topic 13.A.4(b) Question 5 (formerly Question 27 of the FAQ) is added.

o. The subheading *Contingent rental income* is added.

p. Topic 13.A.4(c) Question is formerly Question 8.

q. The subheading *Claims processing and billing services* is added.

r. Topic 13.A.4(d) Question (formerly Question 28 of the FAQ) is added. The facts are modified to reflect to evaluation in the context of a single unit of accounting.

5. Topic 13.A.5 is deleted. This topic provided guidance on income statement presentation and whether transactions should be presented on a gross as a principal or net as an agent basis. EITF Issue 99-19, *"Reporting Revenue Gross as a Principal versus Net as an Agent"*, which was issued subsequent to SAB 101, provides such guidance. Therefore, this guidance is no longer necessary.

6. Topic 13.B is modified as follows:

a. The interpretive response to Question 1 is modified to reference multiple units of accounting in lieu of multiple elements.

b. Question 2 is modified to delete the reference to Question 10 of Topic 13.A and Topic 8.A.

c. Question 3 (formerly Question 29 of the FAQ) is added.

d. Question 4 (formerly Question 30 of the FAQ) is added.

e. Question 5 (formerly Question 31 of the FAQ) is added.

[For the text of Topics 1—13, See ¶ 39,101—39,221. CCH]

[¶ 39,071]   RELEASE NO. 105, March 9, 2004

Application of Accounting Principles to Loan Commitments

AGENCY: Securities and Exchange Commission

ACTION: Publication of Staff Accounting Bulletin

SUMMARY: This staff accounting bulletin summarizes the views of the staff regarding the application of generally accepted accounting principles to loan commitments accounted for as derivative instruments.

DATE: March 9, 2004

FOR FURTHER INFORMATION CONTACT: John James, Greg Cross or Eric Schuppenhauer, Office of the Chief Accountant (202) 942-4400, or Louise Dorsey, Division of Corporation Finance (202) 942-2960, Securities and Exchange Commission, 450 Fifth Street, NW, Washington, DC 20549.

SUPPLEMENTARY INFORMATION: The statements in staff accounting bulletins are not rules or interpretations of the Commission, nor are they published as bearing the Commission's official approval. They represent interpretations and practices followed by the Division of Corporation Finance and the Office

of the Chief Accountant in administering the disclosure requirements of the Federal securities laws.

Jill M. Peterson

Assistant Secretary

Date: March 9, 2004

Part 211 - (AMEND)

Accordingly, Part 211 of Title 17 of the Code of Federal Regulations is amended by adding Staff Accounting Bulletin No. 105 to the table found in Subpart B.

STAFF ACCOUNTING BULLETIN NO. 105

The staff hereby adds Section DD to Topic 5 of the Staff Accounting Bulletin Series. Topic 5:DD provides guidance regarding loan commitments accounted for as derivative instruments.

TOPIC 5: MISCELLANEOUS ACCOUNTING

* * * * * * *

DD. Loan Commitments Accounted for as Derivative Instruments

Facts : Bank A enters into a loan commitment with a customer to extend a mortgage loan at a specified rate. Bank A intends to sell the mortgage loan after it is funded. Under Statement No. 133, such a loan commitment should be accounted for as a derivative instrument and measured at fair value.[1] Bank A expects to receive future cash flows related to servicing rights from servicing fees (included in the loan's interest rate or otherwise), late charges, and other ancillary sources, or from selling the servicing rights into the market.

Question 1 : In recognizing the loan commitment, may Bank A consider the expected future cash flows related to the associated servicing of the loan?

Interpretive Response : No. The staff believes that incorporating expected future cash flows related to the associated servicing of the loan essentially results in the immediate recognition of a servicing asset. However, servicing assets are to be recognized only once the servicing asset has been contractually separated from the underlying loan by sale or securitization of the loan with servicing retained.[2]

Further, no other internally-developed intangible assets (such as customer relationship intangible assets) should be recorded as part of the loan commitment derivative. Recognition of such assets would only be appropriate in a third-party transaction (for example, the purchase of a loan commitment either individually, in a portfolio, or in a business combination).

Question 2 : What disclosures should Bank A provide with respect to loan commitments accounted for as derivative instruments?

Interpretive Response : Bank A should disclose its accounting policy for loan commitments pursuant to APB Opinion No. 22, *Disclosure of Accounting Policies*. Bank A should provide disclosures related to loan commitments accounted for as derivatives, including methods and assumptions used to estimate fair value and any associated hedging strategies, as required by Statement No. 107,[3] Statement No. 133 and Item 305 of Regulation S-K. Additionally, Bank A should provide disclosures required by Item 303 of Regulation S-K and any related interpretive guidance.

Question 3 : Will the staff expect retroactive changes by registrants to comply with the accounting described in this bulletin?

Interpretive Response : The staff will not object if registrants that have not been applying the accounting described in this bulletin continue to use their existing accounting policies for loan commitments accounted for as derivatives entered into on or before March 31, 2004. For loan commitments accounted for as derivatives and entered into subsequent to that date, the staff expects all registrants to apply the accounting described in this bulletin. Financial statements filed with the Commission before applying the guidance in this bulletin should include disclosures similar to those described in SAB Topic 11:M.

[For the text of Topic 5, see ¶ 39,141. CCH]

[¶ 39,072] RELEASE No. 106, September 28, 2004

Application of FASB Statement No. 143, *Accounting for Asset Retirement Obligations,* by Oil and Gas Producing Companies Following the Full Cost Accounting Method

SECURITIES AND EXCHANGE COMMISSION

AGENCY: Securities and Exchange Commission.

ACTION: Publication of Staff Accounting Bulletin.

SUMMARY: The interpretations in this staff accounting bulletin express the staff's views regarding the application of FASB Statement No. 143, *Accounting for Asset Retirement Obligations,* by oil and gas producing companies following the full cost accounting method.

DATES: September 28, 2004

FOR FURTHER INFORMATION CONTACT: Cathy J. Cole or John W. Albert, Office of the Chief Accountant (202) 942-4400 or Leslie A. Overton, Division of Corporation Finance (202) 942-2960, Securities and Exchange Commission, 450 Fifth Street, NW, Washington, DC 20549-1103.

SUPPLEMENTARY INFORMATION: The statements in staff accounting bulletins are not rules or interpretations of the Commission, nor are they published as bearing the Commission's official approval. They represent interpretations and practices followed by the Division of Corporation Finance and the Office of the Chief Accountant in administering the disclosure requirements of the Federal securities laws.

Margaret H. McFarland

Deputy Secretary

---

[1] Paragraph 3 of FASB Statement No. 149, *Amendment of Statement 133 on Derivative Instruments and Hedging Activities,* amended paragraph 6(c) of Statement No. 133,*Accounting for Derivative Instruments and Hedging Activities,* to add: "...loan commitments that relate to the origination of mortgage loans that will be held for sale, as discussed in paragraph 21 of FASB Statement No. 65, *Accounting for Mortgage Banking Activities* (as amended), shall be accounted for as derivative instruments by the issuer of the loan commitment (that is, the potential lender)." Similar guidance is provided in Statement 133 Implementation Issue No. C13, *Scope Exceptions: When a Loan Commitment Is Included in the Scope of Statement 133.*

[2] See paragraph 61 of FASB Statement No. 140, *Accounting for Transfers and Servicing of Financial Assets and Extinguishments of Liabilities.*

[3] FASB Statement No. 107, *Disclosures about Fair Value of Financial Instruments.*

Date: September 28, 2004

Part 211—(AMEND)

Accordingly, Part 211 of Title 17 of the Code of Federal Regulations is amended by adding Staff Accounting Bulletin No. 106 to the table found in Subpart B.

STAFF ACCOUNTING BULLETIN NO. 106

The staff hereby adds Section 4 to Topic 12-D of the staff accounting bulletin series. Topic 12-D.4 provides guidance regarding the interaction of Statement of Financial Accounting Standards No. 143, *Accounting for Asset Retirement Obligations*, with the full cost accounting rules in Article 4-10 of Regulation S-X.

TOPIC 12: OIL AND GAS PRODUCING ACTIVITIES

* * * * *

D. Application of Full Cost Method of Accounting

* * * * *

4. Interaction of Statement 143[1] and the Full Cost Rules

a. Impact of Statement 143 on the full cost ceiling test

Facts : A company following the full cost method of accounting under Rule 4-10(c) of Regulation S-X must periodically calculate a limitation on capitalized costs, *i.e.*, the full cost ceiling. Prior to adopting Statement 143, in calculating the full cost ceiling a company reduced the expected future revenues from proved oil and gas reserves by the estimated future expenditures to be incurred in developing and producing such reserves discounted using a factor specified in the rule. While expected future cash flows related to the asset retirement obligation (ARO) were included in the calculation of the ceiling test, no associated asset was recorded. Under Statement 143, a company must recognize a liability for an asset retirement obligation at fair value in the period in which the obligation is incurred, if a reasonable estimate of fair value can be made. The company also must initially capitalize the associated asset retirement costs by increasing long-lived oil and gas assets by the same amount as the liability. Any asset retirement costs capitalized pursuant to Statement 143 are subject to the full cost ceiling limitation under Rule 4-10(c)(4) of Regulation S-X. If after adoption of Statement 143, a company were to continue calculating the full cost ceiling by reducing expected future net revenues by the cash flows required to settle the ARO, then the effect would be to "double-count" such costs in the ceiling test. The assets that must be recovered would be increased while the future net revenues available to recover the assets continue to be reduced by the amount of the ARO settlement cash flows.

Question 1 : After adopting Statement 143, how should a company compute the full cost ceiling to avoid double-counting the expected future cash outflows associated with asset retirement costs? *Interpretive Response* : After adoption of Statement 143, the future cash outflows associated with settling AROs that have been accrued on the balance sheet should be excluded from the computation of the present value of estimated future net revenues for purposes of the full cost ceiling calculation.[2],[3]

Question 2 : What disclosures should the company provide on the interaction of Statement 143 and the full cost rules?

Interpretive Response : In order to inform financial statement users on the interaction of Statement 143 and the full cost rules, a company following such rules is expected to provide appropriate disclosures in the financial statement footnotes and Management's Discussion and Analysis explaining in detail how the adoption of Statement 143 impacts its accounting for oil and gas operations. This disclosure is expected to address each area of accounting that is impacted and expected to be impacted and should specifically address each way that the company's application of full cost accounting has changed as a result of adoption of Statement 143. These disclosures and discussions should include, but are not limited to, how the company's calculation of the ceiling test and depreciation, depletion, and amortization are affected by the adoption of Statement 143.

b. Impact of Statement 143 on the calculation of depreciation, depletion, and amortization

Facts : Regarding the base for depreciation, depletion, and amortization (DD&A) of proved reserves, Rule 4-10(c)(3)(i) of Regulations S-X states that "[c]osts to be amortized shall include (A) all capitalized costs, less accumulated amortization, other than the cost of properties described in paragraph (ii) below;[4] (B) the estimated future expenditures (based on current costs) to be incurred in developing proved reserves; and (C) estimated dismantlement and abandonment costs, net of estimated salvage values."

Statement 143 requires that upon initial recognition of an ARO, the associated asset retirement costs be included in the capitalized costs of the company.

---

[1] Statement of Financial Accounting Standards No. 143 (Statement 143), *Accounting for Asset Retirement Obligations*, is effective for financial statements issued for fiscal years beginning after June 15, 2002.

[2] If an obligation for expected asset retirement costs has not been accrued under Statement 143 for certain asset retirement costs required to be included in the full cost ceiling calculation under Rule 4-10(c)(4), such costs should continue to be included in the full cost ceiling calculation.

[3] This approach is consistent with the guidance in paragraph 12 of Statement 143 on testing for impairment under Statement of

Financial Accounting Standards No. 144, *Accounting for the Impairment or Disposal of Long-Lived Assets*. Under that guidance, the asset tested should include capitalized asset retirement costs. The estimated cash flows related to the associated ARO that has been recognized in the financial statements are to be excluded from both the undiscounted cash flows used to test for recoverability and the discounted cash flows used to measure the asset's fair value.

[4] The reference to "cost of properties described in paragraph (ii) below" relates to the costs of investments in unproved properties and major development projects, as defined. *http://www.sec.gov/ interps/account/sab106.htm*

Therefore, subsequent to the adoption of Statement 143, the estimated dismantlement and abandonment costs described in (C) above may be included in the capitalized costs described in (A) above, at least to the extent that an ARO has been incurred as a result of acquisition, exploration and development activities to date. Future development activities on proved reserves may result in additional asset retirement obligations when such activities are performed and the associated asset retirement costs will be capitalized at that time.

Question: Following the adoption of Statement 143, should the costs to be amortized under Rule 4-10(c)(3) of Regulation S-X include an amount for estimated dismantlement and abandonment costs, net of estimated salvage values, that are expected to result from future development activities?

Interpretive Response : Yes. To the extent that estimated dismantlement and abandonment costs, net of estimated salvage values, have not been included as capitalized costs in the base for computing DD&A because they have not yet been capitalized as asset retirement costs under Statement 143, compliance with Rule 4-10(c)(3) of Regulation S-X continues to require that they be included in the base for computing DD&A. Companies should estimate the amount of dismantlement and abandonment costs that will be incurred as a result of future development activities on proved reserves and include those amounts in the costs to be amortized.

c. Transition

Question : When will registrants be expected to comply with the accounting and disclosures described in this bulletin?

Interpretive Response : All registrants are expected to apply the accounting and disclosures described in this bulletin prospectively as of the beginning of the first fiscal quarter beginning after the publication of this bulletin in the Federal Register. If a registrant files financial statements with the Commission before applying the guidance in this bulletin, disclosures similar to those described in Staff Accounting Bulletin Topic 11-M should be provided.

[For the text of Topic 12, see ¶ 39,211. CCH]

[¶ 39,073]   RELEASE NO. 107, March 29, 2005

Valuation of Share-Based Payment Arrangements for Public Companies

SECURITIES AND EXCHANGE COMMISSION

AGENCY: Securities and Exchange Commission.

ACTION: Publication of Staff Accounting Bulletin.

SUMMARY: The interpretations in this staff accounting bulletin ("SAB") express views of the staff regarding the interaction between Statement of Financial Accounting Standards Statement No. 123 (revised 2004), *Share-Based Payment* ("Statement 123R" or the "Statement") and certain Securities and Exchange Commission ("SEC") rules and regulations and provide the staff's views regarding the valuation of share-based payment arrangements for public companies. In particular, this SAB provides guidance related to share-based payment transactions with nonemployees, the transition from nonpublic to public entity status, valuation methods (including assumptions such as expected volatility and expected term), the accounting for certain redeemable financial instruments issued under share-based payment arrangements, the classification of compensation expense, non-GAAP financial measures, first-time adoption of Statement 123R in an interim period, capitalization of compensation cost related to share-based payment arrangements, the accounting for income tax effects of share-based payment arrangements upon adoption of Statement 123R, the modification of employee share options prior to adoption of Statement 123R and disclosures in Management's Discussion and Analysis ("MD&A") subsequent to adoption of Statement 123R.

DATES: March 29, 2005

FOR FURTHER INFORMATION CONTACT: Shan L. Benedict, Chad A. Kokenge, or Alison T. Spivey, Office of the Chief Accountant (202) 942-4400 or Craig Olinger, Division of Corporation Finance (202) 942-2960, Securities and Exchange Commission, 450 Fifth Street NW, Washington, DC 20549-1103.

SUPPLEMENTARY INFORMATION: The statements in staff accounting bulletins are not rules or interpretations of the Commission, nor are they published as bearing the Commission's official approval. They represent interpretations and practices followed by the Division of Corporation Finance and the Office of the Chief Accountant in administering the disclosure requirements of the Federal securities laws.

Margaret H. McFarland

Deputy Secretary

Date: March 29, 2005

Part 211 - [AMENDED]

Accordingly, Part 211 of Title 17 of the Code of Federal Regulations is amended by adding Staff Accounting Bulletin No. 107 to the table found in Subpart B. [Note: The text of SAB 107 will not appear in the Code of Federal Regulations.]

STAFF ACCOUNTING BULLETIN NO. 107

The staff hereby adds Topic 14 to the staff accounting bulletin series. Topic 14 provides guidance regarding the application of Statement of Financial Accounting Standards No. 123 (revised 2004), *Share-Based Payment*. The staff also hereby amends the following staff accounting bulletins.

1. Topic 4.D.2. is modified to update the references in footnote 4 from APB Opinion No. 25, *Accounting for Stock Issued to Employees*

("Opinion 25") and FASB Statement No. 123, *Accounting for Stock-Based Compensation* ("Statement 123") to Statement 123R. Opinion 25 and Statement 123 were superseded by Statement 123R.

2. Topic 4.E. is modified to delete the references and related guidance to compensation and deferred compensation. Statement 123R requires compensation costs to be recognized in the financial statements as services are provided by employees and does not permit those costs to be recognized as deferred compensation on the balance sheet before services are provided.

3. Topic 5.T. is modified to update the references from "AICPA Interpretation 1 to Opinion 25" to "paragraph 11 of Statement 123R." AICPA Interpretation 1 to Opinion 25 was superseded by Statement 123R.

TOPIC 14: SHARE-BASED PAYMENT

The interpretations in this SAB express views of the staff regarding the interaction between Statement 123R and certain SEC rules and regulations and provide the staff's views regarding the valuation of share-based payment arrangements for public companies. Statement 123R was issued by the Financial Accounting Standards Board ("FASB") on December 16, 2004. Statement 123R is based on the underlying accounting principle that compensation cost resulting from share-based payment transactions be recognized in financial statements at fair value.[1] Recognition of compensation cost at fair value will provide investors and other users of financial statements with more complete and comparable financial information.[2]

Statement 123R addresses a wide range of share-based compensation arrangements including share options, restricted share plans, performance-based awards, share appreciation rights, and employee share purchase plans.

Statement 123R replaces Statement 123 and supersedes Opinion 25. Statement 123, as originally issued in 1995, established as preferable, but did not require, a fair-value-based method of accounting for share-based payment transactions with employees.

The staff believes the guidance in this SAB will assist issuers in their initial implementation of Statement 123R and enhance the information received by investors and other users of financial statements, thereby assisting them in making investment and other decisions. This SAB includes interpretive guidance related to share-based payment transactions with nonemployees, the transition from nonpublic to public entity[3] status, valuation methods (including assumptions such as expected volatility and expected term), the accounting for certain redeemable financial instruments issued under share-based payment arrangements, the classification of compensation expense, non-GAAP financial measures, first-time adoption of Statement 123R in an interim period, capitalization of compensation cost related to share-based payment arrangements, the accounting for income tax effects of share-based payment arrangements upon adoption of Statement 123R, the modification of employee share options prior to adoption of Statement 123R and disclosures in MD&A subsequent to adoption of Statement 123R.

The staff recognizes that there is a range of conduct that a reasonable issuer might use to make estimates and valuations and otherwise implement Statement 123R, and the interpretive guidance provided by this SAB, particularly during the period of the Statement's initial implementation. Thus, throughout this SAB the use of the terms "reasonable" and "reasonably" is not meant to imply a single conclusion or methodology, but to encompass the full range of potential conduct, conclusions or methodologies upon which an issuer may reasonably base its valuation decisions. Different conduct, conclusions or methodologies by different issuers in a given situation does not of itself raise an inference that any of those issuers is acting unreasonably. While the zone of reasonable conduct is not unlimited, the staff expects that it will be rare when there is only one acceptable choice in estimating the fair value of share-based payment arrangements under the provisions of Statement 123R and the interpretive guidance provided by this SAB in any given situation. In addition, as discussed in the Interpretive Response to Question 1 of Section C, Valuation Methods, estimates of fair value are not intended to predict actual future events, and subsequent events are not indicative of the reasonableness of the original estimates of fair value made under Statement 123R. Over time, as issuers and accountants gain more experience in applying Statement 123R and the guidance provided in this SAB, the staff anticipates that particular approaches may begin to emerge as best practices and that the range of reasonable conduct, conclusions and methodologies will likely narrow.

* * * * *

A. Share-Based Payment Transactions with Nonemployees

Question: Are share-based payment transactions with nonemployees included in the scope of Statement 123R?

Interpretive Response: Only certain aspects of the accounting for share-based payment transactions with nonemployees are explicitly addressed by Statement 123R. Statement 123R explicitly:

- Establishes fair value as the measurement objective in accounting for all share-based payments;[4] and

- Requires that an entity record the value of a transaction with a nonemployee based on the more reliably measurable fair value of either

---

[1] Statement 123R, paragraph 1.
[2] Statement 123R, page iv.

[3] Defined in Statement 123R, Appendix E.
[4] Statement 123R, paragraph 7.

the good or service received or the equity instrument issued.[5]

Statement 123R does not supersede any of the authoritative literature that specifically addresses accounting for share-based payments with nonemployees. For example, Statement 123R does not specify the measurement date for sharebased payment transactions with nonemployees when the measurement of the transaction is based on the fair value of the equity instruments issued.[6] For determining the measurement date of equity instruments issued in share-based transactions with nonemployees, a company should refer to Emerging Issues Task Force ("EITF") Issue No. 96-18, *Accounting for Equity Instruments That Are Issued to Other Than Employees for Acquiring, or in Conjunction with Selling, Goods or Services*.

With respect to questions regarding nonemployee arrangements that are not specifically addressed in other authoritative literature, the staff believes that the application of guidance in Statement 123R would generally result in relevant and reliable financial statement information. As such, the staff believes it would generally be appropriate for entities to apply the guidance in Statement 123R by analogy to share-based payment transactions with nonemployees unless other authoritative accounting literature more clearly addresses the appropriate accounting, or the application of the guidance in Statement 123R would be inconsistent with the terms of the instrument issued to a nonemployee in a sharebased payment arrangement.[7] For example, the staff believes the guidance in Statement 123R on certain transactions with related parties or other holders of an economic interest in the entity would generally be applicable to share-based payment transactions with nonemployees. The staff encourages registrants that have additional questions related to accounting for share-based payment transactions with nonemployees to discuss those questions with the staff.

B. Transition from Nonpublic to Public Entity Status

Facts: Company A is a nonpublic entity[8] that first files a registration statement with the SEC to register its equity securities for sale in a public market on January 2, 20X8.[9] As a nonpublic entity, Company A had been assigning value to its share options[10] under the calculated value method prescribed by Statement 123R[11] and had elected to measure its liability awards based on intrinsic value. Company A is considered a public entity on January 2, 20X8 when it makes its initial filing with the SEC in preparation for the sale of its shares in a public market.

Question 1: How should Company A account for the share options that were granted to its employees prior to January 2, 20X8 for which the requisite service has not been rendered by January 2, 20X8?

Interpretive Response: Prior to becoming a public entity, Company A had been assigning value to its share options under the calculated value method. The staff believes that Company A should continue to follow that approach for those share options that were granted prior to January 2, 20X8, unless those share options are subsequently modified, repurchased or cancelled.[12] If the share options are subsequently modified, repurchased or cancelled, Company A would assess the event under the public company provisions of Statement 123R. For example, if Company A modified the share options on February 1, 20X8, any incremental compensation cost would be measured under Statement 123R, paragraph 51(a), as the fair value of the modified share options over the fair value of the original share options measured immediately before the terms were modified.[13]

Question 2: How should Company A account for its liability awards granted to its employees prior to January 2, 20X8 which are fully vested but have not been settled by January 2, 20X8?

Interpretive Response: As a nonpublic entity, Company A had elected to measure its liability awards

---

[5] *Ibid.*

[6] Statement 123R, paragraph 8.

[7] For example, due to the nature of specific terms in employee share options, including nontransferability, nonhedgability and the truncation of the contractual term due to post-vesting service termination, Statement 123R requires that when valuing an employee share option under the Black-Scholes-Merton framework, the fair value of an employee share option be based on the option's expected term rather than the contractual term. If these features (i.e., nontransferability, nonhedgability and the truncation of the contractual term) were not present in a nonemployee share option arrangement, the use of an expected term assumption shorter than the contractual term would generally not be appropriate in estimating the fair value of the nonemployee share options.

[8] Defined in Statement 123R, Appendix E.

[9] For the purposes of these illustrations, assume all of Company A's equity-based awards granted to its employees were granted after the adoption of Statement 123R.

[10] For purposes of this staff accounting bulletin, the phrase "share options" is used to refer to "share options or similar instruments."

[11] Statement 123R, paragraph 23 requires a nonpublic entity to use the calculated value method when it is not able to reasonably estimate the fair value of its equity share options and similar instruments because it is not practicable for it to estimate the expected volatility of its share price. Statement 123R, paragraph A43 indicates that a nonpublic entity may be able to identify similar public entities for which share or option price information is available and may consider the historical, expected, or implied volatility of those entities' share prices in estimating expected volatility. The staff would expect an entity that becomes a public entity and had previously measured its share options under the calculated value method to be able to support its previous decision to use calculated value and to provide the disclosures required by paragraph A240(e)(2)(b) of Statement 123R.

[12] This view is consistent with the FASB's basis for rejecting full retrospective application of Statement 123R as described in Statement 123R, paragraph B251.

[13] Statement 123R, footnote 103. The staff believes that because Company A is a public entity as of the date of the modification, it would be inappropriate to use the calculated value method to measure the original share options immediately before the terms were modified.

subject to Statement 123R at intrinsic value.[14] When Company A becomes a public entity, it should measure the liability awards at their fair value determined in accordance with Statement 123R.[15] In that reporting period there will be an incremental amount of measured cost for the difference between fair value as determined under Statement 123R and intrinsic value. For example, assume the intrinsic value in the period ended December 31, 20X7 was $10 per award. At the end of the first reporting period ending after January 2, 20X8 (when Company A becomes a public entity), assume the intrinsic value of the award is $12 and the fair value as determined in accordance with Statement 123R is $15. The measured cost in the first reporting period after December 31, 20X7 would be $5.[16]

Question 3: After becoming a public entity, may Company A retrospectively apply the fair-value-based method to its awards that were granted prior to the date Company A became a public entity?

Interpretive Response: No. Before becoming a public entity, Company A did not use the fair-value-based method for either its share options or its liability awards granted to the Company's employees. The staff does not believe it is appropriate for Company A to apply the fair-value-based method on a retrospective basis, because it would require the entity to make estimates of a prior period, which, due to hindsight, may vary significantly from estimates that would have been made contemporaneously in prior periods.[17]

Question 4: Upon becoming a public entity, what disclosures should Company A consider in addition to those prescribed by Statement 123R?[18]

Interpretive Response: In the registration statement filed on January 2, 20X8, Company A should clearly describe in MD&A the change in accounting policy that will be required by Statement 123R in subsequent periods and the reasonably likely material future effects.[19] In subsequent filings, Company A should provide financial statement disclosure of the effects of the changes in accounting policy. In addition, Company A should consider the applicability of SEC Release No. FR-60[20] and Section V, "Critical Accounting Estimates," in SEC Release No. FR-72[21] regarding critical accounting policies and estimates in MD&A.

C. Valuation Methods

Statement 123R, paragraph 16, indicates that the measurement objective for equity instruments awarded to employees is to estimate at the grant date the fair value of the equity instruments the entity is obligated to issue when employees have rendered the requisite service and satisfied any other conditions necessary to earn the right to benefit from the instruments. The Statement also states that observable market prices of identical or similar equity or liability instruments in active markets are the best evidence of fair value and, if available, should be used as the basis for the measurement for equity and liability instruments awarded in a share-based payment transaction with employees.[22] However, if observable market prices of identical or similar equity or liability instruments are not available, the fair value shall be estimated by using a valuation technique or model that complies with the measurement objective, as described in Statement 123R.[23]

Question 1: If a valuation technique or model is used to estimate fair value, to what extent will the staff consider a company's estimates of fair value to be materially misleading because the estimates of fair value do not correspond to the value ultimately realized by the employees who received the share options?

Interpretive Response: The staff understands that estimates of fair value of employee share options, while derived from expected value calculations, cannot predict actual future events.[24] The estimate of fair value represents the measurement of the cost of the employee services to the company. The estimate of fair value should reflect the assumptions marketplace participants would use in determining how much to pay for an instrument on the date of the measurement (generally the grant date for equity awards). For example, valuation techniques used in estimating the fair value of employee share options may consider information about a large number of possible share price paths, while, of course, only one share price path will ultimately emerge. If a company makes a good faith fair value estimate in accordance with the provisions of Statement 123R in a way that is designed to take into account the assumptions that underlie the instrument's value that marketplace participants would reasonably make, then subsequent future events that affect the instrument's value do not provide meaningful information about the quality of

---

[14] Statement 123R, paragraph 38.

[15] Statement 123R, paragraph 37.

[16] $15 fair value less $10 intrinsic value equals $5 of incremental cost.

[17] This view is consistent with the FASB's basis for rejecting full retrospective application of Statement 123R as described in Statement 123R, paragraph B251.

[18] Statement 123R disclosure requirements are described in paragraphs 64, 65, A240, A241 and A242.

[19] *See* generally SEC Release No. FR-72, "Commission Guidance Regarding Management's Discussion and Analysis of Financial Condition and Results of Operations."

[20] SEC Release No. FR-60, "Cautionary Advice Regarding Disclosure About Critical Accounting Policies."

[21] SEC Release No. FR-72, "Commission Guidance Regarding Management's Discussion and Analysis of Financial Condition and Results of Operations."

[22] Statement 123R, paragraph A7.

[23] Statement 123R, paragraph A8.

[24] Statement 123R, paragraph A12, states "The fair value of those instruments at a single point in time is not a forecast of what the estimated fair value of those instruments may be in the future."

the original fair value estimate. As long as the share options were originally so measured, changes in an employee share option's value, no matter how significant, subsequent to its grant date do not call into question the reasonableness of the grant date fair value estimate.

Question 2: In order to meet the fair value measurement objective in Statement 123R, are certain valuation techniques preferred over others?

Interpretive Response: Statement 123R, paragraph A14, clarifies that the Statement does not specify a preference for a particular valuation technique or model. As stated in Statement 123R, paragraph A8, in order to meet the fair value measurement objective, a company should select a valuation technique or model that (a) is applied in a manner consistent with the fair value measurement objective and other requirements of Statement 123R, (b) is based on established principles of financial economic theory and generally applied in that field and (c) reflects all substantive characteristics of the instrument.

The chosen valuation technique or model must meet all three of the requirements stated above. In valuing a particular instrument, certain techniques or models may meet the first and second criteria but may not meet the third criterion because the techniques or models are not designed to reflect certain characteristics contained in the instrument. For example, for a share option in which the exercisability is conditional on a specified increase in the price of the underlying shares, the Black-Scholes-Merton closed-form model would not generally be an appropriate valuation model because, while it meets both the first and second criteria, it is not designed to take into account that type of market condition.[25]

Further, the staff understands that a company may consider multiple techniques or models that meet the fair value measurement objective before making its selection as to the appropriate technique or model. The staff would not object to a company's choice of a technique or model as long as the technique or model meets the fair value measurement objective. For example, a company is not required to use a lattice model simply because that model was the most complex of the models the company considered.

Question 3: In subsequent periods, may a company change the valuation technique or model chosen to value instruments with similar characteristics?[26]

Interpretive Response: As long as the new technique or model meets the fair value measurement objective in Statement 123R as described in Question 2

above, the staff would not object to a company changing its valuation technique or model.[27] A change in the valuation technique or model used to meet the fair value measurement objective would not be considered a change in accounting principle. As such, a company would not be required to file a preferability letter from its independent accountants as described in Rule 10-01(b)(6) of Regulation S-X when it changes valuation techniques or models.[28] However, the staff would not expect that a company would frequently switch between valuation techniques or models, particularly in circumstances where there was no significant variation in the form of share-based payments being valued. Disclosure in the footnotes of the basis for any change in technique or model would be appropriate.[29]

Question 4: Must every company that issues share options or similar instruments hire an outside third party to assist in determining the fair value of the share options?

Interpretive Response: No. However, the valuation of a company's share options or similar instruments should be performed by a person with the requisite expertise.

D. Certain Assumptions Used in Valuation Methods

Statement 123R's fair value measurement objective for equity instruments awarded to employees is to estimate the grant-date fair value of the equity instruments that the entity is obligated to issue when employees have rendered the requisite service and satisfied any other conditions necessary to earn the right to benefit from the instruments.[30] In order to meet this fair value measurement objective, management will be required to develop estimates regarding the expected volatility of its company's share price and the exercise behavior of its employees. The staff is providing guidance in the following sections related to the expected volatility and expected term assumptions to assist public entities in applying those requirements.

The staff understands that companies may refine their estimates of expected volatility and expected term as a result of the guidance provided in Statement 123R and in sections (1) and (2) below. Changes in assumptions during the periods presented in the financial statements should be disclosed in the footnotes.[31]

1. Expected Volatility

Statement 123R, paragraph A31, states, "Volatility is a measure of the amount by which a financial variable, such as share price, has fluctuated (histor-

---

[25] *See* Statement 123R, paragraphs A13-17.

[26] Statement 123R, paragraph A14 and footnote 49, indicate that an entity may use different valuation techniques or models for instruments with different characteristics.

[27] The staff believes that a company should take into account the reason for the change in technique or model in determining whether the new technique or model meets the fair value measurement objective. For example, changing a technique or model from

period to period for the sole purpose of lowering the fair value estimate of a share option would not meet the fair value measurement objective of the Statement.

[28] Statement 123R, paragraph A23.

[29] *See* generally Statement 123R, paragraph 64c.

[30] Statement 123R, paragraph A2.

[31] Statement 123R, paragraph A240(e).

ical volatility) or is expected to fluctuate (expected volatility) during a period. Option-pricing models require an estimate of expected volatility as an assumption because an option's value is dependent on potential share returns over the option's term. The higher the volatility, the more the returns on the share can be expected to vary - up or down. Because an option's value is unaffected by expected negative returns on the shares, other things [being] equal, an option on a share with higher volatility is worth more than an option on a share with lower volatility."

Facts: Company B is a public entity whose common shares have been publicly traded for over twenty years. Company B also has multiple options on its shares outstanding that are traded on an exchange ("traded options"). Company B grants share options on January 2, 20X6.

Question 1: What should Company B consider when estimating expected volatility for purposes of measuring the fair value of its share options?

Interpretive Response: Statement 123R does not specify a particular method of estimating expected volatility. However, the Statement does clarify that the objective in estimating expected volatility is to ascertain the assumption about expected volatility that marketplace participants would likely use in determining an exchange price for an option.[32] Statement 123R provides a list of factors entities should consider in estimating expected volatility.[33] Company B may begin its process of estimating expected volatility by considering its historical volatility.[34] However, Company B should also then consider, based on available information, how the expected volatility of its share price may differ from historical volatility.[35] Implied volatility[36] can be useful in estimating expected volatility because it is generally reflective of both historical volatility and expectations of how future volatility will differ from historical volatility.

The staff believes that companies should make good faith efforts to identify and use sufficient information in determining whether taking historical volatility, implied volatility or a combination of both into account will result in the best estimate of expected volatility. The staff believes companies

that have appropriate traded financial instruments from which they can derive an implied volatility should generally consider this measure. The extent of the ultimate reliance on implied volatility will depend on a company's facts and circumstances; however, the staff believes that a company with actively traded options or other financial instruments with embedded options[37] generally could place greater (or even exclusive) reliance on implied volatility. (See the Interpretive Responses to Questions 3 and 4 below.)

The process used to gather and review available information to estimate expected volatility should be applied consistently from period to period. When circumstances indicate the availability of new or different information that would be useful in estimating expected volatility, a company should incorporate that information.

Question 2: What should Company B consider if computing historical volatility?[38]

Interpretive Response: The following should be considered in the computation of historical volatility:

1. Method of Computing Historical Volatility -

   The staff believes the method selected by Company B to compute its historical volatility should produce an estimate that is representative of Company B's expectations about its future volatility over the expected (if using a Black-Scholes-Merton closed-form model) or contractual (if using a lattice model) term[39] of its employee share options. Certain methods may not be appropriate for longer term employee share options if they weight the most recent periods of Company B's historical volatility much more heavily than earlier periods.[40] For example, a method that applies a factor to certain historical price intervals to reflect a decay or loss of relevance of that historical information emphasizes the most recent historical periods and thus would likely bias the estimate to this recent history.[41]

2. Amount of Historical Data -

   Statement 123R, paragraph A32(a), indicates entities should consider historical volatility

---

[32] Statement 123R, paragraph B86.

[33] Statement 123R, paragraph A32.

[34] Statement 123R, paragraph A34.

[35] *Ibid.*

[36] Implied volatility is the volatility assumption inherent in the market prices of a company's traded options or other financial instruments that have option-like features. Implied volatility is derived by entering the market price of the traded financial instrument, along with assumptions specific to the financial options being valued, into a model based on a constant volatility estimate (*e.g.,* the Black-Scholes-Merton closedform model) and solving for the unknown assumption of volatility.

[37] The staff believes implied volatility derived from embedded options can be utilized in determining expected volatility if, in deriving the implied volatility, the company considers all relevant features of the instruments (*e.g.,* value of the host instrument, value of the option, etc.). The staff believes the derivation of implied

volatility from other than simple instruments (*e.g.,* a simple convertible bond) can, in some cases, be impracticable due to the complexity of multiple features.

[38] *See* Statement 123R, paragraph A32.

[39] For purposes of this staff accounting bulletin, the phrase "expected or contractual term, as applicable" has the same meaning as the phrase "expected (if using a Black-Scholes-Merton closed-form model) or contractual (if using a lattice model) term of an employee share option."

[40] Statement 123R, paragraph A32(a), states that entities should consider historical volatility over a period generally commensurate with the expected or contractual term, as applicable, of the share option. Accordingly, the staff believes methods that place extreme emphasis on the most recent periods may be inconsistent with this guidance.

[41] Generalized Autoregressive Conditional Heteroskedasticity ("GARCH") is an example of a method that demonstrates this characteristic.

over a period generally commensurate with the expected or contractual term, as applicable, of the share option. The staff believes Company B could utilize a period of historical data longer than the expected or contractual term, as applicable, if it reasonably believes the additional historical information will improve the estimate. For example, assume Company B decided to utilize a Black-Scholes-Merton closed-form model to estimate the value of the share options granted on January 2, 20X6 and determined that the expected term was six years. Company B would not be precluded from using historical data longer than six years if it concludes that data would be relevant.

3. Frequency of Price Observations -

Statement 123R, paragraph A32(d), indicates an entity should use appropriate and regular intervals for price observations based on facts and circumstances that provide the basis for a reasonable fair value estimate. Accordingly, the staff believes Company B should consider the frequency of the trading of its shares and the length of its trading history in determining the appropriate frequency of price observations. The staff believes using daily, weekly or monthly price observations may provide a sufficient basis to estimate expected volatility if the history provides enough data points on which to base the estimate.[42] Company B should select a consistent point in time within each interval when selecting data points.[43]

4. Consideration of Future Events -

The objective in estimating expected volatility is to ascertain the assumptions that marketplace participants would likely use in determining an exchange price for an option.[44] Accordingly, the staff believes that Company B should consider those future events that it reasonably concludes a marketplace participant would also consider in making the estimation. For example, if Company B has recently announced a merger with a company that would change its business risk in the future, then it should consider the impact of the merger in estimating the expected volatility if it reasonably believes a marketplace participant would also consider this event.

5. Exclusion of Periods of Historical Data -

In some instances, due to a company's particular business situations, a period of historical volatility data may not be relevant in evaluating expected volatility.[45] In these instances, that period should be disregarded. The staff believes that if Company B disregards a period of historical volatility, it should be prepared to support its conclusion that its historical share price during that previous period is not relevant to estimating expected volatility due to one or more discrete and specific historical events and that similar events are not expected to occur during the expected term of the share option. The staff believes these situations would be rare.

Question 3: What should Company B consider when evaluating the extent of its reliance on the implied volatility derived from its traded options?

Interpretive Response: To achieve the objective of estimating expected volatility as stated in paragraph B86 of Statement 123R, the staff believes Company B generally should consider the following in its evaluation: 1) the volume of market activity of the underlying shares and traded options; 2) the ability to synchronize the variables used to derive implied volatility; 3) the similarity of the exercise prices of the traded options to the exercise price of the employee share options; and 4) the similarity of the length of the term of the traded and employee share options.[46]

1. Volume of Market Activity -

The staff believes Company B should consider the volume of trading in its underlying shares as well as the traded options. For example, prices for instruments in actively traded markets are more likely to reflect a marketplace participant's expectations regarding expected volatility.

2. Synchronization of the Variables -

Company B should synchronize the variables used to derive implied volatility. For example, to the extent reasonably practicable, Company B should use market prices (either traded prices or the average of bid and asked quotes) of the traded options and its shares measured at the same point in time. This measurement should also be synchronized with the grant of the employee share options; however, when this is not reasonably practicable, the staff believes Company B should derive implied volatility as of a point in time as close to the grant of the employee share options as reasonably practicable.

3. Similarity of the Exercise Prices -

---

[42] Further, if shares of a company are thinly traded the staff believes the use of weekly or monthly price observations would generally be more appropriate than the use of daily price observations. The volatility calculation using daily observations for such shares could be artificially inflated due to a larger spread between the bid and asked quotes and lack of consistent trading in the market.

[43] Statement 123R, paragraph A34, states that a company should establish a process for estimating expected volatility and apply that

process consistently from period to period. In addition, Statement 123R, paragraph A23, indicates that assumptions used to estimate the fair value of instruments granted to employees should be determined in a consistent manner from period to period.

[44] Statement 123R, paragraph B86.

[45] Statement 123R, paragraph A32(a).

[46] *See generally Options, Futures, and Other Derivatives* by John C. Hull (Prentice Hall, 5th Edition, 2003).

The staff believes that when valuing an at-the-money employee share option, the implied volatility derived from at- or near-the-money traded options generally would be most relevant.[47] If, however, it is not possible to find at- or near-the-money traded options, Company B should select multiple traded options with an average exercise price close to the exercise price of the employee share option.[48]

4. Similarity of Length of Terms -

The staff believes that when valuing an employee share option with a given expected or contractual term, as applicable, the implied volatility derived from a traded option with a similar term would be the most relevant. However, if there are no traded options with maturities that are similar to the share option's contractual or expected term, as applicable, then the staff believes Company B could consider traded options with a remaining maturity of six months or greater.[49] However, when using traded options with a term of less than one year,[50] the staff would expect the company to also consider other relevant information in estimating expected volatility. In general, the staff believes more reliance on the implied volatility derived from a traded option would be expected the closer the remaining term of the traded option is to the expected or contractual term, as applicable, of the employee share option.

The staff believes Company B's evaluation of the factors above should assist in determining whether the implied volatility appropriately reflects the market's expectations of future volatility and thus the extent of reliance that Company B reasonably places on the implied volatility.

Question 4: Are there situations in which it is acceptable for Company B to rely exclusively on either implied volatility or historical volatility in its estimate of expected volatility?

Interpretive Response: As stated above, Statement 123R does not specify a method of estimating ex-

pected volatility; rather, it provides a list of factors that should be considered and requires that an entity's estimate of expected volatility be reasonable and supportable.[51] Many of the factors listed in Statement 123R are discussed in Questions 2 and 3 above. The objective of estimating volatility, as stated in Statement 123R, is to ascertain the assumption about expected volatility that marketplace participants would likely use in determining a price for an option.[52] The staff believes that a company, after considering the factors listed in Statement 123R, could, in certain situations, reasonably conclude that exclusive reliance on either historical or implied volatility would provide an estimate of expected volatility that meets this stated objective.

The staff would not object to Company B placing exclusive reliance on implied volatility when the following factors are present, as long as the methodology is consistently applied:

- Company B utilizes a valuation model that is based upon a constant volatility assumption to value its employee share options;[53]

- The implied volatility is derived from options that are actively traded;

- The market prices (trades or quotes) of both the traded options and underlying shares are measured at a similar point in time to each other and on a date reasonably close to the grant date of the employee share options;

- The traded options have exercise prices that are both (a) near-the-money and (b) close to the exercise price of the employee share options;[54] and

- The remaining maturities of the traded options on which the estimate is based are at least one year.

The staff would not object to Company B placing exclusive reliance on historical volatility when the following factors are present, so long as the methodology is consistently applied:

- Company B has no reason to believe that its future volatility over the expected or contrac-

---

[47] Implied volatilities of options differ systematically over the "moneyness" of the option. This pattern of implied volatilities across exercise prices is known as the "volatility smile" or "volatility skew." Studies such as "Implied Volatility" by Stewart Mayhew, *Financial Analysts Journal*, July-August 1995, have found that implied volatilities based on near-the-money options do as well as sophisticated weighted implied volatilities in estimating expected volatility. In addition, the staff believes that because near-the-money options are generally more actively traded, they may provide a better basis for deriving implied volatility.

[48] The staff believes a company could use a weighted-average implied volatility based on traded options that are either in-the-money or out-of-the-money. For example, if the employee share option has an exercise price of $52, but the only traded options available have exercise prices of $50 and $55, then the staff believes that it is appropriate to use a weighted average based on the implied volatilities from the two traded options; for this example, a 40% weight on the implied volatility calculated from the option with an exercise price of $55 and a 60% weight on the option with an exercise price of $50.

[49] The staff believes it may also be appropriate to consider the entire term structure of volatility provided by traded options with a

variety of remaining maturities. If a company considers the entire term structure in deriving implied volatility, the staff would expect a company to include some options in the term structure with a remaining maturity of six months or greater.

[50] The staff believes the implied volatility derived from a traded option with a term of one year or greater would typically not be significantly different from the implied volatility that would be derived from a traded option with a significantly longer term.

[51] Statement 123R, paragraphs A31-A32.

[52] Statement 123R, paragraph B86.

[53] Statement 123R, paragraphs A15 and A33, discuss the incorporation of a range of expected volatilities into option pricing models. The staff believes that a company that utilizes an option pricing model that incorporates a range of expected volatilities over the option's contractual term should consider the factors listed in Statement 123R, and those discussed in the Interpretive Responses to Questions 2 and 3 above, to determine the extent of its reliance (including exclusive reliance) on the derived implied volatility.

[54] When near-the-money options are not available, the staff believes the use of a weighted-average approach, as noted in a previous footnote, may be appropriate.

tual term, as applicable, is likely to differ from its past;[55]

- The computation of historical volatility uses a simple average calculation method;

- A sequential period of historical data at least equal to the expected or contractual term of the share option, as applicable, is used; and

- A reasonably sufficient number of price observations are used, measured at a consistent point throughout the applicable historical period.[56]

Question 5: What disclosures would the staff expect Company B to include in its financial statements and MD&A regarding its assumption of expected volatility?

Interpretive Response: Statement 123R, paragraph A240, prescribes the minimum information needed to achieve the Statement's disclosure objectives.[57] Under that guidance, Company B is required to disclose the expected volatility and the method used to estimate it.[58] Accordingly, the staff expects that at a minimum Company B would disclose in a footnote to its financial statements how it determined the expected volatility assumption for purposes of determining the fair value of its share options in accordance with Statement 123R. For example, at a minimum, the staff would expect Company B to disclose whether it used only implied volatility, historical volatility, or a combination of both.

In addition, Company B should consider the applicability of SEC Release No. FR-60 and Section V, "Critical Accounting Estimates," in SEC Release No. FR-72 regarding critical accounting policies and estimates in MD&A. The staff would expect such disclosures to include an explanation of the method used to estimate the expected volatility of its share price. This explanation generally should include a discussion of the basis for the company's conclusions regarding the extent to which it used historical volatility, implied volatility or a combination of both. A company could consider summarizing its evaluation of the factors listed in Questions 2 and 3 of this section as part of these disclosures in MD&A.

Facts: Company C is a newly public entity with limited historical data on the price of its publicly traded

shares and no other traded financial instruments. Company C believes that it does not have sufficient company specific information regarding the volatility of its share price on which to base an estimate of expected volatility.

Question 6: What other sources of information should Company C consider in order to estimate the expected volatility of its share price?

Interpretive Response: Statement 123R provides guidance on estimating expected volatility for newly public and nonpublic entities that do not have company specific historical or implied volatility information available.[59] Company C may base its estimate of expected volatility on the historical, expected or implied volatility of similar entities whose share or option prices are publicly available. In making its determination as to similarity, Company C would likely consider the industry, stage of life cycle, size and financial leverage of such other entities.[60]

The staff would not object to Company C looking to an industry sector index (*e.g.*, NASDAQ Computer Index) that is representative of Company C's industry, and possibly its size, to identify one or more similar entities.[61] Once Company C has identified similar entities, it would substitute a measure of the individual volatilities of the similar entities for the expected volatility of its share price as an assumption in its valuation model.[62] Because of the effects of diversification that are present in an industry sector index, Company C should not substitute the volatility of an index for the expected volatility of its share price as an assumption in its valuation model.[63]

After similar entities have been identified, Company C should continue to consider the volatilities of those entities unless circumstances change such that the identified entities are no longer similar to Company C. Until Company C has sufficient information available, the staff would not object to Company C basing its estimate of expected volatility on the volatility of similar entities for those periods for which it does not have sufficient information available.[64] Until Company C has either a sufficient amount of historical information regarding the volatility of its share price or other traded financial instruments are available to derive an implied volatility to support an estimate of expected volatility, it should consistently apply a pro-

---

[55] *See* Statement 123R, paragraph B87. A change in a company's business model that results in a material alteration to the company's risk profile is an example of a circumstance in which the company's future volatility would be expected to differ from its past volatility. Other examples may include, but are not limited to, the introduction of a new product that is central to a company's business model or the receipt of U.S. Food and Drug Administration approval for the sale of a new prescription drug.

[56] If the expected or contractual term, as applicable, of the employee share option is less than three years, the staff believes monthly price observations would not provide a sufficient amount of data.

[57] Statement 123R disclosure requirements are included in paragraphs 64, 65, A240, A241, and A242.

[58] Statement 123R, paragraph A240(e)(2)(b).

[59] Statement 123R, paragraphs A22 and A43.

[60] Statement 123R, paragraph A22.

[61] If a company operates in a number of different industries, it could look to several industry indices. However, when considering the volatilities of multiple companies, each operating only in a single industry, the staff believes a company should take into account its own leverage, the leverages of each of the entities, and the correlation of the entities' stock returns.

[62] Statement 123R, paragraph A45.

[63] Statement 123R, paragraph A22.

[64] Statement 123R, paragraph A32(c). The staff believes that at least two years of daily or weekly historical data could provide a reasonable basis on which to base an estimate of expected volatility if a company has no reason to believe that its future volatility will differ materially during the expected or contractual term, as applicable, from the volatility calculated from this past information. If the expected or contractual term, as applicable, of a share option is shorter than two years, the staff believes a company should use daily or weekly historical data for at least the length of that applicable term.

cess as described above to estimate expected volatility based on the volatilities of similar entities.[65]

2. Expected Term

Statement 123R, paragraph A26, states "The fair value of a traded (or transferable) share option is based on its contractual term because rarely is it economically advantageous to the holder to exercise, rather than sell, a transferable share option before the end of its contractual term. Employee share options generally differ from transferable [or tradable] share options in that employees cannot sell (or hedge) their share options - they can only exercise them; because of this, employees generally exercise their options before the end of the options' contractual term. Thus, the inability to sell or hedge an employee share option effectively reduces the option's value [compared to a transferable option] because exercise prior to the option's expiration terminates its remaining life and thus its remaining time value." Accordingly, Statement 123R requires that when valuing an employee share option under the Black-Scholes-Merton framework the fair value of employee share options be based on the share options' expected term rather than the contractual term.

The staff believes the estimate of expected term should be based on the facts and circumstances available in each particular case. Consistent with our guidance regarding reasonableness immediately preceding Topic 14.A, the fact that other possible estimates are later determined to have more accurately reflected the term does not necessarily mean that the particular choice was unreasonable. The staff reminds registrants of the expected term disclosure requirements described in Statement 123R, paragraph A240(e)(2)(a).

Facts: Company D utilizes the Black-Scholes-Merton closed-form model to value its share options for the purposes of determining the fair value of the options under Statement 123R. Company D recently granted share options to its employees. Based on its review of various factors, Company D determines that the expected term of the options is six years, which is less than the contractual term of ten years.

Question 1: When determining the fair value of the share options in accordance with Statement 123R, should Company D consider an additional discount for nonhedgability and nontransferability?

Interpretive Response: No. Statement 123R, paragraphs A26 and B82, indicates that nonhedgability and nontransferability have the effect of increasing the likelihood that an employee share option will be exercised before the end of its contractual term. Nonhedgability and nontransferability therefore factor into the expected term assumption (in this case reducing the term assumption from ten years to six years), and the expected term reasonably adjusts for the effect of these factors. Accordingly, the staff believes that no additional reduction in the term assumption or other discount to the estimated fair value is appropriate for these particular factors.[66]

Question 2: Should forfeitures or terms that stem from forfeitability be factored into the determination of expected term?

Interpretive Response: No. Statement 123R indicates that the expected term that is utilized as an assumption in a closed-form option-pricing model or a resulting output of a lattice option pricing model when determining the fair value of the share options should not incorporate restrictions or other terms that stem from the pre-vesting forfeitability of the instruments. Under Statement 123R, these prevesting restrictions or other terms are taken into account by ultimately recognizing compensation cost only for awards for which employees render the requisite service.[67]

Question 3: Can a company's estimate of expected term ever be shorter than the vesting period?

Interpretive Response: No. The vesting period forms the lower bound of the estimate of expected term.[68]

Question 4: Statement 123R, paragraph A30, indicates that an entity shall aggregate individual awards into relatively homogenous groups with respect to exercise and post-vesting employment termination behaviors for the purpose of determining expected term, regardless of the valuation technique or model used to estimate the fair value. How many groupings are typically considered sufficient?

Interpretive Response: As it relates to employee groupings, the staff believes that an entity may generally make a reasonable fair value estimate with as few as one or two groupings.[69]

Question 5: What approaches could a company use to estimate the expected term of its employee share options?

---

[65] Statement 123R, paragraph A34.

[66] The staff notes the existence of academic literature that supports the assertion that the Black-Scholes-Merton closed-form model, with expected term as an input, can produce reasonable estimates of fair value. Such literature includes J. Carpenter, "The exercise and valuation of executive stock options," *Journal of Financial Economics*, May 1998, pp.127-158; C. Marquardt, "The Cost of Employee Stock Option Grants: An Empirical Analysis," *Journal of Accounting Research*, September 2002, p. 1191-1217); and J. Bettis, J. Bizjak and M. Lemmon, "Exercise behavior, valuation, and the incentive effect of employee stock options," *Journal of Financial Economics*, forthcoming, 2005.

[67] Statement 123R, paragraph 18.

[68] Statement 123R, paragraph A28a.

[69] The staff believes the focus should be on groups of employees with significantly different expected exercise behavior. Academic research suggests two such groups might be executives and non-executives. A study by S. Huddart found executives and other senior managers to be significantly more patient in their exercise behavior than more junior employees. (Employee rank was proxied for by the number of options issued to that employee.) See S. Huddart, "Patterns of stock option exercise in the United States," in: J. Carpenter and D. Yermack, eds., *Executive Compensation and Shareholder Value: Theory and Evidence* (Kluwer, Boston, MA, 1999), pp. 115-142. See also S. Huddart and M. Lang, "Employee stock option exercises: An empirical analysis," *Journal of Accounting and Economics*, 1996, pp. 5-43.

Interpretive Response: A company should use an approach that is reasonable and supportable under Statement 123R's fair value measurement objective, which establishes that assumptions and measurement techniques should be consistent with those that marketplace participants would be likely to use in determining an exchange price for the share options.[70] If, in developing its estimate of expected term, a company determines that its historical share option exercise experience is the best estimate of future exercise patterns, the staff will not object to the use of the historical share option exercise experience to estimate expected term.[71]

A company may also conclude that its historical share option exercise experience does not provide a reasonable basis upon which to estimate expected term. This may be the case for a variety of reasons, including, but not limited to, the life of the company and its relative stage of development, past or expected structural changes in the business, differences in terms of past equity-based share option grants,[72] or a lack of variety of price paths that the company may have experienced.[73]

Statement 123R describes other alternative sources of information that might be used in those cases when a company determines that its historical share option exercise experience does not provide a reasonable basis upon which to estimate expected term. For example, a lattice model (which by definition incorporates multiple price paths) can be used to estimate expected term as an input into a Black-Scholes-Merton closed-form model.[74] In addition, Statement 123R, paragraph A29, states ". . . expected term might be estimated in some other manner, taking into account whatever relevant and supportable information is available, including industry averages and other pertinent evidence such as published academic research." For example, data about exercise patterns of employees in similar industries and/or situations as the company's might be used. While such comparative information may not be widely available at present, the staff understands that various parties, including actuaries, valuation professionals and others are gathering such data.

Facts: Company E grants equity share options to its employees that have the following basic characteristics:[75]

- The share options are granted at-the-money;

- Exercisability is conditional only on performing service through the vesting date;[76]

- If an employee terminates service prior to vesting, the employee would forfeit the share options;

- If an employee terminates service after vesting, the employee would have a limited time to exercise the share options (typically 30-90 days); and

- The share options are nontransferable and nonhedgeable.

Company E utilizes the Black-Scholes-Merton closed-form model for valuing its employee share options.

Question 6: As share options with these "plain-vanilla" characteristics have been granted in significant quantities by many companies in the past, is the staff aware of any "simple" methodologies that can be used to estimate expected term?

Interpretive Response: As noted above, the staff understands that an entity that chooses not to rely on its historical exercise data may find that certain alternative information, such as exercise data relating to employees of other companies, is not easily obtainable. As such, in the short term, some companies may encounter difficulties in making a refined estimate of expected term. Accordingly, the staff will accept the following "simplified" method for "plain vanilla" options consistent with those in the fact set above: expected term = ((vesting term + original contractual term) / 2). Assuming a ten year original contractual term and graded vesting over four years (25% of the options in each grant vest annually) for the share options in the fact set described above, the resultant expected term would be 6.25 years.[77]

Academic research on the exercise of options issued to executives provides some general support for outcomes that would be produced by the application of this method.[78] If a company elects to use this method,

---

[70] Statement 123R, paragraph A10.

[71] Historical share option exercise experience encompasses data related to share option exercise, postvesting termination, and share option contractual term expiration.

[72] For example, if a company had historically granted share options that were always in-the-money, and will grant at-the-money options prospectively, the exercise behavior related to the in-the-money options may not be sufficient as the sole basis to form the estimate of expected term for the at-the-money grants.

[73] For example, if a company had a history of previous equity-based share option grants and exercises only in periods in which the company's share price was rising, the exercise behavior related to those options may not be sufficient as the sole basis to form the estimate of expected term for current option grants.

[74] Statement 123R, paragraph A27.

[75] Employee share options with these features are sometimes referred to as "plain-vanilla" options.

[76] In this fact pattern the requisite service period equals the vesting period.

[77] Calculated as [[[1 year vesting term (for the first 25% vested) plus 2 year vesting term (for the second 25% vested) plus 3 year vesting term (for the third 25% vested) plus 4 year vesting term (for the last 25% vested)] divided by 4 total years of vesting] plus 10 year contractual life] divided by 2; that is, $(((1+2+3+4)/4) + 10) / 2 = 6.25$ years.

[78] J.N. Carpenter, "The exercise and valuation of executive stock options," *Journal of Financial Economics*, 1998, pp.127-158 studies a sample of 40 NYSE and AMEX firms over the period 1979-1994 with share option terms reasonably consistent to the terms presented in the fact set and example. The mean time to exercise after grant was 5.83 years and the median was 6.08 years. The "mean time to exercise" is shorter than expected term since the study's sample included only exercised options. Other research on executive options includes (but is not limited to) J. Carr Bettis; John M. Bizjak; and Michael L. Lemmon, "Exercise behavior, valuation, and the incentive effects of employee stock options," forthcoming in the *Journal of Financial Economics*. One of the few studies on nonexecutive employee options the staff is aware of is S. Huddart, "Patterns of stock option exercise in the United States," in: J. Carpenter and D. Yermack, eds., *Executive Compensation and*

it should be applied consistently to all "plain vanilla" employee share options, and the company should disclose the use of the method in the notes to its financial statements. Companies that have the information (from whatever source) to make more refined estimates of expected term may choose not to apply this simplified method. In addition, this simplified method is not intended to be applied as a benchmark in evaluating the appropriateness of more refined estimates of expected term.

Also, as noted above, the staff believes that more detailed information about exercise behavior will, over time, become readily available to companies. As such, the staff does not expect that such a simplified method would be used for share option grants after December 31, 2007, as more detailed information should be widely available by then.

E. Statement 123R and Certain Redeemable Financial Instruments

Certain financial instruments awarded in conjunction with share-based payment arrangements have redemption features that require settlement by cash or other assets upon the occurrence of events that are outside the control of the issuer.[79] Statement 123R provides guidance for determining whether instruments granted in conjunction with share-based payment arrangements should be classified as liability or equity instruments. Under that guidance, most instruments with redemption features that are outside the control of the issuer are required to be classified as liabilities; however, some redeemable instruments will qualify for equity classification.[80] SEC Accounting Series Release No. 268, *Presentation in Financial Statements of "Redeemable Preferred Stocks,"*[81] ("ASR 268") and related guidance[82] address the classification and measurement of certain redeemable equity instruments.

Facts: Under a share-based payment arrangement, Company F grants to an employee shares (or share options) that all vest at the end of four years (cliff vest).

The shares (or shares underlying the share options) are redeemable for cash at fair value at the holder's option, but only after six months from the date of share issuance (as defined in Statement 123R). Company F has determined that the shares (or share options) would be classified as equity instruments under the guidance of Statement 123R. However, under ASR 268 and related guidance, the instruments would be considered to be redeemable for cash or other assets upon the occurrence of events (*e.g.*, redemption at the option of the holder) that are outside the control of the issuer.

Question 1: While the instruments are subject to Statement 123R,[83] is ASR 268 and related guidance applicable to instruments issued under share-based payment arrangements that are classified as equity instruments under Statements 123R?

Interpretive Response: Yes. The staff believes that registrants must evaluate whether the terms of instruments granted in conjunction with share-based payment arrangements with employees that are not classified as liabilities under Statement 123R result in the need to present certain amounts outside of permanent equity (also referred to as being presented in "temporary equity") in accordance with ASR 268 and related guidance.[84]

When an instrument ceases to be subject to Statement 123R and becomes subject to the recognition and measurement requirements of other applicable GAAP, the staff believes that the company should reassess the classification of the instrument as a liability or equity at that time and consequently may need to reconsider the applicability of ASR 268.

Question 2: How should Company F apply ASR 268 and related guidance to the shares (or share options) granted under the share-based payment arrangements with employees that may be unvested at the date of grant?

Interpretive Response: Under Statement 123R, when compensation cost is recognized for instruments classified as equity instruments, additional paid-

---

(Footnote Continued)

Shareholder Value: Theory and Evidence (Kluwer, Boston, MA, 1999), pp. 115-142.

[79] The terminology "outside the control of the issuer" is used to refer to any of the three redemption conditions described in Rule 5-02.28 of Regulation S-X that would require classification outside permanent equity. That rule requires preferred securities that are redeemable for cash or other assets to be classified outside of permanent equity if they are redeemable (1) at a fixed or determinable price on a fixed or determinable date, (2) at the option of the holder, or (3) upon the occurrence of an event that is not solely within the control of the issuer.

[80] Statement 123R, paragraphs 28-35 and A225-A232.

[81] ASR 268, July 27, 1979, Rule 5-02.28 of Regulation S-X.

[82] Related guidance includes EITF Abstracts Topic No. D-98, *Classification and Measurement of Redeemable Securities* ("Topic D-98").

[83] Statement 123R, paragraph A231, states that an instrument ceases to be subject to Statement 123R when "the rights conveyed by the instrument to the holder are no longer dependent on the holder being an employee of the entity (that is, no longer dependent on providing service)."

[84] Instruments granted in conjunction with share-based payment arrangements with employees that do not by their terms require redemption for cash or other assets (at a fixed or determinable price on a fixed or determinable date, at the option of the holder, or upon the occurrence of an event that is not solely within the control of the issuer) would not be assumed by the staff to require net cash settlement for purposes of applying ASR 268 in circumstances in which paragraphs 14 - 18 of EITF Issue 00-19, *Accounting for Derivative Financial Instruments Indexed to, and Potentially Settled in, a Company's Own Stock*, would otherwise require the assumption of net cash settlement. *See* Statement 123R, footnote 152 to paragraph B121, which states, in part: ". . . Issue 00-19 specifies that events or actions necessary to deliver registered shares are not controlled by a company and, therefore, except under limited circumstances, such provisions would require a company to assume that the contract would be net-cash settled. . . .Thus, employee share options might be classified as substantive liabilities if they were subject to Issue 00-19; however, for purposes of this Statement, the Board does not believe that employee share options should be classified as liabilities based solely on that notion." *See* also Statement 123R, footnote 20.

incapital[85] is increased. If the award is not fully vested at the grant date, compensation cost is recognized and additional paid-in-capital is increased over time as services are rendered over the requisite service period. A similar pattern of recognition should be used to reflect the amount presented as temporary equity for share-based payment awards that have redemption features that are outside the issuer's control but are classified as equity instruments under Statement 123R. The staff believes Company F should present as temporary equity at each balance sheet date an amount that is based on the redemption amount of the instrument, but takes into account the proportion of consideration received in the form of employee services. Thus, for example, if a nonvested share that qualifies for equity classification under Statement 123R is redeemable at fair value more than six months after vesting, and that nonvested share is 75% vested at the balance sheet date, an amount equal to 75% of the fair value of the share should be presented as temporary equity at that date. Similarly, if an option on a share of redeemable stock that qualifies for equity classification under Statement 123R is 75% vested at the balance sheet date, an amount equal to 75% of the intrinsic[86] value of the option should be presented as temporary equity at that date.

Question 3: Would the methodology described for employee awards in the Interpretive Response to Question 2 above apply to nonemployee awards to be issued in exchange for goods or services with similar terms to those described above?

Interpretive Response: See Topic 14.A for a discussion of the application of the principles in Statement 123R to nonemployee awards. The staff believes it would generally be appropriate to apply the methodology described in the Interpretive Response to Question 2 above to nonemployee awards.

F. Classification of Compensation Expense Associated with Share-Based Payment Arrangements

Facts: Company G utilizes both cash and share-based payment arrangements to compensate its employees and nonemployee service providers. Company G would like to emphasize in its income statement the amount of its compensation that did not involve a cash outlay.

Question: How should Company G present in its income statement the non-cash nature of its expense related to share-based payment arrangements?

Interpretive Response: The staff believes Company G should present the expense related to share-based payment arrangements in the same line or lines as cash compensation paid to the same employees.[87] The staff believes a company could consider disclosing the amount of expense related to share-based payment arrangements included in specific line items in the financial statements. Disclosure of this information might be appropriate in a parenthetical note to the appropriate income statement line items, on the cash flow statement, in the footnotes to the financial statements, or within MD&A.

G. Non-GAAP Financial Measures

Facts: Company H, a calendar year company, adopts Statement 123R as of July 1, 2005. Company H has issued share options to its employees each year since issuing publicly traded stock twenty years ago. In the MD&A section of its 2005 Form 10-K, Company H believes it would be useful to investors to disclose what net income would be before considering the effect of accounting for share-based payment transactions in accordance with Statement 123R.

Question 1: Does the resulting measure, "Net Income Before Share-Based Payment Charge," or an equivalent measure, meet the definition of a non-GAAP measure in Regulation G and Item 10(e) of Regulation S-K?[88]

Interpretive Response: Yes. Because the financial measure Company H is considering excludes an amount (share-based payment expense) that is included in the most directly comparable measure calculated and presented in accordance with GAAP (net income), it would be considered a non-GAAP financial measure pursuant to the provisions of Regulation G and Item 10(e) of Regulation S-K.

Question 2: Is the measure "Net Income Before Share-Based Payment Charge," or an equivalent measure, a prohibited non-GAAP measure pursuant to Item 10(e) of Regulation S-K?

Interpretive Response: Item 10(e) prohibits the inclusion of certain non-GAAP financial measures and also mandates specific disclosures for registrants that include permitted non-GAAP financial measures in filings. Generally, under Item 10(e) of Regulation S-K, a company may not present a non-GAAP performance measure that removes an expense from net income by identifying that expense as non-recurring, infrequent, or unusual if it is reasonably likely that the expense will recur within two years or if the company had a similar expense

---

[85] Depending on the fact pattern, this may be recorded as common stock and additional paid in capital.

[86] The potential redemption amount of the share option in this illustration is its intrinsic value because the holder would pay the exercise price on exercise of the option and then, upon redemption of the underlying shares, the company would pay the holder the fair value of those shares. Thus, the net cash outflow from the arrangement would be equal to the intrinsic value of the share option. In situations where there would be no cash inflows from the share option holder, the cash required to be paid to redeem the

underlying shares upon the exercise of the put option would be the redemption value.

[87] Statement 123R does not identify a specific line item in the income statement for presentation of the expense related to share-based payment arrangements.

[88] 17 CFR 229.10(e). All references to Item 10(e) of Regulation S-K also includes corresponding provisions of Item 10(h) of Regulation S-B with respect to small business issuers as well as US GAAP information of foreign private issuers under General Instruction C(e) of Form 20-F.

within the prior two years. The staff issued Frequently Asked Questions Regarding the Use of Non-GAAP Measures in June of 2003. Question 8 discusses whether it is appropriate to eliminate or smooth an item that is identified as recurring. The staff answered the question in part by stating "Companies should never use a non-GAAP financial measure in an attempt to smooth earnings. Further, while there is no per se prohibition against removing a recurring item, companies must meet the burden of demonstrating the usefulness of any measure that excludes recurring items, especially if the non-GAAP financial measure is used to evaluate performance."

The staff believes that a measure used by the management of Company H that excludes share-based payments internally to evaluate performance may be relevant disclosure for investors. In these cases, if Company H determines that the non-GAAP financial measure "Net Income Before Share-Based Payment Charge" does not violate any of the prohibitions from inclusion in filings with the Commission outlined in Item 10(e) of Regulation S-K, Company H's management would be required to disclose, among other items, the following:

- The reasons that the company's management believes that presentation of the non-GAAP financial measure provides useful information to investors regarding the company's financial condition and results of operations; and

- To the extent material, the additional purposes, if any, for which the company's management uses the non-GAAP financial measure that are not otherwise disclosed.[89]

In addition, the staff's response to Question 8 included in Frequently Asked Questions Regarding the Use of Non-GAAP Measures in June of 2003 notes that the inclusion of a non-GAAP financial measure may be misleading absent the following disclosures:

- The manner in which management uses the non-GAAP measure to conduct or evaluate its business;

- The economic substance behind management's decision to use such a measure;

- The material limitations associated with use of the non-GAAP financial measure as compared to the use of the most directly comparable GAAP financial measure;

- The manner in which management compensates for these limitations when using the non-GAAP financial measure; and

- The substantive reasons why management believes the non-GAAP financial measure provides useful information to investors.

Question 3: How could Company H demonstrate the effect of accounting for share-based payment transactions in accordance with Statement 123R and Regula-

tion G and Item 10(e) of Regulation S-K in its Form 10-K?

Interpretive Response: The staff believes that including a discussion in MD&A addressing significant trends and variability of a company's earnings and changes in the significant components of certain line items is important to assist an investor in understanding the company's performance. The staff also understands that expenses from share-based payments might vary in different ways and for different reasons than would other expenses. In particular, the staff believes Company H's investors would be well served by disclosure in MD&A that explains the components of the company's expenses, including, if material, identification of the amount of expense associated with share-based payment transactions and discussion of the reasons why such amounts have fluctuated from period to period.

Question 4: Would the staff object to Company H including a pro-forma income statement in its SEC filings that removes from net income the effects of accounting for share-based payment arrangements in accordance with Statement 123R?

Interpretive Response: Yes. Removal of the effects of accounting for sharebased payment arrangements in accordance with Statement 123R would not meet any of the conditions in Rule 11-01(a) of Regulation S-X for presentation of pro forma financial information. Further, the removal of the effects of accounting for share-based payment arrangements in accordance with Statement 123R would not meet any of the conditions in Rule 11-02(b)(6) of Regulation S-X to be reflected as a pro forma adjustment in circumstances where pro forma financial information is required under Rule 11-01(a) of Regulation S-X for other transactions such as recent or probable business combinations.

In addition, Item 10(e) of Regulation S-X prohibits presenting non-GAAP financial measures on the face of any pro forma financial information required to be disclosed by Article 11 of Regulation S-X. Further, a company may not present non-GAAP financial measures on the face of the company's financial statements prepared in accordance with GAAP or in the accompanying notes.

H. First Time Adoption of Statement 123R in an Interim Period

Facts: Company I's fiscal year begins on January 1, 2005. Company I plans to adopt Statement 123R on July 1, 2005, which is the beginning of its first interim period following the effective date. Company I previously recognized share-based payment compensation in accordance with Opinion 25.

Question 1: What disclosures are required in Company I's Form 10-Q for the third quarter of 2005?

Interpretive Response: The disclosures required by paragraphs 64-65, 84, and A240-242 of Statement 123R should be included in the Form 10-Q for the interim period when Statement 123R is first

---

[89] 17 CFR 229.10(e)(1).

adopted. If Company I applies the modified retrospective method[90] in other than the first interim period of a fiscal year, the staff believes that the Form 10-Q for the period of adoption should include disclosure of the effects of the adoption of Statement 123R on previously reported interim periods.[91] If Company I applies the modified prospective method,[92] the financial statements for Company I's prior interim periods and fiscal years will not reflect any restated amounts. The staff believes that Company I should disclose this fact. Regardless of the transition method chosen, Company I should also provide the disclosures required by SAB Topic 11M, *Disclosure Of The Impact That Recently Issued Accounting Standards Will Have On The Financial Statements Of The Registrant When Adopted In A Future Period*, in interim and annual financial statements preceding the adoption of Statement 123R.

Facts: Company J plans to adopt Statement 123R by applying the modified retrospective method only to the preceding interim periods of its current fiscal year. Company J anticipates recording an adjustment upon the adoption of Statement 123R to reflect the cumulative effect of reclassifying certain sharebased payment arrangements as liabilities.

Question 2: Would Company J be required to apply the cumulative effect adjustment to the beginning of the fiscal year and to reflect the change in classification from liabilities to equity to its interim periods preceding adoption in accordance with Statement 3,[93] paragraph 10?

Interpretive Response: No. Statement 123R, paragraph 76, limits retrospective application to recording compensation cost for unvested awards based on the amounts previously determined under Statement 123 for pro forma footnote disclosure. Any adjustments to be recorded as a cumulative effect of a change in accounting principle should be recorded as of the date of adoption of Statement 123R, which may occur after the beginning of the fiscal year. Therefore, based on the guidance in Statement 123R, paragraphs 79-82, registrants are not required to apply the provisions of Statement 3, paragraph 10.

I. Capitalization of Compensation Cost Related to Share-Based Payment Arrangements

Facts: Company K is a manufacturing company that grants share options to its production employees. Company K has determined that the cost of the production employees' service is an inventoriable cost. As such, Company K is required to initially capitalize the cost of the share option grants to these production employees as inventory and later recognize the cost in the income statement when the inventory is consumed.[94]

Question: If Company K elects to adjust its period end inventory balance for the allocable amount of share-option cost through a period end adjustment to its financial statements, instead of incorporating the share-option cost through its inventory costing system, would this be considered a deficiency in internal controls?

Interpretive Response: No. Statement 123R does not prescribe the mechanism a company should use to incorporate a portion of share-option costs in an inventory-costing system. The staff believes Company K may accomplish this through a period end adjustment to its financial statements. Company K should establish appropriate controls surrounding the calculation and recording of this period end adjustment, as it would any other period end adjustment. The fact that the entry is recorded as a period end adjustment, by itself, should not impact management's ability to determine that the internal control over financial reporting, as defined by the SEC's rules implementing Section 404 of the Sarbanes-Oxley Act of 2002,[95] is effective.

J. Accounting for Income Tax Effects of Share-Based Payment Arrangements Upon Adoption of Statement 123R

Facts: In accordance with Statement 123R, reporting entities will need to determine whether deductions reported on tax returns for share-based payment awards exceed or are less than the cumulative compensation cost recognized for financial reporting. If the deductions exceed the cumulative compensation cost recognized for financial reporting, the entity generally should record any resulting excess tax benefits as additional paid-in capital. If deductions are less than the cumulative compensation cost recognized for financial reporting, the entity should record the write-off of the deferred tax asset, net of the related valuation allowance, against any remaining additional paid-in capital from previous awards accounted for in accordance with the fair value method of Statement 123 or Statement 123R, as applicable. The remaining balance, if any, of the write-off of the deferred tax asset shall be recognized in the income statement.[96]

Company L is an entity that previously recognized employee share-based payment costs under the intrinsic value method of Opinion 25. In this situation, Statement 123R states that Company L "shall calculate the amount available for offset [in additional paid-in capital] as the net amount of excess tax benefits that would have qualified as such had it instead adopted Statement 123 for recognition purposes pursuant to Statement 123's original effective date and transition method."[97]

Question: When is Company L required to calculate the additional paid-in capital from previous share-

---

[90] Statement 123R, paragraph 76.

[91] *See* Statement 123R, paragraph 77.

[92] Statement 123R, paragraph 74.

[93] Statement of Financial Accounting Standards No. 3, *Reporting Accounting Changes in Interim Financial Statements* ("Statement 3").

[94] Statement 123R, paragraph 5.

[95] Release No. 34-47986, June 5, 2003, *Management's Report on Internal Control Over Financial Reporting and Certification of Disclosure in Exchange Act Period Reports.*

[96] Statement 123R, paragraph 63.

[97] *Ibid.*

based payment awards that is available for offset against the write-off of a deferred tax asset?

Interpretive Response: Statement 123R will necessitate the tracking of tax attributes relating to share-based payment transactions with employees for a number of reasons, including the requirements related to any required write-off of excess deferred tax assets upon settlement of a share option. While it is important that appropriate detailed information be available when needed for consideration, the timing as to when such information actually affects financial reporting will vary from company to company. In preparation for the adoption of Statement 123R, Company L should evaluate the level of detail which may be required considering its particular facts and circumstances.

Statement 123R is silent as to when the additional paid-in capital available for offset should be calculated. However, the staff notes that Company L would not be required to calculate the additional paid-in capital available for offset by the date it adopts Statement 123R. In addition, the staff notes that Statement 123R does not require disclosure of the additional paid-in capital available for offset.[98] The staff believes that Company L need only calculate the additional paid-in capital available for offset if and when Company L faces a situation in which deductions reported on its tax return are less than the relevant deferred tax asset. In addition, Company L need only perform the calculations periodically to the extent necessary to conclude that sufficient paid-in capital is available for the offset of the deduction shortfall.

K. Modification of Employee Share Options Prior to Adoption of Statement 123R

Facts: Company M is a public entity that historically applied the recognition provisions of Opinion 25 and intends to transition to Statement 123R under the modified prospective method of application.[99] In prior periods, Company M granted at-the-money share options to its employees in which the exercisability of the options is conditional only on performing service through the vesting date.[100] Since the time of grant, Company M's share price has fallen such that the share options are out-of-the-money. Prior to adoption of Statement 123R the share options are still unvested, and Company M intends to modify these unvested share options to accelerate the vesting. Company M has determined that the modification to accelerate vesting will not require recognition of compensation cost in its financial statements in the period of the modification under the provisions of Opinion 25.[101] However, Company M intends to reflect the compensation

cost related to the modification in its fair value pro forma disclosures under Statement 123,[102] in the period the modification is made.

Question: Would the staff object to Company M reflecting the remaining compensation cost related to these share options in the fair value pro forma disclosures required under Statement 123 as a result of the modification in the period in which the modification was enacted?

Interpretive Response: No. The staff believes that an acceptable interpretation of Statement 123 is that the modification to accelerate the vesting of such share options would result in the recognition of the remaining amount of compensation cost in the period the modification is made, so long as the acceleration of vesting permits employees to exercise the share options in a circumstance when they would not otherwise have been able to do so absent the modification. The staff notes that the service period definition in Statement 123[103] indicates, "If the service period is not defined as an earlier or shorter period, it shall be presumed to be the vesting period." After the modification, Company M's share options will be vested pursuant to the awards' terms. Accordingly, under this interpretation, there is no remaining service period and any remaining unrecognized service cost for those share options should be recognized at the date of the modification. The staff believes that since the remaining unrecognized compensation cost is accelerated and recognized at the date of modification, no compensation cost would be recognized for these modified share options in the income statement in the periods after adoption of Statement 123R, absent any further modifications.

The staff reminds public entities that Statement 123, paragraph 47, indicates that for each year an income statement is provided, the terms of significant modifications of outstanding awards shall be disclosed. In order to inform investors about modification transactions and management's reasons for entering into those transactions, the staff believes that public entities should specifically disclose any modifications to accelerate the vesting of out-of-the-money share options in anticipation of adopting Statement 123R, including the reasons for modifying the option terms.

L. Application of the Measurement Provisions of Statement 123R to Foreign Private Issuers[104]

Question: Does the staff believe there are differences in the measurement provisions for share-based payment arrangements with employees under International Accounting Standards Board

---

[98] Statement 123R's disclosure requirements are described in paragraphs 64, 65, A240, A241 and A242.

[99] Statement 123R, paragraph 74.

[100] The terms of these share options do not define the service period as being other than the vesting period.

[101] *See* FASB Interpretation No. 44, *Accounting for Certain Transactions Involving Stock Compensation*, paragraph 36, which requires the recognition of compensation expense under Opinion 25 due to a modification of a share-based payment award only if,

absent the acceleration of vesting, the award would have otherwise been forfeited during the vesting period pursuant to its original terms.

[102] Statement 123, paragraph 45, as amended by Statement 148, *Accounting for Stock-Based Compensation - Transition and Disclosure ("Statement 148")*.

[103] Statement 123, Appendix E.

[104] As defined in Regulation C § 230.405.

International Financial Reporting Standard 2, *Share-based Payment* ("IFRS 2") and Statement 123R that would result in a reconciling item under Item 17 or 18 of Form 20-F?

Interpretive Response: The staff believes that application of the guidance provided by IFRS 2 regarding the measurement of employee share options would generally result in a fair value measurement that is consistent with the fair value objective stated in Statement 123R.[105] Accordingly, the staff believes that application of Statement 123R's measurement guidance would not generally result in a reconciling item required to be reported under Item 17 or 18 of Form 20-F for a foreign private issuer that has complied with the provisions of IFRS 2 for share-based payment transactions with employees. However, the staff reminds foreign private issuers that there are certain differences between the guidance in IFRS 2 and Statement 123R that may result in reconciling items.[106]

M. Disclosures in MD&A Subsequent to Adoption of Statement 123R

Question: What disclosures should companies consider including in MD&A to highlight the effects of 1) differences between the accounting for share-based payment arrangements before and after the adoption of Statement 123R and 2) changes to share-based payment arrangements?

Interpretive Response: As stated in SEC Release FR-72, the principal objectives of MD&A are to give readers a view of a company through the eyes of management, to provide the context within which financial information should be analyzed and to provide information about the quality of, and potential variability of, a company's earnings and cash flow, so that investors can ascertain the likelihood that past performance is indicative of future performance. The adoption of Statement 123R may result in significant differences between the financial statements of periods before and after the adoption, especially for companies with significant share-based compensation programs that have followed the recognition provisions of Opinion 25 or that adopted the fair-value-based method for financial statement recognition in accordance with Statement 123 using the prospective method permitted by Statement 148. Furthermore, the staff understands that companies may refine their estimates of assumptions as a result of implementing Statement 123R and the interpretive guidance provided in this SAB. In addition, the staff understands that many companies are evaluating their share-based payment arrangements and making changes to those arrangements.

Each of these situations may affect the comparability of financial statements. Accordingly, to assist investors and other users of financial statements in understanding the financial results of a company that has adopted Statement 123R, the staff believes that companies should consider including in

MD&A material qualitative and quantitative information about any of the following, as well as other information that could affect comparability of financial statements from period to period:

- Transition method selected (*e.g.*, modified prospective application or modified retrospective application) and the resulting financial statement impact in current and future reporting periods;

- Method utilized by the company to account for share-based payment arrangements in periods prior to the adoption of Statement 123R and the impact, or lack thereof, on the prior period financial statements;

- Modifications made to outstanding share options prior to the adoption of Statement 123R and the reason(s) for the modification;

- Differences in valuation methodologies or assumptions compared to those that were used in estimating the fair value of share options under Statement 123;

- Changes in the quantity or type of instruments used in share-based payment programs, such as a shift from share options to restricted shares;

- Changes in the terms of share-based payment arrangements, such as the addition of performance conditions;

- A discussion of the one-time effect, if any, of the adoption of Statement 123R, such as any cumulative adjustments recorded in the financial statements; and

- Total compensation cost related to nonvested awards not yet recognized and the weighted average period over which it is expected to be recognized.

END TOPIC 14

* * * * *

AMENDMENTS TO CODIFICATION OF STAFF ACCOUNTING BULLETINS

The Codification of Staff Accounting Bulletins is amended to revise Question 2 and the related interpretive response in Topic 4.D., all of Topic 4.E., and all of Topic 5.T. as follows:

TOPIC 4: EQUITY ACCOUNTS

* * * * *

D. Earnings Per Share Computations In An Initial Public Offering

* * * * *

Question 2: Does reflecting nominal issuances as outstanding for all historical periods in the computation of earnings per share alter the registrant's responsibility to determine whether compensation

---

[105] Statement 123R, paragraph A2.

[106] Statement 123R, paragraphs B258-B269, identify the more significant differences between IFRS 2 and Statement 123R.

expense must be recognized for such issuances to employees?

Interpretive Response: No. Registrants must follow GAAP in determining whether the recognition of compensation expense for any issuances of equity instruments to employees is necessary.[107] Reflecting nominal issuances as outstanding for all historical periods in the computation of earnings per share does not alter that existing responsibility under GAAP.

* * * * *

E. Receivables From Sale Of Stock

Facts: Capital stock is sometimes issued to officers or other employees before the cash payment is received.

Question: How should the receivables from the officers or other employees be presented in the balance sheet?

Interpretive Response: The amount recorded as a receivable should be presented in the balance sheet as a deduction from stockholders' equity. This is generally consistent with Rule 5-02.30 of Regulation S-X which states that accounts or notes receivable arising from transactions involving the registrant's capital stock should be presented as deductions from stockholders' equity and not as assets.

It should be noted generally that all amounts receivable from officers and directors resulting from sales of stock or from other transactions (other than expense advances or sales on normal trade terms) should be separately stated in the balance sheet irrespective of whether such amounts may be shown as assets or are required to be reported as deductions from stockholders' equity.

The staff will not suggest that a receivable from an officer or director be deducted from stockholders' equity if the receivable was paid in cash prior to the publication of the financial statements and the payment date is stated in a note to the financial statements. However, the staff would consider the subsequent return of such cash payment to the officer or director to be part of a scheme or plan to evade the registration or reporting requirements of the securities laws.

* * * * *

TOPIC 5: MISCELLANEOUS ACCOUNTING

* * * * *

T. Accounting for Expenses or Liabilities Paid by Principal Stockholder(s)

Facts: Company X was a defendant in litigation for which the company had not recorded a liability in accordance with Statement 5. A principal stockholder[108] of the company transfers a portion of his shares to the plaintiff to settle such litigation. If the company had settled the litigation directly, the company would have recorded the settlement as an expense.

Question: Must the settlement be reflected as an expense in the company's financial statements, and if so, how?

Interpretive Response: Yes. The value of the shares transferred should be reflected as an expense in the company's financial statements with a corresponding credit to contributed (paid-in) capital.

The staff believes that such a transaction is similar to those described in paragraph 11 of Statement of Financial Accounting Standards Statement No. 123 (revised 2004), *Share-Based Payment* (Statement 123R), which states that "share-based payments awarded to an employee of the reporting entity by a related party or other holder of an economic interest[109] in the entity as compensation for services provided to the entity are share-based payment transactions to be accounted for under this Statement unless the transfer is clearly for a purpose other than compensation for services to the reporting entity." As explained in paragraph 11 of Statement 123R, the substance of such a transaction is that the economic interest holder makes a capital contribution to the reporting entity, and the reporting entity makes a share-based payment to its employee in exchange for services rendered.

The staff believes that the problem of separating the benefit to the principal stockholder from the benefit to the company cited in Statement 123R is not limited to transactions involving stock compensation. Therefore, similar accounting is required in this and other[110] transactions where a principal stockholder pays an expense for the company, unless the stockholder's action is caused by a relationship or obligation completely unrelated to his position as a stockholder or such action clearly does not benefit the company.

Some registrants and their accountants have taken the position that since Statement 57 applies to these transactions and requires only the disclosure of material related party transactions, the staff should not analogize to the accounting called for by Statement 123R, paragraph 11 for transactions other than those specifically covered by it. The staff

---

[107] As prescribed by Statement 123R.

[108] Statement 57, paragraph 24e, defines principal owners as "owners of record or known beneficial owners of more than 10 percent of the voting interests of the enterprise."

[109] Statement 123R defines an economic interest in an entity as "any type or form of pecuniary interest or arrangement that an entity could issue or be a party to, including equity securities; financial instruments with characteristics of equity, liabilities or both; long-term debt and other debt-financing arrangements;

leases; and contractual arrangements such as management contracts, service contracts, or intellectual property licenses." Accordingly, a principal stockholder would be considered a holder of an economic interest in an entity.

[110] For example, SAB Topic 1.B indicates that the separate financial statements of a subsidiary should reflect any costs of its operations which are incurred by the parent on its behalf. Additionally, the staff notes that AICPA Technical Practice Aids §4160 also indicates that the payment by principal stockholders of a company's debt should be accounted for as a capital contribution.

notes, however, that Statement 57 does not address the measurement of related party transactions and that, as a result, such transactions are generally recorded at the amounts indicated by their terms.[111] However, the staff believes that transactions of the type described above differ from the typical related party transactions.

The transactions for which Statement 57 requires disclosure generally are those in which a company receives goods or services directly from, or provides goods or services directly to, a related party, and the form and terms of such transactions may be structured to produce either a direct or indirect benefit to the related party. The participation of a related party in such a transaction negates the presumption that transactions reflected in the financial statements have been consummated at arm's length. Disclosure is therefore required to compen-

sate for the fact that, due to the related party's involvement, the terms of the transaction may produce an accounting measurement for which a more faithful measurement may not be determinable.

However, transactions of the type discussed in the facts given do not have such problems of measurement and appear to be transacted to provide a benefit to the stockholder through the enhancement or maintenance of the value of the stockholder's investment. The staff believes that the substance of such transactions is the payment of an expense of the company through contributions by the stockholder. Therefore, the staff believes it would be inappropriate to account for such transactions according to the form of the transaction.

[For the text of Topic 4, see ¶ 39,131. For the text of Topic 5, see ¶ 39,141. For the text of Topic 14, see ¶ 39,231.]

[¶ 39,074]   RELEASE NO. 108, September 13, 2006

Considering the Effects of Prior Year Misstatements when Quantifying Misstatements in Current Year Financial Statements

ACTION: Publication of Staff Accounting Bulletin.

SUMMARY: The interpretations in this Staff Accounting Bulletin express the staff's views regarding the process of quantifying financial statement misstatements. The staff is aware of diversity in practice. For example, certain registrants do not consider the effects of prior year errors on current year financial statements, thereby allowing improper assets or liabilities to remain unadjusted. While these errors may not be material if considered only in relation to the balance sheet, correcting the errors could be material to the current year income statement. Certain registrants have proposed to the staff that allowing these errors to remain on the balance sheet as assets or liabilities in perpetuity is an appropriate application of generally accepted accounting principles. The staff believes that approach is not in the best interest of the users of financial statements. The interpretations in this Staff Accounting Bulletin are being issued to address diversity in practice in quantifying financial statement misstatements and the potential under current practice for the build up of improper amounts on the balance sheet.

DATE: September 13, 2006.

FOR FURTHER INFORMATION CONTACT: Mark S. Mahar, Office of the Chief Accountant (202) 551-5300, Todd E. Hardiman, Division of Corporation Finance (202) 551-3400, or Toai P. Cheng (202) 551-6918, Division of Investment Management, Securities and Exchange Commission, 100 F Street NE, Washington, DC 20549.

SUPPLEMENTARY INFORMATION: The statements in staff accounting bulletins are not rules or interpretations of the Commission, nor are they published as bearing the Commission's official approval. They represent interpretations and practices followed by the Division of Corporation Finance, the Division of Investment Management and the Office of the Chief Accountant in administering the disclosure requirements of the Federal securities laws.

Nancy M. Morris

Secretary

Date: September 13, 2006

Part 211 - [AMEND]

Accordingly, Part 211 of Title 17 of the Code of Federal Regulations is amended by adding Staff Accounting Bulletin No. 108 to the table found in Subpart B.

STAFF ACCOUNTING BULLETIN NO. 108

The staff hereby adds Section N to Topic 1, *Financial Statements*, of the Staff Accounting Bulletin Series. Section N provides guidance on the consideration of the effects of prior year misstatements in quantifying current year misstatements for the purpose of a materiality assessment.

Note: The text of SAB 108 will not appear in the Code of Federal Regulations.

Topic 1: Financial Statements

*****

---

[111] However, in some circumstances it is necessary to reflect, either in the historical financial statements or a pro forma presentation (depending on the circumstances), related party transactions at amounts other than those indicated by their terms. Two such circumstances are addressed in Staff Accounting Bulletin Topic 1.B.1, Questions 3 and 4. Another example is where the terms of a material contract with a related party are expected to change upon the completion of an offering (i.e., the principal shareholder requires payment for services which had previously been contributed by the shareholder to the company).

N. Considering the Effects of Prior Year Misstatements when Quantifying Misstatements in Current Year Financial Statements

Facts: During the course of preparing annual financial statements, a registrant is evaluating the materiality of an improper expense accrual (*e.g.*, overstated liability) in the amount of $100, which has built up over 5 years, at $20 per year.[1] The registrant previously evaluated the misstatement as being immaterial to each of the prior year financial statements (*i.e.*, years 1-4). For the purpose of evaluating materiality in the current year (*i.e.*, year 5), the registrant quantifies the error as a $20 overstatement of expenses.

Question 1: Has the registrant appropriately quantified the amount of this error for the purpose of evaluating materiality for the current year?

Interpretive Response: No. In this example, the registrant has only quantified the effects of the identified unadjusted error that arose in the current year income statement. The staff believes a registrant's materiality evaluation of an identified unadjusted error should quantify the effects of the identified unadjusted error on each financial statement and related financial statement disclosure.

Topic 1M notes that a materiality evaluation must be based on all relevant quantitative and qualitative factors.[2] This analysis generally begins with quantifying potential misstatements to be evaluated. There has been diversity in practice with respect to this initial step of a materiality analysis.

The diversity in approaches for quantifying the amount of misstatements primarily stems from the effects of misstatements that were not corrected at the end of the prior year ("prior year misstatements"). These prior year misstatements should be considered in quantifying misstatements in current year financial statements.

The techniques most commonly used in practice to accumulate and quantify misstatements are generally referred to as the "rollover" and "iron curtain" approaches.

The rollover approach, which is the approach used by the registrant in this example, quantifies a misstatement based on the amount of the error originating in the current year income statement. Thus, this approach ignores the effects of correcting the portion of the current year balance sheet misstatement that originated in prior years (*i.e.*, it ignores the "carryover effects" of prior year misstatements).

The iron curtain approach quantifies a misstatement based on the effects of correcting the misstatement existing in the balance sheet at the end of the current year, irrespective of the misstatement's year(s) of origination. Had the registrant in this fact pattern applied the iron curtain approach, the misstatement would have been quantified as a $100 misstatement based on the end of year balance sheet misstatement. Thus, the adjustment needed to correct the financial statements for the end of year error would be to reduce the liability by $100 with a corresponding decrease in current year expense.

As demonstrated in this example, the primary weakness of the rollover approach is that it can result in the accumulation of significant misstatements on the balance sheet that are deemed immaterial in part because the amount that originates in each year is quantitatively small. The staff is aware of situations in which a registrant, relying on the rollover approach, has allowed an erroneous item to accumulate on the balance sheet to the point where eliminating the improper asset or liability would itself result in a material error in the income statement if adjusted in the current year. Such registrants have sometimes concluded that the improper asset or liability should remain on the balance sheet into perpetuity.

In contrast, the primary weakness of the iron curtain approach is that it does not consider the correction of prior year misstatements in the current year (*i.e.*, the reversal of the carryover effects) to be errors. Therefore, in this example, if the misstatement was corrected during the current year such that no error existed in the balance sheet at the end of the current year, the reversal of the $80 prior year misstatement would not be considered an error in the current year financial statements under the iron curtain approach. Implicitly, the iron curtain approach assumes that because the prior year financial statements were not materially misstated, correcting any immaterial errors that existed in those statements in the current year is the "correct" accounting, and is therefore not considered an error in the current year. Thus, utilization of the iron curtain approach can result in a misstatement in the current year income statement not being evaluated as an error at all.

The staff does not believe the exclusive reliance on either the rollover or iron curtain approach appropriately quantifies all misstatements that could be material to users of financial statements.

In describing the concept of materiality, FASB Concepts Statement No. 2, *Qualitative Characteristics of Accounting Information*, indicates that materiality determinations are based on whether "it is probable that the judgment of a reasonable person relying upon the report would have been changed or influenced *by the inclusion or correction of the item*" (emphasis added).[3] The staff believes registrants must quantify the impact of correcting all misstatements, including both the carryover and reversing effects of prior year misstatements, on the current year financial statements. The staff believes that this can be accomplished by quantifying an error under both the rollover and iron curtain approaches as described above and by evalu-

---

[1] For purposes of these facts, assume the registrant properly determined that the overstatement of the liability resulted from an error rather than a change in accounting estimate. See FASB Statement 154, *Accounting Changes and Error Corrections*, paragraph 2, for the distinction between an error and a change in accounting estimate.

[2] Topic 1N addresses certain of these quantitative issues, but does not alter the analysis required by Topic 1M.

[3] Concepts Statement 2, paragraph 132. See also Concepts Statement 2, Glossary of Terms - Materiality.

ating the error measured under each approach. Thus, a registrant's financial statements would require adjustment when either approach results in quantifying a misstatement that is material, after considering all relevant quantitative and qualitative factors.

As a reminder, a change from an accounting principle that is not generally accepted to one that is generally accepted is a correction of an error.[4]

The staff believes that the registrant should quantify the current year misstatement in this example using both the iron curtain approach (*i.e.*, $100) and the rollover approach (*i.e.*, $20). Therefore, if the $100 misstatement is considered material to the financial statements, after all of the relevant quantitative and qualitative factors are considered, the registrant's financial statements would need to be adjusted.

It is possible that correcting an error in the current year could materially misstate the current year's income statement. For example, correcting the $100 misstatement in the current year will:

- Correct the $20 error originating in the current year;
- Correct the $80 balance sheet carryover error that originated in Years 1 through 4; but also
- Misstate the current year income statement by $80.

If the $80 understatement of current year expense is material to the current year, after all of the relevant quantitative and qualitative factors are considered, the prior year financial statements should be corrected, even though such revision previously was and continues to be immaterial to the prior year financial statements. Correcting prior year financial statements for immaterial errors would not require previously filed reports to be amended. Such correction may be made the next time the registrant files the prior year financial statements.

The following example further illustrates the staff's views on quantifying misstatements, including the consideration of the effects of prior year misstatements:

Facts: During the course of preparing annual financial statements, a registrant is evaluating the materiality of a sales cut-off error in which $50 of revenue from the following year was recorded in the current year, thereby overstating accounts receivable by $50 at the end of the current year. In addition, a similar sales cut-off error existed at the end of the prior year in which $110 of revenue from the current year was recorded in the prior year. As a result of the combination of the current year and prior year cut-off errors, revenues in the current year are understated by $60 ($110 understatement of revenues at the beginning of the current year partially offset by a $50 overstatement of revenues at the end of the current year). The prior year error was evaluated in the prior year as being immaterial to those financial statements.

Question 2: How should the registrant quantify the misstatement in the current year financial statements?

Interpretive Response: The staff believes the registrant should quantify the current year misstatement in this example using both the iron curtain approach (*i.e.*, $50) and the rollover approach (*i.e.*, $60). Therefore, assuming a $60 misstatement is considered material to the financial statements, after all relevant quantitative and qualitative factors are considered, the registrant's financial statements would need to be adjusted.

Further, in this example, recording an adjustment in the current year could alter the amount of the error affecting the current year financial statements. For instance:

- If only the $60 understatement of revenues were to be corrected in the current year, then the overstatement of current year end accounts receivable would increase to $110; or,
- If only the $50 overstatement of accounts receivable were to be corrected in the current year, then the understatement of current year revenues would increase to $110.

If the misstatement that exists after recording the adjustment in the current year financial statements is material (considering all relevant quantitative and qualitative factors), the prior year financial statements should be corrected, even though such revision previously was and continues to be immaterial to the prior year financial statements. Correcting prior year financial statements for immaterial errors would not require previously filed reports to be amended. Such correction may be made the next time the registrant files the prior year financial statements.

If the cut-off error that existed in the prior year was not discovered until the current year, a separate analysis of the financial statements of the prior year (and any other prior year in which previously undiscovered errors existed) would need to be performed to determine whether such prior year financial statements were materially misstated. If that analysis indicates that the prior year financial statements are materially misstated, they would need to be restated in accordance with Statement 154.[5]

Facts: When preparing its financial statements for years ending on or before November 15, 2006, a registrant quantified errors by using either the iron curtain approach or the rollover approach, but not both. Based on consideration of the guidance in this Staff Accounting Bulletin, the registrant concludes that errors existing in previously issued financial statements are material.

Question 3: Will the staff expect the registrant to restate prior period financial statements when first applying this guidance?

Interpretive Response: The staff will not object if a registrant[6] does not restate financial statements for

---

[4] Statement 154, paragraph 2h.

[5] Statement 154, paragraph 25.

[6] If a registrant's initial registration statement is not effective on or before November 15, 2006, and the registrant's prior year(s)

fiscal years ending on or before November 15, 2006, if management properly applied its previous approach, either iron curtain or rollover, so long as all relevant qualitative factors were considered.

To provide full disclosure, registrants electing not to restate prior periods should reflect the effects of initially applying the guidance in Topic 1N in their annual financial statements covering the first fiscal year ending after November 15, 2006. The cumulative effect of the initial application should be reported in the carrying amounts of assets and liabilities as of the beginning of that fiscal year, and the offsetting adjustment should be made to the opening balance of retained earnings for that year. Registrants should disclose the nature and amount of each individual error being corrected in the cumulative adjustment. The disclosure should also include when and how each error being corrected arose and the fact that the errors had previously been considered immaterial.

Early application of the guidance in Topic 1N is encouraged in any report for an interim period of the first fiscal year ending after November 15, 2006, filed after the publication of this Staff Accounting Bulletin. In the event that the cumulative effect of application of the guidance in Topic 1N is first reported in an interim period other than the first interim period of the first fiscal year ending after November 15, 2006, previously filed interim reports need not be amended. However, comparative information presented in reports for interim periods of the first year subsequent to initial application should be adjusted to reflect the cumulative effect adjustment as of the beginning of the year of initial application. In addition, the disclosures of selected quarterly information required by Item 302 of Regulation S-K should reflect the adjusted results.

[For the text of Topic 1, see ¶ 39,101.]

[¶ 39,075]   RELEASE NO. 109, November 5, 2007

Written Loan Commitments That Are Accounted for At Fair Value Through Earnings Under Generally Accepted Accounting Principles

ACTION: Publication of Staff Accounting Bulletin.

SUMMARY: This staff accounting bulletin ("SAB") expresses the views of the staff regarding written loan commitments that are accounted for at fair value through earnings under generally accepted accounting principles. SAB No. 105, *Application of Accounting Principles to Loan Commitments* ("SAB 105"), provided the views of the staff regarding derivative loan commitments that are accounted for at fair value through earnings pursuant to Statement of Financial Accounting Standards No. 133, *Accounting for Derivative Instruments and Hedging Activities*. SAB 105 stated that in measuring the fair value of a derivative loan commitment, the staff believed it would be inappropriate to incorporate the expected net future cash flows related to the associated servicing of the loan. This SAB supersedes SAB 105 and expresses the current view of the staff that, consistent with the guidance in Statement of Financial Accounting Standards No. 156, *Accounting for Servicing of Financial Assets*, and Statement of Financial Accounting Standards No. 159, *The Fair Value Option for Financial Assets and Financial Liabilities*, the expected net future cash flows related to the associated servicing of the loan should be included in the measurement of all written loan commitments that are accounted for at fair value through earnings. SAB 105 also indicated that the staff believed that internally-developed intangible assets (such as customer relationship intangible assets) should not be recorded as part of the fair value of a derivative loan commitment. This SAB retains that staff view and broadens its application to all written loan commitments that are accounted for at fair value through earnings.

The staff expects registrants to apply the views in Question 1 of SAB 109 on a prospective basis to derivative loan commitments issued or modified in fiscal quarters beginning after December 15, 2007.

DATE: November 5, 2007.

FOR FURTHER INFORMATION CONTACT: Ashley W. Carpenter, Office of the Chief Accountant (202) 551-5300 or Craig C. Olinger, Division of Corporation Finance (202) 551-3400, Securities and Exchange Commission, 100 F Street NE, Washington, DC 20549.

SUPPLEMENTARY INFORMATION: The statements in staff accounting bulletins are not rules or interpretations of the Commission, nor are they published as bearing the Commission's official approval. They represent interpretations and practices followed by the Division of Corporation Finance and the Office of the Chief Accountant in administering the disclosure requirements of the Federal securities laws.

Florence E. Harmon

Deputy Secretary

Date: November 5, 2007

Part 211 - [AMEND]

Accordingly, Part 211 of Title 17 of the Code of Federal Regulations is amended by adding Staff Accounting Bulletin No. 109 to the table found in Subpart B.

STAFF ACCOUNTING BULLETIN NO. 109

The staff hereby amends and replaces Section DD of Topic 5, *Miscellaneous Accounting*, of the Staff Ac-

---

(Footnote Continued)

financial statements are materially misstated based on consideration of the guidance in this Staff Accounting Bulletin, the prior year financial statements should be restated in accordance with State-

ment 154, paragraph 25. If a registrant's initial registration statement is effective on or before November 15, 2006, the guidance in the interpretive response to Question 3 is applicable.

counting Bulletin Series. Topic 5: DD (as amended) expresses the views of the staff regarding written loan commitments that are accounted for at fair value through earnings under generally accepted accounting principles.

Note: The text of SAB 109 will not appear in the Code of Federal Regulations.

TOPIC 5: MISCELLANEOUS ACCOUNTING

*****

DD. Written Loan Commitments Recorded at Fair Value Through Earnings

Facts: Bank A enters into a loan commitment with a customer to originate a mortgage loan at a specified rate. As part of this written loan commitment, Bank A expects to receive future net cash flows related to servicing rights from servicing fees (included in the loan's interest rate or otherwise), late charges, and other ancillary sources, or from selling the servicing rights to a third party. If Bank A intends to sell the mortgage loan after it is funded, pursuant to paragraph 6 of FASB Statement No. 133, *Accounting for Derivative Instruments and Hedging Activities*, as amended by FASB Statement No. 149, *Amendment of Statement 133 on Derivative Instruments and Hedging Activities* ("Statement 133"), the written loan commitment is accounted for as a derivative instrument and recorded at fair value through earnings (referred to hereafter as a "derivative loan commitment"). If Bank A does not intend to sell the mortgage loan after it is funded, the written loan commitment is not accounted for as a derivative under Statement 133. However, paragraph 7(c) of FASB Statement No. 159, *The Fair Value Option for Financial Assets and Financial Liabilities* ("Statement 159"), permits Bank A to record the written loan commitment at fair value through earnings (referred to hereafter as a "written loan commitment"). Pursuant to Statement 159, the fair value measurement for a written loan commitment would include the expected net future cash flows related to the associated servicing of the loan.

Question 1: In measuring the fair value of a derivative loan commitment accounted for under Statement 133, should Bank A include the expected net future cash flows related to the associated servicing of the loan?

Interpretive Response: Yes. The staff believes that, consistent with the recently issued guidance in FASB Statement No. 156, *Accounting for Servicing of Financial Assets* ("Statement 156")[1], and Statement 159, the expected net future cash flows related to the associated servicing of the loan should be included in the

fair value measurement of a derivative loan commitment. The expected net future cash flows related to the associated servicing of the loan that are included in the fair value measurement of a derivative loan commitment or a written loan commitment should be determined in the same manner that the fair value of a recognized servicing asset or liability is measured under FASB Statement No. 140, *Accounting for Transfers and Servicing of Financial Assets and Extinguishments of Liabilities*, as amended by Statement 156 ("Statement 140"). However, as discussed in paragraphs 61 and 62 of Statement 140, a separate and distinct servicing asset or liability is not recognized for accounting purposes until the servicing rights have been contractually separated from the underlying loan by sale or securitization of the loan with servicing retained.

The views in Question 1 apply to all loan commitments that are accounted for at fair value through earnings. However, for purposes of electing fair value accounting pursuant to Statement 159, the views in Question 1 are not intended to be applied by analogy to any other instrument that contains a nonfinancial element.

Question 2: In measuring the fair value of a derivative loan commitment accounted for under Statement 133 or a written loan commitment accounted for under Statement 159, should Bank A include the expected net future cash flows related to internally-developed intangible assets?

Interpretive Response: No. The staff does not believe that internally-developed intangible assets (such as customer relationship intangible assets) should be recorded as part of the fair value of a derivative loan commitment or a written loan commitment. Such nonfinancial elements of value should not be considered a component of the related instrument. Recognition of such assets would only be appropriate in a third-party transaction. For example, in the purchase of a portfolio of derivative loan commitments in a business combination, a customer relationship intangible asset is recorded separately from the fair value of such loan commitments. Similarly, when an entity purchases a credit card portfolio, EITF Issue No. 88-20, *Difference between Initial Investment and Principal Amount of Loans in a Purchased Credit Card Portfolio*, requires an allocation of the purchase price to a separately recorded cardholder relationship intangible asset.

The view in Question 2 applies to all loan commitments that are accounted for at fair value through earnings.

[For the text of Topic 5, see ¶ 39,141.]

[¶ 39,076]   RELEASE NO. 110, December 21, 2007

---

[1] Statement 156 permits an entity to subsequently measure recognized servicing assets and servicing liabilities (which are nonfinancial instruments) at fair value through earnings.

Use of a Simplified Method in Developing an Estimate of Expected Term of "Plain Vanilla" Share Options

ACTION: Publication of Staff Accounting Bulletin.

SUMMARY: This staff accounting bulletin ("SAB") expresses the views of the staff regarding the use of a "simplified" method, as discussed in SAB No. 107 ("SAB 107"), in developing an estimate of expected term of "plain vanilla" share options in accordance with Statement of Financial Accounting Standards No. 123 (revised 2004), *Share-Based Payment*. In particular, the staff indicated in SAB 107 that it will accept a company's election to use the simplified method, regardless of whether the company has sufficient information to make more refined estimates of expected term. At the time SAB 107 was issued, the staff believed that more detailed external information about employee exercise behavior (e.g., employee exercise patterns by industry and/or other categories of companies) would, over time, become readily available to companies. Therefore, the staff stated in SAB 107 that it would not expect a company to use the simplified method for share option grants after December 31, 2007. The staff understands that such detailed information about employee exercise behavior may not be widely available by December 31, 2007. Accordingly, the staff will continue to accept, under certain circumstances, the use of the simplified method beyond December 31, 2007.

DATES: December 21, 2007

FOR FURTHER INFORMATION CONTACT: Sandie E. Kim or Mark J. Barrysmith, Office of the Chief Accountant (202) 551-5300, or Craig C. Olinger, Division of Corporation Finance (202) 551-3400, Securities and Exchange Commission, 100 F Street NE, Washington, DC 20549.

SUPPLEMENTARY INFORMATION: The statements in staff accounting bulletins are not rules or interpretations of the Commission, nor are they published as bearing the Commission's official approval. They represent interpretations and practices followed by the Division of Corporation Finance and the Office of the Chief Accountant in administering the disclosure requirements of the Federal securities laws.

Nancy M. Morris

Secretary

Date: December 21, 2007

Part 211 - [AMENDED]

Accordingly, Part 211 of Title 17 of the Code of Federal Regulations is amended by adding Staff Accounting Bulletin No. 110 to the table found in Subpart B.

STAFF ACCOUNTING BULLETIN NO. 110

Effective January 1, 2008, the staff hereby amends and replaces Question 6 of Section D.2 of Topic 14, *Share-Based Payment*, of the Staff Accounting Bulletin Series. Question 6 of Topic 14: D.2 (as amended) expresses the views of the staff regarding the use of a "simplified" method in developing an estimate of expected term of "plain vanilla" share options in accordance with Statement of Financial Accounting Standards No. 123 (revised 2004), *Share-Based Payment*.

Note : The text of SAB 110 will not appear in the Code of Federal Regulations.

TOPIC 14: SHARE-BASED PAYMENT

* * * * *

D. Certain Assumptions Used In Valuation Methods

* * * * *

2. Expected Term

* * * * *

Facts: Company E grants equity share options to its employees that have the following basic characteristics:[75]

- The share options are granted at-the-money;

- Exercisability is conditional only on performing service through the vesting date;[76]

- If an employee terminates service prior to vesting, the employee would forfeit the share options;

- If an employee terminates service after vesting, the employee would have a limited time to exercise the share options (typically 30-90 days); and

- The share options are nontransferable and nonhedgeable.

Company E utilizes the Black-Scholes-Merton closed-form model for valuing its employee share options.

Question 6: As share options with these "plain vanilla" characteristics have been granted in significant quantities by many companies in the past, is the staff aware of any "simple" methodologies that can be used to estimate expected term?

Interpretive Response: As noted above, the staff understands that an entity that is unable to rely on its historical exercise data may find that certain alternative information, such as exercise data relating to employees of other companies, is not easily obtainable. As such, some companies may encounter difficulties in making a refined estimate of expected term. Accordingly, if a company concludes that its historical share option exercise experience does not provide a reasonable basis upon which to estimate expected term, the staff will accept the following "simplified" method for "plain vanilla" options consistent with those in the fact set above: expected term = ((vesting

---

[75] Employee share options with these features are sometimes referred to as "plain vanilla" options.

[76] In this fact pattern the requisite service period equals the vesting period.

term + original contractual term) / 2). Assuming a ten year original contractual term and graded vesting over four years (25% of the options in each grant vest annually) for the share options in the fact set described above, the resultant expected term would be 6.25 years.[77] Academic research on the exercise of options issued to executives provides some general support for outcomes that would be produced by the application of this method.[78]

Examples of situations in which the staff believes that it may be appropriate to use this simplified method include the following:

- A company does not have sufficient historical exercise data to provide a reasonable basis upon which to estimate expected term due to the limited period of time its equity shares have been publicly traded.

- A company significantly changes the terms of its share option grants or the types of employees that receive share option grants such that its historical exercise data may no longer provide a reasonable basis upon which to estimate expected term.

- A company has or expects to have significant structural changes in its business such that its historical exercise data may no longer provide a reasonable basis upon which to estimate expected term.

The staff understands that a company may have sufficient historical exercise data for some of its share option grants but not for others. In such cases, the staff will accept the use of the simplified method for only some but not all share option grants. The staff also does not believe that it is necessary for a company to consider using a lattice model before it decides that it is eligible to use this simplified method. Further, the staff will not object to the use of this simplified method in periods prior to the time a company's equity shares are traded in a public market.

If a company uses this simplified method, the company should disclose in the notes to its financial statements the use of the method, the reason why the method was used, the types of share option grants for which the method was used if the method was not used for all share option grants, and the periods for which the method was used if the method was not used in all periods. Companies that have sufficient historical share option exercise experience upon which to estimate expected term may not apply this simplified method. In addition, this simplified method is not intended to be applied as a benchmark in evaluating the appropriateness of more refined estimates of expected term.

Also, as noted above in Question 5, the staff believes that more detailed external information about exercise behavior will, over time, become readily available to companies. As such, the staff does not expect that such a simplified method would be used for share option grants when more relevant detailed information becomes widely available.

[For the text of Topic 14, see ¶ 39,231.]

[¶ 39,077]   RELEASE NO. 111, April 13, 2009

Other Than Temporary Impairment of Certain Investments in Equity Securities

ACTION: Publication of Staff Accounting Bulletin.

SUMMARY: This staff accounting bulletin ("SAB") amends Topic 5.M. in the Staff Accounting Bulletin Series entitled Other Than Temporary Impairment of Certain Investments in Debt and Equity Securities ("Topic 5.M."). On April 9, 2009, the FASB issued FASB Staff Position No. FAS 115-2 and FAS 124-2, Recognition and Presentation of Other-Than-Temporary Impairments ("FSP 115-2") to provide guidance for assessing whether an impairment of a debt security is other than temporary. This SAB maintains the staff's previous views related to equity securities. It also amends Topic 5.M. to exclude debt securities from its scope.

DATES: April 13, 2009.

FOR FURTHER INFORMATION CONTACT: Sandie E. Kim or Mark J. Barrysmith, Office of the Chief Accountant (202) 551-5300, or Craig C. Olinger, Division of Corporation Finance (202) 551-3400, Securities and Exchange Commission, 100 F Street NE, Washington, DC 20549.

SUPPLEMENTARY INFORMATION: The statements in staff accounting bulletins are not rules or interpretations of the Commission, nor are they published as bearing the Commission's official approval. They represent interpretations and practices followed by the Division of Corporation Finance and the Office of the Chief Accountant in administering the disclosure requirements of the Federal securities laws.

Elizabeth M. Murphy

---

[77] Calculated as [[[1 year vesting term (for the first 25% vested) plus 2 year vesting term (for the second 25% vested) plus 3 year vesting term (for the third 25% vested) plus 4 year vesting term (for the last 25% vested)] divided by 4 total years of vesting] plus 10 year contractual life] divided by 2; that is, $(((1+2+3+4)/4) + 10) /2 = 6.25$ years.

[78] J.N. Carpenter, "The exercise and valuation of executive stock options", *Journal of Financial Economics*, 1998, pp.127-158 studies a sample of 40 NYSE and AMEX firms over the period 1979-1994 with share option terms reasonably consistent to the terms presented in the fact set and example. The mean time to exercise after grant was 5.83 years and the median was 6.08 years. The "mean time to exercise" is shorter than expected term since the study's sample included only exercised options. Other research on executive options includes (but is not limited to) J. Carr Bettis; John M. Bizjak; and Michael L. Lemmon, "Exercise behavior, valuation, and the incentive effects of employee stock options," forthcoming in the *Journal of Financial Economics*. One of the few studies on nonexecutive employee options the staff is aware of is S. Huddart, "Patterns of stock option exercise in the United States," in: J. Carpenter and D. Yermack, eds., *Executive Compensation and Shareholder Value: Theory and Evidence* (Kluwer, Boston, MA, 1999), pp. 115-142.

Secretary

Date: April 13, 2009

Part 211 - [AMENDED]

Accordingly, Part 211 of Title 17 of the Code of Federal Regulations is amended by adding Staff Accounting Bulletin No. 110 to the table found in Subpart B.

STAFF ACCOUNTING BULLETIN NO. 111

This staff accounting bulletin ("SAB") amends Topic 5.M. in the Staff Accounting Bulletin Series entitled *Other Than Temporary Impairment of Certain Investments in Debt and Equity Securities* ("Topic 5.M."). On April 9, 2009, the FASB issued FASB Staff Position No. FAS 115-2 and FAS 124-2, *Recognition and Presentation of Other-Than-Temporary Impairments* ("FSP 115-2") to provide guidance for assessing whether an impairment of a debt security is other than temporary. This SAB maintains the staff's previous views related to equity securities. It also amends Topic 5.M. to exclude debt securities from its scope.

Note: The text of SAB 111 will not appear in the Code of Federal Regulations.

TOPIC 5: MISCELLANEOUS ACCOUNTING

* * * * *

M. Other Than Temporary Impairment of Certain Investments in Equity Securities

Facts: FASB Staff Position No. FAS 115-2 and FAS 124-2, *Recognition and Presentation of Other-Than-Temporary Impairments* ("FSP 115-2") does not define the phrase "other than temporary" for available-for-sale equity securities. For its available-for-sale equity securities, Company A has interpreted "other than temporary" to mean permanent impairment. Therefore, because Company A's management has not been able to determine that its investment in Company B's equity securities is permanently impaired, no realized loss has been recognized even though the market price of Company B's equity securities is currently less than one-third of Company A's average acquisition price.

Question: For equity securities classified as available-for-sale, does the staff believe that the phrase "other than temporary" should be interpreted to mean "permanent"?

Interpretive Response: No. The staff believes that the FASB consciously chose the phrase "other than temporary" because it did not intend that the test be "permanent impairment," as has been used elsewhere in accounting practice.[1]

The value of investments in equity securities classified as available-for-sale may decline for various reasons. The market price may be affected by general market conditions which reflect prospects for the economy as a whole or by specific information pertaining to an industry or an individual company. Such declines require further investigation by management. Acting upon the premise that a write-down may be required, management should consider all available evidence to evaluate the realizable value of its investment in equity securities classified as available-for-sale.

There are numerous factors to be considered in such an evaluation and their relative significance will vary from case to case. The staff believes that the following are only a few examples of the factors which, individually or in combination, indicate that a decline in value of an equity security classified as available-for-sale is other than temporary and that a write-down of the carrying value is required:

- The length of the time and the extent to which the market value has been less than cost;

- The financial condition and near-term prospects of the issuer, including any specific events which may influence the operations of the issuer such as changes in technology that may impair the earnings potential of the investment or the discontinuance of a segment of the business that may affect the future earnings potential; or

- The intent and ability of the holder to retain its investment in the issuer for a period of time sufficient to allow for any anticipated recovery in market value.

Unless evidence exists to support a realizable value equal to or greater than the carrying value of the investment in equity securities classified as available-for-sale, a write-down to fair value accounted for as a realized loss should be recorded. Such loss should be recognized in the determination of net income of the period in which it occurs and the written down value of the investment in the company becomes the new cost basis of the investment.

[For the text of Topic 5, see ¶ 39,141.]

[¶ 39,078] RELEASE NO. 112, June 4, 2009

ACTION: Publication of Staff Accounting Bulletin.

SUMMARY: This staff accounting bulletin amends or rescinds portions of the interpretive guidance included in the Staff Accounting Bulletin Series in order to make the relevant interpretive guidance consistent with current authoritative accounting and auditing guidance and Securities and Exchange Commission rules and regulations. Specifically, the staff is updating the Series in order to bring existing guidance into conformity with recent pronouncements by the Financial Accounting Standards Board, namely, Statement of Financial Accounting Standards No. 141 (revised

---

[1] FASB Staff Position No. FAS 115-1 and FAS 124-1, *The Meaning of Other-Than-Temporary Impairment and Its Application to Certain Investments* refers to this SAB for a discussion of considerations applicable to a determination as to whether a decline in market value below cost of an equity security, at a particular point in time, is other than temporary.

2007), *Business Combinations*, and Statement of Financial Accounting Standards No. 160, *Noncontrolling Interests in Consolidated Financial Statements*.

The staff expects registrants to apply the views in Question 1 of SAB 109 on a prospective basis to derivative loan commitments issued or modified in fiscal quarters beginning after December 15, 2007.

DATES: Effective Date: June 10, 2009.

FOR FURTHER INFORMATION CONTACT: Eric C. West, Associate Chief Accountant, Office of the Chief Accountant, at (202) 551-5314, or Steven C. Jacobs, Associate Chief Accountant, Division of Corporation Finance, at (202) 551-3403, Securities and Exchange Commission, 100 F Street, NE, Washington, DC 20549.

SUPPLEMENTARY INFORMATION: The statements in staff accounting bulletins are not rules or interpretations of the Commission, nor are they published as bearing the Commission's official approval. They represent interpretations and practices followed by the Division of Corporation Finance and the Office of the Chief Accountant in administering the disclosure requirements of the Federal securities laws.

Elizabeth M. Murphy

Secretary

Date: June 4, 2009

Part 211 - [AMENDED]

Accordingly, Part 211 of Title 17 of the Code of Federal Regulations is amended by adding Staff Accounting Bulletin No. 112 to the table found in Subpart B.

STAFF ACCOUNTING BULLETIN NO. 112

This staff accounting bulletin amends or rescinds portions of the interpretive guidance included in the Staff Accounting Bulletin Series in order to make the relevant interpretive guidance consistent with current authoritative accounting and auditing guidance and Securities and Exchange Commission ("Commission") rules and regulations. Specifically, the staff is updating the Series in order to bring existing guidance into conformity with recent pronouncements by the Financial Accounting Standards Board ("FASB"), namely, Statement of Financial Accounting Standards No. 141 (revised 2007), *Business Combinations* ("Statement 141(R)"), and Statement of Financial Accounting Standards No. 160, *Noncontrolling Interests in Consolidated Financial Statements* ("Statement 160").

The following describes the changes made to the Staff Accounting Bulletin Series that are presented at the end of this release:

1. Topic 2: Business Combinations

a. Topic 2.A is retitled. It previously referred to the "purchase method," which is a term rendered obsolete by Statement 141(R). That accounting method is now referred to as the "Acquisition Method."

b. Topic 2.A.5 is removed. This topic provided guidance on assigning acquisition cost to loans receivable acquired in a business combination. In a business combination, Statement 141(R) requires an entity to measure acquired receivables, including loans, at their acquisition-date fair value. Paragraph A57 of Statement 141(R) provides new guidance that precludes an acquirer from recognizing a separate valuation allowance as of the acquisition date for assets acquired in a business combination that are measured at their acquisition-date fair values because the effects of uncertainty about future cash flows are included in the fair value measure.

c. Topic 2.A.6 is amended to conform to the requirement in paragraph 59 of Statement 141(R) that acquisition-related costs be accounted for as expenses in the period in which the costs are incurred and services are received, except for costs incurred to issue debt or equity securities which are recognized in accordance with other applicable generally accepted accounting principles ("GAAP").

d. Topic 2.A.7 is removed. This topic provided guidance on how an acquirer should account for and disclose contingent liabilities that have been assumed in a business combination. Statement 141(R), as amended by FASB Staff Position 141(R)-1 ("FSP 141(R)-1"), provides guidance on the recognition, measurement and disclosure of assets and liabilities arising from contingencies.

e. Topic 2.A.8 is amended to remove the reference to Emerging Issues Task Force ("EITF") Issue No. 88-16, *Basis in Leveraged Buyout Transactions*, which was superseded by Statement 141(R).

f. Topic 2.A.9 is removed. This topic provided guidance on cash flow estimates used to determine the fair value of a contingent liability assumed in a business combination and referenced the need for disclosures in Management's Discussion and Analysis ("MD&A") for any adjustments made to the historical financial statements of the acquired entity. This guidance is no longer necessary because: Statement 141(R), as amended by FSP 141(R)-1, provides guidance on the recognition, measurement and disclosure of assets and liabilities arising from contingencies; Statement of Financial Accounting Standards No. 157, *Fair Value Measurements* ("Statement 157"), provides guidance on fair value measurements; Statement of Financial Accounting Standards No.154, *Accounting Changes and Error Corrections*, provides guidance on error correction and disclosure; and Item 303 of Regulation S-K provides guidance on MD&A disclosures.

g. Topic 2.D is amended to remove the guidance on determining the basis of properties in "exchange offers" (also referred to as "roll-ups" or "put-togethers"). This guidance is no longer necessary since Statement 141(R) provides measurement guidance for business combinations.

2. Topic 5: Miscellaneous Accounting

a. Topic 5.E is amended to reflect the issuance of FASB Interpretation No. 45, *Guarantor's Accounting and Disclosure Requirements for Guarantees, Including Indirect Guarantees of Indebtedness of Others* ("FIN 45"), Statement 157, and Statement 160. Topic 5.E (as modified) expresses the views of the staff regarding the accounting for the divestiture of a subsidiary or other business operation.

b. Topic 5.H is removed. This topic provided guidance on the accounting for the direct sale of unissued shares by a consolidated subsidiary that resulted in a decrease in the parent's ownership percentage without resulting in deconsolidation of the subsidiary. Under this guidance, when an offering takes the form of a subsidiary's direct sale of its unissued shares, the parent could adopt an accounting policy whereby the amount in excess of the parent's carrying value received may be reflected as a gain in the parent's consolidated financial statements. Paragraphs 32 and 33 of Accounting Research Bulletin ("ARB") 51, as amended by Statement 160, provide new guidance on the accounting for a change in a parent's ownership interest when the parent retains its controlling financial interest. That guidance requires that changes in a parent's ownership interest that do not result in deconsolidation shall be accounted for as equity transactions. Therefore, no gain or loss shall be recognized on the direct sale of unissued shares by a consolidated subsidiary if the parent does not deconsolidate the subsidiary.

c. Topic 5.J is amended, in response to Statement 160, to clarify the basis of accounting for purchased assets and liabilities that should be used to establish a new accounting basis when a substantially wholly-owned subsidiary presents separate financial statements.

d. Topic 5.U is removed. This topic provided guidance on the recognition of gains in certain exchanges in which the seller received non-cash proceeds, such as securities issued by the buyer, as consideration for the assets transferred. This guidance is no longer necessary due to the issuance of FIN 45, Statement 157, and Statement 160.

3. Topic 6: Interpretations of Accounting Series Releases and Financial Reporting Releases

Topic 6.G.1.a and 2.a is amended to conform terminology to the Technical Amendments to Rules, Forms, Schedules and Codification of Financial Reporting Policies [Release Nos. 33-9026; 34-59775; FR-79 (April 15, 2009)] that the Commission adopted to conform to Statement 141(R) and Statement 160.

Accordingly, the staff hereby amends the Staff Accounting Bulletin Series as follows:

Note: The text of SAB 112 will not appear in the Code of Federal Regulations.

TOPIC 2: BUSINESS COMBINATIONS

A. Acquisition Method

*****

5. Removed by SAB 112

6. Debt Issue Costs

Facts: Company A is to acquire the net assets of Company B in a transaction to be accounted for as a business combination. In connection with the transaction, Company A has retained an investment banker to provide advisory services in structuring the acquisition and to provide the necessary financing. It is expected that the acquisition will be financed on an interim basis using "bridge financing" provided by the investment banker. Permanent financing will be arranged at a later date through a debt offering, which will be underwritten by the investment banker. Fees will be paid to the investment banker for the advisory services, the bridge financing, and the underwriting of the permanent financing. These services may be billed separately or as a single amount.

Question 1: Should total fees paid to the investment banker for acquisition-related services and the issuance of debt securities be allocated between the services received?

Interpretive Response: Yes. Fees paid to an investment banker in connection with a business combination or asset acquisition, when the investment banker is also providing interim financing or underwriting services, must be allocated between acquisition related services and debt issue costs.

When an investment banker provides services in connection with a business combination or asset acquisition and also provides underwriting services associated with the issuance of debt or equity securities, the total fees incurred by an entity should be allocated between the services received on a relative fair value basis. The objective of the allocation is to ascribe the total fees incurred to the actual services provided by the investment banker.

Statement 141(R) provides guidance for the portion of the costs that represent acquisition-related services. The portion of the costs pertaining to the issuance of debt or equity securities should be accounted for in accordance with other applicable GAAP.

Question 2: May the debt issue costs of the interim "bridge financing" be amortized over the anticipated combined life of the bridge and permanent financings?

Interpretive Response: No. Debt issue costs should be amortized by the interest method over the life of the debt to which they relate. Debt issue costs related to the bridge financing should be recognized as interest cost during the estimated interim period preceding the placement of the permanent financing with any unamortized amounts charged to expense if the bridge loan is repaid prior to the expiration of the estimated period. Where the bridged financing consists of increasing rate debt, the consensus reached in EITF Issue 86-15, *Increasing Rate Debt*, should be followed.[1]

---

[1] As noted in the "Status" section of the Abstract to Issue 86-15, the term-extending provisions of the debt instrument should be analyzed to determine whether they constitute an embedded derivative requiring separate accounting in accordance with Statement 133 (as amended).

7. Removed by SAB 112

8. Business Combinations Prior to an Initial Public Offering

Facts: Two or more businesses combine in a single combination just prior to or contemporaneously with an initial public offering.

Question: Does the guidance in SAB Topic 5.G apply to business combinations entered into just prior to or contemporaneously with an initial public offering?

Interpretive Response: No. The guidance in SAB Topic 5.G is intended to address the transfer, just prior to or contemporaneously with an initial public offering, of nonmonetary assets in exchange for a company's stock. The guidance in SAB Topic 5.G is not intended to modify the requirements of Statement 141(R). Accordingly, the staff believes that the combination of two or more businesses should be accounted for in accordance with Statement 141(R).

9. Removed by SAB 112

*****

D. Financial Statements of Oil and Gas Exchange Offers

Facts: The oil and gas industry has experienced periods of time where there have been a significant number of "exchange offers" (also referred to as "roll-ups" or "put-togethers") to form a publicly held company, take an existing private company public, or increase the size of an existing publicly held company. An exchange offer transaction involves a swap of shares in a corporation for interests in properties, typically limited partnership interests. Such interests could include direct interests such as working interests and royalties related to developed or undeveloped properties and indirect interests such as limited partnership interests or shares of existing oil and gas companies. Generally, such transactions are structured to be tax-free to the individual or entity trading the property interest for shares of the corporation. Under certain circumstances, however, part or all of the transaction may be taxable. For purposes of the discussion in this Topic, in each of these situations, the entity (or entities) or property (or properties) are deemed to constitute a business.

One financial reporting issue in exchange transactions involves deciding which prior financial results of the entities should be reported.

Question 1: In Form 10-K filings with the Commission, the staff has permitted limited partnerships to omit certain of the oil and gas reserve value information and the supplemental summary of oil and gas activities disclosures required by Statement 69 in some circumstances. Is it permissible to omit these disclosures from the financial statements included in an exchange offering?

Interpretive Response: No. Normally full disclosures of reserve data and related information are required. The exemptions previously allowed relate only to partnerships where value-oriented data are otherwise available to the limited partners pursuant to the partnership agreement. The staff has previously stated that it will require all of the required disclosures for partnerships which are the subject of exchange offers.[13] These disclosures may, however, be presented on a combined basis if the entities are under common control.

The staff believes that the financial statements in an exchange offer registration statement should provide sufficient historical reserve quantity and value-based disclosures to enable offerees and secondary market public investors to evaluate the effect of the exchange proposal. Accordingly, in all cases, it will be necessary to present information as of the latest year-end on reserve quantities and the future net revenues associated with such quantities. In certain circumstances, where the exchange is accounted for using the acquisition method of accounting, the staff will consider, on a case-by-case basis, granting exemptions from (i) the disclosure requirements for year-to-year reconciliations of reserve quantities, and (ii) the requirements for a summary of oil and gas producing activities and a summary of changes in the net present value of reserves. For instance, the staff may consider requests for exemptions in cases where the properties acquired in the exchange transaction are fully explored and developed, particularly if the management of the emerging company has not been involved in the exploration and development of such properties.

Question 2: If the exchange company will use the full cost method of accounting, does the full cost ceiling limitation apply as of the date of the financial statements reflecting the exchange?

Interpretive Response: Yes. The full cost ceiling limitation on costs capitalized does apply. However, as discussed under Topic 12.D.3, the Commission has stated that in unusual circumstances, registrants may request an exemption if as a result of a major purchase, a write-down would be required even though it can be demonstrated that the fair value of the properties clearly exceeds the unamortized costs.

Question 3: How should "common control accounting" be applied to the specific assets and liabilities of the new exchange company?

Interpretive Response: Consistent with SAB Topic 12.C.2, under "common control accounting" the various accounting methods followed by the offeree entities should be conformed to the methods adopted by the new exchange company. It is not appropriate to combine assets and liabilities accounted for on different bases. Accordingly, all of the oil and gas properties of the new entity must be accounted for on the same basis (either full cost or successful efforts) applied retrospectively.

Question 4: What pro forma financial information is required in an exchange offer filing?

Interpretive Response: The requirements for pro forma financial information in exchange offer filings are the

---

[13] *See* SAB 40, Topic 12.A.3.c.

same as in any other filings with the Commission and are detailed in Article 11 of Regulation S-X.[14] Rule 11-02(b) specifies the presentation requirements, including periods presented and types of adjustments to be made. The general criteria of Rule 11-02(b)(6) are that pro forma adjustments should give effect to events that are (i) directly attributable to the transaction, (ii) expected to have a continuing impact on the registrant, and (iii) factually supportable. In the case of an exchange offer, such adjustments typically are made to:

(1) Show varying levels of acceptance of the offer.

(2) Conform the accounting methods used in the historical financial statements to those to be applied by the new entity.

(3) Recompute the depreciation, depletion and amortization charges, in cases where the new entity will use full-cost accounting, on a combined basis. If this computation is not practicable, and the exchange offer is accounted for as a transaction among entities under common control, historical depreciation, depletion and amortization provisions may be aggregated, with appropriate disclosure.

(4) Reflect the acquisition in the pro forma statements where the exchange offer is accounted for using the acquisition method of accounting, including depreciation, depletion and amortization based on the measurement guidance in Statement 141(R).

(5) Provide pro forma reserve information comparable to the disclosures required by paragraphs 10 through 17 and 30 through 34 of SFAS 69.

(6) Reflect significant changes, if any, in levels of operations (revenues or costs), or in income tax status and to reflect debt incurred in connection with the transaction.

In addition, the depreciation, depletion and amortization rate which will apply for the initial period subsequent to consummation of the exchange offer should be disclosed.

Question 5: Are there conditions under which the presentation of other than full historical financial statements would be acceptable?

Interpretive Response: Generally, full historical financial statements as specified in Rules 3-01 and 3-02 of Regulation S-X are considered necessary to enable offerees and secondary market investors to evaluate the transaction. Where securities are being registered to offer to the security holders (including limited partners and other ownership interests) of the businesses to be acquired, such financial statements are normally required pursuant to Rule 3-05 of Regulation S-X, either individually for each entity or, where appropriate, separately for the offeror and on a combined basis for other entities, generally excluding corporations. However, certain exceptions may apply as explained in the outline below:

A. Acquisition Method Accounting

1. If the registrant can demonstrate that full historical financial statements of the offeree businesses are not reasonably available, the staff may permit presentation of audited Statements of Combined Gross Revenues and Direct Lease Operating Expenses for all years for which an income statement would otherwise be required. In these circumstances, the registrant should also disclose in an unaudited footnote the amounts of total exploration and development costs, and general and administrative expenses along with the reasons why presentation of full historical financial statements is not practicable.

2. The staff will consider requests to waive the requirement for prior year financial statements of the offerees and instead allow presentation of only the latest fiscal year and interim period, if the registrant can demonstrate that the prior years' data would not be meaningful because the offerees had no material quantity of production.

B. Common Control Accounting

The staff would expect that the full historical financial statements as specified in Rules 3-01 and 3-02 of Regulation S-X would be included in the registration statement for exchange offers accounted for as transactions among entities under common control, including all required supplemental reserve information. The presentation of individual or combined financial statements would depend on the circumstances of the particular exchange offer.

Registrants are also reminded that wherever historical results are presented, it may be appropriate to explain the reasons why historical costs are not necessarily indicative of future expenditures.

*****

TOPIC 5: MISCELLANEOUS ACCOUNTING

*****

E. Accounting for Divestiture of a Subsidiary or Other Business Operation

Facts: Company X transferred certain operations (including several subsidiaries) to a group of former employees who had been responsible for managing those operations. Assets and liabilities with a net book value of approximately $8 million were transferred to a newly formed entity — Company Y — wholly owned by the former employees. The consideration received consisted of $1,000 in cash and interest bearing promissory notes for $10 million, payable in equal annual installments of $1 million each, plus interest, beginning two years from the date of the transaction. The former employees possessed insufficient assets to pay the notes and Company X expected the funds for payments to come exclusively from future operations of the transferred business. Company X remained contingently liable for performance on existing contracts transferred and agreed to

---

[14] As announced in Financial Reporting Release No. 2 (July 9, 1982).

guarantee, at its discretion, performance on future contracts entered into by the newly formed entity. Company X also acted as guarantor under a line of credit established by Company Y.

The nature of Company Y's business was such that Company X's guarantees were considered a necessary predicate to obtaining future contracts until such time as Company Y achieved profitable operations and substantial financial independence from Company X.

Question: If deconsolidation of the subsidiaries and business operations is appropriate, can Company X recognize a gain?

Interpretive Response: Before recognizing any gain, Company X should identify all of the elements of the divesture arrangement and allocate the consideration exchanged to each of those elements. In this regard, we believe that Company X would recognize the guarantees at fair value in accordance with FIN 45, *Guarantor's Accounting and Disclosure Requirements for Guarantees, Including Indirect Guarantees of the Indebtedness of Others*; the contingent liability for performance on existing contracts in accordance with Statement 5, *Accounting for Contingencies*; and the promissory notes in accordance with APB 21, *Interest on Receivables and Payables*, and Statements 114, *Accounting by Creditors for Impairment of a Loan*, and 118, *Accounting by Creditors for Impairment of a Loan — Income Recognition and Disclosures.*

*****

H. Removed by SAB 112

*****

J. New Basis of Accounting Required in Certain Circumstances

Facts: Company A (or Company A and related persons) acquired substantially all of the common stock of Company B in one or a series of purchase transactions.

Question 1: Must Company B's financial statements presented in either its own or Company A's subsequent filings with the Commission reflect the new basis of accounting arising from Company A's acquisition of Company B when Company B's separate corporate entity is retained?

Interpretive Response: Yes. The staff believes that purchase transactions that result in an entity becoming substantially wholly owned (as defined in Rule 1-02(aa) of Regulation S-X) establish a new basis of accounting for the purchased assets and liabilities.

When the form of ownership is within the control of the parent, the basis of accounting for purchased assets and liabilities should be the same regardless of

whether the entity continues to exist or is merged into the parent's operations. Therefore, Company B's separate financial statements should reflect the new basis of accounting recorded by Company A upon acquisition (*i.e.,* "pushed down" basis).

Question 2: What is the staff's position if Company A acquired less than substantially all of the common stock of Company B or Company B had publicly held debt or preferred stock at the time Company B became wholly owned?

Interpretive Response: The staff recognizes that the existence of outstanding public debt, preferred stock or a significant noncontrolling interest in a subsidiary might impact the parent's ability to control the form of ownership. Although encouraging its use, the staff generally does not insist on the application of push down accounting in these circumstances.

Question 3: Company A borrows funds to acquire substantially all of the common stock of Company B. Company B subsequently files a registration statement in connection with a public offering of its stock or debt.[6] Should Company B's new basis ("push down") financial statements include Company A's debt related to its purchase of Company B?

Interpretive Response: The staff believes that Company A's debt,[7] related interest expense, and allocable debt issue costs should be reflected in Company B's financial statements included in the public offering (or an initial registration under the Exchange Act) if: (1) Company B is to assume the debt of Company A, either presently or in a planned transaction in the future; (2) the proceeds of a debt or equity offering of Company B will be used to retire all or a part of Company A's debt; or (3) Company B guarantees or pledges its assets as collateral for Company A's debt. Other relationships may exist between Company A and Company B, such as the pledge of Company B's stock as collateral for Company A's debt.[8] While in this latter situation, it may be clear that Company B's cash flows will service all or part of Company A's debt, the staff does not insist that the debt be reflected in Company B's financial statements providing there is full and prominent disclosure of the relationship between Companies A and B and the actual or potential cash flow commitment. In this regard, the staff believes that Statements 5 and 57 as well as Interpretation 45 require sufficient disclosure to allow users of Company B's financial statements to fully understand the impact of the relationship on Company B's present and future cash flows. Rule 4-08(e) of Regulation S-X also requires disclosure of restrictions which limit the payment of dividends.

Therefore, the staff believes that the equity section of Company B's balance sheet and any pro forma financial information and capitalization tables should

---

[6] The guidance in this SAB should also be considered for Company B's separate financial statements included in its public offering following Company B's spin-off or carve-out from Company A.

[7] The guidance in this SAB should also be considered where Company A has financed the acquisition of Company B through the issuance of mandatory redeemable preferred stock.

[8] The staff does not believe Company B's financial statements must reflect the debt in this situation because in the event of default on the debt by Company A, the debt holder(s) would only be entitled to Company B's stock held by Company A. Other equity or debt holders of Company B would retain their priority with respect to the net assets of Company B.

clearly disclose that this arrangement exists.[9] Regardless of whether the debt is reflected in Company B's financial statements, the notes to Company B's financial statements should generally disclose, at a minimum: (1) the relationship between Company A and Company B; (2) a description of any arrangements that result in Company B's guarantee, pledge of assets[10] or stock, etc. that provides security for Company A's debt; (3) the extent (in the aggregate and for each of the five years subsequent to the date of the latest balance sheet presented) to which Company A is dependent on Company B's cash flows to service its debt and the method by which this will occur; and (4) the impact of such cash flows on Company B's ability to pay dividends or other amounts to holders of its securities. Additionally, the staff believes Company B's Management's Discussion and Analysis of Financial Condition and Results of Operations should discuss any material impact of its servicing of Company A's debt on its own liquidity pursuant to Item 303(a)(1) of Regulation S-K.

*****

U. Removed by SAB 112

*****

TOPIC 6: INTERPRETATIONS OF ACCOUNTING SERIES RELEASES AND FINANCIAL REPORTING RELEASES

*****

G. Accounting Series Releases 177 and 286— Relating to Amendments to Form 10-Q, Regulation S-K, and Regulations S-X Regarding Interim Financial Reporting.

*****

1. Selected Quarterly Financial Data (Item 302(a) of Regulation S-K)

a. Disclosure of Selected Quarterly Financial Data

Facts: Item 302(a)(1) of Regulation S-K requires disclosure of net sales, gross profit, income before extraordinary items and cumulative effect of a change in accounting, per share data based upon such income (loss), net income (loss), and net income (loss) attributable to the registrant for each full quarter within the two most recent fiscal years and any subsequent interim period for which financial statements are included. Item 302(a)(3) requires the registrant to describe the effect of any disposals of components of an entity[11] and extraordinary, unusual or infrequently occurring items recognized in each quarter, as well as the aggregate effect and the nature of year-end or other adjustments which are material to the results of

that quarter. Furthermore, Item 302(a)(2) requires a reconciliation of amounts previously reported on Form 10-Q to the quarterly data presented if the amounts differ.

*****

2. Amendments to Form 10-Q

a. Form of Condensed Financial Statements

Facts: Rules 10-01(a)(2) and (3) of Regulation S-X provide that interim balance sheets and statements of income shall include only major captions (i.e., numbered captions) set forth in Regulation S-X, with the exception of inventories where data as to raw materials, work in process and finished goods shall be included, if applicable, either on the face of the balance sheet or in notes thereto. Where any major balance sheet caption is less than 10% of total assets and the amount in the caption has not increased or decreased by more than 25% since the end of the preceding fiscal year, the caption may be combined with others. When any major income statement caption is less than 15% of average net income attributable to the registrant for the most recent three fiscal years and the amount in the caption has not increased or decreased by more than 20% as compared to the corresponding interim period of the preceding fiscal year, the caption may be combined with others. Similarly, the statement of cash flows may be abbreviated, starting with a single figure of cash flows provided by operations and showing other changes individually only when they exceed 10% of the average of cash flows provided by operations for the most recent three years.

Question 1: If a company previously combined captions in a Form 10-Q but is required to present such captions separately in the Form 10-Q for the current quarter, must it retroactively reclassify amounts included in the prior-year financial statements presented for comparative purposes to conform with the captions presented for the current-year quarter?

Interpretive Response: Yes.

Question 2: If a company uses the gross profit method or some other method to determine cost of goods sold for interim periods, will it be acceptable to state only that it is not practicable to determine components of inventory at interim periods?

Interpretive Response: The staff believes disclosure of inventory components is important to investors. In reaching this decision, the staff recognizes that registrants may not take inventories during interim periods and that managements, therefore, will have to estimate the inventory components. However, the staff believes that management will be able to make reasonable estimates of inventory components based

---

[9] For example, the staff has noted that certain registrants have indicated on the face of such financial statements (as part of the stockholder's equity section) the actual or potential financing arrangement and the registrant's intent to pay dividends to satisfy its parent's debt service requirements. The staff believes such disclosures are useful to highlight the existence of arrangements that could result in the use of Company B's cash to service Company A's debt.

[10] A material asset pledge should be clearly indicated on the face of the balance sheet. For example, if all or substantially all of the assets are pledged, the "assets" and "total assets" captions should include parenthetically: "pledged for parent company debt — See Note X."

[11] See question 5 for a discussion of the meaning of components of an entity as used in Item 302(a)(2).

upon their knowledge of the company's production cycle, the costs (labor and overhead) associated with this cycle as well as the relative sales and purchasing volume of the company.

Question 3: If a company has years during which operations resulted in a net outflow of cash and cash equivalents, should it exclude such years from the computation of cash and cash equivalents provided by operations for the three most recent years in determining what sources and applications must be shown separately?

Interpretive Response: Yes. Similar to the determination of average net income, if operations resulted in a net outflow of cash and cash equivalents during any year, such amount should be excluded in making the computation of cash flow provided by operations for the three most recent years unless operations resulted in a net outflow of cash and cash equivalents in all three years, in which case the average of the net outflow of cash and cash equivalents should be used for the test.

[¶ 39,079]　　　　　　　　RELEASE NO. 113, October 29, 2009

AGENCY: Securities and Exchange Commission.

ACTION: Publication of staff accounting bulletin.

SUMMARY: This Staff Accounting Bulletin (SAB) revises or rescinds portions of the interpretive guidance included in the section of the Staff Accounting Bulletin Series titled "Topic 12: Oil and Gas Producing Activities" (Topic 12) and revises a technical reference in "Topic 3: Senior Securities" (Topic 3). This update is intended to make the relevant interpretive guidance consistent with current authoritative accounting and auditing guidance and Commission rules and regulations. The principal changes involve revision or removal of material due to recent Commission rulemaking. Specifically, the staff is updating the Series in order to bring existing guidance into conformity with the contents of Financial Reporting Release No. 78 (Release No. 33-8995), *Modernization of Oil and Gas Reporting*, issued December 31, 2008 (FR-78), and, in the case of the technical amendment to SAB Topic 3, Financial Reporting Release No. 79 (Release Nos. 33-9026; 34-59775), *Technical Amendments to Rules, Forms, Schedules and Codification of Financial Reporting Policies* (FR-79), issued April 15, 2009. This SAB also updates related interpretive responses and examples in Topic 12. The staff expects registrants to apply the updated guidance in this SAB related to Topic 12 on a prospective basis in conjunction with the application of FR-78 and retroactively for the technical amendment to Topic 3 in conjunction with the effective date of FR-79. FR-78 is effective for registration statements filed on or after January 1, 2010, and for annual reports on Forms 10-K and 20-F for fiscal years ending on or after December 31, 2009. FR-79 is effective as of April 23, 2009.

EFFECTIVE DATE: November 4, 2009.

FOR FURTHER INFORMATION CONTACT: Jonathan W. Duersch, Assistant Chief Accountant, Office of the Chief Accountant, at (202) 551-3719, Doug Parker, Professional Accounting Fellow, Office of the Chief Accountant, at (202) 551-5316 or Leslie A. Overton, Associate Chief Accountant, Division of Corporation Finance, at (202) 551-3518, Securities and Exchange Commission, 100 F Street, NE, Washington, DC 20549.

SUPPLEMENTARY INFORMATION: The statements in staff accounting bulletins are not rules or interpretations of the Commission, nor are they published as bearing the Commission's official approval.

They represent interpretations and practices followed by the Division of Corporation Finance and the Office of the Chief Accountant in administering the disclosure requirements of the Federal securities laws.

Elizabeth M. Murphy

Secretary

Date: October 29, 2009

Part 211 - [AMENDED]

Accordingly, Part 211 of Title 17 of the Code of Federal Regulations is amended by adding Staff Accounting Bulletin No. 113 to the table found in Subpart B.

STAFF ACCOUNTING BULLETIN NO. 113

This staff accounting bulletin revises or rescinds portions of the interpretive guidance in Topic 12, "Oil and Gas Producing Activities," included in the Staff Accounting Bulletin Series, in order to make the relative interpretive guidance consistent with current authoritative accounting and auditing guidance and Financial Reporting Release No. 78 (Release No. 33-8995), *Modernization of Oil and Gas Reporting*, issued December 31, 2008 (2008 Oil & Gas Release). This SAB also updates related interpretive responses and examples. This SAB also includes an amendment to Topic 3 "Senior Securities," for a technical reference revision to conform to Financial Reporting Release No. 79 (Release Nos. 33-9026; 34-59775), *Technical Amendments to Rules, Forms, Schedules and Codification of Financial Reporting Policies*, issued April 15, 2009.

The following describes the changes made to the Staff Accounting Bulletin Series that are presented at the end of this release:

Topic 3: Senior Securities

Topic 3.C, the introductory facts are amended to replace the reference "Rule 5-02.28 of Regulation S-X" with "Rule 5-02.27 of Regulation S-X" to conform to paragraph numbering amendments made by FR-79.

Topic 12: Oil and Gas Producing Activities

a. Topic 12 is amended to update authoritative accounting literature references to the FASB's Accounting Standards Codification (FASB ASC) throughout.

b. Topic 12.A.1, the introductory facts have been amended, and questions 1, 2, and 3 are removed, leaving question 4 in place (without a numerical designation). Questions 1 and 2 are no longer applicable to the amended definition of "reliable technology" in Rule 4-10 of Regulation S-X. Question 3 is removed to conform to Instruction 1 of Item 1204 of Regulation S-K, which no longer addresses reserves attributable to production from processing plant ownership as previously included in Instruction B of Item 3 of former Industry Guide 2.

c. Topic 12.A.2, the facts and the interpretive response to question 1 are amended to conform to changes made by the 2008 Oil & Gas Release by replacing the use of a year-end price when determining reserve quantities with the use of the average price during the 12-month period prior to the ending date of the period covered by the balance sheet, determined as the unweighted arithmetic average of the first-day-of-the-month market price within such period for that oil and gas (the average price). Questions 2 and 3 are removed because the average price is applied in all cases where contractual prices do not exist as specified under Rule 4-10(a)(22) of Regulation S-X.

d. Topic 12.A.3.b is removed to conform to the 2008 Oil & Gas Release which permits the disclosure of probable and possible reserve quantities but does not provide a basis to present estimated values attributed to those reserve quantities.

e. Topic 12.A.3.c, the facts are amended to remove references to Industry Guide 2, which has been replaced by amendments to Regulation S-K and to remove unnecessary references to Regulation S-X and Financial Accounting Standards Board (FASB) Statement No. 69. The interpretive response is amended to replace the term "merger" with the term "business combination" and replace the term "combined" with the term "consolidated or combined".

f. Topic 12.A.3.d is removed to conform to the Commission's rules and regulations which do not require (and the Division of Corporation Finance no longer requests) a balance sheet of the general partner to be included in a registration statement for an offering of limited partnership interests.

g. Topic 12.C.1, the facts are amended to remove a reference to FASB Statement No. 25, which is not included in the FASB ASC. In addition, non-substantive editorial changes are made to Topic 12.C.2.

h. Topic 12.D.1, non-substantive editorial changes are made to question 1 and question 2 is amended to simplify the illustrative example in the interpretive response and thereby promote a clearer understanding of the calculation using the "shortcut" method for determining the tax effects in computing the full cost ceiling limitation and the resulting gross write-off attributed to the full cost pool.

i. Topic 12.D.3.b is amended to conform to changes made by the 2008 Oil & Gas Release by replacing the use of a year-end spot price when determining reserve quantities with the use of the average price during the 12-month period prior to the ending date of the period covered by the balance sheet, determined as the unweighted arithmetic average of the first-day-of-the-month market price within such period for that oil and gas. Additionally, the interpretive response is amended to remove unnecessary references to guidance in FASB Statements 52 and 80, which is now provided in FASB ASC Topic 815, *Derivatives and Hedging,* and to add a reference to Financial Reporting Release No. 72 (Release Nos. 33-8350; 34-48960), *Commission Guidance Regarding Management's Discussion and Analysis of Financial Condition and Results of Operations,* which is more recent guidance pertinent to Management's Discussion and Analysis disclosures.

j. Topic 12.D.3.c is amended to conform to changes made by the 2008 Oil & Gas Release by removing the provision to apply a recovery of oil and gas prices subsequent to period-end, when assessing whether a write-off computed under the full cost ceiling limitation should be recognized. As stated in the 2008 Oil & Gas Release, this guidance is no longer necessary because use of the average price would effectively eliminate anomalies caused by the single-day period-end price.

k. Topic 12.D.4, Footnote 1 is removed to eliminate unnecessary references specifically related to the adoption of FASB Statement 143, which is now referenced to FASB ASC Subtopic 410-20, *Asset Retirement and Environmental Obligations - Asset Retirement Obligations.* Footnotes previously numbered 2, 3 and 4 are renumbered 1, 2 and 3, respectively.

l. Topic 12.D.4.a, question 1 and the facts and interpretive response related to question 1 are amended and question 2 is removed to eliminate unnecessary references and guidance specifically related to the adoption of FASB Statement 143.

m. Topic 12.D.4.b, the facts, question and interpretive response are amended to eliminate unnecessary references and guidance specifically related to the adoption of FASB Statement 143.

n. Topic 12.D.4.c is removed to eliminate unnecessary transition guidance specifically related to the adoption of FASB Statement 143.

o. Topic 12.F, Footnote 4 is added to reference the definition of current prices used in Rule 4-10(c) of Regulation S-X, which was amended to conform to the 2008 Oil & Gas Release. As amended, Rule 4-10(c)(8) of Regulation S-X defines current price as the average price during the 12-month period prior to the ending date of the period covered by the report, determined as an unweighted arithmetic average of the first-day-of-the-month price for each month within such period, unless prices are defined by contractual arrangements, excluding escalations based upon future conditions.

p. Topic 12.G and Footnotes 5 and 6 are removed to conform to changes made by the 2008 Oil & Gas Release. This conforming change reflects the fact that, under amended Rule 4-10(a)(16) the definition of "oil and gas producing activities" includes the extraction of natural gas from coal beds.

[Note: The text of SAB 113 will not appear in the Code of Federal Regulations.]

*****

TOPIC 3: SENIOR SECURITIES

*****

C. Redeemable Preferred Stock

Facts: Rule 5-02.27 of Regulation S-X states that redeemable preferred stocks are not to be included in amounts reported as stockholders' equity, and that their redemption amounts are to be shown on the face of the balance sheet. However, the Commission's rules and regulations do not address the carrying amount at which redeemable preferred stock should be reported, or how changes in its carrying amount should be treated in calculations of earnings per share and the ratio of earnings to combined fixed charges and preferred stock dividends.

*****

TOPIC 12: OIL AND GAS PRODUCING ACTIVITIES

A. Accounting Series Release 257 - Requirements for Financial Accounting and Reporting Practices for Oil and Gas Producing Activities

1. *Estimates of reserve quantities*

Facts: Rule 4-10 of Regulation S-X contains definitions of possible reserves, probable reserves, and proved and developed oil and gas reserves to be used in determining quantities of oil and gas reserves to be reported in filings with the Commission.

Question: What pressure base should be used for reporting gas and production, 14.73 psia or the pressure base specified by the state?

Interpretive Response: The reporting instructions to the Department of Energy's Form EIA-28 specify that natural gas reserves are to be reported at 14.73 psia and 60 degrees F. There is no pressure base specified in Regulation S-X or S-K. At the present time staff will not object to natural gas reserves and production data calculated at other pressure bases, if such pressure bases are identified in the filing.

2. *Estimates of future net revenues*

Facts: U.S. GAAP requires the disclosure of the standardized measure of discounted future net cash flows from production of proved oil and gas reserves.

Question: For purposes of determining reserves and estimated future net revenues, what price should be used for oil and gas which will be produced after an existing contract expires or after the redetermination date in a contract?

Interpretive Response: The price to be used for oil and gas which will be produced after a contract expires or has a redetermination is the average price during the 12-month period prior to the ending date of the period covered by the balance sheet, determined as an unweighted arithmetic average of the first-day-of-the-month price for each month within such period for that oil and gas. This average price, which should be based on the first-day-of-the-month market prices, may be increased thereafter only for additional fixed and determinable escalations, as appropriate. A fixed and determinable escalation is one which is specified in amount and is not based on future events such as rates of inflation.

3. *Disclosure of reserve information*

a. Removed by SAB 103

b. Removed by SAB 113

c. *Limited partnership 10-K reports*

Facts: Item 1201(a) of Regulation S-K contains an exemption from the requirements to disclose certain information relating to oil and gas operations for "limited partnerships or joint ventures that conduct, operate, manage, or report upon oil and gas drilling income programs that acquire properties either for drilling and production, or for production of oil, gas, or geothermal steam . . . ."

Limited partnership agreements often contain buyout provisions under which the general partner agrees to purchase limited partnership interests that are offered for sale, based upon a specified valuation formula. Because of these arrangements, the requirements for disclosure of reserve value information may be of little significance to the limited partners.

Question: Must the financial statements of limited partnerships included in reports on Form 10-K contain the disclosures of estimated future net revenues, present values and changes therein, and supplemental summary of oil and gas activities specified in paragraphs 23 through 36 of FASB Accounting Standards Codification (FASB ASC) Section 932-235-50, *Extractive Activities - Oil and Gas - Notes to Financial Statements - Disclosure*?

Interpretive Response: The staff will not take exception to the omission of these disclosures in a limited partnership Form 10-K if reserve value information is available to the limited partners pursuant to the partnership agreement (even though the valuations may be computed differently and may be as of a date other than year end). However, the staff will require all of the information listed in paragraphs 23 through 36 of FASB ASC Section 932-235-50 for partnerships which are the subject of a business combination or exchange offer under which various limited partnerships are to be consolidated or combined into a single entity.

d. Removed by SAB 113

e. *Rate regulated companies*

Question: If a company has cost-of-service oil and gas producing properties, how should they be treated in the supplemental disclosures of reserve quantities and related future net revenues provided pursuant to paragraphs 29 through 36 of FASB ASC Section 932-235-50, *Extractive Activities - Oil and Gas - Notes to Financial Statements - Disclosure*?

Interpretive Response: Rule 4-10 provides that registrants may give effect to differences arising from the ratemaking process for cost-of-service oil and gas properties. Accordingly, in these circumstances, the staff believes that the company's supplemental reserve quantity disclosures should indicate separately the quantities associated with properties subject to cost-of-service ratemaking, and that it is appropriate to exclude those quantities from the future net revenue disclosures. The company should also disclose the nature and impact of its cost-of-service ratemaking, including the unamortized cost included in the balance sheet.

4. Removed by SAB 103

B. Removed by SAB 103

C. Methods of Accounting by Oil and Gas Producers

1. *First-time registrants*

Facts: In ASR 300, the Commission announced that it would allow registrants to change methods of accounting for oil and gas producing activities so long as such changes were in accordance with GAAP. Accordingly, the Commission stated that changes from the full cost method to the successful efforts method would not require a preferability letter. Changes to full cost, however, would require justification by the company making the change and filing of a preferability letter from the company's independent accountants.

Question: How does this policy apply to a nonpublic company which changes its accounting method in connection with a forthcoming public offering or initial registration under either the 1933 Act or 1934 Act?

Interpretive Response: The Commission's policy that first-time registrants may change their previous accounting methods without filing a preferability letter is applicable. Therefore, such a company may change to the full cost method without filing a preferability letter.

2. *Consistent use of accounting methods within a consolidated entity*

Facts: Rule 4-10(c) of Regulation S-X states in part that "[a] reporting entity that follows the full cost method shall apply that method to all of its operations and to the operations of its subsidiaries . . . "

Question 1: May a subsidiary of the parent use the full cost method if the parent company uses the successful efforts method of accounting for oil and gas producing activities?

Interpretive Response: No. The use of different methods of accounting in the consolidated financial statements by a parent company and its subsidiary would be inconsistent with the full cost requirement that a parent and its subsidiaries all use the same method of accounting.

The staff's general policy is that an enterprise should account for all its like operations in the same manner. However, Rule 4-10 of Regulation S-X provides that oil and gas companies with cost-of-service oil and gas properties may give effect to any differences resulting from the ratemaking process, including regulatory requirements that a certain accounting method be used for the cost-of-service properties.

Question 2: Must the method of accounting (full cost or successful efforts) followed by a registrant for its oil and gas producing activities also be followed by any fifty percent or less owned companies in which the registrant carries its investment on the equity method (equity investees)?

Interpretive Response: No. Conformity of accounting methods between a registrant and its equity investees, although desirable, may not be practicable and thus is not required. However, if a registrant proportionately consolidates its equity investees, it will be necessary to present them all on the same basis of accounting.

D. Application of Full Cost Method of Accounting

1. *Treatment of income tax effects in the computation of the limitation on capitalized costs*

Facts: Item (D) in Rule 4-10(c)(4)(i) of Regulation S-X provides that the income tax effects related to the properties involved should be deducted in computing the full cost ceiling.

Question 1: What specific types of income tax effects should be considered in computing the income tax effects to be deducted from estimated future net revenues?

Interpretive Response: The rule refers to income tax effects generally. Thus, the computation should take into account (i) the tax basis of oil and gas properties, (ii) net operating loss carryforwards, (iii) foreign tax credit carryforwards, (iv) investment tax credits, (v) alternative minimum taxes on tax preference items, and (vi) the impact of statutory (percentage) depletion.

It may often be difficult to allocate a net operating loss (NOL) carryforward between oil and gas assets and other assets. However, to the extent that the NOL is clearly attributable to oil and gas operations and is expected to be realized within the carryforward period, it should be added to tax basis.

Similarly, to the extent that investment tax credit (ITC) carryforwards and foreign tax credit carryforwards are attributable to oil and gas operations and are expected to be realized within the carryforward period, they should be considered as a deduction from the tax effect otherwise computed. Consideration of NOL and ITC or foreign tax credit carryforwards should not, of course, reduce the total tax effect below zero.

Question 2: How should the tax effect be computed considering the various factors discussed above?

Interpretive Response: Theoretically, taxable income and tax could be determined on a year-by-year basis and the present value of the related tax computed. However, the "shortcut" method illustrated below is also acceptable.

ASSUMPTIONS:

Cost of proved properties being amortized	$396,000
Lower of cost or estimated fair value of unproved properties to be amortized	49,000
Cost of properties not being amortized	55,000
Capitalized costs of oil and gas assets	500,000
Accumulated DD&A	(100,000)
Book basis of oil and gas assets	$400,000
Excess of book basis over tax basis ($270,000) of oil and gas assets	$(130,000)
NOL carryforward*	20,000
	(110,000)
Statutory tax rate (percent)	× 46%
	(50,600)
Foreign tax credit carryforward*	1,000
ITC carryforward*	2,000
Related net deferred income tax liability	(47,600)
Net book basis to be recovered	$352,400

Other Assumptions:

Present value of ITC relating to future development costs	$1,500
Present value of statutory depletion attributable to future deductions	$10,000
Estimated preference (minimum) tax on percentage depletion in excess of cost depletion	$500
Present value of future net revenue from proved oil and gas reserves	$272,000

CALCULATION:

Present value of future net revenue	$272,000
Cost of properties not being amortized	55,000
Lower of cost or estimated fair value of unproved properties included in costs being amortized	49,000
Total ceiling limitation before tax effects	$376,000

Tax Effects:

Total ceiling limitation before tax effects		$376,000
Less: Tax basis of properties	$(270,000)	
Statutory depletion	(10,000)	
NOL carryforward	(20,000)	
		(300,000)
Future taxable income		76,000
Tax rate (percent)		× 46%
Tax at statutory rate		(34,960)
ITC (future development costs and carryforward)		3,500
Foreign tax credit carryforward		1,000
Estimated preference tax		(500)
Net tax effects		(30,960)
Cost Center Ceiling		$345,040
Less: Net book basis to be recovered		352,400
REQUIRED WRITE-OFF, net of tax**		$(7,360)

* All carryforward amounts in this example represent amounts which are available for tax purposes and which relate to oil and gas operations.

** For accounting purposes, the gross write-off should be recorded to adjust both the oil and gas properties account and the related deferred income taxes.

CALCULATION OF GROSS PRE-TAX WRITE-OFF:

Required write-off, net of tax	$(7,360)
Divided by (100% minus the statutory rate of 46%)	54%
Gross pre-tax write-off	$ (13,630)

Related Journal Entries	DR	CR
Full cost ceiling impairment	$13,630	
Oil and gas assets		$13,630

Deferred income tax liability	$6,270
Deferred income tax benefit	$6,270

2. Exclusion of costs from amortization

Facts: Rule 4-10(c)(3)(ii) indicates that the costs of acquiring and evaluating unproved properties may be excluded from capitalized costs to be amortized if the costs are unusually significant in relation to aggregate costs to be amortized. Costs of major development projects may also be incurred prior to ascertaining the quantities of proved reserves attributable to such properties.

Question: At what point should amortization of previously excluded costs commence—when proved reserves have been established or when those reserves become marketable? For instance, a determination of proved reserves may be made before completion of an extraction plant necessary to process sour crude or a pipeline necessary to market the reserves. May the costs continue to be excluded from amortization until the plant or pipeline is in service?

Interpretive Response: No. The proved reserves and the costs allocable to such reserves should be transferred into the amortization base on an ongoing (well-by-well or property-by-property) basis as the project is evaluated and proved reserves are established.

Once the determination of proved reserves has been made, there is no justification for continued exclusion from the full cost pool, regardless of whether other factors prevent immediate marketing. Moreover, at the same time that the costs are transferred into the amortization base, it is also necessary in accordance with FASB ASC Subtopic 932-835, *Extractive Activities - Oil and Gas - Interest* and FASB ASC Subtopic 835-20, *Interest - Capitalization of Interest*, to terminate capitalization of interest on such properties.

In this regard, registrants are reminded of their responsibilities not to delay recognizing reserves as proved once they have met the engineering standards.

3. Full cost ceiling limitation

a. Exemptions for purchased properties

Facts: During 20x1, a registrant purchases proved oil and gas reserves in place ("the purchased reserves") in an arm's-length transaction for the sum of $9.8 million. Primarily because the registrant expects oil and gas prices to escalate, it paid $1.2 million more for the purchased reserves than the "Present Value of Estimated Future Net Revenues" computed as defined in Rule 4-10(c)(4)(i)(A) of Regulation S-X. An analysis of the registrant's full cost center in which the purchased reserves are located at December 31, 20x1 is as follows:

(Amounts in thousands)

	Total	Purchased Reserves	Other Proved Properties	Unproved Properties
Present value of estimated future net revenues	$14,100	8,600	5,500	—
Cost, net of amortization	$16,300	9,800	5,500	1,000
Related deferred taxes	$2,300	—	2,000	300
Income tax effects related to properties	$2,500	—	2,500	—

Comparison of capitalized costs with limitation on capitalized costs at December 31, 20x1:	Including Purchased Reserves	Excluding Purchased Reserves
Capitalized costs, net of amortization	$16,300	$6,500
Related deferred taxes	(2,300)	(2,300)
Net book cost	14,000	4,200
Present value of estimated future net revenues	14,100	$5,500

Comparison of capitalized costs with limitation on capitalized costs at December 31, 20x1:

	Including Purchased Reserves	Excluding Purchased Reserves
Lower of cost or market of unproved properties	1,000	1,000
Income tax effects related to properties	(2,500)	(2,500)
Limitation on capitalized costs	12,600	4,000
Excess of capitalized costs over limitation on Capitalized costs, net of tax*	$1,400	$ 200

---

* For accounting purposes, the gross write-off should be recorded to adjust both the oil and gas properties account and the related deferred income taxes

Question: Is it necessary for the registrant to write down the carrying value of its full cost center at December 31, 20x1 by $1,400,000?

Interpretive Response: Although the net carrying value of the full cost center exceeds the cost center's limitation on capitalized costs, the text of ASR 258 provides that a registrant may request an exemption from the rule if as a result of a major purchase of proved properties, a write down would be required even though the registrant believes the fair value of the properties in a cost center clearly exceeds the unamortized costs.

Therefore, to the extent that the excess carrying value relates to the purchased reserves, the registrant may seek a temporary waiver of the full-cost ceiling limitation from the staff of the Commission. Registrants requesting a waiver should be prepared to demonstrate that the additional value exists beyond reasonable doubt.

To the extent that the excess costs relate to properties other than the purchased reserves, however, a write-off should be recorded in the current period. In order to determine the portion of the total excess carrying value which is attributable to properties other than the purchased reserves, it is necessary to perform the ceiling computation on a "with and without" basis as shown in the example above. Thus in this case, the registrant must record a write-down of $200,000 applicable to other reserves. An additional $1,200,000 write-down would be necessary unless a waiver was obtained.

b. Use of cash flow hedges in the computation of the limitation on capitalized costs

Facts: Rule 4-10(c)(4) of Regulation S-X provides, in pertinent part, that capitalized costs, net of accumulated depreciation and amortization, and deferred income taxes, should not exceed an amount equal to the sum of components that include the present value of estimated future net revenues computed by applying current prices of oil and gas reserves (with consideration of price changes only to the extent provided by contractual arrangements) to estimated future production of proved oil and gas reserves as of the date of the latest balance sheet presented.

As of the reported balance sheet date, capitalized costs of an oil and gas producing company exceed the full cost limitation calculated under the above-described rule based on current prices, as defined in Rule 4-10(c)(8) of Regulation S-X, for oil and natural gas. However, prior to the balance sheet date, the company entered into certain hedging arrangements for a portion of its future natural gas and oil production, thereby enabling the company to receive future cash flows that are higher or lower than the estimated future cash flows indicated by use of the average price during the 12-month period prior to the balance sheet date, determined as an unweighted arithmetic average of the first-day-of-the-month price for each month within such period. These arrangements qualify as cash flow hedges under the provisions of FASB ASC Topic 815, *Derivatives and Hedging,* and are documented, designated, and accounted for as such under the criteria of that standard.

Question: Under these circumstances, must the company use the higher or lower prices to be received after taking into account the hedging arrangements ("hedge-adjusted prices") in calculating the estimated cash flows from future production of oil and gas reserves covered by the hedges as of the reported balance sheet date?

Interpretive Response: Yes. Derivative contracts that qualify as a hedging instrument in a cash flow hedge and are accounted for as such pursuant to FASB ASC Topic 815 represent the type of contractual arrangements for which consideration of price changes should be given under the existing rule. While the SEC staff has objected to previous proposals to consider various hedging techniques as being equivalent to the contractual arrangements permitted under the existing rules, the staff's objection was based on concerns that the lack of clear, consistent guidance in the accounting literature would lead to inconsistent application in practice. However, the staff believes that FASB ASC Topic 815 and related guidance (including a more systematic approach to documentation) provides sufficient guidance so that comparable financial reporting in comparable factual circumstances should result.

This interpretive response reflects the SEC staff's view that, assuming compliance with the prerequisite accounting requirements, hedge-adjusted prices represent the best measure of estimated cash flows from future production of the affected oil and gas reserves to use in calculating the ceiling limitation. Nonetheless, the staff expects that oil and gas producing companies subject to the full cost rules will clearly indicate the effects of using cash flow hedges in calculating ceiling limitations within their financial statement footnotes. The staff further expects that disclosures will indicate the portion of future oil and gas production being hedged. The dollar amount that would have been charged to income had the effects of the cash flow hedges not been considered in calculating the ceiling limitation also should be disclosed.

The use of hedge-adjusted prices should be consistently applied in all reporting periods, including periods in which the hedge-adjusted price is more or less than the average price during the 12-month period prior to the balance sheet date, determined as an unweighted arithmetic average of the first-day-of-the-month price for each month within such period. Oil and gas producers whose computation of the ceiling limitation includes hedge-adjusted prices because of the use of cash flow hedges also should consider the disclosure requirements under FASB ASC Section 275-10-50, *Risks and Uncertainties - Overall-Disclosure*. Paragraph 9 of FASB ASC Section 275-10-50 calls for disclosure when it is at least reasonably possible that the effects of cash flow hedges on capitalized costs on the reported balance sheet date will change in the near term due to one or more confirming events, such as potential future changes in commodity prices.

In addition, the use of cash flow hedges in calculating the ceiling limitation may represent a type of critical accounting policy that oil and gas producers should consider disclosing consistent with the cautionary advice provided in Financial Reporting Release No. 60 (Release Nos. 33-8040; 34-45149), *Cautionary Advice Regarding Disclosure about Critical Accounting Policies* (December 12, 2001), and Financial Reporting Release No. 72 (Release Nos. 33-8350; 34-48960), *Commission Guidance Regarding Management's Discussion and Analysis of Financial Condition and Results of Operations* (December 29, 2003). Through these releases, the Commission has encouraged companies to include, within their MD&A disclosures, full explanations, in plain English, of the judgments and uncertainties affecting the application of critical accounting policies, and the likelihood that materially different amounts would be reported under different conditions or using different assumptions.

The staff's guidance on this issue would apply to calculations of ceiling limitations both in interim and annual reporting periods.

c. Effect of subsequent events on the computation of the limitation on capitalized costs

Facts: Rule 4-10(c)(4)(ii) of Regulation S-X provides that an excess of unamortized capitalized costs within a cost center over the related cost ceiling shall be charged to expense in the period the excess occurs.

Question: Assume that at the date of the company's fiscal year-end, its capitalized costs of oil and gas producing properties exceed the limitation prescribed by Rule 4-10(c)(4) of Regulation S-X. Thus, a write-down is indicated. Subsequent to year-end but before the date of the auditor's report on the company's financial statements, assume that additional reserves are proved up (excluding the effect of increased oil and gas prices subsequent to year-end) on properties owned at year-end. The present value of future net revenues from the additional reserves is sufficiently large that if the full cost ceiling limitation were recomputed giving effect to those factors as of year-end, the ceiling would more than cover the costs. Is it necessary to record a write-down?

Interpretive Response: No. In this case, the proving up of additional reserves on properties owned at year-end indicates that the capitalized costs were not in fact impaired at year-end. However, for purposes of the revised computation of the "ceiling," the net book costs capitalized as of year-end should be increased by the amount of any additional costs incurred subsequent to year-end to prove the additional reserves or by any related costs previously excluded from amortization.

While the fact pattern described herein relates to annual periods, the guidance on the effects of subsequent events applies equally to interim period calculations of the ceiling limitation.

The registrant's financial statements should disclose that capitalized costs exceeded the limitation thereon at year-end and should explain why the excess was not charged against earnings. In addition, the registrant's supplemental disclosures of estimated proved reserve quantities and related future net revenues and costs should not give effect to the reserves proved up or the cost incurred after year-end. However, such quantities may be disclosed separately, with appropriate explanations.

Registrants should be aware that oil and gas reserves related to properties acquired after year-end would not justify avoiding a write-off indicated as of year-end. Similarly, the effects of cash flow hedging arrangements entered into after year-end cannot be factored into the calculation of the ceiling limitation at year-end. Such acquisitions and financial arrangements do not confirm situations existing at year-end.

4. Interaction of FASB ASC Subtopic 410-20 Asset Retirement and Environmental Obligations - Asset Retirement Obligations and the Full Cost Rules

a. Impact of FASB ASC Subtopic 410-20 on the full cost ceiling test

Facts: A company following the full cost method of accounting under Rule 4-10(c) of Regulation S-X must periodically calculate a limitation on capitalized costs, i.e., the full cost ceiling. Under FASB ASC Subtopic 410-20, *Asset Retirement and Environmental Obligations - Asset Retirement Obligations*, a company must recognize a liability for an asset retirement obligation (ARO) at fair value in the period in which the obligation is incurred, if a reasonable estimate of fair value can be made. The company also must initially capitalize the associated asset retirement costs by increasing long-lived oil and gas assets by the same amount as the liability. Any asset retirement costs capitalized pursuant to FASB ASC Subtopic 410-20 are subject to the full cost ceiling limitation under Rule 4-10(c)(4) of Regulation S-X. If a company were to calculate the full cost ceiling by reducing expected future net revenues by the cash flows required to settle the ARO, then the effect would be to "double-count" such costs in the ceiling test. The assets that must be recovered would be increased while the future net revenues available to recover the assets continue to be reduced by the amount of the ARO settlement cash flows.

Question: How should a company compute the full cost ceiling to avoid double-counting the expected future cash outflows associated with asset retirement costs?

Interpretive Response: The future cash outflows associated with settling AROs that have been accrued on the balance sheet should be excluded from the computation of the present value of estimated future net revenues for purposes of the full cost ceiling calculation.[1],[2]

b. Impact of FASB ASC Subtopic 410-20 on the calculation of depreciation, depletion, and amortization

Facts: Regarding the base for depreciation, depletion, and amortization (DD&A) of proved reserves, Rule 4-10(c)(3)(i) of Regulation S-X states that "[c]osts to be amortized shall include (A) all capitalized costs, less accumulated amortization, other than the cost of properties described in paragraph (ii) below;[3] (B) the estimated future expenditures (based on current costs) to be incurred in developing proved reserves; and (C) estimated dismantlement and abandonment costs, net of estimated salvage values." FASB ASC Subtopic 410-20 requires that upon initial recognition of an ARO, the associated asset retirement costs be included in the capitalized costs of the company. Therefore, the estimated dismantlement and abandonment costs described in (C) above may be included in the capitalized costs described in (A) above, at least to the extent that an ARO has been incurred as a result of acquisition, exploration and development activities to date. Future development activities on proved reserves may result in additional asset retirement obligations when such activities are performed and the associated asset retirement costs will be capitalized at that time.

Question: Should the costs to be amortized under Rule 4-10(c)(3) of Regulation S-X include an amount for estimated dismantlement and abandonment costs, net of estimated salvage values, that are expected to result from future development activities?

Interpretive Response: Yes. Companies should estimate the amount of dismantlement and abandonment costs that will be incurred as a result of future development activities on proved reserves and include those amounts in the costs to be amortized.

c. Removed by SAB 113

E. Financial Statements of Royalty Trusts

Facts: Several oil and gas exploration and production companies have created "royalty trusts." Typically, the creating company conveys a net profits interest in certain of its oil and gas properties to the newly created trust and then distributes units in the trust to its shareholders. The trust is a passive entity which is prohibited from entering into or engaging in any business or commercial activity of any kind and from acquiring any oil and gas lease, royalty or other mineral interest. The function of the trust is to serve as an agent to distribute the income from the net profits interest. The amount to be periodically distributed to the unitholders is defined in the trust agreement and is typically determined based on the cash received from the net profits interest less expenses of the trustee. Royalty trusts have typically reported their earnings on the basis of cash distributions to unitholders. The net profits interest paid to the trust for any month is based on production from a preceding month; therefore, the method of accounting followed by the trust for the net profits interest income is different from the creating company's method of accounting for the related revenue.

Question: Will the staff accept a statement of distributable income which reflects the amounts to be distributed for the period in question under the terms of the trust agreement in lieu of a statement of income prepared under GAAP?

Interpretive Response: Yes. Although financial statements filed with the Commission are normally required to be prepared in accordance with GAAP, the Commission's rules provide that other presentations may be acceptable in unusual situations. Since the operations of a royalty trust are limited to the distribution of income from the net profits interests contributed to it, the staff believes that the item of primary importance to the reader of the financial statements of the royalty trust is the amount of the cash distributions to the unitholders for the period reported. Should there be any change in the nature of the trust's operations due to revisions in the tax laws or other factors, the staff's interpretation would be reexamined.

A note to the financial statements should disclose the method used in determining distributable income and should also describe how distributable income as

---

[1] If an obligation for expected asset retirement costs has not been accrued under FASB ASC Subtopic 410-20 for certain asset retirement costs required to be included in the full cost ceiling calculation under Rule 4-10(c)(4) of Regulation S-X, such costs should continue to be included in the full cost ceiling calculation.

[2] This approach is consistent with the guidance in FASB ASC Subtopic 410-20 on testing for impairment under FASB ASC Section 360-10-35 *Property, Plant, and Equipment - Overall - Subsequent Measurement*. Under that guidance, the asset tested should include

capitalized asset retirement costs. The estimated cash flows related to the associated ARO that has been recognized in the financial statements are to be excluded from both the undiscounted cash flows used to test for recoverability and the discounted cash flows used to measure the asset's fair value.

[3] The reference to "cost of properties described in paragraph (ii) below" relates to the costs of investments in unproved properties and major development projects, as defined.

reported differs from income determined on the basis of GAAP.

F. Gross Revenue Method of Amortizing Capitalized Costs

Facts: Rule 4-10(c)(3)(iii) of Regulation S-X states in part: "Amortization shall be computed on the basis of physical units, with oil and gas converted to a common unit of measure on the basis of their approximate relative energy content, unless economic circumstances (related to the effects of regulated prices) indicate that use of units of revenue is a more appropriate basis of computing amortization. In the latter case, amortization shall be computed on the basis of current gross revenues (excluding royalty payments and net profits disbursements) from production in relation to future gross revenues based on current prices (including consideration of changes in existing prices provided only by contractual arrangements), from estimated production of proved oil and gas reserves."[4]

Question: May entities using the full cost method of accounting for oil and gas producing activities compute amortization based on the gross revenue method described in the above rule when substantial production is not subject to pricing regulation?

Interpretive Response: Yes. Under the existing rules for cost amortization adopted in ASR 258, the use of the gross revenue method of amortization was permitted in those circumstances where, because of the effect of existing pricing regulations, the use of the units of production method would result in an amortization provision that would be inconsistent with the current sales prices being received. While the effect of regulation on gas prices has lessened, factors other than price regulation (such as changes in typical contract lengths and methods of marketing natural gas) have caused oil and gas prices to be disproportionate to their relative energy content. The staff therefore believes that it may be more appropriate for registrants to compute amortization based on the gross revenue method whenever oil and gas sales prices are disproportionate to their relative energy content to the extent that the use of the units of production method would result in an improper matching of the costs of oil and gas production against the related revenue received. The method should be consistently applied and appropriately disclosed within the financial statements.

G. Removed by SAB 113

---

[4] Rule 4-10(c)(8) of Regulation S-X defines current price as the average price during the 12-month period prior to the ending date of the period covered by the report, determined as an unweighted arithmetic average of the first-day-of-the-month price for each month within such period, unless prices are defined by contractual arrangements, excluding escalations based upon future conditions.

CODIFICATION OF STAFF ACCOUNTING BULLETINS

TOPIC 1: FINANCIAL STATEMENTS

A. Target Companies

Facts: Company X proposes to file a registration statement covering an exchange offer to stockholders of Company Y, a publicly held company. Company X asks Company Y to furnish information about its business, including current audited financial statements, for inclusion in the prospectus. Company Y declines to furnish such information.

Question 1: In filing the registration statement without the required information about Company Y, may Company X rely on Rule 409 in that the information is "unknown or not reasonably available?"

Interpretive Response: Yes, but to determine whether such reliance is justified, the staff requests the registrant to submit as supplemental information copies of correspondence between the registrant and the target company evidencing the request for and the refusal to furnish the financial statements. In addition, the prospectus must include any financial statements which are relevant and available from the Commission's public files and must contain a statement adequately describing the situation and the sources of information about the target company. Other reliable sources of financial information should also be utilized.

Question 2: Would the response change if Company Y was a closely held company?

Interpretive Response: Yes. The staff does not believe that Rule 409 is applicable to negotiated transactions of this type.

B. Allocation Of Expenses And Related Disclosure In Financial Statements Of Subsidiaries, Divisions Or Lesser Business Components Of Another Entity

Facts: A company (the registrant) operates as a subsidiary of another company (parent). Certain expenses incurred by the parent on behalf of the subsidiary have not been charged to the subsidiary in the past. The subsidiary files a registration statement under the Securities Act of 1933 in connection with an initial public offering.

1. Costs reflected in historical financial statements

Question 1: Should the subsidiary's historical income statements reflect all of the expenses that the parent incurred on its behalf?

Interpretive Response: In general, the staff believes that the historical income statements of a registrant should reflect all of its costs of doing business. Therefore, in specific situations, the staff has required the subsidiary to revise its financial statements to include certain expenses incurred by the parent on its behalf. Examples of such expenses may include, but are not necessarily limited to, the following (income taxes and interest are discussed separately below):

1. Officer and employee salaries,

2. Rent or depreciation,

3. Advertising,

4. Accounting and legal services, and

5. Other selling ,general and administrative expenses.

When the subsidiary's financial statements have been previously reported on by independent accountants and have been used other than for internal purposes, the staff has accepted a presentation that shows income before tax as previously reported, followed by adjustments for expenses not previously allocated, income taxes, and adjusted net income.

Question 2: How should the amount of expenses incurred on the subsidiary's behalf by its parent be determined, and what disclosure is required in the financial statements?

Interpretive Response: The staff expects any expenses clearly applicable to the subsidiary to be reflected in its income statements. However, the staff understands that in some situations a reasonable method of allocating common expenses to the subsidiary (e.g., incremental or proportional cost allocation) must be chosen because specific identification of expenses is not practicable. In these situations, the staff has required an explanation of the allocation method used in the notes to the financial statements along with management's assertion that the method used is reasonable.

In addition, since agreements with related parties are by definition not at arms length and may be changed at any time, the staff has required footnote disclosure, when practicable, of management's estimate of what the expenses (other than income taxes and interest discussed separately below) would have been on a stand alone basis, that is, the cost that would have been incurred if the subsidiary had operated as an unaffiliated entity. The disclosure has been presented for each year for which an income statement was required when such basis produced materially different results.

Question 3: What are the staff's views with respect to the accounting for and disclosure of the subsidiary's income tax expense?

Interpretive Response: Recently, a number of parent companies have sold interests in subsidiaries, but have retained sufficient ownership interests to permit continued inclusion of the subsidiaries in their consolidated tax returns. The staff believes that it is material to investors to know what the effect on income would have been if the registrant had not been eligible to be included in a consolidated income tax return with its parent. Some of these subsidiaries have calculated their tax provision on the separate return basis, which the staff believes is the preferable method. Others, however, have used different allocation methods. When the historical income statements in the filing do not reflect the tax provision on the separate return basis, the staff has required a pro forma income statement for the most recent year and interim period reflecting a tax provision calculated on the separate return basis.[1]

Question 4: Should the historical income statements reflect a charge for interest on intercompany debt if no such charge had been previously provided?

Interpretive Response: The staff generally believes that financial statements are more useful to investors if they reflect all costs of doing business, including interest costs. Because of the inherent difficulty in distinguishing the elements of a subsidiary's capital structure, the staff has not insisted that the historical income statements include an interest charge on intercompany debt if such a charge was not provided in the past, except when debt specifically related to the operations of the subsidiary and previously carried on the parent's books will henceforth be recorded in the subsidiary's books. In any case, financing arrangements with the parent must be discussed in a note to the financial statements. In this connection, the staff has taken the position that, where an interest charge on intercompany debt has not been provided, appropriate disclosure would include an analysis of the intercompany accounts as well as the average balance due to or from related parties for each period for which an income statement is required. The analysis of the intercompany accounts has taken the form of a listing of transactions (e.g., the allocation of costs to the subsidiary, intercompany purchases, and cash transfers between entities) for each period for which an income statement was required, reconciled to the intercompany accounts reflected in the balance sheets.

2. *Pro forma financial statements and earnings per share*

Question: What disclosure should be made if the registrant's historical financial statements are not indicative of the ongoing entity (e.g., tax or other cost sharing agreements will be terminated or revised)?

Interpretive Response: The registration statement should include pro forma financial information that is in accordance with Article 11 of Regulation S-X and reflects the impact of terminated or revised cost sharing agreements and other significant changes.

3. *Other matters*

Question: What is the staff's position with respect to dividends declared by the subsidiary subsequent to the balance sheet date?

Interpretive Response: The staff believes that such dividends either be given retroactive effect in the balance sheet with appropriate footnote disclosure, or reflected in a pro forma balance sheet. In addition, when the dividends are to be paid from the proceeds of the offering, the staff believes it is appropriate to include pro forma per share data (for the latest year and interim period only) giving effect to the number of shares whose proceeds were to be used to pay the dividend. A similar presentation is appropriate when dividends exceed earnings in the current year, even though the stated use of proceeds is other than for the payment of dividends. In these situations, pro forma per share data should give effect to the increase in the number of shares which, when multiplied by the offering price, would be sufficient to replace the capital in excess of earnings being withdrawn.

C. Unaudited Financial Statements For A Full Fiscal Year

Facts: Company A, which is a reporting company under the Securities Exchange Act of 1934, proposes to file a registration statement within 90 days of its fiscal year end but does not have audited year-end financial statements available. The company meets the criteria under Rule 3-01(c) of Regulation S-X and is therefore not required to include year-end audited financial statements in its registration statement. However, the Company does propose to include in the prospectus the unaudited results of operations for its entire fiscal year.

Question: Would the staff find this objectionable?

Interpretive Response: The staff recognizes that many registrants publish the results of their most recent year's operations prior to the availability of year-end audited financial statements. The staff will not object to the inclusion of unaudited results for a full fiscal year and indeed would expect such data in the registration statement if the registrant has published such information. When such data is included in a prospectus, it must be covered by a management's representation that all adjustments necessary for a fair statement of the results have been made.

D. Foreign Companies

1. *Disclosures required of companies complying with Item 17 of Form 20-F*

Facts: A foreign private issuer may use Form 20-F as a registration statement under section 12 or as an annual report under section 13(a) or 15(d) of the Exchange Act. The registrant must furnish the financial statements specified in Item 17 of that form. However, in certain circumstances, Forms F-3 and F-2 require that the annual report include financial statements complying with Item 18 of the form. Also, financial statements complying with Item 18 are required for registration of securities under the Securities Act in most circumstances. Item 17 permits the registrant to use its financial statements that are prepared on a comprehensive basis other than U.S. GAAP, but requires quantification of the material dif-

---

[1] Paragraph 40 of Statement 109 states: "The consolidated amount of current and deferred tax expense for a group that files a consolidated tax return shall be allocated among the members of the group when those members issue separate financial statements.... The method adopted ... shall be systematic, rational, and consistent with the broad principles established by [Statement 109]. A method that allocates current and deferred taxes to members of the group by applying [Statement 109] to each member as if it were a separate taxpayer meets those criteria.

ferences in the principles, practices and methods of accounting. An issuer complying with Item 18 must satisfy the requirements of Item 17 and also must provide all other information required by U.S. GAAP and Regulation S-X.

Question: Assuming that the registrant's financial statements include a discussion of material variances from U.S. GAAP along with quantitative reconciliations of net income and material balance sheet items, does Item 17 of Form 20-F require other disclosures in addition to those prescribed by the standards and practices which comprise the comprehensive basis on which the registrant's primary financial statements are prepared?

Interpretive Response: No. The distinction between Items 17 and 18 is premised on a classification of the requirements of U.S. GAAP and Regulation S-X into those that specify the methods of measuring the amounts shown on the face of the financial statements and those prescribing disclosures that explain, modify or supplement the accounting measurements. Disclosures required by U.S. GAAP but not required under the foreign GAAP on which the financial statements are prepared need not be furnished pursuant to Item 17.

Notwithstanding the absence of a requirement for certain disclosures within the body of the financial statements, some matters routinely disclosed pursuant to U.S. GAAP may rise to a level of materiality such that their disclosure is required by Item 5 (Management's Discussion and Analysis) of Form 20-F. Among other things, this item calls for a discussion of any known trends, demands, commitments, events or uncertainties that are reasonably likely to affect liquidity, capital resources or the results of operations in a material way. Also, instruction 2 of this item requires "a discussion of any aspects of the differences between foreign and U.S. GAAP, not discussed in the reconciliation, that the registrant believes is necessary for an understanding of the financial statements as a whole." Matters that may warrant discussion in response to Item 5 include the following:

- material undisclosed uncertainties (such as reasonably possible loss contingencies), commitments (such as those arising from leases), and credit risk exposures and concentrations;

- material unrecognized obligations (such as pension obligations);

- material changes in estimates and accounting methods, and other factors or events affecting comparability;

- defaults on debt and material restrictions on dividends or other legal constraints on the registrant's use of its assets;

- material changes in the relative amounts of constituent elements comprising line items presented on the face of the financial statements;

- significant terms of financings which would reveal material cash requirements or constraints;

- material subsequent events, such as events that affect the recoverability of recorded assets;

- material related party transactions (as addressed by Statement 57) that may affect the terms under which material revenues or expenses are recorded; and

- significant accounting policies and measurement assumptions not disclosed in the financial statements, including methods of costing inventory, recognizing revenues, and recording and amortizing assets, which may bear upon an understanding of operating trends or financial condition.

2. *"Free distributions" by Japanese companies*

Facts: It is the general practice in Japan for corporations to issue "free distributions" of common stock to existing shareholders in conjunction with offerings of common stock so that such offerings may be made at less than market. These free distributions usually are from 5 to 10 percent of outstanding stock and are accounted for in accordance with provisions of the Commercial Code of Japan by a transfer of the par value of the stock distributed from paid-in capital to the common stock account. Similar distributions are sometimes made at times other than when offering new stock and are also designated "free distributions." U.S. accounting practice would require that the fair value of such shares, if issued by U.S. companies, be transferred from retained earnings to the appropriate capital accounts.

Question: Should the financial statements of Japanese corporations included in Commission filings which are stated to be prepared in accordance with U.S. GAAP be adjusted to account for stock distributions of less than 25 percent of outstanding stock by transferring the fair value of such stock from retained earnings to appropriate capital accounts?

Interpretive Response: If registrants and their independent accountants believe that the institutional and economic environment in Japan with respect to the registrant is sufficiently different that U.S. accounting principles for stock dividends should not apply to free distributions, the staff will not object to such distributions being accounted for at par value in accordance with Japanese practice. If such financial statements are identified as being prepared in accordance with U.S. GAAP, then there should be footnote disclosure of the method being used which indicates that U.S. companies issuing shares in comparable amounts would be required to account for them as stock dividends, and including in such disclosure the fair value of any such shares issued during the year and the cumulative amount (either in an aggregate figure or a listing of the amounts by year) of the fair value of shares issued over time.

E. Requirements For Audited Or Certified Financial Statements

1. Deleted by SAB 103

2. *Qualified auditors' opinions*

Facts: The accountants' report is qualified as to scope of audit, or the accounting principles used.

Question: Does the staff consider the requirements for audited or certified financial statements met when the auditors' opinion is so qualified?

Interpretive Response: No. The staff does not accept as consistent with the requirements of Rule 2-02(b) of Regulation S-X financial statements on which the auditors' opinions are qualified because of a limitation on the scope of the audit, since in these situations the auditor was unable to perform all the procedures required by professional standards to support the expression of an opinion. This position was discussed in ASR 90 in connection with representations concerning the verification of prior years' inventories in first audits.

Financial statements for which the auditors' opinions contain qualifications relating to the acceptability of accounting principles used or the completeness of disclosures made are also unacceptable. (See ASR 4, and with respect to a "going concern" qualification, ASR 115.)

F. Financial Statement Requirements In Filings Involving The Formation Of A One-Bank Holding Company

Facts: Holding Company A is organized for the purpose of issuing common stock to acquire all of the common stock of Bank A. Under the plan of reorganization, each share of common stock of Bank A will be exchanged for one share of common stock of the holding company. The shares of the holding company to be issued in the transaction will be registered on Form S-4. The holding company will not engage in any operations prior to consummation of the reorganization, and its only significant asset after the transaction will be its investment in the bank. The bank has been furnishing its shareholders with an annual report that includes financial statements that comply with GAAP.

Item 14 of Schedule 14A of the proxy rules provides that financial statements generally are not necessary in proxy material relating only to changes in legal organization (such as reorganizations involving the issuer and one or more of its totally held subsidiaries).

Question 1: Must the financial statements and the information required by Securities Act Industry Guide ("Guide 3")[2] for Bank A be included in the initial registration statement on Form S-4?

Interpretive Response: No, provided that certain conditions are met. The staff will not take exception to the omission of financial statements and Guide 3 information in the initial registration statement on Form S-4 if all of the following conditions are met:

• There are no anticipated changes in the shareholders' relative equity ownership interest in the underlying bank assets, except for redemption of no more than a nominal number of shares of unaffiliated persons who dissent;

• In the aggregate, only nominal borrowings are to be incurred for such purposes as organizing the holding company, to pay nonaffiliated persons who dissent, or to meet minimum capital requirements;

• There are no new classes of stock authorized other than those corresponding to the stock of Bank A immediately prior to the reorganization;

• There are no plans or arrangements to issue any additional shares to acquire any business other than Bank A; and,

• There has been no material adverse change in the financial condition of the bank since the latest fiscal year-end included in the annual report to shareholders.

If at the time of filing the S-4, a letter is furnished to the staff stating that all of these conditions are met, it will not be necessary to request the Division of Corporation Finance to waive the financial statement or Guide 3 requirements of Form S-4.

Although the financial statements may be omitted, the filing should include a section captioned, "Financial Statements," which states either that an annual report containing financial statements for at least the latest fiscal year prepared in conformity with GAAP was previously furnished to shareholders or is being delivered with the prospectus. If financial statements have been previously furnished, it should be indicated that an additional copy of such report for the latest fiscal year will be furnished promptly upon request without charge to shareholders. The name and address of the person to whom the request should be made should be provided. One copy of such annual report should be furnished supplementally with the initial filing for purposes of staff review.

If any nominal amounts are to be borrowed in connection with the formation of the holding company, a statement of capitalization should be included in the filing which shows Bank A on an historical basis, the pro forma adjustments, and the holding company on a pro forma basis. A note should also explain the pro forma effect, in total and per share, which the borrowings would have had on net income for the latest fiscal year if the transaction had occurred at the beginning of the period.

Question 2: Are the financial statements of Bank A required to be audited for purposes of the initial Form S-4 or the subsequent Form 10-K report?

Interpretive Response: The staff will not insist that the financial statements in the annual report to shareholders used to satisfy the requirement of the initial Form S-4 be audited.

The consolidated financial statements of the holding company to be included in the registrant's initial report on Form 10-K should comply with the applicable financial statement requirements in Regulation S-X at the time such annual report is filed. However, the regulations also provide that the staff may allow one or more of the required statements to be unaudited

---

[2] Item 801 of Regulation S-K.

where it is consistent with the protection of investors.[3] Accordingly, the policy of the Division of Corporation Finance is as follows:

• The registrant should file audited balance sheets as of the two most recent fiscal years and audited statements of income and cash flows for each of the three latest fiscal years, with appropriate footnotes and schedules as required by Regulation S-X unless the financial statements have not previously been audited for the periods required to be filed. In such cases, the Division will not object if the financial statements in the first annual report on Form 10-K (or the special report filed pursuant to Rule 15d-2)[4] are audited only for the two latest fiscal years.[5] This policy only applies to filings on Form 10-K, and not to any Securities Act filings made after the initial S-4 filing.

The above procedure may be followed without making a specific request of the Division of Corporation Finance for a waiver of the financial statement requirements of Form 10-K.

The information required by Guide 3 should also be provided in the Form 10-K for at least the periods for which audited financial statements are furnished. If some of the statistical information for the two most recent fiscal years for which audited financial statements are included (other than information on nonperforming loans and the summary of loan loss experience) is unavailable and cannot be obtained without unwarranted or undue burden or expense, such data may be omitted provided a brief explanation in support of such representation is included in the report on Form 10-K. In all cases, however, information with respect to nonperforming loans and loan loss experience, or reasonably comparable data, must be furnished for at least the two latest fiscal years in the initial 10-K. Thereafter, for subsequent years in reports on Form 10-K, all of the Guide 3 information is required; Guide 3 information which had been omitted in the initial 10-K in accordance with the above procedure can be excluded in any subsequent 10-Ks.

G. Deleted by FRR 55 (Release 33-7878)

H. Deleted by FRR 55 (Release 33-7878)

I. Financial Statements Of Properties Securing Mortgage Loans

Facts: A registrant files a Securities Act registration statement covering a maximum of $100 million of securities. Proceeds of the offering will be used to make mortgage loans on operating residential or commercial property. Proceeds of the offering will be placed in escrow until $1 million of securities are sold at which point escrow may be broken, making the proceeds immediately available for lending, while the selling of securities would continue.

Question 1: Under what circumstances are the financial statements of a property on which the registrant makes or expects to make a loan required to be included in a filing?

Interpretive Response: Rule 3-14 of Regulation S-X specifies the requirements for financial statements when the registrant has acquired one or more properties which in the aggregate are significant, or since the date of the latest balance sheet required has acquired or proposes to acquire one or more properties which in the aggregate are significant.

Included in the category of properties acquired or to be acquired under Rule 3-14 are operating properties underlying certain mortgage loans, which in economic substance represent an investment in real estate or a joint venture rather than a loan. Certain characteristics of a lending arrangement indicate that the "lender" has the same risks and potential rewards as an owner or joint venturer. Those characteristics are set forth in Exhibit I to the Appendix of the American Institute of Certified Public Accountants' Practice Bulletin 1[6] "ADC[7] Arrangements" ("Exhibit I to PB1"). In September 1986 the EITF[8] reached a consensus on this issue[9] to the effect that, although Exhibit I to PB1 was issued to address the real estate ADC arrangements of financial institutions, preparers and auditors should consider the guidance contained in Exhibit I to PB1 in accounting for shared appreciation mortgages, loans on operating real estate and real estate ADC arrangements entered into by enterprises other than financial institutions.

Statement 133 as amended by Statements 137 and 138, generally requires that embedded instruments meeting the definition of a derivative and not clearly and closely related to the host contract be accounted for separately from the host instrument. If the embedded the expected residual profit component of an ADC arrangement need not be separately accounted for as a derivative under Statement 133, then the disclosure requirements discussed below for ADC loans and similar arrangements should be followed.[10]

In certain cases the "lender" has virtually the same potential rewards as those of an owner or a joint

---

[3] Rule 3-13 of Regulation S-X.

[4] Rule 15d-2 would be applicable if the annual report furnished with the Form S-4 was not for the registrant's most recent fiscal year. In such a situation, Rule 15d-2 would require the registrant to file a special report within 90 days after the effective date of the Form S-4 furnishing audited financial statements for the most recent fiscal year.

[5] Unaudited statements of income and cash flows should be furnished for the earliest period.

[6] "ADC Arrangements" was originally issued as a *notice to practitioners* (February 1986, as *p*ublished in the April 1986 issue of the Journal of Accountancy). The notice to practitioners was reprinted without change as Exhibit I to the Appendix of the American

Institute of Certified Public Accountants' *Practice Bulletin 1* (November, 1987).

[7] Acquisition, development and construction.

[8] The Emerging Issues Task Force ("EITF") was formed in 1984 to assist the Financial Accounting Standards Board in the early identification and resolution of emerging accounting issues. Topics to be discussed by the EITF are publicly announced prior to its meetings and minutes of all EITF meetings are available to the public.

[9] See Issue 86-21.

[10] The equity kicker (the expected residual profit) would typically not be separated from the host contract and accounted for as a derivative because paragraph 12(c) of Statement 133 exempts a

venturer by virtue of participating in expected residual profit.[11] In addition, Exhibit I to PB1 includes a number of other characteristics which, when considered individually or in combination, would suggest that the risks of an ADC arrangement are similar to those associated with an investment in real estate or a joint venture or, conversely, that they are similar to those associated with a loan. Among those other characteristics is whether the lender agrees to provide all or substantially all necessary funds to acquire the property, resulting in the borrower having title to, but little or no equity in, the underlying property. The staff believes that the borrower's equity in the property is adequate to support accounting for the transaction as a mortgage loan when the borrower's initial investment meets the criteria in paragraph 11 of Statement 66[12] and the borrower's payments of principal and interest on the loan are adequate to maintain a continuing investment in the property which meets the criteria in paragraph 12 of Statement 66.[13]

The financial statements of properties which will secure mortgage loans made or to be made from the proceeds of the offering which have the characteristics of real estate investments or joint ventures should be included as required by Rule 3-14 in the registration statement when such properties secure loans previously made, or have been identified as security for probable loans prior to effectiveness, and in filings made pursuant to the undertaking in Item 20D of Securities Act Industry Guide 5.

Rule 1-02(w) of Regulation S-X includes the conditions used in determining whether an acquisition is significant. The separate financial statements of an individual property should be provided when a property would meet the requirements for a significant subsidiary under this rule using the amount of the "loan" as a substitute for the "investment in the subsidiary" in computing the specified conditions. The combined financial statements of properties which are not individually significant should also be provided. However, the staff will not object if the combined financial statements of such properties are not included if none of the conditions specified in Rule 1-02(w), with respect to all such properties combined, exceeds 20% in the aggregate.

Under certain circumstances, information may also be required regarding operating properties underlying mortgage loans where the terms do not result in the lender having virtually the same risks and potential rewards as those of owners or joint venturers. Generally, the staff believes that, where investment risks exist due to substantial asset concentration, financial and other information should be included regarding operating properties underlying a mortgage loan that represents a significant amount of the registrant's assets. Such presentation is consistent with Rule 3-13 of Regulation S-X and Rule 408 under the Securities Act of 1933.

Where the amount of a loan exceeds 20% of the amount in good faith expected to be raised in the offering, disclosures would be expected to consist of financial statements for the underlying operating properties for the periods contemplated by Rule 3-14. Further, where loans on related properties are made to a single person or group of affiliated persons which in the aggregate amount to more than 20% of the amount expected to be raised, the staff believes that such lending arrangements result in a sufficient concentration of assets so as to warrant the inclusion of financial and other information regarding the underlying properties.

Question 2: Will the financial statements of the mortgaged properties be required in filings made under the 1934 Act?

Interpretive Response: Rule 3-09 of Regulation S-X specifies the requirement for significant, as defined, investments in operating entities, the operations of which are not included in the registrant's consolidated financial statements.[14] Accordingly, the staff believes that the financial statements of properties securing significant loans which have the characteristics of real estate investments or joint ventures should be included in subsequent filings as required by Rule 3-09. The materiality threshold for determining whether such an investment is significant is the same as set forth in paragraph (a) of that Rule.[15]

Likewise, the staff believes that filings made under the 1934 Act should include the same financial and other information relating to properties underlying

---

(Footnote Continued)

hybrid contract from bifurcation if a separate instrument with the same terms as the embedded equity kicker is not a derivative instrument subject to the requirements of Statement 133.

[11] Expected residual profit is defined in Exhibit I to PB1 as the amount of profit, whether called interest or another name, such as equity kicker, above a reasonable amount of interest and fees expected to be earned by the "lender."

[12] Statement 66 establishes standards for the recognition of profit on real estate sales transactions. Paragraph 11 states that the buyer's initial investment shall be adequate to demonstrate the buyer's commitment to pay for the property and shall indicate a reasonable likelihood that the seller will collect the receivable. Guidance on minimum initial investments in various types of real estate is provided in paragraphs 53 and 54 of Statement 66.

[13] Paragraph 12 of Statement 66 states that the buyer's continuing investment in a real estate transaction shall not qualify unless the buyer is contractually required to pay each year on its total debt for the purchase price of the property an amount at least equal to the level annual payment that would be needed to pay that debt

and interest on the unpaid balance over not more than (a) 20 years for debt for land and (b) the customary amortization term of a first mortgage loan by an independent established lending institution for other real estate.

[14] Rule 3-14 states that the financial statements of an acquired property should be furnished if the acquisition took place during the period for which the registrant's income statements are required. Paragraph (b) of the Rule states that the information required by the Rule is not required to be included in a filing on Form 10-K. That exception is consistent with Item 8 of Form 10-K which excludes acquired company financial statements, which would otherwise be required by Rule 3-05 of Regulation S-X, from inclusion in filings on that Form. Those exceptions are based, in part, on the fact that acquired properties and acquired companies will generally be included in the registrant's consolidated financial statements from the acquisition date.

[15] Rule 3-09(a) states, in part, that "[i]f any of the conditions set forth in [Rule] 1-02(w), substituting 20 percent for 10 percent in the tests used therein to determine significant subsidiary, are met . . . separate financial statements . . . shall be filed."

---

any loans which are significant as discussed in the last paragraph of Question 1, except that in the determination of significance the 20% disclosure threshold should be measured using total assets. The staff believes that this presentation would be consistent with Rule 12b-20 under the Securities Exchange Act of 1934.

Question 3: The interpretive response to question 1 indicates that the staff believes that the borrower's equity in an operating property is adequate to support accounting for the transaction as a mortgage loan when the borrower's initial investment meets the criteria in paragraph 11 of Statement 66 and the borrower's payments of principal and interest on the loan are adequate to maintain a continuing investment in the property which meets the criteria in paragraph 12 of Statement 66. Is it the staff's view that meeting these criteria is the only way the borrower's equity in the property is considered adequate to support accounting for the transaction as a mortgage loan?

Interpretive Response: No. It is the staff's position that the determination of whether loan accounting is appropriate for these arrangements should be made by the registrant and its independent accountants based on the facts and circumstances of the individual arrangements, using the guidance provided in the Exhibit I to the Appendix of the American Institute of Certified Public Accountants Practice Bulletin 1 (November, 1987) ("Exhibit I to PB1"). As stated in Exhibit I to PB1, loan accounting may not be appropriate when the lender participates in expected residual profit and has virtually the same risks as those of an owner, or joint venturer. In assessing the question of whether the lender has virtually the same risks as an owner, or joint venturer, the essential test that needs to be addressed is whether the borrower has and is expected to continue to have a substantial amount at risk in the project.[16] The criteria described in Statement 66 provide a "safe harbor" for determining whether the borrower has a substantial amount at risk in the form of a substantial equity investment. The borrower may have a substantial amount at risk without meeting the criteria described in Statement 66.

Question 4: What financial statements should be included in filings made under the Securities Act regarding investment-type arrangements that individually amount to 10% or more of total assets?

Interpretive Response: In the staff's view, separate audited financial statements should be provided for any investment-type arrangement that constitutes 10% or more of the greater of (i) the amount of minimum proceeds or (ii) the total assets of the registrant, including the amount of proceeds raised, as of the date the filing is required to be made. Of course, the narrative information required by items 14 and 15 of Form S-11 should also be included with respect to these investment-type arrangements.

Question 5: What information must be provided under the Securities Act for investment-type arrangements that individually amount to less than 10%?

Interpretive Response: No specific financial information need be presented for investment-type arrangements that amount to less than 10%. However, where such arrangements aggregate more than 20%, a narrative description of the general character of the properties and arrangements should be included that gives an investor an understanding of the risks and rewards associated with these arrangements. Such information may, for example, include a description of the terms of the arrangements, participation by the registrant in expected residual profits, and property types and locations.

Question 6: What financial statements should be included in annual reports filed under the Exchange Act with respect to investment-type arrangements that constitute 10% or more of the registrant's total assets?

Interpretive Response: In annual reports filed with the Commission, the staff has advised registrants that separate audited financial statements should be provided for each nonconsolidated investment-type arrangement that is 20% or more of the registrant's total assets. While the distribution is on-going, however, the percentage may be calculated using the greater of (i) the amount of the minimum proceeds or (ii) the total assets of the registrant, including the amount of proceeds raised, as of the date the filing is required to be made. In annual reports to shareholders registrants may either include the separate audited financial statements for 20% or more nonconsolidated investment-type arrangements or, if those financial statements are not included, present summarized financial information for those arrangements in the notes to the registrant's financial statements.

The staff has also indicated that separate summarized financial information (as defined in Rule 1-02(bb) of Regulation S-X) should be provided in the footnotes to the registrant's financial statements for each nonconsolidated investment-type arrangement that is 10% or more but less than 20%. Of course, registrants should also make appropriate textural disclosure with respect to material investment-type arrangements in the "business" and "property" sections of their annual reports to the Commission.[17]

Question 7: What information should be provided in annual reports filed under the Exchange Act with respect to investment-type arrangements that do not meet the 10% threshold?

Interpretive Response: The staff believes it will not be necessary to provide any financial information (full

---

[16] Regarding the composition of the borrower's investment, paragraph 9b of Exhibit I to PB1 indicates that the borrower's investment may include the value of land or other assets contributed by the borrower, net of encumbrances. The staff emphasizes that such paragraph indicates, ". . . recently acquired property generally should be valued at no higher than cost . . ." Thus, for such

recently acquired property, appraisals will not be sufficient to justify the use of a value in excess of cost.

[17] Registrants are reminded that in filings on Form 8-K that are triggered in connection with an acquisition of an investment-type arrangement, separate audited financial statements are required for any such arrangement that individually constitutes 10% or more.

or summarized) for investment-type arrangements that do not meet the 10% threshold. However, in the staff's view, where such arrangements aggregate more than 20%, a narrative description of the general character of the properties and arrangements would be necessary. The staff believes that information should be included that would give an investor an understanding of the risks and rewards associated with these arrangements. Such information may, for example, include a description of the terms of the arrangements, participation by the registrant in expected residual profits, and property types and locations. Of course, disclosure regarding the operations of such components should be included as part of the Management's Discussion and Analysis where there is a known trend or uncertainty in the operations of such properties, either individually or in the aggregate, which would be reasonably likely to result in a material impact on the registrant's future operations, liquidity or capital resources.

J. Application Of Rule 3-05 In Initial Public Offerings

Facts: Rule 3-05 of Regulation S-X establishes the financial statement requirements for businesses acquired or to be acquired. If required, financial statements must be provided for one, two or three years depending upon the relative significance of the acquired entity as determined by the application of Rule 1-02(w) of Regulation S-X. The calculations required for these tests are applied by comparison of the financial data of the registrant and acquiree(s) for the fiscal years most recently completed prior to the acquisition. The staff has recognized that these tests literally applied in some initial public offerings may require financial statements for an acquired entity which may not be significant to investors because the registrant has had substantial growth in assets and earnings in recent years.[18]

Question: How should Rules 3-05 and 1-02(w) of Regulation S-X be applied in determining the periods for which financial statements of acquirees are required to be included in registration statements for initial public offerings?

Interpretive Response: It is the staff's view that initial public offerings involving businesses that have been built by the aggregation of discrete businesses that remain substantially intact after acquisition[19] were not contemplated during the drafting of Rule 3-05 and that the significance of an acquired entity in such situations may be better measured in relation to the

size of the registrant at the time the registration statement is filed, rather than its size at the time the acquisition was made. Therefore, for a first time registrant, the staff has indicated that in applying the significance tests in Rule 3-05, the three tests in Rule 1-02(w) generally can be measured against the combined entities, including those to be acquired, which comprise the registrant at the time the registration statement is filed. The staff's policy is intended to ensure that the registration statement will include not less than three, two and one year(s) of audited financial statements for not less than 60%, 80% and 90%, respectively, of the constituent businesses that will comprise the registrant on an ongoing basis. In all circumstances, the audited financial statements of the registrant are required for three years, or since its inception if less than three years. The requirement to provide the audited financial statements of a constituent business in the registration statement is satisfied for the post-acquisition period by including the entity's results in the audited consolidated financial statements of the registrant. If additional periods are required, the entity's separate audited financial statements for the immediate pre-acquisition period(s) should be presented.[20]

In order for the pre-acquisition audited financial statements of an acquiree to be omitted from the registration statement, the following conditions must be met:

a. the combined significance of businesses acquired or to be acquired for which audited financial statements cover a period of less than 9 months[21] may not exceed 10%;

b. the combined significance of businesses acquired or to be acquired for which audited financial statements cover a period of less than 21 months may not exceed 20%; and

c. the combined significance of businesses acquired or to be acquired for which audited financial statements cover a period of less than 33 months may not exceed 40%.

Combined significance is the total, for all included companies, of each individual company's highest level of significance computed under the three tests of significance. The significance tests should be applied to pro forma financial statements of the registrant, prepared in a manner consistent with Article 11 of Regulation S-X. The pro forma balance sheet should be as of the date of the registrant's latest balance sheet included in the registration statement, and

---

[18] An acquisition which was relatively significant in the earliest year for which a registrant is required to file financial statements may be insignificant to its latest fiscal year due to internal growth and/or subsequent acquisitions. Literally applied, Rules 3-05 and 1-02(w) might still require separate financial statements for the now insignificant acquisition.

[19] For example, nursing homes, hospitals or cable TV systems. This interpretation would not apply to businesses for which the relative significance of one portion of the business to the total business may be altered by post-acquisition decisions as to the allocation of incoming orders between plants or locations. This bulletin does not address all possible cases in which similar relief may be appropriate but, rather, attempts to describe a general

framework within which administrative policy has been established. In other distinguishable situations, registrants may request relief as appropriate to their individual facts and circumstances.

[20] If audited pre-acquisition financial statements of a business are necessary pursuant to the alternative tests described here, the interim period following that entity's latest pre-acquisition fiscal year end but prior to its acquisition by the registrant generally would be required to be audited.

[21] As a matter of policy the staff accepts financial statements for periods of not less than 9, 21 and 33 consecutive months (not more than 12 months may be included in any period reported on) as substantial compliance with requirements for financial statements for 1, 2 and 3 years, respectively.

should give effect to businesses acquired subsequent to the end of the latest year or to be acquired as if they had been acquired on that date. The pro forma statement of operations should be for the registrant's most recent fiscal year included in the registration statement and should give effect to all acquisitions consummated during and subsequent to the end of the year and probable acquisitions as if they had been consummated at the beginning of that fiscal year.

The three tests specified in Rule 1-02(w) should be made in comparison to the registrant's pro forma consolidated assets and pretax income from continuing operations. The assets and pretax income of the acquired businesses which are being evaluated for significance should reflect any new cost basis arising from purchase accounting.

Example: On February 20, 20X9 Registrant files Form S-1 containing its audited consolidated financial statements as of and for the three years ended December 31, 20X8. Acquisitions since inception have been:

Acquiree	Fiscal Year End	Date of Acquisition	Highest Significance at Acquisition
A.	3/31	1/1/x7	60%
B.	7/31	4/1/x7	45%
C.	9/30	9/1/x7	40%
D.	12/31	2/1/x8	21%
E.	3/31	11/1/x8	11%
F.	12/31	To be acquired	11%

The following table reflects the application of the significance tests to the combined financial information at the time the registration statement is filed.

Component Entity	Assets	Significance of Earnings	Investment	Highest Level of Significance
A	12%	23%	12%	23%
B	10%	21%	10%	21%
C	21%	3%	4%	21%
D	10%	5%	13%	13%
E	4%	9% loss	3%	9%
F	2%	11%	6%	11%

Year 1 (most recent fiscal year) - Entity E is the only acquiree for which pre-acquisition financial statements may be omitted for the latest year since significance for each other entity exceeds 10% under one or more test.

Year 2 (preceding fiscal year) - Financial statements for E and F may be omitted since their combined significance is 20% and no other combination can be formed with E which would not exceed 20%.

Year 3 (second preceding fiscal year) - Financial statements for D, E and F may be omitted since the combined significance of these entities is 33%[22] and no other combination can be formed with E and F which would not exceed 40%.

The financial statement requirements must be satisfied by filing separate pre-acquisition audited financial statements for each entity that was not included in the consolidated financial statements for the periods set forth above. The following table illustrates the requirements for this example.

---

[22] Combined significance is the sum of the significance of D's investment test (13%), E's earnings test (9%) and F's earnings test (11%).

Component Entity	Date of Acquisition	Minimum Financial Statement Requirement	Period in Consolidated Financial Statements	Separate Pre-acquisition Audited Financial Statement
		(months)		
Registrant	N/A	33	36	—
A	1/1/x7	33	24	9
B	4/1/x7	33	21	12[23]
C	9/1/x7	33	16	17
D	2/1/x8	21	11	10
E	11/1/x8	—	2	—
F	To be acquired	9	—	9

K. Financial Statements Of Acquired Troubled Financial Institutions

Facts: Federally insured depository institutions are subject to regulatory oversight by various federal agencies including the Federal Reserve, Office of the Comptroller of the Currency, Federal Deposit Insurance Corporation and Office of Thrift Supervision. During the 1980s, certain of these institutions experienced significant financial difficulties resulting in their inability to meet necessary capital and other regulatory requirements. The Financial Institutions Reform, Recovery and Enforcement Act of 1989 was adopted to address various issues affecting this industry.

Many troubled institutions have merged into stronger institutions or reduced the scale of their operations through the sale of branches and other assets pursuant to recommendation or directives of the regulatory agencies. In other situations, institutions that were taken over by or operated under the management of a federal regulator have been reorganized, sold or transferred by that federal agency to financial and nonfinancial companies.

A number of registrants have acquired, or are contemplating acquisition of, these troubled financial institutions. Complete audited financial statements of the institutions for the periods necessary to comply fully with Rule 3-05 of Regulation S-X may not be reasonably available in some cases. Some troubled institutions have never obtained an audit while others have been operated under receivership by regulators for a significant period without audit. Auditors' reports on the financial statements of some of these acquirees may not satisfy the requirements of Rule 2-02 of Regulation S-X because they contain qualifications due to audit scope limitations or disclaim an opinion.

A registrant that acquires a troubled financial institution for which complete audited financial statements are not reasonably available may be precluded from raising capital through a public offering of securities for up to three years following the acquisition because of the inability to comply with Rule 3-05.

Question 1: Are there circumstances under which the staff would conclude that financial statements of an acquired troubled financial institution are not required by Rule 3-05?

Interpretive Response: Yes. In some case, financial statements will not be required because there is not sufficient continuity of the acquired entity's operations prior to and after the acquisition, so that disclosure of prior financial information is material to an understanding of future operations, as discussed in Rule 11-01 of Regulation S-X. For example, such a circumstance may exist in the case of an acquisition solely of the physical facilities of a banking branch with assumption of the related deposits if neither income-producing assets (other than treasury bills and similar low-risk investment) nor the management responsible for its historical investment and lending activities transfer with the branch to the registrant. In this and other circumstances, where the registrant can persuasively demonstrate that continuity of operations is substantially lacking and a representation to this effect is included in the filing, the staff will not object to the omission of financial statements. However, applicable disclosures specified by Industry Guide 3, Article 11 of Regulation S-X (pro forma information), and other information which is descriptive of the transaction and of the assets acquired and liabilities assumed should be furnished to the extent reasonably available.

Question 2: If the acquired financial institution is found to constitute a business having material continuity of operations after the transaction, are there circumstances in which the staff will waive the requirements of Rule 3-05?

Interpretive Response: Yes. The staff believes the circumstances surrounding the present restructuring of U.S. depository institutions are unique. Accordingly, the staff has identified situations in which it will grant a waiver of the requirements of Rule 3-05 of Regulation S-X to the extent that audited financial statements are not reasonably available.

For purposes of this waiver a "troubled financial institution" is one which either:

---

[23] The audited pre-acquisition period need not correspond to the acquiree's pre-acquisition fiscal year. However, audited periods must not be for periods in excess of 12 months.

1. Is in receivership, conservatorship or is otherwise operating under a similar supervisory agreement with a federal financial regulatory agency; or

2. Is controlled by a federal regulatory agency; or

3. Is acquired in a federally assisted transaction.

A registrant that acquires a troubled financial institution that is deemed significant pursuant to Rule 3-05 may omit audited financial statements of the acquired entity, if such statements are not reasonably available and the total acquired assets of the troubled institution do not exceed 20% of the registrant's assets before giving effect to the acquisition. The staff will consider requests for waivers in situations involving more significant acquisitions, where federal financial assistance or guarantees are an essential part of the transaction, or where the nature and magnitude of federal assistance is so pervasive as to substantially reduce the relevance of such information to an assessment of future operations. Where financial statements are waived, disclosure concerning the acquired business as outlined in response to Question 3 must be furnished.

Question 3: Where historical financial statements meeting the requirements of Rule 3-05 of Regulation S-X are waived, what financial statements and other disclosures would the staff expect to be provided in filings with the Commission?

Interpretive Response: Where complete audited historical financial statements of a significant acquiree that is a troubled financial institution are not provided, the staff would expect filings to include an audited statement of assets acquired and liabilities assumed if the acquisition is not already reflected in the registrant's most recent audited balance sheet at the time the filing is made. Where reasonably available, unaudited statement of operations and cash flows that are prepared in accordance with GAAP and otherwise comply with Regulation S-X should be filed in lieu of any audited financial statements which are not provided if historical information may be relevant.

In all cases where a registrant succeeds to assets and/or liabilities of a troubled financial institution which are significant to the registrant pursuant to the tests in Rule 1-02(w) of Regulation S-X, narrative description should be required, quantified to the extent practicable, of the anticipated effects of the acquisition on the registrant's financial condition, liquidity, capital resources and operating results. If federal financial assistance (including any commitments, agreements or understandings made with respect to capital, accounting or other forbearances) may be material, the limits, conditions and other variables affecting its availability should be disclosed, along with an analysis of its likely short term and long term effects on cash flows and reported results.

If the transaction will result in the recognition of any significant intangibles that cannot be separately sold, such as goodwill or a core deposit intangible, the discussion of the transaction should describe the amount of such intangibles, the necessarily subjective nature of the estimation of the life and value of such

intangibles, and the effects upon future results of operations, liquidity and capital resources, including any consequences if a recognized intangible will be excluded from the calculation of capital for regulatory purposes. The discussion of the impact on future operations should specifically address the period over which intangibles will be amortized and the period over which any discounts on acquired assets will be taken into income. If amortization of intangibles will be over a period which differs from the period over which income from discounts on acquired assets will be recognized (whether from amortization of discounts or sale of discounted assets), disclosure should be provided concerning the disparate effects of the amortization and income recognition on operating results for all affected periods.

Information specified by Industry Guide 3 should be furnished to the extent applicable and reasonably available. For the categories identified in the Industry Guide, the registrant should disclose the carrying value of loans and investments acquired, as well as their principal amount and average contractual yield and term. Amounts of acquired investments, loans, or other assets that are nonaccrual, past due or restructured, or for which other collectibility problems are indicated should be disclosed. Where historical financial statements of the acquired entity are furnished, pro forma information presented pursuant to Rule 11-02 should be supplemented as necessary with a discussion of the likely effects of any federal assistance and changes in operations subsequent to the acquisition. To the extent historical financial statements meeting all the requirements of Rule 3-05 are not furnished, the filing should include an explanation of the basis for their omission.

Question 4: If an audited statement of assets acquired and liabilities assumed is required, but certain of the assets conveyed in the transaction are subject to rights allowing the registrant to put the assets back to the seller upon completion of a due diligence review, will the staff grant an extension of time for filing the required financial statement until the put period lapses?

Interpretive Response: If it is impracticable to provide an audited statement at the time the Form 8-K reporting the transaction is filed, an extension of time is available under certain circumstances. Specifically, if more than 25% of the acquired assets may be put and the put period does not exceed 120 days, the registrant should timely file a statement of assets acquired and liabilities assumed on an unaudited basis with full disclosure of the terms and amounts of the put arrangement. Within 21 days after the put period lapses, the registrant should furnish an audited statement of assets acquired and liabilities assumed unless the effects of the transaction are already reflected in an audited balance sheet which has been filed with the Commission. However, until the audited financial statement has been filed, certain offerings under the Securities Act of 1933 would be prevented, as described in Instruction 1 to Item 7 of Form 8-K.

L. Deleted by SAB 103

M. Materiality

1. *Assessing materiality*

Facts: During the course of preparing or auditing year-end financial statements, financial management or the registrant's independent auditor becomes aware of misstatements in a registrant's financial statements. When combined, the misstatements result in a 4% overstatement of net income and a $.02 (4%) overstatement of earnings per share. Because no item in the registrant's consolidated financial statements is misstated by more than 5%, management and the independent auditor conclude that the deviation from GAAP is immaterial and that the accounting is permissible.[24]

Question: Each Statement of Financial Accounting Standards adopted by the FASB states, "The provisions of this Statement need not be applied to immaterial items." In the staff's view, may a registrant or the auditor of its financial statements assume the immateriality of items that fall below a percentage threshold set by management or the auditor to determine whether amounts and items are material to the financial statements?

Interpretive Response: No. The staff is aware that certain registrants, over time, have developed quantitative thresholds as "rules of thumb" to assist in the preparation of their financial statements, and that auditors also have used these thresholds in their evaluation of whether items might be considered material to users of a registrant's financial statements. One rule of thumb in particular suggests that the misstatement or omission[25] of an item that falls under a 5% threshold is not material in the absence of particularly egregious circumstances, such as self-dealing or misappropriation by senior management. The staff reminds registrants and the auditors of their financial statements that exclusive reliance on this or any percentage or numerical threshold has no basis in the accounting literature or the law.

The use of a percentage as a numerical threshold, such as 5%, may provide the basis for a preliminary assumption that - without considering all relevant circumstances - a deviation of less than the specified percentage with respect to a particular item on the registrant's financial statements is unlikely to be material. The staff has no objection to such a "rule of thumb" as an initial step in assessing materiality. But quantifying, in percentage terms, the magnitude of a misstatement is only the beginning of an analysis of materiality; it cannot appropriately be used as a substitute for a full analysis of all relevant considerations. Materiality concerns the significance of an item to users of a registrant's financial statements. A matter is "material" if there is a substantial likelihood that a reasonable person would consider it important. In its Concepts Statement 2, the FASB stated the essence of the concept of materiality as follows:

The omission or misstatement of an item in a financial report is material if, in the light of surrounding circumstances, the magnitude of the item is such that it is probable that the judgment of a reasonable person relying upon the report would have been changed or influenced by the inclusion or correction of the item.[26]

This formulation in the accounting literature is in substance identical to the formulation used by the courts in interpreting the federal securities laws. The Supreme Court has held that a fact is material if there is -

a substantial likelihood that the . . . fact would have been viewed by the reasonable investor as having significantly altered the "total mix" of information made available.[27]

Under the governing principles, an assessment of materiality requires that one views the facts in the context of the "surrounding circumstances," as the accounting literature puts it, or the "total mix" of information, in the words of the Supreme Court. In the context of a misstatement of a financial statement item, while the "total mix" includes the size in numerical or percentage terms of the misstatement, it also includes the factual context in which the user of financial statements would view the financial statement item. The shorthand in the accounting and auditing literature for this analysis is that financial management and the auditor must consider both "quantitative" and "qualitative" factors in assessing an item's materiality.[28] Court decisions, Commission rules and enforcement actions, and accounting and auditing literature[29] have all considered "qualitative" factors in various contexts.

---

[24] AU 312 states that the auditor should consider audit risk and materiality both in (a) planning and setting the scope for the audit and (b) evaluating whether the financial statements taken as a whole are fairly presented in all material respects in conformity with GAAP. The purpose of this SAB is to provide guidance to financial management and independent auditors with respect to the evaluation of the materiality of misstatements that are identified in the audit process or preparation of the financial statements (i.e., (b) above). This SAB is not intended to provide definitive guidance for assessing "materiality" in other contexts, such as evaluations of auditor independence, as other factors may apply. There may be other rules that address financial presentation. See, e.g., Rule 2a-4, 17 CFR 270.2a-4, under the Investment Company Act of 1940.

[25] As used in this SAB, "misstatement" or "omission" refers to a financial statement assertion that would not be in conformity with GAAP.

[26] Concepts Statement 2, paragraph 132. See also Concepts Statement 2, Glossary of Terms - Materiality.

[27] TSC Industries v. Northway, Inc., 426 U.S. 438, 449 (1976). See also Basic, Inc. v. Levinson, 485 U.S. 224 (1988). As the Supreme Court has noted, determinations of materiality require "delicate assessments of the inferences a 'reasonable shareholder' would draw from a given set of facts and the significance of those inferences to him . . . ." TSC Industries, 426 U.S. at 450.

[28] See, e.g., Concepts Statement 2, paragraphs 123-124; AU 312A.10 (materiality judgments are made in light of surrounding circumstances and necessarily involve both quantitative and qualitative considerations); AU 312A.34 ("Qualitative considerations also influence the auditor in reaching a conclusion as to whether misstatements are material."). As used in the accounting literature and in this SAB, "qualitative" materiality refers to the surrounding circumstances that inform an investor's evaluation of financial statement entries. Whether events may be material to investors for non-financial reasons is a matter not addressed by this SAB.

[29] See, e.g., Rule 1-02(o) of Regulation S-X, 17 CFR 210.1-02(o), Rule 405 of Regulation C, 17 CFR 230.405, and Rule 12b-2, 17 CFR

The FASB has long emphasized that materiality cannot be reduced to a numerical formula. In its Concepts Statement 2, the FASB noted that some had urged it to promulgate quantitative materiality guides for use in a variety of situations. The FASB rejected such an approach as representing only a "minority view, stating -

The predominant view is that materiality judgments can properly be made only by those who have all the facts. The Board's present position is that no general standards of materiality could be formulated to take into account all the considerations that enter into an experienced human judgment.[30]

The FASB noted that, in certain limited circumstances, the Commission and other authoritative bodies had issued quantitative materiality guidance, citing as examples guidelines ranging from one to ten percent with respect to a variety of disclosures.[31] And it took account of contradictory studies, one showing a lack of uniformity among auditors on materiality judgments, and another suggesting widespread use of a "rule of thumb" of five to ten percent of net income.[32] The FASB also considered whether an evaluation of materiality could be based solely on anticipating the market's reaction to accounting information.[33]

The FASB rejected a formulaic approach to discharging "the onerous duty of making materiality decisions"[34] in favor of an approach that takes into account all the relevant considerations. In so doing, it made clear that -

[M]agnitude by itself, without regard to the nature of the item and the circumstances in which the judgment has to be made, will not generally be a sufficient basis for a materiality judgment.[35]

Evaluation of materiality requires a registrant and its auditor to consider *all* the relevant circumstances, and the staff believes that there are numerous circumstances in which misstatements below 5% could well be material. Qualitative factors may cause misstatements of quantitatively small amounts to be material; as stated in the auditing literature:

As a result of the interaction of quantitative and qualitative considerations in materiality judgments, misstatements of relatively small amounts that come to the auditor's attention could have a material effect on the financial statements.[36]

Among the considerations that may well render material a quantitatively small misstatement of a financial statement item are -

• whether the misstatement arises from an item capable of precise measurement or whether it arises from an estimate and, if so, the degree of imprecision inherent in the estimate[37]

• whether the misstatement masks a change in earnings or other trends

• whether the misstatement hides a failure to meet analysts' consensus expectations for the enterprise

• whether the misstatement changes a loss into income or vice versa

• whether the misstatement concerns a segment or other portion of the registrant's business that has been identified as playing a significant role in the registrant's operations or profitability

• whether the misstatement affects the registrant's compliance with regulatory requirements

• whether the misstatement affects the registrant's compliance with loan covenants or other contractual requirements

• whether the misstatement has the effect of increasing management's compensation - for example, by satisfying requirements for the award of bonuses or other forms of incentive compensation

• whether the misstatement involves concealment of an unlawful transaction.

This is not an exhaustive list of the circumstances that may affect the materiality of a quantitatively small misstatement.[38] Among other factors, the demonstrated volatility of the price of a registrant's securities in response to certain types of disclosures may provide guidance as to whether investors regard quantitatively small misstatements as material. Consideration of potential market reaction to disclosure

---

(Footnote Continued)

240.12b-2; AU 312A.10 - .11, 317.13, 411.04 n. 1, and 508.36; In re Kidder Peabody Securities Litigation, 10 F. Supp. 2d 398 (S.D.N.Y. 1998); Parnes v. Gateway 2000, Inc., 122 F.3d 539 (8th Cir. 1997); In re Westinghouse Securities Litigation, 90 F.3d 696 (3d Cir. 1996); In the Matter of W.R. Grace & Co., Accounting and Auditing Enforcement Release ("AAER") 1140 (June 30, 1999); In the Matter of Eugene Gaughan, AAER 1141 (June 30, 1999); In the Matter of Thomas Scanlon, AAER 1142 (June 30, 1999); and In re Sensormatic Electronics Corporation, Sec. Act Rel. No. 7518 (March 25, 1998).

[30] Concepts Statement 2, paragraph 131.

[31] Concepts Statement 2, paragraphs 131 and 166.

[32] Concepts Statement 2, paragraph 167.

[33] Concepts Statement 2, paragraphs 168-169.

[34] Concepts Statement 2, paragraph 170.

[35] Concepts Statement 2, paragraph 125.

[36] AU 312.11.

[37] As stated in Concepts Statement 2, paragraph 130:

Another factor in materiality judgments is the degree of precision that is attainable in estimating the judgment item. The amount of deviation that is considered immaterial may increase as the attainable degree of precision decreases. For example, accounts payable usually can be estimated more accurately than can contingent liabilities arising from litigation or threats of it, and a deviation considered to be material in the first case may be quite trivial in the second.

This SAB is not intended to change current law or guidance in the accounting literature regarding accounting estimates. *See, e.g.*, Accounting Principles Board Opinion 20, Accounting Changes 10, 11, 31-33 (July 1971).

[38] The staff understands that the Big Five Audit Materiality Task Force ("Task Force") was convened in March of 1998 and has made recommendations to the Auditing Standards Board including suggestions regarding communications with audit committees about unadjusted misstatements. *See* generally Big Five Audit Materiality Task Force. "Materiality in a Financial Statement Audit - Considering Qualitative Factors When Evaluating Audit Findings" (August 1998).

of a misstatement is by itself "too blunt an instrument to be depended on" in considering whether a fact is material.[39] When, however, management or the independent auditor expects (based, for example, on a pattern of market performance) that a known misstatement may result in a significant positive or negative market reaction, that expected reaction should be taken into account when considering whether a misstatement is material.[40]

For the reasons noted above, the staff believes that a registrant and the auditors of its financial statements should not assume that even small intentional misstatements in financial statements, for example those pursuant to actions to "manage" earnings, are immaterial.[41] While the intent of management does not render a misstatement material, it may provide significant evidence of materiality. The evidence may be particularly compelling where management has intentionally misstated items in the financial statements to "manage" reported earnings. In that instance, it presumably has done so believing that the resulting amounts and trends would be significant to users of the registrant's financial statements.[42] The staff believes that investors generally would regard as significant a management practice to over- or understate earnings up to an amount just short of a percentage threshold in order to "manage" earnings. Investors presumably also would regard as significant an accounting practice that, in essence, rendered all earnings figures subject to a management-directed margin of misstatement.

The materiality of a misstatement may turn on where it appears in the financial statements. For example, a misstatement may involve a segment of the registrant's operations. In that instance, in assessing materiality of a misstatement to the financial statements taken as a whole, registrants and their auditors should consider not only the size of the misstatement but also the significance of the segment information to the financial statements taken as a whole.[43] "A misstatement of the revenue and operating profit of a relatively small segment that is represented by management to be important to the future profitability of the entity"[44] is more likely to be material to investors than a misstatement in a segment that management has not identified as especially important. In assessing the materiality of misstatements in segment information - as with materiality generally - situations may

arise in practice where the auditor will conclude that a matter relating to segment information is qualitatively material even though, in his or her judgment, it is quantitatively immaterial to the financial statements taken as a whole.[45]

Aggregating and Netting Misstatements

In determining whether multiple misstatements cause the financial statements to be materially misstated, registrants and the auditors of their financial statements should consider each misstatement separately and the aggregate effect of all misstatements.[46] A registrant and its auditor should evaluate misstatements in light of quantitative and qualitative factors and "consider whether, in relation to individual amounts, subtotals, or totals in the financial statements, they materially misstate the financial statements taken as a whole."[47] This requires consideration of - the significance of an item to a particular entity (for example, inventories to a manufacturing company), the pervasiveness of the misstatement (such as whether it affects the presentation of numerous financial statement items), and the effect of the misstatement on the financial statements taken as a whole . . . .[48]

Registrants and their auditors first should consider whether each misstatement is material, irrespective of its effect when combined with other misstatements. The literature notes that the analysis should consider whether the misstatement of "individual amounts" causes a material misstatement of the financial statements taken as a whole. As with materiality generally, this analysis requires consideration of both quantitative and qualitative factors.

If the misstatement of an individual amount causes the financial statements as a whole to be materially misstated, that effect cannot be eliminated by other misstatements whose effect may be to diminish the impact of the misstatement on other financial statement items. To take an obvious example, if a registrant's revenues are a material financial statement item and if they are materially overstated, the financial statements taken as a whole will be materially misleading even if the effect on earnings is completely offset by an equivalent overstatement of expenses.

Even though a misstatement of an individual amount may not cause the financial statements taken

---

[39] See Concepts Statement 2, paragraph 169.

[40] If management does not expect a significant market reaction, a misstatement still may be material and should be evaluated under the criteria discussed in this SAB.

[41] Intentional management of earnings and intentional misstatements, as used in this SAB, do not include insignificant errors and omissions that may occur in systems and recurring processes in the normal course of business. See notes 37 and 49 infra.

[42] Assessments of materiality should occur not only at year-end, but also during the preparation of each quarterly or interim financial statement. See, e.g., In the Matter of Venator Group, Inc., AAER 1049 (June 29, 1998).

[43] See, e.g., In the Matter of W.R. Grace & Co., AAER 1140 (June 30, 1999).

[44] AU 9326.33.

[45] Id.

[46] The auditing literature notes that the "concept of materiality recognizes that some matters, either individually or in the aggregate, are important for fair presentation of financial statements in conformity with generally accepted accounting principles." AU 312.03. See also AU 312.04.

[47] AU 312.34. Quantitative materiality assessments often are made by comparing adjustments to revenues, gross profit, pretax and net income, total assets, stockholders' equity, or individual line items in the financial statements. The particular items in the financial statements to be considered as a basis for the materiality determination depend on the proposed adjustment to be made and other factors, such as those identified in this SAB. For example, an adjustment to inventory that is immaterial to pretax income or net income may be material to the financial statements because it may affect a working capital ratio or cause the registrant to be in default of loan covenants.

[48] AU 508.36.

as a whole to be materially misstated, it may nonetheless, when aggregated with other misstatements, render the financial statements taken as a whole to be materially misleading. Registrants and the auditors of their financial statements accordingly should consider the effect of the misstatement on subtotals or totals. The auditor should aggregate all misstatements that affect each subtotal or total and consider whether the misstatements in the aggregate affect the subtotal or total in a way that causes the registrant's financial statements taken as a whole to be materially misleading.[49]

The staff believes that, in considering the aggregate effect of multiple misstatements on a subtotal or total, registrants and the auditors of their financial statements should exercise particular care when considering whether to offset (or the appropriateness of offsetting) a misstatement of an estimated amount with a misstatement of an item capable of precise measurement. As noted above, assessments of materiality should never be purely mechanical; given the imprecision inherent in estimates, there is by definition a corresponding imprecision in the aggregation of misstatements involving estimates with those that do not involve an estimate.

Registrants and auditors also should consider the effect of misstatements from prior periods on the current financial statements. For example, the auditing literature states,

Matters underlying adjustments proposed by the auditor but not recorded by the entity could potentially cause future financial statements to be materially misstated, even though the auditor has concluded that the adjustments are not material to the current financial statements.[50]

This may be particularly the case where immaterial misstatements recur in several years and the cumulative effect becomes material in the current year.

2. Immaterial misstatements that are intentional

Facts: A registrant's management intentionally has made adjustments to various financial statement items in a manner inconsistent with GAAP. In each accounting period in which such actions were taken, none of the individual adjustments is by itself material, nor is the aggregate effect on the financial statements taken as a whole material for the period. The registrant's earnings "management" has been effected at the direction or acquiescence of management in the belief that any deviations from GAAP have been immaterial and that accordingly the accounting is permissible.

Question: In the staff's view, may a registrant make intentional immaterial misstatements in its financial statements?

Interpretive Response: No. In certain circumstances, intentional immaterial misstatements are unlawful.

Considerations of the books and records provisions under the Exchange Act

Even if misstatements are immaterial,[51] registrants must comply with Sections 13(b)(2) - (7) of the Securities Exchange Act of 1934 (the "Exchange Act").[52] Under these provisions, each registrant with securities registered pursuant to Section 12 of the Exchange Act,[53] or required to file reports pursuant to Section 15(d),[54] must make and keep books, records, and accounts, which, in reasonable detail, accurately and fairly reflect the transactions and dispositions of assets of the registrant and must maintain internal accounting controls that are sufficient to provide reasonable assurances that, among other things, transactions are recorded as necessary to permit the preparation of financial statements in conformity with GAAP.[55] In this context, determinations of what constitutes "reasonable assurance" and "reasonable detail" are based not on a "materiality" analysis but on the level of detail and degree of assurance that would satisfy prudent officials in the conduct of their own affairs.[56] Accordingly, failure to record accurately immaterial items, in some instances, may result in violations of the securities laws.

The staff recognizes that there is limited authoritative guidance[57] regarding the "reasonableness" standard in Section 13(b)(2) of the Exchange Act. A principal statement of the Commission's policy in this area is set forth in an address given in 1981 by then

---

[49] AU 312.34.

[50] AU 380.09.

[51] FASB Statements generally provide that "[t]he provisions of this Statement need not be applied to immaterial items." This SAB is consistent with that provision of the Statements. In theory, this language is subject to the interpretation that the registrant is free intentionally to set forth immaterial items in financial statements in a manner that plainly would be contrary to GAAP if the misstatement were material. The staff believes that the FASB did not intend this result.

[52] 15 U.S.C. 78m(b)(2) - (7).

[53] 15 U.S.C. 78l.

[54] 15 U.S.C. 78o(d).

[55] Criminal liability may be imposed if a person knowingly circumvents or knowingly fails to implement a system of internal accounting controls or knowingly falsifies books, records or accounts. 15 U.S.C. 78m(4) and (5). See also Rule 13b2-1 under the Exchange Act, 17 CFR 240.13b2-1, which states, "No person shall, directly or indirectly, falsify or cause to be falsified, any book,

record or account subject to Section 13(b)(2)(A) of the Securities Exchange Act."

[56] 15 U.S.C. 78m(b)(7). The books and records provisions of section 13(b) of the Exchange Act originally were passed as part of the Foreign Corrupt Practices Act ("FCPA"). In the conference committee report regarding the 1988 amendments to the FCPA, the committee stated:

The conference committee adopted the prudent man qualification in order to clarify that the current standard does not connote an unrealistic degree of exactitude or precision. The concept of reasonableness of necessity contemplates the weighing of a number of relevant factors, including the costs of compliance.

Cong. Rec. H2116 (daily ed. April 20, 1988).

[57] So far as the staff is aware, there is only one judicial decision that discusses Section 13(b)(2) of the Exchange Act in any detail, SEC v. World-Wide Coin Investments, Ltd., 567 F. Supp. 724 (N.D. Ga. 1983), and the courts generally have found that no private right of action exists under the accounting and books and records provisions of the Exchange Act. See e.g., Lamb v. Phillip Morris Inc., 915 F.2d 1024 (6th Cir. 1990) and JS Service Center Corporation v. General Electric Technical Services Company, 937 F. Supp. 216 (S.D.N.Y. 1996).

Chairman Harold M. Williams.[58] In his address, Chairman Williams noted that, like materiality, "reasonableness" is not an "absolute standard of exactitude for corporate records."[59] Unlike materiality, however, "reasonableness" is not solely a measure of the significance of a financial statement item to investors. "Reasonableness," in this context, reflects a judgment as to whether an issuer's failure to correct a known misstatement implicates the purposes underlying the accounting provisions of Sections 13(b)(2) - (7) of the Exchange Act.[60]

In assessing whether a misstatement results in a violation of a registrant's obligation to keep books and records that are accurate "in reasonable detail," registrants and their auditors should consider, in addition to the factors discussed above concerning an evaluation of a misstatement's potential materiality, the factors set forth below.

• The significance of the misstatement. Though the staff does not believe that registrants need to make finely calibrated determinations of significance with respect to immaterial items, plainly it is "reasonable" to treat misstatements whose effects are clearly inconsequential differently than more significant ones.

• How the misstatement arose. It is unlikely that it is ever "reasonable" for registrants to record misstatements or not to correct known misstatements - even immaterial ones - as part of an ongoing effort directed by or known to senior management for the purposes of "managing" earnings. On the other hand, insignificant misstatements that arise from the operation of systems or recurring processes in the normal course of business generally will not cause a registrant's books to be inaccurate "in reasonable detail."[61]

• The cost of correcting the misstatement. The books and records provisions of the Exchange Act do not require registrants to make major expenditures to correct small misstatements.[62] Conversely, where there is little cost or delay involved in correcting a misstatement, failing to do so is unlikely to be "reasonable."

• The clarity of authoritative accounting guidance with respect to the misstatement. Where reasonable minds may differ about the appropriate accounting treatment of a financial statement item, a failure to correct it may not render the registrant's financial

statements inaccurate "in reasonable detail." Where, however, there is little ground for reasonable disagreement, the case for leaving a misstatement uncorrected is correspondingly weaker.

There may be other indicators of "reasonableness" that registrants and their auditors may ordinarily consider. Because the judgment is not mechanical, the staff will be inclined to continue to defer to judgments that "allow a business, acting in good faith, to comply with the Act's accounting provisions in an innovative and cost-effective way."[63]

The Auditor's Response to Intentional Misstatements

Section 10A(b) of the Exchange Act requires auditors to take certain actions upon discovery of an "illegal act."[64] The statute specifies that these obligations are triggered "whether or not [the illegal acts are] perceived to have a material effect on the financial statements of the issuer . . . ." Among other things, Section 10A(b)(1) requires the auditor to inform the appropriate level of management of an illegal act (unless clearly inconsequential) and assure that the registrant's audit committee is "adequately informed" with respect to the illegal act.

As noted, an intentional misstatement of immaterial items in a registrant's financial statements may violate Section 13(b)(2) of the Exchange Act and thus be an illegal act. When such a violation occurs, an auditor must take steps to see that the registrant's audit committee is "adequately informed" about the illegal act. Because Section 10A(b)(1) is triggered regardless of whether an illegal act has a material effect on the registrant's financial statements, where the illegal act consists of a misstatement in the registrant's financial statements, the auditor will be required to report that illegal act to the audit committee irrespective of any "netting" of the misstatements with other financial statement items.

The requirements of Section 10A echo the auditing literature. See, for example, SAS Nos. 54 and 99. Pursuant to paragraph 77 of SAS 99, if the auditor determines there is evidence that fraud may exist, the auditor must discuss the matter with the appropriate level of management that is at least one level above those involved, and with senior management and the audit committee. The auditor must report directly to the audit committee fraud involving senior manage-

---

[58] The Commission adopted the address as a formal statement of policy in Securities Exchange Act Release No. 17500 (January 29, 1981), 46 FR 11544 (February 9, 1981), 21 SEC Docket 1466 (February 10, 1981).

[59] *Id.* at 46 FR 11546.

[60] *Id.*

[61] For example, the conference report regarding the 1988 amendments to the FCPA stated:

The Conferees intend to codify current Securities and Exchange Commission (SEC) enforcement policy that penalties not be imposed for insignificant or technical infractions or inadvertent conduct. The amendment adopted by the Conferees [Section 13(b)(4)]accomplishes this by providing that criminal penalties shall not be imposed for failing to comply with the FCPA's books and records or accounting provisions. This provision [Section 13(b)(5)] is meant to ensure that criminal penalties would be imposed where acts of commission or omission in keeping books

or records or administering accounting controls have the purpose of falsifying books, records or accounts, or of circumventing the accounting controls set forth in the Act. This would include the deliberate falsification of books and records and other conduct calculated to evade the internal accounting controls requirement.

Cong. Rec. H2115 (daily ed. April 20, 1988).

[62] As Chairman Williams noted with respect to the internal control provisions of the FCPA, "[t]housands of dollars ordinarily should not be spent conserving hundreds." 46 FR 11546.

[63] *Id.*, at 11547.

[64] Section 10A(f) defines, for purposes of Section 10A, an "illegal act" as "an act or omission that violates any law, or any rule or regulation having the force of law." This is broader than the definition of an "illegal act" in AU 317.02, which states, "Illegal acts by clients do not include personal misconduct by the entity's personnel unrelated to their business activities."

ment and fraud that causes a material misstatement of the financial statements. Paragraph 6 of SAS 99 states that "misstatements arising from fraudulent financial reporting are intentional misstatements or omissions of amounts or disclosures in financial statements designed to deceive financial statement users . . ."[65] SAS 99 further states that fraudulent financial reporting may involve falsification or alteration of accounting records; misrepresenting or omitting events, transactions or other information in the financial statements; and the intentional misapplication of accounting principles relating to amounts, classifications, the manner of presentation, or disclosures in the financial statements.[66] The clear implication of SAS 99 is that immaterial misstatements may be fraudulent financial reporting.[67]

Auditors that learn of intentional misstatements may also be required to (1) re-evaluate the degree of audit risk involved in the audit engagement, (2) determine whether to revise the nature, timing, and extent of audit procedures accordingly, and (3) consider whether to resign.[68]

Intentional misstatements also may signal the existence of reportable conditions or material weaknesses in the registrant's system of internal accounting control designed to detect and deter improper accounting and financial reporting.[69] As stated by the National Commission on Fraudulent Financial Reporting, also known as the Treadway Commission, in its 1987 report,

The tone set by top management—the corporate environment or culture within which financial reporting occurs - is the most important factor contributing to the integrity of the financial reporting process. Notwithstanding an impressive set of written rules and procedures, if the tone set by management is lax, fraudulent financial reporting is more likely to occur.[70]

An auditor is required to report to a registrant's audit committee any reportable conditions or material weaknesses in a registrant's system of internal accounting control that the auditor discovers in the course of the examination of the registrant's financial statements.[71]

GAAP precedence over industry practice

Some have argued to the staff that registrants should be permitted to follow an industry accounting practice even though that practice is inconsistent with authoritative accounting literature. This situation might occur if a practice is developed when there are few transactions and the accounting results are clearly inconsequential, and that practice never changes despite a subsequent growth in the number or materiality of such transactions. The staff disagrees with this argument. Authoritative literature takes precedence over industry practice that is contrary to GAAP.[72]

General comments

This SAB is not intended to change current law or guidance in the accounting or auditing literature.[73] This SAB and the authoritative accounting literature cannot specifically address all of the novel and com-

---

[65] An unintentional illegal act triggers the same procedures and considerations by the auditor as a fraudulent misstatement if the illegal act has a direct and material effect on the financial statements. See AU 110 n. 1, 317.05 and 317.07. Although distinguishing between intentional and unintentional misstatements is often difficult, the auditor must plan and perform the audit to obtain reasonable assurance that the financial statements are free of material misstatements in either case.

[66] Although the auditor is not required to plan or perform the audit to detect misstatements that are immaterial to the financial statements, SAS 99 requires the auditor to evaluate several fraud "risk factors" that may bring such misstatements to his or her attention. For example, an analysis of fraud risk factors under SAS 99 must include, among other things, consideration of management's interest in maintaining or increasing the registrant's stock price or earnings trend through the use of unusually aggressive accounting practices, whether management has a practice of committing to analysts or others that it will achieve unduly aggressive or clearly unrealistic forecasts, and the existence of assets, liabilities, revenues, or expenses based on significant estimates that involve unusually subjective judgments or uncertainties.

[67] In requiring the auditor to consider whether fraudulent misstatements are material, and in requiring differing responses depending on whether the misstatement is material, SAS 99 makes clear that fraud can involve immaterial misstatements. Indeed, a misstatement can be "inconsequential" and still involve fraud.

Under SAS 99, assessing whether misstatements due to fraud are material to the financial statements is a "cumulative process" that should occur both during and at the completion of the audit. SAS 99 further states that this accumulation is primarily a "qualitative matter" based on the auditor's judgment. The staff believes that in making these assessments, management and auditors should refer to the discussion in Part 1 of this SAB.

[68] Auditors should document their determinations in accordance with SAS 96, SAS 99, and other appropriate sections of the audit literature.

[69] See, e.g., SAS 99.

[70] Report of the National Commission on Fraudulent Financial Reporting at 32 (October 1987). See also Report and Recommendations of the Blue Ribbon Committee on Improving the Effectiveness of Corporate Audit Committees (February 8, 1999).

[71] AU 325.02. See also AU 380.09, which, in discussing matters to be communicated by the auditor to the audit committee, states:

The auditor should inform the audit committee about adjustments arising from the audit that could, in his judgment, either individually or in the aggregate, have a significant effect on the entity's financial reporting process. For purposes of this section, an audit adjustment, whether or not recorded by the entity, is a proposed correction of the financial statements . . . .

[72] See AU 411.05.

[73] The FASB Discussion Memorandum, "Criteria for Determining Materiality," states that the financial accounting and reporting process considers that "a great deal of the time might be spent during the accounting process considering insignificant matters . . . . If presentations of financial information are to be prepared economically on a timely basis and presented in a concise intelligible form, the concept of materiality is crucial." This SAB is not intended to require that misstatements arising from insignificant errors and omissions (individually and in the aggregate) arising from the normal recurring accounting close processes, such as a clerical error or an adjustment for a missed accounts payable invoice, always be corrected, even if the error is identified in the audit process and known to management. Management and the auditor would need to consider the various factors described elsewhere in this SAB in assessing whether such misstatements are material, need to be corrected to comply with the FCPA, or trigger procedures under Section 10A of the Exchange Act. Because this SAB does not change current law or guidance in the accounting or auditing literature, adherence to the principles described in this SAB should not raise the costs associated with recordkeeping or with audits of financial statements.

plex business transactions and events that may occur. Accordingly, registrants may account for, and make disclosures about, these transactions and events based on analogies to similar situations or other factors. The staff may not, however, always be persuaded that a registrant's determination is the most appropriate under the circumstances. When disagreements occur after a transaction or an event has been reported, the consequences may be severe for registrants, auditors, and, most importantly, the users of financial statements who have a right to expect consistent accounting and reporting for, and disclosure of, similar transactions and events. The staff, therefore, encourages registrants and auditors to discuss on a timely basis with the staff proposed accounting treatments for, or disclosures about, transactions or events that are not specifically covered by the existing accounting literature.

N. Considering the Effects of Prior Year Misstatements when Quantifying Misstatements in Current Year Financial Statements

Facts: During the course of preparing annual financial statements, a registrant is evaluating the materiality of an improper expense accrual (*e.g.*, overstated liability) in the amount of $100, which has built up over 5 years, at $20 per year.[1] The registrant previously evaluated the misstatement as being immaterial to each of the prior year financial statements (*i.e.*, years 1-4). For the purpose of evaluating materiality in the current year (*i.e.*, year 5), the registrant quantifies the error as a $20 overstatement of expenses.

Question 1: Has the registrant appropriately quantified the amount of this error for the purpose of evaluating materiality for the current year?

Interpretive Response: No. In this example, the registrant has only quantified the effects of the identified unadjusted error that arose in the current year income statement. The staff believes a registrant's materiality evaluation of an identified unadjusted error should quantify the effects of the identified unadjusted error on each financial statement and related financial statement disclosure.

Topic 1M notes that a materiality evaluation must be based on all relevant quantitative and qualitative factors.[2] This analysis generally begins with quantifying potential misstatements to be evaluated. There has been diversity in practice with respect to this initial step of a materiality analysis.

The diversity in approaches for quantifying the amount of misstatements primarily stems from the effects of misstatements that were not corrected at the end of the prior year ("prior year misstatements"). These prior year misstatements should be considered in quantifying misstatements in current year financial statements.

The techniques most commonly used in practice to accumulate and quantify misstatements are generally referred to as the "rollover" and "iron curtain" approaches.

The rollover approach, which is the approach used by the registrant in this example, quantifies a misstatement based on the amount of the error originating in the current year income statement. Thus, this approach ignores the effects of correcting the portion of the current year balance sheet misstatement that originated in prior years (*i.e.*, it ignores the "carryover effects" of prior year misstatements).

The iron curtain approach quantifies a misstatement based on the effects of correcting the misstatement existing in the balance sheet at the end of the current year, irrespective of the misstatement's year(s) of origination. Had the registrant in this fact pattern applied the iron curtain approach, the misstatement would have been quantified as a $100 misstatement based on the end of year balance sheet misstatement. Thus, the adjustment needed to correct the financial statements for the end of year error would be to reduce the liability by $100 with a corresponding decrease in current year expense.

As demonstrated in this example, the primary weakness of the rollover approach is that it can result in the accumulation of significant misstatements on the balance sheet that are deemed immaterial in part because the amount that originates in each year is quantitatively small. The staff is aware of situations in which a registrant, relying on the rollover approach, has allowed an erroneous item to accumulate on the balance sheet to the point where eliminating the improper asset or liability would itself result in a material error in the income statement if adjusted in the current year. Such registrants have sometimes concluded that the improper asset or liability should remain on the balance sheet into perpetuity.

In contrast, the primary weakness of the iron curtain approach is that it does not consider the correction of prior year misstatements in the current year (*i.e.*, the reversal of the carryover effects) to be errors. Therefore, in this example, if the misstatement was corrected during the current year such that no error existed in the balance sheet at the end of the current year, the reversal of the $80 prior year misstatement would not be considered an error in the current year financial statements under the iron curtain approach. Implicitly, the iron curtain approach assumes that because the prior year financial statements were not materially misstated, correcting any immaterial errors that existed in those statements in the current year is the "correct" accounting, and is therefore not considered an error in the current year. Thus, utilization of the iron curtain approach can result in a misstatement in the current year income statement not being evaluated as an error at all.

The staff does not believe the exclusive reliance on either the rollover or iron curtain approach appropri-

---

[1] For purposes of these facts, assume the registrant properly determined that the overstatement of the liability resulted from an error rather than a change in accounting estimate. See FASB Statement 154, *Accounting Changes and Error Corrections* , para-

graph 2, for the distinction between an error and a change in accounting estimate.

[2] Topic 1N addresses certain of these quantitative issues, but does not alter the analysis required by Topic 1M.

ately quantifies all misstatements that could be material to users of financial statements.

In describing the concept of materiality, FASB Concepts Statement No. 2, *Qualitative Characteristics of Accounting Information*, indicates that materiality determinations are based on whether "it is probable that the judgment of a reasonable person relying upon the report would have been changed or influenced *by the inclusion or correction of the item*" (emphasis added).[3] The staff believes registrants must quantify the impact of correcting all misstatements, including both the carryover and reversing effects of prior year misstatements, on the current year financial statements. The staff believes that this can be accomplished by quantifying an error under both the rollover and iron curtain approaches as described above and by evaluating the error measured under each approach. Thus, a registrant's financial statements would require adjustment when either approach results in quantifying a misstatement that is material, after considering all relevant quantitative and qualitative factors.

As a reminder, a change from an accounting principle that is not generally accepted to one that is generally accepted is a correction of an error.[4]

The staff believes that the registrant should quantify the current year misstatement in this example using both the iron curtain approach (*i.e.*, $100) and the rollover approach (*i.e.*, $20). Therefore, if the $100 misstatement is considered material to the financial statements, after all of the relevant quantitative and qualitative factors are considered, the registrant's financial statements would need to be adjusted.

It is possible that correcting an error in the current year could materially misstate the current year's income statement. For example, correcting the $100 misstatement in the current year will:

- Correct the $20 error originating in the current year;

  Correct the $80 balance sheet carryover error that originated in Years 1 through 4; but also

  Misstate the current year income statement by $80.

If the $80 understatement of current year expense is material to the current year, after all of the relevant quantitative and qualitative factors are considered, the prior year financial statements should be corrected, even though such revision previously was and continues to be immaterial to the prior year financial statements. Correcting prior year financial statements for immaterial errors would not require previously filed reports to be amended. Such correction may be made the next time the registrant files the prior year financial statements.

The following example further illustrates the staff's views on quantifying misstatements, including the consideration of the effects of prior year misstatements:

Facts: During the course of preparing annual financial statements, a registrant is evaluating the materiality of a sales cut-off error in which $50 of revenue from the following year was recorded in the current year, thereby overstating accounts receivable by $50 at the end of the current year. In addition, a similar sales cut-off error existed at the end of the prior year in which $110 of revenue from the current year was recorded in the prior year. As a result of the combination of the current year and prior year cut-off errors, revenues in the current year are understated by $60 ($110 understatement of revenues at the beginning of the current year partially offset by a $50 overstatement of revenues at the end of the current year). The prior year error was evaluated in the prior year as being immaterial to those financial statements.

Question 2: How should the registrant quantify the misstatement in the current year financial statements?

Interpretive Response: The staff believes the registrant should quantify the current year misstatement in this example using both the iron curtain approach (*i.e.*, $50) and the rollover approach (*i.e.*, $60). Therefore, assuming a $60 misstatement is considered material to the financial statements, after all relevant quantitative and qualitative factors are considered, the registrant's financial statements would need to be adjusted.

Further, in this example, recording an adjustment in the current year could alter the amount of the error affecting the current year financial statements. For instance:

- If only the $60 understatement of revenues were to be corrected in the current year, then the overstatement of current year end accounts receivable would increase to $110; or,

- If only the $50 overstatement of accounts receivable were to be corrected in the current year, then the understatement of current year revenues would increase to $110.

If the misstatement that exists after recording the adjustment in the current year financial statements is material (considering all relevant quantitative and qualitative factors), the prior year financial statements should be corrected, even though such revision previously was and continues to be immaterial to the prior year financial statements. Correcting prior year financial statements for immaterial errors would not require previously filed reports to be amended. Such correction may be made the next time the registrant files the prior year financial statements.

If the cut-off error that existed in the prior year was not discovered until the current year, a separate analysis of the financial statements of the prior year (and any other prior year in which previously undiscovered errors existed) would need to be performed to determine whether such prior year financial statements were materially misstated. If that analysis indicates that the prior year financial statements are

---

[3] Concepts Statement 2, paragraph 132. See also Concepts Statement 2, Glossary of Terms - Materiality.

[4] Statement 154, paragraph 2h.

materially misstated, they would need to be restated in accordance with Statement 154.[5]

Facts: When preparing its financial statements for years ending on or before November 15, 2006, a registrant quantified errors by using either the iron curtain approach or the rollover approach, but not both. Based on consideration of the guidance in this Staff Accounting Bulletin, the registrant concludes that errors existing in previously issued financial statements are material.

Question 3: Will the staff expect the registrant to restate prior period financial statements when first applying this guidance?

Interpretive Response: The staff will not object if a registrant[6] does not restate financial statements for fiscal years ending on or before November 15, 2006, if management properly applied its previous approach, either iron curtain or rollover, so long as all relevant qualitative factors were considered.

To provide full disclosure, registrants electing not to restate prior periods should reflect the effects of initially applying the guidance in Topic 1N in their annual financial statements covering the first fiscal year ending after November 15, 2006. The cumulative effect of the initial application should be reported in the carrying amounts of assets and liabilities as of the beginning of that fiscal year, and the offsetting adjustment should be made to the opening balance of retained earnings for that year. Registrants should disclose the nature and amount of each individual error being corrected in the cumulative adjustment. The disclosure should also include when and how each error being corrected arose and the fact that the errors had previously been considered immaterial.

Early application of the guidance in Topic 1N is encouraged in any report for an interim period of the first fiscal year ending after November 15, 2006, filed after the publication of this Staff Accounting Bulletin. In the event that the cumulative effect of application of the guidance in Topic 1N is first reported in an interim period other than the first interim period of the first fiscal year ending after November 15, 2006, previously filed interim reports need not be amended. However, comparative information presented in reports for interim periods of the first year subsequent to initial application should be adjusted to reflect the cumulative effect adjustment as of the beginning of the year of initial application. In addition, the disclosures of selected quarterly information required by Item 302 of Regulation S-K should reflect the adjusted results.

TOPIC 2: BUSINESS COMBINATIONS

[¶ 39,111]

A. Acquisition Method

1. **Deleted by SAB 103**

2. **Deleted by SAB 103**

3. **Deleted by SAB 103**

4. **Deleted by SAB 103**

5. **Removed by SAB 112**

6. *Debt issue costs*

Facts: Company A is to acquire the net assets of Company B in a transaction to be accounted for as a business combination. In connection with the transaction, Company A has retained an investment banker to provide advisory services in structuring the acquisition and to provide the necessary financing. It is expected that the acquisition will be financed on an interim basis using "bridge financing" provided by the investment banker. Permanent financing will be arranged at a later date through a debt offering, which will be underwritten by the investment banker. Fees will be paid to the investment banker for the advisory services, the bridge financing, and the underwriting of the permanent financing. These services may be billed separately or as a single amount.

Question 1: Should total fees paid to the investment banker for acquisition-related services and the issu-

ance of debt securities be allocated between the services received?

Interpretive Response: Yes. Fees paid to an investment banker in connection with a business combination or asset acquisition, when the investment banker is also providing interim financing or underwriting services, must be allocated between acquisition related services and debt issue costs.

When an investment banker provides services in connection with a business combination or asset acquisition and also provides underwriting services associated with the issuance of debt or equity securities, the total fees incurred by an entity should be allocated between the services received on a relative fair value basis. The objective of the allocation is to ascribe the total fees incurred to the actual services provided by the investment banker.

Statement 141(R) provides guidance for the portion of the costs that represent acquisition-related services. The portion of the costs pertaining to the issuance of debt or equity securities should be accounted for in accordance with other applicable GAAP.

Question 2: May the debt issue costs of the interim "bridge financing" be amortized over the anticipated combined life of the bridge and permanent financings?

---

[5] Statement 154, paragraph 25.

[6] If a registrant's initial registration statement is not effective on or before November 15, 2006, and the registrant's prior year(s) financial statements are materially misstated based on considera-

tion of the guidance in this Staff Accounting Bulletin, the prior year financial statements should be restated in accordance with Statement 154, paragraph 25. If a registrant's initial registration statement is effective on or before November 15, 2006, the guidance in the interpretive response to Question 3 is applicable.

Interpretive Response: No. Debt issue costs should be amortized by the interest method over the life of the debt to which they relate. Debt issue costs related to the bridge financing should be recognized as interest cost during the estimated interim period preceding the placement of the permanent financing with any unamortized amounts charged to expense if the bridge loan is repaid prior to the expiration of the estimated period. Where the bridged financing consists of increasing rate debt, the consensus reached in EITF Issue 86-15, *Increasing Rate Debt*, should be followed.[1]

7. Removed by SAB 112

8. Business Combinations Prior to an Initial Public Offering

Facts: Two or more businesses combine in a single combination just prior to or contemporaneously with an initial public offering.

Question: Does the guidance in SAB Topic 5.G apply to business combinations entered into just prior to or contemporaneously with an initial public offering?

Interpretive Response: No. The guidance in SAB Topic 5.G is intended to address the transfer, just prior to or contemporaneously with an initial public offering, of nonmonetary assets in exchange for a company's stock. The guidance in SAB Topic 5.G is not intended to modify the requirements of Statement 141(R). Accordingly, the staff believes that the combination of two or more businesses should be accounted for in accordance with Statement 141(R).

9. Removed by SAB 112

B. Deleted by SAB 103

C. Deleted by SAB 103

D. Financial Statements of Oil and Gas Exchange Offers

Facts: The oil and gas industry has experienced periods of time where there have been a significant number of "exchange offers" (also referred to as "roll-ups" or "put-togethers") to form a publicly held company, take an existing private company public, or increase the size of an existing publicly held company. An exchange offer transaction involves a swap of shares in a corporation for interests in properties, typically limited partnership interests. Such interests could include direct interests such as working interests and royalties related to developed or undeveloped properties and indirect interests such as limited partnership interests or shares of existing oil and gas companies. Generally, such transactions are structured to be tax-free to the individual or entity trading the property interest for shares of the corporation. Under certain circumstances, however, part or all of the transaction may be taxable. For purposes of the discussion in this Topic, in each of these situations, the entity (or entities) or property (or properties) are deemed to constitute a business.

One financial reporting issue in exchange transactions involves deciding which prior financial results of the entities should be reported.

Question 1: In Form 10-K filings with the Commission, the staff has permitted limited partnerships to omit certain of the oil and gas reserve value information and the supplemental summary of oil and gas activities disclosures required by Statement 69 in some circumstances. Is it permissible to omit these disclosures from the financial statements included in an exchange offering?

Interpretive Response: No. Normally full disclosures of reserve data and related information are required. The exemptions previously allowed relate only to partnerships where value-oriented data are otherwise available to the limited partners pursuant to the partnership agreement. The staff has previously stated that it will require all of the required disclosures for partnerships which are the subject of exchange offers.[13] These disclosures may, however, be presented on a combined basis if the entities are under common control.

The staff believes that the financial statements in an exchange offer registration statement should provide sufficient historical reserve quantity and value-based disclosures to enable offerees and secondary market public investors to evaluate the effect of the exchange proposal. Accordingly, in all cases, it will be necessary to present information as of the latest year-end on reserve quantities and the future net revenues associated with such quantities. In certain circumstances, where the exchange is accounted for using the acquisition method of accounting, the staff will consider, on a case-by-case basis, granting exemptions from (i) the disclosure requirements for year-to-year reconciliations of reserve quantities, and (ii) requirements for a summary of oil and gas producing activities and a summary of changes in the net present value of reserves. For instance, the staff may consider requests for exemptions in cases where the properties acquired in the exchange transaction are fully explored and developed, particularly if the management of the emerging company has not been involved in the exploration and development of such properties.

Question 2: If the exchange company will use the full cost method of accounting, does the full cost ceiling limitation apply as of the date of the financial statements reflecting the exchange?

Interpretive Response: Yes. The full cost ceiling limitation on costs capitalized does apply. However, as discussed under Topic 12.D.3, the Commission has stated that in unusual circumstances, registrants may request an exemption if as a result of a major purchase, a write-down would be required even

---

[1] As noted in the "Status" section of the Abstract to Issue 86-15, the term-extending provisions of the debt instrument should be analyzed to determine whether they constitute an embedded derivative requiring separate accounting in accordance with Statement 133 (as amended).

[13] *See* SAB 40, Topic 12.A.3.c.

though it can be demonstrated that the fair value of the properties clearly exceeds the unamortized costs.

Question 3: How should "common control accounting" be applied to the specific assets and liabilities of the new exchange company?

Interpretive Response: Consistent with SAB Topic 12.C.2, under "common control accounting" the various accounting methods followed by the offeree entities should be conformed to the methods adopted by the new exchange company. It is not appropriate to combine assets and liabilities accounted for on different bases. Accordingly, all of the oil and gas properties of the new entity must be accounted for on the same basis (either full cost or successful efforts) applied retrospectively.

Question 4: What pro forma financial information is required in an exchange offer filing?

Interpretive Response: The requirements for pro forma financial information in exchange offer filings are the same as in any other filings with the Commission and are detailed in Article 11 of Regulation S-X.[14] Rule 11-02(b) specifies the presentation requirements, including periods presented and types of adjustments to be made. The general criteria of Rule 11-02(b)(6) are that pro forma adjustments should give effect to events that are (i) directly attributable to the transaction, (ii) expected to have a continuing impact on the registrant, and (iii) factually supportable. In the case of an exchange offer, such adjustments typically are made to:

(1) Show varying levels of acceptance of the offer.

(2) Conform the accounting methods used in the historical financial statements to those to be applied by the new entity.

(3) Recompute the depreciation, depletion and amortization charges, in cases where the new entity will use full-cost accounting, on a combined basis. If this computation is not practicable, and the exchange offer is accounted for as a transaction among entities under common control, historical depreciation, depletion and amortization provisions may be aggregated, with appropriate disclosure.

(4) Reflect the acquisition in the pro forma statements where the exchange offer is accounted for using the acquisition method of accounting, including depreciation, depletion and amortization based on the measurement guidance in Statement 141(R).

(5) Provide pro forma reserve information comparable to the disclosures required by paragraphs 10 through 17 and 30 through 34 of SFAS 69.

(6) Reflect significant changes, if any, in levels of operations (revenues or costs), or in income tax status and to reflect debt incurred in connection with the transaction.

In addition, the depreciation, depletion and amortization rate which will apply for the initial period

subsequent to consummation of the exchange offer should be disclosed.

Question 5: Are there conditions under which the presentation of other than full historical financial statements would be acceptable?

Interpretive Response: Generally, full historical financial statements as specified in Rules 3-01 and 3-02 of Regulation S-X are considered necessary to enable offerees and secondary market investors to evaluate the transaction. Where securities are being registered to offer to the security holders (including limited partners and other ownership interests) of the businesses to be acquired, such financial statements are normally required pursuant to Rule 3-05 of Regulation S-X, either individually for each entity or, where appropriate, separately for the offeror and on a combined basis for other entities, generally excluding corporations. However, certain exceptions may apply as explained in the outline below:

A. Acquisition Method Accounting

1. If the registrant can demonstrate that full historical financial statements of the offeree businesses are not reasonably available, the staff may permit presentation of audited Statements of Combined Gross Revenues and Direct Lease Operating Expenses for all years for which an income statement would otherwise be required. In these circumstances, the registrant should also disclose in an unaudited footnote the amounts of total exploration and development costs, and general and administrative expenses along with the reasons why presentation of full historical financial statements is not practicable.

2. The staff will consider requests to waive the requirement for prior year financial statements of the offerees and instead allow presentation of only the latest fiscal year and interim period, if the registrant can demonstrate that the prior years' data would not be meaningful because the offerees had no material quantity of production.

B. Common Control Accounting

The staff would expect that the full historical financial statements as specified in Rules 3-01 and 3-02 of Regulation S-X would be included in the registration statement for exchange offers accounted for as transactions among entities under common control, including all required supplemental reserve information. The presentation of individual or combined financial statements would depend on the circumstances of the particular exchange offer.

Registrants are also reminded that wherever historical results are presented, it may be appropriate to explain the reasons why historical costs are not necessarily indicative of future expenditures.

E. Deleted by SAB 103

F. Deleted by SAB 103

---

[14] As announced in Financial Reporting Release No. 2 (July 9, 1982).

[¶ 39,121]   **TOPIC 3: SENIOR SECURITIES**

A. Convertible Securities

Facts : Company B proposes to file a registration statement covering convertible securities.

Question : In registration, what consideration should be given to the dilutive effects of convertible securities?

Interpretive Response : In a registration statement of convertible preferred stock or debentures, the staff believes that disclosure of pro forma earnings per share (EPS) is important to investors when the proceeds will be used to extinguish existing preferred stock or debt and such extinguishments will have a material effect on EPS. That disclosure is required by Article 11, Rule 11-01(a)(8) and Rule 11-02(a)(7) of Regulation S-X, if material.

B. Deleted by ASR 307

C. Redeemable Preferred Stock

Facts: Rule 5-02.27 of Regulation S-X states that redeemable preferred stocks are not to be included in amounts reported as stockholders' equity, and that their redemption amounts are to be shown on the face of the balance sheet. However, the Commission's rules and regulations do not address the carrying amount at which redeemable preferred stock should be reported, or how changes in its carrying amount should be treated in calculations of earnings per share and the ratio of earnings to combined fixed charges and preferred stock dividends.

Question 1 : How should the carrying amount of redeemable preferred stock be determined?

Interpretive Response : The initial carrying amount of redeemable preferred stock should be its fair value

at date of issue. Where fair value at date of issue is less than the mandatory redemption amount, the carrying amount shall be increased by periodic accretions, using the interest method, so that the carrying amount will equal the mandatory redemption amount at the mandatory redemption date. The carrying amount shall be further periodically increased by amounts representing dividends not currently declared or paid, but which will be payable under the mandatory redemption features, or for which ultimate payment is not solely within the control of the registrant (e.g., dividends that will be payable out of future earnings). Each type of increase in carrying amount shall be effected by charges against retained earnings or, in the absence of retained earnings, by charges against paid-in capital.

The accounting described in the preceding paragraph would apply irrespective of whether the redeemable preferred stock may be voluntarily redeemed by the issuer prior to the mandatory redemption date, or whether it may be converted into another class of securities by the holder. Companies also should consider the guidance in EITF Topic D-98.

Question 2 : How should periodic increases in the carrying amount of redeemable preferred stock be treated in calculations of earnings per share and ratios of earnings to combined fixed charges and preferred stock dividends?

Interpretive Response : Each type of increase in carrying amount described in the Interpretive Response to Question 1 should be treated in the same manner as dividends on nonredeemable preferred stock.

[¶ 39,131]   **TOPIC 4: EQUITY ACCOUNTS**

A. Subordinated Debt

Facts : Company E proposes to include in its registration statement a balance sheet showing its subordinate debt as a portion of stockholders' equity.

Question : Is this presentation appropriate?

Interpretive Response : Subordinated debt may not be included in the stockholders' equity section of the balance sheet. Any presentation describing such debt as a component of stockholders' equity must be eliminated. Furthermore, any caption representing the combination of stockholders' equity and only subordinated debts must be deleted.

B. S Corporations

Facts : An S corporation has undistributed earnings on the date its S election is terminated.

Question : How should such earnings be reflected in the financial statements?

Interpretive Response : Such earnings must be included in the financial statements as additional paid-in capital. This assumes a constructive distribution to

the owners followed by a contribution to the capital of the corporation.

C. Change In Capital Structure

Facts : A capital structure change to a stock dividend, stock split or reverse split occurs after the date of the latest reported balance sheet but before the release of the financial statements or the effective date of the registration statement, whichever is later.

Question : What effect must be given to such a change?

Interpretive Response : Such changes in the capital structure must be given retroactive effect in the balance sheet. An appropriately cross-referenced note should disclose the retroactive treatment, explain the change made and state the date the change became effective.

D. Earnings Per Share Computations In An Initial Public Offering

Facts : A registration statement is filed in connection with an initial public offering (IPO) of common stock. During the periods covered by income statements that are included in the registration statement or in the subsequent period prior to the effective date of the IPO, the registrant issued for nominal consideration[1] common stock, options or warrants to purchase common stock or other potentially dilutive instruments (collectively, referred to hereafter as "nominal issuances").

Prior to the effective date of Statement 128, the staff believed that certain stock and warrants[2] should be treated as outstanding for all reporting periods in the same manner as shares issued in a stock split or a recapitalization effected contemporaneously with the IPO. The dilutive effect of such stock and warrants could be measured using the treasury stock method.

Question 1 : Does the staff continue to believe that such treatment for stock and warrants would be appropriate upon adoption of Statement 128?

Interpretive Response : Generally, no. Historical EPS should be prepared and presented in conformity with Statement 128.

In applying the requirements of Statement 128, the staff believes that nominal issuances are recapitalizations in substance. In computing basic EPS for the periods covered by income statements included in the registration statement and in subsequent filings with the SEC, nominal issuances of common stock should be reflected in a manner similar to a stock split or stock dividend for which retroactive treatment is required by paragraph 54 of Statement 128. In computing diluted EPS for such periods, nominal issuances of common stock and potential common stock[3] should be reflected in a manner similar to a stock split or stock dividend.

Registrants are reminded that disclosure about materially dilutive issuances is required outside the financial statements. Item 506 of Regulation S-K requires tabular presentation of the dilutive effects of those issuances on net tangible book value. The effects of dilutive issuances on the registrant's liquidity, capital resources and results of operations should be addressed in Management's Discussion and Analysis.

Question 2: Does reflecting nominal issuances as outstanding for all historical periods in the computation of earnings per share alter the registrant's responsibility to determine whether compensation expense must be recognized for such issuances to employees?

Interpretive Response: No. Registrants must follow GAAP in determining whether the recognition of compensation expense for any issuances of equity instruments to employees is necessary.[4] Reflecting nominal issuances as outstanding for all historical

periods in the computation of earnings per share does not alter that existing responsibility under GAAP.

E. Receivables From Sale Of Stock

Facts: Capital stock is sometimes issued to officers or other employees before the cash payment is received.

Question: How should the receivables from the officers or other employees be presented in the balance sheet?

Interpretive Response: The amount recorded as a receivable should be presented in the balance sheet as a deduction from stockholders' equity. This is generally consistent with Rule 5-02.30 of Regulation S-X which states that accounts or notes receivable arising from transactions involving the registrant's capital stock should be presented as deductions from stockholders' equity and not as assets. It should be noted generally that all amounts receivable from officers and directors resulting from sales of stock or from other transactions (other than expense advances or sales on normal trade terms) should be separately stated in the balance sheet irrespective of whether such amounts may be shown as assets or are required to be reported as deductions from stockholders' equity. The staff will not suggest that a receivable from an officer or director be deducted from stockholders' equity if the receivable was paid in cash prior to the publication of the financial statements and the payment date is stated in a note to the financial statements. However, the staff would consider the subsequent return of such cash payment to the officer or director to be part of a scheme or plan to evade the registration or reporting requirements of the securities laws.

F. Limited Partnerships

Facts : There exist a number of publicly held partnerships having one or more corporate or individual general partners and a relatively larger number of limited partners. There are no specific requirements or guidelines relating to the presentation of the partnership equity accounts in the financial statements. In addition, there are many approaches to the parallel problem of relating the results of operations to the two classes of partnership equity interests.

Question : How should the financial statements of limited partnerships be presented so that the two ownership classes can readily determine their relative participations in both the net assets of the partnership and in the results of its operations?

Interpretive Response : The equity section of a partnership balance sheet should distinguish between amounts ascribed to each ownership class. The

---

[1] Whether a security was issued for nominal consideration should be determined based on facts and circumstances. The consideration the entity receives for the issuance should be compared to the security's fair value to determine whether the consideration is nominal.

[2] The stock and warrants encompassed by the prior guidance were those issuances of common stock at prices below the IPO price and options or warrants with exercise prices below the IPO

price that were issued within a one-year period prior to the initial filing of the registration statement relating to the IPO through the registration statement's effective date.

[3] SFAS 128 defines potential common stock as "a security or other contract that may entitle its holder to obtain common stock during the reporting period or after the end of the reporting period."

[4] As prescribed by Statement 123R.

equity attributed to the general partners should be stated separately from the equity of the limited partners, and changes in the number of equity units authorized and outstanding should be shown for each ownership class. A statement of changes in partnership equity for each ownership class should be furnished for each period for which an income statement is included.

The income statements of partnerships should be presented in a manner which clearly shows the aggregate amount of net income (loss) allocated to the general partners and the aggregate amount allocated to the limited partners. The statement of income should also state the results of operations on a per unit basis.

G. Notes And Other Receivables From Affiliates

Facts : The balance sheet of a corporate general partner is often presented in a registration statement. Frequently, the balance sheet of the general partner discloses that it holds notes or other receivables from a parent or another affiliate. Often the notes or other receivables were created in order to meet the "substantial assets" test which the Internal Revenue Service utilizes in applying its "Safe Harbor" doctrine in the classification of organizations for income tax purposes.

Question : How should such notes and other receivables be reported in the balance sheet of the general partner?

Interpretive Response : While these notes and other receivables evidencing a promise to contribute capital are often legally enforceable, they seldom are actually paid. In substance, these receivables are equivalent to unpaid subscriptions receivable for capital shares which Rule 5-02,30 of Regulation S-X requires to be deducted from the dollar amount of capital shares subscribed.

The balance sheet display of these or similar items is not determined by the quality or actual value of the receivable or other asset "contributed" to the capital of the affiliated general partner, but rather by the relationship of the parties and the control inherent in that relationship. Accordingly, in these situations, the receivable must be treated as a deduction from stockholders' equity in the balance sheet of the corporate general partner.

[¶ 39,141] TOPIC 5: MISCELLANEOUS ACCOUNTING

A. Expenses of Offering

Facts: Prior to the effective date of an offering of equity securities, Company Y incurs certain expenses related to the offering.

Question: Should such costs be deferred?

Interpretive Response: Specific incremental costs directly attributable to a proposed or actual offering of securities may properly be deferred and charged against the gross proceeds of the offering. However, management salaries or other general and administrative expenses may not be allocated as costs of the offering and deferred costs of an aborted offering may not be deferred and charged against proceeds of a subsequent offering. A short postponement (up to 90 days) does not represent an aborted offering.

B. Gain Or Loss From Disposition Of Equipment

Facts: Company A has adopted the policy of treating gains and losses from disposition of revenue producing equipment as adjustments to the current year's provision for depreciation. Company B reflects such gains and losses as a separate item in the statement of income.

Question: Does the staff have any views as to which method is preferable?

Interpretive Response: Gains and losses resulting from the disposition of revenue producing equipment should not be treated as adjustments to the provision for depreciation in the year of disposition, but should be shown as a separate item in the statement of income.

If such equipment is depreciated on the basis of group of composite accounts for fleets of like vehicles, gains (or losses) may be charged (or credited) to accumulated depreciation with the result that depreciation is adjusted over a period of years on an average basis. It should be noted that the latter treatment would not be appropriate for (1) an enterprise (such as an airline) which replaces its fleet on an episodic rather than a continuing basis or (2) an enterprise (such as a car leasing company) where equipment is sold after limited use so that the equipment on hand is both fairly new and carried at amounts closely related to current acquisition cost.

C.1. Deleted by SAB 103

C.2. Deleted by SAB 103

D. Organization And Offering Expenses And Selling Commissions—Limited Partnerships Trading In Commodity Futures

Facts: Partnerships formed for the purpose of engaging in speculative trading in commodity futures contracts sell limited partnership interests to the public and frequently have a general partner who is an affiliate of the partnership's commodity broker or the principal underwriter selling the limited partnership interests. The commodity broker or a subsidiary typically assumes the liability for all or part of the organization and offering expenses and selling commissions in connection with the sale of limited partnership interests. Funds raised from the sale of partnership interests are deposited in a margin account with the commodity broker and are invested in Treasury Bills or similar securities. The arrangement further provides that interest earned on the investments for an initial period is to be retained by the broker until it has been reimbursed for all or a specified portion of the aforementioned expenses and commissions and that thereafter interest earned accrues to the partnership.

In some instances, there may be no reference to reimbursement of the broker for expenses and commissions to be assumed. The arrangements may provide that all interest earned on investments accrues to the partnership but that commissions on commodity transactions paid to the broker are at higher rates for a specified initial period and at lower rates subsequently.

Question 1: Should the partnership recognize a commitment to reimburse the commodity broker for the organization and offering expenses and selling commissions?

Interpretive Response: Yes. A commitment should be recognized by reducing partnership capital and establishing a liability for the estimated amount of expenses and commissions for which the broker is to be reimbursed.

Question 2: Should the interest income retained by the broker for reimbursement of expenses be recognized as income by the partnership?

Interpretive Response: Yes. All the interest income on the margin account investments should be recognized as accruing to the partnership as earned. The portion of income retained by the broker and not actually realized by the partnership in cash should be applied to reduce the liability for the estimated amount of reimbursable expenses and commissions.

Question 3: If the broker retains all of the interest income for a specified period and thereafter it accrues to the partnership, should an equivalent amount of interest income be reflected on the partnership's financial statements during the specified period?

Interpretive Response: Yes. If it appears from the terms of the arrangement that it was the intent of the parties to provide for full or partial reimbursement for the expenses and commissions paid by the broker, then a commitment to reimbursement should be recognized by the partnership and an equivalent amount of interest income should be recognized on the partnership's financial statements as earned.

Question 4: Under the arrangements where commissions on commodity transactions are at a lower rate after a specified period and there is no reference to reimbursement of the broker for expenses and commissions, should recognition be given on the partnership's financial statements to a commitment to reimburse the broker for all or part of the expenses and commissions?

Interpretive Response: If it appears from the terms of the arrangement that the intent of the parties was to provide for full or partial reimbursement of the broker's expenses and commissions, then the estimated commitment should be recognized on the partnership's financial statements. During the specified initial period commissions on commodity transactions should be charged to operations at the lower commission rate with the difference applied to reduce the aforementioned commitment.

E. Accounting for Divestiture of a Subsidiary or Other Business Operation

Facts: Company X transferred certain operations (including several subsidiaries) to a group of former employees who had been responsible for managing those operations. Assets and liabilities with a net book value of approximately $8 million were transferred to a newly formed entity — Company Y — wholly owned by the former employees. The consideration received consisted of $1,000 in cash and interest bearing promissory notes for $10 million, payable in equal annual installments of $1 million each, plus interest, beginning two years from the date of the transaction. The former employees possessed insufficient assets to pay the notes and Company X expected the funds for payments to come exclusively from future operations of the transferred business. Company X remained contingently liable for performance on existing contracts transferred and agreed to guarantee, at its discretion, performance on future contracts entered into by the newly formed entity. Company X also acted as guarantor under a line of credit established by Company Y.

The nature of Company Y's business was such that Company X's guarantees were considered a necessary predicate to obtaining future contracts until such time as Company Y achieved profitable operations and substantial financial independence from Company X.

Question: If deconsolidation of the subsidiaries and business operations is appropriate, can Company X recognize a gain?

Interpretive Response: Before recognizing any gain, Company X should identify all of the elements of the divesture arrangement and allocate the consideration exchanged to each of those elements. In this regard, we believe that Company X would recognize the guarantees at fair value in accordance with FIN 45, *Guarantor's Accounting and Disclosure Requirements for Guarantees, Including Indirect Guarantees of the Indebtedness of Others*; the contingent liability for performance on existing contracts in accordance with Statement 5, *Accounting for Contingencies*; and the promissory notes in accordance with APB 21, *Interest on Receivables and Payables*, and Statements 114, *Accounting by Creditors for Impairment of a Loan*, and 118, *Accounting by Creditors for Impairment of a Loan — Income Recognition and Disclosures*.

F. Accounting Changes Not Retroactively Applied Due To Immateriality

Facts: A registrant is required to adopt an accounting principle by means of restatement of prior periods' financial statements. However, the registrant determines that the accounting change does not have a material effect on prior periods' financial statements and, accordingly, decides not to restate such financial statements.

Question: In these circumstances, is it acceptable to adjust the beginning balance of retained earnings of the period in which the change is made for the cumulative effect of the change on the financial statements of prior periods?

Interpretive Response: No. If prior periods are not restated, the cumulative effect of the change should be included in the statement of income for the period in which the change is made (not to be reported as a cumulative effect adjustment in the manner of APB Opinion 20). Even in cases where the total cumulative effect is not significant, the staff believes that the amount should be reflected in the results of operations for the period in which the change is made. However, if the cumulative effect is material to current operations or to the trend of the reported results of operations, then the individual income statements of the earlier years should be retroactively adjusted.

This position is consistent with the requirements of Statement 5 and Statement 13, which indicate that "the cumulative effect [of the change] on retained earnings at the beginning of the earliest period restated shall be included in determining net income of that period."

G. Transfers Of Nonmonetary Assets By Promoters Or Shareholders

Facts: Nonmonetary assets are exchanged by promoters or shareholders for all or part of a company's common stock just prior to or contemporaneously with a first-time public offering.

Question: Since paragraph 4 of APB Opinion 29 states that Opinion 29 is not applicable to transactions involving the acquisition of nonmonetary assets or services on issuance of the capital stock of an enterprise, what value should be ascribed to the acquired assets by the company?

Interpretive Response: The staff believes that transfers of nonmonetary assets to a company by its promoters or shareholders in exchange for stock prior to or at the time of the company's initial public offering normally should be recorded at the transferors' historical cost basis determined under GAAP.

The staff will not always require that predecessor cost be used to value nonmonetary assets received from an enterprise's promoters or shareholders. However, deviations from this policy have been rare applying generally to situations where the fair value of either the stock issued[3] or assets acquired is objectively measurable and the transferor's stock ownership following the transaction was not so significant that the transferor had retained a substantial indirect interest in the assets as a result of stock ownership in the company.

H. Removed by SAB 112

I. Deleted by SAB 70

J. New Basis of Accounting Required in Certain Circumstances

Facts: Company A (or Company A and related persons) acquired substantially all of the common stock of Company B in one or a series of purchase transactions.

Question 1: Must Company B's financial statements presented in either its own or Company A's subsequent filings with the Commission reflect the new basis of accounting arising from Company A's acquisition of Company B when Company B's separate corporate entity is retained?

Interpretive Response: Yes. The staff believes that purchase transactions that result in an entity becoming substantially wholly owned (as defined in Rule 1-02(aa) of Regulation S-X) establish a new basis of accounting for the purchased assets and liabilities.

When the form of ownership is within the control of the parent, the basis of accounting for purchased assets and liabilities should be the same regardless of whether the entity continues to exist or is merged into the parent's operations. Therefore, Company B's separate financial statements should reflect the new basis of accounting recorded by Company A upon acquisition (*i.e.*, "pushed down" basis).

Question 2: What is the staff's position if Company A acquired less than substantially all of the common stock of Company B or Company B had publicly held debt or preferred stock at the time Company B became wholly owned?

Interpretive Response: The staff recognizes that the existence of outstanding public debt, preferred stock or a significant noncontrolling interest in a subsidiary might impact the parent's ability to control the form of ownership. Although encouraging its use, the staff generally does not insist on the application of push down accounting in these circumstances.

Question 3: Company A borrows funds to acquire substantially all of the common stock of Company B. Company B subsequently files a registration statement in connection with a public offering of its stock or debt.[6] Should Company B's new basis ("push down") financial statements include Company A's debt related to its purchase of Company B?

Interpretive Response: The staff believes that Company A's debt,[7] related interest expense, and allocable debt issue costs should be reflected in Company B's financial statements included in the public offering (or an initial registration under the Exchange Act) if: (1) Company B is to assume the debt of Company A, either presently or in a planned transaction in the future; (2) the proceeds of a debt or equity offering of Company B will be used to retire all or a part of Company A's debt; or (3) Company B guarantees or pledges its assets as collateral for Company A's debt. Other relationships may exist between Company A and Company B, such as the pledge of Company B's

---

[3] Estimating the fair value of the common stock issued, however, is not appropriate when the stock is closely held and/or seldom or ever traded.

[6] The guidance in this SAB should also be considered for Company B's separate financial statements included in its public offering following Company B's spin-off or carve-out from Company A.

[7] The guidance in this SAB should also be considered where Company A has financed the acquisition of Company B through the issuance of mandatory redeemable preferred stock.

stock as collateral for Company A's debt.[8] While in this latter situation, it may be clear that Company B's cash flows will service all or part of Company A's debt, the staff does not insist that the debt be reflected in Company B's financial statements providing there is full and prominent disclosure of the relationship between Companies A and B and the actual or potential cash flow commitment. In this regard, the staff believes that Statements 5 and 57 as well as Interpretation 45 require sufficient disclosure to allow users of Company B's financial statements to fully understand the impact of the relationship on Company B's present and future cash flows. Rule 4-08(e) of Regulation S-X also requires disclosure of restrictions which limit the payment of dividends.

Therefore, the staff believes that the equity section of Company B's balance sheet and any pro forma financial information and capitalization tables should clearly disclose that this arrangement exists.[9] Regardless of whether the debt is reflected in Company B's financial statements, the notes to Company B's financial statements should generally disclose, at a minimum: (1) the relationship between Company A and Company B; (2) a description of any arrangements that result in Company B's guarantee, pledge of assets[10] or stock, etc. that provides security for Company A's debt; (3) the extent (in the aggregate and for each of the five years subsequent to the date of the latest balance sheet presented) to which Company A is dependent on Company B's cash flows to service its debt and the method by which this will occur; and (4) the impact of such cash flows on Company B's ability to pay dividends or other amounts to holders of its securities. Additionally, the staff believes Company B's Management's Discussion and Analysis of Financial Condition and Results of Operations should discuss any material impact of its servicing of Company A's debt on its own liquidity pursuant to Item 303(a)(1) of Regulation S-K.

K. Deleted by SAB 95

L. LIFO Inventory Practices

Facts: On November 30, 1984, AcSEC and its Task Force on LIFO Inventory Problems (task force) issued a paper, "Identification and Discussion of Certain Financial Accounting and Reporting Issues Concerning LIFO Inventories." This paper identifies and discusses certain financial accounting and reporting issues related to the last-in, first-out (LIFO) inventory method for which authoritative accounting literature presently provides no definitive guidance. For some issues, the task force's advisory conclusions recommend changes in current practice to narrow the diversity which the task force believes exists. For other issues, the task force's advisory conclusions recommend that current practice should be continued for financial reporting purposes and that additional accounting guidance is unnecessary. Except as otherwise noted in the paper, AcSEC generally supports the task force's advisory conclusions. As stated in the issues paper, "Issues papers of the AICPA's accounting standards division are developed primarily to identify financial accounting and reporting issues the division believes need to be addressed or clarified by the Financial Accounting Standards Board." On February 6, 1985, the FASB decided not to add to its agenda a narrow project on the subject of LIFO inventory practices.

Question 1: What is the SEC staff's position on the issues paper?

Interpretive Response: In the absence of existing authoritative literature on LIFO accounting, the staff believes that registrants and their independent accountants should look to the paper for guidance in determining what constitutes acceptable LIFO accounting practice.[11] In this connection, the staff considers the paper to be an accumulation of existing acceptable LIFO accounting practices which does not establish any new standards and does not diverge from GAAP.

The staff also believes that the advisory conclusions recommended in the issues paper are generally consistent with conclusions previously expressed by the Commission, such as:

1. Pooling—paragraph 4-6 of the paper discusses LIFO inventory pooling and concludes "establishing separate pools with the principal objective of facilitating inventory liquidations is unacceptable." In Accounting and Auditing Enforcement Release 35, August 13, 1984, the Commission stated that it believes that the Company improperly realigned its LIFO pools in such a way as to maximize the likelihood and magnitude of LIFO liquidations and thus, overstated net income.

---

[8] The staff does not believe Company B's financial statements must reflect the debt in this situation because in the event of default on the debt by Company A, the debt holder(s) would only be entitled to Company B's stock held by Company A. Other equity or debt holders of Company B would retain their priority with respect to the net assets of Company B.

[9] For example, the staff has noted that certain registrants have indicated on the face of such financial statements (as part of the stockholder's equity section) the actual or potential financing arrangement and the registrant's intent to pay dividends to satisfy its parent's debt service requirements. The staff believes such disclosures are useful to highlight the existence of arrangements that could result in the use of Company B's cash to service Company A's debt.

[10] A material asset pledge should be clearly indicated on the face of the balance sheet. For example, if all or substantially all of the assets are pledged, the "assets" and "total assets" captions should include parenthetically: "pledged for parent company debt — See Note X."

[11] In ASR 293 (July 2, 1981) see Financial Reporting Codification § 205, the Commission expressed its concerns about the inappropriate use of Internal Revenue Service (IRS) practices for financial statement preparation. Because the IRS amended its regulations concerning the LIFO conformity rule on January 13, 1981, allowing companies to apply LIFO differently for financial reporting purposes than for tax purposes, the Commission strongly encouraged registrants and their independent accountants to examine their financial reporting LIFO practices. In that release, the Commission acknowledged the "task force which has been established by AcSEC to accumulate information about [LIFO]application problems" and noted that "This type of effort, in addition to self-examination [of LIFO practices] by individual registrants, is appropriate ..."

2. New Items-paragraph 4-27 of the paper discusses determination of the cost of new items and concludes "if the double extension or an index technique is used, the objective of LIFO is achieved by reconstructing the base year cost of new items added to existing pools." In ASR 293, the Commission stated that when the effects of inflation on the cost of new products are measured by making a comparison with current cost as the base-year cost, rather than a reconstructed base-year cost, income is improperly increased.

Question 2: If a registrant utilizes a LIFO practice other than one recommended by an advisory conclusion in the issues paper, must the registrant change its practice to one specified in the paper?

Interpretive Response: Now that the issues paper is available, the staff believes that a registrant and its independent accountants should re-examine previously adopted LIFO practices and compare them to the recommendations in the paper. In the event that the registrant and its independent accountants conclude that the registrant's LIFO practices are preferable in the circumstances, they should be prepared to justify their position in the event that a question is raised by the staff.

Question 3: If a registrant elects to change its LIFO practices to be consistent with the guidance in the issues paper and discloses such changes in accordance with APB Opinion 20 will the registrant be requested by the staff to explain its past practices and its justification for those practices?

Interpretive Response: The staff does not expect to routinely raise questions about changes in LIFO practices which are made to make a company's accounting consistent with the recommendations in the issues paper.

M. Other Than Temporary Impairment Of Certain Investments In Debt And Equity Securities

Facts: FASB Staff Position No. FAS 115-2 and FAS 124-2, *Recognition and Presentation of Other-Than-Temporary Impairments* ("FSP 115-2") does not define the phrase "other than temporary" for available-for-sale equity securities. For its available-for-sale equity securities, Company A has interpreted "other than temporary" to mean permanent impairment. Therefore, because Company A's management has not been able to determine that its investment in Company B's equity securities is permanently impaired, no realized loss has been recognized even though the market price of Company B's equity securities is currently less than one-third of Company A's average acquisition price.

Question: For equity securities classified as available-for-sale, does the staff believe that the phrase "other

than temporary" should be interpreted to mean "permanent"?

Interpretive Response: No. The staff believes that the FASB consciously chose the phrase "other than temporary" because it did not intend that the test be "permanent impairment," as has been used elsewhere in accounting practice.[1]

The value of investments in equity securities classified as available-for-sale may decline for various reasons. The market price may be affected by general market conditions which reflect prospects for the economy as a whole or by specific information pertaining to an industry or an individual company. Such declines require further investigation by management. Acting upon the premise that a write-down may be required, management should consider all available evidence to evaluate the realizable value of its investment in equity securities classified as available-for-sale.

There are numerous factors to be considered in such an evaluation and their relative significance will vary from case to case. The staff believes that the following are only a few examples of the factors which, individually or in combination, indicate that a decline in value of an equity security classified as available-for-sale is other than temporary and that a write-down of the carrying value is required:

- The length of the time and the extent to which the market value has been less than cost;

- The financial condition and near-term prospects of the issuer, including any specific events which may influence the operations of the issuer such as changes in technology that may impair the earnings potential of the investment or the discontinuance of a segment of the business that may affect the future earnings potential; or

- The intent and ability of the holder to retain its investment in the issuer for a period of time sufficient to allow for any anticipated recovery in market value.

Unless evidence exists to support a realizable value equal to or greater than the carrying value of the investment in equity securities classified as available-for-sale, a write-down to fair value accounted for as a realized loss should be recorded. Such loss should be recognized in the determination of net income of the period in which it occurs and the written down value of the investment in the company becomes the new cost basis of the investment.

N. Discounting By Property-Casualty Insurance Companies

Facts: A registrant which is an insurance company discounts certain unpaid claims liabilities related to short-duration[13] insurance contracts for purposes of reporting to state regulatory authorities, using dis-

---

[1] FASB Staff Position No. FAS 115-1 and FAS 124-1, *The Meaning of Other-Than-Temporary Impairment and Its Application to Certain Investments* refers to this SAB for a discussion of considerations applicable to a determination as to whether a decline in market value below cost of an equity security, at a particular point in time, is other than temporary.

[13] The term "short-duration" refers to the period of coverage (see Statement 60, paragraph 7), not the period that the liabilities are expected to be outstanding.

count rates permitted or prescribed by those authorities ("statutory rates") which approximate 3 1/2 percent. The registrant follows the same practice in preparing its financial statements in accordance with GAAP. It proposes to change for GAAP purposes, to using a discount rate related to the historical yield on its investment portfolio ("investment related rate") which is represented to approximate 7 percent, and to account for the change as a change in accounting estimate, applying the investment related rate to claims settled in the current and subsequent years while the statutory rate would continue to be applied to claims settled in all prior years.

Question 1: What is the staff's position with respect to discounting claims liabilities related to short-duration insurance contracts?

Interpretive Response: The staff is aware of efforts by the accounting profession to assess the circumstances under which discounting may be appropriate in financial statements. Pending authoritative guidance resulting from those efforts however, the staff will raise no objection if a registrant follows a policy for GAAP reporting purposes of:

• Discounting liabilities for unpaid claims and claim adjustment expenses at the same rates that it uses for reporting to state regulatory authorities with respect to the same claims liabilities, or

• Discounting liabilities with respect to settled claims under the following circumstances:

• the payment pattern and ultimate cost are fixed and determinable on an individual claim basis, and

• the discount rate used is reasonable on the facts and circumstances applicable to the registrant at the time the claims are settled.

Question 2: Does the staff agree with the registrant's proposal that the change from a statutory rate to an investment related rate be accounted for as a change in accounting estimate?

Interpretive Response: No. The staff believes that such a change involves a change in the method of applying an accounting principle, i.e., the method of selecting the discount rate was changed. The staff therefore believes that the registrant should reflect the cumulative effect of the change in accounting by applying the new selection method retroactively to liabilities for claims settled in all prior years, in accordance with the requirements of APB Opinion 20. Initial adoption of discounting for GAAP purposes would be treated similarly. In either case, in addition to the disclosures required by APB Opinion 20 concerning the change in accounting principle, a preferability letter from the registrant's independent accountant is required.

O. Research And Development Arrangements

Facts: Statement 68 paragraph 7 states that conditions other than a written agreement may exist which create a presumption that the enterprise will repay the funds provided by other parties under a research and development arrangement. Paragraph 8(c) lists as one of those conditions the existence of a "significant related party relationship" between the enterprise and the parties funding the research and development.

Question 1: What does the staff consider a "significant related party relationship" as that term is used in paragraph 8(c) of Statement 68?

Interpretive Response: The staff believes that a significant related party relationship exists when 10 percent or more of the entity providing the funds is owned by related parties.[14] In unusual circumstances, the staff may also question the appropriateness of treating a research and development arrangement as a contract to perform service for others at the less than 10 percent level. In reviewing these matters the staff will consider, among other factors, the percentage of the funding entity owned by the related parties in relationship to their ownership in and degree of influence or control over the enterprise receiving the funds.

Question 2: Paragraph 7 of Statement 68 states that the presumption of repayment "can be overcome only by substantial evidence to the contrary." Can the presumption be overcome by evidence that the funding parties were assuming the risk of the research and development activities since they could not reasonably expect the enterprise to have resources to repay the funds based on its current and projected future financial condition?

Interpretive Response: No. Paragraph 5 of Statement 68 specifically indicates that the enterprise "may settle the liability by paying cash, by issuing securities, or by some other means." While the enterprise may not be in a position to pay cash or issue debt, repayment could be accomplished through the issuance of stock or various other means. Therefore, an apparent or projected inability to repay the funds with cash (or debt which would later be paid with cash) does not necessarily demonstrate that the funding parties were accepting the entire risks of the activities.

P. Restructuring Charges

1. Deleted by SAB 103

2. Deleted by SAB 103

3. *Income statement presentation of restructuring charges*

Facts: Restructuring charges often do not relate to a separate component of the entity, and, as such, they would not qualify for presentation as losses on the disposal of a discontinued operation. Additionally, since the charges are not both unusual and infrequent[15] they are not presented in the income statement as extraordinary items.

Question 1: May such restructuring charges be presented in the income statement as a separate caption after income from continuing operations before

---

[14] Related parties as used herein are as defined in paragraph 24 of Statement 57.

[15] See APB Opinion 30, paragraph 20.

income taxes (i.e., preceding income taxes and/or discontinued operations)?

Interpretive Response: No. Paragraph 26 of APB Opinion 30 states that items that do not meet the criteria for classification as an extraordinary item should be reported as a component of income from continuing operations.[16] Neither Opinion 30 nor Rule 5-03 of Regulation S-X contemplate a category in between continuing and discontinued operations. Accordingly, the staff believes that restructuring charges should be presented as a component of income from continuing operations, separately disclosed if material. Furthermore, the staff believes that a separately presented restructuring charge should not be preceded by a sub-total representing "income from continuing operations before restructuring charge" (whether or not it is so captioned). Such a presentation would be inconsistent with the intent of Opinion 30.

Question 2: Some registrants utilize a classified or "two-step" income statement format (i.e., one which presents operating revenues, expenses and income followed by other income and expense items). May a charge which relates to assets or activities for which the associated revenues and expenses have historically been included in operating income be presented as an item of "other expense" in such an income statement?

Interpretive Response: No. The staff believes that the proper classification of a restructuring charge depends on the nature of the charge and the assets and operations to which it relates. Therefore, charges which relate to activities for which the revenues and expenses have historically been included in operating income should generally be classified as an operating expense, separately disclosed if material. Furthermore, when a restructuring charge is classified as an operating expense, the staff believes that it is generally inappropriate to present a preceding subtotal captioned or representing operating income before restructuring charges. Such an amount does not represent a measurement of operating results under GAAP.

Conversely, charges relating to activities previously included under "other income and expenses" should be similarly classified, also separately disclosed if material.

Question 3: Is it permissible to disclose the effect on net income and earnings per share of such a restructuring charge?

Interpretive Response: Discussions in MD&A and elsewhere which quantify the effects of unusual or infrequent items on net income and earnings per share are beneficial to a reader's understanding of the financial statements and are therefore acceptable.

MD&A also should discuss the events and decisions which gave rise to the restructuring, the nature of the charge and the expected impact of the restructuring on future results of operations, liquidity and sources and uses of capital resources.

4. *Disclosures*

Beginning with the period in which the exit plan is initiated, Statement 146 requires disclosure, in *all* periods, *including interim* periods, until the exit plan is completed, of the following:

a. A description of the exit or disposal activity, including the facts and circumstances leading to the expected activity and the expected completion date

b. For each major type of cost associated with the activity (for example, one-time termination benefits, contract termination costs, and other associated costs):

(1) The total amount expected to be incurred in connection with the activity, the amount incurred in the period, and the cumulative amount incurred to date

(2) A reconciliation of the beginning and ending liability balances showing separately the changes during the period attributable to costs incurred and charged to expense, costs paid or otherwise settled, and any adjustments to the liability with an explanation of the reason(s) therefor

c. The line item(s) in the income statement or the statement of activities in which the costs in (b) above are aggregated

d. For each reportable segment, the total amount of costs expected to be incurred in connection with the activity, the amount incurred in the period, and the cumulative amount incurred to date, net of any adjustments to the liability with an explanation of the reason(s) therefor

e. If a liability for a cost associated with the activity is not recognized because fair value cannot be reasonably estimated, that fact and the reasons therefor.

Question: What specific disclosures about restructuring charges has the staff requested to fulfill the disclosure requirements of Statement 146 and MD&A?

Interpretive Response: The staff often has requested greater disaggregation and more precise labeling when exit and involuntary termination costs are grouped in a note or income statement line item with items unrelated to the exit plan. For the reader's understanding, the staff has requested that discretionary, or decision-dependent, costs of a period, such as exit costs, be disclosed and explained in MD&A separately. Also to improve transparency, the staff has requested disclosure of the nature and amounts of additional types of exit costs and other types of restructuring charges[17] that appear quantitatively or

---

[16] Paragraph 26 of APB Opinion 30 further provides that such items should not be reported on the income statement net of income taxes or in any manner that implies that they are similar to extraordinary items.

[17] Examples of common components of exit costs and other types of restructuring charges which should be considered for separate disclosure include, but are not limited to, involuntary employee terminations and related costs, changes in valuation of current assets such as inventory writedowns, long term asset

qualitatively material, and requested that losses relating to asset impairments be identified separately from charges based on estimates of future cash expenditures.

The staff frequently reminds registrants that in periods subsequent to the initiation date that material changes and activity in the liability balances of each significant type of exit cost and involuntary employee termination benefits[18] (either as a result of expenditures or changes in/reversals of estimates or the fair value of the liability) should be disclosed in the footnotes to the interim and annual financial statements and discussed in MD&A. In the event a company recognized liabilities for exit costs and involuntary employee termination benefits relating to multiple exit plans, the staff believes presentation of separate information for each individual exit plan that has a material effect on the balance sheet, results of operations or cash flows generally is appropriate.

For material exit or involuntary employee termination costs related to an acquired business, the staff has requested disclosure in either MD&A or the financial statements of:

1. When the registrant began formulating exit plans for which accrual may be necessary,

2. The types and amounts of liabilities recognized for exit costs and involuntary employee termination benefits and included in the acquisition cost allocation, and

3. Any unresolved contingencies or purchase price allocation issues and the types of additional liabilities that may result in an adjustment of the acquisition cost allocation.

The staff has noted that the economic or other events that cause a registrant to consider and/or adopt an exit plan or that impair the carrying amount of assets, generally occur over time. Accordingly, the staff believes that as those events and the resulting trends and uncertainties evolve, they often will meet the requirement for disclosure pursuant to the Commission's MD&A rules prior to the period in which the exit costs and liabilities are recorded pursuant to GAAP. Whether or not currently recognizable in the financial statements, material exit or involuntary termination costs that affect a known trend, demand, commitment, event, or uncertainty to management, should be disclosed in MD&A. The staff believes that MD&A should include discussion of the events and decisions which gave rise to the exit costs and exit plan, and the likely effects of management's plans on financial position, future operating results and liquidity unless it is determined that a material effect is not reasonably likely to occur. Registrants should identify the periods in which material cash outlays are anticipated and the expected source of their funding. Regis-

trants should also discuss material revisions to exit plans, exit costs, or the timing of the plan's execution, including the nature and reasons for the revisions.

The staff believes that the expected effects on future earnings and cash flows resulting from the exit plan (for example, reduced depreciation, reduced employee expense, etc.) should be quantified and disclosed, along with the initial period in which those effects are expected to be realized. This includes whether the cost savings are expected to be offset by anticipated increases in other expenses or reduced revenues. This discussion should clearly identify the income statement line items to be impacted (for example, cost of sales; marketing; selling, general and administrative expenses; etc.). In later periods if actual savings anticipated by the exit plan are not achieved as expected or are achieved in periods other than as expected, MD&A should discuss that outcome, its reasons, and its likely effects on future operating results and liquidity.

The staff often finds that, because of the discretionary nature of exit plans and the components thereof, presenting and analyzing material exit and involuntary termination charges in tabular form, with the related liability balances and activity (e.g., beginning balance, new charges, cash payments, other adjustments with explanations, and ending balances) from balance sheet date to balance sheet date, is necessary to explain fully the components and effects of significant restructuring charges. The staff believes that such a tabular analysis aids a financial statement user's ability to disaggregate the restructuring charge by income statement line item in which the costs would have otherwise been recognized, absent the restructuring plan, (for example, cost of sales; selling, general, and administrative; etc.).

Q. Increasing Rate Preferred Stock

Facts: A registrant issues Class A and Class B nonredeemable preferred stock[19] on 1/1/×1. Class A, by its terms, will pay no dividends during the years 20×1 through 20×3. Class B, by its terms, will pay dividends at annual rates of $2, $4 and $6 per share in the years 20×1, 20×2 and 20×3, respectively. Beginning in the year 20×4 and thereafter as long as they remain outstanding, each instrument will pay dividends at an annual rate of $8 per share. In all periods, the scheduled dividends are cumulative.

At the time of issuance, eight percent per annum was considered to be a market rate for dividend yield on Class A, given its characteristics other than scheduled cash dividend entitlements (voting rights, liquidation preference, etc.), as well as the registrant's financial condition and future economic prospects. Thus, the registrant could have expected to receive proceeds of approximately $100 per share for Class A

(Footnote Continued)

disposals, adjustments for warranties and product returns, leasehold termination payments, and other facility exit costs, among others.

[18] The staff would expect similar disclosures for employee termination benefits whether those costs have been recognized pursuant to Statement 88, 112, or 146.

[19] "Nonredeemable" preferred stock, as used in this SAB, refers to preferred stocks which are not redeemable or are redeemable only at the option of the issuer.

if the dividend rate of $8 per share (the "perpetual dividend") had been in effect at date of issuance. In consideration of the dividend payment terms, however, Class A was issued for proceeds of $79 3/8 per share. The difference, $20 5/8, approximated the value of the absence of $8 per share dividends annually for three years, discounted at 8%.

The issuance price of Class B shares was determined by a similar approach, based on the terms and characteristics of the Class B shares.

Question 1: How should preferred stocks of this general type (referred to as "increasing rate preferred stocks") be reported in the balance sheet?

Interpretive Response: As is normally the case with other types of securities, increasing rate preferred stock should be recorded initially at its fair value on date of issuance. Thereafter, the carrying amount should be increased periodically as discussed in the Interpretive Response to Question 2.

Question 2: Is it acceptable to recognize the dividend costs of increasing rate preferred stocks according to their stated dividend schedules?

Interpretive Response: No. The staff believes that when consideration received for preferred stocks reflects expectations of future dividend streams, as is normally the case with cumulative preferred stocks, any discount due to an absence of dividends (as with Class A) or gradually increasing dividends (as with Class B) for an initial period represents prepaid, unstated dividend cost.[20] Recognizing the dividend cost of these instruments according to their stated dividend schedules would report Class A as being cost-free, and would report the cost of Class B at less than its effective cost, from the standpoint of common stock interests (i.e., for purposes of computing income applicable to common stock and earnings per common share) during the years 20×1 through 20×3.

Accordingly, the staff believes that discounts on increasing rate preferred stock should be amortized over the period(s) preceding commencement of the perpetual dividend, by charging imputed dividend cost against retained earnings and increasing the carrying amount of the preferred stock by a corresponding amount. The discount at time of issuance should be computed as the present value of the difference between (a) dividends that will be payable, if any, in the period(s) preceding commencement of the perpetual dividend; and (b) the perpetual dividend amount for a corresponding number of periods; dis-

counted at a market rate for dividend yield on preferred stocks that are comparable (other than with respect to dividend payment schedules) from an investment standpoint. The amortization in each period should be the amount which, together with any stated dividend for the period (ignoring fluctuations in stated dividend amounts that might result from variable rates,[21] results in a constant rate of effective cost vis-a-vis the carrying amount of the preferred stock (the market rate that was used to compute the discount).

Simplified (ignoring quarterly calculations) application of this accounting to the Class A preferred stock described in the "Facts" section of this bulletin would produce the following results on a per share basis:

Carrying amount of preferred stock

	Beginning of Year (BOY)	Imputed Dividend (8% of Carrying Amount at BOY)	End of year
Year 20×1	$79.38	6.35	85.73
Year 20×2	85.73	6.86	92.59
Year 20×3	92.59	7.41	100.00

During 20×4 and thereafter, the stated dividend of $8 measured against the carrying amount of $100[22] would reflect dividend cost of 8%, the market rate at time of issuance.

The staff believes that existing authoritative literature, while not explicitly addressing increasing rate preferred stocks, implicitly calls for the accounting described in this bulletin.

The pervasive, fundamental principle of accrual accounting would, in the staff's view, preclude registrants from recognizing the dividend cost on the basis of whatever cash payment schedule might be arranged. Furthermore, recognition of the effective cost of unstated rights and privileges is well-established in accounting, and is specifically called for by APB Opinion 21 and Topic 3.C of this codification for unstated interest costs of debt capital and unstated dividend costs of redeemable preferred stock capital, respectively. The staff believes that the requirement to recognize the effective periodic cost of capital applies also to nonredeemable preferred stocks because, for that purpose, the distinction between debt capital and preferred equity capital (whether redeemable[23] or

---

[20] As described in the "Facts" section of this issue, a registrant would receive less in proceeds for a preferred stock, if the stock were to pay less than its perpetual dividend for some initial period(s), than if it were to pay the perpetual dividend from date of issuance. The staff views the discount on increasing rate preferred stock as equivalent to a prepayment of dividends by the issuer, as though the issuer had concurrently (a) issued the stock with the perpetual dividend being payable from date of issuance, and (b) returned to the investor a portion of the proceeds representing the present value of certain future dividend entitlements which the investor agreed to forgo.

[21] See Question 3 regarding variable increasing rate preferred stocks.

[22] It should be noted that the $100 per share amount used in this issue is for illustrative purposes, and is not intended to imply that application of this issue will necessarily result in the carrying amount of a nonredeemable preferred stock being accreted to its par value, stated value, voluntary redemption value or involuntary liquidation value.

[23] Application of the interest method with respect to redeemable preferred stocks pursuant to Topic 3.C results in accounting consistent with the provisions of this bulletin irrespective of whether the redeemable preferred stocks have constant or increasing stated dividend rates. The interest method, as described in APB Opinion 21, produces a constant effective periodic rate of cost that is comprised of amortization of discount as well as the stated cost in each period.

nonredeemable) is irrelevant from the standpoint of common stock interests.

Question 3: Would the accounting for discounts on increasing rate preferred stock be affected by variable stated dividend rates?

Interpretive Response: No. If stated dividends on an increasing rate preferred stock are variable, computations of initial discount and subsequent amortization should be based on the value of the applicable index at date of issuance and should not be affected by subsequent changes in the index.

For example, assume that a preferred stock issued $1/1/\times1$ is scheduled to pay dividends at annual rates, applied to the stock's par value, equal to 20% of the actual (fluctuating) market yield on a particular Treasury security in 20×1 and 20×2, and 90% of the fluctuating market yield in 20X3 and thereafter. The discount would be computed as the present value of a two-year dividend stream equal to 70% (90% less 20%) of the $1/1/\times1$ Treasury security yield, annually, on the stock's par value. The discount would be amortized in years 20×1 and 20×2 so that, together with 20% of the $1/1/\times1$ Treasury yield on the stock's par value, a constant rate of cost vis-a-vis the stock's carrying amount would result. Changes in the Treasury security yield during 20×1 and 20×2 would, of course, cause the rate of total reported preferred dividend cost (amortization of discount plus cash dividends) in those years to be more or less than the rate indicated by discount amortization plus 20% of the $1/1/\times1$ Treasury security yield. However, the fluctuations would be due solely to the impact of changes in the index on the stated dividends for those periods.

Question 4: Will the staff expect retroactive changes by registrants to comply with the accounting described in this bulletin?

Interpretive Response: All registrants will be expected to follow the accounting described in this bulletin for increasing rate preferred stocks issued after December 4, 1986.[24] Registrants that have not followed this accounting for increasing rate preferred stocks issued before that date were encouraged to retroactively change their accounting for those preferred stocks in the financial statements next filed with the Commission. The staff did not object if registrants did not make retroactive changes for those preferred stocks, provided that all presentations of and discussions regarding income applicable to common stock and earnings per share in future filings and shareholders' reports are accompanied by equally prominent supplemental disclosures (on the face of the income statement, in presentations of selected financial data, in MD&A, etc.) of the impact of not changing their accounting and an explanation of such impact (e.g., that dividend cost has been recognized on a cash basis).

R. Deleted by SAB 103

S. Quasi-Reorganization

Facts: As a consequence of significant operating losses and/or recent write-downs of property, plant and equipment, a company's financial statements reflect an accumulated deficit. The company desires to eliminate the deficit by reclassifying amounts from paid-in-capital. In addition, the company anticipates adopting a discretionary change in accounting principles[25] that will be recorded as a cumulative-effect type of accounting change. The recording of the cumulative effect will have the result of increasing the company's retained earnings.

Question 1: May the company reclassify its capital accounts to eliminate the accumulated deficit without satisfying all of the conditions enumerated in Section 210[26] of the Codification of Financial Reporting Policies for a quasi-reorganization?

Interpretive Response: No. The staff believes a deficit reclassification of any nature is considered to be a quasi-reorganization. As such, a company may not reclassify or eliminate a deficit in retained earnings unless all requisite conditions set forth in Section 210[27] for a quasi-reorganization are satisfied.[28]

Question 2: Must the company implement the discretionary change in accounting principle simultaneously with the quasi-reorganization or may it adopt the change after the quasi-reorganization has been effected?

Interpretive Response: The staff has taken the position that the company should adopt the anticipated accounting change prior to or as an integral part of the quasi-reorganization. Any such accounting change should be effected by following GAAP with respect to the change.[29]

Chapter 7A of ARB 43 indicates that, following a quasi-reorganization, a "company's accounting should be substantially similar to that appropriate for a new

---

[24] The staff first publicly expressed its view as to the appropriate accounting at the December 3-4, 1986 meeting of the EITF.

[25] Discretionary accounting changes require the filing of a preferability letter by the registrant's independent accountant pursuant to Item 601 of Regulation S-K and Rule 10-01(b)(6) of Regulation S-X, respectively.

[26] ASR 25.

[27] Section 210 (ASR 25) indicates the following conditions under which a quasi-reorganization can be effected without the creation of a new corporate entity and without the intervention of formal court proceedings:

1. Earned surplus, as of the date selected, is exhausted;

2. Upon consummation of the quasi-reorganization, no deficit exists in any surplus account;

3. The entire procedure is made known to all persons entitled to vote on matters of general corporate policy and the appropriate consents to the particular transactions are obtained in advance in accordance with the applicable laws and charter provisions;

4. The procedure accomplishes, with respect to the accounts, substantially what might be accomplished in a reorganization by legal proceedings - namely, the restatement of assets in terms of present considerations as well as appropriate modifications of capital and capital surplus, in order to obviate, so far as possible, the necessity of future reorganization of like nature.

[28] In addition, ARB 43, Chapter 7A, outlines procedures that must be followed in connection with and after a quasi-reorganization.

[29] Opinion 20 provides accounting principles to be followed when adopting accounting changes. In addition, many newly-issued accounting pronouncements provide specific guidance to be followed when adopting the accounting specified in such pronouncements.

company." The staff believes that implicit in this "fresh-start" concept is the need for the company's accounting principles in place at the time of the quasi-reorganization to be those planned to be used following the reorganization to avoid a misstatement of earnings and retained earnings after the reorganization.[30] Chapter 7A of ARB 43 states, in part, ". . . in general, assets should be carried forward as of the date of the readjustment at fair and not unduly conservative amounts, **determined with due regard for the accounting to be employed by the Company thereafter.**" (emphasis added)

In addition, the staff believes that adopting a discretionary change in accounting principle that will be reflected in the financial statements within 12 months following the consummation of a quasi-reorganization leads to a presumption that the accounting change was contemplated at the time of the quasi-reorganization.[31]

Question 3: In connection with a quasi-reorganization, may there be a write-up of net assets?

Interpretive Response: No. The staff believes that increases in the recorded values of specific assets (or reductions in liabilities) to fair value are appropriate providing such adjustments are factually supportable, however, the amount of such increases are limited to offsetting adjustments to reflect decreases in other assets (or increases in liabilities) to reflect their new fair value. In other words, a quasi-reorganization should not result in a write-up of net assets of the registrant.

Question 4: The interpretive response to question 1 indicates that the staff believes that a deficit reclassification of any nature is considered to be a quasi-reorganization, and accordingly, must satisfy all the conditions of Section 210.[32] Assume a company has satisfied all the requisite conditions of Section 210,

and has eliminated a deficit in retained earnings by a concurrent reduction in paid-in capital, but did not need to restate assets and liabilities by a charge to capital because assets and liabilities were already stated at fair values. How should the company reflect the tax benefits of operating loss or tax credit carryforwards for financial reporting purposes that existed as of the date of the quasi-reorganization when such tax benefits are subsequently recognized for financial reporting purposes?

Interpretive Response: The staff believes Statement 109 requires that any subsequently recognized tax benefits of operating loss or tax credit carryforwards that existed as of the date of a quasi-reorganization be reported as a direct addition to paid-in capital. The staff believes that this position is consistent with the "new company" or "fresh-start" concept embodied in Section 210,[33] and in existing accounting literature regarding quasi-reorganizations, and with the FASB staff's justification for such a position when they stated that a "new enterprise would not have tax benefits attributable to operating losses or tax credits that arose prior to its organization date.[34]

The FASB recognized that a practice existed of recording deficit elimination type quasi-reorganizations without evaluating the concurrent need to restate assets and liabilities to fair values, and provided guidance on accounting for the tax benefits of carryforward items subsequent to such an event.[35] This practice and accounting is not permitted by Section 210, and accordingly, is not appropriate for registrants. The staff believes that all registrants that comply with the requirements of Section 210 in effecting a quasi-reorganization should apply the accounting required by the first sentence of paragraph 39 of Statement 109 for the tax benefits of tax carryforward items.[36] Therefore, even though the only effect of a quasi-reorganization is the elimination of a deficit in

---

[30] Certain newly-issued accounting standards do not require adoption until some future date. The staff believes, however, that if the registrant intends or is required to adopt those standards within 12 months following the quasi-reorganization, the registrant should adopt those standards prior to or as an integral part of the quasi-reorganization. Further, registrants should consider early adoption of standards with effective dates more than 12 months subsequent to a quasi-reorganization.

[31] Certain accounting changes require restatement of prior financial statements. The staff believes that if a quasi-reorganization had been recorded in a restated period, the effects of the accounting change on quasi-reorganization adjustments should also be restated to properly reflect the quasi-reorganization in the restated financial statements.

[32] See footnote 3.

[33] Section 210 (ASR 25) discusses the "conditions under which a quasi-reorganization has come to be applied in accounting to the corporate procedures in the course of which a company, without creation of new corporate entity and without intervention of formal court proceedings, is enabled to eliminate a deficit whether resulting from operations or recognition of other losses or both and to establish a new earned surplus account for the accumulation of earnings subsequent to the date selected as the effective date of the quasi-reorganization." It further indicates that "it is implicit in a procedure of this kind that it is not to be employed recurrently, **but only under circumstances which would justify an actual reorganization or formation of a new corporation**, particularly if the sole purpose of the quasi-reorganization is the elimination of a deficit in earned surplus resulting from operating losses." (emphasis added)

[34] FASB Special Report: A Guide to Implementation of Statement 109 on Accounting for Income Taxes: Questions and Answers answer 9 states in part: "ARB 43, Chapter 7, 'Capital Accounts,' states that after a quasi-reorganization, the enterprise's accounting should be substantially similar to that appropriate for a new enterprise. As such, any subsequently recognized tax benefit of an operating loss or tax credit carryforward that existed at the date of a quasi-reorganization should not be included in the determination of income of the 'new' enterprise, regardless of whether losses that gave rise to an operating loss carryforward were charged to income prior to the quasi-reorganization or directly to contributed capital as part of the quasi-reorganization. A new enterprise would not have tax benefits attributable to operating losses or tax credits that arose prior to its organization date."

[35] Statement 109, paragraph 39, states, in part: "The only exception is for enterprises that have previously both adopted Statement 96 and effected a quasi-reorganization that involves only the elimination of a deficit in retained earnings by a concurrent reduction in contributed capital prior to adopting this Statement. For those enterprises, subsequent recognition of the tax benefit of prior deductible temporary differences and carryforwards is included in income and reported as required by paragraph 37 . . . and then reclassified from retained earnings to contributed capital . . . " Also, see Footnote 10.

[36] The first sentence of paragraph 39 of Statement 109 states: "[t]he tax benefit of deductible temporary differences and carryforwards as of the date of a quasi reorganization as defined and contemplated in ARB 43, Chapter 7, ordinarily are reported as a direct addition to contributed capital if the tax benefits are recognized in subsequent years."

retained earnings because assets and liabilities are already stated at fair values and the revaluation of assets and liabilities is unnecessary (or a write-up of net assets is prohibited as indicated in the interpretive response to question 3 above), subsequently recognized tax benefits of operating loss or tax credit carryforward items should be recorded as a direct addition to paid-in capital.

Question 5: If a company had previously recorded a quasi-reorganization that only resulted in the elimination of a deficit in retained earnings, may the company reverse such entry and "undo" its quasi-reorganization?

Interpretive Response: No. The staff believes Opinion 20 would preclude such a change in accounting. It states: "a method of accounting that was previously adopted for a type of transaction or event which is being terminated **or which was a single, nonrecurring event in the past should not be changed**." (emphasis added.)[37]

T. Accounting For Expenses Or Liabilities Paid By Principal Stockholder(s)

Facts: Company X was a defendant in litigation for which the company had not recorded a liability in accordance with Statement 5. A principal stockholder[38] of the company transfers a portion of his shares to the plaintiff to settle such litigation. If the company had settled the litigation directly, the company would have recorded the settlement as an expense.

Question: Must the settlement be reflected as an expense in the company's financial statements, and if so, how?

Interpretive Response: Yes. The value of the shares transferred should be reflected as an expense in the company's financial statements with a corresponding credit to contributed (paid-in) capital.

The staff believes that such a transaction is similar to those described in paragraph 11 of Statement of Financial Accounting Standards Statement No. 123 (revised 2004), *Share-Based Payment* (Statement 123R), which states that "share-based payments awarded to an employee of the reporting entity by a related party or other holder of an economic interest[39] in the entity as compensation for services provided to the entity are share-based payment transactions to be accounted for under this Statement unless the transfer

is clearly for a purpose other than compensation for services to the reporting entity." As explained in paragraph 11 of Statement 123R, the substance of such a transaction is that the economic interest holder makes a capital contribution to the reporting entity, and the reporting entity makes a share-based payment to its employee in exchange for services rendered.

The staff believes that the problem of separating the benefit to the principal stockholder from the benefit to the company cited in Statement 123R is not limited to transactions involving stock compensation. Therefore, similar accounting is required in this and other[40] transactions where a principal stockholder pays an expense for the company, unless the stockholder's action is caused by a relationship or obligation completely unrelated to his position as a stockholder or such action clearly does not benefit the company.

Some registrants and their accountants have taken the position that since Statement 57 applies to these transactions and requires only the disclosure of material related party transactions, the staff should not analogize to the accounting called for by Statement 123R, paragraph 11 for transactions other than those specifically covered by it. The staff notes, however, that Statement 57 does not address the measurement of related party transactions and that, as a result, such transactions are generally recorded at the amounts indicated by their terms.[41] However, the staff believes that transactions of the type described above differ from the typical related party transactions.

The transactions for which Statement 57 requires disclosure generally are those in which a company receives goods or services directly from, or provides goods or services directly to, a related party, and the form and terms of such transactions may be structured to produce either a direct or indirect benefit to the related party. The participation of a related party in such a transaction negates the presumption that transactions reflected in the financial statements have been consummated at arm's length. Disclosure is therefore required to compensate for the fact that, due to the related party's involvement, the terms of the transaction may produce an accounting measurement for which a more faithful measurement may not be determinable.

However, transactions of the type discussed in the facts given do not have such problems of measurement and appear to be transacted to provide a benefit

---

[37] Opinion 20, paragraph 16.

[38] Statement 57, paragraph 24e, defines principal owners as "owners of record or known beneficial owners of more than 10 percent of the voting interests of the enterprise."

[39] Statement 123R defines an economic interest in an entity as "any type or form of pecuniary interest or arrangement that an entity could issue or be a party to, including equity securities; financial instruments with characteristics of equity, liabilities or both; long-term debt and other debt-financing arrangements; leases; and contractual arrangements such as management contracts, service contracts, or intellectual property licenses." Accordingly, a principal stockholder would be considered a holder of an economic interest in an entity.

[40] For example, SAB Topic 1.B indicates that the separate financial statements of a subsidiary should reflect any costs of its

operations which are incurred by the parent on its behalf. Additionally, the staff notes that AICPA Technical Practice Aids § 4160 also indicates that the payment by principal stockholders of a company's debt should be accounted for as a capital contribution.

[41] However, in some circumstances it is necessary to reflect, either in the historical financial statements or a pro forma presentation (depending on the circumstances), related party transactions at amounts other than those indicated by their terms. Two such circumstances are addressed in Staff Accounting Bulletin Topic 1.B.1, Questions 3 and 4. Another example is where the terms of a material contract with a related party are expected to change upon the completion of an offering (i.e., the principal shareholder requires payment for services which had previously been contributed by the shareholder to the company).

to the stockholder through the enhancement or maintenance of the value of the stockholder's investment. The staff believes that the substance of such transactions is the payment of an expense of the company through contributions by the stockholder. Therefore, the staff believes it would be inappropriate to account for such transactions according to the form of the transaction.

U. Removed by SAB 112

V. Certain Transfers Of Nonperforming Assets

Facts: A financial institution desires to reduce its nonaccrual or reduced rate loans and other nonearning assets, including foreclosed real estate (collectively, "nonperforming assets"). Some or all of such nonperforming assets are transferred to a newly-formed entity (the "new entity"). The financial institution, as consideration for transferring the nonperforming assets, may receive (a) the cash proceeds of debt issued by the new entity to third parties, (b) a note or other redeemable instrument issued by the new entity, or (c) a combination of (a) and (b). The residual equity interests in the new entity, which carry voting rights, initially owned by the financial institution, are transferred to outsiders (for example, via distribution to the financial institution's shareholders or sale or contribution to an unrelated third party).

The financial institution typically will manage the assets for a fee, providing necessary services to liquidate the assets, but otherwise does not have the right to appoint directors or legally control the operations of the new entity.

Statement 140 provides guidance for determining when a transfer of financial assets can be recognized as a sale. The interpretive guidance provided in response to Questions 1 and 2 of this SAB does not apply to transfers of financial assets falling within the scope of Statement 140. Because Statement 140 does not apply to distributions of financial assets to shareholders or a contribution of such assets to unrelated third parties, the interpretive guidance provided in response to Questions 1 and 2 of this SAB would apply to such conveyances.

Further, registrants should consider the guidance contained in FASB Interpretation 46 in determining whether it should consolidate the newly-formed entity.

Question 1: What factors should be considered in determining whether such transfer of nonperforming assets can be accounted for as a disposition by the financial institution?

Interpretive Response: The staff believes that determining whether nonperforming assets have been disposed of in substance requires an assessment as to whether the risks and rewards of ownership have been transferred. SAB Topic 5.E[47] discusses some factors that the staff believes should be considered in determining whether the risks of a business have been transferred. Consistent with the factors discussed in SAB Topic 5.E, the staff believes that the transfer described should not be accounted for as a sale or disposition if (a) the transfer of nonperforming assets to the new entity provides for recourse by the new entity to the transferor financial institution, (b) the financial institution directly or indirectly guarantees debt of the new entity in whole or in part, (c) the financial institution retains a participation in the rewards of ownership of the transferred assets, for example through a higher than normal incentive or other management fee arrangement,[48] or (d) the fair value of any material non-cash consideration received by the financial institution (for example, a note or other redeemable instrument) cannot be reasonably estimated. Additionally, the staff believes that the accounting for the transfer as a sale or disposition generally is not appropriate where the financial institution retains rewards of ownership through the holding of significant residual equity interests or where third party holders of such interests do not have a significant amount of capital at risk.

Where accounting for the transfer as a sale or disposition is not appropriate, the nonperforming assets should remain on the financial institution's balance sheet and should continue to be disclosed as nonaccrual, past due, restructured or foreclosed, as appropriate, and the debt of the new entity should be recorded by the financial institution.

Question 2: If the transaction is accounted for as a sale to an unconsolidated party, at what value should the transfer be recorded by the financial institution?

Interpretive Response: The staff believes that the transfer should be recorded by the financial institution at the fair value of assets transferred (or, if more clearly evident, the fair value of assets received) and a loss recognized by the financial institution for any excess of the net carrying value[49] over the fair value.[50] Fair value is the amount that would be realizable in an outright sale to an unrelated third party for

---

[47] SAB Topic 5.E addresses the accounting for the transfer of certain operations whereby there is a continuing involvement by the seller or other evidence that incidents of ownership remain with the seller.

[48] The staff recognizes that the determination of whether the financial institution retains a participation in the rewards of ownership will require an analysis of the facts and circumstances of each individual transaction. Generally, the staff believes that, in order to conclude that the financial institution has disposed of the assets in substance, the management fee arrangement should not enable the financial institution to participate to any significant extent in the potential increases in cash flows or value of the assets, and the terms of the arrangement, including provisions for discontinuance

of services, must be substantially similar to management arrangements with third parties.

[49] The carrying value should be reduced by any allocable allowance for credit losses or other valuation allowances. The staff believes that the loss recognized for the excess of the net carrying value over the fair value should be considered a credit loss and this should not be included by the financial institution as loss on disposition.

[50] The staff notes that the EITF reached a consensus at its November 17, 1988 meeting on Issue 88-25 that the newly created "liquidating bank" should continue to report its assets and liabilities at fair values at the date of the financial statements.

cash.[51] The same concepts should be applied in determining fair value of the transferred assets, i.e., if an active market exists for the assets transferred, then fair value is equal to the market value. If no active market exists, but one exists for similar assets, the selling prices in that market may be helpful in estimating the fair value. If no such market price is available, a forecast of expected cash flows, discounted at a rate commensurate with the risks involved, may be used to aid in estimating the fair value. In situations where discounted cash flows are used to estimate fair value of nonperforming assets, the staff would expect that the interest rate used in such computations will be substantially higher than the cost of funds of the financial institution and appropriately reflect the risk of holding these nonperforming assets. Therefore, the fair value determined in such a way will be lower than the amount at which the assets would have been carried by the financial institution had the transfer not occurred, unless the financial institution had been required under GAAP to carry such assets at market value or the lower of cost or market value.

Question 3: Where the transaction may appropriately be accounted for as a sale to an unconsolidated party and the financial institution receives a note receivable or other redeemable instrument from the new entity, how should such asset be disclosed pursuant to Item III C, "Risk Elements," of Industry Guide 3? What factors should be considered related to the subsequent accounting for such instruments received?

Interpretive Response: The staff believes that the financial institution may exclude the note receivable or other asset from its Risk Elements disclosures under Guide 3 provided that: (a) the receivable itself does not constitute a nonaccrual, past due, restructured, or potential problem loan that would require disclosure under Guide 3, and (b) the underlying collateral is described in sufficient detail to enable investors to understand the nature of the note receivable or other asset, if material, including the extent of any over-collateralization. The description of the collateral normally would include material information similar to that which would be provided if such assets were owned by the financial institution, including pertinent Risk Element disclosures.

The staff notes that, in situations in which the transaction is accounted for as a sale to an unconsolidated party and a portion of the consideration received by the registrant is debt or another redeemable instrument, careful consideration must be given to the appropriateness of recording profits on the management fee arrangement, or interest or dividends on the instrument received, including consideration of whether it is necessary to defer such amounts or to treat such payments on a cost recovery basis. Further, if the new entity incurs losses to the point that its permanent equity based on GAAP is eliminated, it would ordinarily be necessary for the financial institution, at a minimum, to record further operating losses as its best estimate of the loss in realizable value of its investment.[52]

W. Contingency Disclosures Regarding Property-Casualty Insurance Reserves For Unpaid Claim Costs

Facts: A property-casualty insurance company (the "Company") has established reserves, in accordance with Statement 60 for unpaid claim costs, including estimates of costs relating to claims incurred but not reported ("IBNR").[53] The reserve estimate for IBNR claims was based on past loss experience and current trends except that the estimate has been adjusted for recent significant unfavorable claims experience that the Company considers to be nonrecurring and abnormal. The Company attributes the abnormal claims experience to a recent acquisition and accelerated claims processing; however, actuarial studies have been inconclusive and subject to varying interpretations. Although the reserve is deemed adequate to cover all probable claims, there is a reasonable possibility that the abnormal claims experience could continue, resulting in a material understatement of claim reserves.

Statement 5 requires, among other things, disclosure of loss contingencies.[54] However, paragraph 2 of that Statement notes that "[n]ot all uncertainties inherent in the accounting process give rise to contingencies as that term is used in [Statement 5]."

SOP 94-6[55] also provides disclosure guidance regarding certain significant estimates.

Question 1: In the staff's view, do Statement 5 and SOP 94-6 disclosure requirements apply to property-

---

[51] The EITF reached a consensus on issue 11 of Issue 01-02 that an enterprise that distributes loans to its owners should report such distribution at fair value.

[52] Typically, the financial institution's claim on the new entity is subordinate to other debt instruments and thus the financial institution will incur any losses beyond those incurred by the permanent equity holders.

[53] Paragraph 18 of Statement 60 prescribes that "[t]he liability for unpaid claims shall be based on the estimated ultimate cost of settling the claims (including the effects of inflation and other societal and economic factors), using past experience adjusted for current trends, and any other factors that would modify past experience." [Footnote reference omitted]

[54] Paragraph 10 of Statement 5 specified that "[i]f no accrual is made for a loss contingency because one or both of the conditions in paragraph 8 are not met, **or if an exposure to loss exists in excess of the amount accrued** pursuant to the provisions of paragraph 8, disclosure of the contingency shall be made when

there is at least a reasonable possibility that a loss or an additional loss may have been incurred. The disclosure shall indicate the nature of the contingency and shall give an estimate of the possible loss or range of loss or state that such an estimate cannot be made." [Footnote reference omitted and emphasis added.]

[55] SOP 94-6 provides that disclosures regarding certain significant estimates should be made when the following criteria are met. The SOP provides that:

The disclosure should indicate the nature of the uncertainty and include an indication that it is at least reasonably possible that a change in the estimate will occur in the near term. If the estimate involves a loss contingency covered by [Statement] 5, the disclosure also should include an estimate of the possible loss or range of loss, or state that such an estimate cannot be made. Disclosure of the factors that cause the estimate to be sensitive to change is encouraged but not required. (footnote references omitted)

SOP 94-6 requires disclosures regarding current vulnerability due to certain concentrations which may be applicable as well.

casualty insurance reserves for unpaid claim costs? If so, how?

Interpretive Response: Yes. The staff believes that specific uncertainties (conditions, situations and/or sets of circumstances) not considered to be normal and recurring because of their significance and/or nature can result in loss contingencies[56] for purposes of applying Statement 5 and SOP 94-6 disclosure requirements. General uncertainties, such as the amount and timing of claims, that are normal, recurring, and inherent to estimations of property-casualty insurance reserves are not considered subject to the disclosure requirements of Statement 5. Some specific uncertainties that may result in loss contingencies pursuant to Statement 5, depending on significance and/or nature, include insufficiently understood trends in claims activity; judgmental adjustments to historical experience for purposes of estimating future claim costs (other than for normal recurring general uncertainties); significant risks to an individual claim or group of related claims; or catastrophe losses. The requirements of SOP 94-6 apply when "[i]t is at least reasonably possible that the estimate of the effect on the financial statements of a condition, situation, or set of circumstances that existed at the date of the financial statements will change in the near term due to one or more future confirming events . . . [and] the effect of the change would be material to the financial statements."

Question 2: Do the facts presented above describe an uncertainty that requires disclosures under Statement 5 and SOP 94-6?

Interpretive Response: Yes. The staff believes the judgmental adjustments to historical experience for insufficiently understood claims activity noted above results in a loss contingency within the scope of Statement 5 and SOP 94-6. Based on the facts presented above, at a minimum the Company's financial statements should disclose that for purposes of estimating IBNR claim reserves, past experience was adjusted for what management believes to be abnormal claims experience related to the recent acquisition of Company A and accelerated claims processing. It should also be disclosed that there is a reasonable possibility that the claims experience could be the indication of an unfavorable trend which would require additional IBNR claim reserves in the approximate range of $XX-$XX million (alternatively, if Company management is unable to estimate the possible loss or range of loss, a statement to that effect should be disclosed).

Additionally, the staff also expects companies to disclose the nature of the loss contingency and the potential impact on trends in their loss reserve development discussions provided pursuant to Property-Casualty Industry Guides 4 and 6. Consideration should also be given to the need to provide disclosure in MD&A.

Question 3: Does the staff have an example in which specific uncertainties involving an individual claim or group of related claims result in a loss contingency the staff believes requires disclosure?

Interpretive Response: Yes. A property-casualty insurance company (the "Company") underwrites product liability insurance for an insured manufacturer which has produced and sold millions of units of a particular product which has been used effectively and without problems for many years. Users of the product have recently begun to report serious health problems that they attribute to long term use of the product and have asserted claims under the insurance policy underwritten and retained by the Company. To date, the number of users reporting such problems is relatively small, and there is presently no conclusive evidence that demonstrates a causal link between long term use of the product and the health problems experienced by the claimants. However, the evidence generated to date indicates that there is at least a reasonable possibility that the product is responsible for the problems and the assertion of additional claims is considered probable, and therefore the potential exposure of the Company is material. While an accrual may not be warranted since the loss exposure may not be both probable and estimable, in view of the reasonable possibility of material future claim payments, the staff believes that disclosures made in accordance with Statement 5 and SOP 94-6 would be required under these circumstances.

The disclosure concepts expressed in this example would also apply to an individual claim or group of claims that are related to a single catastrophic event or multiple events having a similar effect.

X. Deleted by SAB 103

Y. Accounting And Disclosures Relating To Loss Contingencies

Facts: A registrant believes it may be obligated to pay material amounts as a result of product or environmental remediation liability. These amounts may relate to, for example, damages attributed to the registrant's products or processes, clean-up of hazardous wastes, reclamation costs, fines, and litigation costs. The registrant may seek to recover a portion or all of these amounts by filing a claim against an insurance carrier or other third parties.

Question 1: Assuming that the registrant's estimate of an environmental remediation or product liability meets the conditions set forth in paragraph 132 of SOP 96-1 for recognition on a discounted basis, what discount rate should be applied and what, if any, special disclosures are required in the notes to the financial statements?

Interpretive Response: The rate used to discount the cash payments should be the rate that will produce an amount at which the environmental or product liability could be settled in an arm's-length transaction with a third party. SOP 96-1 further states that the

---

[56] The loss contingency referred to in this document is the potential for a material understatement of reserves for unpaid claims.

discount rate used to discount the cash payments should not exceed the interest rate on monetary assets that are essentially risk free[57] and have maturities comparable to that of the environmental or product liability.

If the liability is recognized on a discounted basis to reflect the time value of money, the notes to the financial statements should, at a minimum, include disclosures of the discount rate used, the expected aggregate undiscounted amount, expected payments for each of the five succeeding years and the aggregate amount thereafter, and a reconciliation of the expected aggregate undiscounted amount to amounts recognized in the statements of financial position. Material changes in the expected aggregate amount since the prior balance sheet date, other than those resulting from pay-down of the obligation, should be explained.

Question 2: What financial statement disclosures should be furnished with respect to recorded and unrecorded product or environmental remediation liabilities?

Interpretive Response: Paragraphs 9 and 10 of Statement 5 identify disclosures regarding loss contingencies that generally are furnished in notes to financial statements. SOP 96-1 identifies disclosures that are required and recommended regarding both recorded and unrecorded environmental remediation liabilities. The staff believes that product and environmental remediation liabilities typically are of such significance that detailed disclosures regarding the judgments and assumptions underlying the recognition and measurement of the liabilities are necessary to prevent the financial statements from being misleading and to inform readers fully regarding the range of reasonably possible outcomes that could have a material effect on the registrant's financial condition, results of operations, or liquidity. In addition to the disclosures required by Statement 5 and SOP 96-1, examples of disclosures that may be necessary include:

• Circumstances affecting the reliability and precision of loss estimates.

• The extent to which unasserted claims are reflected in any accrual or may affect the magnitude of the contingency.

• Uncertainties with respect to joint and several liability that may affect the magnitude of the contingency, including disclosure of the aggregate expected cost to remediate particular sites that are individually material if the likelihood of contribution by the other significant parties has not been established.

• Disclosure of the nature and terms of cost-sharing arrangements with other potentially responsible parties.

• The extent to which disclosed but unrecognized contingent losses are expected to be recoverable through insurance, indemnification arrangements, or other sources, with disclosure of any material limitations of that recovery.

• Uncertainties regarding the legal sufficiency of insurance claims or solvency of insurance carriers.[58]

• The time frame over which the accrued or presently unrecognized amounts may be paid out.

• Material components of the accruals and significant assumptions underlying estimates.

Registrants are cautioned that a statement that the contingency is not expected to be material does not satisfy the requirements of Statement 5 if there is at least a reasonable possibility that a loss exceeding amounts already recognized may have been incurred and the amount of that additional loss would be material to a decision to buy or sell the registrant's securities. In that case, the registrant must either (a) disclose the estimated additional loss, or range of loss, that is reasonably possible, or (b) state that such an estimate cannot be made.

Question 3: What disclosures regarding loss contingencies may be necessary outside the financial statements?

Interpretive Response: Registrants should consider the requirements of Items 101 (Description of Business), 103 (Legal Proceedings), and 303 (MD&A) of Regulations S-K and S-B. The Commission has issued interpretive releases that provide additional guidance with respect to these items.[59] In a 1989 interpretive release, the Commission noted that the availability of insurance, indemnification, or contribution may be relevant in determining whether the criteria for disclosure have been met with respect to a contingency.[60] The registrant's assessment in this regard should include consideration of facts such as the periods in which claims for recovery may be realized, the likelihood that the claims may be contested, and the financial condition of third parties from which recovery is expected.

Disclosures made pursuant to the guidance identified in the preceding paragraph should be sufficiently specific to enable a reader to understand the scope of the contingencies affecting the registrant. For example, a registrant's discussion of historical and anticipated environmental expenditures should, to the extent material, describe separately (a) recurring costs associated with managing hazardous substances and pollution in on-going operations, (b) capital expenditures to limit or monitor hazardous

---

[57] As described in Concepts Statement 7.

[58] The staff believes there is a rebuttable presumption that no asset should be recognized for a claim for recovery from a party that is asserting that it is not liable to indemnify the registrant. Registrants that overcome that presumption should disclose the amount of recorded recoveries that are being contested and dis-

cuss the reasons for concluding that the amounts are probable of recovery.

[59] See Securities Act Release No. 6130, FR 36, Securities Act Release No. 33-8040, Securities Act Release No. 33-8039, and Securities Act Release 33-8176.

[60] See, for example, footnote 30 of FR 36 (footnote 17 of Section 501.02 of the Codification of Financial Reporting Policies).

substances or pollutants, (c) mandated expenditures to remediate previously contaminated sites, and (d) other infrequent or non-recurring clean-up expenditures that can be anticipated but which are not required in the present circumstances. Disaggregated disclosure that describes accrued and reasonably likely losses with respect to particular environmental sites that are individually material may be necessary for a full understanding of these contingencies. Also, if management's investigation of potential liability and remediation cost is at different stages with respect to individual sites, the consequences of this with respect to amounts accrued and disclosed should be discussed.

Examples of specific disclosures typically relevant to an understanding of historical and anticipated product liability costs include the nature of personal injury or property damages alleged by claimants, aggregate settlement costs by type of claim, and related costs of administering and litigating claims. Disaggregated disclosure that describes accrued and reasonably likely losses with respect to particular claims may be necessary if they are individually material. If the contingency involves a large number of relatively small individual claims of a similar type, such as personal injury from exposure to asbestos, disclosure of the number of claims pending at each balance sheet date, the number of claims filed for each period presented, the number of claims dismissed, settled, or otherwise resolved for each period, and the average settlement amount per claim may be necessary. Disclosures should address historical and expected trends in these amounts and their reasonably likely effects on operating results and liquidity.

Question 4: What disclosures should be furnished with respect to site restoration costs or other environmental remediation costs?[61]

Interpretive Response: The staff believes that material liabilities for site restoration, post-closure, and monitoring commitments, or other exit costs that may occur on the sale, disposal, or abandonment of a property as a result of unanticipated contamination of the asset should be disclosed in the notes to the financial statements. Appropriate disclosures generally would include the nature of the costs involved, the total anticipated cost, the total costs accrued to date, the balance sheet classification of accrued amounts, and the range or amount of reasonably possible additional losses. If an asset held for sale or development will require remediation to be performed by the registrant prior to development, sale, or as a condition of sale, a note to the financial statements should describe how the necessary expenditures are considered in the assessment of the asset's value and the possible need to reflect an

impairment loss. Additionally, if the registrant may be liable for remediation of environmental damage relating to assets or businesses previously disposed, disclosure should be made in the financial statements unless the likelihood of a material unfavorable outcome of that contingency is remote.[62] The registrant's accounting policy with respect to such costs should be disclosed in accordance with Opinion 22.

Z. Accounting And Disclosure Regarding Discontinued Operations

1. Deleted by SAB 103

2. Deleted by SAB 103

3. Deleted by SAB 103

4. *Disposal of operation with significant interest retained*

Facts: A Company disposes of its controlling interest in a component of an entity as defined by Statement 144. The Company retains a minority voting interest directly in the component or it holds a minority voting interest in the buyer of the component. Controlling interest includes those controlling interests established through other means, such as variable interests. Because the Company's voting interest enables it to exert significant influence over the operating and financial policies of the investee, the Company is required by Opinion 18 to account for its residual investment using the equity method.[63]

Question: May the historical operating results of the component and the gain or loss on the sale of the majority interest in the component be classified in the Company's statement of operations as "discontinued operations" pursuant to Statement 144?

Interpretive Response: No. A condition necessary for discontinued operations reporting, as indicated in paragraph 42 of Statement 144 is that an entity "not have any significant continuing involvement in the operations of the component after the disposal transaction." In these circumstances, the transaction should be accounted for as the disposal of a group of assets that is not a component of an entity and classified within continuing operations pursuant to Statement 144.[64]

5. *Classification and disclosure of contingencies relating to discontinued operations*

Facts: A company disposed of a component of an entity in a previous accounting period. The Company received debt and/or equity securities of the buyer of the component or of the disposed component as consideration in the sale, but this financial interest is not sufficient to enable the Company to apply the equity method with respect to its investment in the buyer. The Company made certain warranties to the buyer with respect to the discontinued business, or remains

---

[61] Registrants are reminded that Statement 143 provides guidance for accounting and reporting for costs associated with asset retirement obligations.

[62] If the company has a guarantee as defined by Interpretation 45, the entity is required to provide the disclosures and recognize the fair value of the guarantee in the company's financial statements even if the "contingent" aspect of the guarantee is deemed to be remote.

[63] In some circumstances, the seller's continuing interest may be so great that divestiture accounting is inappropriate. See SAB Topic 5.E.

[64] However, a plan of disposal that contemplates the transfer of assets to a limited-life entity created for the single purpose of liquidating the assets of a component of an entity would not necessitate classification within continuing operations solely because the registrant retains control or significant influence over the liquidating entity.

liable under environmental or other laws with respect to certain facilities or operations transferred to the buyer. The disposition satisfied the criteria of Statement 144 for presentation as "discontinued operations." The Company estimated the fair value of the securities received in the transaction for purposes of calculating the gain or loss on disposal that was recognized in its financial statements. The results of discontinued operations prior to the date of disposal or classification as held for sale included provisions for the Company's existing obligations under environmental laws, product warranties, or other contingencies. The calculation of gain or loss on disposal included estimates of the Company's obligations arising as a direct result of its decision to dispose of the component, under its warranties to the buyer, and under environmental or other laws. In a period subsequent to the disposal date, the Company records a charge to income with respect to the securities because their fair value declined materially and the Company determined that the decline was other than temporary. The Company also records adjustments of its previously estimated liabilities arising under the warranties and under environmental or other laws.

Question 1: Should the writedown of the carrying value of the securities and the adjustments of the contingent liabilities be classified in the current period's statement of operations within continuing operations or as an element of discontinued operations?

Interpretive Response: Adjustments of estimates of contingent liabilities or contingent assets that remain after disposal of a component of an entity or that arose pursuant to the terms of the disposal generally should be classified within discontinued operations.[65] However, the staff believes that changes in the carrying value of assets received as consideration in the disposal or of residual interests in the business should be classified within continuing operations.

Paragraph 44 of Statement 144 requires that "adjustments to amounts previously reported in discontinued operations that are directly related to the disposal of a component of an entity in a prior period shall be classified separately in the current period in discontinued operations." The staff believes that the provisions of paragraph 44 apply only to adjustments that are necessary to reflect new information about events that have occurred that becomes available prior to disposal of the component of the entity, to reflect the actual timing and terms of the disposal when it is consummated, and to reflect the resolution of contingencies associated with that component, such as warranties and environmental liabilities retained by the seller.

Developments subsequent to the disposal date that are not directly related to the disposal of the component or the operations of the component prior to disposal are not "directly related to the disposal" as contemplated by paragraph 44 of Statement 144. Subsequent changes in the carrying value of assets received upon disposition of a component do not affect the determination of gain or loss at the disposal date, but represent the consequences of management's subsequent decisions to hold or sell those assets. Gains and losses, dividend and interest income, and portfolio management expenses associated with assets received as consideration for discontinued operations should be reported within continuing operations.

Question 2: What disclosures would the staff expect regarding discontinued operations prior to the disposal date and with respect to risks retained subsequent to the disposal date?

Interpretive Response: MD&A[66] should include disclosure of known trends, events, and uncertainties involving discontinued operations that may materially affect the Company's liquidity, financial condition, and results of operations (including net income) between the date when a component of an entity is classified as discontinued and the date when the risks of those operations will be transferred or otherwise terminated. Disclosure should include discussion of the impact on the Company's liquidity, financial condition, and results of operations of changes in the plan of disposal or changes in circumstances related to the plan. Material contingent liabilities,[67] such as product or environmental liabilities or litigation, that may remain with the Company notwithstanding disposal of the underlying business should be identified in notes to the financial statements and any reasonably likely range of possible loss should be disclosed pursuant to Statement 5. MD&A should include discussion of the reasonably likely effects of these contingencies on reported results and liquidity. If the Company retains a financial interest in the discontinued component or in the buyer of that component that is material to the Company, MD&A should include discussion of known trends, events, and uncertainties, such as the financial condition and operating results of the issuer of the security, that may be reasonably expected to affect the amounts ultimately realized on the investments.

6. Deleted by SAB 103

7. Accounting for the spin-off of a subsidiary

Facts: A Company disposes of a business through the distribution of a subsidiary's stock to the Company's shareholders on a pro rata basis in a transaction that is referred to as a spin-off.

Question: May the Company elect to characterize the spin-off transaction as resulting in a change in the reporting entity and restate its historical financial statements as if the Company never had an investment in the subsidiary, in the manner specified by paragraph 34 of APB Opinion 20?

Interpretive Response: Not ordinarily. If the Company was required to file periodic reports under the Exchange Act within one year prior to the spin-off,

---

[65] Registrants are reminded that Interpretation 45 requires recognition and disclosure of certain guarantees which may impose accounting and disclosure requirements in addition to those discussed in this SAB Topic.

[66] Item 303 of Regulation S-K.

[67] Registrants also should consider the disclosure requirements of Interpretation 45.

the staff believes the Company should reflect the disposition in conformity with Statement 144. This presentation most fairly and completely depicts for investors the effects of the previous and current organization of the Company. However, in limited circumstances involving the initial registration of a company under the Exchange Act or Securities Act, the staff has not objected to financial statements that retroactively reflect the reorganization of the business as a change in the reporting entity if the spin-off transaction occurs prior to effectiveness of the registration statement. This presentation may be acceptable in an initial registration if the Company and the subsidiary are in dissimilar businesses, have been managed and financed historically as if they were autonomous, have no more than incidental common facilities and costs, will be operated and financed autonomously after the spin-off, and will not have material financial commitments, guarantees, or contingent liabilities to each other after the spin-off. This exception to the prohibition against retroactive omission of the subsidiary is intended for companies that have not distributed widely financial statements that include the spun-off subsidiary. Also, dissimilarity contemplates substantially greater differences in the nature of the businesses than those that would ordinarily distinguish reportable segments as defined by Statement 131.

AA. Deleted by SAB 103

BB. Inventory Valuation Allowances

Facts: ARB 43, Chapter 4, Statement 5, specifies that: "[a]departure from the cost basis of pricing the inventory is required when the utility of the goods is no longer as great as its cost. Where there is evidence that the utility of goods, in their disposal in the ordinary course of business, will be less than cost, whether due to physical obsolescence, changes in price levels, or other causes, the difference should be recognized as a loss of the current period. This is generally accomplished by stating such goods at a lower level commonly designated as market."

Footnote 2 to that same chapter indicates that "[i]n the case of goods which have been written down below cost at the close of a fiscal period, such reduced amount is to be considered the cost for subsequent accounting purposes."

Lastly, Opinion 20 provides "inventory obsolescence" as one of the items subject to estimation and changes in estimates under the guidance in paragraphs 10-11 and 31-33 of that Opinion.

Question: Does the write-down of inventory to the lower of cost or market, as required by ARB 43, create a new cost basis for the inventory or may a subsequent change in facts and circumstances allow for restoration of inventory value, not to exceed original historical cost?

Interpretive Response: Based on ARB 43, footnote 2, the staff believes that a write-down of inventory to the lower of cost or market at the close of a fiscal period

creates a new cost basis that subsequently cannot be marked up based on changes in underlying facts and circumstances.[68]

CC. Impairments

Standards for recognizing and measuring impairment of the carrying amount of long-lived assets including certain identifiable intangibles to be held and used in operations are found in Statement 144. Standards for recognizing and measuring impairment of the carrying amount of goodwill and identifiable intangible assets that are not currently being amortized are found in Statement 142.

Facts: Company X has mainframe computers that are to be abandoned in six to nine months as replacement computers are put in place. The mainframe computers were placed in service in January 20X0 and were being depreciated on a straight-line basis over seven years. No salvage value had been projected at the end of seven years and the original cost of the computers was $8,400. The board of directors, with the appropriate authority, approved the abandonment of the computers in March 20X3 when the computers had a remaining carrying value of $4,600. No proceeds are expected upon abandonment. Abandonment cannot occur prior to the receipt and installation of replacement computers, which is expected prior to the end of 20X3. Management had begun reevaluating its mainframe computer capabilities in January 20X2 and had included in its 20X3 capital expenditures budget an estimated amount for new mainframe computers. The 20X3 capital expenditures budget had been prepared by management in August 20X2, had been discussed with the company's board of directors in September 20X2 and was formally approved by the board of directors in March 20X3. Management had also begun soliciting bids for new mainframe computers beginning in the fall of 20X2. The mainframe computers, when grouped with assets at the lowest level of identifiable cash flows, were not impaired on a "held and used" basis throughout this time period. Management had not adjusted the original estimated useful life of the computers (seven years) since 20X0.

Question 1: Company X proposes to recognize an impairment charge under Statement 144 for the carrying value of the mainframe computers of $4,600 in March 20X3. Does Company X meet the requirements in Statement 144 to classify the mainframe computer assets as "to be abandoned?"

Interpretive Response: No. Statement 144, paragraph 28, provides that "a long-lived asset to be abandoned is disposed of when it ceases to be used. If an entity commits to a plan to abandon a long-lived asset before the end of its previously estimated useful life, depreciation estimates shall be revised in accordance with Opinion 20 to reflect the use of the asset over its shortened useful life."

Question 2: Would the staff accept an adjustment to write down the carrying value of the computers to

---

[68] See also disclosure requirement for inventory balances in Rule 5-02(6) of Regulation S-X.

reflect a "normalized depreciation" rate for the period from March 20X3 through actual abandonment (e.g., December 20X3)? Normalized depreciation would represent the amount of depreciation otherwise expected to be recognized during that period without adjustment of the asset's useful life, or $1,000 ($100/month for ten months) in the example fact pattern.

Interpretive Response: No. The mainframe computers would be viewed as "held and used" at March 20X3 under the fact pattern described. There is no basis under Statement 144 to write down an asset to an amount that would subsequently result in a "normalized depreciation" charge through the disposal date, whether disposal is to be by sale, abandonment, or other means. For an asset that meets the requirements to be classified as "held for sale" under Statement 144, paragraph 34 of that standard requires the asset to be valued at the lower of carrying amount or fair value less cost to sell. For assets that are classified as "held and used" under Statement 144, an assessment must first be made as to whether the asset (asset group) is impaired. Paragraph 7 of Statement 144 indicates that an impairment loss shall be recognized only if the carrying amount of a long-lived asset (asset group) is not recoverable and exceeds its fair value. The carrying amount of a long-lived asset (asset group) is not recoverable if it exceeds the sum of the undiscounted cash flows expected to result from the use and eventual disposition of the asset (asset group). The staff would object to a write down of long-lived assets to a "normalized depreciation" value as representing an acceptable alternative to the approaches required in Statement 144.

The staff also believes that registrants must continually evaluate the appropriateness of useful lives assigned to long-lived assets, including identifiable intangible assets and goodwill. In the above fact pattern, management had contemplated removal of the mainframe computers beginning in January 20X2 and, more formally, in August 20X2 as part of compiling the 20X3 capital expenditures budget. At those times, at a minimum, management should have reevaluated the original useful life assigned to the computers to determine whether a seven year amortization period remained appropriate given the company's current facts and circumstances, including ongoing technological changes in the market place. This reevaluation process should have continued at the time of the September 20X2 board of directors' meeting to discuss capital expenditure plans and, further, as the company pursued mainframe computer bids. Given the contemporaneous evidence that management's best estimate during much of 20X2 was that the current mainframe computers would be removed from service in 20X3, the depreciable life of the computers should have been adjusted prior to 20X3 to reflect this new estimate. The staff does not view the recognition of an impairment charge to be an acceptable substitute for choosing the appropriate initial amortization or depreciation period or subsequently adjusting this period as company or industry conditions change. The staff's view applies also to selection of, and changes to, estimated residual values. Conse-

quently, the staff may challenge impairment charges for which the timely evaluation of useful life and residual value cannot be demonstrated.

Question 3: Has the staff expressed any views with respect to company-determined estimates of cash flows used for assessing and measuring impairment of assets under Statement 144?

Interpretive Response: In providing guidance on the development of cash flows for purposes of applying the provisions of Statement 144, paragraph 17 of that Statement indicates that "estimates of future cash flows used to test the recoverability of a long-lived asset (asset group) shall incorporate the entity's own assumptions about its use of the asset (asset group) and shall consider all available evidence. The assumptions used in developing those estimates shall be reasonable in relation to the assumptions used in developing other information used by the entity for comparable periods, such as internal budgets and projections, accruals related to incentive compensation plans, or information communicated to others."

The staff recognizes that various factors, including management's judgments and assumptions about the business plans and strategies, affect the development of future cash flow projections for purposes of applying Statement 144. The staff, however, cautions registrants that the judgments and assumptions made for purposes of applying Statement 144 must be consistent with other financial statement calculations and disclosures and disclosures in MD&A. The staff also expects that forecasts made for purposes of applying Statement 144 be consistent with other forward-looking information prepared by the company, such as that used for internal budgets, incentive compensation plans, discussions with lenders or third parties, and/or reporting to management or the board of directors.

For example, the staff has reviewed a fact pattern where a registrant developed cash flow projections for purposes of applying the provisions of Statement 144 using one set of assumptions and utilized a second, more conservative set of assumptions for purposes of determining whether deferred tax valuation allowances were necessary when applying the provisions of Statement 109. In this case, the staff objected to the use of inconsistent assumptions.

In addition to disclosure of key assumptions used in the development of cash flow projections, the staff also has required discussion in MD&A of the implications of assumptions. For example, do the projections indicate that a company is likely to violate debt covenants in the future? What are the ramifications to the cash flow projections used in the impairment analysis? If growth rates used in the impairment analysis are lower than those used by outside analysts, has the company had discussions with the analysts regarding their overly optimistic projections? Has the company appropriately informed the market and its shareholders of its reduced expectations for the future that are sufficient to cause an impairment charge? The staff believes that cash flow projections used in the impairment analysis must be both internally consistent with the company's other projections and externally consistent with financial statement and other public disclosures.

DD. Written Loan Commitments Recorded at Fair Value Through Earnings

Facts: Bank A enters into a loan commitment with a customer to originate a mortgage loan at a specified rate. As part of this written loan commitment, Bank A expects to receive future net cash flows related to servicing rights from servicing fees (included in the loan's interest rate or otherwise), late charges, and other ancillary sources, or from selling the servicing rights to a third party. If Bank A intends to sell the mortgage loan after it is funded, pursuant to paragraph 6 of FASB Statement No. 133, *Accounting for Derivative Instruments and Hedging Activities*, as amended by FASB Statement No. 149, *Amendment of Statement 133 on Derivative Instruments and Hedging Activities* ("Statement 133"), the written loan commitment is accounted for as a derivative instrument and recorded at fair value through earnings (referred to hereafter as a "derivative loan commitment"). If Bank A does not intend to sell the mortgage loan after it is funded, the written loan commitment is not accounted for as a derivative under Statement 133. However, paragraph 7(c) of FASB Statement No. 159, *The Fair Value Option for Financial Assets and Financial Liabilities* ("Statement 159"), permits Bank A to record the written loan commitment at fair value through earnings (referred to hereafter as a "written loan commitment"). Pursuant to Statement 159, the fair value measurement for a written loan commitment would include the expected net future cash flows related to the associated servicing of the loan.

Question 1: In measuring the fair value of a derivative loan commitment accounted for under Statement 133, should Bank A include the expected net future cash flows related to the associated servicing of the loan?

Interpretive Response: Yes. The staff believes that, consistent with the recently issued guidance in FASB Statement No. 156, *Accounting for Servicing of Financial Assets* ("Statement 156") [69], and Statement 159, the expected net future cash flows related to the associated servicing of the loan should be included in the fair value measurement of a derivative loan commitment. The expected net future cash flows related to the associated servicing of the loan that are included in the fair value measurement of a derivative

loan commitment or a written loan commitment should be determined in the same manner that the fair value of a recognized servicing asset or liability is measured under FASB Statement No. 140, *Accounting for Transfers and Servicing of Financial Assets and Extinguishments of Liabilities*, as amended by Statement 156 ("Statement 140"). However, as discussed in paragraphs 61 and 62 of Statement 140, a separate and distinct servicing asset or liability is not recognized for accounting purposes until the servicing rights have been contractually separated from the underlying loan by sale or securitization of the loan with servicing retained.

The views in Question 1 apply to all loan commitments that are accounted for at fair value through earnings. However, for purposes of electing fair value accounting pursuant to Statement 159, the views in Question 1 are not intended to be applied by analogy to any other instrument that contains a nonfinancial element.

Question 2: In measuring the fair value of a derivative loan commitment accounted for under Statement 133 or a written loan commitment accounted for under Statement 159, should Bank A include the expected net future cash flows related to internally-developed intangible assets?

Interpretive Response: No. The staff does not believe that internally-developed intangible assets (such as customer relationship intangible assets) should be recorded as part of the fair value of a derivative loan commitment or a written loan commitment. Such nonfinancial elements of value should not be considered a component of the related instrument. Recognition of such assets would only be appropriate in a third-party transaction. For example, in the purchase of a portfolio of derivative loan commitments in a business combination, a customer relationship intangible asset is recorded separately from the fair value of such loan commitments. Similarly, when an entity purchases a credit card portfolio, EITF Issue No. 88-20, *Difference between Initial Investment and Principal Amount of Loans in a Purchased Credit Card Portfolio*, requires an allocation of the purchase price to a separately recorded cardholder relationship intangible asset.

The view in Question 2 applies to all loan commitments that are accounted for at fair value through earnings.

[¶ 39,151]   TOPIC 6: INTERPRETATIONS OF ACCOUNTING SERIES RELEASES AND FINANCIAL REPORTING RELEASES

A.1. Deleted by SAB 103

B. Accounting Series Release 280 -General Revision Of Regulation S-X: Income Or Loss Applicable To Common Stock

Facts: A registrant has various classes of preferred stock. Dividends on those preferred stocks and accre-

tions of their carrying amounts cause income applicable to common stock to be less than reported net income.

Question: In ASR 280, the Commission stated that although it had determined not to mandate presentation of income or loss applicable to common stock in

---

[69] Statement 156 permits an entity to subsequently measure recognized servicing assets and servicing liabilities (which are nonfinancial instruments) at fair value through earnings.

all cases, it believes that disclosure of that amount is of value in certain situations. In what situations should the amount be reported, where should it be reported, and how should it be computed?

Interpretive Response: Income or loss applicable to common stock should be reported on the face of the income statement[1] when it is materially different in quantitative terms from reported net income or loss[2] or when it is indicative of significant trends or other qualitative considerations. The amount to be reported should be computed for each period as net income or loss less: (a) dividends on preferred stock, including undeclared or unpaid dividends if cumulative; and (b) periodic increases in the carrying amounts of instruments reported as redeemable preferred stock (as discussed in Topic 3.C) or increasing rate preferred stock (as discussed in Topic 5.Q).

C. Accounting Series Release 180 -Institution Of Staff Accounting Bulletins (SABs)-Applicability Of Guidance Contained In SABs

Facts: The series of SABs was instituted to achieve wide dissemination of administrative interpretations and practices of the Commission's staff. In illustration of certain interpretations and practices, SABs may be written narrowly to describe the circumstances of particular matters which resulted in expression of the staff's views on those particular matters.

Question: How does the staff intend SABs to be applied in circumstances analogous to those addressed in SABs?

Interpretive Response: The staff's purpose in issuing SABs is to disseminate guidance for application not only in the narrowly described circumstances, but also, unless authoritative accounting literature calls for different treatment, in other circumstances where events and transactions have similar accounting and/or disclosure implications.

Registrants and independent accountants are encouraged to consult with the staff if they believe that particular circumstances call for accounting and/or disclosure different from that which would result from application of a SAB addressing those same or analogous circumstances.

D. Redesignated as Topic 12.A by SAB 47

E. Redesignated as Topic 12.B by SAB 47

F. Deleted by SAB 103

G. Accounting Series Releases 177 And 286-Relating To Amendments To Form 10-Q, Regulation S-K, And Regulation S-X Regarding Interim Financial Reporting

General Facts: Disclosure requirements for quarterly data on Form 10-Q were amended in ASR 177 and 286 to include condensed interim financial statements, a narrative analysis of financial condition and results of operations, a letter from the registrant's independent public accountant commenting on any accounting change, and a signature by the registrant's chief financial officer or chief accounting officer.[3] In addition, certain selected quarterly data is required to be disclosed by virtually all registrants (see Item 302(a)(5) of Regulation S-K).

1. Selected quarterly financial data (Item 302(A) of Regulation S-K)

a. Disclosure of selected quarterly financial data

Facts: Item 302(a)(1) of Regulation S-K requires disclosure of net sales, gross profit, income before extraordinary items and cumulative effect of a change in accounting, per share data based upon such income (loss), net income (loss), and net income (loss) attributable to the registrant for each full quarter within the two most recent fiscal years and any subsequent interim period for which financial statements are included. Item 302(a)(3) requires the registrant to describe the effect of any disposals of components of an entity[11] and extraordinary, unusual or infrequently occurring items recognized in each quarter, as well as the aggregate effect and the nature of year-end or other adjustments which are material to the results of that quarter. Furthermore, Item 302(a)(2) requires a reconciliation of amounts previously reported on Form 10-Q to the quarterly data presented if the amounts differ.

Question 1: Are these disclosure requirements applicable to supplemental financial statements included in a filing with the SEC for unconsolidated subsidiaries and 50% or less owned persons?

Interpretive Response: The summarized quarterly financial data required by Item 302(a)(1) need not be included in supplemental financial statements for unconsolidated subsidiaries and 50% or less owned persons unless the financial statements are for a subsidiary or affiliate that is itself a registrant which meets the criteria set forth in Item 302(a)(5).

Question 2: If a company is in a specialized industry where "gross profit" generally is not computed (e.g., banks, insurance companies and finance companies), what disclosure should be made to comply with the requirements of Item 302(a)(1)?

Interpretive Response: Companies in specialized industries should present summarized quarterly financial data which are most meaningful in their

---

[1] If a registrant elects to follow the encouraged disclosure discussed in paragraph 23 of Statement 130, and displays the components of other comprehensive income and the total for comprehensive income using a one-statement approach, the registrant must continue to follow the guidance set forth in the SAB Topic. One approach may be to provide a separate reconciliation of net income to income available to common stock below comprehensive income reported on a statement of income and comprehensive income.

[2] The assessment of materiality is the responsibility of each registrant. However, absent concerns about trends or other qualitative considerations, the staff generally will not insist on the reporting of income or loss applicable to common stock if the amount differs from net income or loss by less than ten percent.

[3] These requirements have been further revised to require the company's CEO and CFO to certify to the information contained in the company's periodic filing.

[11] See question 5 for a discussion of the meaning of components of an entity as used in Item 302(a)(2).

particular circumstances. For example, a bank might present interest income, interest expense, provision for loan losses, security gains or losses and net income. Similarly, an insurance company might present net premiums earned, underwriting costs and expenses, investment income, security gains or losses and net income.

Question 3: If a company wishes to make its quarterly and annual disclosures on the same basis, would disclosure of costs and expenses associated directly with or allocated to products sold or services rendered, or other appropriate data to enable users to compute "gross profit," satisfy the requirements of Item 302(a)(1)?

Interpretive Response: Yes.

Question 4: What is meant by "per-share data based upon such income" as used in Item 302(a)(1)?

Interpretive Response: Item 302(a)(1) only requires disclosure of per share amounts for income before extraordinary items and cumulative effect of a change in accounting. It is expected that when per share data is calculated for each full quarter based upon such income, the per share amounts would be both basic and diluted. Although it is not required by the rule, there are many instances where it would be desirable to disclose other per share figures such as net earnings per share and the per share effect of extraordinary items also. Where such disclosure is made, per share data should be both basic and diluted.

Question 5: What is intended by the requirement set forth in Item 302(a)(3) that registrants "describe the effect of" disposals of segments of a business, etc.?

Interpretive Response: The rule uses the language of segments of a business that was previously found in the authoritative literature. Consistent with the terminology used in Statement 144, as used here, segments of a business is intended to mean components of an entity. The rule is intended to require registrants to "disclose the amount" of such unusual transactions and events included in the results reported for each quarter. Such disclosure would be made in narrative form. However, it would not require that matters covered by MD&A be repeated. In this situation, registrants should disclose the nature and amount of the unusual transaction or event and refer to MD&A for further discussion of the matter.

Question 6: What is intended by the requirement of Item 302(a)(3) to disclose "the aggregate effect and the nature of year-end or other adjustments which are material to the results of that quarter"?

Interpretive Response: This language is taken directly from paragraph 31 of APB Opinion 28 which relates to disclosures required for the fourth quarter of the year. The Opinion indicates that earlier quarters should not be restated to reflect a change in accounting estimate recorded at year end. However, changes in an accounting estimate made in an interim period that materially affect the quarter in which the change occurred are required to be disclosed in order to avoid misleading comparisons. In making such disclosure, registrants may wish to identify (but not

restate) the prior periods in which transactions were recorded which relate to the change in the quarter.

Question 7: If company has filed a Form 10-Q/A amending a previously filed Form 10-Q, is a reconciliation of quarterly data in annual financial statements with the amounts originally reported on Form 10-Q required?

Interpretive Response: Yes. However, if the company publishes quarterly reports to shareholders and has previously made detailed disclosure to shareholders in such reports of the change reported on the Form 10-Q/A, no reconciliation would be required.

b. Financial statements presented on other than a quarterly basis

Facts: Item 302(a)(1) requires disclosure of quarterly financial data for each full quarter of the last two fiscal years and in any subsequent interim period for which an income statement is presented.

Question: If a company reports at interim dates on other than a calendar-quarter basis (e.g., 12-12-16-12 week basis), will it be precluded from reporting on such basis in the future?

Interpretive Response: No, as long as it discloses the basis of interim fiscal period reporting and the interim fiscal periods on which it reports are consistently determined from year to year (or, if not, the lack of comparability is disclosed).

c. Deleted by SAB 103

2. *Amendments to Form 10-Q*

a. Form of condensed financial statements

Facts: Rules 10-01(a)(2) and (3) of Regulation S-X provide that interim balance sheets and statements of income shall include only major captions (i.e., numbered captions) set forth in Regulation S-X, with the exception of inventories where data as to raw materials, work in process and finished goods shall be included, if applicable, either on the face of the balance sheet or in notes thereto. Where any major balance sheet caption is less than 10% of total assets and the amount in the caption has not increased or decreased by more than 25% since the end of the preceding fiscal year, the caption may be combined with others. When any major income statement caption is less than 15% of average net income attributable to the registrant for the most recent three fiscal years and the amount in the caption has not increased or decreased by more than 20% as compared to the corresponding interim period of the preceding fiscal year, the caption may be combined with others. Similarly, the statement of cash flows may be abbreviated, starting with a single figure of cash flows provided by operations and showing other changes individually only when they exceed 10% of the average of cash flows provided by operations for the most recent three years.

Question 1: If a company previously combined captions in a Form 10-Q but is required to present such captions separately in the Form 10-Q for the current quarter, must it retroactively reclassify amounts included in the prior-year financial statements presented for comparative purposes to conform with the captions presented for the current-year quarter?

Interpretive Response: Yes.

Question 2: If a company uses the gross profit method or some other method to determine cost of goods sold for interim periods, will it be acceptable to state only that it is not practicable to determine components of inventory at interim periods?

Interpretive Response: The staff believes disclosure of inventory components is important to investors. In reaching this decision, the staff recognizes that registrants may not take inventories during interim periods and that managements, therefore, will have to estimate the inventory components. However, the staff believes that management will be able to make reasonable estimates of inventory components based upon their knowledge of the company's production cycle, the costs (labor and overhead) associated with this cycle as well as the relative sales and purchasing volume of the company.

Question 3: If a company has years during which operations resulted in a net outflow of cash and cash equivalents, should it exclude such years from the computation of cash and cash equivalents provided by operations for the three most recent years in determining what sources and applications must be shown separately?

Interpretive Response: Yes. Similar to the determination of average net income, if operations resulted in a net outflow of cash and cash equivalents during any year, such amount should be excluded in making the computation of cash flow provided by operations for the three most recent years unless operations resulted in a net outflow of cash and cash equivalents in all three years, in which case the average of the net outflow of cash and cash equivalents should be used for the test.

b. *Reporting requirements for accounting changes*

1. Preferability

Facts: Rule 10-01(b)(6) of Regulation S-X requires that a registrant who makes a material change in its method of accounting shall indicate the date of and the reason for the change. The registrant also must include as an exhibit in the first Form 10-Q filed subsequent to the date of an accounting change, a letter from the registrant's independent accountants indicating whether or not the change is to an alternative principle which in his judgment is preferable under the circumstances. A letter from the independent accountant is not required when the change is made in response to a standard adopted by the Financial Accounting Standards Board which requires such a change.

Question 1: For some alternative accounting principles, authoritative bodies have specified when one

alternative is preferable to another. However, for other alternative accounting principles, no authoritative body has specified criteria for determining the preferability of one alternative over another. In such situations, how should preferability be determined?

Interpretive Response: In such cases, where objective criteria for determining the preferability among alternative accounting principles have not been established by authoritative bodies, the determination of preferability should be based on the particular circumstances described by and discussed with the registrant. In addition, the independent accountant should consider other significant information of which he is aware.[5]

Question 2: Management may offer, as justification for a change in accounting principle, circumstances such as: their expectation as to the effect of general economic trends on their business (e.g., the impact of inflation), their expectation regarding expanding consumer demand for the company's products, or plans for change in marketing methods. Are these circumstances which enter into the determination of preferability?

Interpretive Response: Yes. Those circumstances are examples of business judgment and planning and should be evaluated in determining preferability. In the case of changes for which objective criteria for determining preferability have not been established by authoritative bodies, business judgment and business planning often are major considerations in determining that the change is to a preferable method because the change results in improved financial reporting.

Question 3: What responsibility does the independent accountant have for evaluating the business judgment and business planning of the registrant?

Interpretive Response: Business judgment and business planning are within the province of the registrant. Thus, the independent accountant may accept the registrant's business judgment and business planning and express reliance thereon in his letter. However, if either the plans or judgment appear to be unreasonable to the independent accountant, he should not accept them as justification. For example, an independent accountant should not accept a registrant's plans for a major expansion if he believes the registrant does not have the means of obtaining the funds necessary for the expansion program.

Question 4: If a registrant, who has changed to an accounting method which was preferable under the circumstances, later finds that it must abandon its business plans or change its business judgment because of economic or other factors, is the registrant's justification nullified?

Interpretive Response: No. A registrant must in good faith justify a change in its method of accounting under the circumstances which exist at the time of

---

[5] Registrants also are reminded that paragraph 17 of APB Opinion 20 requires that companies disclose the nature of and justification for the change as well as the effects of the change on net income for the period in which the change is made. Furthermore,

the justification for the change should explain clearly why the newly adopted principle is preferable to the previously-applied principle.

the change. The existence of different circumstances at a later time does not nullify the previous justification for the change.

Question 5: If a registrant justified a change in accounting method as preferable under the circumstances, and the circumstances change, may the registrant revert to the method of accounting used before the change?

Interpretive Response: Any time a registrant makes a change in accounting method, the change must be justified as preferable under the circumstances. Thus, a registrant may not change back to a principle previously used unless it can justify that the previously used principle is preferable in the circumstances as they currently exist.

Question 6: If one client of an independent accounting firm changes its method of accounting and the accountant submits the required letter stating his view of the preferability of the principle in the circumstances, does this mean that all clients of that firm are constrained from making the converse change in accounting (e.g., if one client changes from FIFO to LIFO, can no other client change from LIFO to FIFO)?

Interpretive Response: No. Each registrant must justify a change in accounting method on the basis that the method is preferable under the circumstances of that registrant. In addition, a registrant must furnish a letter from its independent accountant stating that in the judgment of the independent accountant the change in method is preferable under the circumstances of that registrant. If registrants in apparently similar circumstances make changes in opposite directions, the staff has a responsibility to inquire as to the factors which were considered in arriving at the determination by each registrant and its independent accountant that the change was preferable under the circumstances because it resulted in improved financial reporting. The staff recognizes the importance, in many circumstances, of the judgments and plans of management and recognizes that such management judgments may, in good faith, differ. As indicated above, the concern relates to registrants in apparently similar circumstances, no matter who their independent accountants may be.

Question 7: If a registrant changes its accounting to one of two methods specifically approved by the FASB in a Statement of Financial Accounting Standards, need the independent accountant express his view as to the preferability of the method selected?

Interpretive Response: If a registrant was formerly using a method of accounting no longer deemed acceptable, a change to either method approved by the FASB may be presumed to be a change to a preferable method and no letter will be required from the independent accountant. If, however, the registrant was formerly using one of the methods approved by the FASB for current use and wishes to change to an alternative approved method, then the registrant must justify its change as being one to a preferable method in the circumstances and the independent accountant must submit a letter stating that

in his view the change is to a principle that is preferable in the circumstances.

2. Filing of a letter from the accountants

Facts: The registrant makes an accounting change in the fourth quarter of its fiscal year. Rule 10-01(b)(6) of Regulation S-X requires that the registrant file a letter from its independent accountants stating whether or not the change is preferable in the circumstances in the next Form 10-Q. Item 601(b)(18) of Regulation S-K provides that the independent accountant's preferability letter be filed as an exhibit to reports on Forms 10-K or 10-Q.

Question: When the independent accountant's letter is filed with the Form 10-K, must another letter also be filed with the first quarter's Form 10-Q in the following year?

Interpretive Response: No. A letter is not required to be filed with Form 10-Q if it has been previously filed as an exhibit to the Form 10-K.

H. Accounting Series Release 148 -Disclosure Of Compensating Balances And Short-Term Borrowing Arrangements (Adopted November 13, 1973 As Modified By ASR 172 Adopted On June 13, 1975 And ASR 280 Adopted On September 2, 1980)

Facts: ASR 148 (as modified) amends Regulation S-X to include:

1. Disclosure of compensating balance arrangements.

2. Segregation of cash for compensating balance arrangements that are legal restrictions on the availability of cash.

1. *Applicability*

a. *Arrangements with other lending institutions*

Question: In addition to banks, is ASR 148 applicable to arrangements with factors, commercial finance companies or other lending entities?

Interpretive Response: Yes.

b. *Bank holding companies and brokerage firms*

Question: Do the provisions of ASR 148 apply to bank holding companies and to brokerage firms filing under Rule 17a-5?

Interpretive Response: Yes; however, brokerage firms are not expected to meet these requirements when filing Form X-17a-5.

c. *Financial statements of parent company and unconsolidated subsidiaries*

Question: Are the provisions of ASR 148 applicable to parent company financial statements in addition to consolidated financial statements? To financial statements of unconsolidated subsidiaries?

Interpretive Response: ASR 148 data for consolidated financial statements only will generally be sufficient when a filing includes consolidated and parent company financial statements. Such data are required for each unconsolidated subsidiary or other entity when a filing is required to include complete financial statements of those entities. When the filing includes summarized financial data in a footnote about such entities, the disclosures under ASR 148 relating to the consolidated financial statements will be sufficient.

d. Foreign lenders

Question: Are ASR 148 disclosure requirements applicable to arrangements with foreign lenders?

Interpretive Response: Yes.

2. Classification of short-term obligations-Debt related to long-term projects

Facts: Companies engaging in significant long-term construction programs frequently arrange for revolving cover loans which extend until the completion of long-term construction projects. Such revolving cover loans are typically arranged with substantial financial institutions and typically have the following characteristics:

1. A firm long-term mortgage commitment is obtained for each project.

2. Interest rates and terms are in line with the company's normal borrowing arrangements.

3. Amounts are equal to the expected full mortgage amount of all projects.

4. The company may draw down funds at its option up to the maximum amount of the agreement.

5. The company uses short-term interim construction financing (commercial paper, bank loans, etc.) against the revolving cover loan. Such indebtedness is rolled over or drawn down on the revolving cover loan at the company's option. The company typically has regular bank lines of credit, but these generally are not legally enforceable.

Question: Under Statement 6, will the classification of loans such as described above as long-term be acceptable?

Interpretive Response: Where such conditions exist providing for a firm commitment throughout the construction program as well as a firm commitment for permanent mortgage financing, and where there are no contingencies other than the completion of construction, the guideline criteria are met and the borrowing under such a program should be classified as long-term with appropriate disclosure.

3. Compensating balances

a. Compensating balances for future credit availability

Facts: Rule 5-02.1 of Regulation S-X requires disclosure of compensating balances in order to avoid undisclosed commingling of such balances with other funds having different liquidity characteristics and bearing no determinable relationship to borrowing arrangements. It also requires footnote disclosure distinguishing the amounts of such balances maintained under a formal agreement to assure future credit availability.

Question: In disclosing compensating balances maintained to assure future credit availability, is it necessary to segregate compensating balances for an unused portion of a regular line of credit when a total compensating balance amount covering both used and unused amounts of a line of credit is disclosed?

Interpretive Response: No.

b. Changes in compensating balances

Facts: ASR 148 guidelines indicate the need for additional disclosures where compensating balances were materially greater during the period than at the end of the period.

Question: Does this disclosure relate to changes in the arrangement (e.g., the required compensating balance percentage) or changes in borrowing levels?

Interpretive Response: Both.

c. Float

Facts: ASR 148 states that "compensating balance arrangements . . . are normally expressed in terms of collected bank ledger balances but the financial statements are presented on the basis of the company's books. In order to make the disclosure of compensating balance amounts . . . consistent with the cash amounts reflected in the financial statements, the balance figure agreed upon by the bank and the company should be adjusted if possible by the estimated float."

Question: In determining the amount of "float" as suggested by ASR 148 guidelines, frequently an adjustment to the bank balance is required for "uncollected funds." On what basis should this adjustment be estimated?

Interpretive Response: The adjustment should be estimated based upon the method used by the bank or a reasonable approximation of that method. The following is a sample computation of the amount of compensating balances to be disclosed where uncollected funds are involved.

Assumptions: The company has agreed to maintain compensating balances equal to 20% of short-term borrowings.

Short-term borrowings	$10,000,000
Compensating balances per bank balances	2,000,000
Estimated float (approximates the excess of outstanding checks over deposits in transit)	480,000
Estimated uncollected funds	320,000
Computation:	
Compensating balances per bank balances	2,000,000
Estimated uncollected funds	320,000
Estimated float	(480,000)
Compensating balances stated in terms of a book cash balance and to be disclosed	$1,840,000

4. Miscellaneous

a. Periods required

Question: For what periods are ASR 148 disclosures required?

Interpretive Response: Disclosure of compensating balance arrangements and other disclosures called for in ASR 148 are required for the latest fiscal year but are generally not required for any later interim period unless a material change has occurred since year end.

b. 10-Q Disclosures

Question: Are ASR 148 disclosures required in 10-Q's?

Interpretive Response: In general, ASR 148 disclosures are not required in Form 10-Q. However, in some instances material changes in borrowing arrangements or borrowing levels may give rise to the need for disclosure either in Form 10-Q or Form 8-K.

I. Accounting Series Release 149 -Improved Disclosure Of Income Tax Expense (Adopted November 28, 1973 And Modified By ASR 280 Adopted On September 2, 1980)

Facts: ASR 149 and 280 amend Regulation S-X to include:

1. Disclosure of tax effect of timing differences comprising deferred income tax expense.

2. Disclosure of the components of income tax expense, including currently payable and the net tax effects of timing differences.

3. Disclosure of the components of income [loss] before income tax expense [benefit] as either domestic or foreign.

4. Reconciliation between the statutory Federal income tax rate and the effective tax rate.

1. Tax rate

Question 1: In reconciling to the effective tax rate should the rate used be a combination of state and Federal income tax rates?

Interpretive Response: No, the reconciliation should be made to the Federal income tax rate only.

Question 2: What is the "applicable statutory Federal income tax rate"?

Interpretive Response: The applicable statutory Federal income tax rate is the normal rate applicable to the reporting entity. Hence, the statutory rate for a U.S. partnership is zero. If, for example, the statutory rate for U.S. corporations is 22% on the first $25,000 of taxable income and 46% on the excess over $25,000, the "normalized rate" for corporations would fluctuate in the range between 22% and 46% depending on the amount of pretax accounting income a corporation has.

2. Taxes of investee company

Question: If a registrant records its share of earnings or losses of a 50% or less owned person on the equity basis and such person has an effective tax rate which differs by more than 5% from the applicable statutory Federal income tax rate, is a reconciliation as required by Rule 4-08(g) necessary?

Interpretive Response: Whenever the tax components are known and material to the investor's (registrant's) financial position or results of operations, appropriate disclosure should be made. In some instances where 50% or less owned persons are accounted for by the equity method of accounting in the financial statements of the registrant, the registrant may not know the rate at which the various components of income are taxed and it may not be practicable to provide disclosure concerning such components.

It should also be noted that it is generally necessary to disclose the aggregate dollar and per-share effect of situations where temporary tax exemptions or "tax holidays" exist, and that such disclosures are also applicable to 50% or less owned persons. Such disclosures should include a brief description of the factual circumstances and give the date on which the special tax status will terminate. See Topic 11.C.

3. Net of tax presentation

Question: What disclosure is required when an item is reported on a net of tax basis (e.g., extraordinary items, discontinued operations, or cumulative adjustment related to accounting change)?

Interpretive Response: When an item is reported on a net of tax basis, additional disclosure of the nature of the tax component should be provided by reconciling the tax component associated with the item to the applicable statutory Federal income tax rate or rates.

4. Loss years

Question: Is a reconciliation of a tax recovery in a loss year required?

Interpretive Response: Yes, in loss years the actual book tax benefit of the loss should be reconciled to expected normal book tax benefit based on the applicable statutory Federal income tax rate.

5. Foreign registrants

Question 1: Occasionally, reporting foreign persons may not operate under a normal income tax base rate such as the current U.S. Federal corporate income tax rate. What form of disclosure is acceptable in these circumstances?

Interpretive Response: In such instances, reconciliations between year-to-year effective rates or between a weighted average effective rate and the current effective rate of total tax expense may be appropriate in meeting the requirements of Rule 4-08(h)(2). A brief description of how such a rate was determined would be required in addition to other required disclosures. Such an approach would not be acceptable for a U.S. registrant with foreign operations. Foreign registrants with unusual tax situations may find that these guidelines are not fully responsive to their needs. In such instances, registrants should discuss the matter with the staff.

Question 2: Where there are significant reconciling items that relate in significant part to foreign operations as well as domestic operations, is it necessary to disclose the separate amounts of the tax component by geographical area, e.g., statutory depletion allowances provided for by U.S. and by other foreign jurisdictions?

Interpretive Response: It is not practicable to give an all-encompassing answer to this question. However, in many cases such disclosure would seem appropriate.

6. Securities gains and losses

Question: If the tax on the securities gains and losses of banks and insurance companies varies by more than 5% from the applicable statutory Federal income tax rate, should a reconciliation to the statutory rate be provided?

Interpretive Response: Yes.

7. Tax expense components v. "overall" presentation

Facts: Rule 4-08(h) requires that the various components of income tax expense be disclosed, e.g., currently payable domestic taxes, deferred foreign taxes, etc. Frequently income tax expense will be included in more than one caption in the financial statements. For example, income taxes may be allocated to continuing operations, discontinued operations, extraordinary items, cumulative effects of an accounting change and direct charges and credits to shareholders' equity.

Question: In instances where income tax expense is allocated to more than one caption in the financial statements, must the components of income tax expense included in each caption be disclosed or will an "overall" presentation such as the following be acceptable?

The components of income tax expense are:

Currently payable (per tax return):

Federal	$350,000
Foreign	150,000
State	50,000
Deferred:	
Federal	125,000
Foreign	75,000
State	50,000
	$800,000

Income tax expense is included in the financial statements as follows:

Continuing operations	$600,000
Discontinued operations	(200,000)
Extraordinary income	300,000
Cumulative effect of change in accounting principle	100,000
	$800,000

Interpretive Response: An overall presentation of the nature described will be acceptable.

J. Deleted by SAB 47

K. Accounting Series Release 302 - Separate Financial Statements Required By Regulation S-X

1. Deleted by SAB 103

2. Parent company financial information

a. Computation of restricted net assets of subsidiaries

Facts: The revised rules for parent company disclosures adopted in ASR 302 require, in certain circumstances, (1) footnote disclosure in the consolidated financial statements about the nature and amount of significant restrictions on the ability of subsidiaries to transfer funds to the parent through intercompany loans, advances or cash dividends [Rule 4-08(e)(3)], and (2) the presentation of condensed parent company financial information and other data in a schedule (Rule 12-04). To determine which disclosures, if any, are required, a registrant must compute its proportionate share of the net assets of its consolidated and unconsolidated subsidiary companies as of the end of the most recent fiscal year which are restricted as to transfer to the parent company because the consent of a third party (a lender, regulatory agency, foreign government, etc.) is required. If the registrant's proportionate share of the restricted net assets of consolidated subsidiaries exceeds 25% of the registrant's consolidated net assets, both the footnote and schedule information are required. If the amount of such restrictions is less than 25%, but the sum of these restrictions plus the amount of the registrant's proportionate share of restricted net assets of unconsolidated subsidiaries plus the registrant's equity in the undistributed earnings of 50% or less owned persons (investees) accounted for by the equity method exceed 25% of consolidated net assets, the footnote disclosure is required.

Question 1: How are restricted net assets of subsidiaries computed?

Interpretative Response: The calculation of restricted net assets requires an evaluation of each subsidiary to identify any circumstances where third parties may limit the subsidiary's ability to loan, advance or dividend funds to the parent. This evaluation normally comprises a review of loan agreements, statutory and regulatory requirements, etc., to determine the dollar amount of each subsidiary's restrictions. The related amount of the subsidiary's net assets designated as restricted, however, should not exceed the amount of the subsidiary's net assets included in consolidated net assets, since parent company disclosures are triggered when a significant amount of consolidated net assets are restricted. The amount of each subsidiary's net assets included in consolidated net assets is determined by allocating (pushing down) to each subsidiary any related consolidation adjustments such as intercompany balances, intercompany profits, and differences between fair value and historical cost arising from a business combination accounted for as a purchase. This amount is referred to as the subsidiary's adjusted net assets. If the subsidiary's adjusted net assets are less than the amount of its restrictions because the push down of consolidating adjustments reduced its net assets, the subsidiary's adjusted net assets is the amount of the subsidiary's restricted net assets used in the tests.

Registrants with numerous subsidiaries and investees may wish to develop approaches to facilitate the determination of its parent company disclosure requirements. For example, if the parent company's adjusted net assets (excluding any interest in its subsidiaries) exceed 75% of consolidated net assets, or if the total of all of the registrant's consolidated and unconsolidated subsidiaries' restrictions and its equity in investees' earnings is less than 25% of consolidated net assets, then the allocation of consolidating adjustments to the subsidiaries to determine the amount of their adjusted net assets would not be necessary since no parent company disclosures would be required.

Question 2: If a registrant makes a decision that it will permanently reinvest the undistributed earnings of a subsidiary, and thus does not provide for income taxes thereon because it meets the criteria set forth in APB Opinion 23, is there considered to be a restriction for purposes of the test?

Interpretive Response: No. The rules require that only third party restrictions be considered. Restrictions on subsidiary net assets imposed by management are not included.

b. Application of tests for parent company disclosures

Facts: The balance sheet of the registrant's 100%-owned subsidiary at the most recent fiscal year-end is summarized as follows:

Current assets	$120	Current liabilities	$30
Noncurrent assets	45	Long-term debt	60
			90
		Common stock	25
		Retained earnings	50
			75
	$165		$165

Net assets of the subsidiary are $75. Assume there are no consolidating adjustments to be allocated to the subsidiary. Restrictive covenants of the subsidiary's debt agreements provide that:

• Net assets, excluding intercompany loans, cannot be less than $35

• 60% of accumulated earnings must be maintained

Question 1: What is the amount of the subsidiary's restricted net assets?

Interpretive Response:

Current assets	$75
Noncurrent assets	90
	$165

Assume that the registrant's consolidated net assets are $130 and there are no consolidating adjustments to be allocated to the subsidiary. The

Restriction	Computed Restrictions
Net assets: currently $75, cannot be less than $35; therefore	$35
Dividends: 60% of accumulated earnings ($50) cannot be paid out; therefore	$30

Restricted net assets for purposes of the test are $35. The maximum amount that can be loaned or advanced to the parent without violating the net asset covenant is $40 ($75 – 35). Alternatively, the subsidiary could pay a dividend of up to $20 ($50 – 30) without violating the dividend covenant, and loan or advance up to $20, without violating the net asset provision.

Facts: The registrant has one 100%-owned subsidiary. The balance sheet of the subsidiary at the latest fiscal year-end is summarized as follows:

Current liabilities	$23
Long-term debt	57
Redeemable preferred stock	10
Common stock	30
Retained earnings	45
	75
	$165

subsidiary's net assets are $75. The subsidiary's noncurrent assets are comprised of $40 in operating plant and equipment used in the subsidiary's business and a $50 investment in a 30% investee. The subsidiary's equity in this investee's undistributed earnings is $18. Restrictive covenants of the subsidiary's debt agreements are as follows:

1. Net assets, excluding intercompany balances, cannot be less than $20.

2. 80% of accumulated earnings must be reinvested in the subsidiary.

3. Current ratio of 2:1 must be maintained.

Question 2: Are parent company footnote or schedule disclosures required?

Interpretive Response: Only the parent company footnote disclosures are required. The subsidiary's restricted net assets are computed as follows:

Restriction	Computed Restriction
Net assets: currently $75, cannot be less than $20; therefore	$20
Dividends: 80% of accumulated earnings ($45) cannot be paid; therefore	$36
Current ratio: must be at least 2:1 ($46 current assets must be maintained since current liabilities are $23 at fiscal year-end); therefore	$46

Restricted net assets for purposes of the test are $20. The amount computed from the dividend restriction ($36) and the current ratio requirement ($46) are not used because net assets may be transferred by the subsidiary up to the limitation imposed by the requirement to maintain net assets of at least $20, without violating the other restrictions. For example, a transfer to the parent of up to $55 of net assets could be accomplished by a combination of dividends of current assets of $9 ($45-36), and loans or advances of current assets of up to $20 and noncurrent assets of up to $26.

Parent company footnote disclosures are required in this example since the restricted net assets of the subsidiary and the registrant's equity in the earnings of its 100%-owned subsidiary's investee exceed 25% of consolidated net assets [($20 + 18)/$130=29%]. The parent company schedule information is not required since the restricted net assets of the subsidiary are only 15% of consolidated net assets ($20/$130 =15%).

Although the subsidiary's noncurrent assets are not in a form which is readily transferable to the parent company, the illiquid nature of the assets is not relevant for purposes of the parent company tests. The objective of the tests is to require parent company disclosures when the parent company does not have control of its subsidiaries' funds because it does not have unrestricted access to their net assets. The tests trigger parent company disclosures only when there are significant third party restrictions on transfers by subsidiaries of net assets and the subsidiaries' net assets comprise a significant portion of consolidated net assets. Practical limitations, other than third

party restrictions on transferability at the measurement date (most recent fiscal year-end), such as subsidiary illiquidity, are not considered in computing restricted net assets. However, the potential effect of any limitations other than those imposed by third parties should be considered for inclusion in Management's Discussion and Analysis of liquidity.

Facts:

	Net assets
Subsidiary A	$(500)
Subsidiary B	$2,000
Consolidated	$3,700

Subsidiaries A and B are 100% owned by the registrant. Assume there are no consolidating adjustments to be allocated to the subsidiaries. Subsidiary A has restrictions amounting to $200. Subsidiary B's restrictions are $1,000.

Question 3: What parent company disclosures are required for the registrant?

Interpretive Response: Since subsidiary A has an excess of liabilities over assets, it has no restricted net assets for purposes of the test. However, both parent company footnote and schedule disclosures are required, since the restricted net assets of subsidiary B exceed 25% of consolidated net assets ($1,000/3,700=27%).

Facts:

	Net assets
Subsidiary A	$850
Subsidiary B	$300
Consolidated	$3,700

The registrant owns 80% of subsidiary A. Subsidiary A owns 100% of subsidiary B. Assume there are no consolidating adjustments to be allocated to the subsidiaries. A may not pay any dividends or make any affiliate loans or advances. B has no restrictions. A's net assets of $850 do not include its investment in B.

Question 4: Are parent company footnote or schedule disclosures required for this registrant?

Interpretive Response: No. All of the registrant's share of subsidiary A's net assets ($680) are restricted. Although B may pay dividends and loan or advance funds to A, the parent's access to B's funds through A is restricted. However, since there are no limitations on B's ability to loan or advance funds to the parent, none of the parent's share of B's net assets are restricted. Since A's restricted net assets are less than 25% of consolidated net assets ($680/3700=18%), no parent company disclosures are required.

Facts: The consolidating balance sheet of the registrant at the latest fiscal year-end is summarized as follows:

	Registrant	Subsidiary	Consolidating Adjustments	Consolidated
Current assets	$800	$700	$0	$1,500
30% investment in affiliate .	175	0	0	175
Investment in subsidiary . .	350	0	(350)	0
Other noncurrent assets . .	625	300	(100)	825
	$1,950	$1,000	$(450)	$2,500
Current liabilities	$600	$400	$0	$1,000
Concurrent liabilities	375	150	0	525
Redeemable preferred stock	275	0	0	275
Common stock	110	1	(1)	110
Paid-in capital	290	49	(49)	290
Retained earnings	300	400	(400)	300
	700	450	(450)	700
	$1,950	$1,000	$(450)	$2,500

The acquisition of the 100%-owned subsidiary was consummated on the last day of the most recent fiscal year. Immediately preceding the acquisition, the registrant had net assets of $700, which included its equity in the undisputed earnings of its 30% investee of $75. Immediately after acquiring the subsidiary's net assets, which had an historical cost of $450 and a fair value of $350, the registrant's net assets were still $700 since debt and preferred stock totaling $350 were issued in the purchase. The subsidiary has debt covenants which permit dividends, loans or advances, to the extent, if any, that net assets exceed an amount which is determined by the sum of $100 plus 75% of the subsidiary's accumulated earnings.

Question 5: What is the amount of the subsidiary's restricted net assets? Are parent company footnote or schedule disclosures required?

Interpretive Response: Restricted net assets for purposes of the test are $350, and both the parent company footnote and schedule disclosures are required.

The amount of the subsidiary's restrictions at year-end is $400 [$100 + (75%×$400)]. The subsidiary's adjusted net assets after the push down of the consolidation entry to the subsidiary to record the noncurrent assets acquired at their fair value is $350 ($450 – $100). Since the subsidiary's adjusted net assets ($350) are less than the amount of its restrictions ($400), restricted net assets are $350. The computed percentages applicable to each of the disclosure tests is in excess of 25%. Therefore, both parent company footnote and schedule information are required. The percentage applicable to the footnote disclosure test is 61% [($75 + 350)/$700]. The computed percentage for the schedule disclosure is 50% ($350/$700).

3. Undistributed earnings of 50% or less owned persons

Facts: Rule 4-08(e)(2) of Regulation SX requires footnote disclosures of the amount of consolidated retained earnings which represents undistributed earnings of 50% or less owned persons (investee)

accounted for by the equity method. The test adopted in ASR 302 to trigger disclosures about the registrant's restricted net assets (Rule 4-08(e)(3)) includes the parent's equity in the undistributed earnings of investees.

Question: Is the amount required for footnote disclosure the same as the amount included in the test to determine disclosures about restrictions?

Interpretive Response: Yes. The amount used in the test in Rule 4-08(e)(3) should be the same as the amount required to be disclosed by Rule 4-08(e)(2). This is the portion of the registrant's consolidated retained earnings which represents the undistributed earnings of an investee since the date(s) of acquisition. It is computed by determining the registrant's cumulative equity in the investee's earnings, adjusted by any dividends received, related goodwill amortized, and any related income taxes provided.

4. Application of significant subsidiary test to investees and unconsolidated subsidiaries

a. Separate financial statement requirements

Facts: Rule 3-09 of Regulation SX requires the presentation of separate financial statements of unconsolidated subsidiaries and of 50% or less owned persons (investee) accounted for by the equity method either by the registrant or by a subsidiary of the registrant in filings with the Commission if any of the tests of a significant subsidiary are met at a 20% level.

Question 1: Are the requirements for separate financial statements also applicable to an investee accounted for by the equity method by an investee of the registrant?

Interpretive Response: Yes. Rule 3-09 is intended to apply to all investees which are material to the financial position or results of operations of the registrant, regardless of whether the investee is held by the registrant, a subsidiary or another investee. Separate financial statements should be provided for any lower tier investee where such an entity is significant to the registrant's consolidated financial statements.

Question 2: How is the significant subsidiary test applied to the lower tier investee in the situation described in Question 1?

Interpretive Response: Since the disclosures provided by separate financial statements of an investee are considered necessary to evaluate the overall financial condition of the registrant, the significant subsidiary test is computed based on the materiality of the lower tier investee to the registrant consolidated. An example of the application of the assets test of the significant subsidiary rules to such an investee situation will illustrate the materiality measurement. A registrant with total consolidated assets of $5,000 owns 50% of Investee A, whose total assets are $3,800. Investee A has a 45% investment in Investee B, whose total assets are $4,800. There are no intercompany eliminations. Separate financial statements are required for Investee A, and they are required for Investee B because the registrant's share of B's total assets exceeds 20% of consolidated assets [(50%×45%× $4800)/$5000 = 22%].

b. Summarized financial statement requirements

Facts: Rule 4-08(g) of Regulation S-X requires summarized financial information about unconsolidated subsidiaries and 50% or less owned persons (investee) to be included in the footnotes to the financial statements if, in the aggregate, they meet the tests of a significant subsidiary set forth in Rule 1-02(w).

Question 1: Must a registrant which includes separate financial statements or condensed financial statements for unconsolidated subsidiaries or investees in its annual report to shareholders also include in such report the summarized financial information for these entities pursuant to Rule 4-08(g)?

Interpretive Response: No. The purpose of the summarized information is to provide minimum standards of disclosure when the impact of such entities on the consolidated financial statements is significant. If the registrant furnishes more information in the annual report than is required by these minimum disclosure standards, such as condensed financial information or separate audited financial statements, the summarized data can be excluded. The Commission's rules are not intended to conflict with the provisions of APB Opinion 18, par 20(c) and (d), which provide that either separate financial statements of investees be presented with the financial statements of the reporting entity or that summarized information be included in the reporting entity's financial statement footnotes.

Question 2: Can summarized information be omitted for individual entities as long as the aggregate information for the omitted entity(s) does not exceed 10% under any of the significance tests of Rule 1-02(w)?

Interpretive Response: The 10% measurement level of the significant subsidiary rule was not intended to establish a materiality criteria for omission, and the arbitrary exclusion of summarized information for selected entities up to a 10% level is not appropriate. Rule 4-08(g) requires that the summarized information be included for all unconsolidated subsidiaries and investees. However, the staff recognizes that exclusion of the summarized information for certain entities is appropriate in some circumstances where it is impracticable to accumulate such information and the summarized information to be excluded is de minimis.

L. Financial Reporting Release 28 -Accounting For Loan Losses By Registrants Engaged In Lending Activities

1. Accounting for loan losses

General: GAAP for recognition of loan losses is provided by Statements 5 and 114.[6] An estimated loss from a loss contingency, such as the collectibility of receivables, should be accrued when, based on information available prior to the issuance of the financial statements, it is probable that an asset has been impaired or a liability has been incurred at the date of the financial statements and the amount of the loss can be reasonably estimated.[7] Statement 114 provides more specific guidance on measurement of loan impairment and related disclosures but does not change the fundamental recognition criteria for loan losses provided by Statement 5. Additional guidance on the recognition, measurement, and disclosure of loan losses is provided by EITF Topic D-80, Interpretation 14, and the AICPA Audit and Accounting Guide, Banks and Savings Institutions.

Further guidance for SEC registrants is provided by FRR 28, which added subsection (b), Procedural Discipline in Determining the Allowance and Provision for Loan Losses to be Reported, of Section 401.09, Accounting for Loan Losses by Registrants Engaged in Lending Activities, to the Codification of Financial Reporting Policies (hereafter referred to as FRR 28). Additionally, public companies are required to comply with the books and records provisions of the Securities Exchange Act of 1934 (Exchange Act). Under Sections 13(b)(2) - (7) of the Exchange Act, registrants must make and keep books, records, and accounts, which, in reasonable detail, accurately and fairly reflect the transactions and dispositions of assets of the registrant. Registrants also must maintain internal accounting controls that are sufficient to provide reasonable assurances that, among other things, transactions are recorded as necessary to permit the preparation of financial statements in conformity with GAAP.

This staff interpretation applies to all registrants that are creditors in loan transactions that, individually or in the aggregate, have a material effect on the registrant's financial statements.[8]

---

[6] As amended by Statement 118.

[7] Paragraph 8 of Statement 5.

[8] For purposes of this interpretation, a loan is defined (consistent with paragraph 4 of Statement 114) as a contractual right to receive

money on demand or on fixed or determinable dates that is recognized as an asset in the creditor's statement of financial position. For purposes of this interpretation, loans do not include trade

2. Developing and documenting a systematic methodology

a. Developing a systematic methodology

Facts: Registrant A, or one of its consolidated subsidiaries, engages in lending activities and is developing or performing a review of its loan loss allowance methodology.

Question: What are some of the factors or elements that the staff normally would expect Registrant A to consider when developing (or subsequently performing an assessment of) its methodology for determining its loan loss allowance under GAAP?

Interpretive Response: The staff normally would expect a registrant that engages in lending activities to develop and document a systematic methodology[9] to determine its provision for loan losses and allowance for loan losses as of each financial reporting date. It is critical that loan loss allowance methodologies incorporate management's current judgments about the credit quality of the loan portfolio through a disciplined and consistently applied process. A registrant's loan loss allowance methodology is influenced by entity-specific factors, such as an entity's size, organizational structure, business environment and strategy, management style, loan portfolio characteristics, loan administration procedures, and management information systems.

However, as indicated in the AICPA Audit and Accounting Guide, Banks and Savings Institutions (Audit Guide), "[w]hile different institutions may use different methods, there are certain common elements that should be included in any [loan loss allowance] methodology for it to be effective."[10] A registrant's loan loss allowance methodology generally should:[11]

- Include a detailed analysis of the loan portfolio, performed on a regular basis;

- Consider all loans (whether on an individual or group basis);

- Identify loans to be evaluated for impairment on an individual basis under Statement 114 and segment the remainder of the portfolio into groups of loans with similar risk characteristics for evaluation and analysis under Statement 5;

- Consider all known relevant internal and external factors that may affect loan collectibility;

- Be applied consistently but, when appropriate, be modified for new factors affecting collectibility;

- Consider the particular risks inherent in different kinds of lending;

- Consider current collateral values (less costs to sell), where applicable;

- Require that analyses, estimates, reviews and other loan loss allowance methodology functions be performed by competent and well-trained personnel;

- Be based on current and reliable data;

- Be well documented, in writing, with clear explanations of the supporting analyses and rationale (see Question 2 below for staff views on documenting a loan loss allowance methodology); and

- Include a systematic and logical method to consolidate the loss estimates and ensure the loan loss allowance balance is recorded in accordance with GAAP.

For many entities engaged in lending activities, the allowance and provision for loan losses are significant elements of the financial statements.

Therefore, the staff believes it is appropriate for an entity's management to review, on a periodic basis, its methodology for determining its allowance for loan losses.[12] Additionally, for registrants that have audit committees, the staff believes that oversight of the financial reporting and auditing of the loan loss allowance by the audit committee can strengthen the registrant's control system and process for determining its allowance for loan losses.[13]

A systematic methodology that is properly designed and implemented should result in a registrant's best estimate of its allowance for loan losses.[14] Accordingly, the staff normally would expect regis-

---

(Footnote Continued)

accounts receivable or notes receivable with terms less than one year or debt securities subject to the provisions of Statement 115.

[9] FRR 28 states that "the Commission's staff normally would expect to find that the books and records of registrants engaged in lending activities include documentation of [the]: (a) systematic methodology to be employed each period in determining the amount of the loan losses to be reported, and (b) rationale supporting each period's determination that the amounts reported were adequate."

[10] See paragraph 7.05 of the Audit Guide.

[11] *Ibid.*

[12] For federally insured depository institutions, the December 21, 1993 "Interagency Policy Statement on the Allowance for Loan and Lease Losses (ALLL)" (the 1993 Interagency Policy Statement) indicates that boards of directors and management have certain responsibilities for the ALLL process and amounts reported. For example, as indicated on page 4 of that statement, "the board of directors and management are expected to: Ensure that the institution has an effective loan review system and controls[;] Ensure the prompt charge-off of loans, or portions of loans, that available information confirms to be uncollectible[; and] Ensure that the

institution's process for determining an adequate level for the ALLL is based on a comprehensive, adequately documented, and consistently applied analysis of the institution's loan and lease portfolio."

[13] SAS 61 (as amended by SAS 90) states, in part: "In connection with each SEC engagement the auditor should discuss with the audit committee the auditor's judgments about the quality, not just the acceptability, of the entity's accounting principles as applied in its financial reporting. The discussion should include items that have a significant impact on the representational faithfulness, verifiability, and neutrality of the accounting information included in the financial statements. [Footnote omitted.] Examples of items that may have such an impact are the following:

- Selection of new or changes to accounting policies
- Estimates, judgments, and uncertainties
- Unusual transactions
- Accounting policies relating to significant financial statement items, including the timing or transactions and the period in which they are recorded."

[14] Registrants should also refer to Interpretation 14, which provides accounting and disclosure guidance for situations in which a range of loss can be reasonably estimated but no single amount

trants to adjust their loan loss allowance balance, either upward or downward, in each period for differences between the results of the systematic determination process and the unadjusted loan loss allowance balance in the general ledger.[15]

b. Documenting a systematic methodology

Question 1: Assume the same facts as in Question 1. What would the staff normally expect Registrant A to include in its documentation of its loan loss allowance methodology?

Interpretive Response: In FRR 28, the Commission provided guidance for documentation of loan loss provisions and allowances for registrants engaged in lending activities. The staff believes that appropriate written supporting documentation for the loan loss provision and allowance facilitates review of the loan loss allowance process and reported amounts, builds discipline and consistency into the loan loss allowance determination process, and improves the process for estimating loan losses by helping to ensure that all relevant factors are appropriately considered in the allowance analysis.

The staff, therefore, normally would expect a registrant to document the relationship between the findings of its detailed review of the loan portfolio and the amount of the loan loss allowance and the provision for loan losses reported in each period.[16]

The staff normally would expect to find that registrants maintain written supporting documentation for the following decisions, strategies, and processes:[17]

• Policies and procedures:

• Over the systems and controls that maintain an appropriate loan loss allowance, and

• Over the loan loss allowance methodology;

• Loan grading system or process;

• Summary or consolidation of the loan loss allowance balance;

• Validation of the loan loss allowance methodology; and

• Periodic adjustments to the loan loss allowance process.

Question 2: The Interpretive Response to Question 2 indicates that the staff normally would expect to find that registrants maintain written supporting documentation for their loan loss allowance policies and procedures. In the staff's view, what aspects of a registrant's loan loss allowance internal accounting control systems and processes would appropriately be addressed in its written policies and procedures?

Interpretive Response: The staff is aware that registrants utilize a wide range of policies, procedures, and control systems in their loan loss allowance processes, and these policies, procedures, and systems are tailored to the size and complexity of the registrant and its loan portfolio. However, the staff believes that, in order for a registrant's loan loss allowance methodology to be effective, the registrant's written policies and procedures for the systems and controls that maintain an appropriate loan loss allowance would likely address the following:

• The roles and responsibilities of the registrant's departments and personnel (including the lending function, credit review, financial reporting, internal audit, senior management, audit committee, board of directors, and others, as applicable) who determine or review, as applicable, the loan loss allowance to be reported in the financial statements;[18]

• The registrant's accounting policies for loans and loan losses, including the policies for charge-offs and recoveries and for estimating the fair value of collateral, where applicable;[19]

• The description of the registrant's systematic methodology, which should be consistent with the registrant's accounting policies for determining its loan loss allowance (see Question 4 below for further discussion);[20] and

---

(Footnote Continued)

within the range appears to be a better estimate than any other amount within the range.

[15] Registrants should refer to the guidance on materiality in SAB 99 (SAB Topic 1.M).

[16] FRR 28 states: "The specific rationale upon which the [loan loss allowance and provision] amount actually reported is based-i.e., the bridge between the findings of the detailed review [of the loan portfolio]and the amount actually reported in each period—would be documented to help ensure the adequacy of the reported amount, to improve auditability, and to serve as a benchmark for exercise of prudent judgment in future periods."

[17] The Paragraph 7.39 in the Audit Guide outlines specific aspects of effective internal control related to the allowance for loan losses. These specific aspects include the control environment ("management communication of the need for proper reporting of the allowance"); management reports that summarize loan activity and the institution's procedures and controls ("accumulation of relevant, sufficient, and reliable data on which to base management's estimate of the allowance"); "independent loan review;" review of information and assumptions ("adequate review and approval of the allowance estimates by the individuals specified in management's written policy"); assessment of the process ("com-

parison of prior estimates related to the allowance with subsequent results to assess the reliability of the process used to develop the allowance"); and "consideration by management of whether the allowance is consistent with the operational plans of the institution."

[18] Paragraph 7.39 of the Audit Guide discusses "management communication of the need for proper reporting of the allowance." As indicated in that paragraph, the "control environment strongly influences the effectiveness of the system of controls and reflects the overall attitude, awareness, and action of the board of directors and management concerning the importance of control."

[19] Paragraph 7.33 of the Audit Guide refers to the documentation, for disclosure purposes, that an entity should include in the notes to the financial statements describing the accounting policies the entity used to estimate its allowance and related provision for loan losses.

[20] *Ibid.* As indicated in paragraph 7.33, "[s]uch a description should identify the factors that influenced management's judgment (for example, historical losses and existing economic conditions) and may also include discussion of risk elements relevant to particular categories of financial instruments."

• The system of internal controls used to ensure that the loan loss allowance process is maintained in accordance with GAAP.[21]

The staff normally would expect an internal control system[22] for the loan loss allowance estimation process to:

• Include measures to provide assurance regarding the reliability[23] and integrity of information and compliance with laws, regulations, and internal policies and procedures;[24]

• Reasonably assure that the registrant's financial statements are prepared in accordance with GAAP; and

• Include a well-defined loan review process.[25]

A well-defined loan review process[26] typically contains:

• An effective loan grading system that is consistently applied, identifies differing risk characteristics and loan quality problems accurately and in a timely manner, and prompts appropriate administrative actions;[27]

• Sufficient internal controls to ensure that all relevant loan review information is appropriately considered in estimating losses. This includes maintaining appropriate reports, details of reviews performed, and identification of personnel involved;[28] and

• Clear formal communication and coordination between a registrant's credit administration function, financial reporting group, management, board of directors, and others who are involved in the loan loss allowance determination or review process, as applicable (e.g., written policies and procedures, management reports, audit programs, and committee minutes).[29]

Question 3: The Interpretive Response to Question 3 indicates that the staff normally would expect a registrant's written loan loss allowance policies and procedures to include a description of the registrant's systematic allowance methodology, which should be consistent with its accounting policies for determining its loan loss allowance. What elements of a registrant's loan loss allowance methodology would the staff normally expect to be described in the registrant's written policies and procedures?

Interpretive Response: The staff normally would expect a registrant's written policies and procedures to describe the primary elements of its loan loss allowance methodology, including portfolio segmentation and impairment measurement. The staff normally would expect that, in order for a registrant's loan loss allowance methodology to be effective, the registrant's written policies and procedures would describe the methodology:

• For segmenting the portfolio:

• How the segmentation process is performed (i.e., by loan type, industry, risk rates, etc.);[30]

• When a loan grading system is used to segment the portfolio:

• The definitions of each loan grade;

• A reconciliation of the internal loan grades to supervisory loan grades, if applicable; and

• The delineation of responsibilities for the loan grading system.

• For determining and measuring impairment under Statement 114:[31]

• The methods used to identify loans to be analyzed individually;

• For individually reviewed loans that are impaired, how the amount of any impairment is determined and measured, including:

• Procedures describing the impairment measurement techniques available; and

• Steps performed to determine which technique is most appropriate in a given situation.

• The methods used to determine whether and how loans individually evaluated under Statement

---

[21] *See* also paragraph 7.39 in the Audit Guide which provides information about specific aspects of effective internal control related to the allowance for loan losses.

[22] *Ibid.* Public companies are required to comply with the books and records provisions of the Exchange Act. Under Sections 13(b)(2) - (7) of the Exchange Act, registrants must make and keep books, records, and accounts, which, in reasonable detail, accurately and fairly reflect the transactions and dispositions of assets of the registrant. Registrants also must maintain internal accounting controls that are sufficient to provide reasonable assurances that, among other things, transactions are recorded as necessary to permit the preparation of financial statements in conformity with GAAP.

[23] Concepts Statement 2 provides guidance on "reliability" as a primary quality of accounting information.

[24] Section 13(b)(2) -(7) of the Exchange Act.

[25] As indicated in paragraph 7.05, item a, in the Audit Guide, a loan loss allowance methodology should "include a detailed and regular analysis of the loan portfolio." Paragraphs 7.06 to 7.13 provide additional information on how creditors traditionally identify and review loans on an individual basis and review or analyze loans on a group or pool basis.

[26] *Ibid.* Additionally, paragraph 7.39 in the Audit Guide provides guidance on the loan review process. As stated in that paragraph,

"[m]anagement reports summarizing loan activity, renewals, and delinquencies are vital to the timely identification of problem loans." The paragraph further states: "Loan reviews should be conducted by institution personnel who are independent of the underwriting, supervision, and collections functions. The specific lines of reporting depend on the complexity of the institution's organizational structure, but the loan reviewers should report to a high level of management that is independent from the lending process in the institution."

[27] *Ibid.*

[28] *Ibid.*

[29] *Ibid.*

[30] Paragraph 7.07 in the Audit Guide states that "creditors have traditionally identified loans that are to be evaluated for collectibility by dividing the loan portfolio into different segments. Each segment should contain loans with similar characteristics, such as risk classification, past-due status, and type of loan." Paragraph 7.08 provides additional guidance on classifying individual loans and paragraph 7.13 indicates considerations for groups or pools of loans.

[31] *See* Statement 114, paragraphs 8 through 10 on recognition of impairment and paragraphs 11 through 16 on measurement of impairment. *See* also the guidance in EITF Topic D-80.

114, but not considered to be individually impaired, should be grouped with other loans that share common characteristics for impairment evaluation under Statement 5.[32]

• For determining and measuring impairment under Statement 5:[33]

• How loans with similar characteristics are grouped to be evaluated for loan collectibility (such as loan type, past-due status, and risk);

• How loss rates are determined (e.g., historical loss rates adjusted for environmental factors or migration analysis) and what factors are considered when establishing appropriate time frames over which to evaluate loss experience; and

• Descriptions of qualitative factors (e.g., industry, geographical, economic, and political factors) that may affect loss rates or other loss measurements.

3. *Applying a systematic methodology - measuring and documenting loan losses under Statement 114*

a. *Measuring and documenting loan losses under Statement 114 - general*

Facts: Approximately one-third of Registrant B's commercial loan portfolio consists of large balance, non-homogeneous loans. Due to their large individual balances, these loans meet the criteria under Registrant B's policies and procedures for individual review for impairment under Statement 114.

Upon review of the large balance loans, Registrant B determines that certain of the loans are impaired as defined by Statement 114.[34]

Question: or the commercial loans reviewed under Statement 114 that are individually impaired, how would the staff normally expect Registrant B to measure and document the impairment on those loans? Can it use an impairment measurement method other than the methods allowed by Statement 114?

Interpretive Response: For those loans that are reviewed individually under Statement 114 and considered individually impaired, Registrant B must use one of the methods for measuring impairment that is specified by Statement 114 (that is, the present value of expected future cash flows, the loan's observable market price, or the fair value of collateral).[35] Accordingly, in the circumstances described above, for the

loans considered individually impaired under Statement 114, it would not be appropriate for Registrant B to choose a measurement method not prescribed by Statement 114. For example, it would not be appropriate to measure loan impairment by applying a loss rate to each loan based on the average historical loss percentage for all of its commercial loans for the past five years.

The staff normally would expect Registrant B to maintain as sufficient, objective evidence[36] written documentation to support its measurement of loan impairment under Statement 114.[37] If Registrant B uses the present value of expected future cash flows to measure impairment of a loan, it should document the amount and timing of cash flows, the effective interest rate used to discount the cash flows, and the basis for the determination of cash flows, including consideration of current environmental factors[38] and other information reflecting past events and current conditions. If Registrant B uses the fair value of collateral to measure impairment, the staff normally would expect to find that Registrant B had documented how it determined the fair value, including the use of appraisals, valuation assumptions and calculations, the supporting rationale for adjustments to appraised values, if any, and the determination of costs to sell, if applicable, appraisal quality, and the expertise and independence of the appraiser.[39] Similarly, the staff normally would expect to find that Registrant B had documented the amount, source, and date of the observable market price of a loan, if that method of measuring loan impairment is used.

b. *Measuring and documenting loan losses under Statement 114 for a collateral dependent loan*

Facts: Registrant C has a $10 million loan outstanding to Company X that is secured by real estate, which Registrant C individually evaluates under Statement 114 due to the loan's size. Company X is delinquent in its loan payments under the terms of the loan agreement. Accordingly, Registrant C determines that its loan to Company X is impaired, as defined by Statement 114. Because the loan is collateral dependent, Registrant C measures impairment of the loan based on the fair value of the collateral. Registrant C determines that the most recent valuation of the collateral was performed by an appraiser eighteen months ago and, at that time, the estimated

---

[32] *See* EITF Topic D-80, Exhibit D-80A, Question #10.

[33] *See* Statement 5, paragraphs 8(a) and 8(b) on accrual of loss contingencies and paragraphs 22 and 23 on collectibility of receivables. See also the guidance in EITF Topic D-80.

[34] Paragraph 8 of Statement 114 provides that a loan is impaired when, based on current information and events, it is probable that all amounts due will not be collected pursuant to the terms of the loan agreement.

[35] *See* paragraph 13 of Statement 114.

[36] Under GAAS, auditors should obtain "sufficient competent evidential matter" to support its audit opinion. See AU Section 326. The staff normally would expect registrants to maintain such evidential matter for its allowances for loan losses for use by the auditors in conducting their annual audit.

[37] Paragraph 7.45 in the Audit Guide outlines sources of information, available from management, that the independent account-

ant should consider in identifying loans that contain high credit risk or other significant exposures and concentrations. These sources of information would also likely include documentation of loan impairment under Statement 114 or Statement 5. Additionally, as indicated in paragraphs 7.56 to 7.68 of the Audit Guide, the independent accountant, in conducting an audit, may perform a detailed loan file review for selected loans. A registrant's loan files may contain documentation about borrowers' financial resources and cash flows (see paragraph 7.63) or about the collateral securing the loans, if applicable (see paragraphs 7.65 and 7.66).

[38] Question #16 in Exhibit D-80A of EITF Topic D-80 indicates that environmental factors include existing industry, geographical, economic, and political factors.

[39] *See* paragraphs 7.65 and 7.66 in the Audit Guide for additional information about documentation of loan collateral.

value of the collateral (fair value less costs to sell) was $12 million.

Registrant C believes that certain of the assumptions that were used to value the collateral eighteen months ago do not reflect current market conditions and, therefore, the appraiser's valuation does not approximate current fair value of the collateral.

Several buildings, which are comparable to the real estate collateral, were recently completed in the area, increasing vacancy rates, decreasing lease rates, and attracting several tenants away from the borrower. Accordingly, credit review personnel at Registrant C adjust certain of the valuation assumptions to better reflect the current market conditions as they relate to the loan's collateral.[40] After adjusting the collateral valuation assumptions, the credit review department determines that the current estimated fair value of the collateral, less costs to sell, is $8 million.[41] Given that the recorded investment in the loan is $10 million, Registrant C concludes that the loan is impaired by $2 million and records an allowance for loan losses of $2 million.

Question: What documentation would the staff normally expect Registrant C to maintain to support its determination of the allowance for loan losses of $2 million for the loan to Company X?

Interpretive Response: The staff normally would expect Registrant C to document that it measured impairment of the loan to Company X by using the fair value of the loan's collateral, less costs to sell, which it estimated to be $8 million.[42] This documentation[43] should include the registrant's rationale and basis for the $8 million valuation, including the revised valuation assumptions it used, the valuation calculation, and the determination of costs to sell, if applicable.

Because Registrant C arrived at the valuation of $8 million by modifying an earlier appraisal, it should document its rationale and basis for the changes it made to the valuation assumptions that resulted in the collateral value declining from $12 million eighteen months ago to $8 million in the current period.

c. Measuring and documenting loan losses under Statement 114—fully collateralized loans

Question: In the staff's view, what is an example of an acceptable documentation practice for a registrant to adequately support its determination that no allowance for loan losses should be recorded for a group of loans because the loans are fully collateralized?

Interpretive Response: Consider the following fact pattern: Registrant D has $10 million in loans that are fully collateralized by highly rated debt securities with readily determinable market values. The loan agreement for each of these loans requires the borrower to provide qualifying collateral sufficient to maintain a loan-to-value ratio with sufficient margin to absorb volatility in the securities' market prices. Registrant D's collateral department has physical control of the debt securities through safekeeping arrangements. In addition, Registrant D perfected its security interest in the collateral when the funds were originally distributed. On a quarterly basis, Registrant D's credit administration function determines the market value of the collateral for each loan using two independent market quotes and compares the collateral value to the loan carrying value. If there are any collateral deficiencies, Registrant D notifies the borrower and requests that the borrower immediately remedy the deficiency. Due in part to its efficient operation, Registrant D has historically not incurred any material losses on these loans. Registrant D believes these loans are fully-collateralized and therefore does not maintain any loan loss allowance balance for these loans.

Registrant D's management summary of the loan loss allowance includes documentation indicating that, in accordance with its loan loss allowance policy, the collateral protection on these loans has been verified by the registrant, no probable loss has been incurred, and no loan loss allowance is necessary.

Documentation in Registrant D's loan files includes the two independent market quotes obtained each quarter for each loan's collateral amount, the documents evidencing the perfection of the security interest in the collateral, and other relevant supporting documents. Additionally, Registrant D's loan loss allowance policy includes a discussion of how to determine when a loan is considered "fully collateralized" and does not require a loan loss allowance. Registrant D's policy requires the following factors to be considered and its findings concerning these factors to be fully documented:

- Volatility of the market value of the collateral;

- Recency and reliability of the appraisal or other valuation;

- Recency of the registrant's or third party's inspection of the collateral;

- Historical losses on similar loans;

- Confidence in the registrant's lien or security position including appropriate:

- Type of security perfection (e.g., physical possession of collateral or secured filing);

- Filing of security perfection (i.e., correct documents and with the appropriate officials); and

- Relationship to other liens; and

- Other factors as appropriate for the loan type.

---

[40] When reviewing collateral dependent loans, Registrant C may often find it more appropriate to obtain an updated appraisal to estimate the effect of current market conditions on the appraised value instead of internally estimating an adjustment.

[41] An auditor who uses the work of a specialist, such as an appraiser, in performing an audit in accordance with GAAS should refer to the guidance in SAS 73 (AU Section 336).

[42] See paragraphs 7.65 to 7.66 in the Audit Guide for further information about documentation of loan collateral and associated audit procedures that may be performed by the independent accountant.

[43] As stated in paragraph 7.14 of the Audit Guide, "[t]he institution's conclusions about the appropriate amount [of loan impairment and the allowance for loan losses] should be well documented."

In the staff's view, Registrant D's documentation supporting its determination that certain of its loans are fully collateralized, and no loan loss allowance should be recorded for those loans, is acceptable under FRR 28.

4. Applying a systematic methodology—measuring and documenting loan losses under Statement 5

a. Measuring and documenting loan losses under Statement 5—general

Question 1: In the staff's view, what are some general considerations for a registrant in applying its systematic methodology to measure and document loan losses under Statement 5?

Interpretive Response: For loans evaluated on a group basis under Statement 5, the staff believes that a registrant should segment the loan portfolio by identifying risk characteristics that are common to groups of loans.[44] Registrants typically decide how to segment their loan portfolios based on many factors, which vary with their business strategies as well as their information system capabilities. Regardless of the segmentation method used, the staff normally would expect a registrant to maintain documentation to support its conclusion that the loans in each segment have similar attributes or characteristics. As economic and other business conditions change, registrants often modify their business strategies, which may result in adjustments to the way in which they segment their loan portfolio for purposes of estimating loan losses. The staff normally would expect registrants to maintain documentation to support these segmentation adjustments.[45]

Based on the segmentation of the loan portfolio, a registrant should estimate the Statement 5 portion of its loan loss allowance. For those segments that require an allowance for loan losses,[46] the registrant should estimate the loan losses, on at least a quarterly basis, based upon its ongoing loan review process and analysis of loan performance.[47] The registrant should follow a systematic and consistently applied approach to select the most appropriate loss measurement methods and support its conclusions and rationale with written documentation.[48]

Facts: After identifying certain loans for evaluation under Statement 114, Registrant E segments its remaining loan portfolio into five pools of loans. For three of the pools, it measures loan impairment under Statement 5 by applying historical loss rates, adjusted for relevant environmental factors, to the pools' aggregate loan balances. For the remaining two pools of loans, Registrant E uses a loss estimation model that is consistent with GAAP to measure loan impairment under Statement 5.

Question 2: What documentation would the staff normally expect Registrant E to prepare to support its loan loss allowance for its pools of loans under Statement 5?

Interpretive Response: Regardless of the method used to determine loan loss measurements under Statement 5, Registrant E should demonstrate and document that the loss measurement methods used to estimate the loan loss allowance for each segment of its loan portfolio are determined in accordance with GAAP as of the financial statement date.[49]

As indicated for Registrant E, one method of estimating loan losses for groups of loans is through the application of loss rates to the groups' aggregate loan balances. Such loss rates typically reflect the registrant's historical loan loss experience for each group of loans, adjusted for relevant environmental factors (e.g., industry, geographical, economic, and political factors) over a defined period of time. If a registrant does not have loss experience of its own, it may be appropriate to reference the loss experience of other companies in the same business, provided that the registrant demonstrates that the attributes of the loans in its portfolio segment are similar to those of the loans included in the portfolio of the registrant providing the loss experience.[50] Registrants should maintain supporting documentation for the technique used to develop their loss rates, including the period of time over which the losses were incurred. If a range of loss is determined, registrants should maintain documentation to support the identified range and the rationale used for determining which estimate is the best estimate within the range of loan losses.[51]

---

[44] Paragraph 7.07 of the Audit Guide indicates that "[e]ach segment [of the loan portfolio] should contain loans with similar characteristics, such as risk classification, past-due status, and type of loan."

[45] Segmentation of the loan portfolio is a standard element in a loan loss allowance methodology. As indicated in paragraph 7.05 of the Audit Guide, the loan loss allowance methodology "should be well documented, with clear explanations of the supporting analyses and rationale."

[46] An example of a loan segment that does not generally require an allowance for loan losses is a group of loans that are fully secured by deposits maintained at the lending institution.

[47] FRR 28 refers to a "systematic methodology to be employed each period" in determining provisions and allowances for loan losses. As indicated in FRR 28, the staff normally would expect that the systematic methodology would be documented "to help ensure that all matters affecting loan collectibility will consistently be identified in the detailed [loan] review process."

[48] *Ibid.* Also, as indicated in paragraph 7.05 of the Audit Guide, the loan loss allowance methodology "should be well documented,

with clear explanations of the supporting analyses and rationale." Further, as indicated in paragraph 7.14 of the Audit Guide, "[t]he institution's conclusions about the appropriate amount [of the allowance] should be well documented."

[49] Refer to paragraph 8(b) of Statement 5. Also, as indicated in Exhibit D-80A of EITF Topic D-80, "[t]he approach for determination of the allowance should be well documented and applied consistently from period to period." (See the overview section of Exhibit D-80A and Question #18.)

[50] Refer to paragraph 23 of Statement 5.

[51] Registrants should also refer to Interpretation 14, which provides guidance for situations in which a range of loss can be reasonably estimated but no single amount within the range appears to be a better estimate than any other amount within the range. Also, paragraph 7.14 of the Audit Guide notes the use of "a method that results in a range of estimates for the allowance," except for impairment measurement under Statement 114, which is based on "a single best estimate and not a range of estimates." Paragraph 7.14 also states that "[t]he institution's conclusions about the appropriate amount should be well documented."

The staff normally would expect that, before employing a loss estimation model, a registrant would evaluate and modify, as needed, the model's assumptions to ensure that the resulting loss estimate is consistent with GAAP. In order to demonstrate consistency with GAAP, registrants that use loss estimation models should typically document the evaluation, the conclusions regarding the appropriateness of estimating loan losses with a model or other loss estimation tool, and the objective support for adjustments to the model or its results.[52]

In developing loss measurements, registrants should consider the impact of current environmental factors and then document which factors were used in the analysis and how those factors affected the loss measurements. Factors that should be considered in developing loss measurements include the following:[53]

- Levels of and trends in delinquencies and impaired loans;

- Levels of and trends in charge-offs and recoveries;

- Trends in volume and terms of loans;

- Effects of any changes in risk selection and underwriting standards, and other changes in lending policies, procedures, and practices;

- Experience, ability, and depth of lending management and other relevant staff;

- National and local economic trends and conditions;

- Industry conditions; and

- Effects of changes in credit concentrations.

For any adjustment of loss measurements for environmental factors, a registrant should maintain sufficient, objective evidence[54] (a) to support the amount of the adjustment and (b) to explain why the adjustment is necessary to reflect current information, events, circumstances, and conditions in the loss measurements.

b. Measuring and documenting loan losses under Statement 5—adjusting loss rates

Facts: Registrant F's lending area includes a metropolitan area that is financially dependent upon the profitability of a number of manufacturing businesses. These businesses use highly specialized equipment and significant quantities of rare metals in the manufacturing process. Due to increased low-cost foreign competition, several of the parts suppliers servicing these manufacturing firms declared bankruptcy. The foreign suppliers have subsequently increased prices and the manufacturing firms have suffered from increased equipment maintenance costs and smaller profit margins.

Additionally, the cost of the rare metals used in the manufacturing process increased and has now stabilized at double last year's price. Due to these events, the manufacturing businesses are experiencing financial difficulties and have recently announced downsizing plans.

Although Registrant F has yet to confirm an increase in its loss experience as a result of these events, management knows that it lends to a significant number of businesses and individuals whose repayment ability depends upon the long-term viability of the manufacturing businesses. Registrant F's management has identified particular segments of its commercial and consumer customer bases that include borrowers highly dependent upon sales or salary from the manufacturing businesses. Registrant F's management performs an analysis of the affected portfolio segments to adjust its historical loss rates used to determine the loan loss allowance. In this particular case, Registrant F has experienced similar business and lending conditions in the past that it can compare to current conditions.

Question: How would the staff normally expect Registrant F to document its support for the loss rate adjustments that result from considering these manufacturing firms' financial downturns?[55]

Interpretive Response: The staff normally would expect Registrant F to document its identification of the particular segments of its commercial and consumer loan portfolio for which it is probable that the manufacturing business' financial downturn has resulted in loan losses. In addition, the staff normally would expect Registrant F to document its analysis that resulted in the adjustments to the loss rates for the affected portfolio segments.[56] The staff normally would expect that, as part of its documentation, Registrant F would maintain copies of the documents supporting the analysis, which may include relevant economic reports, economic data, and information from individual borrowers.

Because in this case Registrant F has experienced similar business and lending conditions in the past, it should consider including in its supporting documentation an analysis of how the current conditions compare to its previous loss experiences in similar circumstances. The staff normally would expect that, as part of Registrant F's effective loan loss allowance methodology, it would create a summary of the amount and rationale for the adjustment factor for

---

[52] The systematic methodology (including, if applicable, loss estimation models) used to determine loan loss provisions and allowances should be documented in accordance with FRR 28, paragraph 7.05 of the Audit Guide, and EITF Topic D-80.

[53] Refer to paragraph 7.13 in the Audit Guide.

[54] AU 326 describes the "sufficient competent evidential matter" that auditors must consider in accordance with GAAS.

[55] This question and response would also apply to other registrant fact patterns in which the registrant adjusts loss rates for environmental factors.

[56] Paragraph 7.33 of the Audit Guide refers to the documentation, for disclosure purposes, that an entity should include in the notes to the financial statements describing the accounting policies and methodology the entity used to estimate its allowance and related provision for loan losses. As indicated in paragraph 7.33, "[s]uch a description should identify the factors that influenced management's judgment (for example, historical losses and existing economic conditions) and may also include discussion of risk elements relevant to particular categories of financial instruments."

review by management prior to the issuance of the financial statements.[57]

c. Measuring and documenting loan losses under Statement 5—estimating losses on loans individually reviewed for impairment but not considered individually impaired

Facts: Registrant G has outstanding loans of $2 million to Company Y and $1 million to Company Z, both of which are paying as agreed upon in the loan documents. The registrant's loan loss allowance policy specifies that all loans greater than $750,000 must be individually reviewed for impairment under Statement 114. Company Y's financial statements reflect a strong net worth, good profits, and ongoing ability to meet debt service requirements. In contrast, recent information indicates Company Z's profitability is declining and its cash flow is tight. Accordingly, this loan is rated substandard under the registrant's loan grading system. Despite its concern, management believes Company Z will resolve its problems and determines that neither loan is individually impaired as defined by Statement 114.

Registrant G segments its loan portfolio to estimate loan losses under Statement 5. Two of its loan portfolio segments are Segment 1 and Segment 2. The loan to Company Y has risk characteristics similar to the loans included in Segment 1 and the loan to Company Z has risk characteristics similar to the loans included in Segment 2.[58]

In its determination of its loan loss allowance under Statement 5, Registrant G includes its loans to Company Y and Company Z in the groups of loans with similar characteristics (i.e., Segment 1 for Company Y's loan and Segment 2 for Company Z's loan).[59] Management's analyses of Segment 1 and Segment 2 indicate that it is probable that each segment includes some losses, even though the losses cannot be identified to one or more specific loans. Management estimates that the use of its historical loss rates for these two segments, with adjustments for changes in environmental factors, provides a reasonable estimate of the registrant's probable loan losses in these segments.

Question: How would the staff normally expect Registrant G to adequately document a loan loss allowance under Statement 5 for these loans that were individually reviewed for impairment but are not considered individually impaired?

Interpretive Response: The staff normally would expect that, as part of Registrant G's effective loan loss allowance methodology, it would document its decision to include its loans to Company Y and Company Z in its determination of its loan loss allowance under Statement 5.[60] The staff also normally would expect that Registrant G would document the specific characteristics of the loans that were the basis for grouping these loans with other loans in Segment 1 and Segment 2, respectively.[61] Additionally, the staff normally would expect Registrant G to maintain documentation to support its method of estimating loan losses for Segment 1 and Segment 2, which typically would include the average loss rate used, the analysis of historical losses by loan type and by internal risk rating, and support for any adjustments to its historical loss rates.[62] The registrant would typically maintain copies of the economic and other reports that provided source data.

When measuring and documenting loan losses, Registrant G should take steps to prevent layering loan loss allowances. Layering is the inappropriate practice of recording in the allowance more than one amount for the same probable loan loss. Layering can happen when a registrant includes a loan in one segment, determines its best estimate of loss for that loan either individually or on a group basis (after taking into account all appropriate environmental factors, conditions, and events), and then includes the loan in another group, which receives an additional loan loss allowance amount.

5. Documenting the results of a systematic methodology

a. Documenting the results of a systematic methodology—general

Facts: Registrant H has completed its estimation of its loan loss allowance for the current reporting period, in accordance with GAAP, using its established systematic methodology.

Question: What summary documentation would the staff normally expect Registrant H to prepare to support the amount of its loan loss allowance to be reported in its financial statements?

Interpretive Response: The staff normally would expect that, to verify that loan loss allowance balances are presented fairly in accordance with GAAP and are auditable, management would prepare a document that summarizes the amount to be reported in the financial statements for the loan loss allowance.[63]

---

[57] Paragraph 7.39 in the Audit Guide indicates that effective internal control related to the allowance for loan losses should include "accumulation of relevant, sufficient, and reliable data on which to base management's estimate of the allowance."

[58] These groups of loans do not include any loans that have been individually reviewed for impairment under Statement 114 and determined to be impaired as defined by Statement 114.

[59] Question #10 in Exhibit D-80A of EITF Topic D-80 states that if a creditor concludes that an individual loan specifically identified for evaluation is not impaired under Statement 114, that loan may be included in the assessment of the allowance for loan losses under Statement 5, but only if specific characteristics of the loan indicate that it is probable that there would be an incurred loss in a group of loans with those characteristics.

[60] Paragraph 7.05 in the Audit Guide indicates that an entity's method of estimating credit losses should "include a detailed and regular analysis of the loan portfolio," "consider all loans (whether on an individual or pool-of-loans basis)," "be based on current and reliable data," and "be well documented, with clear explanations of the supporting analyses and rationale." Question #10 in Exhibit D-80A of EITF Topic D-80 provides guidance as to the analysis to be performed when determining whether a loan that is not individually impaired under Statement 114 should be included in the assessment of the loan loss allowance under Statement 5.

[61] *Ibid.*

[62] *Ibid.*

[63] FRR 28 states: "[t]he specific rationale upon which the [loan loss allowance and provision] amount actually reported is based-

Common elements that the staff normally would expect to find documented in loan loss allowance summaries include:[64]

- The estimate of the probable loss or range of loss incurred for each category evaluated (e.g., individually evaluated impaired loans, homogeneous pools, and other groups of loans that are collectively evaluated for impairment);

- The aggregate probable loss estimated using the registrant's methodology;

- A summary of the current loan loss allowance balance;

- The amount, if any, by which the loan loss allowance balance is to be adjusted;[65] and

- Depending on the level of detail that supports the loan loss allowance analysis, detailed subschedules of loss estimates that reconcile to the summary schedule.

Generally, a registrant's review and approval process for the loan loss allowance relies upon the data provided in these consolidated summaries. There may be instances in which individuals or committees that review the loan loss allowance methodology and resulting allowance balance identify adjustments that need to be made to the loss estimates to provide a better estimate of loan losses. These changes may be due to information not known at the time of the initial loss estimate (e.g., information that surfaces after determining and adjusting, as necessary, historical loss rates, or a recent decline in the marketability of property after conducting a Statement 114 valuation based upon the fair value of collateral). It is important that these adjustments are consistent with GAAP and are reviewed and approved by appropriate personnel.[66] Additionally, it would typically be appropriate for the summary to provide each subsequent reviewer with an understanding of the support behind these adjustments. Therefore, the staff normally would expect management to document the nature of any adjustments and the underlying rationale for making the changes.[67]

The staff also normally would expect this documentation to be provided to those among management making the final determination of the loan loss allowance amount.[68]

b. Documenting the results of a systematic methodology—allowance adjustments

Facts: Registrant I determines its loan loss allowance using an established systematic process. At the end of each reporting period, the accounting department prepares a summary schedule that includes the amount of each of the components of the loan loss allowance, as well as the total loan loss allowance amount, for review by senior management, including the Credit Committee. Members of senior management meet to discuss the loan loss allowance. During these discussions, they identify changes that are required by GAAP to be made to certain of the loan loss allowance estimates. As a result of the adjustments made by senior management, the total amount of the loan loss allowance changes. However, senior management (or its designee) does not update the loan loss allowance summary schedule to reflect the adjustments or reasons for the adjustments. When performing their audit of the financial statements, the independent accountants are provided with the original loan loss allowance summary schedule reviewed by senior management, as well as a verbal explanation of the changes made by senior management when they met to discuss the loan loss allowance.

Question: In the staff's view, are Registrant I's documentation practices related to the balance of its loan loss allowance in compliance with existing documentation guidance in this area?

Interpretive Response: No. A registrant should maintain supporting documentation for the loan loss allowance amount reported in its financial statements.[69] As illustrated above, there may be instances in which loan loss allowance reviewers identify adjustments that need to be made to the loan loss estimates. The staff normally would expect the nature of the adjustments, how they were measured or determined, and the underlying rationale for making the changes to the loan loss allowance balance to be documented.[70] The staff also normally would expect appropriate documentation of the adjustments to be provided to management for review of the final loan loss allowance amount to be reported in the financial statements. This documentation should also be made available to the independent accountants. If changes frequently occur during management or credit committee reviews of the loan loss allowance, management may find it appropriate to analyze the reasons for the frequent changes and to reassess the methodology the registrant uses.[71]

6. Validating a systematic methodology

(Footnote Continued)

i.e., the bridge between the findings of the detailed review [of the loan portfolio] and the amount actually reported in each period would be documented to help ensure the adequacy of the reported amount, to improve auditability, and to serve as a benchmark for exercise of prudent judgment in future periods."

[64] *See* also paragraph 7.14 of the Audit Guide.

[65] Subsequent to adjustments, the staff normally would expect that there would be no material differences between the consolidated loss estimate, as determined by the methodology, and the final loan loss allowance balance reported in the financial statements. Registrants should refer to SAB 99 and SAS 89 and its amendments to AU Section 310.

[66] Paragraph 7.39 in the Audit Guide indicates that effective internal control related to the allowance for loan losses should

include "adequate review and approval of the allowance estimates by the individuals specified in management's written policy."

[67] *See* the guidance in paragraph 7.14 of the Audit Guide ("the institution's conclusions about the appropriate amount should be well documented") and in FRR 28 ("he specific rationale upon which the amount actually reported in each individual period is based would be documented").

[68] *Ibid.*

[69] *Ibid.*

[70] *Ibid.*

[71] As outlined in paragraph 7.39 of the Audit Guide, effective internal controls related to the allowance for loan losses should include adequate review and approval of allowance estimates, in-

Question: What is the staff's guidance to a registrant on validating, and documenting the validation of, its systematic methodology used to estimate loan loss allowances?

Interpretive Response: The staff believes that a registrant's loan loss allowance methodology is considered valid when it accurately estimates the amount of loss contained in the portfolio. Thus, the staff normally would expect the registrant's methodology to include procedures that adjust loan loss estimation methods to reduce differences between estimated losses and actual subsequent charge-offs, as necessary. To verify that the loan loss allowance methodology is valid and conforms to GAAP, the staff believes it is appropriate for management to establish internal control policies,[72] appropriate for the size of the registrant and the type and complexity of its loan products. These policies may include procedures for a review, by a party who is independent of the allowance for loan losses estimation process, of the allowance for loan losses methodology and its application in order to confirm its effectiveness.

In practice, registrants employ numerous procedures when validating the reasonableness of their loan loss allowance methodology and determining whether there may be deficiencies in their overall methodology or loan grading process. Examples are:

• A review of trends in loan volume, delinquencies, restructurings, and concentrations.

• A review of previous charge-off and recovery history, including an evaluation of the timeliness of the entries to record both the charge-offs and the recoveries.

• A review by a party that is independent of the loan loss allowance estimation process. This often involves the independent party reviewing, on a test basis, source documents and underlying assumptions to determine that the established methodology develops reasonable loss estimates.

• An evaluation of the appraisal process of the underlying collateral. This may be accomplished by periodically comparing the appraised value to the actual sales price on selected properties sold.

It is the staff's understanding that, in practice, management usually supports the validation process with the workpapers from the loan loss allowance review function. Additional documentation often includes the summary findings of the independent reviewer. The staff normally would expect that, if the methodology is changed based upon the findings of the validation process, documentation that describes and supports the changes would be maintained.[73]

[¶ 39,161]   TOPIC 7: REAL ESTATE COMPANIES

A. Deleted by SAB 103

B. Deleted by SAB 103

C. Schedules Of Real Estate And Accumulated Depreciation, And Of Mortgage Loans On Real Estate

Facts : Whenever investments in real estate or mortgage loans on real estate are significant, the schedules of such items (see Rules 12-28 and 12-29 of Regulation S-X) are required in a prospectus.

Question : Is such information also required in annual reports to shareholders?

Interpretive Response : Although Rules 14a-3 and 14c-3 permit the omission of financial statement schedules from annual reports to shareholders, the staff is of the view that the information required by these schedules is of such significance within the real estate industry that the information should be included in the financial statements in the annual report to shareholders.

D. Income Before Depreciation

Facts : Occasionally an income statement format will contain a subtitle or caption titled "Income before depreciation and depletion."

Question : Is this caption appropriate?

Interpretive Response : The staff objects to this presentation because in the staff's view the presentation may suggest to the reader that the amount so captioned represents cash flow for the period, which is rarely the case (see ASR 142).

[¶ 39,171]   TOPIC 8: RETAIL COMPANIES

A. Sales of Leased or Licensed Departments

Facts: At times, department stores and other retailers have included the sales of leased or licensed departments in the amount reported as "total revenues."

Question: Does the staff have any objection to this practice?

Interpretive Response: In November 1975 the staff issued SAB 1 that addressed this issue. In that SAB the staff did not object to retailers presenting sales of leased or licensed departments in the amount re-

---

(Footnote Continued)

cluding review of sources of relevant information, review of development of assumptions, review of reasonableness of assumptions and resulting estimates, and consideration of changes in previously established methods to arrive at the allowance.

[72] *Ibid.*

[73] *See* paragraph 7.39 of the Audit Guide.

ported as "total revenues" because of industry practice. Subsequently, in November 1976 the FASB issued Statement 13. In June 1995, the AICPA staff amended its Technical Practice Aid (TPA) section 5100.16 based upon an interpretation of Statement 13 that leases of departments within a retail establishment are leases of tangible assets within the scope of Statement 13.[1] Consistent with the interpretation in TPA section 5100.16, the staff believes that Statement 13 requires department stores and other retailers that lease or license store space to account for rental income from leased departments in accordance with Statement 13. Accordingly, it would be inappropriate for a department store or other retailer to include in its revenue the sales of the leased or licensed departments. Rather, the department store or other retailer should include the rental income as part of its gross revenue. The staff would not object to disclosure in the footnotes to the financial statements of the amount of the lessee's sales from leased departments. If the arrangement is not a lease but rather a service arrangement that provides for payment of a fee or commission, the retailer should recognize the fee or commission as revenue when earned. If the retailer

assumes the risk of bad debts associated with the lessee's merchandise sales, the retailer generally should present bad debt expense in accordance with Rule 5-03(b)(5) of Regulation S-X.

B. Finance Charges

Facts: Department stores and other retailers impose finance charges on credit sales.

Question: How should such charges be disclosed?

Interpretive Response: As a minimum, the staff requests that the amount of gross revenue from such charges be stated in a footnote and that the income statement classification which includes such revenue be identified. The following are examples of acceptable disclosure:

Example 1

Consumer Credit Operations:

The results of the Consumer Credit Operations which are included in the Statement of Earnings as a separate line item are as follows for the fiscal year ended January 31, 20x0:

Service charges	$167,000,000
Operating expenses	
Interest	60,000,000
Payroll	35,000,000
Provision for uncollected accounts	29,000,000
All other credit and collection expenses	32,000,000
Provision for Federal income taxes	5,000,000
Total operating expenses	$161,000,000
Consumer credit operations earnings	$6,000,000

Example 2

Service charges on retail credit accounts are netted against selling, general and administrative expense.

The cost of administering retail credit program continued to exceed service charges on customer receivables as follows:

(in millions)	20×2	20×1	Percent Increase (decrease)
Costs:			
Regional office operations	$45	$42	9
Interest	51	44	13
Provision for doubtful accounts	21	15	34
Total	$117	$102	15
Less service charge income	96	79	22
Net cost of credit	$21	$23	(10)
Net cost as percent of credit sales	1.4%	1.6%	

The above results do not reflect either "in store" costs related to credit operations or any allocation of corporate overhead expenses.

This SAB is not intended to change current guidance in the accounting literature. For this reason, adherence to the principles described in this SAB

---

[1] Statement 13, paragraph 1 defines a lease as "the right to use property, plant, or equipment (land or depreciable assets or both) usually for a stated period of time."

should not raise the costs associated with record-keeping or with audits of financial statements.

[¶ 39,181] TOPIC 9: FINANCE COMPANIES

A. Deleted by SAB 103

B. Deleted by ASR 307

[¶ 39,191] TOPIC 10: UTILITY COMPANIES

A. Financing By Electric Utility Companies Through Use Of Construction Intermediaries

Facts : Some electric utility companies finance construction of a generating plant or their share of a jointly owned plant through the use of a "construction intermediary" which may be organized as a trust or a corporation. Typically the utility assigns its interest in property and other contract rights to the construction intermediary with the latter authorized to obtain funds to finance construction with term loans, bank loans, commercial paper and other sources of funds and that may be available. The intermediary's borrowings are guaranteed in part of the work in progress but more significantly, although indirectly, by the obligation of the utility to purchase the project upon completion and assume or otherwise settle the borrowings. The utility may be committed to provide any deficiency of funds which the intermediary cannot obtain and excess funds may be loaned to the utility by the intermediary. (In one case involving construction of an entire generating plant, the intermediary appointed the utility as its agent to complete construction.) On the occurrence of an event such as commencement of the testing period for the plant or placing the plant in commercial service (but not later than a specified date) the interest in the plant reverts to the utility and concurrently the utility must either assume the obligations issued by the intermediary or purchase them from the holders. The intermediary also may be authorized to borrow amounts for accrued interest when due and those amounts are added to the balance of the outstanding indebtedness. Interest is thus capitalized during the construction period at rates being charged by the lenders; however, it is deductible by the utility for tax purposes in the year of accrual.

Question : How should construction work in progress and related liabilities and interest expense being financed through a construction intermediary be reflected in an electric utility's financial statements?

Interpretive Response : The balance sheet of an electric utility company using a construction intermediary to finance construction should include the intermediary's work in progress in the appropriate caption under utility plant. The related debt should be included in long-term liabilities and disclosed either on the balance sheet or in a note.

The amount of interest cost incurred and the respective amounts expensed or capitalized shall be disclosed for each period for which an income statement is presented. Consequently, capitalized interest included as part of an intermediary's construction work in progress on the balance sheet should be recognized on the current income statement as interest expense with a corresponding offset to allowance for borrowed funds used during construction. Income statements for prior periods should also be restated. The amounts may be shown separately on the statement or included with interest expense and allowance for borrowed funds used during construction.

A note to the financial statements should describe briefly the organization and purpose of the intermediary and the nature of its authorization to incur debt to finance construction. The note should disclose the rate at which interest on this debt has been capitalized and the dollar amount for each period for which an income statement is presented.

B. Deleted by SAB 103

C. Jointly Owned Electric Utility Plants

Facts : Groups of electric utility companies have been building and operating utility plants under joint ownership agreements or arrangements which do not create legal entities for which separate financial statements are presented.[1] Under these arrangements, a participating utility has an undivided interest in a utility plant and is responsible for its proportionate share of the costs of construction and operation and its entitled to its proportionate share of the energy produced.

During the construction period a participating utility finances its own share of a utility plant using its own financial resources and not the combined resources of the group. Allowance for funds used during construction is provided in the same manner and at the same rates as for plants constructed to be used entirely by the participant utility.

When a joint-owned plant becomes operational, one of the participant utilities acts as operator and bills the other participants for their proportionate share of the direct expenses incurred. Each individual participant incurs other expenses related to transmission, distribution, supervision and control which cannot be

---

[1] Before considering the guidance in this SAB Topic, registrants are reminded that the arrangement should be evaluated in accordance with the provisions of Interpretation 46.

related to the energy generated or received from any particular source. Many companies maintain depreciation records on a composite basis for each class of property so that neither the accumulated allowance for depreciation nor the periodic expense can be allocated to specific generating units whether jointly or wholly owned.

Question : What disclosure should be made on the financial statements or in the notes concerning interests in jointly owned utility plants?

Interpretive Response : A participating utility should include information concerning the extent of its interests in jointly owned plants in a note to its financial statements. The note should include a table showing separately for each interest in a jointly owned plant the amount of utility plant in service, the accumulated provision for depreciation (if available), the amount of plant under construction, and the proportionate share. The amounts presented for plant in service or plant under construction may be further subdivided to show amounts applicable to plant subcategories such as production, transmission, and distribution. The note should include statements that the dollar amounts represent the participating utility's share in each joint plant and that each participant must provide its own financing. Information concerning two or more generating plants on the same site may be combined if appropriate.

The note should state that the participating utility's share of direct expenses of the joint plants is included in the corresponding operating expenses on its income statement (e.g., fuel, maintenance of plant, other operating expense). If the share of direct expenses is charged to purchased power then the note should disclose the amount so charged and the proportionate amounts charged to specific operating expenses on the records maintained for the joint plants.

D. Long-Term Contracts For Purchase Of Electric Power

Facts : Under long-term contracts with public utility districts, cooperatives or other organizations, a utility company receives a portion of the output of a production plant constructed and financed by the district or cooperative. The utility has only a nominal or no investment at all in the plant but pays a proportionate part of the plant's costs, including debt service. The contract may be in the form of a sale of a generating plant and its immediate lease back. The utility is obligated to pay certain minimum amounts which cover debt service requirements whether or not the plant is operating. At the option of other parties to the contract and in accordance with a predetermined schedule, the utility's proportionate share of the output may be reduced. Separate agreements may exist for the transmission of power to the utility's system.[2]

Question : How should the cost of power obtained under long-term purchase contracts be reflected on the financial statements and what supplemental disclosures should be made in notes to the statements?

Interpretive Response : The cost of power obtained under long-term purchase contracts, including payments required to be made when a production plant is not operating, should be included in the operating expenses section of the income statement. A note to the financial statements should present information concerning the terms and significance of such contracts to the utility company including date of contract expiration, share of plant output being purchased, estimated annual cost, annual minimum debt service payment required and amount of related long-term debt or lease obligations outstanding.

Additional disclosure should be given if the contract provides, or is expected to provide, in excess of five percent of current or estimated future system capability. This additional disclosure may be in the form of separate financial statements of the vendor entity or inclusion of the amount of the obligation under the contract as a liability on the balance sheet with a corresponding amount as an asset representing the right to purchase power under the contract.

The note to the financial statements should disclose the allocable portion of interest included in charges under such contracts.

E. Classification Of Charges For Abandonments And Disallowances

Facts : A public utility company abandons the construction of a plant and, under the provisions of Statement 90, must charge a portion of the costs of the abandoned plant to expense.[3] Also, the utility determines that it is probable that certain costs of a recently completed plant will be disallowed, and charges those costs to expense as required by Statement 90.

Question : May such charges for abandonments and disallowances be reported as extraordinary items in the statement of income?

Interpretive Response : No. The staff does not believe that such charges meet the requirements of APB Opinion 30 that an item be both unusual and infrequent to be classified as an extraordinary item. Accordingly, the public utility was advised by the staff that such charges should be reported as a component of income from continuing operations, separately presented, if material.[4]

---

[2] Registrants are reminded that the arrangement may contain a guarantee that is within the scope of Interpretation 45. Further, registrants should consider the guidance of Interpretation 46. Also, registrants would need to consider whether the arrangement contains a derivative that should be accounted for according to Statement 133.

[3] Paragraph 3 of Statement 90 requires that costs of abandoned plants in excess of the present value of the future revenues expected to be provided to recover any allowable costs be charged to expense in the period that the abandonment becomes probable. Also, paragraph 7 of Statement 90 requires that disallowed costs for recently completed plants be charged to expense when the disallowance becomes probable and can be reasonably estimated.

[4] Additionally, the registrant was reminded that paragraph 26 of APB Opinion 30 provides that items which are not reported as extraordinary should not be reported on the income statement net of income taxes or in any manner that implies that they are similar to extraordinary items.

Paragraph 20 of APB Opinion 30 indicates that to be unusual, an item must "possess a high degree of abnormality and be of a type clearly unrelated to, or only incidentally related to, the ordinary and typical activities of the entity, taking into account the environment in which the entity operates." Similarly, that paragraph indicates that, to be infrequent, an event should "not reasonably be expected to recur in the foreseeable future."

Electric utilities operate under a franchise that requires them to furnish adequate supplies of electricity for their service area. That undertaking requires utilities to continually forecast the future demand for electricity, and the costs to be incurred in constructing the plants necessary to meet that demand. Abandonments and disallowances result from the failure of demand to reach projected levels and/or plant construction costs that exceed anticipated amounts. Neither event qualifies as being both unusual and infrequent in the environment in which electric utilities operate.

Accordingly, the staff believes that charges for abandonments and disallowances under Statement 90 should not be presented as extraordinary items.[5]

F. Presentation Of Liabilities For Environmental Costs

Facts : A public utility company determines that it is obligated to pay material amounts as a result of an environmental liability. These amounts may relate to, for example, damages attributed to clean-up of hazardous wastes, reclamation costs, fines, and litigation costs.

Question 1 : May a rate-regulated enterprise present on its balance sheet the amount of its estimated liability for environmental costs net of probable future revenue resulting from the inclusion of such costs in allowable costs for rate-making purposes?

Interpretive Response : No. Statement 71 specifies the conditions under which rate actions of a regulator can provide reasonable assurance of the existence of an asset. The staff believes that environmental costs meeting the criteria of paragraph 9[6] of Statement 71 should be presented on the balance sheet as an asset and should not be offset against the liability. Contingent recoveries through rates that do not meet the criteria of paragraph 9 should not be recognized either as an asset or as a reduction of the probable liability.

Question 2 : May a rate-regulated enterprise delay recognition of a probable and estimable liability for environmental costs which it has incurred at the date of the latest balance sheet until the regulator's deliberations have proceeded to a point enabling management to determine whether this cost is likely to be included in allowable costs for rate-making purposes?

Interpretive Response : No. Statement 5 states that an estimated loss from a loss contingency shall be accrued by a charge to income if it is probable that a liability has been incurred and the amount of the loss can be reasonably estimated.[7] The staff believes that actions of a regulator can affect whether an incurred cost is capitalized or expensed pursuant to Statement 71, but the regulator's actions cannot affect the timing of the recognition of the liability.

[¶ 39,201] TOPIC 11: MISCELLANEOUS DISCLOSURE

A. Operating-Differential Subsidies

Facts : Company A has received an operating-differential subsidy pursuant to the Merchant Marine Act of 1936, as amended.

Question : How should such subsidies be displayed in the income statement?

Interpretive Response : Revenue representing an operating-differential subsidy under the Merchant Marine Act of 1936, as amended, must be set forth as a separate line item in the income statement either under a revenue caption or as credit in the costs and expenses section.

B. Depreciation And Depletion Excluded From Cost Of Sales

Facts : Company B excludes depreciation and depletion from cost of sales in its income statement.

Question : How should this exclusion be disclosed?

Interpretive Response : If cost of sales or operating expenses exclude charges for depreciation, depletion and amortization of property, plant and equipment, the description of the line item should read somewhat as follows: "Cost of goods sold (exclusive of items shown separately below)" or "Cost of goods sold (exclusive of depreciation shown separately below)." To avoid placing undue emphasis on "cash flow," depreciation, depletion and amortization should not be positioned in the income statement in a manner which results in reporting a figure for income before depreciation.

C. Tax Holidays

Facts : Company C conducts business in a foreign jurisdiction which attracts industry by granting a "holiday" from income taxes for a specified period.

---

[5] The staff also notes that paragraphs 3 and 7 of Statement 90, in requiring that such costs be "recognized as a loss," do not specify extraordinary item treatment. The staff believes that it generally has been the FASB's practice to affirmatively require extraordinary item treatment when it believes that it is appropriate for charges or credits to income specifically required by a provision of a statement.

[6] Paragraph 9 of Statement 71 requires a rate-regulated enterprise to capitalize all or part of an incurred cost that would otherwise be charged to expense if it is probable that future revenue will be provided to recover the previously incurred cost from inclusion of the costs in allowable costs for rate-making purposes.

[7] Registrants also should apply the guidance of SOP 96-1 in determining the appropriate recognition of environmental remediation costs.

Question : Does the staff generally request disclosure of this fact?

Interpretive Response : Yes. In such event, a note must (1) disclose the aggregate dollar and per share effects of the tax holiday and (2) briefly describe the factual circumstances including the date on which the special tax status will terminate.

D. Deleted by SAB 103

E. Chronological Ordering Of Data

Question : Does the staff have any preference in what order data are presented (e.g., the most current data displayed first, etc.)?

Interpretive Response : The staff has no preference as to order; however, financial statements and other data presented in tabular form should read consistently from left to right in the same chronological order throughout the filing. Similarly, numerical data included in narrative sections should be consistently ordered.

F. LIFO Liquidations

Facts : Registrant on LIFO basis of accounting liquidates a substantial portion of its LIFO inventory and as a result includes a material amount of income in its income statement which would not have been recorded had the inventory liquidation not taken place.

Question : Is disclosure required of the amount of income realized as a result of the inventory liquidation?

Interpretive Response : Yes. Such disclosure would be required in order to make the financial statements not misleading. Disclosure may be made either in a footnote or parenthetically on the face of the income statement.

G. Tax Equivalent Adjustment In Financial Statements Of Bank Holding Companies

Facts : Bank subsidiaries of bank holding companies frequently hold substantial amounts of state and municipal bonds, interest income from which is exempt from Federal income taxes. Because of the tax exemption the stated yield on these securities is lower than the yield on securities with similar risk and maturity characteristics whose interest is subject to Federal tax. In order to make the interest income and resultant yields on tax exempt obligations comparable to those on taxable investments and loans, a "tax equivalent adjustment" is often added to interest income when presented in analytical tables or charts. When the data presented also includes income taxes, a corresponding amount is added to income tax expense so that there is no effect on net income. Adjustment may also be made for the tax equivalent effect of exemption from state and local taxes.

Question 1 : Is the concept of the tax equivalent adjustment appropriate for inclusion in financial statements and related notes?

Interpretive Response : No. The tax equivalent adjustment represents a credit to interest income which is not actually earned and realized and a corresponding charge to taxes (or other expense) which will never be paid. Consequently, it should not be reflected on the income statement or in notes to financial statements included in reports to shareholders or in a report or registration statement filed with the Commission.

Question 2 : May amounts representing tax equivalent adjustments be included in the body of a statement of income provided they are designated as not being included in the totals and balances on the statement?

Interpretive Response : No. The tabular format of a statement develops information in an orderly manner which becomes confusing when additional numbers not an integral part of the statement are inserted into it.

Question 3 : May revenues on a tax equivalent adjusted basis be included in selected financial data?

Interpretive Response : Revenues may be included in selected financial data on a tax equivalent basis if the respective captions state which amounts are tax equivalent adjusted and if the corresponding unadjusted amounts are also reported in the selected financial data.

Because of differences among registrants in making the tax equivalency computation, a brief note should describe the extent of recognition of exemption from Federal, state and local taxes and the combined marginal or incremental rate used. Where net operating losses exist, the note should indicate the nature of the tax equivalency adjustment made.

Question 4 : May information adjusted to a tax equivalent basis be included in management's discussion and analysis of financial condition and results of operations?

Interpretive Response : One of the purposes of MD&A is to enable investors to appraise the extent that earnings have been affected by changes in business activity and accounting principles or methods. Material changes in items of revenue or expense should be analyzed and explained in textual discussion and statistical tables. It may be appropriate to use amounts or to present yields on a tax equivalent basis. If appropriate, the discussion should include a comment on material changes in investment securities positions that affect tax exempt interest income. For example, there might be a comment on a change from investments in tax exempt securities because of the availability of net operating losses to offset taxable income of current and future periods, or a comment on a change in the quality level of the tax exempt investments resulting in increased interest income and risk and a corresponding increase in the tax equivalent adjustment.

Tax equivalent adjusted amounts should be clearly identified and related to the corresponding unadjusted amounts in the financial statements. A descriptive note similar to that suggested to accompany adjusted amounts included in selected financial data should be provided.

H. Disclosures By Bank Holding Companies Regarding Certain Foreign Loans

1. *Deposit/relending arrangements*

Facts : Certain foreign countries experiencing liquidity problems, by agreement with U.S. banks, have instituted arrangements whereby borrowers in the foreign country may remit local currency to the foreign country's central bank, in return for the central bank's assumption of the borrowers' non-local currency obligations to the U.S. banks. The local currency is held on deposit at the central bank, for the account of the U.S. banks, and may be subject to relending to other borrowers in the country. Ultimate repayment of the obligations to the U.S. banks, in the requisite non-local currency, may not be due until a number of years hence.

Question : What disclosures are appropriate regarding deposit/relending arrangements of this general type?

Interpretive Response : The staff emphasizes that it is the responsibility of each registrant to determine the appropriate financial statement treatment and classification of foreign outstandings. The facts and circumstances surrounding deposit/relending arrangements should be carefully analyzed to determine whether the local currency payments to the foreign central bank represent collections of outstandings for financial reporting purposes, and whether such outstandings should be classified as nonaccrual, past due or restructured loans pursuant to Item III.C.1. of Industry Guide 3, Statistical Disclosure by Bank Holding Companies ("Guide 3").

The staff believes, however, that the impact of deposit/relending arrangements covering significant amounts of outstandings to a foreign country should be disclosed pursuant to Guide 3, Item III.C.3., Instruction (6)(a).[1] The disclosures should include a general description of the arrangements and, if significant, the amounts of interest income recognized for financial reporting purposes which has not been remitted in the requisite non-local currency to the U.S. bank.

2. *Accounting and disclosures by bank holding companies for a "Mexican Debt Exchange" transaction*

Facts : Inquiries have been made of the staff regarding certain accounting and disclosure issues raised by a proposed "Mexican Debt Exchange" transaction which could involve numerous bank holding companies with existing obligations of the United Mexican States ("Mexico") or other Mexican public sector entities (collectively, "Existing Obligations"). The key elements of the Mexican Debt Exchange are as follows:

Mexico will offer for sale bonds ("Bonds"), denominated in U.S. dollars, which will pay interest at a LIBOR-based floating rate and mature in twenty years. Mexico will undertake to list the Bonds on the Luxembourg Stock Exchange. The Bonds will be secured, as to their ultimate principal value only, by non-interest bearing securities of the U.S. Treasury ("Zero Coupon Treasury Securities") which will be purchased by Mexico. The Zero Coupon Treasury Securities will be pledged to holders of the Bonds and held in custody at the Federal Reserve Bank of New York and will have a maturity date and ultimate principal value which match the maturity date and principal value of the Bonds. While the Bonds will have default and acceleration provisions, the holder of a Bond will not be permitted to have access to the collateral prior to the final scheduled maturity date, at which time the proceeds of the collateral will be available to pay the full principal amount of the Bonds. As such, the holder of a Bond ultimately will be secured as to principal at maturity; however, the interest payments will not be secured. The Bonds will not be subject to future restructurings of Mexico's Existing Obligations, and Mexico has indicated that neither the Bonds nor the Existing Obligations exchanged therefor will be considered part of a base amount with respect to any future requests by Mexico for new money.

The Mexican Debt Exchange will be structured in such a way that potential purchasers of the Bonds will submit bids on a voluntary basis to the auction agent. These bids will specify the face dollar amount of existing restructured commercial bank obligations of Mexico or of other Mexican public sector entities that the potential purchaser is willing to tender and the face dollar amount of Bonds that the purchaser is willing to accept in exchange for the Existing Obligations. Following the auction date, Mexico will determine the face dollar amount of Bonds to be issued and will exchange the Bonds for Existing Obligations taking first the offer of the largest face dollar amount of Existing Obligations per face dollar amount of Bonds, and so on, until all Bonds which Mexico is willing to issue have been subscribed. It is therefore possible that a greater amount of Existing Obligations could be tendered than Mexico is willing to accept.

The lender has appropriately accounted for the transaction as a troubled debt restructuring in accordance with the provisions of Statement 15 as amended by Statement 114.

Question 1 : What financial statement and other disclosure issues regarding the Mexican Debt Exchange and the Bonds received should be considered by registrants?

Interpretive Response : The staff believes that disclosure of the nature of the transaction would be necessary, including:

• Carrying value and terms of Existing Obligations exchanged;

---

[1] Instruction (6)(a) calls for description of the nature and impact of developments in countries experiencing liquidity problems which are expected to have a material impact on timely repayment of principal or interest. Additionally, Instruction (6)(d)(ii) to Item III.C.3. calls for disclosure of commitments to relend, or to maintain on deposit, arising in connection with certain restructurings of foreign outstanding.

• Face value, carrying value, market value and terms of Bonds received;

• The effect of the transaction on the allowance for loan losses and the provision for losses in the current period; and

• Annual interest income on Existing Obligations exchanged and annual interest income on Bonds received.

On an ongoing basis, the staff believes that the terms, carrying value and market value of the Bonds should be disclosed, if material, due to their unique features.[2]

Question 2 : What disclosure with respect to the Bonds received would be acceptable under Industry Guide 3?

Interpretive Response : Instruction (4) to Item III.C.3. of Industry Guide 3 states: "The value of any tangible, liquid collateral may also be netted against cross-border outstandings of a country if it is held and realizable by the lender outside of the borrower's country." Given the unique features of the Bonds in that the ultimate repayment of the principal amount (but not interest) at maturity is assured, the staff will not object to either of two presentations. Under the first presentation, the carrying value of the Bonds, including any accrued but unpaid interest, would be included as a "cross-border outstanding" to the extent it exceeds the current fair value of the Zero Coupon Treasury Securities which collateralize the bonds. Alternatively, under the second presentation, the carrying value of the Bond principal would be excluded from Mexican cross-border outstandings provided (a) disclosure is made of the exclusion, (b) for purposes of determining the 1% and .75% of total assets disclosure thresholds of Item III.C.3. of Industry Guide 3, such carrying values are not excluded, and (c) all the Guide 3 disclosures relating to cross-border outstandings continue to be made, as discussed further below.

For registrants that adopt the alternative disclosure approach and whose Mexican cross-border outstandings (excluding the carrying value of the Bond principal) exceed 1% of total assets, appropriate footnote disclosure of the exclusions should be made. Such footnote should indicate the face amount and carrying value of the Bonds excluded, the market value of such Bonds, and the face amount and current fair value of the Zero Coupon Treasury Securities which secure the Bonds.

If the Mexican cross-border outstandings (excluding the carrying value of the Bond principal) are less than 1% of total assets but with the addition of the carrying value of the Bond principal would exceed 1%, the carrying value of the Mexican cross-border outstandings may be excluded from the list of countries whose cross-border outstandings exceed 1% of total assets provided that a footnote discloses the amount

of Mexican cross-border outstandings (excluding the carrying value of the Bond principal) along with the footnote-type disclosure concerning the Bonds discussed in the previous paragraph. This disclosure and any other material disclosure specified by Item III.C.3. of Industry Guide 3 would continue to be made as long as Mexican exposure, including the carrying value of the Bond principal, exceeded 1%.

If the Mexican cross-border outstandings (excluding the carrying value of the Bond principal) are less than .75% of total assets but with the addition of the carrying value of the Mexican Bond principal would exceed .75% but be less than 1%, cross-border outstandings disclosed pursuant to Instruction (7) to Item III.C.3. of Industry Guide 3 may exclude Mexico provided a footnote is added to the aggregate disclosure which discloses the amount of Mexican cross-border outstandings and the fact that they have not been included. The carrying value of the Bond principal may be excluded from the amount of Mexican cross-border outstandings disclosed in the footnote provided the footnote-type disclosure discussed in the second preceding paragraph is also made.

In essence, the alternative discussed herein results in a change only in the method of presenting information, not in the total information required.[3]

The appropriate disclosure would depend on the level of Mexican cross-border outstandings as follows:

A. Assuming that the remaining Mexican cross-border outstandings are in excess of 1% of total assets:

• Mexican cross-border outstandings (which excludes the total amount of the carrying value of Bond principal) would be disclosed in the table presenting all such outstandings in excess of 1%.

• Proposed footnote disclosure -

Not included in this amount is $___ million of Mexican Government Bonds maturing in 2008, with a carrying value of $___ million [if different from face value]. These Mexican Government Bonds had a market value of $___ million on [reporting date]. The principal amount of these bonds is fully secured, at maturity, by $___ million face value of U.S. zero coupon treasury securities that mature on the same date. The current fair value of these U.S. Government securities is $___ million at [reporting date]. This collateral is pledged to holders of the bonds and held in custody at the Federal Reserve Bank of New York. The details of the transaction in which these bonds were acquired was reported in the Corporation's Form (8-K, 10-Q or 10-K) for (date). Accrued interest on the bonds, which is not secured, is included in the outstandings reported [amount to be disclosed if material]. Future interest on the bonds remains a cross-border risk.

---

[2] Registrants also are reminded that if the security received in the exchange constitutes a debt security within the scope of Statement 115, the disclosures required by Statement 115 also would need to be provided.

[3] The following represents proposed disclosure using the alternative method discussed above. Of course, it would be necessary to supplement this disclosure with the additional disclosures regarding foreign outstandings that are called for by Guide 3 (e.g., an analysis of the changes in aggregate outstandings), and the disclosures called for by the Interpretive Responses to Question 1.

B. Assuming that remaining Mexican cross-border outstandings are less than 1% of total assets but with the addition of the carrying value of the Mexican Bond principal would exceed 1%:

• There would not be any disclosure included in any cross-border table.

• The total amount of remaining cross-border Mexican outstandings would be disclosed in a footnote to the table. Such footnote would also explain that the Mexican outstandings are excluded from the table.

• Additional footnote disclosure - (same disclosure in A above)

• The disclosure required under this paragraph (plus any other disclosure required by Item III.C.3. of Guide 3) would continue so long as Mexican exposure, including the carrying value of the Mexican Bond principal, exceeded 1%.

C. Assuming that the remaining Mexican cross-border outstandings is less than .75% of total assets but with the addition of the carrying value of the Mexican Bond principal is greater than .75% but less than 1%:

• Mexico would not be included in the list of names of countries required by Instruction 7 to Item III.C.3. of Industry Guide 3 and the amount of Mexican cross-border outstandings would not be included in the aggregate amount of outstandings attributable to all such countries.

• A footnote would be added to this disclosure of aggregate outstandings which discusses the Mexican outstandings and the Mexican Bonds. An example follows:

Not included in the above aggregate outstandings are the Corporation's cross-border outstandings to Mexico which totaled $___ million at (reporting date). This amount is less than .75% of total assets. (The remaining portion of this footnote is the same disclosure in A above.)

D. Assuming that the total of the Mexican cross-border outstanding plus the carrying value of the Bond principal is less than the .75% of total assets:

• No disclosure would be required.

• However, same disclosure as in A above would be provided if any other aspects of the financial statements are materially affected by this transaction (such as the allowance for loan losses).

Changes in aggregate outstandings to certain countries experiencing liquidity problems are required to be presented in tabular form in compliance with Instruction (6)(b) to Item III.C.3. In this table, Existing Obligations exchanged for the Bonds would generally be included in the aggregate cross-border outstandings at the beginning of the period during which the exchange occurred. For registrants using the alternative method, the amount of Existing Obligations which were exchanged would be included as a deduction in the "other changes" caption in the table. In addition, a footnote will be provided to the table as follows:

• Relates primarily to the exchange of unsecured Mexican outstandings for Mexican bonds. The principal amount of these bonds is secured at maturity by $___ face U.S. Zero Coupon Treasury Securities which mature on the same date and have a current fair value of $___. Future interest on the bonds remains a cross-border risk.]

I. Reporting Of An Allocated Transfer Risk Reserve In Filings Under The Federal Securities Laws

Facts : The Comptroller of the Currency, Board of Governors of the Federal Reserve System and Federal Deposit Insurance Corporation jointly issued final rules, pursuant to the International Lending Supervision Act of 1983, requiring banking institutions to establish special reserves (Allocated Transfer Risk Reserve "ATRR") against the risks presented in certain international assets when the Federal banking agencies determine that such reserves are necessary. The rules provide that the ATRR is to be accounted for separately from the General Allowances for Possible Loan Losses, and shall not be included in the banking institution's capital or surplus. The rules also provide that no ATRR provisions are required if the banking institution writes down the assets in the requisite amount.

Question : How should the ATRR be reported in filings under the Federal Securities Laws?

Interpretive Response : It is the staff's understanding that the three banking agencies believe that those bank holding companies that have not written down the designated assets by the requisite amount and, therefore, are required to establish an ATRR should disclose the amount of the ATRR. The staff believes that such disclosure should be part of the discussion of Loan Loss Experience, Item IV of Guide 3. Part A under Item IV calls for an analysis of loss experience in the form of a reconciliation of the allowance for loan losses, and the staff believes that it would be appropriate to show and discuss separately the ATRR in the context of that reconciliation.

Registrants should recognize that the amount provided as an ATRR, or the write off of the requisite amount, represents the identification of an amount which those regulatory agencies have determined should not be included as a part of the institution's capital or surplus for purposes of administration of the regulatory and supervisory functions of those agencies. In this context, the staff believes that disclosure of the ATRR, as part of the footnote required to be presented in a registrant's financial statements by Item 7(d) of Rule 9-03 of Regulation S-X, may provide a more complete explanation of charge offs and provisions for loan losses. It should be noted, however, that the ATRR amount to be excluded from the institution's capital and surplus does not address the more general issue of the adequacy of allowances for any particular bank holding company's loans. It is still the responsibility of each registrant to determine whether GAAP require an additional provision for losses in excess of the amount required to be included in an ATRR (or the requisite amount written off).

J. Deleted by SAB 103

K. Application Of Article 9 And Guide 3

Facts : Article 9 of Regulation S-X specifies the form and content of and requirements for financial statements for bank holding companies filing with the Commission. Similarly, bank holding companies disclose supplemental statistical disclosures in filings, pursuant to Industry Guide 3. No specific guidance as to the form and content of financial statements or supplemental disclosures has been promulgated for registrants which are not bank holding companies but which are engaged in similar lending and deposit activities.[4]

Question : Should non-bank holding company registrants with material amounts of lending and deposit activities file financial statements and make disclosures called for by Article 9 of Regulation S-X and Industry Guide 3?

Interpretive Response : In the staff's view, Article 9 and Guide 3, while applying literally only to bank holding companies, provide useful guidance to certain other registrants, including savings and loan holding companies, on certain disclosures relevant to an understanding of the registrant's operations. Thus, to the extent particular guidance is relevant and material to the operations of an entity, the staff believes the specified information, or comparable data, should be provided.

For example, in accordance with Guide 3, bank holding companies disclose information about yields and costs of various assets and liabilities. Further, bank holding companies provide certain information about maturities and repricing characteristics of various assets and liabilities. Such companies also disclose risk elements, such as nonaccrual and past due items in the lending portfolio. The staff believes that this information and other relevant data would be material to a description of business of other registrants with material lending and deposit activities and accordingly, the specified information and/or comparable data (such as scheduled item disclosure for risk elements) should be provided.

In contrast, other requirements of Article 9 and Guide 3 may not be material or relevant to an understanding of the financial statements of some financial institutions. For example, bank holding companies present average balance sheet information, because period-end statements might not be representative of bank activity throughout the year. Some financial institutions other than bank holding companies may determine that average balance sheet disclosure does not provide significant additional information. Others may determine that assets and liabilities are subject to sufficient volatility that average balance information should be presented.

Pursuant to Article 9, the income statements of bank holding companies use a "net interest income" presentation. Similarly, bank holding companies present the aggregate market value, at the balance sheet date, of investment securities, on the face of the balance sheet. The staff believes that such disclosures and other relevant information should also be provided by other registrants with material lending and deposit activities.

L. Income Statement Presentation Of Casino-Hotels

Facts : Registrants having casino-hotel operations present separately within the income statement amounts of revenue attributable to casino, hotel and restaurant operations, respectively.

Question : What is the appropriate income statement presentation of expenses attributable to casino-hotel activities?

Interpretive Response : The staff believes that the expenses attributable to each of the separate revenue producing activities of casino, hotel and restaurant operations should be separately presented on the face of the income statement. Such a presentation is consistent with the general reporting format for income statement presentation under Regulation S-X (Rules 5-03.1 and 5-03.2) which requires presentation of amounts of revenues and related costs and expenses applicable to major revenue providing activities. This detailed presentation affords an analysis of the relative contribution to operating profits of each of the revenue producing activities of a typical casino-hotel operation.

M. Disclosure Of The Impact That Recently Issued Accounting Standards Will Have On The Financial Statements Of The Registrant When Adopted In A Future Period

Facts : An accounting standard has been issued[5] that does not require adoption until some future date. A registrant is required to include financial statements in filings with the Commission after the issuance of the standard but before it is adopted by the registrant.

Question 1 : Does the staff believe that these filings should include disclosure of the impact that the recently issued accounting standard will have on the financial position and results of operations of the registrant when such standard is adopted in a future period?

Interpretive Response : Yes. The Commission addressed a similar issue with respect to Statement 52 and concluded that "The Commission also believes that registrants that have not yet adopted Statement 52 should discuss the potential effects of adoption in registration statements and reports filed with the

---

[4] The Commission staff has been considering the need for more specific guidance in the area but believes that the FASB project on financial instruments may make Commission action in this area unnecessary. In the interim, this bulletin provides the staff's views with respect to filings by similar entities such as saving and loan holding companies.

[5] Some registrants may want to disclose the potential effects of proposed accounting standards not yet issued, (e.g., exposure drafts). Such disclosures, which generally are not required because the final standard may differ from the exposure draft, are not addressed by this SAB. See also FRR 26.

Commission."[6] The staff believes that this disclosure guidance applies to all accounting standards which have been issued but not yet adopted by the registrant unless the impact on its financial position and results of operations is not expected to be material.[7] MD&A[8] requires registrants to provide information with respect to liquidity, capital resources and results of operations and such other information that the registrant believes to be necessary to understand its financial condition and results of operations. In addition, MD&A requires disclosure of presently known material changes, trends and uncertainties that have had or that the registrant reasonably expects will have a material impact on future sales, revenues or income from continuing operations. The staff believes that disclosure of impending accounting changes is necessary to inform the reader about expected impacts on financial information to be reported in the future and, therefore, should be disclosed in accordance with the existing MD&A requirements. With respect to financial statement disclosure, GAAS[9] specifically address the need for the auditor to consider the adequacy of the disclosure of impending changes in accounting principles if (a) the financial statements have been prepared on the basis of accounting principles that were acceptable at the financial statement date but that will not be acceptable in the future and (b) the financial statements will be restated in the future as a result of the change. The staff believes that recently issued accounting standards may constitute material matters and, therefore, disclosure in the financial statements should also be considered in situations where the change to the new accounting standard will be accounted for in financial statements of future periods, prospectively or with a cumulative catch-up adjustment.

Question 2 : Does the staff have a view on the types of disclosure that would be meaningful and appropriate when a new accounting standard has been issued but not yet adopted by the registrant?

Interpretive Response : The staff believes that the registrant should evaluate each new accounting standard to determine the appropriate disclosure and recognizes that the level of information available to the registrant will differ with respect to various standards and from one registrant to another. The objectives of the disclosure should be to (1) notify the reader of the disclosure documents that a standard has been issued which the registrant will be required to adopt in the future and (2) assist the reader in assessing the

significance of the impact that the standard will have on the financial statements of the registrant when adopted. The staff understands that the registrant will only be able to disclose information that is known.

The following disclosures should generally be considered by the registrant:

• A brief description of the new standard, the date that adoption is required and the date that the registrant plans to adopt, if earlier.

• A discussion of the methods of adoption allowed by the standard and the method expected to be utilized by the registrant, if determined.

• A discussion of the impact that adoption of the standard is expected to have on the financial statements of the registrant, unless not known or reasonably estimable. In that case, a statement to that effect may be made.

• Disclosure of the potential impact of other significant matters that the registrant believes might result from the adoption of the standard (such as technical violations of debt covenant agreements, planned or intended changes in business practices, etc.) is encouraged.

N. Disclosures Of The Impact Of Assistance From Federal Financial Institution Regulatory Agencies

Facts : An entity receives financial assistance from a federal regulatory agency in conjunction with either an acquisition of a troubled financial institution, transfer of nonperforming assets to a newly-formed entity, or other reorganization.

Question : What are the disclosure implications of the existence of regulatory assistance?

Interpretive Response : The staff believes that users of financial statements must be able to assess the impact of credit and other risks on a company following a regulatory assisted acquisition, transfer or other reorganization on a basis comparable to that disclosed by other institutions, i.e., as if the assistance did not exist. In this regard, the staff believes that the amount of regulatory assistance should be disclosed separately and should be separately identified in the statistical information furnished pursuant to Industry Guide 3, to the extent it impacts such information.[10][11] Further, the nature, extent and impact of such assistance needs to be fully discussed in Management's Discussion and Analysis.[12]

---

[6] FRR 6, Section 2.

[7] In those instances where a recently issued standard will impact the preparation of, but not materially affect, the financial statements, the registrant is encouraged to disclose that a standard has been issued and that its adoption will not have a material effect on its financial position or results of operations.

[8] Item 303 of Regulation S-K.

[9] See AU 9410.13-18.

[10] The staff has previously expressed its views regarding acceptable methods of compliance with this principle in the minutes of EITF Issue 88-19, and an announcement by the SEC Observer to the EITF at the February 23, 1989 meeting.

[11] See EITF Issue 88-19 for guidance on the appropriate period in which to record certain types of regulatory assistance.

[12] See Section 501.06.c. of the Financial Reporting Codification for further discussion of the MD&A disclosures of the effects of regulatory assistance.

A. Accounting Series Release 257 - Requirements for Financial Accounting and Reporting Practices for Oil and Gas Producing Activities

1. *Estimates of reserve quantities*

Facts: Rule 4-10 of Regulation S-X contains definitions of possible reserves, probable reserves, and proved and developed oil and gas reserves to be used in determining quantities of oil and gas reserves to be reported in filings with the Commission.

Question: What pressure base should be used for reporting gas and production, 14.73 psia or the pressure base specified by the state?

Interpretive Response: The reporting instructions to the Department of Energy's Form EIA-28 specify that natural gas reserves are to be reported at 14.73 psia and 60 degrees F. There is no pressure base specified in Regulation S-X or S-K. At the present time staff will not object to natural gas reserves and production data calculated at other pressure bases, if such pressure bases are identified in the filing.

2. *Estimates of future net revenues*

Facts: U.S. GAAP requires the disclosure of the standardized measure of discounted future net cash flows from production of proved oil and gas reserves.

Question: For purposes of determining reserves and estimated future net revenues, what price should be used for oil and gas which will be produced after an existing contract expires or after the redetermination date in a contract?

Interpretive Response: The price to be used for oil and gas which will be produced after a contract expires or has a redetermination is the average price during the 12-month period prior to the ending date of the period covered by the balance sheet, determined as an unweighted arithmetic average of the first-day-of-the-month price for each month within such period for that oil and gas. This average price, which should be based on the first-day-of-the-month market prices, may be increased thereafter only for additional fixed and determinable escalations, as appropriate. A fixed and determinable escalation is one which is specified in amount and is not based on future events such as rates of inflation.

3. *Disclosure of reserve information*

a. Removed by SAB 103

b. Removed by SAB 113

c. *Limited partnership 10-K reports*

Facts: Item 1201(a) of Regulation S-K contains an exemption from the requirements to disclose certain information relating to oil and gas operations for "limited partnerships or joint ventures that conduct, operate, manage, or report upon oil and gas drilling income programs that acquire properties either for drilling and production, or for production of oil, gas, or geothermal steam ...."

Limited partnership agreements often contain buyout provisions under which the general partner agrees to purchase limited partnership interests that are offered for sale, based upon a specified valuation formula. Because of these arrangements, the requirements for disclosure of reserve value information may be of little significance to the limited partners.

Question: Must the financial statements of limited partnerships included in reports on Form 10-K contain the disclosures of estimated future net revenues, present values and changes therein, and supplemental summary of oil and gas activities specified in paragraphs 23 through 36 of FASB Accounting Standards Codification (FASB ASC) Section 932-235-50, *Extractive Activities - Oil and Gas - Notes to Financial Statements - Disclosure*?

Interpretive Response: The staff will not take exception to the omission of these disclosures in a limited partnership Form 10-K if reserve value information is available to the limited partners pursuant to the partnership agreement (even though the valuations may be computed differently and may be as of a date other than year end). However, the staff will require all of the information listed in paragraphs 23 through 36 of FASB ASC Section 932-235-50 for partnerships which are the subject of a business combination or exchange offer under which various limited partnerships are to be consolidated or combined into a single entity.

d. Removed by SAB 113

e. *Rate regulated companies*

Question: If a company has cost-of-service oil and gas producing properties, how should they be treated in the supplemental disclosures of reserve quantities and related future net revenues provided pursuant to paragraphs 29 through 36 of FASB ASC Section 932-235-50, *Extractive Activities - Oil and Gas - Notes to Financial Statements - Disclosure*?

Interpretive Response: Rule 4-10 provides that registrants may give effect to differences arising from the ratemaking process for cost-of-service oil and gas properties. Accordingly, in these circumstances, the staff believes that the company's supplemental reserve quantity disclosures should indicate separately the quantities associated with properties subject to cost-of-service ratemaking, and that it is appropriate to exclude those quantities from the future net revenue disclosures. The company should also disclose the nature and impact of its cost-of-service ratemaking, including the unamortized cost included in the balance sheet.

4. Removed by SAB 103

B. Removed by SAB 103

C. Methods of Accounting by Oil and Gas Producers

1. *First-time registrants*

Facts: In ASR 300, the Commission announced that it would allow registrants to change methods of accounting for oil and gas producing activities so long as such changes were in accordance with GAAP. Accordingly, the Commission stated that changes from the full cost method to the successful efforts method would not require a preferability letter. Changes to full cost, however, would require justification by the company making the change and filing of a preferability letter from the company's independent accountants.

Question: How does this policy apply to a nonpublic company which changes its accounting method in connection with a forthcoming public offering or initial registration under either the 1933 Act or 1934 Act?

Interpretive Response: The Commission's policy that first-time registrants may change their previous accounting methods without filing a preferability letter is applicable. Therefore, such a company may change to the full cost method without filing a preferability letter.

2. *Consistent use of accounting methods within a consolidated entity*

Facts: Rule 4-10(c) of Regulation S-X states in part that "[a] reporting entity that follows the full cost method shall apply that method to all of its operations and to the operations of its subsidiaries . . ."

Question 1: May a subsidiary of the parent use the full cost method if the parent company uses the successful efforts method of accounting for oil and gas producing activities?

Interpretive Response: No. The use of different methods of accounting in the consolidated financial statements by a parent company and its subsidiary would be inconsistent with the full cost requirement that a parent and its subsidiaries all use the same method of accounting.

The staff's general policy is that an enterprise should account for all its like operations in the same manner. However, Rule 4-10 of Regulation S-X provides that oil and gas companies with cost-of-service oil and gas properties may give effect to any differences resulting from the ratemaking process, including regulatory requirements that a certain accounting method be used for the cost-of-service properties.

ASSUMPTIONS:

Question 2: Must the method of accounting (full cost or successful efforts) followed by a registrant for its oil and gas producing activities also be followed by any fifty percent or less owned companies in which the registrant carries its investment on the equity method (equity investees)?

Interpretive Response: No. Conformity of accounting methods between a registrant and its equity investees, although desirable, may not be practicable and thus is not required. However, if a registrant proportionately consolidates its equity investees, it will be necessary to present them all on the same basis of accounting.

D. Application of Full Cost Method of Accounting

1. *Treatment of income tax effects in the computation of the limitation on capitalized costs*

Facts: Item (D) in Rule 4-10(c)(4)(i) of Regulation S-X provides that the income tax effects related to the properties involved should be deducted in computing the full cost ceiling.

Question 1: What specific types of income tax effects should be considered in computing the income tax effects to be deducted from estimated future net revenues?

Interpretive Response: The rule refers to income tax effects generally. Thus, the computation should take into account (i) the tax basis of oil and gas properties, (ii) net operating loss carryforwards, (iii) foreign tax credit carryforwards, (iv) investment tax credits, (v) alternative minimum taxes on tax preference items, and (vi) the impact of statutory (percentage) depletion.

It may often be difficult to allocate a net operating loss (NOL) carryforward between oil and gas assets and other assets. However, to the extent that the NOL is clearly attributable to oil and gas operations and is expected to be realized within the carryforward period, it should be added to tax basis.

Similarly, to the extent that investment tax credit (ITC) carryforwards and foreign tax credit carryforwards are attributable to oil and gas operations and are expected to be realized within the carryforward period, they should be considered as a deduction from the tax effect otherwise computed. Consideration of NOL and ITC or foreign tax credit carryforwards should not, of course, reduce the total tax effect below zero.

Question 2: How should the tax effect be computed considering the various factors discussed above?

Interpretive Response: Theoretically, taxable income and tax could be determined on a year-by-year basis and the present value of the related tax computed. However, the "shortcut" method illustrated below is also acceptable.

Cost of proved properties being amortized $396,000

Lower of cost or estimated fair value of unproved properties to be amortized	49,000	
Cost of properties not being amortized	55,000	
Capitalized costs of oil and gas assets	500,000	
Accumulated DD&A	(100,000)	
Book basis of oil and gas assets		$400,000
Excess of book basis over tax basis ($270,000) of oil and gas assets	$(130,000)	
NOL carryforward*	20,000	
	(110,000)	
Statutory tax rate (percent)	× 46%	
	(50,600)	
Foreign tax credit carryforward*	1,000	
ITC carryforward*	2,000	
	(47,600)	
Net book basis to be recovered		$352,400

Other Assumptions:

Present value of ITC relating to future development costs	$1,500
Present value of statutory depletion attributable to future deductions	$10,000
Estimated preference (minimum) tax on percentage depletion in excess of cost depletion	$500
Present value of future net revenue from proved oil and gas reserves	$272,000

CALCULATION:

Present value of future net revenue	272,000	
Cost of properties not being amortized	55,000	
Lower of cost or estimated fair value of unproved properties included in costs being amortized	49,000	
Total ceiling limitation before tax effects		$376,000

Tax Effects:

Total ceiling limitation before tax effects	$376,000

Less: Tax basis of properties	$(270,000)
Statutory depletion	(10,000)
NOL carryforward	(20,000)
	(300,000)
Future taxable income	76,000
Tax rate (percent)	× 46%
Tax at statutory rate	(34,960)
ITC (future development costs and carryforward)	3,500
Foreign tax credit carryforward	1,000
Estimated preference tax	(500)
Net tax effects	(30,960)
Cost Center Ceiling	$345,040
Less: Net book basis to be recovered	352,400
REQUIRED WRITE-OFF, net of tax**	$(7,360)

* All carryforward amounts in this example represent amounts which are available for tax purposes and which relate to oil and gas operations.

** For accounting purposes, the gross write-off should be recorded to adjust both the oil and gas properties account and the related deferred income taxes.

CALCULATION OF GROSS PRE-TAX WRITE-OFF:

Required write-off, net of tax	$(7,360)
Divided by (100% minus the statutory rate of 46%)	54%
Gross pre-tax write-off	$ (13,630)

Related Journal Entries	DR	CR
Full cost ceiling impairment	$13,630	
Oil and gas assets		$13,630
Deferred income tax liability	$6,270	
Deferred income tax benefit		$6,270

2. *Exclusion of costs from amortization*

Facts: Rule 4-10(c)(3)(ii) indicates that the costs of acquiring and evaluating unproved properties may be excluded from capitalized costs to be amortized if the costs are unusually significant in relation to aggregate costs to be amortized. Costs of major development projects may also be incurred prior to ascertaining the quantities of proved reserves attributable to such properties.

Question: At what point should amortization of previously excluded costs commence—when proved reserves have been established or when those reserves become marketable? For instance, a determination of proved reserves may be made before completion of an extraction plant necessary to process sour crude or a pipeline necessary to market the reserves. May the costs continue to be excluded from amortization until the plant or pipeline is in service?

Interpretive Response: No. The proved reserves and the costs allocable to such reserves should be transferred into the amortization base on an ongoing (well-by-well or property-by-property) basis as the project is evaluated and proved reserves are established.

Once the determination of proved reserves has been made, there is no justification for continued exclusion from the full cost pool, regardless of whether other factors prevent immediate marketing. Moreover, at the same time that the costs are transferred into the amortization base, it is also necessary in accordance with FASB ASC Subtopic 932-835, *Extractive Activities - Oil and Gas - Interest* and FASB ASC Subtopic 835-20, *Interest - Capitalization of Interest,* to terminate capitalization of interest on such properties.

In this regard, registrants are reminded of their responsibilities not to delay recognizing reserves as proved once they have met the engineering standards.

3. *Full cost ceiling limitation*

a. *Exemptions for purchased properties*

Facts: During 20x1, a registrant purchases proved oil and gas reserves in place ("the purchased reserves") in an arm's-length transaction for the sum of $9.8 million. Primarily because the registrant expects oil and gas prices to escalate, it paid $1.2 million more for the purchased reserves than the "Present Value of Estimated Future Net Revenues" computed as defined in Rule 4-10(c)(4)(i)(A) of Regulation S-X. An analysis of the registrant's full cost center in which the purchased reserves are located at December 31, 20x1 is as follows:

(Amounts in thousands)

	Total	Purchased Reserves	Other Proved Properties	Unproved Properties
Present value of estimated future net revenues	$14,100	8,600	5,500	—
Cost, net of amortization	$16,300	9,800	5,500	1,000
Related deferred taxes	$2,300	—	2,000	300
Income tax effects related to properties	$2,500	—	2,500	—

Comparison of capitalized costs with limitation on capitalized costs at December 31, 20x1:	Including Purchased Reserves	Excluding Purchased Reserves
Capitalized costs, net of amortization	$16,300	$6,500
Related deferred taxes	(2,300)	(2,300)
Net book cost	14,000	4,200
Present value of estimated future net revenues	14,100	$5,500
Lower of cost or market of unproved properties	1,000	1,000
Income tax effects related to properties	(2,500)	(2,500)

Comparison of capitalized costs with limitation on capitalized costs at December 31, 20x1:

	Including Purchased Reserves	Excluding Purchased Reserves
Limitation on capitalized costs	12,600	4,000
Excess of capitalized costs over limitation on Capitalized costs, net of tax*	$1,400	$ 200

---

* For accounting purposes, the gross write-off should be recorded to adjust both the oil and gas properties account and the related deferred income taxes

Question: Is it necessary for the registrant to write down the carrying value of its full cost center at December 31, 20x1 by $1,400,000?

Interpretive Response: Although the net carrying value of the full cost center exceeds the cost center's limitation on capitalized costs, the text of ASR 258 provides that a registrant may request an exemption from the rule if as a result of a major purchase of proved properties, a write down would be required even though the registrant believes the fair value of the properties in a cost center clearly exceeds the unamortized costs.

Therefore, to the extent that the excess carrying value relates to the purchased reserves, the registrant may seek a temporary waiver from the full-cost ceiling limitation from the staff of the Commission. Registrants requesting a waiver should be prepared to demonstrate that the additional value exists beyond reasonable doubt.

To the extent that the excess costs relate to properties other than the purchased reserves, however, a write-off should be recorded in the current period. In order to determine the portion of the total excess carrying value which is attributable to properties other than the purchased reserves, it is necessary to perform the ceiling computation on a "with and without" basis as shown in the example above. Thus in this case, the registrant must record a write-down of $200,000 applicable to other reserves. An additional $1,200,000 write-down would be necessary unless a waiver was obtained.

b. Use of cash flow hedges in the computation of the limitation on capitalized costs

Facts: Rule 4-10(c)(4) of Regulation S-X provides, in pertinent part, that capitalized costs, net of accumulated depreciation and amortization, and deferred income taxes, should not exceed an amount equal to the sum of components that include the present value of estimated future net revenues computed by applying current prices of oil and gas reserves (with consideration of price changes only to the extent provided by contractual arrangements) to estimated future production of proved oil and gas reserves as of the date of the latest balance sheet presented.

As of the reported balance sheet date, capitalized costs of an oil and gas producing company exceed the full cost limitation calculated under the above-described rule based on current prices, as defined in Rule 4-10(c)(8) of Regulation S-X, for oil and natural gas. However, prior to the balance sheet date, the company entered into certain hedging arrangements for a portion of its future natural gas and oil production, thereby enabling the company to receive future cash flows that are higher or lower than the estimated future cash flows indicated by use of the average price during the 12-month period prior to the balance sheet date, determined as an unweighted arithmetic average of the first-day-of-the-month price for each month within such period. These arrangements qualify as cash flow hedges under the provisions of FASB ASC Topic 815, *Derivatives and Hedging,* and are documented, designated, and accounted for as such under the criteria of that standard.

Question: Under these circumstances, must the company use the higher or lower prices to be received after taking into account the hedging arrangements ("hedge-adjusted prices") in calculating the estimated cash flows from future production of oil and gas reserves covered by the hedges as of the reported balance sheet date?

Interpretive Response: Yes. Derivative contracts that qualify as a hedging instrument in a cash flow hedge and are accounted for as such pursuant to FASB ASC Topic 815 represent the type of contractual arrangements for which consideration of price changes should be given under the existing rule. While the SEC staff has objected to previous proposals to consider various hedging techniques as being equivalent to the contractual arrangements permitted under the existing rules, the staff's objection was based on concerns that the lack of clear, consistent guidance in the accounting literature would lead to inconsistent application in practice. However, the staff believes that FASB ASC Topic 815 and related guidance (including a more systematic approach to documentation) provides sufficient guidance so that comparable financial reporting in comparable factual circumstances should result.

This interpretive response reflects the SEC staff's view that, assuming compliance with the prerequisite accounting requirements, hedge-adjusted prices represent the best measure of estimated cash flows from future production of the affected oil and gas reserves to use in calculating the ceiling limitation. Nonetheless, the staff expects that oil and gas producing companies subject to the full cost rules will clearly indicate the effects of using cash flow hedges in calculating ceiling limitations within their financial statement footnotes. The staff further expects that disclosures will indicate the portion of future oil and gas production being hedged. The dollar amount that would have been charged to income had the effects of the cash flow hedges not been considered in calculating the ceiling limitation also should be disclosed.

The use of hedge-adjusted prices should be consistently applied in all reporting periods, including periods in which the hedge-adjusted price is more or less than the average price during the 12-month period prior to the balance sheet date, determined as an unweighted arithmetic average of the first-day-of-the-month price for each month within such period. Oil and gas producers whose computation of the ceiling limitation includes hedge-adjusted prices because of the use of cash flow hedges also should consider the disclosure requirements under FASB ASC Section 275-10-50, *Risks and Uncertainties - Overall-Disclosure*. Paragraph 9 of FASB ASC Section 275-10-50 calls for disclosure when it is at least reasonably possible that the effects of cash flow hedges on capitalized costs on the reported balance sheet date will change in the near term due to one or more confirming events, such as potential future changes in commodity prices.

In addition, the use of cash flow hedges in calculating the ceiling limitation may represent a type of critical accounting policy that oil and gas producers should consider disclosing consistent with the cautionary advice provided in Financial Reporting Release No. 60 (Release Nos. 33-8040; 34-45149), *Cautionary Advice Regarding Disclosure about Critical Accounting Policies* (December 12, 2001), and Financial Reporting Release No. 72 (Release Nos. 33-8350; 34-48960), *Commission Guidance Regarding Management's Discussion and Analysis of Financial Condition and Results of Operations* (December 29, 2003). Through these releases, the Commission has encouraged companies to include, within their MD&A disclosures, full explanations, in plain English, of the judgments and uncertainties affecting the application of critical accounting policies, and the likelihood that materially different amounts would be reported under different conditions or using different assumptions.

The staff's guidance on this issue would apply to calculations of ceiling limitations both in interim and annual reporting periods.

c. Effect of subsequent events on the computation of the limitation on capitalized costs

Facts: Rule 4-10(c)(4)(ii) of Regulation S-X provides that an excess of unamortized capitalized costs within a cost center over the related cost ceiling shall be charged to expense in the period the excess occurs.

Question: Assume that at the date of the company's fiscal year-end, its capitalized costs of oil and gas producing properties exceed the limitation prescribed by Rule 4-10(c)(4) of Regulation S-X. Thus, a write-down is indicated. Subsequent to year-end but before the date of the auditor's report on the company's financial statements, assume that additional reserves are proved up (excluding the effect of increased oil and gas prices subsequent to year-end) on properties owned at year-end. The present value of future net revenues from the additional reserves is sufficiently large that if the full cost ceiling limitation were recomputed giving effect to those factors as of year-end, the ceiling would more than cover the costs. Is it necessary to record a write-down?

Interpretive Response: No. In this case, the proving up of additional reserves on properties owned at year-end indicates that the capitalized costs were not in fact impaired at year-end. However, for purposes of the revised computation of the "ceiling," the net book costs capitalized as of year-end should be increased by the amount of any additional costs incurred subsequent to year-end to prove the additional reserves or by any related costs previously excluded from amortization.

While the fact pattern described herein relates to annual periods, the guidance on the effects of subsequent events applies equally to interim period calculations of the ceiling limitation.

The registrant's financial statements should disclose that capitalized costs exceeded the limitation thereon at year-end and should explain why the excess was not charged against earnings. In addition, the registrant's supplemental disclosures of estimated proved reserve quantities and related future net revenues and costs should not give effect to the reserves proved up or the cost incurred after year-end. However, such quantities may be disclosed separately, with appropriate explanations.

Registrants should be aware that oil and gas reserves related to properties acquired after year-end would not justify avoiding a write-off indicated as of year-end. Similarly, the effects of cash flow hedging arrangements entered into after year-end cannot be factored into the calculation of the ceiling limitation at year-end. Such acquisitions and financial arrangements do not confirm situations existing at year-end.

4. Interaction of FASB ASC Subtopic 410-20 Asset Retirement and Environmental Obligations - Asset Retirement Obligations and the Full Cost Rules

a. Impact of FASB ASC Subtopic 410-20 on the full cost ceiling test

Facts: A company following the full cost method of accounting under Rule 4-10(c) of Regulation S-X must periodically calculate a limitation on capitalized costs, i.e., the full cost ceiling. Under FASB ASC Subtopic 410-20, *Asset Retirement and Environmental Obligations - Asset Retirement Obligations*, a company must recognize a liability for an asset retirement obligation (ARO) at fair value in the period in which the obligation is incurred, if a reasonable estimate of fair value can be made. The company also must initially capitalize the associated asset retirement costs by increasing long-lived oil and gas assets by the same amount as the liability. Any asset retirement costs capitalized pursuant to FASB ASC Subtopic 410-20 are subject to the full cost ceiling limitation under Rule 4-10(c)(4) of Regulation S-X. If a company were to calculate the full cost ceiling by reducing expected future net revenues by the cash flows required to settle the ARO, then the effect would be to "double-count" such costs in the ceiling test. The assets that must be recovered would be increased while the future net revenues available to recover the assets continue to be reduced by the amount of the ARO settlement cash flows.

Question: How should a company compute the full cost ceiling to avoid double-counting the expected future cash outflows associated with asset retirement costs?

Interpretive Response: The future cash outflows associated with settling AROs that have been accrued on the balance sheet should be excluded from the computation of the present value of estimated future net revenues for purposes of the full cost ceiling calculation.[1],[2]

b. Impact of FASB ASC Subtopic 410-20 on the calculation of depreciation, depletion, and amortization

Facts: Regarding the base for depreciation, depletion, and amortization (DD&A) of proved reserves, Rule 4-10(c)(3)(i) of Regulation S-X states that "[c]osts to be amortized shall include (A) all capitalized costs, less accumulated amortization, other than the cost of properties described in paragraph (ii) below;[3] (B) the estimated future expenditures (based on current costs) to be incurred in developing proved reserves; and (C) estimated dismantlement and abandonment costs, net of estimated salvage values." FASB ASC Subtopic 410-20 requires that upon initial recognition of an ARO, the associated asset retirement costs be included in the capitalized costs of the company. Therefore, the estimated dismantlement and abandonment costs described in (C) above may be included in the capitalized costs described in (A) above, at least to the extent that an ARO has been incurred as a result of acquisition, exploration and development activities to date. Future development activities on proved reserves may result in additional asset retirement obligations when such activities are performed and the associated asset retirement costs will be capitalized at that time.

Question: Should the costs to be amortized under Rule 4-10(c)(3) of Regulation S-X include an amount for estimated dismantlement and abandonment costs, net of estimated salvage values, that are expected to result from future development activities?

Interpretive Response: Yes. Companies should estimate the amount of dismantlement and abandonment costs that will be incurred as a result of future development activities on proved reserves and include those amounts in the costs to be amortized.

c. Removed by SAB 113

E. Financial Statements of Royalty Trusts

Facts: Several oil and gas exploration and production companies have created "royalty trusts." Typically, the creating company conveys a net profits interest in certain of its oil and gas properties to the newly created trust and then distributes units in the trust to its shareholders. The trust is a passive entity which is prohibited from entering into or engaging in any business or commercial activity of any kind and from acquiring any oil and gas lease, royalty or other mineral interest. The function of the trust is to serve as an agent to distribute the income from the net profits interest. The amount to be periodically distributed to the unitholders is defined in the trust agreement and is typically determined based on the cash received from the net profits interest less expenses of the trustee. Royalty trusts have typically reported their earnings on the basis of cash distributions to unitholders. The net profits interest paid to the trust for any month is based on production from a preceding month; therefore, the method of accounting followed by the trust for the net profits interest income is different from the creating company's method of accounting for the related revenue.

Question: Will the staff accept a statement of distributable income which reflects the amounts to be distributed for the period in question under the terms of the trust agreement in lieu of a statement of income prepared under GAAP?

Interpretive Response: Yes. Although financial statements filed with the Commission are normally required to be prepared in accordance with GAAP, the Commission's rules provide that other presentations may be acceptable in unusual situations. Since the operations of a royalty trust are limited to the distribution of income from the net profits interests contributed to it, the staff believes that the item of primary importance to the reader of the financial statements of the royalty trust is the amount of the cash distributions to the unitholders for the period reported. Should there be any change in the nature of the trust's operations due to revisions in the tax laws or other factors, the staff's interpretation would be reexamined.

A note to the financial statements should disclose the method used in determining distributable income and should also describe how distributable income as reported differs from income determined on the basis of GAAP.

---

[1] If an obligation for expected asset retirement costs has not been accrued under FASB ASC Subtopic 410-20 for certain asset retirement costs required to be included in the full cost ceiling calculation under Rule 4-10(c)(4) of Regulation S-X, such costs should continue to be included in the full cost ceiling calculation.

[2] This approach is consistent with the guidance in FASB ASC Subtopic 410-20 on testing for impairment under FASB ASC Section 360-10-35 *Property, Plant, and Equipment - Overall - Subsequent Measurement*. Under that guidance, the asset tested should include

capitalized asset retirement costs. The estimated cash flows related to the associated ARO that has been recognized in the financial statements are to be excluded from both the undiscounted cash flows used to test for recoverability and the discounted cash flows used to measure the asset's fair value.

[3] The reference to "cost of properties described in paragraph (ii) below" relates to the costs of investments in unproved properties and major development projects, as defined.

F. Gross Revenue Method of Amortizing Capitalized Costs

Facts: Rule 4-10(c)(3)(iii) of Regulation S-X states in part: "Amortization shall be computed on the basis of physical units, with oil and gas converted to a common unit of measure on the basis of their approximate relative energy content, unless economic circumstances (related to the effects of regulated prices) indicate that use of units of revenue is a more appropriate basis of computing amortization. In the latter case, amortization shall be computed on the basis of current gross revenues (excluding royalty payments and net profits disbursements) from production in relation to future gross revenues based on current prices (including consideration of changes in existing prices provided only by contractual arrangements), from estimated production of proved oil and gas reserves."[4]

Question: May entities using the full cost method of accounting for oil and gas producing activities compute amortization based on the gross revenue method described in the above rule when substantial production is not subject to pricing regulation?

Interpretive Response: Yes. Under the existing rules for cost amortization adopted in ASR 258, the use of the gross revenue method of amortization was permitted in those circumstances where, because of the effect of existing pricing regulations, the use of the units of production method would result in an amortization provision that would be inconsistent with the current sales prices being received. While the effect of regulation on gas prices has lessened, factors other than price regulation (such as changes in typical contract lengths and methods of marketing natural gas) have caused oil and gas prices to be disproportionate to their relative energy content. The staff therefore believes that it may be more appropriate for registrants to compute amortization based on the gross revenue method whenever oil and gas sales prices are disproportionate to their relative energy content to the extent that the use of the units of production method would result in an improper matching of the costs of oil and gas production against the related revenue received. The method should be consistently applied and appropriately disclosed within the financial statements.

G. Removed by SAB 113

[¶ 39,221]   **TOPIC 13—REVENUE RECOGNITION**

A. Selected Revenue Recognition Issues

1. *Revenue recognition - general*

The accounting literature on revenue recognition includes both broad conceptual discussions as well as certain industry-specific guidance.[1] If a transaction is within the scope of specific authoritative literature that provides revenue recognition guidance, that literature should be applied. However, in the absence of authoritative literature addressing a specific arrangement or a specific industry, the staff will consider the existing authoritative accounting standards as well as the broad revenue recognition criteria specified in the FASB's conceptual framework that contain basic guidelines for revenue recognition.

Based on these guidelines, revenue should not be recognized until it is realized or realizable and earned.[2] Concepts Statement 5, paragraph 83(b) states that "an entity's revenue-earning activities involve delivering or producing goods, rendering services, or other activities that constitute its ongoing major or central operations, and revenues are consid-ered to have been earned when the entity has substantially accomplished what it must do to be entitled to the benefits represented by the revenues" [footnote reference omitted]. Paragraph 84(a) continues "the two conditions (being realized or realizable and being earned) are usually met by the time product or merchandise is delivered or services are rendered to customers, and revenues from manufacturing and selling activities and gains and losses from sales of other assets are commonly recognized at time of sale (usually meaning delivery)" [footnote reference omitted]. In addition, paragraph 84(d) states that "If services are rendered or rights to use assets extend continuously over time (for example, interest or rent), reliable measures based on contractual prices established in advance are commonly available, and revenues may be recognized as earned as time passes."

The staff believes that revenue generally is realized or realizable and earned when all of the following criteria are met:

- Persuasive evidence of an arrangement exists,[3]

---

[4] Rule 4-10(c)(8) of Regulation S-X defines current price as the average price during the 12-month period prior to the ending date of the period covered by the report, determined as an unweighted arithmetic average of the first-day-of-the-month price for each month within such period, unless prices are defined by contractual arrangements, excluding escalations based upon future conditions.

[1] The February 1999 AICPA publication "Audit Issues in Revenue Recognition" provides an overview of the authoritative accounting literature and auditing procedures for revenue recognition and identifies indicators of improper revenue recognition.

[2] Concepts Statement 5, paragraphs 83-84; ARB 43, Chapter 1A, paragraph 1; Opinion 10, paragraph 12. The citations provided herein are not intended to present the complete population of citations where a particular criterion is relevant. Rather, the citations are intended to provide the reader with additional reference material.

[3] Concepts Statement 2, paragraph 63 states "Representational faithfulness is correspondence or agreement between a measure or description and the phenomenon it purports to represent." The staff believes that evidence of an exchange arrangement must exist to determine if the accounting treatment represents faithfully the transaction. See also SOP 97-2, paragraph 8. The use of the term "arrangement" in this SAB Topic is meant to identify the final understanding between the parties as to the specific nature and terms of the agreed-upon transaction.

- Delivery has occurred or services have been rendered,[4]
- The seller's price to the buyer is fixed or determinable,[5] and
- Collectibility is reasonably assured.[6]

Some revenue arrangements contain multiple revenue-generating activities. The staff believes that the determination of the units of accounting within an arrangement should be made prior to the application of the guidance in this SAB Topic by reference to the applicable accounting literature.[7]

2. *Persuasive evidence of an arrangement*

Question 1

Facts: Company A has product available to ship to customers prior to the end of its current fiscal quarter. Customer Beta places an order for the product, and Company A delivers the product prior to the end of its current fiscal quarter. Company A's normal and customary business practice for this class of customer is to enter into a written sales agreement that requires the signatures of the authorized representatives of the Company and its customer to be binding. Company A prepares a written sales agreement, and its authorized representative signs the agreement before the end of the quarter. However, Customer Beta does not sign the agreement because Customer Beta is awaiting the requisite approval by its legal department. Customer Beta's purchasing department has orally agreed to the sale and stated that it is highly likely that the contract will be approved the first week of Company A's next fiscal quarter.

Question: May Company A recognize the revenue in the current fiscal quarter for the sale of the product to Customer Beta when (1) the product is delivered by the end of its current fiscal quarter and (2) the final written sales agreement is executed by Customer Beta's authorized representative within a few days after the end of the current fiscal quarter?

Interpretive Response: No. Generally the staff believes that, in view of Company A's business practice of requiring a written sales agreement for this class of customer, persuasive evidence of an arrangement would require a final agreement that has been executed by the properly authorized personnel of the customer. In the staff's view, Customer Beta's execution of the sales agreement after the end of the quarter causes the transaction to be considered a transaction of the subsequent period.[8] Further, if an arrangement is subject to subsequent approval (*e.g.*, by the management committee or board of directors)

or execution of another agreement, revenue recognition would be inappropriate until that subsequent approval or agreement is complete.

Customary business practices and processes for documenting sales transactions vary among companies and industries. Business practices and processes may also vary within individual companies (*e.g.*, based on the class of customer, nature of product or service, or other distinguishable factors). If a company does not have a standard or customary business practice of relying on written contracts to document a sales arrangement, it usually would be expected to have other forms of written or electronic evidence to document the transaction. For example, a company may not use written contracts but instead may rely on binding purchase orders from third parties or on-line authorizations that include the terms of the sale and that are binding on the customer. In that situation, that documentation could represent persuasive evidence of an arrangement.

The staff is aware that sometimes a customer and seller enter into "side" agreements to a master contract that effectively amend the master contract. Registrants should ensure that appropriate policies, procedures, and internal controls exist and are properly documented so as to provide reasonable assurances that sales transactions, including those affected by side agreements, are properly accounted for in accordance with GAAP and to ensure compliance with Section 13 of the Securities Exchange Act of 1934 (*i.e.*, the Foreign Corrupt Practices Act). Side agreements could include cancellation, termination, or other provisions that affect revenue recognition. The existence of a subsequently executed side agreement may be an indicator that the original agreement was not final and revenue recognition was not appropriate.

Question 2

Facts: Company Z enters into an arrangement with Customer A to deliver Company Z's products to Customer A on a consignment basis. Pursuant to the terms of the arrangement, Customer A is a consignee, and title to the products does not pass from Company Z to Customer A until Customer A consumes the products in its operations. Company Z delivers product to Customer A under the terms of their arrangement.

Question: May Company Z recognize revenue upon delivery of its product to Customer A?

Interpretive Response: No. Products delivered to a consignee pursuant to a consignment arrangement

---

[4] Concepts Statement 5, paragraph 84(a), (b), and (d). Revenue should not be recognized until the seller has substantially accomplished what it must do pursuant to the terms of the arrangement, which usually occurs upon delivery or performance of the services.

[5] Concepts Statement 5, paragraph 83(a); Statement 48, paragraph 6(a); SOP 97-2, paragraph 8. SOP 97-2 defines a "fixed fee" as a "fee required to be paid at a set amount that is not subject to refund or adjustment. A fixed fee includes amounts designated as minimum royalties." Paragraphs 26-33 of SOP 97-2 discuss how to apply the fixed or determinable fee criterion in software transactions. The staff believes that the guidance in paragraphs 26 and

30-33 is appropriate for other sales transactions where authoritative guidance does not otherwise exist. The staff notes that paragraphs 27 through 29 specifically consider software transactions, however, the staff believes that guidance should be considered in other sales transactions in which the risk of technological obsolescence is high.

[6] ARB 43, Chapter 1A, paragraph 1 and Opinion 10, paragraph 12. See also Concepts Statement 5, paragraph 84(g) and SOP 97-2, paragraph 8.

[7] See EITF Issue 00-21 paragraph 4 for additional discussion.

[8] AU Section 560.05.

are not sales and do not qualify for revenue recognition until a sale occurs. The staff believes that revenue recognition is not appropriate because the seller retains the risks and rewards of ownership of the product and title usually does not pass to the consignee.

Other situations may exist where title to delivered products passes to a buyer, but the substance of the transaction is that of a consignment or a financing. Such arrangements require a careful analysis of the facts and circumstances of the transaction, as well as an understanding of the rights and obligations of the parties, and the seller's customary business practices in such arrangements. The staff believes that the presence of one or more of the following characteristics in a transaction precludes revenue recognition even if title to the product has passed to the buyer:

1. The buyer has the right to return the product and:

    (a) the buyer does not pay the seller at the time of sale, and the buyer is not obligated to pay the seller at a specified date or dates.[9]

    (b) the buyer does not pay the seller at the time of sale but rather is obligated to pay at a specified date or dates, and the buyer's obligation to pay is contractually or implicitly excused until the buyer resells the product or subsequently consumes or uses the product,[10]

    (c) the buyer's obligation to the seller would be changed (*e.g.*, the seller would forgive the obligation or grant a refund) in the event of theft or physical destruction or damage of the product,[11]

    (d) the buyer acquiring the product for resale does not have economic substance apart from that provided by the seller,[12] or

    (e) the seller has significant obligations for future performance to directly bring about resale of the product by the buyer.[13]

2. The seller is required to repurchase the product (or a substantially identical product or processed goods of which the product is a component) at specified prices that are not subject to change except for fluctuations due to finance and holding costs,[14] and the amounts to be paid by the seller will be adjusted, as necessary, to cover substantially all fluctuations in costs incurred by the buyer in purchasing and holding the product (including interest).[15] The staff believes that indicators of the latter condition include:

    (a) the seller provides interest-free or significantly below market financing to the buyer beyond the seller's customary sales terms and until the products are resold,

    (b) the seller pays interest costs on behalf of the buyer under a thirdparty financing arrangement, or

    (c) the seller has a practice of refunding (or intends to refund) a portion of the original sales price representative of interest expense for the period from when the buyer paid the seller until the buyer resells the product.

3. The transaction possesses the characteristics set forth in EITF Issue 95-1 and does not qualify for sales-type lease accounting.

4. The product is delivered for demonstration purposes.[16]

This list is not meant to be a checklist of all characteristics of a consignment or a financing arrangement, and other characteristics may exist. Accordingly, the staff believes that judgment is necessary in assessing whether the substance of a transaction is a consignment, a financing, or other arrangement for which revenue recognition is not appropriate. If title to the goods has passed but the substance of the arrangement is not a sale, the consigned inventory should be reported separately from other inventory in the consignor's financial statements as "inventory consigned to others" or another appropriate caption.

Question 3

Facts: The laws of some countries do not provide for a seller's retention of a security interest in goods in the same manner as established in the U.S. Uniform Commercial Code (UCC). In these countries, it is common for a seller to retain a form of title to goods delivered to customers until the customer makes payment so that the seller can recover the goods in the event of customer default on payment.

Question: Is it acceptable to recognize revenue in these transactions before payment is made and title has transferred?

Interpretive Response: Presuming all other revenue recognition criteria have been met, the staff would not object to revenue recognition at delivery if the only rights that a seller retains with the title are those enabling recovery of the goods in the event of customer default on payment. This limited form of ownership may exist in some foreign jurisdictions where, despite technically holding title, the seller is not entitled to direct the disposition of the goods, cannot rescind the transaction, cannot prohibit its customer from moving, selling, or otherwise using the goods in

---

[9] Statement 48, paragraphs 6(b) and 22.

[10] Statement 48, paragraphs 6(b) and 22. The arrangement may not specify that payment is contingent upon subsequent resale or consumption. However, if the seller has an established business practice permitting customers to defer payment beyond the specified due date(s) until the products are resold or consumed, then the staff believes that the seller's right to receive cash representing the sales price is contingent.

[11] Statement 48, paragraph 6(c).

[12] Statement 48, paragraph 6(d).

[13] Statement 48, paragraph 6(e).

[14] Statement 49, paragraph 5(a). Paragraph 5(a) provides examples of circumstances that meet this requirement. As discussed further therein, this condition is present if (a) a resale price guarantee exists, (b) the seller has an option to purchase the product, the economic effect of which compels the seller to purchase the product, or (c) the buyer has an option whereby it can require the seller to purchase the product.

[15] Statement 49, paragraph 5(b).

[16] See SOP 97-2, paragraph 25.

the ordinary course of business, and has no other rights that rest with a titleholder of property that is subject to a lien under the U.S. UCC. On the other hand, if retaining title results in the seller retaining rights normally held by an owner of goods, the situation is not sufficiently different from a delivery of goods on consignment. In this particular case, revenue should not be recognized until payment is received. Registrants and their auditors may wish to consult legal counsel knowledgeable of the local law and customs outside the U.S. to determine the seller's rights.

3. *Delivery and performance*

a. Bill and hold arrangements

Facts: Company A receives purchase orders for products it manufactures. At the end of its fiscal quarters, customers may not yet be ready to take delivery of the products for various reasons. These reasons may include, but are not limited to, a lack of available space for inventory, having more than sufficient inventory in their distribution channel, or delays in customers' production schedules.

Question: May Company A recognize revenue for the sale of its products once it has completed manufacturing if it segregates the inventory of the products in its own warehouse from its own products?

May Company A recognize revenue for the sale if it ships the products to a third-party warehouse but (1) Company A retains title to the product and (2) payment by the customer is dependent upon ultimate delivery to a customer-specified site?

Interpretative Response: Generally, no. The staff believes that delivery generally is not considered to have occurred unless the customer has taken title and assumed the risks and rewards of ownership of the products specified in the customer's purchase order or sales agreement. Typically this occurs when a product is delivered to the customer's delivery site (if the terms of the sale are "FOB destination") or when a product is shipped to the customer (if the terms are "FOB shipping point").

The Commission has set forth criteria to be met in order to recognize revenue when delivery has not occurred.[17] These include:

1. The risks of ownership must have passed to the buyer;

2. The customer must have made a fixed commitment to purchase the goods, preferably in written documentation;

3. The buyer, not the seller, must request that the transaction be on a bill and hold basis.[18] The buyer must have a substantial business purpose for ordering the goods on a bill and hold basis;

4. There must be a fixed schedule for delivery of the goods. The date for delivery must be reasonable and must be consistent with the buyer's business purpose (*e.g.*, storage periods are customary in the industry);

5. The seller must not have retained any specific performance obligations such that the earning process is not complete;

6. The ordered goods must have been segregated from the seller's inventory and not be subject to being used to fill other orders; and

7. The equipment [product] must be complete and ready for shipment.

The above listed conditions are the important conceptual criteria that should be used in evaluating any purported bill and hold sale. This listing is not intended as a checklist. In some circumstances, a transaction may meet all factors listed above but not meet the requirements for revenue recognition. The Commission also has noted that in applying the above criteria to a purported bill and hold sale, the individuals responsible for the preparation and filing of financial statements also should consider the following factors:[19]

1. The date by which the seller expects payment, and whether the seller has modified its normal billing and credit terms for this buyer;[20]

2. The seller's past experiences with and pattern of bill and hold transactions;

3. Whether the buyer has the expected risk of loss in the event of a decline in the market value of goods;

4. Whether the seller's custodial risks are insurable and insured;

5. Whether extended procedures are necessary in order to assure that there are no exceptions to the buyer's commitment to accept and pay for the goods sold (*i.e.*, that the business reasons for the bill and hold have not introduced a contingency to the buyer's commitment).

Delivery generally is not considered to have occurred unless the product has been delivered to the customer's place of business or another site specified by the customer. If the customer specifies an intermediate site but a substantial portion of the sales price is not payable until delivery is made to a final site, then revenue should not be recognized until final delivery has occurred.[21]

---

[17] See In the Matter of Stewart Parness, AAER 108 (August 5, 1986); SEC v. Bollinger Industries, Inc., et al, LR 15093 (September 30, 1996); In the Matter of Laser Photonics, Inc., AAER 971 (September 30, 1997); In the Matter of Cypress Bioscience Inc., AAER 817 (September 19, 1996). Also see Concepts Statement 5, paragraph 84(a). and SOP 97-2, paragraph 22.

[18] Such requests typically should be set forth in writing by the buyer.

[19] See Note 17, supra.

[20] Such individuals should consider whether Opinion 21 pertaining to the need for discounting the related receivable, is applicable. Opinion 21, paragraph 3(a), indicates that the requirements of that Opinion to record receivables at a discounted value are not intended to apply to "receivables and payables arising from transactions with customers or suppliers in the *normal course of business which are due in customary trade terms* not exceeding approximately one year" (emphasis added).

[21] SOP 97-2, paragraph 22.

b. Customer acceptance

After delivery of a product or performance of a service, if uncertainty exists about customer acceptance, revenue should not be recognized until acceptance occurs.[22] Customer acceptance provisions may be included in a contract, among other reasons, to enforce a customer's rights to (1) test the delivered product, (2) require the seller to perform additional services subsequent to delivery of an initial product or performance of an initial service (*e.g.*, a seller is required to install or activate delivered equipment), or (3) identify other work necessary to be done before accepting the product. The staff presumes that such contractual customer acceptance provisions are substantive, bargained-for terms of an arrangement. Accordingly, when such contractual customer acceptance provisions exist, the staff generally believes that the seller should not recognize revenue until customer acceptance occurs or the acceptance provisions lapse.

Question 1

Question: Do circumstances exist in which formal customer sign-off (that a contractual customer acceptance provision is met) is unnecessary to meet the requirements to recognize revenue?

Interpretive Response:

Yes. Formal customer sign-off is not always necessary to recognize revenue provided that the seller objectively demonstrates that the criteria specified in the acceptance provisions are satisfied. Customer acceptance provisions generally allow the customer to cancel the arrangement when a seller delivers a product that the customer has not yet agreed to purchase or delivers a product that does not meet the specifications of the customer's order. In those cases, revenue should not be recognized because a sale has not occurred. In applying this concept, the staff observes that customer acceptance provisions normally take one of four general forms. Those forms, and how the staff generally assesses whether customer acceptance provisions should result in revenue deferral, are described below:

(a) *Acceptance provisions in arrangements that purport to be for trial or evaluation purposes.*[23] In these arrangements, the seller delivers a product to a customer, and the customer agrees to receive the product, solely to give the customer the ability to evaluate the delivered product prior to acceptance. The customer does not agree to purchase the delivered product until it accepts the product. In some cases, the acceptance provisions lapse by the passage of time without the customer rejecting the delivered product, and in other cases affirmative acceptance from the

customer is necessary to trigger a sales transaction. Frequently, the title to the product does not transfer and payment terms are not established prior to customer acceptance. These arrangements are, in substance, consignment arrangements until the customer accepts the product as set forth in the contract with the seller. Accordingly, in arrangements where products are delivered for trial or evaluation purposes, revenue should not be recognized until the earlier of when acceptance occurs or the acceptance provisions lapse.

In contrast, other arrangements do not purport to be for trial or evaluation purposes. In these instances, the seller delivers a specified product pursuant to a customer's order, establishes payment terms, and transfers title to the delivered product to the customer. However, customer acceptance provisions may be included in the arrangement to give the purchaser the ability to ensure the delivered product meets the criteria set forth in its order. The staff evaluates these provisions as follows:

(b) *Acceptance provisions that grant a right of return or exchange on the basis of subjective matters*. An example of such a provision is one that allows the customer to return a product if the customer is dissatisfied with the product.[24] The staff believes these provisions are not different from general rights of return and should be accounted for in accordance with Statement 48. Statement 48 requires that the amount of future returns must be reasonably estimable in order for revenue to be recognized prior to the expiration of return rights.[25] That estimate may not be made in the absence of a large volume of homogeneous transactions or if customer acceptance is likely to depend on conditions for which sufficient historical experience is absent.[26] Satisfaction of these requirements may vary from product-to-product, location-to-location, customer-to-customer, and vendor-to-vendor.

(c) *Acceptance provisions based on seller-specified objective criteria*. An example of such a provision is one that gives the customer a right of return or replacement if the delivered product is defective or fails to meet the vendor's published specifications for the product.[27] Such rights are generally identical to those granted to all others within the same class of customer and for which satisfaction can be generally assured without consideration of conditions specific to the customer. Provided the seller has previously demonstrated that the product meets the specified criteria, the staff believes that these provisions are not different from general or specific warranties and should be accounted for as warranties in accordance with Statement 5. In this case, the cost of potentially defective goods must be reliably estimable based on a demonstrated history of substantially similar transac-

---

[22] SOP 97-2, paragraph 20. Also, Concepts Statement 5, paragraph 83(b) states "revenues are considered to have been earned when the entity has substantially accomplished what it must do to be entitled to the benefits represented by the revenues." If an arrangement expressly requires customer acceptance, the staff generally believes that customer acceptance should occur before the entity has substantially accomplished what it must do to be

entitled to the benefits represented by the revenues, especially when the seller is obligated to perform additional steps.

[23] See, for example, SOP 97-2, paragraph 25.

[24] Statement 48, paragraph 13.

[25] Statement 48, paragraph 6(f).

[26] Statement 48, paragraphs 8(c) and 8(d).

[27] Statement 5, paragraph 24 and Statement 48, paragraph 4(c).

tions.[28] However, if the seller has not previously demonstrated that the delivered product meets the seller's specifications, the staff believes that revenue should be deferred until the specifications have been objectively achieved.

(d) *Acceptance provisions based on customer-specified objective criteria.* These provisions are referred to in this document as "customer-specific acceptance provisions" against which substantial completion and contract fulfillment must be evaluated. While formal customer sign-off provides the best evidence that these acceptance criteria have been met, revenue recognition also would be appropriate, presuming all other revenue recognition criteria have been met, if the seller reliably demonstrates that the delivered products or services meet all of the specified criteria prior to customer acceptance. For example, if a seller reliably demonstrates that a delivered product meets the customerspecified objective criteria set forth in the arrangement, the delivery criterion would generally be satisfied when title and the risks and rewards of ownership transfers unless product performance may reasonably be different under the customer's testing conditions specified by the acceptance provisions. Further, the seller should consider whether it would be successful in enforcing a claim for payment even in the absence of formal signoff. Whether the vendor has fulfilled the terms of the contract before customer acceptance is a matter of contract law, and depending on the facts and circumstances, an opinion of counsel may be necessary to reach a conclusion.

Question 2

Facts: Consider an arrangement that calls for the transfer of title to equipment upon delivery to a customer's site. However, customer-specific acceptance provisions permit the customer to return the equipment unless the equipment satisfies certain performance tests. The arrangement calls for the vendor to perform the installation. Assume the equipment and the installation are separate units of accounting under EITF Issue 00-21.[29]

Question: Must revenue allocated to the equipment always be deferred until installation and on-site testing are successfully completed?

Interpretive Response: No. The staff would not object to revenue recognition for the equipment upon delivery (presuming all other revenue recognition criteria have been met for the equipment) if the seller demonstrates that, at the time of delivery, the equipment already meets all of the criteria and specifications in the customer-specific acceptance provisions. This may be demonstrated if conditions under which the customer intends to operate the equipment are replicated in pre-shipment testing, unless the performance of the equipment, once installed and operated at the customer's facility, may reasonably be different from that tested prior to shipment.

Determining whether the delivered equipment meets all of a product's criteria and specifications is a matter of judgment that must be evaluated in light of the facts and circumstances of a particular transaction. Consultation with knowledgeable project managers or engineers may be necessary in such circumstances.

For example, if the customer acceptance provisions were based on meeting certain size and weight characteristics, it should be possible to determine whether those criteria have been met before shipment. Historical experience with the same specifications and functionality of a particular machine that demonstrates that the equipment meets the customer's specifications also may provide sufficient evidence that the currently shipped equipment satisfies the customer-specific acceptance provisions.

If an arrangement includes customer acceptance criteria or specifications that cannot be effectively tested before delivery or installation at the customer's site, the staff believes that revenue recognition should be deferred until it can be demonstrated that the criteria are met. This situation usually will exist when equipment performance can vary based on how the equipment works in combination with the customer's other equipment, software, or environmental conditions. In these situations, testing to determine whether the criteria are met cannot be reasonably performed until the products are installed or integrated at the customer's facility.

Although the following questions provide several examples illustrating how the staff evaluates customer acceptance, the determination of when customer-specific acceptance provisions of an arrangement are met in the absence of the customer's formal notification of acceptance depends on the weight of the evidence in the particular circumstances. Different conclusions could be reached in similar circumstances that vary only with respect to a single variable, such as complexity of the equipment, nature of the interface with the customer's environment, extent of the seller's experience with the same type of transactions, or a particular clause in the agreement. The staff believes management and auditors are uniquely positioned to evaluate the facts and arrive at a reasoned conclusion. The staff will not object to a determination that is well reasoned on the basis of this guidance.

Question 3

Facts: Company E is an equipment manufacturer whose main product is generally sold in a standard model. The contracts for sale of that model provide for customer acceptance to occur after the equipment is received and tested by the customer. The acceptance provisions state that if the equipment does not perform to Company E's published specifications, the customer may return the equipment for a full refund or a replacement unit, or may require Company E to repair the equipment so that it performs up to pub-

---

[28] Statement 5, paragraph 25.

[29] This fact is provided as an assumption to facilitate an analysis of revenue recognition in this fact pattern. No interpretation of Issue 00-21 is intended.

lished specifications. Customer acceptance is indicated by either a formal sign-off by the customer or by the passage of 90 days without a claim under the acceptance provisions. Title to the equipment passes upon delivery to the customer. Company E does not perform any installation or other services on the equipment it sells and tests each piece of equipment against its specifications before shipment. Payment is due under Company E's normal payment terms for that product 30 days after customer acceptance.

Company E receives an order from a new customer for a standard model of its main product. Based on the customer's intended use of the product, location and other factors, there is no reason that the equipment would operate differently in the customer's environment than it does in Company E's facility.

Question: Assuming all other revenue recognition criteria are met (other than the issue raised with respect to the acceptance provision), when should Company E recognize revenue from the sale of this piece of equipment?

Interpretive Response : While the staff presumes that customer acceptance provisions are substantive provisions that generally result in revenue deferral, that presumption can be overcome as discussed above. Although the contract includes a customer acceptance clause, acceptance is based on meeting Company E's published specifications for a standard model. Company E demonstrates that the equipment shipped meets the specifications before shipment, and the equipment is expected to operate the same in the customer's environment as it does in Company E's. In this situation, Company E should evaluate the customer acceptance provision as a warranty under Statement 5. If Company E can reasonably and reliably estimate the amount of warranty obligations, the staff believes that it should recognize revenue upon delivery of the equipment, with an appropriate liability for probable warranty obligations.

Question 4

Facts: Assume the same facts about Company E's equipment, contract terms and customary practices as in Question 3 above. Company E enters into an arrangement with a new customer to deliver a version of its standard product modified as necessary to fit into a space of specific dimensions while still meeting all of the published vendor specifications with regard to performance. In addition to the customer acceptance provisions relating to the standard performance specifications, the customer may reject the equipment if it does not conform to the specified dimensions. Company E creates a testing chamber of the exact same dimensions as specified by the customer and makes simple design changes to the product so that it fits into the testing chamber. The equipment still meets all of the standard performance specifications.

Question: Assuming all other revenue recognition criteria are met (other than the issue raised with respect to the acceptance provision), when should

Company E recognize revenue from the sale of this piece of equipment?

Interpretive Response: Although the contract includes a customer acceptance clause that is based, in part, on a customer specific criterion, Company E demonstrates that the equipment shipped meets that objective criterion, as well as the published specifications, before shipment. The staff believes that the customer acceptance provisions related to the standard performance specifications should be evaluated as a warranty under Statement 5. If Company E can reasonably and reliably estimate the amount of warranty obligations, it should recognize revenue upon delivery of the equipment, with an appropriate liability for probable warranty obligations.

Question 5

Facts: Assume the same facts about Company E's equipment, contract terms and customary practices as in Question 3 above. Company E enters into an arrangement with a new customer to deliver a version of its standard product modified as necessary to be integrated into the customer's new assembly line while still meeting all of the standard published vendor specifications with regard to performance. The customer may reject the equipment if it fails to meet the standard published performance specifications or cannot be satisfactorily integrated into the new line. Company E has never modified its equipment to work on an integrated basis in the type of assembly line the customer has proposed. In response to the request, Company E designs a version of its standard equipment that is modified as believed necessary to operate in the new assembly line. The modified equipment still meets all of the standard published performance specifications, and Company E believes the equipment will meet the requested specifications when integrated into the new assembly line. However, Company E is unable to replicate the new assembly line conditions in its testing.

Question: Assuming all other revenue recognition criteria are met (other than the issue raised with respect to the acceptance provision), when should Company E recognize revenue from the sale of this piece of equipment?

Interpretive Response: This contract includes a customer acceptance clause that is based, in part, on a customer specific criterion, and Company E cannot demonstrate that the equipment shipped meets that criterion before shipment. Accordingly, the staff believes that the contractual customer acceptance provision has not been met at shipment. Therefore, the staff believes that Company E should wait until the product is successfully integrated at its customer's location and meets the customer-specific criteria before recognizing revenue. While this is best evidenced by formal customer acceptance, other objective evidence that the equipment has met the customer-specific criteria may also exist (*e.g.*, confirmation from the customer that the specifications were met).

c. Inconsequential or perfunctory performance obligations

Question 1

Question: Does the failure to complete all activities related to a unit of accounting preclude recognition of revenue for that unit of accounting?

Interpretive Response: No. Assuming all other recognition criteria are met, revenue for the unit of accounting may be recognized in its entirety if the seller's remaining obligation is inconsequential or perfunctory.

A seller should substantially complete or fulfill the terms specified in the arrangement related to the unit of accounting at issue in order for delivery or performance to have occurred.[30] When applying the substantially complete notion, the staff believes that only inconsequential or perfunctory actions may remain incomplete such that the failure to complete the actions would not result in the customer receiving a refund or rejecting the delivered products or services performed to date. In addition, the seller should have a demonstrated history of completing the remaining tasks in a timely manner and reliably estimating the remaining costs. If revenue is recognized upon substantial completion of the terms specified in the arrangement related to the unit of accounting at issue, all related costs of performance or delivery should be accrued.

Question 2

Question: What factors should be considered in the evaluation of whether a remaining obligation related to a unit of accounting is inconsequential or perfunctory?

Interpretive Response: A remaining performance obligation is not inconsequential or perfunctory if it is essential to the functionality of the delivered products or services. In addition, remaining activities are not inconsequential or perfunctory if failure to complete the activities would result in the customer receiving a full or partial refund or rejecting (or a right to a refund or to reject) the products delivered or services performed to date. The terms of the sales contract regarding both the right to a full or partial refund and the right of return or rejection should be considered when evaluating whether a portion of the purchase price would be refundable. If the company has a historical pattern of granting such rights, that historical pattern should also be considered even if the current contract expressly precludes such rights. Further, other factors should be considered in assessing whether remaining obligations are inconsequential or perfunctory. For example, the staff also considers the following factors, which are not all-inclusive, to be indicators that a remaining performance obligation is substantive rather than inconsequential or perfunctory:

- The seller does not have a demonstrated history of completing the remaining tasks in a timely manner and reliably estimating their costs.

- The cost or time to perform the remaining obligations for similar contracts historically has varied significantly from one instance to another.

- The skills or equipment required to complete the remaining activity are specialized or are not readily available in the marketplace.

- The cost of completing the obligation, or the fair value of that obligation, is more than insignificant in relation to such items as the contract fee, gross profit, and operating income allocable to the unit of accounting.

- The period before the remaining obligation will be extinguished is lengthy. Registrants should consider whether reasonably possible variations in the period to complete performance affect the certainty that the remaining obligations will be completed successfully and on budget.

- The timing of payment of a portion of the sales price is coincident with completing performance of the remaining activity.

Registrants' determinations of whether remaining obligations are inconsequential or perfunctory should be consistently applied.

Question 3

Facts: Consider a unit of accounting that includes both equipment and installation because the two deliverables do not meet the separation criteria under EITF Issue 00-21. This may be because the equipment does not have value to the customer on a standalone basis, there is no objective and reliable evidence of fair value for the installation or there is a general right of return when the installation is not considered probable and in control of the vendor.

Question: In this situation, must all revenue be deferred until installation is performed?

Interpretive Response: Yes, if installation is essential to the functionality of the equipment.[31] Examples of indicators that installation is essential to the functionality of equipment include:

- The installation involves significant changes to the features or capabilities of the equipment or building complex interfaces or connections;

- The installation services are unavailable from other vendors.[32]

Conversely, examples of indicators that installation is not essential to the functionality of the equipment include:

- The equipment is a standard product;

---

[30] Concepts Statement 5, paragraph 83(b) states "revenues are considered to have been earned when the entity has substantially accomplished what it must do to be entitled to the benefits represented by the revenues."

[31] See SOP 97-2, paragraph 13.

[32] See SOP 97-2, paragraphs 68-71 for analogous guidance.

- Installation does not significantly alter the equipment's capabilities;

- Other companies are available to perform the installation.[33]

If it is determined that the undelivered service is not essential to the functionality of the delivered product but a portion of the contract fee is not payable until the undelivered service is delivered, the staff would not consider that obligation to be inconsequential or perfunctory. Generally, the portion of the contract price that is withheld or refundable should be deferred until the outstanding service is delivered because that portion would not be realized or realizable.[34]

d. License fee revenue

Facts: Assume that intellectual property is physically delivered and payment is received on December 20, upon the registrant's consummation of an agreement granting its customer a license to use the intellectual property for a term beginning on the following January 1.

Question: Should the license fee be recognized in the period ending December 31?

Interpretive Response: No. In licensing and similar arrangements (*e.g.*, licenses of motion pictures, software, technology, and other intangibles), the staff believes that delivery does not occur for revenue recognition purposes until the license term begins.[35] Accordingly, if a licensed product or technology is physically delivered to the customer, but the license term has not yet begun, revenue should not be recognized prior to inception of the license term. Upon inception of the license term, revenue should be recognized in a manner consistent with the nature of the transaction and the earnings process.

e. Layaway sales arrangements

Facts: Company R is a retailer that offers "layaway" sales to its customers. Company R retains the merchandise, sets it aside in its inventory, and collects a cash deposit from the customer. Although Company R may set a time period within which the customer must finalize the purchase, Company R does not require the customer to enter into an installment note or other fixed payment commitment or agreement when the initial deposit is received. The merchandise generally is not released to the customer until the customer pays the full purchase price. In the event that the customer fails to pay the remaining purchase price, the customer forfeits its cash deposit. In the event the merchandise is lost, damaged, or destroyed, Company R either must refund the cash deposit to the customer or provide replacement merchandise.

Question: In the staff's view, when may Company R recognize revenue for merchandise sold under its layaway program?

Interpretive Response: Provided that the other criteria for revenue recognition are met, the staff believes that Company R should recognize revenue from sales made under its layaway program upon delivery of the merchandise to the customer. Until then, the amount of cash received should be recognized as a liability entitled such as "deposits received from customers for layaway sales" or a similarly descriptive caption. Because Company R retains the risks of ownership of the merchandise, receives only a deposit from the customer, and does not have an enforceable right to the remainder of the purchase price, the staff would object to Company R recognizing any revenue upon receipt of the cash deposit. This is consistent with item two (2) in the Commission's criteria for bill-and-hold transactions which states "the customer must have made a fixed commitment to purchase the goods."

f. Nonrefundable up-front fees

Question 1

Facts: Registrants may negotiate arrangements pursuant to which they may receive nonrefundable fees upon entering into arrangements or on certain specified dates. The fees may ostensibly be received for conveyance of a license or other intangible right or for delivery of particular products or services. Various business factors may influence how the registrant and customer structure the payment terms. For example, in exchange for a greater up-front fee for an intangible right, the registrant may be willing to receive lower unit prices for related products to be delivered in the future. In some circumstances, the right, product, or service conveyed in conjunction with the nonrefundable fee has no utility to the purchaser separate and independent of the registrant's performance of the other elements of the arrangement. Therefore, in the absence of the registrant's continuing involvement under the arrangement, the customer would not have paid the fee. Examples of this type of arrangement include the following:

- A registrant sells a lifetime membership in a health club. After paying a nonrefundable "initiation fee," the customer is permitted to use the health club indefinitely, so long as the customer also pays an additional usage fee each month. The monthly usage fees collected from all customers are adequate to cover the operating costs of the health club.

- A registrant in the biotechnology industry agrees to provide research and development activities for a customer for a specified term. The customer needs to use certain technology owned by the registrant for use in the research and development activities. The technology is not sold or licensed separately without the research and development activities. Under the terms of the arrangement, the customer is required to pay a nonrefundable "technology

---

[33] Ibid.

[34] Concepts Statement 5, paragraph 83(a) and Statement 48, paragraph 6(b).

[35] SOP 00-2, paragraph 7.

access fee" in addition to periodic payments for research and development activities over the term of the contract.

- A registrant requires a customer to pay a nonrefundable "activation fee" when entering into an arrangement to provide telecommunications services. The terms of the arrangement require the customer to pay a monthly usage fee that is adequate to recover the registrant's operating costs. The costs incurred to activate the telecommunications service are nominal.

- A registrant charges users a fee for non-exclusive access to its web site that contains proprietary databases. The fee allows access to the web site for a one-year period. After the customer is provided with an identification number and trained in the use of the database, there are no incremental costs that will be incurred in serving this customer.

- A registrant charges a fee to users for advertising a product for sale or auction on certain pages of its web site. The company agrees to maintain the listing for a period of time. The cost of maintaining the advertisement on the web site for the stated period is minimal.

- A registrant charges a fee for hosting another company's web site for one year. The arrangement does not involve exclusive use of any of the hosting company's servers or other equipment. Almost all of the projected costs to be incurred will be incurred in the initial loading of information on the host company's internet server and setting up appropriate links and network connections.

Question: Assuming these arrangements qualify as single units of accounting under EITF Issue 00-21[36], when should the revenue relating to nonrefundable, up-front fees in these types of arrangements be recognized?

Interpretive Response: The staff believes that registrants should consider the specific facts and circumstances to determine the appropriate accounting for nonrefundable, upfront fees. Unless the up-front fee is in exchange for products delivered or services performed that represent the culmination of a separate earnings process,[37] the deferral of revenue is appropriate.

In the situations described above, the staff does not view the activities completed by the registrants (*i.e.*, selling the membership, signing the contract, enroll-

ing the customer, activating telecommunications services or providing initial set-up services) as discrete earnings events.[38] The terms, conditions, and amounts of these fees typically are negotiated in conjunction with the pricing of all the elements of the arrangement, and the customer would ascribe a significantly lower, and perhaps no, value to elements ostensibly associated with the up-front fee in the absence of the registrant's performance of other contract elements. The fact that the registrants do not sell the initial rights, products, or services separately (*i.e.*, without the registrants' continuing involvement) supports the staff's view. The staff believes that the customers are purchasing the ongoing rights, products, or services being provided through the registrants' continuing involvement. Further, the staff believes that the earnings process is completed by performing under the terms of the arrangements, not simply by originating a revenuegenerating arrangement.

While the incurrence of nominal up-front costs helps make it clear that there is not a separate earnings event in the telecommunications example above, incurrence of substantive costs, such as in the web hosting example above, does not necessarily indicate that there is a separate earnings event. Whether there is a separate earnings event should be evaluated on a case-by-case basis. Some have questioned whether revenue may be recognized in these transactions to the extent of the incremental direct costs incurred in the activation. Because there is no separable deliverable or earnings event, the staff would generally object to that approach, except where it is provided for in the authoritative literature (*e.g.*, Statement 51).

Supply or service transactions may involve the charge of a nonrefundable initial fee with subsequent periodic payments for future products or services. The initial fees may, in substance, be wholly or partly an advance payment for future products or services. In the examples above, the on-going rights or services being provided or products being delivered are essential to the customers receiving the expected benefit of the up-front payment. Therefore, the up-front fee and the continuing performance obligation related to the services to be provided or products to be delivered are assessed as an integrated package. In such circumstances, the staff believes that up-front fees, even if nonrefundable, are earned as the products and/or services are delivered and/or performed over the term of the arrangement or the expected period of performance[39] and generally should be deferred and recognized systematically over the periods that the fees are earned.[40]

---

[36] The staff believes that the vendor activities associated with the up-front fee, even if considered a deliverable to be evaluated under EITF Issue 00-21, will rarely provide value to the customer on a standalone basis.

[37] See Concepts Statement 5, footnote 51, for a description of the "earning process."

[38] In a similar situation, lenders may collect nonrefundable loan origination fees in connection with lending activities. The FASB concluded in Statement 91 that loan origination is not a separate revenue-producing activity of a lender, and therefore, those nonrefundable fees collected at the outset of the loan arrangement

are not recognized as revenue upon receipt but are deferred and recognized over the life of the loan (paragraphs 5 and 37).

[39] The revenue recognition period should extend beyond the initial contractual period if the relationship with the customer is expected to extend beyond the initial term and the customer continues to benefit from the payment of the up-front fee (*e.g.*, if subsequent renewals are priced at a bargain to the initial up-front fee).

[40] A systematic method would be on a straight-line basis, unless evidence suggests that revenue is earned or obligations are fulfilled in a different pattern, in which case that pattern should be followed.

Some propose that revenue should be recognized when the initial set-up is completed in cases where the on-going obligation involves minimal or no cost or effort and should, therefore, be considered perfunctory or inconsequential. However, the staff believes that the substance of each of these transactions indicates that the purchaser is paying for a service that is delivered over time. Therefore, revenue recognition should occur over time, reflecting the provision of service.[41]

Question 2

Facts: Company A provides its customers with activity tracking or similar services (*e.g.*, tracking of property tax payment activity, sending delinquency letters on overdue accounts, etc.) for a ten-year period. Company A requires customers to prepay for all the services for the term specified in the arrangement. The on-going services to be provided are generally automated after the initial customer set-up. At the outset of the arrangement, Company A performs set-up procedures to facilitate delivery of its on-going services to the customers. Such procedures consist primarily of establishing the necessary records and files in Company A's pre-existing computer systems in order to provide the services. Once the initial customer set-up activities are complete, Company A provides its services in accordance with the arrangement. Company A is not required to refund any portion of the fee if the customer terminates the services or does not utilize all of the services to which it is entitled. However, Company A is required to provide a refund if Company A terminates the arrangement early. Assume Company A's activities are not within the scope of Statement 91 and that this arrangement qualifies as a single unit of accounting under EITF Issue 00-21.[42]

Question: When should Company A recognize the service revenue?

Interpretive Response: The staff believes that, provided all other revenue recognition criteria are met, service revenue should be recognized on a straight-line basis, unless evidence suggests that the revenue is earned or obligations are fulfilled in a different pattern, over the contractual term of the arrangement or the expected period during which those specified services will be performed,[43] whichever is longer. In this case, the customer contracted for the on-going activity tracking service, not for the set-up activities. The staff notes that the customer could not, and would not, separately purchase the set-up services without the on-going services. The services specified in the arrangement are performed continuously over the contractual term of the arrangement (and any subsequent renewals). Therefore, the staff believes that Company A should recognize revenue on a straight-line basis, unless evidence suggests that the revenue is earned or obligations are fulfilled in a different pattern, over the contractual term of the arrangement or the expected period during which

those specified services will be performed, whichever is longer.

In this situation, the staff would object to Company A recognizing revenue in proportion to the costs incurred because the set-up costs incurred bear no direct relationship to the performance of services specified in the arrangement. The staff also believes that it is inappropriate to recognize the entire amount of the prepayment as revenue at the outset of the arrangement by accruing the remaining costs because the services required by the contract have not been performed.

Question 3

Facts: Assume the same facts as in Question 2 above.

Question: Are the initial customer set-up costs incurred by Company A within the scope of SOP 98-5?

Interpretive Response: Footnote 1 of SOP 98-5 states that "this SOP does not address the financial reporting of costs incurred related to ongoing customer acquisition, such as policy acquisition costs in Statement 60 . . . and loan origination costs in Statement 91 . . . The SOP addresses the more substantive one-time efforts to establish business with an entirely new class of customers (for example, a manufacturer who does all of its business with retailers attempts to sell merchandise directly to the public)." As such, the set-up costs incurred in this example are not within the scope of SOP 98-5.

The staff believes that the incremental direct costs (Statement 91 provides an analogous definition) incurred related to the acquisition or origination of a customer contract in a transaction that results in the deferral of revenue, unless specifically provided for in the authoritative literature, may be either expensed as incurred or accounted for in accordance with paragraph 4 of Technical Bulletin 90-1 or paragraph 5 of Statement 91. The staff believes the accounting policy chosen for these costs should be disclosed and applied consistently.

Question 4

Facts: Assume the same facts as in Question 2 above.

Question: What is the staff's view of the pool of contract acquisition and origination costs that are eligible for capitalization?

Interpretive Response: As noted in Question 3 above, Statement 91 includes a definition of incremental direct costs in its glossary. Paragraph 6 of Statement 91 provides further guidance on the types of costs eligible for capitalization as customer acquisition costs indicating that only costs that result from successful loan origination efforts are capitalized. The FASB staff has published an Implementation Guide on Statement 91 that provides additional guidance on the costs that qualify for capitalization as customer acquisition costs. Further, Technical Bulletin 90-1 also requires

---

[41] Concepts Statement 5, paragraph 84(d).

[42] See Note 36, supra.

[43] See Note 39, supra.

capitalization of incremental direct customer acquisition costs and requires that those costs be "identified consistent with the guidance in paragraph 6 of Statement 91." Although the facts of a particular situation should be analyzed closely to capture those costs that are truly direct and incremental, the staff generally would not object to an accounting policy that results in the capitalization of costs in accordance with paragraph 6(a) and (b) of Statement 91 or Technical Bulletin 90-1. Registrants should disclose their policies for determining which costs to capitalize as contract acquisition and origination costs.

Question 5

Facts: Assume the same facts as in Question 2 above. Based on the guidance in Questions 2, 3 and 4 above, Company A has capitalized certain direct and incremental customer set-up costs associated with the deferred revenue.

Question: Over what period should Company A amortize these costs?

Interpretive Response: When both costs and revenue (in an amount equal to or greater than the costs) are deferred, the staff believes that the capitalized costs should be charged to expense proportionally and over the same period that deferred revenue is recognized as revenue.[44]

g. Deliverables within an arrangement

Question: If a company (the seller) has a patent to its intellectual property which it licenses to customers, the seller may represent and warrant to its licensees that it has a valid patent, and will defend and maintain that patent. Does that obligation to maintain and defend patent rights, in and of itself, constitute a deliverable to be evaluated under EITF Issue 00-21?

Interpretive Response: No. Provided the seller has legal and valid patents upon entering the license arrangement, existing GAAP on licenses of intellectual property (*e.g.*, SOP 97-2, SOP 00-2, and SFAS No. 50) does not indicate that an obligation to defend valid patents represents an additional deliverable to which a portion of an arrangement fee should be allocated in an arrangement that otherwise qualifies for sales-type accounting. While this clause may obligate the licenser to incur costs in the defense and maintenance of the patent, that obligation does not involve an additional deliverable to the customer. Defending the patent is generally consistent with the seller's representation in the license that such patent is legal and valid. Therefore, the staff would not consider a clause like this to represent an additional deliverable in the arrangement.[45]

4. *Fixed or determinable sales price*

a. Refundable fees for services

A company's contracts may include customer cancellation or termination clauses. Cancellation or termination provisions may be indicative of a demonstration period or an otherwise incomplete transaction. Examples of transactions that financial management and auditors should be aware of and where such provisions may exist include "side" agreements and significant transactions with unusual terms and conditions. These contractual provisions raise questions as to whether the sales price is fixed or determinable. The sales price in arrangements that are cancelable by the customer is neither fixed nor determinable until the cancellation privileges lapse.[46] If the cancellation privileges expire ratably over a stated contractual term, the sales price is considered to become determinable ratably over the stated term.[47] Short-term rights of return, such as thirty-day money-back guarantees, and other customary rights to return products are not considered to be cancellation privileges, but should be accounted for in accordance with Statement 48.[48]

Question 1

Facts: Company M is a discount retailer. It generates revenue from annual membership fees it charges customers to shop at its stores and from the sale of products at a discount price to those customers. The membership arrangements with retail customers require the customer to pay the entire membership fee (*e.g.*, $35) at the outset of the arrangement. However, the customer has the unilateral right to cancel the arrangement at any time during its term and receive a full refund of the initial fee. Based on historical data collected over time for a large number of homogeneous transactions, Company M estimates that approximately 40% of the customers will request a refund before the end of the membership contract term. Company M's data for the past five years indicates that significant variations between actual and estimated cancellations have not occurred, and Company M does not expect significant variations to occur in the foreseeable future.

Question: May Company M recognize in earnings the revenue for the membership fees and accrue the costs to provide membership services at the outset of the arrangement?

Interpretive Response: No. In the staff's view, it would be inappropriate for Company M to recognize the membership fees as earned revenue upon billing or receipt of the initial fee with a corresponding accrual for estimated costs to provide the membership services. This conclusion is based on Company M's remaining and unfulfilled contractual obligation to perform services (*i.e.*, make available and offer products for sale at a discounted price) throughout the membership period. Therefore, the earnings process,

---

[44] Technical Bulletin 90-1, paragraph 4.

[45] Note, however, the staff believes that this obligation qualifies as a guarantee within the scope of FIN 45, subject to a scope exception from the initial recognition and measurement provisions.

[46] SOP 97-2, paragraph 31.

[47] Ibid.

[48] Ibid.

irrespective of whether a cancellation clause exists, is not complete.

In addition, the ability of the member to receive a full refund of the membership fee up to the last day of the membership term raises an uncertainty as to whether the fee is fixed or determinable at any point before the end of the term. Generally, the staff believes that a sales price is not fixed or determinable when a customer has the unilateral right to terminate or cancel the contract and receive a cash refund. A sales price or fee is variable until the occurrence of future events (other than product returns that are within the scope of Statement 48) generally is not fixed or determinable until the future event occurs. The revenue from such transactions should not be recognized in earnings until the sales price or fee becomes fixed or determinable. Moreover, revenue should not be recognized in earnings by assessing the probability that significant, but unfulfilled, terms of a contract will be fulfilled at some point in the future. Accordingly, the revenue from such transactions should not be recognized in earnings prior to the refund privileges expiring. The amounts received from customers or subscribers (*i.e.*, the $35 fee mentioned above) should be credited to a monetary liability account such as "customers' refundable fees."

The staff believes that if a customer has the unilateral right to receive both (1) the seller's substantial performance under an arrangement (*e.g.*, providing services or delivering product) and (2) a cash refund of prepaid fees, then the prepaid fees should be accounted for as a monetary liability. In consideration of whether the monetary liability can be derecognized, Statement 140 provides that liabilities may be derecognized only if (1) the debtor pays the creditor and is relieved of its obligation for the liability (paying the creditor includes delivery of cash, other financial assets, goods, or services or reacquisition by the debtor of its outstanding debt securities) or (2) the debtor is legally released from being the primary obligor under the liability.[49] If a customer has the unilateral right to receive both (1) the seller's substantial performance under the arrangement and (2) a cash refund of prepaid fees, then the refund obligation is not relieved upon performance of the service or delivery of the products. Rather, the seller's refund obligation is relieved only upon refunding the cash or expiration of the refund privilege.

Some have argued that there may be a limited exception to the general rule that revenue from membership or other service transaction fees should not be recognized in earnings prior to the refund privileges expiring. Despite the fact that Statement 48 expressly does not apply to the accounting for service revenue if part or all of the service fee is refundable under cancellation privileges granted to the buyer,[50]

they believe that in certain circumstances a potential refund of a membership fee may be seen as being similar to a right of return of products under Statement 48. They argue that revenue from membership fees, net of estimated refunds, may be recognized ratably over the period the services are performed whenever pertinent conditions of Statement 48 are met, namely, there is a large population of transactions that grant customers the same unilateral termination or cancellation rights and reasonable estimates can be made of how many customers likely will exercise those rights.

The staff believes that, because service arrangements are specifically excluded from the scope of Statement 48, the most direct authoritative literature to be applied to the extinguishment of obligations under such contracts is Statement 140. As noted above, because the refund privilege extends to the end of the contract term irrespective of the amount of the service performed, Statement 140 indicates that the liability would not be extinguished (and therefore no revenue would be recognized in earnings) until the cancellation or termination and related refund privileges expire. Nonetheless, the staff recognizes that over the years the accounting for membership refunds evolved based on analogy to Statement 48 and that practice did not change when Statement 140 became effective. Reasonable people held, and continue to hold, different views about the application of the accounting literature.

Pending further action in this area by the FASB, the staff will not object to the recognition of refundable membership fees, net of estimated refunds, as earned revenue over the membership term in the limited circumstances where all of the following criteria have been met:[51]

- The estimates of terminations or cancellations and refunded revenues are being made for a large pool of homogeneous items (*e.g.*, membership or other service transactions with the same characteristics such as terms, periods, class of customers, nature of service, etc.).

- Reliable estimates of the expected refunds can be made on a timely basis.[52] Either of the following two items would be considered indicative of an inability to make reliable estimates: (1) recurring, significant differences between actual experience and estimated cancellation or termination rates (*e.g.*, an actual cancellation rate of 40% versus an estimated rate of 25%) even if the impact of the difference on the amount of estimated refunds is not material to the consolidated financial statements[53] or (2) recurring variances between the actual and estimated amount of refunds that are material

---

[49] Statement 140, paragraph 16.

[50] Statement 48, paragraph 4.

[51] The staff will question further analogies to the guidance in Statement 48 for transactions expressly excluded from its scope.

[52] Reliability is defined in Concepts Statement 2 as "the quality of information that assures that information is reasonably free from error and bias and faithfully represents what it purports to rep-

resent." Paragraph 63 of Concepts Statement 5 reiterates the definition of reliability, requiring that "the information is representationally faithful, verifiable, and neutral."

[53] For example, if an estimate of the expected cancellation rate varies from the actual cancellation rate by 100% but the dollar amount of the error is immaterial to the consolidated financial statements, some would argue that the estimate could still be viewed as reliable. The staff disagrees with that argument.

to either revenue or net income in quarterly or annual financial statements. In addition, the staff believes that an estimate, for purposes of meeting this criterion, would not be reliable unless it is remote[54] that material adjustments (both individually and in the aggregate) to previously recognized revenue would be required. The staff presumes that reliable estimates cannot be made if the customer's termination or cancellation and refund privileges exceed one year.

- There is a sufficient company-specific historical basis upon which to estimate the refunds,[55] and the company believes that such historical experience is predictive of future events. In assessing these items, the staff believes that estimates of future refunds should take into consideration, among other things, such factors as historical experience by service type and class of customer, changing trends in historical experience and the basis thereof (*e.g.*, economic conditions), the impact or introduction of competing services or products, and changes in the customer's "accessibility" to the refund (*i.e.*, how easy it is for customers to obtain the refund).

- The amount of the membership fee specified in the agreement at the outset of the arrangement is fixed, other than the customer's right to request a refund.

If Company M does not meet all of the foregoing criteria, the staff believes that Company M should not recognize in earnings any revenue for the membership fee until the cancellation privileges and refund rights expire.

If revenue is recognized in earnings over the membership period pursuant to the above criteria, the initial amounts received from customer or subscribers (*i.e.*, the $35 fee mentioned above) should be allocated to two liability accounts. The amount of the fee representing estimated refunds should be credited to a monetary liability account, such as "customers' refundable fees," and the remaining amount of the fee representing unearned revenue should be credited to a nonmonetary liability account, such as "unearned revenues." For each income statement presented, registrants should disclose in the footnotes to the financial statements the amounts of (1) the unearned revenue and (2) refund obligations as of the beginning of each period, the amount of cash received from customers, the amount of revenue recognized in earnings, the amount of refunds paid, other adjustments (with an explanation thereof), and the ending balance of (1) unearned revenue and (2) refund obligations.

If revenue is recognized in earnings over the membership period pursuant to the above criteria, the staff believes that adjustments for changes in estimated refunds should be recorded using a retrospective approach whereby the unearned revenue and refund obligations are remeasured and adjusted at each balance sheet date with the offset being recorded as earned revenue.[56]

Companies offering memberships often distribute membership packets describing and discussing the terms, conditions, and benefits of membership. Packets may include vouchers, for example, that provide new members with discounts or other benefits from third parties. The costs associated with the vouchers should be expensed when distributed. Advertising costs to solicit members should be accounted for in accordance with SOP 93-7. Incremental direct costs incurred in connection with enrolling customers (*e.g.*, commissions paid to agents) should be accounted for as follows: (1) if revenue is deferred until the cancellation or termination privileges expire, incremental direct costs should be either (a) charged to expense when incurred if the costs are not refundable to the company in the event the customer obtains a refund of the membership fee, or (b) if the costs are refundable to the company in the event the customer obtains a refund of the membership fee, recorded as an asset until the earlier of termination or cancellation or refund; or (2) if revenue, net of estimated refunds, is recognized in earnings over the membership period, a like percentage of incremental direct costs should be deferred and recognized in earnings in the same pattern as revenue is recognized, and the remaining portion should be either (a) charged to expense when incurred if the costs are not refundable to the company in the event the customer obtains a refund of the membership fee, or (b) if the costs are refundable to the company in the event the customer obtains a refund of the membership fee, recorded as an asset until the refund occurs.[57] All costs other than incremental direct costs (*e.g.*, indirect costs) should be expensed as incurred.

Question 2

Question: Will the staff accept an analogy to Statement 48 for service transactions subject to customer

---

[54] The term "remote" is used here with the same definition as used in Statement 5.

[55] Paragraph 8 of Statement 48 notes various factors that may impair the ability to make a reasonable estimate of returns, including the lack of sufficient historical experience. The staff typically expects that the historical experience be based on the particular registrant's historical experience for a service and/or class of customer. In general, the staff typically expects a start-up company, a company introducing new services, or a company introducing services to a new class of customer to have at least two years of experience to be able to make reasonable and reliable estimates.

[56] The staff believes deferred costs being amortized on a basis consistent with the deferred revenue should be similarly adjusted.

Such an approach is generally consistent with the amortization methodology in Statement 91, paragraph 19.

[57] Statement 91, paragraph 5 and Technical Bulletin 90-1, paragraph 4 both provide for the deferral of incremental direct costs associated with acquiring a revenue-producing contract. Even though the revenue discussed in this example is refundable, if a registrant meets the aforementioned criteria for revenue recognition over the membership period, the staff would analogize to this guidance. However, if neither a nonrefundable contract nor a reliable basis for estimating net cash inflows under refundable contracts exists to provide a basis for recovery of incremental direct costs, the staff believes that such costs should be expensed as incurred. See SAB Topic 13.A.3.f. Question 3.

cancellation privileges other than those specifically addressed in the previous question?

Interpretive Response: The staff has accepted the analogy in limited circumstances due to the existence of a large pool of homogeneous transactions and satisfaction of the criteria in the previous question. Examples of other arrangements involving customer cancellation privileges and refundable service fees that the staff has addressed include the following:

- a leasing broker whose commission from the lessor upon a commercial tenant's signing of a lease agreement is refundable (or in some cases, is not due) under lessor cancellation privileges if the tenant fails to move into the leased premises by a specified date.

- a talent agent whose fee receivable from its principal (*i.e.*, a celebrity) for arranging a celebrity endorsement for a five-year term is cancelable by the celebrity if the celebrity breaches the endorsement contract with its customer.

- an insurance agent whose commission received from the insurer upon selling an insurance policy is refundable in whole for the 30-day period that state law permits the consumer to repudiate the contract and then refundable on a declining pro rata basis until the consumer has made six monthly payments.

In the first two of these cases, the staff advised the registrants that the portion of revenue subject to customer cancellation and refund must be deferred until no longer subject to that contingency because the registrants did not have an ability to make reliable estimates of customer cancellations due to the lack of a large pool of homogeneous transactions. In the case of the insurance agent, however, the particular registrant demonstrated that it had a sufficient history of homogeneous transactions with the same characteristics from which to reliably estimate contract cancellations and satisfy all the criteria specified in the previous question. Accordingly, the staff did not object to that registrant's policy of recognizing its sales commission as revenue when its performance was complete, with an appropriate allowance for estimated cancellations.

Question 3

Question: Must a registrant analogize to Statement 48, or may it choose to defer all revenue until the refund period lapses as suggested by Statement 140 even if the criteria above for analogy to Statement 48 are met?

Interpretive Response: The analogy to Statement 48 is presented as an alternative that would be acceptable to the staff when the listed conditions are met. However, a registrant may choose to defer all revenue until the refund period lapses. The policy chosen should be disclosed and applied consistently.

Question 4

Question: May a registrant that meets the above criteria for reliable estimates of cancellations choose at some point in the future to change from the Statement 48 method to the Statement 140 method of accounting for these refundable fees? May a registrant change from the Statement 140 method to the Statement 48 method?

Interpretive Response: The staff believes that Statement 140 provides a preferable accounting model for service transactions subject to potential refunds. Therefore, the staff would not object to a change from the Statement 48 method to the Statement 140 method. However, if a registrant had previously chosen the Statement 140 method, the staff would object to a change to the Statement 48 method.

Question 5

Question: Is there a minimum level of customers that must be projected not to cancel before use of Statement 48 type accounting is appropriate?

Interpretive Response: Statement 48 does not include any such minimum. Therefore, the staff does not believe that a minimum must apply in service transactions either. However, as the refund rate increases, it may be increasingly difficult to make reasonable and reliable estimates of cancellation rates.

Question 6

Question: When a registrant first determines that reliable estimates of cancellations of service contracts can be made (*e.g.*, two years of historical evidence becomes available), how should the change from the complete deferral method to the method of recognizing revenue, net of estimated cancellations, over time be reflected?

Interpretive Response: Changes in the ability to meet the criteria set forth above should be accounted for in the manner described in paragraph 6 of Statement 48, which addresses the accounting when a company experiences a change in the ability to make reasonable estimates of future product returns.

b. Estimates and changes in estimates

Accounting for revenues and costs of revenues requires estimates in many cases; those estimates sometimes change. Registrants should ensure that they have appropriate internal controls and adequate books and records that will result in timely identification of necessary changes in estimates that should be reflected in the financial statements and notes thereto.

Question 1

Facts: Paragraph 8 of Statement 48 lists a number of factors that may impair the ability to make a reasonable estimate of product returns in sales transactions when a right of return exists.[58] The paragraph

---

[58] These factors include "a) the susceptibility of the product to significant external factors, such as technological obsolescence or changes in demand, b) relatively long periods in which a particular product may be returned, c) absence of historical experience with similar types of sales of similar products, or inability to apply such experience because of changing circumstances, for example,

concludes by stating "other factors may preclude a reasonable estimate."

Question: What "other factors," in addition to those listed in paragraph 8 of Statement 48, has the staff identified that may preclude a registrant from making a reasonable and reliable estimate of product returns?

Interpretive Response: The staff believes that the following additional factors, among others, may affect or preclude the ability to make reasonable and reliable estimates of product returns: (1) significant increases in or excess levels of inventory in a distribution channel (sometimes referred to as "channel stuffing"), (2) lack of "visibility" into or the inability to determine or observe the levels of inventory in a distribution channel and the current level of sales to end users, (3) expected introductions of new products that may result in the technological obsolescence of and larger than expected returns of current products, (4) the significance of a particular distributor to the registrant's (or a reporting segment's) business, sales and marketing, (5) the newness of a product, (6) the introduction of competitors' products with superior technology or greater expected market acceptance, and (7) other factors that affect market demand and changing trends in that demand for the registrant's products. Registrants and their auditors should carefully analyze all factors, including trends in historical data, which may affect registrants' ability to make reasonable and reliable estimates of product returns.

The staff reminds registrants that if a transaction fails to meet all of the conditions of paragraphs 6 and 8 in Statement 48, no revenue may be recognized until those conditions are subsequently met or the return privilege has substantially expired, whichever occurs first.[59] Simply deferring recognition of the gross margin on the transaction is not appropriate.

Question 2

Question: Is the requirement cited in the previous question for "reliable" estimates meant to imply a new, higher requirement than the "reasonable" estimates discussed in Statement 48?

Interpretive Response: No. "Reliability" of financial information is one of the qualities of accounting information discussed in Concepts Statement 2. The staff's expectation that estimates be reliable does not change the existing requirement of Statement 48. If management cannot develop an estimate that is sufficiently reliable for use by investors, the staff believes it cannot make a reasonable estimate meeting the requirements of that standard.

Question 3

Question: Does the staff expect registrants to apply the guidance in Question 1 of Topic 13.A.4(a) above to sales of tangible goods and other transactions specifically within the scope of Statement 48?

Interpretive Response: The specific guidance above does not apply to transactions within the scope of Statement 48. The views set forth in Question 1 of Topic 13.A.4(a) are applicable to the service transactions discussed in that Question. Service transactions are explicitly outside the scope of Statement 48.

Question 4

Question: Question 1 of Topic 13.A.4(a) above states that the staff would expect a two-year history of selling a new service in order to be able to make reliable estimates of cancellations. How long a history does the staff believe is necessary to estimate returns in a product sale transaction that is within the scope of Statement 48?

Interpretive Response: The staff does not believe there is any specific length of time necessary in a product transaction. However, Statement 48 states that returns must be subject to reasonable estimation. Preparers and auditors should be skeptical of estimates of product returns when little history with a particular product line exists, when there is inadequate verifiable evidence of historical experience, or when there are inadequate internal controls that ensure the reliability and timeliness of the reporting of the appropriate historical information. Start-up companies and companies selling new or significantly modified products are frequently unable to develop the requisite historical data on which to base estimates of returns.

Question 5

Question: If a company selling products subject to a right of return concludes that it cannot reasonably estimate the actual return rate due to its limited history, but it can conservatively estimate the maximum possible returns, does the staff believe that the company may recognize revenue for the portion of the sales that exceeds the maximum estimated return rate?

Interpretive Response: No. If a reasonable estimate of future returns cannot be made, Statement 48 requires that revenue not be recognized until the return period lapses or a reasonable estimate can be made.[60] Deferring revenue recognition based on the upper end of a wide range of potential return rates is inconsistent with the provisions of Statement 48.

c. Contingent rental income

Facts: Company A owns and leases retail space to retailers. Company A (lessor) renews a lease with a customer (lessee) that is classified as an operating lease. The lease term is one year and provides that the lease payments are $1.2 million, payable in equal monthly installments on the first day of each month, plus one percent of the lessee's net sales in excess of $25 million if the net sales exceed $25 million during the lease term (*i.e.*, contingent rental). The lessee has historically experienced annual net sales in excess of

---

(Footnote Continued)

changes in the selling enterprise's marketing policies and relationships with its customers, and d) absence of a large volume of relatively homogeneous transactions."

[59] Statement 48, paragraph 6.
[60] Statement 48, paragraph 6(f).

$25 million in the particular space being leased, and it is probable that the lessee will generate in excess of $25 million net sales during the term of the lease.

Question: In the staff's view, should the lessor recognize any rental income attributable to the one percent of the lessee's net sales exceeding $25 million before the lessee actually achieves the $25 million net sales threshold?

Interpretive Response: No. The staff believes that contingent rental income "accrues" (*i.e.*, it should be recognized as revenue) when the changes in the factor(s) on which the contingent lease payments is (are) based actually occur.[61]

Statement 13 paragraph 19(b) states that lessors should account for operating leases as follows: "Rent shall be reported in income over the lease term as it becomes receivable according to the provisions of the lease. However, if the rentals vary from a straight-line basis, the income shall be recognized on a straight-line basis unless another systematic and rational basis is more representative of the time pattern in which use benefit from the leased property is diminished, in which case that basis shall be used."

Statement 29 amended Statement 13 and clarifies that "lease payments that depend on a factor that does not exist or is not measurable at the inception of the lease, such as future sales volume, would be contingent rentals in their entirety and, accordingly, would be excluded from minimum lease payments and included in the determination of income as they accrue." [Summary] Paragraph 17 of Statement 29 provides the following example of determining contingent rentals:

A lease agreement for retail store space could stipulate a monthly base rental of $200 and a monthly supplemental rental of one-fourth of one percent of monthly sales volume during the lease term. Even if the lease agreement is a renewal for store space that had averaged monthly sales of $25,000 for the past 2 years, minimum lease payments would include only the $200 monthly base rental; the supplemental rental is a contingent rental that is excluded from minimum lease payments. The future sales for the lease term do not exist at the inception of the lease, and future rentals would be limited to $200 per month if the store were subsequently closed and no sales were made thereafter.

Technical Bulletin 85-3 addresses whether it is appropriate for lessors in operating leases to recognize scheduled rent increases on a basis other than as required in Statement 13, paragraph 19(b). Paragraph 2 of Technical Bulletin 85-3 states "using factors such as the time value of money, anticipated inflation, or *expected future revenues* [emphasis added] to allocate scheduled rent increases is inappropriate because these factors do not relate to the *time pattern* of the physical usage of the leased property. However, such factors may affect the periodic reported rental income

or expense if the lease agreement involves contingent rentals, which are excluded from minimum lease payments and accounted for separately under Statement 13, as amended by Statement 29." In developing the basis for why scheduled rent increases should be recognized on a straight-line basis, the FASB distinguishes the accounting for scheduled rent increases from contingent rentals. Paragraph 13 states "There is an important substantive difference between lease rentals that are contingent upon some specified future event and scheduled rent increases that are unaffected by future events; the accounting under Statement 13 reflects that difference. If the lessor and lessee eliminate the risk of variable payments by agreeing to scheduled rent increases, the accounting should reflect those different circumstances."

The example provided in Statement 29 implies that contingent rental income in leases classified as sales-type or direct-financing leases becomes "accruable" when the changes in the factors on which the contingent lease payments are based actually occur. Technical Bulletin 85-3 indicates that contingent rental income in operating leases should not be recognized in a manner consistent with scheduled rent increases (*i.e.*, on a straight-line basis over the lease term or another systematic and rational allocation basis if it is more representative of the time pattern in which the leased property is physically employed) because the risk of variable payments inherent in contingent rentals is substantively different than scheduled rent increases. The staff believes that the reasoning in Technical Bulletin 85-3 supports the conclusion that the risks inherent in variable payments associated with contingent rentals should be reflected in financial statements on a basis different than rental payments that adjust on a scheduled basis and, therefore, operating lease income associated with contingent rents would not be recognized as time passes or as the leased property is physically employed. Furthermore, prior to the lessee's achievement of the target upon which contingent rentals are based, the lessor has no legal claims on the contingent amounts. Consequently, the staff believes that it is inappropriate to anticipate changes in the factors on which contingent rental income in operating leases is based and recognize rental income prior to the resolution of the lease contingencies.

Because Company A's contingent rental income is based upon whether the customer achieves net sales of $25 million, the contingent rentals, which may not materialize, should not be recognized until the customer's net sales actually exceed $25 million. Once the $25 million threshold is met, Company A would recognize the contingent rental income as it becomes accruable, in this case, as the customer recognizes net sales. The staff does not believe that it is appropriate to recognize revenue based upon the probability of a factor being achieved. The contingent revenue should be recorded in the period in which the contingency is resolved.

---

[61] Lessees should follow the guidance established in EITF Issue 98-9.

d. Claims processing and billing services

Facts: Company M performs claims processing and medical billing services for healthcare providers. In this role, Company M is responsible for preparing and submitting claims to third-party payers, tracking outstanding billings, and collecting amounts billed. Company M's fee is a fixed percentage (*e.g.*, five percent) of the amount collected. If no collections are made, no fee is due to Company M. Company M has historical evidence indicating that the third-party payers pay 85 percent of the billings submitted with no further effort by Company M. Company M has determined that the services performed under the arrangement are a single unit of accounting.

Question: May Company M recognize as revenue its five percent fee on 85 percent of the gross billings at the time it prepares and submits billings, or should it wait until collections occur to recognize any revenue?

Interpretive Response: The staff believes that Company M must wait until collections occur before recognizing revenue. Before the third-party payer has remitted payment to Company M's customers for the services billed, Company M is not entitled to any revenue. That is, its revenue is not yet realized or realizable.[62] Until Company M's customers collect on the billings, Company M has not performed the requisite activity under its contract to be entitled to a fee.[63] Further, no amount of the fee is fixed or determinable or collectible until Company Ms' customers collect on the billings.

B. Disclosures

Question 1

Question: What disclosures are required with respect to the recognition of revenue?

Interpretive Response: A registrant should disclose its accounting policy for the recognition of revenue pursuant to Opinion 22. Paragraph 12 thereof states that "the disclosure should encompass important judgments as to appropriateness of principles relating to recognition of revenue . . . ." Because revenue recognition generally involves some level of judgment, the staff believes that a registrant should always disclose its revenue recognition policy. If a company has different policies for different types of revenue transactions, including barter sales, the policy for each material type of transaction should be disclosed. If sales transactions have multiple units of accounting, such as a product and service, the accounting policy should clearly state the accounting policy for each unit of accounting as well as how units of accounting are determined and valued. In addition, the staff believes that changes in estimated returns recognized in accordance with Statement 48 should be disclosed, if material (*e.g.*, a change in estimate from two percent of sales to one percent of sales).

Regulation S-X requires that revenue from the sales of products, services, and other products each be separately disclosed on the face of the income statement.[64] The staff believes that costs relating to each type of revenue similarly should be reported separately on the face of the income statement.

MD&A requires a discussion of liquidity, capital resources, results of operations and other information necessary to an understanding of a registrant's financial condition, changes in financial condition and results of operations.[65] This includes unusual or infrequent transactions, known trends or uncertainties that have had, or might reasonably be expected to have, a favorable or unfavorable material effect on revenue, operating income or net income and the relationship between revenue and the costs of revenue. Changes in revenue should not be evaluated solely in terms of volume and price changes, but should also include an analysis of the reasons and factors contributing to the increase or decrease. The Commission stated in FRR 36 that MD&A should "give investors an opportunity to look at the registrant through the eyes of management by providing a historical and prospective analysis of the registrant's financial condition and results of operations, with a particular emphasis on the registrant's prospects for the future."[66]

Examples of such revenue transactions or events that the staff has asked to be disclosed and discussed in accordance with FRR 36 are:

- Shipments of product at the end of a reporting period that significantly reduce customer backlog and that reasonably might be expected to result in lower shipments and revenue in the next period.

- Granting of extended payment terms that will result in a longer collection period for accounts receivable (regardless of whether revenue has been recognized) and slower cash inflows from operations, and the effect on liquidity and capital resources. (The fair value of trade receivables should be disclosed in the footnotes to the financial statements when the fair value does not approximate the carrying amount.)[67]

- Changing trends in shipments into, and sales from, a sales channel or separate class of customer that could be expected to have a significant effect on future sales or sales returns.

- An increasing trend toward sales to a different class of customer, such as a reseller distribution channel that has a lower gross profit margin than existing sales that are principally made to end users. Also, increasing service revenue that has a higher profit margin than product sales.

- Seasonal trends or variations in sales.

---

[62] Concepts Statement 5, paragraph 83(a).

[63] Concepts Statement 5, paragraph 83(b).

[64] See Regulation S-X, Article 5-03(b)(1) and (2).

[65] See Regulation S-K, Article 303 and FRR 36.

[66] FRR 36, also see In the Matter of Caterpillar Inc., AAER 363 (March 31, 1992).

[67] Statement 107.

- A gain or loss from the sale of an asset(s).[68]

Question 2

Question: Will the staff expect retroactive changes by registrants to comply with the accounting described in this bulletin?

Interpretive Response: All registrants are expected to apply the accounting and disclosures described in this bulletin. The staff, however, will not object if registrants that have not applied this accounting do not restate prior financial statements provided they report a change in accounting principle in accordance with Opinion 20 and Statement 3 no later than the fourth fiscal quarter of the fiscal year beginning after December 15, 1999. In periods subsequent to transition, registrants should disclose the amount of revenue (if material to income before income taxes) recognized in those periods that was included in the cumulative effect adjustment. If a registrant files financial statements with the Commission before applying the guidance in this bulletin, disclosures similar to those described in SAB Topic 11.M should be provided.

However, if registrants have not previously complied with GAAP, for example, by recording revenue for products prior to delivery that did not comply with the applicable bill-and-hold guidance, those registrants should apply the guidance in Opinion 20 for the correction of an error.[69] In addition, registrants should be aware that the Commission may take enforcement action where a registrant in prior financial statements has violated the antifraud or disclosure provisions of the securities laws with respect to revenue recognition.

Question 3

Question: The previous question indicates that the staff will not object to cumulative effect-type transition so long as the prior accounting does not represent an error. Could a company whose prior accounting does not represent an error voluntarily adopt a new

method consistent with this SAB Topic by restatement of prior periods, rather than through a cumulative catch-up adjustment?

Interpretive Response: In most instances, no. Opinion 20 does not permit restatement of financial statements for a change in accounting principle that does not represent correction of an error, except in very rare circumstances.[70] An exception is a company that is filing publicly for the first time. As stated in paragraph 29 of Opinion 20, those companies are permitted to reflect the adoption of the new policy via a restatement, and the staff believes that approach is usually necessary to avoid confusing investors in an initial public offering.

Question 4

Question: Should a registrant reporting a change in accounting principle as a result of this SAB Topic file a preferability letter?

Interpretive Response: No preferability letter is required if an accounting change is made in response to a newly issued Staff Accounting Bulletin.

Question 5

Question: If a company had not previously adjusted sales revenues, but deferred recognition of the gross margin of estimated returns for a transaction subject to Statement 48, how should it present a current change in accounting to reduce revenue and cost of sales for estimated returns?

Interpretive Response: Paragraph 7 of Statement 48 states that "sales revenue and cost of sales reported in the income statement *shall be reduced* to reflect estimated returns." Statement 48 does not provide for recognition of sales and costs of sales while deferring gross margin under any circumstance. This SAB Topic provides no new guidance on this point. If a registrant has failed to comply with GAAP, the registrant should retroactively revise prior financial statements in the manner set forth in Opinion 20 and Statement 16.

[¶ 39,231]   TOPIC 14—SHARE-BASED PAYMENT

The interpretations in this SAB express views of the staff regarding the interaction between Statement 123R and certain SEC rules and regulations and provide the staff's views regarding the valuation of share-based payment arrangements for public companies. Statement 123R was issued by the Financial Accounting Standards Board ("FASB") on December 16, 2004. Statement 123R is based on the underlying accounting principle that compensation cost resulting from share-based payment transactions be recog-

nized in financial statements at fair value.[1] Recognition of compensation cost at fair value will provide investors and other users of financial statements with more complete and comparable financial information.[2]

Statement 123R addresses a wide range of share-based compensation arrangements including share options, restricted share plans, performance-based awards, share appreciation rights, and employee share purchase plans.

---

[68] Gains or losses from the sale of assets should be reported as "other general expenses" pursuant to Regulation S-X, Article 5-03(b)(6). Any material item should be stated separately.

[69] Opinion 20, paragraph 13 and paragraphs 36-37 describe and provide the accounting and disclosure requirements applicable to the correction of an error in previously issued financial statements. Because the term "error" as used in Opinion 20 includes "oversight

or misuse of facts that existed at the time that the financial statements were prepared," that term includes both unintentional errors as well as intentional fraudulent financial reporting and misappropriation of assets as described in SAS 99.

[70] See, for example, Opinion 20, paragraph 27.

[1] Statement 123R, paragraph 1.

[2] Statement 123R, page iv.

Statement 123R replaces Statement 123 and supersedes Opinion 25. Statement 123, as originally issued in 1995, established as preferable, but did not require, a fair-value-based method of accounting for share-based payment transactions with employees.

The staff believes the guidance in this SAB will assist issuers in their initial implementation of Statement 123R and enhance the information received by investors and other users of financial statements, thereby assisting them in making investment and other decisions. This SAB includes interpretive guidance related to share-based payment transactions with nonemployees, the transition from nonpublic to public entity[3] status, valuation methods (including assumptions such as expected volatility and expected term), the accounting for certain redeemable financial instruments issued under share-based payment arrangements, the classification of compensation expense, non-GAAP financial measures, first-time adoption of Statement 123R in an interim period, capitalization of compensation cost related to share-based payment arrangements, the accounting for income tax effects of share-based payment arrangements upon adoption of Statement 123R, the modification of employee share options prior to adoption of Statement 123R and disclosures in MD&A subsequent to adoption of Statement 123R.

The staff recognizes that there is a range of conduct that a reasonable issuer might use to make estimates and valuations and otherwise implement Statement 123R, and the interpretive guidance provided by this SAB, particularly during the period of the Statement's initial implementation. Thus, throughout this SAB the use of the terms "reasonable" and "reasonably" is not meant to imply a single conclusion or methodology, but to encompass the full range of potential conduct, conclusions or methodologies upon which an issuer may reasonably base its valuation decisions. Different conduct, conclusions or methodologies by different issuers in a given situation does not of itself raise an inference that any of those issuers is acting unreasonably. While the zone of reasonable conduct is not unlimited, the staff expects that it will be rare when there is only one acceptable choice in estimating the fair value of share-based payment arrangements under the provisions of Statement 123R and the interpretive guidance provided by this SAB in any given situation. In addition, as discussed in the Interpretive Response to Question 1 of Section C, Valuation Methods, estimates of fair value are not intended to predict actual future events, and subsequent events are not indicative of the reasonableness of the original estimates of fair value made under Statement 123R. Over time, as issuers and accountants gain more experience in applying Statement 123R and the guidance provided in this SAB, the staff anticipates that particu-

lar approaches may begin to emerge as best practices and that the range of reasonable conduct, conclusions and methodologies will likely narrow.

* * * * *

A. Share-Based Payment Transactions with Nonemployees

Question: Are share-based payment transactions with nonemployees included in the scope of Statement 123R?

Interpretive Response: Only certain aspects of the accounting for share-based payment transactions with nonemployees are explicitly addressed by Statement 123R. Statement 123R explicitly:

- Establishes fair value as the measurement objective in accounting for all share-based payments;[4] and

- Requires that an entity record the value of a transaction with a nonemployee based on the more reliably measurable fair value of either the good or service received or the equity instrument issued.[5]

Statement 123R does not supersede any of the authoritative literature that specifically addresses accounting for share-based payments with nonemployees. For example, Statement 123R does not specify the measurement date for sharebased payment transactions with nonemployees when the measurement of the transaction is based on the fair value of the equity instruments issued.[6] For determining the measurement date of equity instruments issued in share-based transactions with nonemployees, a company should refer to Emerging Issues Task Force ("EITF") Issue No. 96-18, *Accounting for Equity Instruments That Are Issued to Other Than Employees for Acquiring, or in Conjunction with Selling, Goods or Services.*

With respect to questions regarding nonemployee arrangements that are not specifically addressed in other authoritative literature, the staff believes that the application of guidance in Statement 123R would generally result in relevant and reliable financial statement information. As such, the staff believes it would generally be appropriate for entities to apply the guidance in Statement 123R by analogy to share-based payment transactions with nonemployees unless other authoritative accounting literature more clearly addresses the appropriate accounting, or the application of the guidance in Statement 123R would be inconsistent with the terms of the instrument issued to a nonemployee in a sharebased payment arrangement.[7] For example, the staff believes the guidance in Statement 123R on certain transactions with related parties or other holders of an economic interest in the

---

[3] Defined in Statement 123R, Appendix E.

[4] Statement 123R, paragraph 7.

[5] *Ibid.*

[6] Statement 123R, paragraph 8.

[7] For example, due to the nature of specific terms in employee share options, including nontransferability, nonhedgability and truncation of the contractual term due to post-vesting service termi-

nation, Statement 123R requires that when valuing an employee share option under the Black-Scholes-Merton framework, the fair value of an employee share option be based on the option's expected term rather than the contractual term. If these features (i.e., nontransferability, nonhedgability and the truncation of the contractual term) were not present in a nonemployee share option arrangement, the use of an expected term assumption shorter than the contractual term would generally not be appropriate in estimating the fair value of the nonemployee share options.

entity would generally be applicable to share-based payment transactions with nonemployees. The staff encourages registrants that have additional questions related to accounting for share-based payment transactions with nonemployees to discuss those questions with the staff.

B. Transition from Nonpublic to Public Entity Status

Facts: Company A is a nonpublic entity[8] that first files a registration statement with the SEC to register its equity securities for sale in a public market on January 2, 20X8.[9] As a nonpublic entity, Company A had been assigning value to its share options[10] under the calculated value method prescribed by Statement 123R[11] and had elected to measure its liability awards based on intrinsic value. Company A is considered a public entity on January 2, 20X8 when it makes its initial filing with the SEC in preparation for the sale of its shares in a public market.

Question 1: How should Company A account for the share options that were granted to its employees prior to January 2, 20X8 for which the requisite service has not been rendered by January 2, 20X8?

Interpretive Response: Prior to becoming a public entity, Company A had been assigning value to its share options under the calculated value method. The staff believes that Company A should continue to follow that approach for those share options that were granted prior to January 2, 20X8, unless those share options are subsequently modified, repurchased or cancelled.[12] If the share options are subsequently modified, repurchased or cancelled, Company A would assess the event under the public company provisions of Statement 123R. For example, if Company A modified the share options on February 1, 20X8, any incremental compensation cost would be measured under Statement 123R, paragraph 51(a), as the fair value of the modified share options over the fair value of the original share options measured immediately before the terms were modified.[13]

Question 2: How should Company A account for its liability awards granted to its employees prior to

January 2, 20X8 which are fully vested but have not been settled by January 2, 20X8?

Interpretive Response: As a nonpublic entity, Company A had elected to measure its liability awards subject to Statement 123R at intrinsic value.[14] When Company A becomes a public entity, it should measure the liability awards at their fair value determined in accordance with Statement 123R.[15] In that reporting period there will be an incremental amount of measured cost for the difference between fair value as determined under Statement 123R and intrinsic value. For example, assume the intrinsic value in the period ended December 31, 20X7 was $10 per award. At the end of the first reporting period ending after January 2, 20X8 (when Company A becomes a public entity), assume the intrinsic value of the award is $12 and the fair value as determined in accordance with Statement 123R is $15. The measured cost in the first reporting period after December 31, 20X7 would be $5.[16]

Question 3: After becoming a public entity, may Company A retrospectively apply the fair-value-based method to its awards that were granted prior to the date Company A became a public entity?

Interpretive Response: No. Before becoming a public entity, Company A did not use the fair-value-based method for either its share options or its liability awards granted to the Company's employees. The staff does not believe it is appropriate for Company A to apply the fair-value-based method on a retrospective basis, because it would require the entity to make estimates of a prior period, which, due to hindsight, may vary significantly from estimates that would have been made contemporaneously in prior periods.[17]

Question 4: Upon becoming a public entity, what disclosures should Company A consider in addition to those prescribed by Statement 123R?[18]

Interpretive Response: In the registration statement filed on January 2, 20X8, Company A should clearly describe in MD&A the change in accounting policy that will be required by Statement 123R in subsequent periods and the reasonably likely material

---

[8] Defined in Statement 123R, Appendix E.

[9] For the purposes of these illustrations, assume all of Company A's equity-based awards granted to its employees were granted after the adoption of Statement 123R.

[10] For purposes of this staff accounting bulletin, the phrase "share options" is used to refer to "share options or similar instruments."

[11] Statement 123R, paragraph 23 requires a nonpublic entity to use the calculated value method when it is not able to reasonably estimate the fair value of its equity share options and similar instruments because it is not practicable for it to estimate the expected volatility of its share price. Statement 123R, paragraph A43 indicates that a nonpublic entity may be able to identify similar public entities for which share or option price information is available and may consider the historical, expected, or implied volatility of those entities' share prices in estimating expected volatility. The staff would expect an entity that becomes a public entity and had previously measured its share options under the calculated value method to be able to support its previous decision to use calculated

value and to provide the disclosures required by paragraph A240(e)(2)(b) of Statement 123R.

[12] This view is consistent with the FASB's basis for rejecting full retrospective application of Statement 123R as described in Statement 123R, paragraph B251.

[13] Statement 123R, footnote 103. The staff believes that because Company A is a public entity as of the date of the modification, it would be inappropriate to use the calculated value method to measure the original share options immediately before the terms were modified.

[14] Statement 123R, paragraph 38.

[15] Statement 123R, paragraph 37.

[16] $15 fair value less $10 intrinsic value equals $5 of incremental cost.

[17] This view is consistent with the FASB's basis for rejecting full retrospective application of Statement 123R as described in Statement 123R, paragraph B251.

[18] Statement 123R disclosure requirements are described in paragraphs 64, 65, A240, A241 and A242.

future effects.[19] In subsequent filings, Company A should provide financial statement disclosure of the effects of the changes in accounting policy. In addition, Company A should consider the applicability of SEC Release No. FR-60[20] and Section V, "Critical Accounting Estimates," in SEC Release No. FR-72[21] regarding critical accounting policies and estimates in MD&A.

C. Valuation Methods

Statement 123R, paragraph 16, indicates that the measurement objective for equity instruments awarded to employees is to estimate at the grant date the fair value of the equity instruments the entity is obligated to issue when employees have rendered the requisite service and satisfied any other conditions necessary to earn the right to benefit from the instruments. The Statement also states that observable market prices of identical or similar equity or liability instruments in active markets are the best evidence of fair value and, if available, should be used as the basis for the measurement for equity and liability instruments awarded in a share-based payment transaction with employees.[22] However, if observable market prices of identical or similar equity or liability instruments are not available, the fair value shall be estimated by using a valuation technique or model that complies with the measurement objective, as described in Statement 123R.[23]

Question 1: If a valuation technique or model is used to estimate fair value, to what extent will the staff consider a company's estimates of fair value to be materially misleading because the estimates of fair value do not correspond to the value ultimately realized by the employees who received the share options?

Interpretive Response: The staff understands that estimates of fair value of employee share options, while derived from expected value calculations, cannot predict actual future events.[24] The estimate of fair value represents the measurement of the cost of the employee services to the company. The estimate of fair value should reflect the assumptions marketplace participants would use in determining how much to pay for an instrument on the date of the measurement (generally the grant date for equity awards). For example, valuation techniques used in estimating the fair value of employee share options may consider information about a large number of possible share price paths, while, of course, only one share price path will ultimately emerge. If a company makes a good faith fair value estimate in accordance with the provi-

sions of Statement 123R in a way that is designed to take into account the assumptions that underlie the instrument's value that marketplace participants would reasonably make, then subsequent future events that affect the instrument's value do not provide meaningful information about the quality of the original fair value estimate. As long as the share options were originally so measured, changes in an employee share option's value, no matter how significant, subsequent to its grant date do not call into question the reasonableness of the grant date fair value estimate.

Question 2: In order to meet the fair value measurement objective in Statement 123R, are certain valuation techniques preferred over others?

Interpretive Response: Statement 123R, paragraph A14, clarifies that the Statement does not specify a preference for a particular valuation technique or model. As stated in Statement 123R, paragraph A8, in order to meet the fair value measurement objective, a company should select a valuation technique or model that (a) is applied in a manner consistent with the fair value measurement objective and other requirements of Statement 123R, (b) is based on established principles of financial economic theory and generally applied in that field and (c) reflects all substantive characteristics of the instrument.

The chosen valuation technique or model must meet all three of the requirements stated above. In valuing a particular instrument, certain techniques or models may meet the first and second criteria but may not meet the third criterion because the techniques or models are not designed to reflect certain characteristics contained in the instrument. For example, for a share option in which the exercisability is conditional on a specified increase in the price of the underlying shares, the Black-Scholes-Merton closed-form model would not generally be an appropriate valuation model because, while it meets both the first and second criteria, it is not designed to take into account that type of market condition.[25]

Further, the staff understands that a company may consider multiple techniques or models that meet the fair value measurement objective before making its selection as to the appropriate technique or model. The staff would not object to a company's choice of a technique or model as long as the technique or model meets the fair value measurement objective. For example, a company is not required to use a lattice model simply because that model was the most complex of the models the company considered.

---

[19] *See* generally SEC Release No. FR-72, "Commission Guidance Regarding Management's Discussion and Analysis of Financial Condition and Results of Operations."

[20] SEC Release No. FR-60, "Cautionary Advice Regarding Disclosure About Critical Accounting Policies."

[21] SEC Release No. FR-72, "Commission Guidance Regarding Management's Discussion and Analysis of Financial Condition and Results of Operations."

[22] Statement 123R, paragraph A7.

[23] Statement 123R, paragraph A8.

[24] Statement 123R, paragraph A12, states "The fair value of those instruments at a single point in time is not a forecast of what the estimated fair value of those instruments may be in the future."

[25] *See* Statement 123R, paragraphs A13-17.

Question 3: In subsequent periods, may a company change the valuation technique or model chosen to value instruments with similar characteristics?[26]

Interpretive Response: As long as the new technique or model meets the fair value measurement objective in Statement 123R as described in Question 2 above, the staff would not object to a company changing its valuation technique or model.[27] A change in the valuation technique or model used to meet the fair value measurement objective would not be considered a change in accounting principle. As such, a company would not be required to file a preferability letter from its independent accountants as described in Rule 10-01(b)(6) of Regulation S-X when it changes valuation techniques or models.[28] However, the staff would not expect that a company would frequently switch between valuation techniques or models, particularly in circumstances where there was no significant variation in the form of share-based payments being valued. Disclosure in the footnotes of the basis for any change in technique or model would be appropriate.[29]

Question 4: Must every company that issues share options or similar instruments hire an outside third party to assist in determining the fair value of the share options?

Interpretive Response: No. However, the valuation of a company's share options or similar instruments should be performed by a person with the requisite expertise.

D. Certain Assumptions Used in Valuation Methods

Statement 123R's fair value measurement objective for equity instruments awarded to employees is to estimate the grant-date fair value of the equity instruments that the entity is obligated to issue when employees have rendered the requisite service and satisfied any other conditions necessary to earn the right to benefit from the instruments.[30] In order to meet this fair value measurement objective, management will be required to develop estimates regarding the expected volatility of its company's share price and the exercise behavior of its employees. The staff is providing guidance in the following sections related to the expected volatility and expected term assumptions to assist public entities in applying those requirements.

The staff understands that companies may refine their estimates of expected volatility and expected term as a result of the guidance provided in Statement 123R and in sections (1) and (2) below. Changes in assumptions during the periods presented in the financial statements should be disclosed in the footnotes.[31]

1. Expected Volatility

Statement 123R, paragraph A31, states, "Volatility is a measure of the amount by which a financial variable, such as share price, has fluctuated (historical volatility) or is expected to fluctuate (expected volatility) during a period. Option-pricing models require an estimate of expected volatility as an assumption because an option's value is dependent on potential share returns over the option's term. The higher the volatility, the more the returns on the share can be expected to vary - up or down. Because an option's value is unaffected by expected negative returns on the shares, other things [being] equal, an option on a share with higher volatility is worth more than an option on a share with lower volatility."

Facts: Company B is a public entity whose common shares have been publicly traded for over twenty years. Company B also has multiple options on its shares outstanding that are traded on an exchange ("traded options"). Company B grants share options on January 2, 20X6.

Question 1: What should Company B consider when estimating expected volatility for purposes of measuring the fair value of its share options?

Interpretive Response: Statement 123R does not specify a particular method of estimating expected volatility. However, the Statement does clarify that the objective in estimating expected volatility is to ascertain the assumption about expected volatility that marketplace participants would likely use in determining an exchange price for an option.[32] Statement 123R provides a list of factors entities should consider in estimating expected volatility.[33] Company B may begin its process of estimating expected volatility by considering its historical volatility.[34] However, Company B should also then consider, based on available information, how the expected volatility of its share price may differ from historical volatility.[35] Implied volatility[36] can be useful in estimating expected volatility because it is generally reflective of both historical volatility and

---

[26] Statement 123R, paragraph A14 and footnote 49, indicate that an entity may use different valuation techniques or models for instruments with different characteristics.

[27] The staff believes that a company should take into account the reason for the change in technique or model in determining whether the new technique or model meets the fair value measurement objective. For example, changing a technique or model from period to period for the sole purpose of lowering the fair value estimate of a share option would not meet the fair value measurement objective of the Statement.

[28] Statement 123R, paragraph A23.

[29] *See* generally Statement 123R, paragraph 64c.

[30] Statement 123R, paragraph A2.

[31] Statement 123R, paragraph A240(e).

[32] Statement 123R, paragraph B86.

[33] Statement 123R, paragraph A32.

[34] Statement 123R, paragraph A34.

[35] *Ibid.*

[36] Implied volatility is the volatility assumption inherent in the market prices of a company's traded options or other financial instruments that have option-like features. Implied volatility is derived by entering the market price of the traded financial instrument, along with assumptions specific to the financial options being valued, into a model based on a constant volatility estimate (*e.g.*, the Black-Scholes-Merton closedform model) and solving for the unknown assumption of volatility.

expectations of how future volatility will differ from historical volatility.

The staff believes that companies should make good faith efforts to identify and use sufficient information in determining whether taking historical volatility, implied volatility or a combination of both into account will result in the best estimate of expected volatility. The staff believes companies that have appropriate traded financial instruments from which they can derive an implied volatility should generally consider this measure. The extent of the ultimate reliance on implied volatility will depend on a company's facts and circumstances; however, the staff believes that a company with actively traded options or other financial instruments with embedded options[37] generally could place greater (or even exclusive) reliance on implied volatility. (See the Interpretive Responses to Questions 3 and 4 below.)

The process used to gather and review available information to estimate expected volatility should be applied consistently from period to period. When circumstances indicate the availability of new or different information that would be useful in estimating expected volatility, a company should incorporate that information.

Question 2: What should Company B consider if computing historical volatility?[38]

Interpretive Response: The following should be considered in the computation of historical volatility:

1. Method of Computing Historical Volatility -

   The staff believes the method selected by Company B to compute its historical volatility should produce an estimate that is representative of Company B's expectations about its future volatility over the expected (if using a Black-Scholes-Merton closed-form model) or contractual (if using a lattice model) term[39] of its employee share options. Certain methods may not be appropriate for longer term employee share options if they weight the most recent periods of Company B's historical volatility much more heavily than earlier periods.[40] For example, a method that applies a factor to certain historical price intervals to reflect a decay or loss of relevance of that

historical information emphasizes the most recent historical periods and thus would likely bias the estimate to this recent history.[41]

2. Amount of Historical Data -

   Statement 123R, paragraph A32(a), indicates entities should consider historical volatility over a period generally commensurate with the expected or contractual term, as applicable, of the share option. The staff believes Company B could utilize a period of historical data longer than the expected or contractual term, as applicable, if it reasonably believes the additional historical information will improve the estimate. For example, assume Company B decided to utilize a Black-Scholes-Merton closed-form model to estimate the value of the share options granted on January 2, 20X6 and determined that the expected term was six years. Company B would not be precluded from using historical data longer than six years if it concludes that data would be relevant.

3. Frequency of Price Observations -

   Statement 123R, paragraph A32(d), indicates an entity should use appropriate and regular intervals for price observations based on facts and circumstances that provide the basis for a reasonable fair value estimate. Accordingly, the staff believes Company B should consider the frequency of the trading of its shares and the length of its trading history in determining the appropriate frequency of price observations. The staff believes using daily, weekly or monthly price observations may provide a sufficient basis to estimate expected volatility if the history provides enough data points on which to base the estimate.[42] Company B should select a consistent point in time within each interval when selecting data points.[43]

4. Consideration of Future Events -

   The objective in estimating expected volatility is to ascertain the assumptions that marketplace participants would likely use in determining an exchange price for an op-

---

[37] The staff believes implied volatility derived from embedded options can be utilized in determining expected volatility if, in deriving the implied volatility, the company considers all relevant features of the instruments (*e.g.*, value of the host instrument, value of the option, etc.). The staff believes the derivation of implied volatility from other than simple instruments (*e.g.*, a simple convertible bond) can, in some cases, be impracticable due to the complexity of multiple features.

[38] *See* Statement 123R, paragraph A32.

[39] For purposes of this staff accounting bulletin, the phrase "expected or contractual term, as applicable" has the same meaning as the phrase "expected (if using a Black-Scholes-Merton closed-form model) or contractual (if using a lattice model) term of an employee share option."

[40] Statement 123R, paragraph A32(a), states that entities should consider historical volatility over a period generally commensurate with the expected or contractual term, as applicable, of the share option. Accordingly, the staff believes methods that place extreme

emphasis on the most recent periods may be inconsistent with this guidance.

[41] Generalized Autoregressive Conditional Heteroskedasticity ("GARCH") is an example of a method that demonstrates this characteristic.

[42] Further, if shares of a company are thinly traded the staff believes the use of weekly or monthly price observations would generally be more appropriate than the use of daily price observations. The volatility calculation using daily observations for such shares could be artificially inflated due to a larger spread between the bid and asked quotes and lack of consistent trading in the market.

[43] Statement 123R, paragraph A34, states that a company should establish a process for estimating expected volatility and apply that process consistently from period to period. In addition, Statement 123R, paragraph A23, indicates that assumptions used to estimate the fair value of instruments granted to employees should be determined in a consistent manner from period to period.

tion.[44] Accordingly, the staff believes that Company B should consider those future events that it reasonably concludes a marketplace participant would also consider in making the estimation. For example, if Company B has recently announced a merger with a company that would change its business risk in the future, then it should consider the impact of the merger in estimating the expected volatility if it reasonably believes a marketplace participant would also consider this event.

5. Exclusion of Periods of Historical Data -

In some instances, due to a company's particular business situations, a period of historical volatility data may not be relevant in evaluating expected volatility.[45] In these instances, that period should be disregarded. The staff believes that if Company B disregards a period of historical volatility, it should be prepared to support its conclusion that its historical share price during that previous period is not relevant to estimating expected volatility due to one or more discrete and specific historical events and that similar events are not expected to occur during the expected term of the share option. The staff believes these situations would be rare.

Question 3: What should Company B consider when evaluating the extent of its reliance on the implied volatility derived from its traded options?

Interpretive Response: To achieve the objective of estimating expected volatility as stated in paragraph B86 of Statement 123R, the staff believes Company B generally should consider the following in its evaluation: 1) the volume of market activity of the underlying shares and traded options; 2) the ability to synchronize the variables used to derive implied volatility; 3) the similarity of the exercise prices of the traded options to the exercise price of the employee share options; and 4) the similarity of the length of the term of the traded and employee share options.[46]

1. Volume of Market Activity -

The staff believes Company B should consider the volume of trading in its underlying shares as well as the traded options. For example, prices for instruments in actively traded markets are more likely to reflect a marketplace participant's expectations regarding expected volatility.

2. Synchronization of the Variables -

Company B should synchronize the variables used to derive implied volatility. For example, to the extent reasonably practicable, Company B should use market prices (either traded prices or the average of bid and asked quotes) of the traded options and its shares measured at the same point in time. This measurement should also be synchronized with the grant of the employee share options; however, when this is not reasonably practicable, the staff believes Company B should derive implied volatility as of a point in time as close to the grant of the employee share options as reasonably practicable.

3. Similarity of the Exercise Prices -

The staff believes that when valuing an at-the-money employee share option, the implied volatility derived from at- or near-the-money traded options generally would be most relevant.[47] If, however, it is not possible to find at- or near-the-money traded options, Company B should select multiple traded options with an average exercise price close to the exercise price of the employee share option.[48]

4. Similarity of Length of Terms -

The staff believes that when valuing an employee share option with a given expected or contractual term, as applicable, the implied volatility derived from a traded option with a similar term would be the most relevant. However, if there are no traded options with maturities that are similar to the share option's contractual or expected term, as applicable, then the staff believes Company B could consider traded options with a remaining maturity of six months or greater.[49] However, when using traded options with a term of less than one year,[50] the staff would expect the company to also consider other relevant information in estimating expected volatility.

---

[44] Statement 123R, paragraph B86.

[45] Statement 123R, paragraph A32(a).

[46] *See* generally *Options, Futures, and Other Derivatives* by John C. Hull (Prentice Hall, 5th Edition, 2003).

[47] Implied volatilities of options differ systematically over the "moneyness" of the option. This pattern of implied volatilities across exercise prices is known as the "volatility smile" or "volatility skew." Studies such as "Implied Volatility" by Stewart Mayhew, *Financial Analysts Journal*, July-August 1995, have found that implied volatilities based on near-the-money options do as well as sophisticated weighted implied volatilities in estimating expected volatility. In addition, the staff believes that because near-the-money options are generally more actively traded, they may provide a better basis for deriving implied volatility.

[48] The staff believes a company could use a weighted-average implied volatility based on traded options that are either in-the-money or out-of-the-money. For example, if the employee share option has an exercise price of $52, but the only traded options available have exercise prices of $50 and $55, then the staff believes that it is appropriate to use a weighted average based on the implied volatilities from the two traded options; for this example, a 40% weight on the implied volatility calculated from the option with an exercise price of $55 and a 60% weight on the option with an exercise price of $50.

[49] The staff believes it may also be appropriate to consider the entire term structure of volatility provided by traded options with a variety of remaining maturities. If a company considers the entire term structure in deriving implied volatility, the staff would expect a company to include some options in the term structure with a remaining maturity of six months or greater.

[50] The staff believes the implied volatility derived from a traded option with a term of one year or greater would typically not be significantly different from the implied volatility that would be derived from a traded option with a significantly longer term.

In general, the staff believes more reliance on the implied volatility derived from a traded option would be expected the closer the remaining term of the traded option is to the expected or contractual term, as applicable, of the employee share option.

The staff believes Company B's evaluation of the factors above should assist in determining whether the implied volatility appropriately reflects the market's expectations of future volatility and thus the extent of reliance that Company B reasonably places on the implied volatility.

Question 4: Are there situations in which it is acceptable for Company B to rely exclusively on either implied volatility or historical volatility in its estimate of expected volatility?

Interpretive Response: As stated above, Statement 123R does not specify a method of estimating expected volatility; rather, it provides a list of factors that should be considered and requires that an entity's estimate of expected volatility be reasonable and supportable.[51] Many of the factors listed in Statement 123R are discussed in Questions 2 and 3 above. The objective of estimating volatility, as stated in Statement 123R, is to ascertain the assumption about expected volatility that marketplace participants would likely use in determining a price for an option.[52] The staff believes that a company, after considering the factors listed in Statement 123R, could, in certain situations, reasonably conclude that exclusive reliance on either historical or implied volatility would provide an estimate of expected volatility that meets this stated objective.

The staff would not object to Company B placing exclusive reliance on implied volatility when the following factors are present, as long as the methodology is consistently applied:

- Company B utilizes a valuation model that is based upon a constant volatility assumption to value its employee share options;[53]

- The implied volatility is derived from options that are actively traded;

- The market prices (trades or quotes) of both the traded options and underlying shares are measured at a similar point in time to each other and on a date reasonably close to the grant date of the employee share options;

- The traded options have exercise prices that are both (a) near-the-money and (b) close to the exercise price of the employee share options;[54] and

- The remaining maturities of the traded options on which the estimate is based are at least one year.

The staff would not object to Company B placing exclusive reliance on historical volatility when the following factors are present, so long as the methodology is consistently applied:

- Company B has no reason to believe that its future volatility over the expected or contractual term, as applicable, is likely to differ from its past;[55]

- The computation of historical volatility uses a simple average calculation method;

- A sequential period of historical data at least equal to the expected or contractual term of the share option, as applicable, is used; and

- A reasonably sufficient number of price observations are used, measured at a consistent point throughout the applicable historical period.[56]

Question 5: What disclosures would the staff expect Company B to include in its financial statements and MD&A regarding its assumption of expected volatility?

Interpretive Response: Statement 123R, paragraph A240, prescribes the minimum information needed to achieve the Statement's disclosure objectives.[57] Under that guidance, Company B is required to disclose the expected volatility and the method used to estimate it.[58] Accordingly, the staff expects that at a minimum Company B would disclose in a footnote to its financial statements how it determined the expected volatility assumption for purposes of determining the fair value of its share options in accordance with Statement 123R. For example, at a minimum, the staff would expect Company B to disclose whether it used only implied volatility, historical volatility, or a combination of both.

In addition, Company B should consider the applicability of SEC Release No. FR-60 and Section V, "Critical Accounting Estimates," in SEC Release No. FR-72 regarding critical accounting policies and estimates in MD&A. The staff would expect such disclosures to

---

[51] Statement 123R, paragraphs A31-A32.

[52] Statement 123R, paragraph B86.

[53] Statement 123R, paragraphs A15 and A33, discuss the incorporation of a range of expected volatilities into option pricing models. The staff believes that a company that utilizes an option pricing model that incorporates a range of expected volatilities over the option's contractual term should consider the factors listed in Statement 123R, and those discussed in the Interpretive Responses to Questions 2 and 3 above, to determine the extent of its reliance (including exclusive reliance) on the derived implied volatility.

[54] When near-the-money options are not available, the staff believes the use of a weighted-average approach, as noted in a previous footnote, may be appropriate.

[55] *See* Statement 123R, paragraph B87. A change in a company's business model that results in a material alteration to the company's risk profile is an example of a circumstance in which the company's future volatility would be expected to differ from its past volatility. Other examples may include, but are not limited to, the introduction of a new product that is central to a company's business model or the receipt of U.S. Food and Drug Administration approval for the sale of a new prescription drug.

[56] If the expected or contractual term, as applicable, of the employee share option is less than three years, the staff believes monthly price observations would not provide a sufficient amount of data.

[57] Statement 123R disclosure requirements are included in paragraphs 64, 65, A240, A241, and A242.

[58] Statement 123R, paragraph A240(e)(2)(b).

include an explanation of the method used to estimate the expected volatility of its share price. This explanation generally should include a discussion of the basis for the company's conclusions regarding the extent to which it used historical volatility, implied volatility or a combination of both. A company could consider summarizing its evaluation of the factors listed in Questions 2 and 3 of this section as part of these disclosures in MD&A.

Facts: Company C is a newly public entity with limited historical data on the price of its publicly traded shares and no other traded financial instruments. Company C believes that it does not have sufficient company specific information regarding the volatility of its share price on which to base an estimate of expected volatility.

Question 6: What other sources of information should Company C consider in order to estimate the expected volatility of its share price?

Interpretive Response: Statement 123R provides guidance on estimating expected volatility for newly public and nonpublic entities that do not have company specific historical or implied volatility information available.[59] Company C may base its estimate of expected volatility on the historical, expected or implied volatility of similar entities whose share or option prices are publicly available. In making its determination as to similarity, Company C would likely consider the industry, stage of life cycle, size and financial leverage of such other entities.[60]

The staff would not object to Company C looking to an industry sector index (*e.g.,* NASDAQ Computer Index) that is representative of Company C's industry, and possibly its size, to identify one or more similar entities.[61] Once Company C has identified similar entities, it would substitute a measure of the individual volatilities of the similar entities for the expected volatility of its share price as an assumption in its valuation model.[62] Because of the effects of diversification that are present in an industry sector index, Company C should not substitute the volatility of an index for the expected volatility of its share price as an assumption in its valuation model.[63]

After similar entities have been identified, Company C should continue to consider the volatilities of those entities unless circumstances change such that the identified entities are no longer similar to Company C. Until Company C has sufficient information available, the staff would not object to Company C basing its estimate of expected volatility on the volatility of similar entities for those periods for which it does not have sufficient information available.[64] Until Com-

pany C has either a sufficient amount of historical information regarding the volatility of its share price or other traded financial instruments are available to derive an implied volatility to support an estimate of expected volatility, it should consistently apply a process as described above to estimate expected volatility based on the volatilities of similar entities.[65]

2. Expected Term

Statement 123R, paragraph A26, states "The fair value of a traded (or transferable) share option is based on its contractual term because rarely is it economically advantageous to the holder to exercise, rather than sell, a transferable share option before the end of its contractual term. Employee share options generally differ from transferable [or tradable] share options in that employees cannot sell (or hedge) their share options - they can only exercise them; because of this, employees generally exercise their options before the end of the options' contractual term. Thus, the inability to sell or hedge an employee share option effectively reduces the option's value [compared to a transferable option] because exercise prior to the option's expiration terminates its remaining life and thus its remaining time value." Accordingly, Statement 123R requires that when valuing an employee share option under the Black-Scholes-Merton framework the fair value of employee share options be based on the share options' expected term rather than the contractual term.

The staff believes the estimate of expected term should be based on the facts and circumstances available in each particular case. Consistent with our guidance regarding reasonableness immediately preceding Topic 14.A, the fact that other possible estimates are later determined to have more accurately reflected the term does not necessarily mean that the particular choice was unreasonable. The staff reminds registrants of the expected term disclosure requirements described in Statement 123R, paragraph A240(e)(2)(a).

Facts: Company D utilizes the Black-Scholes-Merton closed-form model to value its share options for the purposes of determining the fair value of the options under Statement 123R. Company D recently granted share options to its employees. Based on its review of various factors, Company D determines that the expected term of the options is six years, which is less than the contractual term of ten years.

Question 1: When determining the fair value of the share options in accordance with Statement 123R,

---

[59] Statement 123R, paragraphs A22 and A43.

[60] Statement 123R, paragraph A22.

[61] If a company operates in a number of different industries, it could look to several industry indices. However, when considering the volatilities of multiple companies, each operating only in a single industry, the staff believes a company should take into account its own leverage, the leverages of each of the entities, and the correlation of the entities' stock returns.

[62] Statement 123R, paragraph A45.

[63] Statement 123R, paragraph A22.

[64] Statement 123R, paragraph A32(c). The staff believes that at least two years of daily or weekly historical data could provide a reasonable basis on which to base an estimate of expected volatility if a company has no reason to believe that its future volatility will differ materially during the expected or contractual term, as applicable, from the volatility calculated from this past information. If the expected or contractual term, as applicable, of a share option is shorter than two years, the staff believes a company should use daily or weekly historical data for at least the length of that applicable term.

[65] Statement 123R, paragraph A34.

should Company D consider an additional discount for nonhedgability and nontransferability?

Interpretive Response: No. Statement 123R, paragraphs A26 and B82, indicates that nonhedgability and nontransferability have the effect of increasing the likelihood that an employee share option will be exercised before the end of its contractual term. Nonhedgability and nontransferability therefore factor into the expected term assumption (in this case reducing the term assumption from ten years to six years), and the expected term reasonably adjusts for the effect of these factors. Accordingly, the staff believes that no additional reduction in the term assumption or other discount to the estimated fair value is appropriate for these particular factors.[66]

Question 2: Should forfeitures or terms that stem from forfeitability be factored into the determination of expected term?

Interpretive Response: No. Statement 123R indicates that the expected term that is utilized as an assumption in a closed-form option-pricing model or a resulting output of a lattice option pricing model when determining the fair value of the share options should not incorporate restrictions or other terms that stem from the pre-vesting forfeitability of the instruments. Under Statement 123R, these prevesting restrictions or other terms are taken into account by ultimately recognizing compensation cost only for awards for which employees render the requisite service.[67]

Question 3: Can a company's estimate of expected term ever be shorter than the vesting period?

Interpretive Response: No. The vesting period forms the lower bound of the estimate of expected term.[68]

Question 4: Statement 123R, paragraph A30, indicates that an entity shall aggregate individual awards into relatively homogenous groups with respect to exercise and post-vesting employment termination behaviors for the purpose of determining expected term, regardless of the valuation technique or model used to estimate the fair value. How many groupings are typically considered sufficient?

Interpretive Response: As it relates to employee groupings, the staff believes that an entity may generally make a reasonable fair value estimate with as few as one or two groupings.[69]

Question 5: What approaches could a company use to estimate the expected term of its employee share options?

Interpretive Response: A company should use an approach that is reasonable and supportable under Statement 123R's fair value measurement objective, which establishes that assumptions and measurement techniques should be consistent with those that marketplace participants would be likely to use in determining an exchange price for the share options.[70] If, in developing its estimate of expected term, a company determines that its historical share option exercise experience is the best estimate of future exercise patterns, the staff will not object to the use of the historical share option exercise experience to estimate expected term.[71]

A company may also conclude that its historical share option exercise experience does not provide a reasonable basis upon which to estimate expected term. This may be the case for a variety of reasons, including, but not limited to, the life of the company and its relative stage of development, past or expected structural changes in the business, differences in terms of past equity-based share option grants,[72] or a lack of variety of price paths that the company may have experienced.[73]

Statement 123R describes other alternative sources of information that might be used in those cases when a company determines that its historical share option exercise experience does not provide a reasonable basis upon which to estimate expected term. For example, a lattice model (which by definition incorporates multiple price paths) can be used to estimate expected term as an input into a Black-Scholes-Merton closed-form model.[74] In addition, Statement 123R, paragraph A29, states " . . . expected term might be estimated in some other manner, taking into account whatever relevant and supportable information is available, including industry averages and other pertinent evidence such

---

[66] The staff notes the existence of academic literature that supports the assertion that the Black-Scholes-Merton closed-form model, with expected term as an input, can produce reasonable estimates of fair value. Such literature includes J. Carpenter, "The exercise and valuation of executive stock options," *Journal of Financial Economics*, May 1998, pp.127-158; C. Marquardt, "The Cost of Employee Stock Option Grants: An Empirical Analysis," *Journal of Accounting Research*, September 2002, p. 1191-1217); and J. Bettis, J. Bizjak and M. Lemmon, "Exercise behavior, valuation, and the incentive effect of employee stock options," *Journal of Financial Economics*, forthcoming, 2005.

[67] Statement 123R, paragraph 18.

[68] Statement 123R, paragraph A28a.

[69] The staff believes the focus should be on groups of employees with significantly different expected exercise behavior. Academic research suggests two such groups might be executives and non-executives. A study by S. Huddart found executives and other senior managers to be significantly more patient in their exercise behavior than more junior employees. (Employee rank was proxied for by the number of options issued to that employee.) See S. Huddart, "Patterns of stock option exercise in the United States,"

in: J. Carpenter and D. Yermack, eds., *Executive Compensation and Shareholder Value: Theory and Evidence* (Kluwer, Boston, MA, 1999), pp. 115-142. See also S. Huddart and M. Lang, "Employee stock option exercises: An empirical analysis," *Journal of Accounting and Economics*, 1996, pp. 5-43.

[70] Statement 123R, paragraph A10.

[71] Historical share option exercise experience encompasses data related to share option exercise, postvesting termination, and share option contractual term expiration.

[72] For example, if a company had historically granted share options that were always in-the-money, and will grant at-the-money options prospectively, the exercise behavior related to the in-the-money options may not be sufficient as the sole basis to form the estimate of expected term for the at-the-money grants.

[73] For example, if a company had a history of previous equity-based share option grants and exercises only in periods in which the company's share price was rising, the exercise behavior related to those options may not be sufficient as the sole basis to form the estimate of expected term for current option grants.

[74] Statement 123R, paragraph A27.

as published academic research." For example, data about exercise patterns of employees in similar industries and/or situations as the company's might be used. While such comparative information may not be widely available at present, the staff understands that various parties, including actuaries, valuation professionals and others are gathering such data.

Facts: Company E grants equity share options to its employees that have the following basic characteristics:[75]

- The share options are granted at-the-money;

- Exercisability is conditional only on performing service through the vesting date;[76]

- If an employee terminates service prior to vesting, the employee would forfeit the share options;

- If an employee terminates service after vesting, the employee would have a limited time to exercise the share options (typically 30-90 days); and

- The share options are nontransferable and nonhedgeable.

Company E utilizes the Black-Scholes-Merton closed-form model for valuing its employee share options.

Question 6: As share options with these "plain vanilla" characteristics have been granted in significant quantities by many companies in the past, is the staff aware of any "simple" methodologies that can be used to estimate expected term?

Interpretive Response: As noted above, the staff understands that an entity that is unable to rely on its historical exercise data may find that certain alternative information, such as exercise data relating to employees of other companies, is not easily obtainable. As such, some companies may encounter difficulties in making a refined estimate of expected term. Accordingly, if a company concludes that its historical share option exercise experience does not provide a reasonable basis upon which to estimate expected term, the staff will accept the following "simplified" method for "plain vanilla" options consistent with those in the fact set above: expected term = ((vesting term + original contractual term) / 2). Assuming a ten year original contractual term and graded vesting over four years (25% of the options in each grant vest annually) for the

share options in the fact set described above, the resultant expected term would be 6.25 years.[77] Academic research on the exercise of options issued to executives provides some general support for outcomes that would be produced by the application of this method.[78]

Examples of situations in which the staff believes that it may be appropriate to use this simplified method include the following:

- A company does not have sufficient historical exercise data to provide a reasonable basis upon which to estimate expected term due to the limited period of time its equity shares have been publicly traded.

- A company significantly changes the terms of its share option grants or the types of employees that receive share option grants such that its historical exercise data may no longer provide a reasonable basis upon which to estimate expected term.

- A company has or expects to have significant structural changes in its business such that its historical exercise data may no longer provide a reasonable basis upon which to estimate expected term.

The staff understands that a company may have sufficient historical exercise data for some of its share option grants but not for others. In such cases, the staff will accept the use of the simplified method for only some but not all share option grants. The staff also does not believe that it is necessary for a company to consider using a lattice model before it decides that it is eligible to use this simplified method. Further, the staff will not object to the use of this simplified method in periods prior to the time a company's equity shares are traded in a public market.

If a company uses this simplified method, the company should disclose in the notes to its financial statements the use of the method, the reason why the method was used, the types of share option grants for which the method was used if the method was not used for all share option grants, and the periods for which the method was used if the method was not used in all periods. Companies that have sufficient historical share option exercise experience upon which to estimate expected term may not apply this simplified method. In addition, this simplified method is not intended to be applied

---

[75] Employee share options with these features are sometimes referred to as "plain vanilla" options.

[76] In this fact pattern the requisite service period equals the vesting period.

[77] Calculated as [[[1 year vesting term (for the first 25% vested) plus 2 year vesting term (for the second 25% vested) plus 3 year vesting term (for the third 25% vested) plus 4 year vesting term (for the last 25% vested)] divided by 4 total years of vesting] plus 10 year contractual life] divided by 2; that is, $(((1+2+3+4)/4) + 10) / 2 = 6.25$ years.

[78] J.N. Carpenter, "The exercise and valuation of executive stock options," *Journal of Financial Economics*, 1998, pp.127-158 studies a sample of 40 NYSE and AMEX firms over the period

1979-1994 with share option terms reasonably consistent to the terms presented in the fact set and example. The mean time to exercise after grant was 5.83 years and the median was 6.08 years. The "mean time to exercise" is shorter than expected term since the study's sample included only exercised options. Other research on executive options includes (but is not limited to) J. Carr Bettis; John M. Bizjak; and Michael L. Lemmon, "Exercise behavior, valuation, and the incentive effects of employee stock options," forthcoming in the *Journal of Financial Economics*. One of the few studies on nonexecutive employee options the staff is aware of is S. Huddart, "Patterns of stock option exercise in the United States," in: J. Carpenter and D. Yermack, eds., *Executive Compensation and Shareholder Value: Theory and Evidence* (Kluwer, Boston, MA, 1999), pp. 115-142.

as a benchmark in evaluating the appropriateness of more refined estimates of expected term.

Also, as noted above in Question 5, the staff believes that more detailed external information about exercise behavior will, over time, become readily available to companies. As such, the staff does not expect that such a simplified method would be used for share option grants when more relevant detailed information becomes widely available.

E. Statement 123R and Certain Redeemable Financial Instruments

Certain financial instruments awarded in conjunction with share-based payment arrangements have redemption features that require settlement by cash or other assets upon the occurrence of events that are outside the control of the issuer.[79] Statement 123R provides guidance for determining whether instruments granted in conjunction with share-based payment arrangements should be classified as liability or equity instruments. Under that guidance, most instruments with redemption features that are outside the control of the issuer are required to be classified as liabilities; however, some redeemable instruments will qualify for equity classification.[80] SEC Accounting Series Release No. 268, *Presentation in Financial Statements of "Redeemable Preferred Stocks,"*[81] ("ASR 268") and related guidance[82] address the classification and measurement of certain redeemable equity instruments.

Facts: Under a share-based payment arrangement, Company F grants to an employee shares (or share options) that all vest at the end of four years (cliff vest).

The shares (or shares underlying the share options) are redeemable for cash at fair value at the holder's option, but only after six months from the date of share issuance (as defined in Statement 123R). Company F has determined that the shares (or share options) would be classified as equity instruments under the guidance of Statement 123R. However, under ASR 268 and related guidance, the

instruments would be considered to be redeemable for cash or other assets upon the occurrence of events (*e.g.*, redemption at the option of the holder) that are outside the control of the issuer.

Question 1: While the instruments are subject to Statement 123R,[83] is ASR 268 and related guidance applicable to instruments issued under share-based payment arrangements that are classified as equity instruments under Statements 123R?

Interpretive Response: Yes. The staff believes that registrants must evaluate whether the terms of instruments granted in conjunction with share-based payment arrangements with employees that are not classified as liabilities under Statement 123R result in the need to present certain amounts outside of permanent equity (also referred to as being presented in "temporary equity") in accordance with ASR 268 and related guidance.[84]

When an instrument ceases to be subject to Statement 123R and becomes subject to the recognition and measurement requirements of other applicable GAAP, the staff believes that the company should reassess the classification of the instrument as a liability or equity at that time and consequently may need to reconsider the applicability of ASR 268.

Question 2: How should Company F apply ASR 268 and related guidance to the shares (or share options) granted under the share-based payment arrangements with employees that may be unvested at the date of grant?

Interpretive Response: Under Statement 123R, when compensation cost is recognized for instruments classified as equity instruments, additional paid-incapital[85] is increased. If the award is not fully vested at the grant date, compensation cost is recognized and additional paid-in-capital is increased over time as services are rendered over the requisite service period. A similar pattern of recognition should be used to reflect the amount presented as temporary equity for share-based payment awards that have redemption features that are outside the issuer's control but are classified as equity instru-

---

[79] The terminology "outside the control of the issuer" is used to refer to any of the three redemption conditions described in Rule 5-02.28 of Regulation S-X that would require classification outside permanent equity. That rule requires preferred securities that are redeemable for cash or other assets to be classified outside of permanent equity if they are redeemable (1) at a fixed or determinable price on a fixed or determinable date, (2) at the option of the holder, or (3) upon the occurrence of an event that is not solely within the control of the issuer.

[80] Statement 123R, paragraphs 28-35 and A225-A232.

[81] ASR 268, July 27, 1979, Rule 5-02.28 of Regulation S-X.

[82] Related guidance includes EITF Abstracts Topic No. D-98, *Classification and Measurement of Redeemable Securities* ("Topic D-98").

[83] Statement 123R, paragraph A231, states that an instrument ceases to be subject to Statement 123R when "the rights conveyed by the instrument to the holder are no longer dependent on the holder being an employee of the entity (that is, no longer dependent on providing service)."

[84] Instruments granted in conjunction with share-based payment arrangements with employees that do not by their terms require

redemption for cash or other assets (at a fixed or determinable price on a fixed or determinable date, at the option of the holder, or upon the occurrence of an event that is not solely within the control of the issuer) would not be assumed by the staff to require net cash settlement for purposes of applying ASR 268 in circumstances in which paragraphs 14 - 18 of EITF Issue 00-19, *Accounting for Derivative Financial Instruments Indexed to, and Potentially Settled in, a Company's Own Stock*, would otherwise require the assumption of net cash settlement. *See* Statement 123R, footnote 152 to paragraph B121, which states, in part: ". . . Issue 00-19 specifies that events or actions necessary to deliver registered shares are not controlled by a company and, therefore, except under limited circumstances, such provisions would require a company to assume that the contract would be net-cash settled . . . .Thus, employee share options might be classified as substantive liabilities if they were subject to Issue 00-19; however, for purposes of this Statement, the Board does not believe that employee share options should be classified as liabilities based solely on that notion." *See* also Statement 123R, footnote 20.

[85] Depending on the fact pattern, this may be recorded as common stock and additional paid in capital.

ments under Statement 123R. The staff believes Company F should present as temporary equity at each balance sheet date an amount that is based on the redemption amount of the instrument, but takes into account the proportion of consideration received in the form of employee services. Thus, for example, if a nonvested share that qualifies for equity classification under Statement 123R is redeemable at fair value more than six months after vesting, and that nonvested share is 75% vested at the balance sheet date, an amount equal to 75% of the fair value of the share should be presented as temporary equity at that date. Similarly, if an option on a share of redeemable stock that qualifies for equity classification under Statement 123R is 75% vested at the balance sheet date, an amount equal to 75% of the intrinsic[86] value of the option should be presented as temporary equity at that date.

Question 3: Would the methodology described for employee awards in the Interpretive Response to Question 2 above apply to nonemployee awards to be issued in exchange for goods or services with similar terms to those described above?

Interpretive Response: See Topic 14.A for a discussion of the application of the principles in Statement 123R to nonemployee awards. The staff believes it would generally be appropriate to apply the methodology described in the Interpretive Response to Question 2 above to nonemployee awards.

F. Classification of Compensation Expense Associated with Share-Based Payment Arrangements

Facts: Company G utilizes both cash and share-based payment arrangements to compensate its employees and nonemployee service providers. Company G would like to emphasize in its income statement the amount of its compensation that did not involve a cash outlay.

Question: How should Company G present in its income statement the non-cash nature of its expense related to share-based payment arrangements?

Interpretive Response: The staff believes Company G should present the expense related to share-based payment arrangements in the same line or lines as cash compensation paid to the same employees.[87] The staff believes a company could consider disclosing the amount of expense related to share-based payment arrangements included in specific line items in the financial statements. Disclosure of this information might be appropriate in

a parenthetical note to the appropriate income statement line items, on the cash flow statement, in the footnotes to the financial statements, or within MD&A.

G. Non-GAAP Financial Measures

Facts: Company H, a calendar year company, adopts Statement 123R as of July 1, 2005. Company H has issued share options to its employees each year since issuing publicly traded stock twenty years ago. In the MD&A section of its 2005 Form 10-K, Company H believes it would be useful to investors to disclose what net income would be before considering the effect of accounting for share-based payment transactions in accordance with Statement 123R.

Question 1: Does the resulting measure, "Net Income Before Share-Based Payment Charge," or an equivalent measure, meet the definition of a non-GAAP measure in Regulation G and Item 10(e) of Regulation S-K?[88]

Interpretive Response: Yes. Because the financial measure Company H is considering excludes an amount (share-based payment expense) that is included in the most directly comparable measure calculated and presented in accordance with GAAP (net income), it would be considered a non-GAAP financial measure pursuant to the provisions of Regulation G and Item 10(e) of Regulation S-K.

Question 2: Is the measure "Net Income Before Share-Based Payment Charge," or an equivalent measure, a prohibited non-GAAP measure pursuant to Item 10(e) of Regulation S-K?

Interpretive Response: Item 10(e) prohibits the inclusion of certain non-GAAP financial measures and also mandates specific disclosures for registrants that include permitted non-GAAP financial measures in filings. Generally, under Item 10(e) of Regulation S-K, a company may not present a non-GAAP performance measure that removes an expense from net income by identifying that expense as non-recurring, infrequent, or unusual if it is reasonably likely that the expense will recur within two years or if the company had a similar expense within the prior two years. The staff issued Frequently Asked Questions Regarding the Use of Non-GAAP Measures in June of 2003. Question 8 discusses whether it is appropriate to eliminate or smooth an item that is identified as recurring. The staff answered the question in part by stating "Companies should never use a non-GAAP financial measure in an attempt to smooth earnings. Further, while there is no per se prohibition against

---

[86] The potential redemption amount of the share option in this illustration is its intrinsic value because the holder would pay the exercise price upon exercise of the option and then, upon redemption of the underlying shares, the company would pay the holder the fair value of those shares. Thus, the net cash outflow from the arrangement would be equal to the intrinsic value of the share option. In situations where there would be no cash inflows from the share option holder, the cash required to be paid to redeem the underlying shares upon the exercise of the put option would be the redemption value.

[87] Statement 123R does not identify a specific line item in the income statement for presentation of the expense related to share-based payment arrangements.

[88] 17 CFR 229.10(e). All references to Item 10(e) of Regulation S-K also includes corresponding provisions of Item 10(h) of Regulation S-B with respect to small business issuers as well as US GAAP information of foreign private issuers under General Instruction C(e) of Form 20-F.

removing a recurring item, companies must meet the burden of demonstrating the usefulness of any measure that excludes recurring items, especially if the non-GAAP financial measure is used to evaluate performance."

The staff believes that a measure used by the management of Company H that excludes share-based payments internally to evaluate performance may be relevant disclosure for investors. In these cases, if Company H determines that the non-GAAP financial measure "Net Income Before Share-Based Payment Charge" does not violate any of the prohibitions from inclusion in filings with the Commission outlined in Item 10(e) of Regulation S-K, Company H's management would be required to disclose, among other items, the following:

- The reasons that the company's management believes that presentation of the non-GAAP financial measure provides useful information to investors regarding the company's financial condition and results of operations; and

- To the extent material, the additional purposes, if any, for which the company's management uses the non-GAAP financial measure that are not otherwise disclosed.[89]

In addition, the staff's response to Question 8 included in Frequently Asked Questions Regarding the Use of Non-GAAP Measures in June of 2003 notes that the inclusion of a non-GAAP financial measure may be misleading absent the following disclosures:

- The manner in which management uses the non-GAAP measure to conduct or evaluate its business;

- The economic substance behind management's decision to use such a measure;

- The material limitations associated with use of the non-GAAP financial measure as compared to the use of the most directly comparable GAAP financial measure;

- The manner in which management compensates for these limitations when using the non-GAAP financial measure; and

- The substantive reasons why management believes the non-GAAP financial measure provides useful information to investors.

Question 3: How could Company H demonstrate the effect of accounting for share-based payment transactions in accordance with Statement 123R and Regulation G and Item 10(e) of Regulation S-K in its Form 10-K?

Interpretive Response: The staff believes that including a discussion in MD&A addressing significant trends and variability of a company's earnings and changes in the significant components of certain line items is important to assist an investor in understanding the company's performance. The staff also understands that expenses from share-based payments might vary

in different ways and for different reasons than would other expenses. In particular, the staff believes Company H's investors would be well served by disclosure in MD&A that explains the components of the company's expenses, including, if material, identification of the amount of expense associated with share-based payment transactions and discussion of the reasons why such amounts have fluctuated from period to period.

Question 4: Would the staff object to Company H including a pro-forma income statement in its SEC filings that removes from net income the effects of accounting for share-based payment arrangements in accordance with Statement 123R?

Interpretive Response: Yes. Removal of the effects of accounting for sharebased payment arrangements in accordance with Statement 123R would not meet any of the conditions in Rule 11-01(a) of Regulation S-X for presentation of pro forma financial information. Further, the removal of the effects of accounting for share-based payment arrangements in accordance with Statement 123R would not meet any of the conditions in Rule 11-02(b)(6) of Regulation S-X to be reflected as a pro forma adjustment in circumstances where pro forma financial information is required under Rule 11-01(a) of Regulation S-X for other transactions such as recent or probable business combinations.

In addition, Item 10(e) of Regulation S-X prohibits presenting non-GAAP financial measures on the face of any pro forma financial information required to be disclosed by Article 11 of Regulation S-X. Further, a company may not present non-GAAP financial measures on the face of the company's financial statements prepared in accordance with GAAP or in the accompanying notes.

H. First Time Adoption of Statement 123R in an Interim Period

Facts: Company I's fiscal year begins on January 1, 2005. Company I plans to adopt Statement 123R on July 1, 2005, which is the beginning of its first interim period following the effective date. Company I previously recognized share-based payment compensation in accordance with Opinion 25.

Question 1: What disclosures are required in Company I's Form 10-Q for the third quarter of 2005?

Interpretive Response: The disclosures required by paragraphs 64-65, 84, and A240-242 of Statement 123R should be included in the Form 10-Q for the interim period when Statement 123R is first adopted. If Company I applies the modified retrospective method[90] in other than the first interim period of a fiscal year, the staff believes that the Form 10-Q for the period of adoption should include disclosure of the effects of the adoption of Statement 123R on previously reported interim periods.[91] If Company I applies the modified prospective method,[92] the financial statements for

---

[89] 17 CFR 229.10(e)(1).

[90] Statement 123R, paragraph 76.

[91] *See* Statement 123R, paragraph 77.

[92] Statement 123R, paragraph 74.

Company I's prior interim periods and fiscal years will not reflect any restated amounts. The staff believes that Company I should disclose this fact. Regardless of the transition method chosen, Company I should also provide the disclosures required by SAB Topic 11M, *Disclosure Of The Impact That Recently Issued Accounting Standards Will Have On The Financial Statements Of The Registrant When Adopted In A Future Period*, in interim and annual financial statements preceding the adoption of Statement 123R.

Facts: Company J plans to adopt Statement 123R by applying the modified retrospective method only to the preceding interim periods of its current fiscal year. Company J anticipates recording an adjustment upon the adoption of Statement 123R to reflect the cumulative effect of reclassifying certain sharebased payment arrangements as liabilities.

Question 2: Would Company J be required to apply the cumulative effect adjustment to the beginning of the fiscal year and to reflect the change in classification from liabilities to equity to its interim periods preceding adoption in accordance with Statement 3,[93] paragraph 10?

Interpretive Response: No. Statement 123R, paragraph 76, limits retrospective application to recording compensation cost for unvested awards based on the amounts previously determined under Statement 123 for pro forma footnote disclosure. Any adjustments to be recorded as a cumulative effect of a change in accounting principle should be recorded as of the date of adoption of Statement 123R, which may occur after the beginning of the fiscal year. Therefore, based on the guidance in Statement 123R, paragraphs 79-82, registrants are not required to apply the provisions of Statement 3, paragraph 10.

I. Capitalization of Compensation Cost Related to Share-Based Payment Arrangements

Facts: Company K is a manufacturing company that grants share options to its production employees. Company K has determined that the cost of the production employees' service is an inventoriable cost. As such, Company K is required to initially capitalize the cost of the share option grants to these production employees as inventory and later recognize the cost in the income statement when the inventory is consumed.[94]

Question: If Company K elects to adjust its period end inventory balance for the allocable amount of share-option cost through a period end adjustment to its financial statements, instead of incorporating the share-option cost through its inventory costing system, would this be considered a deficiency in internal controls?

Interpretive Response: No. Statement 123R does not prescribe the mechanism a company should use to incorporate a portion of share-option costs in an inventory-costing system. The staff believes Company K may accomplish this through a period end adjustment to its financial statements. Company K should establish appropriate controls surrounding the calculation and recording of this period end adjustment, as it would any other period end adjustment. The fact that the entry is recorded as a period end adjustment, by itself, should not impact management's ability to determine that the internal control over financial reporting, as defined by the SEC's rules implementing Section 404 of the Sarbanes-Oxley Act of 2002,[95] is effective.

J. Accounting for Income Tax Effects of Share-Based Payment Arrangements Upon Adoption of Statement 123R

Facts: In accordance with Statement 123R, reporting entities will need to determine whether deductions reported on tax returns for share-based payment awards exceed or are less than the cumulative compensation cost recognized for financial reporting. If the deductions exceed the cumulative compensation cost recognized for financial reporting, the entity generally should record any resulting excess tax benefits as additional paid-in capital. If deductions are less than the cumulative compensation cost recognized for financial reporting, the entity should record the write-off of the deferred tax asset, net of the related valuation allowance, against any remaining additional paid-in capital from previous awards accounted for in accordance with the fair value method of Statement 123 or Statement 123R, as applicable. The remaining balance, if any, of the write-off of the deferred tax asset shall be recognized in the income statement.[96]

Company L is an entity that previously recognized employee share-based payment costs under the intrinsic value method of Opinion 25. In this situation, Statement 123R states that Company L "shall calculate the amount available for offset [in additional paid-in capital] as the net amount of excess tax benefits that would have qualified as such had it instead adopted Statement 123 for recognition purposes pursuant to Statement 123's original effective date and transition method."[97]

Question: When is Company L required to calculate the additional paid-in capital from previous share-based payment awards that is available for offset against the write-off of a deferred tax asset?

Interpretive Response: Statement 123R will necessitate the tracking of tax attributes relating to share-based payment transactions with employees for a number of reasons, including the requirements related to any required write-off of excess deferred tax assets upon settlement of a share option. While

---

[93] Statement of Financial Accounting Standards No. 3, *Reporting Accounting Changes in Interim Financial Statements* ("Statement 3").

[94] Statement 123R, paragraph 5.

[95] Release No. 34-47986, June 5, 2003, *Management's Report on Internal Control Over Financial Reporting and Certification of Disclosure in Exchange Act Period Reports.*

[96] Statement 123R, paragraph 63.

[97] *Ibid.*

it is important that appropriate detailed information be available when needed for consideration, the timing as to when such information actually affects financial reporting will vary from company to company. In preparation for the adoption of Statement 123R, Company L should evaluate the level of detail which may be required considering its particular facts and circumstances.

Statement 123R is silent as to when the additional paid-in capital available for offset should be calculated. However, the staff notes that Company L would not be required to calculate the additional paid-in capital available for offset by the date it adopts Statement 123R. In addition, the staff notes that Statement 123R does not require disclosure of the additional paid-in capital available for offset.[98] The staff believes that Company L need only calculate the additional paid-in capital available for offset if and when Company L faces a situation in which deductions reported on its tax return are less than the relevant deferred tax asset. In addition, Company L need only perform the calculations periodically to the extent necessary to conclude that sufficient paid-in capital is available for the offset of the deduction shortfall.

K. Modification of Employee Share Options Prior to Adoption of Statement 123R

Facts: Company M is a public entity that historically applied the recognition provisions of Opinion 25 and intends to transition to Statement 123R under the modified prospective method of application.[99] In prior periods, Company M granted at-the-money share options to its employees in which the exercisability of the options is conditional only on performing service through the vesting date.[100] Since the time of grant, Company M's share price has fallen such that the share options are out-of-the-money. Prior to adoption of Statement 123R the share options are still unvested, and Company M intends to modify these unvested share options to accelerate the vesting. Company M has determined that the modification to accelerate vesting will not require recognition of compensation cost in its financial statements in the period of the modification under the provisions of Opinion 25.[101] However, Company M intends to reflect the compensation cost related to the modification in its fair value pro forma disclosures under Statement 123,[102] in the period the modification is made.

Question: Would the staff object to Company M reflecting the remaining compensation cost related to these share options in the fair value pro forma disclosures required under Statement 123 as a re-

sult of the modification in the period in which the modification was enacted?

Interpretive Response: No. The staff believes that an acceptable interpretation of Statement 123 is that the modification to accelerate the vesting of such share options would result in the recognition of the remaining amount of compensation cost in the period the modification is made, so long as the acceleration of vesting permits employees to exercise the share options in a circumstance when they would not otherwise have been able to do so absent the modification. The staff notes that the service period definition in Statement 123[103] indicates, "If the service period is not defined as an earlier or shorter period, it shall be presumed to be the vesting period." After the modification, Company M's share options will be vested pursuant to the awards' terms. Accordingly, under this interpretation, there is no remaining service period and any remaining unrecognized service cost for those share options should be recognized at the date of the modification. The staff believes that since the remaining unrecognized compensation cost is accelerated and recognized at the date of modification, no compensation cost would be recognized for these modified share options in the income statement in the periods after adoption of Statement 123R, absent any further modifications.

The staff reminds public entities that Statement 123, paragraph 47, indicates that for each year an income statement is provided, the terms of significant modifications of outstanding awards shall be disclosed. In order to inform investors about modification transactions and management's reasons for entering into those transactions, the staff believes that public entities should specifically disclose any modifications to accelerate the vesting of out-of-the-money share options in anticipation of adopting Statement 123R, including the reasons for modifying the option terms.

L. Application of the Measurement Provisions of Statement 123R to Foreign Private Issuers[104]

Question: Does the staff believe there are differences in the measurement provisions for share-based payment arrangements with employees under International Accounting Standards Board International Financial Reporting Standard 2, *Share-based Payment* ("IFRS 2") and Statement 123R that would result in a reconciling item under Item 17 or 18 of Form 20-F?

Interpretive Response: The staff believes that application of the guidance provided by IFRS 2 regarding the measurement of employee share options

---

[98] Statement 123R's disclosure requirements are described in paragraphs 64, 65, A240, A241 and A242.

[99] Statement 123R, paragraph 74.

[100] The terms of these share options do not define the service period as being other than the vesting period.

[101] *See* FASB Interpretation No. 44, *Accounting for Certain Transactions Involving Stock Compensation,* paragraph 36, which requires the recognition of compensation expense under Opinion 25 due to a modification of a share-based payment award only if,

absent the acceleration of vesting, the award would have otherwise been forfeited during the vesting period pursuant to its original terms.

[102] Statement 123, paragraph 45, as amended by Statement 148, *Accounting for Stock-Based Compensation - Transition and Disclosure* ("Statement 148").

[103] Statement 123, Appendix E.

[104] As defined in Regulation C § 230.405.

would generally result in a fair value measurement that is consistent with the fair value objective stated in Statement 123R.[105] Accordingly, the staff believes that application of Statement 123R's measurement guidance would not generally result in a reconciling item required to be reported under Item 17 or 18 of Form 20-F for a foreign private issuer that has complied with the provisions of IFRS 2 for share-based payment transactions with employees. However, the staff reminds foreign private issuers that there are certain differences between the guidance in IFRS 2 and Statement 123R that may result in reconciling items.[106]

M. Disclosures in MD&A Subsequent to Adoption of Statement 123R

Question: What disclosures should companies consider including in MD&A to highlight the effects of 1) differences between the accounting for share-based payment arrangements before and after the adoption of Statement 123R and 2) changes to share-based payment arrangements?

Interpretive Response: As stated in SEC Release FR-72, the principal objectives of MD&A are to give readers a view of a company through the eyes of management, to provide the context within which financial information should be analyzed and to provide information about the quality of, and potential variability of, a company's earnings and cash flow, so that investors can ascertain the likelihood that past performance is indicative of future performance. The adoption of Statement 123R may result in significant differences between the financial statements of periods before and after the adoption, especially for companies with significant share-based compensation programs that have followed the recognition provisions of Opinion 25 or that adopted the fair-value-based method for financial statement recognition in accordance with Statement 123 using the prospective method permitted by Statement 148. Furthermore, the staff understands that companies may refine their estimates of assumptions as a result of implementing Statement 123R and the interpretive guidance provided in this SAB. In addition, the staff understands that many companies are evaluating their share-based payment arrangements and making changes to those arrangements.

Each of these situations may affect the comparability of financial statements. Accordingly, to assist investors and other users of financial statements in understanding the financial results of a company that has adopted Statement 123R, the staff believes that companies should consider including in MD&A material qualitative and quantitative information about any of the following, as well as other information that could affect comparability of financial statements from period to period:

- Transition method selected (*e.g.*, modified prospective application or modified retrospective application) and the resulting financial statement impact in current and future reporting periods;

- Method utilized by the company to account for share-based payment arrangements in periods prior to the adoption of Statement 123R and the impact, or lack thereof, on the prior period financial statements;

- Modifications made to outstanding share options prior to the adoption of Statement 123R and the reason(s) for the modification;

- Differences in valuation methodologies or assumptions compared to those that were used in estimating the fair value of share options under Statement 123;

- Changes in the quantity or type of instruments used in share-based payment programs, such as a shift from share options to restricted shares;

- Changes in the terms of share-based payment arrangements, such as the addition of performance conditions;

- A discussion of the one-time effect, if any, of the adoption of Statement 123R, such as any cumulative adjustments recorded in the financial statements; and

- Total compensation cost related to nonvested awards not yet recognized and the weighted average period over which it is expected to be recognized.

---

[105] Statement 123R, paragraph A2.

[106] Statement 123R, paragraphs B258-B269, identify the more significant differences between IFRS 2 and Statement 123R.

PROXY RULES

PROXY RULES

TABLE OF CONTENTS

PROXY RULES

REGULATION 14A—SOLICITATION OF PROXIES

ATTENTION ELECTRONIC FILERS
THIS REGULATION SHOULD BE READ IN CONJUNCTION WITH REGULATION S- T (PART 232
OF THIS CHAPTER), WHICH GOVERNS THE PREPARATION AND SUBMISSION OF DOCU-
MENTS IN ELECTRONIC FORMAT. MANY PROVISIONS RELATING TO THE PREPARATION AND
SUBMISSION OF DOCUMENTS IN PAPER FORMAT CONTAINED IN THIS REGULATION ARE
SUPERSEDED BY THE PROVISIONS OF REGULATION S-T FOR DOCUMENTS REQUIRED TO BE
FILED IN ELECTRONIC FORMAT.

[¶ 40,001] Definitions

Reg. § 240.14a-1. Unless the context otherwise requires, all terms used in this regulation have
the same meanings as in the Act or elsewhere in the general rules and regulations thereunder. In
addition, the following definitions apply unless the context otherwise requires:

(a) *Associate.* The term "associate," used to indicate a relationship with any person, means (1) any
corporation or organization (other than the registrant or a majority owned subsidiary of the registrant)
of which such person is an officer or partner or is, directly or indirectly, the beneficial owner of 10
percent or more of any class of equity securities; (2) any trust or other estate in which such person has a
substantial beneficial interest or as to which such person serves as trustee or in a similar fiduciary
capacity; and (3) any relative or spouse of such person, or any relative of such spouse, who has the same
home as such person or who is a director or officer of the registrant or any of its parents or subsidiaries.

(b) *Employee benefit plan.* For purposes of §§ 240.14a-13, 240.14b-1 and 240.14b-2, the term
"employee benefit plan" means any purchase, savings, option, bonus, appreciation, profit sharing, thrift,
incentive, pension or similar plan primarily for employees, directors, trustees or officers.

(c) *Entity that exercises fiduciary powers.* The term "entity that exercises fiduciary powers" means
any entity that holds securities in nominee name or otherwise on behalf of a beneficial owner but does
not include a clearing agency registered pursuant to section 17A of the Act or a broker or a dealer.

(d) *Exempt employee benefit plan securities.* For purposes of §§ 240.14a-13, 240.14b-1 and 240.14b-2,
the term "exempt employee benefit plan securities" means: (1) securities of the registrant held by an
employee benefit plan, as defined in paragraph (b) of this section, where such plan is established by the
registrant; or (2) if notice regarding the current solicitation has been given pursuant to
§ 240.14a-13(a)(1)(ii)(C) or if notice regarding the current request for a list of names, addresses and
securities positions of beneficial owners has been given pursuant to § 240.14a-13(b)(3), securities of the
registrant held by an employee benefit plan, as defined in paragraph (b) of this section, where such plan
is established by an affiliate of the registrant.

(e) *Last fiscal year.* The term "last fiscal year" of the registrant means the last fiscal year of the
registrant ending prior to the date of the meeting for which proxies are to be solicited or if the
solicitation involves written authorizations or consents in lieu of a meeting, the earliest date they may be
used to effect corporate action.

(f) *Proxy.* The term "proxy" includes every proxy, consent or authorization within the meaning of
section 14(a) of the Act. The consent or authorization may take the form of failure to object or to dissent.

(g) *Proxy statement.* The term "proxy statement" means the statement required by § 240.14a-3(a)
whether or not contained in a single document.

(h) *Record date.* The term "record date" means the date as of which the record holders of securities
entitled to vote at a meeting or by written consent or authorization shall be determined.

(i) *Record holder.* For purposes of §§ 240.14a-13, 240.14b-1 and 240.14b-2, the term "record holder"
means any broker, dealer, voting trustee, bank, association or other entity that exercises fiduciary
powers which holds securities of record in nominee name or otherwise or as a participant in a clearing
agency registered pursuant to section 17A of the Act.

(j) *Registrant.* The term "registrant" means the issuer of the securities in respect of which proxies
are to be solicited.

(k) *Respondent bank.* For purposes of §§ 240.14a-13, 240.14b-1 and 240.14b-2, the term "respondent
bank" means any bank, association or other entity that exercises fiduciary powers which holds securities
on behalf of beneficial owners and deposits such securities for safekeeping with another bank, association or other entity that exercises fiduciary powers.

(l) *Solicitation.* (1) The terms "solicit" and "solicitation" include:

(i) Any request for a proxy whether or not accompanied by or included in a form of proxy;

(ii) Any request to execute or not to execute, or to revoke, a proxy; or

(iii) The furnishing of a form of proxy or other communication to security holders under circumstances reasonably calculated to result in the procurement, withholding or revocation of a proxy.

(2) The terms do not apply, however, to:

(i) The furnishing of a form of proxy to a security holder upon the unsolicited request of such security holder;

(ii) The performance by the registrant of acts required by § 240.14a-7;

(iii) The performance by any person of ministerial acts on behalf of a person soliciting a proxy; or

(iv) A communication by a security holder who does not otherwise engage in a proxy solicitation (other than a solicitation exempt under § 240.14a-2) starting how the security holder intends to vote and the reasons therefor, provided that the communication:

(A) is made by means of speeches in public forums, press releases, published or broadcast opinions, statements, or advertisements appearing in a broadcast media, or newspaper, magazine or other bona fide publication disseminated on a regular basis,

(B) is directed to persons to whom the security holder owes a fiduciary duty in connection with the voting of securities of a registrant held by the security holder, or

(C) is made in response to unsolicited requests for additional information with respect to a prior communication by the security holder made pursuant to this paragraph (*l*) (2) (iv).

[As last amended in Release No. 34-31326, October 16, 1992, 57 F.R. 48276.]

≫→ *CCH Note: **The SEC has stayed the effectiveness of proxy rule amendments adopted in Release 33-9136 pending resolution of a challenge filed by the Business Roundtable and the U.S. Chamber of Commerce in the U.S. Court of Appeals for the District of Columbia Circuit. See Release No. 33-9149, October 4, 2010.***

≫→ *Amended by Release No. 33-9136, effective November 15, 2010, 75 F.R. 56668.*

[¶ 40,011] Solicitations to Which § 240.14a-3 to § 240.14a-15 Apply

Reg. § 240.14a-2. Sections 240.14a-3 to 240.14a-15, except as specified below, apply to every solicitation of a proxy with respect to securities registered pursuant to section 12 of the Act, whether or not trading in such securities has been suspended. To the extent specified below, certain of these sections also apply to roll-up transactions that do not involve an entity with securities registered pursuant to Section 12 of the Act.

(a) Sections 240.14a-3 to 240.14a-15 do not apply to the following:

(1) Any solicitation by a person in respect to securities carried in his name or in the name of his nominee (otherwise than as voting trustee) or held in his custody, if such person—

(i) Receives no commission or remuneration for such solicitation, directly or indirectly, other than reimbursement of reasonable expenses,

(ii) Furnishes promptly to the person solicited (or such person's household in accordance with § 240.14a-3(e)(1)) a copy of all soliciting material with respect to the same subject matter or meeting received from all persons who shall furnish copies thereof for such purpose and who shall, if requested, defray the reasonable expenses to be incurred in forwarding such material, and

(iii) In addition, does no more than impartially instruct the person solicited to forward a proxy to the person, if any, to whom the person solicited desires to give a proxy, or impartially request from the person solicited instructions as to the authority to be conferred by the proxy and state that a proxy will be given if no instructions are received by a certain date.

(2) Any solicitation by a person in respect of securities of which he is the beneficial owner;

(3) Any solicitation involved in the offer and sale of securities registered under the Securities Act of 1933: *Provided,* That this paragraph shall not apply to securities to be issued in any transaction of the character specified in paragraph (a) of Rule 145 under that Act;

(4) Any solicitation with respect to a plan of reorganization under Chapter 11 of the Bankruptcy Reform Act of 1978, as amended, if made after the entry of an order approving the written disclosure statement concerning a plan of reorganization pursuant to section 1125 of said Act and after, or concurrently with, the transmittal of such disclosure statement as required by section 1125 of said Act;

(5) [Removed and reserved.]

(6) Any solicitation through the medium of a newspaper advertisement which informs security holders of a source from which they may obtain copies of a proxy statement, form of proxy and any other soliciting material and does no more than (i) name the registrant, (ii) state the reason for the advertisement, and (iii) identify the proposal or proposals to be acted upon by security holders.

(b) Sections 240.14a-3 to 240.14a-6 (other than 14a-6(g)), 240.14a-8, and 240.14a-10 to 14a-15 do not apply to the following:

(b) Sections 240.14a-3 to 240.14a-6 (other than paragraphs 14a-6(g) and 14a-6(p)), § 240.14a-8, § 240.14a-10, and §§ 240.14a-12 to 240.14a-15 do not apply to the following:

(1) Any solicitation by or on behalf of any person who does not, at any time during such solicitation, seek directly or indirectly, either on its own or another's behalf, the power to act as proxy for a security holder and does not furnish or otherwise request, or act on behalf of a person who furnishes or requests, a form of revocation, abstention, consent or authorization. *Provided, however,* that the exemption set forth in this paragraph shall not apply to:

(i) the registrant or an affiliate or associate of the registrant (other than an officer or director or any person serving in a similar capacity);

(ii) an officer or director of the registrant or any person serving in a similar capacity engaging in a solicitation financed directly or indirectly by the registrant;

(iii) an officer, director, affiliate or associate of a person that is ineligible to rely on the exemption set forth in this paragraph (other than persons specified in paragraph (b)(1)(i) of this section), or any person serving in a similar capacity;

(iv) any nominee for whose election as a director proxies are solicited;

(v) any person soliciting in opposition to a merger, recapitalization, reorganization, sale of assets or other extraordinary transaction recommended or approved by the board of directors of the registrant who is proposing or intends to propose an alternative transaction to which such person or one of its affiliates is a party;

(vi) any person who is required to report beneficial ownership of the registrant's equity securities on a Schedule 13D [§240.13d-101], unless such person has filed a Schedule 13D and has not disclosed pursuant to Item 4 thereto an intent, or reserved the right, to engage in a control transaction, or any contested solicitation for the election of directors;

(vii) any person who receives compensation from an ineligible person directly related to the solicitation of proxies, other than pursuant to §240.14a-13;

(viii) where the registrant is an investment company registered under the Investment Company Act of 1940 [15 U.S.C. 80a-1 et seq.], an "interested person" of that investment company, as that term is defined in Section 2(a)(19) of the Investment Company Act [15 U.S.C. 80a-2];

(ix) any person who, because of a substantial interest in the subject matter of the solicitation, is likely to receive a benefit from a successful solicitation that would not be shared pro rata by all other holders of the same class of securities, other than a benefit arising from the person's employment with the registrant; and

(x) any person acting on behalf of any of the foregoing.

(2) Any solicitation made otherwise than on behalf of the registrant where the total number of persons solicited is not more than ten; and

(3) The furnishing of proxy voting advice by any person (the "advisor") to any other person with whom the advisor has a business relationship, if:

(i) The advisor renders financial advice in the ordinary course of his business;

(ii) The advisor discloses to the recipient of the advice any significant relationship with the registrant or any of its affiliates, or a security holder proponent of the matter on which advice is given, as well as any material interests of the advisor in such matter;

(iii) The advisor receives no special commission or remuneration for furnishing the proxy voting advice from any person other than a recipient of the advice and other persons who receive similar advice under this subsection; and

(iv) The proxy voting advice is not furnished on behalf of any person soliciting proxies or on behalf of a participant in an election subject to the provisions of §240.14a-12(c); and

(4) Any solicitation in connection with a roll-up transaction as defined in Item 901(c) of Regulation S-K (§229.901 of this chapter) in which the holder of a security that is the subject of a proposed roll-up transaction engages in preliminary communications with other holders of securities that are the subject of the same limited partnership roll-up transaction for the purpose of determining whether to solicit proxies, consents, or authorizations in opposition to the proposed limited partnership roll-up transaction; *provided, however,* that:

(i) This exemption shall not apply to a security holder who is an affiliate of the registrant or general partner or sponsor; and

(ii) This exemption shall not apply to a holder of five percent (5%) or more of the outstanding securities of a class that is the subject of the proposed roll-up transaction who engages in the business of buying and selling limited partnership interests in the secondary market unless that holder discloses to the persons to whom the communications are made such ownership interest and any relations of the holder to the parties of the transaction or to the transaction itself, as required by § 240.14a-6(n)(1) and specified in the Notice of Exempt Preliminary Roll-up Communication (§ 240.14a-104). If the communication is oral, this disclosure may be provided to the security holder orally. Whether the communication is written or oral, the notice required by § 240.14a-6(n) and § 240.14a-104 shall be furnished to the Commission.

(5) Publication or distribution by a broker or a dealer of a research report in accordance with Rule 138 (§ 230.138 of this chapter) or Rule 139 (§ 230.139 of this chapter) during a transaction in which the broker or dealer or its affiliate participates or acts in an advisory role.

(6) Any solicitation by or on behalf of any person who does not seek directly or indirectly, either on its own or another's behalf, the power to act as proxy for a shareholder and does not furnish or otherwise request, or act on behalf of a person who furnishes or requests, a form of revocation, abstention, consent, or authorization in an electronic shareholder forum that is established, maintained or operated pursuant to the provisions of § 240.14a-17, provided that the solicitation is made more than 60 days prior to the date announced by a registrant for its next annual or special meeting of shareholders. If the registrant announces the date of its next annual or special meeting of shareholders less than 60 days before the meeting date, then the solicitation may not be made more than two days following the date of the registrant's announcement of the meeting date. Participation in an electronic shareholder forum does not eliminate a person's eligibility to solicit proxies after the date that this exemption is no longer available, or is no longer being relied upon, provided that any such solicitation is conducted in accordance with this regulation.

Amendment

(7) Any solicitation by or on behalf of any shareholder in connection with the formation of a nominating shareholder group pursuant to § 240.14a-11, provided that:

(i) The soliciting shareholder is not holding the registrant's securities with the purpose, or with the effect, of changing control of the registrant or to gain a number of seats on the board of directors that exceeds the maximum number of nominees that the registrant could be required to include under § 240.14a-11(d);

(ii) Each written communication includes no more than:

(A) A statement of each soliciting shareholder's intent to form a nominating shareholder group in order to nominate one or more directors under § 240.14a-11;

(B) Identification of, and a brief statement regarding, the potential nominee or nominees or, where no nominee or nominees have been identified, the characteristics of the nominee or nominees that the shareholder intends to nominate, if any;

(C) The percentage of voting power of the registrant's securities that are entitled to be voted on the election of directors that each soliciting shareholder holds or the aggregate percentage held by any group to which the shareholder belongs; and

(D) The means by which shareholders may contact the soliciting party.

(iii) Any written soliciting material published, sent or given to shareholders in accordance with this paragraph must be filed by the shareholder with the Commission, under the registrant's Exchange Act file number, or, in the case of a registrant that is an investment company registered under the Investment Company Act of 1940 (15 U.S.C. 80a-1 *et seq.*), under the registrant's Investment Company Act file number, no later than the date the material is first published, sent or given to shareholders. Three copies of the material must at the same time be filed with, or mailed for filing to, each national securities exchange upon which any class of securities of the registrant is listed and registered. The soliciting material must include a cover page in the form set forth in Schedule 14N (§ 240.14n-101) and the appropriate box on the cover page must be marked.

(iv) In the case of an oral solicitation made in accordance with the terms of this section, the nominating shareholder must file a cover page in the form set forth in Schedule 14N (§ 240.14n-101), with the appropriate box on the cover page marked, under the registrant's Exchange Act file number (or in the case of an investment company registered under the Investment Company Act of 1940 (15 U.S.C. 80a-1 *et seq.*), under the registrant's Investment Company Act file number), no later than the date of the first such communication.

Instruction to paragraph (b)(7). The exemption provided in paragraph (b)(7) of this section shall not apply to a shareholder that subsequently engages in soliciting or other nominating activities outside the scope of § 240.14a-2(b)(8) and § 240.14a-11 in connection with the subject election of directors or is or becomes a member of any other group, as determined under section 13(d)(3) of the Act (15 U.S.C. 78m(d)(3) and § 240.13d-5(b)), or otherwise, with persons engaged in soliciting or other nominating activities in connection with the subject election of directors.

(8) Any solicitation by or on behalf of a nominating shareholder or nominating shareholder group in support of its nominee that is included or that will be included on the registrant's form of proxy in accordance with § 240.14a-11 or for or against the registrant's nominee or nominees, provided that:

(i) The soliciting party does not, at any time during such solicitation, seek directly or indirectly, either on its own or another's behalf, the power to act as proxy for a shareholder and does not furnish or otherwise request, or act on behalf of a person who furnishes or requests, a form of revocation, abstention, consent or authorization;

(ii) Any written communication includes:

(A) The identity of each nominating shareholder and a description of his or her direct or indirect interests, by security holdings or otherwise;

(B) A prominent legend in clear, plain language advising shareholders that a shareholder nominee is or will be included in the registrant's proxy statement and that they should read the registrant's proxy statement when available because it includes important information (or, if the registrant's proxy statement is publicly available, advising shareholders of that fact and encouraging shareholders to read the registrant's proxy statement because it includes important information). The legend also must explain to shareholders that they can find the registrant's proxy statement, other soliciting material, and any other relevant documents at no charge on the Commission's Web site; and

(iii) Any written soliciting material published, sent or given to shareholders in accordance with this paragraph must be filed by the nominating shareholder or nominating shareholder group with the Commission, under the registrant's Exchange Act file number, or, in the case of a registrant that is an investment company registered under the Investment Company Act of 1940 (15 U.S.C. 80a-1 *et seq.*), under the registrant's Investment Company Act file number, no later than the date the material is first published, sent or given to shareholders. Three copies of the material must at the same time be filed with, or mailed for filing to, each national securities exchange upon which any class of securities of the registrant is listed and registered. The soliciting material must include a cover page in the form set forth in Schedule 14N (§ 240.14n-101) and the appropriate box on the cover page must be marked.

Instruction 1 to paragraph (b)(8). A nominating shareholder or nominating shareholder group may rely on the exemption provided in paragraph (b)(8) of this section only after receiving notice from the registrant in accordance with § 240.14a-11(g)(1) or § 240.14a-11(g)(3)(iv) that the registrant will include the nominating shareholder's or nominating shareholder group's nominee or nominees in its form of proxy.

Instruction 2 to paragraph (b)(8). Any solicitation by or on behalf of a nominating shareholder or nominating shareholder group in support of its nominee included or to be included on the registrant's form of proxy in accordance with § 240.14a-11 or for or against the registrant's nominee or nominees must be made in reliance on the exemption provided in paragraph (b)(8) of this section and not on any other exemption.

Instruction 3 to paragraph (b)(8). The exemption provided in paragraph (b)(8) of this section shall not apply to a person that subsequently engages in soliciting or other nominating activities outside the scope of § 240.14a-11 in connection with the subject election of directors or is or becomes a member of any other group, as determined under section 13(d)(3) of the Act (15 U.S.C. 78m(d)(3) and § 240.13d-5(b)), or otherwise, with persons engaged in soliciting or other nominating activities in connection with the subject election of directors.

End of Amendment

[As last amended in Release No. 33-9136, effective November 15, 2010, 75 F.R. 56668.]

[¶ 40,021] Information to Be Furnished Security Holders

Reg. § 240.14a-3. (a) No solicitation subject to this regulation shall be made unless each person solicited is concurrently furnished or has previously been furnished with:

(1) A publicly-filed preliminary or definitive proxy statement, in the form and manner described in § 240.14a-16, containing the information specified in Schedule 14A (§ 240.14a–101);

(2) A preliminary or definitive written proxy statement included in a registration statement filed under the Securities Act of 1933 on Form S-4 or F-4 (§ 239.25 or § 239.34 of this chapter) or Form N–14 (§ 239.23 of this chapter) and containing the information specified in such Form; or

(3) A publicly-filed preliminary or definitive proxy statement, not in the form and manner described in § 240.14a-16, containing the information specified in Schedule 14A (§ 240.14a–101), if:

(i) The solicitation relates to a business combination transaction as defined in § 230.165 of this chapter, as well as transactions for cash consideration requiring disclosure under Item 14 of § 240.14a-101.

(ii) The solicitation may not follow the form and manner described in § 240.14a-16 pursuant to the laws of the state of incorporation of the registrant:

(b) If the solicitation is made on behalf of the registrant, other than an investment company registered under the Investment Company Act of 1940, and relates to an annual (or special meeting in lieu of the annual) meeting of security holders, or written consent in lieu of such meeting, at which directors are to be elected, each proxy statement furnished pursuant to paragraph (a) of this section shall be accompanied or preceded by an annual report to security holders as follows:

(1) The report shall include, for the registrant and its subsidiaries, consolidated and audited balance sheets as of the end of the two most recent fiscal years and audited statements of income and cash flows for each of the three most recent fiscal years prepared in accordance with Regulation S-X (part 210 of this chapter), except that the provisions of Article 3 (other than §§ 210.3-03(e), 210.3-04 and 210.3-20) and Article 11 shall not apply. Any financial statement schedules or exhibits or separate financial statements which may otherwise be required in filings with the Commission may be omitted. If the financial statements of the registrant and its subsidiaries consolidated in the annual report filed or to be filed with the Commission are not required to be audited, the financial statements required by this paragraph may be unaudited. A smaller reporting company may provide the information in Article 8 of Regulation S-X (§ 210.8 of this chapter) in lieu of the financial information required by this paragraph 9(b)(1).

Note 1 to Paragraph (b)(1): If the financial statements for a period prior to the most recently completed fiscal year have been examined by a predecessor accountant, the separate report of the predecessor accountant may be omitted in the report to security holders, provided the registrant has obtained from the predecessor accountant a reissued report covering the prior period presented and the successor accountant clearly indicates in the scope paragraph of his or her report (a) that the financial statements of the prior period were examined by other accountants, (b) the date of their report, (c) the type of opinion expressed by the predecessor accountant and (d) the substantive reasons therefore, if it was other than unqualified. It should be noted, however, that the separate report of any predecessor accountant is required in filings with the Commission. If, for instance, the financial statements in the annual report to security holders are incorporated by reference in a Form 10-K, the separate report of a predecessor accountant shall be filed in Part II or in Part IV as a financial statement schedule.

Note 2 to Paragraph (b)(1): For purposes of complying with § 240.14a-3, if the registrant has changed its fiscal closing date, financial statements covering two years and one period of nine to 12 months shall be deemed to satisfy the requirements for statements of income and cash flows for the three most recent fiscal years.

(2)(i) Financial statements and notes thereto shall be presented in roman type at least as large and as legible as 10-point modern type. If necessary for convenient presentation, the financial statements may be in roman type as large and as legible as 8-point modern type. All type shall be leaded at least 2-point.

(ii) Where the annual report to security holders is delivered through an electronic medium, issuers may satisfy legibility requirements applicable to printed documents, such as type size and font, by presenting all required information in a format readily communicated to investors.

(3) The report shall contain the supplementary financial information required by Item 302 of Regulation S-K (§ 229.302 of this chapter).

(4) The report shall contain information concerning changes in and disagreements with accountants on accounting and financial disclosure required by Item 304 of Regulation S-K (§ 229.304 of this chapter).

(5)(i) The report shall contain the selected financial data required by Item 301 of Regulation S-K (§ 229.301 of this chapter).

(ii) The report shall contain management's discussion and analysis of financial condition and results of operations required by Item 303 of Regulation S-K (§ 229.303 of this chapter).

(iii) The report shall contain the quantitative and qualitative disclosures about market risk required by Item 305 of Regulation S-K (§ 229.305 of this chapter).

(6) The report shall contain a brief description of the business done by the registrant and its subsidiaries during the most recent fiscal year which will, in the opinion of management, indicate the general nature and scope of the business of the registrant and its subsidiaries.

(7) The report shall contain information relating to the registrant's industry segments, classes of similar products or services, foreign and domestic operations and exports sales required by paragraphs (b), (c)(1)(i) and (d) of Item 101 of Regulation S-K (§ 229.101 of this chapter).

(8) The report shall identify each of the registrant's directors and executive officers, and shall indicate the principal occupation or employment of each such person and the name and principal business of any organization by which such person is employed.

(9) The report shall contain the market price of and dividends on the registrant's common equity and related security holder matters required by Items 201(a), (b) and (c) of Regulation S-K

(§ 229.201(a), (b) and (c) of this chapter). If the report precedes or accompanies a proxy statement or information statement relating to an annual meeting of security holders at which directors are to be elected (or special meeting or written consents in lieu of such meeting), furnish the performance graph required by Item 201(e) (§ 229.201(e) of this chapter).

(10) The registrant's proxy statement, or the report, shall contain an undertaking in bold face or otherwise reasonably prominent type to provide without charge to each person solicited upon the written request of any such person, a copy of the registrant's annual report on Form 10-K, including the financial statements and the financial statement schedules, required to be filed with the Commission pursuant to Rule 13a-1 (§ 240.13a-1 of this chapter) under the Act for the registrant's most recent fiscal year, and shall indicate the name and address (including title or department) of the person to whom such a written request is to be directed. In the discretion of management, a registrant need not undertake to furnish without charge copies of all exhibits to its Form 10-K, provided that the copy of the annual report on Form 10-K furnished without charge to requesting security holders is accompanied by a list briefly describing all the exhibits not contained therein and indicating that the registrant will furnish any exhibit upon the payment of a specified reasonable fee, which fee shall be limited to the registrant's reasonable expenses in furnishing such exhibit. If the registrant's annual report to security holders complies with all of the disclosure requirements of Form 10-K and is filed with the Commission in satisfaction of its Form 10-K filing requirements, such registrant need not furnish a separate Form 10-K to security holders who receive a copy of such annual report.

Note to Paragraph (b)(10): Pursuant to the undertaking required by paragraph (b)(10) of this section, a registrant shall furnish a copy of its annual report on Form 10-K (§ 249.310 of this chapter) to a beneficial owner of its securities upon receipt of a written request from such person. Each request must set forth a good faith representation that, as of the record date for the solicitation requiring the furnishing of the annual report to security holders pursuant to paragraph (b) of this section, the person making the request was a beneficial owner of securities entitled to vote.

(11) Subject to the foregoing requirements, the report may be in any form deemed suitable by management and the information required by paragraphs (b)(5) to (b)(10) of this section may be presented in an appendix or other separate section of the report, provided that the attention of security holders is called to such presentation.

Note: Registrants are encouraged to utilize tables, schedules, charts and graphic illustrations of present financial information in an understandable manner. Any presentation of financial information must be consistent with the data in the financial statements contained in the report and, if appropriate, should refer to relevant portions of the financial statements and notes thereto.

(12) [Removed and reserved in Release No. 34-34832, effective November 23, 1994, 59 F.R. 52689.]

(13) Paragraph (b) of this section shall not apply, however, to solicitations made on behalf of the registrant before the financial statements are available if a solicitation is being made at the same time in opposition to the registrant and if the registrant's proxy statement includes an undertaking in bold face type to furnish such annual report to all persons being solicited at least 20 calendar days before the date of the meeting or, if the solicitation refers to a written consent or authorization in lieu of a meeting, at least 20 calendar days prior to the earliest date on which it may be used to effect corporate action.

(c) Seven copies of the report sent to security holders pursuant to this rule shall be mailed to the Commission, solely for its information, not later than the date on which such report is first sent or given to security holders or the date on which preliminary copies, or definitive copies, if preliminary filing was not required, of solicitation material are filed with the Commission pursuant to Rule 14a-6, whichever date is later. The report is not deemed to be "soliciting material" or to be "filed" with the Commission or subject to this regulation otherwise than as provided in this Rule, or to the liabilities of section 18 of the Act, except to the extent that the registrant specifically requests that it be treated as a part of the proxy soliciting material or incorporates it in the proxy statement or other filed report by reference.

(d) An annual report to security holders prepared on an integrated basis pursuant to General Instruction H to Form 10-K (§ 249.310 of this chapter) may also be submitted in satisfaction of this section. When filed as the annual report on Form 10-K, responses to the Items of that form are subject to section 18 of the Act notwithstanding paragraph (c) of this section.

(e) Notwithstanding paragraphs (a) and (b) of this section:

(e)(1)(i) A registrant will be considered to have delivered an annual report to security holders, proxy statement or Notice of Internet Availability of Proxy Materials, as described in § 240.14a-16, to all security holders of record who share an address if:

(A) The registrant delivers one annual report to security holders, proxy statement or Notice of Internet Availability of Proxy Materials, as applicable, to the shared address;

(B) The registrant addresses the annual report to security holders, proxy statement or Notice of Internet Availability of Proxy Materials, as applicable, to the security holders as a group (for example, "ABC Fund [or Corporation] Security Holders," "Jane Doe and Household," "The Smith Family"), to each of the security holders individually (for example, "John Doe and Richard Jones") or to the security holders in a form to which each of the security holders has consented in writing;

Note to paragraph (e)(1)(i)(B): Unless the registrant addresses the annual report to security holders, proxy statement or Notice of Internet Availability of Proxy Materials to the security holders as a group or to each of the security holders individually, it must obtain, from each security holder to be included in the householded group, a separate affirmative written consent to the specific form of address the registrant will use.

(C) The security holders consent, in accordance with paragraph (e)(1)(ii) of this section, to delivery of one annual report to security holders or proxy statement, as applicable;

(D) With respect to delivery of the proxy statement or Notice of Internet Availability of Proxy Materials, the registrant delivers, together with or subsequent to delivery of the proxy statement, a separate proxy card for each security holder at the shared address; and

(E) The registrant includes an undertaking in the proxy statement to deliver promptly upon written or oral request a separate copy of the annual report to security holders, proxy statement or Notice of Internet Availability of Proxy Materials, as applicable, to a security holder at a shared address to which a single copy of the document was delivered.

(ii) *Consent.* (A) *Affirmative written consent.* Each security holder must affirmatively consent, in writing, to delivery of one annual report to security holders or proxy statement, as applicable. A security holder's affirmative written consent will be considered valid only if the security holder has been informed of:

(*1*) The duration of the consent;

(*2*) The specific types of documents to which the consent will apply;

(*3*) The procedures the security holder must follow to revoke consent; and

(*4*) The registrant's obligation to begin sending individual copies to a security holder within thirty days after the security holder revokes consent.

(B) *Implied consent.* The registrant need not obtain affirmative written consent from a security holder for purposes of paragraph (e)(1)(ii)(A) of this section if all of the following conditions are met:

(*1*) The security holder has the same last name as the other security holders at the shared address or the registrant reasonably believes that the security holders are members of the same family;

(*2*) The registrant has sent the security holder a notice at least 60 days before the registrant begins to rely on this section concerning delivery of annual reports to security holders, proxy statements or Notices of Internet Availability of Proxy Materials to that security holder. The notice must:

(*i*) Be a separate written document;

(*ii*) State that only one annual report to security holders, proxy statement or Notice of Internet Availability of Proxy Materials, as applicable, will be delivered to the shared address unless the registrant receives contrary instructions;

(*iii*) Include a toll-free telephone number, or be accompanied by a reply form that is pre-addressed with postage provided, that the security holder can use to notify the registrant that the security holder wishes to receive a separate annual report to security holders, proxy statement or Notice of Internet Availability of Proxy Materials;

(*iv*) State the duration of the consent;

(*v*) Explain how a security holder can revoke consent;

(*vi*) State that the registrant will begin sending individual copies to a security holder within thirty days after the security holder revokes consent; and

(*vii*) Contain the following prominent statement, or similar clear and understandable statement, in bold-face type: "Important Notice Regarding Delivery of Security Holder Documents." This statement also must appear on the envelope in which the notice is delivered. Alternatively, if the notice is delivered separately from other communications to security holders, this statement may appear either on the notice or on the envelope in which the notice is delivered.

Note to paragraph (e)(1)(ii)(B)(2):

The notice should be written in plain English. See § 230.421(d)(2) of this chapter for a discussion of plain English principles.

(*3*) The registrant has not received the reply form or other notification indicating that the security holder wishes to continue to receive an individual copy of the annual report to security holders, proxy statement or Notice of Internet Availability of Proxy Materials, as applicable, within 60 days after the registrant sent the notice required by paragraph (e)(1)(ii)(B)(2) of this section; and

(*4*) The registrant delivers the document to a post office box or residential street address.

Note to paragraph (e)(1)(ii)(B)(4):

The registrant can assume that a street address is residential unless the registrant has information that indicates the street address is a business.

(iii) *Revocation of consent.* If a security holder, orally or in writing, revokes consent to delivery of one annual report to security holders, proxy statement or Notice of Internet Availability of Proxy Materials to a shared address, the registrant must begin sending individual copies to that security holder within 30 days after the registrant receives revocation of the security holder's consent.

(iv) *Definition of address.* Unless otherwise indicated, for purposes of this section, *address* means a street address, a post office box number, an electronic mail address, a facsimile telephone number or other similar destination to which paper or electronic documents are delivered, unless otherwise provided in this section. If the registrant has reason to believe that the address is a street address of a multi-unit building, the address must include the unit number.

Note to paragraph (e) (1).

A person other than the registrant making a proxy solicitation may deliver a single proxy statement to security holders of record or beneficial owners who have separate accounts and share an address if: (a) the registrant or intermediary has followed the procedures in this section; and (b) the registrant or intermediary makes available the shared address information to the person in accordance with § 240.14a-7(a)(2)(i) and (ii).

(2) Notwithstanding paragraphs (a) and (b) of this section, unless state law requires otherwise, a registrant is not required to send an annual report to security holders, proxy statement or Notice of Internet Availability of Proxy Materials to a security holder if:

(i) An annual report to security holders and a proxy statement, or a Notice of Internet of Availability of Proxy Materials, for two consecutive annual meetings; or

(ii) All, and at least two, payments (if sent by first class mail) of dividends or interest on securities, or dividend reinvestment confirmations, during a twelve month period, have been mailed to such security holder's address and have been returned as undeliverable. If any such security holder delivers or causes to be delivered to the registrant written notice setting forth his then current address for security holder communications purposes, the registrant's obligation to deliver an annual report to security holders, a proxy statement or a Notice of Internet Availability of Proxy Materials under this section is reinstated.

(f) The provisions of paragraph (a) of this section shall not apply to a communication made by means of speeches in public forums, press releases, published or broadcast opinions, statements, or advertisements appearing in a broadcast media, newspaper, magazine or other bona fide publication disseminated on a regular basis, provided that:

(1) No form of proxy, consent or authorization or means to execute the same is provided to a security holder in connection with the communication; and

(2) At the time the communication is made, a definitive proxy statement is on file with the Commission pursuant to § 240.14a-6(b).

[As last amended in Release No. 34-55146A, effective April 1, 2008, 73 F.R. 17809 (technical correction).]

»»→ *CCH Note: The SEC has stayed the effectiveness of proxy rule amendments adopted in Release 33-9136 pending resolution of a challenge filed by the Business Roundtable and the U.S. Chamber of Commerce in the U.S. Court of Appeals for the District of Columbia Circuit. See Release No. 33-9149, October 4, 2010.*

»»→ *Amended by Release No. 33-9136, effective November 15, 2010, 75 F.R. 56668.*

[¶ 40,031] Requirements as to Proxy

Reg. § 240.14a-4. (a) The form of proxy (1) shall indicate in bold-face type whether or not the proxy is solicited on behalf of the registrant's board of directors or, if provided other than by a majority of the board of directors, shall indicate in bold-face type on whose behalf the solicitation is made; (2) shall provide a specifically designated blank space for dating the proxy card; and (3) shall identify clearly and impartially each separate matter intended to be acted upon, whether or not related to or conditioned on the approval of other matters, and whether proposed by the registrant or by security holders. No reference need be made, however, to proposals as to which discretionary authority is conferred pursuant to paragraph (c) of this section.

Note to paragraph (a) (3) (electronic filers): Electronic filers shall satisfy the filing requirements of Rule 14a-6(a) or (b) (§ 240.14a-6(a) or (b)) with respect to the form of proxy by filing the form of proxy as an appendix at the end of the proxy statement. Forms of proxy shall not be filed as exhibits or separate documents within an electronic submission.

(b)(1) Means shall be provided in the form of proxy whereby the person solicited is afforded an opportunity to specify by boxes a choice between approval or disapproval of, or abstention with respect to each separate matter referred to therein as intended to be acted upon, other than elections to office. A proxy may confer discretionary authority with respect to matters as to which a choice is not specified by the security holder provided that the form of proxy states in bold-face type how it is intended to vote the shares represented by the proxy in each such case.

(2) A form of proxy which provides for the election of directors shall set forth the names of persons nominated for election as directors. Such form of proxy shall clearly provide any of the following means for security holders to withhold authority to vote for each nominee:

*Amendment*_____

(2) A form of proxy that provides for the election of directors shall set forth the names of persons nominated for election as directors, including any person whose nomination by a shareholder or shareholder group satisfies the requirements of § 240.14a-11, an applicable state or foreign law provision, or a registrant's governing documents as they relate to the inclusion of shareholder director nominees in the registrant's proxy materials. Such form of proxy shall clearly provide any of the following means for security holders to withhold authority to vote for each nominee:

*End of Amendment*_____

(i) a box opposite the name of each nominee which may be marked to indicate that authority to vote for such nominee is withheld; or

(ii) an instruction in bold-face type which indicates that the security holder may withhold authority to vote for any nominee by lining through or otherwise striking out the name of any nominee; or

(iii) designated blank spaces in which the security holder may enter the names of nominees with respect to whom the shareholder chooses to withhold authority to vote; or

(iv) any other similar means, provided that clear instructions are furnished indicating how the security holder may withhold authority to vote for any nominee.

Such form of proxy also may provide a means for the security holder to grant authority to vote for the nominees set forth, as a group, provided that there is a similar means for the security holder to withhold authority to vote for such group of nominees. Any such form of proxy which is executed by the security holder in such manner as not to withhold authority to vote for the election of any nominee shall be deemed to grant such authority, provided that the form of proxy so states in bold-face type.

*Amendment*_____

Such form of proxy also may provide a means for the security holder to grant authority to vote for the nominees set forth, as a group, provided that there is a similar means for the security holder to withhold authority to vote for such group of nominees. Any such form of proxy which is executed by the security holder in such manner as not to withhold authority to vote for the election of any nominee shall be deemed to grant such authority, provided that the form of proxy so states in bold-face type. Means to grant authority to vote for any nominees as a group or to withhold authority for any nominees as a group may not be provided if the form of proxy includes one or more shareholder nominees in accordance with § 240.14a-11, an applicable state or foreign law provision, or a registrant's governing documents as they relate to the inclusion of shareholder director nominees in the registrant's proxy materials.

*End of Amendment*_____

Instructions. 1. Paragraph (2) does not apply in the case of a merger, consolidation or other plan if the election of directors is an integral part of the plan.

2. If applicable state law gives legal effect to votes cast against a nominee, then in lieu of, or in addition to, providing a means for security holders to withhold authority to vote, the issuer should provide a similar means for security holders to vote against each nominee.

(c) A proxy may confer discretionary authority to vote on any of the following matters:

(1) For an annual meeting of shareholders, if the registrant did not have notice of the matter at least 45 days before the date on which the registrant first sent its proxy materials for the prior year's annual meeting of shareholders (or date specified by an advance notice provision), and a specific statement to that effect is made in the proxy statement or form of proxy. If during the prior year the registrant did not hold an annual meeting, or if the date of the meeting has changed more than 30 days from the prior year, then notice must not have been received a reasonable time before the registrant sends its proxy materials for the current year.

(2) In the case in which the registrant has received timely notice in connection with an annual meeting of shareholders (as determined under paragraph (c)(1) of this section), if the registrant includes, in the proxy statement, advice on the nature of the matter and how the registrant intends to exercise its discretion to vote on each matter. However, even if the registrant includes this information in its proxy statement, it may not exercise discretionary voting authority on a particular proposal if the proponent:

(i) Provides the registrant with a written statement, within the time-frame determined under paragraph (c)(1) of this section, that the proponent intends to deliver a proxy statement and form of proxy to holders of at least the percentage of the company's voting shares required under applicable law to carry the proposal;

(ii) Includes the same statement in its proxy materials filed under § 240.14a-6; and

(iii) Immediately after soliciting the percentage of shareholders required to carry the proposal, provides the registrant with a statement from any solicitor or other person with knowledge that the necessary steps have been taken to deliver a proxy statement and form of proxy to holders of at least the percentage of the company's voting shares required under applicable law to carry the proposal.

(3) For solicitations other than for annual meetings or for solicitations by persons other than the registrant, matters which the persons making the solicitation do not know, a reasonable time before the solicitation, are to be presented at the meeting, if a specific statement to that effect is made in the proxy statement or form of proxy.

(4) Approval of the minutes of the prior meeting if such approval does not amount to ratification of the action taken at that meeting;

(5) The election of any person to any office for which a bona fide nominee is named in the proxy statement and such nominee is unable to serve or for good cause will not serve.

(6) Any proposal omitted from the proxy statement and form of proxy pursuant to § 240.14a-8 or § 240.14a-9 of this chapter.

(7) Matters incident to the conduct of the meeting.

(d) No proxy shall confer authority (1) to vote for the election of any person to any office for which a bona fide nominee is not named in the proxy statement, (2) to vote at any annual meeting other than the next annual meeting (or any adjournment thereof) to be held after the date on which the proxy statement and form of proxy are first sent or given to security holders, (3) to vote with respect to more than one meeting (and any adjournment thereof) or more than one consent solicitation or (4) to consent to or authorize any action other than the action proposed to be taken in the proxy statement, or matters referred to in paragraph (c) of this rule. A person shall not be deemed to be a bona fide nominee and he shall not be named as such unless he has consented to being named in the proxy statement and to serve if elected. *Provided, however,* that nothing in this section 240.14a-4 shall prevent any person soliciting in support of nominees who, if elected, would constitute a minority of the board of directors, from seeking authority to vote for nominees named in the registrant's proxy statement, so long as the soliciting party:

(i) seeks authority to vote in the aggregate for the number of director positions then subject to election;

(ii) represents that it will vote for all the registrant nominees, other than those registrant nominees specified by the soliciting party;

(iii) provides the security holder an opportunity to withhold authority with respect to any other registrant nominee by writing the name of that nominee on the form of proxy; and

(iv) states on the form of proxy and in the proxy statement that there is no assurance that the registrant's nominees will serve if elected with any of the soliciting party's nominees.

(e) The proxy statement or form of proxy shall provide, subject to reasonable specified conditions, that the shares represented by the proxy will be voted and that where the person solicited specifies by means of a ballot provided pursuant to paragraph (b) a choice with respect to any matter to be acted upon, the shares will be voted in accordance with the specifications so made.

(f) No person conducting a solicitation subject to this regulation shall deliver a form of proxy, consent or authorization to any security holder unless the security holder concurrently receives, or has previously received, a definitive proxy statement that has been filed with the Commission pursuant to § 240.14a-6(b).

[As last amended in Release No. 33-9136, effective November 15, 2010, 75 F.R. 56668.]

⫸ *CCH Note: The SEC has stayed the effectiveness of proxy rule amendments adopted in Release 33-9136 pending resolution of a challenge filed by the Business Roundtable and the U.S. Chamber of Commerce in the U.S. Court of Appeals for the District of Columbia Circuit. See Release No. 33-9149, October 4, 2010.*

⫸ *Amended by Release No. 33-9136, effective November 15, 2010, 75 F.R. 56668.*

[¶ 40,041] Presentation of Information in Proxy Statement

Reg. § 240.14a-5. (a) The information included in the proxy statement shall be clearly presented and the statements made shall be divided into groups according to subject matter and the various groups of statements shall be preceded by appropriate headings. The order of items and sub-items in the schedule need not be followed. Where practicable and appropriate, the information shall be presented in tabular form. All amounts shall be stated in figures. Information required by more than one applicable item need not be repeated. No statement need be made in response to any item or sub-item which is inapplicable.

(b) Any information required to be included in the proxy statement as to terms of securities or other subject matter which from a standpoint of practical necessity must be determined in the future may be stated in terms of present knowledge and intention. To the extent practicable, the authority to be conferred concerning each such matter shall be confined within limits reasonably related to the need for discretionary authority. Subject to the foregoing, information which is not known to the persons on whose behalf the solicitation is to be made and which it is not reasonably within the power of such persons to ascertain or procure may be omitted, if a brief statement of the circumstances rendering such information unavailable is made.

(c) Any information contained in any other proxy soliciting material which has been furnished to each person solicited in connection with the same meeting or subject matter may be omitted from the proxy statement, if a clear reference is made to the particular document containing such information.

(d) (1) All printed proxy statements shall be in roman type at least as large and as legible as 10-point modern type, except that to the extent necessary for convenient presentation financial statements and other tabular data, but not the notes thereto, may be in roman type at least as large and as legible as 8-point modern type. All such type shall be leaded at least 2 points.

(2) Where a proxy statement is delivered through an electronic medium, issuers may satisfy legibility requirements applicable to printed documents, such as type size and font, by presenting all required information in a format readily communicated to investors.

(e) All proxy statements shall disclose, under an appropriate caption, the following dates:

(1) The deadline for submitting shareholder proposals for inclusion in the registrant's proxy statement and form of proxy for the registrant's next annual meeting, calculated in the manner provided in § 240.14a-8(e) (Question 5); and

(2) The date after which notice of a shareholder proposal submitted outside the processes of § 240.14a-8 is considered untimely, either calculated in the manner provided by § 240.14a-4(c) (1) or as established by the registrant's advance notice provision, if any, authorized by applicable state law.

*Amendment*_____

(e) All proxy statements shall disclose, under an appropriate caption, the following dates:

(1) The deadline for submitting shareholder proposals for inclusion in the registrant's proxy statement and form of proxy for the registrant's next annual meeting, calculated in the manner provided in § 240.14a-8(e) (Question 5);

(2) The date after which notice of a shareholder proposal submitted outside the processes of § 240.14a-8 is considered untimely, either calculated in the manner provided by § 240.14a-4(c) (1) or as established by the registrant's advance notice provision, if any, authorized by applicable state law; and

(3) The deadline for submitting nominees for inclusion in the registrant's proxy statement and form of proxy pursuant to § 240.14a-11, an applicable state or foreign law provision, or a registrant's governing documents as they relate to the inclusion of shareholder director nominees in the registrant's proxy materials for the registrant's next annual meeting of shareholders.

*End of Amendment*_____

(f) If the date of the next annual meeting is subsequently advanced or delayed by more than 30 calendar days from the date of the annual meeting to which the proxy statement relates, the registrant shall, in a timely manner, inform shareholders of such change, and the new dates referred to in paragraphs (e) (1) and (e) (2) of this section, by including a notice, under Item 5, in its earliest possible quarterly report on Form 10-Q (§ 249.308a of this chapter), or, in the case of investment companies, in a shareholder report under § 270.30d-1 of this chapter under the Investment Company Act of 1940, or, if impracticable, any means reasonably calculated to inform shareholders.

[As last amended in Release No. 33-9136, effective November 15, 2010, 75 F.R. 56668.]

⫸→ *CCH Note: The SEC has stayed the effectiveness of proxy rule amendments adopted in Release 33-9136 pending resolution of a challenge filed by the Business Roundtable and the U.S. Chamber of Commerce in the U.S. Court of Appeals for the District of Columbia Circuit. See Release No. 33-9149, October 4, 2010.*

⫸→ *Amended by Release No. 33-9136, effective November 15, 2010, 75 F.R. 56668.*

[¶ 40,051] Filing Requirements

Reg. § 240.14a-6. (a) *Preliminary proxy statement.* Five preliminary copies of the proxy statement and form of proxy shall be filed with the Commission at least 10 calendar days prior to the date definitive copies of such material are first sent or given to security holders, or such shorter period prior to that date as the Commission may authorize upon a showing of good cause thereunder. A registrant, however, shall not file with the Commission a preliminary proxy statement, form of proxy or other soliciting material to be furnished to security holders concurrently therewith if the solicitation relates to an annual (or special meeting in lieu of the annual) meeting, or for an investment company registered under the Investment Company Act of 1940 [15 U.S.C. 80a-1 *et seq.*] or a business development company, if the solicitation relates to any meeting of security holders at which the only matters to be acted upon are:

(1) the election of directors;

(2) the election, approval or ratification of accountant(s);

(3) a security holder proposal included pursuant to Rule 14a-8 [§ 240.14a-8 of this chapter];

(4) The approval or ratification of a plan as defined in paragraph (a)(6)(ii) of Item 402 of Regulation S-K (§ 229.402(a)(6)(ii) of this chapter) or amendments to such a plan;

(5) with respect to an investment company registered under the Investment Company Act of 1940 or a business development company, a proposal to continue, without change, any advisory or other contract or agreement that previously has been the subject of a proxy solicitation for which proxy material was filed with the Commission pursuant to this rule;

(6) with respect to an open-end investment company registered under the Investment Company Act of 1940, a proposal to increase the number of shares authorized to be issued; and/or

(7) A vote to approve the compensation of executives as required pursuant to Section 111(e)(1) of the Emergency Economic Stabilization Act of 2008 (12 U.S.C. 5221(e)(1)) and § 240.14a-20.

*Amendment*_____

(4) A shareholder nominee for director included pursuant to § 240.14a-11, an applicable state or foreign law provision, or a registrant's governing documents as they relate to the inclusion of shareholder director nominees in the registrant's proxy materials.

(5) The approval or ratification of a plan as defined in paragraph (a)(6)(ii) of Item 402 of Regulation S-K (§ 229.402(a)(6)(ii) of this chapter) or amendments to such a plan;

(6) with respect to an investment company registered under the Investment Company Act of 1940 or a business development company, a proposal to continue, without change, any advisory or other contract or agreement that previously has been the subject of a proxy solicitation for which proxy material was filed with the Commission pursuant to this rule;

(7) with respect to an open-end investment company registered under the Investment Company Act of 1940, a proposal to increase the number of shares authorized to be issued; and/or

(8) A vote to approve the compensation of executives as required pursuant to Section 111(e)(1) of the Emergency Economic Stabilization Act of 2008 (12 U.S.C. 5221(e)(1)) and § 240.14a-20.

*End of Amendment*_____

This exclusion from filing preliminary proxy material does not apply if the registrant comments upon or refers to a solicitation in opposition in connection with the meeting in its proxy material.

Note 1: The filing of revised material does not recommence the ten day time period unless the revised material contains material revisions or material new proposal(s) that constitute a fundamental change in the proxy material.

Note 2: The official responsible for the preparation of the proxy material should make every effort to verify the accuracy and completeness of the information required by the applicable rules. The preliminary material should be filed with the Commission at the earliest practicable date.

Note 3. *Solicitation in Opposition.* For purposes of the exclusion from filing preliminary proxy material, a "solicitation in opposition" includes: (a) any solicitation opposing a proposal supported by the registrant; and (b) any solicitation supporting a proposal that the registrant does not expressly support, other than a security holder proposal included in the registrant's proxy material pursuant to Rule 14a-8 [§ 240.14a-8 of this chapter]. The inclusion of a security holder proposal in the registrant's proxy material pursuant to Rule 14a-8 does not constitute a "solicitation in opposition," even if the registrant opposes the proposal and/or includes a statement in opposition to the proposal.

*Amendment*_____

Note 3. *Solicitation in Opposition.* For purposes of the exclusion from filing preliminary proxy material, a "solicitation in opposition" includes: (a) any solicitation opposing a proposal supported by the registrant; and (b) any solicitation supporting a proposal that the registrant does not expressly support, other than a security holder proposal included in the registrant's proxy material pursuant to Rule 14a-8 [§ 240.14a-8 of this chapter]. The inclusion of a security holder proposal in the registrant's proxy material pursuant to Rule 14a-8 does not constitute a "solicitation in opposition," even if the registrant opposes the proposal and/or includes a statement in opposition to the proposal. The inclusion of a shareholder nominee in the registrant's proxy materials pursuant to § 240.14a-11, an applicable state or foreign law provision, or a registrant's governing documents as they relate to the inclusion of shareholder director nominees in the registrant's proxy materials does not constitute a "solicitation in opposition" for purposes of Rule 14a-6(a) (§ 240.14a-6(a)), even if the registrant opposes the shareholder nominee and solicits against the shareholder nominee and in favor of a registrant nominee.

End of Amendment

Note 4. A registrant that is filing proxy material in preliminary form only because the registrant has commented on or referred to a solicitation in opposition should indicate that fact in a transmittal letter when filing the preliminary material with the Commission.

(b) *Definitive proxy statement and other soliciting material.* Eight definitive copies of the proxy statement, form of proxy and all other soliciting materials, in the same form as the materials sent to security holders, must be filed with the Commission no later than the date they are first sent or given to security holders. Three copies of these materials also must be filed with, or mailed for filing to, each national securities exchange on which the registrant has a class of securities listed and registered.

(c) *Personal solicitation materials.* If part or all of the solicitation involves personal solicitation, then eight copies of all written instructions or other materials that discuss, review or comment on the merits of any matter to be acted on, that are furnished to persons making the actual solicitation for their use directly or indirectly in connection with the solicitation, must be filed with the Commission no later than the date the materials are first sent or given to these persons.

(d) *Release dates.* All preliminary proxy statements and forms of proxy filed pursuant to paragraph (a) of this section shall be accompanied by a statement of the date on which definitive copies thereof filed pursuant to paragraph (b) of this section are intended to be released to security holders. All definitive material filed pursuant to paragraph (b) of this section shall be accompanied by a statement of the date on which copies of such material were released to security holders, or, if not released, the date on which copies thereof are intended to be released. All material filed pursuant to paragraph (c) of this section shall be accompanied by a statement of the date on which copies thereof were released to the individual who will make the actual solicitation or if not released, the date on which copies thereof are intended to be released.

(e)(1) *Public Availability of Information.* All copies of preliminary proxy statements and forms of proxy filed pursuant to paragraph (a) of this section shall be clearly marked "Preliminary Copies," and shall be deemed immediately available for public inspection unless confidential treatment is obtained pursuant to paragraph (e)(2) of this section.

(2) *Confidential treatment.* If action will be taken on any matter specified in Item 14 of Schedule 14A (§ 240.14a-101), all copies of the preliminary proxy statement and form of proxy filed under paragraph (a) of this section will be for the information of the Commission only and will not be deemed available for public inspection until filed with the Commission in definitive form so long as:

(i) The proxy statement does not relate to a matter or proposal subject to § 240.13e-3 or a roll-up transaction as defined in Item 901(c) of Regulation S-K (§ 229.901(c) of this chapter);

(ii) Neither the parties to the transaction nor any persons authorized to act on their behalf have made any public communications relating to the transaction except for statements where the content is limited to the information specified in § 230.135 of this chapter; and

(iii) The materials are filed in paper and marked "Confidential, For Use of the Commission Only." In all cases, the materials may be disclosed to any department or agency of the United States Government and to the Congress, and the Commission may make any inquiries or investigation into the materials as may be necessary to conduct an adequate review by the Commission.

Instruction to paragraph (e)(2): If communications are made publicly that go beyond the information specified in § 230.135 of this chapter, the preliminary proxy materials must be re-filed promptly with the Commission as public materials.

(f) *Communications not required to be filed.* Copies of replies to inquiries from security holders requesting further information and copies of communications which do no more than request that forms of proxy theretofore solicited be signed and returned need not be filed pursuant to this rule.

(g) *Solicitations subject to § 240.14a-2(b)(1).*

(1) Any person who:

(i) engages in a solicitation pursuant to § 240.14a-2(b)(1), and

(ii) at the commencement of that solicitation owns beneficially securities of the class which is the subject of the solicitation with a market value of over $5 million, shall furnish or mail to the Commission, not later than three days after the date this written solicitation is first sent or given to any security holder, five copies of a statement containing the information specified in the Notice of Exempt Solicitation [§ 240.14a-103] which statement shall attach as an exhibit all written soliciting materials. Five copies of an amendment to such statement shall be furnished or mailed to the Commission, in connection with dissemination of any additional communications, not later than three days after the date the additional material is first sent or given to any security holder. Three copies of the Notice of Exempt Proxy Solicitation and amendments thereto shall, at the same time the materials are furnished or mailed to the Commission, be furnished or mailed to each national securities exchange upon which any class of securities of the registrant is listed and registered.

(2) Notwithstanding paragraph (g)(1) of this section, no such submission need be made with respect to oral solicitations (other than with respect to scripts used in connection with such oral solicitations), speeches delivered in a public forum, press releases, published or broadcast opinions, statements, and advertisements appearing in a broadcast media, or a newspaper, magazine or other bona fide publication disseminated on a regular basis.

(h) *Revised material.* Where any proxy statement, form of proxy or other material filed pursuant to this rule is amended or revised, two of the copies of such amended or revised material filed pursuant to this rule (or in the case of investment companies registered under the Investment Company Act of 1940, three of such copies) shall be marked to indicate clearly and precisely the changes effected therein. If the amendment or revision alters the text of the material the changes in such text shall be indicated by means of underscoring or in some other appropriate manner.

(i) *Fees.* At the time of filing the proxy solicitation material, the persons upon whose behalf the solicitation is made, other than investment companies registered under the Investment Company Act of 1940, shall pay to the Commission the following applicable fee:

(1) For preliminary proxy material involving acquisitions, mergers, spinoffs, consolidations or proposed sales or other dispositions of substantially all the assets of the company, a fee established in accordance with Rule 0-11 (§ 240.0-11 of this chapter) shall be paid. No refund shall be given.

(2) For all other proxy submissions and submissions made pursuant to § 240.14a-6(g), no fee shall be required.

(j) *Merger proxy materials.* Any proxy statement, form of proxy or other soliciting material required to be filed by this section that also is either: (i) included in a registration statement filed under the Securities Act of 1933 on Forms S-4 (§ 239.25 of this chapter), F-4 (§ 239.34 of this chapter) or N-14 (§ 239.23 of this chapter); or (ii) filed under § 230.424, § 230.425 or § 230.497 of this chapter is required to be filed only under the Securities Act, and is deemed filed under this section. In that case, the fee required under paragraph (i) of this section need not be paid.

(k) *Computing time periods.* In computing time periods beginning with the filing date specified in Regulation 14A (§§ 240.14a-1 to 240.14b-1 of this chapter), the filing date shall be counted as the first day of the time period and midnight of the last day shall constitute the end of the specified time period.

(l) *Roll-up transactions.* If a transaction is a roll-up transaction as defined in Item 901(c) of Regulation S-K (17 CFR 229.901(c)) and is registered (or authorized to be registered) on Form S-4 (17 CFR 229.25) or Form F-4 (17 CFR 229.34), the proxy statement of the sponsor or the general partner as defined in Item 901(d) and Item 901(a), respectively, of Regulation S-K (17 CFR 229.901) must be distributed to security holders no later than the lesser of 60 calendar days prior to the date on which the meeting of security holders is held or action is taken, or the maximum number of days permitted for giving notice under applicable state law.

(m) *Cover Page.* Proxy materials filed with the Commission shall include a cover page in the form set forth in Schedule 14A (§ 240.14a-101 of this chapter). The cover page required by this paragraph need not be distributed to security holders.

(n) *Solicitations subject to § 240.14a-2(b)(4).* Any person who:

(1) Engages in a solicitation pursuant to § 240.14a-2(b)(4), and

(2) At the commencement of that solicitation both owns five percent (5%) or more of the outstanding securities of a class that is the subject of the proposed roll-up transaction, and engages in the business of buying and selling limited partnership interests in the secondary market, shall furnish or mail to the Commission, not later than three days after the date an oral or written solicitation by that person is first made, sent or provided to any security holder, five copies of a statement containing the information specified in the Notice of Exempt Preliminary Roll-up Communication (§ 240.14a-104). Five copies of any amendment to such statement shall be furnished or mailed to the Commission not later than three days after a communication containing revised material is first made, sent or provided to any security holder.

(o) *Solicitations before furnishing a definitive proxy statement.* Solicitations that are published, sent or given to security holders before they have been furnished a definitive proxy statement must be made in accordance with § 240.14a-12 unless there is an exemption available under § 240.14a-2.

Amendment_____

(p) *Solicitations subject to § 240.14a-11.* Any soliciting material that is published, sent or given to shareholders in connection with § 240.14a-2(b)(7) or (b)(8) must be filed with the Commission as specified in that section.

End of Amendment_____

[As last amended in Release No. 33-9136, effective November 15, 2010, 75 F.R. 56668.]

[¶ 40,061] Obligations of Registrants to Provide a List of, or Mail Soliciting Material to, Security Holders

Reg. § 240.14a-7. (a) If the registrant has made or intends to make a proxy solicitation in connection with a security holder meeting or action by consent or authorization, upon the written request by any record or beneficial holder of securities of the class entitled to vote at the meeting or to execute a consent or authorization to provide a list of security holders or to mail the requesting security holder's materials, regardless of whether the request references this section, the registrant shall:

(1) deliver to the requesting security holder within five business days after receipt of the request:

(i) notification as to whether the registrant has elected to mail the security holder's soliciting materials or provide a security holder list if the election under paragraph (b) is to be made by the registrant;

(ii) a statement of the approximate number of record holders and beneficial holders, separated by type of holder and class, owning securities in the same class or classes as holders which have been or are to be solicited on management's behalf, or any more limited group of such holders designated by the security holder if available or retrievable under the registrant's or its transfer agent's security holder data systems; and

(iii) the estimated cost of mailing a proxy statement, form of proxy or other communication to such holders, including to the extent known or reasonably available, the estimated costs of any bank, broker, and similar person through whom the registrant has solicited or intends to solicit beneficial owners in connection with the security holder meeting or action.

(2) perform the acts set forth in either paragraphs (a)(2)(i) or (a)(2)(ii) of this section, at the registrant's or requesting security holder's option, as specified in paragraph (b) of this section:

(i) Send copies of any proxy statement, form of proxy, or other soliciting material, including a Notice of Internet Availability of Proxy Materials (as described in § 240.14a-16), furnished by the security holder to the record holders, including banks, brokers, and similar entities, designated by the security holder. A sufficient number of copies must be sent to the banks, brokers, and similar entities for distribution to all beneficial owners designated by the security holder. The security holder may designate only record holders and/or beneficial owners who have not requested paper and/or e-mail copies of the proxy statement. If the registrant has received affirmative written or implied consent to deliver a single proxy statement to security holders at a shared address in accordance with the procedures in § 240.14a-3(e)(1), a single copy of the proxy statement or Notice of Internet Availability of Proxy Materials furnished by the security holder shall be sent to that address, provided that if multiple copies of the Notice of Internet Availability of Proxy Materials are furnished by the security holder for that address, the registrant shall deliver those copies in a single envelope to that address. The registrant shall send the security holder material with reasonable promptness after tender of the material to be sent, envelopes or other containers therefore, postage or payment for postage and other reasonable expenses of effecting such distribution. The registrant shall not be responsible for the content of the material; or

(ii) Deliver the following information to the requesting security holder within five business days of receipt of the request:

(A) A reasonably current list of the names, addresses and security positions of the record holders, including banks, brokers and similar entities holding securities in the same class or classes as holders which have been or are to be solicited on management's behalf, or any more limited group of such holders designated by the security holder if available or retrievable under the registrant's or its transfer agent's security holder data systems;

(B) The most recent list of names, addresses and security positions of beneficial owners as specified in § 240.14a-13(b), in the possession, or which subsequently comes into the possession, of the registrant;

(C) The names of security holders at a shared address that have consented to delivery of a single copy of proxy materials to a shared address, if the registrant has received written or implied consent in accordance with § 240.14a-3(e)(1); and

(D) If the registrant has relied on § 240.14a-16, the names of security holders who have requested paper copies of the proxy materials for all meetings and the names of security holders who, as of the date that the registrant receives the request, have requested paper copies of the proxy materials only for the meeting to which the solicitation relates.

(iii) All security holder list information shall be in the form requested by the security holder to the extent that such form is available to the registrant without undue burden or expense. The registrant shall furnish the security holder with updated record holder information on a daily basis or, if not available on a daily basis, at the shortest reasonable intervals; provided, however, the registrant need not provide beneficial or record holder information more current than the record date for the meeting or action.

(b) (1) The requesting security holder shall have the options set forth in paragraph (a) (2) of this section, and the registrant shall have corresponding obligations, if the registrant or general partner or sponsor is soliciting or intends to solicit with respect to:

(i) A proposal that is subject to § 240.13e-3;

(ii) A roll-up transaction as defined in Item 901(c) of Regulation S-K (§ 229.901(c) of this chapter) that involves an entity with securities registered pursuant to Section 12 of the Act (15 U.S.C. 78*l*); or

(iii) A roll-up transaction as defined in Item 901(c) of Regulation S-K (§ 229.901(c) of this chapter) that involves a limited partnership, unless the transaction involves only:

(A) Partnership whose investors will receive new securities or securities in another entity that are not reported under a transaction reporting plan declared effective before December 17, 1993 by the Commission under Section 11A of the Act (15 U.S.C. 78k-1); or

(B) Partnerships whose investors' securities are reported under a transaction reporting plan declared effective before December 17, 1993 by the Commission under Section 11A of the Act (15 U.S.C. 78k-1).

(2) With respect to all other requests pursuant to this section, the registrant shall have the option to either mail the security holder's material or furnish the security holder list as set forth in this section.

(c) At the time of a list request, the security holder making the request shall:

(1) if holding the registrant's securities through a nominee, provide the registrant with a statement by the nominee or other independent third party, or a copy of a current filing made with the Commission and furnished to the registrant, confirming such holder's beneficial ownership; and

(2) provide the registrant with an affidavit, declaration, affirmation or other similar document provided for under applicable state law identifying the proposal or other corporate action that will be the subject of the security holder's solicitation or communication and attesting that:

(i) the security holder will not use the list information for any purpose other than to solicit security holders with respect to the same meeting or action by consent or authorization for which the registrant is soliciting or intends to solicit or to communicate with security holders with respect to a solicitation commenced by the registrant; and

(ii) the security holder will not disclose such information to any person other than a beneficial owner for whom the request was made and an employee or agent to the extent necessary to effectuate the communication or solicitation.

(d) The security holder shall not use the information furnished by the registrant pursuant to paragraph (a) (2) (ii) of this section for any purpose other than to solicit security holders with respect to the same meeting or action by consent or authorization for which the registrant is soliciting or intends to solicit or to communicate with security holders with respect to a solicitation commenced by the registrant; or disclose such information to any person other than an employee, agent, or beneficial owner for whom a request was made to the extent necessary to effectuate the communication or solicitation. The security holder shall return the information provided pursuant to paragraph (a) (2) (ii) of this section and shall not retain any copies thereof or of any information derived from such information after the termination of the solicitation.

(e) The security holder shall reimburse the reasonable expenses incurred by the registrant in performing the acts requested pursuant to paragraph (a) of this section.

Notes to § 240.14a-7.

Note 1. to § 240.14a-7. Reasonably prompt methods of distribution to security holders may be used instead of mailing. If an alternative distribution method is chosen, the costs of that method should be considered where necessary rather than the costs of mailing.

Note 2. to § 240.14a-7. When providing the information required by § 240.14a-7(a) (1) (ii), if the registrant has received affirmative written or implied consent to delivery of a single copy of proxy materials to a shared address in accordance with § 240.14a-3(e) (1), it shall exclude from the number of record holders those to whom it does not have to deliver a separate proxy statement.

[As last amended in Release No. 34–56135, effective January 1, 2008, 72 F.R. 42222.]

>»→ *CCH Note: The SEC has stayed the effectiveness of proxy rule amendments adopted in Release 33-9136 pending resolution of a challenge filed by the Business Roundtable and the U.S. Chamber of Commerce in the U.S. Court of Appeals for the District of Columbia Circuit. See Release No. 33-9149, October 4, 2010.*

>»→ *Amended by Release No. 33-9136, effective November 15, 2010, 75 F.R. 56668.*

[¶ 40,071] Shareholder Proposals

Reg. § 240.14a-8. This section addresses when a company must include a shareholder's proposal in its proxy statement and identify the proposal in its form of proxy when the company holds an annual or special meeting of shareholders. In summary, in order to have your shareholder proposal included on a company's proxy card, and included along with any supporting statement in its proxy statement, you must be eligible and follow certain procedures. Under a few specific circumstances, the company is permitted to exclude your proposal, but only after submitting its reasons to the Commission. We structured this section in a question-and-answer format so that it is easier to understand. The references to "you" are to a shareholder seeking to submit the proposal.

(a) **Question 1: What is a proposal?**

A shareholder proposal is your recommendation or requirement that the company and/or its board of directors take action, which you intend to present at a meeting of the company's shareholders. Your proposal should state as clearly as possible the course of action that you believe the company should follow. If your proposal is placed on the company's proxy card, the company must also provide in the form of proxy means for shareholders to specify by boxes a choice between approval or disapproval, or abstention. Unless otherwise indicated, the word "proposal" as used in this section refers both to your proposal, and to your corresponding statement in support of your proposal (if any).

(b) **Question 2: Who is eligible to submit a proposal, and how do I demonstrate to the company that I am eligible?**

(1) In order to be eligible to submit a proposal, you must have continuously held at least $2,000 in market value, or 1%, of the company's securities entitled to be voted on the proposal at the meeting for at least one year by the date you submit the proposal. You must continue to hold those securities through the date of the meeting.

(2) If you are the registered holder of your securities, which means that your name appears in the company's records as a shareholder, the company can verify your eligibility on its own, although you will still have to provide the company with a written statement that you intend to continue to hold the securities through the date of the meeting of shareholders. However, if like many shareholders you are not a registered holder, the company likely does not know that you are a shareholder, or how many shares you own. In this case, at the time you submit your proposal, you must prove your eligibility to the company in one of two ways:

(i) The first way is to submit to the company a written statement from the "record" holder of your securities (usually a broker or bank) verifying that, at the time you submitted your proposal, you continuously held the securities for at least one year. You must also include your own written statement that you intend to continue to hold the securities through the date of the meeting of shareholders; or

(ii) The second way to prove ownership applies only if you have filed a Schedule 13D (§ 240.13d-101), Schedule 13G (§ 240.13d-102), Form 3 (§ 249.103 of this chapter), Form 4 (§ 249.104 of this chapter) and/or Form 5 (§ 249.105 of this chapter), or amendments to those documents or updated forms, reflecting your ownership of the shares as of or before the date on which the one-year eligibility period begins. If you have filed one of these documents with the SEC, you may demonstrate your eligibility by submitting to the company:

(A) A copy of the schedule and/or form, and any subsequent amendments reporting a change in your ownership level;

(B) Your written statement that you continuously held the required number of shares for the one-year period as of the date of the statement; and

(C) Your written statement that you intend to continue ownership of the shares through the date of the company's annual or special meeting.

(c) **Question 3: How many proposals may I submit?**

Each shareholder may submit no more than one proposal to a company for a particular shareholders' meeting.

(d) **Question 4: How long can my proposal be?**

The proposal, including any accompanying supporting statement, may not exceed 500 words.

(e) **Question 5: What is the deadline for submitting a proposal?** (1) If you are submitting your proposal for the company's annual meeting, you can in most cases find the deadline in last year's proxy statement. However, if the company did not hold an annual meeting last year, or has changed the date of its meeting for this year more than 30 days from last year's meeting, you can usually find the deadline in one of the company's quarterly reports on Form 10-Q (§ 249.308a of this chapter), or in shareholder reports of investment companies under § 270.30d-1 of this chapter of the Investment Company Act of 1940. In order to avoid controversy, shareholders should submit their proposals by means, including electronic means, that permit them to prove the date of delivery.

(2) The deadline is calculated in the following manner if the proposal is submitted for a regularly scheduled annual meeting. The proposal must be received at the company's principal executive offices not less than 120 calendar days before the date of the company's proxy statement released to shareholders in connection with the previous year's annual meeting. However, if the company did not hold an annual meeting the previous year, or if the date of this year's annual meeting has been changed by more than 30 days from the date of the previous year's meeting, then the deadline is a reasonable time before the company begins to print and send its proxy materials.

(3) If you are submitting your proposal for a meeting of shareholders other than a regularly scheduled annual meeting, the deadline is a reasonable time before the company begins to print and send its proxy materials.

(f) **Question 6: What if I fail to follow one of the eligibility or procedural requirements explained in answers to Questions 1 through 4 of this section?**

(1) The company may exclude your proposal, but only after it has notified you of the problem, and you have failed adequately to correct it. Within 14 calendar days of receiving your proposal, the company must notify you in writing of any procedural or eligibility deficiencies, as well as of the time frame for your response. Your response must be postmarked, or transmitted electronically, no later than 14 days from the date you received the company's notification. A company need not provide you such notice of a deficiency if the deficiency cannot be remedied, such as if you fail to submit a proposal by the company's properly determined deadline. If the company intends to exclude the proposal, it will later have to make a submission under § 240.14a-8 and provide you with a copy under Question 10 below, § 240.14a-8(j).

(2) If you fail in your promise to hold the required number of securities through the date of the meeting of shareholders, then the company will be permitted to exclude all of your proposals from its proxy materials for any meeting held in the following two calendar years.

(g) **Question 7: Who has the burden of persuading the Commission or its staff that my proposal can be excluded?**

Except as otherwise noted, the burden is on the company to demonstrate that it is entitled to exclude a proposal.

(h) **Question 8: Must I appear personally at the shareholders' meeting to present the proposal?**

(1) Either you, or your representative who is qualified under state law to present the proposal on your behalf, must attend the meeting to present the proposal. Whether you attend the meeting yourself or send a qualified representative to the meeting in your place, you should make sure that you, or your representative, follow the proper state law procedures for attending the meeting and/or presenting your proposal.

(2) If the company holds its shareholder meeting in whole or in part via electronic media, and the company permits you or your representative to present your proposal via such media, then you may appear through electronic media rather than traveling to the meeting to appear in person.

(3) If you or your qualified representative fail to appear and present the proposal, without good cause, the company will be permitted to exclude all of your proposals from its proxy materials for any meetings held in the following two calendar years.

(i) **Question 9: If I have complied with the procedural requirements, on what other bases may a company rely to exclude my proposal?**

(1) *Improper under state law:* If the proposal is not a proper subject for action by shareholders under the laws of the jurisdiction of the company's organization;

Note to paragraph (i)(1): Depending on the subject matter, some proposals are not considered proper under state law if they would be binding on the company if approved by shareholders. In our experience, most proposals that are cast as recommendations or requests that the board of directors take specified action are proper under state law. Accordingly, we will assume that a proposal drafted as a recommendation or suggestion is proper unless the company demonstrates otherwise.

(2) *Violation of law:* If the proposal would, if implemented, cause the company to violate any state, federal, or foreign law to which it is subject;

Note to paragraph (i)(2): We will not apply this basis for exclusion to permit exclusion of a proposal on grounds that it would violate foreign law if compliance with the foreign law would result in a violation of any state or federal law.

(3) *Violation of proxy rules:* If the proposal or supporting statement is contrary to any of the Commission's proxy rules, including §240.14a-9, which prohibits materially false or misleading statements in proxy soliciting materials;

(4) *Personal grievance; special interest:* If the proposal relates to the redress of a personal claim or grievance against the company or any other person, or if it is designed to result in a benefit to you, or to further a personal interest, which is not shared by the other shareholders at large;

(5) *Relevance:* If the proposal relates to operations which account for less than 5 percent of the company's total assets at the end of its most recent fiscal year, and for less than 5 percent of its net earnings and gross sales for its most recent fiscal year, and is not otherwise significantly related to the company's business;

(6) *Absence of power/authority:* If the company would lack the power or authority to implement the proposal;

(7) *Management functions:* If the proposal deals with a matter relating to the company's ordinary business operations;

(8) *Relates to election:* If the proposal relates to a nomination or an election for membership on the company's board of directors or analogous governing body or a procedure for such nomination or election;

Amendment

(8) *Director elections:* If the proposal:

(i) Would disqualify a nominee who is standing for election;

(ii) Would remove a director from office before his or her term expired;

(iii) Questions the competence, business judgment, or character of one or more nominees or directors;

(iv) Seeks to include a specific individual in the company's proxy materials for election to the board of directors; or

(v) Otherwise could affect the outcome of the upcoming election of directors.

End of Amendment

(9) *Conflicts with company's proposal:* If the proposal directly conflicts with one of the company's own proposals to be submitted to shareholders at the same meeting;

Note to paragraph (i)(9): A company's submission to the Commission under this section should specify the points of conflict with the company's proposal.

(10) *Substantially implemented:* If the company has already substantially implemented the proposal;

(11) *Duplication:* If the proposal substantially duplicates another proposal previously submitted to the company by another proponent that will be included in the company's proxy materials for the same meeting;

(12) *Resubmissions:* If the proposal deals with substantially the same subject matter as another proposal or proposals that has or have been previously included in the company's proxy materials within the preceding 5 calendar years, a company may exclude it from its proxy materials for any meeting held within 3 calendar years of the last time it was included if the proposal received:

(i) Less than 3% of the vote if proposed once within the preceding 5 calendar years;

(ii) Less than 6% of the vote on its last submission to shareholders if proposed twice previously within the preceding 5 calendar years; or

(iii) Less than 10% of the vote on its last submission to shareholders if proposed three times or more previously within the preceding 5 calendar years; and

(13) *Specific amount of dividends:* If the proposal relates to specific amounts of cash or stock dividends.

(j) Question 10: What procedures must the company follow if it intends to exclude my proposal?

(1) If the company intends to exclude a proposal from its proxy materials, it must file its reasons with the Commission no later than 80 calendar days before it files its definitive proxy statement and form of proxy with the Commission. The company must simultaneously provide you with a copy of its submission. The Commission staff may permit the company to make its submission later than 80 days before the company files its definitive proxy statement and form of proxy, if the company demonstrates good cause for missing the deadline.

(2) The company must file six paper copies of the following:

(i) The proposal;

(ii) An explanation of why the company believes that it may exclude the proposal, which should, if possible, refer to the most recent applicable authority, such as prior Division letters issued under the rule; and

(iii) A supporting opinion of counsel when such reasons are based on matters of state or foreign law.

(k) Question 11: May I submit my own statement to the Commission responding to the company's arguments?

Yes, you may submit a response, but it is not required. You should try to submit any response to us, with a copy to the company, as soon as possible after the company makes its submission. This way, the Commission staff will have time to consider fully your submission before it issues its response. You should submit six paper copies of your response.

(l) Question 12: If the company includes my shareholder proposal in its proxy materials, what information about me must it include along with the proposal itself?

(1) The company's proxy statement must include your name and address, as well as the number of the company's voting securities that you hold. However, instead of providing that information, the company may instead include a statement that it will provide the information to shareholders promptly upon receiving an oral or written request.

(2) The company is not responsible for the contents of your proposal or supporting statement.

(m) Question 13: What can I do if the company includes in its proxy statement reasons why it believes shareholders should not vote in favor of my proposal, and I disagree with some of its statements?

(1) The company may elect to include in its proxy statement reasons why it believes shareholders should vote against your proposal. The company is allowed to make arguments reflecting its own point of view, just as you may express your own point of view in your proposal's supporting statement.

(2) However, if you believe that the company's opposition to your proposal contains materially false or misleading statements that may violate our anti-fraud rule, § 240.14a-9, you should promptly send to the Commission staff and the company a letter explaining the reasons for your view, along with a copy of the company's statements opposing your proposal. To the extent possible, your letter should include specific factual information demonstrating the inaccuracy of the company's claims. Time permitting, you may wish to try to work out your differences with the company by yourself before contacting the Commission staff.

(3) We require the company to send you a copy of its statements opposing your proposal before it sends its proxy materials, so that you may bring to our attention any materially false or misleading statements, under the following timeframes:

(i) If our no-action response requires that you make revisions to your proposal or supporting statement as a condition to requiring the company to include it in its proxy materials, then the company must provide you with a copy of its opposition statements no later than 5 calendar days after the company receives a copy of your revised proposal; or

(ii) In all other cases, the company must provide you with a copy of its opposition statements no later than 30 calendar days before its files definitive copies of its proxy statement and form of proxy under § 240.14a-6.

[As last amended in Release No. 33-9136, effective November 15, 2010, 75 F.R. 56668.]

≫→ *CCH Note: **The SEC has stayed the effectiveness of proxy rule amendments adopted in Release 33-9136 pending resolution of a challenge filed by the Business Roundtable and the U.S. Chamber of Commerce in the U.S. Court of Appeals for the District of Columbia Circuit. See Release No. 33-9149, October 4, 2010.***

≫→ *Amended by Release No. 33-9136, effective November 15, 2010, 75 F.R. 56668.*

[¶ 40,081] False or Misleading Statements

Reg. § 240.14a-9. (a) No solicitation subject to this regulation shall be made by means of any proxy statement, form of proxy, notice of meeting or other communication, written or oral, containing any statement which, at the time and in the light of the circumstances under which it is made, is false or misleading with respect to any material fact, or which omits to state any material fact necessary in order to make the statements therein not false or misleading or necessary to correct any statement in any earlier communication with respect to the solicitation of a proxy for the same meeting or subject matter which has become false or misleading.

(b) The fact that a proxy statement, form of proxy or other soliciting material has been filed with or examined by the Commission shall not be deemed a finding by the Commission that such material is accurate or complete or not false or misleading, or that the Commission has passed upon the merits of or approved any statement contained therein or any matter to be acted upon by security holders. No representation contrary to the foregoing shall be made.

Amendment

(c) No nominee, nominating shareholder or nominating shareholder group, or any member thereof, shall cause to be included in a registrant's proxy materials, either pursuant to the federal proxy rules, an applicable state or foreign law provision, or a registrant's governing documents as they relate to including shareholder nominees for director in a registrant's proxy materials, include in a notice on Schedule 14N (§ 240.14n-101), or include in any other related communication, any statement which, at the time and in the light of the circumstances under which it is made, is false or misleading with respect to any material fact, or which omits to state any material fact necessary in order to make the statements therein not false or misleading or necessary to correct any statement in any earlier communication with respect to a solicitation for the same meeting or subject matter which has become false or misleading.

*End of Amendment*_____

Note: The following are some examples of what, depending upon particular facts and circumstances, may be misleading within the meaning of this section.

a. Predictions as to specific future market values.

b. Material which directly or indirectly impugns character, integrity or personal reputation, or directly or indirectly makes charges concerning improper, illegal or immoral conduct or associations, without factual foundation.

c. Failure to so identify a proxy statement, form of proxy and other soliciting material as to clearly distinguish it from the soliciting material of any other person or persons soliciting for the same meeting or subject matter.

d. Claims made prior to a meeting regarding the results of a solicitation.

[As last amended in Release No. 33-9136, effective November 15, 2010, 75 F.R. 56668.]

[¶ 40,091] Prohibition of Certain Solicitations

Reg. § 240.14a-10. No person making a solicitation which is subject to §§ 240.14a-1 to 240.14a-10 shall solicit:

(a) any undated or post-dated proxy, or

(b) any proxy which provides that it shall be deemed to be dated as of any date subsequent to the date on which it is signed by the security holder.

[As adopted in Release No. 34-4775, December 11, 1952, 17 F.R. 11431.]

≫→ CCH Note: The SEC has stayed the effectiveness of proxy rule amendments adopted in Release 33-9136 pending resolution of a challenge filed by the Business Roundtable and the U.S. Chamber of Commerce in the U.S. Court of Appeals for the District of Columbia Circuit. See Release No. 33-9149, October 4, 2010.

≫→ Added in Release No. 33-9136, effective November 15, 2010, 75 F.R. 56668.

[¶ 40,101] Shareholder Nominations

Reg. § 240.14a-11. (a) *Applicability*. In connection with an annual (or a special meeting in lieu of an annual) meeting of shareholders, or a written consent in lieu of such meeting, at which directors are elected, a registrant will be required to include in its proxy statement and form of proxy the name of a person or persons nominated by a shareholder or group of shareholders for election to the board of directors and include in its proxy statement the disclosure about such nominee or nominees and the nominating shareholder or members of the nominating shareholder group as specified in Item 5 of Schedule 14N (§ 240.14n-101), provided that the conditions set forth in paragraph (b) of this section are satisfied. This rule will not apply to a registrant if:

(1) The registrant is subject to the proxy rules solely because it has a class of debt securities registered under section 12 of the Exchange Act (15 U.S.C. 78l); or

(2) Applicable state or foreign law or a registrant's governing documents prohibit the registrant's shareholders from nominating a candidate or candidates for election as director.

(b) *Eligibility*. A shareholder nominee or nominees shall be included in a registrant's proxy statement and form of proxy if the following requirements are satisfied:

(1) The nominating shareholder individually, or the nominating shareholder group in the aggregate, holds at least 3% of the total voting power of the registrant's securities that are entitled to be voted on the election of directors at the annual (or a special meeting in lieu of the annual) meeting of shareholders or on a written consent in lieu of such meeting, on the date the nominating shareholder or nominating shareholder group files the notice on Schedule 14N (§ 240.14n-101) with the Commission and transmits the notice to the registrant;

(2) The nominating shareholder or each member of the nominating shareholder group has held the amount of securities that are used for purposes of satisfying the minimum ownership requirement of paragraph (b)(1) of this section continuously for at least three years as of the date the notice on

Schedule 14N (§ 240.14n-101) is filed with the Commission and transmitted to the registrant and must continue to hold that amount of securities through the date of the subject election of directors;

(3) The nominating shareholder or each member of the nominating shareholder group provides proof of ownership of the amount of securities that are used for purposes of satisfying the ownership and holding period requirements of paragraphs (b)(1) and (b)(2) of this section. If the nominating shareholder or each member of the nominating shareholder group is not the registered holder of the securities, the nominating shareholder or each member of the nominating shareholder group must provide proof of ownership in the form of one or more written statements from the registered holder of the nominating shareholder's securities (or the brokers or banks through which those securities are held) verifying that, as of a date within seven calendar days prior to filing the notice on Schedule 14N (§ 240.14n-101) with the Commission and transmitting the notice to the registrant, the nominating shareholder or each member of the nominating shareholder group, continuously held the amount of securities being used to satisfy the ownership threshold for a period of at least three years. The written statement or statements proving ownership must be attached as an appendix to Schedule 14N on the date the notice is filed with the Commission and transmitted to the registrant, and provide the information specified in Item 4 of Schedule 14N. In the alternative, if the nominating shareholder or member of the nominating shareholder group has filed a Schedule 13D (§ 240.13d-101), Schedule 13G (§ 240.13d-102), Form 3 (§ 249.103 of this chapter), Form 4 (§ 249.104 of this chapter), and/or Form 5 (§ 249.105 of this chapter), or amendments to those documents, reflecting ownership of the securities as of or before the date on which the three-year eligibility period begins, the nominating shareholder or member of the nominating shareholder group may attach the filing as an appendix to the Schedule 14N or incorporate the filing by reference into the Schedule 14N;

(4) The nominating shareholder or each member of the nominating shareholder group provides a statement, as specified in Item 4(b) of Schedule 14N (§ 240.14n-101), on the date the notice on Schedule 14N is filed with the Commission and transmitted to the registrant, that the nominating shareholder or each member of the nominating shareholder group intends to continue to hold the amount of securities that are used for purposes of satisfying the minimum ownership requirement of paragraph (b)(1) of this section through the date of the meeting;

(5) The nominating shareholder or each member of the nominating shareholder group provides a statement, as specified in Item 4(b) of Schedule 14N (§ 240.14n-101), on the date the notice on Schedule 14N is filed with the Commission and transmitted to the registrant, regarding the nominating shareholder's or group's intent with respect to continued ownership of the registrant's securities after the election;

(6) The nominating shareholder (or where there is a nominating shareholder group, each member of the nominating shareholder group) is not holding any of the registrant's securities with the purpose, or with the effect, of changing control of the registrant or to gain a number of seats on the board of directors that exceeds the maximum number of nominees that the registrant could be required to include under paragraph (d) of this section;

(7) Neither the nominee nor the nominating shareholder (or where there is a nominating shareholder group, any member of the nominating shareholder group) has an agreement with the registrant regarding the nomination of the nominee;

(8) The nominee's candidacy or, if elected, board membership would not violate controlling federal law, state law, foreign law, or rules of a national securities exchange or national securities association (other than rules regarding director independence) or, in the case that the nominee's candidacy or, if elected, board membership would violate such laws or rules, such violation could not be cured by the time provided in paragraph (g)(2) of this section;

(9) In the case of a registrant other than an investment company, the nominee meets the objective criteria for "independence" of the national securities exchange or national securities association rules applicable to the registrant, if any, or, in the case of a registrant that is an investment company, the nominee is not an "interested person" of the registrant as defined in section 2(a)(19) of the Investment Company Act of 1940 (15 U.S.C. 80a-2(a)(19));

(10) The nominating shareholder or nominating shareholder group provides notice to the registrant on Schedule 14N (§ 240.14n-101), as specified by § 240.14n-1, of its intent to require that the registrant include that shareholder's or group's nominee in the registrant's proxy statement and form of proxy. This notice must be transmitted to the registrant on the date it is filed with the Commission. The notice must be filed with the Commission and transmitted to the registrant no earlier than 150 calendar days, and no later than 120 calendar days, before the anniversary of the date that the registrant mailed its proxy materials for the prior year's annual meeting, except that, if the registrant did not hold an annual meeting during the prior year, or if the date of the meeting has changed by more than 30 calendar days from the prior year, or if the registrant is holding a special meeting or conducting an election of directors by written consent, then the nominating shareholder or nominating shareholder group must

transmit the notice to the registrant and file its notice with the Commission a reasonable time before the registrant mails its proxy materials, as specified by the registrant in a Form 8-K (§ 249.308 of this chapter) filed pursuant to Item 5.08 of Form 8-K; and

(11) The nominating shareholder or nominating shareholder group provides the certifications required by Schedule 14N (§ 240.14n-101) on the date the notice on Schedule 14N is filed with the Commission and transmitted to the registrant.

Instruction to paragraph (b). A registrant will not be required to include a nominee or nominees submitted by a nominating shareholder or nominating shareholder group pursuant to this section if the nominating shareholder or any member of the nominating shareholder group also submits any other nomination to that registrant and/or is participating in more than one nominating shareholder group for that registrant. In addition, a registrant will not be required to include a nominee or nominees if a nominating shareholder or member of a nominating shareholder group:

a. Is or becomes a member of any other group, as determined under section 13(d)(3) of the Act (15 U.S.C. 78m(d)(3) and § 240.13d-5(b)), or otherwise, with persons engaged in soliciting or other nominating activities in connection with the subject election of directors;

b. Is separately conducting a solicitation in connection with the subject election of directors other than a solicitation subject to § 240.14a-2(b)(8) in relation to those nominees it has nominated pursuant to this section or for or against the registrant's nominees; or

c. Is acting as a participant in another person's solicitation in connection with the subject election of directors.

Instruction 1 to paragraph (b)(1). In the case of a registrant other than an investment company registered under the Investment Company Act of 1940 (15 U.S.C. 80a-1 *et seq.*), for purposes of (b)(1) of this section, in determining the total voting power of the registrant's securities that are entitled to be voted on the election of directors, the nominating shareholder or nominating shareholder group may rely on information set forth in the registrant's most recent quarterly or annual report, and any current report subsequent thereto, filed with the Commission pursuant to this Act, unless the nominating shareholder or nominating shareholder group knows or has reason to know that the information contained therein is inaccurate. In the case of a registrant that is an investment company registered under the Investment Company Act of 1940, for purposes of (b)(1) of this section, in determining the total voting power of the registrant's securities that are entitled to be voted on the election of directors, the nominating shareholder or nominating shareholder group may rely on information set forth in the following documents, unless the nominating shareholder or nominating shareholder group knows or has reason to know that the information contained therein is inaccurate:

a. In the case of a registrant that is a series company as defined in Rule 18f-2(a) under the Investment Company Act of 1940 (§ 270.18f-2(a) of this chapter), the Form 8-K (§ 249.308 of this chapter) described in Instruction 2 to paragraph (b)(1) of this section; or

b. In the case of other investment companies, the registrant's most recent annual or semi-annual report filed with the Commission on Form N-CSR (§ 249.331 and § 274.128 of this chapter).

Instruction 2 to paragraph (b)(1). If the registrant is an investment company that is a series company (as defined in § 270.18f-2(a) of this chapter), the registrant must disclose pursuant to Item 5.08 of Form 8-K (§ 249.308 of this chapter) the total number of shares of the registrant outstanding and entitled to be voted (or if the votes are to be cast on a basis other than one vote per share, then the total number of votes entitled to be voted and the basis for allocating such votes) on the election of directors as of the end of the most recent calendar quarter.

Instruction 3 to paragraph (b)(1).

a. When determining the total voting power of the registrant's securities, which is the denominator in the calculation of the percentage of voting power held by the nominating shareholder individually or the nominating shareholder group in the aggregate, calculate the aggregate number of votes derived from all classes of securities of the registrant that are entitled to vote on the election of directors regardless of whether solicitation of a proxy with respect to those securities would require compliance with Exchange Act Regulation 14A (§ 240.14a-1 *et seq.*).

b. When determining the total voting power of the registrant's securities held by the nominating shareholder or any member of the nominating shareholder group, which is the numerator in the calculation of the percentage:

1. Calculate the number of votes derived only from securities with respect to which solicitation of a proxy would require compliance with Exchange Act Regulation 14A (§ 240.14a1 *et seq.*) and over which the nominating shareholder or any the member of the nominating shareholder group, as the case may be, has voting power and investment power, either directly or through any person acting on their behalf;

2. Notwithstanding the voting power calculation specified in paragraph b.1. of this instruction, add to the result of the calculation specified in paragraph b.1. of this instruction any votes attributable to securities with respect to which solicitation of a proxy would require compliance with Exchange Act Regulation 14A (§ 240.14a-1 *et seq.*) that have been loaned by or on behalf of the nominating shareholder or any member of the nominating shareholder group to another person, if the nominating shareholder or member of the nominating shareholder group, as the case may be, or any person acting on their behalf, has the right to recall the loaned securities, and will recall the loaned securities upon being notified that any of the nominating shareholder's or group's nominees will be included in the registrant's proxy statement and proxy card; and

3. Subtract from the result of the calculation specified in paragraphs b.1. and b.2. of this instruction the number of votes attributable to securities of the registrant entitled to vote on the election of directors, regardless of whether solicitation of a proxy with respect to those securities would require compliance Exchange Act Regulation 14A (§ 240.14a-1 *et seq.*), that the nominating shareholder or any member of the nominating shareholder group, as the case may be, or any person acting on their behalf, has sold in a short sale, as defined in 17 CFR 242.200(a), that is not closed out, or has borrowed for purposes other than a short sale.

c. For purposes of the voting power calculation in paragraph b.1. of this instruction:

1. A shareholder has voting power directly only when the shareholder has the power to vote or direct the voting, and investment power directly only when the shareholder has the power to dispose or direct the disposition, of the securities; and

2. A securities intermediary (as defined in § 240.17Ad-20(b)) shall not have voting power or investment power over securities for purposes of paragraph b.1. of this instruction solely because such intermediary holds such securities by or on behalf of another person, notwithstanding that pursuant to the rules of a national securities exchange such intermediary may vote or direct the voting of such securities without instruction.

Instruction 4 to paragraph (b)(1). If a registrant has more than one class of outstanding securities entitled to vote on the election of directors and those classes do not vote together in the election of all directors, then the voting power of the registrant's securities for purposes of the calculation of both the numerator and denominator specified in Instruction 3 to paragraph (b)(1) should be determined only on the basis of the voting power of the class or classes of securities that would be voting together on the election of the person or persons sought to be nominated by the nominating shareholder or the nominating shareholder group.

Instruction to paragraph (b)(2). To determine whether the amount of securities that are used for purposes of satisfying the minimum ownership requirement of paragraph (b)(1) has been held continuously during the three year period prior to the date the Schedule 14N (§ 240.14n-101) is filed and during the period after the Schedule 14N is filed through the date of the subject election of directors, and with respect to all points in time during those periods:

a. Include only the amount of securities with respect to which a solicitation of a proxy would require compliance with Exchange Act Regulation 14A (§ 240.14a-1 *et seq.*) and over which the nominating shareholder or the member of the nominating shareholder group, as the case may be, has voting power and investment power, either directly or through any person acting on their behalf;

b. Notwithstanding the voting power determination specified in paragraph a. of this instruction, include the amount of securities that have been loaned by or on behalf of the nominating shareholder or any member of the nominating shareholder group to another person, if the nominating shareholder or member of the nominating shareholder group, as the case may be, or any person acting on their behalf:

1. Has the right to recall the loaned securities; and

2. With respect to the period from the date the Schedule 14N (§ 240.14n-101) is filed through the date of the subject election of directors, will recall the loaned securities upon being notified that any of the person's nominees will be included in the registrant's proxy statement and proxy card;

c. Reduce the amount of securities held by the amount of securities, on a class basis, that the nominating shareholder or any member of the nominating shareholder group, as the case may be, or any person acting on their behalf, sold in a short sale, as defined in 17 CFR 242.200(a), during the periods, or borrowed for purposes other than a short sale; and

d. Adjust the amount of securities held to give effect to any changes in the amount of securities during the periods resulting from stock splits, reclassifications or other similar adjustments by the registrant.

Instruction to paragraph (b)(3). If the nominating shareholder or member of the nominating shareholder group must provide proof of ownership in the form of a written statement with respect to securities held through a broker or bank that is a participant in the Depository Trust Company or other clearing agency acting as a securities depository, then a statement from such broker or bank will satisfy the requirements of paragraph (b)(3) of this section. If the securities are held through a broker or bank (*e.g.,* in an omnibus account) that is not a participant in a clearing agency acting as a securities depository, the nominating shareholder or member of the nominating shareholder group must also obtain and submit a separate written statement specified in the Instruction to Item 4 of Schedule 14N (§ 240.14n101).

Instruction to paragraph (b)(7). Negotiations between the nominee, the nominating shareholder or nominating shareholder group and the nominating committee or board of the registrant to have the nominee included in the registrant's proxy statement and form of proxy as a registrant nominee, where those negotiations are unsuccessful, or negotiations that are limited to whether the registrant is required to include the shareholder nominee in the registrant's proxy statement and form of proxy in accordance with this section, will not represent a direct or indirect agreement with the registrant.

Instruction to paragraph (b)(9). For purposes of this provision, the nominee would be required to meet the definition of "independence" that is generally applicable to directors of the registrant and not any particular definition of independence applicable to members of the audit committee of the registrant's board of directors. To the extent a national securities exchange or national securities association rule imposes a standard regarding independence that requires a subjective determination by the board or a group or committee of the board (for example, requiring that the board of directors or any group or committee of the board of directors make a determination regarding the existence of factors material to a determination of a nominee's independence), the nominee would not be required to meet the subjective determination of independence as part of the shareholder nomination process.

Instruction 1 to paragraph (b)(10). If the registrant held a meeting the previous year and the date of the current year's annual meeting has not changed by more than 30 calendar days from the date of the previous year's annual meeting, the window period for filing a notice on Schedule 14N (§ 240.14n-101) with the Commission and transmitting that notice to the registrant should be calculated by determining the release date disclosed in the registrant's previous year's proxy statement, increasing the year by one, and counting back 150 calendar days and 120 calendar days for the beginning and end of the window period, respectively. Where the 120 calendar day deadline falls on a Saturday, Sunday or holiday, the deadline will be treated as the first business day following the Saturday, Sunday or holiday.

Instruction 2 to paragraph (b)(10). If the registrant did not hold an annual meeting the previous year, or if the date of the current year's annual meeting has been changed by more than 30 calendar days from the date of the previous year's annual meeting, or if the registrant is holding a special meeting or conducting the election of directors by written consent, the registrant must disclose pursuant to Item 5.08 of Form 8-K (§ 249.308 of this chapter) the date by which a shareholder or group must submit the notice required pursuant to paragraph (b)(10) of this section, which date shall be a reasonable time prior to the date the registrant mails its proxy materials for the meeting.

(c) *Statement of support.* A registrant will be required to include a statement of support submitted by a nominating shareholder or nominating shareholder group in Item 5(i) of the notice on Schedule 14N (§ 240.14n-101), provided that the statement of support does not exceed 500 words per nominee. If a statement of support submitted by a nominating shareholder or nominating shareholder group exceeds 500 words per nominee, the registrant will be required to include the nominee or nominees, provided that the eligibility requirements and other conditions of the rule are satisfied, but the registrant may exclude the supporting statement(s).

(d) *Maximum number of shareholder nominees.* (1) A registrant will be required to include in its proxy statement and form of proxy one shareholder nominee or the number of nominees that represents 25% of the total number of the registrant's board of directors, whichever is greater, submitted by a nominating shareholder or nominating shareholder group pursuant to this section, subject to the limitations in paragraphs (d)(2), (d)(3), (d)(4), and (d)(5) of this section. A registrant may exclude a nominee or nominees if including the nominee or nominees would result in the registrant exceeding the maximum number of nominees it is required to include in its proxy statement and form of proxy pursuant to this provision.

(2) Where the registrant has one or more directors currently serving on its board of directors who were elected as a shareholder nominee pursuant to this section, and the term of that director or directors extends past the election of directors for which it is soliciting proxies, the registrant will not be required to include in the proxy statement and form of proxy more shareholder nominees than could result in the total number of directors who were elected as shareholder nominees pursuant to this section and serving on the board being more than one shareholder nominee or 25% of the total number of the registrant's board of directors, whichever is greater.

(3) Where the registrant has multiple classes of securities and each class is entitled to elect a specified number of directors, the registrant will be required to include the lesser of the number of nominees that the nominating shareholder's or group's class is entitled to elect or 25% of the registrant's board of directors, but in no case less than one nominee.

(4) Where the registrant agrees to include in its proxy statement and form of proxy, as an unopposed registrant nominee, the nominee or nominees of the nominating shareholder or nominating shareholder group that otherwise would be eligible under this section to have its nominees included in the registrant's proxy materials, the nominee will be considered a shareholder nominee for purposes of calculating the maximum number of shareholder nominees that must be included in the registrant's proxy statement and form of proxy, provided that the nominating shareholder or nominating shareholder group filed its notice on Schedule 14N (§ 240.14n-101) before beginning communications with the registrant about the nomination.

(5) A nominee included in a registrant's proxy statement and form of proxy as a result of an agreement between the nominee or nominating shareholder (or where there is a nominating shareholder group, any member of the nominating shareholder group) and the registrant, other than as specified in paragraph (d)(4) of this section, will not be counted as a shareholder nominee for purposes of calculating the maximum number of shareholder nominees that the registrant is required to include in its proxy statement and form of proxy.

Instruction to paragraph (d)(1). Depending on board size, 25% of the board may not result in a whole number. In those instances, the registrant will round down to the closest whole number below 25% to determine the maximum number of shareholder nominees for director that the registrant is required to include in its proxy statement and form of proxy.

Instruction to paragraph (d)(5). Negotiations between the nominee, the nominating shareholder or nominating shareholder group and the nominating committee or board of the registrant to have the nominee included in the registrant's proxy statement and form of proxy as a registrant nominee, where those negotiations are unsuccessful, or negotiations that are limited to whether the registrant is required to include the shareholder nominee in the registrant's proxy statement and form of proxy in accordance with this section, will not represent a direct or indirect agreement with the registrant.

(e) *Order of priority for shareholder nominees.* (1) In the event that more than one eligible shareholder or group of shareholders submits a nominee or nominees for inclusion in the registrant's proxy materials pursuant to this section, the registrant shall include in the proxy statement and form of proxy the nominee or nominees of the nominating shareholder or nominating shareholder group with the highest qualifying voting power percentage disclosed as of the date of filing the Schedule 14N (§ 240.14n-101) (as determined in calculating ownership to satisfy the requirement as specified in paragraph (b)(1) of this section) from which the registrant received a notice filed and transmitted as specified in paragraph (b)(10) of this section, up to and including the total number of nominees required to be included by the registrant pursuant to this section. Where the nominating shareholder or nominating shareholder group with the highest qualifying voting power percentage that is otherwise eligible to rely on this section and that filed and transmitted the notice as specified in paragraph (b)(10) of this section does not nominate the maximum number of individuals required to be included by the registrant, the nominee or nominees of the nominating shareholder or nominating shareholder group with the next highest qualifying voting power percentage from which the registrant received the notice filed and transmitted as specified in paragraph (b)(10) of this section would be included in the registrant's proxy statement and form of proxy, if any, up to and including the total number required to be included by the registrant. This process would continue until the registrant has included the maximum number of nominees it is required to include in its proxy statement and form of proxy pursuant to paragraph (d) of this section or the registrant exhausts the list of eligible nominees.

(2) Prior to the time a registrant has commenced printing its proxy statement and form of proxy, if a nominating shareholder or nominating shareholder group withdraws or is disqualified, a registrant will be required to include in its proxy statement and form of proxy the nominee or nominees of the nominating shareholder or nominating shareholder group with the next highest qualifying voting power percentage, disclosed as of the date of filing the Schedule 14N (§ 240.14n-101) (as determined in calculating ownership to satisfy the requirement as specified in paragraph (b)(1) of this section), from which the registrant received a notice filed and transmitted as specified in paragraph (b)(10) of this section, if any, up to and including the total number required to be included by the registrant. This process would continue until the registrant included the maximum number of nominees it is required to include in its proxy statement and form of proxy pursuant to paragraph (d) of this section or the registrant exhausts the list of eligible nominees. If the registrant has commenced printing its proxy statement and form of proxy, the registrant will not be required to include a nominee or nominees in its proxy statement and form of proxy in place of a nominee or nominees that has withdrawn or has been disqualified.

(3) If a nominee or nominees withdraws or is disqualified after the registrant provides notice to the nominating shareholder or nominating shareholder group of the registrant's intent to include the nominee or nominees in its proxy statement and form of proxy, the registrant will be required to include in its proxy statement and form of proxy any other eligible nominee submitted by that nominating shareholder or nominating shareholder group. If that nominating shareholder or nominating shareholder group did not include any other eligible nominees in its notice filed on Schedule 14N (§ 240.14n-101), then the registrant will be required to include the nominee or nominees of the nominating shareholder or nominating shareholder group with the next highest voting power percentage, disclosed as of the date of filing the Schedule 14N (§ 240.14n-101) (as determined in calculating ownership to satisfy the requirement as specified in paragraph (b)(1) of this section), from which the registrant received a notice filed and transmitted as specified in paragraph (b)(10) of this section, if any, up to and including the total number required to be included by the registrant. This process would continue until the registrant included the maximum number of nominees it is required to include in its proxy statement and form of proxy pursuant to paragraph (d) of this section or the registrant exhausts the list of eligible nominees. If the registrant has commenced printing its proxy statement and form of proxy, the registrant will not be required to include a nominee or nominees in its proxy statement and form of proxy in place of a nominee or nominees that has withdrawn or has been disqualified.

(4) Notwithstanding the other provisions of this paragraph, if a registrant has multiple classes of securities and each class is entitled to elect a specified number of directors, and nominating shareholders or groups of nominating shareholders of more than one of those classes submit a number of eligible nominees for inclusion in the registrant's proxy materials pursuant to this section that is greater than 25% of the total number of the registrant's board of directors, the registrant shall include in the proxy statement and form of proxy the nominee or nominees of the nominating shareholders or groups on the basis of the proportion of total voting power in the election of directors attributable to each class, rounding to the closest whole number, if necessary, and otherwise in accordance with paragraph (e) of this section.

Instruction 1 to paragraph (e). In determining the priority of the nominee or nominees to be included in the registrant's proxy materials, the registrant will be required to consider only the nominee or nominees that would otherwise be required to be included under the provisions of this section.

Instruction 2 to paragraph (e). If the registrant is including shareholder director nominees from more than one nominating shareholder or nominating shareholder group, as described in this paragraph, and including all of the shareholder director nominees of the nominating shareholder or nominating shareholder group that is last in priority would result in exceeding the maximum number required under paragraph (d) of this section, the nominating shareholder or nominating shareholder group that is last in priority may specify which of its nominees are to be included in the registrant's proxy materials.

(f) *False or misleading statements.* The registrant is not responsible for any information in the notice from the nominating shareholder or nominating shareholder group submitted as required by paragraph (b)(10) of this section or otherwise provided by the nominating shareholder or nominating shareholder group that is included in the registrant's proxy materials.

(g) *Determinations regarding eligibility.* (1) If the registrant determines that it will include a shareholder nominee, it must notify the nominating shareholder or nominating shareholder group (or their authorized representative) upon making this determination. In no event should the notification be postmarked or transmitted electronically later than 30 calendar days before it files its definitive proxy statement and form of proxy with the Commission.

(2) If the registrant determines that it may exclude a shareholder nominee pursuant to a provision in paragraph (a), (b), (d), or (e) of this section, or exclude a statement of support pursuant to paragraph (c) of this section, the registrant must notify in writing the nominating shareholder or nominating shareholder group (or their authorized representative) of this determination. This notice must be postmarked or transmitted electronically to the nominating shareholder or nominating shareholder group (or their authorized representative) no later than 14 calendar days after the close of the period for submission specified in paragraph (b)(10) of this section.

(i) The registrant's notice to the nominating shareholder or nominating shareholder group (or their authorized representative) that it has determined that it may exclude a shareholder nominee or statement of support must include an explanation of the registrant's basis for determining that it may exclude the nominee or statement of support.

(ii) The nominating shareholder or nominating shareholder group shall have 14 calendar days after receipt of the registrant's notice pursuant to paragraph (g)(2)(i) of this section to respond to the registrant's notice and correct any eligibility or procedural deficiencies identified in that notice. The nominating shareholder's or nominating shareholder group's response must be postmarked or transmitted electronically to the registrant no later than 14 calendar days after receipt of the registrant's notice.

(3) If the registrant intends to exclude a shareholder nominee or statement of support, after providing the requisite notice of and time for the nominating shareholder or nominating shareholder group to remedy any eligibility or procedural deficiencies in the nomination or statement, the registrant must provide notice of the basis for its determination to the Commission no later than 80 calendar days before it files its definitive proxy statement and form of proxy with the Commission. The Commission staff may permit the registrant to make its submission later than 80 calendar days before the registrant files its definitive proxy statement and form of proxy if the registrant demonstrates good cause for missing the deadline.

(i) The registrant's notice to the Commission shall include:

(A) Identification of the nominating shareholder or each member of the nominating shareholder group, as applicable;

(B) The name of the nominee or nominees;

(C) An explanation of the registrant's basis for determining that the registrant may exclude the nominee or nominees or a statement of support; and

(D) A supporting opinion of counsel when the registrant's basis for excluding a nominee or nominees relies on a matter of state or foreign law.

(ii) The registrant must file its notice to the Commission and simultaneously provide a copy to the nominating shareholder or each member of the nominating shareholder group (or their authorized representative). At the time the registrant files its notice, the registrant also may seek an informal statement of the Commission staff's views with regard to its determination to exclude from its proxy materials a nominee or nominees or a statement of support. The Commission staff may provide an informal statement of its views to the registrant along with a copy to the nominating shareholder or nominating shareholder group (or their authorized representative);

(iii) The nominating shareholder or nominating shareholder group may submit a response to the registrant's notice to the Commission. This response must be postmarked or transmitted electronically to the Commission no later than 14 calendar days after the nominating shareholder's or nominating shareholder group's receipt of the registrant's notice to the Commission. The nominating shareholder or nominating shareholder group must simultaneously provide to the registrant a copy of its response to the Commission.

(iv) If the registrant seeks an informal statement of the Commission staff's views with regard to its determination to exclude a shareholder nominee or nominees, the registrant shall provide the nominating shareholder or nominating shareholder group (or their authorized representative) with notice, either postmarked or transmitted electronically, promptly following receipt of the staff's response, of whether it will include or exclude the shareholder nominee; and

(v) The exclusion of a shareholder nominee or a statement of support by a registrant where that exclusion is not permissible under paragraph (a), (b), (c), (d), or (e) of this section shall be a violation of this section.

Instruction 1 to paragraph (g). When a registrant must provide a notice to a nominating shareholder, member of a nominating shareholder group, or authorized representative of a nominating shareholder group, the registrant is responsible for providing the notice in a manner that evidences timely transmission. Where a nominating shareholder, member of a nominating shareholder group, or authorized representative of a nominating shareholder group responds to a notice, the nominating shareholder, member of a nominating shareholder group, or authorized representative of a nominating shareholder group is responsible for providing the response in a manner that evidences timely transmission.

Instruction 2 to paragraph (g). Neither the composition of the nominating shareholder group nor the shareholder nominee may be changed as a means to correct a deficiency identified in the registrant's notice to the nominating shareholder or nominating shareholder group under paragraph (g)(2) of this section; however, where a nominating shareholder or nominating shareholder group submits a number of nominees that exceeds the maximum number required to be included by the registrant under the circumstances set forth in paragraph (d) of this section, the nominating shareholder or nominating shareholder group may specify which nominee or nominees are not to be included in the registrant's proxy materials.

Instruction 3 to paragraph (g). Unless otherwise indicated in this section, the burden is on the registrant to demonstrate that it may exclude a nominee or statement of support.

[Added in Release No. 33-9136, effective November 15, 2010, 75 F.R. 56668.]

⋙→ *CCH Note: The SEC has stayed the effectiveness of proxy rule amendments adopted in Release 33-9136 pending resolution of a challenge filed by the Business Roundtable and the U.S. Chamber of Commerce in the U.S. Court of Appeals for the District of Columbia Circuit. See Release No. 33-9149, October 4, 2010.*

⋙→ *Amended by Release No. 33-9136, effective November 15, 2010, 75 F.R. 56668.*

[¶ 40,111] Solicitation Before Furnishing a Proxy Statement

Reg. § 240.14a-12. (a) Notwithstanding the provisions of § 240.14a-3(a), a solicitation may be made before furnishing security holders with a proxy statement meeting the requirements of Reg. 240.14a-3(a) if:

(1) Each written communication includes:

(i) The identity of the participants in the solicitation (as defined in Instruction 3 to Item 4 of Schedule 14A (§ 240.14a-101)) and a description of their direct or indirect interests, by security holdings or otherwise, or a prominent legend in clear, plain language advising security holders where they can obtain that information; and

(ii) A prominent legend in clear, plain language advising security holders to read the proxy statement when it is available because it contains important information. The legend also must explain to investors that they can get the proxy statement, and any other relevant documents, for free at the Commission's web site and describe which documents are available free from the participants; and

(2) A definitive proxy statement meeting the requirements of § 240.14a-3(a) is sent or given to security holders solicited in reliance on this section before or at the same time as the forms of proxy, consent or authorization are furnished to or requested from security holders.

(b) Any soliciting material published, sent or given to security holders in accordance with paragraph (a) of this section must be filed with the Commission no later than the date the material is first published, sent or given to security holders. Three copies of the material must at the same time be filed with, or mailed for filing to, each national securities exchange upon which any class of securities of the registrant is listed and registered. The soliciting material must include a cover page in the form set forth in Schedule 14A (§ 240.14a-101) and the appropriate box on the cover page must be marked. Soliciting material in connection with a registered offering is required to be filed only under § 230.424 or § 230.425 of this chapter, and will be deemed filed under this section.

(c) Solicitations by any person or group of persons for the purpose of opposing a solicitation subject to this regulation by any other person or group of persons with respect to the election or removal of directors at any annual or special meeting of security holders also are subject to the following provisions:

(1) *Application of this rule to annual report to security holders.* Notwithstanding the provisions of § 240.14a-3(b) and (c), any portion of the annual report to security holders referred to in § 240.14a-3(b) that comments upon or refers to any solicitation subject to this rule, or to any participant in the solicitation, other than the solicitation by the management, must be filed with the Commission as proxy material subject to this regulation. This must be filed in electronic format unless an exemption is available under Rules 201 or 202 of Regulation S-T (§ 232.201 or § 232.202 of this chapter).

(2) *Use of reprints or reproductions.* In any solicitation subject to this § 240.14a-12(c), soliciting material that includes, in whole or part, any reprints or reproductions of any previously published material must:

(i) State the name of the author and publication, the date of prior publication, and identify any person who is quoted without being named in the previously published material.

(ii) Except in the case of a public or official document or statement, state whether or not the consent of the author and publication has been obtained to the use of the previously published material as proxy soliciting material.

(iii) If any participant using the previously published material, or anyone on his or her behalf, paid, directly or indirectly, for the preparation or prior publication of the previously published material, or has made or proposes to make any payments or give any other consideration in connection with the publication or republication of the material, state the circumstances.

1. If paper filing is permitted, file eight copies of the soliciting material with the Commission, except that only three copies of the material specified by § 240.14a-12(c)(1) need be filed.

2. Any communications made under this section after the definitive proxy statement is on file but before it is disseminated also must specify that the proxy statement is publicly available and the anticipated date of dissemination.

Amendment

Instruction 1 to § 240.14a-12. If paper filing is permitted, file eight copies of the soliciting material with the Commission, except that only three copies of the material specified by § 240.14a-12(c)(1) need be filed.

Instruction 2 to § 240.14a-12. Any communications made under this section after the definitive proxy statement is on file but before it is disseminated also must specify that the proxy statement is publicly available and the anticipated date of dissemination.

Instruction 3 to § 240.14a-12. Inclusion of a nominee pursuant to § 240.14a-11, an applicable state or foreign law provision, or a registrant's governing documents as they relate to the inclusion of shareholder director nominees in the registrant's proxy materials, or solicitations by a nominating shareholder or nominating shareholder group that are made in connection with that nomination constitute solicitations in opposition subject to § 240.14a-12(c), except for purposes of § 240.14a-6(a).

End of Amendment_____

[As last amended in Release No. 33-9136, effective November 15, 2010, 75 F.R. 56668.]

[¶ 40,121] Obligation of Registrants in Communicating with Beneficial Owners

Reg. § 240.14a-13. (a) If the registrant knows that securities of any class entitled to vote at a meeting (or by written consents or authorizations if no meeting is held) with respect to which the registrant intends to solicit proxies, consents or authorizations are held of record by a broker, dealer, voting trustee, bank, association, or other entity that exercises fiduciary powers in nominee name or otherwise, the registrant shall:

(1) By first class mail or other equally prompt means: (i) inquire of each such record holder: (A) whether other persons are the beneficial owners of such securities and if so, the number of copies of the proxy and other soliciting material necessary to supply such material to such beneficial owners; (B) in the case of an annual (or special meeting in lieu of the annual) meeting, or written consents in lieu of such meeting, at which directors are to be elected, the number of copies of the annual report to security holders necessary to supply such report to beneficial owners to whom such reports are to be distributed by such record holder or its nominee and not by the registrant; and (C) if the record holder has an obligation under § 240.14b-1(b)(3) or § 240.14b-2(b)(4)(ii) and (iii), whether an agent has been designated to act on its behalf in fulfilling such obligation and, if so, the name and address of such agent; and (D) whether it holds the registrant's securities on behalf of any respondent bank and, if so, the name and address of each such respondent bank; and (ii) indicate to each such record holder: (A) whether the registrant, pursuant to paragraph (c) of this section, intends to distribute the annual report to security holders to beneficial owners of its securities whose names, addresses and securities positions are disclosed pursuant to § 240.14b-1(c) and § 240.14b-2(e)(2) and (3); (B) the record date; and (C) at the option of the registrant, any employee benefit plan established by an affiliate of the registrant that holds securities of the registrant that the registrant elects to treat as exempt employee benefit plan securities;

(2) Upon receipt of a record holder's or respondent bank's response indicating, pursuant to § 240.14b-2(b)(1)(i), the names and addresses of its respondent banks, within one business day after the date such response is received, make an inquiry of and give notification to each such respondent bank in the same manner required by paragraph (a)(1) of this section; *Provided, however,* the inquiry required by paragraphs (a)(1) and (a)(2) of this section shall not cover beneficial owners of exempt employee benefit plan securities;

(3) Make the inquiry required by paragraph (a)(1) of this section at least 20 business days prior to the record date of the meeting of security holders, or (i) if such inquiry is impracticable 20 business days prior to the record date of a special meeting, as many days before the record date of such meeting as is practicable or, (ii) if consents or authorizations are solicited, and such inquiry is impracticable 20 business days before the earliest date on which they may be used to effect corporate action, as many days before that date as is practicable, or (iii) at such later time as the rules of a national securities exchange on which the class of securities in question is listed may permit for good cause shown; *Provided, however,* that if a record holder or respondent bank has informed the registrant that a designated office(s) or department(s) is to receive such inquiries, the inquiry shall be made to such designated office(s) or department(s); and

(4) Supply, in a timely manner, each record holder and respondent bank of whom the inquiries required by paragraphs (a)(1) and (a)(2) of this section are made with copies of the proxy, other proxy soliciting material, and/or the annual report to security holders, in such quantities, assembled in such form and at such place(s), as the record holder or respondent bank may reasonably request in order to send such material to each beneficial owner of securities who is to be furnished with such material by the record holder or respondent bank; and

(5) Upon the request of any record holder or respondent bank that is supplied with proxy soliciting material and/or annual reports to security holders pursuant to paragraph (a)(4) of this section, pay its reasonable expenses for completing the sending of such material to beneficial owners.

Note 1.—If the registrant's list of security holders indicates that some of its securities are registered in the name of a clearing agency registered pursuant to section 17A of the Act (*e.g.*, "Cede & Co.," nominee for the Depository Trust Company), the registrant shall make appropriate inquiry of the clearing agency and thereafter of the participants in such clearing agency who may hold on behalf of a beneficial owner or respondent bank, and shall comply with the above paragraph with respect to any such participant (see § 240.14a-1 (i)).

Note 2: The attention of registrants is called to the fact that each broker, dealer, bank, association, and other entity that exercises fiduciary powers has an obligation pursuant to § 240.14b-1 and § 240.14b-2 (except as provided therein with respect to exempt employee benefit plan securities held in nominee name) and, with respect to brokers and dealers, applicable self-regulatory organization requirements to obtain and forward, within the time periods prescribed therein, (a) proxies (or in lieu thereof requests for voting instructions) and proxy soliciting materials to be beneficial owners on whose behalf it holds securities, and (b) annual reports to security holders to beneficial owners on whose behalf it holds securities, unless the registrant has notified the record holder or respondent bank that it has assumed responsibility to send such material to beneficial owners whose names, addresses, and securities positions are disclosed pursuant to § 240.14b-1 (b) (3) and § 240.14b-2 (b) (4) (ii) and (iii).

Note 3.—The attention of registrants is called to the fact that registrants have an obligation, pursuant to paragraph (d) of this section, to cause proxies (or in lieu thereof requests for voting instructions), proxy soliciting material and annual reports to security holders to be furnished, in a timely manner, to beneficial owners of exempt employee benefit plan securities.

(b) Any registrant requesting pursuant to § 240.14b-1 (c) and § 240.14b-2 (e) (2) and (3) a list of names, addresses and securities positions of beneficial owners of its securities who either have consented or have not objected to disclosure of such information shall:

(1) By first class mail or other equally prompt means, inquire of each record holder and each respondent bank identified to the registrant pursuant to § 240.14b-2 (b) (4) (i) whether such record holder or respondent bank holds the registrant's securities on behalf of any respondent banks and, if so, the name and address of each such respondent bank.

(2) Request such list to be compiled as of a date no earlier than five business days after the date the registrant's request is received by the record holder or respondent bank; *Provided, however,* that if the record holder or respondent bank has informed the registrant that a designated office(s) or department(s) is to receive such requests, the request shall be made to such designated office(s) or department(s);

(3) Make such request to the following persons that hold the registrant's securities on behalf of beneficial owners: all brokers, dealers, banks, associations and other entities that exercise fiduciary powers; *Provided, however,* such request shall not cover beneficial owners of exempt employee benefit plan securities as defined in § 240.14a-1 (d) (1); and, at the option of the registrant, such request may give notice of any employee benefit plan established by an affiliate of the registrant that holds securities of the registrant that the registrant elects to treat as exempt employee benefit plan securities;

(4) Use the information furnished in response to such request exclusively for purposes of corporate communications; and

(5) Upon the request of any record holder or respondent bank to whom such request is made, pay the reasonable expenses, both direct and indirect, of providing beneficial owner information.

Note.—A registrant will be deemed to have satisfied its obligations under paragraph (b) of this section by requesting consenting and non-objecting beneficial owner lists from a designated agent acting on behalf of the record holder or respondent bank and paying to that designated agent the reasonable expenses of providing the beneficial owner information.

(c) A registrant, at its option, may send its annual report to security holders to the beneficial owners whose identifying information is provided by record holders and respondent banks, pursuant to § 240.14b-1 (b) (3) and § 240.14b-2 (b) (4) (ii) and (iii), provided that such registrant notifies the record holders and respondent banks, at the time it makes the inquiry required by paragraph (a) of this section, that the registrant will send the annual report to security holders to the beneficial owners so identified.

(d) If a registrant solicits proxies, consents or authorizations from record holders and respondent banks who hold securities on behalf of beneficial owners, the registrant shall cause proxies (or in lieu thereof requests for voting instructions), proxy soliciting material and annual reports to security holders to be furnished, in a timely manner, to beneficial owners of exempt employee benefit plan securities.

[As last amended in Release No. 34-55146, effective March 30, 2007, 72 F.R. 4147.]

[¶ 40,125] Modified or Superseded Documents

Reg. § 240.14a-14. (a) Any statement contained in a document incorporated or deemed to be incorporated by reference shall be deemed to be modified or superseded, for purposes of the proxy statement, to the extent that a statement contained in the proxy statement or in any other subsequently filed document that also is or is deemed to be incorporated by reference modifies or replaces such statement.

(b) The modifying or superseding statement may, but need not, state it has modified or superseded a prior statement or include any other information set forth in the document that is not so modified or superseded. The making of a modifying or superseding statement shall not be deemed an admission that the modified or superseded statement, when made, constituted an untrue statement of a material fact, an omission to state a material fact necessary to make a statement not misleading, or the employment of a manipulative, deceptive, or fraudulent device, contrivance, scheme, transaction, act, practice, course of business or artifice to defraud, as those terms are used in the Securities Act of 1933, the Securities Exchange Act of 1934 ("the Act"), the Investment Company Act of 1940, or the rules and regulations thereunder.

(c) Any statement so modified shall not be deemed in its unmodified form to constitute part of the proxy statement for purposes of the Act. Any statement so superseded shall not be deemed to constitute a part of the proxy statement for purposes of the Act.

[As last amended in Release No. 34-55146A, effective April 1, 2008, 73 F.R. 17809 (technical correction).]

[¶ 40,131] Differential and Contingent Compensation in Connection With Roll-Up Transactions

Reg. § 240.14a-15. (a) It shall be unlawful for any person to receive compensation for soliciting proxies, consents, or authorizations directly from security holders in connection with a roll-up transaction as provided in paragraph (b) of this section, if the compensation is:

(1) Based on whether the solicited proxy, consent, or authorization either approves or disapproves the proposed roll-up transaction; or

(2) Contingent on the approval, disapproval, or completion of the roll-up transaction.

(b) This section is applicable to a roll-up transaction as defined in Item 901(c) of Regulation S-K (§ 229.901(c) of this chapter), except for a transaction involving only:

(1) Finite-life entities that are not limited partnerships;

(2) Partnerships whose investors will receive new securities or securities in another entity that are not reported under a transaction reporting plan declared effective before December 17, 1993 by the Commission under Section 11A of the Act (15 U.S.C. 78k-1);or

(3) Partnerships whose investors' securities are reported under a transaction reporting plan declared effective before December 17, 1993 by the Commission under Section 11A of the Act (15 U.S.C. 78k-1).

[As adopted in Release No. 34-35036, December 1, 1994, 59 F.R. 63676.]

[¶ 40,141] Internet Availability of Proxy Materials

Reg. § 240.14a-16. (a)(1) A registrant shall furnish a proxy statement pursuant to § 240.14a-3(a), or an annual report to security holders pursuant to § 240.14a-3(b), to a security holder by sending the security holder a Notice of Internet Availability of Proxy Materials, as described in this section, 40 calendar days or more prior to the security holder meeting date, or if no meeting is to be held, 40 calendar days or more prior to the date the votes, consents or authorizations may be used to effect the corporate action, and complying with all other requirements of this section.

(2) Unless the registrant chooses to follow the full set delivery option set forth in paragraph (n) of this section, it must provide the record holder or respondent bank with all information listed in paragraph (d) of this section in sufficient time for the record holder or respondent bank to prepare, print and send a Notice of Internet Availability of Proxy Materials to beneficial owners at least 40 calendar days before the meeting date.

(b)(1) All materials identified in the Notice of Internet Availability of Proxy Materials must be publicly accessible, free of charge, at the Web site address specified in the notice on or before the time that the notice is sent to the security holder and such materials must remain available on that Web site through the conclusion of the meeting of security holders.

(2) All additional soliciting materials sent to security holders or made public after the Notice of Internet Availability of Proxy Materials has been sent must be made publicly accessible at the specified Web site address no later than the day on which such materials are first sent to security holders or made public.

(3) The Web site address relied upon for compliance under this section may not be the address of the Commission's electronic filing system.

(4) The registrant must provide security holders with a means to execute a proxy as of the time the Notice of Internet Availability of Proxy Materials is first sent to security holders.

(c) The materials must be presented on the Web site in a format, or formats, convenient for both reading online and printing on paper.

(d) The Notice of Internet Availability of Proxy Materials must contain the following:

(1) A prominent legend in bold-face type that states "Important Notice Regarding the Availability of Proxy Materials for the Shareholder Meeting To Be Held on [insert meeting date]";

(2) An indication that the communication is not a form for voting and presents only an overview of the more complete proxy materials, which contain important information and are available on the Internet or by mail, and encouraging a security holder to access and review the proxy materials before voting;

(3) The Internet Web site address where the proxy materials are available;

(4) Instructions regarding how a security holder may request a paper or email copy of the proxy materials at no charge, including the date by which they should make the request to facilitate timely delivery, and an indication that they will not otherwise receive a paper or email copy;

(5) The date, time, and location of the meeting, or if corporate action is to be taken by written consent, the earliest date on which the corporate action may be effected;

(6) A clear and impartial identification of each separate matter intended to be acted on and the soliciting person's recommendations, if any, regarding those matters, but no supporting statements;

(7) A list of the materials being made available at the specified Web site;

(8) A toll-free telephone number, an e-mail address, and an Internet Web site where the security holder can request a copy of the proxy statement, annual report to security holders, and form of proxy, relating to all of the registrant's future security holder meetings and for the particular meeting to which the proxy materials being furnished relate;

(9) Any control/identification numbers that the security holder needs to access his or her form of proxy;

(10) Instructions on how to access the form of proxy, provided that such instructions do not enable a security holder to execute a proxy without having access to the proxy statement and, if required by § 240.14a-3(b), the annual report to security holders; and

(11) Information on how to obtain directions to be able to attend the meeting and vote in person.

(e)(1) The Notice of Internet Availability of Proxy Materials may not be incorporated into, or combined with, another document, except that it may be incorporated into, or combined with, a notice of security holder meeting required under state law, unless state law prohibits such incorporation or combination.

(2) The Notice of Internet Availability of Proxy Materials may contain only the information required by paragraph (d) of this section and any additional information required to be included in a notice of security holders meeting under state law; provided that:

(i) The registrant must revise the information on the Notice of Internet Availability of Proxy Materials, including any title to the document, to reflect the fact that:

(A) The registrant is conducting a consent solicitation rather than a proxy solicitation; or

(B) The registrant is not soliciting proxy or consent authority, but is furnishing an information statement pursuant to § 240.14c-2; and

(ii) The registrant may include a statement on the Notice to educate security holders that no personal information other than the identification or control number is necessary to execute a proxy.

(f)(1) Except as provided in paragraph (h) of this section, the Notice of Internet Availability of Proxy Materials must be sent separately from other types of security holder communications and may not accompany any other document or materials, including the form of proxy.

(2) Notwithstanding paragraph (f)(1) of this section, the registrant may accompany the Notice of Internet Availability of Proxy Materials with:

(i) A pre-addressed, postage-paid reply card for requesting a copy of the proxy materials;

(ii) A copy of any notice of security holder meeting required under state law if that notice is not combined with the Notice of Internet Availability of Proxy Materials; and

(iii) In the case of an investment company registered under the Investment Company Act of 1940, the company's prospectus, a summary prospectus that satisfies the requirements of § 230.498(b) of this chapter, or a report that is required to be transmitted to stockholders by section 30(e) of the Investment Company Act (15 U.S.C. 80a-29(e)) and the rules thereunder; and

(iv) An explanation of the reasons for a registrant's use of the rules detailed in this section and the process of receiving and reviewing the proxy materials and voting as detailed in this section.

(g) *Plain English.*

(1) To enhance the readability of the Notice of Internet Availability of Proxy Materials, the registrant must use plain English principles in the organization, language, and design of the notice.

(2) The registrant must draft the language in the Notice of Internet Availability of Proxy Materials so that, at a minimum, it substantially complies with each of the following plain English writing principles:

(i) Short sentences;

(ii) Definite, concrete, everyday words;

(iii) Active voice;

(iv) Tabular presentation or bullet lists for complex material, whenever possible;

(v) No legal jargon or highly technical business terms; and

(vi) No multiple negatives.

(3) In designing the Notice of Internet Availability of Proxy Materials, the registrant may include pictures, logos, or similar design elements so long as the design is not misleading and the required information is clear.

(h) The registrant may send a form of proxy to security holders if:

(1) At least 10 calendar days or more have passed since the date it first sent the Notice of Internet Availability of Proxy Materials to security holders and the form of proxy is accompanied by a copy of the Notice of Internet Availability of Proxy Materials; or

(2) The form of proxy is accompanied or preceded by a copy, via the same medium, of the proxy statement and any annual report to security holders that is required by § 240.14a-3(b).

(i) The registrant must file a form of the Notice of Internet Availability of Proxy Materials with the Commission pursuant to § 240.14a-6(b) no later than the date that the registrant first sends the notice to security holders.

(j) *Obligation to provide copies.*

(1) The registrant must send, at no cost to the record holder or respondent bank and by U.S. first class mail or other reasonably prompt means, a paper copy of the proxy statement, information statement, annual report to security holders, and form of proxy (to the extent each of those documents is applicable) to any record holder or respondent bank requesting such a copy within three business days after receiving a request for a paper copy.

(2) The registrant must send, at no cost to the record holder or respondent bank and via e-mail, an electronic copy of the proxy statement, information statement, annual report to security holders, and form of proxy (to the extent each of those documents is applicable) to any record holder or respondent bank requesting such a copy within three business days after receiving a request for an electronic copy via e-mail.

(3) The registrant must provide copies of the proxy materials for one year after the conclusion of the meeting or corporate action to which the proxy materials relate, provided that, if the registrant receives the request after the conclusion of the meeting or corporate action to which the proxy materials relate, the registrant need not send copies via First Class mail and need not respond to such request within three business days.

(4) The registrant must maintain records of security holder requests to receive materials in paper or via e-mail for future solicitations and must continue to provide copies of the materials to a security holder who has made such a request until the security holder revokes such request.

(k) *Security holder information.*

(1) A registrant or its agent shall maintain the Internet Web site on which it posts its proxy materials in a manner that does not infringe on the anonymity of a person accessing such Web site.

(2) The registrant and its agents shall not use any e-mail address obtained from a security holder solely for the purpose of requesting a copy of proxy materials pursuant to paragraph (j) for any purpose other than to send a copy of those materials to that security holder. The registrant shall not disclose such information to any person other than an employee or agent to the extent necessary to send a copy of the proxy materials pursuant to paragraph (j).

(*l*) A person other than the registrant may solicit proxies pursuant to the conditions imposed on registrants by this section, provided that:

(1) A soliciting person other than the registrant is required to provide copies of its proxy materials only to security holders to whom it has sent a Notice of Internet Availability of Proxy Materials; and

(2) A soliciting person other than the registrant must send its Notice of Internet Availability of Proxy Materials by the later of:

(i) 40 calendar days prior to the security holder meeting date or, if no meeting is to be held, 40 calendar days prior to the date the votes, consents, or authorizations may be used to effect the corporate action; or

(ii) The date on which it files its definitive proxy statement with the Commission, provided its preliminary proxy statement is filed no later than 10 calendar days after the date that the registrant files its definitive proxy statement.

(3) *Content of the soliciting person's Notice of Internet Availability of Proxy Materials.*

(i) If, at the time a soliciting person other than the registrant sends its Notice of Internet Availability of Proxy Materials, the soliciting person is not aware of all matters on the registrant's agenda for the meeting of security holders, the soliciting person's Notice on Internet Availability of Proxy Materials must provide a clear and impartial identification of each separate matter on the agenda to the extent known by the soliciting person at that time. The soliciting person's notice also must include a clear statement indicating that there may be additional agenda items of which the soliciting person is not aware and that the security holder cannot direct a vote for those items on the soliciting person's proxy card provided at that time.

(ii) If a soliciting person other than the registrant sends a form of proxy not containing all matters intended to be acted upon, the Notice of Internet Availability of Proxy Materials must clearly state whether execution of the form of proxy will invalidate a security holder's prior vote on matters not presented on the form of proxy.

(m) This section shall not apply to a proxy solicitation in connection with a business combination transaction, as defined in § 230.165 of this chapter, as well as transactions for cash consideration requiring disclosure under Item 14 of § 240.14a-101.

(n) *Full Set Delivery Option.*

(1) For purposes of this paragraph (n), the term full set of proxy materials shall include all of the following documents:

(i) A copy of the proxy statement;

(ii) A copy of the annual report to security holders if required by § 240.14a-3 (b); and

(iii) A form of proxy.

(2) Notwithstanding paragraphs (e) and (f) (2) of this section, a registrant or other soliciting person may:

(i) Accompany the Notice of Internet Availability of Proxy Materials with a full set of proxy materials; or

(ii) Send a full set of proxy materials without a Notice of Internet Availability of Proxy Materials if all of the information required in a Notice of Internet Availability of Proxy Materials pursuant to paragraphs (d) and (n) (4) is incorporated in the proxy statement and the form of proxy.

(3) A registrant or other soliciting person that sends a full set of proxy materials to a security holder pursuant to this paragraph (n) need not comply with

(i) The timing provisions of paragraphs (a) and (l) (2); and

(ii) The obligation to provide copies pursuant to paragraph (j).

(4) A registrant or other soliciting person that sends a full set of proxy materials to a security holder pursuant to this paragraph (n) need not include in its Notice of Internet Availability of Proxy Materials, proxy statement, or form of proxy the following disclosures:

(i) Instructions regarding the nature of the communication pursuant to paragraph (d) (2) of this section;

(ii) Instructions on how to request a copy of the proxy materials; and

(iii) Instructions on how to access the form of proxy pursuant to paragraph (d) (10).

[As amended in Release No. 33-9108, effective March 29, 2010, 75 F.R. 9074.]

[¶ 40,143] Electronic Shareholder Forums

Reg. § 240.14a-17. (a) A shareholder, registrant, or third party acting on behalf of a shareholder or registrant may establish, maintain, or operate an electronic shareholder forum to facilitate interaction among the registrant's shareholders and between the registrant and its shareholders as the shareholder or registrant deems appropriate. Subject to paragraphs (b) and (c) of this section, the forum must comply with the federal securities laws, including Section 14 (a) of the Act and its associated regulations, other applicable federal laws, applicable state laws, and the registrant's governing documents.

(b) No shareholder, registrant, or third party acting on behalf of a shareholder or registrant, by reason of establishing, maintaining, or operating an electronic shareholder forum, will be liable under the federal securities laws for any statement or information provided by another person to the electronic shareholder forum. Nothing in this section prevents or alters the application of the federal securities laws, including the provisions for liability for fraud, deception, or manipulation, or other applicable federal and state laws to the person or persons that provide a statement or information to an electronic shareholder forum.

(c) Reliance on the exemption in § 240.14a-2 (b) (6) to participate in an electronic shareholder forum does not eliminate a person's eligibility to solicit proxies after the date that the exemption in § 240.14a-2 (b) (6) is no longer available, or is no longer being relied upon, provided that any such solicitation is conducted in accordance with this regulation.

[Added in Release No. 34-57172, effective February 25, 2008, 73 F.R. 4450.]

⟫⟶ *CCH Note: The SEC has stayed the effectiveness of proxy rule amendments adopted in Release 33-9136 pending resolution of a challenge filed by the Business Roundtable and the U.S. Chamber of Commerce in the U.S. Court of Appeals for the District of Columbia Circuit. See Release No. 33-9149, October 4, 2010.*

⟫⟶ *Added in Release No. 33-9136, effective November 15, 2010, 75 F.R. 56668.*

[¶ 40,145] Disclosure Regarding Nominating Shareholders and Nominees Submitted for Inclusion in a Registrant's Proxy Materials Pursuant to Applicable State or Foreign Law, or a Registrant's Governing Documents

Reg. § 240.14a-18. To have a nominee included in a registrant's proxy materials pursuant to a procedure set forth under applicable state or foreign law, or the registrant's governing documents addressing the inclusion of shareholder director nominees in the registrant's proxy materials, the nominating shareholder or nominating shareholder group must provide notice to the registrant of its intent to do so on a Schedule 14N (§ 240.14n-101) and file that notice, including the required disclosure, with the Commission on the date first transmitted to the registrant. This notice shall be postmarked or transmitted electronically to the registrant by the date specified by the registrant's advance notice provision or, where no such provision is in place, no later than 120 calendar days before the anniversary of the date that the registrant mailed its proxy materials for the prior year's annual meeting, except that, if the registrant did not hold an annual meeting during the prior year, or if the date of the meeting has changed by more than 30 calendar days from the prior year, then the nominating shareholder or nominating shareholder group must provide notice a reasonable time before the registrant mails its proxy materials, as specified by the registrant in a Form 8-K (§ 249.308 of this chapter) filed pursuant to Item 5.08 of Form 8-K.

Instruction to § 240.14a-18. The registrant is not responsible for any information provided in the Schedule 14N (§ 240.14n-101) by the nominating shareholder or nominating shareholder group, which is submitted as required by this section or otherwise provided by the nominating shareholder or nominating shareholder group that is included in the registrant's proxy materials.

[Added in Release No. 33-9136, effective November 15, 2010, 75 F.R. 56668.]

[¶ 40,150] Shareholder Approval of Executive Compensation of TARP Recipients

Reg. § 240.14a-20. If a solicitation is made by a registrant that is a *TARP recipient,* as defined in section 111(a)(3) of the Emergency Economic Stabilization Act of 2008 (12 U.S.C. 5221(a)(3)), during the period in which any obligation arising from financial assistance provided under the TARP, as defined in section 3(8) of the Emergency Economic Stabilization Act of 2008 (12 U.S.C. 5202(8)), remains outstanding and the solicitation relates to an annual (or special meeting in lieu of the annual) meeting of security holders for which proxies will be solicited for the election of directors, as required pursuant to section 111(e)(1) of the Emergency Economic Stabilization Act of 2008 (12 U.S.C. 5221(e)(1)), the registrant shall provide a separate shareholder vote to approve the compensation of executives, as disclosed pursuant to Item 402 of Regulation S-K (§ 229.402 of this chapter), including the compensation discussion and analysis, the compensation tables, and any related material.

Note to § 240.14a-20: TARP recipients that are smaller reporting companies entitled to provide scaled disclosure pursuant to Item 402(l) of Regulation S-K are not required to include a compensation discussion and analysis in their proxy statements in order to comply with this section. In the case of these smaller reporting companies, the required vote must be to approve the compensation of executives as disclosed pursuant to Item 402(m) through (q) of Regulation S-K.

[Added in Release No. 34-61335, effective February 18, 2010, 75 F.R. 2789.]

SCHEDULE 14A

⟫⟶ *CCH Note: The SEC has stayed the effectiveness of proxy rule amendments adopted in Release 33-9136 pending resolution of a challenge filed by the Business Roundtable and the U.S. Chamber of Commerce in the U.S. Court of Appeals for the District of Columbia Circuit. See Release No. 33-9149, October 4, 2010.*

⟫⟶ *Amended by Release No. 33-9136, effective November 15, 2010, 75 F.R. 56668.*

[¶ 40,151] Reg. § 240.14a-101. Information Required in Proxy Statement

Proxy Statement Pursuant to Section 14(a) of the Securities Exchange Act of 1934 (Amendment No.   )

Filed by the Registrant [ ]

Filed by a Party other than the Registrant [ ]

Check the appropriate box:

[ ] Preliminary Proxy Statement

[ ] Confidential, for Use of the Commission Only (as permitted by Rule 14a-6(e)(2))
[ ] Definitive Proxy Statement
[ ] Definitive Additional Materials
[ ] Soliciting Material Pursuant to § 240.14a-12

. . . .
(Name of Registrant as Specified In Its Charter)

. . . .
(Name of Person(s) Filing Proxy Statement if other than the Registrant)

Payment of Filing Fee (Check the appropriate box):
[ ] No fee required.
[ ] Fee computed on table below per Exchange Act Rules 14a-6(i)(1) and 0-11.

    1) Title of each class of securities to which transaction applies:

. . . .

    2) Aggregate number of securities to which transaction applies:

. . . .

    3) Per unit price or other underlying value of transaction computed pursuant to Exchange Act Rule 0-11 (Set forth the amount on which the filing fee is calculated and state how it was determined):

. . . .

    4) Proposed maximum aggregate value of transaction:

. . . .

    5) Total fee paid:

. . . .

[ ] Fee paid previously with preliminary materials.
[ ] Check box if any part of the fee is offset as provided by Exchange Act Rule 240.0-11 and identify the filing for which the offsetting fee was paid previously. Identify the previous filing by registration statement number, or the Form or Schedule and the date of its filing.

    1) Amount Previously Paid:

    _____

    2) Form, Schedule or Registration Statement No.:

    _____

    3) Filing Party:

    _____

    4) Date Filed:

    _____

    Notes.—A. Where any item calls for information with respect to any matter to be acted upon and such matter involves other matters with respect to which information is called for by other items of this schedule, the information called for by such other items also shall be given. For example, where a solicitation of security holders is for the purpose of approving the authorization of additional securities which are to be used to acquire another specified company, and the registrants' security holders will not have a separate opportunity to vote upon the transaction, the solicitation to authorize the securities is also a solicitation with respect to the acquisition. Under those facts, information required by Items 11, 13 and 14 shall be furnished.

    B. Where any item calls for information with respect to any matter to be acted upon at the meeting, such item need be answered in the registrant's soliciting material only with respect to proposals to be made by or on behalf of the registrant.

    C. Except as otherwise specifically provided, where any item calls for information for a specified period with regard to directors, executive officers, officers or other persons holding specified positions or relationships, the information shall be given with regard to any person who held any of the specified positions or relationship at any time during the period. Information, other than information required by Item 404 of Regulation S-K (§ 229.404 of this chapter), need not be included for any portion of the period during which such person did not hold any such position or relationship, provided a statement to that effect is made.

    D. Information may be incorporated by reference only in the manner and to the extent specifically permitted in the items of this schedule. Where incorporation by reference is used, the following shall apply:

    1. Any incorporation by reference of information pursuant to the provisions of this schedule shall be subject to the provisions of § 229.10(d) of this chapter restricting incorporation by reference of

documents that incorporate by reference other information. A registrant incorporating any documents, or portions of documents, shall include a statement on the last page(s) of the proxy statement as to which documents, or portions of documents, are incorporated by reference. Information shall not be incorporated by reference in any case where such incorporation would render the statement incomplete, unclear or confusing.

2. If a document is incorporated by reference but not delivered to security holders, include an undertaking to provide, without charge, to each person to whom a proxy statement is delivered, upon written or oral request of such person and by first class mail or other equally prompt means within one business day of receipt of such request, a copy of any and all of the information that has been incorporated by reference in the proxy statement (not including exhibits to the information that is incorporated by reference unless such exhibits are specifically incorporated by reference into the information that the proxy statement incorporates), and the address (including title or department) and telephone numbers to which such a request is to be directed. This includes information contained in documents filed subsequent to the date on which definitive copies of the proxy statement are sent or given to security holders, up to the date of responding to the request.

3. If a document or portion of a document other than an annual report sent to security holders pursuant to the requirements of Rule 14a-3 (§ 240.14a-3 of this chapter) with respect to the same meeting or solicitation of consents or authorizations as that to which the proxy statement relates is incorporated by reference in the manner permitted by Item or 13 or 14 of this schedule, the proxy statement must be sent to security holders no later than 20 business days prior to the date on which the meeting of such security holders is held or, if no meeting is held, at least 20 business days prior to the date the votes, consents or authorizations may be used to effect the corporate action.

4. *Electronic filings.* If any of the information required by Items 13 or 14 of this Schedule is incorporated by reference from an annual or quarterly report to security holders, such report, or any portion thereof incorporated by reference, shall be filed in electronic format with the proxy statement. This provision shall not apply to registered investment companies.

E. In Item 13 of this Schedule, the reference to "meets the requirement of Form S-3" shall refer to a registrant who meets the following requirements:

(1) the registrant meets the requirements of General Instruction I.A. of Form S-3 (§ 239.13 of this chapter); and

(2) one of the following is met:

(i) the registrant meets the aggregate market value requirement of General Instruction I.B.1 of Form S-3; or

(ii) action is to be taken as described in Items 11, 12 and 14 of this schedule which concerns non-convertible debt or preferred securities which are "investment grade securities" as defined in General Instruction I.B.2 of Form S-3, except that the time by which the rating must be assigned shall be the date on which definitive copies of the proxy statement are first sent or given to security holders; or

(iii) the registrant is a majority-owned subsidiary and one of the conditions of General Instruction I.C. of Form S-3 is met.

Item 1. Date, Time and Place Information

(a) State the date, time and place of the meeting of security holders, and the complete mailing address, including ZIP Code, of the principal executive offices of the registrant, unless such information is otherwise disclosed in material furnished to security holders with or preceding the proxy statement. If action is to be taken by written consent, state the date by which consents are to be submitted if state law requires that such a date be specified or if the person soliciting intends to set a date.

(b) On the first page of the proxy statement, as delivered to security holders, state the approximate date on which the proxy statement and form of proxy are first sent or given to security holders.

(c) Furnish the information required to be in the proxy statement by Rule 14a-5(e) (§ 240.14a-5(e) of this chapter).

Item 2. Revocability of Proxy

State whether or not the person giving the proxy has the power to revoke it. If the right of revocation before the proxy is exercised is limited or is subject to compliance with any formal procedure, briefly describe such limitation or procedure.

Item 3. Dissenters' Right of Appraisal

Outline briefly the rights of appraisal or similar rights of dissenters with respect to any matter to be acted upon and indicate any statutory procedure required to be followed by dissenting security holders in order to perfect such rights. Where such rights may be exercised only within a limited time after the date of adoption of a proposal, the filing of a charter amendment or other similar act, state whether the persons solicited will be notified of such date.

Instructions. 1. Indicate whether a security holder's failure to vote against a proposal will constitute a waiver of his appraisal or similar rights and whether a vote against a proposal will be deemed to satisfy any notice requirements under State law with respect to appraisal rights. If the State law is unclear, state what position will be taken in regard to these matters.

2. Open-end investment companies registered under the Investment Company Act of 1940 are not required to respond to this item.

Item 4. Persons Making the Solicitation

(a) *Solicitations not subject to Rule 14a-12(c) (§240.14a-12(c) of this chapter.)* (1) If the solicitation is made by the registrant, so state. Give the name of any director of the registrant who has informed the registrant in writing that he intends to oppose any action intended to be taken by the registrant and indicate the action which he intends to oppose.

(2) If the solicitation is made otherwise than by the registrant, so state and give the names of the participants in the solicitation, as defined in paragraphs (a)(iii), (iv), (v) and (vi) of Instruction 3 to this Item.

(3) If the solicitation is to be made otherwise than by the use of the mails or pursuant to §240.14a-16, describe the methods to be employed. If the solicitation is to be made by specially engaged employees or paid solicitors, state (i) the material features of any contract or arrangement for such solicitation and identify the parties, and (ii) the cost or anticipated cost thereof.

(4) State the names of the persons by whom the cost of solicitation has been or will be borne, directly or indirectly.

(b) *Solicitations subject to Rule 14a-12(c) (§240.14a-12(c)).* (1) State by whom the solicitation is made and describe the methods employed and to be employed to solicit security holders.

(2) If regular employees of the registrant or any other participant in a solicitation have been or are to be employed to solicit security holders, describe the class or classes of employees to be so employed, and the manner and nature of their employment for such purpose.

(3) If specially engaged employees, representatives or other persons have been or are to be employed to solicit security holders, state (i) the material features of any contract or arrangement for such solicitation and the identity of the parties, (ii) the cost or anticipated cost thereof, and (iii) the approximate number of such employees or employees of any other person (naming such other person) who will solicit security holders).

(4) State the total amount estimated to be spent and the total expenditures to date for, in furtherance of, or in connection with the solicitation of security holders.

(5) State by whom the cost of the solicitation will be borne. If such cost is to be borne initially by any person other than the registrant, state whether reimbursement will be sought from the registrant, and, if so, whether the question of such reimbursement will be submitted to a vote of security holders.

(6) If any such solicitation is terminated pursuant to a settlement between the registrant and any other participant in such solicitation, describe the terms of such settlement, including the cost or anticipated cost thereof to the registrant.

Instructions. 1. With respect to solicitations subject to Rule 14a-12(c) (§240.14a-12(c)), costs and expenditures within the meaning of this Item 4 shall include fees for attorneys, accountants, public relations or financial advisers, solicitors, advertising, printing, transportation, litigation and other costs incidental to the solicitation, except that the registrant may exclude the amount of such costs represented by the amount normally expended for a solicitation for an election of directors in the absence of a contest, and costs represented by salaries and wages of regular employees and officers, provided a statement to that effect is included in the proxy statement.

2. The information required pursuant to paragraph (b)(6) of this Item should be included in any amended or revised proxy statement or other soliciting materials relating to the same meeting or subject matter furnished to security holders by the registrant subsequent to the date of settlement.

3. For purposes of this Item 4 and Item 5 of this Schedule 14A: (a) The terms "participant" and "participant in a solicitation" include the following:

(i) the registrant;

(ii) any director of the registrant, and any nominee for whose election as a director proxies are solicited;

(iii) any committee or group which solicits proxies, any member of such committee or group, and any person whether or not named as a member who, acting alone or with one or more other persons, directly or indirectly takes the initiative, or engages, in organizing, directing, or arranging for the financing of any such committee or group;

(iv) any person who finances or joins with another to finance the solicitation of proxies, except persons who contribute not more than $500 and who are not otherwise participants;

(v) any person who lends money or furnishes credit or enters into any other arrangements, pursuant to any contract or understanding with a participant, for the purpose of financing or otherwise inducing the purchase, sale, holding or voting of securities of the registrant by any participant or other persons, in support of or in opposition to a participant; except that such terms do not include a bank, broker or dealer who, in the ordinary course of business, lends money or executes orders for the purchase or sale of securities and who is not otherwise a participant; and

(vi) any person who solicits proxies.

(b) The terms "participant" and "participant in a solicitation" do not include:

(i) any person or organization retained or employed by a participant to solicit security holders and whose activities are limited to the duties required to be performed in the course of such employment;

(ii) any person who merely transmits proxy soliciting material or performs other ministerial or clerical duties;

(iii) any person employed by a participant in the capacity of attorney, accountant, or advertising, public relations or financial adviser, and whose activities are limited to the duties required to be performed in the course of such employment;

(iv) any person regularly employed as an officer or employee of the registrant or any of its subsidiaries who is not otherwise a participant; or

(v) any officer or director of, or any person regularly employed by, any other participant, if such officer, director or employee is not otherwise a participant.

Item 5. Interest of Certain Persons in Matters to Be Acted Upon

(a) *Solicitations not subject to Rule 14a-12(c) (§ 240.14a-12(c) of this chapter)*. Describe briefly any substantial interest, direct or indirect, by security holdings or otherwise, of each of the following persons in any matter to be acted upon, other than elections to office:

(1) If the solicitation is made on behalf of the registrant, each person who has been a director or executive officer of the registrant at any time since the beginning of the last fiscal year.

(2) If the solicitation is made otherwise than on behalf of the registrant, each participation in the solicitation, as defined in paragraphs in the solicitation, as defined in paragraphs (a)(iii), (iv), (v), and (vi) of Instruction 3 to Item 4 of This Schedule 14A.

(3) Each nominee for election as a director of the registrant.

(4) Each associate of any of the foregoing persons.

Instruction. Except in the case of a solicitation subject to this regulation made in opposition to another solicitation subject to this regulation, the sub-item (a) shall not apply to any interest arising from the ownership of securities of the registrant where the security holder receives no extra or special benefit not shared on a pro rata basis by all other holders of the same class.

(b) *Solicitation subject to Rule 14a-12c (§ 240.14a-12(c) of this chapter)*. With respect to any solicitation subject to Rule 14a-12(c) (§ 240.14a-12(c)):

(1) Describe briefly any substantial interest, direct or indirect, by security holdings or otherwise, of each participant as defined in paragraphs (a)(ii), (iii), (iv), (v) and (vi) of Instruction 3 to Item 4 of this Schedule 14A, in any matter to be acted upon at the meeting, and include with respect to each participant the following information, or a fair and accurate summary thereof:

(i) Name and business address of the participant.

(ii) The participant's present principal occupation or employment and the name, principal business and address of any corporation or other organization in which such employment is carried on.

(iii) State whether or not, during the past ten years, the participant has been convicted in a criminal proceeding (excluding traffic violations or similar misdemeanors) and, if so, give dates, nature of conviction, name and location of court, and penalty imposed or other disposition of the case. A negative answer need not be included in the proxy statement or other soliciting material.

(iv) State the amount of each class of securities of the registrant which the participant owns beneficially, directly or indirectly.

(v) State the amount of each class of securities of the registrant which the participant owns of record but not beneficially.

(vi) State with respect to all securities of the registrant purchased or sold within the past two years, the dates on which they were purchased or sold and the amount purchased or sold on each such date.

(vii) If any part of the purchase price or market value of any of the shares specified in paragraph (b)(1)(vi) of this Item is represented by funds borrowed or otherwise obtained for the purpose of acquiring or holding such securities, so state and indicate the amount of the indebtedness as of the latest practicable date. If such funds were borrowed or obtained otherwise than pursuant to a margin account or bank loan in the regular course of business of a bank, broker or dealer, briefly describe the transaction, and state the names of the parties.

(viii) State whether or not the participant is, or was within the past year, a party to any contract, arrangements or understandings with any person with respect to any securities of the registrant, including, but not limited to joint ventures, loan or option arrangements, puts or calls, guarantees against loss or guarantees of profit, division of losses or profits, or the giving or withholding of proxies. If so, name the parties to such contracts, arrangements or understandings and give the details thereof.

(ix) State the amount of securities of the registrant owned beneficially, directly or indirectly, by each of the participant's associates and the name and address of each such associate.

(x) State the amount of each class of securities of any parent or subsidiary of the registrant which the participant owns beneficially, directly or indirectly.

(xi) Furnish for the participant and associates of the participant the information required by Item 404(a) of Regulation S-K (§ 229.404(a) of this chapter).

(xii) State whether or not the participant or any associates of the participant have any arrangement or understanding with any person—

(A) with respect to any future employment by the registrant or its affiliates; or

(B) with respect to any future transactions to which the registrant or any of its affiliates will or may be a party.

If so, describe such arrangement or understanding and state the names of the parties thereto.

(2) With respect to any person, other than a director or executive officer of the registrant acting solely in that capacity, who is a party to an arrangement or understanding pursuant to which a nominee for election as director is proposed to be elected, describe any substantial interest, direct or indirect, by security holdings or otherwise, that such person has in any matter to be acted upon at the meeting, and furnish the information called for by paragraphs (b)(1)(xi) and (xii) of this Item.

Instruction: For purposes of this Item 5, beneficial ownership shall be determined in accordance with Rule 13d-3 under the Act (Section 240.13d-3 of this chapter).

Item 6. Voting Securities and Principal Holders Thereof

(a) As to each class of voting securities of the registrant entitled to be voted at the meeting (or by written consents or authorizations if no meeting is held), state the number of shares outstanding and the number of votes to which each class is entitled.

(b) State the record date, if any, with respect to this solicitation. If the right to vote or give consent is not to be determined, in whole or in part, by reference to a record date, indicate the criteria for the determination of security holders entitled to vote or give consent.

(c) If action is to be taken with respect to the election of directors and if the persons solicited have cumulative voting rights: (1) Make a statement that they have such rights, (2) briefly describe such rights, (3) state briefly the conditions precedent to the exercise thereof, and (4) if discretionary authority to cumulate votes is solicited, so indicate.

(d) Furnish the information required by Item 403 of Regulation S-K (§ 229.403 of this chapter) to the extent known by the persons on whose behalf the solicitation if made.

(e) If, to the knowledge of the persons on whose behalf the solicitation is made, a change in control of the registrant has occurred since the beginning of its last fiscal year, state the name of the person(s) who acquired such control, the amount and the source of the consideration used by such person or persons; the basis of the control, the date and a description of the transaction(s) which resulted in the change of control and the percentage of voting securities of the registrant now beneficially owned directly or indirectly by the person(s) who acquired control; and the identity of the person(s) from whom control was assumed. If the source of all or any part of the consideration used is a loan made in the ordinary course of business by a bank as defined by section 3(a)(6) of the Act, the identity of such bank shall be omitted provided a request for confidentiality has been made pursuant to section 13(d)(1)(B) of the Act by the person(s) who acquired control. In lieu thereof, the material shall indicate that the identity of the bank has been so omitted and filed separately with the Commission.

Instruction. 1. State the terms of any loans or pledges obtained by the new control group for the purposes of acquiring control, and the names of the lenders or pledgees.

2. Any arrangements or understandings among members of both the former and new control groups and their associates with respect to election of directors or other matters should be described.

Item 7. Directors and Executive Officers

If action is to be taken with respect to the election of directors, furnish the following information in tabular form to the extent practicable. If, however, the solicitation is made on behalf of persons other than the registrant, the information required need be furnished only as to nominees of the persons making the solicitation.

(a) The information required by instruction 4 to Item 103 of Regulation S-K (§ 229.103 of this chapter) with respect to directors and executive officers.

(b) The information required by Items 401, 404(a) and (b), 405 and 407(d)(4), (d)(5) and (h) of Regulation S–K (§ 229.401, § 229.404(a) and (b),§ 229.405 and § 229.407(d)(4), (d)(5) and (h) of this chapter).

(c) The information required by Item 407(a) of Regulation S-K (§ 229.407 of this chapter).

(d) The information required by Item 407(b), (c)(1), (c)(2), (d)(1), (d)(2), (d)(3), (e)(1), (e)(2), (e)(3) and (f) of Regulation S-K (§ 229.407(b), (c)(1), (c)(2), (d)(1), (d)(2), (d)(3), (e)(1), (e)(2), (e)(3) and (f) of this chapter).

(e) In lieu of the information required by this Item 7, investment companies registered under the Investment Company Act of 1940 (15 U.S.C. 80a) must furnish the information required by Item 22(b) of this Schedule 14A.

Amendment

(e) If a shareholder nominee or nominees are submitted to the registrant for inclusion in the registrant's proxy materials pursuant to § 240.14a-11 and the registrant is not permitted to exclude the nominee or nominees pursuant to the provisions of § 240.14a-11, the registrant must include in its proxy statement the disclosure required from the nominating shareholder or nominating shareholder group under Item 5 of § 240.14n-101 with regard to the nominee or nominees and the nominating shareholder or nominating shareholder group.

Instruction to Item 7(e). The information disclosed pursuant to paragraph (e) of this Item will not be deemed incorporated by reference into any filing under the Securities Act of 1933 (15 U.S.C. 77a *et seq.*), the Securities Exchange Act of 1934 (15 U.S.C. 78a *et seq.*), or the Investment Company Act of 1940 (15 U.S.C. 80a-1 *et seq.*), except to the extent that the registrant specifically incorporates that information by reference.

(f) If a registrant is required to include a shareholder nominee or nominees submitted to the registrant for inclusion in the registrant's proxy materials pursuant to a procedure set forth under applicable state or foreign law, or the registrant's governing documents providing for the inclusion of shareholder director nominees in the registrant's proxy materials, the registrant must include in its proxy statement the disclosure required from the nominating shareholder or nominating shareholder group under Item 6 of § 240.14n-101 with regard to the nominee or nominees and the nominating shareholder or nominating shareholder group.

Instruction to Item 7(f). The information disclosed pursuant to paragraph (f) of this Item will not be deemed incorporated by reference into any filing under the Securities Act of 1933 (15 U.S.C. 77a *et seq.*), the Securities Exchange Act of 1934 (15 U.S.C. 78a *et seq.*), or the Investment Company Act of 1940 (15

U.S.C. 80a-1 *et seq.*), except to the extent that the registrant specifically incorporates that information by reference.

(g) In lieu of the information required by this Item 7, investment companies registered under the Investment Company Act of 1940 (15 U.S.C. 80a) must furnish the information required by Item 22(b) of this Schedule 14A.

End of Amendment

Item 8. Compensation of Directors and Executive Officers

Furnish the information required by Item 402 of Regulation S-K (§ 229.402 of this chapter) and paragraphs (e)(4) and (e)(5) of Item 407 of Regulation S-K (§ 229.407(e)(4) and (e)(5) of this chapter) if action is to be taken with regard to:

(a) the election of directors;

(b) any bonus, profit sharing or other compensation plan, contract or arrangement in which any director, nominee for election as a director, or executive officer of the registrant will participate;

(c) any pension or retirement plan in which any such person will participate; or

(d) the granting or extension to any such person of any options, warrants or rights to purchase any securities, other than warrants or rights issued to security holders as such, on a pro rata basis. However, if the solicitation is made on behalf of persons other than the registrant, the information required need be furnished only as to nominees of the persons making the solicitation and associates of such nominees. In the case of investment companies registered under the Investment Company Act of 1940 (15 U.S.C. 80a), furnish the information required by Item 22(b)(13) of this Schedule 14A.

Instruction. If an otherwise reportable compensation plan became subject to such requirements because of an acquisition or merger and, within one year of the acquisition or merger, such plan was terminated for purposes of prospective eligibility, the registrant may furnish a description of its obligation to the designated individuals pursuant to the compensation plan. Such description may be furnished in lieu of a description of the compensation plan in the proxy statement.

Item 9. Independent Public Accountants

If the solicitation is made on behalf of the registrant and relates to (1) the annual (or special meeting in lieu of annual) meeting of security holders at which directors are to be elected, or a solicitation of consents or authorizations in lieu of such meeting or (2) the election, approval or ratification of the registrant's accountant, furnish the following information describing the registrant's relationship with its independent public accountant:

(a) The name of the principal accountant selected or being recommended to security holders for election, approval or ratification for the current year. If no accountant has been selected or recommended, so state and briefly describe the reasons therefor.

(b) The name of the principal accountant for the fiscal year most recently completed if different from the accountant selected or recommended for the current year of if no accountant has yet been selected or recommended for the current year.

(c) The proxy statement shall indicate (1) whether or not representatives of the principal accountant for the current year and for the most recently completed fiscal year are expected to be present at the security holders' meeting, (2) whether or not they will have the opportunity to make a statement if they desire to do so and (3) whether or not such representatives are expected to be available to respond to appropriate questions.

(d) If during the registrant's two most recent fiscal years or any subsequent interim period, (1) an independent accountant who was previously engaged as the principal accountant to audit the registrant's financial statements, or an independent accountant on whom the principal accountant expressed reliance in its report regarding a significant subsidiary, has resigned (or indicated it has declined to stand for re-election after the completion of the current audit) or was dismissed, or (2) a new independent accountant has been engaged as either the principal accountant to audit the registrant's financial statements or as an independent accountant on whom the principal accountant has expressed or is expected to express reliance in its report regarding a significant subsidiary, then, notwithstanding any previous disclosure, provide the information required by Item 304(a) of Regulation S-K (§ 229.304 of this chapter).

(e) (1) Disclose, under the caption *Audit Fees*, the aggregate fees billed for each of the last two fiscal years for professional services rendered by the principal accountant for the audit of the registrant's annual financial statements and review of financial statements included in the registrant's Form 10-Q (17 CFR 249.308a) or services that are normally provided by the accountant in connection with statutory and regulatory filings or engagements for those fiscal years.

(2) Disclose, under the caption *Audit-Related Fees*, the aggregate fees billed in each of the last two fiscal years for assurance and related services by the principal accountant that are reasonably related to the performance of the audit or review of the registrant's financial statements and are not reported under paragraph (e)(1) of this section. Registrants shall describe the nature of the services comprising the fees disclosed under this category.

(3) Disclose, under the caption *Tax Fees*, the aggregate fees billed in each of the last two fiscal years for professional services rendered by the principal accountant for tax compliance, tax advice, and tax planning. Registrants shall describe the nature of the services comprising the fees disclosed under this category.

(4) Disclose, under the caption *All Other Fees*, the aggregate fees billed in each of the last two fiscal years for products and services provided by the principal accountant, other than the services reported in paragraphs (e)(1) through (e)(3) of this section. Registrants shall describe the nature of the services comprising the fees disclosed under this category.

(5)(i) Disclose the audit committee's pre-approval policies and procedures described in 17 CFR 210.2-01(c)(7)(i).

(ii) Disclose the percentage of services described in each of paragraphs (e)(2) through (e)(4) of this section that were approved by the audit committee pursuant to 17 CFR 210.2-01(c)(7)(i)(C).

(6) If greater than 50 percent, disclose the percentage of hours expended on the principal accountant's engagement to audit the registrant's financial statements for the most recent fiscal year that were attributed to work performed by persons other than the principal accountant's full-time, permanent employees.

(7) If the registrant is an investment company, disclose the aggregate non-audit fees billed by the registrant's accountant for services rendered to the registrant, and to the registrant's investment adviser (not including any subadviser whose role is primarily portfolio management and is subcontracted with or overseen by another investment adviser), and any entity controlling, controlled by, or under common control with the adviser that provides ongoing services to the registrant for each of the last two fiscal years of the registrant.

(8) If the registrant is an investment company, disclose whether the audit committee of the board of directors has considered whether the provision of non-audit services that were rendered to the registrant's investment adviser (not including any subadviser whose role is primarily portfolio management and is subcontracted with or overseen by another investment adviser), and any entity controlling, controlled by, or under common control with the investment adviser that provides ongoing services to the registrant that were not pre-approved pursuant to 17 CFR 210.2-01(c)(7)(ii) is compatible with maintaining the principal accountant's independence.

Instruction to Item 9(e).

For purposes of Item 9(e)(2), (3), and (4), registrants that are investment companies must disclose fees billed for services rendered to the registrant and separately, disclose fees required to be approved by the investment company registrant's audit committee pursuant to 17 CFR 210.2-01(c)(7)(ii). Registered investment companies must also disclose the fee percentages as required by Item 9(e)(5)(ii) for the registrant and separately, disclose the fee percentages as required by Item 9(e)(5)(ii) for the fees required to be approved by the investment company registrant's audit committee pursuant to 17 CFR 210.2-01(c)(7)(ii).

Item 10. Compensation Plans

If action is to be taken with respect to any plan pursuant to which cash or noncash compensation may be paid or distributed, furnish the following information:

(a) *Plans Subject to Securityholder Action.*

(1) Describe briefly the material features of the plan being acted upon, identify each class of persons who will be eligible to participate therein, indicate the approximate number of persons in each such class and state the basis of such participation.

(2)(i) In the tabular format specified below, disclose the benefits or amounts that will be received by or allocated to each of the following under the plan being acted upon, if such benefits or amounts are determinable:

NEW PLAN BENEFITS
Plan Name

Name and Position	Dollar Value ($)	Number of Units
CEO		
A		
B		
C		
D		
Executive Group		
Non-Executive Director Group		
Non-Executive Officer Employee Group		

(ii) The table required by paragraph (a)(2)(i) of this Item shall provide information as to the following persons:

(A) Each person (stating name and position) specified in paragraph (a)(3) of Item 402 of Regulation S-K (§ 229.402(a)(3) of this chapter);

Instruction: In the case of investment companies registered under the Investment Company Act of 1940, furnish the information for Compensated Persons as defined in Item 22(b)(13) of this Schedule in lieu of the persons specified in paragraph (a)(3) of Item 402 of Regulation S-K (§ 229.402(a)(3) of this chapter).

(B) All current executive officers as a group;

(C) All current directors who are not executive officers as a group; and

(D) All employees, including all current officers who are not executive officers, as a group.

Instruction to New Plan Benefits Table.

Additional columns should be added for each plan with respect to which securityholder action is to be taken.

(iii) If the benefits or amounts specified in paragraph (a)(2)(i) of this Item are not determinable, state the benefits or amounts which would have been received by or allocated to each of the following for the last completed fiscal year if the plan had been in effect, if such benefits or amounts may be determined in the table specified in paragraph (a)(2)(i) of this Item:

(A) Each person (stating name and position) specified in paragraph (a)(3) of Item 402 of Regulation S-K (§ 229.402(a)(3) of this chapter);

(B) All current executive officers as a group;

(C) All current directors who are not executive officers as a group; and

(D) All employees, including all current officers who are not executive officers, as a group.

(3) If the plan to be acted upon can be amended, otherwise than by a vote of securityholders, to increase the cost thereof to the registrant or to alter the allocation of the benefits as between the persons and groups specified in paragraph (2)(a) of this item, state the nature of the amendments which can be so made.

(b) *Additional Information Regarding Specific Plans Subject to Securityholder Action.*

(1) With respect to any pension or retirement plan submitted for securityholder action, state:

(i) The approximate total amount necessary to fund the plan with respect to past services, the period over which such amount is to be paid and the estimated annual payments necessary to pay the total amount over such period; and

(ii) The estimated annual payment to be made with respect to current services. In the case of a pension or retirement plan, information called for by paragraph (a)(2) of this Item may be furnished in the format specified by paragraph (h)(2) of Item 402 of Regulation S-K (§ 229.402(h)(2) of this chapter).

Instruction to paragraph (b)(1)(ii).

In the case of investment companies registered under the Investment Company Act of 1940 (15 U.S.C. 80a), refer to Instruction 4 in Item 22(b)(13)(i) of this Schedule in lieu of paragraph (h)(2) of Item 402 of Regulation S-K (§ 229.402(h)(2) of this chapter).

(2)(i) With respect to any specific grant of or any plan containing options, warrants or rights submitted for security holder action, state:

(A) The title and amount of securities underlying such options, warrants or rights;

(B) The prices, expiration dates and other material conditions upon which the options, warrants or rights may be exercised;

(C) The consideration received or to be received by the registrant or subsidiary for the granting or extension of the options, warrants or rights;

(D) The market value of the securities underlying the options, warrants or rights as of the latest practicable date; and

(E) In the case of options, the federal income tax consequences of the issuance and exercise of such options to the recipient and the registrant; and

(ii) State separately the amount of such options received or to be received by the following persons if such benefits or amounts are determinable:

(A) Each person (stating name and position) specified in paragraph (a)(3) of Item 402 of Regulation S-K (§ 229.402(a)(3) of this chapter);

(B) All current executive officers as a group;

(C) All current directors who are not executive officers as a group;

(D) Each nominee for election as a director;

(E) Each associate of any of such directors, executive officer or nominees;

(F) Each other person who received or is to receive 5 percent of such options, warrants or rights; and

(G) All employees, including all current officers who are not executive officers, as a group.

(c) *Information regarding plans and other arrangements not subject to security holder action.* Furnish the information required by Item 201(d) of Regulation S-K (§ 229.201(d) of this chapter).

Instructions to paragraph (c).

1. If action is to be taken as described in paragraph (a) of this Item with respect to the approval of a new compensation plan under which equity securities of the registrant are authorized for issuance, information about the plan shall be disclosed as required under paragraphs (a) and (b) of this Item and shall not be included in the disclosure required by Item 201(d) of Regulation S-K (§ 229.201(d) of this chapter). If action is to be taken as described in paragraph (a) of this Item with respect to the amendment or modification of an existing plan under which equity securities of the registrant are authorized for issuance, the registrant shall include information about securities previously authorized for issuance under the plan (including any outstanding options, warrants and rights previously granted pursuant to the plan and any securities remaining available for future issuance under the plan) in the disclosure required by Item 201(d) of Regulation S-K (§ 229.201(d) of this chapter). Any additional securities that are the subject of the amendments or modification of the existing plan shall be disclosed as required under paragraphs (a) and (b) of this Item and shall not be included in the Item 201(d) disclosure.

Instructions

1. The term *plan* as used in this Item means any plan as defined in paragraph (a)(6)(ii) of Item 402 of Regulation S-K (§ 229.402(a)(6)(ii) of this chapter).

2. If action is to be taken with respect to a material amendment or modification of an existing plan, the item shall be answered with respect to the plan as proposed to be amended or modified and shall indicate any material differences from the existing plan.

3. If the plan to be acted upon is set forth in a written document, three copies thereof shall be filed with the Commission at the time copies of the proxy statement and form of proxy are first filed pursuant to paragraph (a) or (b) of § 240.14a-6. Electronic filers shall file with the Commission a copy of such written plan document in electronic format as an appendix to the proxy statement. It need not be provided to security holders unless it is a part of the proxy statement.

4. Paragraphs (b)(2)(ii) does not apply to warrants or rights to be issued to security holders as such on a pro rata basis.

5. The Commission should be informed, as supplemental information, when the proxy statement is first filed, as to when the options, warrants, or rights and the shares called for thereby will be registered under the Securities Act or, if such registration is not contemplated, the section of the Securities Act or rule of the Commission under which exemption from such registration is claimed and the facts relied upon to make the exemption available.

Item 11. Authorization or Issuance of Securities Otherwise than for Exchange

If action is to be taken with respect to the authorization or issuance of any securities otherwise than for exchange for outstanding securities of the registrant, furnish the following information:

(a) State the title and amount of securities to be authorized or issued.

(b) Furnish the information required by Item 202 of Regulation S-K (§ 229.202 of this chapter). If the terms of the securities cannot be stated or estimated with respect to any or all of the securities to be authorized, because no offering thereof is contemplated in the proximate future, and if no further authorization by security holders for the issuance thereof is to be obtained, it should be stated that the terms of the securities to be authorized, including dividend or interest rates, conversion prices, voting rights, redemption prices, maturity dates, and similar matters will be determined by the board of directors. If the securities are additional shares of common stock of a class outstanding, the description may be omitted except for a statement of the preemptive rights, if any. Where the statutory provisions with respect to preemptive rights are so indefinite or complex that they cannot be stated in summarized form, it will suffice to make a statement in the form of an opinion of counsel as to the existence and extent of such rights.

(c) Describe briefly the transaction in which the securities are to be issued including a statement as to (1) the nature and approximate amount of consideration received or to be received by the registrant and (2) the approximate amount devoted to each purpose so far as determinable for which the net proceeds have been or are to be used. If it is impracticable to describe the transaction in which the securities are to be issued, state the reason, indicate the purpose of the authorization of the securities, and state whether further authorization for the issuance of the securities by a vote of security holders will be solicited prior to such issuance.

(d) If the securities are to be issued otherwise than in a public offering for cash, state the reasons for the proposed authorization or issuance and the general effect thereof upon the rights of existing security holders.

(e) Furnish the information required by Item 13(a) of this schedule.

Item 12. Modification or Exchange of Securities

If action is to be taken with respect to the modification of any class of securities of the registrant, or the issuance or authorization for issuance of securities of the registrant in exchange for outstanding securities of the registrant furnish the following information:

(a) If outstanding securities are to be modified, state the title and amount thereof. If securities are to be issued in exchange for outstanding securities, state the title and amount of securities to be so issued, the title and amount of outstanding securities to be exchanged therefor and the basis of the exchange.

(b) Describe any material differences between the outstanding securities and the modified or new securities in respect of any of the matters concerning which information would be required in the description of the securities in Item 202 of Regulation S-K (§ 229.202 of this chapter).

(c) State the reasons for the proposed modification or exchange and the general effect thereof upon the rights of existing security holders.

(d) Furnish a brief statement as to arrears in dividends or as to defaults in principal or interest in respect to the outstanding securities which are to be modified or exchanged and such other information as may be appropriate in the particular case to disclose adequately the nature and effect of the proposed action.

(e) Outline briefly any other material features of the proposed modification or exchange. If the plan of proposed action is set forth in a written document, file copies thereof with the Commission in accordance with § 240.14a-8.

(f) Furnish the information required by Item 13(a) of this Schedule.

Instruction. If the existing security is presently listed and registered on a national securities exchange, state whether the registrant intends to apply for listing and registration of the new or reclassified security on such exchange or any other exchange. If the registrant does not intend to make such application, state the effect of the termination of such listing and registration.

Item 13. Financial and Other Information

(*See* Notes D and E at the beginning of this Schedule.)

(a) Information required. If action is to be taken with respect to any matter specified in Item 11 or 12, furnish the following information:

(1) Financial statements meeting the requirements of Regulation S-X, including financial information required by Rule 3-05 and Article 11 of Regulation S-X with respect to transactions other than pursuant to which action is to be taken as described in this proxy statement (A smaller reporting company may provide the information in Rules 8-04 and 8-05 of Regulation S-X (§ 210.8-04 and § 210.8-05 of this chapter) in lieu of the financial information required by Rule 3-05 and Article 11 of Regulation S-X);

(2) Item 302 of Regulation S-K, supplementary financial information;

(3) Item 303 of Regulation S-K, management's discussion and analysis of financial condition and results of operations;

(4) Item 304 of Regulation S-K, changes in and disagreements with accountants on accounting and financial disclosure;

(5) Item 305 of Regulation S-K, quantitative and qualitative disclosures about market risk; and

(6) A statement as to whether or not representatives of the principal accountants for the current year and for the most recently completed fiscal year:(i) are expected to be present at the security holders' meeting;

(ii) will have the opportunity to make a statement if they desire to do so; and

(iii) are expected to be available to respond to appropriate questions.

(b) Incorporation by reference. The information required pursuant to paragraph (a) of this Item may be incorporated by reference into the proxy statement as follows:

(1) S-3 registrants. If the registrant meets the requirements of Form S-3 (*see* Note E to this Schedule), it may incorporate by reference to previously-filed documents any of the information required by paragraph (a) of this Item, provided that the requirements of paragraph (c) are met. Where the registrant meets the requirements of Form S-3 and has elected to furnish the required information by incorporation by reference, the registrant may elect to update the information so incorporated by reference to information in subsequently-filed documents.

(2) All registrants. The registrant may incorporate by reference any of the information required by paragraph (a) of this Item, provided that the information is contained in an annual report to security holders or a previously-filed statement or report, such report or statement is delivered to security holders with the proxy statement and the requirements of paragraph (c) are met.

(c) *Certain conditions applicable to incorporation by reference.* Registrants eligible to incorporate by reference into the proxy statement the information required by paragraph (a) of this Item in the manner specified by paragraphs (b)(1) and (b)(2) may do so only if:

(1) the information is not required to be included in the proxy statement pursuant to the requirement of another Item;

(2) the proxy statement identifies on the last page(s) the information incorporated by reference; and

(3) the material incorporated by reference substantially meets the requirements of this Item or the appropriate portions of this Item.

Instructions to Item 13 1. Notwithstanding the provisions of this Item, any or all of the information required by paragraph (a) of this Item, not material for the exercise of prudent judgment in regard to the matter to be acted upon may be omitted. In the usual case the information is deemed material to the exercise of prudent judgment where the matter to be acted upon is the authorization or issuance of a material amount of senior securities, but the information is not deemed material where the matter to be acted upon is the authorization or issuance of common stock, otherwise than in an exchange, merger, consolidation, acquisition or similar transaction, the authorization of preferred stock without present intent to issue or the authorization of preferred stock for issuance for cash in an amount constituting fair value.

2. In order to facilitate compliance with Rule 2-02(a) of Regulation S-X, one copy of the definitive proxy statement filed with the Commission shall include a manually signed copy of the accountant's report. If the financial statements are incorporated by reference, a manually signed copy of the accountant's report shall be filed with the definitive proxy statement.

3. Notwithstanding the provisions of Regulation S-X, no schedules other than those prepared in accordance with Rules 12-15, 12-28and 12-29 (or, for management investment companies, Rules 12-12 through 12-14) of that regulation need be furnished in the proxy statement.

4. Unless registered on a national securities exchange or otherwise required to furnish such information, registered investment companies need not furnish the information required by paragraphs (a)(2) or (3) of this Item.

5. If the registrant submits preliminary proxy material incorporating by reference financial statements required by this Item, the registrant should furnish a draft of the financial statements if the document from which they are incorporated has not been filed with or furnished to the Commission.

6. A registered investment company need not comply with items (a)(2), (a)(3), and (a)(5) of this Item 13.

Item 14. Mergers, Consolidations, Acquisitions and Similar Matters

(See Notes A and D at the beginning of this Schedule.)

Instructions to Item 14.

1. In transactions in which the consideration offered to security holders consists wholly or in part of securities registered under the Securities Act of 1933, furnish the information required by Form S-4 (§239.25 of this chapter), Form F-4 (§239.34 of this chapter), or Form N-14 (§239.23 of this chapter), as applicable, instead of this Item. Only a Form S-4, Form F-4, or Form N-14 must be filed in accordance with §240.14a-6(j).

2. (a) In transactions in which the consideration offered to security holders consists wholly of cash, the information required by paragraph (c)(1) of this Item for the acquiring company need not be provided unless the information is material to an informed voting decision (*e.g.*, the security holders of the target company are voting and financing is not assured).

(b) Additionally, if only the security holders of the target company are voting:

i. The financial information in paragraphs (b)(8) - (11) of this Item for the acquiring company and the target need not be provided; and

ii. The information in paragraph (c)(2) of this Item for the target company need not be provided.

If, however, the transaction is a going-private transaction (as defined by §240.13e-3), then the information required by paragraph (c)(2) of this Item must be provided and to the extent that the going-private rules require the information specified in paragraph (b)(8) - (b)(11) of this Item, that information must be provided as well.

3. In transactions in which the consideration offered to security holders consists wholly of securities exempt from registration under the Securities Act of 1933 or a combination of exempt securities and cash, information about the acquiring company required by paragraph (c)(1) of this Item need not be provided if only the security holders of the acquiring company are voting, unless the information is material to an informed voting decision. If only the security holders of the target company are voting, information about the target company in paragraph (c)(2) of this Item need not be provided. However, the information required by paragraph (c)(2) of this Item must be provided if the transaction is a going-private (as defined by §240.13e-3) or roll-up (as described by Item 901 of Regulation S-K (§229.901 of this chapter)) transaction.

4. The information required by paragraphs (b)(8) - (11) and (c) need not be provided if the plan being voted on involves only the acquiring company and one or more of its totally held subsidiaries and does not involve a liquidation or a spin-off.

5. To facilitate compliance with Rule 2-02(a) of Regulation S-X (§210.2-02(a) of this chapter) (technical requirements relating to accountants' reports), one copy of the definitive proxy statement filed with the Commission must include a signed copy of the accountant's report. If the financial statements are incorporated by reference, a signed copy of the accountant's report must be filed with the definitive

proxy statement. Signatures may be typed if the document is filed electronically on EDGAR. *See* Rule 302 of Regulation S-T (§ 232.302 of this chapter).

6. Notwithstanding the provisions of Regulation S-X, no schedules other than those prepared in accordance with § 210.12-15, § 210.12-28 and § 210.12-29 of this chapter (or, for management investment companies, § § 210.12-12 through 210.12-14 of this chapter) of that regulation need be furnished in the proxy statement.

7. If the preliminary proxy material incorporates by reference financial statements required by this Item, a draft of the financial statements must be furnished to the Commission staff upon request if the document from which they are incorporated has not been filed with or furnished to the Commission.

(a) *Applicability.* If action is to be taken with respect to any of the following transactions, provide the information required by this Item:

(1) A merger or consolidation;

(2) An acquisition of securities of another person;

(3) An acquisition of any other going business or the assets of a going business;

(4) A sale or other transfer of all or any substantial part of assets; or

(5) A liquidation or dissolution.

(b) *Transaction information.* Provide the following information for each of the parties to the transaction unless otherwise specified:

(1) *Summary term sheet.* The information required by Item 1001 of Regulation M-A (§ 229.1001 of this chapter).

(2) *Contact information.* The name, complete mailing address and telephone number of the principal executive offices.

(3) *Business conducted.* A brief description of the general nature of the business conducted.

(4) *Terms of the transaction.* The information required by Item 1004(a)(2) of Regulation M-A (§ 229.1004 of this chapter).

(5) *Regulatory approvals.* A statement as to whether any federal or state regulatory requirements must be complied with or approval must be obtained in connection with the transaction and, if so, the status of the compliance or approval.

(6) *Reports, opinions, appraisals.* If a report, opinion or appraisal materially relating to the transaction has been received from an outside party, and is referred to in the proxy statement, furnish the information required by Item 1015(b) of Regulation M-A (§ 229.1015 of this chapter).

(7) *Past contacts, transactions or negotiations.* The information required by Items 1005(b) and 1011(a)(1) of Regulation M-A (§ 229.1005 of this chapter and § 229.1011 of this chapter), for the parties to the transaction and their affiliates during the periods for which financial statements are presented or incorporated by reference under this Item.

(8) *Selected financial data.* The selected financial data required by Item 301 of Regulation S-K (§ 229.301 of this chapter).

(9) *Pro forma selected financial data.* If material, the information required by Item 301 of Regulation S-K (§ 229.301 of this chapter) for the acquiring company, showing the pro forma effect of the transaction.

(10) *Pro forma information.* In a table designed to facilitate comparison, historical and pro forma per share data of the acquiring company and historical and equivalent pro forma per share data of the target company for the following Items:

(i) Book value per share as of the date financial data is presented pursuant to Item 301 of Regulation S-K (§ 229.301 of this chapter);

(ii) Cash dividends declared per share for the periods for which financial data is presented pursuant to Item 301 of Regulation S-K (§ 229.301 of this chapter); and

(iii) Income (loss) per share from continuing operations for the periods for which financial data is presented pursuant to Item 301 of Regulation S-K (§ 229.301 of this chapter).

Instructions to paragraphs (b)(8), (b)(9) and (b)(10):

1. For a business combination, present the financial information required by paragraphs (b)(9) and (b)(10) only for the most recent fiscal year and interim period. For a combination between entities under common control, present the financial information required by paragraphs (b)(9) and (b)(10) (except for information with regard to book value) for the most recent three fiscal years and interim period. For purposes of these paragraphs, book value information need only be provided for the most recent balance sheet date.

2. Calculate the equivalent pro forma per share amounts for one share of the company being acquired by multiplying the exchange ratio times each of:

(i) The pro forma income (loss) per share before non-recurring charges or credits directly attributable to the transaction;

(ii) The pro forma book value per share; and

(iii) The pro forma dividends per share of the acquiring company.

3. Unless registered on a national securities exchange or otherwise required to furnish such information, registered investment companies need not furnish the information required by paragraphs (b)(8) and (b)(9) of this Item.

(11) *Financial information.* If material, financial information required by Article 11 of Regulation S-X (§§ 210.10-01 through 229.11-03 of this chapter) with respect to this transaction.

Instructions to paragraph (b)(11):

1. Present any Article 11 information required with respect to transactions other than those being voted upon (where not incorporated by reference) together with the pro forma information relating to the transaction being voted upon. In presenting this information, you must clearly distinguish between the transaction being voted upon and any other transaction.

2. If current pro forma financial information with respect to all other transactions is incorporated by reference, you need only present the pro forma effect of this transaction.

(c) *Information about the parties to the transaction.*

(1) *Acquiring company.* Furnish the information required by Part B (Registrant Information) of Form S-4 (§ 239.25 of this chapter) or Form F-4 (§ 239.34 of this chapter), as applicable, for the acquiring company. However, financial statements need only be presented for the latest two fiscal years and interim periods.

(2) *Acquired company.* Furnish the information required by Part C (Information with Respect to the Company Being Acquired) of Form S-4 (§ 239.25 of this chapter) or Form F-4 (§ 239.34 of this chapter), as applicable.

(d) *Information about parties to the transaction: registered investment companies and business development companies.*

If the acquiring company or the acquired company is an investment company registered under the Investment Company Act of 1940 or a business development company as defined by Section 2(a)(48) of the Investment Company Act of 1940, provide the following information for that company instead of the information specified by paragraph (c) of this Item:

(1) Information required by Item 101 of Regulation S-K (§ 229.101 of this chapter), description of business;

(2) Information required by Item 102 of Regulation S-K (§ 229.102 of this chapter), description of property;

(3) Information required by Item 103 of Regulation S-K (§ 229.103 of this chapter), legal proceedings;

(4) Information required by Item 201(a), (b) and (c) of Regulation S-K (§ 229.201(a), (b) and (c) of this chapter), market price of and dividends on the registrant's common equity and related stockholder matters;

(5) Financial statements meeting the requirements of Regulation S-X, including financial information required by Rule 3-05 and Article 11 of Regulation S-X (§ 210.3-05 and § 210.11-01 through § 210.11-03 of this chapter) with respect to transactions other than that as to which action is to be taken as described in this proxy statement;

(6) Information required by Item 301 of Regulation S-K (§ 229.301 of this chapter), selected financial data;

(7) Information required by Item 302 of Regulation S-K (§ 229.302 of this chapter), supplementary financial information;

(8) Information required by Item 303 of Regulation S-K (§ 229.303 of this chapter), management's discussion and analysis of financial condition and results of operations; and

(9) Information required by Item 304 of Regulation S-K (§ 229.304 of this chapter), changes in and disagreements with accountants on accounting and financial disclosure.

Instruction to paragraph (d) of Item 14:

Unless registered on a national securities exchange or otherwise required to furnish such information, registered investment companies need not furnish the information required by paragraphs (d)(6), (d)(7) and (d)(8) of this Item.

(e) *Incorporation by reference.*

(1) The information required by paragraph (c) of this section may be incorporated by reference into the proxy statement to the same extent as would be permitted by Form S-4 (§ 239.25 of this chapter) or Form F-4 (§ 239.34 of this chapter), as applicable.

(2) Alternatively, the registrant may incorporate by reference into the proxy statement the information required by paragraph (c) of this Item if it is contained in an annual report sent to security holders in accordance with§ 240.14a-3 of this chapter with respect to the same meeting or solicitation of consents or authorizations that the proxy statement relates to and the information substantially meets the disclosure requirements of Item 14 or Item 17 of Form S-4 (§ 239.25 of this chapter) or Form F-4 (§ 239.34 of this chapter), as applicable.

Item 15. Acquisition or Disposition of Property

If action is to be taken with respect to the acquisition or disposition of any property, furnish the following information:

(a) Describe briefly the general character and location of the property.

(b) State the nature and amount of consideration to be paid or received by the registrant or any subsidiary. To the extent practicable, outline briefly the facts bearing upon the question of the fairness of the consideration.

(c) State the name and address of the transferer or transferee, as the case may be and the nature of any material relationship of such person to the registrant or any affiliate of the registrant.

(d) Outline briefly any other material features of the contract or transaction.

Item 16. Restatement of Accounts

If action is to be taken with respect to the restatement of any asset, capital, or surplus account of the registrant, furnish the following information:

(a) State the nature of the restatement and the date as of which it is to be effective.

(b) Outline briefly the reasons for the restatement and for the selection of the particular effective date.

(c) State the name and amount of each account (including any reserve accounts) affected by the restatement and the effect of the restatement thereon. Tabular presentation of the amounts shall be made when appropriate, particularly in the case of recapitalizations.

(d) To the extent practicable, state whether and the extent, if any, to which the restatement will, as of the date thereof, alter the amount available for distribution to the holders of equity securities.

Item 17. Action with Respect to Reports

If action is to be taken with respect to any report of the registrant or of its directors, officers or committees or any minutes of a meeting of its security holders furnish the following information:

(a) State whether or not such action is to constitute approval or disapproval of any of the matters referred to in such reports or minutes.

(b) Identify each of such matters which it is intended will be approved or disapproved, and furnish the information required by the appropriate item or items of this schedule with respect to each such matter.

Item 18. Matters Not Required to Be Submitted

If action is to be taken with respect to any matter which is not required to be submitted to a vote of security holders, state the nature of such matter, the reasons for submitting it to a vote of security holders and what action is intended to be taken by the registrant in the event of a negative vote on the matter by the security holders.

Item 19. Amendment of Charter, Bylaws or Other Documents

If action is to be taken with respect to any amendment of the registrant's charter, bylaws or other documents as to which information is not required above, state briefly the reasons for and the general effect of such amendment.

Instructions. 1. Where the matter to be acted upon is the classification of directors, state whether vacancies which occur during the year may be filled by the board of directors to serve only until the next annual meeting or may be so filled for the remainder of the full term.

2. Attention is directed to the discussion of disclosure regarding anti-takeover and similar proposals in Release No. 34-15230 (October 13, 1978).

Item 20. Other Proposed Action

If action is to be taken on any matter not specifically referred to in this Schedule 14A, describe briefly the substance of each such matter in substantially the same degree of detail as is required by Items 5 to 19, inclusive, of this Schedule, and, with respect to investment companies registered under the Investment Company Act of 1940, Item 22 of this Schedule. Registrants required to provide a separate shareholder vote pursuant to section 111(e)(1) of the Emergency Economic Stabilization Act of 2008 (12 U.S.C. 5221(e)(1)) and § 240.14a-20 shall disclose that they are providing such a vote as required pursuant to the Emergency Economic Stabilization Act of 2008, and briefly explain the general effect of the vote, such as whether the vote is non-binding.

Item 21. Voting Procedures

As to each matter which is to be submitted to a vote of security holders, furnish the following information:

(a) State the vote required for approval or election, other than for the approval of auditors.

(b) Disclose the method by which votes will be counted, including the treatment and effect of abstentions and broker non-votes under applicable state law as well as registrant charter and by-law provisions.

Item 22. Information Required in Investment Company Proxy Statement

(a) *General.*

(1) *Definitions.* Unless the context otherwise requires, terms used in this Item that are defined in § 240.14a-1 (with respect to proxy soliciting material), in § 240.14c-1 (with respect to information statements), and in the Investment Company Act of 1940 shall have the same meanings provided therein and the following terms shall also apply:

(i) *Administrator.* The term "Administrator" shall mean any person who provides significant administrative or business affairs management services to a Fund.

(ii) *Affiliated Broker.* The term "Affiliated Broker" shall mean any broker:

(A) That is an affiliated person of the Fund;

(B) That is an affiliated person of such person; or

(C) An affiliated person of which is an affiliated person of the Fund, its investment adviser, principal underwriter, or Administrator.

(iii) *Distribution Plan.* The term "Distribution Plan" shall mean a plan adopted pursuant to Rule 12b-1 under the Investment Company Act of 1940 (§ 270.12b-1 of this chapter).

(iv) *Family of Investment Companies.* The term "Family of Investment Companies" shall mean any two or more registered investment companies that:

(A) Share the same investment adviser or principal underwriter; and

(B) Hold themselves out to investors as related companies for purposes of investment and investor services.

(v) *Fund.* The term "Fund" shall mean a Registrant or, where the Registrant is a series company, a separate portfolio of the Registrant.

(vi) *Fund Complex.* The term "Fund Complex" shall mean two or more Funds that:

(A) Hold themselves out to investors as related companies for purposes of investment and investor services; or

(B) Have a common investment adviser or have an investment adviser that is an affiliated person of the investment adviser of any of the other Funds.

(vii) *Immediate Family Member.* The term "Immediate Family Member" shall mean a person's spouse; child residing in the person's household (including step and adoptive children); and any dependent of the person, as defined in section 152 of the Internal Revenue Code (26 U.S.C. 152).

(viii) *Officer.* The term "Officer" shall mean the president, vice-president, secretary, treasurer, controller, or any other officer who performs policy-making functions.

(ix) *Parent.* The term "Parent" shall mean the affiliated person of a specified person who controls the specified person directly or indirectly through one or more intermediaries.

(x) *Registrant.* The term "Registrant" shall mean an investment company registered under the Investment Company Act of 1940 (15 U.S.C. 80a) or a business development company as defined by section 2(a)(48) of the Investment Company Act of 1940 (15 U.S.C. 80a-2(a)(48)).

(xi) *Sponsoring Insurance Company.* The term "Sponsoring Insurance Company" of a Fund that is a separate account shall mean the insurance company that establishes and maintains the separate account and that owns the assets of the separate account.

(xii) *Subsidiary.* The term "Subsidiary" shall mean an affiliated person of a specified person who is controlled by the specified person directly, or indirectly through one or more intermediaries.

(2) [Removed and reserved in Release No. 34-37692, effective October 7, 1996, 61 F.R. 49957.]

(3) *General Disclosure.* Furnish the following information in the proxy statement of a Fund or Funds:

(i) State the name and address of the Fund's investment adviser, principal underwriter, and Administrator.

(ii) When a Fund proxy statement solicits a vote on proposals affecting more than one Fund or class of securities of a Fund (unless the proposal or proposals are the same and affect all Fund or class shareholders), present a summary of all of the proposals in tabular form on one of the first three pages of the proxy statement and indicate which Fund or class shareholders are solicited with respect to each proposal.

(iii) Unless the proxy statement is accompanied by a copy of the Fund's most recent annual report, state prominently in the proxy statement that the Fund will furnish, without charge, a copy of the annual report and the most recent semi-annual report succeeding the annual report, if any, to a shareholder upon request providing the name, address, and toll-free telephone number of the person to whom such request shall be directed (or, if no toll-free telephone number is provided, a self-addressed postage paid card for requesting the annual report). The Fund should provide a copy of the annual report and the most recent semi-annual report succeeding the annual report, if any, to the requesting shareholder by first class mail, or other means designed to assure prompt delivery, within three business days of the request.

(iv) If the action to be taken would, directly or indirectly, establish a new fee or expense or increase any existing fee or expense to be paid by the Fund or its shareholders, provide a table showing the current and pro forma fees (with the required examples) using the format prescribed in the appropriate registration statement form under the Investment Company Act of 1940 (for open-end management investment companies, Item 2 of Form N-1A (§239.15A); for closed-end management investment companies, Item 3 of Form N-2 (§239.14); and for separate accounts that offer variable annuity contracts, Item 3 of Form N-3 (§239.17a)).

Instructions. 1. Where approval is sought only for a change in asset breakpoints for a pre-existing fee that would not have increased the fee for the previous year (or have the effect of increasing fees or expenses, but for any other reason would not be reflected in a pro forma fee table), describe the likely effect of the change in lieu of providing pro forma fee information.

2. An action would indirectly establish or increase a fee or expense where, for example, the approval of a new investment advisory contract would result in higher custodial or transfer agency fees.

3. The tables should be prepared in a manner designed to facilitate understanding of the impact of any change in fees or expenses.

4. A Fund that offers its shares exclusively to one or more separate accounts and thus is not required to include a fee table in its prospectus (*see* Item 2(a)(ii) of Form N-1A (§ 239.15A)) should nonetheless prepare a table showing current and pro forma expenses and disclose that the table does not reflect separate account expenses, including sales load.

(v) If action is to be taken with respect to the election of directors or the approval of an advisory contract, describe any purchases or sales of securities of the investment adviser or its Parents, or Subsidiaries of either, since the beginning of the most recently completed fiscal year by any director or any nominee for election as a director of the Fund.

Instructions. 1. Identify the parties, state the consideration, the terms of payment and describe any arrangement or understanding with respect to the composition of the board of directors of the Fund or of the investment adviser, or with respect to the selection of appointment of any person to any office with either such company.

2. Transactions involving securities in an amount not exceeding one percent of the outstanding securities of any class of the investment adviser or any of its Parents or Subsidiaries may be omitted.

(b) *Election of Directors.* If action is to be taken with respect to the election of directors of a Fund, furnish the following information in the proxy statement in addition to, in the case of business development companies, the information (and in the format) required by Item 7 and Item 8 of this Schedule 14A.

Instructions to introductory text of paragraph (b). 1. Furnish information with respect to a prospective investment adviser to the extent applicable.

2. If the solicitation is made by or on behalf of a person other than the Fund or an investment adviser of the Fund, provide information only as to nominees of the person making the solicitation.

3. When providing information about directors and nominees for election as directors in response to this Item 22(b), furnish information for directors or nominees who are or would be "interested persons" of the Fund within the meaning of section 2(a)(19) of the Investment Company Act of 1940 (15 U.S.C. 80a-2(a)(19)) separately from the information for directors or nominees who are not or would not be interested persons of the Fund. For example, when furnishing information in a table, you should provide separate tables (or separate sections of a single table) for directors and nominees who are or would be interested persons and for directors or nominees who are not or would not be interested persons. When furnishing information in narrative form, indicate by heading or otherwise the directors or nominees who are or would be interested persons and the directors or nominees who are not or would not be interested persons.

4. No information need be given about any director whose term of office as a director will not continue after the meeting to which the proxy statement relates.

(1) Provide the information required by the following table for each director, nominee for election as director, Officer of the Fund, person chosen to become an Officer of the Fund, and, if the Fund has an advisory board, member of the board.

Explain in a footnote to the table any family relationship between the persons listed.

(1)	(2)	(3)	(4)	(5)	(6)
Name, Address, and Age	Position(s) Held with Fund	Term of Office and Length of Time Served	Principal Occupation(s) During Past 5 Years	Number of Portfolios in Fund Complex Overseen by Director or Nominee for Director	Other Directorships Held by Director or Nominee for Director

Instructions to paragraph (b)(1). 1. For purposes of this paragraph, the term "family relationship" means any relationship by blood, marriage, or adoption, not more remote than first cousin.

2. No nominee or person chosen to become a director or Officer who has not consented to act as such may be named in response to this Item. In this regard, see Rule 14a-4(d) under the Exchange Act (§ 240.14a-4(d)).

3. If fewer nominees are named than the number fixed by or pursuant to the governing instruments, state the reasons for this procedure and that the proxies cannot be voted for a greater number of persons than the number of nominees named.

4. For each director or nominee for election as director who is or would be an "interested person" of the Fund within the meaning of section 2(a)(19) of the Investment Company Act of 1940 (15 U.S.C. 80a-2(a)(19)), describe, in a footnote or otherwise, the relationship, events, or transactions by reason of which the director or nominee is or would be an interested person.

5. State the principal business of any company listed under column (4) unless the principal business is implicit in its name.

6. Include in column (5) the total number of separate portfolios that a nominee for election as director would oversee if he were elected.

7. Indicate in column (6) directorships not included in column (5) that are held by a director or nominee for election as director in any company with a class of securities registered pursuant to section 12 of the Exchange Act (15 U.S.C. 78l), or subject to the requirements of section 15(d) of the Exchange Act (15 U.S.C. 78o(d)), or any company registered as an investment company under the Investment Company Act of 1940 (15 U.S.C. 80a), as amended, and name the companies in which the directorships are held.

Where the other directorships include directorships overseeing two or more portfolios in the same Fund Complex, identify the Fund Complex and provide the number of portfolios overseen as a director in the Fund Complex rather than listing each portfolio separately.

(2) For each individual listed in column (1) of the table required by paragraph (b)(1) of this Item, except for any director or nominee for election as director who is not or would not be an "interested person" of the Fund within the meaning of section 2(a)(19) of the Investment Company Act of 1940 (15 U.S.C. 80a-2(a)(19)), describe any positions, including as an officer, employee, director, or general partner, held with affiliated persons or principal underwriters of the Fund.

Instruction to paragraph (b)(2). When an individual holds the same position(s) with two or more registered investment companies that are part of the same Fund Complex, identify the Fund Complex and provide the number of registered investment companies for which the position(s) are held rather than listing each registered investment company separately.

(3)(i) For each director or nominee for election as director, briefly discuss the specific experience, qualifications, attributes, or skills that led to the conclusion that the person should serve as a director for the Fund at the time that the disclosure is made in light of the Fund's business and structure. If material, this disclosure should cover more than the past five years, including information about the person's particular areas of expertise or other relevant qualifications.

(ii) Describe briefly any arrangement or understanding between any director, nominee for election as director, Officer, or person chosen to become an Officer, and any other person(s) (naming the person(s)) pursuant to which he was or is to be selected as a director, nominee, or Officer.

Instruction to paragraph (b)(3)(ii). Do not include arrangements or understandings with directors or Officers acting solely in their capacities as such.

(4)(i) Unless disclosed in the table required by paragraph (b)(1) of this Item, describe any positions, including as an officer, employee, director, or general partner, held by any director or nominee for election as director, who is not or would not be an "interested person" of the Fund within the meaning of section 2(a)(19) of the Investment Company Act of 1940 (15 U.S.C. 80a-2(a)(19)), or Immediate Family Member of the director or nominee, during the past five years, with:

(A) The Fund;

(B) An investment company, or a person that would be an investment company but for the exclusions provided by sections 3(c)(1) and 3(c)(7) of the Investment Company Act of 1940 (15 U.S.C. 80a-3(c)(1) and (c)(7)), having the same investment adviser, principal underwriter, or Sponsoring Insurance Company as the Fund or having an investment adviser, principal underwriter, or Sponsoring Insurance Company that directly or indirectly controls, is controlled by, or is under common control with an investment adviser, principal underwriter, or Sponsoring Insurance Company of the Fund;

(C) An investment adviser, principal underwriter, Sponsoring Insurance Company, or affiliated person of the Fund; or

(D) Any person directly or indirectly controlling, controlled by, or under common control with an investment adviser, principal underwriter, or Sponsoring Insurance Company of the Fund.

(ii) Unless disclosed in the table required by paragraph (b)(1) of this Item or in response to paragraph (b)(4)(i) of this Item, indicate any directorships held during the past five years by each director or nominee for election as director in any company with a class of securities registered pursuant to section 12 of the Exchange Act (15 U.S.C. 78l) or subject to the requirements of section 15(d) of the Exchange Act (15 U.S.C. 78o(d)) or any company registered as an investment company under the Investment Company Act of 1940 (15 U.S.C. 80a-1 et seq.), as amended, and name the companies in which the directorships were held.

Instruction to paragraph (b)(4). When an individual holds the same position(s) with two or more portfolios that are part of the same Fund Complex, identify the Fund Complex and provide the number of portfolios for which the position(s) are held rather than listing each portfolio separately.

(5) For each director or nominee for election as director, state the dollar range of equity securities beneficially owned by the director or nominee as required by the following table:

(i) In the Fund; and

(ii) On an aggregate basis, in any registered investment companies overseen or to be overseen by the director or nominee within the same Family of Investment Companies as the Fund.

(1)	*(2)*	*(3)*
Name of Director or Nominee	*Dollar Range of Equity Securities in the Fund*	*Aggregate Dollar Range of Equity Securities in All Funds Overseen or to be Overseen by Director or Nominee in Family of Investment Companies*

Instructions to paragraph (b)(5). 1. Information should be provided as of the most recent practicable date. Specify the valuation date by footnote or otherwise.

2. Determine "beneficial ownership" in accordance with rule 16a-1(a)(2) under the Exchange Act (§ 240.16a-1(a)(2)).

3. If action is to be taken with respect to more than one Fund, disclose in column (2) the dollar range of equity securities beneficially owned by a director or nominee in each such Fund overseen or to be overseen by the director or nominee.

4. In disclosing the dollar range of equity securities beneficially owned by a director or nominee in columns (2) and (3), use the following ranges: none, $1-$10,000, $10,001-$50,000, $50,001-$100,000, or over $100,000.

(6) For each director or nominee for election as director who is not or would not be an "interested person" of the Fund within the meaning of section 2(a)(19) of the Investment Company Act of 1940 (15 U.S.C. 80a-2(a)(19), and his Immediate Family Members, furnish the information required by the following table as to each class of securities owned beneficially or of record in:

(i) An investment adviser, principal underwriter, or Sponsoring Insurance Company of the Fund; or

(ii) A person (other than a registered investment company) directly or indirectly controlling, controlled by, or under common control with an investment adviser, principal underwriter, or Sponsoring Insurance Company of the Fund:

(1)	*(2)*	*(3)*	*(4)*	*(5)*	*(6)*
Name of Director or Nominee	*Name of Owners and Relationships to Director or Nominee*	*Company*	*Title of Class*	*Value of Securities*	*Percent of Class*

Instructions to paragraph (b)(6). 1. Information should be provided as of the most recent practicable date. Specify the valuation date by footnote or otherwise.

2. An individual is a "beneficial owner" of a security if he is a "beneficial owner" under either rule 13d-3 or rule 16a-1(a)(2) under the Exchange Act (§§ 240.13d-3 or 240.16a-1(a)(2)).

3. Identify the company in which the director, nominee, or Immediate Family Member of the director or nominee owns securities in column (3). When the company is a person directly or indirectly controlling, controlled by, or under common control with an investment adviser, principal underwriter,

or Sponsoring Insurance Company, describe the company's relationship with the investment adviser, principal underwriter, or Sponsoring Insurance Company.

4. Provide the information required by columns (5) and (6) on an aggregate basis for each director (or nominee) and his Immediate Family Members.

(7) Unless disclosed in response to paragraph (b)(6) of this Item, describe any direct or indirect interest, the value of which exceeds $120,000, of each director or nominee for election as director who is not or would not be an "interested person" of the Fund within the meaning of section 2(a)(19) of the Investment Company Act of 1940 (15 U.S.C. 80a-2(a)(19)), or Immediate Family Member of the director or nominee, during the past five years, in:

(i) An investment adviser, principal underwriter, or Sponsoring Insurance Company of the Fund; or

(ii) A person (other than a registered investment company) directly or indirectly controlling, controlled by, or under common control with an investment adviser, principal underwriter, or Sponsoring Insurance Company of the Fund.

Instructions to paragraph (b)(7). 1. A director, nominee, or Immediate Family Member has an interest in a company if he is a party to a contract, arrangement, or understanding with respect to any securities of, or interest in, the company.

2. The interest of the director (or nominee) and the interests of his Immediate Family Members should be aggregated in determining whether the value exceeds $120,000.

(8) Describe briefly any material interest, direct or indirect, of any director or nominee for election as director who is not or would not be an "interested person" of the Fund within the meaning of section 2(a)(19) of the Investment Company Act of 1940 (15 U.S.C. 80a-2(a)(19)), or Immediate Family Member of the director or nominee, in any transaction, or series of similar transactions, since the beginning of the last two completed fiscal years of the Fund, or in any currently proposed transaction, or series of similar transactions, in which the amount involved exceeds $120,000 and to which any of the following persons was or is to be a party:

(i) The Fund;

(ii) An Officer of the Fund;

(iii) An investment company, or a person that would be an investment company but for the exclusions provided by sections 3(c)(1) and 3(c)(7) of the Investment Company Act of 1940 (15 U.S.C. 80a-3(c)(1) and (c)(7)), having the same investment adviser, principal underwriter, or Sponsoring Insurance Company as the Fund or having an investment adviser, principal underwriter, or Sponsoring Insurance Company that directly or indirectly controls, is controlled by, or is under common control with an investment adviser, principal underwriter, or Sponsoring Insurance Company of the Fund;

(iv) An Officer of an investment company, or a person that would be an investment company but for the exclusions provided by sections 3(c)(1) and 3(c)(7) of the Investment Company Act of 1940 (15 U.S.C. 80a-3(c)(1) and (c)(7)), having the same investment adviser, principal underwriter, or Sponsoring Insurance Company as the Fund or having an investment adviser, principal underwriter, or Sponsoring Insurance Company that directly or indirectly controls, is controlled by, or is under common control with an investment adviser, principal underwriter, or Sponsoring Insurance Company of the Fund;

(v) An investment adviser, principal underwriter, or Sponsoring Insurance Company of the Fund;

(vi) An Officer of an investment adviser, principal underwriter, or Sponsoring Insurance Company of the Fund;

(vii) A person directly or indirectly controlling, controlled by, or under common control with an investment adviser, principal underwriter, or Sponsoring Insurance Company of the Fund; or

(viii) An Officer of a person directly or indirectly controlling, controlled by, or under common control with an investment adviser, principal underwriter, or Sponsoring Insurance Company of the Fund.

Instructions to paragraph (b)(8). 1. Include the name of each director, nominee, or Immediate Family Member whose interest in any transaction or series of similar transactions is described and the nature of the circumstances by reason of which the interest is required to be described.

2. State the nature of the interest, the approximate dollar amount involved in the transaction, and, where practicable, the approximate dollar amount of the interest.

3. In computing the amount involved in the transaction or series of similar transactions, include all periodic payments in the case of any lease or other agreement providing for periodic payments.

4. Compute the amount of the interest of any director, nominee, or Immediate Family Member of the director or nominee without regard to the amount of profit or loss involved in the transaction(s).

5. As to any transaction involving the purchase or sale of assets, state the cost of the assets to the purchaser and, if acquired by the seller within two years prior to the transaction, the cost to the seller. Describe the method used in determining the purchase or sale price and the name of the person making the determination.

6. If the proxy statement relates to multiple portfolios of a series Fund with different fiscal years, then, in determining the date that is the beginning of the last two completed fiscal years of the Fund, use the earliest date of any series covered by the proxy statement.

7. Disclose indirect, as well as direct, material interests in transactions. A person who has a position or relationship with, or interest in, a company that engages in a transaction with one of the persons listed in paragraphs (b)(8)(i) through (b)(8)(viii) of this Item may have an indirect interest in the transaction by reason of the position, relationship, or interest. The interest in the transaction, however, will not be deemed "material" within the meaning of paragraph (b)(8) of this Item where the interest of the director, nominee, or Immediate Family Member arises solely from the holding of an equity interest (including a limited partnership interest, but excluding a general partnership interest) or a creditor interest in a company that is a party to the transaction with one of the persons specified in paragraphs (b)(8)(i) through (b)(8)(viii) of this Item, and the transaction is not material to the company.

8. The materiality of any interest is to be determined on the basis of the significance of the information to investors in light of all the circumstances of the particular case. The importance of the interest to the person having the interest, the relationship of the parties to the transaction with each other, and the amount involved in the transaction are among the factors to be considered in determining the significance of the information to investors.

9. No information need be given as to any transaction where the interest of the director, nominee, or Immediate Family Member arises solely from the ownership of securities of a person specified in paragraphs (b)(8)(i) through (b)(8)(viii) of this Item and the director, nominee, or Immediate Family Member receives no extra or special benefit not shared on a pro rata basis by all holders of the class of securities.

10. Transactions include loans, lines of credit, and other indebtedness. For indebtedness, indicate the largest aggregate amount of indebtedness outstanding at any time during the period, the nature of the indebtedness and the transaction in which it was incurred, the amount outstanding as of the latest practicable date, and the rate of interest paid or charged.

11. No information need be given as to any routine, retail transaction. For example, the Fund need not disclose that a director has a credit card, bank or brokerage account, residential mortgage, or insurance policy with a person specified in paragraphs (b)(8)(i) through (b)(8)(viii) of this Item unless the director is accorded special treatment.

(9) Describe briefly any direct or indirect relationship, in which the amount involved exceeds $120,000, of any director or nominee for election as director who is not or would not be an "interested person" of the Fund within the meaning of section 2(a)(19) of the Investment Company Act of 1940 (15 U.S.C. 80a-2(a)(19)), or Immediate Family Member of the director or nominee, that exists, or has existed at any time since the beginning of the last two completed fiscal years of the Fund, or is currently proposed, with any of the persons specified in paragraphs (b)(8)(i) through (b)(8)(viii) of this Item. Relationships include:

(i) Payments for property or services to or from any person specified in paragraphs (b)(8)(i) through (b)(8)(viii) of this Item;

(ii) Provision of legal services to any person specified in paragraphs (b)(8)(i) through (b)(8)(viii) of this Item;

(iii) Provision of investment banking services to any person specified in paragraphs (b)(8)(i) through (b)(8)(viii) of this Item, other than as a participating underwriter in a syndicate; and

(iv) Any consulting or other relationship that is substantially similar in nature and scope to the relationships listed in paragraphs (b)(9)(i) through (b)(9)(iii) of this Item.

Instructions to paragraph (b)(9). 1. Include the name of each director, nominee, or Immediate Family Member whose relationship is described and the nature of the circumstances by reason of which the relationship is required to be described.

2. State the nature of the relationship and the amount of business conducted between the director, nominee, or Immediate Family Member and the person specified in paragraphs (b)(8)(i) through

(b)(8)(viii) of this Item as a result of the relationship since the beginning of the last two completed fiscal years of the Fund or proposed to be done during the Fund's current fiscal year.

3. In computing the amount involved in a relationship, include all periodic payments in the case of any agreement providing for periodic payments.

4. If the proxy statement relates to multiple portfolios of a series Fund with different fiscal years, then, in determining the date that is the beginning of the last two completed fiscal years of the Fund, use the earliest date of any series covered by the proxy statement.

5. Disclose indirect, as well as direct, relationships. A person who has a position or relationship with, or interest in, a company that has a relationship with one of the persons listed in paragraphs (b)(8)(i) through (b)(8)(viii) of this Item may have an indirect relationship by reason of the position, relationship, or interest.

6. In determining whether the amount involved in a relationship exceeds $120,000, amounts involved in a relationship of the director (or nominee) should be aggregated with those of his Immediate Family Members.

7. In the case of an indirect interest, identify the company with which a person specified in paragraphs (b)(8)(i) through (b)(8)(viii) of this Item has a relationship; the name of the director, nominee, or Immediate Family Member affiliated with the company and the nature of the affiliation; and the amount of business conducted between the company and the person specified in paragraphs (b)(8)(i) through (b)(8)(viii) of this Item since the beginning of the last two completed fiscal years of the Fund or proposed to be done during the Fund's current fiscal year.

8. In calculating payments for property and services for purposes of paragraph (b)(9)(i) of this Item, the following may be excluded:

A. Payments where the transaction involves the rendering of services as a common contract carrier, or public utility, at rates or charges fixed in conformity with law or governmental authority; or

B. Payments that arise solely from the ownership of securities of a person specified in paragraphs (b)(8)(i) through (b)(8)(viii) of this Item and no extra or special benefit not shared on a pro rata basis by all holders of the class of securities is received.

9. No information need be given as to any routine, retail relationship. For example, the Fund need not disclose that a director has a credit card, bank or brokerage account, residential mortgage, or insurance policy with a person specified in paragraphs (b)(8)(i) through (b)(8)(viii) of this Item unless the director is accorded special treatment.

(10) If an Officer of an investment adviser, principal underwriter, or Sponsoring Insurance Company of the Fund, or an Officer of a person directly or indirectly controlling, controlled by, or under common control with an investment adviser, principal underwriter, or Sponsoring Insurance Company of the Fund, serves, or has served since the beginning of the last two completed fiscal years of the Fund, on the board of directors of a company where a director of the Fund or nominee for election as director who is not or would not be an "interested person" of the Fund within the meaning of section 2(a)(19) of the Investment Company Act of 1940 (15 U.S.C. 80a-2(a)(19)), or Immediate Family Member of the director or nominee, is, or was since the beginning of the last two completed fiscal years of the Fund, an Officer, identify:

(i) The company;

(ii) The individual who serves or has served as a director of the company and the period of service as director;

(iii) The investment adviser, principal underwriter, or Sponsoring Insurance Company or person controlling, controlled by, or under common control with the investment adviser, principal underwriter, or Sponsoring Insurance Company where the individual named in paragraph (b)(10)(ii) of this Item holds or held office and the office held; and

(iv) The director of the Fund, nominee for election as director, or Immediate Family Member who is or was an Officer of the company; the office held; and the period of holding the office.

Instruction to paragraph (b)(10). If the proxy statement relates to multiple portfolios of a series Fund with different fiscal years, then, in determining the date that is the beginning of the last two completed fiscal years of the Fund, use the earliest date of any series covered by the proxy statement.

(11) Provide in tabular form, to the extent practicable, the information required by Items 401(f) and (g), 404(a), 405, and 407(h) of Regulation S-K (§§ 229.401(f) and (g), 229.404(a), 229.405, and 229.407(h) of this chapter).

Instruction to paragraph 22(b)(11). Information provided under paragraph (b)(8) of this Item 22 is deemed to satisfy the requirements of Item 404(a) of Regulation S-K for information about directors, nominees for election as directors, and Immediate Family Members of directors and nominees, and need not be provided under this paragraph (b)(11).

(12) Describe briefly any material pending legal proceedings, other than ordinary routine litigation incidental to the Fund's business, to which any director or nominee for director or affiliated person of such director or nominee is a party adverse to the Fund or any of its affiliated persons or has a material interest adverse to the Fund or any of its affiliated persons. Include the name of the court where the case is pending, the date instituted, the principal parties, a description of the factual basis alleged to underlie the proceeding, and the relief sought.

(13) In the case of a Fund that is an investment company registered under the Investment Company Act of 1940 (15 U.S.C. 80a), for all directors, and for each of the three highest-paid Officers that have aggregate compensation from the Fund for the most recently completed fiscal year in excess of $60,000 ("Compensated Persons"):

(i) Furnish the information required by the following table for the last fiscal year:

Compensation Table

(1)	(2)	(3)	(4)	(5)
Name of Person, Position	Aggregate Compensation From Fund	Pension or Retirement Benefits Accrued as Part of Fund Expenses	Estimated Annual Benefits Upon Retirement	Total Compensation From Fund and Fund Complex Paid to Directors

Instructions to paragraph (b)(13)(i). 1. For column (1), indicate, if necessary, the capacity in which the remuneration is received. For Compensated Persons that are directors of the Fund, compensation is amounts received for service as a director.

2. If the Fund has not completed its first full year since its organization, furnish the information for the current fiscal year, estimating future payments that would be made pursuant to an existing agreement or understanding. Disclose in a footnote to the Compensation Table the period for which the information is furnished.

3. Include in column (2) amounts deferred at the election of the Compensated Person, whether pursuant to a plan established under Section 401(k) of the Internal Revenue Code (26 U.S.C. 401(k)) or otherwise, for the fiscal year in which earned. Disclose in a footnote to the Compensation Table the total amount of deferred compensation (including interest) payable to or accrued for any Compensated Person.

4. Include in columns (3) and (4) all pension or retirement benefits proposed to be paid under any existing plan in the event of retirement at normal retirement date, directly or indirectly, by the Fund or any of its Subsidiaries, or by other companies in the Fund Complex. Omit column (4) where retirement benefits are not determinable.

5. For any defined benefit or actuarial plan under which benefits are determined primarily by final compensation (or average final compensation) and years of service, provide the information required in column (4) in a separate table showing estimated annual benefits payable upon retirement (including amounts attributable to any defined benefit supplementary or excess pension award plans) in specified compensation and years of service classifications. Also provide the estimated credited years of service for each Compensated Person.

6. Include in column (5) only aggregate compensation paid to a director for service on the board and other boards of investment companies in a Fund Complex specifying the number of such other investment companies.

(ii) Describe briefly the material provisions of any pension, retirement, or other plan or any arrangement other than fee arrangements disclosed in paragraph (b)(13)(i) of this Item pursuant to which Compensated Persons are or may be compensated for any services provided, including amounts paid, if any, to the Compensated Person under any such arrangements during the most recently completed fiscal year. Specifically include the criteria used to determine amounts payable under any plan, the length of service or vesting period required by the plan, the retirement age or other event that gives rise to payments under the plan, and whether the payment of benefits is secured or funded by the Fund

(14) State whether or not the Fund has a separately designated audit committee established in accordance with section 3(a)(58)(A) of the Act (15 U.S.C. 78c(a)(58)(A)). If the entire board of directors is acting as the Fund's audit committee as specified in section 3(a)(58)(B) of the Act (15 U.S.C. 78c(a)(58)(B)), so state. If applicable, provide the disclosure required by§ 240.10A-3(d) regarding an exemption from the listing standards for audit committees. Identify the other standing committees of the Fund's board of directors, and provide the following information about each committee, including any separately designated audit committee and any nominating committee:

(i) A concise statement of the functions of the committee;

(ii) The members of the committee and, in the case of a nominating committee, whether or not the members of the committee are "interested persons" of the Fund as defined in section 2(a)(19) of the Investment Company Act of 1940 (15 U.S.C. 80a-2(a)(19)); and

(iii) The number of committee meetings held during the last fiscal year.

Instruction to paragraph (b)(14): For purposes of Item 22(b)(14), the term "nominating committee" refers not only to nominating committees and committees performing similar functions, but also to groups of directors fulfilling the role of a nominating committee, including the entire board of directors.

(15)(i) Provide the information (and in the format) required by Items 407(b)(1), (b)(2) and (f) of Regulation S-K (§ 229.407(b)(1), (b)(2) and (f) of this chapter); and

(ii) Provide the following regarding the requirements for the director nomination process:

(A) The information (and in the format) required by Items 407(c)(1) and (c)(2) of Regulation S-K (§ 229.407(c)(1) and (c)(2) of this chapter); and

(B) If the Fund is a listed issuer (as defined in§ 240.10A-3 of this chapter) whose securities are listed on a national securities exchange registered pursuant to section 6(a) of the Act (15 U.S.C. 78f(a)) or in an automated inter-dealer quotation system of a national securities association registered pursuant to section 15A of the Act (15 U.S.C. 78o-3(a)) that has independence requirements for nominating committee members, identify each director that is a member of the nominating committee that is not independent under the independence standards described in this paragraph. In determining whether the nominating committee members are independent, use the Fund's definition of independence that it uses for determining if the members of the nominating committee are independent in compliance with the independence standards applicable for the members of the nominating committee in the listing standards applicable to the Fund. If the Fund does not have independence standards for the nominating committee, use the independence standards for the nominating committee in the listing standards applicable to the Fund.

Instruction to paragraph (b)(15)(ii)(B).

If the national securities exchange or inter-dealer quotation system on which the Fund's securities are listed has exemptions to the independence requirements for nominating committee members upon which the Fund relied, disclose the exemption relied upon and explain the basis for the Fund's conclusion that such exemption is applicable.

(16) In the case of a Fund that is a closed-end investment company:

(i) Provide the information (and in the format) required by Item 407(d)(1), (d)(2) and (d)(3) of Regulation S-K (§ 229.407(d)(1), (d)(2) and (d)(3) of this chapter); and

(ii) Identify each director that is a member of the Fund's audit committee that is not independent under the independence standards described in this paragraph. If the Fund does not have a separately designated audit committee, or committee performing similar functions, the Fund must provide the disclosure with respect to all members of its board of directors.

(A) If the Fund is a listed issuer (as defined in§ 240.10A-3 of this chapter) whose securities are listed on a national securities exchange registered pursuant to section 6(a) of the Act (15 U.S.C. 78f(a)) or in an automated inter-dealer quotation system of a national securities association registered pursuant to section 15A of the Act (15 U.S.C. 78o-3(a)) that has independence requirements for audit committee members, in determining whether the audit committee members are independent, use the Fund's definition of independence that it uses for determining if the members of the audit committee are independent in compliance with the independence standards applicable for the members of the audit committee in the listing standards applicable to the Fund. If the Fund does not have independence standards for the audit committee, use the independence standards for the audit committee in the listing standards applicable to the Fund.

(B) If the Fund is not a listed issuer whose securities are listed on a national securities exchange registered pursuant to section 6(a) of the Act (15 U.S.C. 78f(a)) or in an automated inter-dealer quotation system of a national securities association registered pursuant to section 15A of the Act (15 U.S.C. 78o-3(a)), in determining whether the audit committee members are independent, use a definition of independence of a national securities exchange registered pursuant to section 6(a) of the Act (15 U.S.C. 78f(a)) or an automated inter-dealer quotation system of a national securities association registered pursuant to section 15A of the Act (15 U.S.C. 780-3(a)) which has requirements that a majority of the board of directors be independent and that has been approved by the Commission, and state which definition is used. Whatever such definition the Fund chooses, it must use the same definition with respect to all directors and nominees for director. If the national securities exchange or national securities association whose standards are used has independence standards for the members of the audit committee, use those specific standards.

Instruction to paragraph (b)(16)(ii).

If the national securities exchange or inter-dealer quotation system on which the Fund's securities are listed has exemptions to the independence requirements for nominating committee members upon which the Fund relied, disclose the exemption relied upon and explain the basis for the Fund's conclusion that such disclosure is applicable. The same disclosure should be provided if the Fund is not a listed issuer and the national securities exchange or inter-dealer quotation system selected by the Fund has exemptions that are applicable to the Fund.

(17) In the case of a Fund that is an investment company registered under the Investment Company Act of 1940 (15 U.S.C. 80a), if a director has resigned or declined to stand for re-election to the board of directors since the date of the last annual meeting of security holders because of a disagreement with the registrant on any matter relating to the registrant's operations, policies or practices, and if the director has furnished the registrant with a letter describing such disagreement and requesting that the matter be disclosed, the registrant shall state the date of resignation or declination to stand for re-election and summarize the director's description of the disagreement. If the registrant believes that the description provided by the director is incorrect or incomplete, it may include a brief statement presenting its view of the disagreement.

Amendment

(18) If a shareholder nominee or nominees are submitted to the Fund for inclusion in the Fund's proxy materials pursuant to § 240.14a-11 and the Fund is not permitted to exclude the nominee or nominees pursuant to the provisions of § 240.14a-11, the Fund must include in its proxy statement the disclosure required from the nominating shareholder or nominating shareholder group under Item 5 of § 240.14n-101 with regard to the nominee or nominees and the nominating shareholder or nominating shareholder group.

Instruction to paragraph (b)(18). The information disclosed pursuant to paragraph (b)(18) of this Item will not be deemed incorporated by reference into any filing under the Securities Act of 1933 (15 U.S.C. 77a *et seq.*), the Securities Exchange Act of 1934 (15 U.S.C. 78a *et seq.*), or the Investment Company Act of 1940 (15 U.S.C. 80a-1 *et seq.*), except to the extent that the Fund specifically incorporates that information by reference.

(19) If a Fund is required to include a shareholder nominee or nominees submitted to the Fund for inclusion in the Fund's proxy materials pursuant to a procedure set forth under applicable state or foreign law or the Fund's governing documents providing for the inclusion of shareholder director nominees in the Fund's proxy materials, the Fund must include in its proxy statement the disclosure required from the nominating shareholder or nominating shareholder group under Item 6 of § 240.14n-101 with regard to the nominee or nominees and the nominating shareholder or nominating shareholder group.

Instruction to paragraph (b)(19). The information disclosed pursuant to paragraph (b)(19) of this Item will not be deemed incorporated by reference into any filing under the Securities Act of 1933 (15 U.S.C. 77a *et seq.*), the Securities Exchange Act of 1934 (15 U.S.C. 78a *et seq.*), or the Investment Company Act of 1940 (15 U.S.C. 80a-1 *et seq.*), except to the extent that the Fund specifically incorporates that information by reference.

End of Amendment

(c) *Approval of Investment Advisory Contract.* If action is to be taken with respect to an investment advisory contract, include the following information in the proxy statement.

Instruction. Furnish information with respect to a prospective investment adviser to the extent applicable (including the name and address of the prospective investment adviser).

(1) With respect to the existing investment advisory contract:

(i) State the date of the contract and the date on which it was last submitted to a vote of security holders of the Fund, including the purpose of such submission;

(ii) Briefly describe the terms of the contract, including the rate of compensation of the investment adviser;

(iii) State the aggregate amount of the investment adviser's fee and the amount and purpose of any other material payments by the Fund to the investment adviser, or any affiliated person of the investment adviser, during the last fiscal year of the Fund;

(iv) If any person is acting as an investment adviser of the Fund other than pursuant to a written contract that has been approved by the security holders of the company, identify the person and describe the nature of the services and arrangements;

(v) Describe any action taken with respect to the investment advisory contract since the beginning of the Fund's last fiscal year by the board of directors of the Fund (unless described in response to paragraph (c)(1)(vi)) of this Item 22); and

(vi) If an investment advisory contract was terminated or not renewed for any reason, state the date of such termination or non-renewal, identify the parties involved, and describe the circumstances of such termination or non-renewal.

(2) State the name, address and principal occupation of the principal executive officer and each director or general partner of the investment adviser.

Instruction. If the investment adviser is a partnership with more than ten general partners, name:

(i) the general partners with the five largest economic interests in the partnership, and, if different, those general partners comprising the management or executive committee of the partnership or exercising similar authority;

(ii) the general partners with significant management responsibilities relating to the fund.

(3) State the names and addresses of all Parents of the investment adviser and show the basis of control of the investment adviser and each Parent by its immediate Parent.

Instructions. 1. If any person named is a corporation, include the percentage of its voting securities owned by its immediate Parent.

2. If any person named is a partnership, name the general partners having the three largest partnership interests (computed by whatever method is appropriate in the particular case).

(4) If the investment adviser is a corporation and if, to the knowledge of the persons making the solicitation or the persons on whose behalf the solicitation is made, any person not named in answer to paragraph (c)(3) of this Item 22 owns, of record or beneficially, ten percent or more of the outstanding voting securities of the investment adviser, indicate that fact and state the name and address of each such person.

(5) Name each officer or director of the Fund who is an officer, employee, director, general partner or shareholder of the investment adviser. As to any officer or director who is not a director or general partner of the investment adviser and who owns securities or has any other material direct or indirect interest in the investment adviser or any other person controlling, controlled by or under common control with the investment adviser, describe the nature of such interest.

(6) Describe briefly and state the approximate amount of, where practicable, any material interest, direct or indirect, of any director of the Fund in any material transactions since the beginning of the most recently completed fiscal year, or in any material proposed transactions, to which the investment adviser of the Fund, any Parent or Subsidiary of the investment adviser (other than another Fund), or any Subsidiary of the Parent of such entities was or is to be a party.

Instructions. 1. Include the name of each person whose interest in any transaction is described and the nature of the relationship by reason of which such interest is required to be described. Where it is not practicable to state the approximate amount of the interest, indicate the approximate amount involved in the transaction.

2. As to any transaction involving the purchase or sale of assets by or to the investment adviser, state the cost of the assets to the purchaser and the cost thereof to the seller if acquired by the seller within two years prior to the transaction.

3. If the interest of any person arises from the position of the person as a partner in a partnership, the proportionate interest of such person in transactions to which the partnership is a party need not be set forth, but state the amount involved in the transaction with the partnership.

4. No information need be given in response to this paragraph (c)(6) of Item 22 with respect to any transaction that is not related to the business or operations of the Fund and to which neither the Fund nor any of its Parents or Subsidiaries is a party.

(7) Disclose any financial condition of the investment adviser that is reasonably likely to impair the financial ability of the adviser to fulfill its commitment to the fund under the proposed investment advisory contract.

(8) Describe the nature of the action to be taken on the investment advisory contract and the reasons therefor, the terms of the contract to be acted upon, and, if the action is an amendment to, or a replacement of, an investment advisory contract, the material differences between the current and proposed contract.

(9) If a change in the investment advisory fee is sought, state:

(i) The aggregate amount of the investment adviser's fee during the last year;

(ii) The amount that the adviser would have received had the proposed fee been in effect; and

(iii) The difference between the aggregate amounts stated in response to paragraphs (i) and (ii) of this item (c)(9) as a percentage of the amount stated in response to paragraph (i) of this item (c)(9).

(10) If the investment adviser acts as such with respect to any other Fund having a similar investment objective, identify and state the size of such other Fund and the rate of the investment adviser's compensation. Also indicate for any Fund identified whether the investment adviser has waived, reduced, or otherwise agreed to reduce its compensation under any applicable contract.

Instruction. Furnish the information in response to this paragraph (c)(10) of Item 22 in tabular form.

(11) Discuss in reasonable detail the material factors and the conclusions with respect thereto that form the basis for the recommendation of the board of directors that the shareholders approve an investment advisory contract. Include the following in the discussion:

(i) Factors relating to both the board's selection of the investment adviser and approval of the advisory fee and any other amounts to be paid by the Fund under the contract. This would include, but not be limited to, a discussion of the nature, extent, and quality of the services to be provided by the investment adviser; the investment performance of the Fund and the investment adviser; the costs of the services to be provided and profits to be realized by the investment adviser and its affiliates from the relationship with the Fund; the extent to which economies of scale would be realized as the Fund grows; and whether fee levels reflect these economies of scale for the benefit of Fund investors. Also indicate in the discussion whether the board relied upon comparisons of the services to be rendered and the amounts to be paid under the contract with those under other investment advisory contracts, such as contracts of the same and other investment advisers with other registered investment companies or other types of clients (*e.g.*, pension funds and other institutional investors). If the board relied upon such comparisons, describe the comparisons that were relied on and how they assisted the board in determining to recommend that the shareholders approve the advisory contract; and

(ii) If applicable, any benefits derived or to be derived by the investment adviser from the relationship with the Fund such as soft dollar arrangements by which brokers provide research to the Fund or its investment adviser in return for allocating Fund brokerage.

Instructions. 1. Conclusory statements or a list of factors will not be considered sufficient disclosure. Relate the factors to the specific circumstances of the Fund and the investment advisory contract for which approval is sought and state how the board evaluated each factor. For example, it is not sufficient to state that the board considered the amount of the investment advisory fee without stating what the board concluded about the amount of the fee and how that affected its determination to recommend approval of the contract.

2. If any factor enumerated in paragraph (c)(11)(i) of this Item 22 is not relevant to the board's evaluation of the investment advisory contract for which approval is sought, note this and explain the reasons why that factor is not relevant.

(12) Describe any arrangement or understanding made in connection with the proposed investment advisory contract with respect to the composition of the board of directors of the Fund or the investment adviser or with respect to the selection or appointment of any person to any office with either such company.

(13) For the most recently completed fiscal year, state:

(i) The aggregate amount of commissions paid to any Affiliated Broker; and

(ii) The percentage of the Fund's aggregate brokerage commissions paid to any such Affiliated Broker.

Instruction. Identify each Affiliated Broker and the relationships that cause the broker to be an Affiliated Broker.

(14) Disclose the amount of any fees paid by the Fund to the investment adviser, its affiliated persons or any affiliated person of such person during the most recent fiscal year for services provided to the Fund (other than under the investment advisory contract or for brokerage commissions). State whether these services will continue to be provided after the investment advisory contract is approved.

(d) *Approval of Distribution Plan.* If action is to be taken with respect to a Distribution Plan, include the following information in the proxy statement.

Instruction. Furnish information on a prospective basis to the extent applicable.

(1) Describe the nature of the action to be taken on the Distribution Plan and the reason therefor, the terms of the Distribution Plan to be acted upon, and, if the action is an amendment to, or a replacement of, a Distribution Plan, the material differences between the current and proposed Distribution Plan.

(2) If the Fund has a Distribution Plan in effect:

(i) Provide the date that the Distribution Plan was adopted and the date of the last amendment, if any;

(ii) Disclose the persons to whom payments may be made under the Distribution Plan, the rate of the distribution fee and the purposes for which such fee may be used;

(iii) Disclose the amount of distribution fees paid by the Fund pursuant to the plan during its most recent fiscal year, both in the aggregate and as a percentage of the Fund's average net assets during the period;

(iv) Disclose the name of, and the amount of any payments made under the Distribution Plan by the Fund during its most recent fiscal year to, any person who is an affiliated person of the Fund, its investment adviser, principal underwriter, or Administrator, an affiliated person of such person, or a person that during the most recent fiscal year received 10% or more of the aggregate amount paid under the Distribution Plan by the Fund;

(v) Describe any action taken with respect to the Distribution Plan since the beginning of the Fund's most recent fiscal year by the board of directors of the Fund; and

(vi) If a Distribution Plan was or is to be terminated or not renewed for any reason, state the date or prospective date of such termination or non-renewal, identify the parties involved, and describe the circumstances of such termination or non-renewal.

(3) Describe briefly and state the approximate amount of, where practicable, any material interest, direct or indirect, of any director or nominee for election as a director of the Fund in any material transactions since the beginning of the most recently completed fiscal year, or in any material proposed transactions, to which any person identified in response to Item 22(d)(2)(iv) was or is to be a party.

Instructions. 1. Include the name of each person whose interest in any transaction is described and the nature of the relationship by reason of which such interest is required to be described. Where it is not practicable to state the approximate amount of the interest, indicate the approximate amount involved in the transaction.

2. As to any transaction involving the purchase or sale of assets, state the cost of the assets to the purchaser and the cost thereof to the seller if acquired by the seller within two years prior to the transaction.

3. If the interest of any person arises from the position of the person as a partner in a partnership, the proportionate interest of such person in transactions to which the partnership is a party need not be set forth but state the amount involved in the transaction with the partnership.

4. No information need be given in response to this paragraph (d)(3) of Item 22 with respect to any transaction that is not related to the business or operations of the Fund and to which neither the Fund nor any of its Parents or Subsidiaries is a party.

(4) Discuss in reasonable detail the material factors and the conclusions with respect thereto which form the basis for the conclusion of the board of directors that there is a reasonable likelihood that the proposed Distribution Plan (or amendment thereto) will benefit the Fund and its shareholders.

Instruction. Conclusory statements or a list of factors will not be considered sufficient disclosure.

Item 23. Delivery of Documents to Security Holders Sharing an Address

If one annual report to security holders, proxy statement, or Notice of Internet Availability of Proxy Materials is being delivered to two or more security holders who share an address in accordance with § 240.14a-3(e)(1), furnish the following information:

(a) State that only one annual report to security holders, proxy statement, or Notice of Internet Availability of Proxy Materials, as applicable, is being delivered to multiple security holders sharing an address unless the registrant has received contrary instructions from one or more of the security holders;

(b) Undertake to deliver promptly upon written or oral request a separate copy of the annual report to security holders, proxy statement, or Notice of Internet Availability of Proxy Materials, as applicable, to a security holder at a shared address to which a single copy of the documents was delivered and provide instructions as to how a security holder can notify the registrant that the security holder wishes to receive a separate copy of an annual report to security holders, proxy statement, or Notice of Internet Availability of Proxy Materials, as applicable;

(c) Provide the phone number and mailing address to which a security holder can direct a notification to the registrant that the security holder wishes to receive a separate annual report to security holders, proxy statement, or Notice of Internet Availability of Proxy Materials, as applicable, in the future; and

(d) Provide instructions how security holders sharing an address can request delivery of a single copy of annual reports to security holders, proxy statements, or Notices of Internet Availability of Proxy Materials if they are receiving multiple copies of annual reports to security holders, proxy statements, or Notices of Internet Availability of Proxy Materials.

[As last amended by Release No. 33-9136, effective November 15, 2010, 75 F.R. 56668.]

[¶ 40,301] Reg. § 240.14a-103. Notice of Exempt Solicitation. Information to Be Included in Statements Submitted by or on Behalf of a Person Pursuant to § 240.14a-6(g)

U.S. Securities and Exchange Commission
Washington, D.C. 20549
Notice of Exempt Solicitation

1. Name of the Registrant:

. . . .

2. Name of person relying on exemption:

. . . .

3. Address of person relying on exemption:

. . . .

4. Written materials. Attach written material required to be submitted pursuant to Rule 14a-6(g)(1) [§ 240.14a-6(g)(1)].

[As adopted in Release No. 34-31326, October 16, 1992, 57 F.R. 48276.]

[¶ 40,311] Reg. § 240.14a-104. Notice of Exempt Preliminary Roll-up Communication. Information Regarding Ownership Interests and any Potential Conflicts of Interest to Be Included in Statements Submitted by or on Behalf of a Person Pursuant to § 240.14a-2(b)(4) and § 240.14a-6(n)

UNITED STATES SECURITIES AND EXCHANGE COMMISSION
Washington, D.C. 20549
Notice of Exempt Preliminary Roll-Up Communication

1. Name of registrant appearing on Securities Act of 1933 registration statement for the roll-up transaction (or, if registration statement has not been filed, name of entity into which partnerships are to be rolled up):

. . . .

2. Name of partnership that is the subject of the proposed roll-up transaction:

. . . .

3. Name of person relying on exemption:

. . . .

4. Address of person relying on exemption:

. . . .

5. Ownership interest of security holder in partnership that is the subject of the proposed roll-up transaction:

. . . .

. . . .

Note: To the extent that the holder owns securities in any other entities involved in this roll-up transaction, disclosure of these interests also should be made.

6. Describe any and all relations of the holder to the parties to the transaction or to the transaction itself:

a. The holder is engaged in the business of buying and selling limited partnership interests in the secondary market would be adversely affected if the roll-up transaction were completed.

. . . .

. . . .

. . . .

b. The holder would suffer direct (or indirect) material financial injury if the roll-up transaction were completed since it is a service provider to an affected limited partnership.

. . . .

. . . .

. . . .

c. The holder is engaged in another transaction that may be competitive with the pending roll-up transaction.

. . . .

. . . .

. . . .

d. Any other relations to the parties involved in the transaction or to the transaction itself, or any benefits enjoyed by the holder not shared on a pro rata basis by all other holders of the same class of securities of the partnership that is the subject of the proposed roll-up transaction.

. . . .

. . . .

. . . .

[As adopted in Release No. 34-35036, December 1, 1994, 59 F.R. 63676.]

[¶ 40,350] Obligation of Registered Brokers and Dealers in Connection With the Prompt Forwarding of Certain Communications to Beneficial Owners

Reg. § 240.14b-1. (a) *Definitions.* Unless the context otherwise requires, all terms used in this section shall have the same meanings as in the Act and, with respect to proxy soliciting material, as in § 240.14a-1 thereunder and, with respect to information statements, as in § 240.14c-1 thereunder. In addition, as used in this section, the term "registrant" means:

(1) The issuer of a class of securities registered pursuant to Section 12 of the Act; or

(2) An investment company registered under the Investment Company Act of 1940.

(b) *Dissemination and beneficial owner information requirements.* A broker or dealer registered under Section 15 of the Act shall comply with the following requirements for disseminating certain communications to beneficial owners and providing beneficial owner information to registrants.

(1) The broker or dealer shall respond, by first class mail or other equally prompt means, directly to the registrant no later than seven business days after the date it receives an inquiry made in accordance with § 240.14a-13(a) or § 240.14c-7(a) by indicating, by means of a search card or otherwise:

(i) The approximate number of customers of the broker or dealer who are beneficial owners of the registrant's securities that are held of record by the broker, dealer, or its nominee;

(ii) The number of customers of the broker or dealer who are beneficial owners of the registrant's securities who have objected to disclosure of their names, addresses, and securities positions if the registrant has indicated, pursuant to § 240.14a-13(a)(1)(ii)(A) or § 240.14c-7(a)(1)(ii)(A), that it will distribute the annual report to security holders to beneficial owners of its securities whose names, addresses and securities positions are disclosed pursuant to paragraph (b)(3) of this section; and

(iii) The identity of the designated agent of the broker or dealer, if any, acting on its behalf in fulfilling its obligations under paragraph (b)(3) of this section; *Provided, however,* that if the broker or dealer has informed the registrant that a designated office(s) or department(s) is to receive such inquiries, receipt for purposes of paragraph (b)(1) of this section shall mean receipt by such designated office(s) or department(s).

(2) The broker or dealer shall, upon receipt of the proxy, other proxy soliciting material, information statement, and/or annual report to security holders from the registrant or other soliciting person, forward such materials to its customers who are beneficial owners of the registrant's securities no later than five business days after receipt of the proxy material, information statement or annual report to security holders.

Note to Paragraph (b)(2): At the request of a registrant, or on its own initiative so long as the registrant does not object, a broker or dealer may, but is not required to, deliver one annual report to security holders, proxy statement, information statement, or Notice of Internet Availability of Proxy Materials to more than one beneficial owner sharing an address if the requirements set forth in § 240.14a-3(e)(1) (with respect to annual reports to security holders, proxy statements, and Notices of Internet Availability of Proxy Materials) and § 240.14c-3(c) (with respect to annual reports to security holders, information statements, and Notices of Internet Availability of Proxy Materials) applicable to registrants, with the exception of § 240.14a-3(e)(1)(i)(E), are satisfied instead by the broker or dealer.

(3) The broker or dealer shall, through its agent or directly:

(i) Provide the registrant, upon the registrant's request, with the names, addresses, and securities positions, compiled as of a date specified in the registrant's request which is no earlier than five business days after the date the registrant's request is received, of its customers who are beneficial owners of the registrant's securities and who have not objected to disclosure of such information; *Provided, however,* that if the broker or dealer has informed the registrant that a designated office(s) or department(s) is to receive such requests, receipt shall mean receipt by such designated office(s) or department(s); and

(ii) Transmit the data specified in paragraph (b)(3)(i) of this section to the registrant no later than five business days after the record date or other date specified by the registrant.

Note 1: Where a broker or dealer employs a designated agent to act on its behalf in performing the obligations imposed on the broker or dealer by paragraph (b)(3) of this section, the five business day time period for determining the date as of which the beneficial owner information is to be compiled is calculated from the date the designated agent receives the registrant's request. In complying with the registrant's request for beneficial owner information under paragraph (b)(3) of this section, a broker or dealer need only supply the registrant with the names, addresses, and securities positions of non-objecting beneficial owners.

Note 2: If a broker or dealer receives a registrant's request less than five business days before the requested compilation date, it must provide a list compiled as of a date that is no more than five business days after receipt and transmit the list within five business days after the compilation date.

(c) *Exceptions to dissemination and beneficial owner information requirements.* A broker or dealer registered under Section 15 of the Act shall be subject to the following with respect to its dissemination and beneficial owner information requirements.

(1) With regard to beneficial owners of exempt employee benefit plan securities, the broker or dealer shall:

(i) Not include information in its response pursuant to paragraph (b)(1) of this section or forward proxies (or in lieu thereof requests for voting instructions), proxy soliciting material, information statements, or annual reports to security holders pursuant to paragraph (b)(2) of this section to such beneficial owners; and

(ii) Not include in its response, pursuant to paragraph (b)(3) of this section, data concerning such beneficial owners.

(2) A broker or dealer need not satisfy:

(i) Its obligations under paragraphs (b)(2), (b)(3) and (d) of this section if the registrant or other soliciting person, as applicable, does not provide assurance of reimbursement of the broker's or dealer's reasonable expenses, both direct and indirect, incurred in connection with performing the obligations imposed by paragraphs (b)(2), (b)(3) and (d) of this section; or

(ii) Its obligation under paragraph (b)(2) of this section to forward annual reports to security holders to non-objecting beneficial owners identified by the broker or dealer, through its agent or directly, pursuant to paragraph (b)(3) of this section if the registrant notifies the broker or dealer pursuant to §240.14a-13(c) or §240.14c-7(c) that the registrant will send the annual report to security holders to such non-objecting beneficial owners identified by the broker or dealer and delivered in a list to the registrant pursuant to paragraph (b)(3) of this section.

(3) In its response pursuant to paragraph (b)(1) of this section, a broker or dealer shall not include information about annual reports to security holders, proxy statements or information statements that will not be delivered to security holders sharing an address because of the broker or dealer's reliance on the procedures referred to in the Note to paragraph (b)(2) of this section.

(d) Upon receipt from the soliciting person of all of the information listed in §240.14a-16(d), the broker or dealer shall:

(1) Prepare and send a Notice of Internet Availability of Proxy Materials containing the information required in paragraph (e) of this section to beneficial owners no later than:

(i) With respect to a registrant, 40 calendar days prior to the security holder meeting date or, if no meeting is to be held, 40 calendar days prior to the date the votes, consents, or authorizations may be used to effect the corporate action; and

(ii) With respect to a soliciting person other than the registrant, the later of:

(A) 40 calendar days prior to the security holder meeting date or, if no meeting is to be held, 40 calendar days prior to the date the votes, consents, or authorizations may be used to effect the corporate action; or

(B) 10 calendar days after the date that the registrant first sends its proxy statement or Notice of Internet Availability of Proxy Materials to security holders.

(2) Establish a Web site at which beneficial owners are able to access the broker or dealer's request for voting instructions and, at the broker or dealer's option, establish a Web site at which beneficial owners are able to access the proxy statement and other soliciting materials, provided that such Web sites are maintained in a manner consistent with paragraphs (b), (c), and (k) of §240.14a-16;

(3) Upon receipt of a request from the registrant or other soliciting person, send to security holders specified by the registrant or other soliciting person a copy of the request for voting instructions accompanied by a copy of the intermediary's Notice of Internet Availability of Proxy Materials 10 calendar days or more after the broker or dealer sends its Notice of Internet Availability of Proxy Materials pursuant to paragraph (d)(1); and

(4) Upon receipt of a request for a copy of the materials from a beneficial owner:

(i) Request a copy of the soliciting materials from the registrant or other soliciting person, in the form requested by the beneficial owner, within three business days after receiving the beneficial owner's request;

(ii) Forward a copy of the soliciting materials to the beneficial owner, in the form requested by the beneficial owner, within three business days after receiving the materials from the registrant or other soliciting person; and

(iii) Maintain records of security holder requests to receive a paper or e-mail copy of the proxy materials in connection with future proxy solicitations and provide copies of the proxy materials to a security holder who has made such a request for all securities held in the account of that security holder until the security holder revokes such request.

(5) Notwithstanding any other provisions in this paragraph (d), if the broker or dealer receives copies of the proxy statement and annual report to security holders (if applicable) from the soliciting person with instructions to forward such materials to beneficial owners, the broker or dealer:

(i) Shall either:

(A) Prepare a Notice of Internet Availability of Proxy Materials and forward it with the proxy statement and annual report to security holders (if applicable); or

(B) Incorporate any information required in the Notice of Internet Availability of Proxy Materials that does not appear in the proxy statement into the broker or dealer's request for voting instructions to be sent with the proxy statement and annual report (if applicable);

(ii) Need not comply with the following provisions:

(A) The timing provisions of paragraph (d)(1)(ii); and

(B) Paragraph (d)(4); and

(iii) Need not include in its Notice of Internet Availability of Proxy Materials or request for voting instructions the following disclosures:

(A) Legends 1 and 3 in § 240.14a-16(d)(1); and

(B) Instructions on how to request a copy of the proxy materials.

(e) *Content of Notice of Internet Availability of Proxy Materials.* The broker or dealer's Notice of Internet Availability of Proxy Materials shall:

(1) Include all information, as it relates to beneficial owners, required in a registrant's Notice of Internet Availability of Proxy Materials under § 240.14a-16(d), provided that the broker or dealer shall provide its own, or its agent's, toll-free telephone number, an e-mail address, and an Internet Web site to service requests for copies from beneficial owners;

(2) Include a brief description, if applicable, of the rules that permit the broker or dealer to vote the securities if the beneficial owner does not return his or her voting instructions; and

(3) Otherwise be prepared and sent in a manner consistent with paragraphs (e), (f), and (g) of § 240.14a-16.

[As last amended in Release No. 34-55146A, effective April 1, 2008, 73 F.R. 17809 (technical correction).]

[¶ 40,351] Obligation of Banks, Associations and Other Entities that Exercise Fiduciary Powers in Connection With the Prompt Forwarding of Certain Communications to Beneficial Owners

Reg. § 240.14b-2. (a) *Definitions.* Unless the context otherwise requires, all terms used in this section shall have the same meanings as in the Act and, with respect to proxy soliciting material, as in § 240.14a-1 thereunder and, with respect to information statements, as in § 240.14c-1 thereunder. In addition, as used in this section, the following terms shall apply:

(1) The term *bank* means a bank, association, or other entity that exercises fiduciary powers.

(2) The term *beneficial owner* includes any person who has or shares, pursuant to an instrument, agreement, or otherwise, the power to vote, or to direct the voting of a security.

Note 1: If more than one person shares voting power, the provisions of the instrument creating that voting power shall govern with respect to whether consent to disclosure of beneficial owner information has been given.

Note 2: If more than one person shares voting power or if the instrument creating that voting power provides that such power shall be exercised by different persons depending on the nature of the corporate action involved, all persons entitled to exercise such power shall be deemed beneficial owners; *Provided, however,* that only one such beneficial owner need be designated among the beneficial owners to receive proxies or requests for voting instructions, other proxy soliciting material, information statements, and/or annual reports to security holders, if the person so designated assumes the obligation to disseminate, in a timely manner, such materials to the other beneficial owners.

(3) The term *registrant* means:

(i) The issuer of a class of securities registered pursuant to Section 12 of the Act; or

(ii) An investment company registered under the Investment Company Act of 1940.

(b) *Dissemination and beneficial owner information requirements.* A bank shall comply with the following requirements for disseminating certain communications to beneficial owners and providing beneficial owner information to registrants.

(1) The bank shall:

(i) Respond, by first class mail or other equally prompt means, directly to the registrant, no later than one business day after the date it receives an inquiry made in accordance with § 240.14a-13(a) or § 240.14c-7(a) by indicating the name and address of each of its respondent banks that holds the registrant's securities on behalf of beneficial owners, if any; and

(ii) Respond, by first class mail or other equally prompt means, directly to the registrant no later than seven business days after the date it receives an inquiry made in accordance with § 240.14a-13(a) or § 240.14c-7(a) by indicating, by means of a search card or otherwise:

(A) The approximate number of customers of the bank who are beneficial owners of the registrant's securities that are held of record by the bank or its nominee;

(B) If the registrant has indicated, pursuant to § 240.14a-13(a)(1)(ii) (A) or § 240.14c-7(a)(1)(ii) (A), that it will distribute the annual report to security holders to beneficial owners of its securities whose names, addresses, and securities positions are disclosed pursuant to paragraphs (b)(4)(ii) and (iii) of this section:

(1) With respect to customer accounts opened on or before December 28, 1986, the number of beneficial owners of the registrant's securities who have affirmatively consented to disclosure of their names, addresses, and securities positions; and

(2) With respect to customer accounts opened after December 28, 1986, the number of beneficial owners of the registrant's securities who have not objected to disclosure of their names, addresses, and securities positions; and

(C) The identity of its designated agent, if any, acting on its behalf in fulfilling its obligations under paragraphs (b)(4)(ii) and (iii) of this section;

Provided, however, that, if the bank or respondent bank has informed the registrant that a designated office(s) or department(s) is to receive such inquiries, receipt for purposes of paragraphs (b)(1)(i) and (ii) of this section shall mean receipt by such designated office(s) or department(s).

(2) Where proxies are solicited, the bank shall, within five business days after the record date:

(i) Execute an omnibus proxy, including a power of substitution, in favor of its respondent banks and forward such proxy to the registrant; and

(ii) Furnish a notice to each respondent bank in whose favor an omnibus proxy has been executed that it has executed such a proxy, including a power of substitution, in its favor pursuant to paragraph (b)(2)(i) of this section.

(3) Upon receipt of the proxy, other proxy soliciting material, information statement, and/or annual report to security holders from the registrant or other soliciting person, the bank shall forward such materials to each beneficial owner on whose behalf it holds securities, no later than five business days after the date it receives such material and, where a proxy is solicited, the bank shall forward, with the other proxy soliciting material and/or the annual report to security holders, either:

(i) A properly executed proxy:

(A) indicating the number of securities held for such beneficial owner;

(B) bearing the beneficial owner's account number or other form of identification, together with instructions as to the procedures to vote the securities;

(C) briefly stating which other proxies, if any, are required to permit securities to be voted under the terms of the instrument creating that voting power or applicable state law; and

(D) being accompanied by an envelope addressed to the registrant or its agent, if not provided by the registrant; or

(ii) A request for voting instructions (for which registrant's form of proxy may be used and which shall be voted by the record holder bank or respondent bank in accordance with the instructions received), together with an envelope addressed to the record holder bank or respondent bank.

Note to Paragraph (b)(3): At the request of a registrant, or on its own initiative so long as the registrant does not object, a bank may, but is not required to, deliver one annual report to security holders, proxy statement, information statement, or Notice of Internet Availability of Proxy Materials to more than one beneficial owner sharing an address if the requirements set forth in § 240.14a-3(e)(1) (with respect to annual reports to security holders, proxy statements, and Notices of Internet Availability of Proxy Materials) and § 240.14c-3(c) (with respect to annual reports to security holders, information statements, and Notices of Internet Availability of Proxy Materials) applicable to registrants, with the exception of § 240.14a-3(e)(1)(i)(E), are satisfied instead by the bank.

(4) The bank shall:

(i) Respond, by first class mail or other equally prompt means, directly to the registrant no later than one business day after the date it receives an inquiry made in accordance with § 240.14a-13(b)(1) or § 240.14c-7(b)(1) by indicating the name and address of each of its respondent banks that holds the registrant's securities on behalf of beneficial owners, if any;

(ii) Through its agent or directly, provide the registrant, upon the registrant's request, and within the time specified in paragraph (b)(4)(iii) of this section, with the names, addresses, and securities position, compiled as of a date specified in the registrant's request which is no earlier than five business days after the date the registrant's request is received, of:

(A) With respect to customer accounts opened on or before December 28, 1986, beneficial owners of the registrant's securities on whose behalf it holds securities who have consented affirmatively to disclosure of such information, subject to paragraph (b)(5) of this section; and

(B) With respect to customer accounts opened after December 28, 1986, beneficial owners of the registrant's securities on whose behalf it holds securities who have not objected to disclosure of such information;

Provided, however, that if the record holder bank or respondent bank has informed the registrant that a designated office(s) or department(s) is to receive such requests, receipt for purposes of paragraphs (b)(4)(i) and (ii) of this section shall mean receipt by such designated office(s) or department(s); and

(iii) Through its agent or directly, transmit the data specified in paragraph (b)(4)(ii) of this section to the registrant no later than five business days after the date specified by the registrant.

Note 1: Where a record holder bank or respondent bank employs a designated agent to act on its behalf in performing the obligations imposed on it by paragraphs (b)(4)(ii) and (iii) of this section, the five business day time period for determining the date as of which the beneficial owner information is to be compiled is calculated from the date the designated agent receives the registrant's request. In complying with the registrant's request for beneficial owner information under paragraphs (b)(4)(ii) and (iii) of this section, a record holder bank or respondent bank need only supply the registrant with the names, addresses and securities positions of affirmatively consenting and non-objecting beneficial owners.

Note 2: If a record holder bank or respondent bank receives a registrant's request less than five business days before the requested compilation date, it must provide a list compiled as of a date that is no more than five business days after receipt and transmit the list within five business days after the compilation date.

(5) For customer accounts opened on or before December 28, 1986, unless the bank has made a good faith effort to obtain affirmative consent to disclosure of beneficial owner information pursuant to paragraph (b)(4)(ii) of this section, the bank shall provide such information as to beneficial owners who do not object to disclosure of such information. A good faith effort to obtain affirmative consent to disclosure of beneficial owner information shall include, but shall not be limited to, making an inquiry:

(i) Phrased in neutral language, explaining the purpose of the disclosure and the limitations on the registrant's use thereof;

(ii) Either in at least one mailing separate from other account mailings or in repeated mailings; and

(iii) In a mailing that includes a return card, postage paid enclosure.

(c) *Exceptions to dissemination and beneficial owner information requirements.* The bank shall be subject to the following with respect to its dissemination and beneficial owner requirements.

(1) With regard to beneficial owners of exempt employee benefit plan securities, the bank shall not:

(i) Include information in its response pursuant to paragraph (b)(1) of this section; or forward proxies (or in lieu thereof requests for voting instructions), proxy soliciting material, information statements, or annual reports to security holders pursuant to paragraph (b)(3) of this section to such beneficial owners; or

(ii) Include in its response pursuant to paragraphs (b)(4) and (b)(5) of this section data concerning such beneficial owners.

(2) The bank need not satisfy:

(i) Its obligations under paragraphs (b)(2), (b)(3), (b)(4) and (d) of this section if the registrant or other soliciting person, as applicable, does not provide assurance of reimbursement of its reasonable expenses, both direct and indirect, incurred in connection with performing the obligations imposed by paragraphs (b)(2), (b)(3), (b)(4) and (d) of this section; or

(ii) Its obligation under paragraph (b)(3) of this section to forward annual reports to security holders to consenting and non-objecting beneficial owners identified pursuant to paragraphs (b)(4)(ii) and (iii) of this section if the registrant notifies the record holder bank or respondent bank, pursuant to § 240.14a-13(c) or § 240.14c-7(c), that the registrant will send the annual report to security holders to beneficial owners whose names addresses and securities positions are disclosed pursuant to paragraphs (b)(4)(ii) and (iii) of this section.

(3) For the purposes of determining the fees which may be charged to registrants pursuant to § 240.14a-13(b)(5), § 240.14c-7(a)(5), and paragraph (c)(2) of this section for performing obligations under paragraphs (b)(2), (b)(3), and (b)(4) of this section: an amount no greater than that permitted to be charged by brokers or dealers for reimbursement of their reasonable expenses, both direct and indirect, incurred in connection with performing the obligations imposed by paragraphs (b)(2) and (b)(3) of § 240.14b-1, shall be deemed to be reasonable.

(4) In its response pursuant to paragraph (b)(1)(ii)(A) of this section, a bank shall not include information about annual reports to security holders, proxy statements or information statements that will not be delivered to security holders sharing an address because of the bank's reliance on the procedures referred to in the Note to paragraph (b)(3) of this section.

(d) Upon receipt from the soliciting person of all of the information listed in § 240.14a-16(d), the bank shall:

(1) Prepare and send a Notice of Internet Availability of Proxy Materials containing the information required in paragraph (e) of this section to beneficial owners no later than:

(i) With respect to a registrant, 40 calendar days prior to the security holder meeting date or, if no meeting is to be held, 40 calendar days prior to the date the votes, consents, or authorizations may be used to effect the corporate action; and

(ii) With respect to a soliciting person other than the registrant, the later of:

(A) 40 calendar days prior to the security holder meeting date or, if no meeting is to be held, 40 calendar days prior to the date the votes, consents, or authorizations may be used to effect the corporate action; or

(B) 10 calendar days after the date that the registrant first sends its proxy statement or Notice of Internet Availability of Proxy Materials to security holders.

(2) Establish a Web site at which beneficial owners are able to access the bank's request for voting instructions and, at the bank's option, establish a Web site at which beneficial owners are able to access the proxy statement and other soliciting materials, provided that such Web sites are maintained in a manner consistent with paragraphs (b), (c), and (k) of § 240.14a-16;

(3) Upon receipt of a request from the registrant or other soliciting person, send to security holders specified by the registrant or other soliciting person a copy of the request for voting instructions accompanied by a copy of the intermediary's Notice of Internet Availability of Proxy Materials 10 days or more after the bank sends its Notice of Internet Availability of Proxy Materials pursuant to paragraph (d)(1); and

(4) Upon receipt of a request for a copy of the materials from a beneficial owner:

(i) Request a copy of the soliciting materials from the registrant or other soliciting person, in the form requested by the beneficial owner, within three business days after receiving the beneficial owner's request;

(ii) Forward a copy of the soliciting materials to the beneficial owner, in the form requested by the beneficial owner, within three business days after receiving the materials from the registrant or other soliciting person; and

(iii) Maintain records of security holder requests to receive a paper or e-mail copy of the proxy materials in connection with future proxy solicitations and provide copies of the proxy materials to a security holder who has made such a request for all securities held in the account of that security holder until the security holder revokes such request.

(e) *Content of Notice of Internet Availability of Proxy Materials.* The bank's Notice of Internet Availability of Proxy Materials shall:

(1) Include all information, as it relates to beneficial owners, required in a registrant's Notice of Internet Availability of Proxy Materials under § 240.14a-16(d), provided that the bank shall provide its own, or its agent's, toll-free telephone number, e-mail address, and Internet Web site to service requests for copies from beneficial owners; and

(2) Otherwise be prepared and sent in a manner consistent with paragraphs (e), (f), and (g) of § 240.14a-16.

(5) Notwithstanding any other provisions in this paragraph (d), if the bank receives copies of the proxy statement and annual report to security holders (if applicable) from the soliciting person with instructions to forward such materials to beneficial owners, the bank:

(i) Shall either:

(A) Prepare a Notice of Internet Availability of Proxy Materials and forward it with the proxy statement and annual report to security holders (if applicable); or

(B) Incorporate any information required in the Notice of Internet Availability of Proxy Materials that does not appear in the proxy statement into the bank's request for voting instructions to be sent with the proxy statement and annual report (if applicable);

(ii) Need not comply with the following provisions:

(A) The timing provisions of paragraph (d)(1)(ii); and

(B) Paragraph (d)(4); and

(iii) Need not include in its Notice of Internet Availability of Proxy Materials or request for voting instructions the following disclosures:

(A) Legends 1 and 3 in § 240.14a-16(d)(1); and

(B) Instructions on how to request a copy of the proxy materials.

[As last amended in Release No. 34-55146A, effective April 1, 2008, 73 F.R. 17809 (technical correction).]

REGULATION 14C—DISTRIBUTION OF INFORMATION PURSUANT TO SECTION 14(c)

ATTENTION ELECTRONIC FILERS
THIS REGULATION SHOULD BE READ IN CONJUNCTION WITH REGULATION S- T (PART 232 OF THIS CHAPTER), WHICH GOVERNS THE PREPARATION AND SUBMISSION OF DOCUMENTS IN ELECTRONIC FORMAT. MANY PROVISIONS RELATING TO THE PREPARATION AND SUBMISSION OF DOCUMENTS IN PAPER FORMAT CONTAINED IN THIS REGULATION ARE SUPERSEDED BY THE PROVISIONS OF REGULATION S-T FOR DOCUMENTS REQUIRED TO BE FILED IN ELECTRONIC FORMAT.

[¶ 40,401] Definitions

Reg. § 240.14c-1. Unless the context otherwise requires, all terms used in this regulation have the same meanings as in the Act or elsewhere in the general rules and regulations thereunder. In addition, the following definitions apply unless the context otherwise requires:

(a) *Associate.* The term "associate" used to indicate a relationship with any person, means (1) any corporation or organization (other than the registrant or a majority owned subsidiary of the registrant) of which such person is an officer or partner or is, directly or indirectly, the beneficial owner of 10 percent or more of any class of equity securities; (2) any trust or other estate in which such person has a substantial beneficial interest or as to which such person serves as trustee or in a similar fiduciary capacity; and (3) any relative or spouse of such person, or any relative of such spouse, who has the same home as such person or who is a director or officer of the registrant or any of its parents or subsidiaries.

(b) *Employee benefit plan.* For purposes of § 240.14c-7, the term "employee benefit plan" means any purchase, savings, option, bonus, appreciation, profit sharing, thrift, incentive, pension or similar plan primarily for employees, directors, trustees or officers.

(c) *Entity that exercises fiduciary powers.* The term "entity that exercises fiduciary powers" means any entity that holds securities in nominee name or otherwise on behalf of a beneficial owner but does not include a clearing agency registered pursuant to section 17A of the Act, or a broker or a dealer.

(d) *Exempt employee benefit plan securities.* For purposes of § 240.14c-7, the term "exempt employee benefit plan securities" means: (1) securities of the registrant held by an employee benefit plan, as defined in paragraph (b) of this section, where such plan is established by the registrant; or (2) if notice regarding the current distribution of information statements has been given pursuant to § 240.14c-7(a)(1)(ii)(C) or if notice regarding the current request for a list of names, addresses and securities positions of beneficial owners has been given pursuant to § 240.14c-7(b)(3), securities of the registrant held by an employee benefit plan, as defined in paragraph (b) of this section, where such plan is established by an affiliate of the registrant.

(e) *Information statement.* The term "information statement" means the statement required by § 240.14c-2, whether or not contained in a single document.

(f) *Last fiscal year.* The term "last fiscal year" of the registrant means the last fiscal year of the registrant ending prior to the date of the meeting with respect to which an information statement is required to be distributed, or if the information statement involves consents or authorizations in lieu of a meeting, the earliest date on which they may be used to effect corporate action.

(g) *Proxy.* The term "proxy" includes every proxy, consent or authorization within the meaning of section 14(a) of the Act. The consent or authorization may take the form of failure to object or to dissent.

(h) *Record date.* The term "record date" means the date as of which the record holders of securities entitled to vote at a meeting or by written consent or authorization shall be determined.

(i) *Record holder.* For purposes of § 240.14c-7, the term "record holder" means any broker, dealer, voting trustee, bank, association or other entity that exercises fiduciary powers which holds securities of record in nominee name or otherwise or as a participant in a clearing agency registered pursuant to section 17A of the Act.

(j) *Registrant.* The term "registrant" means:

(1) The issuer of a class of securities registered pursuant to Section 12 of the Act; or

(2) An investment company registered under the Investment Company Act of 1940 that has made a public offering of its securities.

(k) *Respondent bank.* For purposes of § 240.14c-7, the term "respondent bank" means any bank, association or other entity that exercises fiduciary powers which holds securities on behalf of beneficial owners and deposits such securities for safekeeping with another bank, association or other entity that exercises fiduciary powers.

[As last amended in Release No. 34-30147, January 6, 1992, effective with respect to shareholder meetings held, or corporate action taken by consent or authorization, on or after March 31, 1992, that have a record date on or after February 10, 1992, 57 F.R. 1096.]

[¶ 40,411] Distribution of Information Statement

Reg. § 240.14c-2. (a) (1) In connection with every annual or other meeting of the holders of the class of securities registered pursuant to section 12 of the Act or of a class of securities issued by an investment company registered under the Investment Company Act of 1940 that has made a public offering of securities, including the taking of corporate action by the written authorization or consent of security holders, the registrant shall transmit to every security holder of the class that is entitled to vote or give an authorization or consent in regard to any matter to be acted upon and from whom proxy authorization or consent is not solicited on behalf of the registrant pursuant to section 14(a) of the Act:

(i) A written information statement containing the information specified in Schedule 14C (§ 240.14c-101);

(ii) A publicly-filed information statement, in the form and manner described in § 240.14c-3(d), containing the information specified in Schedule 14C (§ 240.14c-101); or

(iii) A written information statement included in a registration statement filed under the Securities Act of 1933 on Form S-4 or F-4 (§ 239.25 or § 239.34 of this chapter) or Form N-14 (§ 239.23 of this chapter) and containing the information specified in such Form.

(2) Notwithstanding paragraph (a) (1) of this section:

(i) In the case of a class of securities in unregistered or bearer form, such statements need to be transmitted only to those security holders whose names are known to the registrant; and

(ii) No such statements need to be transmitted to a security holder if a registrant would be excused from delivery of an annual report to security holders or a proxy statement under § 240.14a-3(e) (2) if such section were applicable.

(b) The information statement shall be sent or given at least 20 calendar days prior to the meeting date or, in the case of corporate action taken pursuant to the consents or authorizations of security holders, at least 20 calendar days prior to the earliest date on which the corporate action may be taken.

(c) If a transaction is a roll-up transaction as defined in Item 901(c) of Regulation S-K (17 CFR 229.901(c)) and is registered (or authorized to be registered) on Form S-4 (17 CFR 229.25) or Form F-4 (17 CFR 229.34), the information statement must be distributed to security holders no later than the lesser of 60 calendar days prior to the date on which the meeting of security holders is held or action is taken, or the maximum number of days permitted for giving notice under applicable state law.

(d) A registrant shall transmit an information statement to security holders pursuant to paragraph (a) of this section by satisfying the requirements set forth in § 240.14a-16; provided, however, that the registrant shall revise the information required in the Notice of Internet Availability of Proxy Materials, including changing the title of that notice, to reflect the fact that the registrant is not soliciting proxies for the meeting.

[As last amended in Release No. 34–56135, effective January 1, 2008, 72 F.R. 42222.]

[¶ 40,421] Annual Report to Be Furnished Security Holders

Reg. § 240.14c-3. (a) If the information statement relates to an annual (or special meeting in lieu of the annual) meeting, or written consent in lieu of such meeting, of security holders at which directors of the registrant, other than an investment company registered under the Investment Company Act of 1940, are to be elected, it shall be accompanied or preceded by an annual report to security holders:

(1) The annual report to security holders shall contain the information specified in paragraphs (b) (1) through (b) (11) of § 240.14a-3.

(2) [Reserved in Release No. 34-34832, effective November 23, 1994, 59 F.R. 52689.]

(b) Seven copies of the report sent to security holders pursuant to this rule shall be mailed to the Commission, solely for its information, not later than the date on which such report is first sent or given to security holders or the date on which preliminary copies, or definitive copies, if preliminary filing was not required, of the information statement are filed with the Commission pursuant to Rule 14c-5, whichever date is later. The report is not deemed to be "filed" with the Commission or subject to this regulation otherwise than as provided in this rule, or to the liabilities of Section 18 of the Act, except to the extent that the registrant specifically requests that it be treated as a part of the information statement or incorporates it in the information statement or other filed report by reference.

(c) A registrant will be considered to have delivered a Notice of Internet Availability of Proxy Materials, annual report to security holders or information statement to security holders of record who share an address if the requirements set forth in § 240.14a-3(e)(1) are satisfied with respect to the Notice of Internet Availability of Proxy Materials, annual report to security holders or information statement, as applicable.

(d) A registrant shall furnish an annual report to security holders pursuant to paragraph (a) of this section by satisfying the requirements set forth in § 240.14a-16.

[As last amended in Release No. 33-8876, effective February 4, 2008, 73 F.R. 934.]

[¶ 40,431] Presentation of Information in Information Statement

Reg. § 240.14c-4. (a) The information included in the information statement shall be clearly presented and the statements made shall be divided into groups according to subject matter and the various groups of statements shall be preceded by appropriate headings. The order of items and sub-items in the schedule need not be followed. Where practicable and appropriate, the information shall be presented in tabular form. All amounts shall be stated in figures. Information required by more than one applicable item need not be repeated. No statement need be made in response to any item or sub-item which is inapplicable.

(b) Any information required to be included in the information statement as to terms of securities or other subject matter which from a standpoint of practical necessity must be determined in the future may be stated in terms of present knowledge and intention. Subject to the foregoing, information which is not known to the registrant and which it is not reasonably within the power of the registrant to ascertain or procure may be omitted if a brief statement of the circumstances rendering such information unavailable is made.

(c) All printed information statements shall be in roman type at least as large and as legible as 10-point modern type except that to the extent necessary for convenient presentation financial statements and other tabular data, but not the notes thereto, may be in roman type at least as large and as legible as 8-point modern type. All such types shall be leaded at least 2 points.

(d) Where an information statement is delivered through an electronic medium, issuers may satisfy legibility requirements applicable to printed documents, such as type size and font, by presenting all required information in a format readily communicated to investors.

[As last amended in Release No. 34-37183, May 9, 1996, effective June 14, 1996, 61 F.R. 24652.]

[¶ 40,441] Filing Requirements

Reg. § 240.14c-5. (a) *Preliminary information statement.* Five preliminary copies of the information statement shall be filed with the Commission at least 10 calendar days prior to the date definitive copies of such statement are first sent or given to security holders, or such shorter period prior to that date as the Commission may authorize upon a showing of good cause therefor. In computing the 10-day period, the filing date of the preliminary copies is to be counted as the first day and the 11th day is the date on which definitive copies of the information statement may be sent to security holders. A registrant, however, shall not file with the Commission a preliminary information statement if it relates to an annual (or special meeting in lieu of the annual) meeting, of security holders at which the only matters to be acted upon are:

(1) the election of directors;

(2) the election, approval or ratification of accountant(s);

(3) a security holder proposal identified in the registrant's information statement pursuant to Item 4 of Schedule 14C [§ 240.14c-101 of this chapter; and/or

(4) The approval or ratification of a plan as defined in paragraph (a)(6)(ii) of Item 402 of Regulation S-K (§ 229.402(a)(6)(ii) of this chapter) or amendments to such a plan.

This exclusion from filing a preliminary information statement does not apply if the registrant comments upon or refers to a solicitation in opposition in connection with the meeting in its information statement.

Note 1: The filing of revised material does not recommence the ten day time period unless the revised material contains material revisions or material new proposal(s) that constitute a fundamental change in the information statement.

Note 2: The officials responsible for the preparation of the information statement should make every effort to verify the accuracy and completeness of the information required by the applicable rules. The preliminary statement should be filed with the Commission at the earliest practicable date.

Note 3. *Solicitation in Opposition.* For purposes of the exclusion from filing a preliminary information statement, a "solicitation in opposition" includes: (a) any solicitation opposing a proposal supported by the registrant; and (b) any solicitation supporting a proposal that the registrant does not expressly support, other than a security holder proposal identified in the registrant's information statement pursuant to Item 4 of Schedule 14C [§ 240.14c-101 of this chapter]. The identification of a security holder proposal in the registrant's information statement does not constitute a "solicitation in opposition," even if the registrant opposes the proposal and/or includes a statement in opposition to the proposal.

Note 4. A registrant that is filing an information statement in preliminary form only because the registrant has commented on or referred to an opposing solicitation should indicate that fact in a transmittal letter when filing the preliminary material with the Commission.

(b) *Definitive information statement.* Eight definitive copies of the information statement, in the form in which it is furnished to security holders, must be filed with the Commission no later than the date the information statement is first sent or given to security holders. Three copies of these materials also must be filed with, or mailed for filing to, each national securities exchange on which the registrant has a class of securities listed and registered.

(c) *Release dates.* All preliminary material filed pursuant to paragraph (a) of this section shall be accompanied by a statement of the date on which copies thereof filed pursuant to paragraph (b) of this section are intended to be released to security holders. All definitive material filed pursuant to paragraph (b) of this section shall be accompanied by a statement of the date on which copies of such material have been released to security holders or, if not released, the date on which copies thereof are intended to be released.

(d)(1) *Public Availability of Information.* All copies of material filed pursuant to paragraph (a) of this section shall be clearly marked "Preliminary Copies," and shall be deemed immediately available for public inspection unless confidential treatment is obtained pursuant to paragraph (d)(2) of this section.

(2) *Confidential treatment.* If action will be taken on any matter specified in Item 14 of Schedule 14A (§ 240.14a-101), all copies of the preliminary information statement filed under paragraph (a) of this section will be for the information of the Commission only and will not be deemed available for public inspection until filed with the Commission in definitive form so long as:

(i) The information statement does not relate to a matter or proposal subject to § 240.13e-3 or a roll-up transaction as defined in Item 901(c) of Regulation S-K (§ 229.901(c) of this chapter);

(ii) Neither the parties to the transaction nor any persons authorized to act on their behalf have made any public communications relating to the transaction except for statements where the content is limited to the information specified in § 230.135 of this chapter; and

(iii) The materials are filed in paper and marked "Confidential, For Use of the Commission Only." In all cases, the materials may be disclosed to any department or agency of the United States Government and to the Congress, and the Commission may make any inquiries or investigation into the materials as may be necessary to conduct an adequate review by the Commission.

Instruction to paragraph (d)(2): If communications are made publicly that go beyond the information specified in § 230.135, the materials must be re-filed publicly with the Commission.

(e) *Revised information statements.* Where any information statement filed pursuant to this section is amended or revised, two of the copies of such amended or revised material filed pursuant to this section shall be marked to indicate clearly and precisely the changes effected therein. If the amendment or revision alters the text of the material, the changes in such text shall be indicated by means of underscoring or in some other appropriate manner.

(f) *Merger material.* Notwithstanding the foregoing provisions of this section, any information statement or other material included in a registration statement filed under the Securities Act of 1933 on Form N-14, S-4, or F-4 (§ 239.23, 25 or 34 of this chapter) shall be deemed filed both for the purposes of that Act and for the purposes of this section, but separate copies of such material need not be furnished pursuant to this section, nor shall any fee be required under paragraph (a) of this section. However, any additional material used after the effective date of the registration statement on Form N-14, S-4, or F-4 shall be filed in accordance with this section, unless separate copies of such material are required to be filed as an amendment of such registration statement.

(g) *Fees.* At the time of filing a preliminary information statement regarding an acquisition, merger, spinoff, consolidation or proposed sale or other disposition of substantially all the assets of the company, the registrant shall pay the Commission a fee, no part of which shall be refunded, established in accordance with § 240.0-11.

(h) *Cover page.* Each information statement filed with the Commission shall include a cover page in the form set forth in Schedule 14C (§ 240.14c-101 of this chapter). The cover page required by this paragraph need not be distributed to security holders.

[As last amended in Release No. 34-55146, effective March 30, 2007, 72 F.R. 4147.]

[¶ 40,451] False or Misleading Statements

Reg. § 240.14c-6. (a) No information statement shall contain any statement which, at the time and in the light of the circumstances under which it is made, is false or misleading with respect to any material fact, or which omits to state any material fact necessary in order to make the statements therein not false or misleading or necessary to correct any statement in any earlier communications with respect to the same meeting or subject matter which has become false or misleading.

(b) The fact that an information statement has been filed with or examined by the Commission shall not be deemed a finding by the Commission that such material is accurate or complete or not false or misleading, or that the Commission has passed upon the merits of or approved any statement contained therein or any matter to be acted upon by security holders. No representation contrary to the foregoing shall be made.

[As adopted in Release No. 34-7774, December 30, 1965, 31 F.R. 262.]

[¶ 40,461] Providing Copies of Material for Certain Beneficial Owners

Reg. § 240.14c-7. (a) If the registrant knows that securities of any class entitled to vote at a meeting, or by written authorizations or consents if no meeting is held, are held of record by a broker, dealer, voting trustee, or bank, association, or other entity that exercises fiduciary powers in nominee name or otherwise, the registrant shall:

(1) By first class mail or other equally prompt means: (i) Inquire of each such record holder: (A) whether other persons are the beneficial owners of such securities and, if so, the number of copies of the information statement necessary to supply such material to such beneficial owners; and (B) in the case of an annual (or special meeting in lieu of the annual) meeting, or written consents in lieu of such meeting, at which directors are to be elected, the number of copies of the annual report to security holders, necessary to supply such report to such beneficial owners for whom proxy material has not been and is not to be made available and to whom such reports are to be distributed by such record holder or its nominee and not by the registrant; (C) If the record holder or respondent bank has an obligation under § 240.14b-1(b)(3) or § 240.14b-2(b)(4)(ii) and (iii), whether an agent has been designated to act on its behalf in fulfilling such obligation, and, if so, the name and address of such agent; and (D) whether it holds the registrant's securities on behalf of any respondent bank and, if so, the name and address of each such respondent bank; and (ii) indicate to each such record holder: (A) whether the registrant pursuant to paragraph (c) of this section, intends to distribute the annual report to security holders to beneficial owners of its securities whose names, addresses and securities positions are disclosed pursuant to § 240.14b-1(b)(3) and § 240.14b-2(b)(4)(ii) and (iii); (B) the record date; and (C) at the option of the registrant, any employee benefit plan established by an affiliate of the registrant that holds securities of the registrant that the registrant elects to treat as exempt employee benefit plan securities;

(2) Upon receipt of a record holder's or respondent bank's response indicating, pursuant to § 240.14b-2(b)(1)(i), the names and addresses of its respondent banks, within one business day after the date such response is received, make an inquiry of and give notification to each such respondent bank in the same manner required by paragraph (a)(1) of this section; *Provided, however,* the inquiry required by paragraphs (a)(1) and (a)(2) of this section shall not cover beneficial owners of exempt employee benefit plan securities;

(3) Make the inquiry required by paragraph (a)(1) of this section on the earlier of:

(i) At least 20 business days prior to the record date of the meeting of security holders or the record date of written consents in lieu of a meeting; or

(ii) At least 20 business days prior to the date the information statement is required to be sent or given pursuant to § 240.14c-2(b);

Provided, however, That, if a record holder or respondent bank has informed the registrant that a designated office(s) or department(s) is to receive such inquiries, the inquiry shall be made to such designated office(s) or department(s);

(4) Supply, in a timely manner, each record holder and respondent bank of whom the inquiries required by paragraphs (a)(1) and (a)(2) of this section are made with copies of the information statement and/or the annual report to security holders, in such quantities, assembled in such form and at such place(s), as the record holder or respondent bank may reasonably request in order to send such

material to each beneficial owner of securities who is to be furnished with such material by the record holder or respondent bank; and

(5) Upon the request of any record holder or respondent bank that is supplied with Notices of Internet Availability of Proxy Materials, information statements and/or annual reports to security holders pursuant to paragraph (a)(3) of this section, pay its reasonable expenses for completing the sending of such material to beneficial owners.

Note 1.—If the registrant's list of security holders indicates that some of its securities are registered in the name of a clearing agency registered pursuant to section 17A of the Act (*e.g.,* "Cede & Co.," nominee for the Depository Trust Company), the registrant shall make appropriate inquiry of the clearing agency and thereafter of the participants in such a clearing agency who may hold on behalf of a beneficial owner or respondent bank, and shall comply with the above paragraph with respect to any such participant (*see* § 240.14c-1(h)).

Note 2.—The attention of registrants is called to the fact that each broker, dealer , bank, association, and other entity that exercises fiduciary powers has an obligation pursuant to § 240.14b-1 and§ 240.14b-2 (except as provided therein with respect to exempt employee benefit plan securities held in nominee name) and with respect to brokers and dealers, applicable self-regulatory organization requirements to obtain and forward, within the time periods prescribed therein, (a) information statements to beneficial owners on whose behalf it holds securities, and (b) annual reports to security holders to beneficial owners on whose behalf it holds securities, unless the registrant has notified the record holder or respondent bank that it has assumed responsibility to send such material to beneficial owners whose names, addresses and securities positions are disclosed pursuant to § 240.14b-1(b)(3) and § 240.14b-2(b)(4)(ii) and (iii).

Note 3.—The attention of registrants is called to the fact that registrants have an obligation, pursuant to paragraph (d) of this section, to cause information statements and annual reports to security holders to be furnished, in accordance with § 240.14c-2, to beneficial owners of exempt employee benefit plan securities.

(b) Any registrant requesting pursuant to § 240.14b-1(b)(3) and § 240.14b-2(b)(4)(ii) and (iii) a list of names, addresses and securities positions of beneficial owners of its securities who either have consented or have not objected to disclosure of such information shall:

(1) By first class mail or other equally prompt means, inquire of each record holder and each respondent bank identified to the registrant pursuant to § 240.14b-2(b)(4)(i) whether such record holder or respondent bank holds the registrant's securities on behalf of any respondent banks and, if so, the name and address of each such respondent bank;

(2) Request such list be compiled as of a date no earlier than five business days after the date the registrant's request is received by the record holder or respondent bank; *Provided, however,* that if the record holder or respondent bank has informed the registrant that a designated office(s) or depart-ment(s) is to receive such requests, the request shall be made to such designated office(s) or department(s):

(3) Make such request to the following persons that hold the registrant's securities on behalf of beneficial owners: all brokers, dealers, banks, associations and other entities that exercise fiduciary powers: *Provided, however,* such request shall not cover beneficial owners of exempt employee benefit plan securities as defined in § 240.14a-1(d)(1); and, at the option of the registrant, such request may give notice of any employee benefit plan established by an affiliate of the registrant that holds securities of the registrant that the registrant elects to treat as exempt employee benefit plan securities;

(4) Use the information furnished in response to such request exclusively for purposes of corporate communications; and

(5) Upon the request of any record holder or respondent bank to whom such request is made, pay the reasonable expenses, both direct and indirect, of providing beneficial owner information.

Note.—A registrant will be deemed to have satisfied its obligations under paragraph (b) of this section by requesting consenting and non-objecting beneficial owner lists from a designated agent acting on behalf of the record holder or respondent bank and paying to that designated agent the reasonable expenses of providing the beneficial owner information.

(c) A registrant, at its option, may send by mail or other equally prompt means, its annual report to security holders to the beneficial owners whose identifying information is provided by record holders and respondent banks, pursuant to § 240.14b-1(b)(3) and § 240.14b-2(b)(4)(ii) and (iii), provided that such registrant notifies the record holders and respondent banks at the time it makes the inquiry required by paragraph (a) of this section that the registrant will send the annual report to security holders to the beneficial owners so identified.

(d) If a registrant furnishes information statements to record holders and respondent banks who hold securities on behalf of beneficial owners, the registrant shall cause information statements and annual reports to security holders to be furnished, in accordance with § 240.14c-2, to beneficial owners of exempt employee benefit plan securities.

[As last amended in Release No. 34-55146, effective March 30, 2007, 72 F.R. 4147.]

SCHEDULE 14C

[¶ 40,501]   Reg. § 240.14c-101.   Information Required in Information Statement

SCHEDULE 14C INFORMATION

Information Statement Pursuant to Section 14(c) of the Securities Exchange Act of 1934
(Amendment No.)

Check the appropriate box:

[ ] Preliminary Information Statement

[ ] Confidential, for Use of the Commission Only (as permitted by Rule 14c-5(d)(2))

[ ] Definitive Information Statement

. . . .

(Name of Registrant As Specified In Its Charter)

Payment of Filing Fee (Check the appropriate box):

     [ ] No fee required.

     [ ] Fee computed on table below per Exchange Act Rules 14c-5(g) and 0-11.

     1) Title of each class of securities to which transaction applies:

. . . .

     2) Aggregate number of securities to which transaction applies:

. . . .

     3) Per unit price or other underlying value of transaction computed pursuant to Exchange Act Rule 0-11 (Set forth the amount on which the filing fee is calculated and state how it was determined):

. . . .

     4) Proposed maximum aggregate value of transaction:

. . . .

     5) Total fee paid:

. . . .

[ ] Fee paid previously with preliminary materials.

[ ] Check box if any part of the fee is offset as provided by Exchange Act Rule 0-11(a)(2) and identify the filing for which the offsetting fee was paid previously. Identify the previous filing by registration statement number, or the Form or Schedule and the date of its filing.

     1) Amount Previously Paid:

. . . .

     2) Form, Schedule or Registration Statement No.:

. . . .

     3) Filing Party:

. . . .

     4) Date Filed:

. . . .

Note to Cover Page: Where any item, other than Item 4, calls for information with respect to any matter to be acted upon at the meeting or, if no meeting is being held, by written authorization or consent, such item need be answered only with respect to proposals to be made by the registrant. Registrants and acquirees that meet the definition of "smaller reporting company" under Rule 12b-2 of the Exchange Act (§ 240.12b-2) shall refer to the disclosure items in Regulation S-K (§ § 229.10 through 229.1123 of this chapter) with specific attention to the scaled disclosure requirements for smaller reporting companies, if any. A smaller reporting company may provide the information in Article 8 of Regulation S-X in lieu of any financial statements required by Item 1 of § 240.14c-101.

Item 1. Information Required by Items of Schedule 14A (17 CFR 240.14a-101.)

Furnish the information called for by all of the items of Schedule 14A of Regulation 14A (17 CFR 240.14a-101) (other than Items 1(c). 2, 4 and 5 thereof) which would be applicable to any matter to be acted upon at the meeting if proxies were to be solicited in connection with the meeting. Notes A, C, D, and E to Schedule 14A are also applicable to Schedule 14C.

Item 2. Statement That Proxies Are Not Solicited

The following statement shall be set forth on the first page of the information statement in bold-face type:

We Are Not Asking You for a Proxy and You are Requested Not To Send Us a Proxy

Item 3. Interest of Certain Persons in or Opposition to Matters to Be Acted Upon

(a) Describe briefly any substantial interest, direct or indirect, by security holdings or otherwise, of each of the following persons in any matter to be acted upon, other than elections to office:

(1) each person who has been a director or officer of the registrant at any time since the beginning of the last fiscal year;

(2) each nominee for election as a director of the registrant;

(3) each associate of any of the foregoing persons.

(b) Give the name of any director of the registrant who has informed the registrant in writing that he intends to oppose any action to be taken by the registrant at the meeting and indicate the action which he intends to oppose.

Item 4. Proposals by Security Holders

If any security holder entitled to vote at the meeting or by written authorization or consent has submitted to the registrant a reasonable time before the information statement is to be transmitted to security holders a proposal, other than elections to office, which is accompanied by notice of his intention to present the proposal for action at the meeting the registrant shall, if a meeting is held, make a statement to that effect, identify the proposal and indicate the disposition proposed to be made of the proposal by the registrant at the meeting.

Instructions. 1. This item need not be answered as to any proposal submitted with respect to an annual meeting if such proposal is submitted less than 60 days in advance of a day corresponding to the date of sending a proxy statement or information statement in connection with the last annual meeting of security holders.

2. If the registrant intends to rule a proposal out of order, the Commission shall be so advised 20 calendar days prior to the date the definitive copies of the information statement are filed with the Commission, together with a statement of the reasons why the proposal is not deemed to be a proper subject for action by security holders.

Item 5. Delivery of Documents to Security Holders Sharing an Address

If one annual report to security holders, information statement, or Notice of Internet Availability of Proxy Materials is being delivered to two or more security holders who share an address, furnish the following information in accordance with § 240.14a-3(e)(1):

(a) State that only one annual report to security holders, information statement, or Notice of Internet Availability of Proxy Materials, as applicable, is being delivered to multiple security holders sharing an address unless the registrant has received contrary instructions from one or more of the security holders;

(b) Undertake to deliver promptly upon written or oral request a separate copy of the annual report to security holders, information statement, or Notice of Internet Availability of Proxy Materials, as applicable, to a security holder at a shared address to which a single copy of the documents was delivered and provide instructions as to how a security holder can notify the registrant that the security holder wishes to receive a separate copy of an annual report to security holders, information statement, or Notice of Internet Availability of Proxy Materials, as applicable;

(c) Provide the phone number and mailing address to which a security holder can direct a notification to the registrant that the security holder wishes to receive a separate annual report to security holders, information statement, or Notice of Internet Availability of Proxy Materials, as applicable, in the future; and

(d) Provide instructions how security holders sharing an address can request delivery of a single copy of annual reports to security holders, information statements, or Notices of Internet Availability of Proxy Materials if they are receiving multiple copies of annual reports to security holders, information statements, or Notices of Internet Availability of Proxy Materials.

[As last amended in Release No. 33-8876, effective February 4, 2008, 73 F.R. 934.]

REGULATION 14D

ATTENTION ELECTRONIC FILERS
THIS REGULATION SHOULD BE READ IN CONJUNCTION WITH REGULATION S- T (PART 232 OF THIS CHAPTER), WHICH GOVERNS THE PREPARATION AND SUBMISSION OF DOCU- MENTS IN ELECTRONIC FORMAT. MANY PROVISIONS RELATING TO THE PREPARATION AND SUBMISSION OF DOCUMENTS IN PAPER FORMAT CONTAINED IN THIS REGULATION ARE SUPERSEDED BY THE PROVISIONS OF REGULATION S-T FOR DOCUMENTS REQUIRED TO BE FILED IN ELECTRONIC FORMAT.

Disclosure Requirements and Minimum Time for Tender Offers

[¶ 40,601] Scope of and Definitions Applicable to Regulations 14D and 14E

Reg. § 240.14d-1. (a) *Scope.* Regulation 14D (§§ 240.14d-1 through 240.14d-101) shall apply to any tender offer that is subject to section 14(d)(1) of the Act (15 U.S.C. 78n(d)(1)), including, but not limited to, any tender offer for securities of a class described in that section that is made by an affiliate of the issuer of such class. Regulation 14E (§§ 240.14e-1 through 240.14e-8) shall apply to any tender offer for securities (other than exempted securities) unless otherwise noted therein.

(b) The requirements imposed by sections 14(d)(1) through 14(d)(7) of the Act, Regulation 14D and Schedules TO and 14D-9 thereunder, and Rule 14e-1 of Regulation 14E under the Act, shall be deemed satisfied with respect to any tender offer, including any exchange offer, for the securities of an issuer incorporated or organized under the laws of Canada or any Canadian province or territory, if such issuer is a foreign private issuer and is not an investment company registered or required to be registered under the Investment Company Act of 1940, if less than 40 percent of the class of securities outstanding that is the subject of the tender offer is held by U.S. holders, and the tender offer is subject to, and the bidder complies with, the laws, regulations and policies of Canada and/or any of its provinces or territories governing the conduct of the offer (unless the bidder has received an exemption(s) from, and the tender offer does not comply with, requirements that otherwise would be prescribed by Regulation 14D or 14E), *provided that:*

(1) In the case of tender offers subject to section 14(d)(1) of the Act, where the consideration for a tender offer subject to this section consists solely of cash, the entire disclosure document or documents required to be furnished to holders of the class of securities to be acquired shall be filed with the Commission on Schedule 14D-1F (§ 240.14d-102) and disseminated to shareholders of the subject company residing in the United States in accordance with such Canadian laws, regulations and policies; or

(2) Where the consideration for a tender offer subject to this section includes securities of the bidder to be issued pursuant to the offer, any registration statement and/or prospectus relating thereto shall be filed with the Commission along with the Schedule 14D-1F referred to in paragraph (b)(1) of this section, and shall be disseminated, together with the home jurisdiction document(s) accompanying such Schedule, to shareholders of the subject company residing in the United States in accordance with such Canadian laws, regulations and policies.

NOTES: 1. For purposes of any tender offer, including any exchange offer, otherwise eligible to proceed in accordance with Rule 14d-1(b) under the Act, the issuer of the subject securities will be presumed to be a foreign private issuer and U.S. holders will be presumed to hold less than 40 percent of such outstanding securities, *unless* (a) the aggregate trading volume of that class on national securities exchanges in the United States and on NASDAQ exceeded its aggregate trading volume on securities exchanges in Canada and on the Canadian Dealing Network, Inc. ("CDN") over the 12 calendar month period prior to commencement of this offer, or if commenced in response to a prior offer, over the 12 calendar month period prior to the commencement of the initial offer (based on volume figures published by such exchanges and NASDAQ and CDN); (b) the most recent annual report or annual information form filed or submitted by the issuer with securities regulators of Ontario, Quebec, British Columbia or Alberta (or, if the issuer of the subject securities is not a reporting issuer in any of such provinces, with any other Canadian securities regulator) or with the Commission indicates that U.S. holders hold 40 percent or more of the outstanding subject class of securities; or (c) the offeror has actual knowledge that the level of U.S. ownership equals or exceeds 40 percent of such securities.

2. Notwithstanding the grant of an exemption from one or more of the applicable Canadian regulatory provisions imposing requirements that otherwise would be prescribed by Regulation 14D or 14E, the tender offer will be eligible to proceed in accordance with the requirements of this section if the Commission by order determines that the applicable Canadian regulatory provisions are adequate to protect the interest of investors.

(c) *Tier I.* Any tender offer for the securities of a foreign private issuer as defined in §240.3b-4 is exempt from the requirements of Sections 14(d)(1) through 14(d)(7) of the Act (15 U.S.C. 78n(d)(1) through 78n(d)(7)), Regulation 14D (§240.14d-1 through §240.14d-10) and Schedules TO (§240.14d-100) and 14D-9 (§240.14d-101) thereunder, and §240.14e-1 and §240.14e-2 of Regulation 14E under the Act if the following conditions are satisfied:

(1) *U.S. ownership limitation.* Except the in case of a tender offer that is commenced during the pendency of a tender offer made by a prior bidder in reliance on this paragraph or § 240.13e-4(h)(8), U.S. holders do not hold more than 10 percent of the class of securities sought in the offer (as determined under Instructions 2 or 3 to paragraphs (c) and (d) of this section).

(2) *Equal treatment.* The bidder must permit U.S. holders to participate in the offer on terms at least as favorable as those offered any other holder of the same class of securities that is the subject of the tender offer; however:

(i) *Registered exchange offers.* If the bidder offers securities registered under the Securities Act of 1933 (15 U.S.C. 77a *et seq.*), the bidder need not extend the offer to security holders in those states or jurisdictions that prohibit the offer or sale of the securities after the bidder has made a good faith effort to register or qualify the offer and sale of securities in that state or jurisdiction, except that the bidder must offer the same cash alternative to security holders in any such state or jurisdiction that it has offered to security holders in any other state or jurisdiction.

(ii) *Exempt exchange offers.* If the bidder offers securities exempt from registration under §230.802 of this chapter, the bidder need not extend the offer to security holders in those states or jurisdictions that require registration or qualification, except that the bidder must offer the same cash alternative to security holders in any such state or jurisdiction that it has offered to security holders in any other state or jurisdiction.

(iii) *Cash only consideration.* The bidder may offer U.S. holders only a cash consideration for the tender of the subject securities, notwithstanding the fact that the bidder is offering security holders outside the United States a consideration that consists in whole or in part of securities of the bidder, so long as the bidder has a reasonable basis for believing that the amount of cash is substantially equivalent to the value of the consideration offered to non-U.S. holders, and either of the following conditions are satisfied:

(A) The offered security is a "margin security" within the meaning of Regulation T (12 CFR 220.2) and the issuer undertakes to provide, upon the request of any U.S. holder or the Commission staff, the closing price and daily trading volume of the security on the principal trading market for the security as of the last trading day of each of the six months preceding the announcement of the offer and each of the trading days thereafter; or

(B) If the offered security is not a "margin security" within the meaning of Regulation T (12 CFR 220.2) the issuer undertakes to provide, upon the request of any U.S. holder or the Commission staff, an opinion of an independent expert stating that the cash consideration offered to U.S. holders is substantially equivalent to the value of the consideration offered security holders outside the United States.

(iv) *Disparate tax treatment.* If the bidder offers loan notes solely to offer sellers tax advantages not available in the United States and these notes are neither listed on any organized securities market nor registered under the Securities Act of 1933 (15 U.S.C. 77a *et seq.*), the loan notes need not be offered to U.S. holders.

(3) *Informational documents.* (i) The bidder must disseminate any informational document to U.S. holders, including any amendments thereto, in English, on a comparable basis to that provided to security holders in the home jurisdiction.

(ii) If the bidder disseminates by publication in its home jurisdiction, the bidder must publish the information in the United States in a manner reasonably calculated to inform U.S. holders of the offer.

(iii) In the case of tender offers for securities described in Section 14(d)(1) of the Act (15 U.S.C. 78n(d)(1)), if the bidder publishes or otherwise disseminates an informational document to the holders of the securities in connection with the tender offer, the bidder must furnish that informational document, including any amendments thereto, in English, to the Commission on Form CB (§249.480 of this chapter) by the first business day after publication or dissemination. If the bidder is a foreign company, it must also file a Form F-X (§239.42 of this chapter) with the Commission at the same time as the submission of Form CB to appoint an agent for service in the United States.

(4) *Investment companies.* The issuer of the securities that are the subject of the tender offer is not an investment company registered or required to be registered under the Investment Company Act of 1940 (15 U.S.C. 80a-1 *et seq.*), other than a registered closed-end investment company.

(d) *Tier II.* A person conducting a tender offer (including any exchange offer) that meets the conditions in paragraph (d)(1) of this section shall be entitled to the exemptive relief specified in paragraph (d)(2) of this section, provided that such tender offer complies with all the requirements of this section other than those for which an exemption has been specifically provided in paragraph (d)(2) of this section. In addition, a person conducting a tender offer subject only to the requirements of section 14(e) of the Act (15 U.S.C. 78n(e)) and Regulation 14E thereunder that meets the conditions in paragraph (d)(1) of the section also shall be entitled to the exemptive relief specified in paragraph (d)(2) of this section, to the extent needed under the requirements of Regulation 14E, so long as the tender offer complies with all requirements of Regulation 14E other than those for which an exemption has been specifically provided in paragraph (d)(2) of this section:

(1) *Conditions.* (i) The subject company is a foreign private issuer as defined in § 240.3b-4 and is not an investment company registered or required to be registered under the Investment Company Act of 1940 (15 U.S.C. 80a-1 *et seq.*), other than a registered closed-end investment company;

(ii) Except in the case of a tender offer that is commenced during the pendency of a tender offer made by a prior bidder in reliance on this paragraph or § 240.13e-4(i), U.S. holders do not hold more than 40 percent of the class of securities sought in the offer (as determined under Instructions 2 or 3 to paragraphs (c) and (d) of this section); and

(iii) The bidder complies with all applicable U.S. tender offer laws and regulations, other than those for which an exemption has been provided for in paragraph (d)(2) of this section.

(2) *Exemptions.* (i) *Equal treatment - loan notes.* If the bidder offers loan notes solely to offer sellers tax advantages not available in the United States and these notes are neither listed on any organized securities market nor registered under the Securities Act of 1933 (15 U.S.C. 77a *et seq.*), the loan notes need not be offered to U.S. holders, notwithstanding § 240.14d-10.

(ii) *Equal treatment-separate U.S. and foreign offers.* Notwithstanding the provisions of § 240.14d-10, a bidder conducting a tender offer meeting the conditions of paragraph (d)(1) of this section may separate the offer into multiple offers: one offer made to U.S. holders, which also may include all holders of American Depositary Shares representing interests in the subject securities, and one or more offers made to non-U.S. holders. The U.S. offer must be made on terms at least as favorable as those offered any other holder of the same class of securities that is the subject of the tender offers. U.S. holders may be included in the foreign offer(s) only where the laws of the jurisdiction governing such foreign offer(s) expressly preclude the exclusion of U.S. holders from the foreign offer(s) and where the offer materials distributed to U.S. holders fully and adequately disclose the risks of participating in the foreign offer(s).

(iii) *Notice of extensions.* Notice of extensions made in accordance with the requirements of the home jurisdiction law or practice will satisfy the requirements of § 240.14e-1(d).

(iv) *Prompt payment.* Payment made in accordance with the requirements of the home jurisdiction law or practice will satisfy the requirements of § 240.14e-1(c). Where payment may not be made on a more expedited basis under home jurisdiction law or practice, payment for securities tendered during any subsequent offering period within 20 business days of the date of tender will satisfy the prompt payment requirements of § 240.14d-11(e). For purposes of this paragraph, a business day is determined with reference to the target's home jurisdiction.

(v) *Subsequent offering period/Withdrawal rights.* A bidder will satisfy the announcement and prompt payment requirements of § 240.14d-11(d), if the bidder announces the results of the tender offer, including the approximate number of securities deposited to date, and pays for tendered securities in accordance with the requirements of the home jurisdiction law or practice and the subsequent offering period commences immediately following such announcement. Notwithstanding Section 14(d)(5) of the Act (15 U.S.C. 78n(d)(5)), the bidder need not extend withdrawal rights following the close of the offer and prior to the commencement of the subsequent offering period.

(vi) *Payment of interest on securities tendered during subsequent offering period.* Notwithstanding the requirements of § 240.14d-11(f), the bidder may pay interest on securities tendered during a subsequent offering period, if required under applicable foreign law. Paying interest on securities tendered during a subsequent offering period in accordance with this section will not be deemed to violate § 240.14d-10(a)(2).

(vii) *Suspension of withdrawal rights during counting of tendered securities.* The bidder may suspend withdrawal rights required under section 14(d)(5) of the Act (15 U.S.C. 78n(d)(5)) at the end of the offer and during the period that securities tendered into the offer are being counted, provided that:

(A) The bidder has provided an offer period including withdrawal rights for a period of at least 20 U.S. business days;

(B) At the time withdrawal rights are suspended, all offer conditions have been satisfied or waived, except to the extent that the bidder is in the process of determining whether a minimum acceptance condition included in the terms of the offer has been satisfied by counting tendered securities; and

(C) Withdrawal rights are suspended only during the counting process and are reinstated immediately thereafter, except to the extent that they are terminated through the acceptance of tendered securities.

(viii) *Mix and match elections and the subsequent offering period.* Notwithstanding the requirements of § 240.14d-11(b), where the bidder offers target security holders a choice between different forms of consideration, it may establish a ceiling on one or more forms of consideration offered. Notwithstanding the requirements of § 240.14d-11(f), a bidder that establishes a ceiling on one or more forms of consideration offered pursuant to this subsection may offset elections of tendering security holders against one another, subject to proration, so that elections are satisfied to the greatest extent possible and pro rated to the extent that they cannot be satisfied in full. Such a bidder also may separately offset and pro rate securities tendered during the initial offering period and those tendered during any subsequent offering period, notwithstanding the requirements of § 240.14d-10(c).

(ix) *Early termination of an initial offering period.* A bidder may terminate an initial offering period, including a voluntary extension of that period, if at the time the initial offering period and withdrawal rights terminate, the following conditions are met:

(A) The initial offering period has been open for at least 20 U.S. business days;

(B) The bidder has adequately discussed the possibility of and the impact of the early termination in the original offer materials;

(C) The bidder provides a subsequent offering period after the termination of the initial offering period;

(D) All offer conditions are satisfied as of the time when the initial offering period ends; and

(E) The bidder does not terminate the initial offering period or any extension of that period during any mandatory extension required under U.S. tender offer rules.

Instructions to paragraphs (c) and (d):

1. Home jurisdiction means both the jurisdiction of the subject company's incorporation, organization or chartering and the principal foreign market where the subject company's securities are listed or quoted.

2. *U.S. holder* means any security holder resident in the United States. Except as otherwise provided in Instruction 3 below, to determine the percentage of outstanding securities held by U.S. holders:

i. Calculate the U.S. ownership as of a date no more than 60 before and no more than 30 days after public announcement of the tender offer. If you are unable to calculate as of a date within these time frames, the calculation may be made as of the most recent practicable date before public announcement, but in no event earlier than 120 days before announcement;

ii. Include securities underlying American Depositary Shares convertible or exchangeable into the securities that are the subject of the tender offer when calculating the number of subject securities outstanding, as well as the number held by U.S. holders. Exclude from the calculations other types of securities that are convertible or exchangeable into the securities that are the subject of the tender offer, such as warrants, options and convertible securities. Exclude from those calculations securities held by the bidder;

iii. Use the method of calculating record ownership in Rule 12g3-2(a) under the Act (§ 240.12g3-2(a) of this chapter), except that your inquiry as to the amount of securities represented by accounts of customers resident in the United States may be limited to brokers, dealers, banks and other nominees located in the United States, the subject company's jurisdiction of incorporation or that of each participant in a business combination, and the jurisdiction that is the primary trading market for the subject securities, if different than the subject company's jurisdiction of incorporation;

iv. If, after reasonable inquiry, you are unable to obtain information about the amount of securities represented by accounts of customers resident in the United States, you may assume, for purposes of this definition, that the customers are residents of the jurisdiction in which the nominee has its principal place of business; and

v. Count securities as beneficially owned by residents of the United States as reported on reports of beneficial ownership that are provided to you or publicly filed and based on information otherwise provided to you.

3. In a tender offer by a bidder other than an affiliate of the issuer of the subject securities that is not made pursuant to an agreement with the issuer of the subject securities, the issuer of the subject securities will be presumed to be a foreign private issuer and U.S. holders will be presumed to hold less than 10 percent (40 percent in the case of paragraph (d) of this section) of such outstanding securities, unless paragraphs i., ii., or iii. of this section indicate otherwise. In addition, where the bidder is unable to conduct the analysis of U.S. ownership set forth in Instruction 2 above, the bidder may presume that the percentage of securities held by U.S. holders is less than 10 percent (40 percent in the case of paragraph (d) of this section) of the outstanding securities so long as there is a primary trading market for the subject securities outside the U.S., as defined in Rule 12h-6(f)(5), unless:

i. Average daily trading volume of the subject securities in the United States for a recent twelve-month period ending on a date no more than 60 days before the public announcement of the offer exceeds 10 percent (40 percent in the case of paragraph (d) of this section) of the average daily trading volume of that class of securities on a worldwide basis for the same period; or

ii. The most recent annual report or annual information filed or submitted by the issuer with securities regulators of the home jurisdiction or with the Commission or any jurisdiction in which the subject securities trade before the public announcement of the offer indicates that U.S. holders hold more than 10 percent (40 percent in the case of paragraph (d) of this section) of the outstanding subject class of securities; or

iii. The bidder knows or has reason to know, before the public announcement of the offer, that the level of U.S. ownership exceeds 10 percent (40 percent in the case of paragraph (d) of this section) of such securities. As an example, a bidder is deemed to know information about U.S. ownership of the subject class of securities that is publicly available and that appears in any filing with the Commission or any regulatory body in the issuer's jurisdiction of incorporation or (if different) the non-U.S. jurisdiction in which the primary trading market for the subject securities is located. The bidder is deemed to know information about U.S. ownership available from the issuer or obtained or readily available from any other source that is reasonably reliable, including from persons it has retained to advise it about the transaction, as well as from third-party information providers. These examples are not intended to be exclusive.

4. *United States* means the United States of America, its territories and possessions, any State of the United States, and the District of Columbia.

5. The exemptions provided by paragraphs (c) and (d) of this section are not available for any securities transaction or series of transactions that technically complies with paragraph (c) or (d) of this section but are part of a plan or scheme to evade the provisions of Regulations 14D or 14E.

(e) Notwithstanding paragraph (a) of this section, the requirements imposed by sections 14(d)(1) through 14(d)(7) of the Act [15 U.S.C. 78n(d)(1) through 78n(d)(7)], Regulation 14D promulgated thereunder (§§ 240.14d-1 through 240.14d-10), and §§ 240.14e-1 and 240.14e-2 shall not apply by virtue of the fact that a bidder for the securities of a foreign private issuer, as defined in § 240.3b-4, the subject company of such a tender offer, their representatives, or any other person specified in § 240.14d-9(d), provides any journalist with access to its press conferences held outside of the United States, to meetings with its representatives conducted outside of the United States, or to written press-related materials released outside the United States, at or in which a present or proposed tender offer is discussed, if:

(1) Access is provided to both U.S. and foreign journalists; and

(2) With respect to any written press-related materials released by the bidder or its representatives that discuss a present or proposed tender offer for equity securities registered under Section 12 of the Act [15 U.S.C. 78l], the written press-related materials must state that these written press-related materials are not an extension of a tender offer in the United States for a class of equity securities of the subject company. If the bidder intends to extend the tender offer in the United States at some future time, a statement regarding this intention, and that the procedural and filing requirements of the Williams Act will be satisfied at that time, also must be included in these written press-related materials. No means to tender securities, or coupons that could be returned to indicate interest in the tender offer, may be provided as part of, or attached to, these written press-related materials.

(f) For the purpose of § 240.14d-1(c), a bidder may presume that a target company qualifies as a foreign private issuer if the target company is a foreign issuer and files registration statements or reports on the disclosure forms specifically designated for foreign private issuers, claims the exemption from registration under the Act pursuant to § 240.12g3-2(b), or is not reporting in the United States.

(g) *Definitions.* Unless the context otherwise requires, all terms used in Regulation 14D and Regulation 14E have the same meaning as in the Act and in Rule 12b-2 (§ 240.12b-2) promulgated thereunder. In addition, for purposes of section 14(d) and 14(e) of the Act and Regulations 14D and 14E, the following definitions apply:

(1) The term "beneficial owner" shall have the same meaning as that set forth in Rule 13d-3: *Provided, however,* That, except with respect to Rule 14d-3 and Rule 14d-9(d), the term shall not include a person who does not have or share investment power or who is deemed to be a beneficial owner by virtue of Rule 13d-3(d)(1) (§ 240.13d-3(d)(1));

(2) The term "bidder" means any person who makes a tender offer or on whose behalf a tender offer is made: *Provided, however,* That the term does not include an issuer which makes a tender offer for securities of any class of which it is the issuer;

(3) The term "business day" means any day, other than Saturday, Sunday or a federal holiday, and shall consist of the time period from 12:01 a.m. through 12:00 midnight Eastern time. In computing any time period under section 14(d)(5) or section 14(d)(6) of the Act or under Regulation 14D or Regulation 14E, the date of the event which begins the running of such time period shall be included *except that* if

such event occurs on other than a business day such period shall begin to run on and shall include the first business day thereafter; and

(4) The term *initial offering period* means the period from the time the offer commences until all minimum time periods, including extensions, required by Regulations 14D (§§ 240.14d-1 through 240.14d-103) and 14E (§§ 240.14e-1 through 240.14e-8) have been satisfied and all conditions to the offer have been satisfied or waived within these time periods.

(5) The term "security holders" means holders of record and beneficial owners of securities which are the subject of a tender offer;

(6) The term "security position listing" means, with respect to securities of any issuer held by a registered clearing agency in the name of the clearing agency or its nominee, a list of those participants in the clearing agency on whose behalf the clearing agency holds the issuer's securities and of the participants' respective positions in such securities as of a specified date.

(7) The term "subject company" means any issuer of securities which are sought by a bidder pursuant to a tender offer;

(8) The term *subsequent offering period* means the period immediately following the initial offering period meeting the conditions specified in § 240.14d-11.

(9) The term "tender offer material" means:

(i) The bidder's formal offer, including all the material terms and conditions of the tender offer and all amendments thereto;

(ii) The related transmittal letter (whereby securities of the subject company which are sought in the tender offer may be transmitted to the bidder or its depositary) and all amendments thereto; and

(iii) Press releases, advertisements, letters and other documents published by the bidder or sent or given by the bidder to security holders which, directly or indirectly, solicit, invite or request tenders of the securities being sought in the tender offer;

(h) *Signatures.* Where the Act or the rules, forms, reports or schedules thereunder require a document filed with or furnished to the Commission to be signed, such document shall be manually signed, or signed using either typed signatures or duplicated or facsimile versions of manual signatures. Where typed, duplicated or facsimile signatures are used, each signatory to the filing shall manually sign a signature page or other document authenticating, acknowledging or otherwise adopting his or her signature that appears in the filing. Such document shall be executed before or at the time the filing is made and shall be retained by the filer for a period of five years. Upon request, the filer shall furnish to the Commission or its staff a copy of any or all documents retained pursuant to this section.

[As last amended in Release No. 33-8957, effective December 8, 2008, 73 F.R. 60049.]

[¶ 40,611] Commencement of a Tender Offer

Reg. § 240.14d-2. (a) *Date of commencement.* A bidder will have commenced its tender offer for purposes of section 14(d) of the Act (15 U.S.C. 78n) and the rules under that section at 12:01 a.m. on the date when the bidder has first published, sent or given the means to tender to security holders. For purposes of this section, the means to tender includes the transmittal form or a statement regarding how the transmittal form may be obtained.

(b) *Pre-commencement communications.* A communication by the bidder will not be deemed to constitute commencement of a tender offer if:

(1) It does not include the means for security holders to tender their shares into the offer; and

(2) All written communications relating to the tender offer, from and including the first public announcement, are filed under cover of Schedule TO (§ 240.14d-100) with the Commission no later than the date of the communication. The bidder also must deliver to the subject company and any other bidder for the same class of securities the first communication relating to the transaction that is filed, or required to be filed, with the Commission.

Instructions to paragraph (b)(2): 1. The box on the front of Schedule TO indicating that the filing contains pre-commencement communications must be checked.

2. Any communications made in connection with an exchange offer registered under the Securities Act of 1933 need only be filed under § 230.425 of this chapter and will be deemed filed under this section.

3. Each pre-commencement written communication must include a prominent legend in clear, plain language advising security holders to read the tender offer statement when it is available because it contains important information. The legend also must advise investors that they can get the tender offer statement and other filed documents for free at the Commission's web site and explain which documents are free from the offeror.

4. See Regs. 230.135, 230.165 and 230.166 of this chapter for pre-commencement communications made in connection with registered exchange offers.

5. "Public announcement" is any oral or written communication by the bidder, or any person authorized to act on the bidder's behalf, that is reasonably designed to, or has the effect of, informing the public or security holders in general about the tender offer.

(c) *Filing and other obligations triggered by commencement.* As soon as practicable on the date of commencement, a bidder must comply with the filing requirements of § 240.14d-3(a), the dissemination requirements of § 240.14d-4(a) or (b), and the disclosure requirements of § 240.14d-6(a).

[As last amended in Release No. 33-7760, effective January 24, 2000, 64 F.R. 61408.]

[¶ 40,621] Filing and Transmission of Tender Offer Statement

Reg. § 240.14d-3. (a) *Filing and transmittal.* No bidder shall make a tender offer if, after consummation thereof, such bidder would be the beneficial owner of more than 5 percent of the class of the subject company's securities for which the tender offer is made, unless as soon as practicable on the date of the commencement of the tender offer such bidder:

(1) Files with the Commission a Tender Offer Statement on Schedule TO (§ 240.14d-100), including all exhibits thereto;

(2) Delivers a copy of such Schedule TO, including all exhibits thereto:

(i) To the subject company at its principal executive office; and

(ii) To any other bidder, which has filed a Schedule TO with the Commission relating to a tender offer which has not yet terminated for the same class of securities of the subject company, at such bidder's principal executive office or at the address of the person authorized to receive notices and communications (which is disclosed on the cover sheet of such other bidder's Schedule TO);

(3) Gives telephonic notice of the information required by Rule 14d-6(d)(2)(i) and (ii) (§ 240.14d-6(d)(2)(i) and (ii)) and mails by means of first class mail a copy of such Schedule TO, including all exhibits thereto:

(i) To each national securities exchange where such class of the subject company's securities is registered and listed for trading (which may be based upon information contained in the subject company's most recent Annual Report on Form 10-K (§ 249.310 of this chapter) filed with the Commission unless the bidder has reason to believe that such information is not current), which telephonic notice shall be made when practicable before the opening of each such exchange; and

(ii) To the National Association of Securities Dealers, Inc. ("NASD") if such class of the subject company's securities is authorized for quotation in the NASDAQ interdealer quotation system.

(b) *Post-commencement amendments and additional materials.* The bidder making the tender offer must file with the Commission:

(1) An amendment to Schedule TO (§ 240.14d-100) reporting promptly any material changes in the information set forth in the schedule previously filed and including copies of any additional tender offer materials as exhibits; and

(2) A final amendment to Schedule TO (§ 240.14d-100) reporting promptly the results of the tender offer.

Instruction to paragraph (b):

A copy of any additional tender offer materials or amendment filed under this section must be sent promptly to the subject company and to any exchange and/or NASD, as required by paragraph (a) of this section, but in no event later than the date the materials are first published, sent or given to security holders.

(c) *Certain announcements.* Notwithstanding the provisions of paragraph (b) of this section, if the additional tender offer material or an amendment to Schedule TO discloses only the number of shares deposited to date, and/or announces an extension of the time during which shares may be tendered, then the bidder may file such tender offer material or amendment and send a copy of such tender offer material or amendment to the subject company, any exchange and/or the NASD, as required by paragraph (a) of this section, promptly after the date such tender offer material is first published or sent or given to security holders.

[As last amended in Release No. 34-55146A, effective April 1, 2008, 73 F.R.17809 (technical correction).]

[¶ 40,631] Dissemination of Tender Offers to Security Holders

Reg. § 240.14d-4. As soon as practicable on the date of commencement of a tender offer, the bidder must publish, send or give the disclosure required by § 240.14d-6 to security holders of the class of securities that is the subject of the offer, by complying with all of the requirements of any of the following:

(a) *Cash tender offers and exempt securities offers.* For tender offers in which the consideration consists solely of cash and/or securities exempt from registration under section 3 of the Securities Act of 1933 (15 U.S.C. 77c):

(1) *Long-form publication.* The bidder makes adequate publication in a newspaper or newspapers of long-form publication of the tender offer.

(2) *Summary publication.*

(i) If the tender offer is not subject to Rule 13e-3 (§ 240.13e-3), the bidder makes adequate publication in a newspaper or newspaper of a summary advertisement of the tender offer; and

(ii) Mails by first class mail or otherwise furnishes with reasonable promptness the bidder's tender offer materials to any security holder who requests such tender offer materials pursuant to the summary advertisement or otherwise.

(3) *Use of stockholder lists and security position listings.* Any bidder using stockholder lists and security position listings under § 240.14d-5 must comply with paragraph (a)(1) or (2) of this section on or before the date of the bidder's request under § 240.14d-5(a).

Instruction to paragraph (a): Tender offers may be published or sent or given to security holders by other methods, but with respect to summary publication and the use of stockholder lists and security position listings under § 240.14d-5, paragraphs (a)(2) and (a)(3) of this section are exclusive.

(b) *Registered securities offers.* For tender offers in which the consideration consists solely or partially of securities registered under the Securities Act of 1933, a registration statement containing all of the required information, including pricing information, has been filed and a preliminary prospectus or a prospectus that meets the requirements of Section 10(a) of the Securities Act (15 U.S.C. 77j(a)), including a letter of transmittal, is delivered to security holders. However, for going-private transactions (as defined by § 240.13e-3) and roll-up transactions (as described by Item 901 of Regulation S-K (§ 229.901 of this chapter)), a registration statement registering the securities to be offered must have become effective and only a prospectus that meets the requirements of Section 10(a) of the Securities Act may be delivered to security holders on the date of commencement.

Instructions to paragraph (b): 1. If the prospectus is being delivered by mail, mailing on the date of commencement is sufficient.

2. A preliminary prospectus used under this section may not omit information under § 230.430 or § 230.430A of this chapter.

3. If a preliminary prospectus is used under this section and the bidder must disseminate material changes, the tender offer must remain open for the period specified in paragraph (d)(2) of this section.

4. If a preliminary prospectus is used under this section, tenders may be requested in accordance with § 230.162(a) of this chapter.

(c) *Adequate publication.* Depending on the facts and circumstances involved, adequate publication of a tender offer pursuant to this section may require publication in a newspaper with a national circulation or may only require publication in a newspaper with metropolitan or regional circulation or may require publication in a combination thereof: *Provided, however,* That publication in all editions of a daily newspaper with a national circulation shall be deemed to constitute adequate publication.

(d)(1) *Publication of changes and extension of the offer.* If a tender offer has been published or sent or given to security holders by one or more of the methods enumerated in this section, a material change in the information published, sent or given to security holders shall be promptly disseminated to security holders in manner reasonably designed to inform security holders of such change; *Provided, however,* That if the bidder has elected pursuant to Rule 14d-5(f)(1) of this section to require the subject company to disseminate amendments disclosing material changes to the tender offer materials pursuant to Rule 14d-5, the bidder shall disseminate material changes in the information published or sent or given to security holders at least pursuant to Rule 14d-5.

(2) In a registered securities offer where the bidder disseminates the preliminary prospectus as permitted by paragraph (b) of this section, the offer must remain open from the date that material changes to the tender offer materials are disseminated to security holders, as follows:

(i) Five business days for a prospectus supplement containing a material change other than price or share levels;

(ii) Ten business days for a prospectus supplement containing a change in price, the amount of securities sought, the dealer's soliciting fee, or other similarly significant change;

(iii) Ten business days for a prospectus supplement included as part of a post-effective amendment; and

(iv) Twenty business days for a revised prospectus when the initial prospectus was materially deficient.

[As last amended Release No. 33-7760, effective January 24, 2000, 64 F.R. 61408.]

[¶ 40,641] Dissemination of Certain Tender Offers by the Use of Stockholder Lists and Security Position Listings

Reg. § 240.14d-5. (a) *Obligations of the subject company.* Upon receipt by a subject company at its principal executive offices of a bidder's written request, meeting the requirements of paragraph (e) of this section, the subject company shall comply with the following sub-paragraphs.

(1) The subject company shall notify promptly transfer agents and any other person who will assist the subject company in complying with the requirements of this section of the receipt by the subject company of a request by a bidder pursuant to this section.

(2) The subject company shall promptly ascertain whether the most recently prepared stockholder list, written or otherwise, within the access of the subject company was prepared as of a date earlier than ten business days before the date of the bidder's request and, if so, the subject company shall promptly prepare or cause to be prepared a stockholder list as of the most recent practicable date which shall not be more than ten business days before the date of the bidder's request.

(3) The suject company shall make an election to comply and shall comply with all of the provisions of either paragraph (b) or paragraph (c) of this section. The subject company's election once made shall not be modified or revoked during the bidder's tender offer and extensions thereof.

(4) No later than the second business day after the date of the bidder's request, the subject company shall orally notify the bidder, which notification shall be confirmed in writing, of the subject company's election made pursuant to paragraph (a)(3) of this section. Such notification shall indicate (i) the approximate number of security holders of the class of securities being sought by the bidder and, (ii) if the subject company elects to comply with paragraph (b) of this section, appropriate information concerning the location for delivery of the bidder's tender offer materials and the approximate direct costs incidental to the mailing to security holders of the bidder's tender offer materials computed in accordance with paragraph (g)(2) of this section.

(b) *Mailing of tender offer materials by the subject company.* A subject company which elects pursuant to paragraph (a)(3) of this section to comply with the provisions of this paragraph shall perform the acts prescribed by the following subparagraphs.

(1) The subject company shall promptly contact each participant named on the most recent security position listing of any clearing agency within the access of the subject company and make inquiry of each such participant as to the approximate number of beneficial owners of the subject company securities being sought in the tender offer held by each such participant.

(2) No later than the third business day after delivery of the bidder's tender offer materials pursuant to paragraph (g)(1) of this section, the subject company shall begin to mail or cause to be mailed by means of first class mail a copy of the bidder's tender offer materials to each person whose name appears as a record holder of the class of securities for which the offer is made on the most recent stockholder list referred to in paragraph (a)(2) of this section. The subject company shall use its best efforts to complete the mailing in a timely manner but in no event shall such mailing be completed in a substantially greater period of time than the subject company would complete a mailing to security holders of its own materials relating to the tender offer.

(3) No later than the third business day after the delivery of the bidder's tender offer materials pursuant to paragraph (g)(1) of this section, the subject company shall begin to transmit or cause to be transmitted a sufficient number of sets of the bidder's tender offer materials to the participants named on the security position listings described in paragraph (b)(1) of this section. The subject company shall use its best efforts to complete the transmittal in a timely manner but in no event shall such transmittal be completed in a substantially greater period of time than the subject company would complete a transmittal to such participants pursuant to security position listings of clearing agencies of its own material relating to the tender offer.

(4) The subject company shall promptly give oral notification to the bidder, which notification shall be confirmed in writing, of the commencement of the mailing pursuant to paragraph (b)(2) of this section and of the transmittal pursuant to paragraph (b)(3) of this section.

(5) During the tender offer and any extension thereof the subject company shall use reasonable efforts to update the stockholder list and shall mail or cause to be mailed promptly following each update a copy of the bidder's tender offer materials (to the extent sufficient sets of such materials have been furnished by the bidder) to each person who has become a record holder since the later of (i) the date of preparation of the most recent stockholder list referred to in paragraph (a)(2) of this section or (ii) the last preceding update.

(6) If the bidder has elected pursuant to paragraph (f)(1) of this section to require the subject company to disseminate amendments disclosing material changes to the tender offer materials pursuant to this section, the subject company, promptly following delivery of each such amendment, shall mail or cause to be mailed a copy of each such amendment to each record holder whose name appears on the

shareholder list described in paragraphs (a)(2) and (b)(5) of this section and shall transmit or cause to be transmitted sufficient copies of such amendment to each participant named on security position listings who received sets of the bidder's tender offer materials pursuant to paragraph (b)(3) of this section.

(7) The subject company shall not include any communication other than the bidder's tender offer materials or amendments thereto in the envelopes or other containers furnished by the bidder.

(8) Promptly following the termination of the tender offer, the subject company shall reimburse the bidder the excess, if any, of the amounts advanced pursuant to paragraph (f)(3)(iii) over the direct costs incidental to compliance by the subject company and its agents in performing the acts required by this section computed in accordance with paragraph (g)(2) of this section.

(c) *Delivery of stockholder lists and security position listings.* A subject company which elects pursuant to paragraph (a)(3) of this section to comply with the provisions of this paragraph shall perform the acts prescribed by the following subparagraphs.

(1) No later than the third business day after the date of the bidder's request, the subject company must furnish to the bidder at the subject company's principal executive office a copy of the names and addresses of the record holders on the most recent stockholder list referred to in paragraph (a) (2) of this section; the names and addresses of participants identified on the most recent security position listing of any clearing agency that is within the access of the subject company; and the most recent list of names, addresses and security positions of beneficial owners as specified in §240.14a-13(b), in the possession of the subject company, or that subsequently comes into its possession. All security holder list information must be in the format requested by the bidder to the extent the format is available to the subject company without undue burden or expense.

(2) If the bidder has elected pursuant to paragraph (f)(1) of this section to require the subject company to disseminate amendments disclosing material changes to the tender offer materials, the subject company shall update the stockholder list by furnishing the bidder with the name and address of each record holder named on the stockholder list, and not previously furnished to the bidder, promptly after such information becomes available to the subject company during the tender offer and any extensions thereof.

(d) *Liability of subject company and others.* Neither the subject company nor any affiliate or agent of the subject company nor any clearing agency shall be:

(1) Deemed to have made a solicitation or recommendation respecting the tender offer within the meaning of section 14(d)(4) based solely upon the compliance or noncompliance by the subject company or any affiliate or agent of the subject company with one or more requirements of this section;

(2) Liable under any provision of the Federal securities laws to the bidder or to any security holder based solely upon the inaccuracy of the current names or addresses on the stockholder list or security position listing, unless such inaccuracy results from a lack of reasonable care on the part of the subject company or any affiliate or agent of the subject company;

(3) Deemed to be an "underwriter" within the meaning of section (2)(11) of the Securities Act of 1933 for any purpose of that Act or any rule or regulation promulgated thereunder based solely upon the compliance or noncompliance by the subject company or any affiliate or agent of the subject company with one or more of the requirements of this section;

(4) Liable under any provision of the Federal securities laws for the disclosure in the bidder's tender offer materials, including any amendment thereto, based solely upon the compliance or noncompliance by the subject company or any affiliate or agent of the subject company with one or more of the requirements of this section.

(e) *Content of the bidder's request.* The bidder's written request referred to in paragraph (a) of this section shall include the following:

(1) The identity of the bidder;

(2) The title of the class of securities which is the subject of the bidder's tender offer;

(3) A statement that the bidder is making a request to the subject company pursuant to paragraph (a) of this section for the use of the stockholder list and security position listings for the purpose of disseminating a tender offer to security holders;

(4) A statement that the bidder is aware of and will comply with the provisions of paragraph (f) of this section;

(5) A statement as to whether or not it has elected pursuant to paragraph (f)(1) of this section to disseminate amendments disclosing material changes to the tender offer materials pursuant to this section; and

(6) The name, address and telephone number of the person whom the subject company shall contact pursuant to paragraph (a)(4) of this section.

(f) *Obligations of the bidder.* Any bidder who requests that a subject company comply with the provisions of paragraph (a) of this section shall comply with the following subparagraphs.

(1) The bidder shall make an election whether or not to require the subject company to disseminate amendments disclosing material changes to the tender offer materials pursuant to this section, which election shall be included in the request referred to in paragraph (a) of this section and shall not be revocable by the bidder during the tender offer and extensions thereof.

(2) With respect to a tender offer subject to section 14(d)(1) of the Act in which the consideration consists solely of cash and/or securities exempt from registration under section 3 of the Securities Act of 1933, the bidder shall comply with the requirements of Rule 14d-4(a)(3).

(3) If the subject company elects to comply with paragraph (b) of this section,

(i) The bidder shall promptly deliver the tender offer materials after receipt of the notification from the subject company as provided in paragraph (a)(4) of this section;

(ii) The bidder shall promptly notify the subject company of any amendment to the bidder's tender offer materials requiring compliance by the subject company with paragraph (b)(6) of this section and shall promptly deliver such amendment to the subject company pursuant to paragraph (g)(1) of this section;

(iii) The bidder shall advance to the subject company an amount equal to the approximate cost of conducting mailings to security holders computed in accordance with paragraph (g)(2) of this section;

(iv) The bidder shall promptly reimburse the subject company for the direct costs incidental to compliance by the subject company and its agents in performing the acts required by this section computed in accordance with paragraph (g)(2) of this section which are in excess of the amount advanced pursuant to paragraph (f)(2)(iii) of this section; and

(v) The bidder shall mail by means of first class mail or otherwise furnish with reasonable promptness the tender offer materials to any security holder who requests such materials.

(4) If the subject company elects to comply with paragraph (c) of this section,

(i) The subject company shall use the stockholder list and security position listings furnished to the bidder pursuant to paragraph (c) of this section exclusively in the dissemination of tender offer materials to security holders in connection with the bidder's tender offer and extensions thereof;

(ii) The bidder shall return the stockholder lists and security position listings furnished to the bidder pursuant to paragraph (c) of this section promptly after the termination of the bidder's tender offer;

(iii) The bidder shall accept, handle and return the stockholder lists and security position listings furnished to the bidder pursuant to paragraph (c) of this section to the subject company on a confidential basis;

(iv) The bidder shall not retain any stockholder list or security position listing furnished by the subject company pursuant to paragraph (c) of this section, or any copy thereof, nor retain any information derived from any such list or listing or copy thereof after the termination of the bidder's tender offer;

(v) The bidder shall mail by means of first class mail, at its own expense, a copy of its tender offer materials to each person whose identity appears on the stockholder list as furnished and updated by the subject company pursuant to paragraphs (c)(1) and (c)(2) of this section;

(vi) The bidder shall contact the participants named on the security position listing of any clearing agency, make inquiry of each participant as to the approximate number of sets of tender offer materials required by each such participant, and furnish, at its own expense, sufficient sets of tender offer materials and any amendment thereto to each such participant for subsequent transmission to the beneficial owners of the securities being sought by the bidder;

(vii) The bidder shall mail by means of first class mail or otherwise furnish with reasonable promptness the tender offer materials to any security holder who requests such materials; and

(viii) The bidder shall promptly reimburse the subject company for direct costs incidental to compliance by the subject company and its agents in performing the acts required by this section computed in accordance with paragraph (g)(2) of this section.

(g) *Delivery of materials, computation of direct costs.*

(1) Whenever the bidder is required to deliver tender offer materials or amendments to tender offer materials, the bidder shall deliver to the subject company at the location specified by the subject company in its notice given pursuant to paragraph (a)(4) of this section a number of sets of the materials or of the amendment, as the case may be, at least equal to the approximate number of security holders specified by the subject company in such notice, together with appropriate envelopes or other containers therefor: *Provided, however,* That such delivery shall be deemed not to have been made unless the bidder has complied with paragraph (f)(3)(iii) of this section at the time the materials or amendments, as the case may be, are delivered.

(2) The approximate direct cost of mailing the bidder's tender offer materials shall be computed by adding (i) the direct cost incidental to the mailing of the subject company's last annual report to shareholders (excluding employee time), less the cost of preparation and printing of the report, and postage, plus (ii) the amount of first class postage required to mail the bidder's tender offer materials. The approximate direct costs incidental to the mailing of the amendments to the bidder's tender offer materials shall be computed by adding (iii) the estimated direct costs of preparing mailing labels, of updating shareholder lists and of third party handling charges plus (iv) the amount of first class postage required to mail the bidder's amendment. Direct costs incidental to the mailing of the bidder's tender offer materials and amendments thereto when finally computed may include all reasonable charges paid by the subject company to third parties for supplies or services, including costs attendant to preparing shareholder lists, mailing labels, handling the bidder's materials, contacting participants named on security position listings and for postage, but shall exclude indirect costs, such as employee time which is devoted to either contesting or supporting the tender offer on behalf of the subject company. The final billing for direct costs shall be accompanied by an appropriate accounting in reasonable detail.

    Note to § 240.14d-5. Reasonably prompt methods of distribution to security holders may be used instead of mailing. If alternative methods are chosen, the approximate direct costs of distribution shall be computed by adding the estimated direct costs of preparing the document for distribution through the chosen medium (including updating of shareholder lists) plus the estimated reasonable cost of distribution through that medium. Direct costs incidental to the distribution of tender offer materials and amendments thereto may include all reasonable charges paid by the subject company to third parties for supplies or services, including costs attendant to preparing shareholder lists, handling the bidder's materials, and contacting participants named on security position listings, but shall not include indirect costs, such as employee time which is devoted to either contesting or supporting the tender offer on behalf of the subject company.

    [As last amended in Release No. 33-7760, effective January 24, 2000, 64 F.R. 61408.]

[¶ 40,651] Disclosure of Tender Offer Information to Security Holders

    Reg. § 240.14d-6.   (a) *Information required on date of commencement.*

    (1) *Long-form publication.* If a tender offer is published, sent or given to security holders on the date of commencement by means of long-form publication under § 240.14d-4(a)(1), the long-form publication must include the information required by paragraph (d)(1) of this section.

    (2) *Summary publication.* If a tender offer is published, sent or given to security holders on the date of commencement by means of summary publication under § 240.14d-4(a)(2):

    (i) The summary advertisement must contain at least the information required by paragraph (d)(2) of this section; and

    (ii) The tender offer materials furnished by the bidder upon request of any security holder must include the information required by paragraph (d)(1) of this section.

    (3) *Use of stockholder lists and security position listings.* If a tender offer is published, sent or given to security holders on the date of commencement by the use of stockholder lists and security position listings under § 240.14d-4(a)(3):

    (i) The summary advertisement must contain at least the information required by paragraph (d)(2) of this section; and

    (ii) The tender offer materials transmitted to security holders pursuant to such lists and security position listings and furnished by the bidder upon the request of any security holder must include the information required by paragraph (d)(1) of this section.

    (4) *Other tender offers.* If a tender offer is published or sent or given to security holders other than pursuant to § 240.14d-4(a), the tender offer materials that are published or sent or given to security holders on the date of commencement of such offer must include the information required by paragraph (d)(1) of this section.

    (b) *Information required in other tender offer materials published after commencement.* Except for tender offer materials described in paragraphs (a)(2)(ii) and (a)(3)(ii) of this section, additional tender offer materials published, sent or given to security holders after commencement must include:

    (1) The identities of the bidder and subject company;

    (2) The amount and class of securities being sought;

    (3) The type and amount of consideration being offered; and

    (4) The scheduled expiration date of the tender offer, whether the tender offer may be extended and, if so, the procedures for extension of the tender offer.

    Instruction to paragraph (b): If the additional tender offer materials are summary advertisements, they also must include the information required by paragraphs (d)(2)(v) of this section.

(c) *Material changes.* A material change in the information published or sent or given to security holders must be promptly disclosed to security holders in additional tender offer materials.

(d) *Information to be included.*

(1) *Tender offer materials other than summary publication.* The following information is required by paragraphs (a)(1), (a)(2)(ii), (a)(3)(ii) and (a)(4) of this section:

(i) The information required by Item 1 of Schedule TO (§ 240.14d-100) (Summary Term Sheet); and

(ii) The information required by the remaining items of Schedule TO (§ 240.14d-100) for third-party tender offers, except for Item 12 (exhibits) of Schedule TO (§ 240.14d-100), or a fair and adequate summary of the information.

(2) *Summary Publication.* The following information is required in a summary advertisement under paragraphs (a)(2)(i) and (a)(3)(i) of this section:

(i) The identity of the bidder and the subject company;

(ii) The information required by Item 1004(a)(1) of Regulation M-A (§ 229.1004(a)(1) of this chapter);

(iii) If the tender offer is for less than all of the outstanding securities of a class of equity securities, a statement as to whether the purpose or one of the purposes of the tender offer is to acquire or influence control of the business of the subject company;

(iv) A statement that the information required by paragraph (d)(1) of this section is incorporated by reference into the summary advertisement;

(v) Appropriate instructions as to how security holders may obtain promptly, at the bidder's expense, the bidder's tender offer materials; and

(vi) In a tender offer published or sent or given to security holders by use of stockholder lists and security position listings under § 240.14d-4(a)(3), a statement that a request is being made for such lists and listings. The summary publication also must state that tender offer materials will be mailed to record holders and will be furnished to brokers, banks and similar persons whose name appears or whose nominee appears on the list of security holders or, if applicable, who are listed as participants in a clearing agency's security position listing for subsequent transmittal to beneficial owners of such securities. If the list furnished to the bidder also included beneficial owners pursuant to § 240.14d-5(c)(1) and tender offer materials will be mailed directly to beneficial holders, include a statement to that effect.

(3) *No transmittal letter.* Neither the initial summary advertisement nor any subsequent summary advertisement may include a transmittal letter (the letter furnished to security holders for transmission of securities sought in the tender offer) or any amendment to the transmittal letter.

[As last amended in Release No. 33-7760, effective January 24, 2000, 64 F.R. 61408.]

[¶ 40,661] Additional Withdrawal Rights

Reg. § 240.14d-7. (a)(1) *Rights.* In addition to the provisions of section 14(d)(5) of the Act, any person who has deposited securities pursuant to a tender offer has the right to withdraw any such securities during the period such offer request or invitation remains open.

(a)(2) *Exemption during subsequent offering period.* Notwithstanding the provisions of Section 14 (d)(5) of the Act (15 U.S.C. 78n(d)(5)) and paragraph (a) of this section, the bidder need not offer withdrawal rights during a subsequent offering period.

(b) *Notice of withdrawal.* Notice of withdrawal pursuant to this section shall be deemed to be timely upon the receipt by the bidder's depositary of a written notice of withdrawal specifying the name(s) of the tendering stockholder(s), the number or amount of the securities to be withdrawn and the name(s) in which the certificate(s) is (are) registered, if different from that of the tendering security holder(s). A bidder may impose other reasonable requirements, including certificate numbers and a signed request for withdrawal accompanied by a signature guarantee, as conditions precedent to the physical release of withdrawn securities.

[As last amended in Release No. 33-7760, effective January 24, 2000, 64 F.R. 61408.]

[¶ 40,671] Exemption from Statutory Pro Rata Requirement

Reg. § 240.14d-8. Notwithstanding the pro rata provisions of Section 14(d)(6) of the Act, if any person makes a tender offer or request or invitation for tenders, for less than all of the outstanding equity securities of a class, and if a greater number of securities are deposited pursuant thereto than such person is bound or willing to take up and pay for, the securities taken up and paid for shall be taken up and paid for as nearly as may be pro rata, disregarding fractions, according to the number of securities deposited by each depositor during the period such offer, request or invitation remains open.

[As last amended in Release No. 34-19336, December 15, 1982, 47 F.R. 57679.]

[¶ 40,681] Recommendation or Solicitation by the Subject Company and Others

Reg. § 240.14d-9. (a) *Pre-commencement communications.*

A communication by a person described in paragraph (e) of this section with respect to a tender offer will not be deemed to constitute a recommendation or solicitation under this section if:

(1) The tender offer has not commenced under § 240.14d-2; and

(2) The communication is filed under cover of Schedule 14D-9 (§ 240.14d-101) with the Commission no later than the date of the communication.

Instructions to paragraph (a)(2):

1. The box on the front of Schedule 14D-9 (§ 240.14d-101) indicating that the filing contains pre-commencement communications must be checked.

2. Any communications made in connection with an exchange offer registered under the Securities Act of 1933 need only be filed under § 230.425 of this chapter and will be deemed filed under this section.

3. Each pre-commencement written communication must include a prominent legend in clear, plain language advising security holders to read the company's solicitation/ recommendation statement when it is available because it contains important information. The legend also must advise investors that they can get the recommendation and other filed documents for free at the Commission's web site and explain which documents are free from the filer.

4. See Sections 230.135, 230.165 and 230.166 of this chapter for pre-commencement communications made in connection with registered exchange offers.

(b) *Post-commencement communications.*

After commencement by a bidder under § 240.14d-2, no solicitation or recommendation to security holders may be made by any person described in paragraph (e) of this section with respect to a tender offer for such securities unless as soon as practicable on the date such solicitation or recommendation is first published or sent or given to security holders such person complies with the following:

(1) Such person shall file with the Commission a Tender Offer Solicitation/ Recommendation Statement on Schedule 14D-9 (240.14d-101), including all exhibits thereto; and

(2) If such person is either the subject company or an affiliate of the subject company,

(i) Such person shall hand deliver a copy of the Schedule 14D-9 to the bidder at its principal office or at the address of the person authorized to receive notices and communications (which is set forth on the cover sheet of the bidder's Schedule TO (§ 240.14d-100) filed with the Commission; and

(ii) Such person shall give telephonic notice (which notice to the extent possible shall be given prior to the opening of the market) of the information required by Items 1003(d) and 1012(a) of Regulation M-A (§ 229.1005(d) and § 229.1012(a)) and shall mail a copy of the Schedule to each national securities exchange where the class of securities is registered and listed for trading and, if the class is authorized for quotation in the NASDAQ interdealer quotation system, to the National Association of Securities Dealers, Inc. ("NASD").

(3) If such person is neither the subject company nor an affiliate of the subject company,

(i) Such person shall mail a copy of the schedule to the bidder at its principal office or at the address of the person authorized to receive notices and communications (which is set forth on the cover sheet of the bidder's Schedule TO (§ 240.14d-100) filed with the Commission); and

(ii) Such person shall mail a copy of the Schedule to the subject company at its principal office.

(c) *Amendments.* If any material change occurs in the information set forth in the Schedule 14D-9 (§ 240.14d-101) required by this section, the person who filed such Schedule 14D-9 shall:

(1) File with the Commission an amendment on Schedule 14D-9 (§ 240.14d-101) disclosing such change promptly, but not later than the date such material is first published, sent or given to security holders; and

(2) Promptly deliver copies and give notice of the amendment in the same manner as that specified in paragraph (b)(2) or (3) of this section, whichever is applicable; and

(3) Promptly disclose and disseminate such change in a manner reasonably designed to inform security holders of such change.

(d) *Information required in solicitation or recommendation.*

Any solicitation or recommendation to holders of a class of securities referred to in section 14(d)(1) of the Act with respect to a tender offer for such securities shall include the name of the person making such solicitation or recommendation and the information required by Items 1 through 8 of Schedule 14D-9 (§ 240.14d-101) or a fair and adequate summary thereof: *Provided, however,* That such solicitation or recommendation may omit any of such information previously furnished to security holders of such class of securities by such person with respect to such tender offer.

(e) *Applicability.*

(1) Except as is provided in paragraphs (e)(2) and (f) of this section, this section shall only apply to the following persons:

(i) The subject company, any director, officer, employee, affiliate or subsidiary of the subject company;

(ii) Any record holder or beneficial owner of any security issued by the subject company, by the bidder, or by any affiliate of either the subject company or the bidder; and

(iii) Any person who makes a solicitation or recommendation to security holders on behalf of any of the foregoing or on behalf of the bidder other than by means of a solicitation or recommendation to security holders which has been filed with the Commission pursuant to this section or Rule 14d-3 (§ 240.14d-3).

(2) Notwithstanding paragraph (e)(1) of this section, this section shall not apply to the following persons:

(i) A bidder who has filed a Schedule TO (§ 240.14d-100) pursuant to Rule 14d-3 (§ 240.14d-3);

(ii) Attorneys, banks, brokers, fiduciaries or investment advisers who are not participating in a tender offer in more than a ministerial capacity and who furnish information and/or advice regarding such tender offer to their customers or clients on the unsolicited request of such customers or clients or solely pursuant to a contract or a relationship providing for advice to the customer or client to whom the information and/or advice is given.

(iii) Any person specified in paragraph (e)(1) of this section if:

(A) The subject company is the subject of a tender offer conducted under § 240.14d-1(c);

(B) Any person specified in paragraph (e)(1) of this section furnishes to the Commission on Form CB (§ 249.480 of this chapter) the entire informational document it publishes or otherwise disseminates to holders of the class of securities in connection with the tender offer no later than the next business day after publication or dissemination;

(C) Any person specified in paragraph (e)(1) of this section disseminates any informational document to U.S. holders, including any amendments thereto, in English, on a comparable basis to that provided to security holders in the issuer's home jurisdiction; and

(D) Any person specified in paragraph (e)(1) of this section disseminates by publication in its home jurisdiction, such person must publish the information in the United States in a manner reasonably calculated to inform U.S. security holders of the offer.

(f) *Stop-look-and-listen communication.* This section shall not apply to the subject company with respect to a communication by the subject company to its security holders which only:

(1) Identifies the tender offer by the bidder;

(2) States that such tender offer is under consideration by the subject company's board of directors and/or management;

(3) States that on or before a specified date (which shall be no later than 10 business days from the date of commencement of such tender offer) the subject company will advise such security holders of (i) whether the subject company recommends acceptance or rejection of such tender offer; expresses no opinion and remains neutral toward such tender offer; or is unable to take a position with respect to such tender offer and (ii) the reason(s) for the position taken by the subject company with respect to the tender offer (including the inability to take a position); and

(4) Requests such security holders to defer making a determination whether to accept or reject such tender offer until they have been advised of the subject company's position with respect thereto pursuant to paragraph (f)(3) of this section.

(g) *Statement of management's position.* A statement by the subject company of its position with respect to a tender offer which is required to be published or sent or given to security holders pursuant to Rule 14e-2 shall be deemed to constitute a solicitation or recommendation within the meaning of this section and section 14(d)(4) of the Act.

[As last amended in Release No. 34-55146A, effective April 1, 2008, 73 F.R.17809 (technical correction).]

[¶ 40,691] Equal Treatment of Security Holders

Reg. § 240.14d-10. (a) No bidder shall make a tender offer unless:

(1) The tender offer is open to all security holders of the class of securities subject to the tender offer; and

(2) The consideration paid to any security holder for securities tendered in the tender offer is the highest consideration paid to any other security holder for securities tendered in the tender offer.

(b) Paragraph (a)(1) of this section shall not:

(1) Affect dissemination under Rule 14d-4 (§ 240.14d-4); or

(2) Prohibit a bidder from making a tender offer excluding all security holders in a state where the bidder is prohibited from making the tender offer by administrative or judicial action pursuant to a state statute after a good faith effort by the bidder to comply with such statute.

(c) Paragraph (a)(2) of this section shall not prohibit the offer of more than one type of consideration in a tender offer, provided that:

(1) Security holders are afforded equal right to elect among each of the types of consideration offered; and

(2) The highest consideration of each type paid to any security holder is paid to any other security holder receiving that type of consideration.

(d)(1) Paragraph (a)(2) of this section shall not prohibit the negotiation, execution or amendment of an employment compensation, severance or other employee benefit arrangement, or payments made or to be made or benefits granted or to be granted according to such an arrangement, with respect to any security holder of the subject company, where the amount payable under the arrangement:

(i) Is being paid or granted as compensation for past services performed, future services to be performed, or future services to be refrained from performing, by the security holder (and matters incidental thereto); and

(ii) Is not calculated based on the number of securities tendered or to be tendered in the tender offer by the security holder.

(2) The provisions of paragraph (d)(1) of this section shall be satisfied and, therefore, pursuant to this non-exclusive safe harbor, the negotiation, execution or amendment of an arrangement and any payments made or to be made or benefits granted or to be granted according to that arrangement shall not be prohibited by paragraph (a)(2) of this section, if the arrangement is approved as an employment compensation, severance or other employee benefit arrangement solely by independent directors as follows:

(i) The compensation committee or a committee of the board of directors that performs functions similar to a compensation committee of the subject company approves the arrangement, regardless of whether the subject company is a party to the arrangement, or, if the bidder is a party to the arrangement, the compensation committee or a committee of the board of directors that performs functions similar to a compensation committee of the bidder approves the arrangement; or

(ii) If the subject company's or bidder's board of directors, as applicable, does not have a compensation committee or a committee of the board of directors that performs functions similar to a compensation committee or if none of the members of the subject company's or bidder's compensation committee or committee that performs functions similar to a compensation committee is independent, a special committee of the board of directors formed to consider and approve the arrangement approves the arrangement; or

(iii) If the subject company or bidder, as applicable, is a foreign private issuer, any or all members of the board of directors or any committee of the board of directors authorized to approve employment compensation, severance or other employee benefit arrangements under the laws or regulations of the home country approves the arrangement.

Instructions to paragraph (d)(2): For purposes of determining whether the members of the committee approving an arrangement in accordance with the provisions of paragraph (d)(2) of this section are independent, the following provisions shall apply:

1. If the bidder or subject company, as applicable, is a listed issuer (as defined in § 240.10A-3 of this chapter) whose securities are listed either on a national securities exchange registered pursuant to section 6(a) of the Exchange Act (15 U.S.C. 78f(a)) or in an inter-dealer quotation system of a national securities association registered pursuant to section 15A(a) of the Exchange Act (15 U.S.C. 78o-3(a)) that has independence requirements for compensation committee members that have been approved by the Commission (as those requirements may be modified or supplemented), apply the bidder's or subject company's definition of independence that it uses for determining that the members of the compensation committee are independent in compliance with the listing standards applicable to compensation committee members of the listed issuer.

2. If the bidder or subject company, as applicable, is not a listed issuer (as defined in § 240.10A-3 of this chapter), apply the independence requirements for compensation committee members of a national securities exchange registered pursuant to section 6(a) of the Exchange Act (15 U.S.C. 78f(a)) or an inter-dealer quotation system of a national securities association registered pursuant to section 15A(a) of the Exchange Act (15 U.S.C. 78o-3(a)) that have been approved by the Commission (as those requirements may be modified or supplemented). Whatever definition the bidder or subject company, as applicable, chooses, it must apply that definition consistently to all members of the committee approving the arrangement.

3. Notwithstanding Instructions 1 and 2 to paragraph (d)(2), if the bidder or subject company, as applicable, is a closed-end investment company registered under the Investment Company Act of 1940, a director is considered to be independent if the director is not, other than in his or her capacity as a member of the board of directors or any board committee, an "interested person" of the investment company, as defined in section 2(a)(19) of the Investment Company Act of 1940 (15 U.S.C. 80a-2(a)(19)).

4. If the bidder or the subject company, as applicable, is a foreign private issuer, apply either the independence standards set forth in Instructions 1 and 2 to paragraph (d)(2) or the independence requirements of the laws, regulations, codes or standards of the home country of the bidder or subject company, as applicable, for members of the board of directors or the committee of the board of directors approving the arrangement.

5. A determination by the bidder's or the subject company's board of directors, as applicable, that the members of the board of directors or the committee of the board of directors, as applicable, approving an arrangement in accordance with the provisions of paragraph (d)(2) are independent in accordance with the provisions of this instruction to paragraph (d)(2) shall satisfy the independence requirements of paragraph (d)(2).

Instruction to paragraph (d): The fact that the provisions of paragraph (d) of this section extend only to employment compensation, severance and other employee benefit arrangements and not to other arrangements, such as commercial arrangements, does not raise any inference that a payment under any such other arrangement constitutes consideration paid for securities in a tender offer.

(e) If the offer and sale of securities constituting consideration offered in a tender offer is prohibited by the appropriate authority of a state after a good faith effort by the bidder to register or qualify the offer and sale of such securities in such state:

(1) The bidder may offer security holders in such state an alternative form of consideration; and

(2) Paragraph (c) of this section shall not operate to require the bidder to offer or pay the alternative form of consideration to security holders in any other state.

(f) This section shall not apply to any tender offer with respect to which the Commission, upon written request or upon its own motion, either unconditionally or on specified terms and conditions, determines that compliance with this section is not necessary or appropriate in the public interest or for the protection of investors.

[As last amended in amended by Release No. 34-54684, effective December 8, 2006, 71 F.R. 65393.]

[¶ 40,695] Subsequent Offering Period

Reg. § 240.14d-11. A bidder may elect to provide a subsequent offering period of at least three business days during which tenders will be accepted if:

(a) The initial offering period of at least 20 business days has expired;

(b) The offer is for all outstanding securities of the class that is the subject of the tender offer, and if the bidder is offering security holders a choice of different forms of consideration, there is no ceiling on any form of consideration offered;

(c) The bidder immediately accepts and promptly pays for all securities tendered during the initial offering period;

(d) The bidder announces the results of the tender offer, including the approximate number and percentage of securities deposited to date, no later than 9:00 a.m. Eastern time on the next business day after the expiration date of the initial offering period and immediately begins the subsequent offering period;

(e) The bidder immediately accepts and promptly pays for all securities as they are tendered during the subsequent offering period; and

(f) The bidder offers the same form and amount of consideration to security holders in both the initial and the subsequent offering period.

Note § 240.14d-11: No withdrawal rights apply during the subsequent offering period in accordance with § 240.14d-7(a)(2).

[As last amended by Release No. 33-8957, effective December 8, 2008, 73 F.R. 60049.]

SCHEDULE TO

[¶ 40,701] Schedule TO

Reg. § 240.14d-100. Tender offer statement pursuant to section 14(d)(1) of the Securities Exchange Act of 1934.

SECURITIES AND EXCHANGE COMMISSION
Washington, D.C. 20549
SCHEDULE TO

Tender Offer Statement under Section 14(d)(1) or 13(e)(1) of the Securities Exchange Act of 1934 (Amendment No. ___)*

_____

(Name of Subject Company (issuer))

_____

(Names of Filing Persons (identifying status as offeror, issuer or other person))

_____

(Title of Class of Securities)

_____

(CUSIP Number of Class of Securities)

(Name, address, and telephone numbers of person authorized to receive notices and communications on behalf of filing persons)

Calculation of Filing Fee

Transaction valuation*	Amount of filing fee

* Set forth the amount on which the filing fee is calculated and state how it was determined.

[ ] Check the box if any part of the fee is offset as provided by Rule 0-11(a)(2) and identify the filing with which the offsetting fee was previously paid. Identify the previous filing by registration statement number, or the Form or Schedule and the date of its filing.

Amount Previously Paid:_____

Form or Registration No.:_____

Filing Party:_____

Date Filed:_____

[ ] Check the box if the filing relates solely to preliminary communications made before the commencement of a tender offer.

Check the appropriate boxes below to designate any transactions to which the statement relates:

[ ] third-party tender offer subject to Rule 14d-1.

[ ] issuer tender offer subject to Rule 13e-4.

[ ] going-private transaction subject to Rule 13e-3.

[ ] amendment to Schedule 13D under Rule 13d-2.

Check the following box if the filing is a final amendment reporting the results of the tender offer:[ ]

General Instructions:

A. File eight copies of the statement, including all exhibits, with the Commission if paper filing is permitted.

B. This filing must be accompanied by a fee payable to the Commission as required by § 240.0-11.

C. If the statement is filed by a general or limited partnership, syndicate or other group, the information called for by Items 3 and 5—8 for a third-party tender offer and Items 5—8 for an issuer tender offer must be given with respect to: (i) each partner of the general partnership; (ii) each partner who is, or functions as, a general partner of the limited partnership; (iii) each member of the syndicate or group; and (iv) each person controlling the partner or member. If the statement is filed by a corporation or if a person referred to in (i), (ii), (iii) or (iv) of this Instruction is a corporation, the information called for by the items specified above must be given with respect to: (a) each executive officer and director of the corporation; (b) each person controlling the corporation; and (c) each executive officer and director of any corporation or other person ultimately in control of the corporation.

D. If the filing contains only preliminary communications made before the commencement of a tender offer, no signature or filing fee is required. The filer need not respond to the items in the schedule. Any pre-commencement communications that are filed under cover of this schedule need not be incorporated by reference into the schedule.

E. If an item is inapplicable or the answer is in the negative, so state. The statement published, sent or given to security holders may omit negative and not applicable responses. If the schedule includes any information that is not published, sent or given to security holders, provide that information or specifically incorporate it by reference under the appropriate item number and heading in the schedule. Do not recite the text of disclosure requirements in the schedule or any document published, sent or given to security holders. Indicate clearly the coverage of the requirements without referring to the text of the items.

F. Information contained in exhibits to the statement may be incorporated by reference in answer or partial answer to any item unless it would render the answer misleading, incomplete, unclear or confusing. A copy of any information that is incorporated by reference or a copy of the pertinent pages of a document containing the information must be submitted with this statement as an exhibit, unless it was previously filed with the Commission electronically on EDGAR. If an exhibit contains information responding to more than one item in the schedule, all information in that exhibit may be incorporated by reference once in response to the several items in the schedule for which it provides an answer. Information incorporated by reference is deemed filed with the Commission for all purposes of the Act.

G. A filing person may amend its previously filed Schedule 13D (§ 240.13d-101) on Schedule TO (§ 240.14d-100) if the appropriate box on the cover page is checked to indicate a combined filing and the information called for by the fourteen disclosure items on the cover page of Schedule 13D (§ 240.13d-101) is provided on the cover page of the combined filing with respect to each filing person.

H. The final amendment required by § 240.14d-3(b)(2) and § 240.13e-4(c)(4) will satisfy the reporting requirements of section 13(d) of the Act with respect to all securities acquired by the offeror in the tender offer.

I. Amendments disclosing a material change in the information set forth in this statement may omit any information previously disclosed in this statement.

J. If the tender offer disclosed on this statement involves a going-private transaction, a combined Schedule TO (§ 240.14d-100) and Schedule 13E-3 (§ 240.13e-100) may be filed with the Commission under cover of Schedule TO. The Rule 13e-3 box on the cover page of the Schedule TO must be checked to indicate a combined filing. All information called for by both schedules must be provided except that Items 1–3, 5, 8 and 9 of Schedule TO may be omitted to the extent those items call for information that duplicates the item requirements in Schedule 13E-3.

K. For purposes of this statement, the following definitions apply:

(1) The term *offeror* means any person who makes a tender offer or on whose behalf a tender offer is made;

(2) The term *issuer tender offer* has the same meaning as in Rule 13e-4(a)(2); and

(3) The term *third-party tender offer* means a tender offer that is not an issuer tender offer.

SPECIAL INSTRUCTIONS FOR COMPLYING WITH SCHEDULE TO:

Under Sections 13(e), 14(d) and 23 of the Act and the rules and regulations of the Act, the Commission is authorized to solicit the information required to be supplied by this schedule.

Disclosure of the information specified in this schedule is mandatory. The information will be used for the primary purpose of disclosing tender offer and going-private transactions. This statement will be made a matter of public record. Therefore, any information given will be available for inspection by any member of the public.

Because of the public nature of the information, the Commission can use it for a variety of purposes, including referral to other governmental authorities or securities self-regulatory organizations for investigatory purposes or in connection with litigation involving the federal securities laws or other civil, criminal or regulatory statutes or provisions.

Failure to disclose the information required by this schedule may result in civil or criminal action against the persons involved for violation of the federal securities laws and rules.

Item 1. *Summary Term Sheet.*

Furnish the information required by Item 1001 of Regulation M-A (§ 229.1001 of this chapter) unless information is disclosed to security holders in a prospectus that meets the requirements of § 230.421(d) of this chapter.

Item 2. *Subject Company Information.*

Furnish the information required by Item 1002(a) through (c) of Regulation M-A (§ 229.1002 of this chapter).

Item 3. *Identity and Background of Filing Person.*

Furnish the information required by Item 1003(a) through (c) of Regulation M-A (§ 229.1003 of this chapter) for a third-party tender offer and the information required by Item 1003(a) of Regulation M-A (§ 229.1003 of this chapter) for an issuer tender offer.

Item 4. *Terms of the Transaction.*

Furnish the information required by Item 1004(a) of Regulation M-A (§ 229.1004 of this chapter) for a third-party tender offer and the information required by Item 1004(a) through (b) of Regulation M-A (§ 229.1004 of this chapter) for an issuer tender offer.

Item 5. *Past Contacts, Transactions, Negotiations and Agreements.*

Furnish the information required by Item 1005(a) and (b) of Regulation M-A (§ 229.1005 of this chapter) for a third-party tender offer and the information required by Item 1005(e) of Regulation M-A (§ 229.1005) for an issuer tender offer.

Item 6. *Purposes of the Transaction and Plans or Proposals.*

Furnish the information required by Item 1006(a) and (c)(1) through (7) of Regulation M-A (§ 229.1006 of this chapter) for a third-party tender offer and the information required by Item 1006(a) through (c) of Regulation M-A (§ 229.1006 of this chapter) for an issuer tender offer.

Item 7. *Source and Amount of Funds or Other Consideration.*

Furnish the information required by Item 1007(a), (b) and (d) of Regulation M-A (§ 229.1007 of this chapter).

Item 8. *Interest in Securities of the Subject Company.*

Furnish the information required by Item 1008 of Regulation M-A (§ 229.1008 of this chapter).

Item 9. *Persons/Assets, Retained, Employed, Compensated or Used.*

Furnish the information required by Item 1009(a) of Regulation M-A (§ 229.1009 of this chapter).

Item 10. *Financial Statements.*

If material, furnish the information required by Item 1010(a) and (b) of Regulation M-A (§ 229.1010 of this chapter) for the issuer in an issuer tender offer and for the offeror in a third-party tender offer.

Instructions to Item 10:

1. Financial statements must be provided when the offeror's financial condition is material to security holder's decision whether to sell, tender or hold the securities sought. The facts and circumstances of a tender offer, particularly the terms of the tender offer, may influence a determination as to whether financial statements are material, and thus required to be disclosed.

2. Financial statements are *not* considered material when: (a) the consideration offered consists solely of cash; (b) the offer is not subject to any financing condition; *and* either: (c) the offeror is a public reporting company under Section 13(a) or 15(d) of the Act that files reports electronically on EDGAR, or (d) the offer is for all outstanding securities of the subject class. Financial information may be required, however, in a two-tier transaction. *See* Instruction 5 below.

3. The filing person may incorporate by reference financial statements contained in any document filed with the Commission, solely for the purposes of this schedule, if: (a) the financial statements substantially meet the requirements of this item; (b) an express statement is made that the financial statements are incorporated by reference; (c) the information incorporated by reference is clearly identified by page, paragraph, caption or otherwise; and (d) if the information incorporated by reference is not filed with this schedule, an indication is made where the information may be inspected and copies obtained. Financial statements that are required to be presented in comparative form for two or more fiscal years or periods may not be incorporated by reference unless the material incorporated by reference includes the entire period for which the comparative data is required to be given. *See* General Instruction F to this schedule.

4. If the offeror in a third-party tender offer is a natural person, and such person's financial information is material, disclose the net worth of the offeror. If the offeror's net worth is derived from material amounts of assets that are not readily marketable or there are material guarantees and contingencies, disclose the nature and approximate amount of the individual's net worth that consists of illiquid assets and the magnitude of any guarantees or contingencies that may negatively affect the natural person's net worth.

5. Pro forma financial information is required in a negotiated third-party cash tender offer when securities are intended to be offered in a subsequent merger or other transaction in which remaining target securities are acquired and the acquisition of the subject company is significant to the offeror under § 210.11-01(b)(1) of this chapter. The offeror must disclose the financial information specified in Item 3(f) and Item 5 of Form S-4 (§ 239.25 of this chapter) in the schedule filed with the Commission, but may furnish only the summary financial information specified in Item 3(d), (e) and (f) of Form S-4 in the disclosure document sent to security holders. If pro forma financial information is required by this instruction, the historical financial statements specified in Item 1010 of Regulation M-A (§ 229.1010 of this chapter) are required for the bidder.

6. The disclosure materials disseminated to security holders may contain the summarized financial information specified by Item 1010(c) of Regulation M-A (§ 229.1010 of this chapter) instead of the financial information required by Item 1010(a) and (b). In that case, the financial information required by Item 1010(a) and (b) of Regulation M-A must be disclosed in the statement. If summarized financial information is disseminated to security holders, include appropriate instructions on how more complete financial information can be obtained. If the summarized financial information is prepared on the basis of

a comprehensive body of accounting principles other than U.S. GAAP, the summarized financial information must be accompanied by a reconciliation as described in Instruction 8 of this Item.

7. If the offeror is not subject to the periodic reporting requirements of the Act, the financial statements required by this Item need not be audited if audited financial statements are not available or obtainable without unreasonable cost or expense. Make a statement to that effect and the reasons for their unavailability.

8. If the financial statements required by this Item are prepared on the basis of a comprehensive body of accounting principles other than U.S. GAAP, provide a reconciliation to U.S. GAAP in accordance with Item 17 of Form 20-F (§ 249.220f of this chapter), unless a reconciliation is unavailable or not obtainable without unreasonable cost or expense. At a minimum, however, when financial statements are prepared on a basis other than U.S. GAAP, a narrative description of all material variations in accounting principles, practices and methods used in preparing the non-U.S. GAAP financial statements from those accepted in the U.S. must be presented.

Item 11. *Additional Information.*

Furnish the information required by Item 1011 of Regulation M-A (§ 229.1011 of this chapter).

Item 12. *Exhibits.*

File as an exhibit to the Schedule all documents specified by Item 1016(a), (b), (d), (g) and (h) of Regulation M-A (§ 229.1016 of this chapter).

Item 13. *Information Required by Schedule 13E-3.*

If the Schedule TO is combined with Schedule 13E-3 (§ 240.13e-100), set forth the information required by Schedule 13E-3 that is not included or covered by the items in Schedule TO.

Signature. After due inquiry and to the best of my knowledge and belief, I certify that the information set forth in this statement is true, complete and correct.

_____
(Signature)

_____
(Name and title)

_____
(Date)

Instruction to Signature:

The statement must be signed by the filing person or that person's authorized representative. If the statement is signed on behalf of a person by an authorized representative (other than an executive officer of a corporation or general partner of a partnership), evidence of the representative's authority to sign on behalf of the person must be filed with the statement. The name and any title of each person who signs the statement must be typed or printed beneath the signature. See § § 240.12b-11 and 240.14d-1(h) with respect to signature requirements.

The original statement shall be signed by each person on whose behalf the statement is filed or his authorized representative. If the statement is signed on behalf of a person by his authorized representative (other than an executive officer or general partner of the bidder), evidence of the representative's authority to sign on behalf of such person shall be filed with the statement. The name and any title of each person who signs the statement shall be typed or printed beneath his signature.

[As last amended by Release No. 34-55146A, effective April 1, 2008, 73 F.R.17809 (technical correction).]

SCHEDULE 14D-9

[¶ 40,751] Schedule 14D-9

Reg. § 240.14d-101. Schedule 14D-9.

SECURITIES AND EXCHANGE COMMISSION

Washington, D.C. 20549

SCHEDULE 14D-9

Solicitation/Recommendation Statement under Section 14(d)(4) of the Securities Exchange Act of 1934

(Amendment No.___)

_____
(Name of Subject Company)

_____
(Names of Persons Filing Statement)

(Title of Class of Securities)

(CUSIP Number of Class of Securities)

(Name, address, and telephone numbers of person authorized to receive notices and communications on behalf of the persons filing statement)

[ ] Check the box if the filing relates solely to preliminary communications made before the commencement of a tender offer.

General Instructions:

A. File eight copies of the statement, including all exhibits, with the Commission if paper filing is permitted.

B. If the filing contains only preliminary communications made before the commencement of a tender offer, no signature is required. The filer need not respond to the items in the schedule. Any pre-commencement communications that are filed under cover of this schedule need not be incorporated by reference into the schedule.

C. If an item is inapplicable or the answer is in the negative, so state. The statement published, sent or given to security holders may omit negative and not applicable responses. If the schedule includes any information that is not published, sent or given to security holders, provide that information or specifically incorporate it by reference under the appropriate item number and heading in the schedule. Do not recite the text of disclosure requirements in the schedule or any document published, sent or given to security holders. Indicate clearly the coverage of the requirements without referring to the text of the items.

D. Information contained in exhibits to the statement may be incorporated by reference in answer or partial answer to any item unless it would render the answer misleading, incomplete, unclear or confusing. A copy of any information that is incorporated by reference or a copy of the pertinent pages of a document containing the information must be submitted with this statement as an exhibit, unless it was previously filed with the Commission electronically on EDGAR. If an exhibit contains information responding to more than one item in the schedule, all information in that exhibit may be incorporated by reference once in response to the several items in the schedule for which it provides an answer. Information incorporated by reference is deemed filed with the Commission for all purposes of the Act.

E. Amendments disclosing a material change in the information set forth in this statement may omit any information previously disclosed in this statement.

Item 1. *Subject Company Information.*

Furnish the information required by Item 1002(a) and (b) of Regulation M-A (§ 229.1002 of this chapter).

Item 2. *Identity and Background of Filing Person.*

Furnish the information required by Item 1003(a) and (d) of Regulation M-A (§ 229.1003 of this chapter).

Item 3. *Past Contacts, Transactions, Negotiations and Agreements.*

Furnish the information required by Item 1005(d) of Regulation M-A (§ 229.1005 of this chapter).

Item 4. *The Solicitation or Recommendation.*

Furnish the information required by Item 1012(a) through (c) of Regulation M-A (§ 229.1012 of this chapter).

Item 5. *Person/Assets, Retained, Employed, Compensated or Used.*

Furnish the information required by Item 1009(a) of Regulation M-A (§ 229.1009 of this chapter).

Item 6. *Interest in Securities of the Subject Company.*

Furnish the information required by Item 1008(b) of Regulation M-A (§ 229.1008 of this chapter).

Item 7. *Purposes of the Transaction and Plans or Proposals.*

Furnish the information required by Item 1006(d) of Regulation M-A (§ 229.1006 of this chapter).

Item 8. *Additional Information.*

Furnish the information required by Item 1011(b) of Regulation M-A (§ 229.1011 of this chapter).

Item 9. *Exhibits.*

File as an exhibit to the Schedule all documents specified by Item 1016(a), (e) and (g) of Regulation M-A (§ 229.1016 of this chapter).

Signature. After due inquiry and to the best of my knowledge and belief, I certify that the information set forth in this statement is true, complete and correct.

_____

(Signature)

_____

(Name and title)

_____

(Date)

Instruction to Signature:

The statement must be signed by the filing person or that person's authorized representative. If the statement is signed on behalf of a person by an authorized representative (other than an executive officer of a corporation or general partner of a partnership), evidence of the representative's authority to sign on behalf of the person must be filed with the statement. The name and any title of each person who signs the statement must be typed or printed beneath the signature. See § 240.14d-1(h) with respect to signature requirements.

[As last amended in Release No. 34-55146A, effective April 1, 2008, 73 F.R.17809 (technical correction).]

[¶ 40,771] SCHEDULE 14D-1F

Reg. § 240.14d-102. Tender offer statement pursuant to rule 14d-1(b) under the Securities Exchange Act of 1934.

U.S. Securities and Exchange Commission
Washington, D.C. 20549

Schedule 14D-1F

TENDER OFFER STATEMENT PURSUANT TO RULE 14d-1(b) UNDER THE SECURITIES EXCHANGE ACT OF 1934

(AMENDMENT NO. . . . . . .)

. . . .

(Name of Subject Company [Issuer])

. . . .

(Translation of Subject Company's [Issuer's] name into English (if applicable))

. . . .

(Jurisdiction of Subject Company's [Issuer's]Incorporation or Organization)

. . . .

(Bidder)

. . . .

(Title of Class of Securities)

. . . .

(CUSIP Number of Class of Securities (if applicable))

. . . .

(Name, address (including zip code) and telephone number (including area code of person(s) authorized to receive notices and communications on behalf of bidder)

. . . .

(Date tender offer first published, sent or given to securityholders)

CALCULATION OF FILING FEE*

Transaction Valuation	Amount of Filing Fee

* Set forth the amount on which the filing fee is calculated and state how it was determined. See General Instruction II.C. for rules governing the calculation of the filing fee.

[ ] Check box if any part of the fee is offset as provided by Rule 0-11(a)(2) and identify the filing with which the offsetting fee was previously paid. Identify the previous filing by registration statement number, or the Form or Schedule and the date of its filing.

Amount Previously Paid: . . . . Registration No.: . . . .

Filing Party: . . . .

Form: . . . . Date Filed: . . . .

GENERAL INSTRUCTIONS

I. Eligibility Requirements for Use of Schedule 14D-1F

A. Schedule 14D-1F may be used by any person making a cash tender or exchange offer (the "bidder") for securities of any issuer incorporated or organized under the laws of Canada or any Canadian province or territory that is a foreign private issuer, where less than 40 percent of the outstanding class of such issuer's securities that is the subject of the offer is held by U.S. holders. The calculation of U.S. holders shall be made as of the end of the subject issuer's last quarter or, if such quarter terminated within 60 days of the filing date, as of the end of such issuer's preceding quarter.

Instructions

1. For purposes of this schedule, "foreign private issuer" shall be construed in accordance with Rule 405 under the Securities Act.

2. For purposes of this Schedule, the term "U.S. holder" shall mean any person whose address appears on the records of the issuer, any voting trustee, any depositary, any share transfer agent or any person acting in a similar capacity on behalf of the issuer as being located in the United States.

3. With respect to any tender offer, including any exchange offer, otherwise eligible to proceed in accordance with Rule 14d-1(b) under the Securities Exchange Act of 1934 (the "Exchange Act"), the

issuer of the subject securities will be presumed to be a foreign private issuer and U.S. holders will be presumed to hold less than 40 percent of such outstanding securities, *unless* (a) the aggregate trading volume of that class on national securities exchanges in the United States and on NASDAQ exceeded its aggregate trading volume on securities exchanges in Canada and on the Canadian Dealing Network, Inc. ("CDN") over the 12 calendar month period prior to commencement of this offer, or if commenced in response to a prior offer, over the calendar month period prior to commencement of the initial offer (based on volume figures published by such exchanges and NASDAQ and CDN); (b) the most recent annual report or annual information form filed or submitted by the issuer with securities regulators of Ontario, Quebec, British Columbia or Alberta (or, if the issuer of the subject securities is not a reporting issuer in any of such provinces, with any other Canadian securities regulator) or with the Commission indicates that U.S. holders hold 40 percent or more of the subject class of securities; or (c) the offeror has actual knowledge that the level of U.S. ownership equals or exceeds 40 percent of such securities.

4. If this Schedule is filed during the pendency of one or more ongoing cash tender or exchange offers for securities of the class subject to this offer that was commenced or was eligible to be commenced on Schedule 13E-4F, Schedule 14D-1F and/or Form F-8 or Form F-80, the date for calculation of U.S. ownership for purposes of this Schedule shall be the same as that date used by the initial bidder or issuer.

5. For purposes of this Schedule, the class of subject securities shall not include any securities that may be converted into or are exchangeable for the subject securities.

B. Any bidder using this Schedule must extend the cash tender or exchange offer to U.S. holders of securities of the subject company upon terms and conditions not less favorable than those extended to any other holder of such securities, and must comply with the requirements of any Canadian federal, provincial and/or territorial law, regulation or policy relating to the terms and conditions of the offer.

C. This Schedule shall not be used if the subject company is an investment company registered or required to be registered under the Investment Company Act of 1940.

D. This Schedule shall not be used to comply with the reporting requirements of Section 13(d) of the Exchange Act. Persons using this Schedule are reminded of their obligation to file or update a Schedule 13D where required by Section 13(d)(1) of the Exchange Act and the Commission's rules and regulations thereunder.

II. Filing Instructions and Fee

A.(1) The bidder must file this Schedule and any amendment to the Schedule (see Part I, Item 1.(b)), including all exhibits and other documents filed as part of the Schedule or amendment, in electronic format via the Commission's Electronic Data Gathering, Analysis, and Retrieval (EDGAR) system in accordance with the EDGAR rules set forth in Regulation S-T (17 CFR Part 232). For assistance with technical questions about EDGAR or to request an access code, call the EDGAR Filer Support Office at (202) 551-8900. For assistance with the EDGAR rules, call the Office of EDGAR and Information Analysis at (202) 551-3610.

(2) If filing the Schedule in paper under a hardship exemption in 17 CFR 232.201 or 232.202 of Regulation S-T, or as otherwise permitted, the bidder must file with the Commission at its principal office five copies of the complete Schedule and any amendment, including exhibits and all other documents filed as a part of the Schedule or amendment. The bidder must bind, staple or otherwise compile each copy in one or more parts without stiff covers. The bidder must further bind the Schedule or amendment on the side or stitching margin in a manner that leaves the reading matter legible. The bidder must provide three additional copies of the Schedule or amendment without exhibits to the Commission.

B. An electronic filer must provide the signatures required for the Schedule or amendment in accordance with 17 CFR 232.302 of Regulation S-T. A bidder filing in paper must have the original and at least one copy of the Schedule and any amendment signed in accordance with Exchange Act Rule 12b-11(d) (17 CFR 12b-11(d)) by the persons whose signatures are required for this Schedule or amendment. The bidder must also conform the unsigned copies.

C. At the time of filing this Schedule with the Commission, the bidder shall pay to the Commission in accordance with Rule 0-11 of the Exchange Act, a fee in U.S. dollars in the amount prescribed by Section 14(g)(3) of the Exchange Act. See also Rule 0-9 under the Exchange Act.

(1) Where the bidder is offering securities or other non-cash consideration for some or all of the securities to be acquired, whether or not in combination with a cash payment for the same securities, the value of the consideration shall be based on the market value of the securities to be received by the bidder as established by paragraph 3 of this section.

(2) If there is no market for the securities to be acquired by the bidder, the book value of such securities computed as of the latest practicable date prior to the date of filing the Schedule shall be used, unless the issuer of such securities is in bankruptcy or receivership or has an accumulated capital

deficit, in which case one-third of the principal amount, par value or stated value of such securities shall be used.

(3) When the fee is based upon the market value of the securities, such market value shall be calculated upon the basis of either the average of the high and low prices reported in the consolidated reporting system (for exchange traded securities and last sale reported for over-the-counter securities) or the average of the bid and asked price (for other over-the-counter securities) as of a specified date within five business days prior to the date of filing the Schedule.

D. If at any time after the initial payment of the fee the aggregate consideration offered is increased, an additional filing fee based upon such increase shall be paid with the required amended filing.

E. The bidder must file the Schedule or amendment in electronic format in the English language in accordance with 17 CFR 232.306 of Regulation S-T. The bidder may file part of the Schedule or amendment, or exhibit or other attachment to the Schedule or amendment, in both French and English if the bidder included the French text to comply with the requirements of the Canadian securities administrator or other Canadian authority and, for an electronic filing, if the filing is an HTML document, as defined in 17 CFR 232.11 of Regulation S-T. For both an electronic filing and a paper filing, the bidder may provide an English translation or English summary of a foreign language document as an exhibit or other attachment to the Schedule or amendment as permitted by the rules of the applicable Canadian securities administrator.

F. A paper filer must number sequentially the signed original of the Schedule or amendment (in addition to any internal numbering that otherwise may be present) by handwritten, typed, printed or other legible form of notation from the first page through the last page of the Schedule or amendment, including any exhibits or attachments. A paper filer must disclose the total number of pages on the first page of the sequentially numbered Schedule or amendment.

III. Compliance with the Exchange Act

A. Pursuant to Rule 14d-1(b) under the Exchange Act, the bidder shall be deemed to comply with the requirements of Sections 14(d)(1) through 14(d)(7) of the Exchange Act, Regulation 14D under the Exchange Act and Schedule TO thereunder, and Rule 14e-1 under Regulation 14E of the Exchange Act, in connection with a cash tender or exchange offer for securities that may be made pursuant to this Schedule; *provided that,* if an exemption has been granted from requirements of Canadian federal, provincial, and/or territorial laws, regulations or policies, and the tender offer does not comply with requirements that otherwise would be prescribed by Regulation 14D or 14E, the bidder (absent an order from the Commission) shall comply with the provisions of Sections 14(d)(1) through 14(d)(7) of the Exchange Act, Regulation 14D and Schedule TO thereunder, and Rule 14e-1 under Regulation 14E.

B. Any cash tender or exchange offer made pursuant to this Schedule is not exempt from the antifraud provisions of Section 10(b) of the Exchange Act and Rule 10b-5 thereunder, and Section 14(e) of the Exchange Act and Rule 14e-3 thereunder, and this Schedule shall be deemed "filed" for purposes of Section 18 of the Exchange Act.

C. The issuer's attention is directed to Regulation M (§§ 242.100 through 242.105 of this chapter), in the case of an issuer exchange offer, and to Rule 14e-5 under the Exchange Act (§ 240.14e-5), in the case of an issuer cash tender offer or issuer exchange offer. [*See* Exchange Act Release No. 29355 (June 21, 1991) containing an exemption from Rule 10b-13, the predecessor to Rule 14e-5.]

PART I INFORMATION REQUIRED TO BE SENT TO SHAREHOLDERS

Item 1. Home Jurisdiction Documents

(a) This Schedule shall be accompanied by the entire disclosure document or documents required to be delivered to holders of securities to be acquired in the proposed transaction by the bidder pursuant to the laws, regulations or policies of Canada and/or any of its provinces or territories governing the conduct of the tender offer. It shall not include any documents incorporated by reference into such disclosure document(s) and not distributed to offerees pursuant to any such law, regulation or policy.

(b) Any amendment made by the bidder to a home jurisdiction document or documents shall be filed with the Commission under cover of this Schedule, which must indicate on the cover page the number of the amendment.

(c) In an exchange offer where securities of the bidder have been or are to be offered or cancelled in the transaction, such securities shall be registered on forms promulgated by the Commission under the Securities Act of 1933 including, where available, the Commission's Form F-8 or F-80 providing for inclusion in that registration statement of the home jurisdiction prospectus.

Item 2. Informational Legends

The following legends, to the extent applicable, shall appear on the outside front cover page of the home-jurisdiction document(s) in bold-face roman type at least as high as ten-point modern type and at least two points leaded:

"This tender offer is made for the securities of a foreign issuer and while the offer is subject to disclosure requirements of the country in which the subject company is incorporated or organized, investors should be aware that these requirements are different from those of the United States. Financial statements included herein, if any, have been prepared in accordance with foreign generally accepted accounting principles and thus may not be comparable to financial statements of United States companies.

"The enforcement by investors of civil liabilities under the federal securities laws may be affected adversely by the fact that the subject company is located in a foreign country, and that some or all of its officers and directors are residents of a foreign country.

"Investors should be aware that the bidder or its affiliates, directly or indirectly, may bid for or make purchases of the issuer's securities subject to the offer, or of the issuer's related securities, during the period of the tender offer, as permitted by applicable Canadian laws or provincial laws or regulations."

In the case of an exchange offer:

"Investors should be aware that the bidder or its affiliates, directly or indirectly, may bid for or make purchases of the issuer's securities subject to the offer or of the issuer's related securities, or of the bidder's securities to be distributed or of the bidder's related securities, during the period of the tender offer, as permitted by applicable Canadian laws or provincial laws or regulations."

Note to Item 2. If the home-jurisdiction document(s) are delivered through an electronic medium, the issuer may satisfy the legibility requirements for the required legends relating to type size and font by presenting the legend in any manner reasonably calculated to draw security holder attention to it.

PART II INFORMATION NOT REQUIRED TO BE SENT TO SHAREHOLDERS

The exhibits specified below shall be filed as part of the Schedule, but are not required to be sent to shareholders unless so required pursuant to the laws, regulations or policies of Canada and/or any of its provinces or territories. Exhibits shall be appropriately lettered or numbered for convenient reference.

(1) File any reports or information that, in accordance with the requirements of the home jurisdiction(s), must be made publicly available by the bidder in connection with the transaction but need not be disseminated to shareholders.

(2) File copies of any documents incorporated by reference into the home jurisdiction document(s).

(3) If any name is signed to this Schedule pursuant to power of attorney, manually signed copies of any such power of attorney shall be filed. If the name of any officer signing on behalf of the bidder is signed pursuant to a power of attorney, certified copies of the bidder's board of directors authorizing such signature also shall be filed.

PART III UNDERTAKINGS AND CONSENT TO SERVICE OF PROCESS

1. Undertakings

The Schedule shall set forth the following undertakings of the bidder:

a. The bidder undertakes to make available, in person or by telephone, representatives to respond to inquiries made by the Commission staff, and to furnish promptly, when requested to do so by the Commission staff, information relating to this Schedule or to transactions in said securities.

b. The bidder undertakes to disclose in the United States, on the same basis as it is required to make such disclosure pursuant to applicable Canadian federal and/or provincial or territorial laws, regulations or policies, or otherwise discloses, information regarding purchases of the issuer's securities in connection with the cash tender or exchange offer covered by this Schedule. Such information shall be set forth in amendments to this Schedule.

c. In the case of an exchange offer:

The bidder undertakes to disclose in the United States, on the same basis as it is required to make such disclosure pursuant to any applicable Canadian federal and/or provincial or territorial law, regulation or policy, or otherwise discloses, information regarding purchases of the issuer's or bidder's securities in connection with the offer.

2. Consent to Service of Process

(a) At the time of filing this Schedule, the bidder (if a non-U.S. person) shall file with the Commission a written irrevocable consent and power of attorney on Form F-X.

(b) Any change to the name or address of a registrant's agent for service shall be communicated promptly to the Commission by amendment to Form F-X referencing the file number of the registrant.

PART IV   SIGNATURES

A. The Schedule shall be signed by each person on whose behalf the Schedule is filed or its authorized representative. If the Schedule is signed on behalf of a person by his authorized representative (other than an executive officer or general partner of the bidder), evidence of the representative's authority shall be filed with the Schedule.

B. The name and any title of each person who signs the Schedule shall be typed or printed beneath his signature.

C. By signing this Schedule, the bidder consents without power of revocation that any administrative subpoena may be served, or any administrative proceeding, civil suit or civil action where the cause of action arises out of or relates to or concerns any offering made or purported to be made in connection with the filing on Schedule 14D-1F or any purchases or sales of any security in connection therewith, may be commenced against it in any administrative tribunal or in any appropriate court in any place subject to the jurisdiction of any state or of the United States by service of said subpoena or process upon the registrant's designated agent.

After due inquiry and to the best of my knowledge and belief, I certify that the information set forth in this statement is true, complete and correct.

(Signature) . . . .

(Name and Title) . . . .

(Date) . . . .

[As last amended in Release No. 34-55146A, effective April 1, 2008, 73 F.R.17809 (technical correction).]

[¶ 40,775]   Schedule 14D-9F

Reg. § 240.14d-103. Solicitation/recommendation statement pursuant to section 14(d)(4) of the Securities Exchange Act of 1934 and rules 14d-1(b) and 14e-2(c) thereunder.

U.S. Securities and Exchange Commission
Washington, D.C. 20549

Schedule 14D-9F

SOLICITATION/RECOMMENDATION STATEMENT PURSUANT TO SECTION 14(d)(4) OF THE SECURITIES EXCHANGE ACT OF 1934 AND RULES 14d-1(b) AND 14e-2(c) THEREUNDER

(Amendment No. . . . . . .)

. . . .
(Name of Subject Company [Issuer])

. . . .
(Translation of Subject Company's [Issuer's] Name into English (if applicable))

. . . .
(Jurisdiction of Subject Company's [Issuer's]incorporation or Organization)

. . . .
(Name(s) of Person(s) Filing Statement)

. . . .
(Title of Class of Securities)

. . . .
(CUSIP Number of Class of Securities (if applicable))

. . . .
(Name, address (including zip code) and telephone number (including area code) of person(s) authorized to receive notices and communications on behalf of the person(s) filing statement)

GENERAL INSTRUCTIONS

I. Eligibility Requirements for Use of Schedule 14D-9F

A. Schedule 14D-9F is used by any issuer incorporated or organized under the laws of Canada or any Canadian province or territory that is a foreign private issuer (the "subject company"), or by any director or officer of such issuer, where the issuer is the subject of a cash tender or exchange offer for a class of its securities filed on Schedule 14D-1F.

For purposes of this Schedule, "foreign private issue" shall be construed in accordance with Rule 405 under the Securities Act.

B. Any person(s) using this Schedule must comply with the requirements of any Canadian federal, provincial and/or territorial law, regulation or policy relating to a recommendation by the subject issuer's board of directors, or any director or officer thereof, with respect to the offer.

II. Filing Instructions

A.(1) The subject issuer must file this Schedule and any amendment to the Schedule (see Part I, Item 1.(b)), including all exhibits and other documents filed as part of the Schedule or amendment, in electronic format via the Commission's Electronic Data Gathering, Analysis, and Retrieval (EDGAR) system in accordance with the EDGAR rules set forth in Regulation S-T (17 CFR Part 232). For assistance with technical questions about EDGAR or to request an access code, call the EDGAR Filer Support Office at (202) 551-8900. For assistance with the EDGAR rules, call the Office of EDGAR and Information Analysis at (202) 551-3610.

(2) If filing the Schedule in paper under a hardship exemption in 17 CFR 232.201 or 232.202 of Regulation S-T, or as otherwise permitted, the subject issuer must file with the Commission at its principal office five copies of the complete Schedule and any amendment, including exhibits and all other documents filed as a part of the Schedule or amendment. The subject issuer must bind, staple or otherwise compile each copy in one or more parts without stiff covers. The subject issuer must further bind the Schedule or amendment on the side or stitching margin in a manner that leaves the reading matter legible. The subject issuer must provide three additional copies of the Schedule or amendment without exhibits to the Commission.

B. An electronic filer must provide the signatures required for the Schedule or amendment in accordance with 17 CFR 232.302 of Regulation S-T. A subject issuer filing in paper must have the original and at least one copy of the Schedule and any amendment signed in accordance with Exchange Act Rule 12b-11(d) (17 CFR 12b-11(d)) by the persons whose signatures are required for this Schedule or amendment. The subject issuer must also conform the unsigned copies.

C. The subject issuer must file the Schedule or amendment in electronic format in the English language in accordance with 17 CFR 232.306 of Regulation S-T. The subject issuer may file part of the Schedule or amendment, or exhibit or other attachment to the Schedule or amendment, in both French and English if the bidder included the French text to comply with the requirements of the Canadian securities administrator or other Canadian authority and, for an electronic filing, if the filing is an HTML document, as defined in 17 CFR 232.11 of Regulation S-T. For both an electronic filing and a paper filing, the subject issuer may provide an English translation or English summary of a foreign language document as an exhibit or other attachment to the Schedule or amendment as permitted by the rules of the applicable Canadian securities administrator.

D. A paper filer must number sequentially the signed original of the Schedule or amendment (in addition to any internal numbering that otherwise may be present) by handwritten, typed, printed or other legible form of notation from the first page through the last page of the Schedule or amendment, including any exhibits or attachments. A paper filer must disclose the total number of pages on the first page of the sequentially numbered Schedule or amendment.

III. Compliance with the Exchange Act

A. Pursuant to Rule 14e-2(c) under the Securities Exchange Act of 1934 (the "Exchange Act"), this Schedule shall be filed by an issuer, a class of the securities of which is the subject of a cash tender or exchange offer filed on Schedule 14D-1F, and may be filed by any director or officer of such issuer.

B. Any recommendation with respect to a cash tender or exchange offer for a class of securities of the subject company made pursuant to this Schedule is not exempt from the antifraud provisions of Section 10(b) of the Exchange Act and Rule 10b-5 thereunder and Section 14(e) of the Exchange Act and Rule 14e-3 thereunder, and this Schedule shall be deemed "filed" with the Commission for purposes of Section 18 of the Exchange Act.

PART I   INFORMATION REQUIRED TO BE SENT TO SHAREHOLDERS

Item 1. Home Jurisdiction Documents

(a) This Schedule shall be accompanied by the entire disclosure document or documents required to be delivered to holders of securities to be acquired in the proposed transaction pursuant to the laws, regulations or policies of Canada and/or any of its provinces or territories governing the conduct of the offer. It shall not include any documents incorporated by reference into such disclosure document(s) and not distributed to offerees pursuant to any such law, regulation or policy.

(b) Any amendment made to a home jurisdiction document or documents shall be filed with the Commission under cover of this Schedule, which must indicate on the cover page the number of the amendment.

Item 2. Informational Legends

The following legends, to the extent applicable, shall appear on the outside front cover page of the home jurisdiction document(s) in bold-face roman type at least as high as ten-point modern type and at least two points leaded:

"This tender offer is made for the securities of a foreign issuer and while the offer is subject to disclosure requirements of the country in which the subject issuer is incorporated or organized, investors should be aware that these requirements are different from those of the United States. Financial statements included herein, if any, have been prepared in accordance with foreign generally accepted accounting principles and thus may not be comparable to financial statements of United States companies.

"The enforcement by investors of civil liabilities under the federal securities laws may be affected adversely by the fact that the issuer is located in a foreign country, and that some or all of its officers and directors are residents of a foreign country."

Note to Item 2. If the home-jurisdiction document(s) are delivered through an electronic medium, the issuer may satisfy the legibility requirements for the required legends relating to type size and font by presenting the legend in any manner reasonably calculated to draw security holder attention to it.

PART II   INFORMATION NOT REQUIRED TO BE SENT TO SHAREHOLDERS

The exhibits specified below shall be filed as part of the Schedule, but are not required to be sent to shareholders unless so required pursuant to the laws, or regulations or policies of Canada and/or any of its provinces or territories. Exhibits shall be appropriately lettered or numbered for convenient reference.

(1) File any reports or information that, in accordance with the requirements of the home jurisdictions(s), must be made publicly available by the person(s) filing this Schedule in connection with the transaction, but need not be disseminated to shareholders.

(2) File copies of any documents incorporated by reference into the home jurisdiction document(s).

(3) If any name is signed to the Schedule pursuant to power of attorney, manually signed copies of any such power of attorney shall be filed. If the name of any officer signing on behalf of the issuer is signed pursuant to a power of attorney, certified copies of a resolution of the issuer's board of directors authorizing such signature also shall be filed.

PART III   UNDERTAKING AND CONSENT TO SERVICE OF PROCESS

1. Undertaking

The Schedule shall set forth the following undertaking of the person filing it:

The person(s) filing this Schedule undertakes to make available, in person or by telephone, representatives to respond to inquiries made by the Commission staff, and to furnish promptly, when requested to do so by the Commission staff, information relating to this Schedule or to transactions in said securities.

2. Consent to Service of Process

(a) At the time of filing this Schedule, the person(s) (if a non-U.S. person) so filing shall file with the Commission a written irrevocable consent and power of attorney on Form F-X.

(b) Any change to the name or address of a registrant's agent for service shall be communicated promptly to the Commission by amendment to Form F-X referencing the file number of the registrant.

PART IV   SIGNATURES

A. The Schedule shall be signed by each person on whose behalf the Schedule is filed or its authorized representative. If the Schedule is signed on behalf of a person by his authorized representative (other than an executive officer or general partner of the subject company), evidence of the representative's authority shall be filed with the Schedule.

B. The name and any title of each person who signs the Schedule shall be typed or printed beneath his signature.

C. By signing this Schedule, the persons signing consent without power of revocation that any administrative subpoena may be served, or any administrative proceeding, civil suit or civil action where the cause of action arises out of or relates to or concerns any offering made or purported to be made in connection with filing on this Schedule 14D-9F or any purchases or sales of any security in connection therewith, may be commenced against them in any administrative tribunal or in any appropriate court in any place subject to the jurisdiction of any state or of the United States by service of said subpoena or process upon the registrant's designated agent.

After due inquiry and to the best of my knowledge and belief, I certify that the information set forth in this statement is true, complete and correct.

(Signature) . . . .

(Name and Title) . . . .

(Date) . . . .

[As last amended in Release No. 34-55146A, effective April 1, 2008, 73 F.R.17809 (technical correction).]

REGULATION 14E

Note: For the scope of and definitions applicable to Regulation 14E refer to § 240.14d-1.

[¶ 40,801] Unlawful Tender Offer Practices

Reg. § 240.14e-1. As a means reasonably designed to prevent fraudulent, deceptive or manipulative acts or practices within the meaning of section 14(e) of the Act, no person who makes a tender offer shall:

(a) Hold such tender offer open for less than twenty business days from the date such tender offer is first published or sent to security holders; provided, however, that if the tender offer involves a roll-up transaction as defined in Item 901(c) of Regulation S-K (17 CFR 229.901(c)) and the securities being offered are registered (or authorized to be registered) on Form S-4 (17 CFR 229.25) or Form F-4 (17 CFR 229.34), the offer shall not be open for less than sixty calendar days from the date the tender offer is first published or sent to security holders;

(b) Increase or decrease the percentage of the class of securities being sought or the consideration offered or the dealer's soliciting fee to be given in a tender offer unless such tender offer remains open for at least ten business days from the date that notice of such increase or decrease is first published or sent or given to security holders;

Provided, however, That, for purposes of this paragraph, the acceptance for payment of an additional amount of securities not to exceed two percent of the class of securities that is the subject of the tender offer shall not be deemed to be an increase. For purposes of this paragraph, the percentage of a class of securities shall be calculated in accordance with section 14(d)(3) of the Act.

(c) Fail to pay the consideration offered or return the securities deposited by or on behalf of security holders promptly after the termination or withdrawal of a tender offer. This paragraph does not prohibit a bidder electing to offer a subsequent offering period under § 240.14d-11 from paying for securities during the subsequent offering period in accordance with that section.

(d) Extend the length of a tender offer without issuing a notice of such extension by press release or other public announcement, which notice shall include disclosure of the approximate number of securities deposited to date and shall be issued no later than the earlier of (i) 9:00 a.m. Eastern time, on the next business day after the scheduled expiration date of the offer or (ii), if the class of securities which is the subject of the tender offer is registered on one or more national securities exchanges, the first opening of any one of such exchanges on the next business day after the scheduled expiration date of the offer.

(e) The periods of time required by paragraphs (a) and (b) of this section shall be tolled for any period during which the bidder has failed to file in electronic format, absent a hardship exemption (§§ 232.201 and 232.202 of this chapter), the Schedule TO Tender Offer Statement (§ 240.14d-100), any tender offer material required to be filed by Item 12 of that Schedule pursuant to paragraph (a) of Item 1016 of Regulation M-A (§ 229.1016(a) of this chapter), and any amendments thereto. If such documents were filed in paper pursuant to a hardship exemption (*see* § 232.201 and § 232.202(d)), the minimum offering periods shall be tolled for any period during which a required confirming electronic copy of such Schedule and tender offer material is delinquent.

[As last amended in Release No. 34-55146A, effective April 1, 2008, 73 F.R.17809 (technical correction).]

[¶ 40,811] Position of a Subject Company with Respect to a Tender Offer

Reg. § 240.14e-2. (a) *Position of subject company.* As a means reasonably designed to prevent fraudulent, deceptive or manipulative acts or practices within the meaning of section 14(e) of the Act, the subject company, no later than 10 business days from the date the tender offer is first published or sent or given, shall publish, send or give to security holders a statement disclosing that the subject company:

(1) Recommends acceptance or rejection of the bidder's tender offer;

(2) Expresses no opinion and is remaining neutral toward the bidder's tender offer; or

(3) Is unable to take a position with respect to the bidder's tender offer.

Such statement shall also include the reason(s) for the position (including the inability to take a position) disclosed therein.

(b) *Material change.* If any material change occurs in the disclosure required by paragraph (a) of this section, the subject company shall promptly publish, send or give a statement disclosing such material change to security holders.

(c) Any issuer, a class of the securities of which is the subject of a tender offer filed with the Commission on Schedule 14D-1F and conducted in reliance upon and in conformity with Rule 14d-1(b) under the Act, and any director or officer of such issuer where so required by the laws, regulations and policies of Canada and/or any of its provinces or territories, in lieu of the statements called for by paragraph (a) of this section and Rule 14d-9 under the Act, shall file with the Commission on Schedule 14D-9F the entire disclosure document(s) required to be furnished to holders of securities of the subject issuer by the laws, regulations and policies of Canada and/or any of its provinces or territories governing the conduct of the tender offer, and shall disseminate such document(s) in the United States in accordance with such laws, regulations and policies.

(d) *Exemption for cross-border tender offers.* The subject company shall be exempt from this section with respect to a tender offer conducted under § 240.14d-1(c).

[As last amended in Release No. 33-7759, effective January 24, 2000, 64 F.R. 61382.]

[¶ 40,815] Transactions in Securities on the Basis of Material, Nonpublic Information in the Context of Tender Offers

Reg. § 240.14e-3. (a) If any person has taken a substantial step or steps to commence, or has commenced, a tender offer (the "offering person"), it shall constitute a fraudulent, deceptive or manipulative act or practice within the meaning of section 14(e) of the Act for any other person who is in possession of material information relating to such tender offer which information he knows or has reason to know is nonpublic and which he knows or has reason to know has been acquired directly or indirectly from (1) the offering person, (2) the issuer of the securities sought or to be sought by such tender offer, or (3) any officer, director, partner or employee or any other person acting on behalf of the offering person or such issuer, to purchase or sell or cause to be purchased or sold any of such securities or any securities convertible into or exchangeable for any such securities or any option or right to obtain or to dispose of any of the foregoing securities, unless within a reasonable time prior to any purchase or sale such information and its source are publicly disclosed by press release or otherwise.

(b) A person other than a natural person shall not violate paragraph (a) of this section if such persons shows that:

(1) The individual(s) making the investment decision on behalf of such person to purchase or sell any security described in paragraph (a) or to cause any such security to be purchased or sold by or on behalf of others did not know the material, nonpublic information; and

(2) Such person had implemented one or a combination of policies and procedures, reasonable under the circumstances, taking into consideration the nature of the person's business, to ensure that individual(s) making investment decision(s) would not violate paragraph (a), which policies and procedures may include, but are not limited to, (i) those which restrict any purchase, sale and causing any purchase and sale of any such security or (ii) those which prevent such individual(s) from knowing such information.

(c) Notwithstanding anything in paragraph (a) to the contrary, the following transactions shall not be violations of paragraph (a) of this section:

(1) Purchase(s) of any security described in paragraph (a) by a broker or by another agent on behalf of an offering person; or

(2) Sale(s) by any person of any security described in paragraph (a) to the offering person.

(d)(1) As a means reasonably designed to prevent fraudulent, deceptive or manipulative acts or practices within the meaning of section 14(e) of the Act, it shall be unlawful for any person described in paragraph (d)(2) of this section to communicate material, nonpublic information relating to a tender offer to any other person under circumstances in which it is reasonably foreseeable that such communication is likely to result in a violation of this section *except* that this paragraph shall not apply to a communication made in good faith,

(i) To the officers, directors, partners or employees of the offering person, to its advisors or to other persons, involved in the planning, financing, preparation or execution of such tender offer;

(ii) To the issuer whose securities are sought or to be sought by such tender offer, to its officers, directors, partners, employees or advisors or to other persons, involved in the planning, financing, preparation or execution of the activities of the issuer with respect to such tender offer; or

(iii) To any person pursuant to a requirement of any statute or rule or regulation promulgated thereunder.

(2) The persons referred to in paragraph (d)(1) of this section are:

(i) The offering person or its officers, directors, partners, employees or advisers;

(ii) The issuer of the securities sought or to be sought by such tender offer or its officers, directors, partners, employees or advisors;

(iii) Anyone acting on behalf of the persons in paragraph (d)(2)(i) or the issuer or persons in paragraph (d)(2)(ii); and

(iv) Any person in possession of material information relating to a tender offer which information he knows or has reason to know is nonpublic and which he knows or has reason to know has been acquired directly or indirectly from any of the above.

[As adopted in Release No. 34-17120, effective October 14, 1980, 45 F.R. 60410.]

[¶ 40,816] Prohibited Transactions In Connection With Partial Tender Offers

Reg. § 240.14e-4. (a) Definitions. For purposes of this section:

(1) The amount of a person's "net long position" in a subject security shall equal the excess, if any, of such person's "long position" over such person's "short position." For the purposes of determining the net long position as of the end of the proration period and for tendering concurrently to two or more partial tender offers, securities that have been tendered in accordance with the Rule and not withdrawn are deemed to be part of the person's long position.

(i) Such person's "long position," is the amount of subject securities that such person:

(A) or his agent has title to or would have title to but for having lent such securities; or

(B) has purchased, or has entered into an unconditional contract, binding on both parties thereto, to purchase but has not yet received; or

(C) has exercised a standardized call option for; or

(D) has converted, exchanged, or exercised an equivalent security for; or

(E) is entitled to receive upon conversion, exchange, or exercise of an equivalent security.

(ii) Such person's "short position," is the amount of subject securities or subject securities underlying equivalent securities that such person:

(A) has sold, or has entered into an unconditional contract, binding on both parties thereto, to sell; or

(B) has borrowed; or

(C) has written a non-standardized call option, or granted any other right pursuant to which his shares may be tendered by another person; or

(D) is obligated to deliver upon exercise of a standardized call option sold on or after the date that a tender offer is first publicly announced or otherwise made known by the bidder to holders of the security to be acquired, if the exercise price of such option is lower than the highest tender offer price or stated amount of the consideration offered for the subject security. For the purpose of this paragraph, if one or more tender offers for the same security are ongoing on such date, the announcement date shall be that of the first announced offer.

(2) The term "equivalent security" means (i) any security (including any option, warrant, or other right to purchase the subject security), issued by the person whose securities are the subject of the offer, that is immediately convertible into, or exchangeable or exercisable for, a subject security, or (ii) any other right or option (other than a standardized call option) that entitles the holder thereof to acquire a subject security, but only if the holder thereof reasonably believes that the maker or writer of the right or option has title to and possession of the subject security and upon exercise will promptly deliver the subject security.

(3) The term "subject security" means a security that is the subject of any tender offer or request or invitation for tenders.

(4) For purposes of this rule, a person shall be deemed to "tender" a security if he (i) delivers a subject security pursuant to an offer, (ii) causes such delivery to be made, (iii) guarantees delivery of a subject security pursuant to a tender offer, (iv) causes a guarantee of such delivery to be given by another person, or (v) uses any other method by which acceptance of a tender offer may be made.

(5) The term "partial tender offer" means a tender offer or request or invitation for tenders for less than all of the outstanding securities subject to the offer in which tenders are accepted either by lot or on a *pro rata* basis for a specified period, or a tender offer for all of the outstanding shares that offers a choice of consideration in which tenders for different forms of consideration may be accepted either by lot or on a *pro rata* basis for a specified period.

(6) The term "standardized call option" means any call option that is traded on an exchange, or for which quotation information is disseminated in an electronic interdealer quotation system of a registered national securities association.

(b) It shall be unlawful for any person acting alone or in concert with others, directly or indirectly, to tender any subject security in a partial tender offer:

(1) For his own account unless at the time of tender, and at the end of the proration period or period during which securities are accepted by lot (including any extensions thereof), he has a net long position equal to or greater than the amount tendered in:

(i) the subject security and will deliver or cause to be delivered such security for the purpose of tender to the person making the offer within the period specified in the offer; or

(ii) an equivalent security and, upon the acceptance of his tender will acquire the subject security by conversion, exchange, or exercise of such equivalent security to the extent required by the terms of the offer, and will deliver or cause to be delivered the subject security so acquired for the purpose of tender to the person making the offer within the period specified in the offer; or

(2) For the account of another person unless the person making the tender (i) possesses the subject security or an equivalent security, or (ii) has a reasonable belief that, upon information furnished by the person on whose behalf the tender is made, such person owns the subject security or an equivalent security and will promptly deliver the subject security or such equivalent security for the purpose of tender to the person making the tender.

(c) This rule shall not prohibit any transaction or transactions which the Commission, upon written request or upon its own motion, exempts, either unconditionally or on specified terms and conditions.

[As last amended in Release No. 34-28660, November 30, 1990, 55 F.R. 50316.]

[¶ 40,817] Prohibiting Purchases Outside of a Tender Offer

Reg. § 240.14e-5. (a) *Unlawful activity.* As a means reasonably designed to prevent fraudulent, deceptive or manipulative acts or practices in connection with a tender offer for equity securities, no covered person may directly or indirectly purchase or arrange to purchase any subject securities or any related securities except as part of the tender offer. This prohibition applies from the time of public announcement of the tender offer until the tender offer expires. This prohibition does not apply to any purchases or arrangements to purchase made during the time of any subsequent offering period as provided for in § 240.14d-11 if the consideration paid or to be paid for the purchases or arrangements to purchase is the same in form and amount as the consideration offered in the tender offer.

(b) *Excepted activity.* The following transactions in subject securities or related securities are not prohibited by paragraph (a) of this section:

(1) *Exercises of securities.* Transactions by covered persons to convert, exchange, or exercise related securities into subject securities, if the covered person owned the related securities before public announcement;

(2) *Purchases for plans.* Purchases or arrangements to purchase by or for a plan that are made by an agent independent of the issuer;

(3) *Purchases during odd-lot offers.* Purchases or arrangements to purchase if the tender offer is excepted under § 240.13e-4(h)(5);

(4) *Purchases as intermediary.* Purchases by or through a dealer-manager or its affiliates that are made in the ordinary course of business and made either:

(i) On an agency basis not for a covered person; or

(ii) As principal for its own account if the dealer-manager or its affiliate is not a market maker, and the purchase is made to offset a contemporaneous sale after having received an unsolicited order to buy from a customer who is not a covered person;

(5) *Basket transactions.* Purchases or arrangements to purchase a basket of securities containing a subject security or a related security if the following conditions are satisfied:

(i) The purchase or arrangement to purchase is made in the ordinary course of business and not to facilitate the tender offer;

(ii) The basket contains 20 or more securities; and

(iii) Covered securities and related securities do not comprise more than 5% of the value of the basket;

(6) *Covering transactions.* Purchases or arrangements to purchase that are made to satisfy an obligation to deliver a subject security or a related security arising from a short sale or from the exercise of an option by a non-covered person if:

(i) The short sale or option transaction was made in the ordinary course of business and not to facilitate the offer;

(ii) In the case of a short sale, the short sale was entered into before public announcement of the tender offer; and

(iii) In the case of an exercise of an option, the covered person wrote the option before public announcement of the tender offer;

(7) *Purchases pursuant to contractual obligations.* Purchases or arrangements to purchase pursuant to a contract if the following conditions are satisfied:

(i) The contract was entered into before public announcement of the tender offer;

(ii) The contract is unconditional and binding on both parties; and

(iii) The existence of the contract and all material terms including quantity, price and parties are disclosed in the offering materials;

(8) *Purchases or arrangements to purchase by an affiliate of the dealer-manager.* Purchases or arrangements to purchase by an affiliate of a dealer-manager if the following conditions are satisfied:

(i) The dealer-manager maintains and enforces written policies and procedures reasonably designed to prevent the flow of information to or from the affiliate that might result in a violation of the federal securities laws and regulations;

(ii) The dealer-manager is registered as a broker or dealer under Section 15(a) of the Act;

(iii) The affiliate has no officers (or persons performing similar functions) or employees (other than clerical, ministerial, or support personnel) in common with the dealer-manager that direct, effect, or recommend transactions in securities; and

(iv) The purchases or arrangements to purchase are not made to facilitate the tender offer;

(9) *Purchases by connected exempt market makers or connected exempt principal traders.* Purchases or arrangements to purchase if the following conditions are satisfied:

(i) The issuer of the subject security is a foreign private issuer, as defined in § 240.3b-4(c);

(ii) The tender offer is subject to the United Kingdom's City Code on Takeovers and Mergers;

(iii) The purchase or arrangement to purchase is effected by a connected exempt market maker or a connected exempt principal trader, as those terms are used in the United Kingdom's City Code on Takeovers and Mergers;

(iv) The connected exempt market maker or the connected exempt principal trader complies with the applicable provisions of the United Kingdom's City Code on Takeovers and Mergers; and

(v) The tender offer documents disclose the identity of the connected exempt market maker or the connected exempt principal trader and disclose, or describe how U.S. security holders can obtain, information regarding market making or principal purchases by such market maker or principal trader to the extent that this information is required to be made public in the United Kingdom; and

(10) *Purchases during cross-border tender offers.* Purchases or arrangements to purchase if the following conditions are satisfied:

(i) The tender offer is excepted under § 240.13e-4(h)(8) or § 240.14d-1(c);

(ii) The offering documents furnished to U.S. holders prominently disclose the possibility of any purchases, or arrangements to purchase, or the intent to make such purchases;

(iii) The offering documents disclose the manner in which any information about any such purchases or arrangements to purchase will be disclosed;

(iv) The offeror discloses information in the United States about any such purchases or arrangements to purchase in a manner comparable to the disclosure made in the home jurisdiction, as defined in § 240.13e-4(i)(3); and

(v) The purchases comply with the applicable tender offer laws and regulations of the home jurisdiction; and

(11) *Purchases or arrangements to purchase pursuant to a foreign tender offer(s).* Purchases or arrangements to purchase pursuant to a foreign offer(s) where the offeror seeks to acquire subject securities through a U.S. tender offer and a concurrent or substantially concurrent foreign offer(s), if the following conditions are satisfied:

(i) The U.S. and foreign tender offer(s) meet the conditions for reliance on the Tier II cross-border exemptions set forth in § 240.14d-1(d);

(ii) The economic terms and consideration in the U.S. tender offer and foreign tender offer(s) are the same, provided that any cash consideration to be paid to U.S. security holders may be converted from the currency to be paid in the foreign tender offer(s) to U.S. dollars at an exchange rate disclosed in the U.S. offering documents;

(iii) The procedural terms of the U.S. tender offer are at least as favorable as the terms of the foreign tender offer(s);

(iv) The intention of the offeror to make purchases pursuant to the foreign tender offer(s) is disclosed in the U.S. offering documents; and

(v) Purchases by the offeror in the foreign tender offer(s) are made solely pursuant to the foreign tender offer(s) and not pursuant to an open market transaction(s), a private transaction(s), or other transaction(s); and

(12) *Purchases or arrangements to purchase by an affiliate of the financial advisor and an offeror and its affiliates.*

(i) Purchases or arrangements to purchase by an affiliate of a financial advisor and an offeror and its affiliates that are permissible under and will be conducted in accordance with the applicable laws of the subject company's home jurisdiction, if the following conditions are satisfied:

(A) The subject company is a foreign private issuer as defined in § 240.3b-4(c);

(B) The covered person reasonably expects that the tender offer meets the conditions for reliance on the Tier II cross-border exemptions set forth in § 240.14d-1(d);

(C) No purchases or arrangements to purchase otherwise than pursuant to the tender offer are made in the United States;

(D) The United States offering materials disclose prominently the possibility of, or the intention to make, purchases or arrangements to purchase subject securities or related securities outside of the tender offer, and if there will be public disclosure of purchases of subject or related securities, the manner in which information regarding such purchases will be disseminated;

(E) There is public disclosure in the United States, to the extent that such information is made public in the subject company's home jurisdiction, of information regarding all purchases of subject securities and related securities otherwise than pursuant to the tender offer from the time of public announcement of the tender offer until the tender offer expires;

(F) Purchases or arrangements to purchase by an offeror and its affiliates must satisfy the following additional condition: the tender offer price will be increased to match any consideration paid outside of the tender offer that is greater than the tender offer price; and

(G) Purchases or arrangements to purchase by an affiliate of a financial advisor must satisfy the following additional conditions:

(*1*) The financial advisor and the affiliate maintain and enforce written policies and procedures reasonably designed to prevent the transfer of information among the financial advisor and affiliate that might result in a violation of U.S. federal securities laws and regulations through the establishment of information barriers;

(*2*) The financial advisor has an affiliate that is registered as a broker or dealer under section 15(a) of the Act (15 U.S.C. 78o(a));

(*3*) The affiliate has no officers (or persons performing similar functions) or employees (other than clerical, ministerial, or support personnel) in common with the financial advisor that direct, effect, or recommend transactions in the subject securities or related securities who also will be involved in providing the offeror or subject company with financial advisory services or dealer-manager services; and

(*4*) The purchases or arrangements to purchase are not made to facilitate the tender offer.

(ii) Reserved.

(c) *Definitions.* For purposes of this section, the term:

(1) *Affiliate* has the same meaning as in § 240.12b-2;

(2) *Agent independent of the issuer* has the same meaning as in § 242.100(b) of this chapter;

(3) *Covered person* means:

(i) The offeror and its affiliates;

(ii) The offeror's dealer-manager and its affiliates;

(iii) Any advisor to any of the persons specified in paragraph (c)(3)(i) and (ii) of this section, whose compensation is dependent on the completion of the offer; and

(iv) Any person acting, directly or indirectly, in concert with any of the persons specified in this paragraph (c)(3) in connection with any purchase or arrangement to purchase any subject securities or any related securities;

(4) *Plan* has the same meaning as in § 242.100(b) of this chapter;

(5) *Public announcement* is any oral or written communication by the offeror or any person authorized to act on the offeror's behalf that is reasonably designed to, or has the effect of, informing the public or security holders in general about the tender offer;

(6) *Related securities* means securities that are immediately convertible into, exchangeable for, or exercisable for subject securities; and

(7) *Subject securities* has the same meaning as in § 229.1000 of this chapter; and

(8) *Subject company* has the same meaning as in § 229.1000 of this chapter; and

(9) *Home jurisdiction* has the same meaning as in the Instructions to paragraphs (c) and (d) of § 240.14d-1.

(d) *Exemptive authority.* Upon written application or upon its own motion, the Commission may grant an exemption from the provisions of this section, either unconditionally or on specified terms or conditions, to any transaction or class of transactions or any security or class of security, or any person or class of persons.

[As last amended by Release No. 33-8957, effective December 8, 2008, 73 F.R. 60049.]

[¶ 40,818] Repurchase Offers by Certain Closed-End Registered Investment Companies

Reg. § 240.14e-6. Sections 240.14e-1 and 240.14e-2 shall not apply to any offer by a closed-end management investment company to repurchase equity securities of which it is the issuer pursuant to § 270.23c-3 of this chapter.

[As adopted in Release No. 34-32116, April 7, 1993, effective May 14, 1993, 58 F.R. 19330.]

[¶ 40,819] Unlawful Tender Offer Practices in Connection With Roll-Ups

Reg. § 240.14e-7. In order to implement Section 14(h) of the Act (15 U.S.C. 78n(h)):

(a)(1) It shall be unlawful for any person to receive compensation for soliciting tenders directly from security holders in connection with a roll-up transaction as provided in paragraph (a)(2) of this section, if the compensation is:

(i) Based on whether the solicited person participates in the tender offer; or

(ii) Contingent on the success of the tender offer.

(2) Paragraph (a)(1) of this section is applicable to a roll-up transaction as defined in Item 901(c) of Regulation S-K (§ 229.901(c) of this chapter), structured as a tender offer, except for a transaction involving only:

(i) Finite-life entities that are not limited partnerships;

(ii) Partnerships whose investors will receive new securities or securities in another entity that are not reported under a transaction reporting plan declared effective before December 17, 1993 by the Commission under Section 11A of the Act (15 U.S.C. 78k-1); or

(iii) Partnerships whose investors' securities are reported under a transaction reporting plan declared effective before December 17, 1993 by the Commission under Section 11A of the Act (15 U.S.C. 78k-1).

(b)(1) It shall be unlawful for any finite-life entity that is the subject of a roll-up transaction as provided in paragraph (b)(2) of this section to fail to provide a security holder list or mail communications related to a tender offer that is in furtherance of the roll-up transaction, at the option of a requesting security holder, pursuant to the procedures set forth in § 240.14a-7.

(2) Paragraph (b)(1) of this section is applicable to a roll-up transaction as defined in Item 901(c) of Regulation S-K (§ 229.901(c) of this chapter), structured as a tender offer, that involves:

(i) An entity with securities registered pursuant to Section 12 of the Act (15 U.S.C. 78*l*); or

(ii) A limited partnership, unless the transaction involves only:

(A) Partnerships whose investors will receive new securities or securities in another entity that are not reported under a transaction reporting plan declared effective before December 17, 1993 by the Commission under Section 11A of the Act (15 U.S.C. 78k-1); or

(B) Partnerships whose investors' securities are reported under a transaction reporting plan declared effective before December 17, 1993 by the Commission under Section 11A of the Act (15 U.S.C. 78k-1).

[As adopted in Release No. 34-35036, December 1, 1994, 59 F.R. 63676.]

[¶ 40,820] Prohibited Conduct in Connection with Pre-Commencement Communications

Reg. § 240.14e-8. It is a fraudulent, deceptive or manipulative act or practice within the meaning of section 14(e) of the Act (15 U.S.C. 78n) for any person to publicly announce that the person (or a party on whose behalf the person is acting) plans to make a tender offer that has not yet been commenced, if the person:

(a) Is making the announcement of a potential tender offer without the intention to commence the offer within a reasonable time and complete the offer;

(b) Intends, directly or indirectly, for the announcement to manipulate the market price of the stock of the bidder or subject company; or

(c) Does not have the reasonable belief that the person will have the means to purchase securities to complete the offer.

[As adopted in Release No. 33-7760, effective January 24, 2000, 64 F.R. 61408.]

[¶ 40,821] Change in Majority of Directors

Reg. § 240.14f-1. If, pursuant to any arrangement or understanding with the person or persons acquiring securities in a transaction subject to section 13(d) or 14(d) of the Act, any persons are to be elected or designated as directors of the issuer, otherwise than at a meeting of security holders, and the persons so elected or designated will constitute a majority of the directors of the issuer, then, not less than 10 days prior to the date any such person take office as a director, or such shorter period prior to that date as the Commission may authorize upon a showing of good cause therefor, the issuer shall file with the Commission and transmit to all holders of record of securities of the issuer who would be entitled to vote at a meeting for election of directors, information substantially equivalent to the information which would be required by Items 6(a), (d) and (e), 7 and 8 of Schedule 14A of Regulation 14A (§ 240.14a-101 of this chapter) to be transmitted if such person or persons were nominees for election as directors at a meeting of such security holders.

Eight copies of such information shall be filed with the Commission.

[As last amended in Release No. 34-23789, November 10, 1986, 51 F.R. 42048.]

REGULATION 14N—FILINGS REQUIRED BY CERTAIN NOMINATING SHAREHOLDERS

⟫⟫→ CCH Note: The SEC has stayed the effectiveness of proxy rule amendments adopted in Release 33-9136 pending resolution of a challenge filed by the Business Roundtable and the U.S. Chamber of Commerce in the U.S. Court of Appeals for the District of Columbia Circuit. See Release No. 33-9149, October 4, 2010.

[¶ 40,901] Filing of Schedule 14N

Reg. § 240.14n-1. (a) A shareholder or group of shareholders that submits a nominee or nominees in accordance with § 240.14a-11 or a procedure set forth under applicable state or foreign law, or a registrant's governing documents providing for the inclusion of shareholder director nominees in the registrant's proxy materials shall file with the Commission a statement containing the information required by Schedule 14N (§ 240.14n-101) and simultaneously provide the notice on Schedule 14N to the registrant.

(b)(1) Whenever two or more persons are required to file a statement containing the information required by Schedule 14N (§ 240.14n-101), only one statement need be filed. The statement must identify all such persons, contain the required information with regard to each such person, indicate that the statement is filed on behalf of all such persons, and include, as an appendix, their agreement in writing that the statement is filed on behalf of each of them. Each person on whose behalf the statement is filed is responsible for the timely filing of that statement and any amendments thereto, and for the completeness and accuracy of the information concerning such person contained therein; such person is not responsible for the completeness or accuracy of the information concerning the other persons making the filing.

(2) If the group's members elect to make their own filings, each filing should identify all members of the group but the information provided concerning the other persons making the filing need only reflect information which the filing person knows or has reason to know.

[As added in Release No. 33-9136, effective November 15, 2010, 75 F.R. 56668.]

⟫⟫→ CCH Note: The SEC has stayed the effectiveness of proxy rule amendments adopted in Release 33-9136 pending resolution of a challenge filed by the Business Roundtable and the U.S. Chamber of Commerce in the U.S. Court of Appeals for the District of Columbia Circuit. See Release No. 33-9149, October 4, 2010.

[¶ 40,903] Filing of amendments to Schedule 14N

Reg. § 240.14n-2. (a) If any material change occurs with respect to the nomination, or in the disclosure or certifications set forth in the Schedule 14N (§ 240.14n-101) required by § 240.14n-1(a), the person or persons who were required to file the statement shall promptly file or cause to be filed with the Commission an amendment disclosing that change.

(b) An amendment shall be filed within 10 calendar days of the final results of the election being announced by the registrant stating the nominating shareholder's or the nominating shareholder group's intention with regard to continued ownership of their shares.

[As added in Release No. 33-9136, effective November 15, 2010, 75 F.R. 56668.]

⟫⟫→ CCH Note: The SEC has stayed the effectiveness of proxy rule amendments adopted in Release 33-9136 pending resolution of a challenge filed by the Business Roundtable and the U.S. Chamber of Commerce in the U.S. Court of Appeals for the District of Columbia Circuit. See Release No. 33-9149, October 4, 2010.

[¶ 40,905] Dissemination

Reg. § 240.14n-3. One copy of Schedule 14N (§ 240.14n-101) filed pursuant to §§ 240.14n-1 and 240.14n2 shall be mailed by registered or certified mail or electronically transmitted to the registrant at its principal executive office. Three copies of the material must at the same time be filed with, or mailed for filing to, each national securities exchange upon which any class of securities of the registrant is listed and registered.

[As added in Release No. 33-9136, effective November 15, 2010, 75 F.R. 56668.]

≫→ *CCH Note: The SEC has stayed the effectiveness of proxy rule amendments adopted in Release 33-9136 pending resolution of a challenge filed by the Business Roundtable and the U.S. Chamber of Commerce in the U.S. Court of Appeals for the District of Columbia Circuit. See Release No. 33-9149, October 4, 2010.*

[¶ 40,910] Reg. § 240.14n-101. Schedule 14N

SCHEDULE 14N: Information to Be Included in Statements Filed pursuant to § 240.14n-1 and Amendments thereto Filed Pursuant to § 240.14n-2

Securities and Exchange Commission, Washington, D.C. 20549

(Amendment No._)

_____

(Name of Issuer)

_____

(Title of Class of Securities)

_____

(CUSIP Number)

_____

[ ] Solicitation pursuant to § 240.14a-2(b)(7)

[ ] Solicitation pursuant to § 240.14a-2(b)(8)

[ ] Notice of Submission of a Nominee or Nominees in Accordance with § 240.14a-11

[ ] Notice of Submission of a Nominee or Nominees in Accordance with Procedures Set Forth Under Applicable State or Foreign Law, or the Registrant's Governing Documents

*The remainder of this cover page shall be filled out for a reporting person's initial filing on this form, and for any subsequent amendment containing information which would alter the disclosures provided in a prior cover page.

The information required in the remainder of this cover page shall not be deemed to be "filed" for the purpose of Section 18 of the Securities Exchange Act of 1934 ("Act") or otherwise subject to the liabilities of that section of the Act but shall be subject to all other provisions of the Act.

(1) Names of reporting persons: _____

(2) Mailing address and phone number of each reporting person (or, where applicable, the authorized representative): _____

(3) Amount of securities held that are entitled to be voted on the election of directors held by each reporting person (and, where applicable, amount of securities held in the aggregate by the nominating shareholder group), but including loaned securities and net of securities sold short or borrowed for purposes other than a short sale: _____

(4) Number of votes attributable to the securities entitled to be voted on the election of directors represented by amount in Row (3) (and, where applicable, aggregate number of votes attributable to the securities entitled to be voted on the election of directors held by group):

_____

Instructions for Cover Page:

(1) *Names of Reporting Persons* - Furnish the full legal name of each person for whom the report is filed - *i.e.*, each person required to sign the schedule itself - including each member of a group. Do not include the name of a person required to be identified in the report but who is not a reporting person.

(3) and (4) *Amount Held by Each Reporting Person* -Rows (3) and (4) are to be completed in accordance with the provisions of Item 3 of Schedule 14N.

Notes: Attach as many copies of parts one through three of the cover page as are needed, one reporting person per copy.

Filing persons may, in order to avoid unnecessary duplication, answer items on Schedule 14N by appropriate cross references to an item or items on the cover page(s). This approach may only be used where the cover page item or items provide all the disclosure required by the schedule item. Moreover, such a use of a cover page item will result in the item becoming a part of the schedule and accordingly being considered as "filed" for purposes of Section 18 of the Act or otherwise subject to the liabilities of that section of the Act.

SPECIAL INSTRUCTIONS FOR COMPLYING WITH SCHEDULE 14N

Under Sections 14 and 23 of the Securities Exchange Act of 1934 and the rules and regulations thereunder, the Commission is authorized to solicit the information required to be supplied by this Schedule. The information will be used for the primary purpose of determining and disclosing the holdings and interests of a nominating shareholder or nominating shareholder group. This statement will be made a matter of public record. Therefore, any information given will be available for inspection by any member of the public.

Because of the public nature of the information, the Commission can use it for a variety of purposes, including referral to other governmental authorities or securities self-regulatory organizations for investigatory purposes or in connection with litigation involving the Federal securities laws or other civil, criminal or regulatory statutes or provisions. Failure to disclose the information requested by this schedule may result in civil or criminal action against the persons involved for violation of the Federal securities laws and rules promulgated thereunder, or in some cases, exclusion of the nominee from the registrant's proxy materials.

General instructions to item requirements.

The item numbers and captions of the items shall be included but the text of the items is to be omitted. The answers to the items shall be prepared so as to indicate clearly the coverage of the items without referring to the text of the items. Answer every item. If an item is inapplicable or the answer is in the negative, so state.

Item 1(a). Name of registrant

Item 1(b). Address of registrant's principal executive offices

Item 2(a). Name of person filing

Item 2(b). Address or principal business office or, if none, residence

Item 2(c). Title of class of securities

Item 2(d). CUSIP No.

Item 3. Ownership

Provide the following information, in accordance with Instruction 3 to § 240.14a11(b)(1):

(a) Amount of securities held and entitled to be voted on the election of directors (and, where applicable, amount of securities held in the aggregate by the nominating shareholder group): _____.

(b) The number of votes attributable to the securities referred to in paragraph (a) of this Item: _____.

(c) The number of votes attributable to securities that have been loaned but which the reporting person:

(i) has the right to recall; and

(ii) will recall upon being notified that any of the nominees will be included in the registrant's proxy statement and proxy card: _____.

(d) The number of votes attributable to securities that have been sold in a short sale that is not closed out, or that have been borrowed for purposes other than a short sale: _____.

(e) The sum of paragraphs (b) and (c), minus paragraph (d) of this Item, divided by the aggregate number of votes derived from all classes of securities of the registrant that are entitled to vote on the election of directors, and expressed as a percentage: _____.

Item 4. Statement of Ownership from a Nominating Shareholder or Each Member of a Nominating Shareholder Group Submitting this Notice Pursuant to § 240.14a-11

(a) If the nominating shareholder, or each member of the nominating shareholder group, is the registered holder of the shares, please so state. Otherwise, attach to the Schedule 14N one or more written statements from the persons (usually brokers or banks) through which the nominating share-holder's securities are held, verifying that, within seven calendar days prior to filing the shareholder notice on Schedule 14N with the Commission and transmitting the notice to the registrant, the nominating shareholder continuously held the amount of securities being used to satisfy the ownership threshold for a period of at least three years. In the alternative, if the nominating shareholder has filed a Schedule 13D (§ 240.13d-101), Schedule 13G (§ 240.13d102), Form 3 (§ 249.103 of this chapter), Form 4 (§ 249.104 of this chapter), and/or Form 5 (§ 249.105 of this chapter), or amendments to those documents, reflecting ownership of the securities as of or before the date on which the three-year eligibility period begins, so state and incorporate that filing or amendment by reference.

(b) Provide a written statement that the nominating shareholder, or each member of the nominat-ing shareholder group, intends to continue to hold the amount of securities that are used for purposes of satisfying the minimum ownership requirement of § 240.14a-11(b)(1) through the date of the meeting of shareholders, as required by § 240.14a-11(b)(4). Additionally, provide a written statement from the nominating shareholder or each member of the nominating shareholder group regarding the nominat-ing shareholder's or nominating shareholder group member's intent with respect to continued owner-ship after the election of directors, as required by § 240.14a-11(b)(5).

Instruction to Item 4. If the nominating shareholder or any member of the nominating shareholder group is not the registered holder of the securities and is not proving ownership for purposes of §

240.14a-11(b)(3) by providing previously filed Schedules 13D or 13G or Forms 3, 4, or 5, and the securities are held in an account with a broker or bank that is a participant in the Depository Trust Company ("DTC") or other clearing agency acting as a securities depository, a written statement or statements from that participant or participants in the following form will satisfy § 240.14a-11(b)(3):

As of [date of this statement], [name of nominating shareholder or member of the nominating shareholder group] held at least [number of securities owned continuously for at least three years] of the [registrant's] [class of securities], and has held at least this amount of such securities continuously for [at least three years]. [Name of clearing agency participant] is a participant in [name of clearing agency] whose nominee name is [nominee name].

[name of clearing agency participant]

By: [name and title of representative]

Date:_____

If the securities are held through a broker or bank (*e.g.* in an omnibus account) that is not a participant in a clearing agency acting as a securities depository, the nominating shareholder or member of the nominating shareholder group must (a) obtain and submit a written statement or statements (the "initial broker statement") from the broker or bank with which the nominating shareholder or member of the nominating shareholder group maintains an account that provides the information about securities ownership set forth above and (b) obtain and submit a separate written statement from the clearing agency participant through which the securities of the nominating shareholder or member of the nominating shareholder group are held, that (i) identifies the broker or bank for whom the clearing agency participant holds the securities, and (ii) states that the account of such broker or bank has held, as of the date of the separate written statement, at least the number of securities specified in the initial broker statement, and (iii) states that this account has held at least that amount of securities continuously for at least three years.

If the securities have been held for less than three years at the relevant entity, provide written statements covering a continuous period of three years and modify the language set forth above as appropriate.

For purposes of complying with § 240.14a-11(b)(3), loaned securities may be included in the amount of securities set forth in the written statements.

Item 5. Disclosure Required for Shareholder Nominations Submitted Pursuant to § 240.14a-11

If a nominating shareholder or nominating shareholder group is submitting this notice in connection with the inclusion of a shareholder nominee or nominees for director in the registrant's proxy materials pursuant to § 240.14a-11, provide the following information:

(a) A statement that the nominee consents to be named in the registrant's proxy statement and form of proxy and, if elected, to serve on the registrant's board of directors;

(b) Disclosure about the nominee as would be provided in response to the disclosure requirements of Items 4(b), 5(b), 7(a), (b) and (c) and, for investment companies, Item 22(b) of Schedule 14A (§ 240.14a-101), as applicable;

(c) Disclosure about the nominating shareholder or each member of a nominating shareholder group as would be required of a participant in response to the disclosure requirements of Items 4(b) and 5(b) of Schedule 14A (§ 240.14a-101), as applicable;

(d) Disclosure about whether the nominating shareholder or any member of a nominating shareholder group has been involved in any legal proceeding during the past ten years, as specified in Item 401(f) of Regulation S-K (§ 229.10 of this chapter). Disclosure pursuant to this paragraph need not be provided if provided in response to Item 5(c) of this section;

Instruction 1 to Item 5 (c) and (d). Where the nominating shareholder is a general or limited partnership, syndicate or other group, the information called for in paragraphs (c) and (d) of this Item must be given with respect to:

a. Each partner of the general partnership;

b. Each partner who is, or functions as, a general partner of the limited partnership;

c. Each member of the syndicate or group; and

d. Each person controlling the partner or member.

Instruction 2 to Item 5 (c) and (d). If the nominating shareholder is a corporation or if a person referred to in a., b., c. or d. of Instruction 1 to paragraphs (c) and (d) of this Item is a corporation, the information called for in paragraphs (c) and (d) of this Item must be given with respect to:

a. Each executive officer and director of the corporation;

b. Each person controlling the corporation; and

c. Each executive officer and director of any corporation or other person ultimately in control of the corporation.

(e) Disclosure about whether, to the best of the nominating shareholder's or group's knowledge, the nominee meets the director qualifications, if any, set forth in the registrant's governing documents;

(f) A statement that, to the best of the nominating shareholder's or group's knowledge, in the case of a registrant other than an investment company, the nominee meets the objective criteria for "independence" of the national securities exchange or national securities association rules applicable to the registrant, if any, or, in the case of a registrant that is an investment company, the nominee is not an "interested person" of the registrant as defined in section 2(a)(19) of the Investment Company Act of 1940 (15 U.S.C. 80a-2(a)(19)).

Instruction to Item 5(f). For this purpose, the nominee would be required to meet the definition of "independence" that is generally applicable to directors of the registrant and not any particular definition of independence applicable to members of the audit committee of the registrant's board of directors. To the extent a national securities exchange or national securities association rule imposes a standard regarding independence that requires a subjective determination by the board or a group or committee of the board (for example, requiring that the board of directors or any group or committee of the board of directors make a determination regarding the existence of factors material to a determination of a nominee's independence), the nominee would not be required to meet the subjective determination of independence as part of the shareholder nomination process.

(g) The following information regarding the nature and extent of the relationships between the nominating shareholder or nominating shareholder group, the nominee, and/or the registrant or any affiliate of the registrant:

(1) Any direct or indirect material interest in any contract or agreement between the nominating shareholder or any member of the nominating shareholder group, the nominee, and/or the registrant or any affiliate of the registrant (including any employment agreement, collective bargaining agreement, or consulting agreement);

(2) Any material pending or threatened legal proceeding in which the nominating shareholder or any member of the nominating shareholder group and/or the nominee is a party or a material participant, and that involves the registrant, any of its executive officers or directors, or any affiliate of the registrant; and

(3) Any other material relationship between the nominating shareholder or any member of the nominating shareholder group, the nominee, and/or the registrant or any affiliate of the registrant not otherwise disclosed;

Note to Item 5(g)(3). Any other material relationship of the nominating shareholder or any member of the nominating shareholder group or nominee with the registrant or any affiliate of the registrant may include, but is not limited to, whether the nominating shareholder or any member of the nominating shareholder group currently has, or has had in the past, an employment relationship with the registrant or any affiliate of the registrant (including consulting arrangements).

(h) The Web site address on which the nominating shareholder or nominating shareholder group may publish soliciting materials, if any; and

(i) Any statement in support of the shareholder nominee or nominees, which may not exceed 500 words for each nominee, if the nominating shareholder or nominating shareholder group elects to have such statement included in the registrant's proxy materials.

Item 6. Disclosure Required by § 240.14a-18

If a nominating shareholder or nominating shareholder group is submitting this notice in connection with the inclusion of a shareholder nominee or nominees for director in the registrant's proxy materials pursuant to a procedure set forth under applicable state or foreign law, or the registrant's governing documents provide the following disclosure:

(a) A statement that the nominee consents to be named in the registrant's proxy statement and form of proxy and, if elected, to serve on the registrant's board of directors;

(b) Disclosure about the nominee as would be provided in response to the disclosure requirements of Items 4(b), 5(b), 7(a), (b) and (c) and, for investment companies, Item 22(b) of Schedule 14A (§ 240.14a-101), as applicable;

(c) Disclosure about the nominating shareholder or each member of a nominating shareholder group as would be required in response to the disclosure requirements of Items 4(b) and 5(b) of Schedule 14A (§ 240.14a-101), as applicable;

(d) Disclosure about whether the nominating shareholder or any member of a nominating shareholder group has been involved in any legal proceeding during the past ten years, as specified in Item 401(f) of Regulation S-K (§ 229.10 of this chapter). Disclosure pursuant to this paragraph need not be provided if provided in response to Item 6(c) of this section;

Instruction 1 to Item 6(c) and (d). Where the nominating shareholder is a general or limited partnership, syndicate or other group, the information called for in paragraphs (c) and (d) of this Item must be given with respect to:

   a. Each partner of the general partnership;

   b. Each partner who is, or functions as, a general partner of the limited partnership;

   c. Each member of the syndicate or group; and

   d. Each person controlling the partner or member.

Instruction 2 to Item 6(c) and (d). If the nominating shareholder is a corporation or if a person referred to in a., b., c. or d. of Instruction 1 to paragraphs (c) and (d) of this Item is a corporation, the information called for in paragraphs (c) and (d) of this Item must be given with respect to:

   a. Each executive officer and director of the corporation;

   b. Each person controlling the corporation; and

   c. Each executive officer and director of any corporation or other person ultimately in control of the corporation.

(e) The following information regarding the nature and extent of the relationships between the nominating shareholder or nominating shareholder group, the nominee, and/or the registrant or any affiliate of the registrant:

(1) Any direct or indirect material interest in any contract or agreement between the nominating shareholder or any member of the nominating shareholder group, the nominee, and/or the registrant or any affiliate of the registrant (including any employment agreement, collective bargaining agreement, or consulting agreement);

(2) Any material pending or threatened legal proceeding in which the nominating shareholder or any member of the nominating shareholder group and/or nominee is a party or a material participant, involving the registrant, any of its executive officers or directors, or any affiliate of the registrant; and

(3) Any other material relationship between the nominating shareholder or any member of the nominating shareholder group, the nominee, and/or the registrant or any affiliate of the registrant not otherwise disclosed; and

Instruction to Item 6(e)(3). Any other material relationship of the nominating shareholder or any member of the nominating shareholder group with the registrant or any affiliate of the registrant may include, but is not limited to, whether the nominating shareholder or any member of the nominating shareholder group currently has, or has had in the past, an employment relationship with the registrant or any affiliate of the registrant (including consulting arrangements).

(f) The Web site address on which the nominating shareholder or nominating shareholder group may publish soliciting materials, if any.

Item 7. Notice of Dissolution of Group or Termination of Shareholder Nomination

Notice of dissolution of a nominating shareholder group or the termination of a shareholder nomination shall state the date of the dissolution or termination.

Item 8. Signatures

(a) The following certifications shall be provided by the filing person submitting this notice pursuant to § 240.14a-11, or in the case of a group, each filing person whose securities are being aggregated for purposes of meeting the ownership threshold set out in § 240.14a-11(b)(1) exactly as set forth below:

I, [identify the certifying individual], after reasonable inquiry and to the best of my knowledge and belief, certify that:

(1) I [or if signed by an authorized representative, the name of the nominating shareholder or each member of the nominating shareholder group, as appropriate] am [is] not holding any of the registrant's securities with the purpose, or with the effect, of changing control of the registrant or to gain a number of seats on the board of directors that exceeds the maximum number of nominees that the registrant could be required to include under § 240.14a-11(d);

(2) I [or if signed by an authorized representative, the name of the nominating shareholder or each member of the nominating shareholder group, as appropriate] otherwise satisfy [satisfies] the requirements of § 240.14a-11(b), as applicable;

(3) The nominee or nominees satisfies the requirements of § 240.14a-11(b), as applicable; and

(4) The information set forth in this notice on Schedule 14N is true, complete and correct.

(b) The following certification shall be provided by the filing person or persons submitting this notice in connection with the submission of a nominee or nominees in accordance with procedures set forth under applicable state or foreign law or the registrant's governing documents:

I, [identify the certifying individual], after reasonable inquiry and to the best of my knowledge and belief, certify that the information set forth in this notice on Schedule 14N is true, complete and correct.

Dated: _____

Signature: _____

Name/Title: _____

The original statement shall be signed by each person on whose behalf the statement is filed or his authorized representative. If the statement is signed on behalf of a person by his authorized representative other than an executive officer or general partner of the filing person, evidence of the representative's authority to sign on behalf of such person shall be filed with the statement, *provided, however*, that a power of attorney for this purpose which is already on file with the Commission may be incorporated by reference. The name and any title of each person who signs the statement shall be typed or printed beneath his signature.

Attention: Intentional misstatements or omissions of fact constitute Federal criminal violations (see 18 U.S.C. 1001).

[As added in Release No. 33-9136, effective November 15, 2010, 75 F.R. 56668.]

STAFF LEGAL BULLETINS (SELECTED)

STAFF LEGAL BULLETINS (SELECTED)

STAFF LEGAL BULLETINS

RELEASES

[¶ 43,001]   Staff Legal Bulletin No. 1A (CF)

"Confidential Treatment Requests"

Action: Publication of CF Staff Legal Bulletin

Date: February 28, 1997 (*Addendum included: July 11, 2001*)

Summary: This staff legal bulletin sets forth views of the Division of Corporation Finance ("Division") regarding the requirements a registrant must satisfy when requesting confidential treatment of information that otherwise is required to be disclosed in registration statements, periodic reports and other documents filed with the Securities and Exchange Commission ("Commission"). The procedures are contained in Rule 406 under the Securities Act of 1933 and Rule 24b-2 under the Securities Exchange Act of 1934.

Supplementary Information: The statements in this legal bulletin represent the views of the staff of the Division of Corporation Finance. This bulletin is not a rule, regulation or statement of the Securities and Exchange Commission. Further, the Commission has neither approved nor disapproved its content.

Contact Person: For further information, please contact L. Jacob Fien-Helfman, Special Counsel at (202) 942-2997; the Special Counsel of the office in the Division to which the company is assigned; or, for small business issuers, the Special Counsel in the Office of Small Business.

I. Background

In recent years, the number of confidential treatment requests ("CTRs" or "applications") processed by the Division has increased steadily from approximately 540 in fiscal year 1992 to more than 1,000 in fiscal year 1996. Applications as initially filed often lack the information and analysis necessary for the staff to evaluate compliance with the requirements of the rules. Consequently, the staff frequently issues deficiency letters which require the applicant to amend its application. Often the applicant also must amend the filing covered by the application.

This legal bulletin provides guidance on the substantive and procedural requirements contained in

Rule 406[1] under the Securities Act of 1933 ("Securities Act")[2] and Rule 24b-2[3] under the Securities Exchange Act of 1934 ("Exchange Act").[4] The bulletin also suggests procedures that, while not required, would facilitate the staff's processing of CTRs. This guidance should help issuers prepare complete confidential treatment applications and thereby reduce the time and costs incurred by issuers and the Division in processing confidential treatment applications.

Failure to comply with either the substantive or procedural aspects of the Commission's confidential treatment process may result in a denial of an application. In this regard, the Commission has delegated authority to the Division to grant and deny requests for confidential treatment.[5]

II. Substantive and Procedural Requirements

A. General Discussion

The federal securities laws generally require any company that is publicly held or that is registering its securities for public sale to disclose a broad range of financial and non-financial information in registration statements, annual reports and other filings made with the Commission. The disclosure requirements for financial and non-financial information primarily are found in Regulation S-K and, for small business issuers, Regulation SB.[6] Regulation S-X sets forth the financial statement disclosure requirements.[7]

Sometimes disclosure of information required by the regulations can adversely affect a company's business and financial condition because of the competitive harm that could result from the disclosure. This issue frequently arises in connection with the requirement that a registrant file publicly all contracts material to its business other than those it enters into in the ordinary course of business.[8] Typical examples of the information that raises this concern include pricing terms, technical specifications and milestone payments. To address the potential disclosure hardship, the Commission has a system allowing companies to request confidential treatment of information filed under the Securities Act and the Exchange Act.

---

[1] 17 CFR 230.406.

[2] 15 U.S.C. 77a et seq.

[3] 17 CFR 24b-2.

[4] 15 U.S.C. 78a et seq.

[5] See 17 CFR 200.30-1(a)(3) and 17 CFR 200.30-1(f)(3).

[6] See 17 CFR 229.10 et seq. and 17 CFR 228.10 et seq. For purposes of this staff legal bulletin, references to specific item of Regulation S-K also pertain to analogous provisions of Regulation S-B.

[7] 17 CFR 210.1-01 et seq.

[8] See Item 601(b)(10) of Regulation S-K [17 CFR 29.601(b)(10)]. Item 601(b)(10) requires that: Every contract not made in the ordinary course of business which is material to the registrant and is to be performed in whole or in part at or after the filing of the registration statement or report or was entered into not more than two years before such filing.

While Rule 406 under the Securities Act of 1933, in particular, appears to contemplate confidential treatment for portions of filed documents, this Bulletin will address requests made with respect to exhibits to filings only. Issuers requesting confidential treatment with respect to other portions of filings should bring such requests to the attention of the staff before public filing.

Specifically, Rules 406 and 24b-2 set forth the exclusive means for obtaining confidential treatment of information contained in a document filed under the Securities Act and under the Exchange Act, respectively,[9] that would be exempt from disclosure under the Freedom of Information Act ("FOIA").[10]

The rules incorporate the criteria for non-disclosure set forth in FOIA and the Commission's FOIA rules.[11] FOIA requires all federal agencies to make specified information available to the public, including the information required to be filed publicly by Commission rules. FOIA contains, however, nine specific exemptions.[12] The rules require that CTRs contain an analysis of the applicable FOIA exemption. Most applicants rely on the exemption that covers "trade secrets and commercial or financial information obtained from a person and privileged or confidential" which is commonly referred to as "the (b)(4) exemption."[13]

B. Substantive Requirements: General

1. Confidential treatment cannot be granted if the information is publicly disclosed

The applicant must make every effort not to disclose any of the confidential information. For example, the applicant should safeguard carefully copies of agreements and restrict access to only those who have a need to know the information or who are under a duty to keep the information confidential. The application must include an affirmative representation as to the confidentiality of the information it covers.

Based on the staff's experience, there are a few common mistakes that result in the inadvertent disclosure of the information that is the subject of the application.[14] The following points illustrate typical mistakes.

- For paper filings, the text can be read through the marking used to delete the information.

- For filings by the Commission's electronic filing system, EDGAR,[15] the applicant fails to remove all of the confidential information from the electronic version of the document.

- The applicant omits the information, such as pricing terms, from one part of the document, but not

from another part of that document or another document or report. Applicants should be aware that information may appear in more than one place in a document. For example, a section heading may appear in the table of contents of an agreement as well as in the agreement itself. In addition, preparers of applications should pay particular attention to the description of the business of the company, the financial statement footnotes and the Management's Discussion and Analysis of Financial Condition and Results of Operations section of disclosure documents.

- Another party to the agreement has disclosed (or intends to disclose) the information publicly.

- The company has included the information in a press release or news article or has provided the information to one or more analysts.

- The company has disclosed the information in documents filed publicly with other regulators, such as insurance, banking, utility or environmental regulators.

The staff understands, however, that an applicant may in a general manner inform the market about, for example, a newly negotiated contract. This may occur through various methods such as the issuance of a press release. General disclosure about a contract should not prevent an applicant from requesting confidential treatment of selected terms of the contract that remain undisclosed.

2. Required and/or material information must be disclosed, even if confidential

In some instances the Commission's specific disclosure requirements cover information that could be withheld under FOIA. Except in unusual circumstances, disclosure required by Regulation S-K or any other applicable disclosure requirement is not an appropriate subject for confidential treatment, regardless of the availability of an exemption under FOIA. This type of information includes, for example,

- the identity of a 10% customer;

- the dollar amount of firm backlog orders;

- interest expense and other similar terms in a material credit agreement;

---

[9] This staff legal bulletin is not intended to include an exhaustive discussion of all Commission rules relating to confidential treatment of information submitted to the Commission. For example, Rule 418 of Regulation C under the Securities Act of 1933 [17 CFR 230.418] and Rule 12b-4 under the Securities Exchange Act of 1934 [17 CFR 240.12b-4] cover specific types of supplemental information requested by the staff in processing registrant filings with the Commission. Rule 171 under the Securities Act [17 CFR 230.171] and Rule 0-6 under the Exchange Act [17 CFR 240.0-6] cover the disclosure of information detrimental to the national security of the United States. Public availability of no- action and interpretive letters is governed by Rule 81 under the Rules of Practice [17 CFR 200.81]. Confidential treatment of other information not required to be filed under either Act is covered by Rule 83 under the Rules of Practice [17 CFR 200.83]. Confidential treatment of the CTR and supplemental information provided to the

staff in connection with the processing of the CTR should be requested pursuant to Rule 83.

[10] 5 U.S.C. 552.

[11] 17 CFR 200.80 et seq.

[12] See 5 U.S.C. 552(b) for the list of information that is exempt from disclosure under FOIA.

[13] 5 U.S.C. 552(b)(4); 17 CFR 200.80(b)(4).

[14] Even if the disclosure is made in error, whether by the issuer or its agent, the staff will not attempt to edit a filed document and will not grant confidential treatment for any of the disclosed information. See Release No. 33-6977 (February 23, 1993) [58 FR 14628].

[15] Regulation S-T [17 CFR 232 et seq.] requires most filings made with the Commission to be made via the Electronic Data Gathering, Analysis, and Retrieval ("EDGAR") system.

• "... the duration and effect of all patents, trademarks, licenses, franchises and concessions held";[16]

• required disclosure in the Management's Discussion and Analysis of Financial Condition and Results of Operations section[17] relating for instance to loan arrangements and installment payment obligations on debt; and

• disclosure about related party transactions.[18]

In addition, confidential treatment is generally not appropriate for information that is material to investors. Depending on the facts and circumstances, examples of material information could include the name of a key supplier, material contingency clauses, indemnification clauses, anti-assignability clauses, take-or-pay clauses, and financial covenants in material financing or credit agreements. Materiality must be analyzed in the context of the issuer's business, financial condition and financial results. Where there is any question about the materiality of the information, the application must address the issue and provide factual support for the issuer's belief that the information is not material to investors.[19]

C. Substantive Requirements: Specific

In addition to complying with the general substantive requirements discussed above, an application for confidential treatment must comply with several more specific substantive requirements. In the staff's experience, however, applications often do not.

1. The application should not be overly broad

Applicants should be selective when identifying the information covered by their application. Frequently, applications are overly broad and attempt to cover information that is not confidential under FOIA and the Commission's confidential treatment system. The information covered by an application should include no more text than necessary to prevent competitive harm to the issuer. A CTR should cover only those words and phrases for which confidentiality is necessary and supported by FOIA and applicable Commission rules.

The staff will comment on applications that cover lengthy portions of agreements. Absent a satisfactory demonstration that such extensive omissions are appropriate under the Commission's confidential treatment rules, the CTR will be denied. For example, the omission of an entire section is not appropriate without an analysis that specifically addresses:

(i) why the disclosure of the existence of the section would be commercially harmful; and

(ii) why its disclosure is not necessary for the protection of investors.

2. Applicants must set forth their analysis of the exemption

The rules require that the application include a "statement of the grounds of the objection referring to and analyzing the applicable exemption(s) from disclosure under ... the Commission's rule adopted under [FOIA]."[20] Applicants should note that an agreement between the parties to keep information confidential does not itself provide adequate justification for confidential treatment. The Commission's confidential treatment system is premised on the disclosure requirements of the federal securities laws and FOIA, and does not contemplate non-disclosure based on a private contractual provision between the parties.

The application should avoid conclusory statements and must include a sufficient legal analysis, including case law references. Two seminal cases covering the definition of "confidential" information are National Parks and Conservation *Association v. Morton*, 498 F.2d 765 (D.C. Cir. 1974) and *National Parks and Conservation Association v. Kleppe*, 547 F.2d 673 (D.C. Cir. 1976).

The application also should include a factual analysis of the basis for the exemption requested (for example, commercial harm to the filing party) with respect to the specific information that is the subject of the request. Where the application relates to different types of information (for example, trade secrets and financial provisions), the application should address each type separately.

Finally, the application should describe anything about the issuer's business or the specific contract that would help the staff evaluate the sensitivity and importance of the information to the issuer.

3. Applicants must specify a particular duration

The application must request a specific date (year, month and day) for the termination of confidential treatment of the subject information. Further, the application must include an analysis that supports the period requested.[21] This analysis must be specific to the confidential information and to the company and its business. The application should tie the term to specific provisions of, anticipated performance under, or other facts related to, the contract from which the confidential information is omitted.

Confidential treatment beyond the minimum term of an agreement usually is inappropriate, as the value of the information typically is associated with the effective period of an agreement. Where continued confidential treatment after the term of the agreement is justified, the staff will consider applications to extend the period. This bulletin addresses applications for extension in Section III below ("Other Matters").

---

[16] See Item 101(c)(1)(iv) of Regulation S-K [17 CFR 229.101(c)(1)(iv)].

[17] See Item 303 of Regulation S-K [17 CFR 229.303].

[18] See Item 404 of Regulation S-K [17 CFR 229.404].

[19] See Rule 406(b)(2)(iii) [17 CFR 230.406(b)(2)(iii)].

[20] Rule 406(b)(2)(ii) [17 CFR 230.406(b)(2)(ii)]. Rule 24b-2(b)(2)(ii) [17 CF 240.24b-2(b)(2)(ii)]contains similar language.

[21] See Rule 406(b)(2)(ii) [CFR 230.406(b)(2)(ii)] and Rule 24b-2(b)(2)(ii) [240.24b-2(b)(2)(ii)].

4. Applicants must identify clearly the information that is the subject of the application

Applicants must identify clearly the information that is the subject of a request for confidential treatment. To make sure there is a complete record as to which information has been granted confidential treatment, the application should describe each item or category of information omitted pursuant to the CTR. The staff will question any inconsistencies between the material identified in the application and the material deleted from the public file.

5. Applicants must consent to the release of the information for official purposes

The application must include a written consent to the furnishing of the confidential portion "to other government agencies, offices or bodies and to the Congress."[22] Conditions to this consent—which have appeared most frequently when the applicant demands notification if the Commission releases the subject information to any of the institutions listed—are not consistent with the requirement of the rules. Applicants should recognize that in granting any order for confidential treatment pursuant to delegated authority, the staff of the Commission is not explicitly or implicitly agreeing to furnish notice other than as required under the applicable rules and regulations.

D. Procedural Requirements

1. Applicants must file the application with the Office of the Secretary

Applicants must send every application for confidential treatment to the Office of the Secretary in an envelope marked "confidential" which is separate from the envelope for any materials which are to be or have been filed publicly.[23] Applicants should send to the filing desk only documents that they mean to have on public file.

2. Applicants, including EDGAR filers, must file the application in paper form

Both rules require, in introductory notes, that applicants file CTRs in paper form, not by EDGAR, the electronic filing system.[24] This paper filing requirement applies regardless of whether the applicant files other documents electronically. Once an applicant files electronically by mistake information meant to be covered by a CTR, such information is immediately available to the public and is no longer confidential.[25]

3. Applicants should file the application at the same time they file the material from which they have omitted the confidential information

The confidential treatment process contemplates that issuers file CTRs at the same time that they file the publicly disclosed portions.[26] The staff will not process the application unless and until the material from which information is omitted has been filed publicly. There is only one exception to that general rule with respect to domestic registrants. In the case of joint proxy statements/prospectuses filed confidentially pursuant to Rule 14a-6(e)(2) of Regulation 14A, the registrant customarily files the wrap registration statement on Form S-4 only after the staff has completed its review of the non-public proxy statement/prospectus.[27] The staff must review the CTR on a preliminary basis at the same time it is reviewing the proxy statement/prospectus to avoid delays in the acceleration of effectiveness at the time the registrant files the Form S-4.

4. Applicants must omit from the public filings all of the information that is the subject of the application

As discussed above, the grant of confidential treatment is premised on the subject information being non-public. See Section II.B.1 of this bulletin. The release of the information by the issuer, even if inadvertent, precludes the grant of confidential treatment.

5. Applicants must adequately mark the confidential portions of publicly filed documents

The applicant must "indicate at the appropriate place in the material filed that the confidential portion has been so omitted and filed separately with the Commission."[28] An application will be considered incomplete unless the publicly-filed document has been marked to indicate both that the material has been omitted pursuant to a request for confidential treatment and that the material has been filed separately.

A recommended method of marking is to place an asterisk or other mark in the precise places in the document where the applicant deletes information. If the registrant uses this method of marking, it should key the mark to a legend which includes the required language on the page from which material is omitted and/or on the first page of the exhibit. In the unusual case where the confidential information consists of multiple pages, the publicly-filed document also must include an indication of the number of pages omitted pursuant to the CTR.

---

[22] Rule 406(b)(2)(iv) [17 CFR 230.406(b)(2)(iv)] and Rule 24b-2(b)(2)(iii) [17 CFR 240.24b-2(b)(2)(iii)].

[23] Rule 406(b)(3) [17 CFR 230.406(b)(3)] and Rule 24b-2(b)(3) [17 CFR 240.24b-2(b)(3)].

[24] In a release issued on December 6, 1996 (Release No. 33-7369) [61 FR 65440], the Commission solicited comment as to whether the EDGAR system should be enhanced to allow confidential treatment requests to be filed electronically.

[25] See note 14, supra.

[26] See Rule 406(b) [17 CFR 230.406(b)] and Rule 24b-2(b) [17 CFR 240.24b-2(b)]. As an accommodation to foreign private issuers, the Division developed an informal procedure whereby the staff will review and comment on draft registration statements. Typically, a foreign private issuer will formally file a CTR concurrently with its submission of its draft registration statement. This bulletin does not change the procedures applicable to foreign private issuers.

[27] 17 CFR 240.14a-6(e)(2).

[28] Rule 406(b) [17 CFR 230.406(b)] and Rule 24b-2(b) [17 CFR 240.24b-2(b)].

Finally, the applicant should mark the exhibit index to indicate that portions of the exhibit or exhibits have been omitted pursuant to a request for confidential treatment.

6. Applicants should show clearly which portions of the complete documents filed with the application are the subject of the CTR

The application must include one complete copy of the document clearly marked to show those portions of the document covered by the CTR. The applicant must submit the complete marked copy "in the same form as the remainder of the material filed."[29] The confidential segments should be underlined, highlighted, circled or otherwise clearly marked in that copy.

7. Applicants should indicate to whom correspondence, orders and notices should be sent

Rule 406(b)(2)(v) requires the application to include "the name, address and telephone number of the person to whom all notices and orders issued under [the] rule should be directed."[30] If an application filed pursuant to Rule 24b-2 does not specifically include this information, the service list for the order will include the person who prepared the application.

III. Other Matters

A. Requests for extension of previously granted orders for confidential treatment

An applicant requesting the extension of a previously granted order for confidential treatment should submit the application before the expiration date of the earlier order. After the expiration date of an order, the subject information is publicly available upon request under FOIA.

The request for extension (including the substantive supporting argument) must comply with the disclosure and confidential treatment rules at the time the applicant submits the extension request. The application should include a complete copy of the agreement or agreements, a copy of the original order, and copies of the original application and correspondence with the Commission, if available.

The substantive and procedural requirements discussed in this bulletin are equally applicable to any extension request. Therefore, the applicant should represent that (a) none of the confidential information has been disclosed, (b) disclosure of the information will cause substantial competitive harm to the issuer, and (c) disclosure of the confidential information is not necessary for protection of investors.

To the extent that the applicant cannot make these representations, the applicant should refile the agreement to disclose the information that no longer satisfies the requirements. The applicant should refile the agreement with the first filing it makes after the order expires. The extension application should include a request for confidential treatment of the information in the newly filed document as well as continuing confidential treatment for the document that the issuer filed earlier. The applicant should take care to cite the appropriate rule for each part of the application.

B. Timing of CTR Submission

1. Initial public offerings

The staff processes confidential treatment requests filed with initial public offerings pursuant to Rule 406 concurrently with the review of the registration statement. All issues must be resolved, and the CTR must be complete, before the acceleration of effectiveness of the registration statement. Issuers are advised to file the CTR at the time they initially file the registration statement, rather than waiting to file the agreements and the CTR with later amendments to the registration statement. See Section II.D.3. of this bulletin regarding the need to file the application and the agreements at the same time. In addition, because the issuer files the CTR and the registration statement separately, the staff may not be aware that a CTR has been filed at the time of the filing of the registration statement. The applicant should include a reference to the related application for confidential treatment in its cover letter to the registration statement.

2. Registered offerings by reporting companies

Regardless of whether the staff selects a registration statement for review, the staff must act on a confidential treatment request filed in connection with a registration statement pursuant to Rule 406 before the acceleration of effectiveness of a pending registration statement.

Please note that the same restriction applies to registration statements that incorporate by reference periodic reports. All CTRs filed pursuant to Rule 24b-2 must be completed before the effectiveness of the registration statement can be accelerated. The applicant should include in its cover letter to the registration statement a reference to the pending CTR, and issuers should allow enough time in their offering schedules for processing of the CTR by the staff.

3. Applications pursuant to Rule 24b-2 when no registration statement is pending

The goal of the Division is to complete the initial review of confidential treatment requests filed pursuant to Rule 24b-2 within 28 days from the filing date. Comments will usually be issued within this period. If the staff has no comments, an order will be issued granting the CTR. If the staff issues comments, applicants must respond to those comments within 21 days of the date of the comment letter. If the applicant does not respond within this period, the staff will consider, pursuant to its delegated authority from the Commission, what action is warranted, including

---

[29] Rule 406(b)(1) [17 CFR 230.406(b)(1)]and Rule 24b2(b)(1) [17 CFR 240.24b-2(b)(1)].

[30] 17 CFR 406(b)(2)(v) [17 CFR 230.406(b)(2)(v)].

whether to grant, deny, or grant and deny in part confidential treatment applications based on the record before it. The staff will base its action on the initial application and all amendments and supplemental information received.

Addendum to Staff Legal Bulletin No. 1

Dated July 11, 2001

This addendum updates Staff Legal Bulletin No. 1, dated February 28, 1997, relating to the Division's processing of confidential treatment requests. The first matter discussed below represents a change from the original bulletin and the second represents an addition to it.

• In *footnote 9* to the original bulletin, we stated that issuers should request confidential treatment for the application itself, as well as for any supplemental materials provided during the processing of the request, under Rule 83 of the Commission's Rules of Practice. Rule 83 governs applications for confidential treatment of information not required to be filed under the Securities Act or the Exchange Act. We have recently changed our position to be consistent with the practices of the Division of Investment Management. Requests for confidential treatment of the application and other supporting supplemental information should be submitted under Securities Act Rule 406 or Exchange Act Rule 24b-2, whichever is appropriate for the underlying filing.

• In *Section II.C.3* of the original bulletin, we stated that confidential treatment beyond the minimum term of an agreement is usually inappropriate. We stated in *Section III.A* that if an issuer wanted confidential treatment beyond the term originally granted, it should file an application for extension before the expiration of the earlier order to justify continued confidential treatment. However, we gave no guidance with respect to the length of time we would consider appropriate for continued confidential treatment. We believe the following guidelines will assist issuers in preparing their extension applications:

—If the remaining term of the contract is greater than 10 years from the date of the extension application, we generally will only grant confidential treatment for 10 years;

—If the remaining term of the contract is less than 10 years from the date of the extension application, we will consider a request for the remaining term of the contract;

—If the remaining term of the contract is less than five years from the date of the application, but there is a possibility that it will be extended beyond its stated term, we will consider granting confidential treatment for a period of up to five years.

These guidelines assume that the applicant provides adequate support for any period requested.

[¶ 43,002]   Staff Legal Bulletin No. 2 (CF)

ACTION: Publication of CF Staff Legal Bulletin

DATE: April 15, 1997

SUMMARY: This staff legal bulletin provides the Division of Corporation Finance's views on requests to modify the Securities Exchange Act of 1934 periodic reporting of issuers that are either reorganizing or liquidating under the provisions of the United States Bankruptcy Code.

SUPPLEMENTARY INFORMATION: The statements in this legal bulletin represent the views of the Division's staff. This bulletin is not a rule, regulation, or statement of the Securities and Exchange Commission. Further, the Commission has neither approved nor disapproved its content.

CONTACT PERSON: For further information please contact Anne M. Krauskopf, Special Counsel, at (202) 942-2900.

I. Background

Issuers are required to file current and periodic reports with the Commission pursuant to Sections 13(a)[1] or 15(d)[2] of the Exchange Act[3] if they have:

* securities listed on a national securities exchange;[4]

* securities registered under Section 12(g)[5] of the Exchange Act; or

* a registration statement that has become effective under the Securities Act of 1933.[6]

In June 1972, the Commission published Exchange Act Release No. 9660, which addressed how the Exchange Act reporting requirements apply to "[i]ssuers which have ceased or severely curtailed their operations." In the release, the Commission emphasized the importance of Exchange Act reporting in preserving free, fair, and informed securities markets. The Commission stated, however, that "when not inconsistent with the protection of investors, [it] would modify the reporting requirements as they apply to particular issuers."

Companies in bankruptcy are not relieved of their reporting obligations. Neither the United States Bankruptcy Code[7] nor the federal securities laws provide an exemption from Exchange Act periodic reporting for issuers that have filed for bankruptcy. In the release, however, the Commission expressed the

---

[1] 15 U.S.C. 78m(a).
[2] 15 U.S.C. 78o(d).
[3] 15 U.S.C. 78a et seq.
[4] See Section 12(b) of the Exchange Act (15 U.S.C. 78l(b)).

[5] 15 U.S.C. 78l(g).
[6] 15 U.S.C. 77a et seq.
[7] 11 U.S.C. 101 et seq.

general position that, with respect to issuers subject to the jurisdiction of the Bankruptcy Court, it generally would accept reports which "differ in form or content from reports required to be filed under the Exchange Act."

The release also states that, in deciding whether to accept modified Exchange Act reports, the Commission will consider the following: (1) how difficult it is for the issuer to obtain the information necessary to complete those reports;[8] (2) the issuer's financial condition; (3) the issuer's efforts to advise its security holders and the public of its financial condition and activities; and (4) the nature and extent of the trading in the issuer's securities.

The release provides the Commission's general position on accepting modified Exchange Act reports from issuers subject to the jurisdiction of the Bankruptcy Court. An issuer relying on that general interpretive guidance should take all steps possible to inform its security holders and the market of its ongoing financial condition and the status of its bankruptcy proceedings, including filing any available information with the Commission.

II. Requests for Modified Exchange Act Reporting

An issuer in bankruptcy may request a "no-action" position from the Division that applies the positions in the release to the issuer's facts.[9] In providing a no-action position, the Division determines whether modified reporting is consistent with the protection of investors. In its request, the issuer should present a clear demonstration of its inability to continue reporting, its efforts to inform its security holders and the market, and the absence of a market in its securities.

Requests often do not provide all of the information necessary for the Division's analysis. This staff legal bulletin identifies factors the Division considers when acting on these requests. This guidance will help issuers prepare requests and make the process more efficient and less costly.

III. Information Required in Requests

A. Information Regarding Disclosure of Financial Condition

The first factor the Division considers is whether the issuer made efforts to inform its security holders and the market of its financial condition. The Division also looks at the issuer's Exchange Act reporting history. The request should include the following information.

1. Whether the issuer complied with its Exchange Act reporting obligations before its Bankruptcy Code filing

Because the issuer's efforts to inform the market of its financial condition are important, an issuer submitting a request should have been current in its Exchange Act reports for the 12 months before its Bankruptcy Code filing.[10] Accordingly, the issuer should discuss its Exchange Act reporting history for that period.

2. When the issuer filed its Form 8-K announcing its bankruptcy filing; whether the issuer made any other efforts to advise the market of its financial condition

The Division considers the timeliness of the issuer's Form 8-K announcing its bankruptcy filing when determining whether to grant the request.[11] The Division does not have a specific, objective test concerning the timing of the Form 8-K filing. However, the issuer should state the date the Form 8-K was due and filed. If the issuer filed the Form 8-K after the due date, it should explain why. The issuer also should discuss any other efforts that it made to inform its security holders and the market of its financial condition.

3. Whether the issuer is able to continue Exchange Act reporting; whether the information in modified reports is adequate to protect investors

The issuer should discuss the reasons why it is unable to continue Exchange Act reporting. The request should discuss specifically: (1) whether the issuer has ceased its operations or the extent to which the issuer has curtailed operations; (2) why filing periodic reports would present an undue hardship to the issuer; (3) why the issuer cannot comply with the disclosure requirements; and (4) why the issuer believes granting the request is consistent with the protection of investors.

Management of the issuer also should represent, if true, that: (1) the filing of periodic reports would present an undue hardship; and (2) the information contained in the reports filed with the Bankruptcy Court pursuant to the Bankruptcy Code is sufficient for the protection of investors while the issuer is subject to the jurisdiction of the Bankruptcy Court.

B. Information Regarding the Market for the Issuer's Securities

The Division also considers the nature and extent of trading in the issuer's securities. The issuer should discuss in detail the market for its securities. Trading of the issuer's securities on a national securities exchange or the Nasdaq Stock Market is, by itself, sufficient evidence that there is an active market for those securities. The Division will not issue a

---

[8] See Exchange Act Rule 12b-21.

[9] The Division has granted nine no-action requests since January 1995. E.g., Comptronix Corporation (April 4, 1997); Cray Computer Corporation (May 16, 1996); I.C.H. Corporation (May 10, 1996); F&M Distributors, Inc. (May 1, 1996).

[10] Focus Surgery, Inc. (October 3, 1996).

[11] Item 3 of Form 8-K requires the issuer to file a current report on that form within 15 calendar days of specified events related to a bankruptcy filing.

favorable response to a request for modification of Exchange Act reporting for those securities.[12]

Issuers that do not have securities traded on a national securities exchange or the Nasdaq Stock Market should quantify the effect of the Bankruptcy Code filing on the trading in the issuer's securities.[13] This information should demonstrate that there is minimal trading in the securities.[14]

The issuer should state the number of market makers for its securities. The issuer also should provide detailed information regarding the number of shares traded and the number of trades per month for each of the three months before the issuer's Bankruptcy Code filing and each month after that filing.[15]

General statements in the request that trading has been "minimal" or "insignificant" are not sufficient to enable the Division to reach a conclusion on the request. An unequivocal statement that there is "no trading" in the issuer's securities is sufficient.[16]

C. The Timing of the Issuer's Request for Modified Reporting

An issuer should submit its request promptly after it has entered bankruptcy, not when it is preparing to emerge from bankruptcy.[17] The Division will consider a request as submitted "promptly" if it is filed before the date the issuer's first periodic report is due following the issuer's filing for bankruptcy.[18]

IV. Positions Taken by the Division in Granting Requests

A. Reports Required While Bankruptcy Proceedings are Pending

Generally, the Division will accept, instead of Form 10-K and 10-Q filings, the monthly reports an issuer must file with the Bankruptcy Court under Rule 2015.[19] The issuer must file each monthly report with the Commission on a Form 8-K within 15 calendar days after the monthly report is due to the Bankruptcy Court.

Notably, the relief given applies only to filing Forms 10-K and 10-Q.[20] The issuer still must satisfy all other provisions of the Exchange Act, including filing the current reports required by Form 8-K and satisfying the proxy, issuer tender offer and going-private provisions.[21]

Issuers reorganizing under the jurisdiction of the Bankruptcy Court must file a Form 8-K to disclose any material events relating to the reorganization. Issuers liquidating under the jurisdiction of the Bankruptcy Court must file a Form 8-K to disclose whether any liquidation payments will be made to security holders, the amount of any liquidation payments, the amount of any expenses incurred, and any other material events relating to the liquidation.[22]

B. Reports Required Upon Emergence From Bankruptcy

1. An issuer that is reorganized under its bankruptcy plan

When an issuer's reorganization plan becomes effective, the issuer must file an appropriate Form 8-K. That Form 8-K should include the issuer's audited balance sheet. From then on, the issuer must file Exchange Act periodic reports for all periods that begin after the plan becomes effective.[23]

Any post-reorganization filings under the Securities Act or the Exchange Act must include audited financial statements prepared in accordance with generally accepted accounting principles for all periods for which audited financial statements are required even though the issuer may have been subject to bankruptcy proceedings during some portion of those periods.[24]

2. An issuer that is liquidated under its bankruptcy plan

After the issuer's liquidation plan becomes effective, the issuer must continue to disclose material events relating to the liquidation on Form 8-K. At the

---

[12] If the issuer remains current in its Exchange Act reporting requirements until trading on a national securities exchange or the Nasdaq Stock Market stops, it may then request modified reporting. F&C International, Inc. (October 15, 1993).

[13] An issuer's securities are not considered to be "traded" on a national securities exchange or the Nasdaq Stock Market if: (1) those securities have been delisted; or (2) trading in those securities on those markets has formally been suspended.

[14] E.g., Sea Galley Stores, Inc. (March 24, 1995) (tabular presentation demonstrated decreased trading volume in the issuer's securities).

[15] If national securities exchange or Nasdaq Stock Market trading stopped during one of these months, the issuer should show separately within that month the information for the periods before and after trading stopped.

[16] E.g., Numerica Financial Corporation (April 1, 1996) (noting that no transfers of issuer stock occurred for a two-year period and that transfer agent was given instructions to prohibit further transfers); F&M Distributors, Inc., supra, and Focus Surgery, Inc., supra (stating there was no trading in the issuer's stock).

[17] Selectors, Inc. (September 18, 1990) and AorTech, Inc. (September 14, 1990).

[18] Focus Surgery, Inc., supra. The staff also will consider a request to be submitted "promptly" if the issuer is current in its Exchange Act reporting after filing its Bankruptcy Code petition and through the date of its request. United Merchants and Manufacturers, Inc. (November 19, 1996).

[19] Fed. R. Bankr. P. 2015.

[20] If, as a result of a "hardship," an issuer wants to file in paper format rather than electronically on EDGAR, it should contact the Division's Office of Edgar Policy at (202) 9422940.

[21] Transactions in the issuer's securities also continue to be subject to the requirements of the Exchange Act, including tender offer and short-swing profit provisions.

[22] BSD Bancorp, Inc. (March 30, 1994); Cray Computer Company, supra; I.C.H. Corporation, supra.

[23] Famous Restaurants, Inc. (June 4, 1993); Sea Galley Stores, Inc., supra; Diversified Industries, Inc., supra.

[24] Any requests for relief from financial statement obligations should be sent to the Division's Office of Chief Accountant.

time the liquidation is complete, the issuer must file a final Form 8-K to report that event.[25]

C. Effect on Short-Form Registration, Rule 144 and Regulation S

An issuer that has filed modified reports would not be considered "current" in its Exchange Act reporting, with respect to those reports due while its bankruptcy proceedings were pending, for purposes of: (1) determining eligibility to use Securities Act Form S-2 or S-3; (2) satisfying the current public information requirement of Securities Act Rule 144(c)(1); or (3) satisfying the reporting issuer definition of Rule 902(l) of Regulation S.

D. Availability of Rule 12h-3

Exchange Act Rule 12h-3 provides a means to suspend an issuer's obligation to file periodic reports under Section 15(d) of the Exchange Act. The Division has taken the position that modified Exchange Act reporting in accordance with a grant of a request would be sufficient for purposes of meeting the reporting requirement of Rule 12h-3.[26] Accordingly, an issuer that otherwise satisfies the conditions of Rule 12h-3 may suspend reporting upon emergence from its bankruptcy proceedings if it has been granted relief in response to a request and has satisfied the conditions of that grant.

[¶ 43,003] Staff Legal Bulletin No. 3A (CF)

Action: Publication of CF Staff Legal Bulletin

Date: June 18, 2008

Summary: This staff legal bulletin provides the Division of Corporation Finance's views regarding the Section 3(a)(10) exemption from the Securities Act of 1933's registration requirements. The bulletin also expresses the Division's views regarding the Securities Act resale status of securities that are received in certain transactions exempt from registration pursuant to Section 3(a)(10).[1]

Supplementary Information: The statements in this legal bulletin represent the views of the Division of Corporation Finance. This bulletin is not a rule, regulation, or statement of the Securities and Exchange Commission. Further, the Commission has neither approved nor disapproved its content.

Contacts: For further information, please contact the Office of Chief Counsel in the Division of Corporation Finance at (202) 551-3500.

1. Overview

Section 3(a)(10)[2] of the Securities Act[3] is an exemption from Securities Act registration for offers and sales of securities in specified exchange transactions.[4] Before the issuer can rely on the exemption, the following conditions must be met.[5]

- The securities must be issued in exchange for securities, claims, or property interests; they cannot be offered for cash.[6]

- A court or authorized governmental entity[7] must approve the fairness of the terms and conditions of the exchange.

- The reviewing court or authorized governmental entity must:

- find, before approving the transaction, that the terms and conditions of the exchange are fair to those to whom securities will be issued;[8] and

- be advised before the hearing that the issuer will rely on the Section 3(a)(10) exemption based on

---

[25] E.g., Cray Computer Company, supra; I.C.H. Corporation, supra.

[26] Union Valley Corporation (November 2, 1993).

[1] The bulletin was originally issued on July 25, 1997 and revised on October 20, 1999 to provide the Division's views on the availability of the Section 3(a)(10) exemption after the enactment of Section 302 of the Securities Litigation Uniform Standards Act of 1998. The bulletin is now further revised to express the Division's views regarding the Securities Act resale status of securities that are received in transactions exempt from registration pursuant to Section 3(a)(10) in light of Securities Act Release No. 8869 (Dec. 6, 2007) [72 FR 71546], which amended Securities Act Rules 144 and 145. This bulletin replaces the two prior bulletins in their entirety.

[2] 15 U.S.C. §77c(a)(10). Section 3(a)(10) reads as follows: "Except with respect to a security exchanged in a case under title 11 of the United States Code, any security which is issued in exchange for one or more bona fide outstanding securities, claims or property interests, or partly in such exchange and partly for cash, where the terms and conditions of such issuance and exchange are approved, after a hearing upon the fairness of such terms and conditions at which all persons to whom it is proposed to issue securities in such exchange shall have the right to appear, by any court, or by any official or agency of the United States, or by any State or Territorial banking or insurance commission or other governmental authority expressly authorized by law to grant such approval."

[3] 15 U.S.C. §77a et seq.

[4] The Trust Indenture Act of 1939 does not include an exemption that is the equivalent of Section 3(a)(10) of the Securities Act. If an issuer is relying on Section 3(a)(10) to offer and sell debt securities without Securities Act registration, it should note that the Trust Indenture Act would still apply to that offering.

[5] The staff derives these conditions from the language of Section 3(a)(10) and positions expressed by John J. Burns, the General Counsel of the Commission, in a letter excerpted in Securities Act Release No. 312 (Mar. 15, 1935) [11 FR 10953].

[6] Section 3(a)(10) also exempts sales of securities that are "partly in such exchange and partly for cash. . . ." It is the Division's view that Section 3(a)(10) exempts transactions that are predominantly exchanges and that the "partly for cash" language is intended merely to permit flexibility in structuring those exchanges. Because this analysis necessarily would be very fact-specific, the Division is not able to give specific guidance on the issue in this staff legal bulletin. To the extent the issue is presented in a transaction, an issuer may wish to request a no-action position from the staff on that particular transaction.

[7] Authorized governmental entities may include state insurance commissions, state corporation or securities commissions, state banking agencies, etc.

[8] In the Division's view, the reviewing court or authorized governmental entity must find the terms and conditions of the exchange to be fair both procedurally and substantively.

the court's or authorized governmental entity's approval of the transaction.

- The court or authorized governmental entity must hold a hearing before approving the fairness of the terms and conditions of the transaction.

- A governmental entity must be expressly authorized by law to hold the hearing, although it is not necessary that the law require the hearing.

- The fairness hearing must be open to everyone to whom securities would be issued in the proposed exchange.

- Adequate notice must be given to all those persons.

- There cannot be any improper impediments to the appearance by those persons at the hearing.

The Section 3(a)(10) exemption is available without any action by the Division or the Commission. Issuers that are unsure of whether the exemption is available for a specific contemplated transaction may, however, seek the Division's views by requesting a "no-action" position from the Division.

This bulletin discusses the issues that commonly arise in those "no-action" requests. The Division believes that, by making its views on these issues more widely known, issuers will better understand when the exemption is available. Also, by making the Division's views more widely known, this bulletin should decrease those situations in which an issuer is uncertain whether the exemption is available for a contemplated transaction.

2. Timing of No-Action Requests

The Division will not issue a no-action response concerning a transaction after the fairness hearing has been held. An issuer must, therefore, submit its no-action request *before* the fairness hearing. If an issuer submits a no-action request very close to the fairness hearing date, the Division may not have adequate time to consider the issues presented and respond before the fairness hearing.[9]

3. Timing of Security Holders' Votes

When an issuer solicits security holders' votes on the transaction before the fairness hearing, it is offering the securities to be issued in the transaction. This solicitation ordinarily requires either registration or an exemption.

A practical issue arises because many statutes governing fairness hearings require security holders to vote before the hearing, at a time when the issuer cannot be certain that it will be able to rely on the Section 3(a)(10) exemption. In these situations, the Division has not objected to a vote before the fairness hearing, even though this means an investment decision is made before the fairness hearing. The Division takes this view because the timing is required by the governing statute and, under that statute, the transaction is not effected unless the court or authorized governmental entity approves it. In the Division's view, the issuer should submit to the court or authorized governmental entity the disclosure materials offering the securities before it mails them to the offerees.

4. Division Analysis of the Requirements Underlying the Exemption

A. The Securities Must Be Issued in Exchange for Securities, Claims, or Property Interests

This requirement generally does not raise interpretive issues.[10] However, it is important to note that when options, warrants, or other convertible securities are issued in the Section 3(a)(10) transaction, Section 3(a)(10) does not exempt the later exercise or conversion.[11]

This is different than transactions that are exempt under Section 1145 of the U.S. Bankruptcy Code. Section 1145 specifically exempts the later exercise or conversion from Securities Act registration.[12]

B. A Court or Authorized Governmental Entity Must Approve the Exchange's Terms and Conditions

1. Appropriate Authorization for Governmental Entity Approval

If a governmental entity is approving the exchange, that entity must be authorized by statute:

- to hold a hearing on the transaction, although it is not necessary that the statute require the hearing; and

- to approve the fairness of the exchange's terms and conditions.[13]

In this analysis, the statute must require the entity to conclude affirmatively that the exchange is fair to the *security holders participating in the exchange.*[14] For example, the statute must require the governmental

---

[9] Generally, the Division strives to respond to requests for no-action within 30 days of receipt. It makes every effort to satisfy the time schedule of the requestor but may not be able to accommodate a very short deadline.

[10] Despite the "exchange" requirement of Section 3(a)(10), the Division has not objected, in limited circumstances, to the issuance of securities as attorneys' fees without registration in reliance on the Section 3(a)(10) exemption, such as when those securities amount to no more than one-third of the securities issued in the settlement. *See, e.g., Hanover Compressor Co.* (Jan. 27, 2004); *Sprint Corp.* (Aug. 25, 2003); *Sulcus Corp.* (June 19, 1996); and *The Score Board* (Nov. 3, 1995). For a discussion of exchanges that are "partly for cash," see footnote 6.

[11] *See, e.g., Canadian Conquest Exploration, Inc.* (Apr. 6, 1989); and *Allied Leisure Industries, Inc.* (Oct. 4, 1979).

[12] 11 U.S.C. § 1145(a)(2).

[13] Where an issuer will use court approval as a basis for relying on the Section 3(a)(10) exemption, the court also must make this finding. It is not necessary, however, that the court be expressly authorized by statute to do so. *See* Securities Act Release No. 312, *supra* note 5. See also the discussion in the *Foreign Courts* subsection of this bulletin for the requirements for a foreign court to approve the exchange.

[14] In 1938, the staff of the Commission stated its view that:

entity to conclude that the terms and conditions of the exchange are "in the best interest of shareholders" or "fair" to shareholders, *not* that the exchange is "not unfair," "not unreasonable," "not prejudicial," or "not counter to the best interest of shareholders."[15] Moreover, the governmental entity must find the terms and conditions to be fair both procedurally and substantively.

If there is a question as to whether the statute authorizes the governmental entity to hold a hearing on the transaction and to approve the fairness of the exchange's terms and conditions, it may be clear from the actual practice of the authorized governmental entity. For example, in *State Mutual Life Assurance Company* (Mar. 23, 1995), the Division relied on an opinion from counsel to the Division of Insurance of the Commonwealth of Massachusetts that the relevant statute authorized the Massachusetts Insurance Commissioner to make the requisite fairness determination.

If an issuer intends to rely on the Section 3(a)(10) exemption, it may want to look at prior Division no-action responses and see if the particular statute has ever been the basis for a Division no-action position. If the statute has been the basis for a Division no-action position, the issuer should consider whether the language of the statute has changed since the Division took that no-action position.

2. Information That Must Be Available to the Court or Authorized Governmental Entity When It Makes Its Fairness Determination

The issuer must advise the court or authorized governmental entity before the hearing that the issuer will rely on the Section 3(a)(10) exemption based on the court's or authorized governmental entity's approval of the exchange. It is the Division's view that the reviewing court or authorized governmental entity making the fairness determination "must have sufficient information before it to determine the value of both the securities, claims or interests to be surrendered and the securities to be issued in the proposed transaction."[16]

3. Fairness Hearings Conducted under State Securities Laws

Under Section 18 of the Securities Act, securities that otherwise would be covered securities, and therefore exempt from the registration or qualification provisions of state securities laws, are removed from the definition of "covered securities" if they are offered and sold in reliance on the Section 3(a)(10) exemption.[17] Accordingly, an issuer may rely upon a fairness hearing conducted under state securities law to perfect an exemption under Section 3(a)(10) for securities that otherwise would be covered securities.[18]

(Footnote Continued)

"[A] commission or authority must be authorized to grant approval of the fairness of the terms and conditions of the issuance and exchange, *from the point of view of the persons to whom the securities are issued in the exchange*, and this authority must be express. This seems to be the proper interpretation if the requirement of a hearing upon the fairness of the terms and conditions is not to be rendered meaningless. As a result many commissions, such as public service commissions, whose authorization may be required for the reorganization of certain companies, will be found not to have the requisite authority because [they are] not authorized to pass upon the interest of the security holders." (emphasis added)

—Milton V. Freeman, A Summary of Administrative Interpretations of the Securities Act of 1933, As Amended at 280-81 (draft of May 1, 1938) (citations omitted). This position was restated in the Report of the Task Force on Disclosure Simplification (Mar. 5, 1996), available at *http://www.sec.gov/news/studies/smpl.htm* (the "Task Force Report"). *See also* Securities Act Release No. 312, *supra* note 5 ("In my opinion a State governmental authority . . . must possess express authority of law to approve the fairness of the terms and conditions of the issuance and exchange of the securities in question. This interpretation seems necessary to give meaning to the express requirement of a hearing upon the fairness of such terms and conditions, which must subsume authority in the supervisory body to pass upon the fairness from the standpoint of the investor, as well as the issuer and consumer, and to disapprove terms and conditions because unfair either to those who are to receive the securities or to other security holders of the issuer, or to the public.").

[15] Examples of appropriate statutory standards in favorable Division responses to no-action requests include requirements that the entity determine that the transaction:

(1) is one where "an intelligent and honest man, a member of the class concerned and acting in respect of his interest, might reasonably approve" (*Transocean Inc.*, Sept. 26, 2007); (2) "adequately protects the interests of depositors, other creditors and shareholders" (*Minowa Bancshares, Inc.*, Nov. 26, 1990); (3) is "fair and equitable" to shareholders (*Farm Family Mutual Insurance Co.*, Apr. 2, 1996); and (4) promotes the "public convenience and

advantage and the interest of [the merging] institutions, their members, stockholders and depositors" (*CFX Corp.*, Apr. 19, 1996).

[16] *See* Task Force Report, *supra* note 14, at page 80. *See also ICICI Bank Limited* (Dec. 13, 2001); *Information Resources, Inc.* (Feb. 27, 1995); and *Applied Magnetics Corp.* (May 30, 1995).

[17] *See* 15 U.S.C. § 77r(b)(4)(C). The National Securities Markets Improvements Act, Pub. L. No. 104-290 (1996) ("NSMIA"), amended Section 18 of the Securities Act to preclude any state from requiring registration or qualification of "covered securities." "Covered securities" are defined in Section 18 and Securities Act Rule 146 to include, among others, securities listed or approved for listing on the New York Stock Exchange, the American Stock Exchange, or The NASDAQ Stock Market. The effect of this amendment was to preempt any state law that authorized a state fairness hearing relating to the registration, or exemption from registration, of securities that were "covered securities" before the hearing. An issuer, therefore, could not use such a hearing as a basis for relying on the Section 3(a)(10) exemption. (Of course, as noted in the original SLB 3, not all state fairness hearings relating to exchanges of securities were preempted by NSMIA. The preemption did not apply to state fairness hearing procedures outside the scope of state securities laws, such as those authorized by state corporation, banking or insurance law and not relating to registration, or an exemption from registration, of securities. Issuers were never precluded from using such hearings as a basis for relying on the Section 3(a)(10) exemption.)

NSMIA's prohibition of reliance on certain state fairness hearings to perfect a Section 3(a)(10) claim of exemption with respect to "covered securities" was inadvertent. *See* 144 Cong. Rec. H6052, H6060 (daily ed. July 21, 1998) (statement of Rep. Cox). To correct this, Section 302 of the Securities Litigation Uniform Standards Act of 1998, Pub. L. No. 105-353 (1998), was enacted to amend Section 18(b)(4)(C) to add securities issued under Section 3(a)(10) of the Securities Act as a category of securities exempt from the definition of "covered securities."

[18] The Division first published its views regarding this matter in letters to *Food Lion, Inc.* (Jan. 13, 1999) and *Maverick Networks* (Jan. 25, 1999).

Because Section 18 exempts all securities issued in reliance on Section 3(a)(10) from the definition of "covered securities," such securities are no longer exempt from the registration or qualification provisions of any state securities laws.

4. Foreign Courts

It is the Division's view that the term "any court" in Section 3(a)(10) may include a foreign court.[19]

In connection with no-action requests in these situations:

- all requirements that apply to exchanges approved by U.S. courts must be met; and

- the issuer must provide the Division with an opinion from counsel licensed to practice in the foreign jurisdiction that says that, before the foreign court can give its approval, it must approve the fairness of the proposed exchange to persons receiving securities in the exchange.[20]

C. Before Approval, the Court or Authorized Governmental Entity Must Hold a Hearing on the Fairness of the Exchange; This Hearing Must Be Open to Everyone to Whom Securities Would Be Issued in the Proposed Exchange

The court or authorized governmental entity must:

- hold a hearing to determine whether the proposed exchange's terms and conditions are fair to all those who will receive securities in the exchange; and

- approve the fairness of the terms and conditions of the proposed exchange.

The hearing must be open to everyone to whom securities would be issued in the proposed exchange.

The issuer must provide appropriate notice of the hearing in a timely manner.[21] Section 3(a)(10) does not specify the information that must be included in the required notice.

Although the anti-fraud requirements of the federal securities laws would govern disclosure, the Division does not address the adequacy or appropriateness of the information provided to persons who have a right to appear at the hearing. In connection with no-action

requests, the Division will consider the adequacy of the notice only to the extent that it:

- adequately advises those who are proposed to be issued securities in the exchange of their right to attend the hearing; and

- gives them the information necessary to exercise that right.

An issuer that intends to rely on the Section 3(a)(10) exemption should consider whether, as a practical matter, imposing prerequisites to appearance will prevent those persons from having a meaningful opportunity to appear at that hearing.[22]

5. Resale Status of Securities Received in a Transaction Exempt From Securities Act Registration Pursuant to Section 3(a)(10)

In Securities Act Release No. 8869 (Dec. 6, 2007), the Commission amended Securities Act Rule 145 to eliminate the presumptive underwriter provision in Rule 145(c) except for transactions involving a shell company, other than a business combination related shell company.

Accordingly, it is the Division's view that securities received in a Rule 145(a) transaction not involving a shell company that was exempt under Section 3(a)(10) may generally be resold without regard to Rule 144 if the sellers are not affiliates of the issuer of the Section 3(a)(10) securities and have not been affiliates within 90 days of the date of the Section 3(a)(10)-exempt transaction, as such securities would not constitute "restricted securities" within the meaning of Rule 144(a)(3) under the Securities Act. In the event that the securities are held by affiliates of the issuer, those holders may be able to resell the securities in accordance with the provisions of Rule 144.[23]

When a Rule 145(a) transaction is exempt from Securities Act registration under Section 3(a)(10) and any party to that transaction is a shell company, other than a business combination related shell company, then the Rule 145(c) and (d) resale limitations apply to any party to that transaction (other than the issuer of the Section 3(a)(10) securities) and to any person who is an affiliate of such party at the time such transaction is submitted for vote or consent.[24] In those situations, holders who are deemed to be underwriters under Rule 145(c) may resell their securi-

---

[19] *See, e.g., SanDisk Corp.* (Sept. 21, 2006); *AngloGold Ltd.* (Jan. 15, 2004); *Constellation Brands, Inc.* (Jan. 29, 2003); *Galen Holdings PLC* (Aug. 7, 2000); *Lucas Industries plc* (Aug. 20, 1996); *Symantec Corp.* (Nov. 22, 1995); and *Orbital Sciences Corp.* (Oct. 13, 1995).

[20] The Division requires this additional opinion because the fairness standard in foreign jurisdictions often is derived from case law that interprets and applies the statute(s), rather than from the specific language of the statute(s). The opinion of foreign counsel should state clearly that:

- under applicable law, the court cannot approve the exchange unless it finds the transaction to be fair to the persons who will receive the securities;

- those persons will receive notice of, and have the right to appear at, the fairness hearing; and

- the issuer will advise the court *before* the hearing that it will rely on the Section 3(a)(10) exemption and not register the ex-

change under the Securities Act based on the court's approval of the exchange.

[21] For example, if the securities are held in bearer form, there must be appropriate publication of the notice.

[22] The Division has not objected to the mere requirement to file a notice of an intention to appear. For examples of favorable staff responses to no-action requests where the filing of a notice of an intention to appear was required, see *ICICI Bank Ltd.* (Dec. 13, 2001); *Digicon Inc.* (Aug. 19, 1996); and *Canadian Pacific Ltd.*, (June 26, 1996).

[23] *See* Rule 144(b)(2) under the Securities Act.

[24] In computing the holding period of the Section 3(a)(10) securities for purposes of Rule 145(d)(2)(ii) or (d)(2)(iii), such persons may not "tack" the holding period of the securities exchanged for the Section 3(a)(10) securities in the Section 3(a)(10)-exempt transaction.

ties without registration in the manner permitted by Rule 145(d).[25]

http://www.sec.gov/interps/legal/cfslb3a.htm

[¶ 43,004] Staff Legal Bulletin No. 4 (CF)

ACTION: Publication of CF Staff Legal Bulletin

DATE: September 16, 1997

SUMMARY: This staff legal bulletin states the Division of Corporation Finance's views regarding whether Section 5 of the Securities Act of 1933 applies to spin-offs. This bulletin also addresses related matters, including how securities received in spin-offs may be resold under the Securities Act.

SUPPLEMENTARY INFORMATION: The statements in this legal bulletin represent the views of the staff of the Division of Corporation Finance. This bulletin is not a rule, regulation or statement of the Securities and Exchange Commission. Further, the Commission has neither approved nor disapproved its content.

CONTACT PERSON: For further information, please contact Mark W. Green, Deputy Chief Counsel at (202) 942-2900. For further information regarding foreign company spin-offs, please contact Felicia Kung, Special Counsel, Office of International Corporate Finance at (202) 942-2990.

1. What Is A "Spin-Off"?

In a "spin-off," a parent company distributes shares of a subsidiary to the parent company's shareholders.

2. What Is This Bulletin's Purpose?

Even though companies do not have to request the Division's views on a proposed spin-off, many companies do. This bulletin discusses our views on issues that commonly arise in those requests.[1]

The Division will no longer respond to requests for its views on the issues we address in this bulletin. We will respond when a company asks for our views on novel or unusual issues in a proposed spin-off.

3. What Are the Basic Concerns About Spin-Offs?

A subsidiary must register a spin-off of shares under the Securities Act if the spin-off is a "sale" of the securities by the parent.[2] Also, when a company

that reports under the Exchange Act spins-off shares of a company that does not report under the Exchange Act, the spin-off raises concerns because it may:

• result in an active trading market for the spun-off shares without adequate public information about their issuer; and

• violate the anti-fraud provisions of the Securities Act and the Exchange Act.[3]

4. Does the Subsidiary Have to Register the Spin-Off Under the Securities Act?

A. The Subsidiary Does Not Have to Register the Spin-Off if Five Conditions are Met

It is the Division's view that the subsidiary does not have to register a spin-off under the Securities Act when:[4]

• the parent shareholders do not provide consideration for the spun-off shares;

• the spin-off is pro-rata to the parent shareholders;

• the parent provides adequate information about the spin-off and the subsidiary to its shareholders and to the trading markets;

• the parent has a valid business purpose for the spin-off; and

• if the parent spins-off "restricted securities," it has held those securities for at least two years.

B. An Explanation Of The Conditions

1. The parent shareholders do not provide consideration for the spun-off shares

If the parent shareholders provide consideration for the spun-off shares, the parent would be transferring the spun-off securities for value. This transfer of securities for value is a "sale" under the Securities Act. So, when shareholders provide consideration, the subsidiary must register the spin-off unless an exemption is available.

---

[25] However, Rule 145(d) is not available with respect to any transactions or series of transactions that, although in technical compliance with the rule, are part of a plan or scheme to evade the Securities Act registration requirements. Note to Rule 145(c) and (d) under the Securities Act.

[1] This bulletin does not address:

* whether the anti-fraud provisions of the Securities Act and the Securities Exchange Act of 1934 apply to spin-offs; or

* those spin-offs where the parent distributes securities whose value is determined, at least in part, by reference to a distinct part of the parent's business (for example, "targeted stock"). These spin-offs differ from traditional spin-offs because the parent retains the part of the business that determines the return on the distributed securities.

[2] The term "sale" is defined in Section 2(a)(3) of the Securities Act. Even though the parent is the seller of the securities in a spin-off, the subsidiary has to file the registration statement because it is the issuer of the securities.

[3] The Commission discussed these spin-offs and the concerns they raise in Release No. 33-4982 (July 2, 1969).

[4] If the spin-off does not meet these conditions and the subsidiary registers the spin-off, it should look to Securities Act Rule 457(f) to determine the filing fee. Although that rule does not specifically mention spin-offs, it contains provisions that help to determine the proper fee. Consistent with Rule 457(f)(1), the Securities Act filing fee is based on the market value of the spun-off securities as specified in Rule 457(c). If there is no market for those securities, consistent with Rule 457(f)(2), the filing fee is based on the book value of the spun-off subsidiary's assets.

2. The spin-off must be pro rata

When the spin-off is pro rata, the parent shareholders have the same proportionate interest in the parent and the subsidiary both before and after the spin-off. If a spin-off is not pro rata, the shareholders' relative interests change and some shareholders give up value for the spun-off shares. Ordinarily, Securities Act registration would be required if a spin-off is not pro rata.

3. The parent must provide adequate information to its shareholders and the trading markets

Whether the parent provides adequate information about the spin-off and the subsidiary to its shareholders and the trading markets depends on whether the subsidiary is an Exchange Act reporting company or a non-reporting company before and after the spin-off. In this discussion, we assume the parent is a reporting company.[5]

a. Non-reporting subsidiary

If the subsidiary is a non-reporting company, the parent provides adequate information if, by the date it spins-off the securities:

- it gives its shareholders an information statement that describes the spin-off and the subsidiary and that substantially complies with Regulation 14A or Regulation 14C under the Exchange Act; and

- the subsidiary registers the spun-off securities under the Exchange Act.[6]

b. Reporting Subsidiary

If the subsidiary is a reporting company, the parent may provide less information about the spin-off to its shareholders. In this situation, the parent provides adequate information if, by the date it spins-off the securities:

- the subsidiary has been subject to the Exchange Act reporting requirements for at least 90 days;

- the subsidiary is current in its Exchange Act reporting; and

- the parent gives its shareholders information about the ratio it used to compute the number of shares distributed for each share held, how it will treat fractional shares, and the spin-off's expected tax consequences.[7]

If the reporting subsidiary has not been reporting for 90 days or is not current in its Exchange Act reporting, the parent may provide adequate information in the same manner as for a non-reporting company.[8]

c. Foreign companies

When the parent and subsidiary are foreign, the parent provides adequate information if, by the date it spins-off the securities:

- it gives its U.S. shareholders an information statement that describes the spin-off and the subsidiary and that substantially complies with Regulation 14A or Regulation 14C; and

- the subsidiary registers the spun-off securities under the Exchange Act.

There may be situations where the subsidiary will not register the spun-off securities under the Exchange Act (for example, the Rule 12g3-2(a) or 12g3-2(b) exemption from registration may be available). Whether the parent provides adequate information in these situations requires an analysis of all of the facts and circumstances.[9] We will continue to consider requests for "no-action" positions from foreign companies that do not intend to register the spun-off shares under the Exchange Act.

4. Valid Business Purpose for Spin-Off

When there is a valid business purpose for a spin-off, it is less likely that the parent indirectly will receive value for the spun-off shares through the creation of a market in those securities.[10] The Division has recognized the following as examples of valid business purposes for a spin-off:

- allowing management of each business to focus solely on that business;

---

[5] In five situations over the last ten years, the Division has provided its views to a non-reporting U.S. parent that proposed to spin-off a non-reporting subsidiary. In these situations, the parent provides adequate information if, by the date it spins-off the securities:

* the parent shareholders get an information statement that describes the spin-off and that substantially complies with Regulation 14A or Regulation 14C;

* the holders of the spun-off securities can only transfer the securities in specific, limited situations (this is to make sure that no public market develops in those securities before the subsidiary registers them under the Exchange Act);

* the information statement tells the holders about the transfer limits;

* the spun-off securities have a legend on them that describes the transfer limits; and

* the spun-off subsidiary's stock transfer books include stop transfer instructions that indicate the transfer limits.

Our no-action letter to Axion Inc. (September 17, 1996) discusses these transfer limits and how they apply to later purchasers.

We will continue to provide our views on non-reporting company spin-offs when requested.

[6] See Collins & Aikman Corporation (February 5, 1997) and WMS Industries, Inc. (February 25, 1997).

[7] See Trinity Industries, Inc. (February 27, 1997).

[8] Under appropriate circumstances involving a reporting subsidiary that has not been reporting for 90 days, the parent or the subsidiary may use other methods to provide adequate information to the parent's shareholders and to the trading markets. For example, it may be appropriate for:

* the parent to provide the subsidiary's initial public offering prospectus to the parent's shareholders upon their request (Signet Banking Corp. (February 14, 1995)); or

* the subsidiary to file a Form 10-K before the spin-off (Pacific Telesis Group (February 14, 1994)).

[9] See, e.g., AB Electrolux (April 28, 1997) and British Gas plc (December 4, 1996).

[10] This concern is addressed in SEC v. Datronics Engineers, Inc., 490 F.2d 250 (4th Cir. 1973), cert. denied 416 U.S. 937 (1974) and SEC v. Harwyn Industries, 326 F.Supp. 943 (S.D.N.Y. 1971).

• providing employees of each business stock-based incentives linked solely to his or her employer;

• enhancing access to financing by allowing the financial community to focus separately on each business; or

• enabling the companies to do business with each other's competitors.

In our view, there is not a valid business purpose for a spin-off when the purpose is:

• creating a market in the spun-off securities without providing adequate information to the shareholders or to the trading markets;

• the creation of a public market in the shares of a company that has minimal operations or assets; or

• the creation of a public market in the shares of a company that is a development stage company that has no specific business plan or whose business plan is to engage in a merger or acquisition with an unidentified company.

Other than the business purposes discussed above, the facts of a particular situation will determine whether the business purpose is valid. Accordingly, the parent must determine whether there is a valid business purpose for the spin-off.

5. If the parent spins-off "restricted securities," the parent must have held those securities for at least two years

A company that spins-off "restricted securities" may be an underwriter in the public distribution of those securities.[11] The Division believes, however, that the parent would not be an underwriter of the spun-off securities and the subsidiary would not have to register the spin-off under the Securities Act when:

• the parent has held the "restricted securities" at least two years; and

• the spin-off satisfies the conditions described above.[12]

This two-year holding period position does not apply where the parent formed the subsidiary being spun-off, rather than acquiring the business from a third-party.

5. Does Securities Act Rule 145 Require the Subsidiary To Register A Spin-Off?

Securities Act Rule 145 requires specified transactions to be registered under the Securities Act when investors decide whether to accept a new or different security in exchange for their existing security. For example, when shareholders vote on a plan or an agreement for the transfer of assets in consideration for the issuance of securities, Rule 145(a)(3) may deem that vote to be a "sale" under the Securities Act.

Parent companies often ask their shareholders to vote on proposed spin-offs. Further, spin-offs may include the transfer of assets to the subsidiary.

Based on Rule 145(a)(3), the Division generally has refused to say that the subsidiary does not have to register a spin-off where the parent's shareholders vote on an asset transfer from the parent to the subsidiary.[13] However, we have reconsidered this position where the parent wholly owns the subsidiary. In this situation, we will no longer require Securities Act registration of a spin-off solely as a result of a shareholder vote on the asset transfer. The reason for the change in our view is that, when the other conditions described in response to Question 4, immediately above, are met, the vote on the asset transfer does not change the overall nature of the transaction.[14]

6. When an Independent Agent Aggregates and Sells Fractional Shares, Does the Subsidiary Have to Register those Sales?

The distribution ratio in many spin-offs would result in many shareholders receiving fractional shares. Rather than issue fractional shares, the parent often hires an independent agent to combine the fractions, sell the shares and provide the proceeds to shareholders.

We believe that the subsidiary need not register an independent agent's sales of combined fractional shares if the spin-off meets the conditions described in response to Question 4, above, and:[15]

• the independent agent makes the sales in the open market;

• the independent agent, in its sole discretion (that is, without influence by the parent or the subsidiary), determines when, how, through which broker-dealer and at what price to make its sales; and

• the independent agent and the broker-dealers it uses are not affiliates of the parent or the subsidiary.

7. Are Spun-Off Securities "Restricted Securities" Under Rule 144?

It is the Division's view that securities received by shareholders in a spin-off that meets the conditions described in response to Question 4, above, generally are not "restricted securities."[16]

In rare situations, however, a large shareholder of the parent so controls the parent that the shareholder essentially decides whether to do the spin-off. In

---

[11] The term "restricted securities" is defined in Securities Act Rule 144(a)(3).

[12] If the parent is a closely-held investment entity, Rule 144 permits distributees to "tack" their holding period to that of the parent. The position discussed in this section does not affect this interpretation of Rule 144.

[13] See Summit Energy, Inc. (March 29, 1988).

[14] Of course, if a parent company is subject to the Exchange Act proxy rules, it will have to comply with those rules in connection with the shareholders' vote.

[15] See Alco Standard Corporation (February 14, 1997).

[16] See Alco Standard Corporation (February 14, 1997). Sales by the spun-off company's affiliates, however, would be subject to Rule 144, except for the holding period requirement of Rule 144(d), absent registration or another appropriate exemption.

these infrequent situations, we view the spin-off as a privately negotiated transaction between the parent and that shareholder, with that shareholder getting restricted securities.[17] The other shareholders get securities that are not restricted.

8. Can The Subsidiary Consider Itself To Meet the Exchange Act Reporting Requirements of Rule 144 On The Date Of The Spin-Off, Rather Than Wait 90 Days?

Affiliates of a spun-off company may want to sell securities that they received in the spin-off. Absent registration under the Securities Act, affiliates must sell these securities under Rule 144 or another appropriate exemption.

These affiliates can only rely on Rule 144 if the subsidiary has been a reporting company for at least 90 days.[18] We believe that the subsidiary satisfies this reporting requirement on the date the parent spins-off the securities (that is, before 90 days have passed) if:[19]

- the spin-off meets the conditions described in response to Question 4, above;

- the parent is current in its Exchange Act reporting;

- the subsidiary will have substantially the same assets, business, and operations as a segment or subsidiary about which the parent has reported extensive segment data[20] and other financial and narrative disclosure in its Exchange Act periodic reports for at least 12 months before the date it spins-off the securities.[21]

9. Can the Subsidiary Consider the Parent's Reporting History When Determining Whether It Is Eligible to Use Form S-3?

A spun-off company may want to register offers and sales of securities on a Form S-3. Generally, one requirement a company must meet to use Form S-3 is that it has timely filed required Exchange Act reports for at least 12 months.[22] If a spun-off subsidiary meets the conditions described in response to Question 8, immediately above, we believe that it also may consider its former parent's Exchange Act reports in determining whether it satisfies Form S-3's reporting history requirement.[23]

10. Can The Subsidiary Use Form S-8 To Register Offers and Sales to Parent Employees Before the Spin-Off?

Form S-8 permits a reporting company to register offers and sales of securities to specified people under employee benefit plans. These people include:

- employees of the reporting company's parent;

- employees of the reporting company's subsidiaries; and

- former employees of these companies if the Form S-8 registers the offer and sale of shares underlying non-transferable options that were granted during their employment.[24]

After the subsidiary becomes a reporting company - but before the spin-off occurs - the subsidiary may want to grant options to parent employees who will not be employees of the subsidiary after the spin-off. It will want to grant these options to make the parent employees financially "whole," because the parent options those employees hold may lose value in the spin-off. A spun-off subsidiary often will want to use Form S-8 to register its shares underlying these options.

We believe that the subsidiary may use Form S-8 to register the offer and sale of securities underlying these "make-whole" options if the spin-off meets the conditions described in response to Question 4, above and:[25]

- the options are not transferable;[26]

- the parent has not had any unusual grant activity under its option plans; and

- the employees of the parent and the subsidiary will receive the same information about the subsidiary's stock option plans under which it grants the options.

11. Does Exchange Act Section 16 Apply to Spin-Offs?

Exchange Act Section 16 applies to the officers, directors, and principal security holders of most companies with a class of equity securities registered under the Exchange Act. Section 16 requires these people to file ownership reports and subjects them to potential "short-swing" profit liability for their purchases and sales of the company's equity securities. Exchange Act Rule 16a-9(a) exempts the receipt

---

[17] See Valhi, Inc. (December 23, 1994).

[18] Rule 144(c)(1).

[19] See Alco Standard Corporation (February 14, 1997).

[20] The segment data reported must include at least: revenues; operating profit or loss; identifiable assets; expenses from depreciation, depletion and amortization; capital expenditures; and any other information required by Statement of Financial Accounting Standards ("FAS") No. 14 (Financial Reporting for Segments of a Business Enterprise) or, for fiscal years beginning after December 15, 1997, FAS No. 131 (Disclosures about Segments of an Enterprise and Related Information). Further, the parent's Exchange Act reports must have discussed the spun-off segment as a separate segment in the Description of Business and MD&A sections.

[21] It is not adequate if the parent has included "liquidated operations" or "discontinued operations" information regarding the spun-off segment.

[22] General Instruction I.A.3. to Form S-3.

[23] See Alco Standard Corporation (February 14, 1997).

[24] See General Instruction A.1.a. to Form S-8. A company that is a subsidiary can only use Form S-8 to offer and sell securities to employees of another subsidiary of that company's ultimate parent if the other subsidiary also is a parent of the company or is a subsidiary of the company.

[25] See Getty Petroleum Corp. (December 9, 1996).

[26] For this purpose, these options are still considered not transferable if holders can transfer them only to the limited extent described in Merrill Lynch & Co., Inc. (May 16, 1996).

of securities in a spin-off from Section 16 if all holders of a class of securities participate in the spin-off on a pro rata basis.

Anyone subject to Section 16 still would have to file a Form 3 when the subsidiary registers a class of spun-off equity securities under the Exchange Act.

[¶ 43,007]   Staff Legal Bulletin No. 7A (CF)

Action: Publication of the Division of Corporation Finance

Date: June 7, 1999

Summary

This updates the staff legal bulletin we issued on September 4, 1998 to provide information on the plain English rule and amendments as they apply to companies filing with the Division of Corporation Finance. This rule and the amendments apply to Securities Act of 1933 registration statements filed on or after October 1, 1998.

Questions and Answers

The original staff legal bulletin no. 7 answered the questions we had been asked most frequently from the date the rule and amendments were adopted to the date we published the bulletin. In this update, we eliminated the questions and answers that applied to the phase-in period for the new rule and amendments because this period ended October 1, 1998. Also, we added a question and answer on when Form S-3 post-effective amendments must comply with the plain English rule and amendments. *See Q&A no. 10.*

Risk Factor Guidance

Amended Item 503(c) of Regulation S-K specifies that issuers should not present risks that could apply to any issuer or any offering. Further, the subheadings must adequately describe the risk that follows. Item 503(c) seems to be the least understood of the plain English requirements. We have provided sample risk factor disclosures and subheadings to help preparers comply with Rule 421(d) of Regulation C and Item 503(c) of Regulation S-K.

Sample Comments

Now that the staff has gained several months' experience issuing plain English comments under the new rule and amendments, we thought it would be helpful to list the comments we have been issuing most frequently. By alerting issuers to these comments before they file their next registration statement, we hope to enable them to avoid receiving these comments. Of course, these are not the only plain English comments we issue; each prospectus is different and many of the comments we issue are unique to the organization of and disclosure in individual prospectuses.

Supplementary Information: The statements in this legal bulletin represent the views of the staff of the Division of Corporation Finance. This bulletin is not a rule, regulation, or statement of the Securities and Exchange Commission. Further, the Commission has neither approved nor disapproved its content.

Contact Person: For further information regarding the plain English rule and amendments, please contact Carolyn A. Miller, Attorney-Adviser, at (202) 942-2890. For information regarding the comments the Division raises on a specific registration statement, contact the staff members identified in your comment letter.

Brief Description of the New Plain English Rule and Amendments

As of October 1, 1998, companies filing registration statements under the Securities Act of 1933 must:

- write the forepart of these registration statements in plain English;

- write the remaining portions of these registration statements in a clear, understandable manner; and

- design these registration statements to be visually inviting and easy to read.

The Commission adopted new Rule 421(d) and amendments to Rule 421(b), numerous Regulation S-K and Regulation S-B item requirements, and numerous disclosure form requirements.

Rule 421(d)—The New Plain English Rule

Issuers must use plain English writing principles in the organization, language, and design of the front and back cover pages, the summary, and the risk factors section. Also, when drafting the language in these parts of the prospectus, issuers must substantially comply with these plain English principles:

- short sentences;

- definite, concrete everyday language;

- active voice;

- tabular presentation of complex information;

- no legal jargon; and

- no multiple negatives.

In designing these and other parts of the prospectus, issuers may include pictures, logos, charts, graphs, or other design elements so long as the design is not misleading and the required information is clear.

Amended Rule 421(b)

When writing the remaining portions of their registration statements, issuers must use these standards:

- clear, concise sections, paragraphs, and sentences—using, whenever possible, short explanatory sentences and bullet lists; and

- descriptive headings and subheadings.

In addition, issuers must avoid:

• legal and highly technical business terminology; and

• frequent reliance on glossaries or defined terms as the primary means of explaining information. Define terms in a glossary or other section of the prospectus only if the meaning is unclear from the context. Use a glossary only if it facilitates understanding of the disclosure.

Finally, issuers should avoid:

• legalistic or overly complex presentations that make the substance of the disclosure difficult to understand;

• vague "boilerplate" explanations that are imprecise and readily subject to different interpretations;

• complex information copied directly from legal documents without any clear and concise explanation of the provision(s); and

• repetitive disclosure that does not enhance the quality of the information.

Questions and Answers

1. Scope of New Rule and Amendments

Q: Which filings do the new plain English rule and amendments apply to?

A: They apply only to prospectuses filed under the Securities Act of 1933.

2. Glossaries and Defined Terms

Q: Rule 421(b) specifies that we "must avoid frequent reliance on glossaries or defined terms as the primary means of explaining information in the prospectus. Define terms in a glossary or other section of the prospectus only if the meaning is unclear from the context. Use a glossary only if it facilitates understanding of the disclosure." When should we use a glossary?

A: You should use a glossary only if:

• you must include terms in your prospectus that are understood only by industry experts; and

• you cannot make the meanings of these terms clear from the context or explain them concisely where you first use them.

You should not use a glossary to define commonly understood abbreviations, like SEC, or acronyms, like NASDAQ. Further, you should not use a glossary to define terms that you have created solely for the purpose of your registration statement. We urge you not to create a vocabulary that is unique to your offering, with the exception of brand or trade names you use to identify the type of security you are offering.

3. Documents Incorporated by Reference

Q: Are all the documents we incorporate by reference into our registration statements subject to the new plain English rule and amendments?

A: No. The information you incorporate by reference in response to a general requirement need not comply. For example, Item 12 on Form S-3 requires you to incorporate by reference your recent Exchange Act reports in their entirety.

However, any information you incorporate by reference to satisfy a specific disclosure requirement must comply with the applicable plain English rule and amendments. For example, on Form S-3, if you incorporate by reference risk factors from a Form 10-K to satisfy Item 3, the risk factors must comply with Rule 421(d). Similarly, on Form S-3, if you incorporate by reference the description of securities to be registered from a Form 8-A, this description must comply with Rule 421(b).

4. Information Physically Included in a Prospectus

Q: If we reprint in our registration statement information from our 1934 Act filings, do we need to revise it to comply with the plain English rules?

A: Yes. Any information that you physically include in a prospectus must comply.

5. Plain English "Monitors"

Q: Will the staff randomly select registration statements to review them only for plain English?

A: Possibly. We may choose to review a filing solely for compliance with the new rule and amendments. We call this spot check a "monitor." The number of monitors we conduct depends on many factors, such as work load.

6. Staff Members Who Issue Plain English Comments

Q: Who on the staff will issue plain English comments on our registration statements?

A: The same staff member who is assigned to review your registration statement will also conduct the plain English review. Plain English comments you receive, if any, will appear in your regular comment letter.

7. Nature of Plain English Comments

Q: What will the staff be looking for when reviewing a prospectus for compliance with the new plain English rule and amendments? Will you be issuing "grammar" comments?

A: The staff will read the registration statements for clarity. The standards in Rule 421(d) and the guidance in the amendments to Rule 421(b) give issuers the tools they need to write clear disclosure documents. While the staff generally will not issue grammar comments, it may cite these rules in comments that are issued to help clarify issuers' disclosure.

8. Issuer's Business Is Highly Technical

Q: Because Rule 421(d) substantially curbs the use of technical terms in the forepart of the prospectus, how should issuers whose businesses are highly technical describe their companies?

A: An issuer with a highly technical business should provide a brief, general description of its business with, if necessary, concrete examples to illus-

Computational Systems, Inc. 10-K[1]

The Company primarily designs, produces and markets an integrated family of advanced predictive maintenance products and services for use in large scale, continuous run manufacturing facilities. The Company's Reliability-Based Maintenance products and services help customers detect potentially disruptive conditions in the operation of their machinery before damage or complete mechanical failure occurs, thereby allowing maintenance to be scheduled at the most appropriate time.

trate the description. Compare the following two descriptions of Computational Systems, Inc. The first is from CSI's 1996 10-K, which is not subject to the plain English rules. The other is from the summary of a merger proxy that CSI filed during the Division's plain English pilot program:

Computational Systems, Inc./Emerson Electric Company's merger proxy[2]

CSI's primary business is the design manufacture, and sale of a family of high-tech instruments that help companies determine when their industrial machines are in need of repair or adjustment. CSI also offers services to help its customers better manage the maintenance of their equipment. CSI's products and services help its customers keep their production lines running and maintain the quality of their products which may be adversely affected by an improperly functioning production line machine. CSI's customers are primarily large manufacturing, processing or power generating companies.

---

[1] Form 10-K for the fiscal year ended December 31, 1996, File No. 0-26596.
[2] Emerson Electric Co. Merger Proxy/Form S-4, File No. 333-40871.

9. Limited Partnership Offerings and Redundant Risk Factor

Disclosure

Q: In your proposing and adopting plain English rule releases, you emphasize how important it is to eliminate redundant information in registration statements. Why then does Securities Act Release No. 6900 require limited partnership offering prospectuses and similar offerings to list key risks on the cover page and repeat them in the risk factors section?

A: We believe the unique nature of these offerings and the risks they present to investors warrant requiring the issuer to highlight these risks on the cover page. Of course, the cover page, summary, and risk factors section must otherwise comply with the plain English rule and amendments.

10. When Plain English Applies to Post-Effective Amendments to Form S-3 Registration Statements

Q: When does a post-effective amendment to a Form S-3 that, when first filed was not subject to plain English, trigger the plain English requirements?

A: Now that the plain English rule and amendments are effective, there are two instances in which you must rewrite your post-effective amendment to comply. You must rewrite your post-effective amendment to comply if:

• it incorporates by reference audited financials that are more recent than those incorporated in any earlier post-effective amendment or the original registration statement; or

• enough time has lapsed since your last post-effective amendment or the original registration statement that you are required to post-effectively amend

your prospectus under Section 10(a)(3) of the Securities Act of 1933.

11. Plain English is Clarity, Not Brevity

Q: In our efforts to write the disclosure in plain English, should we focus on making the disclosure brief?

A: No—not at the expense of completeness or accuracy. The goal of plain English is clarity, not brevity. Writing disclosure in plain English can sometimes increase the length of particular sections of your prospectus. You will likely reduce the length of your plain English prospectus by writing concisely and eliminating redundancies— not by eliminating substance.

12. When Electronic Filers Also Submit Paper Copies to the Staff for Review

Q: Recently, the Division of Corporation Finance announced that, because issuers are required to file their registration statements electronically on ED-GAR, the staff did not want issuers to send paper copies of their filings. However, in the plain English adopting release, you say if a registration statement that is subject to the new plain English rule is selected for review, the staff will need paper copies. Why?

A: As many people know, when issuers file their registration statements electronically on our EDGAR system, the document's layout is lost. Because the new plain English rule is intended to enhance the readability of the prospectus through language and design, we need to see the layout of the plain English sections as you are delivering them to investors.

The staff member assigned to your filing will call to request paper copies of the prospectus. We are working to upgrade our EDGAR system to give issuers the option of filing of an exact duplicate of the paper copy sent to investors but this may not occur for some time.

13. Plain English and Acceleration Requests

Q: Can the staff ask the Commission to deny acceleration of a registration statement where the issuer has not made a good faith effort to comply with the new plain English rule and amendments?

A: Yes. Under Rule 461(b)(1), the staff may ask the Commission to deny acceleration "[w]here there has not been a bona fide effort to make the prospectus reasonably concise, readable, and in compliance with the plain English requirements of Rule 421(d)."

Risk Factor Guidance

Risk factors loosely fall into three broad categories:

• **Industry Risk** - risks companies face by virtue of the industry they're in. For example, many REITs run the risk that, despite due diligence, they will acquire properties with significant environmental issues.

• **Company Risk** - risks that are specific to the company. For example, a REIT owns four properties with significant environmental issues and cleaning up these properties will be a serious financial drain.

• **Investment Risk** - risks that are specifically tied to a security. For example, in a debt offering, the debt being offered is the most junior subordinated debt of the company.

When drafting risk factors, be sure to specifically link each risk to your industry, company, or investment, as applicable. See the two examples of before and after risk factors, below.

Before:

Competition

The lawn care industry is highly competitive. The Company competes for commercial and retail customers with national lawn care service providers, lawn care product manufacturers with service components, and other local and regional producers and operators. Many of these competitors have substantially greater financial and other resources than the Company.

After:

Because we are significantly smaller than the majority of our national competitors, we may lack the financial resources needed to capture increased market share.

Based on total assets and annual revenues, we are significantly smaller than the majority of our national competitors: we are one-third the size of our next largest national competitor. If we compete with them for the same geographical markets, their financial strength could prevent us from capturing those markets.

For example, our largest competitor did the following when it aggressively expanded five years ago:

• launched extensive print and television campaigns to advertise their entry into new markets;

• discounted their services for extended periods of time to attract new customers; and

• provided enhanced customer service during the initial phases of these new relationships.

Our national competitors likely have the financial resources to do the same, and we do not have the financial resources needed to compete on this level.

Because our local competitors are better positioned to capitalize on the industry's fastest growing markets, we may emerge from this period of growth with only a modest increase in market share, at best.

Industry experts predict that the smaller, secondary markets throughout the mid-west will soon experience explosive growth. We have forecasted that about 17% of our future long-term growth will come from these markets. However, because it is common practice for lawn care companies in smaller markets to acquire customers through personal relationships, our competitors in nearly half of these mid-west markets are better positioned to capitalize on this anticipated explosive growth. Unlike us, these local competitors live and work in the same communities as their and our potential customers.

For the foreseeable future, the majority of our sales people who cover these markets will work out of our two mid-west regional offices because we lack the financial resources to open local offices at this time. As a result, we may substantially fail to realize our forecasted 17% long-term growth from these markets.

Before:

Shares Eligible for Future Sale

Sales of substantial amounts of privately held Common Stock in the public market following the Offering could have an adverse effect on the price of the Company's Common Stock. Upon completion of the Offering, the Company will have outstanding 24,000,000 shares of Common Stock. Of these shares, the 6,000,000 shares offered hereby will be freely tradable without restriction under the Securities Act of 1933, as amended (the "Securities Act"). The remaining 18,000,000 shares of Common Stock held by existing stockholders (the "Restricted Shares") are restricted securities as that term is defined in Rule 144 ("Rule 144") under the Securities Act. Approximately 10,000,000 Restricted Shares will become eligible for sale beginning 90 days after the effectiveness of the Registration Statement of which this prospectus is a part (the "Effective Date") pursuant to Rule 144 under the Securities Act. Holders of approximately 8,000,000 additional Restricted Shares (the "Lock-up Shares") are subject to agreements not to sell or otherwise transfer their shares for a period of 180 days following the Effective Date. The Underwriters, in their sole discretion and at anytime without notice, may release any or all of the holders of Lock-up Shares from any or all of their obligations under the agreements not to sell.

After:

Eighteen million, or 75%, of our total outstanding shares are restricted from immediate resale but may be sold into the market in the near future. This could cause the market price of our common stock to drop significantly, even if our business is doing well.

After this offering, we will have outstanding 24,000,000 shares of common stock. This includes the

6,000,000 we are selling in this offering, which may be resold in the public market immediately. The remaining 75%, or 18,000,000 shares, of our total outstanding shares will become available for resale in the public market as shown in the chart below.

As restrictions on resale end, the market price could drop significantly if the holders of these restricted shares sell them or are perceived by the market as intending to sell them.

Number of shares/%	Date of availability for resale into public market of total outstanding
8,000,000 / 33%	180 days after the date of this prospectus due to an agreement these shareholders have with the underwriters. However, the underwriters can waive this restriction and allow these shareholders to sell their shares at any time.
10,000,000 / 42%	Between 90 and 365 days after the date of this prospectus due to the requirements of the federal securities laws.

For a more detailed description, see "Shares Eligible for Future Sale," on page 79

Sample Comments

The order in which we provide these sample comments follows the order in which we issue comments in our comment letters to issuers.

Comments applicable to entire prospectus

#1 Rather than use "Company" to refer to your company, use your actual company name or a shortened version of it throughout your prospectus.

#2 Throughout your prospectus, you are capitalizing terms that you are using for their common meanings. For example, you capitalize "Common Stock," "Preferred Stock," "Registration Statement," "Prospectus," "Merger Agreement," etc. Because you are using these terms for their common meanings, you could safely eliminate the initial capital letters without causing confusion.

#3 The meanings of the terms in parenthetical phrases are clear from their context. For example, you define The X Company, Inc., as ("X Company"). It's highly unlikely that anyone reading your prospectus will think you are referring to any other company when you use the shortened name "X Company." Similarly, you define the Securities and Exchange Commission as ("SEC"), the Internal Revenue Service as ("IRS"), and Securities Exchange Act as (the "Exchange Act"). Parenthetical definitions such as these are unnecessary. Therefore, delete these and all other unnecessary parenthetical definitions from your prospectus.

#4 Many of the terms you use are unique to this prospectus. By creating terms that exist only for use in this prospectus, you are forcing investors to learn a new vocabulary before they can understand your disclosure. Eliminate this over-reliance on defined terms. Instead, disclose material information in a clear, concise, and understandable manner. See Rule 421(b) of Regulation C.

#5 If you choose a shortened name or abbreviation, ensure its meaning is clear from the context. For example, consider using "Hard Disk Drive Group" as the shortened name of "Hard Disk Drive Group Company, Inc." rather than "HDDG" since the meaning of this abbreviation is unclear without the benefit of a parenthetical definition. See Rule 421(b) of Regulation C.

#6 The term "such" is typically legalese for "this," "these," or "the." Please replace this term throughout your prospectus with a concrete, everyday word that means the same thing.

#7 Many sentences throughout your prospectus are too long to understand on the first reading because you have embedded lists of information in paragraph form. See, for example, pages X, Y, and Z. Rather than include these lists in the paragraph, break them out into bullet points, with one bullet point for each list item. Also, use bullet points, regular numbers, or letters instead of small Roman numerals in parentheses. See Rule 421(b) of Regulation C.

#8 Many sentences throughout your prospectus contain parenthetical phrases that disrupt the flow of information and make these sentences very long. As a result, investors may have to read them several times to understand the disclosure. See, for example, pages A, B, C, and D. Eliminate parenthetical phrases throughout your prospectus. If the information in the parenthetical phrase is part of the sentence, merely set it off by commas. If the parenthetical phrase does not fit as part of the sentence, include it in its own sentence.

#9 Minimize the use of footnote treatment, where possible. For example, if the text in a footnote applies to the entire table, include the text in the narrative discussion that precedes the table. Also, if a number of footnotes repeat the same text, consider moving this text to the introductory paragraph or adding a column to the table that includes this information.

#10 The organization of your prospectus is driven by the mechanics of the transaction, not by how the transaction can affect your shareholders' investments. For example, the first page of your summary describes the merger subsidiary that exists solely to effect the merger. Will shareholders base their investment decisions on this? The organization of your prospectus should be from the shareholders' perspectives and explain how the proposed transactions affect their investments.

#11 Eliminate all unnecessary redundancy throughout your prospectus. For example, by page 5, you have repeated 3 times what the Company X shareholders will receive in the transaction. It is appropriate:

- to briefly introduce topics on the cover page;

- to expand on these topics in a summary fashion and summarize other key aspects of the transaction in the summary; and

- discuss these and the remaining topics in greater detail in the body of the prospectus.

This is the only type of repetition that is appropriate in the prospectus.

#12 Your subheadings do not state and characterize succinctly the information that follows. For example:

- The subheading "Costs" on page 2 does not adequately describe the subsection's contents. This subsection also describes how you may solicit proxies.

Jargon/technical terms

    proprietary drug

    intravenous solutions

    logistics capabilities

    coordinated manufacturing and distribution efforts

    proprietary medicines

    vertically integrated costefficient providers

    revenue synergies

    lower margin

    products utilization realigning sales forces

    centralized management information systems

    profit-enhancing synergies

    global platform

Eliminate the legalese and industry jargon from the forepart of your prospectus. Instead, explain these concepts in concrete, everyday language. Further, place any industry terms you use in context so those potential investors who do not work in your industry can understand the disclosure. See Rule 421(d) of Regulation C.

#15 **Note: this comment does NOT apply to registration statements filed on**

Form S-4 because that form requires specific information on the inside front cover page.

- The subheading "General Instructions" on page 3 applies to a subsection that describes the proxy card.

Informative subheadings provide readers with helpful navigational cues. Rewrite your subheadings to be more descriptive and specific to this prospectus. If your subheadings would work equally well in any other company's disclosure document, they are probably too vague to be helpful. See Rule 421(b) of Regulation C.

#13 Currently, your prospectus is written from the perspective of someone who is already quite familiar with the transaction and the entities involved. For example, throughout your prospectus, you make several references to "certain circumstances," "certain matters," "certain amendments," "certain persons," and "certain extraordinary matters." Presumably, someone who is already familiar with these transactions will know what you're referring to. But, what should these phrases mean to your shareholders, who are first learning of the proposed transaction through this prospectus? Replace the term "certain" with a brief description of what makes the information qualify as "certain."

Comments applicable to the forepart of the prospectus: cover page, summary, and risk factors section

#14 The forepart of your prospectus contains a lot of jargon, technical terms, and legalese. You have not used words for their common meanings. For example, these words and phrases appear in the first 10 pages of your prospectus:

Legalese

    definitive agreement

    consummation

    those preceded by

    herein

    set forth under

    by such forward-looking statements

    without limitations

    cease to conduct

    completion of the combination

    commencing

    hereinafter so surrendered

    defeased

    as amended qualified in its entirety

Organize the forepart of your prospectus from your investors' perspectives. For example, on the inside front cover you advise investors as to where they can find more information but you haven't provided them with any other information yet. Move this information so it appears somewhere after the risk factors section or, if you did not include a risk factors section, the summary.

#16 The forepart of your prospectus contains many defined terms. The meanings of the terms you use in the forepart of your prospectus must be clear from the context. Accordingly, eliminate the defined terms throughout the forepart of your prospectus and use terms whose meanings are clear from the context instead. See Rule 421(d) of Regulation C.

Cover page comments

#17 Your cover page exceeds the one page limit imposed by Item 501 of Regulation

S-K. Much of the information you include here is very detailed and is repeated in the summary. Move the information that is not required by Item 501 or is not key to an investment decision off the cover page. This will enable you to limit the cover to one page.

#18 Limit the cover page to the information that is required by Item 501 of Regulation S-K and other information that is key to an investment decision. Your cover page contains superfluous information such as the par value of common stock. Will potential investors base their investment decisions on the par value? Also, how should investors use the information in [the last paragraph]? Is this information key to an investment decision?

#19 Using [all capital letters] [and][cascading margins] impedes the readability of the text on the cover page. Since Item 501 limits this page to information that is key to an investment decision, it is very important that it be readable. See part IV.A. of Securities Act Release No. 7497. Revise text written in all capital letters and eliminate cascading margins from your cover page.

#20 Item 501(a)(5) of Regulation S-K requires you to highlight the cross reference to the risk factors section by prominent type or in another manner. Your cross reference is not visually distinctive from the other text on your cover page. Highlight this cross reference using, for example, bold-faced and italicized type. Note that placing this cross reference in all capital letters will impede its readability, not highlight it.

#21 The text on your cover page is dense and the margins are quite narrow. This is because you are including much more information than is required by Item 501 of Regulation S-K. As a result, your cover page is not visually inviting. The layout of your cover page must highlight the information required by Item 501 and encourage investors to read your prospectus. Move any information that is not required by Item 501 or is not key to an investment decision off the cover page. Then, surround the remaining information with ample white space and use wider left and right hand margins. See Rule 421(d) of Regulation C.

#22 The cover page should focus shareholders on the information that is key to their investment decision. On your cover page, this key information is obscured by a technical, detailed description of the transaction. For example, before you tell shareholders what they will receive in the merger, you introduce the merger subsidiary that exists solely to effect the merger. Before you provide the date, time, and location of the meeting, you tell shareholders that the acquiring company needs to amend its certificate of incorporation before it can complete the transaction.

Reorganize your cover page to highlight the information that is key to your shareholders' investment decisions. Also, move the information that is not required by Item 501 of Regulation S-K or is not key to an investment decision off the cover page.

Q&A section comments

Some issuers choose to include a "Questions and Answers" section in their merger proxy/prospectuses even though this section is not required by any of our rules. The staff neither encourages nor discourages the use of a Q&A section. However, we do not consider it a suitable replacement for the summary. If you include a Q&A section, it must not be a mere repetition of portions of the summary in a different format.

#23 You currently repeat a lot of information in both your Q&A and summary section. The Q&A should not repeat any information that appears in the summary, and *vice versa*. For purposes of eliminating redundancies and grouping like information together, view your Q&A and summary section as one section.

#24 Answer each question directly. Currently, you begin many answers with a discussion of related matters and don't provide the answer until the end of the paragraph. For example, Question #3 asks when you intend to complete the merger. Your answer begins with a discussion of the steps you must take before you may complete the merger. The answer—by the end of the next fiscal quarter—appears at the end of the paragraph. Put the answer first. Then, if necessary, describe the contingencies.

Further, if the question calls for a "yes" or "no" answer, state "yes" or "no" first, then explain why.

Summary comments

#25 The introductory paragraph to your summary states that the summary is not complete. A summary, by its very nature, does not and is not required to contain all of the detailed information that is in the prospectus. However, if you have elected to include a summary in your prospectus, it must be complete. Do you mean to say that, because this is a summary, it may not contain all of the information that is important to your investors? Delete the reference to an incomplete summary from your prospectus.

#26 Group like information together. Currently, your summary separates the items that discuss how the transaction directly affects shareholders with information on other topics. For example, the exchange ratio appears on page 3 and the tax consequences for payments on fractional shares appears on page 7. In between are discussions of regulatory matters, termination fees, conditions to the merger, etc.

#27 It is not clear in the summary which information you intend to highlight for shareholders. For example, in the first several pages in your summary, you explain at length the technical steps the companies must take, such as creating a merger subsidiary, to effect the merger. Further, you discuss the boards of directors' reasons for the merger and the conflicts of interest that may result before you explain how the proposed transaction directly affects shareholders. For example, the exchange ratio does not appear until page 36. Is this a logical order of information? Also, do shareholders need a summary of the technical steps to make an investment decision?

#28 We note your summary contains a lengthy description of the company's business and business strategy. Further, we note the identical disclosure appears later in your prospectus. In the summary, you are to carefully consider and identify those aspects of the offering that are the most significant and determine how to best highlight those points in clear, plain language. The summary should not include a lengthy description of the company's business and business strategy. This detailed information is better suited for the body of the prospectus. If you want to highlight key aspects of your business strategy, consider listing these in a bullet-point format, with one sentence per bullet point. See Item 503(a) of Regulation S-K and part IV.C. of Securities Act Release No. 7497.

#29 The amount of detail you include in the summary overwhelms the most significant aspects of the offering. For example, currently you include detail such as [insert example]. Do [shareholders] [potential investors] need this degree of detail in the summary? Also, much of this detail is repeated in the body of the prospectus. In the summary, you must carefully consider and identify those aspects of the offering that are the most significant and determine how to best highlight those points in clear, plain language.

Risk factor comments

See also the *Risk Factor Guidance* section.

#30 We note in the introductory paragraph to your risk factors section you state that this section is not complete, that there may be risks that you do not consider material now but may become material, or there may be risks that you have not yet identified. You must disclose all risks that you believe are material at this time. Delete this language from your introductory paragraph.

#31 Currently, it appears you are including more than one risk factor under one subheading. For example, is the second paragraph under "Recent Operating Results" a significant risk factor of this offering that needs to stand alone under an explanatory subheading? Other examples of "bundled" risk factors include . . . In order to give the proper prominence to each risk you present, we suggest you assign each risk its own descriptive subheading.

#32 Present the risks in more concrete terms. For example, in the first risk factor on page 12, you discuss the risks due to the "costs" associated with the benefit plans. So investors can better understand these risks, clearly state that the "costs" are not expenses of running those plans, but rather the added compensation expense that stems from the shares purchased or granted to employees and executives under those plans.

#33 In each risk factor, get to the risk as quickly as possible and provide only enough detail to place the risk in context. In some of your risk factors, the actual risk you are trying to convey does not stand out from the extensive detail you provide. For example, what specifically is the risk in the first risk factor? The first paragraph explains in detail Company X's past losses without any reference to a current risk.

Also, this discussion of past losses appears elsewhere in the prospectus. Where you repeat later in the prospectus the details you currently include in your risk factors section, eliminate the extensive detail here. Instead, include a very brief overview to place the risk in context and provide a specific cross reference to the more detailed discussion elsewhere in the prospectus.

#34 Provide the information investors need to assess the magnitude of the risk. For example, in the second risk factor on page 4, you state that increases in short-term interest rates could have a material adverse effect on XYZ Bank's profitability. Explain why. Are a substantial percentage of XYZ's interest-earning assets in long-term investments that pay fixed rates while the interest you pay to your depositors fluctuates? If so, what percentage of your interest-earning assets are in long-term investments?

#35 Item 503(c) of Regulation S-K states that issuers should not "present risk factors that could apply to any issuer or to any offering." For example, the risk you disclose under "Dependence on Key Personnel" could apply to nearly any issuer in your industry and even in other industries. If you elect to retain these and other general risk factors in your prospectus, you must clearly explain how they apply to your industry, company, or offering. For example, explain why you are concerned you could lose these key personnel. Are they about to retire? Do you not have employment contracts with them?

#36 Revise each subheading to ensure it reflects the risk that you discuss in the text. Many of your subheadings currently either merely state a fact about your business, such as "Our capacity to borrow is limited" and "The services we provide are regulated," or describe an event that may occur in the future, such as "We may not be able to obtain the necessary regulatory approvals," and "We expect competition in our industry to increase." Succinctly state in your subheadings the risks that result from the facts or uncertainties.

#37 The subheadings in your risk factors section are too vague and generic to adequately describe the risk that follows. For example, on page X, you use the subheading "Competition." Because all companies operating in a free market economy are subject to competition, this subheading is not descriptive.

Revise your risk factor subheadings so they reflect the risk that follows. As a general rule, your revised subheadings should work only in this prospectus. If they are readily transferable to other companies' offering documents, they are probably too generic. See Item 503(c) of Regulation S-K.

#38 To the extent possible, avoid the generic conclusion you make in most of your risk factors that the risk discussed would have a material adverse effect on your [operations] [financial condition][business]. Instead, replace this language with specific disclosure of how your [operations] [financial condition] [business] would be affected.

Comments applicable to body of prospectus

#39 Rule 421(b) of Regulation C requires you to avoid relying on defined terms as a primary means of explaining information in the prospectus. We note that the body of your prospectus contains a large number of defined terms. For example, page 32 alone contains over 20 defined terms. Most of these are terms that you created solely for use in this prospectus. While this practice provides a useful shortcut for the writer, potential investors must memorize a new vocabulary—whose usefulness is limited to this prospectus—before they can understand your disclosure. Revise your prospectus to eliminate your over-reliance on defined terms, as required by Rule 421(b).

#40 If you must include technical terms in the body of your prospectus that are understood only by industry experts, you must make every effort to concisely explain these terms where you first use them. Where this is simply not possible, explain these terms in a glossary. In addition, do not use technical terms or industry jargon in your concise explanations.

You should not use a glossary to define commonly understood abbreviations, like SEC, or acronyms, like NASDAQ. Further, you should not use a glossary to define terms that you have created solely for the purpose of your registration statement. We urge you not to create a vocabulary that is unique to your offering.

#41 Under Rule 421(b) of Regulation C, you must avoid copying complex information directly from legal documents without any clear and concise explanation of this information. It appears that much of the language in the body of the prospectus was taken directly from the underlying [indenture] [shareholder agreements] [rights plan] [merger agreement][statute on dissenters rights] [employment agreement]. Rewrite this disclosure so it is clear, concise, and understandable. If you believe the language as it appears in the underlying legal documents is indispensable to your prospectus, you must:

- present it clearly, using bullet lists and concise sections and paragraphs as described in Rule 421(b); and

- explain what it means to investors.

http://www.sec.gov/offices/corpfin/cfslb7a.htm

Last update: 06/04/1999

[¶ 43,014] Staff Legal Bulletin No. 14 (CF)

Action: Publication of CF Staff Legal Bulletin

Date: July 13, 2001

Summary: This staff legal bulletin provides information for companies and shareholders on rule 14a-8 of the Securities Exchange Act of 1934.

Supplementary Information: The statements in this legal bulletin represent the views of the Division of Corporation Finance. This bulletin is not a rule, regulation or statement of the Securities and Exchange Commission. Further, the Commission has neither approved nor disapproved its content.

Contact Person: For further information, please contact Jonathan Ingram, Michael Coco, Lillian Cummins or Keir Gumbs at (202) 942-2900.

A. What is the purpose of this bulletin?

The Division of Corporation Finance processes hundreds of rule 14a-8 no-action requests each year. We believe that companies and shareholders may benefit from information that we can provide based on our experience in processing these requests. Therefore, we prepared this bulletin in order to

- explain the rule 14a-8 no-action process, as well as our role in this process;

- provide guidance to companies and shareholders by expressing our views on some issues and questions that commonly arise under rule 14a-8; and

- suggest ways in which both companies and shareholders can facilitate our review of no-action requests.

Because the substance of each proposal and no-action request differs, this bulletin primarily addresses procedural matters that are common to companies and shareholders. However, we also discuss some substantive matters that are of interest to companies and shareholders alike.

We structured this bulletin in a question and answer format so that it is easier to understand and we can more easily respond to inquiries regarding its contents. The references to "we," "our" and "us" are to the Division of Corporation Finance. You can find a copy of rule 14a-8 in Release No. 34-40018, dated May 21, 1998, which is located on the Commission's website at *www.sec.gov/rules/final/34-40018.htm*.

B. Rule 14a-8 and the no-action process

1. What is rule 14a-8?

Rule 14a-8 provides an opportunity for a shareholder owning a relatively small amount of a company's securities to have his or her proposal placed alongside management's proposals in that company's proxy materials for presentation to a vote at an annual or special meeting of shareholders. It has become increasingly popular because it provides an avenue for communication between shareholders and companies, as well as among shareholders themselves. The rule generally requires the company to include the proposal unless the shareholder has not complied with the rule's procedural requirements or the proposal falls within one of the 13 substantive bases for exclusion described in the table below.

Substantive Basic	Description
Rule 14a-8(i)(1)	The proposal is not a proper subject for action by shareholders under the laws of the jurisdiction of the company's organization.
Rule 14a-8(i)(2)	The proposal would, if implemented, cause the company to violate any state, federal or foreign law to which it is subject.
Rule 14a-8(i)(3)	The proposal or supporting statement is contrary to any of the Commission's proxy rules, including rule 14a-9, which prohibits materially false or misleading statements in proxy soliciting materials.
Rule 14a-8(i)(4)	The proposal relates to the redress of a personal claim or grievance against the company or any other person, or is designed to result in a benefit to the shareholder, or to further a personal interest, which is not shared by the other shareholders at large.
Rule 14a-8(i)(5)	The proposal relates to operations that account for less than 5% of the company's total assets at the end of its most recent fiscal year, and for less than 5% of its net earnings and gross sales for its most recent fiscal year, and is not otherwise significantly related to the company's business.
Rule 14a-8(i)(6)	The company would lack the power or authority to implement the proposal.
Rule 14a-8(i)(7)	The proposal deals with a matter relating to the company's ordinary business operations.
Rule 14a-8(i)(8)	The proposal relates to an election for membership on the company's board of directors or analogous governing body.
Rule 14a-8(i)(9)	The proposal directly conflicts with one of the company's own proposals to be submitted to shareholders at the same meeting.
Rule 14a-8(i)(10)	The company has already substantially implemented the proposal.
Rule 14a-8(i)(11)	The proposal substantially duplicates another proposal previously submitted to the company by another shareholder that will be included in the company's proxy materials for the same meeting.
Rule 14a-8(i)(12)	The proposal deals with substantially the same subject matter as another proposal or proposals that previously has or have been included in the company's proxy materials within a specified time frame and did not receive a specified percentage of the vote. Please refer to questions and answers F.2, F.3 and F.4 for more complete descriptions of this basis.
Rule 14a-8(i)(13)	The proposal relates to specific amounts of cash or stock dividends.

2. How does rule 14a-8 operate?

The rule operates as follows:

• the shareholder must provide a copy of his or her proposal to the company by the deadline imposed by the rule;

• if the company intends to exclude the proposal from its proxy materials, it must submit its reason(s) for doing so to the Commission and simultaneously provide the shareholder with a copy of that submission. This submission to the Commission of reasons for excluding the proposal is commonly referred to as a no-action request;

• the shareholder may, but is not required to, submit a reply to us with a copy to the company; and

• we issue a no-action response that either concurs or does not concur in the company's view regarding exclusion of the proposal.

3. What are the deadlines contained in rule 14a-8?

Rule 14a-8 establishes specific deadlines for the shareholder proposal process. The following table briefly describes those deadlines.

120 days before the release date disclosed in the previous year's proxy statement	Proposals for a regularly scheduled annual meeting must be received at the company's principal executive offices not less than 120 calendar days before the release date of the previous year's annual meeting proxy statement. Both the release date and the deadline for receiving rule 14a-8 proposals for the next annual meeting should be identified in that proxy statement.
14-day notice of defect(s)/response to notice of defect(s)	If a company seeks to exclude a proposal because the shareholder has not complied with an eligibility or procedural requirement of rule 14a-8, generally, it must notify the shareholder of the alleged defect(s) within 14 calendar days of receiving the proposal. The shareholder then has 14 calendar days after receiving the notification to respond. Failure to cure the defect(s) or respond in a timely manner may result in exclusion of the proposal.
80 days before the company files its definitive proxy statement and form of proxy	If a company intends to exclude a proposal from its proxy materials, it must submit its no-action request to the Commission no later than 80 calendar days before it files its definitive proxy statement and form of proxy with the Commission unless it demonstrates "good cause" for missing the deadline. In addition, a company must simultaneously provide the shareholder with a copy of its no-action request.
30 days before the company files its definitive proxy statement and form of proxy	If a proposal appears in a company's proxy materials, the company may elect to include its reasons as to why shareholders should vote against the proposal. This statement of reasons for voting against the proposal is commonly referred to as a statement in opposition. Except as explained in the box immediately below, the company is required to provide the shareholder with a copy of its statement in opposition no later than 30 calendar days before it files its definitive proxy statement and form of proxy.
Five days after the company has received a revised proposal	If our no-action response provides for shareholder revision to the proposal or supporting statement as a condition to requiring the company to include it in its proxy materials, the company must provide the shareholder with a copy of its statement in opposition no later than five calendar days after it receives a copy of the revised proposal.

In addition to the specific deadlines in rule 14a-8, our informal procedures often rely on timely action. For example, if our no-action response requires that the shareholder revise the proposal or supporting statement, our response will afford the shareholder seven calendar days from the date of receiving our response to provide the company with the revisions. In this regard, please refer to questions and answers B.12.a and B.12.b.

4. What is our role in the no-action process?

Our role begins when we receive a no-action request from a company. In these no-action requests, companies often assert that a proposal is excludable under one or more parts of rule 14a-8. We analyze each of the bases for exclusion that a company asserts, as well as any arguments that the shareholder chooses to set forth, and determine whether we concur in the company's view.

The Division of Investment Management processes rule 14a-8 no-action requests submitted by registered investment companies and business development companies.

Rule 14a-8 no-action requests submitted by registered investment companies and business development companies, as well as shareholder responses to those requests, should be sent to

U.S. Securities and Exchange Commission
Division of Investment Management
Office of Chief Counsel
450 Fifth Street, N.W.
Washington, D.C. 20549

All other rule 14a-8 no-action requests and shareholder responses to those requests should be sent to

U.S. Securities and Exchange Commission
Division of Corporation Finance
Office of Chief Counsel
450 Fifth Street, N.W.
Washington, D.C. 20549

5. What factors do we consider in determining whether to concur in a company's view regarding exclusion of a proposal from the proxy statement?

The company has the burden of demonstrating that it is entitled to exclude a proposal, and we will not consider any basis for exclusion that is not advanced by the company. We analyze the prior no-action letters that a company and a shareholder cite in support of their arguments and, where appropriate, any applicable case law. We also may conduct our own research to determine whether we have issued additional letters that support or do not support the company's and shareholder's positions. Unless a company has demonstrated that it is entitled to exclude a proposal, we will not concur in its view that it may exclude that proposal from its proxy materials.

6. Do we base our determinations solely on the subject matter of the proposal?

No. We consider the specific arguments asserted by the company and the shareholder, the way in which the proposal is drafted and how the arguments and our prior no-action responses apply to the specific proposal and company at issue. Based on these considerations, we may determine that company X may exclude a proposal but company Y cannot exclude a proposal that addresses the same or similar subject matter. The following chart illustrates this point by showing that variations in the language of a proposal, or different bases cited by a company, may result in different responses.

As shown below, the first and second examples deal with virtually identical proposals, but the different company arguments resulted in different responses. In the second and third examples, the companies made similar arguments, but differing language in the proposals resulted in different responses.

Company	Proposal	Bases for exclusion that the company cited	Date of our response	Our response
PG&E Corp.	Adopt a policy that independent directors are appointed to the audit, compensation and nomination committees.	Rule 14a-8(b) only	Feb. 21, 2000	We did not concur in PG&E's view that it could exclude the proposal. PG&E did not demonstrate that the shareholder failed to satisfy the rule's minimum ownership requirements. PG&E included the proposal in its proxy materials.
PG&E Corp.	Adopt a bylaw that independent directors are appointed for all future openings on the audit, compensation and nomination committees.	Rule 14a-8(i)(6) only	Jan. 22, 2001	We concurred in PG&E's view that it could exclude the proposal. PG&E demonstrated that it lacked the power or authority to implement the proposal. PG&E did not include the proposal in its proxy materials.

Company	Proposal	Bases for exclusion that the company cited	Date of our response	Our response
General Motors Corp.	Adopt a bylaw requiring a *transition to* independent directors for each seat on the audit, compensation and nominating committees as openings occur (emphasis added).	Rules 14a-8(i)(6) and 14a-8(i)(10)	Mar. 22, 2001	We did not concur in GM's view that it could exclude the proposal. GM did not demonstrate that it lacked the power or authority to implement the proposal or that it had substantially implemented the proposal. GM included the proposal in its proxy materials.

7. Do we judge the merits of proposals?

No. We have no interest in the merits of a particular proposal. Our concern is that shareholders receive full and accurate information about all proposals that are, or should be, submitted to them under rule 14a-8.

8. Are we required to respond to no-action requests?

No. Although we are not required to respond, we have, as a convenience to both companies and shareholders, engaged in the informal practice of expressing our enforcement position on these submissions through the issuance of no-action responses. We do this to assist both companies and shareholders in complying with the proxy rules.

9. Will we comment on the subject matter of pending litigation?

No. Where the arguments raised in the company's no-action request are before a court of law, our policy is not to comment on those arguments. Accordingly, our no-action response will express no view with respect to the company's intention to exclude the proposal from its proxy materials.

10. How do we respond to no-action requests?

We indicate either that there appears to be some basis for the company's view that it may exclude the proposal or that we are unable to concur in the company's view that it may exclude the proposal. Because the company submits the no-action request, our response is addressed to the company. However, at the time we respond to a no-action request, we provide all related correspondence to both the company and the shareholder. These materials are available in the Commission's Public Reference Room and on commercially available, external databases.

11. What is the effect of our no-action response?

Our no-action responses only reflect our informal views regarding the application of rule 14a-8. We do not claim to issue "rulings" or "decisions" on proposals that companies indicate they intend to exclude, and our determinations do not and cannot adjudicate the merits of a company's position with respect to a proposal. For example, our decision not to recommend enforcement action does not prohibit a shareholder from pursuing rights that he or she may have against the company in court should management exclude a proposal from the company's proxy materials.

12. What is our role after we issue our no-action response?

Under rule 14a-8, we have a limited role after we issue our no-action response. In addition, due to the large number of no-action requests that we receive between the months of December and February, the no-action process must be efficient. As described in answer B.2, above, rule 14a-8 envisions a structured process under which the company submits the request, the shareholder may reply and we issue our response. When shareholders and companies deviate from this structure or are unable to resolve differences, our time and resources are diverted and the process breaks down. Based on our experience, this most often occurs as a result of friction between companies and shareholders and their inability to compromise. While we are always available to facilitate the fair and efficient application of the rule, the operation of the rule, as well as the no-action process, suffers when our role changes from an issuer of responses to an arbiter of disputes. The following questions and answers are examples of how we view our limited role after issuance of our no-action response.

a. If our no-action response affords the shareholder additional time to provide documentation of ownership or revise the proposal, but the company does not believe that the documentation or revisions comply with our no-action response, should the company submit a new no-action request?

No. For example, our no-action response may afford the shareholder seven days to provide documentation demonstrating that he or she satisfies the minimum ownership requirements contained in rule 14a-8(b). If the shareholder provides the required documentation eight days after receiving our no-action response, the company should not submit a new no-action request in order to exclude the proposal. Similarly, if we indicate in our response that the shareholder must provide factual support for a sentence in the supporting statement, the company and the shareholder should work together to determine whether the revised sentence contains appropriate factual support.

b. If our no-action response affords the shareholder an additional seven days to provide documentation of ownership or revise the proposal, who should keep track of when the seven-day period begins to run?

When our no-action response gives a shareholder time, it is measured from the date the shareholder receives our response. As previously noted in answer B.10, we send our response to both the company and the shareholder. However, the company is responsible for determining when the seven-day period begins to run. In order to avoid controversy, the company should forward a copy of our response to the shareholder by a means that permits the company to prove the date of receipt.

13. Does rule 14a-8 contemplate any other involvement by us after we issue a no-action response?

Yes. If a shareholder believes that a company's statement in opposition is materially false or misleading, the shareholder may promptly send a letter to us and the company explaining the reasons for his or her view, as well as a copy of the proposal and statement in opposition. Just as a company has the burden of demonstrating that it is entitled to exclude a proposal, a shareholder should, to the extent possible, provide us with specific factual information that demonstrates the inaccuracy of the company's statement in opposition. We encourage shareholders and companies to work out these differences before contacting us.

14. What must a company do if, before we have issued a no-action response, the shareholder withdraws the proposal or the company decides to include the proposal in its proxy materials?

If the company no longer wishes to pursue its no-action request, the company should provide us with a letter as soon as possible withdrawing its no-action request. This allows us to allocate our resources to other pending requests. The company should also provide the shareholder with a copy of the withdrawal letter.

15. If a company wishes to withdraw a no-action request, what information should its withdrawal letter contain?

In order for us to process withdrawals efficiently, the company's letter should contain

- a statement that either the shareholder has withdrawn the proposal or the company has decided to include the proposal in its proxy materials;

- if the shareholder has withdrawn the proposal, a copy of the shareholder's signed letter of withdrawal, or some other indication that the shareholder has withdrawn the proposal;

- if there is more than one eligible shareholder, the company must provide documentation that all of the eligible shareholders have agreed to withdraw the proposal;

- if the company has agreed to include a revised version of the proposal in its proxy materials, a statement from the shareholder that he or she accepts the revisions; and

- an affirmative statement that the company is withdrawing its no-action request.

C. Questions regarding the eligibility and procedural requirements of the rule

Rule 14a-8 contains eligibility and procedural requirements for shareholders who wish to include a proposal in a company's proxy materials. Below, we address some of the common questions that arise regarding these requirements.

1. To be eligible to submit a proposal, rule 14a-8(b) requires the shareholder to have continuously held at least $2,000 in market value, or 1%, of the company's securities entitled to be voted on the proposal at the meeting for at least one year by the date of submitting the proposal. Also, the shareholder must continue to hold those securities through the date of the meeting. The following questions and answers address issues regarding shareholder eligibility.

a. How do you calculate the market value of the shareholder's securities?

Due to market fluctuations, the value of a shareholder's investment in the company may vary throughout the year before he or she submits the proposal. In order to determine whether the shareholder satisfies the $2,000 threshold, we look at whether, on any date within the 60 calendar days before the date the shareholder submits the proposal, the shareholder's investment is valued at $2,000 or greater, based on the average of the bid and ask prices. Depending on where the company is listed, bid and ask prices may not always be available. For example, bid and ask prices are not provided for companies listed on the New York Stock Exchange. Under these circumstances, companies and shareholders should determine the market value by multiplying the number of securities the shareholder held for the one-year period by the highest selling price during the 60 calendar days before the shareholder submitted the proposal. For purposes of this calculation, it is important to note that a security's highest selling price is not necessarily the same as its highest closing price.

b. What type of security must a shareholder own to be eligible to submit a proposal?

A shareholder must own company securities entitled to be voted on the proposal at the meeting.

Example

A company receives a proposal relating to executive compensation from a shareholder who owns only shares of the company's class B common stock. The company's class B common stock is entitled to vote only on the election of directors. Does the shareholder's ownership of only class B stock provide a basis for the company to exclude the proposal?

Yes. This would provide a basis for the company to exclude the proposal because the shareholder does not own securities entitled to be voted on the proposal at the meeting.

c. How should a shareholder's ownership be substantiated?

Under rule 14a-8(b), there are several ways to determine whether a shareholder has owned the minimum amount of company securities entitled to be voted on the proposal at the meeting for the required time period. If the shareholder appears in the company's records as a registered holder, the company can verify the shareholder's eligibility independently. However, many shareholders hold their securities indirectly through a broker or bank. In the event that the shareholder is not the registered holder, the shareholder is responsible for proving his or her eligibility to submit a proposal to the company. To do so, the shareholder must do one of two things. He or she can submit a written statement from the record holder of the securities verifying that the shareholder has owned the securities continuously for one year as of the time the shareholder submits the proposal. Alternatively, a shareholder who has filed a Schedule 13D, Schedule 13G, Form 4 or Form 5 reflecting ownership of the securities as of or before the date on which the one-year eligibility period begins may submit copies of these forms and any subsequent amendments reporting a change in ownership level, along with a written statement that he or she has owned the required number of securities continuously for one year as of the time the shareholder submits the proposal.

(1) Does a written statement from the shareholder's investment adviser verifying that the shareholder held the securities continuously for at least one year before submitting the proposal demonstrate sufficiently continuous ownership of the securities?

The written statement must be from the record holder of the shareholder's securities, which is usually a broker or bank. Therefore, unless the investment adviser is also the record holder, the statement would be insufficient under the rule.

(2) Do a shareholder's monthly, quarterly or other periodic investment statements demonstrate sufficiently continuous ownership of the securities?

No. A shareholder must submit an affirmative written statement from the record holder of his or her securities that specifically verifies that the shareholder owned the securities *continuously* for a period of one year as of the time of submitting the proposal.

(3) If a shareholder submits his or her proposal to the company on June 1, does a statement from the record holder verifying that the shareholder owned the securities continuously for one year as of May 30 of the same year demonstrate sufficiently continuous ownership of the securities as of the time he or she submitted the proposal?

No. A shareholder must submit proof from the record holder that the shareholder continuously owned the securities for a period of one year as of the time the shareholder submits the proposal.

d. Should a shareholder provide the company with a written statement that he or she intends to continue holding the securities through the date of the shareholder meeting?

Yes. The shareholder must provide this written statement regardless of the method the shareholder uses to prove that he or she continuously owned the securities for a period of one year as of the time the shareholder submits the proposal.

2. In order for a proposal to be eligible for inclusion in a company's proxy materials, rule 14a-8(d) requires that the proposal, including any accompanying supporting statement, not exceed 500 words. The following questions and answers address issues regarding the 500-word limitation.

a. May a company count the words in a proposal's "title" or "heading" in determining whether the proposal exceeds the 500-word limitation?

Any statements that are, in effect, arguments in support of the proposal constitute part of the supporting statement. Therefore, any "title" or "heading" that meets this test may be counted toward the 500-word limitation.

b. Does referencing a website address in the proposal or supporting statement violate the 500-word limitation of rule 14a-8(d)?

No. Because we count a website address as one word for purposes of the 500-word limitation, we do not believe that a website address raises the concern that rule 14a-8(d) is intended to address. However, a website address could be subject to exclusion if it refers readers to information that may be materially false or misleading, irrelevant to the subject matter of the proposal or otherwise in contravention of the proxy rules. In this regard, please refer to question and answer F.1.

3. Rule 14a-8(e)(2) requires that proposals for a regularly scheduled annual meeting be received at the company's principal executive of-

fices by a date not less than 120 calendar days before the date of the company's proxy statement released to shareholders in connection with the previous year's annual meeting. The following questions and answers address a number of issues that come up in applying this provision.

a. How do we interpret the phrase "before the date of the company's proxy statement released to shareholders?"

We interpret this phrase as meaning the approximate date on which the proxy statement and form of proxy were first sent or given to shareholders. For example, if a company having a regularly scheduled annual meeting files its definitive proxy statement and form of proxy with the Commission dated April 1, 2001, but first sends or gives the proxy statement to shareholders on April 15, 2001, as disclosed in its proxy statement, we will refer to the April 15, 2001 date as the release date. The company and shareholders should use April 15, 2001 for purposes of calculating the 120-day deadline in rule 14a-8(e)(2).

b. How should a company that is planning to have a regularly scheduled annual meeting calculate the deadline for submitting proposals?

The company should calculate the deadline for submitting proposals as follows:

• start with the release date disclosed in the previous year's proxy statement;

• increase the year by one; and

• count back 120 calendar days.

Examples

If a company is planning to have a regularly scheduled annual meeting in May of 2003 and the company disclosed that the release date for its 2002 proxy statement was April 14, 2002, how should the company calculate the deadline for submitting rule 14a-8 proposals for the company's 2003 annual meeting?

• The release date disclosed in the company's 2002 proxy statement was April 14, 2002.

• Increasing the year by one, the day to begin the calculation is April 14, 2003.

• "Day one" for purposes of the calculation is April 13, 2003.

• "Day 120" is December 15, 2002.

• The 120-day deadline for the 2003 annual meeting is December 15, 2002.

• A rule 14a-8 proposal received after December 15, 2002 would be untimely.

If the 120th calendar day before the release date disclosed in the previous year's proxy statement is a Saturday, Sunday or federal holiday, does this change the deadline for receiving rule 14a-8 proposals?

No. The deadline for receiving rule 14a-8 proposals is always the 120th calendar day before the release date disclosed in the previous year's proxy statement. Therefore, if the deadline falls on a Saturday, Sunday or federal holiday, the company must disclose this date in its proxy statement, and rule 14a-8 proposals received after business reopens would be untimely.

c. How does a shareholder know where to send his or her proposal?

The proposal must be received at the company's principal executive offices. Shareholders can find this address in the company's proxy statement. If a shareholder sends a proposal to any other location, even if it is to an agent of the company or to another company location, this would not satisfy the requirement.

d. How does a shareholder know if his or her proposal has been received by the deadline?

A shareholder should submit a proposal by a means that allows him or her to determine when the proposal was received at the company's principal executive offices.

4. Rule 14a-8(h)(1) requires that the shareholder or his or her qualified representative attend the shareholders' meeting to present the proposal. Rule 14a-8(h)(3) provides that a company may exclude a shareholder's proposals for two calendar years if the company included one of the shareholder's proposals in its proxy materials for a shareholder meeting, neither the shareholder nor the shareholder's qualified representative appeared and presented the proposal and the shareholder did not demonstrate "good cause" for failing to attend the meeting or present the proposal. The following questions and answers address issues regarding these provisions.

a. Does rule 14a-8 require a shareholder to represent in writing before the meeting that he or she, or a qualified representative, will attend the shareholders' meeting to present the proposal?

No. The Commission stated in Release No. 34-20091 that shareholders are no longer required to provide the company with a written statement of intent to appear and present a shareholder proposal. The Commission eliminated this requirement because it "serve[d] little purpose" and only encumbered shareholders. We, therefore, view it as inappropriate for companies to solicit this type of written statement from shareholders for purposes of rule 14a-8. In particular, we note that shareholders who are unfamiliar with the proxy rules may be misled, even unintentionally, into believing that a written statement of intent is required.

b. What if a shareholder provides an unsolicited, written statement that neither his or her qualified representative will attend the meeting to present the proposal? May the company exclude the proposal under this circumstance?

Yes. Rule 14a-8(i)(3) allows companies to exclude proposals that are contrary to the proxy rules, including rule 14a-8(h)(1). If a shareholder voluntarily provides a written statement evidencing his or her intent to act contrary to rule 14a-8(h)(1), rule 14a-8(i)(3) may serve as a basis for the company to exclude the proposal.

c. If a company demonstrates that it is entitled to exclude a proposal under rule 14a-8(h)(3), can the company request that we issue a no-action response that covers both calendar years?

Yes. For example, assume that, without "good cause," neither the shareholder nor the shareholder's representative attended the company's 2001 annual meeting to present the shareholder's proposal, and the shareholder then submits a proposal for inclusion in the company's 2002 proxy materials. If the company seeks to exclude the 2002 proposal under rule 14a-8(h)(3), it may concurrently request forward-looking relief for any proposal(s) that the shareholder may submit for inclusion in the company's 2003 proxy materials. If we grant the company's request and the company receives a proposal from the shareholder in connection with the 2003 annual meeting, the company still has an obligation under rule 14a-8(j) to notify us and the shareholder of its intention to exclude the shareholder's proposal from its proxy materials for that meeting. Although we will retain that notice in our records, we will not issue a no-action response.

5. In addition to rule 14a-8(h)(3), are there any other circumstances in which we will grant forward-looking relief to a company under rule 14a-8?

Yes. Rule 14a-8(i)(4) allows companies to exclude a proposal if it relates to the redress of a personal claim or grievance against the company or any other person or is designed to result in a benefit to the shareholder, or to further a personal interest, that is not shared by the other shareholders at large. In rare circumstances, we may grant forward-looking relief if a company satisfies its burden of demonstrating that the shareholder is abusing rule 14a-8 by continually submitting similar proposals that relate to a particular personal claim or grievance. As in answer C.4.c, above, if we grant this relief, the company still has an obligation under rule 14a-8(j) to notify us and the shareholder of its intention to exclude the shareholder's proposal(s) from its proxy materials. Although will retain that notice in our records, we will not issue a no-action response.

6. What must a company do in order to exclude a proposal that fails to comply with the eligibility or procedural requirements of the rule?

If a shareholder fails to follow the eligibility or procedural requirements of rule 14a-8, the rule provides procedures for the company to follow if it wishes to exclude the proposal. For example, rule 14a-8(f) provides that a company may exclude a proposal from its proxy materials due to eligibility or procedural defects if

• within 14 calendar days of receiving the proposal, it provides the shareholder with written notice of the

defect(s), including the time frame for responding; and

• the shareholder fails to respond to this notice within 14 calendar days of receiving the notice of the defect(s) or the shareholder timely responds but does not cure the eligibility or procedural defect(s).

Section G.3 - Eligibility and Procedural Issues, below, contains information that companies may want to consider in drafting these notices. If the shareholder does not timely respond or remedy the defect(s) and the company intends to exclude the proposal, the company still must submit, to us and to the shareholder, a copy of the proposal and its reasons for excluding the proposal.

a. Should a company's notices of defect(s) give different levels of information to different shareholders depending on the company's perception of the shareholder's sophistication in rule 14a-8?

No. Companies should not assume that any shareholder is familiar with the proxy rules or give different levels of information to different shareholders based on the fact that the shareholder may or may not be a frequent or "experienced" shareholder proponent.

b. Should companies instruct shareholders to respond to the notice of defect(s) by a specified date rather than indicating that shareholders have 14 calendar days after receiving the notice to respond?

No. Rule 14a-8(f) provides that shareholders must respond within 14 calendar days of receiving notice of the alleged eligibility or procedural defect(s). If the company provides a specific date by which the shareholder must submit his or her response, it is possible that the deadline set by the company will be shorter than the 14-day period required by rule 14a-8(f). For example, events could delay the shareholder's receipt of the notice. As such, if a company sets a specific date for the shareholder to respond and that date does not result in the shareholder having 14 calendar days after receiving the notice to respond, we do not believe that the company may rely on rule 14a-8(f) to exclude the proposal.

c. Are there any circumstances under which a company does not have to provide the shareholder with a notice of defect(s)? For example, what should the company do if the shareholder indicates that he or she does not own at least $2,000 in market value, or 1%, of the company's securities?

The company does not need to provide the shareholder with a notice of defect(s) if the defect(s) cannot be remedied. In the example provided in the question, because the shareholder cannot remedy this defect after the fact, no notice of the defect would be required. The same would apply, for example, if

• the shareholder indicated that he or she had owned securities entitled to be voted on the proposal for a period of less than one year before submitting the proposal;

• the shareholder indicated that he or she did not own securities entitled to be voted on the proposal at the meeting;

• the shareholder failed to submit a proposal by the company's properly determined deadline; or

• the shareholder, or his or her qualified representative, failed to attend the meeting or present one of the shareholder's proposals that was included in the company's proxy materials during the past two calendar years.

In all of these circumstances, the company must still submit its reasons regarding exclusion of the proposal to us and the shareholder. The shareholder may, but is not required to, submit a reply to us with a copy to the company.

D. Questions regarding the inclusion of shareholder names in proxy statements

1. If the shareholder's proposal will appear in the company's proxy statement, is the company required to disclose the shareholder's name?

No. A company is not required to disclose the identity of a shareholder proponent in its proxy statement. Rather, a company can indicate that it will provide the information to shareholders promptly upon receiving an oral or written request.

2. May a shareholder request that the company not disclose his or her name in the proxy statement?

Yes. However, the company has the discretion not to honor the request. In this regard, if the company chooses to include the shareholder proponent's name in the proxy statement, rule 14a-8(l)(1) requires that the company also include that shareholder proponent's address and the number of the company's voting securities that the shareholder proponent holds.

3. If a shareholder includes his or her e-mail address in the proposal or supporting statement, may the company exclude the e-mail address?

Yes. We view an e-mail address as equivalent to the shareholder proponent's name and address and, under rule 14a-8(l)(1), a company may exclude the shareholder's name and address from the proxy statement.

E. Questions regarding revisions to proposals and supporting statements

In this section, we first discuss the purpose for allowing shareholders to revise portions of a proposal and supporting statement. Second, we express our views with regard to revisions that a shareholder makes to his or her proposal before we receive a company's no-action request, as well as during the course of our review of a no-action request. Finally, we address the circumstances under which our responses may allow shareholders to make revisions to their proposals and supporting statements.

1. Why do our no-action responses sometimes permit shareholders to make revisions to their proposals and supporting statements?

There is no provision in rule 14a-8 that allows a shareholder to revise his or her proposal and supporting statement. However, we have a long-standing practice of issuing no-action responses that permit shareholders to make revisions that are minor in nature and do not alter the substance of the proposal. We adopted this practice to deal with proposals that generally comply with the substantive requirements of the rule, but contain some relatively minor defects that are easily corrected. In these circumstances, we believe that the concepts underlying Exchange Act section 14(a) are best served by affording an opportunity to correct these kinds of defects.

Despite the intentions underlying our revisions practice, we spend an increasingly large portion of our time and resources each proxy season responding to no-action requests regarding proposals or supporting statements that have obvious deficiencies in terms of accuracy, clarity or relevance. This is not beneficial to all participants in the process and diverts resources away from analyzing core issues arising under rule 14a-8 that are matters of interest to companies and shareholders alike. Therefore, when a proposal and supporting statement will require detailed and extensive editing in order to bring them into compliance with the proxy rules, we may find it appropriate for companies to exclude the entire proposal, supporting statement, or both, as materially false or misleading.

2. If a company has received a timely proposal and the shareholder makes revisions to the proposal before the company submits its no-action request, must the company accept those revisions?

No, but it *may* accept the shareholder's revisions. If the changes are such that the revised proposal is actually a different proposal from the original, the revised proposal could be subject to exclusion under

• rule 14a-8(c), which provides that a shareholder may submit no more than one proposal to a company for a particular shareholders' meeting; and

• rule 14a-8(e), which imposes a deadline for submitting shareholder proposals.

3. If the shareholder decides to make revisions to his or her proposal after the company has submitted its no-action request, must the company address those revisions?

No, but it *may* address the shareholder's revisions. We base our no-action response on the proposal included in the company's no-action request. Therefore, if the company indicates in a letter to us and the shareholder that it acknowledges and accepts the shareholder's changes, we will base our response on the revised proposal. Otherwise, we will base our response on the proposal contained in the company's original no-action request. Again, it is important for shareholders to note that, depending on the nature and timing of the changes, a revised proposal could be subject to exclusion under rule 14a-8(c), rule 14a-8(e), or both.

4. If the shareholder decides to make revisions to his or her proposal after the company has submitted its no-action request, should the shareholder provide a copy of the revisions to us?

Yes. All shareholder correspondence relating to the no-action request should be sent to us and the company. However, under rule 14a-8, no-action requests and shareholder responses to those requests are submitted to us. The proposals themselves are not submitted to us. Because proposals are submitted to companies for inclusion in their proxy materials, we will not address revised proposals unless the company chooses to acknowledge the changes.

5. When do our responses afford shareholders an opportunity to revise their proposals and supporting statements?

We may, under limited circumstances, permit shareholders to revise their proposals and supporting statements. The following table provides examples of the rule 14a-8 bases under which we typically allow revisions, as well as the types of permissible changes:

Basis	Type of revision that we may permit
Rule 14a-8(i)(1)	When a proposal would be binding on the company if approved by shareholders, we may permit the shareholder to revise the proposal to a recommendation or request that the board of directors take the action specified in the proposal.
Rule 14a-8(i)(2)	If implementing the proposal would require the company to breach existing contractual obligations, we may permit the shareholder to revise the proposal so that it applies only to the company's future contractual obligations.
Rule 14a-8(i)(3)	If the proposal contains specific statements that may be materially false or misleading or irrelevant to the subject matter of the proposal, we may permit the shareholder to revise or delete these statements. Also, if the proposal or supporting statement contains vague terms, we may, in rare circumstances, permit the shareholder to clarify these terms.
Rule 14a-8(i)(6)	Same as rule 14a-8(i)(2), above.
Rule 14a-8(i)(7)	If it is unclear whether the proposal focuses on senior executive compensation or director compensation, as opposed to general employee compensation, we may permit the shareholder to make this clarification.
Rule 14a-8(i)(8)	If implementing the proposal would disqualify directors previously elected from completing their terms on the board or disqualify nominees for directors at the upcoming shareholder meeting, we may permit the shareholder to revise the proposal so that it will not affect the unexpired terms of directors elected to the board at or prior to the upcoming shareholder meeting.
Rule 14a-8(i)(9)	Same as rule 14a-8(i)(8), above.

F. Other questions that arise under rule 14a-8

1. May a reference to a website address in the proposal or supporting statement be subject to exclusion under the rule?

Yes. In some circumstances, we may concur in a company's view that it may exclude a website address under rule 14a-8(i)(3) because information contained on the website may be materially false or misleading, irrelevant to the subject matter of the proposal or otherwise in contravention of the proxy rules. Companies seeking to exclude a website address under rule 14a-8(i)(3) should specifically indicate why they believe information contained on the particular website is materially false or misleading, irrelevant to the subject matter of the proposal or otherwise in contravention of the proxy rules.

2. Rule 14a-8(i)(12) provides a basis for a company to exclude a proposal dealing with substantially the same subject matter as another proposal or proposals that previously has or have been included in the company's proxy materials. How does rule 14a-8(i)(12) operate?

Rule 14a-8(i)(12) operates as follows:

a. First, the company should look back three calendar years to see if it previously included a proposal or proposals dealing with substantially the same subject matter. If it has not, rule 14a-8(i)(12) is not available as a basis to exclude a proposal from this year's proxy materials.

b. If it has, the company should then count the number of times that a proposal or proposals dealing with substantially the same subject matter was or were included over the preceding five calendar years.

c. Finally, the company should look at the percentage of the shareholder vote that a proposal dealing with substantially the same subject matter received the last time it was included.

- If the company included a proposal dealing with substantially the same subject matter only once in the preceding five calendar years, the company may exclude a proposal from this year's proxy materials under rule 14a-8(i)(12)(i) if it received less than 3% of the vote the last time that it was voted on.

- If the company included a proposal or proposals dealing with substantially the same subject matter twice in the preceding five calendar years, the company may exclude a proposal from this year's proxy materials under rule 14a-8(i)(12)(ii) if it received less than 6% of the vote the last time that it was voted on.

- If the company included a proposal or proposals dealing with substantially the same subject matter

three or more times in the preceding five calendar years, the company may exclude a proposal from this year's proxy materials under rule 14a-8(i)(12)(iii) if it received less than 10% of the vote the last time that it was voted on.

3. Rule 14a-8(i)(12) refers to calendar years. How do we interpret calendar years for this purpose?

Because a calendar year runs from January 1 through December 31, we do not look at the specific dates of company meetings. Instead, we look at the calendar year in which a meeting was held. For example, a company scheduled a meeting for April 25, 2002. In looking back three calendar years to determine if it previously had included a proposal or proposals dealing with substantially the same subject matter, any meeting held in calendar years 1999, 2000 or 2001 - which would include any meetings held between January 1, 1999 and December 31, 2001 - would be relevant under rule 14a-8(i)(12).

Examples

A company receives a proposal for inclusion in its 2002 proxy materials dealing with substantially the same subject matter as proposals that were voted on at the following shareholder meetings:

Calendar Year	1997	1998	1999	2000	2001	2002	2003
Voted on?	Yes	No	No	Yes	No	—	—
Percentage	4%	N/A	N/A	4%	N/A	—	—

May the company exclude the proposal from its 2002 proxy materials in reliance on rule 14a-8(i)(12)?

Yes. The company would be entitled to exclude the proposal under rule 14a-8(i)(12)(ii). First, calendar year 2000, the last time the company included a proposal dealing with substantially the same subject matter, is within the prescribed three calendar years. Second, the company included proposals dealing with substantially the same subject matter twice within the preceding five calendar years, specifically, in 1997 and 2000. Finally, the proposal received less than 6% of the vote on its last submission to shareholders in 2000. Therefore, rule 14a-8(i)(12)(ii), which permits exclusion when a company has included a proposal or proposals dealing with substantially the same subject matter twice in the preceding five calendar years and that proposal received less than 6% of the shareholder vote the last time it was voted on, would serve as a basis for excluding the proposal.

If the company excluded the proposal from its 2002 proxy materials and then received an identical proposal for inclusion in its 2003 proxy materials, may the company exclude the proposal from its 2003 proxy materials in reliance on rule 14a-8(i)(12)?

No. Calendar year 2000, the last time the company included a proposal dealing with substantially the same subject matter, is still within the prescribed

three calendar years. However, 2000 was the only time within the preceding five calendar years that the company included a proposal dealing with substantially the same subject matter, and it received more than 3% of the vote at the 2000 meeting. Therefore, the company would not be entitled to exclude the proposal under rule 14a-8(i)(12)(i).

4. How do we count votes under rule 14a-8(i)(12)?

Only votes for and against a proposal are included in the calculation of the shareholder vote of that proposal. Abstentions and broker non-votes are not included in this calculation.

Example

A proposal received the following votes at the company's last annual meeting:

- **5,000 votes for the proposal;**
- **3,000 votes against the proposal;**
- **1,000 broker non-votes; and**
- **1,000 abstentions.**

How is the shareholder vote of this proposal calculated for purposes of rule 14a-8(i)(12)?

This percentage is calculated as follows:

formula: votes for proposal divided by the sum of votes against the proposal and votes for the proposal equals voting percentage

Applying this formula to the facts above, the proposal received 62.5% of the vote.

example using previous formula: five thousand divided by the sum of three

G. How can companies and shareholders facilitate our processing of no-action requests or take steps to avoid the submission of no-action requests?

Eligibility and procedural issues

1. Before submitting a proposal to a company, a shareholder should look in the company's most recent proxy statement to find the deadline for submitting rule 14a-8 proposals. To avoid exclusion on the basis of untimeliness, a shareholder should submit his or her proposal well in advance of the deadline and by a means that allows the shareholder to demonstrate the date the proposal was received at the company's principal executive offices.

2. A shareholder who intends to submit a written statement from the record holder of the shareholder's securities to verify continuous ownership of the securities should contact the record holder before submitting a proposal to ensure that the record holder will provide the written statement and knows how to provide a written statement that will satisfy the requirements of rule 14a-8(b).

3. Companies should consider the following guidelines when drafting a letter to notify a shareholder of perceived eligibility or procedural defects:

- provide adequate detail about what the shareholder must do to remedy all eligibility or procedural defects;

- although not required, consider including a copy of rule 14a-8 with the notice of defect(s);

- explicitly state that the shareholder must respond to the company's notice within 14 calendar days of receiving the notice of defect(s); and

- send the notification by a means that allows the company to determine when the shareholder received the letter.

4. Rule 14a-8(f) provides that a shareholder's response to a company's notice of defect(s) must be postmarked, or transmitted electronically, no later than 14 days from the date the shareholder received the notice of defect(s). Therefore, a shareholder should respond to the company's notice of defect(s) by a means that allows the shareholder to demonstrate when he or she responded to the notice.

5. Rather than waiting until the deadline for submitting a no-action request, a company should submit a no-action request as soon as possible after it receives a proposal and determines that it will seek a no-action response.

6. Companies that will be submitting multiple no-action requests should submit their requests individually or in small groups rather than waiting and sending them all at once. We receive the heaviest volume of no-action requests between December and February of each year. Therefore, we are not able to process no-action requests as quickly during this period. Our experience shows that we often receive 70 to 80 no-action requests a week during our peak period and, at most, we can respond to 30 to 40 requests in any given week. Therefore, companies that wait until December through February to submit all of their requests will have to wait longer for a response.

7. Companies should provide us with all relevant correspondence when submitting the no-action request, including the shareholder proposal, any cover letter that the shareholder provided with the proposal, the shareholder's address and any other correspondence the company has exchanged with the shareholder relating to the proposal. If the company provided the shareholder with notice of a perceived eligibility or procedural defect, the company should include a copy of the notice, documentation demonstrating when the company notified the shareholder, documentation demonstrating when the shareholder received the notice and any shareholder response to the notice.

8. If a shareholder intends to reply to the company's no-action request, he or she should try to send the reply as soon as possible after the company submits its no-action request.

9. Both companies and shareholders should promptly forward to each other copies of all correspondence that is provided to us in connection with no-action requests.

10. Due to the significant volume of no-action requests and phone calls we receive during the proxy season, companies should limit their calls to us regarding the status of their no-action request.

11. Shareholders who write to us to object to a company's statement in opposition to the shareholder's proposal also should provide us with copies of the proposal as it will be printed in the company's proxy statement and the company's proposed statement in opposition.

Substantive issues

1. When drafting a proposal, shareholders should consider whether the proposal, if approved by shareholders, would be binding on the company. In our experience, we have found that proposals that are binding on the company face a much greater likelihood of being improper under state law and, therefore, excludable under rule 14a-8(i)(1).

2. When drafting a proposal, shareholders should consider what actions are within a company's power or authority. Proposals often request or require action by the company that would violate law or would not be within the power or authority of the company to implement.

3. When drafting a proposal, shareholders should consider whether the proposal would require the company to breach existing contracts. In our experience, we have found that proposals that would result in the company breaching existing contractual obligations face a much greater likelihood of being excluda-

ble under rule 14a-8(i)(2), rule 14a-8(i)(6), or both. This is because implementing the proposals may require the company to violate law or may not be within the power or authority of the company to implement.

4. In drafting a proposal and supporting statement, shareholders should avoid making unsupported assertions of fact. To this end, shareholders should provide factual support for statements in the proposal and supporting statement or phrase statements as their opinion where appropriate.

5. Companies should provide a supporting opinion of counsel when the reasons for exclusion are based on matters of state or foreign law. In determining how much weight to afford these opinions, one factor we consider is whether counsel is licensed to practice law in the jurisdiction where the law is at issue.

[¶ 43,014A]   Staff Legal Bulletin No. 14A (CF)

Shareholder Proposals

Action: Publication of CF Staff Legal Bulletin

Date: July 12, 2002

Summary: This staff legal bulletin provides information for companies and shareholders regarding rule 14a-8 of the Securities Exchange Act of 1934.

Supplementary Information: The statements in this staff legal bulletin represent the views of the Division of Corporation Finance. This bulletin is not a rule, regulation or statement of the Securities and Exchange Commission. Further, the Commission has neither approved nor disapproved its content.

Contact Person: For further information, please contact Keir D. Gumbs at (202) 942-2900.

Rule 14a-8 provides an opportunity for a shareholder owning a relatively small amount of a company's securities to have his or her proposal placed alongside management's proposals in that company's proxy materials for presentation to a vote at an annual or special meeting of shareholders. The rule generally requires the company to include the proposal unless the shareholder has not complied with the rule's procedural requirements or the proposal falls within one of the rule's 13 substantive bases for exclusion.

Rule 14a-8(i)(7) is one of the substantive bases for exclusion in rule 14a-8. It provides a basis for excluding a proposal that deals with a matter relating to the company's ordinary business operations. The fact that a proposal relates to ordinary business matters does not conclusively establish that a company may exclude the proposal from its proxy materials. As the Commission stated in Exchange Act Release No.

Shareholders who wish to contest a company's reliance on a legal opinion as to matters of state or foreign law should, but are not required to, submit an opinion of counsel supporting their position.

H. Conclusion

Whether or not you are familiar with rule 14a-8, we hope that this bulletin helps you gain a better understanding of the rule, the no-action request process and our views on some issues and questions that commonly arise during our review of no-action requests. While not exhaustive, we believe that the bulletin contains information that will assist both companies and shareholders in ensuring that the rule operates more effectively. Please contact us with any questions that you may have regarding information contained in the bulletin.

40018, proposals that relate to ordinary business matters but that focus on "sufficiently significant social policy issues . . . would not be considered to be excludable because the proposals would transcend the day-to-day business matters."[1]

In the 2001-2002 proxy season, shareholders submitted proposals to several companies relating to equity compensation plans. Some of these proposals requested that the companies submit for shareholder approval all equity compensation plans that potentially would result in material dilution to existing shareholders. We received four no-action requests from companies seeking to exclude these proposals from their proxy materials in reliance on rule 14a-8(i)(7). In each instance, we took the view that the proposal could be excluded in reliance on rule 14a-8(i)(7) because the proposal related to general employee compensation, an ordinary business matter.[2]

The Commission has stated that proposals involving "the management of the workforce, such as the hiring, promotion, and termination of employees," relate to ordinary business matters.[3] Our position to date with respect to equity compensation proposals is consistent with this guidance and the Division's historical approach to compensation proposals. Since 1992, we have applied a bright-line analysis to proposals concerning equity or cash compensation:

• We agree with the view of companies that they may exclude proposals that relate to general employee compensation matters in reliance on rule 14a-8(i)(7);[4] and

• We do not agree with the view of companies that they may exclude proposals that concern *only* senior

---

[1] *See* Amendments to Rules on Shareholder Proposals, Exchange Act Release No. 40018 (May 21, 1998).

[2] *See Adobe Systems* (February 1, 2002) (proposal requesting that Adobe's Board of Directors "submit all equity compensation plans (other than those that would not result in material potential dilu-

tion) to shareholders for approval"); *see also Cadence Design Systems* (March 20, 2002); *AutoDesk, Inc.* (April 1, 2002); *Synopsys, Inc.* (April 1, 2002).

[3] *See* Exchange Act Release No. 40018 (May 21, 1998).

[4] *See e.g., Bio-Technology General Corporation* (April 28, 2000).

executive and director compensation in reliance on rule 14a-8(i)(7).[5]

The Commission has previously taken the position that proposals relating to ordinary business matters "but focusing on sufficiently significant social policy issues . . . generally would not be considered to be excludable, because the proposals would transcend the day-to-day business matters and raise policy issues so significant that it would be appropriate for a shareholder vote."[6] The Division has noted many times that the presence of widespread public debate regarding an issue is among the factors to be considered in determining whether proposals concerning that issue "transcend the day-to-day business matters."[7]

We believe that the public debate regarding shareholder approval of equity compensation plans has become significant in recent months.

Consequently, in view of the widespread public debate regarding shareholder approval of equity compensation plans and consistent with our historical analysis of the "ordinary business" exclusion, we are modifying our treatment of proposals relating to this topic.[8] Going forward, we will take the following approach to rule 14a-8(i)(7) submissions concerning proposals that relate to shareholder approval of equity compensation plans:[9]

• *Proposals that focus on equity compensation plans that may be used to compensate only senior executive officers and directors.* As has been our position since 1992, companies may not rely on rule 14a-8(i)(7) to omit these proposals from their proxy materials.

• *Proposals that focus on equity compensation plans that may be used to compensate senior executive officers, directors and the general workforce.* If the proposal seeks to obtain shareholder approval of all such equity compensation plans, without regard to their potential dilutive effect, a company may rely on rule 14a-8(i)(7) to omit the proposal from its proxy materials. If the proposal seeks to obtain shareholder approval of all such equity compensation plans that potentially would result in material dilution to existing shareholders, a company may not rely on rule 14a-8(i)(7) to omit the proposal from its proxy materials.

• *Proposals that focus on equity compensation plans that may be used to compensate the general workforce only, with no senior executive officer or director participation.* If the proposal seeks to obtain shareholder approval of all such equity compensation plans, without regard to their potential dilutive effect, a company may rely on rule 14a-8(i)(7) to omit the proposal from its proxy materials. If the proposal seeks to obtain shareholder approval of all such equity compensation plans that potentially would result in material dilution to existing shareholders, a company may not rely on rule 14a-8(i)(7) to omit the proposal from its proxy materials.

Companies and shareholders with questions about this bulletin are encouraged to call Keir D. Gumbs, Office of Chief Counsel of the Division of Corporation Finance, at (202) 942-2900.

[¶ 43,014B]   Staff Legal Bulletin No. 14B (CF)

Shareholder Proposals

Action: Publication of CF Staff Legal Bulletin

Date: September 15, 2004

Summary: This staff legal bulletin provides information for companies and shareholders regarding rule 14a-8 of the Securities Exchange Act of 1934.

Supplementary Information: The statements in this legal bulletin represent the views of the Division of Corporation Finance. This bulletin is not a rule, regulation, or statement of the Securities and Exchange Commission. Further, the Commission has neither approved nor disapproved its content.

Contacts: For further information, please contact the Office of Chief Counsel in the Division of Corporation Finance at (202) 942-2900.

A. What is the purpose of this bulletin?

On July 13, 2001, the Division of Corporation Finance published SLB No. 14 in order to:

• explain the rule 14a-8 no-action process, as well as our role in this process;

• provide guidance to companies and shareholders by expressing our views on some issues and questions that arise commonly under rule 14a-8; and

• suggest ways in which both companies and shareholder proponents can facilitate our review of no-action requests.

SLB No. 14 addressed primarily those procedural matters that are common to companies and shareholder proponents and discussed some substantive matters that are of interest to companies and shareholder proponents alike.

---

[5] *See e.g., Battle Mountain Gold Company* (February 13, 1992).
[6] *See* Exchange Act Release No. 40018 (May 21, 1998).
[7] *See e.g., Transamerica Corporation* (January 10, 1990) and *Aetna Life and Casualty Company* (February 13, 1992).
[8] This bulletin addresses only the specific matter of shareholder proposals relating to shareholder approval of equity compensation plans. We are not addressing or commenting on any other posi-

tions concerning shareholder proposals relating to equity compensation or cash compensation.
[9] We recognize that the New York Stock Exchange and the Nasdaq Stock Market have, or are in the process of adopting, rules to require companies listed or quoted by them to provide for shareholder approval of some equity compensation plans. This bulletin does not address those rules.

On July 12, 2002, the Division of Corporation Finance published SLB No. 14A. SLB No. 14A clarified our position on shareholder proposals related to equity compensation plans.

The purpose of this bulletin is to clarify and update some of the guidance that is included in SLB No. 14 and to provide additional guidance on issues that arise commonly under rule 14a-8. Specifically, this bulletin contains our views regarding:

- the application of rule 14a-8(i)(3);

- common issues regarding a company's notice of defect(s) to a shareholder proponent under rule 14a-8(f);

- the application of the 80-day requirement in rule 14a-8(j);

- opinions of counsel under rule 14a-8(j)(2)(iii); and

- processing matters relating to the availability of submitted materials and the mailing and public availability of our responses.

This bulletin includes a discussion of rule 14a-9 and its interaction with the operation of rule 14a-8. This discussion applies to our review of rule 14a-8 no-action requests only; it does not apply to other contexts, such as our review of disclosure contained in proxy statement filings and additional soliciting materials that may be considered materially false or misleading under rule 14a-9.

The references to "we," "our," and "us" are to the Division of Corporation Finance. You can find a copy of rule 14a-8 in Exchange Act Release No. 34-40018 (May 21, 1998), which is located on the Commission's website at www.sec.gov/rules/final/34-40018.htm. You can find a copy of SLB No. 14 on the Commission's website at www.sec.gov/interps/legal/cfslb14.htm. You can find a copy of SLB No. 14A on the Commission's website at www.sec.gov/interps/legal/cfslb14a.htm.

B. Under rule 14a-8(i)(3), when will the staff grant requests to exclude either all or part of a proposal or supporting statement based on false or misleading statements?

1. Rule 14a-8(i)(3)

Question 9 in rule 14a-8 reads, "If I have complied with the procedural requirements, on what other bases may a company rely to exclude my proposal?" Thirteen bases are then listed as answers to Question 9. The third basis, which is cited as rule 14a-8(i)(3), provides:

Violation of proxy rules: If the proposal or supporting statement is contrary to any of the Commission's proxy rules, including §240.14a-9, which prohibits materially false or misleading statements in proxy materials.

It is important to note that rule 14a-8(i)(3), unlike the other bases for exclusion under rule 14a-8, refers explicitly to the supporting statement as well as the proposal as a whole. Accordingly, companies have relied on rule 14a-8(i)(3) to exclude portions of the supporting statement, even if the balance of the proposal and the supporting statement may not be excluded. Companies have requested that the staff concur in the appropriateness of excluding statements in reliance on rule 14a-8(i)(3) for a number of reasons, including the following:

- *Vagueness* —Companies have argued that the proposal may be excluded in its entirety if the language of the proposal or the supporting statement render the proposal so vague and indefinite that neither the stockholders voting on the proposal, nor the company in implementing the proposal (if adopted), would be able to determine with any reasonable certainty exactly what actions or measures the proposal requires.

- *Impugning Statements* —Companies have argued that they may exclude statements in a supporting statement because they fall within Note (b) to rule 14a-9, which states that "[m]aterial which directly or indirectly impugns character, integrity or personal reputation or directly or indirectly makes charges concerning improper, illegal or immoral conduct or associations, without factual foundation" is an example of "what, depending upon particular facts and circumstances, may be misleading within the meaning of [rule 14a-9]."

- *Irrelevant Statements* —Companies have argued that they may exclude statements in a supporting statement because they are irrelevant to the subject matter of the proposal being presented. It is argued that it is appropriate to exclude these statements because they mislead shareholders by making unclear the nature of the matter on which they are being asked to vote.

- *Opinions Presented as Fact* —Companies have argued that they may exclude statements in a supporting statement because they are presented as fact when they are the opinion of the shareholder proponent. It is argued that it is appropriate to exclude these statements because they are contrary to rule 14a-9 in that they may mislead shareholders into believing that the statements are fact and not opinion.

- *Statements Without Factual Support* —Companies have argued that they may exclude statements in a supporting statement because they are presented as fact, but do not cite to a source that proves that statement. It is argued that it is appropriate to exclude these statements because they are contrary to rule 14a-9 in that they may be false and misleading and should be accompanied by a citation to permit shareholders to assess the context in which the source presented the information. As we noted in SLB No. 14, we spend an increasingly large portion of our time and resources each proxy season responding to no-action requests regarding asserted deficiencies in terms of clarity, relevance, or accuracy in proposals and supporting statements.

2. Our approach to rule 14a-8(i)(3) no-action requests

As we noted in SLB No. 14, there is no provision in rule 14a-8 that allows a shareholder to revise his or her proposal and supporting statement. We have had, however, a long-standing practice of issuing no-action responses that permit shareholders to make revisions that are minor in nature and do not alter the substance of the proposal. We adopted this practice to deal with proposals that comply generally with the substantive requirements of rule 14a-8, but contain some minor defects that could be corrected easily. Our intent to limit this practice to minor defects was evidenced by our statement in SLB No. 14 that we may find it appropriate for companies to exclude the entire proposal, supporting statement, or both as materially false or misleading if a proposal or supporting statement would require detailed and extensive editing in order to bring it into compliance with the proxy rules.

3. The need to clarify our views under rule 14a-8(i)(3)

Unfortunately, our discussion of rule 14a-8(i)(3) in SLB No. 14 has caused the process for company objections and the staff's consideration of those objections to evolve well beyond its original intent. The discussion in SLB No. 14 has resulted in an unintended and unwarranted extension of rule 14a-8(i)(3), as many companies have begun to assert deficiencies in virtually every line of a proposal's supporting statement as a means to justify exclusion of the proposal in its entirety. Our consideration of those requests requires the staff to devote significant resources to editing the specific wording of proposals and, especially, supporting statements. During the last proxy season, nearly half the no-action requests we received asserted that the proposal or supporting statement was wholly or partially excludable under rule 14a-8(i)(3).

We believe that the staff's process of becoming involved in evaluating wording changes to proposals and/or supporting statements has evolved well beyond its original intent and resulted in an inappropriate extension of rule 14a-8(i)(3). In addition, we believe the process is neither appropriate under nor consistent with rule 14a-8(l)(2), which reads, "The company is not responsible for the contents of [the shareholder proponent's] proposal or supporting statement." Finally, we believe that current practice is not beneficial to participants in the process and diverts resources away from analyzing core issues arising under rule 14a-8.

4. Clarification of our views regarding the application of rule 14a-8(i)(3)

Accordingly, we are clarifying our views with regard to the application of rule 14a-8(i)(3). Specifically, because the shareholder proponent, and not the company, is responsible for the content of a proposal and its supporting statement, we do not believe that exclusion or modification under rule 14a-8(i)(3) is appropriate for much of the language in supporting statements to which companies have objected. Accordingly, going forward, we believe that it would not be appropriate for companies to exclude supporting statement language and/or an entire proposal in reliance on rule 14a-8(i)(3) in the following circumstances:

- the company objects to factual assertions because they are not supported;

- the company objects to factual assertions that, while not materially false or misleading, may be disputed or countered;

- the company objects to factual assertions because those assertions may be interpreted by shareholders in a manner that is unfavorable to the company, its directors, or its officers; and/or

- the company objects to statements because they represent the opinion of the shareholder proponent or a referenced source, but the statements are not identified specifically as such.

We believe that it is appropriate under rule 14a-8 for companies to address these objections in their statements of opposition.

There continue to be certain situations where we believe modification or exclusion may be consistent with our intended application of rule 14a-8(i)(3). In those situations, it may be appropriate for a company to determine to exclude a statement in reliance on rule 14a-8(i)(3) and seek our concurrence with that determination. Specifically, reliance on rule 14a-8(i)(3) to exclude or modify a statement may be appropriate where:

- statements directly or indirectly impugn character, integrity, or personal reputation, or directly or indirectly make charges concerning improper, illegal, or immoral conduct or association, without factual foundation;

- the company demonstrates objectively that a factual statement is materially false or misleading;

- the resolution contained in the proposal is so inherently vague or indefinite that neither the stockholders voting on the proposal, nor the company in implementing the proposal (if adopted), would be able to determine with any reasonable certainty exactly what actions or measures the proposal requires—this objection also may be appropriate where the proposal and the supporting statement, when read together, have the same result; and

- substantial portions of the supporting statement are irrelevant to a consideration of the subject matter of the proposal, such that there is a strong likelihood that a reasonable shareholder would be uncertain as to the matter on which she is being asked to vote.

In this regard, rule 14a-8(i)(3) permits the company to exclude a proposal or a statement that is contrary to any of the proxy rules, including rule 14a-9, which prohibits *materially* false or misleading statements. Further, rule 14a-8(g) makes clear that the company bears the burden of demonstrating that a proposal or statement may be excluded. As such, the staff will concur in the company's reliance on rule 14a-8(i)(3) to exclude or modify a proposal or statement only where that company has demonstrated objectively that the proposal or statement is *materially* false or misleading.

C. What are common issues regarding companies' notices of defect(s)?

1. How should companies draft notices of defect(s)?

We put forth the following guidance in SLB No. 14 for companies to consider when drafting letters to notify shareholder proponents of eligibility or procedural defects:

- provide adequate detail about what the shareholder proponent must do to remedy the eligibility or procedural defect(s);

- although not required, consider including a copy of rule 14a-8 with the notice of defect(s);

- explicitly state that the shareholder proponent must transmit his or her response to the company's notice within 14 calendar days of receiving the notice of defect(s); and

- send the notification by a means that allows the company to determine when the shareholder proponent received the letter.

We believe that this guidance continues to be of significant benefit to companies, and we urge all companies to consider it when drafting notices of defect(s) under rule 14a-8.

2. Is there any further guidance to companies with regard to what their notices of defect(s) should state about demonstrating proof of the shareholder proponent's ownership?

Yes. If the company cannot determine whether the shareholder satisfies the rule 14a-8 minimum ownership requirements, the company should request that the shareholder provide proof of ownership that satisfies the requirements of rule 14a-8. The company should use language that tracks rule 14a-8(b), which states that the shareholder proponent "must" prove its eligibility by submitting:

- the shareholder proponent's written statement that he or she intends to continue holding the shares through the date of the company's annual or special meeting; and

- either:

- a written statement from the "record" holder of the securities (usually a broker or bank) verifying that, at the time the shareholder proponent submitted the proposal, the shareholder proponent continuously held the securities for at least one year; or

- a copy of a filed Schedule 13D, Schedule 13G, Form 3, Form 4, Form 5, or amendments to those documents or updated forms, reflecting the shareholder proponent's ownership of shares as of or before the date on which the one-year eligibility period begins and the shareholder proponent's written statement that he or she continuously held the required number of shares for the one-year period as of the date of the statement.

We have expressed the view consistently that a company does not meet its obligation to provide appropriate notice of defects in a shareholder proponent's proof of ownership where the company refers the shareholder proponent to rule 14a-8(b) but does not either:

- address the specific requirements of that rule in the notice; or

- attach a copy of rule 14a-8(b) to the notice.

D. What are the consequences if the staff denies a company's request for a waiver of rule 14a-8(j)'s 80-day requirement? Will the company have to wait 80 days to file its definitive proxy materials?

No, the company is not required to wait 80 days to file its definitive proxy materials. Rule 14a-8(j) provides that if the company intends to exclude a proposal from its proxy materials, it must file its reasons with the Commission no later than 80 calendar days before it files its definitive proxy statement and form of proxy with the Commission. Rule 14a-8(j) also requires the company to simultaneously provide the shareholder proponent with a copy of its submission. The staff may permit the company to make its submission later than 80 days before the company files its definitive proxy statement and form of proxy if the company demonstrates "good cause" for missing the deadline. In that instance, the failure to comply with rule 14a-8(j) would not require the company to delay its filing date until the expiration of 80 days from the date that it submits its no-action request. The most common basis for the company's showing of good cause is that the proposal was not submitted timely and the company did not receive the proposal until after the 80-day deadline had passed.

There are instances in which the staff will not agree that a company has demonstrated good cause for failing to make its rule 14a-8 submission at least 80 days before the intended filing of its definitive proxy materials. In those instances, we generally will consider the bases upon which the company intends to exclude a proposal, as we believe that is an appropriate exercise of our responsibilities under rule 14a-8. When we advise such a company and the shareholder proponent of our views regarding the application of rule 14a-8 to the proposal, we also will advise them of our view that the company has not followed the appropriate procedure under rule 14a-8. As noted above, our response in that situation would not require the company to wait to file its proxy materials until 80 days after its rule 14a-8 submission. Companies that have not demonstrated good cause for failing to make a timely rule 14a-8 submission should be aware that, despite our expression of a view with regard to the application of the eligibility or substantive requirements of rule 14a-8 to a proposal, the filing of their definitive proxy materials before the expiration of the 80-day time period in that situation may not be in accordance with the procedural requirements of rule 14a-8. Further, companies should note that, in issuing such a response, we are making no determination as to the appropriateness of filing definitive proxy materials less than 80 days after the date of the rule 14a-8(j) submission.

We will consider the timeliness of a rule 14a-8 no-action request in determining whether to respond. We reserve the right to decline to respond to rule 14a-8 no-action requests if the company does not comply with the time frame in rule 14a-8(j).

E. When should companies and shareholder proponents provide a supporting opinion of counsel and what should counsel to companies and shareholder proponents consider in drafting such an opinion?

Rule 14a-8(i)(1) and rule 14a-8(i)(2) permit the company to exclude a proposal if it meets its burden of demonstrating that the proposal is improper under state law or that the proposal, if implemented, would cause the company to violate any state, federal, or foreign law to which it is subject. Rule 14a-8(i)(6) permits the company to exclude a proposal if it meets its burden of demonstrating that the company would lack the power or authority to implement the proposal. Rule 14a-8(j)(2)(iii) requires the company to provide the Commission with a supporting opinion of counsel when the asserted reasons for exclusion are based on matters of state or foreign law. In submitting such an opinion of counsel, the company and its counsel should consider whether the law underlying the opinion of counsel is unsettled or unresolved and, whenever possible, the opinion of counsel should cite relevant legislative authority or judicial precedents regarding the opinion of counsel. Proposals that would result in the company breaching existing contractual obligations may be excludable under rule 14a-8(i)(2), rule 14a-8(i)(6), or both, because implementing the proposal would require the company to violate applicable law or would not be within the power or authority of the company to implement. If a company asserts either of these bases for exclusion in its rule 14a-8 submission, it expedites the staff's review and often assists the company in meeting its burden of demonstrating that it may exclude the proposal when the company provides a copy of the relevant contract, cites specific provisions of the contract that would be violated, and explains how implementation of the proposal would cause the company to breach its obligations under that contract. The submission also should provide a supporting opinion of counsel or indicate that the arguments advanced under state or foreign law constitute the opinion of counsel.

In analyzing an opinion of counsel that is submitted under rule 14a-8(j)(2)(iii), we consider whether counsel is licensed to practice law in the jurisdiction where the law is at issue. We also consider the extent to which the opinion makes assumptions about the operation of the proposal that are not called for by the language of the proposal. Shareholder proponents who wish to contest a company's reliance on an opinion of counsel as to matters of state or foreign law may, but are not required to, submit an opinion of counsel supporting their position.

F. What should companies and shareholder proponents know about how we process no-action requests?

1. Availability of materials provided to us

Commission rule 82, which can be found at 17 CFR § 200.82, reads as follows (citations are omitted):

Materials filed with the Commission pursuant to rule 14a-8(d) under the Securities Exchange Act of 1934 [the predecessor of current rule 14a-8(j)], written communications related thereto received from any person, and each related no-action letter or other written communication issued by the staff of the Commission, shall be made available to any person upon request for inspection or copying.

In adopting rule 82, the Commission stated, "all materials required to be filed with the Commission pursuant to proxy rule 14a-8[j] will be considered public records of the Commission. [Rule 82] also provides for the public availability of written communications related to the materials filed pursuant to rule 14a-8[(j)] which may be voluntarily submitted by shareholder-proponents or other persons." See Exchange Act Release No. 9785 (September 22, 1972). As such, when a company submits a no-action request, we forward a copy of the request to the Commission's Public Reference Room immediately.

In order to ensure that the staff's process is fair to all parties, we base our determinations on the written materials provided to us. While we will respond to telephone questions from the company or the shareholder proponent regarding the status of a request, we do not discuss the substantive nature of any specific no-action request with either the company or the shareholder proponent. Therefore, we request that any additional information that the company or the shareholder proponent would like to provide be submitted to us and the other party in writing.

2. Availability of responses

After we have completed our review of a no-action request, we generally send our response to the request by mail to both the shareholder proponent who submitted the proposal and the company that submitted the request. In addition, we forward a copy of our response, along with the relevant correspondence, to the Commission's Public Reference Room at the time that we issue the response. Commercial databases that check the Public Reference Room routinely for new no-action responses issued by the Division often upload the responses to their systems. As a result, the company or the shareholder proponent often may find our response in the Public Reference Room or on a commercial database prior to their receipt of that response.

3. Facilitating prompt, consistent delivery of responses to companies and shareholder proponents

During the highest volume periods of the rule 14a-8 season, the mailing of our no-action responses may be delayed and the company and the shareholder proponent may not receive the copies that are sent by mail immediately after the issuance of our no-action response. As such, we may fax copies of our responses in order to ensure that shareholder proponents and companies are given timely responses and to avoid prejudicing either party unnecessarily in resolving disputes that may arise in connection with the rule 14a-8 no-action requests. When we have a fax number for both the company and the shareholder proponent, we will fax our response to each if we are unable to mail the response promptly; when we have a fax number for the company but not for the shareholder proponent, we will fax the response to the company where the company agrees to forward promptly our response to the shareholder proponent. It is important to note that the practice of faxing copies of our no-action responses is a courtesy and is not required by Commission rules.

In order to facilitate the prompt delivery of our responses by providing us as much contact information regarding the shareholder proponent as possible, companies should provide us with all relevant correspondence when submitting a no-action request. In this regard, our review is facilitated best when a company's correspondence with us includes the shareholder proposal, any cover letter that the shareholder proponent provided with the proposal, the shareholder's address and fax number, and any other correspondence the company has exchanged with the shareholder relating to the proposal.

G. Conclusion

We hope that this bulletin, along with SLB No. 14 and SLB No. 14A, helps you gain a better understanding of rule 14a-8, the no-action request process, and our views on some significant issues and questions that arise commonly during our review of rule 14a-8 no-action requests. We believe that these bulletins contain information that will assist in the efficient operation of the rule 14a-8 process for both companies and shareholders.

[¶ 43,014C] Staff Legal Bulletin No. 14C (CF)

Shareholder Proposals

Action: Publication of CF Staff Legal Bulletin

Date: June 28, 2005

Summary: This staff legal bulletin provides information for companies and shareholders regarding rule 14a-8 under the Securities Exchange Act of 1934.

Supplementary Information: The statements in this legal bulletin represent the views of the Division of Corporation Finance. This bulletin is not a rule, regulation, or statement of the Securities and Exchange Commission. Further, the Commission has neither approved nor disapproved its content. The references to "we," "our," and "us" are to the Division of Corporation Finance.

Contacts: For further information, please contact the Office of Chief Counsel in the Division of Corporation Finance at (202) 551-3500.

A. What is the purpose of this bulletin?

This bulletin is part of a continuing effort by the Division of Corporation Finance to identify and provide guidance on issues that arise commonly under rule 14a-8. Specifically, this bulletin contains information regarding:

- the addresses for submitting no-action requests and shareholder responses to those requests;
- the application of rule 14a-8(i)(6) to proposals calling for director independence;
- the application of rule 14a-8(i)(7) to proposals referencing environmental or public health issues;
- the application of rule 14a-8(l);

- the company facsimile number shareholder proponents should rely on when transmitting proposals and responses to notices of defects;
- the written materials that should accompany a no-action request;
- the withdrawal of a proposal submitted by multiple shareholder proponents; and
- the circumstances under which we will transmit our no-action responses by facsimile.

The following additional guidance regarding rule 14a-8 is available on the Commission's website:

- the text of rule 14a-8, which is in Exchange Act Release No. 40018 (May 21, 1998), at *www.sec.gov/rules/final/34-40018.htm*;
- SLB No. 14, which explains the rule 14a-8 no-action process and addresses matters of interest to companies and shareholder proponents, at *www.sec.gov/interps/legal/cfslb14.htm*;
- SLB No. 14A, which clarifies our position on shareholder proposals related to equity compensation plans, at *www.sec.gov/interps/legal/cfslb14a.htm*; and
- SLB No. 14B, which clarifies and updates some of the guidance contained in SLB No. 14, at *www.sec.gov/interps/legal/cfslb14b.htm*.

B. Have the addresses for submitting no-action requests and shareholder responses to those requests changed from those published in SLB No. 14?

Yes. The Commission has moved its headquarters. As a result, you should use the following addresses:

- rule 14a-8 no-action requests submitted by registered investment companies and business development companies, as well as shareholder responses to those requests, should be sent to:

U.S. Securities and Exchange Commission

Division of Investment Management

Office of Legal and Disclosure

901 E Street, N.W.

Washington, D.C. 20549

- all other rule 14a-8 no-action requests and shareholder responses to those requests should be sent to:

U.S. Securities and Exchange Commission

Division of Corporation Finance

Office of Chief Counsel

100 F Street, N.E.

Washington, D.C. 20549

C. Under rule 14a-8(i)(6), when do we concur with a company's view that there is a basis for excluding a proposal calling for director independence?

1. Rule 14a-8(i)(6)

Rule 14a-8(i)(6) is one of the substantive bases for exclusion in rule 14a-8. It permits a company to exclude a proposal that the company would lack the power or authority to implement.

2. Our analysis of no-action requests from companies that intend to rely on rule 14a-8(i)(6) to exclude proposals calling for director independence

Our analysis of whether a proposal that seeks to impose independence qualifications on directors is beyond the power or authority of the company to implement focuses primarily on whether the proposal requires continued independence at all times. In this regard, although we would not agree with a company's argument that it is unable to ensure the election of independent directors, we would agree with the argument that a board of directors lacks the power to ensure that its chairman or any other director will retain his or her independence at all times. As such, when a proposal is drafted in a manner that would require a director to maintain his or her independence at all times, we permit the company to exclude the proposal under rule 14a-8(i)(6) on the basis that the proposal does not provide the board with an opportunity or mechanism to cure a violation of the standard requested in the proposal. In contrast, if the proposal does not require a director to maintain independence at all times or contains language permitting the company to cure a director's loss of independence, any such loss of independence would not result in an automatic violation of the standard in the proposal and we, therefore, do not permit the company to exclude the proposal under rule 14a-8(i)(6).

We believe that our approach is consistent with Commission rules relating to director independence. Specifically, Exchange Act rule 10A-3, adopted pursuant to Exchange Act Section 10A(m), mandates various audit committee requirements for most exchange-listed issuers, including a requirement that audit committees consist entirely of independent directors. Although rule 10A-3 requires entirely independent audit committees for most listed issuers, the rule also contemplates that a director may cease to be independent. In addition, both Section 10A(m) and rule 10A-3 require that an issuer have an opportunity to cure any non-compliance with the applicable audit committee independence requirements before such non-compliance may serve as a basis for prohibiting the listing of the issuer's securities. Therefore, we believe that our view that a board lacks the power to ensure that a director maintains his or her independence at all times is consistent with Section 10A(m) and rule 10A-3, which not only contemplate that a board member may lose independence, but require that mechanisms exist to allow an issuer to cure such a loss.

The following chart illustrates our analysis of the application of rule 14a-8(i)(6) to proposals calling for director independence, and demonstrates that, as we indicated in question and answer B.6 of SLB No. 14, differing language in proposals may result in different no-action responses.

Company	Proposal	Date of our response	Our response
Allied Waste Industries, Inc.	"The shareholders . . . urge the Board of Directors . . . to amend the by-laws to require that an independent director who has not served as the chief executive of the Company serve as Board Chair."	Mar. 21, 2005	We concurred in Allied Waste's view that it could exclude the proposal under rule 14a-8(i)(6). In doing so, our response noted that the proposal did not provide the board with an opportunity or mechanism to cure a violation of the independence standard requested in the proposal.

Company	Proposal	Date of our response	Our response
Merck & Co., Inc.	"The shareholders ... request that the Board of Directors establish a policy of separating the roles of Board Chair and Chief Executive Officer (CEO) whenever possible, so that an independent director who has not served as an executive officer of the Company serves as Chair of the Board of Directors."	Dec. 29, 2004	We did not concur in Merck's view that it could exclude the proposal under rule 14a-8(i)(6). The proposal provided the board with an opportunity or mechanism to cure a violation of the independence standard requested in the proposal.
The Walt Disney Co.	"[T]he shareholders ... urge the Board of Directors to amend the Corporate Governance Guidelines, and take what ever other actions are necessary to set as a company policy that the Chairman of the Board of Directors will always be an independent member of the Board of Directors, except in rare and explicitly spelled out, extraordinary circumstances."	Nov. 24, 2004	We did not concur in Disney's view that it could exclude the proposal under rule 14a-8(i)(6). The proposal provided the board with an opportunity or mechanism to cure a violation of the independence standard requested in the proposal.

D. Under rule 14a-8(i)(7), when do we concur with a company's view that there is a basis for excluding a proposal referencing environmental or public health issues as relating to the ordinary business matter of evaluating risk?

1. Rule 14a-8(i)(7)

Rule 14a-8(i)(7) is another of the substantive bases for exclusion in rule 14a-8. It permits a company to exclude a proposal that deals with a matter relating to the company's ordinary business operations. The fact that a proposal relates to ordinary business matters does not conclusively establish that a company may exclude the proposal from its proxy materials. As the Commission stated in Exchange Act Release No. 40018, proposals that relate to ordinary business matters but that focus on "sufficiently significant social policy issues . . . would not be considered to be excludable, because the proposals would transcend the day-to-day business matters . . . ."

2. Our analysis of no-action requests from companies that intend to rely on rule 14a-8(i)(7)

to exclude proposals as relating to an evaluation of risk

Each year, we are asked to analyze numerous proposals that make reference to environmental or public health issues. In determining whether the focus of these proposals is a significant social policy issue, we consider both the proposal and the supporting statement as a whole. To the extent that a proposal and supporting statement focus on the company engaging in an internal assessment of the risks or liabilities that the company faces as a result of its operations that may adversely affect the environment or the public's health, we concur with the company's view that there is a basis for it to exclude the proposal under rule 14a-8(i)(7) as relating to an evaluation of risk. To the extent that a proposal and supporting statement focus on the company minimizing or eliminating operations that may adversely affect the environment or the public's health, we do not concur with the company's view that there is a basis for it to exclude the proposal under rule 14a-8(i)(7). The following chart illustrates this distinction.

Company	Proposal	Date of our response	Our response
Xcel Energy Inc.	"That the Board of Directors report . . . on (a) the economic risks associated with the Company's past, present, and future emissions of carbon dioxide, sulphur dioxide, nitrogen oxide and mercury emissions, and the public stance of the company regarding efforts to reduce these emissions and (b) the economic benefits of committing to a substantial reduction of those emissions related to its current business activities (i.e. potential improvement in competitiveness and profitability)."	Apr. 1, 2003	We concurred in Xcel's view that it could exclude the proposal under rule 14a-8(i)(7), as relating to an evaluation of risks and benefits.
Exxon Mobil Corp.	"[S]hareholders request . . . a report . . . on the potential environmental damage that would result from the company drilling for oil and gas in protected areas . . . ."	Mar. 18, 2005	We did not concur in ExxonMobil's view that it could exclude the proposal under rule 14a-8(i)(7).

E. Must a company submit a no-action request to exclude a shareholder proponent's name or address from its proxy statement under rule 14a-8(l)?

No. Rule 14a-8(l) is a self-executing provision of the rule that permits a company to exclude from its proxy statement a shareholder proponent's name, address, and number of voting securities held, as long as the company includes a statement that it will provide this information to shareholders promptly upon receiving an oral or written request.

F. What company facsimile number should a shareholder proponent rely on when transmitting a proposal or transmitting a response to a notice of defects?

A shareholder proponent is encouraged to submit a proposal or a response to a notice of defects by a means that allows him or her to determine when the proposal or response was received by the company, such as by facsimile. However, if the shareholder proponent transmits these materials by facsimile, the shareholder proponent should ensure that he or she has obtained the correct facsimile number for making such submissions. For example, if the shareholder proponent obtains the company's facsimile number from a third-party website, and the facsimile number is incorrect, the shareholder proponent's proposal may be subject to exclusion on the basis that the shareholder proponent failed to submit the proposal or response in a timely manner. As such, shareholder proponents should use the facsimile number for submitting proposals that the company disclosed in its most recent proxy statement. In those instances where the company does not disclose in its proxy statement a facsimile number for submitting proposals, we encourage shareholder proponents to contact the company to obtain the correct facsimile number for submitting proposals and responses to notices of defects.

G. When submitting a no-action request, should a company provide us with all relevant correspondence exchanged with the shareholder proponent(s)?

Yes. As we indicated in question and answer G.7 of SLB No. 14 and question and answer F.3 of SLB No. 14B, a company should provide us with all relevant correspondence when submitting a no-action request. In this regard, we wish to reiterate that our process may be delayed unless the company provides with its no-action request:

- a copy of the shareholder proposal;

- copies of any cover letters that the shareholder proponent(s) provided with the proposal;

- any addresses and facsimile numbers of the shareholder proponent(s); and

- any other correspondence the company has exchanged with the shareholder proponent(s) relating to the proposal, such as any notices of defects and any shareholder responses to the notices.

H. When a company submits a letter withdrawing a no-action request for a proposal submitted by multiple proponents, should the company include documentation demonstrating that each

shareholder proponent has agreed to withdraw the proposal?

Yes. As we indicated in question and answer B.15 of SLB No. 14, when a proposal is submitted by multiple shareholder proponents and the proposal is withdrawn, the company should include with its withdrawal letter documentation demonstrating that each shareholder proponent has agreed to withdraw the proposal. In this regard, if each shareholder proponent has designated a lead individual to act on its behalf, and the company is able to demonstrate that the individual is authorized to act on behalf of all of the shareholder proponents, the company need only provide a letter from that lead individual indicating that it is withdrawing the proposal on behalf of all of the shareholder proponents. You can find additional guidance regarding withdrawals of no-action requests in questions and answers B.14 and B.15 of SLB No. 14.

I. Will we transmit our no-action responses by facsimile to companies and shareholder proponents?

Yes. As we indicated in question and answer F.3 of SLB No. 14B, we may transmit our responses by facsimile during the highest volume periods of the rule 14a-8 season to ensure that companies and shareholder proponents are given timely responses. If we are unable to mail our response promptly, we will transmit our response by facsimile if the company requests such a transmission and provides facsimile numbers for both the company and the shareholder proponent. We will not transmit the response to the company by facsimile when we have a facsimile number for the company but not for the shareholder proponent.

We wish to reiterate that the practice of transmitting copies of our no-action responses by facsimile is a courtesy and is not required by Commission rules. In addition, we remind companies and shareholder proponents that commercial databases check the Commission's Public Reference Room routinely for new no-action responses issued by the Division and upload the responses to their systems. As a result, the company or the shareholder proponent often may find our response in the Public Reference Room or on a commercial database prior to their receipt of that response.

J. Conclusion

We hope that this bulletin, along with SLB No. 14, SLB No. 14A, and SLB No. 14B, helps you gain a better understanding of rule 14a-8, the no-action request process, and our views on some significant issues that arise commonly during our review of rule 14a-8 no-action requests. We believe that these bulletins contain information that will assist in the efficient operation of the rule 14a-8 process for both companies and shareholders.

[¶ 43,014D] Staff Legal Bulletin No. 14D (CF)

Action: Publication of CF Staff Legal Bulletin

Date: November 7, 2008

Summary: This staff legal bulletin provides information for companies and shareholders regarding rule 14a-8 under the Securities Exchange Act of 1934.

Supplementary Information: The statements in this legal bulletin represent the views of the Division of Corporation Finance. This bulletin is not a rule, regulation, or statement of the Securities and Exchange Commission. Further, the Commission has neither approved nor disapproved its content. The references to "we," "our," and "us" are to the Division of Corporation Finance.

Contacts: For further information, please contact the Office of Chief Counsel in the Division of Corporation Finance at (202) 551-3500.

A. What is the purpose of this bulletin?

This bulletin is part of a continuing effort by the Division of Corporation Finance to identify and provide guidance on issues that commonly arise under rule 14a-8. Specifically, this bulletin contains information regarding:

- shareholder proposals that recommend, request, or require a board of directors to unilaterally amend the company's articles or certificate of incorporation;

- a new e-mail address established for the receipt of rule 14a-8 no-action requests and related correspondence;

- whether a company must send a notice of defect if the company's records indicate that the proponent has not owned the minimum amount of securities for the required period of time as set forth in rule 14a-8(b); and

- the requirement that a proponent send copies of correspondence to the company and the manner in which the company and a proponent should provide additional correspondence to us and to each other.

The following additional guidance regarding rule 14a-8 is available on the Commission's web site:

- *SLB No. 14*, which explains the rule 14a-8 no-action process and addresses matters of interest to companies and proponents;

- *SLB No. 14A*, which clarifies our position on shareholder proposals related to equity compensation plans;

- *SLB No. 14B*, which clarifies and updates some of the guidance contained in SLB No. 14; and

- *SLB No. 14C*, which addresses additional matters of interest to companies and proponents, and clarifies and updates some of the guidance contained in SLB No. 14 and SLB No. 14B.

B. A shareholder proposal recommends, requests, or requires that the board of directors amend the company's charter. If, under applicable state law, the charter can be amended only if the amendment is initiated by the board and subsequently approved by the shareholders, may a company exclude a proposal under rule 14a-8(i)(1), rule 14a-8(i)(2), or rule 14a-8(i)(6) based solely on the argument that the board does not have the unilateral authority or power under state law to amend the charter?

If a proposal recommends, requests, or requires the board of directors to amend the company's charter, we may concur that there is some basis for the company to omit the proposal in reliance on rule 14a-8(i)(1), rule 14a-8(i)(2), or rule 14a-8(i)(6) if the company meets its burden of establishing that applicable state law requires any such amendment to be initiated by the board and then approved by shareholders in order for the charter to be amended as a matter of law. In accordance with longstanding staff practice, however, our response may permit the proponent to revise the proposal to provide that the board of directors "take the steps necessary" to amend the company's charter. If the proponent revises the proposal in this manner within the time frame specified in our response letter, we do not believe there would be a basis for the company to exclude the proposal under rule 14a-8(i)(1), rule 14a-8(i)(2), or rule 14a-8(i)(6). The chart below includes examples of revisions that we have previously permitted in response to no-action requests similar to those discussed in this question and answer.

Company	Proposal	Date of our response	Our response
SBC Communications Inc.	Resolved that as of December 31, 2005 the number of SBC Board of Director seats will be reduced from twenty one (21) to fourteen (14).	Jan. 11, 2004	We concurred in the company's view that the proposal could be excluded under rules 14a-8(i)(2) and 14a-8(i)(6), unless the proponent revised the proposal as a recommendation or request that the board of directors take the steps necessary to implement the proposal.
Gyrodyne Co. of America, Inc.	It is proposed that the classified board be abolished and all Directors, effective after the election of Directors in 1999, be elected annually.	Aug. 18, 1999	We concurred in the company's view that the proposal could be excluded under rule 14a-8(i)(1), unless the proponent revised the proposal as a recommendation or request that the board of directors take the steps necessary to implement the proposal.
Sears, Roebuck and Co.	Resolved: That the stockholders ... urge the Board of Directors to amend the Company's Restated Certificate of Incorporation to declassify the Board of Directors for the purpose of Director elections.	Feb. 17, 1989	We concurred in the company's view that the proposal could be excluded under rules 14a-8(c)(2) and 14a-8(c)(6) [now rules 14a-8(i)(2) and 14a-8(i)(6)], unless the proponent revised the proposal to urge that the board of directors take the steps necessary to effect the proposed amendment to the certificate of incorporation.

C. May companies and shareholders e-mail us rule 14a-8 no-action requests and related correspondence?

Yes. We have established a new e-mail address for the receipt of no-action requests and correspondence related to rule 14a-8. Companies and proponents may submit requests for no-action relief under rule 14a-8 and related correspondence to us at *shareholderproposals@sec.gov*. This mailbox should not be used to submit other types of no-action requests or correspondence. Please include your name and telephone number in any submission directed to this mailbox. Remember that your e-mail is not confidential, and others may intercept and read your e-mail. We will process no-action requests and related correspondence received through this mailbox in the same manner as requests and correspondence submitted in paper.

D. If a proponent is listed in a company's records as a registered holder, and the records indicate that the proponent has not owned the minimum amount of securities for the required period of time as set forth in rule 14a-8(b), must the company send the proponent a notice of defect if it wishes to exclude the proposal on eligibility grounds?

Yes. If a proponent is listed in a company's records as a registered holder, the company can confirm that the proponent's holdings satisfy the ownership eligibility requirements of rule 14a-8(b). Because the proponent can also hold the company's securities by other means, however, such as through a broker or bank, the company's records do not prove conclusively that the proponent fails to meet the ownership eligibility requirement. As a result, in situations in which a company's records indicate that the proponent does not satisfy the ownership eligibility requirement in rule 14a-8(b), the company must inform the proponent that the proponent must provide proof of ownership that satisfies the requirements of rule 14a-8(b) if the company intends to exclude the proposal based upon the proponent's failure to satisfy the requirements of rule 14a-8(b).

E. Does rule 14a-8 require proponents to provide companies with any correspondence they send to us? If so, how should the correspondence be transmitted?

Yes. Rule 14a-8(k) requires a proponent to provide the company with a copy of any correspondence submitted in response to the company's no-action request. In addition, as stated in section G.9 of SLB No. 14, both the company and the proponent should promptly forward to each other copies of all correspondence provided to us in connection with rule 14a-8 no-action requests. We encourage companies and proponents to use the same means of transmitting correspondence to each other as they use to transmit materials to us. For example, if a company transmits correspondence to us via overnight mail, the company should transmit a copy to the proponent via overnight mail as well.

F. Conclusion

We hope that this bulletin, along with SLB No. 14, SLB No. 14A, SLB No. 14B, and SLB No. 14C, helps you gain a better understanding of rule 14a-8, the no-action request process, and our views on some significant issues that commonly arise during our review of rule 14a-8 no-action requests. We believe that these bulletins contain information that will assist in the efficient operation of the rule 14a-8 process for both companies and shareholders.

[¶ 43,014E]　Staff Legal Bulletin No. 14E (OF)

Action: Publication of CF Staff Legal Bulletin

Date: October 27, 2009

Summary: This staff legal bulletin provides information for companies and shareholders regarding Rule 14a-8 under the Securities Exchange Act of 1934.

Supplementary Information: The statements in this legal bulletin represent the views of the Division of Corporation Finance. This bulletin is not a rule, regulation or statement of the Securities and Exchange Commission. Further, the Commission has neither approved nor disapproved its content. The references to "we," "our" and "us" are to the Division of Corporation Finance.

Contacts: For further information, please contact the Office of Chief Counsel in the Division of Corporation Finance at (202) 551-3500.

A. What is the purpose of this bulletin?

This bulletin is part of a continuing effort by the Division of Corporation Finance to provide guidance on important issues arising under Rule 14a-8. Specifically, this bulletin contains information regarding:

- the application of Rule 14a-8(i)(7) to proposals relating to risk;

- the application of Rule 14a-8(i)(7) to proposals focusing on succession planning for a company's chief executive officer (CEO); and

- the manner in which shareholder proponents and companies can notify us that they will be submitting correspondence in connection with a no-action request.

You can find additional guidance regarding Rule 14a-8 in the following bulletins that are available on the Commission's web site: *SLB No. 14, SLB No. 14A, SLB No. 14B, SLB No. 14C* and *SLB No. 14D*.

B. What analytical framework will we apply in determining whether a company may exclude a proposal related to risk under Rule 14a-8(i)(7)?

Over the past decade, we have received numerous no-action requests from companies seeking to exclude proposals relating to environmental, financial or health risks under Rule 14a-8(i)(7). As we explained in SLB No. 14C, in analyzing such requests, we have sought to determine whether the proposal and supporting statement as a whole relate to the company engaging in an evaluation of risk, which is a matter we have viewed as relating to a company's ordinary business operations. To the extent that a proposal and supporting statement have focused on a company engaging in an internal assessment of the risks and liabilities that the company faces as a result of its operations, we have permitted companies to exclude these proposals under Rule 14a-8(i)(7) as relating to an evaluation of risk. To the extent that a proposal and supporting statement have focused on a company minimizing or eliminating operations that may adversely affect the environment or the public's health, we have not permitted companies to exclude these proposals under Rule 14a-8(i)(7).

We have recently witnessed a marked increase in the number of no-action requests in which companies seek to exclude proposals as relating to an evaluation of risk. In these requests, companies have frequently argued that proposals that do not explicitly request an evaluation of risk are nonetheless excludable under Rule 14a-8(i)(7) because they would require the company to engage in risk assessment.

Based on our experience in reviewing these requests, we are concerned that our application of the analytical framework discussed in SLB No. 14C may have resulted in the unwarranted exclusion of proposals that relate to the evaluation of risk but that focus on significant policy issues. Indeed, as most corporate decisions involve some evaluation of risk, the evaluation of risk should not be viewed as an end in itself, but rather, as a means to an end. In addition, we have become increasingly cognizant that the adequacy of risk management and oversight can have major consequences for a company and its shareholders. Accordingly, we have reexamined the analysis that we have used for risk proposals, and upon reexamination, we believe that there is a more appropriate framework to apply for analyzing these proposals.

On a going-forward basis, rather than focusing on whether a proposal and supporting statement relate to the company engaging in an evaluation of risk, we will instead focus on the subject matter to which the risk pertains or that gives rise to the risk. The fact that a proposal would require an evaluation of risk will not be dispositive of whether the proposal may be excluded under Rule 14a-8(i)(7). Instead, similar to the way in which we analyze proposals asking for the preparation of a report,[1] the formation of a committee[2] or the inclusion of disclosure in a Commission-prescribed document[3] - where we look to the underlying subject matter of the report, committee or disclosure to determine whether the proposal relates to ordinary business - we will consider whether the underlying subject matter of the risk evaluation involves a matter of ordinary business to the company. In those cases in which a proposal's underlying subject matter transcends the day-to-day business matters of the company and raises policy issues so significant that it would be appropriate for a shareholder vote, the proposal generally will not be excludable under Rule 14a-8(i)(7) as long as a sufficient nexus exists between the nature of the proposal and the company.[4] Conversely, in those cases in which a proposal's underlying subject matter involves an ordinary business matter to the company, the proposal generally will be excludable under Rule 14a-8(i)(7). In determining whether the subject matter raises significant policy issues and has a sufficient nexus to the company, as described above, we will apply the same standards that we apply to other types of proposals under Rule 14a-8(i)(7).[5]

In addition, we note that there is widespread recognition that the board's role in the oversight of a company's management of risk is a significant policy matter regarding the governance of the corporation. In light of this recognition, a proposal that focuses on the board's role in the oversight of a company's management of risk may transcend the day-to-day business matters of a company and raise policy issues so significant that it would be appropriate for a shareholder vote.

C. May a company rely on Rule 14a-8(i)(7) to exclude a proposal that focuses on CEO succession planning?

During the past two proxy seasons, we received a number of no-action requests from companies seeking to exclude proposals relating to CEO succession planning in reliance on Rule 14a-8(i)(7). These pro-

---

[1] See Exchange Act Release No. 20091 (Aug. 16, 1983) [48 FR 38218] ("In the past, the staff has taken the position that proposals requesting issuers to prepare reports on specific aspects of their business or to form special committees to study a segment of their business would not be excludable under Rule 14a-8(c)(7). Because this interpretation raises form over substance and renders the provisions of paragraph (c)(7) largely a nullity, the Commission has determined to adopt the interpretative change set forth in the Proposing Release. Henceforth, the staff will consider whether the subject matter of the special report or the committee involves a matter of ordinary business; where it does, the proposal will be excludable under Rule 14a-8(c)(7).").

[2] See id.

[3] See Johnson Controls, Inc. (Oct. 26, 1999) ("Similar to our previous change in position regarding the excludability of proposals requesting preparation and dissemination of special reports to shareholders on specific aspects of a registrant's business (see

Release 34-20091 (Aug. 16, 1983)), we have determined that proposals requesting additional disclosures in Commission-prescribed documents should not be omitted under the 'ordinary business' exclusion solely because they relate to the preparation and content of documents filed with or submitted to the Commission. We now believe that our prior interpretation elevated form over substance. Beginning today, we therefore will consider whether the subject matter of the additional disclosure sought in a particular proposal involves a matter of ordinary business; where it does, we believe it may be excluded under rule 14a-8(i)(7).").

[4] The determination as to whether a proposal deals with a matter relating to a company's ordinary business operations is made on a case-by-case basis, taking into account factors such as the nature of the proposal and the circumstances of the company to which it is directed. See Exchange Act Release No. 40018 (May 21, 1998) [63 FR 29106].

[5] See id.; see, e.g., Lowe's Companies, Inc. (Feb. 1, 2008).

posals generally requested that the companies adopt and disclose written and detailed CEO succession planning policies with specified features, including that the board develop criteria for the CEO position, identify and develop internal candidates, and use a formal assessment process to evaluate candidates. We expressed the view that these proposals could be excluded in reliance on Rule 14a-8(i)(7) because the proposals related to the termination, hiring or promotion of employees.[6]

The Commission stated in Exchange Act Release No. 40018 (May 21, 1998) that proposals involving "the management of the workforce, such as the hiring, promotion, and termination of employees" relate to ordinary business matters. Our position to date with respect to CEO succession planning proposals was based on this guidance and the Division's historical approach to proposals relating to employee hiring and promotion. In the same release, however, the Commission recognized that a proposal relating to ordinary business matters may transcend the company's day-to-day business matters and raise policy issues so significant that it would be appropriate for a shareholder vote.[7]

One of the board's key functions is to provide for succession planning so that the company is not adversely affected due to a vacancy in leadership. Recent events have underscored the importance of this board function to the governance of the corporation. We now recognize that CEO succession planning raises a significant policy issue regarding the governance of the corporation that transcends the day-to-day business matter of managing the workforce. As such, we have reviewed our position on CEO succession

planning proposals and have determined to modify our treatment of such proposals. Going forward, we will take the view that a company generally may not rely on Rule 14a-8(i)(7) to exclude a proposal that focuses on CEO succession planning.[8]

D. May companies and shareholder proponents alert us that they intend to submit correspondence related to a no-action request?

Yes. If a company or a shareholder proponent intends to submit correspondence in connection with a no-action request, we encourage them to contact us so that, if possible, we can review the correspondence prior to issuing our no-action response. We also encourage companies and shareholder proponents to provide us with the date by which they intend to submit their correspondence. Companies and shareholder proponents can either call us at (202) 551-3500 or e-mail us at *shareholderproposals@sec.gov* to notify us of the pending submission. As we stated in SLB No. 14, if a shareholder proponent intends to reply to the company's no-action request, he or she should try to send the reply as soon as possible after the company submits its no-action request.

E. Conclusion

We hope that this bulletin, along with our other bulletins, helps you gain a better understanding of Rule 14a-8, the no-action request process, and our views on some significant issues that commonly arise during our review of Rule 14a-8 no-action requests. We believe that these bulletins contain information that will assist in the efficient operation of the Rule 14a-8 process for both companies and shareholders.

[¶ 43,018] Staff Legal Bulletin No. 18 (CF)

Exchange Act Rule 12h-3

Action: Publication of CF Staff Legal Bulletin

Date: March 15, 2010

Summary: This staff legal bulletin provides the Division of Corporation Finance's views regarding certain situations in which issuers may utilize Rule 12h-3 under the Securities Exchange Act of 1934 to suspend their reporting obligations under Section 15(d) of the Exchange Act.

Supplementary Information: The statements in this legal bulletin represent the views of the Division of Corporation Finance. This bulletin is not a rule, regulation or statement of the Securities and Exchange

Commission. Further, the Commission has neither approved nor disapproved its content.

Contacts: For further information, please contact the Office of Chief Counsel in the Division of Corporation Finance at (202) 551-3500.

I. Introduction

Over the past several years, the staff of the Division of Corporation Finance has responded to an increasing number of routine no-action requests from issuers seeking to suspend their reporting obligations under Section 15(d) of the Exchange Act by relying on Rule 12h-3 under the Exchange Act.[1] The purpose of this legal bulletin is to:

---

[6] *See, e.g., National Instruments Corp.* (Mar. 5, 2009).

[7] The Commission also noted that, "[f]rom time to time, in light of experience dealing with proposals in specific subject areas, and reflecting changing societal views, the Division adjusts its view with respect to 'social policy' proposals involving ordinary business." Exchange Act Release No. 40018.

[8] Such a proposal could be excluded under Rule 14a-8(i)(7), however, if it seeks to micro-manage the company by probing too deeply into matters of a complex nature upon which shareholders,

as a group, would not be in a position to make an informed judgment. *See* Exchange Act Release No. 40018.

[1] Excluding requests for no-action letters under Exchange Act Rule 14a-8, the shareholder proposal rule, approximately one-third of all interpretive, no-action and exemptive requests acted on by the Office of Chief Counsel during fiscal year 2009 involved the application of Rule 12h-3. In fiscal year 2010 to date, approximately 60% of such requests acted on by the Office have involved Rule 12h-3.

- explain the operation of Section 15(d) and Rule 12h-3;

- identify two common situations that give rise to favorable no-action responses under Rule 12h-3;

- set forth the conditions that must be satisfied in these situations in order for an issuer to avail itself of the reporting suspension provided by Rule 12h-3; and

- discuss the Division's approach to processing Rule 12h-3 no-action requests on a going-forward basis.

II. The Operation of Section 15(d) and Rule 12h-3

When an issuer's registration statement under the Securities Act of 1933 becomes effective, Section 15(d) requires the issuer to file the reports required by Section 13(a) of the Exchange Act with respect to each class of securities covered by the registration statement. As the Commission has explained, the purpose of periodic reporting under Section 15(d) is "to assure a stream of current information about an issuer for the benefit of purchasers in the registered offering, and for the public, in situations where Section 13 of the Exchange Act would not otherwise apply."[2] The issuer must continue to file these reports until the Section 15(d) reporting obligation for each class of securities is suspended.

The Section 15(d) reporting obligation is suspended while a class of securities is registered under Section 12 of the Exchange Act. In addition, there are two other ways in which a Section 15(d) reporting obligation may be suspended. First, Section 15(d) provides for an automatic statutory suspension of this reporting obligation if, on the first day of any fiscal year other than the fiscal year in which a Securities Act registration statement became effective, there are fewer than 300 record holders of the class of securities offered under the Securities Act registration statement. Second, an issuer may seek to avail itself of the suspension provided by Rule 12h-3 at any time *during* the issuer's fiscal year if it meets the conditions of the rule.

In order to rely on Rule 12h-3, the issuer:

- must be current in its Exchange Act reporting obligations;[3]

- must have (1) fewer than 300 record holders of the class of securities offered under the Securi-

ties Act registration statement; or (2) fewer than 500 record holders and its assets must not have exceeded $10 million on the last day of each of the issuer's three most recent fiscal years;[4] and

- must not have had a Securities Act registration statement relating to that class of securities become effective in the fiscal year for which the issuer seeks to suspend reporting, or have had a registration statement that was required to be updated by Section 10(a)(3) of the Securities Act during the fiscal year for which the issuer seeks to suspend reporting, and, if the issuer is relying on the fewer than 500 record holder and $10 million in assets threshold noted above, during the two preceding fiscal years.

It is this last requirement, contained in Rule 12h-3(c), that has prompted issuers to seek no-action relief from the staff.[5]

In order to avail itself of the suspension provided by Rule 12h-3, the issuer must also file a certification of termination on Form 15. If the certification of termination on Form 15 is subsequently withdrawn or denied, the company must file all reports that would have been required if the Form 15 had not been filed.[6] Similarly, if in the future the issuer no longer satisfies the requirements under which it was able to cease reporting under Section 15(d), the suspension ends and the reporting obligation returns without any action by the issuer.[7]

III. Two Common Situations That Give Rise to Favorable No-Action Responses Under Rule 12h-3

In the following two situations, the Division has repeatedly expressed the view that Rule 12h-3(c) does not preclude an issuer from filing a Form 15 to suspend its Section 15(d) reporting obligation with respect to a class of securities, even though a Securities Act registration statement relating to that class became effective or was required to be updated by Section 10(a)(3) during the time period specified in Rule 12h-3(c).

- *Abandoned Initial Public Offering:* An issuer with no Exchange Act reporting obligations has a Securities Act registration statement become effective, but does not sell any securities pursuant to the registration statement. The issuer files an application to withdraw the registration state-

---

[2] *See* Exchange Act Release No. 20263 (Oct. 5, 1983).

[3] More specifically, the issuer must have filed all reports required by Section 13(a) for the shorter of its most recent three fiscal years and the portion of its current year, or the period since it became subject to a Section 15(d) reporting obligation. *See* Rule 12h-3(a). In addition, if the issuer obtained an extension of time under Rule 12b-25 under the Exchange Act to file a required periodic report, it still would have to file the periodic report in question before availing itself of the suspension provided by Rule 12h-3. *See* Exchange Act Release No. 20263 at II.2.

[4] *See* paragraphs (b)(1)(i) and (ii) of Rule 12h-3. In addition, paragraph (b)(2) of Rule 12h-3 requires that the class of securities not be registered under Section 12.

[5] For example, an issuer may have an effective Form S-3 or Form S-8. The automatic incorporation by reference of its annual report on Form 10-K into the Form S-3 or Form S-8 serves as the Section 10(a)(3) update for those registration statements, thus calling into question the availability of Rule 12h-3 to suspend reporting.

[6] *See* Rule 12h-3(a).

[7] If on the first day of any subsequent fiscal year the thresholds in Rule 12h-3(b)(1) are exceeded, the suspension of reporting obligations under Section 15(d) will lapse, and the issuer would be required to resume periodic and current reporting under Section 15(d) in the manner specified in Rule 12h-3(e).

ment pursuant to Securities Act Rule 477, and the staff consents to the withdrawal.[8]

- *Acquired Issuer:* An issuer has been acquired by another entity, resulting in the class or classes of securities for which the issuer has a Section 15(d) reporting obligation being either: (1) extinguished; or (2) held or assumed by only one recordholder, the acquiring entity.[9]

In these two situations, subject to the conditions noted below, the Division has repeatedly expressed the view that continued Exchange Act reporting no longer serves the purposes underlying Section 15(d) and Rule 12h-3 because there are either no public shareholders or no longer any public shareholders of the class of securities for which there is a Section 15(d) reporting obligation, thereby making the benefits of periodic reporting not commensurate with the burdens imposed.[10] Consequently, the Division has agreed with issuers that Rule 12h-3(c) would not preclude them from filing Forms 15 to suspend their reporting obligations under Section 15(d) in these two situations.

IV. Conditions That Must Be Satisfied in These Two Situations in Order for an Issuer to Avail Itself of the Reporting Suspension Provided by Rule 12h-3

When an issuer fits within either situation described in Part III above, and satisfies the conditions discussed below, the Division has repeatedly expressed the view that the application of Rule 12h-3(c) would not preclude the issuer from filing a Form 15 to suspend its reporting obligation for a class of securities under Section 15(d), even though a Securities Act registration statement relating to that class became effective or was required to be updated by Section 10(a)(3) during the time period specified in Rule 12h-3(c).

1. The issuer must not have a class of securities registered under Section 12 of the Exchange Act

An issuer may not rely on Rule 12h-3 to suspend its Section 15(d) reporting obligation if it has a class of securities registered, or required to be registered, under Section 12 of the Exchange Act. Section 15(d) provides that the obligation to file reports under Section 15(d) is automatically suspended if and so long as any class of securities of an issuer is registered pursuant to Section 12. Accordingly, any Forms 25 and 15 to terminate Section 12 registration for any class of securities registered under Section 12 must be properly filed before suspension of a Section 15(d) reporting obligation may be effected pursuant to Rule 12h-3.[11]

2. The issuer must comply with the other requirements of Rule 12h-3

The issuer may not exceed the recordholder and asset thresholds in Rule 12h-3(b)(1). The issuer must file a Form 15 and be current in its Exchange Act reporting obligations as of the date of filing the Form 15.

3. The issuer must deregister any unsold securities from Securities Act registration statements and withdraw any registration statements if there were no sales

The issuer must have terminated all registered securities offerings and cannot have any unsold securities remaining on any Securities Act registration statement. In this regard, the issuer must have filed post-effective amendments to deregister all unsold securities under Securities Act registration statements or, if there were no sales made pursuant to a registration statement, an application to withdraw the registration statement. These post-effective amendments or applications to withdraw must be effective or consented to before filing the Form 15.[12] Also, the issuer may not have any pre-effective Securities Act registration statements on file with the Commission that have not been withdrawn.

---

[8] *See, e.g., Liberty Lane Acquisition Corp.* (July 28, 2008).

[9] *See, e.g., Wyeth* (Nov. 4, 2009). In proposing to adopt former Rule 12h-4 under the Exchange Act, the predecessor to Rule 12h-3, the Commission noted that: "Recent acquisition activity has given rise to many . . . applications [for reporting relief] in situations where a corporation is the sole holder of a class of an acquired company's securities subject to a section 15(d) duty to file reports [and that] any benefit of requiring corporations to either file reports . . . or to apply for exemption . . . is generally outweighed both by the burden of compliance imposed upon such corporations and by the burden placed upon the staff in processing routine . . . applications." *See* Exchange Act Release No. 15757 (Apr. 23, 1979). Similarly, less than one year after the Commission adopted paragraph (c) of Rule 12h-3 in 1984, the Division indicated that Rule 12h-3(c) was not intended to require a company that was acquired in a merger to remain subject to the reporting requirements of Section 15(d) solely because the company had a Form S-8 that was updated pursuant to Section 10(a)(3) during the fiscal year in which the merger was consummated. *See C. Michael Harrington* (Jan. 4, 1985).

[10] As the Commission has observed, Congress allowed the Section 15(d) reporting obligation to be suspended out of the recognition that "with respect to Section 15(d) . . . the benefits of periodic

reporting by an issuer might not always be commensurate with the burdens imposed." *See* Exchange Act Release No. 20263.

[11] See Exchange Act Rules Compliance and Disclosure Interpretations 144.01 and 144.02 regarding the timing for filing forms when a Section 12 registration is being terminated.

[12] *See* Item 512(a)(3) of Regulation S-K. Post-effective amendments to Forms S-8 filed for the purpose of removing unsold securities from registration are effective upon filing, while post-effective amendments to most other registration statements for such purpose must be declared effective by the Division. *See* Securities Act Rule 464. Similarly, the staff must consent to applications to withdraw registration statements. *See* Securities Act Rule 477. Note that the requirement to file a post-effective amendment to deregister unsold securities does not apply to registration statements that have expired under Securities Act Rule 415(a)(5). Under Rule 415(a)(5), if three years have elapsed since the initial effective date of the registration statement under which they were being offered and sold, and a new registration statement has not been filed under Rule 415(a)(6), the offering of securities on the registration statement has expired. The registration statement will not be required to be updated under Item 512(a)(3) of Regulation S-K and will not need to be post-effectively amended to deregister unsold securities.

4. The issuer must not otherwise file Exchange Act reports during the time period in which it seeks to avail itself of the suspension provided by Rule 12h-3

If the issuer will continue to have any outstanding debt, neither the indenture nor any documents related thereto may require the issuer to submit, provide, furnish or file reports under the Exchange Act with the Commission or the indenture trustee during the time period in which the issuer seeks to avail itself of the suspension provided by Rule 12h-3. Otherwise, suspending the issuer's obligation to file reports under Section 15(d) would have no practical effect on the issuer's preparation of Exchange Act reports.

V. The Division's Approach to Processing Rule 12h-3 No-Action Requests on a Going-Forward Basis

The Division has issued an extensive number of no-action responses regarding the ability of an issuer to rely on Rule 12h-3 for a class of securities, notwithstanding the fact that a Securities Act registration statement relating to that class became effective or was required to be updated by Section 10(a)(3) during the time period specified in Rule 12h-3(c). Because of the routine nature of these requests, the large body of no-action precedent and the guidance in this legal bulletin, the Division is of the view that, on a going-forward basis, an issuer that fits within either of the two situations identified above and satisfies the conditions set forth in this legal bulletin does not need a no-action response from the Division before filing a Form 15 to suspend its Section 15(d) reporting obligation in reliance on Rule 12h-3. In order to cease reporting, an issuer must file a Form 15 for each class of securities for which there is a Section 15(d) reporting obligation.

The Division will continue to entertain questions regarding the availability of Rule 12h-3 for situations that fall outside the facts and conditions discussed in this legal bulletin.[13]

---

[13] For example, an issuer with a "going dark" fact pattern — in which the number of record holders of the class of securities subject to the Section 15(d) reporting obligation has fallen below the thresholds in Rule 12h-3(b)(1), and there have been no sales pursuant to Securities Act registration statements during the fiscal year with respect to which the issuer seeks to suspend reporting — must continue to seek no-action relief to suspend its Section 15(d) reporting obligation if it does not meet the requirements of Rule 12h-3. *See, e.g., International Wire Group, Inc.* (Nov. 6, 2009).

Compliance & Disclosure Interpretations—Form 8-K

[To view the full collection of Compliance & Disclosure Interpretations, and any updates to the Form 8-K interpretations issued after publication of this book, visit: *http://www.sec.gov/divisions/corpfin/cfguidance.shtml*]

Compliance and Disclosure Interpretations—Form 8-K

TABLE OF CONTENTS

QUESTIONS and ANSWERS of GENERAL APPLICABILITY

General Guidance

Item 1.01—Entry into a Material Definitive Agreement

Item 1.02—Termination of a Material Definitive Agreement

Item 1.03—Bankruptcy or Receivership

Item 2.01—Completion of Acquisition or Disposition of Assets

Item 2.02—Results of Operations and Financial Condition

Item 2.03—Creation of a Direct Financial Obligation under an Off-Balance Sheet Arrangement of a Registrant

Item 2.04—Triggering Events That Accelerate or Increase a Direct Financial Obligation or an Obligation under an Off-Balance Sheet Arrangement

Item 2.05—Costs Associated with Exit or Disposal Activities

CONTENTS

CONTENTS

Item 5.06—Change in Shell Company Status

Item 6.01—ABS Information and Computational Material

Item 6.02—Change of Servicer or Trustee

Item 6.03—Change in Credit Enhancement or Other External Support

Item 6.04—Failure to Make a Required Distribution

Item 6.05—Securities Act Updating Disclosure

Item 7.01—Regulation FD Disclosure

Item 8.01—Other Events

Item 9.01—Financial Statements and Exhibits

COMPLIANCE AND DISCLOSURE INTERPRETATIONS—FORM 8-K

QUESTIONS and ANSWERS of GENERAL APPLICABILITY

Section 101. General Guidance

¶ 50,001 [Disclosure in Periodic Reports]

Question 101.01

Question: If a triggering event specified in one of the items of Form 8-K occurs within four business days before a registrant's filing of a periodic report, may the registrant disclose the event in its periodic report rather than a separate Form 8-K? If so, under what item of the periodic report should the event be disclosed? Item 5 of Part II of Form 10-Q and Item 9B of Form 10-K appear to be limited to events that were required to be disclosed during the period covered by those reports.

Answer: Yes, a triggering event occurring within four business days before the registrant's filing of a periodic report may be disclosed in that periodic report, except for filings required to be made under Item 4.01 of Form 8-K, Changes in Registrant's Certifying Accountant and Item 4.02 of Form 8-K, Non-Reliance on Previously Issued Financial Statements or a Related Audit Report or Completed Interim Review. The registrant may disclose triggering events, other than Items 4.01 and 4.02 events, on the periodic report under Item 5 of Part II of Form 10-Q or Item 9B of Form 10-K, as applicable. All Item 4.01 and Item 4.02 events must be reported on Form 8-K. Of course, amendments to previously filed Forms 8-K must be filed on a Form 8-K/A. See also Exchange Act Form 8-K Question 106.04 regarding the ability to rely on Item 2.02 of Form 8-K.

Reference: Form 8-K

History: Issued April 2008.

¶ 50,002 [Triggering Events—Registrants and Subsidiaries]

Question 101.02

Question: Some items of Form 8-K are triggered by the specified event occurring in relation to the "registrant" (such as Items 1.01, 1.02, 2.03, 2.04). Other items of Form 8-K refer also to majority-owned subsidiaries (such as Item 2.01). Should registrants interpret all Form 8-K Items as applying the triggering event to the registrant and subsidiaries, other than items that obviously apply only at the registrant level, such as changes in directors and principal officers?

Answer: Yes. Triggering events apply to registrants and subsidiaries. For example, entry by a subsidiary into a non-ordinary course definitive agreement that is material to the registrant is reportable under Item 1.01 and termination of such an agreement is reportable under Item 1.02. Similarly, Item 2.03 disclosure is triggered by definitive obligations or off-balance sheet arrangements of the registrant and/or its subsidiaries that are material to the registrant.

Reference: Form 8-K

History: Issued April 2008.

¶ 50,003 ["Exchange" Defined]

Question 101.03

Question: General Instruction E to Form 8-K requires that a copy of the report be filed with each exchange where the registrant's securities are listed. Does the term "exchange" as used in the instruction refer only to domestic exchanges?

Answer: Yes. The term "exchange" as used in the instruction refers only to domestic exchanges and, accordingly, Form 8-K reports need be furnished only to domestic exchanges.

Reference: Form 8-K

History: Issued July 1997; modified April 2008.

¶ 50,004 [Voluntary Filing of Interactive Data]

Question 101.04

Question: If a Form 8-K contains audited annual financial statements that are a revised version of financial statements previously filed with the Commission and have been revised to reflect the effects of certain subsequent events, such as discontinued operations, a change in reportable segments or a change in accounting principle, then under Item 601(b)(101)(i) of Regulation S-K, the filer must submit an interactive data file with the Form 8-K for those revised audited annual financial statements. Paragraph 6(a) of General Instruction C of Form 6-K contains a similar requirement. Item 601(b)(101)(ii) of Regulation S-K and Paragraph 6(b) of General Instruction C of Form 6-K permit a filer to voluntarily submit an interactive data file with a Form 8-K or 6-K, respectively, under specified conditions. Is a filer permitted to voluntarily submit an interactive data file with a Form 8-K or 6-K for other financial statements that may be included in the Form 8-K or 6-K, but for which an interactive data file is not required to be submitted? For example, if the 6-K contains interim financial statements other than pursuant to the nine-month updating requirement of Item 8.A.5 of Form 20-F?

Answer: Yes, if the filer otherwise complies with Item 601(b)(101)(ii) of Regulation S-K and Paragraph 6(b) of General Instruction C of 6-K, as applicable.

Reference: Item 601 of Regulation S-K; Form 6-K and Form 8-K

History: Issued September 2009.

¶ 50,005 [Proper Form Requirement]

Question 101.05

Question: If a Form 8-K contains audited annual financial statements that are a revised version of financial statements previously filed with the Commission and have been revised to reflect the effects of certain subsequent events, such as discontinued operations, a change in reportable segments or a change in accounting principle, then under Item 601(b)(101)(i) of Regulation S-K, the filer must submit an interactive data file with the Form 8-K for those revised audited annual financial statements. Paragraph 6(a) of General Instruction C of Form 6-K contains a similar requirement. Item 601(b)(101)(ii) of Regulation S-K and Paragraph 6(b) of General Instruction C of Form 6-K permit a filer to voluntarily submit an interactive data file with a Form 8-K or 6-K, respectively, under specified conditions. Is a filer permitted to voluntarily submit an interactive data file with a Form 8-K or 6-K for other financial statements that may be included in the Form 8-K or 6-K, but for which an interactive data file is not required to be submitted? For example, if the 6-K contains interim financial statements other than pursuant to the nine-month updating requirement of Item 8.A.5 of Form 20-F?

Answer: Yes, if the filer otherwise complies with Item 601(b)(101)(ii) of Regulation S-K and Paragraph 6(b) of General Instruction C of 6-K, as applicable.

Reference: Item 601 of Regulation S-K; Form 6-K and Form 8-K

History: Issued September 2009.

Section 102. Item 1.01—Entry into a Material Definitive Agreement

¶ 50,006 [Materiality]

Question: If an agreement that was not material at the time the registrant entered into it becomes material at a later date, must the registrant file an Item 1.01 Form 8-K at the time the agreement becomes material?

Answer: No. If an agreement becomes material to the registrant but was not material to the registrant when it entered into, or amended, the agreement, the registrant need not file a Form 8-K under Item 1.01. In any event, the registrant must file the agreement as an exhibit to the periodic report relating to the reporting period in which the agreement became material if, at any time during that period, the agreement was material to the registrant. In this regard, the registrant would apply the requirements of Item 601 of Regulation S-K to determine if the agreement must be filed with the periodic report.

Reference: Form 8-K, Item 1.01

History: Issued April 2008.

¶ 50,007 [Underwriting Agreements]

Question 102.02

Question: Is a placement agency or underwriting agreement a material definitive agreement for purposes of Item 1.01? If so, does the requirement to disclose the parties to the agreement require disclosure of the name of the placement agent or underwriter? Would such disclosure render the safe harbor from the definition of an "offer" included in Securities Act Rule 135c not available for the Form 8-K filing?

Answer: The registrant must determine whether specific agreements are material using established standards of materiality and with reference to Instruction 1 to Item 1.01. If the registrant determines that such an agreement requires filing under Item 1.01, it may, as under Item 3.02, omit the identity of the underwriters from the disclosure in the Form 8-K to remain within the safe harbor of Rule 135c.

Reference: Form 8-K, Item 1.01

History: Issued April 2008.

¶ 50,008 [Exhibits]

Question: Must a material definitive agreement be summarized in the body of the Form 8-K if it is filed as an exhibit to the Form 8-K?

Answer: Yes. Item 1.01 requires "a brief description of the material terms and conditions of the agreement or amendment that are material to the registrant." Therefore, incorporation by reference of the actual agreement would not satisfy this disclosure requirement. In some cases, the agreement may be so brief that it may make sense to disclose all the terms of the agreement into the body of the Form 8-K.

Reference: Form 8-K, Item 1.01

History: Issued April 2008.

Section 103. Item 1.02—Termination of a Material Definitive Agreement

¶ 50,009 [Termination Notice]

Question 103.01

Question: A material definitive agreement has an advance notice provision that requires 180 days advance notice to terminate. The counterparty delivers to the registrant written advance notice of termination. Even though the registrant intends to negotiate with the counterparty and believes in good faith that the agreement will ultimately not be terminated, is an Item 1.02 Form 8-K required when the registrant receives the appropriate advance notice of termination?

Answer: Yes. Although Instruction 1 to Item 1.02 notes that no disclosure is required solely by reason of that item during negotiations or discussions regarding termination of a material definitive agreement unless and until the agreement has been terminated, and Instruction 2 indicates that no disclosure is required if the registrant believes in good faith that the material definitive agreement has not been terminated, Instruction 2 clarifies that, once notice of termination pursuant to the terms of the agreement has been received, the Form 8-K is required, notwithstanding the registrant's continued efforts to negotiate a continuation of the contract.

Reference: Form 8-K, Item 1.02

History: Issued April 2008.

¶ 50,010 [Automatic Renewals]

Question 103.02

Question: A material definitive agreement expires automatically on June 30, 200X, but is continued for successive one-year terms until the next June 30th unless one party sends a non-renewal notice during a 30-day window period six months before the automatic renewal – in other words, January. Does non-renewal of this type of agreement by sending the notice in January trigger Item 1.02 disclosure?

Answer: Yes. The triggering event is the sending of the notice in January, not the termination of the agreement on June 30th. However, automatic renewal in accordance with the terms of the agreement (in other words, when no non-renewal notice is sent) does not trigger the filing of an Item 1.01 Form 8-K.

Reference: Form 8-K, Item 1.02

History: Issued April 2008.

¶ 50,011 [Termination Date]

Question 103.03

Question: A material definitive agreement expires on June 30, 200X. It provides that either party may renew the agreement for another one-year term ending on June 30th if it sends a renewal notice to the other party during January, and the other party does not affirmatively reject that notice in February. If neither party sends a renewal notice during January, which means that the agreement terminates on June 30th, is an Item 1.02 Form 8-K filing required?

Answer: No. This would be a termination on the agreement's stated termination date that does not trigger an Item 1.02 filing. If one party sends a renewal notice that is not rejected, an Item 1.01 Form 8-K is required. Such a filing would be triggered by the passage of the rejection deadline on February 28th, and not the sending of the renewal notice in January.

Reference: Form 8-K, Item 1.02

History: Issued April 2008.

Section 104. Item 1.03—Bankruptcy or Receivership

¶ 50,012 [Reserved]

None.

Section 105. Item 2.01—Completion of Acquisition or Disposition of Assets

¶ 50,013 [Reserved]

None.

Section 106. Item 2.02—Results of Operations and Financial Condition

¶ 50,014 [Broadcasts of Earnings Information]

Question 106.01

Question: Item 2.02 of Form 8-K contains a conditional exemption from its requirement to furnish a Form 8-K where earnings information is presented orally, telephonically, by webcast, by broadcast or by similar means. Among other conditions, the company must provide on its web site any financial and other statistical information contained in the presentation, together with any information that would be required by Regulation G. Would an audio file of the initial webcast satisfy this condition to the exemption?

Answer: Yes, provided that: (1) the audio file contains all material financial and other statistical information included in the presentation that was not previously disclosed, and (2) investors can access it and replay it through the company's web site. Alternatively, slides or a similar presentation posted on the web site at the time of the presentation containing the required, previously undisclosed, material financial and other statistical information would satisfy the condition. In each case, the company must provide all previously undisclosed material financial and other statistical information, including information provided in connection with any questions and answers. Regulation FD also may impose disclosure requirements in these circumstances.

Reference: Form 8-K, Item 2.02

History: Issued April 2008; modified January 11, 2010.

¶ 50,015 [Conference Calls]

Question 106.02

Question: A company issues its earnings release after the close of the market and holds a properly noticed conference call to discuss its earnings two hours later. That conference call contains material, previously undisclosed, information of the type described under Item 2.02 of Form 8-K. Because of this timing, the company is unable to furnish its earnings release on a Form 8-K before its conference call. Accordingly, the company cannot rely on the exemption from the requirement to furnish the information in the conference call on a Form 8-K. What must the company file with regard to its conference call?

Answer: The company must furnish the material, previously non-public, financial and other statistical information required to be furnished on Item 2.02 of Form 8-K as an exhibit to a Form 8-K and satisfy the other requirements of Item 2.02 of Form 8-K. A transcript of the portion of the conference call or slides or a similar presentation including such information will satisfy this requirement. In each case, all material, previously undisclosed, financial and other statistical information, including that provided in connection with any questions and answers, must be provided.

Reference: Form 8-K, Item 2.02

History: Issued April 2008; modified January 11, 2010.

¶ 50,016 [Web Site Disclosure]

Question 106.03

Question: Item 2.02 of Form 8-K contains a conditional exemption from its requirement to furnish a Form 8-K where earnings information is presented orally, telephonically, by webcast, by broadcast or by similar means. Among other conditions, the company must provide on its web site any material financial and other statistical information not previously disclosed and contained in the presentation, together with any information that would be required by Regulation G. When must all of this information appear on the company's web site?

Answer: The required information must appear on the company's web site at the time the oral presentation is made. In the case of information that is not provided in a presentation itself but, rather, is disclosed unexpectedly in connection with the question and answer session that was part of that oral presentation, the information must be posted on the company's web site promptly after it is disclosed. Any requirements of Regulation FD also must be satisfied. A webcast of the oral presentation would be sufficient to meet this requirement.

Reference: Form 8-K, Item 2.02

History: Issued April 2008; modified January 11, 2010.

¶ 50,017 [Form 10-Q Exhibits]

Question 106.04

Question: Company X files its quarterly earnings release as an exhibit to its Form 10-Q on Wednesday morning, prior to holding its earnings conference call Wednesday afternoon. Assuming that all of the other conditions of Item 2.02(b) are met, may the company rely on the exemption for its conference call even if it does not also furnish the earnings release in an Item 2.02 Form 8-K?

Answer: Yes. Company X's filing of the earnings release as an exhibit to its Form 10-Q, rather than in an Item 2.02 Form 8-K, before the conference call takes place, would not preclude reliance on the exemption for the conference call.

Reference: Form 8-K, Item 2.02

History: Issued April 2008; modified January 11, 2010.

¶ 50,018 [Timeliness]

Question 106.05

Question: Does a company's failure to furnish to the Commission the Form 8-K required by Item 2.02 in a timely manner affect the company's eligibility to use Form S-3?

Answer: No. Form S-3 requires the company to have filed in "a timely manner all reports required to be filed in twelve calendar months and any portion of a month immediately preceding the filing of the registration statement." Because an Item 2.02 Form 8-K is furnished to the Commission, rather than filed with the Commission, failure to furnish such a Form 8-K in a timely manner would not affect a company's eligibility to use Form S-3. While not affecting a company's Form S-3 eligibility, failure to comply with Item 2.02 of Form 8-K would, of course, be a violation of Section 13(a) of the Exchange Act and the rules thereunder.

Reference: Form 8-K, Item 2.02

History: Issued April 2008; modified January 11, 2010.

¶ 50,019 [Press Releases]

Question 106.06

Question: Company A issues a press release announcing its results of operations for a just-completed fiscal quarter, including its expected adjusted earnings (a non-GAAP financial measure) for the fiscal period. Would this press release be subject to Item 2.02 of Form 8-K?

Answer: Yes, because it contains material, non-public information regarding its results of operations for a completed fiscal period. The adjusted earnings range presented would be subject to the requirements of Item 2.02 applicable to non-GAAP financial measures.

Reference: Form 8-K, Item 2.02

History: Issued April 2008; modified January 11, 2010.

¶ 50,020 [Preliminary Earnings Report]

Question 106.07

Question: A registrant reports "preliminary" earnings and results of operations for a completed quarterly period, and some of these amounts may even be estimates. In issuing this preliminary earnings release, must the registrant comply with all of the requirements of, and instructions to, Item 2.02 of Form 8-K?

Answer: Yes.

Reference: Form 8-K, Item 2.02

History: Issued April 2009.

Section 107. Item 2.03—Creation of a Direct Financial Obligation under an Off-Balance Sheet Arrangement of a Registrant

¶ 50,021 [Four Business Day Period]

Question 107.01

Question: Instruction 2 to Item 2.03 states that if the registrant is not a party to the transaction creating the contingent obligation arising under the off-balance sheet arrangement, the four business day period begins on the "earlier of" (1) the fourth business day after the contingent obligation is created or arises, and (2) the day on which an executive officer becomes aware. How can a registrant disclose something of which it is not aware?

Answer: A registrant must maintain disclosure and internal controls and procedures designed to ensure that information required to be disclosed by the issuer in the reports that it files under the Exchange Act, including Current Reports on Form 8-K, is recorded, processed, summarized and reported within the required time frames. Instruction 2 to Item 2.03 provides for an additional four business days as a "grace" period given the nature of the requirement.

Reference: Form 8-K, Item 2.03

History: Issued April 2008.

¶ 50,022 [Long-Term Debt Issues]

Question 107.02

Question: If a registrant has a long-term debt issuance in a private placement that is coming due, and replaces it or refunds it with another long term debt issuance of the same principal amount and with similar terms in another private placement, is a Form 8-K required to be filed under Item 2.03?

Answer: Item 2.03 requires disclosure of a direct financial obligation that is material to the registrant. Materiality is a facts and circumstances determination. Whether the financial obligation is a refinancing on similar terms is one such fact; the amount of the obligation is another. Depending on other facts and circumstances (including but not limited to factors such as current impact on covenants, liquidity and debt capacity and other debt requirements), a registrant may be able to conclude that a financial obligation in this situation is not material.

Reference: Form 8-K, Item 2.03

History: Issued April 2008.

Section 108. Item 2.04—Triggering Events That Accelerate or Increase a Direct Financial Obligation or an Obligation under an Off-Balance Sheet Arrangement

¶ 50,023 [Conditions]

Question: Is an Item 2.04 Form 8-K required if all conditions necessary to an event triggering acceleration or an increase in a direct financial obligation under an agreement have occurred but the counterparty has not declared, or provided notice of, a default?

Answer: It depends on how the agreement is written. If, as is often the case, such declaration or notice is necessary prior to the increase or the acceleration of the obligation, then Item 2.04 is not triggered. If no such declaration or notice is necessary and the increase or acceleration is triggered automatically on the occurrence of an event without declaration or notice and the consequences of the event are material to the registrant, then disclosure is required under Item 2.04.

Reference: Form 8-K, Item 2.04

History: Issued April 2008.

Section 109. Item 2.05—Costs Associated with Exit or Disposal Activities

¶ 50,024 [Definitions]

Question: Are costs associated with an exit activity limited to those addressed in FASB Statement of Financial Accounting Standards No. 146, Accounting for Costs Associated with Exit or Disposal Activities (SFAS 146)?

Answer: No. SFAS 146 addresses certain costs associated with an exit activity. Paragraph 2 of SFAS 146 states that such costs include, but are not limited to, those costs addressed by the SFAS. Other costs that may need to be disclosed pursuant to Item 2.05 of Form 8-K are addressed by FASB Statements of Financial Accounting Standards Nos. 87, 88, 106 and 112.

Reference: Form 8-K, Item 2.05

History: Issued April 2008.

¶ 50,025 [Filing Date]

Question 109.02

Question: If a registrant, in connection with an exit activity, is terminating employees, must it file the Form 8-K when the registrant commits to the plan, or can it wait until it has informed its employees?

Answer: Item 2.05 was intended to be generally consistent with SFAS 146. SFAS 146 states that, if a registrant is terminating employees as part of a plan to exit an activity, it need not disclose the commitment to the plan until it has informed affected employees. Similarly, a Form 8-K need not be filed until those employees have been informed. See paragraphs 8, 20 and 21 of SFAS 146.

Reference: Form 8-K, Item 2.05

History: Issued April 2008.

Section 110. Item 2.06—Material Impairments

¶ 50,026 [Reserved]

None.

Section 111. Item 3.01—Notice of Delisting or Failure to Satisfy a Continued Listing Rule or Standard; Transfer of Listing

¶ 50,027 [Reserved]

None.

Section 112. Item 3.02—Unregistered Sales of Equity Securities

¶ 50,028 [Stock Options]

Question 112.01

Question: Does the grant of stock options pursuant to an employee stock option plan require disclosure under Item 3.02 of Form 8-K?

Answer: If a grant of stock options pursuant to an employee stock option plan does not constitute a "sale" or "offer to sell" under Securities Act Section 2(a)(3), the grant need not be reported under Item 3.02 of Form 8-K. See, e.g., *Millennium Pharmaceuticals, Inc.* (May 21, 1998).

Reference: Form 8-K, Item 3.02

History: Issued April 2008.

¶ 50,029 [Volume Threshold]

Question 112.02

Question: If a registrant sells, in an unregistered transaction, shares of a class of equity securities that is not currently outstanding, would the volume threshold under Item 3.02 of Form 8-K be exceeded by such sale?

Answer: Yes. As such, in these circumstances, an Item 3.02 Form 8-K filing requirement would be triggered.

Reference: Form 8-K, Item 3.02

History: Issued April 2008.

Section 113. Item 3.03—Material Modification to Rights of Security Holders

¶ 50,030 [Reserved]

None.

Section 114. Item 4.01—Changes in Registrant's Certifying Accountant

¶ 50,031 [Reserved]

None.

Section 115. Item 4.02—Non-Reliance on Previously Issued Financial Statements or a Related Audit Report or Completed Interim Review

¶ 50,032 [Filing Requirements]

Question 115.01

Question: If a registrant has taken appropriate action to prevent reliance on the financial statements and also has filed a Form 8-K under Item 4.02(a), must the registrant file a second Form 8-K under Item 4.02(b) if it is separately advised by, or receives notice from, its auditor that the auditor has reached the same conclusion?

Answer: No. If the registrant has reported that reliance should not be placed on previously issued financial statements because of an error in such financial statements, the issuer does not need to file a second Form 8-K to indicate that the auditor also has concluded that future reliance should not be placed on its audit report, unless the auditor's conclusion relates to an error or matter different from that which triggered the registrant's filing under Item 4.02(a).

Reference: Form 8-K, Item 4.02

History: Issued April 2008.

¶ 50,033 [Financial Statement Errors]

Question 115.02

Question: Does the Item 4.02 requirement to file a Form 8-K if a company concludes that any previously issued financial statements should no longer be relied upon because of an error in such financial statements, as addressed in FASB Statement of Financial Accounting Standards No. 154, Accounting Changes and Error Corrections, apply to pro forma financial information?

Answer: No. The Item 4.02 requirement does not apply to pro forma financial information. If an error is detected in pro forma financial information, an amendment to the form containing such information may be required to correct the error.

Reference: Form 8-K, Item 4.02

History: Issued April 2008.

¶ 50,034 [Errors in Interactive Data Files]

Question 115.03

Question: Must a filer provide disclosures under Item 4.02(a) of Form 8-K when it discovers a material error in its Interactive Data File while the financial statements upon which they are based do not contain an error and may continue to be relied on?

Answer: No. Item 4.02(a) requires a Form 8-K only when the filer determines that previously issued financial statements should no longer be relied upon because of an error in those financial statements. If a filer wants to voluntarily provide non-reliance disclosure similar to Item 4.02(a) that pertains only to the interactive data, it can do so under either Item 7.01 or Item 8.01 of Form 8-K. In any event, if a filer finds a material error in its Interactive Data File, it must file an amendment to correct the error. In addition, once a filer becomes aware of the error in its Interactive Data File, it must correct the error promptly in order for the Interactive Data File to be eligible for the modified treatment under the federal securities laws provided by Rule 406T of Regulation S-T.

Reference: Form 8-K, Item 4.02

History: Issued May 2009.

Section 116. Item 5.01—Changes in Control of Registrant

¶ 50,035 [Reserved]

None.

Section 117. Item 5.02—Departure of Directors or Certain Officers; Election of Directors; Appointment of Certain Officers; Compensatory Arrangements of Certain Officers

¶ 50,036 [Triggering Event]

Question 117.01

Question: When is the obligation to report an event specified in Item 5.02(b) of Form 8-K triggered? Must the Form 8-K filed to report an Item 5.02(b) event disclose the effective date of the resignation or other event?

Answer: With respect to any resignation, retirement or refusal to stand for re-election reportable under Item 5.02(b), other than in the corporate governance policy situations addressed in Question 117.15, the Form 8-K reporting obligation is triggered by a notice of a decision to resign, retire or refuse to stand for re-election provided by the director, whether or not such notice is written, and regardless of whether the resignation, retirement or refusal to stand for re-election is conditional or subject to acceptance. The disclosure shall specify the effective date of the resignation or retirement. In the case of a refusal to stand for re-election, the registrant must disclose when the election in question will occur, for example, at the registrant's next annual meeting. No disclosure is required solely by reason of Item

5.02(b) of discussions or consideration of resignation, retirement or refusal to stand for re-election. Whether communications represent discussion or consideration, on the one hand, or notice of a decision, on the other hand, is a facts and circumstances determination. A registrant should ensure that it has appropriate disclosure controls and procedures in place—for example, a board policy that all directors must provide any such notice directly to the corporate secretary—to determine when a notice of resignation, retirement or refusal has been communicated to the registrant.

Reference: Form 8-K, Item 5.02

History: Issued April 2008; modified June 2008.

¶ 50,037 [Named Executive Officers]

Question 117.02

Question: Item 5.02(b) of Form 8-K requires current disclosure when any named executive officer retires, resigns or is terminated from that position. Since status as a named executive officer is determined based on the level of total compensation under Item 402(a)(3) of Regulation S-K, does this mean that disclosure on Form 8-K is triggered when the person is no longer required to be included in the Summary Compensation Table because of the executive officer's level of total compensation?

Answer: No. Under Instruction 4 to Item 5.02, the term "named executive officer" refers to those executive officers for whom disclosure under Item 402(c) of Regulation S-K was required in the most recent Commission filing. A Form 8-K is triggered under Item 5.02(b) when one of those officers retires, resigns or is terminated from the position that the executive officer is listed as holding in the most recent filing including executive compensation disclosure under Item 402(c) of Regulation S-K.

Reference: Form 8-K, Item 5.02

History: Issued April 2008.

¶ 50,038 [Change in Officer's Duties]

Question 117.03

Question: A registrant's principal operating officer has his duties and responsibilities as principal operating officer removed and reassigned to other personnel in the organization; however, the person remains employed by the registrant, and the person's title remains the same. Is the registrant required to file a Form 8-K under Item 5.02 to report the principal operating officer's termination?

Answer: Yes. The term "termination" includes situations where an officer identified in Item 5.02 has been demoted or has had his or her duties and responsibilities removed such that he or she no longer functions in the position of that officer.

Reference: Form 8-K, Item 5.02

History: Issued April 2008.

¶ 50,039 [Director Renomination]

Question 117.04

Question: If a registrant decides not to nominate a director for re-election at its next annual meeting, is a Form 8-K required?

Answer: No. That situation is not covered under the phrase "is removed." However, if the director, upon receiving notice from the registrant that it does not intend to nominate him or her for re-election, then resigns his or her position as a director, then a Form 8-K would be required pursuant to Item 5.02. If the director tells the registrant that he or she refuses to stand for re-election, a Form 8-K is required because the director has communicated a "refusal to stand for re-election," whether or not in response to an offer by the registrant to be nominated.

Reference: Form 8-K, Item 5.02

History: Issued April 2008.

¶ 50,040 [Appointment of New Officer as Director]

Question 117.05

Question: If a registrant appoints a new executive officer, it may delay disclosure until it makes a public announcement of the event under the Instruction to Item 5.02(c). If the new executive officer were simultaneously appointed to the board of directors of the registrant, would the registrant have to disclose such appointment pursuant to Item 5.02(d) within four business days following such appointment, even if that date is before the public announcement of the officer's appointment?

Answer: No. In these circumstances, disclosures under paragraph (d) of Item 5.02 may be delayed to the time of public announcement consistent with Item 5.02(c). Similarly, any disclosure required under paragraph (e) of Item 5.02 may be delayed to the time of public announcement consistent with Item 5.02(c).

Reference: Form 8-K, Item 5.02

History: Issued April 2008.

¶ 50,041 [Principal Accounting Officer]

Question 117.06

Question: If the registrant does not consider its principal accounting officer an executive officer for purposes of Items 401 or 404 of Regulation S-K, must the registrant make all of the disclosures required by Item 5.02(c)(2) of Form 8-K?

Answer: Yes. All of the information required by Item 5.02(c)(2) regarding specified newly appointed officers, including a registrant's principal accounting officer, is required to be reported on Form 8-K even if the information was not required to be disclosed in the Form 10-K because the position does not fall within the definition of an executive officer for purposes of Items 401 or 404 of Regulation S-K.

Reference: Form 8-K, Item 5.02

History: Issued April 2008.

¶ 50,042 [Directors Not Elected by Shareholders]

Question 117.07

Question: If a director is elected to the board of directors other than by a vote of security holders at a meeting, but the director's term will begin on a later date, when is the reporting requirement under Item 5.02(d) of Form 8-K triggered?

Answer: The reporting requirement is triggered as of the date of the director's election to the board. The Item 5.02(d) Form 8-K should disclose the date on which the director's term begins.

Reference: Form 8-K, Item 5.02

History: Issued April 2008.

¶ 50,043 [Adoption of Equity Compensation Plan]

Question 117.08

Question: The board of directors of the registrant adopts a material equity compensation plan in which named executive officers are eligible to participate. No awards have been made under the plan. Does board adoption of the plan trigger disclosure under Item 5.02(e)? Does the fact that adoption of the plan is subject to shareholder approval affect the timing of disclosure under Item 5.02(e)?

Answer: Adoption by the registrant's board of directors of a material equity compensation plan in which named executive officers are eligible to participate requires current disclosure pursuant to Item 5.02(e) of Form 8-K. Where the registrant's board adopts a compensation plan subject to shareholder approval, the obligation to file a Form 8-K pursuant to Item 5.02(e) is triggered upon receipt of shareholder approval of the plan. Similarly, if a reportable plan amendment or stock option grant is adopted subject to shareholder approval, the obligation to file a Form 8-K pursuant to Item 5.02 is triggered upon receipt of shareholder approval of the plan amendment or grant.

Reference: Form 8-K, Item 5.02

History: Issued April 2008.

¶ 50,044 [Adoption of Cash Bonus Plan]

Question 117.09

Question: The board of directors of the registrant adopts a material cash bonus plan under which named executive officers participate. No specific performance criteria, performance goals or bonus opportunities have been communicated to plan participants. Does the adoption of such a plan require disclosure pursuant to Item 5.02(e) of Form 8-K?

Answer: Yes. Moreover, if the plan is adopted and is also subject to shareholder approval, the receipt of shareholder approval—and not the plan's adoption—triggers the obligation to file a Form 8-K pursuant to Item 5.02(e).

Reference: Form 8-K, Item 5.02

History: Issued April 2008.

¶ 50,045 [Performance Goals]

Question 117.10

Question: After the adoption of a material cash bonus plan has been disclosed in an Item 5.02(e) Form 8-K, the board of directors sets specific performance goals and business criteria for named executive officers during the performance period. Does this action require disclosure pursuant to Item 5.02(e) of Form 8-K if the specific performance goals and business criteria set for the performance period are materially consistent with the previously disclosed terms of the plan?

Answer: No. In reliance on Instruction 2 to Item 5.02(e), the registrant is not required to file an Item 5.02(e) Form 8-K to report this action if the specific performance goals and business criteria set for the performance period are materially consistent with the previously disclosed terms of the plan, for example if the specific goals and criteria are among the previously disclosed performance goals and business criteria (such as EBITDA, return on equity or other applicable measure) that the plan may apply or has applied.

Reference: Form 8-K, Item 5.02

History: Issued April 2008.

¶ 50,046 [Cash Bonus Plan Award]

Question 117.11

Question: A registrant pays out a material cash award pursuant to a cash bonus plan for which disclosure previously was filed consistent with Exchange Act Form 8-K Questions 117.09 and 117.10. Does payment of the award require disclosure pursuant to Item 5.02(e) of Form 8-K?

Answer: Disclosure under Item 5.02(e) depends on the circumstances relating to the payment of the cash award. If the registrant pays out a cash award upon determining that the performance criteria have been satisfied, pursuant to Instruction 2 to Item 5.02(e), a Form 8-K reporting such a payment would not be required under Item 5.02(e) because the payment was materially consistent with the previously disclosed terms of the plan. However, if the registrant exercised discretion to pay the bonus even though the specified performance criteria were not satisfied, a Form 8-K reporting such a payment would be required under Item 5.02(e) because the payment was not materially consistent with the previously disclosed terms of the plan, even if the plan provided for the exercise of such discretion.

Reference: Form 8-K, Item 5.02

History: Issued April 2008.

¶ 50,047 [Non-Equity Incentive Plan Award Target Levels]

Question 117.12

Question: If an Item 5.02(e) Form 8-K is filed to disclose an annual non-equity incentive plan award, does the disclosure have to include the specific target levels?

Answer: The registrant is not required to provide disclosure pursuant to Item 5.02(e) of target levels with respect to specific quantitative or qualitative performance related-factors, or any other factors or criteria involving confidential trade secrets or confidential commercial or financial information, the disclosure of which would result in competitive harm for the registrant. This position is consistent with the treatment of similar information under Instruction 4 to Item 402(b) of Regulation S-K and Instruction 2 to Item 402(e)(1) of Regulation S-K.

Reference: Form 8-K, Item 5.02

History: Issued April 2008; modified April 2009.

¶ 50,048 [Previously-Disclosed Employment Agreements]

Question 117.13

Question: If a previously-disclosed employment agreement provides that the principal executive officer is entitled to receive a cash bonus in an amount determined by the compensation committee in its discretion, would an Item 5.02(e) Form 8-K be required when the committee makes an ad hoc determination of the amount of the principal executive officer's bonus at the end of the first year that the contract is in effect? Would an Item 5.02(e) Form 8-K be required if the committee makes an ad hoc determination of the amount of the CEO's bonus at the end of the second year in which the contract is in effect?

Answer: No. In both cases, no Item 5.02(e) Form 8-K would be required to report the discretionary bonus amount. Disclosure regarding material information about the bonus should be included in the registrant's Compensation Discussion and Analysis and related disclosures under Item 402 of Regulation S-K.

Reference: Form 8-K, Item 5.02

History: Issued April 2008.

¶ 50,049 [Plan Terminations]

Question: A registrant intends to terminate an executive compensation plan. Item 5.02(e) requires that material amendments or modifications of compensatory arrangements be disclosed on Form 8-K. Does this item require disclosure of plan terminations?

Answer: Yes. A termination should be disclosed if it constitutes a material amendment or modification of the executive compensation plan. Release No. 33-8732A stated that "[i]nstead of being required to be disclosed based on the general requirements with regard to material definitive agreements in Item 1.01 and Item 1.02 of Form 8-K, employment compensation arrangements will now be covered under Item 5.02 of Form 8-K, as amended."

Reference: Form 8-K, Item 5.02

History: Issued April 2008.

¶ 50,050 [Resignation Pursuant to Governance Policy]

Question 117.15

Question: If a company has a corporate governance policy that requires a director to tender her resignation from the board of directors upon the occurrence of an event — such as reaching mandatory retirement age, changing jobs or failing to receive a majority of votes cast for election of directors at the annual meeting of shareholders — when must a company file a Form 8-K under Item 5.02(b)?

Answer: Under these circumstances, in which a director tenders her resignation only because she is required to do so in order to comply with a corporate governance policy, the company must file a Form 8-K under Item 5.02(b) within four business days of the board's decision to accept the director's tender of resignation. If the board does not accept the director's tender of resignation—and thus, the director remains on the board—the company should consider informing shareholders as to whether and to what extent corporate governance policies are being followed and enforced.

Reference: Form 8-K, Item 5.02

History: Issued June 2008.

¶ 50,051 [New Director's Compensation]

Question 117.16

Question: A registrant appoints a new director, triggering the obligation to file a Form 8-K pursuant to Item 5.02(d). The newly appointed director enters into the standard compensatory and other agreements and arrangements that the company provides its non-employee directors (e.g., an equity award, annual cash compensation and an indemnification agreement). Pursuant to Item 5.02(d)(5), must the Form 8-K describe these compensatory and other agreements and arrangements?

Answer: Yes. Item 5.02(d)(5) requires a brief description of the newly appointed director's compensatory and other agreements and arrangements, even if they are consistent with the registrant's previously disclosed standard agreements and arrangements for non-employee directors. In lieu of describing any material plan, contract or arrangement to which the director is a party or in which he or she participates, (but not material amendments or grants or awards or modifications thereto), the registrant may cross-reference the description of such plan, contract or arrangement from the Item 402 disclosure in the company's most recent annual report on Form 10-K or proxy statement.

Reference: Form 8-K, Item 5.02

History: Issued May 2009.

Section 118. Item 5.03—Amendments to Articles of Incorporation or Bylaws; Change in Fiscal Year

¶ 50,052 [Restatement of Articles of Incorporation]

Question 118.01

Question: Does the restatement of a registrant's articles of incorporation, without any substantive amendments to those articles or any requirement to be approved by security holders, trigger a Form 8-K filing requirement?

Answer: No. An Item 5.03 Form 8-K is not required to be filed when the registrant is merely restating its articles of incorporation (e.g., a restatement that merely consolidates previous amendments without any substantive changes to the articles of incorporation). However, the Division staff recommends that a registrant refile its complete articles of incorporation, if restated, in its next periodic report for ease of reference by investors.

Reference: Form 8-K, Item 5.03

History: Issued April 2008.

Section 119. Item 5.04—Temporary Suspension of Trading Under Registrant's Employee Benefit Plans

¶ 50,053 "Blackout Period"

Question 119.01

Question: Is a Form 8-K filing required for the notice of any time period that constitutes a "blackout period" for purposes of the notice requirements under ERISA, without regard to whether it is also a "blackout period" for purposes of Section 306(a) of the Sarbanes-Oxley Act of 2002 and Regulation BTR?

Answer: No. Item 5.04 applies only to a notice of a "blackout period" under Section 306(a) of Sarbanes-Oxley and Regulation BTR.

Reference: Form 8-K, Item 5.04

History: Issued May 2009.

Section 120. Item 5.05—Amendments to the Registrant's Code of Ethics, or Waiver of a Provision of the Code of Ethics

¶ 50,054 [Reserved]

None.

Section 121. Item 5.06—Change in Shell Company Status

¶ 50,055 [Reserved]

None.

Section 121A. Item 5.07—Submission of Matters to a Vote of Security Holders

¶ 50,055A [Filing Period]

Question 121A.01

Question: How should an issuer calculate the four business day filing period for an Item 5.07 Form 8-K?

Answer: Pursuant to Instruction 1 to Item 5.07, the date on which the shareholder meeting ends is the triggering event for an Item 5.07 Form 8-K. Day one of the four-business day filing period is the day after the date on which the shareholder meeting ends. For example, if the meeting ends on Tuesday, day one would be Wednesday, and the four-business day filing period would end on Monday.

Reference: Form 8-K, Item 5.07

History: Issued February 16, 2010.

¶ 50,055B [Shareholder Vote Results]

Question 121A.02

Question: Does the Item 5.07(b) requirement to report the number of shareholder votes cast for, against or withheld with respect to a matter apply only to matters voted upon at a meeting that involves the election of directors?

Answer: No. This reporting obligation applies with respect to any matter submitted to a vote of security holders, through the solicitation of proxies or otherwise.

Reference: Form 8-K, Item 5.07

History: Issued June 4, 2010.

Section 122. Item 6.01—ABS Information and Computational Material

¶ 50,056 [Reserved]

None.

Section 123. Item 6.02—Change of Servicer or Trustee

¶ 50,057 [Reserved]

None.

Section 124. Item 6.03—Change in Credit Enhancement or Other External Support

¶ 50,058 [Reserved]

None.

Section 125. Item 6.04—Failure to Make a Required Distribution

¶ 50,059 [Reserved]

None.

Section 126. Item 6.05—Securities Act Updating Disclosure

¶ 50,060 [Reserved]

None.

Section 127. Item 7.01—Regulation FD Disclosure

¶ 50,061 [Reserved]

None.

Section 128. Item 8.01—Other Events

¶ 50,062 [Reserved]

None.

Section 129. Item 9.01—Financial Statements and Exhibits

¶ 50,063 [Dispositions and Automatic Extensions]

Question 129.01

Question Is the automatic 71-day extension of time in Item 9.01 of Form 8-K available with respect to dispositions?

Answer: No. The automatic 71-day extension of time in Item 9.01 of Form 8-K is available only with respect to acquisitions, not dispositions. The Division's Office of the Chief Accountant will continue to address questions regarding dispositions on a case-by-case basis.

Reference: Form 8-K, Item 5.03

History: Issued July 1997; modified April 2008.

INTERPRETIVE RESPONSES REGARDING PARTICULAR SITUATIONS

Section 201. General Guidance

¶ 50,064 [Reserved]

None.

Section 202. Item 1.01—Entry into a Material Definitive Agreement

¶ 50,065 [Exhibits]

202.01

If an Item 1.01 Form 8-K filing requirement is triggered in early April for a registrant with a calendar year fiscal year (i.e., after the end of the registrant's first quarter but before the registrant is required to file its Form 10-Q for that quarter), and the registrant timely files the Item 1.01 Form 8-K but does not file the agreement (to which the Item 1.01 Form 8-K relates) as an exhibit to that Form 8-K, the registrant is required to file the agreement as an exhibit to its first quarter Form 10-Q. The disclosure requirement under Item 1.01 of Form 8-K does not alter the existing requirements for the filing of exhibits under Item 601 of Regulation S-K.

Reference: Form 8-K, Item 1.01

History: Issued April 2008.

Section 203. Item 1.02—Termination of a Material Definitive Agreement

¶ 50,066 [Reserved]

None.

Section 204. Item 1.03—Bankruptcy or Receivership

¶ 50,067 [Reserved]

None.

Section 205. Item 2.01—Completion of Acquisition or Disposition of Assets

¶ 50,068 [Contract for Acquisition or Disposition of Assets]

205.01

Item 2.01 of Form 8-K, which calls for disclosure of the acquisition or disposition of a significant amount of assets, does not require disclosure of the execution of a contract to acquire or dispose of the assets. Disclosure under Item 2.01 is specifically required only when such an acquisition or disposition is consummated. Nevertheless, the filing of a Form 8-K reporting the execution of a contract for the acquisition or disposition of assets may be required earlier by Item 1.01 of Form 8-K if the registrant has entered into a material definitive agreement not made in the ordinary course of business of the registrant (or an amendment of such agreement that is material). Even if Item 1.01 and Item 2.01 do not require disclosure, if the registrant deems the contract to be of importance to security holders, then the registrant may voluntarily disclose it pursuant to Item 8.01. The financial statement requirement of Item 9.01 is triggered by Item 2.01, but is not triggered by Item 1.01 or 8.01.

Reference: Form 8-K, Item 2.01

History: Issued July 1997; modified April 2008.

¶ 50,069 [Minority Interest Stock Purchase]

205.02

The purchase by a reporting company of a minority stock interest in a business from an independent third party (which is accounted for under the cost method) would not require the filing of the financial statements of that business with any Form 8-K filed to report the transaction, so long as that minority position did not result in the reporting company's control of the assets.

Reference: Form 8-K, Item 2.01

History: Issued July 1997; modified April 2008.

¶ 50,070 [Subsidiaries]

205.03

A wholly-owned subsidiary acquires a significant amount of assets from its parent. Both the subsidiary and the parent are reporting companies. The term "any person" found in Instruction 1 to Item 2.01 of Form 8-K refers to the company that has the obligation to file the report. Therefore, while Instruction 1 would not require a filing by the parent, the subsidiary would be required to file the report.

Reference: Form 8-K, Item 2.01

History: Issued July 1997; modified April 2008.

¶ 50,071 [Closing of Portion of Business]

205.04

An indefinite closing of a portion of a company's restaurant facilities, coupled with a write-down of its assets in excess of 10 percent, constitutes an "other disposition" for purposes of Instruction 2 to Item 2.01 of Form 8-K, and thus requires the filing of a Form 8-K report.

Reference: Form 8-K, Item 2.01

History: Issued July 1997; modified April 2008.

¶ 50,072 [Sale of Securities]

205.05

Paragraph (iii) of Instruction 1 to Item 2.01 of Form 8-K indicates that a Form 8-K filing is not required to report the redemption or acquisition of securities from the public, or the sale or other disposition of securities to the public, by the issuer of such securities or by a wholly-owned subsidiary of that issuer. This instruction does not apply to the sale of a subsidiary's equity, because the subsidiary would not be wholly-owned after the transaction is completed.

Reference: Form 8-K, Item 2.01

History: Issued April 2008.

Section 206—Item 2.02 Results of Operations and Financial Condition

¶ 50,073 [Earnings Disclosures]

206.01

Item 2.02(b) provides that a Form 8-K is not required to report the disclosure of material nonpublic information that is disclosed orally, telephonically, by webcast, broadcast or similar means if, among other things, that presentation is complementary to and initially occurs within 48 hours following a related written announcement or release that has been furnished on an Item 2.02 Form 8-K. This 48-hour safe harbor is construed literally and is not the equivalent of two business or calendar days.

Reference: Form 8-K, Item 2.02

History: Issued April 2008.

Section 207. Item 2.03—Creation of a Direct Financial Obligation under an Off-Balance Sheet Arrangement of a Registrant

¶ 50,074 [Reserved]

None.

Section 208. Item 2.04—Triggering Events That Accelerate or Increase a Direct Financial Obligation or an Obligation under an Off-Balance Sheet Arrangement

¶ 50,075 [Redemption of Convertible Notes]

208.01

A voluntary redemption of convertible notes by a registrant is not a triggering event for purposes of Item 2.04 of Form 8-K.

Reference: Form 8-K, Item 2.04

History: Issued April 2008.

¶ 50,076 [Default Notices]

208.02

A company disagrees with the legitimacy of a notice of default and brings the matter to arbitration, pursuant to its rights under the terms of the applicable loan agreement. The matter is pending with an arbitrator. Notwithstanding its good faith belief that no event of default has taken place and the fact that the arbitrator has yet to rule on the legitimacy of the event of default, the notice of default is a triggering event under Item 2.04. When the company files the Form 8-K, it may include a discussion of the basis for its belief that no event of default has occurred.

Reference: Form 8-K, Item 2.04

History: Issued April 2008.

Section 209—Item 2.05 Costs Associated with Exit or Disposal Activities

¶ 50,077 [Plan of Termination]

209.01

An Item 2.05 Form 8-K filing requirement is triggered when a registrant's board or board committee, or the registrant's officer(s) authorized to take such action if board action is not required, commits the registrant to a "plan of termination" that meets the description of such a plan in paragraph 8 of SFAS No. 146, under which material charges will be incurred under generally accepted accounting principles applicable to the registrant under the plan. The "plan of termination" need not fall within an "exit activity," as defined in SFAS No. 146, or otherwise constitute an "exit or disposal plan" (or part of one), to trigger an Item 2.05 Form 8-K filing requirement.

Reference: Form 8-K, Item 2.05

History: Issued April 2008.

Section 210—Item 2.06 Material Impairments

¶ 50,078 [Reserved]

None.

Section 211. Item 3.01—Notice of Delisting or Failure to Satisfy a Continued Listing Rule or Standard; Transfer of Listing

¶ 50,079 [Listing Application]

211.01

A registrant's common stock is traded on the OTC Bulletin Board, which is not an automated inter-dealer quotation system of a registered national securities association, and is not otherwise traded on an exchange. The registrant has applied to list its common stock on the American Stock Exchange. In this instance, an Item 3.01 Form 8-K filing requirement is not triggered upon the registrant's application for listing on the American Stock Exchange, or upon the approval of the application.

Reference: Form 8-K, Item 3.01

History: Issued April 2008.

Section 212. Item 3.02—Unregistered Sales of Equity Securities

¶ 50,080 [Unregistered Securities Issued for Services]

212.01

An Item 3.02 Form 8-K filing requirement is triggered when a registrant enters into an agreement enforceable against the registrant to issue unregistered equity securities to a third party in exchange for services and the applicable volume threshold is exceeded.

Reference: Form 8-K, Item 3.02

History: Issued April 2008.

¶ 50,081 [Subsidiaries]

212.02

If an Exchange Act reporting, wholly-owned subsidiary receives an additional equity investment from its Exchange Act reporting parent and the volume threshold under Item 3.02 of Form 8-K is exceeded, the wholly-owned subsidiary is required to file an Item 3.02 Form 8-K to report the additional equity investment, regardless of whether the wholly-owned subsidiary meets the conditions for the filing of abbreviated periodic reports under General Instruction H of Form 10-Q and General Instruction I of Form 10-K.

Reference: Form 8-K, Item 3.02

History: Issued April 2008.

¶ 50,082 [Warrants]

212.03

An Item 3.02 Form 8-K filing requirement is triggered upon an unregistered sale of warrants to purchase equity securities (or an unregistered sale of options outside a stock option plan), if the volume threshold under Item 3.02 is exceeded, or upon an unregistered sale of convertible notes (convertible into equity securities), if the volume threshold under Item 3.02 of the underlying equity security issuable upon conversion is exceeded. Pursuant to Item 701(e) of Regulation S-K, the registrant must disclose the terms of, as applicable, the exercise of the warrants or the options or the conversion of the convertible notes in the Item 3.02 Form 8-K. If the Item 3.02 Form 8-K that discloses the initial sale of the warrants, the options, or the convertible notes also discloses the maximum amount of the underlying securities that may be issued through, as applicable, the exercise of the warrants or the options or the conversion of the convertible notes, then a subsequent Item 3.02 Form 8-K filing requirement is not triggered upon the exercise of the warrants or the options or the conversion of the notes.

Reference: Form 8-K, Item 3.02

History: Issued April 2008.

Section 213. Item 3.03—Material Modifications to Rights of Security Holders

¶ 50,083 [Shareholder Rights Plans]

213.01

Upon adoption of a shareholder rights plan, a registrant undertook to make a dividend of a preferred share purchase right for each outstanding share of common stock. The Plan was adopted by the board on August 9. The certificate of designation related to the preferred share purchase right was filed with the state on August 25. The dividend, not yet declared, will occur only upon certain change in control events. Under Item 3.03(b) of Form 8-K, the triggering event related to the plan occurs not upon adoption of the plan or upon filing of the certificate of designation with the state, but rather upon the issuance of the dividend. The rights of the holders of the registered common stock are not materially limited or qualified until the issuance of, in this case, the preferred share purchase rights. The preferred share purchase rights are not issued until the dividend is declared and the rights are distributed. Although the registrant is not required to file an Item 3.03 Form 8-K until the issuance of the dividend, the registrant must file an Item 1.01 Form 8-K when it enters into the shareholder rights plan if the plan constitutes a material definitive agreement not made in the ordinary course of business.

Reference: Form 8-K, Item 3.03

History: Issued April 2008.

Section 214. Item 4.01—Changes in Registrant's Certifying Accountant

¶ 50,084 [Statement by Former Accountant]

214.01

Item 4.01 of Form 8-K requires an issuer to report a change in its certifying accountant. The item also requires that the issuer request the former accountant to furnish a letter stating whether the former accountant agrees with the issuer's statements concerning the reasons for the change. Where the former accountant declines to provide such a letter, the issuer should indicate that fact in the Form 8-K.

Reference: Form 8-K, Item 4.01

History: Issued July 1997; modified April 2008.

¶ 50,085 [Amendments]

214.02

Item 4.01 of Form 8-K requires a registrant to report changes in its certifying accountant. The company must file the report on a Form 8-K and must file any required amendments to the report on a Form 8-K/A. It is not sufficient to report the event in a periodic report. See Exchange Act Form 8-K Question 101.01.

Reference: Form 8-K, Item 4.01

History: Issued April 2008.

Section 215. Item 4.02—Non-Reliance on Previously Issued Financial Statements or a Related Audit Report or Completed Interim Review

¶ 50,086 [Periodic Reports Insufficient]

215.01

Item 4.02 of Form 8-K requires an issuer to report a decision that its past financial statements should no longer be relied upon. The company must file the report on a Form 8-K and file any required amendments on a Form 8-K/A. It is not sufficient to report the event in a periodic report. See Exchange Act Form 8-K Question 101.01.

Reference: Form 8-K, Item 4.02

History: Issued April 2008.

Section 216. Item 5.01—Changes in Control of Registrant

¶ 50,087 [Reserved]

None.

Section 217. Item 5.02—Departure of Certain Directors or Certain Officers; Election of Directors; Appointment of Certain Officers; Compensatory Arrangements of Certain Officers

¶ 50,088 [Director Resignations]

217.01

Item 5.02(a) of Form 8-K requires registrants to describe the circumstances of a director's resignation when he or she resigned "because of a disagreement with the registrant . . . on any matter related to the registrant's operations, policies or practices." A disagreement with the process chosen by the Chairman and other board members to address a director's alleged violation of a company's policy regarding unauthorized public disclosures and the board's related decision to ask the director to resign is a disagreement on matters "related to the registrant's operations, policies or practices." See *In the Matter of Hewlett Packard Company*, Release 34-55801 (May 23, 2007).

Reference: Form 8-K, Item 5.02

History: Issued April 2008.

¶ 50,089 [Transfer of Duties]

217.02

When a principal financial officer temporarily turns his or her duties over to another person, a company must file a Form 8-K under Item 5.02(b) to report that the original principal financial officer has temporarily stepped down and under Item 5.02(c) to report that the replacement principal financial officer has been appointed. If the original principal financial officer returns to the position, then the company must file a Form 8-K under Item 5.02(b) to report the departure of the temporary principal financial officer and under Item 5.02(c) to report the "re-appointment" of the original principal financial officer.

Reference: Form 8-K, Item 5.02

History: Issued April 2008.

¶ 50,090 [Resignation of Designee of Majority Shareholder]

217.03

A director who is designated by an issuer's majority shareholder gives notice that he will resign if the majority shareholder sells its entire holdings of issuer stock. This notice triggers an obligation to file an Item 5.02(b) Form 8-K, which should state clearly the nature of the contingency and the extent to which the resigning director can control occurrence of the contingency.

Reference: Form 8-K, Item 5.02

History: Issued April 2008.

¶ 50,091 [Death of Director or Listed Officer]

217.04

Item 5.02(b) of Form 8-K does not require a registrant to report the death of a director or listed officer.

Reference: Form 8-K, Item 5.02

History: Issued April 2008.

¶ 50,092 [Notice of Termination]

217.05

If, pursuant to a contractual provision in a named executive officer's employment contract or otherwise, the registrant must notify the named executive officer of the termination of his or her employment a specified number of days prior to the date on which the named executive officer's employment would end, an Item 5.02(b) Form 8-K filing requirement is triggered on the date the registrant notifies the named executive officer of his or her termination, not on the date the named executive officer's employment actually ends.

Reference: Form 8-K, Item 5.02

History: Issued April 2008.

¶ 50,093 [Change of Principal Accounting Officer]

217.06

A registrant appoints a new principal accounting officer, which triggers an Item 5.02(c) Form 8-K filing requirement. The registrant can decide to delay the filing of the Item 5.02(c) Form 8-K until it makes a public announcement of the appointment of the new principal accounting officer, pursuant to the Instruction to paragraph (c) of Item 5.02. The new principal accounting officer replaces the old principal accounting officer, who retired, resigned, or was terminated from that position. The retirement, resignation, or termination of the old principal accounting officer triggers an Item 5.02(b) Form 8-K filing requirement. The registrant may not delay the filing of the Item 5.02(b) Form 8-K 8-K until the filing of the Form 5.02(c) Form 8-K. Rather, the Item 5.02(b) Form 8-K filing obligation is triggered by the old principal accounting officer's notice of a decision to retire or resign or by the notice of termination, whether or not such notice is written.

Reference: Form 8-K, Item 5.02

History: Issued April 2008.

¶ 50,094 [Committee Appointments]

217.07

A director was appointed by board vote and, at the same time, named to the audit committee. Both the appointment of the director to the board and the committee assignment were disclosed under Item 5.02(d) of Form 8-K. Three months later, the board rotates committee assignments, and the new director is moved from the audit committee to the compensation committee. No new Form 8-K or amendment to the Item 5.02(d) Form 8-K is required by Instruction 2 to Item 5.02 in this situation, provided that the change in committee assignment was not contemplated at the time of the director's initial election to the board and appointment to the audit committee.

Reference: Form 8-K, Item 5.02

History: Issued April 2008.

¶ 50,095 [Renewal of Employment Agreements]

217.08

In the past, a named executive officer entered into an employment agreement that will, pursuant to its terms, expire after two years. The employment agreement automatically extends for an additional two-year term, unless the registrant or the named executive officer affirmatively gives notice that it is not renewing the agreement. The automatic renewal of the employment agreement (i.e., when the original two-year term of the employment agreement expires and neither party gives notice that it does not wish to renew the agreement) does not trigger an Item 5.02(e) Form 8-K filing requirement.

Reference: Form 8-K, Item 5.02

History: Issued April 2008.

¶ 50,096 [Foreign Private Issuers]

217.09

Foreign private issuers that satisfy the Item 402 of Regulation S-K disclosure requirement by providing compensation disclosure in accordance with Item 402(a)(1) should refer to Instruction 4 to

Item 5.02 to determine who is a "named executive officer." The named executive officers will be those individuals for whom disclosure was provided in the last Securities Act or Exchange Act filing pursuant to Item 6.B or 6.E.2 of Form 20-F.

Reference: Form 8-K, Item 5.02

History: Issued April 2008.

Section 218. Item 5.03—Amendments to Articles of Incorporation or Bylaws; Changes in Fiscal Year

¶ 50,097 [Change in Fiscal Year]

218.01

Release No. 34-26589, which significantly amended Rule 15d-10, states that "[a] change from a fiscal year ending as of the last day of the month to a 52-53 week fiscal year commencing within seven days of the month end (or from a 52-53 week to a month end) is not deemed a change in fiscal year for purposes of reporting subject to Rule 13a-10 or 15d-10 if the new fiscal year commences with the end of the old fiscal year. In such cases, a transition report would not be required. Either the old or new fiscal year could, therefore, be as short as 359 days, or as long as 371 days (372 in a leap year)." While a transition report would not be required in such a situation, an Item 5.03(b) Form 8-K would have to be filed to report the change in fiscal year-end.

Reference: Form 8-K, Item 5.03

History: Issued July 1997: modified April 2008.

Section 219. Item 5.04—Temporary Suspension of Trading Under Registrant's Employee Benefit Plans

¶ 50,098 [Reserved]

None.

Section 220. Item 5.05—Amendments to the Registrant's Code of Ethics, or Waiver of a Provision of the Code of Ethics

¶ 50,099 [Reserved]

None.

Section 221. Item 5.06—Change in Shell Company Status

¶ 50,100 [Reserved]

None.

Section 222. Item 6.01—ABS Information and Computational Material

¶ 50,101 [Reserved]

None.

Section 223. Item 6.02—Change of Servicer or Trustee

¶ 50,102 [Reserved]

None.

Section 224. Item 6.03—Change in Credit Enhancement or Other External Support

¶ 50,103 [Reserved]

None.

Section 225. Item 6.04—Failure to Make a Required Distribution

¶ 50,104 [Reserved]

None.

Section 226. Item 6.05—Securities Act Updating Disclosure

¶ 50,105 [Reserved]

None.

Section 227. Item 7.01—Regulation FD Disclosure

¶ 50,106 [Reserved]

None.

Section 228. Item 8.01—Other Events

¶ 50,107 [Reserved]

None.

Section 229. Item 9.01—Financial Statements and Exhibits

¶ 50,108 [Acquired Properties' Financials]

229.01

Item 20.D. of Industry Guide 5 requires, *inter alia*, an undertaking to file every three months post-effective amendments containing financial statements of acquired properties. Even if the automatic 71-day extension of time to file the financial statements for an acquired property is applicable to a Form 8-K, this extension does not apply to the Guide 5 post-effective amendment. Accordingly, the post-effective amendment must be filed when required by Item 20 of Guide 5, and must contain the required financial statements. This is the same position as that taken before the Form 8-K extensions were made automatic.

Reference: Form 8-K, Item 9.01; Industry Guide 5

History: Issued July 1997; modified April 2008.

¶ 50,109 [Limited Partnerships]

229.02

During the pendency of a 71-day extension applicable to a Form 8-K, Securities Act offerings may not be made except as provided in the Instruction to Item 9.01 of Form 8-K. The Division staff has been asked whether this provision applies to real estate limited partnership offerings, thus prohibiting sales from being made until financial statements for properties acquired during the offering period have been filed (even when the quarterly post-effective amendment is not yet due). The amendment to Form 8-K was not intended to change the procedure established in Item 20.D. of Guide 5. Accordingly, when properties are acquired during the offering period, the registrant may continue sales activities notwithstanding the pendency of an 8-K extension, so long as the quarterly post-effective amendments containing the financial statements are filed when required.

Reference: Form 8-K, Item 9.01; Industry Guide 5

History: Issued July 1997; modified April 2008.

¶ 50,110 [Waiver of Financial Statement Requirement]

229.03

The Instruction to Item 9.01 of Form 8-K addresses the status of transactions in securities registered under the Securities Act and Rule 144 and sales during the pendency of an extension, but does not address the status of such sales after a denial of a request for waiver of financial statements. This question will be dealt with on a case-by-case basis.

Reference: Form 8-K, Item 9.01

History: Issued July 1997; modified April 2008.

¶ 50,111 [Acquired Companies' Financials]

229.04

Item 17(b)(7) of Form S-4 states generally that the financial statements of acquired companies that were not previously Exchange Act reporting companies need be audited only to the extent practicable, unless the Form S-4 prospectus is to be used for resales by any person deemed an underwriter within the meaning of Rule 145(c), in which case such financial statements must be audited. The Division staff was asked whether a resale pursuant to Rule 145(d), in lieu of the Form S-4 prospectus, would require the financial statements to be audited. The Division staff noted that Rule 145(d) is not included in the Instruction to Item 9.01 of Form 8-K regarding sales pursuant to Rule 144 during the 71-day extension period for filing financial statements. As the audited financial statements for the acquired company would be required pursuant to Item 9.01 of Form 8-K, a resale pursuant to Rule 145(d) would not be permitted until they are filed.

Reference: Form 8-K, Item 9.01

History: Issued July 1997; modified April 2008.

Compliance & Disclosure Interpretations—Non-GAAP Financial Measures

[To view the full collection of Compliance & Disclosure Interpretations, and any updates to Non-GAAP Financial Measures issued after publication of this book, visit: *http://www.sec.gov/divisions/corpfin/cfguidance.shtml*]

Compliance and Disclosure Interpretations—Non-GAAP Financial Measures

TABLE OF CONTENTS

CONTENTS

COMPLIANCE AND DISCLOSURE INTERPRETATIONS—NON-GAAP FINANCIAL MEASURES

QUESTIONS and ANSWERS of GENERAL APPLICABILITY

Section 101. Business Combination Transactions

¶ 51,000 [Use of Non-GAAP Information in Other Documents]

Question 101.01

Question: Does the exemption from Regulation G and Item 10(e) of Regulation S-K for non-GAAP financial measures disclosed in communications relating to a business combination transaction extend to the same non-GAAP financial measures disclosed in registration statements, proxy statements and tender offer materials?

Answer: No. There is an exemption from Regulation G and Item 10(e) of Regulation S-K for non-GAAP financial measures disclosed in communications subject to Securities Act Rule 425 and Exchange Act Rules 14a-12 and 14d-2(b)(2); it is also intended to apply to communications subject to Exchange Act Rule 14d-9(a)(2). This exemption does not extend beyond such communications. Consequently, if the same non-GAAP financial measure that was included in a communication filed under one of those rules is also disclosed in a Securities Act registration statement or a proxy statement or tender offer statement, no exemption from Regulation G and Item 10(e) of Regulation S-K would be available for that non-GAAP financial measure.

In addition, there is an exemption from Regulation G and Item 10(e) of Regulation S-K for non-GAAP financial measures disclosed pursuant to Item 1015 of Regulation M-A, which applies even if such non-GAAP financial measures are included in Securities Act registration statements, proxy statements and tender offer statements.

Reference: Regulation G; Item 10(e) of Regulation S-K

History: Issued January 11, 2010.

¶ 51,005 [Reconciliation]

Question 101.02

Question: If reconciliation of a non-GAAP financial measure is required and the most directly comparable measure is a "pro forma" measure prepared and presented in accordance with Article 11 of Regulation S-X, may companies use that measure for reconciliation purposes, in lieu of a GAAP financial measure?

Answer: Yes.

Reference: Regulation G; Item 10(e) of Regulation S-K; Article 11 of Regulation S-X

History: Issued January 11, 2010.

Section 102. Item 10(e) of Regulation S-K

¶ 51,010 ["Funds from Operations" Defined]

Question 102.01

Question: What measure was contemplated by "funds from operations" in footnote 50 to Exchange Act Release No. 47226, *Conditions for Use of Non-GAAP Financial Measures,* which indicates that companies may use "funds from operations per share" in earnings releases and materials that are filed or furnished to the Commission, subject to the requirements of Regulation G and Item 10(e) of Regulation S-K?

Answer: The reference to "funds from operations" in footnote 50 refers to the measure as defined and clarified, as of January 1, 2000, by the National Association of Real Estate Investment Trusts. The staff accepts this definition of FFO as a performance measure and, as a performance measure, it may be presented on a per share basis.

Reference: Regulation G; Item 10(e) of Regulation S-K

History: Issued January 11, 2010.

¶ 51,015 [Funds from Operations Calculation]

Question 102.02

Question: May a registrant present "funds from operations" on a basis other than as defined and clarified, as of January 1, 2000, by the National Association of Real Estate Investment Trusts?

Answer: Yes, provided that any adjustments made to "funds from operations," as defined in footnote 50 of Exchange Act Release No. 47226, comply with Item 10(e) of Regulation S-K. Any adjustments made to "funds from operations" as defined in footnote 50 must comply with the requirements of Item 10(e) of Regulation S-K for a performance measure or a liquidity measure, depending on how it is presented. If the adjusted measure is a performance measure, it may be presented on a per share basis; if it is a liquidity measure, it may not be.

Reference: Regulation G; Item 10(e) of Regulation S-K

History: Issued January 11, 2010.

¶ 51,020 [Non-Recurring and Similar Events]

Question 102.03

Question: Item 10(e) of Regulation S-K prohibits adjusting a non-GAAP financial performance measure to eliminate or smooth items identified as non-recurring, infrequent or unusual, when the nature of the charge or gain is such that it is reasonably likely to recur within two years or there was a similar charge or gain within the prior two years. Is this prohibition based on the description of the charge or gain, or is it based on the nature of the charge or gain?

Answer: The prohibition is based on the description of the charge or gain that is being adjusted. It would not be appropriate to state that a charge or gain is non-recurring, infrequent or unusual unless it meets the specified criteria. The fact that a registrant cannot describe a charge or gain as non-recurring, infrequent or unusual, however, does not mean that the registrant cannot adjust for that charge or gain. Registrants can make adjustments they believe are appropriate, subject to Regulation G and the other requirements of Item 10(e) of Regulation S-K.

Reference: Regulation G; Item 10(e) of Regulation S-K

History: Issued January 11, 2010.

¶ 51,025 [Use of Non-GAAP Measures]

Question 102.04

Question: Is the registrant required to use the non-GAAP measure in managing its business or for other purposes in order to be able to disclose it?

Answer: No. Item 10(e)(1)(i)(D) of Regulation S-K states only that, "[t]o the extent material," there should be a statement disclosing the additional purposes, "if any," for which the registrant's management uses the non-GAAP financial measure. There is no prohibition against disclosing a non-GAAP financial measure that is not used by management in managing its business.

Reference: Regulation G; Item 10(e) of Regulation S-K

History: Issued January 11, 2010.

¶ 51,030 [Per Share Non-GAAP Measures]

Question 102.05

Question: While Item 10(e)(1)(ii) of Regulation S-K does not prohibit the use of per share non-GAAP financial measures, the adopting release for Item 10(e), Exchange Act Release No. 47226, states that "per share measures that are prohibited specifically under GAAP or Commission rules continue to be prohibited in materials filed with or furnished to the Commission." In light of Commission guidance, specifically Accounting Series Release No. 142, *Reporting Cash Flow and Other Related Data*, and Accounting Standards Codification 230, are non-GAAP earnings per share numbers prohibited in documents filed or furnished with the Commission?

Answer: No. Item 10(e) recognizes that certain non-GAAP per share performance measures may be meaningful from an operating standpoint. Non-GAAP per share performance measures should be reconciled to GAAP earnings per share. On the other hand, non-GAAP liquidity measures, such as cash flow, should not be presented on a per share basis in documents filed or furnished with the Commission, consistent with Accounting Series Release No. 142.

Reference: Regulation G; Item 10(e) of Regulation S-K

History: Issued January 11, 2010.

¶ 51,035 [Comparable GAAP Measures]

Question 102.06

Question: Is Item 10(e)(1)(i) of Regulation S-K, which requires the prominent presentation of, and reconciliation to, the most directly comparable GAAP financial measure or measures, intended to change the staff's practice of requiring the prominent presentation of amounts for the three major categories of the statement of cash flows when a non-GAAP liquidity measure is presented?

Answer: No. The requirements in Item 10(e)(1)(i) are consistent with the staff's practice. The three major categories of the statement of cash flows should be presented when a non-GAAP liquidity measure is presented.

Reference: Regulation G; Item 10(e) of Regulation S-K

History: Issued January 11, 2010.

¶ 51,040 [Free Cash Flow]

Question 102.07

Question: Some companies present a measure of "free cash flow," which is typically calculated as cash flows from operating activities as presented in the statement of cash flows under GAAP, less capital expenditures. Does Item 10(e)(1)(ii) of Regulation S-K prohibit this measure in documents filed with the Commission?

Answer: No. The deduction of capital expenditures from the GAAP financial measure of cash flows from operating activities would not violate the prohibitions in Item 10(e)(1)(ii). However, companies should be aware that this measure does not have a uniform definition and its title does not describe how it is calculated. Accordingly, a clear description of how this measure is calculated, as well as the necessary reconciliation, should accompany the measure where it is used. Companies should also avoid inappropriate or potentially misleading inferences about its usefulness. For example, "free cash flow" should not be used in a manner that inappropriately implies that the measure represents the residual cash flow available for discretionary expenditures, since many companies have mandatory debt service requirements or other non-discretionary expenditures that are not deducted from the measure.

Reference: Regulation G; Item 10(e) of Regulation S-K

History: Issued January 11, 2010.

¶ 51,045 [Free Writing Prospectuses]

Question 102.08

Question: Does Item 10(e) of Regulation S-K apply to filed free writing prospectuses?

Answer: Regulation S-K applies to registration statements filed under the Securities Act, as well as registration statements, periodic and current reports and other documents filed under the Exchange Act. A free writing prospectus is not filed as part of the issuer's registration statement, unless the issuer files it on Form 8-K or otherwise includes it or incorporates it by reference into the registration statement. Therefore, Item 10(e) of Regulation S-K does not apply to a filed free writing prospectus unless the free writing prospectus is included in or incorporated by reference into the issuer's registration statement or included in an Exchange Act filing.

Reference: Regulation G; Item 10(e) of Regulation S-K

History: Issued January 11, 2010.

¶ 51,050 [Adjusted EBITDA]

Question 102.09

Question: Item 10(e)(1)(ii)(A) of Regulation S-K prohibits "excluding charges or liabilities that required, or will require, cash settlement, or would have required cash settlement absent an ability to settle in another manner, from non-GAAP liquidity measures, other than the measures earnings before interest and taxes (EBIT) and earnings before interest, taxes, depreciation and amortization (EBITDA)." A company's credit agreement contains a material covenant regarding the non-GAAP financial measure "Adjusted EBITDA." If disclosed in a filing, the non-GAAP financial measure "Adjusted EBITDA" would violate Item 10(e), as it excludes charges that are required to be cash settled. May a company nonetheless disclose this non-GAAP financial measure?

Answer: Yes. The prohibition in Item 10(e) notwithstanding, because MD&A requires disclosure of material items affecting liquidity, if management believes that the credit agreement is a material agreement, that the covenant is a material term of the credit agreement and that information about the covenant is material to an investor's understanding of the company's financial condition and/or liquidity, then the company may be required to disclose the measure as calculated by the debt covenant as part of its MD&A. In disclosing the non-GAAP financial measure in this situation, a company should consider also disclosing the following:

- the material terms of the credit agreement including the covenant;
- the amount or limit required for compliance with the covenant; and
- the actual or reasonably likely effects of compliance or non-compliance with the covenant on the company's financial condition and liquidity.

Reference: Regulation G; Item 10(e) of Regulation S-K

History: Issued January 11, 2010.

¶ 51,055 [Full Non-GAAP Income Statements]

Question 102.10

Question: Is it appropriate to present a full non-GAAP income statement for purposes of reconciling non-GAAP measures to the most directly comparable GAAP measures?

Answer: Generally, no. Presenting a full non-GAAP income statement may attach undue prominence to the non-GAAP information.

Reference: Regulation G; Item 10(e) of Regulation S-K

History: Issued January 11, 2010.

¶ 51,060 [Tax Effects]

Question 102.11

Question: May a registrant present an adjustment "net of tax" when reconciling a non-GAAP performance measure to the most directly comparable GAAP measure?

Answer: Yes, provided that the tax effect of each reconciling item is disclosed parenthetically or in a footnote to the reconciliation. Alternatively, the company can present the tax effect in one line in the reconciliation. Regardless of the format of the presentation, registrants should disclose how the tax effect was calculated.

Reference: Regulation G; Item 10(e) of Regulation S-K

History: Issued January 11, 2010.

¶ 51,061 [Non-Mandatory Government or SRO Guidance]

Question 102.12

Question: A registrant discloses a financial measure or information that is not in accordance with GAAP or calculated exclusively from amounts presented in accordance with GAAP. In some circumstances, this financial information may have been prepared in accordance with guidance published by a government, governmental authority or self-regulatory organization that is applicable to the registrant, although the information is not required disclosure by the government, governmental authority or self-regulatory organization. Is this information considered to be a "non-GAAP financial measure" for purposes of Regulation G and Item 10 of Regulation S-K?

Answer: Yes. Unless this information is required to be disclosed by a system of regulation that is applicable to the registrant, it is considered to be a "non-GAAP financial measure" under Regulation G and Item 10 of Regulation S-K. Registrants that disclose such information must provide the disclosures required by Regulation G or Item 10 of Regulation S-K, if applicable, including the quantitative reconciliation from the non-GAAP financial measure to the most comparable measure calculated in accordance with GAAP. This reconciliation should be in sufficient detail to allow a reader to understand the nature of the reconciling items.

Reference: Regulation G; Item 10(e) of Regulation S-K

History: Issued April 24, 2009.

Section 103. EBIT and EBITDA

¶ 51,065 ["Earnings"]

Question 103.01

Question: Exchange Act Release No. 47226 describes EBIT as "earnings before interest and taxes" and EBITDA as "earnings before interest, taxes, depreciation and amortization." What GAAP measure is intended by the term "earnings?" May measures other than those described in the release be characterized as "EBIT" or "EBITDA?" Does the exception for EBIT and EBITDA from the prohibition in Item 10(e)(1)(ii)(A) of Regulation S-K apply to these other measures?

Answer: "Earnings" means net income as presented in the statement of operations under GAAP. Measures that are calculated differently than those described as EBIT and EBITDA in Exchange Act Release No. 47226 should not be characterized as "EBIT" or "EBITDA" and their titles should be distinguished from "EBIT" or "EBITDA," such as "Adjusted EBITDA." These measures are not exempt from the prohibition in Item 10(e)(1)(ii)(A) of Regulation S-K, with the exception of measures addressed in Question 102.09.

Reference: Regulation G; Item 10(e) of Regulation S-K

History: Issued January 11, 2010.

¶ 51,070 [Performance Measures]

Question 103.02

Question: If EBIT or EBITDA is presented as a performance measure, to which GAAP financial measure should it be reconciled?

Answer: If a company presents EBIT or EBITDA as a performance measure, such measures should be reconciled to net income as presented in the statement of operations under GAAP. Operating income would not be considered the most directly comparable GAAP financial measure because EBIT and EBITDA make adjustments for items that are not included in operating income.

Reference: Regulation G; Item 10(e) of Regulation S-K

History: Issued January 11, 2010.

Section 104. Segment Information

¶ 51,080 [Segment Profitability]

Question 104.01

Question: Is segment information that is presented in conformity with Accounting Standards Codification 280, pursuant to which a company may determine segment profitability on a basis that differs from the amounts in the consolidated financial statements determined in accordance with GAAP, considered to be a non-GAAP financial measure under Regulation G and Item 10(e) of Regulation S-K?

Answer: No. Non-GAAP financial measures do not include financial measures that are required to be disclosed by GAAP. Exchange Act Release No. 47226 lists "measures of profit or loss and total assets for each segment required to be disclosed in accordance with GAAP" as examples of such measures. The measure of segment profit or loss and segment total assets under Accounting Standards Codification 280 is the measure reported to the chief operating decision maker for purposes of making decisions about allocating resources to the segment and assessing its performance.

The list of examples in Exchange Act Release No. 47226 is not exclusive. As an additional example, because Accounting Standards Codification 280 requires or expressly permits the footnotes to the company's consolidated financial statements to include specific additional financial information for each segment, that information also would be excluded from the definition of non-GAAP financial measures.

Reference: Regulation G; Item 10(e) of Regulation S-K

History: Issued January 11, 2010.

¶ 51,085 [MD&A]

Question 104.02

Question: Does Item 10(e)(1)(ii) of Regulation S-K prohibit the discussion in MD&A of segment information determined in conformity with Accounting Standards Codification 280?

Answer: No. Where a company includes in its MD&A a discussion of segment profitability determined consistent with Accounting Standards Codification 280, which also requires that a footnote to the company's consolidated financial statements provide a reconciliation, the company also should include in the segment discussion in the MD&A a complete discussion of the reconciling items that apply to the particular segment being discussed. In this regard, see Financial Reporting Codification Section 501.06.a, footnote 28.

Reference: Regulation G; Item 10(e) of Regulation S-K

History: Issued January 11, 2010.

¶ 51,090 [Non-Compliance with Accounting Standards Codification 280]

Question 104.03

Question: Is a measure of segment profit/loss or liquidity that is not in conformity with Accounting Standards Codification 280 a non-GAAP financial measure under Regulation G and Item 10(e) of Regulation S-K?

Answer: Yes. Segment measures that are adjusted to include amounts excluded from, or to exclude amounts included in, the measure reported to the chief operating decision maker for purposes of making decisions about allocating resources to the segment and assessing its performance do not comply with Accounting Standards Codification 280. Such measures are, therefore, non-GAAP financial measures and subject to all of the provisions of Regulation G and Item 10(e) of Regulation S-K.

Reference: Regulation G; Item 10(e) of Regulation S-K

History: Issued January 11, 2010.

¶ 51,095 [Footnote Reconciliation]

Question 104.04

Question: In the footnote that reconciles the segment measures to the consolidated financial statements, a company may total the profit or loss for the individual segments as part of the Accounting Standards Codification 280 required reconciliation. Would the presentation of the total segment profit or loss measure in any context other than the Accounting Standards Codification 280 required reconciliation in the footnote be the presentation of a non-GAAP financial measure?

Answer: Yes. The presentation of the total segment profit or loss measure in any context other than the Accounting Standards Codification 280 required reconciliation in the footnote would be the presentation of a non-GAAP financial measure because it has no authoritative meaning outside of the Accounting Standards Codification 280 required reconciliation in the footnotes to the company's consolidated financial statements.

Reference: Regulation G; Item 10(e) of Regulation S-K

History: Issued January 11, 2010.

¶ 51,100 [Table Illustrating Revenues by Certain Products]

Question 104.05

Question: Company X presents a table illustrating a breakdown of revenues by certain products, but does not sum this to the revenue amount presented on Company X's financial statements. Is the information in the table considered a non-GAAP financial measure under Regulation G and Item 10(e) of Regulation S-K?

Answer: No, assuming the product revenue amounts are calculated in accordance with GAAP. The presentation would be considered a non-GAAP financial measure, however, if the revenue amounts are adjusted in any manner.

Reference: Regulation G; Item 10(e) of Regulation S-K

History: Issued January 11, 2010.

¶ 51,105 [Exchange Rates]

Question 104.06

Question: Company X has operations in various foreign countries where the local currency is used to prepare the financial statements which are translated into the reporting currency under the applicable accounting standards. In preparing its MD&A, Company X will explain the reasons for changes in various financial statement captions. A portion of these changes will be attributable to changes in exchange rates between periods used for translation. Company X wants to isolate the effect of exchange rate differences and will present financial information in a constant currency—e.g., assume a constant exchange rate between periods for translation. Would such a presentation be considered a non-GAAP measure under Regulation G and Item 10(e) of Regulation S-K?

Answer: Yes. Company X may comply with the reconciliation requirements of Regulation G and Item 10(e) by presenting the historical amounts and the amounts in constant currency and describing the process for calculating the constant currency amounts and the basis of presentation.

Reference: Regulation G; Item 10(e) of Regulation S-K

History: Issued January 11, 2010.

Section 105. Item 2.02 of Form 8-K

¶ 51,110 [Audio Files]

Question 105.01

Question: Item 2.02 of Form 8-K contains a conditional exemption from its requirement to furnish a Form 8-K where earnings information is presented orally, telephonically, by webcast, by broadcast or by similar means. Among other conditions, the company must provide on its web site any financial and other statistical information contained in the presentation, together with any information that would be required by Regulation G. Would an audio file of the initial webcast satisfy this condition to the exemption?

Answer: Yes, provided that: (1) the audio file contains all material financial and other statistical information included in the presentation that was not previously disclosed, and (2) investors can access it and replay it through the company's web site. Alternatively, slides or a similar presentation posted on the web site at the time of the presentation containing the required, previously undisclosed, material financial and other statistical information would satisfy the condition. In each case, the company must provide all previously undisclosed material financial and other statistical information, including information provided in connection with any questions and answers. Regulation FD also may impose disclosure requirements in these circumstances.

Reference: Regulation G; Item 10(e) of Regulation S-K; Item 2.02 of Form 8-K

History: Issued January 11, 2010.

¶ 51,115 [Timeliness]

Question 105.02

Question: Item 2.02 of Form 8-K contains a conditional exemption from its requirement to furnish a Form 8-K where earnings information is presented orally, telephonically, by webcast, by broadcast or by similar means. Among other conditions, the company must provide on its web site any material financial and other statistical information not previously disclosed and contained in the presentation, together with any information that would be required by Regulation G. When must all of this information appear on the company's web site?

Answer: The required information must appear on the company's web site at the time the oral presentation is made. In the case of information that is not provided in a presentation itself but, rather, is disclosed unexpectedly in connection with the question and answer session that was part of that oral presentation, the information must be posted on the company's web site promptly after it is disclosed. Any requirements of Regulation FD also must be satisfied. A webcast of the oral presentation would be sufficient to meet this requirement.

Reference: Regulation G; Item 10(e) of Regulation S-K; Item 2.02 of Form 8-K

History: Issued January 11, 2010.

¶ 51,120 [Form S-3 Eligibility]

Question 105.03

Question: Does a company's failure to furnish to the Commission the Form 8-K required by Item 2.02 in a timely manner affect the company's eligibility to use Form S-3?

Answer: No. Form S-3 requires the company to have filed in "a timely manner all reports required to be filed in twelve calendar months and any portion of a month immediately preceding the filing of the registration statement." Because an Item 2.02 Form 8-K is furnished to the Commission, rather than filed with the Commission, failure to furnish such a Form 8-K in a timely manner would not affect a company's eligibility to use Form S-3. While not affecting a company's Form S-3 eligibility, failure to comply with Item 2.02 of Form 8-K would, of course, be a violation of Section 13(a) of the Exchange Act and the rules thereunder.

Reference: Regulation G; Item 10(e) of Regulation S-K; Item 2.02 of Form 8-K; Form S-3

History: Issued January 11, 2010.

¶ 51,125 [Withdrawn]

Question 105.04

Question: A company issues its quarterly earnings release within 48 hours of its quarterly earnings conference call. However, on the conference call the company discloses material non-public information relating to its results of operations for the quarter that was not disclosed in the earnings release, and thus does not satisfy the exemption in Item 2.02(b) of Form 8-K with respect to that information. Is the company required to furnish an Item 2.02 Form 8-K with respect to all responsive information disclosed on the conference call, or just the information omitted from the earnings release?

Answer: The company will have an Item 2.02 Form 8-K filing obligation only with respect to the material non-public information relating to its results of operations for the quarter that was disclosed on the earnings call but not disclosed in the earnings release. A transcript of this portion of the conference call will satisfy this requirement. Regulation FD also may impose disclosure requirements in these circumstances.

Reference: Regulation G; Item 10(e) of Regulation S-K; Item 2.02 of Form 8-K; Form S-3

History: Issued January 11, 2010; withdrawn January 15, 2010.

¶ 51,130 [Form 10-Q Exhibits]

Question 105.05

Question: Company X files its quarterly earnings release as an exhibit to its Form 10-Q on Wednesday morning, prior to holding its earnings conference call Wednesday afternoon. Assuming that all of the other conditions of Item 2.02(b) are met, may the company rely on the exemption for its conference call even if it does not also furnish the earnings release in an Item 2.02 Form 8-K?

Answer: Yes. Company X's filing of the earnings release as an exhibit to its Form 10-Q, rather than in an Item 2.02 Form 8-K, before the conference call takes place, would not preclude reliance on the exemption for the conference call.

Reference: Regulation G; Item 10(e) of Regulation S-K; Item 2.02 of Form 8-K; Form S-3

History: Issued January 11, 2010.

¶ 51,135 [Press Release]

Question 105.06

Question: Company A issues a press release announcing its results of operations for a just-completed fiscal quarter, including its expected adjusted earnings (a non-GAAP financial measure) for the fiscal period. Would this press release be subject to Item 2.02 of Form 8-K?

Answer: Yes, because it contains material, non-public information regarding its results of operations for a completed fiscal period. The adjusted earnings range presented would be subject to the requirements of Item 2.02 applicable to non-GAAP financial measures.

Reference: Regulation G; Item 10(e) of Regulation S-K; Item 2.02 of Form 8-K; Form S-3

History: Issued January 11, 2010.

¶ 51,137 [Conference Calls]

Question 105.07

Question: A company issues its earnings release after the close of the market and holds a properly noticed conference call to discuss its earnings two hours later. That conference call contains material, previously undisclosed, information of the type described under Item 2.02 of Form 8-K. Because of this timing, the company is unable to furnish its earnings release on a Form 8-K before its conference call. Accordingly, the company cannot rely on the exemption from the requirement to furnish the information in the conference call on a Form 8-K. What must the company file with regard to its conference call?

Answer: The company must furnish the material, previously non-public, financial and other statistical information required to be furnished on Item 2.02 of Form 8-K as an exhibit to a Form 8-K and satisfy the other requirements of Item 2.02 of Form 8-K. A transcript of the portion of the conference call or slides or a similar presentation including such information will satisfy this requirement. In each case, all material, previously undisclosed, financial and other statistical information, including that provided in connection with any questions and answers, must be provided.

Reference: Regulation G; Item 10(e) of Regulation S-K; Item 2.02 of Form 8-K

History: Issued January 15, 2010.

Section 106. Foreign Private Issuers

¶ 51,140 ["Expressly Permitted"]

Question 106.01

Question: The Note to Item 10(e) of Regulation S-K permits a foreign private issuer to include in its filings a non-GAAP financial measure that otherwise would be prohibited by Item 10(e)(1)(ii) if, among other things, the non-GAAP financial measure is required or expressly permitted by the standard setter that is responsible for establishing the GAAP used in the company's primary financial statements included in its filing with the Commission. What does "expressly permitted" mean?

Answer: A measure is "expressly permitted" if the particular measure is clearly and specifically identified as an acceptable measure by the standard setter that is responsible for establishing the GAAP used in the company's primary financial statements included in its filing with the Commission.

The concept of "expressly permitted" can be also be demonstrated with explicit acceptance of a presentation by the primary securities regulator in the foreign private issuer's home country jurisdiction or market. Explicit acceptance by the regulator would include (1) published views of the regulator or members of the regulator's staff or (2) a letter from the regulator or its staff to the foreign private issuer indicating the acceptance of the presentation—which would be provided to the Commission's staff upon request.

Reference: Regulation G; Item 10(e) of Regulation S-K

History: Issued January 11, 2010.

¶ 51,145 [Press Releases]

Question 106.02

Question: A foreign private issuer furnishes a press release on Form 6-K that includes a section with non-GAAP financial measures. Can a foreign private issuer incorporate by reference into a Securities Act registration statement only those portions of the furnished press release that do not include the non-GAAP financial measures?

Answer: Yes. Reports on Form 6-K are not incorporated by reference automatically into Securities Act registration statements. In order to incorporate a Form 6-K into a Securities Act registration statement, a foreign private issuer must specifically provide for such incorporation by reference in the registration statement and in any subsequently submitted Form 6-K. See Item 6(c) of Form F-3. Where a foreign private issuer wishes to incorporate by reference a portion or portions of the press release provided on a Form 6-K, the foreign private issuer should either: (1) specify in the Form 6-K those portions of the press release to be incorporated by reference, or (2) furnish two Form 6-K reports, one that contains the full press release and another that contains the portions that would be incorporated by reference (and specifies that the second Form 6-K is so incorporated). Using a separate report on Form 6-K containing the portions that would be incorporated by reference may provide more clarity for investors in most circumstances. A company must also consider whether its disclosure is rendered misleading if it incorporates only a portion (or portions) of a press release.

Reference: Regulation G; Item 10(e) of Regulation S-K; Form 6-K

History: Issued January 11, 2010.

¶ 51,150 [Incorporation by Reference]

Question 106.03

Question: A foreign private issuer publishes a non-GAAP financial measure that does not comply with Regulation G, in reliance on Rule 100(c), and then furnishes the information in a report on Form 6-K. Must the foreign private issuer comply with Item 10(e) of Regulation S-K with respect to that information if the company chooses to incorporate that Form 6-K report into a filed Securities Act registration statement (other than an MJDS registration statement)?

Answer: Yes, the company must comply with all of the provisions of Item 10(e) of Regulation S-K.

Reference: Regulation G; Item 10(e) of Regulation S-K; Form 6-K

History: Issued January 11, 2010.

¶ 51,155 [Canadian Issuers]

Question 106.04

Question: If a Canadian company includes a non-GAAP financial measure in an annual report on Form 40-F, does the company need to comply with Regulation G or Item 10(e) of Regulation S-K with respect to that information if the company files a non-MJDS Securities Act registration statement that incorporates by reference the Form 40-F?

Answer: No. Information included in a Form 40-F is not subject to Regulation G or Item 10(e) of Regulation S-K.

Reference: Regulation G; Item 10(e) of Regulation S-K; Form 40-F

History: Issued January 11, 2010.

Section 107. Voluntary Filers

¶ 51,160 [Suspension of Reporting Obligations]

Question 107.01

Question: Section 15(d) of the Exchange Act suspends automatically its application to any company that would be subject to the filing requirements of that section where, if other conditions are met, on the first day of the company's fiscal year it has fewer than 300 holders of record of the class of securities that created the Section 15(d) obligation. This suspension, which relates to the fiscal year in which the fewer than 300 record holders determination is made on the first day thereof, is automatic and does not require any filing with the Commission. The Commission adopted Rule 15d-6 under the Exchange Act to require the filing of a Form 15 as a notice of the suspension of a company's reporting obligation under Section 15(d). Such a filing, however, is not a condition to the suspension. A number of companies whose Section 15(d) reporting obligation is suspended automatically by the statute choose not to file the notice required by Rule 15d-6 and continue to file Exchange Act reports as though they continue to be required. Must a company whose reporting obligation is suspended automatically by Section 15(d) but continues to file periodic reports as though it were required to file periodic reports comply with Regulation G and the requirements of Item 10(e) of Regulation S-K?

Answer: Yes. Regulation S-K relates to filings with the Commission. Accordingly, a company that is making filings as described in this question must comply with Regulation S-K or Form 20-F, as applicable, in its filings.

As to other public communications, any company "that has a class of securities registered under Section 12 of the Securities Exchange Act of 1934, or is required to file reports under Section 15(d) of the Securities Exchange Act of 1934" must comply with Regulation G. The application of this standard to those companies that no longer are "required" to report under Section 15(d) but choose to continue to report presents a difficult dilemma, as those companies technically are not subject to Regulation G but their continued filing is intended to and does give the appearance that they are a public company whose disclosure is subject to the Commission's regulations. It is reasonable that this appearance would cause shareholders and other market participants to expect and rely on a company's required compliance with the requirements of the federal securities laws applicable to companies reporting under Section 15(d). Accordingly, while Regulation G technically does not apply to a company such as the one described in this question, the failure of such a company to comply with all requirements (including Regulation G) applicable to a Section 15(d)-reporting company can raise significant issues regarding that company's compliance with the anti-fraud provisions of the federal securities laws.

Reference: Exchange Act Section 15(d); Regulation G; Item 10(e) of Regulation S-K

History: Issued January 11, 2010.

SARBANES-OXLEY ACT OF 2002

SARBANES-OXLEY ACT OF 2002

[¶ 64,001]

SARBANES-OXLEY ACT OF 2002

H.R.3763

One Hundred Seventh Congress

of the

United States of America

AT THE SECOND SESSION

Begun and held at the City of Washington on Wednesday,
the twenty-third day of January, two thousand and two

An Act

To protect investors by improving the accuracy and reliability of corporate disclosures made pursuant to the securities laws, and for other purposes.

Be it enacted by the Senate and House of Representatives of the United States of America in Congress assembled,

[¶ 64,001C]   SEC. 1. [15 USC 7201] SHORT TITLE; TABLE OF CONTENTS.

(a) SHORT TITLE—This Act may be cited as the 'Sarbanes-Oxley Act of 2002'.

(b) TABLE OF CONTENTS—The table of contents for this Act is as follows:

Sec. 1101. Short title.

Sec. 1102. Tampering with a record or otherwise impeding an official proceeding.

Sec. 1103. Temporary freeze authority for the Securities and Exchange Commission.

Sec. 1104. Amendment to the Federal Sentencing Guidelines.

Sec. 1105. Authority of the Commission to prohibit persons from serving as officers or directors.

Sec. 1106. Increased criminal penalties under Securities Exchange Act of 1934.

Sec. 1107. Retaliation against informants.

[¶ 64,011]   SEC. 2. [15 USC 7201] DEFINITIONS.

(a) IN GENERAL—Except as otherwise specifically provided in this Act, in this Act, the following definitions shall apply:

(1) APPROPRIATE STATE REGULATORY AUTHORITY- The term 'appropriate State regulatory authority' means the State agency or other authority responsible for the licensure or other regulation of the practice of accounting in the State or States having jurisdiction over a registered public accounting firm or associated person thereof, with respect to the matter in question.

(2) AUDIT—The term 'audit' means an examination of the financial statements of any issuer by an independent public accounting firm in accordance with the rules of the Board or the Commission (or, for the period preceding the adoption of applicable rules of the Board under section 103, in accordance with then-applicable generally accepted auditing and related standards for such purposes), for the purpose of expressing an opinion on such statements.

(3) AUDIT COMMITTEE—The term 'audit committee' means—

(A) a committee (or equivalent body) established by and amongst the board of directors of an issuer for the purpose of overseeing the accounting and financial reporting processes of the issuer and audits of the financial statements of the issuer; and

(B) if no such committee exists with respect to an issuer, the entire board of directors of the issuer.

(4) AUDIT REPORT—The term 'audit report' means a document or other record—

(A) prepared following an audit performed for purposes of compliance by an issuer with the requirements of the securities laws; and

(B) in which a public accounting firm either—

(i) sets forth the opinion of that firm regarding a financial statement, report, or other document; or

(ii) asserts that no such opinion can be expressed.

(5) BOARD—The term 'Board' means the Public Company Accounting Oversight Board established under section 101.

(6) COMMISSION—The term 'Commission' means the Securities and Exchange Commission.

(7) ISSUER—The term 'issuer' means an issuer (as defined in section 3 of the Securities Exchange Act of 1934 (15 U.S.C. 78c)), the securities of which are registered under section 12 of that Act (15 U.S.C. 78l), or that is required to file reports under section 15(d) (15 U.S.C. 78o(d)), or that files or has filed a registration statement that has not yet become effective under the Securities Act of 1933 (15 U.S.C. 77a et seq.), and that it has not withdrawn.

(8) NON-AUDIT SERVICES—The term 'non-audit services' means any professional services provided to an issuer by a registered public accounting firm, other than those provided to an issuer in connection with an audit or a review of the financial statements of an issuer.

(9) PERSON ASSOCIATED WITH A PUBLIC ACCOUNTING FIRM

(A) IN GENERAL—The terms 'person associated with a public accounting firm' (or with a 'registered public accounting firm') and 'associated person of a public accounting firm' (or of a 'registered public accounting firm') mean any individual proprietor, partner, shareholder, principal, accountant, or other professional employee of a public accounting firm, or any other independent contractor or entity that, in connection with the preparation or issuance of any audit report—

(i) shares in the profits of, or receives compensation in any other form from, that firm; or

(ii) participates as agent or otherwise on behalf of such accounting firm in any activity of that firm.

(B) EXEMPTION AUTHORITY—The Board may, by rule, exempt persons engaged only in ministerial tasks from the definition in subparagraph (A), to the extent that the Board determines that any such exemption is consistent with the purposes of this Act, the public interest, or the protection of investors.

(C) Investigative and Enforcement Authority—For purposes of sections 3(c), 101(c), 105, and 107(c) and the rules of the Board and Commission issued thereunder, except to the extent specifically excepted by such rules, the terms defined in subparagraph (A) shall include any person associated, seeking to become associated, or formerly associated with a public accounting firm, except that—

(i) the authority to conduct an investigation of such person under section 105(b) shall apply only with respect to any act or practice, or omission to act, by the person while such person was associated or seeking to become associated with a registered public accounting firm; and

(ii) the authority to commence a disciplinary proceeding under section 105(c)(1), or impose sanctions under section 105(c)(4), against such person shall apply only with respect to—

(I) conduct occurring while such person was associated or seeking to become associated with a registered public accounting firm; or

(II) non-cooperation, as described in section 105(b)(3), with respect to a demand in a Board investigation for testimony, documents, or other information relating to a period when such person was associated or seeking to become associated with a registered public accounting firm.

(10) PROFESSIONAL STANDARDS—The term 'professional standards' means—

(A) accounting principles that are—

(i) established by the standard setting body described in section 19(b) of the Securities Act of 1933, as amended by this Act, or prescribed by the Commission under section 19(a) of that Act (15 U.S.C. 17a(s)) or section 13(b) of the Securities Exchange Act of 1934 (15 U.S.C. 78a(m)); and

(ii) relevant to audit reports for particular issuers, or dealt with in the quality control system of a particular registered public accounting firm; and

(B) auditing standards, standards for attestation engagements, quality control policies and procedures, ethical and competency standards, and independence standards (including rules implementing title II) that the Board or the Commission determines—

(i) relate to the preparation or issuance of audit reports for issuers; and

(ii) are established or adopted by the Board under section 103(a), or are promulgated as rules of the Commission.

(11) PUBLIC ACCOUNTING FIRM—The term 'public accounting firm' means—

(A) a proprietorship, partnership, incorporated association, corporation, limited liability company, limited liability partnership, or other legal entity that is engaged in the practice of public accounting or preparing or issuing audit reports; and

(B) to the extent so designated by the rules of the Board, any associated person of any entity described in subparagraph (A).

(12) REGISTERED PUBLIC ACCOUNTING FIRM- The term 'registered public accounting firm' means a public accounting firm registered with the Board in accordance with this Act.

(13) RULES OF THE BOARD—The term 'rules of the Board' means the bylaws and rules of the Board (as submitted to, and approved, modified, or amended by the Commission, in accordance with section 107), and those stated policies, practices, and interpretations of the Board that the Commission, by rule, may deem to be rules of the Board, as necessary or appropriate in the public interest or for the protection of investors.

(14) SECURITY—The term 'security' has the same meaning as in section 3(a) of the Securities Exchange Act of 1934 (15 U.S.C. 78c(a)).

(15) SECURITIES LAWS—The term 'securities laws' means the provisions of law referred to in section 3(a)(47) of the Securities Exchange Act of 1934 (15 U.S.C. 78c(a)(47)), as amended by this Act, and includes the rules, regulations, and orders issued by the Commission thereunder.

(16) STATE—The term 'State' means any State of the United States, the District of Columbia, Puerto Rico, the Virgin Islands, or any other territory or possession of the United States.

(b) CONFORMING AMENDMENT—Section 3(a)(47) of the Securities Exchange Act of 1934 (15 U.S.C. 78c(a)(47)) is amended by inserting 'the Sarbanes-Oxley Act of 2002,' before 'the Public'.

(17) FOREIGN AUDITOR OVERSIGHT AUTHORITY—The term 'foreign auditor oversight authority' means any governmental body or other entity empowered by a foreign government to conduct inspections of public accounting firms or otherwise to administer or enforce laws related to the regulation of public accounting firms.

[¶ 64,021]   SEC. 3. [15 USC 7202] COMMISSION RULES AND
ENFORCEMENT.

(a) REGULATORY ACTION—The Commission shall promulgate such rules and regulations, as may be necessary or appropriate in the public interest or for the protection of investors, and in furtherance of this Act.

(b) ENFORCEMENT

(1) IN GENERAL—A violation by any person of this Act, any rule or regulation of the Commission issued under this Act, or any rule of the Board shall be treated for all purposes in the same manner as a violation of the Securities Exchange Act of 1934 (15 U.S.C. 78a et seq.) or the rules and regulations issued thereunder, consistent with the provisions of this Act, and any such person shall be subject to the same penalties, and to the same extent, as for a violation of that Act or such rules or regulations.

(2) INVESTIGATIONS, INJUNCTIONS, AND PROSECUTION OF OFFENSES—Section 21 of the Securities Exchange Act of 1934 (15 U.S.C. 78u) is amended—

(A) in subsection (a)(1), by inserting 'the rules of the Public Company Accounting Oversight Board, of which such person is a registered public accounting firm or a person associated with such a firm,' after 'is a participant,';

(B) in subsection (d)(1), by inserting 'the rules of the Public Company Accounting Oversight Board, of which such person is a registered public accounting firm or a person associated with such a firm,' after 'is a participant,';

(C) in subsection (e), by inserting 'the rules of the Public Company Accounting Oversight Board, of which such person is a registered public accounting firm or a person associated with such a firm,' after 'is a participant,'; and

(D) in subsection (f), by inserting 'or the Public Company Accounting Oversight Board' after 'self-regulatory organization' each place that term appears.

(3) CEASE-AND-DESIST PROCEEDINGS—Section 21C(c)(2) of the Securities Exchange Act of 1934 (15 U.S.C. 78u-3(c)(2)) is amended by inserting 'registered public accounting firm (as defined in section 2 of the Sarbanes-Oxley Act of 2002),' after 'government securities dealer,'.

(4) ENFORCEMENT BY FEDERAL BANKING AGENCIES. Section 12(i) of the Securities Exchange Act of 1934 (15 U.S.C. 78l(i)) is amended by—

(A) striking 'sections 12,' each place it appears and inserting 'sections 10A(m), 12,'; and

(B) striking 'and 16,' each place it appears and inserting 'and 16 of this Act, and sections 302, 303, 304, 306, 401(b), 404, 406, and 407 of the Sarbanes-Oxley Act of 2002,'.

(c) EFFECT ON COMMISSION AUTHORITY- Nothing in this Act or the rules of the Board shall be construed to impair or limit—

(1) the authority of the Commission to regulate the accounting profession, accounting firms, or persons associated with such firms for purposes of enforcement of the securities laws;

(2) the authority of the Commission to set standards for accounting or auditing practices or auditor independence, derived from other provisions of the securities laws or the rules or regulations thereunder, for purposes of the preparation and issuance of any audit report, or otherwise under applicable law; or

(3) the ability of the Commission to take, on the initiative of the Commission, legal, administrative, or disciplinary action against any registered public accounting firm or any associated person thereof.

TITLE I—PUBLIC COMPANY ACCOUNTING OVERSIGHT BOARD

[¶ 64,031] SEC. 101. [15 USC 7211] ESTABLISHMENT; ADMINISTRATIVE PROVISIONS.

(a) ESTABLISHMENT OF BOARD—There is established the Public Company Accounting Oversight Board, to oversee the audit of companies that are subject to the securities laws, and related matters, in order to protect the interests of investors and further the public interest in the preparation of informative, accurate, and independent audit reports. The Board shall be a body corporate, operate as a nonprofit corporation, and have succession until dissolved by an Act of Congress.

(b) STATUS—The Board shall not be an agency or establishment of the United States Government, and, except as otherwise provided in this Act, shall be subject to, and have all the powers conferred upon a nonprofit corporation by, the District of Columbia Nonprofit Corporation Act. No member or person employed by, or agent for, the Board shall be deemed to be an officer or employee of or agent for the Federal Government by reason of such service.

(c) DUTIES OF THE BOARD—The Board shall, subject to action by the Commission under section 107, and once a determination is made by the Commission under subsection (d) of this section—

(1) register public accounting firms that prepare audit reports for issuers, brokers, and dealers, in accordance with section 102;

(2) establish or adopt, or both, by rule, auditing, quality control, ethics, independence, and other standards relating to the preparation of audit reports for issuers, brokers, and dealers, in accordance with section 103;

(3) conduct inspections of registered public accounting firms, in accordance with section 104 and the rules of the Board;

(4) conduct investigations and disciplinary proceedings concerning, and impose appropriate sanctions where justified upon, registered public accounting firms and associated persons of such firms, in accordance with section 105;

(5) perform such other duties or functions as the Board (or the Commission, by rule or order) determines are necessary or appropriate to promote high professional standards among, and improve the quality of audit services offered by, registered public accounting firms and associated persons thereof, or otherwise to carry out this Act, in order to protect investors, or to further the public interest;

(6) enforce compliance with this Act, the rules of the Board, professional standards, and the securities laws relating to the preparation and issuance of audit reports and the obligations and liabilities of accountants with respect thereto, by registered public accounting firms and associated persons thereof; and

(7) set the budget and manage the operations of the Board and the staff of the Board.

(d) COMMISSION DETERMINATION—The members of the Board shall take such action (including hiring of staff, proposal of rules, and adoption of initial and transitional auditing and other professional standards) as may be necessary or appropriate to enable the Commission to determine, not later than 270 days after the date of enactment of this Act, that the Board is so organized and has the capacity to carry out the requirements of this title, and to enforce compliance with this title by registered public accounting firms and associated persons thereof. The Commission shall be responsible, prior to the appointment of the Board, for the planning for the establishment and administrative transition to the Board's operation.

(e) BOARD MEMBERSHIP

(1) COMPOSITION—The Board shall have 5 members, appointed from among prominent individuals of integrity and reputation who have a demonstrated commitment to the interests of investors and the public, and an understanding of the responsibilities for and nature of the financial disclosures required of issuers, brokers, and dealers under the securities laws and the obligations of accountants with respect to the preparation and issuance of audit reports with respect to such disclosures.

(2) LIMITATION—Two members, and only 2 members, of the Board shall be or have been certified public accountants pursuant to the laws of 1 or more States, provided that, if 1 of those 2 members is the chairperson, he or she may not have been a practicing certified public accountant for at least 5 years prior to his or her appointment to the Board.

(3) FULL-TIME INDEPENDENT SERVICE—Each member of the Board shall serve on a full-time basis, and may not, concurrent with service on the Board, be employed by any other person or engage in any other professional or business activity. No member of the Board may share in any of the profits of, or receive payments from, a public accounting firm (or any other person, as determined by rule of the Commission), other than fixed continuing payments, subject to such conditions as the Commission may impose, under standard arrangements for the retirement of members of public accounting firms.

(4) APPOINTMENT OF BOARD MEMBERS

(A) INITIAL BOARD—Not later than 90 days after the date of enactment of this Act, the Commission, after consultation with the Chairman of the Board of Governors of the Federal Reserve System and the Secretary of the Treasury, shall appoint the chairperson and other initial members of the Board, and shall designate a term of service for each.

(B) VACANCIES—A vacancy on the Board shall not affect the powers of the Board, but shall be filled in the same manner as provided for appointments under this section.

(5) TERM OF SERVICE

(A) IN GENERAL—The term of service of each Board member shall be 5 years, and until a successor is appointed, except that—

(i) the terms of office of the initial Board members (other than the chairperson) shall expire in annual increments, 1 on each of the first 4 anniversaries of the initial date of appointment; and

(ii) any Board member appointed to fill a vacancy occurring before the expiration of the term for which the predecessor was appointed shall be appointed only for the remainder of that term.

(B) TERM LIMITATION—No person may serve as a member of the Board, or as chairperson of the Board, for more than 2 terms, whether or not such terms of service are consecutive.

(6) REMOVAL FROM OFFICE—A member of the Board may be removed by the Commission from office, in accordance with section 107(d)(3), for good cause shown before the expiration of the term of that member.

(f) POWERS OF THE BOARD—In addition to any authority granted to the Board otherwise in this Act, the Board shall have the power, subject to section 107—

(1) to sue and be sued, complain and defend, in its corporate name and through its own counsel, with the approval of the Commission, in any Federal, State, or other court;

(2) to conduct its operations and maintain offices, and to exercise all other rights and powers authorized by this Act, in any State, without regard to any qualification, licensing, or other provision of law in effect in such State (or a political subdivision thereof);

(3) to lease, purchase, accept gifts or donations of or otherwise acquire, improve, use, sell, exchange, or convey, all of or an interest in any property, wherever situated;

(4) to appoint such employees, accountants, attorneys, and other agents as may be necessary or appropriate, and to determine their qualifications, define their duties, and fix their salaries or other compensation (at a level that is comparable to private sector self-regulatory, accounting, technical, supervisory, or other staff or management positions);

(5) to allocate, assess, and collect accounting support fees established pursuant to section 109, for the Board, and other fees and charges imposed under this title; and

(6) to enter into contracts, execute instruments, incur liabilities, and do any and all other acts and things necessary, appropriate, or incidental to the conduct of its operations and the exercise of its obligations, rights, and powers imposed or granted by this title.

(g) RULES OF THE BOARD—The rules of the Board shall, subject to the approval of the Commission—

(1) provide for the operation and administration of the Board, the exercise of its authority, and the performance of its responsibilities under this Act;

(2) permit, as the Board determines necessary or appropriate, delegation by the Board of any of its functions to an individual member or employee of the Board, or to a division of the Board, including functions with respect to hearing, determining, ordering, certifying, reporting, or otherwise acting as to any matter, except that—

(A) the Board shall retain a discretionary right to review any action pursuant to any such delegated function, upon its own motion;

(B) a person shall be entitled to a review by the Board with respect to any matter so delegated, and the decision of the Board upon such review shall be deemed to be the action of the Board for all purposes (including appeal or review thereof); and

(C) if the right to exercise a review described in subparagraph (A) is declined, or if no such review is sought within the time stated in the rules of the Board, then the action taken by the holder of such delegation shall for all purposes, including appeal or review thereof, be deemed to be the action of the Board;

(3) establish ethics rules and standards of conduct for Board members and staff, including a bar on practice before the Board (and the Commission, with respect to Board-related matters) of 1 year for former members of the Board, and appropriate periods (not to exceed 1 year) for former staff of the Board; and

(4) provide as otherwise required by this Act.

(h) ANNUAL REPORT TO THE COMMISSION- The Board shall submit an annual report (including its audited financial statements) to the Commission, and the Commission shall transmit a copy of that report to the Committee on Banking, Housing, and Urban Affairs of the Senate, and the Committee on Financial Services of the House of Representatives, not later than 30 days after the date of receipt of that report by the Commission.

[¶ 64,041]   SEC. 102. [15 USC 7212] REGISTRATION WITH THE BOARD.

(a) MANDATORY REGISTRATION—It shall be unlawful for any person that is not a registered public accounting firm to prepare or issue, or to participate in the preparation or issuance of, any audit report with respect to any issuer, broker, or dealer.

(b) APPLICATIONS FOR REGISTRATION

(1) FORM OF APPLICATION—A public accounting firm shall use such form as the Board may prescribe, by rule, to apply for registration under this section.

(2) CONTENTS OF APPLICATIONS—Each public accounting firm shall submit, as part of its application for registration, in such detail as the Board shall specify—

(A) the names of all issuers, brokers, and dealers for which the firm prepared or issued audit reports during the immediately preceding calendar year, and for which the firm expects to prepare or issue audit reports during the current calendar year;

(B) the annual fees received by the firm from each such issuer, broker, or dealer for audit services, other accounting services, and non-audit services, respectively;

(C) such other current financial information for the most recently completed fiscal year of the firm as the Board may reasonably request;

(D) a statement of the quality control policies of the firm for its accounting and auditing practices;

(E) a list of all accountants associated with the firm who participate in or contribute to the preparation of audit reports, stating the license or certification number of each such person, as well as the State license numbers of the firm itself;

(F) information relating to criminal, civil, or administrative actions or disciplinary proceedings pending against the firm or any associated person of the firm in connection with any audit report;

(G) copies of any periodic or annual disclosure filed by an issuer, broker, or dealer with the Commission during the immediately preceding calendar year which discloses accounting disagreements between such issuer, broker, or dealer and the firm in connection with an audit report furnished or prepared by the firm for such issuer, broker, or dealer; and

(H) such other information as the rules of the Board or the Commission shall specify as necessary or appropriate in the public interest or for the protection of investors.

(3) CONSENTS—Each application for registration under this subsection shall include—

(A) a consent executed by the public accounting firm to cooperation in and compliance with any request for testimony or the production of documents made by the Board in the furtherance of its authority and responsibilities under this title (and an agreement to secure and enforce similar consents from each of the associated persons of the public accounting firm as a condition of their continued employment by or other association with such firm); and

(B) a statement that such firm understands and agrees that cooperation and compliance, as described in the consent required by subparagraph (A), and the securing and enforcement of such consents from its associated persons, in accordance with the rules of the Board, shall be a condition to the continuing effectiveness of the registration of the firm with the Board.

(c) ACTION ON APPLICATIONS

(1) TIMING—The Board shall approve a completed application for registration not later than 45 days after the date of receipt of the application, in accordance with the rules of the Board, unless the Board, prior to such date, issues a written notice of disapproval to, or requests more information from, the prospective registrant.

(2) TREATMENT—A written notice of disapproval of a completed application under paragraph (1) for registration shall be treated as a disciplinary sanction for purposes of sections 105(d) and 107(c).

(d) PERIODIC REPORTS—Each registered public accounting firm shall submit an annual report to the Board, and may be required to report more frequently, as necessary to update the information contained in its application for registration under this section, and to provide to the Board such additional information as the Board or the Commission may specify, in accordance with subsection (b)(2).

(e) PUBLIC AVAILABILITY—Registration applications and annual reports required by this subsection, or such portions of such applications or reports as may be designated under rules of the Board, shall be made available for public inspection, subject to rules of the Board or the Commission, and to applicable laws relating to the confidentiality of proprietary, personal, or other information contained in such applications or reports, provided that, in all events, the Board shall protect from public disclosure information reasonably identified by the subject accounting firm as proprietary information.

(f) REGISTRATION AND ANNUAL FEES—The Board shall assess and collect a registration fee and an annual fee from each registered public accounting firm, in amounts that are sufficient to recover the costs of processing and reviewing applications and annual reports.

[¶ 64,051] SEC. 103. [15 USC 7213] AUDITING, QUALITY CONTROL, AND INDEPENDENCE STANDARDS AND RULES.

(a) AUDITING, QUALITY CONTROL, AND ETHICS STANDARDS

(1) IN GENERAL—The Board shall, by rule, establish, including, to the extent it determines appropriate, through adoption of standards proposed by 1 or more professional groups of accountants designated pursuant to paragraph (3)(A) or advisory groups convened pursuant to paragraph (4), and amend or otherwise modify or alter, such auditing and related attestation standards, such quality control standards, such ethics standards, and such independence standards to be used by registered public accounting firms in the preparation and issuance of audit reports, as required by this Act or the rules of the Commission, or as may be necessary or appropriate in the public interest or for the protection of investors.

(2) RULE REQUIREMENTS—In carrying out paragraph (1), the Board—

(A) shall include in the auditing standards that it adopts, requirements that each registered public accounting firm shall—

(i) prepare, and maintain for a period of not less than 7 years, audit work papers, and other information related to any audit report, in sufficient detail to support the conclusions reached in such report;

(ii) provide a concurring or second partner review and approval of such audit report (and other related information), and concurring approval in its issuance, by a qualified person (as prescribed by the Board) associated with the public accounting firm, other than the person in charge of the audit, or by an independent reviewer (as prescribed by the Board); and

(iii) in each audit report for an issuer, describe the scope of the auditor's testing of the internal control structure and procedures of the issuer, required by section 404(b), and present (in such report or in a separate report)—

(I) the findings of the auditor from such testing;

(II) an evaluation of whether such internal control structure and procedures—

(aa) include maintenance of records that in reasonable detail accurately and fairly reflect the transactions and dispositions of the assets of the issuer;

(bb) provide reasonable assurance that transactions are recorded as necessary to permit preparation of financial statements in accordance with generally accepted accounting principles, and that receipts and expenditures of the issuer are being made only in accordance with authorizations of management and directors of the issuer; and

(III) a description, at a minimum, of material weaknesses in such internal controls, and of any material noncompliance found on the basis of such testing.

(B) shall include, in the quality control standards that it adopts with respect to the issuance of audit reports, requirements for every registered public accounting firm relating to—

(i) monitoring of professional ethics and independence from issuers, brokers, and dealers on behalf of which the firm issues audit reports;

(ii) consultation within such firm on accounting and auditing questions;

(iii) supervision of audit work;

(iv) hiring, professional development, and advancement of personnel;

(v) the acceptance and continuation of engagements;

(vi) internal inspection; and

(vii) such other requirements as the Board may prescribe, subject to subsection (a)(1).

(3) AUTHORITY TO ADOPT OTHER STANDARDS

(A) IN GENERAL—In carrying out this subsection, the Board—

(i) may adopt as its rules, subject to the terms of section 107, any portion of any statement of auditing standards or other professional standards that the Board determines satisfy the requirements of paragraph (1), and that were proposed by 1 or more professional groups of accountants that shall be designated or recognized by the Board, by rule, for such purpose, pursuant to this paragraph or 1 or more advisory groups convened pursuant to paragraph (4); and

(ii) notwithstanding clause (i), shall retain full authority to modify, supplement, revise, or subsequently amend, modify, or repeal, in whole or in part, any portion of any statement described in clause (i).

(B) INITIAL AND TRANSITIONAL STANDARDS- The Board shall adopt standards described in subparagraph (A)(i) as initial or transitional standards, to the extent the Board determines necessary, prior to a determination of the Commission under section 101(d), and such standards shall be separately approved by the Commission at the time of that determination, without regard to the procedures required by section 107 that otherwise would apply to the approval of rules of the Board.

(4) ADVISORY GROUPS—The Board shall convene, or authorize its staff to convene, such expert advisory groups as may be appropriate, which may include practicing accountants and other experts, as well as representatives of other interested groups, subject to such rules as the Board may prescribe to prevent conflicts of interest, to make recommendations concerning the content (including proposed drafts) of auditing, quality control, ethics, independence, or other standards required to be established under this section.

(b) INDEPENDENCE STANDARDS AND RULES- The Board shall establish such rules as may be necessary or appropriate in the public interest or for the protection of investors, to implement, or as authorized under, title II of this Act.

(c) COOPERATION WITH DESIGNATED PROFESSIONAL GROUPS OF ACCOUNTANTS AND ADVISORY GROUPS

(1) IN GENERAL—The Board shall cooperate on an ongoing basis with professional groups of accountants designated under subsection (a)(3)(A) and advisory groups convened under subsection (a)(4) in the examination of the need for changes in any standards subject to its authority under subsection (a), recommend issues for inclusion on the agendas of such designated professional groups of accountants or advisory groups, and take such other steps as it deems appropriate to increase the effectiveness of the standard setting process.

(2) BOARD RESPONSES—The Board shall respond in a timely fashion to requests from designated professional groups of accountants and advisory groups referred to in paragraph (1) for any changes in standards over which the Board has authority.

(d) EVALUATION OF STANDARD SETTING PROCESS- The Board shall include in the annual report required by section 101(h) the results of its standard setting responsibilities during the period to which the report relates, including a discussion of the work of the Board with any designated professional groups of accountants and advisory groups described in paragraphs (3)(A) and (4) of subsection (a), and its pending issues agenda for future standard setting projects.

[¶ 64,061]   SEC. 104. [15 USC 7214] INSPECTIONS OF REGISTERED PUBLIC ACCOUNTING FIRMS.

(a) IN GENERAL

(1) INSPECTIONS GENERALLY—The Board shall conduct a continuing program of inspections to assess the degree of compliance of each registered public accounting firm and associated persons of that firm with this Act, the rules of the Board, the rules of the Commission, or professional standards, in connection with its performance of audits, issuance of audit reports, and related matters involving issuers.

(2) INSPECTIONS OF AUDIT REPORTS FOR BROKERS AND DEALERS—(A) The Board may, by rule, conduct and require a program of inspection in accordance with paragraph (1), on a basis to be determined by the Board, of registered public accounting firms that provide one or more audit reports for a broker or dealer. The Board, in establishing such a program, may allow for differentiation among classes of brokers and dealers, as appropriate.

(B) If the Board determines to establish a program of inspection pursuant to subparagraph (A), the Board shall consider in establishing any inspection schedules whether differing schedules would be appropriate with respect to registered public accounting firms that issue audit reports only for one or more brokers or dealers that do not receive, handle, or hold customer securities or cash or are not a member of the Securities Investor Protection Corporation.

(C) Any rules of the Board pursuant to this paragraph shall be subject to prior approval by the Commission pursuant to section 107(b) before the rules become effective, including an opportunity for public notice and comment.

(D) Notwithstanding anything to the contrary in section 102 of this Act, a public accounting firm shall not be required to register with the Board if the public accounting firm is exempt from the inspection program which may be established by the Board under subparagraph (A).

(b) INSPECTION FREQUENCY

(1) IN GENERAL—Subject to paragraph (2), inspections required by this section shall be conducted—

(A) annually with respect to each registered public accounting firm that regularly provides audit reports for more than 100 issuers; and

(B) not less frequently than once every 3 years with respect to each registered public accounting firm that regularly provides audit reports for 100 or fewer issuers.

(2) ADJUSTMENTS TO SCHEDULES—The Board may, by rule, adjust the inspection schedules set under paragraph (1) if the Board finds that different inspection schedules are consistent with the purposes of this Act, the public interest, and the protection of investors. The Board may conduct special inspections at the request of the Commission or upon its own motion.

(c) PROCEDURES—The Board shall, in each inspection under this section, and in accordance with its rules for such inspections—

(1) identify any act or practice or omission to act by the registered public accounting firm, or by any associated person thereof, revealed by such inspection that may be in violation of this Act, the rules of the Board, the rules of the Commission, the firm's own quality control policies, or professional standards;

(2) report any such act, practice, or omission, if appropriate, to the Commission and each appropriate State regulatory authority; and

(3) begin a formal investigation or take disciplinary action, if appropriate, with respect to any such violation, in accordance with this Act and the rules of the Board.

(d) CONDUCT OF INSPECTIONS—In conducting an inspection of a registered public accounting firm under this section, the Board shall—

(1) inspect and review selected audit and review engagements of the firm (which may include audit engagements that are the subject of ongoing litigation or other controversy between the firm and 1 or more third parties), performed at various offices and by various associated persons of the firm, as selected by the Board;

(2) evaluate the sufficiency of the quality control system of the firm, and the manner of the documentation and communication of that system by the firm; and

(3) perform such other testing of the audit, supervisory, and quality control procedures of the firm as are necessary or appropriate in light of the purpose of the inspection and the responsibilities of the Board.

(e) RECORD RETENTION—The rules of the Board may require the retention by registered public accounting firms for inspection purposes of records whose retention is not otherwise required by section 103 or the rules issued thereunder.

(f) PROCEDURES FOR REVIEW—The rules of the Board shall provide a procedure for the review of and response to a draft inspection report by the registered public accounting firm under inspection. The Board shall take such action with respect to such response as it considers appropriate (including revising the draft report or continuing or supplementing its inspection activities before issuing a final report), but the text of any such response, appropriately redacted to protect information reasonably identified by the accounting firm as confidential, shall be attached to and made part of the inspection report.

(g) REPORT—A written report of the findings of the Board for each inspection under this section, subject to subsection (h), shall be—

(1) transmitted, in appropriate detail, to the Commission and each appropriate State regulatory authority, accompanied by any letter or comments by the Board or the inspector, and any letter of response from the registered public accounting firm; and

(2) made available in appropriate detail to the public (subject to section 105(b)(5)(A), and to the protection of such confidential and proprietary information as the Board may determine to be appropriate, or as may be required by law), except that no portions of the inspection report that deal with criticisms of or potential defects in the quality control systems of the firm under inspection shall be made public if those criticisms or defects are addressed by the firm, to the satisfaction of the Board, not later than 12 months after the date of the inspection report.

(h) INTERIM COMMISSION REVIEW

(1) REVIEWABLE MATTERS—A registered public accounting firm may seek review by the Commission, pursuant to such rules as the Commission shall promulgate, if the firm—

(A) has provided the Board with a response, pursuant to rules issued by the Board under subsection (f), to the substance of particular items in a draft inspection report, and disagrees with the assessments contained in any final report prepared by the Board following such response; or

(B) disagrees with the determination of the Board that criticisms or defects identified in an inspection report have not been addressed to the satisfaction of the Board within 12 months of the date of the inspection report, for purposes of subsection (g)(2).

(2) TREATMENT OF REVIEW—Any decision of the Commission with respect to a review under paragraph (1) shall not be reviewable under section 25 of the Securities Exchange Act of 1934 (15 U.S.C. 78y), or deemed to be 'final agency action' for purposes of section 704 of title 5, United States Code.

(3) TIMING—Review under paragraph (1) may be sought during the 30-day period following the date of the event giving rise to the review under subparagraph (A) or (B) of paragraph (1).

[¶ 64,071]   SEC. 105. [15 USC 7215] INVESTIGATIONS AND DISCIPLINARY PROCEEDINGS.

(a) IN GENERAL—The Board shall establish, by rule, subject to the requirements of this section, fair procedures for the investigation and disciplining of registered public accounting firms and associated persons of such firms.

(b) INVESTIGATIONS

(1) AUTHORITY—In accordance with the rules of the Board, the Board may conduct an investigation of any act or practice, or omission to act, by a registered public accounting firm, any associated person of such firm, or both, that may violate any provision of this Act, the rules of the Board, the provisions of the securities laws relating to the preparation and issuance of audit reports and the obligations and liabilities of accountants with respect thereto, including the rules of the Commission issued under this Act, or professional standards, regardless of how the act, practice, or omission is brought to the attention of the Board.

(2) TESTIMONY AND DOCUMENT PRODUCTION- In addition to such other actions as the Board determines to be necessary or appropriate, the rules of the Board may—

(A) require the testimony of the firm or of any person associated with a registered public accounting firm, with respect to any matter that the Board considers relevant or material to an investigation;

(B) require the production of audit work papers and any other document or information in the possession of a registered public accounting firm or any associated person thereof, wherever domiciled, that the Board considers relevant or material to the investigation, and may inspect the books and records of such firm or associated person to verify the accuracy of any documents or information supplied;

(C) request the testimony of, and production of any document in the possession of, any other person, including any client of a registered public accounting firm that the Board considers relevant or material to an investigation under this section, with appropriate notice, subject to the needs of the investigation, as permitted under the rules of the Board; and

(D) provide for procedures to seek issuance by the Commission, in a manner established by the Commission, of a subpoena to require the testimony of, and production of any document in the possession of, any person, including any client of a registered public accounting firm, that the Board considers relevant or material to an investigation under this section.

(3) NONCOOPERATION WITH INVESTIGATIONS

(A) IN GENERAL—If a registered public accounting firm or any associated person thereof refuses to testify, produce documents, or otherwise cooperate with the Board in connection with an investigation under this section, the Board may—

(i) suspend or bar such person from being associated with a registered public accounting firm, or require the registered public accounting firm to end such association;

(ii) suspend or revoke the registration of the public accounting firm; and

(iii) invoke such other lesser sanctions as the Board considers appropriate, and as specified by rule of the Board.

(B) PROCEDURE—Any action taken by the Board under this paragraph shall be subject to the terms of section 107(c).

(4) COORDINATION AND REFERRAL OF INVESTIGATIONS

(A) COORDINATION—The Board shall notify the Commission of any pending Board investigation involving a potential violation of the securities laws, and thereafter coordinate its work with the work of the Commission's Division of Enforcement, as necessary to protect an ongoing Commission investigation.

(B) REFERRAL—The Board may refer an investigation under this section—

(i) to the Commission;

(ii) to a self-regulatory organization, in the case of an investigation that concerns an audit report for a broker or dealer that is under the jurisdiction of such self-regulatory organization;

(iii) to any other Federal functional regulator (as defined in section 509 of the Gramm-Leach-Bliley Act (15 U.S.C. 6809)), in the case of an investigation that concerns an audit report for an institution that is subject to the jurisdiction of such regulator; and

(iv) at the direction of the Commission, to—

(I) the Attorney General of the United States;

(II) the attorney general of 1 or more States; and

(III) the appropriate State regulatory authority.

(5) USE OF DOCUMENTS

(A) CONFIDENTIALITY—Except as provided in subparagraphs (B) and (C), all documents and information prepared or received by or specifically for the Board, and deliberations of the Board and its employees and agents, in connection with an inspection under section 104 or with an investigation under this section, shall be confidential and privileged as an evidentiary matter (and shall not be subject to civil discovery or other legal process) in any proceeding in any Federal or State court or administrative agency, and shall be exempt from disclosure, in the hands of an agency or establishment of the Federal Government, under the Freedom of Information Act (5

U.S.C. 552a), or otherwise, unless and until presented in connection with a public proceeding or released in accordance with subsection (c).

(B) AVAILABILITY TO GOVERNMENT AGENCIES- Without the loss of its status as confidential and privileged in the hands of the Board, all information referred to in subparagraph (A) may—

(i) be made available to the Commission; and

(ii) in the discretion of the Board, when determined by the Board to be necessary to accomplish the purposes of this Act or to protect investors, be made available to—

(I) the Attorney General of the United States;

(II) the appropriate Federal functional regulator (as defined in section 509 of the Gramm-Leach Bliley Act (15 U.S.C. 6809)), other than the Commission, and the Director of the Federal Housing Finance Agency, with respect to an audit report for an institution subject to the jurisdiction of such regulator;

(III) State attorneys general in connection with any criminal investigation;

(IV) any appropriate State regulatory authority; and

(V) a self-regulatory organization, with respect to an audit report for a broker or dealer that is under the jurisdiction of such self-regulatory organization,

each of which shall maintain such information as confidential and privileged.

(C) AVAILABILITY TO FOREIGN OVERSIGHT AUTHORITIES—Without the loss of its status as confidential and privileged in the hands of the Board, all information referred to in subparagraph (A) that relates to a public accounting firm that a foreign government has empowered a foreign auditor oversight authority to inspect or otherwise enforce laws with respect to, may, at the discretion of the Board, be made available to the foreign auditor oversight authority, if—

(i) the Board finds that it is necessary to accomplish the purposes of this Act or to protect investors;

(ii) the foreign auditor oversight authority provides —

(I) such assurances of confidentiality as the Board may request;

(II) a description of the applicable information systems and controls of the foreign auditor oversight authority; and

(III) a description of the laws and regulations of the foreign government of the foreign auditor oversight authority that are relevant to information access; and

(iii) the Board determines that it is appropriate to share such information.

(6) IMMUNITY—Any employee of the Board engaged in carrying out an investigation under this Act shall be immune from any civil liability arising out of such investigation in the same manner and to the same extent as an employee of the Federal Government in similar circumstances.

(c) DISCIPLINARY PROCEDURES

(1) NOTIFICATION; RECORDKEEPING—The rules of the Board shall provide that in any proceeding by the Board to determine whether a registered public accounting firm, or an associated person thereof, should be disciplined, the Board shall—

(A) bring specific charges with respect to the firm or associated person;

(B) notify such firm or associated person of, and provide to the firm or associated person an opportunity to defend against, such charges; and

(C) keep a record of the proceedings.

(2) PUBLIC HEARINGS—Hearings under this section shall not be public, unless otherwise ordered by the Board for good cause shown, with the consent of the parties to such hearing.

(3) SUPPORTING STATEMENT—A determination by the Board to impose a sanction under this subsection shall be supported by a statement setting forth—

(A) each act or practice in which the registered public accounting firm, or associated person, has engaged (or omitted to engage), or that forms a basis for all or a part of such sanction;

(B) the specific provision of this Act, the securities laws, the rules of the Board, or professional standards which the Board determines has been violated; and

(C) the sanction imposed, including a justification for that sanction.

(4) SANCTIONS—If the Board finds, based on all of the facts and circumstances, that a registered public accounting firm or associated person thereof has engaged in any act or practice, or omitted to act, in violation of this Act, the rules of the Board, the provisions of the securities laws relating to the preparation and issuance of audit reports and the obligations and liabilities of accountants with respect thereto, including the rules of the Commission issued under this Act, or professional standards, the Board may impose such disciplinary or remedial sanctions as it determines appropriate, subject to applicable limitations under paragraph (5), including—

(A) temporary suspension or permanent revocation of registration under this title;

(B) temporary or permanent suspension or bar of a person from further association with any registered public accounting firm;

(C) temporary or permanent limitation on the activities, functions, or operations of such firm or person (other than in connection with required additional professional education or training);

(D) a civil money penalty for each such violation, in an amount equal to—

(i) not more than $100,000 for a natural person or $2,000,000 for any other person; and

(ii) in any case to which paragraph (5) applies, not more than $750,000 for a natural person or $15,000,000 for any other person;

(E) censure;

(F) required additional professional education or training; or

(G) any other appropriate sanction provided for in the rules of the Board.

(5) INTENTIONAL OR OTHER KNOWING CONDUCT- The sanctions and penalties described in subparagraphs (A) through (C) and (D) (ii) of paragraph (4) shall only apply to—

(A) intentional or knowing conduct, including reckless conduct, that results in violation of the applicable statutory, regulatory, or professional standard; or

(6) FAILURE TO SUPERVISE

(A) IN GENERAL—The Board may impose sanctions under this section on a registered accounting firm or upon any person who is, or at the time of the alleged failure reasonably to supervise was, a supervisory person of such firm, if the Board finds that—

(i) the firm has failed reasonably to supervise an associated person, either as required by the rules of the Board relating to auditing or quality control standards, or otherwise, with a view to preventing violations of this Act, the rules of the Board, the provisions of the securities laws relating to the preparation and issuance of audit reports and the obligations and liabilities of accountants with respect thereto, including the rules of the Commission under this Act, or professional standards; and

(ii) such associated person commits a violation of this Act, or any of such rules, laws, or standards.

(B) RULE OF CONSTRUCTION—No current or former supervisory person of a registered public accounting firm shall be deemed to have failed reasonably to supervise any associated person for purposes of subparagraph (A), if—

(i) there have been established in and for that firm procedures, and a system for applying such procedures, that comply with applicable rules of the Board and that would reasonably be expected to prevent and detect any such violation by such associated person; and

(ii) such person has reasonably discharged the duties and obligations incumbent upon that person by reason of such procedures and system, and had no reasonable cause to believe that such procedures and system were not being complied with.

(7) EFFECT OF SUSPENSION

(A) ASSOCIATION WITH A PUBLIC ACCOUNTING FIRM —It shall be unlawful for any person that is suspended or barred from being associated with a registered public accounting firm under this subsection willfully to become or remain associated with any registered public accounting firm, or for any registered public accounting firm that knew, or, in the exercise of reasonable care should have known, of the suspension or bar, to permit such an association, without the consent of the Board or the Commission.

(B) ASSOCIATION WITH AN ISSUER, BROKER, OR DEALER — It shall be unlawful for any person that is suspended or barred from being associated with a registered public accounting firm under this subsection willfully to become or remain associated with any issuer, broker, or dealer in an accountancy or a financial management capacity, and for any issuer, broker, or dealer that knew, or in the exercise of reasonable care should have known, of such suspension or bar, to permit such an association, without the consent of the Board or the Commission.

(d) REPORTING OF SANCTIONS

(1) RECIPIENTS—If the Board imposes a disciplinary sanction, in accordance with this section, the Board shall report the sanction to—

(A) the Commission;

(B) any appropriate State regulator authority or any foreign accountancy licensing board with which such firm or person is licensed or certified; and

(C) the public (once any stay on the imposition of such sanction has been lifted).

(2) CONTENTS—The information reported under paragraph (1) shall include—

(A) the name of the sanctioned person;

(B) a description of the sanction and the basis for its imposition; and

(C) such other information as the Board deems appropriate.

(e) STAY OF SANCTIONS

(1) IN GENERAL—Application to the Commission for review, or the institution by the Commission of review, of any disciplinary action of the Board shall operate as a stay of any such disciplinary action, unless and until the Commission orders (summarily or after notice and opportunity for hearing on the question of a stay, which hearing may consist solely of the submission of affidavits or presentation of oral arguments) that no such stay shall continue to operate.

(2) EXPEDITED PROCEDURES—The Commission shall establish for appropriate cases an expedited procedure for consideration and determination of the question of the duration of a stay pending review of any disciplinary action of the Board under this subsection.

[¶ 64,081]   SEC. 106. [15 USC 7216] FOREIGN PUBLIC ACCOUNTING FIRMS.

(a) APPLICABILITY TO CERTAIN FOREIGN FIRMS

(1) IN GENERAL—Any foreign public accounting firm that prepares or furnishes an audit report with respect to any issuer, broker, or dealer, shall be subject to this Act and the rules of the Board and the Commission issued under this Act, in the same manner and to the same extent as a public accounting firm that is organized and operates under the laws of the United States or any State, except that registration pursuant to section 102 shall not by itself provide a basis for subjecting such a foreign public accounting firm to the jurisdiction of the Federal or State courts, other than with respect to controversies between such firms and the Board.

(2) BOARD AUTHORITY—The Board may, by rule, determine that a foreign public accounting firm (or a class of such firms) that does not issue audit reports nonetheless plays such a substantial role in the preparation and furnishing of such reports for particular issuers, brokers, or dealers, that it is necessary or appropriate, in light of the purposes of this Act and in the public interest or for the protection of investors, that such firm (or class of firms) should be treated as a public accounting firm (or firms) for purposes of registration under, and oversight by the Board in accordance with, this title.

(b) PRODUCTION OF DOCUMENTS.—

(1) PRODUCTION BY FOREIGN FIRMS—If a foreign public accounting firm performs material services upon which a registered public accounting firm relies in the conduct of an audit or interim review, issues an audit report, performs audit work, or conducts interim reviews, the foreign public accounting firm shall—

(A) produce the audit work papers of the foreign public accounting firm and all other documents of the firm related to any such audit work or interim review to the Commission or the Board, upon request of the Commission or the Board; and

(B) be subject to the jurisdiction of the courts of the United States for purposes of enforcement of any request for such documents.

(2) OTHER PRODUCTION—Any registered public accounting firm that relies, in whole or in part, on the work of a foreign public accounting firm in issuing an audit report, performing audit work, or conducting an interim review, shall—

(A) produce the audit work papers of the foreign public accounting firm and all other documents related to any such work in response to a request for production by the Commission or the Board; and

(B) secure the agreement of any foreign public accounting firm to such production, as a condition of the reliance by the registered public accounting firm on the work of that foreign public accounting firm.

(c) EXEMPTION AUTHORITY—The Commission, and the Board, subject to the approval of the Commission, may, by rule, regulation, or order, and as the Commission (or Board) determines necessary or appropriate in the public interest or for the protection of investors, either unconditionally or upon specified terms and conditions exempt any foreign public accounting firm, or any class of such firms, from any provision of this Act or the rules of the Board or the Commission issued under this Act.

(d) SERVICE OF REQUESTS OR PROCESS—

(1) IN GENERAL—Any foreign public accounting firm that performs work for a domestic registered public accounting firm shall furnish to the domestic registered public accounting firm a written irrevocable consent and power of attorney that designates the domestic registered public accounting firm as an agent upon whom may be served any request by the Commission or the Board under this section or upon whom may be served any process, pleadings, or other papers in any action brought to enforce this section.

(2) SPECIFIC AUDIT WORK—Any foreign public accounting firm that performs material services upon which a registered public accounting firm relies in the conduct of an audit or interim review, issues an audit report, performs audit work, or, performs interim reviews, shall designate to the Commission or the Board an agent in the United States upon whom may be served any request by the Commission or the Board under this section or upon whom may be served any process, pleading, or other papers in any action brought to enforce this section.

(e) SANCTIONS—A willful refusal to comply, in whole in or in part, with any request by the Commission or the Board under this section, shall be deemed a violation of this Act.

(f) OTHER MEANS OF SATISFYING PRODUCTION OBLIGATIONS—Notwithstanding any other provisions of this section, the staff of the Commission or the Board may allow a foreign public accounting firm that is subject to this section to meet production obligations under this section through alternate means, such as through foreign counterparts of the Commission or the Board.

(g) DEFINITION—In this section, the term 'foreign public accounting firm' means a public accounting firm that is organized and operates under the laws of a foreign government or political subdivision thereof.

[¶ 64,091]   SEC. 107. [15 USC 7217] COMMISSION OVERSIGHT OF THE BOARD.

(a) GENERAL OVERSIGHT RESPONSIBILITY- The Commission shall have oversight and enforcement authority over the Board, as provided in this Act. The provisions of section 17(a)(1) of the Securities Exchange Act of 1934 (15 U.S.C. 78q(a)(1)), and of section 17(b)(1) of the Securities Exchange Act of 1934 (15 U.S.C. 78q(b)(1)) shall apply to the Board as fully as if the Board were a 'registered securities association' for purposes of those sections 17(a)(1) and 17(b)(1).

(b) RULES OF THE BOARD

(1) DEFINITION—In this section, the term 'proposed rule' means any proposed rule of the Board, and any modification of any such rule.

(2) PRIOR APPROVAL REQUIRED—No rule of the Board shall become effective without prior approval of the Commission in accordance with this section, other than as provided in section 103(a)(3)(B) with respect to initial or transitional standards.

(3) APPROVAL CRITERIA—The Commission shall approve a proposed rule, if it finds that the rule is consistent with the requirements of this Act and the securities laws, or is necessary or appropriate in the public interest or for the protection of investors.

(4) PROPOSED RULE PROCEDURES—The provisions of paragraphs (1) through (3) of section 19(b) of the Securities Exchange Act of 1934 (15 U.S.C. 78s(b)) shall govern the proposed rules of the Board, as fully as if the Board were a 'registered securities association' for purposes of that section 19(b), except that, for purposes of this paragraph—

(A) the phrase 'consistent with the requirements of this title and the rules and regulations thereunder applicable to such organization' in section 19(b)(2) of that Act shall be deemed to read 'consistent with the requirements of title I of the Sarbanes-Oxley Act of 2002, and the rules and regulations issued thereunder applicable to such organization, or as necessary or appropriate in the public interest or for the protection of investors'; and

(B) the phrase 'otherwise in furtherance of the purposes of this title' in section 19(b)(3)(C) of that Act shall be deemed to read 'otherwise in furtherance of the purposes of title I of the Sarbanes-Oxley Act of 2002'.

(5) COMMISSION AUTHORITY TO AMEND RULES OF THE BOARD—The provisions of section 19(c) of the Securities Exchange Act of 1934 (15 U.S.C. 78s(c)) shall govern the abrogation, deletion, or addition to portions of the rules of the Board by the Commission as fully as if the Board were a 'registered securities association' for purposes of that section 19(c), except that the phrase 'to conform its rules to the requirements of this title and the rules and regulations thereunder applicable to such organization, or otherwise in furtherance of the purposes of this title' in section 19(c) of that Act shall, for purposes of this paragraph, be deemed to read 'to assure the fair administration of the Public Company Accounting Oversight Board, conform the rules promulgated by that Board to the requirements of title I of the Sarbanes-Oxley Act of 2002, or otherwise further the purposes of that Act, the securities laws, and the rules and regulations thereunder applicable to that Board'.

(c) COMMISSION REVIEW OF DISCIPLINARY ACTION TAKEN BY THE BOARD

(1) NOTICE OF SANCTION—The Board shall promptly file notice with the Commission of any final sanction on any registered public accounting firm or on any associated person thereof, in such form and containing such information as the Commission, by rule, may prescribe.

(2) REVIEW OF SANCTIONS—The provisions of sections 19(d)(2) and 19(e)(1) of the Securities Exchange Act of 1934 (15 U.S.C. 78s (d)(2) and (e)(1)) shall govern the review by the Commission of final disciplinary sanctions imposed by the Board (including sanctions imposed under section 105(b)(3) of this Act for noncooperation in an investigation of the Board), as fully as if the Board were a self-regulatory organization and the Commission were the appropriate regulatory agency for such organization for purposes of those sections 19(d)(2) and 19(e)(1), except that, for purposes of this paragraph—

(A) section 105(e) of this Act (rather than that section 19(d)(2)) shall govern the extent to which application for, or institution by the Commission on its own motion of, review of any disciplinary action of the Board operates as a stay of such action;

(B) references in that section 19(e)(1) to 'members' of such an organization shall be deemed to be references to registered public accounting firms;

(C) the phrase 'consistent with the purposes of this title' in that section 19(e)(1) shall be deemed to read 'consistent with the purposes of this title and title I of the Sarbanes-Oxley Act of 2002';

(D) references to rules of the Municipal Securities Rulemaking Board in that section 19(e)(1) shall not apply; and (E) the reference to section 19(e)(2) of the Securities Exchange Act of 1934 shall refer instead to section 107(c)(3) of this Act.

(3) COMMISSION MODIFICATION AUTHORITY- The Commission may enhance, modify, cancel, reduce, or require the remission of a sanction imposed by the Board upon a registered public accounting firm or associated person thereof, if the Commission, having due regard for the public interest and the protection of investors, finds, after a proceeding in accordance with this subsection, that the sanction—

(A) is not necessary or appropriate in furtherance of this Act or the securities laws; or

(B) is excessive, oppressive, inadequate, or otherwise not appropriate to the finding or the basis on which the sanction was imposed.

(d) CENSURE OF THE BOARD; OTHER SANCTIONS

(1) RESCISSION OF BOARD AUTHORITY—The Commission, by rule, consistent with the public interest, the protection of investors, and the other purposes of this Act and the securities

laws, may relieve the Board of any responsibility to enforce compliance with any provision of this Act, the securities laws, the rules of the Board, or professional standards.

(2) CENSURE OF THE BOARD; LIMITATIONS- The Commission may, by order, as it determines necessary or appropriate in the public interest, for the protection of investors, or otherwise in furtherance of the purposes of this Act or the securities laws, censure or impose limitations upon the activities, functions, and operations of the Board, if the Commission finds, on the record, after notice and opportunity for a hearing, that the Board—

(A) has violated or is unable to comply with any provision of this Act, the rules of the Board, or the securities laws; or

(B) without reasonable justification or excuse, has failed to enforce compliance with any such provision or rule, or any professional standard by a registered public accounting firm or an associated person thereof.

(3) CENSURE OF BOARD MEMBERS; REMOVAL FROM OFFICE—The Commission may, as necessary or appropriate in the public interest, for the protection of investors, or otherwise in furtherance of the purposes of this Act or the securities laws, remove from office or censure any person who is, or at the time of the alleged misconduct was, a member of the Board, if the Commission finds, on the record, after notice and opportunity for a hearing, that such member—

(A) has willfully violated any provision of this Act, the rules of the Board, or the securities laws;

(B) has willfully abused the authority of that member; or

(C) without reasonable justification or excuse, has failed to enforce compliance with any such provision or rule, or any professional standard by any registered public accounting firm or any associated person thereof.

[¶ 64,101] SEC. 108. [15 USC 7218] [15 USC 77s] [15 USC 7219] ACCOUNTING STANDARDS.

(a) AMENDMENT TO SECURITIES ACT OF 1933- Section 19 of the Securities Act of 1933 (15 U.S.C. 77s) is amended—

(1) by redesignating subsections (b) and (c) as subsections (c) and (d), respectively; and

(2) by inserting after subsection (a) the following:

'(b) RECOGNITION OF ACCOUNTING STANDARDS

'(1) IN GENERAL—In carrying out its authority under subsection (a) and under section 13(b) of the Securities Exchange Act of 1934, the Commission may recognize, as 'generally accepted' for purposes of the securities laws, any accounting principles established by a standard setting body—

'(A) that—

'(i) is organized as a private entity;

'(ii) has, for administrative and operational purposes, a board of trustees (or equivalent body) serving in the public interest, the majority of whom are not, concurrent with their service on such board, and have not been during the 2-year period preceding such service, associated persons of any registered public accounting firm;

'(iii) is funded as provided in section 109 of the Sarbanes-Oxley Act of 2002;

'(iv) has adopted procedures to ensure prompt consideration, by majority vote of its members, of changes to accounting principles necessary to reflect emerging accounting issues and changing business practices; and

'(v) considers, in adopting accounting principles, the need to keep standards current in order to reflect changes in the business environment, the extent to which international convergence on high quality accounting standards is necessary or appropriate in the public interest and for the protection of investors; and

'(B) that the Commission determines has the capacity to assist the Commission in fulfilling the requirements of subsection (a) and section 13(b) of the Securities Exchange Act of 1934, because, at a minimum, the standard setting body is capable of improving the accuracy and effectiveness of financial reporting and the protection of investors under the securities laws.

'(2) ANNUAL REPORT—A standard setting body described in paragraph (1) shall submit an annual report to the Commission and the public, containing audited financial statements of that standard setting body.'.

(b) COMMISSION AUTHORITY—The Commission shall promulgate such rules and regulations to carry out section 19(b) of the Securities Act of 1933, as added by this section, as it deems necessary or appropriate in the public interest or for the protection of investors.

(c) NO EFFECT ON COMMISSION POWERS—Nothing in this Act, including this section and the amendment made by this section, shall be construed to impair or limit the authority of the Commission to establish accounting principles or standards for purposes of enforcement of the securities laws.

(d) STUDY AND REPORT ON ADOPTING PRINCIPLES-BASED ACCOUNTING

(1) STUDY

(A) IN GENERAL—The Commission shall conduct a study on the adoption by the United States financial reporting system of a principles-based accounting system.

(B) STUDY TOPICS—The study required by subparagraph (A) shall include an examination of—

(i) the extent to which principles-based accounting and financial reporting exists in the United States;

(ii) the length of time required for change from a rules-based to a principles-based financial reporting system;

(iii) the feasibility of and proposed methods by which a principles-based system may be implemented; and

(iv) a thorough economic analysis of the implementation of a principles-based system.

(2) REPORT—Not later than 1 year after the date of enactment of this Act, the Commission shall submit a report on the results of the study required by paragraph (1) to the Committee on Banking, Housing, and Urban Affairs of the Senate and the Committee on Financial Services of the House of Representatives.

[¶ 64,111]   SEC. 109. [15 USC 78m] [15 USC 7231] FUNDING.

(a) IN GENERAL—The Board, and the standard setting body designated pursuant to section 19(b) of the Securities Act of 1933, as amended by section 108, shall be funded as provided in this section.

(b) ANNUAL BUDGETS—The Board and the standard setting body referred to in subsection (a) shall each establish a budget for each fiscal year, which shall be reviewed and approved according to their respective internal procedures not less than 1 month prior to the commencement of the fiscal year to which the budget pertains (or at the beginning of the Board's first fiscal year, which may be a short fiscal year). The budget of the Board shall be subject to approval by the Commission. The budget for the first fiscal year of the Board shall be prepared and approved promptly following the appointment of the initial five Board members, to permit action by the Board of the organizational tasks contemplated by section 101(d).

(c) SOURCES AND USES OF FUNDS

(1) RECOVERABLE BUDGET EXPENSES—The budget of the Board (reduced by any registration or annual fees received under section 102(e) for the year preceding the year for which the budget is being computed), and all of the budget of the standard setting body referred to in subsection (a), for each fiscal year of each of those 2 entities, shall be payable from annual accounting support fees, in accordance with subsections (d) and (e). Accounting support fees and other receipts of the Board and of such standard-setting body shall not be considered public monies of the United States.

(2) FUNDS GENERATED FROM THE COLLECTION OF MONETARY PENALTIES— Subject to the availability in advance in an appropriations Act, and notwithstanding subsection (j), all funds collected by the Board as a result of the assessment of monetary penalties shall be used to fund a merit scholarship program for undergraduate and graduate students enrolled in accredited accounting degree programs, which program is to be administered by the Board or by an entity or agent identified by the Board.

(d) ANNUAL ACCOUNTING SUPPORT FEE FOR THE BOARD

(1) ESTABLISHMENT OF FEE—The Board shall establish, with the approval of the Commission, a reasonable annual accounting support fee (or a formula for the computation thereof), as may be necessary or appropriate to establish and maintain the Board. Such fee may also cover costs incurred in the Board's first fiscal year (which may be a short fiscal year), or may be levied separately with respect to such short fiscal year.

(2) ASSESSMENTS—The rules of the Board under paragraph (1) shall provide for the equitable allocation, assessment, and collection by the Board (or an agent appointed by the Board) of the fee established under paragraph (1), among issuers, in accordance with subsection (g), and among brokers and dealers, in accordance with subsection (h), and allowing for differentiation among classes of issuers, brokers and dealers, as appropriate.

(3) BROKERS AND DEALERS—The Board shall begin the allocation, assessment, and collection of fees under paragraph (2) with respect to brokers and dealers with the payment of support fees to fund the first full fiscal year beginning after the date of enactment of the Investor Protection and Securities Reform Act of 2010.

(e) ANNUAL ACCOUNTING SUPPORT FEE FOR STANDARD SETTING BODY—The annual accounting support fee for the standard setting body referred to in subsection (a)—

(1) shall be allocated in accordance with subsection (g), and assessed and collected against each issuer, on behalf of the standard setting body, by 1 or more appropriate designated collection agents, as may be necessary or appropriate to pay for the budget and provide for the expenses of that standard setting body, and to provide for an independent, stable source of funding for such body, subject to review by the Commission; and

(2) may differentiate among different classes of issuers.

(f) LIMITATION ON FEE—The amount of fees collected under this section for a fiscal year on behalf of the Board or the standards setting body, as the case may be, shall not exceed the recoverable budget expenses of the Board or body, respectively (which may include operating, capital, and accrued items), referred to in subsection (c)(1).

(g) ALLOCATION OF ACCOUNTING SUPPORT FEES AMONG ISSUERS–Any amount due from issuers (or a particular class of issuers) under this section to fund the budget of the Board or the standard setting body referred to in subsection (a) shall be allocated among and payable by each issuer (or each issuer in a particular class, as applicable) in an amount equal to the total of such amount, multiplied by a fraction—

(1) the numerator of which is the average monthly equity market capitalization of the issuer for the 12-month period immediately preceding the beginning of the fiscal year to which such budget relates; and

(2) the denominator of which is the average monthly equity market capitalization of all such issuers for such 12-month period.

(h) ALLOCATION OF ACCOUNTING SUPPORT FEES AMONG BROKERS AND DEALERS—

(1) OBLIGATION TO PAY—Each broker or dealer shall pay to the Board the annual accounting support fee allocated to such broker or dealer under this section.

(2) ALLOCATION—Any amount due from a broker or dealer (or from a particular class of brokers and dealers) under this section shall be allocated among brokers and dealers and payable by the broker or dealer (or the brokers and dealers in the particular class, as applicable).

(3) PROPORTIONALITY—The amount due from a broker or dealer shall be in proportion to the net capital of the broker or dealer (before or after any adjustments), compared to the total net capital of all brokers and dealers (before or after any adjustments), in accordance with rules issued by the Board.

(i) CONFORMING AMENDMENTS—Section 13(b)(2) of the Securities Exchange Act of 1934 (15 U.S.C. 78m(b)(2)) is amended—

(1) in subparagraph (A), by striking 'and' at the end; and

(2) in subparagraph (B), by striking the period at the end and inserting the following: '; and '(C) notwithstanding any other provision of law, pay the allocable share of such issuer of a reasonable annual accounting support fee or fees, determined in accordance with section 109 of the Sarbanes-Oxley Act of 2002.'.

(j) RULE OF CONSTRUCTION—Nothing in this section shall be construed to render either the Board, the standard setting body referred to in subsection (a), or both, subject to procedures in Congress to authorize or appropriate public funds, or to prevent such organization from utilizing additional sources of revenue for its activities, such as earnings from publication sales, provided that each additional source of revenue shall not jeopardize, in the judgment of the Commission, the actual and perceived independence of such organization.

(k) START-UP EXPENSES OF THE BOARD—From the unexpended balances of the appropriations to the Commission for fiscal year 2003, the Secretary of the Treasury is authorized to advance to the Board not to exceed the amount necessary to cover the expenses of the Board during its first fiscal year (which may be a short fiscal year).

[¶ 64,113]   **SEC. 110. DEFINITIONS.**

For the purposes of this title, the following definitions shall apply:

(1) AUDIT—The term 'audit' means an examination of the financial statements, reports, documents, procedures, controls, or notices of any issuer, broker, or dealer by an independent public accounting firm in accordance with the rules of the Board or the Commission, for the purpose of expressing an opinion on the financial statements or providing an audit report.

(2) AUDIT REPORT—The term 'audit report' means a document, report, notice, or other record—

(A) prepared following an audit performed for purposes of compliance by an issuer, broker, or dealer with the requirements of the securities laws; and

(B) in which a public accounting firm either—

(i) sets forth the opinion of that firm regarding a financial statement, report, notice, or other document, procedures, or controls; or

(ii) asserts that no such opinion can be expressed.

(3) BROKER—The term 'broker' means a broker (as such term is defined in section 3(a)(4) of the Securities Exchange Act of 1934 (15 U.S.C. 78c(a)(4))) that is required to file a balance sheet, income statement, or other financial statement under section 17(e)(1)(A) of such Act (15 U.S.C. 78q(e)(1)(A)), where such balance sheet, income statement, or financial statement is required to be certified by a registered public accounting firm.

(4) DEALER—The term 'dealer' means a dealer (as such term is defined in section 3(a)(5) of the Securities Exchange Act of 1934 (15 U.S.C. 78c(a)(5))) that is required to file a balance sheet, income statement, or other financial statement under section 17(e)(1)(A) of such Act (15 U.S.C. 78q(e)(1)(A)), where such balance sheet, income statement, or financial statement is required to be certified by a registered public accounting firm.

(5) PROFESSIONAL STANDARDS—The term 'professional standards' means—

(A) accounting principles that are—

(i) established by the standard setting body described in section 19(b) of the Securities Act of 1933, as amended by this Act, or prescribed by the Commission under section 19(a) of that Act (15 U.S.C. 17a(s)) or section 13(b) of the Securities Exchange Act of 1934 (15 U.S.C. 78a(m)); and

(ii) relevant to audit reports for particular issuers, brokers, or dealers, or dealt with in the quality control system of a particular registered public accounting firm; and

(B) auditing standards, standards for attestation engagements, quality control policies and procedures, ethical and competency standards, and independence standards (including rules implementing title II) that the Board or the Commission determines—

(i) relate to the preparation or issuance of audit reports for issuers, brokers, or dealers; and

(ii) are established or adopted by the Board under section 103(a), or are promulgated as rules of the Commission.

(6) SELF-REGULATORY ORGANIZATION—The term 'self-regulatory organization' has the same meaning as in section 3(a) of the Securities Exchange Act of 1934 (15 U.S.C. 78c(a)).

TITLE II—AUDITOR INDEPENDENCE

[¶ 64,121] SEC. 201. [15 USC 78j-1] SERVICES OUTSIDE THE SCOPE OF PRACTICE OF AUDITORS.

(a) PROHIBITED ACTIVITIES—Section 10A of the Securities Exchange Act of 1934 (15 U.S.C. 78j-1) is amended by adding at the end the following: '(g) PROHIBITED ACTIVITIES-Except as provided in subsection (h), it shall be unlawful for a registered public accounting firm (and any associated person of that firm, to the extent determined appropriate by the Commission) that performs for any issuer any audit required by this title or the rules of the Commission under this title or, beginning 180 days after the date of commencement of the operations of the Public Company Accounting Oversight Board established under section 101 of the Sarbanes-Oxley Act of 2002 (in this section referred to as the 'Board'), the rules of the Board, to provide to that issuer, contemporaneously with the audit, any non-audit service, including—

'(1) bookkeeping or other services related to the accounting records or financial statements of the audit client;

'(2) financial information systems design and implementation;

'(3) appraisal or valuation services, fairness opinions, or contribution-in-kind reports;

'(4) actuarial services;

'(5) internal audit outsourcing services;

'(6) management functions or human resources;

'(7) broker or dealer, investment adviser, or investment banking services;

'(8) legal services and expert services unrelated to the audit; and

'(9) any other service that the Board determines, by regulation, is impermissible.

'(h) PREAPPROVAL REQUIRED FOR NON-AUDIT SERVICES—A registered public accounting firm may engage in any nonaudit service, including tax services, that is not described in any of paragraphs (1) through (9) of subsection (g) for an audit client, only if the activity is approved in advance by the audit committee of the issuer, in accordance with subsection (i).'.

(b) EXEMPTION AUTHORITY—The Board may, on a case by case basis, exempt any person, issuer, public accounting firm, or transaction from the prohibition on the provision of services under section 10A(g) of the Securities Exchange Act of 1934 (as added by this section), to the extent that such exemption is necessary or appropriate in the public interest and is consistent with the protection of investors, and subject to review by the Commission in the same manner as for rules of the Board under section 107.

[¶ 64,131] SEC. 202. [15 USC 78j-1] PREAPPROVAL REQUIREMENTS.

Section 10A of the Securities Exchange Act of 1934 (15 U.S.C. 78j-1), as amended by this Act, is amended by adding at the end the following:

'(i) PREAPPROVAL REQUIREMENTS

'(1) IN GENERAL

'(A) AUDIT COMMITTEE ACTION—All auditing services (which may entail providing comfort letters in connection with securities underwritings or statutory audits required for insurance companies for purposes of State law) and non-audit services, other than as provided in subparagraph (B), provided to an issuer by the auditor of the issuer shall be preapproved by the audit committee of the issuer.

'(B) DE MINIMUS EXCEPTION—The preapproval requirement under subparagraph (A) is waived with respect to the provision of non-audit services for an issuer, if—

'(i) the aggregate amount of all such non-audit services provided to the issuer constitutes not more than 5 percent of the total amount of revenues paid by the issuer to its auditor during the fiscal year in which the nonaudit services are provided;

'(ii) such services were not recognized by the issuer at the time of the engagement to be non-audit services; and

'(iii) such services are promptly brought to the attention of the audit committee of the issuer and approved prior to the completion of the audit by the audit committee or by 1 or more members of the audit committee who are members of the board of directors to whom authority to grant such approvals has been delegated by the audit committee.

'(2) DISCLOSURE TO INVESTORS- Approval by an audit committee of an issuer under this subsection of a non-audit service to be performed by the auditor of the issuer shall be disclosed to investors in periodic reports required by section 13(a).

'(3) DELEGATION AUTHORITY—The audit committee of an issuer may delegate to 1 or more designated members of the audit committee who are independent directors of the board of directors, the authority to grant preapprovals required by this subsection. The decisions of any member to whom authority is delegated under this paragraph to preapprove an activity under this subsection shall be presented to the full audit committee at each of its scheduled meetings.

'(4) APPROVAL OF AUDIT SERVICES FOR OTHER PURPOSES —In carrying out its duties under subsection (m)(2), if the audit committee of an issuer approves an audit service within the scope of the engagement of the auditor, such audit service shall be deemed to have been preapproved for purposes of this subsection.'.

[¶ 64,141]   **SEC. 203. [15 USC 78j-1] AUDIT PARTNER ROTATION.**

Section 10A of the Securities Exchange Act of 1934 (15 U.S.C. 78j-1), as amended by this Act, is amended by adding at the end the following:

'(j) AUDIT PARTNER ROTATION—It shall be unlawful for a registered public accounting firm to provide audit services to an issuer if the lead (or coordinating) audit partner (having primary responsibility for the audit), or the audit partner responsible for reviewing the audit, has performed audit services for that issuer in each of the 5 previous fiscal years of that issuer.'.

[¶ 64,151]   **SEC. 204. [15 USC 78j-1] AUDITOR REPORTS TO AUDIT COMMITTEES.**

Section 10A of the Securities Exchange Act of 1934 (15 U.S.C. 78j-1), as amended by this Act, is amended by adding at the end the following:

'(k) REPORTS TO AUDIT COMMITTEES- Each registered public accounting firm that performs for any issuer any audit required by this title shall timely report to the audit committee of the issuer—

'(1) all critical accounting policies and practices to be used;

'(2) all alternative treatments of financial information within generally accepted accounting principles that have been discussed with management officials of the issuer, ramifications of the use of such alternative disclosures and treatments, and the treatment preferred by the registered public accounting firm; and

'(3) other material written communications between the registered public accounting firm and the management of the issuer, such as any management letter or schedule of unadjusted differences.'.

[¶ 64,161]   **SEC. 205. [15 USC 78c] [15 USC 78j-1] CONFORMING AMENDMENTS.**

(a) DEFINITIONS—Section 3(a) of the Securities Exchange Act of 1934 (15 U.S.C. 78c(a)) is amended by adding at the end the following:

'(58) AUDIT COMMITTEE—The term 'audit committee' means—

'(A) a committee (or equivalent body) established by and amongst the board of directors of an issuer for the purpose of overseeing the accounting and financial reporting processes of the issuer and audits of the financial statements of the issuer; and

'(B) if no such committee exists with respect to an issuer, the entire board of directors of the issuer.

'(59) REGISTERED PUBLIC ACCOUNTING FIRM—The term 'registered public accounting firm' has the same meaning as in section 2 of the Sarbanes-Oxley Act of 2002.'.

(b) AUDITOR REQUIREMENTS—Section 10A of the Securities Exchange Act of 1934 (15 U.S.C. 78j-1) is amended—

(1) by striking 'an independent public accountant' each place that term appears and inserting 'a registered public accounting firm';

(2) by striking 'the independent public accountant' each place that term appears and inserting 'the registered public accounting firm';

(3) in subsection (c), by striking 'No independent public accountant' and inserting 'No registered public accounting firm'; and

(4) in subsection (b)—

(A) by striking 'the accountant' each place that term appears and inserting 'the firm';

(B) by striking 'such accountant' each place that term appears and inserting 'such firm'; and

(C) in paragraph (4), by striking 'the accountant's report' and inserting 'the report of the firm'.

(c) OTHER REFERENCES—The Securities Exchange Act of 1934 (15 U.S.C. 78a et seq.) is amended—

(1) in section 12(b)(1) (15 U.S.C. 78l(b)(1)), by striking 'independent public accountants' each place that term appears and inserting 'a registered public accounting firm'; and

(2) in subsections (e) and (i) of section 17 (15 U.S.C. 78q), by striking 'an independent public accountant' each place that term appears and inserting 'a registered public accounting firm'.

(d) CONFORMING AMENDMENT—Section 10A(f) of the Securities Exchange Act of 1934 (15 U.S.C. 78k(f)) is amended—

(1) by striking 'DEFINITION' and inserting 'DEFINITIONS'; and

(2) by adding at the end the following: 'As used in this section, the term 'issuer' means an issuer (as defined in section 3), the securities of which are registered under section 12, or that is required to file reports pursuant to section 15(d), or that files or has filed a registration statement that has not yet become effective under the Securities Act of 1933 (15 U.S.C. 77a et seq.), and that it has not withdrawn.'.

[¶ 64,171] SEC. 206. [15 USC 78j-1] CONFLICTS OF INTEREST.

Section 10A of the Securities Exchange Act of 1934 (15 U.S.C. 78j-1), as amended by this Act, is amended by adding at the end the following:

'(l) CONFLICTS OF INTEREST—It shall be unlawful for a registered public accounting firm to perform for an issuer any audit service required by this title, if a chief executive officer, controller, chief financial officer, chief accounting officer, or any person serving in an equivalent position for the issuer, was employed by that registered independent public accounting firm and participated in any capacity in the audit of that issuer during the 1-year period preceding the date of the initiation of the audit.'.

[¶ 64,181] SEC. 207. [15 USC 7232] STUDY OF MANDATORY ROTATION OF REGISTERED PUBLIC ACCOUNTING FIRMS.

(a) STUDY AND REVIEW REQUIRED—The Comptroller General of the United States shall conduct a study and review of the potential effects of requiring the mandatory rotation of registered public accounting firms.

(b) REPORT REQUIRED—Not later than 1 year after the date of enactment of this Act, the Comptroller General shall submit a report to the Committee on Banking, Housing, and Urban Affairs of the Senate and the Committee on Financial Services of the House of Representatives on the results of the study and review required by this section.

(c) DEFINITION—For purposes of this section, the term 'mandatory rotation' refers to the imposition of a limit on the period of years in which a particular registered public accounting firm may be the auditor of record for a particular issuer.

[¶ 64,191] SEC. 208. [15 USC 7233] COMMISSION AUTHORITY.

(a) COMMISSION REGULATIONS—Not later than 180 days after the date of enactment of this Act, the Commission shall issue final regulations to carry out each of subsections (g) through (l) of section 10A of the Securities Exchange Act of 1934, as added by this title.

(b) AUDITOR INDEPENDENCE—It shall be unlawful for any registered public accounting firm (or an associated person thereof, as applicable) to prepare or issue any audit report with respect to any issuer, if the firm or associated person engages in any activity with respect to that issuer prohibited by any of subsections (g) through (l) of section 10A of the Securities Exchange Act of 1934, as added by this title, or any rule or regulation of the Commission or of the Board issued thereunder.

[¶ 64,201]   SEC. 209. [15 USC 7234] CONSIDERATIONS BY APPROPRIATE STATE REGULATORY AUTHORITIES.

In supervising nonregistered public accounting firms and their associated persons, appropriate State regulatory authorities should make an independent determination of the proper standards applicable, particularly taking into consideration the size and nature of the business of the accounting firms they supervise and the size and nature of the business of the clients of those firms. The standards applied by the Board under this Act should not be presumed to be applicable for purposes of this section for small and medium sized nonregistered public accounting firms.

TITLE III—CORPORATE RESPONSIBILITY

[¶ 64,211] SEC. 301. [15 USC 78j-1] PUBLIC COMPANY AUDIT COMMITTEES.

Section 10A of the Securities Exchange Act of 1934 (15 U.S.C. 78f) is amended by adding at the end the following:

'(m) STANDARDS RELATING TO AUDIT COMMITTEES.

'(1) COMMISSION RULES

'(A) IN GENERAL—Effective not later than 270 days after the date of enactment of this subsection, the Commission shall, by rule, direct the national securities exchanges and national securities associations to prohibit the listing of any security of an issuer that is not in compliance with the requirements of any portion of paragraphs (2) through (6).

'(B) OPPORTUNITY TO CURE DEFECTS—The rules of the Commission under subparagraph (A) shall provide for appropriate procedures for an issuer to have an opportunity to cure any defects that would be the basis for a prohibition under subparagraph (A), before the imposition of such prohibition.

'(2) RESPONSIBILITIES RELATING TO REGISTERED PUBLIC ACCOUNTING FIRMS— The audit committee of each issuer, in its capacity as a committee of the board of directors, shall be directly responsible for the appointment, compensation, and oversight of the work of any registered public accounting firm employed by that issuer (including resolution of disagreements between management and the auditor regarding financial reporting) for the purpose of preparing or issuing an audit report or related work, and each such registered public accounting firm shall report directly to the audit committee.

'(3) INDEPENDENCE

'(A) IN GENERAL—Each member of the audit committee of the issuer shall be a member of the board of directors of the issuer, and shall otherwise be independent.

'(B) CRITERIA—In order to be considered to be independent for purposes of this paragraph, a member of an audit committee of an issuer may not, other than in his or her capacity as a member of the audit committee, the board of directors, or any other board committee—

'(i) accept any consulting, advisory, or other compensatory fee from the issuer; or

'(ii) be an affiliated person of the issuer or any subsidiary thereof.

'(C) EXEMPTION AUTHORITY—The Commission may exempt from the requirements of subparagraph

(B) a particular relationship with respect to audit committee members, as the Commission determines appropriate in light of the circumstances.

'(4) COMPLAINTS—Each audit committee shall establish procedures for—

'(A) the receipt, retention, and treatment of complaints received by the issuer regarding accounting, internal accounting controls, or auditing matters; and

'(B) the confidential, anonymous submission by employees of the issuer of concerns regarding questionable accounting or auditing matters.

'(5) AUTHORITY TO ENGAGE ADVISERS- Each audit committee shall have the authority to engage independent counsel and other advisers, as it determines necessary to carry out its duties.

'(6) FUNDING—Each issuer shall provide for appropriate funding, as determined by the audit committee, in its capacity as a committee of the board of directors, for payment of compensation—

'(A) to the registered public accounting firm employed by the issuer for the purpose of rendering or issuing an audit report; and

'(B) to any advisers employed by the audit committee under paragraph (5).'.

SEC. 302. [15 USC 7241] CORPORATE RESPONSIBILITY FOR FINANCIAL REPORTS.

(a) REGULATIONS REQUIRED—The Commission shall, by rule, require, for each company filing periodic reports under section 13(a) or 15(d) of the Securities Exchange Act of 1934 (15 U.S.C. 78m, 78o(d)), that the principal executive officer or officers and the principal financial officer or officers, or persons performing similar functions, certify in each annual or quarterly report filed or submitted under either such section of such Act that—

(1) the signing officer has reviewed the report;

(2) based on the officer's knowledge, the report does not contain any untrue statement of a material fact or omit to state a material fact necessary in order to make the statements made, in light of the circumstances under which such statements were made, not misleading;

(3) based on such officer's knowledge, the financial statements, and other financial information included in the report, fairly present in all material respects the financial condition and results of operations of the issuer as of, and for, the periods presented in the report;

(4) the signing officers—

(A) are responsible for establishing and maintaining internal controls;

(B) have designed such internal controls to ensure that material information relating to the issuer and its consolidated subsidiaries is made known to such officers by others within those entities, particularly during the period in which the periodic reports are being prepared;

(C) have evaluated the effectiveness of the issuer's internal controls as of a date within 90 days prior to the report; and

(D) have presented in the report their conclusions about the effectiveness of their internal controls based on their evaluation as of that date;

(5) the signing officers have disclosed to the issuer's auditors and the audit committee of the board of directors (or persons fulfilling the equivalent function)—

(A) all significant deficiencies in the design or operation of internal controls which could adversely affect the issuer's ability to record, process, summarize, and report financial data and have identified for the issuer's auditors any material weaknesses in internal controls; and

(B) any fraud, whether or not material, that involves management or other employees who have a significant role in the issuer's internal controls; and

(6) the signing officers have indicated in the report whether or not there were significant changes in internal controls or in other factors that could significantly affect internal controls subsequent to the date of their evaluation, including any corrective actions with regard to significant deficiencies and material weaknesses.

(b) FOREIGN REINCORPORATIONS HAVE NO EFFECT—Nothing in this section 302 shall be interpreted or applied in any way to allow any issuer to lessen the legal force of the statement required under this section 302, by an issuer having reincorporated or having engaged in any other transaction that resulted in the transfer of the corporate domicile or offices of the issuer from inside the United States to outside of the United States.

(c) DEADLINE—The rules required by subsection (a) shall be effective not later than 30 days after the date of enactment of this Act.

SEC. 303. [15 USC 7242] IMPROPER INFLUENCE ON CONDUCT OF AUDITS.

(a) RULES TO PROHIBIT—It shall be unlawful, in contravention of such rules or regulations as the Commission shall prescribe as necessary and appropriate in the public interest or for the protection of investors, for any officer or director of an issuer, or any other person acting under the direction thereof, to take any action to fraudulently influence, coerce, manipulate, or mislead any independent public or certified accountant engaged in the performance of an audit of the financial statements of that issuer for the purpose of rendering such financial statements materially misleading.

(b) ENFORCEMENT—In any civil proceeding, the Commission shall have exclusive authority to enforce this section and any rule or regulation issued under this section.

(c) NO PREEMPTION OF OTHER LAW—The provisions of subsection (a) shall be in addition to, and shall not supersede or preempt, any other provision of law or any rule or regulation issued thereunder.

(d) DEADLINE FOR RULEMAKING—The Commission shall—

(1) propose the rules or regulations required by this section, not later than 90 days after the date of enactment of this Act; and

(2) issue final rules or regulations required by this section, not later than 270 days after that date of enactment.

[¶ 64,241]   SEC. 304. [15 USC 7243] FORFEITURE OF CERTAIN BONUSES AND PROFITS.

(a) ADDITIONAL COMPENSATION PRIOR TO NONCOMPLIANCE WITH COMMISSION FINANCIAL REPORTING REQUIREMENTS—If an issuer is required to prepare an accounting restatement due to the material noncompliance of the issuer, as a result of misconduct, with any financial reporting requirement under the securities laws, the chief executive officer and chief financial officer of the issuer shall reimburse the issuer for—

(1) any bonus or other incentive-based or equity-based compensation received by that person from the issuer during the 12-month period following the first public issuance or filing with the Commission (whichever first occurs) of the financial document embodying such financial reporting requirement; and

(2) any profits realized from the sale of securities of the issuer during that 12-month period.

(b) COMMISSION EXEMPTION AUTHORITY- The Commission may exempt any person from the application of subsection (a), as it deems necessary and appropriate.

[¶ 64,251]   SEC. 305. [15 USC 78u] [15 USC 77t] OFFICER AND DIRECTOR BARS AND PENALTIES.

(a) UNFITNESS STANDARD

(1) SECURITIES EXCHANGE ACT OF 1934- Section 21(d)(2) of the Securities Exchange Act of 1934 (15 U.S.C. 78u(d)(2)) is amended by striking 'substantial unfitness' and inserting 'unfitness'.

(2) SECURITIES ACT OF 1933—Section 20(e) of the Securities Act of 1933 (15 U.S.C. 77t(e)) is amended by striking 'substantial unfitness' and inserting 'unfitness'.

(b) EQUITABLE RELIEF—Section 21(d) of the Securities Exchange Act of 1934 (15 U.S.C. 78u(d)) is amended by adding at the end the following:

'(5) EQUITABLE RELIEF—In any action or proceeding brought or instituted by the Commission under any provision of the securities laws, the Commission may seek, and any Federal court may grant, any equitable relief that may be appropriate or necessary for the benefit of investors.'.

[¶ 64,261]   SEC. 306. [15 USC 7244] INSIDER TRADES DURING PENSION FUND BLACKOUT PERIODS.

(a) PROHIBITION OF INSIDER TRADING DURING PENSION FUND BLACKOUT PERIODS

(1) IN GENERAL—Except to the extent otherwise provided by rule of the Commission pursuant to paragraph (3), it shall be unlawful for any director or executive officer of an issuer of any equity security (other than an exempted security), directly or indirectly, to purchase, sell, or otherwise acquire or transfer any equity security of the issuer (other than an exempted security) during any blackout period with respect to such equity security if such director or officer acquires such equity security in connection with his or her service or employment as a director or executive officer.

(2) REMEDY

(A) IN GENERAL—Any profit realized by a director or executive officer referred to in paragraph (1) from any purchase, sale, or other acquisition or transfer in violation of this subsection shall inure to and be recoverable by the issuer, irrespective of any intention on the part of such director or executive officer in entering into the transaction.

(B) ACTIONS TO RECOVER PROFITS—An action to recover profits in accordance with this subsection may be instituted at law or in equity in any court of competent jurisdiction by the issuer, or by the owner of any security of the issuer in the name and in behalf of the issuer if the issuer fails or refuses to bring such action within 60 days after the date of request, or fails diligently to prosecute the action thereafter, except that no such suit shall be brought more than 2 years after the date on which such profit was realized.

(3) RULEMAKING AUTHORIZED—The Commission shall, in consultation with the Secretary of Labor, issue rules to clarify the application of this subsection and to prevent evasion thereof. Such rules shall provide for the application of the requirements of paragraph (1) with respect to entities treated as a single employer with respect to an issuer under section 414(b), (c), (m), or (o) of the Internal Revenue Code of 1986 to the extent necessary to clarify the application of such requirements and to prevent evasion thereof. Such rules may also provide for appropriate exceptions from the requirements of this subsection, including exceptions for purchases pursuant to an automatic dividend reinvestment program or purchases or sales made pursuant to an advance election.

(4) BLACKOUT PERIOD—For purposes of this subsection, the term 'blackout period', with respect to the equity securities of any issuer—

(A) means any period of more than 3 consecutive business days during which the ability of not fewer than 50 percent of the participants or beneficiaries under all individual account plans maintained by the issuer to purchase, sell, or otherwise acquire or transfer an interest in any equity of such issuer held in such an individual account plan is temporarily suspended by the issuer or by a fiduciary of the plan; and

(B) does not include, under regulations which shall be prescribed by the Commission—

(i) a regularly scheduled period in which the participants and beneficiaries may not purchase, sell, or otherwise acquire or transfer an interest in any equity of such issuer, if such period is—

(I) incorporated into the individual account plan; and

(II) timely disclosed to employees before becoming participants under the individual account plan or as a subsequent amendment to the plan; or

(ii) any suspension described in subparagraph (A) that is imposed solely in connection with persons becoming participants or beneficiaries, or ceasing to be participants or beneficiaries, in an individual account plan by reason of a corporate merger, acquisition, divestiture, or similar transaction involving the plan or plan sponsor.

(5) INDIVIDUAL ACCOUNT PLAN—For purposes of this subsection, the term 'individual account plan' has the meaning provided in section 3(34) of the Employee Retirement Income Security Act of 1974 (29 U.S.C. 1002(34), except that such term shall not include a one-participant retirement plan (within the meaning of section 101(i)(8)(B) of such Act (29 U.S.C. 1021(i)(8)(B))).

(6) NOTICE TO DIRECTORS, EXECUTIVE OFFICERS, AND THE COMMISSION—In any case in which a director or executive officer is subject to the requirements of this subsection in connection with a blackout period (as defined in paragraph (4)) with respect to any equity securities, the issuer of such equity securities shall timely notify such director or officer and the Securities and Exchange Commission of such blackout period.

(b) NOTICE REQUIREMENTS TO PARTICIPANTS AND BENEFICIARIES UNDER ERISA

(1) IN GENERAL—Section 101 of the Employee Retirement Income Security Act of 1974 (29 U.S.C. 1021) is amended by redesignating the second subsection (h) as subsection (j), and by inserting after the first subsection (h) the following new subsection:

'(i) NOTICE OF BLACKOUT PERIODS TO PARTICIPANT OR BENEFICIARY UNDER INDIVIDUAL ACCOUNT PLAN

'(1) DUTIES OF PLAN ADMINISTRATOR- In advance of the commencement of any blackout period with respect to an individual account plan, the plan administrator shall notify the plan participants and beneficiaries who are affected by such action in accordance with this subsection.

'(2) NOTICE REQUIREMENTS

'(A) IN GENERAL—The notices described in paragraph (1) shall be written in a manner calculated to be understood by the average plan participant and shall include—

'(i) the reasons for the blackout period,

'(ii) an identification of the investments and other rights affected,

'(iii) the expected beginning date and length of the blackout period, '(iv) in the case of investments affected, a statement that the participant or beneficiary should evaluate the appropriateness of their current investment decisions in light of their inability to direct or diversify assets credited to their accounts during the blackout period, and

'(v) such other matters as the Secretary may require by regulation.

'(B) NOTICE TO PARTICIPANTS AND BENEFICIARIES —Except as otherwise provided in this subsection, notices described in paragraph

(1) shall be furnished to all participants and beneficiaries under the plan to whom the blackout period applies at least 30 days in advance of the blackout period.

'(C) EXCEPTION TO 30-DAY NOTICE REQUIREMENT —In any case in which—

'(i) a deferral of the blackout period would violate the requirements of subparagraph (A) or (B) of section 404(a)(1), and a fiduciary of the plan reasonably so determines in writing, or

'(ii) the inability to provide the 30-day advance notice is due to events that were unforeseeable or circumstances beyond the reasonable control of the plan administrator, and a fiduciary of the plan reasonably so determines in writing,

subparagraph (B) shall not apply, and the notice shall be furnished to all participants and beneficiaries under the plan to whom the blackout period applies as soon as reasonably possible under the circumstances unless such a notice in advance of the termination of the blackout period is impracticable.

'(D) WRITTEN NOTICE—The notice required to be provided under this subsection shall be in writing, except that such notice may be in electronic or other form to the extent that such form is reasonably accessible to the recipient.

'(E) NOTICE TO ISSUERS OF EMPLOYER SECURITIES SUBJECT TO BLACKOUT PE-RIOD—In the case of any blackout period in connection with an individual account plan, the plan administrator shall provide timely notice of such blackout period to the issuer of any employer securities subject to such blackout period.

'(3) EXCEPTION FOR BLACKOUT PERIODS WITH LIMITED APPLICABILITY—In any case in which the blackout period applies only to 1 or more participants or beneficiaries in connection with a merger, acquisition, divestiture, or similar transaction involving the plan or plan sponsor and occurs solely in connection with becoming or ceasing to be a participant or beneficiary under the plan by reason of such merger, acquisition, divestiture, or transaction, the requirement of this subsection that the notice be provided to all participants and beneficiaries shall be treated as met if the notice required under paragraph (1) is provided to such participants or beneficiaries to whom the blackout period applies as soon as reasonably practicable.

'(4) CHANGES IN LENGTH OF BLACKOUT PERIOD—If, following the furnishing of the notice pursuant to this subsection, there is a change in the beginning date or length of the blackout period (specified in such notice pursuant to paragraph (2)(A)(iii)), the administrator shall provide affected participants and beneficiaries notice of the change as soon as reasonably practicable. In relation to the extended blackout period, such notice shall meet the requirements of paragraph (2)(D) and shall specify any material change in the matters referred to in clauses (i) through (v) of paragraph (2)(A).

'(5) REGULATORY EXCEPTIONS—The Secretary may provide by regulation for additional exceptions to the requirements of this subsection which the Secretary determines are in the interests of participants and beneficiaries.

'(6) GUIDANCE AND MODEL NOTICES—The Secretary shall issue guidance and model notices which meet the requirements of this subsection.

'(7) BLACKOUT PERIOD—For purposes of this subsection—

'(A) IN GENERAL—The term 'blackout period' means, in connection with an individual account plan, any period for which any ability of participants or beneficiaries under the plan, which is otherwise available under the terms of such plan, to direct or diversify assets credited to their accounts, to obtain loans from the plan, or to obtain distributions from the plan is temporarily suspended, limited, or restricted, if such suspension, limitation, or restriction is for any period of more than 3 consecutive business days.

'(B) EXCLUSIONS—The term 'blackout period' does not include a suspension, limitation, or restriction—

'(i) which occurs by reason of the application of the securities laws (as defined in section 3(a)(47) of the Securities Exchange Act of 1934),

'(ii) which is a change to the plan which provides for a regularly scheduled suspension, limitation, or restriction which is disclosed to participants or beneficiaries through any summary of material modifications, any materials describing specific investment alternatives under the plan, or any changes thereto, or

'(iii) which applies only to 1 or more individuals, each of whom is the participant, an alternate payee (as defined in section 206(d)(3)(K)), or any other beneficiary pursuant to a qualified domestic relations order (as defined in section 206(d)(3)(B)(i)).

'(8) INDIVIDUAL ACCOUNT PLAN

'(A) IN GENERAL—For purposes of this subsection, the term 'individual account plan' shall have the meaning provided such term in section 3(34), except that such term shall not include a one-participant retirement plan.

'(B) ONE-PARTICIPANT RETIREMENT PLAN—For purposes of subparagraph (A), the term 'one-participant retirement plan' means a retirement plan that—

'(i) on the first day of the plan year—

'(I) covered only the employer (and the employer's spouse) and the employer owned the entire business (whether or not incorporated), or

'(II) covered only one or more partners (and their spouses) in a business partnership (including partners in an S or C corporation (as defined in section 1361(a) of the Internal Revenue Code of 1986)),

'(ii) meets the minimum coverage requirements of section 410(b) of the Internal Revenue Code of 1986 (as in effect on the date of the enactment of this paragraph) without being combined with any other plan of the business that covers the employees of the business,

'(iii) does not provide benefits to anyone except the employer (and the employer's spouse) or the partners (and their spouses),

'(iv) does not cover a business that is a member of an affiliated service group, a controlled group of corporations, or a group of businesses under common control, and

'(v) does not cover a business that leases employees.'.

(2) ISSUANCE OF INITIAL GUIDANCE AND MODEL NOTICE—The Secretary of Labor shall issue initial guidance and a model notice pursuant to section 101(i)(6) of the Employee Retirement Income Security Act of 1974 (as added by this subsection) not later than January 1, 2003. Not later than 75 days after the date of the enactment of this Act, the Secretary shall promulgate interim final rules necessary to carry out the amendments made by this subsection.

(3) CIVIL PENALTIES FOR FAILURE TO PROVIDE NOTICE —Section 502 of such Act (29 U.S.C. 1132) is amended—

(A) in subsection (a)(6), by striking '(5), or (6)' and inserting '(5), (6), or (7)';

(B) by redesignating paragraph (7) of subsection (c) as paragraph (8); and

(C) by inserting after paragraph (6) of subsection (c) the following new paragraph:

'(7) The Secretary may assess a civil penalty against a plan administrator of up to $100 a day from the date of the plan administrator's failure or refusal to provide notice to participants and beneficiaries in accordance with section 101(i). For purposes of this paragraph, each violation with respect to any single participant or beneficiary shall be treated as a separate violation.'.

(3) PLAN AMENDMENTS—If any amendment made by this subsection requires an amendment to any plan, such plan amendment shall not be required to be made before the first plan year beginning on or after the effective date of this section, if—

(A) during the period after such amendment made by this subsection takes effect and before such first plan year, the plan is operated in good faith compliance with the requirements of such amendment made by this subsection, and

(B) such plan amendment applies retroactively to the period after such amendment made by this subsection takes effect and before such first plan year.

(c) EFFECTIVE DATE—The provisions of this section (including the amendments made thereby) shall take effect 180 days after the date of the enactment of this Act. Good faith compliance with the requirements of such provisions in advance of the issuance of applicable regulations thereunder shall be treated as compliance with such provisions.

[¶ 64,271] SEC. 307. [15 USC 7245] RULES OF PROFESSIONAL RESPONSIBILITY FOR ATTORNEYS.

Not later than 180 days after the date of enactment of this Act, the Commission shall issue rules, in the public interest and for the protection of investors, setting forth minimum standards of professional conduct for attorneys appearing and practicing before the Commission in any way in the representation of issuers, including a rule—

(1) requiring an attorney to report evidence of a material violation of securities law or breach of fiduciary duty or similar violation by the company or any agent thereof, to the chief legal counsel or the chief executive officer of the company (or the equivalent thereof); and

(2) if the counsel or officer does not appropriately respond to the evidence (adopting, as necessary, appropriate remedial measures or sanctions with respect to the violation), requiring the attorney to report the evidence to the audit committee of the board of directors of the issuer or to another committee of the board of directors comprised solely of directors not employed directly or indirectly by the issuer, or to the board of directors.

[¶ 64,281] SEC. 308. [15 USC 7246] [15 USC 7261] FAIR FUNDS FOR INVESTORS.

(a) CIVIL PENALTIES TO BE USED FOR THE RELIEF OF VICTIMS—If, in any judicial or administrative action brought by the Commission under the securities laws, the Commission obtains a civil penalty against any person for a violation of such laws, or such person agrees, in settlement of any such action, to such civil penalty, the amount of such civil penalty shall, on the motion or at the direction of the Commission, be added to and become part of a disgorgement fund or other fund established for the benefit of the victims of such violation.

(b) ACCEPTANCE OF ADDITIONAL DONATIONS—The Commission is authorized to accept, hold, administer, and utilize gifts, bequests and devises of property, both real and personal, to the United States for a disgorgement fund or other fund described in subsection (a). Such gifts, bequests, and devises of money and proceeds from sales of other property received as gifts, bequests, or devises shall be deposited in such fund and shall be available for allocation in accordance with subsection (a).

(c) STUDY REQUIRED

(1) SUBJECT OF STUDY—The Commission shall review and analyze—

(A) enforcement actions by the Commission over the five years preceding the date of the enactment of this Act that have included proceedings to obtain civil penalties or disgorgements to identify areas where such proceedings may be utilized to efficiently, effectively, and fairly provide restitution for injured investors; and

(B) other methods to more efficiently, effectively, and fairly provide restitution to injured investors, including methods to improve the collection rates for civil penalties and disgorgements.

(2) REPORT REQUIRED—The Commission shall report its findings to the Committee on Financial Services of the House of Representatives and the Committee on Banking, Housing, and Urban Affairs of the Senate within 180 days after of the date of the enactment of this Act, and shall use such findings to revise its rules and regulations as necessary. The report shall include a discussion of regulatory or legislative actions that are recommended or that may be necessary to address concerns identified in the study.

(d) CONFORMING AMENDMENTS—Each of the following provisions is amended by inserting ', except as otherwise provided in section 308 of the Sarbanes-Oxley Act of 2002' after 'Treasury of the United States':

(1) Section 21(d)(3)(C)(i) of the Securities Exchange Act of 1934 (15 U.S.C. 78u(d)(3)(C)(i)).

(2) Section 21A(d)(1) of such Act (15 U.S.C. 78u1(d)(1)).

(3) Section 20(d)(3)(A) of the Securities Act of 1933 (15 U.S.C. 77t(d)(3)(A)).

(4) Section 42(e)(3)(A) of the Investment Company Act of 1940 (15 U.S.C. 80a-41(e)(3)(A)).

(5) Section 209(e)(3)(A) of the Investment Advisers Act of 1940 (15 U.S.C. 80b-9(e)(3)(A)).

[(e) Removed.]

TITLE IV—ENHANCED FINANCIAL DISCLOSURES

[¶ 64,291]   SEC. 401.   [15 USC 78m] DISCLOSURES IN PERIODIC REPORTS.

(a) DISCLOSURES REQUIRED—Section 13 of the Securities Exchange Act of 1934 (15 U.S.C. 78m) is amended by adding at the end the following:

'(i) ACCURACY OF FINANCIAL REPORTS- Each financial report that contains financial statements, and that is required to be prepared in accordance with (or reconciled to) generally accepted accounting principles under this title and filed with the Commission shall reflect all material correcting adjustments that have been identified by a registered public accounting firm in accordance with generally accepted accounting principles and the rules and regulations of the Commission.

'(j) OFF-BALANCE SHEET TRANSACTIONS- Not later than 180 days after the date of enactment of the Sarbanes-Oxley Act of 2002, the Commission shall issue final rules providing that each annual and quarterly financial report required to be filed with the Commission shall disclose all material off-balance sheet transactions, arrangements, obligations (including contingent obligations), and other relationships of the issuer with unconsolidated entities or other persons, that may have a material current or future effect on financial condition, changes in financial condition, results of operations, liquidity, capital expenditures, capital resources, or significant components of revenues or expenses.'.

(b) COMMISSION RULES ON PRO FORMA FIGURES- Not later than 180 days after the date of enactment of the Sarbanes-Oxley Act fo 2002, the Commission shall issue final rules providing that pro forma financial information included in any periodic or other report filed with the Commission pursuant to the securities laws, or in any public disclosure or press or other release, shall be presented in a manner that—

(1) does not contain an untrue statement of a material fact or omit to state a material fact necessary in order to make the pro forma financial information, in light of the circumstances under which it is presented, not misleading; and

(2) reconciles it with the financial condition and results of operations of the issuer under generally accepted accounting principles.

(c) STUDY AND REPORT ON SPECIAL PURPOSE ENTITIES

(1) STUDY REQUIRED—The Commission shall, not later than 1 year after the effective date of adoption of off-balance sheet disclosure rules required by section 13(j) of the Securities Exchange Act of 1934, as added by this section, complete a study of filings by issuers and their disclosures to determine—

(A) the extent of off-balance sheet transactions, including assets, liabilities, leases, losses, and the use of special purpose entities; and

(B) whether generally accepted accounting rules result in financial statements of issuers reflecting the economics of such off-balance sheet transactions to investors in a transparent fashion.

(2) REPORT AND RECOMMENDATIONS—Not later than 6 months after the date of completion of the study required by paragraph (1), the Commission shall submit a report to the President, the Committee on Banking, Housing, and Urban Affairs of the Senate, and the Committee on Financial Services of the House of Representatives, setting forth—

(A) the amount or an estimate of the amount of off-balance sheet transactions, including assets, liabilities, leases, and losses of, and the use of special purpose entities by, issuers filing periodic reports pursuant to section 13 or 15 of the Securities Exchange Act of 1934;

(B) the extent to which special purpose entities are used to facilitate off-balance sheet transactions;

(C) whether generally accepted accounting principles or the rules of the Commission result in financial statements of issuers reflecting the economics of such transactions to investors in a transparent fashion;

(D) whether generally accepted accounting principles specifically result in the consolidation of special purpose entities sponsored by an issuer in cases in which the issuer has the majority of the risks and rewards of the special purpose entity; and

(E) any recommendations of the Commission for improving the transparency and quality of reporting off-balance sheet transactions in the financial statements and disclosures required to be filed by an issuer with the Commission.

[¶ 64,301] SEC. 402. [15 USC 78m] ENHANCED CONFLICT OF INTEREST PROVISIONS.

(a) PROHIBITION ON PERSONAL LOANS TO EXECUTIVES

Section 13 of the Securities Exchange Act of 1934 (15 U.S.C. 78m), as amended by this Act, is amended by adding at the end the following:

'(k) PROHIBITION ON PERSONAL LOANS TO EXECUTIVES

'(1) IN GENERAL—It shall be unlawful for any issuer (as defined in section 2 of the Sarbanes-Oxley Act of 2002), directly or indirectly, including through any subsidiary, to extend or maintain credit, to arrange for the extension of credit, or to renew an extension of credit, in the form of a personal loan to or for any director or executive officer (or equivalent thereof) of that issuer. An extension of credit maintained by the issuer on the date of enactment of this subsection shall not be subject to the provisions of this subsection, provided that there is no material modification to any term of any such extension of credit or any renewal of any such extension of credit on or after that date of enactment.

'(2) LIMITATION—Paragraph (1) does not preclude any home improvement and manufactured home loans (as that term is defined in section 5 of the Home Owners' Loan Act (12 U.S.C. 1464)), consumer credit (as defined in section 103 of the Truth in Lending Act (15 U.S.C. 1602)), or any extension of credit under an open end credit plan (as defined in section 103 of the Truth in Lending Act (15 U.S.C. 1602)), or a charge card (as defined in section 127(c)(4)(e) of the Truth in Lending Act (15 U.S.C. 1637(c)(4)(e)), or any extension of credit by a broker or dealer registered under section 15 of this title to an employee of that broker or dealer to buy, trade, or carry securities, that is permitted under rules or regulations of the Board of Governors of the Federal Reserve System pursuant to section 7 of this title (other than an extension of credit that would be used to purchase the stock of that issuer), that is—

'(A) made or provided in the ordinary course of the consumer credit business of such issuer;

'(B) of a type that is generally made available by such issuer to the public; and

'(C) made by such issuer on market terms, or terms that are no more favorable than those offered by the issuer to the general public for such extensions of credit.

'(3) RULE OF CONSTRUCTION FOR CERTAIN LOANSParagraph (1) does not apply to any loan made or maintained by an insured depository institution (as defined in section 3 of the Federal Deposit Insurance Act (12 U.S.C. 1813)), if the loan is subject to the insider lending restrictions of section 22(h) of the Federal Reserve Act (12 U.S.C. 375b).'.

[¶ 64,311] SEC. 403. [15 USC 78p] DISCLOSURES OF TRANSACTIONS INVOLVING MANAGEMENT AND PRINCIPAL STOCKHOLDERS.

(a) AMENDMENT—Section 16 of the Securities Exchange Act of 1934 (15 U.S.C. 78p) is amended by striking the heading of such section and subsection (a) and inserting the following:

'SEC. 16. DIRECTORS, OFFICERS, AND PRINCIPAL STOCKHOLDERS.

'(a) DISCLOSURES REQUIRED

'(1) DIRECTORS, OFFICERS, AND PRINCIPAL STOCKHOLDERS REQUIRED TO FILE— Every person who is directly or indirectly the beneficial owner of more than 10 percent of any class of any equity security (other than an exempted security) which is registered pursuant to section 12, or who is a director or an officer of the issuer of such security, shall file the statements required by this subsection with the Commission (and, if such security is registered on a national securities exchange, also with the exchange).

'(2) TIME OF FILING—The statements required by this subsection shall be filed—

'(A) at the time of the registration of such security on a national securities exchange or by the effective date of a registration statement filed pursuant to section 12(g);

'(B) within 10 days after he or she becomes such beneficial owner, director, or officer;

'(C) if there has been a change in such ownership, or if such person shall have purchased or sold a security-based swap agreement (as defined in section 206(b) of the Gramm-Leach-Bliley Act (15 U.S.C. 78c note)) involving such equity security, before the end of the second business day following the day on which the subject transaction has been executed, or at such other time as the

Commission shall establish, by rule, in any case in which the Commission determines that such 2-day period is not feasible.

'(3) CONTENTS OF STATEMENTS—A statement filed—

'(A) under subparagraph (A) or (B) of paragraph (2) shall contain a statement of the amount of all equity securities of such issuer of which the filing person is the beneficial owner; and

'(B) under subparagraph (C) of such paragraph shall indicate ownership by the filing person at the date of filing, any such changes in such ownership, and such purchases and sales of the security-based swap agreements as have occurred since the most recent such filing under such subparagraph.

'(4) ELECTRONIC FILING AND AVAILABILITY—Beginning not later than 1 year after the date of enactment of the Sarbanes-Oxley Act of 2002—

'(A) a statement filed under subparagraph (C) of paragraph (2) shall be filed electronically;

'(B) the Commission shall provide each such statement on a publicly accessible Internet site not later than the end of the business day following that filing; and

'(C) the issuer (if the issuer maintains a corporate website) shall provide that statement on that corporate website, not later than the end of the business day following that filing.'.

(b) EFFECTIVE DATE—The amendment made by this section shall be effective 30 days after the date of the enactment of this Act.

[¶ 64,321]   SEC. 404. [15 USC 7262] MANAGEMENT ASSESSMENT OF INTERNAL CONTROLS.

(a) RULES REQUIRED—The Commission shall prescribe rules requiring each annual report required by section 13(a) or 15(d) of the Securities Exchange Act of 1934 (15 U.S.C. 78m or 78o(d)) to contain an internal control report, which shall—

(1) state the responsibility of management for establishing and maintaining an adequate internal control structure and procedures for financial reporting; and

(2) contain an assessment, as of the end of the most recent fiscal year of the issuer, of the effectiveness of the internal control structure and procedures of the issuer for financial reporting.

(b) INTERNAL CONTROL EVALUATION AND REPORTING—With respect to the internal control assessment required by subsection (a), each registered public accounting firm that prepares or issues the audit report for the issuer shall attest to, and report on, the assessment made by the management of the issuer. An attestation made under this subsection shall be made in accordance with standards for attestation engagements issued or adopted by the Board. Any such attestation shall not be the subject of a separate engagement.

(c) EXEMPTION FOR SMALLER ISSUERS—Subsection (b) shall not apply with respect to any audit report prepared for an issuer that is neither a 'large accelerated filer' nor an 'accelerated filer' as those terms are defined in Rule 12b-2 of the Commission (17 C.F.R. 240.12b-2).

[¶ 64,331]   SEC. 405. [15 USC 7263] EXEMPTION.

Nothing in section 401, 402, or 404, the amendments made by those sections, or the rules of the Commission under those sections shall apply to any investment company registered under section 8 of the Investment Company Act of 1940 (15 U.S.C. 80a-8).

[¶ 64,341]   SEC. 406. [15 USC 7264] CODE OF ETHICS FOR SENIOR FINANCIAL OFFICERS.

(a) CODE OF ETHICS DISCLOSURE—The Commission shall issue rules to require each issuer, together with periodic reports required pursuant to section 13(a) or 15(d) of the Securities Exchange Act of 1934, to disclose whether or not, and if not, the reason therefor, such issuer has adopted a code of ethics for senior financial officers, applicable to its principal financial officer and comptroller or principal accounting officer, or persons performing similar functions.

(b) CHANGES IN CODES OF ETHICS—The Commission shall revise its regulations concerning matters requiring prompt disclosure on Form 8-K (or any successor thereto) to require the immediate disclosure, by means of the filing of such form, dissemination by the Internet or by other electronic means, by any issuer of any change in or waiver of the code of ethics for senior financial officers.

(c) DEFINITION—In this section, the term 'code of ethics' means such standards as are reasonably necessary to promote—

(1) honest and ethical conduct, including the ethical handling of actual or apparent conflicts of interest between personal and professional relationships;

(2) full, fair, accurate, timely, and understandable disclosure in the periodic reports required to be filed by the issuer; and

(3) compliance with applicable governmental rules and regulations.

(d) DEADLINE FOR RULEMAKING—The Commission shall—

(1) propose rules to implement this section, not later than 90 days after the date of enactment of this Act; and

(2) issue final rules to implement this section, not later than 180 days after that date of enactment.

[¶ 64,351]   SEC. 407. [15 USC 7265] DISCLOSURE OF AUDIT COMMITTEE FINANCIAL EXPERT.

(a) RULES DEFINING 'FINANCIAL EXPERT'—The Commission shall issue rules, as necessary or appropriate in the public interest and consistent with the protection of investors, to require each issuer, together with periodic reports required pursuant to sections 13(a) and 15(d) of the Securities Exchange Act of 1934, to disclose whether or not, and if not, the reasons therefor, the audit committee of that issuer is comprised of at least 1 member who is a financial expert, as such term is defined by the Commission.

(b) CONSIDERATIONS—In defining the term 'financial expert' for purposes of subsection (a), the Commission shall consider whether a person has, through education and experience as a public accountant or auditor or a principal financial officer, comptroller, or principal accounting officer of an issuer, or from a position involving the performance of similar functions—

(1) an understanding of generally accepted accounting principles and financial statements;

(2) experience in—

(A) the preparation or auditing of financial statements of generally comparable issuers; and

(B) the application of such principles in connection with the accounting for estimates, accruals, and reserves;

(3) experience with internal accounting controls; and

(4) an understanding of audit committee functions.

(c) DEADLINE FOR RULEMAKING—The Commission shall—

(1) propose rules to implement this section, not later than 90 days after the date of enactment of this Act; and

(2) issue final rules to implement this section, not later than 180 days after that date of enactment.

[¶ 64,361] SEC. 408. [15 USC 7266] ENHANCED REVIEW OF PERIODIC DISCLOSURES BY ISSUERS.

(a) REGULAR AND SYSTEMATIC REVIEW—The Commission shall review disclosures made by issuers reporting under section 13(a) of the Securities Exchange Act of 1934 (including reports filed on Form 10-K), and which have a class of securities listed on a national securities exchange or traded on an automated quotation facility of a national securities association, on a regular and systematic basis for the protection of investors. Such review shall include a review of an issuer's financial statement.

(b) REVIEW CRITERIA—For purposes of scheduling the reviews required by subsection (a), the Commission shall consider, among other factors—

(1) issuers that have issued material restatements of financial results;

(2) issuers that experience significant volatility in their stock price as compared to other issuers;

(3) issuers with the largest market capitalization;

(4) emerging companies with disparities in price to earning ratios;

(5) issuers whose operations significantly affect any material sector of the economy; and

(6) any other factors that the Commission may consider relevant.

(c) MINIMUM REVIEW PERIOD—In no event shall an issuer required to file reports under section 13(a) or 15(d) of the Securities Exchange Act of 1934 be reviewed under this section less frequently than once every 3 years.

[¶ 64,371] SEC. 409. [15 USC 78m] REAL TIME ISSUER DISCLOSURES.

Section 13 of the Securities Exchange Act of 1934 (15 U.S.C. 78m), as amended by this Act, is amended by adding at the end the following:

'(l) REAL TIME ISSUER DISCLOSURES- Each issuer reporting under section 13(a) or 15(d) shall disclose to the public on a rapid and current basis such additional information concerning material changes in the financial condition or operations of the issuer, in plain English, which may include trend and qualitative information and graphic presentations, as the Commission determines, by rule, is necessary or useful for the protection of investors and in the public interest.'.

TITLE V—ANALYST CONFLICTS OF INTEREST

[¶ 64,381] SEC. 501. [15 USC 78o-6] TREATMENT OF SECURITIES ANALYSTS BY REGISTERED SECURITIES ASSOCIATIONS AND NATIONAL SECURITIES EXCHANGES.

(a) RULES REGARDING SECURITIES ANALYSTS- The Securities Exchange Act of 1934 (15 U.S.C. 78a et seq.) is amended by inserting after section 15C the following new section:

'SEC. 15D. SECURITIES ANALYSTS AND RESEARCH REPORTS.

'(a) ANALYST PROTECTIONS—The Commission, or upon the authorization and direction of the Commission, a registered securities association or national securities exchange, shall have adopted, not later than 1 year after the date of enactment of this section, rules reasonably designed to address conflicts of interest that can arise when securities analysts recommend equity securities in research reports and public appearances, in order to improve the objectivity of research and provide investors with more useful and reliable information, including rules designed—

'(1) to foster greater public confidence in securities research, and to protect the objectivity and independence of securities analysts, by—

'(A) restricting the prepublication clearance or approval of research reports by persons employed by the broker or dealer who are engaged in investment banking activities, or persons not directly responsible for investment research, other than legal or compliance staff;

'(B) limiting the supervision and compensatory evaluation of securities analysts to officials employed by the broker or dealer who are not engaged in investment banking activities; and

'(C) requiring that a broker or dealer and persons employed by a broker or dealer who are involved with investment banking activities may not, directly or indirectly, retaliate against or threaten to retaliate against any securities analyst employed by that broker or dealer or its affiliates as a result of an adverse, negative, or otherwise unfavorable research report that may adversely affect the present or prospective investment banking relationship of the broker or dealer with the issuer that is the subject of the research report, except that such rules may not limit the authority of a broker or dealer to discipline a securities analyst for causes other than such research report in accordance with the policies and procedures of the firm;

'(2) to define periods during which brokers or dealers who have participated, or are to participate, in a public offering of securities as underwriters or dealers should not publish or otherwise distribute research reports relating to such securities or to the issuer of such securities;

'(3) to establish structural and institutional safeguards within registered brokers or dealers to assure that securities analysts are separated by appropriate informational partitions within the firm from the review, pressure, or oversight of those whose involvement in investment banking activities might potentially bias their judgment or supervision; and

'(4) to address such other issues as the Commission, or such association or exchange, determines appropriate.

'(b) DISCLOSURE—The Commission, or upon the authorization and direction of the Commission, a registered securities association or national securities exchange, shall have adopted, not later than 1 year after the date of enactment of this section, rules reasonably designed to require each securities analyst to disclose in public appearances, and each registered broker or dealer to disclose in each research report, as applicable, conflicts of interest that are known or should have been known by the securities analyst or the broker or dealer, to exist at the time of the appearance or the date of distribution of the report, including—

'(1) the extent to which the securities analyst has debt or equity investments in the issuer that is the subject of the appearance or research report;

'(2) whether any compensation has been received by the registered broker or dealer, or any affiliate thereof, including the securities analyst, from the issuer that is the subject of the appearance or research report, subject to such exemptions as the Commission may determine appropriate and necessary to prevent disclosure by virtue of this paragraph of material non-public information regarding specific potential future investment banking transactions of such issuer, as is appropriate in the public interest and consistent with the protection of investors;

'(3) whether an issuer, the securities of which are recommended in the appearance or research report, currently is, or during the 1-year period preceding the date of the appearance or date of distribution of the report has been, a client of the registered broker or dealer, and if so, stating the types of services provided to the issuer;

'(4) whether the securities analyst received compensation with respect to a research report, based upon (among any other factors) the investment banking revenues (either generally or specifically earned from the issuer being analyzed) of the registered broker or dealer; and

'(5) such other disclosures of conflicts of interest that are material to investors, research analysts, or the broker or dealer as the Commission, or such association or exchange, determines appropriate.

'(c) DEFINITIONS—In this section—

'(1) the term 'securities analyst' means any associated person of a registered broker or dealer that is principally responsible for, and any associated person who reports directly or indirectly to a securities analyst in connection with, the preparation of the substance of a research report, whether or not any such person has the job title of 'securities analyst'; and

'(2) the term 'research report' means a written or electronic communication that includes an analysis of equity securities of individual companies or industries, and that provides information reasonably sufficient upon which to base an investment decision.'.

(b) ENFORCEMENT—Section 21B(a) of the Securities Exchange Act of 1934 (15 U.S.C. 78u-2(a)) is amended by inserting '15D,' before '15B'.

(c) COMMISSION AUTHORITY—The Commission may promulgate and amend its regulations, or direct a registered securities association or national securities exchange to promulgate and amend its rules, to carry out section 15D of the Securities Exchange Act of 1934, as added by this section, as is necessary for the protection of investors and in the public interest.

TITLE VI—COMMISSION RESOURCES AND AUTHORITY

[¶ 64,391] SEC. 601. [15 USC 78kk] AUTHORIZATION OF APPROPRIATIONS.

Section 35 of the Securities Exchange Act of 1934 (15 U.S.C. 78kk) is amended to read as follows:

'SEC. 35. AUTHORIZATION OF APPROPRIATIONS.

'In addition to any other funds authorized to be appropriated to the Commission, there are authorized to be appropriated to carry out the functions, powers, and duties of the Commission, $776,000,000 for fiscal year 2003, of which—

'(1) $102,700,000 shall be available to fund additional compensation, including salaries and benefits, as authorized in the Investor and Capital Markets Fee Relief Act (Public Law 107123; 115 Stat. 2390 et seq.);

'(2) $108,400,000 shall be available for information technology, security enhancements, and recovery and mitigation activities in light of the terrorist attacks of September 11, 2001; and

'(3) $98,000,000 shall be available to add not fewer than an additional 200 qualified professionals to provide enhanced oversight of auditors and audit services required by the Federal securities laws, and to improve Commission investigative and disciplinary efforts with respect to such auditors and services, as well as for additional professional support staff necessary to strengthen the programs of the Commission involving Full Disclosure and Prevention and Suppression of Fraud, risk management, industry technology review, compliance, inspections, examinations, market regulation, and investment management.'.

[¶ 64,401] SEC. 602. [15 USC 78d-3] APPEARANCE AND PRACTICE BEFORE THE COMMISSION.

The Securities Exchange Act of 1934 (15 U.S.C. 78a et seq.) is amended by inserting after section 4B the following:

'SEC. 4C. APPEARANCE AND PRACTICE BEFORE THE COMMISSION.

'(a) AUTHORITY TO CENSURE—The Commission may censure any person, or deny, temporarily or permanently, to any person the privilege of appearing or practicing before the Commission in any way, if that person is found by the Commission, after notice and opportunity for hearing in the matter—

'(1) not to possess the requisite qualifications to represent others;

'(2) to be lacking in character or integrity, or to have engaged in unethical or improper professional conduct; or

'(3) to have willfully violated, or willfully aided and abetted the violation of, any provision of the securities laws or the rules and regulations issued thereunder.

'(b) DEFINITION—With respect to any registered public accounting firm or associated person, for purposes of this section, the term 'improper professional conduct' means—

'(1) intentional or knowing conduct, including reckless conduct, that results in a violation of applicable professional standards; and

'(2) negligent conduct in the form of—

'(A) a single instance of highly unreasonable conduct that results in a violation of applicable professional standards in circumstances in which the registered public accounting firm or associated person knows, or should know, that heightened scrutiny is warranted; or

'(B) repeated instances of unreasonable conduct, each resulting in a violation of applicable professional standards, that indicate a lack of competence to practice before the Commission.'.

[¶ 64,411] SEC. 603. [15 USC 78u] [15 USC 78t] [15 USC 78o] FEDERAL COURT AUTHORITY TO IMPOSE PENNY STOCK BARS.

(a) SECURITIES EXCHANGE ACT OF 1934—Section 21(d) of the Securities Exchange Act of 1934 (15 U.S.C. 78u(d)), as amended by this Act, is amended by adding at the end the following:

'(6) AUTHORITY OF A COURT TO PROHIBIT PERSONS FROM PARTICIPATING IN AN OFFERING OF PENNY STOCK

'(A) IN GENERAL—In any proceeding under paragraph (1) against any person participating in, or, at the time of the alleged misconduct who was participating in, an offering of penny stock, the court may prohibit that person from participating in an offering of penny stock, conditionally or unconditionally, and permanently or for such period of time as the court shall determine.

'(B) DEFINITION—For purposes of this paragraph, the term 'person participating in an offering of penny stock' includes any person engaging in activities with a broker, dealer, or issuer for purposes of issuing, trading, or inducing or attempting to induce the purchase or sale of, any penny stock. The Commission may, by rule or regulation, define such term to include other activities, and may, by rule, regulation, or order, exempt any person or class of persons, in whole or in part, conditionally or unconditionally, from inclusion in such term.'.

(b) SECURITIES ACT OF 1933—Section 20 of the Securities Act of 1933 (15 U.S.C. 77t) is amended by adding at the end the following:

'(g) AUTHORITY OF A COURT TO PROHIBIT PERSONS FROM PARTICIPATING IN AN OFFERING OF PENNY STOCK

'(1) IN GENERAL—In any proceeding under subsection (a) against any person participating in, or, at the time of the alleged misconduct, who was participating in, an offering of penny stock, the court may prohibit that person from participating in an offering of penny stock, conditionally or unconditionally, and permanently or for such period of time as the court shall determine.

'(2) DEFINITION—For purposes of this subsection, the term 'person participating in an offering of penny stock' includes any person engaging in activities with a broker, dealer, or issuer for purposes of issuing, trading, or inducing or attempting to induce the purchase or sale of, any penny stock. The Commission may, by rule or regulation, define such term to include other activities, and may, by rule, regulation, or order, exempt any person or class of persons, in whole or in part, conditionally or unconditionally, from inclusion in such term.'.

[¶ 64,421]   SEC. 604. [15 USC 80b-3] QUALIFICATIONS OF ASSOCIATED PERSONS OF BROKERS AND DEALERS.

(a) BROKERS AND DEALERS—Section 15(b)(4) of the Securities Exchange Act of 1934 (15 U.S.C. 78o) is amended—

(1) by striking subparagraph (F) and inserting the following:

'(F) is subject to any order of the Commission barring or suspending the right of the person to be associated with a broker or dealer;'; and

(2) in subparagraph (G), by striking the period at the end and inserting the following: '; or

'(H) is subject to any final order of a State securities commission (or any agency or officer performing like functions), State authority that supervises or examines banks, savings associations, or credit unions, State insurance commission (or any agency or office performing like functions), an appropriate Federal banking agency (as defined in section 3 of the Federal Deposit Insurance Act (12 U.S.C. 1813(q))), or the National Credit Union Administration, that—

'(i) bars such person from association with an entity regulated by such commission, authority, agency, or officer, or from engaging in the business of securities, insurance, banking, savings association activities, or credit union activities; or

'(ii) constitutes a final order based on violations of any laws or regulations that prohibit fraudulent, manipulative, or deceptive conduct.'.

(b) INVESTMENT ADVISERS—Section 203(e) of the Investment Advisers Act of 1940 (15 U.S.C. 80b-3(e)) is amended—

(1) by striking paragraph (7) and inserting the following:

'(7) is subject to any order of the Commission barring or suspending the right of the person to be associated with an investment adviser;';

(2) in paragraph (8), by striking the period at the end and inserting '; or'; and

(3) by adding at the end the following:

'(9) is subject to any final order of a State securities commission (or any agency or officer performing like functions), State authority that supervises or examines banks, savings associations, or credit unions, State insurance commission (or any agency or office performing like functions), an appropriate Federal banking agency (as defined in section 3 of the Federal Deposit Insurance Act (12 U.S.C. 1813(q))), or the National Credit Union Administration, that—

'(A) bars such person from association with an entity regulated by such commission, authority, agency, or officer, or from engaging in the business of securities, insurance, banking, savings association activities, or credit union activities; or

'(B) constitutes a final order based on violations of any laws or regulations that prohibit fraudulent, manipulative, or deceptive conduct.'.

(c) CONFORMING AMENDMENTS

(1) SECURITIES EXCHANGE ACT OF 1934—The Securities Exchange Act of 1934 (15 U.S.C. 78a et seq.) is amended—

(A) in section 3(a)(39)(F) (15 U.S.C. 78c(a)(39)(F))—

(i) by striking 'or (G)' and inserting '(H), or (G)'; and

(ii) by inserting ', or is subject to an

order or finding,' before 'enumerated'; (B) in each of section 15(b)(6)(A)(i) (15 U.S.C. 78o(b)(6)(A)(i)), paragraphs (2) and (4) of section 15B(c) (15 U.S.C. 78o-4(c)), and subparagraphs (A) and (C) of section 15C(c)(1) (15 U.S.C. 78o-5(c)(1))—

(i) by striking 'or (G)' each place that term appears and inserting '(H), or (G)'; and

(ii) by striking 'or omission' each place that term appears, and inserting ', or is subject to an order or finding,'; and

(C) in each of paragraphs (3)(A) and (4)(C) of section 17A(c) (15 U.S.C. 78q-1(c))—

(i) by striking 'or (G)' each place that term appears and inserting '(H), or (G)'; and

(ii) by inserting ', or is subject to an order or finding,' before 'enumerated' each place that term appears.

(2) INVESTMENT ADVISERS ACT OF 1940- Section 203(f) of the Investment Advisers Act of 1940 (15 U.S.C. 80b-3(f)) is amended—

(A) by striking 'or (8)' and inserting '(8), or (9)'; and

(B) by inserting 'or (3)' after 'paragraph (2)'.

TITLE VII—STUDIES AND REPORTS

[¶ 64,431]   SEC. 701. [15 USC 7201] GAO STUDY AND REPORT REGARDING CONSOLIDATION OF PUBLIC ACCOUNTING FIRMS.

(a) STUDY REQUIRED—The Comptroller General of the United States shall conduct a study—

(1) to identify—

(A) the factors that have led to the consolidation of public accounting firms since 1989 and the consequent reduction in the number of firms capable of providing audit services to large national and multinational business organizations that are subject to the securities laws;

(B) the present and future impact of the condition described in subparagraph (A) on capital formation and securities markets, both domestic and international; and

(C) solutions to any problems identified under subparagraph (B), including ways to increase competition and the number of firms capable of providing audit services to large national and multinational business organizations that are subject to the securities laws;

(2) of the problems, if any, faced by business organizations that have resulted from limited competition among public accounting firms, including—

(A) higher costs;

(B) lower quality of services;

(C) impairment of auditor independence; or

(D) lack of choice; and

(3) whether and to what extent Federal or State regulations impede competition among public accounting firms.

(b) CONSULTATION—In planning and conducting the study under this section, the Comptroller General shall consult with—

(1) the Commission;

(2) the regulatory agencies that perform functions similar to the Commission within the other member countries of the Group of Seven Industrialized Nations;

(3) the Department of Justice; and

(4) any other public or private sector organization that the Comptroller General considers appropriate.

(c) REPORT REQUIRED—Not later than 1 year after the date of enactment of this Act, the Comptroller General shall submit a report on the results of the study required by this section to the Committee on Banking, Housing, and Urban Affairs of the Senate and the Committee on Financial Services of the House of Representatives.

[¶ 64,441]   SEC. 702. COMMISSION STUDY AND REPORT REGARDING CREDIT RATING AGENCIES.

(a) STUDY REQUIRED

(1) IN GENERAL—The Commission shall conduct a study of the role and function of credit rating agencies in the operation of the securities market.

(2) AREAS OF CONSIDERATION—The study required by this subsection shall examine—

(A) the role of credit rating agencies in the evaluation of issuers of securities;

(B) the importance of that role to investors and the functioning of the securities markets;

(C) any impediments to the accurate appraisal by credit rating agencies of the financial resources and risks of issuers of securities;

(D) any barriers to entry into the business of acting as a credit rating agency, and any measures needed to remove such barriers;

(E) any measures which may be required to improve the dissemination of information concerning such resources and risks when credit rating agencies announce credit ratings; and

(F) any conflicts of interest in the operation of credit rating agencies and measures to prevent such conflicts or ameliorate the consequences of such conflicts.

(b) REPORT REQUIRED—The Commission shall submit a report on the study required by subsection (a) to the President, the Committee on Financial Services of the House of Representatives, and the Committee on Banking, Housing, and Urban Affairs of the Senate not later than 180 days after the date of enactment of this Act.

[¶ 64,451]   SEC. 703. STUDY AND REPORT ON VIOLATORS AND VIOLATIONS.

(a) STUDY—The Commission shall conduct a study to determine, based upon information for the period from January 1, 1998, to December 31, 2001—

(1) the number of securities professionals, defined as public accountants, public accounting firms, investment bankers, investment advisers, brokers, dealers, attorneys, and other securities professionals practicing before the Commission—

(A) who have been found to have aided and abetted a violation of the Federal securities laws, including rules or regulations promulgated thereunder (collectively referred to in this section as 'Federal securities laws'), but who have not been sanctioned, disciplined, or otherwise penalized as a primary violator in any administrative action or civil proceeding, including in any settlement of such an action or proceeding (referred to in this section as 'aiders and abettors'); and

(B) who have been found to have been primary violators of the Federal securities laws;

(2) a description of the Federal securities laws violations committed by aiders and abettors and by primary violators, including—

(A) the specific provision of the Federal securities laws violated;

(B) the specific sanctions and penalties imposed upon such aiders and abettors and primary violators, including the amount of any monetary penalties assessed upon and collected from such persons;

(C) the occurrence of multiple violations by the same person or persons, either as an aider or abettor or as a primary violator; and

(D) whether, as to each such violator, disciplinary sanctions have been imposed, including any censure, suspension, temporary bar, or permanent bar to practice before the Commission; and

(3) the amount of disgorgement, restitution, or any other fines or payments that the Commission has assessed upon and collected from, aiders and abettors and from primary violators.

(b) REPORT—A report based upon the study conducted pursuant to subsection (a) shall be submitted to the Committee on Banking, Housing, and Urban Affairs of the Senate, and the Committee on Financial Services of the House of Representatives not later than 6 months after the date of enactment of this Act.

[¶ 64,461]   SEC. 704. STUDY OF ENFORCEMENT ACTIONS.

(a) STUDY REQUIRED—The Commission shall review and analyze all enforcement actions by the Commission involving violations of reporting requirements imposed under the securities laws, and restatements of financial statements, over the 5-year period preceding the date of enactment of this Act, to identify areas of reporting that are most susceptible to fraud, inappropriate manipulation, or inappropriate earnings management, such as revenue recognition and the accounting treatment of off-balance sheet special purpose entities.

(b) REPORT REQUIRED—The Commission shall report its findings to the Committee on Financial Services of the House of Representatives and the Committee on Banking, Housing, and Urban Affairs of the Senate, not later than 180 days after the date of enactment of this Act, and shall use such findings to revise its rules and regulations, as necessary. The report shall include a discussion of regulatory or legislative steps that are recommended or that may be necessary to address concerns identified in the study.

[¶ 64,471]   SEC. 705. STUDY OF INVESTMENT BANKS.

(a) GAO STUDY—The Comptroller General of the United States shall conduct a study on whether investment banks and financial advisers assisted public companies in manipulating their earnings and obfuscating their true financial condition. The study should address the role of investment banks and financial advisers—

(1) in the collapse of the Enron Corporation, including with respect to the design and implementation of derivatives transactions, transactions involving special purpose vehicles, and other financial arrangements that may have had the effect of altering the company's reported financial statements in ways that obscured the true financial picture of the company;

(2) in the failure of Global Crossing, including with respect to transactions involving swaps of fiberoptic cable capacity, in the designing transactions that may have had the effect of altering the company's reported financial statements in ways that obscured the true financial picture of the company; and

(3) generally, in creating and marketing transactions which may have been designed solely to enable companies to manipulate revenue streams, obtain loans, or move liabilities off balance sheets without altering the economic and business risks faced by the companies or any other mechanism to obscure a company's financial picture.

(b) REPORT—The Comptroller General shall report to Congress not later than 180 days after the date of enactment of this Act on the results of the study required by this section. The report shall include a discussion of regulatory or legislative steps that are recommended or that may be necessary to address concerns identified in the study.

TITLE VIII—CORPORATE AND CRIMINAL FRAUD ACCOUNTABILITY

[¶ 64,481] SEC. 801. [18 USC 1501] SHORT TITLE.

This title may be cited as the 'Corporate and Criminal Fraud Accountability Act of 2002'.

[¶ 64,491] SEC. 802. [18 USC 1519] CRIMINAL PENALTIES FOR ALTERING DOCUMENTS.

(a) IN GENERAL—Chapter 73 of title 18, United States Code, is amended by adding at the end the following:

'Sec. 1519. Destruction, alteration, or falsification of records in Federal investigations and bankruptcy

'Whoever knowingly alters, destroys, mutilates, conceals, covers up, falsifies, or makes a false entry in any record, document, or tangible object with the intent to impede, obstruct, or influence the investigation or proper administration of any matter within the jurisdiction of any department or agency of the United States or any case filed under title 11, or in relation to or contemplation of any such matter or case, shall be fined under this title, imprisoned not more than 20 years, or both.

'Sec. 1520. Destruction of corporate audit records

'(a)(1) Any accountant who conducts an audit of an issuer of securities to which section 10A(a) of the Securities Exchange Act of 1934 (15 U.S.C. 78j-1(a)) applies, shall maintain all audit or review workpapers for a period of 5 years from the end of the fiscal period in which the audit or review was concluded.

'(2) The Securities and Exchange Commission shall promulgate, within 180 days, after adequate notice and an opportunity for comment, such rules and regulations, as are reasonably necessary, relating to the retention of relevant records such as workpapers, documents that form the basis of an audit or review, memoranda, correspondence, communications, other documents, and records (including electronic records) which are created, sent, or received in connection with an audit or review and contain conclusions, opinions, analyses, or financial data relating to such an audit or review, which is conducted by any accountant who conducts an audit of an issuer of securities to which section 10A(a) of the Securities Exchange Act of 1934 (15 U.S.C. 78j-1(a)) applies. The Commission may, from time to time, amend or supplement the rules and regulations that it is required to promulgate under this section, after adequate notice and an opportunity for comment, in order to ensure that such rules and regulations adequately comport with the purposes of this section.

'(b) Whoever knowingly and willfully violates subsection (a)(1), or any rule or regulation promulgated by the Securities and Exchange Commission under subsection (a)(2), shall be fined under this title, imprisoned not more than 10 years, or both.

'(c) Nothing in this section shall be deemed to diminish or relieve any person of any other duty or obligation imposed by Federal or State law or regulation to maintain, or refrain from destroying, any document.'.

(b) CLERICAL AMENDMENT—The table of sections at the beginning of chapter 73 of title 18, United States Code, is amended by adding at the end the following new items:

'1519. Destruction, alteration, or falsification of records in Federal investigations and bankruptcy.

'1520. Destruction of corporate audit records.'.

[¶ 64,501] SEC. 803. [11 USC 523] DEBTS NONDISCHARGEABLE IF INCURRED IN VIOLATION OF SECURITIES FRAUD LAWS.

Section 523(a) of title 11, United States Code, is amended—

(1) in paragraph (17), by striking 'or' after the semicolon;

(2) in paragraph (18), by striking the period at the end and inserting '; or'; and

(3) by adding at the end, the following:

'(19) that—

'(A) is for—

'(i) the violation of any of the Federal securities laws (as that term is defined in section 3(a)(47) of the Securities Exchange Act of 1934), any of the State securities laws, or any regulation or order issued under such Federal or State securities laws; or

'(ii) common law fraud, deceit, or manipulation in connection with the purchase or sale of any security; and

'(B) results from—

'(i) any judgment, order, consent order, or decree entered in any Federal or State judicial or administrative proceeding;

'(ii) any settlement agreement entered into by the debtor; or

'(iii) any court or administrative order for any damages, fine, penalty, citation, restitutionary payment, disgorgement payment, attorney fee, cost, or other payment owed by the debtor.'.

[¶ 64,511] SEC. 804. [28 USC 1658] STATUTE OF LIMITATIONS FOR SECURITIES FRAUD.

(a) IN GENERAL—Section 1658 of title 28, United States Code, is amended—

(1) by inserting '(a)' before 'Except'; and

(2) by adding at the end the following:

'(b) Notwithstanding subsection (a), a private right of action that involves a claim of fraud, deceit, manipulation, or contrivance in contravention of a regulatory requirement concerning the securities laws, as defined in section 3(a)(47) of the Securities Exchange Act of 1934 (15 U.S.C. 78c(a)(47)), may be brought not later than the earlier of—

'(1) 2 years after the discovery of the facts constituting the violation; or

'(2) 5 years after such violation.'.

(b) EFFECTIVE DATE—The limitations period provided by section 1658(b) of title 28, United States Code, as added by this section, shall apply to all proceedings addressed by this section that are commenced on or after the date of enactment of this Act.

(c) NO CREATION OF ACTIONS—Nothing in this section shall create a new, private right of action.

[¶ 64,521] SEC. 805. [28 USC 944] REVIEW OF FEDERAL SENTENCING GUIDELINES FOR OBSTRUCTION OF JUSTICE AND EXTENSIVE CRIMINAL FRAUD.

(a) ENHANCEMENT OF FRAUD AND OBSTRUCTION OF JUSTICE SENTENCES—Pursuant to section 994 of title 28, United States Code, and in accordance with this section, the United States Sentencing Commission shall review and amend, as appropriate, the Federal Sentencing Guidelines and related policy statements to ensure that—

(1) the base offense level and existing enhancements contained in United States Sentencing Guideline 2J1.2 relating to obstruction of justice are sufficient to deter and punish that activity;

(2) the enhancements and specific offense characteristics relating to obstruction of justice are adequate in cases where—

(A) the destruction, alteration, or fabrication of evidence involves—

(i) a large amount of evidence, a large number of participants, or is otherwise extensive;

(ii) the selection of evidence that is particularly probative or essential to the investigation; or

(iii) more than minimal planning; or

(B) the offense involved abuse of a special skill or a position of trust;

(3) the guideline offense levels and enhancements for violations of section 1519 or 1520 of title 18, United States Code, as added by this title, are sufficient to deter and punish that activity;

(4) a specific offense characteristic enhancing sentencing is provided under United States Sentencing Guideline 2B1.1 (as in effect on the date of enactment of this Act) for a fraud offense that endangers the solvency or financial security of a substantial number of victims; and

(5) the guidelines that apply to organizations in United States Sentencing Guidelines, chapter 8, are sufficient to deter and punish organizational criminal misconduct.

(b) EMERGENCY AUTHORITY AND DEADLINE FOR COMMISSION ACTION—The United States Sentencing Commission is requested to promulgate the guidelines or amendments provided for under this section as soon as practicable, and in any event not later than 180 days after the date of enactment of this Act, in accordance with the procedures set forth in section 219(a) of the Sentencing Reform Act of 1987, as though the authority under that Act had not expired.

[¶ 64,531]   SEC. 806. [18 USC 1514A] PROTECTION FOR EMPLOYEES OF PUBLICLY TRADED COMPANIES WHO PROVIDE EVIDENCE OF FRAUD.

(a) IN GENERAL—Chapter 73 of title 18, United States Code, is amended by inserting after section 1514 the following:

'Sec. 1514A. Civil action to protect against retaliation in fraud cases

'(a) WHISTLEBLOWER PROTECTION FOR EMPLOYEES OF PUBLICLY TRADED COMPANIES—No company with a class of securities registered under section 12 of the Securities Exchange Act of 1934 (15 U.S.C. 78l), or that is required to file reports under section 15(d) of the Securities Exchange Act of 1934 (15 U.S.C. 78o(d)) including any subsidiary or affiliate whose financial information is included in the consolidated financial statements of such company, or nationally recognized statistical rating organization (as defined in section 3(a) of the Securities Exchange Act of 1934 (15 U.S.C. 78c), or any officer, employee, contractor, subcontractor, or agent of such company or nationally recognized statistical rating organization, may discharge, demote, suspend, threaten, harass, or in any other manner discriminate against an employee in the terms and conditions of employment because of any lawful act done by the employee—

'(1) to provide information, cause information to be provided, or otherwise assist in an investigation regarding any conduct which the employee reasonably believes constitutes a violation of section 1341, 1343, 1344, or 1348, any rule or regulation of the Securities and Exchange Commission, or any provision of Federal law relating to fraud against shareholders, when the information or assistance is provided to or the investigation is conducted by—

'(A) a Federal regulatory or law enforcement agency;

'(B) any Member of Congress or any committee of Congress; or

'(C) a person with supervisory authority over the employee (or such other person working for the employer who has the authority to investigate, discover, or terminate misconduct); or

'(2) to file, cause to be filed, testify, participate in, or otherwise assist in a proceeding filed or about to be filed (with any knowledge of the employer) relating to an alleged violation of section 1341, 1343, 1344, or 1348, any rule or regulation of the Securities and Exchange Commission, or any provision of Federal law relating to fraud against shareholders.

'(b) ENFORCEMENT ACTION

'(1) IN GENERAL—A person who alleges discharge or other discrimination by any person in violation of subsection (a) may seek relief under subsection (c), by—

'(A) filing a complaint with the Secretary of Labor; or

'(B) if the Secretary has not issued a final decision within 180 days of the filing of the complaint and there is no showing that such delay is due to the bad faith of the claimant, bringing an action at law or equity for de novo review in the appropriate district court of the United States, which shall have jurisdiction over such an action without regard to the amount in controversy.

'(2) PROCEDURE

'(A) IN GENERAL—An action under paragraph (1)(A) shall be governed under the rules and procedures set forth in section 42121(b) of title 49, United States Code.

'(B) EXCEPTION—Notification made under section 42121(b)(1) of title 49, United States Code, shall be made to the person named in the complaint and to the employer.

'(C) BURDENS OF PROOF—An action brought under paragraph (1)(B) shall be governed by the legal burdens of proof set forth in section 42121(b) of title 49, United States Code.

'(D) STATUTE OF LIMITATIONS—An action under paragraph (1) shall be commenced not later than 180 days after the date on which the violation occurs, or after the date on which the employee became aware of the violation.

'(E) JURY TRIAL—party to an action brought under paragraph (1)(B) shall be entitled to trial by jury.

'(c) REMEDIES

'(1) IN GENERAL—An employee prevailing in any action under subsection (b)(1) shall be entitled to all relief necessary to make the employee whole.

'(2) COMPENSATORY DAMAGES—Relief for any action under paragraph (1) shall include—

'(A) reinstatement with the same seniority status that the employee would have had, but for the discrimination;

'(B) the amount of back pay, with interest; and

'(C) compensation for any special damages sustained as a result of the discrimination, including litigation costs, expert witness fees, and reasonable attorney fees.

'(d) RIGHTS RETAINED BY EMPLOYEE- Nothing in this section shall be deemed to diminish the rights, privileges, or remedies of any employee under any Federal or State law, or under any collective bargaining agreement.'.

'(e) NONENFORCEABILITY OF CERTAIN PROVISIONS WAIVING RIGHTS AND REMEDIES OR REQUIRING ARBITRATION OF DISPUTES

'(1) WAIVER OF RIGHTS AND REMEDIES—The rights and remedies provided for in this section may not be waived by any agreement, policy form, or condition of employment, including by a predispute arbitration agreement.

'(2) PREDISPUTE ARBITRATION AGREEMENTS—No predispute arbitration agreement shall be valid or enforceable, if the agreement requires arbitration of a dispute arising under this section.

(b) CLERICAL AMENDMENT—The table of sections at the beginning of chapter 73 of title 18, United States Code, is amended by inserting after the item relating to section 1514 the following new item:

'1514A. Civil action to protect against retaliation in fraud cases.'.

[¶ 64,541]   SEC. 807. [18 USC 1348] CRIMINAL PENALTIES FOR
DEFRAUDING SHAREHOLDERS OF PUBLICLY TRADED COMPANIES.

(a) IN GENERAL—Chapter 63 of title 18, United States Code, is amended by adding at the end the following:

'Sec. 1348. Securities and commodities fraud

'Whoever knowingly executes, or attempts to execute, a scheme or artifice—

'(1) to defraud any person in connection with any commodity for future delivery, or any option on a commodity for future delivery, or any security of an issuer with a class of securities registered under section 12 of the Securities Exchange Act of 1934 (15 U.S.C. 78l) or that is required to file reports under section 15(d) of the Securities Exchange Act of 1934 (15 U.S.C. 78o(d)); or

'(2) to obtain, by means of false or fraudulent pretenses, representations, or promises, any money or property in connection with the purchase or sale of any commodity for future delivery, or any option on a commodity for future delivery, or any security of an issuer with a class of securities registered under section 12 of the Securities Exchange Act of 1934 (15 U.S.C. 78l) or that is required to file reports under section 15(d) of the Securities Exchange Act of 1934 (15 U.S.C. 78o(d));

shall be fined under this title, or imprisoned not more than 25 years, or both.'.

(b) CLERICAL AMENDMENT—The table of sections at the beginning of chapter 63 of title 18, United States Code, is amended by adding at the end the following new item:

'1348. Securities fraud.'.

TITLE IX—WHITE-COLLAR CRIME PENALTY ENHANCEMENTS

[¶ 64,551] SEC. 901. [18 USC 1341] SHORT TITLE.

This title may be cited as the 'White-Collar Crime Penalty Enhancement Act of 2002'.

[¶ 64,561] SEC. 902. [18 USC 1349] ATTEMPTS AND CONSPIRACIES TO COMMIT CRIMINAL FRAUD OFFENSES.

(a) IN GENERAL—Chapter 63 of title 18, United States Code, is amended by inserting after section 1348 as added by this Act the following:

'Sec. 1349. Attempt and conspiracy

'Any person who attempts or conspires to commit any offense under this chapter shall be subject to the same penalties as those prescribed for the offense, the commission of which was the object of the attempt or conspiracy.

(b) CLERICAL AMENDMENT—The table of sections at the beginning of chapter 63 of title 18, United States Code, is amended by adding at the end the following new item:

'1349. Attempt and conspiracy.'.

[¶ 64,571] SEC. 903. [18 USC 1341] CRIMINAL PENALTIES FOR MAIL AND WIRE FRAUD.

(a) MAIL FRAUD—Section 1341 of title 18, United States Code, is amended by striking 'five' and inserting '20'.

(b) WIRE FRAUD—Section 1343 of title 18, United States Code, is amended by striking 'five' and inserting '20'.

[¶ 64,581] SEC. 904. [29 USC 1131] CRIMINAL PENALTIES FOR VIOLATIONS OF THE EMPLOYEE RETIREMENT INCOME SECURITY ACT OF 1974.

Section 501 of the Employee Retirement Income Security Act of 1974 (29 U.S.C. 1131) is amended—

(1) by striking '$5,000' and inserting '$100,000';

(2) by striking 'one year' and inserting '10 years'; and

(3) by striking '$100,000' and inserting '$500,000'.

[¶ 64,591] SEC. 905. [28 USC 994] AMENDMENT TO SENTENCING GUIDELINES RELATING TO CERTAIN WHITE-COLLAR OFFENSES.

(a) DIRECTIVE TO THE UNITED STATES SENTENCING COMMISSION—Pursuant to its authority under section 994(p) of title 18, United States Code, and in accordance with this section, the United States Sentencing Commission shall review and, as appropriate, amend the Federal Sentencing Guidelines and related policy statements to implement the provisions of this Act.

(b) REQUIREMENTS—In carrying out this section, the Sentencing Commission shall—

(1) ensure that the sentencing guidelines and policy statements reflect the serious nature of the offenses and the penalties set forth in this Act, the growing incidence of serious fraud offenses which are identified above, and the need to modify the sentencing guidelines and policy statements to deter, prevent, and punish such offenses;

(2) consider the extent to which the guidelines and policy statements adequately address whether the guideline offense levels and enhancements for violations of the sections amended by this Act are sufficient to deter and punish such offenses, and specifically, are adequate in view of the statutory increases in penalties contained in this Act;

(3) assure reasonable consistency with other relevant directives and sentencing guidelines;

(4) account for any additional aggravating or mitigating circumstances that might justify exceptions to the generally applicable sentencing ranges;

(5) make any necessary conforming changes to the sentencing guidelines; and

(6) assure that the guidelines adequately meet the purposes of sentencing, as set forth in section 3553(a)(2) of title 18, United States Code.

(c) EMERGENCY AUTHORITY AND DEADLINE FOR COMMISSION ACTION—The United States Sentencing Commission is requested to promulgate the guidelines or amendments provided for under this section as soon as practicable, and in any event not later than 180 days after the date of enactment of this Act, in accordance with the procedures set forth in section 219(a) of the Sentencing Reform Act of 1987, as though the authority under that Act had not expired.

[¶ 64,601]   SEC. 906. [18 USC 1350] CORPORATE RESPONSIBILITY FOR FINANCIAL REPORTS.

(a) IN GENERAL—Chapter 63 of title 18, United States Code, is amended by inserting after section 1349, as created by this Act, the following:

'Sec. 1350. Failure of corporate officers to certify financial reports

(a) CERTIFICATION OF PERIODIC FINANCIAL REPORTS—Each periodic report containing financial statements filed by an issuer with the Securities Exchange Commission pursuant to section 13(a) or 15(d) of the Securities Exchange Act of 1934 (15 U.S.C. 78m(a) or 78o(d)) shall be accompanied by a written statement by the chief executive officer and chief financial officer (or equivalent thereof) of the issuer.

'(b) CONTENT—The statement required under subsection (a) shall certify that the periodic report containing the financial statements fully complies with the requirements of section 13(a) or 15(d) of the Securities Exchange Act of 1934 (15 U.S.C. 78m or 78o(d)) and that information contained in the periodic report fairly presents, in all material respects, the financial condition and results of operations of the issuer.

'(c) CRIMINAL PENALTIES—Whoever—

'(1) certifies any statement as set forth in subsections (a) and (b) of this section knowing that the periodic report accompanying the statement does not comport with all the requirements set forth in this section shall be fined not more than $1,000,000 or imprisoned not more than 10 years, or both; or

'(2) willfully certifies any statement as set forth in subsections (a) and (b) of this section knowing that the periodic report accompanying the statement does not comport with all the requirements set forth in this section shall be fined not more than $5,000,000, or imprisoned not more than 20 years, or both.'.

(b) CLERICAL AMENDMENT—The table of sections at the beginning of chapter 63 of title 18, United States Code, is amended by adding at the end the following:

'1350. Failure of corporate officers to certify financial reports.'.

TITLE X—CORPORATE TAX RETURNS

[¶ 64,611]   SEC. 1001. SENSE OF THE SENATE REGARDING THE SIGNING OF CORPORATE TAX RETURNS BY CHIEF EXECUTIVE OFFICERS.

It is the sense of the Senate that the Federal income tax return of a corporation should be signed by the chief executive officer of such corporation.

TITLE XI—CORPORATE FRAUD ACCOUNTABILITY

[¶ 64,621]   SEC. 1101. [15 USC 78a] SHORT TITLE.

This title may be cited as the 'Corporate Fraud Accountability Act of 2002'.

[¶ 64,631]   SEC. 1102. [18 USC 1512] TAMPERING WITH A RECORD OR OTHERWISE IMPEDING AN OFFICIAL PROCEEDING.

Section 1512 of title 18, United States Code, is amended—

(1) by redesignating subsections (c) through (i) as subsections (d) through (j), respectively; and

(2) by inserting after subsection (b) the following new subsection:

'(c) Whoever corruptly—

'(1) alters, destroys, mutilates, or conceals a record, document, or other object, or attempts to do so, with the intent to impair the object's integrity or availability for use in an official proceeding; or

'(2) otherwise obstructs, influences, or impedes any official proceeding, or attempts to do so, shall be fined under this title or imprisoned not more than 20 years, or both.'.

[¶ 64,641] SEC. 1103. [15 USC 78u-3] TEMPORARY FREEZE AUTHORITY FOR THE SECURITIES AND EXCHANGE COMMISSION.

(a) IN GENERAL—Section 21C(c) of the Securities Exchange Act of 1934 (15 U.S.C. 78u-3(c)) is amended by adding at the end the following:

'(3) TEMPORARY FREEZE

'(A) IN GENERAL

'(i) ISSUANCE OF TEMPORARY ORDER—Whenever, during the course of a lawful investigation involving possible violations of the Federal securities laws by an issuer of publicly traded securities or any of its directors, officers, partners, controlling persons, agents, or employees, it shall appear to the Commission that it is likely that the issuer will make extraordinary payments (whether compensation or otherwise) to any of the foregoing persons, the Commission may petition a Federal district court for a temporary order requiring the issuer to escrow, subject to court supervision, those payments in an interest-bearing account for 45 days.

'(ii) STANDARD—A temporary order shall be entered under clause (i), only after notice and opportunity for a hearing, unless the court determines that notice and hearing prior to entry of the order would be impracticable or contrary to the public interest.

'(iii) EFFECTIVE PERIOD—A temporary order issued under clause (i) shall—

'(I) become effective immediately;

'(II) be served upon the parties subject to it; and

'(III) unless set aside, limited or suspended by a court of competent jurisdiction, shall remain effective and enforceable for 45 days.

'(iv) EXTENSIONS AUTHORIZED—The effective period of an order under this subparagraph may be extended by the court upon good cause shown for not longer than 45 additional days, provided that the combined period of the order shall not exceed 90 days.

'(B) PROCESS ON DETERMINATION OF VIOLATIONS

'(i) VIOLATIONS CHARGED—If the issuer or other person described in subparagraph (A) is charged with any violation of the Federal securities laws before the expiration of the effective period of a temporary order under subparagraph (A) (including any applicable extension period), the order shall remain in effect, subject to court approval, until the conclusion of any legal proceedings related thereto, and the affected issuer or other person, shall have the right to petition the court for review of the order.

'(ii) VIOLATIONS NOT CHARGED- If the issuer or other person described in subparagraph (A) is not charged with any violation of the Federal securities laws before the expiration of the effective period of a temporary order under subparagraph (A) (including any applicable extension period), the escrow shall terminate at the expiration of the 45-day effective period (or the expiration of any extension period, as applicable), and the disputed payments (with accrued interest) shall be returned to the issuer or other affected person.'.

(b) TECHNICAL AMENDMENT—Section 21C(c)(2) of the Securities Exchange Act of 1934 (15 U.S.C. 78u-3(c)(2)) is amended by striking 'This' and inserting 'paragraph (1)'.

[¶ 64,651] SEC. 1104. [28 USC 994] AMENDMENT TO THE FEDERAL SENTENCING GUIDELINES.

(a) REQUEST FOR IMMEDIATE CONSIDERATION BY THE UNITED STATES SENTENCING COMMISSION- Pursuant to its authority under section 994(p) of title 28, United States Code, and in accordance with this section, the United States Sentencing Commission is requested to—

(1) promptly review the sentencing guidelines applicable to securities and accounting fraud and related offenses;

(2) expeditiously consider the promulgation of new sentencing guidelines or amendments to existing sentencing guidelines to provide an enhancement for officers or directors of publicly traded corporations who commit fraud and related offenses; and

(3) submit to Congress an explanation of actions taken by the Sentencing Commission pursuant to paragraph (2) and any additional policy recommendations the Sentencing Commission may have for combating offenses described in paragraph (1).

(b) CONSIDERATIONS IN REVIEW—In carrying out this section, the Sentencing Commission is requested to—

(1) ensure that the sentencing guidelines and policy statements reflect the serious nature of securities, pension, and accounting fraud and the need for aggressive and appropriate law enforcement action to prevent such offenses;

(2) assure reasonable consistency with other relevant directives and with other guidelines;

(3) account for any aggravating or mitigating circumstances that might justify exceptions, including circumstances for which the sentencing guidelines currently provide sentencing enhancements;

(4) ensure that guideline offense levels and enhancements for an obstruction of justice offense are adequate in cases where documents or other physical evidence are actually destroyed or fabricated;

(5) ensure that the guideline offense levels and enhancements under United States Sentencing Guideline 2B1.1 (as in effect on the date of enactment of this Act) are sufficient for a fraud offense when the number of victims adversely involved is significantly greater than 50;

(6) make any necessary conforming changes to the sentencing guidelines; and

(7) assure that the guidelines adequately meet the purposes of sentencing as set forth in section 3553(a)(2) of title 18, United States Code.

(c) EMERGENCY AUTHORITY AND DEADLINE FOR COMMISSION ACTION—The United States Sentencing Commission is requested to promulgate the guidelines or amendments provided for under this section as soon as practicable, and in any event not later than the 180 days after the date of enactment of this Act, in accordance with the procedures sent forth in section 21(a) of the Sentencing Reform Act of 1987, as though the authority under that Act had not expired.

[¶ 64,661]   SEC. 1105. [15 USC 78u-3] AUTHORITY OF THE COMMISSION TO PROHIBIT PERSONS FROM SERVING AS OFFICERS OR DIRECTORS.

(a) SECURITIES EXCHANGE ACT OF 1934—Section 21C of the Securities Exchange Act of 1934 (15 U.S.C. 78u-3) is amended by adding at the end the following:

'(f) AUTHORITY OF THE COMMISSION TO PROHIBIT PERSONS FROM SERVING AS OFFICERS OR DIRECTORS—In any cease-and-desist proceeding under subsection (a), the Commission may issue an order to prohibit, conditionally or unconditionally, and permanently or for such period of time as it shall determine, any person who has violated section 10(b) or the rules or regulations thereunder, from acting as an officer or director of any issuer that has a class of securities registered pursuant to section 12, or that is required to file reports pursuant to section 15(d), if the conduct of that person demonstrates unfitness to serve as an officer or director of any such issuer.'.

(b) SECURITIES ACT OF 1933—Section 8A of the Securities Act of 1933 (15 U.S.C. 77h-1) is amended by adding at the end of the following:

'(f) AUTHORITY OF THE COMMISSION TO PROHIBIT PERSONS FROM SERVING AS OFFICERS OR DIRECTORS—In any cease-and-desist proceeding under subsection (a), the Commission may issue an order to prohibit, conditionally or unconditionally, and permanently or for such period of time as it shall determine, any person who has violated section 17(a)(1) or the rules or regulations thereunder, from acting as an officer or director of any issuer that has a class of securities registered pursuant to section 12 of the Securities Exchange Act of 1934, or that is required to file reports pursuant to section 15(d) of that Act, if the conduct of that person demonstrates unfitness to serve as an officer or director of any such issuer.'.

[¶ 64,671]   SEC. 1106. [15 USC 78ff] INCREASED CRIMINAL PENALTIES UNDER SECURITIES EXCHANGE ACT OF 1934.

Section 32(a) of the Securities Exchange Act of 1934 (15 U.S.C. 78ff(a)) is amended—

(1) by striking '$1,000,000, or imprisoned not more than 10 years' and inserting '$5,000,000, or imprisoned not more than 20 years'; and

(2) by striking '$2,500,000' and inserting '$25,000,000'.

[¶ 64,681] SEC. 1107. [18 USC 1513] RETALIATION AGAINST INFORMANTS.

(a) IN GENERAL—Section 1513 of title 18, United States Code, is amended by adding at the end the following:

'(e) Whoever knowingly, with the intent to retaliate, takes any action harmful to any person, including interference with the lawful employment or livelihood of any person, for providing to a law enforcement officer any truthful information relating to the commission or possible commission of any Federal offense, shall be fined under this title or imprisoned not more than 10 years, or both.'.

Speaker of the House of Representatives.

Vice President of the United States and

President of the Senate.

END

TOPICAL INDEX

TOPICAL INDEX

References are to paragraph (¶) numbers.